ABOUT THE AUTHORS

MIKE DOUCHANT

Douchant was a basketball editor for *The Sporting News* from 1977 to 1991. He also contributed to *The Sporting News Basketball Yearbooks, Official NBA Register,* and *Lindy's College Basketball Yearbook.* During the 1996 NCAA Tournament, Douchant ventured into cyberspace with CBS.SPORTSLINE.COM to offer his expertise in a basketball Q & A forum. He is also an analyst for College Sports Exchange, an information provider for online services.

BILLY PACKER

Billy Packer has covered 23 NCAA Division I Men's Basketball Championships as an analyst, the last 16 for CBS Sports. In 1993, he won the Sports Emmy Award for Outstanding Sports Personality/Analyst. Packer's love of college basketball developed while growing up as the son of the Lehigh University coach. He attended Wake Forest University where he was an All-Atlanctic Coast Conference guard from 1960 to 1962 and participated in the 1962 Final Four. After graduating that year with an economics degree, he became an assistant coach for his alma mater until 1969. Packer's illustrious broadcasting career began in 1972 when he filled in as an analyst for a regionally televised ACC game. He became a regular the next season. Over the years, he has worked with an array of broadcasting all-stars such as Curt Gowdy, Dick Enberg, Al McGuire, and currently with Jim Nantz.

ALSO FROM VISIBLE INK PRESS

Bud Collins' Tennis Encyclopedia

"Bud Collins, the walking tennis encyclopedia, has finally put himself between hard covers."—*Mary Carillo, CBS-TV*

In this new edition, *Bud Collins' Tennis Encyclopedia,* (formerly Bud Collins' Modern Encyclopedia of Tennis) considered the Bible of the tennis world, provides thorough statistics and presents a history of the sport from its country club beginnings in 1876 to the billion-dollar industry it is today.

Bud Collins and Zander Hollander   700 pages   230 photos   ISBN: 1-57859-000-0

Inside Sports Hockey 1998

"For the newcomer, this is a splendid primer... for the long-time fan, this is tremendous grist to start or settle arguments."—*Mike Emerick, FOX NHL Broadcaster*

In *Inside Sports Hockey,* exciting game action, vital stats, fascinating history, Stanley Cup highlights and much more are artfully combined for thorough coverage of one of America's favorite sports. This expanded new annual edition is updated with first-time coverage of the International and Canadian Junior Leagues, as well as great hockey announcers throughout history.

Zander Hollander   750 pages   300 photos   ISBN: 1-57859-019-1

Inside Sports Golf

"The best reference book on golf history."—*amazon.com*

With a broad range and in-depth approach that other golf books simply can't par, *Inside Sports Golf* will satisfy novices and fanatics alike with a host of player profiles, PGA, SPGA, LPGA, international, and amateur tournament results and previews, as well as commentary on the greatest golf shots of all time and golf in popular culture.

Roger Matuz   640 pages   200 photos   ISBN: 1-57859-007-8

Coming soon: NASCAR: The Ultimate Fan Book

The first affordable guide to auto racing, the sport with the highest average attendance of any sporting event, *NASCAR: The Ultimate Fan Book* provides a complete overview, including race results on every past NASCAR season, extensive bios and photos, and a directory of racing teams.

Al Pearce and Bill Fleischman   600 pages   200 photos   ISBN: 1-57859-033-7

INSIDE SPORTS MAGAZINE

COLLEGE BASKETBALL

INSIDE SPORTS MAGAZINE
COLLEGE BASKETBALL

Mike Douchant

Foreword by
Billy Packer

VISIBLE
INK
PRESS

Detroit • New York • Toronto • London

INSIDE SPORTS COLLEGE BASKETBALL

Copyright © 1995, 1998 by Michael Douchant

Published by **Visible Ink Press**™
A division of Gale Research
835 Penobscot Building
Detroit, MI 48226-4094

Visible Ink Press™ is a trademark of Gale Research

Inside Sports Magazine ©1998 is a registered trademark of Inside Sports Inc.

Most Visible Ink Press™ books are available at quantity discounts when purchased in bulk by corporations, organizations, or groups. Customized printings, special imprints, messages, and excerpts can be produced to meet your needs. For more information, contact Special Markets Manager, Gale Research, 835 Penobscot Building, Detroit, MI 48226. Or call 1-800-877-4253.

Art Director: Michelle DiMercurio
Front cover photograph of Tim Duncan: AP/Wide World Photos
Back cover photograph of Kara Wolters: AP/Wide World Photos

Library of Congress Cataloging-in-Publication Data
Douchant, Mike, 1951-
  Inside Sports college basketball / Mike Douchant. — 3rd ed.
     p.   cm.
  Includes bibliographical references and index.
  ISBN 1-57859-009-4
  1. Basketball—United States—History. 2. College sports—United States—History. I. Inside sports. II. Title.
GV885.7.D68   1997
796.2323'0973—dc21

                      97-23449
                        CIP

Printed in the United States of America
All rights reserved

10 9 8 7 6 5 4 3 2 1

Inside Sports College Basketball Pocket Guide—© Inside Sports Inc. 1998.

High fives to two passionate basketball players wearing uniform No. 23 I'm most fond of watching—the high-flying man virtually everyone on earth knows and the high-spirited lady who knows how to keep me down-to-earth. No one can stop him and no one can top her.

CONTENTS

Pre-Game Warm-Up

Foreword by Billy Packer xiii
Introduction by Mike Douchant xvii

Full-Court Press

1   The Early Years: 1891–1937 1
The game's evolution, pioneering individuals, & trend-setting schools

2   The Start of National Tournaments 1938–49 25
Season summaries & highlights, statistical leaders, final polls & rankings, all-decade team profiles & post-season tournament coverage

3   The "Great Players" Era: The 1950s 69
Season summaries & highlights, statistical leaders, final polls & rankings, all-decade team profiles & post-season tournament coverage

4   The UCLA Dynasty: The 1960s 129
Season summaries & highlights, statistical leaders, final polls & rankings, all-decade team profiles & post-season tournament coverage

5   Explosion of National Popularity: The 1970s 195
Season summaries & highlights, statistical leaders, final polls & rankings, all-decade team profiles & post-season tournament coverage

6   The Emergence of Parity: The 1980s 273
Season summaries & highlights, statistical leaders, final polls & rankings, all-decade team profiles & post-season tournament coverage

7   The South Rises Again: The 1990s 349
Season summaries & highlights, statistical leaders, final polls & rankings, all-decade team profiles & post-season tournament coverage

8   **National Invitation Tournament (NIT)** 419
Statistics & highlights about the former premier postseason competition including results from every past tournament

9   **All-Stars and All-Americans** 435
The cream of the crop for next season and All-Americans from seasons past

10 **Coach Directory** 455
The eminent X's-&-O's men of college hoops today

11 **Fascination With Freshmen** 469
Great freshman and their performances, by conference, school and year

12 **Women's Hoops** 499
The history of women's basketball and bios on the premier players and coaches

13 **Small Colleges: J.C., Divisions II & III, and NAIA** 537
Highlights, small-school standouts, & NJCAA & NAIA/NAIB tournament records

14 **What's Ahead in 1997-98** 553
A preview of the upcoming season, highlighting players, coaches, and schools to watch

15 **Conference Directory** 565
Details on Division I basketball leagues

16 **School Directory** 603
Vital facts about NCAA's major schools

17 **Pioneers of the Game** 649
Profiles the players who broke the color barriers at schools across the nation

18 **The Questions & Answers of 1997-98** 655
Takes a look at 35 thought-provoking issues that will affect the upcoming season

19 **NCAA Honors** 665
Individual and team accomplishments for both the regular season and the NCAA tournament

Post-Season Festivities

Index 675
Photo Credits 711

FOREWORD

by Billy Packer

It's hard to believe that anyone could be so fortunate to spend the course of a lifetime being involved with a sport that he enjoys, as I have with basketball. There are so many years of wonderful memories.

My father was a basketball coach, and about the time I was able to reach the rim with a shot attempt he became the head coach at Lehigh University in Bethlehem, Pa. I became a gym rat, developing my game along with school-boy friends like Al Senavitis, who later became a star player at Seton Hall. I attended Lehigh practices and games, and I saw great players like Tom Gola of La Salle and Guy Rodgers of Temple go against my dad's teams. I'll never forget sitting on my living room floor listening on radio to the 1955 NCAA championship game between La Salle and a team called San Francisco. "Bill Russell? Who's he?'" I thought. "No one can play with Gola.'" How wrong I was.

Things were different back then. There was no national TV, no Inside Sports preseason preview, very little national coverage of either the collegiate or the professional game. The explosion was yet to come.

The opportunity to play the game opened many doors. I earned a scholarship to Wake Forest University, which gave me the opportunity to play for the legendary "Bones'" McKinney. Every kid hopes to someday play on a championship team, and I was very fortunate at Wake to be with a number of topnotch players, like Len Chappell, a great scorer and rebounder who led us to two Atlantic Coast Conference crowns and great runs in the NCAA Tournament, including a trip to the Final Four in 1962.

Although we didn't win it all that season, I have great memories of the competition in Louisville. We faced one of the top collegiate teams of all time in Ohio State, with future Hall-of-Famers Jerry Lucas and John Havlicek. Interestingly, the very first college game for my class, some three years earlier, was also against the Buckeyes, who beat us on all three occasions we faced them in our careers, including the 1962 Final Four semifinal game. Ohio State had a better team—but as is the case today, on any given night anyone can be defeated. The Buckeyes found that out when they were defeated by a great Cincinnati team for the championship.

In those days, the tournament held a consolation game to determine third and fourth place. Our opponent in 1962 was a team called UCLA, coached by a man named John Wooden. Despite having coached at UCLA for 14 years, it was Coach Wooden's first Final Four, and our victory over his team would be the last time he was defeated in Final Four play until 1974, when David Thompson and North Carolina State pulled off the upset. Imagine—after the loss to our team in 1962, UCLA won 10 national championships in 12 years and had a Final Four record of 21-1 under Coach Wooden during the period.

After college I worked as an assistant coach for Bones McKinney and for Jack McCloskey, the man who later orchestrated two world championships for the Detroit Pistons as their general manager. It was a great time to study the game from a different perspective: to watch the genius of great coaches like Everett Case, Vic Bubas, Frank McGuire, and "Big House'" Gaines; and to see legends-to-be like Bob Knight and Dean Smith begin their illustrious careers. It's hard to imagine that I was a senior at Wake Forest when Coach Smith began his career at North Carolina. Dean, the surprising choice to succeed Frank McGuire, had some early difficulties but has become the winningest coach in the history of the collegiate game. It has been a thrill to watch him every step of the way—as an opposing player, a coach, and now as a broadcaster.

Over the years I've watched the fascinating development of talent, from the likes of a Cleo Hill (a player who came before his time) to the ultimate gym rat in Pete Maravich, to the "first Michael Jordan,'" David Thompson—and yes, to Michael himself, whom I first covered as a high school player.

The game has exploded. The NCAA Tournament, the NBA playoffs, and the Olympic Games themselves have made basketball a truly global game. One of its many allies has been television. Basketball is the perfect sport for TV: a two-hour program confined to a small space where the players can be identified for their skill and personalities. The story line is ever-changing—the game can be played by so many teams so many different ways. Next year's Final Four will be my 24th as a broadcaster, and I've been very fortunate to have so many great partners: Curt Gowdy, Dick Enberg, Al McGuire, Gary Bender, Brent Musburger, and now Jim Nantz. I've also been privileged to be involved with many key games, tournaments, and special occasions for the sport: John Wooden's final game in 1975; Bird vs. Magic in 1979; Dean Smith's first crown in 1982; the "perfect game,'" Villanova-Georgetown in 1985; Bob Knight's third title in 1987; Duke's back-to-back championships in 1991 and '92; and Arizona's run for the crown last year. Each year provides a new story line, with the unexpected supplying the by-line of the day.

As I see it, the 1997 season started a new era for the college game. As more underclassmen leave school early, experienced superstars and dominant veteran teams won't appear as often as they have in the past. In the short term this change created a stir in the college ranks, myself included, but 1997 proved that the college game has great resiliency. The fans, coaches, and players reacted in a very positive fashion, to the point where you might say last year's NCAA Tournament was one of the best ever.

The NCAA champs are not necessarily the best team in the college game for the full season, but rather the best team in a "one-and-done'" shootout held over three weeks. In my estimation, Kansas would have won a best-of-seven series, but on that one special day Arizona proved to be better club. The Wildcats' win added to the legacy of the nation's greatest sports playoff, pro or college.

The 1998 season looks like another special one for Lute Olson's team, which has everyone back—but who knows if the Cats can win their own conference, with the likes of UCLA and Stanford ready to challenge? As I look around the country, a number of teams jump out: Duke and North Carolina are powers to be reckoned with, and darkhorse challengers like Fresno State and Xavier will have a major impact. How about Kansas, the team we all expected to win last year?

Roy Williams may pull it off, with All-Americans Raef LaFrentz and Paul Pierce returning. In any case, there is plenty to think about as we get ready for another season.

As a person who loves the game—its history, its strategy, its stars, and its coaches—I have found that those who study the game and truly understand it are those who most appreciate and enjoy the time they get to spend with it. Having been associated with the sport for so long, I know most of the people who cover the game as writers, broadcasters, and historians: guys like "Hoops'" Wiess, Larry Donald, Dick O'Connell, Bob Ryan, Dick Vitale, and the man who has put together the volume you are about to read, Mike Douchant. Mike has collaborated on many outstanding yearbooks and historical and statistical publications. He knows his business, and he knows the game, and I know you will be educated and amazed as you read this year's edition of *Inside Sports College Basketball.*

INTRODUCTION

by Mike Douchant

Occasionally when you're in the middle of things, circumstances change, sometimes dramatically. For instance, Michael Jordan didn't earn a spot on his high school varsity basketball team in Wilmington, N.C., as a sophomore. A mere four years later, I was principally responsible for the North Carolina sophomore guard receiving college player of the year honors from a national magazine while every other media outlet tabbed ACC counterpart Ralph Sampson of Virginia. The entire country, of course, finally got on Jordan's bandwagon his junior season.

It feels great when your gut instincts prove correct, although you could have just joined the crowd to avoid the wrath, of say, Virginia zealots annoyed because they felt their celebrated center was shortchanged. On the other hand, I've made more than my share of mistakes in assessing what's important about the game and have received justifiable criticism. But it's always been gratifying to be involved in helping create relevant stories analyzing the wacky world of college hoops, including the following:

• Encouraging noted author John Feinstein to write a feature in a national publication about Georgetown's "Hoya Paranoia" and then feeling somewhat responsible for him being disciplined by his sports editor at the Washington Post.

• Assigning a feature on Bob Knight's former assistant coaches in *The Sporting News'* inaugural basketball yearbook that probably helped pave the way for Feinstein gaining access to Indiana's program, resulting in the best-selling sports book in history (*A Season on the Brink*).

• Providing the first significant national exposure for David Robinson (Navy), Charles Barkley (Auburn) and Karl Malone (Louisiana Tech) before they became household names.

• Acknowledging the diamond-in-the-rough skills of an unheralded foreign center named Akeem Olajuwon before he became "The Dream" for the University of Houston.

• Giving fans the national leaders in assists, steals and blocked shots before they became official NCAA statistics.

• Citing ascending stars in the coaching profession such as Tim Floyd and Pete Gillen before they became marquee names.

• Critiquing graduation ratios across the country long before it became fashionable and emphasizing textbook student-athletes who aren't ashamed of their grade-point averages.

• Supplying extensive historical perspective for the March Mania online environment at

CBS.SPORTSLINE.COM.

• Compiling a comprehensive off-season weekly notes column from a national perspective.

In other words, I'm not afraid of taking a risk to assemble a more pertinent product. That explains many of the noticeable changes in this year's volume.

The genesis for this publication, titled the *Encyclopedia of College Basketball* when first published in 1994, came while browsing through periodicals at book stores. There, I noticed long-standing respected encyclopedias covering major league baseball, the NFL, and NBA. I was surprised that a similar comprehensive volume on college basketball wasn't available. After all, "Final Four" has ascended to a spotlight previously reserved for such marquee events as the Masters, Super Bowl, World Series, Indianapolis 500, Kentucky Derby and major New Year's Day football bowl games.

I was on the ground floor in helping create products such as *The Sporting News Basketball Yearbooks, Official NBA Register,* and *Lindy's College Basketball Yearbook.* So I'm well aware that a "repeat" publication needs to be refined in subsequent editions in order to continue to be distinctive and edify diehard fans. I think readers already exposed to this book, let alone newcomers, will be pleased by much of the fine-tuning. Any suggestions from readers on how to improve the content are welcome.

College basketball in general also needs modification, although the engaging sport remains grand and has become essential to the world of sports. In all modesty, I believe whatever level of interest you possess will be piqued and you'll enjoy the vigor of college hoops even more by making yourself familiar with this handy guide.

What's in the Book?

Obviously, the bulk of a much-needed source on college hoops needs to accentuate major college basketball and the incredibly popular NCAA Division I Tournament. I also envisioned that an enterprising edition would be more authoritative by including pertinent material on other significant levels of competition such as the NIT, small colleges (NAIA, NCAA Divisions II and III, and junior colleges) and women's basketball.

I am enamored by the diverse approaches with which the history of college hoops could be portrayed if the information was packaged properly. Thus, in the pages that follow I've tried to deliver a variety of highly readable points to ponder plus relevant statistics and facts that college basketball fans require in order to be properly illuminated about the sport.

Inside Sports College Basketball contains 19 chapters of historical facts, individual and team profiles, an assortment of relevant statistics, enlightening trivia, and other pertinent information.

The 1998 edition features brand new chapters covering a broad range of important topics.

• The 25th anniversary of freshmen eligibility is celebrated with a chapter detailing the accomplishments and influence that freshmen have had on college basketball.

• I've compiled an exhaustive list of several hundred All-Americans, including their alma maters, positions, and years and organizations of recognition.

• I've closely examined the upcoming season and made bold predictions on everything from All-Americans to conference and national champions.

• This year marks the 50th anniversary of Jackie Robinson breaking the color barrier in major league baseball. This important event prompted me to compile a list of African American men who were the first to break the color barriers of their universities and play college basketball. This chapter is appropriately named "Pioneers of the Game."

Inside Sports College Basketball also contains hundreds of photos, a multitude of statistical tables, and a smattering of sidebar features on rules and famous games. And we've also included a special portable pocket guide from Inside Sports to help you enjoy the game more.

Acknowledgments

This treasure trove of facts and statistics is unique only because it catalogs the matchless performances of uncommon participants. It couldn't have been achieved without securing input from a variety of basketball aficionados. Therefore, I offer hearty thank-yous to the following contributors for their mix of clean prose and pertinent stats:

John Duxbury—His painstaking research enlightened year-by-year reviews and made player/coaching records more comprehensive. Dux, the nation's premier sports historian, is and always will be "The Answer Man."

Andy Geerken and Gary Johnson—Their work on many of the coaches' profiles was especially efficient. Here is how I think effervescent Dick Vitale would describe Andy, the director of communications for the National Association of Basketball Coaches, and Gary, a statistics coordinator for the NCAA: "They're the 3-R Men, baby! They're Reputable, Reliable and Resourceful."

Michael Johnson—The author of "The Juco Classic" knows more about the history of junior college basketball than anyone with a pulse. His labor of love in researching J.C. hoops is beyond compare.

Roland Lazenby—As with any subject delving into archival material, this book is dependent on precise and relevant analysis on the pioneers of the sport. Roland capitalized on his extensive experience as a sports book author to supply an incisive look at "The Early Years."

Walt Meyer—I value his keen insight and still can't believe some of the salient statistical research he conducted.

Wendy Parker—She has honed a witty and well-informed writing style that helps individuals such as myself to shed our male basketball chauvinism. In Wendy's whirlwind way, she consistently captures how the ladies have improved immeasurably this decade while the men's game has suffered from inattention to fundamentals such as competent free-throw shooting. The team-oriented women look for passing angles while many self-indulging men look for camera angles to display individualistic "flashdance" routines.

Patrick Premo—A Naismith Memorial Basketball Hall of Fame recommendation proved accurate as Patrick supplied invaluable perspective of teams playing the first half of this century with pre-wire service national polls.

I'm also indebted to college sports information directors from across the country for providing the vast majority of the photographs and title team statistics.

Of course, Christopher Scanlon, editor, Michelle Dimercurio, art director, Wendy Blurton, production, and the other folks at Visible Ink Press have my genuine respect for allowing the creativity to deviate somewhat from traditional encyclopedia-like volumes yet providing a necessary focus to keep me from going off on too many tangents. I believe the end result is an exceptional reader-friendly edition. And a special thanks to Roger Janecke, special markets manager at Visible Ink and *Inside Sports* Magazine editor Ken Leiker, publisher Jerry Croft, and Vice President of Everything Else, Howard Fisher, for their help and continued support.

1

THE EARLY YEARS:

1891–1937

As the well-worn legend goes, James Naismith, a young physical education instructor at the YMCA's School for Christian Workers in Springfield, Massachusetts, invented the game of basketball in 1891 to relieve boredom in his winter gym classes.

The school in Springfield trained its students to become managers in the YMCA's network of health clubs around the world. Every winter, the students grew weary of the routine of gymnastics and calisthenics used in their "physical training." They often complained bitterly. In the fall of 1891, the mood seemed nastier than usual, and two instructors had quit rather than deal with the headache. Naismith announced at a faculty meeting that he would take on the problem. He said the students needed an indoors game, one they could learn easily and play in the gym by artificial light.

At first Naismith tried a combination of soccer, lacrosse, and football, but it was too rough. He turned to other options but none worked. "I tried all games that seemed to offer any hope, and studied each one," he later explained in a letter to a friend, "but kept the idea of lacrosse always in mind."

Then, Naismith recalled a childhood game, "Duck on a Rock," where the players attempted to knock a larger, melon-sized rock off a boulder by throwing smaller rocks at it. There seemed to be something to that concept. Plus, he remembered how a rugby team he once played on spent winter days indoors throwing rugby balls into a box.

So he tinkered with a new idea. In late December of 1891 he gave the idea a try, and posted the rules on a bulletin board outside the gym. He first envisioned a game where the players would attempt to throw a soccer ball into a box suspended above the gym floor. But the school janitor, Pops Stebbins, couldn't find any boxes, so he brought Naismith two peach baskets. The railing around the school gym happened to be 10 feet off the floor, so the baskets were set at that height. And because his class held 18 students, Naismith divided them into nine on a side.

"The first words were not very encouraging, when one of the class made the remark, 'Humph, a new game,'" Naismith recalled. "I asked the boys to try it once as a favor to me. They started, and after the ball was first thrown up there was no need of further coaxing."

Naismith's Game Is a Hit

The elements meshed together rather loosely, but all in all the effort was a rousing success. The first hoopsters had been bitten by the bug. One student even suggested that the instructor label the new game "Naismith ball," which Naismith rejected. The student, Frank Mahon, then offered another suggestion "basket ball."

It wasn't long before lunchtime crowds began gathering to watch the frenetic action of "basket ball" in Naismith's class. It was an awkward game with two teams of nine students attempting to heave a soccer ball into peach baskets suspended 10 feet above the gym floor. But even in its rudimentary stage, it held a peculiar magic. It was fun to play and, almost as important, fun to watch. Basketball rather quickly became a spectator sport. Aided by the YMCA's missionary nature and its network of centers, Naismith's invention soon spread.

On February 12, 1892, the central and Armory Hill branches of the Springfield YMCA staged a boys game that drew a crowd of 100 or so and resulted in a 2-2 tie. "The game is a very pretty one to watch," reported the *Springfield Daily Republican.*

By March 12, Naismith's idea was refined enough to weather another public display. The school's faculty took on the students in a game that drew 200 spectators. The students won, 5-1, and Amos Alonzo Stagg, who would go on to fame coaching college football, scored the faculty's only goal. "The most conspicuous figure on the floor was Stagg in the blue Yale uniform, who managed to have a hand in every scrimmage," the

James Naismith: The father of basketball.

Republican reported. "His football training hampered him and he was perpetually making fouls by shoving his opponents."

Later that same month, Naismith took a team on a tour of exhibition games in Troy, Albany, and Schenectady, New York, and Newport and Providence, Rhode Island. In April, the Brooklyn YMCA was playing games against other New York branches.

Something of a fad, the game was on its way to rapid distribution. Its popularity among YMCA members and high school athletes grew from there. By the winter of 1893-94, the YMCA in Hartford, Connecticut, had organized a five-team league. The public was invited in to see the games. No admission was charged, except 10 cents for reserved seats. By the end of the winter, more than 10,000 spectators had come to watch the action and the YMCA had collected a $250 profit.

Soon, athletic clubs and high schools took up basketball; then the colleges followed. Women, too, were soon won over by the new game's charm. And before long, "professionals" were attempting to make a few dollars on weekends playing on courts enclosed by wire cages (thus, early basketballers were called "cagers"). By the turn of the century, barnstorming pro teams playing in small Northeastern cities were drawing a few hundred paying fans.

But the real growth in popularity came with the college sport. The early 20th century brought a refinement of rules, and by the 1920s, promoters found they could earn a tidy profit staging college games, the only problem being that the crowds demanded more action and less stalling and fouling and free-throw shooting. The rules makers eventually complied, and the sport bounced along toward a new level of popularity. In 1938 and 1939, with the founding of the National Invitation and the National Collegiate Athletic Association tournaments, basketball found a format that would open the way to mass appeal.

Yet much of the success of the modern game can be traced to the sport's early decades, a fasci-

THE FIRST RULES On January 15, 1892, James Naismith's "basket ball" rules were printed in the Springfield (Mass.) YMCA School for Christian Workers newspaper, the *Triangle*. They read as follows:

1. The ball may be thrown in any direction with one or both hands.

2. The ball may be batted in any direction with one or both hands (never with the fist).

3. A player cannot run with the ball. The player must throw it from the spot on which he catches it; allowance to be made for a man who catches the ball when running at a good speed.

4. The ball must be held in or between the hands; the arms or body must not be used for holding it.

5. No shouldering, holding, pushing, tripping or striking, in any way the person of an opponent shall be allowed; the first infringement of this rule by any person shall count as a foul, the second shall disqualify him until the next goal is made; or, if there was evident intent to injure the person for the whole of the game, no substitute shall be allowed.

6. A foul is striking at the ball with the fist, violation of Rules 3, 4, and such as described in Rule 5.

7. If either side makes three consecutive fouls, it shall count a goal for the opponents. (Consecutive means without the opponents in the meantime making a foul.)

8. A goal shall be made when the ball is thrown or batted from the ground into the basket and stays there, providing those defending the goal do not touch or disturb the goal. If the ball rests on the edge and the opponent moves the basket, it shall count as a goal.

9. When the ball goes out of bounds, it shall be thrown into the field and played by the person first touching it. In case of a dispute, the umpire shall throw it straight into the field. The thrower-in is allowed five seconds. If he holds it longer, it shall go to the opponent. If any side persists in delaying the game, the umpire shall call a foul on them.

10. The umpire shall be the judge of the men and shall note the fouls and notify the referee when three consecutive fouls have been made. He shall have power to disqualify men according to Rule 5.

11. The referee shall be the judge of the ball and shall decide when the ball is in play, in bounds, to which side it belongs, and shall keep the time. He shall decide when a goal has been made, and keep account of the goals, with any other duties that are usually performed by a referee.

12. The time shall be two fifteen minute halves, with five minutes rest between.

13. The side making the most goals in that time shall be declared the winners. In case of a draw, the game may, by agreement of the captains, be continued until another goal is made.

nating time, complete with strange stories, hot competition, and constantly changing rules.

The New Century

Basketball was born in a time of bicycles and penny arcades and Sunday school picnics. Women wore corsets and full skirts; men sported straw hats, slightly tilted. Community brass bands were a favorite. "There'll Be a Hot Time in the Old Town Tonight" was the hit song. Yet all around there were signs of change in 1891. The newly invented wonders of the world were the trolley car and electric elevator. Ragtime music marked America's quickening, nervous rhythm.

To fill leisure time brought on by industrialization, people hungered for more diversion, and sports provided cheap, quick alternatives. In the spring and summer, they had baseball, and in the fall they had the newfangled game of football. But winters were the dark ages, until quite suddenly in 1891, Naismith introduced some light.

Seemingly overnight, basketball was being played in every YMCA in America.

"It is doubtful if the history of competitive games contains an example of more rapid growth than that shown by basket ball during the first two or three years of its existence," wrote Dr. Joseph E. Raycroft, the coach of the University of Chicago's great early teams. "Even the remarkable spread of baseball in the years immediately following the Civil War was second to this."

Basketball fit just the need for a rigorous indoor game, plus it had the evangelistic fervor of "muscular Christianity" on its side. From Naismith's first class, one student introduced the game in India; another took it to China, and another to Japan. Everywhere the YMCA reached, basketball touched the population. And through students who belonged to YMCAs, the sport eventually worked its way into the colleges. In 1893, W. O. Black left the YMCA's school in Springfield

RULES CHANGES DURING THE EARLY YEARS

1895: The free-throw line is moved from 20 feet to 15.

1896: A field goal changes from three to two points, and free throws from three points to one point.

1897: Backboards are first installed.

1901: A dribbler cannot shoot for a field goal and may dribble only once, and then with two hands.

1909: A dribbler is permitted to shoot. The double dribble is made illegal.

1911: Players are disqualified upon committing their fourth personal foul. No coaching is permitted during the progress of a game by anybody connected with their team. A warning is given for the first violation and a free throw is awarded after that.

1914: The bottom of the net is left open.

1915: College, YMCA, and AAU rules are made the same for the first time.

1921: A player is permitted to reenter the game once. Previously, a player could not reenter for the remainder of the game if he exited the contest. Backboards are moved two feet from the wall of the court. Previously, players would "climb" up the padded wall to sink baskets.

1922: Running with the ball changes from a foul to a violation.

1924: A fouled player must shoot his own free throws. Previously, one person usually shot all of his team's foul shots.

1929: The charging foul is introduced.

1931: A "held ball" can be assessed when a closely guarded player is keeping the ball from play for five seconds. The result will be a jump ball.

1933: The 10-second center line is introduced to de-emphasize stalling.

1934: A player is permitted to reenter a game twice.

1936: No offensive player can remain in the free-throw lane, with or without the ball, for longer than three seconds. Following a successful free throw, the team scored upon shall put the ball in play at the end of the court where the goal was scored.

and took the game to Stanford University. A classmate, W. H. Anderson, introduced basketball at Yale. Another Springfield alumnus, Charles Bemus, reportedly started a team at little Geneva College in Pennsylvania as early as 1892. The University of Toronto and Vanderbilt University also reportedly had teams as early as 1893. That same year Amos Alonzo Stagg left Springfield and went to the University of Chicago, where he founded a team in 1894 that played a seven-game schedule against local athletic clubs. Early written accounts indicate that during 1894 students at Yale and Cornell formed teams to play against New England athletic clubs. Temple University, Ohio

State University, and Haverford College all started teams shortly thereafter.

The First College Game?

In February of 1895, a team from the Minnesota School of Agriculture and Mining beat Hamline College, 9-3, in what is generally considered the first game between two college teams. Each side, however, played nine players at a time. A month later, a Haverford College team beat Temple, 6-4. In 1896, Stagg's Chicago team defeated a YMCA team composed of University of Iowa students, 15-12, in a game that featured five men on a side. But Penn athletic director Ralph Morgan claimed the first real intercollegiate game occurred when Yale defeated Penn, 32-10, in 1897.

As it had for early football, Yale played a large role in the development of basketball. It was there that the five-man game found its footing, and there that the dribble gained popularity as both a defensive and offensive weapon.

"Yale continued to put a team on the floor in 1898, 1899 and 1900," Morgan wrote, "but no college team was again met until 1899, when Yale played and defeated Cornell in Poughkeepsie, N.Y., by the score of 49-7. In 1900, Yale took a Western trip and played, among other teams, Ohio State and Wisconsin."

Morgan's opinion that Yale and Penn played the first intercollegiate game may reflect an Eastern bias because historians have found it difficult to determine exactly who played the first game. After a time, it mattered little anyway. Each passing season brought more schools into the fold. After all, basketball was the new game for the new age. Its rapid pace appealed to the young.

"In playing it comes the joy of a quickened pulse and fast-working lungs, the health-giving exercise to all our muscles, the forgetting of all troubles," wrote an elated Southerner in 1902. "There is no game which requires more wind or endurance nor which needs greater agility and deftness."

Despite the game's appeal, a large number of colleges still had no team, leaving basketball to

those schools that had gymnasiums. Other colleges, eager to begin the sport, played their games outdoors. Hiram College won an exhibition tournament played outdoors at the 1904 Olympic games in St. Louis. Some colleges continued outdoor competition well into the next decade, and international competition would retain that format even longer.

Some traditionally strong football teams, such as Harvard and Princeton, couldn't seem to get the knack of the new game. Others found almost instant success. The University of Nebraska started a team and created an early dynasty of sorts by closing out the century with 19 wins in a row from 1898-1900. Notre Dame, the most recognized football power in college history, has an unusual historical footnote involving its first basketball captain, John Shillington. Most people know that the sinking of the *Maine* led to the United States' involvement in the Spanish-American War. Few, however, know that Shillington was among those who went down with the ship in the Havana harbor on February 15, 1898. A monument to him—a mounted shell taken from the sunken ship—was erected in front of Brownson Hall, his last home on Notre Dame's campus.

Rules Made to Order

The more colleges became involved in basketball, the more they wanted to have a say in the rules, a situation that grew increasingly awkward early in the new century. The YMCA and the Athletic Amateur Union (AAU) had run the rules committee together, but this arrangement didn't last long. The AAU forbade Yale to play during the 1904-5 season because it was an "unregistered" team, but the school persisted anyway. The AAU then told Penn that it, too, would lose official sanction if it played a scheduled game against Yale. Penn athletic director Ralph Morgan, then still an undergraduate, was angered by the AAU's position and called a series of meetings in 1905, leading to the formation of the Intercollegiate Athletic Association, the forerunner of the NCAA, and the establishing of a separate set of college rules. Soon afterward, college and AAU officials made peace and began meeting to discuss the rules of their respective games, but they would not merge as a joint rules organization until 1915.

This organizing of the college game helped bring a surge of growth. In 1905, there were an estimated 88 colleges engaged in basketball, with the bulk of them in Pennsylvania, New York, and Ohio. By 1914, these ranks had swelled to 366, with substantial growth in Illinois, Indiana, Iowa, Kansas, Michigan, Minnesota, Missouri, Virginia, and Wisconsin.

This overwhelming acceptance left basketball's earliest promoters both amazed and proud. "More men and boys are playing Basket Ball than are playing any organized sport in America, with the exception of baseball," declared the YMCA's Dr. Luther Gulick in the 1908-9 issue of *Spalding's Guide,* the sport's early yearbook. "It has become the American indoor game."

But, as *Spalding's* editors explained, there simply weren't enough qualified and seasoned officials to keep up with the pace of expansion. Other difficulties stemmed from the evolution of the rules. Drastic changes were made yearly, requiring officials to have the skills of a lawyer to keep pace.

"During 1908, 1909 and 1910, considerable criticism of the game was made, principally from New England, where President (Charles) Eliot of Harvard was a particular foe," wrote Ralph Morgan in 1914. One player acquired 15 fouls in a game against Harvard, which hastened Eliot's complaints. The criticism was answered with a series of revisions, but not to Eliot's liking. Declaring that "basket ball has become even more brutal than football," Eliot barred the sport at Harvard in 1909. In its official reasoning, the university stated, "The games more closely resembled free fights than friendly athletic contests between amateur teams."

Opponents of Harvard's action suggested the school was merely frustrated by a poor record. But such criticism hastened the sport away from unnecessary roughness. There was little question that Eastern basketball had developed a reputation for forwards who powered and shoved their way near the goal for a score. There was no three-second violation in those days, which left the floor open to sumo-style struggles underneath the hoop.

To counteract the criticism, the rules committee in 1909-10 rescinded its 1908 five-foul rule. Instead, players would be disqualified after four fouls, which reduced the violence somewhat. Some areas of the country even saw the addition of a second referee in 1910.

Playing style was another factor in moving basketball away from brutishness. Observers were already noting the different styles Western teams played. The Mississippi Valley style focused on solid defense, fast-breaking offense and one-handed shots, wrote E. P. O'Neill in the 1906-7 *Spalding's Guide*. "Long, swift passes replace excessive footwork, and the forwards depend on backward one-foot pivots and one-handed throws for shots at goal rather than numerous passes to obtain an unguarded throw. A one-handed shot is more inaccurate than a two-handed shot, but it is not to be guarded without a foul."

Another help in alleviating the inside struggle was the development of the outside shooter. The early game featured forwards and centers as the big scorers, until players such as 5-4 guard Barney Sedran came along. He led City College of New York in scoring from 1909 to 1911. The first of the great set shooters, Sedran would heave 20- and 30-footers into goals without backboards, a skill that carried him on to a celebrated professional career.

Bucknell's John Anderson, one of few players to score 50 or more points in a game until George Mikan in 1945, had 80 vs. Philadelphia College of Pharmacy in 1903. No team averaged at least 80 points in a season until 1952.

East Meets West

Perhaps the most important development in the college game was the founding of leagues or conferences. That brought organization and scheduling to the competition. More important, the leagues began setting up training classes for officials.

In May 1901, several schools, including Yale, Harvard, Trinity, Holy Cross, Amherst, and Williams, formed the New England Intercollegiate Basketball League. However, Yale and Harvard dropped out later that year to join the newly formed Eastern Intercollegiate League, the fore-runner of the Ivy League. The New England League lasted just one season before folding.

The formation of leagues added a new element of competitiveness to college basketball, setting up the potential for intersectional rivalries. This potential was realized in 1905 when teams from the universities of Wisconsin and Minnesota barnstormed east to take on Columbia, the undefeated champion of the Eastern League.

Emmett Angell coached Wisconsin; his team featured Christian Steinmetz, the first college player to score one thousand points (1903-5), and Bob Zuppke, who would go on to fame as a college football coach. Steinmetz had gained notoriety by scoring what then was the incredible total of 44 points in an 80-10 win over Beloit. In 1905, he would score 50 points in another game. But even his firepower didn't help on the Eastern road trip. The Badgers "played a number of minor games on their trip from the West," reported the 1905-6 edition of *Spalding's*, "and consequently were in excellent condition when they met the Columbia University Five in New York City. As had been predicted by the Eastern critics, the Westerners could not cope with the accurate passing and shooting, or the speedy play of the Blue and White Five, and were handily defeated by the respective scores of 21-15 and 27-15. The victories in these two contests and the winning of the championship of the Eastern colleges gives Columbia the undisputed title of "Intercollegiate Champions of the United States."

If nothing else, the games reflected just how differently the regions approached the game. "Western" teams were used to closely called games, while the Eastern players were glad to mix it up.

"The Minnesota and Wisconsin men played in the style prevalent among most of the girl colleges in the East, that is, the 'no contact' game," sneered Yale's W. C. Hyatt.

Such pettiness aside, Steinmetz was named to the Naismith Memorial Basketball Hall of Fame in 1961. He scored 462 points in a single season, an amazing total in the early years. Harry Fisher,

Columbia's leading scorer between 1902 and 1905, was elected to the Hall of Fame in 1973. He scored 13 field goals in a game in 1905, a collegiate record that stood for 45 years. After college, Fisher went on to an esteemed coaching career at Columbia and Army.

Early Conferences

In the 1905-6 season, the big schools of the Midwest met in Chicago to form the "Western Conference," the forerunner of the Big Ten. Members included the universities of Chicago, Minnesota, Wisconsin, Illinois, and Purdue. Similar alliances appeared around the country. The Southern Intercollegiate Athletic Association, featuring Georgia Tech, Auburn, Howard College, Tulane, Vanderbilt, and the University of Georgia, formed for the 1905-6 season and entertained Yale's Southern tour.

The 1908-9 season brought two more major conferences plus the expansion of the Western with Indiana, Iowa, and Northwestern joining the league. The Missouri Valley Conference formed two divisions, with Kansas, Missouri, and Washington College in the Southern and Nebraska, Ames (Iowa State), and Drake in the Northern.

The Northwest College Conference formed that same season (1908-9) with Oregon Agricultural (Oregon State), Whitman College, Washington State, and the University of Idaho. The next season, the universities of Washington and Oregon also joined the group.

The top program in basketball during the era was the University of Chicago, which compiled a 78-12 record from 1900 to 1909. Chicago's best player was 6-3 center John Schommer, who led the Western League in scoring for three years, averaging just over 10 points per game. A three-time Helms Foundation All-American, he was selected national player of the year in 1909 and would become known in later life for inventing the modern backboard.

"Head and shoulders above all players in the league" is how Wisconsin great Chris Steinmetz described Schommer, who, according to *Spald-*

ing's, had all the assets of a great center—speed, strength, reach, and size. Plus, he could shoot and never loafed on defense, Steinmetz said.

In the backcourt, Chicago had H. O. "Pat" Page, a quick guard and two-time All-American who went on to coaching fame at both Chicago and Butler. Page was named national player of the year in 1910.

Chicago was also one of the first colleges to have a paid coach, Dr. Joseph E. Raycroft. The combination of a paid coach, quick guard, and star center carried Chicago to a 21-2 record and the "national" championship in 1908. But before claiming national honors, Chicago had to battle the University of Wisconsin in Madison before a crowd of 1,500 for the Western title. Chicago won on a last-minute shot by Page, 18-16. The prize was a berth in a two-game playoff with the Eastern champion, Penn. At 8-0, Penn was projected by basketball's Eastern establishment to be the favorite.

But Chicago beat Penn in a two-game series. Although his team lost, Penn's all-conference forward Charles Keinath dazzled a *Spalding's* writer, who reported "his dribbling electrified the crowd, many of whom before had never seen such fancy footwork."

Other conferences, particularly the resuscitated New England League, scoffed that a playoff between two leagues hardly amounted to a national championship. With college leagues springing up in every region of the country, schools were tiring of the Eastern bias. With the help of the New York newspapers, the Eastern League pretentiously announced an "All-America" team each year featuring only Eastern players.

Still, the college game was young and already thirsting to declare a national champion. "The 1908 series had a very good effect on basket ball," declared *Spalding's,* "and the contending teams showed tremendous crowds in Philadelphia and Chicago what a good, wholesome, sportsmanlike game basket ball is."

Chicago finished the 1908-9 season undefeated at 12-0, but despite a clamoring for a championship match against Columbia, the Eastern champion, none could be scheduled. Instead, *Spalding's* listed the various regional league champions, including Georgetown in the Southern, Kansas in the Middle West, Oregon Agriculture in the Northwest, and Williams in New England. The no-championship stalemate would remain for many seasons. Chicago won the Western and Columbia the Eastern again in 1910, but no national championship series between the two leagues could be scheduled.

"The question of intercollegiate supremacy arose, bringing in its wake volumes of idle words, footless arguments and bootless discussions," wrote Oswald Tower, a member of the rules committee, in 1910, "and when all was said and done, no impartial critic could say with any certainty that the best team of this section was better than the best team of any other section."

Great Teams Emerge

The first decade of the new century brought a stunning evolution in basketball. Several teams emerged as powerhouses. Joining the ranks of prominent winners were Dayton, Oregon State, Michigan State, Montana, and Wisconsin. Minnesota won a whopping 107 games during the period.

The next 10 years brought the rise of the Naval Academy with a record of 109-9 from 1910-19, a .924 winning percentage. The University of Texas won 102 games during that period, including a 44-game winning streak beginning in 1913. Other big winners included Virginia, Creighton, California, Virginia Polytechnic, Wisconsin, Illinois, Texas A&M, Kansas State, Syracuse, and numerous other schools.

Despite the flowering of these regional college basketball cultures, the establishment of an annual national champion was further complicated by the difficulties of travel and changes in rules and equipment. Some teams played outdoors. Some used old rules, some new. The official joining of the YMCA, NCAA, and AAU in a rules

committee in 1915 helped, but the question of a national champion remained cloudy. Some teams took turns trumpeting their greatness through friendly newspaper editors. Other college teams entered the national AAU competition, hoping that the national title there would stand as evidence that they were the best.

Allen and the Rise of Coaches

The 1908-10 seasons marked a major turning point for the college game. Glass backboards were allowed; out-of-bounds rules were firmed up to eliminate the mad scrambles for the ball out of play; traveling rules were tightened to allow the ball handler only one step; and the double dribble was eliminated.

Despite complaints about roughness, the game was opening up. James Naismith, who had since obtained his degree in medicine and retreated to the faculty at the University of Kansas where he coached that school's team for nine seasons, was particularly pleased with the effect dribbling had on the game.

"The restoration of the dribble has made the game more enjoyable from the standpoint of the spectators as well as the players," he observed. "It has done away with some of the negative features and helped make the game cleaner. This is especially true on large floors, for the chief cause of the roughness was the attempt of the guard to prevent the player with the ball from getting a good, clean throw, and as the player was unable to move, he was unmercifully crowded, and this individual crowding was so evident to the spectators that it made it appear as if the game was exceedingly rough. But with the dribble, if there is no one to whom a player can pass, he can get away from the crowding. The dribble gives the opportunity for the exhibition of skill of the highest order, and spectators show their appreciation of this by bursts of applause that greet the performance of some favorite expert."

With its early success, the college game was beginning to show tinges of commerce. Many programs found they could be self-supporting, even

CANN'S CAN

NYU coach Howard Cann led his alma mater to the 1920 AAU championship. He was an all-around athlete who participated in the 1920 Olympic Games in Antwerp, Belgium, placing eighth in the shot put.

He and his brother, Ted Cann, also a NYU alumnus, were the first members of the same family ever chosen for the U.S. Olympic team. In 1920, Ted, a Medal of Honor winner in World War I, set three world records and won three national championships in different distances in swimming. Unfortunately, Ted was in a serious automobile accident prior to the Olympics and had to drop off the U.S. squad.

profitable, from ticket sales alone. Dr. Raycroft, Chicago's paid coach, created a stir when he accepted a similar job at Princeton because that school, eager for a winning, big-time program, made him a better offer.

From the game's earliest days, Naismith had believed coaches were unnecessary. "The game isn't meant to be coached; it's meant to be played," he said. But experience proved him wrong. Naismith coached with a philosophy of letting his players play. To this date, he is the only coach in Kansas history with a losing career record.

As schools became more competitive, they wanted men who could make them winners. Yale hired its first professional coach in 1907. About that time Naismith learned what effect a good coach could have. An undergraduate named Forrest "Phog" Allen coached Baker University to an undefeated season, including wins over Kansas and Missouri. Naismith agreed to turn the Kansas coaching job over to Allen for 1907-8. That season Allen coached both Baker and Kansas, and the following season, 1908-9, he added the coaching job at Haskell Institute to his duties. Over two busy seasons, Allen won 116 games. Kansas alone went to a 26-3 record under the young coach in 1908-9 and won the Missouri Valley Conference championship.

Allen earned his medical degree over the next four years at the Kansas City School of Osteopathy, then returned to coaching at Warrensburg Teachers College, where he ran up a 107-7 record and won seven Missouri College Conference championships in seven years. He then returned to Kansas and compiled a career record of 746-233, a .768 winning percentage, good enough for fourth on the all-time list of winningest college coaches.

An autocratic man, Allen pushed college basketball toward the concepts of recruiting and professionalism. Naismith, of course, opposed these things, believing instead in the supremacy of amateurism. He supported the notion of basketball for the fun of it. He and Allen often disagreed over rule changes, but the two men worked together amicably on the Kansas campus for a number of years.

Something of a self-promoter, Allen fancied himself as a "father of basketball coaches." His innovations included a blending of man-to-man and zone defenses, what he called a man defense "with zone principle." His teams ran the standard pattern offense, but Allen believed deeply that the formula for victory in basketball was coaching strategy. His record suggests that he knew what he was talking about.

There were several other excellent coaches in college basketball's formative era. Among them were:

Doc Meanwell: He never played basketball but became one of the early game's most innovative coaches. Meanwell received his medical degree from the University of Maryland in 1909, and became interested in the game while teaching it to children in Baltimore's slums. He became the coach at the University of Wisconsin in 1911 and earned a doctorate in public health there in 1915. In 20 years at Wisconsin and two at the University of Missouri, he won 290 games and six conference titles. He also helped direct the development of the valve-free, hidden-lace ball. As a coach, he believed fiercely that, using the short pass in a pattern offense, a team could work for the right shot.

His teams were patient and ran up a 44-1 record in his first three years at Wisconsin. He disdained the dribble and taught tight, tight defense.

Cam Henderson: He coached at two West Virginia colleges, Davis & Elkins first, then at Marshall. From about 1916 to 1930, the standing zone was the defense that ruled college basketball. Henderson's teams played it so well that other coaches copied his innovations. His 611 career victories still rank him among the all-time winningest college coaches.

Doc Carlson: He earned his medical degree at the University of Pittsburgh in 1920, then became basketball coach there in 1922. Carlson invented the "Figure 8" offense and directed two Pitt teams (1928 and 1930) to the mythical national championship. He won 371 games in 31 years at Pitt. Known as one of early basketball's more colorful figures, he was never too consumed with a game to carry on with spectators. A fan in Morgantown, West Virginia, once dumped a bucket of water on Carlson, after the coach continually complained of bad officiating by saying, "This burns me up."

The Fans Arrive

The college game got a glimpse at its future in 1920 when 10,000 fans packed the 168th Street Regimental Armory in New York to see a tournament featuring City College of New York and New York University. The rival New York teams were off to big seasons, and just like that, entrepreneurs saw where the money was. Instead of the usual 1,500 to 2,000 spectators (NYU didn't have a gym and played some games on a Hudson River barge), the game was standing room only. Led by star (and future college coaching legend) Howard Cann, NYU won 39-21 and went on to capture the national AAU title in Atlanta later in the year.

The game helped show college basketball its future—big crowds. The 1920s brought the construction of numerous arenas, many of them in the Midwest. The University of Iowa, for example, built a 16,000-seat facility.

The decade brought more good teams. Montana State led the charge, winning 213 games against 44 defeats between 1920 and 1929. Army, Navy, North Carolina, Cal, Creighton, Oklahoma, Penn State, and CCNY all produced excellent teams.

At Kansas, Phog Allen won six Missouri Valley conference championships in the 1920s, leading Kansas partisans to claim at least two national championships. In 1928, Pittsburgh went 21-0. The Panthers were led by forward Chuck Hyatt and guard Sykes Reed. Hyatt, a three-time college All-American, led the nation in scoring his senior year, 1929-30, and Pitt again earned top rankings with a 23-2 season. During his career, Pitt rang up a 60-7 record. He went on to become an AAU All-American, playing nine seasons for the Phillips 66 Oilers.

Other great players of the 1920s included:

Paul Endacott: Named Helms Foundation Player of the Year in 1923, Endacott was the heart of Phog Allen's undefeated 1923 Kansas team. In 1924, Dr. Naismith declared Endacott the best ever at Kansas. A quarter century later, the appraisals were still high. Allen named him to the national All-Time College Team.

Victor A. Hanson: A three-time All-American for Syracuse, 1925-27, Hanson led the

Orangemen to a 48-7 record during his college career and the 1925-26 national championship. He was named national player of the year in 1927, and Grantland Rice named him to the All-Time All-American team in 1952. Hanson played pro basketball with the Cleveland Rosenblums and organized baseball in the New York Yankees' organization. He even coached football at Syracuse from 1930 to 1936 (see Chapter 9).

Branch McCracken: Led Indiana to basketball prominence in the late 1920s. An All-Big Ten selection three years running, he set the conference scoring record his senior year and was named All-American. He later coached the Hoosiers to national championships in 1940 and 1953.

John Roosma: A key player on the great Passaic (N.J.) High School "Wonder Team," Roosma went on to play at the U.S. Military Academy, where he led the Cadets to 33 consecutive wins and an undefeated season. Over three years, he carried Army to a 70-3 record. Later he achieved the rank of colonel in the Army.

Charles Murphy: He led his high school team to the Indiana state title in 1926, then went on to two-time All-America honors at Purdue.

Forrest S. DeBernardi: He scored 50 points in a game for Westminster College in 1920, then went on to become an AAU All-American in 1921, 1922, and 1923. He played three different positions and earned All-American honors at each of them.

John A. "Cat" Thompson: The player largely responsible for Montana State's great success in the 1920s, Thompson was named Helms Foundation player of the year in 1929. During his career, Montana State compiled a 72-4 record. Thompson scored 1,539 points in three years of college play, astronomical numbers for the era.

Harold "Bud" Foster: One of Doc Meanwell's key charges at Wisconsin, Foster led the Badgers to the Western Conference championship in 1929 and was named All-American in 1930.

Early Integration and African-American Teams

African Americans took up basketball shortly after the game's invention, and by the turn of the century were beginning to gain limited prominence. By 1906, black athletic clubs in Brooklyn, New Jersey, and New York had begun sponsoring teams. Soon college programs followed. By 1910, Lincoln University, Howard University, Hampton Institute, and Union University entered the competition.

The 1920s brought limited integration of some college teams. At Columbia, sophomore George Gregory gained notoriety as the All-Eastern Conference center for 1928-29. Described in *Spalding's* as "the tall colored boy who played center" and as "the graceful Columbia center," Gregory ranked fourth in the conference in scoring and second in free throws made.

Penn athletic director Ralph Morgan wrote, "Gregory had height; he got the tap; he was fast and could shoot. The coaches were clearly right when they selected him (to the all-conference team)."

That same season Western Illinois State Teacher's College had two black players, one of whom, a guard named Page, was selected all-conference. For 1928-29, Southern Cal, the Brooklyn College of Pharmacy, and the Columbia College of Pharmacy teams all had an African-American player.

High school and junior high teams in Pennsylvania showed extensive integration in 1928-29. Elsewhere, from Yankton, South Dakota to Peoria, Illinois, to Warwick, New York, incidents of integration were isolated. But they eventually helped break down the sturdy racial barriers in the college game. In the 1920s, 1930s, and 1940s, noted African-American players began to appear, including Paul Robeson (the future actor and pro football player) at Rutgers, Wilbur Woods at Nebraska, Sadat Singh at Syracuse, and Dolly King at Long Island University.

The Last Great Dribble Debate

Basketball seemed to be heading briskly toward its future in the late 1920s, but it paused in 1927 and flirted briefly with the past. Urged on by Wisconsin's Doc Meanwell, who loved the notion of moving the ball only with the short pass, the Joint Rules Committee voted 9-8 to eliminate the dribble. The committee then adjourned to watch the Original Celtics use the passing game to whip the Cleveland Rosenblums for the professional championship. After the game, the committee reconvened, and Meanwell further praised the passing game. But Nat Holman, a member of the Celtics who also coached at CCNY, urged a reconsideration. College players, he argued passionately, were not pros and needed the dribble to maneuver. Upon hearing Holman, the committee voted to keep the dribble in college basketball.

Surviving this threat, the college game was up and running—or off and bouncing—with its big games drawing big crowds. Unknown to many, its greatest legend was already afoot. John Wooden, a quietly determined young guard, had entered Purdue after playing on a high school state championship team in Martinsville, Indiana.

Star Purdue guard and future UCLA coaching legend John Wooden.

The City Game and the Wonder Five

The moment that college basketball hit the big time isn't exactly clear, but there is little doubt as to the location. The game had kept New York City in its grip since Naismith invented it. Basketball was just the sport to suit Gotham's aggressive nature; it spread quickly across the boroughs, through the YMCAs and athletic clubs. Goals and dirt courts soon appeared on playgrounds around the city, and the neighborhoods came alive with this new competition. Basketball hadn't been born to New Yorkers, but they adopted it as their own.

These feelings only deepened with time. As the game moved into the colleges, the whole city seemed to burn with interest. First came Columbia's big success in 1905. Then dawned the age of "professional" coaches, and New York got its share. Nat Holman, the playmaker for New York's

NO MEXICAN SIESTA

Wichita won most of its games in three years of Mexican tours in the early 1930s. The Mexicans, however, employed a new innovation.

"They chased us all over the floor and upset us so badly," Wichita coach Gene Johnson told The Wichita Eagle-Beacon. "I said, 'If a bunch of punks like those Mexicans can drive us crazy doing that, what can we do if we adapt it with some safety measures?'"

A couple of adjustments later and Johnson had pioneered full-court defensive pressure. In those days, they called it "fire department" basketball and labeled Johnson "a renegade."

But the pressure, most often used in a 2-2-1 zone press, usually worked. Johnson became an assistant coach for the first U.S. Olympic basketball team in 1936. "I sort of feel like I invented the modern game," he said three years before his death in 1989.

Original Celtics, started at City College of New York in 1919 while still playing pro ball. Ed Kelleher took the coaching job at Fordham in 1922, and Howard Cann went to work at NYU a year later. St. John's hired Buck Freeman, and Lew Andreas took over at upstate Syracuse. Each of these coaches built winning programs, and that in turn built excitement. Within a matter of years, games in small college gyms were packed with 1,500 fans craning their necks for a view of the floor.

The more crowded the games, the more obvious it became that the sport was bursting at the seams. On January 1, 1927, the Palestra opened in Philadelphia, and soon 10,000 spectators crowded inside to see Penn play Princeton. "The Palestra (built for the princely sum of $750,000) was constructed for basketball," wrote Penn's Ralph Morgan.

College basketball, the business, was waiting to be born. All it needed was someone to slap it on the fanny and make it breathe. That someone was a Penn undergraduate, Ned Irish, who witnessed the Palestra phenomenon first hand. A New Yorker, Irish had been working as a part-time sportswriter since high school, making as much as $100 a week from the local papers. When he headed off to college, the New York papers hired him to cover the Philadelphia sports scene. He also worked full time for the *Philadelphia Record*.

Irish returned to New York in 1929 as a sportswriter for the *World-Telegram* and soon made that paper the leader in college basketball coverage (most New York papers virtually ignored the game). For Irish and basketball, the timing couldn't have been better, although the first quake of the Great Depression had already struck. Clair Bee was coaching little Rider College to an 18-3 record, and Freeman had assembled "The Wonder Five" at St. John's. Maturing together for four years, from freshmen to seniors, the "Wonder Five" included 6-5 center Matty Begovich and forward Mack Posnack. The three guards were 5-8 dribble king Mac Kinsbrunner, quick-shooting Allie Schuckman, and defensive specialist Rip Gerson. Freeman packed them into a nifty, Celtics-style post game and let 'em go. In their sophomore season, 1928-29, they ran off an 18-game winning streak on their way to a 23-2 record. They opened the next season, 1929-30, with a 13-game streak, lost a few games, then closed with another run of victories.

Early in the 1930-31 season, the string had grown to 20-something games. The Redmen had grown immensely popular but still played most nights in a packed gym before 1,200 fans. Then, early in 1931, the "Wonder Five" beat CCNY at the 106th Infantry Armory with a record New York crowd of 12,000 watching. Within weeks, Mayor Jimmy Walker was calling on sportswriters to help promote a tripleheader at Madison Square Garden to benefit the Unemployment Relief Fund. Columbia, Fordham, CCNY, Manhattan, St. John's, and NYU were the draw. All had good teams and good records, and 15,000 fans paid to see them play. The Wonder Five beat CCNY again that night to push their win streak to 22. They went on to win 27 in a row and compile a four-year record of 86-8. From there, they toured two years independently, then played five years as the Jewels in the old American League. But the Wonder Five's biggest impact on basketball was the excitement they brought to the city. They had given Irish a hint of things to come.

In 1933, Mayor Walker again set up a basketball benefit, a seven-game extravaganza that attracted 20,000 fans to the Garden, which gave Irish more pause to think. According to some accounts, Irish first hatched the idea of staging big-time games one night as he tore his pants while crawling through a window of a little gym in Riverdale to cover a sold-out Manhattan College game. The next season, 1933-34, found the 28-year-old sportswriter plotting to promote a game between NYU and CCNY. He had hoped to play the game at the Garden but a conflict with a boxing match killed the deal. Still, Irish decided to move ahead with his promotional plans. He lined up six dates at the Garden for the following season.

Irish's frantic planning conflicted with his job, and he left the *World-Telegram* a month before the first event. He staked his future on a December 29 doubleheader at the Garden featuring St. John's vs. Westminster and NYU vs. Notre Dame. A sell-out crowd of 16,000 watched, and college basketball, the business, was on its way. Irish's next seven doubleheaders drew 100,000 fans, and he became a rich young man.

From New York, he branched out to Philadelphia, then Buffalo, then other venues. He made vast sums promoting college games. Soon, other promoters picked up his lead with big games from Atlanta to Boston to Chicago.

Bee's Blackbirds vs. Hank's One-Hander

In his writing, author Clair Bee created an ideal athlete, the fictional character Chip Hilton who had it all. Intelligence. Diligence. Honesty. And a nose for victory.

Bee sought to instill those same qualities in the college basketball teams he coached. For the most part, he was overwhelmingly successful. His teams lost just seven games in his seven years of coaching at Rider College. From there, he established a powerhouse at Long Island University from 1931 to 1951. Over those 18 years (Bee missed two seasons

Stanford star Hank Luisetti was best known for his one-handed shooting style.

while in the service during World War II), his teams won 95 percent of their games, including two NIT titles. LIU's record consisted of winning streaks of 43, 38, 28, and 26 games.

Bee, a small, intense man, was a gentle, scholarly sort, but he could seize on opponents' weaknesses like a mongoose. A thinking man's coach, he held five degrees and authored 44 books, including 23 Chip Hilton volumes. He created the 1-3-1 zone defense and even played a role in bringing the 24-second shot clock to pro basketball (he coached the Baltimore Bullets after leaving LIU in 1951). A native of Grafton, West Virginia, Bee overcame tuberculosis as a child, and his rehabilitation led to an intense involvement with sports.

In his third year at LIU, 1933-34, the Blackbirds finished 27-1, losing only to St. John's and scoring 1,000 points, a benchmark in those days of center jumps after each basket. The next season they ran up a 24-2 record, and suddenly Bee was the toast of New York. In 1935-36, his Blackbirds finished 26-0 with a lineup that featured Marius Russo (who later pitched for the Yankees), Willie Schwartz, Art Hillhouse, Leo Merson, and Jules Bender. Their one close call on the schedule came against Duquesne in the Garden. Down five points with four minutes to play, the Blackbirds survived on Russo's bucket at the buzzer.

LIU opened the next season on the same note, stretching their winning streak to 43 straight before running into the college game's newest sensation. He was a West Coast player, Stanford's Hank Luisetti, whose polished, running, one-handed shooting style created a stir in those days of set-shooters. Luisetti was 6-3 and handsome, which made him a hero to youngsters on the West Coast. On the East Coast, however, he was virtually unknown until Irish lured Stanford to the Garden.

An invitation from Irish to play at the Garden quickly become a status symbol in 1930s college basketball, and Stanford was definitely among the elite. Luisetti's freshman team went undefeated in 1934-35, and the next year he led Stanford to the Pacific Coast Conference championship. Luisetti's team came East in December of 1936. First, Stanford stopped off in Philadelphia to beat Temple. Then, on December 29, the Indians (called Cardinal now) met Bee's top-ranked LIU team in the Garden. Plump with confidence from their 43-game streak, the Blackbirds were the darlings of the 17,623 spectators. Luisetti didn't open the game with a flashy show of play, but it wasn't long before he wooed the crowd.

Early on, while being guarded by LIU All-American Art Hillhouse, Luisetti fired up his one-hander on the run. "I'll never forget that look on Hillhouse's face," he said years later. "He'd never seen a shot like that. When it hit, I could just see him saying, 'Boy, is this guy lucky.'"

Luisetti went on to score 15, but it was his floor game, passing, and defense that made the difference. Stanford ended LIU's streak that night, 45-31, and the Garden crowd gave Luisetti a

standing ovation when he left the floor. "It seemed Luisetti could do nothing wrong," the *New York Times* reported the next morning. "Some of his shots would have been deemed foolhardy if attempted by somebody else, but with Luisetti shooting, these were accepted by the crowd as a matter of course."

The subsequent media attention made Luisetti the darling of college basketball over the remainder of the season and the following year. Stanford traveled about the country, drawing large crowds wherever Luisetti played. And although their coaches frowned on it, schoolboys everywhere began trying to heave up Hank's one-hander.

Stanford returned to New York later that season for a game against CCNY. "I'll quit coaching if I have to teach the one-handed shot to win," declared CCNY coach Nat Holman. "Nobody can convince me that a shot predicated on a prayer is smart basketball."

If Luisetti's shots were prayers, they seemed to get answers. At one point, he popped in 13 consecutive points, and Stanford won, 45-42. The New York newspapers again trumpeted his greatness. Yet Luisetti remained an unselfish player, until finally against Duquesne in Cleveland in 1938, his teammates refused to take shots, feeding his own passes back to him. Luisetti scored 50 that night as Stanford won, 92-27.

Luisetti was twice named national player of the year and led Stanford to three consecutive Pacific titles. He left Stanford in 1938 and was offered a Hollywood deal to make a film, *Campus Confessions,* with Betty Grable. It bombed, and worse, the AAU suspended his amateur status for a season, ruling that he had profited from basketball. Luisetti returned from suspension and went on to star in AAU basketball, but he never followed up his college success with a pro career. He played service ball while in the Navy during World War II and contracted meningitis. Although he won an AAU national championship in 1951 as a coach, the illness shortened his playing career.

One of the schoolboys affected by Luisetti's example was Jim Pollard, who played at Stanford and later starred with the Minneapolis Lakers. Pollard greatly admired Luisetti: "He was a great guy to watch. He had that charisma about him that everybody liked. Because he was such a graceful ball player and such a great one everybody tried to copy the greatness he had. But Hank was not primarily a scorer. He was a great defensive ball player and an excellent passer. Everybody gives him credit for popularizing the one-hander, which he did. I admit I freely copied it because he was my hero when I was a kid.

"I got to see Hank play a number of times and even played against him frequently in the service for a couple of years. Then when I got out of the service we were going to play together in the Oakland area. I was dying to play with him. He had been hurt during the war when he got spinal meningitis. We scrimmaged about 10 minutes one day. Hank and I took the next three best ball players and just wiped them. Hank was marvelous. But he walked off the floor just like he was drunk. He was weaving; he'd lost his sense of balance. I don't think he ever got on the court again to play."

Tournament Time

Off and on since 1897, the AAU had run a national basketball tournament. The event attracted big interest in Atlanta in 1920, then settled into Kansas City for 1921 and stayed there the next 14 years. But no tournament was held in 1936, and the event moved to Denver.

Angered at the loss of the tournament, Kansas City civic leaders enlisted the help of Dr. Naismith (who was still on the faculty at Kansas) in founding a "national" tournament. The first event in Kansas City in 1937 was actually an eight-team playoff of Midwest conference champions. This tournament organization later flowered into the National Association of Intercollegiate Athletics. As such, the NAIA is credited with staging the first national collegiate tournament. Its initial champion in March 1937 was Warrensburg (later to become Central Missouri), a 45-30 winner over Washburn College. The trophy was named for Naismith's wife, Maude.

MINE EYES HAVE SEEN THE GORY

The quality of the competition might have been suspect, but the first quarter of this century supplied many of the most lopsided results in college basketball history. For instance, an unheard of feat occurred on January 23, 1907, when Dayton blanked Cedarville, 80-0.

In an era where most people believe a ponderous brand of ball was performed, here is a list of some of the obscene margins of more than 70 points:

MARGIN	WINNER	LOSER	SEASON
120	Georgia 122	S.E. Christian 2	1917-18
106	Purdue 112	Indiana State 6	1910-11
101	Texas 10	San Marcos Baptist 1	1915-16
100	California 108	Pomona American Legion 8	1921-22
96	Western Ky. 103	Adairville Independents 7	1922-23
93	Washington 100	Puget Sound 7	1920-21
91	Niagara 100	Rochester YMCA 9	1911-12
90	Niagara 105	Ellicottville YMCA 15	1911-12
88	Georgia 100	Davidson 12	1908-09
83	Texas 89	Southwest Texas 6	1918-19
80	Dayton 80	Cedarville 0	1906-07
80*	Georgia 92	Auburn 12	1912-13
79	Auburn 92	White's Business College 13	1927-28
78	Butler 92	Indiana Law School 14	1921-22
78	Colgate 90	Alfred 12	1921-22
78	Texas 92	Deaf School 14	1909-10
75	Mississippi St. 75	Brownsville Athletic Club 0	1908-09
74	Dayton 75	Lafayette 1	1912-13
74	Delaware 80	Lebanon Valley 6	1909-10
73	Texas 80	St. Edward's 7	1915-16
72	Georgia 90	Auburn 18	1916-17
72	Ottawa 80	Wichita State 8	1912-13
71	Columbus YMCA 74	Auburn 3	1913-14

*Georgia defeated Auburn twice by the same score that season.

But, as usual, the "big time" was in New York. Doubleheaders in the larger arenas meant that money was pouring into college basketball. That, in turn, meant that college teams could afford to travel. Figuring there should be a national tournament, the Metropolitan Basketball Writer's Association, a New York sportswriters group, organized the National Invitation Tournament (NIT) to close the 1937-38 season. They hoped to attract the big-name teams and players. Little did they realize they were opening college basketball's billion-dollar future.

PREMO POWER POLL The first wire-service national poll wasn't conducted until the 1948–49 season by the Associated Press. In an attempt to recognize some of the premier teams in the history of men's college basketball before that time, Patrick M. Premo, a professor of accounting at St. Bonaventure, analyzed every season since 1892–93. Not only did Premo look at each team's opponents and the final scores of each game, but he also reviewed as many of those opponents' games as possible in an attempt to derive a "strength of schedule" for each team.

In the early years, there were often no common opponents, making the evaluations of teams from different regions of the country very difficult. In addition, obtaining information on some schools in the early years was impossible in a number of cases; this accounts for why only a smattering of teams were rankable in the early years. Consequently, some subjectivity was necessary to complete Premo's analysis in reviewing the early years of the sport. Once teams began to oppose clubs outside of their geographic regions, the task of comparing squads became somewhat easier.

In order to avoid confusion, the current name for each school is cited in practically all cases. Premo does not claim that his polls are definitive. They are simply his opinion. But the Premo Power Polls provide a nostalgic trip through the early history of men's college basketball! (See the end of each season's regular-season account in Chapter 2 for the Premo Power Polls in the late 1930s and 1940s. A Premo Power Poll for best teams of each decade is also included at the end of Chapters 1 through 6.)

1892–93

RANKING	TEAM
1	Iowa (2-0-1)7
2	Geneva (1-0)

1893–94

RANKING	TEAM
1	Hiram (Ohio) (1-0)

1894–95

RANKING	TEAM
1	Temple (8-3)

1895–96

RANKING	TEAM
1	Temple (15-7)
2	Yale (8-5)
3	Chicago (5-2)
4	Minnesota (3-2)
5	Bucknell (1-3)

1896–97

RANKING	TEAM
1	Yale (11-5-1)
2	Temple (10-11)
3	Chicago (5-2)
4	Bucknell (4-1)
5	Wabash (1-0)

1897–98

RANKING	TEAM
1	Mount Union (8-1)
2	Yale (12-9)
3	Westminster (Penn.) (4-2)
4	Temple (20-5)
5	Hiram (Ohio) (3-2)

1898–99

RANKING	TEAM
1	Yale (9-1)
2	Allegheny (8-1)
3	Nebraska (4-0)
4	Temple (18-6)
5	Minnesota (7-2)
6	Ohio St. (12-4)
7	Wabash (2-0)
8	Hiram (Ohio) (4-1)
9	Kansas (7-4)
10	Syracuse (1-0-1)

1899–1900

RANKING	TEAM
1	Yale (9-6)
2	Dartmouth (22-4-1)
3	Allegheny (10-4)
4	Nebraska (5-0)
5	Penn St. (7-1)
6	Geneva (8-3)
7	Illinois St. (5-0)
8	Hiram (Ohio) (7-1)
9	Bucknell (6-3)
10	Temple (13-9)

1900–1

RANKING	TEAM
1	Bucknell (12-1)
2	Purdue (12-0)
3	Penn St. (5-1)
4	Yale (10-6)
5	Amherst (4-0)
6	Allegheny (14-2)
7	Minnesota (11-1)
8	Hiram (Ohio) (9-1)
9	Williams (9-2)
10	Dartmouth (11-8)
11	Geneva (10-2)
12	Western Reserve (5-2)
13	Princeton (7-5)
14	Harvard (11-8)
15	Lafayette (4-3)
16	Mount Union (10-6)
17	Syracuse (2-1)
18	Wisc.-Superior (8-2)
19	Michigan St. (3-0)
20	Illinois St. (4-1)

1901–2

RANKING	TEAM
1	Minnesota (15-0)
2	Purdue (11-3)
3	Allegheny (12-1)
4	Amherst (8-0)
5	Iowa (10-2)
6	Williams (12-3)
7	Bucknell (12-2)
8	Wisconsin (7-3)
9	Dartmouth (11-5)
10	Yale (13-8)
11	Penn St. (9-2)
12	Washington (7-0)
13	Colgate (7-2)
14	Harvard (9-5)
15	Pennsylvania (7-2-1)
16	Mount Union (10-2)
17	Lehigh (9-5)
18	Grove City (13-3)
19	Michigan St. (5-0)
20	St. Francis (13-1)

1902–3

RANKING	TEAM
1	Minnesota (13-0)
2	Yale (15-1)
3	Purdue (8-0)
4	Bucknell (10-0)
5	Colgate (7-1)
6	Grove City (13-1)
7	Geneva (10-1)
8	Allegheny (10-2-1)
9	Williams (18-2)
10	Ohio St. (5-2)
11	Columbia (10-6)
12	Princeton (9-6)
13	Wabash (12-3)
14	Hiram (Ohio) (4-1)
15	Wisconsin (5-2)
16	Lehigh (4-2-1)
17	Michigan St. (6-0)
18	Latter Day Sts. (15-1)
19	Wheaton (Ill.) (8-1)
20	Vanderbilt (6-0)

PREMO POWER POLL (CONTD.)

1903–4

RANKING	TEAM
1	Columbia (17-1)
2	Minnesota (11-2)
3	Allegheny (12-2)
4	Purdue (11-2)
5	Holy Cross (10-2)
6	Pennsylvania (10-4)
7	Princeton (10-5)
8	Ohio St. (10-4)
9	Hiram (Ohio) (9-3)
10	Wisconsin (11-4)
11	Williams (15-7)
12	Colgate (12-5)
13	Chicago (7-0)
14	Wheaton (Ill.) (10-3-1)
15	Iowa (6-2)
16	Lehigh (5-2)
17	Washington (5-1)
18	Oregon St. (7-3)
19	Maine (8-2)
20	Illinois St. (7-1)

1904–5

RANKING	TEAM
1	Columbia (19-1)
2	Williams (20-2)
3	Ohio St. (12-2)
4	Allegheny (10-2)
5	Syracuse (16-7)
6	Brown (12-6)
7	Harvard (11-5)
8	Wabash (8-1)
9	Dartmouth (20-10-1)
10	Chicago (9-2)
11	Holy Cross (6-4)
12	Princeton (8-5)
13	Colgate (10-7)
14	Yale (22-13)
15	Butler (6-1)
16	Augustana (Ill.) (9-0)
17	Nebraska (11-5)
18	Penn St. (6-2)
19	Cincinnati (6-3)
20	Dayton (6-1)

1905–6

RANKING	TEAM
1	Wabash (17-1)
2	Dartmouth (16-2)
3	Minnesota (13-2)
4	Wisconsin (12-2)
5	Westminster (Pa.) (12-2)
6	Williams (14-3-1)
7	Pennsylvania (16-4)
8	Bucknell (10-2)
9	Allegheny (13-4)
10	Ohio St. (9-1)
11	Columbia (12-4)
12	Nebraska (12-3)
13	Syracuse (9-3)
14	Harvard (12-4)
15	Holy Cross (12-3)
16	Michigan St. (11-2)
17	Western Reserve (13-3)
18	Wooster (7-3)
19	Oregon St. (10-0)
20	Denison (Ohio) (12-2)

1906–7

RANKING	TEAM
1	Chicago (20-2)
2	Williams (15-1)
3	Wabash (17-2)
4	Columbia (14-4)
5	Allegheny (10-1)
6	Yale (30-6-1)
7	Dartmouth (13-4)
8	Minnesota (10-2)
9	Wisconsin (11-3)
10	Oregon St. (17-1)
11	Westminster (Pa.) (7-1)
12	Bucknell (10-1)
13	Michigan St. (14-2)
14	Dayton (14-0)
15	Grinnell (9-2)
16	Akron (5-2)
17	Lehigh (9-2)
18	CCNY (8-1)
19	Buffalo (6-2)
20	Vanderbilt (6-1)

1907–8

RANKING	TEAM
1	Wabash (24-0)
2	Chicago (21-2)
3	Pennsylvania (23-4)
4	Allegheny (12-0)
5	Wisconsin (10-2)
6	Bucknell (12-0)
7	Grinnell (14-3)
8	Notre Dame (12-4)
9	Syracuse (11-2)
10	Michigan St. (15-5)
11	Dartmouth (11-4)
12	CCNY (9-2)
13	Penn St. (10-4)
14	St. Lawrence (9-2)
15	Lehigh (6-1)
16	Georgetown (5-1)
17	Haskell (24-11)
18	Mount Union (17-3)
19	Washington St. (12-3)
20	Cincinnati (9-0)

1908–9

RANKING	TEAM
1	Chicago (12-0)
2	Swarthmore (12-0)
3	NYU (13-0)
4	Williams (13-1)
5	Columbia (16-1)
6	Ohio St. (11-1)
7	Notre Dame (33-7)
8	Allegheny (11-2)
9	Army (9-2)
10	Grinnell (12-1)
11	Wooster (10-2)
12	Bucknell (9-3)
13	Oregon St. (10-1)
14	Vanderbilt (11-4)
15	Kansas (25-3)
16	Georgia (6-2)
17	Washington (9-1)
18	Dayton (12-2)
19	Illinois St. (9-0)
20	MIT (10-6)

1909–10

RANKING	TEAM
1	Williams (11-0)
2	Columbia (11-1)
3	Army (14-1)
4	Kansas (18-1)
5	VPI (11-0)
6	Cotner (Neb.) (11-0)
7	Centre (Ky.) (20-3)
8	Minnesota (10-3)
9	Kansas St. (11-2-1)
10	Chicago (9-3)
11	Navy (10-1)
12	Ohio St. (11-1)
13	Grinnell (12-1)
14	Iowa (11-3)
15	Allegheny (9-3)
16	NYU (13-4)
17	Swarthmore (9-3)
18	Niagara (13-3)
19	Oberlin (10-3)
20	Oklahoma (8-0)

1910–11

RANKING	TEAM
1	St. John's (14-0)
2	Columbia (13-1)
3	Navy (10-1)
4	Dayton (10-0)
5	Wabash (10-1)
6	Ohio St. (7-2)
7	VPI (11-1)
8	Notre Dame (7-3)
9	Allegheny (9-2)
10	Wesleyan (Conn.) (10-3)
11	Army (9-3)
12	Oberlin (10-2)
13	Washington (11-1)
14	N. Central College (14-2)
15	Grinnell (13-1)
16	Williams (8-2)
17	Wooster (16-4)
18	Oregon (9-3)
19	CCNY (7-2)
20	Union (7-2)

1911–12

RANKING	TEAM
1	Wisconsin (15-0)
2	Purdue (12-0)
3	Grove City (13-0)
4	Allegheny (11-1)
5	Swarthmore (11-1)
6	Wesleyan (Conn.) (13-0)
7	Notre Dame (15-2)
8	Navy (7-1)
9	Beloit (6-2)
10	Columbia (10-2)
11	Dayton (13-0)
12	Oregon St. (16-3)
13	Washington (12-4)
14	Nebraska (14-1)
15	Oregon (9-3)
16	Kentucky (9-0)
17	Syracuse (11-3)
18	St. Lawrence (12-3)
19	Mississippi St. (9-0)
20	Mississippi (10-2)

PREMO POWER POLL (CONTD.)

1912–13

RANKING	TEAM
1	Navy (9-0)
2	Denison (Ohio) (13-1)
3	Dayton (11-0)
4	Wisconsin (14-1)
5	Detroit Mercy (13-0)
6	Georgia (10-1)
7	Akron (7-1)
8	Grinnell (11-0)
9	Army (11-2)
10	Nebraska (17-2)
11	Wesleyan (Conn.) (14-2)
12	Notre Dame (13-2)
13	Catholic (14-3)
14	Penn St. (8-3)
15	Lehigh (12-2)
16	Allegheny (9-2)
17	Virginia (12-3)
18	Utah (21-3)
19	Springfield (6-1)
20	Mississippi St. (11-1)

1913–14

RANKING	TEAM
1	Wisconsin (15-0)
2	Denison (Ohio) (15-1)
3	Navy (10-0)
4	Syracuse (12-0)
5	Cornell (14-2)
6	Lehigh (12-2)
7	St. Mary's (Cal.) (15-0)
8	Nebraska (15-3)
9	Virginia (12-1-1)
10	Grinnell (10-1)
11	Georgia (9-1)
12	Kansas (17-1)
13	Oberlin (7-3)
14	Kentucky (12-2)
15	Duquesne (7-2)
16	Washington (12-2)
17	Catholic (13-4)
18	Tennessee (15-2)
19	Utah (12-2)
20	BYU (10-1)

1914–15

RANKING	TEAM
1	Illinois (16-0)
2	Army (11-2)
3	Navy (9-2)
4	Virginia (17-0)
5	Yale (14-3)
6	Syracuse (10-1)
7	Chicago (9-3)
8	Notre Dame (15-2)
9	Cornell (12-4)
10	Allegheny (10-1)
11	Wabash (7-2)
12	Penn St. (10-3)
13	Seton Hall (15-2)
14	Kansas (16-1)
15	Denison (Ohio) (12-2)
16	Washington (17-2)
17	Whittier (17-3)
18	Texas (14-0)
19	Wisconsin (13-4)
20	Duquesne (12-2)

1915–16

RANKING	TEAM
1	Wisconsin (20-1)
2	Allegheny (10-1)
3	Pittsburgh (16-2)
4	Illinois (13-3)
5	Princeton (16-4)
6	Swarthmore (10-2)
7	Navy (12-2)
8	Nebraska (13-1)
9	Utah (10-0)
10	Missouri (13-3)
11	Kansas St. (13-3)
12	Texas (12-0)
13	Wabash (17-4)
14	Washington St. (18-3)
15	Virginia (11-2)
16	Texas A&M (11-2)
17	Catholic (10-4)
18	Tennessee (12-0)
19	Ripon (15-3)
20	Montana St. (10-1)

1916–17

RANKING	TEAM
1	Washington St. (25-1)
2	California (15-1)
3	Wabash (19-2)
4	Minnesota (15-2)
5	Illinois (13-3)
6	Wisconsin (15-3)
7	Kansas St. (15-2)
8	Navy (11-0)
9	CCNY (15-3)
10	Purdue (11-3)
11	Yale (19-5)
12	Lehigh (15-4)
13	Penn St. (12-2)
14	Syracuse (13-3)
15	Montana St. (19-1)
16	Washington & Lee (13-0)
17	Central Missouri St. (13-2)
18	Georgia (8-1)
19	VPI (17-2)
20	Case Tech (12-1)

1917–18

RANKING	TEAM
1	Syracuse (16-1)
2	Oregon St. (15-0)
3	Penn St. (12-1)
4	Pennsylvania (18-2)
5	Geneva (13-3)
6	Navy (14-2)
7	Princeton (12-3)
8	Stevens (14-0)
9	Wash. & Jefferson (10-2)
10	Union (14-1)
11	Idaho (11-1)
12	Missouri (17-1)
13	Wisconsin (14-3)
14	Springfield (13-3)
15	Virginia (7-1)
16	Centre (10-1)
17	Utah St. (9-0)
18	LSU (12-1)
19	Kentucky (9-2-1)
20	North Carolina St. (12-2)

1918–19

RANKING	TEAM
1	Navy (16-0)
2	Minnesota (13-0)
3	Pennsylvania (15-1)
4	Georgetown (9-1)
5	Penn St. (11-2)
6	Wabash (13-3)
7	Cornell (11-3)
8	Oregon (13-3)
9	Yale (7-2)
10	Idaho (13-2)
11	VPI (18-4)
12	Kansas St. (17-2)
13	Santa Clara (14-1)
14	Missouri (14-3)
15	Bucknell (13-3)
16	Delaware (8-2)
17	Chicago (10-2)
18	Oklahoma (12-0)
19	Washington & Lee (10-3)
20	Texas (17-3)

1918–19 TOP SERVICE TEAMS

RANKING	TEAM
1	Great Lakes NTS (23-7)
2	Camp Dodge (10-1)

1919–20

RANKING	TEAM
1	Pennsylvania (22-1)
2	Missouri (17-1)
3	Penn St. (12-1)
4	NYU (16-1)
5	Georgetown (13-1)
6	Purdue (16-4)
7	Delaware (13-2)
8	Wisconsin (15-1)
9	Navy (14-3)
10	Chicago (11-4)
11	Army (12-2)
12	Westminster (Mo.) (17-0)
13	Texas A&M (19-0)
14	Nebraska (22-2)
15	Syracuse (15-3)
16	Montana St. (13-0)
17	Millikin (22-1)
18	CCNY (13-3)
19	Ripon (11-2)
20	Wyoming (10-1)

1920–21

RANKING	TEAM
1	Missouri (17-1)
2	Pennsylvania (21-2)
3	Navy (18-1)
4	NYU (12-1)
5	Penn St. (14-2)
6	Grove City (15-0)
7	VMI (16-1)
8	Stanford (15-3)
9	Nebraska (12-3)
10	Arizona (7-0)
11	Virginia (11-3)
12	Wisconsin (13-4)
13	Ohio Northern (21-3)
14	Michigan (16-4)
15	Central Mo. St. (22-2)
16	Wabash (21-4)
17	Denison (Ohio) (14-3)
18	Ohio University (16-2)
19	DePauw (12-3)
20	Oberlin (11-1)

PREMO POWER POLL (CONTD.)

1921–22

RANKING	TEAM
1	Missouri (16-1)
2	Kansas (16-2)
3	Army (17-2)
4	Idaho (19-1)
5	Oregon St. (21-2)
6	Wabash (21-3)
7	Holy Cross (14-3)
8	Purdue (15-3)
9	Michigan (15-4)
10	CCNY (10-2)
11	Butler (23-4)
12	Princeton (20-5)
13	Illinois (14-5)
14	Wisconsin (14-5)
15	Pennsylvania (24-3)
16	Texas A&M (18-3)
17	Navy (15-3)
18	Wooster (14-1)
19	Beloit (12-0)
20	Texas (20-4)

1922–23

RANKING	TEAM
1	Army (17-0)
2	Kansas (17-1)
3	Missouri (15-3)
4	Springfield (15-1)
5	Butler (16-4)
6	Iowa (13-2)
7	Penn St. (13-1)
8	N. Texas St. (13-1)
9	Hardin-Simmons (13-1)
10	Marquette (19-2)
11	Grove City (15-2)
12	Idaho (14-3)
13	Wisconsin (12-3)
14	Texas A&M (16-4)
15	West Texas St. (12-4)
16	Navy (14-4)
17	Colgate (14-4)
18	Akron (12-1)
19	Washington (13-3)
20	Denison (Ohio) (12-1)

1923–24

RANKING	TEAM
1	North Carolina (26-0)
2	Kansas (16-3)
3	Navy (15-3)
4	Penn St. (13-2)
5	Texas (23-0)
6	Oklahoma (15-3)
7	Columbia (15-4)
8	Cornell (13-3)
9	Vermont (15-2)
10	USC (15-4)
11	Tulane (22-1)
12	Army (16-2)
13	CCNY (12-1)
14	Beloit (14-0)
15	Creighton (13-2)
16	California (7-3)
17	Alabama (12-4)
18	RPI (11-1)
19	Springfield (13-3)
20	Washington (12-4)

1924–25

RANKING	TEAM
1	Princeton (21-2)
2	Wabash (18-1)
3	Ohio St. (14-2)
4	Kansas (17-1)
5	Syracuse (15-2)
6	Fordham (15-1)
7	Butler (20-4)
8	Oklahoma St. (15-3)
9	Army (12-3)
10	Washburn (15-0)
11	Penn St. (12-2)
12	Creighton (13-2)
13	CCNY (12-2)
14	Dartmouth (12-5)
15	Grove City (15-2)
16	Pennsylvania (17-5)
17	Harvard (11-2)
18	Evansville (11-2)
19	TCU (14-5)
20	Navy (18-5)

1925–26

RANKING	TEAM
1	Syracuse (19-1)
2	Notre Dame (19-1)
3	Kansas (16-2)
4	Columbia (16-2)
5	California (14-0)
6	Oklahoma (11-4)
7	Purdue (13-4)
8	Michigan (12-5)
9	Indiana (12-5)
10	Iowa (12-5)
11	Cincinnati (17-2)
12	Maryland (14-3)
13	Butler (16-5)
14	Oregon (18-4)
15	UCLA (14-2)
16	Lehigh (13-1)
17	North Carolina (20-5)
18	Navy (12-5)
19	Arkansas (15-1)
20	Mississippi (16-2)

1926–27

RANKING	TEAM
1	Notre Dame (19-1)
2	California (13-0)
3	Michigan (14-3)
4	Fordham (18-2)
5	Indiana (13-4)
6	Evansville (16-4)
7	Butler (17-4)
8	Kansas (15-2)
9	Navy (15-2)
10	Oregon (24-4)
11	Vanderbilt (20-4)
12	Syracuse (15-4)
13	West Texas St. (23-3)
14	Western Michigan (16-2)
15	Furman (16-4)
16	Montana St. (30-7)
17	Loyola (Ill.) (15-4)
18	Washington (15-4)
19	Creighton (14-5)
20	Xavier (Ohio) (11-3)

1927–28

RANKING	TEAM
1	Pittsburgh (21-0)
2	Montana St. (36-2)
3	Indiana (15-2)
4	Purdue (15-2)
5	Butler (19-3)
6	Notre Dame (18-4)
7	Arkansas (19-1)
8	Oklahoma (18-0)
9	Fordham (12-1)
10	Springfield (18-2)
11	Georgetown (12-1)
12	Auburn (20-2)
13	Pennsylvania (22-5)
14	USC (22-4)
15	Westminster (Pa.) (17-3)
16	Evansville (14-3)
17	St. John's (18-4)
18	LSU (14-4)
19	Oregon (18-3)
20	Wayne St. (18-1)

1928–29

RANKING	TEAM
1	Montana St. (36-2)
2	San Francisco (21-2)
3	Arkansas (16-1)
4	Michigan (13-3)
5	Butler (17-2)
6	Oklahoma (13-2)
7	Texas (18-2)
8	California (16-4)
9	Wisconsin (15-2)
10	Purdue (13-4)
11	Washington (18-2)
12	Fordham (18-1)
13	West Texas St. (16-2)
14	Loyola (Ill.) (16-0)
15	Notre Dame (15-5)
16	Northwestern (12-5)
17	Pittsburgh (16-5)
18	Westminster (Pa.) (15-2)
19	Washington & Lee (15-1)
20	Creighton (13-4)

1929–30

RANKING	TEAM
1	Alabama (20-0)
2	Syracuse (18-2)
3	Pittsburgh (23-2)
4	Wisconsin (15-2)
5	Duke (18-2)
6	Purdue (13-2)
7	Missouri (15-3)
8	St. John's (23-1)
9	Furman (16-1)
10	USC (15-5)
11	NYU (13-3)
12	Kansas (14-4)
13	Michigan St. (12-4)
14	Western Michigan (17-0)
15	Washington (21-7)
16	Kentucky (16-3)
17	Notre Dame (14-6)
18	Columbia (17-5)
19	CCNY (10-3)
20	Temple (18-3)

PREMO POWER POLL (CONTD.)

1930–31

RANKING	TEAM
1	Northwestern (16-1)
2	St. John's (21-1)
3	Washington (25-3)
4	Columbia (21-2)
5	Georgia (23-2)
6	Pittsburgh (20-4)
7	Syracuse (16-4)
8	Michigan (13-4)
9	Minnesota (13-4)
10	Purdue (12-5)
11	Illinois (12-5)
12	Manhattan (17-2)
13	Furman (15-2)
14	Michigan St. (16-1)
15	Kansas (15-3)
16	Butler (17-2)
17	West Texas St. (17-3)
18	Williams (12-3)
19	Army (12-3)
20	Santa Clara (16-3)

1931–32

RANKING	TEAM
1	Purdue (17-1)
2	Notre Dame (18-2)
3	Minnesota (15-3)
4	Kentucky (15-2)
5	CCNY (16-1)
6	Santa Clara (15-4)
7	St. John's (22-4)
8	Princeton (18-4)
9	Washington St. (22-5)
10	Butler (14-5)
11	Wyoming (18-2)
12	Northwestern (12-5)
13	Creighton (17-4)
14	Arizona (18-2)
15	Providence (19-5)
16	North Carolina (16-5)
17	Michigan St. (12-5)
18	West Texas St. (20-3)
19	Westminster (Pa.) (16-2)
20	Mount Union (16-1)

1932–33

RANKING	TEAM
1	Texas (22-1)
2	South Carolina (21-2)
3	Ohio St. (17-3)
4	Kentucky (20-3)
5	Princeton (19-3)
6	Yale (19-3)
7	Navy (14-2)
8	Syracuse (14-2)
9	Iowa (15-5)
10	St. John's (23-4)
11	Marquette (14-3)
12	TCU (16-4)
13	Northwestern (15-4)
14	Duquesne (15-1)
15	Butler (16-5)
16	Notre Dame (16-6)
17	Creighton (12-5)
18	West Texas St. (20-4)
19	CCNY (13-1)
20	Morgan (28-1)

1933–34

RANKING	TEAM
1	South Carolina (18-1)
2	Kentucky (16-1)
3	Duquesne (19-2)
4	NYU (16-0)
5	Wyoming (26-3)
6	Purdue (17-3)
7	Notre Dame (20-4)
8	Pittsburgh (18-4)
9	Alabama (16-2)
10	Pennsylvania (16-3)
11	DePaul (17-0)
12	Syracuse (15-2)
13	CCNY (14-1)
14	Navy (11-2)
15	LIU-Brooklyn (26-1)
16	Westminster (Pa.) (22-4)
17	North Carolina (18-4)
18	St. John's (16-3)
19	Kansas (16-1)
20	Marquette (15-4)

1934–35

RANKING	TEAM
1	Richmond (20-0)
2	NYU (19-1)
3	Duquesne (18-1)
4	Kentucky (19-2)
5	North Carolina (23-2)
6	Purdue (17-3)
7	LSU (14-1)
8	LIU-Brooklyn (24-2)
9	DePaul (15-1)
10	USC (20-6)
11	Pittsburgh (18-6)
12	Navy (11-3)
13	Pennsylvania (16-4)
14	SMU (14-3)
15	Syracuse (15-2)
16	Illinois (15-5)
17	Wisconsin (15-5)
18	Ohio Wesleyan (17-2)
19	Rutgers (13-3)
20	Westminster (Pa.) (19-3)

1935–36

RANKING	TEAM
1	LIU-Brooklyn (25-0)
2	Notre Dame (22-2-1)
3	Kansas (21-2)
4	Indiana (18-2)
5	Arkansas (24-3)
6	Washington (25-7)
7	DePaul (18-4)
8	Manhattan (17-2)
9	Washington & Lee (18-2)
10	NYU (15-4)
11	Stanford (22-7)
12	St. John's (18-4)
13	Purdue (16-4)
14	Columbia (19-3)
15	George Washington (16-3)
16	Northwestern (13-6-1)
17	Western Kentucky (26-4)
18	Temple (18-6)
19	Duquesne (14-3)
20	Murray St. (23-2)

1936–37

RANKING	TEAM
1	Stanford (25-2)
2	Notre Dame (20-3)
3	LIU-Brooklyn (28-3)
4	Michigan (16-4)
5	Purdue (15-5)
6	Pennsylvania (17-3)
7	Illinois (14-4)
8	George Washington (16-4)
9	USC (19-6)
10	Western Kentucky (21-2)
11	Temple (17-6)
12	Kentucky (17-5)
13	Rhode Island (18-3)
14	Hardin-Simmons (16-1)
15	Oklahoma St. (20-3)
16	Springfield (18-3)
17	Washington St. (24-8)
18	Loyola (Ill.) (16-3)
19	Murray St. (22-3)
20	Ohio Univ. (18-3)

PREMO POWER POLL: BEST TEAMS BY DECADE

1890–99

RANKING	SEASON	TEAM
1	1898–99	Yale (9-1)
2	1898–99	Allegheny (Pa.) (8-1)
3	1898–99	Nebraska (4-0)
4	1897–98	Mt. Union (Ohio) (8-1)
5	1898–99	Temple (18-6)
6	1896–97	Yale (11-5-1)
7	1898–99	Minnesota (7-2)
8	1897–98	Yale (12-9)
9	1897–98	Westminster (Pa.) (4-2)
10	1894–95	Temple (8-3)

1900–9

RANKING	SEASON	TEAM
1	1907–8	Wabash (Ind.) (24-0)
2	1902–3	Minnesota (13-0)
3	1907–8	Chicago (21-2)
4	1901–2	Minnesota (15-0)
5	1906–7	Chicago (20-2)
6	1904–5	Columbia (19-1)
7	1908–9	Chicago (12-0)
8	1902–3	Yale (15-1)
9	1905–6	Wabash (Ind.) (17-1)
10	1903–4	Columbia (17-1)
11	1908–9	Swarthmore (Pa.) (12-0)
12	1906–7	Williams (Mass.) (15-1)
13	1904–5	Williams (Mass.) (20-2)
14	1907–8	Pennsylvania (23-4)
15	1907–8	Allegheny (Pa.) (12-0)
16	1908–9	New York Univ. (13-0)
17	1902–3	Purdue (8-0)
18	1906–7	Wabash (Ind.) (17-2)
19	1904–5	Ohio St. (12-2)
20	1906–7	Columbia (14-4)

PREMO POWER POLL (CONTD.)

1910–19

RANKING	SEASON	TEAM
1	1918–19	Navy (16-0)
2	1912–13	Navy (9-0)
3	1911–12	Wisconsin (15-0)
4	1913–14	Wisconsin (15-0)
5	1918–19	Minnesota (13-0)
6	1914–15	Illinois (16-0)
7	1910–11	St. John's (14-0)
8	1916–17	Washington St. (25-1)
9	1911–12	Purdue (12-0)
10	1913–14	Denison (Ohio) (15-1)
11	1912–13	Denison (Ohio) (13-1)
12	1909–10	Williams (Mass.) (11-0)
13	1915–16	Wisconsin (20-1)
14	1916–17	California (15-1)
15	1913–14	Navy (10-0)
16	1917–18	Syracuse (16-1)
17	1910–11	Columbia (13-1)
18	1911–12	Grove City (Pa.) (13-0)
19	1918–19	Pennsylvania (15-1)
20	1916–17	Wabash (Ind.) (19-2)

1920–29

RANKING	SEASON	TEAM
1	1928–29	Montana St. (36-2)
2	1927–28	Pittsburgh (21-0)
3	1922–23	Army (17-0)
4	1919–20	Pennsylvania (22-1)
5	1925–26	Syracuse (19-1)
6	1927–28	Montana St. (36-2)
7	1923–24	North Carolina (26-0)
8	1926–27	Notre Dame (19-1)
9	1920–21	Missouri (17-1)
10	1925–26	Notre Dame (19-1)
11	1922–23	Kansas (17-1)
12	1919–20	Missouri (17-1)
13	1928–29	San Francisco (21-2)
14	1924–25	Princeton (21-2)
15	1921–22	Missouri (16-1)
16	1919–20	Penn St. (12-1)
17	1920–21	Pennsylvania (21-2)
18	1921–22	Kansas (16-2)
19	1928–29	Arkansas (16-1)
20	1927–28	Indiana (15-2)

1930–39

RANKING	SEASON	TEAM
1	1938–39	LIU-Brooklyn# (23-0)
2	1936–37	Stanford (25-2)
3	1935–36	LIU-Brooklyn (25-0)
4	1931–32	Purdue (17-1)
5	1937–38	Temple# (23-2)
6	1934–35	Richmond (20-0)
7	1929–30	Alabama (20-0)
8	1932–33	Texas (22-1)
9	1935–36	Notre Dame (22-2-1)
10	1936–37	Notre Dame (20-3)
11	1933–34	South Carolina (18-1)
12	1930–31	Northwestern (16-1)
13	1934–35	NYU (19-1)
14	1931–32	Notre Dame (18-2)
15	1937–38	Stanford (21-3)
16	1938–39	Bradley (19-3)
17	1930–31	St. John's (21-1)
18	1933–34	Kentucky (16-1)
19	1932–33	South Carolina (21-2)
20	1934–35	Duquesne (18-1)
	1935–36	Kansas (21-2)

#–NIT Champion

EARLY AWARD WINNERS

NCAA CONSENSUS FIRST-TEAM ALL-AMERICANS FROM 1929 TO 1937

1928–29: Thomas Churchill, Oklahoma; Vern Corbin, California; Chuck Hyatt, Pittsburgh; Charles Murphy, Purdue; Joe Schaaf, Pennsylvania; John Thompson, Montana State

1929–30: Chuck Hyatt, Pittsburgh; Charles Murphy, Purdue; Branch McCracken, Indiana; John Thompson, Montana State; Frank Ward, Montana State; John Wooden, Purdue

1930–31: Wes Fesler, Ohio State; George Gregory, Columbia; Joe Reiff, Northwestern; Elwood Romney, Brigham Young; John Wooden, Purdue

1931–32: Louis Berger, Maryland; Ed Krause, Notre Dame; Forest Sale, Kentucky; Les Witte, Wyoming; John Wooden, Purdue

1932–33: Ed Krause, Notre Dame; Elliott Loughlin, Navy; Jerry Nemer, Southern Cal; Joe Reiff, Northwestern; Forest Sale, Kentucky; Don Smith, Pittsburgh

1933–34: Norman Cottom, Purdue; Claire Cribbs, Pittsburgh; Ed Krause, Notre Dame; Hal Lee, Washington; Les Witte, Wyoming

1934–35: Bud Browning, Oklahoma; Claire Cribbs, Pittsburgh; Leroy Edwards, Kentucky; Jack Gray, Texas; Lee Guttero, Southern Cal

1935–36: Vern Huffman, Indiana; Bob Kessler, Purdue; Bill Kinner, Utah; Hank Luisetti, Stanford; John Moir, Notre Dame; Paul Nowak, Notre Dame; Ike Poole, Arkansas

1936–37: Jules Bender, Long Island; Hank Luisetti, Stanford; John Moir, Notre Dame; Paul Nowak, Notre Dame; Jewell Young, Purdue

---

HELMS FOUNDATION CHAMPIONS FROM 1901 TO 1937 The Helms Foundation of Los Angeles, under the guidance of founder Bill Schroeder, chose national college champions from 1942 to 1982 and researched retroactive No. 1 selections from 1901 to 1941. There are four years when the Helms picks differ from the actual champion since the NIT commenced in 1938–39 (Helms selected LIU), 1940 (Southern Cal), 1944 (Army), and 1954 (Kentucky). Army had a policy against postseason play until accepting a bid to the 1961 NIT. Kentucky rejected a bid to the 1954 NCAA Tournament after the NCAA declared three seniors ineligible.

Multiple Helms national championships from 1901 to 1937 include Chicago (3), Columbia (3), Wisconsin (3), Kansas (2), Minnesota (2), Notre Dame (2), Penn (2), Pittsburgh (2), Syracuse (2), and Yale (2). Only two of these 10 schools won an NCAA Tournament since it started in 1939—Wisconsin (1941) and Kansas (1952 and 1988).

YEAR	CHAMPION (RECORD)	HEAD COACH	TOP PLAYER, POS.
1901	Yale (10-6)	No coach	G. M. Clark, F
1902	Minnesota (15-0)	Louis Cooke	W. C. Deering, F
1903	Yale (15-1)	W. H. Murphy	R. B. Hyatt, F
1904	Columbia (17-1)	No coach	Harry Fisher, F
1905	Columbia (19-1)	No coach	Harry Fisher, F
1906	Dartmouth (16-2)	No coach	George Grebenstein, F
1907	Chicago (22-2)	Joseph Raycroft	John Schommer, C
1908	Chicago (21-2)	Joseph Raycroft	John Schommer, C
1909	Chicago (12-0)	Joseph Raycroft	John Schommer, C
1910	Columbia (11-1)	Harry Fisher	Ted Kiendl, F
1911	St. John's (14-0)	Claude Allen	John Keenan, F-C
1912	Wisconsin (15-0)	Doc Meanwell	Otto Stangel, F
1913	Navy (9-0)	Louis Wenzel	Laurence Wild, F
1914	Wisconsin (15-0)	Doc Meanwell	Gene Van Gent, C
1915	Illinois (16-0)	Ralph Jones	Ray Woods, G
1916	Wisconsin (20-1)	Doc Meanwell	George Lewis, F
1917	Washington State (25-1)	Doc Bohler	Ray Bohler, G
1918	Syracuse (16-1)	Edmund Dollard	Joe Schwarzer, G
1919	Minnesota (13-0)	Louis Cooke	Arnold Oss, F
1920	Penn (22-1)	Lon Jourdet	George Sweeney, F
1921	Penn (21-2)	Edward McNichol	Danny McNichol, G
1922	Kansas (16-2)	Phog Allen	Paul Endacott, G
1923	Kansas (17-1)	Phog Allen	Paul Endacott, G
1924	North Carolina (26-0)	Bo Shepard	Jack Cobb, F
1925	Princeton (21-2)	Al Wittmer	Art Loeb, G
1926	Syracuse (19-1)	Lew Andreas	Vic Hanson, F
1927	Notre Dame (19-1)	George Keagan	John Nykas, C
1928	Pittsburgh (21-0)	Doc Carlson	Chuck Hyatt, F
1929	Montana State (36-2)	Schubert Dyche	John Thompson, F
1930	Pittsburgh (23-2)	Doc Carlson	Chuck Hyatt, F
1931	Northwestern (16-1)	Dutch Lonborg	Joe Reiff, C
1932	Purdue (17-1)	Piggy Lambert	John Wooden, G
1933	Kentucky (20-3)	Adolph Rupp	Forest Sale, F
1934	Wyoming (26-3)	Willard Witte	Les Witte, G
1935	NYU (19-1)	Howard Cann	Sid Gross, F
1936	Notre Dame (22-2-1)	George Keogan	John Moir, F
1937	Stanford (25-2)	John Bunn	Hank Luisetti, F

2

START OF THE NATIONAL TOURNAMENTS:

1938-49

The NCAA's prize product, the Division I Men's Basketball Tournament, wasn't the NCAA's idea and was literally dumped into the governing body's lap by the National Association of Basketball Coaches. A group of New York sportswriters staged the first major college tournament, the National Invitation Tournament in 1938 in New York. But a coalition of NABC members, particularly coaches from the Midwest, felt if there was to be a national tourney, it should be sponsored by a collegiate organization and not scribes, especially those possessing what they perceived to be a "biased" Eastern influence.

Harold Olsen, a former Wisconsin player and coach at Ohio State, is accorded much of the credit for unveiling the NCAA Tournament to the American sports scene. The first NCAA Tournament was conducted in 1939, sponsored not by the NCAA but by the NABC. Oddly, Olsen's Ohio State team reached the final of the eight-team event (one from each district) before losing to Oregon, 46-33.

Total attendance for the inaugural NCAA playoff was a meager 15,025, and the venture produced $2,531 worth of red ink. Because the NABC was out of funds, it asked the NCAA to assume responsibility.

"We were darn lucky to get out of debt," said former Wisconsin coach Harold (Bud) Foster, a past president of the NABC. "When the NCAA bailed us out, they provided tickets for all our members. It was interesting that Wisconsin played a major role in pulling the basketball tournament out of debt. We had the NCAA boxing tournament in Madison in '39 and drew packed houses. The university turned over $18,000 to the NCAA, and that was the biggest amount the NCAA had received from any source up to that time."

Unbelievably, the NCAA sponsored a boxing tournament before it chose to promote basketball in a similar fashion. And wouldn't you know boxing is no longer an NCAA-sanctioned sport?

A more vital fighting led to the following universities among others choosing not to field teams at least one season during World War II: Alabama, Auburn, Ball State, Bradley, Butler, Colorado, Colorado State, Creighton, Dayton, Duquesne, Eastern Kentucky, Florida, Fordham, Furman, Georgetown, George Washington, Hawaii, Kent, Loyola of Chicago, Loyola Marymount, Manhat-

LUISETTI EXPLODES FOR 50 POINTS Stanford's star player Hank Luisetti ushered in 1938 with a bang. On New Year's Day, Stanford trounced Duquesne, 92-27, in Cleveland, thanks to Luisetti's 50-point outburst. Luisetti was best known for his running one-handed shot.

STANFORD (92)	FG	FT	PTS.
Lafaille	1	0	2
P. Zonne	7	1	15
Huff	1	0	2
Luisetti	23	4	50
Stoefen	5	3	13
Calderwood	1	0	2
Lyon	0	2	2
Lee	0	0	0
Burnett	3	0	6
B. Zonne	0	0	0
Rapp	0	0	0
Heath	0	0	0
TOTALS	**41**	**10**	**92**

DUQUESNE (27)	FG	FT	PTS.
Cristofack	0	1	1
Weitzel	3	1	7
Fortney	3	0	6
Yankitis	2	0	4
Scarry	0	0	0
O'Malley	0	1	1
Neiderberger	0	0	0
Kreilling	1	2	4
Adams	2	0	4
TOTALS	**11**	**5**	**27**

Halftime: Stanford 55-12.

tan, Massachusetts, Memphis, Miami (Fla.), Mississippi, Mississippi State, New Hampshire, Niagara, Oklahoma City, St. Bonaventure, St. Francis (Pa.), St. Louis, San Francisco, San Jose State, Santa Clara, Seton Hall, Southern Mississippi, Stanford, Syracuse, Tennessee, Utah State, Vermont, Wake Forest, Wichita State, Wyoming, Xavier and Youngstown State.

Consequently, numerous schools were forced to schedule games against club teams and Armed Forces squads. In fact, four consecutive NCAA champions from 1942 through 1945 incurred defeats to such non-traditional opponents. Another example of the upheaval caused by the war was South Carolina, which had five different coaches in as many seasons from 1941-42 through 1945-46. Only four of the 17 winningest programs in the 1940s had the same coach during the entire decade.

Numerous standout players had their college playing careers interrupted by the conflict. For instance, all 11 regulars on Pittsburgh's 1941 Final Four team served in the U.S. military during WWII, and one of them, guard Bob Artman, was killed in action. Here is a list of the total of seven two-time first- and second-team NCAA consensus All-Americas who had their college careers interrupted while serving in the U.S. Armed Forces: Air Force-Charles Black (Kansas);Army-Vince Boryla (Notre Dame/Denver), Arnie Ferrin (Utah), Alex Groza (Kentucky), and Gerry Tucker (Okla-homa); Marine Corps-Andy Phillip (Illinois); Navy-Leo Klier (Notre Dame).

Conflict on the basketball court in the mid-1940s focused on an argument regarding which of the first two imposing big men was best: Oklahoma A&M's Bob Kurland (7'0") or DePaul's George Mikan (6'10"). Each of them set school single-game scoring records that still exist. There has been an infatuation with tall players ever since.

It doesn't take a genius to deduce All-America players are all-important to teams, but sheer standouts do not guarantee success in postseason competition. None of the first six two-time NCAA consensus first-team All-Americas in the 1940s reached the NCAA Tournament national semifinals-Dartmouth's Gus Broberg ('40 and '41), North Carolina's George Glamack ('40 and '41), Notre Dame's Leo Klier ('44 and '46), Illinois' Andy Phillip ('42 and '43), NYU's Sid Tanenbaum ('46 and '47) and St. Louis' Ed Macauley ('48 and '49).

The state of Kentucky supplied three of the nation's five winningest programs in the 1940s-Kentucky (1st), Eastern Kentucky (4th) and Western Kentucky (5th). Kansas was the only school west of the Mississippi River to rank among the top 10 programs in winning percentage in the 1930s and Oklahoma A&M was the only institution west of the Mississippi to rank among the top 19 in winning percentage in the 1940s.

Toledo was one of the 10 winningest programs in the '40s despite having five different head coaches in that period. Toledo was among eight of the 12 winningest programs in the '40s (joining Seton Hall, Rhode Island, Eastern Kentucky, Tennessee, Bowling Green, Notre Dame and St. John's) to fail to appear in the NCAA playoffs during the decade as the NCAA Tournament struggled with the NIT regarding national postseason tourney supremacy. The NCAA began making substantial inroads to stealing some of the NIT's thunder, however, after the first Eastern school (Holy Cross) won the NCAA in 1947.

Holy Cross' coach was Alvin "Doggie" Julian, who previously directed Muhlenberg (Pa.) to the NIT. Muhlenberg had a Navy V-12 program, which resulted in the assignment of many great players to campus. The 1944-45 squad, which fought 15-to-1 favorite St. John's to a one-point game (34-33) in the first round of the NIT, was completely different from the 1943-44 team because of military reassignments. Only one player, Oscar "Red" Baldwin, who played a year for Union (Ky.) College, had any previous college basketball experience.

Several days before Muhlenberg was selected to play in the 1945 NIT, Julian was named head basketball and assistant football coach at Holy Cross. Bud Barker, selected as Julian's replacement, could not coach in 1945-46 because he had to complete some service duty. That made Lee Coker one of the best fill-in coaches in college basketball history. In Coker's first (and only) year as head coach, he led the Mules not only to a 22-3 regular-season record but also to a first-round win in the NIT against Syracuse. What made Coker's achievement all the more amazing was his roster consisted of a senior, two sophomores and the rest freshmen-all the military men had been discharged when the war ended. Muhlenberg, after earning three consecutive NIT appearances with three radically different teams, eventually disappeared from the major-college ranks.

The beginning of separating the haves from the have-nots occurred in 1948, the first year of official classification of schools when 160 universities were designated as major colleges.

Coaches frequently did double duty in this era. In the wake of World War II, Virginia coach Gus Tebell also served as the duly elected mayor of Charlottesville, Va.

1937-38

AT A GLANCE

NIT Champion: Temple (23-2; coached by James Usilton; won Eastern Intercollegiate Conference by three games with a 9-1 record).

New Conference: New England (forerunner of Yankee disbanded in 1976).

New Rule: Center jump after every basket is rescinded.

NCAA Consensus First-Team All-Americans: Meyer (Mike) Bloom, C, Sr., Temple; Angelo (Hank) Luisetti, F, Sr., Stanford; John Moir, F, Sr., Notre Dame; Paul Nowak, C, Sr., Notre Dame; Fred Pralle, G, Sr., Kansas; Jewell Young, F, Sr., Purdue.

Perhaps no player had more of an effect on basketball than Stanford's Hank Luisetti. A couple of decades ahead of his time, he is credited with revolutionizing basketball by introducing his running one-handed shot. Luisetti led Stanford to three consecutive Pacific Coast Conference championships and to a 46-5 record in his final two seasons. Regrettably, it wasn't until the year after his graduation that the NCAA staged its first tourney. The same year of the initial NCAA playoffs, Luisetti starred with legendary actress Betty Grable in a film called "Campus Confessions." The movie earned him $10,000 from Paramount Pictures.

Luisetti (50 points vs. Duquesne at Cleveland) and Brown sophomore Harry Platt (48 vs. Northeastern) established what are still single-game school scoring records. Luisetti almost doubled Duquesne's output in a 92-27 victory, contributing to the Dukes' only losing season (6-11) in a 37-year span from 1920-21 through 1956-57.

New York's Madison Square Garden was the mecca of college basketball at the time, however. Long Island University, which had a 43-game winning streak snapped by Stanford (45-31) the previous year, was featured in six of the 12 doubleheaders played in the Garden.

Joe Hagan's 48-foot shot with 12 seconds remaining enabled Kentucky to edge Marquette, 35-33. Showing the state's obsession with hoops success after the game, Gov. Happy Chandler pounded a nail into the floor to mark the spot of the decisive shot. Hagan went to Kentucky to play football, tried out for the basketball team uninvited by coach Adolph Rupp and was captain of the Wildcats' 1937 football squad.

In the Big Ten, Illinois junior forward Lou Boudreau was declared ineligible for further intercollegiate competition in early February because his mother had been given monthly payments by the Cleveland Indians. John Kundla, who later coached the Minneapolis Lakers to six league titles, was the second-leading scorer for a Minnesota squad that finished second in the Big Ten. Michigan's John Townsend was named to the first five on the Converse All-American team. Fifty-six seasons later (1993-94), his grandson, North Carolina center Eric Montross, would be selected to the first five on the National Association of Basketball Coaches All-American team. Purdue had a 50-10 record against archrival Indiana after twice defeating the Hoosiers.

All-Americans John Moir and Paul Nowak were joined on Notre Dame's frontcourt by senior captain Ray Meyer, who later became a Hall of Fame coach for DePaul. They helped the Irish compile a 62-8-1 record in their three-year varsity careers. . . . Western Michigan suffered its first losing record (6-12) since its initial competitive season in 1913-14.

Oklahoma A&M lost its Missouri Valley opener to Grinnell before winning 13 consecutive

1937–38 PREMO POWER POLL

RANKING	SCHOOL
1	Temple# (23-2)
2	Stanford (21-3)
3	Purdue (18-2)
4	Notre Dame (20-3)
5	Oklahoma St. (25-3)
6	Bradley (18-2)
7	Western Kentucky (30-3)
8	Minnesota (16-4)
9	Kansas (18-2)
10	LIU-Brooklyn (23-5)
11	Central Missouri St.+ (24-3)
12	Roanoke (19-2)
13	Rhode Island (19-2)
14	Murray St. (27-4)
15	New Mexico St. (22-3)
16	Oregon (25-8)
17	Arkansas (19-3)
18	Villanova (25-5)
19	Marshall (28-4)
20	Centenary (13-1)

–NIT champion
+ –NAIA champion

league games en route to the conference crown. . . . Coach Phog Allen guided Kansas to its seventh title in the last eight seasons of the 10-year history of the Big Six Conference. . . . Gail Goodrich of Southern California finished sixth in scoring in the Pacific Coast Conference Southern Division. His son, Gail Goodrich Jr., became an All-American for UCLA in the mid-1960s. . . . Four starters for New Mexico A&M (now New Mexico State) were named to the first five on the All-Border Conference team after their school went undefeated (18-0) in league competition. . . . Coach Forrest Twogood guided Idaho to an 11-9 record for the Vandals' only winning season in a 16-year stretch from 1929-30 through 1944-45.

Maryland bowed to Washington & Lee nine consecutive times in their series until defeating the Generals, 36-32. . . . Georgetown was the only team to defeat Temple in Eastern Intercollegiate Conference competition. But the Hoyas lost for the fifth consecutive time in their series with Carnegie Tech, 54-31. Carnegie Tech's Melvin Cratsley set a league single-game scoring record with 34 points against West Virginia.

Western Kentucky, one of the nation's seven winningest programs in the 1930s and 1940s, began a streak of 10 consecutive triumphs over

Louisville. . . . Western Kentucky (30-3/coached by Ed Diddle) lost twice to Bradley but finished with its most victories in school history. Mississippi (22-12/George Bohler) had its winningest season in school history by posting 11 consecutive victories before losing to Georgia Tech in the SEC Tournament final. Ole Miss had just one winning record in its next 12 seasons (14-8 in 1944-45 after not fielding a squad the previous year because of World War II). . . . Alabama's 4-13 record was the school's lone losing mark in a 21-year span from 1927-28 through 1948-49 (did not field a team in 1943-44 because of WWII). . . . South Carolina (3-21) lost more than 20 games for the only time in school history.

1938-39

AT A GLANCE

NCAA Champion: Oregon (29-5; coached by Howard Hobson; won PCC North Division by three games with a 14-2 record).

NIT Champion: Long Island (23-0; coached by Clair Bee).

New Rules: Ball thrown in from out of bounds at mid-court by the team shooting a free throw following a technical foul. Previously, the ball was put into play with a center jump following a technical. . . . The circumference of the ball is established as 30 inches.

NCAA First-Team All-Americans: Ernie Andres, G, Sr., Indiana; Jimmy Hull, F, Sr., Ohio State; Chet Jaworski, G, Sr., Rhode Island; Irving Torgoff, F, Sr., Long Island; Urgel (Slim) Wintermute, C, Sr., Oregon.

It hasn't always been a pleasant spotlight near or at the top of the national polls for marquee schools Duke, North Carolina and UCLA.

Duke incurred its only losing record (10-12) in a 45-year span from 1927-28 through 1971-72. Meanwhile, rival North Carolina sustained its only losing mark (10-11) in a 30-year stretch from 1920-21 through 1949-50.

UCLA, the most successful school in NCAA Tournament history, was a playoff pretender instead of contender the first year of the national tourney. The Bruins won a non-league game by 57 points (76-19 over LaVerne), but they finished winless in the Pacific Coast Conference's Southern Division for the second straight season. Their senior captain and leading scorer was Bob (Ace) Calkins. During World War II as a navigator on a Flying Fortress, Calkins' plane was shot down and he later died in an Italian prison camp from wounds sustained in the air attack.

Texas toppled Manhattan, 54-32, at Madison Square Garden in front of 18,000 fans, the largest crowd to see a basketball game up to that point. It was the worst defeat dealt to a New York school in the Garden to that time. . . . Intercollegiate doubleheaders, with Loyola and DePaul serving as hosts, made their debut in Chicago with five twinbills at the 132nd Infantry Armory on West Madison Street (capacity 6,000).

Clemson, after recovering from a 2-5 start in regular-season league competition, won the Southern Conference Tournament championship although the Tigers never led at halftime in any of their four tourney games. Tigers athletic director Jess Neely, who also happened to be the school's football coach, rejected an invitation to the NIT because several of the key players were members of the football squad that had to return for spring practice. The extra workouts on the gridiron might have been the difference in helping Clemson earn an invitation to the Cotton Bowl that year.

LIU went unbeaten for the second time in four years. . . . The seven-year-old Eastern Intercollegiate Conference agreed to disband at the end of the season. The AP described the league as "one of the best in the nation." Geographical problems had made scheduling difficult for the six members-Carnegie Tech, Georgetown, Penn State, Pittsburgh, Temple and West Virginia. Penn State was the only member never to win outright or share a league regular-season title.

Panzer College of East Orange, N.J., compiled a 20-1 record, losing only to unbeaten LIU

The 1938–39 champion Oregon Ducks were dubbed "The Tall Firs" due to their size.

(41-35) early in the season. NIT champion LIU played only one game outside New York (vs. La Salle in Philadelphia). . . . Penn State's Max Corbin hit a shot from three quarters length of the floor against West Virginia to send their game into overtime. Penn State wound up winning, 46-43, in triple overtime. . . . Defending NIT champion Temple compiled a 10-12 record for coach James Usilton's second losing season in 13 years. Just three days after the end of the campaign, he died of a heart ailment. . . . Rhode Island's school-record 22-game winning streak under coach Frank Keaney ended with a 62-50 defeat against Tufts. . . . Brown had a school-record 11-game winning streak in George Allen's

first season as head coach en route to its highest winning percentage in history (16-4, .800). . . . Lehigh (10-5), coached by Paul Calvert, managed a double-digit victory total for the only season in a 24-year span from 1928-29 through 1951-52. . . . Connecticut lost 16 consecutive games to Rhode Island in their series until the Huskies prevailed, 68-67.

Stanford's school-record 17-game winning streak was snapped by Dartmouth, 48-47, in the fourth contest of the season. Everett Dean was in his first season as coach of Stanford, which won 55 of its previous 60 games since the end of the 1935-36 campaign. . . . Emphasis on foreigners

1938–39 PREMO POWER POLL

RANKING	SCHOOL
1	LIU-Brooklyn# (23-0)
2	Bradley (19-3)
3	Loyola (Ill.) (21-1)
4	Oregon* (29-5)
5	St. John's (18-4)
6	Indiana (17-3)
7	USC (20-5)
8	New Mexico St. (20-4)
9	Kentucky (16-4)
10	Ohio St. (16-7)
11	California (24-8)
12	Army (13-2)
13	Duquesne (14-4)
14	Villanova (20-5)
15	Marquette (12-5)
16	Washington (20-5)
17	Colorado (14-4)
18	Notre Dame (15-6)
19	Western Kentucky (22-3)
20	Roanoke (21-3)

#–NIT champion
*–NCAA champion

isn't a recent phenomenon. Francisco "Kiko" Martinez, a member of the 1936 bronze-medal winning Mexican Olympic team, was the leading scorer for New Mexico A&M (now New Mexico State), which finished with a 20-4 record after losing to NIT champion-to-be LIU in the opening round. . . . Junior college transfer Jesse "Cab" Renick, a full-blooded Choctaw Indian, played guard, center and forward for Missouri Valley co-champion Oklahoma A&M. He was named to the first five on the all-conference team and finished third in the league in scoring. Renick also lettered for the Aggies' football squad. In 1948, while playing for the Phillips 66 Oilers, he was a member of the gold-medal winning U.S. Olympic basketball team. . . . Baylor posted its lone victory over Oklahoma A&M (30-28) in a 19-game stretch of their series from 1923 through 1956.

Virginia Tech edged North Carolina, 36-35, for the Hokies' lone victory in a 30-game stretch of their series from 1931 through 1949. . . . Alabama, coached by Hank Crisp, finished atop the SEC standings just one year after placing 12th in the 13-team league. . . . Tennessee started a 17-game winning streak in its series with Mississippi State that extended through 1949. . . . Northwestern compiled its first losing record (7-13) in 12 seasons under coach Dutch Lonborg. . . . Grinnell (Ia.) finished in a tie for third place in the Missouri Valley in its final season as a member of the conference. . . . On the same day (March 11, 1939), Idaho State defeated the University of Mexico City, 32-23, in Pocatello, then lost, 32-30, to the Murtaugh Savages in Rupert, Idaho.

1938–39 NCAA CHAMPION: OREGON

SEASON STATISTICS OF OREGON REGULARS

PLAYER	POS.	CL.	G	PPG
Laddie Gale	F	Sr.	34	12.0
Slim Wintermute	C	Sr.	31	10.0
John Dick	F	Jr.	34	6.7
Wally Johansen	G	Sr.	34	5.7
Bobby Anet	G	Sr.	33	5.4
Bob Hardy	F	Jr.	30	3.8
Ted Sarpola	F	Jr.	27	3.4
Matt Pavalunas	G	Jr.	33	2.7
Ford Mullen	G	Jr.	29	1.2
TEAM TOTALS			**34**	**49.5**

1939 CHAMPIONSHIP GAME

EVANSTON, IL

OREGON (46)	FG	FT-A	PF	PTS.
Gale	2	4-5	1	8
Dick	5	5-5	3	15
Wintermute	2	0-1	1	4
Anet	4	2-3	3	10
Johansen	4	1-2	1	9
Mullen	0	0-0	0	0
Pavalunas	0	0-0	0	0
TOTALS	**17**	**12-16**	**9**	**46**
FT%: .750.				

OHIO STATE (33)	FG	FT-A	PF	PTS.
Hull	5	2-2	2	12
Baker	0	0-1	0	0
Schick	1	0-0	1	2
Dawson	1	0-0	4	2
Lynch	3	1-3	3	7
Maag	0	0-0	0	0
Scott	0	1-1	1	1
Boughner	1	0-0	0	2
Sattler	3	1-2	0	7
Mickelson	0	0-0	2	0
Stafford	0	0-0	0	0
TOTALS	**14**	**5-9**	**13**	**33**
FT%: .556.				
Halftime: Oregon 21-16.				

MOST OUTSTANDING PLAYER
None selected.

1939 NCAA Tournament

Summary: Four native Oregonians and one Washingtonian comprised the starting lineup for Oregon coach Howard Hobson. Guards Bobby Anet and Wally Johansen had been teammates since their grade school days in Astoria. Different brands of play and refereeing dominated an era when college basketball was basically a regional game. Intersectional contests were rare, although Oregon scheduled games in eight Eastern and Midwest cities (New York, Philadelphia, Buffalo, Cleveland, Detroit, Chicago, Peoria, Ill., and Des Moines). Oregon's rigorous slate might have made the Ducks more prepared for the inaugural NCAA Tournament. Another factor was Oregon's height. The Ducks, nicknamed "The Tall Firs" by a sportswriter because they had a 6-8 center and a pair of 6-4 1/2 forwards, boasted more size than most teams.

One and Only: John Dick is the only leading scorer in an NCAA Tournament final (15 points as a junior forward for champion Oregon in 1939 against Ohio State) to subsequently serve as an admiral in the U.S. Navy. Dick commanded the aircraft carrier Saratoga for two years and served as chief of staff for all carrier forces in the Western Pacific. . . . Oregon is the only NCAA champion to never have a player on its roster play in the NBA or the league's predecessor.

Numbers Game: Only two players scored at least 20 points in the eight tourney games. Ohio State's Jimmy Hull had the high game with 28 points in a 53-36 victory over Villanova in the Eastern Regional final. . . . Ohio State reached the NCAA championship game despite losing five of its first 10 outings. . . . Oklahoma trailed Oregon by only three points early in the second half of the national semifinals before the Ducks pulled away to win, 55-37.

Putting Things in Perspective: Oregon State, which compiled a 6-10 record in the PCC, defeated Oregon, 50-31. Oregon State was coming off a victory over Washington that snapped the Beavers' 13-game North Division losing streak.

Scoring Leader: Jimmy Hull, Ohio State (58 points, 19.3 ppg).

1939 CHAMPIONSHIP BRACKET

WINNINGEST PROGRAMS OF THE 1930s

RK.	SCHOOL	W.	L.	PCT.
1.	Long Island	198	38	.839
2.	Kentucky	162	34	.827
3.	St. John's	181	40	.819
4.	Kansas	153	37	.805
5.	Syracuse	143	37	.794
6.	Purdue	148	39	.791
7.	Western Kentucky	197	52	.791
8.	Rhode Island	142	39	.785
9.	Notre Dame	170	49	.776
10.	CCNY	120	35	.774

ALL-DECADE TEAM - 1930s

LeRoy (Cowboy) Edwards, C, Kentucky
Chuck Hyatt, F, Pittsburgh
Hank Luisetti, F, Stanford
John Moir, F, Notre Dame
Fred Pralle, G, Kansas
Joe Reiff, F, Northwestern
Forest (Aggie) Sale, F-C, Kentucky
Les Witte, F, Wyoming
John Wooden, G, Purdue
Jewell Young, F, Purdue
Co-Coaches: Phog Allen, Kansas and Clair Bee, Rider/LIU

LeRoy (Cowboy) Edwards

Kentucky
6-5 - C
Indianapolis, Ind. (Tech)

NCAA consensus All-American in 1935.

SEASON	G.	PTS.	AVG.
1934-35	21	343	16.3

(Dropped out of college following sophomore season.)

Chuck Hyatt

Pittsburgh
6-0 - F
Uniontown, Pa.

NCAA consensus first-team All-American in 1929 and 1930. . . . Elected to Naismith Memorial Basketball Hall of Fame in 1959.

SEASON	FGM	FTM	PTS.
1927-28	110	46	266
1928-29	118	64	300
1929-30	138	38	314
Totals	366	148	880

Angelo (Hank) Luisetti

Stanford
6-2 - F
San Francisco, Calif. (Galileo H.S.)

NCAA consensus All-American in 1936, 1937 and 1938. . . . Led the nation in scoring in 1936 and 1937. . . . Did not play in NCAA Tournament or NIT. . . . Elected to Naismith Memorial Basketball Hall of Fame in 1959.

SEASON	G.	PTS.	AVG.
1935-36	29	416	14.3
1936-37	24	410	17.1
1937-38	27	465	17.2
Totals	80	1291	16.1

John Moir

Notre Dame
6-2 - F
Niagara Falls, N.Y. (Trott Vocational)

NCAA consensus first-team All-American in 1936, 1937 and 1938.

SEASON	G.	PTS.	AVG.
1935-36	23	260	11.3
1936-37	22	290	13.2
1937-38	22	230	10.5
Totals	67	317	11.6

Ferdinand (Fred) Pralle

Kansas
6-3 - G
St. Louis, Mo. (Beaumont H.S.)

NCAA consensus All-American in 1938.

SEASON	G.	PTS.	AVG.
1935-36	23	152	6.6
1936-37	18	160	8.8
1937-38	20	214	10.7
Totals	61	526	8.6

Joe Reiff

Northwestern
6-2 - F
Chicago, Ill. (Crane H.S.)

NCAA consensus first-team All-American in 1931 and 1933.

SEASON	G.	PTS.	AVG.
1930-31	12	123	10.3
1931-32	12	104	8.7
1932-33	12	167	13.9
Totals	36	394	10.9

NOTE: Statistics are for Big Ten Conference games only.

Forest (Aggie) Sale

Kentucky
6-4 - F/C
Lawrenceburg, Ky. (Kavanaugh H.S.)

NCAA consensus first-team All-American in 1932 and 1933.

SEASON	G.	PTS.	AVG.
1930-31	..	62	....
1931-32	17	235	13.8
1932-33	23	324	14.0
Totals	..	621	....

Les Witte

Wyoming
6-0 - F
Lincoln, Neb.

NCAA consensus first-team All-American in 1932 and 1934.

SEASON	G.	PTS.	AVG.
1930-31	23	274	11.9
1931-32	20	238	11.9
1932-33	23	234	10.2
1933-34	27	323	12.0
Totals	93	1069	11.5

John Wooden

Purdue
5-10 - G
Martinsville, Ind.

NCAA consensus first-team All-American in 1930, 1931 and 1932. . . . Elected to Naismith Memorial Basketball Hall of Fame as a player in 1960.

SEASON	G.	PTS.	AVG.
1929-30	13	116	8.9
1930-31	17	140	8.2
1931-32	18	219	12.2
Totals	48	475	9.9

Jewell Young

Purdue
6-0 - F
Lafayette, Ind. (Jefferson H.S.)

NCAA consensus first-team All-American in 1937 and 1938.

SEASON	G.	PTS.	AVG.
1935-36	20	177	8.9
1936-37	20	243	12.2
1937-38	20	289	14.5
Totals	60	709	11.8

FORREST (PHOG) ALLEN

Kansas '06
Independence, Mo.

Elected to Naismith Memorial Basketball Hall of Fame in 1959. . . . U.S. Olympic team assistant coach in 1952. . . . Reached NCAA Final Four three times-1940 (2nd), 1952 (1st) and 1953 (2nd). . . . His 1922 and 1923 Kansas teams were selected as national champions by the Helms Foundation. . . . Holds the NCAA career record for most years coached.

SEASON	SCHOOL	OVERALL	LEAGUE	FINISH	POSTSEASON
1905-06	Baker	18-3	......	......	
1906-07	Baker	14-0	......	......	
1907-08	Baker	13-6	......	......	
1907-08	Kansas	18-6	6-0	1st (MVC)	
1908-09	Kansas	25-3	8-2	1st (MVC)	
1908-09	Haskell	27-5	......	......	
1912-13	Central Mo. St.	11-7	......	......	
1913-14	Central Mo. St.	15-4	......	......	
1914-15	Central Mo. St.	13-4	......	......	
1915-16	Central Mo. St.	9-4	......	......	
1916-17	Central Mo. St.	13-2	......	......	
1917-18	Central Mo. St.	9-4	......	......	
1918-19	Central Mo. St.	14-6	......	......	
1919-20	Kansas	10-7	9-7	3rd (MVC)	
1920-21	Kansas	10-8	10-8	4th (MVC)	
1921-22	Kansas	16-2	15-1	T1st (MVC)	
1922-23	Kansas	17-1	16-0	1st (MVC)	
1923-24	Kansas	16-3	15-1	1st (MVC)	
1924-25	Kansas	17-1	15-1	1st (MVC)	
1925-26	Kansas	16-2	16-2	1st (MVC)	
1926-27	Kansas	15-2	10-2	1st (MVC)	
1927-28	Kansas	9-9	9-9	4th (MVC)	
1928-29	Kansas	3-15	2-8	T5th (Big Six)	
1929-30	Kansas	14-4	7-3	2nd (Big Six)	
1930-31	Kansas	15-3	7-3	1st (Big Six)	
1931-32	Kansas	13-5	7-3	1st (Big Six)	
1932-33	Kansas	13-4	8-2	1st (Big Six)	
1933-34	Kansas	16-1	9-1	1st (Big Six)	
1934-35	Kansas	15-5	12-1	2nd (Big Six)	
1935-36	Kansas	21-2	10-0	1st (Big Six)	Olympic Playoffs (3-2)
1936-37	Kansas	15-4	8-2	T1st (Big Six)	
1937-38	Kansas	18-2	9-1	1st (Big Six)	DNP
1938-39	Kansas	13-7	6-4	3rd (Big Six)	DNP
1939-40	Kansas	19-6	8-2	T1st (Big Six)	NCAA (2-1)
1940-41	Kansas	12-6	7-3	T1st (Big Six)	DNP
1941-42	Kansas	17-5	8-2	T1st (Big Six)	NCAA (1-1)
1942-43	Kansas	22-6	10-0	1st (Big Six)	DNP
1943-44	Kansas	17-9	5-5	3rd (Big Six)	DNP
1944-45	Kansas	12-5	7-3	2nd (Big Six)	DNP
1945-46	Kansas	19-2	10-0	1st (Big Six)	DNP
1946-47	Kansas*	8-5	5-5	T3rd (Big Six)	DNP
1947-48	Kansas	9-15	4-8	T6th (Big Seven)	DNP
1948-49	Kansas	12-12	3-9	T6th (Big Seven)	DNP
1949-50	Kansas	14-11	8-4	T1st (Big Seven)	DNP
1950-51	Kansas	16-8	8-4	T2nd (Big Seven)	DNP
1951-52	Kansas	26-2	11-1	1st (Big Seven)	NCAA (4-0)
1952-53	Kansas	19-6	10-2	1st (Big Seven)	NCAA (3-1)
1953-54	Kansas	16-5	10-2	T1st (Big Seven)	DNP
1954-55	Kansas	11-10	5-7	5th (Big Seven)	DNP
1955-56	Kansas	14-9	6-6	5th (Big Seven)	DNP

*Howard Engleman finished out the season with an 8-6 record as coach when Allen was ordered to take a rest.
48-Year Coaching Record: 746-264 (.739) overall; 45-9 (.833) in three years at Baker; 27-5 (.844) in one year at Haskell; 84-31 (.730) in seven years at Central Missouri State; 588-218 (.730) in 39 years at Kansas; 115-31 (.788) in Missouri Valley Conference; 210-94 (.691) in Big Eight Conference; 10-3 (.769) in NCAA Tournament.

CLAIR BEE

Waynesburg '25
Grafton, W. Va.

Elected to Naismith Memorial Basketball Hall of Fame in 1967. . . . Coached LIU-Brooklyn to NIT titles in 1939 and 1941. . . . Second on the all-time coaches list for career winning percentage. . . . Compiled a 34-116 record with the NBA's Baltimore Bullets from 1952-53 through 1954-55.

SEASON	SCHOOL	OVERALL	POSTSEASON
1928-29	Rider	19-3	......
1929-30	Rider	17-2	......
1930-31	Rider	17-2	......
1931-32	LIU-Brooklyn	16-4	......
1932-33	LIU-Brooklyn	6-11	......
1933-34	LIU-Brooklyn	26-1	......

1934-35	LIU-Brooklyn	24-2	......
1935-36	LIU-Brooklyn	25-0	......
1936-37	LIU-Brooklyn	28-3	......
1937-38	LIU-Brooklyn	23-5	NIT (0-1)
1938-39	LIU-Brooklyn	23-0	NIT (3-0)
1939-40	LIU-Brooklyn	19-4	NIT (0-1)
1940-41	LIU-Brooklyn	25-2	NIT (3-0)
1941-42	LIU-Brooklyn	25-3	NIT (0-1)
1942-43	LIU-Brooklyn	13-6	DNP
1945-46	LIU-Brooklyn	14-9	DNP
1946-47	LIU-Brooklyn	17-5	NIT (0-1)
1947-48	LIU-Brooklyn	17-4	DNP
1948-49	LIU-Brooklyn	18-12	DNP
1949-50	LIU-Brooklyn	20-5	NIT (0-1)
1950-51	LIU-Brooklyn	20-4	DNP

21-Year Coaching Record: 412-87 (.826) overall; 53-7 (.883) in three years at Rider; 359-80 (.818) in 18 years at LIU-Brooklyn; 6-5 (.545) in NIT.

1939-40

AT A GLANCE

NCAA Champion: Indiana (20-3; coached by Branch McCracken; finished in second place in Big Ten with a 9-3 record, which was one game behind Purdue).

NIT Champion: Colorado (17-4; coached by Frosty Cox; won Mountain States Conference by three games with an 11-1 record).

New Rules: Teams have the choice of whether to shoot a free throw or take the ball out-of-bounds at midcourt. If two or more free throws are awarded, the option applies to the final free throw. . . . The backboards move from two to four feet from the end line to permit more movement under the goal.

NCAA First-Team All-Americans: Gus Broberg, G-F, Jr., Dartmouth; John Dick, F, Sr., Oregon; George Glamack, C, Jr., North Carolina; Bill Hapac, F, Sr., Illinois; Ralph Vaughn, F, Sr., Southern California.

Dr. James Naismith, the inventor of basketball who was born in Canada (Ontario), died at his home in Lawrence, Kan. He was 78. The previous season, Naismith criticized the zone defense in a talk before New York writers, saying: "I have no sympathy with it. The defensive team is stalling which lays back and waits for the offense to come to it. If a soccer team hung back and grouped itself in front of the goal, what could the other team do? The zone is much like that."

Clair Bee, the director of LIU's Department of Physical Education, coached the school's football, basketball and baseball teams. A New York Times article announcing the resumption of football at LIU pointed out that "Bee prefers football to basketball." On Thanksgiving Day, LIU's Dolly King started at center for the basketball team in a 59-41 victory over the alumni after starting at left end for the football squad and catching a touchdown pass that afternoon at Ebbets Field in a 35-14 defeat to Catholic University. King went on to become a consultant to President Johnson's Council on Physical Fitness.

North Carolina All-American George Glamack was an inspiration to those fond of individuals overcoming adversity. The Spalding Guide noted that "Glamack, who is ambidextrous when on the court, is also so nearsighted that the ball is merely a dim object, but apparently he never looked where he was shooting, depending upon his sense of distance and direction." The secret of "The Blind Bomber" was looking at the black lines on the court. By doing that he knew where he was in reference to the basket and could measure his shot. . . . Duke, coached by Eddie Cameron, became the 12th different school to win the Southern Conference championship in the first 19 years of the league.

Seton Hall's "Wonder Five" finished the season undefeated (19-0), but the Pirates, coached by Honey Russell, didn't participate in either the NCAA Tournament or NIT. . . . The first basketball game telecast was on February 28, 1940, when W2XBS carried a doubleheader from Madison Square Garden (Pittsburgh vs. Fordham and NYU vs. Georgetown). . . . NYU defeated St. John's for the 15th time in their first 18 meetings. . . . Future NBA coaching legend Arnold "Red" Auerbach was George Washington's leading scorer, averaging 8.5 points per game. . . . Dartmouth's school-record 38-game homecourt winning streak was snapped by Army, 44-36. . . . Navy's streak of consecutive non-losing seasons since the school's initial campaign in 1907-08 ended at 33 when the Midshipmen compiled a 3-11 record. They entered the season having won more than 80 percent of their games.

1939-40 PREMO POWER POLL

RANKING	SCHOOL
1	Indiana* (20-3)
2	USC (20-3)
3	Colorado# (17-4)
4	Duquesne (20-3)
5	Oklahoma St. (26-3)
6	Purdue (16-4)
7	NYU (18-1)
8	Rice (25-4)
9	Kansas (19-6)
10	DePaul (22-6)
11	LIU-Brooklyn (19-4)
12	Seton Hall (19-0)
13	Utah (18-4)
14	St. John's (15-5)
15	Western Kentucky (24-6)
16	Villanova (17-2)
17	Marshall (25-4)
18	Santa Clara (17-3)
19	Rhode Island (19-3)
20	Toledo (24-6)

#–NIT champion
*–NCAA champion

Ohio Wesleyan defeated Dayton twice in a single season for the third consecutive year. . . . Tennessee sophomore Bernie Mehen, described by Kentucky coach Adolph Rupp as "one of the greatest first-year men of all-time," earned a berth as a forward on the SEC All-Tournament team. . . . Kentucky began a streak of 19 consecutive victories over Vanderbilt that ended in 1951. . . . Sewanee (Tenn.) dropped out of the SEC after its sixth winless league record in eight years as a member of the conference. . . . Rice (25-4/coached by Buster Brannon) and Toledo (24-6/Harold Anderson) had their winningest season in school history. . . . Texas-El Paso ended a 20-game losing streak to archrival New Mexico A&M in their series. . . . Washington, coached by Hec Edmundson, registered its only losing record (10-15) in a 28-year stretch from 1920-21 through 1947-48. . . . Oregon State lost 13 consecutive games at Washington until defeating the Huskies in Seattle, 46-31, to clinch the PCC championship. Earlier, Oregon State ended a 13-game losing streak in its series with Washington State.

1940 NCAA Tournament

Summary: Indiana's "Hurryin' Hoosiers" were noted for their fastbreak emphasizing quick ball movement because coach Branch McCracken detested dribbling. If that didn't keep him awake, something else certainly did because McCracken had a habit of drinking about 30 cups of coffee a day. The Hoosiers' 60-42 victory over Kansas in the NCAA final marked the highest output for the winner in the championship game until 1950. Kansas newspapers called the blitzing IU team a

1939-40 UNDEFEATED TEAM: SETON HALL (19-0)

COACH: HONEY RUSSELL

SH	OPPONENT	PIRATES HIGH SCORER
45	Alumni 29	Parpan 12
58	Mount St. Mary's 32	Sadowski 13
53	Tulane 25	Davies 9
43	Florida 41	Davies/Sadowski 13
51	William & Mary 35	Sadowski 17
48	at Scranton 32	Sadowski 17
69	Becker 29	Sadowski 14
42	at Kutztown 34	Sadowski 15
50	Loyola (Md.) 40	Sadowski 13
55	at St. Peter's 27	Coyle 13
51	at Brooklyn 34	Fischer 13
44	Rider 32	Davies/Ruthenberg 8
48	St. Francis (Pa.) 36	Davies 17
46	St. Bonaventure 41	Davies 19
53	Kutztown 33	Davies 15
52	Canisius 46	Davies 17
53	Catholic 27	Ryan 13
43	Brooklyn 41	Delany 16
68	Scranton 39	Davies 16

Note: Seton Hall played its home games at five different arenas-East Orange High School, Elizabeth Armory, Orange Armory, Orange High School and Dickinson High School (Jersey City).

INDIVIDUAL STATISTICS FOR SETON HALL REGULARS

PLAYER	POS.	CL.	G.	PPG
Ed Sadowski*	C	Sr.	9	12.2
Bob Davies	F	So.	18	11.8
Bob Fischer	F	So.	18	4.9
John Ruthenberg	G-C	So.	19	4.7
Bob Holm	G	So.	17	4.2
Frank Delany	G-F	Sr.	19	3.8
Bernie Coyle	G-F	Sr.	18	3.7
Nick Parpan	G-F	Jr.	14	3.4
Ken Pine	C	So.	16	3.2
Ray Studwell	F-G	So.	18	1.2

*Sadowski missed half of the season because of a broken kneecap.

"tornado" in the wake of the one-sided final. "That tornado was us," boasted Hoosiers guard Marv Huffman, "and we just blew them out of the stadium!"

Outcome for Defending Champion: Oregon (19-12) finished second in the North Division of the Pacific Coast Conference. The Ducks' defeats were by an average margin of just 4.25 points with only two of them by more than six.

Biggest Upset: Heavily favored Southern Cal blew a six-point lead in the closing minutes of a 43-42 setback against Kansas in a national semifinal.

Star Gazing: Huffman, the only senior among Indiana's regulars and the younger brother of former Hoosiers standout Vern Huffman (NCAA consensus All-American in 1936 in basketball and football), was named Final Four Most Outstanding Player despite his lowly 4.3-point scoring average for the season. The only game all year when Marv Huffman managed double-digits in scoring was the NCAA final when he tied Jay

McCreary with a team-high 12 points. McCreary went on to become LSU's head coach for eight seasons from 1957-58 through 1964-65 before serving as an assistant under Press Maravich when his son, Pete, set national scoring records that might never be matched. McCreary's Muncie, Ind., High School team won the 1952 state championship and was runner-up in 1954 to Milan, the later game depicted in the hit movie "Hoosiers."

One and Only: McCracken is the only NCAA consensus first-team All-American (1930) to later coach his alma mater to an NCAA championship. He is one of six NCAA consensus first-team All-Americans to later coach in the NCAA Tournament.

Numbers Game: Bob Allen is the only player to lead an NCAA championship game in scoring while playing for his father. Phog Allen was coach of the Kansas squad that lost the championship game to Indiana despite his son's game-high total of 13 points. . . . Kansas' Howard Engleman had a tourney-high 21 points in a 50-44

1939–40 NCAA CHAMPION: INDIANA

SEASON STATISTICS OF INDIANA REGULARS

PLAYER	POS.	CL.	G	PPG
Curly Armstrong	F	Jr.	23	8.9
Herman Schaefer	G-F	Jr.	23	8.0
Bill Menke	C	Jr.	23	7.7
Bob Dro	F-G	Jr.	23	6.3
Jay McCreary	F	Jr.	21	4.5
Marv Huffman	G	Sr.	23	4.3
Andy Zimmer	C	So.	18	1.8
Chet Francis	F	Jr.	14	1.4
Bob Menke	C-F	Jr.	18	1.4
Ralph Dorsey	F	Sr.	20	1.2
James Gridley	G	Jr.	18	1.1
Bill Torphy	G	So.	12	1.0
TEAM TOTALS			**23**	**45.6**

1940 CHAMPIONSHIP GAME

KANSAS CITY, MO

INDIANA (60)	FG	FT-A	PF	PTS.
Schaefer	4	1-1	1	9
McCreary	6	0-0	2	12
W. Menke	2	1-2	3	5
Huffman	5	2-3	4	12
Dro	3	1-1	4	7
Armstrong	4	2-3	3	10
Gridley	0	0-0	0	0
R. Menke	0	0-0	0	0
Zimmer	2	1-1	1	5
Dorsey	0	0-0	0	0
Francis	0	0-0	1	0
TOTALS	**26**	**8-11**	**19**	**60**
FT%: .723.				

KANSAS (42)	FG	FT-A	PF	PTS.
Ebling	1	2-5	0	4
Engleman	5	2-3	3	12
Allen	5	3-4	3	13
Miller	0	2-2	4	2
Harp	2	1-3	1	5
Hunter	0	1-1	0	1
Hogben	2	0-0	0	4
Kline	0	0-0	0	0
Voran	0	1-2	0	1
Sands	0	0-0	0	0
Johnson	0	0-0	0	0
TOTALS	**15**	**12-20**	**11**	**42**
FT%: .600.				
Halftime: Indiana 32-19.				

ALL-TOURNAMENT TEAM
Bob Allen, C, Jr., Kansas
Howard Engleman, F, Jr., Kansas
Marvin Huffman, G-F, Sr., Indiana*
Jay McCreary, G-F, Jr., Indiana
Bill Menke, C, Jr., Indiana
 * Most Outstanding Tournament Player

victory over Rice in a Western Regional semifinal. . . . Winning teams usually shot about 30 percent from the floor at this time in the sport's history, but Springfield's 12.7 percent shooting (8 for 63) in an 48-24 opening-round loss to Indiana was particularly paltry. . . . Colorado, coached by Frosty Cox, won the NIT by extending its school-record winning streak to 12 games in a row before the Buffaloes lost both of their outings in the NCAA Tournament.

What Might Have Been: Indiana would not have appeared in the tourney if Big Ten champion Purdue participated in the event instead of staying home because Boilermakers coach Piggy Lambert wasn't fond of postseason play. The Hoosiers, 9-3 in Big Ten competition, became the only NCAA kingpin with more than two conference defeats until Michigan State in 1979.

Scoring Leader: Howard Engleman, Kansas (39 points, 13 ppg).

All-Tournament Team

Bob Allen, C, Jr., Kansas (21 points in final two games)
Howard Engleman, F, Jr., Kansas (18 points)
*Marv Huffman, G-F, Sr., Indiana (18 points)
Jay McCreary, G-F, Jr., Indiana (12 points)
Bill Menke, C, Jr., Indiana (15 points)

   *Named Most Outstanding Player.

1940 CHAMPIONSHIP BRACKET

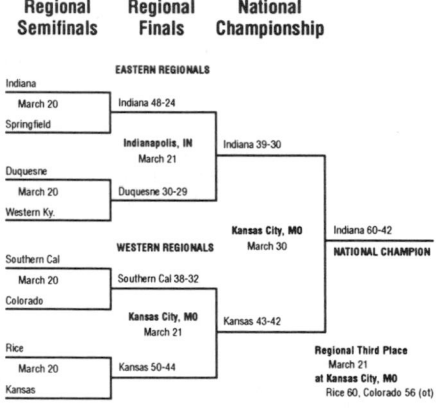

Regional Semifinals	Regional Finals	National Championship
	EASTERN REGIONALS	

Indiana
March 20 — Indiana 48-24
Springfield
   Indianapolis, IN — Indiana 39-30
   March 21
Duquesne
March 20 — Duquesne 30-29
Western Ky.
      Kansas City, MO — Indiana 60-42
      March 30 — NATIONAL CHAMPION
  WESTERN REGIONALS
Southern Cal
March 20 — Southern Cal 38-32
Colorado
   Kansas City, MO — Kansas 43-42
   March 21
Rice
March 20 — Kansas 50-44
Kansas

Regional Third Place
March 21
at Kansas City, MO
Rice 60, Colorado 56 (ot)

1940-41

AT A GLANCE

NCAA Champion: Wisconsin (20-3; coached by Bud Foster; won Big Ten title by one game with an 11-1 record).

NIT Champion: Long Island (25-2; coached by Clair Bee).

New Rule: Fan-shaped backboards are legalized.

NCAA First-Team All-Americans: John Adams, F, Sr., Arkansas; Gus Broberg, G-F, Sr., Dartmouth; Howard Engleman, F, Sr., Kansas; Gene Englund, C, Sr., Wisconsin; George Glamack, C, Sr., North Carolina.

Postseason conference tournaments haven't always filled big-time league coffers. According to the *Official Basketball Guide,* the SEC Tournament "for the first time in history was a complete financial success, paying the entire expenses of all twelve schools and leaving a substantial amount in the conference treasury. The gross gate was slightly over $15,000."

Dartmouth's Gus Broberg became the first of five players in Ivy League history to win three consecutive scoring championships (conference was known at the time as the Eastern Intercollegiate League). Broberg played professional basketball briefly before World War II. After enlisting in the Marines as an aviator, he lost his right arm in a plane crash. Broberg went on to study law and become a respected judge in Florida.

Seton Hall's 42-game winning streak under coach Honey Russell ended when the Pirates were leveled by Long Island, 49-26, in the NIT. . . . Army compiled its first losing record (5-11) in 22 years. . . . Rhode Island was undefeated through 16 games before bowing to Springfield, 59-50.

St. Louis, winless in seven games before meeting Oklahoma A&M, stunned the defending Missouri Valley Conference champion, 32-29, in perhaps the biggest upset of the season. . . . Iowa State, coached by Louis Menze, earned a share of the Big Six Conference championship after finishing in a tie for last place the previous year. . . . Kansas State's Nichols Gymnasium was packed with legislators when students at the Wildcats' game against archrival Kansas chose to illustrate the danger of cramped seating conditions in the old building by dropping a ketchup-stained dummy from the rafters. . . . Kansas State posted its lone victory over Oklahoma (41-36) in an 18-game stretch of their series from 1936 through 1944 and Nebraska notched its lone triumph over the Sooners (43-42) in a 17-game span of their series from 1939 to 1947. . . . Washburn (Kan.) dropped out of the Missouri Valley after its seventh non-winning record in as many seasons in the league. . . . Wittenberg (O.) defeated Dayton for the eighth consecutive year and Mount Union (O.) beat the Flyers for the fourth straight campaign. . . . Creighton defeated Marquette for the 18th time in their last 25 meetings.

Stanford ended Southern Cal's school-record 20-game homecourt winning streak. . . . UCLA sustained 20 defeats for the third time in four years. . . . Washington State (26-6/coached by Jack Friel) had its winningest season in school history. . . . New Mexico lost 19 consecutive

1940–41 PREMO POWER POLL

RANKING	SCHOOL
1	LIU-Brooklyn# (25-2)
2	Wisconsin* (20-3)
3	Washington St. (26-6)
4	Indiana (17-3)
5	Stanford (21-5)
6	Ohio Univ. (18-4)
7	Arkansas (20-3)
8	Duquesne (17-3)
9	Westminster (Pa.) (20-2)
10	Western Kentucky (22-4)
11	Toledo (21-3)
12	Dartmouth (19-5)
13	CCNY (17-5)
14	Washington & Jefferson (15-3)
15	San Diego St. (24-7)
16	Murray St. (25-5)
17	Seton Hall (20-2)
18	Penn St. (15-5)
19	Oregon St. (19-9)
20	Xavier (La.) (29-0)

#–NIT champion
*–NCAA champion

games to archrival New Mexico State until defeating the Aggies, 44-29.

Duke opened the season with a 43-39 defeat to Lincoln Memorial and had a 6-9 record after 15 games. The Blue Devils, however, won their last seven games, including two victories over Southern Conference regular-season champion North Carolina, and captured the league tournament. . . .

1940–41 NCAA CHAMPION: WISCONSIN

SEASON STATISTICS OF WISCONSIN REGULARS

PLAYER	POS.	CL.	G	PPG
Gene Englund	C	Sr.	23	13.2
John Kotz	F	So.	23	9.0
Ted Strain	G	Sr.	23	4.8
Charlie Epperson	F	Jr.	22	4.5
Fred Rehm	G	So.	21	3.7
Bob Alwin	G	Jr.	21	2.7
Don Timmerman	C	Sr.	22	1.9
Ed Scheiwe	G	Jr.	17	1.4
TEAM TOTALS			**23**	**43.7**

1941 CHAMPIONSHIP GAME

KANSAS CITY, MO

WISCONSIN (39)	FG	FT-A	PF	PTS.
Epperson	2	0-0	3	4
Schrage	0	0-0	1	0
Kotz	5	2-3	2	12
Englund	5	3-4	2	13
Timmerman	1	0-0	1	2
Rehm	2	0-1	2	4
Strain	0	2-2	1	2
Alwin	1	0-0	0	2
TOTALS	**16**	**7-10**	**12**	**39**

FG%: .254; FT%: .700.

WASHINGTON STATE (34)	FG	FT-A	PF	PTS.
Gentry	0	1-2	1	1
Gilberg	1	0-2	1	2
Butts	1	1-1	1	3
Lindeman	0	3-4	1	3
Zimmerman	0	0-0	0	0
Gebert	10	1-2	1	21
Hunt	0	0-0	0	0
Sundquist	2	0-1	3	4
Hooper	0	0-0	0	0
TOTALS	**14**	**6-12**	**8**	**34**

FG%: .215; FT%: .500.
Halftime: Wisconsin 21-17.

MOST OUTSTANDING PLAYER
John Kotz, F, Soph., Wisconsin

Maryland (1-21) won its season finale to avoid going winless. . . . North Carolina State started a 15-game winning streak in its series with Clemson that extended through 1956. Meanwhile, N.C. State started a 15-game losing streak in its series with Duke that ran to 1947. . . . Florida's second-place finish in the SEC was the Gators' highest in the league until 1966-67. . . . Tulane posted its first winning record (8-6) in 11 seasons.

1941 NCAA Tournament

Summary: Wisconsin, capitalizing on a homecourt advantage to overcome halftime deficits in the first two rounds of the tourney, captured the crown in a fairy tale script resembling the hit movie "Hoosiers". In 1940, Wisconsin finished a dismal ninth in the Big Ten and the Badgers' overall record of 5-15 represented their worst mark since joining the Big Ten in 1906. They became the only school to finish more than two games below .500 one season and win the national championship the next year. The 20-3 Badgers, coached by Bud Foster, tied a school single-season record for most victories.

Outcome for Defending Champion: Indiana (17-3), an eight-point loser to Wisconsin, finished runner-up to the Badgers in the Big Ten. The Hoosiers' two other defeats were by a total of six points (at Southern Cal and Purdue).

Star Gazing: Wisconsin limited Washington State center Paul Lindeman (6-7, 230 pounds) to three points (all free throws) in the final after he averaged 20 points in the Cougars' first two games. Lindeman scored 26 of the Cougars' points in a 48-39 decision over Creighton in the opening round.

One and Only: Howard "Red" Hickey is the only individual to appear in the Final Four before playing and coaching in the NFL at least five seasons apiece. Hickey, a first-team All-Southwest Conference forward for Arkansas, was sufficiently skilled as a tackle in football to make the Razorbacks' all-decade team. A lineman for six seasons

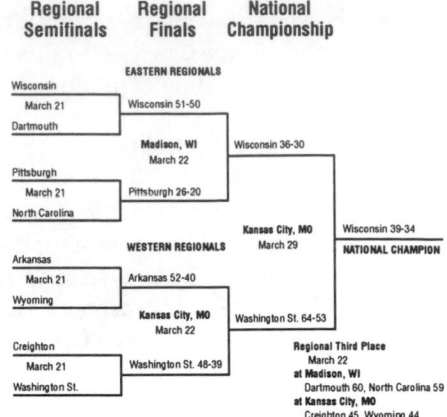

1941 CHAMPIONSHIP BRACKET

in the NFL with two different franchises from 1941 through 1948, he coached the San Francisco 49ers for five years from 1959 through 1963, compiling a 27-27-1 record.

Numbers Game: The only player to score more than 30 points in a playoff game the first 11 years of the event was North Carolina's George Glamack, who supplied 31 points in a 60-59 loss to Dartmouth in the East Regional third-place game. Glamack had a game-high nine points when the Tar Heels succumbed to Pittsburgh, 26-20, in the opening round in the lowest-scoring contest in NCAA playoff history. . . . Washington State hit an anemic 21.5 percent of its field-goal attempts (14 of 65) in the national final.

Putting Things in Perspective: Amazingly, Wisconsin lost its conference opener by 17 points at Minnesota when the Badgers failed to make a single field goal in the second half before going undefeated through the remainder of their league schedule and the playoffs.

Scoring Leader: John Adams, Arkansas (48 points, 24 ppg).

Most Outstanding Player: John Kotz, F, Soph., Wisconsin (22 points in final two games).

1941-42

AT A GLANCE

NCAA Champion: Stanford (27-4; coached by Everett Dean; won PCC South Division by four games with an 11-1 record).

NIT Champion: West Virginia (19-4; coached by Dyke Raese).

NCAA First-Team All-Americans: Price Brookfield, C, Sr., West Texas State; Bob Davies, G, Sr., Seton Hall; Bob Kinney, C, Sr., Rice; John Kotz, F, Jr., Wisconsin; Andy Phillip, F, Soph., Illinois.

Everett Dean was Stanford's basketball coach from 1938 to 1951 and baseball coach from 1950 to 1955.

Long Island's Clair Bee was the cream of the crop in the coaching profession, improving his career winning percentage to an astonishing 87.7 (291-41 record) when the Blackbirds compiled a 25-3 mark. It was the seventh time in nine years that they lost fewer than four games.

Tennessee held LIU to nine points in the second half in a 36-33 victory in the Sugar Bowl Tournament, snapping LIU's 23-game winning streak. LIU was seeded No. 1 in the NIT, but the Blackbirds bowed in the opening round to eventual champion West Virginia, 58-49.

UCLA continued to struggle, compiling a losing league record for the 15th time in as many seasons as a member of the Pacific Coast Conference. Southern Cal defeated UCLA four times, extending the Trojans' winning streak against the Bruins to 40 games. . . . Arizona's 9-13 record marked the Wildcats' first losing season in the last 16 years under coach Fred Enke. . . . Brigham Young, coached by Floyd Millet, compiled its best winning percentage in school history (17-3, .850). Two of the Cougars' defeats were to Colorado and the other setback was at Wyoming.

Bob Faught, a 6-5 sophomore center, joined Notre Dame's basketball team in an effort to keep in shape for tennis. He proceeded to lead the Irish in scoring with 9.5 points per game, including 26 in a 55-43 victory over NYU at Madison Square Garden. . . . Rhode Island defeated New Hampshire, 127-50, in a game where the URI regulars played just the first 16 minutes. . . . Dartmouth (22-4/coached by Ozzie Cowles) had its winningest season in school history. . . . Penn's Lou Jourdet coached the son (Larry Davis) of a player (Lardie Davis) he had on his Penn roster in 1918 and 1919. . . . Western Kentucky finished going full circle in national postseason competition. WKU was runner-up in the NIT after participating in the NAIA Tournament in 1938 and NCAA Tournament in 1940.

Iowa, coached by Rollie Williams, won six consecutive conference games late in the season to end a streak of eight straight non-winning Big Ten records. . . . Wittenberg (O.) defeated Bowling Green for the seventh straight season. . . . Texas Christian notched its first winning record in eight years (13-10). . . . Kansas' Ralph Miller, who would later be elected to the Naismith Memorial Basketball Hall of Fame after winning 657 games in 38 seasons at three major universities, led the Big Six Conference in scoring after missing the previous season following knee surgery. Kansas was eliminated in the NCAA Tournament by Colorado, a school that had four starters who grew up in Kansas. Colorado won its first 14 games (existing school record) before bowing at Wyoming, 40-39.

1941–42 PREMO POWER POLL

RANKING	SCHOOL
1	Stanford* (28-4)
2	LIU-Brooklyn (25-3)
3	Rice (22-5)
4	Colorado (16-2)
5	West Virginia# (19-4)
6	Dartmouth (22-4)
7	Western Kentucky (29-5)
8	Penn State (18-3)
9	West Texas St. (28-3)
10	Duke (22-2)
11	Tennessee (19-3)
12	BYU (17-3)
13	Toledo (23-5)
14	Kentucky (19-6)
15	Kansas (17-5)
16	Arkansas (19-4)
17	Illinois (18-5)
18	Creighton (18-5)
19	CCNY (16-3)
20	Mount Union (17-1)

#–NIT champion
*–NCAA champion

1942 NCAA Tournament

Summary: Stanford overcame the title game absence of flu-ridden standout Jim Pollard, who scored 43.4 percent of his team's points in its first two tourney contests. Was it worth it? Stanford (28-4/coached by Everett Dean) took home a meager check for $93.75 to cover its stay in Kansas City to climax the school's all-time winningest season. Pollard popped in a tourney-high 26 points in a 53-47 opening-game victory over Rice.

Outcome for Defending Champion: Wisconsin (14-7) finished in a three-way tie for second place in the Big Ten despite losing its first three conference contests.

Star Gazing: Three Stanford starters-co-captains Don Burness and Bill Cowden and sophomore Howie Dallmar-attended the same high school in San Francisco. . . . Kentucky's first game in an NCAA Tournament resulted in a 46-44 verdict over Big Ten titlist Illinois.

One and Only: Dallmar, a 6-5 guard, became the only Final Four Most Outstanding Player to complete his collegiate playing career attending another university (NCAA consensus first-team All-American with Penn in 1945). Sent to Philadelphia by the Navy toward the end of World

1942 NCAA CHAMPION: STANFORD

SEASON STATISTICS OF STANFORD REGULARS

PLAYER	POS.	CL.	G	PPG
Jim Pollard	F	Jr.	23	10.5
Ed Voss	C	Jr.	29	8.7
Don Burness	F	Sr.	26	8.5
Howie Dallmar	G	So.	31	7.3
Bill Cowden	G	Sr.	31	5.5
Jack Dana	F	Jr.	27	3.7
Freddie Linari	F	Jr.	25	2.0
Leo McCaffrey	G	Jr.	22	1.0
TEAM TOTALS			**31**	**39.8**

1942 CHAMPIONSHIP GAME

KANSAS CITY, MO

STANFORD (53)	MIN.	FG	FT-A	PF	PTS.
Dana	40	7	0-0	0	14
Burness	9	0	0-0	0	0
Linari	31	3	0-0	0	6
Voss	40	6	1-1	2	13
Cowden	40	2	1-2	3	5
Dallmar	40	6	3-5	0	15
TOTALS	**200**	**24**	**5-8**	**5**	**53**

FT%: .625.

DARTMOUTH (38)	MIN.	FG	FT-A	PF	PTS.
Myers	29	4	0-1	1	8
Parmer	11	1	0-0	0	2
Munroe	40	5	2-2	1	12
Olsen	40	4	0-1	0	8
Pearson	40	2	2-2	3	6
Skaug	40	1	0-0	2	2
TOTALS	**200**	**17**	**4-6**	**7**	**38**

FT%: .667.
Halftime: Stanford 24-22.

MOST OUTSTANDING PLAYER
Howie Dallmar, G, Soph., Stanford

1942 CHAMPIONSHIP BRACKET

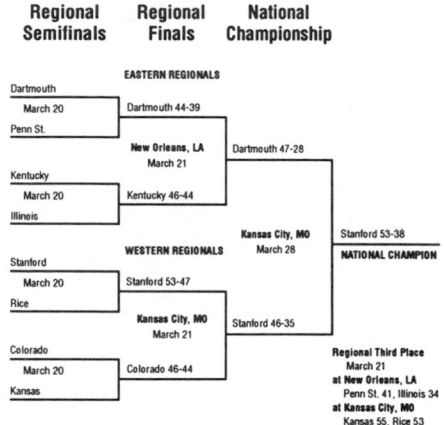

Regional Semifinals	Regional Finals	National Championship

EASTERN REGIONALS

Dartmouth
March 20 — Dartmouth 44-39
Penn St.

New Orleans, LA
March 21 — Dartmouth 47-28

Kentucky
March 20 — Kentucky 46-44
Illinois

Kansas City, MO
March 28 — Stanford 53-38
NATIONAL CHAMPION

WESTERN REGIONALS

Stanford
March 20 — Stanford 53-47
Rice

Kansas City, MO
March 21 — Stanford 46-35

Colorado
March 20 — Colorado 46-44
Kansas

Regional Third Place
March 21
at New Orleans, LA
Penn St. 41, Illinois 34
at Kansas City, MO
Kansas 55, Rice 53

War II to attend pre-flight training school, Dallmar enrolled at Penn to complete his undergraduate work and to use his final season of sports eligibility (NCAA consensus first-team All-American in 1945). He is also the only Most Outstanding Player to guide a school other than his alma mater to the playoffs. Dallmar posted a 1-1 tourney record with Penn in 1953 before coaching Stanford for 21 years without directing his alma mater to the NCAA playoffs. The principal culprit in denying Dallmar an NCAA appearance with the Cardinal was UCLA's dynasty under John Wooden. Both coaches retired at the end of the 1974-75 season. One of the three defeats for the NCAA champion Bruins that year was at Stanford. Dallmar, an All-NBA first-team selection in 1947-48 when he led the league in assists with the defending champion Philadelphia Warriors, moonlighted in sports the next season in a way practically never done. He played professionally for the Warriors while compiling a 15-8 record in his rookie campaign as coach of Penn.

Numbers Game: Stanford's Dean, compiling a 3-0 tournament record, is the only unbeaten coach in NCAA playoff history. He is also the only NCAA basketball championship coach to win a College World Series baseball game for the same school (1953). . . . . Kentucky's output in a 47-28 loss to Dartmouth in the national semifinals is an all-time Final Four-low.

Scoring Leaders: Stanford's Jim Pollard and Rice's Chet Palmer (43 points, 21.5 ppg).

Most Outstanding Player: Howie Dallmar, G, Soph., Stanford (20 points in final two games).

1942-43

AT A GLANCE

NCAA Champion: Wyoming (31-2; coached by Everett Shelton; won Big Seven Conference by three games with an 11-1 record).

NIT Champion: St. John's (21-3; coached by Joe Lapchick).

New Conference: Metropolitan New York (disbanded after 1962-63 season)

New Rule: Any player eligible to start an overtime period is allowed an extra personal foul, increasing the total for disqualification to five fouls.

NCAA First-Team All-Americans: Ed Beisser, C, Sr., Creighton; Charles Black, F, Soph., Kansas; Harry Boykoff, C, Soph., St. John's; Bill Closs, C-F, Sr., Rice; Andy Phillip, F, Jr., Illinois; George Senesky, F, Sr., St. Joseph's.

Illinois, undefeated in Big Ten competition (12-0) after having four sophomore starters on a league championship squad dubbed "The Whiz Kids" the previous season, placed four players on the first five of the all-conference team-forward Andy Phillip, center Art Mathisen and guards Gene Vance and Jack Smiley. The fifth Illini starter was named to the second five-forward Ken Menke. Phillip was the first player to average more than 20 points per game for a full season in Big Ten play (21.3). All but Mathisen went on to play professionally.

This is the only year when the Big Ten wasn't represented in the NCAA Tournament. Illinois, the only Big Ten team to go undefeated in league play in a 30-year span from 1930-31 through 1959-60, didn't participate in a postseason tournament although it ranked first in the final Dunkel Ratings. The school's athletic director declined a bid because he thought it would be unfair to his players to keep them away from their classes for three weeks. The Illini's lone loss was to Camp Grant at Rockford, Ill., where coach Doug Mills played a mostly substitute lineup. Something more pressing dismantled the team at the end of the school year when all five starters headed to active duty in the armed forces. Before entering the service, however, Phillip led the Illini's baseball squad in innings pitched with 64.

RED CROSS GAMES

For three consecutive years during World War II, the NCAA and NIT champions met in a benefit game at Madison Square Garden in New York to raise money for the Red Cross. The NCAA champions won all three games.

YEAR	OUTCOME
1943	Wyoming (NCAA) 52, St. John's (NIT) 47
1944	Utah (NCAA) 43, St. John's (NIT) 36
1945	Oklahoma A&M (NCAA) 52, DePaul (NIT) 44

Wyoming head coach Ev Shelton.

1942–43 NCAA CHAMPION: WYOMING

SEASON STATISTICS OF WYOMING REGULARS

PLAYER	POS.	CL.	G	PPG
Milo Komenich	C	Jr.	33	16.7
Kenny Sailors	F	Jr.	33	15.0
Jim Weir	F	Jr.	33	10.1
Floyd Volker	F-G	Jr.	33	6.4
Jimmie Reese	F	So.	23	4.3
Lew Roney	G	Jr.	30	2.7
Jim Collins	G	So.	31	2.5
Antone Katana	C	So.	24	1.5
Earl Ray	G	Jr.	19	0.8
TEAM TOTALS			**33**	**59.4**

1943 CHAMPIONSHIP GAME

NEW YORK, NY

WYOMING (46)	FG	FT-A	PF	PTS.
Sailors	6	4-5	2	16
Collins	4	0-0	1	8
Weir	2	1-3	2	5
Waite	0	0-0	0	0
Komenich	4	1-4	2	9
Volker	2	1-2	3	5
Roney	0	1-2	1	1
Reese	1	0-0	0	2
TOTALS	**19**	**8-16**	**11**	**46**

FT%: .500.

GEORGETOWN (40)	FG	FT-A	PF	PTS.
Reilly	1	0-0	0	2
Potolicchio	1	2-3	1	4
Gabbianelli	1	2-3	3	4
Hyde	0	0-0	0	0
Mahnken	2	2-3	2	6
Hassett	3	0-3	4	6
Finnerty	0	0-0	0	0
Kraus	2	0-1	3	4
Feeney	4	0-0	1	8
Duffey	0	0-0	0	0
TOTALS	**14**	**6-13**	**14**	**34**

FT%: .462.
Halftime: Wyoming 18-16.

MOST OUTSTANDING PLAYER
Kenny Sailors, F, Jr., Wyoming

Purdue's streak of winning seasons stopped at 23 when the Boilermakers lost six of seven games in a mid-season stretch to finish with a 9-11 record. . . . St. Louis (11-10), coached by Bob Klenck, ended a string of seven straight losing seasons and began a streak of 19 consecutive winning records. . . . Notre Dame coach George Keogan died of a heart attack on February 17, 1943. In 24 seasons as a college coach (20 with the Irish), he never had a losing record. Keogan passed away before ever appearing in the NIT or NCAA Tournament. . . . Kentucky lost seven consecutive games to Notre Dame until defeating the Irish, 60-55.

Center Ed Beisser, forward Ralph Langer and guard Dick Nolan finished their three-year varsity careers at Creighton with two Missouri Valley Conference undisputed championships and one co-championship. The Bluejays were undefeated entering postseason competition but were nipped by Washington & Jefferson, 43-42, in the first round of the NIT. . . . Toledo's undefeated home-court streak reached 40 games before it was snapped by DePaul, 49-40. . . . Valparaiso, compiling a 17-4 record, claimed to possess the tallest team in the country with a starting lineup averaging 6-6.

St. Joseph's George Senesky (23.4 ppg) became the only non-Rhode Island State player to lead the nation in scoring in a seven-year span from 1937-38 through 1943-44. . . . Manhattan, boasting eight freshmen among its first 10 players, registered an 18-3 record, including a 42-38 victory over eventual NIT champion St. John's. . . . Syracuse's streak of 18 consecutive winning records under coach Lew Andreas ended when the Orangemen compiled an 8-10 mark. . . . Davidson defeated North Carolina, 57-41, for the Wildcats' lone victory in a 19-game stretch of their series from 1939 through 1948.

Western Kentucky, coached by Ed Diddle, became the first school to compile 10 consecutive 20-win seasons. . . . Center Don Barksdale's 18-point effort helped UCLA end USC's 42-game winning streak in their series with the Bruins, 42-

1942–43 PREMO POWER POLL

RANKING	SCHOOL
1	Illinois (17-1)
2	Wyoming* (31-2)
3	Notre Dame (18-2)
4	St. John's# (21-3)
5	Indiana (18-2)
6	Georgetown (22-5)
7	DePaul (19-5)
8	Creighton (19-2)
9	Dartmouth (20-3)
10	Western Kentucky (24-3)
11	Toledo (22-4)
12	Kentucky (17-6)
13	Manhattan (18-3)
14	Penn St. (15-4)
15	Arizona (22-2)
16	Washington & Jefferson (18-5)
17	Kansas (22-6)
18	Detroit (15-5)
19	Fordham (17-6)
20	Tennessee (14-5)

#–NIT champion
*–NCAA champion

37. UCLA finished with a 14-7 overall mark for its first winning record in 12 years.

1943 NCAA Tournament

Summary: Virtually every university anticipated having players enter the military in the aftermath of the tourney. Wyoming (31-2/coached by Everett Shelton) had its winningest season in school history despite playing just nine home games during the year. After losing at Duquesne in the fourth contest of the campaign, the Cowboys did not lose a game to another college team the remainder of the year. Their only other setback was to the Denver legion squad. Wyoming would have become the only champion to trail at half-time in every tournament game if the Cowboys didn't score the last three baskets of the first half in the national final to lead Georgetown at intermission (18-16). The Hoyas couldn't hold a five-point edge with six minutes remaining.

Outcome for Defending Champion: Stanford (10-11 overall; 4-4 in conference competition) became one of only two defending champions to compile a losing record. Only two teams in the nine-member PCC posted a worse league mark.

Star Gazing: Wyoming's Kenny Sailors became the fourth consecutive Most Outstanding

1943 CHAMPIONSHIP BRACKET

	Regional Semifinals	Regional Finals	National Championship

EASTERN REGIONALS

Georgetown
March 24
New York U.
  → Georgetown 55-36
  New York, NY
  March 25
    → Georgetown 53-49

DePaul
March 24
Dartmouth
  → DePaul 46-35

WESTERN REGIONALS

Texas
March 26
Washington
  → Texas 59-55
  Kansas City, MO
  March 27
    → Wyoming 58-54

Wyoming
March 26
Oklahoma
  → Wyoming 53-50

New York, NY
March 30
  → Wyoming 46-34
  NATIONAL CHAMPION

Regional Third Place
March 25
at New York, NY
Dartmouth 51, New York U. 49
March 27
at Kansas City, MO
Oklahoma 48, Washington 43

Player not to be his team's leading scorer for the season. The jump shot that Sailors is credited with inventing is commonplace in today's game, but was unheard of in his day. "If your feet left the floor," Sailors said, "you were a freak."

Biggest Upset: Wyoming went to New York and defeated homestanding St. John's in overtime, 52-47, in a benefit game for the American Red Cross between the NCAA and NIT champions. Center Milo Komenich scored a game-high 20 points for Wyoming, which recovered after blowing an eight-point lead in the last two minutes of regulation.

One and Only: Wyoming's Shelton later became the only coach to guide teams to the championship game in both the Division I and Division II Tournaments. Shelton directed Sacramento State to a second-place finish in the 1962 Division II Tournament. . . . Sam Mele is the only individual to lead the American League in doubles as a player and manage an A.L. team to a pennant (Minnesota Twins in 1965) after leading a school in scoring in an NCAA Tournament (total of 18 points for NYU in two losses).

Numbers Game: The only team to fail to have at least one player score in double figures in the championship game was Georgetown, a 46-

34 loser against Wyoming. . . . DePaul's Ray Meyer became the first individual to reach the national semifinals in his initial season as a head coach. . . . Texas' John Hargis had a tourney-high 30 points in a 59-55 opening-game victory over Washington.

Scoring Leader: John Hargis, Texas (59 points, 29.5 ppg).

Most Outstanding Player: Kenny Sailors, F, Jr., Wyoming (28 points in final two games).

1943-44

AT A GLANCE

NCAA Champion: Utah (22-4; coached by Vadal Peterson).

NIT Champion: St. John's (18-5; coached by Joe Lapchick).

NCAA First-Team All-Americans: Bob Brannum, C, Fr., Kentucky; Audley Brindley, C, Jr., Dartmouth; Otto Graham, F, Sr., Northwestern; Leo Klier, F, Jr., Notre Dame; Bob Kurland, C, Soph., Oklahoma A&M; George Mikan, C, Soph., DePaul; Alva (Allie) Paine, G, Jr., Oklahoma.

NCAA champion-to-be Utah was invited to the NCAA playoffs following Arkansas' withdrawal after two of its best players were injured in a horrific automobile accident. The SWC representative declined to participate because of the auto mishap involving the Razorbacks' five starters. Their station wagon, driven by physical education instructor Eugene Norris, had a flat left rear tire about 20 miles outside Fayetteville, Ark., while returning from a tune-up game against a military team in Fort Smith. Norris stopped in the right lane on U.S. 71 because the shoulder was too narrow. Norris and two of the starters-Deno Nichols and Ben Jones-were putting the flat in the back of the wagon when a car driven by a local undertaker plowed into the vehicle at full speed.

The 28-year-old Norris, escorting the team for the first time, was pronounced dead of internal

The 1944 champion Utah Utes, with star freshman and Final Four Most Outstanding Player Arnie Ferrin in back row center (#22).

injuries and extreme shock after arriving at a nearby hospital. Nichols' right leg was broken in two places and both of Jones' legs were broken and his back fractured. Nichols' leg became gangrenous and was amputated just two months after he was married. Jones spent the next two years in various casts and braces.

Times were different in 1944. All-SWC guard "Parson" Bill Flynt had dropped out of Arkansas to become a full-time minister at a Baptist church in Perryville, Ark., just before the NCAA Tournament.

The Razorbacks tied for the SWC title with Rice, which withdrew from playoff consideration because of military commitments and regulations. Arkansas' only league loss was by 26 points (67-41) at Rice.

St. John's guard Dick McGuire became the first freshman to win the award given by the New York Basketball Writers Association to the outstanding college player in the metropolitan area. McGuire, Cornell center Bob Gale, NYU forward Harry Leggat and Fordham guard Walter Mercer finished the season playing for Dartmouth, where they underwent military training as Navy trainees stationed at the Hanover, N.H., college under the wartime V-12 program. St. John's won the NIT while Dartmouth finished runner-up to Utah in the NCAA Tournament.

Rhode Island State (New England) and Dartmouth (Ivy League) each captured its seventh consecutive conference championship. Dartmouth compiled a 19-2 record (.905) under Earl Brown in his only year as coach of the Big Green. The influx of trainees at Dartmouth for the largest V-12 program in the country also included St. John's forward Lionel Baxter, NYU guard Joe Fater and Vermont forward Tom Killick during the regular season before they were shipped out.

Rhode Island State's Ernie Calverley averaged 26.7 points per game, a mark that remained a national record until 1951 and still is a school standard. No individual has had a season scoring average remain intact longer. He became the first major-college player to score at least 45 points twice in a single season (48 vs. Northwestern and 45 vs. Maine).

The University of Havana became the first foreign team to play at Madison Square Garden, losing to LIU, 40-37. Havana displayed "the most spectacular ballhandling seen in New York in many years," according to the *Official Basketball Guide*. . . . Rider registered its lone victory over Villanova (42-27) in their first 20 meetings through the 1994-95 campaign.

The final Converse-Dunkel Ratings for the season had Army in first, followed by Utah, Kentucky, DePaul and Western Michigan. Army, under first-year coach Ed Kelleher after going 5-10 the previous season, compiled a 15-0 record with three starters (Dale Hall, Doug Kenna and John Hennessey) who had lettered for the school's football squad. The U.S. Military Academy's closest game was its season finale (47-40 over archrival Navy) and its largest margin of victory was its next-to-last game (85-22 over Maryland). Army's basketball arena is named after team captain Edward C. Christl, a first lieutenant the next year when he was killed in Austria. Christl was third in scoring average for the undefeated team. . . . Kelleher left the Army program after the next season. He is among the last 16 Army head coaches who have an average tenure there of less than four years.

The University of Chicago's Frank Whittaker became the first African American ever to play for a Big Ten Conference team. . . . Northwestern forward Otto Graham, a quarterback on the school's football squad, became the first athlete ever to earn first-team All-American status in both sports in the same school year. . . . Toledo, after winning more than 20 games each of the previous four seasons, compiled a 5-13 mark for its only losing record in a 20-year span from 1934-35 through 1953-54. . . . Nebraska, 2-13, posted its fewest victories in a season since the 1897-98 campaign.

North Carolina, in Bill Lange's final season as coach of the Tar Heels, posted the best record in

1943-44 UNDEFEATED TEAM: ARMY (15-0)

COACH: ED KELLEHER

ARMY	OPPONENT	ARMY'S HIGH SCORER
80	Swarthmore 29	Faas 20
69	Colgate 44	Hall 18
49	St. John's 36	Hall 21
55	at Columbia 37	Hall 17
49	Penn State 38	Hall 14
55	Coast Guard 37	Kenna 11
58	West Virginia 31	Hall 18
57	at Rochester 43	Hall 23
66	Pittsburgh 32	Christl 16
69	Hobart 36	Hall/Kenna 20
55	Pennsylvania 38	Hall 18
34	Villanova 22	Hall 23
46	New York Univ. 36	Hall 18
85	Maryland 22	Hall 32
47	Navy 40	Kenna 17

INDIVIDUAL STATISTICS FOR ARMY REGULARS

PLAYER	POS.	CL.	G.	PPG
Dale Hall	F	Jr.	15	18.2
Doug Kenna	G	Jr.	15	10.1
Ed Christl	C	Sr.	12	8.3
Bob Faas	F	Sr.	15	7.1
Bill Ekberg	C	Jr.	15	4.7
Jack Hennessey	G	Sr.	15	1.7

1943–44 PREMO POWER POLL

RANKING	SCHOOL
1	Army (15-0)
2	Utah* (21-4)
3	Kentucky (19-2)
4	DePaul (22-4)
5	Dartmouth (19-2)
6	St. John's# (18-5)
7	Oklahoma St. (27-6)
8	Bowling Green (22-4)
9	Rice (15-5)
10	Ohio St. (14-7)
11	Western Michigan (15-4)
12	Iowa St. (14-4)
13	Gonzaga (22-4)
14	Washington (26-6)
15	Muhlenberg (20-5)
16	Denison (18-2)
17	Northwestern (12-7)
18	Illinois (11-9)
19	Miami (Ohio) (10-2)
20	Navy (10-4)

#–NIT champion
*–NCAA champion

the Southern Conference (9-1) just one year after compiling the league's 11th-best mark (8-9).

Washington State sustained its only losing mark (8-19) in a 23-year stretch from 1929-30 through 1951-52 during Jack Friel's 30 seasons as head coach of the Cougars. . . . Southern Cal dropped its last seven games to suffer the Trojans' first losing record in 12 years (8-12).

George Edwards became the only coach to direct Missouri to the NCAA Tournament in the first 37 years of the event. Edwards was a classic example showing the assortment of duties coaches had in the "old" days. He was also the school's sports information director at the time and probably encountered difficulty drumming up much publicity because the Tigers had non-winning records seven of the previous nine seasons. Edwards, a former president of the National Association of Basketball Coaches, wrote the NABC creed the organization still embraces.

1944 NCAA Tournament

Summary: With so many upperclassmen enlisting or being drafted during World War II, Utah had to rely almost entirely on freshmen and sophomores. Utah, entering the NCAA Tournament through the back door after losing to Kentucky in the first round of the NIT, won the NCAA championship game against Dartmouth in overtime (42-40) on freshman Herb Wilkinson's basket from far beyond the top of the key. Utah freshman Arnie Ferrin scored 22 points in the final to help end Dartmouth's school-record 17-game winning streak. Two nights later in a benefit game at Madison Square Garden for the American Red Cross, the Utes defeated yet another favorite, beating NIT titlist St. John's, 43-36, when Ferrin tal-

1943–44 NCAA CHAMPION: UTAH

SEASON STATISTICS OF UTAH REGULARS

PLAYER	POS.	CL.	G	PPG
Arnie Ferrin	F	Fr.	21	13.2
Fred Sheffield	C	So.	21	10.4
Herb Wilkinson	G-F	Fr.	21	7.9
Wat Misaka	G	Fr.	20	6.9
Bob Lewis	G	Fr.	20	5.5
Dick Smuin	F-G	Fr.	19	3.7
Bill Kastelic	F	Fr.	14	2.8

TEAM TOTALS | | | 26 | 52.8

Note: Statistics are unavailable for Utah's first four games of the season.

1944 CHAMPIONSHIP GAME

NEW YORK, NY

UTAH (42)	MIN.	FG	FT-A	PF	PTS.
Ferrin	45	8	6-7	0	22
Smuin	45	0	0-0	2	0
Sheffield	4	1	0-0	1	2
Misaka	41	2	0-0	1	4
Wilkinson	45	3	1-4	0	7
B. Lewis	45	2	3-3	2	7
TOTALS	225	16	10-14	6	42

FT%: .714.

DARTMOUTH (40)	MIN.	FG	FT-A	PF	PTS.
Gale	37	5	0-2	1	10
Mercer	19	0	1-1	3	1
Leggat	34	4	0-0	1	8
Nordstrom	8	0	0-0	0	0
Brindley	39	5	1-1	3	11
McGuire	38	3	0-1	3	6
Murphy	17	0	0-0	0	0
Vancisin	19	2	0-0	3	4
Goering	14	0	0-0	0	0
TOTALS	225	19	2-5	14	40

FT%: .400.

Halftime: Dartmouth 18-17. **Regulation:** Tied 36-36.

MOST OUTSTANDING PLAYER
Arnie Ferrin, F, Fr., Utah

All-American center George Mikan of DePaul.

lied a game-high 17 points. St. John's had edged Utah's initial postseason opponent, Kentucky, in the NIT semifinals. Utah's players, all raised within 35 miles of the campus, had an average age of 18 years, six months. Among the four freshman starters was Wat Misaka, a spirited Japanese-American whose country was at war with the homeland of his ancestors. Utah lost its last eight games and 11 of its last 12 the previous season when it compiled a 10-12 record, the Utes' only losing mark in a 16-year span from 1936-37 through 1951-52.

Outcome for Defending Champion: Wyoming, the only school to win the NCAA championship one season and not compete in basketball the next year, did not field a team because of the war. In 1944-45, Wyoming lost its first nine games en route to compiling a 10-18 record.

Star Gazing: Ferrin, Misaka and Fred Sheffield were the only three of this group to earn any more letters with the Utes, which lost both of their NCAA playoff games in 1945. Ferrin was a second-team consensus All-American in 1947, when Utah won the NIT as the 5-8 Misaka restricted unanimous first-team All-American Ralph Beard to two points in a 49-45 triumph over Kentucky in the championship game. Wilkinson played the next three seasons for Iowa, where he was an NCAA consensus second-team All-American in 1945. Bob Lewis transferred to Stanford, where he was a three-year letterman from 1947-49.

One and Only: Sheffield, Utah's starting center, is the only Final Four player to finish among the top two high jumpers in four NCAA national track meets. Sheffield, the first athlete to place in the NCAA high jump four consecutive years, was first in 1943 with a best jump of 6-8, second in 1944, tied for first in 1945 and tied for second in 1946.

Numbers Game: Utah is the only championship team to have as many as four freshman starters. Lyman Condie, a second-year medical student, was an original starter for the team. Condie was invited by coach Vadal Peterson to try out for the squad because of a manpower shortage stemming from the war. Condie had a free block of time in the afternoons to practice during the fall quarter. However, when the winter quarter started his afternoons were no longer free and he had to make a choice between basketball or medical school. He chose medical school and left the team. His place as a starter was taken by Dick Smuin. . . . Iowa State, coached by Louis Menze, made its only NCAA Tournament appearance until 1985. . . . National runner-up Dartmouth won at least one NCAA playoff game for the fourth consecutive year. The Big Green beat Ohio State, 60-53, in the Eastern Regional final behind Aud Brindley's tourney-high 28 points.

Scoring Leader: Aud Brindley, Dartmouth (52 points, 17.3 ppg).

Highest Scoring Average: Nick Buzolich, Pepperdine (45 points, 22.5 ppg).

1944 CHAMPIONSHIP BRACKET

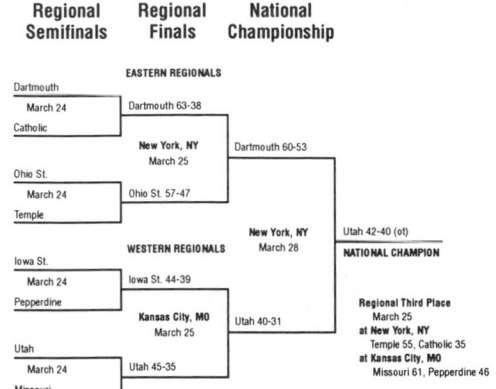

Regional Semifinals | Regional Finals | National Championship

EASTERN REGIONALS

Dartmouth
March 24
Catholic
— Dartmouth 63-38
New York, NY
March 25
— Dartmouth 60-53
Ohio St.
March 24
Temple
— Ohio St. 57-47

New York, NY
March 28
— Utah 42-40 (ot)
NATIONAL CHAMPION

WESTERN REGIONALS

Iowa St.
March 24
Pepperdine
— Iowa St. 44-39
Kansas City, MO
March 25
— Utah 40-31
Utah
March 24
Missouri
— Utah 45-35

Regional Third Place
March 25
at New York, NY
Temple 55, Catholic 35
at Kansas City, MO
Missouri 61, Pepperdine 46

Most Outstanding Player: Arnie Ferrin, F, Fr., Utah (28 points in final two games).

1944-45

AT A GLANCE

NCAA Champion: Oklahoma A&M (27-4; coached by Hank Iba).

NIT Champion: DePaul (21-3; coached by Ray Meyer).

New Rules: Defensive goaltending is banned, five personal fouls now disqualifies a player (had been four since 1910), an extra foul is not allowed in overtime games, and unlimited substitution is introduced.

NCAA First-Team All-Americans: Howie Dallmar, G, Sr., Penn; Arnie Ferrin, F, Soph., Utah; Wyndol Gray, F, Soph., Bowling Green; Billy Hassett, G, Jr., Notre Dame; Bill Henry, C-F, Sr., Rice; Walt Kirk, G, Jr., Illinois; Bob Kurland, C, Jr., Oklahoma A&M; George Mikan, C, Jr., DePaul.

NCAA champion Oklahoma A&M defeated NIT kingpin DePaul, 52-44, at Madison Square Garden in an American Red Cross War Fund benefit game featuring the nation's two premier pivotmen-DePaul's George Mikan and A&M's Bob Kurland. Mikan fouled out of the contest after 14 minutes with the Blue Demons leading, 21-14. Cecil Hankins, the top pass receiver for A&M's Cotton Bowl winner, scored a game-high 20 points and Kurland contributed 14. Mikan had set a school record by pouring in 53 points against Rhode Island State in the NIT semifinals.

Incredibly, three of the NCAA consensus first-team All-Americans previously or later played an entire season for other four-year universities-Penn's Howie Dallmar (previously attended Stanford), Bowling Green's Wyndol Gray (played next season for Harvard) and Notre Dame's Billy Hassett (previously attended Georgetown).

Rice, coached by Joe Davis, managed its most lopsided victory in history (95-22 over Baylor) en route to a school-best 20-1 record. The Owls' lone defeat was against NCAA champion-to-be Oklahoma A&M, 42-28, in the All-College Tournament in Oklahoma City. . . . Winless Baylor (0-17) lost back-to-back games at Arkansas by a total of 126 points (90-30 and 94-28). . . . Nebraska (2-17) ended a school-record streak of 12 consecutive conference defeats by defeating Kansas, 59-45.

In a gigantic mismatch, Kentucky overwhelmed Arkansas State, 75-6, although Alex Groza, the Wildcats' standout freshman center, did not play in the game. Groza led Kentucky to an 11-0 start with an average of 16.5 points per game before he was inducted into the Army. . . . Mississippi coach Edwin Hale concluded his two-year stint with the Rebels. Hale is the last coach to finish his tenure at Ole Miss with a winning record (22-18).

Big Ten champion Iowa, coached by Pops Harrison, compiled its best winning percentage in school history (.944) with a 17-1 overall record but declined an invitation to the NCAA Tournament. . . . NCAA consensus second-team All-American Max Morris of Northwestern led the Big Ten in scoring in league games (15.8 points per game) after earning MVP honors for the Wildcats' football squad the previous fall as an end. . . .

DePauw (Ind.) defeated Indiana for the second straight season.

Temple outlasted Penn State, 63-60, in five overtimes. . . . Dartmouth suffered its first losing record (6-8) in 25 years. . . . St. John's (21-3), coached by Joe Lapchick, finished in third place in the NIT although standouts Harry Boykoff, Dick McGuire and Max Zaslofsky were serving in the U.S. military. . . . Princeton started playing home games in a different arena after University Gymnasium was destroyed by fire.

Oregon (30-13/coached by John Warren) had its winningest season in school history. . . . North Carolina began a stretch during which the Tar Heels defeated South Carolina 23 times in 25 meetings to 1960. . . . Davidson compiled a .500 record (9-9), but sustained its most lopsided defeat in school history (89-20 at North Carolina). . . . Maryland also incurred its most lopsided defeat in history (85-22 to Bainbridge Navy). . . . Rensselaer Polytechnic Institute claimed to be the only undefeated college team during the regular season, compiling a 13-0 record before losing to Bowling Green, 60-45, in the opening round of the NIT. . . . Five members of Brooklyn's team admit they received $1,000 each and were promised $2,000

1944–45 PREMO POWER POLL

RANKING	SCHOOL
1	Iowa (17-1)
2	Oklahoma St.* (27-4)
3	DePaul# (21-3)
4	Rice (20-1)
5	Army (14-1)
6	Ohio St. (15-5)
7	Navy (12-2)
8	Kentucky (22-4)
9	Notre Dame (15-5)
10	Bowling Green (24-4)
11	St. John's (21-3)
12	NYU (16-8)
13	Akron (21-2)
14	Muhlenberg (24-4)
15	Rhode Island (20-5)
16	Arkansas (17-9)
17	South Carolina (19-3)
18	Hamline (20-4)
19	Tennessee (18-5)
20	RPI (13-1)

#–NIT champion
*–NCAA champion

more if they lost a game against Akron. The gamblers were arrested and the game cancelled.

1945 NCAA Tournament

Summary: The era of the big man arrived. Bob Kurland, continuing his vast improvement in just a couple of years after showing up at Oklahoma A&M as the sterotyped awkward seven-footer, led the Aggies to the NCAA title with 17.1 points per game. They prevailed although Kurland

1944–45 NCAA CHAMPION: OKLA. A&M

SEASON STATISTICS OF OKLAHOMA A&M REGULARS

PLAYER	POS.	CL.	G	PPG
Bob Kurland	C	Jr.	31	17.1
Cecil Hankins*	F	Sr.	23	13.3
Weldon Kern	F	Jr.	31	9.8
Doyle Parrack	G	Sr.	19	7.6
J. L. Parks	F	Fr.	31	4.0
Blake Williams	G	Fr.	31	3.8
John Wylie	G	Fr.	28	1.8
Joe Halbert	C	Fr.	20	0.6
TEAM TOTALS			**31**	**54.1**

*First-semester senior.

1945 CHAMPIONSHIP GAME

NEW YORK, NY

OKLAHOMA A&M (49)	FG	FT-A	PF	PTS.
Hankins	6	3-6	3	15
Parks	0	0-0	3	0
Kern	3	0-4	3	6
Wylie	0	0-0	0	0
Kurland	10	2-3	3	22
Parrack	2	0-1	3	4
Williams	1	0-1	1	2
TOTALS	**22**	**5-15**	**16**	**49**

FT%: .333.

NEW YORK UNIV. (45)	FG	FT-A	PF	PTS.
Grenert	5	2-3	3	12
Forman	5	1-2	1	11
Goldstein	0	2-2	2	2
Schayes	2	2-6	2	6
Walsh	0	0-0	2	0
Tanenbaum	2	0-0	2	4
Mangiapane	2	2-4	3	6
Most	1	2-3	2	4
TOTALS	**17**	**11-20**	**17**	**45**

FT%: .550.
Halftime: Oklahoma A&M 26-21.

MOST OUTSTANDING PLAYER
Bob Kurland, C, Jr., Oklahoma A&M

was their only returning letterman. Oklahoma A&M won the national final against New York University, 49-45, although the Aggies hit just 5 of 15 free-throw attempts.

Outcome for Defending Champion: Utah (17-4) was eliminated in the opening round, 62-37, when Kurland scored a tourney-high 28 points for A&M. One of the Utes' other three setbacks was by 28 points to Ohio State.

Biggest Upset: NYU, featuring just one senior on its roster, erased a 10-point deficit in the final two minutes of regulation on its way to frustrating Ohio State, 70-65, in overtime in the national semifinals.

Numbers Game: Dolph Schayes became the Doogie Howser of Final Four players. He is believed to be the youngest Hall of Famer to appear in an NCAA championship game, joining NYU's varsity lineup in midseason as a 16-year-old freshman and helping the Violets reach the NCAA final against Oklahoma A&M two months before his 17th birthday.

What Might Have Been: Kentucky (22-4) could have fared better in the playoffs if standout center Alex Groza wasn't inducted into the Army in mid-season.

Putting Things in Perspective: Arkansas' 79-76 victory over Oregon in the opening round shattered the previous two-team tourney scoring record by 36 points.

Scoring Leader: Bob Kurland, Oklahoma A&M (65 points, 21.7 ppg).

Highest Scoring Average: Dick Wilkins, Oregon (44 points, 22 ppg).

Most Outstanding Player: Bob Kurland, C, Jr., Oklahoma A&M (37 points in final two games).

1945-46

AT A GLANCE

NCAA Champion: Oklahoma A&M (31-2; coached by Hank Iba; won Missouri Valley title by five games with a 12-0 record).

NIT Champion: Kentucky (28-2; coached by Adolph Rupp; went undefeated in SEC along with LSU).

NCAA First-Team All-Americans: Leo Klier, F, Sr., Notre Dame; Bob Kurland, C, Sr., Oklahoma A&M; George Mikan, C, Sr., DePaul; Max Morris, F-C, Sr., Northwestern; Sid Tannenbaum, G, Jr., NYU.

Clarence "Nibs" Price completed a unique Rose Bowl-NCAA Tournament double when his California basketball team finished in fourth place in the NCAA playoffs with a 30-6 record one year after going 7-8. On January 1, 1929, Price had coached the Cal football squad in its 8-7 defeat to Georgia Tech in the Rose Bowl game that is famous for Roy Riegels' wrong-way run for the Bears.

Purdue's Ward "Piggy" Lambert ended his 29-year coaching career with a 371-152 record. Lambert directed the Boilermakers to six Big Ten titles and five co-championships and holds the conference record for longevity. His final season marked the school's first losing league mark (4-8) since 1919.

1945 CHAMPIONSHIP BRACKET

Regional Semifinals	Regional Finals	National Championship

EASTERN REGIONALS

New York U.
March 22
Tufts
→ New York U. 59-44
→ New York, NY March 24

Ohio St.
March 22
Kentucky
→ Ohio St. 45-37

New York U. 70-65 (ot)

WESTERN REGIONALS

Arkansas
March 23
Oregon
→ Arkansas 79-76
→ Kansas City, MO March 24

Oklahoma St.
March 23
Utah
→ Oklahoma St. 62-37

Oklahoma St. 68-41

New York, NY March 27 → Oklahoma St. 49-45 **NATIONAL CHAMPION**

Regional Third Place
March 24
at New York, NY
Kentucky 66, Tufts 56
at Kansas City, MO
Oregon 69, Utah 66

George Ratterman, a quarterback for Notre Dame's football team, scored the last 11 points for the Irish in a 56-47 upset of a Kentucky squad that eventually won the NIT. Ratterman averaged 8.6 points per game as a starting forward.

Oklahoma A&M's Bob Kurland authored a school-record 58 points in an 86-33 rout of St. Louis. Kurland, a native of Jennings, Mo., doubled the Billikens' output in the first half on his way to powering A&M to a 38-16 lead at intermission. . . . Oklahoma A&M (31-2/coached by Hank Iba), California (30-6/Nibs Price) and Harvard (19-3/Floyd Stahl) had their winningest seasons in school history. . . . All five starters for Oklahoma A&M were named to the 10-man All-Missouri Valley Conference team. . . . Harvard, which was 4-25 the previous two seasons under Stahl, set a school standard with 14 consecutive victories.

A then college-record crowd of 22,822 watched Ohio State defeat Northwestern, 53-46, and DePaul upend Notre Dame, 63-47, in a doubleheader at Chicago Stadium. The victory enabled Ohio State to clinch the Big Ten crown in the Buckeyes' regular-season finale. . . . Defending Big Ten champion Iowa won its first two games by a total of 127 points (87-25 over Augustana and 91-26 over South Dakota) and its first five outings by an average margin of 43.6 points. . . . The University of Chicago dropped out of the Big Ten Conference after its fifth consecutive winless league record.

SWC champion Baylor sported its winningest season (25-5) in school history in Bill Henderson's initial full season as the Bears' head coach just one year after they were winless. . . . Texas A&M posted its lone triumph over Texas (50-44) in a 16-game stretch from 1943 through 1950. . . . Guy Lewis became the first Houston player to crack the 30-point plateau in a game. He later became the Cougars' all-time winningest coach. . . . Kansas State lost a school-record 11 consecutive games en route to a school-worst 4-20 mark. It was the Wildcats' 15th straight non-winning season. They were 3-5 at home for their last losing

record there before setting an NCAA record for consecutive home winning seasons that was extended to 50 through 1995-96. . . . Elmore Morgenthaler, a 7-1 center for New Mexico School of Mines, was called the "tallest player in the world" by the Converse Basketball Yearbook. The Boston College transfer scored 12 field goals in an 84-61 victory over Drury (Mo.) in an exhibition game with 12-foot baskets at Kansas City. Field goals counted for three points in the contest.

Ozzie Cowles captured his seventh Ivy League championship in his last eight seasons as Dartmouth's coach. At one point, Dartmouth won 72 of 76 home games with Cowles at the helm. None of the 11 coaches since him compiled a winning career with the Big Green. . . . Boston College fielded its first intercollegiate basketball team since the 1924-25 season and notched a 3-10 record. . . . Connecticut's losing streak against the Coast Guard reached seven consecutive games. . . . Yale compiled a 14-1 record in Red Rolfe's fourth and final season as its coach. He had become Yale's coach in 1942 after playing in the World Series with the New York Yankees earlier that year. . . . Manhattan defeated Villanova 10 consecutive times in their series until losing to the Wildcats, 42-40. . . . The U.S. Merchant Marine Academy (Kings Point) compiled a modest 5-11 record, but two of its victories came against Villanova (43-38) and Maryland (52-25). . . . La Salle lost its last five games to finish with the Explorers' only losing record (9-14) in a 29-year span from 1936-37 through 1964-65. . . . George Washington compiled its only losing mark (7-8) in a 25-season stretch from 1929-30 through 1955-56 (GWU did not field squads in 1943-44 and 1944-45 because of World War II).

The Official Basketball Guide reported that "a record-breaking crowd of 8,800 paid admissions" saw Duke's second game with North Carolina "in Duke's big indoor stadium." The Guide went on to note that "this is reputed to be the largest crowd ever to see a game in the South."

Georgia Tech freshman Jim Nolan led the SEC in scoring with 14.6 points per game. He was the fourth different individual in as many

1945–46 PREMO POWER POLL

RANKING	SCHOOL
1	Oklahoma St.* (31-2)
2	Kentucky# (28-2)
3	North Carolina (30-5)
4	Indiana (18-3)
5	DePaul (19-5)
6	Rhode Island (21-3)
7	Ohio St. (16-5)
8	Notre Dame (17-4)
9	West Virginia (24-3)
10	Bowling Green (27-5)
11	NYU (19-3)
12	Kansas (19-2)
13	Illinois (14-7)
14	Wyoming (22-4)
15	Northwestern (15-5)
16	Baylor (25-5)
17	Iowa (14-4)
18	California (30-6)
19	Tennessee St. (26-2)
20	Yale (14-1)

\#–NIT champion
*–NCAA champion

years to lead the SEC in scoring from two schools (also Tulane) that are no longer members of the league. . . . Clemson defeated intrastate rival South Carolina, 47-42, for the Tigers' lone victory in a 22-game stretch of their series from 1941 to 1951. . . . Richmond registered its only triumph over George Washington in their first 20 meetings to 1954.

1946 NCAA Tournament

Summary: Oklahoma A&M's Bob Kurland was the only player for the first repeat champion to score in double figures in any of the Aggies' three playoff games. He tallied a tourney-high 29 points in a 52-39 victory over California in the Western Regional final. Twenty-six different players appeared in A&M's 33 games, but only three scored more than five points in either of the two Final Four frays.

Star Gazing: Sam Aubrey, who had been seriously wounded in the war, came back to be a regular for A&M although there had been some doubt whether he would ever walk again.

One and Only: Kurland became the only player to score more than half of a championship team's points in a single tournament (total of 72 points accounted for 51.8 percent of Oklahoma A&M's output in three games). . . . The only member of the champion Aggies' roster to later play in the NBA was freshman guard Joe Bradley, who averaged 3.4 points per game. Bradley averaged 1.9 points per game for the Chicago Stags in 1949-50.

Numbers Game: Bones McKinney, who averaged 9.8 points per game as a junior center for

1945–46 NCAA CHAMPION: OKLAHOMA A&M

SEASON STATISTICS OF OKLAHOMA A&M REGULARS

PLAYER	POS.	CL.	G	PPG
Bob Kurland	C	Sr.	33	19.5
Weldon Kern	F	Jr.	25	8.2
J. L. Parks	G	So.	33	5.7
Blake Williams	G	So.	33	4.5
A. L. Bennett	F	So.	22	3.8
Joe Bradley	G	Fr.	30	3.4
Sam Aubrey	F	Sr.	33	3.3
Joe Pitts	F	Fr.	25	1.9
Joe Halbert	C	So.	27	1.3
Paul Geymann	F	Sr.	21	1.0
TEAM TOTALS			**33**	**50.4**

1946 CHAMPIONSHIP GAME

NEW YORK, NY

OKLAHOMA A&M (43)	FG	FT-A	PF	PTS.
Aubrey	0	1-2	1	1
Bennett	3	0-0	4	6
Kern	3	1-3	2	7
Bradley	1	1-2	1	3
Kurland	9	5-9	5	23
Halbert	0	0-0	0	0
Williams	0	2-4	2	2
Bell	0	1-1	1	1
Parks	0	0-0	2	0
TOTALS	**16**	**11-21**	**18**	**43**

FT%: .524.

NORTH CAROLINA (40)	FG	FT-A	PF	PTS.
Dillon	5	6-6	5	16
Anderson	3	2-3	3	8
Paxton	2	0-0	4	4
McKinney	2	1-3	5	5
White	0	1-1	0	1
Thorne	1	0-0	2	2
Jordan	0	4-8	3	4
TOTALS	**13**	**14-21**	**22**	**40**

FT%: .667.
Halftime: Oklahoma A&M 23-17.

MOST OUTSTANDING PLAYER
Bob Kurland, C, Sr., Oklahoma A&M

NCAA runner-up North Carolina, is the only one of the five individuals to play for and coach a team in the Final Four to average more than 5.5 points per game in the season his alma mater reached the national semifinals. McKinney, who averaged 9.8 points per game for Carolina, coached Wake Forest to the 1962 Final Four. . . . Harvard, coached by Floyd Stahl, made its only appearance in an NCAA Tournament.

What Might Have Been: Ohio State captured the Big Ten Conference crown but was edged by national runnerup-to-be North Carolina (60-57 in overtime) in the East Regional final to finish the season with a 16-5 record. The Buckeyes might have had sufficient firepower to prevent Oklahoma A&M from repeating as NCAA champion if their top two scorers from Final Four teams the previous two years had still been around. But Don Grate, a two-time NCAA consensus second-team All-American forward, signed a pro baseball contract as a pitcher with the Philadelphia Phillies prior to his senior year, and center Arnie Risen played just six games in the first semester before becoming academically ineligible and ending the season with a pro franchise in Indianapolis. Risen led the NBA in field-goal percentage three years later when he was the Rochester Royals' top scorer and an All-NBA second team selection.

Putting Things in Perspective: George Mikan-led DePaul defeated Oklahoma A&M in both 1945 and 1946.

Scoring Leader: Bob Kurland, Oklahoma A&M (72 points, 24 ppg).

Most Outstanding Player: Bob Kurland, C, Sr., Oklahoma A&M (52 points in final two games).

1946-47

AT A GLANCE

NCAA Champion: Holy Cross (27-3; coached by Doggie Julian).

NIT Champion: Utah (19-5; coached by Vadal Peterson; finished in second place with a 12-2 record behind Wyoming in the Big Seven Conference).

New Conference: Mid-American.

New Rule: Transparent backboards are authorized.

NCAA First-Team All-Americans: Ralph Beard, G, Soph., Kentucky; Alex Groza, C, Soph., Kentucky; Ralph Hamilton, F, Sr., Indiana; Sid Tannenbaum, G, Sr., NYU; Gerry Tucker, C, Sr., Oklahoma.

1946 CHAMPIONSHIP BRACKET

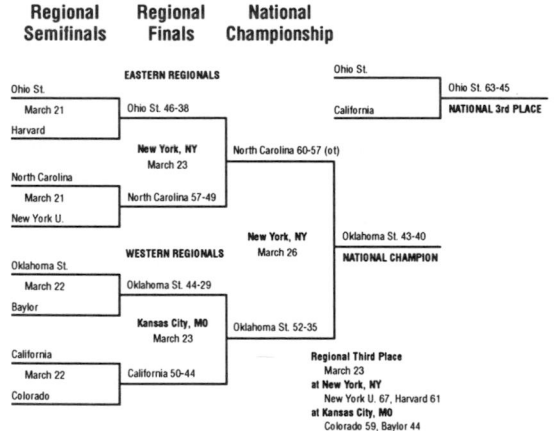

Regional Semifinals	Regional Finals	National Championship		
	EASTERN REGIONALS	Ohio St.		
Ohio St. March 21 Harvard	Ohio St. 46-38		Ohio St. 63-45 **NATIONAL 3rd PLACE**	
	New York, NY March 23	North Carolina 60-57 (ot)	California	
North Carolina March 21 New York U.	North Carolina 57-49			
	WESTERN REGIONALS	**New York, NY** March 26	Oklahoma St. 43-40 **NATIONAL CHAMPION**	
Oklahoma St. March 22 Baylor	Oklahoma St. 44-29			
	Kansas City, MO March 23	Oklahoma St. 52-35		
California March 22 Colorado	California 50-44			

Regional Third Place
March 23
at New York, NY
New York U. 67, Harvard 61
at Kansas City, MO
Colorado 59, Baylor 44

Which enterprise was deemed Bob Davies' second job when he pulled off one of the most amazing feats in college basketball history? Davies coached Seton Hall, his alma mater, to a 24-3 record the same season he also earned National Basketball League Most Valuable Player honors (averaged 14.3 points in 43 regular-season and playoff games with the Rochester Royals). The "Blonde Bomber" is credited with inventing the behind-the-back dribble. He was 26 years old in his only season as coach of the Pirates.

Kentucky standout center Alex Groza saw limited action in the SEC Tournament because of a back injury, but the Wildcats cruised to victories over Vanderbilt (98-29), Auburn (84-18), Georgia Tech (75-53) and Tulane (55-38). The all-tourney team (considered the All-SEC team that season) included five Wildcats on the first five-forwards Jack Tingle and Joe Holland, center Wallace "Wah Wah" Jones and guards Ken Rollins and Ralph Beard. Sophomores Beard and Groza are the only set of underclassmen teammates named NCAA consensus first-team All-Americans in the same year since the start of the NCAA Tournament.

Wisconsin, after finishing in ninth place the previous season, won three league games by one point en route to its last Big Ten Conference championship. Defending Big Ten champion Ohio State fell to a tie for sixth place. Wisconsin, involved in a bizarre late-season game to determine the title, was locked in a battle with Purdue atop the standings when the Badgers visited Lafayette, Ind., on February 24. At halftime, newly-installed wooden bleachers at Lambert Fieldhouse's east grandstand collapsed under the overflow crowd of more than 11,000, crushing three student spectators and injuring hundreds of other patrons. The second half of the ill-fated contest was suspended for more than two weeks until being completed at a neutral site (Evanston, Ill., High School), where Wisconsin outscored Purdue, 39-26, to claim a belated 72-60 triumph. The Badgers were coached by Bud Foster.

Oklahoma center Gerry Tucker became an NCAA consensus first-team All-American after having his career interrupted for three years while serving in the U.S. Army. He later became coach of the 1956 U.S. Olympic team.

Texas, the "Mighty Mice" team featuring three starters 5-10 or shorter, compiled a 26-2 record with both of its defeats coming by one point (40-39 to defending NCAA champion Oklahoma A&M and 55-54 to Oklahoma in the NCAA Tournament Western Regional finals). The Longhorns were coached by Jack Gray, who was hired in the 1936-37 season when he was only 25. In an era of slow, deliberate play, Gray's squads were known for their innovative running, pressing style and were one of the first to don white sneakers.

Holy Cross coach Alvin F. (Doggie) Julian.

UCLA's Don Barksdale, a second-team selection, became the first African American player named to an NCAA consensus All-American squad. After a three-year stint in the U.S. Army, he led the Pacific Coast Conference Southern Division in scoring. . . . The top major-college single-game output of the season was a 54-point effort by St. John's Harry Boykoff against St. Francis (N.Y.). . . . Creighton compiled a 17-8 mark in Eddie Hickey's final season as the Bluejays' coach before they suffered nine consecutive non-winning records.

Bowling Green (28-7/coached by Harold Anderson), Holy Cross (27-3/Doggie Julian), Texas (26-2/Jack Gray) and Eastern Kentucky (21-4/Paul McBrayer) had their winningest seasons in school major-college history. It was McBrayer's first year as coach of the Colonels.

Cincinnati, winning more than 10 games for the first time in eight years, compiled a 17-9 record in John Wiethe's first season as coach of the Bearcats.. . . Illinois' famed "Whiz Kids," who won Big Ten titles in 1942 and 1943, returned after missing three seasons while in military service and tied Indiana for second place.

RANKING	SCHOOL
1	Kentucky (34-3)
2	Holy Cross* (27-3)
3	Texas (26-2)
4	Duquesne (20-2)
5	Utah# (19-5)
6	Oklahoma (24-7)
7	Western Kentucky (25-4)
8	Notre Dame (20-4)
9	Navy (16-3)
10	Oregon St. (28-5)
11	N. Carolina St. (26-5)
12	Oklahoma St. (24-8)
13	West Virginia (19-3)
14	Arizona (21-3)
15	CCNY (17-6)
16	Wyoming (22-6)
17	LIU-Brooklyn (17-5)
18	Seton Hall (24-3)
19	Wisconsin (16-6)
20	Santa Clara (21-4)

#–NIT champion
*–NCAA champion

Whiz Kids Jack Smiley, Gene Vance, Andy Phillip and Ken Menke were joined in the Illini starting lineup by Fred Green. Branch McCracken also returned to coach Indiana after taking a three-year leave of absence serving in World War II. . . . Miami of Ohio notched its most lopsided victory in history by overwhelming Wright State, 89-32.

North Carolina State, in Everett Case's first season as a college coach, posted the best record in the 16-team Southern Conference (11-2) just one year after finishing in a tie for ninth place. The Wolfpack squad was comprised of nine freshmen and a sophomore. . . . Western Kentucky won its first meeting with Miami (Fla.), starting an 11-game winning streak against the Hurricanes. . . . Washington's Hec Edmundson ended his 29-year coaching career with a 508-204 record. In an 18-year span from 1927-28 through 1944-45, he notched 20-win seasons 11 times.

Kansas posted a 16-11 mark, but Howard Engleman concluded the campaign as coach when Phog Allen was ordered to take a rest after he had difficulty shaking the flu in mid-season when the Jayhawks were in the midst of a five-game losing streak. . . . Kansas' 22-game winning streak in its series with Kansas State ended with a 48-45 setback against the Wildcats. . . . Kansas State started a streak of 18 consecutive winning seasons by compiling a 14-10 record in the initial campaign of Jack Gardner's second go-around as the Wildcats' coach. Meanwhile, Maryland registered the same 14-10 mark for its only winning season in a

1946–47 NCAA CHAMPION: HOLY CROSS

SEASON STATISTICS OF HOLY CROSS REGULARS

PLAYER	POS.	CL.	G	PPG
George Kaftan	F-C	So.	28	11.1
Dermie O'Connell	F	So.	29	9.0
Bob Cousy	G-F	Fr.	30	7.6
Ken Haggerty	G	Sr.	29	5.7
Andy Laska	G-F	Fr.	30	5.6
Joe Mullaney	G	So.	30	5.0
Frank Oftring	C-F	Fr.	29	4.6
Bob Curran	F-C	Jr.	30	4.4
Charlie Bollinger	C	So.	26	4.0
Bobbie McMullen	G-F	Fr.	29	3.8
TEAM TOTALS			30	60.9

1947 CHAMPIONSHIP GAME

NEW YORK, NY

HOLY CROSS (58)	FG	FT-A	PF	PTS.
Kaftan	7	4-9	4	18
O'Connell	7	2-4	3	16
Oftring	6	2-3	5	14
Mullaney	0	0-0	2	0
Haggerty	0	0-0	0	0
Laska	0	0-0	0	0
Curran	0	0-1	2	0
Riley	0	0-0	1	0
McMullen	2	4-4	0	8
Cousy	0	2-2	1	2
Bollinger	0	0-0	0	0
Graver	0	0-0	0	0
TOTALS	22	14-23	18	58

FT%: .609.

OKLAHOMA (47)	FG	FT-A	PF	PTS.
Reich	3	2-2	3	8
Courty	3	2-3	4	8
Tucker	6	10-12	3	22
Paine	2	2-2	0	6
Landon	1	0-1	4	2
Waters	0	0-0	0	0
Day	0	0-0	0	0
Pryor	0	1-1	2	1
Merchant	0	0-0	1	0
TOTALS	15	17-21	17	47

FT%: .810.
Halftime: Oklahoma 31-28.

MOST OUTSTANDING PLAYER
George Kaftan, F-C, Soph., Holy Cross

10-year span from 1940-41 through 1949-50. . . . Drake notched its lone victory over Oklahoma A&M (42-34) in a 24-game stretch of their series from 1939 to 1958.

1947 NCAA Tournament

Summary: Holy Cross, entering the tourney with 20 consecutive victories, fell behind early in all three playoff contests (against Navy, CCNY and Oklahoma) before rallying to win the title. It was an incredible turnaround for the Crusaders, who compiled a meager 4-9 record two years earlier.

Outcome for Defending Champion: Oklahoma A&M compiled a 24-8 record. The Aggies' only double-digit defeat was to visiting St. Louis, 38-20.

Star Gazing: The lowest team-leading scoring average for an individual in the season he was named Final Four Most Outstanding Player was compiled by George Kaftan, a forward-center with an 11.1-point average for Holy Cross' NCAA champion after becoming the first player to score 30 points in a Final Four game (tourney-high 30 in a 60-45 victory over CCNY in East Regional final before tossing in a team-high 18 in a 58-47 triumph over Oklahoma in the national final).

One and Only: Alvin (Doggie) Julian is the only coach of a championship team to subsequently coach another university and compile a winning NCAA playoff record at his last major college job. Julian captured a national title in the middle of his three seasons as coach at Holy Cross before compiling a 4-3 playoff record in three tournament appearances with Dartmouth from 1956-59.

Numbers Game: Seldom-used Ken Pryor's only basket in the tourney, a long jumper in the closing seconds, gave Oklahoma a 55-54 victory over Texas in the national semifinals. . . . Wisconsin made its last NCAA playoff appearance until 1994.

Putting Things in Perspective: Holy Cross suffered its three defeats in successive early-season games. The Crusaders' first two setbacks were by a total of 26 points.

1947 CHAMPIONSHIP BRACKET

Scoring Leader: George Kaftan, Holy Cross (63 points, 21 ppg).

Most Outstanding Player: George Kaftan, F-C, Soph., Holy Cross (48 points in final two games).

1947-48

AT A GLANCE

NCAA Champion: Kentucky (36-3; coached by Adolph Rupp; compiled 9-0 record in SEC to finish with a better winning percentage than Tulane, which was 13-1).

NIT Champion: St. Louis (24-3; coached by Eddie Hickey; finished in second place in Missouri Valley two games behind Oklahoma A&M).

New Rule: Clock stopped on every dead ball the last three minutes of the second half and of every overtime period. This includes every time a basket is scored because the ball is considered dead until put into play again (rule was abolished in 1951).

NCAA First-Team All-Americans: Ralph Beard, G, Jr., Kentucky; Ed Macauley, C-F, Jr., St. Louis; Jim McIntyre, C, Jr., Minnesota; Kevin O'Shea, G, Soph., Notre Dame; Murray Wier, G, Sr., Iowa.

Long before multi-sport standouts Bo Jackson and Deion Sanders were hailed as jacks-of-all-trades, there was three-sport whiz Dike Eddleman, possibly the most amazing all-around athlete to participate in the Final Four. Eddleman, a 6-3, 180-pound guard-forward for Illinois, was named the Big Ten Most Valuable Player by the Chicago Tribune in 1949 when he was the leading scorer for the national third-place finisher in basketball. In football, he played both offense and defense, punted and returned kicks, and played in the 1947 Rose Bowl for a team that overwhelmed UCLA, 45-14. He set school season records in 1948 for highest punting average (43 yards per kick) and punt return average (32.8). Eddleman, interrupting his collegiate career by joining the U.S. Army Air Corps during World War II, earned an amazing 11 varsity letters at Illinois. He won three Big Ten high jump titles. But his greatest athletic achievement might have been winning a silver medal in the high jump in the 1948 Olympics in London. The Olympics climaxed an outstanding academic school year for Eddleman. He won the NCAA high jump crown and led Illinois' football and basketball teams in scoring.

North Carolina State, runner-up to Rhode Island State in team offense with 75.3 points per game, became the first school other than the Rhodies ever to average more than 75. The Wolfpack, undefeated in Southern Conference competition (12-0), finished the season with a 29-3 mark when its leading scorer, sophomore Dick Dickey, was sidelined with the mumps in an NIT opening-round defeat to DePaul. . . . Virginia defeated Duke, 49-39, for the Cavaliers' only victory over the Blue Devils in a 23-game stretch of their series from 1929-30 through 1955-56. Duke swept Wake Forest to give the Blue Devils 40 triumphs in their last 42 meetings.

Michigan, coached by Ozzie Cowles, compiled a 10-2 Big Nine mark for its first winning league record in 11 years and first conference title in 19

1947–48 INDIVIDUAL LEADERS

SCORING

PLAYER	PTS.	AVG.
Hankins, Lawrence Tech	630	22.5
Wier, Iowa	399	21.0
Lavelli, Yale	554	20.5
Kudelka, St. Mary's	489	20.4
Vandeweghe, Colgate	385	20.3
Haskins, Hamline	605	19.5
Kok, Arkansas	469	19.5
McIntyre, Minnesota	360	18.9
Hatchett, Rutgers	201	18.3
Berce, Marquette	390	17.7

FIELD GOAL PERCENTAGE

PLAYER	FGM	FGA	PCT.
Petersen, Oregon St.	89	187	.476
Mackin, Muhlenberg	158	338	.467
Coleman, Louisville	136	292	.466
Compton, Louisville	109	241	.452
Karpiak, Colorado A&M	77	176	.438
Mann, Bradley	87	199	.437
Brown, Miami (Ohio)	178	417	.427
Walker, Akron	135	316	.427
Dobler, Colorado A&M	106	251	.422
Richter, Cincinnati	122	294	.415
Harman, Kansas St.	76	183	.415

FREE THROW PERCENTAGE

PLAYER	FTM	FTA	PCT.
Urzetta, St. Bonaventure	59	64	.922
Sterling, West Virginia	40	45	.889
Shannon, Kansas St.	55	66	.879
Sharman, USC	38	44	.864
Wylie, Ohio U.	88	102	.863
L. Malamed, CCNY	55	66	.833
Line, Kentucky	48	58	.828
McMullen, Mississippi	70	86	.814
Woodcock, Bucknell	39	48	.813
Nelson, Brigham Young	111	138	.804

1947–48 TEAM LEADERS

SCORING OFFENSE

SCHOOL	PTS.	AVG.
Rhode Island St.	1755	76.3
North Carolina St.	2409	75.3
Bowling Green	2327	70.5
Lawrence Tech	1961	70.0
Bradley	2157	69.6

SCORING DEFENSE

SCHOOL	PTS.	AVG.
Oklahoma A&M	1006	32.5
Alabama	1070	39.6
Creighton	925	40.2
Wyoming	1101	40.8
Siena	1161	41.5

FREE THROW PERCENTAGE

SCHOOL	FTM	FTA	PCT.
Texas	351	481	.730
Michigan	280	411	.681
St. Bonaventure	286	421	.679
DePaul	468	698	.670
New York University	433	646	.670

FIELD GOAL PERCENTAGE

SCHOOL	FGM	FGA	PCT.
Oregon St.	668	1818	.367
Muhlenberg	655	1822	.359
Akron	571	1617	.353
Louisville	709	2028	.350
Bowling Green	918	2639	.348

seasons. . . . Iowa's Murray Wier is acknowledged as the shortest player (5-9) to lead the nation in scoring (21 points per game) although Norm Hankins of Lawrence Tech in Detroit was designated as the major-college scoring leader (22.5 ppg). Wier was the only senior among the consensus NCAA first-team All-American selections. Ten of the 14 consensus NCAA first- and second-team choices were undergraduates. . . . Purdue posted its lone victory over Ohio State (69-64) in a 13-game stretch of their series from 1945 through 1954.

Jim Lacy of Loyola (Md.) finished 12th in the nation in scoring with 17.5 points per game but had the nation's single-game high of 44 points against Western Maryland. . . . St. Bonaventure's Sam Urzetta (92.2 percent) became the only player to convert more than 90 percent of his free throws in a single season until 1962. . . . Notre Dame (17-7), coached by Moose Krause, defeated two teams ranked No. 1 in the country in the final month of the regular season-NCAA champion-to-be Kentucky and NIT runner-up NYU. But Notre Dame's school-record

homecourt winning streak was snapped at 38 by eventual NIT kingpin St. Louis. NYU's school-record 19-game winning streak came to an end when it sustained its first loss of the year to the Irish at Madison Square Garden. . . . Duquesne's Chick Davies ended a 21-year coaching career with a 314-106 record.

Arkansas, coached by Gene Lambert, became the first school to compile 25 consecutive winning seasons. . . . Kansas State, coached by Jack Gardner, ended its streak of 21 consecutive non-winning conference records by capturing the Big Seven title with a 9-3 league mark. It was the Wildcats' first conference crown in 29 seasons. . . . Kansas' streak of 18 consecutive winning records under coach Phog Allen came to a halt when the Jayhawks lost 10 straight games the second half of the season en route to a 9-15 mark. It was the school's only losing record in a 29-year span through 1957-58.

Washington's Jack Nichols finished his fifth season of varsity competition in the Pacific Coast

1947–48 NCAA CHAMPION: KENTUCKY

SEASON STATISTICS OF KENTUCKY REGULARS

PLAYER	POS.	CL.	G	FG%	FT%	PPG
Alex Groza	C	Jr.	39	.377	.629	12.5
Ralph Beard	G	Jr.	38	.362	.591	12.5
Wallace Jones	F-C	Jr.	36	.311	.670	9.3
James Line	F	So.	38	.361	.823	7.0
Ken Rollins	G	Sr.	39	.279	.728	6.6
Cliff Barker	F	Jr.	38	.309	.559	6.5
Dale Barnstable	F	So.	38	.271	.571	4.6
Joe Holland	F	Jr.	38	.280	.511	3.7
Jack Parkinson	G	Sr.	29	.201	.455	3.3
Walt Hirsch	F-G	Fr.	13	.291	.556	2.8
Albert Cummins	G	So.	17	.351	.667	1.9
Jim Jordan	F	So.	30	.148	.720	1.5
Garland Townes	G	Fr.	13	.318	.455	1.5
Roger Day	F	Fr.	11	.278	.778	1.5
Albert Campbell	C	Sr.	15	.222	.571	1.1
Johnny Stough	G	So.	23	.211	.500	0.9
TEAM TOTALS			39	.312	.626	70.0

Note: Statistics include three games in Olympic Trials after the NCAA Tournament.

1948 CHAMPIONSHIP GAME

NEW YORK, NY

KENTUCKY (58)	FG	FT-A	PF	PTS.
Jones	4	1-1	3	9
Barker	2	1-3	4	5
Groza	6	2-4	4	14
Beard	4	4-4	1	12
Rollins	3	3-5	3	9
Line	3	1-1	3	7
Holland	1	0-0	1	2
Barnstable	0	0-1	0	0
TOTALS	23	12-19	19	58

FT%: .632.

BAYLOR (42)	FG	FT-A	PF	PTS.
Owens	2	1-2	0	5
DeWitt	3	2-4	3	8
Heathington	3	2-4	5	8
Johnson	3	4-7	5	10
Robinson	3	2-4	4	8
Pulley	0	1-1	0	1
Hickman	1	0-0	0	2
Preston	0	0-2	2	0
Srack	0	0-0	0	0
TOTALS	15	12-24	19	42

FT%: .500.
Halftime: Kentucky 29-16.

MOST OUTSTANDING PLAYER
Alex Groza, C, Jr., Kentucky

1947–48 PREMO POWER POLL

RANKING	SCHOOL
1	Kentucky* (36-3)
2	St. Louis# (24-3)
3	Holy Cross (26-4)
4	Western Kentucky (28-2)
5	N. Carolina St. (29-3)
6	NYU (22-4)
7	DePaul (22-8)
8	West Virginia (17-3)
9	Michigan (16-6)
10	Oklahoma St. (27-4)
11	Baylor (24-8)
12	Tennessee (20-5)
13	Bowling Green (27-6)
14	Tulane (23-3)
15	Bradley (28-3)
16	Iowa (15-4)
17	Texas (20-5)
18	Illinois (15-5)
19	CCNY (18-3)
20	Columbia (21-3)

#–NIT champion
*–NCAA champion

Conference (three with the Huskies and two as a military trainee during World War II with Southern California). . . . Montana's Bob Cope set a school single-game scoring record by firing in 40 points against Gonzaga (mark later tied). . . . Hamline (Minn.), Lawrence Tech (Minn.), Scranton (Pa.) and Texas Wesleyan competed in their final season at the major-college level. . . . Georgetown posted its lone victory against St. John's in a 17-game stretch of their series from 1931 to 1973. . . . Muhlenberg (Pa.) defeated Villanova for the seventh consecutive time, 67-60. The average margin of victory in the previous six games with the Wildcats was 16.7.

1948 NCAA Tournament

Summary: Ken Rollins, the lone senior among coach Adolph Rupp's "Fabulous Five," held standout guard Bob Cousy, the leading scorer for defending champion Holy Cross, to just five points in the semifinals. Kentucky's winningest team in school history (36-3 under coach Adolph Rupp) had an excessive amount of maturity since Rollins, Alex Groza, Dale Barnstable, Jim Line and Cliff Barker were World War II service veterans. Barker, a defensive specialist, was in a German prisoner-of-war camp for 16 months after the crewman's B-17 was shot down in Europe.

Outcome for Defending Champion: Holy Cross finished with a 26-4 record when Kentucky ended the Crusaders' 19-game winning streak. Their most lopsided defeat was to NIT champion-to-be St. Louis, 61-46. Eddie Hickey was SLU's first-year coach.

One and Only: Michigan's Pete Elliott became the only player to score a team-high point total in his school's first NCAA Tournament victory the same year he earned All-American honors as a quarterback for a national football champion. Elliott, a second-team pick on the Helms All-American team scored a team-high 15 points in a 66-49 decision over Columbia in the Eastern Regional third-place game. Elliott also earned All-American honors as a quarterback for the Wolverines' 1948 national football champion. He was executive director of the Pro Football Hall of Fame after serving as head football coach at Nebraska (1956), California (1957-59) and Illinois (1960-66), leading Cal and the Illini to Rose Bowl berths.

Numbers Game: Columbia entered the playoffs with just one defeat (59-54 against Princeton in overtime), but Kentucky's Wallace Jones (21), Groza (17) and Beard (15) combined to equal the Lions' entire output as the Wildcats prevailed, 76-53, in the opening round. . . . Michigan made its only NCAA Tournament appearance in the first 25 years of the event. Michigan's Ozzie Cowles became the initial coach to direct two different schools to the NCAA playoffs for the initial time. He guided Dartmouth to its first tourney appearance in 1941. . . . Wyoming's John Pilch scored a tourney-high 24 points in a 57-47 loss to Washington in the Western Regional third-place game.

Scoring Leader: Alex Groza, Kentucky (54 points, 18 ppg).

Highest Scoring Average: Jack Nichols, Washington (39 points, 19.5 ppg).

Most Outstanding Player: Alex Groza, C, Jr., Kentucky (37 points in final two games).

1948 CHAMPIONSHIP BRACKET

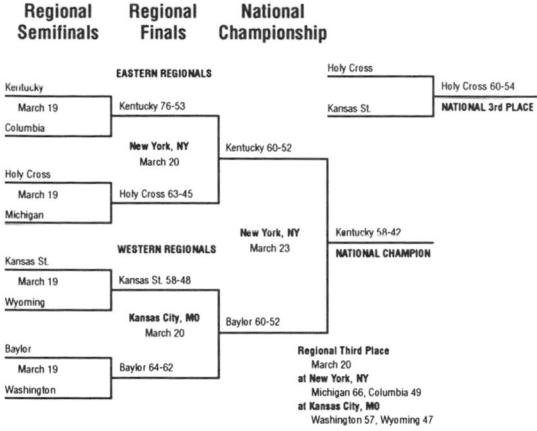

Regional Semifinals	Regional Finals	National Championship		

EASTERN REGIONALS

Kentucky
March 19
Columbia

Kentucky 76-53

New York, NY
March 20

Holy Cross
March 19
Michigan

Holy Cross 63-45

Holy Cross

Holy Cross 60-54

Kansas St.

NATIONAL 3rd PLACE

Kentucky 60-52

WESTERN REGIONALS

Kansas St.
March 19
Wyoming

Kansas St. 58-48

Kansas City, MO
March 20

Baylor
March 19
Washington

Baylor 64-62

Baylor 60-52

New York, NY
March 23

Kentucky 58-42

NATIONAL CHAMPION

Regional Third Place
March 20
at New York, NY
Michigan 66, Columbia 49
at Kansas City, MO
Washington 57, Wyoming 47

1948-49

AT A GLANCE

NCAA Champion: Kentucky (32-2; coached by Adolph Rupp; compiled 13-0 SEC record to finish two games ahead of Tulane).

NIT Champion: San Francisco (25-5; coached by Pete Newell).

New Conference: Ohio Valley.

New Rules: Coaches allowed to converse while mingling with players during a timeout. . . . NIT field expanded from eight teams to 12.

NCAA First-Team All-Americans: Ralph Beard, G, Sr., Kentucky; Vince Boryla, F, Sr., Denver; Alex Groza, C, Sr., Kentucky; Tony Lavelli, F, Sr., Yale; Ed Macauley, C-F, Sr., St. Louis.

A weekly ritual began when the Associated Press announced the results of the first weekly basketball poll on January 18, 1949. St. Louis was ranked first in the initial poll, followed by Kentucky, Western Kentucky, Minnesota, Oklahoma A&M, San Francisco, Illinois, Hamline (Minn.), Villanova and Utah.

Kentucky, unbeaten in SEC competition for the third consecutive season en route to becoming the only school to win more than 30 games overall in three consecutive campaigns, finished sixth nationally in both team offense and defense. Kentucky coach Adolph Rupp needed every single one of the victories to finish one win ahead of Harold Anderson (248 with Toledo and Bowling Green) for most triumphs in the decade.

The season's most shocking defeat was the Wildcats' 67-56 setback against Loyola of Chicago in the opening round of the NIT. The defending NCAA champions entered the game ranked No. 1 in the nation in the AP poll. Later, it was disclosed that the Kentucky-Loyola game was one in which UK players allegedly were bribed by gamblers to keep the winning margin under 10 points.

Western Kentucky won 32 consecutive regular-season games until bowing to Eastern Kentucky, 42-40. . . . Oklahoma A&M captured the Missouri Valley title, extending the Aggies' streak of finishing first or second in the MVC to 12 consecutive seasons. . . . Texas-El Paso posted its lone triumph over Arizona in an 18-game stretch of their series from 1942 through 1951.

Jim Lacy of Loyola (Md.) became the first player to finish his career cracking the 2,000-point plateau. . . . Villanova's Paul Arizin erupted for a school-record 85 points in a 117-25 pounding of Philadelphia NAMC (Naval Air Material Center) after the Wildcats played their previous eight games on the road. But the only player to score at least 40 points in two games was Yale's Tony Lavelli. A 52-point uprising by Lavelli against Williams remains a school record. . . . Lafayette's first 20-win season came in Bill Anderson's 11th and final year as its coach. He had been a student-coach in 1917-18 and 1918-19 on his way to becoming the school's first 1,000-point scorer. . . . Dartmouth defeated Holy Cross, 50-44, in a major upset. Holy Cross' average annual record in a 10-year span from 1946-47 through 1955-56 was 23-5.

Muhlenberg (Pa.) registered seven straight victories over Villanova in their series until succumbing to the Wildcats, 62-49. . . . Colgate's Ernie Vandeweghe finished among the nation's top five scorers for the third consecutive season. His son, Kiki, became a standout at UCLA and averaged more than 20 points per game seven consecutive seasons in the NBA from 1981-82 through 1987-88. . . . West Virginia's school-record homecourt winning streak ended at 57 consecutive games with a 34-32 overtime loss to Pittsburgh in the closing contest on the Mountaineers' schedule.

Cliff Wells, Tulane's all-time winningest coach, guided the Green Wave to its only Top 20 appearance in a final wire-service poll by compiling a school-record 24-4 record. Three of Tulane's four defeats were to Kentucky. The only other setback for the Green Wave was by two points at Vanderbilt. It was the third consecutive Tulane team with more than 20 victories. The following excerpt of a letter written by Wells to a high school coach might explain the drive behind Green Wave teams of the Wells era:

"I am a firm believer that condition means stamina. Stamina demands training. Training spells sacrifice. Sacrifice is the highway to desire. If a boy is traveling another road he is lost in every sense of the word. I would not have him on my squad. The athlete at his best learns something different. Not comfortable, ease. Not idleness. Not self-indulgence. Not jaunty contempt for authority. These never win any game. Instead, these: obedience, self-denial, team play and always the inner cry-'I must, I MUST and I will!'"

Another school to register its winningest season in history was William & Mary (24-10/coached by Bernard Wilson).

Ohio University went 6-16 for its first losing season in 15 years. . . . Miami of Ohio suffered

1948–49 INDIVIDUAL LEADERS

SCORING

PLAYER	PTS.	AVG.
Lavelli, Yale	671	22.4
Arizin, Villanova	594	22.0
Giermak, William & Mary	740	21.8
Senesky, St. Joseph's	483	21.0
Vandeweghe, Colgate	397	20.9
Groza, Kentucky	698	20.5
Goodwin, Rhode Island	433	19.7
Noertker, Virginia	442	19.2
Boryla, Denver	624	18.9
Schaus, West Virginia	442	18.4

FIELD GOAL PERCENTAGE

PLAYER	FGM	FGA	PCT.
Macauley, St. Louis	144	275	.524
Goodwin, Rhode Island	145	291	.498
Brawley, Maryland	78	161	.484
Leverte, Seton Hall	101	210	.481
Boven, Western Michigan	123	257	.479
Share, Bowling Green	193	410	.471
Coleman, Louisville	188	404	.465
Kerris, Loyola (Ill.)	175	382	.458
White, Texas	83	185	.449
Grover, Bradley	98	212	.462

FREE THROW PERCENTAGE

PLAYER	FTM	FTA	PCT.
Schroer, Valparaiso	59	68	.868
Line, Kentucky	43	51	.843
Oftring, Holy Cross	47	56	.839
Dolnics, TCU	99	119	.832
Goodwin, Rhode Island	143	172	.831
Lavelli, Yale	215	261	.824
Palcheff, Washington (Mo.)	65	80	.813
Alston, Xavier	52	64	.813
Cheek, Davidson	75	94	.798
Westerfeld, Cincinnati	50	63	.794

1948–49 TEAM LEADERS

SCORING OFFENSE

SCHOOL	PTS.	AVG.
Rhode Island St.	1575	71.6
Western Kentucky	2028	69.9
Yale	2089	69.6
Bowling Green	2139	69.0
Colgate	1297	68.3

FIELD GOAL PERCENTAGE

SCHOOL	FGM	FGA	PCT.
Muhlenberg	593	1512	.392
Wyoming	674	1777	.379
Loyola (Ill.)	720	1918	.375
Seton Hall	566	1509	.375
Bradley	889	2372	.375

SCORING MARGIN

SCHOOL	OWN	OPP.	MAR.
Kentucky	68.2	43.9	24.3
Tulane	65.6	48.8	16.8
Rhode Island St.	71.6	56.0	15.6
Loyola (Ill.)	61.3	45.7	15.5
Western Kentucky	69.9	54.4	15.5

SCORING DEFENSE

SCHOOL	PTS.	AVG.
Oklahoma A&M	985	35.2
Siena	1215	41.9
Wyoming	1509	43.1
Minnesota	912	43.4
St. Bonaventure	1137	43.7

FREE THROW PERCENTAGE

SCHOOL	FTM	FTA	PCT.
Davidson	347	489	.710
Kentucky	514	728	.706
Utah	489	704	.695
Denver	505	730	.692
Valparaiso	340	496	.687

its most lopsided defeat in history when the Redskins were clobbered at Cincinnati, 94-36. . . . Bowling Green hasn't won more than 20 games in a season since compiling a 24-7 mark as third-place finisher in the NIT. The Falcons averaged 24.3 victories annually over the last seven seasons in the 1940s despite sustaining losses in that span to Muskingum, Great Lakes, Denison and Baldwin-Wallace. . . . St. Louis' Ed Macauley finished his career as a two-time first-team All-American after averaging a modest 6.8 points per game in his three-year varsity career at a local high school. . . . Wisconsin had a career 35-15 record against Indiana after defeating the Hoosiers, 58-48.

Texas' Slater Martin set a school record (subsequently tied) with 49 points against TCU. Martin more than tripled his season scoring average of 16 points per game. His career scoring average was a modest 12.7 ppg. . . . Pacific lost 17 consecutive games in its series with Santa Clara until defeating the Broncos, 60-52. . . . John Wooden began his coaching career at UCLA with a 22-7 record, breaking the Bruins' previous single-season mark of 18 victories, which was set two years earlier under his prede-

1948-49 FINAL NATIONAL POLL

AP	SCHOOL(RECORD)	HEAD COACH
1	Kentucky (32-2)	Adolph Rupp
2	Oklahoma St. (23-5)	Hank Iba
3	St. Louis (22-4)	Eddie Hickey
4	Illinois (21-4)	Harry Combes
5	Western Kentucky (25-4)	Ed Diddle
6	Minnesota (18-3)	Ozzie Cowles
7	Bradley (27-8)	Forddy Anderson
8	San Francisco (25-5)	Pete Newell
9	Tulane (24-4)	Cliff Wells
10	Bowling Green St. (24-7)	Harold Anderson

cessor, Wilbur Johns. Wooden, who coached two seasons at Indiana State in his home state, had also caught the eye of Minnesota but UCLA put its offer on the table first and he accepted a first-year salary of $6,000.

1949 NCAA Tournament

Summary: Despite returning seven of his top eight scorers from an NCAA titlist, Kentucky coach Adolph Rupp experimented with the Wildcats' lineup until he achieved the chemistry he sought. Cliff Barker was moved from forward to guard and forward Dale Barnstable also played some guard. After an early-season defeat to St. Louis on a last-second tip-in, Kentucky won all of

1948–49 NCAA CHAMPION: KENTUCKY

SEASON STATISTICS OF KENTUCKY REGULARS

PLAYER	POS.	CL.	G	FG%	FT%	PPG
Alex Groza	C	Sr.	34	.423	.726	20.5
Ralph Beard	G	Sr.	34	.299	.713	10.9
Wallace Jones	F-C	Sr.	32	.295	.653	9.7
Cliff Barker	G-F	Sr.	34	.298	.682	7.3
Dale Barnstable	F-G	Jr.	34	.272	.719	6.1
Jim Line	F	Jr.	32	.359	.843	5.7
Walt Hirsch	F-G	So.	34	.321	.688	4.6
Roger Day	F	So.	19	.538	.529	2.7
Garland Townes	G	So.	16	.208	.550	1.9
Johnny Stough	G	Jr.	25	.232	.857	1.5
TEAM TOTALS			**34**	**.328**	**.706**	**68.2**

1949 CHAMPIONSHIP GAME

SEATTLE, WA

KENTUCKY (46)	FG	FT-A	PF	PTS.
Jones	1	1-3	3	3
Line	2	1-2	3	5
Groza	9	7-8	5	25
Beard	1	1-2	4	3
Barker	1	3-3	4	5
Barnstable	1	1-1	1	3
Hirsch	1	0-0	1	2
TOTALS	**16**	**14-19**	**21**	**46**

FT%: .737.

OKLAHOMA A&M (36)	FG	FT-A	PF	PTS.
Yates	1	0-0	1	2
Shelton	3	6-7	4	12
Harris	3	1-1	5	7
Bradley	0	3-6	3	3
Parks	2	3-4	5	7
Jaquet	0	1-2	0	1
McArthur	0	2-2	1	2
Pilgrim	0	2-2	1	2
Smith	0	0-0	1	0
TOTALS	**9**	**18-24**	**21**	**36**

FT%: .750.
Halftime: Kentucky 25-20.

MOST OUTSTANDING PLAYER
Alex Groza, C, Sr., Kentucky

its games until bowing in the NIT to eventual finalist Loyola of Chicago. A couple of years later, Alex Groza, Ralph Beard and Barnstable admitted in sworn testimony that they accepted $1,500 in bribes to throw the NIT game against Loyola. There was also testimony that bribes from gamblers were accepted to shave points in other contests. Each received a suspended sentence in return for cooperating with federal officials and were banned by the NBA. Beard and Groza are the only two of the 10 players who started the first NBA All-Star Game in 1951 not to be in the Naismith Memorial Basketball Hall of Fame. Beard admits to taking $700, but not even the gambler, a student who sat on Kentucky's bench, said Beard agreed to shave points. "It's like I told the grand jury," Beard says. "I said, 'I would like to know what constitutes guilt. If taking money constitutes guilt, I'm guilty. But if influencing the point spread constitutes guilt, I'm as innocent as anybody ever was.' I was too selfish as a player, too proud of who I was, to ever play less than my best."

Star Gazing: Groza is the brother of football Hall of Famer Lou Groza. . . . Interestingly, a reserve on Kentucky's team early in the season, Joe B. Hall, didn't make the trip to Seattle because he had transferred to the University of the South. Later, he was the Wildcats' coach when they made a trip to the "Emerald City" at the 1984 Final Four.

One and Only: Groza, the Final Four Most Outstanding Player in 1948 and 1949, is the only player to appear at a minimum of two Final Fours and be the game-high scorer in every Final Four contest he played in. Despite missing 13 minutes of the second half because of foul trouble, Groza scored 25 points to lead the Wildcats to a 46-36 decision over Oklahoma A&M in the title game. . . . Wyoming, coached by Everett Shelton, became the only school to fall one victory shy of reaching the Final Four three consecutive years. . . . Oklahoma A&M, coached by Hank Iba, became the only school to reach the NCAA championship game in its first three playoff appearances-won titles in 1945 and 1946.

Numbers Game: Groza and Villanova's Paul Arizin each scored a tourney-high 30 points when

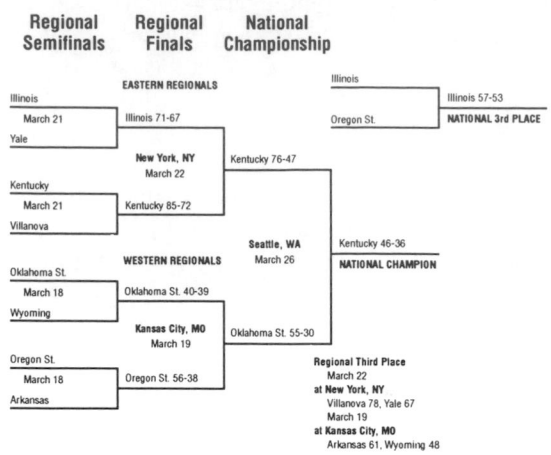

1949 CHAMPIONSHIP BRACKET

Kentucky defeated Villanova, 85-72, in their Eastern Regional opener. It was the only playoff game in which two players scored at least 30 in the same game until 1953.

Scoring Leader: Alex Groza, Kentucky (82 points, 27.3 ppg).

Most Outstanding Player: Alex Groza, C, Sr., Kentucky (52 points in final two games).

WINNINGEST PROGRAMS OF THE 1940s

RK.	SCHOOL	W.	L.	PCT.
1.	Kentucky	239	42	.851
2.	Oklahoma A&M	237	55	.812
3.	Rhode Island	178	44	.802
4.	Eastern Kentucky	143	37	.794
5.	Western Kentucky	222	66	.771
6.	Tennessee	152	46	.768
7.	Bowling Green	204	66	.756
8.	Notre Dame	162	55	.747
9.	Toledo	176	65	.730
10.	St. John's	162	60	.730

Note: Seton Hall (128-22 record, .853) and Duquesne (118-32, .787) competed in only seven seasons during the decade.

ALL-DECADE TEAM - 1940s

Ralph Beard, G, Kentucky
Gus Broberg, G-F, Dartmouth
Arnie Ferrin, F, Utah
George Glamack, C, North Carolina
Alex Groza, C, Kentucky
Bob Kurland, C, Oklahoma A&M
Ed Macauley, C-F, St. Louis
George Mikan, C, DePaul
Andy Phillip, F, Illinois
Sid Tannenbaum, G, NYU

Coach: Hank Iba, Oklahoma A&M

Ralph Beard

Kentucky
5-11 - G
Hardinsburg, Ky., and Louisville, Ky. (Male H.S.)

NCAA unanimous first-team All-American in 1947 and 1948, and consensus first-team All-American in 1949. . . . Second-leading scorer for NCAA champions in 1948 (36-3 record) and 1949 (32-2). . . . Averaged 9.2 points in six NCAA Tournament games in 1948 and 1949 (6-0 record). . . . Averaged 12 points in seven NIT games in 1946 (champion), 1947 (runner-up) and 1949 (opening-game loser). . . . Member of 1948 U.S. Olympic team (3.7 ppg). . . . Selected by the Chicago Stags in first round of 1949 BAA draft but a corporation including him and several Kentucky teammates was granted an NBL franchise (the Indianapolis Olympians). When the BAA and NBL merged that summer to form the NBA, the Olympians represented one of the franchises involved in the merger.

SEASON	G.	FGM-FGA	FG%	FTM-FTA	FT%	PTS.	AVG.
1945-46	30	111-	-	57-110	.518	279	9.3
1946-47	37	157-469	.335	78-115	.678	392	10.6
1947-48	38	194-536	.362	88-149	.591	476	12.5
1948-49	34	144-481	.299	82-115	.713	370	10.9
Totals	139	606-	-	305-489	.624	1517	10.9

Gus Broberg

Dartmouth
6-1 - G/F
Torrington, Conn.

NCAA consensus first-team All-American in 1940 and 1941. . . . Averaged 19 points in two NCAA Tournament games in 1941 (1-1 record).

SEASON	G.	FGM	FTM-FTA	FT%	PTS.	AVG.
1938-39	23	127	64-76	.842	318	13.8
1939-40	21	124	57-60	.950	305	14.5
1940-41	23	141	61-76	.803	343	14.9
Totals	67	392	182-212	.858	966	14.4

Arnie Ferrin

Utah
6-4 - F
Ogden, Utah

NCAA consensus first-team All-American in 1945 and second-team All-American in 1944, 1947 and 1948. . . . Final Four Most Outstanding Player in 1944. . . . Leading scorer with 13.3 points per game during 1944 tournament for NCAA champion (22-4 record). Did not play in the 1945 playoffs after entering military service the day following the end of the regular season. . . . Averaged 13.5 points in four NIT games in 1944 (first-round loser) and 1947 (champion).

SEASON	G.	FGM	FTM	PTS.	AVG.
1943-44	24	127	47	301	12.5
1944-45	18	-	-	315	17.4
1945-46	Military Service (Army)				
1946-47	20	82	63	227	11.4
1947-48	20	96	90	282	14.1
Totals	82	-	-	1125	13.7

George Glamack

North Carolina
6-6 - C
Allentown, Pa. (Preparatory H.S.)

NCAA consensus first-team All-American in 1940 and 1941. . . . Averaged 20 points in two NCAA Tournament games in 1941 (0-2 record).

SEASON	G.	FGM	FTM	PTS.	AVG.
1938-39	-	-	-	-	-
1939-40	-	-	-	-	-
1940-41	28	-	-	578	20.6
Totals	-	-	-	-	-

Alex Groza

Kentucky
6-7 - C
Martins Ferry, Ohio

NCAA consensus first-team All-American in 1947 and 1949, and consensus second-team All-American in 1948. . . . Final Four Most Outstanding Player in 1948 (37 points in final two games) and 1949 (52 points). . . . Ranked 6th in the nation in scoring in 1949. . . . Leading scorer for NCAA champions in 1948 (36-3 record) and 1949 (32-2). . . . Averaged 22.7 points in six NCAA Tournament games in 1948 and 1949 (6-0 record). . . . Averaged 13.3 points in four NIT games in 1947 (runner-up) and 1949 (opening-game loser). . . . Leading scorer (11.1 points per game) for 1948 U.S. Olympic team. . . . Selected by the Indianapolis Olympians in 1949 NBA draft.

SEASON	G.	FGM-FGA	FG%	FTM-FTA	FT%	PTS.	AVG.
1944-45	10	62-		41-	-	165	16.5
1945-46		Military Service (Army)					
1946-47	37	146-372	.392	101-160	.631	393	10.6
1947-48	39	200-530	.377	88-140	.629	488	12.5
1948-49	34	259-612	.423	180-248	.726	698	20.5
Totals	120	667-		410-		1744	14.5

NOTE: Groza missed more than half of the 1944-45 season because he was inducted into the Army.

Bob Kurland

Oklahoma A&M
7-0 - C
Jennings, Mo.

NCAA consensus first-team All-American in 1944, 1945 and 1946. . . . Final Four Most Outstanding Player in 1945 (37 points in final two games) and 1946 (52 points). . . . Leading scorer for NCAA Tournament champions in 1945 (27-4 record) and 1946 (31-2). . . . Averaged 22.8 points in six NCAA Tournament games in 1945 and 1946 (6-0 record). . . . Averaged 13.7 points in three games for fourth-place team in 1944 NIT (1-2 record). . . . Member of U.S. Olympic teams in 1948 (9.3 ppg) and 1952 (9.6 ppg). . . . Elected to Naismith Memorial Basketball Hall of Fame in 1961.

SEASON	G.	FGM	FTM	PTS.	AVG.
1942-43	21	22	9	53	2.5
1943-44	33	182	80	444	13.5
1944-45	31	214	101	529	17.1
1945-46	33	257	129	643	19.5
Totals	118	675	319	1669	14.1

Ed Macauley

St. Louis
6-8 - C/F
St. Louis, Mo. (University H.S.)

NCAA unanimous first-team All-American in 1949 and consensus first-team All-American in 1948. . . . Led the nation in field-goal percentage in 1949. . . . Ranked among the nation's leaders in scoring (38th) and free-throw percentage (32nd) in 1949. . . . Did not play in NCAA Tournament. . . . NIT Most Valuable Player in 1948. . . . Averaged 16.5 points in four NIT games in 1948 (champion) and 1949 (first-round loser). . . . Selected as a territorial pick by the St. Louis Bombers of the Basketball Association of American in 1949. . . . Elected to Naismith Memorial Basketball Hall of Fame in 1960.

SEASON	G.	FGM-FGA	FG%	FTM-FTA	FT%	PTS.	AVG.
1945-46	23	94-		71-	-	259	11.3
1946-47	28	141-		104-	-	386	13.8
1947-48	27	132-324	.407	104-159	.654	368	13.6
1948-49	26	144-275	.524	116-153	.758	404	15.5
Totals	104	511-		395-	-	1417	13.6

George Mikan

DePaul
6-10 - C
Joliet, Ill. (Catholic H.S.) and Chicago, Ill. (Quigley Prep)

NCAA consensus first-team All-American in 1944, 1945 and 1946. . . . Led the nation in scoring in 1945 and 1946. . . . Leading scorer for national semifinalist in 1943 NCAA Tournament (19-5 record). . . . Averaged 15.5 points in two NCAA Tournament games in 1943 (1-1 record). . . . NIT Most Valuable Player in 1945. . . . Leading scorer in NIT in 1944 and 1945 when he averaged 28.2 points in six games. . . . Signed by the Chicago Stags of National Basketball League in 1946. . . . Elected to Naismith Memorial Basketball Hall of Fame in 1959.

SEASON	G.	FGM	FTM-FTA	FT%	PTS.	AVG.
1942-43	24	97	77-111	.694	271	11.3
1943-44	26	188	110-169	.651	486	18.7
1944-45	24	218	122-199	.613	558	23.3
1945-46	24	206	143-186	.769	555	23.1
Totals	98	709	452-665	.680	1870	19.1

Andy Phillip

Illinois
6-2 - F
Granite City, Ill.

NCAA consensus first-team All-American in 1942 and 1943, and consensus second-team All-American in 1947. . . . Averaged 5.5 points in two NCAA Tournament games in 1942 (0-2 record). . . . Elected to Naismith Memorial Basketball Hall of Fame in 1961.

SEASON	G.	FGM	FTM-FTA	FT%	PTS.	AVG.
1941-42	23	87	58-	-	232	10.1
1942-43	18	131	43-57	.754	305	16.9
1943-44, 1944-45 and 1945-46			Military Service (Marines)			
1946-47	20	81	30-61	.492	192	9.6
Totals	61	299	131-	-	729	12.0

Sid Tannenbaum

New York University
6-0 - G
Brooklyn, N.Y. (Thomas Jefferson H.S.)

NCAA consensus first-team All-American in 1946 and 1947. . . . Second-leading scorer for 1945 NCAA Tournament runner-up (16-8 record). . . . Averaged 9.8 points in five NCAA Tournament games in 1945 and 1946 (3-2 record).

SEASON	G.	FGM	FTM	PTS.	AVG.
1943-44	16	88	34	210	13.1
1944-45	24	121	60	302	12.6
1945-46	22	113	58	284	12.9
1946-47	21	117	44	278	13.2
Totals	83	439	196	1074	12.9

HENRY (HANK) IBA

Westminster, Mo. '28
Easton, Mo.

Elected to Naismith Memorial Basketball Hall of Fame in 1968. . . . U.S. Olympic Team coach in 1964, 1968 and 1972. . . . Reached Final Four on four occasions-1945 (1st), 1946 (1st), 1949 (2nd) and 1951 (4th). . . . Coach of three teams that reached NIT semifinals-1938 (3rd), 1940 (3rd) and 1944 (4th).

SEASON	SCHOOL	OVERALL	LEAGUE	FINISH	POSTSEASON
1929-30	NW Missouri St.	31-0	16-0	1st (MIAA)	-
1930-31	NW Missouri St.	32-6	3-5	T3rd (MIAA)	-
1931-32	NW Missouri St.	26-2	7-1	1st (MIAA)	-
1932-33	NW Missouri St.	12-6	6-2	1st (MIAA)	-
1933-34	Colorado	11-8	7-5	2nd (RMC)	-
1934-35	Oklahoma State	9-9	5-7	T5th (MVC)	-
1935-36	Oklahoma State	16-8	8-4	T1st (MVC)	-
1936-37	Oklahoma State	20-3	11-1	1st (MVC)	-
1937-38	Oklahoma State	25-3	13-1	1st (MVC)	NIT (1-1)
1938-39	Oklahoma State	19-8	11-3	T1st (MVC)	DNP
1939-40	Oklahoma State	26-3	12-0	1st (MVC)	NIT (1-1)
1940-41	Oklahoma State	18-7	8-4	2nd (MVC)	DNP
1941-42	Oklahoma State	20-6	9-1	T1st (MVC)	DNP
1942-43	Oklahoma State	14-10	7-3	T2nd (MVC)	DNP
1943-44	Oklahoma State	27-6	-	Mo. Valley	NIT (1-2)
1944-45	Oklahoma State	27-4	-	Mo. Valley	NCAA (3-0)
1945-46	Oklahoma State	31-2	12-0	1st (MVC)	NCAA (3-0)
1946-47	Oklahoma State	24-8	8-4	T2nd (MVC)	DNP
1947-48	Oklahoma State	27-4	10-0	1st (MVC)	DNP
1948-49	Oklahoma State	23-5	9-1	1st (MVC)	NCAA (2-1)
1949-50	Oklahoma State	18-9	7-5	T3rd (MVC)	DNP
1950-51	Oklahoma State	29-6	12-2	1st (MVC)	NCAA (2-2)
1951-52	Oklahoma State	19-8	7-3	2nd (MVC)	DNP
1952-53	Oklahoma State	23-7	8-2	1st (MVC)	NCAA (1-1)
1953-54	Oklahoma State	24-5	9-1	1st (MVC)	NCAA (1-1)
1954-55	Oklahoma State	12-13	5-5	3rd (MVC)	DNP
1955-56	Oklahoma State	18-9	8-4	T2nd (MVC)	NIT (0-1)
1956-57	Oklahoma State	17-9	8-6	T3rd (MVC)	DNP
1957-58	Oklahoma State	21-8	-		NCAA (2-1)
1958-59	Oklahoma State	11-14	5-9	T5th (Big Eight)	DNP
1959-60	Oklahoma State	10-15	4-10	T7th (Big Eight)	DNP
1960-61	Oklahoma State	15-10	9-5	3rd (Big Eight)	DNP
1961-62	Oklahoma State	14-11	7-7	4th (Big Eight)	DNP
1962-63	Oklahoma State	16-9	7-7	5th (Big Eight)	DNP
1963-64	Oklahoma State	15-10	7-7	T4th (Big Eight)	DNP
1964-65	Oklahoma State	20-7	12-2	1st (Big Eight)	NCAA (1-1)
1965-66	Oklahoma State	4-21	2-12	7th (Big Eight)	DNP
1966-67	Oklahoma State	7-18	2-12	7th (Big Eight)	DNP
1967-68	Oklahoma State	10-16	3-11	T7th (Big Eight)	DNP
1968-69	Oklahoma State	12-13	5-9	T6th (Big Eight)	DNP
1969-70	Oklahoma State	14-12	5-9	T7th (Big Eight)	DNP

41-Year Coaching Record: 767-338 (.694) overall; 101-14 (.878) in four years at Northwest Missouri State; 11-8 (.579) in one year at Colorado; 655-316 (.675) in 36 years at Oklahoma State; 32-8 (.800) in Missouri Intercollegiate Athletic Association; 7-5 (.583) in Rocky Mountain Conference; 187-57 (.766) in Missouri Valley Conference; 68-100 (.405) in Big Eight Conference; 15-7 (.682) in NCAA Tournament; 3-5 (.375) in NIT.

3

THE "GREAT PLAYERS" ERA:

THE 1950s

Kentucky, after closing out the 1940s with back-to-back NCAA crowns, continued to excel but represented the best and worst of the 1950s. The Wildcats were virtually invincible on the court, winning at least 20 games every season they competed in the decade. On the other hand, they were party to a widespread gambling-related scandal that barred them from participating one season.

Kentucky coach Adolph Rupp's average record in a 15-year span from 1944-59 was an incredible 27-3. An example of the Wildcats' SEC dominance was their five victories over Florida from 1948-54 when they won four of the outings by at least 42 points.

Manhattan's Junius Kellogg became perhaps the most courageous player in history. Kellogg stood up to the mob and exposed gambling scandals infecting the sport. Later, he fought back against a crippling automobile accident to lead an exemplary life.

The '50s also marked the emergence of dominating African American players such as Elgin Baylor, Wilt Chamberlain, Oscar Robertson and Bill Russell. The athleticism of big men like

Chamberlain and Russell was amazing and altered the scope of the game. Chamberlain became the only seven-foot center to lead a Final Four in scoring (55 points in two games for 1957 runner-up Kansas) and win a conference high jump title in the same year (Big Eight outdoor meet at a height of 6'5"). Russell, 6-10, did more than lead San Francisco to back-to-back NCAA basketball championships. He was ranked as the world's No. 7 high jumper in Track and Field News rankings for 1956 after winning titles in the West Coast Relays, Pacific AAU meet and Central California AAU meet. Baylor and Robertson were equally impressive physical specimens.

Chamberlain, who grew up in Philadelphia, headlined an impressive string of All-Americas from Pennsylvania. He and eight other natives of the Quaker State became NCAA consensus first-team All-Americas a total of 12 times from 1950-58. Joining Chamberlain on this list were Paul Arizin (Villanova), Bill Mlkvy (Temple), Dick Groat (Duke), Ernie Beck (Penn), Tom Gola (La Salle), Dick Ricketts (Duquesne), Don Hennon (Pitt) and Guy Rodgers (Temple). Gola and Ricketts were among freshmen declared eligible for varsity competition in the 1951-52 season by most colleges because of the manpower shortage stemming from the Korean War.

The Atlantic Coast Conference, the NCAA Tournament's most dominant league the vast majority of the time since 1981, got off to a lackluster start in its first three years in the NCAA playoffs, compiling a modest 2-3 tourney record from 1954 through 1956. Star-crossed North Carolina State was the only ACC school to finish among the nation's 20 winningest programs of the decade. The untimely deaths of four N.C. State players from the mid- to late-1950s (Ronnie Shavlik, Cliff Dwyer, John Richter and Bob Seitz) would eventually cast an unfortunate pall on that otherwise successful stretch. Seitz died in 1967 at age 33 of a rare gland disease, Dwyer succumbed to a heart attack in 1975, Shavlik was felled by cancer in 1983 and Richter committed suicide in 1985.

Coach Frank McGuire, a native of New York, was able to make North Carolina's program prosper in the last half of the decade by creating a New York/New Jersey pipeline that delivered Tar Heel stars Lennie Rosenbluth, Tommy Kearns, York Larese, Lou Brown, Doug Moe and Larry Brown.

The '50s are the long lost glory years for many schools. More than half of the decade's Top 20 teams in final wire-service polls failed to appear among the Top 20 in comparable rankings the first half of the 1990s. Three schools in the '50s went from the Final Four one year to at least 10 games below .500 the next season.

1949-50

AT A GLANCE

NCAA/NIT Champion: CCNY (24-5; coached by Nat Holman).

NCAA Consensus First-Team All-Americans: Paul Arizin, F, Sr., Villanova; Bob Cousy, G, Sr., Holy Cross; Dick Schnittker, F, Sr., Ohio State; Bill Sharman, G, Sr., Southern California; Paul Unruh, F, Sr., Bradley.

Senior Paul Arizin, who couldn't earn a spot on his high school squad and didn't bother to try out as a Villanova freshman, led the nation in scoring average (25.3). Arizin's outbursts helped Villanova end Rhode Island State's streak of 14 consecutive seasons leading the nation in offense. The Wildcats averaged 72.8 points per game.

Bob Zawoluk's school-record 65 points for St. John's against St. Peter's was the top one-game barrage during the season. . . . Frank Adams concluded his six-year stint at Fordham with a 68-71 record. He was the first of Fordham's initial 15 coaches to compile a losing career mark at the school. . . . Butler's Ralph "Buckshot" O'Brien, a 5-9, 150-pound guard, averaged 25.3 points per game in seven games against Big Nine teams. . . . St. Bonaventure's Sam Urzetta led the nation in free-throw accuracy for the second time in three seasons. Urzetta also went on to win the U.S. Amateur golf title. . . . St. Francis (N.Y.) compiled a 6-18 record for its only losing season in a 26-year span from 1932-33 through 1957-58. . . . Chet Giermak finished his William & Mary career with 2,052 points. He has the longest running all-time scoring record for a school that has always been classified as a major college.

Ohio State forward Dick Schnittker earned consensus All-American honors after starting as an end for Ohio State's conference co-championship football squad that defeated California, 17-14, in the Rose Bowl. . . . Michigan defeated archrival Michigan State for the 37th time in their last 49 meetings. . . . Northwestern posted its lone victory over Notre Dame (66-56) in a 21-game stretch of their series from 1946 through 1956. . . . Cincinnati, coached by John Wiethe, became the only Mid-American team to ever go undefeated in conference competition since the league's inception in 1947. . . . Bradley (32-5/coached by Forddy Anderson) had its winningest season in school history. Holy Cross (27-4/Buster Sheary) tied its school record for most victories in a single season.

Two future teammates with the Boston Celtics led the Pacific Coast Conference in scoring for four seasons. Washington State's Gene

Conley paced the Northern Division with 13.8 points per game while Southern Cal's Bill Sharman led the Southern Division with a 19.8 mark. Both Conley and Sharman also played professional baseball. Speaking of the Celtics, Red Auerbach was an assistant coach and heir apparent to Gerry Gerard at Duke for three months before leaving for a pro job with Tri-Cities. Auerbach was given much credit for grooming Duke All-American Dick Groat.

TCU finished with a losing record in SWC competition but became the first major-college team to hit 40 percent of its field-goal attempts in a single season. . . . Baylor captured its third straight and final SWC championship. Bears coach Bill Henderson had only two winning records in the next 11 seasons. . . . Tulane's school-record 42-game homecourt winning streak under coach Clifford Wells ended when Arkansas edged the Green Wave, 42-41. Arkansas got off to a 3-8 start, however, and finished with its first non-winning record in 26 years (12-12). . . . Kansas (14-11) tied for the Big Seven Conference crown after finishing in last place the previous

1949-50 FINAL NATIONAL POLL

AP	SCHOOL (RECORD)	HEAD COACH
1	Bradley (32-5)	Forddy Anderson
2	Ohio State (22-4)	Tippy Dye
3	Kentucky (25-5)	Adolph Rupp
4	Holy Cross (27-4)	Buster Sheary
5	N.C. State (27-6)	Everett Case
6	Duquesne (23-6)	Dudey Moore
7	UCLA (24-7)	John Wooden
8	Western Kentucky (25-6)	Ed Diddle
9	St. John's (24-5)	Frank McGuire
10	La Salle (21-4)	Ken Loeffler
11	Villanova (25-4)	Al Severance
12	San Francisco (19-7)	Pete Newell
13	Long Island (20-5)	Clair Bee
14	Kansas State (17-7)	Jack Gardner
15	Arizona (26-5)	Fred Enke
16	Wisconsin (17-5)	Bud Foster
17	San Jose State (21-7)	Walter McPherson
18	Washington State (19-13)	Jack Friel
19	Kansas (14-11)	Phog Allen
20	Indiana (17-5)	Branch McCracken

1949-50 INDIVIDUAL LEADERS

SCORING

PLAYER	PTS.	AVG.
Arizin, Villanova	735	25.3
Senesky, St. Joseph's	537	22.4
White, Long Island	551	22.0
Lovellette, Kansas	545	21.8
Lavoy, Western Kentucky	671	21.6
Schnittker, Ohio St.	469	21.3
Giermak, William & Mary	646	20.8
Handlan, Washington & Lee	406	20.3
Zawoluk, St. John's	588	20.3
Noertker, Virginia	503	20.1

FIELD GOAL PERCENTAGE

PLAYER	FGM	FGA	PCT.
Moran, Niagara	98	185	.530
Toft, Denver	146	281	.520
McDonald, Toledo	102	200	.510
Arizin, Villanova	260	527	.493
Skendrovich, Duquesne	108	220	.491
Mann, Bradley	135	291	.464
Share, Bowling Green	204	444	.459
Meineke, Dayton	194	424	.458
Beck, Bowling Green	84	186	.452
Pilch, Wyoming	143	317	.451

FREE THROW PERCENTAGE

PLAYER	FTM	FTA	PCT.
Urzetta, St. Bonaventure	54	61	.885
Morrill, Michigan	41	48	.854
Ballots, Temple	73	86	.849
Popp, Baldwin-Wallace	69	83	.831
Sermersheim, Georgia Tech	68	82	.829
Gardiner, St. Louis	53	64	.828
Brawner, Auburn	49	60	.817
Turner, Western Kentucky	84	103	.816
Davis, Pennsylvania	44	54	.815
Norris, Colgate	79	97	.814

1949-50 TEAM LEADERS

SCORING OFFENSE

SCHOOL	PTS.	AVG.
Villanova	2111	72.8
Holy Cross	2251	72.6
St. John's	2093	72.2
Muhlenberg	1651	71.8
Western Kentucky	2216	71.5

SCORING DEFENSE

SCHOOL	PTS.	AVG.
Oklahoma A&M	1059	39.2
Wyoming	1491	41.4
Tulsa	1027	44.7
Washington (Mo.)	1066	46.3
San Francisco	1237	47.6

FIELD GOAL PERCENTAGE

SCHOOL	FGM	FGA	PCT.
Texas Christian	476	1191	.400
Bowling Green	808	2070	.390
Toledo	633	1631	.388
Bradley	999	2588	.386
Akron	676	1752	.386
Wyoming	629	1631	.386

FREE THROW PERCENTAGE

SCHOOL	FTM	FTA	PCT.
Temple	342	483	.708
Colorado	395	576	.686
Auburn	390	574	.679
Duquesne	418	616	.679
Washington St.	456	673	.678

SCORING MARGIN

SCHOOL	OWN	OPP.	MAR.
Holy Cross	72.6	55.4	17.2
Villanova	72.8	55.7	17.1
St. John's	72.2	56.7	15.5
La Salle	69.8	54.8	15.0
North Carolina St.	65.3	51.7	13.7

year. The Jayhawks shared the title after losing an early-season game to Creighton, which was in the midst of nine consecutive non-winning seasons. . . . Nebraska registered the largest ever winning margin in an overtime game with an 85-67 triumph over Iowa State. . . . Clarence Iba became Tulsa's ninth head coach in 12 years. . . . Wichita's only victory in its last 18 outings (38-37 over Oklahoma A&M) was the Shockers' lone triumph in the first 19 times they opposed Aggies coach Hank Iba from 1935 to 1953.

Coach Lee Patton, who holds the second-best winning percentage in West Virginia history, died in an auto accident late in the season. . . . Lyles Alley, en route to becoming Furman's all-time winningest coach, missed the season while taking a one-year sabbatical to work on his masters degree at Columbia. . . . Kentucky claimed its seventh consecutive SEC Tournament title. The Wildcats sustained just 15 defeats in the last five seasons, with the third setback in that span to Notre Dame, 64-51. . . . Georgia's 71-60 success over Kentucky was the Bulldogs' lone victory in a 31-game stretch of their series from 1940 through 1966. Tennessee's 66-53 decision over UK was the Volunteers' lone triumph in a 33-game span of their series from 1945 to 1960. . . . Mississippi's Jack Marshall finished his fifth season of varsity competition with an 11.2-point scoring average.

Alabama, coached by Floyd Burdette, sustained its only losing record (9-12) in a 19-year stretch from 1938-39 through 1957-58 (Bama did not field a squad in 1943-44 because of World War II). . . . Wisconsin (coached by Bud Foster), Long Island (Clair Bee), San Jose State (Walt McPherson) and Washington State (Jack Friel) made their lone appearance in the Top 20 of a final wire-service poll. . . . Wayne State (Mich.) competed in its final season at the major-college level.

1950 NCAA Tournament

Summary: City College of New York became the only school to win the NCAA playoffs and NIT in the same year. It is also the only former major college to compile a winning playoff record in the NCAA Division I Tournament. The ultimate "Cinderella" squad won the NCAA crown by defeating three teams ranked in the AP top five (second-ranked Ohio State, fifth-ranked

1949–50 NCAA CHAMPION: CCNY

SEASON STATISTICS OF CCNY REGULARS

PLAYER	POS.	CL.	G.	FG%	FT%	PPG
Ed Roman	C	So.	29	.416	.642	16.4
Ed Warner	F	So.	29	.430	.567	14.8
Irwin Dambrot	F	Sr.	29	.371	.580	10.2
Floyd Layne	G	So.	29	.280	.606	6.9
Al Roth	G	So.	29	.288	.515	6.4
Herb Cohen	G	So.	24	.410	.526	5.4
Norm Mager	F	Sr.	29	.353	.629	3.6
Ronald Nadell	G	Jr.	19	.386	.650	2.5
Mike Wittlin	G	Sr.	22	.314	.600	1.7
Joe Galiber	C	Sr.	24	.239	.522	1.4
TEAM TOTALS			29	.363	.577	68.7

1950 CHAMPIONSHIP GAME

NEW YORK, NY

CCNY (71)	FG-A	FT-A	A	PF	PTS.
Dambrot	7-14	1-2	2	0	15
Roman	6-17	0-2	1	5	12
Warner	4-9	6-14	3	2	14
Roth	2-7	1-5	3	2	5
Mager	4-10	6-6	2	3	14
Galiber	0-0	0-0	0	1	0
Layne	3-7	5-6	4	3	11
Nadell	0-0	0-0	1	1	0
TOTALS	**26-64**	**19-35**	**16**	**17**	**71**

FG%: .406. **FT%:** .543.

BRADLEY (68)	FG-A	FT-A	A	PF	PTS.
Grover	0-10	2-3	3	3	2
Schlictman	0-3	0-0	0	2	0
Unruh	4-9	0-0	2	5	8
Behnke	3-10	3-3	2	4	9
Kelly	0-1	0-2	0	0	0
Mann	2-7	5-5	1	5	9
Preece	6-11	0-0	0	5	12
D. Melchiorre	0-0	0-0	0	0	0
G. Melchiorre	7-16	2-4	5	4	16
Chianakas	5-7	1-3	1	4	11
Stowell	0-0	1-1	0	0	1
TOTALS	**27-74**	**14-21**	**14**	**32**	**68**

FG%: .365. **FT%:** .667.
Halftime: CCNY 39-32.

MOST OUTSTANDING PLAYER
Irwin Dambrot, F, Sr., CCNY

North Carolina State and top-ranked Bradley) although five of CCNY's six leading scorers were sophomores. CCNY, coached by Nat Holman, also defeated 12th-ranked San Francisco, third-ranked Kentucky, sixth-ranked Duquesne and Bradley a second time the same year on its way to the NIT title. "Nat was a great coach," said Red Holzman, who played for Holman at CCNY from 1940-42. "He had a lot to do with the development of the game. His philosophy of basketball was great. He preached team basketball, passing the ball to the open man, moving without the ball, unselfishness, defense. He taught me a lot of things that I preached later on (coaching the Knicks to their only two NBA titles)."

Outcome for Defending Champion: Kentucky (25-5) was embarrassed by CCNY, 89-50, in the Wildcats' NIT opener. Their other four defeats were each by more than 10 points.

Star Gazing: CCNY was the first NCAA champion to have black players in its starting line-up—Floyd Layne, Joe Galiber and Ed Warner. Alas, midnight struck for the Beavers following their storybook season when four CCNY regulars and other New York-based players were indicted in a point-shaving scandal rocking the sport the following year. After the investigation revealed scholastic records were falsified to allow several recruits admission to CCNY, the school de-emphasized its program in 1953.

One and Only: CCNY is the only former NCAA Tournament champion not to win at least one playoff game since capturing the title.

Numbers Game: The worst winning percentage for a Final Four team was compiled by Baylor, which finished with a 14-13 record (.519) after losing both of its Final Four games (to Bradley and North Carolina State). The Bears lost three outings by at least 33 points, including a whopping 48-point setback at Kansas State. The 78-30 blowout is the most lopsided loss ever for a team to reach the national semifinals. . . . UCLA, making its playoff debut under coach John Wooden, led mighty Bradley by seven points with five minutes remaining before the Braves went on a 23-2 spurt to end the game. . . . North Carolina State's Sam Ranzino scored a tourney-high 32 points in an 87-74 victory over Holy Cross in their Eastern Regional opener. . . . N.C. State won the national third-place game over Baylor, 53-41, although the Wolfpack hit a Final Four-low 19.5 percent of its field-goal attempts (15 of 77).

What Might Have Been: Bob Cousy and Frank Oftring, members of Holy Cross' 1947 NCAA titlist as freshmen, were senior co-captains when the Crusaders won their first 26 games to earn the No. 1 ranking nationally by the AP. But they lost four of their last five contests, including both outings in the NCAA playoffs when Cousy went 17 for 61 from the floor (27.9 percent).

Putting Things in Perspective: Would CCNY have been able to become the only school to win the NIT and NCAA playoffs in the same season if both of the national postseason tournaments weren't staged in New York? Most observers thought CCNY was out of the playoff picture after the Beavers lost three of five games late in the season.

Scoring Leader: Sam Ranzino, North Carolina State (77 points, 25.7 ppg).

Most Outstanding Player: Irwin Dambrot, F, Sr., CCNY (28 points in final two games).

1950 CHAMPIONSHIP BRACKET

1950-51

AT A GLANCE

NCAA Champion: Kentucky (32-2; coached by Adolph Rupp; compiled 14-0 record in SEC to finish four games ahead of Alabama and Vanderbilt).

NIT Champion: Brigham Young (28-9; coached by Stan Watts; finished in first place in Rocky Mountain Conference with a 15-5 record).

New Rule: NCAA Tournament field expands from eight to 16 teams, with 10 conference champions qualifying automatically for the first time (Big Seven, Big Ten, Border, Ivy League, Missouri Valley, Pacific Coast, Skyline, Southeastern, Southern, and Southwest).

NCAA Consensus First-Team All-Americans: Clyde Lovellette, C, Jr., Kansas; Gene Melchiorre, G, Sr., Bradley; Bill Mlkvy, F, Jr., Temple; Sam Ranzino, F, Sr., North Carolina State; Bill Spivey, C, Jr., Kentucky.

Long Island University's Clair Bee ended his 21-year college coaching career with a 412-87 record when LIU dropped its program in the wake of a fixing scandal. Star center Sherman White, who had scored 63 points against John Marshall the previous season, and two other Blackbird regulars were implicated and later prosecuted. In all, by the time the investigation was completed, 32 players at seven schools were cited in a plot to fix 86 games played at Madison Square Garden and 22 other arenas in 17 states. White spent eight months in prison for conspiracy to commit bribery.

Other prominent players implicated in fixing games were Ed Warner and Ed Roman of City College of New York; Gene Melchiorre of Bradley; and Frank Beard, Bill Spivey and Alex Groza of Kentucky. Gamblers paid bribes estimated at more than $72,000.

"In the first half of the century, Bee was basketball," said Bob Knight, who was befriended by Bee when Knight was at Army and Bee at a local military school. "There wasn't a thing he did that didn't affect the game, and there wasn't a thing that affected the game that he didn't do. He was one of the most singularly brilliant minds ever involved with athletics, and one of the greatest analytical basketball minds we've ever had. He had such a clear, brilliant grasp of what had to be done. He was a coach in the truest sense of the word."

LIU was undefeated at home in its last 13 seasons, compiling an overall 225-3 record at the 800-seat Brooklyn College of Pharmacy. Bee refused to employ a zone defense at home because

1950–51 INDIVIDUAL LEADERS

SCORING

PLAYER	PTS.	AVG.
Mlkvy, Temple	731	29.2
Handlan, Washington & Lee	656	26.2
Workman, West Virginia	705	26.1
Groat, Duke	831	25.2
Lovellette, Kansas	548	22.8
Slaughter, South Carolina	569	22.8
Hennessey, Villanova	703	22.0
Ove, Valparaiso	469	21.3
Zawoluk, St. John's	654	21.1
Ranzino, N.C. St.	706	20.8

REBOUNDING

PLAYER	REB.	AVG.
Beck, Pennsylvania	556	20.6
Mlkvy, Temple	472	18.9
Christ, Fordham	493	18.4
Payton, Tulane	426	17.8
Darling, Iowa	387	17.6
Nolen, Texas Tech	492	17.6
Deasy, North Carolina	399	17.3

Spivey, Kentucky	567	17.2
Slaughter, South Carolina	413	16.5
Corizzi, Rutgers	339	16.1

ASSISTS

PLAYER	AST.	AVG.
Walker, Toledo	210	7.2
Mlkvy, Temple	176	7.0
Birch, Niagara	193	6.9
Chadwick, Cornell	170	6.8
Regan, Seton Hall	158	5.6
Markham, Wisconisn	99	5.5
Becker, New York	87	5.4
Baird, Holy Cross	114	5.4
Stratton, Colgate	119	5.4
Cox, South Carolina	135	5.4

FIELD GOAL PERCENTAGE

PLAYER	FGM	FGA	PCT.
Meineke, Dayton	240	469	.512
Maguire, Villanova	86	170	.506
Workman, West Virginia	273	558	.489
Rogers, Texas Western	154	317	.486
Slaughter, South Carolina	222	458	.485
Jennerich, Manhattan	76	157	.484
Chambers, William & Mary	199	413	.482
Koffenberger, Maryland	97	202	.480
Sullivan, Alabama	136	284	.479
Jones, Virginia Tech	184	388	.474

FREE THROW PERCENTAGE

PLAYER	FTM	FTA	PCT.
Handlan, Washington & Lee	158	184	.859
McMurray, Wichita	81	95	.853
Preece, Bradley	62	73	.849
Gordon, Temple	53	63	.841
Skoog, Minnesota	52	63	.825
Davis, Pennsylvania	61	74	.824
Matthews, Hardin-Simmons	60	73	.822
Sayre, Virginia Tech	128	156	.821
Travis, Texas Western	84	103	.816
Stange, Iowa St.	66	81	.815

he thought it would give his team an unfair advantage on a court that was 24 feet shorter than regulation, putting the 10-second line at the rear free-throw line instead of at midcourt. LIU's average record in its last 16 seasons under Bee was 21-4.

The only regular-season defeat for NCAA champion-to-be Kentucky was against St. Louis (43-42) in the opening round of the Sugar Bowl in New Orleans. The Wildcats also bowed to Vanderbilt in the SEC Tournament final (61-57) although the championship trophy already had "Kentucky" engraved on it.

Temple's Bill Mlkvy concluded the season with a school-record 73 points, including 54 consecutive, at Wilkes College to finish with a national-leading 29.2 points per game. He averaged an amazing 39 field-goal attempts per game on his way to setting a school record for highest scoring average in a single season (29.2 points per game). Mlkvy, dubbed the Owl without a vowel, was also national runner-up in rebounding (18.9) and assists (7.0). Washington & Lee's Jay Handlan, runner-up to Mlkvy in scoring, set an NCAA record with 71 field-goal attempts (30 made) when he scored 66 points in a game against Furman.

Duke, coached by Harold Bradley, manufactured the greatest comeback in NCAA history in a 74-72 victory over Tulane in the consolation game of the Dixie Classic at Raleigh, N.C. The Blue Devils trailed by 32 points with two minutes remaining in the first half (54-22) and by 29 points at halftime (56-27). Bradley was appointed Duke's coach shortly before the start of the season after Gerry Gerard's cancer no longer was in remission.

North Carolina State, coached by Everett Case, won both the Southern Conference regular-season and postseason tourney titles for the fifth consecutive year. . . . North Carolina lost the first six times the Tar Heels opposed George Washington until clipping the Colonials, 66-60. . . . Clemson, coached by Banks McFadden, compiled its first winning season (11-7) in 12 years. . . . Navy, coached by Ben Carnevale, defeated Maryland for the 13th time in 14 games, 51-47.

Columbia, coached by first-year mentor Lou Rossini after Gordon Ridings was sidelined by illness, became the first team in the 50-year history of the Eastern Intercollegiate League to finish its regular season undefeated (22-0), but the Lions lost to Illinois, 79-71, in the opening round of the NCAA Tournament. Columbia's leading scorer was 6-4 1/2 sophomore Jack Molinas (14.4 points per game), who later served five years in prison for his role as "master fixer" in point-shaving scandals. Molinas, barred from the NBA for betting on his own team, was subsequently murdered at his home in California.

Eastern schools supplied 18 consecutive national team scoring leaders until Cincinnati moved atop the list with a 77-point average. The Bearcats captured their fifth Mid-American Conference championship in as many years with coach John Wiethe at their helm. . . . Eleven players

1950–51 TEAM LEADERS

SCORING OFFENSE

SCHOOL	PTS.	AVG.
Cincinnati	1694	77.0
North Carolina St.	2748	76.3
Kentucky	2540	74.7
Virginia Tech	2149	74.1
Gettysburg (Pa.)	1623	73.8

SCORING DEFENSE

SCHOOL	PTS.	AVG.
Texas A&M	1275	44.0
Arkansas	1101	45.9
Oklahoma A&M	1616	46.2
Texas	1256	46.5
Oklahoma City	1423	47.4

FIELD GOAL PERCENTAGE

SCHOOL	FGM	FGA	PCT.
Maryland	481	1210	.398
Virginia Tech	805	2029	.397
Washington & Lee (Va.)	639	1613	.396
Toledo	725	1852	.391
Bradley	941	2427	.388

FREE THROW PERCENTAGE

SCHOOL	FTM	FTA	PCT.
Minnesota	287	401	.716
Virginia Tech	539	756	.713
Oklahoma	383	547	.700
Duke	619	888	.697
Baylor	371	533	.696

SCORING MARGIN

SCHOOL	OWN	OPP.	MAR.
Kentucky	74.7	52.5	22.3
Columbia	72.9	52.7	20.1
Cincinnati	77.0	58.1	18.9
Arizona	69.5	55.4	14.1
Kansas St.	68.8	55.1	13.8

fouled out of a first-round NIT game when St. Bonaventure outlasted Cincinnati, 70-67, in double overtime. NIT champion Brigham Young attempted to duplicate CCNY's feat the previous year of winning both the NIT and NCAA, but BYU was eliminated by Kansas State, 64-54, in an NCAA Western Regional final. . . . Connecticut's Bill Corley set a school record when he tallied 51 points against New Hampshire. . . . Rhode Island lost six of its first seven games en route to a 13-15 record for Rams' first losing season in 29 years.

Brigham Young (28-9/coached by Stan Watts), Kansas State (25-4/Jack Gardner) and Cornell (20-5/Roy Greene) had their winningest seasons in school history. Bradley (32-6/Forddy Anderson) tied its school record for most victories in a single season.

Tulane's Mel Payton (31 vs. Mississippi State) and Purdue's Carl McNulty (27 vs. Minnesota) set school single-game rebounding records. . . . Murray State made its lone appearance in the Top 20 of a final wire-service poll. . . . Penn lost its first 14 meetings with Notre Dame until defeating the Irish, 71-60. Notre Dame,

which finished 13-11, dealt St. Louis (23-4) a shocking 77-70 defeat. The Irish raced to a 46-20 lead at intermission. . . . Northwestern's Ray Ragelis became the last Big Ten individual scoring champ to average fewer than 20 points per

1950-51 FINAL NATIONAL POLLS

AP	UPI	SCHOOL (RECORD)	HEAD COACH
1	1	Kentucky (32-2)	Adolph Rupp
2	2	Oklahoma A&M (29-6)	Hank Iba
3	5	Columbia (23-1)	Lou Rossini*
4	3	Kansas State (25-4)	Jack Gardner
5	4	Illinois (22-5)	Harry Combes
6	6	Bradley (32-6)	Forddy Anderson
7	8	Indiana (19-3)	Branch McCracken
8	7	N.C. State (30-7)	Everett Case
9	9	St. John's (26-5)	Frank McGuire
10	11	St. Louis (22-8)	Eddie Hickey
11	10	Brigham Young (28-9)	Stan Watts
12	12	Arizona (24-6)	Fred Enke
13	18	Dayton (27-5)	Tom Blackburn
14	-	Toledo (23-8)	Jerry Bush
15	13	Washington (24-6)	Tippy Dye
16	-	Murray State (21-6)	Harlan Hodges
17	17	Cincinnati (18-4)	John Wiethe
18	-	Siena (19-8)	Dan Cunha
19	-	Southern Cal (21-6)	Forrest Twogood
20	14	Villanova (25-7)	Al Severance
-	14	Beloit, Wis. (18-5)	Dolph Stanley
-	16	UCLA (19-10)	John Wooden
-	18	St. Bonaventure (19-6)	Ed Melvin
-	18	Seton Hall (24-7)	Honey Russell
-	18	Texas A&M (17-12)	John Floyd

*Rossini handled coaching duties at Columbia because of Gordon Ridings' illness.

1950-51 NCAA CHAMPION: KENTUCKY

SEASON STATISTICS OF KENTUCKY REGULARS

PLAYER	POS.	CL.	G.	FG%	FT%	PPG	RPG
Bill Spivey	C	Jr.	33	.399	.621	19.2	17.2
Shelby Linville	F	Jr.	34	.389	.757	10.4	9.1
Bobby Watson	G	Jr.	34	.328	.750	10.4	2.5
Frank Ramsey	G	So.	34	.327	.610	10.1	12.8
Cliff Hagan	F-C	So.	20	.367	.738	9.2	8.5
Walt Hirsch*	F	Sr.	30	.285	.706	9.1	8.0
Skip Whitaker	G	Jr.	31	.342	.600	5.2	2.0
Lou Tsioropoulos	F-C	So.	27	.311	.533	3.4	4.8
Dwight Price	F	So.	20	.277	.444	1.7	2.2
C. M. Newton	G	Jr.	18	.229	.454	1.2	0.7
TEAM TOTALS			34	.342	.648	74.7	62.0

*Ineligible for NCAA Tournament as a fourth-year varsity player.

1951 CHAMPIONSHIP GAME

MINNEAPOLIS, MN

KENTUCKY (68)	FG-A	FT-A	REB.	PF	PTS.
Whitaker	4-5	1-1	2	2	9
Linville	2-7	4-8	8	5	8
Spivey	9-29	4-6	21	2	22
Ramsey	4-10	1-3	4	5	9
Watson	3-8	2-4	3	3	8
Hagan	5-6	0-2	4	5	10
Tsioropoulos	1-4	0-0	3	1	2
Newton	0-0	0-0	0	0	0
TOTALS	28-69	12-24	45	23	68

FG%: .406. FT%: .500.

KANSAS STATE (58)	FG-A	FT-A	REB.	PF	PTS.
Head	3-11	2-2	3	2	8
Stone	3-8	6-8	6	2	12
Hitch	6-15	1-1	9	3	13
Barrett	2-12	0-2	3	1	4
Iverson	3-12	1-2	0	3	7
Rousey	2-10	0-0	2	3	4
Gibson	0-2	1-1	1	5	1
Upson	0-1	0-0	2	1	0
Knostman	1-4	1-2	3	1	3
Peck	2-3	0-1	0	0	4
Schuyler	1-2	0-1	1	2	2
TOTALS	23-80	12-20	30	23	58

FG%: .288. FT%: .600.
Halftime: Kansas State 29-27.

MOST OUTSTANDING PLAYER
None selected.

game (19.8). . . . Bradley won 32 games for the second straight season.

Texas finished in a tie for first place in the SWC despite compiling its first overall losing record (13-14) in 21 years. One of the two teams to tie Texas was Texas A&M, which posted its only winning mark (17-12) in a 20-year span from 1938-39 through 1957-58. . . . Arizona established an NCAA record for highest rebound margin in a single game by grabbing 84 more rebounds (102-18) than Northern Arizona. The Wildcats, coached by Fred Enke, captured their sixth consecutive Border Conference championship.

New Washington coach Tippy Dye became the first coach to guide two different schools to a Top 20 appearance in a final wire-service poll in back-to-back seasons. Washington, the PCC champion, sustained six setbacks by an average of only 4.5 points. The previous year, Dye directed Ohio State to a 22-4 record and Big Ten title.

So many players fouled out of a game against Tennessee Tech that Morehead State had only three men on the court in the final minutes. Morehead coach Ellis Johnson chose to play the remaining few minutes after referees let him participate only after he had conceded the contest. "What bothered me most," said Johnson after his club lost 90-88, "was that my players wouldn't pass the ball to me."

1951 NCAA Tournament

Summary: The scandal surrounding college basketball had not yet focused intensely on Kentucky when the Wildcats captured their third NCAA title in four years. Kansas State led at halftime (29-27) in the championship game, but guard Ernie Barrett, the Wildcats' leading scorer, was hampered by a sore shoulder and finished with just four points on two of 12 field-goal shooting. Kentucky had edged Illinois, 76-74, in the East Regional final behind center Bill Spivey's tourney-high 28 points. The Wildcats were the only NCAA champion to have six players finish the season with scoring averages higher than nine points per game until UCLA duplicated the feat in 1995.

Outcome for Defending Champion: City College of New York posted a 12-7 record before its last two games (against Manhattan and NYU) were canceled after a fix scandal broke. One of the games CCNY agreed to shave points in was at Madison Square Garden, where the school bowed to visiting Missouri, 54-37.

Star Gazing: Columbia, undefeated entering the tourney (21-0), blew a seven-point, halftime lead and lost in the first round of East Regional against eventual national third-place finisher Illinois (79-71). The Lions' John Azary was outscored by the Illini's Don Sunderlage (25-13) in a battle of All-American candidates. Sunderlage finished the season with 471 points, breaking the Illinois single-season record by 138 points.

Biggest Upset: Oklahoma A&M, entering the tourney with a No. 2 national ranking, fell behind 37-14 at intermission when it was eliminated by Kansas State, 68-44.

Numbers Game: Four teammates outrebounded Kentucky center Bill Spivey in the Wildcats' 79-68 opening-game victory over Louisville before he averaged 16 rebounds per game in their last three tourney contests. . . . Arizona made its only NCAA Tournament appearance until 1976 and San Jose State participated for the only time until 1980.

Putting Things in Perspective: North Carolina State, returning the nucleus of a national third-place team, had a 29-4 record after winning the Southern Conference Tournament. But without three standouts (Sam Ranzino, Paul Horvath and Vic Bubas) ineligible for the NCAA playoffs because they were in their fourth year of varsity competition, N.C. State was eliminated in the second round by Illinois (84-70).

Scoring Leader: Don Sunderlage, Illinois (83 points, 20.75 ppg).

Highest Scoring Average: Bill Kukoy, North Carolina State (69 points, 23 ppg).

Rebounding Leader: Bill Spivey, Kentucky (65 rebounds, 16.3 rpg).

1951 CHAMPIONSHIP BRACKET

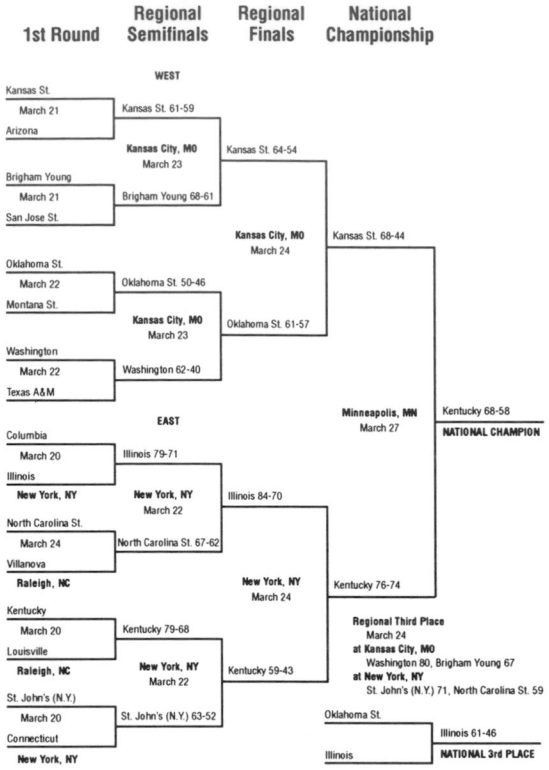

1st Round	Regional Semifinals	Regional Finals	National Championship

WEST

Kansas St.
March 21
Arizona
— Kansas St. 61-59

Kansas City, MO
March 23
— Kansas St. 64-54

Brigham Young
March 21
San Jose St.
— Brigham Young 68-61

Kansas City, MO
March 24
— Kansas St. 68-44

Oklahoma St.
March 22
Montana St.
— Oklahoma St. 50-46

Kansas City, MO
March 23
— Oklahoma St. 61-57

Washington
March 22
Texas A&M
— Washington 62-40

Minneapolis, MN
March 27
— Kentucky 68-58
NATIONAL CHAMPION

EAST

Columbia
March 20
Illinois
— Illinois 79-71

New York, NY
March 22
— Illinois 84-70

North Carolina St.
March 24
Villanova
Raleigh, NC
— North Carolina St. 67-62

New York, NY
March 24
— Kentucky 76-74

Kentucky
March 20
Louisville
Raleigh, NC
— Kentucky 79-68

New York, NY
March 22
— Kentucky 59-43

St. John's (N.Y.)
March 20
Connecticut
New York, NY
— St. John's (N.Y.) 63-52

Regional Third Place
March 24
at Kansas City, MO
Washington 80, Brigham Young 67
at New York, NY
St. John's (N.Y.) 71, North Carolina St. 59

Oklahoma St.
— Illinois 61-46
Illinois
NATIONAL 3rd PLACE

1951-52

AT A GLANCE

NCAA Champion: Kansas (26-2; coached by Phog Allen; won Big Seven title by one game with an 11-1 record).

NIT Champion: La Salle (25-7; coached by Ken Loeffler).

New Rule: Games are played in four 10-minute quarters. Previously, games were played in two 20-minute halves.

NCAA Consensus First-Team All-Americans: Chuck Darling, C, Sr., Iowa; Rod Fletcher, G, Sr., Illinois; Dick Groat, G, Sr., Duke; Cliff Hagan, F, Jr., Kentucky; Clyde Lovellette, C, Sr., Kansas.

Freshmen, thrust to the varsity level because of a manpower shortage stemming from the Korean War, made an impact long before the first half of the 1970s when they permanently gained eligibility. Freshman center Tom Gola led NIT champion La Salle in scoring (17.2 ppg) and rebounding (16.5 rpg). Another standout freshman was Wichita forward Cleo Littleton, who was named to the first five on the All-Missouri Valley Conference team with an 18.5-point scoring average.

Littleton matriculated to Wichita from a local high school when the university hired his prep coach (Ralph Miller). Here is an alphabetical list of other freshmen of influenced during the season:

- Center Jesse Arnelle (Penn State's leading scorer and rebounder).
- Center Art Bunte (Colorado's second-leading scorer and rebounder).
- Guard Ed Fleming (Niagara's second-leading scorer).
- Center Dick Hemric (Wake Forest's leading scorer and rebounder).
- Forward-center John Horan (Averaged 10.1 points and 7.1 rebounds per game for a @main body: Dayton team that participated in both the NCAA Tournament and NIT).
- Guard Al Lifson (North Carolina's leading scorer).
- Center Bob McKeen (California's leading rebounder and second-leading scorer).
- Guard Chuck Mencel (Minnesota's second-leading scorer).
- Forward Dick Ricketts (Duquesne's second-leading scorer).
- Center Don Schlundt (Indiana's leading scorer and rebounder).
- Forward Ken Sears (Starter for Santa Clara's Final Four team).

Kansas' Clyde Lovellette became the only Big Eight Conference player ever to lead the nation in scoring (28.4 ppg). Defending scoring champion Bill Mlkvy of Temple plummeted to 42nd (17.4 ppg) by incurring the largest decrease in scoring average (11.8) from one season to the next for any underclassman who ever led the nation in scoring.

Duke's Dick Groat, who later become an All-Star shortstop in the majors, was national runner-up in scoring and assists. He is the only individual to win an MVP award in major league baseball (1960 with the Pittsburgh Pirates) after becoming an NCAA consensus first-team basketball All-America. Duke teammate Bernie Janicki set a school single-game record by grabbing 31 rebounds against North Carolina.

Seattle's 5-8 Johnny O'Brien became the first college player to score 1,000 or more points in a season when he amassed 1,051 points in 37 games for a 28.4 average. He had 43 points in a shocking 84-81 victory over the Harlem Globe-trotters in a special game played to raise money for the U.S. Olympic Games Fund. The mighty Globetrotters, in an era before they went exclusively to entertainment, usually opened a big lead before going into their crowd-pleasing antics. However, they were without ball-handling wizard Marques Haynes against Seattle because he had to appear at his draft board. O'Brien scored most of his points against Globetrotters great Goose Tatum.

Army sophomore Bill Hannon became the shortest player (6-3) ever to lead the nation in rebounding. He averaged 20.9 rebounds per game. . . . Colgate's Al Antinelli fouled out of 15 of 22 games. . . . Dale Hall was in his only season as coach of New Hampshire when the school compiled its only winning record (11-9) in a 26-season span from 1941-42 through 1968-69 (cancelled 1943-44 and 1944-45 campaigns because of World War II).

Field-goal accuracy was only 33.7 percent per game despite an all-time high 140.64 field-goal attempts per outing for both teams.

LSU's Bob Pettit recorded the biggest one-game scoring output of the season with 50 points against Georgia. . . . Kentucky's Cliff Hagan established SEC Tournament records for most points in a single game (42 against Tennessee) and

1951-52 FINAL NATIONAL POLLS

AP	UPI	SCHOOL (RECORD)	HEAD COACH
1	1	Kentucky (29-3)	Adolph Rupp
2	2	Illinois (22-4)	Harry Combes
3	6	Kansas State (19-5)	Jack Gardner
4	4	Duquesne (23-4)	Dudey Moore
5	7	St. Louis (23-8)	Eddie Hickey
6	5	Washington (25-6)	Tippy Dye
7	8	Iowa (19-3)	Bucky O'Connor
8	3	Kansas (28-3)	Phog Allen
9	14	West Virginia (23-4)	Red Brown
10	9	St. John's (25-6)	Frank McGuire
11	18	Dayton (28-5)	Tom Blackburn
12	–	Duke (24-6)	Harold Bradley
13	15	Holy Cross (24-4)	Buster Sheary
14	12	Seton Hall (25-3)	Honey Russell
15	11	St. Bonaventure (21-6)	Ed Melvin
16	10	Wyoming (28-7)	Everett Shelton
17	19	Louisville (20-6)	Peck Hickman
18	–	Seattle (29-8)	Al Brightman
19	20	UCLA (19-12)	John Wooden
20	–	SW Texas State (30-1)	Milton Jowers
–	13	Texas Christian (24-4)	Buster Brannon
–	16	Western Kentucky (26-5)	Ed Diddle
–	17	La Salle (25-7)	Ken Loeffler
–	20	Indiana (16-6)	Branch McCracken

in an entire tourney (110 in four games). . . . Tennessee's Herb Neff set a SEC single-game standard with a school-record 36 rebounds against Georgia Tech. . . . West Virginia's Mack Isner (31 vs. Virginia Tech) and Iowa's Charles Darling (30 vs. Wisconsin) established school single-game rebounding records.

North Carolina lost its last five games to finish with a 12-15 record for the second consecutive season. The Tar Heels then lured coach Frank McGuire away from St. John's after he had guided the Redmen to an average of 25 victories the past three years. . . . Arkansas' streak of non-losing seasons ended at 28 when the Razorbacks dropped five of six SWC games down the stretch to finish with a 10-14 record. . . . Tulsa lost 21 consecutive games to Oklahoma A&M until defeating the Aggies, 39-33. . . . Dayton (28-5/coached by Tom Blackburn) and Texas Christian (24-4/Buster Brannon) had their winningest seasons in school history.

Illinois became the only school to lead the Big Ten in scoring five consecutive seasons in league competition. The Illini achieved the feat in Harry Combes' first five years as coach. . . . Arizona's 81-game homecourt winning streak, which started in 1945, was snapped by Kansas State, 76-57. . . . Arizona's 17-game winning streak in its series with archrival Arizona State also came to an end. . . . Idaho State (coached by Steve Belko) won its eighth consecutive Rocky Mountain Conference crown and North Carolina State (Everett Case) captured its sixth consecutive Southern Conference Tournament championship. . . . N.C. State's bid to win its sixth consecutive regular-season Southern Conference crown suffered a devastating blow when the Wolfpack lost at William & Mary, 70-61. N.C. State had whipped William & Mary by 36 points earlier in the year. . . . Clemson improved its Southern Conference record for the fifth consecutive season under coach Banks McFadden, but the Tigers still finished in fourth place.

1952 NCAA Tournament

Summary: Legendary coach Phog Allen, running out of time in his quest to capture an elusive national championship, achieved his goal on the broad shoulders of Clyde Lovellette although his star player got lost in the fog. The night before the semifinals, one of Lovellette's Sigma Chi fraternity brothers, who was in the Coast Guard and stationed on a cutter anchored in Puget Sound, invited Lovellette to dinner on the ship. By the time they were finished, a dense fog moved in and they were unable to make it back to shore. Lovellette spent the night on the ship and didn't get back to his team's hotel until after dawn. Unfazed, he became

1951–52 INDIVIDUAL LEADERS

SCORING

PLAYER	PTS.	AVG.
Lovellette, Kansas	795	28.4
Groat, Duke	780	26.0
Pettit, Louisiana St.	612	25.5
Darling, Iowa	561	25.5
Selvy, Furman	591	24.6
Workman, West Virginia	577	23.1
Retherford, Baldwin-Wallace	457	21.8
Hemric, Wake Forest	629	21.7
Hagan, Kentucky	692	21.6
Clune, Navy	487	21.2

REBOUNDING

PLAYER	REB.	AVG.
Hannon, Army	355	20.9
Dukes, Seton Hall	513	19.7
Beck, Pennsylvania	551	19.0
Tuttle, Creighton	396	18.9
Chambers, William & Mary	509	18.2
Molinas, Columbia	234	18.0
Hemric, Wake Forest	510	17.5
Workman, West Virginia	437	17.5
Gola, La Salle	497	17.1
Peterson, Oregon	465	16.6

ASSISTS

PLAYER	AST.	AVG.
O'Toole, Boston College	213	7.9
Groat, Duke	229	7.6
McLean, Davidson	187	7.5
Friedman, Muhlenberg	168	7.3
Chadwick, Cornell	171	6.9
Simms, Xavier	150	6.3
Holmes, West Virginia	160	6.2
Heim, Xavier	145	6.0
Burch, Pittsburgh	131	6.0
Rhodes, Western Kentucky	182	5.9

FIELD GOAL PERCENTAGE

PLAYER	FGM	FGA	PCT.
Spoelstra, Western Kentucky	178	345	.516
Rogers, Texas Western	136	270	.504
Swanson, Detroit	172	342	.503
Klinar, Virginia Military	98	199	.492
Marshall, Western Kentucky	189	385	.491
Workman, West Virginia	207	430	.481
Lovellette, Kansas	315	660	.477
Patton, Denver	93	198	.470
Daukas, Boston College	136	290	.469
Preston, Hardin-Simmons	117	250	.468

FREE THROW PERCENTAGE

PLAYER	FTM	FTA	PCT.
Chadroff, Miami (Fla.)	99	123	.805
Kenney, Kansas	110	137	.803
Turner, St. Mary's	81	101	.802
Bartlett, Tennessee	93	116	.802
Rerucha, Colorado A&M	76	95	.800
Moore, West Virginia	68	85	.800
Tuttle, New Mexico	87	110	.791
Meineke, Dayton	194	246	.789
Bunt, New York Univ.	85	108	.787
Feiereisel, DePaul	113	144	.785

1951–52 TEAM LEADERS

SCORING OFFENSE

SCHOOL	PTS.	AVG.
Kentucky	2635	82.3
West Virginia	2172	80.4
Louisville	2080	80.0
Duke	2320	77.3
Western Kentucky	2388	77.0

SCORING DEFENSE

SCHOOL	PTS.	AVG.
Oklahoma A&M	1228	45.5
Oklahoma City	1287	47.7
Texas A&M	1159	48.3
New Mexico A&M	1514	48.8
Texas Christian	1395	49.8

FIELD GOAL PERCENTAGE

SCHOOL	FGM	FGA	PCT.
Boston College	787	1893	.416
Western Kentucky	959	2339	.410
Seton Hall	783	1941	.403
Stanford	743	1889	.393
Kansas	748	1906	.392
Furman	691	1761	.392

FREE THROW PERCENTAGE

SCHOOL	FTM	FTA	PCT.
Kansas	491	707	.6944
Pennsylvania	454	654	.6941
Kansas St.	473	684	.692
South Carolina	400	582	.687
Syracuse	430	626	.687

1951–52 NCAA CHAMPION: KANSAS

SEASON STATISTICS OF KANSAS REGULARS

PLAYER	POS.	CL.	G.	FG%	FT%	PPG	RPG
Clyde Lovellette	C	Sr.	31	.474	.728	28.6	13.2
Bob Kenney	F	Sr.	30	.360	.789	13.1	3.8
Bill Hougland	G	Sr.	30	.391	.742	6.8	5.6
Dean Kelley	G	Jr.	31	.397	.605	6.5	3.3
Bill Lienhard	F	Sr.	29	.303	.700	5.8	3.3
Charlie Hoag	F-G	Jr.	21	.303	.564	5.2	3.0
John Keller	F-G	Sr.	27	.388	.767	2.3	2.7
B. H. Born	C	So.	27	.304	.613	1.7	1.2
Bill Heitholt	G-F	Fr.	28	.237	.454	1.5	1.9
Dean Smith	G	Jr.	19	.455	.500	1.5	0.6
Larry Davenport	F	Fr.	22	.324	.700	1.4	1.0
TEAM TOTALS			31	.390	.692	71.3	37.8

Note: Statistics include three games in Olympic Trials after NCAA Tournament.

1952 CHAMPIONSHIP GAME

SEATTLE, WA

Kansas (80)	FG-A	FT-A	REB.	PF	PTS.
Kenney	4-11	4-6	4	2	12
Keller	1-1	0-0	4	2	2
Lovellette	12-25	9-11	17	4	33
Lienhard	5-8	2-2	4	4	12
Kelley	2-5	3-6	3	5	7
Hoag	2-6	5-7	4	5	9
Houghland	2-5	1-3	6	2	5
Davenport	0-0	0-0	0	1	0
Heitholt	0-0	0-0	0	0	0
Born	0-0	0-0	0	0	0
Kelley	0-2	0-0	1	0	0
TOTALS	**28-63**	**24-35**	**43**	**25**	**80**

FG%: .444. **FT%:** .686.

St. John's (63)	FG-A	FT-A	REB.	PF	PTS.
McMahon	6-12	1-4	2	4	13
Davis	1-4	2-3	2	4	4
Zawoluk	7-12	6-11	9	5	20
Duckett	2-5	2-2	2	4	6
MacGilvray	3-8	2-5	10	3	8
Walsh	3-6	0-0	4	3	6
Walker	0-2	0-0	2	4	0
McMorrow	1-3	0-0	0	3	2
Sagona	2-2	0-0	0	5	4
Giancontieri	0-0	0-2	1	0	0
Peterson	0-1	0-0	0	0	0
TOTALS	**25-55**	**13-27**	**32**	**35**	**63**

FG%: .455. **FT%:** .481.
Halftime: Kansas State 41-27.

ALL-TOURNAMENT TEAM

Dean Kelley, G, Jr., Kansas (17 points in final two games)
John Kerr, C, Soph., Illinois (34 points)
*Clyde Lovellette, C, Sr., Kansas (66 points)
Ron MacGilvray, G, Sr., St. John's (14 points)
Bob Zawoluk, C, Sr., St. John's (44 points)

*Named Most Outstanding Player.

the only player to crack the 30-point plateau in the national semifinals and final in the same season (33 points against both Santa Clara in the semifinals and St. John's in the final). In a West Regional final, Lovellette poured in a tourney-high 44 points in a 74-55 triumph over St. Louis.

Outcome for Defending Champion: Kentucky (29-3), the first school to lead the nation in scoring with an average of more than 80 points per game (82.3), claimed its ninth consecutive SEC regular-season title. The Wildcats' two regular-season defeats were in non-league play (61-57 at Minnesota and 61-60 vs. St. Louis in the Sugar Bowl final in New Orleans). It was the third time in four years for SLU to defeat a top-ranked Kentucky club. No other school beat the Wildcats more than twice in an eight-season stretch from 1946-47 through 1954-55.

Biggest Upset: St. John's gained sweet revenge against the nation's No. 1 team. Kentucky humiliated the Redmen by 41 points (81-40) early in the season when the Catholic institution became the first to have a black player on the floor at Lexington, Ky., despite Kentucky coach Adolph Rupp's protests. The African American in question, Solly Walker, played only a few minutes before he took a hit sidelining him for three weeks. But St. John's, sparked by center Bob Zawoluk's 32 points, avenged the rout by eliminating the Wildcats (64-57) in the East Regional, ending their 23-game winning streak.

One and Only: Lovellette is the only player to lead the nation in scoring average (28.4 ppg) while playing for a team reaching the NCAA Tournament championship game. . . . St. John's is the only school to reach the Final Four after losing a regular-season game by more than 40 points. . . . Princeton forward Dave Sisler is the only son of a member of one of the early classes of baseball Hall of Fame selections (first baseman George Sisler) to start for a school in its first NCAA Tournament appearance. . . . New Mexico A&M (now New Mexico State) became the only current Division I school to participate in the same season in the NAIA Tournament at Kansas City (eliminated by Southwest Texas State) and the NCAA Tournament (also in Kansas City; eliminated by St. Louis).

Numbers Game: St. Louis' Eddie Hickey became the first coach to direct two different schools to NCAA playoff victories in their initial tourney appearances. He guided Creighton to the

1952 CHAMPIONSHIP BRACKET

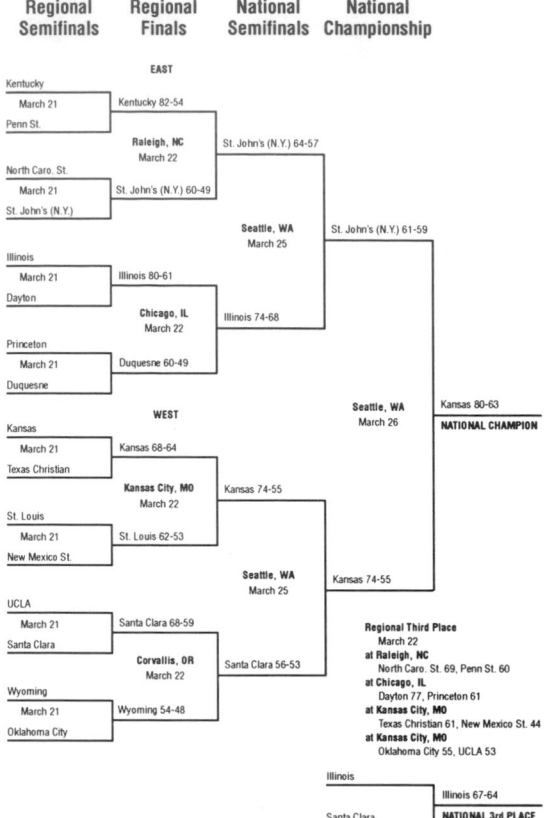

Regional Semifinals	Regional Finals	National Semifinals	National Championship

EAST

Kentucky / March 21 / Penn St. → Kentucky 82-54

Raleigh, NC — March 22 → St. John's (N.Y.) 64-57

North Caro. St. / March 21 / St. John's (N.Y.) → St. John's (N.Y.) 60-49

Seattle, WA — March 25 → St. John's (N.Y.) 61-59

Illinois / March 21 / Dayton → Illinois 80-61

Chicago, IL — March 22 → Illinois 74-68

Princeton / March 21 / Duquesne → Duquesne 60-49

Seattle, WA — March 26 → Kansas 80-63 — **NATIONAL CHAMPION**

WEST

Kansas / March 21 / Texas Christian → Kansas 68-64

Kansas City, MO — March 22 → Kansas 74-55

St. Louis / March 21 / New Mexico St. → St. Louis 62-53

Seattle, WA — March 25 → Kansas 74-55

UCLA / March 21 / Santa Clara → Santa Clara 68-59

Corvallis, OR — March 22 → Santa Clara 56-53

Wyoming / March 21 / Oklahoma City → Wyoming 54-48

Regional Third Place
March 22
at Raleigh, NC
North Caro. St. 69, Penn St. 60
at Chicago, IL
Dayton 77, Princeton 61
at Kansas City, MO
Texas Christian 61, New Mexico St. 44
at Kansas City, MO
Oklahoma City 55, UCLA 53

Illinois → Illinois 67-64
Santa Clara → **NATIONAL 3rd PLACE**

1941 NCAA Tournament. . . . Elmer Gross became the first individual to coach his alma mater in the NCAA playoffs after playing in the tourney (Penn State '42). . . . All five Dayton starters fouled out when the Flyers committed an NCAA playoff-record 41 fouls in an 80-61 loss to Illinois in the East Regional semifinals.

What Might Have Been: Kansas State finished runner-up in the Big Seven Conference to NCAA champion-to-be Kansas, a team the Wildcats defeated at home in Manhattan by 17 points. K-State, ranked 3rd by AP and 6th by UPI after finishing as national runner-up to Kentucky the previous year, lost another matchup against the Jayhawks on a neutral court in overtime.

Scoring Leader: Clyde Lovellette, Kansas (141 points, 35.25 ppg).

1952-53

AT A GLANCE

NCAA Champion: Indiana (23-3; coached by Branch McCracken; won Big Ten title by three games with a 17-1 record).

NIT Champion: Seton Hall (31-2; coached by Honey Russell).

New Conference: California Basketball Association (forerunner of West Coast).

New Rules: Teams no longer waive free throws in favor of taking the ball out of bounds. . . . The one-and-one free-throw rule is introduced although the bonus is used only if the first shot misfires. The rule will be in effect the entire game except the last three minutes, when every foul is two shots. . . . The NCAA Tournament bracket expanded from 16 teams to 22 and fluctuated between 22 and 25 until 1974.

NCAA Probation: Bradley, Kentucky

NCAA Consensus First-Team All-Americans: Ernie Beck, F, Sr., Penn; Walter Dukes, C, Jr., Seton Hall; Tom Gola, C-F, Soph., La Salle; Bob Houbregs, C, Sr., Washington; Johnny O'Brien, G, Sr., Seattle.

The season marked the greatest increase in points per game from one year to the next (126.6 to 138.1). College basketball's record book was overhauled when intercollegiate competition was interpreted as being between varsity teams of four-year, degree-granting universities. In effect, the ruling negated games against AAU, service, junior college, alumni and freshman teams. The decision stemmed from 100-point plus outings by Rio Grande's Clarence "Bevo" Francis and Los Angeles State's John Barber. In response to Francis' 113-point performance, Los Angeles State coach Sax Elliott scheduled a game for his team with the Chapman junior varsity and had his players concentrate on scoring and feeding Barber, a 6-6 center. Los Angeles State won, 206-82, as Barber scored 188 points.

Furman (21-6 record/coached by Lyles Alley) became the first school to average more than 90 points per game (90.2). Furman's Frank Selvy supplied the season's top scoring effort with 63 points against Mercer.

A couple of major rebounding records were established. Seton Hall's Walter Dukes set an NCAA single-season record by retrieving a total of 734 missed shots. William & Mary's Bill Chambers grabbed an NCAA-record 51 rebounds in a 105-84 victory against Virginia on Valentine's Day. Chambers later became his alma mater's all-time winningest coach in a nine-year coaching career with the Tribe from 1957-58 through 1965-66.

Niagara outlasted Siena, 88-81, in a six-over-time game. Niagara's Ed Fleming played all 70 minutes and teammate Larry Costello played all but 20 seconds before fouling out. As a result,

Fleming had his uniform number changed to 70 and Costello's was changed to 69. Oddly, one of the referees in the game was Max Tabbachi, who had officiated a five-overtime NBA game between Rochester and Indianapolis two seasons ago.

The University of Chicago, a former power-house, ended a 45-game losing streak with a 65-52 victory over Illinois-Navy Pier. . . . Cincinnati compiled an 11-13 overall record but finished in a tie for second place in the Mid-American Conference (9-3) in its final year as a member of the league. . . . Seattle's Johnny O'Brien finished among the top six in both field-goal shooting (53.3 percent) and free-throw accuracy (80.8). . . . Western Kentucky's Art Spoelstra, who led the nation in field-goal marksmanship (51.6 percent) the previous season, improved to 52.8 percent yet finished sixth. Three severe heart attacks sidelined Western Kentucky coach Ed Diddle for a time.

1952-53 INDIVIDUAL LEADERS

SCORING

PLAYER	PTS.	AVG.
Selvy, Furman	738	29.5
Hennessey, Villanova	438	29.2
J. O'Brien, Seattle	884	28.5
Dukes, Seton Hall	861	26.1
Beck, Pennsylvania	673	25.9
Houbregs, Washington	800	25.8
Schlundt, Indiana	661	25.4
Hemric, Wake Forest	623	24.9
Dalton, John Carroll	669	24.8
Pettit, Louisiana St.	519	24.7

REBOUNDING

PLAYER	REB.	AVG.
Conlin, Fordham	612	23.5
Dukes, Seton Hall	734	22.2

Chambers, William & Mary	480	21.8
Quimby, Connecticut	430	20.5
Virostek, Pittsburgh	424	20.2
Estergard, Bradley	540	20.0
Hannon, Army	365	19.2
Holup, George Washington	396	18.0
Lange, Navy	374	17.8
Tuttle, Creighton	438	17.5

FIELD GOAL PERCENTAGE

PLAYER	FGM	FGA	PCT.
Stokes, St. Francis (NY)	147	247	.595
Houbregs, Washington	306	564	.543
E. O'Brien, Seattle	176	325	.542
J. O'Brien, Seattle	276	518	.533
Hoxie, Niagara	125	235	.532
Spoelstra, W. Kentucky	188	356	.528
Gordon, Furman	249	483	.516

Holup, G. Washington	154	301	.512
Nathanic, Seton Hall	111	222	.500
Glowaski, Seattle	199	405	.491

FREE THROW PERCENTAGE

PLAYER	FTM	FTA	PCT.
Weber, Yale	117	141	.830
Dohner, Virginia	96	117	.821
Sharp, Wyoming	163	200	.815
Sheets, Oklahoma A&M	87	107	.813
Matheny, California	101	125	.808
J. O'Brien, Seattle	332	411	.808
Schlundt, Indiana	249	310	.803
Perry, Holy Cross	101	126	.802
Ollrich, Drake	137	171	.801
Beck, Pennsylvania	183	229	.799

1952-53 TEAM LEADERS

SCORING OFFENSE

SCHOOL	PTS.	AVG.
Furman	2435	90.2
Seattle	2818	88.1
George Washington	1890	85.9
Duke	2093	83.7
Miami (Ohio)	1916	83.3

SCORING DEFENSE

SCHOOL	PTS.	AVG.
Oklahoma A&M	1614	53.8
Maryland	1256	54.6

Oklahoma City	1338	55.8
Wyoming	1676	55.9
San Jose St.	1293	56.2

FIELD GOAL PERCENTAGE

SCHOOL	FGM	FGA	PCT.
Furman	936	2106	.444
Niagara	718	1640	.438
Seattle	1019	2350	.434
Seton Hall	914	2129	.429
William & Mary	603	1410	.428

FREE THROW PERCENTAGE

SCHOOL	FTM	FTA	PCT.
George Washington	502	696	.721
Pennsylvania	502	702	.715
Oklahoma City	548	771	.711
Loyola (Ill.)	525	743	.707
Fordham	493	699	.705

The Citadel's Jerry Varn (51 points vs. Piedmont), Washington's Bob Houbregs (49 vs. Idaho) and Penn's Ernie Beck (47 vs. Duke in Dixie Classic at Raleigh, N.C.) set school single-game scoring records. Villanova's Larry Hennessy (29.2 ppg), Beck (25.9) and Houbregs (25.6) set school records for highest scoring average in a single season. Houbregs' outbursts helped Washington finish with a 30-3 mark for its winningest season in history (coached by Tippy Dye).

Northern Arizona set an NCAA record by attempting 79 free throws (46 made) in a game against Arizona. A new free-throw rule increased attempts from the charity stripe to a staggering 65.8 per game for both teams. . . . LSU established a SEC standard for most lopsided victory by smothering Southwestern (Tenn.), 124-33. . . . Arizona State, coached by Bill Kajikawa, overcame a 1-10 start to finish with its only winning record (13-12) in a 10-year span from 1948-49 through 1957-58. . . . Oklahoma A&M captured its 14th team defense title in 19 seasons although it was the first time a Hank Iba-coached squad allowed as many as 50 points per game (53.8). . . . Colorado's Burdette Haldorson collected 31 points and a school-record 31 rebounds against Oklahoma in the Big Eight Christmas Tournament at Kansas City.

Fordham's Ed Conlin (36 vs. Colgate), Richmond's Walt Lysaght (35 vs. North Carolina in double overtime), Seton Hall's Dukes (34 vs. King's, Pa.), St. Joseph's John Doogan (34 vs. West Chester State), Columbia's Jack Molinas (31 vs. Brown), Wisconsin's Paul Morrow (30 vs. Purdue), Rutgers' Swede Sundstrom (30 vs. Johns Hopkins), Georgia Tech's Eric Crake (27 vs. Georgia) and Pittsburgh's Don Virostek (26 vs. Westminster) also set school single-game rebounding records. It was one of five times in Conlin's career that he grabbed more than 30 rebounds. Sundstrom tied his record the next season against Army.

Coach Frank McGuire lost six of his first seven games against North Carolina State after leaving St. John's for North Carolina. But McGuire's first contest against the Wolfpack with Carolina was a 70-69 success at Raleigh, ending the Tar Heels' 15-game losing streak against their big rival. Later, Wake Forest ended N.C. State's streak of six consecutive Southern Conference

1952–53 NCAA CHAMPION: INDIANA

SEASON STATISTICS OF INDIANA REGULARS

PLAYER	POS.	CL.	G.	FG%	FT%	PPG	RPG
Don Schlundt	C	So.	26	.432	.803	25.4	8.5
Bob Leonard	G	Jr.	26	.326	.667	16.3	...
Dick Farley	F	Jr.	26	.443	.694	10.1	...
Burke Scott	G	So.	26	.369	.647	8.0	...
Charles Kraak	F	Jr.	26	.356	.588	7.2	...
Dick White	F	So.	22	.313	.741	5.6	...
Phil Byers	G	So.	23	.347	.542	2.7	...
James DeaKyne	G	Jr.	20	.230	.417	2.3	...
TEAM TOTALS			26	.365	.701	81.2	...

1953 CHAMPIONSHIP GAME

KANSAS CITY, MO

INDIANA (69)	FG-A	FT-A	PF	PTS.
Kraak	5-8	7-10	5	17
DeaKyne	0-0	0-0	1	0
Farley	1-8	0-0	5	2
Schlundt	11-26	8-11	3	30
White	1-5	0-0	2	2
Leonard	5-15	2-4	2	12
Poff	0-1	0-0	0	0

	FG-A	FT-A	PF	PTS.
Scott	2-4	2-3	3	6
Byers	0-2	0-0	1	0
TOTALS	**25-69**	**19-28**	**22**	**69**

FG%: .362. FT%: .679.

KANSAS (68)	FG-A	FT-A	PF	PTS.
Patterson	1-3	7-8	3	9
A. Kelley	7-20	6-8	3	20
Davenport	0-1	0-0	0	0
Born	8-27	10-12	5	26
Smith	0-0	1-1	1	1
Alberts	0-1	0-0	1	0
D. Kelley	3-4	2-4	2	8
Reich	2-9	0-0	2	4
TOTALS	**21-65**	**26-33**	**17**	**68**

FG%: .323. FT%: .788.
Halftime: Tied 41-41.

ALL-TOURNAMENT TEAM

*B.H. Born, C, Jr., Kansas (51 points in final two games)
Bob Houbregs, C, Sr., Washington (60 points)
Dean Kelley, G, Sr., Kansas (24 points)
Bob Leonard, G, Jr., Indiana (34 points)
Don Schlundt, C, Soph., Indiana (59 points)

*Named Most Outstanding Player.

Tournament championships with a 71-70 victory over the Wolfpack. It was the final Southern Conference tourney before seven of the league's members broke away to form the Atlantic Coast Conference.

Maryland lost to Penn for the 12th straight time in their series. . . . Tony Packer, the father of former Wake Forest star and current CBS analyst Billy Packer, posted his only winning record (12-8) in 16 years as coach at Lehigh. It was the Engineers' lone winning season in a 28-year span from 1939-40 through 1966-67.

Dayton, struggling to stay above .500 in its only campaign in an eight-year span through 1957-58 to fail to finish among the nation's Top 20 in a final wire-service poll, pulled off the biggest upset of the season when the Flyers toppled top-ranked Seton Hall, 71-65. The Pirates, who would go on to capture the NIT, entered the road game with a 27-0 record. Seton Hall also lost its next outing (73-67 at Louisville) en route to finishing with a 31-2 mark, a school record for most victories.

Pete Mullins, the sixth-place finisher in the 1948 Olympic decathlon while competing for Australia, finished his career as Washington

B.H. Born was named the Most Outstanding Player during the 1952-53 NCAA Tournament.

State's leading scorer with 13.3 points per game. He had been the Cougars' second-leading scorer as a sophomore and third-leading scorer as a junior. . . . Big Ten charter member Indiana captured its first undisputed conference championship. Hoosiers coach Branch McCracken had been denied a Big Ten title in his first 11 years at his alma mater despite winning more than 70 percent of his games. . . . Baldwin-Wallace (O.) and CCNY competed in their final season at the major-college level.

Utah's Vadal Peterson ended his 26-year coaching career with a 386-223 record. Pitt posted its first winning record (12-11) in eight seasons as Dr. H.C. Carlson ended his 31-year coaching career at the school with a 367-250 record.

Carlson's distaste for recruiting soured him on the game and he retired. One of his last recruit-

1952–53 FINAL NATIONAL POLLS

AP	UPI	SCHOOL	HEAD COACH
1	1	Indiana (23-3)	Branch McCracken
2	2	Seton Hall (31-2)	Honey Russell
3	5	Kansas (19-6)	Phog Allen
4	3	Washington (30-3)	Tippy Dye
5	6	Louisiana State (22-3)	Harry Rabenhorst
6	4	La Salle (25-3)	Ken Loeffler
7	–	St. John's (17-6)	Al DeStefano
8	7	Oklahoma A&M (23-7)	Hank Iba
9	20	Duquesne (21-8)	Dudey Moore
10	13	Notre Dame (19-5)	John Jordan
11	10	Illinois (18-4)	Harry Combes
12	9	Kansas State (17-4)	Jack Gardner
13	17	Holy Cross (20-6)	Buster Sheary
14	–	Seattle (29-4)	Al Brightman
15	–	Wake Forest (22-7)	Murray Greason
16	–	Santa Clara (20-7)	Bob Feerick
17	11	Western Kentucky (25-6)	Ed Diddle
18	8	N.C. State (26-6)	Everett Case
19	14	DePaul (19-9)	Ray Meyer
20	–	SW Missouri State (24-4)	Bob Vanatta
–	12	California (16-10)	Nibs Price
–	14	Wyoming (20-10)	Everett Shelton
–	16	St. Louis (16-11)	Eddie Hickey
–	18	Oklahoma City (18-6)	Doyle Parrack
–	19	Brigham Young (22-8)	Stan Watts

Stars of the 50's decade: Clyde Lovellette and Oscar Robertson.

ing acts would prove costly to Bob Timmons, his successor, for the next four years. Carlson, looking to break the color line at Pitt, couldn't make up his mind between Ernie Bryant and Maurice Stokes. Carlson chose Bryant, who quit after his freshman year and never played varsity ball. Stokes went on to put St. Francis (Pa.) on the basketball map and became an instant star in the NBA before a disabling disease ended his career.

1953 NCAA Tournament

Summary: Junior guard Bob Leonard supplied the decisive point by hitting one of two free throws with 27 seconds remaining to give Indiana a 69-68 victory over defending champion Kansas in the final. Don Schlundt, averaging 25.4 points per game for the Hoosiers as a sophomore center, is the only player to never appear in the NBA or ABA after averaging more than 20 for a team reaching the NCAA championship game. Schlundt, a 1955 draft choice of the Syracuse Nationals, became successful in the insurance business after rejecting their contract offer of $6,000.

Outcome for Defending Champion: Big Seven champion Kansas finished with a 19-6 record. The Jayhawks' two league losses were by 15 points at Oklahoma and 21 at Oklahoma State.

Star Gazing: Bertram "B.H." Born, the only Kansas starter taller than 6-1, scored more points in two Final Four games (51) for the national runner-up Jayhawks than he did the entire previous season when he averaged just 1.7 points per game as a sophomore backup to Clyde Lovellette, who was named Most Outstanding Player in powering KU to the 1952 title.

Biggest Upset: George "Rinso" Marquette, the first-year coach at Lebanon Valley (Pa.), guided the Flying Dutchmen to the NCAA Tournament when they received an invitation after La Salle and Seton Hall had chosen to go to the NIT. Lebanon Valley's "Seven Dwarfs"—no player was taller than 6-1—won the Middle Atlantic Conference and led the nation in field-goal shooting (47.2 percent). They flogged Fordham, 80-67, in the first round of the East Regional before bowing to Bob Pettit-led LSU, an eventual Final Four team. Lebanon Valley, with a current enrollment of 900 after having 425 students in 1953, remains

1953 CHAMPIONSHIP BRACKET

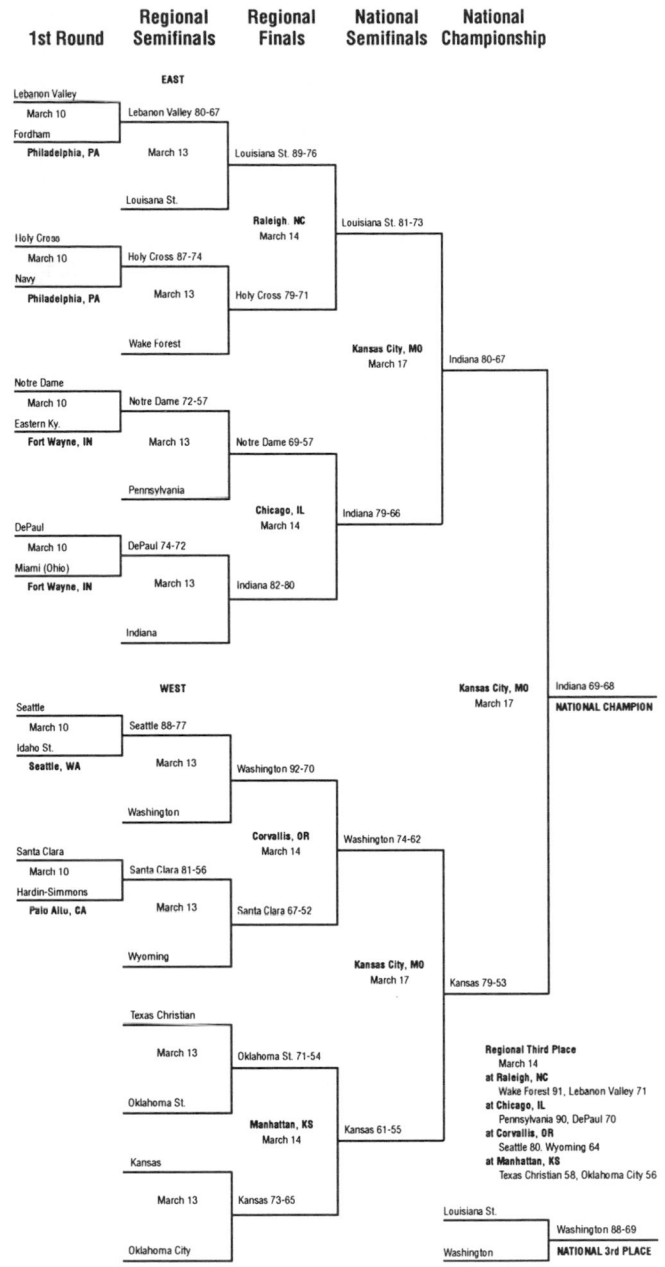

	Regional	Regional	National	National
1st Round	Semifinals	Finals	Semifinals	Championship

EAST

Lebanon Valley
March 10
Fordham
Philadelphia, PA

Lebanon Valley 80-67
March 13

Louisiana St.

Louisiana St. 89-76

Raleigh, NC
March 14

Louisiana St. 81-73

Holy Cross
March 10
Navy
Philadelphia, PA

Holy Cross 87-74
March 13

Wake Forest

Holy Cross 79-71

Kansas City, MO
March 17

Indiana 80-67

Notre Dame
March 10
Eastern Ky.
Fort Wayne, IN

Notre Dame 72-57
March 13

Pennsylvania

Notre Dame 69-57

Chicago, IL
March 14

Indiana 79-66

DePaul
March 10
Miami (Ohio)
Fort Wayne, IN

DePaul 74-72
March 13

Indiana

Indiana 82-80

Kansas City, MO
March 17

Indiana 69-68

NATIONAL CHAMPION

WEST

Seattle
March 10
Idaho St.
Seattle, WA

Seattle 88-77
March 13

Washington

Washington 92-70

Corvallis, OR
March 14

Washington 74-62

Santa Clara
March 10
Hardin-Simmons
Palo Alto, CA

Santa Clara 81-56
March 13

Wyoming

Santa Clara 67-52

Kansas City, MO
March 17

Kansas 79-53

Texas Christian
March 13
Oklahoma St.

Oklahoma St. 71-54

Manhattan, KS
March 14

Kansas 61-55

Kansas
March 13
Oklahoma City

Kansas 73-65

Regional Third Place
March 14
at Raleigh, NC
Wake Forest 91, Lebanon Valley 71
at Chicago, IL
Pennsylvania 90, DePaul 70
at Corvallis, OR
Seattle 80, Wyoming 64
at Manhattan, KS
Texas Christian 58, Oklahoma City 56

Louisiana St.

Washington

Washington 88-69

NATIONAL 3rd PLACE

the smallest school ever to play in the tournament. The leading scorer for Lebanon Valley was Howie Landa, who went on to coach nationally-ranked Mercer County (N.J.) Community College and then serve as an assistant to both the men's and women's teams at UNLV.

One and Only: Kansas' Dean Kelley became the only player to have season scoring averages of fewer than 10 points per game in back-to-back years in which he was named to the All-NCAA Tournament team. He and fellow guard Allen Kelley are the only set of brothers to play together in two NCAA playoff title games.

Numbers Game: Of the nearly 50 coaches reaching the national semifinals at least twice, Indiana's Branch McCracken is the only one to compile an undefeated Final Four record. He also won the championship in 1940. . . . Seattle's Johnny O'Brien, a 5-8 unanimous first-team All-America, became the only player to score more than 40 points in his first playoff game. He had 42 in an 88-77 victory over Idaho State. . . . Washington's Bob Houbregs had a tourney-high 45 points in a 92-70 scorching of Seattle in the West Regional semifinals. He poured in 42 in an 88-69 trouncing of LSU in the national third-place game.

What Might Have Been: Mighty Kentucky was barred from playing a competitive schedule.

Putting Things in Perspective: Indiana almost finished undefeated, losing three games during the regular season by a total of five points on field goals scored with fewer than five seconds remaining.

Scoring Leader: Bob Houbregs, Washington (139 points, 34.75 ppg).

1953-54

AT A GLANCE

NCAA Champion: La Salle (26-4; coached by Ken Loeffler).

NIT Champion: Holy Cross (26-2; coached by Buster Sheary).

New Conference: ACC.

New Rule: The Tuesday-Wednesday format for the NCAA Tournament semifinals and final changes to Friday-Saturday.

NCAA Probation: Arizona State.

NCAA Consensus First-Team All-Americans: Tom Gola, C-F, Jr., La Salle; Cliff Hagan, F, Sr., Kentucky; Bob Pettit, C, Sr., Louisiana State; Don Schlundt, C, Jr., Indiana; Frank Selvy, F, Sr., Furman.

The Southern Conference wound up on center stage although seven members left the league to form the nucleus of the now acclaimed Atlantic Coast Conference. Furman forward Frank Selvy was the principal reason the Southern Conference was in the limelight.

Selvy scored 100 points vs. Newberry (S.C.) on his way to becoming the first three-year player to reach 2,000 points, finishing with 2,538. Selvy (41.7 ppg) and Darrell Floyd (24.3) combined for 66 points per game during the season and are the highest-scoring duo in major-college history. Selvy scored 50 or more in seven games.

Making Selvy's 100-point outburst even more amazing was the fact that his mother, watching her son play for the initial time, was among several hundred fans from his hometown of Corbin, Ky., who made the trip to Greenville, S.C., to watch the game. An early indication that something special was in the offing came less than three minutes into the game when Newberry's Bobby Bailey, who helped hold Selvy to a season-low 25 points two weeks earlier, fouled out.

Selvy's last three field goals came in the game's closing 30 seconds, and the crowning moment was his final basket. "It (the 100-point game) was something that was just meant to be," Selvy said. "My last basket was from past half-court just before the final buzzer." Selvy hit 41 of 66 shots from the floor and 18 of 22 from the free-throw line. He played every minute of every game his senior season to help Furman finish with a 20-9 record after the Paladins lost six of their first seven outings.

Selvy and Iona's Richie Guerin (24.7) set school records for highest scoring average in a single season. Despite Selvy's Southern Conference-record scoring average, scoring decreased nationally for the first time in 19 years from 138.1 the previous season to 137.9. . . . George Washington, unbeaten in Southern Conference regular-season competition including a 102-97 victory at Furman, also won the league's postseason tournament to advance to the NCAA playoffs.

San Francisco's Bill Russell collected 23 points and 13 blocked shots in his varsity debut, a 51-33 victory over California. . . . Teammates Joe Holup (57.2 percent) and Elliott Karver (56.1) finished one-two in the country in field-goal accuracy to help George Washington lead the nation in that category. It is the only time in NCAA history that a pair of teammates claimed the top two spots nationally. . . . A pair of four-game losing streaks led to St. John's incurring its first losing record (9-11) in 32 years.

La Salle's Tom Gola

Undefeated Kentucky (25-0/coached by Adolph Rupp) finished among the top 10 in team offense and won at least 25 games for the eighth consecutive season in which it participated (barred from playing in 1952-53 as the result of an NCAA ruling regarding improper payments to players). Cliff Hagan and Frank Ramsey combined for 43.6 points per game and either one or both of them led the Wildcats in scoring in each of their 25 contests. . . . LSU tied Kentucky for the SEC championship by going undefeated in league competition for the second straight season. Two years later, LSU lost its season opener to obscure visitor Louisiana College, 84-79.

Western Kentucky won 21 consecutive games, an Ohio Valley Conference record, en route to Ed Diddle becoming the first coach to reach the 600-win plateau. The Hilltoppers (29-3) set an OVC standard for most victories in a single season. . . . Eastern Kentucky (7-16 under coach Paul McBrayer) sustained its first losing mark after 17 consecutive winning seasons (did not compete in 1943-44 because of World War II).

Virginia junior guard Buzz Wilkinson set ACC Tournament records for most field-goal attempts (13 of 44) and free-throw attempts (16 of 22) when he scored 42 points in a 76-68 first-round defeat against Duke. . . . The ACC's inaugural season marked the only time North Carolina finished fifth or worse in the league standings. . . . Coach Everett Case and his staff for ACC Tournament champion North Carolina State produced quite possibly the first ever all-color highlight film. N.C. State finished in fourth place in the regular season before winning its first of three straight ACC Tournament titles. . . . Maryland started a 13-game winning streak in its series with nearby rival Georgetown.

Marshall's Charlie Slack became one of four major-college players in history to grab at least 40 rebounds in a single game when he retrieved 43 missed shots against Morris Harvey. . . . Bradley's Dick Estergard, a 6-4, 192-pound forward referred to as "Mr. Rebound," finished his career with an average of 16.1 rebounds per game.

St. Louis' Jerry Koch (38 vs. Bradley), VMI's Bill Ralph (31 vs. Hampden-Sydney), Western Kentucky's Tom Marshall (29 at Louisville), St. Mary's Mike Wadsworth (26 vs. California Aggies) and Nebraska's Bill Johnson (26 vs. Iowa State) set school single-game rebounding records.

Wichita compiled a 27-4 mark under coach Ralph Miller just two years after incurring its sixth consecutive losing season. Wichita, Duquesne (26-3/coached by Dudey Moore) and St. Francis, N.Y. (23-5/Daniel Lynch) had their winningest seasons in school history. . . . Rice, coached by Don Suman, made its lone appearance in the Top 20 of a final wire-service poll. . . . St. Louis sustained its only losing Missouri Valley record (4-6) in the first 16 years after World War II from 1945-46 through 1960-61.

Wade "Swede" Halbrook, a 7-3, 245-pound sophomore, averaged 21.2 points and 11.9 rebounds per game for Oregon State. He was called "the largest man in basketball history" by the *NCAA Basketball Guide*. . . . Washington com-

---

SELVY SCORES RECORD 100 POINTS   On February 13, 1954, Furman forward Frank Selvy scored 100 points vs. Newberry on his way to becoming the first three-year player to reach 2,000 points. (He wound up with a career total of 2,538.) Making Selvy's 100-point outburst even more amazing was the fact that his mother, watching her son play for the first time, was among several hundred fans from his hometown of Corbin, Kentucky, who made the trip to Furman, located in Greenville, South Carolina, to watch the game. An early indication that something special was in the offing came less than three minutes into the game when the Newberry player (Bobby Bailey) assigned to defend Selvy fouled out.

Selvy's last three field goals came in the game's closing 30 seconds, and the crowning moment was his final basket. "It (the 100-point game) was something that was just meant to be," Selvy said. "My last basket was from past halfcourt just before the final buzzer." Selvy hit 41 of 66 shots from the floor and 18 of 22 from the free-throw line. He played every minute of every game that season.

FURMAN (149)	FG	FT-A	PTS.
Bennett	0	1-1	1
Floyd	12	1-1	25
Fraley	3	0-2	6
Poole	0	0-0	0
Thomas	5	1-1	11
Kyber	0	0-2	0
Roth	0	0-0	0
Gordon	0	0-0	0
Selvy	41	18-22	100
Deardorff	1	1-1	3
Wright	0	0-0	0
Jones	0	1-1	1
Gilreath	1	0-0	2
TOTALS	**63**	**23-31**	**149**

NEWBERRY (95)	FG	FT-A	PTS.
Boland	0	0-0	0
Warner	2	0-4	4
Leitner	6	4-7	16
Bailey	0	1-2	1
Blanko	14	7-10	35
Cone	1	0-0	2
Roth	0	3-4	3
McKlven	1	0-0	2
Davis	13	6-7	32
TOTALS	**37**	**21-34**	**95**

Halftime: Furman 77-44.

1953-54 FINAL NATIONAL POLLS

AP	UPI	SCHOOL(RECORD)	HEAD COACH
1	2	Kentucky (25-0)	Adolph Rupp
2	11	La Salle (26-4)	Ken Loeffler
3	9	Holy Cross (26-2)	Buster Sheary
4	1	Indiana (20-4)	Branch McCracken
5	3	Duquesne (26-3)	Dudey Moore
6	5	Notre Dame (22-3)	John Jordan
7	–	Bradley (19-13)	Forddy Anderson
8	6	Western Kentucky (29-3)	Ed Diddle
9	–	Penn State (18-6)	Elmer Gross
10	4	Oklahoma A&M (24-5)	Hank Iba
11	14	Southern Cal (19-14)	Forrest Twogood
12	–	George Washington (23-3)	Bill Reinhart
13	10	Iowa (17-5)	Bucky O'Connor
14	8	Louisiana State (20-5)	Harry Rabenhorst
15	20	Duke (22-6)	Harold Bradley
16	–	Niagara (24-6)	Taps Gallagher
17	17	Seattle (26-2)	Al Brightman
18	7	Kansas (16-5)	Phog Allen
19	12	Illinois (17-5)	Harry Combes
20	–	Maryland (23-7)	Bud Millikan
–	13	Colorado State (22-7)	Bill Strannigan
–	14	N.C. State (26-7)	Everett Case
–	16	Oregon State (19-10)	Slats Gill
–	17	Dayton (25-7)	Tom Blackburn
–	19	Rice (23-5)	Don Suman

Furman's Frank Selvy shoots for 2, on his way to 100 points vs. Newberry.

piled an 8-18 mark after finishing among the top 15 the previous three seasons in final wire-service polls. The Huskies, a Final Four team the previous year when they were 30-3, lost their first nine games and 14 of their first 15. . . . Guard Ron Livingston, UCLA's leading scorer with 12.5 points per game, won the 1954 NCAA Doubles title in tennis and advanced to the finals in the singles division. He was the first outstanding two-fisted tennis player in college.

Colorado State's 22-7 record under coach Bill Strannigan marked the first winning season in eight years for the Rams. . . . NIT champion Holy Cross compiled its highest winning percentage in school history (.929). . . . Seton Hall failed to advance to the NIT for the only time in a seven-year span from 1951 through 1957. . . . Notre Dame defeated Purdue for the 15th time in their last 17 meetings, 78-58.

1954 NCAA Tournament

Summary: After a one-year schedule boycott, Kentucky's undefeated squad declined a bid to the NCAA playoffs because its three fifth-year (postgraduate) stars—Cliff Hagan, Frank Ramsey and Lou Tsioropoulos—were ineligible. The Wildcats defeated national champion-to-be La Salle by 13 points in the UK Invitation Tournament final on their way to being ranked 1st by AP and 2nd by UPI. UK had just two games tighter than a 12-point decision (77-71 over Xavier and 63-56 over LSU). Sandwiched between those two contests were 16 victories by an average margin of 33.7 points. Without UK, La Salle's achievement lost some of its significance.

Outcome for Defending Champion: Big Ten champion Indiana (20-4) lost its tourney opener to Notre Dame, 65-64. Former Notre Dame athletic director Dick Rosenthal collected 25 points and 15 rebounds for the Irish and helped limit Hoosiers All-American Don Schlundt to one field goal. Indiana's first three defeats were by a total of 44 points.

Star Gazing: Tom Gola is the only individual to be named both NCAA Final Four Most Outstanding Player and NIT Most Valuable Player in

his career. Gola led La Salle to the 1954 NCAA crown with a 23-point average. Two years earlier as a freshman when the Explorers won the NIT, he shared the MVP award with teammate Norm Grekin.

Biggest Upset: Penn State, supposedly the final team selected for the NCAA playoffs, reached the Final Four by winning its first three tourney games by at least eight points—knocking off Toledo and Bob Pettit-led LSU before snapping Notre Dame's 18-game winning streak. The Nittany Lions' 62-50 triumph over Toledo came despite 4 of 19 field-goal shooting by star Jesse Arnelle. Phil Martin scored more than half of Toledo's points (26) in a losing effort.

One and Only: The worst composite winning percentage when four teams arrived at the national semifinals was this year as La Salle (24-4), Bradley (18-12), Penn State (17-5) and Southern California (19-12) combined for a 78-33 record (.703). Southern Cal lost both of its Final Four games (against Bradley and Penn State) to become the only national semifinalist with as many as 14 defeats. Bradley lost the championship game against La Salle to become one of only three Final Four squads to finish a season with more than a

Junior center Jesse Arnelle led Cinderella-story Penn State to the NCAA Final Four.

1953-54 UNDEFEATED TEAM: UNIVERSITY OF KENTUCKY (25-0)

COACH: ADOLPH RUPP

UK	OPPONENT	UK'S HIGH SCORER
86	Temple 59	Hagan 51
81	at Xavier 66	Ramsey 27
101	Wake Forest 69	Hagan 18
71	at St. Louis 59	Ramsey 21
85	Duke 69	Hagan 27
73	La Salle 60	Hagan 28
74	Minnesota 59	Ramsey 23
77	Xavier 71	Hagan 20
105	Georgia Tech 53	Hagan 34
81	DePaul 63	Hagan/Ramsey 22
94	Tulane 43	Ramsey 26
97	at Tennessee 71	Ramsey 37
85	at Vanderbilt 63	Ramsey 24
99	Georgia Tech* 48	Hagan 23
106	Georgia 55	Ramsay 29
100	Georgia* 68	Unavailable
97	at Florida 55	Hagan 22
88	Mississippi 62	Hagan 38
81	Mississippi State 49	Hagan 26
90	Tennessee 63	Hagan 24
76	at DePaul 61	Unavailable
100	Vanderbilt 64	Hagan 22
109	Auburn* 79	Unavailable
68	at Alabama 43	Hagan 24

SEC PLAYOFF

UK	OPPONENT	UK'S HIGH SCORER
63	Louisiana State* 56	Ramsey 30

*Neutral court games.

INDIVIDUAL STATISTICS FOR KENTUCKY REGULARS

PLAYER	POS.	CL.	G.	PPG
Cliff Hagan	F-C	Sr.	25	24.0
Frank Ramsey	G	Sr.	25	19.6
Lou Tsioropoulos	F	Sr.	25	14.5
Billy Evans	F-G	Jr.	25	8.4
Gayle Rose	G	Jr.	23	6.7
Phil Grawemeyer	F-C	So.	25	5.9
Linville Puckett	G	So.	24	5.1
Bill Bibb	F	So.	16	1.7

1953–54 INDIVIDUAL LEADERS

SCORING

PLAYER	PTS.	AVG.
Selvy, Furman	1209	41.7
Pettit, Louisiana St.	785	31.4
Wilkinson, Virginia	814	30.1
Short, Oklahoma City	696	27.8
Schafer, Villanova	836	27.0
Walowac, Marshall	548	26.1
Marshall, W. Kentucky	829	25.9
Kerr, Illinois	556	25.3
Bianchi, Bowling Green	600	25.0
Palazzi, Holy Cross	670	24.8

REBOUNDING

PLAYER	REB.	AVG.
Quimby, Connecticut	588	22.6
Slack, Marshall	466	22.2

Gola, La Salle	652	21.7
Sundstrom, Rutgers	494	20.6
Koch, St. Louis	502	20.1
Tuttle, Creighton	601	20.0
Russell, San Francisco	403	19.2
Holup, George Washington	484	18.6
Conlin, Fordham	417	17.4
Hannon, Army	381	17.3

FIELD GOAL PERCENTAGE

PLAYER	FGM	FGA	PCT.
Holup, G. Wash.	179	313	.572
Karver, G. Wash.	124	221	.561
Mattick, Okla. A&M	199	358	.556
Hoxie, Niagara	115	211	.545
Spoelstra, W. Kentucky	202	381	.530
Carpenter, Texas Tech	110	214	.514
Shue, Maryland	237	469	.505

Hemric, Wake Forest	225	446	.504
Heim, Xavier	139	277	.502
Schlundt, Indiana	177	354	.500

FREE THROW PERCENTAGE

PLAYER	FTM	FTA	PCT.
Daugherty, Arizona St.	75	86	.872
Kelley, Kansas	75	87	.862
Powell, Florida	166	195	.851
Dalton, John Carroll	189	225	.840
Nystedt, New Mexico	98	118	.831
Short, Oklahoma City	232	282	.823
Costello, Niagara	125	152	.822
Lamkin, DePaul	105	128	.820
Williams, San Jose St.	184	225	.818
Devlin, G. Wash.	115	141	.816

1953–54 TEAM LEADERS

SCORING OFFENSE

SCHOOL	PTS.	AVG.
Furman	2658	91.7
Kentucky	2187	87.5
W. Kentucky	2730	85.3
Duke	2250	83.3
Holy Cross	2329	83.2

SCORING DEFENSE

SCHOOL	PTS.	AVG.
Oklahoma A&M	1539	53.1

Duquesne	1551	53.5
Wyoming	1522	54.4
Oregon State	1585	54.7
Oklahoma City	1370	54.8

FIELD GOAL PERCENTAGE

SCHOOL	FGM	FGA	PCT.
George Washington	744	1632	.456
Holy Cross	871	2018	.432
Niagara	778	1817	.428
Maryland	669	1564	.428
Furman	990	2370	.418

FREE THROW PERCENTAGE

SCHOOL	FTM	FTA	PCT.
Wake Forest	734	1010	.727
Florida	540	746	.724
Tulane	422	583	.724
New Mexico	444	614	.723
Niagara	667	929	.718

1953–54 NCAA CHAMPION: LA SALLE

SEASON STATISTICS OF LA SALLE REGULARS

PLAYER	POS.	CL.	G.	FG%	FT%	PPG	RPG
Tom Gola	C-G	Jr.	30	.407	.732	23.0	21.7
Charlie Singley	F	So.	30	.382	.654	10.7	5.1
Frank Blatcher	F	So.	27	.374	.640	10.4	4.6
Frank O'Hara	G	Sr.	30	.406	.708	9.6	3.7
Fran O'Malley	G-F	So.	30	.345	.697	7.4	4.6
Bob Maples	C-F	So.	30	.404	.554	6.9	4.7
Charles Greenberg	F-G	So.	26	.311	.545	4.7	3.0
John Yodsnukis	C	So.	18	.304	.625	4.6	5.7
Bob Ames	F	So.	14	.300	.769	2.0	0.9
Manuel Gomez	C	So.	16	.167	.462	0.6	0.8
TEAM TOTALS			30	.378	.667	75.4	51.1

1954 CHAMPIONSHIP GAME

KANSAS CITY, MO

LA SALLE (92)	FG	FT-A	PF	PTS.
Singley	8	7-10	4	23
Greenberg	2	1-2	1	5
Maples	2	0-0	4	4
Blatcher	11	1-2	4	23
Gola	7	5-5	5	19
O'Malley	5	1-1	4	11
Yodsnukis	0	0-0	5	0
O'Hara	2	2-3	1	7
TOTALS	37	18-24	28	92

FT%: .750.

BRADLEY (76)	FG	FT-A	PF	PTS.
Petersen	4	2-2	2	10
Babetch	0	0-0	0	0
King	3	6-7	4	12
Gower	0	1-2	1	1
Estergard	3	11-12	1	17
Carney	3	11-17	4	17
Utt	0	0-0	1	0
Kent	8	0-2	2	16
Riley	1	1-2	1	3
TOTALS	22	32-44	16	76

FT%: .727.
Halftime: Bradley 43-42.

ALL-TOURNAMENT TEAM

Jesse Arnelle, C, Jr., Penn State (43 points in final two games)
Bob Carney, G, Sr., Bradley (37 points)
*Tom Gola, C-F, Jr., La Salle (38 points)
Roy Irvin, C, Jr., Southern Cal (35 points)
Chuck Singley, F, Soph., La Salle (33 points)

*Named Most Outstanding Player.

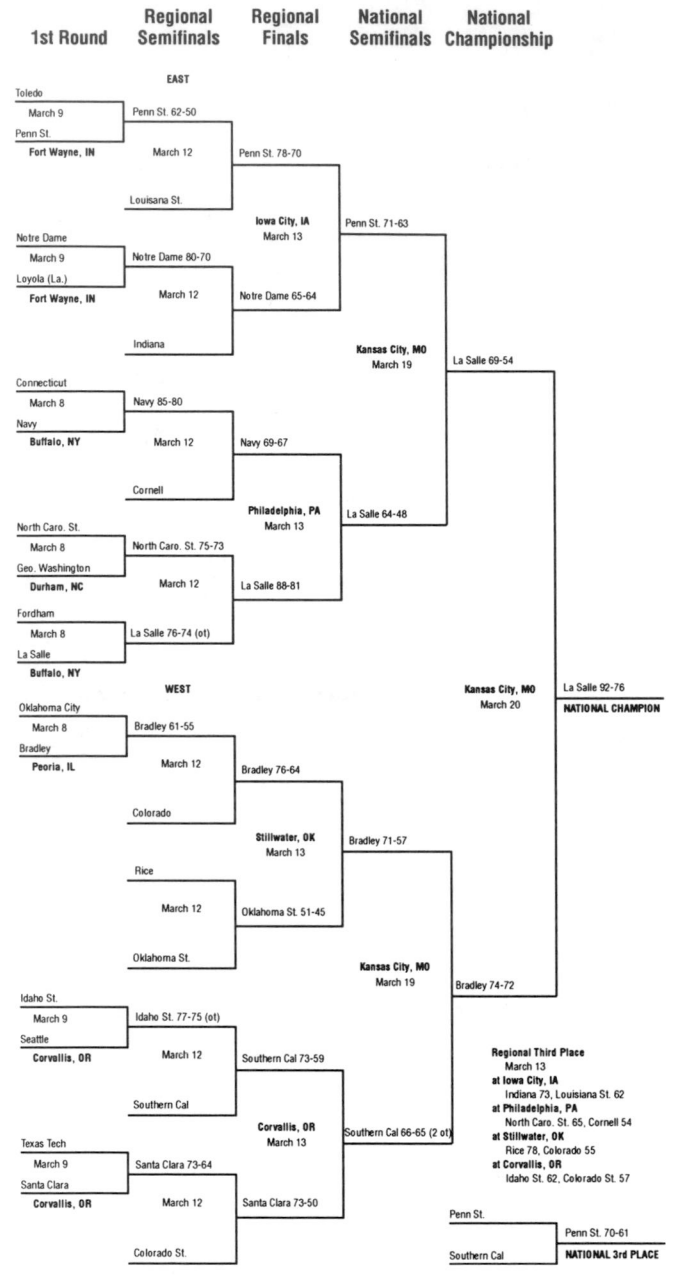

	1st Round	Regional Semifinals	Regional Finals	National Semifinals	National Championship

EAST

Toledo
March 9
Penn St.
Fort Wayne, IN

Penn St. 62-50
March 12

Louisana St.

Penn St. 78-70

Iowa City, IA
March 13

Notre Dame
March 9
Loyola (La.)
Fort Wayne, IN

Notre Dame 80-70
March 12

Indiana

Notre Dame 65-64

Penn St. 71-63

Kansas City, MO
March 19

Connecticut
March 8
Navy
Buffalo, NY

Navy 85-80
March 12

Cornell

Navy 69-67

Philadelphia, PA
March 13

North Caro. St.
March 8
Geo. Washington
Durham, NC

North Caro. St. 75-73
March 12

La Salle 88-81

Fordham
March 8
La Salle
Buffalo, NY

La Salle 76-74 (ot)

La Salle 64-48

La Salle 69-54

La Salle 92-76
NATIONAL CHAMPION

Kansas City, MO
March 20

WEST

Oklahoma City
March 8
Bradley
Peoria, IL

Bradley 61-55
March 12

Colorado

Bradley 76-64

Stillwater, OK
March 13

Rice
March 12
Oklahoma St.

Oklahoma St. 51-45

Bradley 71-57

Kansas City, MO
March 19

Idaho St.
March 9
Seattle
Corvallis, OR

Idaho St. 77-75 (ot)
March 12

Southern Cal

Southern Cal 73-59

Corvallis, OR
March 13

Texas Tech
March 9
Santa Clara
Corvallis, OR

Santa Clara 73-64
March 12

Colorado St.

Santa Clara 73-50

Southern Cal 66-65 (2 ot)

Bradley 74-72

Regional Third Place
March 13
at Iowa City, IA
Indiana 73, Louisiana St. 62
at Philadelphia, PA
North Caro. St. 65, Cornell 54
at Stillwater, OK
Rice 78, Colorado 55
at Corvallis, OR
Idaho St. 62, Colorado St. 57

Penn St.

Penn St. 70-61

Southern Cal

NATIONAL 3rd PLACE

Four squads to finish a season with more than a dozen defeats.

Numbers Game: Of the more than 40 different players to score more than 225 points in the playoffs and/or average over 25 points per tournament game (minimum of six games), Pettit is the only one to score more than 22 points in every postseason contest (six games in 1953 and 1954). He is the only player from that select group to have a single-digit differential between his high game (36 points) and his low game (27). . . . La Salle's output in a 92-76 victory over Bradley in the final represented the most points by a team in a championship game until UCLA's first national crown in 1964. . . . Navy's Jack Clune collected a tourney-high 42 points in an 85-80 opening-game victory over Connecticut. . . . Bradley's Bob Carney became the only player ever to make at least 50 free throws in a single tourney. He was 55 of 70 from the foul line in five games, including a 23 of 26 effort from the charity stripe against Colorado in the Midwest Regional semifinals.

What If: San Francisco (14-7) might have been the California Basketball Association representative instead of Santa Clara if USF guard K.C. Jones didn't miss the majority of the season after undergoing an appendectomy.

Putting Things in Perspective: Niagara (24-6) defeated La Salle twice by a total of 27 points before finishing in third place in the NIT.

Scoring Leader: Tom Gola, La Salle (114 points, 22.8 ppg).

Highest Scoring Average: Bob Pettit, LSU (61 points, 30.5 ppg).

1954-55

AT A GLANCE

NCAA Champion: San Francisco (28-1; coached by Phil Woolpert; won California Basketball Association by five games with a 12-0 record).

NIT Champion: Duquesne (22-4; coached by Dudey Moore).

New Rules: Games changed back to two 20-minute halves. . . . The one-and-one free-throw is altered so that the bonus shot is given only if the first shot is converted.

NCAA Probation: Miami (Fla.), North Carolina State.

NCAA Consensus First-Team All-Americans: Dick Garmaker, F, Sr., Minnesota; Tom Gola, C-F, Sr., La Salle; Si Green, G, Jr., Duquesne; Dick Ricketts, F-C, Sr., Duquesne; Bill Russell, C, Jr., San Francisco.

National Player of the Year: Gola (24.2 ppg, 19.9 rpg).

National Coach of the Year: Phil Woolpert, San Francisco (28-1/UPI).

David slew Goliath twice in a 23-day period. Kentucky's NCAA-record 129-game homecourt winning streak was snapped by Georgia Tech, 59-58, on January 8. Tech guard Joe Helms scored a game-high 23 points, including a one-handed, 12-footer with 11 seconds remaining to end the Wildcats' 54-game regular-season winning streak and 16-year unbeaten streak at home in the SEC. The Jackets, 2-22 the previous season and 22-73 the previous four years, had lost to Sewanee, 67-66, one game prior to venturing to Lexington, where they had lost 10 times during UK's streak by an average margin of 35 points. Later in January, Tech became the first team to twice defeat Kentucky coach Adolph Rupp in the same season, leading the Wildcats all the way in a 65-59 decision.

Georgia Tech, coached by Whack Hyder, used only five players in both upsets after losing its previous 28 games to UK. Despite the pair of setbacks to a team that finished with a losing record (12-13), Rupp improved his career mark to 520-86 (85.8 winning percentage) as the Wildcats went 23-3.

Alabama's George Linn grabbed a rebound in the closing seconds of the first half of a game against North Carolina, turned and made an overhand throw to the basket at the opposite end of the court and made the shot, which was measured at 84 feet, 11 inches.

Alabama was also involved in a bizarre pregame fight at Kentucky. The Wildcats had a disconserting tactic of sending their backups to mid-

1954 ACC Player-of-the-Year Dickie Hemric of Wake Forest.

court, where they stood and tried to give their opponents an inferiority complex by staring at them warming up. Bama coach Johnny Dee, however, fought glare with glare. Dee dispatched his reserves to disdainfully assess UK. After exchanging words, players soon were swinging away in a pileup in the middle of the floor and had to be separated by state troopers. The Crimson Tide led midway through the second half before faltering down the stretch and losing, 66-52, providing Kentucky with the one-game cushion the Wildcats needed to stay ahead of 'Bama in the SEC regular-season race.

Brown's Ed Tooley established an NCAA record for most free-throw attempts in a game with 36 against Amherst (see accompanying box). . . . Marshall's Charlie Slack set an NCAA single-season record for highest rebounding average with 25.6 boards per game. . . . Holy Cross' Tom Heinsohn (42 vs. Boston College) and Connecticut's

Art Quimby (40 vs. Boston University) became two of four major-college players in history to grab at least 40 rebounds in a single game. Quimby's boardwork helped Connecticut set an NCAA single-season record for highest rebounding average with 70 per game.

Wake Forest started a stretch where it won 22 of 24 games against ACC member Virginia through 1965. . . . Wake Forest's Dickie Hemric, one of only three starters in the ACC to measure 6-7 or better the previous year in the league's inaugural season, set an ACC single-game record by grabbing a school-record 36 rebounds against Clemson. . . . Dick Ricketts, Duquesne's all-time leading scorer, grabbed 28 rebounds in a game against Villanova. That's the highest rebounding total for any Dukes player against a major college.

San Francisco's Bill Russell (35 vs. Loyola Marymount), North Carolina State's Ronnie Shavlik (35 vs. Villanova), Penn's Barton Leach (32 vs. Harvard), Harvard's Bob Canty (31 vs. Boston College), Clemson's Tommy Smith (30 vs. Georgia), Rice's Joe Durrenberger (30 vs. Baylor), Santa Clara's Ken Sears (30 vs. Pacific), Penn State's Jesse Arnelle (27 at Temple) and Missouri's Bob Reiter (27 at Kansas State) set school single-game rebounding records. Sears was annointed California Basketball Association MVP over Russell although the USF center was a first-team All-America.

Oregon's Jim Loscutoff established what remains a Pacific-10 Conference record by averaging 17.2 rebounds per game, including a school-record 32 rebounds against Brigham Young. Oregon State's Swede Halbrook set a league mark with 36 rebounds in a game against Idaho. . . . La Salle's Tom Gola finished his career with 2,462 points and 2,201 rebounds. His total of points and rebounds (4,663) is the highest in NCAA history. Gola, who grabbed a school-record 37 rebounds in a 112-70 victory over Lebanon Valley, later became a state legislator and ran for mayor of Philadelphia. . . . Coach Ken Loeffler, after guiding NCAA runner-up La Salle to more than 20 victories each of his six years with the Explorers, left after the season for a similar position at Texas A&M.

Furman's Darrell Floyd, the nation's leading scorer, poured in a national-high 67 points against Morehead State. Floyd's fireworks helped Furman led the nation in scoring for the third consecutive season. . . . Minnesota defeated Purdue, 59-56, in six overtimes in the longest game in Big Ten history. Each team used only six players. . . . Purdue lost 13 consecutive games to archrival Indiana in their series until the Boilermakers blasted the Hoosiers, 92-67. . . . Bowling Green's school record of 12 consecutive winning seasons ended with a 6-16 worksheet, including the most lopsided defeat in the Falcons' history (109-39 against Dayton).

Virginia guard Buzz Wilkinson set an ACC single-season scoring average record by averaging 32.1 points per game, becoming the first major-college player to crack 30 points per game in back-to-back years. Wilkinson still has seven of the eight games in Cavaliers history with more than 42 points.

TCU's Dick O'Neal (49 points vs. Rice) and Kent State's Dan Potopsky (49 vs. Western Michigan) established school single-game scoring records. Potopsky scored 20 of the Flashes' 22 points in the first quarter against WMU. . . . Virginia's Wilkinson, Clemson's Bill Yarborough (28.3 ppg), William & Mary's Johnny Mahoney (27.3), Penn State's Arnelle (26.1) and Kent State's Potopsky (23.4) set school records for highest scoring average in a single season.

Texas sophomore Raymond Downs averaged 26.1 points per game in Southwest Conference

1954–55 INDIVIDUAL LEADERS

SCORING

PLAYER	PTS.	AVG.
Floyd, Furman	897	35.9
Wilkinson, Virginia	898	32.1
Freeman, Ohio St.	409	31.5
Yarbrough, Clemson	651	28.3
O'Neal, Texas Christian	676	28.2
Hemric, Wake Forest	746	27.6
Patterson, Tulsa	773	27.6
Mahoney, William & Mary	656	27.3
Brackeen, Mississippi	599	27.2
Arnelle, Penn St.	731	26.1

REBOUNDING

PLAYER	REB.	PCT.
Slack, Marshall	538	.264
Russell, San Francisco	594	.258

Conlin, Fordham	578	.241
Boldebuck, Houston	453	.221
Sparrow, Detroit	489	.218
Harper, Alabama	456	.205
Holup, G. Wash.	546	.203
Gola, La Salle	618	.203
Quimby, Connecticut	611	.196
McCarvill, Iona	422	.189

FIELD GOAL PERCENTAGE

PLAYER	FGM	FGA	PCT.
O'Connor, Manhattan	147	243	.605
Holup, G. Wash.	223	373	.598
Glowaski, Seattle	144	245	.588
Francis, Dartmouth	117	204	.574
Carpenter, Texas Tech	129	227	.568
Crosthwaite, W. Ky.	156	285	.547
Russell, San Fran.	229	423	.541

Young, Lafayette	143	266	.538
Devlin, G. Wash.	263	490	.537
McCarty, Virginia	236	444	.532

FREE THROW PERCENTAGE

PLAYER	FTM	FTA	PCT.
Scott, W. Texas St.	153	171	.895
Walczak, Marquette	104	118	.881
Barnes, SMU	83	97	.856
Williams, San Jose St.	181	214	.846
Forte, Columbia	187	222	.842
Ryan, Hardin-Simmons	105	125	.840
Blackshear, Texas Tech	83	99	.838
Sears, Santa Clara	197	235	.838
Murdock, Wake Forest	101	121	.835
Stewart, Missouri	88	106	.830

1954–55 TEAM LEADERS

SCORING OFFENSE

SCHOOL	PTS.	AVG.
Furman	2572	95.3
Connecticut	2252	90.1
Virginia	2605	89.8
North Carolina St.	2839	88.7
Marshall	1834	87.3

SCORING DEFENSE

SCHOOL	PTS.	AVG.
San Francisco	1511	52.1
Oklahoma A&M	1333	53.3
Oregon State	1660	55.3
Duquesne	1512	58.2
Santa Clara	1427	59.5

FIELD GOAL PERCENTAGE

SCHOOL	FGM	FGA	PCT.
George Washington	867	1822	.476
Wake Forest	803	1745	.460
Lafayette	760	1700	.447
Manhattan	604	1351	.447
Virginia	935	2115	.442

FREE THROW PERCENTAGE

SCHOOL	FTM	FTA	PCT.
Wake Forest	709	938	.756
Arizona State	832	627	.754
George Washington	615	819	.751
Missouri	550	747	.736
Richmond	641	879	.729

REBOUNDING

SCHOOL	TOTAL REB.	REB.	PCT.
Niagara	2417	1507	.624
St. Louis	2499	1512	.605
Seattle	2219	1336	.602
Kentucky	2800	1680	.600
North Carolina St.	3111	1864	.599

competition, but failed to earn a spot among the first five on the all-league team after the Longhorns lost a school-record 15 consecutive games. . . . Kansas dedicated Allen Fieldhouse on March 1 with a 77-66 victory over Kansas State before a crowd of 17,228. Season tickets the first full season the next year cost $16, which included free parking close to the arena. The Jayhawks had previously played their home games at Hoch Auditorium, which had a seating capacity of 3,800 for basketball. . . . Wichita's Cleo Littleton became the initial player west of the Mississippi to finish his career with more than 2,000 points. . . . Hank Iba absorbed his first losing record (12-13) in 21 seasons as coach at Oklahoma A&M/State.

Seattle didn't finish among the Top 20 in a final wire-service poll for the only time in an eight-year span through 1958-59. . . . New Mexico lost back-to-back games at Southern Cal (103-39) and UCLA (106-41) by a total of 129 points. The defeats are the two most lopsided in Lobos history. . . . George Washington (24-6/coached by Bill Reinhart) and Lafayette (23-3/Butch van Breda Kolff) had their winningest seasons in school history. Lafayette won its last 20 regular-season games, a winning streak that remains a school record.

Manhattan's Ed O'Connor became the first player to lead the nation in field-goal shooting with a mark above 60 percent (60.5). . . . The California Basketball Association, the forerunner of the West Coast Conference, was led in free-throw shooting by San Jose State's Carroll Williams (81.3 percent

ANYTHING BUT FREE

Brown vs. Amherst
December 4, 1954

Brown could have avoided a one-point loss to Amherst if Ed Tooley had hit 69 percent of his foul shots, but he missed 13 of his NCAA-record 36 free-throw attempts. Tooley would have set a school single-game scoring standard of 49 points by canning 33 of his charity tosses instead of 23.

BROWN (70): Tooley 8 **23-36** 39, Kincade 4 1 9, Lubin 2 2 6, Campisi 0 5 5, Popp 0 4 4, Gerould 1 2 4, Arnold 0 2 2, Pendergast 0 1 1, Malkiewicz 0 0 0, Merritt 0 0 0, Smith 0 0 0, Ewing 0 0 0. Team 15 40 70.

AMHERST (71): Scott 9 8 26, Hawkins 6 12 24, Allen 3 3 9, Benson 2 0 4, Anderson 2 0 4, Rumrill 1 0 2, Boley 0 1 1, Knight 0 1 1, Gould 0 0 0, Symmes 0 0 0, Ascari 0 0 0, Tooman 0 0 0. Team 23 25 71.

AP	UPI	SCHOOL(RECORD)	HEAD COACH
1	1	San Francisco (28-1)	Phil Woolpert
2	2	Kentucky (23-3)	Adolph Rupp
3	3	La Salle (26-5)	Ken Loeffler
4	6	N.C. State (28-4)	Everett Case
5	5	Iowa (19-7)	Bucky O'Connor
6	7	Duquesne (22-4)	Dudey Moore
7	4	Utah (24-4)	Jack Gardner
8	9	Marquette (24-3)	Jack Nagle
9	10	Dayton (25-4)	Tom Blackburn
10	8	Oregon State (22-8)	Slats Gill
11	13	Minnesota (15-7)	Ozzie Cowles
12	–	Alabama (19-5)	Johnny Dee
13	12	UCLA (21-5)	John Wooden
14	15	George Washington (24-6)	Bill Reinhart
15	11	Colorado (19-6)	Bebe Lee
16	14	Tulsa (21-7)	Clarence Iba
17	–	Vanderbilt (16-6)	Bob Polk
18	16	Illinois (17-5)	Harry Combes
19	–	West Virginia (19-11)	Fred Schaus
20	18	St. Louis (20-8)	Eddie Hickey
–	17	Niagara (20-7)	Taps Gallagher
–	19	Holy Cross (19-7)	Buster Sheary
–	20	Cincinnati (21-8)	George Smith

accuracy). Williams later became the league's all-time winningest coach in 22 seasons at Santa Clara. . . . Connecticut compiled a 20-5 record, which matched the Huskies' average number of defeats annually in a nine-year span from 1946-47. . . . Western Kentucky's 67-game homecourt winning streak was snapped by Xavier (82-80 in overtime). . . . A pair of Ohio universities, Case Western Reserve and John Carroll, competed in their final season at the major-college level.

1955 NCAA Tournament

Summary: Bill Russell retrieved 25 missed shots in the final while defensive specialist K.C. Jones, 6-1, held La Salle's three-time consensus first-team All-American Tom Gola, 6-6, without a basket during one 21-minute stretch and outscored him, 24-16, in San Francisco's 77-63 triumph.

Outcome for Defending Champion: La Salle (26-5) won its first three tourney games by an average of 32 points. The Explorers had lost three of their last six outings the first month of the season.

Biggest Upset: Kentucky, ranked second in the country entering the tourney, lost its opener to Marquette, 79-71. Marquette had losing records in 12 of the previous 15 seasons before compiling a 24-3 mark.

1955 CHAMPIONSHIP BRACKET

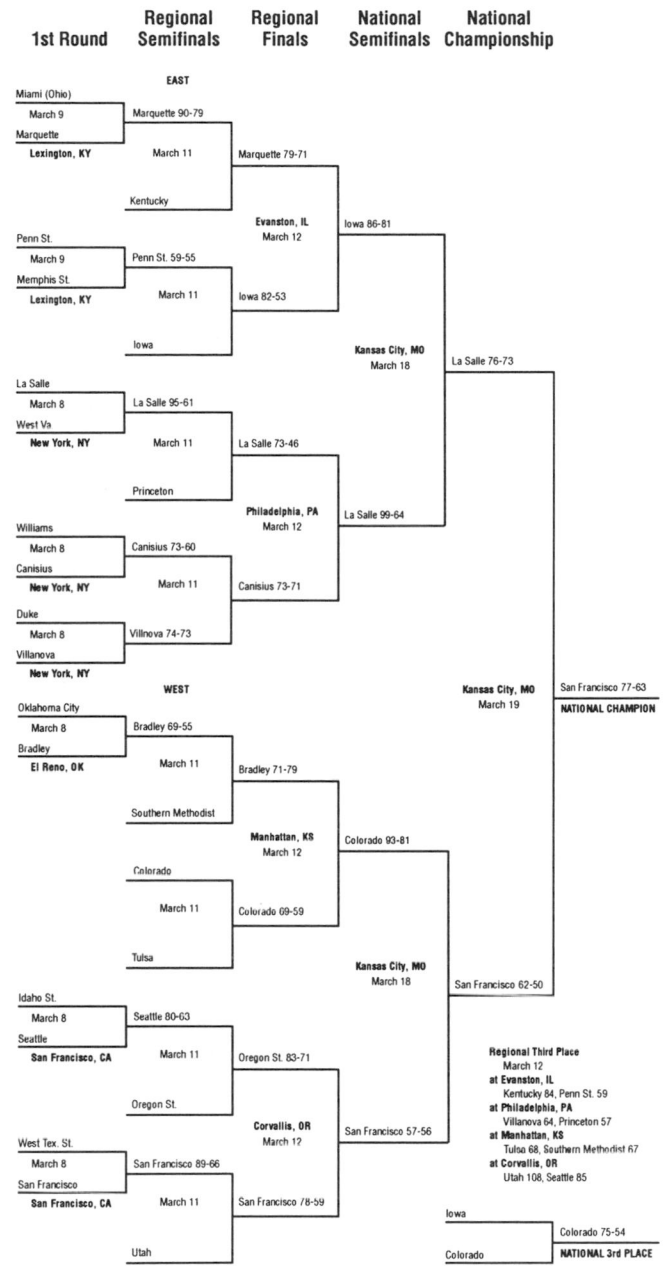

	Regional Semifinals	Regional Finals	National Semifinals	National Championship

1st Round

EAST

Miami (Ohio)
March 9
Marquette
Lexington, KY

Marquette 90-79
March 11

Kentucky

Marquette 79-71

Evanston, IL
March 12

Iowa 86-81

Penn St.
March 9
Memphis St.
Lexington, KY

Penn St. 59-55
March 11

Iowa

Iowa 82-53

Kansas City, MO
March 18

La Salle 76-73

La Salle
March 8
West Va
New York, NY

La Salle 95-61
March 11

Princeton

La Salle 73-46

Philadelphia, PA
March 12

La Salle 99-64

Williams
March 8
Canisius
New York, NY

Canisius 73-60
March 11

Canisius 73-71

Duke
March 8
Villanova
New York, NY

Villnova 74-73

Kansas City, MO
March 19

San Francisco 77-63
NATIONAL CHAMPION

WEST

Oklahoma City
March 8
Bradley
El Reno, OK

Bradley 69-55
March 11

Southern Methodist

Bradley 71-79

Manhattan, KS
March 12

Colorado 93-81

Colorado
March 11

Colorado 69-59

Tulsa

Kansas City, MO
March 18

San Francisco 62-50

Idaho St.
March 8
Seattle
San Francisco, CA

Seattle 80-63
March 11

Oregon St.

Oregon St. 83-71

Corvallis, OR
March 12

San Francisco 57-56

West Tex. St.
March 8
San Francisco
San Francisco, CA

San Francisco 89-66
March 11

San Francisco 78-59

Utah

Regional Third Place
March 12
at Evanston, IL
Kentucky 84, Penn St. 59
at Philadelphia, PA
Villanova 64, Princeton 57
at Manhattan, KS
Tulsa 68, Southern Methodist 67
at Corvallis, OR
Utah 108, Seattle 85

Iowa

Colorado

Colorado 75-54
NATIONAL 3rd PLACE

1954–55 NCAA CHAMPION: SAN FRANCISCO

SEASON STATISTICS OF SAN FRANCISCO REGULARS

PLAYER	POS.	CL.	G.	FG%	FT%	PPG	RPG
Bill Russell	C	Jr.	29	.541	.590	21.4	20.5
Jerry Mullen	F	Sr.	27	.379	.729	13.6	7.1
K. C. Jones	G	Jr.	29	.358	.674	10.6	5.1
Hal Perry	G	Jr.	29	.372	.750	6.9	1.9
Stan Buchanan	F	Sr.	29	.302	.711	5.2	3.2
Bob Wiebusch	F	Sr.	28	.322	.714	3.6	2.1
Rudy Zannini	G	Sr.	27	.300	.724	1.9	0.4
Dick Lawless	F	Sr.	26	.270	.600	1.8	1.1
Warren Baxter	G	Jr.	19	.524	.706	1.8	0.5
Bill Bush	G	Jr.	25	.333	.556	1.6	1.0
Jack King	F	So.	16	.333	.700	0.9	0.4
Gordon Kirby	C	Sr.	20	.200	.200	0.4	0.7
TEAM TOTALS			29	.396	.657	67.3	45.7

1955 CHAMPIONSHIP GAME

KANSAS CITY, MO

SAN FRANCISCO (77)	FG	FT-A	PF	PTS.
Mullen	4	2-5	5	10
Buchanan	3	2-2	1	8
Russell	9	5-7	1	23
Jones	10	4-4	2	24
Perry	1	2-2	4	4
Wiebusch	2	0-0	0	4
Zannini	1	0-0	0	2
Lawless	1	0-0	0	2
Kirby	0	0-0	1	0
TOTALS	**31**	**15-20**	**14**	**77**

FG%: .373. FT%: .750.

LA SALLE (63)	FG	FT-A	PF	PTS.
O'Malley	4	2-3	1	10
Singley	8	4-4	1	20
Gola	6	4-5	4	16
Lewis	1	4-9	1	6
Greenberg	1	1-2	4	3
Blatcher	4	0-0	1	8
Maples	0	0-0	0	0
Fredricks	0	0-0	0	0
TOTALS	**24**	**15-23**	**12**	**63**

FG%: .353. FT%: .652.
Halftime: San Francisco 35-24.

ALL-TOURNAMENT TEAM

Carl Cain, F, Jr., Iowa (31 points in final two games)
Tom Gola, C, Sr., La Salle (39 points)
K.C. Jones, G, Jr., San Francisco (32 points)
Jim Ranglos, F, Jr., Colorado (22 points)
*Bill Russell, C, Jr., San Francisco (47 points, 34 rebounds)

*Named Most Outstanding Player.

One and Only: Bradley is the only school to win at least one playoff game in a year it entered the tournament with a losing record. The Braves were the only team to enter the playoffs with a record of more than 10 games under the .500 mark (7-19). They are the only school to go from the Final Four one year to 20 defeats the next season.

Numbers Game: Colorado reached the national semifinals despite an early-season four-game losing streak. . . . Utah, which defeated Seattle (108-85) in the West Regional third-place game, was the only school to reach triple figures in scoring in the first 20 tournaments. . . . Terry Rand set a Marquette record for most points in an NCAA playoff game when he poured in a tourney-high 37 in a 90-79 victory over Miami of Ohio. . . . Oklahoma City's Gerald Bullard became the first player to appear in four consecutive NCAA Tournaments. He scored a total of seven points in five playoff games.

What Might Have Been: ACC regular-season and tournament champion North Carolina State, which defeated eventual national runner-up La Salle, was ineligible to participate in the NCAA Tournament because it was on probation. . . . Kentucky forward Phil Grawemeyer was averaging 13 points per game when he broke his leg against DePaul and missed the Wildcats' last six contests, including a 79-71 defeat to Marquette in their NCAA Tournament opener. UK (23-3) defeated NCAA playoff runner-up La Salle by nine points early in the season.

Putting Things in Perspective: The first of San Francisco's back-to-back champions survived a scare in a West Regional and won by one point at Oregon State (57-56). The Beavers would have avenged a 26-point defeat earlier in the season against the Dons if they hadn't missed a last-second shot. A 60-34 verdict over Oregon State was the first of USF's 60 consecutive victories, the longest winning streak in major-college history until UCLA won 88 games in a row from 1971-74.

Scoring Leader: Bill Russell, San Francisco (118 points, 23.6 ppg).

Highest Scoring Average: Bob Patterson, Tulsa (57 points, 28.5 ppg).

1955-56

AT A GLANCE

NCAA Champion: San Francisco (29-0; coached by Phil Woolpert; won WCAC by five games with a 14-0 record).

NIT Champion: Louisville (26-3; coached by Peck Hickman).

New Rules: The two-shot penalty in the last three minutes of a game is eliminated. The one-and-one is put in effect the entire game. . . . The NCAA Tournament went from two regionals to four.

NCAA Probation: Cincinnati.

NCAA Consensus First-Team All-Americans: Robin Freeman, G, Sr., Ohio State; Si Green, G, Sr., Duquesne; Tom Heinsohn, F, Sr., Holy Cross; Bill Russell, C, Sr., San Francisco; Ronnie Shavlik, C, Sr., North Carolina State.

National Player of the Year: Russell (20.6 ppg, 21 rpg, 51.3 FG%).

Alabama was ranked 5th by AP and UPI but didn't participate in the NCAA Tournament because of a rules technicality stemming from varsity participation as freshmen by several of the "Rocket 8" star players in 1953. Alabama's squad, dominated by Midwest recruits who didn't survive tryouts to receive scholarships from Notre Dame, became the first opponent to score 100 points against Kentucky. The 20-6 Wildcats, the SEC's representative to the NCAA Tournament, were whipped by 24 points (101-77 in the Massacre in Montgomery) as 'Bama went on a 27-2 second-half spurt en route to finishing the season with 16 consecutive victories. It was Alabama's lone vic-

1955–56 INDIVIDUAL LEADERS

SCORING LEADERS

PLAYER	PTS.	AVG.
Floyd, Furman	946	33.8
Freeman, Ohio St.	723	32.9
Swartz, Morehead St.	828	28.6
Heinsohn, Holy Cross	740	27.4
McCoy, Michigan St.	600	27.3
Rosenbluth, North Carolina	614	26.7
Hundley, West Virginia	798	26.6
Downs, Texas	580	26.4
Ray, Toledo	563	25.6
Sigler, Louisiana St.	501	25.1

REBOUNDING

PLAYER	REB.	PCT.
Holup, G. Wash.	604	.256
Tyra, Louisville	645	.235

Harper, Alabama	517	.232
Russell, San Francisco	609	.231
Slack, Marshall	520	.215
Inniss, St. Francis (NY)	465	.196
Shavlik, North Carolina St.	545	.193
Heinsohn, Holy Cross	549	.188
Sobieszczyk, DePaul	316	.182
McLaughlin, St. Louis	455	.181

FIELD GOAL PERCENTAGE

PLAYER	FGM	FGA	PCT.
Holup, G. Wash.	200	309	.647
Greer, Marshall	128	213	.601
Johnson, St. Mary's	134	238	.563
Downs, Texas	167	309	.540
Lombardo, Manhattan	172	322	.534
Roberson, Cornell	117	224	.522
Ellis, Niagara	133	255	.522

O'Shea, Alabama	112	218	.514
Russell, San Francisco	246	480	.513
Choice, Indiana	148	290	.510

FREE THROW PERCENTAGE

PLAYER	FTM	FTA	PCT.
Von Weyhe, Rhode Island	180	208	.865
Murdock, Wake Forest	203	237	.857
Molodet, N. Carolina St.	167	196	.852
Miani, Miami (Fla.)	139	166	.837
McCarty, Virginia	163	196	.832
Petcavich, G. Wash.	138	166	.831
Gaudin, Loyola (La.)	130	157	.828
Plump, Butler	94	114	.825
Downs, Texas	246	290	.823
Forte, Columbia	114	139	.820

1955–56 TEAM LEADERS

SCORING OFFENSE

SCHOOL	PTS.	AVG.
Morehead St.	2782	95.9
Marshall	2145	93.3
Illinois	1996	90.7
Furman	2492	89.0
Memphis St.	2385	88.3

SCORING DEFENSE

SCHOOL	PTS.	AVG.
San Francisco	1514	52.2
Oklahoma A&M	1428	52.9
New Mexico A&M	1358	59.0
Tulsa	1537	59.1
San Jose St.	1485	59.4

FIELD GOAL PERCENTAGE

SCHOOL	FGM	FGA	PCT.
George Washington	725	1451	.500
Manhattan	698	1519	.460
DePaul	659	1456	.453
Niagara	739	1653	.447
Wake Forest	777	1754	.443

FREE THROW PERCENTAGE

SCHOOL	FTM	FTA	PCT.
Southern Methodist	701	917	.764
Murray State	590	791	.746
Texas Western	517	698	.741
Illinois	534	725	.737
North Carolina St.	639	869	.735

REBOUNDING

SCHOOL	TOTAL REB.	REB.	PCT.
George Washington	2356	1451	.616
Niagara	2008	1198	.597
San Francisco	2642	1573	.595
St. Louis	2529	1503	.594
Rice	2181	1294	.593

tory over UK in a 23-game stretch of their series from 1943 through 1963.

The Crimson Tide's three defeats—at North Carolina and St. John's and against Notre Dame on a neutral court—were in a span of four games. As incredible as it might seem today, Johnny Dee left Alabama after such a splendid season to coach an amateur team sponsored by the Denver-Chicago Trucking Company. The school wound up failing to participate in the NCAA Tournament for the first time until 1975. Dee later coached at Notre Dame for seven seasons.

Jerry Harper, who set a conference record by averaging 21.5 rebounds per game, garnered 37 points and 26 rebounds for Alabama in its big win over Kentucky. Earlier, he collected 41 points and a school-record 33 rebounds in a 105-71 triumph over Louisiana College.

Alabama's last loss was to Notre Dame (86-80) in the semifinals of the Sugar Bowl Tournament at New Orleans. The Irish defeated Utah, a Top 20 team most of the season, the next evening. The Sugar Bowl was the high point of the campaign for Notre Dame, which absorbed its first losing record (9-15) in 33 years.

Ronnie Shavlik still owns 12 of the top 13 rebounding efforts in North Carolina State history. He cleaned the glass with 25 or more boards six times in his career. His 19.5 rebounds per game average as a senior is still an ACC record. . . . N.C. State, coached by Everett Case, captured its sixth Dixie Classic title in the first seven years of the eight-team event. The original showcase of "Big Four" basketball was considered the No. 1 Christmas holiday tournament in the nation. During the Dixie Classic's heyday, the reams of copy moved nationally prompted Western Union officials to call it "the biggest sporting event in the South." The final year for the Classic was 1960. . . . Case won at least 24 games each of his first 10 seasons with the Wolfpack.

North Carolina ended its streak of at least 10 defeats in six consecutive seasons by compiling an 18-5 record. . . . Clemson lost its first 26 games in ACC regular-season play, a league record, before upending Virginia, 75-73. It was the "toothless" Tigers' only victory in their first 42 meetings against ACC competition.

Ohio State's streak of consecutive non-winning seasons ended at five when the Buckeyes compiled a 16-6 record. They ended a 12-game losing streak to Illinois by outlasting the Illini, 87-84. . . . Ohio State guard Robin Freeman's only sub-20 point game all season (12 against Illinois) cost him the national scoring title in a battle with Furman's Darrell Floyd (33.8 points per game). Freeman, who finished at 32.9, was 34.3 in all contests except the mediocre contests against the Illini. Floyd poured in a national-high 62 points against The Citadel. However, The Citadel's NCAA-record 37-game losing streak was snapped when the Bulldogs defeated Charleston.

In perhaps the biggest upset of the season, Big Ten runner-up Illinois bowed to Northwestern, 83-82, in the closing game of the season for both teams. Northwestern finished with a 2-20 record. . . . Detroit, mired in the midst of a streak of nine straight seasons with more than 10 defeats, lost its first 24 meetings with Notre Dame until beating the Irish, 77-71. Notre Dame also incurred its lone defeat to Loyola of Chicago (71-65) in the first 26 games of their series from 1924 through 1993. . . . DePaul lost 15 consecutive games to Kentucky in their series before edging the visiting Wildcats, 81-79. . . . The Air Force Academy competed in its inaugural season of basketball, compiling an 11-9 record against freshman teams as Bob Beckel led the way with a 28.1-point scoring average.

Wyoming's Joe Capua (51 points vs. Montana), Texas' Raymond Downs (tied with 49 at Baylor), Eastern Kentucky's Jack Adams (49 vs. Union) and George Washington's Joe Holup (49 vs. Furman) set school single-game scoring records. Downs, a 78.5 percent career free-throw shooter, missed three foul shots in the final seconds of the record-tying outburst, any one of which would have put him at the 50-point plateau. Holup had set GWU's standard the previous week with a 47-point spree against Richmond.

Ohio State's Freeman, Morehead State's Dan Swartz (28.6), Alabama's Harper (27.3), Texas' Downs (26.4), Toledo's Jim Ray (25.6), Louisville's Charlie Tyra (23.8) and Cornell's Chuck Rolles (23) set school records for highest scoring average in a single season.

George Washington, coached by Bill Reinhart, led the nation's teams in field-goal shooting for the third consecutive season as Holup finished among the top two individuals in that category for the third straight year. He was eighth as a freshman in 1952-53. Holup also established a Southern Conference single-season standard by averaging 23.2 rebounds per game. . . . Marshall's Charlie Slack, 6-5, finished his career as the only major-college player to average more than 22 rebounds per game in three consecutive seasons. Marshall became the first major college to have at least three players average more than 20 points per game—Slack (22.5), Cebe Price (21.2) and Paul Underwood (20.2). . . . Al Inniss of St. Francis (N.Y.) set an NIT and Madison Square Garden college record with 37 rebounds in an NIT first-round game vs. Lafayette.

Louisville's Charlie Tyra (38 at Canisius), Kentucky's Bob Burrow (34 in a loss to Temple), Yale's Ed Robinson (32 vs. Harvard), Bradley's Barney Cable (28 at Canisius) and Texas Tech's Jim Reed (27 vs. Eastern New Mexico and Texas) set school single-game rebounding records.

The Philadelphia Big Five—an unsanctioned alliance including La Salle, Penn, St. Joseph's, Temple and Villanova—began annual round-robin competition at The Palestra. Villanova is the only one of the five schools to fail to rank among the top 10 nationally in winning percentage in a decade since the start of the Big Five—La Salle (4th in '50s), St. Joseph's (7th in '60s), Penn (3rd in '70s) and Temple (5th in '80s). Villanova's highest finish in a decade was 15th in the '60s.

Norm Stewart, finishing 15th in the nation in scoring, averaged 24.1 points per game for Missouri. He would later become his alma mater's all-time winningest coach. . . . Oklahoma lost 14 consecutive games to Kansas State in their series until nipping the Wildcats, 67-64. . . . Texas posted its lone victory over Oklahoma A&M (59-56) in a 15-game stretch of their series from 1945 through 1964. . . . Tennessee Tech, coached by John Oldham, tied for the Ohio Valley Conference regular-season title in its initial season at the major-college level. . . . Boston College bowed to Brandeis (90-64) and LeMoyne (92-76) for the fourth consecutive season. . . . St. Bonaventure lost its last five games to finish with its only losing record (11-12) in a 37-year span from 1947-48 through 1983-84.

UCLA had a string of outstanding front-courters during coach John Wooden's career. Sur-

1955-56 UNDEFEATED TEAM: SAN FRANCISCO (29-0)

COACH: PHIL WOOLPERT

USF	OPPONENT	USF'S HIGH SCORER	USF	OPPONENT	USF'S HIGH SCORER
70	Chico State 39	Russell 15	79	Fresno State 46	Russell 23
58	Southern California 42	Russell 24	76	at San Jose State 52	Russell 21
72	San Francisco State 47	Russell 20	76	at St. Mary's 63	Russell 28
65	Marquette* 58	Russell 16	80	at Santa Clara 44	Russell 29
82	at DePaul 59	Jones 23	87	Pacific 49	Russell 28
75	at Wichita 65	Russell 17	68	at Pepperdine 40	Boldt 14
61	at Loyola of New Orleans 43	Russell 20	65	at Loyola of Los Angeles 48	Russell 24
79	La Salle* 62	Russell 26	82	St. Mary's 49	Russell 22
67	Holy Cross* 51	Russell 24			
70	UCLA* 53	Russell 17	**NCAA TOURNAMENT**		
62	Pepperdine 51	Russell 20			
74	Santa Clara 56	Farmer 18	72	UCLA* 61	Brown 23
69	at Fresno State 50	Russell 22	92	Utah* 77	Russell 27
33	at California 24	Jones 15	86	Southern Methodist* 68	Farmer 26
67	San Jose State 40	Russell 21	83	Iowa* 71	Russell 26
68	Loyola of Los Angeles 46	Boldt 20			
77	at Pacific 60	Russell 24	*Neutral court games.		

prisingly, the one setting the school record for most rebounds in a single-game was Willie Naulls, who retrieved 28 missed shots against Arizona State. . . . There was a drought of sorts in the Arizona desert. Utah defeated Arizona in back-to-back games by a total of 104 points. A 119-45 setback to the Utes is the most lopsided defeat in Arizona history. Meanwhile, Arizona State also suffered its most lopsided loss (113-63 to Texas Tech). . . . Wyoming, after averaging 22 victories annually the previous 10 years, compiled a 7-19 mark to start a streak of nine consecutive losing records. New Mexico defeated Wyoming, 80-71, for the Lobos' lone victory over the Cowboys in their first 16 meetings from 1951 through 1958.

Kansas coach Phog Allen retired after 48 seasons with a 746-264 record. His final varsity squad lost a preseason game to the school's freshman team when Philadelphia native Wilt Chamberlain collected 42 points and 29 rebounds for the frosh. . . . Yale's Howard Hobson, who guided Oregon to a title in the first NCAA Tournament in 1939, retired after a 23-year coaching career with a 400-257 record.

1956 NCAA Tournament

Summary: San Francisco won the national championship by an average of 14 points after winning all but two of its regular-season games by double-digit margins. Marquette, 13-11 that season, came closest to USF in a 65-58 decision on a neutral court in the DePaul Invitational. Unanimous first-team All-America Bill Russell averaged 22.8 points in four tournament games as the Dons won each of them by more than 10 points. Their 86-68 victory over SMU in the national semifinals snapped the Mustangs' school-record 20-game winning streak. K.C. Jones was ineligible for the playoffs because he had played one game two years earlier before an appendectomy ended his season, but USF still became the first undefeated champion in NCAA history (29-0/coached by Phil Woolpert). It remains the winningest season in USF history.

Star Gazing: Temple mighty mites Hal Lear (5-11) and backcourtmate Guy Rodgers (6-0)

combined to score 73.5 percent of the Owls' points in two Final Four games. Lear manufactured 61.5 percent of Temple's offense by scoring 40 points in the Owls' 65-59 victory against Connecticut in the East Regional semifinals. He tallied a tourney-high 48 points in a 90-81 triumph over SMU in the national third-place game.

Biggest Upset: North Carolina State, ranked No. 2 in the nation entering the tourney, was stunned in four overtimes in the first round by Canisius, 79-78.

One and Only: Russell became the only player to grab more than 41 rebounds at a Final Four (50) and more than 21 in a championship game (Final Four-record 27 against Iowa).

Numbers Game: The most rebounds in a playoff game were corralled by Temple's Fred Cohen when he grabbed a school-record 34 caroms in the victory against Connecticut. Cohen grabbed just five rebounds in the Owls' next contest, a 60-58 win over Canisius.

What If: National runner-up Iowa might have been able to give San Francisco more of a frontcourt battle if sixth man Tom Payne didn't miss the tournament because of a leg ailment. Payne was leading the Hawkeyes in scoring and

1956 CHAMPIONSHIP BRACKET

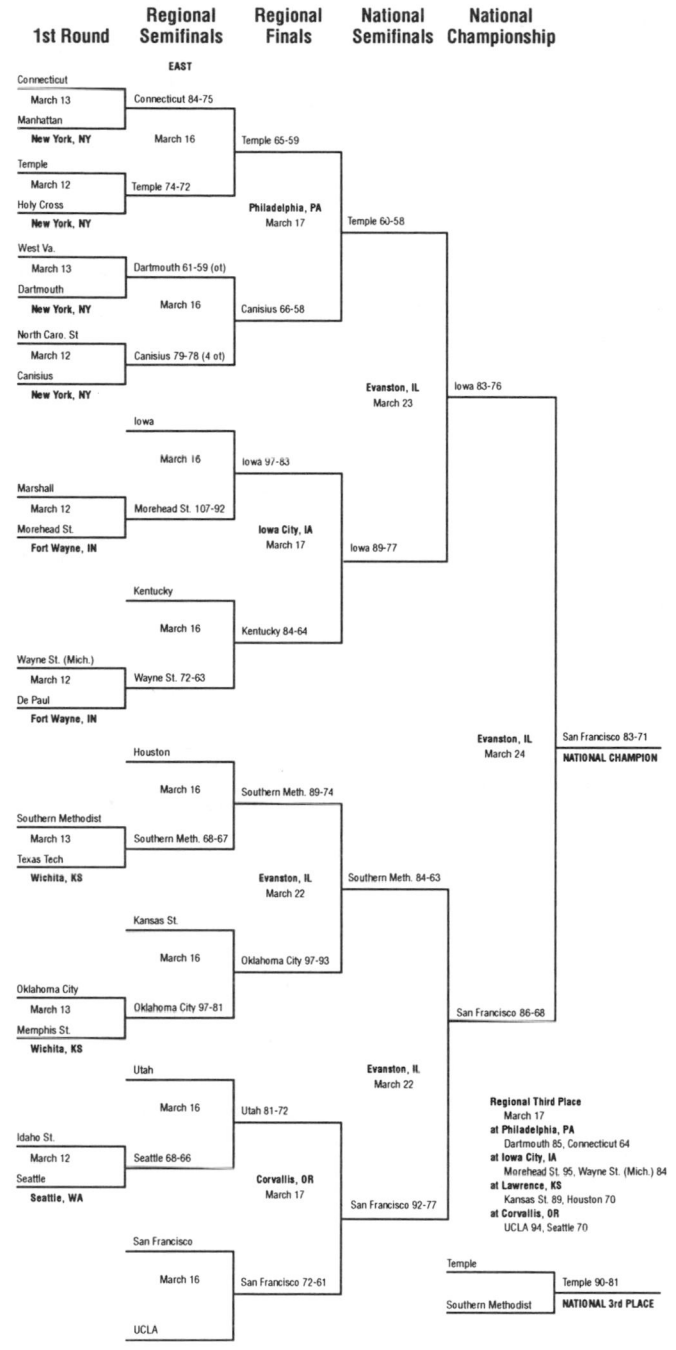

1st Round	Regional Semifinals	Regional Finals	National Semifinals	National Championship

EAST

Connecticut
March 13
Manhattan
New York, NY

Connecticut 84-75
March 16

Temple 65-59

Temple
March 12
Holy Cross
New York, NY

Temple 74-72

Philadelphia, PA
March 17

Temple 60-58

West Va.
March 13
Dartmouth
New York, NY

Dartmouth 61-59 (ot)
March 16

Canisius 66-58

North Caro. St
March 12
Canisius
New York, NY

Canisius 79-78 (4 ot)

Evanston, IL
March 23

Iowa 83-76

Iowa
March 16

Iowa 97-83

Marshall
March 12
Morehead St.
Fort Wayne, IN

Morehead St. 107-92

Iowa City, IA
March 17

Iowa 89-77

Kentucky
March 16

Kentucky 84-64

Wayne St. (Mich.)
March 12
De Paul
Fort Wayne, IN

Wayne St. 72-63

Evanston, IL
March 24

San Francisco 83-71
NATIONAL CHAMPION

Houston
March 16

Southern Meth. 89-74

Southern Methodist
March 13
Texas Tech
Wichita, KS

Southern Meth. 68-67

Evanston, IL
March 22

Southern Meth. 84-63

Kansas St.
March 16

Oklahoma City 97-93

Oklahoma City
March 13
Memphis St.
Wichita, KS

Oklahoma City 97-81

San Francisco 86-68

Utah
March 16

Utah 81-72

Evanston, IL
March 22

Idaho St.
March 12
Seattle
Seattle, WA

Seattle 68-66

Corvallis, OR
March 17

San Francisco 92-77

San Francisco
March 16

San Francisco 72-61

UCLA

Regional Third Place
March 17
at Philadelphia, PA
Dartmouth 85, Connecticut 64
at Iowa City, IA
Morehead St. 95, Wayne St. (Mich.) 84
at Lawrence, KS
Kansas St. 89, Houston 70
at Corvallis, OR
UCLA 94, Seattle 70

Temple

Temple 90-81

Southern Methodist

NATIONAL 3rd PLACE

1955–56 NCAA CHAMPION: SAN FRANCISCO

SEASON STATISTICS OF SAN FRANCISCO REGULARS

PLAYER	POS.	CL.	G.	FG%	FT%	PPG	RPG
Bill Russell	C	Sr.	29	.513	.495	20.6	21.0
K. C. Jones*	G	Sr.	25	.365	.655	9.8	5.2
Hal Perry	G	Sr.	29	.365	.729	9.1	2.0
Carl Boldt	F	Jr.	28	.326	.783	8.6	5.0
Mike Farmer	F	So.	28	.371	.548	8.4	7.8
Gene Brown	G	So.	29	.377	.641	7.1	4.4
Mike Preaseau	F	So.	29	.366	.609	4.1	3.1
Warren Baxter	G	Sr.	26	.301	.667	2.2	0.7
Bill Bush	G	Sr.	22	.208	.625	0.9	0.8
Jack King	F	Jr.	22	.162	.462	0.8	1.0
TEAM TOTALS			29	.388	.604	72.2	54.2

*Ineligible for NCAA Tournament as a fifth-year player.

1956 FINAL FOUR CHAMPIONSHIP GAME

EVANSTON, IL

SAN FRANCISCO (83)	FG	FT-A	PF	PTS.
Boldt	7	2-2	4	16
Farmer	0	0-0	2	0
Preaseau	3	1-2	3	7
Russell	11	4-5	2	26
Nelson	0	0-0	0	0
Perry	6	2-2	2	14
Brown	6	4-4	0	16
Baxter	2	0-0	0	4
TOTALS	35	13-15	13	83

FG%: .402. FT%: .867. Rebounds: 60 (Russell 27).

IOWA (71)	FG	FT-A	PF	PTS.
Cain	7	3-4	1	17
Schoof	5	4-4	3	14
Logan	5	2-2	3	12
George	0	0-0	0	0
Scheuerman	4	3-4	2	11
Seaberg	5	7-10	1	17
Martel	0	0-0	0	0
McConnell	0	0-0	0	0
TOTALS	26	19-24	10	71

FG%: .325. FT%: .792. Rebounds: 48 (Logan 15).
Halftime: San Francisco 38-33.

NATIONAL SEMIFINALS

IOWA (83): Cain 8 4 20, Schoof 5 8 18, Logan 13 10 36, Seaberg 1 0 2, Scheuerman 1 2 4, Martel 1 1 3. Team 29 25 83.

TEMPLE (76): Reinfeld 1 0 2, Norman 1 0 2, Fleming 2 0 4, Cohen 3 0 6, Van Patton 1 2 4, Rodgers 12 4 28, Lear 15 2 32. Team 35 6 76.

Halftime: Iowa 39-36.

SAN FRANCISCO (86): Boldt 3 1 7, Farmer 11 4 26, Preaseau 1 0 2, King 0 0 0, Russell 8 1 17, Perry 6 2 14, Brown 5 2 12, Baxter 4 0 8. Team 38 10 86.

SOUTHERN METHODIST (68): Showalter 4 0 8, Krog 3 0 6, McGregor 1 1 3, Krebs 10 4 24, Miller 1 0 2, Miller 1 9 11, Morris 4 2 10, Herrscher 1 2 4. Team 25 18 68.

Halftime: San Francisco 44-32.

ALL-TOURNAMENT TEAM

Carl Cain, F, Sr., Iowa (39 points, 27 rebounds in final two games)
*Hal Lear, G, Sr., Temple (80 points)
Bill Logan, C, Sr., Iowa (48 points, 23 rebounds)
Hal Perry, G, Sr., San Francisco (28 points)
Bill Russell, C, Sr., San Francisco (43 points, 50 rebounds)

*Named Most Outstanding Player.

rebounding at the end of the first semester the next season as a junior when he was declared academically ineligible. Incidentally, Payne is the father of Michael Payne, a star for Iowa in the early 1980s.

Putting Things in Perspective: Iowa lost four consecutive games and five of six before reeling off 17 straight victories until bowing to San Francisco in the NCAA final, 83-71. Each of the Hawkeyes' starters compiled double-figure scoring averages as they became known as the "Fabulous Five"—Carl Cain (15.8 ppg), Bill Logan (17.7), Sharm Scheuerman (10.1), Bill Schoof (10.8) and Bill Seaberg (13.9). They were the only set of starters to achieve that double-digit distinction and reach the NCAA championship game until 1960 NCAA kingpin Ohio State.

Scoring Leader: Hal Lear, Temple (160 points, 32 ppg; Kentucky's Bob Burrow also averaged 32 ppg).

1956-57

AT A GLANCE

NCAA Champion: North Carolina (32-0; coached by Frank McGuire; won ACC title by five games with a 14-0 record).

NIT Champion: Bradley (22-7; coached by Chuck Orsborn; finished in second place in the Missouri Valley with a 9-5 record, which was three games behind St. Louis).

New Rules: The free-throw lane is increased from six feet to 12 feet. . . . On the lineup for a free throw, the two spaces adjacent to the end line must be occupied by opponents of the free thrower. Previously, one space was marked "H" for a home team player to occupy, and across the lane the first space was marked "V" for a visiting team player to stand in. . . . Grasping the goal is now classified as a technical foul under unsportsmanlike tactics.

NCAA Probation: Auburn, Florida, Louisville, North Carolina State, Ohio State, Southern Cal, Texas A&M, UCLA, Washington.

NCAA Consensus First-Team All-Americans: Wilt Chamberlain, C, Soph., Kansas; Chet Forte, G, Sr., Columbia; Rod Hundley, G-F, Sr., West Virginia; Jim Krebs, C, Sr., Southern Methodist; Lennie Rosenbluth, F, Sr., North Carolina; Charlie Tyra, C, Sr., Louisville.

National Player of the Year: Chet Forte (28.9 ppg, 4.5 rpg, 85.2 FT%).

National Coach of the Year: Frank McGuire, North Carolina (27-0/UPI).

Wilt Chamberlain's coming-out party at Kansas was an immense success as he poured in a school-record 52 points against Northwestern. It is the only existing single-game scoring record achieved in a varsity debut. Chamberlain scored many of the points in his inaugural against fellow sophomore Joe Ruklick. They would later be NBA teammates after becoming the first two draft choices for the Philadelphia Warriors in 1959. Ruklick averaged only 3.5 points per game in his three-year career as Chamberlain's backup, but supplied one of the most worthy yet long-forgotten assists in hoops history. Ruklick fed Wilt a pass in the closing seconds of a memorable March 1, 1962, game in Hershey, Pa., that resulted in Chamberlain scoring his 99th and 100th points of the evening.

Chamberlain, who averaged 29.6 points per game in his initial collegiate campaign, would have had a good chance at leading the nation in scoring except for three contests against Iowa State, which limited him to 16 points per game en route to a .500 league record (6-6). He set a Big Eight Conference record by averaging 18.7 rebounds per contest.

South Carolina's Grady Wallace became the only ACC player to ever lead the nation in scoring (31.2 ppg). It was the fifth consecutive season the scoring title remained in the Palmetto State. Wallace's predecessors were Furman's Frank Selvy and Darell Floyd. Oddly, none of the three were South Carolina natives. Selvy and Wallace were from Kentucky while Floyd was from North Carolina.

The top eight scorers in the country were separated by fewer than 3 1/2 points. The national

West Virginia All-American guard-forward Hot Rod Hundley.

runner-up in scoring was Mississippi's Joe Gibbon (30), who later pitched in the majors. A couple of other prominent hoopsters to end up in the majors were Ohio State's Frank Howard and Morehead State's Steve Hamilton. Howard was one of the nation's premier rebounders with 15.3 boards per game, including a school-record 32 against Brigham Young. Hamilton led the Eagles in scoring and rebounding. Hamilton became the only athlete to appear in the NCAA Tournament before playing in a World Series (New York Yankees in 1963 and 1964) and an NBA Finals (Minneapolis Lakers rookie in 1959 when they were swept by the Boston Celtics).

Hamilton's boardwork helped Morehead State set an NCAA single-season record for rebounding margin with an average of 25 more caroms per game than its opponents. He set a school single-game standard by retrieving 38 missed shots against Florida State.

Miami of Ohio's Wayne Embry grabbed a school-record 34 rebounds in each of back-to-back games against Eastern Kentucky and Kent State. Niagara's Alex Ellis hauled down a school-record 31 rebounds in two games separated by 10 days (vs. Villanova and Kent State). NYU's Cal Ramsey (34 vs. Boston College), Cincinnati's Connie Dierking (33 vs. Loyola of New Orleans) and San Jose State's Marv Branstrom (28 at Arizona State) also established school single-game rebounding standards.

Illinois, coached by Harry Combes, ended San Francisco's 60-game winning streak, 62-33. The Illini, however, finished out of the final wire-service Top 20 polls for the first time in seven years and posted a non-winning Big Ten record (7-7) for the first time since 1944. . . . Michigan, coached by Bill Perigo, compiled a 13-9 overall record to snap its streak of seven consecutive non-winning seasons. The Wolverines, 8-6 in the Big Ten, finished ahead of Illinois in the conference race for just the second time in 19 years. They posted their lone victory (87-86) over Indiana in a 17-game stretch of their series from 1951 to 1962.

Columbia's 5-9 Chet Forte became the first Ivy League player to score more than 400 points in a conference campaign by pouring in 403 points in 14 games (28.8 per league contest). . . . Harvard (12-9 mark under coach Floyd Wilson) notched a double-digit victory total for the first time in 10 years. Bucknell compiled a 16-8 record under coach Benton Kribbs to end its streak of nine consecutive losing seasons. . . . St. Joseph's (17-7) posted its fewest victories in Jack Ramsay's 11 years as coach of the Hawks from 1955-56 through 1965-66. . . . Canisius (22-6/coached by Joseph Curran) had its winningest season in school history.

West Virginia's Hot Rod Hundley (54 points vs. Furman) and Pitt's Don Hennon (45 at Duke) set school single-game scoring records. Hundley's output tied Wallace (vs. Georgia) for the highest single-game outburst during the season. . . . Mississippi State's Jim Ashmore (28.3) and Bailey Howell (25.9) became the first set of teammates in

1956-57 FINAL NATIONAL POLLS

AP	UPI	SCHOOL (RECORD)	HEAD COACH
1	1	North Carolina (32-0)	Frank McGuire
2	2	Kansas (24-3)	Dick Harp
3	3	Kentucky (23-5)	Adolph Rupp
4	4	SMU (22-4)	Doc Hayes
5	5	Seattle (24-3)	John Castellani
6	8	Louisville (21-5)	Peck Hickman
7	11	West Virginia (25-5)	Fred Schaus
8	16	Vanderbilt (17-5)	Bob Polk
9	16	Oklahoma City (19-9)	Abe Lemons
10	10	St. Louis (19-9)	Eddie Hickey
11	7	Michigan State (16-10)	Forddy Anderson
12	–	Memphis State (24-6)	Bob Vanatta
13	6	California (21-5)	Pete Newell
14	9	UCLA (22-4)	John Wooden
15	–	Mississippi State (17-8)	Babe McCarthy
16	–	Idaho State (25-4)	John Grayson
17	19	Notre Dame (20-8)	John Jordan
18	–	Wake Forest (19-9)	Murray Greason
19	–	Canisius (22-6)	Joe Curran
19	–	Oklahoma A&M (17-9)	Hank Iba
–	12	Dayton (19-9)	Tom Blackburn
–	13	Bradley (22-7)	Chuck Orsborn
–	14	Brigham Young (19-9)	Stan Watts
–	15	Indiana (14-8)	Branch McCracken
–	16	Xavier (20-8)	Ned Wulk
–	20	Kansas State (15-8)	Tex Winter

NCAA history to average more than 25 points per game in a single season. Howell (37) and Ashmore (24) combined for 61 points in MSU's first victory over Kentucky in 33 years (89-81) as the Wildcats missed their first 13 field-goal attempts. Howell grabbed a school-record 34 rebounds in a game against LSU.

Wake Forest teammates Ernie Wiggins and Jackie Murdock, deadlocked for the national lead in free-throw shooting entering the postseason, finished 1-2 in the country. Wiggins won by hitting all four of his tournament tosses. . . . Clemson lost 15 consecutive games in its series with N.C. State until outlasting the Wolfpack in overtime, 96-94. . . . North Carolina's Lennie Rosenbluth scored an ACC Tournament-record 45 points in a quarterfinal victory over Clemson. He led the NCAA champion-to-be Tar Heels in scoring in 14 of their last 15 outings. . . . South Carolina's Wallace, Columbia's Forte (28.9 ppg), Mississippi State's Ashmore (28.3) and North Carolina's Rosenbluth (28) set school records for highest scoring average in a single season.

Georgia Tech (18-8 under coach Whack Hyder) won its last five games to end a streak of 11 consecutive seasons with more than 10 defeats. . . . Detroit and Oklahoma State competed in the

Missouri Valley Conference for the final season. . . . Creighton (15-6) compiled its first winning record in 10 years. . . . Idaho State made its lone appearance in the Top 20 of a final wire-service poll. . . . Seattle coach John Castellani was hung in effigy on the school's campus after the Elgin Baylor-led Chieftains, seeded No. 1 in the NIT, lost its postseason opener to St. Bonaventure, 85-68.

In one of the strangest games in NIT history, Bradley erased a 21-point deficit to defeat Xavier, 116-81, in the quarterfinals. The Braves outscored Xavier, 72-29, in the second half, setting NIT and Madison Square Garden college records for most points in a half. . . . Bradley wound up winning the NIT with an 84-83 triumph over Memphis State College in the championship game. Memphis State, competing in just its second season as a major college, defeated Mississippi State twice, Western Kentucky twice and highly-ranked Louisville. . . . Mississippi State lost 17 consecutive contests to Kentucky in their series until defeating the Wildcats, 89-81.

1957 NCAA Tournament

Summary: A championship game frequently misconstrued as an enormous upset was North Carolina's 54-53 triple-overtime victory against Wilt Chamberlain-led Kansas. After all, Carolina was undefeated that season (32-0), winning 22 games by at least nine points, and the Tar Heels' top three scorers wound up playing in the NBA albeit briefly—forwards Lennie Rosenbluth and Pete Brennan and guard Tommy Kearns. Junior center Joe Quigg sank two free throws with six

1956–57 INDIVIDUAL LEADERS

SCORING

PLAYER	PTS.	AVG.
Wallace, South Carolina	906	31.2
Gibbon, Mississippi	631	30.0
Baylor, Seattle	743	29.7
Chamberlain, Kansas	800	29.6
Forte, Columbia	694	28.9
Ashmore, Mississippi St.	708	28.3
Rosenbluth, North Carolina	895	28.0
Ebben, Detroit	724	27.8
Howell, Mississippi St.	647	25.9
Dees, Indiana	550	25.0

REBOUNDING

PLAYER	REB.	PCT.
Baylor, Seattle	508	.235
Ellis, Niagara	502	.234

Tyra, Louisville	520	.229
Chamberlain, Kansas	510	.227
Guarilia, G. Wash.	447	.218
Howell, Mississippi St.	492	.212
Ramsey, New York	372	.202
Howard, Ohio State	336	.201
Freeman, Xavier	526	.195
Hamilton, Morehead St.	543	.194

FIELD GOAL PERCENTAGE

PLAYER	FGM	FGA	PCT.
Howell, Mississippi St.	217	382	.568
Inniss, St. Francis (NY)	189	337	.561
Roth, Muhlenberg	162	298	.544
Holtsma, William & Mary	117	216	.542
Ellis, Niagara	209	389	.537
Crosthwaite, Western Ky.	185	349	.530
Francis, Dartmouth	127	243	.523

Downs, Texas	155	298	.520
Richter, N.C. St.	136	262	.519
Nymeyer, Arizona	153	298	.513
Embry, Miami (Ohio)	224	437	.513

FREE THROW PERCENTAGE

PLAYER	FTM	FTA	PCT.
Wiggins, Wake Forest	93	108	.877
Murdock, Wake Forest	161	184	.875
Seitz, N.C. St.	95	109	.872
Ricketts, Duquesne	150	174	.862
Plump, Butler	160	186	.860
Forte, Columbia	224	263	.852
Novalesi, St. Francis (Pa.)	90	106	.849
Simmons, Idaho	101	119	.849
Steinke, Brigham Young	105	124	.847
Dees, Indiana	176	209	.842

1956–57 TEAM LEADERS

SCORING OFFENSE

SCHOOL	PTS.	AVG.
Connecticut	2183	87.3
Ohio	2004	87.1
Marshall	2070	86.3
Memphis St.	2562	85.4
Morehead St.	2301	85.2

SCORING DEFENSE

SCHOOL	PTS.	AVG.
Oklahoma A&M	1420	54.6
San Francisco	1560	55.7
California	1484	57.1
Santa Clara	1260	57.3
Kansas	1583	58.6

FIELD GOAL PERCENTAGE

SCHOOL	FGM	FGA	PCT.
Manhattan	679	1489	.456
Seattle	742	1644	.451
Western Kentucky	802	1788	.449
Lafayette	776	1736	.447
Niagara	756	1693	.447

FREE THROW PERCENTAGE

SCHOOL	FTM	FTA	PCT.
Oklahoma A&M	569	752	.757
Auburn	479	648	.739
Tulane	459	622	.738
Wake Forest	610	827	.738
Memphis St.	714	971	.735
Louisville	513	698	.735

REBOUNDING

SCHOOL	TOT. REB.	REB.	PCT.
Morehead St.	2796	1735	.621
Seattle	2165	1307	.604
Dartmouth	2381	1414	.594
Louisville	2270	1327	.585
Dayton	2871	1676	.584

1956-57 UNDEFEATED TEAM: NORTH CAROLINA (32-0)

COACH: FRANK MCGUIRE

UNC	OPPONENT		UNC'S HIGH SCORER	UNC	OPPONENT		UNC'S HIGH SCORER
94	Furman	66	Rosenbluth 47	86	North Carolina State	57	Rosenbluth 28
94	Clemson*	75	Brennan 28	75	South Carolina	62	Brennan 26
82	George Washington	55	Rosenbluth 27	69	at Wake Forest	64	Rosenbluth 30
90	at South Carolina	86	Kearns 29	86	at Duke	72	Rosenbluth 40
70	Maryland	61	Rosenbluth 26				
64	at New York University	59	Cunningham 16	**ACC TOURNAMENT**			
89	Dartmouth*	61	Rosenbluth 30	81	Clemson*	61	Rosenbluth 45
83	Holy Cross*	70	Rosenbluth 23	61	Wake Forest*	59	Rosenbluth 23
97	Utah*	76	Rosenbluth 36	95	South Carolina*	75	Rosenbluth 38
87	Duke*	71	Rosenbluth 32				
63	Wake Forest*	55	Rosenbluth 18	**NCAA TOURNAMENT**			
71	at William & Mary	61	Brennan 20	90	Yale*	74	Rosenbluth 29
86	Clemson	54	Rosenbluth 34	87	Canisius*	75	Rosenbluth 39
102	Virginia	90	Rosenbluth 30	67	Syracuse*	58	Rosenbluth 23
83	at North Carolina St.	57	Rosenbluth 29	74	Michigan State* (3OT)	70	Rosenbluth 31
77	at Western Carolina	59	Rosenbluth 26	54	Kansas* (3OT)	53	Rosenbluth 20
65	at Maryland (2OT)	61	Rosenbluth 25	*Neutral court games.			
75	Duke	73	Rosenbluth 35				
68	at Virginia	59	Rosenbluth 23				
72	Wake Forest	69	Rosenbluth 24				

seconds remaining in the third overtime to tie the score and provide the decisive point as North Carolina nipped Kansas, 54-53. Carolina won the national championship by an average of 8.4 points after winning five of its last 11 games against ACC competition by five points or less. The Tar Heels didn't outscore their opponents in both halves of any of their five playoff victories, but Rosenbluth bailed them out by scoring at least 20 points in every game. Rosenbluth was Carolina's leading scorer in 27 of their 32 contests, although the Tar Heels won the triple-overtime final after he fouled out with 1:45 remaining in regulation.

Outcome for Defending Champion: San Francisco (22-7) was clobbered by Kansas, 80-56, in the national semifinals. The Dons won their first five games of the season before losing five of their next six.

Star Gazing: Carolina coach Frank McGuire became the first coach to take two different schools to the NCAA championship game. He guided St. John's to a second-place finish in 1952. In a psychological ploy, McGuire let Kearns (5-11) jump center at the start of the final against Chamberlain (7-0).

Biggest Upset: Kentucky, ranked No. 3 entering the tourney, blew a 12-point halftime lead at home in an 80-68 setback to Michigan State in the

Mideast Regional final. It was only the Wildcats' fifth defeat on their homecourt since 1943.

One and Only: North Carolina, with all of its starters coming from the New York City area, became the only school to play in back-to-back triple-overtime games in the playoffs. The lead in the Tar Heels' 74-70 triumph over Michigan State in the national semifinals changed hands 31 times and the score was tied on 21 occasions. The Spartans' Jack Quiggle made a halfcourt shot that came just after the final buzzer in regulation. Teammate Johnny Green missed a free throw with 11 seconds remaining in the first overtime that would have sealed the verdict for MSU. Brennan grabbed Green's miss. Instead of tossing the ball out to a guard as Brennan normally would do, he dribbled downcourt and hit a game-tying jumper just to the right of the foul line at the buzzer.

Numbers Game: Dick Harp became the only individual to play in an NCAA Tournament championship game (with Kansas in 1940 when the Jayhawks lost to Indiana) and later coach his alma mater to a final (KU lost to North Carolina). . . . Michigan State outrebounded San Francisco (47-26) yet lost the national third-place game to USF, 67-60. The Spartans reached the Final Four despite losing five of six games in a mid-season swoon. . . . Oklahoma City became the first school to participate in six consecutive NCAA playoffs. .

. . Rosenbluth fired in a tourney-high 39 points in North Carolina's 87-75 victory over Canisius in the East Regional semifinals. His 42 field-goal attempts (hit 11) in the national semifinals against Michigan State is a Final Four record. . . . Lafayette, coached by George Davidson, made its lone NCAA Tournament appearance. . . . Syracuse, coached by Marc Guley, participated in the NCAA playoffs for the only time in the first 27 years of the event.

Putting Things in Perspective: Kansas was fortunate SMU shot just 32.1 percent from the floor in their Midwest Regional opener at Dallas.

Long before Georgetown tried to minimize distractions, the Jayhawks stayed 30 miles out of town, but some bigots still burned a cross in a yard across from their lodging quarters. And narrow-minded fans at the game punctuated the contest with racial slurs.

Scoring Leader: Lennie Rosenbluth, North Carolina (140 points, 28 ppg).

Highest Scoring Average: Wilt Chamberlain, Kansas (121 points, 30.25 ppg).

Rebounding Leader: Johnny Green, Michigan State (77 rebounds, 19.3 rpg).

1956–57 NCAA CHAMPION: N. CAROLINA

SEASON STATISTICS OF NORTH CAROLINA REGULARS

PLAYER	POS.	CL.	G.	FG%	FT%	PPG	RPG
Lennie Rosenbluth	F	Sr.	32	.483	.758	28.0	8.8
Pete Brennan	F	Jr.	32	.394	.706	14.7	10.4
Tommy Kearns	G	Jr.	32	.434	.711	12.8	3.1
Joe Quigg	C	Jr.	31	.434	.719	10.3	8.6
Bob Cunningham	G	Jr.	32	.393	.598	7.2	6.7
Tony Radovich	G	Sr.	16	.525	.769	3.9	1.8
Bill Hathaway	C	So.	15	.333	.417	2.8	5.0
Stan Groll	G	So.	12	.370	.556	2.1	1.5
Bob Young	C	Sr.	15	.256	.538	1.9	2.1
Ken Rosemond	G	Jr.	15	.400	.556	1.1	0.6
Danny Lotz	F	So.	24	.350	.391	1.0	1.6
TEAM TOTALS			32	.431	.701	79.3	46.7

1957 FINAL FOUR CHAMPIONSHIP GAME

KANSAS CITY, MO

NORTH CAROLINA (54)	FG-A	FT-A	REB.	PF	PTS.
Rosenbluth	8-15	4-4	5	5	20
Cunningham	0-3	0-1	5	4	0
Brennan	4-8	3-7	11	3	11
Kearns	4-8	3-7	1	4	11
Quigg	4-10	2-3	9	4	10
Lotz	0-0	0-0	2	0	0
Young	1-1	0-0	3	1	2
Team			6		
TOTALS	**21-45**	**12-22**	**42**	**21**	**54**

FG%: .467. FT%: .545.

KANSAS (53)	FG-A	FT-A	REB.	PF	PTS.
Chamberlain	6-13	11-16	14	3	23
King	3-12	5-6	4	4	11
Elstun	4-12	3-6	4	2	11
Parker	2-4	0-0	0	0	4
Loneski	0-5	2-3	3	2	2
L. Johnson	0-1	2-2	0	1	2
Billings	0-0	0-0	0	2	0
Team			3		
TOTALS	**15-47**	**23-33**	**28**	**14**	**53**

FG%: .319. FT%: .697.
Halftime: North Carolina 29-22. **Regulation:** Tied 46-46. **First Overtime:** Tied 48-48. **Second Overtime:** Tied 48-48.

NATIONAL SEMIFINALS

NORTH CAROLINA (74): Rosenbluth 11-42 7-9 29, Cunningham 9-18 3-5 21, Brennan 6-16 2-4 14, Kearns 1-8 4-5 6, Quigg 0-1 2-3 2, Lotz 0-1 0-0 0, Young 1-3 0-1 2, Searcy 0-0 0-0 0. Team 28-89 (.315) 18-27 (.667) 74.

MICHIGAN STATE (70): Quiggle 6-21 8-10 20, Green 4-12 3-6 11, Ferguson 4-8 2-3 10, Hedden 4-20 6-7 14, Wilson 0-3 2-2 2, Anderg 2-7 3-6 7, Bencie 1-6 0-0 2, Scott 2-3 0-2 4. Team 23-80 (.288) 24-36 (.667) 70.

Halftime: Tied 29-29. **Regulation:** Tied 58-58. **First Overtime:** Tied 64-64. **Second Overtime:** Tied 66-66.

KANSAS (80): M. King 6-8 1-1 13, Elstun 8-12 0-0 16, Chamberlain 12-22 8-11 32, Parker 1-1 0-0 2, Loneski 2-6 3-4 7, L. Johnson 1-3 0-0 2, Billings 0-1 0-0 0, Hollinger 1-1 0-1 2, Dater 1-1 0-0 2, Green 1-1 0-0 2, Kindred 0-0 0-2 0, M. Johnson 1-1 0-0 2. Team 34-57 (.597) 12-19 (.632) 80.

SAN FRANCISCO (56): Day 3-14 3-8 9, Dunbar 2-8 0-0 4, Brown 5-14 0-0 10, Farmer 6-15 2-2 14, Preaseau 5-8 2-2 12, Mallen 0-2 0-0 0, Lillevand 1-3 0-0 2, Koljian 0-1 3-4 3, J. King 0-3 0-0 0, Russell 0-0 0-0 0, Radanovich 0-1 0-0 0, Mancasola 1-2 0-0 2. Team 23-71 (.324) 10-16 (.625) 56.

Halftime: Kansas 38-34.

ALL-TOURNAMENT TEAM

Pete Brennan, F, Jr., North Carolina (25 points, 28 rebounds in final two games)
Gene Brown, G, Jr., San Francisco (32 points, nine rebounds)
*Wilt Chamberlain, C, Soph., Kansas (55 points, 25 rebounds)
Johnny Green, C, Soph., Michigan State (20 points, 32 rebounds)
Lennie Rosenbluth, F, Sr., North Carolina (49 points, eight rebounds)

*Named Most Outstanding Player.

1957 CHAMPIONSHIP BRACKET

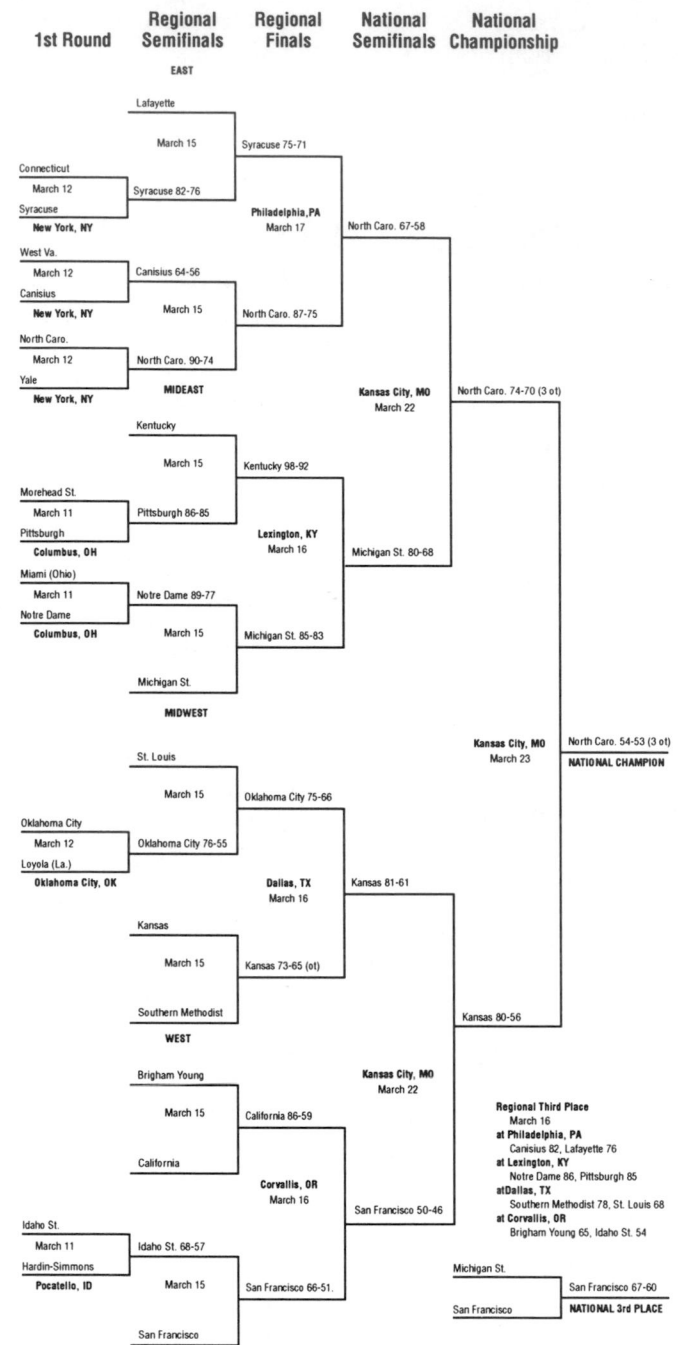

	Regional Semifinals	Regional Finals	National Semifinals	National Championship

1st Round | Regional Semifinals | Regional Finals | National Semifinals | National Championship

EAST

Lafayette

March 15 — Syracuse 75-71

Connecticut
March 12
Syracuse — Syracuse 82-76
New York, NY

Philadelphia, PA
March 17 — North Caro. 67-58

West Va.
March 12 — Canisius 64-56
Canisius
New York, NY

March 15 — North Caro. 87-75

North Caro.
March 12 — North Caro. 90-74
Yale
New York, NY

MIDEAST

Kansas City, MO
March 22 — North Caro. 74-70 (3 ot)

Kentucky
March 15 — Kentucky 98-92

Morehead St.
March 11
Pittsburgh — Pittsburgh 86-85
Columbus, OH

Lexington, KY
March 16

Miami (Ohio)
March 11
Notre Dame — Notre Dame 89-77
Columbus, OH

March 15 — Michigan St. 85-83

Michigan St.

MIDWEST

St. Louis
March 15 — Oklahoma City 75-66

Oklahoma City
March 12
Loyola (La.) — Oklahoma City 76-55
Oklahoma City, OK

Dallas, TX
March 16 — Kansas 81-61

Kansas
March 15 — Kansas 73-65 (ot)

Southern Methodist

WEST

Brigham Young
March 15 — California 86-59

California

Corvallis, OR
March 16 — San Francisco 50-46

Idaho St.
March 11
Hardin-Simmons — Idaho St. 68-57
Pocatello, ID

March 15 — San Francisco 66-51.

San Francisco

Kansas City, MO
March 22 — Kansas 80-56

Kansas City, MO
March 23 — North Caro. 54-53 (3 ot) **NATIONAL CHAMPION**

Regional Third Place
March 16
at Philadelphia, PA
Canisius 82, Lafayette 76
at Lexington, KY
Notre Dame 86, Pittsburgh 85
atDallas, TX
Southern Methodist 78, St. Louis 68
at Corvallis, OR
Brigham Young 65, Idaho St. 54

Michigan St.

San Francisco 67-60

San Francisco

NATIONAL 3rd PLACE

1957-58

AT A GLANCE

NCAA Champion: Kentucky (23-6; coached by Adolph Rupp; won SEC title with a 12-2 record, which was one game ahead of Auburn).

NIT Champion: Xavier (19-11; coached by Jim McCafferty).

New Rules: Offensive goaltending is banned. . . . One free throw for each common foul is taken the first six personal fouls by one team in each half, and the one-and-one is employed thereafter. . . . Uniform numbers "1," "2," and any digit greater than "5" are prohibited.

NCAA Probation: Auburn, Florida, Louisville, Memphis State, Montana State, North Carolina State, UCLA, Washington.

NCAA Consensus First-Team All-Americans: Elgin Baylor, F-C, Jr., Seattle; Bob Boozer, F, Jr., Kansas State; Wilt Chamberlain, C, Jr., Kansas; Don Hennon, G, Jr., Pittsburgh; Oscar Robertson, F, Soph., Cincinnati; Guy Rodgers, G, Sr., Temple.

National Player of the Year: Robertson (35.1 ppg, 15.2 rpg, 57.1 FG%).

National Coach of the Year: Tex Winter, Kansas State (22-5/UPI).

Undergraduates stole the spotlight from seniors. Temple guard Guy Rodgers was the only senior among the six NCAA consensus first-team All-Americans.

The three major-college players to average more than 30 points per game this season—Cincinnati's Oscar Robertson (35.1), Seattle's Elgin Baylor (32.5) and Kansas' Wilt Chamberlain (30.1)—each went on to become an All-NBA selection at least 10 times. Baylor finished his college career with an amazing average of more than 50 points and rebounds per game.

Baylor and Robertson each had four games during the year with at least 47 points. Baylor's 60-point uprising against Portland was the highest in the nation. Robertson, Baylor and Chamberlain all averaged more than 15 rebounds per game. Chamberlain set Big Eight Conference records with 36 rebounds against Iowa State (also a school standard) and for scoring average. Robertson is one of only two individuals to be named national player of the year in his first season of varsity competition. The Big O outscored Seton Hall by himself with 56 points in a 118-54 verdict that represents the Pirates' most lopsided defeat in history.

Chamberlain's final college season included one of the most amazing turnarounds in NCAA annals. Nebraska, in the midst of 15 consecutive losing seasons, suffered its most lopsided defeat in school history (margin of 56 points in a 102-46 decision at Kansas) before upsetting the Jayhawks (43-41) four games later in Omaha when backup guard Jim Kubacki hit a 15-foot basket with two seconds remaining. Kubacki, a senior, spent all but the final seven minutes of the game sitting on the bench in street clothes because of a knee

---

HUSKERS AVENGE 56-POINT DEFEAT   Was it a magic potion? The sad-sack Nebraska Cornhuskers, suffering through another losing season, had been walloped by the Kansas Jayhawks four games earlier, 102-46. But playing in front of their home crowd on February 22, 1958, the Huskers upset the Jayhawks, 43-41. Maybe they had something against the state of Kansas—in their next game, they beat up on No. 1-ranked Kansas State, 55-48.

KANSAS (41)	FG	FT-A	PTS.	NEBRASKA (43)	FG	FT-A	PTS.
Chamberlain	7	4-8	18	Arwood	0	0-1	0
Cleland	0	0-0	0	Fitzpatrick	3	1-1	7
Donaghue	4	1-2	9	Harry	1	0-3	2
Hickman	0	0-0	0	Kubacki	1	0-0	2
J. Johnson	1	1-1	3	Reimers	4	6-8	14
Kindred	1	0-0	2	Smidt	1	4-4	6
Loneski	3	3-6	9	Turner	4	4-7	12
Thompson	0	0-0	0	**TOTALS**	**14**	**15-24**	**43**
TOTALS	**16**	**9-17**	**41**				

Halftime: Nebraska 27-21.

injury. When teammate Gary Reimers left the game with leg cramps, Kubacki convinced coach Jerry Bush to let him suit up. Four minutes later, Kubacki entered the game. Nearly three minutes after that, he furnished the fairytale ending. In the Cornhuskers' next outing, they defeated top-ranked Kansas State (55-48), a team that had overwhelmed them by a total of 46 points in two previous matchups.

In Kansas' ensuing contest, the Jayhawks were saddled with their most lopsided defeat in Chamberlain's two-year varsity career when they bowed at Iowa State by six points (48-42). KU's other seven setbacks with Wilt were by two points or in overtime.

Oklahoma, coached by Doyle Parrack, lost its last three games but compiled a 13-10 record to end a streak of six consecutive losing seasons. . . . Indiana, coached by Branch McCracken, entered Big Ten competition with a 1-6 record yet won the conference championship. . . . Drake's Red Murrell (51 points vs. Houston in overtime), Lafayette's Bobby Mantz (47 vs. Wilkes) and Marquette's Mike Moran (44 vs. Creighton/later tied) set school single-game scoring records.

Cincinnati's Robertson, Kansas' Chamberlain, Pittsburgh's Don Hennon (26 ppg) and Fordham's Jim Cunningham (25.1) established school records for highest scoring average in a single season. . . . Furman's Steve Ross (32 vs. Presbyterian), Northwestern's Joe Ruklick (31 vs. Kansas), Auburn's Rex Frederick (27 at SMU), Toledo's Ned Miklovic (27 at Ohio/later tied), Montana's Russ Sheriff (26 vs. Gonzaga) and Mississippi's Ivan Richmann (25 vs. Tulane) set school rebounding records for a single game.

North Carolina's ACC-record 37-game winning streak ended when the Tar Heels lost to West Virginia, 75-64, in the championship game of the Kentucky Invitational. . . . Maryland, coached by Bud Millikan, became the only school outside the state of North Carolina to win the ACC Tournament in the first 17 years of the event (1954 through 1970). . . . Tennessee Tech, coached by John Oldham, captured the Ohio Valley Confer-

1957-58 FINAL NATIONAL POLLS

AP	UPI	SCHOOL (RECORD)	HEAD COACH
1	1	West Virginia (26-2)	Fred Schaus
2	2	Cincinnati (25-3)	George Smith
3	4	Kansas State (22-5)	Tex Winter
4	3	San Francisco (25-2)	Phil Woolpert
5	5	Temple (27-3)	Harry Litwack
6	6	Maryland (22-7)	Bud Millikan
7	8	Kansas (18-5)	Dick Harp
8	7	Notre Dame (24-5)	John Jordan
9	14	Kentucky (23-6)	Adolph Rupp
10	13	Duke (18-7)	Harold Bradley
11	9	Dayton (25-4)	Tom Blackburn
12	10	Indiana (13-11)	Branch McCracken
13	12	North Carolina (19-7)	Frank McGuire
14	11	Bradley (20-7)	Chuck Orsborn
15	–	Mississippi State (20-5)	Babe McCarthy
16	–	Auburn (16-6)	Joel Eaves
17	19	Michigan State (16-6)	Forddy Anderson
18	19	Seattle (24-7)	John Castellani
19	15	Oklahoma State (21-8)	Hank Iba
20	16	N.C. State (18-6)	Everett Case
–	16	Oregon State (20-6)	Slats Gill
–	18	St. Bonaventure (21-5)	Eddie Donovan
–	19	Wyoming (13-14)	Everett Shelton

ence crown just one season after finishing in last place. . . . Tulane, coached by Clifford Wells, suffered its first losing record (8-15) in 13 seasons.

Dartmouth's Rudy LaRusso grabbed an Ivy League-record 32 rebounds in a game against Columbia. . . . Duquesne defeated Villanova nine consecutive times until bowing to the Wildcats, 69-58. . . . Canisius compiled a 2-19 mark just one year after going 22-6. . . . Seton Hall incurred its only losing record (7-19) in a 14-year span from 1950-51 through 1963-64.

Xavier upset the top three seeds on its way to the NIT title—No. 2 Bradley (72-62), No. 3 St. Bonaventure (72-53) and top-seeded Dayton (78-74 in overtime). It was the fifth time in eight seasons that Dayton reached the NIT final and lost. The championship game marked one of only two NIT finals matching two schools from the same state (Indiana-Purdue in 1979 was the other). . . . Air Force (17-6/coached by Bob Spear) notched its winningest season in school history. Dartmouth (22-5/Doggie Julian) tied its school record for most victories in a single season. "The name on your jersey doesn't say Jones or Smith or Johnson," Julian said. "It says Dartmouth! And that's what we're striving for—not individual scoring titles but a win, a team win for Dartmouth!" . . . Wyoming (13-14) became the only school with a losing record ever to finish in the Top 20 of a final wire-service poll (19th in UPI). . . . NYU's Howard Cann ended his 35-year coaching career with a 409-232 record.

1958 NCAA Tournament

Summary: Would Kentucky's storied "Fiddlin' Five," a team equaling the most defeats (six) of any Wildcats squad in the previous 15 seasons, have snared the title if it didn't enjoy a home-state edge throughout the playoffs (Mideast Regional at Lexington and Final Four at Louisville)? Didn't a highly-partisan crowd give them an emotional lift in the national semifinals when they trailed Temple by four points and the Owls had the ball with less than a minute and half remaining? UK benefitted from a sub-par performance by Seattle's Elgin Baylor in the national final, where he went 9 for 32 from the floor. Baylor was named Final Four Most Outstanding Player although the award could have gone to Kentucky's Johnny Cox, who collected 22 points and 13 rebounds in a 61-60 victory over Temple and 24 points and 16 rebounds in an 84-72 triumph over Seattle.

Outcome for Defending Champion: North Carolina (19-7) tied for second place in the ACC after starting center Joe Quigg was sidelined his entire senior season following a leg injury in the team's first big scrimmage. Six of the Tar Heels' defeats were by more than 10 points.

Biggest Upset: West Virginia, ranked No. 1 in the country at the end of the regular season, was upset by Manhattan in the opening round of the East Regional at New York. Jack Powers, the cur-

1957–58 INDIVIDUAL LEADERS

SCORING

PLAYER	PTS.	AVG.
Robertson, Cincinnati	984	35.1
Baylor, Seattle	943	32.5
Chamberlain, Kansas	633	30.1
Howell, Mississippi St.	695	27.8
Murrell, Drake	668	26.7
Coleman, Ky. Wesleyan	639	26.6
Hennon, Pittsburgh	651	26.0
Reed, Oklahoma City	666	25.6
Dees, Indiana	613	25.5
Flora, Washington & Lee	634	25.4

REBOUNDING

PLAYER	REB.	PCT.
Ellis, Niagara	536	.262
Inniss, St. Francis (NY)	477	.248

Baylor, Seattle	559	.235
Chamberlain, Kansas	367	.216
Cincebox, Syracuse	345	.206
McCadney, Fordham	351	.205
Embry, Miami (Ohio)	488	.202
Green, Michigan St.	392	.199
Howell, Mississippi St.	406	.198
Hamilton, Morehead St.	440	.195

FIELD GOAL PERCENTAGE

PLAYER	FGM	FGA	PCT.
Crosthwaite, W. Ky.	202	331	.610
Robertson, Cincinnati	352	617	.571
Brunone, Manhattan	100	178	.562
Goodall, Tulsa	108	194	.557
Greer, Marshall	236	432	.546
Clark, Oklahoma St.	171	317	.539
Mantz, Lafayette	190	354	.537

Aston, St. Francis (Pa.)	120	226	.531
Cunningham, Fordham	176	332	.530
McDonald, G. Wash.	165	314	.525

FREE THROW PERCENTAGE

PLAYER	FTM	FTA	PCT.
Mintz, Davidson	105	119	.882
Myers, Texas Tech	107	123	.870
Clark, Oklahoma St.	160	185	.865
Hobbs, Florida	98	114	.860
Reed, Oklahoma City	206	242	.851
Sidwell, Tennessee Tech	100	118	.847
McCarthy, Notre Dame	132	156	.846
Kennedy, Temple	112	133	.842
Walsh, Detroit	99	118	.839
Adair, Oklahoma St.	97	116	.836
Hennon, Pittsburgh	117	140	.836

1957–58 TEAM LEADERS

SCORING OFFENSE

SCHOOL	PTS.	AVG.
Marshall	2113	88.0
West Virginia	2433	86.9
Cincinnati	2422	86.5
Kentucky Wesleyan	1993	83.0
Notre Dame	2374	81.9

SCORING DEFENSE

SCHOOL	PTS.	AVG.
San Francisco	1363	50.5
Oklahoma St.	1500	51.7
Kansas	1273	55.3
Providence	1332	55.5
Oregon St.	1449	55.7

FIELD GOAL PERCENTAGE

SCHOOL	FGM	FGA	PCT.
Fordham	693	1440	.481
Cincinnati	910	1895	.480
Marshall	817	1740	.470
Seattle	938	2014	.466
Oklahoma St.	620	1346	.461

FREE THROW PERCENTAGE

SCHOOL	FTM	FTA	PCT.
Oklahoma St.	488	617	.791
Marshall	479	608	.788
Oklahoma City	503	667	.754
Stanford	448	603	.743
Kentucky	502	680	.738

REBOUNDING

SCHOOL	TOTAL REB.	REB.	PCT.
Manhattan	2430	1437	.591
Morehead St.	2262	1331	.588
Seattle	2380	1400	.588
Texas Christian	2162	1253	.580
Muhlenberg	2143	1239	.578

rent executive director of the NIT, collected 29 points and 15 rebounds to carry Manhattan (16-10) to an 89-84 victory. Jerry West scored just 10 points in his first NCAA Tournament game for West Virginia, which finished the season with the best winning percentage in school history (26-2, .929).

One and Only: Cox, a 6-4 forward, is the shortest player to lead an NCAA Tournament champion in rebounding (12.6 per game) since the NCAA began keeping rebounding statistics in the early 1950s.

Numbers Game: Arkansas' lone tournament appearance in a 35-year span from 1942 through 1976 was a disaster when the Razorbacks became the only school ever to lose back-to-back games by at least 25 points in the same tourney. They shot 26.5 percent from the floor in bowing to Oklahoma State, 65-40, and Cincinnati, 97-62. Cincinnati's Oscar Robertson poured in 56 points

in the blowout of the Hogs in the Midwest Regional third-place game. . . . Notre Dame grabbed an NCAA playoff-record 86 rebounds in a 94-61 trouncing of Tennessee Tech in the opening round of the Mideast Regional. The Irish had six players with at least eight rebounds, including a game-high 21 by John McCarthy. Later, Notre Dame coach John Jordan lost his third regional final in six years. . . . Maryland, coached by Bud Millikan, made its only appearance in the first 33 NCAA Tournaments.

What If: West Virginia captain Don Vincent, averaging 12.8 points per game, broke his left leg in the Southern Conference Tournament. The Mountaineers had won by seven points against NCAA champion-to-be Kentucky, handing the Wildcats just their fifth homecourt defeat in 15 years. . . . SEC runner-up Auburn might have gotten off to a better league start and finished ahead

1957–58 NCAA CHAMPION: KENTUCKY

SEASON STATISTICS OF KENTUCKY REGULARS

PLAYER	POS.	CL.	G.	FG%	FT%	PPG	RPG
Vern Hatton	G	Sr.	29	.419	.778	17.1	5.0
Johnny Cox	F	Jr.	29	.367	.748	14.9	12.6
John Crigler	F	Sr.	28	.405	.707	13.6	9.9
Adrian Smith	G	Sr.	29	.371	.765	12.4	3.5
Ed Beck	C	Sr.	29	.283	.722	5.6	11.6
Earl Adkins	G	Sr.	19	.453	.742	5.3	1.5
Don Mills	C	So.	20	.253	.625	3.5	5.0
Phil Johnson	F-C	Jr.	22	.306	.517	3.4	5.7
TEAM TOTALS			29	.373	.738	74.7	53.9

1958 FINAL FOUR CHAMPIONSHIP GAME

LOUISVILLE, KY

KENTUCKY (84)	FG-A	FT-A	REB.	PF	PTS.
Cox	10-23	4-4	16	3	24
Crigler	5-12	4-7	14	4	14
Beck	0-1	0-1	3	4	0
Mills	4-9	1-4	5	3	9
Hatton	9-20	12-15	3	3	30
Smith	2-8	3-5	6	4	7
Team			8		
TOTALS	**30-73**	**24-36**	**55**	**21**	**84**

FG%: .411. FT%: .667.

SEATTLE (72)	FG-A	FT-A	REB.	PF	PTS.
Frizzell	4-6	8-11	5	3	16
Ogorek	4-7	2-2	11	5	10
Baylor	9-32	7-9	19	4	25
Harney	2-5	0-1	1	1	4
Brown	6-17	5-7	5	5	17
Saunders	0-2	0-0	2	3	0
Piasecki	0-0	0-0	0	0	0
Team			3		
TOTALS	**25-69**	**22-30**	**46**	**21**	**72**

FG%: .362. FT%: .733.
Halftime: Seattle 39-36.

NATIONAL SEMIFINALS

KENTUCKY (61): Crigler 3-11 0-2 6, Cox 6-17 10-11 22, Collinsworth 0-0 0-0 0, Beck 3-9 2-2 8, Hatton 5-16 3-4 13, Smith 2-10 8-9 12. Team 19-63 (.302) 23-28 (.821) 61.

TEMPLE (60): Norman 7-17 2-3 16, Brodsky 2-5 0-2 4, Van Patton 1-1 1-2 3, Fleming 3-7 3-6 9, Rodgers 9-24 4-6 22, Kennedy 3-7 0-1 6. Team 25-61 (.410) 10-20 (.500) 60.

Halftime: Tied 31-31.

SEATTLE (73): Ogorek 3-9 1-2 7, Frizzell 2-4 6-7 10, Petrie 0-0-0-0 0, Baylor 9-21 5-7 23, Humphries 0-0 0-0 0. Harney 0-4 0-0 0, Brown 5-6 4-5 14, Saunders 5-11 2-3 12, Piasecki 1-1 3-4 5, Kootnekoff 1-1 0-0 2. Team 26-57 (.456) 21-28 (.750) 73.

KANSAS STATE (51): Boozer 6-15 3-5 15, Frank 6-12 3-4 12, Abbott 0-4 0-0 0, Long 2-6 0-1 4, Fischer 0-1 0-0 0, Parr 2-11 0-1 4, Matuszak 3-8 1-3 7, DeWitz 2-7 2-3 6, Holwerda 0-2 0-0 0. Team 21-66 (.318) 9-17 (.529) 51.

Halftime: Seattle 37-32.

ALL-TOURNAMENT TEAM

*Elgin Baylor, C, Jr., Seattle (48 points, 41 rebounds in final two games)
Charley Brown, G, Jr., Seattle (31 points, 18 rebounds)
Johnny Cox, F, Jr., Kentucky (46 points, 29 rebounds)
Vern Hatton, G, Sr., Kentucky (43 points)
Guy Rodgers, G, Sr., Temple (39 points, nine rebounds)

*Named Most Outstanding Player.

1958 CHAMPIONSHIP BRACKET

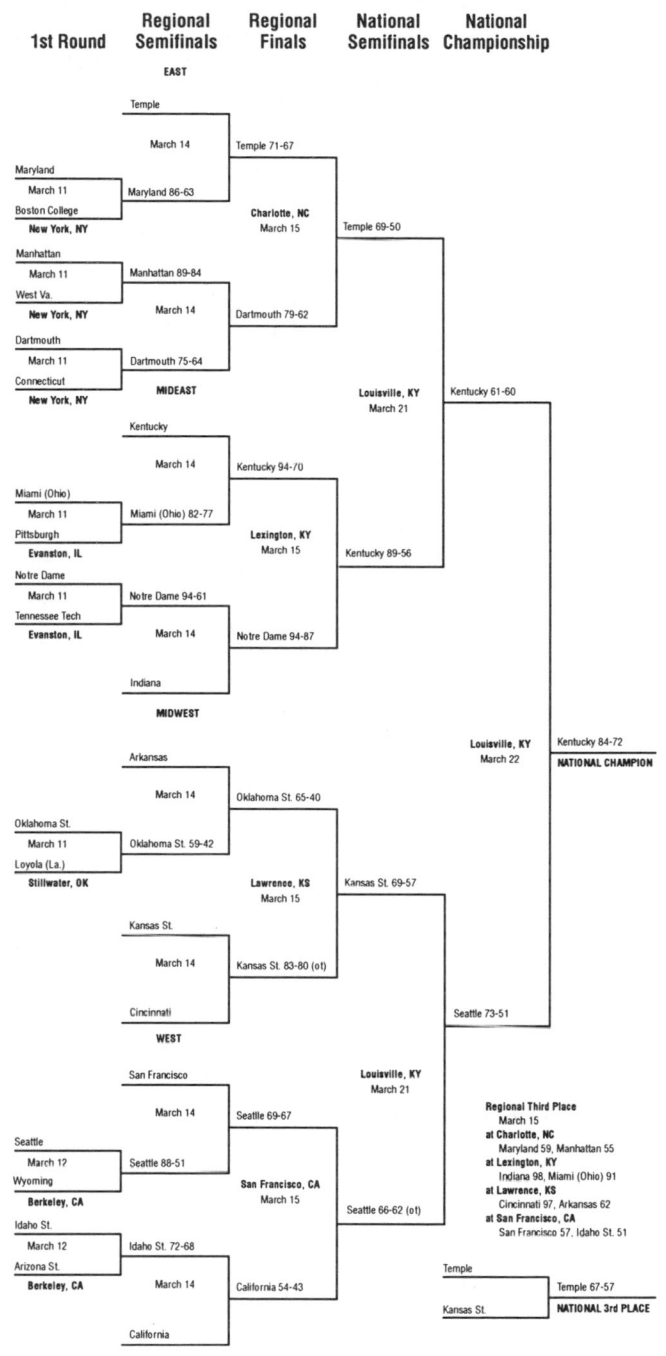

	Regional Semifinals	Regional Finals	National Semifinals	National Championship
1st Round				

EAST

Temple

March 14   Temple 71-67

Maryland
March 11   Maryland 86-63
Boston College
New York, NY

Charlotte, NC
March 15   Temple 69-50

Manhattan
March 11   Manhattan 89-84
West Va.
New York, NY   March 14   Dartmouth 79-62

Dartmouth
March 11   Dartmouth 75-64
Connecticut
New York, NY

MIDEAST

Louisville, KY
March 21   Kentucky 61-60

Kentucky

March 14   Kentucky 94-70

Miami (Ohio)
March 11   Miami (Ohio) 82-77
Pittsburgh
Evanston, IL

Lexington, KY
March 15   Kentucky 89-56

Notre Dame
March 11   Notre Dame 94-61
Tennessee Tech
Evanston, IL   March 14   Notre Dame 94-87

Indiana

MIDWEST

Louisville, KY
March 22   Kentucky 84-72
NATIONAL CHAMPION

Arkansas

March 14   Oklahoma St. 65-40

Oklahoma St.
March 11   Oklahoma St. 59-42
Loyola (La.)
Stillwater, OK

Lawrence, KS
March 15   Kansas St. 69-57

Kansas St.

March 14   Kansas St. 83-80 (ot)

Cincinnati

WEST

Seattle 73-51

San Francisco

March 14   Seattle 69-67

Seattle
March 12   Seattle 88-51
Wyoming
Berkeley, CA

San Francisco, CA
March 15   Seattle 66-62 (ot)

Idaho St.
March 12   Idaho St. 72-68
Arizona St.
Berkeley, CA   March 14   California 54-43

California

Louisville, KY
March 21

Regional Third Place
March 15
at Charlotte, NC
Maryland 59, Manhattan 55
at Lexington, KY
Indiana 98, Miami (Ohio) 91
at Lawrence, KS
Cincinnati 97, Arkansas 62
at San Francisco, CA
San Francisco 57, Idaho St. 51

Temple
Temple 67-57
Kansas St.   **NATIONAL 3rd PLACE**

of Kentucky in the standings if guard Henry Hart didn't redshirt because of a knee injury. Hart averaged 14.2 points and 6.7 rebounds per game the previous season as a sophomore. Auburn lost its first 13 assignments against Kentucky in their series until edging the Wildcats, 64-63.

Scoring Leader: Elgin Baylor, Seattle (135 points, 27 ppg).

Highest Scoring Average: Oscar Robertson, Cincinnati (86 points, 43 ppg).

Rebounding Leader: Elgin Baylor, Seattle (91 rebounds, 18.2 rpg).

1958-59

AT A GLANCE

NCAA Champion: California (25-4; coached by Pete Newell; won PCC title with a 14-2 record, which was three games ahead of Washington).

NIT Champion: St. John's (20-6; coached by Joe Lapchick).

New Conference: Middle Atlantic (disbanded in 1975 when ECC is formed).

NCAA Probation: Auburn, Memphis State, North Carolina State, Seattle, Southern Cal, UCLA.

NCAA Consensus First-Team All-Americans: Bob Boozer, F, Sr., Kansas State; Johnny Cox, F, Sr., Kentucky; Bailey Howell, F, Sr., Mississippi State; Oscar Robertson, F, Jr., Cincinnati; Jerry West, F, Jr., West Virginia.

National Player of the Year: Robertson (32.6 ppg, 16.3 rpg, 6.9 apg, 50.9 FG%).

National Coach of the Year: Eddie Hickey, Marquette (23-6/USBWA).

Cincinnati's Oscar Robertson became the first player to lead the nation's scorers in both his sophomore and junior seasons. Robertson's brilliance wasn't enough to prevent the Bearcats from losing against California (64-58) in the national semifinals when he was held to one point in the second half. Guard Mike Mendenhall, the team's co-captain and third-leading scorer (13.5-point average) as one of the nation's top 15 field-goal shooters (51.3 percent), was declared ineligible for the playoffs by the NCAA because he played briefly in the 1955-56 season before missing the remainder of the year nursing a kidney ailment.

Mississippi State, coached by Babe McCarthy, won its first SEC title with a 13-1 record and finished 24-1 overall, but was forced to bypass the NCAA Tournament because of the opposition of several state officials to inter-racial games. Mississippi State's Bailey Howell set a school record with 47 points against Union.

The season's highest single-game output was 50 points by Air Force's Bob Beckel (school record vs. Arizona) and Rhode Island's Tom Harrington (Brandeis/school record was later tied). Tennessee Tech's Jimmy Hagan established a school mark with 48 points against East Tennessee State (later tied). . . . Marshall's Leo Byrd (29.3 ppg) and Kansas State's Bob Boozer (25.6) set school records for highest scoring average in a single season.

Virginia Tech's Chris Smith (36 vs. Washington & Lee), Ohio University's Dave Scott (34 vs. Marietta), Tennessee Tech's Hagan (30 vs. Morehead State) and Princeton's Carl Belz (29 vs. Rutgers) established school single-game rebounding standards.

Oklahoma State senior Arlen Clark set an NCAA record for most successful free throws in a game without a miss when he sank all 24 of his foul shots in a 42-point outburst against Colorado on his way to leading the nation in free-throw accuracy (see accompanying box). Clark, 6-8, is one of the best free-throw shooting big men in NCAA history, hitting 84.9 percent of his charity tosses. . . . Kansas, minus All-America center Wilt Chamberlain after he bypassed his senior year of eligibility to join the Harlem Globetrotters, lost seven consecutive games in December. . . . Texas A&M (15-9 under coach Bob Rogers) compiled a winning record for the first time in eight years.

Virginia nipped North Carolina, 69-68, for the Cavaliers' lone victory over the Tar Heels in a 19-

Cincinnati's national scoring leader Oscar Robertson comes down with a rebound.

game stretch of their series from 1956 to 1964. . . . North Carolina State coach Everett Case, compiling a 320-81 record through 13 seasons, had more victories than any coach in history from his second year through his 13th. . . . West Virginia (29-5/coached by Fred Schaus) went unbeaten in Southern Conference competition for the third consecutive year en route to its winningest season in school history. Kansas State (25-2/Tex Winter) and Dartmouth (22-6/Doggie Julian) tied their school records for most victories in a single season.

A 22-3 Marquette squad that eventually reached the Mideast Regional final held the ball for the first 11 minutes of a game at Notre Dame. Tom Hawkins scored 18 of his game-high 19

points in the second half to carry the Irish to a 51-35 victory and conclude the campaign with a 12-13 record. The Warriors finished the season with a 23-6 worksheet in their first year with Eddie Hickey as head coach. After Hickey guided St. Louis to a 24-3 mark in his first season in 1947-48, the Billikens finished in the Top 20 of a final wire-service poll seven times in the next nine years. . . . St. Louis, in its first season under coach John Benington, defeated NCAA champion-to-be California, 55-43, and NIT champion-to-be St. John's, 72-63.

Auburn, the only school to rank among the top 35 in both offense and defense, dealt Mississippi State its lone defeat (97-66). The Tigers won their first 19 games under coach Joel Eaves before

North Carolina State coach Everett Case and his Wolfpack were on NCAA probation in 1958–59.

bowing at Kentucky and Tennessee. Auburn's loss at Kentucky snapped the Tigers' school-record 30-game winning streak.... Vanderbilt and visiting Baylor play the season finale using experimental rules such as the 24-second shot clock. Vanderbilt trailed by as many as 11 points in the second half, but Doug Yates' jumper from the top of the circle gives the Commodores a 61-60 triumph. "Frankly, I doubt we would have won the game had we been playing under existing rules," Vandy coach Roy Skinner said.

For the first time, Providence fans were able to follow their favorites on radio and the Friars made the most of the road opportunity, defeating nationally-ranked Villanova in four overtimes, 90-83, behind Johnny Egan's 39 points.... Villanova's George Raveling, who would go on to become one

1958–59 INDIVIDUAL LEADERS

SCORING

PLAYER	PTS.	AVG.
Robertson, Cincinnati	978	32.6
Byrd, Marshall	704	29.3
Hagan, Tennessee Tech	720	28.8
Howell, Mississippi St.	688	27.5
West, West Virginia	903	26.6
Ayersman, Virginia Tech	556	26.5
Hennon, Pittsburgh	617	25.7
Boozer, Kansas St.	691	25.6
Windis, Wyoming	463	24.4
Hawkins, Notre Dame	514	23.4

REBOUNDING

PLAYER	REB.	PCT.
Wright, Pacific	652	.238

Howell, Mississippi St.	379	.220
Smith, Virginia Tech	429	.202
Mealy, Manhattan	240	.201
Cohen, William & Mary	413	.200
Tormohlen, Tennessee	372	.192
Cincebox, Syracuse	365	.188
Danzig, Bucknell	386	.184
Washington, Boston	382	.183

FIELD GOAL PERCENTAGE

PLAYER	FGM	FGA	PCT.
Crosthwaite, W. Ky.	191	296	.645
Carter, Iona	137	225	.609
Kessler, Muhlenberg	153	271	.565
Herdelin, La Salle	144	256	.563
Sanders, New York	131	236	.555
Stith, St. Bonaventure	162	295	.549

Wilson, Furman	157	289	.543
McCraw, Oklahoma City	119	220	.541
Moses, Oklahoma City	158	293	.539
Price, New Mexico St.	209	401	.521

FREE THROW PERCENTAGE

PLAYER	FTM	FTA	PCT.
Clark, Oklahoma St.	201	236	.852
Burgess, Gonzaga	151	178	.848
Neumann, Stanford	127	150	.847
Kaiser, Georgia Tech	106	127	.835
Wendel, Tulsa	185	222	.833
Kennedy, Temple	184	221	.833
Guarilia, G. Wash.	99	119	.832
Siegfried, Ohio St.	136	164	.829
Hagan, Tennessee Tech	212	256	.828
Mills, Kentucky	101	122	.828

1958–59 TEAM LEADERS

SCORING OFFENSE

SCHOOL	PTS.	AVG.
Miami (Fla.)	2190	87.6
West Virginia	2884	84.8
Cincinnati	2519	84.0
Virginia Tech	1758	83.7
Illinois	1815	82.5

SCORING DEFENSE

SCHOOL	PTS.	AVG.
California	1480	51.0
Oklahoma St.	1319	52.8
Idaho St.	1504	53.7
San Jose St.	1352	56.3
Maryland	1296	56.4

FIELD GOAL PERCENTAGE

SCHOOL	FGM	FGA	PCT.
Auburn	593	1216	.488
Cincinnati	970	2062	.470
Oklahoma City	769	1680	.458
St. Bonaventure	724	1584	.457
West Virginia	1075	2355	.456
Mississippi St.	663	1453	.456

FREE THROW PERCENTAGE

SCHOOL	FTM	FTA	PCT.
Tulsa	446	586	.761
Mississippi St.	532	700	.760
George Washington	402	534	.753
Kentucky	570	758	.752
Marshall	472	631	.748

REBOUND PERCENTAGE

SCHOOL	TOT. REB.	REB.	PCT.
Mississippi St.	1719	1012	.589
Iona	1087	1856	.586
Michigan St.	2597	1508	.581
Eastern Kentucky	2346	1361	.580
Gonzaga	2473	1426	.577

of the nation's most visible coaches, ranked among the top 25 players in the country in field-goal shooting (50.6 percent) and rebounding (15.5 per game). . . . Temple suffered its worst winning percentage in history (6-19, .240) just one year after winning 25 consecutive games en route to the Final Four. . . . Boston University lost 25 of its first 26 games against Holy Cross in their series until the visiting Terriers prevailed, 74-57. . . . Washington & Lee's final season at the Division I level was marred by a 105-24 defeat against Virginia Tech. . . . American, after losing the first 19 games in its series with Georgetown, whipped the Hoyas, 92-67. . . . Dick Bavetta, who would go on to become a prominent NBA referee, was a member of a St. Francis (N.Y.) squad that compiled an anemic 5-18 record.

Eastern Kentucky, coached by Paul McBrayer, won the Ohio Valley Conference crown after finishing in sixth place the previous year. . . . Tennessee Tech and St. Mary's made their lone appearance in the Top 20 of a final wire-service poll. . . . Northwestern, coached by William Rohr, wound up in a tie for second place in the Big Ten standings with an 8-6 league record. That represents the Wildcats' highest finish since 1934.

Washington won at Iowa, 81-68, to shatter the Hawkeyes' 77-game homecourt winning streak against non-conference opponents. . . . Pacific's Leroy Wright set a West Coast Conference record by averaging 25 rebounds per game. . . . Idaho, in coach Harlan Hodges' fifth and final season with the Vandals, defeated first-division teams Stanford and UCLA while competing in their last season as a member of the Pacific Coast Conference. . . . Arizona State lost more than 10 games in 13 consecutive seasons until stopping the hemorrhaging by compiling a 17-9 mark in Ned Wulk's second year as the Sun Devils' head coach. . . . Arizona lost a school-record 16 consecutive games in coach Fred Enke's 34th season with the Wildcats.

Harold (Bud) Foster stepped down after 25 seasons as Wisconsin's coach on a negative note with a 3-19 record. He was 44 games under .500 in his last four years to become the only major-college

CLARK IS SUPERMAN FROM LINE

Colorado at Oklahoma State
March 7, 1959

Oklahoma State's Arlen Clark established an NCAA standard for most successful free throws in a game without a miss when he converted all 24 of his foul shots in a game against Colorado. Clark, a senior center, led the nation in free-throw accuracy (85.2 percent).

OKLAHOMA STATE (66): Soergel 4-8 4-5 12, Clarahan 0-2 0-1 0, Clark 9-10 **24-24** 42, Heffington 2-5 2-3 6, Wade 0-2 1-1 1, Walker 2-4 1-1 5, Miller 0-0 0-0 0. **Team 17-31 (.548) 32-35 (.914) 66.**

COLORADO (51): Musciano 6-11 3-6 15, Olson 2-4 2-4 6, Walker 3-8 6-8 12, Lind 0-6 2-2 2, Lewis 0-1 1-2 1, Javernick 0-0 0-0 0, Mansfield 0-0 0-0 0, Anderson 0-2 0-0 0, Beckner 0-1 0-0 0, Piper 0-1 0-0 0, Baskin 0-0 3-4 3. Team 16-34 (.471) 19-29 (.655) 51.

Halftime: Oklahoma State 31-26.

coach to stay at a school that long and finish with a losing career record (265-267) at that institution.

1959 NCAA Tournament

Summary: Two-time first-team All-American swingman Jerry West was denied an NCAA championship ring when Cal junior center Darrall Imhoff, West's teammate with the Los Angeles Lakers for four seasons in the mid-1960s, tipped in a basket with 17 seconds remaining to give California a 71-70 victory over West Virginia in the NCAA final.

Outcome for Defending Champion: Second-ranked Kentucky (24-3) hit less than one-third of

1958-59 FINAL NATIONAL POLLS

AP	UPI	SCHOOL (RECORD)	HEAD COACH
1	1	Kansas St. (25-2)	Tex Winter
2	2	Kentucky (24-3)	Adolph Rupp
3	6	Mississippi St. (24-1)	Babe McCarthy
4	8	Bradley (25-4)	Chuck Orsborn
5	4	Cincinnati (26-4)	George Smith
6	5	North Carolina St. (22-4)	Everett Case
7	3	Michigan St. (20-4)	Forddy Anderson
8	10	Auburn (20-2)	Joel Eaves
9	6	North Carolina (20-5)	Frank McGuire
10	11	West Virginia (29-5)	Fred Schaus
11	9	California (25-4)	Pete Newell
12	13	St. Louis (20-6)	John Bennington
13	–	Seattle (23-6)	Vince Cazzetta
14	20	St. Joseph's (22-5)	Jack Ramsay
15	18	St. Mary's (19-6)	Jim Weaver
16	12	Texas Christian (20-6)	Buster Brannon
17	–	Oklahoma City (20-7)	Abe Lemons
18	14	Utah (25-7)	Jack Gardner
19	–	St. Bonaventure (20-3)	Eddie Donovan
20	15	Marquette (23-6)	Eddie Hickey
–	16	Tennessee Tech (16-9)	John Oldham
–	17	St. John's (20-6)	Joe Lapchick
–	18	Navy (18-6)	Ben Carnevale

1958–59 NCAA CHAMPION: CALIFORNIA

SEASON STATISTICS OF CALIFORNIA REGULARS

PLAYER	POS.	CL.	G.	FG%	FT%	PPG	RPG
Denny Fitzpatrick	G	Sr.	29	.456	.854	13.3	2.8
Darrall Imhoff	C	Jr.	29	.424	.535	11.3	11.0
Al Buch	G	Sr.	29	.358	.646	9.2	2.8
Bill McClintock	F	So.	28	.416	.561	7.8	7.3
Bob Dalton	F	Sr.	29	.367	.663	7.3	4.6
Jack Grout	F	Sr.	28	.464	.639	5.5	3.7
Dick Doughty	C	Jr.	29	.423	.581	3.4	2.6
Jim Langley	F	Sr.	27	.427	.333	2.6	1.5
Bernie Simpson	G	Sr.	28	.295	.688	2.1	1.3
TEAM TOTALS			**29**	**.406**	**.634**	**63.9**	**45.1**

1959 FINAL FOUR CHAMPIONSHIP GAME

LOUISVILLE, KY

WEST VIRGINIA (70)	FG-A	FT-A	REB.	PF	PTS.
West	10-21	8-12	11	4	28
Akers	5-8	0-1	6	0	10
Clousson	4-7	2-3	4	4	10
Smith	2-5	1-1	2	3	5
Bolyard	1-4	4-4	3	4	6
Retton	0-0	2-2	0	0	2
Ritchie	1-4	2-2	4	0	4
Patrone	2-6	1-2	4	1	5
Team			7		
TOTALS	**25-55**	**20-27**	**41**	**16**	**70**

FG%: .455. FT%: .741.

CALIFORNIA (71)	FG-A	FT-A	REB.	PF	PTS.
McClintock	4-13	0-1	10	1	8
Dalton	6-11	3-4	2	4	15
Imhoff	4-13	2-2	9	3	10
Buch	0-4	2-2	2	3	2
Fitzpatrick	8-13	4-7	2	1	20
Simpson	0-1	0-0	2	2	0
Grout	4-5	2-2	3	1	10
Doughty	3-6	0-0	1	3	6
Team			7		
TOTALS	**29-66**	**13-18**	**38**	**18**	**71**

FG%: .439. FT%: .722.
Halftime: California 39-33.

NATIONAL SEMIFINALS

CALIFORNIA (64): McClintock 2-11 2-4 6, Dalton 2-4 3-4 7, Imhoff 10-25 2-5 22, Fitzpatrick 2-9 0-0 4, Buch 7-15 4-6 18, Grout 2-7 1-2 5, Simpson 1-2 0-0 2. Team 26-73 (.356) 12-21 (.571) 64.

CINCINNATI (58): Robertson 5-16 9-11 19, Wiesenhahn 5-11 0-0 10, Tenwick 2-6 1-1 5, Davis 6-15 1-2 13, Whitaker 4-7 0-2 8, Landfried 0-1 3-5 3, Bouldin 0-0 0-1 0. Team 22-56 (.393) 14-22 (.636) 58.

Halftime: Cincinnati 33-29.

WEST VIRGINIA (94): West 12-21 14-20 38, Akers 2-5 1-2 5, Clousson 5-5 2-2 12, Smith 5-9 2-4 12, Bolyard 4-10 5-7 13, Ritchie 2-6 0-2 4, Patrone 1-4 0-0 2, Retton 3-4 0-0 6, Scherzniger 0-0 0-0 0, Posch 1-2 0-0 2, Goode 0-0 0-0 0, Visnic 0-0 0-0 0. Team 35-66 (.530) 24-37 (.649) 94.

LOUISVILLE (79): Goldstein 6-10 9-9 21, Turner 8-16 2-5 18, Sawyer 2-6 3-4 7, Tieman 1-7 1-1 3, Andrews 9-15 1-1 19, Kitchen 3-7 0-0 6, Leathers 2-8 1-1 5, Geiling 0-0 0-0 0, Stacey 0-0 0-0 0. Team 31-69 (.449) 17-21 (.810) 79.

Halftime: West Virginia 48-32.

ALL-TOURNAMENT TEAM

Denny Fitzpatrick, G, Sr., California (24 points in final two games)
Don Goldstein, F, Sr., Louisville (42 points, 17 rebounds)
Darrall Imhoff, C, Jr., California (32 points, 25 rebounds)
Oscar Robertson, F, Jr., Cincinnati (58 points, 36 rebounds, 19 assists)
*Jerry West, F, Jr., West Virginia (66 points, 26 rebounds)

*Named Most Outstanding Player.

its field-goal attempts in blowing a 15-point lead and absorbing a 76-61 setback against Louisville (19-12). The Wildcats' other two defeats were by a minimum of eight points at Vanderbilt and Mississippi State. Kentucky clobbered Marquette, 98-69, in the Mideast Regional consolation game to become the first school to win at least one game in five consecutive NCAA Tournaments.

Star Gazing: West collected a total of 66 points and 26 rebounds for West Virginia in the national semifinals and final.

Biggest Upset: Kansas State, an 85-75 loser against Cincinnati in the Midwest Regional final, is one of only two teams ranked No. 1 by both AP and UPI entering the tourney to lose by a double-digit margin before the Final Four.

One and Only: Pete Newell became the only U.S. Olympic basketball coach to win the NCAA

1950–59 PREMO POWER POLL: BEST TEAMS BY DECADE

RANK	SEASON	SCHOOL
1	1955–56	San Francisco* (29-0)
2	1953–54	Kentucky (25-0)
3	1956–57	North Carolina* (32-0)
4	1954–55	San Francisco* (28-1)
5	1950–51	Kentucky* (32-2)
6	1958–59	Kansas St. (25-2)
7	1951–52	Kentucky (29-3)
8	1957–58	Cincinnati (25-3)
9	1952–53	Indiana* (23-3)
10	1956–57	Kansas (24-3)
11	1953–54	Holy Cross# (26-2)
12	1957–58	West Virginia (26-2)
13	1951–52	Kansas* (28-3)
14	1958–59	California* (25-4)
15	1949–50	CCNY#* (24-5)
16	1952–53	Seton Hall# (31-2)
17	1950–51	Illinois (22-5)
18	1957–58	San Francisco (25-2)
19	1953–54	Duquesne (26-3)
20	1950–51	Indiana (19-3)
	1958–59	Cincinnati (26-4)

#–NIT Champion
*–NCAA Tournament Champion

West Virginia's Jerry West whizzes past Louisville's John Turner in the 1959 NCAA Tournament semifinals.

Kansas great Wilt Chamberlain.

Kansas coaching greats Dick Harp (left) and Phog Allen.

and NIT titles with different schools. Newell was the 1960 U.S. Olympic basketball coach after capturing national titles with San Francisco (NIT in 1949) and California.

Numbers Game: North Carolina, which won 17 of its first 18 games, lost to Navy, 76-63, in the Tar Heels' only NCAA playoff contest in a nine-year span from 1958 through 1966. The victory improved Navy's record against Carolina to 14-5 since 1919-20, including six triumphs for the Midshipmen in their last seven meetings. . . . Cincinnati's Oscar Robertson scored a tourney-high 39 points in a 98-85 victory over Louisville in the national third-place game. . . . TCU's H.E. Kirchner grabbed a tourney-high 24 rebounds in a 71-65 victory over DePaul in the Midwest Regional third-place game. . . . Michigan State's Johnny Green hauled down 23 rebounds in an 88-81 defeat to Louisville in the Mideast Regional final. Green finished his career with an NCAA Tourna-

WINNINGEST PROGRAMS OF THE 1950s

RK.	SCHOOL	W.	L.	PCT.
1.	Kentucky	224	33	.872
2.	N.C. State	240	65	.787
3.	Seattle	233	69	.772
4.	La Salle	209	65	.763
5.	Dayton	228	71	.763
6.	Holy Cross	199	65	.754
7.	Kansas State	179	63	.740
8.	Connecticut	187	67	.736
9.	West Virginia	205	74	.735
10.	Louisville	202	77	.724

ment-record rebounding average of 19.7 per game in six playoff contests. . . . St. Mary's, coached by James Weaver, made its lone NCAA playoff appearance in the first 50 years of the event.

What If: ACC regular-season co-champion and tournament kingpin North Carolina State, which defeated Final Four teams Louisville and Cincinnati, was ineligible for the tourney because of NCAA probation.

1959 CHAMPIONSHIP BRACKET

1st Round	Regional Semifinals	Regional Finals	National Semifinals	National Championship

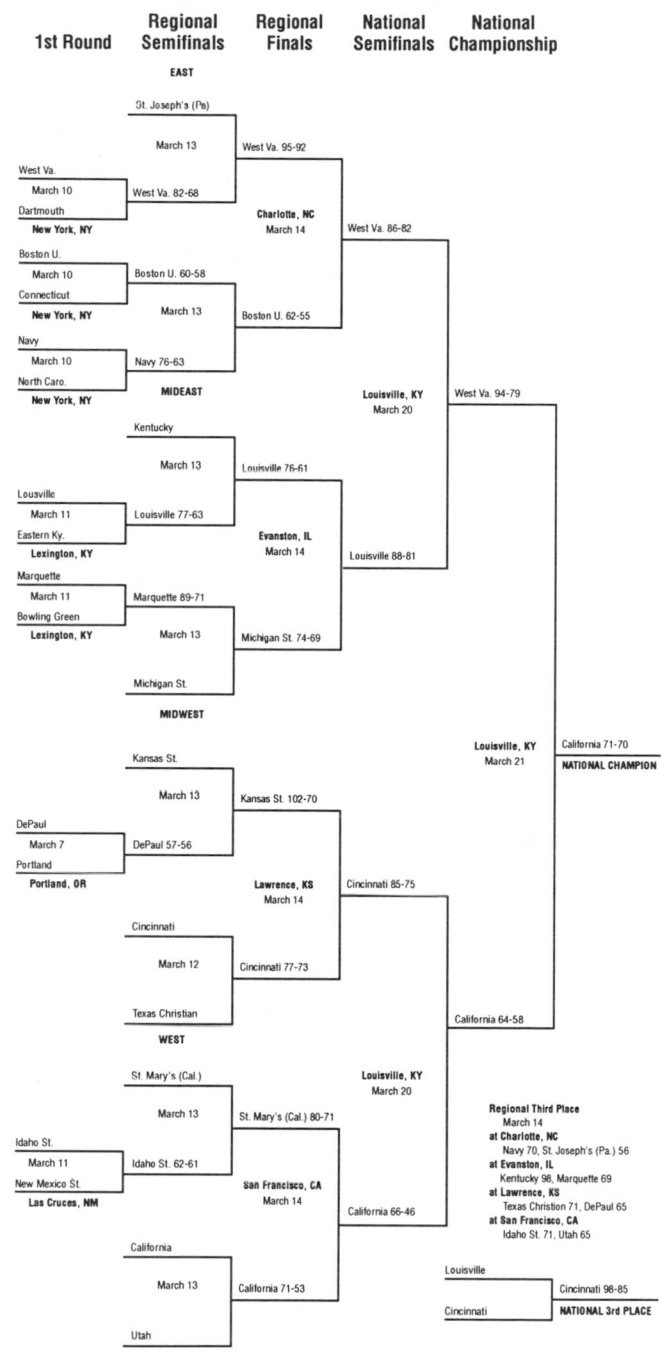

EAST

St. Joseph's (Pa)

March 13 — West Va. 95-92

West Va.
March 10
Dartmouth
New York, NY — West Va. 82-68

Charlotte, NC
March 14 — West Va. 86-82

Boston U.
March 10
Connecticut
New York, NY — Boston U. 60-58

March 13 — Boston U. 62-55

Navy
March 10
North Caro.
New York, NY — Navy 76-63

West Va. 94-79

MIDEAST

Kentucky
March 13 — Louisville 76-61

Lousville
March 11
Eastern Ky.
Lexington, KY — Louisville 77-63

Evanston, IL
March 14 — Louisville 88-81

Louisville, KY
March 20

Marquette
March 11
Bowling Green
Lexington, KY — Marquette 89-71

March 13 — Michigan St. 74-69

Michigan St.

MIDWEST

Louisville, KY
March 21 — California 71-70
NATIONAL CHAMPION

Kansas St.
March 13 — Kansas St. 102-70

DePaul
March 7
Portland
Portland, OR — DePaul 57-56

Lawrence, KS
March 14 — Cincinnati 85-75

Cincinnati
March 12 — Cincinnati 77-73

Texas Christian

California 64-58

WEST

St. Mary's (Cal.)
March 13 — St. Mary's (Cal.) 80-71

Louisville, KY
March 20

Idaho St.
March 11
New Mexico St.
Las Cruces, NM — Idaho St. 62-61

San Francisco, CA
March 14 — California 66-46

California
March 13 — California 71-53

Utah

Regional Third Place
March 14
at Charlotte, NC
Navy 70, St. Joseph's (Pa.) 56
at Evanston, IL
Kentucky 98, Marquette 69
at Lawrence, KS
Texas Christian 71, DePaul 65
at San Francisco, CA
Idaho St. 71, Utah 65

Louisville
Cincinnati — Cincinnati 98-85
NATIONAL 3rd PLACE

Putting Things in Perspective: Oregon, which compiled a 3-13 record in the PCC and 9-16 overall, defeated California, 59-57. . . . Louisville reached the national semifinals despite losing its season opener to Georgetown (Ky.) College, 84-78.

Scoring Leader: Jerry West, West Virginia (160 points, 32 ppg).

Rebounding Leader: Jerry West, West Virginia (73 rebounds, 14.6 rpg).

Highest Rebounding Average: H.E. Kirchner, TCU (42 rebounds, 21 rpg).

ALL-DECADE TEAM — 1950s

Elgin Baylor, F, College of Idaho/Seattle
Wilt Chamberlain, C, Kansas
Tom Gola, F-C, La Salle
Cliff Hagan, F-C, Kentucky
Clyde Lovellette, C, Kansas
Bob Pettit, F-C, Louisiana State
Oscar Robertson, F, Cincinnati
Bill Russell, C, San Francisco
Don Schlundt, C, Indiana
Jerry West, F, West Virginia
Co-Coaches: Everett Case, N.C. State and Adolph Rupp, Kentucky

Elgin Baylor

Seattle
6–6 — F
Washington, D.C. (Phelps Vocational and Spingarn H.S.)

NCAA unanimous first-team All-American in 1958 and consensus second-team All-American in 1957. . . . Led the nation in rebounding in 1957 and finished 3rd in 1958. . . . Ranked among the nation's leading scorers in 1957 (3rd) and 1958 (2nd). . . . Leading scorer and rebounder for 1958 national runner-up (24-7 record). . . . Final Four Most Outstanding Player in 1958 (48 points, 41 rebounds). . . . Averaged 27 points in five NCAA Tournament games in 1958 (4-1 record). . . . Selected as a junior eligible by the Minneapolis Lakers in first round of 1958 NBA draft. . . . Elected to Naismith Memorial Basketball Hall of Fame in 1976.

SEASON	G.	FGM-FGA	FG%	FTM-FTA	FT%	REB.	AVG.	PTS.	AVG.
1954-55*	26	332-651	.510	150-232	.647	492	20.5	814	31.3
1955-56	Sat out the season after transferring from College of Idaho.								
1956-57	25	271-555	.488	201-251	.801	508	20.3	743	29.7
1957-58	29	353-697	.506	237-308	.769	559	19.3	943	32.5
Totals	80	956-1903	.502	588-791	.743	1559	20.0	2500	31.3

*Rebounds available for 24 of 26 games he played for the College of Idaho his freshman season, which was at the small college level.

Wilt Chamberlain

Kansas
7-1 — C
Philadelphia, Pa. (Overbrook H.S.)

NCAA unanimous first-team All-American in 1957 and 1958. . . . Ranked among the nation's scoring leaders in 1957 (4th) and 1958 (3rd). . . . Ranked 4th in the nation in rebounding percentage in 1957 and 1958. . . . Leading scorer and rebounder for 1957 NCAA Tournament runner-up (24-3 record). . . . Final Four Most Outstanding Player in 1957 (55 points, 25 rebounds). . . . Named to 1957 All-NCAA Tournament team. . . . Averaged 30.3 points and 15.5 rebounds in four NCAA Tournament games in 1957 (3-1 record). . . .

Selected as a territorial choice by the Philadelphia Warriors in first round of 1959 NBA draft after he played one season with the Harlem Globetrotters. . . . Elected to Naismith Memorial Basketball Hall of Fame in 1978.

SEASON	G.	FGM-FGA	FG%	FTM-FTA	FT%	REB.	AVG.	PTS.	AVG.
1956-57	27	275-588	.468	250-399	.627	510	18.9	800	29.6
1957-58	21	228-482	.473	177-291	.608	367	17.5	633	30.1
Totals	48	503-1070	.470	427-690	.619	877	18.3	1433	29.9

Tom Gola

La Salle
6-6 — F
Philadelphia, Pa. (La Salle H.S.)

Named national player of the year by UPI in 1955. . . . NCAA unanimous first-team All-American in 1954 and 1955, and consensus first-team All-American in 1953. . . . Ranked among the nation's leading rebounders in 1952 (9th), 1953 (19th), 1954 (3rd) and 1955 (6th). . . . Ranked among the nation's leading scorers in 1952 (41st), 1953 (55th), 1954 (21st) and 1955 (18th). . . . Leading scorer and rebounder for 1954 NCAA Tournament champion (26-4 record) and 1955 national runner-up (26-5). . . . Final Four Most Outstanding Player in 1954 (38 points in final two games). . . . Named to All-NCAA Tournament team in 1954 and 1955. . . . Averaged 22.9 points in 10 NCAA Tournament games in 1954 and 1955 (9-1 record). . . . Co-Most Valuable Player of 1952 NIT with teammate Norm Grekin. . . . Averaged 14 points in five NIT games in 1952 (champion) and 1953 (opening-game loser). . . . Selected as a territorial choice by the Philadelphia Warriors in 1955 NBA draft. . . . Elected to Naismith Memorial Basketball Hall of Fame in 1975.

SEASON	G.	FGM-FGA	FG%	FTM-FTA	FT%	REB.	AVG.	PTS.	AVG.
1951-52	29	192-528	.364	121-170	.712	497	17.1	505	17.4
1952-53	28	186-451	.412	145-186	.780	434	15.5	517	18.5
1953-54	30	252-619	.407	186-254	.732	652	21.7	690	23.0
1954-55	31	274-624	.439	202-267	.757	618	19.9	750	24.2
Totals	118	904-2222	.407	654-877	.746	2201	18.7	2462	20.9

Cliff Hagan

Kentucky
6-4 — F/C
Owensboro, Ky.

NCAA consensus first-team All-American in 1952 and 1954. . . . Ranked among the nation's leading scorers in 1952 (9th) and 1954 (17th). . . . Ranked among the nation's leading rebounders in 1952 (12th) and 1954 (30th). . . . Leading scorer for 1954 undefeated team that chose not to participate in national postseason competition (25-0 record). . . . Fifth-leading scorer for 1951 NCAA champion (32-2). . . . Averaged 12 points in six NCAA Tournament games in 1951 and 1952 (5-1 record). . . . Selected by the Boston Celtics in third round of 1953 NBA draft. Draft rights traded to St. Louis Hawks after he served two years in the military. . . Elected to Naismith Memorial Basketball Hall of Fame in 1977.

SEASON	G.	FGM-FGA	FG%	FTM-FTA	FT%	REB.	AVG.	PTS.	AVG.
1950-51	20	69-188	.367	45-61	.738	169	8.5	183	9.2
1951-52	32	264-633	.417	164-235	.698	528	16.5	692	21.6
1952-53	Kentucky prohibited from playing because of NCAA probation.								
1953-54	25	234-514	.455	132-191	.691	338	13.5	600	24.0
Totals	77	567-1335	.425	341-487	.700	1035	13.4	1475	19.2

Clyde Lovellette

Kansas
6-9 — C
Terre Haute, Ind. (Garfield H.S.)

NCAA consensus first-team All-American in 1951 and 1952. . . . Led the nation in scoring in 1952 after finishing 4th in 1950 and 5th in 1951. . . . Leading scorer and rebounder for 1952 NCAA Tournament champion (28-3 record). . . . Final Four Most Outstanding Player in 1952 (66 points in final two games). . . . Named to All-NCAA Tournament team in 1952 when he averaged 35.3 points in four games. . . . Leading scorer (14.1 points per game) for 1952 U.S. Olympic team. . . . Selected by the Minneapolis Lakers in 1952 NBA draft. . . . Elected to Naismith Memorial Basketball Hall of Fame in 1987.

SEASON	G.	FGM-FGA	FG%	FTM-FTA	FT%	REB.	AVG.	PTS.	AVG.
1949-50	25	214-499	.429	117-181	.646	192	7.7	545	21.8
1950-51	24	245-554	.442	58-89	.652	237	9.9	548	22.8
1951-52	28	315-660	.477	165-224	.737	357	12.8	795	28.4
Totals	77	774-1713	.452	340-494	.688	786	10.2	1888	24.5

Bob Pettit

Louisiana State
6-9 — F/C
Baton Rouge, La.

NCAA consensus first-team All-American in 1954 and consensus second-team All-American in 1953. . . . Ranked among the nation's leading scorers in 1952 (3rd), 1953 (9th) and 1954 (2nd). . . . Ranked among the nation's leaders in field-goal percentage in 1953 (9th) and 1954 (13th). . . . Ranked 11th in the nation in rebounding in 1954. . . . Leading scorer and rebounder for fourth-place team in 1953 NCAA Tournament (22-3 record). . . . Averaged 30.5 points in six NCAA Tournament games in 1953 and 1954 (3-3 record). . . . Selected by the Milwaukee Hawks in first round of 1954 NBA draft. . . . Elected to Naismith Memorial Basketball Hall of Fame in 1970.

SEASON	G.	FGM-FGA	FG%	FTM-FTA	FT%	REB.	AVG.	PTS.	AVG.
1951-52	23	237-549	.432	115-192	.599	315	13.1	589	25.6
1952-53	21	193-394	.490	133-215	.619	263	16.3	519	24.7
1953-54	25	281-573	.490	223-308	.724	432	17.3	785	31.4
Totals	69	711-1516	.469	471-715	.659	1010	14.6	1893	27.4

Oscar Robertson

Cincinnati
6-5 — G/F
Indianapolis, Ind. (Crispus Attucks H.S.)

Named national player of the year by UPI and USBWA in 1958, 1959 and 1960. . . . NCAA unanimous first-team All-American in 1958, 1959 and 1960. . . . Led the nation in scoring in 1958, 1959 and 1960. . . . Ranked among the nation's leaders in rebound percentage in 1958 (16th), 1959 (14th) and 1960 (20th). . . . Ranked among the nation's leaders in field-goal percentage in 1958 (2nd), 1959 (19th) and 1960 (15th). . . . Ranked among the nation's leaders in free-throw percentage in 1958 (33rd) and 1959 (35th). . . . Leading scorer and rebounder for NCAA Tournament third-place teams in 1959 (26-4 record) and 1960 (28-2). . . . Named to All-NCAA Tournament team in 1959 and 1960. . . . Averaged 32.4 points and 13.1 rebounds in 10 NCAA Tournament games from 1958-60 (7-3 record). . . . Tied with Jerry Lucas for scoring leadership (17 points per game) on 1960 U.S. Olympic team. . . . Selected as a territorial pick by the Cincinnati Royals in 1960 NBA draft. . . . Elected to Naismith Memorial Basketball Hall of Fame in 1979.

SEASON	G.	FGM-FGA	FG%	FTM-FTA	FT%	REB.	AVG.	PTS.	AVG.
1957-58	28	352-617	.571	280-355	.789	425	15.2	984	35.1
1958-59	30	331-650	.509	316-398	.794	489	16.3	978	32.6
1959-60	30	369-701	.526	273-361	.756	424	14.1	1011	33.7
Totals	88	1052-1968	.535	869-1114	.780	1338	15.2	2973	33.8

Bill Russell

San Francisco
6-9 — C
Oakland, Calif. (McClymonds H.S.)

Named national player of the year by UPI in 1956. . . . NCAA unanimous first-team All-American in 1956 and consensus first-team All-American in 1955. . . . One of six players to average more than 20 points and 20 rebounds per game in his career. . . . Ranked among the nation's leading rebounders in 1954 (7th), 1955 (4th) and 1956 (4th). . . . Ranked among the nation's leaders in field-goal percentage in 1954 (15th), 1955 (7th) and 1956 (9th). . . . Ranked among the nation's leading scorers in 1954 (48th), 1955 (42nd) and 1956 (58th). . . . Leading scorer and rebounder for NCAA Tournament champions in 1955 (28-1 record) and 1956 (29-0). . . . Final Four Most Outstanding Player in 1955 (47 points, 34 rebounds). . . . Named to All-NCAA Tournament team in 1955 and 1956. . . . Averaged 23.2 points in nine NCAA Tournament games in 1955 and 1956 (9-0 record). . . . Leading scorer (14.1 points per game) for 1956 U.S. Olympic team. . . . Selected by the Boston Celtics in first round of 1956 NBA draft (3rd pick overall). . . . Elected to Naismith Memorial Basketball Hall of Fame in 1974.

SEASON	G.	FGM-FGA	FG%	FTM-FTA	FT%	REB.	AVG.	PTS.	AVG.
1953-54	21	150-309	.485	117-212	.552	403	19.2	417	19.9
1954-55	29	229-423	.541	164-278	.590	594	20.5	622	21.4
1955-56	29	246-480	.513	105-212	.495	609	21.0	597	20.6
Totals	79	625-1212	.516	386-702	.550	1606	20.3	1636	20.7

Don Schlundt

Indiana
6-10 — C
South Bend, Ind. (Washington-Clay Township H.S.)

NCAA consensus first-team All-American in 1954 and consensus second-team All-American in 1953. . . . Ranked among the nation's leading scorers in 1952 (44th), 1953 (7th), 1954 (15th) and 1955 (11th). . . . Ranked among the nation's leaders in free-throw percentage in 1953 (7th) and 1955 (40th). . . . Leading scorer and rebounder for 1953 NCAA Tournament champion (23-3 record). . . . Named to 1953 All-NCAA Tournament team. . . . Averaged 27 points in six NCAA Tournament games in 1953 and 1954 (5-1 record). . . . Selected by the Syracuse Nationals in 1955 NBA draft (never played in league).

SEASON	G.	FGM-FGA	FG%	FTM-FTA	FT%	REB.	AVG.	PTS.	AVG.
1951-52	22	131-289	.453	114-171	.667	158	7.2	376	17.1
1952-53	26	206-477	.432	249-310	.803	220	8.5	661	25.4
1953-54	24	177-354	.500	229-296	.774	267	11.1	583	24.3
1954-55	22	169-377	.448	234-299	.783	215	9.8	572	26.0
Totals	94	683-1497	.456	826-1076	.768	860	9.1	2192	23.3

Jerry West

West Virginia
6-3 — G/F
Cabin Creek, W. Va.

NCAA unanimous first-team All-American in 1959 and 1960. . . . Ranked among the nation's leading scorers in 1958 (65th), 1959 (5th) and 1960 (4th). . . . Ranked among the nation's leaders in field-goal percentage in 1958 (23rd) and 1959 (13th). . . . Ranked 21st in the nation in rebound percentage in 1960. . . . Leading scorer and rebounder for 1959 NCAA Tournament runner-up (29-5 record). . . . Final Four Most Outstanding Player in 1959 (66 points, 25 rebounds, 66.7 FG%). . . . Named to 1959 All-NCAA Tournament team. . . . Averaged 30.6 points and 13.8 rebounds in nine NCAA Tournament games from 1958-60 (6-3 record). . . . Member of 1960 U.S. Olympic team (13.8 ppg). . . . Selected by the Los Angeles Lakers in first round of 1960 NBA draft (2nd pick overall). . . . Elected to Naismith Memorial Basketball Hall of Fame in 1979.

SEASON	G.	FGM-FGA	FG%	FTM-FTA	FT%	REB.	AVG.	PTS.	AVG.
1957-58	28	178-359	.496	142-194	.732	311	11.1	498	17.8
1958-59	34	340-656	.518	223-320	.697	419	12.3	903	26.6
1959-60	31	325-645	.504	258-337	.766	510	16.5	908	29.3
Totals	93	843-1660	.508	623-851	.732	1240	13.3	2309	24.8

Everett Case

Wisconsin '23 (after attending Canterbury from 1916-18)
Anderson, Ind.

Elected to Naismith Memorial Basketball Hall of Fame in 1981. . . . Reached Final Four in 1950 (3rd). . . . Coach of six Southern Conference Tournament champions—1947, 1948, 1949, 1950, 1951 and 1953. . . . Coach of four Atlantic Coast Conference Tournament champions—1954, 1955, 1956 and 1959. . . . Assistant coach at Southern Cal under Sam Barry in 1933-34.

SEASON	SCHOOL	OVERALL	LEAGUE	FINISH	POSTSEASON
1946-47	N.C. St.	26-5	11-2	1st (Southern)	NIT (2-1)
1947-48	N.C. St.	29-3	12-0	1st (Southern)	NIT (0-1)
1948-49	N.C. St.	25-8	14-1	1st (Southern)	DNP
1949-50	N.C. St.	27-6	12-2	1st (Southern)	NCAA (2-1)
1950-51	N.C. St.	30-7	13-1	1st (Southern)	NCAA (1-2); NIT (0-1)
1951-52	N.C. St.	24-10	12-2	2nd (Southern)	NCAA (1-1)
1952-53	N.C. St.	26-6	13-3	1st (Southern)	DNP
1953-54	N.C. St.	26-7	5-3	4th (ACC)	NCAA (2-1)
1954-55	N.C. St.	28-4	12-2	1st (ACC)	DNP
1955-56	N.C. St.	24-4	11-3	T1st (ACC)	(ACC) NCAA (0-1)

1956-57	N.C. St.	15-11	7-7	T4th (ACC)	DNP
1957-58	N.C. St.	18-6	10-4	T2nd (ACC)	DNP
1958-59	N.C. St.	22-4	12-2	T1st (ACC)	DNP
1959-60	N.C. St.	11-15	5-9	6th (ACC)	DNP
1960-61	N.C. St.	16-9	8-6	4th (ACC)	DNP
1961-62	N.C. St.	11-6	10-4	3rd (ACC)	DNP
1962-63	N.C. St.	10-11	5-9	T4th (ACC)	DNP
1963-64	N.C. St.	8-11	4-10	T7th (ACC)	DNP
1964-65	N.C. St.	—	1-1	—	DNP

19-Year Coaching Record: 377-134 (.738) overall; 87-11 (.888) in Southern Conference; 89-60 (.597) in Atlantic Coast Conference; 20-1 (.952) in Southern Conference Tournament; 15-7 (.682) in ACC Tournament; 6-6 (.500) in NCAA Tournament; 2-3 (.400) in NIT.

Adolph Rupp

Kansas '23
Halstead, Kan.

Coached teams to four NCAA titles (1948, 1949, 1951 and 1958). . . . His 1942 squad finished tied for third in the 1942 NCAA Tournament and his 1966 team was runner-up to Texas Western. . . . Elected to Naismith Memorial Basketball Hall of Fame in 1968. . . . Named national coach of the year by UPI in 1959 and 1966, and by the USBWA in 1966. . . . Directed Kentucky to 1946 NIT title. Coached UK to NIT championship game again in 1947. His 1944 UK team finished fourth at NIT. . . . Coach of 1933 Kentucky team that was selected as national champion by the Helms Foundation. . . . Holds NCAA career record for most victories. . . . Coached Kentucky to a SEC-record 24 conference and 13 tournament titles. . . . Played college ball for Phog Allen at Kansas.

SEASON	SCHOOL	OVERALL	LEAGUE	FINISH	POSTSEASON
1930-31	Kentucky	15-3	—	—	—
1931-32	Kentucky	15-2	—	—	—
1932-33	Kentucky	21-3	8-0	1st (SEC)	—
1933-34	Kentucky	16-1	11-0	—	—
1934-35	Kentucky	19-2	11-0	T1st (SEC)	—
1935-36	Kentucky	15-6	6-2	—	—
1936-37	Kentucky	17-5	5-3	1st (SEC)	—

1937-38	Kentucky	13-5	6-0	—	DNP
1938-39	Kentucky	16-4	5-2	1st (SEC)	DNP
1939-40	Kentucky	15-6	4-4	1st (SEC)	DNP
1940-41	Kentucky	17-8	8-1	—	DNP
1941-42	Kentucky	19-6	6-2	1st (SEC)	NCAA (1-1)
1942-43	Kentucky	17-6	8-1	—	DNP
1943-44	Kentucky	19-2	—	1st (SEC)	NIT (2-1)
1944-45	Kentucky	22-4	4-1	1st (SEC)	NCAA (1-1)
1945-46	Kentucky	28-2	6-0	1st (SEC)	NIT (3-0)
1946-47	Kentucky	34-3	11-0	1st (SEC)	NIT (2-1)
1947-48	Kentucky	36-3	9-0	1st (SEC)	NCAA (3-0)
1948-49	Kentucky	32-2	13-0	1st (SEC)	NIT (0-1), NCAA (3-0)
1949-50	Kentucky	25-5	11-2	1st (SEC)	NIT (0-1)
1950-51	Kentucky	32-2	14-0	1st (SEC)	NCAA (4-0)
1951-52	Kentucky	29-3	14-0	1st (SEC)	NCAA (1-1)
1953-54	Kentucky	25-0	14-0	T1st (SEC)	DNP
1954-55	Kentucky	23-3	12-2	1st (SEC)	NCAA (1-1)
1955-56	Kentucky	20-6	12-2	2nd (SEC)	NCAA (1-1)
1956-57	Kentucky	23-5	12-2	1st (SEC)	NCAA (1-1)
1957-58	Kentucky	23-6	12-2	1st (SEC)	NCAA (4-0)
1958-59	Kentucky	24-3	12-2	T2nd (SEC)	NCAA (1-1)
1959-60	Kentucky	18-7	10-4	3rd (SEC)	DNP
1960-61	Kentucky	19-9	10-4	T2nd (SEC)	NCAA (1-1)
1961-62	Kentucky	23-3	13-1	T1st (SEC)	NCAA (1-1)
1962-63	Kentucky	16-9	8-6	5th (SEC)	DNP
1963-64	Kentucky	21-6	11-3	1st (SEC)	NCAA (0-2)
1964-65	Kentucky	15-10	10-6	5th (SEC)	DNP
1965-66	Kentucky	27-2	15-1	1st (SEC)	NCAA (3-1)
1966-67	Kentucky	13-13	8-10	T5th (SEC)	DNP
1967-68	Kentucky	22-5	15-3	1st (SEC)	NCAA (1-1)
1968-69	Kentucky	23-5	16-2	1st (SEC)	NCAA (1-1)
1969-70	Kentucky	26-2	17-1	1st (SEC)	NCAA (1-1)
1970-71	Kentucky	22-6	16-2	1st (SEC)	NCAA (0-2)
1971-72	Kentucky	21-7	14-4	T1st (SEC)	NCAA (1-1)

NOTE: Kentucky did not field a team in 1952-53. From 1933-50 the SEC champion was determined by a tournament, except for 1935.

41-Year Coaching Record: 876-190 (.822) at Kentucky; 397-75 (.845) in Southeastern Conference; 57-6 (.905) in SEC Tournament; 30-18 (.625) in NCAA Tournament; 7-4 (.636) in NIT.

4

THE UCLA DYNASTY:
THE 1960s

The 1960s marked the beginning of perhaps the greatest dynasty in the history of sports as UCLA began its march toward 10 NCAA championships in a 12-year span. Center Lew Alcindor staked a claim as the most influential player of all time by propelling the Bruins to 88 victories in 90 games the last three years of the decade. Both of UCLA's defeats with Alcindor manning the middle were by two points.

North Carolina began to assert itself under coach Dean Smith. From 1967 through 1969, the Tar Heels finished first in the ACC standings and also captured the league tournament title to become the only school ever to win both championships three consecutive years.

The South was behind the times but African Americans were finally allowed to play in the ACC, SEC and SWC. Southwestern Louisiana was the first school among Louisiana state-supported institutions to have black players and actually got in hot water from Gulf States Conference officials in 1966-67 for signing black players. The Big Ten had embraced African American players for some time but the only conference member to

win more than 70 percent of its games during the decade was Ohio State.

The end of the decade supplied not only Alcindor's dominance but the marvelous showmanship of the M Boys—guards Pete Maravich, Rick Mount and Calvin Murphy. The combination of their influences dictated that college hoops would never be the same again. It's difficult to comprehend how many points Maravich, Mount and Murphy would have scored if there had been a three-point arc during their college days.

Surprisingly, Davidson was the only school other than UCLA to have as many as three different players become an NCAA consensus first- or second-team All-American the last half of the decade (1965 through 1969).

Bradley was one of the 10 winningest programs by percentage in the '60s, but the Braves didn't appear in the NCAA Tournament during the decade. They were perennial bridesmaids, finishing among the top three in the Missouri Valley Conference standings 10 consecutive years from 1957 through 1966 yet never winning an undisputed league crown in that span.

1959-60

AT A GLANCE

NCAA Champion: Ohio State (25-3; coached by Fred Taylor; won Big Ten title with a 13-1 record, which was two games ahead of Indiana).

NIT Champion: Bradley (27-2; coached by Chuck Orsborn; finished in second place in Missouri Valley with a 12-2 record, which was one game behind Cincinnati).

NCAA Probation: Arizona State, Auburn, Montana State, North Carolina State, Seattle.

NCAA Consensus First-Team All-Americans: Darrall Imhoff, C, Sr., California; Jerry Lucas, C, Soph., Ohio State; Oscar Robertson, F, Sr., Cincinnati; Tom Stith, F, Jr., St. Bonaventure; Jerry West, F, Sr., West Virginia.

National Player of the Year: Robertson (33.7 ppg, 14.1 rpg, 7.3 apg, 52.6 FG%).

National Coach of the Year: Pete Newell, California (28-2/UPI, USBWA).

Wake Forest's team captain Dave Budd (left) and Billy Packer.

Tom and Sam Stith combined to average 52 points per game, an NCAA single-season record for brothers on the same team. Tom Stith, runner-up in scoring nationally to Cincinnati's Oscar Robertson, improved from ranking 71st in the country the previous year.

Tom Stith averaged more points per game than Robertson over the last two-thirds of the campaign, but the Big O hung on for the title after averaging over 40 points per game through his senior season's first 10 contests. The season's single-game scoring high was Robertson's school- and Missouri Valley Conference-record 62 points against North Texas State.

Robertson's reputation was further enhanced because of his willingness to distribute the ball. He went on to become the first NBA player to average more than 10 assists per game in a season. His greatest assist, however, came in April 1997 when he donated a kidney to his ailing daughter, Tia, who suffered from lupus and needed a transplant.

St. Bonaventure's Tom Stith (31.5 ppg), Tennessee Tech's Jimmy Hagan (28.8) and Montana State's Larry Chanay (23.7) set school records for highest scoring average in a single season. . . . Tom Stith poured in 46 points, including a jumper with 15 seconds remaining in triple overtime, in a 90-89 triumph over Providence to extend the Bonnies' homecourt winning streak to 91 consecutive games. . . . Chanay, originally from Pine Bluff, Ark., became MSU's all-time scoring leader after a military stint. . . . Ohio State's Jerry Lucas had the largest-ever margin over the national runner-up in field-goal shooting. Lucas hit 63.7 percent of his shots compared to 57.6 percent for Cincinnati's Paul Hogue. . . . William & Mary defeated West Virginia, 94-86, to end the Mountaineers' streak of 56 consecutive victories against Southern Conference competition. . . . West Virginia's Jerry West finished his career as the shortest player (6-3) to score more than 2,300 points and grab more than 1,200 rebounds. West, the Mountaineers' all-time leading rebounder (1,240), tied a

1959–60 INDIVIDUAL LEADERS

SCORING

PLAYER	PTS.	AVG.
Robertson, Cincinnati	1011	33.7
T. Stith, St. Bonaventure	819	31.5
Darrow, Bowling Green	705	29.4
West, West Virginia	908	29.3
Burgess, Gonzaga	751	28.9
Butler, Niagara	714	28.6
Dischinger, Purdue	605	26.3
Lucas, Ohio St.	710	26.3
DeBusschere, Detroit	691	25.6
Mudd, N. Texas St.	605	25.2

REBOUNDING

PLAYER	REB.	PCT.
Wright, Pacific	380	.234
DeBusschere, Detroit	540	.198

Mortell, Virginia	350	.194
Cohen, William & Mary	471	.194
Smith, Virginia Tech	495	.190
Jones, Niagara	383	.190
Hadnot, Providence	473	.186
Kojis, Marquette	384	.186
Farley, Cornell	466	.185
Jolliff, Ohio	445	.180

FIELD GOAL PERCENTAGE

PLAYER	FGM	FGA	PCT.
Lucas, Ohio St.	283	444	.637
Hogue, Cincinnati	152	264	.576
Gunter, Seton Hall	128	224	.571
Walker, Bradley	244	436	.560
Nordmann, St. Louis	173	310	.558
Dischinger, Purdue	201	368	.546
Hughes, Texas	111	205	.541

Johnson, Minnesota	186	346	.538
Fibbe, Auburn	108	201	.537
Hart, Auburn	108	201	.537

FREE THROW PERCENTAGE

PLAYER	FTM	FTA	PCT.
Waters, Mississippi	103	118	.873
Larese, N. Carolina	131	151	.868
Kaiser, Georgia Tech	164	190	.863
Carl, DePaul	135	158	.854
Smith, Middle Tenn.	144	170	.847
Butler, Niagara	158	187	.845
Pipczynski, Connecticut	102	122	.836
Names, Washington	90	108	.833
Clarke, St. Joseph's	100	121	.826
Adkins, Virginia	109	132	.826

1959–60 TEAM LEADERS

SCORING OFFENSE

SCHOOL	PTS.	AVG.
Ohio St.	2532	90.4
Miami (Fla.)	2427	89.9
West Virginia	2775	89.5
Cincinnati	2602	86.7
Arizona St.	1930	83.9

SCORING DEFENSE

SCHOOL	PTS.	AVG.
California	1486	49.5
Oklahoma St.	1304	52.2
Stanford	1376	55.0
Oregon St.	1458	56.1
Providence	1632	56.3

FIELD GOAL PERCENTAGE

SCHOOL	FGM	FGA	PCT.
Auburn	532	1022	.521
Cincinnati	1035	2025	.511
Ohio St.	1044	2101	.497
Texas	713	1503	.474
Bradley	921	1969	.468

FREE THROW PERCENTAGE

SCHOOL	FTM	FTA	PCT.
Auburn	424	549	.772
Tulane	438	573	.764
North Carolina	542	715	.758
Mississippi	451	600	.752
East Tennessee St.	438	585	.749

REBOUNDING

SCHOOL	TOTAL REB.	REB.	PCT.
Iona	1736	1054	.607
Cornell	2522	1492	.592
Ohio St.	2447	1415	.578
St. Francis (Pa.)	2472	1429	.578
Loyola (Calif.)	2355	1359	.577

school record when he retrieved 31 missed shots in a game against George Washington.

South Carolina lost 14 consecutive games to North Carolina in their series until the Gamecocks prevailed, 85-81. . . . Virginia posted its lone victory over North Carolina State (53-48) in a 17-game stretch of their series from 1955 through 1962. . . . Kentucky's streak of 20-win seasons ended at 14 when the Wildcats compiled an 18-7 record. Excluding the 1952-53 campaign when the Wildcats were banned by the NCAA from competing, it was the first time they didn't finish among the top 10 in a final wire-service poll. . . . Auburn (19-3) became the first school to lead the nation in field-goal shooting by hitting more than half of its shots (52.1 percent). The Tigers also paced the country in free-throw accuracy (77.2 percent) en route to their only SEC regular-season

championship. Their biggest victory was a 61-60 decision over Kentucky when Jimmy Fibbe converted both ends of a one-and-one free-throw opportunity with four seconds remaining and backup center John Helmlinger blocked a last-second shot by UK's Allen Feldhaus. Auburn's team was fondly dubbed "Snow White and the Seven Dwarfs" because white-haired coach Joel Eaves' starting lineup didn't feature a player taller than 6-4. . . . Harbin (Red) Lawson, who coached Georgia for 14 seasons from 1951-52 through 1964-65, came as close as he ever did to avoiding a losing season with the Bulldogs when they went 12-13. It's the longest stint at a major college with nothing but losing records.

Bowling Green's James Darrow (52 points vs. Toledo in overtime and 52 vs. Marshall), Manhattan's Bob Mealy (51 vs. CCNY), Cornell's George

Farley (47 at Princeton) and Arizona's Ernie McCray (46 vs. Los Angeles State) set school single-game scoring records. Darrow contributed 16 of Bowling Green's 17 field goals after intermission against Toledo. . . . Houston competed as a member of the Missouri Valley for the final season. . . . Future broadcaster Billy Packer was 6 for 35 from the floor for Wake Forest in three ACC Tournament games. It was the last year that no ACC school finished among the Top 10 in a final wire-service poll.

Sophomore Dave DeBusschere grabbed a school-record 39 rebounds for Detroit against Central Michigan. It was one of four games in his career that DeBusschere topped the 30-rebound plateau. . . . Dayton's Garry Roggenburk (32 vs. Miami of Ohio), New Mexico's Tom King (26 vs. Wyoming) and Virginia's Bob Mortell (25 vs. Washington & Lee) set school single-game rebounding records. Michigan State's Horace Walker retrieved 28 missed shots in a Big Ten game against Iowa on his way to setting a league record for highest single-season rebound average (18.3 rpg).

Toledo, coached by Eddie Melvin, notched an 18-6 record to end its streak of five consecutive losing marks and start a string of 26 straight winning seasons. . . . Iowa State registered a 15-9 mark in Glen Anderson's first year as head coach. It was the Cyclones' last season with fewer than 10 defeats. . . . Lafayette's streak of consecutive winning seasons ended at 17 when the Leopards compiled a 12-13 record. . . . Hofstra (23-1/coached by Butch van Breda Kolff) posted the best record of any team in the nation, but failed to win the Middle Atlantic Conference College Division-North because its only defeat came against first-place Wagner. . . . Rutgers defeated Penn, 51-44, for the Scarlet Knights' only victory in their first 17 meetings with the Quakers through 1965-66. . . . St. Joseph's achieved its average of 20 victories over the last five years, but one of the Hawks' seven defeats was the most lopsided in school history—by 44 points at Cincinnati (123-79). . . . Connecticut, coached by Hugh Greer, captured its 10th consecutive Yankee Conference championship despite

1959-60 FINAL NATIONAL POLLS

AP	UPI	SCHOOL (RECORD)	HEAD COACH
1	2	Cincinnati (28-2)	George Smith
2	1	California (28-2)	Pete Newell
3	3	Ohio State (25-3)	Fred Taylor
4	4	Bradley (27-2)	Chuck Orsborn
5	6	West Virginia (26-5)	Fred Schaus
6	5	Utah (26-3)	Jack Gardner
7	10	Indiana (20-4)	Branch McCracken
8	7	Utah State (24-5)	Cecil Baker
9	11	St. Bonaventure (21-5)	Eddie Donovan
10	–	Miami (Fla.) (23-4)	Bruce Hale
11	17	Auburn (19-3)	Joel Eaves
12	12	NYU (22-5)	Lou Rossini
13	8	Georgia Tech (22-6)	John Hyder
14	18	Providence (24-5)	Joe Mullaney
15	19	St. Louis (19-9)	John Bennington
16	–	Holy Cross (20-6)	Roy Leenig
17	9	Villanova (20-6)	Al Severance
18	15	Duke (17-11)	Vic Bubas
19	–	Wake Forest (21-7)	Bones McKinney
20	–	St. John's (17-5)	Joe Lapchick
–	13	Texas (19-8)	Harold Bradley
–	14	North Carolina (18-6)	Frank McGuire
–	16	Kansas State (16-10)	Tex Winter
–	20	Dayton (21-7)	Tom Blackburn

having its 28-game winning streak against Maine snapped by the Black Bears. . . . Georgetown lost 12 consecutive games in its series with Maryland until defeating the Terrapins, 66-51.

Texas, which finished in the SWC cellar the previous year when its only league triumphs were against Rice, captured the conference crown in Harold Bradley's first season as head coach of the Longhorns. . . . The SWC conducted its final preconference tournament, an event that started in the 1951-52 season. . . . John Evans was in his first year as coach for Idaho State when the school won its eighth consecutive Rocky Mountain Conference championship. It was the final season of the league. Evans was the third different Idaho State coach in five years to capture a Rocky Mountain crown. . . . Utah State (24-5/coached by Cecil Baker) and Miami, Fla. (23-4/Bruce Hale) had their winningest seasons in school history. . . . UCLA's Gary Cunningham, who would later coach his alma mater, sank all 28 of his free-throw attempts in conference competition.

Washington (Mo.) competed in its final season at the major-college level. . . . NYU made its lone appearance in the Top 20 of a final wire-service poll. . . . CCNY's Nat Holman ended his 37-year coaching career early in the season with a 423-190 record. . . . Pete Newell, who coached San Francis-

SEASON STATISTICS OF OHIO STATE REGULARS

PLAYER	POS.	CL.	G.	FG%	FT%	PPG	RPG
Jerry Lucas	C	So.	27	.637	.770	26.3	16.4
Larry Siegfried	G	Jr.	28	.466	.750	13.3	3.8
Mel Nowell	G	So.	28	.473	.767	13.1	2.6
John Havlicek	F	So.	28	.462	.716	12.2	7.3
Joe Roberts	F	Sr.	28	.480	.679	11.0	6.9
Richard Furry	F	Sr.	28	.455	.606	5.1	3.3
Bob Knight	F-G	So.	21	.405	.630	3.7	2.0
Howard Nourse	C	Sr.	17	.511	1.000	3.1	2.7
Gary Gearhart	G	So.	19	.404	.438	2.6	1.2
Richie Hoyt	G	Sr.	23	.423	.778	2.5	0.8
David Barker	G	Sr.	16	.407	.167	1.4	0.8
TEAM TOTALS			28	.497	.717	90.4	50.5

1960 FINAL FOUR CHAMPIONSHIP GAME

KANSAS CITY, MO

OHIO STATE (75)	FG-A	FT-A	REB.	PF	PTS.
Havlicek	4-8	4-5	6	2	12
Roberts	5-6	0-1	5	1	10
Lucas	7-9	2-2	10	2	16
Nowell	6-7	3-3	4	2	15
Siegfried	5-6	3-6	1	2	13
Gearhart	0-1	0-0	1	0	0
Cedargren	0-0	1-2	1	1	1
Furry	2-4	0-0	3	1	4
Hoyt	0-1	0-0	0	0	0
Barker	0-0	0-0	0	0	0
Knight	0-1	0-0	0	1	0
Nourse	2-3	0-0	3	1	4
Team			1		
TOTALS	31-46	13-19	35	13	75

FG%: .674. FT%: .684.

CALIFORNIA (55)	FG-A	FT-A	REB.	PF	PTS.
McClintock	4-15	2-3	3	3	10
Gillis	4-9	0-0	1	1	8
Imhoff	3-9	2-2	5	2	8
Wendell	0-6	4-4	0	2	4
Shultz	2-8	2-2	4	4	6
Mann	3-5	1-1	0	0	7
Doughty	4-5	3-3	6	1	11
Stafford	0-1	1-2	0	1	1
Morrison	0-0	0-0	1	1	0
Averbuck	0-0	0-1	1	0	0
Pearson	0-1	0-0	0	0	0
Alexander	0-0	0-0	0	0	0
Team			7		
TOTALS	20-59	15-18	28	15	55

FG%: .339. FT%: .833.
Halftime: Ohio State 37-19.

NATIONAL SEMIFINALS

CALIFORNIA (64): McClintock 2-11 2-4 6, Dalton 2-4 3-4 7, Imhoff 10-25 2-5 22, Fitzpatrick 2-9 0-0 4, Buch 7-15 4-6 18, Grout 2-7 1-2 5, Simpson 1-2 0-0 2. Team 26-73 (.356) 12-21 (.571) 64.

CINCINNATI (58): Robertson 5-16 9-11 19, Wiesenhahn 5-11 0-0 10, Tenwick 2-6 1-1 5, Davis 6-15 1-2 13, Whitaker 4-7 0-2 8, Landfried 0-1 3-5 3, Bouldin 0-0 0-1 0. Team 22-56 (.393) 14-22 (.636) 58.

Halftime: Cincinnati 33-29.

WEST VIRGINIA (94): West 12-21 14-20 38, Akers 2-5 1-2 5, Clousson 5-5 2-2 12, Smith 5-9 2-4 12, Bolyard 4-10 5-7 13, Ritchie 2-6 0-2 4, Patrone 1-4 0-0 2, Retton 3-4 0-0 6, Schertzniger 0-0 0-0 0, Posch 1-2 0-0 2, Goode 0-0 0-0 0, Visnic 0-0 0-0 0. Team 35-66 (.530) 24-37 (.649) 94.

LOUISVILLE (79): Goldstein 6-10 9-9 21, Turner 8-16 2-5 18, Sawyer 2-6 3-4 7, Tieman 1-7 1-3 3, Andrews 9-15 1-1 19, Kitchen 3-7 0-6 6, Leathers 2-8 1-1 5, Geiling 0-0 0-0 0, Stacey 0-0 0-0 0. Team 31-69 (.449) 17-21 (.810) 79.

Halftime: West Virginia 48-32.

ALL-TOURNAMENT TEAM

Darrall Imhoff, C, Sr., California (33 points, 16 rebounds in final two games)
*Jerry Lucas, C, Soph., Ohio State (35 points, 23 rebounds)
Mel Nowell, G, Soph., Ohio State (21 points)
Oscar Robertson, F, Sr., Cincinnati (50 points, 24 rebounds)
Tom Sanders, C, Sr., New York University (35 points, 33 rebounds)

*Named Most Outstanding Player.

co, Michigan State and California, retired after a 14-year coaching career with a 234-123 record. Newell stepped down despite being named national coach of the year and guiding Cal to a second-place finish in the NCAA Tournament.

1960 NCAA Tournament

Summary: Ohio State became the only titlist to win all of its tournament games by more than 15 points. Center Jerry Lucas, a first-team All-American as a sophomore, averaged 24 points and 16 rebounds in four playoff contests for the Buckeyes. He collected 36 points and 25 rebounds to help them erase a six-point halftime deficit in their Mideast Regional opener against Western Kentucky. Ohio State, playing in the Bay Area (San

Francisco) against the nation's top defensive team (California), hit a sizzling 84.2 percent of their first-half field-goal attempts (16-19) en route to a 75-55 victory over the defending champion Bears. Bear in mind this season marked the first time a school led the major-college ranks by hitting more than half of its shots from the floor (52.1 percent by Auburn). Ohio State's five starters—sophomores Lucas, John Havlicek, and Mel Nowell, senior Joe Roberts and junior Larry Siegfried—were all high school centers. They each scored in double figures in the NCAA final before eventually playing at least two seasons in the NBA or ABA or both.

Outcome for Defending Champion: The only regular-season defeat for California (28-2)

1960 CHAMPIONSHIP BRACKET

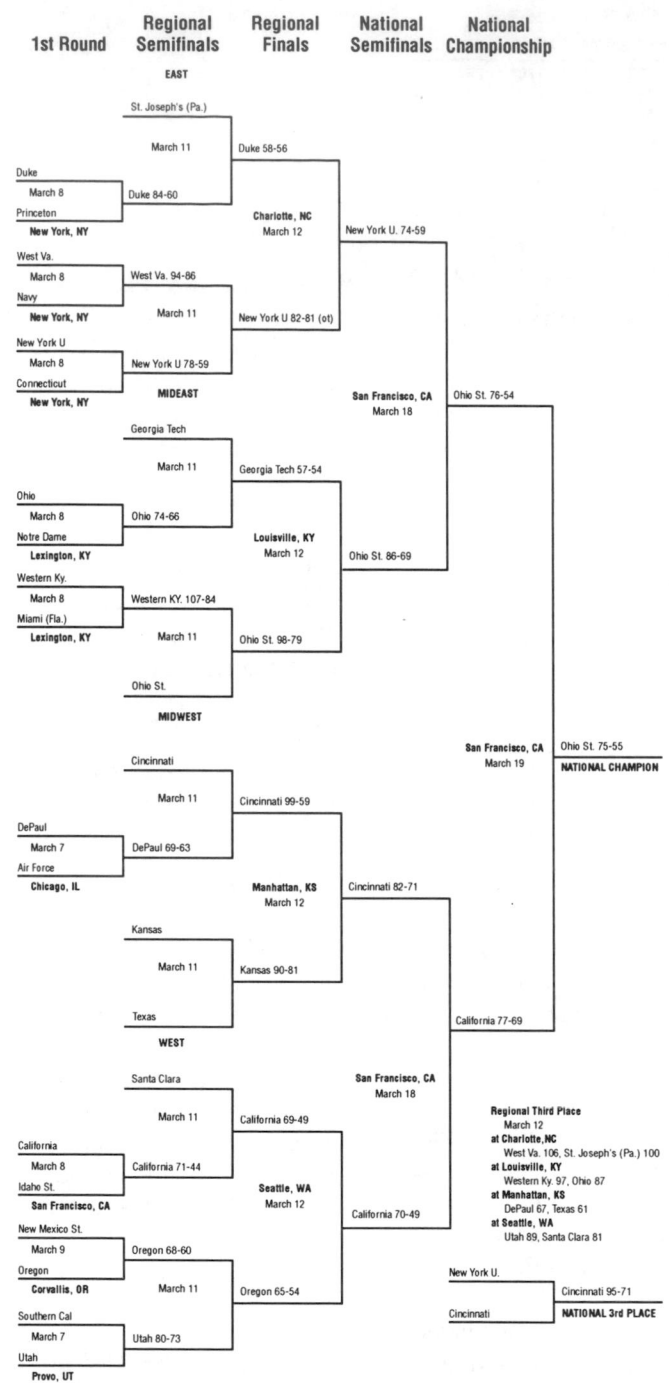

	Regional Semifinals	Regional Finals	National Semifinals	National Championship
1st Round				

EAST

St. Joseph's (Pa.)

March 11 — Duke 58-56

Duke
March 8 — Duke 84-60
Princeton
New York, NY

Charlotte, NC
March 12 — New York U. 74-59

West Va.
March 8 — West Va. 94-86
Navy
New York, NY
March 11 — New York U 82-81 (ot)

New York U
March 8 — New York U 78-59
Connecticut
New York, NY

MIDEAST

San Francisco, CA
March 18 — Ohio St. 76-54

Georgia Tech
March 11 — Georgia Tech 57-54

Ohio
March 8 — Ohio 74-66
Notre Dame
Lexington, KY

Louisville, KY
March 12 — Ohio St. 86-69

Western Ky.
March 8 — Western KY. 107-84
Miami (Fla.)
Lexington, KY
March 11 — Ohio St. 98-79

Ohio St.

MIDWEST

San Francisco, CA
March 19 — Ohio St. 75-55
NATIONAL CHAMPION

Cincinnati
March 11 — Cincinnati 99-59

DePaul
March 7 — DePaul 69-63
Air Force
Chicago, IL

Manhattan, KS
March 12 — Cincinnati 82-71

Kansas
March 11 — Kansas 90-81

Texas

WEST

San Francisco, CA
March 18 — California 77-69

Santa Clara
March 11 — California 69-49

California
March 8 — California 71-44
Idaho St.
San Francisco, CA

Seattle, WA
March 12 — California 70-49

New Mexico St.
March 9 — Oregon 68-60
Oregon
Corvallis, OR
March 11 — Oregon 65-54

Southern Cal
March 7 — Utah 80-73
Utah
Provo, UT

Regional Third Place
March 12
at Charlotte, NC
West Va. 106, St. Joseph's (Pa.) 100
at Louisville, KY
Western Ky. 97, Ohio 87
at Manhattan, KS
DePaul 67, Texas 61
at Seattle, WA
Utah 89, Santa Clara 81

New York U.
Cincinnati 95-71
Cincinnati
NATIONAL 3rd PLACE

was at Southern Cal (65-57), ending the Bears' 30-game winning streak.

Star Gazing: Oscar Robertson, who generated glittering averages of 32.6 points per game and 33.7 in leading Cincinnati to the national semifinals in 1959 and 1960, respectively, before the Bearcats were beaten both years by California. The Bears restricted the Big O to a total of 37 points in the two Final Four games when he was just nine of 32 from the floor. He had poured in a tourney-high 43 points in an 82-71 triumph over Kansas in the Midwest Regional final.

Biggest Upset: Oregon, which lost seven of its last 12 regular-season games, defeated Utah, 65-54, in the West Regional semifinals. Utah, ranked No. 5 by UPI and No. 6 by AP entering the tourney, didn't have a player score more than 10 points against the Ducks.

One and Only: Idaho State became the only school to make as many as eight consecutive NCAA Tournament appearances from the year it participated in the event for the first time (since 1953 under three different coaches). . . . Ohio State's Fred Taylor became the only coach of an NCAA titlist to previously play major league baseball (first baseman for the Washington Senators in parts of three seasons from 1950 through 1952).

Numbers Game: Ohio State, the only team to lead the nation in scoring offense and win the NCAA championship in the same season, is also the only champion to win all of its tournament games by more than 15 points. . . . Lucas scored his playoff career-high 36 points in his tournament debut (98-79 victory over Western Kentucky in Mideast Regional semifinal). . . . West Virginia swingman Jerry West became the only player to score at least 25 points in eight consecutive tournament games (1959 and 1960). West is also the only player to rank among the top five in scoring average in both the NCAA Tournament (30.6 points per game) and NBA playoffs (29.1 ppg). . . . Georgia Tech, coached by Whack Hyder, made its only NCAA playoff appearance prior to 1985 and Miami (Fla.), coached by Bruce Hale, participated in its lone NCAA Tournament.

Scoring Leader: Oscar Robertson, Cincinnati (122 points, 30.5 ppg).

Highest Scoring Average: Jerry West, West Virginia (105 points, 35 ppg).

Rebounding Leader: Tom Sanders, NYU (83 rebounds, 16.6 rpg).

Highest Rebounding Average: Howard Jolliff, Ohio University (65 rebounds, 21.7 rpg).

1960-61

AT A GLANCE

NCAA Champion: Cincinnati (27-3; coached by Ed Jucker; won Missouri Valley title with a 10-2 record, which was one game ahead of Bradley).

NIT Champion: Providence (24-5; coached by Joe Mullaney).

NCAA Probation: Auburn, Indiana, Kansas, Loyola (La.), Montana State, North Carolina.

NCAA Consensus First-Team All-Americans: Terry Dischinger, F, Jr., Purdue; Roger Kaiser, G, Sr., Georgia Tech; Jerry Lucas, C, Jr., Ohio State; Tom Stith, F, Sr., St. Bonaventure; Chet Walker, F, Jr., Bradley.

National Player of the Year: Lucas (24.9 ppg, 17.4 rpg, 62.3 FG%).

National Coach of the Year: Fred Taylor, Ohio State (27-1/UPI, USBWA).

Scandal reared its ugly head again. The only player to score 40 or more points in a Final Four contest and not eventually play in the NBA was St. Joseph's forward Jack Egan, who scored a tourney-high 42 points in a four-overtime, 127-120 triumph against Utah in the national third-place game. Egan became a third-round draft choice of Philadelphia but forfeited the opportunity to play in the pros when he was implicated in a game-fixing scandal. Egan, who scored a school-record 47 points at Gettysburg earlier in the season (mark subsequently tied), was susceptible to such shenanigans inasmuch as he was the father of two children and his wife had suffered a miscarriage just before the campaign started.

North Carolina State forward Don Gallagher was also an ideal target for gamblers' enticements, given his poor-class family background and the fact he was a married man struggling to make ends meet. After his life was threatened by underworld figures, Gallagher was pressured into enlisting three teammates to help alter the outcomes of games (Brooklyn natives Anton Muehlbauer and Stan Niewierowski and Louisville product Terry Litchfield).

A total of 37 players from 22 schools, including legendary Brooklyn playground heroes Roger Brown and Connie Hawkins, who spent their freshman years at Dayton and Iowa, respectively, were implicated in point-shaving transgressions. While in high school, Brown and Hawkins reportedly associated with gambler Jack Molinas, who bought them a few meals and let them use his automobile.

"We just knew him from the playgrounds," Brown recalled. "How did we know he was a gambler? People don't just walk up to you and say, 'Hi, I'm a known gambler.' We had not reason to question him because he was a practicing attorney."

Brown and Hawkins were banned from the NBA, but the ban was later rescinded and their "blackball" suit against the NBA was settled out of court. "They found me guilty without even a trial," Brown said sharply. "I was led to believe that's not the way it's done in the United States."

Indiana's Walt Bellamy set a Big Ten Conference mark with a school-record 33 rebounds in a game against Michigan when the Hoosiers (95) and the Wolverines (57) combined for an NCAA-record 152 rebounds (see accompanying box score). . . . Bowling Green's Nate Thurmond established a Mid-American Conference single-season standard by averaging 18.7 rebounds per game.

Gonzaga's Frank Burgess closed his season with a 37-point outburst to win the scoring title with a 32.38 average, edging East Tennessee State's Tom Chilton, who was second with a 32.13

Georgia Tech All-American Roger Kaiser.

average. Burgess (against UC Davis), Chilton (Austin Peay) and Purdue's Terry Dischinger (Michigan State) tied for the national high in scoring with 52 points. The outbursts for Burgess and Chilton were school records. . . . Burgess, Chilton, Pacific's Ken Stanley (24 ppg) and Bucknell's Joe Steiner (22) set school records for highest scoring average in a single season. Chilton's average is the highest in Ohio Valley Conference history.

William & Mary's Jeff Cohen (49 points vs. Richmond), Missouri's Joe Scott (46 vs. Nebraska) and Tulane's Jim Kerwin (45 vs. Southeastern Louisiana) set school single-game scoring records. . . . Oklahoma State didn't finish among the top three in national defense rankings for the first time in 26 years. The top four defensive teams were all from the San Francisco Bay Area—Santa Clara (48.7), San Jose State (50.3), San Francisco (51.4) and California (54.2).

1960-61 INDIVIDUAL LEADERS

SCORING

PLAYER	PTS.	AVG.
Burgess, Gonzaga	842	32.4
Chilton, E. Tennessee St.	771	32.1
Stith, St. Bonaventure	830	29.6
Dischinger, Purdue	648	28.2
McGill, Utah	862	27.8
Chappell, Wake Forest	745	26.6
Foley, Holy Cross	688	26.5
Walker, Bradley	656	25.2
Heyman, Duke	629	25.2
Warner, Gettysburg	623	24.9
Lucas, Ohio St.	671	24.9

REBOUNDING

PLAYER	REB.	PCT.
Lucas, Ohio St.	470	.198

Thurmond, Bowling Green	449	.196
Cohen, William & Mary	424	.185
DeBusschere, Detroit	514	.180
Hadnot, Providence	475	.178
Chilton, E. Tennessee St.	403	.175
Bellamy, Indiana	428	.171
Ardon, Tulane	392	.168
Kojis, Marquette	462	.167
Smith, Virginia Tech	362	.164

FIELD GOAL PERCENTAGE

PLAYER	FGM	FGA	PCT.
Lucas, Ohio St.	256	411	.623
Gunter, Seton Hall	200	325	.615
Youngkin, Duke	146	253	.577
Dischinger, Purdue	215	373	.576
Lundy, Lafayette	174	303	.574
Havlicek, Ohio St.	183	321	.570

Ward, Boston College	115	202	.569
Walker, Bradley	238	423	.563
Weiss, Rhode Island	111	199	.558
Hull, Wake Forest	114	206	.553

FREE THROW PERCENTAGE

PLAYER	FTM	FTA	PCT.
Sherard, Army	135	154	.877
Carl, DePaul	161	184	.875
Kaiser, Georgia Tech	176	203	.867
Thompson, Morehead St.	180	208	.865
Carlton, Arkansas	101	117	.863
Siegfried, Ohio St.	123	143	.860
Strickland, Oregon	90	106	.849
Patterson, Clemson	146	173	.844
Zeller, Miami (Ohio)	172	205	.839
Pursiful, Kentucky	99	118	.839

1960-61 TEAM LEADERS

SCORING OFFENSE

SCHOOL	PTS.	AVG.
St. Bonaventure	2479	88.5
Loyola (Ill.)	1989	86.5
West Virginia	2325	86.1
Virginia Tech	1874	85.2
Ohio St.	2383	85.1

SCORING DEFENSE

SCHOOL	PTS.	AVG.
Santa Clara	1314	48.7
San Jose St.	1254	50.2
San Francisco	1440	51.4
California	1192	54.2
Portland	1415	56.6

FIELD GOAL PERCENTAGE

SCHOOL	FGM	FGA	PCT.
Ohio St.	939	1886	.498
St. Bonaventure	1010	2041	.495
Bradley	798	1622	.492
Auburn	500	1018	.491
Utah	1008	2069	.487

FREE THROW PERCENTAGE

SCHOOL	FTM	FTA	PCT.
Tulane	459	604	.760
Ohio St.	505	671	.753
West Texas St.	421	561	.750
W. Kentucky	554	742	.747
Arkansas	428	574	.746

REBOUNDING

SCHOOL	TOTAL REB.	REB.	PCT.
Bradley	2247	1330	.592
Memphis St.	2332	1366	.586
Niagara	1796	1048	.584
Cornell	2406	1384	.575
Cincinnati	2706	1553	.574

Tom Meschery, the West Coast Athletic Conference player of the year, finished his career as St. Mary's all-time leading rebounder. Meschery was born in China in 1938, and placed in a Japanese concentration camp at the beginning of World War II. His father was a white Russian military officer and his mother an employee at the American Consulate in China. The Meschery family was reunited after the war in San Francisco by the Christian Brothers priests. "I went into basketball because it was the fastest way to become accepted," Meschery said. "I was a foreign kid who didn't speak English very well. One of the best ways to be accepted by your playmates is to be good as an athlete."

Sylvester Blye, a 6-5, 220-pound sophomore forward, collected 23 points and 11 rebounds for Seattle in his debut and farewell game, an 86-81 loss to Memphis State. The following day it was discovered that he had played briefly the previous season with the New York Clowns, a touring pro team, and he was declared ineligible for further college competition.

Manhattan, coached by Ken Norton, compiled its first losing record (8-11) in 25 competitive seasons (did not field teams in 1943-44 and 1944-45 because of World War II). . . . Connecticut's streak of consecutive winning seasons ended at 15 when the Huskies lost their last five games to finish with an 11-13 mark. They suffered their only defeat to New Hampshire in a 50-game stretch of their series from 1939 through 1968. . . . Rutgers (11-10) registered its first winning record in 12 seasons. . . . St. Bonaventure's 99-game homecourt winning streak, which started in 1948, was snapped by Niagara, 87-77. Drake stopped

1960–61 NCAA CHAMPION: CINCINNATI

SEASON STATISTICS OF CINCINNATI REGULARS

PLAYER	POS.	CL.	G.	FG%	FT%	PPG	RPG
Bob Wiesenhahn	F	Sr.	30	.481	.678	17.1	10.0
Paul Hogue	C	Jr.	30	.532	.518	16.8	12.5
Tom Thacker	G-F	So.	30	.396	.684	12.3	9.5
Carl Bouldin	G	Sr.	30	.428	.800	11.7	2.8
Tony Yates	G	So.	30	.486	.602	7.4	3.5
Dale Heidotting	F-C	So.	26	.429	.652	3.6	3.7
Fred Dierking	F-C	Jr.	25	.483	.467	2.6	2.2
Jim Calhoun	G	Jr.	17	.378	.538	2.1	0.5
Tom Sizer	G	Jr.	24	.375	.750	2.0	1.0
Larry Shingleton	G	So.	20	.292	.400	0.9	0.6
Mark Altenau	F	So.	18	.429	.444	0.9	0.6
TEAM TOTALS			30	.457	.633	75.0	51.8

1961 FINAL FOUR CHAMPIONSHIP GAME

KANSAS CITY, MO

CINCINNATI (70)	FG-A	FT-A	REB.	PF	PTS.
Wiesenhahn	8-15	1-1	9	3	17
Thacker	7-21	1-4	7	0	15
Hogue	3-8	3-6	7	3	9
Yates	4-8	5-5	2	3	13
Bouldin	7-12	2-3	4	4	16
Sizer	0-0	0-0	1	0	0
Heidotting	0-0	0-0	0	0	0
Team			6		
TOTALS	29-64	12-19	36	13	70

FG%: .453. FT%: .632.

OHIO STATE (65)	FG-A	FT-A	REB.	PF	PTS.
Havlicek	1-5	2-2	4	2	4
Hoyt	3-5	1-1	1	3	7
Lucas	10-17	7-7	12	4	27
Nowell	3-9	3-3	3	1	9
Siegfried	6-10	2-3	3	2	14
Knight	1-3	0-0	1	1	2
Gearhart	1-1	0-0	0	1	2
Team			8		
TOTALS	25-50	15-16	32	14	65

FG%: .500. FT%: .938.
Halftime: Ohio State 39-38. Regulation: Tied 61-61.

NATIONAL SEMIFINALS

CINCINNATI (82): Wiesenhahn 5-7 4-6 14, Thacker 1-7 5-6 7, Hogue 9-16 0-4 18, Bouldin 7-14 7-8 21, Yates 4-6 5-7 13, Heidotting 3-8 1-1 7, Sizer 1-1 0-0 2, Dierking 0-0 0-0 0, Altenau 0-0 0-0 0, Shingleton 0-0 0-0 0, Calhoun 0-0 0-0 0. Team 30-59 (.508) 22-32 (.688) 82.

UTAH (67): Ruffell 6-11 2-2 14, Rhead 2-5 4-6 8, McGill 11-31 3-4 25, Morton 3-9 1-1 7, Rowe 1-3 0-0 2, Crain 2-5 0-1 4, Aufderheide 2-3 2-2 6, Cozby 0-0 0-0 0, Thomas 0-0 1-2 1, Jenson 0-0 0-0 0. Team 27-67 (.403) 13-18 (.722) 67.

Halftime: Cincinnati 35-20.

OHIO STATE (95): Nowell 7-11 1-1 15, Havlicek 5-6 1-2 11, Lucas 10-11 9-10 29, Hoyt 2-6 0-0 4, Siegfried 8-11 5-7 21, Knight 2-5 1-2 5, McDonald 1-4 0-0 2, Gearhart 0-2 2-2 2, Reasbeck 0-1 0-1 0, Lee 1-1 0-0 2, Landes 2-2 0-0 4. Team 38-60 (.633) 19-25 (.760) 95.

ST. JOSEPH'S (69): Lynam 2-5 3-4 7, Hoy 6-17 1-1 13, Majewski 4-12 5-7 13, Egan 3-15 2-3 8, Kempton 5-9 8-8 18, Wynne 1-9 2-2 4, Booth 0-3 2-2 2, Gormley 1-5 2-2 4, Westhead 0-1 0-1 0, Bugey 0-0 0-0 0, Dickey 0-0 0-0 0. Team 22-76 (.289) 25-30 (.833) 69.

Halftime: Ohio State 45-28.

ALL-TOURNAMENT TEAM

Carl Bouldin, G, Sr., Cincinnati (37 points, seven rebounds in final two games)
John Egan, F, Sr., St. Joseph's (50 points, 21 rebounds)
*Jerry Lucas, C, Jr., Ohio State (56 points, 25 rebounds)
Larry Siegfried, G, Sr., Ohio State (35 points, 12 rebounds)
Bob Wiesenhahn, F, Sr., Cincinnati (31 points, 14 rebounds)

*Named Most Outstanding Player.

Bradley's 46-game homecourt winning streak, 86-76. Mississippi State ended Auburn's 36-game homecourt winning streak, 56-48. . . . Lehigh lost 34 consecutive games in its series with Lafayette until edging the Leopards, 60-58. VMI lost 32 straight games to Virginia until defeating the Cavaliers, 75-63.

Louisiana State posted a losing record (11-14), but the Tigers managed their lone victory over Kentucky (73-59) in the first 36 games of their series from 1933 to 1972. . . . The Citadel's Keith Stowers set a school single-game record by grabbing 23 rebounds against Richmond. . . . George Washington ended West Virginia's streak of six consecutive Southern Conference Tournament championships. GWU entered the tourney with a 6-16 record. Jon Feldman, 5-10, scored 45 points for the Colonials in the championship game against William & Mary.

. . . Providence defeated St. Louis in the NIT final, 62-59. It was the third consecutive year for the Friars to beat SLU in the NIT.

Ohio State (27-1/coached by Fred Taylor) had its winningest season in school history. . . . Illinois, coached by Harry Combes, dropped seven of its last eight games to finish with a losing record (9-15) for the first time in 33 seasons. Jerry Colangelo, who went on to become an executive with several pro sports franchises in Phoenix, led the Illini in field-goal percentage (128 of 279, .459). Among Colangelo's colleagues the previous year at Illinois were guard Mannie Jackson, who became a Honeywell executive and owner of the Harlem Globetrotters, and team manager Dennis Swanson, who became president of ABC Sports. . . . Wichita State's Gene Wiley set a Missouri Valley Conference record by blocking 15 shots

GANG(S) THAT COULDN'T SHOOT STRAIGHT

Michigan at Indiana
March 11, 1961

An NCAA-record total of 152 rebounds was the byproduct of Indiana and Michigan combining to shoot a meager 31.3 percent from the floor and 54.7 percent from the foul line in their Big Ten Conference game. Indiana guard Gary Long was the only one of 22 players to shoot from the floor in the contest to make more than half of his field-goal attempts (7 of 12).

MICHIGAN (67)	FG-A	FT-A	REB.	PTS.
Charles Higgs	2-6	2-3	4	6
Scott Maentz	3-10	0-0	7	6
Tom Cole	6-17	5-6	15	17
John Tidwell	8-32	3-11	12	19
Jon Hall	4-9	2-4	6	10
Bob Brown	1-2	0-0	1	2
Steve Schoenherr	0-2	0-0	0	0
Richard Donley	1-3	2-3	6	4
Tom Eveland	0-2	3-4	2	3
Totals	**25-83**	**17-31**	**57**	**67**
	FG%—.301. FT%—.548.			

INDIANA (82)	FG-A	FT-A	REB.	PTS.
Tom Bolyard	3-18	3-6	13	9
Chuck Hall	3-12	1-1	7	7
Walt Bellamy	10-26	8-15	33	28
Gary Long	7-12	0-1	5	14
Jerome Bass	7-15	4-4	9	18
Dave Porter	1-5	2-3	8	4
Ray Pavy	0-1	0-1	0	0
Ernie Wilhoit	0-1	0-0	0	0
Jimmy Rayl	0-0	0-2	2	0
Bill Altman	1-1	0-0	0	2
Winston Fairfield	0-2	0-0	1	0
Gordon Mickey	0-2	0-0	4	0
Charles Roush	0-3	0-0	2	0
Dan Prickett	0-1	0-0	0	0
Totals	**32-99**	**18-33**	**95**	**82**
	FG%—.323. FT%—.545.			

Halftime: Indiana 46-23.

against Purdue. . . . Creighton's Dick Hartmann, one of the nation's top rebounders the previous season with 15.1 per game, died in a traffic accident prior to the start of his senior campaign. . . . Colorado State lost to Regis (Colo.) for the fifth straight season.

1961 NCAA Tournament

Summary: Paul Hogue, a 6-9 center who hit just 51.8 percent of his free-throw attempts during the season, sank only two of 10 foul shots in his two previous games before putting Cincinnati ahead to stay with a pair of pivotal free throws in overtime in a 70-65 championship game victory. Ohio State, undefeated entering the tourney, lost the national final against Cincinnati (70-65 in

1960-61 FINAL NATIONAL POLLS

AP	UPI	SCHOOL (RECORD)	HEAD COACH
1	1	Ohio St. (27-1)	Fred Taylor
2	2	Cincinnati (27-3)	Ed Jucker
3	3	St. Bonaventure (24-4)	Eddie Donovan
4	4	Kansas St. (23-4)	Tex Winter
5	6	North Carolina (19-4)	Frank McGuire
6	7	Bradley (21-5)	Chuck Orsborn
7	5	Southern Cal (21-8)	Forrest Twogood
8	10	Iowa (18-6)	Sham Scheueman
9	12	West Virginia (23-4)	George King
10	9	Duke (22-6)	Vic Bubas
11	13	Utah (24-7)	Jack Gardner
12	18	Texas Tech (15-10)	Polk Robison
13	–	Niagara (16-5)	Taps Gallagher
14	20	Memphis St. (20-3)	Bob Vanatta
15	10	Wake Forest (19-11)	Bones McKinney
16	8	St. John's (20-5)	Joe Lapchick
17	16	St. Joseph's (25-5)	Jack Ramsay
18	–	Drake (19-7)	Maury John
19	–	Holy Cross (22-5)	Roy Leenig
20	18	Kentucky (19-9)	Adolph Rupp
–	14	St. Louis (21-9)	John Benington
–	15	Louisville (21-8)	Peck Hickman
–	17	Dayton (20-9)	Tom Blackburn

overtime) after almost getting upset in its opening playoff game at Louisville. Cincinnati's Ed Jucker became the only individual to win an NCAA title in his first full season as head coach at a major university.

Outcome for Defending Champion: Ohio State entered the playoffs undefeated, but needed to overcome a five-point deficit with less than three minutes remaining to escape with a 56-55 triumph at Louisville in the Mideast Regional semifinals. The closest the Buckeyes came to a setback during the regular season were games against St. Bonaventure (84-82 in holiday tournament at Madison Square Garden) and at Iowa (62-61).

Star Gazing: Three-time unanimous first-team All-American Jerry Lucas registered game highs of 27 points and 12 rebounds for the Buckeyes in the championship contest while teammate John Havlicek was limited to four points. Lucas outrebounded Kentucky by himself when he retrieved a tourney-high 30 missed shots in an 87-74 triumph over the Wildcats in the Mideast Regional final.

Biggest Upset: Tom Stith's 29 points weren't enough to keep third-ranked St. Bonaventure from bowing to Wake Forest, 78-73, in the East Regional semifinals.

One and Only: Guard Carl Bouldin became the only athlete to lead his championship team in scoring at the Final Four and play major league baseball in the same year. He helped Cincinnati win the NCAA title with a total of 37 points in two games at Kansas City before pitching in two games later that year for the Washington Senators. . . . Rhode Island's Ernie Calverley became the only individual to coach a team in the playoffs after leading the nation in scoring as a player (26.7 points per game for Rhode Island in 1943-44).

Numbers Game: St. Joseph's Jack Ramsay became the only coach to win an NBA championship (Portland Trail Blazers '77) after directing a college squad to the Final Four. . . . Wake Forest, coached by Bones McKinney, became the only team to ever trail by as many as 10 points at halftime of a tournament game and then win the contest by more than 20. The Demon Deacons were behind at intermission (46-36) in the first round of the East Regional before rallying to defeat St. John's (97-74). St. John's, coached by Joe Lapchick, was making its lone NCAA playoff appearance in a 14-year stretch from 1953 through 1966.

What If: ACC regular-season champion North Carolina, which defeated NCAA representative Wake Forest twice by a total of 24 points, was ineligible for postseason competition because of an NCAA probation. The Tar Heels didn't participate in the ACC Tournament in order to prevent of possibility of the league being shut out of the NCAA playoffs. . . . Utah, coming off a 26-3 season and with twin towers Billy "The Hill" McGill and

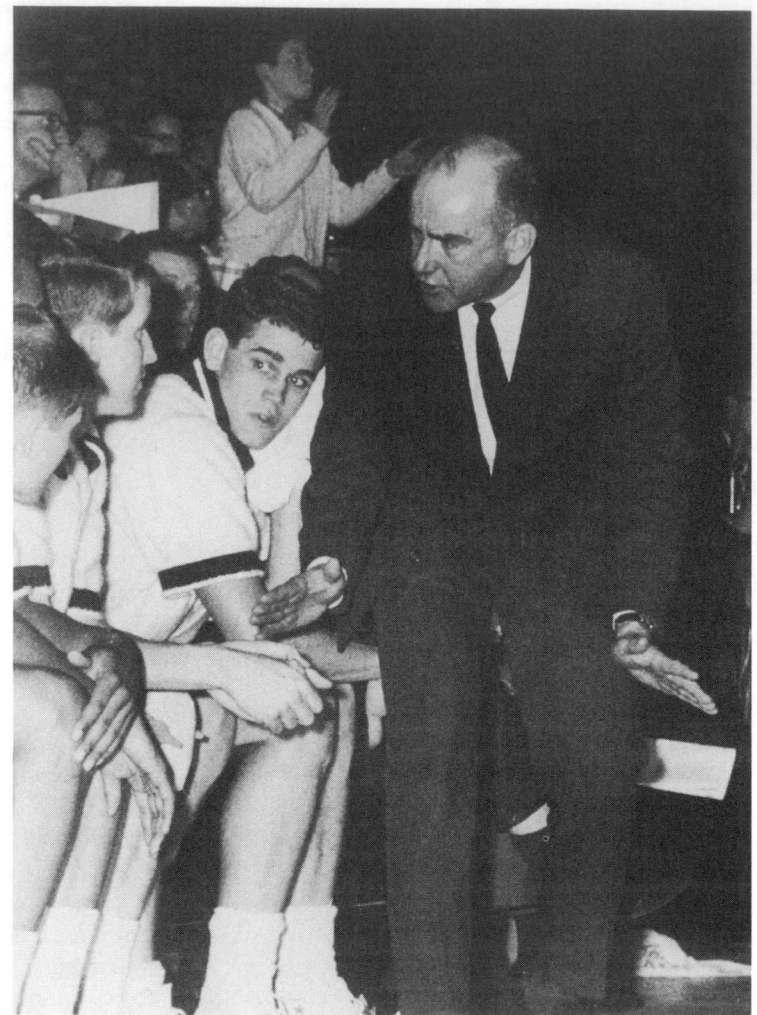

St. Joseph's (Pa.) coach Jack Ramsay instructs his players.

Allen Holmes slated to return, was a strong candidate to win it all. The Utes reached the Final Four although Holmes, the 1959 NJCAA Tournament MVP, didn't play after nearly losing his right leg in a summer auto accident. . . . St. Louis finished in a tie for third place in the Missouri Valley after losing All-MVC first-team center Bob "Bevo" Nordmann because of a severe knee injury. The Billikens, who defeated NCAA champion-to-be Cincinnati by 17 points (57-40), lost the NIT final to Providence.

1961 CHAMPIONSHIP BRACKET

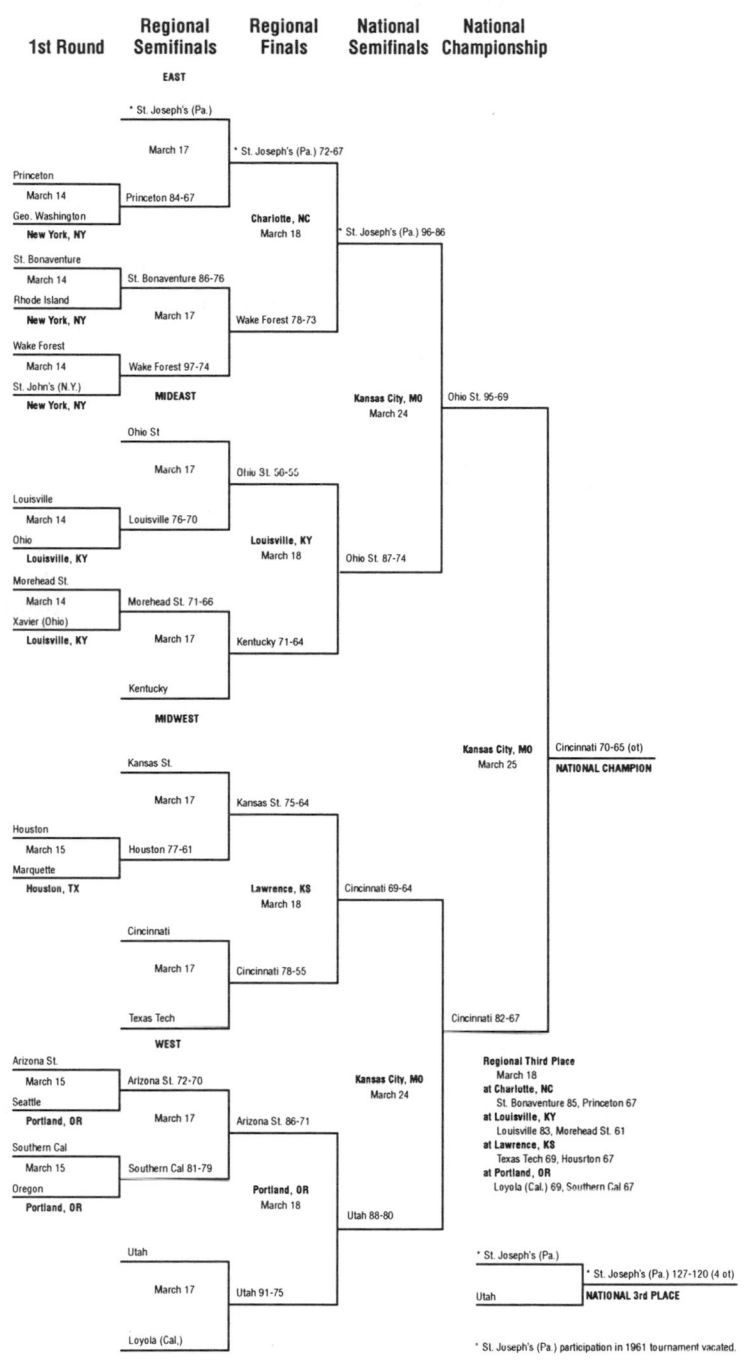

1st Round	Regional Semifinals	Regional Finals	National Semifinals	National Championship

EAST

* St. Joseph's (Pa.)

March 17

Princeton
March 14
Geo. Washington
New York, NY

Princeton 84-67

* St. Joseph's (Pa.) 72-67

Charlotte, NC
March 18

St. Bonaventure
March 14
Rhode Island
New York, NY

St. Bonaventure 86-76

March 17

Wake Forest 78-73

Wake Forest
March 14
St. John's (N.Y.)
New York, NY

Wake Forest 97-74

* St. Joseph's (Pa.) 96-86

MIDEAST

Ohio St

March 17

Louisville
March 14
Ohio
Louisville, KY

Louisville 76-70

Ohio St. 56-55

Kansas City, MO
March 24

Ohio St. 95-69

Louisville, KY
March 18

Morehead St.
March 14
Xavier (Ohio)
Louisville, KY

Morehead St. 71-66

March 17

Kentucky 71-64

Ohio St. 87-74

Kentucky

MIDWEST

Kansas St.

March 17

Houston
March 15
Marquette
Houston, TX

Houston 77-61

Kansas St. 75-64

Lawrence, KS
March 18

Cincinnati

March 17

Cincinnati 78-55

Cincinnati 69-64

Texas Tech

WEST

Arizona St.
March 15
Seattle
Portland, OR

Arizona St. 72-70

March 17

Southern Cal
March 15
Oregon
Portland, OR

Southern Cal 81-79

Arizona St. 86-71

Kansas City, MO
March 24

Cincinnati 82-67

Portland, OR
March 18

Utah 88-80

Utah

March 17

Loyola (Cal.)

Utah 91-75

Kansas City, MO
March 25

Cincinnati 70-65 (ot)

NATIONAL CHAMPION

Regional Third Place
March 18
at Charlotte, NC
St. Bonaventure 85, Princeton 67
at Louisville, KY
Louisville 83, Morehead St. 61
at Lawrence, KS
Texas Tech 69, Houston 67
at Portland, OR
Loyola (Cal.) 69, Southern Cal 67

* St. Joseph's (Pa.)

* St. Joseph's (Pa.) 127-120 (4 ot)

Utah

NATIONAL 3rd PLACE

* St. Joseph's (Pa.) participation in 1961 tournament vacated.

Putting Things in Perspective: Cincinnati lost three times by a total of 44 points in a five-game stretch early in the season, including the Bearcats' first two Missouri Valley Conference contests.

Scoring Leader: Billy McGill, Utah (119 points, 29.75 ppg).

Rebounding Leader: Jerry Lucas, Ohio State (73 rebounds, 18.3 rpg).

1961-62

AT A GLANCE

NCAA Champion: Cincinnati (29-2; coached by Ed Jucker; won Missouri Valley playoff title game, 61-46, after tying Bradley with a 10-2 record).

NIT Champion: Dayton (24-6; coached by Tom Blackburn).

NCAA Probation: Indiana, Kansas, Tennessee Tech, Utah.

NCAA Consensus First-Team All-Americans: Len Chappell, C, Sr., Wake Forest; Terry Dischinger, F, Sr., Purdue; Jerry Lucas, C, Sr., Ohio State; Billy McGill, C, Sr., Utah; Chet Walker, F, Sr., Bradley.

National Player of the Year: Lucas (21.8 ppg, 17.8 rpg, 61.1 FG%).

National Coach of the Year: Fred Taylor, Ohio State (26-2/UPI, USBWA).

Ohio State's Jerry Lucas finished his career with the three best single-season rebounding totals in Big Ten Conference history. Lucas became the first player to ever gain five individual national statistical titles in a career (two for rebounding and three for shooting).

National scoring leader Billy McGill (38.8 points per game) accounted for 45.8 percent of Utah's output. That figure was especially impressive because the Utes were sixth in the country in team offense. McGill's season included 12 of the 19 games in school history of more than 40 points

and all four contests of at least 50, including a school-record and national-high 60 at Brigham Young.

A deadeye duo—Arkansas' Tommy Boyer (93.3 percent) and Jerry Carlton (88.1)—became the only set of teammates to rank one-two in free-throw accuracy. Boyer's margin of victory in free-throw shooting was the largest in NCAA history. . . . One of the nation's premier field-goal shooters was Iowa's Don Nelson (55.5 percent), who would go on to play and coach in the NBA. . . . Davidson, in the Wildcats' second season under coach Lefty Driesell, posted their first winning record (14-11) since 1948-49.

Wake Forest, coached by Bones McKinney, captured its only undisputed ACC regular-season championship with a 12-2 league record. The Demon Deacons reached the Final Four despite losing eight of their first 17 contests. Wake Forest's Len Chappell scored 30 points or more in an ACC-record eight consecutive games, including an ACC-game mark of 50 against Virginia. A sell-out crowd watching a non-league game between Wake and another top 10 ACC rival, Duke, was enthralled by the Blue Devils' flashy new uniforms as they became the first college team to have player names on the back of the jerseys. Chappell's 37 points weren't enough to prevent a 75-73 loss to Duke, which received 33 points from Art Heyman.

The two highest-scoring teams in the nation were separated by a single basket of compiling duplicate records. Loyola of Chicago and Arizona State both posted 23-4 records, but Loyola scored two more points than the Sun Devils (2,436 to 2,434). . . . Purdue's Terry Dischinger finished his three-year varsity career with a 28.3-point average, but he is the only one of more than 50 two-time consensus first-team All-Americans since 1946 to never participate in the NCAA Tournament or the NIT.

Indiana guard Jimmy Rayl, after averaging a modest four points per game the previous season as a sophomore, exploded for a 29.8-point average to finish sixth in the country. He scored a school-

Purdue forward Terry Dischinger.

1961–62 INDIVIDUAL LEADERS

SCORING

PLAYER	PTS.	AVG.
McGill, Utah	1009	38.8
Foley, Holy Cross	866	33.3
Werkman, Seton Hall	793	33.0
Dischinger, Purdue	726	30.3
Chappell, Wake Forest	932	30.1
Rayl, Indiana	714	29.8
Smith, Furman	728	27.0
DeBusschere, Detroit	696	26.8
Duffy, Colgate	611	26.6
Walker, Bradley	687	26.4

REBOUNDING

PLAYER	REB.	PCT.
Lucas, Ohio St.	499	.2112
Silas, Creighton	563	.2108

Glur, Furman	488	.209
Lundy, Lafayette	437	.200
DeBusschere, Detroit	498	.189
Ellis, St. John's	430	.187
Jennings, Murray St.	431	.181
Luyk, Florida	352	.179
Thompson, DePaul	354	.178
Thurmond, Bowling Green	394	.176

FIELD GOAL PERCENTAGE

PLAYER	FGM	FGA	PCT.
Lucas, Ohio St.	237	388	.611
Johns, Auburn	129	221	.584
Green, Colorado St.	203	348	.583
Swain, Florida St.	157	274	.573
Beckman, Memphis St.	206	361	.571
Harger, Houston	145	258	.562
Russell, Nebraska	136	243	.560

McGill, Utah	394	705	.559
Cerkvenik, Arizona St.	101	181	.558
Hadnot, Providence	198	357	.555
Nelson, Iowa	193	348	.555

FREE THROW PERCENTAGE

PLAYER	FTM	FTA	PCT.
Boyer, Arkansas	125	134	.933
Carlton, Arkansas	140	159	.881
Chappelle, Maine	132	151	.874
Foley, Holy Cross	222	256	.867
Williams, Morehead St.	138	160	.863
Sherard, Army	112	130	.862
Komives, Bowling Green	134	156	.859
Loudermilk, SMU	203	239	.849
Reynolds, TCU	100	118	.847
Stroud, Mississippi St.	116	137	.847

1961–62 TEAM LEADERS

SCORING OFFENSE

SCHOOL	PTS.	AVG.
Loyola (Ill.)	2436	90.2
Arizona St.	2434	90.1
Seton Hall	2115	88.1
Indiana	2089	87.0
West Virginia	2562	85.4

SCORING DEFENSE

SCHOOL	PTS.	AVG.
Santa Clara	1302	52.1
Auburn	1254	52.3
San Jose St.	1262	52.6
Cincinnati	1707	55.1
Texas Western	1343	56.0

FIELD GOAL PERCENTAGE

SCHOOL	FGM	FGA	PCT.
Florida St.	709	1386	.512
Utah	883	1812	.487
Ohio St.	952	1961	.485
Memphis St.	736	1530	.481
Bradley	887	1849	.480

FREE THROW PERCENTAGE

SCHOOL	FTM	FTA	PCT.
Arkansas	502	647	.776
Southern Methodist	552	718	.769
Holy Cross	497	650	.765
Memphis St.	367	482	.761
Western Kentucky	538	713	.755

REBOUNDING

SCHOOL	TOTAL REB.	REB.	PCT.
Cornell	2481	1463	.590
Ohio St.	2362	1391	.589
Creighton	2791	1640	.588
DePaul	1989	1161	.584
Delaware	2077	1204	.580

record 56 points against Minnesota. . . . Other players who set school single-game scoring records were Holy Cross' Jack Foley (56 points vs. Connecticut), Brigham Young's Bob Skousen (47 vs. UCLA), Penn State's Gene Harris (46 vs. Holy Cross in Quaker City Classic at Philadelphia) and Minnesota's Eric Magdanz (42 at Michigan/later tied). . . . Utah's McGill, Holy Cross' Foley (33.3), Wake Forest's Chappell (30.1), Indiana's Rayl (29.8) and The Citadel's Gary Daniels (23.9) set school records for highest scoring average in a single season.

Syracuse and Georgetown haven't always been among the Beasts of the East. Syracuse finished with a 2-22 record, the worst mark in university history. The Orangemen lost their first 22 games, including a 63-point setback against NYU (122-59), before ending a school-record 27-game

losing streak with a 73-72 success at Boston College. Meanwhile, Georgetown's streak of seasons with at least 10 defeats ended at eight in a row with a 14-9 mark. The Hoyas, however, lost to Navy for the eighth consecutive time, 64-56, giving them a career 7-31 worksheet against the Midshipmen.

Delaware, coached by Irvin Wisniewski, snapped a streak of eight consecutive losing seasons by compiling an 18-5 record. . . . For the second time in four years, Mississippi State didn't participate in the NCAA Tournament despite compiling the best record in the country (24-1). Mississippi State's only defeat was at Vanderbilt, which finished the season with a .500 mark (12-12). . . . LSU registered its only winning record (13-11 under coach Jay McCreary) in a 13-year span until legendary Pete Maravich joined the Tigers' varsity in the late 1960s.

1961–62 NCAA CHAMPION: CINCINNATI

SEASON STATISTICS OF CINCINNATI REGULARS

PLAYER	POS.	CL.	G.	FG%	FT%	PPG	RPG
Paul Hogue	C	Sr.	31	.498	.566	16.8	12.4
Ron Bonham	F	So.	31	.455	.760	14.3	5.0
Tom Thacker	G-F	Jr.	31	.405	.612	11.0	8.6
George Wilson	F-C	So.	31	.505	.663	9.2	8.0
Tony Yates	G	Jr.	31	.383	.670	8.2	3.0
Fred Dierking	F	Sr.	28	.433	.588	4.1	2.9
Larry Shingleton	G	Jr.	25	.416	.560	3.9	1.4
Dale Heidotting	F	Jr.	22	.511	.571	3.1	2.3
Tom Sizer	G	Sr.	25	.456	.625	2.7	1.3
Jim Calhoun	G	Sr.	18	.368	.667	1.7	0.4
TEAM TOTALS			31	**.447**	**.632**	72.2	49.5

1962 FINAL FOUR CHAMPIONSHIP GAME

LOUISVILLE, KY

OHIO STATE (59)	FG-A	FT-A	REB.	PF	PTS.
Havlicek	5-14	1-2	9	1	11
McDonald	0-1	3-3	1	2	3
Lucas	5-17	1-2	16	3	11
Reasbeck	4-6	0-0	0	4	8
Nowell	4-16	1-1	6	2	9
Doughty	0-1	0-0	2	2	0
Gearhart	1-4	0-0	4	3	0
Bradds	5-7	5-6	4	2	15
TOTALS	**24-66**	**11-14**	**42**	**19**	**59**

FG%: .364. FT%: .786. Turnovers: 9.

CINCINNATI (71)	FG-A	FT-A	REB.	PF	PTS.
Bonham	3-12	4-4	6	3	10
Wilson	1-6	4-4	11	2	6
Hogue	11-18	0-2	19	2	22
Thacker	6-14	9-11	6	2	21
Yates	4-8	4-7	1	1	12
Sizer	0-0	0-0	0	0	0
TOTALS	**25-58**	**21-28**	**43**	**10**	**71**

FG%: .431. FT%: .750. Turnovers: 8.
Halftime: Cincinnati 37-29.

NATIONAL SEMIFINALS

WAKE FOREST (68): Chappell 10-24 7-11 27, Christie 0-2 1-1 1, Woollard 1-3 1-2 3, Wiedeman 5-16 3-6 13, Packer 8-14 1-2 17, Hull 0-2 0-0 0, McCoy 0-1 2-2 2, Carmichael 0-0 0-0 0, Hassell 1-2 0-0 2, Zawacki 0-0 1-3 1, Koehler 0-1 0-0 0, Brooks 0-1 2-2 2. Team 25-66 (.379) 18-29 (.621) 68.

OHIO STATE (84): Havlicek 9-19 7-9 25, McDonald 5-10 1-2 11, Lucas 8-16 3-4 19, Nowell 2-11 0-0 4, Reasbeck 5-7 0-0 10, Gearhart 2-5 0-0 4, Doughty 2-4 4-4 8, Bradds 0-0 0-1 0, Knight 0-2 0-0 0, Flatt 0-0 1-2 1, Taylor 0-0 0-0 0, Frazier 1-1 0-0 2. Team 34-75 (.453) 16-22 (.727) 84.

Halftime: Ohio State 46-34.

UCLA (70): Blackman 2-3 0-0 4, Cunningham 8-14 3-3 19, Slaughter 1-4 0-0 2, Green 9-16 9-11 27, Hazzard 5-10 2-3 12, Waxman 2-3 2-3 6, Stewart 0-0 0-0 0. Team 27-50 (.540) 16-20 (.800) 70.

CINCINNATI (72): Bonham 8-14 3-6 19, Wilson 1-6 1-2 3, Hogue 12-18 12-17 36, Thacker 1-7 0-0 2, Yates 4-10 2-3 10, Sizer 1-3 0-0 2. Team 27-58 (.466) 18-28 (.643) 72.

Halftime: Tied 37-37.

ALL-TOURNAMENT TEAM

Len Chappell, F-C, Sr., Wake Forest (53 points, 29 rebounds in final two games)
John Havlicek, F, Sr., Ohio State (36 points, 25 rebounds)
*Paul Hogue, C, Sr., Cincinnati (58 points, 38 rebounds)
Jerry Lucas, C, Sr., Ohio State (30 points, 32 rebounds)
Tom Thacker, F-G, Jr., Cincinnati (23 points, 10 rebounds)

*Named Most Outstanding Player.

1961-62 FINAL NATIONAL POLLS

AP	UPI	SCHOOL (RECORD)	HEAD COACH
1	1	Ohio St. (26-2)	Fred Taylor
2	2	Cincinnati (29-2)	Ed Jucker
3	3	Kentucky (23-3)	Adolph Rupp
4	4	Mississippi State (24-1)	Babe McCarthy
5	6	Bradley (21-7)	Chuck Orsborn
6	5	Kansas State (22-3)	Tex Winter
7	10	Utah (23-3)	Jack Gardner
8	9	Bowling Green St. (21-4)	Harold Anderson
9	8	Colorado (19-7)	Sox Walseth
10	13	Duke (20-5)	Vic Bubas
11	13	Loyola of Chicago (23-4)	George Ireland
12	12	St. John's (21-5)	Joe Lapchick
13	7	Wake Forest (22-9)	Bones McKinney
14	11	Oregon State (24-5)	Slats Gill
15	16	West Virginia (24-6)	George King
16	15	Arizona State (23-4)	Ned Wulk
17	18	Duquesne (22-7)	Red Manning
18	19	Utah State (22-7)	Ladell Andersen
19	17	UCLA (18-11)	John Wooden
20	20	Villanova (21-7)	Jack Kraft

The San Francisco Bay Area supplied the leader in team defense for the seventh time in eight years—Santa Clara (52.1). . . . San Francisco's Bob Gaillard, who would coach his alma mater to a national No. 1 ranking in 1977, led the West Coast Athletic Conference in free-throw accuracy for the second time in three seasons. . . . Pepperdine, coached by Duck Dowell, captured the WCAC championship just one year after finishing in sixth place. . . . Creighton's Paul Silas (38 vs. Centenary), St. John's LeRoy Ellis (30 vs. NYU), Washington's Ed Corell (30 vs. Oregon) and Utah's McGill (24 at UCLA) set school single-game rebounding records.

NIT champion Dayton compiled a 24-6 mark but didn't finish the season in the Top 20 of a final wire-service poll. The Tom Blackburn-coached Flyers resided there nine times in the previous 11 years. NIT MVP Bill Chmielewski, Dayton's leading scorer and rebounder as a sophomore, left school and played the next year with Philadelphia in the ABL. . . . Butler made its only NCAA Tournament appearance and enjoyed its last season with fewer than 10 defeats (22-6 record) until 1997.

Wayne Hightower, the Big Eight Conference's leading scorer the previous two seasons, did not play his senior year for Kansas after joining the Harlem Globetrotters. . . . Oklahoma State lost 17 consecutive games to Kansas State until defeating the Wildcats, 78-68. . . . Virginia Tech posted its lone victory over West Virginia (85-82) in a 19-game stretch of their series from 1952 through 1964.

Wichita State ended defending champion Cincinnati's 27-game winning streak, 52-51, on Lanny Van Eman's jumper with three seconds remaining. . . . The Border and Skyline conferences disbanded after the season to make way for the Western Athletic Conference. . . . New Mexico lost its first 22 meetings with Brigham Young until defeating the Cougars, 80-70. . . . North Carolina's Dean Smith kicked off his illustrious head coaching career with a modest $9,500 annual salary and an inauspicious 8-9 record. The Tar Heels lost their first four ACC games in February by an average of 18.5 points in Smith's only losing season. Earlier, they bowed to Indiana, 76-70, at Greensboro, N.C., before a meager crowd of 3,000.

1962 NCAA Tournament

Summary: Ohio State All-American center Jerry Lucas wrenched his left knee in the national semifinals against Wake Forest, limiting his effectiveness against Cincinnati counterpart Paul Hogue in the Bearcats' 71-59 triumph in the final. In the 1962 national semifinals against UCLA, Hogue scored 14 consecutive points for the Bearcats down the stretch to finish with 36 before Thacker's desperation long-range basket, his only points of the game, gave them a 72-70 triumph. Cincinnati (29-2/coached by Ed Jucker), setting a school single-season record for most victories, is the only school to capture an NCAA championship after earning a berth in the tourney by winning a conference title playoff game (tied atop the Missouri Valley standings with Bradley).

Outcome for Defending Champion: The only Ohio State regular-season defeat in the last two years of the Lucas/John Havlicek era after they won the 1960 NCAA title was at Wisconsin

(86-67), ending the Buckeyes' 47-game regular-season winning streak and 27-game Big Ten winning string. Havlicek hit just 3 of 15 field-goal attempts in the contest.

Star Gazing: Tom Thacker, a 6-2 swingman who averaged nine rebounds per game for Cincinnati's back-to-back titlists, is the only individual to play for an NCAA champion, NBA champion (Boston Celtics '68) and ABA champion (Indiana Pacers '70).

One and Only: Dave DeBusschere became the only player to post the highest-scoring game in a single tournament the same year he played major league baseball. DeBusschere scored a tourney-high 38 points for Detroit in a 90-81 defeat against Western Kentucky in the first round of the Mideast Regional. He pitched that summer for the Chicago White Sox. . . . Wake Forest forward Bill Hull became the only individual to play in the Final Four the same year he intercepted a pass in overtime of an AFL championship game (23-yard return by defensive end helped set up game-winning field goal for the Dallas Texans in a 20-17 decision over the Houston Oilers).

Numbers Game: Utah State's Cornell Green became the only athlete to compile one of the top five scoring averages in an NCAA Tournament before playing for an NFL champion. Green, a five-time Pro Bowl defensive back during his 13-year career with the Dallas Cowboys from 1962 through 1973, tied for fourth in scoring average in the '62 playoffs (24.3 points per game in three games). But the Aggies were eliminated by coach John Wooden's first Final Four team at UCLA despite Green's game-high 26 points (73-62 in West Regional semifinals). . . . Wooden's initial Final Four squad (18-11 record) was the only national semifinalist in 20 years from 1960 through 1979 to finish a season with double-digit defeats. The Bruins lost seven of their first 11 games. . . . Ohio State became the only school to reach the Final Four three consecutive years on two separate occasions (1944 through 1946 and 1960 through 1962). . . . Wake Forest became the only school to win back-to-back tourney games by

1962 CHAMPIONSHIP BRACKET

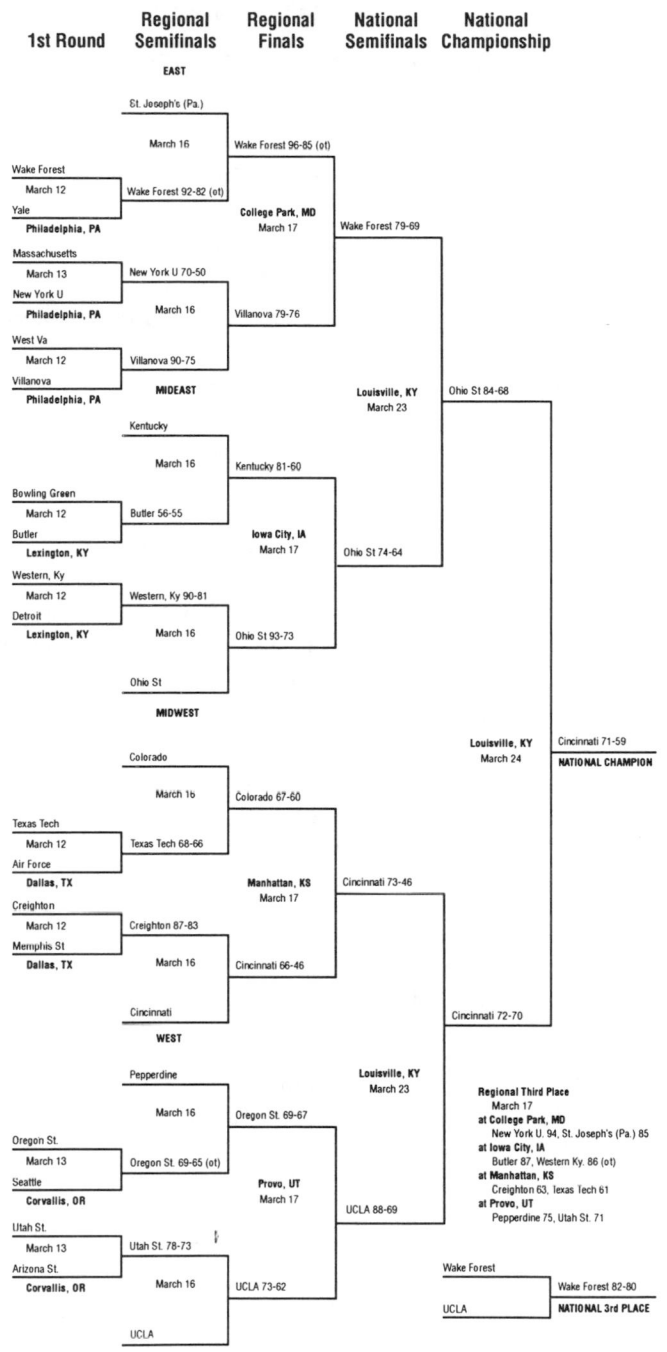

1st Round	Regional Semifinals	Regional Finals	National Semifinals	National Championship

EAST

St. Joseph's (Pa.)

March 16 — Wake Forest 96-85 (ot)

Wake Forest
March 12 — Wake Forest 92-82 (ot)
Yale
Philadelphia, PA

College Park, MD
March 17 — Wake Forest 79-69

Massachusetts
March 13 — New York U 70-50
New York U
Philadelphia, PA
March 16 — Villanova 79-76

West Va
March 12 — Villanova 90-75
Villanova
Philadelphia, PA

Louisville, KY
March 23 — Ohio St 84-68

MIDEAST

Kentucky
March 16 — Kentucky 81-60

Bowling Green
March 12 — Butler 56-55
Butler
Lexington, KY

Iowa City, IA
March 17 — Ohio St 74-64

Western, Ky
March 12 — Western, Ky 90-81
Detroit
Lexington, KY
March 16 — Ohio St 93-73

Ohio St

Louisville, KY
March 24 — Cincinnati 71-59
NATIONAL CHAMPION

MIDWEST

Colorado
March 16 — Colorado 67-60

Texas Tech
March 12 — Texas Tech 68-66
Air Force
Dallas, TX

Manhattan, KS
March 17 — Cincinnati 73-46

Creighton
March 12 — Creighton 87-83
Memphis St
Dallas, TX
March 16 — Cincinnati 66-46

Cincinnati

Cincinnati 72-70

WEST

Pepperdine
March 16 — Oregon St. 69-67

Oregon St.
March 13 — Oregon St. 69-65 (ot)
Seattle
Corvallis, OR

Provo, UT
March 17 — UCLA 88-69

Louisville, KY
March 23

Utah St.
March 13 — Utah St. 78-73
Arizona St.
Corvallis, OR
March 16 — UCLA 73-62

UCLA

Regional Third Place
March 17
at College Park, MD
New York U. 94, St. Joseph's (Pa.) 85
at Iowa City, IA
Butler 87, Western Ky. 86 (ot)
at Manhattan, KS
Creighton 63, Texas Tech 61
at Provo, UT
Pepperdine 75, Utah St. 71

Wake Forest
Wake Forest 82-80
UCLA
NATIONAL 3rd PLACE

double-digit margins in overtime (10-point victory against Yale and 11-point triumph against St. Joseph's in East Regional). . . . Massachusetts, coached by Matt Zunic, made its lone NCAA Tournament appearance until 1992.

What Might Have Been: Utah (23-3), denied a national postseason tournament appearance for the eighth straight year because it was on NCAA probation, won by nine points at UCLA, an eventual Final Four team. The Utes won 80 percent of their games in that eight-year span. . . . Kansas State, ranked 5th by UPI and 6th by AP the year after being eliminated from the NCAA Tournament by eventual national champion Cincinnati, finished runner-up in the Big Eight Conference to Colorado. The Wildcats' three defeats were in road games against Colorado, Kentucky and Oklahoma State.

Putting Things in Perspective: Cincinnati would have gone undefeated if not for two setbacks by a total of three points in Missouri Valley Conference road games (at Wichita State and Bradley). On the other hand, the Bearcats might not have participated in the NCAA playoffs if Bradley standout Mack Herndon didn't miss the season after becoming ineligible and dropping out of school for a year. They tied the Braves for the MVC regular-season championship before defeating them in a league playoff game, 61-46, at Evansville, Ind. Herndon led the MVC in scoring the next season.

Scoring Leader: Len Chappell, Wake Forest (134 points, 26.8 ppg).

Rebounding Leader: Len Chappell, Wake Forest (86 rebounds, 17.2 rpg).

Highest Rebounding Average: Mel Counts, Oregon State (53 rebounds, 17.7 rpg).

1962-63

AT A GLANCE

NCAA Champion: Loyola, Ill. (29-2; coached by George Ireland).

NIT Champion: Providence (24-4; coached by Joe Mullaney).

New Conference: Western Athletic.

NCAA Probation: Dayton, Indiana, New Mexico State

NCAA Consensus First-Team All-Americans: Ron Bonham, F, Jr., Cincinnati; Jerry Harkness, F, Sr., Loyola (Ill.); Art Heyman, F, Sr., Duke; Barry Kramer, F, Jr., NYU; Tom Thacker, F-G, Sr., Cincinnati.

National Player of the Year: Heyman (24.9 ppg, 10.8 rpg).

National Coach of the Year: Ed Jucker, Cincinnati (26-2/UPI, USBWA).

Mississippi State became the first school other than Kentucky to win outright or share three consecutive SEC championships. But Mississippi State coach Babe McCarthy had to sneak out of town in the middle of the night to enable his alma mater to participate in the NCAA playoffs for the first time. He left before he was served injunction papers stemming from two segregationist state legislators seeking to prohibit the team from leaving Mississippi and using state funds to travel to the tournament.

Billy Mitts, one of the "Jim Crow" state senators, was a former Mississippi State student body president, but his influence waned when a county sheriff apparently sympathetic to the players' plight graciously left an airport in time for them to board their plane and evade an unpleasant scene.

Mississippi State, an all-white school at the time, had captured SEC championships under McCarthy in 1959, 1961 and 1962. But the Bulldogs—then more popularly known as the Maroons—declined automatic bids to play in the NCAA Tournament those three years because of an unwritten bigoted policy forbidding Mississippi State or Ole Miss athletes to compete in racially integrated contests. Eventual champion Loyola of Chicago, featuring four black starters, fell behind Mississippi State 7-0, but wound up winning the Mideast Regional semifinal game (61-51) in East Lansing, Mich. Incidentally, the next time Mississippi State appeared in the NCAA playoffs was

1991, when the Bulldogs' 13-man roster had 10 blacks.

Loyola of Chicago (29-2/coached by George Ireland) and Arizona State (26-3/Ned Wulk) had their winningest seasons in school history. Miami, Fla. (23-5/Bruce Hale) tied its school record for most victories in a single season. . . . Three of the country's top five point producers were from the East as Seton Hall's Nick Werkman became the first Easterner in 13 years to lead the nation in scoring (29.5 points per game). . . . Duke's Art Heyman finished his three-year varsity career as "Mr. Consistency." He averaged a career-low 24.9 points per game as a senior after averaging 25.2 as a sophomore and 25.3 as a junior. His rebounding averages were equally consistent (10.9, 11.2 and 10.8).

Dean Smith, in his second year as North Carolina's coach, won at Kentucky, 68-66. The 12th victory of his career came against legendary Kentucky coach Adolph Rupp, who was bypassed by Smith as the all-time winningest major-college coach 34 seasons later. . . . Five of the eight ACC members finished with losing records—Clemson (12-13), N.C. State (10-11), South Carolina (9-15), Maryland (8-13) and Virginia (5-20).

One-eyed Tommy Boyer of Arkansas became the first player to win two consecutive free-throw shooting titles. . . . Bowling Green's Howard Komives set a Mid-American Conference record by hitting 50 consecutive free throws. . . . Two of the nation's top six rebounders—Idaho's Gus Johnson (2nd with 20.3 rpg) and Bowling Green's Nate Thurmond (6th with 16.7 rpg)—had been teammates at Central Hower High School in Akron, O. "In my opinion, he (Johnson) was the forerunner to Dr. J (Julius Erving)," Thurmond said. "He was the first guy who was so big (6-6, 235 pounds) and could do so much with the ball." Johnson grabbed a school-record 31 rebounds in a victory over Oregon. He died of brain cancer on April 29, 1987, at the age of 48.

Wichita State, coached by Ralph Miller, defeated eventual NCAA finalists Loyola of Chicago and Cincinnati although they each finished with only two losses. Wichita State ended

Wichita State's Dave Stallworth.

Cincinnati's 37-game winning streak, 65-64, when Dave Stallworth poured in 46 points for the Shockers. Cincinnati, however, still captured its sixth Missouri Valley Conference championship in as many years as a member of the league. . . . Bradley lost six of eight games in a mid-season tailspin to finish with a 17-9 record, the only season in coach Chuck Orsborn's nine-year stint with the Braves when they didn't win at least two-thirds of their contests. . . . Texas, the epitome of a balanced attack under coach Harold Bradley, lost just one SWC game although it didn't have one of the top 10 scorers in the league. Seven Longhorn players averaged seven or more points per game in SWC competition and three other teammates had at least one game of 10 points or more.

Gary Bradds, the successor to Jerry Lucas as Ohio State's principal scoring threat, averaged 28 points per game after posting a 4.7 average the previous season as a sophomore. . . . Indiana

1962–63 INDIVIDUAL LEADERS

SCORING

PLAYER	PTS.	AVG.
Werkman, Seton Hall	650	29.5
Kramer, New York Univ.	675	29.3
Green, Colorado St.	649	28.2
Bradds, Ohio St.	672	28.0
Bradley, Princeton	682	27.3
Robinson, Wyoming	682	26.2
Miles, Seattle	697	25.8
Rayl, Indiana	608	25.3
Heyman, Duke	747	24.9
Crump, Idaho St.	595	24.8

REBOUNDING

PLAYER	REB.	AVG.
Silas, Creighton	557	20.6
Johnson, Idaho	466	20.3

Pokley, Morehead St.	323	17.0
Petersen, Rutgers	389	16.9
Sahm, Notre Dame	438	16.8
Thurmond, Bowling Green	452	16.7
Barnes, Texas Western	428	16.5
Pelkington, Xavier	454	16.2
Jennings, Murray St.	339	16.1
Cunningham, N. Carolina	339	16.1

FIELD GOAL PERCENTAGE

PLAYER	FGM	FGA	PCT.
Harger, Houston	193	294	.656
Raftery, St. Francis (N.Y.)	115	186	.615
Buckley, Duke	130	217	.599
Green, Colorado St.	215	371	.580
Johnson, San Francisco	178	314	.567
Johns, Auburn	119	210	.567
Blackwell, Auburn	123	219	.562
Becker, Arizona St.	225	404	.557
Mullins, Duke	256	466	.549
Cerkvanik, Arizona St.	123	225	.547

FREE THROW PERCENTAGE

PLAYER	FTM	FTA	PCT.
Boyer, Arkansas	147	161	.913
Bradley, Princeton	258	289	.893
Bonham, Cincinnati	173	194	.892
Batchelor, BYU	104	119	.874
Rayl, Indiana	178	204	.873
Stroud, Miss. St.	120	138	.870
Hyland, Princeton	112	129	.868
Ward, South Carolina	118	136	.868
Vadset, Washington St.	119	138	.862
Smith, Furman	204	238	.857

1962–63 TEAM LEADERS

SCORING OFFENSE

SCHOOL	PTS.	AVG.
Loyola (Ill.)	2847	91.8
Miami (Fla.)	2509	89.6
Indiana	2032	84.7
Illinois	2201	84.7
Duke	2496	83.2

SCORING DEFENSE

SCHOOL	PTS.	AVG.
Cincinnati	1480	52.9
Oklahoma St.	1328	53.1
Texas Western	1419	54.6
San Jose St.	1383	57.6
New Mexico	1447	57.9

FIELD GOAL PERCENTAGE

SCHOOL	FGM	FGA	PCT.
Duke	984	1926	.511
Auburn	601	1188	.506
St. Francis (N.Y.)	553	1109	.499
Memphis St.	773	1553	.498
Colorado St.	593	1193	.497

FREE THROW PERCENTAGE

SCHOOL	FTM	FTA	PCT.
Tulane	390	492	.793
Furman	539	708	.761
Princeton	531	699	.760
Cornell	378	498	.759
Florida	533	703	.758

REBOUNDING

SCHOOL	TOTAL REB.	OWN	PCT.
Texas Western	1975	1167	.591
Auburn	1737	1018	.586
Delaware	2116	1239	.586
Davidson	2171	1254	.578
Regis (Colo.)	2089	1205	.577

guard Jimmy Rayl scored a national-high 56 points against Michigan State, tying a school record he established the previous year.

Illinois' Dave Downey (53 points at Indiana) and Colorado State's Bill Green (48 vs. Denver) set school single-game scoring records. NYU's Barry Kramer (29.3 ppg), CSU's Green (28.2) and St. Mary's Steve Gray (23.8) established school single-season records for highest scoring average. Green was an award-winning educator in the Bronx, N.Y., at the time of his death in 1994.

Bob Starnes' 50-foot heave at the buzzer enabled Illinois to edge Northwestern, 78-76, helping the Fighting Illini tie Ohio State for the Big Ten title. . . . Kansas finished in the second division of the Big Eight, but managed a four-overtime victory against regular-season co-champion Kansas State in the Big Eight Holiday Tour-

nament. . . . Tulsa posted its lone triumph over Bradley (67-62) in an 18-game stretch of their series from 1957 through 1965.

St. John's (9-15) endured its worst winning percentage since going winless in 1918-19 despite ending an eight-game losing streak in its series with St. Louis, 54-48. . . . Syracuse had lost 50 of 59 games when its mid-season record fell to 3-7. . . . Vermont's Benny Becton (29 vs. Maine) and Utah State's Wayne Estes (28 vs. Regis) set school single-game rebounding records. . . . Duquesne star guard Willie Somerset missed the season because of an injury to the tibia bone of his left leg. He averaged 24.7 points per game each of the next two years to finish with the highest scoring average in school history (22.7 ppg). . . . Navy had a 29-5 record in its series with Virginia after defeating the Cavaliers, 78-66.

1962-63 FINAL NATIONAL POLLS

AP	UPI	SCHOOL (RECORD)	HEAD COACH
1	1	Cincinnati (26-2)	Ed Jucker
2	2	Duke (27-3)	Vic Bubas
3	4	Loyola of Chicago (29-2)	George Ireland
4	3	Arizona State (26-3)	Ned Wulk
5	6	Wichita (19-8)	Ralph Miller
6	7	Mississippi State (22-6)	Babe McCarthy
7	8	Ohio State (20-4)	Fred Taylor
8	5	Illinois (20-6)	Harry Combes
9	11	NYU (18-5)	Lou Rossini
10	9	Colorado (19-7)	Sox Walseth
–	10	Stanford (16-9)	Howie Dallmar
–	12	Texas (20-7)	Harold Bradley
–	13	Providence (24-4)	Joe Mullaney
–	14	Oregon State (22-9)	Slats Gill
–	15	UCLA (20-9)	John Wooden
–	16	St. Joseph's (23-5)	Jack Ramsay
–	16	West Virginia (23-8)	George King
–	18	Bowling Green St. (19-8)	Harold Anderson
–	19	Kansas State (16-9)	Tex Winter
–	19	Seattle (21-8)	Clair Markey*

• Markey coached the Seattle Chieftains in the NCAA Tournament after Vince Cazetta's resignation.

West Virginia, coached by George King, earned its eighth Southern Conference championship in nine years. . . . Kentucky's streak of consecutive season-opener victories ended at 37 when the Wildcats bowed to visiting Virginia Tech, 80-77. Despite the splendid start, the Hokies finished 12-12 for their only non-winning record in a 14-year span from 1955-56 through 1968-69. . . . Tennessee, coming off a dismal 4-19 campaign, posted a respectable 13-11 mark in Ray Mears' initial season as coach of the Volunteers. It was the only season in Mears' 21 years as a coach that he reached double digits in defeats.

Brigham Young incurred its fourth losing record in six seasons. . . . New Mexico compiled a 16-9 record in Bob King's initial year as coach of the Lobos after posting an average mark of 5-19

1962–63 NCAA CHAMPION: LOYOLA

SEASON STATISTICS OF LOYOLA OF CHICAGO REGULARS

PLAYER	POS.	CL.	G.	FG%	FT%	PPG	RPG
Jerry Harkness	F	Sr.	31	.504	.725	21.4	7.6
Les Hunter	C	Jr.	31	.530	.731	17.0	11.4
John Egan	G	Jr.	31	.361	.789	13.7	3.6
Vic Rouse	F	Jr.	31	.404	.730	13.5	12.1
Ron Miller	G	Jr.	31	.406	.696	13.3	5.4
Jim Reardon	F	Sr.	14	.321	.813	2.2	2.1
Dan Connaughton	G	So.	17	.424	.625	1.9	1.1
Chuck Wood	F-G	Jr.	17	.393	.714	1.9	1.9
Rich Rochelle	C	Jr.	14	.360	.375	1.5	1.4
TEAM TOTALS			31	.439	.722	91.8	57.7

1963 FINAL FOUR CHAMPIONSHIP GAME

LOUISVILLE, KY

LOYOLA (ILL.) (60)	MIN.	FG-A	FT-A	REB.	A	PF	PTS.
Harkness	45	5-18	4-8	6	0	4	14
Rouse	45	6-22	3-4	12	0	4	15
Hunter	45	6-22	4-4	11	1	3	16
Egan	45	3-8	3-5	3	0	3	9
Miller	45	3-14	0-0	2	0	3	6
Team				11			
TOTALS	225	23-84	14-21	45	1	17	60

FG%: .274. **FT%:** .667. **Turnovers:** 3.

CINCINNATI (58)	MIN.	FG-A	FT-A	REB.	A	PF	PTS.
Bonham	45	8-16	6-6	4	0	3	22
Thacker	45	5-12	3-4	15	3	4	13
Wilson	41	4-8	2-3	13	0	4	10
Yates	45	4-6	1-4	8	1	4	9
Shingleton	45	1-3	2-3	4	0	4	4
Heidotting	4	0-0	0-0	1	0	2	0
Team				7			
TOTALS	225	22-45	14-20	52	4	17	58

FG%: .489. **FT%:** .700. **Turnovers:** 16 (Thacker 7).
Halftime: Cincinnati 29-21. **Regulation:** Tied 54-54.

NATIONAL SEMIFINALS

CINCINNATI (80): Bonham 3-12 8-9 14, Thacker 5-8 4-8 14, Wilson 8-9 8-12 24, Yates 5-9 2-3 12, Shingleton 1-2 0-0 2, Heidotting 0-0 1-2 1, Cunningham 2-3 0-0 4, Meyer 1-1 1-2 3, Smith 1-3 0-2 2, Elasser 1-2 0-1 2, Abernethy 1-2 0-0 2. Team 28-51 (.549) 24-39 (.615) 80.

OREGON STATE (46): Pauly 2-8 0-1 4, Kraus 1-6 1-1 3, Counts 8-14 4-4 20, Peters 1-5 2-4 4, Baker 0-9 0-1 0, Jarvis 1-6 3-4 5, Rossi 1-3 0-0 2, Campbell 0-2 1-1 1, Torgerson 1-2 0-0 2, Hayward 0-2 1-1 1, Benner 2-2 0-0 4. Team 17-59 (.288) 12-15 (.800) 46.

Halftime: Cincinnati 30-27.

LOYOLA OF CHICAGO (94): Harkness 7-18 6-9 20, Rouse 6-12 1-2 13, Hunter 11-20 7-9 29, Egan 4-9 6-7 14, Miller 8-11 2-2 18, Wood 0-1 0-0 0, Rochelle 0-0 0-0 0, Reardon 0-0 0-0 0, Cannaughton 0-0 0-0 0. Team 36-71 (.5-7) 22-29 (.759) 94.

DUKE (75): Heyman 11-30 7-9 29, Mullins 10-20 1-3 21, Buckley 4-10 2-4 10, Schmidt 0-2 0-0 0, Harrison 0-3 2-3 2, Herbster 0-2 0-0 0, Ferguson 1-2 0-0 2, Jamieson 0-0 0-0 0, Cox 0-0 0-0 0, Mann 0-1 0-0 0, Tison 5-12 1-3 11. Team 31-82 (.378) 13-22 (.591) 75.

Halftime: Loyola of Chicago 44-31.

ALL-TOURNAMENT TEAM

Ron Bonham, F, Jr., Cincinnati (36 points, nine rebounds in final two games)
*Art Heyman, F, Sr., Duke (51 points, 19 rebounds)
Les Hunter, C, Jr., Loyola of Chicago (35 points, 29 rebounds)
Tom Thacker, F-G, Sr., Cincinnati (27 points, 26 rebounds)
George Wilson, C, Jr., Cincinnati (34 points, 26 rebounds)

*Named Most Outstanding Player.

the previous eight seasons. They ended an 18-game losing streak in their series with Utah, 84-71. . . . San Francisco, coached by Pete Pelleta, captured the West Coast Athletic Conference title just one year after finishing in sixth place. . . . Muhlenberg (Pa.) competed in its final season at the major-college level. . . . Connecticut's Hugh Greer ended a 17-year coaching career with a 286-112 record.

1963 NCAA Tournament

Summary: Even some teams outside the South adhered to an accepted standard of "start no more than two blacks at home, or three on the road." When Loyola, featuring four African American starters, upset Cincinnati and the Bearcats' three black starters in the championship game, it was the first time a majority of African American players participated in the title game. Junior forward Vic Rouse leaped high to redirect center Les Hunter's shot from the free-throw line into the basket to climax the Ramblers' first year in the playoffs. Loyola of

Idaho's Gus Johnson in action.

Chicago, overcoming 27.4 percent field-goal shooting by committing just three turnovers, won the final against defending NCAA champion Cincinnati (60-58 in overtime). The Ramblers trailed by 15 points in the second half before knotting the score at 54-54 when Jerry Harkness hit a 12-foot jumper with four seconds remaining in regulation. "I never thought we'd lose it," Rouse said. "We came too far to lose it."

One and Only: Oregon State's Terry Baker became the only football Heisman Trophy winner to play in the basketball Final Four. Baker, a quar- terback on Oregon State's football squad that defeated Villanova (6-0) in the 1962 Liberty Bowl on his school-record 99-yard run from scrimmage, was the second-leading scorer for the Beavers' basketball team that finished fourth in the national tourney the same academic school year. Teammate Steve Pauly, Oregon State's second-leading rebounder and third-leading scorer, was the only Final Four player to become AAU national cham- pion in the decathlon the same year.

Numbers Game: Loyola of Chicago, using its starting lineup the entire final, is the only

1963 CHAMPIONSHIP BRACKET

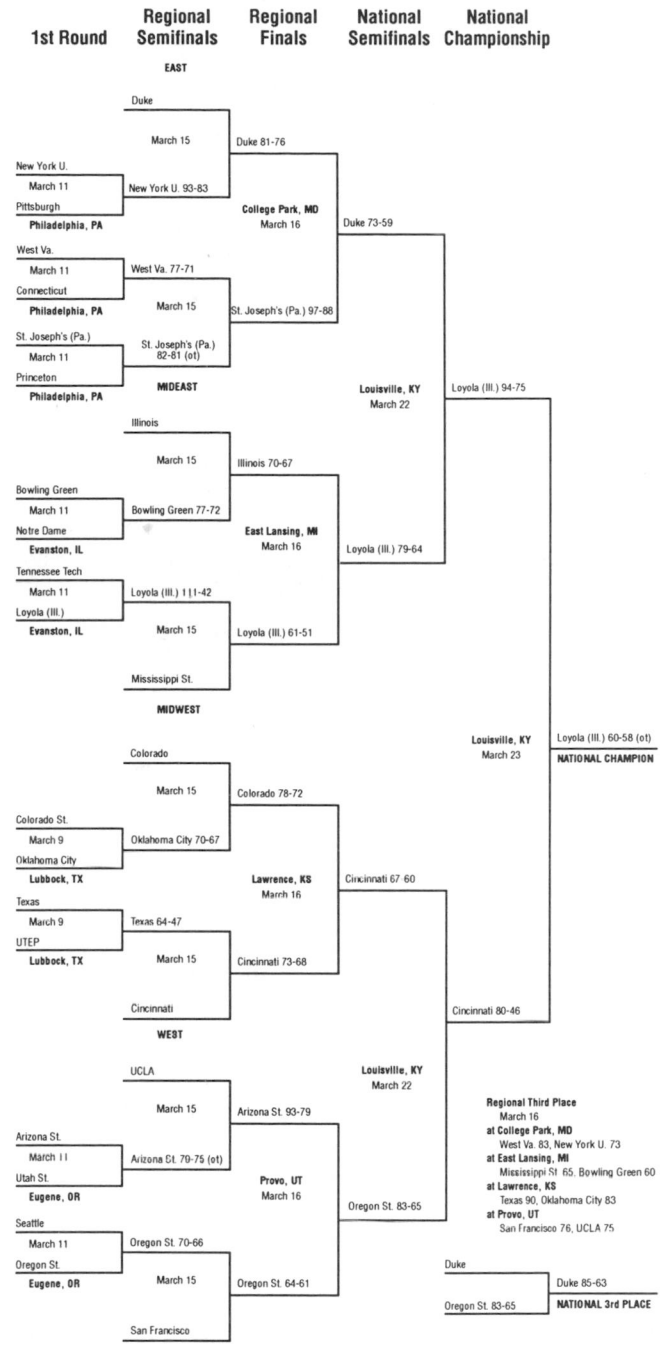

1st Round	Regional Semifinals	Regional Finals	National Semifinals	National Championship

EAST

Duke
March 15
Duke 81-76

New York U.
March 11
Pittsburgh
Philadelphia, PA
New York U. 93-83

College Park, MD
March 16
Duke 73-59

West Va.
March 11
Connecticut
Philadelphia, PA
West Va. 77-71
March 15

St. Joseph's (Pa.)
March 11
Princeton
Philadelphia, PA
St. Joseph's (Pa.) 82-81 (ot)
St. Joseph's (Pa.) 97-88

Louisville, KY
March 22
Loyola (Ill.) 94-75

MIDEAST

Illinois
March 15
Illinois 70-67

Bowling Green
March 11
Notre Dame
Evanston, IL
Bowling Green 77-72

East Lansing, MI
March 16
Loyola (Ill.) 79-64

Tennessee Tech
March 11
Loyola (Ill.)
Evanston, IL
Loyola (Ill.) 111-42
March 15
Loyola (Ill.) 61-51

Mississippi St.

MIDWEST

Colorado
March 15
Colorado 78-72

Colorado St.
March 9
Oklahoma City
Lubbock, TX
Oklahoma City 70-67

Lawrence, KS
March 16
Cincinnati 67-60

Texas
March 9
UTEP
Lubbock, TX
Texas 64-47
March 15
Cincinnati 73-68

Cincinnati

Louisville, KY
March 23
Loyola (Ill.) 60-58 (ot)
NATIONAL CHAMPION

Cincinnati 80-46

WEST

UCLA
March 15
Arizona St. 93-79

Arizona St.
March 11
Utah St.
Eugene, OR
Arizona St. 70-75 (ot)

Provo, UT
March 16
Oregon St. 83-65

Seattle
March 11
Oregon St.
Eugene, OR
Oregon St. 70-66
March 15
Oregon St. 64-61

San Francisco

Louisville, KY
March 22
Oregon St. 83-65

Regional Third Place
March 16
at College Park, MD
West Va. 83, New York U. 73
at East Lansing, MI
Mississippi St. 65, Bowling Green 60
at Lawrence, KS
Texas 90, Oklahoma City 83
at Provo, UT
San Francisco 76, UCLA 75

Duke
Duke 85-63
Oregon St. 83-65
NATIONAL 3rd PLACE

school to deploy just five players in a championship game. The starters all averaged more than 13 points per game, making them the lone group to achieve that feat for an NCAA titlist. The Ramblers are the only team to overcome a halftime deficit of as many as eight points (29-21) to win a title game. Loyola of Chicago became the only team to defeat an opponent by at least 50 points in a tournament game (111-42 over Tennessee Tech in the first round of Mideast Regional). . . . Cincinnati coach Ed Jucker won his first 11 NCAA Tournament games before bowing in the final to finish his career with an all-time best playoff winning percentage (.917 in minimum of 10 games). . . . Bowling Green's Nate Thurmond grabbed the most rebounds ever in a losing effort in the playoffs when he retrieved a tourney-high 31 missed shots in a 65-60 defeat to Mississippi State in the Southeast Regional third-place game. . . . Rod Thorn tossed in a tourney-high 44 points for West Virginia, but it wasn't enough to prevent a 97-88 setback against St. Joseph's in the East Regional semifinals. . . . Cincinnati swingman Tom Thacker was named to the All-Tournament Team despite committing a total of 13 turnovers at the Final Four.

Putting Things in Perspective: Thurmond collected 24 points and 12 rebounds and teammate Howard Komives poured in 32 points in a 92-75 regular-season triumph over NCAA champion-to-be Loyola of Chicago. But Thurmond shot a paltry 29.8 percent from the floor (17 of 57) in three postseason games although the Falcons registered their only NCAA tourney triumph in history (77-72 over Notre Dame).

Scoring Leader: Mel Counts, Oregon State (123 points, 24.6 ppg).

Highest Scoring Average: Barry Kramer, NYU (100 points, 33.3 ppg).

Rebounding Leaders: Bowling Green's Nate Thurmond (70 rebounds, 23.3 rpg) and Loyola's Vic Rouse (70 rebounds, 14 rpg).

1963-64

AT A GLANCE

NCAA Champion: UCLA (30-0; coached by John Wooden; won AAWU title by six games with a 15-0 record).

NIT Champion: Bradley (23-6; coached by Chuck Orsborn; finished in third place in Missouri Valley with a 7-5 record, which was three games behind Wichita State and Drake).

New Conference: Big Sky.

NCAA Probation: Dayton, Indiana, New Mexico State

NCAA Consensus First-Team All-Americans: Gary Bradds, C, Sr., Ohio State; Bill Bradley, F, Jr., Princeton; Walt Hazzard, G, Sr., UCLA; Cotton Nash, F, Sr., Kentucky; Dave Stallworth, F, Jr., Wichita State.

National Players of the Year: Bradds (30.6 ppg, 13.4 rpg, 52.4 FG%/AP, UPI) and Hazzard (18.6 ppg, 4.7 rpg/USBWA).

National Coach of the Year: John Wooden, UCLA (30-0/UPI, USBWA).

Undefeated UCLA won its first of 10 NCAA titles in 12 years, a stretch of dominance that many believe ranks among the greatest achievements in the history of competitive sports. The Bruins had never won a Final Four game despite finishing in a final Top 20 wire-service poll eight times in the previous 14 seasons under coach John Wooden.

UCLA's closest homecourt decision was an 83-79 victory over Illinois despite a school-record 24 rebounds by the Illini's Skip Thoren.

Kentucky set an NCAA single-game record with 108 rebounds in a 102-59 mauling of Mississippi (see accompanying box). Don Kessinger finished among the top three scorers in the SEC for the third consecutive year despite hitting just one of 19 field-goal attempts for Ole Miss against the Rebels. Kessinger was playing major league baseball by the end of the summer. . . . Georgia Tech, coached by Whack Hyder, finished in a tie for second place behind Kentucky in the Southeastern

1963–64 INDIVIDUAL LEADERS

SCORING

PLAYER	PTS.	AVG.
Komives, Bowling Green	844	36.7
Werkman, Seton Hall	830	33.2
Newsome, W. Michigan	653	32.7
Bradley, Princeton	936	32.3
Barry, Miami (Fla.)	870	32.2
Bradds, Ohio St.	735	30.6
Thomas, Xavier	779	30.0
Austin, Boston College	614	29.2
Barnes, Texas Western	816	29.1
Estes, Utah St.	821	28.3

REBOUNDING

PLAYER	REB.	AVG.
Pelkington, Xavier	567	21.80
Silas, Creighton	631	21.75

Dzik, Detroit	521	20.8
Isaac, Iona	403	20.2
Barnes, Texas Western	537	19.2
Reed, Notre Dame	318	17.7
Sahm, Notre Dame	315	17.5
Kimball, Connecticut	466	17.3
Counts, Oregon St.	489	16.9
Johnson, San Francisco	467	16.7

FIELD GOAL PERCENTAGE

PLAYER	FGM	FGA	PCT.
Holland, Davidson	135	214	.631
DeBerardinis, St. Fr. (Pa.)	112	181	.619
Fisher, Texas	136	222	.613
Nightingale, Rhode I.	139	229	.607
Johnson, San Francisco	206	346	.595
Buckley, Duke	160	271	.590
Thompson, Providence	260	442	.588
Pierce, W. Texas St.	123	210	.586
Bustion, Colorado St.	110	188	.585
Richards, Syracuse	177	305	.580

FREE THROW PERCENTAGE

PLAYER	FTM	FTA	PCT.
Park, Tulsa	121	134	.903
Schultz, Tennessee	101	113	.894
Lee, San Francisco	108	121	.893
Izor, Dayton	95	107	.888
Bailey, N. Texas St.	136	156	.872
Murphy, DePaul	93	107	.869
Geiger, Xavier	119	137	.869
Newsome, W. Michigan	129	149	.866
Vrankovich, Santa Clara	165	191	.864
Perry, Alabama	87	101	.861

1963–64 TEAM LEADERS

SCORING OFFENSE

SCHOOL	PTS.	AVG.
Detroit	2402	96.1
Miami (Fla.)	2575	95.4
Michigan St.	2211	92.1
Weber St.	2288	91.5
Loyola (Ill.)	2556	91.3

SCORING DEFENSE

SCHOOL	PTS.	AVG.
San Jose St.	1307	54.5
Texas Western	1548	55.3
Gettysburg (Pa.)	1363	56.8
New Mexico	1660	57.2
Oklahoma St.	1449	58.0

FIELD GOAL PERCENTAGE

SCHOOL	FGM	FGA	PCT.
Davidson	894	1644	.544
West Texas St.	681	1356	.502
Rhode Island	910	1854	.491
Wichita St.	817	1688	.484
San Francisco	764	1581	.483

FREE THROW PERCENTAGE

SCHOOL	FTM	FTA	PCT.
Miami (Fla.)	593	780	.760
Bowling Green	430	571	.753
Utah	578	769	.752
Kentucky	454	605	.750
Lafayette	454	608	.747

REBOUNDING

SCHOOL	TOTAL REB.	OWN	PCT.
Iona	1673	1071	.640
San Francisco	2343	1410	.602
Cornell	2674	1580	.591
Texas Western	2386	1407	.590
New Mexico	2188	1284	.587

Conference in the Yellow Jackets' final season as a member of the league. . . . Cincinnati's 86-game homecourt winning streak, which started in 1957, was snapped by Kansas, 51-47. Cincinnati finished out of the top 10 of the final AP poll for the first time in seven years.

Defending national scoring champion Nick Werkman of Seton Hall scored almost four points per game more than he did the previous season (from 29.5 to 33.2), but finished runner-up to Bowling Green's Howard Komives, a 6-1 guard who averaged 36.7 points per game after hitting 50 consecutive free throws in his last five games. Komives finished 45th in the country in scoring the previous year with a 20.2 norm. Werkman and Komives were among five players to score more than 32 points per game. Werkman's 52 points against Scranton is still a school record.

Princeton's Bill Bradley set a mark for most points in an Ivy League contest when he poured in 51 against Harvard. Harvard's only victory in one seven-game conference stretch was an 88-82 verdict over Princeton, which might be the biggest upset in Crimson history. . . . Setting school single-game scoring records were Texas Western's Jim Barnes (51 points vs. Western New Mexico), Xavier's Steve Thomas (50 vs. Detroit), Ohio State's Gary Bradds (49 vs. Illinois), Boston College's John Austin (49 vs. Georgetown) and Northwestern's Rich Falk (49 vs. Iowa). . . . Barnes also grabbed a school-record 36 rebounds in the Western New Mexico contest. Bradds' outburst was one of six consecutive 40-point games for him in Big Ten competition.

Komives, Werkman, Western Michigan's Manny Newsome (32.7 ppg), Princeton's Bradley

(32.3), Xavier's Steve Thomas (30), Boston College's John Austin (29.2), Texas Western's Barnes (29.2), Davidson's Fred Hetzel (27.3), Sandy Williams (27.3) of St. Francis (Pa.), Oregon State's Mel Counts (26.7), Yale's Rick Kaminsky (24.9), Manhattan's Larry Lembo (24.5), Delaware's Dave Sysko (23.9) and Santa Clara's Russ Vrankavich (22.5) set school records for highest scoring average in a single season.

Komives' average is the highest in Mid-American Conference history. Two of Western Michigan's three defeats in its first four games came at Michigan State (101-100) despite Newsome's 45 points, and against defending NCAA champion Loyola of Chicago (105-102) despite Newsome's 44 points.

Texas A&M, coached by Shelby Metcalf, captured its first outright Southwest Conference championship since 1923. A&M's Bennie Lenox set a school and Southwest Conference record with a national single-game high of 53 points against Wyoming in the All-College Tournament at Oklahoma City. He was one of 10 different players to score 50 or more in a single game during the season. . . . Creighton's Paul Silas finished his varsity career as the only player in Division I history to average more than 20 rebounds each season of a career that lasted at least three years. He had 13 games with at least 27 rebounds.

Ohio State, coached by Fred Taylor, captured an unprecedented fifth consecutive Big Ten title. The Buckeyes, however, saw their 50-game home-court winning streak snapped when they were dumped by Davidson, 95-73. . . . Senior Terry Holland's nation-leading 63.1 percent field-goal shooting helped Davidson pace the country at 54.4 percent. Holland, who would coach Virginia to the Final Four in 1981 and 1984, is the only Final Four coach to previously lead the nation in a statistical category as a major-college player.

Another player who would become a prominent coach was Providence center John Thompson, who ranked among the nation's top 20 in scoring (26.2 ppg), rebounding (14.5 rpg) and field-goal shooting (58.8 percent). . . . Digger Phelps was a graduate assistant coach at Rider when the Broncs stunned NYU, ending the Violets' homecourt winning streak that dated back to 1941.

Forward Joe Caldwell became the only player in Arizona State history to earn first-team all-conference honors on three different occasions—Border (1962) and WAC (1963 and 1964). Jumpin' Joe cleared 6 feet-7 inches in the high jump as a member of the school's track squad. . . . Arizona lost its last three games but registered the Wildcats' first winning record in 10 seasons (15-11).

Duke won a league-record 27 consecutive games against ACC competition (subsequently tied) until bowing at Wake Forest, 72-71. Duke, coached by Vic Bubas, captured the ACC Tournament by an average margin of 23 points. The Blue Devils' trek to the Final Four was unnerving when their 85-seat charter airplane skidded off a rain-slick runway upon landing at Kansas City's Municipal Airport. . . . Clemson, coached by Bobby Roberts, won four of its last five games to compile the Tigers' first winning record (13-12) in 12 years. A pair of double-overtime triumphs over North Carolina enabled the Tigers to end a 25-game losing streak in their series with the Tar Heels. Clemson notched its first winning record in ACC competition (8-6) since the league's inaugural season in 1953-54. . . . North Carolina junior Billy Cunningham reached double digits in scoring and rebounding in the same game a total of 22 times during the season and on 60 occasions in his three-year varsity career.

Tulane was winless through 22 games until winning its season finale against LSU, 80-68. . . . Kansas State finished first or second in the Big Eight Conference standings for the ninth consecutive season. The Wildcats lost twice to undefeated UCLA by a total of just nine points. . . . Drake, coached by Maury John, earned a share of the Missouri Valley Conference regular-season title after finishing in last place the previous year.

Detroit, coached by Bob Calihan, became the only Michigan Division I team ever to lead the nation in scoring. The 14-11 Titans averaged 96.1 points per game, which was well above the national average of 74.4. . . . Minnesota, coached by John Kundla, compiled a 17-7 record to snap a streak of six consecutive non-winning seasons. . . . DePaul, coached by Ray Meyer, finished in the Top 20 of a final wire-service poll for the only time in a 22-year span from 1953-54 through 1974-75. Texas A&M, in Shelby Metcalf's first season as coach of the Aggies, finished in the Top 20 of a final wire-service poll for the only time in a 28-year span from 1951-52 through 1978-79. . . . Xavier's Bob Pelkington grabbed a school-record 31 rebounds in a game against St. Francis (Pa.). . . . Dayton coach Tom Blackburn died one day before the Flyers' final game. Assistant coach Don Donoher handled the team in the last three contests.

Idaho's Tom Moreland set a Big Sky Conference single-game standard by tying a school mark with 31 rebounds against Whitworth. . . . Ben Carnevale was in his 18th season as Navy's coach when the Midshipmen posted their first losing record in 21 years (10-12). . . . Oklahoma State's Hank Iba posted the 700th victory of his college coaching career with an 80-47 triumph over Oklahoma in State's final game of the season.

Pacific ended a streak of seven consecutive losing seasons and started a string of 11 straight winning campaigns by compiling a 15-11 record under first-year coach Dick Edwards. . . . Western Kentucky's Ed Diddle retired after a 42-year coaching career with a 759-302 record. Diddle's teams won an amazing 31 conference championships (13 in the KIAC, 8 in the SIAA and 10 in the OVC). . . . Oregon State's Slats Gill ended his

UCLA's Walt Hazzard dishes one off to a teammate.

36-year coaching career with a 599-392 mark. . . . Marquette's Eddie Hickey, who previously coached Creighton and St. Louis, ended his 26-year career with a 435-231 record. Marquette compiled a 5-21 mark, ending Hickey's streak of 21 consecutive winning records.

1964 NCAA Tournament

Summary: UCLA's Kenny Washington was instrumental in helping venerable coach John Wooden capture his first NCAA Tournament championship. Washington, the only player with a

1963–64 NCAA CHAMPION: UCLA

SEASON STATISTICS OF UCLA REGULARS

PLAYER	POS.	CL.	G.	FG%	FT%	PPG	RPG
Gail Goodrich	G	Jr.	30	.458	.711	21.5	5.2
Walt Hazzard	G	Sr.	30	.445	.718	18.6	4.7
Jack Hirsch	F	Sr.	30	.528	.664	14.0	7.6
Keith Erickson	F	Jr.	30	.403	.623	10.7	9.1
Fred Slaughter	C	Sr.	30	.466	.484	7.9	8.1
Kenny Washington	F-G	So.	30	.458	.627	6.1	4.2
Doug McIntosh	C	So.	30	.519	.500	3.6	4.4
Kim Stewart	F	Sr.	23	.393	.467	2.2	2.0
Rich Levin	F	Jr.	19	.372	.500	2.0	0.6
Mike Huggins	G	Sr.	23	.382	.478	1.6	1.0
Chuck Darrow	G	So.	23	.379	.583	1.6	1.2
Vaughn Hoffman	C	So.	21	.476	.500	1.2	1.3
TEAM TOTALS			**30**	**.455**	**.644**	**88.9**	**55.7**

1964 FINAL FOUR CHAMPIONSHIP GAME

KANSAS CITY, MO

UCLA (98)	FG-A	FT-A	REB.	A	PF	PTS.
Goodrich	9-18	9-9	3	1	1	27
Slaughter	0-1	0-0	1	2	0	0
Hazzard	4-10	3-5	3	8	5	11
Hirsch	5-9	3-5	6	6	3	13
Erickson	2-7	4-4	5	1	5	8
McIntosh	4-9	0-0	11	1	2	8
Washington	11-16	4-4	12	1	4	26
Darrow	0-1	3-4	1	0	2	3
Stewart	0-1	0-0	0	0	1	0
Huggins	0-1	0-1	1	2	2	0
Hoffman	1-2	0-0	0	0	0	2
Levin	0-1	0-0	0	0	0	0
TOTALS	**36-76**	**26-32**	**43**	**22**	**25**	**98**

FG%: .474. FT%: .813. Turnovers: 19.

DUKE (83)	FG-A	FT-A	REB.	A	PF	PTS.
Ferguson	2-6	0-1	1	4	3	4
Buckley	5-8	8-12	9	0	4	18
Tison	3-8	1-1	1	2	2	7
Harrison	1-1	0-0	1	1	2	2
Mullins	9-21	4-4	4	1	5	22
Marin	8-16	0-1	10	1	3	16
Vacendak	2-7	3-3	6	0	4	7
Herbster	1-4	0-2	0	0	0	2
Kitching	1-1	0-0	1	0	0	2
Mann	0-0	3-4	2	0	1	3
Harscher	0-0	0-0	0	0	0	0
Cox	0-0	0-0	0	0	0	0
TOTALS	**32-72**	**19-28**	**35**	**9**	**24**	**83**

FG%: .444. FT%: .679. Turnovers: 24.
Halftime: UCLA 50-38.

NATIONAL SEMIFINALS

UCLA (90): Goodrich 7-18 0-0 14, Slaughter 2-6 0-0 4, Hazzard 7-10 5-7 19, Hirsch 2-11 0-0 4, Erickson 10-21 8-9 28, McIntosh 3-5 2-3 8, Washington 5-11 3-4 13. Team 36-82 (.439) 18-23 (.783) 90.

KANSAS STATE (84): Moss 3-9 1-1 7, Robinson 2-7 0-1 4, Simons 10-17 4-6 24, Suttner 3-9 0-5 6, Murrell 13-22 3-5 29, Paradis 5-9 0-0 10, Williams 1-1 2-3 4, Nelson 0-1 0-0 0, Gottfrid 0-0 0-0 0, Barnard 0-1 0-0 0. Team 37-76 (.487) 10-21 (.476) 84.

Halftime: UCLA 43-41.

DUKE (91): Ferguson 6-11 0-1 12, Buckley 11-16 3-5 25, Tison 3-10 6-10 12, Harrison 6-15 2-3 14, Mullins 8-19 5-6 21, Marin 1-2 0-0 2, Vacendak 2-5 1-2 5, Herbster 0-0 0-0 0. Team 37-78 (.474) 17-27 (.630) 91.

MICHIGAN (80): Buntin 8-18 3-3 19, Cantrell 6-10 0-0 12, Russell 13-19 5-6 31, Tregoning 3-11 2-2 8, Darden 2-6 1-1 5, Myers 2-5 0-0 4, Pomey 0-1 1-2 1, Herner 0-1 0-0 0. Team 34-71 (.479) 12-14 (.857) 80.

Halftime: Duke 48-39.

ALL-TOURNAMENT TEAM

Bill Buntin, C, Jr., Michigan (52 points, 23 rebounds in final two games)
Gail Goodrich, G, Jr., UCLA (41 points, nine rebounds)
*Walt Hazzard, G, Sr., UCLA (30 points, 10 rebounds)
Jeff Mullins, F, Sr., Duke (43 points, 12 rebounds)
Willie Murrell, F, Sr., Kansas State (49 points, 23 rebounds)

*Named Most Outstanding Player.

1963-64 UNDEFEATED TEAM: UCLA (30-0)

COACH: JOHN WOODEN

UCLA	OPPONENT	UCLA'S HIGH SCORER
113	Brigham Young 71	Hazzard 20
80	Butler 65	Hazzard 21
78	Kansas State* 75	Goodrich 21
74	Kansas* 54	Goodrich 23
112	Baylor* 61	Hazzard 23
95	Creighton* 79	Hazzard 26
95	Yale 65	Goodrich 25
98	Michigan 80	Goodrich 30
83	Illinois 79	Goodrich 21
88	at Washington State 83	Goodrich 28
121	at Washington State 77	Goodrich 21
79	Southern California 59	Hazzard 21
78	Southern California 71	Goodrich 23
84	Stanford 71	Goodrich 23
80	Stanford* 61	Hazzard 31
107	UC Santa Barbara 76	Goodrich/Hazzard 21
87	UC Santa Barbara* 59	Goodrich 31
87	at California 67	Goodrich 26
58	at California 56	Hazzard 17
73	Washington 58	Hazzard 17
88	Washington 60	Goodrich 22
100	at Stanford 88	Hazzard 27
78	at Washington 64	Erickson/Hazzard 21
93	Washington State 56	Hazzard 19
87	California 57	Goodrich 23
91	Southern California 81	Goodrich 23

NCAA TOURNAMENT

95	Seattle* 90	Hazzard 26
76	San Francisco* 72	Hazzard 23
90	Kansas State* 84	Erickson 28
98	Duke* 83	Goodrich 27

*Neutral court games.

POUNDING THE BOARDS

Mississippi at Kentucky
February 8, 1964

Kentucky's five starters had a modest average height of 6-3 1/2, but they each grabbed more than 10 rebounds when the Wildcats established an NCAA single-game record by retrieving 108 missed shots in a 102-59 victory over Mississippi. The two teams combined to hit a meager 34 percent of their field-goal attempts. All-America Cotton Nash tied his career high by hauling down 30 rebounds, the most ever by a UK player against a Southeastern Conference opponent.

OLE MISS (59)	FG-A	FT-A	REB.	PTS.
Jack Steinhart	4-14	2-2	4	10
Robert Kreilein	3-6	0-1	4	6
Ron Davidson	3-14	3-5	8	9
Don Kessinger	1-19	3-3	6	5
Glenn Lusk	9-16	1-2	5	19
Charles Huffstatler	0-2	1-1	1	1
John Partridge	0-0	0-0	1	0
James Bobe	3-7	1-1	3	7
Spencer Schreiter	1-5	0-1	1	2
Eddie Dunn	0-1	0-0	0	0
Totals	**24-84**	**11-16**	**40**	**59**

FG%—.286. FT%—.647.

KENTUCKY (102)	FG-A	FT-A	REB.	PTS.
Ted Deeken	9-27	1-1	17	19
Larry Conley	8-14	0-1	12	16
Cotton Nash	9-28	5-6	30	23
Terry Mobley	3-13	1-3	12	7
Tommy Kron	8-17	0-0	11	16
?. Gibson	3-7	0-0	8	6
Charles Ishmael	0-5	0-0	2	0
Randy Embry	2-4	0-0	3	4
Sam Harper	5-9	1-2	6	11
John Adams	0-1	0-0	1	0
Totals	**47-125**	**8-13**	**108**	**102**

FG%—.376. FT%—.615.

Halftime: Kentucky 47-27.

single-digit season scoring average (6.1) to tally more than 25 points in a championship game, scored 26 points in a 98-83 triumph over Duke in the final. Washington became the only player to score 25 or more points in a final and not be named to the All-Tournament team. The Bruins won the national championship by a modest average of 7.5 points after gifted guards Gail Goodrich and Walt Hazzard sparked them to 12 double-digit margin victories in their last 13 regular-season games. Goodrich (21.5 points per game) and Hazzard (18.6 ppg) represent the only backcourt twosome to be the top two scorers on the season for an NCAA championship team. Despite shooting a meager 40.3 percent from the floor and 52.9 percent from the free-throw line, UCLA overcame a 13-point deficit to end San Francisco's 19-game winning streak (76-72) in the West Regional final.

1963-64 FINAL NATIONAL POLLS

AP	UPI	SCHOOL (RECORD)	HEAD COACH
1	1	UCLA (30-0)	John Wooden
2	2	Michigan (23-5)	Dave Strack
3	4	Duke (26-5)	Vic Bubas
4	3	Kentucky (21-6)	Adolph Rupp
5	6	Wichita (23-6)	Ralph Miller
6	5	Oregon State (25-4)	Slats Gill
7	7	Villanova (24-4)	Jack Kraft
8	8	Loyola of Chicago (22-6)	George Ireland
9	11	DePaul (21-4)	Ray Meyer
10	10	Davidson (22-4)	Lefty Driesell
–	9	Texas Western (25-3)	Don Haskins
–	12	Kansas State (22-7)	Tex Winter
–	13	Drake (21-7)	Maury John
–	13	San Francisco (23-5)	Pete Peletta
–	15	Utah State (21-8)	Ladell Andersen
–	16	New Mexico (23-6)	Bob King
–	16	Ohio State (16-8)	Fred Taylor
–	18	Texas A&M (18-7)	Shelby Metcalf
–	19	Arizona State (16-11)	Ned Wulk
–	19	Providence (20-6)	Joe Mullaney

Eight of their 30 victories were by seven points or less, including a 58-56 triumph at California. The Bruins became the only school to win an NCAA title one year after appearing in the playoffs and losing their tournament opener by a double-digit margin (93-79 to Arizona State in 1963).

Outcome for Defending Champion: Loyola of Chicago compiled a 22-6 record. The Ramblers' first defeat was in their seventh game (69-58 against Georgetown). Loyola, eliminated in the second round of the national tournament by Michigan, became the only team in the era of three-year eligibility to have four teammates finish their careers at the same time with more than 1,000 points—center Les Hunter (1,472), guards John Egan (1,315) and Ron Miller (1,299), and forward Vic Rouse (1,169).

Star Gazing: Hazzard, the second-leading scorer over the entire season for UCLA's first championship team in 1964 with an average of 18.6 points per game, was named Most Outstanding Player although he was the Bruins' fourth-leading scorer at the Final Four that year. "I never had a better man on the fast break than Walt," UCLA coach John Wooden said. Hazzard had a two-game total of 30 points, finishing behind the scoring aggregates compiled by teammates Goodrich (41), Washington (39) and Keith Erickson (36). Erickson's 28-point outburst in a 90-84 national semifinal victory over Kansas State was the only one of UCLA's 30 games when neither

Goodrich nor Hazzard at least shared the Bruins' scoring lead.

Biggest Upset: Kentucky, ranked No. 3 by UPI and No. 4 by AP entering the tourney, dropped its opener to Ohio, 85-69, when the Wildcats fell behind by 16 points at intermission.

One and Only: Goodrich, a 6-1 junior, became the shortest undergraduate to average more than 20 points per game for an NCAA titlist (21.5 ppg). He was the only non-Southern Cal player in a six-year span from 1961 through 1966 to lead the Pacific-8 Conference in scoring. . . . UCLA's Washington became the only championship team player to have a season scoring average of less than six points per game entering a Final Four but accumulate at least 30 points in the national semifinals and final. Washington had a season scoring average of 5.2 points per game entering the Final Four before erupting for a total of 39 points in victories over Kansas State and Duke. He is the only player with a single-digit season scoring average to score more than 25 points in a championship game (26 against Duke to finish the year with a 6.1-point average). Goodrich scored 27 in the final when he and Washington combined to become the only teammate duo to each score more than 25 in an NCAA final.

Numbers Game: Of the individuals to both play and coach in the NCAA Tournament, Jeff Mullins leads that group in both scoring and rebounding totals. He managed a tourney-high 43 points in an 87-73 victory over Villanova in the East Regional semifinals. Mullins, who later guided UNC Charlotte to the tourney, garnered 200 points and 63 rebounds in eight playoff games to help Duke twice reach the Final Four. . . . Jim "Bad News" Barnes accounted for 61.8 percent of Texas Western's offense by scoring 42 points in the Miners' 68-62 victory against Texas A&M in the first round of the Midwest Regional. In the Miners next game, Barnes was whistled for three quick personal fouls in the opening minutes against Kansas State and spent almost the entire first half on the bench. He was assessed fouls No. 4 and No. 5 early in the second half and fouled out

UCLA's Gail Goodrich shoots a jumper in the 1964 NCAA Final against Duke.

with four points in their 64-60 defeat. . . . Michigan became the only Final Four team ever to have a duo each average more than 23 points per game—guard Cazzie Russell (24.8) and center Bill Buntin (23.2). . . . UCLA had seven players average more than four rebounds per game. . . . Creighton's Paul Silas outrebounded Oklahoma City's Eddie Jackson, 27-24, in the Bluejays' 89-78 victory over OCU in the first round of the Midwest Regional.

What Might Have Been: Wichita (23-6) reached the Midwest Regional final before bowing to Kansas State, 94-86. The Shockers were without standout senior guard Ernie Moore, who was averaging 17.4 points per game when declared ineligible for postseason play.

Scoring Leader: Jeff Mullins, Duke (116 points, 29 ppg).

1964 CHAMPIONSHIP BRACKET

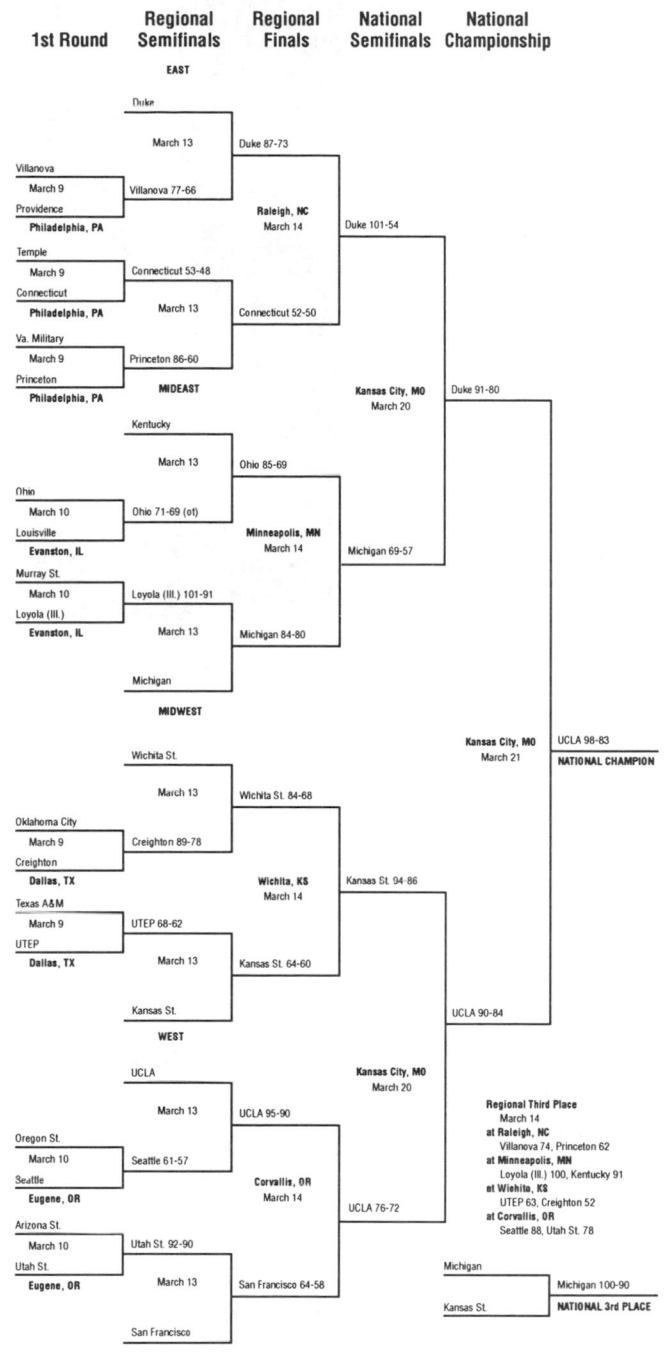

1st Round	Regional Semifinals	Regional Finals	National Semifinals	National Championship

EAST

Duke
March 13 — Duke 87-73

Villanova
March 9
Providence — Villanova 77-66
Philadelphia, PA

Raleigh, NC
March 14 — Duke 101-54

Temple
March 9
Connecticut — Connecticut 53-48
Philadelphia, PA
March 13 — Connecticut 52-50

Va. Military
March 9
Princeton — Princeton 86-60
Philadelphia, PA

Kansas City, MO
March 20 — Duke 91-80

MIDEAST

Kentucky
March 13 — Ohio 85-69

Ohio
March 10
Louisville — Ohio 71-69 (ot)
Evanston, IL

Minneapolis, MN
March 14 — Michigan 69-57

Murray St.
March 10
Loyola (Ill.) — Loyola (Ill.) 101-91
Evanston, IL
March 13 — Michigan 84-80

Michigan

MIDWEST

Wichita St.
March 13 — Wichita St. 84-68

Oklahoma City
March 9
Creighton — Creighton 89-78
Dallas, TX

Wichita, KS
March 14 — Kansas St. 94-86

Texas A&M
March 9
UTEP — UTEP 68-62
Dallas, TX
March 13 — Kansas St. 64-60

Kansas St.

WEST

Kansas City, MO
March 20 — UCLA 90-84

Kansas City, MO
March 21 — UCLA 98-83
NATIONAL CHAMPION

UCLA
March 13 — UCLA 95-90

Oregon St.
March 10
Seattle — Seattle 61-57
Eugene, OR

Corvallis, OR
March 14 — UCLA 76-72

Arizona St.
March 10
Utah St. — Utah St. 92-90
Eugene, OR
March 13 — San Francisco 64-58

San Francisco

Kansas City, MO
March 20

Regional Third Place
March 14
at Raleigh, NC
Villanova 74, Princeton 62
at Minneapolis, MN
Loyola (Ill.) 100, Kentucky 91
at Wichita, KS
UTEP 63, Creighton 52
at Corvallis, OR
Seattle 88, Utah St. 78

Michigan
Kansas St. — Michigan 100-90
NATIONAL 3rd PLACE

Highest Scoring Average: Dave Stallworth, Wichita State (59 points, 29.5 ppg).

Rebounding Leader: Paul Silas, Creighton (57 rebounds, 19 rpg).

Highest Rebounding Average: Dave Stallworth, Wichita State (39 rebounds, 19.5 rpg).

1964-65

AT A GLANCE

NCAA Champion: UCLA (28-2; coached by John Wooden; won AAWU title by five games with a 14-0 record).

NIT Champion: St. John's (21-8; coached by Joe Lapchick).

New Rules: Coaches must remain seated on the bench except while the clock is stopped or to direct or encourage players on the court. This rule was to try to help prevent coaches from inciting undesirable crowd behavior toward the referees. . . . NIT field expanded from 12 to 14 teams.

NCAA Probation: Miami (Fla.).

NCAA Consensus First-Team All-Americans: Rick Barry, F, Sr., Miami (Fla.); Bill Bradley, F, Sr., Princeton; Gail Goodrich, G, Sr., UCLA; Fred Hetzel, F-C, Sr., Davidson; Cazzie Russell, G, Jr., Michigan.

National Player of the Year: Bradley (30.5 ppg, 11.8 rpg, 53.3 FG%, 88.6 FT%).

National Coaches of the Year: Michigan's Dave Strack (24-4/UPI) and Princeton's Butch van Breda Kolff (23-6/USBWA).

Miami of Florida's Rick Barry led the country in scoring in 1964–65.

Wayne Estes, runner-up to Rick Barry of Miami (Fla.) for the national scoring championship, was electrocuted in a freak accident the evening of February 8. The tragedy occurred less than three hours after Estes scored 48 points against Denver to become Utah State's first player to reach the 2,000-point plateau in his career.

En route back and forth to his off-campus apartment and then a restaurant, Estes was with teammate Delano Lyons and another friend when they passed the scene of an auto accident that had killed a Utah State student. The group stopped and inspected the scene briefly. They were returning to their car when Lyons, who is 6-2, noticed a live high-voltage wire dangling in front of him after being dislodged when the victim's car hit a utility pole. Lyons ducked and hollered "Watch it!" to the 6-6 Estes, who was walking behind him. But Estes didn't react quickly enough and the wire carrying 2,700 volts of electricity brushed against his forehead, killing him instantly.

Barry, the only Miami player ever to become an NCAA consensus first- or second-team All-American, was able to stay ahead of Estes in the scoring race by amassing six 50-point games, including a national-high and school record 59 against Rollins. Barry finished the season with an amazing average of 55.7 points and rebounds per contest. He hauled down a school-record 29 rebounds against Oklahoma City.

Western Kentucky's Clem Haskins (55 vs. Middle Tennessee State), Davidson's Fred Hetzel (53 vs. Furman), Utah State's Estes (52 vs. Boston College in overtime at Rainbow Classic in Honolulu), Iona's Warren Isaac (50 vs. Bates), Georgetown's Jim Barry (46 at Fairleigh Dickinson), Middle Tennessee State's Mike Milholland (44 vs. Austin Peay), St. Mary's Jim Moore (43 vs. Sacramento State) and Wisconsin's Ken Barnes (42 vs. Indiana/subsequently tied) established school single-game scoring records.

Haskins' outburst was an Ohio Valley Conference standard. Davidson's Hetzel also grabbed a school-record 27 rebounds in the contest against Furman. MTSU's Miholland grabbed a school-record 32 rebounds in the APSU game. . . . Miami's Barry (37.4 ppg), Utah State's Estes (33.7), Wyoming's Flynn Robinson (27) and Dayton's Henry Finkel (25.3) set school records for highest scoring average in a single season.

Dave Stallworth became the only Wichita State player in history to supply back-to-back 40-point games with 45 and 40 against Loyola of Chicago in overtime and Louisville, respectively, in the last two games of his college career. The midseason graduate was named an NCAA consensus second-team All-American despite playing in just 16 of WSU's 30 games. . . . Wichita State's only No. 1 ranking in school history ended in mid-December when the Shockers were nipped at Michigan, 87-85, on Cazzie Russell's 35-foot basket for the Wolverines at the buzzer.

Princeton's Bill Bradley, who would become a U.S. Senator (D-N.J.), led the country in free-

1964–65 INDIVIDUAL LEADERS

SCORING

PLAYER	PTS.	AVG.
Barry, Miami (Fla.)	973	37.4
Estes, Utah St.	641	33.7
Bradley, Princeton	885	30.5
Schellhase, Purdue	704	29.3
Thomas, Xavier	405	28.9
Robinson, Wyoming	701	27.0
Austin, Boston College	673	26.9
Hetzel, Davidson	689	26.5
Beasley, Texas A&M	619	25.8
Russell, Michigan	694	25.7

REBOUNDING

PLAYER	REB.	AVG.
Kimball, Connecticut	483	21.0
Isaac, Iona	480	20.9

Woods, E. Tennessee St.	450	19.6
Barry, Miami (Fla.)	475	18.3
Swagerty, Pacific	473	18.2
Sahm, Notre Dame	393	16.4
Johnson, San Francisco	469	16.2
Branch, Fairfield	208	16.0
Washington, Villanova	442	15.8
Anderson, St. Joseph's	450	15.5

FIELD GOAL PERCENTAGE

PLAYER	FGM	FGA	PCT.
Kehoe, St. Peter's	138	209	.660
Finkel, Dayton	293	450	.651
McKendrick, Rice	152	250	.608
Newton, Auburn	126	208	.606
Johnson, San Francisco	242	405	.598
Hetzel, Davidson	273	471	.580
Kimball, Connecticut	177	311	.569

Chambers, Utah	199	355	.561
Thoren, Illinois	219	391	.560
Stallworth, Wichita St.	153	275	.556
Ritch, Army	140	252	.556

FREE THROW PERCENTAGE

PLAYER	FTM	FTA	PCT.
Bradley, Princeton	272	308	.886
Banko, UC Santa Barbara	156	177	.881
Park, Tulsa	145	165	.879
Estes, Utah St.	137	156	.878
K. McIntyre, St. John's	144	164	.878
Lloyd, Rutgers	127	145	.876
Neuman, Penn	112	129	.868
Barry, Georgetown	110	127	.866
Anderson, W. Michigan	158	183	.863
Barry, Miami (Fla.)	293	341	.859

1964–65 TEAM LEADERS

SCORING OFFENSE

SCHOOL	PTS.	AVG.
Miami (Fla.)	2558	98.4
Brigham Young	2639	94.3
Duke	2310	92.4
Illinois	2213	92.2
Indiana	2200	91.7

SCORING DEFENSE

SCHOOL	PTS.	AVG.
Tennessee	1391	55.64
Oklahoma St.	1503	55.66
New Mexico	1504	55.7
Texas Western	1468	56.5
Oregon St.	1525	58.7

FIELD GOAL PERCENTAGE

SCHOOL	FGM	FGA	PCT.
St. Peter's	579	1089	.532
Davidson	908	1784	.509
San Francisco	931	1893	.492
Duke	942	1921	.490
Manhattan	677	1382	.490

FREE THROW PERCENTAGE

SCHOOL	FTM	FTA	PCT.
Miami (Fla.)	642	807	.796
Morehead St.	487	620	.785
Indiana	464	604	.768
Kentucky	517	675	.766
UC Santa Barbara	482	633	.761

REBOUNDING

SCHOOL	TOTAL REB.	OWN	PCT.
Iona	1896	1191	.628
Tennessee	1997	1207	.604
Florida	1749	1041	.595
Connecticut	2439	1432	.587
New Mexico	2286	1342	.587

1964–65 NCAA CHAMPION: UCLA

SEASON STATISTICS OF UCLA REGULARS

PLAYER	POS.	CL.	G.	FG%	FT%	PPG	RPG
Gail Goodrich	G	Sr.	30	.525	.717	24.8	5.3
Keith Erickson	F	Sr.	29	.443	.725	12.9	8.8
Fred Goss	G	Jr.	30	.442	.729	12.2	3.3
Edgar Lacey	F	So.	30	.469	.579	11.6	10.2
Kenny Washington	F	Jr.	30	.425	.653	9.2	5.0
Mike Lynn	C	So.	30	.503	.581	6.7	5.1
Doug McIntosh	C	Jr.	30	.429	.737	6.5	5.6
TEAM TOTALS			30	.463	.665	86.3	52.0

1965 FINAL FOUR CHAMPIONSHIP GAME

PORTLAND, OR

UCLA (91)	FG-A	FT-A	REB.	PF	PTS.
Erickson	1-1	1-2	1	1	3
Lacey	5-7	1-2	7	3	11
McIntosh	1-2	1-2	0	2	3
Goodrich	12-22	18-20	4	4	42
Goss	4-12	0-0	3	1	8
Washington	7-9	3-4	5	2	17
Lynn	2-3	1-2	6	1	5
Lyons	0-0	0-0	0	1	0
Galbraith	0-0	0-0	0	0	0
Hoffman	1-1	0-0	1	0	2
Levin	0-1	0-0	1	0	0
Chambers	0-0	0-1	0	0	0
Team			6		
TOTALS	33-58	25-33	34	15	91

FG%: .569. FT%: .758. Assists: 4.

MICHIGAN (80)	FG-A	FT-A	REB.	PF	PTS.
Darden	8-10	1-1	4	5	17
Pomey	2-5	0-0	2	2	4
Buntin	6-14	2-4	6	5	14
Russell	10-16	8-10	5	2	28
Tregoning	2-7	1-1	5	5	5
Myers	0-4	0-0	3	2	0
Brown	0-0	0-0	0	0	0

	FG-A	FT-A	REB		PTS
Ludwig	1-2	0-0	0	0	2
Thompson	0-0	0-0	0	0	0
Bankey	0-0	0-0	0	0	0
Clawson	3-4	0-0	0	2	6
Dill	1-2	2-2	1	1	4
Team			7		
TOTALS	33-64	14-18	33	24	80

FG%: .516. FT%: .778. Assists: 2.
Halftime: UCLA 47-34.

NATIONAL SEMIFINALS

MICHIGAN (93): Tregoning 6-9 1-1 13, Darden 6-13 1-3 13, Buntin 7-13 8-10 22, Russell 10-21 8-9 28, Pomey 2-8 2-2 6, Myers 1-4 0-0 2, Thompson 0-1 2-2 2, Ludwig 0-0 0-0 0, Clawson 2-2 0-1 4. Team 34-71 (.479) 25-32 (.781) 93.

PRINCETON (76): Bradley 12-25 5-5 29, Haarlow 4-10 1-4 9, Brown 2-6 0-0 4, Walters 5-10 1-2 11, Rodenbach 2-5 2-2 6, Hummer 4-10 4-5 12, Koch 1-4 1-2 3, Kingston 0-1 2-2 2. Team 30-71 (.423) 16-22 (.727) 76.

Halftime: Michigan 40-36.

WICHITA STATE (89): Smith 4-11 0-1 8, Thompson 13-19 10-11 36, Leach 6-14 0-1 12, Pete 6-11 5-5 17, Criss 4-13 0-0 8, Reed 2-3 1-1 5, Davis 1-2 0-0 2, Trope 0-1 0-0 0, Nosich 0-0 1-3 1, Reimond 0-1 0-0 0. Team 36-75 (.480) 17-22 (.773) 89.

UCLA (108): Lacey 9-13 6-10 24, Erickson 1-6 0-0 2, McIntosh 4-5 3-4 11, Goodrich 11-21 6-8 28, Goss 8-13 3-3 19, Washington 4-13 2-4 10, Lynn 5-9 0-0 10, Chambers 0-5 0-0 0, Lyons 2-3 0-0 4, Levin 0-1 0-0 0, Galbraith 0-0 0-0 0, Hoffman 0-0 0-0 0. Team 44-89 (.494) 20-29 (.690) 108.

Halftime: UCLA 65-38.

ALL-TOURNAMENT TEAM

*Bill Bradley, F, Sr., Princeton (87 points, 24 rebounds in final two games)
Gail Goodrich, G, Sr., UCLA (70 points, 13 rebounds)
Edgar Lacey, F, Soph., UCLA (35 points, 20 rebounds)
Cazzie Russell, G, Jr., Michigan (56 points, 15 rebounds)
Kenny Washington, F, Jr., UCLA (27 points, 12 rebounds)

*Named Most Outstanding Player.

throw shooting. He is the only Princeton player to score 40 or more points in a game, a feat he achieved 11 times. In one of the most memorable college games in Madison Square Garden history, the Tigers lost to Michigan, 80-78, in the semifinals of the Holiday Festival. Bradley fouled out with with 4 1/2 minutes remaining with 41 points and Princeton leading, 76-63. Russell led Michigan's comeback and hit the game-winning basket from 15 feet away with three seconds left to finish with 27 points. Four of Princeton's five regular-season defeats were by one or two points.

Russell's teammate, Bill Buntin, became the first Michigan player to be chosen in the opening round of an NBA draft. . . . Nebraska suffered its 15th consecutive losing season, but upset top-ranked Michigan, 74-73, on Fred Hare's buzzer-beater. . . . Missouri lost 23 consecutive games to Kansas State in their series until defeating the Wildcats, 80-68. . . . Tennessee (55.64), Oklahoma State (55.66) and New Mexico (55.70) finished one-two-three in team defense in the closest race ever in point prevention. The tight defense helped Oklahoma State captured its only undisputed Big Eight regular-season championship.

North Carolina State's Everett Case retired because of illness early in the 19th season of his coaching career with a 377-134 record. Among the innovations attributed to him were the time clock, introducing players before a game and cutting down the nets after a big tournament victory. . . . Case's successor was Press Maravich, the father of future All-American Pete Maravich. N.C. State reserve forward Larry Worsley entered the ACC

1964-65 FINAL NATIONAL POLLS

AP	UPI	SCHOOL (RECORD)	HEAD COACH
1	1	Michigan (24-4)	Dave Strack
2	2	UCLA (28-2)	John Wooden
3	3	St. Joseph's (26-3)	Jack Ramsay
4	4	Providence (24-2)	Joe Mullaney
5	5	Vanderbilt (24-4)	Roy Skinner
6	7	Davidson (24-2)	Lefty Driesell
7	8	Minnesota (19-5)	John Kundla
8	11	Villanova (23-5)	Jack Kraft
9	6	Brigham Young (21-7)	Stan Watts
10	9	Duke (20-5)	Vic Bubas
–	10	San Francisco (24-5)	Pete Peletta
–	12	N.C. State (21-5)	Press Maravich
–	13	Oklahoma State (20-7)	Hank Iba
–	14	Wichita State (21-9)	Gary Thompson
–	15	Connecticut (23-3)	Fred Shabel
–	16	Illinois (18-6)	Harry Combes
–	17	Tennessee (20-5)	Ray Mears
–	18	Indiana (19-5)	Branch McCracken
–	19	Miami, Fla. (22-4)	Bruce Hale
–	20	Dayton (22-7)	Don Donoher

Tournament with a modest 5.2 scoring average. In three tourney games, all of which he entered as a substitute, he scored 12, 15 and 30 points to pace the Wolfpack to the title and earn the Outstanding Player Award. He hit 14 of 19 field-goal attempts in a 91-85 championship game victory over Duke.

Maryland posted its lone victory over Duke (85-82) in a 17-game stretch of their series from 1962 through 1969. . . . Virginia ended an 11-game losing streak in its series with Clemson. . . . Richmond lost 22 consecutive games to Wake Forest until defeating the Demon Deacons, 74-71. . . . Florida defeated Kentucky, 84-68, for the Gators' first victory over the Wildcats since 1934. Florida had lost 18 games to Kentucky in that span. UK also was defeated by St. Louis for the fifth time in the last six seasons, 80-75, although the Billikens' average record in that span was just 16-11. SLU also defeated Notre Dame for the 13th time in their last 15 meetings, 75-67, after pounding Final Four-bound Princeton, 90-71.

St. Joseph's (26-3/coached by Jack Ramsay) had its winningest season in school history. Two of St. Joseph's defeats were to Providence. . . . West Virginia (14-15) posted its first losing mark since 1943-44 but still finished in the first division of the Southern Conference. Virginia Tech was runner-up to Davidson in the Southern Conference in the Hokies' final season as a member of the league. . . . Davidson, winless in the Southern

Conference in 1960, went undefeated in league competition to improve its conference mark for the fifth consecutive campaign under coach Lefty Driesell. . . . Pacific's Keith Swagerty set a West Coast Athletic Conference standard by grabbing a school-record 39 rebounds in a game against UC Santa Barbara.

East Tennessee State's Tommy Woods (38 vs. Middle Tennessee State) and Notre Dame's Walt Sahm (30 vs. Ball State/later tied) set school single-game rebounding records. . . . Illinois' Skip Thoren grabbed more than 20 rebounds three times in a five-game stretch (at Kentucky, at Villanova and vs. Indiana). . . . Wyoming (16-10) chalked up its first winning record in 10 seasons. . . . Arizona State's 15-game winning streak in its series with archrival Arizona came to a halt. . . . Oregon's 81-74 decision over USC was the Ducks' lone victory against the Trojans in an 18-game stretch of their series from 1956 to 1969.

Texas Western bowed to New Mexico, 55-47, for the Miners' only homecourt defeat in a 68-game span at home from 1961 through 1966. . . . Utah coach Jack Gardner had a team finish in last place for the first time in his 29 seasons of coaching. The Utes were in the basement of the six-team WAC with a 3-7 record despite finishing with a 17-9 overall mark. . . . St. John's Joe Lapchick concluded his 20-year coaching career with a 335-129 record after winning the NIT. Indiana's Branch McCracken, who previously coached Ball State, retired after a 32-year coaching career with a 450-231 record.

1965 NCAA Tournament

Summary: Defending champion UCLA, returning only two starters, was overwhelmed in its season opener at Illinois, 110-83. But the Bruins finished the campaign with a 91-80 victory over another Big Ten team, Michigan, in the NCAA final. The Bruins' only other defeat was to another Big Ten squad—87-82 against Iowa in Chicago. Oddly, Michigan didn't lose to either Illinois or Iowa in Big Ten competition. UCLA averaged an even 100 points in its four tourney games to become the only champion to average triple digits in scoring.

Star Gazing: Princeton's Bill Bradley holds the career playoff record for highest free-throw percentage (minimum of 50 attempts). He was 89 of 96 from the foul line (90.6 percent) from 1963 through 1965. In five of his nine playoff games, Bradley made at least 10 free throws while missing no more than one attempt from the charity stripe. He made 16 of 16 free throws against St. Joseph's in the first round of the 1963 East Regional and 13 of 13 foul shots against Providence in the 1965 East Regional final to become the only player to twice convert more than 12 free throws without a miss in a playoff game. Bradley also holds the mark for most points in a single Final Four game (school-record 58 against Wichita State in national third-place game). He scored 39 points in the second half of the consolation contest. The Rhodes Scholar was the only player to have a double-digit season scoring average (30.5 points per game) for Princeton's Final Four team.

One and Only: UCLA's Gail Goodrich became the only guard to score more than 35 points in an NCAA final, erupting for 42 points on 12 of 22 field-goal shooting and 18 of 20 free-throw shooting in a 91-80 triumph over Michigan. His free throws made and attempted remain championship game records. Goodrich averaged 24.6 points per game, a UCLA school record for guards.

Numbers Game: Princeton's Butch van Breda Kolff went on to become the only coach to direct teams to the NCAA Final Four and the NBA Finals (Lakers in 1968 and 1969) and compile a winning NCAA playoff career record (7-5). . . . Wichita State's Gary Thompson became perhaps the first-year coach overcoming the biggest obstacle to reach the national semifinals. The Shockers' roster was depleted in the second half of Thompson's inaugural season after the departures of both of their high NBA draft picks—All-American forward Dave (The Rave) Stallworth and first-round draft choice center Nate Bowman. Stallworth completed his eligibility after the first

University of Michigan's Cazzie Russell.

16 games and Bowman was declared ineligible for the second semester. Nonetheless, the Missouri Valley Conference champion's roster of primarily local players emerged victorious out of a relatively feeble Midwest Regional field. . . . Michigan's Cazzie Russell became the only player to score more than 25 points in Final Four defeats in back-to-back years. . . . Tony Kimball's 29 rebounds for Connecticut weren't enough to prevent a 67-61 setback against St. Joseph's in their East Regional opener. . . . Vanderbilt, coached by Roy Skinner, made its initial playoff appearance and recorded its lone NCAA Tournament triumph until 1988.

What Might Have Been: Rick Barry-led Miami (Fla.) defeated NCAA playoff first-round winners Houston and Oklahoma City by a total of 35 points, but the Hurricanes were ineligible because of NCAA probation. It was Miami's lone appearance in the Top 20 of a final wire-service poll.

1965 CHAMPIONSHIP BRACKET

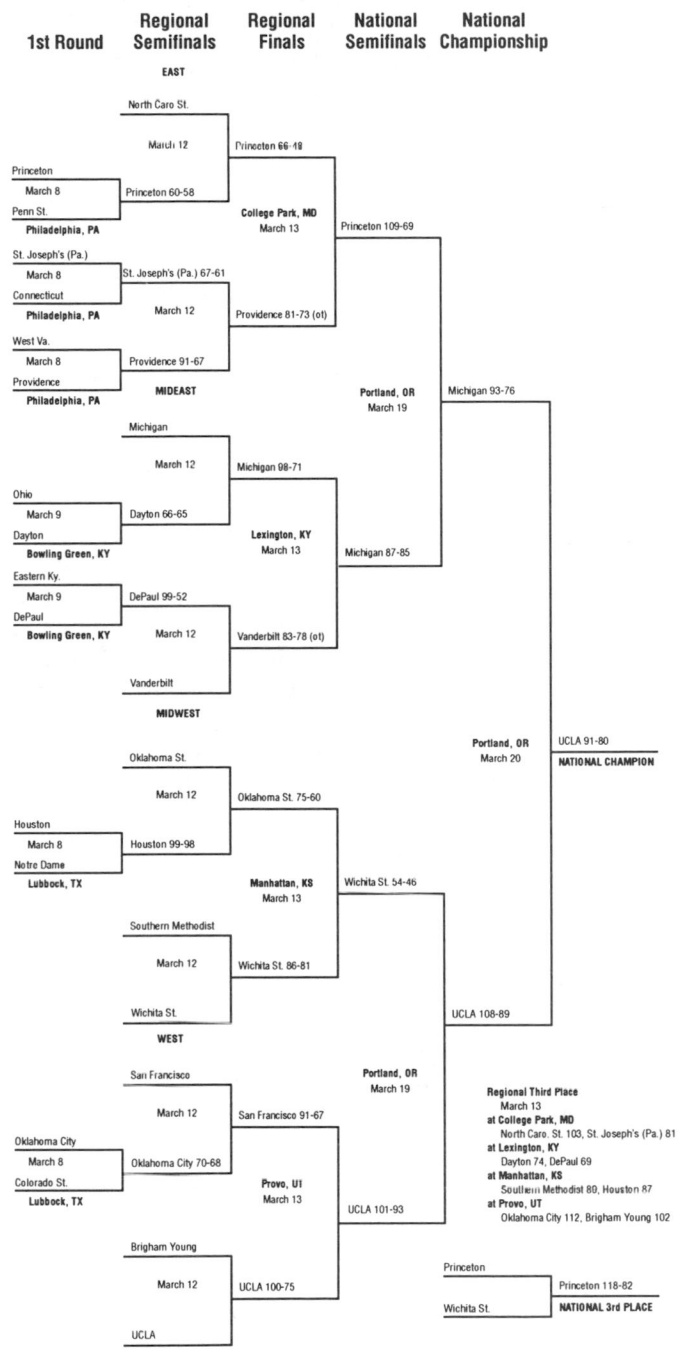

1st Round	Regional Semifinals	Regional Finals	National Semifinals	National Championship

EAST

North Caro St.
March 12
Princeton 66-48
Princeton
March 8
Princeton 60-58
Penn St.
Philadelphia, PA
College Park, MD
March 13
Princeton 109-69
St. Joseph's (Pa.)
March 8
St. Joseph's (Pa.) 67-61
Connecticut
Philadelphia, PA
March 12
Providence 81-73 (ot)
West Va.
March 8
Providence 91-67
Providence
Philadelphia, PA

MIDEAST

Michigan
March 12
Michigan 98-71
Ohio
March 9
Dayton 66-65
Dayton
Bowling Green, KY
Lexington, KY
March 13
Michigan 87-85
Eastern Ky.
March 9
DePaul 99-52
DePaul
Bowling Green, KY
March 12
Vanderbilt 83-78 (ot)
Vanderbilt

Portland, OR
March 19
Michigan 93-76

MIDWEST

Oklahoma St.
March 12
Oklahoma St. 75-60
Houston
March 8
Houston 99-98
Notre Dame
Lubbock, TX
Manhattan, KS
March 13
Wichita St. 54-46
Southern Methodist
March 12
Wichita St. 86-81
Wichita St.

Portland, OR
March 20
UCLA 91-80
NATIONAL CHAMPION

UCLA 108-89

WEST

San Francisco
March 12
San Francisco 91-67
Oklahoma City
March 8
Oklahoma City 70-68
Colorado St.
Lubbock, TX
Provo, UT
March 13
UCLA 101-93
Brigham Young
March 12
UCLA 100-75
UCLA

Portland, OR
March 19

Regional Third Place
March 13
at College Park, MD
North Caro. St. 103, St. Joseph's (Pa.) 81
at Lexington, KY
Dayton 74, DePaul 69
at Manhattan, KS
Southern Methodist 89, Houston 87
at Provo, UT
Oklahoma City 112, Brigham Young 102

Princeton
Princeton 118-82
Wichita St.
NATIONAL 3rd PLACE

Scoring Leader: Bill Bradley, Princeton (177 points, 35.4 ppg).

Highest Scoring Average: Ollie Johnson, San Francisco (72 points, 36 ppg).

Rebounding Leader: Bill Bradley, Princeton (57 rebounds, 11.4 rpg).

Highest Rebounding Average: Ollie Johnson, San Francisco (37 rebounds, 18.5 rpg).

1965-66

AT A GLANCE

NCAA Champion: Texas Western (28-1; coached by Don Haskins).

NIT Champion: Brigham Young (20-5; coached by Stan Watts; finished in second place in WAC with a 6-4 record, which was one game behind Utah).

New Conference: Metropolitan Collegiate (disbanded after four years).

NCAA Consensus First-Team All-Americans: Dave Bing, G, Sr., Syracuse; Clyde Lee, C, Sr., Vanderbilt; Cazzie Russell, G, Sr., Michigan; Dave Schellhase, F, Sr., Purdue; Jimmy Walker, G, Jr., Providence.

National Player of the Year: Russell (30.8 ppg, 8.4 rpg, 51.8 FG%, 82.5 FT%).

National Coach of the Year: Adolph Rupp, Kentucky (27-2/UPI, USBWA).

The best team in the country might have been UCLA's freshman squad. The Bruins' frosh, led by 7-1 Lew Alcindor's 31 points and 21 rebounds, defeated the two-time NCAA champion UCLA varsity, 75-60. The yearlings compiled a 21-0 record, outscoring their opponents 113.2 points per game to 56.6. Starters for what is considered by some as the best freshman team in NCAA history included Alcindor (33.1 ppg and 21.5 rpg), forwards Lynn Shackelford (20.9 ppg and 9.3 rpg) and Kent Taylor (7.2 ppg) and guards Lucius Allen (22.4 ppg and 7.8 rpg) and Kenny Heitz (14.3 ppg).

It was a version of Dave's World for the national scoring championship. Purdue forward Dave Schellhase (32.54) edged Idaho State guard Dave Wagnon (32.50) in the closest race in major-college history. Wagnon, who averaged a modest 14.6 points per game the previous season as a junior, averaged 36.4 the second half of his senior campaign before falling one basket short of overhauling Schellhase. Purdue posted an 8-16 record, leaving Schellhase with the worst mark ever for an NCAA consensus first-team All-American. He had a national single-game high of 57 points against Michigan.

Cazzie Russell set a Michigan record for most points in a regulation game with 48 against Northwestern. Also establishing school single-game scoring standards were Rutgers' Bob Lloyd (51 points at Delaware/later tied), Texas Tech's Dub Malaise (50 at Texas), North Carolina's Bob Lewis (49 vs. Florida State), Tennessee Tech's Ron Filipek (tied with 48 vs. Middle Tennessee State), Rice's Doug McKendrick (47 vs. Georgia Tech), Southern Cal's John Block (45 vs. Washington) and Murray State's Herb McPherson (44 vs. Middle Tennessee State). Lewis' outburst for Carolina capped a six-game stretch during which he averaged 36.1 points per game.

Wagnon, Russell (30.8 ppg), Syracuse's Dave Bing (28.4), Centenary's Tom Kerwin (27.9), Illinois' Don Freeman (27.8) and Texas A&M's John Beasley (27.8) set school records for highest scoring average in a single season. Utah's Jerry Chambers established a Western Athletic Conference single-season record by averaging 28.8 points per game.

Syracuse, after failing to finish among the top 30 in the previous 12 scoring races, won its first national scoring title. Bing grabbed a school-record 25 rebounds in a game against Cornell. . . . One of the most fabled shots in St. Joseph's history came at the Palestra when seldom-used Steve Donches connected on a prayer at the final buzzer to give the Hawks a 71-69 victory over archrival Villanova. . . . Nebraska's string of losing records ended at 15 when the 20-5 Cornhuskers finished

1965-66 INDIVIDUAL LEADERS

SCORING

PLAYER	PTS.	AVG.
Schellhase, Purdue	781	32.54
Wagnon, Idaho St.	845	32.50
Russell, Michigan	800	30.8
Chambers, Utah	892	28.8
Bing, Syracuse	794	28.4
Kerwin, Centenary	726	27.9
Freeman, Illinois	668	27.8
Beasley, Texas A&M	668	27.8
Melchionni, Villanova	801	27.6
Lewis, North Carolina	740	27.4

REBOUNDING

PLAYER	REB.	AVG.
Ware, Oklahoma City	607	20.9
Unseld, Louisville	505	19.4

Swagerty, Pacific	514	18.4
Woods, East Tennessee St.	361	17.2
Hayes, Houston	490	16.9
Murrey, Detroit	416	16.6
Wolters, Boston College	431	16.6
Lee, Vanderbilt	412	15.8
Cunningham, Murray St.	390	15.6
Williams, Temple	421	15.0

FIELD GOAL PERCENTAGE

PLAYER	FGM	FGA	PCT.
Hammond, Tulsa	172	261	.659
McKendrick, Rice	168	265	.634
Finkel, Dayton	248	397	.625
Lewis, Duke	161	271	.594
Stephenson, Rhode I.	128	216	.593
Lechman, Gonzaga	145	246	.589
Williams, Temple	195	336	.580

Murrey, Detroit	195	341	.572
Dean, Syracuse	125	219	.571
Hayes, Houston	323	570	.567

FREE THROW PERCENTAGE

PLAYER	FTM	FTA	PCT.
Blair, Providence	101	112	.902
Morawski, Seton Hall	136	153	.889
Lloyd, Rutgers	161	183	.880
Jones, Miami (Fla.)	134	153	.876
Long, Wake Forest	153	176	.869
Beasley, SMU	137	158	.867
Baumann, The Citadel	91	105	.867
Wetzel, Virginia Tech	123	142	.866
Butler, Memphis St.	114	132	.864
Heroman, LSU	132	153	.863

1965-66 TEAM LEADERS

SCORING OFFENSE

SCHOOL	PTS.	AVG.
Syracuse	2773	99.0
Houston	2845	98.1
Oklahoma City	2829	97.6
Loyola (Ill.)	2438	97.5
Brigham Young	2388	95.5

SCORING DEFENSE

SCHOOL	PTS.	AVG.
Oregon St.	1527	54.5
Tennessee	1499	57.7
Oklahoma St.	1523	60.9
Princeton	1425	62.0
Texas Western	1817	62.7

Kansas	1692	62.7
Pennsylvania	1568	62.7

FIELD GOAL PERCENTAGE

SCHOOL	FGM	FGA	PCT.
North Carolina	838	1620	.517
Davidson	877	1713	.512
Syracuse	1132	2271	.498
Brigham Young	946	1898	.498
Seattle	849	1722	.493

FREE THROW PERCENTAGE

SCHOOL	FTM	FTA	PCT.
Auburn	476	601	.792
Austin Peay St.	463	591	.783

Rhode Island	596	770	.774
Murray St.	488	640	.763
Davidson	563	739	.762

REBOUNDING

SCHOOL	TOTAL REB.	OWN	PCT.
Texas Western	2480	1430	.577
Duke	2598	1490	.574
Tennessee	2193	1255	.572
Detroit	2384	1356	.569

in the Top 20 of a final wire-service poll for the only time until 1991. Their coach was Joe Cipriano. . . . Cincinnati, in Tay Baker's first year as coach of the Bearcats, captured the the Missouri Valley Conference crown after finishing in seventh place the previous season. . . . The MVC didn't have a team reach the NCAA Final Four or win the NIT for the first time in eight years. Louisville's Wes Unseld set a MVC single-season record by averaging 19.4 rebounds per game.

Ron Widby punted for Tennessee's football squad in the afternoon in its 27-6 triumph over Tulsa in the Bluebonnet Bowl and then flew to Shreveport, La., where he scored 18 points that for the Volunteers' basketball team in a 49-43 victory over Centenary in the championship game of the Gulf South Classic. Tennessee handed Kentucky its only regular-season defeat in their SEC finale

(69-62). . . . Vanderbilt's Clyde Lee grabbed a school-record 28 rebounds against Mississippi. . . . Tulane competed as a member of the Southeastern Conference for the final season. . . . Jacksonville posted its lone victory over intrastate opponent Miami (Fla.) in a 22-game stretch of their series from 1959 through 1969. . . . Richmond registered its only triumph over Virginia Tech in a 17-game span of their series from 1962 to 1969 and Virginia notched its lone win over Virginia Tech in a 14-game stretch of their series from 1959 through 1969. . . . Rutgers lost 18 consecutive contests to Princeton until edging the Tigers, 68-66.

Bob Knight embarked on his acclaimed coaching career with an 18-8 record at Army, leading the Cadets to the NIT for the first of four times under him through 1970. Another head coaching

1965–66 NCAA CHAMPION: TEXAS WESTERN

SEASON STATISTICS OF TEXAS WESTERN REGULARS

PLAYER	POS.	CL.	G.	FG%	FT%	PPG	RPG
Bobby Joe Hill	G	Jr.	28	.411	.610	15.0	3.0
David Lattin	C	So.	29	.495	.703	14.0	8.6
Orsten Artis	G	Sr.	28	.470	.867	12.6	3.5
Nevil Shed	F-C	Jr.	29	.494	.755	10.6	7.9
Harry Flournoy	F	Sr.	29	.500	.649	8.3	10.7
Willie Worsley	G	So.	29	.403	.719	8.0	2.3
Willie Cager	F	So.	29	.410	.680	6.6	4.0
Louis Baudoin	F	Jr.	16	.386	.200	2.2	1.3
Jerry Armstrong	F	Sr.	24	.279	.875	1.9	1.4
TEAM TOTALS			**29**	**.445**	**.700**	**77.9**	**49.3**

1966 FINAL FOUR CHAMPIONSHIP GAME

COLLEGE PARK, MD

KENTUCKY (65)	FG-A	FT-A	REB.	PF	PTS.
Dampier	7-18	5-5	9	4	19
Kron	3-6	0-0	7	2	6
Conley	4-9	2-2	8	5	10
Riley	8-22	3-4	4	4	19
Jaracz	3-8	1-2	5	5	7
Berger	2-3	0-0	0	0	4
Gamble	0-0	0-0	0	1	0
LeMaster	0-1	0-0	0	1	0
Tallent	0-3	0-0	0	1	0
TOTALS	**27-70**	**11-13**	**33**	**23**	**65**

FG%: .386. **FT%:** .846.

TEXAS WESTERN (72)	FG-A	FT-A	REB.	PF	PTS.
Hill	7-17	6-9	3	3	20
Artis	5-13	5-5	8	1	15
Shed	1-1	1-1	3	1	3
Lattin	5-10	6-6	9	4	16
Cager	1-3	6-7	6	3	8
Flournoy	1-1	0-0	2	0	2
Worsley	2-4	4-6	4	0	8
TOTALS	**22-49**	**28-34**	**35**	**12**	**72**

FG%: .449. **FT%:** .824.
Halftime: Texas Western 34-31.

NATIONAL SEMIFINALS

DUKE (79): Marin 11-18 7-10 29, Riedy 2-7 2-2 6, Lewis 9-13 3-3 21, Verga 2-7 0-0 4, Vacendak 7-16 3-3 17, Wendelin 1-4 0-1 2, Liccardo 0-1 0-0 0, Barone 0-0 0-0 0. Team 32-66 (.485) 15-19 (.789) 79.

KENTUCKY (83): Conley 3-5 4-4 10, Riley 8-17 3-4 19, Jaracz 3-5 2-3 8, Dampier 11-20 1-2 23, Kron 5-13 2-2 12, Tallent 1-2 2-2 4, Berger 1-4 5-6 7, Gamble 0-0 0-1 0. Team 32-66 (.485) 19-24 (.792) 83.

Halftime: Duke 42-41.

TEXAS WESTERN (85): Hill 5-20 8-10 18, Artis 10-20 2-3 22, Shed 2-3 5-6 9, Lattin 5-7 1-1 11, Flournoy 3-6 2-2 8, Cager 2-5 1-1 5, Worsley 5-8 2-3 12, Armstrong 0-2 0-1 0. Team 32-71 (.451) 21-27 (.778) 85.

UTAH (78): Tate 0-4 1-3 1, Jackson 3-9 2-2 8, MacKay 4-10 6-9 14, Ockel 1-1 3-3 5, Chambers 14-31 10-12 38, Black 3-8 2-4 8, Lake 1-1 0-0 2, Day 1-2 0-0 2. Team 27-66 (.409) 24-33 (.727) 78.

Halftime: Texas Western 42-39.

ALL-TOURNAMENT TEAM

*Jerry Chambers, F, Sr., Utah (70 points, 35 rebounds in final two games)
Louie Dampier, G, Jr., Kentucky (42 points, 13 rebounds)
Bobby Joe Hill, G, Jr., Texas Western (31 points, seven rebounds)
Jack Marin, F, Sr., Duke (52 points, 15 rebounds)
Pat Riley, F, Jr., Kentucky (38 points, 12 rebounds)

*Named Most Outstanding Player.

1965-66 FINAL NATIONAL POLLS

AP	UPI	SCHOOL (RECORD)	HEAD COACH
1	1	Kentucky (27-2)	Adolph Rupp
2	2	Duke (26-4)	Vic Bubas
3	3	Texas Western (28-1)	Don Haskins
4	4	Kansas (23-4)	Ted Owens
5	6	St. Joseph's (24-5)	Jack Ramsay
6	5	Loyola of Chicago (22-3)	George Ireland
7	9	Cincinnati (21-7)	Tay Baker
8	8	Vanderbilt (22-4)	Roy Skinner
9	7	Michigan (18-8)	Dave Strack
10	–	Western Kentucky (25-3)	John Oldham
–	10	Providence (22-5)	Joe Mullaney
–	11	Nebraska (20-5)	Joe Cipriano
–	12	Utah (23-8)	Jack Gardner
–	13	Oklahoma City (24-5)	Abe Lemons
–	14	Houston (23-6)	Guy Lewis
–	15	Oregon State (21-7)	Paul Valenti
–	16	Syracuse (22-6)	Fred Lewis
–	17	Pacific (22-6)	Dick Edwards
–	18	Davidson (21-7)	Lefty Driesell
–	19	Brigham Young (20-5)	Stan Watts
–	19	Dayton (23-6)	Don Donoher

newcomer with an 18-8 record was Lou Carnesecca at St. John's. . . . Maryland guard Billy Jones became the first African American to compete in the ACC. . . . Steve Vacendak was named ACC player of the year despite being voted second team all-league. Vacendak finished ninth in the All-ACC balloting after averaging 13.3 points and four rebounds per game for Duke's 26-4 squad.

North Carolina attempted a slowdown game in an effort to upend heavily-favored Duke in the ACC Tournament semifinals but lost, 21-20. The Tar Heels trailed at halftime, 7-5. Entering the tourney, Duke was ranked No. 3 in the AP poll and No. 2 by UPI. No other ACC team was in the Top 20. Duke won its fourth consecutive undisputed regular-season championship although both of its ACC losses were to teams that finished in a three-way tie for last place (South Carolina and Wake Forest).

Rice's only victory of the season (82-70 verdict over Baylor) ended a school-record 28-game losing streak. . . . Washington State, coached by Marv Harshman, compiled a 15-11 record for its first winning season in 14 years. . . . Oregon's 79-

72 decision over UCLA was the Ducks' lone victory against the Bruins in a 21-game stretch of their series from 1954 to 1970. Meanwhile, UCLA began a 17-game winning streak in its series with Stanford. . . . Montana, coached by Ron Nord, won 10 of 11 games down the stretch to finish with a 14-10 record and the Grizzlies' only winning season in a 10-year span from 1961-62 through 1970-71. . . . Utah, coached by Jack Gardner, won the WAC title after finishing in last place the previous season. . . . Hawaii was winless against a major-college schedule (0-18) although the Rainbows weren't officially classified as Division I until the 1970-71 season. . . . Holy Cross compiled its first losing season in 21 years (10-13) under new coach Jack Donohue, who had guided Power Memorial Academy in New York to a 163-30 record, including 71 consecutive victories with a center named Lew Alcindor.

1966 NCAA Tournament

Summary: Texas Western, now called Texas-El Paso, put the finishing touches on dismantling the prejudiced myth that black athletes couldn't play disciplined basketball by capturing the 1966 title. Texas Western (28-1) had its winningest season in school history. The Miners' Don Haskins was a demanding coach who wouldn't let forward-center Nevil Shed ride back to the hotel with the team after Shed was thrown out in the first half of their 78-76 overtime victory against Cincinnati in the second round. UTEP, featuring an all-black starting lineup with three players 6-1 or shorter in the NCAA final, stunned top-ranked and all-white Kentucky (72-65). Junior college transfer Bobby Joe Hill, one of the Miners' tiny trio, converted steals into layups on consecutive trips down the floor by flustered Kentucky guards to give them a lead they never relinquished. Acclaimed writer Frank Deford, covering the game for Sports Illustrated, said Wildcats coach Adolph Rupp allowed him "into the locker room with the understanding that if Kentucky lost, I wouldn't report on what I saw. Unfortunately, in his anger, Rupp referred to the Texas Western players as 'coons.'" In the wake of UTEP's sterling performance, major Southern

UCLA's Lew Alcindor goes high for a rebound.

schools started modifying their unwritten directives by recruiting more African American players.

Outcome for Defending Champion: UCLA (18-8) finished second in the AAWU, failing to win the conference title for the only time in an 18-year span. The Bruins lost back-to-back games to Duke early in the season by a total of 35 points.

Star Gazing: Utah forward Jerry Chambers became the only Final Four Most Outstanding Player to play for a national fourth-place team. He scored a tourney-high 40 points in an 83-74 triumph over Pacific in the West Regional semifinals. . . . Kentucky starting forward Larry Conley didn't later achieve the name recognition of Dick Vitale, but Conley was the other hoops analyst with ESPN from the cable network's inception.

One and Only: Hill, a 5-10, is the shortest player to lead an NCAA champion in scoring

1966 CHAMPIONSHIP BRACKET

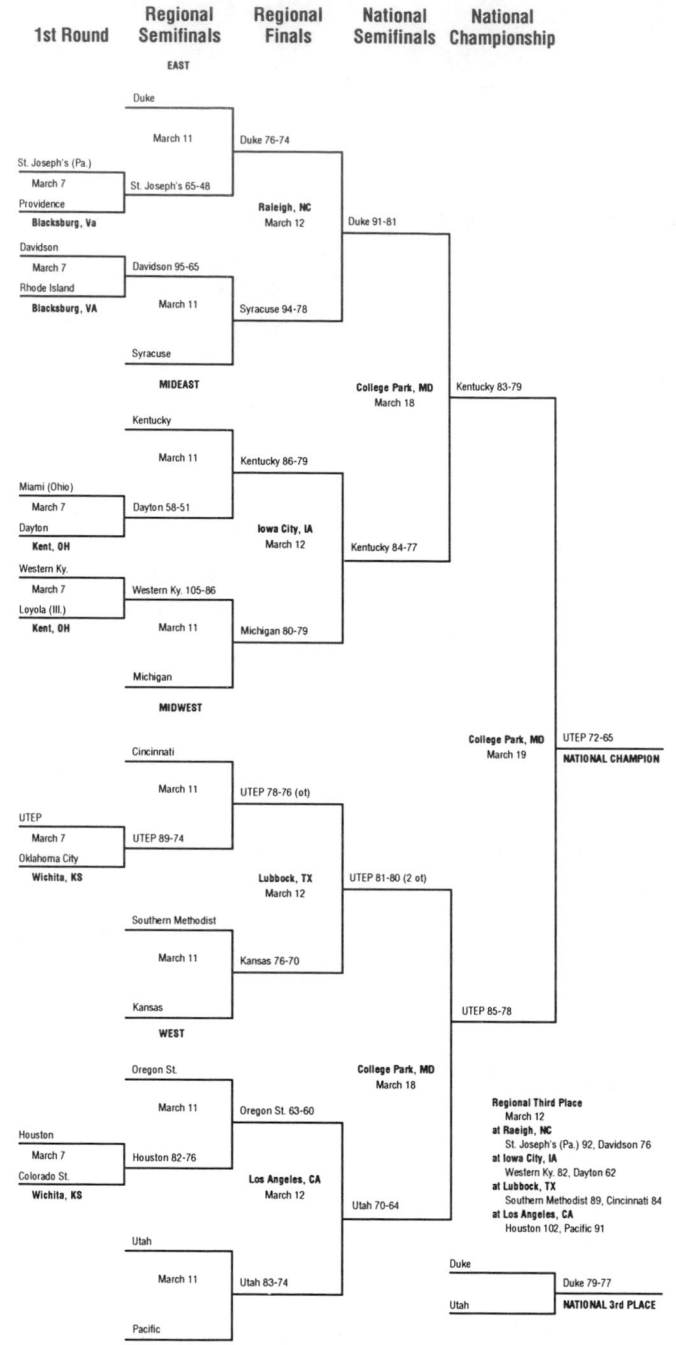

	1st Round	Regional Semifinals	Regional Finals	National Semifinals	National Championship

EAST

Duke
March 11 — Duke 76-74
St. Joseph's (Pa.)
March 7 — St. Joseph's 65-48
Providence
Blacksburg, Va
Raleigh, NC March 12 — Duke 91-81
Davidson
March 7 — Davidson 95-65
Rhode Island
Blacksburg, VA
March 11 — Syracuse 94-78
Syracuse

College Park, MD March 18 — Kentucky 83-79

MIDEAST

Kentucky
March 11 — Kentucky 86-79
Miami (Ohio)
March 7 — Dayton 58-51
Dayton
Kent, OH
Iowa City, IA March 12 — Kentucky 84-77
Western Ky.
March 7 — Western Ky. 105-86
Loyola (Ill.)
Kent, OH
March 11 — Michigan 80-79
Michigan

MIDWEST

College Park, MD March 19 — UTEP 72-65 **NATIONAL CHAMPION**

Cincinnati
March 11 — UTEP 78-76 (ot)
UTEP
March 7 — UTEP 89-74
Oklahoma City
Wichita, KS
Lubbock, TX March 12 — UTEP 81-80 (2 ot)
Southern Methodist
March 11 — Kansas 76-70
Kansas

UTEP 85-78

WEST

Oregon St.
March 11 — Oregon St. 63-60
Houston
March 7 — Houston 82-76
Colorado St.
Wichita, KS
Los Angeles, CA March 12 — Utah 70-64
Utah
March 11 — Utah 83-74
Pacific

College Park, MD March 18

Regional Third Place
March 12
at Raeigh, NC
St. Joseph's (Pa.) 92, Davidson 76
at Iowa City, IA
Western Ky. 82, Dayton 62
at Lubbock, TX
Southern Methodist 89, Cincinnati 84
at Los Angeles, CA
Houston 102, Pacific 91

Duke
Duke 79-77
Utah
NATIONAL 3rd PLACE

average (15 points per game). Hill's 20.2-point average in five tournament games in 1966 doubled the regular-season mark in his career. . . . Utah, the only Western Athletic Conference school ever to reach the Final Four, lost in the national semifinals to future WAC member Texas-El Paso. . . . UTEP is the only current Division I school never to have an NCAA consensus first- or second-team All-American in its history yet capture an NCAA Tournament title.

Numbers Game: Jack Gardner became the only coach to direct two different schools to the Final Four at least twice apiece—Kansas State (4th in 1948 and 2nd in 1951) and Utah (4th in 1961 and 4th in 1966). . . . Elvin Hayes outrebounded Pacific's Keith Swagerty, 28-23, in Houston's 102-91 victory in the West Regional third-place game.

What Might Have Been: Utah lost two Final Four games by a total of just nine points despite the absence of second-leading scorer and rebounder George Fisher, who sustained a broken leg late in the season. Fisher finished the year with averages of 13.1 points and 9.2 rebounds per game. . . . Texas Western had to go into double overtime to nip Kansas, 81-80, in the Midwest Regional final. Jayhawks guard Jo Jo White drilled a 30-footer at the buzzer of the first overtime, but the shot was disallowed when a referee trailing the play saw him step out of bounds moments before releasing the ball.

Scoring Leader: Jerry Chambers, Utah (143 points, 35.75 ppg).

Rebounding Leader: Jerry Chambers, Utah (56 rebounds, 14 rpg).

Highest Rebounding Average: Keith Swagerty, Pacific (42 rebounds, 21 rpg).

1966-67

AT A GLANCE

NCAA Champion: UCLA (30-0; coached by John Wooden; won AAWU title by six games with a 14-0 record).

Providence guard Jimmy Walker after winning the 1966 MVP Award at 1966 Holiday Basketball Festival.

NIT Champion: Southern Illinois (24-2; coached by Jack Hartman).

NCAA Probation: South Carolina.

NCAA Consensus First-Team All-Americans: Lew Alcindor, C, Soph., UCLA; Clem Haskins, G-F, Sr., Western Kentucky; Elvin Hayes, F-C, Jr., Houston; Bob Lloyd, G, Sr., Rutgers; Wes Unseld, C, Jr., Louisville; Bob Verga, G, Sr., Duke; Jimmy Walker, G, Sr., Providence.

National Player of the Year: Alcindor (29 ppg, 15.5 rpg, 66.7 FG%).

National Coach of the Year: John Wooden, UCLA (30-0/AP, UPI, USBWA).

UCLA's Lew Alcindor scored 56 points in his varsity debut against Southern California. Alcindor's opening-game outburst was topped just once all season—by his school record 61 against Washington State. He finished his sophomore season

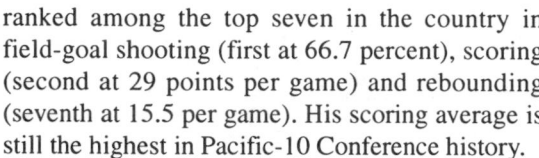
Junior forward Don May was instrumental in leading Dayton to the NCAA Final Four.

Houston's mid-sixties teams, coached by Guy Lewis (center), included future NBA stars Elvin Hayes (left) and Don Chaney.

ranked among the top seven in the country in field-goal shooting (first at 66.7 percent), scoring (second at 29 points per game) and rebounding (seventh at 15.5 per game). His scoring average is still the highest in Pacific-10 Conference history.

Alcindor was one of seven players to finish within three points of each other for the national scoring lead. Never have so many major collegians finished so close to the top. Providence's Jimmy Walker won the scoring race with a 30.4 average.

Kent's Doug Grayson set an NCAA record for most consecutive successful field goals in a single game with 16 when he went 18 of 19 from the floor against North Carolina. . . . Rutgers' Bob Lloyd converted 60 consecutive free throws. One of Lloyd's teammates was Jim Valvano, who later made a name for himself as a coach at Iona and North Carolina State. Lloyd went on to serve as coach at his alma mater, where one of his assis-

tants was a low-key individual by the name of Dick Vitale. . . . Rutgers ended a 23-game losing streak to NYU with a 68-57 triumph.

Santa Clara's Bud Ogden (55 points at Pepperdine), Alabama's Mike Nordholz (50 vs. Southern Mississippi in Birmingham Classic) and Montana State's Tom Storm (44 vs. Portland State) established school single-game scoring records. . . . Providence's Jimmy Walker (30.4 ppg), UCLA's Alcindor, Connecticut's Wes Bialosuknia (28), Lloyd (27.9), St. Joseph's Cliff Anderson (26.5) and Duke's Bob Verga (26.1) set school records for highest scoring average in a single season. . . . South Carolina's streak of years with at least 10 defeats ended at 16 when the Frank McGuire-coached Gamecocks compiled a 16-7 record to start a string of 15 consecutive winning seasons. Their two regular-season ACC

1966-67 UNDEFEATED TEAM: UCLA (30-0)

COACH: JOHN WOODEN

UCLA	OPPONENT	BRUINS HIGH SCORER
105	Southern California 90	Alcindor 56
88	Duke 54	Alcindor/Allen 19
107	Duke 87	Alcindor 38
84	Colorado State 74	Alcindor 34
96	Notre Dame 67	Alcindor 25
100	Wisconsin 56	Alcindor 24
91	Georgia Tech 72	Alcindor 18
107	Southern California 83	Alcindor 25
76	at Washington State 67	Alcindor 28
83	at Washington 68	Alcindor 28
96	California 78	Alcindor 26
116	Stanford 78	Alcindor 37
122	Portland 57	Alcindor 27
119	UC Santa Barbara 75	Alcindor 37
82	at Loyola of Chicago 67	Alcindor 35
120	Illinois* 82	Alcindor 45
40	at Southern Cal (OT) 35	Alcindor 13
76	Oregon State 44	Alcindor/Allen 22
100	Oregon 66	Allen 20
34	at Oregon 25	Alcindor 12
72	at Oregon State 50	Alcindor 28
71	Washington 43	Alcindor 37
100	Washington State 78	Alcindor 61
75	at Stanford 47	Alcindor 20
103	at California 66	Alcindor 30
83	Southern California 55	Alcindor 26

NCAA TOURNAMENT

109	Wyoming* 60	Alcindor 29
80	Pacific* 64	Alcindor 38
73	Houston* 58	Shackelford 22
79	Dayton* 64	Alcindor 20

* Neutral court games.

1966-67 INDIVIDUAL LEADERS

SCORING

PLAYER	PTS.	AVG.
Walker, Providence	851	30.4
Alcindor, UCLA	870	29.0
Graham, New York Univ.	688	28.7
Hayes, Houston	881	28.4
Bialosuknia, Connecticut	673	28.0
Lloyd, Rutgers	809	27.9
Gray, Oklahoma City	715	27.5
Anderson, St. Joseph's	690	26.5
Verga, Duke	705	26.1
Tillman, Loyola (Ill.)	553	25.1

REBOUNDING

PLAYER	REB.	AVG.
Cunningham, Murray St.	479	21.8
Beatty, American	458	19.1

Unseld, Louisville	533	19.0
Swagerty, Pacific	518	18.5
May, Dayton	519	16.7
Hayes, Houston	488	15.7
Alcindor, UCLA	466	15.5
Powers, VMI	318	15.1
Lewis, St. Francis (Pa.)	386	14.8
Dove, St. John's	415	14.8

FIELD GOAL PERCENTAGE

PLAYER	FGM	FGA	PCT.
Alcindor, UCLA	346	519	.667
Allen, Bradley	232	373	.622
Lechman, Gonzaga	196	316	.620
Lewis, St. Francis (Pa.)	181	295	.614
Youngblood, Georgia	140	237	.591
Ogden, Santa Clara	186	322	.578
Wagner, Georgia Tech	164	291	.564

Mix, Toledo	227	403	.563
White, Hofstra	161	288	.559
Ware, Virginia Tech	128	230	.557

FREE THROW PERCENTAGE

PLAYER	FTM	FTA	PCT.
Lloyd, Rutgers	255	277	.921
Sandfoss, Morehead St.	106	117	.906
Thompson, Wichita St.	124	137	.905
Sutherland, Clemson	104	116	.897
Cornwall, Syracuse	103	117	.880
Coleman, Missouri	131	150	.873
McPherson, Murray St.	103	118	.873
Chapman, Iowa	114	131	.870
Fritz, Oregon St.	130	150	.867
Heiser, Princeton	93	108	.861

1966-67 TEAM LEADERS

SCORING OFFENSE

SCHOOL	PTS.	AVG.
Oklahoma City	2496	96.0
Northwestern	2009	91.3
UCLA	2687	89.6
Murray St.	2058	89.5
Houston	2765	89.2

SCORING DEFENSE

SCHOOL	PTS.	AVG.
Tennessee	1511	54.0
Memphis St.	1470	56.5
Army	1206	57.4
Princeton	1619	57.8
Kansas	1607	59.5

FIELD GOAL PERCENTAGE

SCHOOL	FGM	FGA	PCT.
UCLA	1082	2081	.520
St. Peter's	773	1498	.516
Bradley	832	1641	.507
Vanderbilt	834	1654	.504
Tulane	843	1679	.502

FREE THROW PERCENTAGE

SCHOOL	FTM	FTA	PCT.
West Texas St.	400	518	.772
Santa Clara	571	742	.770
Kentucky	429	559	.767
Rice	493	648	.761
Georgia	454	598	.759

REBOUNDING

SCHOOL	TOTAL REB.	OWN	PCT.
Florida	2124	1275	.600
Houston	3224	1862	.578
St. Francis (Pa.)	2266	1298	.573
New Mexico	2278	1304	.572
Princeton	2235	1270	.568

1966–67 NCAA CHAMPION: UCLA

SEASON STATISTICS OF UCLA REGULARS

PLAYER	POS.	CL.	G.	FG%	FT%	PPG	RPG
Lew Alcindor	C	So.	30	.667	.650	29.0	15.5
Lucius Allen	G	So.	30	.479	.713	15.5	5.8
Mike Warren	G	Jr.	30	.465	.758	12.7	4.5
Lynn Shackelford	F	So.	30	.480	.821	11.4	5.9
Ken Heitz	F-G	So.	30	.506	.600	6.1	3.2
Bill Sweek	G	So.	30	.479	.565	4.7	2.8
Jim Nielsen	F-C	So.	27	.519	.455	4.6	3.4
Don Saffer	G	Jr.	27	.451	.542	2.9	0.8
Gene Sutherland	G	Jr.	20	.455	.583	1.9	0.8
Neville Saner	F-C	Jr.	24	.308	.667	1.4	1.9
Joe Chrisman	F	Jr.	19	.320	.364	1.1	1.5
TEAM TOTALS			30	.520	.653	89.6	49.8

1967 FINAL FOUR CHAMPIONSHIP GAME

LOUISVILLE, KY

UCLA (79)	MIN.	FG-A	FT-A	REB.	A	PF	PTS.
Heitz	27	2-7	0-0	6	1	2	4
Shackelford	35	5-10	0-2	3	1	1	10
Alcindor	35	8-12	4-11	18	3	0	20
Allen	36	7-15	5-8	9	2	2	19
Warren	35	8-16	1-1	7	0	1	17
Nielsen	4	0-1	0-1	1	0	3	0
Sweek	8	1-1	0-0	0	0	1	2
Saffer	5	2-5	0-0	0	0	1	4
Saner	5	1-1	0-0	2	0	2	2
Chrisman	4	0-0	1-2	1	0	2	1
Sutherland	4	0-0	0-0	0	0	0	0
Lynn	2	0-1	0-0	0	0	0	0
Team				7			
TOTALS	200	34-69	11-25	54	7	15	79

FG%: .493. FT%: .440.

DAYTON (64)	MIN.	FG-A	FT-A	REB.	A	PF	PTS.
May	40	9-23	3-4	17	3	4	21
Sadlier	26	2-5	1-2	7	0	5	5
Obrovac	5	0-2	0-0	2	1	1	0
Klaus	22	4-7	0-0	0	0	1	8
Hooper	34	2-7	2-4	5	2	2	6
Torain	23	3-14	0-0	4	0	3	6
Waterman	23	4-11	2-3	1	2	3	10
Sharpenter	23	2-5	4-5	5	0	1	8
Samanich	1	0-2	0-0	2	0	0	0
Beckman	1	0-0	0-0	0	0	0	0
Inderrieden	1	0-0	0-0	0	0	0	0
Wannemacher	1	0-0	0-0	0	0	0	0
Team				8			
TOTALS	200	26-76	12-18	51	8	20	64

FG%: .342. FT%: .667.
Halftime: UCLA 38-20.

NATIONAL SEMIFINALS

UCLA (73): Heitz 0-0 1-1 1, Shackelford 11-19 0-1 22, Alcindor 6-11 7-13 19, Allen 6-15 5-5 17, Warren 4-10 6-7 14, Nielsen 0-3 0-0 0, Sweek 0-4 0-0 0, Saffer 0-0 0-0 0. Team 27-62 (.435) 19-27 (.704) 73.

HOUSTON (58): Hayes 12-31 1-2 25, Bell 3-11 4-7 10, Kruse 2-5 1-1 5, Grider 2-7 0-0 4, Chaney 3-11 0-2 6, Lentz 1-2 0-3 2, Spain 1-5 0-0 2, Lewis 0-0 0-1 0, Lee 2-3 0-0 4. Team 26-75 (.347) 6-16 (.375) 58.

Halftime: UCLA 39-28.

DAYTON (76): May 16-22 2-6 34, Sadlier 4-7 0-1 8, Obrovac 0-0 0-0 0, Klaus 3-6 9-10 15, Hooper 1-7 3-4 5, Torain 4-14 6-8 14, Wannemacher 0-0 0-2 0, Waterman 0-0 0-0 0. Team 28-56 (.500) 20-31 (.645) 76.

NORTH CAROLINA (62): Miller 6-18 1-1 13, Buntin 1-3 1-1 3, Clark 8-14 3-5 19, Lewis 5-18 1-1 11, Grubar 2-7 3-3 7, Gauntlett 1-4 0-2 2, Brown 0-3 0-0 0, Tuttle 3-5 1-1 7. Team 26-72 (.361) 10-12 (.833) 62.

Halftime: Dayton 29-23.

ALL-TOURNAMENT TEAM

*Lew Alcindor, C, Soph., UCLA (39 points, 38 rebounds in final two games)
Lucius Allen, G, Soph., UCLA (36 points, 18 rebounds)
Elvin Hayes, F, Jr., Houston (48 points, 40 rebounds)
Don May, F, Jr., Dayton (55 points, 32 rebounds)
Mike Warren, G, Jr., UCLA (31 points, 16 rebounds)

*Named Most Outstanding Player.

---

games with Duke were cancelled by the Blue Devils because of USC was on NCAA probation. Duke finished out of the top 10 of the final AP poll for the first time in seven years.

Murray State's Dick Cunningham (36 vs. MacMurray), South Carolina's Gary Gregor (35 vs. Elon at Charlotte), Marquette's Pat Smith (28 vs. Loyola of Chicago), Washington State's Jim McKean (27 vs. West Virginia) and Portland's Don Lawson (26 vs. Nevada Southern) established school single-game rebounding marks. Cunningham set a single-season Ohio Valley Conference standard by averaging 21.8 rebounds per game.

TCU center James Cash became the first African American to play varsity basketball in the SWC. Cash is now chairman of the Harvard Business School MBA program. . . . Tennessee, coached by Ray Mears, captured its first SEC regular-season championship in 25 years. . . . Georgia's Jim Youngblood became the first non-Auburn player to lead the SEC in field-goal accuracy in eight years (59.1 percent). . . . Kentucky suffered its only non-winning record in coach Adolph Rupp's 41 seasons at the helm when the Wildcats went 13-13. They were 8-10 in league competition for their only losing SEC mark in history until UK duplicated that record under Eddie Sutton in 1988-89. Kentucky's defeats included a 92-77 setback to visiting Cornell, the only Ivy League team to beat the Wildcats since 1942. The Cornell contest was one of a school-record seven homecourt defeats for Kentucky. Georgia's 49-40 success over UK was the Bulldogs' lone victory in a 29-game stretch of

AP	UPI	SCHOOL (RECORD)	HEAD COACH
1	1	UCLA (30-0)	John Wooden
2	2	Louisville (23-5)	Peck Hickman
3	4	Kansas (23-4)	Ted Owens
4	3	North Carolina (26-6)	Dean Smith
5	5	Princeton (25-3)	Butch van Breda Kolff
6	7	Western Kentucky (23-3)	John Oldham
7	6	Houston (27-4)	Guy Lewis
8	9	Tennessee (21-7)	Ray Mears
9	10	Boston College (23-3)	Bob Cousy
10	8	Texas Western (22-7)	Don Haskins
–	11	Toledo (23-2)	Bob Nichols
–	12	St. John's (23-5)	Lou Carnesecca
–	13	Tulsa (19-8)	Joe Swank
–	14	Utah State (22-6)	Ladell Andersen
–	14	Vanderbilt (21-5)	Roy Skinner
–	16	Pacific (24-4)	Dick Edwards
–	17	Providence (21-7)	Joe Mullaney
–	18	New Mexico (19-8)	Bob King
–	19	Duke (18-9)	Vic Bubas
–	20	Florida (21-4)	Tommy Bartlett

UCLA's Lew Alcindor shoots over a Dayton defender in the NCAA Tournament final.

their series from 1950 through 1971. . . . North Carolina finished in the Top 20 of a final wire-service poll for the first time with Dean Smith as head coach. He was in his sixth season as bench boss of the Tar Heels. Carolina defeated Kentucky, 64-55. It was the second of four consecutive victories for Smith against Rupp from 1964-65 through 1968-69. . . . Davidson was runner-up to West Virginia in the Southern Conference, but the Wildcats finished out of the national Top 20 for the only time in a seven-year span from 1964 through 1970. They lost to Richmond, 72-69, for the only time in a 27-game stretch of their series from 1962 to 1973.

Indiana, coached by Lou Watson, won the Big Ten Conference title after finishing in last place the previous year. . . . The only regular-season defeat for Toledo (23-2) was at Marshall, 96-81. The best season by percentage in the Rockets' history ended with an 82-76 opening-round loss in the NCAA Tournament against Virginia Tech, an opponent they had defeated by 19 points (90-71) in their regular-season finale. . . . Tulsa, coached by Joe Swank, finished in the Top 20 of a final wire-service poll for the only time in a 26-year span from 1955-56 through 1980-81. . . . Oklahoma posted its lone victory over Nebraska (99-87) in a 14-game stretch of their series from 1965 through 1970.

Princeton (25-3/coached by Butch van Breda Kolff) and Pacific (24-4/Dick Edwards) had their winningest seasons in school history. . . . Peck

Hickman ended his 23-year coaching career at Louisville with a 443-183 record. He never sustained a losing season. . . . E.C. "Doc" Hayes retired as SMU's coach. The Mustangs did not have a losing record in their last 14 years with him at the helm. In 20 seasons at SMU, Hayes won outright or shared eight SWC titles. No other SWC coach won more than six league championships.

1967 NCAA Tournament

Summary: UCLA, starting four sophomores and one junior, won the national championship by a record average of 23.75 points. The Bruins' toughest test was in the West Regional final, where Pacific trailed by fewer than 10 points in the closing minutes until UCLA pulled away to win by 16 (80-64) behind Lew Alcindor's tourney-high 38 points. The Bruins breezed in the final against Dayton, 79-64, despite hitting just 11 of

1967 CHAMPIONSHIP BRACKET

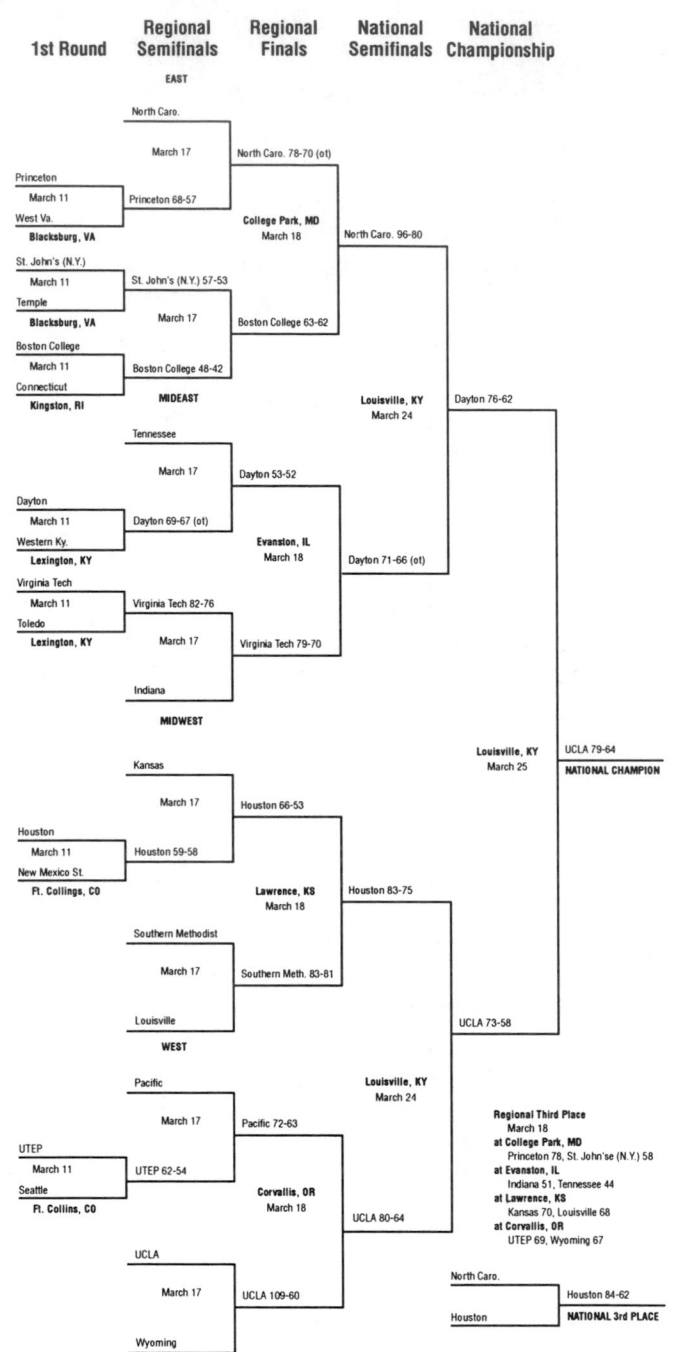

	1st Round	Regional Semifinals	Regional Finals	National Semifinals	National Championship

EAST

North Caro.

North Caro. 78-70 (ot)
March 17

Princeton
March 11
West Va.
Blacksburg, VA

Princeton 68-57

College Park, MD
March 18

North Caro. 96-80

St. John's (N.Y.)
March 11
Temple
Blacksburg, VA

St. John's (N.Y.) 57-53
March 17

Boston College 63-62

Boston College
March 11
Connecticut
Kingston, RI

Boston College 48-42

Louisville, KY
March 24

Dayton 76-62

MIDEAST

Tennessee
March 17

Dayton 53-52

Dayton
March 11
Western Ky.
Lexington, KY

Dayton 69-67 (ot)

Evanston, IL
March 18

Dayton 71-66 (ot)

Virginia Tech
March 11
Toledo
Lexington, KY

Virginia Tech 82-76
March 17

Virginia Tech 79-70

Indiana

MIDWEST

Kansas
March 17

Houston 66-53

Houston
March 11
New Mexico St.
Ft. Collings, CO

Houston 59-58

Lawrence, KS
March 18

Houston 83-75

Southern Methodist
March 17

Southern Meth. 83-81

Louisville

WEST

Louisville, KY
March 24

UCLA 73-58

Pacific
March 17

Pacific 72-63

UTEP
March 11
Seattle
Ft. Collins, CO

UTEP 62-54

Corvallis, OR
March 18

UCLA 80-64

UCLA
March 17

UCLA 109-60

Wyoming

Louisville, KY
March 25

UCLA 79-64
NATIONAL CHAMPION

Regional Third Place
March 18
at College Park, MD
Princeton 78, St. John'se (N.Y.) 58
at Evanston, IL
Indiana 51, Tennessee 44
at Lawrence, KS
Kansas 70, Louisville 68
at Corvallis, OR
UTEP 69, Wyoming 67

North Caro.

Houston 84-62

Houston

NATIONAL 3rd PLACE

25 free-throw attempts. They won 26 of their 30 games by at least 15 points with the only contest in doubt being a 40-35 overtime triumph at Southern Cal in mid-season.

Outcome for Defending Champion: Texas Western compiled a 22-7 record with two of the defeats by double-digit margins against New Mexico State. Bobby Joe Hill, the leading scorer for the Miners' title team, averaged an anemic 4.9 points per game in eight contests.

Biggest Upsets: Dayton wasn't ranked in the UPI top twenty when the Flyers opened the playoffs with a 69-67 overtime triumph against seventh-ranked Western Kentucky as Hilltoppers first-team All-American Clem Haskins, playing with his broken wrist in a cast, was limited to eight points. Dayton also defeated two other top ten teams—Tennessee (ranked ninth by UPI) and North Carolina (third)—before getting clobbered by top-ranked UCLA in the national final. . . . Charles Beasley was limited to nine points, but fellow SWC first-team selection Denny Holman picked up the slack with 30 points, including a decisive basket with three seconds remaining, to spark SMU (20-6) to an 83-81 victory over second-ranked Louisville (23-5). Wes Unseld and Butch Beard combined for 32 points and 21 rebounds, but it wasn't enough for the Cardinals, who hit just 5 of their 14 free throws.

One and Only: UCLA is the only NCAA champion since World War II not to have a senior on its roster. . . . Houston is the only school to reach the Final Four (third place) and College World Series championship game (runner-up to Arizona State) in the same year.

Numbers Game: National field-goal accuracy leader UCLA finished among the top 30 teams in that category for the first time in 12 years. . . . Toledo was eliminated in its opener by Virginia Tech when the Rockets' one-two punch of Steve Mix and John Brisker, a pair of forwards who went on to distinguished pro careers, combined to shoot 36.4 percent from the floor (12 of 33). . . . Tennessee, leading the nation in team defense for the second time in three seasons under coach Ray Mears, made its first appearance in the NCAA Tournament. . . . Elvin Hayes' game-high 25 points and tourney-high 24 rebounds weren't enough to prevent Houston's 73-58 setback against UCLA in the national semifinals.

Scoring Leader: Elvin Hayes, Houston (128 points, 25.6 ppg).

Highest Scoring Average: Lew Alcindor, UCLA (106 points, 26.5 ppg).

Rebounding Leader: Don May, Dayton (82 rebounds, 16.4 rpg).

1967-68

AT A GLANCE

NCAA Champion: UCLA (29-1; coached by John Wooden; won AAWU title by three games with a 14-0 record).

NIT Champion: Dayton (21-9; coached by Don Donoher).

New Rules: The dunk shot is deemed illegal during the game and pregame warmup. . . . NIT field expands from 14 teams to 16.

NCAA Probation: Illinois, Mississippi State, South Carolina.

NCAA Consensus First-Team All-Americans: Lew Alcindor, C, Jr., UCLA; Elvin Hayes, F-C, Sr., Houston; Pete Maravich, G, Soph., Louisiana State; Larry Miller, F, Sr., North Carolina; Wes Unseld, C, Sr., Louisville.

National Player of the Year: Hayes (36.8 ppg, 18.9 rpg, 54.9 FG%).

National Coach of the Year: Guy Lewis, Houston (31-2/AP, UPI, NABC, USBWA).

Houston ended UCLA's 47-game winning streak, 71-69, at the Astrodome in what has been called the "Game of the Century." Houston's Elvin Hayes (39 points and 15 rebounds) outdueled injured UCLA center Lew Alcindor (15 points and 12 rebounds while hampered by a scratched left cornea). The contest was the first in a domed stadium, the first occasion that a regular-season game was national televised by a network and the first

Louisville's Wes Unseld fights off a defender for a rebound.

time in NCAA history that a crowd larger than 50,000 people witnessed a game (52,693). Hayes, who hit just 59 percent of his free throws in his career, sank two foul shots with 28 seconds remaining to snap a 69-69 deadlock.

Sophomore Pete Maravich scored an amazing 49.3 percent of LSU's points in compiling a 43.8-point average. When Maravich was a prep player, his father, Press, coached at North Carolina State. At the time, the ACC required incoming freshmen to score 800 on their SAT. When Pete apparently had difficulty reaching 800, his father decided that coaching his son was more important than remaining in the ACC. So father and son went to LSU in the SEC. During the 1960s it was widely assumed that the 800 score was the ACC's way of perpetuating segregation. But it wound up costing the league one of the most famous white players in history. . . . Maravich's 59-point uprising against Alabama was not the season's single-game high.

Houston's Hayes poured in a school-record 62 against Valparaiso. Hayes finished the season with an amazing average of 55.7 points and rebounds per game.

Florida's Neal Walk became the first Southerner in major-college history and the last Caucasian to pace the nation in rebounding. Walk's school-record tying 31-rebound effort against Alabama was his third game of the season with at least 27 boards. . . . Duke managed just two field goals in a 12-10 defeat against North Carolina State. It was the lowest-scoring game involving at least one major team in 26 years, marking the first time a squad won with fewer than 20 points since 1944. . . . For the only time in ACC history, two members finished the season with at least 20 defeats—Wake Forest (5-21) and Clemson (4-20). . . . North Carolina was unbeaten in ACC competition until losing its last two regular-season games by the same score (87-86 to South Carolina and Duke).

Georgia, coached by Ken Rosemond, compiled a 17-8 record to snap a streak of 16 consecutive losing seasons. . . . Tennessee's school-record 33-game homecourt winning streak ended when the Volunteers lost to Auburn, 53-52. . . . Vanderbilt, coached by Roy Skinner, upset three nationally-ranked teams (North Carolina, Davidson, Duke) within a week. But the biggest news at Vanderbilt was Perry Wallace breaking the racial barrier and becoming the first African American to play varsity basketball in the SEC. Wallace is now a Professor of Law at American University. . . . West Virginia finished runner-up to Davidson in the Southern Conference in the Mountaineers' final season as a member of the league.

Establishing school single-game scoring records were Creighton's Bob Portman (51 points vs. Wisconsin-Milwaukee), Connecticut's Bill Corley (51 vs. New Hampshire), Duquesne's Ron Guziak (50 vs. St. Francis, Pa., at Altoona), Southern Illinois' Dick Garrett (46 vs. Centenary), Louisville's Wes Unseld (45 vs. Georgetown, Ky., College) and Massachusetts' Billy Tindall (41 vs. Vermont). . . . Niagara's Calvin Murphy, a 5-9 sophomore, posted the highest single-season scor-

1967–68 INDIVIDUAL LEADERS

SCORING

PLAYER	PTS.	AVG.
Maravich, LSU	1138	43.8
Murphy, Niagara	916	38.2
Hayes, Houston	1214	36.8
Travis, Oklahoma City	808	29.9
Portman, Creighton	738	29.5
Mount, Purdue	683	28.5
Hill, W. Texas St.	573	27.3
Halimon, Utah St.	671	26.8
Foster, Miami (Ohio)	617	26.8
Walk, Florida	663	26.5

REBOUNDING

PLAYER	REB.	AVG.
Walk, Florida	494	19.8
Smith, E. Kentucky	472	19.7

Hayes, Houston	624	18.9
Unseld, Louisville	513	18.3
Cunningham, Murray St.	410	17.8
Lewis, St. Francis (Pa.)	443	17.7
Wilson, Idaho St.	420	17.5
Cowens, Florida St.	456	16.9
Alcindor, UCLA	461	16.5
Stephenson, Rhode Island	420	16.2

FIELD GOAL PERCENTAGE

PLAYER	FGM	FGA	PCT.
Allen, Bradley	258	304	.655
Hunt, Army	154	248	.621
Alcindor, UCLA	294	480	.613
Unseld, Louisville	294	480	.613
Sorenson, Ohio St.	196	329	.596
Sidle, Oklahoma	189	321	.589
Webster, St. Peter's	279	477	.585

Lanier, St. Bon.	272	466	.584
Bowen, Bradley	185	317	.584
Lienhard, Georgia	213	366	.582

FREE THROW PERCENTAGE

PLAYER	FTM	FTA	PCT.
Heiser, Princeton	117	130	.900
Ward, Centenary	94	106	.887
Carpenter, Pacific	96	109	.881
Luchini, Marquette	107	124	.863
Williams, Rice	113	131	.863
Garrett, S. Ill.	100	116	.862
Montgomery, W. Forest	134	157	.854
Wininger, Butler	97	114	.851
Moeser, Tulane	125	147	.850
Warren, St. John's	102	120	.850
Washington, Miss. St.	96	113	.850

1967–68 TEAM LEADERS

SCORING OFFENSE

SCHOOL	PTS.	AVG.
Houston	3226	97.8
St. Peter's	2630	93.9
UCLA	2802	93.4
Oklahoma City	2492	92.3
Florida St.	2438	90.3

SCORING DEFENSE

SCHOOL	PTS.	AVG.
Army	1448	57.9
Oklahoma St.	1528	58.8
Tennessee	1548	59.5
Villanova	1696	60.6
Princeton	1579	60.7

SCORING MARGIN

SCHOOL	OFF.	DEF.	MAR.
UCLA	93.4	67.2	26.2

Houston	97.8	72.5	25.3
St. Peter's	93.9	76.1	17.8
Columbia	78.8	61.7	17.1
Boston College	88.8	74.9	13.9

WON-LOST PERCENTAGE

SCHOOL	W-L	PCT.
UCLA	29-1	.967
Houston	31-2	.939
St. Bonaventure	23-2	.920
North Carolina	28-4	.875
St. Peter's	24-4	.857

FIELD GOAL PERCENTAGE

SCHOOL	FGM	FGA	PCT.
Bradley	927	1768	.524
St. Peter's	1019	1953	.522
St. Bonaventure	875	1732	.505
UCLA	1161	2321	.500
Louisville	881	1770	.498

FREE THROW PERCENTAGE

SCHOOL	FTM	FTA	PCT.
Vanderbilt	527	684	.770
Mississippi St.	496	645	.769
Nebraska	504	660	.764
Tulane	528	692	.763
Georgia Tech	404	531	.761

REBOUNDS

SCHOOL	REB.	AVG.
Houston	2074	62.8
Northern Illinois	1383	57.6
St. Francis (Pa.)	1434	57.4
Eastern Kentucky	1348	56.2
American	1459	56.1

ing average for a major-college player shorter than 6-0 (38.2 points per game). . . . Murphy, Houston's Hayes (36.8 ppg), Creighton's Bob Portman (29.5) and Miami of Ohio's Fred Foster (26.8) set school records for highest scoring average in a single season.

Rudy Tomjanovich, playing his first varsity game for Michigan when the Wolverines christened Crisler Arena, grabbed a still-existing arena record of 27 rebounds in a 96-79 defeat against Kentucky. . . . Houston's Hayes (37 at Centenary), Eastern Kentucky's Garfield Smith (33 vs. Marshall), North Carolina's Rusty Clark (30 vs. Maryland), Notre Dame's Bob Whitmore (tied with 30 vs. St. Norbert), Idaho State's Ed Wilson (30 vs.

Pan American), Georgetown's Charlie Adrion (29 vs. George Washington), Bucknell's Craig Greenwood (28 vs. DePauw), Rhode Island's Art Stephenson (28 vs. Brown), St. Bonaventure's Bob Lanier (27 vs. Loyola, Md.), California's Bob Presley (27 vs. St. Mary's) and Western Michigan's Reggie Lacefield (26 at Illinois State) established school single-game rebounding records. Wilson set a Big Sky Conference standard by averaging 17.5 rebounds per game.

St. Peter's (24-4/coached by Don Kennedy) and Columbia (23-5/Jack Rohan) had their winningest seasons in school history. St. Peter's pounded Duke by 29 points (100-71) to reach the NIT semifinals. . . . Providence's streak of consec-

UCLA coaching guru John Wooden.

utive 20-win seasons under coach Joe Mullaney ended at nine when the Friars lost nine of their last 13 games to finish with an 11-14 record. . . . Long Island, winner of two of the first four NIT titles (1939 and 1941), participated in the NIT for the first time since 1950.

Army (20-5) lost its NIT opener to Notre Dame but the Bob Knight-coached Cadets finished in the top 20 of a final wire-service poll for the only time in school history. . . . Lehigh, coached by Roy Heckman, registered its only winning record (12-11) in a 27-year span from 1953-54 through 1979-80. . . . Marquette, after losing seven of its previous eight contests with DePaul, started a 19-game winning streak against the Blue Demons.

1967-68 FINAL NATIONAL POLLS

AP	UPI	SCHOOL (RECORD)	HEAD COACH
1	1	Houston (31-2)	Guy Lewis
2	2	UCLA (29-1)	John Wooden
3	3	St. Bonaventure (23-2)	Larry Weise
4	4	North Carolina (28-4)	Dean Smith
5	5	Kentucky (22-5)	Adolph Rupp
6	7	New Mexico (23-5)	Bob King
7	6	Columbia (23-5)	Jack Rohan
8	9	Davidson (24-5)	Lefty Driesell
9	8	Louisville (21-7)	John Dromo
10	11	Duke (22-6)	Vic Bubas
–	10	Marquette (23-6)	Al McGuire
–	12	New Mexico State (23-6)	Lou Henson
–	13	Vanderbilt (20-6)	Roy Skinner
–	14	Kansas State (19-9)	Tex Winter
–	15	Princeton (20-6)	Pete Carril
–	16	Army (20-5)	Bob Knight
–	17	Santa Clara (23-4)	Dick Garibaldi
–	18	Utah (17-9)	Jack Gardner
–	19	Bradley (19-9)	Joe Stowell
–	20	Iowa (16-9)	Ralph Miller

Houston's Elvin Hayes (left) and UCLA's Lew Alcindor go head to head in the 1967–68 NCAA Semifinals.

St. Bonaventure's Bob Lanier stretches to block a shot.

Oklahoma City coach Abe Lemons, upset when his team trailed Duke, 49-38, at intermission of its NIT opener, kept his squad on the Madison Square Garden floor for a 10-minute workout. It didn't help as OCU lost, 97-81. . . . Indiana tied for last place in the Big Ten with a 4-10 league record one season after tying for the title with a 10-4 mark.. . . Forward Joe Franklin became Wisconsin's only All-Big Ten first-team selection in a 38-year span from 1952-53 through 1989-90. He averaged 22.7 points per game and a league-high 13.9 rebounds per contest. . . . Miami of Ohio suffered a season-ending defeat at home against Dayton to finish with the Redskins' only losing record (11-12) in a 16-year stretch from 1962-63 through 1977-78. . . . Texas Christian compiled its first winning mark in nine seasons (15-11) in Johnny Swaim's initial year as coach of the Horned Frogs.

1968 NCAA Tournament

Summary: "I've never come out and said it," UCLA coach John Wooden said, "but it would be hard to pick a team over the 1968 team. I will say it would be the most difficult team to prepare for and play against offensively and defensively. It created so many problems. It had such great balance. We had the big center (Alcindor) who is the most valuable player of all time. Mike Warren was a three-year starter who may have been the most intelligent floor leader ever, going eight complete games once without a turnover. Lucius Allen was a very physical, talented individual who was extremely quick. Lynn Shackleford was a great shooter out of the corner who didn't allow defenses to sag on Jabbar. Mike Lynn didn't have power, but he had as fine a pair of hands around the boards as I have ever seen."

1967–68 NCAA CHAMPION: UCLA

SEASON STATISTICS OF UCLA REGULARS

PLAYER	POS.	CL.	G.	FG%	FT%	PPG	RPG
Lew Alcindor	C	Jr.	28	.613	.616	26.2	16.5
Lucius Allen	G	Jr.	30	.462	.678	15.1	6.0
Mike Warren	G	Sr.	30	.431	.763	12.1	3.7
Lynn Shackelford	F	Jr.	30	.498	.848	10.7	5.0
Mike Lynn	F	Sr.	30	.457	.684	10.3	5.2
Ken Heitz	G	Jr.	27	.500	.743	5.3	2.3
Jim Nielsen	F	Jr.	30	.496	.657	4.6	3.3
Bill Sweek	G	Jr.	27	.471	.654	3.6	1.2
Gene Sutherland	G	Sr.	27	.417	.885	1.6	0.6
Neville Saner	F	Sr.	24	.372	.600	1.5	1.6
TEAM TOTALS			30	.500	.684	93.4	53.4

1968 FINAL FOUR CHAMPIONSHIP GAME

LOS ANGELES, CA

UCLA (78)	MIN.	FG-A	FT-A	REB.	A	PF	PTS.
Shackelford	26	3-5	0-1	2	4	2	6
Lynn	22	1-7	5-7	6	4	2	7
Alcindor	37	15-21	4-4	16	1	4	34
Warren	35	3-7	1-1	3	1	2	7
Allen	35	3-7	5-7	5	5	4	11
Nielsen	10	1-1	0-0	1	0	1	2
Heitz	20	3-6	1-1	2	2	1	7
Sutherland	5	1-2	0-0	2	1	2	2
Sweek	5	0-1	0-0	2	0	0	0
Saner	5	1-3	0-0	2	1	0	2
Team				9			
TOTALS	200	31-60	16-21	48	19	16	78

FG%: .517. **FT%:** .762. **Turnovers:** 26.

N. CAROLINA (55)	MIN.	FG-A	FT-A	REB.	A	PF	PTS.
Miller	37	5-13	4-6	6	3	3	14
Bunting	15	1-3	1-2	2	1	5	3
Clark	37	4-12	1-3	8	1	3	9
Scott	35	6-17	0-1	3	2	3	12
Grubar	35	2-5	1-2	0	1	2	5
Fogler	16	1-4	2-2	0	2	0	4
Brown	13	2-5	2-2	5	0	1	6

Tuttle	2	0-0	0-0	0	1	0	0
Frye	3	1-2	0-1	1	0	0	2
Whitehead	1	0-0	0-0	0	0	0	0
Delany	3	0-1	0-0	0	0	0	0
Fletcher	3	0-1	0-0	0	0	0	0
Team				10			
TOTALS	200	22-63	11-19	35	11	17	55

FG%: .349. **FT%:** .579. **Turnovers:** 23.
Halftime: UCLA 32-22.

NATIONAL SEMIFINALS

OHIO STATE (66): Howell 6-17 1-2 13, Hosket 4-11 6-9 14, Sorenson 5-17 1-3 11, Schnabel 0-1 0-0 0, Meadors 3-13 2-2 8, Finney 8-13 0-2 16, Smith 2-6 0-0 4, Andreas 0-0 0-0 0, Barclay 0-1 0-0 0, Geddes 0-0 0-0 0. Team 28-79 (.354) 10-18 (.556) 66.

NORTH CAROLINA (80): Miller 10-23 0-1 20, Bunting 4-7 9-10 17, Clark 7-9 1-1 15, Scott 6-16 1-4 13, Grubar 4-9 3-3 11, Fogler 1-2 0-0 2, Brown 0-4 0-0 0, Tuttle 1-1 0-1 2. Team 33-71 (.465) 14-20 (.700) 80.

Halftime: North Carolina 34-27.

HOUSTON (69): Lee 2-15 0-0 4, Hayes 3-10 4-7 10, Spain 4-12 7-10 15, Chaney 5-13 5-7 15, Lewis 2-8 2-2 6, Hamood 3-5 4-6 10, Gribben 0-5 0-1 0, Bell 3-8 3-4 9, Taylor 0-0 0-0 0, Cooper 0-2 0-0 0. Team 22-78 (.282) 25-37 (.676) 69.

UCLA (101): Shackelford 6-10 5-5 17, Lynn 8-10 3-3 19, Alcindor 7-14 5-6 19, Warren 7-18 0-0 14, Allen 9-18 1-2 19, Nielsen 2-3 0-0 4, Heitz 3-6 1-1 7, Sweek 1-1 0-1 2, Sutherland 0-1 0-0 0, Saner 0-2 0-0 0. Team 43-83 (.518) 15-18 (.833) 101.

Halftime: UCLA 53-31.

ALL-TOURNAMENT TEAM

*Lew Alcindor, C, Jr., UCLA (53 points, 34 rebounds in final two games)
Lucius Allen, G, Jr., UCLA (30 points, 14 rebounds, 17 assists)
Larry Miller, F, Sr., North Carolina (34 points, 12 rebounds)
Lynn Shackelford, F, Jr., UCLA (23 points)
Mike Warren, G, Sr., UCLA (21 points, eight rebounds, 10 assists)

*Named Most Outstanding Player.

The roster for UCLA's 1968 national champion included six players with double-digit season scoring averages, but senior forward Edgar Lacey dropped off the team with an 11.9-point average following a dispute with Wooden after a highly-publicized mid-season defeat against Houston before 52,693 fans at the Astrodome. Lacey, assigned to defend Cougars star Elvin Hayes early in the game, was annoyed with Wooden for singling him out following Hayes' 29-point first-half outburst. Lacey, the leading rebounder for the Bruins' 1965 NCAA titlist when he was an All-Tournament team selection, missed the 1966-67 campaign because of a fractured left kneecap. Houston, entering the tourney undefeated, lost in the national semifinals against UCLA (101-69)

when Hayes, averaging 37.6 points per game entering the Final Four, was restricted to 10 as the Bruins neutralized him by employing a "diamond-and-one" defense with Lynn Shackelford assigned to cover Hayes.

Star Gazing: St. Bonaventure, undefeated entering the tourney (22-0), lost in the East Regional semifinals against North Carolina (91-72) despite 23 points and nine rebounds by consensus second-team All-American Bob Lanier of the Bonnies.

One and Only: Hayes became the only player to lead the playoffs in scoring and rebounding in back-to-back years. Hayes became the only player to lead a tournament in scoring by more

1968 CHAMPIONSHIP BRACKET

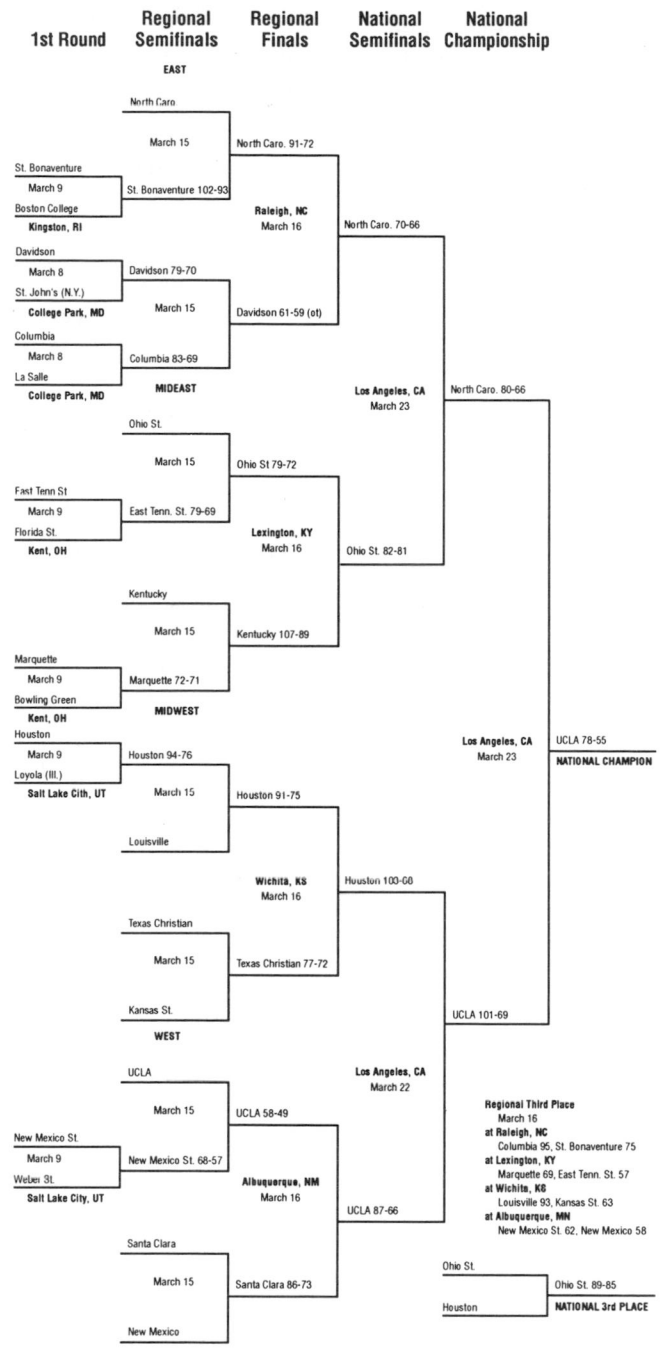

1st Round	Regional Semifinals	Regional Finals	National Semifinals	National Championship

EAST

North Caro.

March 15 — North Caro. 91-72

St. Bonaventure
March 9 — St. Bonaventure 102-93
Boston College
Kingston, RI

Raleigh, NC March 16 — North Caro. 70-66

Davidson
March 8 — Davidson 79-70
St. John's (N.Y.)
College Park, MD March 15 — Davidson 61-59 (ot)

Columbia
March 8 — Columbia 83-69
La Salle
College Park, MD

North Caro. 80-66

MIDEAST

Ohio St.
March 15 — Ohio St 79-72

East Tenn St
March 9 — East Tenn. St. 79-69
Florida St.
Kent, OH

Lexington, KY March 16 — Ohio St. 82-81

Kentucky
March 15 — Kentucky 107-89

Marquette
March 9 — Marquette 72-71
Bowling Green
Kent, OH

Los Angeles, CA March 23 — North Caro. 80-66

MIDWEST

Houston
March 9 — Houston 94-76
Loyola (Ill.)
Salt Lake Cith, UT March 15 — Houston 91-75

Louisville

Wichita, KS March 16 — Houston 100-68

Texas Christian
March 15 — Texas Christian 77-72

Kansas St.

Los Angeles, CA March 23 — UCLA 78-55

NATIONAL CHAMPION

UCLA 101-69

WEST

UCLA
March 15 — UCLA 58-49

New Mexico St.
March 9 — New Mexico St. 68-57
Weber St.
Salt Lake City, UT

Albuquerque, NM March 16 — UCLA 87-66

Santa Clara
March 15 — Santa Clara 86-73

New Mexico

Los Angeles, CA March 22

Regional Third Place
March 16
at Raleigh, NC
Columbia 95, St. Bonaventure 75
at Lexington, KY
Marquette 69, East Tenn. St. 57
at Wichita, KS
Louisville 93, Kansas St. 63
at Albuquerque, MN
New Mexico St. 62, New Mexico 58

Ohio St. — Ohio St. 89-85
Houston — **NATIONAL 3rd PLACE**

than 60 points. Alcindor and his UCLA teammates helped hold Hayes to 10 points in the 1968 national semifinals, but the Big E finished with 167 points in five games. Alcindor, runner-up with 103 points in four games, committed six turnovers in each of the Final Four games. Hayes became the only player in tournament history to collect more than 40 points and 25 rebounds in the same game when he had tourney highs of 49 points and 27 rebounds in a 94-76 decision over Loyola of Chicago in the opening round of the Midwest Regional. Hayes holds the records for most rebounds in a playoff series (97 in five games as a senior) and career (222 in 13 games). He had five games with at least 24 rebounds, including the first three playoff games in 1968, before being held to five in a 101-69 national semifinal loss against UCLA. Hayes also holds the record for most playoff field goals in a career with 152. He averaged almost 24 field goal attempts per game in helping the Cougars win nine of 13 contests.

Numbers Game: UCLA became the only champion to win its two Final Four games by a total of more than 50 points. The Bruins' 78-55 decision over North Carolina was the most lopsided triumph in championship game history until UNLV demolished Duke in 1990 (103-73). The Tar Heels reached the final despite shooting a modest 45.5 percent from the floor for the season. . . . This year marked the only time as many as three Final Four teams returned to the national semifinals for a second consecutive season— UCLA (champion both years under Wooden), Houston (third in '67 and fourth in '68 under Guy Lewis) and North Carolina (fourth in '67 and runner-up in '68 under Dean Smith). . . . Hayes led the tournament in scoring and rebounding by wide margins for fourth-place Houston, but he wasn't named to the all-tournament team.

Putting Things in Perspective: Houston excelled although forward Melvin Bell, the third-leading scorer and second-leading rebounder for the '67 Final Four team, missed the season after undergoing knee surgery. . . . New Mexico defeated New Mexico State twice during the regular season, but lost at home to the Aggies, 62-58, in the

West Regional third-place game. Both schools were ranked among the top 12 in the country.

Scoring Leader: Elvin Hayes, Houston (167 points, 33.4 ppg).

Rebounding Leader: Elvin Hayes, Houston (97 rebounds, 19.4 rpg).

Highest Rebounding Average: Wes Unseld, Louisville (20.5 rpg).

1968-69

AT A GLANCE

NCAA Champion: UCLA (29-1; coached by John Wooden; won Pacific-8 title by two games with a 13-1 record, which was two games ahead of Washington State).

NIT Champion: Temple (22-8; coached by Harry Litwack).

NCAA Probation: Florida State, Illinois, La Salle, Mississippi State, St. Bonaventure, Texas-Pan American, Utah State.

NCAA Consensus First-Team All-Americans: Lew Alcindor, C, Sr., UCLA; Spencer Haywood, F-C, Jr., Detroit; Pete Maravich, G, Jr., Louisiana State; Rick Mount, G, Jr., Purdue; Calvin Murphy, G, Jr., Niagara.

National Player of the Year: Alcindor (24 ppg, 14.7 rpg, 63.5 FG%).

National Coaches of the Year: Drake's Maury John (26-5/USBWA) and UCLA's John Wooden (29-1/AP, UPI, NABC).

LSU's Pete Maravich, averaging 44.2 points per game, won the national scoring championship by a larger margin than any player in history (10.9 points higher than Purdue guard Rick Mount). Duquesne, one of the nation's top defensive teams, was unbeaten through nine contests by limiting opponents to 57.3 points per game entering the Dukes' outing against LSU in the All-College Tournament final at Oklahoma City. Maravich erupted for 53 points in a 94-91 triumph over Duquesne to give LSU a 7-1 record at that juncture. The Tigers,

1968–69 INDIVIDUAL LEADERS

SCORING

PLAYER	PTS.	AVG.
Maravich, LSU	1148	44.2
Mount, Purdue	932	33.3
Murphy, Niagara	778	32.4
Haywood, Detroit	699	31.8
B. Tallent, G. Washington	723	28.9
Roberts, Utah St.	718	27.6
Curnutt, Miami (Fla.)	661	27.5
Lanier, St. Bonaventure	654	27.3
Travis, Oklahoma City	729	27.0
Morgan, Jacksonville	613	26.7

REBOUNDING

PLAYER	REB.	AVG.
Haywood, Detroit	472	21.5
Lewis, St. Francis (Pa.)	495	20.6

Green, Morehead St.	483	17.9
Walk, Florida	481	17.8
Driscoll, Boston College	498	17.8
Cowens, Florida St.	437	17.5
Brown, Middle Tenn. St.	429	16.5
Ladner, S. Mississippi	411	16.4
Grosso, Louisville	432	16.0
Cross, San Francisco	400	16.0

FIELD GOAL PERCENTAGE

PLAYER	FGM	FGA	PCT.
Alcindor, UCLA	303	477	.635
Bunting, N. Carolina	217	363	.598
Wilkes, Virginia	153	256	.598
Awtrey, Santa Clara	240	406	.591
Lanier, St. Bonaventure	270	460	.587
Lienhard, Georgia	235	404	.582
Smith, Syracuse	177	307	.577

Hayes, Boston Univ.	200	351	.570
Dodds, Wyoming	165	290	.569
Gayeska, Massachusetts	142	250	.568

FREE THROW PERCENTAGE

PLAYER	FTM	FTA	PCT.
Justus, Tennessee	133	147	.905
Finney, Ohio St.	99	110	.900
Thomforde, Princeton	123	137	.898
Ward, Centenary	99	112	.884
Davis, Wake Forest	194	220	.882
Mitchell, W. Texas St.	131	149	.879
Powell, Loyola (La.)	106	121	.876
B. Tallent, G. Washington	155	177	.876
Hagan, Vanderbilt	116	133	.872
Mitchell, VMI	99	114	.868

1968–69 TEAM LEADERS

SCORING OFFENSE

SCHOOL	PTS.	AVG.
Purdue	2605	93.0
Hardin-Simmons	2387	91.9
Kentucky	2542	90.8
Michigan	2153	89.7
Louisiana St.	2316	89.1

SCORING DEFENSE

SCHOOL	PTS.	AVG.
Army	1498	53.5
Tennessee	1651	59.0
Oklahoma St.	1482	59.3
Long Island	1372	59.7
Kansas	1625	60.2

SCORING MARGIN

SCHOOL	OFF.	DEF.	MAR.
UCLA	84.7	63.8	20.9
La Salle	89.0	70.9	18.1

Columbia	77.0	61.3	15.7
Santa Clara	77.0	61.3	15.7
Purdue	93.0	79.1	13.9

WON-LOST PERCENTAGE

SCHOOL	W-L	PCT.
UCLA	29-1	.967
La Salle	23-1	.958
Santa Clara	27-2	.931
Weber St.	27-3	.900
Davidson	27-3	.900

FIELD GOAL PERCENTAGE

SCHOOL	FGM	FGA	PCT.
UCLA	1027	1999	.514
Auburn	734	1461	.502
Southern Mississippi	855	1710	.500
Columbia	689	1380	.499
St. Peter's	913	1847	.494

FREE THROW PERCENTAGE

SCHOOL	FTM	FTA	PCT.
Jacksonville	574	733	.783
Purdue	571	730	.782
Tennessee	438	563	.778
Iowa	573	743	.771
Wake Forest	642	833	.771

REBOUNDING

SCHOOL	REB.	AVG.
Middle Tennessee St.	1685	64.8
St. Francis (Pa.)	1411	58.8
Morehead St.	1583	58.6
Indiana	1354	56.4
Maine	1286	55.9

however, lost their next six SEC assignments despite Maravich's prolific production.

Incredibly, Maravich averaged 46.5 points in 15 road games, compared to 41 at home. Needing 49 in the Tigers' finale at Georgia to set an all-time single-season record, he exploded for 58, including 11 in a second overtime when he climaxed the outburst with a hook shot from midcourt.

A coach who might have wondered about all of the fuss over Maravich was Tennessee's Ray Mears, whose "Chinese" defense restricted Pistol Pete to a 19.8 average in four games over two seasons. No other team held Maravich under 30 points in his first 52 games.

Maravich had three consecutive games with at least 50 points against Division I opponents (66-50-54). His 66-point outburst at Tulane was not the season's single-game high. Niagara's Calvin Murphy claimed that distinction by pouring in a school-record 68 in a 118-110 victory against Syracuse, which finished with its fifth losing record of the decade (9-16).

Mount joined guard Bob Lloyd (Rutgers '67) and forward Larry Miller (North Carolina '68) in an odd category by becoming the third NCAA consensus first-team All-American in as many years to go straight to the ABA and never play in the NBA. . . . Michigan's Rudy Tomjanovich, who

1968–69 NCAA CHAMPION: UCLA

SEASON STATISTICS OF UCLA REGULARS

PLAYER	POS.	CL.	G.	FG%	FT%	PPG	RPG
Lew Alcindor	C	Sr.	30	.635	.612	24.0	14.7
Curtis Rowe	F	So.	30	.502	.678	12.9	7.9
John Vallely	G	Jr.	28	.496	.755	11.0	3.3
Sidney Wicks	F	So.	30	.435	.580	7.5	5.1
Lynn Shackelford	F	Sr.	30	.463	.500	7.0	4.0
Ken Heitz	G	Sr.	30	.467	.684	6.5	2.3
Bill Sweek	G	Sr.	30	.506	.625	6.3	2.2
Steve Patterson	C	So.	29	.527	.750	5.0	3.9
Terry Schofield	G	So.	24	.415	.611	2.7	1.6
John Ecker	F	So.	20	.500	.667	1.6	1.2
Bill Seibert	F	So.	15	.261	.714	1.1	0.8
TEAM TOTALS			30	.513	.648	84.7	50.4

1969 FINAL FOUR CHAMPIONSHIP GAME

LOUISVILLE, KY

UCLA (92)	MIN.	FG-A	FT-A	REB.	A	PF	PTS.
Shackelford	35	3-8	5-8	9	0	3	11
Rowe	37	4-10	4-4	12	3	2	12
Alcindor	36	15-20	7-9	20	0	2	37
Heitz	34	0-3	0-1	3	4	4	0
Vallely	31	4-9	7-10	4	0	3	15
Sweek	10	3-3	0-1	1	0	3	6
Wicks	6	0-1	3-6	4	1	1	3
Schofield	3	1-2	0-0	0	0	0	2
Patterson	5	1-1	2-2	2	0	0	4
Seibert	1	0-0	0-0	1	0	0	0
Farmer	1	0-0	0-0	0	0	1	0
Ecker	1	1-1	0-0	0	0	0	2
Team				5			
TOTALS	200	32-58	28-41	61	8	19	92

FG%: .552. FT%: .683. **Turnovers:** 19.

PURDUE (72)	MIN.	FG-A	FT-A	REB.	A	PF	PTS.
Gilliam	32	2-14	3-3	11	3	2	7
Faerber	17	1-2	0-0	3	0	5	2
Johnson	27	4-9	3-4	9	0	2	11
Mount	37	12-36	4-5	1	0	3	28
Keller	32	4-17	3-4	4	3	5	11
Kaufman	13	0-0	2-2	5	0	5	2
Bedford	25	3-8	1-3	8	0	3	7
Weatherford	15	1-5	2-2	1	0	3	4
Reasoner	1	0-1	0-1	1	0	2	0
Taylor	1	0-0	0-0	0	0	0	0
Team				5			
TOTALS	200	27-92	18-24	48	6	30	72

FG%: .293. FT%: .750. **Turnovers:** 4.
Halftime: UCLA 50-41.

NATIONAL SEMIFINALS

NORTH CAROLINA (65): Bunting 7-13 5-7 19, Scott 6-19 4-6 16, Clark 7-9 6-10 20, Fogler 1-4 0-0 2, G. Tuttle 2-4 0-1 4, Delany 0-2 0-0 0, Dedmon 0-1 0-1 0, Brown 1-4 0-0 2, Gipple 0-3 0-0 0, Chadwick 1-2 0-0 2, R. Tuttle 0-1 0-0 0, Eggleston 0-0 0-0 0. Team 25-62 (.403) 15-25 (.600) 65.

PURDUE (92): Gilliam 3-11 0-0 6, Faerber 3-3 2-2 8, Johnson 2-5 1-3 5, Mount 14-28 8-9 36, Keller 9-19 2-3 20, Kaufman 0-1 2-3 2, Weatherford 3-6 1-1 7, Bedford 3-3 0-0 6, Taylor 1-1 0-1 2, Longfellow 0-1 0-0 0, Reasoner 0-0 0-0 0, Young 0-0 0-0 0. Team 38-78 (.487) 16-22 (.727) 92.

Halftime: Purdue 53-30.

DRAKE (82): Pulliam 4-4 4-5 12, Williams 0-1 0-0 0, Wise 5-7 3-4 13, McCarter 10-27 4-4 24, Draper 5-13 2-2 12, Odom 0-2 0-1 0, Wanamaker 4-7 1-1 9, Zeller 4-12 4-6 12, Gwin 0-0 0-1 0. Team 32-83 (.386) 18-24 (.667) 82.

UCLA (85): Shackelford 2-5 2-3 6, Rowe 6-9 2-2 14, Alcindor 8-14 9-16 25, Heitz 3-6 1-3 7, Vallely 9-11 11-14 29, Wicks 0-2 0-0 0, Sweek 0-0 0-0 0, Patterson 0-0 2-2 2, Schofield 0-3 2-4 2. Team 28-50 (.560) 29-44 (.660) 85.

Halftime: UCLA 44-43.

ALL-TOURNAMENT TEAM

*Lew Alcindor, C, Sr., UCLA (62 points, 41 rebounds in final two games)
Willie McCarter, G, Sr., Drake (52 points, 13 assists)
Rick Mount, G, Jr., Purdue (64 points)
Charlie Scott, F-G, Jr., North Carolina (51 points, 10 rebounds)
John Vallely, G, Jr., UCLA (44 points, 10 rebounds)

*Named Most Outstanding Player.

coached the Houston Rockets to NBA championships in 1994 and 1995, set a Chicago Stadium college record and school standard with 30 rebounds in a 112-100 overtime defeat to Loyola of Chicago. Earlier in the season in another overtime game, he established a Michigan field-goal record with 21 baskets and tied Cazzie Russell's scoring standard with 48 points in an 89-87 overtime victory against Indiana.

Maine's Jim Stephenson (54 points vs. Colby), Wake Forest's Charlie Davis (51 vs. American University), St. Bonaventure's Bob Lanier (51 vs. Seton Hall), Larry Lewis of St. Francis, Pa. (46 vs. St. Vincent), Western Michigan's Gene Ford (46 vs. Loyola of Chicago), Vanderbilt's Tom Hagan (44 at Mississippi State) and Pacific's Bill Stricker (44 vs. Port-

land) also set school single-game scoring marks. . . . Detroit's Spencer Haywood (32.1 ppg), George Washington's Bob Tallent (28.9), Boston University's Jim Hayes (25.7), Tulane's Johnny Arthurs (25.6), John Conforti (24.3) of St. Francis (N.Y.), Vanderbilt's Hagan (23.4) and Middle Tennessee State's Willie Brown (23.3) set school records for highest scoring average in a single season.

Larry Mikan, the son of Hall of Famer George Mikan, led Minnesota in scoring (18.4 ppg) and rebounding (10.5 rpg). . . . Purdue, coached by George King, captured its first Big Ten title in 29 years. . . . Illinois, which didn't have a winning record in any of the previous three seasons, won its first nine contests under coach Harv Schmidt, including a 97-84 victory at Hous-

LSU's Pete Maravich (left) was a scoring machine, a three-time All-American—and wore floppy socks!

ton to snap the Cougars' 59-game homecourt winning streak. . . . Kent State, coached by Frank Truitt, compiled a 14-10 record to end a streak of 16 consecutive losing seasons.

Kentucky became the first school to win 1,000 games. . . . Florida made its only appearance in a national postseason tournament until 1984. The Gators lost to Temple, 82-66, in the first round of the NIT. . . . Notre Dame finished in the Top 20 of a final wire-service poll for the first time since 1958. The Irish dropped its NCAA Tournament opener to Miami of Ohio when guard Austin Carr broke his foot early in the contest.

Southern Cal ended UCLA's 41-game winning streak, 46-44. It was one of only two defeats for the Bruins during Lew Alcindor's three-year varsity career with both of the setbacks by two points. . . . Santa Clara (27-2/coached by Dick Garibaldi), Davidson (27-3/Lefty Driesell), Weber State (27-3/Phil Johnson) and Drake (26-5/Maury John) had their winningest seasons in school history. . . . Santa Clara won its first 21 games before the Broncos absorbed their lone regular-season defeat, a 73-69 decision in double overtime against San Jose State. Weber State became the only Big Sky team ever to go undefeated in conference competition since the league's inception in 1964. Colorado captured the Big Eight Conference crown after finishing in a tie for last place the previous year.

Texas Tech did not have a player selected to at least All-SWC second-team honors for the only time from 1957-58 through 1993-94. . . . North Texas State (15-10 under coach Dan Spika) posted its first winning record in 12 years at the Division I level. . . . Wyoming, coached by Bill Strannigan, finished in the Top 20 of a final wire-service poll for the only time in a 22-year span from 1958-59 through 1979-80.

George Washington, coached by Wayne Dobbs, ended a streak of eight consecutive losing seasons by compiling a 14-11 record. . . . Georgia's Bob Leinhard (32 vs. Sewanee) and Boston College's Terry Driscoll (31 vs. Fordham) set school single-game rebounding records. . . . Duke's Vic Bubas retired after a 10-year coaching career with a 213-67 record. The Blue Devils logged a 15-13 mark in their only season under Bubas without finishing in a final wire-service Top 20 poll. His first-year salary was $9,000. He later became commissioner of the Sun Belt Conference. . . . Virginia lost 22 consecutive games in its series with Duke until defeating the Blue Devils, 81-75. . . . Bigotry seemed to rear its ugly head when junior Charlie Scott, the first African American on North Carolina's varsity roster, didn't become a consensus All-ACC first-team selection and lost the conference player of the year vote to South Carolina's John Roche by a wide margin.

San Diego's Phil Woolpert, who gained national acclaim as coach of San Francisco's back-to-back NCAA champions in the mid-1950s, retired after a 16-year coaching career with a 239-164 record. Woolpert spent much of his post-coaching years as a bus driver in the Northwest. . . . Jerry Tarkanian embarked on his major-college coaching career with a 23-3 record (.885) at Long Beach State. Two other first-year head coaches had even higher winning percentages—La Salle's Tom Gola (23-1, .958) and Weber State's Phil Johnson (27-3, .900). . . . Stanley Ward finished his 15-year stint at Brown as the school's all-time winningest coach although he won barely over one-third of his games (133-261 record, .338). . . . Dartmouth, coached by Dave Gavitt, compiled its highest victory total in nine seasons (10-15 mark)

1968-69 FINAL NATIONAL POLLS

AP	UPI	SCHOOL (RECORD)	HEAD COACH
1	1	UCLA (29-1)	John Wooden
2	6	La Salle (23-1)	Tom Gola
3	4	Santa Clara (27-2)	Dick Garibaldi
4	2	North Carolina (27-5)	Dean Smith
5	3	Davidson (27-3)	Lefty Driesell
6	7	Purdue (23-5)	George King
7	5	Kentucky (23-5)	Adolph Rupp
8	8	St. John's (23-6)	Lou Carnesecca
9	10	Duquesne (21-5)	Red Manning
10	15	Villanova (21-5)	Jack Kraft
11	11	Drake (26-5)	Maury John
12	9	New Mexico State (24-5)	Lou Henson
13	20	South Carolina (21-7)	Frank McGuire
14	14	Marquette (24-5)	Al McGuire
15	13	Louisville (21-6)	John Dromo
16	15	Boston College (24-4)	Bob Cousy
17	–	Notre Dame (20-7)	Johnny Dee
18	12	Colorado (21-7)	Sox Walseth
19	20	Kansas (20-7)	Ted Owens
20	–	Illinois (19-5)	Harvey Schmidt
–	17	Weber State (27-3)	Phil Johnson
–	17	Wyoming (19-9)	Bill Strannigan
–	19	Colorado State (17-7)	Jim Williams

despite losing seven games by a total of 14 points. Gavitt was named New England Coach of the Year for that performance before moving on to greater acclaim in a similar position at Providence.

1969 NCAA Tournament

Summary: UCLA's Lew Alcindor, climaxing a streak when he became the only player to earn three consecutive Final Four Most Outstanding Player awards, collected 37 points and 20 rebounds in his final college game, a victory against Purdue (92-72). The 37-point outburst was a tourney high and is the fourth-highest point total in championship game history. Teammate Ken Heitz was scoreless in the final but his defense was instrumental in making Boilermakers standout Rick Mount miss 14 consecutive field-goal attempts in one stretch. UCLA coasted despite committing 19 turnovers to four for Purdue. Guard John Vallely, averaging a modest 10.2 points per game entering the Final Four, erupted for 29 points in the national semifinals and the Bruins needed all of them. They had a nine-point lead with 70 seconds remaining dwindle to one before defeating Drake (85-82) after the Bulldogs missed a go-ahead basket in the waning moments. Alcindor grabbed a tourney-high 21 rebounds in the Drake game. "Drake gave us as much trouble—maybe more—than any team we ever played

1960-69 PREMO POWER POLL: BEST TEAMS BY DECADE

RANK	SEASON	SCHOOL
1	1967–68	UCLA* (29-1)
2	1966–67	UCLA* (30-0)
3	1968–69	UCLA* (29-1)
4	1959–60	Ohio St.* (25-3)
5	1963–64	UCLA* (30-0)
6	1960–61	Ohio St. (27-1)
7	1959–60	California (28-2)
8	1961–62	Cincinnati* (29-2)
9	1964–65	UCLA* (28-2)
10	1959–60	Cincinnati (28-2)
11	1962–63	Loyola (Ill.)* (29-2)
12	1967–68	Houston (31-2)
13	1961–62	Ohio St. (26-2)
14	1965–66	Texas Western* (28-1)
15	1960–61	Cincinnati* (27-3)
16	1962–63	Cincinnati (26-2)
17	1968–69	La Salle (23-1)
18	1964–65	Michigan (24-4)
19	1960–61	St. Bonaventure (24-4)
20	1965–66	Kentucky (27-2)
	1963–64	Duke (26-5)

*–NCAA Tournament Champion

in the tournament," UCLA coach John Wooden said. "They were a very quick team, and played tough man-to-man (defense)."

One and Only: Alcindor, who later changed his name to Kareem Abdul-Jabbar, is the only individual selected the Final Four's Most Outstanding Player three times (1967 through 1969). Alcindor is the only player to couple three unanimous first-team All-American seasons with three NCAA titles. He is also the only player to hit better than 70 percent of his field-goal attempts in two different NCAA title games ('68 and '69). . . . North Carolina became the only school to lose two games by at least 20 points apiece in a single Final Four.

Numbers Game: Mount, who scored 122 points in four playoff games in Purdue's first NCAA Tournament appearance, is the only player to lead a single tourney in scoring with more than 120 points and not eventually play in the NBA. He played five seasons in the ABA with four different franchises. Mount (36 points) and Billy Keller (20) accounted for the highest-scoring starting backcourt in a single Final Four game in history when they combined for 56 points in a 92-65 rout of North Carolina in the semifinals. . . . Mount's 36 field-goal attempts against UCLA is an NCAA championship game record. . . . Charlie Scott's second-half heroics enabled Carolina to reach the Final

Four for the third consecutive year. Scott connected on 12 of 13 field-goal attempts after intermission in a come-from-behind 85-74 victory over Duke in the ACC Tournament final. The next week in the East Regional final, the 6-5 guard hit 10 of 14 shots from the floor in the second half, including a game-winning 20-foot jumper with three seconds remaining in an 87-85 verdict over Davidson. . . . Santa Clara's outstanding frontline of Dennis Awtrey, Bud Ogden and Ralph Ogden combined for 53 points per game before collaborating for just 27 in a 90-52 setback against UCLA in the West Regional final. . . . St. John's lost two of three playoff games despite hitting a tourney series record 87 percent from the free-throw line (47 of 54). The Orangemen were eliminated for the second straight year by Davidson when Wildcats star Mike Maloy hit all 13 of his foul shots in a 79-69 decision. Maloy's accuracy from the charity stripe during his three-year varsity career was less than 70 percent. . . . Backup center Garry Odom averaged a modest 3.8 points and 4.5 rebounds per game on the season, but collected a total of 18 points and 18 rebounds in Drake's two Midwest Regional victories. . . . Texas A&M managed its first NCAA playoff victory (81-66 over Trinity in first round of Midwest Regional).

What Might Have Been: La Salle, which defeated NCAA Tournament entrants Villanova, St. Joseph's and Duquesne by a total of 38 points on its way to a No. 2 ranking by AP, was ineligible for the tourney because of NCAA probation.

Putting Things in Perspective: North Carolina starting guard Dick Grubar, averaging 13 points per game, injured a knee in the ACC Tournament and was lost for the NCAA playoffs. A standout defensive player, the senior would have drawn the assignment of facing the explosive Mount, a 36-point scorer in a national semifinal victory over Carolina. . . . Drake nearly pulled off a gigantic upset against UCLA in the national semifinals although the Bulldogs shot just 38.6 percent from the floor.

Scoring Leader: Rick Mount, Purdue (122 points, 30.5 ppg).

Rebounding Leader: Lew Alcindor, UCLA (64 rebounds, 16 rpg).

1969 CHAMPIONSHIP BRACKET

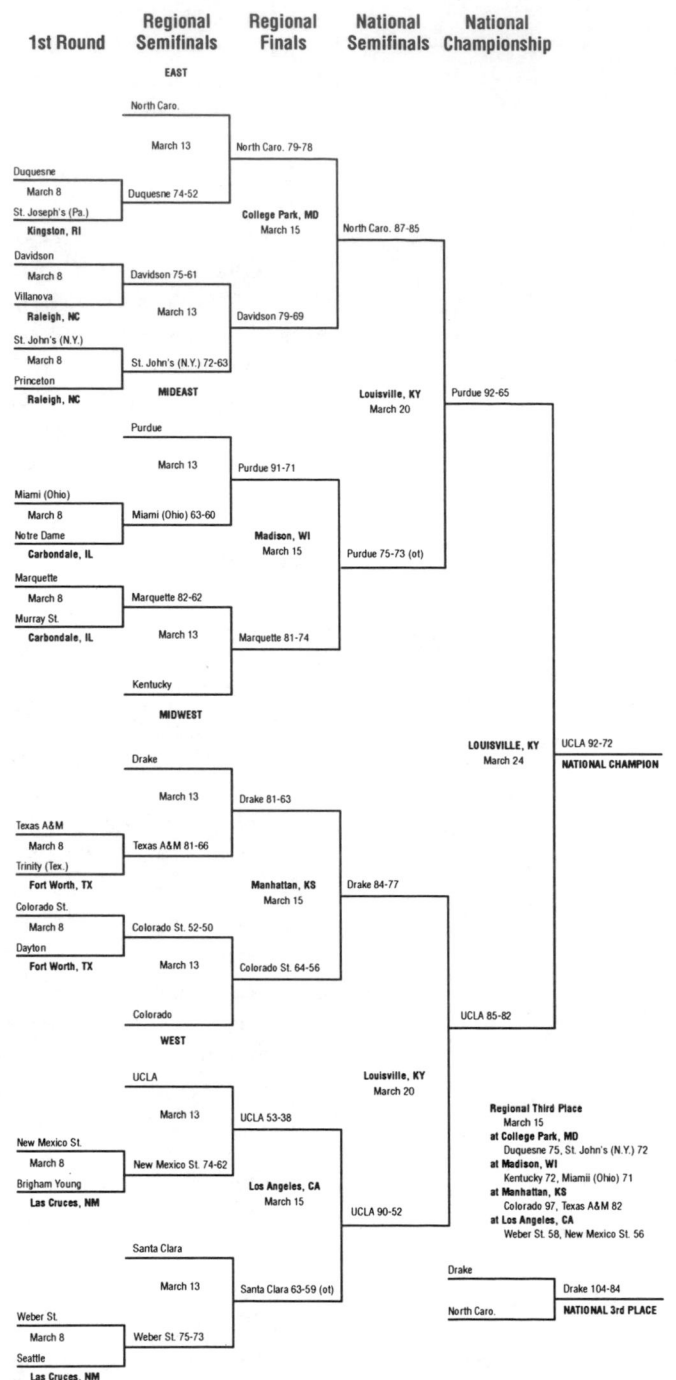

1st Round	Regional Semifinals	Regional Finals	National Semifinals	National Championship

EAST

North Caro.

March 13 — North Caro. 79-78

Duquesne
March 8
St. Joseph's (Pa.) — Duquesne 74-52
Kingston, RI

College Park, MD
March 15 — North Caro. 87-85

Davidson
March 8
Villanova — Davidson 75-61
Raleigh, NC

March 13 — Davidson 79-69

St. John's (N.Y.)
March 8
Princeton — St. John's (N.Y.) 72-63
Raleigh, NC

MIDEAST

Purdue

March 13 — Purdue 91-71

Miami (Ohio)
March 8
Notre Dame — Miami (Ohio) 63-60
Carbondale, IL

Madison, WI
March 15 — Purdue 75-73 (ot)

Marquette
March 8
Murray St. — Marquette 82-62
Carbondale, IL

March 13 — Marquette 81-74

Kentucky

Louisville, KY
March 20 — Purdue 92-65

MIDWEST

Drake

March 13 — Drake 81-63

Texas A&M
March 8
Trinity (Tex.) — Texas A&M 81-66
Fort Worth, TX

Manhattan, KS
March 15 — Drake 84-77

Colorado St.
March 8
Dayton — Colorado St. 52-50
Fort Worth, TX

March 13 — Colorado St. 64-56

Colorado

WEST

UCLA

March 13 — UCLA 53-38

New Mexico St.
March 8
Brigham Young — New Mexico St. 74-62
Las Cruces, NM

Los Angeles, CA
March 15 — UCLA 90-52

Santa Clara

March 13 — Santa Clara 63-59 (ot)

Weber St.
March 8
Seattle — Weber St. 75-73
Las Cruces, NM

Louisville, KY
March 20 — UCLA 85-82

LOUISVILLE, KY
March 24 — UCLA 92-72
NATIONAL CHAMPION

Regional Third Place
March 15
at College Park, MD
Duquesne 75, St. John's (N.Y.) 72
at Madison, WI
Kentucky 72, Miami (Ohio) 71
at Manhattan, KS
Colorado 97, Texas A&M 82
at Los Angeles, CA
Weber St. 58, New Mexico St. 56

Drake

North Caro. — Drake 104-84
NATIONAL 3rd PLACE

WINNINGEST PROGRAMS OF THE 1960s

RK.	SCHOOL	W.	L.	PCT.
1.	UCLA	234	52	.818
2.	Cincinnati	214	63	.773
3.	Providence	204	64	.761
4.	Duke	213	67	.761
5.	Kentucky	197	69	.741
6.	Ohio State	188	69	.732
7.	St. Joseph's	201	74	.731
8.	Dayton	207	77	.729
9.	Bradley	197	74	.727
10.	Princeton	188	71	.726

Note: Weber State compiled a 147-36 record (.803) in only seven major-college seasons during the decade.

ALL-DECADE TEAM — 1960s

Lew Alcindor, C, UCLA
Bill Bradley, F, Princeton
Elvin Hayes, F-C, Houston
Dan Issel, F-C, Kentucky
Jerry Lucas, C, Ohio State
Pete Maravich, G, Louisiana State
Rick Mount, G, Purdue
Cazzie Russell, G, Michigan
Wes Unseld, C, Louisville
Chet Walker, F, Bradley
Coach: John Wooden, UCLA

Lew Alcindor

UCLA
7-2 — C
New York, N.Y. (Power Memorial H.S.)

Named national player of the year by AP, UPI and the USBWA in 1967 and 1969. . . . Naismith Award winner in 1969. . . . NCAA unanimous first-team All-American in 1967, 1968 and 1969. . . . Led the nation in field-goal percentage in 1967 and 1969. Finished fourth in 1968. . . . Ranked among the nation's leading scorers in 1967 (2nd), 1968 (12th) and 1969 (29th). . . . Ranked among the nation's leading rebounders in 1967 (39 points, 38 rebounds, 60.9 FG%), 1968 (9th) and 1969 (16th). . . . Leading scorer and rebounder for NCAA champions in 1967 (30-0 record), 1968 (29-1) and 1969 (29-1). . . . Final Four Most Outstanding Player in 1967 (39 points, 38 rebounds, 60.9 FG%), 1968 (53 points, 34 rebounds, 62.9 FG%, 90.0 FT%) and 1969 (62 points, 41 rebounds, 67.6 FG%). . . . Named to All-NCAA Tournament team in 1967, 1968 and 1969. . . . Averaged 25.3 points and 16.8 rebounds in 12 NCAA Tournament games from 1967-69 (12-0 record). . . . Selected by the Milwaukee Bucks in first round of 1969 NBA draft (1st pick overall). . . . Changed his name to Kareem Abdul-Jabbar. . . . Elected to Naismith Memorial Basketball Hall of Fame in 1995.

SEASON	G.	FGM-FGA	FG%	FTM-FTA	FT%	REB.	AVG.	PTS.	AVG.
1966-67	30	346-519	.667	178-274	.650	466	15.5	870	29.0
1967-68	28	294-480	.613	146-237	.616	461	16.5	734	26.2
1968-69	30	303-477	.635	115-188	.612	440	14.7	721	24.0
Totals	88	943-1476	.639	439-699	.628	1367	15.5	2325	26.4

Bill Bradley

Princeton
6-5 — F
Crystal City, Mo.

Named national player of the year by AP, UPI and USBWA in 1965. . . . NCAA unanimous first-team All-American in 1964 and 1965. . . . Led the nation in free-throw percentage in 1965 after finishing 2nd in 1963 and 14th in 1964. . . . Ranked among the nation's leading scorers in 1963 (5th), 1964 (4th) and 1965 (3rd). . . . Leading scorer and rebounder for third-place team in 1965 NCAA Tournament (23-6 record). . . . Final Four Most Outstanding Player in 1965 (87 points, 24 rebounds, 63.0 FG%, 95.0 FT%). . . . Named to 1965 All-NCAA Tournament team. . . . Averaged 33.7 points and 12 rebounds in nine NCAA Tournament games from 1963-65 (5-4 record). . . . Member of 1964 U.S. Olympic team (10.1 ppg, 95.8 FT%). . . . Selected as

a territorial pick by the New York Knicks in 1965 NBA draft. . . . Elected to Naismith Memorial Basketball Hall of Fame in 1982.

SEASON	G.	FGM-FGA	FG%	FTM-FTA	FT%	REB.	AVG.	PTS.	AVG.
1962-63	25	212-445	.476	258-289	.893	306	12.2	682	27.3
1963-64	29	338-648	.522	260-306	.850	360	12.4	936	32.3
1964-65	29	306-574	.533	273-308	.886	342	11.8	885	30.5
Totals	83	856-1667	.513	791-903	.876	1008	12.1	2503	30.2

Elvin Hayes

Houston
6-9 — F
Rayville, La. (Eula D. Britton H.S.)

Named national player of the year by AP, UPI and USBWA in 1968. . . . NCAA unanimous first-team All-American in 1967 and 1968. . . . Ranked among the nation's leading rebounders in 1966 (5th), 1967 (6th) and 1968 (3rd). . . . Ranked among the nation's leading scorers in 1966 (11th), 1967 (4th) and 1968 (3rd). . . . Ranked 10th in the nation in field-goal percentage in 1966. . . . Leading scorer and rebounder for third-place team in 1967 NCAA Tournament (27-4 record) and fourth-place team in 1968 NCAA Tournament (31-2). . . . Named to 1967 All-NCAA Tournament team. . . . Averaged 27.5 points and 17.4 rebounds in 13 NCAA Tournament games from 1966-68 (9-4 record). . . . Selected by the San Diego Rockets in first round of 1968 NBA draft (1st pick overall). . . . Elected to Naismith Memorial Basketball Hall of Fame in 1989.

SEASON	G.	FGM-FGA	FG%	FTM-FTA	FT%	REB.	AVG.	PTS.	AVG.
1965-66	29	323-570	.567	143-257	.556	490	16.9	789	27.2
1966-67	31	373-750	.497	135-227	.595	488	15.7	881	28.4
1967-68	33	519-945	.549	176-285	.618	624	18.9	1214	36.8
Totals	93	1215-2265	.536	454-769	.590	1602	17.2	2884	31.0

Dan Issel

Kentucky
6-9 — F/C
Batavia, Ill.

NCAA unanimous first-team All-American in 1970 and consensus second-team All-American in 1969. . . . Ranked among the nation's leading scorers in 1969 (11th) and 1970 (4th). . . . Averaged 29.3 points and 11.3 rebounds in six NCAA Tournament games from 1968-70 (3-3 record). . . . Selected by the Kentucky Colonels in first round of 1970 ABA draft. . . . Elected to Naismith Memorial Basketball Hall of Fame in 1993.

SEASON	G.	FGM-FGA	FG%	FTM-FTA	FT%	REB.	AVG.	PTS.	AVG.
1967-68	27	171-390	.438	102-154	.662	328	12.1	444	16.4
1968-69	28	285-534	.534	176-232	.759	381	13.6	746	26.6
1969-70	28	369-667	.553	210-275	.764	369	13.0	948	33.9
Totals	83	825-1591	.519	488-661	.738	1078	13.0	2138	25.8

Jerry Lucas

Ohio State
6-8 — C
Middletown, Ohio

Named national player of the year by AP, UPI and USBWA in 1961 and 1962. . . . NCAA unanimous first-team All-American in 1960, 1961 and 1962. . . . Led the nation in field-goal percentage in 1960, 1961 and 1962. . . . Led the nation in rebounding in 1961 and 1962 after finishing 11th in 1960. . . . Ranked among the nation's leading scorers in 1960 (8th), 1961 (11th) and 1962 (38th). . . . Leading scorer and rebounder for 1960 NCAA Tournament champion (25-3 record) and national runners-up in 1961 (27-1) and 1962 (26-2). . . . Final Four Most Outstanding Player in 1960 (35 points, 23 rebounds, 66.7 FG%) and 1961 (56 points, 25 rebounds, 71.4 FG%, 94.1 FT%). . . . Named to All-NCAA Tournament team in 1960, 1961 and 1962. . . . Averaged 22.2 points and 16.4 rebounds in 12 NCAA Tournament games from 1960-62 (10-2 record). . . . Tied with Oscar Robertson for scoring leadership (17 points per game) on 1960 U.S. Olympic team. . . . Selected as a territorial pick by the Cincinnati Royals in first round of 1962 NBA draft (did not play professionally in 1962-63 after signing with the Cleveland Pipers before they dropped out of the American Basketball League prior to the start of the season). . . . Elected to Naismith Memorial Basketball Hall of Fame in 1979.

SEASON	G.	FGM-FGA	FG%	FTM-FTA	FT%	REB.	AVG.	PTS.	AVG.
1959-60	27	283-444	.637	144-187	.770	442	16.4	710	26.3
1960-61	27	256-411	.623	159-208	.764	470	17.4	671	24.9

SEASON	G.	FGM-FGA	FG%	FTM-FTA	FT%	REB.	AVG.	PTS.	AVG.
1961-62	28	237-388	.611	135-169	.799	499	17.8	609	21.8
Totals	82	776-1243	.624	438-564	.777	1411	17.2	1990	24.3

Pete Maravich

Louisiana State
6-5 — G
Clemson, S.C. (Daniels H.S.); Raleigh, N.C. (Needham Broughton H.S.), and Salemburg, N.C. (Edwards Military Institute)

NCAA unanimous first-team All-American in 1968, 1969 and 1970. . . . Named national player of the year by AP, UPI and USBWA in 1970. . . . Naismith Award winner in 1970. . . . Led the nation in scoring in 1968, 1969 and 1970. . . . Did not play in NCAA Tournament. . . . Averaged 25.7 points, five rebounds and 7.7 assists in three NIT games for 1970 fourth-place team (did not play in one contest). . . . Selected by the Atlanta Hawks in first round of 1970 NBA draft (3rd pick overall). . . . Elected to Naismith Memorial Basketball Hall of Fame in 1986.

SEASON	G.	FGM-FGA	FG%	FTM-FTA	FT%	REB.	AVG.	PTS.	AVG.
1967-68	26	432-1022	.423	274-338	.811	195	7.5	1138	43.8
1968-69	26	433-976	.444	282-378	.746	169	6.5	1148	44.2
1969-70	31	522-1168	.447	337-436	.773	164	5.3	1381	44.5
Totals	83	1387-3166	.438	893-1152	.775	528	6.4	3667	44.2

Rick Mount

Purdue
6-4 — G
Lebanon, Ind.

NCAA unanimous first-team All-American in 1969 and 1970. . . . Ranked among the nation's leading scorers in 1968 (6th), 1969 (2nd) and 1970 (3rd). . . . Ranked 15th in the nation in free-throw percentage in 1969. . . . Leading scorer with a 30.5-point average in four NCAA Tournament games for 1969 national runner-up (23-5 record). . . . Named to 1969 All-NCAA Tournament team. . . . Selected by the Indiana Pacers in 1970 ABA draft.

SEASON	G.	FGM-FGA	FG%	FTM-FTA	FT%	REB.	AVG.	PTS.	AVG.
1967-68	24	259-593	.437	165-195	.846	67	2.8	683	28.5
1968-69	28	366-710	.515	200-236	.847	90	3.2	932	33.3
1969-70	20	285-582	.490	138-166	.831	54	2.7	708	35.4
Totals	72	910-1885	.483	503-597	.843	211	2.9	2323	32.3

Cazzie Russell

Michigan
6-5 — G
Chicago, Ill. (Carver H.S.)

Named national player of the year by AP, UPI and USBWA in 1966. . . . NCAA unanimous first-team All-American in 1965 and 1966, and consensus second-team All-American in 1964. . . . Ranked among the nation's leading scorers in 1964 (24th), 1965 (10th) and 1966 (3rd). . . . Ranked among the nation's leaders in free-throw percentage in 1964 (20th), 1965 (33rd) and 1966 (28th). . . . Leading scorer and third-leading rebounder for third-place team in 1964 NCAA Tournament (23-5 record) and 1965 national runner-up (24-4). . . . Named to 1965 All-NCAA Tournament team. . . . Averaged 24.6 points and 7.4 rebounds in eight NCAA Tournament games from 1964-66 (5-3 record); didn't play in 1964 national third-place game because of a swollen ankle). . . . Selected by the New York Knicks in first round of 1966 NBA draft (1st pick overall).

SEASON	G.	FGM-FGA	FG%	FTM-FTA	FT%	REB.	AVG.	PTS.	AVG.
1963-64	27	260-507	.513	150-178	.843	244	9.0	670	24.8
1964-65	27	271-558	.486	152-186	.817	213	7.9	694	25.7
1965-66	26	308-595	.518	184-223	.825	219	8.4	800	30.8
Totals	80	839-1660	.505	486-587	.828	676	8.5	2164	27.1

Wes Unseld

Louisville
6-7 — C
Louisville, Ky. (Seneca H.S.)

NCAA unanimous first-team All-American in 1967 and 1968. . . . Ranked among the nation's leading rebounders in 1966 (2nd), 1967 (3rd) and 1968 (4th). . . . Ranked 4th in the nation in field-goal percentage and 31st in scor-

ing in 1968. . . . Averaged 20.5 points and 17.5 rebounds in four NCAA Tournament games in 1967 and 1968 (1-3 record). . . . Collected 35 points and 26 rebounds in one NIT game in 1966. . . . Selected by the Baltimore Bullets in first round of 1968 NBA draft (2nd pick overall). . . . Elected to the Naismith Memorial Basketball Hall of Fame in 1987.

SEASON	G.	FGM-FGA	FG%	FTM-FTA	FT%	REB.	AVG.	PTS.	AVG.
1965-66	26	195-374	.521	128-202	.634	505	19.4	518	19.9
1966-67	28	201-374	.537	121-177	.684	533	19.0	523	18.7
1967-68	28	234-382	.613	177-275	.644	513	18.3	645	23.0
Totals	82	630-1130	.558	426-654	.651	1551	18.9	1686	20.6

Chet Walker

Bradley
6-6 — F
Benton Harbor, Mich.

NCAA unanimous first-team All-American in 1962 and consensus first-team All-American in 1961. . . . Ranked among the nation's leading scorers in 1960 (27th), 1961 (8th) and 1962 (10th). . . . Ranked among the nation's leaders in field-goal percentage in 1960 (4th), 1961 (8th) and 1962 (18th). . . . Ranked among the nation's leaders in rebound percentage in 1960 (16th) and 1961 (26th). . . . Did not play in NCAA Tournament. . . . Averaged 23.5 points in four NIT games in 1960 (champion) and 1962 (first-round loser). . . . Selected by the Syracuse Nationals in second round of 1962 NBA draft (14th pick overall).

SEASON	G.	FGM-FGA	FG%	FTM-FTA	FT%	REB.	AVG.	PTS.	AVG.
1959-60	29	244-436	.560	144-234	.615	388	13.4	632	21.8
1960-61	26	238-423	.563	180-250	.720	327	12.6	656	25.2
1961-62	26	268-500	.536	151-236	.640	321	12.3	687	26.4
Totals	81	750-1359	.552	475-720	.660	1036	12.8	1975	24.4

John Wooden

Purdue '32
Martinsville, Ind.

From 1964 to 1975, UCLA won an NCAA-record 10 national titles, including seven straight from 1967 though 1973. . . . Elected to Naismith Memorial Basketball Hall of Fame as a coach in 1972. . . . Named national coach of the year by AP in 1967, 1969, 1970, 1972 and 1973; by UPI in 1964, 1967, 1969, 1970, 1972 and 1973, by the USBWA in 1964, 1967, 1970, 1972, and 1973, and by the NABC in 1969, 1970 and 1972. . . . His 1962 team finished fourth in the NCAA Tournament and his 1974 squad finished third. . . . Won 13 conference titles in his last 14 years.

SEASON	SCHOOL	OVERALL	LEAGUE	FINISH	POSTSEASON
1946-47	Indiana State	17-8	—		DNP
1947-48	Indiana State	27-7	—		NAIA (4-1)
1948-49	UCLA	22-7	10-2	1st-S (PCC)	DNP
1949-50	UCLA	24-7	10-2	1st-S (PCC)	NCAA (0-2)
1950-51	UCLA	19-10	9-4	T1st-S (PCC)	DNP
1951-52	UCLA	19-12	8-4	1st-S (PCC)	NCAA (0-2)
1952-53	UCLA	16-8	6-6	3rd-S (PCC)	DNP
1953-54	UCLA	18-7	7-5	2nd-S (PCC)	DNP
1954-55	UCLA	21-5	11-1	1st-S (PCC)	DNP
1955-56	UCLA	22-6	16-0	1st (PCC)	NCAA (1-1)
1956-57	UCLA	22-4	13-3	T2nd (PCC)	Probation
1957-58	UCLA	16-10	10-6	3rd (PCC)	DNP
1958-59	UCLA	16-9	10-6	T3rd (PCC)	DNP
1959-60	UCLA	14-12	7-5	2nd (AAWU)	DNP
1960-61	UCLA	18-8	7-5	2nd (AAWU)	DNP
1961-62	UCLA	18-11	10-2	1st (AAWU)	NCAA (2-2)
1962-63	UCLA	20-9	8-5	T1st (AAWU)	NCAA (0-2)
1963-64	UCLA	30-0	15-0	1st (AAWU)	NCAA (4-0)
1964-65	UCLA	28-2	14-0	1st (AAWU)	NCAA (4-0)
1965-66	UCLA	18-8	10-4	2nd (AAWU)	DNP
1966-67	UCLA	30-0	14-0	1st (AAWU)	NCAA (4-0)
1967-68	UCLA	29-1	14-0	1st (AAWU)	NCAA (4-0)
1968-69	UCLA	29-1	13-1	1st (Pac-8)	NCAA (4-0)
1969-70	UCLA	28-2	12-2	1st (Pac-8)	NCAA (4-0)
1970-71	UCLA	29-1	14-0	1st (Pac-8)	NCAA (4-0)
1971-72	UCLA	30-0	14-0	1st (Pac-8)	NCAA (4-0)
1972-73	UCLA	30-0	14-0	1st (Pac-8)	NCAA (4-0)
1973-74	UCLA	26-4	12-2	1st (Pac-8)	NCAA (3-1)
1974-75	UCLA	28-3	12-2	1st (Pac-8)	NCAA (5-0)

29-Year Coaching Record: 664-162 (.804) overall; 44-15 (.746) in two years at Indiana State; 620-147 (.808) in 27 years at UCLA; 304-74 (.810) In Pacific-10 Conference; 47-10 (.825) in NCAA Tournament; 4-1 (.800) in NAIA Tournament.

5

EXPLOSION OF NATIONAL POPULARITY:

THE 1970s

Three coaching legends who combined for 2,306 victories and 16 NCAA Tournament titles retired in a six-year stretch from 1970 through 1975—Oklahoma State's Hank Iba ('70), Kentucky's Adolph Rupp ('72) and UCLA's John Wooden ('75). Meanwhile, a crop of younger coaches began to establish themselves for ultra successful stints of longer than 20 years at one university—Denny Crum (first season at Louisville was 1971-72), Bob Knight (1971-72 at Indiana), Dale Brown (1972-73 at LSU), John Thompson (1972-73 at Georgetown) and Jim Boeheim (1976-77 at Syracuse).

UCLA's invincibility began to erode midway through the 1970s after Wooden's departure although the Bruins had an unprecedented six different players become NCAA consensus first-team All-Americans in a five-year span from 1974 through 1978 (Bill Walton, Keith Wilkes, Dave Meyers, Richard Washington, Marques Johnson and David Greenwood).

The pressure to win a national crown was obscenely high for Wooden's successors. Gene Bartow (.852) and Gary Cunningham (.862) each stayed at UCLA just two seasons although they compiled higher winning percentages with the Bruins than Wooden (.808).

UCLA was the only school to have a better record than Marquette during the decade. Marquette flourished despite having three key front-court players leave school early to turn pro in consecutive seasons in the mid-'70s—Jim Chones (drafted in '72), Larry McNeill ('73) and Maurice Lucas ('74). The Warriors finished in the Top 10 of a final wire-service poll all 10 years although Al McGuire was another prominent coach who retired (after 1977 NCAA title).

The NCAA embraced a rule allowing freshman eligibility, accelerating the development of numerous standout players. Parity became more evident as many regal recruits began to bypass illustrious programs to enroll at schools where they could make significant contributions immediately.

The fresh faces became crucial to the game's popularity because of a growing exodus of standouts leaving college with eligibility remaining to join the pros. Following a lawsuit filed by Detroit's Spencer Haywood, the NBA was required by the courts to grant admission to underclassmen. Accordingly, in 1971 the league conducted a separate draft for underclassmen wishing to enter the league because of financial hardship. The next year, such players were included in the regular draft. In 1976, the hardship requirement was eliminated and the current early entry process was implemented whereby any athlete with remaining college eligibility who desires to enter the NBA draft may do so by renouncing his eligibility in a letter to the commissioner postmarked 45 days before the draft.

There wasn't always a pot of gold at the end of the rainbow for standout undergraduates. Early defectors drafted by NBA teams yet never playing in the NBA or ABA included Creighton's Cyril Baptiste (selected by San Francisco in 1971), Jacksonville's David Brent (Los Angeles in 1973), Los Angeles State's Raymond Lewis (Philadelphia in 1973), Long Beach State's Roscoe Pondexter (Boston in 1974), Ohio University's Walter Luckett (Detroit in 1975) and Illinois State's Cyrus Mann (Boston in 1975).

Scholarship limitations (ceiling of 18 in 1973 was further reduced to 15 in 1977) and the flexibility of another year of eligibility fostered player unrest as transferring escalated when athletes didn't receive as much playing time as they thought they should. Transfer players, previously regarded as untouchable lepers, fast became a symbol of the age of instant gratification. The Big Ten was hit hard by defections when Kyle Macy left Purdue for Kentucky and Larry Bird enrolled at Indiana State after leaving Indiana. By the end of the decade, there was an explosion of interest in the NCAA Tournament, highlighted by a dream duel between Bird and fellow first-team All-American Magic Johnson of Michigan State.

Illinois is one of the 10 schools with the most Top 20 appearances, but the Illini did not finish in the Top 20 of a final wire-service poll in the 1970s.

North Carolina, starting what eventually became an NCAA Tournament record for consecutive appearances in the playoffs, earned a spot as one of the nation's 10 winningest programs in a decade for the first time by finishing in the Top 20 each year. UCLA, Marquette and North Carolina were the only schools to finish in the Top 20 more often during the decade than Penn, which reached that plateau on seven occasions.

More colleges moved up to the Division I level than any other decade. The majority of them didn't have longstanding success like they enjoyed as a small school but a select circle went on to eventually reach the national semifinals of the NCAA Tournament or NIT (UAB, Fresno State, Indiana State, Louisiana Tech, UNC Charlotte, Southern Mississippi, Southwestern Louisiana and UNLV). Louisiana Tech and USL were among eight universities in the state to move up to Division I in a seven-year span from 1972-78.

There was a college arena building boom in the '70s with around 200 arenas constructed in the decade for major colleges, helping college basketball attendance reach 30 million for the first time in the 1978-79 campaign. The Big Ten has led the nation's conferences every season since 1976-77.

The remainder of the Southeastern Conference finally emerged from the dark ages and joined Vanderbilt by having African American players on their varsity rosters.

The Missouri Valley Conference suffered a series of major defections the first half of the decade. Two-time NCAA champion Cincinnati abandoned ship after the 1969-70 campaign. Memphis State (1973) and Louisville (1975) left in the aftermath of seasons when they captured MVC titles before reaching the Final Four. St. Louis finished in the first division of the MVC three consecutive years (1971 through 1973) before departing after the 1973-74 season.

The first reference to "Final Four" in an NCAA publication was an offhand comment in the national preview-review of the 1975 *Official Collegiate Basketball Guide.* The first time Final Four was capitalized was in the 1978 NCAA guide.

The decade closed with Indiana coach Bob Knight in the spotlight for one of a series of occasions in the hot seat. He was charged, and later tried and convicted in absentia, for hitting a Puerto Rican policeman before a practice at the Pan American Games. Knight was sentenced to six months in jail, but the government of Puerto Rico decided in 1987 to drop efforts to extradite him.

1969-70

NCAA Champion: UCLA (28-2; coached by John Wooden; won the Pacific-8 title by three games with a 12-2 record).

NIT Champion: Marquette (26-3; coached by Al McGuire).

New Conference: Pacific Coast Athletic Association (forerunner of Big West).

NCAA Probation: Centenary, Florida State, La Salle, Yale.

NCAA Consensus First-Team All-Americans: Dan Issel, F-C, Sr., Kentucky; Bob Lanier, C, Sr., St. Bonaventure; Pete Maravich, G, Sr., Louisiana State; Rick Mount, G, Sr., Purdue; Calvin Murphy, G, Sr., Niagara.

National Player of the Year: Maravich (44.5 ppg, 5.3 rpg, 6.2 apg).

National Coach of the Year: John Wooden, UCLA (28-2/AP, UPI, NABC, USBWA).

Purdue All-American guard Rick Mount scores two of his Big Ten record 61 points against Iowa. The Hawkeyes' Fred Brown (left) and John Johnson can only watch.

Duke, North Carolina and North Carolina State haven't always dominated the ACC. South Carolina, ranked No. 1 in preseason polls and considered the favorite to upend UCLA, lost its season opener to visiting Tennessee (55-54) before going unbeaten in ACC regular-season competition and finishing a league-record five games ahead of the Gamecocks' closest rival.

The ACC selected its representative to the NCAA playoffs at the time through its own post-season tourney and seven of the eight previous winners reached the Final Four. But the Game-cocks, featuring a starting lineup with current Georgia Tech coach Bobby Cremins as its only senior, lost against N.C. State in the ACC Tournament final (42-39 in double overtime) when Cremins collected two points, no assists and no rebounds in 49 minutes. Consensus second-team All-American John Roche, entering the ACC Tournament with a 23.8-point average, sustained a severely sprained ankle in the semifinals and

wound up averaging just nine points per contest in three ACC tourney outings. . . . South Carolina edged Notre Dame, 84-83, in the championship game of the Sugar Bowl Classic despite an almost perfect game by Irish guard Austin Carr, who hit 14 consecutive field goals in one stretch to go 19 of 24 from the floor, sank all five of his free throws, grabbed six rebounds and did not commit a turnover.

LSU's Pete Maravich set NCAA single-season records for most points (1,381) and highest average (44.5), finishing his career with NCAA career marks for most points (3,667) and highest average (44.2). He also established an NCAA record for most successful free throws in a game when he converted 30 of 31 foul shots against Oregon State. Maravich is the only player in NCAA Division I history to score more than 1,000 points and average over 40 points per game in each of three seasons. He had 56 games with at least 40 points in his three-year career, including a school- and SEC-record 69 in a 106-104 defeat at Alabama. No other player has had more than 21 games with a minimum of 40. He averaged more than 50 points per game in a 10-game stretch spanning the last three games of 1968-69 and the first seven games of 1969-70. Incredibly, Maravich improved his field-goal accuracy and assists average each year. Combining scoring and assists, Maravich was responsible for a whopping 59.4 percent of LSU's offense during his career.

Maravich (64) and Kentucky's Dan Issel (51) each scored more than 50 points in the same game on February 21 when the Wildcats won, 121-105. It was one of eight times in Issel's senior season that he scored at least 40 to help Kentucky become the most prolific scoring team in SEC history (96.8 points per game). His high was a school-record 53 at Mississippi.

Purdue's Rick Mount set a Big Ten Conference record with 61 points (13 of his 27 field goals would have been behind the current three-point line), but it wasn't enough to prevent a 108-107 setback against visiting Iowa as the Hawkeyes went unbeaten in league play in coach Ralph Miller's final season at their helm before moving to Oregon State. They compiled a 5-9 Big Ten record the previous season.

Iowa had four players average more than 17 points per game on the Hawkeyes' way to a Big Ten-record 102.9-point average. They went undefeated in the league just one year after finishing in a tie for eighth place. Iowa's John Johnson set a school single-game standard with 49 points against Northwestern. . . . Also setting school single-game scoring records were Auburn's John Mengelt (60 points vs. archrival Alabama), NYU's James Signorile (50 vs. Herbert Lehman), Boston University's Jim Hayes (47 vs. Springfield) and John Conforti of St. Francis, N.Y. (45 vs. Wagner). . . . Maravich, Notre Dame's Austin Carr (38.1 ppg), Purdue's Mount (35.4), Kentucky's Issel (33.9), SMU's Gene Phillips (28.5), Iowa's John Johnson (27.9), Butler's Billy Shepherd (27.8), Florida's Andy Owens (27), Northwestern's Dale Kelley (24.3) and Arizona State's Seabern Hill (22.8) set school records for highest scoring average in a single season. . . . Niagara's Calvin Murphy, 5-9, finished his career as the only major-college player in history shorter than 6-0 to score more than 2,500 points. He has accounted for 19 of the 21 games with more than 40 points in Purple Eagles' history.

Vanderbilt, coached by Roy Skinner, suffered its first losing record (12-14) in 22 seasons. . . . Georgia Tech center Rich Yunkus, a three-time NCAA Academic All-American, twice scored 47 points in a game (vs. Furman and North Carolina). His outburst against the Tar Heels is the highest-ever individual total versus a Dean Smith-coached team. . . . North Carolina lost five of its last seven outings to finish with an 18-9 record. It was the Tar Heels' only season in the last 30 years that

MORE THAN 50-50 Two of college basketball's most explosive guns met in a classic high-scoring affair on February 21, 1970. Kentucky, led by Dan Issel, travelled to Louisiana State, led by Pistol Pete Maravich. Although the home team lost, 121-105, fans saw Maravich pump in 64 and Issel "settle" for 51 in a winning effort.

KENTUCKY (121)	FG	FT-A	PTS.	LSU (105)	FG	FT-A	PTS.
Dinwiddie	1	2-2	4	Maravich	23	18-22	64
Parker	9	0-0	18	Sanders	5	1-3	11
Pratt	11	5-8	27	Tribbett	0	2-3	2
Key	1	5-7	7	Hester	8	1-2	17
Issel	19	13-17	51	Newton	4	1-1	9
Mills	6	2-3	14	Hickman	1	0-0	2
Hollenbeck	0	0-0	0	Lang	0	0-0	0
TOTALS	**47**	**27-37**	**121**	**TOTALS**	**41**	**23-31**	**105**

Halftime: Kentucky 56-48. **Fouled Out:** Newton.

1969–70 INDIVIDUAL LEADERS

SCORING

PLAYER	PTS.	AVG.
Maravich, LSU	1381	44.5
Carr, Notre Dame	1106	38.1
Mount, Purdue	708	35.4
Issel, Kentucky	948	33.9
Humes, Idaho St.	733	30.5
Yunkus, Georgia Tech	814	30.1
Tomjanovich, Michigan	722	30.1
Murphy, Niagara	854	29.4
Lanier, St. Bonaventure	757	29.1
Simpson, Michigan St.	667	29.0

REBOUNDING

PLAYER	REB.	AVG.
Gilmore, Jacksonville	621	22.2
Erving, Massachusetts	522	20.9

Cross, San Francisco	467	18.0
Cowens, Florida St.	447	17.2
Stiles, American	378	17.2
Childress, Colorado St.	392	17.0
Haderlein, Loyola Marymount	442	17.0
Brunson, Furman	401	16.0
Lanier, St. Bonaventure	416	16.0

FIELD GOAL PERCENTAGE

PLAYER	FGM	FGA	PCT.
Williams, Florida St.	185	291	.636
Lienhard, Georgia	215	340	.632
Bartolome, Oregon St.	178	286	.622
Chatmon, Baylor	207	345	.600
Cleamons, Ohio St.	211	353	.598
Newton, LSU	143	242	.591
Schoepfer, Boston U.	160	271	.590
Bell, Hofstra	206	353	.584
Cobb, Marquette	158	272	.581
Gilmore, Jacksonville	307	529	.580

FREE THROW PERCENTAGE

PLAYER	FTM	FTA	PCT.
Kaplan, Rutgers	102	110	.927
England, Tennessee	131	146	.897
Finney, Ohio St.	119	134	.888
Murphy, Niagara	222	252	.881
Davis, Wake Forest	196	224	.875
Vidnovic, Iowa	133	152	.875
Newlin, Utah	245	281	.872
Curnutt, Miami (Fla.)	143	166	.861
Foster, Arizona	100	117	.855
Howard, BYU	122	143	.853

1969–70 TEAM LEADERS

SCORING OFFENSE

SCHOOL	PTS.	AVG.
Jacksonville	2809	100.3
Iowa	2467	98.7
Kentucky	2709	96.8
St. Peter's	2247	93.6
Notre Dame	2711	93.5

SCORING DEFENSE

SCHOOL	PTS.	AVG.
Army	1515	54.1
South Carolina	1606	57.4
Fairleigh Dickinson	1409	61.3
Long Island	1532	61.3
Miami (Ohio)	1497	62.4

SCORING MARGIN

SCHOOL	OFF.	DEF.	MAR.
St. Bonaventure	88.4	65.9	22.5

Jacksonville	100.3	78.5	21.8
UCLA	92.0	73.4	18.6
South Carolina	74.0	57.4	16.6
Florida St.	91.7	75.2	16.5

WON-LOST PERCENTAGE

SCHOOL	W-L	PCT.
UCLA	28-2	.933
Jacksonville	27-2	.931
Kentucky	26-2	.929
Pennsylvania	25-2	.926
New Mexico St.	27-3	.900

FIELD GOAL PERCENTAGE

SCHOOL	FGM	FGA	PCT.
Ohio St.	831	1527	.544
Jacksonville	1118	2137	.523
Iowa	959	1834	.523
Georgia Tech	841	1647	.511
Columbia	748	1481	.505

FREE THROW PERCENTAGE

SCHOOL	FTM	FTA	PCT.
Ohio St.	452	559	.809
Iowa	549	704	.780
Rutgers	430	560	.768
Wake Forest	542	706	.768
Boston College	442	581	.761

REBOUNDING

SCHOOL	REB.	AVG.
Florida St.	1451	55.8
Jacksonville	1561	55.8
Western Kentucky	1386	55.4
UNLV	1421	54.7
New Mexico St.	1632	54.4

they failed to win more than 20 games. . . . Sophomore Julius Erving set a Massachusetts record with 20.9 rebounds per game in powering the 18-7 Minutemen to their most victories in 60 years of basketball. . . . New Hampshire's streak of consecutive losing seasons ended at 17 when Gerry Friel compiled a 12-11 record in his first year as coach of the Wildcats.

Jacksonville (27-2/coached by Joe Williams), New Mexico State (27-3/Lou Henson), St. Bonaventure (25-3/Larry Weise), South Carolina (25-3/Frank McGuire) and Army (22-6/Bob Knight) had their winningest seasons in school history. . . . Jacksonville became the first universi-ty to average more than 100 points per game (100.3). The Dolphins also finished runner-up in four categories—field-goal shooting, rebounding scoring margin and won-lost percentage.

Ohio State, coached by Fred Taylor, led the country in both field-goal shooting (54.4 percent) and free-throw shooting (80.9). The Buckeyes were the first team to hit at least 80 percent of its foul shots in a single season. They were the first team in Big Ten history to have three players aver-age more than 20 points per game—Dave Sorenson (24.2), Jim Cleamons (21.6) and Jody Finney (20.6). . . . Indiana finished in last place in the Big Ten for the fourth time in five seasons. . . . Memphis State finished in the Missouri Valley cellar for the third time in as many seasons, but ended its MVC losing streak at 27 games with an 85-81 victory over Wichita State. Cincinnati was runner-up to Drake in the MVC race in the Bearcats' final season as a member of the league.

Davidson of the Southern Conference became the only school since the start of the NCAA Tournament to go undefeated in back-to-back league seasons with different coaches. Terry Holland succeeded Lefty Driesell after Driesell accepted a similar position at Maryland. . . . Western Kentucky, coached by John Oldham, went unbeaten in Ohio Valley Conference competition for the second time in five seasons. . . . Virginia Tech,

coached by Howie Shannon, dropped five of its first six contests en route to compiling its only losing record (10-12) in a 31-year span from 1955-56 through 1985-86. The Hokies suffered their lone defeat to William & Mary (84-79) in a 21-game stretch of their series from 1966 through 1974. . . . Pitt, coached by Buzz Ridl, compiled a 12-12 record for its first season in six years with more than seven victories.

Southern Mississippi's Wendell Ladner (32 vs. Pan American), Minnesota's Larry Mikan (28 vs. Michigan), DePaul's Ken Warzynski (28 vs. Harvard), St. Peter's Juan Jiminez (28 vs. Upsala), New Mexico State's Sam Lacey (27 vs. Hardin-Simmons), Brigham Young's Scott Warner (27 at

1969-70 NCAA CHAMPION: UCLA

SEASON STATISTICS OF UCLA REGULARS

PLAYER	POS.	CL.	G.	FG%	FT%	PPG	RPG
Sidney Wicks	F	Jr.	30	.533	.632	18.6	11.9
John Vallely	G	Sr.	30	.486	.721	16.3	3.7
Henry Bibby	G	So.	30	.501	.833	15.6	3.5
Curtis Rowe	F	Jr.	30	.554	.641	15.3	8.7
Steve Patterson	C	Jr.	30	.496	.741	12.5	10.0
John Ecker	F	Jr.	30	.500	.774	3.5	2.5
Kenny Booker	F-G	Jr.	28	.449	.649	3.1	1.5
Terry Schofield	G	Jr.	29	.395	.850	2.7	0.8
Andy Hill	G	So.	24	.289	.714	1.8	0.6
Jon Chapman	C-F	So.	20	.344	.867	1.8	1.7
Rick Betchley	G	So.	23	.462	.625	1.5	0.7
Bill Seibert	F	Jr.	21	.316	.400	1.4	1.6
TEAM TOTALS			30	.496	.696	92.0	50.6

1970 FINAL FOUR CHAMPIONSHIP GAME

COLLEGE PARK, MD

JACKSONVILLE (69)	MIN.	FG-A	FT-A	REB.	A	PF	PTS.
Wedeking	37	6-11	0-0	2	3	2	12
Blevins	19	1-2	1-2	0	1	1	3
Morgan	37	5-11	0-0	4	11	5	10
Burrows	24	6-9	0-0	6	0	1	12
Gilmore	38	9-29	1-1	16	1	5	19
Nelson	16	3-9	2-2	5	0	1	8
Dublin	18	0-5	2-2	1	1	4	2
Baldwin	2	0-0	0-0	0	0	0	0
McIntyre	6	1-3	0-0	3	0	4	2
Hawkins	2	0-1	1-1	1	0	1	1
Selke	1	0-0	0-0	0	0	0	0
Team				2			
TOTALS	200	31-80	7-8	40	17	24	69

FG%: .388. FT%: .875. Turnovers: 18 (Morgan 8).

UCLA (80)	MIN.	FG-A	FT-A	REB.	A	PF	PTS.
Rowe	38	7-15	5-5	8	1	4	19
Patterson	38	8-15	1-4	11	2	1	17
Wicks	38	5-9	7-10	18	3	3	17
Vallely	38	5-10	5-7	7	5	2	15
Bibby	38	2-11	4-4	4	2	1	8
Booker	1	0-0	2-3	0	0	0	2
Seibert	2	0-1	0-0	1	0	1	0
Ecker	2	1-1	0-0	0	0	0	2
Betchley	1	0-0	0-1	0	0	0	0
Chapman	2	0-1	0-0	1	0	0	0
Hill	1	0-0	0-1	0	0	0	0
Schofield	1	0-0	0-0	0	0	0	0
Team				3			
TOTALS	200	28-63	24-35	53	13	12	80

FG%: .444. FT%: .686. Turnovers: 23 (Vallely 7).
Halftime: UCLA 41-36.

NATIONAL SEMIFINALS

JACKSONVILLE (91): Wedeking 7-15 1-1 15, Morgan 6-15 5-6 17, Burrows 2-4 1-1 5, McIntyre 0-3 0-0 0, Gilmore 9-14 11-15 29, Dublin 1-3 9-9 11, Nelson 1-7 10-12 12, Blevins 1-1 0-0 2, R. Baldwin 0-1 0-1 0. Team 27-63 (.429) 37-45 (.822) 91.

ST. BONAVENTURE (83): Kalbaugh 5-8 2-2 12, Hoffman 4-14 2-4 10, Gary 2-7 5-8 9, T. Baldwin 2-10 1-2 5, Gantt 8-17 0-0 16, Kull 4-7 0-0 8, Thomas 7-17 1-2 15, Grys 1-5 2-2 4, Tepas 0-0 2-2 2, Fahey 1-1 0-0 2. Team 34-86 (.395) 15-22 (.682) 83.

Halftime: Jacksonville 42-34.

UCLA (93): Rowe 4-7 7-11 15, Patterson 5-9 2-2 12, Wicks 10-12 2-5 22, Vallely 7-19 9-10 23, Bibby 8-13 3-3 19, Betchley 0-0 0-0 0, Schofield 0-0 0-0 0, Ecker 0-0 0-0 0, Seibert 0-1 0-0 0, Hill 0-0 0-1 0, Chapman 1-1 0-0 2. Team 35-63 (.556) 23-32 (.719) 93.

NEW MEXICO STATE (77): Criss 6-16 7-9 19, Collins 13-23 2-3 28, Burgess 1-6 0-0 2, Smith 4-11 2-3 10, Lacey 3-9 2-3 8, Reyes 1-6 0-0 2, Neal 2-4 0-0 4, Horne 0-4 2-2 2, Moore 1-1 0-0 2, Lefevre 0-0 0-0 0, Franco 0-0 0-0 0, McCarthy 0-0 0-0 0. Team 31-80 (.388) 15-20 (.750) 77.

Halftime: UCLA 48-41.

ALL-TOURNAMENT TEAM

Jimmy Collins, G, Sr., New Mexico State (46 points in final two games)
Artis Gilmore, C, Jr., Jacksonville (48 points, 37 rebounds)
Curtis Rowe, F, Jr., UCLA (34 points, 23 rebounds)
John Vallely, G, Sr., UCLA (38 points, 11 rebounds)
*Sidney Wicks, F, Jr., UCLA (39 points, 34 rebounds)

*Named Most Outstanding Player.

AP	UPI	SCHOOL (RECORD)	HEAD COACH
1	1	Kentucky (26-2)	Adolph Rupp
2	2	UCLA (28-2)	John Wooden
3	3	St. Bonaventure (25-3)	Larry Weise
4	5	Jacksonville (27-2)	Joe Williams
5	4	New Mexico State (27-3)	Lou Henson
6	6	South Carolina (25-3)	Frank McGuire
7	7	Iowa (20-5)	Ralph Miller
8	10	Marquette (26-3)	Al McGuire
9	8	Notre Dame (21-8)	Johnny Dee
10	12	N.C. State (23-7)	Norman Sloan
11	14	Florida State (23-3)	Hugh Durham
12	11	Houston (25-5)	Guy Lewis
13	13	Pennsylvania (25-2)	Dick Harter
14	9	Drake (22-7)	Maury John
15	–	Davidson (22-5)	Terry Holland
16	17	Utah State (22-6)	Ladell Andersen
17	17	Niagara (22-7)	Frank Layden
18	17	Western Kentucky (22-3)	John Oldham
19	15	Long Beach State (24-5)	Jerry Tarkanian
20	–	Southern Cal (18-8)	Bob Boyd
–	15	Villanova (22-7)	Jack Kraft
–	20	Cincinnati (21-6)	Tay Baker
–	20	Texas-El Paso (17-8)	Don Haskins

Texas Tech), Tulsa's Dana Lewis (26 vs. McMurry, Tex.), Iowa State's Bill Cain (26 vs. Minnesota) and Weber State's Willie Sojourner (25 vs. West Texas State) set school single-game records for most rebounds.

Idaho State, coached by Dan Miller, won its last four games to compile a 13-11 record for the Bengals' first winning season in eight years. . . . Oklahoma (19-9/coached by John MacLeod), which tied a school record for most defeats the previous season (7-19), lost fewer than 10 games for the first time in 21 years. . . . Oklahoma State's Hank Iba (767-338 record) and Butler's Tony Hinkle (557-393) retired after 41-year coaching careers. Iba served as the United States' head coach for the 1964, 1968 and 1972 Olympic Teams.

Iba, the only coach with six or more NCAA Tournament appearances to reach the regional finals every time, is hailed as the patriarch of basketball's first family of coaches. He had seven of his former Oklahoma State players eventually coach teams into the NCAA playoffs—John Floyd (Texas A&M), Jack Hartman (Kansas State), Don Haskins (Texas-El Paso), Moe Iba (Nebraska), Bud Millikan (Maryland), Doyle Parrack (Oklahoma City) and Eddie Sutton (Creighton, Arkansas, Kentucky, Oklahoma State).

Five generations of major college coaches emanate from Iba, encompassing those coaches who were either players or assistant coaches for Iba or later generations of coaches with ties to the sage. More than 40 active Division I coaches annually are branches of Iba's coaching tree. "Mr. Iba's system was so sound and he inspired such confidence that there was never any question in my mind that his philosophy offered the best opportunity to be successful," Sutton said. "The things he gave us are as valid today as they were 30 years ago."

1970 NCAA Tournament

Summary: Kentucky, after absorbing just one regular-season defeat (at Vanderbilt), was ranked No. 1 in the nation entering the tourney although starting guard Mike Casey missed the entire campaign in the wake of injuries suffered in an auto accident. UK lost to eventual NCAA Tournament runner-up Jacksonville, 106-100, in the Mideast Regional final. Casey was the Wildcats' leading scorer as a sophomore in 1967-68 with 20 points per game and their second-leading scorer as a junior the next year with a 19.1-point average. JU wound up losing to UCLA in the championship game, 80-69, when the Bruins' Sidney Wicks, 6-8, blocked five shots of 7-2 All-American center Artis Gilmore to help them overcome a nine-point deficit midway through the first half. UCLA enjoyed a 35 to 8 advantage in free-throw attempts, including a 19-2 edge in the opening half. UCLA is the only NCAA titlist to have four players who averaged more than 15 points per game—Wicks (18.6), John Vallely (16.3), Henry Bibby (15.6) and Curtis Rowe (15.3).

Star Gazing: LSU's Pete Maravich became the only three-time first-team All-American to fail to appear in the NCAA playoffs. LSU lost to UCLA by 49 points (133-84) just before Christmas.

One and Only: Notre Dame guard Austin Carr became the only player to score more than 60 points in a single playoff game and the only player to score more than 43 points at least twice. Carr, who tallied a school-record 61 points against Ohio University (Southeast Regional first round),

1970 CHAMPIONSHIP BRACKET

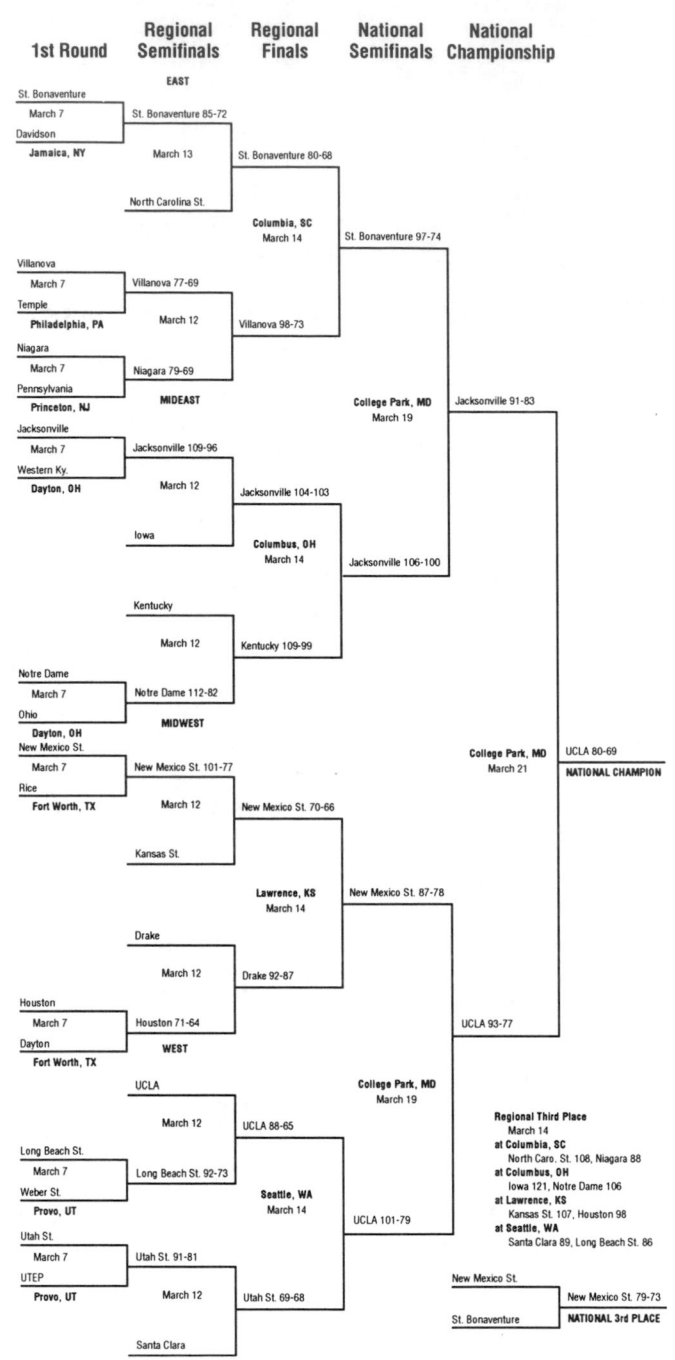

1st Round	Regional Semifinals	Regional Finals	National Semifinals	National Championship

EAST

St. Bonaventure
March 7 — St. Bonaventure 85-72
Davidson
Jamaica, NY
March 13 — St. Bonaventure 80-68
North Carolina St.

Columbia, SC
March 14 — St. Bonaventure 97-74

Villanova
March 7 — Villanova 77-69
Temple
Philadelphia, PA
March 12 — Villanova 98-73
Niagara
March 7 — Niagara 79-69
Pennsylvania
Princeton, NJ

MIDEAST

College Park, MD
March 19 — Jacksonville 91-83

Jacksonville
March 7 — Jacksonville 109-96
Western Ky.
Dayton, OH
March 12 — Jacksonville 104-103
Iowa

Columbus, OH
March 14 — Jacksonville 106-100

Kentucky
March 12 — Kentucky 109-99
Notre Dame
March 7 — Notre Dame 112-82
Ohio
Dayton, OH

MIDWEST

College Park, MD
March 21 — UCLA 80-69
NATIONAL CHAMPION

New Mexico St.
March 7 — New Mexico St. 101-77
Rice
Fort Worth, TX
March 12 — New Mexico St. 70-66
Kansas St.

Lawrence, KS
March 14 — New Mexico St. 87-78

Drake
March 12 — Drake 92-87
Houston
March 7 — Houston 71-64
Dayton
Fort Worth, TX

WEST

College Park, MD
March 19 — UCLA 93-77

UCLA
March 12 — UCLA 88-65
Long Beach St.
March 7 — Long Beach St. 92-73
Weber St.
Provo, UT

Seattle, WA
March 14 — UCLA 101-79

Utah St.
March 7 — Utah St. 91-81
UTEP
Provo, UT
March 12 — Utah St. 69-68
Santa Clara

Regional Third Place
March 14
at **Columbia, SC**
North Caro. St. 108, Niagara 88
at **Columbus, OH**
Iowa 121, Notre Dame 106
at **Lawrence, KS**
Kansas St. 107, Houston 98
at **Seattle, WA**
Santa Clara 89, Long Beach St. 86

New Mexico St.
New Mexico St. 79-73
St. Bonaventure
NATIONAL 3rd PLACE

Niagara All-American guard Calvin Murphy helped his team reach the Mideast Regional semifinals.

accounted for half of the eight games in NCAA Tournament history of more than 46 points. He scored 52 points in the next round, but it wasn't enough to prevent a 109-99 defeat against Kentucky as the Wildcats' Dan Issel scored 44 points in the only tourney game in history to have two players score more than 40. Carr's 52-point play-off outburst is the highest ever in a losing effort.

Numbers Game: The best composite winning percentage when four teams arrived at a Final Four occurred as UCLA (26-2), New Mexico State (26-2), Jacksonville (26-1) and St. Bonaventure (25-1) combined for a 103-6 record (.945). . . . New Mexico State's Sam Lacey grabbed a tourney-high 24 rebounds in an 87-78 triumph over Drake in the Midwest Regional final.

What Might Have Been: Dave Cowens-led Florida State, which split two games with national runner-up Jacksonville (losing at JU by just four points), was ineligible for the tourney because of NCAA probation. . . . St. Bonaventure's only regular-season defeat was by two points at Villanova. But the Bonnies' biggest loss against Villanova was in a 23-point victory over the Wildcats in the East Regional final when All-American center Bob Lanier tore a knee ligament in a freak accident. He was clipped accidentally by future Detroit Pistons teammate Chris Ford, who later became coach of the Boston Celtics.

Scoring Leader: Austin Carr, Notre Dame (158 points, 52.7 ppg).

Rebounding Leader: Artis Gilmore, Jacksonville (93 rebounds, 18.6 rpg).

Highest Rebounding Average: David Hall, Kansas State (40 rebounds, 20 rpg).

1970-71

AT A GLANCE

NCAA Champion: UCLA (29-1; coached by John Wooden; won the Pacific-8 title with a 14-0 record, which was two games ahead of Southern Cal).

NIT Champion: North Carolina (26-6; coached by Dean Smith; won ACC regular-season title with an 11-3 record).

New Rules: A non-jumper may not change his position during a jump ball from the time a referee is ready to make the toss until after the ball is tapped. . . . Any school offered an NCAA Tournament bid must accept it or be prohibited from participating in postseason competition.

NCAA Probation: Centenary, Florida State, Yale.

NCAA Consensus First-Team All-Americans: Austin Carr, G, Sr., Notre Dame; Artis Gilmore, C, Sr., Jacksonville; Jim McDaniels, C, Sr., Western Kentucky; Dean Meminger, G, Sr., Marquette; Sidney Wicks, F, Sr., UCLA.

National Players of the Year: Carr (38 ppg, 7.4 rpg, 51.7 FG%, 81.1 FT%/AP, UPI, Naismith) and Wicks (21.3 ppg, 12.8 rpg, 52.4 FG%/USBWA).

National Coaches of the Year: Villanova's Jack Kraft (23-6/NABC) and Marquette's Al McGuire (28-1/AP, UPI, USBWA).

Jacksonville center Artis Gilmore.

UCLA's starting frontcourt of Sidney Wicks, Curtis Rowe and Steve Patterson combined to average 51.7 points and 32.6 rebounds per game, making it more productive statistically than any of the Bruins' starting frontcourts with all-time great centers Lew Alcindor and Bill Walton.

UCLA's only defeat was an 89-82 setback at Notre Dame when the Bruins' 48-game nonconference winning streak ended. Notre Dame guard Austin Carr scored 46 points, including 15 of the Irish's last 17.

Over his final two seasons, covering 58 games, Carr scored over 40 points 23 times, broke the 30-point plateau on 46 occasions and was never held under 20. Several of Carr's finest performances came against mighty Kentucky. In four meetings with the Wildcats, he averaged 43 points and shot over 70 percent from the floor. "The fact that he (Carr) could go inside or outside and his ability to shoot with either hand is what made him such a great player," said UK coach Adolph Rupp.

Carr, runner-up to LSU's Pete Maravich in scoring the previous season with a 38-point average, was runner-up again at 38.1 to become the most prolific non-champion ever. Mississippi's Johnny Neumann averaged 40.1 points per game to become the only sophomore in NCAA history other than Maravich (43.8 in 1967-68) to average more than 40. Neumann, bolstered by a school-record 63-point outburst at LSU, was threatening Maravich's first-year mark until falling off to a 29.4 average his last five contests. Neumann, the only Ole Miss player ever to become an NCAA consensus first- or second-team All-American, had eight games with at least 46 points in his lone varsity campaign.

Neumann, Georgia Tech's Rich Yunkus (30.1 ppg), Western Kentucky's Jim McDaniels (29.3), St. Peter's Rich Rinaldi (28.6), Auburn's John Mengelt (28.4), Colorado's Cliff Meely (28), Massachusetts' Julius Erving (26.9), Boise State's Ron Austin (24.5), Wisconsin's Clarence Sherrod (23.8) and Lamar's Luke Adams (23) set school Division I records for highest scoring average in a single season.

Bill Smith isn't among the top 15 career scorers in Syracuse history, but the 7-0 center tossed in a school-record 47 points against Lafayette. Also establishing school single-game scoring standards were South Carolina's John Roche (56 points vs. Furman), St. Peter's Rich Rinaldi (54 vs. St. Francis, N.Y.), Idaho State's Willie Humes (53 at Montana State), SMU's Gene Phillips (51 at Texas), Colorado's Meely (47 vs. Oklahoma), Florida State's Ron King (46 at Georgia Southern), Fordham's Charlie Yelverton (46 at Rochester/mark tied the next year), Long Beach State's Ed Ratleff (45 vs. St. Mary's), Boise State's Ron Austin (42 vs. Montana) and Minnesota's Ollie Shannon (tied with 42 against Wisconsin). Humes' outburst is a Big Sky Conference record and Phillips' output is the highest ever in a contest between two Southwest Conference teams.

1970–71 INDIVIDUAL LEADERS

SCORING

PLAYER	PTS.	AVG.
Neumann, Mississippi	923	40.1
Carr, Notre Dame	1101	38.0
Humes, Idaho St.	777	32.4
McGinnis, Indiana	719	30.0
McDaniels, W. Kentucky	878	29.3
Rinaldi, St. Peter's	687	28.6
Mengelt, Auburn	738	28.4
Phillips, SMU	737	28.3
Meely, Colorado	729	28.0
Brown, Iowa	662	27.6

REBOUNDING

PLAYER	REB.	AVG.
Gilmore, Jacksonville	603	23.2
Washington, American	512	20.5

Erving, Massachusetts	527	19.5
Gianelli, Pacific	509	18.2
Davis, St. John's	479	17.7
Martin, Loyola (Ill.)	387	17.6
Benton, Wichita St.	437	16.8
Kennedy, TCU	416	16.6
Harris, Hardin-Simmons	205	15.8
Frazer, Fairfield	377	15.7

FIELD GOAL PERCENTAGE

PLAYER	FGM	FGA	PCT.
Belcher, Arkansas St.	174	275	.633
Wuycik, North Carolina	182	300	.607
Smith, Syracuse	222	366	.607
Kennedy, TCU	202	340	.594
Szczerbiak, G. Wash.	225	379	.594
Bush, Drake	177	299	.592
Jura, Nebraska	181	306	.592

Sanders, LSU	209	355	.589
Williams, Hardin-Simmons	191	326	.586
Penebacker, Hawaii	165	284	.581

FREE THROW PERCENTAGE

PLAYER	FTM	FTA	PCT.
Starrick, S. Illinois	119	132	.902
Tyler, Brown	128	147	.871
England, Tennessee	143	165	.867
Kaplan, Rutgers	102	118	.864
Davis, Wake Forest	188	218	.862
Wuycik, North Carolina	169	197	.858
Thomason, Pacific	118	138	.855
Bryant, E. Kentucky	122	143	.853
Lowery, Texas Tech	121	143	.846
Phillips, SMU	213	252	.845

1970–71 TEAM LEADERS

SCORING OFFENSE

SCHOOL	PTS.	AVG.
Jacksonville	2598	99.9
Kentucky	2670	95.4
Northern Illinois	2132	92.7
St. Peter's	2221	92.5
Loyola (La.)	2394	92.1

SCORING DEFENSE

SCHOOL	PTS.	AVG.
Fairleigh Dickinson	1236	53.7
Army	1403	58.5
Marquette	1820	62.8
Miami (Ohio)	1591	63.6

SCORING MARGIN

SCHOOL	OFF.	DEF.	MAR.
Jacksonville	99.9	79.0	20.9

Marquette	81.7	62.8	18.9
UCLA	83.5	68.5	15.0
Pennsylvania	81.4	66.8	14.6
Massachusetts	79.7	65.1	14.6

WON-LOST PERCENTAGE

SCHOOL	W-L	PCT.
UCLA	29-1	.967
Marquette	28-1	.966
Pennsylvania	28-1	.966
Southern California	24-2	.923
Kansas	27-3	.900

FIELD GOAL PERCENTAGE

SCHOOL	FGM	FGA	PCT.
Jacksonville	1077	2008	.536
North Carolina	1010	1935	.522
Louisiana St.	897	1725	.520
Loyola (La.)	956	1880	.509
Kentucky	1077	2129	.506

FREE THROW PERCENTAGE

SCHOOL	FTM	FTA	PCT.
Tennessee	538	679	.792
Southern Illinois	460	597	.771
Southern Methodist	552	719	.768
Duke	539	704	.766

REBOUNDING

SCHOOL	REB.	AVG.
Pacific	1643	58.7
West Texas St.	1502	57.8
Hawaii	1596	57.0
Arizona St.	1477	56.8
Los Angeles St.	1458	56.1

Artis Gilmore, a junior college transfer, finished his two-year career at Jacksonville with an NCAA career rebounding average of 22.7 per game. He is the only player in major-college history to finish his career with averages of more than 22 points and 22 rebounds per game. Gilmore, who grabbed a school-record 34 rebounds against St. Peter's, helped Jacksonville win an unprecedented three national team statistical titles—offense (99.9-point average), scoring margin (20.9) and field-goal shooting (53.6 percent). . . . Also causing something of a sensation at JU was freshman David Brent, a 7-0 center from St. Louis who averaged 36 points and 17 rebounds in head-to-head duels with Gilmore in two frosh-varsity games. Brent, however, never played varsity college basketball.

Big Ten champion Ohio State's only league loss was to visiting Michigan State, 82-70, although the Spartans sustained their fourth of six consecutive losing records in conference competition. . . . Indiana, after losing its previous seven outings against Iowa, started an 11-game winning streak in their series. The Hoosiers also began a 20-game winning streak in their series with Northwestern. . . . Eldon Miller was in his first season as coach at Western Michigan when the Broncos registered a 14-10 mark for their first winning record in nine years.

Defending ACC regular-season champion South Carolina lost its first four league road games, including a 31-30 overtime verdict at Maryland. The Terrapins, finishing in the ACC's second division for the sixth consecutive year, hit 15 of 18 field-goal attempts (83.3 percent) against South Carolina. The Gamecocks finished runner-up to North Carolina in their final season as a member of the ACC. . . . North Carolina forward Dennis Wuycik was second from the floor nationally at 60.7 percent and sixth from the foul line at 85.8 percent. . . . North Carolina started a 20-game winning streak in its series with Georgia Tech that extended through 1984. . . . Virginia, coached by Bill Gibson, won 11 of its first 13 games to crack the Top 20 for the first time ever. The Cavaliers faded down the stretch to finish with a 15-11 record, but it was their first winning season in 17 years.

TCU's Eugene "Goo" Kennedy set a SWC standard by grabbing a school-record 28 rebounds against Arkansas. Kennedy finished the season with a league-record average of 16 rebounds per game. He was one of five different TCU players in as many years from 1968-72 to lead the SWC in rebounding. . . . Arkansas sustained a school-record nine consecutive SWC defeats. The Razorbacks were 1-13 in the SWC despite losing just two league games by a double-digit margin. One of their setbacks was in overtime against Baylor, 111-110. . . . Memphis State compiled an 18-8 record in Gene Bartow's first season as coach of the Tigers. They had sustained at least 17 defeats each of the previous three years.

Fairleigh Dickinson shattered Army's streak of three consecutive scoring defense championships. FDU coach Al LoBalbo previously served as an assistant at Army under Bob Knight. . . . Harvard, which has never captured an Ivy League title, posted its only undisputed second-place finish with an 11-3 conference record under coach Robert Harrison.

Arizona State, coached by Ned Wulk, ended a streak of six consecutive losing seasons by compiling a 16-10 record. . . . Colorado State's Mike Childress set a Western Athletic Conference single-season standard by averaging 14.1 rebounds per game.

LaRue Martin's school-record 34 rebounds against Valparaiso weren't enough to keep Loyola of Chicago from losing its 14th consecutive game. Also establishing school single-game rebounding records were Lafayette's Ron Moyer (33 at Gettysburg), UMass' Erving (32 vs. Syracuse), Wichita State's Terry Benton (29 vs. North Texas State), Memphis State's Ronnie Robinson (28 vs. Tulsa), Kansas State's David Hall (27 vs. Oklahoma), Toledo's Doug Hess (tied with 27 vs. Marshall) and Texas' Lynn Howden (24 vs. Florida State). Hall later became a professor of law at Northeastern.

Miami (Fla.) dropped its program at the conclusion of the campaign because of dwindling success and finances. The Hurricanes, coached by Ron Godfrey, had their first losing record in 15 years the previous season. . . . Alabama suffered its most lopsided defeat in history (122-75 at Southern Cal) but later won at Mississippi, 101-91, for the Crimson Tide's first road victory in four seasons. . . . Five of Western Kentucky's six defeats were by three points or less.

Guard Dean Meminger became the first Marquette player to become an NCAA consensus first- or second-team All-American. . . . Marquette (28-1/coached by Al McGuire), Pennsylvania (28-1/Dick Harter), Fordham (26-3/Digger Phelps) and Southern California (24-2/Bob Boyd) had their winningest seasons in school history.

Forward Howard Porter was the first Villanova player since 1950 to become an NCAA consensus first- or second-team All-American. He grabbed a school single-game record of 30 rebounds against St. Peter's. . . . NYU competed in its final season at the major-college level.

Joe Williams became the only person to be coach of two different universities in back-to-back years when each school made its initial playoff appearance—Jacksonville '70 and Furman '71. Furman compiled a 15-12 record to end a streak of eight consecutive non-winning seasons.

1970–71 NCAA CHAMPION: UCLA

SEASON STATISTICS OF UCLA REGULARS

PLAYER	POS.	CL.	G.	FG%	FT%	PPG	RPG
Sidney Wicks	F	Sr.	30	.524	.661	21.3	12.8
Curtis Rowe	F	Sr.	30	.523	.627	17.5	10.0
Steve Patterson	C	Sr.	30	.420	.620	13.0	9.8
Henry Bibby	G	Jr.	30	.376	.835	11.8	3.5
Terry Schofield	G	Sr.	30	.432	.561	6.2	2.4
Kenny Booker	G	Sr.	30	.441	.480	5.5	2.6
Larry Farmer	F	So.	22	.402	.481	3.6	3.7
John Ecker	F	Sr.	26	.438	.882	2.8	2.0
Rick Betchley	G	Jr.	20	.538	.467	1.8	0.7
Larry Hollyfield	F-G	So.	11	.273	.250	1.7	0.7
Andy Hill	G	Jr.	19	.438	.850	1.6	0.2
Jon Chapman	F-C	Jr.	18	.200	.000	0.4	1.3
TEAM TOTALS			30	.453	.651	83.5	52.5

1971 FINAL FOUR CHAMPIONSHIP GAME

HOUSTON, TX

VILLANOVA (62)	MIN.	FG-A	FT-A	REB.	A	PF	PTS.
Smith	40	4-11	1-1	2	0	4	9
Porter	40	10-21	5-6	8	0	1	25
Siemiontkowski	37	9-16	1-2	6	0	3	19
Inglesby	40	3-9	1-1	4	7	2	7
Ford	40	0-4	2-3	5	10	4	2
McDowell	3	0-1	0-0	2	1	0	0
Team				4			
TOTALS	200	26-62	10-13	31	18	14	62

FG%: .419. FT%: .769. **Turnovers:** 10 (Ford 7).

UCLA (68)	MIN.	FG-A	FT-A	REB.	A	PF	PTS.
Rowe	40	2-3	4-5	8	2	0	8
Wicks	40	3-7	1-1	9	7	2	7
Patterson	40	13-18	3-5	8	4	1	29
Bibby	40	6-12	5-5	2	3	1	17
Booker	5	0-0	0-0	0	0	0	0
Schofield	26	3-9	0-0	1	4	4	6
Betchley	9	0-0	1-2	1	0	1	1
Team				5			
TOTALS	200	27-49	14-18	34	20	9	68

FG%: .551. **FT%:** .778. **Turnovers:** 13.
Halftime: UCLA 45-37.

NATIONAL SEMIFINALS

WESTERN KENTUCKY (89): Glover 5-15 2-4 12, Dunn 11-33 3-6 25, McDaniels 10-24 2-4 22, Rose 8-21 2-3 18, Bailey 5-11 2-3 12, Witt 0-1 0-0 0, Sundmacker 0-0 0-0 0. Team 39-105 (.371) 11-20 (.550) 89.

VILLANOVA (92): Smith 5-14 3-6 13, Porter 10-20 2-3 22, Siemiontkowski 11-20 9-10 31, Inglesby 5-10 4-7 14, Ford 3-6 2-2 8, McDowell 2-3 0-3 4. Team 36-73 (.493) 20-31 (.645) 92.

Halftime: Western Kentucky 38-35. **Regulation:** Tied 74-74. **First Overtime:** Tied 85-85.

KANSAS (60): Robisch 7-19 3-6 17, Russell 5-12 2-2 12, Brown 3-8 1-3 7, Stallworth 5-10 2-4 12, Nash 3-9 1-2 7, Kivisto 1-1 1-4 3, Canfield 0-0 0-0 0, Williams 0-1 2-2 2, Mathews 0-0 0-0 0, Douglas 0-0 0-0 0. Team 24-60 (.400) 12-23 (.522) 60.

UCLA (68): Rowe 7-10 2-4 16, Wicks 5-9 11-13 21, Patterson 3-11 0-0 6, Bibby 6-9 6-6 18, Booker 1-2 1-2 3, Schofield 1-3 0-1 2, Farmer 0-2 0-1 0, Betchley 0-0 0-1 0, Ecker 0-1 2-2 2, Hill 0-0 0-0 0, Chapman 0-0 0-0 0. Team 23-47 (.489) 22-30 (.733) 68.

Halftime: UCLA 32-25.

ALL-TOURNAMENT TEAM

Jim McDaniels, C, Sr., Western Kentucky (58 points, 36 rebounds in final two games)
Steve Patterson, C, Sr., UCLA (35 points, 14 rebounds)
*Howard Porter, F, Sr., Villanova (47 points, 24 rebounds)
Hank Siemiontkowski, C, Jr., Villanova (50 points, 21 rebounds)
Sidney Wicks, F, Sr., UCLA (28 points, 17 rebounds, 10 assists)

*Named Most Outstanding Player.

1970-71 FINAL NATIONAL POLLS

AP	UPI	SCHOOL (RECORD)	HEAD COACH
1	1	UCLA (29-1)	John Wooden
2	2	Marquette (28-1)	Al McGuire
3	3	Pennsylvania (28-1)	Dick Harter
4	4	Kansas (27-3)	Ted Owens
5	5	Southern Cal (24-2)	Bob Boyd
6	6	South Carolina (23-6)	Frank McGuire
7	7	Western Kentucky (24-6)	John Oldham
8	8	Kentucky (22-6)	Adolph Rupp
9	9	Fordham (26-3)	Digger Phelps
10	10	Ohio State (20-6)	Fred Taylor
11	11	Jacksonville (22-4)	Tom Wasdin
12	14	Notre Dame (20-9)	Johnny Dee
13	13	North Carolina (26-6)	Dean Smith
14	18	Houston (22-7)	Guy Lewis
15	18	Duquesne (21-4)	Red Manning
16	14	Long Beach State (23-5)	Jerry Tarkanian
17	–	Tennessee (21-7)	Ray Mears
18	17	Villanova (23-6)	Jack Kraft
19	16	Drake (21-8)	Maury John
20	11	Brigham Young (18-11)	Stan Watts
–	20	Weber State (21-6)	Phil Johnson

Brigham Young, coached by Stan Watts, captured the WAC title after finishing in seventh place the previous year. . . . Utah's Jack Gardner, who previously coached at Kansas State, ended his 28-year coaching career with a 486-235 record.

1971 NCAA Tournament

Summary: UCLA became the only team to win a national title although its season-leading scorer was held more than 10 points below his average in the championship game, a 68-62 victory over Villanova. Eight of the 10 starters played the entire final. Sidney Wicks, named national player of the year by the U.S. Basketball Writers Association, managed just seven points in a 68-62 victory over Villanova to finish the campaign with a 21.3-point average. The Final Four was tainted when it was disclosed that Villanova star Howard Porter and Western Kentucky standout Jim McDaniels had signed pro contracts before the tourney.

Star Gazing: Julius Erving, leaving Massachusetts with one season of eligibility remaining, didn't participate in the NCAA playoffs despite helping the Minutemen to a composite 41-11 record in 1970 and 1971. He is the only player to score more than 30,000 points in his pro career after never appearing in the NCAA playoffs. UMass was mauled in the first round of the NIT by eventual champion North Carolina, 90-49. . . . Jacksonville blew a 14-point halftime cushion and lost in the first round of the Mideast Regional against eventual Final Four team Western Kentucky (74-72). Western Kentucky's McDaniels outscored Jacksonville's Artis Gilmore, 23-12, in a battle of seven-foot first-team All-Americans.

Biggest Upsets: Marquette, undefeated entering the tourney (26-0), lost in the Mideast Regional semifinals against Ohio State (60-59) after the Warriors' playmaker, unanimous first-team All-American Dean "The Dream" Meminger, fouled out with five minutes remaining. Teammate Allie McGuire, the coach's son, committed a costly turnover in the closing seconds before Buckeyes guard Allan Hornyak converted a pair of crucial free throws to end Marquette's 39-game winning streak. . . . Penn, undefeated entering the tourney (26-0) under coach Dick Harter, lost in the East Regional final against Villanova (90-47) when none of the Quakers' players scored more than eight points. Porter, the Final Four Most Outstanding Player, scored 35 points for the Wildcats to more than double the output (16) of

UCLA's Sidney Wicks takes careful aim over the outstretched arm of a New Mexico State defender.

three Penn players who wound up in the NBA—Corky Calhoun, Phil Hankinson and Dave Wohl.

One and Only: UCLA center Steve Patterson became the only player to have a single-digit point total in a national semifinal game (six vs. Kansas) and then increase his output by more than 20 points in the championship game (career- and game-high 29 vs. Villanova). "It just shows you what a good team can do," Villanova coach Jack Kraft said. "You hold down Wicks and (Curtis)

1971 CHAMPIONSHIP BRACKET

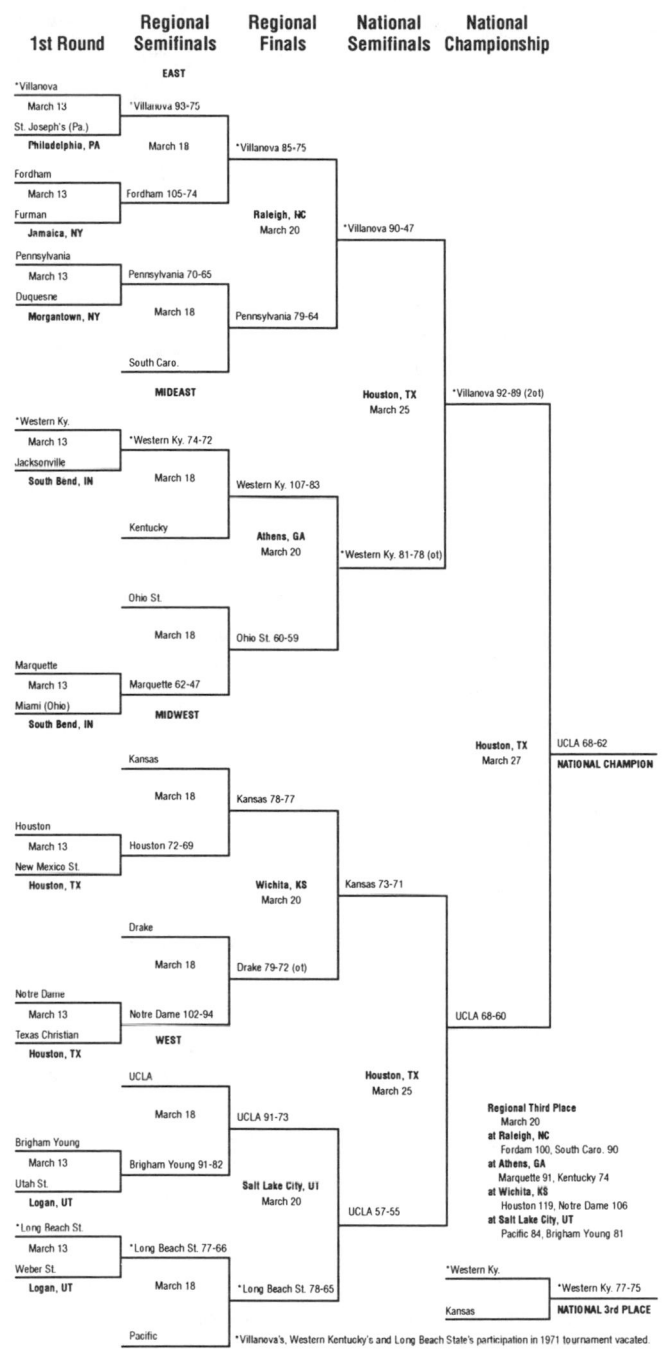

1st Round	Regional Semifinals	Regional Finals	National Semifinals	National Championship

EAST

*Villanova
March 13
St. Joseph's (Pa.)
Philadelphia, PA

*Villanova 93-75
March 18

Fordham
March 13
Furman
Jamaica, NY

Fordham 105-74

*Villanova 85-75

Raleigh, NC
March 20

Pennsylvania
March 13
Duquesne
Morgantown, NY

Pennsylvania 70-65
March 18

Pennsylvania 79-64

South Caro.

*Villanova 90-47

MIDEAST

Houston, TX
March 25

*Villanova 92-89 (2ot)

*Western Ky.
March 13
Jacksonville
South Bend, IN

*Western Ky. 74-72
March 18

Western Ky. 107-83

Kentucky

Athens, GA
March 20

*Western Ky. 81-78 (ot)

Ohio St.

March 18

Ohio St. 60-59

Marquette
March 13
Miami (Ohio)
South Bend, IN

Marquette 62-47

MIDWEST

Kansas

March 18

Kansas 78-77

Houston
March 13
New Mexico St.
Houston, TX

Houston 72-69

Wichita, KS
March 20

Kansas 73-71

Drake

March 18

Drake 79-72 (ot)

Notre Dame
March 13
Texas Christian
Houston, TX

Notre Dame 102-94

WEST

Houston, TX
March 25

UCLA 68-60

UCLA

March 18

UCLA 91-73

Brigham Young
March 13
Utah St.
Logan, UT

Brigham Young 91-82

Salt Lake City, UT
March 20

UCLA 57-55

*Long Beach St.
March 13
Weber St.
Logan, UT

*Long Beach St. 77-66
March 18

*Long Beach St. 78-65

Pacific

Houston, TX
March 27

UCLA 68-62
NATIONAL CHAMPION

UCLA 68-62

Regional Third Place
March 20
at Raleigh, NC
Fordham 100, South Caro. 90
at Athens, GA
Marquette 91, Kentucky 74
at Wichita, KS
Houston 119, Notre Dame 106
at Salt Lake City, UT
Pacific 84, Brigham Young 81

*Western Ky.

*Western Ky. 77-75

Kansas

NATIONAL 3rd PLACE

*Villanova's, Western Kentucky's and Long Beach State's participation in 1971 tournament vacated.

Rowe as well as we did and that third guy (Patterson) kills you." . . . Western Kentucky, coached by John Oldham, became the only Ohio Valley Conference to reach the Final Four. . . . Wicks is the only individual to play for three NCAA titlists after playing in junior college.

Numbers Game: The closest result for UCLA during the Bruins' 38-game tourney winning streak from 1967-73 came in the West Regional final when they had to erase an 11-point deficit despite 29 percent field-goal shooting to edge Long Beach State (57-55). . . . Drake, coached by Maury John, became the only school to appear in at least three NCAA Tournaments and reach a regional final each time. The Bulldogs, who won the national third-place game in 1969, lost in the Midwest Regional finals in 1970 (against New Mexico State) and 1971 (against Kansas) when their opponents each had just two defeats. . . . Three of Kansas' four playoff games were decided by a total of five points. . . . South Carolina appeared in the NCAA Tournament for the first time, becoming the only school to make its inital NCAA playoff appearance in its final year as a league member (ACC) before embracing independent status the next season. The Gamecocks, coached by Frank McGuire, lost the East Regional third-place game to Fordham when the Rams hit all 22 of their free-throw attempts. . . . Notre Dame guard Austin Carr had the two highest-scoring games in the tourney—52 points in a 102-94 triumph over TCU and 47 in a 119-106 setback against Houston. Poo Welch tallied 38 for Houston against the Irish in the Midwest Regional third-place game. . . . BYU's Kresimir Cosic grabbed a playoff-high 23 rebounds in a 91-73 loss to UCLA in the West Regional semifinals.

What Might Have Been: Southern Cal posted its best record in school history (24-2, .923). USC's defeats were by single-digit margins in Pacific-8 Conference competition against national champion-to-be UCLA. The Trojans ranked 5th in both polls. . . . Houston, minus its third-best scorer and top outside threat Jeff Hickman (declared academically ineligible after the first semester), lost to Final Four-bound Kansas by one point (78-77)

in the Midwest Regional semifinals. The Cougars defeated eventual national runner-up Villanova by 15 points on a neutral court early in the season.

Scoring Leader: Jim McDaniels, Western Kentucky (147 points, 29.4 ppg).

Highest Scoring Average: Austin Carr, Notre Dame (125 points, 41.7 ppg).

Rebounding Leader: Clarence Glover, Western Kentucky (89 rebounds, 17.8 rpg).

1971-72

AT A GLANCE

NCAA Champion: UCLA (30-0; coached by John Wooden; won Pacific-8 title with a 14-0 record, which was four games ahead of Washington).

NIT Champion: Maryland (27-5; coached by Lefty Driesell; finished in a tie for second place in ACC with an 8-4 record, which was one game behind North Carolina).

NCAA Consensus First-Team All-Americans: Henry Bibby, G, Sr., UCLA; Jim Chones, C, Jr., Marquette; Dwight "Bo" Lamar, G, Jr., Southwestern Louisiana; Bob McAdoo, C, Jr., North Carolina; Ed Ratleff, F-G, Jr., Long Beach State; Tom Riker, C, Sr., South Carolina; Bill Walton, C, Soph., UCLA.

National Player of the Year: Walton (21.1 ppg, 15.5 rpg, 64.0 FG%).

National Coach of the Year: John Wooden, UCLA (30-0/AP, UPI, NABC, USBWA).

Kentucky's Adolph Rupp, called the "Baron of the Bluegrass," retired after a 41-year coaching career with a 875-190 record. Rupp won four NCAA Tournament championships but had a losing NCAA playoff record (10-12) after capturing his last national title in 1958.

UCLA's Bill Walton joined Oscar Robertson (Cincinnati '58) as the only players in history to be named national player of the year in their first season of varsity competition. UCLA set an NCAA single-season record for highest average scoring margin (30.3). Incredibly, the Bruins' average halftime margin (17.4) was greater than any other team over an entire game excluding North Carolina's 17.7.

Long before premier pivotmen such as Georgetown's Patrick Ewing (Jamaica), Dikembe Mutombo (Zaire), Houston's Hakeem Olajuwon (Nigeria), Marist's Rik Smits (Netherlands), New Mexico's Luc Longley (Australia), George Washington's Yinka Dare (Nigeria) and Wake Forest's Tim Duncan (Virgin Islands) arrived from outposts off the mainland U.S., there was an influential international big man by the name of Kresimir Cosic. The Yugoslavian ranked 42nd in the country by averaging 22.3 points per game as a junior for Brigham Young.

The nation's top three scorers represented teams playing their initial season at the major-college level—Southwestern Louisiana's Bo Lamar (36.3), Oral Roberts' Richie Fuqua (35.9) and Illinois State's Doug Collins (32.6). Fuqua nearly caught Lamar by averaging 41.4 points to Lamar's 38.7 in their last 10 outings. . . . Lamar and fellow junior Ed Ratleff of Long Beach State became the only set of former high school teammates to be named NCAA consensus first-team All-Americans together. USL's 90-83 early-season victory over visiting Long Beach might have been one of the best intersectional matchups few people have ever heard about. Lamar and Ratleff attended East High in Columbus, O., where another one of their teammates was Nick Conner, a starter for Illinois. They were seniors on a 1968-69 high school squad that went undefeated (25-0 record), won the Ohio AA title and extended its winning streak to 49 games. . . . Lamar's explosiveness sparked USL to a 25-4 record for the second consecutive season. He scored 51 points in back-to-back road games at Louisiana Tech and Lamar.

Collins was the star player for Will Robinson, the first black head coach at a predominantly white Division I school. ISU had its first black player before 1920. Oddly, Rich Herrin, Collins' high school coach at Benton (Ill.), never had an opportunity to coach an African American player in his 29 small-town seasons of high-school

Oral Roberts star Richie Fuqua shoots from the outside.

coaching before he was hired by Southern Illinois after the 1984-85 campaign. . . . USL's Lamar, ORU's Fuqua, ISU's Collins, West Virginia's Wil Robinson (29.4 ppg), Central Michigan's Ben Kelso (25.4), Brown's Arnie Berman (25.3), Texas Tech's Greg Lowery (24.5), Georgia Southern's Johnny Mills (24.3) and Harvard's Jim Fitzsimmons (24.2) set school Division I records for highest scoring average in a single season.

Kansas' Bud Stallworth set a Big Eight Conference game record with 50 points against Missouri. Mizzou, however, made its first Top 20 appearance in a final wire-service poll. . . . Jacksonville's Ernie Fleming (national-high 59 points vs. St. Peter's), Florida's Tony Miller (54 vs. Chicago State), Virginia's Barry Parkhill (51 vs. Baldwin-Wallace), New Mexico State's John Williamson (48 at California), Georgia's Ronnie Hogue (46 vs. LSU) and Fairfield's George Groom (41 vs. Assumption) set school single-

1971–72 INDIVIDUAL LEADERS

SCORING

PLAYER	PTS.	AVG.
Lamar, Southwestern La.	1054	36.3
Fuqua, Oral Roberts	1006	35.9
Collins, Illinois St.	847	32.6
Robinson, West Virginia	706	29.4
Averitt, Pepperdine	693	28.9
Williamson, New Mexico St.	678	27.1
Kohls, Syracuse	748	26.7
Miller, Florida	507	26.7
Taylor, Murray St.	538	25.6
Martiniuk, St. Peter's	611	25.5

REBOUNDING

PLAYER	REB.	AVG.
Washington, American	455	19.8
Gianelli, Pacific	466	17.9

Davidson, West Texas St.	420	17.5
Davis, St. John's	460	17.0
Bradley, Northern Illinois	398	15.9
Jones, Loyola Marymount	395	15.8
Barnes, Providence	424	15.7
Martin, Loyola (Ill.)	329	15.7
Walton, UCLA	466	15.5
Hyland, Iona	350	15.2

FIELD GOAL PERCENTAGE

PLAYER	FGM	FGA	PCT.
Martens, Abilene Christian	136	204	.667
Fullarton, Xavier	149	229	.651
Stewart, Santa Clara	202	312	.647
Walton, UCLA	238	372	.640
Shaeffer, St. John's	186	294	.633
Jackson, Los Angeles St.	222	362	.613
Ebron, Southwestern La.	283	464	.610

Wuycik, North Carolina	189	310	.610
Robinson, Memphis St.	170	279	.609
Traylor, South Carolina	174	292	.596
Sanders, LSU	171	287	.596

FREE THROW PERCENTAGE

PLAYER	FTM	FTA	PCT.
Starrick, Southern Ill.	148	160	.925
Denny, South Alabama	117	128	.914
Garrett, Southern Ill.	130	146	.890
Bullington, Ball St.	142	161	.882
Sherwin, Army	110	125	.880
Roberts, New Mexico	118	135	.874
Bush, Indiana St.	107	123	.870
Rogers, St. Louis	124	143	.867
Edwards, Tennessee	103	119	.866
Kohls, Syracuse	222	257	.864

1971–72 TEAM LEADERS

SCORING OFFENSE

SCHOOL	PTS.	AVG.
Oral Roberts	2943	105.1
Southwestern Louisiana	2840	97.9
Northern Illinois	2380	95.2
UCLA	2838	94.6
Furman	2592	92.6
Houston	2499	92.6

SCORING DEFENSE

SCHOOL	PTS.	AVG.
Minnesota	1451	58.0
Fairleigh Dickinson	1410	58.8
Texas-El Paso	1636	60.6
Marquette	1836	63.3
Pennsylvania	1780	63.6
Temple	1973	63.6

SCORING MARGIN

SCHOOL	OFF.	DEF.	MAR.
UCLA	94.6	64.3	30.3

North Carolina	89.1	71.4	17.7
Marshall	92.4	76.4	16.0
Florida St.	86.9	71.4	15.5
Long Beach St.	84.9	69.8	15.1

WON-LOST PERCENTAGE

SCHOOL	W-L	PCT.
UCLA	30-0	1.000
Oral Roberts	26-2	.929
Pennsylvania	25-3	.893
Hawaii	24-3	.889
Marquette	25-4	.862
Long Beach St.	25-4	.862
Southwestern Louisiana	25-4	.862

FIELD GOAL PERCENTAGE

SCHOOL	FGM	FGA	PCT.
North Carolina	1031	1954	.528
Abilene Christian	792	1566	.506
South Carolina	894	1773	.504
UCLA	1140	2262	.504
Southwestern Louisiana	1153	2295	.502

FREE THROW PERCENTAGE

SCHOOL	FTM	FTA	PCT.
Lafayette	656	844	.777
Brown	560	725	.772
Southern Illinois	522	687	.760
St. Louis	507	669	.758
Tennessee	450	594	.758

REBOUNDING

SCHOOL	REB.	AVG.
Oral Roberts	1686	60.2
West Texas St.	1444	57.8
Pacific	1495	57.5
Hawaii	1462	56.2
Houston	1515	56.1

game scoring standards. . . . Parkhill, the first Virginia player to become an NCAA consensus first- or second-team All-American, led the ACC in scoring (21.6 ppg) en route to guiding the Cavaliers to their first-ever Top 20 ranking in a final wire-service poll. Virginia won at Duke for the first time in 32 years and joined the 20-win club for the first time in 44 seasons. The Cavs managed a winning ACC record (8-4) for the only time in the first 25 years of the league's existence.

Southern Illinois' Greg Starrick, who began his college career at Kentucky, finished his career with 90.9 percent free-throw accuracy, an NCAA record. . . . Detroit ended Marquette's 56-game regular-season winning streak, 70-49, and Temple stopped Penn's 48-game regular-season winning streak, 57-52. Marquette's other regular-season defeat was in its regular-season finale at New Mexico State, 73-69. . . . Minnesota center Jim Brewer was annointed as Most Valuable Player in the Big Ten, but he wasn't named to the first- or second-five for either the AP or UPI all-conference teams. Brewer became the only player in the history of the conference's MVP award (first awarded in the 1945-46 season) to capture the honor with a scoring average under 10 points per game (8.5). The Gophers made their initial NCAA

UCLA star Bill Walton blocks a shot.

Tournament appearance after capturing their first Big Ten title in 35 years. Their season, however, was tainted by involvement in a brawl in a game with visiting Ohio State. The contest was stopped with 36 seconds remaining and the Buckeyes leading, 50-44, after a melee so violent that three OSU players were hospitalized. Ohio State junior center Luke Witte was knocked to the floor, kneed in the groin and incurred a concussion when stomped on his head. Minnesota's Corky Taylor and Ron Behagen were suspended for the remainder of the season. Witte eventually became a reverend. . . . Michigan State's Mike Robinson (27.2 points per game) became the third sophomore in five years to lead the Big Ten in scoring.

North Carolina's three ACC defeats were on the road by a total of five points—at Duke, Mary-land (in overtime) and North Carolina State. . . . Maryland, after losing 27 of its previous 33 meetings with North Carolina State, swept the Wolf-pack. . . . Providence's Marvin Barnes notched school records of 34 rebounds and 12 blocked shots in a 76-58 victory over Buffalo State. . . . Dartmouth, coached by George Blaney, defeated Connecticut for the ninth straight time, 107-89.

Pacific's John Gianelli set a single-season Big West Conference record by averaging 17.9 rebounds per game. Pacific (17-9) posted its last season with fewer than 10 defeats. . . . Hawaii's Bob Nash (30 vs. Arizona State) and Southwestern Louisiana's Roy Ebron (28 at Northwestern State) set school single-game rebounding records.

Notre Dame lost back-to-back road games at Indiana (94-29) and UCLA (114-56) by a total of

1971–72 NCAA CHAMPION: UCLA

SEASON STATISTICS OF UCLA REGULARS

PLAYER	POS.	CL.	G.	FG%	FT%	PPG	RPG
Bill Walton	C	So.	30	.640	.704	21.1	15.5
Henry Bibby	G	Sr.	30	.450	.806	15.7	3.5
Keith Wilkes	F	So.	30	.531	.696	13.5	8.2
Larry Farmer	F	Jr.	30	.456	.549	10.7	5.5
Greg Lee	G	So.	29	.492	.824	8.7	2.0
Larry Hollyfield	F	Jr.	30	.514	.651	7.3	3.3
Swen Nater	C	Jr.	29	.535	.609	6.7	4.8
Tommy Curtis	G	So.	30	.437	.636	4.1	2.1
Andy Hill	G	Sr.	26	.356	.709	2.7	0.8
Vince Carson	F	So.	28	.400	.667	2.4	2.6
Jon Chapman	F	Sr.	28	.465	.500	1.6	1.6
Gary Franklin	F	So.	26	.412	.438	1.3	1.0
TEAM TOTALS			30	.504	.695	94.6	54.9

1972 FINAL FOUR CHAMPIONSHIP GAME

LOS ANGELES, CA

FLORIDA STATE (76)	MIN.	FG-A	FT-A	REB.	A	PF	PTS.
Garrett	37	1-9	1-1	5	0	1	3
King	31	12-20	3-3	6	1	1	27
Royals	33	5-7	5-6	10	2	5	15
McCray	23	3-6	2-5	6	3	4	8
Samuel	31	3-10	0-0	1	7	1	6
Harris	26	7-13	2-3	6	1	1	16
Petty	9	0-0	1-1	0	2	1	1
Cole	10	0-2	0-0	2	1	1	0
Team				6			
TOTALS	200	31-67	14-19	42	17	15	76

FG%: .463. FT%: .737.

UCLA (81)	MIN.	FG-A	FT-A	REB.	A	PF	PTS.
Wilkes	38	11-16	1-2	10	3	4	23
Farmer	33	2-6	0-0	6	0	2	4
Walton	34	9-17	6-11	20	2	4	24
Lee	16	0-0	0-0	2	4	0	0
Bibby	40	8-17	2-3	3	1	2	18
Curtis	24	4-14	0-1	4	6	1	8
Hollyfield	9	1-6	0-0	2	3	2	2
Nater	6	1-2	0-1	1	0	0	2
Team				2			
TOTALS	200	36-78	9-18	50	19	15	81

FG%: .462. FT%: .500.
Halftime: UCLA 50-39.

NATIONAL SEMIFINALS

NORTH CAROLINA (75): Jones 4-8 1-1 9, Wuycik 7-16 6-6 20, McAdoo 10-19 4-5 24, Previs 1-5 3-6 5, Karl 5-14 1-3 11, Huband 0-1 0-0 0, Chamberlain 2-5 2-3 6, Johnston 0-1 0-0 0, Chambers 0-1 0-1 0-0. Team 29-70 (.414) 17-25 (.680) 75.

FLORIDA STATE (79): Garrett 4-8 3-7 11, King 6-17 10-10 22, Royals 6-8 6-7 18, McCray 3-6 3-6 9, Samuel 2-4 1-4 5, Harris 1-6 2-2 4, Petty 3-5 4-7 10, Gay 0-1 0-0 0. Team 25-55 (.455) 29-43 (.674) 79.

Halftime: Florida State 45-32.

LOUISVILLE (77): Lawhon 0-7 1-2 1, Thomas 2-4 0-0 4, Vilcheck 3-6 0-0 6, Price 11-23 8-9 30, Bacon 5-11 5-7 15, Carter 4-8 0-0 8, Bunton 1-5 1-1 3, Bradley 1-3 0-0 2, Stallings 1-2 0-1 2, Cooper 0-1 2-2 2, Pry 2-3 0-0 4, Meiman 0-1 0-0 0. Team 30-74 (.405) 17-22 (.773) 77.

UCLA (96): Wilkes 5-11 2-2 12, Farmer 6-12 3-5 15, Walton 11-13 11-12 33, Lee 3-6 4-6 10, Bibby 1-5 0-0 2, Curtis 4-5 0-0 8, Hollyfield 3-6 0-0 6, Carson 1-1 0-0 2, Nater 0-0 2-4 2, Hill 1-1 4-4 6, Chapman 0-0 0-1 0, Franklin 0-1 0-0 0. Team 35-61 (.574) 26-34 (.765) 96.

Halftime: UCLA 39-31.

ALL-TOURNAMENT TEAM

Ron King, G, Jr., Florida State (49 points, 11 rebounds in final two games)
Bob McAdoo, C, Jr., North Carolina (54 points, 34 rebounds)
Jim Price, G, Sr., Louisville (53 points, nine rebounds)
*Bill Walton, C, Soph., UCLA (57 points, 41 rebounds)
Keith Wilkes, F, Soph., UCLA (35 points, 16 rebounds)

*Named Most Outstanding Player.

1971-72 UNDEFEATED TEAM: UCLA (30-0)

COACH: JOHN WOODEN

UCLA	OPPONENT	BRUINS HIGH SCORER
105	The Citadel 49	Bibby 26
106	Iowa 72	Bibby 32
110	Iowa State 81	Walton 24
117	Texas A&M 53	Walton 23
114	Notre Dame 56	Bibby 28
119	Texas Christian 81	Walton 31
115	Texas 65	Walton 28
79	Ohio State 53	Walton 14
78	at Oregon State 72	Bibby 17
93	at Oregon 68	Walton 30
118	Stanford 79	Walton 32
82	California 43	Walton 20
92	Santa Clara 57	Wilkes 16
108	Denver 61	Bibby/Farmer 19
92	at Loyola of Chicago 64	Bibby/Walton 18
57	at Notre Dame 32	Bibby 15
81	Southern California 56	Walton 22
89	Washington State 58	Walton 25
109	Washington 70	Walton 27
100	at Washington 83	Walton 31
85	at Washington State 55	Hollyfield/Wilkes 16
92	Oregon 70	Walton 37
91	Oregon State 72	Walton 26
85	at California 71	Walton 24
102	at Stanford 73	Lee 16
79	at Southern California 66	Walton 20

NCAA TOURNAMENT

90	Weber State* 58	Bibby 16
73	Long Beach State* 57	Bibby 23
96	Louisville* 77	Walton 23
81	Florida State* 76	Walton 24

*Neutral court games.

123 points in coach Digger Phelps' first season at the Irish helm. Two years later, Notre Dame defeated both teams. . . . Kent State was 7-17 overall under coach Frank Truitt, but compiled its only winning Mid-American Conference record (6-4) in the Golden Flashes' first 33 years in the league from 1951-52 through 1983-84. . . . Boston University edged Holy Cross, 65-64, after losing 38 of its previous 40 contests against the Crusaders. . . . Memphis State, after losing its first 11 meetings with Tulsa, swept the Golden Hurricane.

Maryland (27-5/coached by Lefty Driesell), Florida State (27-6/Hugh Durham), Oral Roberts (26-2/Ken Trickey) and Southwestern Louisiana (25-4/Beryl Shipley) had their winningest seasons in school Division I history. ORU's only regular-season defeat was at Murray State, 94-87. . . . Carl Tacy's only season as Marshall's coach resulted in the Thundering Herd finishing in the Top 20 of a final wire-service poll for the lone time in school history. . . . Loyola (La.) competed in its final season at the major-college level.

Brigham Young's Stan Watts ended his 23-year coaching career with a 371-254 record. His final campaign resulted in his highest winning percentage (21-5 mark). . . . Future Hall of Famer Denny Crum launched his head coaching career at Louisville with a 26-5 record and trip to the Final Four. His predecessor, John Dromo, suffered a heart attack after nine games in 1970-71 and did not complete his fourth season. . . . Coach Bob Knight compiled a 17-8 record in his initial season at Indiana. The Hoosiers ended their longest ever drought out of the Top 20 by cracking the select circle for the first time in eight years.

IU's worst defeat was an 85-71 decision at Northern Illinois when Huskies sophomore Jim Bradley collected 24 points and 20 rebounds shortly before they climbed into the AP Top 20. A last-second 86-85 setback against Illinois State probably cost 21-4 NIU a berth in the NCAA Tournament. Two years later, the 6-9, 230-pound Bradley was ruled ineligible during his senior year, finishing his career with averages of 23.1 points and 16.8 rebounds per game. He signed with the ABA's Kentucky Colonels after they purchased his draft rights from San Diego.

Ten years later, Bradley was 29 when he died from a shot in the back in the wee hours of the morning in Portland, Ore., outside a downtown disco two days after his arrest for dealing in a controlled substance. "He was as talented a player as I ever saw," said college and pro standout Dan Issel, who played on two ABA teams with Bradley, "but nobody will ever remember his name because he didn't come close to what he could have been. He could have been as good as anybody who ever played, as far as I'm concerned."

1971-72 FINAL NATIONAL POLLS

AP	UPI	SCHOOL (RECORD)	HEAD COACH
1	1	UCLA (30-0)	John Wooden
2	2	North Carolina (26-5)	Dean Smith
3	3	Pennsylvania (25-3)	Chuck Daly
4	4	Louisville (26-5)	Denny Crum
5	6	Long Beach State (25-4)	Jerry Tarkanian
6	5	South Carolina (24-5)	Frank McGuire
7	7	Marquette (25-4)	Al McGuire
8	8	Southwestern La. (25-4)	Beryl Shipley
9	9	Brigham Young (21-5)	Stan Watts
10	10	Florida State (27-6)	Hugh Durham
11	12	Minnesota (18-7)	Bill Musselman
12	18	Marshall (23-4)	Carl Tacy
13	13	Memphis State (21-7)	Gene Bartow
14	11	Maryland (27-5)	Lefty Driesell
15	15	Villanova (20-8)	Jack Kraft
16	–	Oral Roberts (26-2)	Ken Trickey
17	–	Indiana (17-8)	Bob Knight
18	14	Kentucky (21-7)	Adolph Rupp
19	–	State (18-6)	Fred Taylor
20	–	Virginia (21-7)	Bill Gibson
–	16	State (19-9)	Jack Hartman
–	17	Texas-El Paso (20-7)	Don Haskins
–	19	Missouri (21-6)	Norm Stewart
–	19	Weber State (18-11)	Gene Visscher

1972 NCAA Tournament

Summary: UCLA won the national championship by an average of 18 points. Although the Bill Walton-led Bruins trailed Florida State by a season-high seven points in the first half and the final margin of the championship game was just five (81-76), the outcome never seemed in doubt. Excluding a six-point triumph at Oregon State, they won every other game by at least 13 points.

One and Only: Bo Lamar collected 35 points and a tourney-high 11 assists and Roy Ebron contributed 33 points and 20 rebounds in Division I newcomer Southwestern Louisiana's 112-101 victory over Marshall in the opening round of the Midwest Regional when the Ragin' Cajuns scored the most points in the history of the tourney for a school in its first playoff game. . . . Hawaii coach Red Rocha became the only individual to play and coach in both the NCAA and NBA playoffs. Rocha played for Oregon State in the 1947 NCAA Tournament before appearing in 39 NBA playoff games (including '56 champion Syracuse Nationals) and coaching the Detroit Pistons in the 1959 NBA playoffs.

Numbers Game: Kentucky coach Adolph Rupp's final game was a 73-54 defeat against Florida State in the Mideast Regional final. Rupp is the only coach saddled with more than five regional final losses. Rupp sustained eight such setbacks from 1952 through 1972 by an average margin of 10 points. He also incurred a national quarterfinal reversal in 1945 when the first round of the eight-team event was identified as the regional semifinals. Six of Rupp's first seven "field of eight" defeats were against Big Ten teams, including Ohio State four times. . . . USL's Lamar (36 points vs. Texas) and South Carolina's Tom Riker (36 vs. Villanova) tied for the highest-scoring game in the tourney. . . . Jim Brewer grabbed the most rebounds in a single game (22) to power Minnesota to a 77-72 success against Marquette in the Mideast Regional third-place game.

What Might Have Been: Marquette probably would have been the team with the best chance to unseat UCLA if Warriors All-American Jim Chones didn't terminate his eligibility by signing a professional contract late in the season during the ABA/NBA bidding war. . . . Indiana could have been the Big Ten representative in the NCAA playoffs instead of Minnesota if George McGinnis hadn't left school early for the pros. . . . Kentucky (21-7) might have given runnerup-to-be Florida State more of a challenge in the Mideast Regional if center Tom Payne hadn't left the Wildcats with eligibility remaining to enter the NBA. . . . Duquesne (20-5 under coach Red Manning) probably would have returned to the Top 20 and been in postseason play if forward Mickey Davis didn't depart school early for the ABA.

Scoring Leader: Jim Price, Louisville (103 points, 25.75 ppg).

Highest Scoring Average: Bo Lamar, Southwestern Louisiana (100 points, 33.3 ppg).

Rebounding Leader: Bill Walton, UCLA (64 rebounds, 16 rpg).

Highest Rebounding Average: Jim Brewer, Minnesota (36 rebounds, 18 rpg).

1972 CHAMPIONSHIP BRACKET

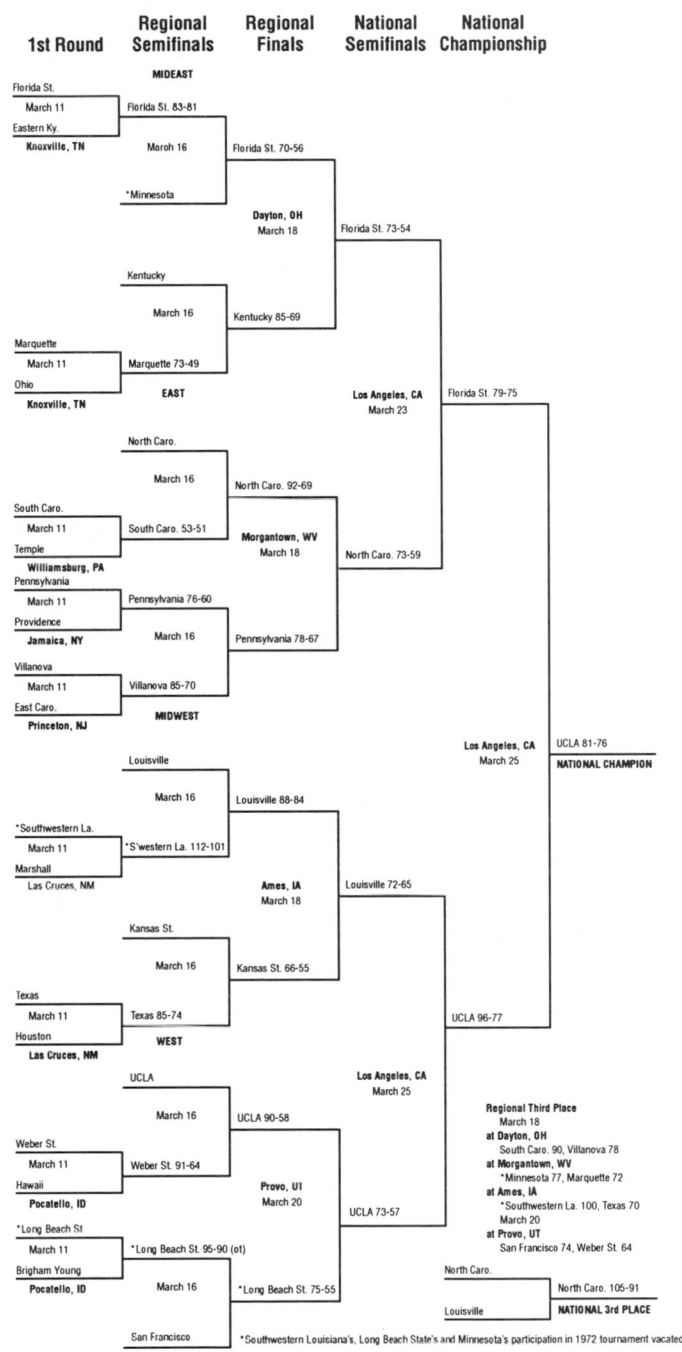

	Regional Semifinals	Regional Finals	National Semifinals	National Championship
1st Round				

MIDEAST

Florida St.
March 11
Eastern Ky.
Knoxville, TN

Florida St. 83-81

March 16

*Minnesota

Florida St. 70-56

Dayton, OH
March 18

Florida St. 73-54

Kentucky

March 16

Kentucky 85-69

Marquette
March 11
Ohio
Knoxville, TN

Marquette 73-49

EAST

Los Angeles, CA
March 23

Florida St. 79-75

North Caro.

March 16

North Caro. 92-69

South Caro.
March 11
Temple
Williamsburg, PA

South Caro. 53-51

Morgantown, WV
March 18

North Caro. 73-59

Pennsylvania
March 11
Providence
Jamaica, NY

Pennsylvania 76-60

March 16

Pennsylvania 78-67

Villanova
March 11
East Caro.
Princeton, NJ

Villanova 85-70

MIDWEST

Los Angeles, CA
March 25

UCLA 81-76

NATIONAL CHAMPION

Louisville

March 16

Louisville 88-84

*Southwestern La.
March 11
Marshall
Las Cruces, NM

*S'western La. 112-101

Ames, IA
March 18

Louisville 72-65

Kansas St.

March 16

Kansas St. 66-55

Texas
March 11
Houston
Las Cruces, NM

Texas 85-74

WEST

UCLA 96-77

UCLA

March 16

UCLA 90-58

Weber St.
March 11
Hawaii
Pocatello, ID

Weber St. 91-64

Provo, UT
March 20

UCLA 73-57

*Long Beach St
March 11
Brigham Young
Pocatello, ID

*Long Beach St. 95-90 (ot)

March 16

*Long Beach St. 75-55

San Francisco

Los Angeles, CA
March 25

Regional Third Place
March 18
at Dayton, OH
South Caro. 90, Villanova 78
at Morgantown, WV
*Minnesota 77, Marquette 72
at Ames, IA
*Southwestern La. 100, Texas 70
March 20
at Provo, UT
San Francisco 74, Weber St. 64

North Caro.

North Caro. 105-91

Louisville

NATIONAL 3rd PLACE

*Southwestern Louisiana's, Long Beach State's and Minnesota's participation in 1972 tournament vacated.

1972-73

AT A GLANCE

NCAA Champion: UCLA (30-0; coached by John Wooden; won Pacific-8 title by five games with a 14-0 record).

NIT Champion: Virginia Tech (22-5; coached by Don DeVoe).

New Rules: The free throw on the first six common fouls each half by a team is eliminated. . . . Players cannot attempt to create the false impression that they have been fouled in charging-guarding situations or while setting a screen when the contact was only "incidental." A referee can charge the "actor" with a technical foul for unsportsmanlike conduct if, in the referee's opinion, the acting is making a travesty of the game. . . . NCAA bylaws make freshmen eligible to play varsity ball. . . . NCAA Tournament first-round byes determined on the basis of an evaluation of the conference's won-lost record over the previous 10 years in playoff competition.

NCAA Probation: Centenary, Duke, Kansas, New Mexico State, North Carolina State, Western Kentucky.

NCAA Consensus First-Team All-Americans: Doug Collins, G, Sr., Illinois State; Ernie DiGregorio, G, Sr., Providence; Dwight "Bo" Lamar, G, Sr., Southwestern Louisiana; Ed Ratleff, F-G, Sr., Long Beach State; David Thompson, F, Soph., North Carolina State; Bill Walton, C, Jr., UCLA; Keith Wilkes, F, Jr., UCLA.

National Player of the Year: Walton (20.4 ppg, 16.9 rpg, 65.0 FG%).

National Coaches of the Year: Memphis State's Gene Bartow (24-6/NABC) and UCLA's John Wooden (30-0/AP, UPI, USBWA).

UCLA, spearheaded by center Bill Walton, became the first major college in history to compile back-to-back perfect-record seasons. "Walton might have been a better all-around player (than Lew Alcindor)," Bruins coach John Wooden said. "If you were grading a player for every fundamental skill, Walton would rank the highest of any center who ever played."

Illinois State guard Doug Collins became the only white NCAA consensus first-team All-American to play for an African American head coach (Will Robinson). . . . Oral Roberts, coached by

Ken Trickey, established an NCAA record for most field-goal attempts per game with 98.5. ORU and Southwestern Louisiana finished 1-2 in the team national scoring race for the second consecutive season. . . . Oklahoma City's Ozie Edwards (28.4) and Marvin Rich (25.3) became one of only four sets of teammates in NCAA history to each average more than 25 points per game in a single season.

Marquette's 81-game homecourt winning streak, which started in 1967, was snapped by Notre Dame, 81-79, on guard Dwight Clay's right corner jumper with four seconds remaining. . . . Freshman James "Fly" Williams, the fifth-leading scorer in the country, became a folk hero of sorts by leading Austin Peay State to the Ohio Valley Conference championship after the school finished in last place the previous year. He set an APSU record with 51 points in two different games (against Georgia Southern in finals of Claxton Fruitcake Classic and against Tennessee Tech). Austin Peay finished in the final top 20 of a wire-service poll for the only time in school history.

Los Angeles State's Raymond Lewis (39.9) and Tulsa's Willie Biles (41.6) had staggering scoring averages in their final five games, but they still finished second and third, respectively, in the national scoring race behind Pepperdine's William "Bird" Averitt, who averaged 38.1 points per game in his last 10 contests. Lewis established a Pacific Coast Athletic Association (now Big West Conference) standard by pouring in 53 points in a double overtime game against Long Beach State on his way to a league record 32.9-point scoring average. . . . Averitt supplied the two highest-scoring games in West Coast Conference history when he poured in a school-record 57 points and later 56 in two separate contests against Nevada-Reno. Averitt, a junior college transfer, had 16 games with 37 or more points in his two-year Pepperdine career.

Biles set a Tulsa scoring record with 48 points against Wichita State. Other school Division I single-game scoring standards were set by Virginia Tech's Allan Bristow (52 points vs. George Washington), Dayton's Donald Smith (52 at Loyola of

1972-73 INDIVIDUAL LEADERS

SCORING

PLAYER	PTS.	AVG.
Averitt, Pepperdine	848	33.9
Lewis, Los Angeles St.	789	32.9
Biles, Tulsa	788	30.3
Stewart, Richmond	574	30.2
Williams, Austin Peay	854	29.4
Lamar, Southwestern La.	808	28.9
Edwards, Oklahoma City	767	28.4
Terry, Arkansas	735	28.3
Williamson, New Mexico St.	490	27.2
Collins, Illinois St.	650	26.0

REBOUNDING

PLAYER	REB.	AVG.
Washington, American	511	20.4
Barnes, Providence	571	19.0
Parish, Centenary	505	18.7

Padgett, Nevada-Reno	462	17.8
Bradley, N. Illinois	426	17.8
Walton, UCLA	506	16.9
Kenon, Memphis St.	501	16.7
Campion, Manhattan	402	15.5
Cash, Bowling Green	396	15.2
Baker, UNLV	424	15.1
Perry, Pan American	388	14.9

Note: Parish's rebounding totals were discounted by the NCAA because Centenary was on probation.

FIELD GOAL PERCENTAGE

PLAYER	FGM	FGA	PCT.
Hayes, Lamar	146	222	.658
Walton, UCLA	277	426	.650
Stewart, Santa Clara	186	291	.639
Schaeffer, St. John's	265	420	.631

Losch, Tulane	151	240	.629
Armstead, Rutgers	143	232	.616
Starks, Murray St.	162	264	.614
Taylor, Jacksonville	191	313	.610
Jones, North Carolina	206	343	.601
Minniefield, New Mexico	156	260	.600

FREE THROW PERCENTAGE

PLAYER	FTM	FTA	PCT.
Smith, Dayton	111	122	.910
Jellison, Northeastern	122	136	.897
Palubinskas, LSU	137	153	.895
Johnson, Denver	108	121	.893
J. Lee, Syracuse	93	105	.886
Ritter, Indiana	117	134	.873
Bullington, Ball St.	147	170	.865
Edwards, Oklahoma City	103	120	.858
Floyd, Texas A&M	96	112	.857
Kruger, Kansas St.	90	105	.857

1972-73 TEAM LEADERS

SCORING OFFENSE

SCHOOL	PTS.	AVG.
Oral Roberts	2626	97.3
Southwestern Louisiana	2800	96.6
Austin Peay St.	2700	93.1
North Carolina St.	2509	92.9
Houston	2472	91.6

SCORING DEFENSE

SCHOOL	PTS.	AVG.
Texas-El Paso	1460	56.2
Pennsylvania	1606	57.4
Fairleigh Dickinson	1523	58.6
Air Force	1420	59.2
UCLA	1802	60.1

SCORING MARGIN

SCHOOL	OFF.	DEF.	MAR.
North Carolina St.	92.9	71.1	21.8

UCLA	81.3	60.1	21.2
Long Beach St.	90.1	72.3	17.8
St. Joseph's	77.8	63.0	14.8
Houston	91.6	77.1	14.5

WON-LOST PERCENTAGE

SCHOOL	W-L	PCT.
UCLA	30-0	1.000
North Carolina St.	27-0	1.000
Long Beach St.	26-3	.897
Providence	27-4	.871
Marquette	25-4	.862

FIELD GOAL PERCENTAGE

SCHOOL	FGM	FGA	PCT.
North Carolina	1150	2181	.527
Maryland	1089	2094	.520
North Carolina St.	1054	2028	.520
UCLA	1054	2032	.519
St. John's	932	1804	.517

FREE THROW PERCENTAGE

SCHOOL	FTM	FTA	PCT.
Duke	496	632	.785
Jacksonville	426	547	.779
Rhode Island	313	405	.773
William & Mary	483	636	.759
Tennessee	281	371	.757

REBOUND MARGIN

SCHOOL	OWN	OPP.	MAR.
Manhattan	56.5	38.0	18.5
American	56.7	40.3	16.4
Oral Roberts	66.9	50.3	15.6
UCLA	49.0	33.9	15.1
Houston	54.7	40.8	13.9

Chicago), Centenary's Robert Parish (50 at Lamar), Memphis State's Larry Finch (48 vs. St. Joseph's, Ind.), Arkansas' Martin Terry (47 vs. SMU), Fordham's Ken Charles (tied with 46 vs. St. Peter's) and Georgia Southern's Johnny Mills (44 vs. Samford). Parish, a freshman, did not convert a free throw in his outburst. . . . Averitt (33.9 ppg), Biles (30.3), Austin Peay's Williams (29.5), Arkansas' Martin Terry (28.3), St. John's Billy Schaeffer (24.7), St. Louis' Harry Rogers (24.5) and Finch (24) set school records for highest scoring average in a single season. Averitt's average is a WCC record. . . . Finch, a guard, was the first Memphis State player to become an NCAA consensus first- or second-team All-American.

Villanova compiled a losing record (11-14) for the only time in Jack Kraft's 12 years as the Wildcats' coach. The Wildcats had defeated Boston College 13 straight times until bowing to the Eagles, 82-81. . . . Brown lost 26 consecutive games to Princeton in their series until upending the Tigers, 68-62. . . . Michigan State started a 14-game winning streak in its series with Ohio State. . . . Bob Knight was in his second season as Indiana's coach when the Hoosiers finished in the Top 10 of a final wire-service poll for the first time since 1960. . . . Kansas State finished in the Top 20 of a final wire-service poll for the 15th time in school history. At the time, intrastate rival Kansas had reached that plateau on 10 occasions.

Davidson (Southern/coached by Terry Holland), Kentucky (SEC/Joe B. Hall) and Weber State (Big Sky/Gene Visscher) each captured its sixth consecutive regular-season league championship. Davidson's crown was its ninth undisputed Southern Conference regular-season title in 10 years. . . . Mississippi lost 39 straight games to Kentucky in their series until Ole Miss prevailed, 61-58. . . . For the first time in ACC Tournament history, the regular-season last-place finisher won a first-round game when Wake Forest (3-9 in the ACC) upset second-place finisher North Carolina State (8-4), 54-52, in overtime.

Houston's only defeat in its last 16 regular-season games was by one point against Eddie Sutton-coached Creighton, 78-77. . . . Arizona's Fred Snowden became the first African American head coach in the Western Athletic Conference. . . . No league benefited more from yearlings than the

---

1972-73 UNDEFEATED TEAM: UCLA (30-0)

COACH: JOHN WOODEN

UCLA	OPPONENT	BRUINS HIGH SCORER
94	Wisconsin 53	Walton 26
73	Bradley 38	Walton 16
81	Pacific 48	Wilkes 18
98	UC Santa Barbara 67	Walton 30
89	Pittsburgh 73	Wilkes 20
82	Notre Dame 56	Wilkes 18
85	Drake* 72	Walton 29
71	Illinois* 64	Walton 22
64	Oregon 38	Farmer/Wilkes 14
87	Oregon State 61	Wilkes 19
82	at Stanford 67	Farmer/Hollyfield/Walton 18
69	at California 50	Farmer/Wilkes 18
92	San Francisco 64	Walton 22
101	Providence 77	Farmer 21
87	at Loyola of Chicago 73	Walton 32
82	at Notre Dame 63	Wilkes 20
79	at Southern California 56	Walton 20
88	at Washington State 50	Walton 17
76	at Washington 67	Walton 29
93	Washington 62	Walton 26
96	Washington State 64	Walton 29
72	at Oregon 61	Wilkes 18
73	at Oregon State 67	Walton 21
90	California 65	Walton/Wilkes 15
51	Stanford 45	Walton 23
76	Southern California 56	Walton/Wilkes 17

NCAA TOURNAMENT

98	Arizona State 81	Walton 28
54	San Francisco 39	Farmer 13
70	Indiana* 59	Curtis 22
87	Memphis State* 66	Walton 44

*Neutral court games.

1972-73 UNDEFEATED TEAM: N.C. STATE (27-0)

COACH: NORMAN SLOAN

NCS	1972-73 OPPONENT	WOLFPACK HIGH SCORER
130	Appalachian State 53	Thompson 33
110	Atlantic Christian 40	Thompson 32
100	Georgia Southern 44	Thompson 40
88	South Florida 25	Thompson 30
88	Wake Forest* 83	Thompson 29
68	North Carolina* 61	Thompson 19
103	Davidson* 90	Cafferky 25
97	at Georgia 83	Thompson 26
68	at Virginia 61	Towe 17
94	Duke 87	Towe/Burleson 20
53	Lehigh 15	Burleson 30
87	at Maryland 85	Thompson 37
86	at Clemson 76	Thompson 24
98	at Furman 73	Thompson 27
89	Maryland 78	Thompson 24
64	Virginia 59	Thompson 18
76	North Carolina 73	Thompson 22
68	Clemson* 61	Thompson 30
118	Georgia Tech* 94	Thompson 36
105	East Carolina 70	Thompson 33
81	at Wake Forest 59	Thompson 21
74	at Duke 50	Thompson 31
100	UNC Charlotte 64	Burleson 26
82	at North Carolina 78	Thompson 18
100	Wake Forest 77	Burleson 27

ACC TOURNAMENT

63	Virginia* 51	Burleson/Thompson 14
76	Maryland* 74	Burleson 14

*Neutral court games.

INDIVIDUAL STATISTICS FOR N.C. STATE REGULARS

Player	POS.	CL.	G.	PPG	RPG
David Thompson	F	So.	27	24.7	8.1
Tom Burleson	C	Jr.	27	17.9	12.0
Monte Towe	G	So.	27	10.0	1.7
Rick Holdt	F	Sr.	27	8.3	3.7
Tim Stoddard	F	So.	27	7.9	5.3
Joe Cafferky	G	Sr.	25	7.2	2.1
Greg Hawkins	F	Jr.	25	5.6	3.3
Mark Moeller	G	So.	27	4.7	1.6
Steve Nuce	F	Jr.	26	4.4	2.1
Craig Kuszmaul	G	So.	19	2.4	.9
TEAM TOTALS			**27**	**92.9**	**46.5**

WAC in the initial season of freshman eligibility. Arizona freshman Coniel Norman led the WAC in scoring (24 ppg), Utah freshman Mike Sojourner paced the WAC in rebounding (12.3 rpg), Arizona freshman guard Eric Money was an all-league second-team selection and Utah freshman guard Luther (Ticky) Burden led the Utes in scoring although they compiled their first losing record (8-18) in 19 years. . . . Long Beach State (26-3/coached by Jerry Tarkanian) had its winningest season in school history. . . . Greg Sten (.819) became the fifth different Gonzaga player in eight years to lead the Big Sky Conference in free-throw percentage.

Bucky Waters' fourth and last season as Duke's coach resulted in the Blue Devils' first losing record in 34 years (12-14). . . . Temple's Harry Litwack ended his 21-year coaching career with a 373-193 record. . . . Georgetown's John Thompson started his college coaching career with a 12-14 record, including defeats to St. John's (by 41 points) and Florida State (31), local rivals Maryland (26), American University (22) and George Washington (13) and small school Roanoke (16).

American's Kermit Washington grabbed at least 26 rebounds in each of his last five games to finish the year with a nation-leading 20.4 rebounds per game. He collected 40 points and 26 rebounds in a 90-68 triumph over Georgetown in the Eagles' regular-season finale to preserve his status as the last Division I player to average more than 20 points and 20 rebounds for an entire season. . . . Sophomore David Vaughn's 34 rebounds for Oral Roberts against Brandeis is the highest single-game total for a major-college player since freshman eligibility was introduced. Centenary's Parish (33 vs. Southern Mississippi), Manhattan's Bill Campion (30 vs. Hofstra), Nevada-Reno's Pete Padgett (30 at Loyola Marymount), Oklahoma's Alvan Adams (28 vs. Indiana State), Oklahoma State's Andy Hopson (27 vs. Missouri), UNLV's Jimmie Baker (26 vs. San Francisco) and Texas A&M's Cedric Joseph (23 vs. Angelo State) set school single-game rebounding records. Joining Parish in the freshman class were Padgett and Adams.

1972-73 FINAL NATIONAL POLLS

AP	UPI	SCHOOL (RECORD)	HEAD COACH
1	1	UCLA (30-0)	John Wooden
2	2	N.C. State (27-0)	Norman Sloan
3	3	Long Beach State (26-3)	Jerry Tarkanian
4	5	Providence (27-4)	Dave Gavitt
5	4	Marquette (25-4)	Al McGuire
6	6	Indiana (22-6)	Bob Knight
7	7	Southwestern La. (24-5)	Beryl Shipley
8	10	Maryland (23-7)	Lefty Driesell
9	7	Kansas State (23-5)	Jack Hartman
10	9	Minnesota (21-5)	Bill Musselman
11	12	North Carolina (25-8)	Dean Smith
12	11	Memphis State (24-6)	Gene Bartow
13	18	Houston (23-4)	Guy Lewis
14	14	Syracuse (24-5)	Roy Danforth
15	17	Missouri (21-6)	Norm Stewart
16	13	Arizona State (19-9)	Ned Wulk
17	15	Kentucky (20-8)	Joe B. Hall
18	20	Pennsylvania (21-7)	Chuck Daly
19	–	Austin Peay State (22-7)	Lake Kelly
20	–	San Francisco (23-5)	Bob Gaillard
–	16	South Carolina (22-7)	Frank McGuire
–	18	Weber State (20-7)	Gene Visscher

Three Texas universities—Abilene Christian, Corpus Christi and Trinity—ended their short stints at the major-college level. Gettysburg (Pa.) also competed in its final season at the major-college level.

1973 NCAA Tournament

Summary: UCLA won the national championship by an average of 16 points. The Bruins' Bill Walton, aided by Greg Lee's tourney-high 14 assists, erupted for a championship game-record 44 points in an 87-66 triumph over Memphis State in the final. Walton had been outscored by fellow center Steve Downing, 26-14, in a 70-59 victory against Indiana in the national semifinals. The Bruins won 26 of their 30 games by a double-digit margin with the closest results being six-point victories against league rivals Oregon State and Stanford.

Star Gazing: This was the last time a champion had just one representative on the All-NCAA Tournament team (Walton).

Biggest Upset: Coach Jerry Tarkanian's fourth consecutive and last tournament team at Long Beach State (26-3) succumbed to San Francisco, 77-67, when two-time consensus first-team All-American Ed Ratleff hit just 4 of 18 field-goal attempts for the 49ers, who were ranked third by UPI.

Providence guard Ernie DiGregorio was a key reason the Friars made it to the 1973 NCAA Final Four.

One and Only: Walton is the only player to have as many as 20 field goals in an NCAA championship game. He was 21 of 22 from the floor against Memphis State.

Numbers Game: Providence's Marvin Barnes hit all 10 of his field-goal attempts in an 87-65 pounding of Pennsylvania in the East Regional semifinals. . . . Memphis State's Larry Kenon had the top two rebounding efforts in the playoffs—22 vs. Providence and 20 vs. South Carolina.

What Might Have Been: Barnes suffered a dislocated right kneecap in the first half of the national semifinals. The Friars, entering the Final Four with just two defeats, didn't have enough firepower to retain a nine-point halftime lead and wound up losing to Memphis State (98-85). According to legendary CCNY coach Nat Holman, they had gotten off to the best eight-minute start he had ever seen with Barnes dominating inside, Kevin Stacom hitting a couple of long jumpers and Ernie DiGregorio displaying his passing wizardry. . . . Undefeated North Carolina State was ineligible for the NCAA Tournament because of NCAA probation. The Wolfpack won its first four games by an average margin of 57 points. . . . North Carolina (25-8) might have been the ACC representative in the NCAA playoffs instead of Maryland if Bob McAdoo hadn't left

1972–73 NCAA CHAMPION: UCLA

SEASON STATISTICS OF UCLA REGULARS

PLAYER	POS.	CL.	G.	FG%	FT%	PPG	RPG
Bill Walton	C	Jr.	30	.650	.569	20.4	16.9
Keith Wilkes	F	Jr.	30	.525	.652	14.8	7.3
Larry Farmer	F	Sr.	30	.511	.701	12.2	5.0
Larry Hollyfield	G	Sr.	30	.466	.492	10.7	2.9
Tommy Curtis	G	Jr.	24	.512	.667	6.4	1.7
Dave Meyers	F	So.	28	.477	.756	4.9	2.9
Greg Lee	G	Jr.	30	.473	.790	4.6	1.3
Swen Nater	C	Sr.	29	.459	.652	3.2	3.3
Pete Trgovich	G-F	So.	25	.382	.400	3.1	1.7
Vince Carson	F	Jr.	26	.514	.471	1.7	2.2
Gary Franklin	F	Jr.	24	.485	.500	1.6	1.3
Bob Webb	G	Jr.	21	.148	.833	0.6	0.2
TEAM TOTALS			30	.519	.632	81.3	49.0

Assists leader: Walton 168.

1973 FINAL FOUR CHAMPIONSHIP GAME

ST. LOUIS, MO

UCLA (87)	MIN.	FG-A	FT-A	REB.	A	PF	PTS.
Wilkes	39	8-14	0-0	7	1	2	16
Farmer	33	1-4	0-0	2	0	2	2
Walton	33	21-22	2-5	13	2	4	44
Lee	34	1-1	3-3	3	14	2	5
Hollyfield	30	4-7	0-0	3	9	4	8
Curtis	11	1-4	2-2	3	0	1	4
Meyers	10	2-7	0-0	3	0	1	4
Nater	7	1-1	0-0	3	0	2	2
Franklin	1	1-2	0-1	1	0	0	2
Carson	1	0-0	0-0	0	0	0	0
Webb	1	0-0	0-0	0	0	0	0
Team				2			
TOTALS	200	40-62	7-11	40	26	18	87

FG%: .645. FT%: .636. **Blocks:** 5. **Turnovers:** 17 (Walton 6). **Steals:** 2.

MEMPHIS ST. (66)	MIN.	FG-A	FT-A	REB.	A	PF	PTS.
Buford	38	3-7	1-2	3	1	1	7
Kenon	34	8-16	4-4	8	3	3	20
Robinson	33	3-6	0-1	7	1	4	6
Laurie	21	0-1	0-0	0	2	0	0
Finch	38	9-21	11-13	1	2	2	29
Westfall	10	0-1	0-0	0	0	5	0
Cook	18	1-4	2-2	0	2	1	4
McKinney	1	0-0	0-0	0	0	0	0
Jones	4	0-0	0-0	0	0	0	0
Tetzlaff	1	0-0	0-2	0	0	1	0
Liss	1	0-1	0-0	0	0	0	0
Andrews	1	0-0	0-0	0	0	0	0
Team				2			
TOTALS	200	24-57	18-24	21	11	17	66

FG%: .421. FT%: .750. **Blocks:** 1. **Turnovers:** 8. **Steals:** 0. **Halftime:** Tied 39-39.

NATIONAL SEMIFINALS

MEMPHIS STATE (98): Buford 3-7 0-0 6, Kenon 14-27 0-4 28, Robinson 11-17 2-3 24, Laurie 1-3 2-3 4, Finch 7-16 7-9 21, Cook 3-6 2-3 8, Westfall 2-3 3-4 7, Jones 0-1 0-0 0. Team 41-80 (.513) 16-26 (.615) 98.

PROVIDENCE (85): Crawford 5-12 0-0 10, Costello 5-5 1-1 11, Barnes 5-7 2-3 12, DiGregorio 15-36 2-2 32, Stacom 6-15 3-3 15, King 2-6 0-0 4, Baker 0-0 0-0 0, Dunphy 0-1 1-2 1, Bello 0-0 0-0 0. Team 38-82 (.463) 9-11 (.818) 85.

Halftime: Providence 49-40.

UCLA (70): Wilkes 5-10 3-4 13, Farmer 3-6 1-2 7, Walton 7-12 0-0 14, Lee 0-1 0-0 0, Hollyfield 5-6 0-0 10, Curtis 9-15 4-7 2, Meyers 2-3 0-0 4, Nater 0-0 0-0 0. Team 31-53 (.585) 8-13 (.615) 70.

INDIANA (59): Buckner 3-10 0-1 6, Crews 4-10 0-0 8, Downing 12-20 2-4 26, Green 1-7 0-0 2, Ritter 6-10 1-1 13, Laskowski 1-8 0-0 2, Abernethy 0-1 0-0 0, Smock 0-0 0-0 0, Noort 0-0 0-0 0, Wilson 0-0 0-0 0, Morris 0-0 0-0 0, Ahlfield 0-0 0-0 0, Allen 1-1 0-0 2, Memering 0-0 0-0 0. Team 28-67 (.418) 3-6 (.500) 59.

Halftime: UCLA 40-22.

ALL-TOURNAMENT TEAM

Ernie DiGregorio, G, Sr., Providence (49 points, nine rebounds, 14 assists in final two games)
Steve Downing, C, Sr., Indiana (47 points, 19 rebounds)
Larry Finch, G, Sr., Memphis State (50 points)
Larry Kenon, F, Jr., Memphis State (48 points, 30 rebounds)
*Bill Walton, C, Jr., UCLA (58 points, 30 rebounds)

*Named Most Outstanding Player.

1973 CHAMPIONSHIP BRACKET

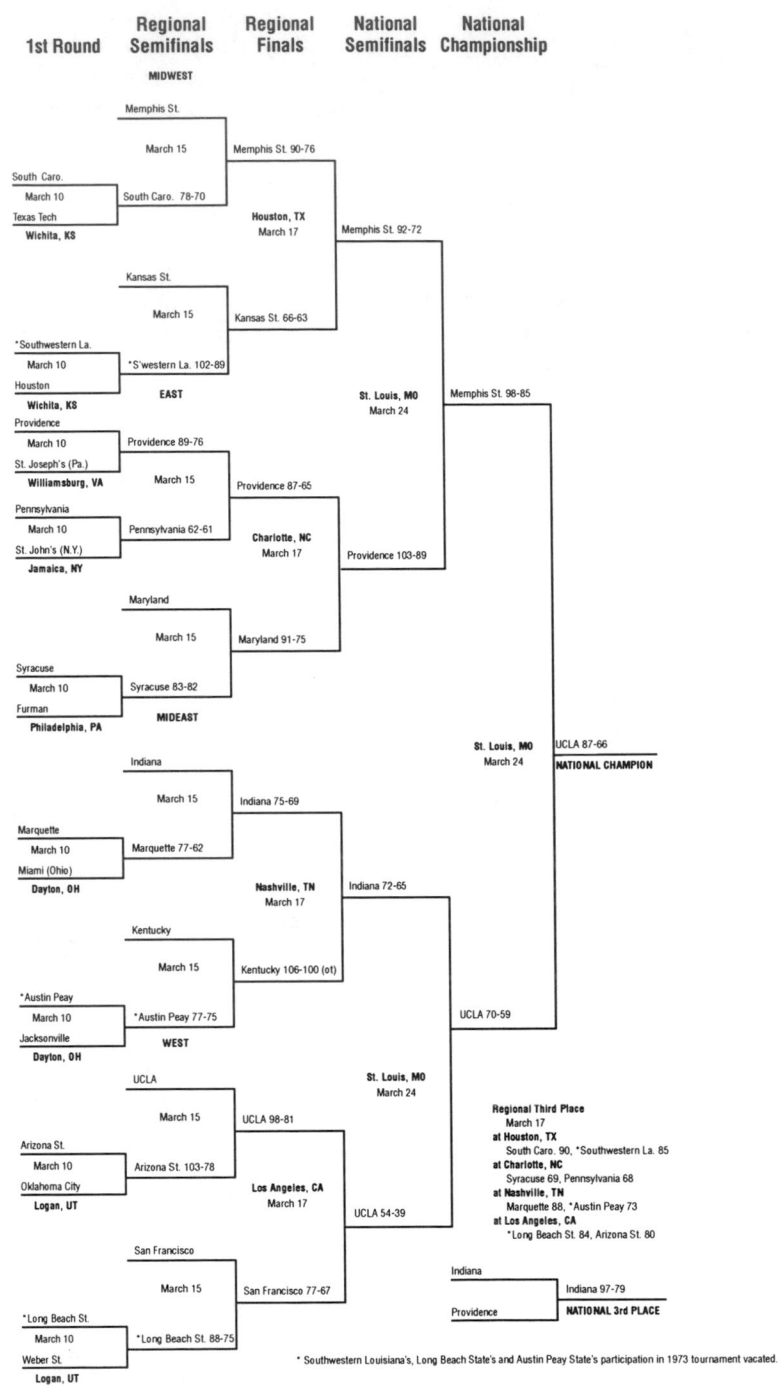

	Regional	Regional	National	National
1st Round	Semifinals	Finals	Semifinals	Championship

MIDWEST

Memphis St.

March 15 — Memphis St. 90-76

South Caro.
March 10 — South Caro. 78-70
Texas Tech
Wichita, KS

Houston, TX
March 17 — Memphis St. 92-72

Kansas St.

March 15 — Kansas St. 66-63

*Southwestern La.
March 10 — *S'western La. 102-89
Houston
Wichita, KS

EAST

St. Louis, MO
March 24 — Memphis St. 98-85

Providence
March 10 — Providence 89-76
St. Joseph's (Pa.)
Williamsburg, VA

March 15 — Providence 87-65

Pennsylvania
March 10 — Pennsylvania 62-61
St. John's (N.Y.)
Jamaica, NY

Charlotte, NC
March 17 — Providence 103-89

Maryland

March 15 — Maryland 91-75

Syracuse
March 10 — Syracuse 83-82
Furman
Philadelphia, PA

MIDEAST

St. Louis, MO
March 24 — UCLA 87-66
NATIONAL CHAMPION

Indiana

March 15 — Indiana 75-69

Marquette
March 10 — Marquette 77-62
Miami (Ohio)
Dayton, OH

Nashville, TN
March 17 — Indiana 72-65

Kentucky

March 15 — Kentucky 106-100 (ot)

*Austin Peay
March 10 — *Austin Peay 77-75
Jacksonville
Dayton, OH

WEST

UCLA 70-59

UCLA

March 15 — UCLA 98-81

Arizona St.
March 10 — Arizona St. 103-78
Oklahoma City
Logan, UT

Los Angeles, CA
March 17 — UCLA 54-39

St. Louis, MO
March 24

San Francisco

March 15 — San Francisco 77-67

*Long Beach St.
March 10 — *Long Beach St. 88-75
Weber St.
Logan, UT

Regional Third Place
March 17
at Houston, TX
South Caro. 90, *Southwestern La. 85
at Charlotte, NC
Syracuse 69, Pennsylvania 68
at Nashville, TN
Marquette 88, *Austin Peay 73
at Los Angeles, CA
*Long Beach St. 84, Arizona St. 80

Indiana

Providence — Indiana 97-79
NATIONAL 3rd PLACE

* Southwestern Louisiana's, Long Beach State's and Austin Peay State's participation in 1973 tournament vacated.

school early for the NBA. . . . Kentucky (20-8) could have possessed the firepower to defeat Indiana in the Mideast Regional final if center Tom Payne hadn't dropped out of college with eligibility remaining. . . . Princeton (16-9) probably would have challenged Penn more to participate in the NCAA playoffs as the Ivy League titlist if guard Brian Taylor hadn't turned pro early. . . . Florida State (18-8) didn't live up to expectations when guard Ron King, the leading scorer for the NCAA Tournament runner-up the previous season, missed the majority of his senior year after dislocating his ankle. . . . St. John's (19-7) probably would have fared better in the tourney if Mel Davis hadn't missed the season because of a knee injury. Davis turned pro early in the 1973-74 campaign.

Putting Things in Perspective: Downing and John Ritter, Indiana's top two scorers, were recruited by coach Bob Knight's predecessor, Lou Watson, who compiled a 17-7 mark in his final season (1970-71) when George McGinnis played his only year in college before turning pro.

Scoring Leader: Ernie DiGregorio, Providence (128 points, 25.6 ppg).

Highest Scoring Average: Larry Finch, Memphis State (107 points, 26.75 ppg).

Rebounding Leader: Bill Walton, UCLA (58 rebounds, 14.5 rpg).

1973-74

AT A GLANCE

NCAA Champion: North Carolina State (30-1; coached by Norman Sloan; won ACC regular-season title by three games with a 12-0 record).

NIT Champion: Purdue (21-9; coached by Fred Schaus; finished in third place in Big Ten with a 10-4 record, which was two games behind co-champions Indiana and Michigan).

CCAT Champion: Indiana (23-5; tied for Big Ten title with a 12-2 record).

New Conferences: ECAC divided to receive multiple automatic qualification berths in the NCAA Tournament.

New Rules: Referees may penalize players for fouls occurring away from the ball (grabbing, illegal screens, etc.). . . . The NCAA Tournament bracket rotation changes for the first time, eliminating East vs. West bracketing in effect since the event's inception. . . . The first public draw to fill oversubscribed orders for Final Four tickets was administered.

NCAA Probation: Centenary, Long Beach State, Louisiana Tech, McNeese State, New Mexico State, Pan American, Western Kentucky, Wichita State

NCAA Consensus First-Team All-Americans: Marvin Barnes, C, Sr., Providence; John Shumate, C-F, Soph., Notre Dame; David Thompson, F, Jr., North Carolina State; Bill Walton, C, Sr., UCLA; Keith Wilkes, F, Sr., UCLA.

National Players of the Year: Thompson (26 ppg, 7.9 rpg, 54.7 FG%/AP) and Walton (19.3 ppg, 14.7 rpg, 66.5 FG%/UPI, USBWA, Naismith).

National Coaches of the Year: Marquette's Al McGuire (26-5/NABC); Notre Dame's Digger Phelps (26-3/UPI), and North Carolina State's Norman Sloan (30-1/AP, USBWA).

UCLA's NCAA-record 88-game winning streak ended at Notre Dame, 71-70, when guard Dwight Clay's fallaway jump shot from the right baseline climaxed a 12-0 spurt in the last three minutes for the Irish. Notre Dame also ended Indiana's 19-game homecourt winning streak, 73-67, and South Carolina's 34-game homecourt winning streak, 72-68. John Shumate scored at least 24 points in all three streak stoppers.

UCLA compiled a 149-2 record at Pauley Pavilion under coach John Wooden, but its streak of Pacific-8 Conference victories ended at 50 when the Bruins bowed at Oregon State, 61-57. It was OSU's lone victory over UCLA in a 26-game stretch of their series from 1967 through 1979. The Bruins then succumbed at Oregon, 56-51, to give them back-to-back defeats for the first time since 1966.

"When you have the same group for three years, they're a little more difficult to work with. They don't mean to be, but they are," Wooden said. "I can't find fault with my team, but I failed to motivate them. And I'm not talking about won-lost record. In many games we won, I didn't think we displayed intensity and didn't play up to our potential."

Maryland's 65-64 setback at UCLA in the Bruins' second game of the season was the closest and one of only three of their 49 home games during the 88-game winning streak decided by fewer than 11 points.

UCLA's Bill Walton finished his career with an amazing field-goal percentage of 65.1 although he never won a single-season shooting title. Walton is the only player to be a three-time first-team NCAA unanimous All-American and first-team Academic All-American. He shot an NCAA Tournament-record 68.6 percent from the floor in 12 playoff games.

Considered in some quarters as the most incredible comeback in major-college history, North Carolina freshman Walter Davis sent the regular-season finale against Duke into overtime with a 30-foot bank shot, climaxing an eight-point rally in the final 17 seconds of regulation. Carolina won in overtime, 96-92, for its first-ever overtime victory against the Blue Devils. . . . In the lowest-scoring game since 1938, Tennessee and Temple combined for a mere 17 points in the Volunteers' 11-6 victory. . . . Jerry Tarkanian, the nation's winningest active Division I coach by percentage, lost his home debut at UNLV (82-76 to Texas Tech) after Tarkanian-coached teams never lost a home game in five years at Long Beach State or in six years in junior college.

The nation's top three scorers grew up in New York City—Canisius' Larry Fogle, Pan American's Bruce "Sky" King and Austin Peay State's

Providence's Marvin Barnes lets it fly.

James "Fly" Williams. Fogle, who set a Canisius record for highest scoring average in a single season (33.4 ppg), enrolled there after Southwestern Louisiana's program was disbanded by the NCAA because of numerous indiscretions. . . . Fogle (55 points vs. St. Peter's) joined the following players who set school single-game scoring records: Appalachian State's Stan Davis (56 at Carson-Newman), Providence's Marvin Barnes (52 vs. Austin Peay), Illinois State's Robert "Bubbles" Hawkins (58 vs. Northern Illinois), Tulsa's Willie Biles (tied own mark with 48 vs. St. Cloud,

Minn.), Eastern Michigan's Gary Tyson (47 vs. Wheaton), Ball State's Larry Bullington (47 vs. Cleveland State), South Alabama's Eugene Oliver (46 at Southern Mississippi) and Fresno State's Charles Bailey (45 in double overtime at North Texas State). . . . The 6-5 Fogle also grabbed 22 rebounds against St. Peter's, which was one of six games during the season when he retrieved at least 20 missed shots in a game, including a school-record 26 against Catholic. . . . North Carolina A&T's James Outlaw set a school Division I record for highest scoring average in a season with 24.9 points per game.

In a remarkable turnaround, Kansas reached the Final Four just one year after compiling an 8-18 record that tied the school standard for most defeats in a single season. The Jayhawks (23-7), coached by Ted Owens, were the nation's most-improved team. They posted their only victory over Kentucky (71-63) in the first 17 meetings of their series from 1950-51 through 1984-85. . . . Mississippi sustained its 14th of 21 consecutive non-winning SEC records but the Rebels handed Arkansas the Hogs' most lopsided defeat in history, 117-66. . . . This season marked won-loss records that were the best (27-2 by Maryland-Eastern Shore) and worst (1-25 by Georgia State) for any first-year Division I schools since classification was first introduced in 1948.

Maryland, ranking fourth in both polls, lost against eventual NCAA champion North Carolina State in the ACC Tournament final (103-100 in overtime) in what some believe might have been the greatest college game ever played. Three players from each team earned All-American honors during their careers—N.C. State's David Thompson, Tom Burleson and Monte Towe and Maryland's John Lucas, Len Elmore and Tom

MOST INCREDIBLE LEAGUE TOURNEY FINAL

MARYLAND VS. NORTH CAROLINA STATE

ACC TOURNAMENT CHAMPIONSHIP GAME (GREENSBORO, NC)

MARCH 9, 1974

Maryland might have been the best team never to appear in the NCAA Tournament. The Terrapins bowed to NCAA champion-to-be North Carolina State, 103-100, in overtime in the ACC Tournament final.

MARYLAND (100)	FG-A	FT-A	REB.	PTS.
Tom McMillen	11-16	0-0	7	22
Owen Brown	7-9	0-0	2	14
Len Elmore	7-12	4-5	13	18
John Lucas	9-20	0-1	3	18
Mo Howard	10-15	2-2	3	22
Tom Roy	3-4	0-0	3	6
Billy Hahn	0-1	0-0	0	0
TOTALS	47-77	6-8	31	100

FG%:.610.FT%:.750.

N.C. STATE (103)	FG-A	FT-A	REB.	PTS.
David Thompson	10-24	9-11	5	29
Tim Stoddard	2-3	0-2	6	4
Tom Burleson	18-2	2-4	13	38
Monte Towe	7-11	3-4	2	17
Moe Rivers	4-13	0-1	5	8
Phil Spence	3-4	1-4	6	7
Mark Moeller	0-0	0-0	0	0
TOTALS	44-80	15-26	37	103

FG%:.550. FT%:.577.

Halftime: Maryland 55-50. **Regulation:** Tied 97-97.

UCLA'S 88-GAME WINNING STREAK ENDS High drama occurred on January 19, 1974 at Notre Dame's Athletic and Convocation Center when the Irish ended UCLA's NCAA-record 88-game winning streak, 71-70. Guard Dwight Clay's fallaway jump shot from the right baseline climaxed a 12-0 spurt in the last three minutes for the Irish. Clay's teammates Gary Brokaw and John Shumate scored 25 and 24 points respectively.

UCLA (70)	FG-A	FT-A	REB.	PTS.
Tommy Curtis	3-11	3-4	1	9
Pete Trgovich	3-5	1-1	0	7
Bill Walton	12-14	0-0	9	24
Dave Meyers	5-10	0-2	7	10
Keith Wilkes	6-16	6-7	5	18
Greg Lee	0-0	2-2	0	2
Marques Johnson	0-0	0-0	0	0
TOTALS	29-56	12-16	27	70

FG%: .518. FT%: .750.

NOTRE DAME (71)	FG-A	FT-A	REB.	PTS.
Gary Brokaw	10-16	5-7	3	25
Dwight Clay	2-5	3-4	6	7
John Shumate	11-22	2-4	11	24
Adrian Dantley	4-12	1-1	8	9
Gary Novak	0-2	0-0	0	0
Bill Paterno	2-4	0-0	1	4
Ray Martin	1-1	0-0	2	2
TOTALS	30-62	11-16	31	71

FG%: .484. FT%: .687.
Halftime: UCLA 43-34.

McMillen. The Terrapins had four players score at least 20 points—Lucas, McMillen, Owen Brown and Mo Howard—in a 20-point victory over 22-6 North Carolina (105-85) in the semifinals. The Terps lost by one point at UCLA in their season opener before dropping both regular-season games against N.C. State by six points and bowing at North Carolina to finish in a tie with the Tar Heels for second place in the ACC standings.

George Washington's Clyde Burwell (33 vs. St. Mary's, Md.), Maine's Bob Warner (28 vs. Trinity), Stanford's Rich Kelley (27 at Kentucky), Southern Illinois' Joe C. Meriweather (27 vs. Indiana State), McNeese State's Henry Ray (27 vs. Texas-Arlington) and Maryland's Elmore (26 at Wake Forest) set school single-game rebounding marks.

South Carolina's school-record 34-game homecourt winning streak ended when the Gamecocks bowed to Notre Dame, 72-68. . . . Rutgers lost 13 consecutive games in its series with Syracuse until defeating the Orangemen, 93-79, in Tom Young's first season as coach of the Scarlet Knights. . . . Providence (28-4/coached by Dave Gavitt), Pittsburgh (25-4/Buzz Ridl) and Brown (17-9/Gerald Alaimo) had their winningest seasons in school history. Southern California (24-5/Bob Boyd) tied its school single-season record for most victories. . . . Pitt, making its only Top 20 appearance in a final wire-service poll until 1987, won a school-record 22 consecutive games after losing its season opener at West Virginia. The Panthers lost at least 10 contests each of the previous nine years when they posted just one winning record. . . . Seton Hall, coached by current network TV analyst Bill Raftery, compiled a 16-11 record to end a streak of nine consecutive losing seasons.

Furman's Fessor Leonard set a Southern Conference standard with 13 blocked shots against St. Peter's. . . . Alabama, coached by C.M. Newton, made its first Top 20 appearance in a final wire-service poll since 1956. . . . Richmond registered its first winning record (16-12/coached by Lewis Mills) in 16 years and St. Mary's posted its first winning mark (15-13/Frank LaPorte) in 11 sea-

1973-74 FINAL NATIONAL POLLS

AP	UPI	SCHOOL (RECORD)	HEAD COACH
1	1	N.C. State (30-1)	Norman Sloan
2	2	UCLA (26-4)	John Wooden
3	5	Marquette (26-5)	Al McGuire
4	4	Maryland (23-5)	Lefty Driesell
5	3	Notre Dame (26-3)	Digger Phelps
6	12	Michigan (22-5)	Johnny Orr
7	10	Kansas (23-7)	Ted Owens
8	6	Providence (28-4)	Dave Gavitt
9	9	Indiana (23-5)	Bob Knight
10	11	Long Beach State (24-2)	Jerry Tarkanian
11	–	Purdue (22-8)	Fred Schaus
12	8	North Carolina (22-6)	Dean Smith
13	7	Vanderbilt (23-5)	Roy Skinner
14	19	Alabama (22-4)	C.M. Newton
15	–	Utah (22-8)	Bill Foster
16	14	Pittsburgh (25-4)	Buzz Ridl
17	13	Southern Cal (24-5)	Bob Boyd
18	–	Oral Roberts (23-6)	Ken Trickey
19	16	South Carolina (22-5)	Frank McGuire
20	19	Dayton (20-9)	Don Donoher
–	15	Louisville (21-7)	Denny Crum
–	17	Creighton (23-7)	Eddie Sutton
–	18	New Mexico (22-7)	Norm Ellenberger

Note: This was one of two years that the AP poll was released after the national postseason tournaments.

sons. . . . Texas posted its lone triumph over Texas Tech (75-74) in a 15-game stretch of their series from 1970 through 1976.

Illinois suffered a school-record 11-game losing streak en route to a 5-18 mark in Harv Schmidt's seventh and final season as coach of the Illini. . . . Lute Olson launched his major college coaching career with a 24-2 record in his lone season at Long Beach State. The only defeats for the probation-shackled 49ers were by two points at Colorado and Marquette. Olson moved on to Iowa after the Hawkeyes went 8-16 in Dick Schultz's fourth and final campaign as their head coach. Schultz, who later became executive director of the NCAA, finished his Iowa career with a 41-55 record and the worst winning percentage (.427) among the 15 men to coach the Hawkeyes at least two years.

1974 NCAA Tournament

Summary: North Carolina State, unbeaten in 27 games the previous season when it was ineligible to participate in the national tournament because of an NCAA probation, defeated Marquette in the championship game (76-64) after Warriors coach Al McGuire was assessed two technical fouls late in the first half. The "T"

N. C. State star forward David Thompson.

UCLA's Keith (Jamaal) Wilkes moves down the court.

helped the Wolfpack score 10 unanswered points in less than a minute and transform a 28-27 deficit into a comfortable 37-28 lead. The final in N.C. State's home state at Greensboro was anticlimatic after the Wolfpack avenged an 18-point loss to UCLA earlier in the season on a neutral court by ending the Bruins' 38-game playoff winning streak (80-77 in overtime). N.C. State erased an 11-point deficit midway through the second half and a seven-point deficit in the extra session behind David Thompson's 28 points and 10 rebounds to halt UCLA's string of seven consecutive NCAA championships. The Bruins were ripe to be knocked off. The (Bill) Walton Gang also blew a 17-point advantage in its playoff opener before regrouping to outlast Dayton (111-100 in triple overtime). "It was the most disappointing, embarrassing event of my life," Walton said. "I think about it almost daily. If I had one week to bring back and live over, that would be it."

Star Gazing: It's inconceivable to think N.C. State would have won the crown if Thompson didn't recover from a nasty fall to the floor after attempting to block a shot by Pitt in the East Regional final. Thompson, cartwheeling over the shoulders of a teammate, landed with a sickening thud on the back of his head and did not move for four minutes. He regained consciousness, was taken to a hospital and, after getting 15 stitches to mend a head wound, was permitted to return to the arena and watch the end of the game. The mild concussion didn't keep him from being ready for the Final Four, where the junior forward was named Most Outstanding Player. "No matter what you say about Thompson and his ability, you can't exaggerate. He's that good," Wolfpack coach Norman Sloan said.

One and Only: N.C. State starting forward Tim Stoddard is the only individual to play for an

1973–74 INDIVIDUAL LEADERS

PLAYER	PTS.	AVG.
Fogle, Canisius	835	33.4
King, Pan American	681	31.0
Williams, Austin Peay	687	27.5
Stewart, Richmond	663	26.5
Thompson, North Carolina St.	805	26.0
Bullington, Ball St.	664	25.5
Oleynick, Seattle	653	25.1
Outlaw, North Carolina A&T	647	24.9
Biles, Tulsa	641	24.7
Shumate, Notre Dame	703	24.2

REBOUNDING

PLAYER	REB.	AVG.
Barnes, Providence	597	18.7
McCullough, Pan American	358	16.3
Robinson, Kent St.	423	16.3
Campion, Manhattan	419	15.5

Parish, Centenary*	382	15.3
Padgett, Nevada-Reno	395	15.2
McKinney, Baylor	375	15.0
Meriweather, Southern Ill.	387	14.9
Walton, UCLA	398	14.7
Elmore, Maryland	412	14.7
Warner, Maine	350	14.6

Note: Parish's rebounding totals were discounted by the NCAA because Centenary was on probation.

FIELD GOAL PERCENTAGE

PLAYER	FGM	FGA	PCT.
Fleming, Arizona	136	204	.667
Walton, UCLA	232	349	.665
Cox, Mississippi	152	242	.628
Shumate, Notre Dame	281	448	.627
Skinner, Massachusetts	196	316	.620

Carroll, Howard	205	332	.617
Fry, Mississippi St.	141	233	.605
Morgan, Samford	214	354	.605
Garrett, Purdue	276	465	.594
C. Pondexter, Long Beach St.	167	283	.590

FREE THROW PERCENTAGE

PLAYER	FTM	FTA	PCT.
Medlock, Arkansas	87	95	.916
Snow, Tennessee	81	91	.890
Ferrell, Marshall	128	145	.883
Compton, Vanderbilt	89	102	.873
Kruger, Kansas St.	122	140	.871
Cook, Memphis St.	119	138	.862
Johnson, Denver	120	140	.857
Palubinskas, LSU	121	142	.852
Cosey, West Texas St.	80	94	.851
Bullington, Ball St.	154	183	.842

1973–74 TEAM LEADERS

SCORING OFFENSE

SCHOOL	PTS.	AVG.
Maryland-Eastern Shore	2831	97.6
Oral Roberts	2744	94.6
Virginia Commonwealth	2266	94.4
North Carolina St.	2833	91.4
Utah	2726	90.9

SCORING DEFENSE

SCHOOL	PTS.	AVG.
Texas-El Paso	1413	56.5
Temple	1417	56.7
Princeton	1520	58.5
Marquette	1857	59.9
St. Joseph's	1807	60.2

SCORING MARGIN

SCHOOL	OFF.	DEF.	MAR.
UNC Charlotte	90.2	69.4	20.8
UCLA	82.3	62.7	19.6

Long Beach St.	80.2	61.1	19.1
Notre Dame	89.9	73.0	16.9
Maryland	85.7	69.0	16.7

WON-LOST PERCENTAGE

SCHOOL	W-L	PCT.
North Carolina St.	30-1	.968
Maryland-Eastern Shore	27-2	.931
Long Beach St.	24-2	.923
Notre Dame	26-3	.897
Providence	28-4	.875

FIELD GOAL PERCENTAGE

SCHOOL	FGM	FGA	PCT.
Notre Dame	1056	1992	.530
Long Beach St.	887	1680	.528
North Carolina	1015	1952	.520
Massachusetts	878	1709	.514
UNC Charlotte	996	1948	.511
Stetson	781	1529	.511

FREE THROW PERCENTAGE

SCHOOL	FTM	FTA	PCT.
Vanderbilt	477	595	.802
Princeton	332	423	.785
Davidson	488	623	.783
Seattle	366	479	.764
Denver	311	410	.759

REBOUND MARGIN

SCHOOL	OWN	OPP.	MAR.
Massachusetts	43.7	30.7	13.0
Virginia Commonwealth	55.1	42.1	13.0
Arkansas St.	50.3	39.2	11.1
Iona	51.0	40.0	11.0
Maryland	47.0	36.1	10.9

NCAA basketball champion and then in a major league baseball World Series (relief pitcher for Baltimore Orioles '79).

Numbers Game: Thompson became the only undergraduate non-center to average more than 23 points per game for a national champion (26 ppg). He tossed in a tourney-high 40 points and teammate Tom Burleson contributed a tourney-high 24 rebounds in a 92-78 victory over Providence in the East Regional semifinals. . . . N.C. State traveled a thorny path during the season to the NCAA title, defeating nine teams that, at the time, were ranked among the nation's Top Five. . . . Texas, winner of just one non-conference game under coach Leon

Black, became the only school with a losing overall record to secure an automatic bid by capturing a regular-season league title.

What Might Have Been: Two-time consensus first-team All-American forward Keith Wilkes shot better than 50 percent from the floor in his three varsity seasons at UCLA before hitting half of his field-goal attempts in a 12-year NBA career. If only he connected on 41 percent of his field-goal attempts instead of 29.4 percent (5 of 17) in the national semifinals, the Bruins could have defeated N.C. State rather than losing 80-77. . . . Marquette (26-5) might have been more of a match for N.C. State in the NCAA final if Larry

1973–74 NCAA CHAMPION: NORTH CAROLINA STATE

SEASON STATISTICS OF N.C. STATE REGULARS

PLAYER	POS.	CL.	G.	FG%	FT%	PPG	RPG
David Thompson	F	Jr.	31	.547	.745	26.0	7.9
Tom Burleson	C	Sr.	31	.516	.654	18.1	12.2
Monte Towe	G	Jr.	31	.517	.811	12.8	2.2
Moe Rivers	G	Jr.	30	.484	.654	12.1	2.9
Phil Spence	F	So.	30	.497	.615	6.0	6.3
Tim Stoddard	F	Jr.	31	.416	.697	5.5	4.5
Steve Nuce	F	Sr.	28	.464	.786	4.4	3.2
Greg Hawkins	F	Sr.	25	.469	.735	2.8	1.4
Mark Moeller	G	Jr.	30	.435	.913	2.7	1.2
TEAM TOTALS			31	.499	.708	91.4	46.8

1974 FINAL FOUR CHAMPIONSHIP GAME

GREENSBORO, NC

MARQUETTE (64)	MIN.	FG-A	FT-A	REB.	A	PF	PTS.
Ellis	39	6-16	0-0	11	1	5	12
Tatum	20	2-7	0-0	3	1	4	4
Lucas	40	7-13	7-9	13	0	4	21
Walton	25	4-10	0-0	2	2	2	8
Washington	35	3-13	5-8	4	0	3	11
Delsman	5	0-0	0-0	0	0	2	0
Daniels	17	1-3	1-2	0	2	3	3
Campbell	12	2-3	0-0	1	0	3	4
Homan	6	0-4	1-2	6	1	2	1
Brennan	1	0-0	0-0	0	0	1	0
Team				3			
TOTALS	200	25-69	14-21	43	7	29	64

FG%: .362. FT%: .667. **Steals:** 9 (Washington 5). **Blocks:** 3.

N.C. STATE (76)	MIN.	FG-A	FT-A	REB.	A	PF	PTS.
Stoddard	26	3-4	2-2	7	2	5	8
Thompson	40	7-12	7-8	7	2	3	21
Burleson	36	6-9	2-6	11	0	4	14
Rivers	40	4-9	6-9	2	5	2	14
Towe	38	5-10	6-7	3	2	1	16
Spence	18	1-2	1-2	3	3	2	3
Moeller	2	0-0	0-0	0	0	0	0
Team				1			
TOTALS	200	26-46	24-34	34	14	17	76

FG%: .565. FT%: .706. **Steals:** 12. **Blocks:** 8 (Burleson 7).
Halftime: North Carolina State 39-30.

NATIONAL SEMIFINALS

UCLA (77): Meyers 6-9 0-1 12, Wilkes 5-17 5-5 15, Walton 13-21 3-3 29, Curtis 4-8 3-4 11, Lee 4-11 0-0 8, Johnson 0-3 0-0 0, McCarter 1-2 0-0 2. Team 33-71 (.465) 11-13 (.846) 77.

NORTH CAROLINA STATE (80): Stoddard 4-11 1-2 9, Thompson 12-25 4-6 28, Burleson 9-20 2-6 20, Rivers 3-8 1-2 7, Towe 4-10 4-4 12, Spence 2-3 0-0 4, Hawkins 0-0 0-0 0. Team 34-77 (.442) 12-20 (.600) 80.

Halftime: Tied 35-35. Regulation: Tied 65-65. First Overtime: Tied 67-67.

KANSAS (51): Cook 1-3 2-4 4, Morningstar 5-13 0-0 10, Knight 0-5 0-0 0, Greenlee 3-7 0-0 6, Kivisto 2-7 2-5 6, Suttle 8-13 3-4 19, Smith 3-4 0-0 6. Team 22-52 (.423) 7-13 (.538) 51.

MARQUETTE (64): Ellis 2-9, 1-2 5, Tatum 5-11 4-6 14, Lucas 7-11 4-4 18, Walton 2-7 3-4 7, Washington 5-12 6-11 16, Daniels 0-2 0-0 0, Campbell 0-1 0-0 0, Homan 1-2 0-0 2, Delsman 0-1 2-2 2, Brennan 0-0 0-0 0, Bryant 0-0 0-0 0, Vollmer 0-0 0-0 0, Johnson 0-0 0-0 0. Team 22-56 (.393) 20-29 (.690) 64.

Halftime: Kansas 24-23.

ALL-TOURNAMENT TEAM

Tom Burleson, C, Sr., North Carolina State (34 points, 25 rebounds, nine blocked shots in final two games)
Maurice Lucas, C, Jr., Marquette (39 points, 27 rebounds)
*David Thompson, F, Jr., North Carolina State (49 points, 17 rebounds)
Monte Towe, G, Jr., North Carolina State (28 points)
Bill Walton, C, Sr., UCLA (35 points, 26 rebounds, eight assists)

*Named Most Outstanding Player.

McNeill hadn't left school early for the NBA. . . . Memphis State (19-11) probably would have wound up in the NCAA playoffs instead of the NIT if Larry Kenon hadn't left school with eligibility remaining to turn pro.

Putting Things in Perspective: Would N.C. State have become kingpin if the Wolfpack didn't play at home (East Regional at Raleigh and nearby Greensboro)?

Scoring Leader: David Thompson, North Carolina State (97 points, 24.25 ppg).

Highest Scoring Average: John Shumate, Notre Dame (86 points, 28.7 ppg).

Rebounding Leader: Tom Burleson, North Carolina State (61 rebounds, 15.25 rpg).

Highest Rebounding Average: Marvin Barnes, Providence (51 rebounds, 17 rpg).

1974 CHAMPIONSHIP BRACKET

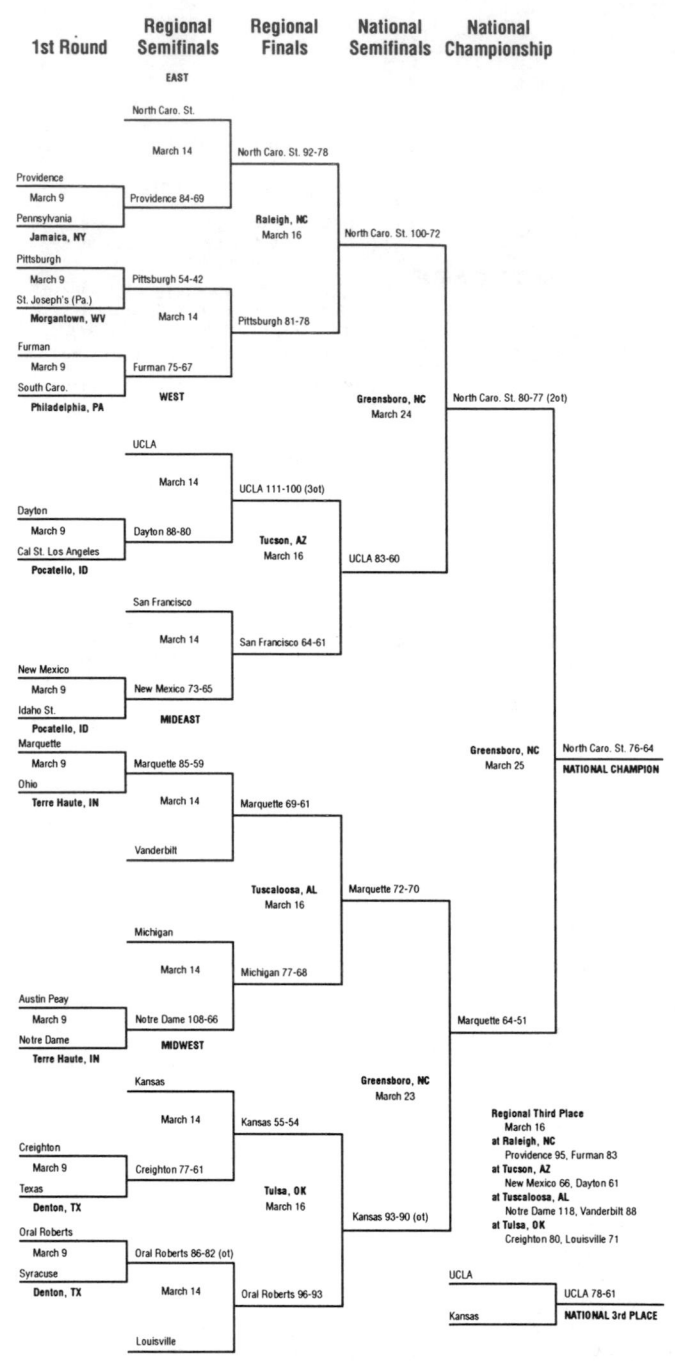

1st Round	Regional Semifinals	Regional Finals	National Semifinals	National Championship

EAST

North Caro. St.
March 14 — North Caro. St. 92-78

Providence
March 9 — Providence 84-69
Pennsylvania
Jamaica, NY

Raleigh, NC
March 16 — North Caro. St. 100-72

Pittsburgh
March 9 — Pittsburgh 54-42
St. Joseph's (Pa.)
Morgantown, WV
March 14 — Pittsburgh 81-78

Furman
March 9 — Furman 75-67
South Caro.
Philadelphia, PA

WEST

Greensboro, NC
March 24 — North Caro. St. 80-77 (2ot)

UCLA
March 14 — UCLA 111-100 (3ot)

Dayton
March 9 — Dayton 88-80
Cal St. Los Angeles
Pocatello, ID

Tucson, AZ
March 16 — UCLA 83-60

San Francisco
March 14 — San Francisco 64-61

New Mexico
March 9 — New Mexico 73-65
Idaho St.
Pocatello, ID

MIDEAST

Marquette
March 9 — Marquette 85-59
Ohio
Terre Haute, IN
March 14 — Marquette 69-61

Vanderbilt

Tuscaloosa, AL
March 16 — Marquette 72-70

Michigan
March 14 — Michigan 77-68

Austin Peay
March 9 — Notre Dame 108-66
Notre Dame
Terre Haute, IN

MIDWEST

Greensboro, NC
March 23 — Marquette 64-51

Kansas
March 14 — Kansas 55-54

Creighton
March 9 — Creighton 77-61
Texas
Denton, TX

Tulsa, OK
March 16 — Kansas 93-90 (ot)

Oral Roberts
March 9 — Oral Roberts 86-82 (ot)
Syracuse
Denton, TX
March 14 — Oral Roberts 96-93

Louisville

Greensboro, NC
March 25 — North Caro. St. 76-64
NATIONAL CHAMPION

Regional Third Place
March 16
at Raleigh, NC
   Providence 95, Furman 83
at Tucson, AZ
   New Mexico 66, Dayton 61
at Tuscaloosa, AL
   Notre Dame 118, Vanderbilt 88
at Tulsa, OK
   Creighton 80, Louisville 71

UCLA
Kansas — UCLA 78-61
NATIONAL 3rd PLACE

1974-75

AT A GLANCE

NCAA Champion: UCLA (28-3; coached by John Wooden; won Pacific-8 title by two games with a 12-2 record).

NIT Champion: Princeton (22-8; coached by Pete Carril; finished in second place in Ivy League with a 12-2 record, which was one game behind Penn).

NCIT Champion: Drake (19-10; finished in third place in Missouri Valley with a 9-5 record).

New Conference: ECC (spinoff of the Middle Atlantic).

New Rules: A non-jumper on the restraining circle during a jump ball may move around after the ball leaves the referee's hand. . . . A player assessed a foul is no longer required to raise his hand. . . . A 32-team bracket is adopted for the NCAA Tournament and teams other than the conference champion can be chosen on an at-large basis from the same league for the first time.

NCAA Probation: Centenary, Illinois, Long Beach State, Louisiana Tech, Maryland-Eastern Shore, McNeese State, Southern Methodist, Texas-Pan American, Western Kentucky, Wichita State.

NCAA Consensus First-Team All-Americans: Adrian Dantley, F, Soph., Notre Dame; John Lucas, G, Jr., Maryland; Scott May, F, Jr., Indiana; Dave Meyers, F, Sr., UCLA; David Thompson, F, Sr., North Carolina State.

National Player of the Year: Thompson (29.9 ppg, 8.2 rpg, 54.6 FG%).

National Coach of the Year: Bob Knight, Indiana (31-1/AP, UPI, NABC, USBWA).

John Wooden, earning a modest $32,500 base salary in his final season, concluded his 29-year coaching career with a 664-162 record. Wooden, the only coach to compile a double-digit total of Final Four victories, notched a 21-3 Final Four record with UCLA in 12 appearances from 1962-75. He won 94 percent of his games in his last 12 seasons (335-22 record), including more than 25 victories each of the final nine campaigns.

"You could probably go back since collegiate basketball first started and never find anyone that has had the impact on the game that he's had," said Hall of Fame Louisville coach Denny Crum, who was an assistant under Wooden. "Not only in style of play, but just in terms of how he approached the game. The way that he dominated college basketball for so many years is mind boggling. You look around and no one can come close to doing what they did at UCLA, and of course Wooden was the architect of all that. He is probably as versatile a teacher as anyone I have ever seen. He was successful with small players, tall players and all different kinds of teams. He was the best. You kind of wish he was still coaching."

Wooden's final defeat was a 103-81 setback at Washington when Huskies reserve Larry Jackson collected 27 points and 14 rebounds. Washington claimed a 52-44 halftime advantage despite being outscored 16-0 at the free-throw line. The victory halted a 25-game losing skid for the Huskies against UCLA dating back to 1963.

Moses Malone, hailed as the country's No. 1 prep player, appeared bound for Maryland to help coach Lefty Driesell fulfill his prophecy of molding the Terrapins into "the UCLA of the East." But to Driesell's chagrin, Malone chose to bypass a collegiate career and went straight from high school to the pros with the Utah Stars of the American Basketball Association.

Richmond's Bob McCurdy won the national scoring title going away with outbursts of 41, 40, 46 and a school-record 53 points (vs. Appalachian State in double overtime) in a 17-day stretch at the end of the season. As a freshman for Virginia, McCurdy scored 42 points against Maryland's Len Elmore-Tom McMillen freshmen, but subsequently transferred.

North Carolina State tied an ACC standard by extending its league winning streak to 27 consecutive games until Wake Forest, sparked by guard Skip Brown's 25 points, ended the Wolfpack's 37-game winning streak overall, 83-78. Later, N.C. State's string of nine consecutive victories in its series with North Carolina ended when the Tar Heels prevailed, 76-74. . . . N.C. State's David Thompson set a school record with 57 points in 34

Gene Bartow (left) became coach of the UCLA Bruins after longtime coach John Wooden retired following the 1974–75 season.

minutes against Buffalo State. UNC Charlotte's George Jackson did likewise with 44 points at Samford. It was deva ju for Jackson, who also hit 21 of 30 field-goal attempts against Samford three weeks earlier when he scored 43 points. . . . Arkansas State's Don Scaife established a school Division I standard by scoring 43 points (vs. Samford and Northeast Louisiana).

McCurdy (32.9 ppg), Thompson (29.9), Iowa State's Hercle Ivy (28.3), Southern Mississippi's Mike Coleman (28.2), New Mexico State's John Williamson (27.2), Arkansas State's Scaife (27.1), Tennessee's Bernard King (26.4), Georgia's Jacky Dorsey (25.8) and UNCC's Jackson (24.5) set

school records for highest scoring average in a single season.

Clemson ended a 17-game losing streak in its series with North Carolina en route to making its lone Top 20 appearance in a final wire-service poll until 1987. The Tigers' Skip Wise became the only freshman to be an All-ACC first-team selection until Kenny Anderson in 1990. No Clemson player has scored at least 35 points in a game since Wise poured in 38 in a 76-75 defeat against Pennsylvania in the IPTAY Tournament. . . . Duke defeated North Carolina (99-96 in overtime) for the Blue Devils' lone victory in a 17-game stretch of their series from 1972 to 1978. . . . North Carolina trailed Wake Forest, 90-82, with only 50 seconds remaining in the first round of the ACC Tournament before the Tar Heels scored the final eight points of regulation and won in overtime, 101-100. Carolina also won the semifinals in overtime against Clemson en route to capturing the ACC Tournament title. . . . Auburn defeated archrival Alabama, 76-70, for the Tigers' lone victory in their series in a 19-game stretch from 1972 to 1981.

Purdue's Bruce Parkinson set a Big Ten Conference record with 18 assists against Minnesota. . . . Indiana's Bob Knight had one of the all-time greatest coaching staffs. His four assistants all eventually became head coaches for at least two different major colleges—Dave Bliss, Bob Donewald, Mike Krzyzewski and Bob Weltlich.

Texas-El Paso led the nation in team defense for the third consecutive season under coach Don Haskins, a disciple of former Oklahoma State coach Hank Iba. . . . Penn, coached by Chuck Daly, won its sixth consecutive Ivy League championship. Penn defeated Villanova for the eighth time in nine meetings before starting a stretch where the Quakers lost to the Wildcats in 12 of 13 outings through 1987. . . . Holy Cross (20-8/coached by George Blaney) was the nation's most-improved team. The Crusaders were 8-18 the previous season. . . . Temple's streak of 15 straight winning seasons ended when the Owls compiled a 7-19 record. Fellow Philadelphia Big 5 member St. Joseph's lost a school-record 12 consecutive games en route to its first losing mark in 20 years (8-17).

An NCAA single-season high of 10 schools were on NCAA probation with sanctions prohibiting them from participating in the NCAA Tournament. . . . Long Beach State's 75-game homecourt winning streak, which started in 1968, was snapped in its home opener by San Francisco, 94-84. Long Beach State won the Pacific Coast Athletic Association title, but the 49ers finished out of the final national Top 20 for the first time in six years. . . . Pepperdine lost more than 10 games in 12 consecutive seasons until the Waves compiled a 17-8 record. . . . Arizona's Fred Snowden became the first African American coach to have a team

appear in the Top 20 of a final wire-service poll (17th in UPI). The Wildcats were 22-7, with their first five defeats by an average of just three points. The Top 20 appearance was also the first for the school.

Centenary (25-4/coached by Larry Little), Middle Tennessee State (23-5/Jimmy Earle), Stetson (22-4/Glenn Wilkes), Central Michigan (22-6/Dick Parfitt), East Carolina (19-9/Dave Patton) and Portland State (18-8/Ken Edwards) had their winningest seasons in school Division I history. . . . Center Leon Douglas became the only Alabama player ever to become an NCAA consensus first- or second-team All-American. . . . Guard Ron Lee was the first Oregon player since 1940 to become an NCAA consensus first- or second-team All-American. . . . Seattle's Frank Oleynick made game-winning shots at the buzzer in games against Penn State (62-60), St. Mary's (72-70) and Pepperdine (72-71 in overtime) but the Chieftains still finished in the second division of the West Coast Athletic Conference. UNLV captured the WCAC championship in the Rebels' final season as a member of the league.

Northern Arizona's Tom DeBerry set a Big Sky Conference record with 12 steals against Portland State. . . . Stanford, which finished 12-14, upset top-ranked and NCAA champion-to-be UCLA, 64-60, in Howie Dallmar's final season as coach. . . . Pacific (12-14) incurred its first losing record in 12 years. . . . Los Angeles State competed in its final season at the major-college level. . . . The West Coast Athletic Conference's freshman of the year was Pepperdine's Ollie Matson, the son of the famous football player with the same name.

George Ireland, Loyola of Chicago's coach when the Ramblers won the NCAA title in 1963, was forced to resign because of ailing health midway through the campaign. . . . South Florida coach Bill Gibson, 47, died of a heart attack following the season after returning from a recruiting trip. He had suffered a severe heart attack before the start of his only season as coach of the Bulls.

1974-75 FINAL NATIONAL POLLS

AP	UPI	SCHOOL (RECORD)	HEAD COACH
1	2	UCLA (28-3)	John Wooden
2	4	Kentucky (26-5)	Joe B. Hall
3	1	Indiana (31-1)	Bob Knight
4	3	Louisville (28-3)	Denny Crum
5	5	Maryland (24-5)	Lefty Driesell
6	–	Syracuse (23-9)	Roy Danforth
7	9	N.C. State (22-6)	Norman Sloan
8	7	Arizona State (25-4)	Ned Wulk
9	10	North Carolina (23-8)	Dean Smith
10	8	Alabama (22-5)	C.M. Newton
11	6	Marquette (23-4)	Al McGuire
12	–	Princeton (22-8)	Pete Carril
13	–	Cincinnati (23-6)	Gale Catlett
14	14	Notre Dame (19-10)	Digger Phelps
15	–	Kansas State (20-9)	Jack Hartman
16	–	Drake (19-10)	Bob Ortegel
17	14	UNLV (24-5)	Jerry Tarkanian
18	–	Oregon State (19-12)	Ralph Miller
19	–	Michigan (19-8)	Johnny Orr
20	11	Pennsylvania (23-5)	Chuck Daly
–	12	Southern Cal (18-8)	Bob Boyd
–	13	Utah State (21-6)	Dutch Belnap
–	16	Creighton (20-7)	Tom Apke
–	17	Arizona (22-7)	Fred Snowden
–	18	New Mexico State (20-7)	Lou Henson
–	19	Clemson (17-11)	Tates Locke
–	20	Texas-El Paso (20-6)	Don Haskins

Note: This was one of two years that the AP poll was released after the national postseason tournaments. Southern Cal (18th) and Centenary (19th) ranked among the AP's Top 20 before the national tourneys.

1975 NCAA Tournament

Summary: John Wooden's farewell resulted in another NCAA title. Richard Washington scored 54 points in two Final Four outings as a sophomore for UCLA after averaging a modest 4.1 points per game the previous season for the national third-place Bruins. UCLA erased a four-point deficit in the last 50 seconds of regulation to send its national semifinal game against Louisville into overtime. Three Louisville regulars shooting better than 52 percent from the floor for the season (swingman Junior Bridgeman, center Ricky Gallon and guard Phillip Bond) combined to hit 25 percent (6 of 24) in a 75-74 loss against UCLA. Adding insult to injury for the Cardinals was reserve guard Terry Howard missing the front end of a one-and-one free-throw opportunity in the closing seconds of overtime after he converted all 28 of his previous foul shots that season. The Bruins led a charmed life throughout the playoffs. They won their opener in overtime after Michigan's C.J. Kupec missed a shot at the end of regulation and defeated Montana by three points (67-64) in the West Regional semifinals when future

pro standout Micheal Ray Richardson scored just two points for the Grizzlies. "I'm sad I'm getting out, but I'm going out pretty happy, too," Wooden said. "I told them (his team) how proud I was of them. I told them they'd won a national championship but to keep it in perspective. There are other things ahead."

Outcome for Defending Champion: N.C. State (22-6) finished in a three-way tie for second place in the ACC. Despite the presence of national player of the year David Thompson, the ACC Tournament runner-up did not compete in the NCAA playoffs after losing twice against regular-season champion Maryland in league play.

Star Gazing: Indiana, undefeated entering the tourney (29-0), lost the Mideast Regional final against Kentucky (92-90) despite Kent Benson's 33 points and tourney-high 23 rebounds. Knight said he made a mistake by playing an offensive player (John Laskowski) substantially more minutes (33 to 3) than defensive standout Tom Abernethy. Kentucky prevailed despite 6-of-19 field-goal shooting by leading scorer Kevin Grevey. UK guards Jimmy Dan Conner and Mike Flynn combined to outscore Indiana counterparts Quinn Buckner and Bobby Wilkerson, 39-22.

One and Only: Louisville is the only school to lead UCLA at halftime in the 20 Final Four games for the Bruins' 10 titlists under Wooden. The Cardinals led UCLA at intermission, 37-33, in the national semifinals before bowing to the Bruins in overtime, 75-74.

Numbers Game: North Carolina, starting its streak of being the only school to participate in the NCAA Tournament every year since conferences were first permitted to have more than one representative, became the only school to hit more than 60 percent from the floor in a playoff series. The Tar Heels, who won the East Regional third-place game, sank 113 of 187 shots from the floor (60.4 percent) in three contests. . . . Carolina was eliminated by Syracuse, 78-76, in the East Regional semifinals although Rudy Hackett, the leading scorer and rebounder for the Orangemen, was limited to six points and one rebound. Hackett had

1974–75 INDIVIDUAL LEADERS

SCORING

PLAYER	PTS.	AVG.
McCurdy, Richmond	855	32.9
Dantley, Notre Dame	883	30.4
Thompson, N.C. St.	838	29.9
Burden, Utah	747	28.7
Ivy, Iowa St.	737	28.3
Coleman, Southern Miss.	564	28.2
Oleynick, Seattle	709	27.3
Scaife, Arkansas St.	678	27.1
Rogers, Pan American	588	26.7
Adams, Oklahoma	691	26.6

REBOUNDING

PLAYER	REB.	AVG.
Parish, Centenary	447	15.4
Irving, Hofstra	323	15.4
Warner, Maine	352	14.1

Roane, Md.-Eastern Shore	356	13.7
Mayes, Furman	394	13.6
Robinzine, DePaul	338	13.5
Barnett, Samford	350	13.5
Sorrell, Middle Tenn. St.	373	13.3
King, Pan American	293	13.3
Adams, Oklahoma	346	13.3
Hayes, Idaho St.	346	13.3

Note: Parish's rebounding totals were discounted by the NCAA because Centenary was on probation.

FIELD GOAL PERCENTAGE

PLAYER	FGM	FGA	PCT.
King, Tennessee	273	439	.622
Fleischer, Duke	178	287	.620
Meriweather, S. Ill.	229	370	.619
Roundfield, Central Mich.	216	353	.612
Glenn, Southern Ill.	196	321	.611

Allison, Arkansas	172	282	.610
Andreas, Ohio St.	210	347	.605
Kupchak, North Carolina	239	397	.602
Tampa, East Tenn. St.	117	195	.600
Cutter, Western Michigan	134	224	.598

FREE THROW PERCENTAGE

PLAYER	FTM	FTA	PCT.
Oleynick, Seattle	135	152	.888
Caldwell, Florida	102	115	.887
Brookins, Creighton	98	111	.883
Johnson, Auburn	102	116	.879
Kraft, Air Force	83	95	.874
Lee, Syracuse	98	114	.860
Hays, Montana	91	106	.858
Johnson, Morehead St.	91	106	.858
Krueger, Texas	102	119	.857
Rose, NE Louisiana	83	97	.856

1974–75 TEAM LEADERS

SCORING OFFENSE

SCHOOL	PTS.	AVG.
South Alabama	2412	92.8
North Carolina St.	2596	92.7
Houston	2407	92.6
Kentucky	2858	92.2
Illinois St.	2375	91.3

SCORING DEFENSE

SCHOOL	PTS.	AVG.
Texas-El Paso	1491	57.3
New Mexico St.	1601	59.3
Minnesota	1577	60.7
Princeton	1835	61.2
Marquette	1679	62.2

SCORING MARGIN

SCHOOL	OFF.	DEF.	MAR.
UNC Charlotte	88.9	65.2	23.7

Indiana	88.0	65.9	22.1
Maryland	89.9	74.6	15.3
North Carolina St.	92.7	77.9	14.8
Pan American	87.0	73.2	13.8

WON-LOST PERCENTAGE

SCHOOL	W-L	PCT.
Indiana	31-1	.969
Pan American	22-2	.917
Louisville	28-3	.903
UCLA	28-3	.903
UNC Charlotte	23-3	.885

FIELD GOAL PERCENTAGE

SCHOOL	FGM	FGA	PCT.
Maryland	1049	1918	.547
North Carolina	1037	1933	.536
Arkansas	807	1524	.530
Tennessee	927	1756	.528
Duke	864	1672	.517

FREE THROW PERCENTAGE

SCHOOL	FTM	FTA	PCT.
Vanderbilt	530	692	.766
Florida	456	596	.765
Seattle	303	399	.759
Maryland	509	672	.757
Drake	402	533	.754

REBOUND MARGIN

SCHOOL	OWN	OPP.	MAR.
Stetson	47.1	34.7	12.4
South Alabama	52.6	42.2	10.4
Pan American	45.6	35.7	9.9
Maryland	43.5	34.4	9.1
Minnesota	39.6	30.8	8.8

three playoff games with at least 28 points and 12 rebounds. . . . Incredibly, Final Four Most Outstanding Players-to-be Jack Givens of Kentucky and Butch Lee of Marquette were blanked in the same game in their freshman season when Kentucky mauled Marquette, 76-54, in the Mideast Regional. . . . Kansas State sustained its third regional final defeat in four years under coach Jack Hartman. Standout Wildcats freshman guard Mike Evans hit only 6 of 21 field-goal attempts in a 95-87 overtime loss to Syracuse in the East Regional final. He was wearing a hockey goalie mask after breaking his nose in the semifinals. . . . Alabama, coached by C.M. Newton, appeared in

the NCAA playoffs for the first time. . . . Kansas had a playoff-record six players disqualified because of fouls in a 77-71 defeat to Notre Dame in the opening round of the Midwest Regional. . . . Louisville's Junior Bridgeman (36 points vs. Rutgers) and Mitch Kupchak (36 vs. Boston College) tied for the highest-scoring game in the playoffs. Rutgers was making its initial NCAA Tournament appearance.

What Might Have Been: Kentucky had four regulars shoot better than 50 percent from the floor during the campaign—forward Kevin Grevey, guard Jimmy Dan Conner, and centers

1974–75 NCAA CHAMPION: UCLA

SEASON STATISTICS OF UCLA REGULARS

PLAYER	POS.	CL.	G.	FG%	FT%	PPG	RPG
Dave Meyers	F	Sr.	31	.484	.736	18.3	7.9
Richard Washington	C-F	So.	31	.576	.724	15.9	7.8
Marques Johnson	F	So.	29	.543	.686	11.6	7.1
Pete Trgovich	G	Sr.	31	.431	.640	10.2	3.3
Ralph Drollinger	C	Jr.	31	.532	.659	8.8	7.4
Andre McCarter	G	Jr.	31	.359	.729	7.0	2.3
Jim Spillane	G	So.	29	.396	.762	4.5	1.2
Wilbert Olinde	F	So.	22	.474	.560	3.1	2.0
Casey Corliss	F	So.	21	.522	.850	3.1	1.3
Ray Townsend	G	Fr.	20	.410	.667	1.9	0.7
TEAM TOTALS			31	.479	.703	84.7	45.7

Assists leader: McCarter 156.

1975 FINAL FOUR CHAMPIONSHIP GAME

SAN DIEGO, CA

UCLA (92)	MIN.	FG-A	FT-A	REB.	A	PF	PTS.
Meyers	40	9-18	6-7	11	1	4	24
M. Johnson	24	3-9	0-1	7	1	2	6
Washington	40	12-23	4-5	12	3	4	28
Trgovich	40	7-16	2-4	5	4	4	16
McCarter	40	3-6	2-3	2	14	1	8
Drollinger	16	4-6	2-5	13	0	4	10
Team				5			
TOTALS	200	38-78	16-25	55	23	19	92

FG%: .487. FT%: .640. Blocks: 7. Turnovers: 13 (Washington 5). Steals: 3.

KENTUCKY (85)	MIN.	FG-A	FT-A	REB.	A	PF	PTS.
Grevey	36	13-30	8-10	5	1	4	34
Guyette	24	7-11	2-2	7	3	3	16
Robey	14	1-3	0-0	9	1	5	2
Conner	38	4-12	1-2	5	6	1	9
Flynn	25	3-9	4-5	3	2	4	10
Givens	25	3-10	2-3	6	1	3	8
Johnson	17	0-3	0-0	3	1	3	0
Phillips	16	1-7	2-3	6	0	4	4
Lee	3	1-1	0-0	1	0	0	2
Hall	2	0-0	0-0	0	1	1	0
Team				4			
TOTALS	200	33-86	19-25	49	16	28	85

FG%: .384. FT%: .760. Blocks: 1. Turnovers: 13. Steals: 6.
Halftime: UCLA 43-40.

NATIONAL SEMIFINALS

SYRACUSE (79): Hackett 4-6 6-9 14, Sease 7-11 4-4 18, Seibert 2-3 0-2 4, Lee 10-17 3-3 23, Williams 2-9 0-1 4, King 2-8 1-3 5, Kindel 1-3 1-2 3, Shaw 0-0 0-0 0, Parker 2-3 4-7 8, Byrnes 0-0 0-1 0, Kelley 0-1 0-0 0, Meadors 0-0 0-0 0. Team 30-61 (.492) 19-32 (.594) 79.

Halftime: Kentucky 44-32.

KENTUCKY (95): Grevey 5-13 4-5 14, Guyette 2-3 3-4 7, Robey 3-8 3-7 9, Conner 5-9 2-4 12, Flynn 4-9 3-5 11, Givens 10-20 4-8 24, Johnson 2-4 0-0 4, Phillips 5-6 0-2 10, Lee 1-4 0-1 2, Haskins 0-0 2-2 2, Hale 0-1 0-0 0, Hall 0-0 0-0 0, Warford 0-0 0-0 0, Smith 0-1 0-0 0. Team 37-78 (.474) 21-38 (.553) 95.

Halftime: Kentucky 44-32.

LOUISVILLE (74): Murphy 14-28 5-7 33, Cox 5-8 4-11 14, Bunton 3-4 1-2 7, Bridgeman 4-15 4-4 12, Bond 2-6 2-2 6, Whitfield 0-0 0-0 0, Gallon 0-3 0-0 0, Brown 1-1 0-0 2, Wilson 0-0 0-0 0, Howard 0-0-0-1 0. Team 29-65 (.446) 16-27 (.593) 74.

UCLA (75): Meyers 6-16 4-16 16, Johnson 5-10, 0-0 10, Washington 11-19 4-6 26, Trgovich 6-12 0-0 12, McCarter 3-12 0-0 6, Drollinger 1-2 1-2 3, Olinde 0-0 0-0 0, Spillane 1-2 0-0 2. Team 33-73 (.452) 9-14 (.643) 75.

Halftime: Louisville 37-33. Regulation: Tied 65-65.

ALL-TOURNAMENT TEAM

Kevin Grevey, F, Sr., Kentucky (48 points, eight rebounds in final two games)
Jim Lee, G, Sr., Syracuse (50 points, eight rebounds)
David Meyers, F, Sr., UCLA (40 points, 18 rebounds)
Allen Murphy, F, Sr., Louisville (53 points, 10 rebounds)
*Richard Washington, C-F, Soph., UCLA (54 points, 20 rebounds)

*Named Most Outstanding Player.

Rick Robey and Mike Phillips. If only they combined to hit 44.2 percent of their field-goal attempts instead of 36.5 percent (19 of 52) in the championship game, the Wildcats could have defeated UCLA rather than losing 92-85. . . . Kentucky could have received more of a challenge from Marquette (23-4) in the Mideast Regional if Maurice Lucas had stayed in college and exercised the remainder of his eligibility. . . . In another opener, Michigan (19-8) might have given UCLA more of a contest in the West Regional if Campy Russell didn't left school early. . . . Notre Dame (19-10) probably would have had more of a chance of advancing beyond the regional semifinals if Gary Brokaw didn't leave school early. . . . Arizona (22-7) might have been one of the WAC representatives in the NCAA playoffs instead of Arizona State or Texas-El Paso if Eric Money and Coniel Norman didn't forsake their remaining eligibility.

Putting Things in Perspective: Consensus first-team All-American forward Scott May's broken arm possibly cost Indiana the national crown. May returned to the lineup against Kentucky, but he was rusty and scored just two points.

Scoring Leader: Jim Lee, Syracuse (119 points, 23.8 ppg).

Highest Scoring Average: Adrian Dantley, Notre Dame (92 points, 30.7 ppg).

Rebounding Leader: Richard Washington, UCLA (60 rebounds, 12 rpg).

Highest Rebounding Average: Mike Franklin, Cincinnati (49 rebounds, 16.3 rpg).

1975 CHAMPIONSHIP BRACKET

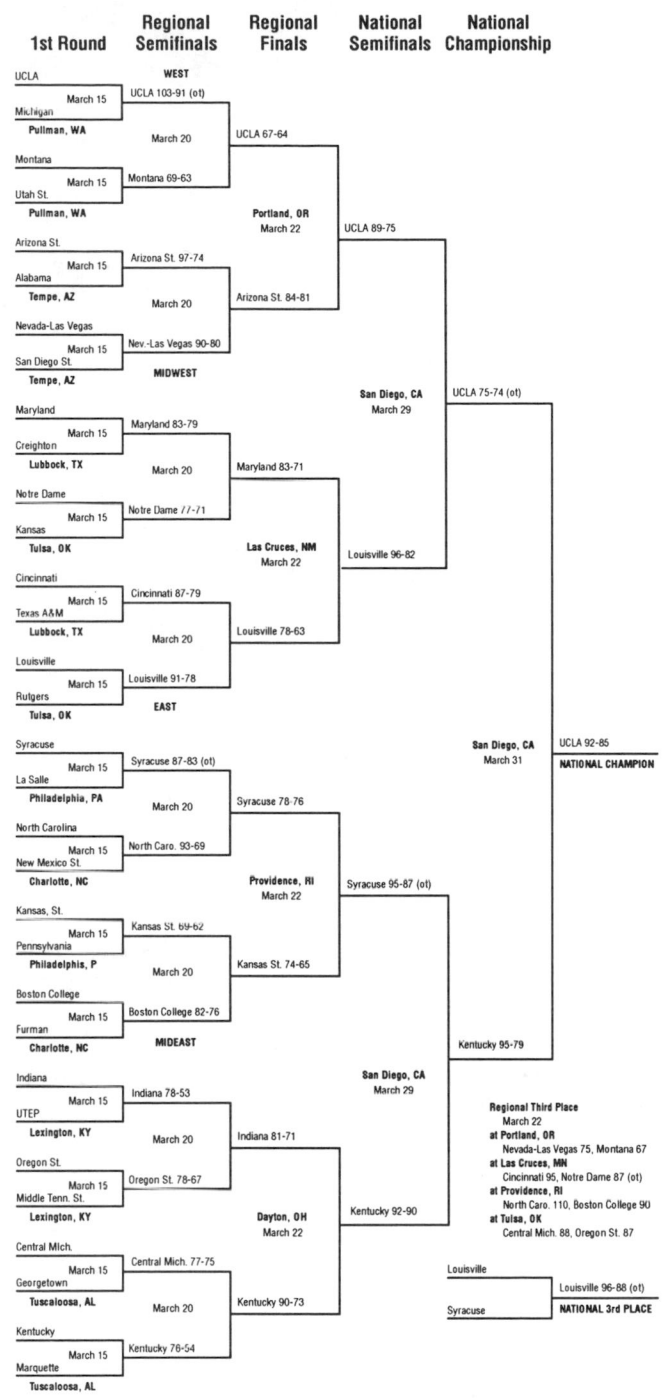

1975-76

AT A GLANCE

NCAA Champion: Indiana (32-0; coached by Bob Knight; won Big Ten title by four games with an 18-0 record).

NIT Champion: Kentucky (20-10; coached by Joe B. Hall; finished in a tie for fourth place in the SEC with an 11-7 record).

New Conferences: Metro, Southland (moved up from Division II).

New Rules: NCAA Tournament regional third-place games are abolished. . . . NIT field reduced from 16 teams to 12 for one year.

NCAA Probation: Canisius, Centenary, Clemson, Long Beach State, Louisiana Tech, Minnesota, Seton Hall, Southwestern Louisiana

NCAA Consensus First-Team All-Americans: Kent Benson, C, Jr., Indiana; Adrian Dantley, F, Jr., Notre Dame; John Lucas, G, Sr., Maryland; Scott May, F, Sr., Indiana; Richard Washington, C-F, Jr., UCLA.

National Players of the Year: Dantley (28.6 ppg, 10.1 rpg, 58.8 FG%/USBWA) and May (23.5 ppg, 7.7 rpg, 52.7 FG%/AP, UPI, NABC, Naismith).

National Coaches of the Year: Indiana's Bob Knight (32-0/AP, USBWA); Michigan's Johnny Orr (25-7/NABC), and Rutgers' Tom Young (31-2/UPI).

Tennessee's Ernie Grunfeld.

Indiana tied North Carolina '57 for the all-time record for victories by an undefeated team (32-0). The Hoosiers' schedule was one of the most difficult of any NCAA kingpin. In 14 games outside the rigorous Big Ten, their opponents combined to win more than three-fourths of their games excluding the contests with Indiana. "I don't think a team should really give a damn who it's playing against," IU coach Bob Knight said. "It doesn't make any difference who you play, how good they are, how poor you are. It's not a game against an opponent; it's a game against your potential. If it is going to be a good team, every time it goes on the floor it is going to try to play against its potential. When it walks off the floor, it need not look at the scorebord to know if

it has played up to its potential or not. It needs only to reflect back on the performance, both individually and collectively, relative to potential, to determine the success of the venture. I think that's the whole essence of athletics."

Joining Indiana for their winningest seasons in school history were Rutgers (31-2/coached by Tom Young), Western Michigan (25-3/Eldon Miller) and North Texas State (22-4/Bill Blakeley). Rutgers made its first Top 20 appearance in a final wire-service poll. North Texas State compiled an anemic 6-20 mark the previous season.

Illinois lost 13 consecutive games against Purdue until the Illini whipped the Boilermakers, 71-63. . . . Purdue (25 of 25) and opponent Wisconsin (22 of 22) combined to sink all 47 of their free-throw attempts on February 7. The Boilermakers won, 85-74, in a game that set an NCAA record for most free throws made by both teams

1975–76 INDIVIDUAL LEADERS

SCORING

PLAYER	PTS.	AVG.
Rogers, Pan American	919	36.8
Williams, Portland St.	834	30.9
Furlow, Michigan St.	793	29.4
Dantley, Notre Dame	829	28.6
Carr, North Carolina St.	798	26.6
Dixon, Hardin-Simmons	707	26.2
Tripucka, Lafayette	679	26.1
Birdsong, Houston	730	26.1
Grunfeld, Tennessee	683	25.3
Smith, Missouri	783	25.3

REBOUNDING

PLAYER	REB.	AVG.
Parish, Centenary*	486	18.0
Pellom, Buffalo	420	16.2
Barnett, Samford	354	15.4

Irving, Hofstra	423	14.6
Thomas, Connecticut	402	13.9
Rudd, McNeese St.	328	13.7
Webster, Indiana St.	339	13.6
Terrell, Southern Methodist	374	13.4
Stephens, Drexel	307	13.3
King, Tennessee	325	13.0
Kyle, Cleveland St.	325	13.0

Note: Parish's rebounding totals were discounted by the NCAA because Centenary was on probation.

FIELD GOAL PERCENTAGE

PLAYER	FGM	FGA	PCT.
Moncrief, Arkansas	149	224	.665
Brown, East Tenn. St.	181	274	.661
Thorpe, Virginia Tech	165	251	.657
Shute, Texas-Arlington	136	209	.651
Abrams, S. Illinois	145	224	.647

Cutter, W. Michigan	140	217	.645
Pierson, Georgia St.	187	291	.643
Davis, Florida St.	143	224	.638
Nordhorn, Stetson	146	234	.624
Hillard, Memphis St.	226	366	.617

FREE THROW PERCENTAGE

PLAYER	FTM	FTA	PCT.
Dufelmeier, Loyola (Ill.)	71	80	.888
O'Connell, Stetson	68	77	.883
Drake, Central Mich.	101	115	.878
Furlow, Michigan St.	177	202	.876
Rood, Hofstra	77	88	.875
Brown, Wake Forest	97	111	.874
Carter, Hawaii	117	136	.860
Macy, Purdue	85	99	.859
Rogers, Pan American	197	230	.857
Evans, Kansas St.	70	82	.854

1975–76 TEAM LEADERS

SCORING OFFENSE

SCHOOL	PTS.	AVG.
UNLV	3426	110.5
North Texas St.	2497	96.0
Pan American	2391	95.6
Rutgers	3079	93.3
Notre Dame	2579	88.9

SCORING DEFENSE

SCHOOL	PTS.	AVG.
Princeton	1427	52.9
Texas-El Paso	1480	56.9
Colgate	1390	57.9
Drexel	1364	59.3
Marquette	1742	60.1

SCORING MARGIN

SCHOOL	OFF.	DEF.	MAR.
UNLV	110.5	89.0	21.5
Indiana	82.1	64.8	17.3

Rutgers	93.3	76.9	16.4
UNC Charlotte	84.5	69.0	15.5
Pan American	95.6	80.7	14.9
Florida St.	83.9	69.0	14.9

WON-LOST PERCENTAGE

SCHOOL	W-L	PCT.
Indiana	32-0	1.000
Rutgers	31-2	.939
UNLV	29-2	.935
Marquette	27-2	.931
Western Michigan	25-3	.893

FIELD GOAL PERCENTAGE

SCHOOL	FGM	FGA	PCT.
Maryland	996	1854	.537
Arkansas	910	1715	.531
Oregon St.	839	1594	.526
North Carolina	966	1838	.526
Duke	968	1853	.522

FREE THROW PERCENTAGE

SCHOOL	FGM	FGA	PCT.
Morehead St.	452	577	.783
Bradley	443	572	.774
Central Michigan	328	425	.772
Ohio	412	534	.772
Michigan St.	443	576	.769

REBOUND MARGIN

SCHOOL	OWN	OPP.	MAR.
Notre Dame	46.3	34.1	12.2
Buffalo	51.5	39.7	11.8
Virginia Tech	45.6	35.3	10.3
Connecticut	43.0	32.8	10.2
UNC Charlotte	44.4	34.2	10.2

without a miss (see accompanying box). It was one of 14 consecutive defeats for the Badgers on the heels of erasing a 22-point deficit in an 82-81 overtime victory against Ohio State. . . . Minnesota's Mychal Thompson established a Big Ten Conference standard with 12 blocked shots in a game against Ohio State. . . . St. Joseph's had an NCAA-record eight players foul out in a 109-96 defeat in double overtime against Xavier. The victory enabled the Musketeers to compile their first winning record (14-12) in 12 years.

Pan American's Marshall Rogers (58 points vs. Texas Lutheran), Michigan State's Terry Furlow (50 vs. Iowa), Louisiana Tech's Mike McConathy (47 vs. Lamar) and Montana's Michael Ray Richardson (tied with 40 vs. Montana State) set school Division I single-game scoring records. Furlow became the only Big Ten player to average more than 30 points per game (32.7) in conference competition in a 23-year span from 1970-71 through 1992-93. . . . Rogers (36.8 ppg), Furlow (29.4), Lafayette's Todd Tripucka (26.1), Minnesota's Mychal Thompson (25.9) and Missouri's Willie Smith (25.3) set school records for highest scoring average in a single season.

Missouri, coached by Norm Stewart, captured its first conference crown since 1930. . . . Oregon guard Ron Lee became the only player in Pacific-

1975-76 UNDEFEATED TEAM: INDIANA (32-0)

COACH: BOB KNIGHT

IU	1975-76 OPPONENT	IU'S HIGH SCORER
84	UCLA* 64	May 33
83	Florida State* 59	May 24
63	Notre Dame 60	May 25
77	Kentucky* (OT) 68	Benson/May 27
93	Georgia 56	May 18
101	Virginia Tech 74	May 27
106	Columbia* 63	Benson 15
97	Manhattan* 61	May 32
76	at St. John's 69	May 29
66	at Ohio State 64	May 24
78	Northwestern 61	Benson 22
80	at Michigan 74	Benson 33
69	at Michigan State 57	Benson 23
83	at Illinois 55	May 27
71	Purdue 67	May 32
85	at Minnesota 76	Abernethy 22
88	at Iowa 73	May 32
114	Wisconsin 61	May 30
72	Michigan (OT) 67	May 27
85	Michigan State 70	Benson 38
58	Illinois 48	Benson 17
74	at Purdue 71	May 26
76	Minnesota 64	Abernethy 22
101	Iowa 81	Buckner 24
96	at Wisconsin 67	May 41
76	at Northwestern 63	May 24
96	Ohio State 67	Benson/May 21

NCAA TOURNAMENT

IU	OPPONENT	IU'S HIGH SCORER
90	St. John's* 70	May 33
74	Alabama* 69	May 25
65	Marquette* 56	Benson 18
65	UCLA* 51	Benson 16
86	Michigan* 68	May 26

*Neutral court games.

8 Conference history to be named to the all-league first team four consecutive years. . . . UNLV's only regular-season defeat was at Pepperdine, 93-91. . . . Arizona, coached by Fred Snowden, posted its lone conference title (WAC) in a 32-year span from 1953-54 through 1984-85 in three different leagues. . . . Neil McCarthy became the fourth different Weber State coach in nine years to capture at least a share of the Big Sky Conference regular-season crown.

Maryland playmaker John Lucas, a U.S. Junior Davis Cup team member as a high school junior, successfully defended his ACC singles tennis championship in the second straight spring he was tabbed an NCAA consensus basketball All-America. . . . Tennessee's Ernie Grunfeld (25.3) and Bernard King (25.2) became one of only four sets of teammates in NCAA history to each average more than 25 points per game in a single season. King was the first Tennessee to become an NCAA consensus first- or second-team All-American. With King idled by a broken right thumb, half of the Bernie-Ernie show was on the sideline and Grunfeld's 36 points weren't enough to prevent an 81-75 defeat against VMI in the first round of the East Regional. The Volunteers, who defeated national runnerup-to-be Michigan early in the season, were in the midst of a span when they beat Kentucky nine times in 11 contests from

1975-76 FINAL NATIONAL POLLS

AP	UPI	SCHOOL (RECORD)	HEAD COACH
1	1	Indiana (32-0)	Bob Knight
2	2	Marquette (27-2)	Al McGuire
3	4	UNLV (29-2)	Jerry Tarkanian
4	3	Rutgers (31-2)	Tom Young
5	5	UCLA (27-5)	Gene Bartow
6	7	Alabama (23-5)	C.M. Newton
7	8	Notre Dame (23-6)	Digger Phelps
8	6	North Carolina (25-4)	Dean Smith
9	9	Michigan (25-7)	Johnny Orr
10	19	Western Michigan (25-3)	Eldon Miller
11	13	Maryland (22-6)	Lefty Driesell
12	16	Cincinnati (25-6)	Gale Catlett
13	14	Tennessee (21-6)	Ray Mears
14	11	Missouri (26-5)	Norm Stewart
15	12	Arizona (24-9)	Fred Snowden
16	–	Texas Tech (25-6)	Gerald Myers
17	–	DePaul (20-9)	Ray Meyer
18	15	Virginia (18-12)	Terry Holland
19	–	Centenary (22-5)	Larry Little
20	–	Pepperdine (22-6)	Gary Colson
–	10	Washington (23-5)	Marv Harshman
–	16	Florida State (21-6)	Hugh Durham
–	18	St. John's (23-6)	Lou Carnesecca
–	19	Princeton (22-5)	Pete Carril

1975 to 1980. . . . Georgia defeated Kentucky, 81-76, for the Bulldogs' lone victory in a 21-game stretch of their series from 1972 through 1982.

Merlin Wilson became the first Georgetown player to finish his career with at least 1,000 points (1,191) and 1,000 rebounds (1,230). . . . Centenary's Robert Parish finished his career as the only player ever to rank among the national top five in rebounding for four seasons. Parish had a total of 16 games with at least 20 rebounds. . . . North Carolina outlasted Tulane, 113-106, in four

Indiana guard Quinn Buckner (left) jumps for the rebound as teammate Scott May looks on.

Rutgers' Phil Sellers hauls down a rebound.

overtimes at the Superdome in New Orleans. . . . The Citadel lost 20 consecutive games in its series with Davidson until upending the Wildcats, 81-77.

Cal State Fullerton's Kerry Davis (27 vs. Central Michigan) and SMU's Ira Terrell (26 vs. New Mexico State) set school single-game rebounding records. . . . Nevada-Reno's Pete Padgett led the West Coast Athletic Conference in rebounding for the fourth consecutive season although his average decreased each year from a high of 17.8 to a low of 10.5. . . . Virginia Military (22-10), posting its first winning record in 33 years, earned its only undisputed Southern Conference regular-season championship. VMI was coached by Bill Blair. . . . Washington (coached by Marv Harshman) finished in the Top 20 of a final wire-service poll for the first time since 1953. Centenary (Larry Little), Pepperdine (Gary Colson) and Western Michigan (Eldon Miller) made

the only appearance in a final wire-service poll in their school history.

Western Michigan compiled a 25-3 record for its only season without at least 10 defeats in a 35-year span from 1956-57 through 1990-91. Meanwhile, Air Force, coached by Hank Egan, posted a 16-9 mark for its only season without at least 10 setbacks in a 34-year stretch from 1962-1963 through 1996-1997.

Ohio State's Fred Taylor ended his 18-year coaching career with a 297-158 record. His final season (6-20 mark) represented the most defeats in the Buckeyes' history until 1994-95. . . . Mike Krzyzewski began his distinguished coaching career at Army with a modest 11-14 record, which was eight games better than the previous season for the Cadets when they posted their worst winning percentage in school history (3-22, .120). In 1976-77, Army reached the 20-win plateau.

FLAWLESS FREE-THROW SHOOTING

Purdue (25) and Wisconsin (22) combined to convert all 47 of their free-throw attempts, an NCAA record for two teams in a single game. Purdue freshman guards Kyle Macy and Jerry Sichting colloborated to sink nine foul shots. Macy, who transferred to Kentucky after the season, and Sichting each went on to hit more than 86 percent of their charity tosses in college and the NBA.

PURDUE (85): Jordan 8-18 3-3 19, Walls 1-7 0-0 2, Scheffler 4-5 0-0 8, Macy 8-14 5-5 21, Parker 8-12 6-6 22, Sichting 0-0 4-4 4, Thomas 1-3 7-7 9, White 0-0 0-0 0, McCarter 0-0 0-0 0, Steele 0-2 0-0 0. Team 30-61 (.492) **25-25** (1.000) 85.

WISCONSIN (74): Koehler 10-19 8-8 28, Pearson 1-3 8-8 10, Johnson 0-2 0-0 0, Colbert 3-6 2-2 8, Paterick 3-6 0-0 6, J. Smith 2-12 0-0 4, Falk 1-6 0-0 2, Brey 3-7 2-2 8, Rudd 3-7 2-2 8, B. Smith 0-0 0-0 0. Team 26-68 (.382) **22-22** (1.000) 74.

Halftime: Purdue 42-31.

1976 NCAA Tournament

Summary: Indiana's Scott May and Kent Benson combined for 40.8 points and 16.5 rebounds per game for team winning national championship by an average of 13.2 points. The Hoosiers kept a perfect record intact despite trailing in the second half of three of their five tournament games, including Mideast Regional contests against Alabama and Marquette accounting for two of the 11 contests they won by single-digit margins. The closest result was a two-point triumph at Ohio State in their Big Ten Conference opener. Knight's alma mater finished in the Big Ten basement that season with a 2-16 league record. Bob Wilkerson collected 19 rebounds and seven assists in a 65-51 victory over UCLA in the national semifinals before captain Quinn Buckner contributed 16 points and eight rebounds in the championship game against Michigan. Trailing by six points at intermission in the final and playing without Wilkerson after the guard sustained a concussion early in the game, the Hoosiers shot 60 percent from the floor in the second half to come from behind and win (86-68). May, Benson and Buckner collaborated for 36 of Indiana's first 38 points in the second half against the Wolverines, an overtime loser at Indiana in Big Ten Conference competition.

Outcome for Defending Champion: UCLA's 98-game homecourt winning streak, which started in 1970, was snapped by Oregon, 65-45. The Bru-

ins (27-5) won the Pacific-8 title by two games although they were upset at Notre Dame for the third year in a row. Their five defeats were by an average of 16.2 points.

Star Gazing: Rutgers, undefeated entering the tourney (28-0), lost in the national semifinals against Michigan (86-70) when the Scarlet Knights hit a paltry 27.5 percent of their field-goal attempts in the first half. Rutgers' top three scorers for the season—forward Phil Sellers and guards Mike Dabney and Eddie Jordan—combined to shoot 31.4 percent from the floor (16 of 51). John Robinson posted game highs of 20 points and 16 rebounds for the Wolverines.

Biggest Upset: UNLV, ranked third by AP and fourth by UPI entering the tourney, lost to Arizona, 114-109, in overtime in the West Regional semifinals. Arizona, coached by Fred Snowden, participated in the tourney for the first time since its debut in 1951. The Wildcats won their opener, 83-76, against John Thompson-coached Georgetown in the first NCAA playoff game where both coaches were African Americans.

One and Only: Buckner was the only one of the Hoosiers' starting quintet to finish his NBA career with a winning playoff record and play for a championship team (Boston Celtics in 1984).

Numbers Game: This year marked the last time more than half of a set of NCAA first-team All-Americans participated in the Final Four. The five-man All-American squad included Indiana's Benson and May and UCLA's Richard Washington. . . . Virginia and Western Michigan appeared in the NCAA Tournament for the first time. Washington participated for the first time in 23 years. . . . Missouri guard Willie Smith scored a tourney-high 43 points in a 95-88 loss to Michigan in the Midwest Regional final.

What Might Have Been: Eventual NBA first-round draft choices Leon Douglas and Reggie King combined to score an average of 31.5 points per game for Alabama in the 1975-76 season. If only this frontcourt duo combined for 22 points instead of 16 in the 1976 Mideast Regional semifinals, the Crimson Tide could have defeated

1975-76 NCAA CHAMPION: INDIANA

SEASON STATISTICS OF INDIANA REGULARS

PLAYER	POS.	CL.	G.	FG%	FT%	PPG	RPG
Scott May	F	Sr.	32	.527	.782	23.5	7.7
Kent Benson	C	Jr.	32	.578	.684	17.3	8.8
Tom Abernethy	F	Sr.	32	.561	.743	10.0	5.3
Quinn Buckner	G	Sr.	32	.441	.488	8.9	2.8
Bobby Wilkerson	G-F	Sr.	32	.493	.630	7.8	4.9
Wayne Radford	G	So.	30	.563	.712	4.7	2.1
Jim Crews	G	Sr.	31	.468	.857	3.3	0.7
Jim Wisman	G	So.	26	.367	.724	2.5	0.8
Rich Valavicius	F	Fr.	28	.483	.625	2.4	1.8
TEAM TOTALS			**32**	**.517**	**.698**	**82.1**	**41.4**

Assists leader: Wilkerson 171. **Steals leader:** Buckner 65.

1976 FINAL FOUR CHAMPIONSHIP GAME

PHILADELPHIA, PA

MICHIGAN (68)	MIN.	FG-A	FT-A	REB.	A	PF	PTS.
Britt	31	5-6	1-1	3	2	5	11
Robinson	38	4-8	0-1	6	5	2	8
Hubbard	31	4-8	2-2	11	0	5	10
Green	39	7-16	4-5	6	2	3	18
Grote	35	4-9	4-6	1	3	4	12
Bergen	5	0-1	0-0	0	0	1	0
Staton	9	2-5	3-4	2	0	3	7
Baxter	6	0-2	0-0	0	0	2	0
Thompson	2	0-0	0-0	0	0	0	0
Hardy	4	1-2	0-0	2	0	0	2
Team				1			
TOTALS	**200**	**27-57**	**14-19**	**32**	**12**	**25**	**68**

FG%: .474. **FT%:** .737. **Blocks:** 3. **Turnovers:** 19 (Robinson 6). **Steals:** 9.

INDIANA (86)	MIN.	FG-A	FT-A	REB.	A	PF	PTS.
Abernethy	35	4-8	3-3	4	1	2	11
May	39	10-17	6-6	8	2	4	26
Benson	39	11-20	3-5	9	2	3	25
Wilkerson	2	0-1	0-0	0	0	1	0
Buckner	39	5-10	6-9	8	4	4	16
Radford	7	0-1	0-0	1	0	0	0
Crews	12	0-1	2-2	1	4	1	2
Wisman	21	0-1	2-3	1	6	4	2
Valavicius	4	1-1	0-0	0	0	0	2

Haymore	1	1-1	0-0	1	0	0	2
Bender	1	0-0	0-0	0	0	0	0
Team				3			
TOTALS	**200**	**32-61**	**22-28**	**36**	**19**	**19**	**86**

FG%: .525. **FT%:** .786. **Blocks:** 2. **Turnovers:** 13. **Steals:** 10 (Buckner 5). **Halftime:** Michigan 35-29.

NATIONAL SEMIFINALS

MICHIGAN (86): Britt 5-9 1-1 11, Robinson 8-13 4-5 20, Hubbard 8-13 0-3 16, Green 7-16 2-2 16, Grote 4-13 6-6 14, Baxter 2-5 1-2 5, Staton 1-1 2-2 4, Bergen 0-0 0-0 0, Thompson 0-0 0-0 0, Schinnerer 0-0 0-0 0, Hardy 0-0 0-0 0, Jones 0-0 0-0 0, Lillard 0-0 0-0 0. Team 35-70 (.500) 16-21 (.762) 86.

RUTGERS (70): Sellers 5-13 1-3 11, Copeland 7-12 1-1 15, Bailey 1-3 4-6 6, Jordan 6-20 4-4 16, Dabney 5-17 0-1 10, Anderson 3-8 0-1 6, Conlin 2-2 0-0 4, Hefele 1-1 0-0 2. Team 30-76 (.395) 10-16 (.625) 70.

Halftime: Michigan 46-29.

UCLA (51): Washington 6-15 3-4 15, Johnson 6-10 0-1 12, Greenwood 2-5 1-2 5, Townsend 2-10 0-0 4, McCarter 2-9 0-0 4, Drollinger 0-3 2-2 2, Holland 0-2 0-0 0, Spillane 0-2 0-0 0, Smith 3-4 0-0 6, Hamilton 0-1 1-2 1, Vroman 0-0 0-0 0, Lippert 0-0 2-2 2, Olinde 0-0 0-0 0. Team 21-61 (.344) 9-13 (.692) 51.

INDIANA (65): Abernethy 7-8 0-1 14, May 5-16 4-6 14, Benson 6-15 4-6 16, Wilkerson 1-5 3-4 5, Buckner 6-14 0-1 12, Crews 1-1 2-3 4. Team 26-59 (.441) 13-21 (.619) 65.

Halftime: Indiana 34-26.

ALL-TOURNAMENT TEAM

Tom Abernethy, F, Sr., Indiana (25 points, 10 rebounds in final two games)
*Kent Benson, C, Jr., Indiana (41 points, 18 rebounds)
Rickey Green, G, Jr., Michigan (34 points, 12 rebounds)
Marques Johnson, F, Jr., UCLA (42 points, 24 rebounds)
Scott May, F, Sr., Indiana (40 points, 12 rebounds, seven assists)

*Named Most Outstanding Player.

unbeaten Indiana rather than losing 74-69. The Hoosiers were also fortunate when eventual NBA players Butch Lee, Lloyd Walton and Jerome Whitehead struggled from the floor for Marquette in the Mideast Regional final. If only Lee, Walton and Whitehead combined to hit 35.1 percent of their field-goal attempts instead of 21.6 percent (8 of 37), the Warriors could have defeated Indiana rather than losing 65-56. . . . Arizona (24-9) could have given UCLA more of a challenge in the West Regional final if Ticky Burden and Coniel Norman had stayed in college and exercised the remainder of their eligibility. . . . Illinois State (20-7) might have made its first NCAA playoff appearance if Bubbles Hawkins didn't leave school early. . . . Utah (19-8) would have had a good chance of appearing in the playoffs for the first time in 10 years if Mike Sojourner had exercised all of his eligibility. . . . Kentucky (20-10) probably would have participated in the NCAA Tournament instead of the NIT if forward-center Rick Robey didn't miss more than half of the season because of a knee injury.

Putting Things in Perspective: North Carolina sophomore playmaker Phil Ford, a second-team consensus All-American, injured a knee in a pickup game after the ACC Tournament and was

1976 CHAMPIONSHIP BRACKET

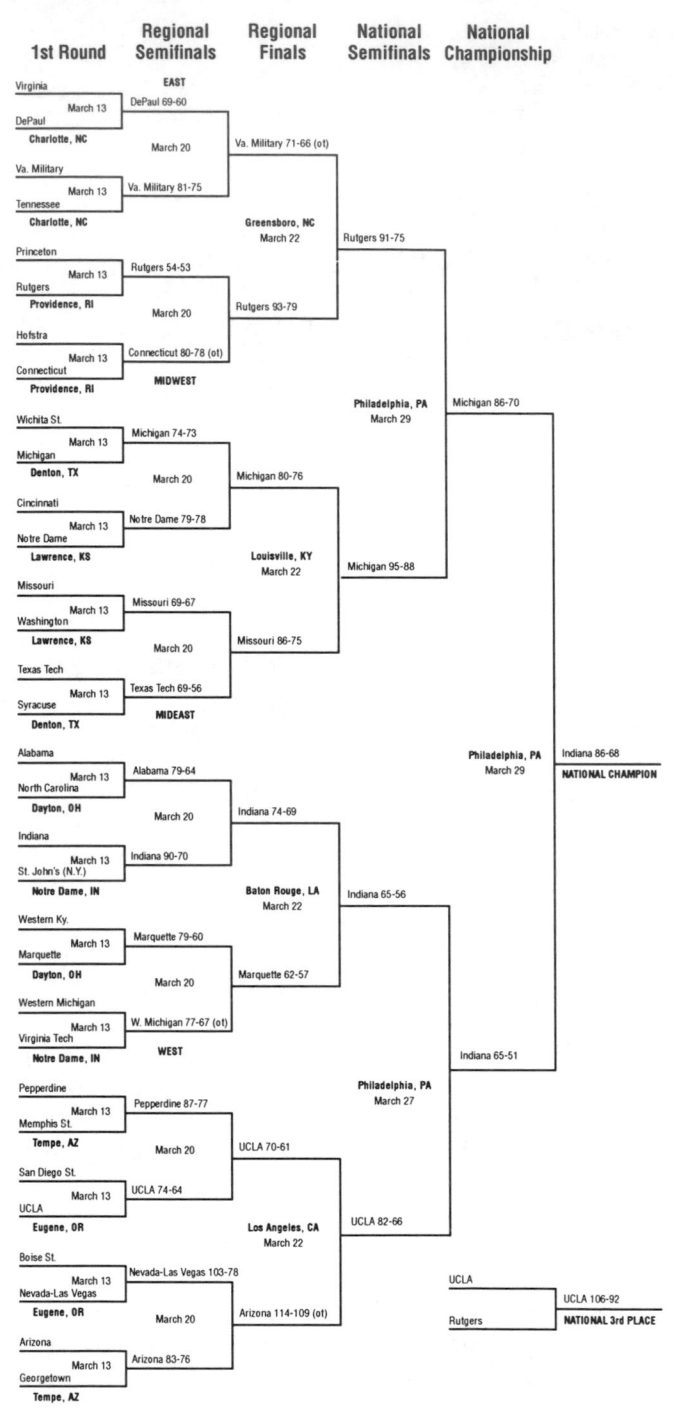

1st Round	Regional Semifinals	Regional Finals	National Semifinals	National Championship

EAST

Virginia
March 13 — DePaul 69-60
DePaul
Charlotte, NC

Va. Military
March 13 — Va. Military 81-75
Tennessee
Charlotte, NC

March 20 — Va. Military 71-66 (ot)

Princeton
March 13 — Rutgers 54-53
Rutgers
Providence, RI

Hofstra
March 13 — Connecticut 80-78 (ot)
Connecticut
Providence, RI

March 20 — Rutgers 93-79

Greensboro, NC
March 22 — Rutgers 91-75

MIDWEST

Wichita St.
March 13 — Michigan 74-73
Michigan
Denton, TX

Cincinnati
March 13 — Notre Dame 79-78
Notre Dame
Lawrence, KS

March 20 — Michigan 80-76

Missouri
March 13 — Missouri 69-67
Washington
Lawrence, KS

Texas Tech
March 13 — Texas Tech 69-56
Syracuse
Denton, TX

March 20 — Missouri 86-75

Louisville, KY
March 22 — Michigan 95-88

Philadelphia, PA
March 29 — Michigan 86-70

MIDEAST

Alabama
March 13 — Alabama 79-64
North Carolina
Dayton, OH

Indiana
March 13 — Indiana 90-70
St. John's (N.Y.)
Notre Dame, IN

March 20 — Indiana 74-69

Western Ky.
March 13 — Marquette 79-60
Marquette
Dayton, OH

Western Michigan
March 13 — W. Michigan 77-67 (ot)
Virginia Tech
Notre Dame, IN

March 20 — Marquette 62-57

Baton Rouge, LA
March 22 — Indiana 65-56

WEST

Pepperdine
March 13 — Pepperdine 87-77
Memphis St.
Tempe, AZ

San Diego St.
March 13 — UCLA 74-64
UCLA
Eugene, OR

March 20 — UCLA 70-61

Boise St.
March 13 — Nevada-Las Vegas 103-78
Nevada-Las Vegas
Eugene, OR

Arizona
March 13 — Arizona 83-76
Georgetown
Tempe, AZ

March 20 — Arizona 114-109 (ot)

Los Angeles, CA
March 22 — UCLA 82-66

Philadelphia, PA
March 27 — Indiana 65-51

Philadelphia, PA
March 29 — Indiana 86-68
NATIONAL CHAMPION

UCLA
Rutgers
UCLA 106-92
NATIONAL 3rd PLACE

ineffective (two points, three assists, five turnovers) in the Tar Heels' 79-64 NCAA Tournament first-round defeat to Alabama.

Scoring Leader: Scott May, Indiana (113 points, 22.6 ppg).

Highest Scoring Average: Willie Smith, Missouri (94 points, 31.3 ppg).

Rebounding Leader: Phil Hubbard, Michigan (61 rebounds, 12.2 rpg).

Highest Rebounding Average: John Thomas, Connecticut (30 rebounds, 15 rpg).

1976-77

AT A GLANCE

NCAA Champion: Marquette (25-7; coached by Al McGuire).

NIT Champion: St. Bonaventure (24-6; coached by Jim Satalin).

New Conference: Eastern Collegiate Basketball League (forerunner of Eastern 8 and Atlantic 10), New Jersey-New York 7 (disbanded three years later), Sun Belt.

New Rules: The dunk shot is allowed again after an eight-year exile. . . . NIT implements format whereby early-round games are played at locations across the country before the four semifinalists advance to New York.

NCAA Probation: Canisius, Centenary, Clemson, Denver, Minnesota, Montana, Nevada, Southwestern Louisiana, West Texas State

NCAA Consensus First-Team All-Americans: Kent Benson, C, Sr., Indiana; Otis Birdsong, G, Sr., Houston; Phil Ford, G, Jr., North Carolina; Rickey Green, G, Sr., Michigan; Marques Johnson, F, Sr., UCLA; Bernard King, F, Jr., Tennessee.

National Player of the Year: Johnson (21.4 ppg, 11.1 rpg, 59.1 FG%).

National Coaches of the Year: San Francisco's Bob Gaillard (29-2/AP, UPI); North Carolina's Dean Smith (28-5/NABC), and Arkansas' Eddie Sutton (26-2/USBWA).

The first 38 NCAA national champions, from Oregon (29-5 record in 1938-39) through

Tennessee forward Bernard King.

Indiana (the last unbeaten team with a 32-0 mark in 1975-76), averaged barely over two defeats per season. None of the titlists sustained more than six setbacks until Marquette's Al McGuire-coached squad won the title with a 25-7 worksheet. It was the final campaign in McGuire's coaching career, which included 20-win seasons each of his last 11 years. His average record in the last 10 years was 25-4. McGuire's eight previous Marquette teams incurred fewer defeats than his lone NCAA titlist. The Warriors' seven defeats were by an average of four points, including a 77-72 double-overtime setback to DePaul that snapped their 19-game winning streak over the Blue Demons.

In an amazing turnaround, New Mexico State trailed 28-0 before rallying to defeat Bradley, 117-109. It was the largest deficit before scoring for a team to overcome and still win a game. New Mexico State coach Ken Hayes replaced his entire

1976-77 INDIVIDUAL LEADERS

SCORING

PLAYER	PTS.	AVG.
Williams, Portland St.	1010	38.8
Roberts, Oral Roberts	951	34.0
Bird, Indiana St.	918	32.8
Birdsong, Houston	1090	30.3
Laurel, Hofstra	908	30.3
Natt, NE Louisiana	782	29.0
McConathy, LSU	716	27.5
Phegley, Bradley	739	27.4
Reynolds, Northwestern (La.)	686	26.4
Hanson, Connecticut	702	26.0

REBOUNDING

PLAYER	REB.	AVG.
Mosley, Seton Hall	473	16.31
Irving, Hofstra	440	16.30
Elmore, Wichita St.	441	15.8

Stephens, Drexel	340	14.8
Landsberger, Arizona St.	359	14.4
King, Tennessee	371	14.3
Bird, Indiana St.	373	13.3
King, Iowa	332	13.3
Jones, Nevada-Reno	355	13.1
Hubbard, Michigan	389	13.0
Hicks, N. Illinois	350	13.0

FIELD GOAL PERCENTAGE

PLAYER	FGM	FGA	PCT.
Senser, W. Chester St.	130	186	.699
Montgomery, VMI	161	247	.652
Moncrief, Arkansas	157	242	.649
Maxwell, UNC Charlotte	244	381	.640
Sowinski, Princeton	163	258	.632
Natt, NE Louisiana	307	493	.623
Cooper, Providence	188	302	.623
Griffin, Wake Forest	198	319	.621

Miller, Cincinnati	180	291	.619
Brewer, Arkansas	199	326	.610
Brown, Iona	150	246	.610

FREE THROW PERCENTAGE

PLAYER	FTM	FTA	PCT.
Smith, UNLV	98	106	.925
Kelly, Vermont	71	77	.922
Thieneman, Va. Tech	98	107	.916
O'Brien, Seattle	89	99	.899
Fagan, Colgate	110	123	.894
DeSantis, Fairfield	116	130	.892
Jonas, Utah	118	133	.887
Mack, Brown	70	79	.886
Hamilton, Iona	68	77	.883
Perry, Holy Cross	156	177	.881
Yoder, Cincinnati	111	126	.881

1976-77 TEAM LEADERS

SCORING OFFENSE

SCHOOL	PTS.	AVG.
UNLV	3426	107.1
Houston	3482	94.1
San Francisco	2904	93.7
North Texas St.	2468	91.4
Detroit	2629	90.7

SCORING DEFENSE

SCHOOL	PTS.	AVG.
Princeton	1343	51.7
Marquette	1900	59.4
Toledo	1604	59.4
Arkansas	1701	60.8
Oregon	1766	60.9

SCORING MARGIN

SCHOOL	OFF.	DEF.	MAR.
UNLV	107.1	87.7	19.4
Clemson	86.6	68.9	17.7
Old Dominion	88.3	70.9	17.4
Detroit	90.7	73.9	16.8
Syracuse	86.9	70.2	16.7

WON-LOST PERCENTAGE

SCHOOL	W-L	PCT.
San Francisco	29-2	.935
Arkansas	26-2	.929
UNLV	29-3	.906
Indiana St.	25-3	.893
Minnesota	24-3	.889

FIELD GOAL PERCENTAGE

SCHOOL	FGM	FGA	PCT.
Arkansas	849	1558	.545
UNC-Wilmington	816	1500	.544
West Texas St.	885	1634	.542
Utah	936	1733	.540
North Carolina	1054	1961	.537

FIELD GOAL PERCENTAGE DEFENSE

SCHOOL	FGM	FGA	PCT.
Minnesota	766	1886	.406
Princeton	548	1336	.410
Oral Roberts	796	1922	.414
Kansas	727	1726	.421
Syracuse	830	1970	.421

FREE THROW PERCENTAGE

SCHOOL	FTM	FTA	PCT.
Utah	499	638	.782
Marquette	446	573	.778
Princeton	391	507	.771
UNLV	610	793	.769
Georgia Tech	434	565	.768

REBOUND MARGIN

SCHOOL	OWN	OPP.	MAR.
Notre Dame	42.4	31.6	10.8
Indiana St.	44.0	33.9	10.1
San Francisco	47.0	37.1	9.9
Arizona	46.7	37.0	9.7
Navy	41.0	32.3	8.7

starting lineup when Bradley raced to a 16-0 lead and didn't reinsert them until the score was 24-0. Twice Hayes called timeout, and on another occasion—when the time clock quit working—he asked the referees for a new ball. "You can't just sit there and do nothing," Hayes said. The Aggies cut the Braves' lead to six at halftime (56-50), but the visitors didn't move in front until there was 3:22 remaining. "It's almost impossible to get a 28-0 lead on a good team," Bradley coach Joe Stowell said, "and it's almost impossible to lose a game once you do."

Transfer Larry Bird, who briefly attended Indiana, began to make a name for himself at Indiana State. He averaged 38.3 points per game in his last 15 outings to finish third in the nation in scoring. Oral Roberts senior Anthony Roberts, who averaged a modest 5.2 points per game as a freshman, finished runner-up in scoring (34 ppg) by averaging 37.3 over the last half of the season, including outbursts of 66 points (school-record vs. North Carolina A&T) and 65 (against Oregon in first round of NIT). The 65-point explosion is the highest-scoring output in NCAA Division I postseason history.

Portland State's Freeman Williams averaged 40.7 ppg from January 9 through the remainder of the season to lead the country with a 38.8 mark.

Williams poured in 71 points against Southern Oregon—the highest total by a major collegian in 23 years. He averaged 35.3 points on a trip to the South when his team ended New Orleans' 21-game homecourt winning streak, North Texas State's 19-game home streak and Pan American's 20-game home streak in a five-day stretch. . . . Williams (38.8 ppg), Bird (32.8), Hofstra's Rich Laurel (30.3), Northeast Louisiana's Calvin Natt (29), Louisiana Tech's Mike McConathy (27.5), Northwestern State's Billy Reynolds (26.4), Nevada-Reno's Edgar Jones (24.7) and Hawaii's Gavin Smith (23.4) set school Division I records for highest scoring average in a single season. . . . Oregon's Greg Ballard set a school record with 43 points at Oral Roberts in the first round of the NIT. It was his third 40-point outing in a month. Also establishing school Division I single-game scoring standards were Stetson's Mel Daniels (48 points vs. UNC-Wilmington), Weber State's Stan Mayhew (45 vs. Utah State), NSU's Reynolds (42 at Lamar) and NE Louisiana's Calvin Natt (39 vs. Northwestern State).

Toledo, en route to its first of five consecutive 20-plus win seasons, ended Indiana's 57-game regular-season winning streak, 59-57, in the inaugural game in the Rockets' Savage Hall. . . . UNC Charlotte (28-5/coached by Lee Rose), Virginia Military (26-4/Charlie Schmaus), Detroit (25-4/Dick Vitale), Old Dominion (25-4/Paul Webb), Idaho State (25-5/Jim Killingsworth), Austin Peay State (24-4/Lake Kelly), Hofstra (23-7/Roger Gaeckler) and Tennessee (22-6/Ray Mears) had their winningest seasons in school Division I history.

The last 16 VMI coaches have all-time losing records at the school. That's what makes the Keydets' lone appearance in the Top 20 of a final wire-service poll so remarkable (20th in AP). UNCC also finished in the Top 20 of a final wire-service poll for the only time in school annals.

Minnesota, which was on NCAA probation, became the only college ever to have three team-

Marquette's Bo Ellis was named to the 1977 All-Tournament Team.

mates later average more than 20 points per game in any NBA season—Kevin McHale (12 ppg as a freshman), Mychal Thompson (22 ppg as a junior) and Ray Williams (18 ppg as a senior). . . . Minnesota transfer Mark Landsberger set an Arizona State single-game record with 27 rebounds against San Diego State. . . . LSU's Rudy Macklin (32 vs. Tulane), Northeast Louisiana's Calvin Natt (tied with 31 vs. Georgia Southern), Drake's Ken Harris (26 vs. Tulsa) and UNC Charlotte's Cedric Maxwell (tied with 24 at Seton Hall) established school single-game rebounding marks.

Wisconsin's Bill Cofield became the first African American head coach in the Big Ten. . . . Houston guard Otis Birdsong set a Southwest Conference record by averaging 30.3 points per game. . . . Texas-El Paso's streak of 16 consecutive winning seasons ended when the Miners compiled an 11-15 record. . . . Southwestern Louisiana

(21-8/coached by Jim Hatfield) was the nation's most-improved team. The Ragin' Cajuns were 7-19 the previous season.

Arkansas, earning its first appearance in the Top 20 of a final wire-service poll, participated in the NCAA Tournament for the first time in 19 years after becoming the first SWC school in 21 seasons to go undefeated in league play. Guards Sidney Moncrief (64.9 percent) and Ron Brewer (61 percent) finished among the top 10 nationally in field-goal shooting to help the Razorbacks lead the country in that category. The Eddie Sutton-coached Hogs clinched the title by shooting 68 percent against Wake Forest in the NCAA Tournament although they lost the game.

UCLA's Marques Johnson, the unanimous national player of the year, didn't mince words when he was asked to express what the return of the dunk meant to him. "It was like I was reborn," Johnson responded.

Notre Dame won at UCLA, 66-63, to snap the Bruins' 115-game nonconference homecourt winning streak. . . . San Francisco, undefeated until its final regular-season game at Notre Dame (93-82), was a first-round NCAA Tournament loser to UNLV. . . . West Virginia forward Bob Huggins, who would later coach Cincinnati to the Final Four, led the fledgling ECBL in free-throw shooting with a mark of 84.4 percent. . . . Forward Rod Griffin became the first Wake Forest player since 1955 to become an NCAA consensus first- or second-team All-American. . . . William & Mary, coached by George Balanis, finished in the first division of the Southern Conference in its final season as a member of the league. Furman, coached by Joe Williams, tied for first place in the SC after finishing in seventh the previous year. . . . George Washington lost 17 consecutive games to Maryland in their series until upending the Terrapins, 86-76. . . . LSU's Kenny Higgs set a still-standing SEC standard for assists per game with an 8.9 mark.

Long Beach State, coached by Dwight Jones, captured its eighth consecutive Pacific Coast Athletic Association championship. . . . Nevada-Reno ended a streak of 10 straight losing seasons by

1976-77 FINAL NATIONAL POLLS

AP	UPI	SCHOOL (RECORD)	HEAD COACH
1	1	Michigan (26-4)	Johnny Orr
2	4	UCLA (24-5)	Gene Bartow
3	5	Kentucky (26-4)	Joe B. Hall
4	6	UNLV (29-3)	Jerry Tarkanian
5	3	North Carolina (28-5)	Dean Smith
6	9	Syracuse (26-4)	Jim Boeheim
7	14	Marquette (25-7)	Al McGuire
8	2	San Francisco (29-2)	Bob Gaillard
9	–	Wake Forest (22-8)	Carl Tacy
10	–	Notre Dame (22-7)	Digger Phelps
11	18	Alabama (25-6)	C.M. Newton
12	19	Detroit (25-4)	Dick Vitale
13	17	Minnesota (24-3)	Jim Dutcher
14	10	Utah (23-7)	Jerry Pimm
15	8	Tennessee (22-6)	Ray Mears
16	11	Kansas State (23-8)	Jack Hartman
17	–	UNC Charlotte (30-5)	Lee Rose
18	7	Arkansas (26-2)	Eddie Sutton
19	13	Louisville (21-7)	Denny Crum
20	–	Virginia Military (26-4)	Charlie Schmaus
–	12	Cincinnati (25-5)	Gale Catlett
–	15	Providence (24-5)	Dave Gavitt
–	16	Indiana State (25-3)	Bob King
–	20	Purdue (20-8)	Fred Schaus

compiling a 15-12 record under first-year Wolf Pack coach Jim Carey. . . . Philadelphia Textile defeated Villanova for the second straight year. . . . Buffalo competed in its final season at the major-college level.

1977 NCAA Tournament

Summary: Tears of joy flowed for coach Al McGuire when Marquette won the championship in his farewell. Marquette overcame halftime deficits to win their first three playoff games against Cincinnati, Kansas State and Wake Forest before trailing most of the second half against UNC Charlotte in the national semifinals. Marquette succeeded in the postseason despite losing five home games, including its last three, to register the Warriors' worst record in 10 years. They lost those home games in Milwaukee Arena, where during one period McGuire's teams were 145-7, including an 81-game winning streak. McGuire, leaving the bench before the game was even over with tears running down his cheeks, pulled away from a hug by long-time assistant Hank Raymonds and made his way to the silence of the locker room. "I want to be alone," McGuire said. "I'm not afraid to cry. All I could think about at the end was—why me? After all the jocks and socks. All the odors in the locker room. All the fights in the gyms. Just the wildness of it all. And to have it end like this ..." McGuire is the only individual to twice direct a school to the Final Four (Marquette also appeared in 1974) after participating as a player in two NBA Finals (1952 and 1953 with the New York Knicks in his first two pro seasons).

Outcome for Defending Champion: Indiana (14-13) finished fourth in the Big Ten although two defeats to Minnesota were later deemed forfeit victories. The Hoosiers had their league-record 37-game winning streak in regular-season Big Ten competition snapped in their conference opener by Purdue, 80-63. They wound up losing their last four conference road games.

Star Gazing: Punctuating UNC Charlotte's 75-68 victory over top-ranked Michigan in the Mideast Regional final was freshman guard Chad Kinch's Jordanesque-type first-half dunk over Wolverines star Phil Hubbard. The slam seemed to send a message to the previous year's national runner-up that the 49ers wouldn't be intimidated.

Biggest Upset: Gene Bartow departed after only two seasons as John Wooden's successor following UCLA's 76-75 setback at Idaho State. The Bruins, ranked fourth by UPI entering the tourney, finished with a 24-5 record when guards Roy Hamilton and Brad Holland combined to hit just 8 of 24 field-goal attempts. Idaho State (25-5), prevailing despite shooting just 40.6 percent from the

1976–77 NCAA CHAMPION: MARQUETTE

SEASON STATISTICS OF MARQUETTE REGULARS

PLAYER	POS.	CL.	G.	FG%	FT%	PPG	RPG
Butch Lee	G	Jr.	32	.477	.872	19.6	3.8
Bo Ellis	F	Sr.	32	.507	.752	15.6	8.3
Jerome Whitehead	C	Jr.	32	.517	.581	10.5	8.2
Gary Rosenberger	G	Jr.	32	.471	.760	7.3	1.4
Jim Boylan	G	Jr.	32	.456	.922	7.0	2.8
Ulice Payne	F-G	Jr.	21	.488	.933	4.5	2.6
Bernard Toone	F-C	So.	32	.410	.711	4.4	2.2
Bill Neary	F	Sr.	32	.328	.769	1.7	2.8
Jim Dudley	F	So.	17	.417	.600	1.5	1.7
TEAM TOTALS			32	.472	.778	70.5	36.6

Assists leaders: Boylan 114, Lee 104.

1977 FINAL FOUR CHAMPIONSHIP GAME

ATLANTA, GA

N. CAROLINA (59)	MIN.	FG-A	FT-A	REB.	A	PF	PTS.
Davis	33	6-13	8-10	8	3	4	20
O'Koren	31	6-10	2-4	11	1	5	14
Yonakor	25	3-5	0-0	4	1	0	6
Ford	38	3-10	0-0	2	5	3	6
Kuester	31	2-6	1-2	0	6	5	5
Krafcisin	10	1-1	0-0	0	0	0	2
Zaliagiris	10	2-3	0-0	0	0	3	4
Bradley	5	1-1	0-0	0	0	2	2
Buckley	10	0-1	0-0	0	0	1	0
Wolf	3	0-1	0-0	1	0	0	0
Colescott	1	0-0	0-0	0	0	0	0
Coley	1	0-0	0-0	0	0	0	0
Doughton	1	0-0	0-0	0	0	0	0
Virgil	1	0-0	0-0	0	0	1	0
Team				2			
TOTALS	200	24-51	11-16	28	16	24	59

FG%: .471. FT%: .688. Blocks: 1. Turnovers: 14. Steals: 6.

MARQUETTE (67)	MIN.	FG-A	FT-A	REB.	A	PF	PTS.
Ellis	39	5-9	4-5	9	3	4	14
Neary	12	0-2	0-0	0	0	1	0
Whitehead	39	2-8	4-4	11	2	2	8
Lee	40	6-14	7-7	3	2	1	19
Boylan	33	5-7	4-4	4	0	3	14
Rosenberger	8	1-1	4-4	1	1	1	6
Toone	29	3-6	0-1	0	0	1	6
Team				1			
TOTALS	200	22-47	23-25	29	8	13	67

FG%: .468. FT%: .920. Blocks: 3. Turnovers: 11. Steals: 5.
Halftime: Marquette 39-27.

NATIONAL SEMIFINALS

NORTH CAROLINA (84): Davis 7-7 5-6 19, O'Koren 14-19 3-5 31, Yonakor 5-7 1-4 11, Ford 4-10 4-5 12, Kuester 2-5 5-7 9, Zaliagiris 0-1 0-0 0, Krafcisin 0-0 0-1 0, Buckley 1-5 0-0 2, Bradley 0-1 0-0 0, Wolf 0-1 0-0 0, Colescott 0-0 0-0 0. Team 33-56 (.589) 18-28 (.643) 84.

UNLV (83): Owens 7-15 0-0 14, Gondrezick 4-8 0-0 8, Moffett 6-9 1-2 13, R. Smith 4-11 0-1 8, S. Smith 10-18 0-0 20, T. Smith 6-8 0-2 12, Theus 4-11 0-0 8, Brown 0-0 0-0 0. Team 41-80 (.513) 1-5 (.200) 83.

Halftime: UNLV 49-43.

UNC CHARLOTTE (49): Massey 7-13 0-0 14, King 2-7 0-0 4, Maxwell 5-6 7-9 17, Kinch 1-7 2-2 4, Watkins 2-4 2-3 6, Gruber 2-6 0-0 4, Scott 0-0 0-0 0. Team 19-43 (.442) 11-14 (.788) 49.

MARQUETTE (51): Ellis 2-8 0-0 4, Neary 0-1 0-0 0, Whitehead 10-16 1-2 21, Lee 5-18 1-1 11, Boylan 4-9 0-0 8, Toone 2-6 2-2 6, Rosenberger 0-0 1-2 1. Team 23-58 (.397) 5-7 (.714) 51.

Halftime: Marquette 25-22.

ALL-TOURNAMENT TEAM

Walter Davis, F, Sr., North Carolina (39 points, 13 rebounds in final two games)
Bo Ellis, F, Sr., Marquette (18 points, 14 rebounds)
*Butch Lee, G, Jr., Marquette (30 points, six rebounds)
Cedric Maxwell, C, Sr., UNC Charlotte (47 points, 28 rebounds)
Jerome Whitehead, C, Jr., Marquette (29 points, 27 rebounds)

*Named Most Outstanding Player.

Marquette coach Al McGuire went out a winner as the Warriors won the NCAA Championship in his last game.

floor, received 27 points and 12 rebounds from Steve Hayes.

One and Only: Cedric "Cornbread" Maxwell is the only player to average more than 20 points and 10 rebounds for an NIT semifinalist one year and an NCAA semifinalist the next season. His UNC Charlotte coach, Lee Rose, became the only individual to coach teams in the NAIA Tournment, NCAA Division III Tournament, NCAA Division II Tournament, NIT and NCAA Division I Tournament. . . . UNLV is the only Final Four team to have as many as six players compile a double-digit season scoring average—forwards Eddie Owens (21.8 points per game) and Sam Smith (14.8); guards Glen Gondrezick (14.6), Reggie Theus (14.5) and Robert Smith (12.8), and center Lewis Brown (10.2). The Rebels, averaging 107.1 points as a team on their way to a national third-place finish, also had two other players come close to a double-figure scoring average—guard Tony Smith (9 ppg) and center Larry Moffett (8). Tony Smith was the only one of the eight players in UNLV's regular rotation to never appear in an NBA game.

Numbers Game: Mike O'Koren became the only freshman to score more than 30 points in a national semifinal or championship game. The North Carolina forward scored 31 in an 84-83 victory over UNLV in the national semifinals. . . . Hubbard hauled in a tourney-high 26 rebounds in Michigan's 86-81 victory over Detroit in the Mideast Regional semifinals. . . . Southern Illinois' Mike Glenn (35 points vs. Arizona), Michigan's Rickey Green (35 vs. Holy Cross) and Hofstra's Rich Laurel (35 vs. Notre Dame) tied for the highest-scoring game in the playoffs. . . . UCLA eliminated Louisville from the playoffs for the third time in six years.

What Might Have Been: Guards Phil Ford and John Kuester combined to score 28.4 points per game on 52.7 percent field-goal shooting for North Carolina in the 1976-77 season. If only they combined for 20 points instead of 11 points on 5 of 16 field-goal shooting (31.3 percent) in the championship game, the Tar Heels could have defeated Marquette rather than losing 67-59. . . .

Notre Dame (22-7) would have sufficient resources to avoid being edged by Carolina in the East Regional semifinals if Adrian Dantley hadn't defected to the NBA. . . . Big Ten runner-up Minnesota, which defeated national champion Marquette on the Warriors' home court, was ineligible for the NCAA Tournament because of an NCAA probation. Minnesota (24-3) could also have had Mark Olberding if he didn't leave school early two years earlier for the ABA after his freshman season. . . . Louisville was flying high with a 19-3 record before forward Larry Williams broke his foot against Tulsa in mid-February. The Cardinals went 2-4 to close out the season, erasing memories of an early-season victory at Marquette. . . . Holy Cross, playing without injured standout freshman guard Ronnie Perry (23 points per game), led top-ranked Michigan with less than five minutes remaining before succumbing in the opening round, 92-81. . . . UCLA (24-5) might not have been upset at Idaho State in the West Regional if Richard Washington didn't leave school early for the NBA. . . . Kansas (18-10) probably would have given Kansas State more of a challenge for the Big Eight title if Norm Cook had stayed in college and not turned pro early.

Putting Things in Perspective: North Carolina senior center Tommy LaGarde was averaging 15.1 points and 7.4 rebounds per game when he injured a knee at midseason and was lost for the remainder of the year. Teammate Phil Ford, a first-team consensus All-American and Carolina's leading scorer, hyperextended his shooting elbow (right) in the East Regional semifinals and scored a total of just 20 points in the team's last three playoff games, including six points on 3 of 10 field-goal shooting in a national final defeat against Marquette.

Scoring Leader: Cedric Maxwell, UNC Charlotte (123 points, 24.6 ppg).

Highest Scoring Average: Mike Glenn, Southern Illinois (65 points, 32.5 ppg).

Rebounding Leader: Cedric Maxwell, UNC Charlotte (64 rebounds, 12.8 rpg).

Highest Rebounding Average: Phil Hubbard, Michigan (45 rebounds, 15 rpg).

1977 CHAMPIONSHIP BRACKET

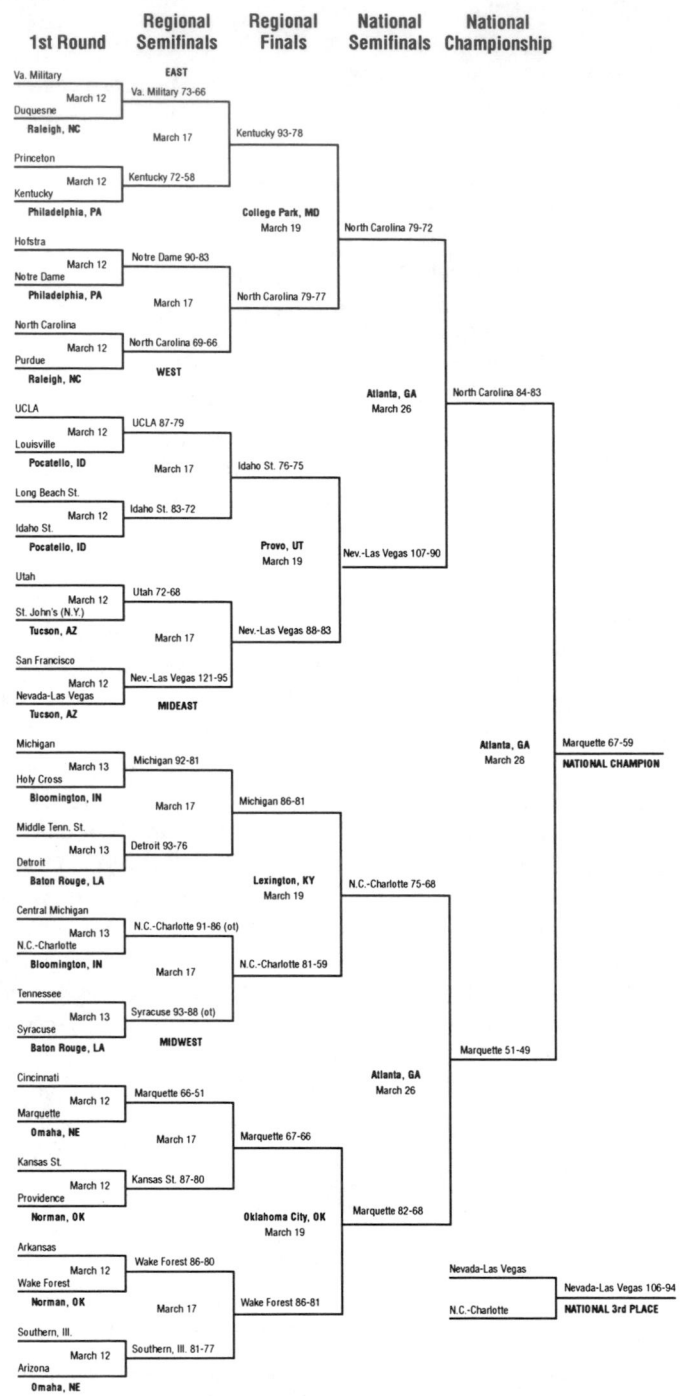

	1st Round	Regional Semifinals	Regional Finals	National Semifinals	National Championship

EAST

Va. Military
March 12
Duquesne
Raleigh, NC
Va. Military 73-66

Princeton
March 12
Kentucky
Philadelphia, PA
Kentucky 72-58

March 17
Kentucky 93-78

Hofstra
March 12
Notre Dame
Philadelphia, PA
Notre Dame 90-83

North Carolina
March 12
Purdue
Raleigh, NC
North Carolina 69-66

March 17
North Carolina 79-77

College Park, MD
March 19
North Carolina 79-72

WEST

UCLA
March 12
Louisville
Pocatello, ID
UCLA 87-79

Long Beach St.
March 12
Idaho St.
Pocatello, ID
Idaho St. 83-72

March 17
Idaho St. 76-75

Utah
March 12
St. John's (N.Y.)
Tucson, AZ
Utah 72-68

San Francisco
March 12
Nevada-Las Vegas
Tucson, AZ
Nev.-Las Vegas 121-95

March 17
Nev.-Las Vegas 88-83

Provo, UT
March 19
Nev.-Las Vegas 107-90

Atlanta, GA
March 26
North Carolina 84-83

North Carolina 84-83

MIDEAST

Michigan
March 13
Holy Cross
Bloomington, IN
Michigan 92-81

Middle Tenn. St.
March 13
Detroit
Baton Rouge, LA
Detroit 93-76

March 17
Michigan 86-81

Central Michigan
March 13
N.C.-Charlotte
Bloomington, IN
N.C.-Charlotte 91-86 (ot)

Tennessee
March 13
Syracuse
Baton Rouge, LA
Syracuse 93-88 (ot)

March 17
N.C.-Charlotte 81-59

Lexington, KY
March 19
N.C.-Charlotte 75-68

MIDWEST

Cincinnati
March 12
Marquette
Omaha, NE
Marquette 66-51

Kansas St.
March 12
Providence
Norman, OK
Kansas St. 87-80

March 17
Marquette 67-66

Arkansas
March 12
Wake Forest
Norman, OK
Wake Forest 86-80

Southern, Ill.
March 12
Arizona
Omaha, NE
Southern, Ill. 81-77

March 17
Wake Forest 86-81

Oklahoma City, OK
March 19
Marquette 82-68

Atlanta, GA
March 26
Marquette 51-49

Marquette 51-49

Atlanta, GA
March 28
Marquette 67-59
NATIONAL CHAMPION

Nevada-Las Vegas
N.C.-Charlotte
Nevada-Las Vegas 106-94
NATIONAL 3rd PLACE

1977-78

AT A GLANCE

NCAA Champion: Kentucky (30-2; coached by Joe B. Hall; won SEC title by three games with a 16-2 record).

NIT Champion: Texas (26-5; coached by Abe Lemons; tied for first place in SWC with a 14-2 record).

New Rule: A seeding process is used in the NCAA Tournament for the first time. A maximum of four automatically-qualifying conference teams are seeded in each of the four regional brackets. These teams are seeded based on their respective conferences' won-lost records in tournament play the previous five years. At-large seeding in each region is based on won-lost records, strength of schedule, and eligibility status of student-athletes for postseason competition.

NCAA Probation: Centenary, Clemson, Hawaii, Idaho, Minnesota, UNLV, Western Carolina.

NCAA Consensus First-Team All-Americans: Larry Bird, F, Jr., Indiana State; Phil Ford, G, Sr., North Carolina; David Greenwood, F, Jr., UCLA; Butch Lee, G, Sr., Marquette; Mychal Thompson, C, Sr., Minnesota.

National Players of the Year: Ford (20.8 ppg, 52.7 FG%, 81.0 FT%/NABC, USBWA, Wooden) and Lee (17.7 ppg, 50.6 FG%, 87.9 FT%).

National Coaches of the Year: Duke's Bill Foster (27-7/shared NABC); Texas' Abe Lemons (26-5/shared NABC); DePaul's Ray Meyer (27-3/USBWA), and Arkansas' Eddie Sutton (32-4/AP, UPI).

Evansville's initial year at the Division I level ended in tragedy when coach Bobby Watson and 13 members of his Purple Aces squad perished in a plane crash just after taking off en route to their fifth game of the season. Their only victory in the first four outings was a 90-83 verdict over Pittsburgh, which finished the season with a winning record (16-11) and tied for third place in the Eastern 8. Watson was hired after former Evansville All-American Jerry Sloan, who went on to a distinguished coaching career with the Utah Jazz, had been named coach of the Purple Aces before abruptly changing his mind. Mike Duff, hailed as Evansville's most promising player, was among those who died. Duff signed with Missouri but changed his mind and was able to immediately

attend Evansville because the Aces weren't affiliated with the national letter of intent. Dick Walters was appointed Watson's successor and guided the Aces to their first NCAA Tournament appearance in 1982.

The North-South Doubleheader in Charlotte, N.C., became a watershed event in Furman history. The Paladins, after losing their first 16 games to North Carolina, defeated the Tar Heels, 89-83. Then, they posted their lone victory over North Carolina State (68-67) in a 29-game stretch of their series from 1940 through 1986. . . . North Carolina set an NCAA record for highest field-goal percentage in a half by hitting 16 of 17 shots (94.1 percent) after intermission against Virginia. . . . Duke's Mike Gminski became the first player in major-college history to score 1,000 points before his 19th birthday. . . . North Carolina A&T, which compiled a 3-24 record the previous season, improved by 16 1/2 games to 20-8. . . . Rutgers started a 15-game winning streak in its series with Massachusetts.

UNLV's 72-game homecourt winning streak, which started in 1974, was snapped by New Mexico, 89-76. Before the season started, Rebels coach Jerry Tarkanian filed suit and was granted an injunction to retain his job after the NCAA placed UNLV on probation for 18 rules violations and recommended that Tarkanian be suspended for two years. . . . New Mexico's Marvin Johnson set a Western Athletic Conference record for most points in a league game with a school-record 50 against Colorado State. CSU, however, compiled its only winning WAC record (8-6) in the Rams' first 14 years in the conference. . . . Arizona and Arizona State each compiled a 6-8 mark in WAC competition in their final season as members of the league.

Portland State guard Freeman Williams became the first major collegian to average more than 30 points per game in his career while playing four seasons in Division I. The senior scored a school-record 81 points against Rocky Mountain. . . . West Chester State's Joe Senser, the country's No. 3 pass receiver in Division II football in the

1977–78 INDIVIDUAL LEADERS

SCORING

PLAYER	PTS.	AVG.
Williams, Portland St.	969	35.9
Bird, Indiana St.	959	30.0
Short, Jackson St.	650	29.5
Mack, East Carolina	699	28.0
Phegley, Bradley	663	27.6
Sanders, Southern (La.)	740	27.4
Carter, VMI	736	26.3
Gerdy, Davidson	670	25.8
Brooks, La Salle	696	24.9
Mitchell, Auburn	671	24.9

REBOUNDING

PLAYER	REB.	AVG.
Williams, N. Texas St.	411	14.7
Taylor, Pan American	368	14.2

Uthoff, Iowa St.	378	14.0
King, Alabama	359	13.3
Natt, NE Louisiana	356	13.2
Searcy, Appalachian St.	359	12.8
Brooks, La Salle	358	12.8
Ruland, Iona	332	12.8
Cooper, New Orleans	343	12.7
Knight, Loyola (Ill.)	343	12.7

FIELD GOAL PERCENTAGE

PLAYER	FGM	FGA	PCT.
Senser, W. Chester St.	135	197	.685
O'Koren, N. Carolina	173	269	.643
Cummings, Cincinnati	212	330	.642
Robey, Kentucky	167	263	.635
Daniels, Stetson	180	284	.634
Young, Fairfield	149	237	.629
Fields, UNC-Wilmington	240	382	.628

Haymore, Mass.	162	259	.625
Macklin, LSU	217	349	.622
Ness, Lafayette	227	368	.617

FREE THROW PERCENTAGE

PLAYER	FTM	FTA	PCT.
Gibson, Marshall	84	89	.944
Tucker, Oklahoma St.	114	125	.912
Williams, J'ville	70	77	.909
Appel, Hofstra	67	74	.905
Perry, Holy Cross	181	201	.900
Macy, Kentucky	115	129	.891
Krivacs, Texas	123	138	.891
Miller, Penn St.	73	82	.890
Stamper, Morehead St.	121	136	.890
Hudson, N. Arizona	92	104	.885

1977–78 TEAM LEADERS

SCORING OFFENSE

SCHOOL	PTS.	AVG.
New Mexico	2731	97.5
Pan American	2487	95.7
Southern (La.)	2653	94.8
Detroit	2730	94.1
Houston	3015	91.4

SCORING DEFENSE

SCHOOL	PTS.	AVG.
Fresno St.	1417	52.5
Princeton	1431	55.0
Marquette	1722	61.5
Arkansas	2218	61.6
Middle Tennessee	1623	62.4

SCORING MARGIN

SCHOOL	OFF.	DEF.	MAR.
UCLA	85.3	67.4	17.9
Detroit	94.1	77.2	16.9
Syracuse	87.8	71.6	16.2
Kansas	81.6	66.4	15.2
Pan American	95.7	80.7	15.0

WON-LOST PERCENTAGE

SCHOOL	W-L	PCT.
Kentucky	30-2	.938
DePaul	27-3	.900
UCLA	25-3	.893
Arkansas	32-4	.889
Detroit	25-4	.862

FIELD GOAL PERCENTAGE

SCHOOL	FGM	FGA	PCT.
Arkansas	1060	1943	.546
Southern (La.)	1107	2031	.545
Kentucky	1040	1922	.541
UNC-Wilmington	809	1499	.540
San Francisco	1020	1907	.535

FIELD GOAL PERCENTAGE DEFENSE

SCHOOL	FGM	FGA	PCT.
Delaware St.	733	1802	.407
Kansas	705	1729	.408
Utah St.	803	1915	.419
Air Force	637	1516	.420
Indiana	723	1720	.420

FREE THROW PERCENTAGE

SCHOOL	FTM	FTA	PCT.
Duke	665	841	.791
Furman	557	721	.773
St. Bonaventure	454	590	.769
Bradley	470	615	.764
Morehead St.	363	475	.764

REBOUND MARGIN

SCHOOL	OWN	OPP.	MAR.
Alcorn St.	52.3	36.0	16.3
Southern (La.)	43.1	31.4	11.7
South Carolina St.	49.1	38.4	10.7
South Alabama	40.0	31.1	8.9
Louisiana St.	46.2	37.5	8.7
Pan American	46.0	37.3	8.7

fall, led the nation in field-goal accuracy for the second consecutive year. . . . Minnesota's Mychal Thompson led the Big Ten Conference in scoring and rebounding, but finished his career as the last NCAA consensus first-team All-American to never participate in the NCAA Tournament.

All five LSU starters fouled out, but the Tigers defeated NCAA champion-to-be Kentucky, 95-94, in overtime. . . . Guard Ron Brewer became the first Arkansas player since 1941 to become an NCAA consensus first- or second-team All-American. . . . South Alabama's stall didn't prevent the Jaguars from losing to New Orleans, 22-20, on Nate Mills' last-second jumper in the final of the Sun Belt Conference Tournament. The next season, the Sun Belt became the first league to experiment with a 45-second shot clock. . . . Fresno State went from last place the previous season in the Pacific Coast Athletic Association to a tie for first under first-year Bulldogs coach Boyd Grant.

Georgetown, coached by John Thompson, earned a spot in the Top 20 of a final wire-service poll for the first time in school history (20th in UPI). Thompson was in his sixth season as bench

Marquette All-American guard Butch Lee works his way through the defense.

boss of the Hoyas. They started what became a 17-game winning streak in their series with Seton Hall after dropping six of their previous seven decisions against the Pirates. . . . St. Francis (N.Y.) compiled its first winning record in 11 seasons (16-9).

East Carolina's Oliver Mack (47 points vs. USC-Aiken), Old Dominion's Ronnie Valentine (44 at Tulane) and Virginia Military's Ron Carter (42 vs. Long Beach State) set school Division I single-game scoring standards. Mack (27.9 ppg), Ron Carter (26.3), Northeastern's Dave Caligaris (24.6), Montana's Michael Ray Richardson (24.2), UNC Wilmington's Denny Fields (22.5) and Northern Arizona's David Henson (19.6) established school Division I records for highest scoring average in a single season. VMI's Carter had 19 consecutive games with 20 points or more.

Michigan State, coached by Jud Heatchote, finished in the Top 20 of a final wire-service poll and participated in the NCAA Tournament for the first time since 1959. . . . Miami of Ohio lost four of five games in a mid-season tailspin but the Redskins (19-9/coached by Darrell Hedric) finished in the final top 20 of a wire-service poll for the only time in school history. . . . Oklahoma State lost 15 consecutive games to Kansas State in their series until edging the Wildcats, 67-65.

Portland, coached by Jack Avina, compiled its only record with fewer than 10 defeats (19-8) since the 1963-64 campaign. . . . Air Force, coached by Hank Egan, registered its last winning season with a 15-10 mark. . . . Northern Colorado competed in its final campaign at the major-college level.

Cal State Fullerton (23-9/coached by Bobby Dye) had its winningest season in school Division I history. Texas (26-5/Abe Lemons), Detroit (25-4/David Gaines), Lafayette (23-8/Roy Chipman) and North Texas (22-6/Bill Blakeley) tied their school records for most victories in a single season.

Southern Cal's Cliff Robinson (28 vs. Portland State) and Appalachian State's Tony Searcy (24 vs. High Point) set school Division I single-game rebounding records. . . . Alabama's Reggie King had a string of 13 consecutive games with at least 10 rebounds. . . . Southern Mississippi, coached by second-year mentor M.K. Turk, ended its streak of seven consecutive losing seasons by compiling a 13-12 record.

Purdue's Fred Schaus, who previously coached West Virginia, chose to enter athletic administration, ending his 12-year coaching career with a 251-96 record. The Boilermakers finished in the first division of the Big Ten but they were drubbed in a non-conference game at Indiana State, 91-63, when the Sycamores' Larry Bird collected 26 points, 17 rebounds and eight assists. . . . Chuck Daly left Penn six weeks before the start of the season to become an assistant coach under Billy Cunningham with the Philadelphia 76ers. The Quakers promoted assistant Bob Weinhauer to succeed Daly. . . . Ray Mears, who never had a losing record in his 21-year career at Wittenberg and Tennessee, did not coach the Volunteers because of exhaustion. He then got out of the coaching profession with a 399-135 record.

1978 NCAA Tournament

Summary: Jack Givens sank 18 of 27 field-goal attempts against Duke's zone defense and scored Kentucky's last 16 points of the first half en route to a 41-point performance in a 94-88 tri-

1977-78 FINAL NATIONAL POLLS

AP	UPI	SCHOOL (RECORD)	HEAD COACH
1	1	Kentucky (30-2)	Joe B. Hall
2	2	UCLA (25-3)	Gary Cunningham
3	7	DePaul (27-3)	Ray Meyer
4	5	Michigan State (25-5)	Jud Heathcote
5	6	Arkansas (32-4)	Eddie Sutton
6	11	Notre Dame (23-8)	Digger Phelps
7	9	Duke (27-7)	Bill Foster
8	3	Marquette (24-4)	Hank Raymonds
9	14	Louisville (23-7)	Denny Crum
10	8	Kansas (24-5)	Ted Owens
11	13	San Francisco (23-6)	Bob Gaillard
12	4	New Mexico (24-4)	Norm Ellenberger
13	15	Indiana (21-8)	Bob Knight
14	18	Utah (23-6)	Jerry Pimm
15	12	Florida State (23-6)	Hugh Durham
16	10	North Carolina (23-8)	Dean Smith
17	19	Texas (26-5)	Abe Lemons
18	–	Detroit (25-4)	Smokey Gaines
19	–	Miami of Ohio (19-9)	Darrell Hedric
20	–	Pennsylvania (20-8)	Bob Weinhauer
–	16	Houston (25-8)	Guy Lewis
–	17	Utah State (21-7)	Dutch Belnap
–	20	Georgetown (23-8)	John Thompson

1977–78 NCAA CHAMPION: KENTUCKY

SEASON STATISTICS OF KENTUCKY REGULARS

PLAYER	POS.	CL.	G.	FG%	FT%	PPG	RPG
Jack Givens	F	Sr.	32	.553	.761	18.1	6.8
Rick Robey	F-C	Sr.	32	.635	.720	14.4	8.2
Kyle Macy	G	So.	32	.536	.891	12.5	2.4
James Lee	F	Sr.	32	.569	.743	10.9	5.2
Mike Phillips	C	Sr.	31	.595	.759	10.2	4.7
Truman Claytor	G	Jr.	32	.466	.774	6.9	0.9
Jay Shidler	G	So.	29	.412	.852	3.7	0.8
Chuck Aleksinas	C	Fr.	27	.569	.694	3.7	2.2
LaVon Williams	F	So.	31	.375	.607	1.9	2.0
Fred Cowan	F	Fr.	19	.500	.667	1.9	0.9
Dwane Casey	G	Jr.	26	.382	.600	1.2	0.7
Tim Stephens	G	So.	19	.333	.857	1.2	0.6
TEAM TOTALS			32	.541	.759	84.2	36.6

Assists leader: Macy 178.

1978 FINAL FOUR CHAMPIONSHIP GAME

ST. LOUIS, MO

DUKE (88)	MIN.	FG-A	FT-A	REB.	A	PF	PTS.
Banks	37	6-12	10-12	8	2	2	22
Dennard	31	5-7	0-0	8	2	5	10
Gminski	37	6-16	8-8	12	2	3	20
Harrell	24	2-2	0-0	0	1	3	4
Spanarkel	40	8-16	5-6	2	3	4	21
Suddath	9	1-3	2-3	2	0	1	4
Bender	16	1-2	5-5	1	4	3	7
Goetsch	6	0-1	0-0	1	0	1	0
Team				1			
TOTALS	200	29-59	30-34	35	14	22	88

FG%: .492. FT%: .882. Blocks: 1. Turnovers: 17. Steals: 6.

KENTUCKY (94)	MIN.	FG-A	FT-A	REB.	A	PF	PTS.
Givens	37	18-27	5-8	8	3	4	41
Robey	32	8-11	4-6	11	0	2	20
Phillips	11	1-4	2-2	2	1	5	4
Macy	38	3-3	3-4	0	8	1	9
Claytor	24	3-5	2-4	0	3	2	8
Lee	20	4-8	0-0	4	2	4	8
Shidler	15	1-5	0-1	1	3	3	2

Aleksinas	1	0-0	0-0	0	0	1	0
Williams	11	1-3	0-0	4	0	2	2
Cowan	8	0-2	0-0	2	0	1	0
Stephens	1	0-0	0-0	0	0	0	0
Courts	1	0-0	0-0	0	0	0	0
Gettelfinger	1	0-0	0-0	0	0	0	0
Casey	0	0-0	0-0	0	0	1	0
TOTALS	200	39-68	16-25	32	20	26	94

FG%: .574. FT%: .573. Blocks: 1. Turnovers: 14. Steals: 9.
Halftime: Kentucky 45-38.

NATIONAL SEMIFINALS

ARKANSAS (59): Counce 2-2 2-3 6, Delph 5-13 5-6 15, Schall 3-5 0-0 6, Brewer 5-12 6-8 16, Moncrief 5-11 3-7 13, Zahn 1-1 1-2 3, Reed 0-0 0-0 0. Team 21-44 (.477) 17-26 (.654) 59.

KENTUCKY (64): Givens 10-16 3-4 23, Robey 3-6 2-2 8, Phillips 1-6 3-4 5, Macy 2-8 3-4 7, Claytor 1-2 0-1 2, Shidler 3-5 0-0 6, Lee 4-8 5-5 13, Casey 0-0 0-0 0, Stephens 0-0 0-0 0, Cowan 0-0 0-0 0, Williams 0-0 0-0 0. Team 24-51 (.471) 16-20 (.800) 64.

Halftime: Kentucky 32-30.

DUKE (90): Banks 8-15 6-7 22, Dennard 2-3 3-5 7, Gminski 13-17 3-4 29, Harrell 0-2 6 6 6, Spanarkel 4-11 12-12 20, Bender 0-1 2-3 2, Goetsch 1-1 0-0 2, Suddath 1-3 0-0 2. Team 29-53 (.547) 32-37 (.865) 90.

NOTRE DAME (86): Tripucka 5-17 2-2 12, Batton 3-6 4-4 10, Flowers 5-8 0-0 10, Branning 4-10 0-0 8, Williams 8-15 0-1 16, Laimbeer 1-5 5-6 7, Hanzlik 3-8 2-2 8, Jackson 5-6 1-2 11, Wilcox 2-2 0-0 4. Team 36-77 (.468) 14-17 (.824) 86.

Halftime: Duke 43-29.

ALL-TOURNAMENT TEAM

Ron Brewer, G, Sr., Arkansas (36 points, 11 rebounds in final two games)
*Jack Givens, F, Sr., Kentucky (64 points, 17 rebounds)
Mike Gminski, C, Soph., Duke (49 points, 17 rebounds)
Rick Robey, F-C, Sr., Kentucky (28 points, 19 rebounds)
Jim Spanarkel, G, Jr., Duke (41 points, eight assists)

*Named Most Outstanding Player.

umph in the final. Duke, after finishing in last place in the ACC regular-season standings the previous four years, improved to second one game behind North Carolina before winning the ACC Tournament and reaching the Final Four.

Outcome for Defending Champion: Marquette (24-4), making its eighth of 10 consecutive tournament appearances, wasted a five-point, halftime lead and lost in the first round of the Mideast Regional against Miami of Ohio (84-81 in overtime). Current Ohio State coach Randy Ayers collected 20 points and 10 rebounds for the Redskins to help offset national player of the year Butch Lee's 27 points for Marquette.

Star Gazing: DePaul center Dave Corzine scored a tourney-high 46 points in a 90-89 victory over Louisville in the Midwest Regional semifinals. Corzine is the only individual ever to score at least 45 points in the NCAA playoffs and never become an NCAA first- or second-team consensus All-American or Final Four Most Outstanding Player. Corzine broke his finger the day before the regional final and the Blue Demons succumbed to Notre Dame, 84-64.

Biggest Upset: Cal State Fullerton (23-9) had four players score from 18 to 23 points and made 62.1 percent of its field-goal attempts to erase a six-point, halftime deficit and upend fourth-ranked New Mexico, 90-85. Future Laker standout

1978 CHAMPIONSHIP BRACKET

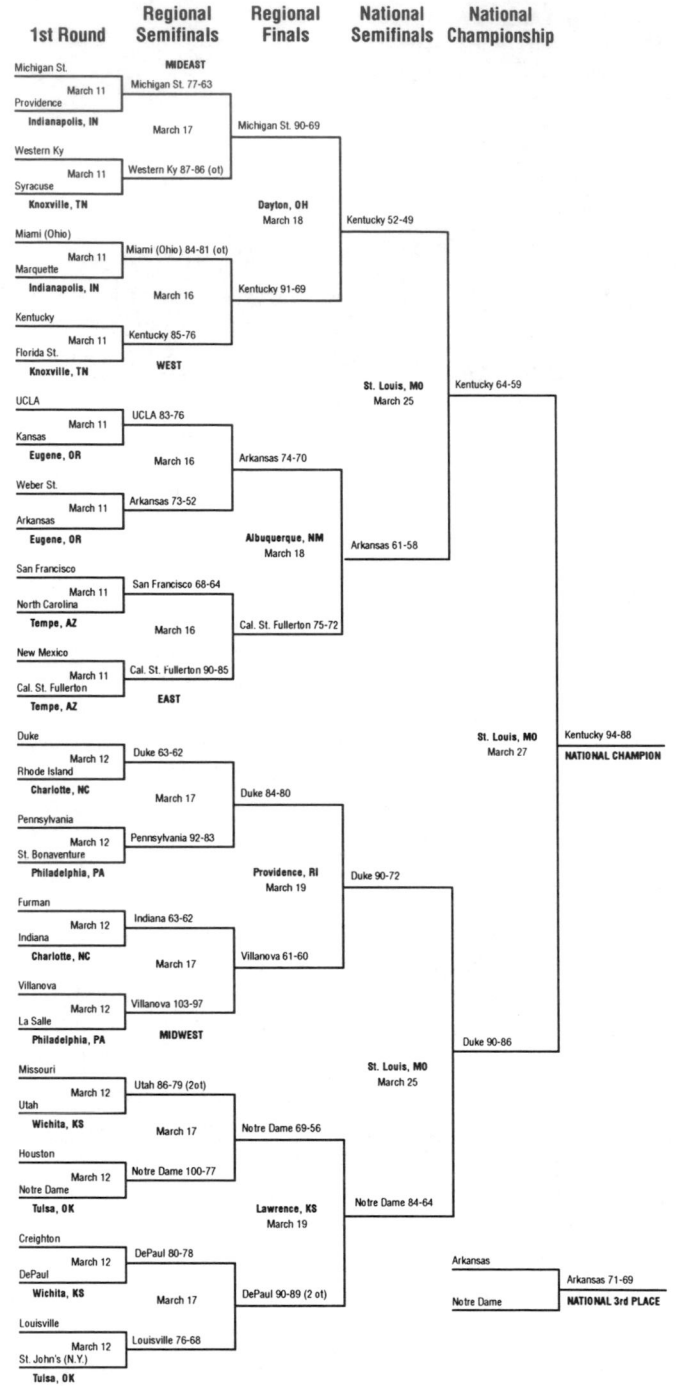

	Regional Semifinals	Regional Finals	National Semifinals	National Championship
1st Round				

MIDEAST

Michigan St.
March 11
Providence
Indianapolis, IN

Michigan St. 77-63

March 17

Western Ky
March 11
Syracuse
Knoxville, TN

Western Ky 87-86 (ot)

Michigan St. 90-69

Dayton, OH
March 18

Miami (Ohio)
March 11
Marquette
Indianapolis, IN

Miami (Ohio) 84-81 (ot)

March 16

Kentucky
March 11
Florida St.
Knoxville, TN

Kentucky 85-76

Kentucky 91-69

Kentucky 52-49

Kentucky 64-59

WEST

UCLA
March 11
Kansas
Eugene, OR

UCLA 83-76

March 16

Weber St.
March 11
Arkansas
Eugene, OR

Arkansas 73-52

Arkansas 74-70

Albuquerque, NM
March 18

San Francisco
March 11
North Carolina
Tempe, AZ

San Francisco 68-64

March 16

New Mexico
March 11
Cal. St. Fullerton
Tempe, AZ

Cal. St. Fullerton 90-85

Cal. St. Fullerton 75-72

Arkansas 61-58

St. Louis, MO
March 25

EAST

Duke
March 12
Rhode Island
Charlotte, NC

Duke 63-62

March 17

Pennsylvania
March 12
St. Bonaventure
Philadelphia, PA

Pennsylvania 92-83

Duke 84-80

Providence, RI
March 19

Furman
March 12
Indiana
Charlotte, NC

Indiana 63-62

March 17

Villanova
March 12
La Salle
Philadelphia, PA

Villanova 103-97

Villanova 61-60

Duke 90-72

Duke 90-86

MIDWEST

Missouri
March 12
Utah
Wichita, KS

Utah 86-79 (2ot)

March 17

Houston
March 12
Notre Dame
Tulsa, OK

Notre Dame 100-77

Notre Dame 69-56

Lawrence, KS
March 19

Creighton
March 12
DePaul
Wichita, KS

DePaul 80-78

March 17

Louisville
March 12
St. John's (N.Y.)
Tulsa, OK

Louisville 76-68

DePaul 90-89 (2 ot)

Notre Dame 84-64

St. Louis, MO
March 25

St. Louis, MO
March 27

Kentucky 94-88

NATIONAL CHAMPION

Arkansas
Notre Dame

Arkansas 71-69

NATIONAL 3rd PLACE

Michael Cooper had an off-game for the Lobos (24-4), sinking just six of 15 field-goal attempts. In the second round, Cal State Fullerton overcame a 12-point deficit at intermission to notch a 75-72 triumph over San Francisco (ranked 11th by AP and 13th by UPI). Incredibly, the Titans almost erased a 15-point, halftime deficit in the regional final before losing, 61-58, against Arkansas (ranked 5th by AP and 6th by UPI). Fullerton, participating in its only NCAA playoff, fell short because of 40.3 percent field-goal shooting compared to 61.7 percent for the Razorbacks.

One and Only: Guard Bob Bender, a member of Indiana's 1976 unbeaten NCAA champion before transferring to Duke, became the only player in NCAA Tournament history to play for two different teams in the championship game.

Numbers Game: None of the five NCAA consensus first-team All-Americans advanced to a regional final, let alone the Final Four. . . . Eight of 11 conference regular-season champions failed to win their league postseason tournament. . . . St. John's George Johnson grabbed a tourney-high 20 rebounds in a 76-68 loss to Louisville in the opening round of the Midwest Regional. . . . UCLA defeated Kansas in the playoffs for the third time in the '70s.

What Might Have Been: Arkansas' acclaimed trio—guards Ron Brewer and Sidney Moncrief and forward Marvin Delph—combined to shoot 55.7 percent from the floor in the 1977-78 season. If only they combined to hit half of their field-goal attempts instead of 41.7 percent (15 of 36) in the national semifinals, the Razorbacks could have defeated eventual champion Kentucky rather than losing 64-59. The Wildcats were fortunate to overcome a five-point halftime deficit in their previous game, a 52-49 victory against Michigan State in the Mideast Regional final. Spartans freshman sensation Magic Johnson hit just two of 10 field-goal attempts and committed six turnovers. Johnson shot a lowly 27.8 percent from the floor (10 of 36) in three tourney games. . . . Phil Hubbard, projected as a first-team All-American for defending Big Ten champion Michigan, missed the season after undergoing

knee surgery. The Wolverines went 16-11. . . . North Carolina State (21-10) might have wound up in the NCAA playoffs instead of the NIT if Kenny Carr didn't forgo his final season of eligibility to turn pro.

Scoring Leader: Mike Gminski, Duke (109 points, 21.8 ppg).

Highest Scoring Average: Dave Corzine, DePaul (82 points, 27.3 ppg).

Rebounding Leader: Gene Banks, Duke (50 rebounds, 10 rpg).

Highest Rebounding Average: Greg Kelser, Michigan State (37 rebounds, 12.3 rpg).

1978-79

AT A GLANCE

NCAA Champion: Michigan State (26-6; coached by Jud Heathcote; tied for first place in Big Ten with a 13-5 record).

NIT Champion: Indiana (22-12; coached by Bob Knight; finished in fifth place in Big Ten with a 10-8 record).

New Rules: The NCAA Tournament bracket expands from 32 teams to 40 and each entrant is seeded for the first time. . . . Three-man officiating crews are assigned to all tournament games. . . . NIT field expands from 16 teams to 24.

NCAA Probation: Cincinnati, Grambling, Hawaii, UNLV.

NCAA Consensus First-Team All-Americans: Larry Bird, F-C, Sr., Indiana State; Mike Gminski, C, Jr., Duke; David Greenwood, F, Sr., UCLA; Earvin "Magic" Johnson, G, Soph., Michigan State; Sidney Moncrief, G-F, Sr., Arkansas.

National Player of the Year: Bird (28.6 ppg, 14.9 rpg, 53.2 FG%, 83.1 FT%).

National Coaches of the Year: Indiana State's Bill Hodges (33-1/AP, UPI); DePaul's Ray Meyer (26-6/NABC), and North Carolina's Dean Smith (23-6/USBWA).

A ballyhooed matchup between Indiana State's Larry Bird and Michigan State's Magic

Michigan State superstar Earvin "Magic" Johnson.

Johnson aroused fans and generated the largest basketball game rating (24.1) and share (38) in television history. A share is the percentage of televisions in use at the time.

Bird was the favorite to lead the nation in scoring until he was limited to four points in a mid-February game against Bradley while Idaho State's Lawrence Butler grabbed the lead with a total of 80 points in two contests. Bird, dubbed the "Hick from French Lick," wasn't able to regain the lead despite pouring in a school-record 49 points against Wichita State in his last regular-season home game. He was instrumental in helping Indiana State become the first Missouri Valley team in 31 years to go unbeaten in conference competition.

Denver's Matt Teahan scored the most points in a single game with 61 against Nebraska Wesleyan. Among the other players who set school

Division I single-game scoring records were James Madison's Steve Stiepler (51 points vs. Robert Morris), Baylor's Vinnie Johnson (50 vs. TCU), Northern Illinois' Paul Dawkins (47 at Western Michigan in overtime), Maryland's Ernest Graham (44 vs. North Carolina State) and Southern Mississippi's Jerome Arnold (41 vs. Missouri-Kansas City). . . . NIU's Dawkins (26.7 ppg), North Texas State's Jon Manning (25.9), Stielper (25.7) and Baylor's Johnson (25.2) set school records for highest scoring average in a single season.

Indiana State (33-1/coached by Bill Hodges), Appalachian State (23-6/Bobby Cremins), Neva-da-Reno (21-7/Jim Carey), Wagner (21-7/P.J. Car-lesimo) and The Citadel (20-7/Les Robinson) had their winningest seasons in school history. Eastern Kentucky (21-8/Ed Byhre) tied its school mark for most victories in a single season. . . . Hodges won his first 33 games, the most ever for any Division I coach at the start of his career before suffering a defeat. . . . Wagner compiled a 7-19 record the previous season. . . . DePaul began a stretch where the Blue Demons defeated Marquette 18 times in 22 games extending to 1992. Meanwhile, Wisconsin ended a 15-game losing streak in its series with Marquette by whipping the Warriors, 65-52.

A point-shaving scandal at Boston College led to a 10-year prison sentence for Eagles player Rick Kuhn. Notorious organized crime figure Henry Hill and New York gambler Richard (The Fixer) Perry masterminded a scheme to fix nine Boston College games in concert with Kuhn and teammates Ernie Cobb and Jim Sweeney. Kuhn, the only player convicted, served 2 1/2 years in prison for conspiracy to commit sports bribery and interstate gambling.

American's Ray Voelkel set an NCAA record for most consecutive successful field goals with 25, covering a nine-game span (see accompanying box). . . . North Texas State's Jon Manning tossed in 41 points against Baylor to become the only player to score 40 or more in a single game for two different schools against Division I opponents. Manning had scored 43 points in January, 1975 as a freshman for Oklahoma City against

Tulsa. . . . UCLA, coached by Gary Cunningham, set an NCAA record with its 13th consecutive regular-season conference championship (Pacific-8/Pacific-10).

Oklahoma finished in the Top 20 of a final wire-service poll for the first time since the AP started its rankings in 1948-49. LSU placed in a final Top 20 for the first time since 1954. . . . The Big Eight Conference sponsored its 33rd and final holiday tournament. The 1946 and 1947 tourneys were conducted prior to Christmas on the second weekend in December. The remainder of the events were held after Christmas. Pairings were based on the previous year's league standings until 1964, but beginning in 1965 the first-round matchups were based on a set rotation. Missouri and Kansas combined to win the last nine Big Eight Holiday Tournament titles.

The Sun Belt became the first conference to sign a long-term contract with the fledgling ESPN cable network. The Sun Belt is the only league to have its championship televised on ESPN every year since the network's inception. . . . South Alabama, coached by Cliff Ellis, went undefeated in Sun Belt competition after compiling a 3-7 league mark the previous year. USA is the only Sun Belt team ever to go undefeated in conference play since the league's inception in 1977. . . . UNLV led the nation in scoring for the third time in four seasons.

Brown lost 38 consecutive games to intracity rival Providence until defeating the Friars, 69-60. Later, Providence gave coach Dave Gavitt a royal send-off in his final homecourt appearance, defeating Rhode Island, 84-77, after losing to the Rams the previous month by 44 points. The next year, Gavitt became commissioner of the wildly successful Big East Conference. . . . Penn, in one of the most remarkable achievements by a school in any decade, had three different coaches guide the Quakers to a Top 20 finish at least twice apiece in the 1970s—Dick Harter, Chuck Daly and Bob Weinhauer. . . . Massachusetts' streak of 11 consecutive winning seasons ended when the Minutemen compiled a 5-22 record. It was their first of 11 straight

Michigan State forward Greg Kelser scores on a slam.

losing seasons. UMass' average annual record in that famine was 8-19. . . . Temple, coached by Don Casey, made its first Top 20 appearance in a final wire-service poll since 1958. . . . The Ivy League permitted freshman eligibility six years after the rest of the nation embraced the rule.

Maryland outlasted N.C. State, 124-110, in the highest-scoring game in ACC history. . . . North Carolina blew a 17-point lead midway through the second half at N.C. State, but Dudley Bradley's steal and dunk in the waning seconds gave the Tar Heels a 70-69 victory. . . . A Carolina player (Al Wood) led the ACC in field-goal percentage for the ninth time in 13 years. . . . Duke's Kenny Dennard set an ACC record with 11 steals in a game against Maryland.

Arizona's Russell Brown established a Pacific-10 Conference record with 19 assists against Grand Canyon. . . . Arizona edged UCLA, 70-69, for the Wildcats' lone victory in a 21-game stretch of their series from 1951 through 1984. . . . Illinois' Derek Holcomb amassed a school-record 11 blocked shots in a 64-57 victory over South Carolina. Illinois had a 15-0 record after edging Michigan State, 57-55, on Eddie Johnson's shot at the buzzer. But the Illini lost 11 of their last 15 games to finish in seventh place in the Big Ten. It was the sixth of seven consecutive second-division finishes for Illinois.

Alcorn State, entering the NIT with an undefeated record, erased a 16-point deficit in an 80-78 victory at Mississippi State in a key intrastate matchup. . . . Mississippi posted its lone victory over Memphis State in a 21-game stretch of their series from 1952 through 1986. . . . Houston didn't have an All-SWC first- or second-team selection for the only time in its first 19 years as a member of the league from 1975-76 through 1993-94. . . . Oklahoma City's Ernie Hill set a Trans America Athletic Conference single-season record by averaging 26.6 points per game. . . . Colorado, coached by Bill Blair, compiled a 14-13 mark for its first winning record in eight campaigns and Brigham Young, coached by Frank Arnold, posted a 20-8 record to snap a streak of five consecutive losing seasons.

Washington went 11-16 for its only losing mark in 14 seasons under coach Marv Harshman.

AMERICAN HERO

American University senior forward Ray Voelkel went on a phenomenal shooting binge in a nine-game stretch from November 24 to December 15, 1978 when he established an NCAA record by hitting 25 straight field-goal attempts. The string of consecutive baskets accounted for almost one-half of Voelkel's field goals for the season (51 of 80). Here is a rundown of his flawless streak:

FG-A	AU OPPONENT	AU RESULT
2-3	St. John's*	L, 72-70
2-2	Alabama	L, 110-87
5-5	Navy	L, 89-78
1-1	Catholic	W, 83-68
7-7	Trenton State	W, 94-50
2-2	Rider	W, 101-72
2-2	Lafayette	W, 63-62
4-4	St. Mary's	W, 105-87
2-3	Delaware*	W, 77-68

*Missed the middle of three field-goal attempts in both the St. John's and Delaware games.

1978-79 FINAL NATIONAL POLLS

AP	UPI	SCHOOL (RECORD)	HEAD COACH
1	1	Indiana State (33-1)	Bill Hodges
2	2	UCLA (25-5)	Gary Cunningham
3	4	Michigan State (26-6)	Jud Heathcote
4	5	Notre Dame (24-6)	Digger Phelps
5	6	Arkansas (25-5)	Eddie Sutton
6	8	DePaul (26-6)	Ray Meyer
7	9	Louisiana State (23-6)	Dale Brown
8	10	Syracuse (26-4)	Jim Boeheim
9	3	North Carolina (23-6)	Dean Smith
10	13	Marquette (22-7)	Hank Raymonds
11	7	Duke (22-8)	Bill Foster
12	17	San Francisco (22-7)	Dan Belluomini
13	19	Louisville (24-8)	Denny Crum
14	–	Pennsylvania (25-7)	Bob Weinhauer
15	14	Purdue (27-8)	Lee Rose
16	–	Oklahoma (21-10)	Dave Bliss
17	–	St. John's (21-11)	Lou Carnesecca
18	–	Rutgers (22-9)	Tom Young
19	–	Toledo (22-7)	Bob Nichols
20	11	Iowa (20-8)	Lute Olson
–	12	Georgetown (24-5)	John Thompson
–	15	Texas (21-8)	Abe Lemons
–	16	Temple (25-4)	Don Casey
–	18	Tennessee (21-12)	Don DeVoe
–	20	Detroit (22-6)	Smokey Gaines

. . . North Carolina State won the first Great Alaska Shootout, which subsequently blossomed into one of the nation's premier in-season tournaments. . . . Paul Lambert, lured by Auburn from Southern Illinois, died in a tragic motel fire. Auburn filled the coaching vacancy by hiring Sonny Smith from East Tennessee State. Another coach who passed away in the offseason was Stu Aberdeen after his second season at Marshall.

1979 NCAA Tournament

Summary: Indiana State, undefeated entering the tourney (29-0), lost the national final against Michigan State (75-64) when the Sycamores' Larry Bird, who hit 53.2 percent of his field-goal attempts on the season, made just one-third of his shots from the floor (7 of 21) as a sore thumb limited his shooting effectiveness. Magic Johnson scored a game-high 24 points for the Spartans. Michigan State dominated the NCAA Tournament, handing every one of its five playoff opponents, a quintet averaging 25.6 victories, their worst defeat of the year—Lamar (31-point margin), LSU (16), Notre Dame (12), Penn (34) and Indiana State (11). Consequently, most observers don't remember the glaring defect of the Spartans earlier in the season when they were defeated by four Big Ten Conference second-divi-

LOWLY NORTHWESTERN STUNS NCAA CHAMPION-TO-BE

MICHIGAN STATE AT NORTHWESTERN

JANUARY 27, 1979

Northwestern has had more than its share of problems in the Big Ten Conference, but the Wildcats were on top of the world when they shocked Michigan State by 18 points, 83-65, in one of the biggest upsets in NCAA history. Eventual NBA forwards Greg Kelser and Jay Vincent combined to hit just four of 15 field-goal attempts for the Spartans.

MICHIGAN STATE (65)	FG-A	FT-A	REB.	PTS.
Greg Kelser	2-10	0-0	4	4
Ron Charles	2-4	1-2	5	5
Jay Vincent	2-5	2-2	2	6
Magic Johnson	7-22	12-16	10	26
Terry Donnelly	1-2	0-0	0	2
Mike Longaker	1-2	2-2	2	4
Greg Lloyd	1-3	2-2	3	4
Mike Brkovich	4-13	1-1	0	9
Rob Gonzalez	1-1	1-2	0	3
Gerald Busby	1-4	0-0	2	2
Jaimie Huffman	0-0	0-0	0	0
Rick Kaye	0-0	0-1	0	0
Don Brkovich	0-1	0-0	0	0
Team:				10
TOTALS	22-67	21-28	38	65

FG%: .328. FT%: .750. Assists: 15 (Johnson 10). Steals: 5. Blocked Shots: 2. Turnovers: 19 (Johnson 5, M. Brkovich 5). Fouled Out: 1 (Vincent).

NORTHWESTERN (83)	FG-A	FT-A	REB.	PTS.
Rod Roberson	6-13	8-9	7	20
Mike Campbell	6-13	4-4	7	16
Brian Jung	1-3	0-2	3	2
Brian Gibson	6-10	4-4	4	16
Jerry Marifke	2-6	8-9	3	12
Bob Klaas	3-7	3-3	7	9
Pete Boeson	1-2	0-0	0	2
Randy Carroll	2-2	0-0	0	4
Bill Fenlon	0-0	0-0	0	0
John Egan	0-0	2-2	1	2
Lyle Dobbins	0-0	0-0	0	0
TOTALS	27-56	29-33	42	83

FG%: .482. FT%: .879. Assists: 19 (Marifke 7). Steals: 2. Blocked Shots: 2. Turnovers: 18 (Roberson 6). Fouled Out: 1 (Klaas).

Halftime: Northwestern 39-29.

sion teams. Michigan State required two overtime victories at home to avoid compiling six Big Ten losses in a seven-game span. Four of the Spartans' five Big Ten defeats were to second-division teams, including an 18-point setback against conference cellar dweller Northwestern, which has more than 25 consecutive losing league records and finished in the Big Ten basement 12 times in one 16-year stretch. Excluding Northwestern, Michigan State's five other defeats were by a total of just eight points.

Outcome for Defending Champion: Kentucky (19-12) incurred its lowest SEC finish (6th) to that point before losing at home in the first round of the NIT to Clemson before an NIT single-game attendance record of 23,522 spectators. The Wildcats bowed three times to Tennessee by an average of 11.3 points.

Star Gazing: Johnson became the only individual to be named Final Four Most Outstanding Player (Michigan State '79) and NBA Finals Most Valuable Player (Los Angeles Lakers '80) in back-to-back seasons.

Biggest Upset: East Regional No. 1 seed North Carolina lost its opener (72-71 against Penn) in the Tar Heels' home state (Raleigh, N.C.).

One and Only: Indiana State is the only school to reach the Final Four in its one and only NCAA Tournament appearance. The Sycamores won the Midwest Regional final against Arkansas, 73-71, when Bob Heaton shifted the ball from his normal right hand to his left for a short shot that bounced twice on the rim before going down. In the regular season, Heaton kept their unbeaten streak intact by hitting a 55-footer that banked off the glass, knotting the score at New Mexico State and forcing an overtime. . . . Bill Hodges of Indiana State is the only individual to win more than 30 games in earning a trip to the national semifinals in his first season as a head coach. Hodges was named interim coach when Bob King was forced to step down four days before practice started after suffering a stroke in the preseason. The Sycamores, who moved up to Division I status in 1972, haven't compiled a winning season since Hodges guided them to a 16-11 mark the year after Bird departed.

Numbers Game: Penn forward Tony Price is the highest scorer in a tourney for a Final Four team to fail to be named All-Tournament. . . . DePaul forward Mark Aguirre became the first freshman to be named to an NCAA All-Tournament team. . . . Michigan State forward Greg Kelser personally outscored (34 to 18) and outrebounded (13 to 11) Notre Dame's vaunted frontcourt of Kelly Tripucka, Orlando Woolridge and Bill Laimbeer in the Mideast Regional final. . . .

1978–79 INDIVIDUAL LEADERS

SCORING

PLAYER	PTS.	AVG.
Butler, Idaho St.	812	30.1
Bird, Indiana St.	973	28.6
Galis, Seton Hall	743	27.5
Tillman, E. Kentucky	780	26.9
Dawkins, N. Illinois	695	26.7
Gerdy, Davidson	721	26.7
Hill, Oklahoma City	771	26.6
Stroud, Mississippi	709	26.3
Manning, N. Texas St.	699	25.9
Stielper, James Madison	668	25.7

REBOUNDING

PLAYER	REB.	AVG.
Davis, Tennessee St.	421	16.2
Cartwright, San Francisco	455	15.7
Garrett, Southern (La.)	433	15.5

Bird, Indiana St.	505	14.9
Knight, Loyola (Ill.)	386	14.3
Smith, Alcorn St.	398	13.7
Brooks, La Salle	347	13.3
Stephens, Drexel	360	13.3
Lawrence, McNeese St.	343	12.7

FIELD GOAL PERCENTAGE

PLAYER	FGM	FGA	PCT.
Brown, Florida St.	237	343	.691
Ruland, Iona	233	347	.671
Johnson, Oregon St.	197	298	.661
Green, Tenn. St.	120	183	.656
Peck, Miss. St.	154	239	.644
Mercer, Georgia	146	227	.643
Spain, Pan American	145	227	.639
Lawrence, McNeese St.	226	356	.635
Bouie, Syracuse	176	279	.631

FREE THROW PERCENTAGE

PLAYER	FTM	FTA	PCT.
Mauldin, Campbell	70	76	.921
Kanaskie, La Salle	55	60	.917
Krivacs, Texas	101	111	.910
Orner, Butler	70	77	.909
Perry, Holy Cross	178	196	.908
Goetz, San Diego St.	74	82	.902
Sienkiewicz, Villanova	78	87	.897
White, Marshall	85	95	.895
Huggins, S. Illinois	76	85	.894
Marifke, Northwestern	63	71	.887

1978–79 TEAM LEADERS

SCORING OFFENSE

SCHOOL	PTS.	AVG.
UNLV	2700	93.1
Alcorn St.	2678	92.3
Wichita St.	2485	88.8
Syracuse	2660	88.7
New Mexico	2567	88.5

SCORING DEFENSE

SCHOOL	PTS.	AVG.
Princeton	1452	55.8
Dartmouth	1486	57.2
Fresno St.	1632	58.3
Montana	1628	60.3
Indiana	2080	61.2
Marquette	1775	61.2

SCORING MARGIN

SCHOOL	OFF.	DEF.	MAR.
Syracuse	88.7	71.5	17.2
Notre Dame	79.7	64.1	15.6
Indiana St.	86.8	72.8	14.0
Alcorn St.	92.3	78.9	13.4
Michigan St.	75.7	62.6	13.1

WON-LOST PERCENTAGE

SCHOOL	W-L	PCT.
Indiana St.	33-1	.971
Alcorn St.	28-1	.966
Syracuse	26-4	.867
Temple	25-4	.862
Arkansas	25-5	.833
UCLA	25-5	.833

FIELD GOAL PERCENTAGE

SCHOOL	FGM	FGA	PCT.
UCLA	1053	1897	.555
Fairfield	792	1468	.540
Arkansas	849	1587	.535
The Citadel	864	1616	.535
Syracuse	1052	1970	.534

FIELD GOAL PERCENTAGE DEFENSE

SCHOOL	FGM	FGA	PCT.
Illinois	738	1828	.404
Tennessee St.	717	1707	.420
Wyoming	667	1582	.422
Indiana	847	2008	.422
Princeton	548	1287	.426

FREE THROW PERCENTAGE

SCHOOL	FTM	FTA	PCT.
St. Francis (Pa.)	350	446	.785
Kentucky	666	858	.776
Fairfield	513	666	.770
Villanova	394	514	.767
DePaul	517	676	.765

REBOUND MARGIN

SCHOOL	OWN	OPP.	MAR.
Alcorn St.	50.1	36.3	13.8
Tennessee St.	49.7	37.9	11.8
Pittsburgh	41.3	30.6	10.7
Indiana St.	48.2	38.1	10.1
Syracuse	44.1	34.8	9.3

MSU guard Terry Donnelly doubled his season scoring average in the second half of the national final with 13 points against Indiana State. . . . David Greenwood's tourney-high 37 points for UCLA weren't enough to prevent a 95-91 setback against DePaul in the West Regional final. . . . St. John's, a No. 10 seed, won three games by an average of three points before losing to Penn by two (64-62) in the East Regional final. . . . Oklahoma, coached by Dave Bliss, made its first NCAA playoff appearance since 1947. . . . Iona, coached by effervescent Jim Valvano, participated in the NCAA playoffs for the initial time. . . . Tennessee notched its first NCAA Tournament victory (97-81 over Eastern Kentucky). In 22 years from 1964-85, the Volunteers finished no worse than fourth in the SEC 18 times and won at least 20 games in 13 of those seasons. . . . Lamar's Clarence Kea collected a game-high 33 points and tourney-high 19 rebounds in a 95-87 triumph over Detroit in the opening round of the Mideast Regional. . . . Southern Cal, coached by Bob Boyd, made its first NCAA Tournament appearance in 18 years. . . . Toledo, coached by Bob

1978–79 NCAA CHAMPION: MICHIGAN STATE

SEASON STATISTICS OF MICHIGAN STATE REGULARS

PLAYER	POS.	CL.	G.	FG%	FT%	PPG	RPG
Greg Kelser	F	Sr.	32	.545	.671	18.8	8.7
Earvin Johnson	G	So.	32	.468	.842	17.1	7.3
Jay Vincent	C	So.	31	.496	.581	12.7	5.2
Ron Charles	F	Jr.	32	.665	.622	8.8	5.1
Mike Brkovich	F	So.	32	.509	.803	7.0	1.8
Terry Donnelly	G	Jr.	32	.535	.754	6.6	1.6
Rob Gonzalez	F	Fr.	28	.581	.800	1.7	1.0
TEAM TOTALS			32	.527	.721	75.7	37.1

Assists leader: Johnson 269.

1979 FINAL FOUR CHAMPIONSHIP GAME

SALT LAKE CITY, UT

MICH. STATE (75)	MIN.	FG-A	FT-A	REB.	A	PF	PTS.
M. Brkovich	39	1-2	3-7	4	1	1	5
Kelser	32	7-13	5-6	8	9	4	19
Charles	31	3-3	1-2	7	0	5	7
Donnelly	39	5-5	5-6	4	0	2	15
Johnson	35	8-15	8-10	7	5	3	24
Vincent	19	2-5	1-2	2	0	4	5
Gonzalez	3	0-0	0-0	0	0	0	0
Longaker	2	0-0	0-0	0	0	0	0
Team				2			
TOTALS	200	26-43	23-33	34	15	19	75

FG%: .605. FT%: .697. Blocks: 2. Turnovers: 16. Steals: 6.

INDIANA STATE (64)	MIN.	FG-A	FT-A	REB.	A	PF	PTS.
Miley	29	0-0	0-1	3	0	1	0
Gilbert	20	2-3	0-4	4	0	4	4
Bird	40	7-21	5-8	13	2	3	19
Nicks	36	7-14	3-6	2	4	5	17
Reed	36	4-9	0-0	0	9	4	8
Heaton	22	4-14	2-2	6	2	2	10
Staley	17	2-2	0-1	3	0	2	4

Nemcek	2	1-1	0-0	0	1	3	2
Team				3			
TOTALS	200	27-64	10-22	34	18	24	64

FG%: .422. FT%: .455. Blocks: 2. Turnovers: 10 (Bird 6). Steals: 6 (Bird 5).

Halftime: Michigan State 37-28.

NATIONAL SEMIFINALS

PENNSYLVANIA (67): Price 7-18 4-4 18, Smith 0-6 0-0 0, White 5-12 3-4 13, Salters 1-5 0-0 2, Willis 4-13 1-3 9, Ross 2-6 0-0 4, Hall 3-8 0-1 6, Reynolds 1-3 0-0 2, Leifsen 0-1 1-2 1, Flick 0-6 6-6 6, Jackson 1-2 4-4 6, Kuhl 0-2 0-0 0, Condon 0-0 0-0 0. Team 24-82 (.293) 19-24 (.792) 67.

MICHIGAN STATE (101): M. Brkovich 6-10 0-0 12, Kelser 12-19 4-6 28, Charles 2-2 0-0 4, Donnelly 3-5 0-0 6, Johnson 9-10 11-12 29, Vincent 0-1 3-4 3, Gonzalez 1-5 0-0 2, Longaker 2-2 0-0 4, Lloyd 0-2 6-7 6, Kaye 2-2 1-3 5, Huffman 0-0 0-1 0, Gilkie 0-1 0-0 0, D. Brkovich 1-1 0-1 2. Team 38-60 (.633) 25-34 (.735) 101.

Halftime: Michigan State 50-17.

DEPAUL (74): Watkins 8-11 0-0 16, Aguirre 9-18 1-2 19, Mitchem 6-11 0-0 12, Bradshaw 4-8 0-0 8, Garland 9-18 1-3 19. Team 36-66 (.545) 2-5 (.400) 74.

INDIANA STATE (76): Miley 2-2 0-0 4, Gilbert 6-7 0-1 12, Bird 16-19 3-4 35, Nicks 4-13 2-2 10, Reed 3-5 0-0 6, Heaton 3-6 0-0 6, Staley 1-4 1-2 3. Team 35-56 (.625) 6-9 (.667) 76.

Halftime: Indiana State 45-42.

ALL-TOURNAMENT TEAM

Mark Aguirre, F, Fr., DePaul (53 points, 19 rebounds in final two games)
Larry Bird, F-C, Sr., Indiana State (54 points, 29 rebounds, 11 assists, six steals)
Gary Garland, G, Sr., DePaul (41 points, 16 rebounds, 13 assists, seven steals)
*Magic Johnson, G, Soph., Michigan State (53 points, 17 rebounds, 15 assists)
Greg Kelser, F, Sr., Michigan State (47 points, 17 rebounds, 12 assists, six blocked shots)
    *Named Most Outstanding Player.

Nichols, overcame a 12-point halftime deficit to nip Iowa, 74-72, for the Rockets' only NCAA playoff victory in school history.

What Might Have Been: LSU won the SEC regular-season title despite the absence of standout forward Rudy Macklin, who missed the majority of the year because of a broken leg. The Tigers were 22-3 entering their regular-season finale but playoff aspirations were defused when leading scorer DeWayne Scales was suspended for repeated conversations with an agent. LSU, making its first NCAA Tournament appearance in 25 years, scored just 19 first-half points in an 87-71 setback against Michigan State in the Mideast Regional semifinals. . . . San Francisco (22-7), not UCLA, might have advanced to the West Regional final against DePaul if Winford Boynes and James

Hardy had remained with the Dons instead of turning pro early.

Putting Things in Perspective: Three players who finished their Duke careers with more than 2,000 points (Gene Banks, Mike Gminski and Jim Spanarkel) each compiled lower scoring averages than they manufactured the previous year, when Duke was national runner-up. In 1978, Banks, Gminski and Spanarkel became the only trio to each score at least 20 points in both Final Four games (total of 71 points in 90-86 victory over Notre Dame in the semifinals and 63 in 94-88 setback against Kentucky in the championship game). Duke is the only national runner-up to score more than 85 points in an NCAA final. Banks, Gminski and Spanarkel all scored at least 16 points when they combined to shoot 53.5 per-

1979 CHAMPIONSHIP BRACKET

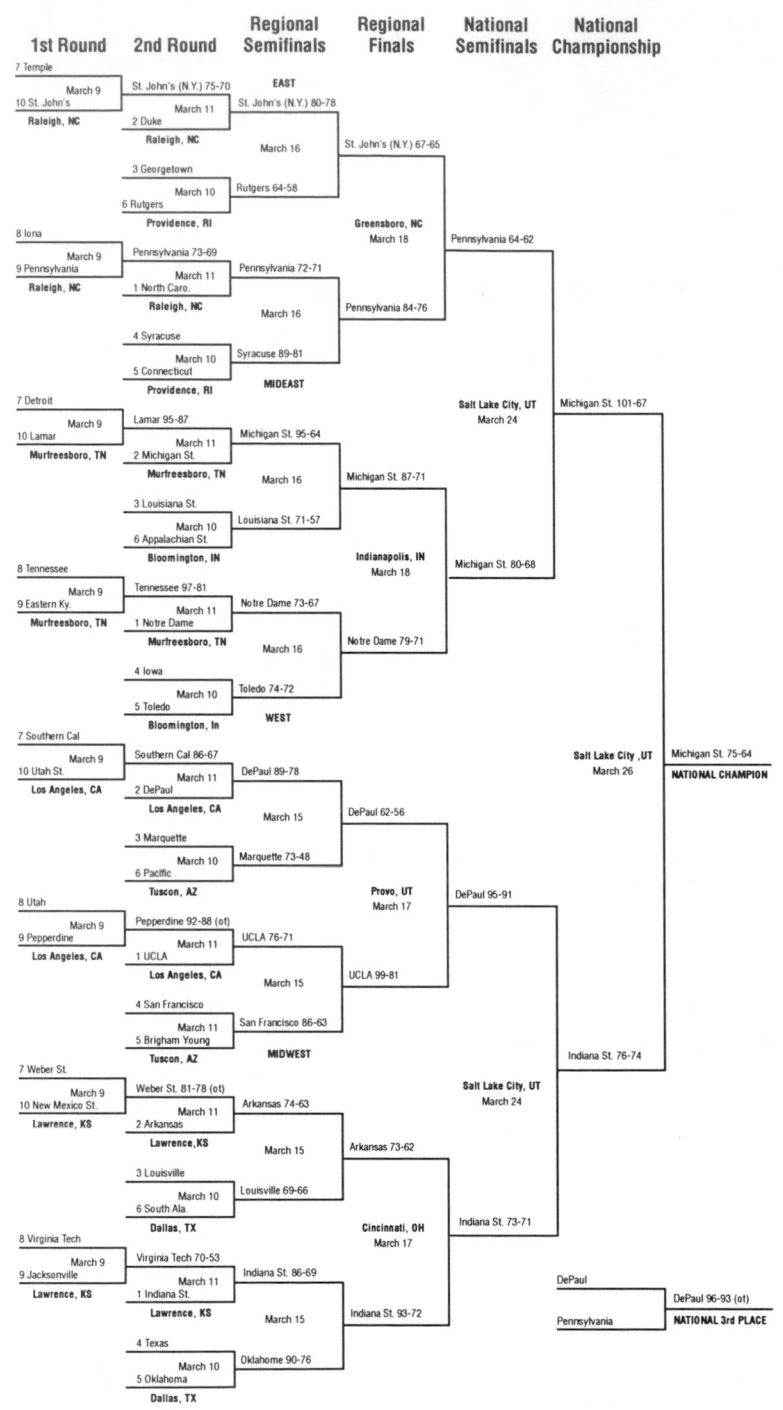

1st Round	2nd Round	Regional Semifinals	Regional Finals	National Semifinals	National Championship

7 Temple
March 9
10 St. John's
Raleigh, NC

St. John's (N.Y.) 75-70
March 11
2 Duke
Raleigh, NC

EAST
St. John's (N.Y.) 80-78

March 16
St. John's (N.Y.) 67-65

3 Georgetown
March 10
6 Rutgers
Providence, RI

Rutgers 64-58

Greensboro, NC
March 18
Pennsylvania 64-62

8 Iona
March 9
9 Pennsylvania
Raleigh, NC

Pennsylvania 73-69
March 11
1 North Caro.
Raleigh, NC

Pennsylvania 72-71

March 16
Pennsylvania 84-76

4 Syracuse
March 10
5 Connecticut
Providence, RI

Syracuse 89-81

MIDEAST

7 Detroit
March 9
10 Lamar
Murfreesboro, TN

Lamar 95-87
March 11
2 Michigan St.
Murfreesboro, TN

Michigan St. 95-64

March 16
Michigan St. 87-71

Salt Lake City, UT
March 24
Michigan St. 101-67

3 Louisiana St.
March 10
6 Appalachian St.
Bloomington, IN

Louisiana St. 71-57

Indianapolis, IN
March 18
Michigan St. 80-68

8 Tennessee
March 9
9 Eastern Ky.
Murfreesboro, TN

Tennessee 97-81
March 11
1 Notre Dame
Murfreesboro, TN

Notre Dame 73-67

March 16
Notre Dame 79-71

4 Iowa
March 10
5 Toledo
Bloomington, In

Toledo 74-72

WEST

7 Southern Cal
March 9
10 Utah St.
Los Angeles, CA

Southern Cal 86-67
March 11
2 DePaul
Los Angeles, CA

DePaul 89-78

March 15
DePaul 62-56

Salt Lake City ,UT
March 26
Michigan St. 75-64
NATIONAL CHAMPION

3 Marquette
March 10
6 Pacific
Tuscon, AZ

Marquette 73-48

Provo, UT
March 17
DePaul 95-91

8 Utah
March 9
9 Pepperdine
Los Angeles, CA

Pepperdine 92-88 (ot)
March 11
1 UCLA
Los Angeles, CA

UCLA 76-71

March 15
UCLA 99-81

4 San Francisco
March 11
5 Brigham Young
Tuscon, AZ

San Francisco 86-63

MIDWEST

Indiana St. 76-74

7 Weber St.
March 9
10 New Mexico St.
Lawrence, KS

Weber St. 81-78 (ot)
March 11
2 Arkansas
Lawrence,KS

Arkansas 74-63

March 15
Arkansas 73-62

Salt Lake City, UT
March 24
Indiana St. 73-71

3 Louisville
March 10
6 South Ala.
Dallas, TX

Louisville 69-66

Cincinnati, OH
March 17

8 Virginia Tech
March 9
9 Jacksonville
Lawrence, KS

Virginia Tech 70-53
March 11
1 Indiana St.
Lawrence, KS

Indiana St. 86-69

March 15
Indiana St. 93-72

4 Texas
March 10
5 Oklahoma
Dallas, TX

Oklahoma 90-76

DePaul
DePaul 96-93 (ot)
Pennsylvania
NATIONAL 3rd PLACE

cent from the floor against St. John's, but none of their teammates managed more than seven points as the Blue Devils blew a five-point halftime lead.

Scoring Leader: Tony Price, Pennsylvania (142 points, 23.7 ppg).

Highest Scoring Average: Bill Cartwright, San Francisco (58 points, 29 ppg).

Rebounding Leader: Larry Bird, Indiana State (67 rebounds, 13.4 rpg).

Highest Rebounding Average: Lionel Green, LSU (31 rebounds, 15.5 rpg).

WINNINGEST PROGRAMS OF THE 1970s

RK.	SCHOOL	W.	L.	PCT.
1.	UCLA	273	27	.910
2.	Marquette	252	40	.863
3.	Pennsylvania	223	56	.799
4.	North Carolina	239	65	.786
5.	Kentucky	223	69	.764
6.	Louisville	224	70	.762
7.	Syracuse	213	69	.755
8.	Long Beach State	203	68	.749
9.	Indiana	208	75	.735
10.	Oral Roberts	161	59	.732

Note: UNC Charlotte compiled a 147-48 record (.754) in seven seasons as a major college during the decade.

1970-79 PREMO POWER POLL: BEST TEAMS BY DECADE

RANK	SEASON	SCHOOL
1	1971–72	UCLA* (30-0)
2	1975–76	Indiana* (32-0)
3	1972–73	UCLA* (30-0)
4	1973–74	North Carolina St.* (30-1)
5	1974–75	Indiana (31-1)
6	1969–70	UCLA* (28-2)
7	1973–74	UCLA (26-4)
8	1970–71	UCLA* (29-1)
9	1977–78	Kentucky* (30-2)
10	1972–73	North Carolina St. (27-0)
11	1969–70	St. Bonaventure (25-3)
12	1970–71	Marquette (28-1)
13	1978–79	Indiana St. (33-1)
14	1976–77	UNLV (29-3)
15	1975–76	Marquette (27-2)
16	1970–71	Pennsylvania (28-1)
17	1969–70	Jacksonville (27-2)
18	1973–74	Maryland (23-5)
19	1974–75	UCLA* (28-3)
20	1977–78	Arkansas (32-4)
	1976–77	North Carolina (28-5)
	1971–72	North Carolina (26-5)
	1978–79	Michigan St.* (26-6)

*–NCAA Tournament Champion

ALL-DECADE TEAM — 1970s

Larry Bird, F, Indiana State
Austin Carr, G, Notre Dame
Adrian Dantley, F, Notre Dame
Phil Ford, G, North Carolina
Artis Gilmore, C, Jacksonville
Magic Johnson, G, Michigan State
John Lucas, G, Maryland
David Thompson, F, North Carolina State
Bill Walton, C, UCLA
Keith Wilkes, F, UCLA
Coach: Al McGuire, Marquette

Larry Bird

Indiana State
6-9 — F
French Lick, Ind. (Spring Valley H.S.)

Named national player of the year by AP, UPI, USBWA and NABC in 1979. . . . Naismith Award and Wooden Award winner in 1979. . . . NCAA unanimous first-team All-American in 1978 and 1979. . . . Ranked among the nation's leading scorers in 1977 (3rd), 1978 (2nd) and 1979 (2nd). . . . Ranked among the nation's leading rebounders in 1977 (7th) and 1979 (4th). . . . Leading scorer and rebounder for 1979 NCAA Tournament runner-up (33-1 record). . . . Named to 1979 All-NCAA Tournament team. . . . Averaged 27.2 points and 13.4 rebounds in five NCAA Tournament games in 1979 (4-1 record). . . . Averaged 31.3 points and 11.7 rebounds in three NIT games in 1977 and 1978 (1-2 record). . . . Member of 1992 U.S. Olympic team (8.4 ppg, 3.8 rpg, 52.1 FG%). . . . Selected as a junior eligible by the Boston Celtics in first round of 1978 NBA draft (6th pick overall).

SEASON	G.	FGM-FGA	FG%	FTM-FTA	FT%	REB.	AVG.	PTS.	AVG.
1974-75	Left Indiana University before the start of the season.								
1975-76	Sat out the season after transferring to Indiana State.								
1976-77	28	375-689	.544	168-200	.840	373	13.3	918	32.8
1977-78	32	403-769	.524	153-193	.793	369	11.5	959	30.0
1978-79	34	376-707	.532	221-266	.831	505	14.9	973	28.6
Totals	94	1154-2165	.533	542-659	.822	1247	13.3	2850	30.3

Austin Carr

Notre Dame
6-3 — G
Washington, D.C. (Mackin H.S.)

Named national player of the year by AP and UPI in 1971. . . . Naismith Award winner in 1971. . . . NCAA unanimous first-team All-American in 1971 and consensus second-team All-American in 1970. . . . Ranked 2nd in the nation in scoring in 1970 and 1971. . . . Averaged 41.3 points and 7.6 rebounds in seven NCAA Tournament games from 1969-71 (2-5 record). . . . Selected by the Cleveland Cavaliers in first round of 1971 NBA draft (1st pick overall).

SEASON	G.	FGM-FGA	FG%	FTM-FTA	FT%	REB.	AVG.	PTS.	AVG.
1968-69	16	143-294	.486	67-85	.788	84	5.3	353	22.1
1969-70	29	444-799	.556	218-264	.826	240	8.3	1106	38.1
1970-71	29	430-832	.517	241-297	.811	214	7.4	1101	38.0
Totals	74	1017-1925	.528	526-646	.814	538	7.3	2560	34.6

Adrian Dantley

Notre Dame
6-5 — F
Hyattsville, Md. (DeMatha Catholic H.S.)

Named national player of the year by USBWA in 1976. . . . NCAA unanimous first-team All-American in 1975 and 1976. . . . Ranked among the nation's leading scorers in 1975 (2nd) and 1976 (4th). . . . Averaged 25.4 points and 8.3 rebounds in eight NCAA Tournament games from 1974-76 (4-4 record). . . . Member of 1976 U.S. Olympic team holds U.S. record for highest scoring average in a single Olympiad (19.3 points per game). . . . Selected as an undergraduate (after junior season) by the Buffalo Braves in first round of 1976 NBA draft (6th pick overall).

SEASON	G.	FGM-FGA	FG%	FTM-FTA	FT%	REB.	AVG.	PTS.	AVG.
1973-74	28	189-339	.558	133-161	.826	255	9.7	511	18.3
1974-75	29	315-581	.542	253-314	.806	296	10.2	883	30.4
1975-76	29	300-510	.588	229-294	.779	292	10.1	829	28.6
Totals	86	804-1430	.562	615-769	.800	843	9.8	2223	25.8

Phil Ford

North Carolina
6-2 — G
Rocky Mount, N.C.

Named national player of the year by NABC and USBWA in 1978. . . . Wooden Award winner in 1978. . . . NCAA unanimous first-team All-American in 1978, consensus first-team All-American in 1977 and consensus second-team All-American in 1977. . . . Leading scorer for 1977 NCAA Tournament runner-up (28-5 record). . . . Averaged 14.7 points and 4.9 assists in 10 NCAA Tournament games from 1975-78 (6-4 record). . . . Member of 1976 U.S. Olympic team (11.3 ppg, 9 apg, 53.7 FG%). . . . Selected by the Kansas City Kings in first round of 1978 NBA draft (2nd pick overall).

SEASON	G.	FGM-FGA	FG%	FTM-FTA	FT%	AST.	AVG.	PTS.	AVG.
1974-75	31	191-370	.516	126-161	.783	161	5.2	508	16.4
1975-76	29	206-387	.532	128-164	.780	203	7.0	540	18.6
1976-77	33	230-431	.534	157-184	.853	217	6.6	617	18.7
1977-78	30	238-452	.527	149-184	.810	172	5.7	625	20.8
Totals	123	865-1640	.527	560-693	.808	753	6.1	2290	18.6

Artis Gilmore

Jacksonville
7-2 — C
Chipley, Fla. (Roulhac H.S.) and Dothan, Ala. (Carver H.S.)

NCAA unanimous first-team All-American in 1971. . . . Only player to average more than 22 points and 22 rebounds per game in his career. . . . Led the nation in rebounding in 1970 and 1971. . . . Ranked among the nation's leading scorers in 1970 (21st) and 1971 (50th). . . . Ranked among the nation's leaders in field-goal percentage in 1970 (10th) and 1971 (14th). . . . Leading scorer and rebounder for 1970 national runner-up (27-2 record). . . . Named to 1970 All-NCAA Tournament team. . . . Averaged 24 points and 19.2 rebounds in six NCAA Tournament games in 1970 and 1971 (4-2 record). . . . Averaged 22.5 points in two junior college seasons at Gardner-Webb (N.C.). . . . Selected by the Chicago Bulls in seventh round of 1971 NBA draft (117th pick overall) and by the Kentucky Colonels in first round of 1971 ABA draft.

SEASON	G.	FGM-FGA	FG%	FTM-FTA	FT%	REB.	AVG.	PTS.	AVG.
1969-70	28	307-529	.580	128-202	.634	621	22.2	742	26.5
1970-71	26	229-405	.565	112-188	.596	603	23.2	570	21.9
Totals	54	536-934	.574	240-390	.615	1224	22.7	1312	24.3

Earvin (Magic) Johnson

Michigan State
6-9 — G
Lansing, Mich. (Everett H.S.)

NCAA unanimous first-team All-American in 1979. . . . Second-leading scorer and rebounder for 1979 NCAA Tournament champion (26-6 record). . . . Final Four Most Outstanding Player in 1979 (53 points, 17 rebounds, 15 assists, 68.0 FG%, 86.4 FT%). . . . Named to 1979 All-NCAA Tournament team. . . . Averaged 17.8 points, eight rebounds and 9.5 assists in eight NCAA Tournament games in 1978 and 1979 (7-1 record). . . . Member of 1992 U.S. Olympic team (8 ppg, 5.5 apg, 56.7 FG%). . . . Selected as an undergraduate (after sophomore season) by the Los Angeles Lakers in first round of 1979 NBA draft (1st pick overall).

SEASON	G.	FGM-FGA	FG%	FTM-FTA	FT%	REB.	AVG.	PTS.	AVG.
1977-78	30	175-382	.458	161-205	.785	237	7.9	511	17.0
1978-79	32	173-370	.468	202-240	.842	234	7.3	548	17.1
Totals	62	348-752	.463	363-445	.816	471	7.6	1059	17.1

John Lucas

Maryland
6-3 — G
Durham, N.C. (Hillside H.S.)

NCAA consensus first-team All-American in 1975 and 1976. . . . Averaged 22.2 points in five NCAA Tournament games in 1973 and 1975 (3-2 record). . . . Selected by the Houston Rockets in first round of 1976 NBA draft (1st pick overall).

SEASON	G.	FGM-FGA	FG%	FTM-FTA	FT%	AST.	AVG.	PTS.	AVG.
1972-73	30	190-353	.538	45-64	.703	178	5.9	425	14.2
1973-74	28	253-495	.511	58-77	.753	159	5.7	564	20.1
1974-75	24	186-339	.549	97-116	.836	91	3.8	469	19.5
1975-76	28	233-456	.511	91-117	.778	86	3.1	557	19.9
Totals	110	862-1643	.525	291-374	.778	514	4.7	2015	18.3

David Thompson

North Carolina State
6-4 — F
Shelby, N.C. (Crest H.S.)

Named national player of the year by UPI, USBWA and NABC in 1975, and by AP in 1974 and 1975. . . . Naismith Award winner in 1975. . . . NCAA unanimous first-team All-American in 1973, 1974 and 1975. . . . Ranked among the nation's leading scorers in 1973 (17th), 1974 (5th) and 1975 (3rd). . . . Leading scorer and second-leading rebounder for 1974 NCAA Tournament champion (30-1 record). . . . Final Four Most Outstanding Player in 1974 (49 points, 17 rebounds). . . . Named to 1974 All-NCAA Tournament team. . . . Averaged 24.3 points and 7.3 rebounds in four NCAA Tournament games in 1974 (4-0 record). . . . Selected by the Virginia Squires in first round of 1975 ABA draft. Rights traded to the Denver Nuggets, July 14, 1975. . . . Elected to Naismith Memorial Basketball Hall of Fame in 1996.

SEASON	G.	FGM-FGA	FG%	FTM-FTA	FT%	REB.	AVG.	PTS.	AVG.
1972-73	27	267-469	.569	132-160	.825	220	8.1	666	24.7
1973-74	31	325-594	.547	155-208	.745	245	7.9	805	26.0
1974-75	28	347-635	.546	144-197	.731	229	8.2	838	29.9
Totals	86	939-1698	.553	431-565	.763	694	8.1	2309	26.8

Bill Walton

UCLA
6-11 — C
La Mesa, Calif. (Helix H.S.)

NCAA unanimous first-team All-American in 1972, 1973 and 1974. . . . Named national player of the year by UPI and USBWA in 1972, 1973 and 1974, and by AP in 1972 and 1973. . . . Naismith Award winner in 1972, 1973 and 1974. . . . Ranked among the nation's leaders in field-goal percentage in 1972 (4th), 1973 (2nd) and 1974 (2nd). . . . Ranked among the nation's rebounding leaders in 1972 (9th), 1973 (6th) and 1974 (9th). . . . Leading scorer and rebounder for undefeated NCAA Tournament champions in 1972 (30-0 record) and 1973 (30-0) and national third-place team in 1974 (26-4). . . . Final Four Most Outstanding Player in 1972 (57 points, 41 rebounds, 69.0 FG%) and 1973 (58 points, 30 rebounds, 82.4 FG%). . . . Named to All-NCAA Tournament team in 1972, 1973 and 1974. . . . Averaged 21.2 points and 14.7 rebounds in 12 NCAA Tournament games from 1972-74 (11-1 record). . . . Selected by the Portland Trail Blazers in first round of 1974 NBA draft (1st pick overall). . . . Elected to Naismith Memorial Basketball Hall of Fame in 1993.

SEASON	G.	FGM-FGA	FG%	FTM-FTA	FT%	REB.	AVG.	PTS.	AVG.
1971-72	30	238-372	.640	157-223	.704	466	15.5	633	21.1
1972-73	30	277-426	.650	58-102	.569	506	16.9	612	20.4
1973-74	27	232-349	.665	58-100	.580	398	14.7	522	19.3
Totals	87	747-1147	.651	273-425	.642	1370	15.7	1767	20.3

Keith Wilkes

UCLA
6-7 — F
Ventura, Calif. and Santa Barbara, Calif.

NCAA unanimous first-team All-American in 1974 and consensus first-team All-American in 1973. . . . Second-leading scorer and rebounder for undefeated 1973 NCAA Tournament champion (30-0 record) and 1974 national third-place team (26-4). . . . Third-leading scorer and second-leading rebounder for undefeated 1972 NCAA Tournament champion (30-0). . . . Named to 1972 All-NCAA Tournament team. . . . Averaged 15 points and 7.2 rebounds in 12 NCAA Tournament games from 1972-74 (11-1 record). . . . Selected by the Golden State Warriors in first round of 1974 NBA draft (11th pick overall). . . . Changed his first name to Jamaal.

SEASON	G.	FGM-FGA	FG%	FTM-FTA	FT%	REB.	AVG.	PTS.	AVG.
1971-72	30	171-322	.531	64-92	.696	245	8.2	406	13.5
1972-73	30	200-381	.525	43-66	.652	220	7.3	443	14.8
1973-74	30	209-426	.491	82-94	.872	198	6.6	500	16.7
Totals	90	580-1129	.514	189-252	.750	663	7.4	1349	15.0

Al McGuire

St. John's '51
Brooklyn, N.Y.

Named national coach of the year by AP, UPI, and the USBWA in 1971, and by the NABC in 1974. . . . Coached Marquette to the NIT title in 1970 and the NCAA championship in 1977. His 1974 Marquette squad finished runner-up to North Carolina State in the NCAA Tournament and his 1967 team lost to Southern Illinois in the NIT final. . . . Elected to Naismith Memorial Basketball Hall of Fame in 1991. . . . Assistant coach at Dartmouth under Doggie Julian.

SEASON	SCHOOL	OVERALL	LEAGUE	FINISH	POSTSEASON
1957-58	Belmont Abbey	24-3	—		—
1958-59	Belmont Abbey	21-2	—		—
1959-60	Belmont Abbey	19-6	—		—
1960-61	Belmont Abbey	17-7	—		—
1961-62	Belmont Abbey	16-9	—		NAIA (0-1)
1962-63	Belmont Abbey	6-19	—		—
1963-64	Belmont Abbey	6-18	—		—
1964-65	Marquette	8-18	—		DNP
1965-66	Marquette	14-12	—		DNP
1966-67	Marquette	21-9	—		NIT (3-1)
1967-68	Marquette	23-6	—		NCAA (2-1)
1968-69	Marquette	24-5	—		NCAA (2-1)
1969-70	Marquette	26-3	—		NIT (4-0)
1970-71	Marquette	28-1	—		NCAA (2-1)
1971-72	Marquette	25-4	—		NCAA (1-2)
1972-73	Marquette	25-4	—		NCAA (2-1)
1973-74	Marquette	26-5	—		NCAA (4-1)
1974-75	Marquette	23-4	—		NCAA (0-1)
1975-76	Marquette	27-2	—		NCAA (2-1)
1976-77	Marquette	26-6	—		NCAA (5-0)

20-Year Coaching Record: 405-143 (.739) overall; 110-63 (.636) in seven years at Belmont Abbey; 295-80 (.787) in 13 years at Marquette; 20-9 (.690) in NCAA Tournament; 7-1 (.875) in NIT; 0-1 in NAIA Tournament.

6

THE EMERGENCE OF PARITY:

THE 1980s

Parity became a buzzword as 10 different schools won NCAA championships in a 10-year stretch beginning in 1982. Tight title games were the rule rather than the exception. Excluding Georgetown's nine-point victory over Houston in the 1984 final, the other seven NCAA championship games from 1982-89 were decided by an average of two points.\

Expansion of the NCAA Tournament field to the magic number of 64 allowed squads to embrace a never-say-die mentality despite struggles during the regular season. Four NCAA champions in a seven-year span from 1983 through 1989 incurred at least five conference defeats. Expansion of the tourney field also helped more and more schools reach the Promised Land for the first time, including long-time major universities such as Auburn, Clemson, Florida, Georgia, Nebraska and Seton Hall. The expansion also enabled elite conferences to dominate the playoffs. For instance, the ACC had 50 entrants in the decade compared to a total of 31 in the league's first 26 years from 1954 through 1979.

The 1980s boasted many of the premier pivotmen in college basketball history—from Ralph Sampson to Patrick Ewing to Hakeem Olajuwon to David Robinson to Alonzo Mourning to the start of Shaquille O'Neal's career. The freshman debuts against major-college competition the first half of the decade by Sampson (4 points/6 rebounds for Virginia in 1979-80), Ewing (7/4 for Georgetown in 1981-82), Olajuwon (2/0 for Houston in 1981-82) and Robinson (0/1 for Navy in 1983-84) weren't harbingers of things to come for these celebrated centers who eventually became All-Americans and first picks overall in NBA drafts.

The '80s represented the first decade since the 1920s that Kentucky failed to finish among the top five programs in winning percentage. The Wildcats lost back-to-back NCAA playoff openers to UAB and Middle Tennessee State in 1981 and 1982, respectively, en route to ranking ninth with a 233-86 record (.730). UCLA, the nation's winningest program each of the two previous decades, didn't finish among the top 20 in the 1980s when the Bruins had six seasons with at least 10 defeats. North Carolina finished in the top 10 of a final wire-service poll every year in the decade except 1980, when the Tar Heels placed 15th. Carolina won at least 27 games an amazing nine consecutive campaigns from 1981 through 1989.

The trite "East is Least" cliche came to an abrupt end with the formation of the Big East Conference. The Big East's arrival highlighted a conference reshuffling that saw 10 new Division I leagues in a four-year span from 1980-83.

Meanwhile, the Big Ten struggled in the NCAA Tournament midway through the decade, compiling a 20-24 playoff record in a five-year stretch from 1982-86. And the Big Eight began to assert itself more nationally when coaches Johnny Orr (Iowa State) and Billy Tubbs (Oklahoma) entered the league and forced conference opponents to change their traditional methodical style of play and embrace a more uptempo brand.

The decade also featured the advent of two key playing rules changes (shot clock and three-point basket) and an increased influx of prominent foreign players. The building of large arenas remained a major growth industry when the '80s closed with 11 conferences having an average seating capacity of at least 10,000.

An obsession in the coaching ranks to have taller players at every position decreased after 5-7 Spud Webb (North Carolina State) and 5-3 Tyrone Bogues (Wake Forest) excelled in the powerful Atlantic Coast Conference. Recruiting also took on a new dimension in November 1982 with the start of an "early" signing period.

Ethical questions hovered over coaches because of the escalating influence of sneaker companies and several prominent mentors receiving "kickbacks" for scheduling non-conference games. Evidence that coaching was becoming more and more of a young man's game was exemplified by three universities hiring a 26-year-old head coach-Siena (John Griffin in 1982), Lehigh (Fran McCaffery in 1985) and Niagara (Jack Armstrong in 1989).

Midway through the 1980s, there was testimony to the explosion of interest in college hoops when "A Season on the Brink" became the best-selling sports book of all time. Written by the Washington Post's John Feinstein, the book chronicled the ins and outs of a season with Indiana's storied program under coach Bob Knight.

1979-80

AT A GLANCE

NCAA Champion: Louisville (33-3; coached by Denny Crum; won Metro title by four games with a 12-0 record).

NIT Champion: Virginia (24-10; coached by Terry Holland; tied for fifth place in ACC with a 7-7 record).

New Conferences: Big East, Midwestern City (forerunner of Midwestern Collegiate), ECAC North (forerunner of North Atlantic and America East), SWAC (moved up to Division I), Trans America Athletic.

New Rules: The NCAA Tournament bracket expands from 40 teams to 48, including 24 automatic qualifiers and 24 at-large teams. . . . The top 16 seeds receive byes to the second round. . . . The limit of two teams from the same conference allowed in the tournament is lifted. . . . The NIT field expands from 24 teams to 32.

NCAA Probation: Auburn, Cincinnati, East Carolina, Memphis State, Oral Roberts, San Francisco.

NCAA Consensus First-Team All-Americans: Mark Aguirre, F, Soph., DePaul; Michael Brooks, F, Sr., La Salle; Joe Barry Carroll, C, Sr., Purdue; Darrell Griffith, G, Sr., Louisville; Kyle Macy, G, Sr., Kentucky.

National Players of the Year: Aguirre (26.8 ppg, 7.6 rpg, 54.0 FG%/AP, UPI, USBWA, Naismith); Brooks (24.1 ppg, 11.5 rpg, 52.4 FG%/NABC), and Griffith (22.9 ppg, 4.8 rpg, 3.8 apg, 55.3 FG%/Wooden).

National Coaches of the Year: DePaul's Ray Meyer (26-2/AP, UPI, USBWA) and Iowa's Lute Olson (23-10/NABC).

Perhaps the greatest single crop of freshman recruits took center stage. An alphabetical list of the standout yearlings for the Class of '83 included John Bagley (Boston College), Thurl Bailey (North Carolina State), Sam Bowie (Kentucky), Antoine Carr (Wichita State), Howard Carter (LSU), Terry Cummings (DePaul), Quintin Dailey (San Francisco), Dale Ellis (Tennessee), Sidney Green (UNLV), Clark Kellogg (Ohio State), Cliff Levingston (Wichita State), Jeff Malone (Mississippi State), Rodney McCray (Louisville), John Paxson (Notre Dame), Ralph Sampson (Virginia), Byron Scott (Arizona State), Steve Stipanovich (Missouri), Isiah Thomas (Indiana), LaSalle

Thompson (Texas), Dominique Wilkins (Georgia), Rob Williams (Houston) and James Worthy (North Carolina).

Worthy was averaging 12.5 points and 7.4 rebounds per game for North Carolina when he sustained a broken ankle at midseason and was lost for the remainder of the year. The Tar Heels lost their NCAA playoff opener in double overtime against Texas A&M. . . . The NCAA Tournament showed the effect of parity and expansion of the field. This was the only year as many as three

Final Four teams finished third or lower in their regular-season league standings—UCLA (fourth in Pacific-10), Purdue (third in Big Ten) and Iowa (fourth in Big Ten). UCLA's streak of 13 consecutive undisputed conference championships was snapped by Oregon State.

Parity also existed among the premier players. La Salle's Michael Brooks scored a national-high 51 points in a 108-106 triple-overtime loss at Brigham Young. Brooks, DePaul's Mark Aguirre and Louisville's Darrell Griffith shared the six national-

1979–80 INDIVIDUAL LEADERS

SCORING

PLAYER	PTS.	AVG.
Murphy, Southern (La.)	932	32.1
Lloyd, Drake	815	30.2
Kelly, Texas Southern	753	29.0
Page, New Mexico	784	28.0
Tillman, E. Kentucky	734	27.2
Belcher, St. Bonaventure	646	26.9
Bowers, American	726	26.9
Nicks, Indiana St.	723	26.8
Aguirre, DePaul	749	26.8
Toney, Southwestern La.	627	26.1

REBOUNDING

PLAYER	REB.	AVG.
Smith, Alcorn St.	392	15.1
Lloyd, Drake	406	15.0

Brown, Mississippi St.	389	14.4
Davis, Tennessee St.	347	13.3
Hooker, Murray St.	356	12.3
Grooms, Kent St.	319	12.3
Schoen, St. Francis (Pa.)	303	12.1
Green, Pan American	337	12.0
Ruland, Iona	407	12.0
Martin, Oral Roberts	334	11.9

FIELD GOAL PERCENTAGE

PLAYER	FGM	FGA	PCT.
Johnson, Oregon St.	211	297	.710
Charles, Mich. St.	169	250	.676
Rhone, Centenary	193	290	.666
Bouie, Syracuse	189	289	.654
Brown, Florida St.	230	356	.646
Manning, Maryland	196	305	.643
Ruland, Iona	256	399	.642

Frazier, Missouri	160	252	.635
McCormick, W. Ky.	165	264	.625
Byrd, Marquette	137	220	.623

FREE THROW PERCENTAGE

PLAYER	FTM	FTA	PCT.
Magid, G. Washington	79	85	.929
Nesbit, The Citadel	74	80	.925
Macy, Kentucky	104	114	.912
Manning, Maryland	79	87	.908
White, Gonzaga	116	130	.892
Matthews, Wisc.	127	143	.888
Salters, Penn	86	97	.887
Nehls, Arizona	108	122	.885
Jones, St. Bon.	84	95	.884
Falconiero, Lafayette	98	111	.883

1979–80 TEAM LEADERS

SCORING OFFENSE

SCHOOL	PTS.	AVG.
Alcorn St.	2729	91.0
Drake	2398	88.8
Oral Roberts	2447	87.4
Utah St.	2329	86.3
Syracuse	2575	85.8

SCORING DEFENSE

SCHOOL	PTS.	AVG.
St. Peter's	1563	50.4
Princeton	1654	55.1
Penn St.	1600	57.1
Wyoming	1644	58.7
Fresno St.	1412	58.8

SCORING MARGIN

SCHOOL	OFF.	DEF.	MAR.
Alcorn St.	91.0	73.6	17.4
Syracuse	85.8	70.4	15.4
South Alabama	76.4	64.5	11.9
Weber St.	75.2	63.3	11.9
Georgetown	80.1	68.8	11.3

WON-LOST PERCENTAGE

SCHOOL	W-L	PCT.
Alcorn St.	28-2	.933
DePaul	26-2	.929
Louisville	33-3	.917
Weber St.	26-3	.897
Oregon St.	26-4	.867
Syracuse	26-4	.867

FIELD GOAL PERCENTAGE

SCHOOL	FGM	FGA	PCT.
Missouri	936	1635	.572
Maryland	985	1789	.551
Oregon St.	943	1732	.544
Syracuse	1025	1902	.539
Toledo	923	1724	.535

FIELD GOAL PERCENTAGE DEFENSE

SCHOOL	FGM	FGA	PCT.
Penn St.	543	1309	.415
St. Peter's	590	1396	.423
UNC-Wilmington	719	1685	.427
Wichita St.	776	1818	.427
Old Dominion	775	1814	.427

FREE THROW PERCENTAGE

SCHOOL	FTM	FTA	PCT.
Oral Roberts	481	610	.789
Southern (La.)	417	537	.777
St. Bonaventure	467	610	.766
Utah St.	605	794	.762
Kentucky	609	802	.759

REBOUND MARGIN

SCHOOL	OWN	OPP.	MAR.
Alcorn St.	49.2	33.8	15.4
Tennessee St.	46.5	34.3	12.2
Wyoming	41.0	30.8	10.2
Northeastern	39.2	31.2	8.0
South Alabama	39.3	31.7	7.6

ly-recognized Player of the Year Awards. It is the only time as many as three individuals shared the principal national awards. . . . Aguirre was the first DePaul player since 1946 to become an NCAA consensus first- or second-team All-American. DePaul won its first 25 games of the season until succumbing at Notre Dame, 76-74, in double overtime. Kelly Tripucka scored 28 points for the Irish.

Since the end of World War II, Kansas and Kansas State had never gone two years in a row without either of them gaining at least a portion of the Big Seven/Eight Conference title until Missouri earned its first of four consecutive undisputed regular-season titles. The Tigers, topping 60 percent in shooting from the floor 12 times, established an NCAA single-season record for field-goal percentage (57.2 percent). . . . Murray State, which compiled a 4-22 record the previous season, improved by 16 1/2 games to 23-8 under coach Ron Greene. . . . Drake's Lewis "Magic" Lloyd finished national runner-up in scoring (30.2) and rebounding (15).

Maryland guard Greg Manning was sixth nationally in field-goal shooting (64.3 percent) and fourth from the free-throw line (90.8 percent). . . . An 89'3" basket at the buzzer by Virginia Tech's Les Henson after he chased down an errant shot, spun and fired the ball the length of the floor, gave the Hokies a 79-77 victory at Florida State. Amazingly, the lefthanded Henson made the shot right-handed!

Lamar's Mike Olliver (50 points at Portland State), San Jose State's Wally Rank (40 vs. Sacramento State) and Robert Morris' Mike Morton (36 vs. Towson State) set school single-game scoring records. . . . Lloyd (30.2 ppg), New Mexico's Kenny Page (28), Eastern Kentucky's James Tillman (27.2), American's Russell Bowers (26.9), Aguirre (26.8), Maine's Rufus Harris (25.6), Cleveland State's Frank Edwards (25.5), Oklahoma State's Ed Odom (24.2) and Washington State's Don Collins (23.1) set school records for highest scoring average in a single season.

Jacksonville's James Ray scored a Sun Belt Conference-record 45 points in a game against South Florida. . . . Syracuse's school-record 57-game homecourt winning streak was snapped in its final game at Manley Field House (52-50 against Georgetown). The Orangemen finished with a 26-4 mark for the third time in Jim Boeheim's first four seasons as their coach. . . . St. Peter's, coached by ex-Princeton assistant Bob Dukiet, dethroned Princeton as the national leader in scoring defense, yielding only 50.4 points per game—the lowest figure in 19 years. . . . Princeton and Penn tied for the Ivy League title with 11-3 conference records. It was the first time in 17 years that an Ivy champion lost more than two league games. Yale dropped all four of its games against Princeton and Penn, but ended a streak of 11 consecutive losing seasons by compiling a 16-10 mark.

Louisville (33-3/coached by Denny Crum), Iona (29-5/Jim Valvano), Texas A&M (26-8/Shelby Metcalf), Furman (23-7/Eddie Holbrook) and Grambling (22-8/Fred Hobdy) had their winningest seasons in school Division I history. Old Dominion (25-5/Paul Webb) tied its school single-season record for most victories. . . . Texas A&M's success stemmed from a formidable frontcourt dubbed "The Wall" (Vernon Smith, Rudy Woods and Rynn Wright). Smith, who concluded his career the next season as the school's all-time leading scorer and rebounder, was murdered in the summer of '92 at the age of 33 when he was fatally shot in Dallas by an angry dice player who apparently mistook him for someone he'd fought with earlier. Smith played piano and organ at the church where his father was minister. . . . SMU posted its lone victory over Arkansas (62-58) in an 18-game stretch of their series from 1976 through 1984.

Iona, coached by Jim Valvano, made its lone appearance in a final wire-service poll. The Gaels leveled NCAA champion-to-be Louisville, 77-60, late in the regular season at Madison Square Garden. Their leading scorer and rebounder for the third consecutive season was center Jeff Ruland. . . . Duquesne, coached by Mike Rice, tied for first place in the Eastern 8 after finishing in seventh the previous year. . . . Massachusetts ended a 29-game

Louisville All-American guard Darrell Griffith sneaks behind the basket for two.

losing streak with a 67-44 triumph over Harvard on a neutral court before the Minutemen snapped a 19-game homecourt losing streak with a 69-63 verdict over New Hampshire.

Bradley, coached by Dick Versace, captured the Missouri Valley Conference crown after finishing in a tie for last place the previous year. . . . Alcorn State, coached by Davey Whitney, led the nation in rebounding margin for the third consecutive season. . . . Clemson, boasting three 6-10 starters along its frontline, defeated six teams that were ranked in the AP Top 20 (prior to the game). The Tigers earned an invitation to the NCAA Tournament for the first time. . . . Ohio State, coached by Eldon Miller, finished in the Top 20 of a final wire-service poll for the only time in an 18-year span from 1972-73 through 1989-90. . . . Wisconsin lost 17 consecutive games to Minneso-

ta until defeating the Gophers, 70-55. . . . Iowa State's Dean Uthoff led the Big Eight Conference in rebounding for the fourth straight season.

Washington State lost 27 consecutive games to UCLA in their series until defeating the Bruins, 80-64. . . . New Mexico averaged 14,344 fans per home date despite incurring its first losing record (6-22) in 18 years. The Lobos lost most of their roster in the aftermath of investigations by the NCAA and FBI revealing serious indiscretions, specifically altering transcripts of transferring students to make them appear eligible. . . . Texas-El Paso, after losing its previous eight assignments with New Mexico, began a stretch of winning 14 of 15 outings against the Lobos through 1986. . . . Idaho, coached by Don Monson, ended a streak of eight consecutive losing seasons by compiling a 17-10 mark.

Weber State (26-3/coached by Neil McCarthy) set a school record with 18 straight victories. . . . Denver and Seattle competed in their final season at the major-college level. . . . South Carolina's Frank McGuire, who previously coached St. John's and North Carolina, retired after a 30-year college coaching career with a 550-235 record. He guided the Gamecocks to six consecutive final Top 20 rankings from 1968-69 through 1973-74.

1979-80 FINAL NATIONAL POLLS

AP	UPI	SCHOOL (RECORD)	HEAD COACH
1	1	DePaul (26-2)	Ray Meyer
2	4	Louisville (33-3)	Denny Crum
3	2	Louisiana State (26-6)	Dale Brown
4	3	Kentucky (29-6)	Joe B. Hall
5	5	Oregon State (26-4)	Ralph Miller
6	6	Syracuse (26-4)	Jim Boeheim
7	7	Indiana (21-8)	Bob Knight
8	8	Maryland (24-7)	Lefty Driesell
9	11	Notre Dame (22-6)	Digger Phelps
10	9	Ohio State (21-8)	Eldon Miller
11	10	Georgetown (26-6)	John Thompson
12	12	Brigham Young (24-5)	Frank Arnold
13	13	St. John's (24-5)	Lou Carnesecca
14	16	Duke (24-9)	Bill Foster
15	15	North Carolina (21-8)	Dean Smith
16	14	Missouri (25-6)	Norm Stewart
17	17	Weber State (26-3)	Neil McCarthy
18	19	Arizona State (22-7)	Ned Wulk
19	–	Iona (29-5)	Jim Valvano
20	–	Purdue (23-10)	Lee Rose
–	18	Texas A&M (26-8)	Shelby Metcalf
–	20	Kansas State (22-9)	Jack Hartman

1979–80 NCAA CHAMPION: LOUISVILLE

SEASON STATISTICS OF LOUISVILLE REGULARS

PLAYER	POS.	CL.	G.	FG%	FT%	PPG	RPG
Darrell Griffith	G	Sr.	36	.553	.713	22.9	4.8
Derek Smith	F	So.	36	.573	.700	14.8	8.3
Wiley Brown	C-F	So.	36	.519	.610	10.4	5.6
Rodney McCray	F-C	Fr.	36	.543	.647	7.8	7.5
Jerry Eaves	G	So.	34	.514	.667	7.7	1.8
Poncho Wright	G-F	So.	36	.450	.729	6.5	2.5
Roger Burkman	G	Jr.	36	.409	.702	3.9	1.7
Tony Branch	G	Sr.	25	.379	.905	1.6	0.1
Greg Deuser	G	So.	22	.360	.682	1.5	0.5
TEAM TOTALS			**36**	**.521**	**.686**	**76.9**	**38.0**

Assists leaders: Griffith 138, Burkman 113, Eaves 82.

1980 FINAL FOUR CHAMPIONSHIP GAME

INDIANAPOLIS, IN

UCLA (54)	MIN.	FG-A	FT-A	REB.	A	PF	PTS.
Wilkes	24	1-4	0-0	6	0	3	2
Vandeweghe	37	4-9	6-6	7	0	3	14
Sanders	34	4-10	2-4	6	0	4	10
Foster	38	6-15	4-4	1	5	3	16
Holton	29	1-3	2-2	2	3	2	4
Pruitt	16	2-8	2-2	6	1	2	6
Daye	13	1-3	0-0	1	2	1	2
Allums	4	0-0	0-0	2	0	0	0
Anderson	5	0-0	0-0	0	0	0	0
Team				3			
TOTALS	**200**	**19-52**	**16-18**	**34**	**11**	**18**	**54**

FG%: .365. **FT%:** .889. **Blocks:** 3. **Turnovers:** 16. **Steals:** 10 (Foster 6).

LOUISVILLE (59)	MIN.	FG-A	FT-A	REB.	A	PF	PTS.
Brown	34	4-12	0-2	7	3	3	8
Smith	36	3-9	3-4	5	1	2	9
R. McCray	36	2-4	3-4	11	2	4	7
Eaves	30	4-7	0-2	3	3	3	8
Griffith	38	9-16	5-8	2	3	3	23
Burkman	11	0-1	0-0	1	1	4	0
Wright	12	2-4	0-0	4	0	1	4
Branch	3	0-0	0-0	0	0	0	0
Team				3			
TOTALS	**200**	**24-53**	**11-20**	**36**	**13**	**20**	**59**

FG%: .453. **FT%:** .550. **Blocks:** 5. **Turnovers:** 17. **Steals:** 8.
Halftime: UCLA 28-26.

NATIONAL SEMIFINALS

IOWA (72): Brookins 6-18 2-2 14, Boyle 0-8 0-0 0, Krafcisin 4-5 4-4 12, Lester 4-4 2-2 10, Arnold 9-17 2-2 20, Waite 4-6 1-1 9, Hansen 2-8 3-4 7, Gannon 0-0 0-0 0, Henry 0-0 0-0 0. Team 29-66 (.439) 14-15 (.933) 72.

LOUISVILLE (80): Brown 1-3 0-2 2, Smith 3-7 7-8 13, R. McCray 5-7 4-4 14, Eaves 2-4 4-5 8, Griffith 14-21 6-8 34, Wright 1-2 0-0 2, Burkman 2-3 3-4 7, Branch 0-0 0-0 0, Deuser 0-0 0-0 0, Cleveland 0-0 0-0 0, Pulliam 0-0 0-0 0. Team 28-47 (.596) 24-31 (.774) 80.

Halftime: Louisville 34-29.

PURDUE (62): Morris 5-14 2-2 12, Hallman 1-7 0-0 2, Carroll 8-14 1-4 17, Edmonson 9-16 5-6 23, B. Walker 1-3 4-5 6, Stallings 0-0 0-0 0, Scearce 0-2 0-0 0, Barnes 1-1 0-0 2, S. Walker 0-1 0-0 0. Team 25-58 (.431) 12-17 (.706) 62.

UCLA (67): Wilkes 2-2 0-0 4, Vandeweghe 9-12 6-6 24, Sanders 3-7 6-6 12, Foster 4-7 1-2 9, Holton 1-3 2-2 4, Allums 0-0 0-2 0, Daye 1-5 4-5 6, Sims 0-3 0-0 0, Pruitt 3-7 2-2 8. Team 23-46 (.500) 21-25 (.840) 67.

Halftime: UCLA 33-25.

ALL-TOURNAMENT TEAM

Joe Barry Carroll, C, Sr., Purdue
Rod Foster, G, Fr., UCLA
Darrell Griffith, G, Sr., Louisville*
Rodney McCray, F-C, Fr., Louisville
Kiki Vandeweghe, F, Sr., UCLA

*Named Most Outstanding Player.

1980 NCAA Tournament

Summary: All-America guard Darrell Griffith hit less than 40 percent of his field-goal attempts when Louisville won its first two tourney games in overtime and played only 18 minutes as the Cardinals overcame an eight-point deficit against LSU in the Midwest Regional final. But the high-leaping Griffith, nicknamed "Dr. Dunkenstein," performed at the top of his game at the Final Four. The Cardinals' only returning starter from the previous season hit 23 of 37 shots from the floor against Iowa (80-72) and UCLA (59-54). "I've guarded other guys who could leap high before," Iowa's Bob Hansen said. "But all of them came down." Louisville forward Wiley Brown left his artificial right thumb on the breakfast table before the championship game and managers had to search through hotel garbage to retrieve it. The Cardinals excelled with 6-7 freshman Rodney McCray, who replaced his brother, Scooter, at the center position after Scooter suffered a season-ending knee injury. Louisville is the last NCAA champion to go undefeated in conference competition (regular season and league tournament).

Outcome for Defending Champion: Michigan State (12-15 overall; ninth place in Big Ten with 6-12 league mark) became one of only two schools to compile a losing record as defending NCAA champion. The Spartans and Indiana State were the last set of title game participants to fail to qualify for the tournament the next season.

Star Gazing: In a 10-year stretch from 1977 through 1986, Griffith (22.9 points per game) was the only player to average more than 20 points the season his school captured a national title. . . . Guard Ronnie Lester, Iowa's leader in scoring average who missed half of the season because of a knee injury, tallied the Hawkeyes' first 10 points in the national semifinals against Louisville before leaving midway through the first half after reinjuring his knee.

Biggest Upset: DePaul was the nation's top-ranked team entering the postseason when the Blue Demons lost their opener (77-71 against UCLA in West Regional).

One and Only: Louisville became the only school to win a Division I championship after capturing a small college national tournament. The Cardinals won the 1948 NAIA Tournament by defeating John Wooden-coached Indiana State in the final. . . . This was the only year no No. 1 seed reached the Final Four.

Numbers Game: Virginia Tech became the only school to erase a halftime deficit of at least 18 points to win a playoff game. The Hokies, Metro Conference runner-up to eventual NCAA champion Louisville, trailed at intermission (48-30) before rallying to edge Western Kentucky (89-85 in overtime) in the first round of the Mideast Regional. . . . Backup swingman Mark Dressler, entering the NCAA playoffs with an eight-point scoring average, erupted for 32 points on 13 of 16 field-goal shooting to spark Missouri to an 87-84 overtime victory against Notre Dame. The short-handed Tigers, playing without starting forward Curtis Berry (knee surgery), lost their next game in the Midwest Regional semifinals to LSU, 68-63. Suspensions had knocked guard Barry Laurie and center Lex Drum off the Tigers' roster, Kirk Shawver quit and Steve Wallace was declared ineligible in mid-season. . . . LSU's Rudy Macklin (19 rebounds vs. Alcorn State) and Notre Dame's Tracy Jackson (19 vs. Missouri) tied for the best single-game rebounding performances in the playoffs. . . . Lamar needed every one of guard Mike Olliver's tourney-high 37 points to nip Weber State, 87-86, in the opening round of the West Regional. . . . Washington State, coached by

George Raveling, made its first playoff appearance since finishing national runner-up in 1941 and San Jose State, coached by Bill Berry, participated in the tourney for the lone time in a 44-year stretch from 1952 through 1995. . . . UCLA reached the NCAA title game despite not finishing among the top 10 in the final AP poll for the first time in 14 seasons. . . . Texas A&M became the only school to participate in back-to-back overtime playoff contests decided by double digits in the same tourney. The Aggies took champion-to-be Louisville to an extra session in a 66-55 loss in the the Midwest Regional semifinals after they posted the largest winning margin in an overtime playoff game (78-61 over North Carolina in double overtime).

What Might Have Been: Forwards Kiki Vandeweghe, Mike Sanders and James Wilkes, guards Rod Foster, Michael Holton and Darren Daye, and center Darrell Allums were proficient enough to eventually play in the NBA after they each shot at least 50 percent from the floor for UCLA in the 1979-80 season. If only they combined to hit 45.5 percent of their field-goal attempts instead of 38.6 percent (17 of 44) in the championship game, the Bruins could have defeated Louisville rather than losing by five points. . . . Big Ten champion Indiana (21-8) might have fared better in the playoffs if guard Randy Wittman didn't miss the majority of the season because of a stress fracture in his right ankle.

Putting Things in Perspective: Louisville lost two of three games in late December, including a 13-point neutral-court defeat to Illinois, which finished with a losing record in Big Ten competition.

Scoring Leader: Joe Barry Carroll, Purdue (158 points, 26.3 ppg).

Highest Scoring Average: Kelvin Ransey, Ohio State (54 points, 27 ppg).

Rebounding Leader: Mike Sanders, UCLA (60 rebounds, 10 rpg).

Highest Rebounding Average: Syracuse's Louis Orr and Maryland's Buck Williams (24 rebounds, 12 rpg).

1980 CHAMPIONSHIP BRACKET

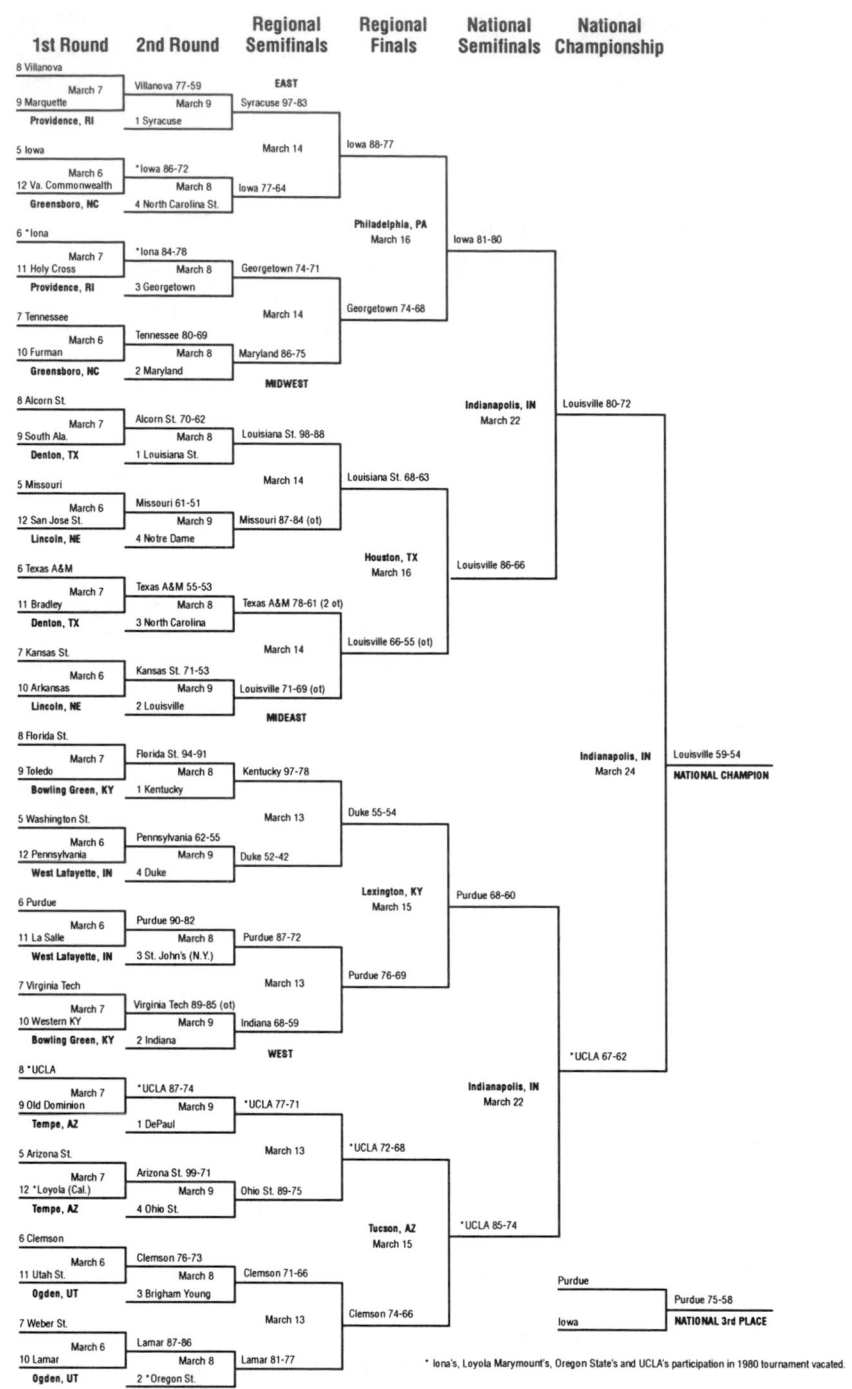

1st Round	2nd Round	Regional Semifinals	Regional Finals	National Semifinals	National Championship

EAST

8 Villanova
March 7
9 Marquette
Providence, RI

Villanova 77-59
March 9
1 Syracuse

Syracuse 97-83

Iowa 88-77

5 Iowa
March 6
12 Va. Commonwealth
Greensboro, NC

*Iowa 86-72
March 8
4 North Carolina St.

Iowa 77-64

March 14

Philadelphia, PA
March 16

Iowa 81-80

6 *Iona
March 7
11 Holy Cross
Providence, RI

*Iona 84-78
March 8
3 Georgetown

Georgetown 74-71

Georgetown 74-68

7 Tennessee
March 6
10 Furman
Greensboro, NC

Tennessee 80-69
March 8
2 Maryland

Maryland 86-75

March 14

MIDWEST

Louisville 80-72

8 Alcorn St.
March 7
9 South Ala.
Denton, TX

Alcorn St. 70-62
March 8
1 Louisiana St.

Louisiana St. 98-88

Louisiana St. 68-63

5 Missouri
March 6
12 San Jose St.
Lincoln, NE

Missouri 61-51
March 9
4 Notre Dame

Missouri 87-84 (ot)

March 14

Houston, TX
March 16

Louisville 86-66

6 Texas A&M
March 7
11 Bradley
Denton, TX

Texas A&M 55-53
March 8
3 North Carolina

Texas A&M 78-61 (2 ot)

Louisville 66-55 (ot)

7 Kansas St.
March 6
10 Arkansas
Lincoln, NE

Kansas St. 71-53
March 9
2 Louisville

Louisville 71-69 (ot)

March 14

Indianapolis, IN
March 22

MIDEAST

Indianapolis, IN
March 24

Louisville 59-54

NATIONAL CHAMPION

8 Florida St.
March 7
9 Toledo
Bowling Green, KY

Florida St. 94-91
March 8
1 Kentucky

Kentucky 97-78

Duke 55-54

5 Washington St.
March 6
12 Pennsylvania
West Lafayette, IN

Pennsylvania 62-55
March 9
4 Duke

Duke 52-42

March 13

Lexington, KY
March 15

Purdue 68-60

6 Purdue
March 6
11 La Salle
West Lafayette, IN

Purdue 90-82
March 8
3 St. John's (N.Y.)

Purdue 87-72

Purdue 76-69

7 Virginia Tech
March 7
10 Western KY
Bowling Green, KY

Virginia Tech 89-85 (ot)
March 9
2 Indiana

Indiana 68-59

March 13

WEST

*UCLA 67-62

8 *UCLA
March 7
9 Old Dominion
Tempe, AZ

*UCLA 87-74
March 9
1 DePaul

*UCLA 77-71

*UCLA 72-68

5 Arizona St.
March 7
12 *Loyola (Cal.)
Tempe, AZ

Arizona St. 99-71
March 9
4 Ohio St.

Ohio St. 89-75

March 13

Indianapolis, IN
March 22

6 Clemson
March 6
11 Utah St.
Ogden, UT

Clemson 76-73
March 8
3 Brigham Young

Clemson 71-66

*UCLA 85-74

7 Weber St.
March 6
10 Lamar
Ogden, UT

Lamar 87-86
March 8
2 *Oregon St.

Lamar 81-77

Clemson 74-66

Tucson, AZ
March 15

Purdue

Iowa

Purdue 75-58

NATIONAL 3rd PLACE

* Iona's, Loyola Marymount's, Oregon State's and UCLA's participation in 1980 tournament vacated.

1980-81

AT A GLANCE

NCAA Champion: Indiana (26-9; coached by Bob Knight; won Big Ten title by one game over Iowa with a 14-4 record).

NIT Champion: Tulsa (26-7; coached by Nolan Richardson; tied for second place in Missouri Valley with an 11-5 record, which was one game behind Wichita State).

New Conference: MEAC (moved up from Division II).

New Rule: No more than 50 percent of the NCAA Tournament berths shall be filled by automatic qualifiers.

NCAA Probation: UC Santa Barbara, New Mexico, West Texas State.

NCAA Consensus First-Team All-Americans: Mark Aguirre, F, Jr., DePaul; Danny Ainge, G, Sr., Brigham Young; Steve Johnson, C, Sr., Oregon State; Ralph Sampson, C, Soph., Virginia; Isiah Thomas, G, Soph., Indiana.

National Players of the Year: Ainge (24.4 ppg, 4.8 rpg, 51.8 FG%, 82.4 FT%/NABC, Wooden) and Sampson (17.7 ppg, 11.5 rpg, 3.1 bpg, 55.7 FG%/AP, UPI, USBWA, Naismith).

National Coaches of the Year: Kansas State's Jack Hartman (24-9/shared NABC) and Oregon State's Ralph Miller (26-2/AP, UPI, shared NABC, USBWA).

Perhaps the national player of the year to struggle the most in a single NCAA Tournament was Virginia sophomore center Ralph Sampson, who had three mediocre playoff games of less than 12 points, including an 11-point outing when the Cavaliers were defeated by North Carolina in the national semifinals. Virginia had captured its only undisputed ACC regular-season title with a 13-1 league record. The Cavaliers sprinted to a 23-0 mark before Notre Dame's Orlando Woolridge ended the streak with a last-second shot, 57-56.

Oregon State's Steve Johnson, who didn't play basketball until his senior year in high school, set an NCAA single-season record by hitting 74.6 percent of his field-goal attempts (235 of 315). He finished his career at 67.8 percent, an NCAA mark with a minimum of 600 baskets.

Johnson, the only player to hit more than 70 percent of his field-goal attempts in two different seasons, led the Pacific-10 in field-goal accuracy all four of his years with the Beavers as they had a player led the conference in that category six consecutive seasons. . . . Oregon State won its first 26 games before the Beavers were blasted in their regular-season finale by visiting Arizona State, 87-67. Guard Byron Scott scored a game-high 25 points for the Sun Devils. Earlier, ASU outlasted UCLA, 78-74, in triple overtime in a game that had nine of its 10 starters go on to NBA careers.

Danny Ainge became the first Brigham Young player since 1953 to earn a spot on an NCAA consensus first- or second-team All-American squad. . . . UC Irvine's Kevin Magee, after an unspectacular high school career in Magnolia, Miss., and brief stints at three colleges, became the first player ever to finish among the top four nationally in scoring, rebounding and field-goal shooting. . . . Colgate's Mike Ferrara (28.6 ppg), UCI's Magee (27.5) and Portland's Jose Slaughter (21.2) set school records for highest scoring average in a single season.

Tulsa became the only school to win more than 25 games the season after a single-digit victory total. The Golden Hurricanes improved to 26-7 from 8-19 after first-year coach Nolan Richardson brought four of his top players from NJCAA champion Western Texas. Tulsa became the first team to capture an NIT title after posting a losing record the previous year. The Golden Hurricanes, after losing their previous eight outings with intracity rival Oral Roberts, began a 13-game winning streak against ORU in their series. They also started a 16-game winning streak against SIU in their series. . . . Oklahoma State, coached by Paul Hansen, compiled an 18-9 record to end a streak of 10 consecutive losing seasons. . . . Nebraska coach Joe Cipriano died after a year-long battle with cancer three days before the Cornhuskers' season opener. . . . TCU's Warren Bridges, Darrell Browder and Deckery Johnson each logged an amazing 60 minutes of action during the Horned Frogs' four-overtime, 78-77 victory over Houston.

... Rice lost 20 consecutive games to Texas until defeating the Longhorns in overtime, 46-40.

South Carolina guard Zam Fredrick, entering his senior season with a career scoring average of just 8.1 points per game, ranked in 20th place at midseason (22.5 ppg) before averaging 36 ppg his last 13 games to finish with a nation-leading mark of 28.9. Fredrick averaged a meager 1.9 ppg as a freshman. South Carolina is the only school in NCAA history to have the nation's leading scorer in basketball and leading rusher in football (Heis-man Trophy-winner George Rogers with 1,891 yards in 1980) in the same school year. . . . Colgate's Ferrara, runner-up to Fredrick in scoring average, had a national-high 50 points against Siena. Ferrara averaged only 2.1 points per game as a freshman at Niagara before transferring.

Michigan's Mike McGee became the only player to score more than 1,500 points in Big Ten Conference competition. . . . Indiana's Ted Kitchel canned all 18 of his free-throw attempts in a 78-61 victory over Illinois, setting a school and Big Ten

1980–81 INDIVIDUAL LEADERS

SCORING

PLAYER	PTS.	AVG.
Fredrick, South Carolina	781	28.9
Ferrara, Colgate	772	28.6
Magee, UC Irvine	743	27.5
Lloyd, Drake	762	26.3
Williams, Houston	749	25.0
Jackson, Oklahoma City	719	24.8
Edwards, Cleveland St.	664	24.6
Belcher, St. Bonaventure	637	24.5
Ainge, Brigham Young	782	24.4
McGee, Michigan	732	24.4

REBOUNDING

PLAYER	REB.	AVG.
Watson, Miss. Valley St.	379	14.0
Sappleton, Loyola (Ill.)	374	13.4

Cage, San Diego St.	355	13.1
Magee, UC Irvine	337	12.5
Thompson, Texas	370	12.3
Kellogg, Ohio St.	324	12.0
Atkins, Duquesne	352	11.7
Williams, Maryland	363	11.7
Henry, Oklahoma City	338	11.7
Sampson, Virginia	378	11.5

FIELD GOAL PERCENTAGE

PLAYER	FGM	FGA	PCT.
Johnson, Oregon St.	235	315	.746
Magee, UC Irvine	280	417	.671
Woolridge, Notre Dame	156	240	.650
Williams, Maryland	183	283	.647
Best, Lafayette	164	255	.643
Johnson, UNLV	152	239	.636
Hopson, Idaho	157	247	.636

Payton, Appa. St.	178	281	.633
Palm, Nevada-Reno	204	323	.632
Aleksinas, Conn.	154	244	.631

FREE THROW PERCENTAGE

PLAYER	FTM	FTA	PCT.
Hildahl, Portland St.	76	82	.927
Moore, Nebraska	118	128	.922
Bontrager, O. Roberts	73	81	.901
Stack, N'western	81	90	.900
Leonard, Manhattan	123	138	.891
Simmons, La. Tech	130	146	.890
Greig, Oregon	82	93	.882
Edwards, Cleve. St.	134	152	.882
Wafer, La. Tech	80	91	.879
Ferrara, Colgate	176	201	.876

1980–81 TEAM LEADERS

SCORING OFFENSE

SCHOOL	PTS.	AVG.
UC Irvine	2332	86.4
West Texas St.	2309	85.5
Oklahoma City	2421	83.5
San Francisco	2579	83.2
Long Island	2390	82.4

SCORING DEFENSE

SCHOOL	PTS.	AVG.
Fresno St.	1470	50.7
Princeton	1438	51.4
St. Peter's	1338	51.5
Air Force	1518	56.2
San Jose St.	1699	56.6

SCORING MARGIN

SCHOOL	OFF.	DEF.	MAR.
Wyoming	73.6	57.5	16.1
Oregon St.	76.6	60.9	15.7
Fresno St.	66.1	50.7	15.4
Wichita St.	80.9	66.5	14.4
DePaul	78.9	66.1	12.8
South Alabama	73.8	61.0	12.8

WON-LOST PERCENTAGE

SCHOOL	W-L	PCT.
DePaul	27-2	.931
Oregon St.	26-2	.929
Virginia	29-4	.879
Fresno St.	25-4	.862
Idaho	25-4	.862

FIELD GOAL PERCENTAGE

SCHOOL	FGM	FGA	PCT.
Oregon St.	862	1528	.564
Notre Dame	824	1492	.552
Idaho	816	1484	.550
UC Irvine	934	1703	.548
Pepperdine	918	1709	.537

FIELD GOAL PERCENTAGE DEFENSE

SCHOOL	FGM	FGA	PTS.
Wyoming	637	1589	.401
Penn St.	547	1338	.409
South Florida	701	1682	.417
St. Peter's	521	1248	.417
Air Force	561	1343	.418

FREE THROW PERCENTAGE

SCHOOL	FTM	FTA	PCT.
Connecticut	487	623	.782
Idaho St.	405	522	.776
Davidson	477	626	.762
St. John's	463	612	.757
Tennessee	424	561	.756

REBOUND MARGIN

SCHOOL	OWN	OPP.	MAR.
Northeastern	44.9	32.0	12.9
Wyoming	42.0	30.3	11.7
Wichita St.	44.1	34.0	10.1
Miss. Valley St.	47.1	39.0	8.1
San Francisco	40.1	32.6	7.5

Lute Olson and his Iowa team went to the Final Four in 1980, but they couldn't match that success when the Hawkeyes fell to Wichita State in the opening round of the 1981 tournament.

standard that still stands. . . . Cleveland State's Frank Edwards set a school single-game scoring record with 49 points at Xavier. . . . Loyola of Chicago's Wayne Sappleton established a Midwestern Collegiate Conference single-season standard by averaging 15.2 rebounds per game. The league was called the Midwestern City at the time. Xavier won the title despite compiling a 12-16 record overall.

Louisiana State (31-5/coached by Dale Brown), South Alabama (25-6/Cliff Ellis), American (24-6/Gary Williams), San Jose State (21-9/Bill Berry) and Texas-Arlington (20-8/Bob LeGrand) had their winningest seasons in school Division I history.

Texas-Arlington's Albert Culton grabbed a school-record 24 rebounds in a game against Northeastern. . . . West Virginia's 23-10 record snapped a streak of losing more than 10 games in 12 consecutive seasons. . . . The three-point goal was an experimental rule in the Southern Conference. Western Carolina's Ronnie Carr made the first three-pointer in history on November 29, 1980, in Reid Gymnasium against Middle Tennessee State. . . . Clem Haskins became the third different Western Kentucky coach in six years to capture an Ohio Valley Conference regular-season crown. He joined Jim Richards ('76) and Gene Keady ('80). . . . Murray State lost 19 consecutive games to intrastate foe Memphis State until defeating the Tigers, 57-52.

Freshman guard John Stockton averaged a modest 3.1 points per game when Gonzaga compiled a 19-8 record for its only season with fewer than 10 defeats in a 25-year span from 1967-68 through 1991-92. Stockton, however, went on to lead the WCAC in assists in 1983 and 1984 to become the only non-Loyola Marymount player to pace the league in that category in a 12-year stretch from 1980-91. . . . National field-goal shooting improved for the eighth consecutive season to 48 percent. . . . Five Mid-American teams tied for first place, the most ever for a Division I conference, with 10-6 league records. . . . Catholic (D.C.) competed in its final season at the major-college level.

1980-81 FINAL NATIONAL POLLS

AP	UPI	SCHOOL (RECORD)	HEAD COACH
1	1	DePaul (27-2)	Ray Meyer
2	2	Oregon State (26-2)	Ralph Miller
3	5	Arizona State (24-4)	Ned Wulk
4	4	Louisiana State (31-5)	Dale Brown
5	3	Virginia (29-4)	Terry Holland
6	6	North Carolina (29-8)	Dean Smith
7	9	Notre Dame (23-6)	Digger Phelps
8	8	Kentucky (22-6)	Joe B. Hall
9	7	Indiana (26-9)	Bob Knight
10	11	UCLA (20-7)	Larry Brown
11	14	Wake Forest (22-7)	Carl Tacy
12	13	Louisville (21-9)	Denny Crum
13	12	Iowa (21-7)	Lute Olson
14	10	Utah (25-5)	Jerry Pimm
15	15	Tennessee (21-8)	Don DeVoe
16	17	Brigham Young (25-7)	Frank Arnold
17	16	Wyoming (24-6)	Jim Brandenburg
18	20	Maryland (21-10)	Lefty Driesell
19	18	Illinois (21-8)	Lou Henson
20	–	Arkansas (24-8)	Eddie Sutton
–	19	Kansas (24-8)	Ted Owens

1981 NCAA Tournament

Summary: North Carolina couldn't cope with two players named Thomas in a 63-50 defeat in the NCAA final. Indiana's Isiah Thomas collected 23 points and five assists and teammate Jim Thomas chipped in with eight assists. Jim Thomas, a defensive standout, became the only player who didn't score a total of more than 10 points in two Final Four games (two points in each game) to be named to an All-NCAA Tournament team.

Star Gazing: Isiah Thomas is the only guard among the eight freshmen and sophomores to lead a national titlist in scoring average.

Outcome for Defending Champion: Louisville (21-9) won the Metro Conference regular-season crown by four games after losing six of its first seven non-league contests.

Biggest Upsets: Louisville and 1980 runner-up UCLA succumbed against Arkansas and Brigham Young, respectively. It was the last time both championship final teams appeared in the tourney again the following season and lost their opening-round games. . . . DePaul was the nation's top-ranked team entering the tourney for the second consecutive season when the Blue Demons lost their playoff opener again (49-48 against St. Joseph's in Mideast Regional). It was the "Year of the Upset" as second-ranked Oregon State suc-

1980–81 NCAA CHAMPION: INDIANA

SEASON STATISTICS OF INDIANA REGULARS

PLAYER	POS.	CL.	G.	FG%	FT%	PPG	RPG
Isiah Thomas	G	So.	34	.554	.742	16.0	3.1
Ray Tolbert	F-C	Sr.	35	.588	.740	12.2	6.4
Randy Wittman	G	Jr.	35	.542	.768	10.4	2.3
Landon Turner	F-C	Jr.	33	.561	.717	9.5	3.7
Ted Kitchel	F	Jr.	34	.465	.854	9.2	3.3
Jim Thomas	G	So.	33	.495	.771	3.7	3.2
Tony Brown	G	So.	28	.458	.536	3.3	1.3
Steve Risley	F	Sr.	31	.452	.651	3.0	2.3
Glen Grunwald	F	Sr.	27	.512	.615	1.9	1.2
Phil Isenbarger	F	Sr.	26	.600	.650	1.7	1.2
Steve Bouchie	F	So.	29	.383	.818	1.6	1.6
Chuck Franz	G	So.	21	.583	.875	1.3	0.3
TEAM TOTALS			35	.530	.744	70.0	32.7

Assists leader: I. Thomas 197. **Blocked shots leader:** Tolbert 35. **Steals leader:** I. Thomas 74.

1981 FINAL FOUR CHAMPIONSHIP GAME

PHILADELPHIA, PA

INDIANA (63)	MIN.	FG-A	FT-A	REB.	A	PF	PTS.
Kitchel	4	0-1	0-0	0	0	3	0
Turner	34	5-8	2-2	6	1	5	12
Tolbert	40	1-4	3-6	11	0	0	5
I. Thomas	40	8-17	7-8	2	5	4	23
Wittman	40	7-13	2-2	4	0	2	16
Risley	13	1-1	3-4	4	0	1	5
J. Thomas	29	1-4	0-0	4	8	2	2
Team				2			
TOTALS	200	23-48	17-22	33	14	17	63

FG%: .479. **FT%:** .773. **Blocks:** 1. **Turnovers:** 14. **Steals:** 8.

NORTH CAROLINA (50)	MIN.	FG-A	FT-A	REB.	A	PF	PTS.
Wood	38	6-13	6-9	6	2	4	18
Worthy	31	3-11	1-2	6	2	5	7
Perkins	39	5-8	1-2	8	1	3	11
Pepper	23	2-5	2-2	1	0	1	6
Black	36	3-4	0-0	2	6	5	6
Budko	1	0-1	0-0	1	0	0	0
Doherty	24	1-2	0-1	4	0	4	2
Braddock	4	0-2	0-0	0	1	1	0
Brust	3	0-0	0-0	0	0	0	0
Kenny	1	0-1	0-0	1	0	0	0
TOTALS	200	20-47	10-16	29	12	23	60

FG%: .426. **FT%:** .625. **Blocks:** 2. **Turnovers:** 19 (Doherty 6). **Steals:** 9. **Halftime:** Indiana 27-26.

NATIONAL SEMIFINALS

INDIANA (67): Kitchel 3-8 4-4 10, Turner 7-19 6-7 20, Tolbert 3-7 1-2 7, I. Thomas 6-8 2-3 14, Wittman 3-10 2-2 8, Risley 0-2 1-2 1, J. Thomas 0-4 2-2 2, Bouchie 0-1 0-0 0, Grunwald 1-2 1-2 3, Brown 0-1 0-1 0, Isenbarger 0-1 0-0 0, Franz 0-0 2-2 2, LaFave 0-0 0-0 0. Team 23-63 (.365) 21-27 (.778) 67.

LOUISIANA STATE (49): Mitchell 3-10 3-4 9, Macklin 2-12 0-0 4, Cook 3-5 0-0 6, Martin 2-8 3-3 7, Carter 5-10 0-0 10, Sims 2-8 1-2 5, Jones 0-2 0-1 0, Tudor 1-3 4-4 6, Bergeron 0-0 0-0 0, Costello 0-0 0-0 0, Black 1-1 0-0 2. Team 19-59 (.322) 11-14 (.786) 49.

Halftime: Louisiana State 30-27.

NORTH CAROLINA (78): Wood 14-19 11-13 39, Worthy 2-8 4-7 8, Perkins 4-7 3-5 11, Pepper 0-4 0-0 0, Black 4-6 2-3 10, Doherty 0-1 8-9 8, Braddock 0-1 0-0 0, Kenny 1-1 0-0 2. Team 25-47 (.532) 28-37 (.757) 78.

VIRGINIA (65): Lamp 7-18 4-4 18, Gates 1-1 0-0 2, Sampson 3-10 5-7 11, Wilson 4-7 0-0 8, Jones 5-13 1-1 11, Stokes 0-2 0-0 0, Raker 5-9 3-3 13, Lattimore 1-1 0-0 2. Team 26-61 (.426) 13-15 (.867) 65.

Halftime: Tied 27-27.

ALL-TOURNAMENT TEAM

Jeff Lamp, G, Sr., Virginia (43 points, 15 rebounds in final two games)
*Isiah Thomas, G, Soph., Indiana (37 points, nine assists)
Jim Thomas, G, Soph., Indiana (four points, 13 rebounds, 10 assists)
Landon Turner, F-C, Jr., Indiana (32 points, 14 rebounds)
Al Wood, F, Sr., North Carolina (57 points, 16 rebounds)

*Named Most Outstanding Player.

---

cumbed to Kansas State, 50-48, and third-ranked Arizona State was clobbered by Kansas, 88-71, in their playoff openers. K-State defeated OSU on Rolando Blackman's 17-foot buzzer beater from the right baseline.

One and Only: DePaul became the only school to be top-ranked entering back-to-back tournaments but lose both opening playoff games. St. Joseph's gained its only lead in the second half when an inexcusably unguarded Hawks player named John Smith sank a layup with three seconds left after DePaul's most accurate foul shooter, Skip Dillard, the guy they called "Money" because when he shot 'em, they were as good as in the bank, missed the front end of a one-and-one with 12 seconds remaining.

DePaul did not score a point or take a shot in the final 6 1/2 minutes. A stunned Aguirre, the national player of the year, didn't even throw the ball inbounds and finished the game with one rebound, one assist, no blocked shots, no steals and the only sub-10 scoring output of his college career (eight points). He must have saved his energy for throwing the game ball into Dayton's Great Miami River after the game.

Smith felt no remorse for Aguirre and venerable DePaul coach Ray Meyer. "Aguirre? Why should I? I know one thing, he didn't light us up, did he? And, he did all the (trash) talking. That made me want to dig in and put it to this guy. Who in the hell does he think he is? He sure wasn't doing anything."

1981 CHAMPIONSHIP BRACKET

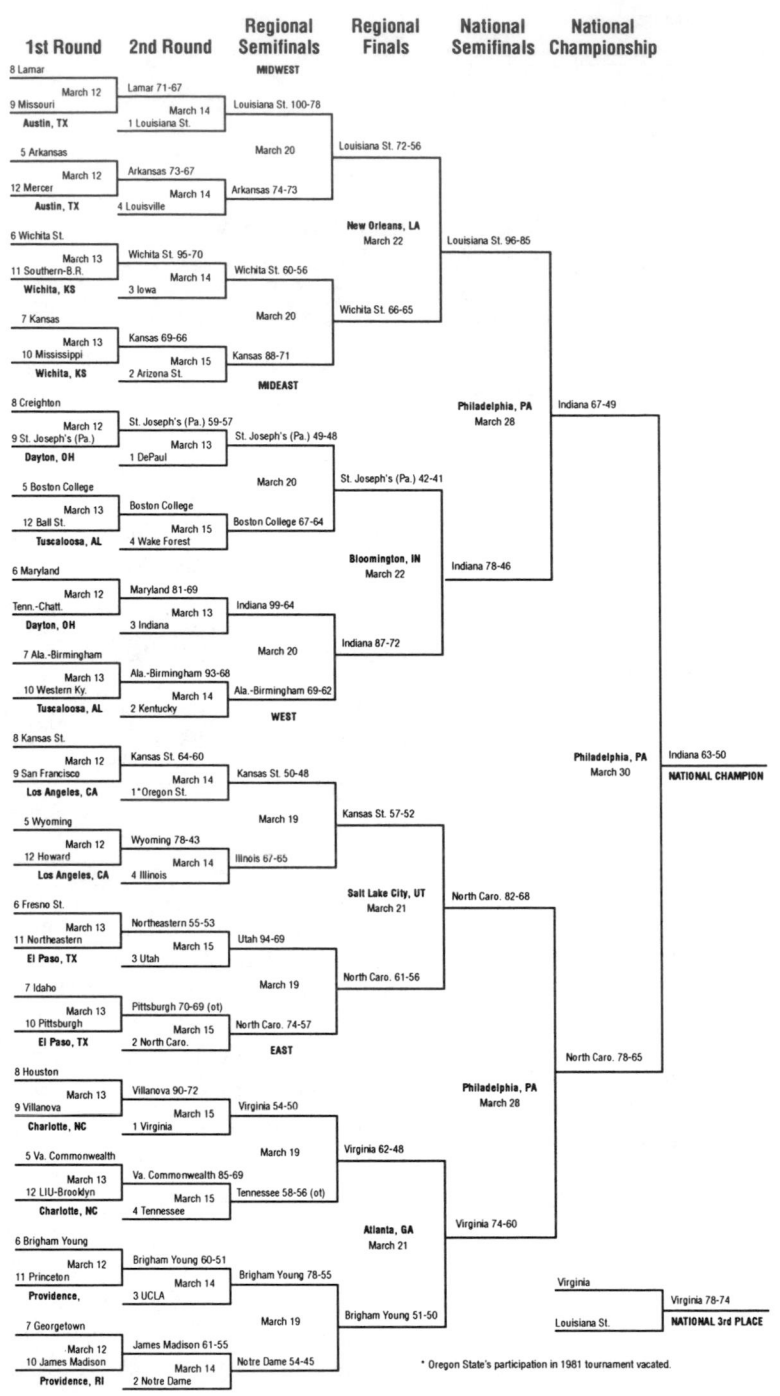

1st Round	2nd Round	Regional Semifinals	Regional Finals	National Semifinals	National Championship

MIDWEST

8 Lamar
March 12 — Lamar 71-67
9 Missouri
Austin, TX
March 14 — 1 Louisiana St. — Louisiana St. 100-78
5 Arkansas
March 12 — Arkansas 73-67
12 Mercer
Austin, TX
March 14 — 4 Louisville — Arkansas 74-73

March 20 — Louisiana St. 72-56

6 Wichita St.
March 13 — Wichita St. 95-70
11 Southern-B.R.
Wichita, KS
March 14 — 3 Iowa — Wichita St. 60-56
7 Kansas
March 13 — Kansas 69-66
10 Mississippi
Wichita, KS
March 15 — 2 Arizona St. — Kansas 88-71

March 20 — Wichita St. 66-65

New Orleans, LA
March 22 — Louisiana St. 96-85

MIDEAST

8 Creighton
March 12 — St. Joseph's (Pa.) 59-57
9 St. Joseph's (Pa.)
Dayton, OH
March 13 — 1 DePaul — St. Joseph's (Pa.) 49-48
5 Boston College
March 13 — Boston College
12 Ball St.
Tuscaloosa, AL
March 15 — 4 Wake Forest — Boston College 67-64

March 20 — St. Joseph's (Pa.) 42-41

6 Maryland
March 12 — Maryland 81-69
Tenn.-Chatt.
Dayton, OH
March 13 — 3 Indiana — Indiana 99-64
7 Ala.-Birmingham
March 13 — Ala.-Birmingham 93-68
10 Western Ky.
Tuscaloosa, AL
March 14 — 2 Kentucky — Ala.-Birmingham 69-62

March 20 — Indiana 87-72

Bloomington, IN
March 22 — Indiana 78-46

Philadelphia, PA
March 28 — Indiana 67-49

WEST

8 Kansas St.
March 12 — Kansas St. 64-60
9 San Francisco
Los Angeles, CA
March 14 — 1*Oregon St. — Kansas St. 50-48
5 Wyoming
March 12 — Wyoming 78-43
12 Howard
Los Angeles, CA
March 14 — 4 Illinois — Illinois 67-65

March 19 — Kansas St. 57-52

6 Fresno St.
March 13 — Northeastern 55-53
11 Northeastern
El Paso, TX
March 15 — 3 Utah — Utah 94-69
7 Idaho
March 13 — Pittsburgh 70-69 (ot)
10 Pittsburgh
El Paso, TX
March 15 — 2 North Caro. — North Caro. 74-57

March 19 — North Caro. 61-56

Salt Lake City, UT
March 21 — North Caro. 82-68

EAST

8 Houston
March 13 — Villanova 90-72
9 Villanova
Charlotte, NC
March 15 — 1 Virginia — Virginia 54-50
5 Va. Commonwealth
March 13 — Va. Commonwealth 85-69
12 LIU-Brooklyn
Charlotte, NC
March 15 — 4 Tennessee — Tennessee 58-56 (ot)

March 19 — Virginia 62-48

6 Brigham Young
March 12 — Brigham Young 60-51
11 Princeton
Providence,
March 14 — 3 UCLA — Brigham Young 78-55
7 Georgetown
March 12 — James Madison 61-55
10 James Madison
Providence, RI
March 14 — 2 Notre Dame — Notre Dame 54-45

March 19 — Brigham Young 51-50

Atlanta, GA
March 21 — Virginia 74-60

Philadelphia, PA
March 28 — North Caro. 78-65

Philadelphia, PA
March 30 — Indiana 63-50 **NATIONAL CHAMPION**

Virginia
Louisiana St. — Virginia 78-74 **NATIONAL 3rd PLACE**

* Oregon State's participation in 1981 tournament vacated.

Numbers Game: The last player to score the most points in a single game of a tournament and play for a Final Four team was Al Wood. He scored a playoff-high 39 points for North Carolina in the Tar Heels' 78-65 victory against Virginia in the national semifinals before they lost to Indiana in the championship game. In the West Regional final, Wood grabbed a tourney-high 17 rebounds to carry Carolina to an 82-68 triumph over Kansas State. . . . Indiana's Ray Tolbert retrieved 11 missed shots in the NCAA final but finished the season with the lowest rebounding average for a player leading a national titlist in that category (6.4 rpg) since the NCAA began charting rebound statistics. . . . LSU's Rudy Macklin, after averaging 20.5 points per game in his first six NCAA playoff contests, scored a total of four points in two Final Four games. . . . Mississippi (coached by Bob Weltlich) made its lone NCAA Tournament appearance until 1997, Idaho (Don Monson) participated in the playoffs for the initial time and Illinois (Lou Henson) appeared for the first time in 18 years. . . . Wichita State's Mike Jones hit two long-range baskets in the last 50 seconds to give the Shockers a 66-65 victory over Kansas in the Midwest Regional semifinals in the first game between the schools in 36 years. . . . Kansas State's Jack Hartman became the only coach to reach a regional final at least four times without ever advancing to the Final Four.

What Might Have Been: Arizona State, ranked third by AP entering the playoffs with a 24-3 record, had the door open to a possible national title when No. 1 seeds DePaul and Oregon State lost their playoff openers at the buzzer. But the Sun Devils, featuring four upperclassmen who combined for a total of more than 35 seasons in the NBA (guards Fat Lever and Byron Scott, center Alton Lister and forward Sam Williams), became one of the biggest busts in tourney history. The door to the Final Four was also slammed shut on them in their opener by Kansas (88-71 in Midwest Regional) when they fell behind by 16 points at intermission. Arizona State had defeated Iowa by eight points early in the season before the Hawkeyes twice upended

eventual national champion Indiana in Big Ten Conference competition.

Putting Things in Perspective: Iowa (21-7) defeated Indiana twice by a total of 16 points before the Hawkeyes lost their NCAA playoff opener in the second round against Wichita State on the Shockers' home court. The Hoosiers got off to a modest 7-5 start, including a defeat on a neutral court against Pan American. . . . Wichita State (26-7) was without starting center Ozell Jones (declared ineligible because of a technicality with his high school transcript) when the Shockers bowed to LSU, 96-85, in the Midwest Regional final at the Louisiana Superdome. . . . LSU (31-5) might have fared better at the Final Four if DeWayne Scales didn't defect early to turn pro.

Scoring Leader: Al Wood, North Carolina (109 points, 21.8 ppg).

Highest Scoring Average: Mike Olliver, Lamar (54 points, 27 ppg).

Rebounding Leader: Cliff Levingston, Wichita State (53 rebounds, 13.25 rpg).

1981-82

AT A GLANCE

NCAA Champion: North Carolina (32-2; coached by Dean Smith; tied for ACC regular-season title with a 12-2 record).

NIT Champion: Bradley (26-10; coached by Dick Versace; won Missouri Valley title by one game with a 13-3 record).

New Conferences: ECAC Metro (forerunner of Northeast), Metro Atlantic Athletic.

New Rules: The jump ball is employed only at the beginning of the game and the start of each overtime. An alternating arrow indicates possession in jump-ball situations during the game, with the arrow first pointing in the direction of the team that didn't gain possession of the initial jump ball. . . . All fouls assessed to bench personnel are charged to the head coach. . . . National third-place game in the NCAA Tournament is abolished.

NCAA Probation: Arkansas State, UC Santa Barbara, New Mexico, UCLA, Wichita State.

NCAA Consensus First-Team All-Americans: Terry Cummings, F-C, Jr., DePaul; Quintin Dailey, G, Jr., San Francisco; Eric "Sleepy" Floyd, G, Sr., Georgetown; Ralph Sampson, C, Jr., Virginia; James Worthy, F, Jr., North Carolina.

National Player of the Year: Sampson (15.8 ppg, 11.4 rpg, 2.7 bpg, 56.1 FG%).

National Coaches of the Year: Oregon State's Ralph Miller (25-5/AP); Idaho's Don Monson (27-3/NABC); Missouri's Norm Stewart (27-4/UPI), and Georgetown's John Thompson (30-7/USBWA).

Georgetown's John Thompson took umbrage to depictions of him as the initial African American coach to direct a team to the Final Four. But the injustices in the past against his race were sufficient reason for placing emphasis on Thompson's achievements with predominantly black rosters. His shooting guard, Sleepy Floyd, became the first Georgetown player to earn a spot on an NCAA consensus first- or second-team All-American squad.

Slowdown tactics that could bore fans to tears embarrassed the prestigious ACC Tournament, helping pave the way for the introduction of a shot clock later in the decade. Despite the presence of standouts such as Michael Jordan, Sam Perkins, James Worthy and Ralph Sampson, only one team scored at least 60 points in the seven ACC Tournament games.

Seton Hall guard Dan Callandrillo averaged 27.4 points per game to set a Big East Conference single-season record. . . . UC Irvine's Kevin Magee became the only player ever to finish two seasons in the top 10 nationally in scoring, rebounding and field-goal shooting. Magee set a school single-game scoring record with 46 points against Loyola Marymount. He also grabbed a school-record 25 rebounds against Long Beach State. . . . Western Illinois' Joe Dykstra set an NCAA record by converting 64 consecutive free throws (eight-game stretch from December 1 to January 4).

In the longest contest in major-college history, Cincinnati outlasted NIT champion-to-be Bradley, 75-73, in seven overtimes. "That was my biggest thrill as a coach," said Tony Barone, an assistant to Bradley's Dick Versace at the time. "One of their subs made a jump shot that he had no business making—a terrible shot—that went in with two seconds left in the seventh overtime. We threw the ball the length of the court and our center caught it, turned around from the top of the key, shot it and the ball went in and out. Otherwise, it would have been eight overtimes." In another wild overtime affair, Dayton scored the

---

LONGEST GAME IN HISTORY Cincinnati and Bradley players anticipating their Christmas break in 1981 had a rude awakening on December 21, 1981. The game between the Braves and the Bearcats went into the seventh overtime before hometeam Bradley lost to Cincinnati, 75-73. Bradley's David Thirdkill and Mitchell Anderson led all scorers with 25 and 20 points, respectively.

CINCINNATI (75)	MIN.	FG-A	FT-A	REB.	PTS.
Gaffney	52	6-16	3-4	8	15
Jones	64	8-14	2-5	15	18
Williams	63	3-11	2-3	15	8
Johnson	63	1-4	0-1	1	2
Austin	73	8-19	2-3	7	18
Schloemer	18	3-3	0-0	3	6
McMillan	13	0-2	0-0	2	0
Robinson	24	2-4	2-3	4	6
Campbell	7	1-1	0-0	1	2
Kecman	1	0-1	0-0	0	0
Team				1	
TOTALS	375	32-75	11-19	57	75

FG%: .427. **FT%:** .579. **Assists:** 18 (Johnson 7). **Steals:** 7. **Blocked Shots:** 0. **Turnovers:** 19. **Fouled Out:** 2 (Gaffney/6th OT, Jones/6th OT).

BRADLEY (73)	MP	FG-A	FT-A	REB.	PTS.
Anderson	65	8-25	4-6	12	20
Thirdkill	68	10-17	5-8	9	25
Reese	73	4-9	6-8	6	14
Scott	68	0-7	2-3	4	2
Mines	6	0-3	0-0	0	0
Winters	69	6-15	0-2	15	12
Cook	10	0-2	0-0	1	0
Mathews	17	0-1	0-0	1	0
Team				2	
TOTALS	375	28-79	17-27	50	73

FG%: .354. **FT%:** .630. **Assists:** 20 (Scott 8). **Steals:** 12. **Blocked Shots:** 2. **Turnovers:** 15. **Fouled Out:** 2 (Anderson/5th OT, Winter/2nd half).

Halftime: Bradley 40-35. **Regulation:** Tied 61-61. **First Overtime:** Tied 63-63. **Second Overtime:** Tied 65-65. **Third Overtime:** Tied 65-65. **Fourth Overtime:** Tied 67-67. **Fifth Overtime:** Tied 71-71. **Sixth Overtime:** Tied 73-73.

1981–82 INDIVIDUAL LEADERS

SCORING

PLAYER	PTS.	AVG.
Kelly, Texas Southern	862	29.7
Pierce, Rice	805	26.8
Callandrillo, Seton Hall	698	25.9
Magee, UC Irvine	732	25.2
Dailey, San Francisco	755	25.2
Jackson, Centenary	693	23.9
Wiggins, Florida St.	523	23.8
Moss, Northeastern	710	23.7
McLaughlin, C. Michigan	581	23.2
Jakubick, Akron	594	22.8

REBOUNDING

PLAYER	REB.	AVG.
Thompson, Texas	365	13.5
Sappleton, Loyola (Ill.)	376	13.0

Tillis, Cleveland St.	346	12.8
McNamara, California	341	12.6
Clarida, Long Island	369	12.3
Norris, Jackson St.	341	12.2
Magee, UC Irvine	353	12.2
Cobb, Pan American	302	12.1
Cummings, DePaul	334	11.9

FIELD GOAL PERCENTAGE

PLAYER	FGM	FGA	PCT.
McNamara, California	231	329	.702
Ellis, Tennessee	257	393	.654
Phillips, Pepperdine	181	280	.646
Culton, Texas-Arl.	200	311	.643
Magee, UC Irvine	272	424	.642
Pinckney, Villanova	169	264	.640
Hopson, Idaho	158	250	.632
Clarida, Long I.	180	285	.632

Jones, Houston Bap.	178	282	.631
Clark, Miss.	251	403	.623

FREE THROW PERCENTAGE

PLAYER	FTA	FTM	PCT.
Foster, UCLA	95	100	.950
Moore, Nebraska	123	131	.939
Dykstra, W. Ill.	147	161	.913
Williams, Idaho St.	70	78	.897
Master, Kentucky	95	106	.896
McGraw, Siena	112	126	.889
Lee, Boise St.	71	80	.888
Carrabino, Harvard	85	97	.876
Gillam, W. Chester St.	85	97	.876
Engelland, Duke	77	88	.875

1981–82 TEAM LEADERS

SCORING OFFENSE

SCHOOL	PTS.	AVG.
Long Island	2605	86.8
Texas Southern	2429	83.8
North Texas St.	2258	83.6
San Francisco	2527	81.5
Houston	2685	81.4

SCORING DEFENSE

SCHOOL	PTS.	AVG.
Fresno St.	1412	47.1
N.C. St.	1570	49.1
Princeton	1277	49.1
Wyoming	1545	51.5
James Madison	1559	52.0

SCORING MARGIN

SCHOOL	OFF.	DEF.	MAR.
Oregon St.	69.6	55.0	14.6
Georgetown	67.6	53.5	14.2
Idaho	71.3	57.5	13.8
Virginia	70.7	57.2	13.5
Tenn.-Chattanooga	72.6	59.9	12.7

WON-LOST PERCENTAGE

SCHOOL	W-L	PCT.
North Carolina	32-2	.941
DePaul	26-2	.929
Fresno St.	27-3	.900
Idaho	27-3	.900
Virginia	30-4	.882

FIELD GOAL PERCENTAGE

SCHOOL	FGM	FGA	PCT.
UC Irvine	920	1639	.561
Mississippi	696	1281	.543
Pepperdine	929	1714	.542
Tennessee	792	1462	.542
Missouri	815	1511	.539

FIELD GOAL PERCENTAGE DEFENSE

SCHOOL	FGM	FGA	PCT.
Wyoming	584	1470	.397
Georgetown	757	1808	.419
Idaho	696	1662	.419
N.C. St.	621	1481	.419
Missouri	742	1766	.420

FREE THROW PERCENTAGE

SCHOOL	FTM	FTA	PCT.
Western Illinois	447	569	.786
Northwestern St. (La.)	489	624	.784
Western Carolina	481	623	.772
Idaho St.	393	522	.753
Ohio St.	415	552	.752

REBOUND MARGIN

SCHOOL	OWN	OPP.	MAR.
Northeastern	41.2	30.8	10.4
Wyoming	36.4	26.7	9.7
Brigham Young	37.3	29.3	8.0
Alabama	37.3	29.5	7.7
Pepperdine	37.7	30.0	7.6

last points in all five extra sessions to outlast Providence, 79-77.

Missouri, coached by Norm Stewart, won its first 19 games and was ranked No. 1 in the country before bowing to visiting Nebraska, 67-51. . . . Texas, coached by Abe Lemons, got off to a sizzling 14-0 start but finished with a modest 16-11 record after forward Mike Wacker sustained a season-ending knee injury. . . . TCU, coached by Jim Killingsworth, compiled a 16-13 mark to end a streak of nine consecutive losing seasons. . . . Texas-El Paso, after losing its previous 10 outings

with Utah, began a stretch where the Miners won 14 of the next 17 meetings in their series.

Oregon State's 14.6-point margin of victory was the lowest ever for a school that led the nation in scoring differential. . . . California compiled a 14-13 record for its only winning season in a 10-year span from 1975-76 through 1984-85. . . . Former NCAA champion San Francisco dropped its program after a 25-6 season because of improprieties frowned upon by the university administration and the NCAA. All-American guard Quintin Dailey, in the course of trying to convince a pro-

The Louisiana Superdome hosts the 1982 NCAA Final Four.

bation officer that he shouldn't go to jail after pleading guilty to one count of assault, revealed he had a $1,000-a-month summer job for which he didn't have to show up. The Dons averaged 22.5 victories annually in their last 11 years. . . . Rice's Ricky Pierce (26.8 ppg) and USF's Dailey (25.2) set school records for highest scoring average in a single season.

Cal State Fullerton, which compiled a 4-23 record the previous season, improved by 11 1/2 games to 18-14 under coach George McQuarn. . . . Montana State's Doug Hashley grabbed a school-record 24 rebounds in a game against Nevada-Reno. . . . West Virginia, coached by Gale Catlett, finished in the Top 20 of a final wire-service poll

for the first time since 1963. The Mountaineers' school-record 23-game winning streak, the longest in the country, was ended at Rutgers, 74-64, in their regular-season finale.

Virginia (30-4/coached by Terry Holland), Fresno State (27-3/Boyd Grant), Idaho (27-3/Don Monson), Tennessee-Chattanooga (27-4/Murray Arnold), James Madison (24-6/Lou Campanelli), UC Irvine (23-7/Bill Mulligan), Western Carolina (19-8/Steve Cottrell) and Northwestern State (19-9/Wayne Yates) had their winningest seasons in school Division I history. . . . Fresno State posted the best scoring defense of any team since 1952 (47.1 points per game). FSU and Alabama-Birmingham, coached by Gene

Bartow, finished in the Top 20 of a final wire-service poll for the only time in school history. . . . Mississippi managed its lone victory over Kentucky in a 28-game stretch of their series from 1975 through 1986.

Western Kentucky competed as a member of the Ohio Valley Conference for the final season. . . . West Chester State (Pa.) competed in its final campaign at the major-college level. . . . Notre Dame, incurring its only losing record (10-17) in an 18-year stretch from 1972-73 through 1989-90, finished out of the top 10 of the final AP poll for the first time in seven seasons. . . . The national scoring average decreased for the seventh consecutive season, reaching the lowest point since 1952 with 135.1 points per game (both teams combined). Texas Southern's Harry Kelly led the country in scoring with a 29.7-point average, including a national-high 51 points against Texas College. . . . North Carolina A&T's Joe Binion set a school Division I record by scoring 41 points against Livingstone (N.C.). . . . Bob Weinhauer won his fifth Ivy League title in as many years as Penn's coach. . . . Temple became the third East Coast Conference member in five years to go undefeated in league competition but fail to receive an at-large bid to the NCAA Tournament after losing in the ECC playoffs.

1981-82 FINAL NATIONAL POLLS

AP	UPI	SCHOOL (RECORD)	HEAD COACH
1	1	North Carolina (32-2)	Dean Smith
2	2	DePaul (26-2)	Ray Meyer
3	3	Virginia (30-4)	Terry Holland
4	4	Oregon State (25-5)	Ralph Miller
5	5	Missouri (27-4)	Norm Stewart
6	7	Georgetown (30-7)	John Thompson
7	6	Minnesota (23-6)	Jim Dutcher
8	8	Idaho (27-3)	Don Monson
9	9	Memphis State (24-5)	Dana Kirk
10	11	Tulsa (24-6)	Nolan Richardson
11	10	Fresno State (27-3)	Boyd Grant
12	13	Arkansas (23-6)	Eddie Sutton
13	12	Alabama (24-7)	Wimp Sanderson
14	17	West Virginia (27-4)	Gale Catlett
15	14	Kentucky (22-8)	Joe B. Hall
16	16	Iowa (21-8)	Lute Olson
17	–	UAB (25-6)	Gene Bartow
18	19	Wake Forest (21-9)	Carl Tacy
19	–	UCLA (21-6)	Larry Farmer
20	20	Louisville (23-10)	Denny Crum
–	15	Wyoming (23-7)	Jim Brandenburg
–	18	Kansas State (23-8)	Jack Hartman

1982 NCAA Tournament

Summary: Georgetown's early 12-6 lead was the biggest of the game. Freshman guard Michael Jordan swished a 16-foot jumper from the left side with 16 seconds remaining to provide the title game's final points as North Carolina edged Georgetown, 63-62. Georgetown guard Fred Brown's errant pass directly to Tar Heels forward James Worthy prevented the Hoyas from attempting a potential game-winning shot in the closing seconds. Georgetown's Patrick Ewing was called for goaltending five times in the opening minutes of the final. Jordan's heroics came after an inauspicious playoff debut when he collected six points, one rebound, no assists and no steals in 37 minutes of a 52-50 opening-round victory against James Madison in the East Regional.

Outcome for Defending Champion: Indiana (19-10), after losing guard Isiah Thomas early to the NBA, was eliminated in the second round of the Mideast Regional by Alabama-Birmingham, 80-70. The Hoosiers had a four-game losing streak after dropping their first two Big Ten assignments but they rebounded to finish in a tie for second place in the league standings.

Star Gazing: Worthy, the Final Four Most Outstanding Player, hit 20 of 27 field-goal attempts in two Final Four games. He scored a career-high 28 points in the championship game. . . . Jordan, the pre-endorsement Airness, donned Converse All-Star sneakers while Georgetown wore Nikes.

Biggest Upsets: DePaul lost its third opener in as many years as a No. 1 seed when the Blue Demons, ranked second nationally, bowed to Boston College, 82-75, in the Midwest Regional. . . . Middle Tennessee State (seeded No. 11) overcame an early 8-0 deficit to defeat Kentucky (No. 6), 50-44, in the first round of the Mideast Regional. No Kentucky player scored more than eight points.

One and Only: Northeastern's Perry Moss was the only player to crack the 30-point plateau in the tourney. He tallied 31 against Villanova.

1981–82 NCAA CHAMPION: N. CAROLINA

SEASON STATISTICS OF NORTH CAROLINA REGULARS

PLAYER	POS.	CL.	G.	FG%	FT%	PPG	RPG
James Worthy	F	Jr.	34	.573	.674	15.6	6.3
Sam Perkins	C	So.	32	.578	.768	14.3	7.8
Michael Jordan	G	Fr.	34	.534	.722	13.5	4.4
Matt Doherty	F	So.	34	.519	.772	9.3	3.0
Jimmy Black	G	Sr.	34	.513	.738	7.6	1.7
Jim Braddock	G	Jr.	34	.452	.833	1.9	0.5
Chris Brust	F	Sr.	33	.622	.455	1.7	1.7
Buzz Peterson	G	Fr.	30	.390	.429	1.2	0.5
Jeb Barlow	F	Sr.	28	.387	.444	1.0	0.8
TEAM TOTALS			34	.537	.692	66.7	29.4

Assists leader: Black 213. **Blocked shots leader:** Perkins 53. **Steals leader:** Black 58.

1982 FINAL FOUR CHAMPIONSHIP GAME

NEW ORLEANS, LA

GEORGETOWN (62)	MIN.	FG-A	FT-A	REB.	A	PF	PTS.
E. Smith	35	6-8	2-2	3	5	5	14
Hancock	8	0-2	0-0	0	0	1	0
Ewing	37	10-15	3-3	11	1	4	23
F. Brown	29	1-2	2-2	2	5	4	4
Floyd	39	9-17	0-0	3	5	2	18
Spriggs	30	0-2	1-2	1	0	2	1
Jones	10	1-3	0-0	0	0	0	2
B. Martin	5	0-2	0-0	0	0	1	0
G. Smith	7	0-0	0-0	0	0	1	0
Team				2			
TOTALS	200	27-51	8-9	22	16	20	62

FG%: .529. **FT%:** .889. **Blocks:** 2. **Turnovers:** 12. **Steals:** 11.

N. CAROLINA (63)	MIN.	FG-A	FT-A	REB.	A	PF	PTS.
Doherty	39	1-3	2-3	3	1	0	4
Worthy	38	13-17	2-7	4	0	3	28
Perkins	38	3-7	4-6	7	1	2	10
Black	38	1-4	2-2	3	7	2	4
Jordan	34	7-13	2-2	9	2	2	16
Peterson	7	0-3	0-0	1	1	0	0
Braddock	2	0-0	0-0	0	1	1	0
Brust	4	0-0	1-2	1	1	1	1
Team				2			
TOTALS	200	25-47	13-22	30	14	11	63

FG%: .532. **FT%:** .591. **Blocks:** 1. **Turnovers:** 13. **Steals:** 7. **Halftime:** Georgetown 32-31.

NATIONAL SEMIFINALS

HOUSTON (63): Drexler 6-12 5-6 17, Young 1-7 0-1 2, Micheaux 8-14 2-3 18, Rose 10-15 0-2 20, R. Williams 0-8 2-2 2, B. Williams 0-1 0-0 0, Olajuwon 1-3 0-0 2, Davis 1-2 0-0 2, Anders 0-2 0-0 0. Team 27-64 (.422) 9-14 (.643) 63.

NORTH CAROLINA (68): Doherty 2-7 1-2 5, Worthy 7-10 0-0 14, Perkins 9-11 7-7 25, Black 1-2 4-6 6, Jordan 7-14 4-4 18, Peterson 0-0 0-0 0, Brust 0-0 0-0 0, W. Martin 0-0 0-0 0, Braddock 0-0 0-0 0. Team 26-44 (.591) 16-19 (.842) 68.

Halftime: North Carolina 31-29.

LOUISVILLE (46): W. Brown 2-5 0-0 4, D. Smith 4-8 2-4 10, R. McCray 2-5 4-4 8, Gordon 1-6 0-0 2, Eaves 4-9, 0-0 8, Wagner 1-4 0-0 2, Jones 4-7 0-2 8, S. McCray 0-1 0-0 0, Wright 1-3 2-2 4. Team 19-48 (.396) 8-12 (.667) 46.

GEORGETOWN (50): E. Smith 6-10 2-4 14, Hancock 1-3 0-0 2, Ewing 3-8 2-2 8, F. Brown 1-3 2-3 4, Floyd 3-11 7-8 13, Spriggs 2-2 1-3 5, G. Smith 0-0 0-0 0, Jones 2-4 0-0 4, B. Martin 0-0 0-0 0. Team 18-41 (.439) 14-20 (.700) 50.

Halftime: Georgetown 24-22.

ALL-TOURNAMENT TEAM

Patrick Ewing, C, Fr., Georgetown (31 points, 21 rebounds in final two games)
Sleepy Floyd, G, Sr., Georgetown (31 points, eight rebounds, eight assists)
Michael Jordan, G, Fr., North Carolina (34 points, 14 rebounds)
Sam Perkins, C, Soph., North Carolina (35 points, 17 rebounds)
*James Worthy, F, Jr., North Carolina (42 points, eight rebounds, five steals)

*Named Most Outstanding Player.

Numbers Game: Junior guard Rob Williams, Houston's leader in scoring with a 21.1-point average, missed all eight of his field-goal attempts against the Tar Heels in the national semifinals. Nonetheless, he still finished as the tourney's leading scorer because he scored at least 25 points in three previous outings. Williams left early for the NBA after the season and was joined in the same category by teammates Clyde Drexler in 1983 and Hakeem Olajuwon in 1984 as the Cougars became the only school to have an undergrad selected in the first round of the NBA draft three consecutive years. . . . Virginia's Ralph Sampson grabbed a tourney-high 21 rebounds, but it was in vain when the Cavaliers bowed to Alabama-Birmingham, 68-66, in the Mideast Regional semifinals. . . . Tulsa, coached by Nolan Richardson, appeared in the playoffs for the first time since 1955.

What Might Have Been: Williams, swingman Michael Young and center Hakeem Olajuwon combined to average 40.3 points per game for Houston. If only they collaborated for 12 points instead of two apiece in the national semifinals, the Cougars could have defeated Carolina rather than losing 68-63. . . . It is unlikely that DePaul (26-2) would have been eliminated right away in the tourney if Mark Aguirre didn't forgo his final season of eligibility. . . . Maryland (16-13) might have wound up in the NCAA playoffs instead of the NIT if rebounder deluxe Buck Williams had remained in school instead of turning pro early. . . . Kentucky (22-8) might have avoided its opening-

1982 CHAMPIONSHIP BRACKET

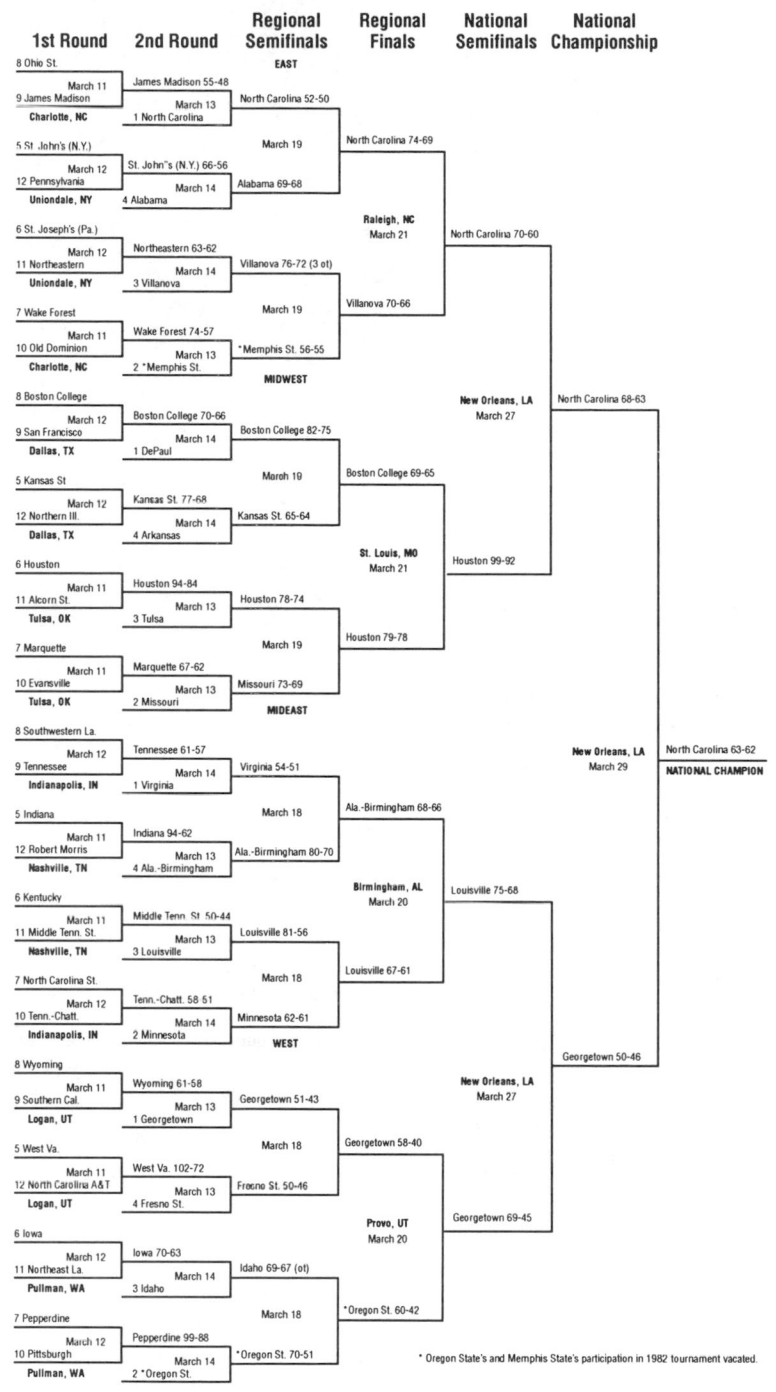

1st Round	2nd Round	Regional Semifinals	Regional Finals	National Semifinals	National Championship

EAST

8 Ohio St.
March 11 — James Madison 55-48
9 James Madison
March 13 — North Carolina 52-50
Charlotte, NC
1 North Carolina

March 19 — North Carolina 74-69

5 St. John's (N.Y.)
March 12 — St. John's (N.Y.) 66-56
12 Pennsylvania
March 14 — Alabama 69-68
Uniondale, NY
4 Alabama

Raleigh, NC
March 21 — North Carolina 70-60

6 St. Joseph's (Pa.)
March 12 — Northeastern 63-62
11 Northeastern
March 14 — Villanova 76-72 (3 ot)
Uniondale, NY
3 Villanova

March 19 — Villanova 70-66

7 Wake Forest
March 11 — Wake Forest 74-57
10 Old Dominion
March 13 — *Memphis St. 56-55
Charlotte, NC
2 *Memphis St.

New Orleans, LA
March 27 — North Carolina 68-63

MIDWEST

8 Boston College
March 12 — Boston College 70-66
9 San Francisco
March 14 — Boston College 82-75
Dallas, TX
1 DePaul

March 19 — Boston College 69-65

5 Kansas St
March 12 — Kansas St. 77-68
12 Northern Ill.
March 14 — Kansas St. 65-64
Dallas, TX
4 Arkansas

St. Louis, MO
March 21 — Houston 99-92

6 Houston
March 11 — Houston 94-84
11 Alcorn St.
March 13 — Houston 78-74
Tulsa, OK
3 Tulsa

March 19 — Houston 79-78

7 Marquette
March 11 — Marquette 67-62
10 Evansville
March 13 — Missouri 73-69
Tulsa, OK
2 Missouri

MIDEAST

8 Southwestern La.
March 12 — Tennessee 61-57
9 Tennessee
March 14 — Virginia 54-51
Indianapolis, IN
1 Virginia

March 18 — Ala.-Birmingham 68-66

5 Indiana
March 11 — Indiana 94-62
12 Robert Morris
March 13 — Ala.-Birmingham 80-70
Nashville, TN
4 Ala.-Birmingham

Birmingham, AL
March 20 — Louisville 75-68

6 Kentucky
March 11 — Middle Tenn. St. 50-44
11 Middle Tenn. St.
March 13 — Louisville 81-56
Nashville, TN
3 Louisville

March 18 — Louisville 67-61

7 North Carolina St.
March 12 — Tenn.-Chatt. 58-51
10 Tenn.-Chatt.
March 14 — Minnesota 62-61
Indianapolis, IN
2 Minnesota

New Orleans, LA
March 29 — North Carolina 63-62
NATIONAL CHAMPION

New Orleans, LA
March 27 — Georgetown 50-46

WEST

8 Wyoming
March 11 — Wyoming 61-58
9 Southern Cal.
March 13 — Georgetown 51-43
Logan, UT
1 Georgetown

March 18 — Georgetown 58-40

5 West Va.
March 11 — West Va. 102-72
12 North Carolina A&T
March 13 — Fresno St. 50-46
Logan, UT
4 Fresno St.

Provo, UT
March 20 — Georgetown 69-45

6 Iowa
March 12 — Iowa 70-63
11 Northeast La.
March 14 — Idaho 69-67 (ot)
Pullman, WA
3 Idaho

March 18 — *Oregon St. 60-42

7 Pepperdine
March 12 — Pepperdine 99-88
10 Pittsburgh
March 14 — *Oregon St. 70-51
Pullman, WA
2 *Oregon St.

Georgetown 50-46

* Oregon State's and Memphis State's participation in 1982 tournament vacated.

THE EMERGENCE OF PARITY: THE 1980s 🏀 **293**

round upset to Middle Tennessee State if center Sam Bowie didn't miss the season because of a leg injury.

Putting Things in Perspective: Would North Carolina have captured the crown if the Tar Heels didn't win three games, two of them by a total of just seven points, in familiar surroundings (second round at Charlotte and East Regional at Raleigh)?

Scoring Leader: Rob Williams, Houston (88 points, 17.6 ppg).

Highest Scoring Average: Perry Moss, Northeastern (55 points, 27.5 ppg).

Rebounding Leader: Clyde Drexler, Houston (41 rebounds, 8.2 rpg).

Highest Rebounding Average: Ralph Sampson, Virginia (30 rebounds, 15 rpg).

1982-83

AT A GLANCE

NCAA Champion: North Carolina State (26-10; coached by Jim Valvano; finished in a tie for third place in ACC with an 8-6 record).

NIT Champion: Fresno State (25-10; coached by Boyd Grant; finished in fourth place in PCAA with a 9-7 record).

New Conferences: Association of Mid-Continent Universities (forerunner of Mid-Continent), ECAC South (forerunner of Colonial Athletic).

New Rules: It is no longer a jump-ball situation when the closely guarded five-second count is reached. It is a violation, and the ball is awarded to the defensive team out of bounds. . . . An opening round was added to the NCAA Tournament, requiring the representatives of eight automatic-qualifying conferences to compete for four positions in the 52-team bracket. . . . The current tourney format was established that begins the event the third weekend in March, regional championships on the fourth Saturday and Sunday, and the national semifinals and final the following Saturday and Monday.

NCAA Probation: Oklahoma City, St. Louis, Wichita State

NCAA Consensus First-Team All-Americans: Dale Ellis, F, Sr., Tennessee; Patrick Ewing, C, Soph., Georgetown; Michael Jordan, G, Soph., North Carolina; Keith

Houston's Clyde Drexler flies past an opponent.

Lee, C, Soph., Memphis State; Sam Perkins, C, Jr., North Carolina; Ralph Sampson, C, Sr., Virginia; Wayman Tisdale, C-F, Fr., Oklahoma.

National Player of the Year: Sampson (19 ppg, 11.7 rpg, 3.1 bpg, 60.4 FG%).

National Coaches of the Year: St. John's Lou Carnesecca (28-5/NABC, USBWA); Houston's Guy Lewis (31-3/AP), and UNLV's Jerry Tarkanian (28-3/UPI).

Parity was more than a rhetorical concept this season. In a game hailed as one of the biggest upsets in college basketball history, Ralph Sampson-led Virginia lost at Chaminade, 77-72, in Hawaii.

Virginia also squandered a 10-point lead in the last 4:12 against North Carolina and bowed to the Tar Heels, 64-63, when they scored the game's last 11 points. A tip-in by Michael Jordan cut their

All-American forward Dale Ellis dunks one for the Tennessee Volunteers.

1982–83 INDIVIDUAL LEADERS

SCORING

PLAYER	PTS.	AVG.
Kelly, Texas Southern	835	28.8
Malone, Miss. St.	777	26.8
Yates, George Mason	723	26.8
Bradley, S. Florida	855	26.7
Jakubick, Akron	774	26.7
Goorjian, Loyola (Cal.)	601	26.1
Hughes, Loyola (Ill.)	744	25.7
Tisdale, Oklahoma	810	24.5
Lyons, N. Texas St.	728	24.3
Jackson, Centenary	697	24.0

REBOUNDING

PLAYER	REB.	AVG.
McDaniel, Wichita St.	403	14.4
Giles, S. Caro. St.	360	12.9
Cage, San Diego St.	354	12.6
Halsel, Northeastern	350	12.5
Cross, Maine	310	11.9
Green, UNLV	368	11.9
Kelly, Texas Southern	340	11.7
Sampson, Virginia	386	11.7
Olajuwon, Houston	388	11.4
Mosley, Nevada-Reno	325	11.2

FIELD GOAL PERCENTAGE

PLAYER	FGM	FGA	PCT.
Mikell, East Tenn. St.	197	292	.675
Phillips, Pepperdine	223	338	.660
McDowell, Florida	203	314	.646
Barkley, Auburn	161	250	.644
Best, St. Peter's	138	215	.642
Thorpe, Providence	204	321	.636
Robinson, Nicholls St.	146	231	.632
Johnson, Grambling	205	325	.631
DeBisschop, Fairfield	203	324	.627
Mosley, Nevada-Reno	184	297	.620

FREE THROW PERCENTAGE

PLAYER	FGM	FGA	PCT.
Gonzalez, Colorado	75	82	.915
Fisher, J. Madison	95	104	.913
Waitkus, Brown	97	108	.898
Cox, Vanderbilt	113	126	.897
Hobdy, Grambling	78	87	.897
Dykstra, W. Ill.	156	176	.886
Allen, Nevada-Reno	117	132	.886
Mullin, St. John's	173	197	.878
Price, Ga. Tech	93	106	.877
Gross, UC S. Barbara	140	160	.875

1982–83 TEAM LEADERS

SCORING OFFENSE

SCHOOL	PTS.	AVG.
Boston College	2697	84.3
Syracuse	2612	84.3
South Carolina St.	2353	84.0
Alabama St.	2352	84.0
Houston	2800	82.4

SCORING DEFENSE

SCHOOL	PTS.	AVG.
Princeton	1507	52.0
Fresno St.	1880	53.7
James Madison	1670	53.9
Notre Dame	1619	55.8
Arkansas St.	1651	56.9

SCORING MARGIN

SCHOOL	OFF.	DEF.	MAR.
Houston	82.4	64.9	17.4
Virginia	81.9	65.0	16.9
Oklahoma	82.3	70.7	11.6
North Carolina	77.0	65.7	11.3
St. John's	75.2	63.9	11.3
Wichita St.	82.3	71.0	11.3

WON-LOST PERCENTAGE

SCHOOL	W-L	PCT.
Houston	31-3	.912
UNLV	28-3	.903
Wichita St.	25-3	.893
Louisville	32-4	.889
Arkansas	26-4	.867

FIELD GOAL PERCENTAGE

SCHOOL	FGM	FGA	PCT.
Kentucky	869	1564	.556
Stanford	752	1373	.548
New Orleans	937	1714	.547
Pepperdine	900	1653	.544
Houston Baptist	712	1319	.540

FIELD GOAL PERCENTAGE DEFENSE

SCHOOL	FGM	FGA	PCT.
Wyoming	599	1441	.416
Virginia	863	2071	.417
Idaho	661	1582	.418
Montana	663	1574	.421
Memphis St.	831	1965	.423

FREE THROW PERCENTAGE

SCHOOL	FTM	FGA	PCT.
Western Illinois	526	679	.775
Dayton	453	586	.773
UC Santa Barbara	413	535	.772
William & Mary	470	609	.772
St. John's	649	843	.770

REBOUND MARGIN

SCHOOL	OWN	OPP.	MAR.
Wichita St.	42.4	33.6	8.8
Virginia	40.6	32.3	8.4
Houston	41.6	33.4	8.1
Wyoming	34.7	27.1	7.6
Alcorn St.	39.8	32.9	6.9

deficit to one before his steal and dunk gave Carolina the triumph.

Wayman Tisdale, the first Oklahoma player since 1947 to become an NCAA consensus first- or second-team All-American, was the first freshman to be named an NCAA consensus first-team All-American. None of the NCAA's seven consensus first-team All-Americans reached the national semifinals. . . . Tisdale (24.5 ppg and 10.3 rpg in Big Eight) and Louisiana Tech's Karl Malone (20.9 ppg and 10.3 rpg in Southland) earned league player of the year honors as freshmen. It was the only season in history that two major conferences had a freshman become player of the year.

Houston's Clyde Drexler set a SWC record with 11 steals against Syracuse. . . . Texas Southern's Harry Kelly led the nation in scoring with a 28.8-point average, including a national-high 60 points against Jarvis Christian. . . . Wichita State's Antoine Carr (47 points vs. Southern Illinois), Akron's Joe Jakubick (47 vs. Murray State), North Texas State's Kenneth Lyons (47 vs. Louisiana Tech in Southland Conference Tournament), Arizona State's Paul Williams (45 at Southern Cal)

1982–83 NCAA CHAMPION: N.C. STATE

SEASON STATISTICS OF N.C. STATE REGULARS

PLAYER	POS.	CL.	G.	FG%	FT%	PPG	RPG
Dereck Whittenburg	G	Sr.	22	.467	.800	17.5	2.7
Thurl Bailey	F-C	Sr.	36	.501	.717	16.7	7.7
Sidney Lowe	G	Sr.	36	.461	.776	11.3	3.7
Ernie Myers	G	Fr.	35	.446	.607	11.2	2.5
Lorenzo Charles	F	So.	36	.542	.670	8.1	6.0
Terry Gannon	G	So.	36	.621	.903	7.3	0.8
Cozell McQueen	C	So.	36	.431	.576	3.5	5.6
Alvin Battle	F	Jr.	33	.419	.520	2.7	2.0
George McClain	G	Fr.	25	.375	.500	2.7	0.5
Harold Thompson	F	Jr.	26	.353	.500	0.5	0.5
TEAM TOTALS			36	.472	.689	74.2	34.4

Assists leader: Lowe 271. **Blocked shots leader:** Bailey 95. **Steals leader:** Lowe 87.

1983 FINAL FOUR CHAMPIONSHIP GAME

ALBUQUERQUE, NM

N.C. STATE (54)	MIN.	FG-A	FT-A	REB.	A	PF	PTS.
Bailey	39	7-16	1-2	5	0	1	15
Charles	25	2-7	0-0	7	0	2	4
McQueen	34	1-5	2-2	12	1	4	4
Whittenburg	39	6-17	2-2	5	1	3	14
Lowe	40	4-9	0-1	0	8	2	8
Battle	4	0-1	2-2	1	1	1	2
Gannon	18	3-4	1-2	1	2	3	7
Myers	1	0-0	0-0	1	0	0	0
Team				2			
TOTALS	200	23-59	8-11	34	13	16	54

FG%: .390. **FT%:** .727. **Blocks:** 2. **Turnovers:** 6. **Steals:** 7 (Lowe 5).

HOUSTON (52)	MIN.	FG-A	FT-A	REB.	A	PF	PTS.
Drexler	25	1-5	2-2	2	0	4	4
Micheaux	18	2-6	0-0	6	0	1	4
Olajuwon	38	7-15	6-7	18	1	1	20
Franklin	35	2-6	0-1	0	3	0	4
Young	30	3-10	0-4	8	1	0	6
Anders	17	4-9	2-5	2	1	2	10
Gettys	20	2-2	0-0	2	2	3	4
Rose	7	0-1	0-0	1	0	2	0
Williams	10	0-1	0-0	4	1	3	0
Team				1			
TOTALS	200	21-55	10-19	44	9	16	52

FG%: .382. **FT%:** .526. **Blocks:** 8 (Olajuwon 7). **Turnovers:** 13. **Steals:** 0. **Halftime:** North Carolina State 33-25.

NATIONAL SEMIFINALS

N.C. STATE (67): Bailey 9-17 2-5 20, Charles 2-2 1-2 5, McQueen 4-5 0-0 8, Whittenburg 8-18, 4-4 20, Lowe 4-6 2-2 10, Battle 0-0 0-0 0, Gannon 1-4 2-2 4. Team 28-52 (.538) 11-15 (.733) 67.

GEORGIA (60): Banks 5-19 3-5 13, Heard 3-5 2-3 8, Fair 2-9 1-2 5, Crosby 5-15 2-2 12, Fleming 7-17 0-0 14, Corhen 3-6 0-1 6, Hartry 1-3 0-0 2, Floyd 0-0 0-0 0. Team 26-74 (.351) 8-13 (.615) 60.

Halftime: North Carolina State 33-32.

LOUISVILLE (81): S. McCray 5-8 0-0 10, R. McCray 3-6 2-8 8, Jones 3-10 6-8 12, Gordon 6-15 5-6 17, Wagner 12-23 0-0 24, Thompson 1-4 4-5 4, Hall 2-4 0-0 4, West 0-0 0-0 0, Valentine 0-0 0-0 0. Team 32-70 (.457) 17-27 (.630) 81.

HOUSTON (94): Drexler 10-15 1-2 21, Micheaux 4-7 0-1 8, Olajuwon 9-14 3-7 21, Franklin 5-8 3-4 13, Young 7-18 2-3 16, Gettys 0-0 0-0 0, Anders 5-9 3-5 13, Rose 0-2 0-0 0, Williams 1-1 0-0 2, Giles 0-0 0-1 0. Team 41-74 (.554) 12-23 (.522) 94.

Halftime: Louisville 41-36.

ALL-TOURNAMENT TEAM

Thurl Bailey, F, Sr., North Carolina State
Sidney Lowe, G, Sr., North Carolina State
Hakeem Olajuwon, C, Soph., Houston*
Milt Wagner, G, Soph., Louisville
Dereck Whittenburg, G, Sr., North Carolina State

*Named Most Outstanding Player.

and South Florida's Charlie Bradley (42 vs. Florida State in semifinals of Florida Four Tournament) established single-game scoring records for their schools. . . . South Florida's Bradley (28.2 ppg) and George Mason's Carlos Yates (26.8) set school records for highest scoring average in a single season.

Washington State (since 1950), Wichita State (1965), Oklahoma State (1965) and Boston College (1969) finished in the Top 20 of a final wire-service poll for the first time in a long time. Georgia finished in the Top 20 for the first of just two times in school history. . . . Boston College (25-7/coached by Gary Williams), Georgia (24-10/Hugh Durham), Robert Morris (23-8/Matt Furjanic), Alabama State (22-6/James Oliver), South Florida (22-10/Lee Rose), Western Illinois (20-11/Jack Margenthaler), Southeastern Louisiana (18-9/Ken Fortenberry) and Northwestern (18-12/Rich Falk) had their winningest seasons in school Division I history. Illinois State (24-7/Bob Donewald) tied its school Division I record for most victories in a single season. Alabama State was in its first year at the Division I level. . . . Northwestern compiled its only winning record in a 24-year span from 1969-70 through 1992-93.

Boston College became the only school since 1952 to lead the nation in scoring with an average under 85 points per game (84.3 ppg). Falk is the only individual to direct a major college to an existing single-season record for most victories after setting the same school's single-game scoring standard as a player. . . . Illinois State and Tennessee-Chattanooga, coached by Murray Arnold,

An explosive Hakeem Olajuwon steals a Louisville pass in the 1983 NCAA Semifinals.

one second remaining in double overtime and drilled an off-balance 25-footer to give the Green Wave an 80-79 victory at Florida State. Two nights earlier, a 30-foot buzzer-beater by Tulane's Daryl Moreau was the difference in a 49-47 victory over nationally ranked Memphis State at Tulane Gym (now Fogelman Arena), a snakepit with one of the smallest seating capacities (3,600) among members of elite leagues.

New Orleans lost three consecutive games to LSU the previous four seasons by an average of 26 points before overcoming a school-record 38 turnovers to prevail at LSU, 99-94, in overtime in the first round of the NIT. LSU, which lost to Tulane, 83-72, in the NIT the previous year, is the only school to be eliminated by visiting intrastate rivals in the opening round of back-to-back NITs.

The nation's top shot blocker before the NCAA began charting the statistic nationally was Old Dominion's Mark West, who finished his career with an average of 3.8 rejections per game. . . . Backup guard Marc Campbell of Clemson connected on seven of seven three-point field goals in back-to-back ACC games. . . . Georgia Tech lost 14 consecutive games in its series with Clemson until topping the Tigers, 71-66. . . . Western Carolina guard Ronnie Carr, the Southern Conference's leading scorer the previous season, suffered career-ending injuries in an auto accident over the summer. . . . Villanova finished in the Top 20 of a final wire-service poll for the only time in a 22-year span from 1972-73 through 1993-94. . . . Defending NCAA champion North Carolina had an 18-game winning streak

made their lone appearances in the Top 20 of a final wire-service poll. . . . Missouri, coached by Norm Stewart, became the only Big Eight school to win four consecutive regular-season championships since the league expanded to eight members in 1959. Center Steve Stipanovich and guard Jon Sundvold became the first Mizzou players to earn spots on an NCAA consensus first- or second-team All-American squad.

Tulane's Paul Thompson took a 90-foot inbounds pass from teammate Lamar Baker with snapped by visiting Villanova, 56-53. The Tar Heels then lost back-to-back ACC road games at Maryland and North Carolina State to post their longest losing streak during All-American Michael Jordan's three-year career.

Manhattan, coached by Gordon Chiesa, posted its only winning mark (15-13) in a 16-year stretch from 1975-76 through 1990-91. The Jaspers won fewer than 10 games in nine of those seasons. . . . St. Bonaventure broke West Virginia's 39-game homecourt winning streak, 64-63. . . . LIU's Carey Scurry grabbed a school-record 26 rebounds in a game against Marist.

Texas Tech's streak of consecutive winning records ended at 13 when the Red Raiders registered an 11-20 mark. . . . Colorado forward Rob Gonzalez paced the nation in free-throw shooting (91.5 percent) to become the only individual ever to lead the country in a major statistical category after previously playing in both games at the Final Four for another four-year school when it captured an NCAA Tournament championship. Gonzalez was a freshman with Michigan State's 1979 titlist.

Wyoming led the nation in field-goal percentage defense for the third consecutive season under coach Jim Brandenburg. . . . Utah State, which compiled a 4-23 record the previous season, improved by 15 games to 20-9 under coach Rod Tueller. . . . Oral Roberts' team voted to boycott when Ken Hayes was fired in mid-season. That put ORU star Mark Acres in the unusual position of having to strike against his father, Dick Acres, who was promoted from assistant to head coach. . . . New Mexico State finished in a tie for third place in the Missouri Valley Conference in the Aggies' final season as a member of the league.

Cal State Fullerton's Leon Wood set a Big West Conference single-season mark by averaging 11 assists per game. UNLV won its first 24 games until bowing at Cal State Fullerton, 86-78. . . . The number of independent schools in Division I decreased from 52 to 19. There had been as many as 79 independents in the mid-1970s. . . . Baltimore competed in its final season at the major-college level.

1982-83 FINAL NATIONAL POLLS

AP	UPI	USA/CNN	SCHOOL (RECORD)	HEAD COACH
1	1	2	Houston (31-3)	Guy Lewis
2	2	3	Louisville (32-4)	Denny Crum
3	3	8	St. John's (28-5)	Lou Carnesecca
4	4	5	Virginia (29-5)	Terry Holland
5	5	9	Indiana (24-6)	Bob Knight
6	6	18	UNLV (28-3)	Jerry Tarkanian
7	7	16	UCLA (23-6)	Larry Farmer
8	8	7	North Carolina (28-8)	Dean Smith
9	9	10	Arkansas (26-4)	Eddie Sutton
10	12	19	Missouri (26-8)	Norm Stewart
11	13	13	Boston College (25-7)	Gary Williams
12	10	6	Kentucky (23-8)	Joe B. Hall
13	11	11	Villanova (24-8)	Rollie Massimino
14	–	15	Wichita State (25-3)	Gene Smithson
15	16	–	UT-Chattanooga (26-4)	Murray Arnold
16	14	1	N.C. State (26-10)	Jim Valvano
17	17	12	Memphis State (23-8)	Dana Kirk
18	15	4	Georgia (24-10)	Hugh Durham
19	19	–	Oklahoma State (24-7)	Paul Hansen
20	20	20	Georgetown (22-10)	John Thompson
–	–	14	Iowa (21-10)	Lute Olson
–	–	17	Ohio State (20-10)	Eldon Miller
–	18	–	Illinois State (24-7)	Bob Donewald
–	–	21	Fresno State (25-10)	Boyd Grant
–	–	22	Utah (18-14)	Jerry Pimm
–	–	23	Syracuse (21-10)	Jim Boeheim
–	–	24	Washington State (23-7)	George Raveling
–	–	25	Tennessee (20-12)	Don DeVoe

1983 NCAA Tournament

Summary: Sophomore forward Lorenzo Charles scored only four points in the title game, but two of them came when he converted guard Dereck Whittenburg's off-line desperation shot from well beyond the top of the free-throw circle into a decisive dunk as North Carolina State upset heavily-favored Houston, 54-52. Houston's 17-2 spurt at the start of the second half was in vain. The Cougars, entering the final with a 26-game winning streak, had a seven-point lead midway through the second half before Houston coach Guy Lewis inexplicably went into a spread offense, a ploy for which he was widely criticized. N.C. State, the first titlist with a double-digit loss total, became the only school to have as many as four playoff games decided by one or two points en route to a championship. The Wolfpack defeated Pepperdine in double overtime after trailing by six points with 24 seconds remaining in regulation, erased a 12-point deficit midway through the second half against UNLV and overcame a 10-point deficit against Virginia in the West Regional final. N.C. State capitalized on its six victims combining to shoot an anemic 56.8 percent from the free-throw line.

Outcome for Defending Champion: North Carolina (28-8) was eliminated in the East Regional final by Georgia, 82-77. The Tar Heels won the ACC regular-season title after recovering from a shaky start when they could have lost four of their first six non-league contests if not for a miraculous 70-68 triple-overtime victory against Tulane.

Star Gazing: Hakeem Olajuwon, who collected 41 points and 40 rebounds (tourney-high 22 vs. Louisville and 18 vs. N.C. State) for national runner-up Houston in two Final Four games, is the only Final Four Most Outstanding Player since 1972 not to play for the championship team.

Biggest Upset: The first meeting between in-state rivals Kentucky and Louisville in more than 24 years was memorable as the Cardinals outscored the Wildcats 18-6 in overtime to reach the Final Four. Kentucky (23-8) might have prevailed if center Sam Bowie didn't miss the season because of a leg injury.

One and Only: This was the only year when all of the Final Four teams won their conference tournaments—North Carolina State (ACC), Houston (SWC), Georgia (SEC) and Louisville (Metro). . . . This was the only year two teams reached the Final Four despite losing an undergraduate player who defected at the end of the previous season to become an NBA first-round draft choice (Georgia forward Dominique Wilkins, the 3rd pick in the 1982 draft and Houston guard Rob Williams, the 19th pick overall). . . . This was also the only year the four No. 2 seeds combined for a losing record (3-4).

Numbers Game: Georgia, seeded No. 4 in the 1983 East Regional in its playoff debut, is the only first-time entrant to be seeded better than fifth since the field expanded to at least 48 teams in 1980. The Bulldogs are the last school to reach the NIT semifinals the season prior to reaching the NCAA Final Four. . . . La Salle's Steve Black scored a tourney-high 31 points in a 76-67 setback against Virginia Commonwealth in the first round of the East Regional.

What Might Have Been: Houston swingmen Clyde Drexler and Michael Young and forward Larry Micheaux combined to score 47 points per game. If only they combined for 17 points instead of 14 points in the championship game, the Cougars could have defeated N.C. State rather than losing by two points. Drexler played only 25 minutes after drawing four fouls in the first half. . . . Boston College (25-7 record/without John Bagley), Indiana (24-6/Isiah Thomas), North Carolina (28-8/James Worthy) and Ohio State (20-10/Clark Kellogg) might have advanced farther in the playoffs if standout players had exercised their remaining eligibility instead of turning pro. . . . DePaul (21-12) probably would have participated in the NCAA Tournament instead of the NIT if Terry Cummings didn't defect early to the NBA. . . . The first NCAA Tournament appearance in 18 years for Oklahoma State (24-7) might have been more successful than one-game-and-out if forward Joe Atkinson didn't miss most of the season because of a broken wrist. Atkinson, a starter as a freshman, was the Cowboys' leading scorer and rebounder the next two years.

Putting Things in Perspective: Maryland (20-10) defeated N.C. State twice by a total of 14 points before losing in the second round against eventual national runner-up Houston. Virginia (29-5) defeated the Wolfpack twice by a total of 19 points before losing against N.C. State by one point in the West Regional final. N.C. State lost six of eight games in one span. Five of the Wolfpack's six ACC losses were by at least eight points, including back-to-back defeats by 18 points apiece.

Scoring Leader: Dereck Whittenburg, North Carolina State (120 points, 20 ppg).

Highest Scoring Average: Steve Black, La Salle (46 points, 23 ppg).

Rebounding Leader: Hakeem Olajuwon, Houston (65 rebounds, 13 rpg).

1983 CHAMPIONSHIP BRACKET

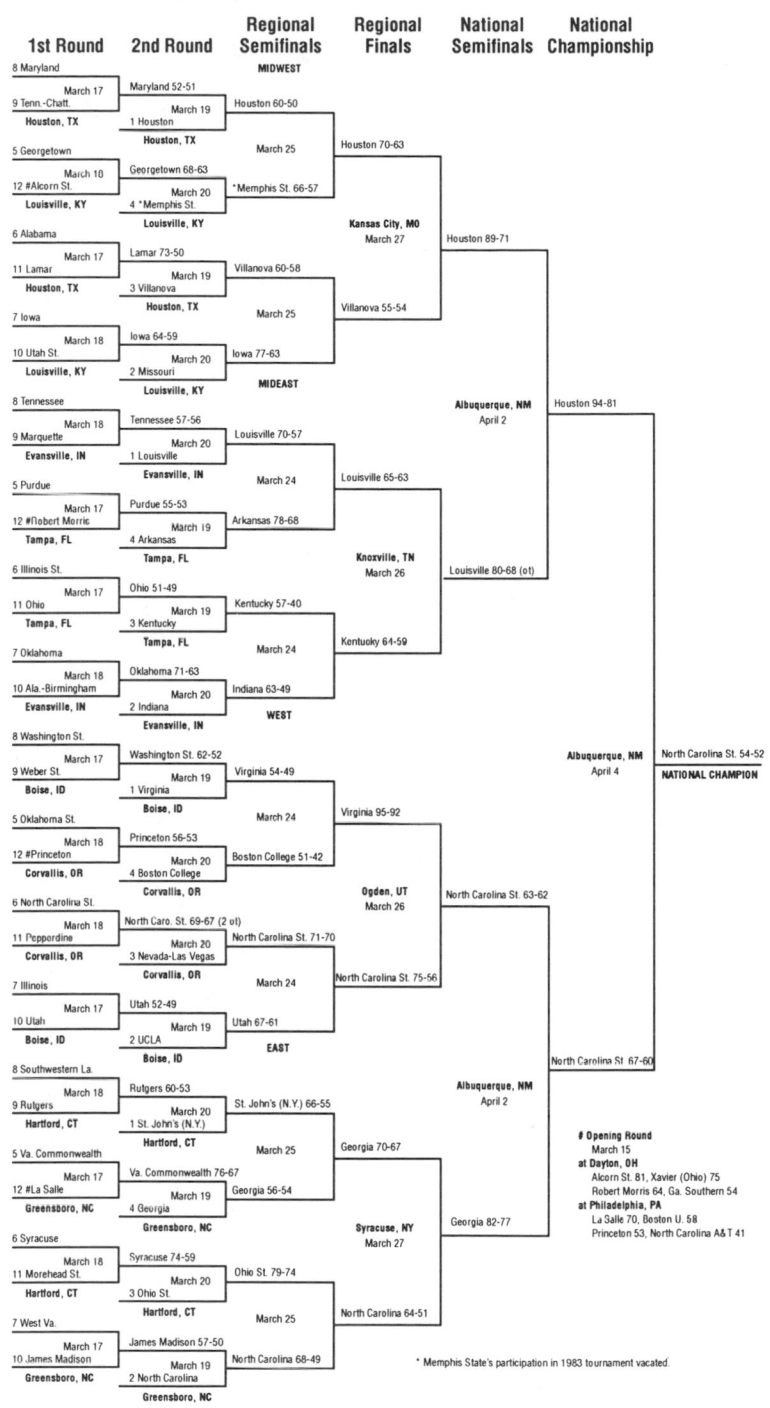

1st Round	2nd Round	Regional Semifinals	Regional Finals	National Semifinals	National Championship

MIDWEST

8 Maryland
March 17
9 Tenn.-Chatt.
Houston, TX

Maryland 52-51
March 19
1 Houston
Houston, TX

Houston 60-50

5 Georgetown
March 10
12 #Alcorn St.
Louisville, KY

Georgetown 68-63
March 20
4 *Memphis St.
Louisville, KY

*Memphis St. 66-57

Houston 70-63

6 Alabama
March 17
11 Lamar
Houston, TX

Lamar 73-50
March 19
3 Villanova
Houston, TX

Villanova 60-58

7 Iowa
March 18
10 Utah St.
Louisville, KY

Iowa 64-59
March 20
2 Missouri
Louisville, KY

Iowa 77-63

Villanova 55-54

Kansas City, MO
March 27

Houston 89-71

MIDEAST

8 Tennessee
March 18
9 Marquette
Evansville, IN

Tennessee 57-56
March 20
1 Louisville
Evansville, IN

Louisville 70-57

5 Purdue
March 17
12 #Robert Morris.
Tampa, FL

Purdue 55-53
March 19
4 Arkansas
Tampa, FL

Arkansas 78-68

Louisville 65-63

6 Illinois St.
March 17
11 Ohio
Tampa, FL

Ohio 51-49
March 19
3 Kentucky
Tampa, FL

Kentucky 57-40

7 Oklahoma
March 18
10 Ala.-Birmingham
Evansville, IN

Oklahoma 71-63
March 20
2 Indiana
Evansville, IN

Indiana 63-49

Kentucky 64-59

Knoxville, TN
March 26

Louisville 80-68 (ot)

WEST

8 Washington St.
March 17
9 Weber St.
Boise, ID

Washington St. 62-52
March 19
1 Virginia
Boise, ID

Virginia 54-49

5 Oklahoma St.
March 18
12 #Princeton
Corvallis, OR

Princeton 56-53
March 20
4 Boston College
Corvallis, OR

Boston College 51-42

Virginia 95-92

6 North Carolina St.
March 18
11 Pepperdine
Corvallis, OR

North Caro. St. 69-67 (2 ot)
March 20
3 Nevada-Las Vegas
Corvallis, OR

North Carolina St. 71-70

7 Illinois
March 17
10 Utah
Boise, ID

Utah 52-49
March 19
2 UCLA
Boise, ID

Utah 67-61

North Carolina St. 75-56

Ogden, UT
March 26

North Carolina St. 63-62

EAST

8 Southwestern La.
March 18
9 Rutgers
Hartford, CT

Rutgers 60-53
March 20
1 St. John's (N.Y.)
Hartford, CT

St. John's (N.Y.) 66-55

5 Va. Commonwealth
March 17
12 #La Salle
Greensboro, NC

Va. Commonwealth 76-67
March 19
4 Georgia
Greensboro, NC

Georgia 56-54

Georgia 70-67

6 Syracuse
March 18
11 Morehead St.
Hartford, CT

Syracuse 74-59
March 20
3 Ohio St.
Hartford, CT

Ohio St. 79-74

7 West Va.
March 17
10 James Madison
Greensboro, NC

James Madison 57-50
March 19
2 North Carolina
Greensboro, NC

North Carolina 68-49

North Carolina 64-51

Syracuse, NY
March 27

Georgia 82-77

Albuquerque, NM
April 2

Houston 94-81

Albuquerque, NM
April 2

Georgia 82-77

Albuquerque, NM
April 4

North Carolina St. 54-52
NATIONAL CHAMPION

North Carolina St. 67-60

 # Opening Round
March 15
at Dayton, OH
 Alcorn St. 81, Xavier (Ohio) 75
 Robert Morris 64, Ga. Southern 54
at Philadelphia, PA
 La Salle 70, Boston U. 58
 Princeton 53, North Carolina A&T 41

* Memphis State's participation in 1983 tournament vacated.

1983-84

AT A GLANCE

NCAA Champion: Georgetown (34-3; coached by John Thompson; won Big East title by two games with a 14-2 record).

NIT Champion: Michigan (23-10; coached by Bill Frieder; finished in fourth place in Big Ten with a 10-8 record).

New Rules: Two free throws are taken for each common foul committed within the last two minutes of the second half and the entire overtime periods, if the bonus rule is in effect (rule was rescinded one month into the season). . . . One additional NCAA Tournament opening-round game was established, requiring 10 automatic-qualifying conferences to compete for five positions in the 53-team bracket.

NCAA Probation: San Diego State.

NCAA Consensus First-Team All-Americans: Patrick Ewing, C, Jr., Georgetown; Michael Jordan, G, Jr., North Carolina; Hakeem Olajuwon, C, Jr., Houston; Sam Perkins, C, Sr., North Carolina; Wayman Tisdale, C-F, Soph., Oklahoma.

National Player of the Year: Jordan (19.6 ppg, 5.3 rpg, 1.6 spg, 55.1 FG%).

National Coaches of the Year: Washington's Marv Harshman (24-7/NABC); Purdue's Gene Keady (22-7/USBWA), and DePaul's Ray Meyer (27-3/AP, UPI).

In one of the most ballyhooed regular-season matchups ever, Ralph Sampson-led Virginia defeated fellow center Patrick Ewing and the Georgetown Hoyas, 68-63. Sampson collected 28 points and 16 rebounds compared to Ewing's 16 points and eight rebounds.

In the first regular-season meeting in 61 years between in-state rivals Kentucky and Louisville, the Wildcats whipped the Cardinals, 65-44. Later, Kentucky's Melvin Turpin tied a SEC Tournament record with 42 points against Georgia.

Houston's Hakeem Olajuwon set a SWC record with 16 blocked shots against Arkansas. . . . North Carolina was ranked No. 1 with a 19-0 record when the Tar Heels succumbed at Arkansas, 65-64, in Pine Bluff on a last-second basket by Charles Balentine. . . . Maryland coach Lefty Driesell won his first ACC Tournament in 15 tries.

Oklahoma's Wayman Tisdale poured in a national-high and school-record 61 points against Texas-San Antonio in the All-College Tournament at Oklahoma City. St. Joseph's Tony Costner tied a school standard with 47 points against Alaska-Anchorage in the Cable Car Classic at San Francisco. . . . Akron's Joe Jakubick became the nation's only player to average more than 30 points per game in a six-year span from 1980-81 through 1985-86. . . . Jakubick (30.1 ppg), Brigham Young's Devin Durrant (27.9), Loyola of Chicago's Alfredrick Hughes (27.6), San Diego State's Michael Cage (24.5) and Cal State Fullerton's Leon Wood (24) set school Division I records for highest scoring average in a single season.

Harvard, coached by Frank McLaughlin, set an NCAA single-season record for free-throw accuracy (82.2 percent). . . . Lamar's 80-game homecourt winning streak, which started in 1978, was snapped by Louisiana Tech, 68-65, in the Southland Conference Tournament.

Duke appeared in the Top 20 of final wire-service polls for the first time under coach Mike Krzyzewski. The Blue Devils were nine games below .500 after his first three years (38-47), including a school-record 43-point loss against Virginia in the first round of the ACC Tournament to end his third season. "I don't think there ever was a time I was afraid for my job," Krzyzewski said in retrospect. "But I was concerned that we'd never achieve what we wanted to achieve at Duke."

Duke, after losing its previous nine games to Virginia, started a streak of 16 consecutives victories over the Cavaliers. . . . Georgia Tech began to assert itself in the Yellow Jackets' fifth year in the ACC. Five ACC home games were decided in the final seconds of play, four of them on the last play of the contest. . . . North Carolina (14-0) and Maryland (9-5) were the only ACC teams to compile winning records in league competition. . . . Massachusetts posted its lone victory over West Virginia (71-60) in a 20-game stretch of their series from

1983–84 INDIVIDUAL LEADERS

SCORING

PLAYER	PTS.	AVG.
Jakubick, Akron	814	30.1
Jackson, Alabama St.	812	29.0
Durrant, Brigham Young	866	27.9
Hughes, Loyola (Ill.)	800	27.6
Tisdale, Oklahoma	919	27.0
Dumars, McNeese St.	817	26.4
Crawford, U.S. Intl.	614	24.6
Cage, San Diego St.	686	24.5
Burtt, Iona	749	24.2
Wood, Cal St. Full.	719	24.0

REBOUNDING

PLAYER	REB.	AVG.
Olajuwon, Houston	500	13.5
Scurry, Long Island	418	13.5
McDaniel, Wichita St.	393	13.1
Newman, Ark.-Little Rock	348	12.9
Cage, San Diego St.	352	12.6
Cross, Maine	339	12.6
Brown, G. Washington	351	12.1
Sanders, Miss. Valley St.	338	12.1
Binion, N. Carolina A&T	335	11.6
Koncak, SMU	378	11.5

ASSISTS

PLAYER	AST.	AVG.
Lathan, Ill.-Chicago	274	9.4
Tarkanian, UNLV	289	8.5
Gettys, Houston	309	8.4
LaFleur, Northeastern	252	7.9
William, Florida St.	215	7.7
Teague, Boston U.	218	7.5
Weingrad, Hofstra	208	7.4
Smith, Massachusetts	212	7.3
Les, Bradley	158	7.2
Stockton, Gonzaga	201	7.2

FIELD GOAL PERCENTAGE

PLAYER	FGM	FGA	PCT.
Olajuwon, Houston	249	369	.675
Hurt, Alabama	168	253	.664
Ewing, Georgetown	242	368	.658
Green, Oregon St.	134	204	.657
Walker, Utica	125	191	.654
Thornton, UC Irvine	151	236	.640
Barkley, Auburn	162	254	.638
Toomer, Florida A&M	149	234	.637
Boldon, C. Mich.	151	238	.634
Burke, Dartmouth	194	306	.634

FREE THROW PERCENTAGE

PLAYER	FTM	FTA	PCT.
Alford, Indiana	137	150	.913
Carrabino, Harvard	153	169	.905
Mullin, St. John's	169	187	.904
Ferry, Harvard	84	93	.903
Cunningham, UTSA	94	107	.879
Golston, Loyola (Ill.)	128	146	.877
Beasley, Arizona St.	112	128	.875
Potter, O. Roberts	82	94	.872
Arnolie, Penn	82	94	.872
White, UT-Chat.	124	143	.867

1983–84 TEAM LEADERS

SCORING OFFENSE

SCHOOL	PTS.	AVG.
Tulsa	2816	90.8
Alabama St.	2485	88.8
Oklahoma	2953	86.9
Marshall	2589	83.5
Oral Roberts	2569	82.9

SCORING DEFENSE

SCHOOL	PTS.	AVG.
Princeton	1403	50.1
Fresno St.	1802	54.6
Tulane	1535	54.8
Oregon St.	1618	55.8
Illinois	1737	56.0

SCORING MARGIN

SCHOOL	OFF.	DEF.	MAR.
Georgetown	74.3	57.9	16.4
North Carolina	80.1	64.8	15.3
Oklahoma	86.9	72.6	14.3
Lamar	78.5	64.8	13.6
UNLV	82.1	68.7	13.4

WON-LOST PERCENTAGE

SCHOOL	W-L	PCT.
Georgetown	34-3	.919
North Carolina	28-3	.903
DePaul	27-3	.900
Texas-El Paso	27-4	.871
Tulsa	27-4	.871

FIELD GOAL PERCENTAGE

SCHOOL	FGM	FGA	PCT.
Houston Baptist	797	1445	.552
North Carolina	966	1779	.543
Southern Methodist	1023	1892	.541
Navy	873	1616	.540
Maryland	941	1745	.539

FIELD GOAL PERCENTAGE DEFENSE

SCHOOL	FGM	FGA	PCT.
Georgetown	799	2025	.395
DePaul	687	1658	.414
Memphis St.	796	1904	.418
Kentucky	796	1894	.420
Southern (La.)	746	1768	.422

FREE THROW PERCENTAGE

SCHOOL	FTM	FTA	PCT.
Harvard	535	651	.822
North Carolina	551	704	.783
Illinois St.	510	659	.774
Fairfield	508	657	.773
St. Louis	400	521	.768

REBOUND MARGIN

SCHOOL	OWN	OPP.	MAR.
Northeastern	40.1	30.3	9.8
Georgetown	40.0	30.5	9.5
St. Joseph's	39.4	30.3	9.1
Auburn	36.9	28.5	8.5
George Washington	38.3	30.8	7.4

1979 through 1989. . . . Temple, coached by John Chaney, went unbeaten in the Atlantic 10 Conference after posting a losing league record the previous year. Northeastern, coached by Jim Calhoun, went unbeaten in North Atlantic Conference competition after finishing in sixth place the previous season with a 4-6 league mark.

Houston (32-5/coached by Guy Lewis), Tulsa (27-4/Nolan Richardson), Northeastern (27-5/Jim Calhoun), Lamar (26-5/Pat Foster), Marshall (25-6/Rick Huckabay), Morehead State (25-6/Wayne Martin), Bucknell (24-5/Charlie Woollum), Miami of Ohio (24-6/Darrell Hedric), Illinois-Chicago (22-7/Willie Little) and George Mason (21-7/Joe Harrington) had their winningest seasons in school Division I history. Alabama State (22-6/James Oliver) tied its school Division I record for most victories in a single season. Bucknell's record-setting campaign came just two years after the worst season in Bison history (7-20).

DePaul coach Ray Meyer (left) retired after the 1983–84 season and was replaced by his son, Joey (right) who was an assistant coach.

Cornell, coached by Tom Miller, compiled a 16-10 record for its first winning season in 17 years. . . . Massachusetts (12-17) lost six of its last seven games but managed to avoid its sixth consecutive season with at least 20 defeats. . . . Richmond, coached by Dick Tarrant, captured the ECAC South title after finishing in last place the previous season.

SMU and Auburn finished in the Top 20 of a final wire-service poll for the first time since 1957 and 1960, respectively. . . . Illinois, coached by Lou Henson, captured its first Big Ten title in 21 years. . . . Kansas suffered its fifth consecutive loss to Oklahoma State in their series before starting a 12-game winning streak against the Cowgboys. . . . Arkansas-Little Rock's Donald Newman set a Trans America Athletic Conference single-game record by grabbing 29 rebounds against Centenary.

DePaul's Ray Meyer retired after a 42-year coaching career with a 724-354 record. Meyer, who compiled a 14-16 record in 13 tournament appearances with DePaul, is the only coach to go more than 40 years from his first appearance in the playoffs to his last (1943 to 1984). He averaged 26 victories his last seven seasons after averaging a modest 14 triumphs annually in a 21-year span from 1957-77.

AP	UPI	USA/CNN	SCHOOL (RECORD)	HEAD COACH
1	1	4	North Carolina (28-3)	Dean Smith
2	2	1	Georgetown (34-3)	John Thompson
3	3	3	Kentucky (29-5)	Joe B. Hall
4	4	6	DePaul (27-3)	Ray Meyer
5	5	2	Houston (32-5)	Guy Lewis
6	6	5	Illinois (26-5)	Lou Henson
7	8	14	Oklahoma (29-5)	Billy Tubbs
8	7	13	Arkansas (25-7)	Eddie Sutton
9	9	20	Texas-El Paso (27-4)	Don Haskins
10	11	17	Purdue (22-7)	Gene Keady
11	10	12	Maryland (24-8)	Lefty Driesell
12	12	21	Tulsa (27-4)	Nolan Richardson
13	13	10	UNLV (29-6)	Jerry Tarkanian
14	14	22	Duke (24-10)	Mike Krzyzewski
15	15	19	Washington (24-7)	Marv Harshman
16	16	9	Memphis State (26-7)	Dana Kirk
17	20	–	Oregon State (22-7)	Ralph Miller
18	16	18	Syracuse (23-9)	Jim Boeheim
19	–	8	Wake Forest (23-9)	Carl Tacy
20	–	25	Temple (26-5)	John Chaney
–	–	7	Virginia (21-12)	Terry Holland
–	18	11	Indiana (22-9)	Bob Knight
–	–	15	Dayton (21-11)	Don Donoher
–	–	16	Louisville (24-11)	Denny Crum
–	19	–	Auburn (20-11)	Sonny Smith
–	–	23	Michigan (24-9)	Bill Frieder
–	–	24	SMU (25-8)	Dave Bliss

1984 NCAA Tournament

Summary: Georgetown's Patrick Ewing and Houston's Hakeem Olajuwon, the nation's two most celebrated centers who lost their previous title bids on last-second freak plays, clashed in the championship game but the head-to-head duel didn't live up to its lofty billing. It was little consolation to Olajuwon when he played Ewing to a standoff on the backboards (each grabbed nine rebounds) and outscored his rival, 15-10. At the end, Olajuwon was on the national runner-up for the second consecutive season as freshmen Reggie Williams and Michael Graham combined for 33 points to spark the Hoyas to a 84-75 triumph. Georgetown became the first Eastern school in 30 years to win an NCAA title. Ewing, the Hoyas' leading scorer on the season, matched the all-time low scoring total for a Final Four Most Outstanding Player with 18 points in two games (fifth on the team), but he was the key component in Georgetown's suffocating defense. The Hoyas led the nation in field-goal percentage defense (39.5 percent) and exhibited their tenacity in the national semifinals when they harassed Kentucky into shooting a dismal 9.1 percent in the second half (3 of 33) en route to a 53-40 victory. George-town's Michael Jackson, a 6-1 guard averaging 1.4 rebounds per game entering the Final Four, retrieved 10 missed shots against Kentucky's formidable frontline to help the Hoyas overcome a seven-point halftime deficit in the national semifinals.

Outcome for Defending Champion: North Carolina State (19-14) finished in seventh place in the ACC before losing at home to Florida State in the first round of the NIT. The Wolfpack twice lost five consecutive ACC regular-season games.

Star Gazing: Ewing, the only individual to fail to score more than 10 points in either the national semifinal or championship game in the year he was named Most Outstanding Player, tallied eight points in a 53-40 triumph over Kentucky in the semifinals and 10 in an 84-75 decision over Houston in the final.

Biggest Upset: Many observers predicted Georgetown would meet top-ranked North Carolina in the national final, but the Tar Heels were upset in the East Regional semifinals by Indiana (72-68) when national player of the year Michael Jordan was limited to 13 points, one rebound and one assist.

One and Only: Virginia became the only school to reach the Final Four despite compiling a losing record in conference competition (6-8 in ACC) and succumbing in the first round of its league tournament. The Cavaliers lost nine of 13 games in a mid-season stretch. . . . Georgetown became the only school to win an NCAA championship after enduring a dry spell of more than 30 years without participating in the playoffs. The Hoyas did not appear in the tourney from 1944 through 1974. . . . Georgetown's John Thompson is the only person to play for an NBA championship team (Boston Celtics '65) before coaching an NCAA titlist.

Numbers Game: Dayton forward Roosevelt Chapman became the only non-guard to be the undisputed leading scorer of an NCAA Tournament and not participate in the Final Four (105 points in four games). He poured in a tourney-high 41 points in an 89-85 victory over Oklahoma

1983–84 NCAA CHAMPION: GEORGETOWN

SEASON STATISTICS OF GEORGETOWN REGULARS

PLAYER	POS.	CL.	G.	FG%	FT%	PPG	RPG
Patrick Ewing	C	Jr.	37	.658	.656	16.4	10.0
David Wingate	G-F	So.	37	.435	.721	11.2	3.6
Michael Jackson	G	So.	31	.509	.816	10.1	1.7
Reggie Williams	G-F	Fr.	37	.433	.768	9.1	3.5
Bill Martin	F	Jr.	37	.509	.705	8.9	5.9
Michael Graham	F	Fr.	35	.561	.459	4.9	4.0
Horace Broadnax	G	So.	35	.434	.853	4.8	1.4
Gene Smith	G	Sr.	36	.511	.592	3.7	2.1
Fred Brown	G	Sr.	36	.486	.646	3.2	2.6
Ralph Dalton	C-F	Jr.	36	.569	.574	2.8	2.2
TEAM TOTALS			37	.509	.678	74.3	40.0

Assists leader: Jackson 137. **Blocked shots leader:** Ewing 133. **Steals leader:** Smith 67.

1984 FINAL FOUR CHAMPIONSHIP GAME

SEATTLE, WA

HOUSTON (75)	MIN.	FG-A	FT-A	REB.	A	PF	PTS.
Winslow	33	0-1	2-2	6	3	4	2
Young	37	8-21	2-3	5	1	3	18
Olajuwon	32	6-9	3-7	9	0	4	15
Franklin	38	8-15	5-6	2	9	3	21
Gettys	29	3-3	0-0	1	7	2	6
Anders	10	2-2	0-2	0	0	0	4
Clark	1	0-0	0-0	0	0	0	0
Anderson	6	1-1	0-0	2	0	0	2
Dickens	6	2-3	1-2	0	0	5	5
Thomas	2	0-0	0-0	0	0	0	0
Giles	2	0-0	0-0	0	0	0	0
Weaver	1	0-0	0-0	0	0	0	0
Orsak	1	1-1	0-0	0	0	0	2
Alexander	1	0-0	0-0	1	0	0	0
Belcher	1	0-0	0-0	0	0	0	0
Team				3			
TOTALS	200	31-56	13-22	29	20	21	75

FG%: .554. **FT%:** .591. **Blocks:** 4. **Turnovers:** 13. **Steals:** 3.

GEORGETOWN (84)	MIN.	FG-A	FT-A	REB.	A	PF	PTS.
Wingate	32	5-10	6-9	1	3	4	16
Dalton	13	0-0	0-0	2	0	1	0
Ewing	30	4-8	2-2	9	3	4	10
Brown	15	1-2	2-2	4	4	4	4
Jackson	35	3-4	5-5	0	6	4	11
Graham	24	7-9	0-2	5	0	4	14
Williams	26	9-18	1-2	7	3	2	19
Broadnax	8	2-3	0-0	0	0	2	4
Martin	16	3-6	0-0	2	0	0	6
Morris	1	0-0	0-0	0	0	0	0
Team				7			
TOTALS	200	34-60	16-22	37	19	25	84

FG%: .567. **FT%:** .727. **Blocks:** 6 (Ewing 4). **Turnovers:** 9. **Steals:** 0. **Halftime:** Georgetown 40-30.

NATIONAL SEMIFINALS

VIRGINIA (47): Miller 6-15 0-0 12, Edelin 1-2 0-0 2, Polynice 4-7 1-1 9, Wilson 5-12 2-2 12, Carlisle 3-14 2-2 8, Stokes 1-1 0-2 2, Sheehey 1-3 0-0 2. Team 21-54 (.389) 5-7 (.714) 47.

HOUSTON (49): Winslow 4-7 0-0 8, Young 8-16 1-4 17, Olajuwon 4-5 4-6 12, Franklin 2-7 2-2 6, Gettys 3-7 0-0 6, Dickens 0-0 0-0 0, Alexander 0-0 0-0 0. Team 21-42 (.500) 7-12 (.583) 49.

Halftime: Houston 25-23. **Regulation:** Tied 43-43.

GEORGETOWN (53): Wingate 5-8 1-2 11, Dalton 0-1 0-0 0, Ewing 4-6 0-0 8, Brown 0-1 0-1 0, Jackson 4-9 4-6 12, Smith 2-4 1-2 5, Martin 1-4 0-0 2, Graham 4-6 0-2 8, Williams 1-7 0-0 2, Broadnax 2-4 1-2 5. Team 23-50 (.460) 7-15 (.467) 53.

KENTUCKY (40): Bowie 3-10 4-4 10, Walker 1-3 2-2 4, Turpin 2-11 1-2 5, Beal 2-8 2-2 6, Master 2-7 2-2 6, Bennett 1-8 0-0 2, Blackmon 2-5 1-2 5, Bearup 0-0 2-2 2, Harden 0-1 0-0 0. Team 13-53 (.245) 14-16 (.875) 40.

Halftime: Kentucky 29-22.

ALL-TOURNAMENT TEAM

*Patrick Ewing, C, Jr., Georgetown (18 points, 18 rebounds in final two games)
Alvin Franklin, G, Soph., Houston (27 points, 16 assists)
Michael Graham, F, Fr., Georgetown (22 points, 11 rebounds)
Hakeem Olajuwon, C, Jr., Houston (27 points, 20 rebounds, seven blocked shots)
Michael Young, F, Sr., Houston (35 points, 12 rebounds)

*Named Most Outstanding Player.

in the second round of the West Regional. . . . Northeastern hit 75 percent from the floor (33 of 44), including 15 of 17 by freshman Reggie Lewis, in the first round, but bowed to Virginia Commonwealth, 70-69. . . . Arkansas' Alvin Robertson finished his career with an average of six steals in four playoff games. . . . The Big Ten compiled its only winning record (4-3) in a five-year span from 1982-86. . . . Oral Roberts' Mark Acres grabbed a tourney-high 18 rebounds in a 92-83 opening-round loss to Memphis State. . . . Auburn, coached by Sonny Smith, and Richmond, coached by Dick Tarrant, appeared in the NCAA playoffs for the first time. . . . In the second and final year of preliminary round competition, Alcorn State (Midwest) and Princeton (West) won games for the second straight season to advance to the first round of their respective regionals.

What Might Have Been: Eventual top six NBA draft choices Sam Bowie, Melvin Turpin and Kenny Walker combined to shoot 56.4 percent from the floor to help Kentucky register 51.5 percent field-goal accuracy as a team in the 1983-84 season. If only the Wildcats managed to hit 30.3 percent of their second-half field-goal attempts instead of 9.1 percent (3 of 33) in the national semifinals, they could have defeated eventual champion Georgetown rather than blowing a seven-point halftime lead. Kentucky's starters

1984 CHAMPIONSHIP BRACKET

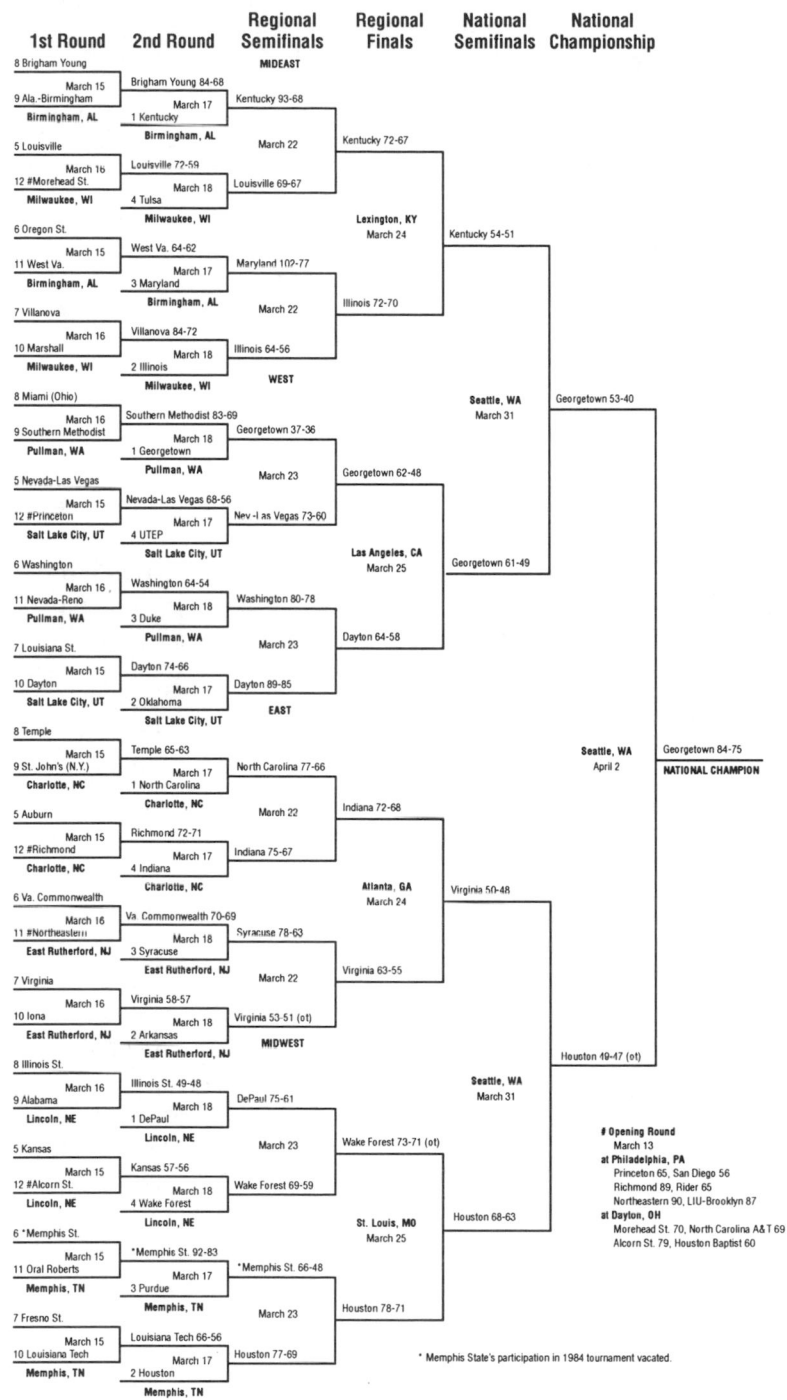

	1st Round	2nd Round	Regional Semifinals	Regional Finals	National Semifinals	National Championship

MIDEAST

8 Brigham Young
March 15
9 Ala.-Birmingham
Birmingham, AL

Brigham Young 84-68
March 17
1 Kentucky
Birmingham, AL

Kentucky 93-68

5 Louisville
March 16
12 #Morehead St.
Milwaukee, WI

Louisville 72-59
March 18
4 Tulsa
Milwaukee, WI

Louisville 69-67

Kentucky 72-67

Lexington, KY
March 24

Kentucky 54-51

6 Oregon St.
March 15
11 West Va.
Birmingham, AL

West Va. 64-62
March 17
3 Maryland
Birmingham, AL

Maryland 102-77

7 Villanova
March 16
10 Marshall
Milwaukee, WI

Villanova 84-72
March 18
2 Illinois
Milwaukee, WI

Illinois 64-56

Illinois 72-70

WEST

8 Miami (Ohio)
March 16
9 Southern Methodist
Pullman, WA

Southern Methodist 83-69
March 18
1 Georgetown
Pullman, WA

Georgetown 37-36

5 Nevada-Las Vegas
March 15
12 #Princeton
Salt Lake City, UT

Nevada-Las Vegas 68-56
March 17
4 UTEP
Salt Lake City, UT

Nev.-Las Vegas 73-60

Georgetown 62-48

Las Angeles, CA
March 25

Georgetown 61-49

Seattle, WA
March 31

Georgetown 53-40

6 Washington
March 16
11 Nevada-Reno
Pullman, WA

Washington 64-54
March 18
3 Duke
Pullman, WA

Washington 80-78

7 Louisiana St.
March 15
10 Dayton
Salt Lake City, UT

Dayton 74-66
March 17
2 Oklahoma
Salt Lake City, UT

Dayton 89-85

Dayton 64-58

EAST

8 Temple
March 15
9 St. John's (N.Y.)
Charlotte, NC

Temple 65-63
March 17
1 North Carolina
Charlotte, NC

North Carolina 77-66

5 Auburn
March 15
12 #Richmond
Charlotte, NC

Richmond 72-71
March 17
4 Indiana
Charlotte, NC

Indiana 75-67

Indiana 72-68

Atlanta, GA
March 24

Virginia 50-48

6 Va. Commonwealth
March 16
11 #Northeastern
East Rutherford, NJ

Va. Commonwealth 70-69
March 18
3 Syracuse
East Rutherford, NJ

Syracuse 78-63

7 Virginia
March 16
10 Iona
East Rutherford, NJ

Virginia 58-57
March 18
2 Arkansas
East Rutherford, NJ

Virginia 53-51 (ot)

Virginia 63-55

Seattle, WA
March 31

Houston 49-47 (ot)

Seattle, WA
April 2

Georgetown 84-75
NATIONAL CHAMPION

MIDWEST

8 Illinois St.
March 16
9 Alabama
Lincoln, NE

Illinois St. 49-48
March 18
1 DePaul
Lincoln, NE

DePaul 75-61

5 Kansas
March 15
12 #Alcorn St.
Lincoln, NE

Kansas 57-56
March 18
4 Wake Forest
Lincoln, NE

Wake Forest 69-59

Wake Forest 73-71 (ot)

St. Louis, MO
March 25

Houston 68-63

6 *Memphis St.
March 15
11 Oral Roberts
Memphis, TN

*Memphis St. 92-83
March 17
3 Purdue
Memphis, TN

*Memphis St. 66-48

7 Fresno St.
March 15
10 Louisiana Tech
Memphis, TN

Louisiana Tech 66-56
March 17
2 Houston
Memphis, TN

Houston 77-69

Houston 78-71

 # Opening Round
March 13
at Philadelphia, PA
  Princeton 65, San Diego 56
  Richmond 89, Rider 65
  Northeastern 90, LIU-Brooklyn 87
at Dayton, OH
  Morehead St. 70, North Carolina A&T 69
  Alcorn St. 79, Houston Baptist 60

* Memphis State's participation in 1984 tournament vacated.

missed all 21 of their field-goal attempts after intermission. The first-round starting frontcourt of Bowie, Turpin and Walker combined to shoot 25 percent from the floor (6 of 24) in the entire game. . . . BYU (20-11) probably would have given Kentucky more of a battle in the second round of the Mideast Regional if Cougars forward Timo Saarelainen didn't sit out the season as a redshirt. Saarelainen became WAC Most Valuable Player the next year. . . . Houston (32-5) might have possessed the firepower necessary to upend Georgetown in the NCAA final if Clyde Drexler didn't turn pro early. . . . Alabama (18-12/without Ennis Whatley), Illinois (26-5/Derek Harper) and Purdue (22-7/Russell Cross) might have advanced farther in the playoffs if standout players had exercised their remaining eligibility instead of defecting to the NBA. . . . Marquette (17-13) probably would have participated in the NCAA Tournament instead of the NIT if Doc Rivers didn't leave school early for the NBA. Ditto for New Mexico (24-11) if two-time WAC field-goal shooting leader George Scott didn't sit out the season as a medical redshirt.

Scoring Leader: Roosevelt Chapman, Dayton (105 points, 26.25 ppg).

Highest Scoring Average: Kevin Mullin, Princeton (56 points, 28 ppg).

Rebounding Leader: Hakeem Olajuwon, Houston (57 rebounds, 11.4 rpg).

Highest Rebounding Average: Keith Lee, Memphis State (37 rebounds, 12.3 rpg).

1984-85

AT A GLANCE

NCAA Champion: Villanova (25-10; coached by Rollie Massimino; tied for third place in Big East with a 9-7 record).

NIT Champion: UCLA (21-12; coached by Walt Hazzard; finished in a three-way tie for third place in Pacific-10 with a 12-6 record).

New Rules: The coaching box is introduced, whereby a coach and all bench personnel must remain in the 28-foot-long coaching box unless seeking information from the scorer's table. . . . The NCAA Tournament bracket was expanded to include 64 teams, eliminating first-round byes.

NCAA Probation: Akron.

NCAA Consensus First-Team All-Americans: Johnny Dawkins, G, Jr., Duke; Patrick Ewing, C, Sr., Georgetown; Keith Lee, C, Sr., Memphis State; Xavier McDaniel, F, Sr., Wichita State; Chris Mullin, G-F, Sr., St. John's; Wayman Tisdale, C-F, Jr., Oklahoma.

National Players of the Year: Ewing (14.6 ppg, 9.2 rpg, 3.6 bpg, 62.5 FG%/AP, NABC, Naismith) and Mullin (19.8 ppg, 4.8 rpg, 2.1 spg, 52.1 FG%, 82.4 FT%/UPI, USBWA, Wooden).

National Coaches of the Year: St. John's Lou Carnesecca (31-4/UPI, USBWA); Michigan's Bill Frieder (26-4/AP), and Georgetown's John Thompson (35-3/NABC).

Chicago product Ben Wilson, named the top player at the Nike/AFBE Camp in Princeton, N.J., entered his senior season of high school generally regarded as the premier recruit in the nation because of his Magic Johnson-like skills. Just a few days prior to the first game of his senior campaign, Wilson was slain by a gunshot within a block of Simeon High's campus.

There is more to the game than scoring. Georgetown center Patrick Ewing compiled the lowest scoring average ever for a wire-service national player of the year. Ewing's forte was intimidation near the basket.

Guard Mark Price became the first Georgia Tech player since 1961 to become an NCAA consensus first- or second-team All-American. . . . Georgia Tech, after finishing in the ACC's second division in its first five seasons in the league, finished in the Top 20 of a final wire-service poll for the first time since 1960. The Yellow Jackets ended a 20-game losing streak in their series with North Carolina en route to earning a three-way share of the league's regular-season title with a 9-5 conference record. No ACC team had previously finished first with more than three defeats. All eight ACC members participated in the two post-

Oklahoma All-American forward Wayman Tisdale racks up some hang time.

season tourneys—five in the NCAA and three in the NIT—but none reached the national semifinals of either event. . . . North Carolina finished in first or second place in the ACC standings for the 19th consecutive year.

North Carolina State, coached by Jim Valvano, finished in a tie for first place in the ACC one year after placing seventh. . . . Wichita State's Xavier McDaniel (27.2 ppg), Oklahoma's Wayman Tisdale (27), Ball State's Dan Palombizio (26.3), South Alabama's Terry Catledge (25.6), Texas-San Antonio's Derrick Gervin (25.6), Nebraska's Dave Hoppen (23.5) and Tennessee-Chattanooga's Gerald Wilkins (21) set school Division I records for highest scoring average in a single season.

Memphis State's Keith Lee averaged 19.7 points per game to finish his four-year career with an 18.8 average. His lowest average was 18.3 as a freshman. Lee is the only major-college player to score more than 2,000 points over four seasons and have his highest and lowest average separated by fewer than two points per game. Lee also led the Metro Conference in rebounding all four campaigns.

Georgetown (35-3/coached by John Thompson), Memphis State (31-4/Dana Kirk), St. John's (31-4/Lou Carnesecca), Louisiana Tech (29-3/Andy Russo), Virginia Commonwealth (26-6/J.D. Barnett), San Diego State (23-8/Smokey Gaines), Mercer (22-9/Bill Bibb), Auburn (22-12/Sonny Smith), Tennessee Tech (19-9/Tom Deaton) and Youngstown State (19-11/Mike Rice) had their winningest seasons in school Division I history. Tennessee (22-15/Don DeVoe), Nevada-Reno (21-10/Sonny Allen) and Southeastern Louisiana (18-9/Newton Chelette) tied their school Division I records for most victories. VCU made its lone appearance in the Top 20 of a final wire-service poll.

Navy center David Robinson began to generate national acclaim by averaging 23.6 points and 11.6 rebounds per game. He averaged a modest 7.6 points and four rebounds per game the previous season as a freshman. . . . Penn State's Craig

Collins set an NCAA single-season record for free-throw accuracy by hitting 94 of 98 foul shots (95.9 percent).

Michigan, which was a total of 16 games under .500 in Big Ten competition over the previous six seasons, captured the conference championship with a 16-2 league mark. The Wolverines won a school record 17 consecutive games before being eliminated in the NCAA Tournament by Villanova. . . . Indiana coach Bob Knight tossed a chair across the court during a game against Purdue. He was ejected and suspended for a game by Big Ten commissioner Wayne Duke. . . . Michigan State guard Sam Vincent (23.7 ppg) followed in his brother Jay's footsteps by leading the Big Ten in scoring. Jay, a forward, paced the league in 1979-80 (22.1) and 1980-81 (24.1). . . . Northwestern posted its lone victory over Iowa in a 24-game stretch of their series from 1978 to 1990.

Syracuse snapped Kentucky's streak of eight consecutive seasons leading the nation in attendance. . . . Fordham fell in the opening round of the NIT for the fifth consecutive year under coach Tom Penders. . . . Loyola of Chicago returned to the Top 20 of a final wire-service poll for the first time since 1966. . . . Cleveland State, coached by Kevin Mackey, captured the Mid-Continent Conference championship one year after finishing in seventh place.

Gervin, the younger brother of pro legend George Gervin, established a Texas-San Antonio mark with 51 points against Baylor. Other players setting school single-game scoring records were Loyola of Chicago's Alfredrick Hughes (47 points vs. Detroit), Miami of Ohio's Ron Harper (45 vs. Ball State in Mid-American Conference Tournament semifinals) and George Mason's Carlos Yates (42 vs. Navy). A Loyola player had won the first six Midwestern City Conference scoring titles after Hughes captured his third in a row. . . . Holy Cross' Jim McCaffrey established a Metro Atlantic Athletic Conference regular-season single-game standard with 46 points against Iona.

LSU was in sixth place in the SEC with a 7-5 record before winning its last six league games to capture the conference crown. The Tigers, coached by Dale Brown, were believed to be the first team ever to win the SEC title with no seniors on its roster. . . . Four Tulane starters, including eventual pro standout John (Hot Rod) Williams, and a reserve were accused of shaving points in two games. Two of the five players, Clyde Eads and Jon Johnson, were granted immunity and testified that the others had also shaved points in exchange for cash and cocaine. Williams was acquitted and nobody served jail time, but university president Eamon Kelly shut down the basketball program for four years. . . . A chartered plane carrying East Tennessee State's team crash landed in Jasper, Ala., after one of its twin engines caught fire. Nine members of the team were treated and released from a nearby medical center, but none of the 33 passengers was injured seriously. The team had been in Birmingham for a game against UAB and was on its way to play in Oxford, Miss., against Mississippi.

Cincinnati, which compiled a 3-25 record the previous season, improved by 12 1/2 games to 17-14 under coach Tony Yates. . . . Princeton lost its first six games against major-college competition to incur its first losing record (11-15) in 32 seasons and St. Bonaventure lost nine of 11 games in a mid-season swoon to sustain its first losing mark (14-15) in 29 years. . . . Army, coached by Les Wothke, posted its only winning record (16-13) since the 1978-79 campaign. . . . Marshall's Bruce Morris hit a basket from 89 feet, 10 inches away as the first-half buzzer sounded against visiting Appalachian State on February 7, 1985. The shot made its way into the Guiness Book of World Records as the longest shot ever recorded in a college game. . . . Oklahoma City competed in its final season at the major-college level.

Southern Cal, coached by Stan Morrison, tied for first place in the Pacific-10 Conference after finishing in eighth the previous year. . . . There were 26 new head coaches at the Division I level, the only year there has been fewer than 34 changes in a season since the number of major universities increased to at least 210 in 1971-72. The changes included Butch van Breda Kolff, who returned to Lafayette

1984-85 FINAL NATIONAL POLLS

AP	UPI	USA/CNN	SCHOOL (RECORD)	HEAD COACH
1	1	2	Georgetown (35-3)	John Thompson
2	2	9	Michigan (26-4)	Bill Frieder
3	3	3	St. John's (31-4)	Lou Carnesecca
4	5	6	Oklahoma (31-6)	Billy Tubbs
5	4	5	Memphis State (31-4)	Dana Kirk
6	6	4	Georgia Tech (27-8)	Bobby Cremins
7	7	7	North Carolina (27-9)	Dean Smith
8	8	8	Louisiana Tech (29-3)	Andy Russo
9	9	20	UNLV (28-4)	Jerry Tarkanian
10	12	13	Duke (23-8)	Mike Krzyzewski
11	11	19	Va. Commonwealth (26-6)	J.D. Barnett
12	10	11	Illinois (26-9)	Lou Henson
13	13	16	Kansas (26-8)	Larry Brown
14	17	12	Loyola of Chicago (27-6)	Gene Sullivan
15	15	17	Syracuse (22-9)	Jim Boeheim
16	18	10	N.C. State (23-10)	Jim Valvano
17	16	–	Texas Tech (23-8)	Gerald Myers
18	14	–	Tulsa (23-8)	Nolan Richardson
19	–	–	Georgia (22-9)	Hugh Durham
20	19	–	Louisiana State (19-10)	Dale Brown
–	–	1	Villanova (25-10)	Rollie Massimino
–	–	14	Auburn (22-12)	Sonny Smith
–	–	15	Boston College (20-11)	Gary Williams
–	–	18	Maryland (25-12)	Lefty Driesell
–	20	–	Michigan State (19-10)	Jud Heathcote
–	–	21	UAB (25-9)	Gene Bartow
–	–	22	Alabama (23-10)	Wimp Sanderson
–	–	23	UCLA (21-12)	Walt Hazzard
–	–	24	Kentucky (18-13)	Joe B. Hall
–	–	25	Arkansas (22-13)	Eddie Sutton

30 years after first coaching at the school from 1951-52 through 1954-55. One of the newcomers was Walt Hazzard, the fifth UCLA coach in 10 years since John Wooden retired. . . . Louisville coach Denny Crum's NCAA record for consecutive 20-win seasons from the start of a coaching career ended at 13. The Cardinals' 17-game winning streak in their series with Cincinnati came to an end. . . . Kentucky's Joe B. Hall retired after a 19-year coaching career with a 373-156 record. Washington's Marv Harshman, who previously coached at Pacific Lutheran and Washington State, retired after a 40-year coaching career with a 642-448 record.

1985 NCAA Tournament

Summary: Villanova became the worst seed (#8 in the Southeast Regional) to win a national championship. The Wildcats shot a championship game-record 78.6 percent from the floor in posting a 66-64 victory against Georgetown, the nation's top-ranked team. The Hoyas' two regular-season defeats were by a total of just three points (against St. John's and Syracuse). Villanova also defeated three other teams with No. 1 or No. 2 seeds (Michigan, North Carolina and Memphis

1984–85 INDIVIDUAL LEADERS

SCORING

PLAYER	PTS.	AVG.
McDaniel, Wichita St.	844	27.2
Hughes, Loyola (Ill.)	868	26.3
Palombizio, Ball St.	762	26.3
Dumars, McNeese St.	697	25.8
Catledge, South Alabama	718	25.6
Gervin, Texas-San Ant.	718	25.6
Tisdale, Oklahoma	932	25.2
Smith, Loyola M'mount	678	25.1
Mitchell, Mercer	774	25.0
Harper, Miami (Ohio)	772	24.9

REBOUNDING

PLAYER	REB.	AVG.
McDaniel, Wichita St.	460	14.8
Benjamin, Creighton	451	14.1
Scurry, Long Island	394	14.1
Towns, Monmouth	319	12.3
Sanders, Miss. Valley St.	344	11.9
Stivrins, Colorado	317	11.7
Robinson, Navy	370	11.6

Catledge, S. Alabama	322	11.5
Neal, Cal St. Full.	326	11.2
Williams, Alabama St.	288	11.1

ASSISTS

PLAYER	AST.	AVG.
Weingard, Hofstra	228	9.5
Golston, Loyola (Ill.)	305	9.2
Les, Bradley	263	8.8
Chisholm, Delaware	224	8.0
Carr, Nebraska	237	7.9
James, Brooklyn	211	7.5
Clarington, Tenn. Tech	210	7.5
Moore, SMU	247	7.5
Teague, Boston	217	7.2
McCarthy, Weber St.	209	7.2

FIELD GOAL PERCENTAGE

PLAYER	FGM	FGA	PCT.
Walker, Utica	154	216	.713
Moore, Creighton	265	393	.674

Hoppen, Nebraska	270	418	.646
Robinson, Navy	302	469	.644
Staves, Southern (La.)	164	257	.638
Salley, Ga. Tech	193	308	.627
Ewing, Georgetown	220	352	.625
Daugherty, N. Carolina	238	381	.625
Bantum, Cornell	163	262	.622
Lavodrama, Houst. Bapt.	186	301	.618

FREE THROW PERCENTAGE

PLAYER	FTM	FTA	PCT.
Collins, Penn St.	94	98	.959
Alford, Indiana	116	126	.921
Eggink, Marist	81	88	.920
Nutt, TCU	77	84	.917
Timko, Youngstown St.	78	86	.907
Hagan, Weber St.	86	95	.905
Burden, St. Louis	93	104	.894
Brooks, Tennessee	146	164	.890
Olson, Wisconsin	73	82	.890
Webster, Harvard	96	108	.889

1984–85 TEAM LEADERS

SCORING OFFENSE

SCHOOL	PTS.	AVG.
Oklahoma	3328	89.9
Alcorn St.	2555	85.2
Southern (La.)	2515	83.8
Loyola (Ill.)	2757	83.5
Utah St.	2292	81.9

SCORING DEFENSE

SCHOOL	PTS.	AVG.
Fresno St.	1696	53.0
Princeton	1429	55.0
Colgate	1451	55.8
Temple	1736	56.0
Illinois	2001	57.2

SCORING MARGIN

SCHOOL	OFF.	DEF.	MAR.
Georgetown	74.3	57.3	17.1
Oklahoma	89.9	75.6	14.4
Navy	78.4	65.3	13.0
Louisiana Tech	77.9	65.1	12.8
Illinois	68.9	57.2	11.7

WON-LOST PERCENTAGE

SCHOOL	W-L	PCT.
Georgetown	35-3	.921
Louisiana Tech	29-3	.906
Memphis St.	31-4	.886
St. John's	31-4	.886
UNLV	28-4	.875

FIELD GOAL PERCENTAGE

SCHOOL	FGM	FGA	PCT.
Navy	946	1726	.548
St. John's	978	1806	.542
North Carolina	1039	1925	.540
Iona	898	1669	.538
Michigan St.	837	1559	.537

FIELD GOAL PERCENTAGE DEFENSE

SCHOOL	FGM	FGA	PCT.
Georgetown	833	2064	.404
Illinois	832	1989	.418
West Virginia	693	1652	.419
Iowa	767	1826	.420
Memphis St.	911	2152	.423

FREE THROW PERCENTAGE

SCHOOL	FTM	FTA	PCT.
Harvard	450	555	.811
Davidson	539	692	.779
Weber St.	495	641	.772
The Citadel	529	688	.769
Texas-San Antonio	454	591	.768

REBOUND MARGIN

SCHOOL	OWN	OPP.	MAR.
Georgetown	39.6	30.5	9.1
Michigan	36.7	28.8	7.9
E. Kentucky	40.8	32.9	7.9
Iowa	41.4	33.8	7.7
Washington	34.3	26.9	7.4

State). The narrow victory over the Hoyas typified Rollie Massimino's NCAA playoff coaching at Villanova as he won 11 of 12 NCAA Tournament games decided by fewer than five points. "It was frustrating," Georgetown guard Horace Broadnax said. "We were right in their faces (on defense) and they kept hitting and hitting." Two years later, it was frustrating and embarrassing for Villanova and Massimino when guard Gary McLain told Sports Illustrated he played the semifinal game against Memphis State while high on cocaine and was also high when the team met President Reagan at the White House.

Outcome for Defending Champion: Georgetown sustained its two Big East defeats by a total of three points in back-to-back games against St. John's and Syracuse.

Star Gazing: Chris Mullin, after averaging 25.5 points in St. John's first four playoff games,

1984–85 NCAA CHAMPION: VILLANOVA

SEASON STATISTICS OF VILLANOVA REGULARS

PLAYER	POS.	CL.	G.	FG%	FT%	PPG	RPG
Ed Pinckney	C	Sr.	35	.600	.730	15.6	8.9
Dwayne McClain	F-G	Sr.	35	.574	.774	14.8	4.1
Harold Pressley	F	Jr.	35	.488	.644	12.0	7.9
Gary McLain	G	Sr.	35	.500	.831	8.0	1.2
Dwight Wilbur	G	Jr.	35	.467	.745	7.5	2.0
Harold Jensen	G	So.	32	.434	.813	4.5	1.2
Mark Plansky	F	Fr.	30	.442	.552	3.3	2.0
Chuck Everson	C	Jr.	32	.514	.565	1.5	1.5
TEAM TOTALS			35	.510	.715	68.7	31.8

Assists leader: McLain 150. Blocked shots leaders: Pinckney 64, Pressley 38. Steals leaders: Pinckney 54, Pressley 53.

1985 FINAL FOUR CHAMPIONSHIP GAME

LEXINGTON, KY

VILLANOVA (66)	MIN.	FG-A	FT-A	REB.	A	PF	PTS.
Pressley	40	4-6	3-4	4	1	1	11
McClain	40	5-7	7-8	1	3	3	17
Pinckney	37	5-7	6-7	6	5	3	16
Wilbur	5	0-0	0-0	0	1	0	0
McLain	40	3-3	2-2	2	2	2	8
Jensen	34	5-5	4-5	1	2	2	14
Plansky	1	0-0	0-1	0	0	1	0
Everson	3	0-0	0-0	0	0	0	0
Team				3			
TOTALS	200	22-28	22-27	17	14	12	66

FG%: .786. FT%: .815. Blocks: 1. Turnovers: 17. Steals: 8.

GEORGETOWN (64)	MIN.	FG-A	FT-A	REB.	A	PF	PTS.
Martin	37	4-6	2-2	5	1	2	10
Williams	29	5-9	0-2	4	2	3	10
Ewing	39	7-13	0-0	5	2	4	14
Jackson	37	4-7	0-0	0	9	4	8

Wingate	39	8-14	0-0	2	2	4	16
McDonald	2	0-1	0-0	0	0	0	0
Broadnax	13	1-2	2-2	1	2	4	4
Dalton	4	0-1	2-2	0	0	1	2
TOTALS	200	29-53	6-8	17	18	22	64

FG%: .547. FT%: .750. Blocks: 1. Turnovers: 11. Steals: 6.
Halftime: Villanova 29-28.

NATIONAL SEMIFINALS

VILLANOVA (52): Pressley 1-8 1-2 3, McClain 6-9 7-7 19, Pinckney 3-7 6-9 12, Wilbur 0-2 0-0 0, McLain 2-5 5-5 9, Plansky 1-1 1-3 3, Jensen 3-6 0-0 6, Everson 0-0 0-0 0. Team 16-38 (.421) 20-26 (.769) 52.

MEMPHIS STATE (45): Lee 3-9 4-4 10, Holmes 4-8 0-0 8, Bedford 4-9 0-0 8, Turner 5-13 1-2 11, Askew 1-3 0-1 2, Wilfong 0-1 0-0 0, Boyd 0-2 0-0 0, Bailey 1-1 0-0 2, Becton 1-4 2-2 4. Team 19-50 (.380) 7-9 (.778) 45.

Halftime: Tied 23-23.

ST. JOHN'S (59): Berry 4-8 4-5 12, Glass 4-4 5-7 13, Wennington 4-7 4-5 12, Mullin 4-8 0-0 8, Moses 3-7 0-0 6, Bross 0-0 0-0 0, Jackson 3-4 0-2 6, Jones 1-4 0-0 2, Stewart 0-0 0-0 0, Shurina 0-0 0-0 0, Cornegy 0-0 0-0 0. Team 23-42 (.548) 13-19 (.684) 59.

GEORGETOWN (77): Martin 4-8 4-4 12, Williams 8-15 4-4 20, Ewing 7-12 2-4 16, Jackson 2-5 0-0 4, Wingate 3-8 6-8 12, McDonald 0-1 0-0 0, Floyd 0-0 0-0 0, Broadnax 3-4 3-4 9, Lockhart 0-0 0-0 0, Highsmith 0-1 0-0 0, Maleen 0-1 0-0 0, Dalton 2-2 0-0 4. Team 29-57 (.509) 19-24 (.792) 77.

Halftime: Georgetown 32-28.

ALL-TOURNAMENT TEAM

Patrick Ewing, C, Sr., Georgetown (30 points, 10 rebounds in final two games)
Harold Jensen, G, Soph., Villanova (20 points)
Dwayne McClain, F-G, Sr., Villanova (36 points)
Gary McLain, G, Sr., Villanova (17 points)
*Ed Pinckney, C, Sr., Villanova (28 points, 15 rebounds)

*Named Most Outstanding Player.

became the only national player of the year (UPI, USBWA and Wooden Award) to score less than 10 points when his school was eliminated in a Final Four contest. The Redmen were routed by Georgetown (77-59) in the national semifinals when Mullin was limited to eight points in 39 minutes.

Biggest Upset: LSU was one of the biggest disappointments in NCAA history. The Tigers, seeded fourth in the Southeast Regional, boasted a roster including eventual NBA first-round draft picks John Williams and Jerry Reynolds and six other players who became NBA draft choices. But they became the only top four seed to lose a opening-round game by more than 20 points when they were trounced by No. 13 seed Navy, 78-55, when David Robinson collected 18 points and a tourney-high 18 rebounds for the Midshipmen.

One and Only: Massimino became the only individual to be more than 10 games below .500 in his initial campaign as a major-college head coach and subsequently guide a team to a national championship. . . . Villanova is the only title team to have a coach with a son on his roster, although guard R.C. Massimino played sparingly.

Numbers Game: St. John's became the only school to defeat a team three times in a season that the opponent captured the NCAA title. The Redmen won their three games against Villanova by a total of 22 points. . . . Nike was crowing when all of the Final Four teams wore its "swoosh" sneakers. . . . Georgetown was the first defending NCAA Tournament champion in 15 years to return to the Final Four the next season. . . . Oklahoma's Wayman Tisdale, who averaged 25.6 points per game in his three-year career, was limit-

1985 CHAMPIONSHIP BRACKET

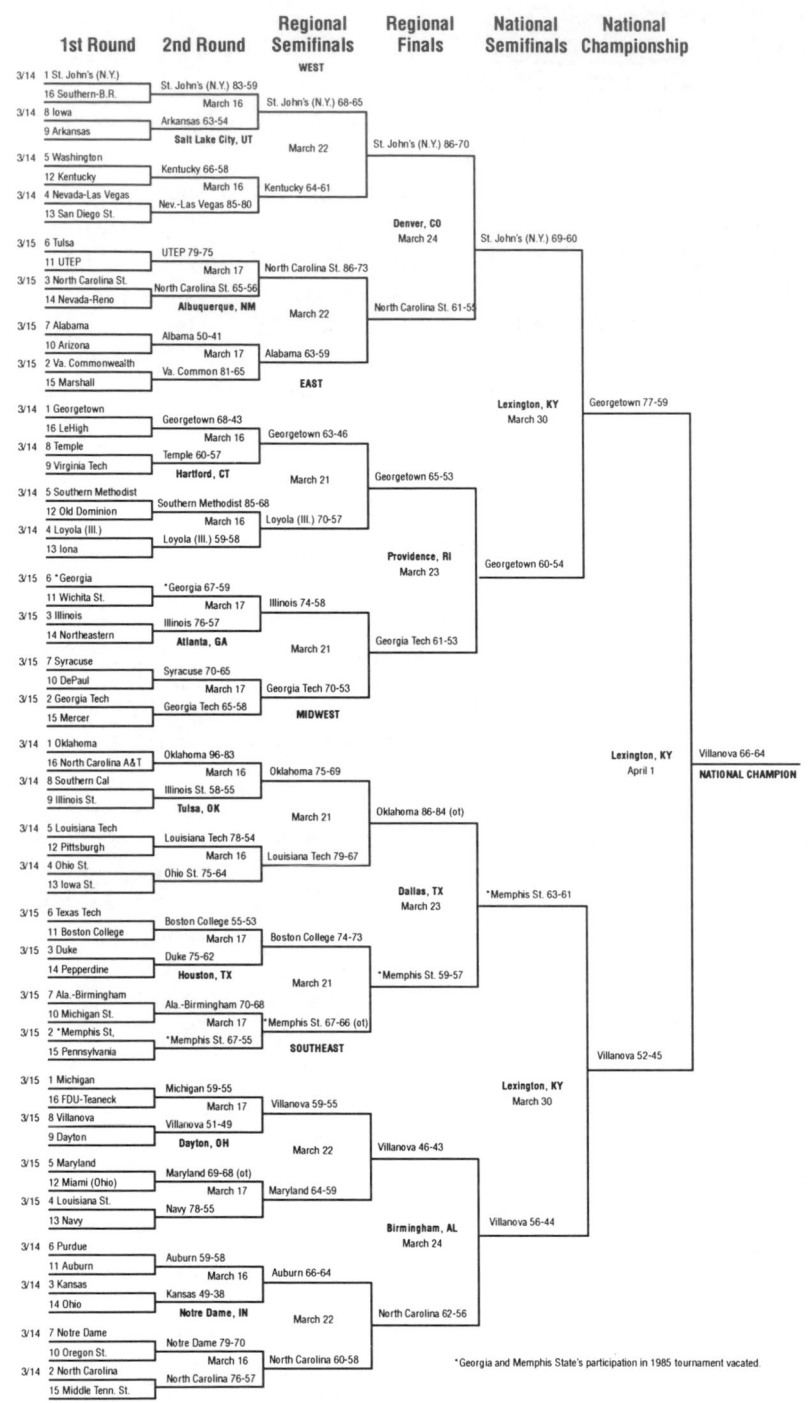

1st Round   **2nd Round**   **Regional Semifinals**   **Regional Finals**   **National Semifinals**   **National Championship**

WEST

3/14 1 St. John's (N.Y.)
16 Southern-B.R.
   St. John's (N.Y.) 83-59
    March 16   St. John's (N.Y.) 68-65
3/14 8 Iowa
9 Arkansas
   Arkansas 63-54
   Salt Lake City, UT   March 22   St. John's (N.Y.) 86-70

3/14 5 Washington
12 Kentucky
   Kentucky 66-58
    March 16   Kentucky 64-61
3/14 4 Nevada-Las Vegas
13 San Diego St.
   Nev.-Las Vegas 85-80

Denver, CO   March 24   St. John's (N.Y.) 69-60

3/15 6 Tulsa
11 UTEP
   UTEP 79-75
    March 17   North Carolina St. 86-73
3/15 3 North Carolina St.
14 Nevada-Reno
   North Carolina St. 65-56
   Albuquerque, NM   March 22   North Carolina St. 61-55

3/15 7 Alabama
10 Arizona
   Alabama 50-41
    March 17   Alabama 63-59
3/15 2 Va. Commonwealth
15 Marshall
   Va. Common 81-65

Lexington, KY   March 30   Georgetown 77-59

EAST

3/14 1 Georgetown
16 LeHigh
   Georgetown 68-43
    March 16   Georgetown 63-46
3/14 8 Temple
9 Virginia Tech
   Temple 60-57
   Hartford, CT   March 21   Georgetown 65-53

3/14 5 Southern Methodist
12 Old Dominion
   Southern Methodist 85-68
    March 16   Loyola (Ill.) 70-57
3/14 4 Loyola (Ill.)
13 Iona
   Loyola (Ill.) 59-58

Providence, RI   March 23   Georgetown 60-54

3/15 6 *Georgia
11 Wichita St.
   *Georgia 67-59
    March 17   Illinois 74-58
3/15 3 Illinois
14 Northeastern
   Illinois 76-57
   Atlanta, GA   March 21   Georgia Tech 61-53

3/15 7 Syracuse
10 DePaul
   Syracuse 70-65
    March 17   Georgia Tech 70-53
3/15 2 Georgia Tech
15 Mercer
   Georgia Tech 65-58

MIDWEST

3/14 1 Oklahoma
16 North Carolina A&T
   Oklahoma 96-83
    March 16   Oklahoma 75-69
3/14 8 Southern Cal
9 Illinois St.
   Illinois St. 58-55
   Tulsa, OK   March 21   Oklahoma 86-84 (ot)

3/14 5 Louisiana Tech
12 Pittsburgh
   Louisiana Tech 78-54
    March 16   Louisiana Tech 79-67
3/14 4 Ohio St.
13 Iowa St.
   Ohio St. 75-64

Dallas, TX   March 23   *Memphis St. 63-61

3/15 6 Texas Tech
11 Boston College
   Boston College 55-53
    March 17   Boston College 74-73
3/15 3 Duke
14 Pepperdine
   Duke 75-62
   Houston, TX   March 21   *Memphis St. 59-57

3/15 7 Ala.-Birmingham
10 Michigan St.
   Ala.-Birmingham 70-68
    March 17   *Memphis St. 67-66 (ot)
3/15 2 *Memphis St.
15 Pennsylvania
   *Memphis St. 67-55

SOUTHEAST

Lexington, KY   April 1   Villanova 66-64   **NATIONAL CHAMPION**

3/15 1 Michigan
16 FDU-Teaneck
   Michigan 59-55
    March 17   Villanova 59-55
3/15 8 Villanova
9 Dayton
   Villanova 51-49
   Dayton, OH   March 22   Villanova 46-43

3/15 5 Maryland
12 Miami (Ohio)
   Maryland 69-68 (ot)
    March 17   Maryland 64-59
3/15 4 Louisiana St.
13 Navy
   Navy 78-55

Lexington, KY   March 30   Villanova 52-45

3/14 6 Purdue
11 Auburn
   Auburn 59-58
    March 16   Auburn 66-64
3/14 3 Kansas
14 Ohio
   Kansas 49-38
   Notre Dame, IN   March 22   Villanova 56-44

3/14 7 Notre Dame
10 Oregon St.
   Notre Dame 79-70
    March 16   North Carolina 60-58
3/14 2 North Carolina
15 Middle Tenn. St.
   North Carolina 76-57

Birmingham, AL   March 24   North Carolina 62-56

*Georgia and Memphis State's participation in 1985 tournament vacated.

ed to 11 in a 63-61 setback against Memphis State in the Midwest Regional final. . . . Michigan State's Sam Vincent (32 points vs. Alabama-Birmingham) and Old Dominion's Mark Davis (32 vs. SMU) tied for the highest output in a playoff game. . . . Lehigh, coached by Tom Schneider, made its first NCAA Tournament appearance. . . . Texas-El Paso tallied its first NCAA playoff victory in 18 years.

What Might Have Been: Center Patrick Ewing, after averaging a modest 13.2 points per game in six Final Four contests with Georgetown, has never averaged fewer than 20 points per game in his eight-year career with the New York Knicks. If only Ewing averaged 14 points per Final Four game by scoring two more points in the 1982 championship game (63-62 defeat against North Carolina) and three more in the 1985 final (66-64 defeat against Villanova), the Hoyas could have captured three national titles in his college career rather than one. They also missed power forward Michael Graham, who dropped out of school. . . . ACC champion Georgia Tech lost to top-ranked Georgetown, 60-54, in the East Regional final. Sophomore Craig Neal, who later became Georgia Tech's all-time assists leader, missed most of the season because of torn wrist ligaments and could have given the Yellow Jackets some depth. . . . Alabama (23-10/without Ennis Whatley), Auburn (22-12/Charles Barkley), Michigan (26-4/Tim McCormick and Eric Turner) and North Carolina (27-9/Michael Jordan) might have advanced farther in the playoffs if standout players had exercised their remaining eligibility instead of defecting to the NBA. . . . UCLA (21-12) probably would have participated in the NCAA Tournament instead of the NIT if center Stuart Gray didn't leave school early for the NBA. Ditto Louisville (19-18) if guard Milt Wagner didn't miss the majority of the season because of an injury.

Putting Things in Perspective: St. John's (31-4) defeated Villanova three times by a total of 22 points before the Redmen lost against Georgetown in the national semifinals. Georgetown (35-3) defeated the Wildcats twice by a total of nine points before losing to Villanova in the national final. Villanova lost four of five Big East Conference games in one span, including three in a row, before dropping its regular-season finale by a whopping 23 points at Pittsburgh. Excluding three setbacks to Georgetown, St. John's only other defeat was by three points to Niagara in Buffalo.

Scoring Leader: Chris Mullin, St. John's (110 points, 22 ppg).

Highest Scoring Average: Rolando Lamb, Virginia Commonwealth (55 points, 27.5 ppg).

Rebounding Leader: Ed Pinckney, Villanova (48 rebounds, 8 rpg).

Highest Rebounding Average: Karl Malone, Louisiana Tech (40 rebounds, 13.3 rpg).

1985-86

AT A GLANCE

NCAA Champion: Louisville (32-7; coached by Denny Crum; won Metro title by one game over Memphis State with a 10-2 record).

NIT Champion: Ohio State (19-14; coached by Eldon Miller; finished in seventh place in Big Ten with an 8-10 record).

New Conference: Big South.

New Rules: The 45-second clock is introduced with the team in control of the ball having to shoot for a goal within 45 seconds after it attains team control. . . . If a shooter is fouled intentionally and the shot is missed, the penalty will be two shots and possession of the ball out of bounds to the team that was fouled. . . . The head coach may stand throughout the game, while all other bench personnel must remain seated. . . . NCAA Tournament regional competition played at neutral sites. If an institution selected to host this level of competition is a participant in the tourney, it will be bracketed in another regional.

NCAA Probation: Baylor, Idaho State, Southern Illinois.

NCAA Consensus First-Team All-Americans: Steve Alford, G, Jr., Indiana; Walter Berry, F, Jr., St. John's; Len Bias, F, Sr., Maryland; Johnny Dawkins, G, Sr., Duke; Kenny Walker, F, Sr., Kentucky.

National Players of the Year: Berry (23 ppg, 11.1 rpg, 2.1 bpg, 59.8 FG%/AP, UPI, NABC, USBWA, Wooden) and Dawkins (20.2 ppg, 3.6 rpg, 3.3 apg, 54.9 FG%, 81.2 FT%/Naismith).

Houston's Guy Lewis bid adieu to coaching after 30 years.

It was one of those moments when time seemed to stand still. The fallout stemming from All-American forward Len Bias' cocaine-induced death just four days after the NBA draft included the ouster of longtime Maryland coach Lefty Driesell.

Another school enduring significant off-the-court transgressions was Minnesota, which was shattered by the arrests of three players on rape charges and the subsequent resignation of coach Jim Dutcher.

Basketball fans in Los Angeles were restless. UCLA fans should have realized something was wrong when Cal ended its 52-game losing streak to the Bruins with a 75-67 success. UCLA's string of 32 consecutive winning records in conference competition terminated when the Bruins finished fourth in the Pacific-10 with a 9-9 mark. They then became the only defending NIT champion to lose an NIT first-round game at home (80-74 to UC Irvine) since the NIT started playing early-round games away from Madison Square Garden. Meanwhile, Southern Cal showed promise with standout freshmen Tom Lewis, Hank Gathers and Bo Kimble. But all three players wound up transferring and finished their careers with more than 2,000 points—Lewis (Pepperdine), Gathers (Loyola Marymount) and Kimble (Loyola Marymount).

Navy's David Robinson blocked 14 shots in a game against North Carolina-Wilmington (see accompanying box score) en route to finishing the season with an NCAA record 207 rejections. Robinson also grabbed a school-record 25 rebounds in a game against Fairfield. . . . Chicago State's Darron Brittman became the only player ever to average as many as five steals per game in a single season.

New Mexico hit 35 of 43 field-goal attempts (81.4 percent) against Oregon State. It was the second-best team shooting from the floor in a sin-gle game in NCAA history. . . . Michigan State led the country in both field-goal shooting (56.1 percent) and free-throw shooting (79.9). When Kansas star Danny Manning fouled out with 2:21 remaining in regulation, the Spartans appeared bound to defeat the Jayhawks in the Midwest Regional semifinals in Kansas City. But the game clock stuck at 2:21 for an estimated 15 seconds, allowing KU to overcome a six-point deficit in the last minute before the Jayhawks won in overtime, 96-86.

St. John's Mark Jackson set a Big East Conference single-season record by averaging 9.4 assists per game. The Redmen won 19 consecutive games on their way to 31 victories for the second straight year. . . . Princeton became the only school to lead the nation in scoring defense (55 points per game) despite compiling a non-winning record (13-13). Meanwhile, U.S. International became the only school to lead the country in scoring offense (90.8 ppg) while posting a losing record (8-20).

Penn and Princeton combined to win the previous 17 Ivy League championships before Brown won its only Ivy title after finishing in seventh

1985–86 INDIVIDUAL LEADERS

SCORING

PLAYER	PTS.	AVG.
Bailey, Wagner	854	29.4
Skiles, Michigan St.	850	27.4
Yezbak, U.S. Intl.	755	27.0
Miller, UCLA	750	25.9
Harper, Miami (Ohio)	757	24.4
Curry, Virginia Tech	722	24.1
Lewis, Northeastern	714	23.8
Bias, Maryland	743	23.2
Ross, American	645	23.0
Berry, St. John's	828	23.0

REBOUNDING

PLAYER	REB.	AVG.
Robinson, Navy	455	13.0
Anderson, Houston	360	12.9
Sellers, Ohio St.	416	12.6
Harper, Miami (Ohio)	362	11.7
Krystkowiak, Montana	364	11.4
Berry, St. John's	399	11.1
Hill, Bethune-Cookman	317	10.9
Carter, Loyola (Md.)	304	10.9
Boone, Marquette	319	10.6
Grant, Clemson	357	10.9

ASSISTS

PLAYER	AST.	AVG.
Jackson, St. John's	328	9.1
Chisholm, Delaware	230	8.5
Bogues, Wake Forest	245	8.4
Lee, Xavier	251	8.4
Thomas, Monmouth	205	8.2
Smith, Old Dominion	253	8.2
Harmon, McNeese St.	243	8.1
Davis, Marist	248	8.0
Paguaga, St. Francis (N.Y.)	223	8.0
Moody, N'western St. (La.)	198	7.9

BLOCKED SHOTS

PLAYER	BLK.	AVG.
Robinson, Navy	207	5.9
Perry, Temple	123	4.0
Blake, St. Joseph's	121	3.8
Fonville, Jackson St.	93	3.2
Kitchen, South Florida	89	3.2
Seikaly, Syracuse	97	3.0
Tarpley, Michigan	97	2.9
Sellers, Ohio St.	97	2.9
Martin, North Carolina	81	2.8
Smith, Pittsburgh	81	2.8

STEALS

PLAYER	STL.	AVG.
Brittman, Chicago St.	139	5.0
Paguaga, St. Francis (N.Y.)	120	4.3
Allen, Hofstra	100	3.6
Harper, Miami (Ohio)	101	3.3
Starks, Providence	84	3.2
Robinson, Md.-E. Shore	69	3.1
Anderson, Pan American	87	3.1
Bogues, Wake Forest	89	3.1
Anderson, Drexel	92	3.0
Ware, Florida A&M	76	2.8

FIELD GOAL PERCENTAGE

PLAYER	FGM	FGA	PCT.
Daugherty, N. Carolina	284	438	.648
Norman, Illinois	216	337	.641
Gattison, Old Dom.	218	342	.637
McKey, Alabama	178	280	.636
Thomas, Centenary	182	288	.632
Duckworth, E. Ill.	250	396	.631
Jones, N'western St. (La.)	130	207	.628
Turner, Brown	199	317	.628
Smits, Marist	216	347	.622
Williams, SMU	150	242	.620

FREE THROW PERCENTAGE

PLAYER	FTM	FTA	PCT.
Barton, Dartmouth	65	69	.942
Goodwin, Dayton	95	102	.931
Suder, Duquesne	135	147	.918
Coval, Wm. & Mary	111	121	.917
Androlewicz, Lehigh	84	93	.903
Skiles, Mich. St.	188	209	.900
Bajusz, Cornell	89	99	.899
Waddy, W. Carolina	70	78	.897
Newman, Richmond	153	172	.890
Rucker, Davidson	103	116	.888

1985–86 TEAM LEADERS

SCORING OFFENSE

SCHOOL	PTS.	AVG.
U.S. International	2542	90.8
Cleveland St.	2934	88.9
Oklahoma	3077	87.9
North Carolina	2945	86.6
Syracuse	2674	83.6

SCORING DEFENSE

SCHOOL	PTS.	AVG.
Princeton	1429	55.0
St. Peter's	1539	55.0
Fresno St.	1708	56.9
North Carolina A&T	1732	57.7
Tulsa	1854	57.9

SCORING MARGIN

SCHOOL	OFF.	DEF.	MAR.
Cleveland St.	88.9	69.6	19.3
North Carolina	86.6	69.0	17.6
Syracuse	83.6	68.3	15.3
Memphis St.	82.4	67.4	15.0
Notre Dame	78.9	64.8	14.1

WON-LOST PERCENTAGE

SCHOOL	W-L	PCT.
Duke	37-3	.925
Bradley	32-3	.914
Kansas	35-4	.897
Kentucky	32-4	.889
Cleveland St.	29-4	.879

FIELD GOAL PERCENTAGE

SCHOOL	FGM	FGA	PCT.
Michigan St.	1043	1860	.561
North Carolina	1197	2140	.559
Kansas	1260	2266	.556
Georgia Tech	1008	1846	.546
Illinois	990	1828	.542

FIELD GOAL PERCENTAGE DEFENSE

SCHOOL	FGM	FGA	PCT.
St. Peter's	574	1395	.411
South Florida	621	1499	.414
Texas Christian	711	1713	.415
Georgetown	789	1885	.419
Navy	932	2215	.421

REBOUND MARGIN

SCHOOL	OWN	OPP.	MAR.
Notre Dame	36.4	27.8	8.6
Michigan	37.4	29.2	8.1
Syracuse	41.0	32.9	8.1
Ark.-Little Rock	44.6	36.5	8.1
Cleveland St.	38.4	31.0	7.5

place the previous year. . . . St. Louis, coached by Rich Grawer, compiled an 18-12 record to end a streak of 12 consecutive losing seasons. . . . Bradley, which posted a 17-13 mark the previous campaign, improved by 12 1/2 games to 32-3 under coach Dick Versace. The Braves made their first Top 20 appearance in a final wire-service poll since 1968. . . . Toledo's streak of 26 consecutive winning seasons ended when the Rockets compiled a 12-17 mark.

Miami (Fla.) and San Francisco resurrected their basketball programs after prolonged absences. . . . Loyola Marymount's streak of non-

On the rebound: Pervis Ellison of Louisville.

Barbara's Scott Fisher (39 at Montana State) set school single-game scoring standards. Bailey (29.4 ppg) established a school record for highest scoring average in a single season. . . . Youngstown State's Tilman Bevely tied an Ohio Valley Conference single-game mark by pouring in 55 points against Tennessee Tech. . . . Georgia Tech had its fourth consecutive ACC Rookie of the Year en route to finishing one game behind Duke. The Yellow Jackets, winless in the ACC in 1981, improved their league record for the fifth consecutive season under coach Bobby Cremins. . . . Texas A&M's Don Marbury led the Southwest Conference in scoring 10 years before one of his brothers, Stephon, took the country by storm as a freshman sensation for Georgia Tech.

Duke (37-3/coached by Mike Krzyzewski), Kansas (35-4/Larry Brown), Navy (30-5/Paul Evans), Cleveland State (29-4/Kevin Mackey), Pepperdine (25-5/Jim Harrick), Fairfield (24-7/Mitch Buonaguro), Akron (22-8/Bob Huggins), Charleston Southern (21-9/Tommy Gaither) and McNeese State (21-11/Glenn Duhon) had their winningest seasons in school Division I history. Bradley (32-3/Dick Versace), St. John's (31-5/Lou Carnesecca), St. Joseph's (26-6/Jim Boyle), Middle Tennessee State (23-11/Bruce Stewart) and Auburn (22-11/Sonny Smith) tied their school records for most victories in a single season.

Navy, coached by Paul Evans, finished in the Top 20 of a final wire-service poll for the first time since 1959. Fairfield, under first-year coach Mitch Buonaguro, won the Metro Atlantic Athlet-

winning seasons ended at 10 in a row when the Lions compiled a 19-11 record in Paul Westhead's first year as their coach. . . . Wyoming, coached by Jim Brandenburg, tied for the WAC regular-season title just one year after finishing in seventh place. . . . Oregon lost 15 consecutive games to archrival Oregon State until defeating the Beavers, 60-47.

San Diego State's Anthony Watson (54 points vs. U.S. International), Wagner's Terrance Bailey (49 vs. Brooklyn in triple overtime), Northeastern's Reggie Lewis (41 vs. Siena) and UC Santa

ROBINSON'S RECORD REJECTIONS

David Robinson blocked an NCAA-record 14 shots in a game against UNC Wilmington on January 4, 1986. UNCW star Brian Rowsom shot 53.6 percent from the floor during the season, but connected on only 13 percent of his field-goal attempts (3 of 23) facing the intimidating Robinson.

NAVY (76)	MP	FG-A	FT-A	REB.	BLK.	PTS.
Vernon Butler	38	10-16	4-5	11	1	24
Tony Wells	18	1-3	0-0	4	0	2
David Robinson	34	9-17	3-6	14	14	21
Kylor Whitaker	31	7-10	1-2	2	0	15
Doug Wojcik	29	2-4	0-0	4	0	4
Cliff Rees	12	2-3	0-0	2	0	4
Craig Prather	7	0-0	0-0	1	0	0
Derrick Turner	5	0-1	0-3	3	0	0
Carl Liebert	12	2-3	0-0	2	0	4
Neal Fenton	11	0-1	0-0	2	0	0
Nathan Bailey	3	1-2	0-0	1	0	2
Carey Manhertz	1	0-0	0-0	0	0	0
TEAM Totals	200	34-60	8-16	47	15	76

FG%—.567. FT%—.500. Steals—8 (Butler 4).

NC WILMINGTON (61)	MP	FG-A	FT-A	REB.	BLK.	PTS.
Greg Bender	35	4-11	2-3	6	0	10
Kevan Miles	24	1-7	0-0	5	0	2
Brian Rowsom	38	3-23	2-2	14	1	8
Sandy Anderson	27	7-14	1-2	4	0	15
Bobby Jo Springer	38	8-21	2-3	3	1	18
Charles Cherry	17	2-2	2-3	5	1	6
Mark Gary	12	0-3	2-2	0	0	2
Ben Pittman	2	0-0	0-0	0	0	0
Rob Wagner	4	0-0	0-0	0	0	0
Dan Porter	1	0-0	0-0	0	0	0
Don Cary	1	0-0	0-0	0	0	0
Kenny Mickens	1	0-0	0-0	0	0	0
TEAM Totals	200	25-81	11-15	38	3	61

FG%—.309. FT%—.733. Steals—11 (Bender 3).

Halftime: Navy 35-28.

ic Conference regular-season and postseason conference titles after finishing in last place the previous year. . . . Nebraska posted its lone victory over Oklahoma in a 16-game stretch of their series from 1983 through 1990. . . . Texas, coached by Bob Weltlich, tied for first place in the Southwest Conference after compiling losing records in league competition the previous five seasons. . . . West Texas State competed in its final campaign at the Division I level. . . . Arkansas' Nolan Richardson became the first African American head coach in the SWC. . . . Houston's Guy Lewis ended his 30-year coaching career with a 592-279 record. He didn't have a losing record in any of his last 27 seasons.

1986 NCAA Tournament

Summary: This is the only time a group of teams arrived at the Final Four with a total of at

1985-86 FINAL NATIONAL POLLS

AP	UPI	USA/CNN	SCHOOL (RECORD)	HEAD COACH
1	1	2	Duke (37-3)	Mike Krzyzewski
2	2	3	Kansas (35-4)	Larry Brown
3	4	4	Kentucky (32-4)	Eddie Sutton
4	3	10	St. John's (31-5)	Lou Carnesecca
5	5	14	Michigan (28-5)	Bill Frieder
6	6	6	Georgia Tech (27-7)	Bobby Cremins
7	7	1	Louisville (32-7)	Denny Crum
8	8	7	North Carolina (28-6)	Dean Smith
9	9	16	Syracuse (26-6)	Jim Boeheim
10	11	21	Notre Dame (23-6)	Digger Phelps
11	10	13	UNLV (33-5)	Jerry Tarkanian
12	12	15	Memphis State (28-6)	Dana Kirk
13	15	19	Georgetown (24-8)	John Thompson
14	13	20	Bradley (32-3)	Dick Versace
15	17	24	Oklahoma (26-9)	Billy Tubbs
16	14	—	Indiana (21-8)	Bob Knight
17	—	8	Navy (30-5)	Paul Evans
18	18	12	Michigan State (23-8)	Jud Heathcote
19	20	25	Illinois (22-10)	Lou Henson
20	16	—	Texas-El Paso (27-6)	Don Haskins
—	—	5	Louisiana State (26-12)	Dale Brown
—	—	9	Auburn (22-11)	Sonny Smith
—	—	11	N.C. State (21-13)	Jim Valvano
—	—	17	Cleveland State (29-4)	Kevin Mackey
—	19	18	Alabama (24-9)	Wimp Sanderson
—	—	22	Iowa State (22-11)	Johnny Orr
—	—	23	DePaul (18-13)	Joey Meyer

least 125 victories with Louisville (30-7), Duke (36-2), Kansas (35-3) and LSU (26-11) combining for a 127-23 record (.847). LSU had lost 10 of its last 17 regular-season games. The two hottest teams of the group—Louisville (16 consecutive victories) and Duke (21)—reached the final, where freshman Pervis Ellison collected 25 points and 11 rebounds to carry the Cardinals to a 72-69 triumph. Louisville's Billy Thompson finished the season with the lowest scoring average to lead an NCAA titlist since 1959 (14.9 points per game). Thompson was the Cardinals' top point producer in the tourncy (total of 110 points) after averaging a modest 4.9 ppg in his first seven playoff contests.

Outcome for Defending Champion: Villanova (23-14) finished in fourth place in the Big East before getting eliminated in the second round of the NCAA Tournament by Georgia Tech, 66-61. The Wildcats lost non-league games by double-digit margins to Lamar, UNLV and Missouri.

Star Gazing: Guard Johnny Dawkins scored 13 of Duke's first 25 points in the final and finished the tourney with 153. No other player scored more than 110.

Biggest Upset: Arkansas-Little Rock, a 17 1/2-point underdog, shocked No. 3 seed Notre

1985–86 NCAA CHAMPION: LOUISVILLE

SEASON STATISTICS OF LOUISVILLE REGULARS

PLAYER	POS.	CL.	G.	FG%	FT%	PPG	RPG
Billy Thompson	F	Sr.	39	.576	.714	14.9	7.8
Milt Wagner	G	Sr.	39	.495	.862	14.8	3.1
Pervis Ellison	C	Fr.	39	.554	.682	13.1	8.2
Herbert Crook	F	So.	39	.528	.688	11.8	6.5
Jeff Hall	G	Sr.	39	.530	.890	10.3	1.7
Tony Kimbro	F	Fr.	39	.572	.591	5.3	2.5
Mark McSwain	F	Jr.	28	.561	.717	3.6	2.9
Kenny Payne	F	Fr.	34	.437	.773	3.6	1.7
Kevin Walls	G	Fr.	27	.444	.750	2.1	0.4
TEAM TOTALS			39	.531	.733	79.4	37.2

Assists leader: Wagner 165. **Blocked shots leader:** Ellison 92. **Steals leader:** Wagner 52.

1986 FINAL FOUR CHAMPIONSHIP GAME

DALLAS, TX

DUKE (69)	MIN.	FG-A	FT-A	REB.	A	PF	PTS.
Henderson	28	5-15	4-4	4	4	5	14
Alarie	33	4-11	4-4	6	0	5	12
Bilas	26	2-3	0-0	3	0	4	4
Amaker	38	3-10	5-6	2	7	3	11
Dawkins	40	10-19	4-4	4	0	1	24
Ferry	20	1-2	2-2	4	0	2	4
Williams	2	0-1	0-0	0	0	0	0
King	13	0-1	0-1	0	1	2	0
Team				4			
TOTALS	200	25-62	19-21	27	12	22	69

FG%: .403. **FT%:** .905. **Blocks:** 0. **Turnovers:** 14. **Steals:** 13 (Amaker 7).

LOUISVILLE (72)	MIN.	FG-A	FT-A	REB.	A	PF	PTS.
Crook	32	5-9	0-3	12	5	2	10
Thompson	31	6-8	1-3	4	2	4	13
Ellison	35	10-14	5-6	11	1	4	25
Wagner	30	2-6	5-5	3	2	4	9
Hall	33	2-4	0-0	2	2	2	4
McSwain	17	2-4	1-2	3	2	1	5
Walls	8	0-1	0-0	1	0	2	0
Kimbro	14	2-4	2-2	2	2	1	6
Team				1			
TOTALS	200	29-50	14-21	39	16	20	72

FG%: .580. **FT%:** .667. **Blocks:** 7. **Turnovers:** 24 (Crook 9). **Steals:** 5. **Halftime:** Duke 37-34.

NATIONAL SEMIFINALS

KANSAS (67): Manning 2-9 0-0 4, Kellogg 11-15 0-0 22, Dreiling 1-7 4-4 6, Hunter 2-5 1-4 5, Thompson 5-12 3-3 13, Turgeon 1-1 0-0 2, Marshall 6-10 1-1 13, Piper 1-1 0-0 2. Team 29-60 (.483) 9-12 (.750) 67.

DUKE (71): Henderson 3-12 7-8 13, Alarie 4-13 4-6 12, Bilas 1-2 5-7 7, Amaker 2-5 3-4 7, Dawkins 11-17 2-4 24, Strickland 0-1 0-0 0, Ferry 4-5 0-1 8, King 0-0 0-0 0. Team 25-55 (.455) 21-30 (.700) 71.

Halftime: Duke 36-33.

LOUISIANA STATE (77): Williams 7-17 0-1 14, Redden 10-20 2-3 22, Blanton 3-5 3-6 9, Taylor 7-17 2-2 16, N. Wilson 7-15 1-1 15, Brown 0-1 1-2 1. Team 34-75 (.453) 9-15 (.600) 77.

LOUISVILLE (88): Crook 8-13 0-1 16, Thompson 10-11 2-5 22, Ellison 5-11 1-2 11, Wagner 8-16 6-6 22, Hall 6-11 2-2 14, McSwain 1-2 1-1 3, Walls 0-2 0-0 0, Kimbro 0-2 0-0 0. Team 38-68 (.559) 12-17 (.708) 88.

Halftime: Louisiana State 44-36.

ALL-TOURNAMENT TEAM

Mark Alarie, F, Sr., Duke (24 points, 14 rebounds in final two games)
Tommy Amaker, G, Jr., Duke (18 points, 13 assists)
Johnny Dawkins, G, Sr., Duke (48 points, seven rebounds)
*Pervis Ellison, F-C, Fr., Louisville (36 points, 24 rebounds)
Billy Thompson, F, Sr., Louisville (35 points, 14 rebounds)

*Named Most Outstanding Player.

Dame in the first round of the Midwest Regional (90-83).

One and Only: Louisville became the only team to win an NCAA crown after setting or tying an existing school record for most defeats the previous season (19-18 mark in 1984-85). . . . Cleveland State became the only school seeded in the bottom of a bracket (13 through 16) to reach a Sweet 16. The Vikings, leading the nation in scoring margin, were seeded No. 14 when they won two East Regional games in their only tourney appearance.

Numbers Game: LSU, the No. 11 seed in the Southeast Regional, is the only double-digit seeded team to reach the Final Four. The Tigers reached the national semifinals after finishing in a tie for fifth place in the SEC with a .500 record (9-9). . . . Maryland earned the best seed (#5) in tourney history for an at-large squad with a losing conference record (6-8 in the ACC). . . . Nebraska, coached by Moe Iba, appeared in the NCAA Tournament for the first time. . . . Temple's Tim Perry grabbed a playoff-high 18 rebounds in a 61-50 first-round triumph over Jacksonville in the Midwest Regional. . . . Navy's David Robinson (35 points vs. Syracuse) and Northeastern's Reggie Lewis (35 vs. Oklahoma) tied for the highest-scoring game in the tourney. . . . Kentucky's Kenny Walker hit all 11 of his field-goal attempts in a 71-64 victory over Western Kentucky in the second round of the Southeast Regional. . . . A record four Sun Belt Conference members—UAB, Jacksonville, Old Dominion and Western Kentuckly—qualified for the NCAA playoffs.

What Might Have Been: Forwards Mark Alarie and David Henderson and guard Tommy

1986 CHAMPIONSHIP BRACKET

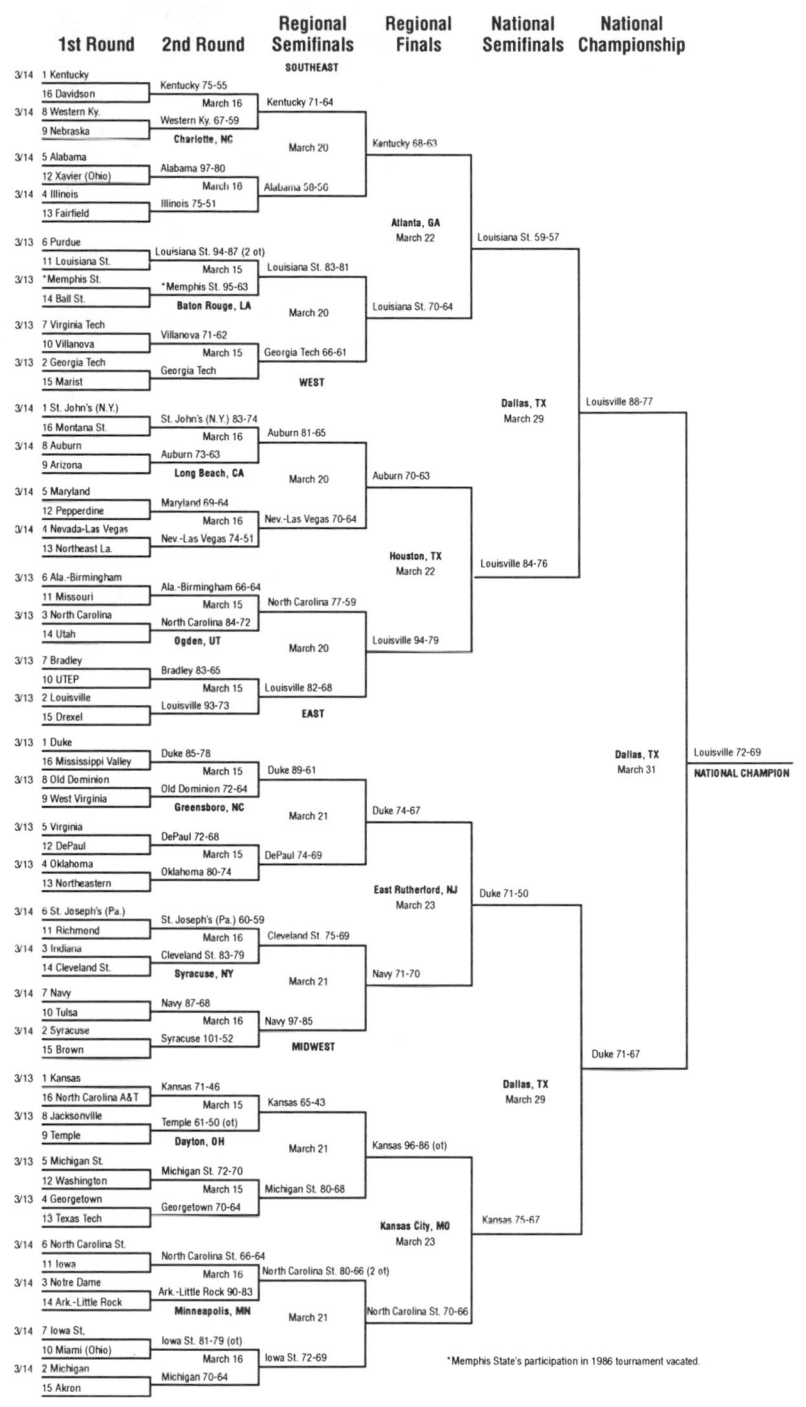

	1st Round	2nd Round	Regional Semifinals	Regional Finals	National Semifinals	National Championship

SOUTHEAST

3/14 1 Kentucky
16 Davidson — Kentucky 75-55
March 16
3/14 8 Western Ky. — Western Ky. 67-59
9 Nebraska
Charlotte, NC
Kentucky 71-64
March 20
3/14 5 Alabama
12 Xavier (Ohio) — Alabama 97-80
March 16
3/14 4 Illinois — Illinois 75-51
13 Fairfield
Alabama 58-56
Kentucky 68-63

Atlanta, GA
March 22

3/13 6 Purdue
11 Louisiana St. — Louisiana St. 94-87 (2 ot)
March 15
3/13 *Memphis St. — *Memphis St. 95-63
14 Ball St.
Baton Rouge, LA
Louisiana St. 83-81
March 20
3/13 7 Virginia Tech
10 Villanova — Villanova 71-62
March 15
3/13 2 Georgia Tech — Georgia Tech
15 Marist
Georgia Tech 66-61
Louisiana St. 70-64

Louisiana St. 59-57

WEST

3/14 1 St. John's (N.Y.)
16 Montana St. — St. John's (N.Y.) 83-74
March 16
3/14 8 Auburn — Auburn 73-63
9 Arizona
Long Beach, CA
Auburn 81-65
March 20
3/14 5 Maryland
12 Pepperdine — Maryland 69-64
March 16
3/14 4 Nevada-Las Vegas — Nev.-Las Vegas 74-51
13 Northeast La.
Nev.-Las Vegas 70-64
Auburn 70-63

Houston, TX
March 22

3/13 6 Ala.-Birmingham
11 Missouri — Ala.-Birmingham 66-64
March 15
3/13 3 North Carolina — North Carolina 84-72
14 Utah
Ogden, UT
North Carolina 77-59
March 20
3/13 7 Bradley
10 UTEP — Bradley 83-65
March 15
3/13 2 Louisville — Louisville 93-73
15 Drexel
Louisville 82-68
Louisville 94-79

Louisville 84-76

Louisville 88-77

Dallas, TX
March 29

EAST

3/13 1 Duke
16 Mississippi Valley — Duke 85-78
March 15
3/13 8 Old Dominion — Old Dominion 72-64
9 West Virginia
Greensboro, NC
Duke 89-61
March 21
3/13 5 Virginia
12 DePaul — DePaul 72-68
March 15
3/13 4 Oklahoma — Oklahoma 80-74
13 Northeastern
DePaul 74-69
Duke 74-67

East Rutherford, NJ
March 23

3/14 6 St. Joseph's (Pa.)
11 Richmond — St. Joseph's (Pa.) 60-59
March 16
3/14 3 Indiana — Cleveland St. 83-79
14 Cleveland St.
Syracuse, NY
Cleveland St. 75-69
March 21
3/14 7 Navy
10 Tulsa — Navy 87-68
March 16
3/14 2 Syracuse — Syracuse 101-52
15 Brown
Navy 97-85
Navy 71-70

Duke 71-50

Duke 71-67

Louisville 72-69
NATIONAL CHAMPION

Dallas, TX
March 31

MIDWEST

3/13 1 Kansas
16 North Carolina A&T — Kansas 71-46
March 15
3/13 8 Jacksonville — Temple 61-50 (ot)
9 Temple
Dayton, OH
Kansas 65-43
March 21
3/13 5 Michigan St.
12 Washington — Michigan St. 72-70
March 15
3/13 4 Georgetown — Georgetown 70-64
13 Texas Tech
Michigan St. 80-68
Kansas 96-86 (ot)

Kansas City, MO
March 23

3/14 6 North Carolina St.
11 Iowa — North Carolina St. 66-64
March 16
3/14 3 Notre Dame — Ark.-Little Rock 90-83
14 Ark.-Little Rock
Minneapolis, MN
North Carolina St. 80-66 (2 ot)
March 21
3/14 7 Iowa St.
10 Miami (Ohio) — Iowa St. 81-79 (ot)
March 16
3/14 2 Michigan — Michigan 70-64
15 Akron
Iowa St. 72-69
North Carolina St. 70-66

Kansas 75-67

Dallas, TX
March 29

*Memphis State's participation in 1986 tournament vacated.

Amaker combined to make more than 50 percent of their field-goal attempts for Duke in the 1985-86 season. If only they combined to hit 39 percent instead of 33.3 percent (12 of 36) in the championship game, the Blue Devils could have defeated Louisville rather than losing 72-69. . . . Oklahoma (26-9) might have advanced farther in the playoffs if Wayman Tisdale had exercised his remaining eligibility instead of defecting to the NBA and if center Stacey King hadn't missed the second semester because of scholastic shortcomings. . . . Louisiana Tech (20-14 without Karl Malone) and SMU (18-11 without Carl Wright) probably would have participated in the NCAA Tournament instead of the NIT if key players didn't leave school early. . . . LSU (26-12) could have fared better at the Final Four if Jerry Reynolds didn't forsake his final year of eligibility to enter the NBA.

Putting Things in Perspective: Kansas (35-4) defeated Louisville twice by a total of seven points before losing to Duke in the national semifinals. The Cardinals lost six of 15 games in one stretch the first half of the season.

Scoring Leader: Johnny Dawkins, Duke (153 points, 25.5 ppg).

Highest Scoring Average: Len Bias, Maryland (57 points, 28.5 ppg).

Rebounding Leader: Pervis Ellison, Louisville (57 rebounds, 9.5 rpg).

Highest Rebounding Average: Tim Perry, Temple (26 rebounds, 13 rpg).

1986-87

AT A GLANCE

NCAA Champion: Indiana (30-4; coached by Bob Knight; tied for first place in Big Ten with Purdue with a 15-3 record).

NIT Champion: Southern Mississippi (23-11; coached by M.K. Turk; tied for third place in Metro with a 6-6 record).

New Rules: The three-point field goal is introduced nationwide and set at 19-feet 9 inches from the center of

Indiana guard Steve Alford tips one in.

the basket. . . . A coach may leave the confines of the bench at any time without penalty to correct a mistake by a scorer or timer. A technical foul is assessed if there is no mistake (rule changed the next year to a timeout). . . . A television replay may be used to prevent or rectify a scorer's or timer's mistake or a malfunction of the clock. . . . All 64 teams selected for the NCAA Tournament are subjected to drug testing for the first time.

NCAA Probation: Bradley, East Tennessee State, Memphis State

NCAA Consensus First-Team All-Americans: Steve Alford, G, Sr., Indiana; Danny Manning, F-C, Jr., Kansas; David Robinson, C, Sr., Navy; Kenny Smith, G, Sr., North Carolina; Reggie Williams, F-G, Sr., Georgetown.

National Player of the Year: Robinson (28.2 ppg, 11.8 rpg, 4.5 bpg, 59.1 FG%).

National Coaches of the Year: Temple's John Chaney (32-4/USBWA); Iowa's Tom Davis (30-5/AP); Indiana's Bob Knight (30-4/Naismith); Providence's Rick Pitino (25-9/NABC), and Georgetown's John Thompson (29-5/UPI).

Controversial legislation affecting academic eligibility was implemented. NCAA Bylaw 5-1-(j), introduced as Proposition 48 at the NCAA Convention in 1983, specified that potential qualifers for an athletic scholarship at A Division I school must meet two requirements:

• An accumulative minimum 2.0 GPA in a core curriculum of at least 11 specified academic courses in the areas of English, math, social science and natural or physical science.

• A score of at least 700 on the verbal and math sections of the SAT or a score of 15 on the ACT.

The most prominent recruits who lost their freshman year of eligibility after failing to meet the new scholastic guidelines were Nick Anderson (Illinois), Chris Brooks (West Virginia), Terry Mills (Michigan), Anthony Pendelton (Iowa), Keith Robinson (Notre Dame) and Rumeal Robinson (Michigan). Pendelton enrolled at Southern Cal after Iowa released him from his letter-of-intent.

Also making an immediate impact was the new three-point field-goal shooting rule. Consider:

• NCAA champion Indiana set an NCAA single-season record by hitting more than half of its three-point field-goal attempts (130 of 256 for 50.8 percent).

• Eastern Kentucky hit 11 consecutive three-point field-goal attempts and was 15 of 18 overall from beyond the arc in a game against North Carolina-Asheville.

• Butler's Darrin Fitzgerald averaged almost 13 three-point field-goal attempts per game on his way to setting an NCAA single-season record for most treys with 158 (see accompanying box).

• Niagara's Gary Bossert set an NCAA record for most consecutive successful three-pointers in a game with 11 vs. Siena.

UNLV's Mark Wade set an NCAA single-season record with 406 assists. . . . Northeastern's Andre LaFleur finished his career as the tallest player (6-3) with more than 800 assists. He had 894. . . . The turnover in the Division I coaching

Syracuse forward Derrick Coleman was named to the 1987 All-Tournament Team.

ranks has never been higher as 66 schools had new mentors. Thirty-five of the new coaches were in their first year at the Division I level. . . . Temple's only Atlantic 10 defeat, a 64-61 setback against West Virginia, snapped the Owls' 33-game McGonigle Hall winning streak.

For the only time in ACC history the league had a team finish undefeated in conference play (North Carolina) and a team finish winless (Maryland) in the same season. . . . Horace Grant (21 ppg) became the only Clemson player to average more than 20 points per game since 1969-70. He is the only player in Clemson history to become an NCAA consensus first- or second-team All-American. . . . Virginia Tech incurred its first losing record (10-18) in 32 seasons. . . . Memphis State erased a seven-point deficit in the last 15 seconds to defeat Oral Roberts, 59-58, although the Tigers fell out of the Top 20 for the first time

1986-87 INDIVIDUAL LEADERS

SCORING

PLAYER	PTS.	AVG.
Houston, Army	953	32.9
Hopson, Ohio St.	958	29.0
Robinson, Navy	903	28.2
Bailey, Wagner	788	28.1
Hawkins, Bradley	788	27.2
Fitzgerald, Butler	734	26.2
Elmore, VMI	713	25.5
Ross, American	683	25.3
Queenan, Lehigh	720	24.8
Larkin, Xavier	792	24.7

REBOUNDING

PLAYER	REB.	AVG.
Lane, Pittsburgh	444	13.5
Dudley, Yale	320	13.3
Moore, Loyola (Ill.)	360	12.4
Robinson, Navy	378	11.8
Rowsom, UNC-Wilm.	345	11.5
Agbejemisin, Wagner	333	11.5
McCann, Morehead St.	317	11.3
Stewart, Texas S.	316	10.9
Besselink, Conn.	300	10.7
Anderson, Houston	318	10.6

ASSISTS

PLAYER	AST.	AVG.
Johnson, Southern (La.)	333	10.7
Wade, UNLV	406	10.7
Fairley, Baptist	270	9.6
Bogues, Wake Forest	276	9.6
Van Drost, Wagner	260	9.3
Washington, Mid. Tenn. St.	255	8.8
Manuel, Bradley	237	8.8
Smith, Old Dominion	229	8.2
Davis, Marist	227	8.1
Chisholm, Delaware	220	7.9

BLOCKED SHOTS

PLAYER	BLK.	AVG.
Robinson, Navy	144	4.5
Lewis, Maryland	114	4.4
Fonville, Jackson St.	112	3.9
Blake, St. Joseph's	87	3.6
Comegys, DePaul	108	3.5
Perry, Temple	116	3.2
Baugh, Howard	90	3.2
Smith, Pittsburgh	106	3.2
Smith, Ball St.	86	3.2
Brow, Virginia Tech	86	3.1

STEALS

PLAYER	STL.	AVG.
Fairley, Baptist	114	4.1
Usitalo, Boise St.	105	3.5
Jeter, Delaware St.	96	3.4
Ford, Texas-Arl.	96	3.4
Washington, Mid. Tenn. St.	93	3.2
Davis, Marist	88	3.1
Anderson, Drexel	85	3.0
Williams, Baylor	93	3.0
Chisholm, Delaware	84	3.0
Blye, Md.-E. Shore	68	3.0

FIELD GOAL PERCENTAGE

PLAYER	FGM	FGA	PCT.
Williams, Princeton	163	232	.703
Howard, E. Ky.	156	230	.678
Grant, Clemson	256	390	.656
Godbolt, La. Tech	191	295	.647
Williams, N.C. A&T	174	273	.637
Tate, Arkansas St.	216	339	.637
Leckner, Wyoming	246	390	.631
Manning, Kansas	347	562	.617
Rebholz, Hofstra	139	226	.615
Himes, Davidson	196	319	.614

FREE THROW PERCENTAGE

PLAYER	FTM	FTA	PCT.
Houston, Army	268	294	.912
Johnson, Mich. St.	111	122	.910
Haffner, Evansville	80	88	.909
Blackwell, Temple	123	136	.904
Smith, BYU	103	114	.904
White, Tennessee	165	183	.902
McPhee, Gonzaga	105	118	.890
Alford, Indiana	160	180	.889
Adams, Hardin-Simm.	87	98	.888
Farmer, Alabama	118	133	.887

THREE-POINT FIELD GOAL PERCENTAGE

PLAYER	FGM	FGA	PCT.
Jones, Pr. View	64	112	.571
Rhodes, S. F. Austin St.	58	106	.547
Davis, G. Mason	45	84	.536
Dimak, S. F. Austin St.	46	86	.535
Alford, Indiana	107	202	.530

THREE-POINT FIELD GOALS PER GAME

PLAYER	FGM	AVG.
Fitzgerald, Butler	158	5.6
Brooks, UC Irvine	111	4.0
Banks, UNLV	152	3.9
Ivory, Miss. Valley St.	109	3.9
Ross, San Diego St.	104	3.7

1986-87 TEAM LEADERS

SCORING OFFENSE

SCHOOL	PTS.	AVG.
UNLV	3612	92.6
North Carolina	3285	91.2
Oklahoma	3028	89.1
Michigan	2821	88.2
Southern (La.)	2706	87.3

SCORING DEFENSE

SCHOOL	PTS.	AVG.
Southwest Missouri St.	1958	57.6
St. Mary's (Calif.)	1766	58.9
Wis.-Green Bay	1714	59.1
Notre Dame	1902	59.4
San Diego	1810	60.3

SCORING MARGIN

SCHOOL	OFF.	DEF.	MAR.
UNLV	92.6	75.5	17.1
North Carolina	91.2	74.9	16.4
Clemson	86.1	71.5	14.6
DePaul	76.2	62.5	13.7
Georgetown	77.8	64.2	13.5

WON-LOST PERCENTAGE

SCHOOL	W-L	PCT.
UNLV	37-2	.949
DePaul	28-3	.903
North Carolina	32-4	.889
Temple	32-4	.889
Indiana	30-4	.882

FIELD GOAL PERCENTAGE

SCHOOL	FGM	FGA	PCT.
Princeton	601	1111	.541
North Carolina	1238	2304	.537
Marshall	946	1777	.532
Clemson	990	1873	.529
Lafayette	813	1544	.527

FIELD GOAL PERCENTAGE DEFENSE

SCHOOL	FGM	FGA	PCT.
San Diego	660	1645	.401
Houston Baptist	740	1835	.403
Jackson St.	703	1721	.408
Navy	814	1961	.415
DePaul	769	1850	.416

FREE THROW PERCENTAGE

SCHOOL	FTM	FTA	PCT.
Alabama	521	662	.787
Army	491	626	.784
Michigan St.	408	529	.771
Northern Iowa	390	507	.769
UC Irvine	532	693	.768

REBOUND MARGIN

SCHOOL	OWN	OPP.	MAR.
Iowa	43.1	31.5	11.5
Pittsburgh	41.5	31.8	9.7
Western Kentucky	39.6	31.5	8.0
Georgetown	40.4	32.4	8.0
Auburn	39.6	32.0	7.6

THREE-POINT FIELD GOAL PERCENTAGE

SCHOOL	FGM	FGA	PCT.
Indiana	130	256	50.8
Miss. Valley St.	161	322	50.0
Stephen F. Austin St.	120	241	49.8
Niagara	128	275	46.5
Eastern Michigan	144	310	46.5

THREE-POINT FIELD GOALS PER GAME

SCHOOL	FGM	AVG.
Providence	280	8.2
UNLV	309	7.9
Eastern Kentucky	216	7.2
Butler	198	7.1
UC Irvine	187	6.7

in six years. Memphis State's new head coach was Larry Finch, who was promoted after Dana Kirk encountered extensive legal problems. Kirk was on the verge of becoming the school's all-time winningest coach after compiling a 158-58 record (.731) in seven seasons.

UNC Charlotte lost 15 consecutive contests to UAB until beating the Blazers, 76-63. . . . James Madison, which compiled a 5-23 record the previous season, improved by 14 games to 20-10 under coach John Thurston. . . . Virginia Military won 29 percent of its contests overall and was 50 games below .500 in Southern Conference competition in the last six seasons despite VMI having five league freshman of the year winners in that span.

Forward Ken Norman became the first Illinois player since 1952 to become an NCAA consensus first- or second-team All-American. . . . Colgate ended its 49-game league losing streak and 32-game losing string overall. . . . Among the schools benefitting from the impact of freshmen was Maryland-Baltimore County, which had three yearlings score more than 13 points per game— forwards Gamel Spencer (13.8 ppg) and Duane Faust (13.7 ppg) and guard Larry Simmons (13.5 ppg). . . . Maryland's Bob Wade and Oklahoma State's Leonard Hamilton became the first African American head coaches in the ACC and Big Eight, respectively. Wade got off on the wrong foot as the Terrapins compiled a 9-17 record for their first losing season in 18 years.

Setting school single-game scoring standards were Butler's Fitzgerald (54 points vs. Detroit), Army's Kevin Houston (53 vs. Fordham in overtime of MAAC Tournament opener), Tennessee's Tony White (51 vs. Auburn), Rutgers' Eric Riggins (tied with 51 vs. Penn State in double overtime), Lehigh's Daren Queenan (49 vs. Bucknell in double overtime in ECC Tournament semifinals), Dartmouth's Jim Barton (48 at Brown in OT), Washington State's Brian Quinnett (45 vs. Loyola Marymount) and UNC Wilmington's Brian Rowsom (39 at East Carolina).

Watson's uprising is the highest in Western Athletic Conference annals and Riggins' outburst

is the highest in Atlantic 10 Conference history. Fitzgerald established a Midwestern Collegiate Conference single-season mark by averaging 31.3 points per game. Queenan's record-setting performance came one night after teammate Mike Polaha had moved atop the school single-game scoring chart with 42 points against Drexel in double overtime in the ECC Tournament quarterfinals. . . . Army's Houston (32.9 ppg), Navy's David Robinson (28.2) and Fairfield's Troy Bradford (22.7) set school records for highest scoring average in a single season. . . . Robinson set a record for most points in a Colonial Athletic Association game when he poured in 45 against James Madison. It was one of five contests during the campaign where Robinson scored at least 43 points.

UNLV (37-2/coached by Jerry Tarkanian), Temple (32-4/John Chaney), Syracuse (31-7/Jim Boeheim), Iowa (30-5/Tom Davis), DePaul (28-3/Joey Meyer), Alabama (28-5/Wimp Sanderson), Southwest Missouri State (28-6/Charlie Spoonhour), New Orleans (26-4/Benny Dees), Arkansas-Little Rock (26-11/Mike Newell), Clemson (25-6/Cliff Ellis), San Diego (24-6/Hank Egan) and Southern Mississippi (23-11/M.K. Turk) had their winningest seasons in school Division I history. Northeastern (27-7/Karl Fogel), Marshall (25-6/Rick Huckabay), Pitt (25-8/Paul Evans), Texas Christian (24-7/Jim Killingsworth), Central Michigan (22-8/Charles Coles) and Charleston Southern (21-9/Tommy Gaither) tied their school Division I records for most victories in a single season. Davis was in his first year as coach of the Hawkeyes.

Central Michigan captured the Mid-American Conference regular-season championship after finishing in a tie for sixth place the previous year. Evansville grabbed a share of the Midwestern Collegiate Conference regular-season crown after finishing in sixth place the previous year. . . . Colorado's 26-game losing streak against Big Eight competition ended when the Buffaloes beat Iowa State, 77-74. . . . Northeast Louisiana lost four of its last five games to suffer its only losing record (13-15) since 1960-61. . . . Texas Christian made its first Top 20 appearance in a final wire-service

BOMBS AWAY

Butler guard Darrin Fitzgerald had at least three baskets from three-point range in all 28 games on his way to establishing NCAA single-season records for highest total of three-pointers (158) and most three-pointers per game (5.8). He averaged an amazing 7.6 treys per contest in a 10-game, mid-season stretch.

OPPONENT	3-POINT FGM-FGA	PCT.
DePauw (Ind.)	5-11	.455
Northwestern	3-8	.375
Ball State	4-8	.500
at Indiana State	4-8	.500
at Valparaiso	4-12	.333
Miss. Valley State	6-9	.667
Ball State	4-11	.364
Indianapolis	4-13	.308
Indiana State	3-10	.300
Nebraska#	3-6	.500
George Mason#	6-10	.600
Western Kentucky	5-15	.333
at Loyola (Ill.)	10-15	.667
at Detroit	6-11	.546
Evansville	9-14	.643
St. Louis	7-15	.467
at Northern Illinois	6-21	.286
at Oral Roberts	7-14	.500
Xavier	7-13	.539
Dayton	7-19	.368
Loyola (Ill.)	5-13	.385
Detroit	12-22	.546
Valparaiso	6-16	.375
at Evansville	3-11	.273
at St. Louis	8-17	.471
at Xavier	4-12	.333
Oral Roberts	5-14	.357
Xavier*	5-14	.357
TOTALS	**158-362**	**.437**

#Rochester (N.Y.) Classic.
*Midwestern Collegiate Conference.

poll since 1959. . . . Texas-San Antonio's Lennell Moore grabbed a school-record 25 rebounds against Centenary. . . . Utica (N.Y.) competed in its final campaign at the Division I level. . . . Arkansas erased a 21-point deficit midway through the second half and edged Arkansas State, 67-64, in overtime in the first round of the NIT.

1987 NCAA Tournament

Summary: Indiana became the first school to win the NCAA championship in four different decades (previous titles were in 1940, 1953 and 1976). Junior college recruit Keith Smart, a guard who was Indiana's fifth-leading scorer, tallied 12 of the Hoosiers' last 15 points, including a 15-foot jumper from the left baseline with five seconds remaining to give them a 74-73 victory over Syracuse in the championship game. Indiana's well-balanced attack featured Smart and the four other

1986-87 FINAL NATIONAL POLLS

AP	UPI	USA/CNN	SCHOOL (RECORD)	HEAD COACH
1	1	2	UNLV (37-2)	Jerry Tarkanian
2	3	4	North Carolina (32-4)	Dean Smith
3	2	1	Indiana (30-4)	Bob Knight
4	4	7	Georgetown (29-5)	John Thompson
5	5	9	DePaul (28-3)	Joey Meyer
6	7	5	Iowa (30-5)	Tom Davis
7	6	13	Purdue (25-5)	Gene Keady
8	8	17	Temple (32-4)	John Chaney
9	9	8	Alabama (28-5)	Wimp Sanderson
10	10	3	Syracuse (31-7)	Jim Boeheim
11	11	20	Illinois (23-8)	Lou Henson
12	12	18	Pittsburgh (25-8)	Paul Evans
13	15	22	Clemson (25-6)	Cliff Ellis
14	14	23	Missouri (24-10)	Norm Stewart
15	13	21	UCLA (25-7)	Walt Hazzard
16	19	–	New Orleans (26-4)	Benny Dees
17	–	11	Duke (24-9)	Mike Krzyzewski
18	18	16	Notre Dame (24-8)	Digger Phelps
19	16	25	Texas Christian (24-7)	Jim Killingsworth
20	–	14	Kansas (25-11)	Larry Brown
–	–	6	Providence (25-9)	Rick Pitino
–	–	10	Louisiana State (24-15)	Dale Brown
–	–	15	Florida (23-11)	Norman Sloan
–	17	19	Wyoming (24-10)	Jim Brandenburg
–	19	12	Oklahoma (24-10)	Billy Tubbs
–	19	–	Texas-El Paso (25-7)	Don Haskins
–	–	24	SW Missouri State (28-6)	Charlie Spoonhour

starters—Steve Alford, Ricky Calloway, Dean Garrett and Daryl Thomas—each having at least one 20-point game and two contests with a minimum of 18 points in the playoffs. IU was fined $10,000 by the NCAA and coach Bob Knight reprimanded after he banged his fist on the scorer's table during the Midwest regional final against LSU.

Outcome for Defending Champion: Louisville (18-14) won the Metro Conference regular-season championship but didn't participate in a national postseason tournament. The Cardinals started the season by losing all three of their assignments in the Great Alaska Shootout.

Star Gazing: Smart, the Final Four Most Outstanding Player, is the only former junior college player to win the award. Indiana looked to Alford for the final shot, but the All-America guard was covered. "I wasn't surprised I got the ball," Smart said. "I was surprised it went in." The biggest surprise might have been that he ever enrolled at a major college. As a junior in high school in Baton Rouge, La., he was only 5-3. He grew to 5-7 as a senior, but that season ended early when Smart broke his arm riding a motorcycle during the season. Before attending Garden City (Kan.) Community College, he spent a year flip-

1986–87 NCAA CHAMPION: INDIANA

SEASON STATISTICS OF INDIANA REGULARS

PLAYER	POS.	CL.	G.	FG%	FT%	PPG	RPG
Steve Alford	G	Sr.	34	.474	.889	22.0	2.6
Daryl Thomas	F	Sr.	34	.538	.786	15.7	5.7
Rick Calloway	F	So.	29	.531	.742	12.6	4.3
Dean Garrett	C	Jr.	34	.542	.635	11.4	8.5
Keith Smart	G	Jr.	34	.517	.841	11.2	2.9
Steve Eyl	F	Jr.	34	.648	.674	3.0	3.4
Joe Hillman	G	Jr.	32	.483	.742	2.5	1.2
Kreigh Smith	G-F	Jr.	25	.500	.857	1.5	0.8
Todd Meier	F-C	Sr.	29	.450	.591	1.1	1.5
TEAM TOTALS			34	.513	.767	82.5	35.0

Three-point field goals leader: Alford (107 of 202, .530). **Assists leader:** Alford 123. **Blocked shots leader:** Garrett 93. **Steals leader:** Thomas 45.

1987 FINAL FOUR CHAMPIONSHIP GAME

NEW ORLEANS, LA

SYRACUSE (73)	MIN.	FG-A	FT-A	REB.	A	PF	PTS.
Triche	32	3-9	2-4	1	1	4	8
Coleman	37	3-7	2-4	19	1	2	8
Seikaly	34	7-13	4-6	10	1	3	18
Monroe	32	5-11	0-1	2	3	1	12
Douglas	39	8-15	2-2	2	7	3	20
Brower	9	3-3	1-3	1	0	3	7
Thompson	17	0-2	0-0	3	1	0	0
TOTALS	200	29-60	11-20	38	14	16	73

FG%: .483. **FT%:** .550. **Three-point goals:** 4 of 10 (Monroe 2-8, Douglas 2-2). **Blocks:** 7. **Turnovers:** 14. **Steals:** 5.

INDIANA (74)	MIN.	FG-A	FT-A	REB.	A	PF	PTS.
Calloway	14	0-3	0-0	2	1	3	0
Thomas	40	8-18	4-7	7	1	1	20
Garrett	33	5-10	0-0	10	0	4	10
Alford	40	8-15	0-0	3	5	2	23
Smart	35	9-15	3-4	5	6	2	21
Meier	4	0-0	0-1	1	0	0	0
Eyl	13	0-0	0-0	1	1	2	0
Smith	1	0-0	0-0	1	0	1	0
Hillman	20	0-1	0-0	2	6	2	0
Team				4			
TOTALS	200	30-62	7-12	35	20	17	74

FG%: .484. **FT%:** .583. **Three-point goals:** 7 of 11 (Alford 7-10, Smart 0-1). **Blocks:** 3. **Turnovers:** 11. **Steals:** 7.
Halftime: Indiana 34-33.

NATIONAL SEMIFINALS

PROVIDENCE (63): Kipfer 4-10 0-1 8, Lewis 2-12 2-2 7, Duda 2-7 0-1 4, Brooks 4-9 0-0 9, Donovan 3-12 1-1 8, Screen 5-6 7-10 18, Shamsid-Deen 1-2 0-0 2, Conlon 1-1 0-0 2, D. Wright 1-4 0-0 3, S. Wright 1-3 0-0 2, Snedeker 0-0 0-0 0. Team 24-66 (.364) 10-15 (.667) 63.

SYRACUSE (77): Triche 4-10 4-5 12, Coleman 4-6 4-7 12, Seikaly 4-11 8-11 16, Monroe 4-9 6-10 17, Douglas 5-11 2-6 12, Brower 0-1 0-0 0, Thompson 3-5 1-3 7, Harried 0-0 1-2 1. Team 24-53 (.453) 26-44 (.591) 77.

Halftime: Syracuse 36-26. **Three-point field goals:** Providence (5-19). Syracuse (3-8).

UNLV (93): Paddio 2-13 0-0 6, Gilliam 14-26 4-6 32, Basnight 3-4 0-1 6, Wade 1-6 1-2 4, Banks 12-23 4-6 38, Robinson 0-0 0-0 0, Graham 0-5 1-4 1, Hudson 3-4 0-0 6, Willard 0-1 0-0 0. Team 35-82 (.427) 10-19 (.526) 93.

INDIANA (97): Alford 10-19 11-13 33, Smart 5-7 4-5 14, Garrett 7-10 4-5 18, Calloway 6-10 0-0 12, Thomas 3-5 0-0 6, Meier 0-0 0-0 0, Eyl 3-3 1-2 7, Smith 0-2 0-0 0, Hillman 3-4 1-3 7. Team 37-60 (.617) 21-28 (.750) 97.

Halftime: Indiana 53-47. **Three-point field goals:** UNLV (13-35). Indiana (2-4).

ALL-TOURNAMENT TEAM

Steve Alford, G, Sr., Indiana (56 points, nine three-pointers in final two games)
Derrick Coleman, F, Fr., Syracuse (20 points, 31 rebounds, five blocked shots)
Sherman Douglas, G, Soph., Syracuse (32 points, 13 rebounds, 13 assists)
Armon Gilliam, F-C, Sr., UNLV (32 points, 10 rebounds/one game)
*Keith Smart, G, Jr., Indiana (35 points, seven rebounds)

*Named Most Outstanding Player.

ping hamburgers at a fast-food restaurant. "I made that same shot on the playground hundreds of times," Smart said. "It was actually nothing special."

Biggest Upsets: Xavier (13th seed) over Missouri (4), 70-69; Southwest Missouri State (13) over Clemson (4), 65-60, and Austin Peay State (14) over Illinois (3), 68-67.

One and Only: Walt Hazzard is the only Final Four Most Outstanding Player (UCLA '64) to later coach his alma mater in the tournament (1-1 playoff record with the Bruins). . . . UNLV became the only school to win a regional final game in which it trailed by more than 12 points at halftime. The Rebels were behind Iowa at intermission in the West Regional final by 16 points

(58-42) before rallying to win (84-81). . . . Iowa became the only school ever to have as many as 14 different players score in a playoff game when the Hawkeyes hammered Santa Clara, 99-76, in the first round of the West Regional.

Numbers Game: Georgetown is the only school to defeat two eventual Final Four teams by double-digit margins in the same conference tournament. The Hoyas whipped Providence by 18 points and Syracuse by 10 to win the Big East Tournament before they were eliminated by Providence in the Southeast Regional final of the NCAA playoffs. . . . Danny Manning is the only player to score more than 62 percent of his team's points in an NCAA Tournament game. He supplied 62.7 percent of Kansas' offense by scoring

1987 CHAMPIONSHIP BRACKET

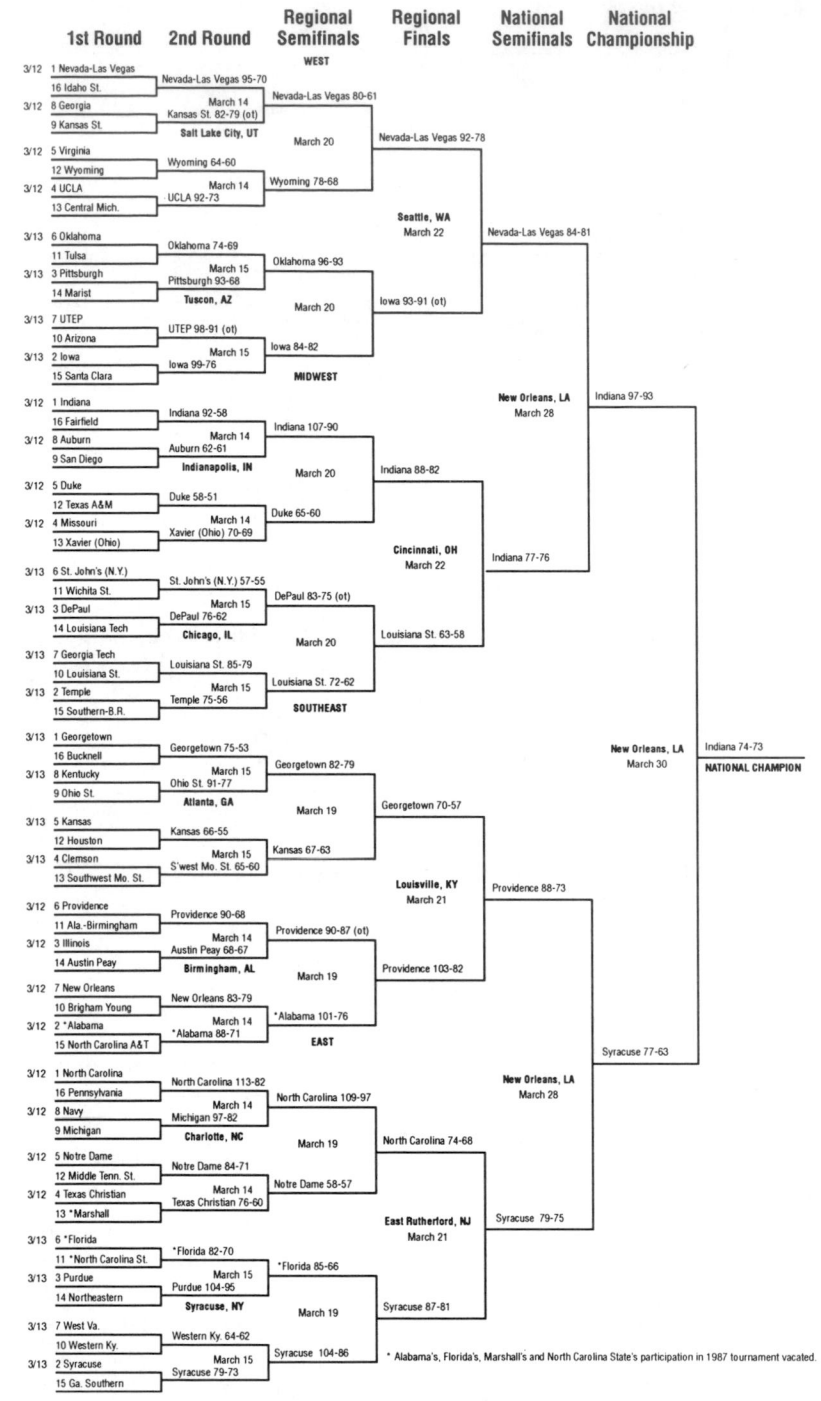

42 points in the Jayhawks' 67-63 victory against Southwest Missouri State in the second round of the Southeast Regional. . . . UNLV guard Freddie Banks scored more points than any player in a Final Four game without being selected to the All-Tournament team (38 in a 97-93 defeat in the national semifinals against eventual champion Indiana). . . . The record for most assists in an NCAA playoff game was set by UNLV playmaker Mark Wade with 18 in a 97-93 loss against Indiana (national semifinals). Wade also established the record for most assists in a single playoff series with 61 in five games. He had at least nine assists in each of the five contests while scoring a total of just 13 points. Wade finished his career with an average of 11.6 assists in eight playoff games. . . . David Robinson furnished 61 percent of Navy's offense by scoring a school-record and tourney-high 50 points in the Middies' 97-82 loss against Michigan in the opening round of the East Regional. . . . Florida, coached by Norman Sloan, appeared in the NCAA Tournament for the first time. . . . Wyoming's Fennis Dembo hit all 16 of his free throws to finish with 41 points in a 78-68 triumph over UCLA in the second round of the West Regional. . . . TCU, coached by Jim Killingsworth, participated in the NCAA playoffs for the first time in 16 years.

What Might Have Been: Forward Derrick Coleman and guards Stephen Thompson and Howard Triche combined to shoot 51.6 percent from the floor for Syracuse in the 1986-87 season. If only they combined to hit 38.9 percent instead of 33.3 percent (six of 18) in the championship game, the Orangemen could have defeated Indiana rather than losing by one point. Coleman's tourney-high 19 rebounds were in vain in the final. . . . Georgia (18-12/without Cedric Henderson), Louisiana State (24-15/John Williams), North Carolina State (20-15/Chris Washburn), St. John's (21-9/Walter Berry) and Syracuse (31-7/Pearl Washington) might have fared better in the playoffs if standout players had exercised their remaining eligibility instead of defecting to the NBA.

Putting Things in Perspective: Pacific-10 runner-up Arizona, minus standout guard Steve Kerr (knee injury), was eliminated in the first round of the West Regional by Texas-El Paso, 98-91, in overtime.

Scoring Leaders: Indiana's Steve Alford and Syracuse's Rony Seikaly (138 points).

Highest Scoring Averages: Wyoming's Fennis Dembo and UCLA's Reggie Miller (28 ppg).

Rebounding Leader: Derrick Coleman, Syracuse (73 rebounds, 12.2 rpg).

Highest Rebounding Average: Tim Perry, Temple (28 rebounds, 14 rpg).

1987-88

AT A GLANCE

NCAA Champion: Kansas (27-11; coached by Larry Brown; finished in third place in Big Eight with a 9-5 record).

NIT Champion: Connecticut (20-14; coached by Jim Calhoun; finished in ninth place in Big East with a 4-12 record).

New Conference: American South (merged with Sun Belt four years later)

New Rule: Each intentional personal foul carries a two-shot penalty plus possession of the ball.

NCAA Probation: Brooklyn, Eastern Washington, Marist, Minnesota, South Carolina, Virginia Tech.

NCAA Consensus First-Team All-Americans: Sean Elliott, F, Jr., Arizona; Gary Grant, G, Sr., Michigan; Hersey Hawkins, G, Sr., Bradley; Danny Manning, F-C, Sr., Kansas; J.R. Reid, C, Soph., North Carolina.

National Players of the Year: Hawkins (36.3 ppg, 7.8 rpg, 2.6 spg, 52.4 FG%, 84.8 FT%/AP, UPI, USBWA) and Manning (24.8 ppg, 9 rpg, 1.8 spg, 58.3 FG%/NABC, Naismith, Wooden).

National Coaches of the Year: Kansas' Larry Brown (27-11/Naismith) and Temple's John Chaney (32-2/AP, UPI, NABC, USBWA).

Loyola Marymount, which finished in last place in the West Coast Conference the previous season, went unbeaten in league competition. The Lions became the only team to ever have four

Bradley's Hersey Hawkins (#33) battles an opponent for a rebound.

Sean Elliott became the first Arizona player ever to become an NCAA consensus first- or second-team All-American. Teammate Steve Kerr finished his career with an NCAA-record 38 consecutive games making a three-point field goal. . . . Holy Cross' Glenn Tropf set an NCAA single-season record for three-point field-goal accuracy by hitting 52 of 82 long-range attempts (63.4 percent). . . . Southern's Avery Johnson set an NCAA single-season record for assists average with 13.3 scoring feeds per game. Johnson, who began his college career at a junior college, averaged 10.7 assists the previous season to become the only player to twice averge double figures in that category. He had 20 or more assists in four games. . . . Oklahoma's Mookie Blaylock, another J.C. transfer, set an NCAA single-season record with 150 steals, including 13 in a game against Centenary. It was one of nine consecutive years from 1985-93 that an OU player led the Big Eight Conference in thefts.

players average more than 17 points per game in a season—Hank Gathers (22.5 ppg), Bo Kimble (22.2), Mike Yoest (17.6) and Corey Gaines (17.4). Loyola Marymount, after compiling a 12-16 record the previous year, improved by 14 games to 28-4 to make its lone appearance in the Top 20 of a final wire-service poll. Oddly, LMU did not have a player lead the WCC in scoring for the only time in an eight-year span from 1985-92 (Pepperdine's Tom Lewis edged Gathers with a 22.9 mark).

Lafester Rhodes isn't among Iowa State's top 20 all-time scorers, but he set a school single-game record with 54 points in overtime against Iowa. Other players establishing school single-game Division I marks were Bradley's Hersey Hawkins (63 points at Detroit), Marshall's Skip Henderson (55 vs. The Citadel in Southern Conference Tournament), Central Michigan's Tommie Johnson (53 at Wright State), Rhode Island's Tom Garrick (tied with 50 vs. Rutgers in Atlantic 10 Tournament quarterfinals), Detroit's Archie Tullos (49 vs. Bradley), San Francisco's Keith Jackson (47 at Loyola Marymount), New Orleans' Ledell Eackles (45 at Florida International), Tennessee

1987–88 INDIVIDUAL LEADERS

SCORING

PLAYER	PTS.	AVG.
Hawkins, Bradley	1125	36.3
Queenan, Lehigh	882	28.5
Mason, Tennessee St.	783	28.0
Hayward, Loyola (Ill.)	756	26.1
Martin, Murray St.	806	26.0
Simmons, Evansvile	750	25.9
Middleton, Southern Ill.	711	25.4
Grayer, Iowa St.	811	25.3
Larkin, Xavier	758	25.3
Henderson, Marshall	804	25.1

REBOUNDING

PLAYER	REB.	AVG.
Miller, Loyola (Ill.)	395	13.6
Mack, S. Carolina St.	387	13.3
Lane, Pittsburgh	378	12.2
Sanders, George Mason	339	11.7
White, La. Tech	359	11.6
Canino, Central Conn. St.	321	11.5
Johnson, Baptist	331	11.4
Simmons, La Salle	386	11.4
West, Texas Southern	322	11.1
Coleman, Syracuse	384	11.0

ASSISTS

PLAYER	AST.	AVG.
Johnson, Southern (La.)	399	13.3
Manuel, Bradley	373	12.0
Neal, Georgia Tech	303	9.5
Gaines, L. Marymount	271	8.7
Evans, Temple	294	8.6
Douglas, Syracuse	288	8.2
Smith, Old Dominion	244	8.1
Williams, Holy Cross	234	8.1
Davis, Marist	207	7.7
Brown, Siena	222	7.7

BLOCKED SHOTS

PLAYER	BLK.	AVG.
Blake, St. Joseph's	116	4.0
Smits, Marist	105	3.9
Brown, Canisius	100	3.7
Perry, Temple	118	3.6
Brow, Virginia Tech	100	3.6
Garrett, Indiana	99	3.4
Butts, Bucknell	91	3.4
Campbell, Clemson	88	3.1
Smith, Pittsburgh	96	3.1
Hopkins, Navy	74	3.1

STEALS

PLAYER	STL.	AVG.
Ware, Florida A&M	142	4.9
Johnson, Towson St.	124	4.1
Blaylock, Oklahoma	150	3.8
Workman, Oral Roberts	103	3.6
Johnson, Southern (La.)	106	3.5
Murdock, Providence	90	3.2
Conway, Montana St.	94	3.1
Robertson, Cleveland St.	90	3.0
McDonald, Texas A&M	90	2.9
Strickland, DePaul	75	2.9

FIELD GOAL PERCENTAGE

PLAYER	FGM	FGA	PCT.
Jones, Boise St.	187	283	.661
Brundy, DePaul	194	295	.658
Holifield, Ill. St.	177	273	.648
Basnight, UNLV	184	284	.648
Leckner, Wyoming	181	281	.644
Stuckey, SW Mo. St.	166	259	.641
White, La. Tech	226	354	.638
Perdue, Vanderbilt	234	369	.634
Ambroise, Baptist	171	270	.633
Campbell, Clemson	217	345	.629

FREE THROW PERCENTAGE

PLAYER	FTM	FTA	PCT.
Henson, Kansas St.	111	120	.925
Tullos, Detroit	139	153	.908
Edwards, Indiana	69	76	.908
Barton, Dartmouth	115	127	.906
Smith, Louisville	143	158	.905
Boyd, Memphis St.	111	124	.895
Willingham, S. F. Austin St.	75	84	.893
Harris, Ill. St.	91	102	.892
Nurnberger, S. Ill.	78	88	.886
Lichti, Stanford	174	198	.879

THREE-POINT FIELD GOAL PERCENTAGE

PLAYER	FGM	FGA	PCT.
Tropf, Holy Cross	52	82	.634
Kerr, Arizona	114	199	.573
Joseph, Bucknell	65	116	.560
Jones, Pr. View	85	155	.548
Orlandini, Princeton	60	110	.545

THREE-POINT FIELD GOALS PER GAME

PLAYER	FGM	AVG.
Pollard, Miss. Valley St.	132	4.7
McGill, E. Ky.	104	3.9
Lancaster, Va. Tech	106	3.7
Mooney, Coastal Carolina	102	3.6
Paddio, UNLV	118	3.5

1987–88 TEAM LEADERS

SCORING OFFENSE

SCHOOL	PTS.	AVG.
Loyola Marymount	3528	110.3
Oklahoma	4012	102.9
Southern (La.)	2965	95.6
Xavier	2840	94.7
Iowa	3181	93.6

SCORING DEFENSE

SCHOOL	PTS.	AVG.
Georgia Southern	1725	55.6
Boise St.	1680	56.0
Princeton	1467	56.4
Colorado St.	2007	57.3
St. Mary's (Calif.)	1640	58.6

SCORING MARGIN

SCHOOL	OFF.	DEF.	MAR.
Oklahoma	102.9	81.0	21.9
Arizona	85.1	64.2	20.9
UNLV	84.3	68.2	16.1
Temple	76.8	61.2	15.6
Xavier	94.7	79.5	15.2

WON-LOST PERCENTAGE

SCHOOL	W-L	PCT.
Temple	32-2	.941
Arizona	35-3	.921
Oklahoma	35-4	.897
North Carolina A&T	26-3	.897
Purdue	29-4	.879

FIELD GOAL PERCENTAGE

SCHOOL	FGM	FGA	PCT.
Michigan	1198	2196	.546
Arizona	1147	2106	.545
North Carolina	1013	1892	.535
Purdue	1018	1912	.532
Brigham Young	976	1839	.531

FIELD GOAL PERCENTAGE DEFENSE

SCHOOL	FGM	FGA	PCT.
Temple	777	1981	.392
Marist	617	1537	.401
Kansas	912	2215	.412
UNLV	841	2012	.418
Georgia Southern	640	1529	.419

FREE THROW PERCENTAGE

SCHOOL	FTM	FTA	PCT.
Butler	413	517	.799
Princeton	315	405	.778
Bucknell	477	617	.773
UNC-Asheville	419	543	.772
Auburn	406	527	.770

REBOUND MARGIN

SCHOOL	OFF.	DEF.	MAR.
Notre Dame	36.0	26.2	9.9
South Carolina St.	42.9	33.5	9.4
Ark.-Little Rock	41.3	32.5	8.8
Georgetown	39.2	31.3	7.9
Missouri	41.9	34.3	7.7

THREE-POINT FIELD GOAL PERCENTAGE

SCHOOL	FGM	FGA	PCT.
Princeton	211	429	.492
Prairie View	129	266	.485
Kansas St.	179	370	.484
Arizona	254	526	.483
Bucknell	154	328	.470

THREE-POINT FIELD GOALS PER GAME

SCHOOL	FGM	AVG.
Princeton	211	8.1
Loyola Marymount	251	7.8
Oklahoma	299	7.7
George Mason	219	7.3
Bradley	224	7.2

State's Anthony Mason (44 at Eastern Kentucky) and Drexel's John Rankin (44 vs. Rider).

Southern Mississippi's John White tied a Division I school record with 41 points at Virginia Tech in double overtime. But White's explosion wasn't enough to offset Virginia Tech guard Bimbo Coles scoring a Metro Conference-record 51 points in a 141-133 victory for the Hokies.

Hawkins' uprising was also a Missouri Valley Conference mark. Henderson's outburst is a SC Tournament standard. . . . Hawkins (36.3 ppg), Lehigh's Daren Queenan (28.5), Evansville's Marty Simmons (25.9), Southern Illinois' Steve Middleton (25.4), Dartmouth's Jim Barton (24.2), San Jose State's Ricky Berry (24.2), Drexel's Michael Anderson (23.9) and Eastern Michigan's Grant Long (23) set school Division I records for highest scoring average in a single season. Hawkins' average is also a MVC single-season record. Middleton had scored a total of just 19 points as a freshman.

Loyola of Chicago's Kenny Miller became the only freshman ever to lead the nation in rebounding (13.6 per game). . . . Central Michigan's Dan Majerle became the fourth different player in as many years to lead the Mid-American Conference in scoring and rebounding. . . . Kansas State's Mitch Richmond poured in 35 points in a 72-61 triumph at Kansas, ending the Jayhawks' school and Big Eight-record 55-game homecourt winning streak. Richmond was the first Kansas State player since 1959 to become an NCAA consensus first- or second-team All-American. . . . Guard Mark Macon was the first Temple player since 1958 to become an NCAA consensus first- or second-team All-American.

Arizona (35-3/coached by Lute Olson), Oklahoma (35-4/Billy Tubbs), Purdue (29-4/Gene Keady), Loyola Marymount (28-4/Paul Westhead), Rhode Island (28-7/Tom Penders), SMU (28-7/Dave Bliss), North Carolina A&T (26-3/Don Corbett), Richmond (26-7/Dick Tarrant), Boise State (24-6/Bobby Dye), Fairleigh Dickinson (23-7/Tom Green), UC Santa Barbara (22-8/Jerry Pimm) and Lehigh (21-10/Fran McCaf-

fery) had their winningest seasons in school Division I history. Temple (32-2/John Chaney), Kansas State (25-9/Lon Kruger) and Middle Tennessee State (23-11/Bruce Stewart) tied their school records for most victories in a single season. . . . Thirteen consecutive coaches finished their careers at Lehigh with losing records until McCaffery arrived. In three seasons with the Engineers, he was 49-39 (.557).

St. John's compiled a 17-12 record. It was the closest Lou Carnesecca ever came to a non-winning mark in his 24 years as head coach of the Redmen. . . . Connecticut lost 13 consecutive games to Georgetown in their series until upending the Hoyas, 66-59. Meanwhile, Boston College posted its lone victory against Georgetown in an 18-game stretch of their series from 1984 through 1991. . . . Pittsburgh, capturing its lone undisputed Big East Conference regular-season championship, became the only school to feature a roster with as many as eight players who would wind up scoring more than 1,000 points before ending their college careers—seniors Charles Smith and Demetreus Gore, junior Jerome Lane, sophomore Rod Brookin and freshmen Bobby Martin, Jason Matthews, Sean Miller and Darelle Porter.

Marquette incurred its first losing record (10-18) in 24 seasons. . . . Rhode Island and Richmond finished in the Top 20 of a final wire-service poll for the only time in their history. Xavier finished in the Top 20 of a final wire-service poll for the first time since 1957. . . . Delaware, coached by Steve Steinwedel, snapped a streak of nine straight losing seasons by notching a 19-9 mark. . . . South Carolina State's Rodney Mack averaged a school Division I single-season standard of 13.2 rebounds per game. . . . Northeastern's Steve Carney collected a school-record 23 rebounds in a contest against Hartford.

Maryland managed its lone victory over Duke (72-69) in a 22-game stretch of their series from 1985 through 1994. . . . Old Dominion's Frank Smith led the Sun Belt Conference in assists and steals for the third consecutive season. . . . North Carolina A&T, coached by Don Corbett, won its seventh consecutive Mid-Eastern Athletic Conference Tournament. . . . Wichita State, coached by Eddie Fogler, finished with a 20-10 record despite losing three consecutive early-season games in overtime. . . . SMU, coached by Dave Bliss, captured the SWC regular-season title just one year after finishing in a tie for sixth place. . . . St. Mary's lost more than 10 games in 26 consecutive seasons until the Gaels compiled a 19-9 record. . . . Long Beach State ended a streak of six consecutive losing seasons by registering a 17-12 ledger in Joe Harrington's initial campaign as coach of the 49ers. . . . UC Santa Barbara swept UNLV after the Gauchos lost their first 16 meetings with the Rebels. Meanwhile, Long Beach State posted its lone victory over UNLV (79-77) in a 25-game stretch of their series from 1982 through 1992.

1988 NCAA Tournament

Summary: The Big Eight went 30 years without winning a Final Four game until Kansas and Oklahoma both won. Kansas won the championship game after losing three previous finals at Kansas City (1940, 1953 and 1957). Danny Manning had a Final Four-record six blocked shots in a 66-59 victory over Duke in the national semifinals. Larry Brown became the only coach to leave an NCAA champion before the next season for another coaching job. After winning the NCAA title, Brown quit the Jayhawks before the start of the next NCAA probation-marred campaign to return to the NBA.

Outcome for Defending Champion: Indiana (19-10) finished fifth in the Big Ten before losing its tourney opener to No. 13 seed Richmond, 72-69. The Hoosiers lost four of their first five league outings.

Star Gazing: Manning became the only one of the more than 60 major-college players to score at least 2,500 career points or average a minimum of 28.5 points per game and play for an NCAA championship team. Manning, the only national player of the year from 1981-91 to play for a national titlist, hit 25 of 45 field-goal attempts and grabbed 28 rebounds at the Final Four.

1987-88 FINAL NATIONAL POLLS

AP	UPI	USA/CNN	SCHOOL (RECORD)	HEAD COACH
1	1	5	Temple (32-2)	John Chaney
2	2	3	Arizona (35-3)	Lute Olson
3	3	6	Purdue (29-4)	Gene Keady
4	4	2	Oklahoma (35-4)	Billy Tubbs
5	5	4	Duke (28-7)	Mike Krzyzewski
6	6	9	Kentucky (27-6)	Eddie Sutton
7	8	7	North Carolina (27-7)	Dean Smith
8	7	13	Pittsburgh (24-7)	Paul Evans
9	9	16	Syracuse (26-9)	Jim Boeheim
10	10	10	Michigan (26-8)	Bill Frieder
11	12	23	Bradley (26-5)	Stan Albeck
12	11	22	UNLV (26-5)	Jerry Tarkanian
13	14	–	Wyoming (26-6)	Benny Dees
14	13	21	N.C. State (24-8)	Jim Valvano
15	16	19	Loyola Marymount (28-4)	Paul Westhead
16	15	20	Illinois (23-10)	Lou Henson
17	18	14	Iowa (24-10)	Tom Davis
18	–	–	Xavier (26-4)	Pete Gillen
19	17	25	Brigham Young (26-6)	Ladell Andersen
20	20	8	Kansas State (25-9)	Lon Kruger
–	–	1	Kansas (27-11)	Larry Brown
–	–	11	Villanova (24-13)	Rollie Massimino
–	–	12	Rhode Island (28-7)	Tom Penders
–	–	15	Louisville (24-11)	Denny Crum
–	–	17	Vanderbilt (20-11)	C.M. Newton
–	–	18	Richmond (26-7)	Dick Tarrant
–	19	–	Indiana (19-10)	Bob Knight
–	–	24	DePaul (22-8)	Joey Meyer

Biggest Upset: Murray State (14th seed) defeated North Carolina State (3), 78-75.

One and Only: Oklahoma became the only school to compete for the national championship in both football and basketball in the same academic school year (1988). The football Sooners lost to Miami (Fla.) in the Orange Bowl, finishing third in the final wire-service polls. . . . Kansas' Brown became the only coach to capture an NCAA crown between NBA divisional titles.

Numbers Game: Temple, a 63-53 loser against Duke in the East Regional final, is one of only two teams ranked No. 1 by both AP and UPI entering the tourney to lose by a double-digit margin before the Final Four. The Owls finished with 32 victories for the second consecutive season. . . . Oklahoma's Mookie Blaylock set the record for most steals in a playoff series (23 in six games). He had seven steals as a junior guard in an 83-79 championship game loss against Kansas. . . . Bradley's Hersey Hawkins poured in a tourney-high 44 points in a 90-86 setback against Auburn in the opening round of the Southwest Regional. . . . Pitt's Jerome Lane grabbed a tourney-high 20 rebounds in an 80-74 defeat against Vanderbilt in

1987–88 NCAA CHAMPION: KANSAS

SEASON STATISTICS OF KANSAS REGULARS

PLAYER	POS.	CL.	G.	FG%	FT%	PPG	RPG
Danny Manning	F-C	Sr.	38	.583	.734	24.8	9.0
Milt Newton	G	Jr.	35	.555	.564	11.6	5.0
Kevin Pritchard	G	So.	37	.486	.739	10.6	2.6
Chris Piper	F	Sr.	34	.537	.705	5.1	3.8
Lincoln Minor	G	Jr.	34	.419	.667	4.8	1.4
Jeff Gueldner	G	So.	34	.422	.681	3.8	2.0
Scooter Barry	G	Jr.	35	.477	.815	3.3	1.3
Keith Harris	F	So.	27	.451	.633	3.1	2.6
Otis Livingston	G	Jr.	27	.650	.613	2.6	1.4
Mike Maddox	F	Fr.	24	.532	.471	2.5	1.5
Mike Masucci	C	Fr.	24	.431	.467	2.1	1.5
TEAM TOTALS			38	.521	.690	75.3	35.6

Three-point field goals leader: Newton (29 of 64, .453). **Assists leader:** Pritchard 113. **Blocked shots leader:** Manning 73. **Steals leaders:** Manning 70, Pritchard 52.

1988 FINAL FOUR CHAMPIONSHIP GAME

KANSAS CITY, MO

KANSAS (83)	MIN.	FG-A	FT-A	REB.	A	PF	PTS.
Piper	37	4-6	0-0	1	2	3	8
Gueldner	15	1-2	0-0	0	1	0	2
Manning	36	13-24	5-7	7	2	3	31
Pritchard	31	6-7	0-0	0	4	1	13
Newton	32	6-6	1-2	0	1	1	15
Barry	9	0-2	1-2	0	2	1	1
Maddox	1	0-0	0-0	0	0	1	0
Harris	12	1-1	0-0	0	0	2	2
Normore	16	3-3	0-1	0	4	3	7
Minor	11	1-4	2-2	0	1	1	4
Team				1			
TOTALS	200	35-55	9-14	8	17	16	83

FG%: .636. **FT%:** .643. **Three-point goals:** 4-6 (Pritchard 1-1, Newton 2-2, Normore 1-1, Gueldner 0-1, Manning 0-1). **Blocks:** 4. **Turnovers:** 23. **Steals:** 11 (Manning 5).

OKLAHOMA (79)	MIN.	FG-A	FT-A	REB.	A	PF	PTS.
Grant	40	6-14	2-3	3	1	4	14
Sieger	40	7-15	1-2	3	7	2	22
King	39	7-14	3-3	2	0	3	17
Blaylock	40	6-13	0-1	3	4	4	14
Grace	34	4-14	3-4	3	7	4	12
Mullins	7	0-0	0-0	0	0	1	0
Team				1			
TOTALS	200	30-70	9-13	14	19	18	79

FG%: .429. **FT%:** .692. **Three-point goals:** 10-24 (Sieger 7-13, Blaylock 2-4, Grace 1-7). **Blocks:** 3. **Turnovers:** 15 (Sieger 6). **Steals:** 13 (Blaylock 7). **Halftime:** Tied 50-50.

NATIONAL SEMIFINALS

KANSAS (66): Piper 3-4 4-4 10, Guelder 0-1 0-0 0, Manning 12-21 1-2 25, Pritchard 2-6 2-2 6, Newton 8-14 2-3 20, Barry 1-2 3-4 5, Maddox 0-0 0-0 0, Harris 0-0 0-0 0, Normore 0-0 0-0 0, Minor 0-0 0-0 0, Mattox 0-0 0-0 0. Team 26-52 (.500) 12-15 (.800) 66.

DUKE (59): Ferry 7-22 4-4 19, King 1-4 1-2 3, Brickey 2-9 2-5 6, Snyder 4-10 1-2 9, Strickland 5-13 0-0 10, Koubek 3-5 0-0 8, Abdelnaby 1-2 2-4 4, Smith 0-0 0-0 0, Henderson 0-2 0-0 0, Cook 0-0 0-0 0. Team 23-67 (.343) 10-17 (.588) 59.

Halftime: Kansas 38-27.
Three-point goals: Kansas 2-4 (.500), Duke 3-14 (.214).

ARIZONA (78): Cook 6-13 4-6 16, Elliott 13-23 3-3 31, Tolbert 5-11 1-2 11, McMillan 3-6 0-0 8, Kerr 2-13 0-0 6, Turner 0-0 0-0 0, Mason 0-0 0-0 0, Buechler 2-2 0-0 4, Lofton 1-4 0-0 2. Team 32-72 (.444) 8-11 (.727) 78.

OKLAHOMA (86): Grant 7-14 7-10 21, Sieger 3-8 3-6 10, King 9-16 3-6 21, Blaylock 3-7 1-2 7, Grace 3-10 5-7 13, Mullins 1-1 0-0 3, Wiley 4-8 3-3 11. Team 30-64 (.469) 22-34 (.647) 86.

Halftime: Oklahoma 39-27.
Three-point goals: Arizona 6-23 (.261), Oklahoma 4-14 (.286).

ALL-TOURNAMENT TEAM

Sean Elliott, F, Jr., Arizona (31 points, 11 rebounds/one Final Four game)
Stacey King, C, Jr., Oklahoma (38 points, 13 rebounds in final two games)
*Danny Manning, F, Sr., Kansas (56 points, 28 rebounds, nine steals, eight blocked shots)
Milt Newton, G-F, Jr., Kansas (35 points, 11 rebounds)
Dave Sieger, F, Sr., Oklahoma (32 points, 11 rebounds, 10 assists, eight three-pointers)

*Named Most Outstanding Player.

the second round of the Midwest Regional. . . . Kansas State guard William Scott finished his playoff career with 65 percent accuracy from three-point range (26 of 40 in five games). . . . North Carolina lost its fourth regional final in six years. . . . Seton Hall, coached by P.J. Carlesimo, made its inaugural NCAA Tournament appearance and Cornell, coached by Mike Dement, participated for the first time in 34 years. . . . Rhode Island, coached by Tom Penders, registered its first NCAA playoff victory with an 87-80 decision over Missouri in the East Regional. . . . Kentucky became the fourth different SEC school in four years to have its NCAA Tournament participation vacated. The previous SEC offenders were Geor-

gia '85, Alabama '87 and Florida '87. . . . Fairleigh Dickinson boasted the best-ever record for a No. 16 seed entering the tourney (23-6).

What Might Have Been: Forwards Danny Ferry and Robert Brickey and guard Phil Henderson combined to shoot 50 percent from the floor in their Duke careers. If only they combined to hit 39.4 percent of their field-goal attempts instead of 27.3 percent (9 of 33) in the national semifinals, the Blue Devils could have defeated eventual champion Kansas rather than losing 66-59. . . . Kansas State (25-9/without Norris Coleman), Louisiana State (16-14/John Williams), Memphis State (20-12/Vincent Askew) and North Carolina State (24-8/Chris

Kansas' Danny Manning (#25) snags a rebound from an opponent.

1988 CHAMPIONSHIP BRACKET

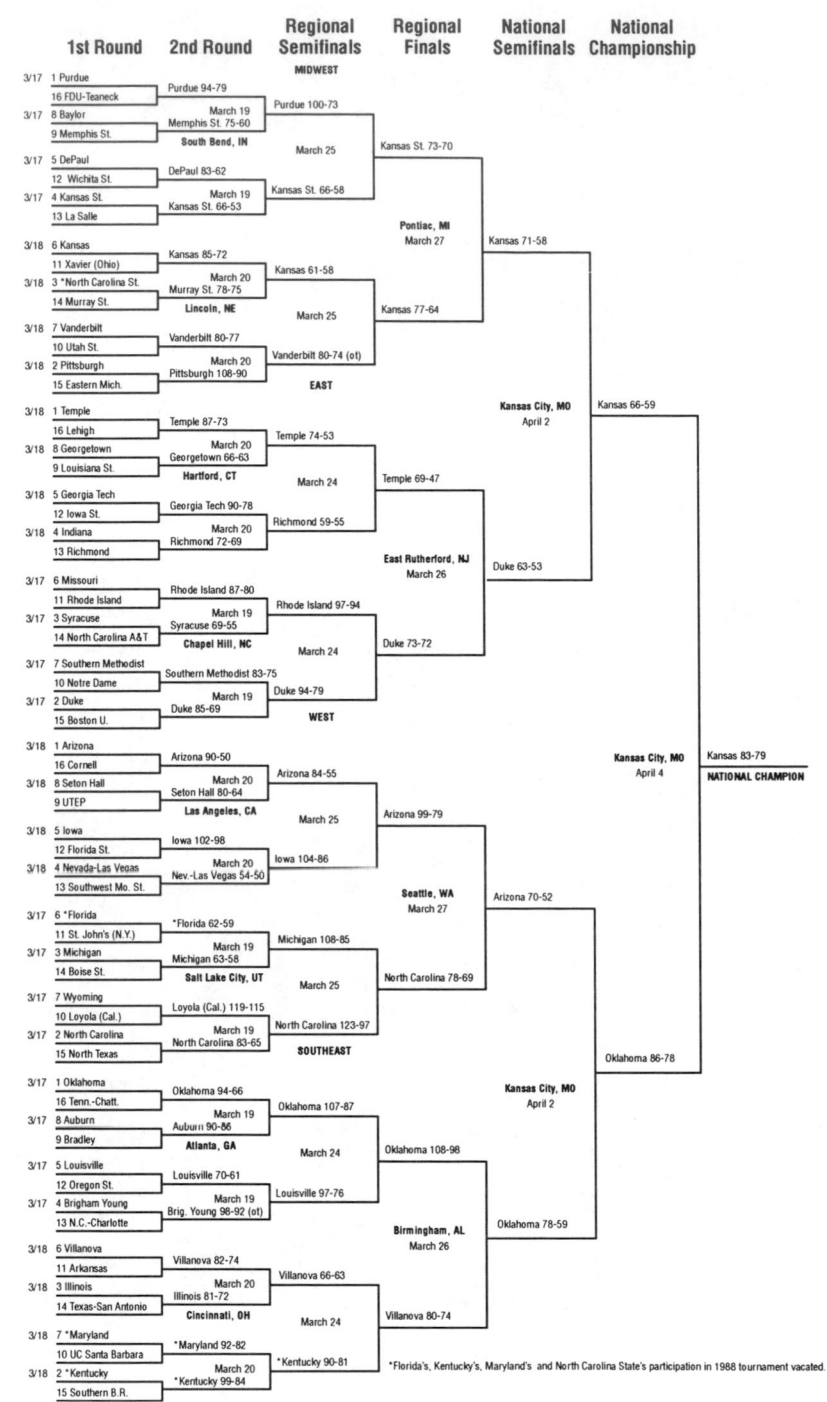

	1st Round	2nd Round	Regional Semifinals	Regional Finals	National Semifinals	National Championship

MIDWEST

3/17 1 Purdue
16 FDU-Teaneck — Purdue 94-79
March 19
3/17 8 Baylor
9 Memphis St. — Memphis St. 75-60
South Bend, IN
Purdue 100-73

3/17 5 DePaul
12 Wichita St. — DePaul 83-62
March 19
3/17 4 Kansas St.
13 La Salle — Kansas St. 66-53
Kansas St. 66-58

March 25 — Kansas St. 73-70

Pontiac, MI March 27 — Kansas 71-58

3/18 6 Kansas
11 Xavier (Ohio) — Kansas 85-72
March 20
3/18 3 *North Carolina St.
14 Murray St. — Murray St. 78-75
Lincoln, NE
Kansas 61-58

3/18 7 Vanderbilt
10 Utah St. — Vanderbilt 80-77
March 20
3/18 2 Pittsburgh
15 Eastern Mich. — Pittsburgh 108-90
Vanderbilt 80-74 (ot)

March 25 — Kansas 77-64

EAST

3/18 1 Temple
16 Lehigh — Temple 87-73
March 20
3/18 8 Georgetown
9 Louisiana St. — Georgetown 66-63
Hartford, CT
Temple 74-53

3/18 5 Georgia Tech
12 Iowa St. — Georgia Tech 90-78
March 20
3/18 4 Indiana
13 Richmond — Richmond 72-69
Richmond 59-55

March 24 — Temple 69-47

East Rutherford, NJ March 26 — Duke 63-53

3/17 6 Missouri
11 Rhode Island — Rhode Island 87-80
March 19
3/17 3 Syracuse
14 North Carolina A&T — Syracuse 69-55
Chapel Hill, NC
Rhode Island 97-94

3/17 7 Southern Methodist
10 Notre Dame — Southern Methodist 83-75
March 19
3/17 2 Duke
15 Boston U. — Duke 85-69
Duke 94-79

March 24 — Duke 73-72

Kansas City, MO April 2 — Kansas 66-59

WEST

3/18 1 Arizona
16 Cornell — Arizona 90-50
March 20
3/18 8 Seton Hall
9 UTEP — Seton Hall 80-64
Las Angeles, CA
Arizona 84-55

3/18 5 Iowa
12 Florida St. — Iowa 102-98
March 20
3/18 4 Nevada-Las Vegas
13 Southwest Mo. St. — Nev.-Las Vegas 54-50
Iowa 104-86

March 25 — Arizona 99-79

Seattle, WA March 27 — Arizona 70-52

3/17 6 *Florida
11 St. John's (N.Y.) — *Florida 62-59
March 19
3/17 3 Michigan
14 Boise St. — Michigan 63-58
Salt Lake City, UT
Michigan 108-85

3/17 7 Wyoming
10 Loyola (Cal.) — Loyola (Cal.) 119-115
March 19
3/17 2 North Carolina
15 North Texas — North Carolina 83-65
North Carolina 123-97

March 25 — North Carolina 78-69

Kansas City, MO April 4 — Kansas 83-79 **NATIONAL CHAMPION**

SOUTHEAST

3/17 1 Oklahoma
16 Tenn.-Chatt. — Oklahoma 94-66
March 19
3/17 8 Auburn
9 Bradley — Auburn 90-86
Atlanta, GA
Oklahoma 107-87

3/17 5 Louisville
12 Oregon St. — Louisville 70-61
March 19
3/17 4 Brigham Young
13 N.C.-Charlotte — Brig. Young 98-92 (ot)
Louisville 97-76

March 24 — Oklahoma 108-98

Birmingham, AL March 26 — Oklahoma 78-59

3/18 6 Villanova
11 Arkansas — Villanova 82-74
March 20
3/18 3 Illinois
14 Texas-San Antonio — Illinois 81-72
Cincinnati, OH
Villanova 66-63

3/18 7 *Maryland
10 UC Santa Barbara — *Maryland 92-82
March 20
3/18 2 *Kentucky
15 Southern B.R. — *Kentucky 99-84
*Kentucky 90-81

March 24 — Villanova 80-74

Kansas City, MO April 2 — Oklahoma 86-78

*Florida's, Kentucky's, Maryland's and North Carolina State's participation in 1988 tournament vacated.

Washburn) might have fared better in the playoffs if standout players had exercised their remaining eligibility instead of defecting to the NBA. . . . Georgia (20-16) probably would have participated in the NCAA Tournament instead of the NIT if Cedric Henderson didn't leave school early for the NBA two years earlier after his sophomore season. Ditto Stanford (21-12) if starting center Eric Reveno didn't miss the campaign because of a back ailment. . . . Louisville (24-11) might have reached the Southeast Regional final instead of Oklahoma if Cardinals swingman Tony Kimbro hadn't missed the season because of academic shortcomings.

Putting Things in Perspective: Kansas State (25-9) defeated Kansas twice by a total of 26 points before losing against KU in the Midwest Regional final, 71-58, when Wildcats star Mitch Richmond was restricted to 11 points and four rebounds. Richmond had averaged 25.8 points and 10.2 rebounds in his first five playoff games. Oklahoma (35-4) defeated the Jayhawks twice by eight points in each Big Eight Conference regular-season game before losing against KU in the national final. Kansas lost five games by double-digit margins. The Jayhawks went almost a month without a victory against a Division I opponent as their only win in a mid-season, six-game stretch was against Hampton (Va.). Nebraska, which was 4-10 in the Big Eight when the Cornhuskers' streak of 14 consecutive winning seasons came to an end, defeated Kansas, 70-68. It was one of four straight league losses for KU.

Scoring Leader: Danny Manning, Kansas (163 points, 27.2 ppg).

Rebounding Leader: Danny Manning, Kansas (56 rebounds, 9.3 rpg).

Highest Rebounding Average: Jerome Lane, Pittsburgh (37 rebounds, 18.5 rpg).

1988-89

AT A GLANCE

NCAA Champion: Michigan (30-7; coached by Bill Frieder and Steve Fisher; finished in third place in Big Ten with a 12-6 record).

NIT Champion: St. John's (20-13; coached by Lou Carnesecca; finished in a tie for seventh place in Big East with a 6-10 record).

New Rules: Neutral courts are used in all rounds of the NCAA Tournament. . . . Bracket rotation for the NCAA tourney was established. . . . Criteria governing automatic qualification for conferences was strengthened.

NCAA Probation: Cincinnati, Cleveland State, Kansas, Marist, Virginia Tech.

NCAA Consensus First-Team All-Americans: Sean Elliott, F, Sr., Arizona; Pervis Ellison, C, Sr., Louisville; Danny Ferry, F-C, Sr., Duke; Chris Jackson, G, Fr., Louisiana State; Stacey King, C, Sr., Oklahoma.

National Players of the Year: Elliott (22.3 ppg, 7.2 rpg, 4.1 apg, 84.1 FT%, 43.7 3FG%/AP, NABC, Wooden) and Ferry (22.6 ppg, 7.4 rpg, 4.7 apg, 52.2 FG%/UPI, USBWA, Naismith).

National Coaches of the Year: Seton Hall's P.J. Carlesimo (31-7/NABC); Indiana's Bob Knight (27-8/AP, UPI, USBWA), and Duke's Mike Krzyzewski (28-8/Naismith).

The proliferation of parity and the wisdom of expanding the postseason field was never more evident than in the 1989 playoffs. All of the Final Four teams would not have qualified for the NCAA Tournament prior to 1975 when more than one league member could be invited—Michigan (finished in third place in Big Ten Conference), Seton Hall (lost in Big East Tournament semifinals after finishing runner-up to Georgetown in regular-season standings), Duke (lost in ACC Tournament final after finishing in three-way tie for second place behind North Carolina State in regular-season standings) and Illinois (runner-up in Big Ten to Indiana).

LSU edged second-ranked Georgetown, 82-80, on Ricky Blanton's last-second rebound basket before 54,321 fans at the Louisiana Superdome (64,144 paid). . . . LSU guard Chris Jackson became the highest-scoring freshman in major-college history when he averaged 30.2 points per game. His 55 points were in vain in a 113-112 overtime loss at Ole Miss when the Rebels' Gerald Glass offset Jackson's outburst with 53 points. . . . Jackson's 48 points weren't enough to prevent a 104-95 defeat against visiting Florida when the

Gators clinched their only SEC regular-season title. Helping Florida along the way was an incredible 81-78 overtime victory at Vanderbilt when the Gators tied the game at the end of regulation after Commodore fans were assessed a two-shot technical for throwing tennis balls at center Dwayne Schintzius, who had previously run afoul of the law while wielding a tennis racket.

Vanderbilt guard Barry Goheen ended his career as one of the premier clutch players in college history. He made six game-winning shots in the closing seconds and sent an NCAA Tournament game into overtime with two three-point baskets in the final five seconds of regulation. . . . Duke's Danny Ferry established an ACC and school single-game record by pouring in 58 points at Miami (Fla.). Also setting school Division I single-game scoring standards were McNeese State's Michael Cutright (51 points at Stephen F. Austin in double overtime), Delaware State's Tom Davis (50 vs. Brooklyn) and Eastern Washington's David Peed (44 at UC Irvine). Cutright's outburst tied a Southland Conference game mark. . . . Virginia Commonwealth's Chris Cheeks tied a school Division I single-game record (42 points against Old Dominion in OT).

Mr. Clutch: Vanderbilt's Barry Goheen.

La Salle's Lionel Simmons (28.4 ppg), Virginia Tech's Bimbo Coles (26.6), Air Force's Raymond Dudley (26.6), Delaware State's Davis (25.2), VCU's Cheeks (23.8), Eastern Illinois' Jay Taylor (23.4), EWU's Peed (20.9) and Morgan

HIGHEST-SCORING GAME IN HISTORY Loyola Marymount's high scorers met U.S. International on January 31, 1989, in what became the highest-scoring game in history. Marymount defeated U.S. International, 181-150. Marymount's high scorer was Hank Gathers; International's top gun was Steve Smith.

USIU (150)	FG-A	FT-A	REB.	PTS.
Williams	9-12	7-12	5	25
Laffitte	12-18	4-5	7	28
Sterner	5-9	0-0	6	10
Wilson	10-21	1-3	3	21
Smith	11-15	8-8	8	32
Davis	3-4	0-1	3	7
Moore	3-5	0-0	4	6
Judd	3-5	0-0	3	6
Hodges	0-2	0-2	0	0
Howard	6-8	1-4	1	13
Banks	1-2	0-0	0	2
Team			9	
TOTALS	**63-101**	**21-35**	**49**	**150**

FG%: .624. **FT%:** .600. **Three-point shooting:** 3 of 7 (Wilson 0-2, Smith 2-2, Davis 1-2, Hodges 0-1).

LMU (181)	FG-A	FT-A	REB.	PTS.
Stumer	4-11	2-3	5	12
Peabody	2-3	1-2	2	5
Gathers	15-24	11-14	29	41
Fryer	10-24	8-10	2	34
Simmons	10-14	3-4	5	25
Lee	2-2	1-3	1	5
Mister	0-0	1-2	2	1
O'Connell	2-3	1-1	1	5
Lowery	5-9	4-4	4	15
Roscoe	0-0	0-0	0	0
Yoest	3-6	0-0	1	6
Kimble	9-15	0-0	4	20
Knight	1-2	2-2	1	4
Veargason	2-3	0-0	4	4
Morley	0-0	0-0	1	0
Slater	2-3	0-0	0	4
Team			1	
TOTALS	**67-119**	**34-45**	**63**	**181**

FG%: .563. **FT%:** .755. **Three-point shooting:** 13 of 34 (Stumer 2-6, Fryer 6-14, Simmons 2-4, Lowery 1-3, Yoest 0-1, Kimble 2-6). **Halftime:** Loyola Marymount 94-76.

Aside from these famous cardboard fans, all spectators were banned from the 1989 North Atlantic Tournament due to a measles outbreak.

State's Anthony Reid (20) set school Division I records for highest scoring average in a single season. . . . Ohio University's Dave Jamerson set an NCAA record for highest percentage of a team's output in a single game vs. a Division I opponent (minimum of 40 points) when his 52 points accounted for 74.3 percent of the Bobcats' total in an 86-70 loss to Kent State.

Memphis State raced to a 24-0 lead at highly-ranked Louisville en route to upending the Cardinals, 72-67. Louisville and Memphis State combined to capture the previous 10 Metro Conference regular-season championships until Florida State moved atop the league standings.

Loyola Marymount junior Hank Gathers became the only player to lead the nation in scoring (32.7 points per game) in a season he shot better than 60 percent from the floor (60.8). Gathers collected 41 points and a school-record 29 rebounds in 30 minutes in a 181-150 victory over U.S. International that set an NCAA record for most total points. The scoring frenzy left the following numbers of note:

• A field goal was attempted an average of every 11 seconds and a basket was scored an average of every 18.5 seconds.

• The longest span between baskets was 59 seconds.

1988–89 INDIVIDUAL LEADERS

SCORING

PLAYER	PTS.	AVG.
Gathers, Loyola Marymount	1015	32.7
Jackson, Louisiana St.	965	30.2
Simmons, La Salle	908	28.4
Glass, Mississippi	841	28.0
Edwards, East Carolina	773	26.7
Dudley, Air Force	746	26.6
Coles, Virginia Tech	717	26.6
Smith, Brigham Young	765	26.4
King, Oklahoma	859	26.0
Taft, Marshall	701	26.0

REBOUNDING

PLAYER	REB.	AVG.
Gathers, Loyola Marymount	426	13.7
Hill, Xavier	403	12.2
Draper, American	336	12.0
Battles, Southern (La.)	360	11.6
Simmons, La Salle	365	11.4
Coleman, Syracuse	422	11.4
Burton, Long Island	309	11.0
Mack, South Carolina St.	361	10.9
Sanders, George Mason	326	10.9
Washington, Weber St.	303	10.8

ASSISTS

PLAYER	AST.	AVG.
Williams, Holy Cross	278	9.9
Corchiani, N.C. St.	266	8.6
Douglas, Syracuse	326	8.6
Payton, Oregon St.	244	8.1
Manuel, Bradley	216	8.0
Timberlake, Boston U.	238	7.9
Overton, La Salle	244	7.6
Richardson, UCLA	236	7.6
Sample, Southern (La.)	234	7.5
McGee, New Mexico	243	7.4

BLOCKED SHOTS

PLAYER	BLK.	AVG.
Mourning, Georgetown	169	5.0
Causwell, Temple	124	4.1
Ogg, UAB	129	3.8
Coleman, Syracuse	127	3.4
Butts, Bucknell	100	3.2
Ellison, Louisville	98	3.2
Henderson, Siena	86	3.1
Green, Rhode Island	85	3.0
West, Texas Southern	90	3.0
Campbell, Clemson	87	3.0
Godfread, Evansville	92	3.0

STEALS

PLAYER	STL.	AVG.
Robertson, Cleveland St.	111	4.0
Blaylock, Oklahoma	131	3.7
Applewhite, Tex. S'thern	105	3.5
Screen, Providence	101	3.5
Lee, Towson St.	98	3.4
Tanner, Rice	94	3.4
Murdock, Providence	97	3.3
Workman, Oral Roberts	93	3.3
Blanks, Texas	111	3.3
Newbern, Minnesota	101	3.3

FIELD GOAL PERCENTAGE

PLAYER	FTM	FTA	PCT.
Davis, Florida	179	248	.722
Burns, Miss. St.	167	249	.671
Davis, Clemson	146	218	.670
Mack, S. Carolina St.	204	306	.667
Parker, Cleve. St.	168	253	.664
Ambroise, Baptist	164	247	.664
Vaught, Michigan	201	304	.661
Stewart, Coppin St.	199	302	.659
Smith, Idaho	185	284	.651
Burke, Wagner	215	331	.650

FREE THROW PERCENTAGE

PLAYER	FTM	FTA	PCT.
Smith, BYU	160	173	.925
Henson, Kansas St.	92	100	.920
Simmons, Md.-Balt. C'nty	83	92	.902
Nurnberger, S. Ill.	129	143	.902
Haffner, Evansville	136	151	.901
Matthews, Pitt	142	158	.899
Blevins, Kent	94	105	.895
Lauritzen, Indiana St.	68	76	.895
Peterson, Yale	111	125	.888
Christian, Appa. St.	76	86	.884

THREE-POINT FIELD GOAL PERCENTAGE

PLAYER	FGM	FGA	PCT.
Calloway, Monmouth	48	82	.585
Tribelhorn, Colo. St.	76	135	.563
Joseph, Bucknell	62	115	.539
Bays, Towson St.	71	132	.538
Anglavar, Marquette	53	99	.535

THREE-POINT FIELD GOALS PER GAME

PLAYER	FGM	AVG.
Pollard, Miss. Vly. St.	124	4.4
Grider, SW La.	122	4.2
Fryer, L. Marymount	126	4.1
Barros, Boston College	112	3.9
McCloud, Florida St.	115	3.8

1988–89 TEAM LEADERS

SCORING OFFENSE

SCHOOL	PTS.	AVG.
Loyola Marymount	3486	112.5
Oklahoma	3680	102.2
Southern (La.)	3015	97.3
Texas	3206	94.3
Louisiana St.	2966	92.7

SCORING DEFENSE

SCHOOL	PTS.	AVG.
Princeton	1430	53.0
St. Mary's (Calif.)	1728	57.6
Boise St.	1767	58.9
Colorado St.	2012	61.0
Idaho	1894	61.1

SCORING MARGIN

SCHOOL	OWN	OPP.	MAR.
St. Mary's (Calif.)	76.1	57.6	18.5
Arizona	84.5	66.9	17.6
Michigan	91.7	74.8	16.9
Duke	86.5	69.8	16.8
Siena	85.0	69.8	15.1

WON-LOST PERCENTAGE

SCHOOL	W-L	PCT.
Ball St.	29-3	.906
Arizona	29-4	.879
Illinois	31-5	.861
Georgetown	29-5	.853
West Virginia	26-5	.839

FIELD GOAL PERCENTAGE

SCHOOL	FGM	FGA	PCT.
Michigan	1325	2341	.566
New Mexico	992	1819	.545
Syracuse	1334	2456	.543
Duke	1163	2166	.537
St. Mary's (Calif.)	859	1606	.535

FIELD GOAL PERCENTAGE DEFENSE

SCHOOL	FGM	FGA	PCT.
Georgetown	795	1993	.399
West Virginia	738	1840	.401
St. Mary's (Calif.)	651	1606	.405
Ball St.	688	1687	.408
Seton Hall	934	2265	.412

FREE THROW PERCENTAGE

SCHOOL	FTM	FTA	PCT.
Brigham Young	527	647	.815
Gonzaga	485	614	.790
Bucknell	590	749	.788
Kent	592	755	.784
Louisiana St.	557	723	.770

REBOUND MARGIN

SCHOOL	OWN	OPP.	MAR.
Iowa	41.4	31.8	9.6
Notre Dame	37.7	28.8	9.0
Missouri	42.1	34.2	7.9
Michigan	37.7	30.3	7.4
Stanford	34.8	27.7	7.1

THREE-POINT FIELD GOAL PERCENTAGE

SCHOOL	FGM	FGA	PCT.
Indiana	121	256	.473
Michigan	196	419	.468
The Citadel	153	328	.466
Colorado St.	141	305	.462
Bucknell	160	347	.461

THREE-POINT FIELD GOALS PER GAME

SCHOOL	FGM	AVG.
Loyola Marymount	287	9.3
Valparaiso	257	8.9
Oral Roberts	216	7.7
Mt. St. Mary's (Md.)	202	7.5
Alabama-Birmingham	247	7.3

1988–89 NCAA CHAMPION: MICHIGAN

SEASON STATISTICS OF MICHIGAN REGULARS

PLAYER	POS.	CL.	G.	FG%	FT%	PPG	RPG
Glen Rice	F	Sr.	37	.577	.832	25.6	6.3
Rumeal Robinson	G	Jr.	37	.557	.656	14.9	3.4
Loy Vaught	F	Jr.	37	.661	.778	12.6	8.0
Terry Mills	C	Jr.	37	.564	.769	11.6	5.9
Sean Higgins	F-G	So.	34	.506	.771	12.4	3.1
Mark Hughes	C-F	Sr.	35	.608	.604	6.8	4.1
Kirk Taylor	G	So.	21	.478	.611	4.5	2.2
Mike Griffin	G-F	Jr.	37	.508	.767	2.7	2.4
J. P. Oosterbaan	C	Jr.	22	.564	.692	2.4	1.2
Demetrius Calip	G	So.	30	.440	.824	2.0	0.6
Rob Pelinka	G	Fr.	26	.360	.700	1.1	0.6
TEAM TOTALS			37	.566	.735	91.7	37.7

Three-point field goals leaders: Rice (99 of 192, .516), Higgins (51 of 110 .464), Robinson (30 of 64, .469). **Assists leaders:** Robinson 233, Mills 104, Griffin 103. **Blocked shots leader:** Mills 49. **Steals leader:** Robinson 70.

1989 FINAL FOUR CHAMPIONSHIP GAME

SEATTLE, WA

MICHIGAN (80)	MIN.	FG-A	FT-A	REB.	A	PF	PTS.
Rice	42	12-25	2-2	1	0	2	31
Hughes	25	1-1	0-0	0	0	2	2
Mills	34	4-8	0-0	3	2	2	8
Griffin	17	0-0	0-0	2	3	4	0
Robinson	43	6-13	9-10	1	11	2	21
Vaught	26	4-8	0-0	2	0	2	8
Calip	11	0-2	0-0	0	1	3	0
Higgins	27	3-10	3-4	2	2	3	10
Team				3			
TOTALS	225	30-67	14-16	14	19	20	80

FG%: .448. **FT%:** .875. **Three-point goals:** 6-16 (Rice 5-12, Higgins 1-4). **Blocks:** 4 (Mills 3). **Turnovers:** 14. **Steals:** 3.

SETON HALL (79)	MIN.	FG-A	FT-A	REB.	A	PF	PTS.
Walker	39	5-9	3-4	3	1	2	13
Gaze	39	1-5	2-2	2	3	3	5
Ramos	33	4-9	1-1	0	1	2	9
Morton	37	11-26	9-10	1	3	3	35
Greene	43	5-13	1-3	0	5	3	13
Avent	11	1-2	0-0	1	1	0	2
Volcy	7	0-0	0-2	0	0	2	0
Cooper	14	0-0	0-0	0	0	1	0
Wigington	2	1-1	0-0	0	0	1	2
Team				2			
TOTALS	225	28-65	16-22	9	14	17	79

FG%: .431. **FT%:** .727. **Three-point goals:** 7-23 (Morton 4-12, Greene 2-5, Gaze 1-5, Walker 0-1). **Blocks:** 2. **Turnovers:** 11. **Steals:** 4.
Halftime: Michigan 37-32. **Regulation:** Tied 71-71.

NATIONAL SEMIFINALS

ILLINOIS (81): Anderson 6-14 5-6 17, Battle 10-17 8-10 29, Hamilton 5-14 1-2 11, Gill 5-9 1-1 11, Bardo 1-7 4-4 7, Smith 3-5 0-0 6, Small 0-0 0-0 0, Liberty 0-1 0-0 0. Team 30-67 (.448) 19-23 (.826) 81.

MICHIGAN (83): Rice 12-24 2-2 28, Hughes 4-5 1-1 9, Mills 4-8 0-0 8, Griffin 0-1 0-0 0, Robinson 6-13 2-5 14, Calip 0-1 0-0 0, Higgins 5-12 3-3 14, Vaught 5-13 0-0 10. Team 36-77 (.468) 8-11 (.727) 83.

Three-point goals: Illinois 2-8 (.25), Michigan 3-8 (.375). **Halftime:** Michigan 39-38.

DUKE (78): Brickey 0-3 2-2 2, Ferry 13-29 7-11 34, Laettner 4-5 5-7 13, Henderson 4-16 5-6 13, Snyder 3-10 0-0 8, Koubek 0-3 0-0 0, Davis 1-2 0-2 2, Abdelnaby 0-0 0-0 0, Smith 1-4 3-4 6, Palmer 0-0 0-0 0, Burgin 0-0 0-0 0, Buckley 0-0 0-0 0. Team 26-72 (.361) 22-32 (.688) 78.

SETON HALL (95): Walker 6-9 7-7 19, Gaze 7-14 2-2 20, Ramos 3-8 3-3 9, Morton 4-8 5-6 13, Greene 5-9 6-6 17, Avent 3-4 0-0 6, Volcy 1-2 0-1 2, Cooper 3-4 0-0 6, Wigington 0-0 0-1 0, Monteserin 0-0 0-0 0, Katsikis 1-1 0-1 3, Crowley 0-1 0-0 0, Rebimias 0-1 0-0 0, Long 0-1 0-0 0. Team 33-62 (.532) 23-27 (.852) 95.

Three-point goals: Duke 4-16 (.250), Seton Hall 6-12 (.500). **Halftime:** Duke 38-33.

ALL-TOURNAMENT TEAM

Danny Ferry, F, Sr., Duke (34 points, 10 rebounds/one Final Four game)
Gerald Greene, G, Sr., Seton Hall (30 points, 10 rebounds, 13 assists in final two games)
John Morton, G, Sr., Seton Hall (48 points)
*Glen Rice, F, Sr., Michigan (59 points, 16 rebounds)
Rumeal Robinson, G, Jr., Michigan (35 points, 23 assists)

*Named Most Outstanding Player.

- A point was scored an average of every 7.25 seconds.

- Seven players amassed more points than minutes played.

Kentucky's NCAA-record streak of consecutive non-losing seasons was stopped at 60 when the Wildcats compiled a 13-19 mark in Eddie Sutton's last year as their coach. They lost their home opener, 85-82, to a rag-tag squad from Northwestern (La.) State that finished the campaign with a 13-16 mark. The following indiscretions left UK's program in turmoil:

- Chris Mills transferred to Arizona in the wake of a Los Angeles newspaper reporting that Emery Worldwide employees had discovered $1,000 in an accidentally opened package sent to Mills' father by Wildcats assistant Dwane Casey. Teammate Leron Ellis, another product from California, transferred to Syracuse.

- Prize recruit Shawn Kemp, a Proposition 48 casualty, dropped out of school after an alleged theft.

- Starter Eric Manuel's ACT score was questioned when it doubled from the second time he took the test to the third. Manuel eventually transferred.

Syracuse's Sherman Douglas (22 assists against Providence) and Georgetown's Dikembe

Mutombo (12 blocked shots against St. John's) set Big East Conference single-game records. . . . Connecticut lost 17 straight games to St. John's in their series until defeating the Redmen, 80-52. The Huskies also snapped a 14-game losing streak in their series with Villanova, 57-55. . . . Rutgers lost 13 consecutive games to Temple in their series until defeating the Owls, 77-64. . . . Mark Macon became the fifth different Temple player in six years to earn the Atlantic 10 Player of the Year award. . . . Seton Hall and Stanford finished in the Top 20 of a final wire-service poll for the first time since 1953 and 1963, respectively. Todd Lichti was the first Stanford player since 1942 to become an NCAA first- or second-team All-American. . . . The North Atlantic Tournament was dubbed the MIT (Measles Invitational Tourney) because all spectators were banned because of a measles outbreak.

Illinois (31-5/coached by Lou Henson), Ball State (29-3/Rick Majerus), Missouri (29-8/Norm Stewart), St. Louis (27-10/Rich Grawer), St. Mary's (25-5/Lynn Nance), Siena (25-5/Mike Deane), Evansville (25-6/Jim Crews), South Carolina State (25-8/Cy Alexander), Colorado State (23-10/Boyd Grant), Maryland-Baltimore County (17-11/Earl Hawkins) and Morgan State (15-14/Nat Frazier) had their winningest seasons in school Division I history. Seton Hall (31-7/P.J. Carlesimo) and Middle Tennessee State (23-8/Bruce Stewart) tied their school single-season records for most victories.

Evansville's Scott Haffner scored a national-high, school-record and Midwestern Collegiate Conference-record 65 points against Dayton. Haffner had averaged only 1.7 points per game as a freshman for Illinois before transferring. . . . Ball State sustained at least 10 defeats in 24 consecutive seasons until compiling a 29-3 record under coach Rick Majerus. The Cardinals, who compiled a 14-14 record the previous season, improved by 13 games en route to their lone appearance in the Top 20 of a final wire-service poll. . . . Illinois State posted winning records in its first 18 seasons in Division I until the Redbirds compiled a 13-17 mark in Bob Donewald's last

year as their coach. . . . Valparaiso lost 29 consecutive games to Notre Dame until defeating the Irish, 71-68. . . . Indiana swept Ohio State to give the Hoosiers 26 victories in the last 32 contests of their series. . . . Wisconsin lost 16 consecutive games to Illinois in their series until overwhelming the Final Four-bound Illini, 72-52. Wisconsin also edged NCAA champion-to-be Michigan, 71-68, for the Badgers' lone triumph over the Wolverines in a 16-game stretch of their series from 1984 to 1992.

A bench-clearing brawl forced referees to eject most of Indiana State's team when the Sycamores lost, 84-69, to visiting Wichita State. ISU was forced to play the second half with only four players, ending the contest with just two on the floor after a couple of them fouled out. . . . Arkansas-Little Rock's Carl Brown had the most points ever in a Trans America Athletic Conference game with 46 against Centenary. . . . Houston Baptist competed in its final season at the Division I level. . . . The Citadel lost 37 consecutive games in its series with intrastate opponent South Carolina until edging the Gamecocks, 88-87. . . . Cal State Fullerton posted its lone triumph over UNLV (93-92) in a 25-game stretch of their series from 1984 to 1993.

The NIT semifinalists all won their third-round games on the road for the only time in the event's history—Alabama-Birmingham (at Connecticut), Michigan State (at Villanova), St. Louis (at New Mexico) and St. John's (at Ohio State). New Mexico sustained its fourth homecourt defeat in the last four years in the NIT, fifth in six seasons and sixth since 1979.

Oregon State's Ralph Miller, who previously coached at Wichita State and Iowa, retired after a 38-year coaching career with a 657-382 record. . . . C.M. Newton, who coached Transylvania, Alabama and Vanderbilt, ended his coaching career with a 509-375 record when he became athletic director at his alma mater (Kentucky). . . . Norman Sloan, who previously coached Presbyterian, The Citadel and North Carolina State, was forced out at Florida, ending his 37-year coaching career

1988-89 FINAL NATIONAL POLLS

AP	UPI	USA/CNN	SCHOOL (RECORD)	HEAD COACH
1	1	7	Arizona (29-4)	Lute Olson
2	2	5	Georgetown (29-5)	John Thompson
3	3	3	Illinois (31-5)	Lou Henson
4	5	12	Oklahoma (30-6)	Billy Tubbs
5	4	8	North Carolina (29-8)	Dean Smith
6	8	11	Missouri (29-8)	Norm Stewart*
7	9	6	Syracuse (30-8)	Jim Boeheim
8	6	10	Indiana (27-8)	Bob Knight
9	7	4	Duke (28-8)	Mike Krzyzewski
10	10	1	Michigan (30-7)	Bill Frieder**
11	11	2	Seton Hall (31-7)	P.J. Carlesimo
12	13	13	Louisville (24-9)	Denny Crum
13	12	21	Stanford (26-7)	Mike Montgomery
14	15	16	Iowa (23-10)	Tom Davis
15	14	9	UNLV (29-8)	Jerry Tarkanian
16	16	22	Florida State (22-8)	Pat Kennedy
17	19	18	West Virginia (26-5)	Gale Catlett
18	–	19	Ball State (29-3)	Rick Majerus
19	18	14	N.C. State (22-9)	Jim Valvano
20	20	–	Alabama (23-8)	Wimp Sanderson
–	–	15	Virginia (22-11)	Terry Holland
–	17	20	Arkansas (25-7)	Nolan Richardson
–	–	17	Minnesota (19-12)	Clem Haskins
–	–	23	Texas-El Paso (26-7)	Don Haskins
–	–	24	South Alabama (23-9)	Ronnie Arrow
–	–	25	UCLA (21-10)	Jim Harrick

* Rich Daly coached Missouri the last 10 games of the season after Stewart became ill.

** Steve Fisher coached Michigan the last six games of the season after replacing Frieder.

with a 624-393 record. . . . Texas A&M's Shelby Metcalf finished his career as the SWC's all-time winningest coach. . . . Coach Gerry Friel concluded his tenure at New Hampshire. He lasted 20 seasons despite winning only 37.4 percent of his games (200-335 mark).

1989 NCAA Tournament

Summary: Michigan, guided by interim coach Steve Fisher, became the NCAA titlist to win its two Final Four games by the fewest total of points (three). Sean Higgins' last-second rebound basket gave the Wolverines an 83-81 victory against Illinois in the national semifinals before Rumeal Robinson sank two free throws with three seconds remaining in overtime in an 80-79 triumph against Seton Hall in the final. In the first overtime final since 1963, Seton Hall guard John Morton had the highest scoring output (35 points with 17 in the last eight minutes of regulation to help the Pirates erase a 12-point deficit) of any player for the losing team in a championship game. Since the introduction of seeding in 1979, this was the only year the championship

game did not include at least one No. 1 or No. 2 seed (Michigan and Seton Hall were both No. 3 seeds). The roster Fisher inherited at the start of the playoffs included four future NBA first-round draft choices—Terry Mills, Glen Rice, Robinson and Loy Vaught. What was the pressure of a one-and-one opportunity for a 65.6 percent free-throw shooter after he had gone one-on-one with the street? Previously, the Jamaican-born Robinson had no place to live at all. He was a 12-year-old street urchin deserted by his mother after they moved to Cambridge, Mass., a Boston suburb.

"Somewhere along the line," Robinson said. "I think I was blessed. I feel no bitterness. I have not been cheated. I do not know why my mother did not want me. I do not know why my biological father died the day before I was to meet him. But I also do not know why I was so lucky to find my adoptive parents. It is not so much bad luck or good luck. It is . . . only how it is. . . . how God wants it."

Outcome for Defending Champion: Kansas (19-12) finished in sixth place in the Big Eight. The Jayhawks suffered their most lopsided defeat ever at home in Allen Fieldhouse (91-66 to Missouri).

Star Gazing: Rice, the Final Four Most Outstanding Player, became the only player to score more than 25 points in two games at a single Final Four from 1975-94. Rice holds the records for most three-point baskets and points in a playoff series (27 treys and 184 points in six games). The senior forward hit 12 of 17 from three-point range on his way to a total of 66 points in Southeast Regional semifinal and final victories over North Carolina (92-87) and Virginia (102-65). Rice's liberal use of the three-pointer enabled him to become the only player from a national champion to average more than 25 points per game in a title season (25.6) since David Thompson finished with a 26-point average for North Carolina State in 1974.

Biggest Upsets: Middle Tennessee State (13th seed) over Florida State (4), 97-83, and Siena (14) over Stanford (3), 80-78. MTSU, sparked by freshman guard Mike Buck's six-for-six shooting from three-point range, overcame a 17-point deficit with 16 minutes remaining. Siena guard Marc Brown poured in 32 points, including a pair of decisive free throws with three seconds remaining, to spoil Stanford's first playoff appearance since 1942.

One and Only: Illinois became the only school to defeat the NCAA champion-to-be twice in one season by at least 12 points when the Illini swept Michigan in Big Ten competition.

Numbers Game: Of the more than 60 different players to score at least 2,500 points and/or rank among the top 25 in career scoring average, Arizona's Sean Elliott finished his career as the only one to have a winning NCAA playoff record in his career plus post higher scoring, rebounding and field-goal shooting career playoff averages than he compiled in the regular season. . . . Xavier, coached by Pete Gillen, became the only school to have the misfortune of opposing eventual national champions in the first round in back-to-back years (Kansas '88 and Michigan '89). . . . Michigan and North Carolina met before a regional final for the third consecutive year. . . . The worst composite conference record in one year of the NCAA playoffs was posted by the SEC, which had all five of its entrants lose their first-round games, with four of them bowing by more than 10 points. Independent South Carolina, a recent addition to the SEC, was also drubbed in its opening-round game, giving the six current SEC members a 13.7-point average margin of defeat. . . . North Carolina State's Rodney Monroe scored a tourney-high 40 points in a 102-96 victory over Iowa in the second round of the East Regional. . . . Notre Dame's LaPhonso Ellis grabbed a tourney-high 18 rebounds in an 81-65 triumph over Vanderbilt in the opening round of the East Regional. . . . Texas, coached by Tom Penders, posted its first NCAA playoff victory in 17 years. . . . In an exciting intra-state battle, South Alabama erased a 16-point halftime deficit in an 86-84 victory over Alabama.

What Might Have Been: Forward Nick Anderson (55.3 percent) and center Lowell Hamilton (53.4 percent) rank among the top five Illinois players in career field-goal shooting. If only they combined for 46.4 percent field-goal shooting instead of 39.3 percent (11 of 28) in the national semifinals, the Illini could have defeated eventual champion Michigan rather than losing 83-81. The Wolverines also dodged a bullet against Seton Hall in their narrow title game victory as Pirates forward Andrew Gaze was restricted to one field goal after contributing at least six baskets in each of the previous four playoff games. . . . DePaul (21-12/without Rod Strickland), Kansas State (19-11/Norris Coleman), Memphis State (21-11/Sylvester Gray), North Carolina State (22-9/Charles Shackleford) and Pittsburgh (17-13/Jerome Lane) might have fared better in the playoffs if standout players had exercised their remaining eligibility instead of defecting to the NBA. . . . There is a good chance that Miami, Fla. (19-12) could have appeared in the tourney for the first time since 1960 if Tito Horford didn't leave school early for the pros. . . . SEC regular-season champion Florida (21-13) might not have made an early exit if prize prospect Stacey Poole didn't miss the season because of a foot injury. . . . Metro Conference regular-season champion Florida State (22-8) might have avoided its upset loss to Middle Tennessee State if forward Michael Polite didn't miss the season because of a neurological disorder. . . . Louisville (24-9) possibly could have advanced farther in the playoffs if regal recruit Jerome Harmon didn't miss the season because of a back problem. Ditto Arkansas (25-7) if swingman Ron Huery wasn't suspended for disciplinary reasons. . . . St. John's probably would have participated in the NCAA playoffs instead of the NIT if standout guard Boo Harvey hadn't been grounded by poor grades.

Putting Things in Perspective: Illinois (31-5) defeated Michigan twice by a total of 28 points before losing to the Wolverines by two points in the national semifinals. Indiana (27-8) defeated the Wolverines twice by a total of two points before losing against eventual national runner-up Seton Hall in the West Regional semifinals.

1989 CHAMPIONSHIP BRACKET

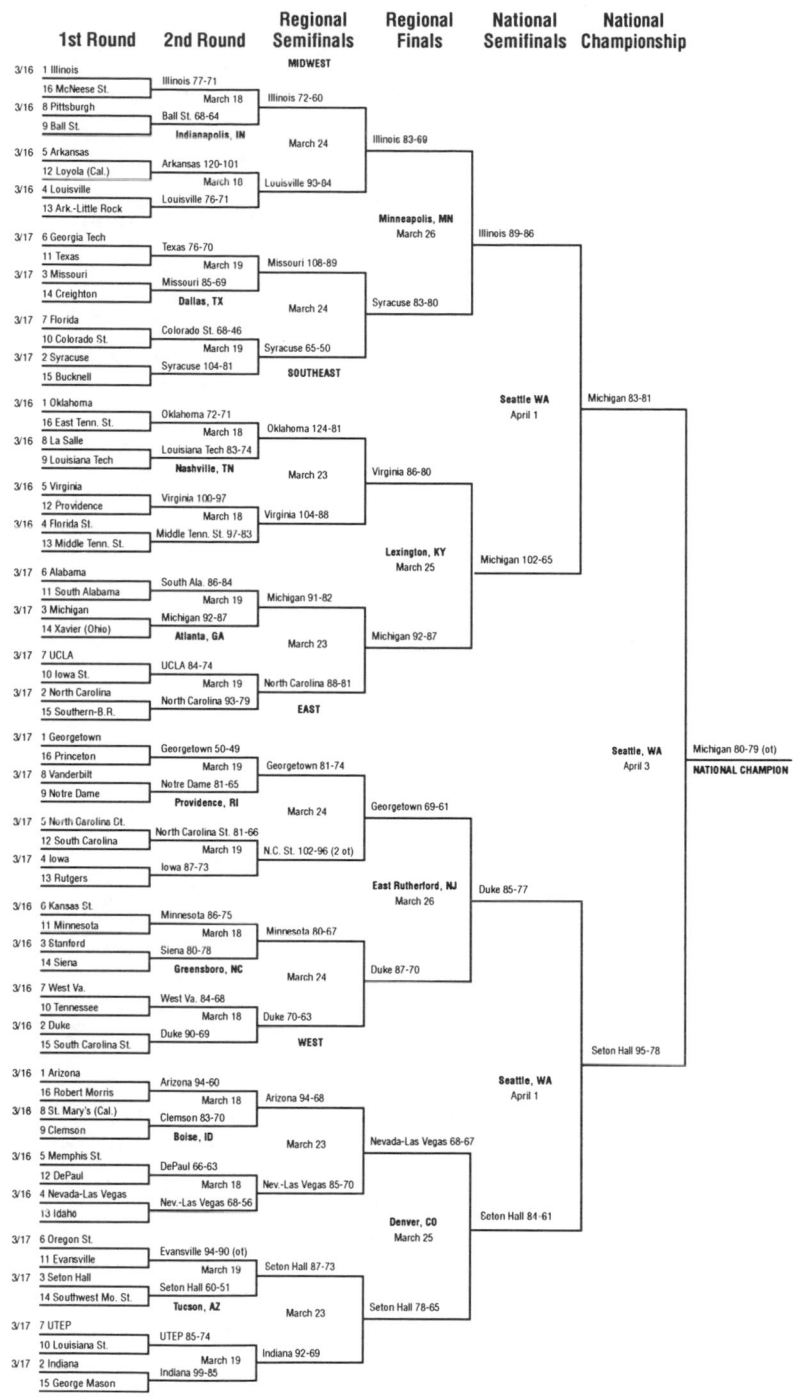

1st Round	2nd Round	Regional Semifinals	Regional Finals	National Semifinals	National Championship

MIDWEST

3/16 1 Illinois
16 McNeese St.
Illinois 77-71
3/16 8 Pittsburgh
9 Ball St.
Ball St. 68-64
March 18
Indianapolis, IN
Illinois 72-60
March 24
Illinois 83-69

3/16 5 Arkansas
12 Loyola (Cal.)
Arkansas 120-101
3/16 4 Louisville
13 Ark.-Little Rock
Louisville 76-71
March 18
Louisville 93-84

Minneapolis, MN
March 26
Illinois 89-86

3/17 6 Georgia Tech
11 Texas
Texas 76-70
3/17 3 Missouri
14 Creighton
Missouri 85-69
March 19
Dallas, TX
Missouri 108-89
March 24
Syracuse 83-80

3/17 7 Florida
10 Colorado St.
Colorado St. 68-46
3/17 2 Syracuse
15 Bucknell
Syracuse 104-81
March 19
Syracuse 65-50

SOUTHEAST

3/16 1 Oklahoma
16 East Tenn. St.
Oklahoma 72-71
3/16 8 La Salle
9 Louisiana Tech
Louisiana Tech 83-74
March 18
Nashville, TN
Oklahoma 124-81
March 23
Virginia 86-80

3/16 5 Virginia
12 Providence
Virginia 100-97
3/16 4 Florida St.
13 Middle Tenn. St.
Middle Tenn. St. 97-83
March 18
Virginia 104-88

Lexington, KY
March 25
Michigan 102-65

Seattle, WA
April 1
Michigan 83-81

3/17 6 Alabama
11 South Alabama
South Ala. 86-84
3/17 3 Michigan
14 Xavier (Ohio)
Michigan 92-87
March 19
Atlanta, GA
Michigan 91-82
March 23
Michigan 92-87

3/17 7 UCLA
10 Iowa St.
UCLA 84-74
3/17 2 North Carolina
15 Southern-B.R.
North Carolina 93-79
March 19
North Carolina 88-81

EAST

3/17 1 Georgetown
16 Princeton
Georgetown 50-49
3/17 8 Vanderbilt
9 Notre Dame
Notre Dame 81-65
March 19
Providence, RI
Georgetown 81-74
March 24
Georgetown 69-61

3/17 5 North Carolina St.
12 South Carolina
North Carolina St. 81-66
3/17 4 Iowa
13 Rutgers
Iowa 87-73
March 19
N.C. St. 102-96 (2 ot)

Seattle, WA
April 3
Michigan 80-79 (ot)
NATIONAL CHAMPION

East Rutherford, NJ
March 26
Duke 85-77

3/16 6 Kansas St.
11 Minnesota
Minnesota 86-75
3/16 3 Stanford
14 Siena
Siena 80-78
March 18
Greensboro, NC
Minnesota 80-67
March 24
Duke 87-70

3/16 7 West Va.
10 Tennessee
West Va. 84-68
3/16 2 Duke
15 South Carolina St.
Duke 90-69
March 18
Duke 70-63

WEST

Seattle, WA
April 1
Seton Hall 95-78

3/16 1 Arizona
16 Robert Morris
Arizona 94-60
3/18 8 St. Mary's (Cal.)
9 Clemson
Clemson 83-70
March 18
Boise, ID
Arizona 94-68
March 23
Nevada-Las Vegas 68-67

3/16 5 Memphis St.
12 DePaul
DePaul 66-63
3/16 4 Nevada-Las Vegas
13 Idaho
Nev.-Las Vegas 68-56
March 18
Nev.-Las Vegas 85-70

Denver, CO
March 25
Seton Hall 84-61

Seton Hall 84-61

3/17 6 Oregon St.
11 Evansville
Evansville 94-90 (ot)
3/17 3 Seton Hall
14 Southwest Mo. St.
Seton Hall 60-51
March 19
Tucson, AZ
Seton Hall 87-73
March 23
Seton Hall 78-65

3/17 7 UTEP
10 Louisiana St.
UTEP 85-74
3/17 2 Indiana
15 George Mason
Indiana 99-85
March 19
Indiana 92-69

Michigan suffered defeats in five of 10 Big Ten games in one span after losing on a neutral court to obscure Alaska-Anchorage, 70-66.

Scoring Leader: Glen Rice, Michigan (184 points, 30.7 ppg).

Rebounding Leader: Daryll Walker, Seton Hall (58 rebounds, 9.7 rpg).

Highest Rebounding Average: Stanley Brundy, DePaul (30 rebounds, 15 rpg).

WINNINGEST PROGRAMS OF THE 1980s

RK.	SCHOOL	W.	L.	PCT.
1.	North Carolina	281	63	.817
2.	UNLV	271	65	.807
3.	Georgetown	269	69	.796
4.	DePaul	235	67	.778
5.	Temple	225	78	.743
6.	Syracuse	243	87	.736
7.	Texas-El Paso	227	82	.735
8.	Oklahoma	245	90	.731
9.	Kentucky	233	86	.730
10.	St. John's	228	85	.728

1980–89 PREMO POWER POLL: BEST TEAMS BY DECADE

RANK	SEASON	SCHOOL
1	1983–84	Georgetown* (34-3)
2	1981–82	North Carolina* (32-2)
3	1984–85	Georgetown (35-3)
4	1982–83	Houston (31-3)
5	1985–86	Duke (37-3)
6	1979–80	Louisville* (33-3)
7	1983–84	North Carolina (28-3)
8	1986–87	Indiana* (30-4)
9	1984–85	St. John's (31-4)
10	1980–81	Oregon St. (26-2)
11	1987–88	Oklahoma (35-4)
12	1988–89	Arizona (29-4)
13	1986–87	UNLV (37-2)
14	1979–80	DePaul (26-2)
15	1981–82	Virginia (30-4)
16	1983–84	DePaul (27-3)
17	1987–88	Arizona (35-3)
18	1980–81	DePaul (27-2)
19	1985–86	Kansas (35-4)
20	1982–83	Louisville (32-4)
	1988–89	Georgetown (29-5)

*–NCAA Tournament Champion

ALL-DECADE TEAM — 1980s

Mark Aguirre, F, DePaul
Steve Alford, G, Indiana
Johnny Dawkins, G, Duke
Patrick Ewing, C, Georgetown
Michael Jordan, G, North Carolina
Danny Manning, F, Kansas
Sam Perkins, F-C, North Carolina
David Robinson, C, Navy
Ralph Sampson, C, Virginia
Wayman Tisdale, C, Oklahoma
Co-Coaches: Dean Smith, North Carolina and Jerry Tarkanian, UNLV

Mark Aguirre

DePaul
6-6 — F
Chicago, Ill. (Austin and Westinghouse H.S.)

Named national player of the year by AP, UPI and USBWA in 1980. . . . Naismith Award winner in 1980. . . . NCAA unanimous first-team All-American in 1980 and 1981. . . . Ranked among the nation's leading scorers in 1979 (18th), 1980 (9th) and 1981 (15th). . . . Leading scorer and second-leading rebounder for third-place team in 1979 NCAA Tournament (26-6 record). . . . Named to 1979 All-NCAA Tournament team. . . . Averaged 20.6 points and 6.1 rebounds in seven NCAA Tournament games from 1979-81 (4-3 record). . . . Member of 1980 U.S. Olympic team (11.3 ppg, 5 rpg). . . . Selected as an undergraduate (after junior season) by the Dallas Mavericks in first round of 1981 NBA draft (1st pick overall).

SEASON	G.	FGM-FGA	FG%	FTM-FTA	FT%	REB.	AVG.	PTS.	AVG.
1978-79	32	302-581	.520	163-213	.765	244	7.6	767	24.0
1979-80	28	281-520	.540	187-244	.766	213	7.6	749	26.8
1980-81	29	280-481	.582	106-137	.774	249	8.6	666	23.0
Totals	89	863-1582	.546	456-594	.768	706	7.9	2182	24.5

Steve Alford

Indiana
6-2 — G
New Castle, Ind. (Chrysler H.S.)

NCAA unanimous first-team All-American in 1987 and consensus first-team All-American in 1986. . . . Led the nation in free-throw percentage in 1984. . . . Finished 2nd in 1985, 21st in 1986 and 8th in 1987. . . . Leading scorer for 1987 NCAA Tournament champion (30-4 record). . . . Named to 1987 All-NCAA Tournament team. . . . Averaged 21.3 points in 10 NCAA Tournament games in 1984, 1986 and 1987 (8-2 record). . . . Averaged 21.6 points in five NIT games for 1985 runner-up. . . . Member of 1984 U.S. Olympic team (10.3 ppg, 3.3 rpg, 64.4 FG%). . . . Selected by the Dallas Mavericks in second round of 1987 NBA draft (26th pick overall).

SEASON	G.	FGM-FGA	FG%	FTM-FTA	FT%	REB.	AVG.	PTS.	AVG.
1983-84	31	171-289	.592	137-150	.913	82	2.6	479	15.5
1984-85	32	232-431	.538	116-126	.921	101	3.2	580	18.1
1985-86	28	254-457	.556	122-140	.871	75	2.7	630	22.5
1986-87	34	241-508	.474	160-180	.889	87	2.6	749	22.0
Totals	125	898-1685	.533	535-596	.898	345	2.8	2438	19.5

Three-point field goals: 107 of 202 (.530) in 1986-87.

Johnny Dawkins

Duke
6-2 — G
Washington, D.C. (Mackin H.S.)

Naismith Award winner in 1986. . . . NCAA unanimous first-team All-American in 1986 and consensus first-team All-American in 1985. . . . Leading scorer, runner-up in assists and third-leading rebounder for 1986 national runner-up (37-3 record). . . . Named to 1986 All-NCAA Tournament team. . . . Averaged 23.8 points and 5.3 rebounds in nine NCAA Tournament games from 1984-86 (6-3 record). . . . Selected by the San Antonio Spurs in first round of 1986 NBA draft (10th pick overall).

SEASON	G.	FGM-FGA	FG%	FTM-FTA	FT%	REB.	AVG.	PTS.	AVG.
1982-83	28	207-414	.500	73-107	.682	115	4.1	506	18.1
1983-84	34	263-547	.481	133-160	.831	138	4.1	659	19.4
1984-85	31	225-455	.495	132-166	.795	141	4.5	582	18.8
1985-86	40	331-603	.549	147-181	.812	142	3.6	809	20.2
Totals	133	1026-2019	.508	485-614	.790	536	4.0	2556	19.2

Three-point field goals: 19 of 54 (.352) in 1982-83.

Patrick Ewing

Georgetown
7-0 — C
Cambridge, Mass. (Rindge & Latin H.S.)

Named national player of the year by AP and NABC in 1985. . . . Naismith Award winner in 1985. . . . NCAA unanimous first-team All-American in 1984 and 1985, and consensus first-team All-American in 1983. . . . Ranked among the nation's leaders in field-goal percentage in 1984 (3rd) and 1985 (7th). . . . Ranked among the nation's leading rebounders in 1983 (24th) and 1984 (27th). . . . Leading scorer and rebounder for 1984 NCAA champion (34-3 record) and 1985 national runner-up (35-3). . . . Second-leading scorer and leading rebounder for 1982 national runner-up (30-7). . . . Final Four Most Outstanding Player in 1984 (18 points, 18 rebounds). . . . Named to All-NCAA Tournament team in 1982, 1984 and 1985. . . . Averaged 14.2 points and eight rebounds in 18 NCAA Tournament games from 1982-85 (15-3 record). . . . Member of U.S. Olympic teams in 1984 (11 ppg, 5.6 rpg, 2.3 bpg, 55.4 FG%) and 1992 (9.5 ppg, 5.3 rpg, 62.3 FG%). . . . Selected by the New York Knicks in first round of 1985 NBA draft (1st pick overall).

SEASON	G.	FGM-FGA	FG%	FTM-FTA	FT%	REB.	AVG.	PTS.	AVG.
1981-82	37	183-290	.631	103-167	.617	279	7.5	469	12.7
1982-83	32	212-372	.570	141-224	.629	325	10.2	565	17.7
1983-84	37	242-368	.658	124-189	.656	371	10.0	608	16.4
1984-85	37	220-352	.625	102-160	.638	341	9.2	542	14.6
Totals	143	857-1382	.620	470-740	.635	1316	9.2	2184	15.3

Michael Jordan

North Carolina
6-6 — G/F
Wilmington, N.C. (Emsley A. Laney H.S.)

NCAA unanimous first-team All-American in 1983 and 1984. . . . Named national player of the year by AP, UPI, USBWA and NABC in 1984. . . . Naismith Award and Wooden Award winner in 1984. . . . Ranked among the nation's leading scorers in 1983 (61st) and 1984 (55th). . . . Third-leading scorer and rebounder for 1982 NCAA Tournament champion (32-2 record). . . . Named to 1982 All-NCAA Tournament team. . . . Averaged 16.5 points and 4.2 rebounds in 10 NCAA Tournament games from 1982-84 (8-2 record). . . . Member of U.S. Olympic teams in 1984 (17.1 ppg, 3 rpg) and 1992 (14.9 ppg, 4.8 apg, 4.6 spg). . . . Selected as an undergraduate (after junior season) by the Chicago Bulls in first round of 1984 NBA draft (3rd pick overall).

SEASON	G.	FGM-FGA	FG%	FTM-FTA	FT%	REB.	AVG.	PTS.	AVG.
1981-82	34	191-358	.534	78-108	.722	149	4.4	460	13.5
1982-83	36	282-527	.535	123-167	.737	197	5.5	721	20.0
1983-84	31	247-448	.551	113-145	.779	163	5.3	607	19.6
Totals	101	720-1333	.540	314-420	.748	509	5.0	1788	17.7

Three-point field goals: 34 of 76 (.447) in 1982-83.

Danny Manning

Kansas
6-10 — F/C
Greensboro, N.C. (Page H.S.) and Lawrence, Kan.

NCAA unanimous first-team All-American in 1987 and 1988, and consensus second-team All-American in 1986. . . . Named national player of the year by NABC in 1988. . . . Naismith Award and Wooden Award winner in 1988. . . . Ranked among the nation's leading scorers in 1987 (15th) and 1988 (12th). . . . Ranked among the nation's leaders in field-goal percentage in 1986 (21st) and 1987 (8th). . . . Leading scorer and rebounder for 1982 NCAA Tournament champion (27-11 record), and leading scorer and second-leading rebounder for 1986 Final Four team (35-4). . . . Named to 1988 All-NCAA Tournament team when he was Final Four Most Outstanding Player (56 points, 17 rebounds, eight blocked shots, 55.6 FG%). . . . Averaged 20.5 points and 7.3 rebounds in 16 NCAA Tournament games from

1985-88 (13-3 record). . . . Member of bronze-medal winning 1988 U.S. Olympic team (11.4 ppg, 6 rpg, 57.1 FG%, 84.6 FT%). . . . Selected by the Los Angeles Clippers in first round of 1988 NBA draft (1st pick overall).

SEASON	G.	FGM-FGA	FG%	FTM-FTA	FT%	REB.	AVG.	PTS.	AVG.
1984-85	34	209-369	.566	78-102	.765	258	7.6	496	14.6
1985-86	39	279-465	.600	95-127	.748	245	6.3	653	16.7
1986-87	36	347-562	.617	165-226	.730	342	9.5	860	23.9
1987-88	38	381-653	.583	171-233	.734	342	9.0	942	24.8
Totals	147	1216-2049	.593	509-688	.740	1187	8.1	2951	20.1

Three-point field goals: 1 of 3 (.333) in 1986-87 and 9 of 26 (.346) in 1987-88. Totals—10 of 29 (.345).

Sam Perkins

North Carolina
6-10 — F/C
Latham, N.Y. (Shaker H.S.)

NCAA consensus first-team All-American in 1983 and 1984, and consensus second-team All-American in 1982. . . . Ranked 12th in the nation in field-goal percentage in 1981. . . . Ranked 20th in the nation in free-throw percentage in 1984. . . . Second-leading scorer and leading rebounder for 1982 NCAA Tournament champion (32-2 record). . . . Second-leading scorer and rebounder for 1981 national runner-up (29-8). . . . Named to 1982 All-NCAA Tournament team. . . . Averaged 15.8 points and 8.6 rebounds in 15 NCAA Tournament games from 1981-84 (12-3 record). . . . Member of 1984 U.S. Olympic team (8.1 ppg, 5.4 rpg, 58.0 FG%). . . . Selected by the Dallas Mavericks in first round of 1984 NBA draft (4th pick overall).

SEASON	G.	FGM-FGA	FG%	FTM-FTA	FT%	REB.	AVG.	PTS.	AVG.
1980-81	37	199-318	.626	152-205	.741	289	7.8	550	14.9
1981-82	32	174-301	.578	109-142	.768	250	7.8	457	14.3
1982-83	35	218-414	.527	145-177	.819	330	9.4	593	16.9
1983-84	31	195-331	.589	155-181	.856	298	9.6	545	17.6
Totals	135	786-1364	.576	561-705	.796	1167	8.6	2145	15.9

Three-point field goals: 12 of 28 (.429) in 1982-83.

David Robinson

Navy
7-0 — C
Manassas, Va. (Osbourn Park H.S.)

Named national player of the year by AP, UPI, USBWA and NABC in 1987. . . . Wooden Award and Naismith Award winner in 1987. . . . NCAA unanimous first-team All-American in 1987 and consensus second-team All-American in 1986. . . . Led the nation in rebounding in 1986. Finished 7th in 1985 and 4th in 1987. . . Led the nation in blocked shots in 1986 (5.9 per game) and 1987 (4.5 per game). . . . Ranked among the nation's leading scorers in 1985 (13th), 1986 (14th) and 1987 (3rd). . . . Ranked among the nation's leaders in field-goal percentage in 1985 (4th), 1986 (16th) and 1987 (19th). . . . Averaged 28.6 points and 12.3 rebounds in seven NCAA Tournament games from 1985-87 (4-3 record). . . . Member of U.S. Olympic team in 1988 (12.8 ppg, 6.8 rpg, 2.4 bpg, 58.0 FG%), 1992 (9 ppg, 4.1 rpg, 57.4 FG%) and 1996. . . . Selected by the San Antonio Spurs in first round of 1987 NBA draft (1st pick overall).

SEASON	G.	FGM-FGA	FG%	FTM-FTA	FT%	REB.	AVG.	PTS.	AVG.
1983-84	28	86-138	.623	42-73	.575	111	4.0	214	7.6
1984-85	32	302-469	.644	152-243	.626	370	11.6	756	23.6
1985-86	35	294-484	.607	208-331	.628	455	13.0	796	22.7
1986-87	32	350-552	.591	202-317	.637	378	11.8	903	28.2
Totals	127	1032-1683	.613	604-964	.627	1314	10.3	2669	21.0

Three-point field goals: 1 for 1 in 1986-87.

NOTE: Missed early action as a plebe because of a broken hand suffered in an Academy boxing class.

Ralph Sampson

Virginia
7-4 — C
Harrisonburg, Va.

Named national player of the year by AP, UPI and USBWA in 1981, 1982 and 1983, and by NABC in 1982 and 1983. . . . Wooden Award winner in 1982 and 1983. . . . Naismith Award winner in 1981, 1982 and 1983. . . .

NCAA unanimous first-team All-American in 1981, 1982 and 1983. . . . Ranked among the nation's leading rebounders in 1980 (15th), 1981 (10th), 1982 (15th) and 1983 (8th). . . . Leading rebounder and second-leading scorer for third-place team in 1981 NCAA Tournament (29-4 record). . . . Averaged 16.4 points and 11.3 rebounds in 10 NCAA Tournament games from 1981-83 (7-3 record). . . . NIT Most Valuable Player in 1980. . . . Averaged 19.2 points and 13.8 rebounds in five NIT games for 1980 champion. . . . Selected by the Houston Rockets in first round of 1983 NBA draft (1st pick overall).

SEASON	G.	FGM-FGA	FG%	FTM-FTA	FT%	REB.	AVG.	PTS.	AVG.
1979-80	34	221-404	.547	66-94	.702	381	11.2	508	14.9
1980-81	33	230-413	.557	125-198	.631	378	11.5	585	17.7
1981-82	32	198-353	.561	110-179	.615	366	11.4	506	15.8
1982-83	33	250-414	.604	126-179	.704	386	11.7	629	19.1
Totals	132	899-1584	.568	427-650	.657	1511	11.4	2228	16.9

Three-point field goals: 3 of 5 (.600) in 1982-83.

Wayman Tisdale

Oklahoma
6-8 — F
Tulsa, Okla. (Booker T. Washington H.S.)

NCAA unanimous first-team All-American in 1984 and 1985, and consensus first-team All-American in 1983. . . . Ranked among the nation's leading scorers in 1983 (8th), 1984 (5th) and 1985 (7th). . . . Ranked among the nation's leading rebounders in 1983 (18th) and 1985 (23rd). . . . Averaged 22.6 points and 9.6 rebounds in seven NCAA Tournament games from 1983-85 (4-3 record). . . . Leading rebounder (6.4 rpg) for 1984 U.S. Olympic team also averaged 8.6 ppg. . . . Selected as an undergraduate (after junior season) by the Indiana Pacers in first round of 1985 NBA draft (2nd pick overall).

SEASON	G.	FGM-FGA	FG%	FTM-FTA	FT%	REB.	AVG.	PTS.	AVG.
1982-83	33	338-583	.580	134-211	.635	341	10.3	810	24.5
1983-84	34	369-639	.577	181-283	.640	329	9.7	919	27.0
1984-85	37	370-640	.578	192-273	.703	378	10.2	932	25.2
Totals	104	1077-1862	.578	507-767	.661	1048	10.1	2661	25.6

Dean Smith

North Carolina

(see active coaches' chapter)

Jerry Tarkanian

UNLV

(see active coaches' chapter)

7

THE SOUTH RISES AGAIN:
THE 1990s

The first half of the 1990s featured the national dominance of two ACC schools—Duke and North Carolina. Developing what many believe is the nation's foremost rivalry, Duke and Carolina or both were represented on the NCAA consensus All-America first- and second-team all but one year (1990) from 1976 through 1995.

The pair of ACC powers combined for more NCAA Tournament victories than the total of over 20 Division I conferences since the playoff field expanded to 64 teams in 1985. Their playoff prowess enabled the ACC to win more than 70 percent of its tourney games with an average of more than 12 victories annually from 1990 through 1995. ACC teams had to be at the top of their games in order to survive the rigorous competition with three league champions this decade going from undisputed first-place finishes to sole possession of last place in back-to-back seasons (Clemson, Duke and Georgia Tech).

North Carolina's Dean Smith passed Adolph Rupp to become the winningest major-college coach in history. Longevity enabled coaches such as Lefty Driesell, Don Haskins, Bob Knight, Norm Stewart and Jerry Tarkanian to already be in

or on the verge of joining the 700 Club in regard to Division I career victories.

The Southeastern Conference compiled the best NCAA playoff record from 1994 through 1996 before the Pacific-10 Conference reigned supreme in 1997 with its second NCAA champion in three years. Meanwhile, the Big Ten struggled with only Indiana among the nation's 20 winningest programs so far in the 1990s to win at least 70 percent of their games.

Several of the nation's premier leagues were extinct by the middle of the decade—Big Eight (merged with four SWC members to form Big 12), Great Midwest (majority of alliance wound up in newly formed Conference USA), Metro (members joined Atlantic 10, Colonial and C-USA) and Southwest (members joined Big 12, C-USA and WAC). Amid all of the conference realigning, Penn State became the first school to twice leave the same league (Atlantic 10).

The impact of Proposition 48's academic requirements for freshman eligibility escalated, leading to more emphasis on junior college recruits. Debate over Proposition 48 among other legislative matters fostered an atmosphere whereby the Black Coaches Association (BCA) threatened boycotts for what it thought was discrimination.

A mass exodus of undergraduates to the NBA, including 40 first-round draft choices in a four-year span from 1993 through 1996, became a constant source of consternation in collegiate circles. The early defections led to a chorus claiming a watered-down product, diluted by NBA migration. Regal high school recruits Kobe Bryant, Kevin Garnett, Tracy McGrady and Jermaine O'Neal bypassed college entirely while prize prospects who did matriculate such as Shareef Abdur-Rahim, Stephon Marbury, Tim Thomas and Dontonio Wingfield exercised only one season of eligibility before turning pro.

1989-90

AT A GLANCE

NCAA Champion: UNLV (35-5; coached by Jerry Tarkanian; tied for first place with New Mexico State in Big West with a 16-2 record).

NIT Champion: Vanderbilt (21-14; coached by Eddie Fogler; tied for seventh place in SEC with a 7-11 record).

NCAA Probation: Cleveland State, Kentucky, North Carolina State

NCAA Consensus First-Team All-Americans: Derrick Coleman, F, Sr., Syracuse; Chris Jackson, G, Soph., Louisiana State; Larry Johnson, F, Jr., UNLV; Gary Payton, G, Sr., Oregon State; Lionel Simmons, F, Sr., La Salle.

National Player of the Year: Simmons (26.5 ppg, 11.1 rpg, 3.6 apg, 1.9 spg, 2 bpg, 51.3 FG%).

Hank Gathers, Loyola Marymount's rising star, collapsed during 1990 NCC Tournament play and tragically died soon after.

National Coaches of the Year: Connecticut's Jim Calhoun (31-6/AP, UPI); Georgia Tech's Bobby Cremins (28-7/Naismith); Michigan State's Jud Heathcote (28-6/NABC), and Kansas' Roy Williams (30-5/USBWA).

The most tragic moment in the history of any league tourney occurred in the semifinals of the West Coast Conference Tournament at Loyola Marymount when Hank Gathers, the league's all-time scoring leader and a two-time tourney MVP, collapsed on his home court during the Lions' game with Portland. He died later that evening of a heart ailment and the tournament was suspended. The Lions still earned an NCAA Tournament bid because of their regular-season crown and advanced to the West Regional final behind the heroics of Bo Kimble, who was Gathers' longtime friend from Philadelphia.

Loyola Marymount, leading the nation in point production for the third consecutive season under coach Paul Westhead, set an NCAA record for highest scoring average per game (122.4). The Lions scored at least 99 points in all but two of their 32 games. They also established a mark for largest-ever margin over the national runner-up (21.1 over Oklahoma). Gathers and Kimble became the only set of teammates to surpass the 2,250-point plateau. Kimble (35.3 ppg), Gathers (29) and Jeff Fryer (22.7) combined for 87 points per game to become the highest-scoring trio in a single season in Division I history. Kimble had four games with at least 50 points.

La Salle's only regular-season defeat was against Loyola Marymount, 121-116. The Explorers made their first Top 20 appearance in a final wire-service poll since 1969. La Salle's Lionel Simmons ended his career with an NCAA-record 115 consecutive games scoring in double figures.

Oregon State's Gary Payton (58 points vs. Southern Cal in OT), LMU's Kimble (54 at St. Joseph's), Nevada-Reno's Kevin Franklin (48 at Loyola Marymount), St. Louis' Anthony Bonner (45 in overtime at Loyola of Chicago) and Harvard's Ralph James (41 at Penn) set school single-game scoring records. Marquette guard Tony Smith tied a school mark with 44 points in an 82-65 loss at Wisconsin. . . . Kimble (35.3 ppg), Ohio's Dave Jamerson (31.2), Duquesne's Mark Stevenson (27.2), Towson State's Kurk Lee (26), Liberty's Bailey Alston (25.5), Marquette's Smith (23.8), Maryland-Baltimore County's Larry Simmons (20.4) and San Diego's John Jerome (19.3) established school Division I records for highest scoring average in a single season.

Northwestern's Todd Leslie set an NCAA record for most consecutive successful three-point

Guard Kenny Anderson-one-third of Georgia Tech's "Lethal Weapon 3"-launches a shot.

baskets with 15 in a span covering four games. . . . OU's Jamerson had 14 treys vs. Charleston (S.C.) in 31 minutes en route to a 60-point outing that is a school and Mid-American Conference record. He contributed five three-pointers in a span of less than four minutes midway through the first half to help the Bobcats increase their lead from two to 16 points.

Georgia Tech's perimeter marksmen Dennis Scott (27.7), Brian Oliver (21.3) and Kenny Anderson (20.6) were known in Hoopdom as Lethal Weapon 3 when they became the first ACC trio to all average more than 20 points per game in the same season. They were also the only three-some ever to achieve the feat for a Final Four team. Anderson, the sixth Tech player in eight years to be named ACC Rookie of the Year, had his best all-around game when he collected 32 points, 12 rebounds and 18 assists in a 93-92 tri-

North Carolina State coach Jim Valvano was one of college basketball's most colorful characters.

umph over Pittsburgh. The Yellow Jackets' six ACC defeats were by a total of 14 points. . . . Georgia, coached by Hugh Durham, captured its lone SEC regular-season title one year after finishing ninth in the 10-team league.

La Salle (30-2/coached by Speedy Morris), Xavier (28-5/Pete Gillen), Michigan State (28-6/Jud Heathcote), Georgia Tech (28-7/Bobby Cremins), Southern Illinois (26-8/Rich Herrin), Southern, La. (25-6/Ben Jobe), Penn State (25-9/Bruce Parkhill), Hawaii (25-10/Riley Wallace), Northern Iowa (23-9/Eldon Miller) and Kent (21-8/Jim McDonald) had their winningest seasons in school Division I history. Tennessee Tech (19-9/Frank Harrell) tied a school single-season mark for most victories.

Seton Hall guard Marko Lokar, a native of Italy making his first college start, scored a Big East Conference-freshman record 41 points against Pittsburgh. In his total of 33 other games with the Pirates this season and a portion of next year, Lokar scored 99 points with only two double-digit outings (15 and 12). Lokar, a pacifist, was opposed to war of any kind and left school because of the reaction he received following his refusal to wear an American flag on his uniform along with the remainder of his teammates during the Gulf War.

Connecticut, improving from a tie for seventh place in the Big East the previous season to a tie for first place under coach Jim Calhoun, made its first appearance in the top 20 of a final wire-service poll for the first time since 1965. . . . Providence lost 21 consecutive games to Syracuse until edging the Orangemen, 87-86. . . . Michigan State, coached by Jud Heathcote, won the Big Ten title just one year after finishing in a tie for eighth place. . . . Kendall Gill (20.4 ppg) became the first Illinois player in 47 years to lead the Big Ten in scoring in conference competition. . . . Oklahoma gave Northeastern Illinois a rude welcome to Division I basketball with a 95-point victory (146-51).

Kentucky had eight different players hit a three-point basket in a 104-73 victory over Furman on December 19, 1989. Four days later, Kentucky (53) and Southwestern Louisiana combined for an NCAA-record 84 three-point field-goal attempts. The Wildcats averaged an NCAA-record 28.9 three-point attempts per game during the season. . . . SEC cellar dweller Florida snapped a 14-game losing streak by leveling LSU, 76-63. Among O'Neal's teammates were two future NBA first-round draft choices—guard Chris Jackson and center Stanley Roberts.

Purdue's Steve Scheffler overcame dyslexia to finish with a Big Ten career record for field-goal shooting (minimum of 400 baskets). He hit 68.5 percent of his field-goal attempts (408 of 596). . . . Clemson, en route to capturing its only ACC regular-season title, closed out its first perfect month of February in 70 years (8-0) with a 97-93 victory over fifth-ranked Duke. The Tigers were coached by Cliff Ellis. . . . North Carolina didn't finish among the top 10 in a final AP poll

1989–90 INDIVIDUAL LEADERS

SCORING

PLAYER	PTS.	AVG.
Kimble, L. Marymount	1131	35.3
Bradshaw, U.S. Intl.	875	31.3
Jamerson, Ohio U.	874	31.2
Ford, Miss. Valley St.	808	29.9
Rogers, Alabama St.	831	29.7
Gathers, L. Marymount	754	29.0
Brooks, Tenn. St.	690	28.8
Jackson, LSU	889	27.8
Scott, Ga. Tech	970	27.7
Stevenson, Duquesne	788	27.2

REBOUNDING

PLAYER	REB.	AVG.
Bonner, St. Louis	456	13.8
McArthur, UC Santa Barb.	377	13.0
Hill, Xavier	402	12.6
Campbell, SW Mo. St.	363	12.5
Ceballos, Cal St. Full.	362	12.5
Shahid, S. Florida	383	12.4
Draper, American	354	12.2
Coleman, Syracuse	398	12.1
O'Neal, LSU	385	12.0
Weatherspoon, S. Miss.	371	11.6

ASSISTS

PLAYER	AST.	AVG.
Lehmann, Drexel	260	9.3
Mitchell, SW La.	264	9.1
Jennings, East Tenn. St.	297	8.7
Livingston, Idaho	262	8.5
Anderson, Ga. Tech	285	8.1
Payton, Oregon St.	235	8.1
Edmond, TCU	234	8.1
Corchiani, N.C. St.	238	7.9
Porter, Pittsburgh	229	7.9
Holt, Prairie View	213	7.9

BLOCKED SHOTS

PLAYER	BLK.	AVG.
Green, Rhode I.	124	4.8
Mutombo, Georgetown	128	4.1
Roberson, Vermont	114	3.8
Williams, Stetson	121	3.8
Roland, Marshall	101	3.6
O'Neal, LSU	115	3.6
Stevenson, Prairie View	97	3.6
Harris, Texas A&M	108	3.5
Longley, New Mexico	117	3.4
Palmer, Dartmouth	85	3.4

STEALS

PLAYER	STL.	AVG.
McMahon, E. Wash.	130	4.5
Dowdell, Coastal Caro.	109	3.8
Henefeld, Conn.	138	3.7
Robinson, Centenary	104	3.5
Payton, Oregon St.	100	3.4
Tanner, Rice	95	3.4
Corchiani, N.C. St.	95	3.2
Rogers, Alabama St.	86	3.1
Giles, Florida A&M	89	3.1
Brown, J'ville	88	3.0

FIELD GOAL PERCENTAGE

PLAYER	FGM	FGA	PCT.
Campbell, SW Mo. St.	192	275	.698
Scheffler, Purdue	173	248	.698
Spencer, Louisville	188	276	.681
Parker, Cleve. St.	155	236	.657
Hill, Evansville	180	278	.647
Stewart, Coppin St.	233	361	.645
Shahid, S. Florida	201	314	.640
French, Hardin-Simm.	212	338	.627
Keefe, Stanford	210	335	.627
Davis, Clemson	205	328	.625

FREE THROW PERCENTAGE

PLAYER	FTM	FTA	PCT.
Robbins, New Mexico	101	108	.935
Joseph, Bucknell	144	155	.929
Jackson, LSU	191	210	.910
Kennedy, UAB	111	123	.902
Henson, Kansas St.	101	112	.902
Matthews, Pittsburgh	141	158	.892
Shreffler, Evansville	84	95	.884
Recasner, Washington	99	112	.884
Venable, Bowling Green	114	129	.884
Franklin, Nevada-Reno	68	77	.883

THREE-POINT FIELD GOAL PERCENTAGE

PLAYER	FGM	FGA	PCT.
Lapin, Princeton	71	133	.534
Iuzzolino, St. Francis (Pa.)	79	153	.516
Oberbrunner, Wisc.-GB	47	93	.505
Mayberry, Arkansas	65	129	.504
Pernell, Holy Cross	81	161	.503

THREE-POINT FIELD GOALS MADE PER GAME

PLAYER	FGM	AVG.
Jamerson, Ohio U.	131	4.7
Grider, SW La.	131	4.5
Alberts, Akron	122	4.4
Fryer, L. Marymount	121	4.3
Brooks, Tenn. St.	95	4.0

1989–90 TEAM LEADERS

SCORING OFFENSE

SCHOOL	PTS.	AVG.
Loyola Marymount	3918	122.4
Oklahoma	3243	101.3
Southern (La.)	3078	99.3
U.S. International	2738	97.8
Centenary	2877	95.9

SCORING DEFENSE

SCHOOL	PTS.	AVG.
Princeton	1378	51.0
Ball St.	1935	58.6
Colorado St.	1778	59.3
Wisc.-Green Bay	1913	59.8
Northern Illinois	1710	61.1

SCORING MARGIN

SCHOOL	OFF.	DEF.	MAR.
Oklahoma	101.3	80.4	21.0
Kansas	92.1	72.3	19.7
Georgetown	81.5	64.8	16.7
Arkansas	95.6	79.8	15.8
Southern (La.)	99.3	84.1	15.2

WON-LOST PERCENTAGE

SCHOOL	W-L	PCT.
La Salle	30-2	.938
UNLV	35-5	.875
Arkansas	30-5	.857
Kansas	30-5	.857
Xavier	28-5	.848

FIELD GOAL PERCENTAGE

SCHOOL	FGM	FGA	PCT.
Kansas	1204	2258	.533
Louisville	1097	2078	.528
Princeton	592	1133	.523
Purdue	778	1491	.522
Loyola Marymount	1456	2808	.519

DEFENSIVE FIELD GOAL PERCENTAGE

SCHOOL	FGM	FGA	PCT.
Georgetown	713	1929	.370
Arizona	780	1990	.392
Ball St.	715	1789	.400
Alabama	784	1952	.402
South Carolina	660	1630	.405

FREE THROW PERCENTAGE

SCHOOL	FTM	FTA	PCT.
Lafayette	461	588	.784
Vanderbilt	742	956	.776
Wisc.-Green Bay	411	532	.773
Murray St.	540	703	.768
Bucknell	502	657	.764

REBOUND MARGIN

SCHOOL	OWN	OPP.	MAR.
Georgetown	44.8	34.0	10.8
Xavier	40.4	30.0	10.4
Ball St.	39.5	30.9	8.6
Michigan St.	38.1	29.8	8.4
Notre Dame	37.9	29.6	8.2

THREE-POINT FIELD GOAL PERCENTAGE

SCHOOL	FGM	FGA	PCT.
Princeton	208	460	45.2
Brigham Young	140	311	45.0
Western Michigan	177	394	44.9
Holy Cross	181	404	44.8
Northwestern	116	260	44.6

THREE-POINT FIELD GOALS MADE

SCHOOL	FGM	AVG.
Kentucky	281	10.0
Loyola Marymount	298	9.3
Southwestern La.	251	8.7
East Tenn. St.	285	8.4
Dayton	261	8.2

UNLV's Anderson Hunt.

Georgia Tech's Brian Oliver reaches for the hoop.

for the first time in 10 years. The Tar Heels, after winning 29 of their previous 34 meetings with Maryland, were swept by the Terrapins.

Texas-El Paso's school-record 31-game home-court winning streak ended when the Miners lost to Indiana, 69-66. UTEP coach Don Haskins missed much of the season when doctors order him to abandon his coaching duties because of an acute case of laryngitis. . . . New Mexico's Rob Robbins set a Western Athletic Conference record by converting 52 consecutive free-throw attempts. . . . New Mexico State nipped UNLV, 83-82, for the Aggies' lone victory over the Rebels in their first 21 meetings from 1984 to 1993. . . . Pacific lost 19 consecutive games to UC Irvine in their series before upending the Anteaters, 70-58. . . . UC Santa Barbara's Eric McArthur set a school single-game record with 28 rebounds against New Mexico State. . . . Oregon State's Payton led the Pacific-10 Conference in assists for the fourth consecutive

season. . . . Oregon outlasted UCLA, 105-99, for the Ducks' lone victory over the Bruins in a 16-game stretch of their series from 1987 to 1994.

Massachusetts (17-14/coached by John Calipari) posted its first winning record in 12 years. . . . Hardin-Simmons (Tex.) competed in its final season at the Division I level. . . . Tennessee's Wade Houston became the first African American head coach in the SEC. . . . National personality Jim Valvano was forced out as coach at N.C. State. The Wolfpack had entered the season on a sour note after the publication of "Personal Fouls," a book alleging a wide range of wrongdoing at the school. Valvano became an ESPN/ABC commentator before dying three years later after a courageous fight against cancer.

1990 NCAA Tournament

Summary: UNLV's 103-73 rout of Duke when the Rebels became the only team to score

1989-90 FINAL NATIONAL POLLS

AP	UPI	USA/CNN	SCHOOL (RECORD)	HEAD COACH
1	1	11	Oklahoma (27-5)	Billy Tubbs
2	2	1	UNLV (35-5)	Jerry Tarkanian
3	3	5	Connecticut (31-6)	Jim Calhoun
4	4	7	Michigan State (28-6)	Jud Heathcote
5	5	14	Kansas (30-5)	Roy Williams
6	6	10	Syracuse (26-7)	Jim Boeheim
7	8	4	Arkansas (30-5)	Nolan Richardson
8	9	15	Georgetown (24-7)	John Thompson
9	7	3	Georgia Tech (28-7)	Bobby Cremins
10	10	6	Purdue (22-8)	Gene Keady
11	11	20	Missouri (26-6)	Norm Stewart
12	13	19	La Salle (30-2)	Speedy Morris
13	15	18	Michigan (23-8)	Steve Fisher
14	12	21	Arizona (25-7)	Lute Olson
15	14	2	Duke (29-9)	Mike Krzyzewski
16	16	24	Louisville (27-8)	Denny Crum
17	17	13	Clemson (26-9)	Cliff Ellis
18	18	–	Illinois (21-8)	Lou Henson
19	–	–	Louisiana State (23-9)	Dale Brown
20	–	8	Minnesota (23-9)	Clem Haskins
21	–	9	Loyola Marymount (26-6)	Paul Westhead
22	–	–	Oregon State (22-7)	Jim Anderson
23	19	16	Alabama (26-9)	Wimp Sanderson
24	20	–	New Mexico State (26-5)	Neil McCarthy
25	–	17	Xavier (28-5)	Pete Gillen
–	–	12	Texas (24-9)	Tom Penders
–	–	22	Ball State (26-7)	Dick Hunsaker
–	–	23	UCLA (22-11)	Jim Harrick
–	–	25	North Carolina (21-13)	Dean Smith

20 WINNINGEST PROGRAMS OF 1990-96

RK.	SCHOOL	W.	L.	PCT.
1.	Kansas	194	44	.815
2.	Kentucky	184	45	.803
3.	Arkansas	195	49	.799
4.	Arizona	179	46	.796
5.	Massachusetts	183	53	.775
6.	Connecticut	175	53	.768
7.	UCLA	170	53	.762
8.	North Carolina	184	58	.760
9.	Wis.-Green Bay	160	53	.751
10.	Syracuse	166	58	.741
11.	Duke	178	63	.739
12.	Indiana	164	60	.732
13.	New Mexico State	159	60	.726
14.	Cincinnati	164	62	.726
15.	Princeton	137	52	.725
16.	Utah	162	63	.720
17.	UNLV	153	61	.715
18.	Purdue	155	63	.711
19.	Montana	145	60	.707
20.	New Mexico	169	72	.701

more than 100 points in a championship game established a record for widest margin of victory in a final. UNLV forced Duke's starting backcourt, Bobby Hurley and Phil Henderson, into a total of 11 turnovers. Larry Johnson, 6-7, finished with the highest rebounding average for a player on an NCAA titlist (11.4 rpg) since North Carolina State's Tom Burleson (12.2 in 1973-74).

Outcome for Defending Champion: Michigan (23-8) finished third in the Big Ten after dropping three of four conference contests late in the season.

Star Gazing: UNLV guard Anderson Hunt is the only Final Four Most Outstanding Players since 1954 to never play in the NBA.

Biggest Upset: Northern Iowa (14th seed) defeated Missouri (3), 74-71.

One and Only: Georgia Tech guard Kenny Anderson became the only freshman on a Final Four team to score more than 20 points in as many as four tournament games.

Numbers Game: Georgia Tech is the only Final Four team to have three players each average more than 20 points per game in the same season. The trio, known as Lethal Weapon 3, included Dennis Scott (27.7), Brian Oliver (21.3) and Anderson (20.6). . . . Each Final Four participant received more than $1.47 million, a whopping increase of about 2,870 percent in just 20 years. Trying to minimize emphasis on the intrinsic dollar value of "six-figure shots" taken by players, the NCAA implemented a new revenue-sharing formula beginning with the next season. . . . The record for most three-point field goals in a playoff game was set by Loyola Marymount senior guard Jeff Fryer with 11 (149-115 victory over defending NCAA champion Michigan in the second round of the West Regional). Fryer (41) and Bo Kimble (37) became the only set of teammates to score more than 35 points in the same tourney game when they combined for 78 vs. Michigan in the highest-scoring game in NCAA playoff history. Kimble had poured in a tourney-high 45 points in a 111-92 triumph over New Mexico State in the opening round. The Lions set an NCAA record for highest scoring average in a playoff series (105.8 in four games). . . . Michigan's Loy Vaught grabbed a tourney-high 21 rebounds in a 76-70 victory over Illinois State in the first round of the West Regional. . . . Louisville's LaBradford Smith finished his playoff career with 95.7 percent accuracy from the free-throw line (45 of 47 in eight games). . . . The four second-round games in the

1989–90 NCAA CHAMPION: UNLV

SEASON STATISTICS OF UNLV REGULARS

PLAYER	POS.	CL.	G.	FG%	FT%	PPG	RPG
Larry Johnson	F	Jr.	40	.624	.767	20.6	11.4
Anderson Hunt	G	So.	39	.481	.663	15.9	2.2
David Butler	C	Sr.	33	.487	.728	15.8	7.4
Stacey Augmon	F	Jr.	39	.553	.671	14.2	6.9
Greg Anthony	G	Jr.	39	.457	.682	11.2	3.0
Moses Scurry	F-C	Sr.	30	.520	.560	7.7	4.1
Travis Bice	G	So.	33	.480	.818	4.3	0.6
Barry Young	F	Jr.	39	.380	.680	4.2	2.0
James Jones	F	Sr.	31	.527	.550	3.9	2.8
Stacey Cvjanovich	G	Sr.	33	.362	.900	2.6	1.1
TEAM TOTALS			40	.508	.699	93.5	41.7

Three-point field goals leaders: Hunt (99 of 258, .384), Anthony (45 of 120 .375), Bice (36 of 75, .480), Young (31 of 96, .323). Assists leaders: Anthony 289, Hunt 158, Augmon 143. Blocked shots leaders: Johnson 56, Augmon 49. Steals leaders: Anthony 106, Augmon 69, Johnson 65.

1990 FINAL FOUR CHAMPIONSHIP GAME

DENVER, CO

UNLV (103)	MIN.	FG-A	FT-A	REB.	A	PF	PTS.
Johnson	30	8-12	4-4	2	2	3	22
Augmon	26	6-7	0-1	2	7	5	12
Butler	27	1-4	2-2	0	3	3	4
Hunt	31	12-16	1-2	0	2	0	29
Anthony	30	5-11	3-4	1	6	3	13
Cvijanovich	10	1-2	2-2	1	2	2	5
Bice	9	0-1	0-0	0	0	0	2
Rice	2	0-2	0-0	0	0	0	0
Young	12	2-2	0-0	0	0	1	5
Jones	8	4-5	0-0	0	0	2	8
Scurry	12	2-5	1-2	3	0	2	5
Jeter	3	0-0	0-0	0	0	0	0
Team				2			
TOTALS	200	41-67	13-17	11	24	23	103

FG%: .612. FT%: .765. Three-point goals: 8-14 (Hunt 4-7, Johnson 2-2, Cvijanovich 1-1, Young 1-1, Rice 0-1, Bice 0-1, Anthony 0-1). Blocks: 3. Turnovers: 17. Steals: 16 (Anthony 5).

DUKE (73)	MIN.	FG-A	FT-A	REB.	A	PF	PTS.
Brickey	24	2-4	0-2	1	2	2	4
Laettner	29	5-12	5-6	5	5	4	15
Abdelnaby	24	5-7	4-6	4	0	3	14
Henderson	32	9-20	2-2	1	0	2	21
Hurley	32	0-3	2-2	0	3	3	2
Hill	8	0-2	0-0	1	1	0	0
Davis	21	2-5	2-3	1	0	1	6
McCaffrey	9	1-3	2-2	0	0	1	4
Koubek	14	1-4	0-0	2	0	0	2
Palmer	2	0-0	3-4	0	0	0	3
Buckley	3	0-0	0-0	0	0	0	0
Cook	2	1-1	0-0	0	0	0	2
Team				6			
TOTALS	200	26-61	20-27	21	11	16	73

FG%: .426. FT%: .741. Three-point goals: 1-11 (Henderson 1-8, Hurley 0-2, Koubek 0-1). Blocks: 3. Turnovers: 23 (Henderson 6, Hurley 5). Steals: 5. Halftime: UNLV 47-35.

NATIONAL SEMIFINALS

GEORGIA TECH (81): Scott 8-17 6-9 29, Mackey 2-3 0-0 4, McNeil 2-4 0-1 4, Anderson 7-14 1-2 16, Oliver 9-18 6-9 24, Brown 2-3 0-0 4, Barnes 0-0 0-0 0. Team 30-59 (.508) 13-21 (.619) 81.

UNLV (90): Johnson 5-11 4-4 15, Augmon 9-16 3-3 22, Butler 6-10 1-3 13, Hunt 7-15 1-2 20, Anthony 4-9 3-7 14, Cvijanovich 0-0 0-0 0, Bice 0-0 0-0 0, Young 0-0 0-0 0, Jones 0-0 0-0 0, Scurry 3-4 0-0 6. Team 34-65 (.523) 12-19 (.632) 90.

Three-point goals: Georgia Tech 8-21 (.381), UNLV 10-15 (.667). Halftime: Georgia Tech 53-46.

DUKE (97): Brickey 8-10 1-3 17, Laettner 5-7 9-12 19, Abdelnaby 8-12 4-5 20, Henderson 10-21 5-5 28, Hurley 0-2 3-6 3, Hill 0-0 0-0 0, Davis 1-4 3-4 5, McCaffrey 0-1 3-4 3, Koubek 1-4 0-0 2, Buckley 0-0 0-0 0, Cook 0-0 0-0 0. Team 33-61 (.541) 28-39 (.718) 97.

ARKANSAS (83): Whitby 0-2 0-0 0, Linn 0-1 0-0 0, Marks 0-0 0-0 0, Day 8-17 7-7 27, Howell 5-9 7-8 18, Credit 2-3 1-4 5, Mayberry 6-18 0-0 12, Bowers 1-6 0-0 2, Murry 2-5 0-0 5, Hawkins 2-4 2-2 6, Miller 1-3 1-2 3, Huery 2-5 1-3 5. Team 29-73 (.397) 19-26 (.731) 83.

Three-point goals: Duke 3-9 (.333), Arkansas 6-21 (.286). Halftime: Duke 46-43.

ALL-TOURNAMENT TEAM

Stacey Augmon, F, Jr., UNLV (34 points, 13 rebounds, 10 assists in final two games)
Phil Henderson, G, Sr., Duke (49 points, 10 rebounds)
*Anderson Hunt, G, Soph., UNLV (49 points, nine assists, nine three-pointers)
Larry Johnson, F, Jr., UNLV (37 points, 16 rebounds)
Dennis Scott, F, Jr., Georgia Tech (29 points/one Final Four game)

*Named Most Outstanding Player.

Midwest Regional were decided by an average of two points.

What Might Have Been: Anderson averaged 27 points per game in his first four tournament contests as a freshman for Georgia Tech. If only he reached that figure in his fifth game instead of scoring 16 points in the national semifinals, the Yellow Jackets could have defeated eventual champion UNLV rather than blowing a seven-point halftime lead and losing 90-81. . . . Illinois (21-8/without Nick Anderson), Indiana (18-11/Jay Edwards) and North Carolina (21-13/J.R. Reid) might have fared better in the playoffs if standout players had exercised their remaining eligibility instead of defecting to the NBA. Ditto Oklahoma (27-5) if forward Jeff Webster didn't miss the majority of the season because of a foot injury. . . . Memphis State (18-12) probably would have participated in the NCAA Tournament instead of the NIT if Sylvester Gray didn't leave school early for the NBA two years earlier after his sophomore season. . . . South Florida (20-11) might have given #2 seed Arizona more of a scare in the Bulls' initial NCAA playoff appearance if forward Gary Alexander didn't miss the season because of

1990 CHAMPIONSHIP BRACKET

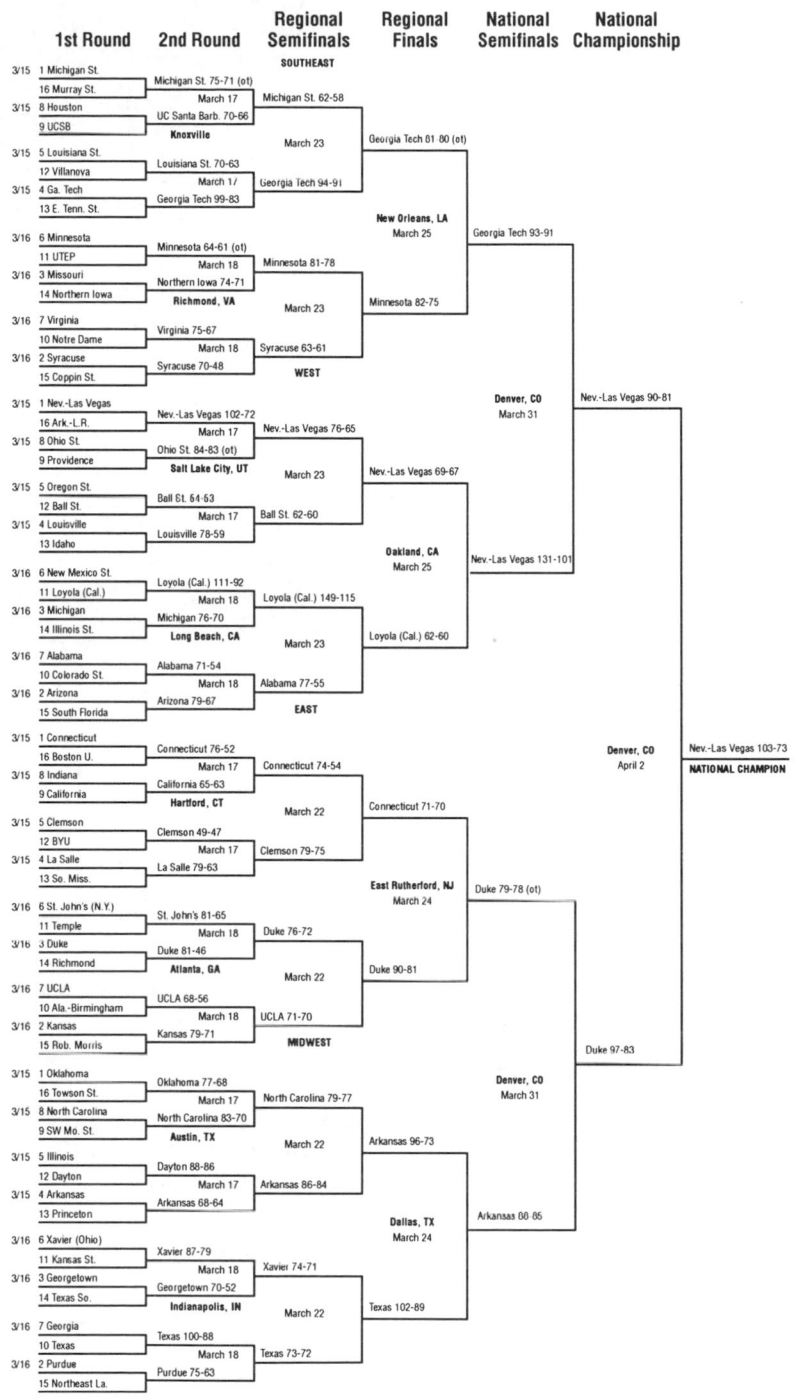

	1st Round	2nd Round	Regional Semifinals	Regional Finals	National Semifinals	National Championship

SOUTHEAST

3/15 1 Michigan St.
16 Murray St.
— Michigan St. 75-71 (ot)
March 17 — Michigan St. 62-58
3/15 8 Houston
9 UCSB
— UC Santa Barb. 70-66
Knoxville
— Georgia Tech 81-80 (ot)
3/15 5 Louisiana St.
12 Villanova
— Louisiana St. 70-63
March 17 — Georgia Tech 94-91
3/15 4 Ga. Tech
13 E. Tenn. St.
— Georgia Tech 99-83
New Orleans, LA March 25 — Georgia Tech 93-91

3/16 6 Minnesota
11 UTEP
— Minnesota 64-61 (ot)
March 18 — Minnesota 81-78
3/16 3 Missouri
14 Northern Iowa
— Northern Iowa 74-71
Richmond, VA
— Minnesota 82-75
3/16 7 Virginia
10 Notre Dame
— Virginia 75-67
March 18 — Syracuse 63-61
3/16 2 Syracuse
15 Coppin St.
— Syracuse 70-48

Georgia Tech 93-91 · **Denver, CO** March 31 · Nev.-Las Vegas 90-81

WEST

3/15 1 Nev.-Las Vegas
16 Ark.-L.R.
— Nev.-Las Vegas 102-72
March 17 — Nev.-Las Vegas 76-65
3/15 8 Ohio St.
9 Providence
— Ohio St. 84-83 (ot)
Salt Lake City, UT
— Nev.-Las Vegas 69-67
3/15 5 Oregon St.
12 Ball St.
— Ball St. 64-63
March 17 — Ball St. 62-60
3/15 4 Louisville
13 Idaho
— Louisville 78-59
Oakland, CA March 25 — Nev.-Las Vegas 131-101

3/16 6 New Mexico St.
11 Loyola (Cal.)
— Loyola (Cal.) 111-92
March 18 — Loyola (Cal.) 149-115
3/16 3 Michigan
14 Illinois St.
— Michigan 76-70
Long Beach, CA
— Loyola (Cal.) 62-60
3/16 7 Alabama
10 Colorado St.
— Alabama 71-54
March 18 — Alabama 77-55
3/16 2 Arizona
15 South Florida
— Arizona 79-67

Denver, CO April 2 · Nev.-Las Vegas 103-73 · **NATIONAL CHAMPION**

EAST

3/15 1 Connecticut
16 Boston U.
— Connecticut 76-52
March 17 — Connecticut 74-54
3/15 8 Indiana
9 California
— California 65-63
Hartford, CT
— Connecticut 71-70
3/15 5 Clemson
12 BYU
— Clemson 49-47
March 17 — Clemson 79-75
3/15 4 La Salle
13 So. Miss.
— La Salle 79-63
East Rutherford, NJ March 24 — Duke 79-78 (ot)

3/16 6 St. John's (N.Y.)
11 Temple
— St. John's 81-65
March 18 — Duke 76-72
3/16 3 Duke
14 Richmond
— Duke 81-46
Atlanta, GA
— Duke 90-81
3/16 7 UCLA
10 Ala.-Birmingham
— UCLA 68-56
March 18 — UCLA 71-70
3/16 2 Kansas
15 Rob. Morris
— Kansas 79-71

Denver, CO March 31 · Duke 97-83

MIDWEST

3/15 1 Oklahoma
16 Towson St.
— Oklahoma 77-68
March 17 — North Carolina 79-77
3/15 8 North Carolina
9 SW Mo. St.
— North Carolina 83-70
Austin, TX
— Arkansas 96-73
3/15 5 Illinois
12 Dayton
— Dayton 88-86
March 17 — Arkansas 86-84
3/15 4 Arkansas
13 Princeton
— Arkansas 68-64
Dallas, TX March 24 — Arkansas 88-85

3/16 6 Xavier (Ohio)
11 Kansas St.
— Xavier 87-79
March 18 — Xavier 74-71
3/16 3 Georgetown
14 Texas So.
— Georgetown 70-52
Indianapolis, IN
— Texas 102-89
3/16 7 Georgia
10 Texas
— Texas 100-88
March 18 — Texas 73-72
3/16 2 Purdue
15 Northeast La.
— Purdue 75-63

a knee injury. Alexander led them in rebounding the next two years to finish his career with the school's best rebound average (9.9 rpg).

Scoring Leader: Dennis Scott, Georgia Tech (153 points, 30.6 ppg).

Highest Scoring Average: Bo Kimble, Loyola Marymount (143 points, 35.75 ppg).

Rebounding Leader: Larry Johnson, UNLV (75 rebounds, 12.5 rpg).

Highest Rebounding Average: Loy Vaught, Michigan (38 rebounds, 19 rpg).

1990-91

AT A GLANCE

NCAA Champion: Duke (32-7; coached by Mike Krzyzewski; won ACC regular-season title by one game over North Carolina with an 11-3 record).

NIT Champion: Stanford (20-13; coached by Mike Montgomery; finished in a five-way tie for fifth place in Pacific-10 with an 8-10 record).

New Conference: Patriot League.

New Rules: Beginning with a team's 10th personal foul in a half, two free throws are awarded for each common foul, except player-control fouls. . . . Three free throws are awarded when a shooter is fouled during an unsuccessful three-point attempt. . . . The definition of "home court" in the NCAA Tournament is amended to include playing no more than three games of a regular-season schedule, excluding league tournaments, in one arena. . . . A preliminary round is used for six of 33 eligible conferences to identify the 30 automatic-qualifying leagues. The conferences with the lowest rankings in the Ratings Percentage Index (RPI) must compete for the available automatic-qualifying positions.

NCAA Probation: Illinois, Kentucky, Marshall, Maryland, Missouri, Northwestern (La.) State, Robert Morris, Southeastern Louisiana

NCAA Consensus First-Team All-Americans: Kenny Anderson, G, Soph., Georgia Tech; Jim Jackson, G-F, Soph., Ohio State; Larry Johnson, F, Sr., UNLV; Shaquille O'Neal, C, Soph., Louisiana State; Billy Owens, F, Jr., Syracuse.

National Players of the Year: Johnson (22.7 ppg, 10.9 rpg, 3 apg, 66.2 FG%, 81.8 FT%/NABC, USBWA, Nai-

UNLV's Larry Johnson in motion.

smith, Wooden) and O'Neal (27.6 ppg, 14.7 rpg, 5 bpg, 62.8 FG%/AP, UPI).

National Coaches of the Year: Ohio State's Randy Ayers (27-4/AP, Naismith, USBWA); Duke's Mike Krzyzewski (32-7/NABC), and Utah's Rick Majerus (30-4/UPI).

Defending champion UNLV, the first team to enter the NCAA Tournament undefeated since Indiana State in 1979, was upset by Duke in the national semifinals. Still, the Rebels will go down as one of the greatest teams in history if only because they're the one squad to have at least four teammates score a minimum of 1,500 points—Stacey Augmon (2,011), Greg Anthony (1,738), Anderson Hunt (1,632) and Larry Johnson (1,617).

U.S. International's Kevin Bradshaw, a Navy veteran who started his college career at Bethune-

1990–91 INDIVIDUAL LEADERS

SCORING

PLAYER	PTS.	AVG.
Bradshaw, U.S. International	1054	37.6
Ford, Miss. Valley St.	915	32.7
McDade, Wisc.-Milw.	830	29.6
Rogers, Alabama St.	852	29.4
Lowery, L. Marymount	884	28.5
Phills, Southern (La.)	795	28.4
O'Neal, LSU	774	27.6
Taft, Marshall	764	27.3
Monroe, N.C. St.	836	27.0
Brandon, Oregon	745	26.6

REBOUNDING

PLAYER	REB.	AVG.
O'Neal, LSU	411	14.7
Jones, Murray St.	469	14.2
Stewart, Coppin St.	403	13.4
Burroughs, J'ville	350	13.0
Kidd, Middle Tenn. St.	370	12.3
Weatherspoon, S'ern Miss.	355	12.2
Johnson, New Orleans	367	12.2
Davis, Delaware St.	366	12.2
Mutombo, Georgetown	389	12.2
Davis, Clemson	340	12.1

ASSISTS

PLAYER	AST.	AVG.
Corchiani, N.C. St.	299	9.6
Tirado, J'ville	259	9.3
Lowery, L. Marymount	283	9.1
Jennings, East Tenn. St.	301	9.1
Anthony, UNLV	310	8.9
Usher, Tenn. Tech	233	8.3
Smart, San Francisco	237	8.2
Johnson, Sam Houston St.	193	8.0

Cody, Texas-Arl. | 229 | 7.9
Bernard, SW Mo. St. | 257 | 7.6

BLOCKED SHOTS

PLAYER	BLK.	AVG.
Bradley, BYU	177	5.2
Lewis, Maryland	143	5.1
O'Neal, LSU	140	5.0
Mutombo, Georgetown	151	4.7
Roberson, Vermont	104	3.7
Williams, Stetson	113	3.6
Earl, Iowa	106	3.3
McIlvaine, Marquette	92	3.3
Longley, New Mexico	95	3.2
Lopez, Fordham	100	3.0

STEALS

PLAYER	STL.	AVG.
Usher, Tenn. Tech	104	3.7
Burrell, Connecticut	112	3.6
Murdock, Providence	111	3.5
McDade, Wisc.-Milw.	97	3.5
Smith, St. Francis (N.Y.)	100	3.4
Davis, Delaware St.	84	3.4
Ellison, Texas-San Ant.	97	3.3
Jennings, East Tenn. St.	109	3.3
Phills, Southern (La.)	90	3.2
Baldwin, N'western	90	3.2

FIELD GOAL PERCENTAGE

PLAYER	FGM	FGA	PCT.
Miller, Arkansas	254	361	.704
Kidd, Middle Tenn. St.	173	247	.700
Freeman, Akron	175	250	.700
James, St. Francis (N.Y.)	149	215	.693
Kennedy, E. Mich.	240	352	.682

Lightfoot, Montana St. | 130 | 196 | .663
Brooks, West Va. | 222 | 335 | .663
Johnson, UNLV | 308 | 465 | .662
Alexander, Iowa St. | 294 | 446 | .659
Longley, New Mex. | 229 | 349 | .656

FREE THROW PERCENTAGE

PLAYER	FTM	FTA	PCT.
Archbold, Butler	187	205	.912
Lewis, Monmouth	91	101	.901
Alexander, Okla. St.	96	107	.897
Jennings, East Tenn. St.	136	152	.895
Monroe, N.C. St.	162	183	.885
Iuzzolino, St. Francis (Pa.)	215	243	.885
Bird, Indiana St.	82	94	.872
Marcelic, S. Utah	81	93	.871
Geter, Ohio	137	158	.867
Kennedy, UAB	167	193	.865

THREE-POINT FIELD GOAL PERCENTAGE

PLAYER	FGM	FGA	PCT.
Jennings, East Tenn. St.	84	142	.592
Bennett, Wisc.-GB	80	150	.533
Iuzzolino, St. Francis (Pa.)	103	195	.528
Richardson, L. Marymount	61	116	.526
Mitchell, Samford	41	78	.526

THREE-POINT FIELD GOALS PER GAME

PLAYER	FGM	AVG.
Phills, Southern (La.)	123	4.4
Schmitz, Mo.-KC	116	4.0
Herdman, UC Irvine	112	3.7
Day, Radford	106	3.7
Jackson, Princeton	95	3.5

1990–91 TEAM LEADERS

SCORING OFFENSE

SCHOOL	PTS.	AVG.
Southern (La.)	2924	104.4
Loyola Marymount	3211	103.6
Arkansas	3783	99.6
UNLV	3420	97.7
Oklahoma	3363	96.1

SCORING DEFENSE

SCHOOL	PTS.	AVG.
Princeton	1320	48.9
Northern Illinois	1781	57.5
Yale	1508	58.0
Wisconsin-Green Bay	1893	61.1
Georgetown	1964	61.4

SCORING MARGIN

SCHOOL	OFF.	DEF.	MAR.
UNLV	97.7	71.0	26.7
Arkansas	99.6	80.4	19.2
East Tennessee St.	94.0	76.8	17.3
Ohio St.	84.6	68.5	16.2
North Carolina	87.6	71.6	16.0

WON-LOST PERCENTAGE

SCHOOL	W-L	PCT.
UNLV	34-1	.971
Arkansas	34-4	.895
Princeton	24-3	.889
Utah	30-4	.882
Ohio St.	27-4	.871

FIELD GOAL PERCENTAGE

SCHOOL	FGM	FGA	PCT.
UNLV	1305	2441	.535
Indiana	1043	1955	.534
New Mexico	868	1644	.528
Brooklyn	656	1262	.520
Kansas	1086	2097	.518

DEFENSIVE FIELD GOAL PERCENTAGE

SCHOOL	FGM	FGA	PCT.
Georgetown	680	1847	.368
Northern Illinois	616	1587	.388
Connecticut	682	1753	.389
New Orleans	725	1837	.395
Middle Tennessee St.	793	2007	.395

FREE THROW PERCENTAGE

SCHOOL	FTM	FTA	PCT.
Butler	725	922	.786
Monmouth	422	547	.771
Air Force	483	627	.770
Northwestern	470	612	.768
Wyoming	654	853	.767

REBOUND MARGIN

SCHOOL	OWN	OPP.	MAR.
New Orleans	41.7	32.4	9.3
Murray St.	43.4	34.6	8.7
Stanford	37.9	29.4	8.5
UNLV	42.5	34.8	7.7
Northern Illinois	35.5	28.0	7.5

THREE-POINT FIELD GOAL PERCENTAGE

SCHOOL	FGM	FGA	PCT.
Wisconsin-Green Bay	189	407	.464
Southern Utah St.	158	353	.448
St. Francis (Pa.)	238	534	.446
Eastern Illinois	200	457	.438
Northern Illinois	133	305	.436

THREE-POINT FIELD GOALS PER GAME

SCHOOL	G.	FGM	AVG.
Texas-Arlington	29	265	9.1
East Tennessee St.	33	301	9.1
Dayton	29	256	8.8
UC Irvine	30	263	8.8
Kentucky	28	242	8.6

Cookman, set a single-game record for most points against a major college opponent with 72 vs. Loyola Marymount. Loyola Marymount, a 186-140 winner in the game, established an NCAA record for most points by a team. Bradshaw, who had three other games with at least 53 points, finished his career as the only player to transfer from one major college to another and score more than 2,750 points. He had 2,804.

Missouri-Kansas City's Ronnie Schmitz (51 points at U.S. International), Georgia Tech's Kenny Anderson (50 vs. Loyola Marymount), Wisconsin-Milwaukee's Von McDade (50 at Illinois in double overtime), Georgia State's Chris Collier (49 vs. Butler), Columbia's Buck Jenkins (47 at Harvard), Radford's Doug Day (43 at Central Connecticut State) and UAB's Andy Kennedy (41 vs. St. Louis) set single-game scoring records for their schools. . . . Schmitz's outburst came in the last game ever for San Diego-based USIU. . . . Collier's barrage is a Trans America Athletic Conference standard. Georgia State shuffled games because his religious convictions as a Worldwide Church of God member prohibited him from normal earthly activities such as playing on the Sabbath (Friday nights or before sundown on Saturdays). . . . McDade (29.6 ppg), Oregon's Terrell Brandon (26.6), Fairleigh Dickinson's Desi Wilson (23.8), Kevin Green of Loyola, Md. (22.1) and UAB's Kennedy (21.8) set school Division I records for highest scoring average in a single season. Wilson went on to play professional baseball as an outfielder.

Providence guard Eric Murdock established a Big East Conference record with 48 points against Pittsburgh. . . . La Salle guards Randy Woods (46) and Doug Overton (45) became the only set of teammates in history to score more than 40 points in a single game when they combined for 91 in a 133-118 victory at Loyola Marymount. . . . A national high of 15 different teams averaged more than 90 points per game. Meanwhile, Princeton, limiting its opponents to 48.9 points per game under coach Pete Carril, set a record for highest-ever margin over the runner-up in team defense (8.6 fewer than Northern Illinois).. . . Connecticut

UNLV's Stacey Augmon prepares to dish it off to a teammate.

set an NCAA mark for largest lead at the start of a game before an opponent scored, racing to a 32-0 advantage in a victory over New Hampshire. Later, New Hampshire's NCAA-record 32 consecutive homecourt defeats was snapped when the Wildcats defeated Holy Cross, 72-56.

Indiana State set an NCAA record for most consecutive successful free throws by converting 49 in a row in two games in mid-February. . . . LSU's Shaquille O'Neal became the only player in SEC history to lead the league in scoring, rebounding, field-goal percentage and blocked shots in the same season. . . . Florida freshman guard Craig Brown scored an NCAA-record 13 points in the second overtime period of the Gators' 91-81 victory at Mississippi. . . . East Tennessee State's Keith "Mister" Jennings (5-7) became the first player under 5-10 to finish his career with more than 900 assists. He had 938

1990-91 NCAA CHAMPION: DUKE

SEASON STATISTICS OF DUKE REGULARS

PLAYER	POS.	CL.	G.	FG%	FT%	PPG	RPG
Christian Laettner	C-F	Jr.	39	.575	.802	19.8	8.7
Billy McCaffrey	G	So.	38	.481	.832	11.6	1.8
Thomas Hill	G-F	So.	39	.552	.743	11.5	3.6
Bobby Hurley	G	So.	39	.423	.728	11.3	2.4
Grant Hill	F-G	Fr.	36	.516	.609	11.2	5.1
Brian Davis	G-F	Jr.	39	.456	.730	7.6	4.1
Greg Koubek	F	Sr.	38	.435	.813	5.9	2.9
Antonio Lang	F-C	Fr.	36	.606	.526	4.3	2.6
Crawford Palmer	C	Jr.	38	.646	.825	3.6	2.0
Marty Clark	G	Fr.	23	.448	.625	2.1	0.7
TEAM TOTALS			**39**	**.511**	**.726**	**87.7**	**36.3**

Three-point field goals leaders: Hurley (76 of 188, .404), Koubek (32 of 76, .421). **Assists leader:** Hurley 289. **Blocked shots leader:** Laettner 44. **Steals leaders:** Laettner 75, T. Hill 59.

1991 FINAL FOUR CHAMPIONSHIP GAME

INDIANAPOLIS, IN

KANSAS (65)	MIN.	FG-A	FT-A	REB.	A.	PF.	PTS.
Jamison	29	1-10	0-0	4	5	4	2
Maddox	19	2-4	0-0	3	4	3	4
Randall	33	7-9	3-6	10	2	4	18
Brown	31	6-15	0-0	4	1	1	16
Jordan	34	4-6	1-2	0	3	0	11
Richey	4	0-1	0-0	1	0	0	0
Woodberry	18	1-4	0-0	4	0	4	2
Tunstall	11	1-5	0-0	1	0	3	2
Wagner	3	1-1	0-0	1	0	0	2
Scott	15	3-9	0-0	2	0	1	6
Johanning	3	1-1	0-0	2	1	1	2
TOTALS	**200**	**27-65**	**4-8**	**32**	**16**	**21**	**65**

FG%: .415. **FT%:** .500. **Three-point goals:** 7 of 18 (Jamison 0-2, Randall 1-1, Brown 4-11, Jordan 2-2, Richey 0-1, Tunstall 0-1). **Blocks:** 2. **Turnovers:** 14. **Steals:** 10 (Jamison 4).

DUKE (72)	MIN.	FG-A	FT-A	REB.	A.	PF.	PTS.
Koubek	17	2-4	0-0	4	0	1	5
G. Hill	28	4-6	2-8	8	3	1	10
Laettner	32	3-8	12-12	10	0	3	18
Hurley	40	3-5	4-4	1	9	1	12
T. Hill	23	1-5	0-0	4	1	2	3
McCaffrey	26	6-8	2-2	1	0	1	16
Lang	1	0-0	0-0	0	0	0	0
Davis	24	4-5	0-2	2	1	4	8
Palmer	9	0-0	0-0	0	0	0	0
Team				1			
TOTALS	**200**	**23-41**	**20-28**	**31**	**14**	**13**	**72**

FG%: .561. **FT%:** .714. **Three-point goals:** 6 of 10 (Koubek 1-2, Hurley 2-4, T. Hill 1-1, McCaffrey 2-3). **Blocks:** 2. **Turnovers:** 18. **Steals:** 6. **Halftime:** Duke 42-34.

NATIONAL SEMIFINALS

DUKE (79): Koubek 1-6 0-0 2, G. Hill 5-8 1-1 11, Laettner 9-14 9-11 28, Hurley 4-7 1-1 12, T. Hill 2-6 2-2 6, McCaffrey 2-3 1-2 5, Lang 0-0 0-0 0, Davis 6-12 3-4 15, Palmer 0-0 0-0 0. Team 29-56 (.518) 17-21 (.810) 79.

UNLV (77): Johnson 5-10 3-4 13, Augmon 3-10 0-1 6, Ackles 3-6 1-2 7, Hunt 11-20 3-5 29, Anthony 8-18 1-1 19, Gray 1-2 0-0 2, Spencer 0-2 1-2 1. Team 31-68 (.456) 9-15 (.600) 77.

Three-point goals: Duke 4-8 (.500), UNLV 6-15 (.400). **Halftime:** UNLV 43-41.

KANSAS (79): Jamison 4-8 1-3 9, Maddox 4-10 2-2 10, Randall 6-11 4-6 16, Brown 1-10 0-0 3, Jordan 4-11 6-13 16, Richey 1-1 2-2 4, Woodberry 0-0 2-2 2, Tunstall 1-5 2-5 5, Wagner 0-1 0-0 0, Scott 6-9 2-3 14, Johanning 0-0 0-0 0. Team 27-66 (.409) 21-36 (.583) 79.

NORTH CAROLINA (73): Lynch 5-8 3-6 13, Fox 5-22 3-3 13, Chilcutt 2-8 0-0 4, Rice 1-6 3-4 5, Davis 9-16 5-5 25, Montross 3-4 0-1 6, Harris 0-2 0-0 0, Rodl 0-1 0-0 0, Phelps 1-1 0-1 2, Reese 2-5 0-3 5, Rozier 0-0 0-0 0, Cherry 0-0 0-0 0, Salvadori 0-0 0-0 0, Wenstrom 0-0 0-0 0. Team 28-73 (.384) 14-23 (.609) 73.

Three-point goals: Kansas 4-14 (.286), North Carolina 3-18 (.167). **Halftime:** Kansas 43-34.

ALL-TOURNAMENT TEAM

Anderson Hunt, G, Jr., UNLV
Bobby Hurley, G, Soph., Duke
*Christian Laettner, C, Jr., Duke (46 points)
Bill McCaffrey, G, Soph., Duke
Mark Randall, F, Sr., Kansas

*Named Most Outstanding Player.

---

after leading the Southern Conference in that category for the fourth straight season.

Arkansas (34-4/coached by Nolan Richardson), Utah (30-4/Rick Majerus), East Tennessee State (28-5/Alan LeForce), Eastern Michigan (26-7/Ben Braun), Nebraska (26-8/Danny Nee), Northern Illinois (25-6/Jim Molinari), Creighton (24-8/Tony Baronc), St. Francis, Pa. (24-8/Jim Baron), Murray State (24-9/Steve Newton), Arkansas State (23-9/Nelson Catalina), Radford (22-7/Oliver Purnell) and Delaware State (19-11/Jeff Jones) had their winningest seasons in Division I school history. Ohio State (27-4/Randy Ayers), Siena (25-10/Mike Deane), St. Peter's (24-7/Ted Fiore) and Texas-Arlington (20-9/Mark Nixon) tied their single-season school Division I records for most victories.

Arkansas authored an Southwest Conference championship in the Razorbacks' final season as a member of the league. . . . Utah captured the WAC championship just one year after finishing in a tie for sixth place. ETSU made its lone appearance in the Top 20 of a final wire-service poll. Nebraska set its school standard on the heels of three consecutive seventh-place Big Eight finishes. . . . Mississippi State and Nebraska finished in the Top 20 of a final wire-service poll for the first time since 1963 and 1966, respectively. Eastern Michigan and

Southern Mississippi made their lone appearance in the Top 25 of a final wire-service poll.

Georgetown (19-13) sustained its most defeats since coach John Thompson's first season in 1972-73, but the Hoyas led the nation in field-goal percentage defense for the third consecutive year. . . . Louisville's NCAA record of consecutive winning seasons was snapped at 46 when the Cardinals went 14-16. . . . Michigan's streak of seven straight 20-win seasons ended when the Wolverines compiled a 14-15 mark. . . . Ohio State, coached by Randy Ayers, captured its first Big Ten title in 20 years. . . . Wisconsin lost 26 consecutive games to Purdue in their series until the Badgers blasted the Boilermakers, 66-44. . . . Northwestern (0-18), finishing in the Big Ten cellar for the seventh straight year, became the first team to go winless in conference competition since the University of Chicago went 0-12 in 1945-46 in its last season as a member of the league.

Rice, coached by Scott Thompson, compiled a 16-14 record for its first winning season in 20 years. . . . St. Francis (N.Y.), coached by Rich Zvosec, ended a streak of 11 consecutive losing records by compiling a 15-14 mark. . . . Vermont's string of consecutive losing seasons was snapped at nine when the Catamounts compiled a 15-13 record under coach Tom Brennan. . . . Radford, which registered a 7-22 record the previous season, improved by 15 games to 22-7 under coach Oliver Purnell.

Drake, with nine freshmen on its roster, pulled off perhaps the biggest upset of the season with a 94-93 victory at Arizona State in Rudy Washington's head coaching debut with the Bulldogs. . . . Brigham Young's Shawn Bradley established a Western Athletic Conference single-game mark and tied the NCAA standard by blocking 14 shots in a 90-86 victory over Eastern Kentucky (see accompanying box). . . . San Diego State posted its lone triumph over Texas-El Paso (58-55) in an 18-game stretch of their series from 1986 to 1994. . . . North Carolina's Dean Smith set a national coaching record with his 24th 20-win season.

Furman, coached by Butch Estes, tied for first place in the Southern Conference after finishing in a tie for sixth the previous season. . . . South Alabama, coached by Ronnie Arrow, captured the Sun Belt Conference crown after finishing in last place the previous year. . . . Tom Young, who previously coached Catholic, American and Rutgers, was forced out at Old Dominion, ending a 31-year coaching career with a 524-328 record.

Long-time Michigan assistant Mike Boyd was appointed head coach at Cleveland State less than a month before the start of official workouts after the Vikings' Kevin Mackey was fired following his confession to substance-abuse and alcohol problems. Mackey had been confronted about rumors concerning his off-the-court activities on numerous occasions, but he denied it all. School officials appeared to wonder how many times

---

RETURN TO SENDER

Eastern Kentucky at Brigham Young in opening round of Cougar Classic
December 7, 1990

Shawn Bradley, a 7-6 freshman center, was playing just his sixth varsity game for BYU when he equaled an NCAA single-game record by blocking 14 shots in a 90-86 triumph over Eastern Kentucky.

E. KENTUCKY (86)	MP	FG-A	FT-A	REB.	BLK.	PTS.
Mike Smith	29	3-10	3-6	7	2	9
Aric Sinclair	25	1-10	4-4	5	0	6
Kirk Greathouse	34	4-11	2-5	3	0	11
Derek Reuben	8	1-1	0-0	0	0	2
Brandon Baker	3	0-0	0-0	0	0	0
Chris Brown	20	5-11	0-0	1	0	12
John Allen	28	9-13	1-2	8	0	22
Jamie Allen	30	7-11	7-8	2	0	24
Toi Bell	17	0-2	0-0	2	2	0
Ken Riley	7	0-1	0-0	0	0	0
Totals	200	30-70	17-25	37	4	86

FG%—.429. FT%—.680. 3-PT%—.600 (9 of 15; Sinclair 0-2, Greathouse 1-5, Brown 2-2, Allen 3-3, Ross 3-3).

BYU (90)	MP	FG-A	FT-A	REB.	BLK.	PTS.
Mark Heslop	23	4-7	0-0	0	0	10
Nathan Call	36	0-2	3-4	3	0	3
Mark Santiago	5	0-1	0-0	0	0	0
Kenneth Roberts	30	3-6	1-2	2	1	7
Jeff Campbell	1	0-0	2-2	0	0	2
Gary Trost	3	1-1	0-0	1	2	2
Steve Schreiner	36	7-10	5-8	6	0	19
Scott Moon	17	3-3	2-2	2	0	9
Shawn Bradley	37	10-15	9-12	8	14	29
Jared Miller	13	4-6	1-2	7	0	9
Totals	200	32-51	23-32	32	17	90

FG%—.627. FT%—.719. 3-PT%—.429 (3 of 7; Heslop 2-5, Call 0-1, Moon 1-1).

Halftime: BYU 44-38.

AP	UPI	USA/CNN	SCHOOL (RECORD)	HEAD COACH
1	1	2	UNLV (34-1)	Jerry Tarkanian
2	2	5	Arkansas (34-4)	Nolan Richardson
3	3	9	Indiana (29-5)	Bob Knight
4	4	4	North Carolina (29-6)	Dean Smith
5	5	8	Ohio State (27-4)	Randy Ayers
6	6	1	Duke (32-7)	Mike Krzyzewski
7	8	16	Syracuse (26-6)	Jim Boeheim
8	7	10	Arizona (28-7)	Lute Olson
9	–	17	Kentucky (22-6)	Rick Pitino
10	10	12	Utah (30-4)	Rick Majerus
11	9	19	Nebraska (26-8)	Danny Nee
12	12	3	Kansas (27-8)	Roy Williams
13	11	6	Seton Hall (25-9)	P.J. Carlesimo
14	13	13	Oklahoma State (24-8)	Eddie Sutton
15	17	22	New Mexico State (23-6)	Neil McCarthy
16	14	25	UCLA (23-9)	Jim Harrick
17	15	24	East Tenn. State (28-5)	Alan LeForce
18	20	–	Princeton (24-3)	Pete Carril
19	16	–	Alabama (23-10)	Wimp Sanderson
20	19	7	St. John's (23-9)	Lou Carnesecca
21	18	–	Mississippi State (20-9)	Richard Williams
22	21	–	Louisiana State (20-10)	Dale Brown
23	25	–	Texas (23-9)	Tom Penders
24	–	–	DePaul (20-9)	Joey Meyer
25	–	–	Southern Miss. (21-8)	M.K. Turk
–	–	15	Connecticut (20-11)	Jim Calhoun
–	–	18	Eastern Michigan (26-7)	Ben Braun
–	23	20	Georgetown (19-13)	John Thompson
–	–	21	Pittsburgh (21-12)	Paul Evans
–	22	–	Michigan State (19-11)	Jud Heathcote
–	24	23	N.C. State (20-11)	Les Robinson

Mackey had lied about other topics, particularly his actions in the recruitment of 7-7 Manute Bol, which resulted in three years of NCAA probation.

1991 NCAA Tournament

Summary: Duke required nine appearances at the Final Four until the resolute Blue Devils finally won a national title. The Blue Devils' Mike Krzyzewski joined UCLA's John Wooden as the only other coach to lead a school to four consecutive Final Fours. Their shocking 79-77 win over defending champion UNLV was the Rebels' lone defeat.

Star Gazing: Christian Laettner became the only player with at least 10 championship game free-throw attempts to convert all of them (12 of 12 against Kansas).

Biggest Upsets: Richmond (15th seed) over Syracuse (2), 73-69; Xavier (14) over Nebraska (3), 89-84, and Penn State (13) over UCLA (4), 74-69. UCLA was without standout freshman forward Ed O'Bannon, who missed the season because of a severe knee injury. After the tourney, Penn State became the first school ever to defect

from a conference for the second time (left Atlantic 10 for the Big Ten).

One and Only: North Carolina's Dean Smith became the only coach to direct teams to Final Fours in four different decades, but the Tar Heels lost against Kansas in the national semifinals to give him nine Final Four defeats. No other coach has more than seven Final Four setbacks. . . . Eddie Sutton became the only coach to guide four different schools to the NCAA Tournament when his alma mater, Oklahoma State, earned a bid.

Numbers Game: Duke became the only school to reach the NCAA Tournament final in back-to-back seasons after losing by double-digit margins in its conference tournament (defeated by 11 points against Georgia Tech in the 1990 ACC Tournament semifinals before getting trounced in the 1991 ACC Tournament final by 22 points against North Carolina). . . . St. John's became the first school to crack the 20-victory plateau in both the NCAA Tournament and NIT. . . . St. Francis (Pa.), coached by Jim Baron, made its lone NCAA playoff appearance.

What Might Have Been: Forward Larry Johnson and guard Stacey Augmon combined for 37 points per game on 61 percent field-goal shooting in their two years together as teammates at UNLV. If only they had combined for 22 points instead of 19 points on 40 percent field-goal shooting (8 of 20) in the national semifinals, the seemingly invincible Rebels could have defeated eventual champion Duke rather than losing 79-77. . . . Georgia Tech (17-13/without Dennis Scott), Indiana (29-5/Jay Edwards), Louisiana State (20-10/Chris Jackson) and Michigan (23-8/Sean Higgins) might have fared better in the playoffs if standout players had exercised their remaining eligibility instead of defecting to the NBA. Ditto Michigan State (19-11) if guard Shawn Respert didn't miss the majority of the season because of a knee injury. . . . Houston (18-11) probably would have participated in the NCAA Tournament instead of the NIT if Carl Herrera didn't leave school early for the NBA. Ditto NIT runner-up Oklahoma (20-15) if forward Jackie Jones and

1991 CHAMPIONSHIP BRACKET

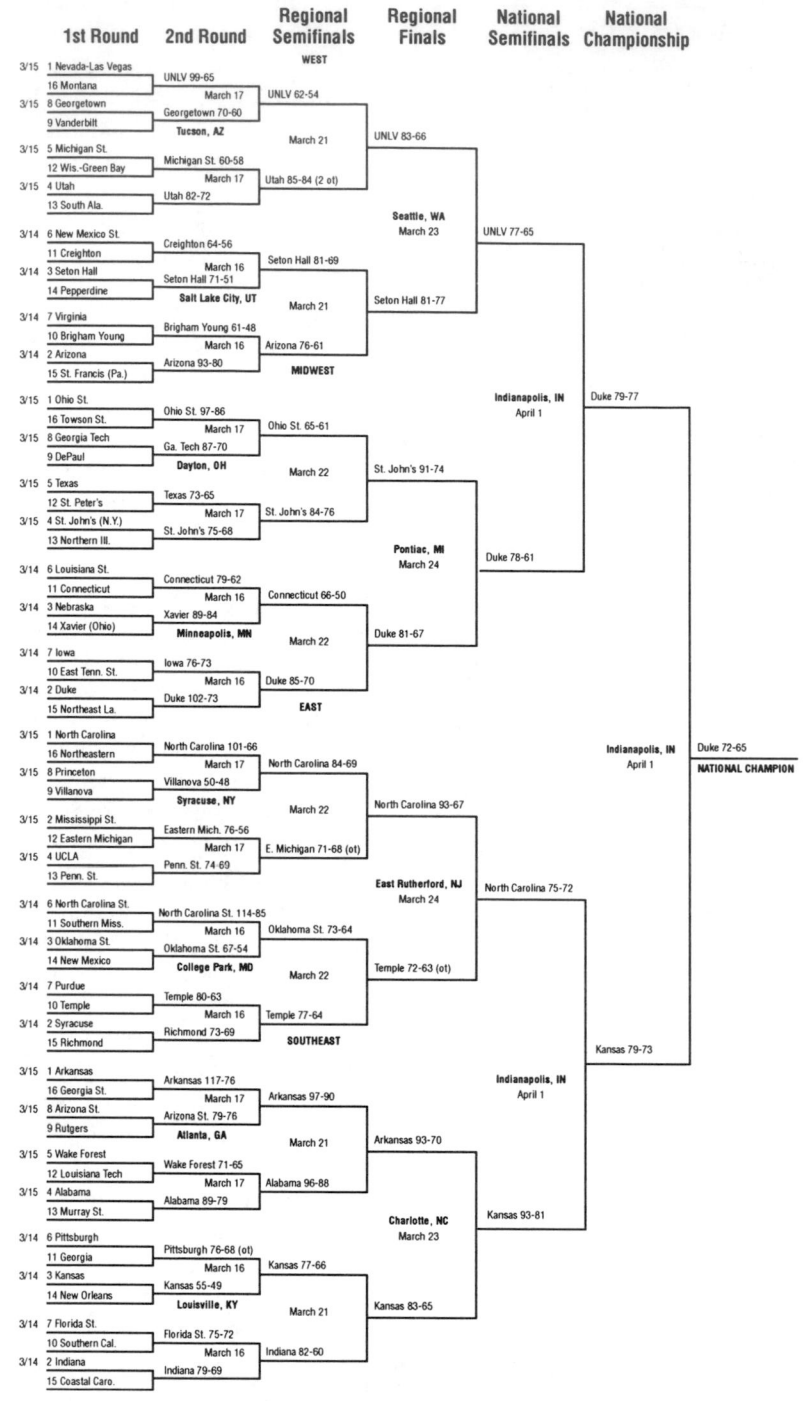

	1st Round	2nd Round	Regional Semifinals	Regional Finals	National Semifinals	National Championship

WEST

3/15 1 Nevada-Las Vegas
16 Montana
UNLV 99-65
March 17
3/15 8 Georgetown
9 Vanderbilt
Georgetown 70-60
UNLV 62-54
Tucson, AZ
March 21

3/15 5 Michigan St.
12 Wis.-Green Bay
Michigan St. 60-58
March 17
3/15 4 Utah
13 South Ala.
Utah 82-72
Utah 85-84 (2 ot)

UNLV 83-66
Seattle, WA
March 23

3/14 6 New Mexico St.
11 Creighton
Creighton 64-56
March 16
3/14 3 Seton Hall
14 Pepperdine
Seton Hall 71-51
Seton Hall 81-69
Salt Lake City, UT
March 21

3/14 7 Virginia
10 Brigham Young
Brigham Young 61-48
March 16
3/14 2 Arizona
15 St. Francis (Pa.)
Arizona 93-80
Arizona 76-61

Seton Hall 81-77

UNLV 77-65

MIDWEST

3/15 1 Ohio St.
16 Towson St.
Ohio St. 97-86
March 17
3/15 8 Georgia Tech
9 DePaul
Ga. Tech 87-70
Ohio St. 65-61
Dayton, OH
March 22

3/15 5 Texas
12 St. Peter's
Texas 73-65
March 17
3/15 4 St. John's (N.Y.)
13 Northern Ill.
St. John's 75-68
St. John's 84-76

St. John's 91-74
Pontiac, MI
March 24

3/14 6 Louisiana St.
11 Connecticut
Connecticut 79-62
March 16
3/14 3 Nebraska
14 Xavier (Ohio)
Xavier 89-84
Connecticut 66-50
Minneapolis, MN
March 22

3/14 7 Iowa
10 East Tenn. St.
Iowa 76-73
March 16
3/14 2 Duke
15 Northeast La.
Duke 102-73
Duke 85-70

Duke 81-67

Duke 78-61

Indianapolis, IN
April 1

Duke 79-77

EAST

3/15 1 North Carolina
16 Northeastern
North Carolina 101-66
March 17
3/15 8 Princeton
9 Villanova
Villanova 50-48
North Carolina 84-69
Syracuse, NY
March 22

3/15 2 Mississippi St.
12 Eastern Michigan
Eastern Mich. 76-56
March 17
3/15 4 UCLA
13 Penn. St.
Penn. St. 74-69
E. Michigan 71-68 (ot)

North Carolina 93-67
East Rutherford, NJ
March 24

3/14 6 North Carolina St.
11 Southern Miss.
North Carolina St. 114-85
March 16
3/14 3 Oklahoma St.
14 New Mexico
Oklahoma St. 67-54
Oklahoma St. 73-64
College Park, MD
March 22

3/14 7 Purdue
10 Temple
Temple 80-63
March 16
3/14 2 Syracuse
15 Richmond
Richmond 73-69
Temple 77-64

Temple 72-63 (ot)

North Carolina 75-72

Indianapolis, IN
April 1

Duke 72-65

NATIONAL CHAMPION

SOUTHEAST

3/15 1 Arkansas
16 Georgia St.
Arkansas 117-76
March 17
3/15 8 Arizona St.
9 Rutgers
Arizona St. 79-76
Arkansas 97-90
Atlanta, GA
March 21

3/15 5 Wake Forest
12 Louisiana Tech
Wake Forest 71-65
March 17
3/15 4 Alabama
13 Murray St.
Alabama 89-79
Alabama 96-88

Arkansas 93-70
Charlotte, NC
March 23

3/14 6 Pittsburgh
11 Georgia
Pittsburgh 76-68 (ot)
March 16
3/14 3 Kansas
14 New Orleans
Kansas 55-49
Kansas 77-66
Louisville, KY
March 21

3/14 7 Florida St.
10 Southern Cal.
Florida St. 75-72
March 16
3/14 2 Indiana
15 Coastal Caro.
Indiana 79-69
Indiana 82-60

Kansas 83-65

Kansas 93-81

Indianapolis, IN
April 1

Kansas 79-73

guard Smokey McCovery didn't flunk out. Jones had led the Big Eight in blocked shots and McCovery had paced the league in steals.

Scoring Leader: Christian Laettner, Duke (125 points, 20.8 ppg).

Highest Scoring Average: Terry Dehere, Seton Hall (97 points, 24.3 ppg).

Rebounding Leader: Larry Johnson, UNLV (51 rebounds, 10.2 rpg).

Highest Rebounding Averages: Ohio State's Perry Carter and Oklahoma State's Byron Houston (36 rebounds, 12 rpg).

1991-92

AT A GLANCE

NCAA Champion: Duke (35-2; coached by Mike Krzyzewski; won ACC regular-season title by three games over Florida State with a 14-2 record).

NIT Champion: Virginia (20-13; coached by Jeff Jones; tied for fourth place in ACC with an 8-8 record).

New Conference: Great Midwest (merged with teams from the Metro to form Conference USA four years later).

New Rules: Contact technical fouls count toward the five fouls for player disqualification and toward team fouls in reaching bonus free-throw situations. . . . The shot clock is reset when the ball strikes the basket ring, not when a shot leaves the shooter's hands as it had been since the rule was introduced in 1986.

NCAA Probation: Auburn, Maryland, UNLV, Northwestern (La.) State, Texas A&M.

NCAA Consensus First-Team All-Americans: Jim Jackson, G-F, Jr., Ohio State; Christian Laettner, F-C, Sr., Duke; Harold Miner, G, Jr., Southern California; Alonzo Mourning, C, Sr., Georgetown; Shaquille O'Neal, C, Jr., Louisiana State.

National Players of the Year: Jackson (22.4 ppg, 6.8 rpg, 4 apg, 81.1 FT%/UPI) and Laettner (21.5 ppg, 7.9 rpg, 57.5 FG%, 81.5 FT%, 55.7 3FG%/AP, NABC, USBWA, Naismith, Wooden).

National Coaches of the Year: Tulane's Perry Clark (21-8/UPI, USBWA); Duke's Mike Krzyzewski (34-2/Naismith); Southern Cal's George Raveling (24-6/NABC), and Kansas' Roy Williams (27-5/AP).

Duke's Christian Laettner hit a dramatic decisive last-second shot against Kentucky in overtime after receiving a long inbounds pass in the East Regional final. The game is acknowledged as one of the most suspenseful in NCAA history (see accompanying box).

Virginia's NIT title enabled Jeff Jones to become the only person to win NIT crowns as a player (Virginia guard in 1980) and as a coach. His father, Bob Jones, had been coach of Kentucky Wesleyan when it won the 1973 NCAA Division II crown. . . . Embattled coach Jerry Tarkanian was forced out at UNLV, but not before the Rebels captured their 10th consecutive Big West Conference championship. Tarkanian's 307 victories in his last 10 seasons is by far the most successful 10-year stretch in major-college history. He won more than 25 games each of those 10 campaigns.

San Francisco's Tomas Thompson set an NCAA standard for most three-pointers in a game without a miss (subsequently tied) when he hit all eight of his attempts from beyond the arc against Loyola Marymount in the West Coast Conference Tournament (see accompanying box).

Georgetown's Alonzo Mourning finished his career with an NCAA record 453 blocked shots (subsequently broken). Joining Ralph Sampson (Virginia), David Robinson (Navy) and J.R. Reid (North Carolina), Mourning became the fourth center in 10 years to earn NCAA consensus first-team All-American recognition after playing high school basketball in Virginia.

LSU's Shaquille O'Neal concluded his three-year career with a total of six games with at least 10 blocked shots. He is the only player to twice average at least five rejections per game in a season. O'Neal was one of six SEC players to be selected in the first round of the NBA draft, including three from conference newcomer Arkansas.

Height doesn't always determine who excels at blocked shots and field-goal shooting. Vermont's Kevin Roberson finished his career as the shortest player (6-7) to block more than three

Cincinnati coach Bob Huggins argues a call.

shots per game (3.65) and Massachusetts' William Herndon finished his career as the shortest player (6-3) to hit more than 63 percent of his field-goal attempts.

Morehead State's Brett Roberts (53 points vs. Middle Tennessee State), Colgate's Jonathan Stone (52 vs. Brooklyn) and Hartford's Vin Baker (44 vs. Lamar in overtime) established school Division I single-game scoring records. . . . Maryland's Walt Williams (26.8 ppg), Southern Cal's Harold Miner (26.3), Stanford's Adam Keefe (25.3) and Georgia State's Phillip Luckydo (21) set school Division I records for highest scoring average in a single season. . . . Alabama State's Steve Rogers (5th with 27.3 ppg) and Butler's

Darrin Archbold (13th with 24.8) finished among the nation's top scorers in their senior seasons. It was a far cry from their freshman campaigns— Rogers (3.1 ppg for Middle Tennessee State before transferring) and Archbold (0.9 for Butler).

Missouri's Jeff Warren established a Big Eight Conference record by hitting 24 consecutive field-goal attempts. . . . Colorado lost 24 consecutive games to Oklahoma in their series until the Buffaloes won in overtime, 70-68. . . . Forward Byron Houston was the first Oklahoma State player since 1954 to become an NCAA consensus first- or second-team All-American. . . . Delaware (27-4/coached by Steve Steinwedel), Montana (27-4/Blaine Taylor), Georgia Southern (25-

MOST EXCITING PLAYOFF GAME FINISH

DUKE VS. KENTUCKY IN EAST REGIONAL FINAL AT THE SPECTRUM, PHILADELPHIA, PA

MARCH 28, 1992

Guard Sean Woods' successful go-ahead bank shot in the waning moments of overtime appeared to have him destined to go down in Kentucky lore. But that was before a miracle pass by Grant Hill and pressure-packed outside jumper by Christian Laettner lifted NCAA champion-to-be Duke to a 104-103 victory over the Wildcats in the NCAA Tournament.

KENTUCKY (103)	MP	FG-A	FT-A	REB.	PTS.
Jamal Mashburn	43	11-16	3-3	10	28
John Pelphrey	25	5-7	3-3	1	16
Gimel Martinez	23	2-4	0-0	0	5
Sean Woods	38	9-15	2-2	2	21
Richie Farmer	15	2-3	4-6	1	9
Deron Feldhaus	37	2-6	1-2	1	5
Dale Brown	30	6-11	3-5	3	18
Travis Ford	7	0-2	0-0	1	0
Aminu Timberlake	5	0-0	1-2	0	1
Andre Riddick	1	0-0	0-0	0	0
Junior Braddy	1	0-1	0-0	0	0
Totals	**225**	**37-65**	**12-22**	**21**	**103**

FG%: .569. **FT%:** .739. 3-PT. **FG:** 12-22 (Mashburn 3-4, Pelphrey 3-4, Brown 3-5, Martinez 1-2, Farmer 1-2, Woods, 1-1, Feldhaus 0-2, Ford 0-1, Braddy 0-1). **Assists:** 24 (Woods 9). **Steals:** 12. **Blocked Shots:** 0. **Turnovers:** 12. **Fouled Out:** 2 (Mashburn, Martinez).

DUKE (104)	MP	FG-A	FT-A	REB.	PTS.
Antonio Lang	21	2-2	0-1	3	4
Brian Davis	38	3-6	7-10	5	13
Christian Laettner	43	10-10	10-10	7	31
Bobby Hurley	45	6-12	5-6	3	22
Thomas Hill	34	6-10	5-5	3	19
Grant Hill	37	5-10	1-2	10	11
Cherokee Parks	6	2-2	0-0	0	4
Marty Clark	1	0-0	0-0	0	0
Totals	**225**	**34-52**	**28-34**	**31**	**104**

FG%: .654. **FT%:** .824. 3-PT. **FG:** 8-16 (Hurley 5-10, T. Hill 2-3, Laettner 1-1, Davis 0-2). **Assists:** 23 (Hurley 10). **Steals:** 8. **Blocked Shots:** 3. **Turnovers:** 20. **Fouled Out:** 1 (Davis).

Halftime: Duke 50-45. **Regulation:** Tied 93-93.

6/Frank Kerns) and Missouri-Kansas City (20-8/Lee Hunt) had their winningest seasons in school Division I history. Southern Cal (24-6/George Raveling) tied its school single-season mark for most victories. . . . Liberty, after compiling a 5-23 record the previous season, improved by 16 1/2 games. . . . Massachusetts, coached by John Calipari, made its initial Top 20 appearance in a final wire-service poll. The Minutemen defeated Temple, 67-52, for the initial time after losing their first 21 meetings with the Owls. . . . Seton Hall lost 23 consecutive games to Syracuse until defeating the Orangemen, 86-76.

Cincinnati (29-5/coached by Bob Huggins), tying its record for most victories in a single season, did not appear in a final wire-service national poll or the NCAA Tournament for 14 consecutive years until highlighting the Great Midwest Conference's inaugural season by reaching the Final Four. It was the first time for a first-year league member to advance to the national semifinals since UNC Charlotte represented the Sun Belt Conference in 1977, which coincidentally was the last year Cincinnati had participated in the event.

Western Michigan, coached by Bob Donewald, compiled a 21-9 record to end a streak of nine consecutive losing seasons. . . . Prairie View (0-28) became the first team to go winless in an entire season since The Citadel went 0-17 in 1955. . . . Miami (Fla.) compiled a 1-17 league record in its inaugural season in the Big East, but the Hurricanes won their Big East Tournament debut with an 83-71 decision over Pittsburgh. . . . Syracuse finished out of the top 10 of a final AP poll for the first time in seven years.

North Carolina, trailing by 20 points with less than 15 minutes remaining, rallied to edge Wake Forest, 80-78, on a last-second shot by Brian Reese. That rates as the largest deficit the Tar Heels have ever had to overcome for a victory. . . . Tulane, coached by Perry Clark, appeared in a final wire-service poll for the first time since the AP's initial rankings in 1949. . . . Tennessee Tech's Van Usher led the nation in assists one year after pacing the country in steals. . . . Radford won 12 games coming from behind in the second half en route to a 20-9 record under coach Ron Bradley.

Wyoming's Reginald Slater (27 against Troy State) and UNC-Wilmington's Matt Fish (20 in triple overtime at American) set school single-game rebounding records. . . . Arizona's 71-game homecourt winning streak, which started in 1987,

1991–92 INDIVIDUAL LEADERS

SCORING

PLAYER	PTS.	AVG.
Roberts, Morehead St.	815	28.1
Baker, Hartford	745	27.6
Ford, Miss. Valley St.	714	27.5
Woods, La Salle	847	27.3
Rogers, Alabama St.	764	27.3
Williams, Maryland	776	26.8
Miner, Southern Cal	789	26.3
Lowery, Loyola Marymount	675	26.0
Cunningham, Bethune-Cookman	744	25.7
Casebier, Evansville	634	25.4

REBOUNDING

PLAYER	REB.	AVG.
Jones, Murray St.	431	14.4
O'Neal, Louisiana St.	421	14.0
Burroughs, Jacksonville	370	13.2
Keefe, Stanford	355	12.2
White, Southern (La.)	367	12.2
Sims, Youngstown St.	327	11.7
Ellis, Notre Dame	385	11.7
Stokes, SW La.	370	11.6
Johnson, San Francisco	309	11.4
Henderson, Fairfield	318	11.4
Smith, TCU	386	11.4

ASSISTS

PLAYER	AST.	AVG.
Usher, Tenn. Tech	254	8.8
Crawford, New Mexico St.	282	8.5
Smart, San Francisco	241	8.3
Soares, Nevada	227	7.8
Evans, Miss. St.	219	7.8
Walker, L. Marymount	218	7.8
Dale, S. Miss.	222	7.7
Hurley, Duke	237	7.6

Miller, Marquette	221	7.6
Yelding, S. Alabama	184	7.1

BLOCKED SHOTS

PLAYER	BLK	AVG.
O'Neal, LSU	157	5.2
Mourning, Georgetown	160	5.0
Roberson, Vermont	139	5.0
Earl, Iowa	121	4.0
Baker, Hartford	100	3.7
Van Dyke, UTEP	116	3.5
Horry, Alabama	121	3.5
Jaxon, New Mexico	109	3.3
Chandler, Nebraska	91	3.1
Outlaw, Houston	97	3.1

STEALS

PLAYER	STL.	AVG.
Snipes, NE Illinois	86	3.4
Burcy, Chicago St.	85	3.3
Corbitt, Cent. Conn. St.	88	3.1
Mitchell, Wisc.-Milw.	78	3.1
Soares, Nevada	90	3.1
White, Southern (La.)	93	3.1
Higgins, Maine	95	3.0
Usher, Tenn. Tech	86	3.0
Evans, Miss. St.	83	3.0
Mee, W. Ky.	94	2.9

FIELD GOAL PERCENTAGE

PLAYER	FGM	FGA	PCT.
Outlaw, Houston	156	228	.684
Kidd, Middle Tenn. St.	156	235	.664
Fish, UNC-Wilm.	206	319	.646
McDowell, Texas-Arl.	184	287	.641
Spencer, UNLV	174	273	.637
Robinson, Mo.-KC	199	314	.634

Peplowski, Mich. St.	168	266	.632
Hupmann, Evansville	159	252	.631
Ellis, Notre Dame	227	360	.631
Solis, Brooklyn	150	238	.630

FREE THROW PERCENTAGE

PLAYER	FTM	FTA	PCT.
MacLean, UCLA	197	214	.921
Adkins, UNC-Wilm.	78	85	.918
Shreffler, Evansville	78	85	.918
Hildebrand, Liberty	114	125	.912
Lauritzen, Indiana St.	82	91	.901
Goodman, Utah St.	82	92	.891
Anderson, Old Dom.	96	108	.889
Schmitz, Mo.-KC	76	86	.884
Breslin, Holy Cross	91	103	.883
Marcelic, S. Utah St.	135	153	.882

THREE-POINT FIELD GOAL PERCENTAGE

PLAYER	FGM	FGA	PCT.
Wightman, W. Mich.	48	76	.632
Laettner, Duke	54	97	.557
Barker, Valparaiso	61	117	.521
Batle, Auburn	71	139	.511
Bennett, Wisc.-GB	95	186	.511

THREE-POINT FIELD GOALS PER GAME

PLAYER	FGM	AVG.
Day, Radford	117	4.0
Alberts, Akron	110	3.9
Woods, La Salle	121	3.9
McKelvey, Portland	106	3.8
Hurd, La Salle	113	3.6

1991–92 TEAM LEADERS

SCORING OFFENSE

SCHOOL	PTS.	AVG.
Northwestern St. (La.)	2660	95.0
Oklahoma	2838	94.6
Southern (La.)	2809	93.6
Georgia Southern	2836	91.5
Loyola Marymount	2552	91.1

SCORING DEFENSE

SCHOOL	PTS.	AVG.
Princeton	1349	48.2
Wisc.-Green Bay	1659	55.3
Southwest Missouri St.	1761	56.8
Monmouth	1701	58.7
Ball St.	1959	59.4

SCORING MARGIN

SCHOOL	OFF.	DEF.	MAR.
Indiana	83.4	65.8	17.6
Kansas	84.5	68.1	16.4
Arizona	84.8	68.8	16.0
Cincinnati	79.0	63.1	15.9
Duke	88.0	72.6	15.3

WON-LOST PERCENTAGE

SCHOOL	W-L	PCT.
Duke	34-2	.944

UNLV	26-2	.929
Delaware	27-4	.871
Montana	27-4	.871
Massachusetts	30-5	.857

FIELD GOAL PERCENTAGE

SCHOOL	FGM	FGA	PCT.
Duke	1108	2069	.536
Liberty	790	1519	.520
UNLV	817	1583	.516
Kansas	975	1892	.515
Wisc.-Green Bay	759	1481	.512

FIELD GOAL PERCENTAGE DEFENSE

SCHOOL	FGM	FGA	PCT.
UNLV	628	1723	.364
Princeton	445	1169	.381
Montana	685	1736	.395
Connecticut	734	1843	.398
Charleston Southern	592	1486	.398
Utah	730	1832	.398

FREE THROW PERCENTAGE

SCHOOL	FTM	FTA	PCT.
Northwestern	497	651	.763
Bucknell	550	722	.762
Monmouth	414	544	.761
Washington St.	554	729	.760
Drexel	524	692	.757

REBOUND MARGIN

SCHOOL	OWN	OPP.	MAR.
Delaware	42.1	33.8	8.3
Montana	40.6	32.4	8.2
Wake Forest	36.8	29.1	7.7
Providence	42.8	35.3	7.5
Michigan	40.4	33.0	7.5

THREE-POINT FIELD GOAL PERCENTAGE

SCHOOL	FGM	FGA	PCT.
Wisc.-Green Bay	204	437	.467
Auburn	182	403	.452
Western Michigan	120	267	.449
Louisiana Tech	161	359	.448
Duke	171	394	.434

THREE-POINT FIELD GOALS PER GAME

SCHOOL	FGM	AVG.
La Salle	294	9.5
Northwestern	259	9.3
N.C. St.	265	8.8
Kentucky	317	8.8
Texas-Arlington	255	8.8

was snapped by UCLA, 89-87. . . . Air Force lost 23 consecutive contests to Texas-El Paso in their series until defeating the Miners, 75-72. . . . Lucius Davis Jr. finished his career at UC Santa Barbara with 1,420 points. He and his father are believed to be the only father-son combination to score more than 1,400 points apiece for schools that are currently at the Division I level. Lucius Davis Sr. scored 1,511 points in three seasons for Fresno State (1968-70) shortly before the Bulldogs moved up to Division I.

St. John's Lou Carnesecca ended his 24-year college coaching career with a 526-200 record. He is the only major-college coach to survive more than 20 seasons with nothing but winning records at least five games above .500. . . . Coach Wimp Sanderson, who coached Alabama to at least 23 victories seven of the last eight seasons, left the Crimson Tide amid allegations of an altercation with his secretary. Just before her sexual discrimination lawsuit went to trial, Sanderson and the former secretary settled out of court.

Grant Hill jumps head and shoulders above Michigan's Jalen Rose in the 1992 NCAA final.

1992 NCAA Tournament

Summary: Christian Laettner became the NCAA Tournament's all-time leading scorer and teammate Bobby Hurley became the tourney's all-time leader in assists as the Blue Devils became the first school since UCLA (1967-73) to repeat as national champion. Hurley took up the slack with 26 points when Laettner was limited to eight points in an 81-78 decision over Indiana in the national semifinals. Laettner closed out his college career with a game-high 19 points in the championship game against Michigan, which became the only school to ever lead an NCAA final at halftime and end up losing the game by at least 20 points. Duke coach Mike Krzyzewski did the unthinkable and temporarily passed UCLA legend John Wooden (47-10, .8246) for the top spot in all-time NCAA playoff winning percentage (minimum of 20 games). Hurley was selected Final Four Most Outstanding Player although dissenters believed that Duke teammate Grant Hill deserved the honor instead. In the two Final Four games,

THOMPSON'S HEROICS

Loyola Marymount vs. San Francisco in WCC Tournament quarterfinals

March 7, 1992

Here is a play-by-play rundown of the NCAA-record setting eight of eight three-point shooting by junior swingman Tomas Thompson for #6 seed San Francisco in a 100-85 victory over #3 seed Loyola Marymount in the first round of the WCC Tournament. He contributed his first six treys in a five-minute span of the first half. Incidentally, Thompson led the WCC in three-point accuracy (48.2 percent), but averaged only 5.6 points per game.

NEUTRAL COURT (PORTLAND) FIRST HALF (6)	TIME	SCORE	MAR
made 3-pointer by Thompson	10:20	26-23	+3
made 3-pointer by Thompson	9:46	29-26	+3
made 3-pointer by Thompson	9:30	32-26	+6
made 3-pointer by Thompson	8:46	35-28	+7
made 3-pointer by Thompson	6:51	40-34	+6
made 3-pointer by Thompson	5:22	47-39	+8
SECOND HALF (2)			
made 3-pointer by Thompson	13:01	63-62	+1
made 3-pointer by Thompson	9:38	75-70	+5

1991-92 FINAL NATIONAL POLLS

AP	UPI	USA/CNN	SCHOOL (RECORD)	HEAD COACH
1	1	1	Duke (34-2)	Mike Krzyzewski
2	2	7	Kansas (27-5)	Roy Williams
3	4	4	Ohio State (26-6)	Randy Ayers
4	3	8	UCLA (28-5)	Jim Harrick
5	6	2	Indiana (27-7)	Bob Knight
6	9	6	Kentucky (29-7)	Rick Pitino
7	–	–	UNLV (26-2)	Jerry Tarkanian
8	7	11	Southern Cal (24-6)	George Raveling
9	8	10	Arkansas (26-8)	Nolan Richardson
10	5	16	Arizona (24-7)	Lute Olson
11	10	9	Oklahoma State (28-8)	Eddie Sutton
12	14	5	Cincinnati (29-5)	Bob Huggins
13	13	19	Alabama (26-9)	Wimp Sanderson
14	11	20	Michigan State (22-8)	Jud Heathcote
15	17	3	Michigan (25-9)	Steve Fisher
16	12	18	Missouri (21-9)	Norm Stewart
17	21	15	Massachusetts (30-5)	John Calipari
18	15	12	North Carolina (23-10)	Dean Smith
19	18	13	Seton Hall (23-9)	P.J. Carlesimo
20	16	14	Florida State (22-10)	Pat Kennedy
21	20	24	Syracuse (22-10)	Jim Boeheim
22	19	23	Georgetown (22-10)	John Thompson
23	22	–	Oklahoma (21-9)	Billy Tubbs
24	23	–	DePaul (20-9)	Joey Meyer
25	–	25	Louisiana State (21-10)	Dale Brown
–	–	17	Memphis State (23-11)	Larry Finch
–	–	21	Georgia Tech (23-12)	Bobby Cremins
–	–	22	Texas-El Paso (27-7)	Don Haskins
–	24	–	St. John's (19-11)	Lou Carnesecca
–	25	–	Tulane (21-8)	Perry Clark

Hill had more field goals than Hurley (14 to 10), outshot him from the floor (61 percent to 41.7), blocked more shots (5 to 0), outrebounded him (16 to 3) and accumulated just as many assists (11 each). Moreover, Hurley's 3 of 12 field-goal shooting in the final against Michigan was the worst marksmanship from the floor for a Final

Indiana's Calbert Cheaney drives through Michigan's Rob Pelinka (left) and Jimmy King.

Four Most Outstanding Player in a championship game since Elgin Baylor of runner-up Seattle went 9 of 32 against Kentucky in 1958. It was the second consecutive year for the Final Four Most Outstanding Player to come from Duke and manage just three baskets and shoot less than 50 percent from the floor in the title game. In 1991, Laettner hit 3 of 8 field-goal attempts against Kansas. Duke became the 18th NCAA Tournament champion to win at least two playoff games by fewer than six points when the Blue Devils edged Kentucky (104-103 in overtime in East Regional final) and Indiana (81-78 in national semifinals). Massachusetts might have been facing Duke instead of Kentucky if not for a critical, and controversial, technical foul assessed to Minutemen coach John Calipari by referee Lenny Wirtz.

Star Gazing: Hurley, 6-0, was the shortest player to be selected Final Four Most Outstanding

SEASON STATISTICS OF DUKE REGULARS

PLAYER	POS.	CL.	G.	FG%	FT%	PPG	RPG
Christian Laettner	C	Sr.	35	.575	.815	21.5	7.9
Thomas Hill	G	Jr.	36	.534	.768	14.6	3.4
Grant Hill	F-G	So.	33	.611	.733	14.0	5.7
Bobby Hurley	G	Jr.	31	.433	.789	13.2	2.0
Brian Davis	F	Sr.	36	.481	.740	11.2	4.5
Antonio Lang	F	So.	34	.562	.657	6.4	4.1
Cherokee Parks	C	Fr.	34	.571	.725	5.0	2.4
Marty Clark	G	So.	34	.541	.778	2.9	0.8
Erik Meek	C	Fr.	25	.579	.500	2.5	1.2
Kenny Blakeney	G	So.	29	.565	.650	1.4	0.8
TEAM TOTALS			36	.536	.748	88.0	34.1

Three-point field goals leaders: Hurley (59 of 140, .421), Laettner (54 of 97, .557), T. Hill (37 of 91, .407). **Assists leaders:** Hurley 237, G. Hill 134. **Blocked shots leaders:** Parks 35, Laettner 32. **Steals leaders:** Laettner 74, T. Hill 60.

1992 FINAL FOUR CHAMPIONSHIP GAME

MINNEAPOLIS, MN

MICHIGAN (51)	MIN.	FG-A	FT-A	REB.	A.	PF.	PTS.
Webber	30	6-12	2-5	11	1	4	14
Jackson	16	0-1	0-0	1	2	1	0
Howard	29	4-9	1-3	3	0	3	9
Rose	37	5-12	1-2	5	4	4	11
King	40	3-10	0-0	2	1	1	7
Riley	19	2-6	0-0	4	1	2	4
Voskuil	15	1-2	2-2	3	3	2	4
Pelinka	10	1-2	0-0	2	1	0	2
Hunter	2	0-0	0-0	0	0	0	0
Talley	1	0-2	0-0	1	0	0	0
Bossard	1	0-1	0-0	0	0	0	0
Seter	1	0-1	0-0	1	0	0	0
Armer	1	0-0	0-0	0	0	0	0
TOTALS	200	22-58	6-12	35	13	17	51

FG%: .379. **FT%:** .500. **Three-point goals:** 1 of 11 (King 1-2, Rose 0-3, Webber 2-9, Howard 0-1, Voskuil 0-1, Talley 0-1, Bossard 0-1). **Blocks:** 3 (Jackson 2). **Turnovers:** 20 (Howard 4, Rose 4). **Steals:** 8 (Webber 2, Rose 2, King 2).

DUKE (71)	MIN.	FG-A	FT-A	REB.	A.	PF.	PTS.
Lang	31	2-3	1-2	4	0	1	5
G. Hill	36	8-14	2-2	10	5	2	18
Laettner	35	6-13	5-6	7	0	1	19
Hurley	36	3-12	2-2	3	7	4	9
T. Hill	34	5-10	5-8	7	0	2	16
Parks	13	1-3	2-2	3	0	3	4
Davis	10	0-2	0-0	0	0	0	0
Ast	1	0-0	0-0	1	0	0	0
Clark	1	0-0	0-0	0	0	0	0
Blakeney	1	0-0	0-0	0	0	0	0
Burt	1	0-0	0-0	0	0	0	0
Meek	1	0-0	0-0	0	0	0	0
TOTALS	200	25-57	17-22	37	12	13	71

FG%: .439. **FT%:** .773. **Three-point goals:** 4 of 9 (Laettner 2-4, Hurley 1-3, T. Hill 1-2). **Blocks:** 4 (G. Hill 2). **Turnovers:** 14 (Laettner 7). **Steals:** 9 (G. Hill 3).

Halftime: Michigan 31-30.

NATIONAL SEMIFINALS

DUKE (81): Lang 1-5 2-2 4, Davis 1-3 3-7 5, Laettner 2-8 4-7 8, T. Hill 3-10 4-5 11, Hurley 7-12 6-8 26, G. Hill 6-9 2-4 14, Parks 3-5 2-3 8, Clark 0-0 5-6 5. Team 23-52 (.442) 28-42 (.667) 81.

INDIANA (76): Cheaney 4-13 2-4 11, Henderson 6-9 2-2 15, Nover 3-4 2-2 9, Bailey 4-8 0-0 9, Reynolds 1-4 0-0 2, Meeks 1-2 1-2 3, Anderson 1-6 0-1 2, G. Graham 6-9 5-5 18, Leary 3-3 0-0 9. Team 29-58 (.500) 12-16 (.750) 78.

Halftime: Indiana 42-37.

MICHIGAN (76): Webber 8-12 0-2 16, Jackson 1-2 1-2 3, Howard 3-9 6-7 12, Rose 4-13 5-6 13, King 5-9 4-4 17, Talley 1-3 2-3 4, Riley 1-1 0-0 2, Voskuil 2-4 4-5 9. Team 25-53 (.471) 22-29 (.758) 76.

CINCINNATI (72): Nelson 2-2 0-0 4, Jones 5-13 2-2 14, Blount 0-3 1-2 1, Buford 6-17 4-4 18, Van Exel 7-15 5-10 21, Martin 4-10 2-3 10, Scott 0-0 0-0 0, Jackson 0-1 0-0 0, Gibson 2-3 0-0 4. Team 26-64 (.406) 14-21 (.667) 72.

Halftime: Cincinnati 41-38.

ALL-TOURNAMENT TEAM

Grant Hill, F, Soph., Duke
*Bobby Hurley, G, Jr., Duke (35 points, 11 assists)
Christian Laettner, C, Sr., Duke
Jalen Rose, G, Fr., Michigan
Chris Webber, F, Fr., Michigan

*Named Most Outstanding Player.

Player since 5-11 Hal Lear led Temple to a national third-place finish in 1956. The only Final Four Most Outstanding Player shorter than Hurley from a championship team was 5-11 Kenny Sailors of Wyoming '43. Hurley shot a mediocre 41 percent from the floor in his career with the Blue Devils, but his playmaking and intangibles helped them win 18 of 20 NCAA playoff games. He holds the career record for most playoff assists (145) although his bid to become the first player to start four consecutive NCAA finals was thwarted when California upset Duke in the second round of the 1993 Midwest Regional despite Hurley's career-high 32 points.

Biggest Upsets: East Tennessee State (14th seed) over Arizona (3), 87-80, and Southwestern Louisiana (13) over Oklahoma (4), 87-83.

One and Only: Guard Jalen Rose is the only freshman to finish with the highest season scoring average for a team reaching the NCAA Tournament championship game. He averaged 17.6 points per game for national runner-up Michigan. Rose and Chris Webber became the only set of freshman teammates to be named to an NCAA All-Tournament team.

Numbers Game: All three Final Four game winners trailed at halftime. . . . Duke defied a

1992 CHAMPIONSHIP BRACKET

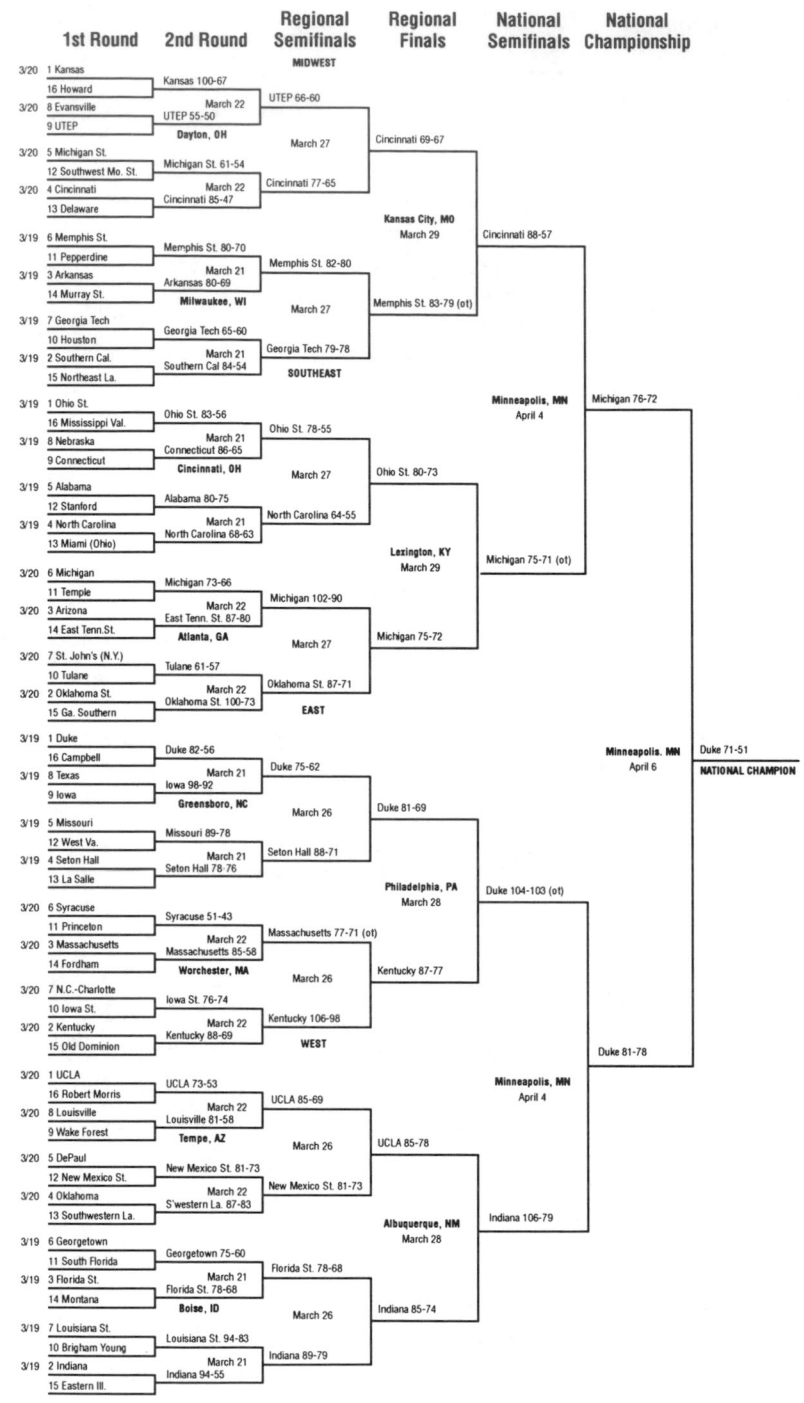

1st Round **2nd Round** **Regional Semifinals** **Regional Finals** **National Semifinals** **National Championship**

MIDWEST

3/20 1 Kansas
16 Howard — Kansas 100-67
3/20 8 Evansville — March 22
9 UTEP — UTEP 55-50 — UTEP 66-60
Dayton, OH — March 27 — Cincinnati 69-67
3/20 5 Michigan St.
12 Southwest Mo. St. — Michigan St. 61-54
3/20 4 Cincinnati — March 22
13 Delaware — Cincinnati 85-47 — Cincinnati 77-65
Kansas City, MO — March 29 — Cincinnati 88-57
3/19 6 Memphis St.
11 Pepperdine — Memphis St. 80-70
3/19 3 Arkansas — March 21
14 Murray St. — Arkansas 80-69 — Memphis St. 82-80
Milwaukee, WI — March 27
3/19 7 Georgia Tech
10 Houston — Georgia Tech 65-60 — Memphis St. 83-79 (ot)
3/19 2 Southern Cal. — March 21
15 Northeast La. — Southern Cal 84-54 — Georgia Tech 79-78

SOUTHEAST

Minneapolis, MN — April 4 — Michigan 76-72
3/19 1 Ohio St.
16 Mississippi Val. — Ohio St. 83-56
3/19 8 Nebraska — March 21
9 Connecticut — Connecticut 86-65 — Ohio St. 78-55
Cincinnati, OH — March 27 — Ohio St. 80-73
3/19 5 Alabama
12 Stanford — Alabama 80-75
3/19 4 North Carolina — March 21
13 Miami (Ohio) — North Carolina 68-63 — North Carolina 64-55
Lexington, KY — March 29 — Michigan 75-71 (ot)
3/20 6 Michigan
11 Temple — Michigan 73-66
3/20 3 Arizona — March 22
14 East Tenn. St. — East Tenn. St. 87-80 — Michigan 102-90
Atlanta, GA — March 27
3/20 7 St. John's (N.Y.)
10 Tulane — Tulane 61-57 — Michigan 75-72
3/20 2 Oklahoma St. — March 22
15 Ga. Southern — Oklahoma St. 100-73 — Oklahoma St. 87-71

EAST

Minneapolis, MN — April 6 — Duke 71-51
NATIONAL CHAMPION
3/19 1 Duke
16 Campbell — Duke 82-56
3/19 8 Texas — March 21
9 Iowa — Iowa 98-92 — Duke 75-62
Greensboro, NC — March 26 — Duke 81-69
3/19 5 Missouri
12 West Va. — Missouri 89-78
3/19 4 Seton Hall — March 21
13 La Salle — Seton Hall 78-76 — Seton Hall 88-71
Philadelphia, PA — March 28 — Duke 104-103 (ot)
3/20 6 Syracuse
11 Princeton — Syracuse 51-43
3/20 3 Massachusetts — March 22
14 Fordham — Massachusetts 85-58 — Massachusetts 77-71 (ot)
Worchester, MA — March 26
3/20 7 N.C.-Charlotte
10 Iowa St. — Iowa St. 76-74 — Kentucky 87-77
3/20 2 Kentucky — March 22
15 Old Dominion — Kentucky 88-69 — Kentucky 106-98

WEST

Minneapolis, MN — April 4 — Duke 81-78
3/20 1 UCLA
16 Robert Morris — UCLA 73-53
3/20 8 Louisville — March 22
9 Wake Forest — Louisville 81-58 — UCLA 85-69
Tempe, AZ — March 26 — UCLA 85-78
3/20 5 DePaul
12 New Mexico St. — New Mexico St. 81-73
3/20 4 Oklahoma — March 22
13 Southwestern La. — S'western La. 87-83 — New Mexico St. 81-73
Albuquerque, NM — March 28 — Indiana 106-79
3/19 6 Georgetown
11 South Florida — Georgetown 75-60
3/19 3 Florida St. — March 21
14 Montana — Florida St. 78-68 — Florida St. 78-68
Boise, ID — March 26
3/19 7 Louisiana St.
10 Brigham Young — Louisiana St. 94-83 — Indiana 85-74
3/19 2 Indiana — March 21
15 Eastern Ill. — Indiana 94-55 — Indiana 89-79

recent trend by becoming the first top-ranked team in 10 years entering the NCAA Tournament to win the national title. The previous five top-ranked teams failed to reach the championship game. . . . The final between Duke and Michigan was the most-watched basketball game in television history. An estimated 53 million viewers took in all or part of the title game in the United States' TV homes covered by the Nielsen ratings. CBS estimated that an additional 10 percent of the total audience watched the 1992 final away from home—in taverns, dormitories and other venues that Nielsen doesn't survey. That's more than 100 times the initial viewing audience estimated at 500,000 in 1946, when the championship game (Oklahoma State defeated North Carolina, 43-40) was televised locally for the first time in New York by WCBS-TV. . . . Four of Michigan's Fab Five Freshmen—Rose (107 points), Webber (98), Jimmy King (83) and Juwan Howard (82)—ranked among the top six freshman scorers in a single tournament in the last 13 years. . . . UNLV's streak of tournament appearances ended at nine when the Rebels were on NCAA probation. . . . Iowa State compiled the worst league record (5-9 in the Big Eight) of any team ever to receive an at-large invitation. . . . Tulane, coached by Perry Clark, appeared in the NCAA playoffs for the first time in school history. . . . Duke won all nine of its NCAA playoff games against Big East and Big Ten teams in a three-year span from 1990-92.

What Might Have Been: Forwards Calbert Cheaney and Eric Anderson shot better than 50 percent from the floor in their careers for Indiana. If only they had combined to hit 36.8 percent of their field-goal attempts instead of 26.3 percent (5 of 19) in the national semifinals, the Hoosiers could have defeated eventual champion Duke rather than having a five-point halftime lead evaporate and losing 81-78. . . . Kentucky coach Rick Pitino was criticized in some quarters for leaving Grant Hill unguarded for his approximate 80-foot pass to Laettner with 2.1 seconds remaining in overtime in the East Regional. . . . Arizona (24-7/without Brian Williams), Georgia Tech (23-12/Kenny Anderson), Louisiana State (21-

10/Chris Jackson), Temple (17-13/Donald Hodge) and Syracuse (22-10/Billy Owens) might have fared better in the playoffs if standout players had exercised their remaining eligibility instead of defecting to the NBA. Ditto Wake Forest (17-12) if guard Randolph Childress didn't miss the season because of a knee injury. . . . Utah (24-11) probably would have participated in the NCAA playoffs instead of the NIT if two-time WAC Player of the Year Josh Grant didn't miss most of the season because of a bum knee. Notre Dame (18-15) is in the same category because of forward Monty Williams' heart problem. . . . New Mexico State (25-8) might have advanced even farther in the West Regional if forward-center Tracey Ware didn't redshirt because of a knee injury. Ware led the Big West Conference in field-goal percentage the next season.

Putting Things in Perspective: Duke came close to becoming the eighth NCAA champion to go undefeated. The Blue Devils' two losses were by a total of just six points (ACC road games against North Carolina and Wake Forest to start and end a stretch of five of six contests away from home from February 5-23).

Scoring Leader: Christian Laettner, Duke (115 points, 19.2 ppg).

Highest Scoring Average: Jamal Mashburn, Kentucky (96 points, 24 ppg).

Rebounding Leader: Chris Webber, Michigan (58 rebounds, 9.7 rpg).

Highest Rebounding Average: Doug Edwards, Florida State (32 rebounds, 10.7 rpg).

1992-93

AT A GLANCE

NCAA Champion: North Carolina (34-4; coached by Dean Smith; won ACC regular-season title by two games over Florida State with a 14-2 record).

NIT Champion: Minnesota (22-10; coached by Clem Haskins; finished in a tie for fifth place in Big Ten with a 9-9 record).

New Rule: Unsportsmanlike technical fouls, in addition to contact technical fouls, count toward the five fouls for player disqualification and the team fouls in reaching bonus free-throw situations.

NCAA Probation: Middle Tennessee State, Syracuse, Texas-Pan American, Tulsa

NCAA Consensus First-Team All-Americans: Calbert Cheaney, F, Sr., Indiana; Anfernee Hardaway, G, Jr., Memphis State; Bobby Hurley, G, Sr., Duke; Jamal Mashburn, F, Jr., Kentucky; Chris Webber, F, Soph., Michigan.

National Player of the Year: Cheaney (22.4 ppg, 6.4 rpg, 54.9 FG%).

National Coaches of the Year: Vanderbilt's Eddie Fogler (28-6/AP, UPI, NABC, USBWA) and North Carolina's Dean Smith (34-4/Naismith).

North Carolina coach Dean Smith goes out of his way to emphasize senior leadership and always has his seniors featured on the cover of the Tar Heels' media guide even if they play sparingly. Carolina had several heroes on its way to capturing the national championship, but none loomed larger than senior forward George Lynch, who turned in double doubles (double figures in scoring and rebounding) in his last four games as the Tar Heels won the East Regional at East Rutherford, N.J., and the Final Four at New Orleans.

One of Carolina's four defeats was at Wake Forest when Demon Deacons guard Randy Childress erupted for 18 second-half points in less than four minutes. Carolina almost had another setback, but the Tar Heels erased a 19-point deficit with less than nine minutes remaining against Florida State to upend the Seminoles, 82-77. The biggest comeback of the season, however, came when Virginia Commonwealth overcame a 26-point deficit midway through the second half to post a 95-91 overtime triumph at South Florida. Guard Kenny Harris, a transfer from North Carolina, tallied 30 points in the final 15 minutes for VCU.

Florida State became the only school in history to have five active 1,000-point career scorers on their roster at the same time (no transfers from other four-year schools)—Douglas Edwards, Rodney Dobard, Sam Cassell, Chuck Graham and Bob

Sura. Cassell was a junior college transfer. . . . Georgia Tech (19-11) averaged 11 defeats annually over the last five seasons despite having an NBA first-round draft choice each year. The Yellow Jackets ended defending NCAA champion Duke's 23-game winning streak, 80-79. . . . Duke's Bobby Hurley finished his career with an NCAA-record 1,076 assists. He had 33 games with at least 10 scoring feeds.

Iowa had a legitimate shot at the Big Ten title until forward Chris Street, the Hawkeyes' leading rebounder, died in an auto accident. . . . Wisconsin's Michael Finley set a Big Ten record with 10 steals against Purdue. . . . Purdue compiled a 9-5 homecourt record for the Boilermakers' worst winning percentage (.643) in Mackey Arena since the 14,123-seat facility opened in 1967-68. One of their homecourt defeats was to Northwestern, 62-59, when the Wildcats snapped a 41-game road losing streak. Purdue had won its previous 19 contests against Northwestern. . . . Indiana coach Bob Knight was suspended for one game after a sideline outburst in a victory against Notre Dame. During the tirade, Knight screamed at his son, Pat, and kicked him in the leg.

Mississippi Valley State guard Alphonso Ford finished his Division I career as the only player to score more than 700 points and average more than 25 points per game in each of four seasons. . . . Connecticut's Scott Burrell finished his career as the tallest player (6-7) to amass more than 300 steals. He had 310. Burrell is the only individual to be a first-round selection by both the NBA (20th pick overall by the Charlotte Hornets) and major league baseball (righthanded pitcher was 26th pick overall by the Seattle Mariners as a high school senior in 1989). . . . Guard Terry Dehere became the first Seton Hall player since 1953 to earn a spot on an NCAA consensus first- or second-team All-American squad. . . . Georgetown, coached by John Thompson, incurred its worst ever finish in the Big East (eighth place) one year after finishing in a tie for first.

Oklahoma State center Bryant Reeves became the first player to lead the Big Eight in scoring,

1992–93 INDIVIDUAL LEADERS

SCORING

PLAYER	PTS.	AVG.
Guy, Texas-Pan Am.	556	29.3
Rider, UNLV	814	29.1
Best, Tenn. Tech	799	28.5
Baker, Hartford	792	28.3
Hunter Jackson St.	907	26.7
Ford, Miss. Valley St.	728	26.0
Edwards, Wright St.	757	25.2
Ross, Appa. St.	683	24.4
Robinson, Purdue	676	24.1
Sykes, Grambling St.	644	23.9

REBOUNDING

PLAYER	REB.	AVG.
Kidd, Middle Tenn. St.	386	14.8
Scales, Southern (La.)	393	12.7
Jackson, Nicholls St.	325	12.5
Dunkley, Delaware	367	12.2
Callahan, Northeastern	340	12.1
Johnson, New Orleans	346	11.9
Rogers, Tenn. St.	339	11.7
Rose, Drexel	330	11.4
Smith, Providence	375	11.4
Brown, Colgate	317	11.3

ASSISTS

PLAYER	AST.	AVG.
Crawford, New Mex. St.	310	9.1
Thomas, UNLV	248	8.6
Woods, Wright St.	253	8.4
Hurley, Duke	262	8.2
Evans, Miss. St.	235	8.1
Kidd, California	222	7.7
Miller, Marquette	213	7.6
Haggerty, Baylor	189	7.3
Browne, Lamar	195	7.2
Capers, Arizona St.	200	7.1

BLOCKED SHOTS

PLAYER	BLK.	AVG.
Ratliff, Wyoming	124	4.4
Wright, Clemson	124	4.1
Outlaw, Houston	114	3.8
Rogers, Tenn. St.	93	3.2
Wilson, E. Mich.	96	3.2
Dunkley, Delaware	96	3.2
Dobard, Florida St.	111	3.2
Popa, Miami (Fla.)	85	3.1
Hart, Iona	80	3.1
Thurman, W. Ill.	83	3.1

STEALS

PLAYER	STL.	AVG.
CALIFORNIA	110	3.8
Goodman, Utah St.	102	3.8
Woods, Wright St.	109	3.6
Bright, Bucknell	94	3.2
Mee, W. Ky.	100	3.1
Myers, St. Francis (N.Y.)	81	3.1
Woods, Charleston	84	3.1
Johnson, Canisius	79	3.0
Peyton, Bucknell	88	3.0
Evans, Oklahoma	97	3.0

FIELD GOAL PERCENTAGE

PLAYER	FGM	FGA	PCT.
Outlaw, Houston	196	298	.658
Grant, Xavier	223	341	.654
Hart, Iona	151	231	.654
Parks, Duke	161	247	.652
Trent, Ohio	194	298	.651
Nahar, Wright St.	190	296	.642
Peplowski, Mich. St.	161	252	.639
Lunsford, Ala. St.	142	223	.637
Kidd, Middle Tenn. St.	167	265	.630
Gay, Winthrop	194	309	.628

FREE THROW PERCENTAGE

PLAYER	FTM	FTA	PCT.
Grant, Utah	104	113	.920
Breslin, Holy Cross	100	111	.901
Lake, Montana	71	79	.899
Schmidt, Valparaiso	70	78	.897
Hartzell, UNC-G'boro	72	81	.889
Holman, Kent	69	78	.885
Ford, Kentucky	104	118	.881
Baldwin, N'western	66	75	.880
Burgess, Radford	109	124	.879
Houston, Tenn.	165	188	.878

THREE-POINT FIELD GOAL PERCENTAGE

PLAYER	FGM	FGA	PCT.
Anderson, Kent	44	82	.537
Moore, S. Houston St.	73	137	.533
Morton, Louisville	51	96	.531
Ford, Kentucky	101	191	.529
Graham, Indiana	57	111	.514

THREE-POINT FIELD GOALS PER GAME

PLAYER	FGM	AVG.
Haslett, S. Miss.	109	4.2
Smith, Arizona St.	113	4.2
Alberts, Akron	107	4.1
Veney, Lamar	106	3.9
Day, Radford	116	3.7

1992–93 TEAM LEADERS

SCORING OFFENSE

SCHOOL	PTS.	AVG.
Southern (La.)	3011	97.1
Northwestern St. (La.)	2357	90.7
UNLV	2592	89.4
Wright St.	2674	89.1
Oklahoma	2850	89.1

SCORING DEFENSE

SCHOOL	PTS.	AVG.
Princeton	1421	54.7
Yale	1444	55.5
Miami (Ohio)	1775	57.3
Cincinnati	1871	58.5
Southwest Missouri St.	1813	58.5

SCORING MARGIN

SCHOOL	OFF.	DEF.	MAR.
North Carolina	86.1	68.3	17.8
Kentucky	87.5	69.8	17.7
Cincinnati	74.5	58.5	16.0
Duke	86.4	71.2	15.2
Indiana	86.5	71.6	14.9

WON-LOST PERCENTAGE

SCHOOL	W-L	PCT.
North Carolina	34-4	.895
Indiana	31-4	.886
Kentucky	30-4	.882
New Orleans	26-4	.867
Michigan	31-5	.861

FIELD GOAL PERCENTAGE

SCHOOL	FGM	FGA	PCT.
Indiana	1076	2062	.522
Northeast Louisiana	1015	1946	.522
James Madison	848	1634	.519
Wright St.	987	1912	.516
Kansas	1109	2154	.515

FIELD GOAL PERCENTAGE DEFENSE

SCHOOL	FGM	FGA	PCT.
Marquette	634	1613	.393
George Washington	708	1794	.395
Arizona	710	1776	.400
Utah	737	1831	.403

FREE THROW PERCENTAGE

SCHOOL	FTM	FTA	PCT.
Utah	476	602	.791
Charleston Southern	408	526	.776
Valparaiso	412	532	.774
Indiana St.	445	580	.767
Brigham Young	697	909	.767

REBOUND MARGIN

SCHOOL	OWN	OPP.	MAR.
Massachusetts	43.9	32.8	11.2
Iowa	42.8	31.7	11.1
Idaho	39.6	29.3	10.3
Arizona	43.1	34.2	9.0
North Carolina	41.1	32.2	8.9

THREE-POINT FIELD GOAL PERCENTAGE

SCHOOL	FGM	FGA	PCT.
Valparaiso	214	500	.428
Princeton	204	479	.426
Indiana	197	464	.425
Kent	162	384	.422
Miami (Ohio)	218	522	.418

THREE-POINT FIELD GOALS PER GAME

SCHOOL	FGM	AVG.
Lamar	271	10.0
Kentucky	340	10.0
Arizona St.	263	9.4
UNC-Asheville	235	8.7
Southern Cal	259	8.6

rebounding and field-goal shooting since Kansas' Wilt Chamberlain achieved the feat in 1956-57. . . . Marquette's Jim McIlvaine blocked 13 shots in a game against Northeastern Illinois. . . . J.R. Rider set a UNLV Division I school record with 44 points against Nevada-Reno. UNLV's 59-game homecourt winning streak was ended by Louisville, 90-86. . . . Jackson State guard Lindsey Hunter, who became a first-round draft choice of the Detroit Pistons, set an NCAA record with 26 three-point field-goal attempts (11 made) in a game vs. Kansas at Honolulu (see accompanying box).

Towson State's Devin Boyd (46 points at Maryland-Baltimore County in double overtime), Wright State's Bill Edwards (45 vs. Morehead State), Hofstra's Demetrius Dudley (44 vs. Central Connecticut State) and Portland's Matt Houle (43 vs. San Francisco) established school Division I single-game scoring standards. Boyd's barrage is a Big South Conference standard and was achieved when he tallied 17 points in the second extra session. . . . Rider (29.1 ppg), Hartford's Vin Baker (28.3), Edwards (25.2), Appalachian State's Billy Ross (24.4), Weber State's Stan Rose (23.2) and Charleston Southern's Darnell Sneed (23) set school Division I records for highest scoring average in a single season. Baker, a senior, had averaged only 4.7 ppg as a freshman. . . . Tennessee Tech senior John Best averaged 28.5 ppg after averaging only 3.1 ppg as a freshman.

Tennessee became the first school ever to have nine successive seasons with one or more players scoring at least 600 points. The Volunteers' principal point producers in that stretch were Michael Brooks, Tony White, Dyron Nix and Allan Houston. Despite the presence of so many prolific scorers, the Vols didn't win an NCAA Tournament game in that span and posted just two winning SEC records. . . . Tennessee State, which compiled a 4-24 record the previous season, improved by 14 1/2 games to 19-10. Tennessee State, coached by Frankie Allen, captured the Ohio Valley Conference regular-season crown after finishing in last place the previous year. . . . George Washington and Western Kentucky finished in the Top 20 of a final wire-service poll for the first time since 1955

and 1971, respectively. GWU, coached by Mike Jarvis, participated in the NCAA Tournament for the first time since 1961 after the Colonial ended a 21-game losing streak in their series with Temple. . . . Western Kentucky lost 12 consecutive times to Louisville in their series until clipping the Cardinals, 78-77. WKU, coached by Ralph Willard, made its first Top 20 appearance in a final wire-service poll since 1971. . . . Forward Tony Dunkin of Coastal Carolina in the Big South Conference became the only player to be named MVP four times in a Division I league. He originally signed with Jacksonville, but left the Dolphins' program before ever playing for them.

North Carolina (34-4/coached by Dean Smith), Michigan (31-5/Steve Fisher), Vanderbilt (28-6/Eddie Fogler), Northeast Louisiana (26-5/Mike Vining) and Colgate (18-10/Jack Bruen) had their winningest seasons in school history. New Orleans (26-4/Tim Floyd) tied its school single-season record for most victories. . . . Vandy made its first Top 20 appearance in a final wire-service poll since 1974. Guard Billy McCaffrey became the first Vanderbilt player since 1966 to earn a spot on an NCAA consensus first- or second-team All-American squad.

Arkansas closed out playing in historic Barnhill Arena on a sour note when the Razorbacks' 36-game conference winning streak at home was snapped by Auburn, 100-89, as the Tigers shot 74 percent from the floor in the second half. . . . Lamar had an NCAA-record 23 three-pointers in a 103-76 victory over Louisiana Tech. Lamar's Keith Veney had two games with 11 three-pointers in a nine-day span in early February against Prairie View A&M and Arkansas-Little Rock. Veney transferred after the season to Marshall. . . . Texas-Pan American's Greg Guy, who averaged a mere 3.3 points per game the previous season in three games for Fresno State before transferring, became the only national scoring champion to average fewer than 14 the season before capturing the scoring title (29.3 ppg).

Drake's Curt Smith became the first player in Missouri Valley Conference history to lead the

A distressed Jason Kidd disputes a call.

JACKSON THREE

Jackson State vs. Kansas in first round of Rainbow Classic at Honolulu

December 27, 1992

Jackson State guard Lindsey Hunter established an NCAA record with 26 three-point field-goal attempts (making 11) in a game vs. Final Four team-to-be Kansas. Hunter finished with 48 points, the most ever against a Kansas squad. Of 1,942 shots from the floor by Hunter in three seasons with Jackson State, 42.2 percent of them came from behind the three-point arc.

JACKSON STATE (85): Whitefield 0-1 0-0 0, **Hunter 17-43 3-4 48,** J. Taylor 5-8 0-0 13, Goodlow 1-6 0-0 2, Simmons 1-3 2-2 4, Lothridge 1-1 2-2 4, R. Taylor 0-0 0-0 0, Harden 0-0 0-0 0, Jones 2-4 0-0 4, Ellis 0-0 0-0 0, Wright 1-3 3-4 5, Hooten 1-1 0-0 2, Thompson 1-2 1-1 3.Team 30-72 (.417) 11-13 (.846) 85.

Three-point shooting: 14 of 34 (Hunter 11-26, J. Taylor 3-6, Jones 0-2).

KANSAS (93): Walters 4-12 2-2 13, Jordan 7-11 4-4 20, Pauley 7-14 2-5 16, Hancock 5-6 0-4 10, Scott 4-5 3-9 11, Rayford 0-0 0-0 0, Richey 2-3 6-6 10, Woodberry 1-4 6-6 8, Pearson 2-5 0-0 5, Gurley 0-0 0-0 0.Team 32-60 (.533) 23-36 (.639) 93.

Three-point shooting: 6 of 16 (Walters 3-8, Jordan 2-4, Woodberry 0-1, Pearson 1-3).

league in scoring, assists and steals in the same season. . . . SMU, coached by John Shumate, captured the SWC regular-season title just one year after finishing in seventh place. . . . Louisiana Tech's string of nine consecutive 20-win seasons ended abruptly when the Bulldogs posted a 7-21 record. . . . New Orleans' Ervin Johnson grabbed a school-record 27 rebounds in a game against Lamar. . . . New Mexico State started a nine-game winning streak against UNLV in their series through 1996. Meanwhile, Pacific ended its 26-game losing streak to UNLV.

Fordham defeated St. John's, 60-55, breaking a 23-game losing streak in the Rams' series with the Redmen. . . . Princeton, coached by Pete Carril, led the nation in team defense for the fifth consecutive season and 11th time in 18 years. . . . Columbia (16-10), coached by Jack Rohan, compiled its first winning record in 11 years. . . . New Hampshire lost more than 20 games for the sev-

enth straight season. . . . Maryland-Eastern Shore's Rob Chavez became a novelty of sorts as the first white coach at a predominantly black Division I school.

A big story was 29-year-old Todd Bozeman, who was promoted at California following a controversial midseason firing of Lou Campanelli. For the first time in its 66-year history, the National Association of Basketball Coaches publicly condemned the dismissal of one of its member coaches. The NABC's principal concern was the absence of due process after Campanelli was accused of verbally abusing the Cal players. Campanelli, who did an outstanding job rejuvenating Cal basketball, subsequently filed a $5 million lawsuit against the school, charging the administration violated due process by not properly warning him that it disapproved of his treatment of players.

1993 NCAA Tournament

Summary: George Lynch, North Carolina's top rebounder and second-leading scorer, made four big plays in the closing moments of the title game. With Michigan leading, 67-66, he and Eric Montross blocked away a driving layup by Jimmy King. That led to a fastbreak basket by Derrick

1992-93 FINAL NATIONAL POLLS

AP	UPI	USA/CNN	SCHOOL (RECORD)	HEAD COACH
1	1	5	Indiana (31-4)	Bob Knight
2	4	3	Kentucky (30-4)	Rick Pitino
3	3	2	Michigan (31-5)	Steve Fisher
4	2	1	North Carolina (34-4)	Dean Smith
5	5	12	Arizona (24-4)	Lute Olson
6	6	11	Seton Hall (28-7)	P.J. Carlesimo
7	7	6	Cincinnati (27-5)	Bob Huggins
8	8	8	Vanderbilt (28-6)	Eddie Fogler
9	9	4	Kansas (29-7)	Roy Williams
10	10	9	Duke (24-8)	Mike Krzyzewski
11	11	7	Florida State (25-10)	Pat Kennedy
12	12	10	Arkansas (22-9)	Nolan Richardson
13	13	19	Iowa (23-9)	Tom Davis
14	16	22	Massachusetts (24-7)	John Calipari
15	14	15	Louisville (22-9)	Denny Crum
16	15	14	Wake Forest (21-9)	Dave Odom
17	18	–	New Orleans (20-10)	Tim Floyd
18	19	–	Georgia Tech (19-11)	Bobby Cremins
19	17	20	Utah (24-7)	Rick Majerus
20	24	16	Western Kentucky (20-11)	Ralph Willard
21	–	–	New Mexico (24-7)	Dave Bliss
22	20	–	Purdue (18-10)	Gene Keady
23	22	–	Oklahoma State (20-9)	Eddie Sutton
24	25	–	New Mexico State (26-8)	Neil McCarthy
25	21	–	UNLV (21-8)	Rollie Massimino
–	–	13	Temple (20-13)	John Chaney
–	–	17	California (21-9)	Todd Bozeman*
–	23	18	Virginia (21-10)	Jeff Jones
–	–	21	George Washington (21-9)	Mike Jarvis
–	–	23	Xavier (24-6)	Pete Gillen
–	–	24	UCLA (22-11)	Jim Harrick
–	–	25	Minnesota (22-10)	Clem Haskins

*Bozeman coached the Bears' last 13 games (11-2 record) after replacing Lou Campanelli.

Phelps and put the Tar Heels ahead to stay with just over three minutes remaining. After a missed Michigan shot, Lynch hit a turnaround jumper from the middle of the lane with 2:28 remaining to increase Carolina's lead to 70-67. On an inbounds play after UNC regained possession, Lynch lofted a perfect pass to Montross for a dunk. The Wolverines rallied to trim the deficit to 73-71 before Lynch and Phelps trapped Chris Webber on the sideline with just 11 seconds remaining and Michigan's consensus first-team All-American called a fateful timeout his team did not have. Donald Williams wrapped the game up with four consecutive free throws.

Outcome for Defending Champion: Duke's streak of five consecutive trips to the Final Four ended when the Blue Devils lost against California in the second round of the Midwest Regional (82-77) despite Grant Hill's eight steals. Duke guard Bobby Hurley was thwarted in his bid to become the first player to start four consecutive NCAA finals, but he is the only player to be cred-

ited with more than 125 assists in the tournament. He had 145 scoring feeds in 20 playoff games. Hurley also has more career three-pointers in the NCAA playoffs than anyone (42).

Star Gazing: Final Four Most Outstanding Player Donald Williams scored 25 points in each Final Four game for North Carolina to become the first guard to score at least 25 in both the national semifinals and final since Rick Mount for runner-up Purdue in 1969. The previous guard for a championship team to score at least 25 points in both the national semifinals and final was UCLA's Gail Goodrich in 1965.

Biggest Upsets: In terms of point spreads, Arizona's 64-61 first-round defeat in the West Regional against 20-point underdog Santa Clara was the biggest upset in NCAA playoff history. The Wildcats, ranked fifth by AP entering the tournament, lost against Santa Clara although they scored 25 consecutive points in a 10-minute span bridging the first and second halves. The setback gave Lute Olson five opening-round defeats as coach at Arizona and lowered his record to 2-8 in down-to-the-wire tourney games decided in overtime or in regulation by fewer than six points. . . . Another first-round shocker was Georgia Tech getting smothered by Southern (93-78), leaving Bobby Cremins of the Yellow Jackets as the only coach to ever lose as many as five playoff games against opponents with double-digit seeds.

One and Only: Williams is the only player to average fewer than four points per game as a freshman and then be named Final Four Most Outstanding Player the next season as a sopho-more. After averaging an unsightly 2.2 points per game for North Carolina in 1991-92, he finished with a 14.3-point average in 1992-93. . . . Dean Smith became the first coach in NCAA Tournament history to reach the 50-win plateau in playoff competition when he raised his record of playoff appearances to 23 and North Carolina won its opening game for the 13th consecutive year.

Quote of Note: Webber's family took his mental lapse in stride and showed time heals all wounds when his father, Mayce, acquired a vanity

1992–93 NCAA CHAMPION: N. CAROLINA

SEASON STATISTICS OF NORTH CAROLINA REGULARS

PLAYER	POS.	CL.	G.	FG%	FT%	PPG	RPG
Eric Montross	C	Jr.	38	.615	.684	15.8	7.6
George Lynch	F	Sr.	38	.501	.667	14.7	9.6
Donald Williams	G	So.	37	.458	.829	14.3	1.9
Brian Reese	F	Jr.	35	.507	.692	11.4	3.6
Derrick Phelps	G	Jr.	36	.457	.675	8.1	4.4
Pat Sullivan	F	Jr.	38	.518	.789	6.4	2.4
Kevin Salvadori	C-F	Jr.	38	.458	.704	4.5	3.6
Henrik Rodl	G	Sr.	38	.496	.658	4.3	1.5
Matt Wenstrom	C	Sr.	33	.557	.593	2.5	1.4
Scott Cherry	G	Sr.	33	.606	.714	2.1	0.7
Dante Calabria	G	Fr.	35	.462	.778	1.8	0.8
TEAM TOTALS			38	.506	.706	86.1	41.1

Three-point field goals leader: Williams (83 of 199, .417). Assists leaders: Phelps 196, Rodl 136, Reese 83. Blocked shots leaders: Montross 47, Salvadori 45. Steals leaders: Lynch 89, Phelps 82.

1993 FINAL FOUR CHAMPIONSHIP GAME

NEW ORLEANS, LA

N. CAROLINA (77)	MIN.	FG-A	FT-A	REB.	A.	PF.	PTS.
Reese	27	2-7	4-4	5	3	1	8
Lynch	28	6-12	0-0	10	1	3	12
Montross	31	5-11	6-9	5	0	2	16
Phelps	36	4-6	1-2	3	6	0	9
Williams	31	8-12	4-4	1	1	1	25
Sullivan	14	1-2	1-2	1	1	2	3
Salvadori	18	0-0	2-2	4	1	1	2
Rodl	11	1-4	0-0	0	0	0	2
Calabria	1	0-0	0-0	0	0	0	0
Wenstrom	2	0-1	0-0	0	0	0	0
Cherry	1	0-0	0-0	0	0	0	0
TOTALS	200	27-55	18-23	29	13	10	77

FG%: .491. FT%: .789. Three-point goals: 5 of 11 (Reese 0-1, Phelps 0-1, Williams 5-7, Rodl 0-2). Blocks: 4. Turnovers: 10 (Phelps 5). Steals: 7.

MICHIGAN (71)	MIN.	FG-A	FT-A	REB.	A.	PF.	PTS.
Webber	33	11-18	1-2	11	1	2	23
Jackson	20	2-3	2-2	1	1	5	6
Howard	34	3-8	1-1	7	3	3	7
Rose	40	5-12	0-0	1	4	3	12
King	34	6-13	2-2	6	4	2	15
Riley	14	1-3	0-0	3	1	1	2
Pelinka	17	2-4	0-0	2	1	1	6
Talley	14	0-0	0-0	0	1	1	0
Voskuil	4	0-1	0-0	0	1	0	0
Team				2			
TOTALS	200	30-62	6-7	33	17	18	71

FG%: .484. FT%: .857. Three-point goals: 5 of 15 (Webber 0-1, Rose 2-6, King 1-5, Pelinka 2-3). Blocks: 4. Turnovers: 14 (Rose 6). Steals: 4. Halftime: North Carolina 42-36.

NATIONAL SEMIFINALS

MICHIGAN (81): Webber 10-17 7-9 27, Jackson 4-7 3-5 11, Howard 6-12 5-7 17, Rose 6-16 6-7 18, King 1-3 0-0 2, Riley 2-4 0-0 4, Pelinka 0-1 2-2 2, Voskuil 0-0 0-0 0. Team 29-61 (.475) 23-30 (.767) 81.

KENTUCKY (78): Mashburn 10-18 5-9 26, Prickett 1-6 7-7 9, Dent 2-6 2-2 6, Ford 3-10 4-4 12, Brown 6-10 0-0 16, Rhodes 0-1 1-2 1, Riddick 2-4 0-1 4, Martinez 0-3 0-0 0, Brassow 0-0 0-0 0, Delk 1-3 2-2 4, Braddy 0-0 0-0 0. Team 25-61 (.410) 21-26 (.808) 78.

Three-point goals: Michigan 0-4, Kentucky 7-21 (.333).
Halftime: Michigan 40-35. Regulation: Tied 71-71.

KANSAS (68): Hancock 2-5 2-2 6, Scott 3-5 2-2 8, Pauley 2-5 1-1 5, Walters 7-15 0-0 19, Jordan 7-13 0-0 19, Rayford 0-0 0-0 0, Woodberry 2-5 0-0 4, Richey 1-4 0-0 2, Ostertag 0-2 2-2 2, Gurley 1-2 0-0 3, Pearson 0-1 0-0 0. Team 25-57 (.439) 7-7 (1.000) 68.

NORTH CAROLINA (78): Lynch 5-12 4-6 14, Reese 3-5 1-2 7, Montross 9-14 5-8 23, Phelps 1-3 1-2 3, Williams 7-11 6-6 25, Sullivan 0-2 0-0 0, Rodl 0-0 0-0 0, Cherry 0-0 0-0 0, Salvadori 3-5 0-0 6, Wenstrom 0-0 0-0 0, Calabria 0-0 0-0 0, Davis 0-0 0-0 0, Stephenson 0-0 0-0 0, Geth 0-0 0-0 0. Team 28-52 (.538) 17-24 (.708) 78.

Three-point goals: Kansas 11-20 (.550), North Carolina 5-7 (.714).
Halftime: North Carolina 40-36.

ALL-TOURNAMENT TEAM

George Lynch, F, Sr., North Carolina
Jamal Mashburn, F, Jr., Kentucky
Eric Montross, C, Jr., North Carolina
Chris Webber, F, Soph., Michigan
*Donald Williams, G, Soph., North Carolina (50 points, 10 three-pointers)

*Named Most Outstanding Player.

license plate that said "Timeout," a reference to his son's excruciating blunder. "It's no big deal," the younger Webber said. "I'm not happy it happened. But I know it's going to help me in some way. It made me a man. It made me grow up a lot faster than if it hadn't happened."

Numbers Game: Purdue forward Glenn Robinson had the highest-scoring game of the tourney when he tossed in 36 points in a first-round loss against Rhode Island. . . . Carolina's Smith and the other three coaches at the Final Four—Michigan's Steve Fisher, Kentucky's Rick Pitino and Kansas' Roy Williams—had all won more than 70 percent of their NCAA playoff games at that stage in their careers. Fisher, improving his tourney record to 17-3 (.850) by reaching the national final for the third time in five years, moved ahead of Hall of Famer John Wooden (47-10, .825) for the highest winning percentage in tournament history (minimum of 20 games). . . . Three No. 1 seeds reached the Final Four for the only time since seeding was introduced in 1979. . . . The Big East suffered a down year when consecutive tourney appearances for Georgetown (14) and Syracuse (10) came to an end. Syracuse was on NCAA probation. . . . California freshman guard Jason Kidd's inside baskets on deft moves in the closing seconds helped boost the Bears to victories over two schools making their 10th consecutive NCAA playoff appearance—Duke and LSU. . . . Florida State's Sam Cassell converted all seven of his three-point field-goal attempts in a 94-63 trouncing of Tulane in the second round of the Southeast Regional. . . . East Carolina became the eighth school to participate in the NCAA Tournament despite entering the playoffs with a losing record (13-16 after winning Colonial Athletic Association Tournament). The Pirates' first-round opponent was North Carolina, which handed them their 39th defeat in as many games against the four schools from their state that were charter members of the ACC. . . . The ACC and Big Eight tied for the most playoff representatives with six apiece. The ACC notched at least 12 tourney triumphs for the fifth consecutive year. . . . Manhattan, coached by Fran Fraschilla, and George Washington, coached by Mike Jarvis, made their first NCAA playoff appearance since 1958 and 1961, respectively. . . . Temple became the first at-large team in seven years to win fewer than 60 percent of its games but still reach a regional semifinal. The Owls advanced all the way to the West Regional final, where they blew an eight-point, second-half lead and lost against Michigan. It was Temple coach John Chaney's third regional final setback in six years. . . . Tennessee's Allan Houston (2,801 points) joined LSU's Pete Maravich (3,667 from 1968-70), Portland State's Freeman Williams (3,249 from 1975-78), Texas Southern's Harry Kelly (3,066 from 1980-83) and Houston's Otis Birdsong (2,832 from 1974-77) as players to score more than 2,800 points in their major-college careers but never participate in the NCAA Tournament. . . . Arkansas' Darrell Hawkins had eight steals in a opening-round victory over Holy Cross.

What Might Have Been: Webber absorbed a good deal of grief after his baffling call for a timeout prevented Michigan from having an opportunity to tie the score or take the lead against North Carolina. But why wasn't a Wolverine guard back to bring the ball up after Webber grabbed a rebound off a missed free throw? Webber became the fourth player to secure NCAA All-Tournament team status in back-to-back seasons without winning a national championship either year as Michigan became the third school to lose two consecutive tourney finals. . . . Indiana was a No. 1 seed entering the tournament, but many experts didn't pick the Hoosiers to reach the Final Four, let alone win the national crown, after star forward Alan Henderson was hampered by a knee injury. . . . Georgia Tech (19-11/without Kenny Anderson), Louisiana State (22-11/Shaquille O'Neal) and UCLA (22-11/Tracy Murray) might have fared better in the playoffs if standout players had exercised their remaining eligibility instead of defecting to the NBA. Ditto Memphis State (20-12 without center David Vaughn/knee injury), New Orleans (26-4 without guard Dedric Willoughby) and Tulane (22-9 without guard Kim Lewis/leg) because of medical redshirt seasons for key players. . . . Ohio State (15-13/without Jim Jackson) and Southern Cal (18-12/Harold Miner) probably would have participated in the NCAA Tournament instead of the NIT if All-Americans didn't leave school early for the NBA. Ditto Arizona State (18-10) if Mario Bennett didn't miss the season because of a knee injury.

Overcoming Adversity: North Carolina, which finished with a 34-4 record, lost back-to-back ACC road games at Wake Forest (88-62) and Duke (81-67) by a total of 40 points. The Tar Heels' other two defeats were against Michigan (79-78 at Rainbow Classic in Honolulu) and Georgia Tech (77-75 in ACC Tournament final when Phelps missed the game because of an injury).

Scoring Leader: Donald Williams, North Carolina (118 points, 19.7 ppg).

Highest Scoring Average: Calbert Cheaney, Indiana (106 points, 26.5 ppg).

Rebounding Leader: Chris Webber, Michigan (68 rebounds, 11.3 rpg).

1993 CHAMPIONSHIP BRACKET

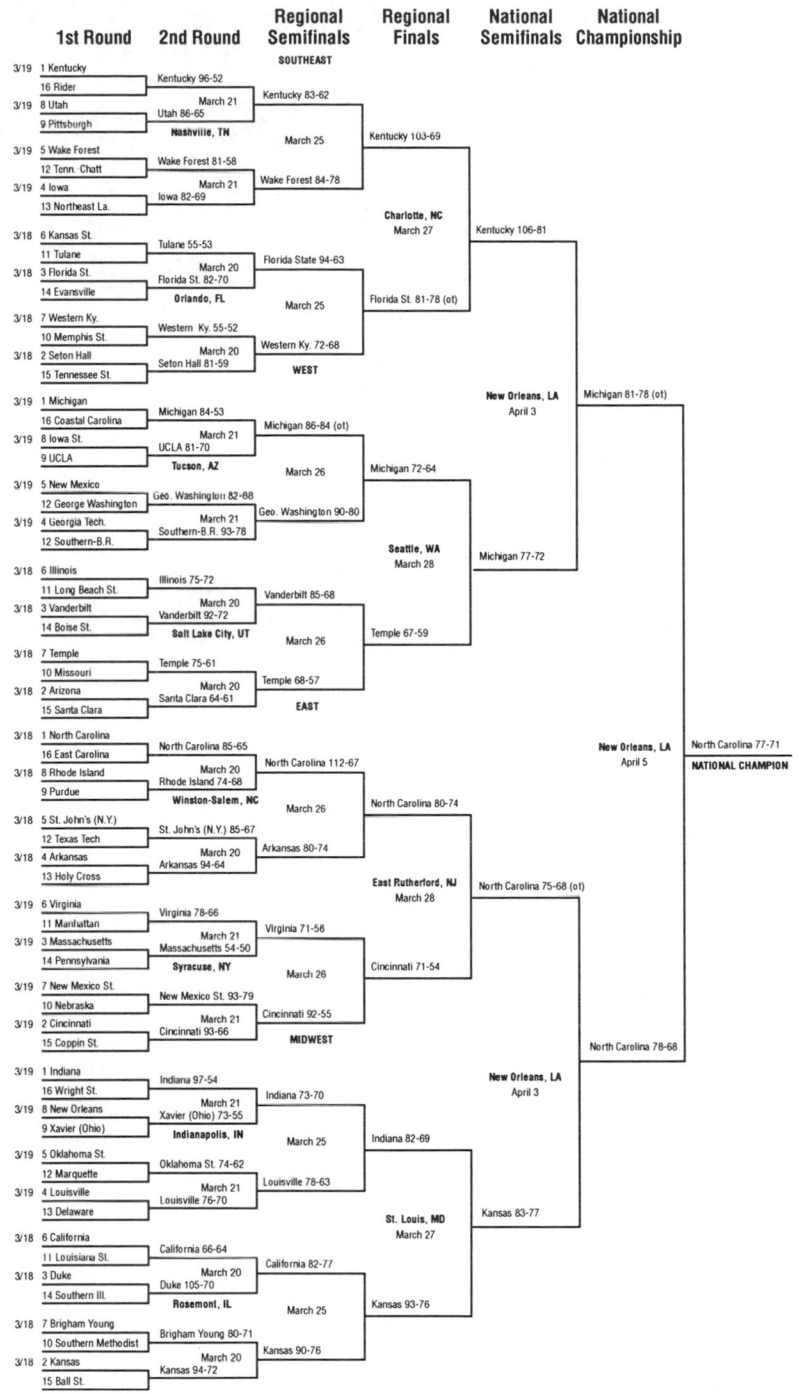

	1st Round	2nd Round	Regional Semifinals	Regional Finals	National Semifinals	National Championship

SOUTHEAST

3/19 1 Kentucky
16 Rider
Kentucky 96-52
3/19 8 Utah
9 Pittsburgh
Utah 86-65
March 21
Nashville, TN
Kentucky 83-62
March 25
3/19 5 Wake Forest
12 Tenn. Chatt
Wake Forest 81-58
3/19 4 Iowa
13 Northeast La.
Iowa 82-69
March 21
Wake Forest 84-78
Kentucky 103-69
Charlotte, NC
March 27

3/18 6 Kansas St.
11 Tulane
Tulane 55-53
3/18 3 Florida St.
14 Evansville
Florida St. 82-70
March 20
Orlando, FL
Florida State 94-63
March 25
3/18 7 Western Ky.
10 Memphis St.
Western Ky. 55-52
3/18 2 Seton Hall
15 Tennessee St.
Seton Hall 81-59
March 20
Western Ky. 72-68
Florida St. 81-78 (ot)
Kentucky 106-81

WEST

3/19 1 Michigan
16 Coastal Carolina
Michigan 84-53
3/19 8 Iowa St.
9 UCLA
UCLA 81-70
March 21
Tucson, AZ
Michigan 86-84 (ot)
March 26
3/19 5 New Mexico
12 George Washington
Geo. Washington 82-68
3/19 4 Georgia Tech.
12 Southern-B.R.
Southern-B.R. 93-78
March 21
Geo. Washington 90-80
Michigan 72-64
Seattle, WA
March 28

3/18 6 Illinois
11 Long Beach St.
Illinois 75-72
3/18 3 Vanderbilt
14 Boise St.
Vanderbilt 92-72
March 20
Salt Lake City, UT
Vanderbilt 85-68
March 26
3/18 7 Temple
10 Missouri
Temple 75-61
3/18 2 Arizona
15 Santa Clara
Santa Clara 64-61
March 20
Temple 68-57
Temple 67-59
Michigan 77-72

New Orleans, LA
April 3

Michigan 81-78 (ot)

EAST

3/18 1 North Carolina
16 East Carolina
North Carolina 85-65
3/18 8 Rhode Island
9 Purdue
Rhode Island 74-68
March 20
Winston-Salem, NC
North Carolina 112-67
March 26
3/18 5 St. John's (N.Y.)
12 Texas Tech
St. John's (N.Y.) 85-67
3/18 4 Arkansas
13 Holy Cross
Arkansas 94-64
March 20
Arkansas 80-74
North Carolina 80-74
East Rutherford, NJ
March 28

3/19 6 Virginia
11 Manhattan
Virginia 78-66
3/19 3 Massachusetts
14 Pennsylvania
Massachusetts 54-50
March 21
Syracuse, NY
Virginia 71-56
March 26
3/19 7 New Mexico St.
10 Nebraska
New Mexico St. 93-79
3/19 2 Cincinnati
15 Coppin St.
Cincinnati 93-66
March 21
Cincinnati 92-55
Cincinnati 71-54
North Carolina 75-68 (ot)

New Orleans, LA
April 3

North Carolina 78-68

MIDWEST

3/19 1 Indiana
16 Wright St.
Indiana 97-54
3/19 8 New Orleans
9 Xavier (Ohio)
Xavier (Ohio) 73-55
March 21
Indianapolis, IN
Indiana 73-70
March 25
3/19 5 Oklahoma St.
12 Marquette
Oklahoma St. 74-62
3/19 4 Louisville
13 Delaware
Louisville 76-70
March 21
Louisville 78-63
Indiana 82-69
St. Louis, MO
March 27

3/18 6 California
11 Louisiana St.
California 66-64
3/18 3 Duke
14 Southern Ill.
Duke 105-70
March 20
Rosemont, IL
California 82-77
March 25
3/18 7 Brigham Young
10 Southern Methodist
Brigham Young 80-71
3/18 2 Kansas
15 Ball St.
Kansas 94-72
March 20
Kansas 90-76
Kansas 93-76
Kansas 83-77

New Orleans, LA
April 5
North Carolina 77-71
NATIONAL CHAMPION

1993-94

AT A GLANCE

NCAA Champion: Arkansas (31-3; coached by Nolan Richardson; won SEC Western Division title by two games over Alabama with a 14-2 record).

NIT Champion: Villanova (20-12; coached by Steve Lappas; finished in a three-way tie for fourth place in Big East with a 10-8 record).

New Rules: Shot clock reduced to 35 seconds from 45, five-second defensive pressure call is eliminated, game clock stopped in the last minute after every basket and trash-talking prohibited.

NCAA Consensus First-Team All-Americans: Grant Hill, F-G, Sr., Duke; Jason Kidd, G, Soph., California; Donyell Marshall, F, Jr., Connecticut; Glenn Robinson, F, Jr., Purdue; Clifford Rozier, C-F, Jr., Louisville.

National Player of the Year: Robinson (30.3 ppg, 10.1 rpg).

National Coaches of the Year: Purdue's Gene Keady (29-5/shared NABC); Arkansas' Nolan Richardson (31-3/Naismith, shared NABC); Saint Louis' Charlie Spoonhour (23-6/USBWA), and Missouri's Norm Stewart (28-4/AP, UPI).

Purdue's Glenn Robinson became the first Big Ten player since 1966 to lead the country in scoring.

A glaring lack of fundamentals was apparent as shooting percentages continued to decrease. Free-throw shooting across the country dipped to 67.1 percent, the lowest mark since 1959. Teams shot an all-time low 34.5 percent from three-point range.

Purdue junior Glenn Robinson became the first Big Ten player to lead the country in scoring (30.3 points per game) since the Boilermakers' Dave Schellhase in 1966. Robinson was at his best against the Big Ten's elite, scoring 73 in two games against Michigan and 72 in two outings against Indiana. Purdue's 29-5 record is that much more impressive when you note that the teams with the other five national scoring leaders from 1991-96 combined for an average mark of 9-17. Robinson's early departure to the NBA left the Patriot League as the only Division I conference in history ever to return two of the top three leading scorers in the country—Holy Cross' Rob Feaster (28 ppg) and Colgate's Tucker Neale (26.6 ppg).

Donyell Marshall, the first Connecticut player ever to become an NCAA consensus first- or second-team All-American, hit 39 of 40 free throws in averaging 37.7 points per game in three contests against St. John's as the Redmen absorbed their first losing record since 1962-63. . . . Houston's streak of 34 consecutive non-losing seasons came to an halt when the Cougars compiled an 8-19 record. . . . Kentucky tied an NCAA record by overcoming a 31-point, second-half deficit in a 99-95 victory at LSU. The deflating defeat contributed to ending LSU's streak of 17 consecutive non-losing records. . . . Louisville's Clifford Rozier set an NCAA record by hitting all 15 of his field-goal attempts in a game against Eastern Kentucky (see accompanying box). Rozier, a transfer from North Carolina, became the first NCAA consensus first-team All-American since the late 1940s to previously play at least one season for

Connecticut forward Donyell Marshall concentrates at the free throw line.

another four-year college. . . . Auburn's Wesley Person finished his career with 2,066 points to join his brother, Chuck (2,311), as the only sibling combination to score more than 2,000 for the same school.

Cleveland State (39) and Kent (36) established an NCAA standard for most points in overtime periods, both teams, when they combined for 75 in the Vikings' 104-101, four-overtime triumph. . . . Southern (La.), coached by Ben Jobe, posted the widest margin of victory in major-college history (97 points) with a 154-57 victory over Patton College. . . . Dartmouth lost by 21 points (94-73) to Boston College, but the Big Green had nine different players hit a three-pointer, an NCAA record (see accompanying box). . . . Providence's Michael Smith set a Big East Conference single-game record by grabbing 26 rebounds against Syracuse. . . . Vermont sophomore guard

Eddie Benton set a school and North Atlantic Conference record with 54 points against Drexel.

Marist's Danny Basile converted all 60 of his free-throw attempts in Northeast Conference regular-season play. Teammate Izett Buchanan set a school record and Northeast Conference standard with 51 points at Long Island University. . . . Also establishing school Division I single-game scoring records were Siena's Doremus Bennerman (51 points vs. Kansas State in NIT third-place game), Idaho's Orlando Lightfoot (50 at Gonzaga), Winthrop's Melvin Branham (45 at Charleston Southern), Arkansas State's Jeff Clifton (tied with 43 vs. Arkansas-Little Rock), Nebraska's Eric Piatkowski (42 vs. Oklahoma in Big Eight Tournament quarterfinals), Liberty's Matt Hildebrand (41 vs. Charleston Southern) and Northern Arizona's Jason Word (40 vs. Southern Utah State in double overtime). Excluding Lightfoot, the remainder of Idaho's team scored just 19 points in a 76-69 setback at Gonzaga. . . . Western Carolina's Frankie King (26.9 ppg), Vermont's Benton (26.4), Missouri-Kansas City's Tony Dumas (26), Siena's Bennerman (26), Marist's Buchanan (25.4), Idaho's Lightfoot (25.4), Arizona's Khalid Reeves (24.2), Northern Iowa's Randy Blocker (23) and Robert Morris' Myron Walker (20.1) set school Division I records for highest scoring average in a single season.

Cal's Murray and teammate Jason Kidd became the first Bears players since 1960 to earn spots on an NCAA consensus first- or second-team All-American squad. It was also the first Top 20 appearance in a final wire-service poll for Cal since 1960. . . . Missouri, coached by Norm Stewart, went unbeaten in the Big Eight after finishing in seventh place the previous year. . . . Guard Donnie Boyce scored 20 consecutive second-half points for Colorado and finished with 46 but it wasn't enough to prevent an 83-68 defeat at Oklahoma State.

Askia Jones exploded for a national-high and Big Eight Conference-record 62 points in boosting Kansas State to a 115-77 rout of visiting Fresno State in the NIT quarterfinals. Jones had 14 three-

1993–94 INDIVIDUAL LEADERS

SCORING

PLAYER	PTS.	AVG.
Robinson, Purdue	1030	30.3
Feaster, Holy Cross	785	28.0
Scales, Southern	733	27.1
King, W. Carolina	752	26.9
Neale, Colgate	771	26.6
Benton, Vermont	687	26.4
Bennerman, Siena	858	26.0
Dumas, Mo.-Kansas City	753	26.0
Jones, Air Force	663	25.5
Buchanan, Marist	685	25.4
Trent, Ohio U.	837	25.4
Lightfoot, Idaho	710	25.4

REBOUNDING

PLAYER	REB.	AVG.
Lambert, Baylor	355	14.8
Scales, Southern	384	14.2
Kubel, N'western (La.)	341	13.1
Warren, Va. C'wealth	336	12.4
Rose, Drexel	371	12.4
Vaughn, Memphis	335	12.0
Jackson, Nicholls St.	311	12.0
Simon, New Orleans	355	11.8
Stewart, UNLV	256	11.6
Rogers, Tennessee St.	358	11.5
Smith, Providence	344	11.5

ASSISTS

PLAYER	AST.	AVG.
Kidd, California	272	9.1
Edwards, Texas A&M	265	8.8
Miller, Marquette	274	8.3
O'Bryant, Nevada	232	8.3
Abdullah, Providence	241	8.0
Nathan, Northeast La.	179	7.8
Smart, San Francisco	204	7.6
Pogue, Campbell	207	7.4

Thomas, UNLV	205	7.3
Haggerty, Baylor	161	7.3

BLOCKED SHOTS

PLAYER	BLK.	AVG.
Livingston, Howard	115	4.4
McIlvaine, Marquette	142	4.3
Ratliff, Wyoming	114	4.1
Vaughn, Memphis	107	3.8
Duncan, Wake Forest	124	3.8
Camby, Massachusetts	105	3.6
Cato, South Alabama	85	3.5
Marshall, Connecticut	111	3.3
McDonald, New Orleans	96	3.2
Fleury, UMBC	80	3.2

STEALS

PLAYER	STL.	AVG.
Griggs, S'western La.	120	4.0
Walker, San Francisco	109	3.9
Cradle, Long Island	79	3.8
Kidd, California	94	3.1
Tyler, Texas	87	3.1
Ceasar, LSU	80	3.0
Black, Texas-Pan Am	80	3.0
Thompson, Oklahoma St.	99	2.9
Robertson, Dayton	78	2.9
Golden, Tennessee	78	2.9
Walton, Alcorn St.	63	2.9

FIELD GOAL PERCENTAGE

PLAYER	FGM	FGA	PCT.
Atkinson, Long Beach St.	141	203	.695
Wade, SW Texas St.	232	356	.652
Miller, Mich. St.	162	249	.651
Thomas, Illinois	207	327	.633
Swinson, Auburn	234	371	.631
Ritter, James Madison	230	366	.628
Williamson, Arkansas	237	436	.626
Ardayfio, Army	180	289	.623
Lunsford, Alabama St.	163	263	.620
Rozier, Louisville	247	400	.618

FREE THROW PERCENTAGE

PLAYER	FGM	FGA	PCT.
Basile, Marist	84	89	.944
Evans, Troy St.	72	77	.935
Schmidt, Valparaiso	75	81	.926
Hildebrand, Liberty	149	161	.925
Culuko, James Madison	117	127	.921
Yoder, Colorado St.	107	117	.915
Ford, Kentucky	103	113	.912
Hoover, Notre Dame	76	84	.905
Cline, Morehead St.	73	81	.901
Tucker, N. Illinois	71	79	.899

THREE-POINT FIELD GOAL PERCENTAGE

PLAYER	FGM	FGA	PCT.
Kell, Evansville	62	123	.504
Santiago, Fresno St.	64	128	.500
Born, Tenn.-Chat.	67	135	.496
Young, Canisius	53	109	.486
Eisley, Boston College	91	188	.484

THREE-POINT FIELD GOALS PER GAME

PLAYER	FGM	AVG.
Brown, UC Irvine	122	4.7
Hicks, Coastal Carolina	115	4.4
Durden, Cincinnati	102	4.1
Haslett, Southern Miss.	112	3.7
Townes, La Salle	100	3.7
Ross, George Mason	99	3.7

pointers, hitting 11 of 14 shots from beyond the arc after intermission to set an NCAA mark for most treys in a half. . . . Texas, coached by Tom Penders, captured the SWC regular-season championship just one year after finishing in seventh place. . . . Texas-Pan American's Greg Guy (29.3 ppg in '93 to 19.2) became the only defending national scoring champion other than Temple's Bill Mlkvy (29.2 in '51 to 17.4 in '52) to have a scoring average decrease of more than 10 points per game.

Florida (29-8/coached by Lon Kruger), Wisconsin-Green Bay (27-7/Dick Bennett), Southwest Texas State (25-7/Jim Wooldridge), Ohio University (25-8/Larry Hunter), Gonzaga (22-8/Dan Fitzgerald), Central Florida (21-9/Kirk Speraw), Rider (21-9/Kevin Bannon), Towson State (21-9/Terry Truax) and Maine (20-9/Rudy Keeling) had their winningest seasons in school Division I history. Purdue (29-5/Gene Keady), Texas (26-8/Tom Penders), Siena (25-8/Mike Deane) and Canisius (22-7/John Beilein) tied their school single-season Division I marks for most victories. . . . Canisius, after finishing in sixth place the previous year, captured the Metro Atlantic Athletic Conference regular-season crown just two seasons after the school suffered an all-time high in losses (8-22 mark in 1991-92). It is believed that Beilein became the only active coach in the country to register 20-win seasons at the junior college, NAIA, NCAA Division II and NCAA Division I levels.

Saint Louis, coached by Charlie Spoonhour, compiled a 23-6 record to finish in a final wire-service poll for the first time since 1961. Fellow

1993-94 TEAM LEADERS

SCORING OFFENSE

SCHOOL	PTS.	AVG.
Southern (La.)	2727	101.0
Troy St.	2634	97.6
Arkansas	3176	93.4
Texas	3119	91.7
Murray St.	2611	90.0

SCORING DEFENSE

SCHOOL	PTS.	AVG.
Princeton	1361	52.3
Temple	1697	54.7
Wisconsin-Green Bay	1872	55.1
Alabama-Birmingham	1806	60.2
Marquette	2040	61.8

SCORING MARGIN

SCHOOL	OFF.	DEF.	MAR.
Arkansas	93.4	75.6	17.9
Connecticut	84.9	68.6	16.3
Arizona	89.3	74.4	14.9
Southern (La.)	101.0	87.7	13.3
North Carolina	85.6	72.4	13.2

WON-LOST PERCENTAGE

TEAM	W-L	PCT.
Arkansas	31-3	.912
Pennsylvania	25-3	.893
Missouri	28-4	.875
Charleston (S.C.)	24-4	.857
Connecticut	29-5	.853
Purdue	29-5	.853

FIELD GOAL PERCENTAGE

SCHOOL	FGM	FGA	PCT.
Auburn	854	1689	.506
Michigan St.	944	1875	.503
Radford	793	1580	.502
James Madison	890	1783	.499
North Carolina	1091	2188	.499

DEFENSIVE FIELD GOAL PERCENTAGE

SCHOOL	FGM	FGA	PCT.
Marquette	750	2097	.358
Temple	621	1686	.368
Wisconsin-Green Bay	664	1777	.374
Kansas	823	2147	.383
Alabama-Birmingham	661	1718	.385

FREE THROW PERCENTAGE

SCHOOL	FTM	FTA	PCT.
Colgate	511	665	.768
Wisconsin-Green Bay	462	607	.761
Iowa St.	521	687	.758
Davidson	529	704	.751
Vanderbilt	557	742	.751

REBOUND MARGIN

SCHOOL	OWN	OPP.	MAR.
Utah St.	38.4	29.8	8.6
North Carolina	43.7	35.3	8.5
Idaho	41.5	33.1	8.4
UCLA	43.9	36.2	7.7
Baylor	50.3	42.7	7.6

THREE-POINT FIELD GOAL PERCENTAGE

SCHOOL	FGM	FGA	PCT.
Indiana	182	401	.454
Robert Morris	139	323	.430
Evansville	244	570	.428
Oklahoma St.	258	619	.417
Montana	150	369	.407

THREE-POINT FIELD GOALS PER GAME

SCHOOL	FGM	AVG.
Troy St.	262	9.7
New Mexico	300	9.7
Vermont	240	8.9
Arkansas	301	8.9
Kentucky	301	8.9

SCORING DEFENSE

SCHOOL	PTS.	AVG.
Oklahoma A&M	1539	53.1
Duquesne	1551	53.5
Wyoming	1522	54.4
Oregon State	1585	54.7
Oklahoma City	1370	54.8

FIELD GOAL PERCENTAGE

SCHOOL	FGM	FGA	PCT.
George Washington	744	1632	.456
Holy Cross	871	2018	.432
Niagara	778	1817	.428
Maryland	669	1564	.428
Furman	990	2370	.418

Great Midwest member Marquette compiled a 24-9 mark under coach Kevin O'Neill to finish in a final national poll for the first time since 1979. . . . Dayton's lone Great Midwest victory came against Saint Louis (82-77 in overtime) when freshman guard Shawn Haughn hit all eight of his shots from beyond the three-point arc. Haughn contributed five of his treys in a four-minute spurt and seven of his three-pointers in an 8:40 stretch bridging the first and second halves to help the Flyers erase a 16-point deficit in that span (see accompanying play-by-play box). . . . Valparaiso, ending its streak of 16 consecutive losing seasons, compiled a 20-8 record. . . . Northwestern coach Ricky Byrdsong was given a leave of absence in the aftermath of his erratic behavior in a loss at Minnesota. Several times during the game, he went into the stands to shake hands with fans.

La Salle went 11-16 for its first losing record in 18 years. . . . New Orleans, coached by Tim Floyd, extended its Sun Belt Conference-record winning streak to 21 consecutive league games before losing. . . . Pepperdine's WCC record of 38 consecutive victories against conference opponents (six in postseason tourney play) ended when the Waves were edged by San Francisco, 75-72. . . . San Jose State and Utah State both lost their first 25 meetings with UNLV until defeating the Rebels.

Appalachian State's Ricky Need finished his four-year career with an NCAA record for field-goal shooting (69 percent, 412 of 597). . . . Davidson lost 34 consecutive games to North Carolina State until edging the Wolfpack, 64-63. . . . Clemson overcame a halftime deficit against North Carolina to defeat the Tar Heels after trailing at intermission against them for the first time since 1954. . . . Former national coaches of the year Butch van Breda Kolff and Johnny Orr retired from Hofstra and Iowa State, respectively.

ROZIER HITS ALL 15 SHOTS

December 11, 1993
Eastern Kentucky at Louisville

Excluding Clifford Rozier, Louisville hit a modest 44.2 percent from the floor but Rozier connected on all 15 of his field-goal attempts to carry the Cardinals to a 90-66 triumph over Eastern Kentucky. Rozier got his 10th basket early in the second half before going over 12 minutes without taking a shot from the floor.

HOME TEAM: LOUISVILLE	TIME	SCORE	MAR
FIRST HALF (9)			
made basket by Rozier (follow)	19:45	2-0	+2
made basket by Rozier (layup)	14:03	11-10	+1
made basket by Rozier (hook flip)	13:47	13-10	+3
made basket by Rozier (layup)	12:51	17-15	+2
made basket by Rozier (alley oop)	10:17	19-17	+2
made basket by Rozier (fast break)	8:36	24-17	+7
made basket by Rozier (layup)	6:42	27-21	+6
made basket by Rozier (alley oop)	4:35	34-27	+7
made basket by Rozier (alley oop)	2:15	42-29	+13
SECOND HALF (6)			
made basket by Rozier (layup)	19:40	47-38	+9
made basket by Rozier (layup)	7:14	70-55	+15
made basket by Rozier (layup)	6:18	72-57	+15
made basket by Rozier (alley oop)	4:13	78-59	+19
made basket by Rozier (alley oop)	1:14	88-63	+25

HAUGHN'S LONG-RANGE HEROICS

February 13, 1994
Saint Louis at Dayton

Here is a play-by-play rundown of the flawless three-point shooting (8 for 8) by freshman guard Shawn Haughn for Dayton in an 82-77 come-from-behind overtime victory against Saint Louis.

HOME TEAM: DAYTON	TIME	SCORE	MAR
FIRST HALF (3)			
made 3-pointer by Haughn	2:29	20-33	-13
made 3-pointer by Haughn	2:02	23-35	-15
made 3-pointer by Haughn	:37	28-40	-12
SECOND HALF (5)			
made 3-pointer by Haughn	19:33	31-40	-9
made 3-pointer by Haughn	15:53	47-52	-5
made 3-pointer by Haughn	15:02	50-52	-2
made 3-pointer by Haughn	13:49	53-52	+1
made 3-pointer by Haughn	6:59	58-63	+5

1994 NCAA Tournament

Summary: Arkansas, boasting a roster with 11 different players who had a season high in scoring of more than 10 points, ended a SEC dry spell in the NCAA playoffs. Despite having an average of three first-round NBA draft choices annually in 15 years since 1979, no current member of the 12-team SEC reached the NCAA Tournament championship game in that span although every school participated in the playoffs at least

TREYS FROM NINE DARTMOUTH PLAYERS ARE IN VAIN

November 30, 1993
Dartmouth at Boston College

Dartmouth set an NCAA record by having nine different players contribute a three-pointer, but the Big Green still lost by 21 points to Boston College, 94-73. Oddly, Dartmouth finished the season with an average of a modest four three-pointers per game and hit only one-third of its shots from beyond the three-point arc.

DARTMOUTH (73): Capps 1-2 2-2 5, Kowalewski 5-7 1-2 14, Gilpin 1-3 0-0 2, Jones 1-3 0-0 3, Frame 2-6 0-0 5, Halligan 3-5 2-2 9, Lonergan 4-8 4-4 12, Butler 1-4 0-0 3, Richards 0-0 1-2 1, Mitchell 2-3 0-0 5, Fisher 2-3 0-0 4, Stanton 2-3 0-0 5, Castillo 1-1 0-0 2, Bush 0-0 0-0 0, Carlson 1-1 0-0 3. Team 26-49 (.531) 10-12 (.833) 73.

Three-point shooting: 11 of 19 (Capps 1-1, Kowalewski 3-4, Jones 1-2, Frame 1-1, Halligan 1-3, Lonergan 0-1, Butler 1-2, Mitchell 1-2, Fisher 0-1, Stanton 1-1, Carlson 1-1).

BOSTON COLLEGE (94): Curley 8-13 8-13 24, Jourdon 1-1 5-8 8, Grant 4-6 0-0 8, Eisley 2-7 3-4 7, Huckaby 4-10 3-5 11, Abrams 3-4 4-5 10, Abram 2-5 0-1 5, Molinsky 3-4 0-0 7, Hrobowski 2-3 3-3 7, Christianson 0-3 2-3 2, Ryan 1-3 3-4 5. Team 30-59 (.508) 31-46 (.674) 94.

Three-point shooting: 3 of 13 (Jourdon 1-1, Eisley 0-2, Huckaby 0-3, Abram 1-4, Molinsky 1-1, Christianson 0-2).

Halftime: Boston College 38-34.

1993-94 FINAL NATIONAL POLLS

AP	UPI	USA/CNN	SCHOOL (RECORD)	HEAD COACH
1	2	9	North Carolina (28-7)	Dean Smith
2	1	1	Arkansas (31-3)	Nolan Richardson
3	3	5	Purdue (29-5)	Gene Keady
4	4	7	Connecticut (29-5)	Jim Calhoun
5	5	6	Missouri (28-4)	Norm Stewart
6	6	2	Duke (28-6)	Mike Krzyzewski
7	8	13	Kentucky (27-7)	Rick Pitino
8	7	15	Massachusetts (28-7)	John Calipari
9	9	3	Arizona (29-6)	Lute Olson
10	10	10	Louisville (28-6)	Denny Crum
11	11	8	Michigan (24-8)	Steve Fisher
12	12	18	Temple (23-8)	John Chaney
13	13	12	Kansas (27-8)	Roy Williams
14	15	4	Florida (29-8)	Lon Kruger
15	14	14	Syracuse (23-7)	Jim Boeheim
16	16	–	California (22-8)	Todd Bozeman
17	17	22	UCLA (21-7)	Jim Harrick
18	18	16	Indiana (21-9)	Bob Knight
19	19	21	Oklahoma State (24-10)	Eddie Sutton
20	21	24	Texas (26-8)	Tom Penders
21	29	17	Marquette (24-9)	Kevin O'Neill
22	24	–	Nebraska (20-10)	Danny Nee
23	23	23	Minnesota (21-12)	Clem Haskins
24	22	–	Saint Louis (23-6)	Charlie Spoonhour
25	–	–	Cincinnati (22-10)	Bob Huggins
–	–	11	Boston College (23-11)	Jim O'Brien
–	–	19	Tulsa (23-8)	Tubby Smith
–	–	20	Maryland (18-12)	Gary Williams
–	25	–	UAB (22-8)	Gene Bartow
–	–	25	Pennsylvania (25-3)	Fran Dunphy

once. Arkansas' title vindicated coach Nolan Richardson, who probably would have been dismissed in 1987 after his second season with the Hogs if they didn't rally from a 21-point second-half deficit in the NIT to edge Arkansas State, 67-

64, in overtime. But that wasn't the most strain he faced that year; his 16-year-old daughter, Yvonne, died of leukemia. Richardson was also a leading figure in a national controversy concerning alleged racial injustices. Pressure was also intense on Scotty Thurman with the shot clock winding down and the score tied with 40 seconds remaining when he lofted a three-point attempt over Duke's Antonio Lang that hit nothing but net. Thurman attributed his ability to get off such a high arc shot to an age-old drill shooting over a defender with a broomstick his coach at Ruston (La.) High School employed during practices. "He made a great play," Duke guard Chris Collins said of Thurman after the Razorbacks' 76-72 victory. "The national championship, less than a minute left, tie game—he made a great shot."

Outcome for Defending Champion: North Carolina's streak of 13 consecutive trips to a regional semifinal ended when the Tar Heels lost to Boston College in the second round. The Tar Heels (28-7) finished in second place in the ACC after incurring at least five league losses for the fourth time in six years. Their only non-conference setback was to Massachusetts in the Preseason NIT.

Star Gazing: Final Four Most Outstanding Player Corliss Williamson of Arkansas briefly surpassed Bill Walton's playoff field-goal shooting record (68.6 percent) before missing his first five shots in the final against Duke's Cherokee Parks and finishing the game 10 of 24 from the floor. Williamson's Final Four heroics overshadowed a brilliant performance against him by Michigan's Juwan Howard in a regional final. Howard outscored Williamson (30-12) and outrebounded him (13-6), but the Wolverines concentrated so much on "Big Nasty" that Arkansas hit 10 three-pointers.

One and Only: Richardson became the only coach to win national championships in junior college (1980 with Western Texas), the NIT (1981 with Tulsa) and the NCAA. . . . Duke guard Chris Collins became the first championship game player to be the son of a former NCAA consensus All-American. His father, NBA analyst Doug Collins, was an All-American for Illinois State the year after playing for the 1972 U.S. Olympic team.

Numbers Game: Skip Prosser of Loyola (Md.) became the only active coach to engineer a turnaround that included an NCAA playoff appear-

UK ERASES HUGE SECOND-HALF DEFICIT ON THE ROAD

KENTUCKY AT LOUISIANA STATE
FEBRUARY 14, 1994

In one of the most amazing comebacks of all time, Kentucky trailed by 31 points (68-37) with 15 1/2 minutes remaining in the second half at LSU before rallying to frustrate the Tigers, 99-95.

KENTUCKY (99)	FG-A	FT-A	REB.	PTS.
Tony Delk	3-8	1-2	7	9
Chris Harrison	3-4	0-1	2	8
Travis Ford	3-8	2-2	2	10
Andre Riddick	4-6	1-2	5	9
Rodrick Rhodes	3-9	4-6	3	11
Jeff Brassow	5-7	0-2	1	14
Jeff Sheppard	0-1	0-0	1	0
Anthony Epps	0-0	0-0	0	0
Jared Prickett	1-4	0-2	0	2
Walter McCarty	9-14	1-2	8	23
Gimel Martinez	6-10	1-2	3	13
Totals	**37-71**	**10-21**	**33**	**99**

FG%: .521. **FT%:** .476. **Three-point shooting:** 15 of 37 (Delk 2-7, Harrison 2-3, Ford 2-5, Rhodes 1-6, Brassow 4-6, McCarty 4-7, Martinez 0-3). **Assists:** 25 (Ford 12). **Steals:** 7. **Blocked Shots:** 4. **Turnovers:** 18 (Delk 5).

LSU (95)	FG-A	FT-A	REB.	PTS.
Jamie Brandon	3-10	6-8	8	13
Andre Owens	1-2	2-2	1	4
Sean Gipson	0-2	0-0	4	0
Ronnie Henderson	12-19	4-4	2	36
Lenear Burns	1-4	0-1	7	2
Clarence Ceasar	10-18	8-11	10	32
Brandon Titus	1-1	3-9	2	5
Glover Jackson	0-0	0-0	0	0
Roman Rubchenko	1-4	1-2	4	3
Totals	**29-60**	**24-37**	**40**	**95**

FG%: .483. **FT%:** .649. **Three-point shooting:** 13 of 24 (Brandon 1-3, Owens 0-1, Henderson 8-13, Ceasar 4-7). **Assists:** 19 (Owens 7). **Steals:** 8. **Blocked Shots:** 3. **Turnovers:** 20.

Halftime: LSU 48-32.

1993 NCAA CHAMPION: ARKANSAS

SEASON STATISTICS OF ARKANSAS REGULARS

PLAYER	POS.	CL.	G.	FG%	FT%	PPG	RPG
Corliss Williamson	F	So.	34	.626	.700	20.4	7.7
Scotty Thurman	G-F	So.	34	.469	.732	15.9	4.5
Al Dillard	G	Jr.	34	.404	.786	8.9	1.1
Corey Beck	G	Jr.	34	.506	.667	8.8	3.9
Clint McDaniel	G	Jr.	31	.407	.754	8.1	2.8
Dwight Stewart	C	Jr.	34	.453	.647	8.0	5.0
Darnell Robinson	C	Fr.	27	.457	.577	7.6	4.7
Roger Crawford	G	Sr.	30	.556	.679	7.4	1.9
Davor Rimac	G	Jr.	34	.455	.786	4.8	1.9
Lee Wilson	C	Fr.	30	.493	.580	3.4	3.1
Ken Biley	F	Sr.	18	.655	.667	2.8	2.1
Elmer Martin	F	Jr.	27	.308	.692	1.3	1.2
Ray Biggers	F	Jr.	18	.172	.438	1.1	2.2
TEAM TOTALS			34	.488	.680	93.4	41.6

Three-point field goals leaders: Thurman (85 of 198, .429), Dillard (75 of 183, .410), McDaniel (38 of 108, .352), Steward (37 of 95, .389), Rimac (32 of 79, .405). **Assists leaders:** Beck 169, Thurman 103. **Blocked shots leader:** Williamson 39. **Steals leaders:** Beck 68, McDaniel 53, Thurman 47.

1994 FINAL FOUR CHAMPIONSHIP GAME

CHARLOTTE, NC

DUKE (72)	MIN.	FG-A	FT-A	REB.	A.	PF.	PTS.
Lang	34	6-9	3-3	5	3	5	15
Hill	38	4-11	3-5	14	6	3	12
Parks	30	7-10	0-1	7	0	3	14
Capel	35	6-16	0-0	5	4	3	14
Collins	34	4-11	0-0	0	1	1	12
Clark	15	1-6	1-2	1	3	2	3
Meek	14	1-2	0-0	7	0	1	2
Team				5			
TOTALS	200	29-65	7-11	44	17	18	72

FG%: .446. **FT%:** .636. **Three-point goals:** 7 of 20 (Hill 1-4, Capel 2-6, Collins 4-8, Clark 0-2). **Blocks:** 7 (Hill 3). **Turnovers:** 23 (Hill 9, Capel 6, Lang 5). **Steals:** 5 (Hill 3).

ARKANSAS (76)	MIN.	FG-A	FT-A	REB.	A.	PF.	PTS.
Biley	3	0-0	0-0	0	0	1	0
Williamson	35	10-24	3-5	8	3	3	23
Stewart	29	3-11	0-0	9	4	3	6
Beck	35	5-11	5-8	10	4	3	15

Thurman	36	6-13	0-0	5	1	2	15
McDaniel	32	2-5	2-4	2	3	2	7
Robinson	12	1-5	0-0	2	0	1	2
Dillard	8	1-5	1-2	1	0	1	4
Rimac	5	0-1	0-0	0	0	0	0
Wilson	5	2-2	0-0	4	0	1	4
Team				3			
TOTALS	200	30-77	11-19	44	15	17	76

FG%: .390. **FT%:** .579. **Three-point goals:** 5 of 18 (Stewart 0-5, Beck 0-1, Thurman 3-5, McDaniel 1-3, Dillard 1-4). **Blocks:** 3. **Turnovers:** 12 (Williamson 5). **Steals:** 11 (Stewart 4). **Halftime:** Arkansas 34-33.

NATIONAL SEMIFINALS

ARIZONA (82): Owes 7-15 2-2 16, Geary 2-6 0-0 4, Blair 4-7 0-1 8, Reeves 6-19 8-9 20, Stoudamire 5-24 4-4 16, Flanagan 1-1 0-0 2, McLean 1-1 0-0 2, Williams 5-7 0-0 14, Rigdon 0-0 0-0 0, Richey 0-0 0-0 0, Brown 0-0 0-0 0, Kelley 0-0 0-0 0. Team 31-80 (.388) 14-16 (.875) 82.

ARKANSAS (91): Stewart 2-5 1-2 7, Williamson 11-18 7-9 29, Robinson 5-9 2-3 12, Beck 2-5 4-8 9, Thurman 5-13 4-6 14, McDaniel 4-10 2-2 12, Dillard 2-7 0-0 6, Wilson 1-2 0-2 2, Rimac 0-1 0-0 0. Team 32-70 (.457) 20-32 (.625) 91.

Three-point goals: Arizona 6-32, Arkansas 7-24 (.292). **Halftime:** Tied 41-41.

FLORIDA (65): Thompson 1-3 2-4 4, DeClercq 7-11 0-2 14, Hill 6-17 4-6 16, Brown 3-9 0-0 8, Cross 3-14 2-4 10, Kuisma 0-2 2-2 2, Anderson 4-6 1-2 9, Dyrkolbotn 0-0 0-0 0, Williams 1-1 0-0 2. Team 25-63 (.397) 11-20 (.550) 65.

DUKE (70): Lang 3-6 6-6 12, Hill 8-13 6-8 25, Parks 4-11 3-4 11, Capel 3-10 1-1 9, Collins 1-4 0-0 2, Clark 3-6 0-0 8, Meek 0-1 3-4 3, Newton 0-0 0-0 0. Team 22-51 (.431) 19-23 (.826) 70.

Three-point goals: Florida 4-9 (.444), Duke 7-14 (.500). **Halftime:** Florida 39-32.

ALL-TOURNAMENT TEAM

Corey Beck, G, Jr., Arkansas
Grant Hill, G, Sr., Duke
Antonio Lang, F, Sr., Duke
Scotty Thurman, G-F, Soph., Arkansas
*Corliss Williamson, F, Soph., Arkansas (52 points, 21 rebounds, eight assists)
*Named Most Outstanding Player.

ance in his first full year at a new job although the school registered a record of more than 20 games below .500 the previous season. The Greyhounds, 2-25 in 1993-94, improved by 13 1/2 games when Prosser assumed control and compiled a 17-13 mark. . . . Gary Williams, leading Maryland to the Midwest Regional semifinals, became the only individual to win games while coaching schools from the three conferences with the best winning percentages in NCAA Tournament history reflecting actual membership—ACC, Big East and Big Ten. He is also the only coach to win games with as many as three different schools (Boston College, Maryland and Ohio State) although they were seeded ninth or worse. . . . Duke's Mike Krzyzewski became the only coach to win his first seven NCAA regional finals. . . . Boston College's Jim O'Brien defeated two of the three coaches with at least 40 tourney victories (North Carolina's Dean Smith and Indiana's Bob Knight in back-to-back East Regional games). . . . Arizona guard Khalid Reeves (20th in scoring with 24.2 points per game) was the only player ranking among the nation's top 60 scorers, top 30 in assists and top 30 rebounders to participate in the Final Four. . . . Fourteen of 17 worst-seeded winners in the tournament shot better behind the three-point arc, by an average of 43.8 percent to 27.5 percent. . . . Wisconsin tied Brown

1994 CHAMPIONSHIP BRACKET

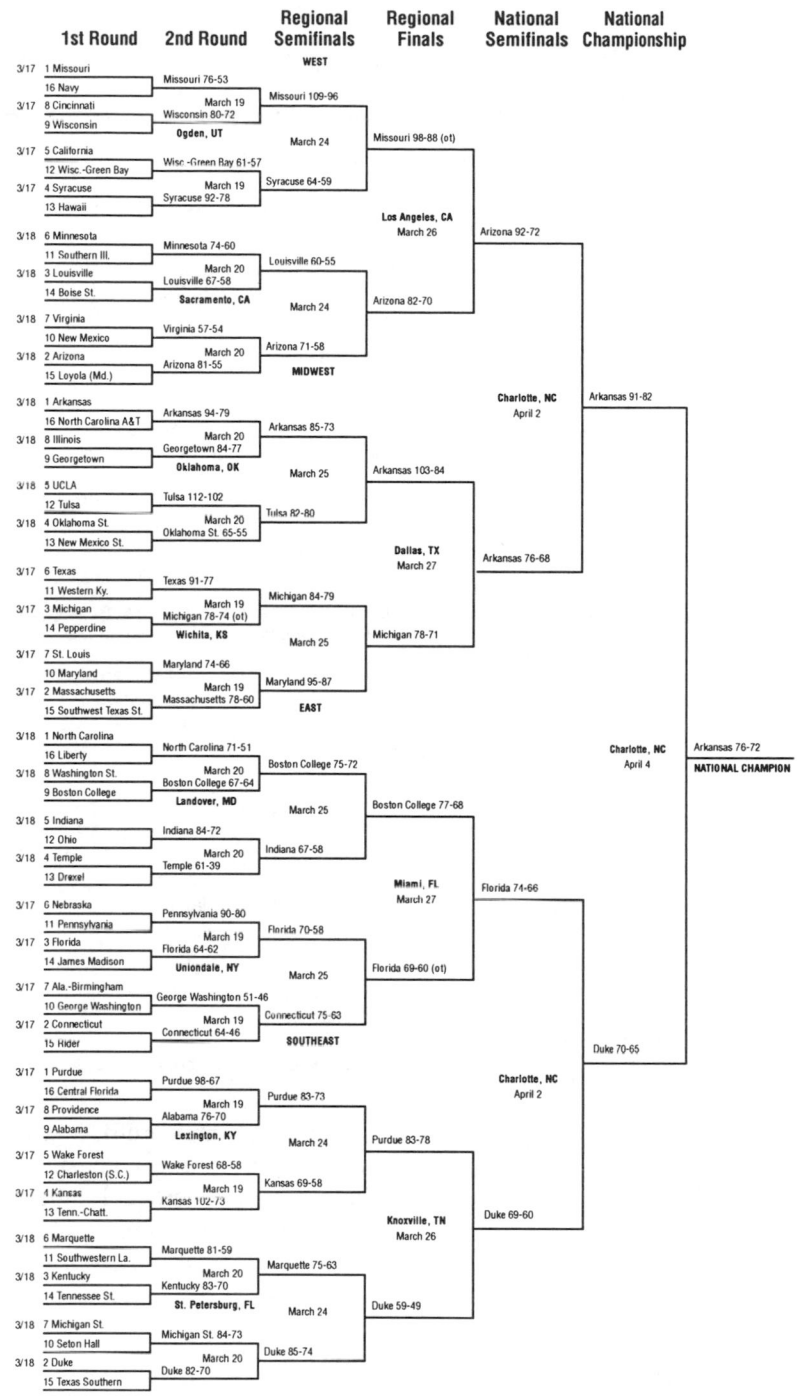

1st Round	2nd Round	Regional Semifinals	Regional Finals	National Semifinals	National Championship

WEST

3/17 1 Missouri
16 Navy
— Missouri 76-53
3/17 8 Cincinnati
9 Wisconsin
— March 19 Wisconsin 80-72
— Missouri 109-96
Ogden, UT

3/17 5 California
12 Wisc.-Green Bay
— Wisc.-Green Bay 61-57
3/17 4 Syracuse
13 Hawaii
— March 19 Syracuse 92-78
— Syracuse 64-59
— March 24 Missouri 98-88 (ot)

Los Angeles, CA
March 26

3/18 6 Minnesota
11 Southern Ill.
— Minnesota 74-60
3/18 3 Louisville
14 Boise St.
— March 20 Louisville 67-58
— Louisville 60-55
— Arizona 92-72

3/18 7 Virginia
10 New Mexico
— Virginia 57-54
3/18 2 Arizona
15 Loyola (Md.)
— March 20 Arizona 81-55
— Arizona 71-58
— March 24 Arizona 82-70

MIDWEST

3/18 1 Arkansas
16 North Carolina A&T
— Arkansas 94-79
3/18 8 Illinois
9 Georgetown
— March 20 Georgetown 84-77
— Arkansas 85-73
Oklahoma, OK

3/18 5 UCLA
12 Tulsa
— Tulsa 112-102
3/18 4 Oklahoma St.
13 New Mexico St.
— March 20 Oklahoma St. 65-55
— Tulsa 82-80
— March 25 Arkansas 103-84

Charlotte, NC
April 2

Arkansas 91-82

Dallas, TX
March 27

3/17 6 Texas
11 Western Ky.
— Texas 91-77
3/17 3 Michigan
14 Pepperdine
— March 19 Michigan 78-74 (ot)
— Michigan 84-79
— Arkansas 76-68

3/17 7 St. Louis
10 Maryland
— Maryland 74-66
3/17 2 Massachusetts
15 Southwest Texas St.
— March 19 Massachusetts 78-60
— Maryland 95-87
— March 25 Michigan 78-71

EAST

3/18 1 North Carolina
16 Liberty
— North Carolina 71-51
3/18 8 Washington St.
9 Boston College
— March 20 Boston College 67-64
— Boston College 75-72
Landover, MD

3/18 5 Indiana
12 Ohio
— Indiana 84-72
3/18 4 Temple
13 Drexel
— March 20 Temple 61-39
— Indiana 67-58
— March 25 Boston College 77-68

Charlotte, NC
April 4

Arkansas 76-72
NATIONAL CHAMPION

Miami, FL
March 27

3/17 6 Nebraska
11 Pennsylvania
— Pennsylvania 90-80
3/17 3 Florida
14 James Madison
— March 19 Florida 64-62
— Florida 70-58
— Florida 74-66

3/17 7 Ala.-Birmingham
10 George Washington
— George Washington 51-46
3/17 2 Connecticut
15 Rider
— March 19 Connecticut 64-46
— Connecticut 75-63
— March 25 Florida 69-60 (ot)

SOUTHEAST

3/17 1 Purdue
16 Central Florida
— Purdue 98-67
3/17 8 Providence
9 Alabama
— March 19 Alabama 76-70
— Purdue 83-73
Lexington, KY

3/17 5 Wake Forest
12 Charleston (S.C.)
— Wake Forest 68-58
3/17 4 Kansas
13 Tenn.-Chatt.
— March 19 Kansas 102-73
— Kansas 69-58
— March 24 Purdue 83-78

Charlotte, NC
April 2

Duke 70-65

Knoxville, TN
March 26

3/18 6 Marquette
11 Southwestern La.
— Marquette 81-59
3/18 3 Kentucky
14 Tennessee St.
— March 20 Kentucky 83-70
— Marquette 75-63
St. Petersburg, FL

3/18 7 Michigan St.
10 Seton Hall
— Michigan St. 84-73
3/18 2 Duke
15 Texas Southern
— March 20 Duke 82-70
— Duke 85-74
— March 24 Duke 59-49

Duke 69-60

for the longest drought in NCAA Tournament history for schools previously participating in the playoffs. The Badgers' last appearance was in 1947. Brown didn't earn a bid from 1940 through 1985. . . . Saint Louis, coached by Charlie Spoonhour, appeared in the NCAA playoffs for the first time since 1957. . . . Tulsa, coached by Tubby Smith, tallied its first NCAA Tournament triumph since 1955.

What Might Have Been: Alabama (20-10/without James Robinson), Kentucky (27-7/Jamal Mashburn), Michigan (24-8/Chris Webber), Seton Hall (17-13/Luther Wright) and Wake Forest (21-12/Rodney Rogers) might have fared better in the playoffs if standout players had exercised their remaining eligibility instead of defecting to the NBA. Ditto Virginia (18-13/without Cory Alexander/broken ankle) and Seton Hall (17-13/Danny Hurley/sabbatical to tend to personal problems) if key guards weren't on the sideline. . . . Brigham Young (22-10) probably would have participated in the NCAA Tournament instead of the NIT if Shawn Bradley didn't leave school early for the NBA.

Overcoming Adversity: Arkansas lost two of three SEC road games from January 8-19 and nearly lost three of four but capitalized on Thurman's three-pointer with nine seconds remaining to escape with a 65-64 victory at Tennessee, which finished with the league's worst record (2-14). Thurman scored a season-low seven points against the Volunteers. The Hogs also almost lost at home to a second-division team, but LSU missed two shots in the final 10 seconds to fall short, 84-83, in the only game at Arkansas' brand new Walton Arena that would be less than a double-digit victory. Later, Arkansas erased a four-point deficit in the last 12 seconds of regulation and two-point deficit with less than 20 seconds remaining in overtime to win at LSU, 108-105.

Scoring Leader: Khalid Reeves, Arizona (137 points, 27.4 ppg).

Highest Scoring Average: Gary Collier, Tulsa (94 points, 31.3 ppg).

Rebounding Leader: Cherokee Parks, Duke (55 rebounds, 9.2 rpg).

Highest Rebounding Average: Juwan Howard, Michigan (51 rebounds, 12.8 rpg).

1994-95

AT A GLANCE

NCAA Champion: UCLA (31-2; coached by Jim Harrick; won Pacific-10 title by three games with a 16-2 record).

NIT Champion: Virginia Tech (25-10; coached by Bill Foster; finished in a tie for fourth place in Metro with a 6-6 record).

New Rules: Voted to restrict scoring to a tap-in when play is resumed by a throw-in and three-tenths (.3) of a second or less remain on the game clock or shot clock. . . . A player whose uniform has blood on it does not have to leave the game if medical personnel judges the uniform to be nonsaturated. . . . Expanded backcourt violation exceptions to a defensive player who receives the ball while in the air. . . . Expanded the fighting rule to include coaches and team personnel. . . . The inner circle at midcourt is eliminated.

NCAA Probation: Alabama State, Coastal Carolina, Northeastern Illinois.

NCAA Consensus First-Team All-Americans: Ed O'Bannon, F, Sr., UCLA; Shawn Respert, G, Sr., Michigan State; Joe Smith, C, Soph., Maryland; Jerry Stackhouse, F, Soph., North Carolina; Damon Stoudamire, G, Sr., Arizona.

National Players of the Year: O'Bannon (20.4 ppg, 8.3 rpg, 1.9 spg, 53.3 FG%, 43.3 3FG%/USBWA, Wooden); Respert (25.6 ppg, 4 rpg, 3 apg, 86.9 FT%, 47.4 3FG%/NABC), and Smith (20.8 ppg, 10.6 rpg, 2.9 bpg, 57.8 FG%/AP, UPI, Naismith).

National Coaches of the Year: Miami's Leonard Hamilton (15-13/UPI); UCLA's Jim Harrick (31-2/NABC, Naismith), and Oklahoma's Kelvin Sampson (23-9/AP, USBWA).

A couple of high profile coaches for Western coaches departed under unusual circumstances before the season started. Southern Cal's George Raveling stepped down in the aftermath of a serious auto accident and UNLV's Rollie Massimino was pressured to resign after a series of questionable activities.

Tim Grgurich, Massimino's successor, left the Rebels after seven games due to health reasons.

1994–95 INDIVIDUAL LEADERS

SCORING

PLAYER	PTS.	AVG.
Thomas, Texas Christian	781	28.9
King, Western Carolina	743	26.5
Sykes, Grambling	684	26.3
Ford, Ill.-Chicago	707	26.2
Roberts, Southern (La.)	680	26.2
Townes, La Salle	699	25.9
Griffin, Long Island	723	25.8
Respert, Michigan St.	716	25.6
Feaster, Holy Cross	672	24.9
Smith, Wis.-Milwaukee	661	24.5

REBOUNDING

PLAYER	REB.	AVG.
Thomas, Texas Christian	393	14.6
Rose, Drexel	404	13.5
Trent, Ohio Univ.	423	12.8
Callahan, Northeastern	364	12.6
Duncan, Wake Forest	401	12.5
Foyle, Colgate	371	12.4
Carpenter, Eastern Mich.	343	11.8
Awojobi, Boston Univ.	365	11.8
Mann, Miss. Valley	317	11.7
Ensminger, Valparaiso	315	11.3

ASSISTS

PLAYER	AST.	AVG.
Haggerty, Baylor	284	10.1
McCants, George Mason	251	9.3
Miglinieks, UC Irvine	245	8.4
Snow, Michigan State	217	7.8
Vaughn, Kansas	238	7.7
Foster, South Alabama	203	7.5
Miller, Marquette	248	7.5
Hassan Sanders, Southern (La.)	179	7.5
Washington, Nicholls State	213	7.3
Stoudamire, Arizona	220	7.3
O'Bryant, Nevada	211	7.3

BLOCKED SHOTS

PLAYER	BLK.	AVG.
Closs, Central Conn.	139	5.3
Ratliff, Wyoming	144	5.1
Foyle, Colgate	147	4.9
Fleury, UMBC	124	4.6
Coleman, Tenn. Tech	122	4.5
Duncan, Wake Forest	135	4.2
Gilpin, Dartmouth	92	3.5
Bennett, Arizona State	115	3.5
Aluma, Liberty	97	3.5
Camby, Massachusetts	103	3.4

STEALS

PLAYER	STL.	AVG.
Anderson, Texas	101	3.4
Black, Tex.-Pan American	94	3.4
Langley, George Mason	87	3.3
Washington, Nicholls St.	88	3.0
Ceasar, LSU	66	3.0
Iverson, Georgetown	89	3.0
McNeil, St. Bonaventure	90	2.9
Young, Fresno State	81	2.9
Strickland, Nebraska	89	2.9
Walker, San Francisco	80	2.9

FIELD-GOAL PERCENTAGE

PLAYER	FGM	FGA	PCT.
Kline-Ruminski, BGSU	181	265	.683
Spain, Davidson	141	210	.671
Wallace, N. Carolina	238	364	.654
Dampier, Mississippi St.	153	239	.640
Koul, George Wash.	160	253	.632
McNaull, Long Beach St.	156	248	.629
Hendrickson, Wash. St.	183	292	.627
McCulloch, Fresno St.	152	244	.623
Coleman, Tenn. Tech	168	270	.622
Robinson, E. Carolina	181	293	.618

FREE-THROW PERCENTAGE

PLAYER	FTM	FTA	PCT.
Bibb, Tennessee Tech	106	117	.906
Hartzell, N.C.-Greensboro	97	108	.898
Brown, Murray State	189	211	.896
Cornett, Texas-Arlington	70	79	.886
Johnson, Eastern Ky.	123	139	.885
Basile, Marist	74	84	.881
Nash, Santa Clara	153	174	.879
Rillie, Gonzaga	87	99	.879
Barker, Valparaiso	72	82	.878
Heary, Navy	105	120	.875

THREE-POINT FG PERCENTAGE

PLAYER	FGM	FGA	PCT.
Jackson, Evansville	53	95	.558
Kegler, Penn	58	114	.509
Westlake, Wis.-Green Bay	87	174	.500
Calabria, N. Carolina	66	133	.496
Hightower, Marshall	46	95	.484
Lake, Montana	76	157	.484

THREE-POINT FIELD GOALS PER GAME

PLAYER	FGM	AVG.
Taylor, Southern (La.)	109	4.4
Respert, Michigan St.	119	4.3
Roberts, Southern (La.)	108	4.2
Rutherford, Okla. St.	146	3.9
Townes, La Salle	103	3.8

Howie Landa and Cleveland Edwards served as interim coaches the remainder of UNLV's sorriest season in history (11-15).

Baylor coach Darrel Johnson was dismissed before the season started because of academic irregularities. Three Baylor assistant coaches—Gary Thomas, Troy Drummond and Kevin Gray—were sentenced to three years probation, assigned 50 hours of community service and fined from $1,000 to $1,500 apiece for helping three recruits cheat. The coaches had been convicted by a federal jury of conspiracy and mail and wire fraud charges. They were found guilty of giving junior college players term papers and of changing their test scores. The mail fraud and wire fraud charges were filed because the Postal Service and fax equipment were used in the process. Johnson was acquitted, but Gray and Thomas said Johnson condoned the wrongdoing. They gave depositions to the NCAA that said the cheating "was always discussed in meetings" with Johnson.

Duke coach Mike Krzyzewski compiled a 9-3 record before missing the remainder of the season recovering from back surgery and exhaustion. Pete Gaudet, a designated restricted-earnings assistant earning an anemic $16,000 annually under NCAA rules, filled in for Krzyzewski. The Blue Devils promptly lost their first nine ACC games for the first time and finished with the most defeats in school history (13-18 mark). Their demise included blowing a 23-point lead with less than 15 minutes remaining against Virginia and bowing to the Cavaliers in double overtime, 91-88.

Tommy Joe Eagles, hired by New Orleans after he was forced out by Auburn at the end of the

1994–95 TEAM LEADERS

SCORING OFFENSE

SCHOOL	PTS.	AVG.
Texas Christian	2529	93.7
Southern (La.)	2425	93.3
Texas	2787	92.9
George Mason	2499	92.6
Troy State	2468	91.4

SCORING DEFENSE

SCHOOL	PTS.	AVG.
Princeton	1501	57.7
Wis.-Green Bay	1767	58.9
Temple	1792	59.7
Miami of Ohio	1827	60.9
Manhattan	1929	62.2

SCORING MARGIN

SCHOOL	OFF.	DEF.	MAR.
Kentucky	87.4	69.0	18.4
Massachusetts	80.9	65.7	15.1
Pennsylvania	82.2	67.5	14.7
UCLA	87.5	73.9	13.7
Montana State	84.2	70.8	13.4

WON-LOST PERCENTAGE

SCHOOL	W-L	PCT.
UCLA	31-2	.939
Western Kentucky	27-4	.871
Massachusetts	29-5	.853
Connecticut	28-5	.848
Kentucky	28-5	.848

FIELD-GOAL PERCENTAGE

SCHOOL	FGM	FGA	PCT.
Washington St.	902	1743	.517
UCLA	1079	2102	.513
North Carolina	1044	2055	.508
Montana State	930	1832	.508
Bowling Green	721	1427	.505

FIELD-GOAL PERCENTAGE DEFENSE

SCHOOL	FGM	FGA	PCT.
Alabama	771	2048	.376
Kansas	768	2032	.378
Marquette	747	1957	.382
Mississippi St.	698	1821	.383
Manhattan	670	1747	.384

FREE-THROW PERCENTAGE

SCHOOL	FTM	FTA	PCT.
Brigham Young	617	798	.773
Murray State	553	719	.769
Wake Forest	475	622	.764
Samford	472	622	.759
Iowa State	610	806	.757

REBOUND MARGIN

SCHOOL	OWN	OPP.	MAR.
Navy	40.6	29.6	11.0
Utah State	40.9	30.4	10.5
Texas Tech	43.3	33.5	9.8
Utah	39.7	30.0	9.8
Miss. Valley	47.0	38.3	8.8

THREE-POINT FIELD GOAL PERCENTAGE

SCHOOL	FGM	FGA	PCT.
Southern Utah	244	571	.427
Evansville	181	424	.427
Wis.-Green Bay	188	451	.417
Arizona	245	593	.413
North Carolina	266	648	.410

THREE-POINT FIELD GOALS PER GAME

SCHOOL	FGM	AVG.
Troy State	287	10.6
Samford	279	10.3
Vermont	268	9.9
Baylor	265	9.5
Marshall	253	9.4

previous season, died of a heart attack during the summer. . . . James Madison's Lefty Driesell became the first coach to register at least 125 victories for three different schools. He previously achieved the feat for Davidson and Maryland. . . . Michigan State's Jud Heathcote, who previously coached Montana, retired with a 420-273 record.

Wisconsin's Michael Finley tied a school single-game record with 42 points in a 92-76 loss at Eastern Michigan. The Badgers trailed EMU by 33 points at halftime (50-17). Finley was among three players on Proviso East's Illinois state Class AA championship in 1991 who were all drafted by NBA teams—Sherell Ford (Illinois-Chicago) and Finley in the first round and Donnie Boyce (Colorado) in the second round. Ford was the nation's fourth-leading scorer as a senior and Boyce finished his career as Colorado's all-time leading scorer.

Corey Beck distributed 30 assists in three

games to spark Arkansas to the Rainbow Classic championship in Hawaii. It was the Razorbacks' first in-season tournament title in 26 years. Rainbow Classic runner-up Iowa defeated Duke in the opening round, ending the Blue Devils' 14-game winning streak against Big Ten teams. . . . Maryland's pair of two-point victories over Duke enabled the Terrapins to gain a share of the ACC regular-season crown and end their streak of nine consecutive defeats in College Park and 15 overall to the Blue Devils. The ACC's four-way tie for the regular-season title was the first in league history. . . . Randolph Childress poured in an ACC Tournament-record 107 points to catapult Wake Forest to its first championship since 1962. . . . Indiana's 50-game homecourt winning streak, which began in 1991, was ended by Michigan, 65-52. . . . A school-record 11 blocked shots by freshman center Samaki Walker helped Louisville nip Kentucky, 88-86, for the Cardinals' first victory over the Wildcats since 1989. . . . Central Connecticut State's Keith Closs had a national-high 13 rejections in a game against St. Francis (Pa.).

Kentucky clobbered Notre Dame, 97-58, handing the Fighting Irish its most lopsided home-court defeat this century. In their next outing, the Wildcats lost at home to Mississippi State, 76-71, for the first time since 1967. . . . In Mississippi State's previous game, the Bulldogs hit five three-pointers in the last 1 1/2 minutes to nearly erase a 12-point deficit against Auburn but they fell short, 70-69. Mississippi State finished with a Top 20 appearance in a final wire-service poll for the first time since 1963. . . . LSU redshirt freshman Randy Livingston was leading the nation with 10 assists per game in mid-season before he was sidelined for the year because of his third knee injury since signing with the Tigers.

Connecticut remained the nation's only unde-feated team through mid-January by overcoming a 25-point deficit in an 85-76 victory at Pittsburgh. The Jim Calhoun-coached Huskies went on to become the only team ever to defeat Georgetown three times in a Big East Conference campaign. . . . Connecticut became the only school to have its men's and women's teams ranked No. 1 at the same time. . . . Miami (Fla.) lost its first 29 Big East road games until upsetting St. John's, 82-79. The Hurricanes, winless in league play the previous year, finished with the greatest one-season turnaround in conference history by compiling a 9-9 Big East record. . . . Kerry Kittles became the first Villanova player since 1971 to earn a spot on an NCAA consensus first- or second-team All-American squad.

Canisius lost 27 consecutive games on St. Bonaventure's home court in Olean, N.Y., until edging the Bonnies, 76-74. Later, St. Bonaventure defeated Temple for the first time in 25 games with a 78-64 triumph in overtime. . . . Eddie Benton became Vermont's all-time leading scorer midway through his junior season.

The Metro, in its final season of existence, was the only conference in the country to have each member post a winning overall record. . . .

Tennessee-Chattanooga's John Oliver averaged a modest 10.9 points per game, but he exploded for a school-record 42 in a game against Georgia Southern. . . . Southern's Tim Roberts scored a national-high 56 points against Faith Baptist. . . . Western Kentucky's Matt Kilcullen became the first coach ever to win back-to-back coach of the year awards at different schools in the same conference (Sun Belt). He was at Jacksonville's helm the previous season. His success enabled WKU to become the first school to have eight different coaches guide teams to the NCAA Tournament.

UCLA (31-2/coached by Jim Harrick), Manhattan (26-5/Fran Fraschilla), Wake Forest (26-6/Dave Odom), Virginia Tech (25-10/Bill Foster), Nicholls State (24-6/Rickey Broussard), UNC-Greensboro (23-6/Mike Dement), Portland (21-8/Rob Chavez) and New Hampshire (19-9/Gib Chapman) had their winningest seasons in school Division I history. Western Illinois (20-8/Jim Kerwin) tied its school single-season Division I mark for most victories. . . . Manhattan was the first school to reach the 20-win plateau. . . . Western Illinois posted the nation's most-improved record, improving from a 7-20 mark the previous year, which represented the Leathernecks' most defeats since moving up to the Division I level. . . . Massachusetts' game at Rutgers was suspended at half-time because of a student protest stemming from racial remarks by the Rutgers president.

Randy Rutherford poured in 45 points in Oklahoma State's regular-season finale at Kansas but the Jayhawks won, 78-62, when Cowboys All-Big Eight center Bryant Reeves went scoreless. Reeves and Rutherford were the nation's only set of teammates to each score more than 700 points during the season. . . . Oregon swept its Pacific-10 series with intra-state rival Oregon State for the first time since 1961. Oregon won more than 16 games for the first time since the 1976-77 campaign. . . . California finished in a tie for eighth place in the Pacific-10 despite becoming the first school in league history to win at UCLA's Pauley Pavilion three consecutive times (100-93). Cal is the only team registering a league record at least eight games under .500 (5-13) to win a road game against a conference rival that later became NCAA champion.

Point guard Steve Nash converted all 21 of his free throws in a 75-71 victory over St. Mary's on his way to becoming the first Santa Clara player to top the WCC in scoring (20.9 points per game) since Mike Gervasoni averaged 20.1 in 1966-67. Nash, a native of British Columbia, scored 40 points, nailing eight three-pointers, to help the Broncos end Gonzaga's 34-game homecourt winning streak, 73-68. They went on to clinch their first WCC regular-season title since 1970.

TCU's Kurt Thomas became the third player to lead the nation in scoring and rebounding. Thomas averaged only 1.9 points per game as a freshman in 1990-91. . . . TCU's Thomas (28.9 ppg), UIC's Ford (26.2) and Nicholls State's Reggie Jackson (21.63) set school Division I records for highest scoring average in a single season. . . . La Salle's Kareem Townes (52 points vs. Loyola of Chicago) and LIU's Joe Griffin (46 at Marist) established school single-game scoring records. . . . Pitt forward Orlando Antigua signed with the Harlem Globetrotters after the season. He became the first non-African American player with the Globetrotters since Bob Karstens in 1942-43.

Marquette's Tony Miller dished out a school single-game record of 17 assists against Memphis en route to finishing his career as the only player at any level of the NCAA to collect 1,000 points, 500 rebounds and 900 assists. . . . Eastern Michigan's Kareem Carpenter set a school single-game rebounding mark with a national-high 27 against Western Michigan. Carpenter also hauled down 26 rebounds in a contest against Central Michigan. . . . Few programs ever unraveled as quickly as Ohio State. The Buckeyes incurred their most defeats in school history (6-22 record) after finishing among the nation's top five teams in final national polls in 1991 and 1992. The core of their sophomore class departed for other schools following the 1993-94 campaign—swingman Derek Anderson (Kentucky), forward Charles Macon (Central Michigan), guard Greg Simpson (West Virginia) and center Nate Wilbourne (South Carolina)—along

1994-95 FINAL NATIONAL POLLS

AP	UPI	USA/NABC	SCHOOL (RECORD)	HEAD COACH
1	1	1	UCLA (31-2)	Jim Harrick
2	2	5	Kentucky (28-5)	Rick Pitino
3	3	9	Wake Forest (26-6)	Dave Odom
4	5	3	North Carolina (28-6)	Dean Smith
5	4	10	Kansas (25-6)	Roy Williams
6	6	2	Arkansas (32-7)	Nolan Richardson
7	7	7	Massachusetts (29-5)	John Calipari
8	8	6	Connecticut (28-5)	Jim Calhoun
9	9	23	Villanova (25-8)	Steve Lappas
10	11	11	Maryland (26-8)	Gary Williams
11	10	20	Michigan State (22-6)	Jud Heathcote
12	12	19	Purdue (25-7)	Gene Keady
13	14	8	Virginia (25-9)	Jeff Jones
14	16	4	Oklahoma State (27-10)	Eddie Sutton
15	13	25	Arizona (23-8)	Lute Olson
16	15	13	Arizona State (24-9)	Bill Frieder
17	19	-	Oklahoma (23-9)	Kelvin Sampson
18	17	12	Mississippi St. (22-8)	Richard Williams
19	18	22	Utah (28-6)	Rick Majerus
20	20	21	Alabama (23-10)	Dave Hobbs
21	-	-	Western Kentucky (27-4)	Matt Kilcullen
22	-	16	Georgetown (21-10)	John Thompson
23	22	18	Missouri (20-9)	Norm Stewart
24	22	-	Iowa State (23-11)	Tim Floyd
25	21	17	Syracuse (20-10)	Jim Boeheim
	24	-	Oregon (19-9)	Jerry Green
	25	-	Stanford (20-9)	Mike Montgomery
-	-	14	Memphis (24-10)	Larry Finch
-	-	15	Tulsa (24-8)	Tubby Smith
-	-	24	Texas (23-7)	Tom Penders

with freshman center Gerald Eaker (Kansas State via junior college). The quintet combined for 56.6 points and 23 rebounds per game as starters for their second major university in 1995-96.

Sacramento State's NCAA-record 55-game losing streak on the road ended with a 68-56 success at Loyola of Chicago. . . . Wyoming's Theo Ratliff blocked 11 shots in each of back-to-back games against Mississippi State and San Diego State. . . . Brad Snyder, Northern Arizona's leading scorer, was killed in a one-vehicle accident late in the season.

1995 NCAA Tournament

Summary: It was a return to glory for UCLA. Playmaker deluxe Tyus Edney played only three minutes in the final because of a sprained right wrist, but his replacement, Cameron Dollar, played like a million dollars. "I was definitely tight and tense at the beginning," said Dollar, who committed just one turnover. "Then I got going and it turned out to be just another game, like any other day in the playground." Edney played the role of Wizard of Westwood II with a series of

1994-95 NCAA CHAMPION: UCLA

SEASON STATISTICS FOR UCLA REGULARS

PLAYER	POS.	CL.	G.	FG%	FT%	PPG	RPG
Ed O'Bannon	F	Sr.	33	.533	.785	20.4	8.3
Tyus Edney	G	Sr.	32	.497	.764	14.3	3.1
Charles O'Bannon	F	So.	33	.554	.739	13.6	6.1
George Zidek	C	Sr.	33	.553	.731	10.6	5.4
Toby Bailey	G	Fr.	33	.484	.564	10.5	4.8
J.R. Henderson	F-C	Fr.	33	.547	.675	9.2	4.2
Cameron Dollar	G	So.	33	.354	.659	3.4	1.9
Ike Nwankwo	C	So.	23	.571	.538	2.7	1.6
Kris Johnson	F	Fr.	21	.420	.706	2.6	1.7
omm'A Givens	F-C	Fr.	25	.381	.563	1.6	1.3
TEAM TOTALS			33	.513	.709	87.5	40.4

Three-point field goals leaders: E. O'Bannon (55 of 127, .433), Edney (25 of 66, .379), Bailey (20 of 73, .274). **Assists leaders:** Edney 216, C. O'Bannon 110, Dollar 103, E. O'Bannon 81. **Blocked shots leader:** C. O'Bannon 38. **Steals leaders:** Edney 74, E. O'Bannon 64, Dollar 54.

1995 FINAL FOUR CHAMPIONSHIP GAME

SEATTLE, WA

UCLA (89)	Min.	FG-A	FT-A	Reb.	A	PF	Pts.
O'Bannon	36	4-10	3-4	9	6	1	11
O'Bannon	40	10-21	9-11	17	3	2	30
Zidek	29	5-8	4-7	6	0	4	14
Edney	3	0-0	0-0	0	0	0	0
Bailey	39	12-20	1-2	9	3	3	26
Dollar	36	1-4	4-5	3	8	4	6
Henderson	17	1-5	0-0	2	1	1	2
Team				4			
TOTALS	200	33-68	21-29	50	21	15	89

FG%: .485. **FT%:** .724. **Three-point goals:** 2 of 7 (E. O'Bannon 1 of 4, Bailey 1 of 2, Dollar 0 of 1). **Blocks:** 4. **Turnovers:** 20 (E. O'Bannon 5). **Steals:** 11 (Dollar 4).

ARKANSAS (78)	MIN.	FG-A	FT-A	REB.	A	PF	PTS.
Thurman	32	2-9	0-0	3	1	2	5
Williamson	33	3-16	6-10	4	6	1	12
Martin	6	1-2	0-0	3	1	2	3
McDaniel	35	5-10	3-4	3	1	5	16
Beck	25	4-6	1-2	3	2	3	11
Stewart	22	5-10	1-2	5	0	4	12
Dillard	15	2-4	0-0	2	1	1	6
Robinson	10	2-3	0-0	2	0	3	4

Rimac	12	1-1	0-0	2	3	0	2
Wilson	7	3-4	1-2	0	0	1	7
Williams	1	0-0	0-0	0	0	0	0
Garrett	2	0-0	0-0	0	0	0	0
Team				4			
TOTALS	200	28-65	12-20	31	15	22	78

FG%: .431. **FT%:** .600. **Three-point goals:** 10 of 28 (Thurman 1 of 7, Martin 1 of 2, McDaniel 3 of 7, Beck 2 of 3, Stewart 1 of 5, Dillard 2 of 3, Robinson 0 of 1). **Blocks:** 4. **Turnovers:** 18. **Steals:** 15 (McDaniel 4, Williamson 4). **Halftime:** UCLA 40-39.

NATIONAL SEMIFINALS

UCLA (74): C. O'Bannon 7-9 5-5 19, E. O'Bannon 6-14 1-2 15, Zidek 2-4 2-2 6, Edney 6-12 9-11 21, Bailey 1-2 0-0 2, Dollar 1-1 7-8 9, Henderson 1-6 0-0 2, Dempsey 0-0 0-0 0, Nwankwo 0-0 0-0 0, Givens 0-0 0-0 0, Johnson 0-1 0-0 0, Myers 0-0 0-0 0. Team 24-49 (.490) 24-28 (.857) 74.

OKLAHOMA STATE (61): Pierce 1-4 0-1 2, Collins 2-6 0-0 6, Reeves 8-16 9-9 25, Rutherford 4-13 3-4 15, Owens 1-4 0-0 3, Roberts 5-7 0-2 10, Skaer 0-0 0-0 0, Alexander 0-0 0-0 0, Baum 0-0 0-0 0, Nelson 0-0 0-0 0, Miles 0-0 0-0 0. Team 21-50 (.420) 12-16 (.750) 61.

Three-point goals: UCLA 2-7 (.286). Oklahoma State 7-19 (.368). **Halftime:** Tied 37-37.

NORTH CAROLINA (68): Stackhouse 4-7 7-10 18, Calabria 1-10 0-0 2, Wallace 4-6 2-4 10, D. Williams 7-19 0-0 19, McInnis 3-9 5-6 13, Sullivan 1-2 2-4 4, Zwikker 0-1 0-0 0, Landry 1-2 0-0 2, S. Williams 0-0 0-0 0. Team 21-56 (.375) 16-24 (.667) 68.

ARKANSAS (75): Thurman 2-10 0-0 6, Williamson 10-17 1-1 21, Martin 1-1 0-0 3, McDaniel 3-7 4-4 13, Beck 2-9 0-0 5, Dillard 0-5 0-0 0, Rimac 2-8 0-0 6, Stewart 6-10 0-2 15, Wilson 1-3 2-2 4, Robinson 1-4 0-0 2. Team 28-74 (.378) 7-9 (.778) 75.

Three-point goals: North Carolina 10-28 (.357). Arkansas 12-34 (.353). **Halftime:** North Carolina 38-34.

ALL-TOURNAMENT TEAM

Toby Bailey, G, Fr., UCLA (28 points, nine rebounds)
Clint McDaniel, G, Sr., Arkansas (29 points, eight rebounds, six three-pointers)
*Ed O'Bannon, F, Sr., UCLA (45 points, 25 rebounds, seven steals)
Bryant Reeves, C, Sr., Oklahoma State (25 points, nine rebounds in one game)
Corliss Williamson, F, Jr., Arkansas (33 points, 14 rebounds)

*Named Most Outstanding Player.

breathtaking drives and baskets in the first five playoff games, including a length-of-the-court game-winner against Missouri in the second round. Teammate Ed O'Bannon collected 30 points and 17 rebounds in an 89-78 victory over Arkansas for one of the best title game performances in history. O'Bannon became only the third different player to amass at least 30 points and 15 rebounds in a championship game, joining Clyde Lovellette (Kansas '52) and Lew Alcindor (UCLA '68 & '69). During a crucial five-game stretch in February, O'Bannon averaged 27.8 points and nine rebounds per game. Toby Bailey became the only freshman to score more than 25 points in a national championship game when he tallied 26 after managing just two in the semifinals against Oklahoma State. UCLA became the only champion other than Kentucky '51 to have six players finish the season with scoring averages higher than nine points per game.

Outcome for Defending Champion: Arkansas reached the NCAA championship game after winning its first two tourney assignments by a total of three points after blowing double-digit second-half leads. The Razorbacks' victory margin entering the Final Four, 3.8, was the slimmest of any team reaching the national semifinals since the tournament expanded to 64 teams in 1985. The Hogs had 13 wins by five or fewer points entering the NCAA final after kicking off the season with a 24-point defeat to Massachusetts in the Tip-Off Classic at Springfield, Mass.

Star Gazing: Alabama center Antonio McDyess had the highest-scoring game in the tourney with 39 points against Penn in overtime in the first round. . . . North Carolina center Rasheed Wallace, the third-leading field-goal shooter in the country (65.4 percent), had just one field-goal attempt in the last 27 minutes as the Tar Heels went more than 12 1/2 minutes without a basket.

Biggest Upset: Old Dominion outlasted Villanova, 89-81, in triple overtime although Monarchs star Odell Hodge missed most of the season because of a severe injury to his left knee.

One and Only: Bob Weltlich became the only coach to earn automatic qualification for two different schools by winning conference tournaments after compiling losing records in regular-season league competition. He was coach of No. 6 seed Mississippi in the 1981 SEC Tournament (8-10) and No. 8 seed Florida International (4-12) in the '95 TAAC Tournament.

Numbers Game: There were six overtime games in the first two rounds of the tourney. Alabama (24) and Penn (18) set a record for most points by both teams in one overtime period when they combined for 42 in Alabama's 91-85 triumph. . . . Michigan coach Steve Fisher won his first 12 NCAA playoff games by fewer than six points or in overtime before bowing to Western Kentucky, 82-76, in overtime in the opening round. . . . The Big Ten didn't have a representative among the final 16 entrants for the first time since the NCAA field expanded to at least 16 teams in 1951. All six Big Ten squads would have been eliminated in the opening round if Wisconsin-Green Bay hadn't missed a last-second shot against Purdue. . . . North Carolina's Southeast Regional final victory over Kentucky was the sixth straight triumph for the Tar Heels over UK in their series, giving Carolina a 16-6 edge. . . . Oregon, coached by Jerry Green, made its first playoff appearance since 1961 and Gonzaga, coached by Dan Fitzgerald, participated for the only time in school history.

What If: Brigham Young (22-10/without Shawn Bradley), Cincinnati (22-12/Dontonio Wingfield), Connecticut (28-5/Donyell Marshall), Louisville (19-14/Cliff Rozier), Michigan (17-14/Juwan Howard, Jalen Rose and Chris Webber) and Purdue (25-7/Glenn Robinson) might have fared better in the playoffs if these standout players had exercised their remaining eligibility instead of defecting to the NBA. . . . Clemson (15-13/without Sharone Wright) and George Washington (18-14/Yinka Dare) probably would have participated in the NCAA Tournament instead of the NIT if prominent big men didn't leave school early for the NBA. . . . California (13-14) likely would have been bound for the NCAA playoffs if Jason Kidd and Lamond Murray didn't forsake their remaining eligibility to turn pro early. . . . Missouri (20-9) might have advanced farther in the NCAA Tournament if forward Kelly Thames wasn't a medical redshirt because of a knee injury.

Putting Things in Perspective: Massachusetts and Virginia were eliminated in regional finals after each of them lost standouts guards. Michael Williams was dismissed from UMass' team for disciplinary reasons. Virginia's Cory Alexander, who became an NBA first-round draft choice as an undergraduate, was injured.

Scoring Leader: Corliss Williamson, Arkansas (125 points, 20.8 ppg).

Highest Scoring Average: Darryl Wilson, Mississippi State (73 points, 24.3 ppg).

Rebounding Leader: Ed O'Bannon, UCLA (54 rebounds, 9 rpg).

Highest Rebounding Average: Tim Duncan, Wake Forest (43 rebounds, 14.3 rpg).

1995 CHAMPIONSHIP BRACKET

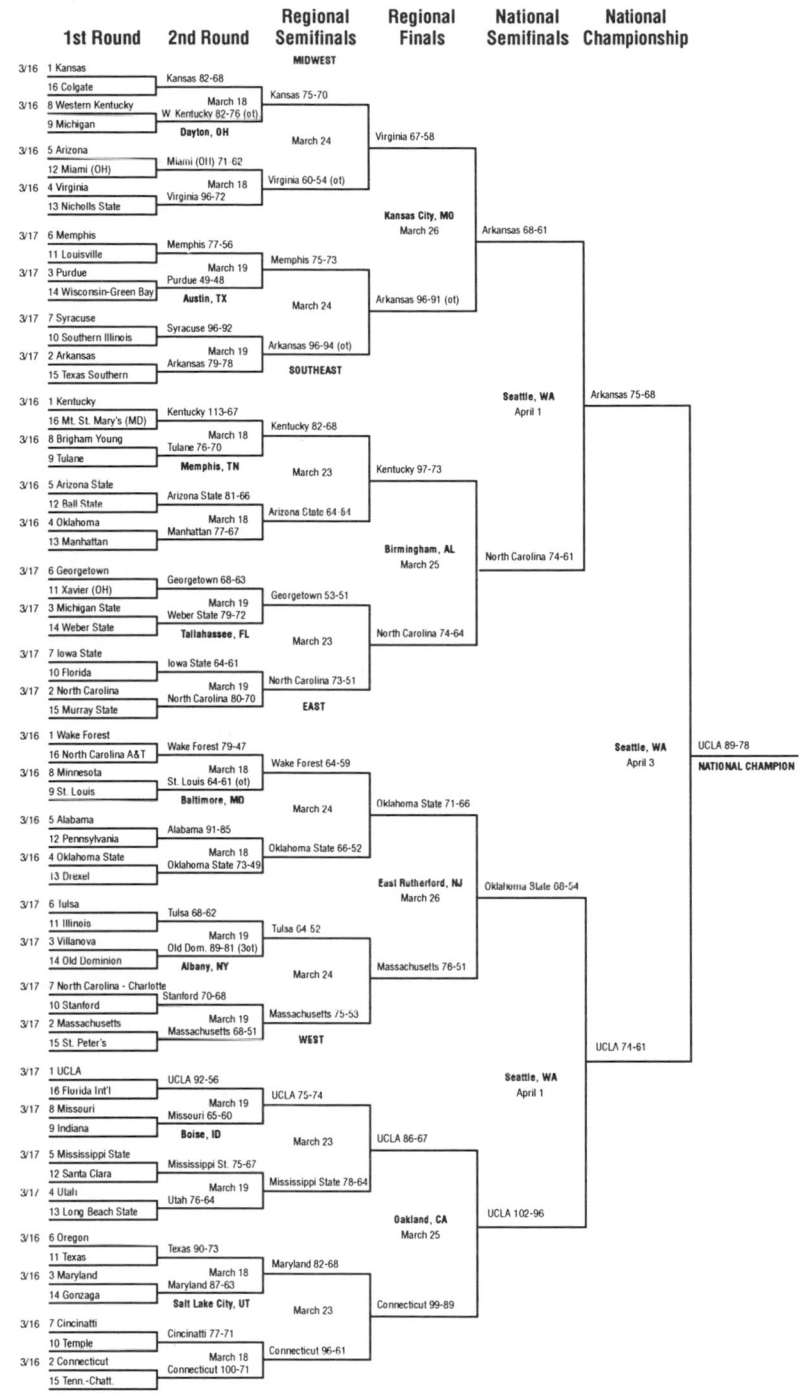

| | 1st Round | 2nd Round | Regional Semifinals | Regional Finals | National Semifinals | National Championship |

MIDWEST

3/16 1 Kansas
16 Colgate — Kansas 82-68
3/16 8 Western Kentucky
9 Michigan — W. Kentucky 82-76 (ot) — March 18 Dayton, OH
Kansas 75-70
3/16 5 Arizona
12 Miami (OH) — Miami (OH) 71-62
3/16 4 Virginia
13 Nicholls State — Virginia 96-72 — March 18
Virginia 60-54 (ot)
Virginia 67-58

Kansas City, MO March 26
Arkansas 68-61

3/17 6 Memphis
11 Louisville — Memphis 77-56
3/17 3 Purdue
14 Wisconsin-Green Bay — Purdue 49-48 — March 19 Austin, TX
Memphis 75-73
3/17 7 Syracuse
10 Southern Illinois — Syracuse 96-92
3/17 2 Arkansas
15 Texas Southern — Arkansas 79-78 — March 19
Arkansas 96-94 (ot)
Arkansas 96-91 (ot)

SOUTHEAST

Seattle, WA April 1
Arkansas 75-68

3/16 1 Kentucky
16 Mt. St. Mary's (MD) — Kentucky 113-67
3/16 8 Brigham Young
9 Tulane — Tulane 76-70 — March 18 Memphis, TN
Kentucky 82-68
3/16 5 Arizona State
12 Ball State — Arizona State 81-66
3/16 4 Oklahoma
13 Manhattan — Manhattan 77-67 — March 18
Arizona State 64-64
Kentucky 97-73

Birmingham, AL March 25
North Carolina 74-61

3/17 6 Georgetown
11 Xavier (OH) — Georgetown 68-63
3/17 3 Michigan State
14 Weber State — Weber State 79-72 — March 19 Tallahassee, FL
Georgetown 53-51
3/17 7 Iowa State
10 Florida — Iowa State 64-61
3/17 2 North Carolina
15 Murray State — North Carolina 80-70 — March 19
North Carolina 73-51
North Carolina 74-64

EAST

Seattle, WA April 3
UCLA 89-78
NATIONAL CHAMPION

3/16 1 Wake Forest
16 North Carolina A&T — Wake Forest 79-47
3/16 8 Minnesota
9 St. Louis — St. Louis 64-61 (ot) — March 18 Baltimore, MD
Wake Forest 64-59
3/16 5 Alabama
12 Pennsylvania — Alabama 91-85
3/16 4 Oklahoma State
13 Drexel — Oklahoma State 73-49 — March 18
Oklahoma State 66-52
Oklahoma State 71-66

East Rutherford, NJ March 26
Oklahoma State 68-54

3/17 6 Tulsa
11 Illinois — Tulsa 68-62
3/17 3 Villanova
14 Old Dominion — Old Dom. 89-81 (3ot) — March 19 Albany, NY
Tulsa 64-52
3/17 7 North Carolina - Charlotte
10 Stanford — Stanford 70-68
3/17 2 Massachusetts
15 St. Peter's — Massachusetts 68-51 — March 19
Massachusetts 75-53
Massachusetts 76-51

WEST

Seattle, WA April 1
UCLA 74-61

3/17 1 UCLA
16 Florida Int'l — UCLA 92-56
3/17 8 Missouri
9 Indiana — Missouri 65-60 — March 19 Boise, ID
UCLA 75-74
3/17 5 Mississippi State
12 Santa Clara — Mississippi St. 75-67
3/1/ 4 Utah
13 Long Beach State — Utah 76-64 — March 19
Mississippi State 78-64
UCLA 86-67

Oakland, CA March 25
UCLA 102-96

3/16 6 Oregon
11 Texas — Texas 90-73
3/16 3 Maryland
14 Gonzaga — Maryland 87-63 — March 18 Salt Lake City, UT
Maryland 82-68
3/16 7 Cincinatti
10 Temple — Cincinatti 77-71
3/16 2 Connecticut
15 Tenn.-Chatt. — Connecticut 100-71 — March 18
Connecticut 96-61
Connecticut 99-89

1995-96

AT A GLANCE

NCAA Champion: Kentucky (34-2; coached by Rick Pitino; won SEC Eastern Division by seven games with a 16-0 record).

NIT Champion: Nebraska (21-14; coached by Danny Nee; finished in seventh place in the Big Eight with a 4-10 record).

New Conference: Conference USA.

New Rules: All unsportsmanlike technical fouls charged to anyone on the bench count toward the team foul total. . . . Teams are allowed one 20-second timeout per half.

NCAA Probation: Alcorn State, Baylor, Georgia Southern, Morgan State, New Mexico State.

NCAA Consensus First-Team All-Americans: Ray Allen, G-F, Jr., Connecticut; Marcus Camby, C, Jr., Massachusetts; Tony Delk, G, Sr., Kentucky; Tim Duncan, C, Jr., Wake Forest; Allen Iverson, G, Soph., Georgetown; Kerry Kittles, G-F, Sr., Villanova.

National Players of the Year: Camby (20.5 ppg, 8.1 rpg, 3.9 bpg/AP, NABC, Naismith, USBWA, Wooden) and Allen (23.4 ppg, 6.5 rpg, 3.3 apg, 81.0 FT%, 46.6 3FG%).

National Coaches of the Year: Purdue's Gene Keady (26-6; 15-3 in Big Ten/AP, UPI, USBWA) and Massachusetts' John Calipari (35-2; 15-1 in Eastern Division of Atlantic 10/NABC, Naismith).

The Big East became the only conference ever to have three different members represented among the NCAA consensus first-team All-American selections. Second-team All-American John Wallace was the only All-Big East standout to appear with his team at the Final Four, however.

Connecticut became the first Big East team to post the league's undisputed best record in back-to-back seasons. . . . St. John's (11-16) compiled its worst mark in 33 years. . . . Murray State's Marcus Brown (26.4 ppg), Georgetown's Allen Iverson (25), New Hampshire's Matt Alosa (24) and Southeastern Louisiana's Sam Bowie (21.9) set school single-season Division I records for highest scoring average. . . . SLU's Bowie (39

points at Central Florida) and New Hampshire's Brad Cirino (39 at Maine in four overtimes) established school Division I single-game scoring records. UNH's Alosa tied Cirino's mark with 39 against Hartford in the first round of the North Atlantic Conference Tournament. Oddly, Cirino was scoreless in eight minutes of the NAC playoff game. . . . West Virginia's 84-63 defeat against Boston College was the Mountaineers' worst homecourt loss since bowing to Westminster, 102-80, in the 1954-55 season. . . . Coach Lefty Driesell sustained his first losing record in 33 seasons when James Madison went 10-20. Davidson, Driesell's first head coaching outpost, became the first Southern Conference school in 21 years to go undefeated in league competition.

Massachusetts (35-2/coached by John Calipari), Connecticut (32-3/Jim Calhoun), Texas Tech (30-2/James Dickey), New Mexico (28-5/Dave Bliss), Drexel (27-4/Bill Herrion), Villanova (26-7/Steve Lappas), Mississippi State (26-8/Richard Williams), Iowa State (24-9/Tim Floyd), Marist (22-7/Dave Magarity) and Mount St. Mary's (21-8/Jim Phelan) had their winningest seasons in school Division I history. Wake Forest (26-6/Dave Odom) tied its school record for most victories in a single season. . . . Texas Tech became only the fourth team in the 82-year history of the Southwest Conference to go undefeated in league competition.

After the season, Calipari accepted a five-year, $15 million deal to coach the NBA's New Jersey Nets. His departure came just a couple of days after a scandal erupted involving national player of the year Marcus Camby and a Hartford, Conn.-based agent. Camby, who exited UMass to make himself available for the NBA draft, admitted receiving improper gifts in college and filed a criminal complaint stemming from allegations he was blackmailed by a would-be agent attempting to woo him as a client. Calipari was also the subject of controversy for giving three Final Four tickets to a long-time acquaintance who was banned from working in Las Vegas casinos because of an alleged link to an organized crime figure. Fulfilling highly unusual requests, prospective agents made

31 requests for complimentary tickets to 11 regular-season UMass home games.

Massachusetts captured both the regular-season and postseason conference tournament titles for the fifth consecutive year. UMass won its first 26 games before bowing to visiting George Washington, 86-76, when Calipari was banished midway through the first half after receiving two technical fouls. Earlier, GWU finally was able to capitalize on its homecourt advantage against Temple by overwhelming the visiting Owls, 64-47. Temple had won its first 13 games at GWU's Smith Center. . . . Mike Jarvis-coached George Washington (21-8, .724) posted its best winning percentage in 41 years. North Carolina lost three homecourt games for the first time in the same time frame.

Duke still had difficulty in the ACC despite the return of coach Mike Krzyzewski. The Blue Devils' blew double-digit leads in their first six ACC defeats and visiting Illinois hit less than half of its free throws but still ended Duke's 95-game homecourt winning streak against non-conference competition, 75-65. Later, however, the Illini lost its first five Big Ten games for the first time since the 1930-31 season. . . . Georgia Tech, despite entering conference play with six defeats in its previous seven non-league games, captured the ACC regular-season championship after winning a school-record seven consecutive league games. Tech's Stephon Marbury became the first freshman to lead an ACC regular-season kingpin in scoring (18.9 ppg). The Yellow Jackets almost overcame an 18-point, second-half deficit in the ACC Tournament final but bowed to Wake Forest, 75-74. . . . Wake Forest's Tim Duncan set an ACC Tournament record with a total of 56 rebounds.

Alabama's Roy Rogers established a SEC record with an NCAA record-tying 14 blocked shots in a game at Georgia but it wasn't enough to prevent a 68-55 setback against the Bulldogs. . . . Kentucky became the first SEC team in 40 years to go undefeated in league regular-season competition. The Wildcats won all but one of their regular-season SEC games by double digits. It was MSU's first-ever SEC Tournament title. . . .

Arkansas' season unraveled when junior college signees Sunday Adebayo and Jesse Pate were forced off the team late in the year because of questions about their academic eligibility. . . . Mississippi State's program came under scrunity when a suspect student and standout forward Dontae' Jones "earned" 36 junior college credits the previous summer (regular classes and correspondence courses) in order to gain his eligibility. . . . South Carolina coach Eddie Fogler won an NIT game with his third different school in eight years. He previously coached Wichita State and Vanderbilt. . . . Mississippi Valley State's Marcus Mann grabbed a national-high 28 rebounds in a game against Jackson State.

Dayton's Chris Daniels ranked second in the nation in field-goal percentage when he died because of a heart ailment. His brother, Antonio, hit a layup in the closing seconds to give Bowling Green a 72-70 victory over Eastern Michigan in Antonio's first game after his sibling's death. . . . Butler's Mike Pflugner fouled out in just 1:38 of a game against Illinois-Chicago.

Marcus Brown set a Murray State single-game scoring record with 45 points against Washington (Mo.). His barrage tied Vermont guard Eddie Benton (45 vs. Hartford) for highest single-game output in the nation. Benton, 5-11, finished his career with 2,474 points, a total second only to Hall of Famer Calvin Murphy (2,548 points for Niagara) in NCAA Division I history for players under six feet tall. . . . Texas Southern's Kevin Granger posted the lowest nation-leading scoring average (27 ppg) since Villanova's Paul Arizin averaged 25.3 in 1950.

New Mexico State recruited a freshman for a scholarship for the first time in the '90s. . . . Arizona refused to play at St. Joseph's because of a snow storm although Philadelphia's airport did not close. St. Joe's coach Phil Martelli said he was so upset by the Wildcats' decision he would not play them again, even if the teams were paired in the NCAA Tournament. The decision cost the Hawks national exposure on a cable network. . . . Cal Poly-San Luis Obispo made the nation's biggest turnaround (from 1-26 to 16-13). . . . Washington ended a 14-game losing streak in its series with Arizona State.

Central Connecticut's Keith Close set a national record for highest average of blocked shots per game when he rejected 6.4 field-goal attempts per outing. . . . Penn's winning streak against Ivy League competition ended at 48 when the Quakers were edged at Dartmouth, 54-53. . . . Penn State closed out 67 years at Rec Hall in style, getting off to its best start in school history (won first 11 games under first-year coach Jerry Dunn) before opening Bryce Jordan Center.

Wisconsin-Green Bay went undefeated in league play, making the Midwestern Collegiate Conference the first non-divisional alliance in 25 years (Princeton and Penn in the Ivy League in 1969 and 1970, respectively) to have two different schools go undefeated in conference competition in back-to-back seasons. Xavier achieved the feat the previous year. . . . Iowa State, despite losing 95 percent of its scoring and rebounding off the previous season's roster, finished in the Top 20 of a final wire-service poll for the first time in school history. Penn State and Marquette reached that plateau for the first time since 1954 and 1979, respectively. . . . Former Indiana All-American Steve Alford became coach at Southwest Missouri State, where his father, Sam, joined him as an assistant in an unusual twist. . . . Minnesota became the first Big Ten team with a winning league record not to receive an at-large bid to the NCAA Tournament.

Venerable coaches Pete Carril (Princeton), Lou Henson (Illinois) and Jim Phelan (Mount St. Mary's) retired with postseason teams. Another high profile coach, UAB's Gene Bartow, also retired. . . . Western Carolina's musical chairs continued when Phil Hopkins became the Catamounts' sixth head coach in 10 years. Hopkins promptly guided WCU to its first NCAA Tournament appearance.

1996 NCAA Tournament

Summary: Kentucky's air of invincibility dissipated when the Wildcats' 27-game winning

1995-96 FINAL NATIONAL POLLS

AP	UPI	USA/NABC	SCHOOL (RECORD)	HEAD COACH
1	1	2	Massachusetts (35-2)	John Calipari
2	2	1	Kentucky (34-2)	Rick Pitino
3	3	8	Connecticut (32-3)	Jim Calhoun
T4	6	7	Georgetown (29-8)	John Thompson
T4	5	5	Kansas (29-5)	Roy Williams
T4	4	15	Purdue (26-6)	Gene Keady
7	7	6	Cincinnati (28-5)	Bob Huggins
8	8	10	Texas Tech (30-2)	James Dickey
9	9	9	Wake Forest (26-6)	Dave Odom
10	12	17	Villanova (26-7)	Steve Lappas
11	11	11	Arizona (26-7)	Lute Olson
12	10	12	Utah (27-7)	Rick Majerus
13	14	13	Georgia Tech (24-12)	Bobby Cremins
14	13	19	UCLA (23-8)	Jim Harrick
15	15	3	Syracuse (29-9)	Jim Boeheim
16	16	–	Memphis (22-8)	Larry Finch
17	18	20	Iowa State (24-9)	Tim Floyd
18	17	–	Penn State (21-7)	Jerry Dunn
19	22	4	Mississippi St. (26-8)	Richard Williams
20	21	23	Marquette (23-8)	Mike Deane
21	19	22	Iowa (23-9)	Tom Davis
22	20	21	Virginia Tech (23-6)	Bill Foster
23	–	25	New Mexico (28-5)	Dave Bliss
24	23	14	Louisville (22-12)	Denny Crum
25	24	24	North Carolina (21-11)	Dean Smith
–	25	–	Stanford (20-9)	Mike Montgomery
–	–	16	Georgia (21-10)	Tubby Smith
–	–	18	Arkansas (20-13)	Nolan Richardson

streak was shattered by Mississippi State in the SEC Tournament final. UK quickly regrouped, however, and the Big Blue showed clearly in the NCAA playoffs that it was the nation's premier team. Kentucky's dominance in the Midwest Regional led some observers to again believe the Wildcats were untouchable, but two rugged games at the Final Four revealed that the principal difference between the Wildcats and the remainder of the field was roster depth brimming with high school All-Americans. UK, entering the Final Four with an opportunity to become the first NCAA kingpin to win all of its playoff games by at least 20 points, won both Final Four games by a single-digit margin. Massachusetts and Syracuse cut double-digit second-half deficits to two against the 'Cats before faltering as they captured their first NCAA title since 1978. National player of the year Marcus Camby finished with 25 points and eight rebounds in the semifinals for UMass, but at one point he went almost 16 minutes without a field goal to impede its "refuse to lose" motto. Freshman Ron Mercer gave Kentucky a big boost with 20 points in the final after scoring just four points in the regional. The Wildcats won the final despite shooting 38 percent from the floor,

1995–96 INDIVIDUAL LEADERS

SCORING

PLAYER	PTS.	AVG.
Granger, Texas Southern	648	27.0
Brown, Murray St.	767	26.4
B. Wells, Austin Peay	789	26.3
Williams, Hampton	669	25.7
B. Wells, Ball St.	712	25.4
McCollum, W. Caro.	751	25.0
Iverson, Georgetown	926	25.0
Benton, Vermont	636	24.5
Alosa, New Hampshire	624	24.0
Allen, Conn.	818	23.4

REBOUNDING

PLAYER	REB.	AVG.
Mann, Miss. Valley St.	394	13.6
Rose, Drexel	409	13.2
Foyle, Colgate	364	12.6
Duncan, Wake Forest	395	12.3
Farley, Mercer	349	12.0
Ensminger, Valparaiso	368	11.5
DeLaney, Charleston	330	11.4
Tomidy, Marist	329	11.3
Lollis, Montana St.	340	11.3
Snowden, Harvard	289	11.1

ASSISTS

PLAYER	AST.	AVG.
Miglinieks, UC Irvine	230	8.5
McCants, George Mason	223	8.3
Pogue, Campbell	183	8.0
Williams, McNeese St.	200	7.4
Sims, Syracuse	281	7.4
Knight, Stanford	212	7.3
Turner, UC Santa Barbara	190	7.3
Geary, Arizona	231	7.0
Fizdale, San Diego	195	7.0
Hutchins, Marquette	215	6.9

BLOCKED SHOTS

PLAYER	BLK.	AVG.
Closs, Central Conn.	178	6.4
Foyle, Colgate	165	5.7
Rogers, Alabama	156	4.9
James, Florida A&M	119	4.4
Tomidy, Marist	113	3.9
Aluma, Liberty	113	3.9
Camby, Mass.	128	3.9
Duncan, Wake Forest	120	3.8

STEALS

PLAYER	STL.	AVG.
Williams, McNeese St.	118	4.4
Rhodes, Maryland	110	3.7
Taylor, Jackson St.	106	3.7
Salahuddin, Long Beach St.	101	3.6
Hoard, NE Ill.	97	3.6

FIELD-GOAL PERCENTAGE

PLAYER	FGM	FGA	PCT.
Lollis, Montana St.	212	314	.675
Watts, Nevada	145	221	.656
Abrams, Centenary	187	286	.654
Koul, George Wash.	163	254	.642
Mott, Coppin St.	208	326	.638
Jamison, North Caro.	201	322	.624
Caldwell, Tennessee St.	110	178	.618
Smith, Delaware	173	282	.613
Mann, Miss. Valley St.	251	415	.605
Fincher, Eastern Ky.	148	245	.604
Potapenko, Wright St.	198	328	.604

FREE-THROW PERCENTAGE

PLAYER	FTM	FTA	PCT.
Dillard, Sam Houston St.	63	68	.926
Cross, Stanford	81	88	.920
Howard, UNCC	93	103	.903
Billet, Rutgers	72	80	.900
Nash, Santa Clara	101	113	.894
Grimm, Missouri	100	113	.885
Wilson, Evansville	75	85	.882
Carter, Middle Tenn. St.	104	118	.881
Simms, UMBC	74	84	.881
Alexander, Stetson	123	140	.879

THREE-POINT FIELD GOAL PERCENTAGE

PLAYER	FGM	FGA	PCT.
Stafford,. W. Caro.	58	110	.527
Peral, Wake Forest	51	100	.510
Tebbs, Weber St.	50	100	.500
Brown, Central Mich.	51	104	.490
Fontaine, Wash. St.	66	136	.485

THREE-POINT FIELD GOALS PER GAME

PLAYER	FGM	AVG.
Young, Fresno St.	120	4.1
McLinton, James Madison	122	4.1
Veney, Marshall	111	4.0
Marshall, Northeast La.	115	3.8
Hudson, Southern Illinois	93	3.7
Lueking, Army	99	3.7

the lowest for a winner in 33 years. Kentucky's Tony Delk tied a championship game record with seven three-pointers. In historical terms, there is probably only one other titlist that had as much depth as UK. Seven players for UCLA's first championship team in 1964 averaged more than four rebounds per game.

Outcome for Defending Champion: UCLA led the nation in field-goal accuracy and won the Pacific-10 championship, but the Bruins committed a conference-worst 554 turnovers and were eliminated in the first round of the NCAA Tournament when Princeton coach Pete Carril bowed out in style with a 43-41 victory reminiscent of how many games were played several decades ago. It was UCLA's lowest-scoring output in 99 playoff outings, and the lowest score for a Bruins team in a regulation game in more than 55 years.

Star Gazing: Coach Jim Boeheim of runner-up Syracuse gave counterpart Rick Pitino of champion Kentucky Pitino's first full-time coaching job in 1976, when Boeheim was promoted to bench boss by the Orangemen. Boeheim came to New York and called Pitino on Pitino's wedding day, offering him an assistant's job, and was so persistent Pitino eventually met with him for 2 1/2 hours at a hotel right after the wedding. "I kept calling my wife every half-hour, telling her I'd be up (to the room)," Pitino recalled.

Biggest Upsets: The biggest upset in the tourney might not have been Princeton over UCLA. It could have been Drexel over Memphis, 75-63. Drexel had an outstanding run the last three seasons, but Memphis had as much talent as any team in the country. . . . Western Carolina missed a three-point shot at the buzzer that would have

1995–96 TEAM LEADERS

SCORING OFFENSE

SCHOOL	PTS.	AVG.
Troy State	2551	94.5
Kentucky	3292	91.4
Marshall	2560	91.4
George Mason	2443	90.5
Southern (La.)	2521	90.0

SCORING DEFENSE

SCHOOL	PTS.	AVG.
Princeton	1498	51.7
Wis.-Green Bay	1620	55.9
South Alabama	1571	58.2
Temple	1922	58.2
N.C.-Wilmington	1694	58.4

SCORING MARGIN

SCHOOL	OFF.	DEF.	MAR.
Kentucky	91.4	69.4	22.1
Connecticut	82.6	64.7	17.9
Drexel	82.6	66.3	16.3
Davidson	84.3	68.2	16.0
Kansas	80.6	65.3	15.4

WON-LOST PERCENTAGE

SCHOOL	W-L	PCT.
Massachusetts	35-2	.946
Kentucky	34-2	.944
Texas Tech	30-2	.938
Connecticut	32-3	.914
Drexel	27-4	.871

FIELD-GOAL PERCENTAGE

SCHOOL	FGM	FGA	PCT.
UCLA	897	1698	.528
Colorado St.	851	1683	.506
Coppin St.	828	1650	.502
Montana St.	898	1800	.499
Weber St.	880	1766	.498

FIELD-GOAL PERCENTAGE DEFENSE

SCHOOL	FGM	FGA	PCT.
Temple	670	1741	.385
Marquette	682	1772	.385
Mississippi St.	803	2084	.385
Connecticut	840	2175	.386
Kansas	777	2008	.387
Massachusetts	812	2098	.387

FREE-THROW PERCENTAGE

SCHOOL	FTM	FTA	PCT.
Utah	649	828	.784
Weber St.	519	675	.769
Brigham Young	587	767	.765
Stanford	558	736	.758
Va. Military	469	623	.753

REBOUND MARGIN

SCHOOL	OWN	OPP.	MAR.
Miss. Valley	48.3	36.8	11.6
Utah St.	39.5	29.5	10.0
Utah	39.6	30.0	9.6
Iowa	40.5	31.4	9.1
Connecticut	43.4	34.4	9.0

THREE-POINT FIELD GOAL PERCENTAGE

SCHOOL	FGM	FGA	PCT.
Weber St.	245	577	.425
Wake Forest	260	618	.421
Penn St.	197	482	.409
Connecticut	258	633	.408
N.C.-Greensboro	205	503	.406

THREE-POINT FIELD GOALS PER GAME

SCHOOL	FGM	AVG.
Troy St.	300	11.1
Marshall	284	10.1
N.C. St.	292	9.4
Southern Ill.	268	9.2
Stanford	243	9.0
Southern (La.)	252	9.0
Auburn	287	9.0

beaten Purdue and made the Catamounts the first No. 16 seed winner in tourney history.

One and Only: First-year Georgia mentor Tubby Smith became the only coach to guide three consecutive teams to regional semifinals despite not being accorded a top four seed during the span. His two previous clubs were at Tulsa.

Numbers Game: Kentucky was a 13 1/2-point favorite in the NCAA final against Syracuse. That is the largest championship game spread since UCLA was a 16-point choice vs. Florida State in 1972 (Bruins won 81-76). . . . UK joined Indiana as the only schools to capture NCAA Tournament crowns in four different decades. The Wildcats were the first NCAA champion since Louisville in 1980 to go unbeaten in conference regular-season competition. . . . The NCAA succumbed to network pressure and moved the title game to 9:22 p.m. ET, but CBS' 18.3 rating for the championship contest was the lowest since 1972. .

. . Central Florida became the second consecutive Trans America Athletic Conference team to enter the NCAA playoffs with an 11-18 record after earning a berth by winning the TAAC Tournament. . . . Canisius made its first appearance in the tourney since 1957. . . . When will the Southeastern Conference receive the respect it deserves? The SEC, boasting two teams at the Final Four for the second time in three years, compiled more NCAA Tournament victories than any league over the last three seasons. . . . The Big Ten came within eight points of going 0-11 in the NCAA playoffs the last two seasons. . . . The last four defeats for Indiana coach Bob Knight were to worse-seeded opponents. . . . Michigan's lack of maturity was exemplified when the Wolverines were assessed a technical for calling yet another timeout in the closing seconds of a playoff game while being out of timeouts. They apparently weren't making a vow to avoid Chris Webber's blunder when several of their standouts had their infamous auto accident

1996 FINAL FOUR CHAMPIONSHIP GAME

SEASON STATISTICS FOR KENTUCKY REGULARS

PLAYER	POS.	CL	G.	FG%	FT%	PPG	RPG
Tony Delk	G	Sr.	36	.494	.800	17.8	4.2
Antoine Walker	F	So.	36	.463	.631	15.2	8.4
Walter McCarty	F-C	Sr.	36	.543	.721	11.3	5.7
Derek Anderson	G-F	Jr.	36	.509	.784	9.4	3.4
Ron Mercer	G-F	Fr.	36	.457	.785	8.0	2.9
Mark Pope	C	Sr.	36	.482	.683	7.6	5.2
Anthony Epps	G	Jr.	36	.438	.817	6.7	3.1
Jeff Sheppard	G	Jr.	34	.520	.621	5.5	2.1
Wayne Turner	G	Fr.	35	.533	.625	4.5	1.5
Allen Edwards	G	So.	35	.463	.739	3.3	1.1
Nazr Mohammed	C	Fr.	16	.448	.458	2.3	1.5
Oliver Simmons	F	Fr.	21	.481	.556	1.8	1.1
TEAM TOTALS			33	.513	.709	87.5	40.4

Three-point field goals leaders: Delk (93 of 210, .443), Epps (43 of 105, .410). **Assists leaders:** Epps 175, Walker 104, McCarty 92, Anderson 88. **Blocked shots leader:** McCarty 51, Pope 44. **Steals leaders:** Delk 67, Anderson 61, Walker 61, Epps 55.

EAST RUTHERFORD, NJ

SYRACUSE (67)	MIN.	FG-A	FT-A	REB.	A.	PF.	PTS.
Burgan	39	7-10	2-5	8	1	5	19
Wallace	38	11-19	5-5	10	1	5	29
Hill	28	3-9	1-1	10	1	2	7
Sims	38	2-5	1-2	2	7	2	6
Cipolla	35	3-8	0-0	1	2	1	6
Reafsnyder	13	0-1	0-0	4	0	0	0
Janulis	8	0-0	0-0	2	0	2	0
Nelson	1	0-0	0-0	0	0	0	0
Team	1						
TOTALS	200	26-52	9-13	37	12	17	67

FG%: .500. **FT%:** .692. **Three-point goals:** 6-15 (Burgan 3-5, Wallace 2-3, Sims 1-4, Cipolla 0-3). **Blocks:** 2. **Turnovers:** 24 (Sims 7, Wallace 6, Burgan 5). **Steals:** 6 (Cipolla 4).

KENTUCKY (76)	MIN.	FG-A	FT-A	REB.	A.	PF.	PTS.
Anderson	16	4-8	1-1	4	1	2	11
Walker	32	4-12	3-6	9	4	2	11
McCarty	19	2-6	0-0	7	3	3	4
Delk	37	8-20	1-2	7	2	2	24
Epps	35	0-6	0-0	4	7	1	0
Pope	27	1-6	2-2	3	2	3	4
Mercer	24	8-12	1-1	2	2	3	20
Sheppard	7	1-2	0-1	2	0	3	2
Edwards	3	0-1	0-0	0	1	0	0
Team	2						
TOTALS	200	28-73	8-13	38	22	19	76

FG%: .384. **FT%:** .615. **Three-point goals:** 12-27 (Delk 7-12, Mercer 3-4, Anderson 2-3, Walker 0-1, Sheppard 0-1, Edwards 0-1, Pope 0-2, Epps 0-3). **Blocks:** 1. **Turnovers:** 15 (Pope 4). **Steals:** 11 (Walker 4).
Halftime: Kentucky 42-33.

NATIONAL SEMIFINALS

MISSISSIPPI STATE (69): Walters 5-9 0-0 10, Jones 6-16 2-2 16, Dampier 4-6 4-4 12, Bullard 4-9 0-0 11, Wilson 7-16 0-0 20, Hughes 0-0 0-0 0, Washington 0-0 0-0 0, Hyche 0-0 0-0 0. Team 26-56 (.464) 6-6 (1.000) 69.

SYRACUSE (77): Burgan 6-11 5-6 19, Wallace 6-14 8-10 21, Hill 7-11 1-2 15, Sims 3-5 4-4 11, Cipolla 3-9 2-2 9, Reafsnyder 1-3 0-0 2, Janulis 0-2 0-0 0. Team 26-55 (.473) 20-24 (.833) 77.

Three-point goals: Mississippi State 11-28 (.393). Syracuse 5-12 (.417).
Halftime: Tied 36-36.

KENTUCKY (81): Walker 5-10 4-5 14, McCarty 4-8 0-0 8, Delk 7-16 5-9 20, Epps 3-6 0-0 7, Pope 1-2 6-6 8, Sheppard 2-2 3-4 7, Turner 1-2 0-0 2, Mercer 4-6 0-1 9, Edwards 0-0 0-0 0. Team 28-55 (.509) 22-30 (.733) 81.

MASSACHUSETTS (74): Dingle 4-6 0-0 8, Bright 7-14 1-2 15, Camby 9-18 7-9 25, E. Padilla 2-10 1-2 6, Travieso 3-7 2-2 10, Weeks 0-2 1-2 s1, Clarke 1-2 1-2 3, Norville 1-1 0-0 2, Nunez 0-0 0-0 0, G. Padilla 2-4 0-0 4. Team 29-64 (.453) 13-19 (.684) 74.

Three-point goals: Kentucky 3-9 (.333). Massachusetts 3-9 (.333).
Halftime: Kentucky 36-28.

ALL-TOURNAMENT TEAM

Todd Burgan, G-F, Soph., Syracuse (38 points, 15 rebounds)
Marcus Camby, C, Jr., Massachusetts (25 points, eight rebounds in one game)
*Tony Delk, G, Sr., Kentucky (44 points, nine rebounds, eight three-pointers)
Ron Mercer, F-G, Fr., Kentucky (29 points)
John Wallace, F, Sr., Syracuse (50 points, 14 rebounds)

*Named Most Outstanding Player.

at 5 a.m. earlier in the season. . . . Texas Tech, after posting the Red Raiders' first NCAA playoff victories in 20 years, had as many players foul out in their 98-90 loss to Georgetown in the East Regional semifinals (three) as they totaled in their first 34 games. . . . None of the first six NCAA champions in the '90s reached a regional final. . . . Eastern Michigan's Brian Tolbert tallied a tourney-high 36 points in a second-round setback against Connecticut in the Southeast Regional. . . . Montana State's Quadre Lollis hit 12 of 13 field-goal attempts in an opening-round loss to Syracuse in the West Regional. . . . Portland, coached by Rob Chavez, participated in the NCAA playoffs for the first time since 1959. . . . The last five times Kentucky won the NCAA crown, the New

York Yankees captured the ensuing major league baseball World Series. UK's first of six titles came in 1948 when the Cleveland Indians claimed the World Series. But since then, the Wildcats won NCAA championships in 1949, 1951, 1958, 1978 and 1996, all followed by Yankee successes.

What Might Have Been: Arkansas (20-13/without Corliss Williamson and Scotty Thurman), Maryland (17-13/Joe Smith), Memphis (22-8/David Vaughn) and North Carolina (21-11/Jerry Stackhouse and Rasheed Wallace) might have fared better in the playoffs if standout players had exercised their remaining eligibility instead of declaring early for the NBA draft. . . . Alabama probably would have participated in the NCAA

1996 CHAMPIONSHIP BRACKET

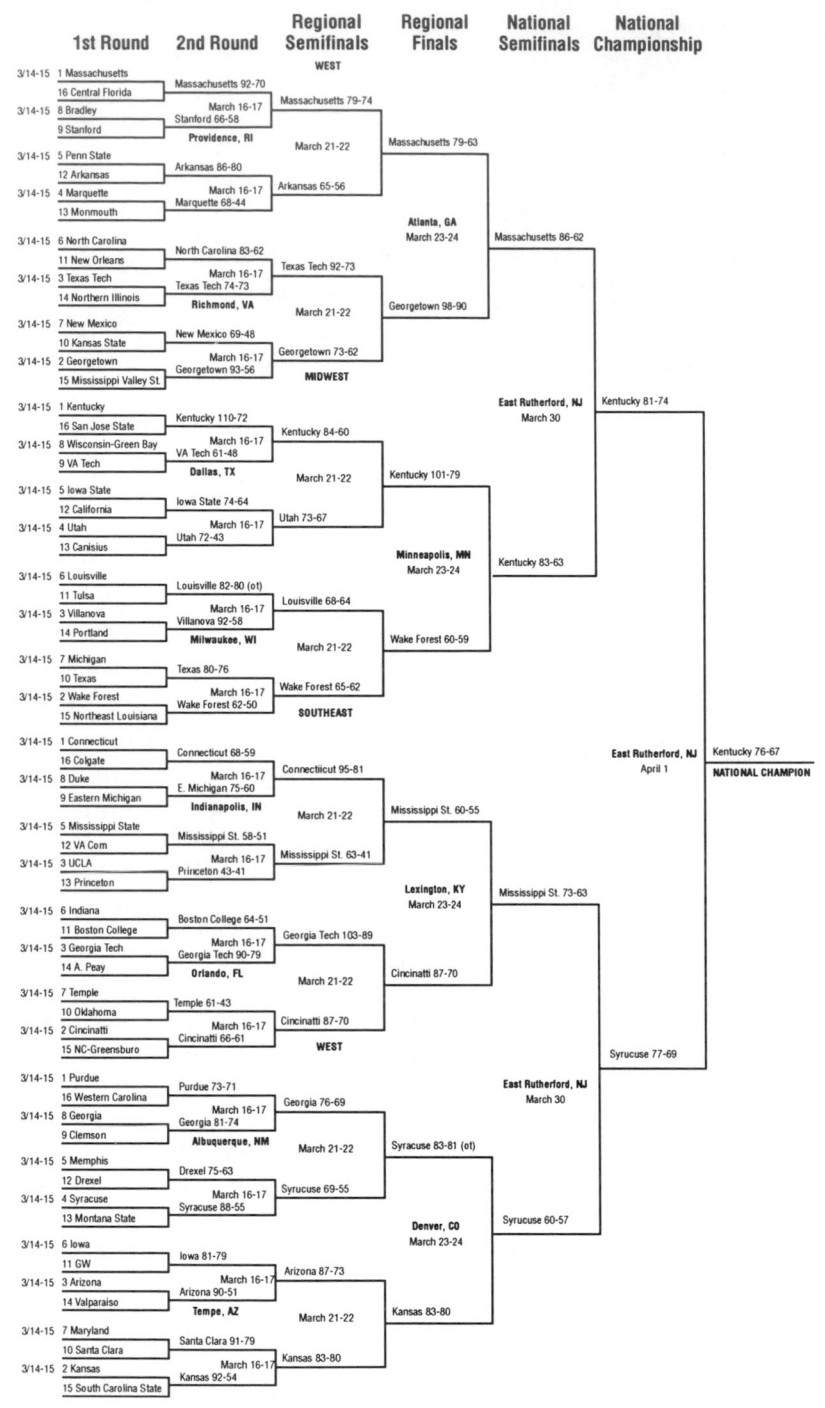

	Regional Semifinals	Regional Finals	National Semifinals	National Championship
1st Round	2nd Round			

WEST

3/14-15 1 Massachusetts
16 Central Florida — Massachusetts 92-70
3/14-15 8 Bradley — March 16-17 Stanford 66-58
9 Stanford — **Providence, RI**
— Massachusetts 79-74
3/14-15 5 Penn State
12 Arkansas — Arkansas 86-80
3/14-15 4 Marquette — March 16-17 Marquette 68-44
13 Monmouth — Arkansas 65-56
— March 21-22 Massachusetts 79-63

3/14-15 6 North Carolina
11 New Orleans — North Carolina 83-62
3/14-15 3 Texas Tech — March 16-17 Texas Tech 74-73
14 Northern Illinois — **Richmond, VA**
— Texas Tech 92-73
3/14-15 7 New Mexico
10 Kansas State — New Mexico 69-48
3/14-15 2 Georgetown — March 16-17 Georgetown 93-56
15 Mississippi Valley St. — Georgetown 73-62
— March 21-22 Georgetown 98-90

Atlanta, GA March 23-24 — Massachusetts 86-62

MIDWEST

3/14-15 1 Kentucky
16 San Jose State — Kentucky 110-72
3/14-15 8 Wisconsin-Green Bay — March 16-17 VA Tech 61-48
9 VA Tech — **Dallas, TX**
— Kentucky 84-60
3/14-15 5 Iowa State
12 California — Iowa State 74-64
3/14-15 4 Utah — March 16-17 Utah 72-43
13 Canisius — Utah 73-67
— March 21-22 Kentucky 101-79

3/14-15 6 Louisville
11 Tulsa — Louisville 82-80 (ot)
3/14-15 3 Villanova — March 16-17 Villanova 92-58
14 Portland — **Milwaukee, WI**
— Louisville 68-64
3/14-15 7 Michigan
10 Texas — Texas 80-76
3/14-15 2 Wake Forest — March 16-17 Wake Forest 62-50
15 Northeast Louisiana — Wake Forest 65-62
— March 21-22 Wake Forest 60-59

Minneapolis, MN March 23-24 — Kentucky 83-63

East Rutherford, NJ March 30 — Kentucky 81-74

SOUTHEAST

3/14-15 1 Connecticut
16 Colgate — Connecticut 68-59
3/14-15 8 Duke — March 16-17 E. Michigan 75-60
9 Eastern Michigan — **Indianapolis, IN**
— Connecticut 95-81
3/14-15 5 Mississippi State
12 VA Com — Mississippi St. 58-51
3/14-15 3 UCLA — March 16-17 Princeton 43-41
13 Princeton — Mississippi St. 63-41
— March 21-22 Mississippi St. 60-55

3/14-15 6 Indiana
11 Boston College — Boston College 64-51
3/14-15 3 Georgia Tech — March 16-17 Georgia Tech 90-79
14 A. Peay — **Orlando, FL**
— Georgia Tech 103-89
3/14-15 7 Temple
10 Oklahoma — Temple 61-43
3/14-15 2 Cincinnati — March 16-17 Cincinnati 66-61
15 NC-Greensboro — Cincinnati 87-70
— March 21-22 Cincinnati 87-70

Lexington, KY March 23-24 — Mississippi St. 73-63

East Rutherford, NJ April 1 — Kentucky 76-67 **NATIONAL CHAMPION**

East Rutherford, NJ March 30 — Syracuse 77-69

WEST

3/14-15 1 Purdue
16 Western Carolina — Purdue 73-71
3/14-15 8 Georgia — March 16-17 Georgia 81-74
9 Clemson — **Albuquerque, NM**
— Georgia 76-69
3/14-15 5 Memphis
12 Drexel — Drexel 75-63
3/14-15 4 Syracuse — March 16-17 Syracuse 88-55
13 Montana State — Syracuse 69-55
— March 21-22 Syracuse 83-81 (ot)

3/14-15 6 Iowa
11 GW — Iowa 81-79
3/14-15 3 Arizona — March 16-17 Arizona 90-51
14 Valparaiso — **Tempe, AZ**
— Arizona 87-73
3/14-15 7 Maryland
10 Santa Clara — Santa Clara 91-79
3/14-15 2 Kansas — March 16-17 Kansas 92-54
15 South Carolina State — Kansas 83-80
— March 21-22 Kansas 83-80

Denver, CO March 23-24 — Syracuse 60-57

After the end of the 1996 season, Calipari accepted a $15 million deal to coach the NBA's New Jersey Nets.

Tournament instead of the NIT if Antonio McDyess didn't defect early for the NBA. Ditto Rhode Island if starting guard Cuttino Mobley didn't miss the season because of an elbow injury. . . . Wake Forest struggled in the tourney when guard Tony Rutland missed his first 15 shots in NCAA playoff play. Rutland eventually underwent reconstructive surgery on his right knee after tearing a ligament in the ACC Tournament title game. . . . UConn's chances of earning its first berth at the Final Four diminished when standout freshman guard Ricky Moore was idled by a shoulder injury. . . . Center Tim Young was out with a bulging disk in his lower back for Stanford, which trailed by just one point in the closing seconds vs. top-ranked UMass. . . . Virginia might have avoided becoming one of the nation's most underachieving teams if guard Cory Alexander hadn't left early for the NBA. . . . Clemson (with-

out Iker Iturbe/shoulder problem) and Penn State (Rahsaan Carlton/knee injury) might have avoided opening-round tourney losses if key forwards didn't sit out the season as medical redshirts. Both players had been starters for 1995 NIT participants. Clemson was also without starting guard Merl Code because of a knee injury.

Putting Things in Perspective: Syracuse finished national runner-up despite losing six times in a nine-game midseason stretch.

Scoring Leader: John Wallace, Syracuse (128 points, 21.3 ppg).

Highest Scoring Average: Allen Iverson, Georgetown (111 points, 27.8 ppg).

Rebounding Leader: Todd Burgan, Syracuse (51 rebounds, 8.5 rpg).

Highest Rebounding Average: Tim Duncan, Wake Forest (39 rebounds, 13 rpg).

1996-97

AT A GLANCE

NCAA Champion: Arizona (25-9; coached by Lute Olson; finished in fifth place in the Pacific-10 with an 11-7 record).

NIT Champion: Michigan (24-11; coached by Steve Fisher; finished in a tie for sixth place in the Big Ten with a 9-9 record).

New Conference: Big 12.

New Rules: Teams warm up and shoot at the end of the court farthest from their own bench for the first half. Previously, the road team had the choice of baskets in the first half. . . . In games not involving commercial electronic media, teams are entitled to four full-length timeouts and two 20-second timeouts per game. In games involving commercial electronic media, teams are entitled to two full-length timeouts and three 20-second timeouts per game.

NCAA Consensus First-Team All-Americans: Tim Duncan, C, Sr., Wake Forest; Danny Fortson, F, Jr., Cincinnati; Raef LaFrentz, F, Jr., Kansas; Ron Mercer, F, Soph., Kentucky; Keith Van Horn, F, Sr., Utah.

National Player of the Year: Duncan (20.8 ppg, 14.7 rpg, 3.2 apg, 3.3 bpg, 60.8 FG%/AP, Naismith, USBWA, Wooden).

National Coach of the Year: Minnesota's Clem Haskins (31-4/AP, NABC, Naismith, USBWA).

The playoff storyline was a good one with an overtime final, but the aesthetics of Arizona's NCAA title underscored a serious erosion of college basketball teams tending to fundamentals. The Wildcats became the first champion since the national tourney went to four regionals in 1956 to shoot less than 40 percent from the floor in both the national semifinals and final. The national numbers weren't pretty either as teams across the country combined to hit 43.5 percent of their field-goal attempts, continuing a decline from an all-time high of 48.1 percent in 1983-84.

It wasn't a good year for some long-time coaches either. UCLA fired coach Jim Harrick two weeks before the season started for what the university described as unethical conduct. Harrick, who won more than 20 games each of his eight seasons with the Bruins, was accused by administrators of breaking a relatively minor NCAA rule, then filing a false expense report and repeatedly lying during an in-house investigation. UCLA incurred its most lopsided defeat in history when the Bruins bowed to Stanford, 109-61, before rebounding to capture the Pacific-10 Conference championship by three games under new coach Steve Lavin.

In another bizarre dismissal, Ralph Underhill was fired by Wright State after the school's all-time winningest coach was arrested for shoplifting five bottles of vitamins. . . . Roger Reid, Brigham Young's winningest coach by percentage since 1925 (152-77, .664), was given an early-season pink slip despite winning more than 20 games each of his first six campaigns with the Cougars from 1989-90 through 1994-95. BYU got off to a slow start after the previous year's scoring leader, Bryon Ruffner, quit school and pleaded guilty to theft in bilking a local computer company. . . . . Joey Meyer was forced out as coach at DePaul after combining with his father, Ray, to win 955 games for the Blue Demons since 1942-43.

Kentucky's Rick Pitino departed of his own volition after the season to return to the NBA. Pitino averaged 30 victories annually his last six years with the Wildcats. . . . Dale Brown, who defeated Kentucky more than any coach in history, stepped down after 25 years at LSU. Brown finished his career with a 448-301 record after averaging only 11 victories annually his last four seasons with the Tigers. . . . Virginia Tech's Bill Foster retired with a 532-325 career record. Previous major-college stops for him during his 30-year career included UNC Charlotte, Clemson and Miami (Fla.).

Helping rebuild his image and LIU's program was freshman forward Richie Parker, a Manhattan product who had a number of prominent programs withdraw scholarship offers to him amid criticism stemming from his being charged with first-degree sodomy in high school. Despite a two-year layoff, Parker averaged more than 15 points and seven rebounds per game on his way to becoming Northeast Conference newcomer of the Year and helping the Blackbirds beat intra-city rival St. John's and win the league's regular-season championship.

Forwards Danny Fortson of Cincinnati and Keith Van Horn of Utah became their schools' first NCAA consensus first-team All-Americans since 1963 and 1962, respectively. . . . St. Joseph's and South Carolina finished in the Top 20 of a final AP poll for the first time in 31 and 23 years, respectively. . . . South Carolina lost non-league home games to UNC Asheville and Charleston Southern before the Gamecocks won all but one of their first 16 Southeastern Conference regular-season assignments. Their victories included a 68-66 win at Kentucky, snapping the Wildcats' streak of winning on Senior Day at 32. . . . Mississippi also defeated Kentucky to help Ole Miss earn its first national ranking in school history. The Rebels went on to capture their first regular-season championship in 65 years as a member of the SEC and their first 20-win season in 59 years.

Cincinnati, the consensus preseason No. 1 pick, was upset in its second game of the season by

SCORING

PLAYER	PTS.	AVG.
Charles Jones, Long Island	903	30.1
Ed Gray, California	644	24.8
Adonal Foyle, Colgate	682	24.4
Raymond Tutt, UC Santa Barbara	649	24.0
Antonio Daniels, Bowling Green	767	24.0
Donnie Carr, La Salle	646	23.9
Olivier Saint-Jean, San Jose State	619	23.8
James Cotton, Long Beach State	634	23.5
Roderick Blakney, S.C. State	655	23.4
Cory Carr, Texas Tech	646	23.1
Victor Page, Georgetown	682	22.7
Randy Bolden, Texas Southern	626	22.4
Kenderick Franklin, Nicholls St.	574	22.1
Keith Van Horn, Utah	705	22.0
Bonzi Wells, Ball State	637	22.0
Isaac Fontaine, Washington State	657	21.9
Vincent Rainey, Murray State	656	21.9
Reggie Freeman, Texas	654	21.8
Danny Fortson, Cincinnati	703	21.3
Greg Smith, Delaware	660	21.3

REBOUNDING

PLAYER	REB.	AVG.
Tim Duncan, Wake Forest	457	14.7
Adonal Foyle, Colgate	368	13.1
Lorenzo Coleman, Tenn. Tech	333	11.9
Tony Battie, Texas Tech	329	11.8
Muntrelle Dobbins, UALR	320	11.4
Eric Taylor, St. Francis (Pa.)	306	11.3
Kory Billups, Chicago State	304	11.3
Nate Huffman, Central Michigan	287	11.0
Greg Smith, Delaware	342	11.0
H.L. Coleman, Wyoming	303	10.8

ASSISTS

PLAYER	AST.	AVG.
Kenny Mitchell, Dartmouth	203	7.8
Brevin Knight, Stanford	234	7.8
Kareem Gilbert, Tenn. State	191	7.6
Jamar Smiley, Illinois State	219	7.3
Chad Peckinpaugh, Eastern Ill.	196	7.3
Anthony Johnson, Charleston	229	7.2
Chad Townsend, Murray State	212	7.1
Ed Cota, North Carolina	234	6.9
Ali Ton, Davidson	190	6.8
Antonio Daniels, Bowling Green	216	6.8

BLOCKED SHOTS

PLAYER	BLK.	AVG.
Adonal Foyle, Colgate	180	6.4
Lorenzo Coleman, Tenn. Tech	134	4.8
Richard Lugo, St. Francis (N.Y.)	125	4.5
Jerome James, Florida A&M	119	4.4
Kelvin Cato, Iowa State	118	4.2
Rodger Farrington, Arizona State	113	4.2
Keon Clark, UNLV	112	3.9
Calvin Booth, Penn State	92	3.4
Erik Nelson, Vermont	73	3.3
Tim Duncan, Wake Forest	102	3.3

STEALS

PLAYER	STL.	AVG.
Joel Hoover, Md.-Eastern Shore	90	3.2
Philip Huyler, Florida Atlantic	86	3.2
Kellii Taylor, Pittsburgh	101	3.2
Moe Segar, St. Peter's	87	3.1
Mustafa Barksdale, Monmouth	81	3.0
Nate Langley, George Mason	80	3.0
Mike Campbell, Long Island	88	2.9
Jason Hart, Syracuse	90	2.8
Shawnta Rogers, George Washington	81	2.8
Juan Sanchez, Temple	86	2.8
Brevin Knight, Stanford	83	2.8
Earl McClellan, Oral Roberts	77	2.8
Shaheen Holloway, Seton Hall	77	2.8

FIELD-GOAL PERCENTAGE

PLAYER	FGM	FGA	PCT.
Todd MacCulloch, Washington	163	241	.676
Sean Scott, Central Conn. St.	128	191	.670
Rosell Ellis, McNeese St.	213	319	.668
Ed Sears, Ohio Univ.	156	241	.647
Lorenzo Coleman, Tenn. Tech	198	307	.645
Chianti Roberts, Oklahoma St.	178	285	.625
Danny Fortson, Cincinnati	243	392	.620
Evan Eschmeyer, Northwestern	147	240	.613
Greg Smith, Delaware	241	396	.609
Tim Duncan, Wake Forest	234	385	.608

FREE-THROW PERCENTAGE

PLAYER	FTM	FTA	PCT.
Aaron Zobrist, Bradley	77	85	.906
Keith Van Horn, Utah	151	167	.904
Jim Williamson, Loyola Marymount	110	122	.902
Marcus Wilson, Evansville	91	101	.901
Trajan Langdon, Duke	113	126	.897
Austin Croshere, Providence	182	205	.888
Scott Gooden, Akron	63	71	.887
M.J. Nodilo, San Francisco	85	96	.885
Bryce Drew, Valparaiso	131	149	.879
Shawnta Rogers, George Wash.	93	106	.877

THREE-POINT FIELD GOAL PERCENTAGE

PLAYER	FGM	FGA	PCT.
Kent McCausland, Iowa	70	134	.522
Bill Slack, Central Michigan	49	96	.510
Ross Land, Northern Arizona	64	126	.508
Marcus Carreno, Fla. International	52	104	.500
Danny Sprinkle, Montana State	61	125	.488
Patrick Lee, Va. Commonwealth	62	130	.477
Corey Reed, Radford	78	164	.476
D.J. Bosse, Kent	86	181	.475
Louis Bullock, Michigan	101	214	.472
Andrew Mavis, Northern Arizona	82	174	.471
Tony Daughtry, UNC Greensboro	64	136	.471

THREE-POINT FIELD GOALS PER GAME

PLAYER	FGM	AVG.
William Fourche, Southern	122	4.5
Keith Veney, Marshall	130	4.5
Troy Hudson, Southern Illinois	134	4.5
Dedric Willoughby, Iowa State	102	3.8
Tom Pipkins, Duquesne	99	3.7
Donnie Carr, La Salle	99	3.7
Charles Jones, Long Island	109	3.6
Nate Erdmann, Oklahoma	105	3.5
John Knox, Jacksonville	98	3.5
Mark Heidersbach, NE Illinois	95	3.4
Cory Carr, Texas Tech	94	3.4

intra-city rival Xavier. It didn't get any better soon thereafter for the Bearcats, who had seven different players suspended or sanctioned at some point during the season. They blew a 16-point lead in a loss to Kansas. . . . Kansas also overcame a 16-point deficit in a victory at Connecticut to halt the Huskies' homecourt winning streak against non-conference competition at 45. Kansas also overcame a 14-point deficit in a triumph at Texas Tech. The Jayhawks' excelled despite stints when Jacque Vaughn (torn ligaments in his right wrist) and Scot Pollard (stress fracture in his left foot) were sidelined with injuries. Another senior starter, Jerod Haase, played much of the season with a broken right wrist. . . . Connecticut struggled after its top two scorers—senior Kirk King and sophomore Ricky Moore—were suspended for receiving improper airline tickets from an agent. . . . St. John's (13-14) had four consecutive non-winning records for the first time in school history.

Villanova's Tim Thomas, one of the nation's premier freshmen, scored a game-high 29 points in his first Big East game, a 75-64 victory over Providence. He declared for the NBA draft after the season. . . . Miami won at Georgetown and

1996–97 TEAM LEADERS

SCORING OFFENSE

SCHOOL	PTS.	AVG.
Long Island	2746	91.5
Kansas	3058	84.9
Arizona	2850	83.8
Texas Christian	2931	83.7
Miss. Valley St.	2413	83.2
Xavier	2413	83.2

SCORING DEFENSE

SCHOOL	PTS.	AVG.
Princeton	1496	53.4
Wis.-Green Bay	1515	54.1
N.C. State	1749	54.72
Wisconsin	1548	55.3
South Alabama	1699	56.6

SCORING MARGIN

SCHOOL	OFF.	DEF.	MAR.
Kentucky	83.1	62.8	20.3
Kansas	84.9	66.1	18.8
Cincinnati	80.7	65.5	15.2
Minnesota	78.3	63.4	14.9
Duke	79.7	66.2	13.5

WON-LOST PERCENTAGE

SCHOOL	W-L	PCT.
Kansas	34-2	.944
Charleston	29-3	.906
Minnesota	31-4	.886
Utah	29-4	.879
Kentucky	35-5	.875

FIELD-GOAL PERCENTAGE

SCHOOL	FGM	FGA	PCT.
UCLA	932	1791	.520
Northern Arizona	763	1478	.516
Princeton	631	1262	.500
Cincinnati	962	1938	.496
Utah	886	1785	.496

FIELD-GOAL PERCENTAGE DEFENSE

SCHOOL	FGM	FGA	PCT.
Marquette	628	1735	.362
Wake Forest	667	1832	.364
Wis.-Green Bay	499	1368	.365
Wisconsin	502	1329	.378
Georgetown	659	1740	.379

FREE-THROW PERCENTAGE

SCHOOL	FTM	FTA	PCT.
Western Kentucky	342	433	.790
Indiana	674	880	.766
Missouri	583	769	.758
Harvard	388	516	.752

REBOUND MARGIN

SCHOOL	OWN	OPP.	MAR.
Utah State	37.4	26.6	10.9
Kansas	42.6	32.2	10.4
Iowa	38.5	28.7	9.8
North Carolina	41.6	32.2	9.4
Cincinnati	39.9	30.6	9.3

THREE-POINT FIELD GOAL PERCENTAGE

SCHOOL	FGM	FGA	PCT.
Northern Arizona	221	527	.419
Texas Tech	201	495	.406
Radford	214	528	.405
Iowa State	149	372	.401

THREE-POINT FIELD GOALS PER GAME

SCHOOL	FGM	AVG.
Miss. Valley State	309	10.7
Long Island	301	10.0
Cal Poly SLO	290	9.7
Morehead State	257	9.5
Fla. International	271	9.3

Villanova in the same week, snapping homecourt winning streaks of 24 and 23, respectively. . . . Providence's Austin Croshere converted a Big East Conference-record 57 consecutive free throws. . . . Boston College advanced to the Big East Conference Tournament semifinals for the first time in 14 years. . . . Last-place seed Fairfield won the MAAC Tournament championship game against Canisius, 78-72, after losing by 46 points to the Golden Griffins earlier in the season. . . . Harvard (17-9) had its best season in 51 years. . . . Maine matched its all-time high for defeats (20) despite posting victories at Marquette and Saint Louis. . . . Robert Morris lost at least 23 games for the third consecutive campaign. . . . Colgate's Adonal Foyle left school early, but not before setting an NCAA standard for career blocked shots.

It was the lowest point total by an opponent during a regular-season game in the 50-year history of Reynolds Coliseum when homestanding North Carolina State whipped visiting Winthrop, 57-28. N.C. State was the #8 seed in the ACC Tournament when the Wolfpack erased a 21-5 deficit and upset top seed Duke. . . . Maryland made its greatest comeback in school history when the Terrapins erased a 22-point deficit with less than 14 1/2 minutes remaining at North Carolina to upend the Tar Heels. Carolina overcame its worst league start in ACC history (0-3) to finish in a tie for second place. . . . Wake Forest beat Duke nine consecutive times until bowing to the Blue Devils, 73-68.

Dairyland defenses were dominant as Wisconsin had three schools ranked among the top four in the country in field-goal percentage defense. Marquette finished first (36.2% shooting by opponents), Wisconsin-Green Bay was third (36.5) and Wisconsin was fourth (37.8). . . . Wisconsin had lost 31 consecutive games to Indiana in their series until the Badgers scored the first 17 points of the contest and committed only five turnovers in a 71-58 victory over the Hoosiers. . . .

1997 FINAL FOUR CHAMPIONSHIP GAME

SEASON STATISTICS FOR ARIZONA REGULARS

PLAYER	POS.	CL.	G.	FG%	FT%	PPG	RPG
Michael Dickerson	F	Jr.	34	.412	.712	18.9	4.5
Miles Simon	G	Jr.	23	.455	.754	18.4	4.1
Mike Bibby	G	Fr.	34	.445	.701	13.5	3.2
Jason Terry	G	So.	34	.443	.713	10.6	2.7
Bennett Davison	F	Jr.	34	.500	.680	9.7	6.4
A.J. Bramlett	C	So.	33	.534	.526	8.1	6.9
Donnell Harris	C	So.	33	.484	.579	5.9	5.9
Jason Lee	F	Sr.	19	.415	.667	3.3	1.8
Eugene Edgerson	F	Fr.	33	.408	.408	2.7	3.7

TEAM TOTALS

Three-point field goals leaders: Bibby (67 of 170, .394), Dickerson (55 of 166, .331), Simon (45 of 111, .405), Terry (40 of 121, .331). **Assists leaders:** Bibby 177, Terry 150, Simon 94. **Blocked shots leader:** Davison 33. **Steals leaders:** Terry 84, Bibby 77, Davison 60.

INDIANAPOLIS, IN

ARIZONA (84)	MIN.	FG-A	FT-A	REB.	A.	PF.	PTS.
Bennett Davison	29	3-9	3-3	7	0	2	9
Michael Dickerson	24	1-8	2-2	4	0	0	5
A.J. Bramlett	27	1-3	1-1	6	1	5	3
Mike Bibby	38	5-12	6-6	9	4	1	19
Miles Simon	40	8-18	14-17	3	1	1	30
Jason Terry	33	2-6	2-2	2	5	1	8
Eugene Edgerson	15	0-0	2-2	5	0	2	2
Donnell Harris	19	2-2	4-8	7	1	4	8
TOTALS	**225**	**22-58**	**34-41**	**43**	**12**	**16**	**84**

FG%: .379. **FT%:** .829. **Three-point goals:** 6-13 (Dickerson 1-3, Bibby 3-5, Simon 0-2, Terry 2-3). **Blocks:** 2 (Bramlett 2). **Turnovers:** 18 (Bibby 8). **Steals:** 7 (Bibby 3, Terry 3).

KENTUCKY (79)	MIN.	FG-A	FT-A	REB.	A.	PF.	PTS.
Ron Mercer	41	5-9	1-1	9	6	5	13
Scott Padgett	30	5-16	4-4	1	0	5	17
Jamaal Magloire	14	0-1	0-0	4	1	4	0
Wayne Turner	28	4-9	0-1	4	5	5	8
Anthony Epps	38	4-13	0-0	5	4	0	11
Allen Edwards	5	0-0	0-0	0	0	0	0
Jared Prickett	21	1-4	4-5	5	1	5	6
Nazr Mohammed	25	6-11	0-6	11	0	3	12
Cameron Mills	22	5-9	0-0	1	1	2	12
Stephen Masiello	1	0-0	0-0	0	0	0	0
TOTALS	**225**	**30-72**	**9-17**	**40**	**18**	**29**	**79**

FG%: .417. **FT%:** .529. **Three-point goals:** 10-30 (Mercer 2-4, Padgett 3-12, Epps 3-8, Mills 2-6). **Blocks:** 7 (Mohammed 3). **Turnovers:** 16 (Mercer 5). **Steals:** 9.
   Halftime: Arizona 33-32. Regulation: Tied 74-74.

NATIONAL SEMIFINALS

ARIZONA (66): Davison 1-2 2-4 4, Dickerson 1-10 2-3 5, Bramlett 0-5 2-2 2, Bibby 7-18 0-0 20, Simon 9-19 3-5 24, Edgerson 1-3 0-0 2, Terry 1-6 0-0 3, Harris 2-3 2-2 6.   Team 22-66 (.333) 11-16 (.688) 66.

NORTH CAROLINA (58): Okalaja 1-8 0-0 3, Jamison 7-17 4-4 18, Zwikker 4-12 0-0 8, Williams 1-13 0-0 3, Carter 8-15 4-5 21, Cota 2-9 0-1 5, Ndiaye 0-0 0-0 00 Team 23-74 (.311) 8-10 (.800) 58.

Three-point goals: Arizona 11-29 (.379), North Carolina 4-21 (.190).
Halftime: Arizona 34-31.

MINNESOTA (69): James 2-3 4-6 8, Jacobson 4-12 2-3 10, J. Thomas 5-6 0-0 10, B. Jackson 8-18 5-6 23, Harris 2-3 0-0 5, Winter 2-3 0-0 4, C. Thomas 2-7 1-2 5, Lewis 1-9 0-0 2, Tarver 1-2 0-2 2, Archambaul 0-0 0-0 0, Stauber 0-1 0-0 0. Team 27-64 (.422) 12-19 (.632) 69.

KENTUCKY (78): Mercer 7-21 4-5 19, Padgett 3-8 0-0 9, Magloire 0-1 1-2 1, Turner 2-6 4 6 8, Epps 3-10 5-6 13, Mills 2-4 4-4 10, Prickett 3-4 1-2 7, Mohammed 2-3 1-5 5, Edwards 1-3 1-2 4, Anderson 0-0 2-2 2. Team 23-60 (.383) 23-34 (.676) 78.

Three-point goals: Minnesota 3-16 (.188), Kentucky 9-23 (.391).
Halftime: Kentucky 36-31.

ALL-TOURNAMENT TEAM

Mike Bibby, G, Fr., Arizona (39 points, 16 rebounds, eight assists, six steals)
Bobby Jackson, G, Sr., Minnesota (23 points, six rebounds in one Final Four game)
Ron Mercer, F, Soph., Kentucky (32 points, 12 rebounds)
Scott Padgett, F, Soph., Kentucky (26 points, six three-point baskets)
*Miles Simon, G, Jr., Arizona (54 points, eight rebounds)

   *Named Most Outstanding Player.

Northwestern posted its most lopsided Big Ten Conference victory since 1944 when the Wildcats whipped Ohio State, 78-47.

   Marshall's Keith Veney set an NCAA record for three-pointers, making 15 of 25 shots from beyond the arc in a 115-93 victory over Morehead State (see accompanying box). . . . Nate Langley scored 22 points in the final 8 1/2 minutes to help George Mason erase a 29-point second-half deficit to edge St. Francis (Pa.), 96-94. . . . Navy improved its conference record for the fifth consecutive season. The top rebounder for the Midshipmen was junior forward Hassan Booker with more than eight per game although he is only 6-2 1/2. . . . Austin Peay's Bubba Wells unofficially led the nation in scoring despite having stainless steel rods implanted in cach leg as a result of stress fractures in 1995 and 1996.

   Northeastern Illinois had back-to-back victories over Pacific-10 Conference teams Oregon State and Arizona State. . . . Pacific upset Georgetown despite the absence of guard Adam Jacobsen, the Tigers' leading scorer the previous season who missed the year after undergoing knee surgery. . . . TCU's Mike Jones scored a WAC Tournament-record 44 points in a 106-81 quarterfinal victory over Fresno State.

   Minnesota (31-4/coached by Clem Haskins), College of Charleston (29-3/John Kresse), Boston University (25-5/Dennis Wolff), Valparaiso (24-

7/Homer Drew), Liberty (23-9/Jeff Meyer), Butler (23-10/Barry Collier), Colorado (22-10/Ricardo Patton) and Northern Arizona (21-7/Ben Howland) had their winningest seasons in school Division I history. St. Joseph's (26-7/Phil Martelli) and Illinois State (24-6/Kevin Stallings) tied their school records for most victories in a single season.

Colorado lost 25 consecutive contests at Missouri until toppling the Tigers. The Buffaloes also ended Texas Tech's 35-game homecourt winning streak on Chauncey Billups' last-second jumper en route to their first double-digit conference victory total and national ranking since 1969. Billups became Colorado's first NCAA consensus All-America in 55 years. . . . Cory Carr became the first Texas Tech player in 21 years to have back-to-back 30-point games. . . . Wyoming mighty mite LaDrell Whitehead (5-9) was leading the WAC in scoring before suffering a season-ending injury (dislocated left elbow) in mid-January. . . . Saint Mary's managed only its second 20-win season in 54 years.

Long Island's Charles Jones (30.1 ppg), California's Ed Gray (24.8), UC Santa Barbara's Raymond Tutt (24), Long Beach State's James Cotton (23.5), South Carolina State's Roderick Blakney (23.4) and Arkansas-Little Rock's Malik Dixon (20.8) set school Division I records for highest scoring average in a single season. . . . Cal's Gray broke his right foot near the end of an 89-87 loss at Washington State when the senior guard scored a school-record 48 points before suffering the season-ending injury on a dunk attempt. Gray finished his career with a school-record 13 consecutive games scoring at least 20 points. . . . LIU's Jones tied a school single-game scoring standard with 46 points in overtime against St. Francis (Pa.). . . . Nicholls State's Kenderick Franklin (40 points vs. Southeastern Louisiana) and Valparaiso's Bryce Drew (38 vs. Western Illinois) set school Division I single-game scoring records.

1997 NCAA Tournament

Summary: Arizona, which came within four points of finishing 9-9 in the Pacific-10 Conference, beat the three winningest programs in the history of major-college basketball (No. 1 seeds Kansas, North Carolina and Kentucky) in its last last three playoff games to capture UA's first NCAA title. Arizona, capitalizing on a 34-9 edge in free throws made, prevailed in the final against Kentucky, 84-79, despite not making a field goal in overtime. Arizona's 37.9 percent field-goal shooting in the final was the worst for a champion since 1963. Speed killed UK, however, as Arizona's quickness among perimeter players negated Kentucky's vaunted press. Neither team gained a double-digit lead in the championship game. The score was tied 16 times, and there were 18 lead changes.

"I think we just wanted it more in the end," said Miles Simon, the Final Four Most Outstanding Player who had missed UA's first 11 games because of academic difficulties. "Their legs were tired. We played with great heart."

Lute Olson, making his fourth Final Four appearance, had been the only coach to go winless at the Final Four among the first 25 to reach the national semifinals at least three times. "I'm very proud of the toughness of this group that no one thought should be here and no one thought could do it," said Olson who had endured three first-round ousters in a four-year span from 1992 through 1995.

It wasn't smooth sailing for Arizona. Leading scorer Michael Dickerson struggled during the tourney, shooting 5 of 28 from three-point range. The Wildcats overcame 10-point second-half deficits against South Alabama and the College of Charleston in the first two rounds. In the Southeast Regional final against Providence, two technical fouls with 6:50 remaining helped push Arizona to a 12-point cushion before the Wildcats blew that lead and nearly lost when the Friars missed a last-second shot in regulation.

Simon and backcourtmate Mike Bibby combined for two-thirds of UA's points in a 66-58 victory over North Carolina in the national semifinals to snap the Tar Heels' 16-game winning streak. Bibby, who committed eight turnovers in the final, is the first freshman point guard to lead a team to a crown since the NCAA made freshmen eligible in the 1972-73 campaign. Center A.J. Bramlett improved immeasurably over the season after failing to reach double digits for rebounds in his first 13 games. Arizona was 9-1 on neutral courts, losing only to NIT champion-to-be Michigan 73-71 in overtime at Auburn Hills, Mich.

Outcome for Defending Champion: Kentucky (35-5/2nd in SEC Eastern Division two games behind behind South Carolina) reached the Final Four for the 12th time despite having only three players available who played in the 1996 title game. All-America Ron Mercer fouled out in the NCAA final when he was held to 13 points.

Star Gazing: Tulsa standout Shea Seals scored only five points when the Golden Hurricane were eliminated in the second round of the Midwest Regional by Clemson. . . . North Carolina guard Shammond Williams missed his last 12 field-goal attempts in the national semifinals against Arizona. . . . Louisville cut a 21-point halftime deficit to three in the East Regional final against Carolina although standout guard DeJuan Wheat was playing with a severely sprained left ankle.

Biggest Upsets: Coppin State became the third No. 15 seed to win a first-round game when the Eagles stunned No. 2 seed South Carolina, 78-65. . . . Fairfield (11-18), had a nine-point lead early in the second half, but the 28-point underdog failed to become the first No. 16 seed to win when the Stags bowed to North Carolina, 82-74. The Tar Heels scored on 26 of 30 second-half possessions, committed only two turnovers and barely won.

One and Only: Arizona became the only team to defeat three #1 seeds in a single tourney (top-ranked Kansas/Southeast, North Carolina/East and Kentucky/West). The Wildcats are also the only team needing at least four games to win the NCAA championship to have all of their playoff games decided by single-digit margins. . . . Minnesota coach Clem Haskins, a graduate of Western Kentucky, is the only individual to coach a team to the Final Four after becoming an NCAA consensus first-team All-America and NBA first-round draft choice (Chicago Bulls in 1967).

Numbers Game: Indianapolis was the ultimate Brickyard. Teams combined to shoot 37.3 percent from the floor in the three Final Four games. . . . A record-tying seven playoff games went into overtime, and 11 of 15 in the final four rounds had single-digit margins. . . . Indiana, ousted in the opening round for the third straight year, sustained its worst loss in 71 tourney games (80-62 to Colorado). . . . Butler made its first playoff appearance in 35 years. . . . Valparaiso guard Bryce Drew hit his first six three-point attempts in the first half, but the Crusaders faded down the stretch and bowed to Boston College, 73-66, in the first round. . . . Marquette was on the verge of setting an NCAA record for lowest field-goal percentage allowed, restricting opponents to 35.7 percent shooting from the floor entering playoff competition, until Providence eliminated the Golden Eagles in the opening round. PC's Austin Croshere connected on a 75-foot shot at the end of the first half en route to a tourney-high 39 points. . . . Tim Duncan grabbed a tourney-high 22 rebounds in a first-round victory over St. Mary's. . . . Arizona ended College of Charleston's 23-game winning streak. . . . Four SEC representatives lost to worst-seeded opponents. . . . The worst-seeded regional matchup in tourney history occurred in the Southeast Regional when #10 Providence met #14 Tennessee-Chattanooga. . . . Top-ranked Kansas didn't exactly set the world on fire before the Jayhawks were eliminated by Arizona. They shot a modest 41 percent from the floor in their first two tourney games.

What Might Have Been: Texas Tech likely would have been invited to the NCAA playoffs as an at-large team, but the Red Raiders had a self-imposed ineligibility because of academic irregularities. . . . Minnesota reached the Final Four although guard Eric Harris suffered a right shoulder contusion in the regional semifinals against Clemson. UCLA center Jelani McCoy sustained a bruised sternum and was ineffective against Minnesota. . . . California (23-9/without Shareef Abdur-Rahim), Cincinnati (26-8, Dontonio Wingfield), Georgetown (20-10/Allen Iverson), Kentucky (34-5/Antoine Walker), Louisville (26-

BOMBS AWAY

Here is a play-by-play rundown of the NCAA-record 15 three-pointers (in 25 attempts from beyond the arc) by Marshall senior guard Keith Veney on December 14, 1996, when he scored 51 points in a 115-93 victory over Morehead State. Veney's barrage included a couple of four-point plays. He clinched the mark with four treys in a 125-second span late in the game.

HOME TEAM: MARSHALL	TIME	SCORE	MAR
FIRST HALF (8)			
made 3-pointer by Veney	19:21	5-0	+5
made 3-pointer by Veney	18:25	11-2	+9
made 3-pointer by Veney	18:14	14-2	+12
made 3-pointer by Veney	12:56	24-12	+12
made 3-pointer by Veney	4:42	46-27	+19
made 3-pointer by Veney	3:54	49-30	+19
made 3-pointer by Veney	1:48	55-34	+21
made 3-pointer by Veney	1:09	58-36	+22
SECOND HALF (7)			
made 3-pointer by Veney	16:26	73-42	+31
made 3-pointer by Veney	10:51	90-55	+35
made 3-pointer by Veney	9:16	95-59	+36
made 3-pointer by Veney	5:26	101-71	+30
made 3-pointer by Veney	4:27	105-75	+30
made 3-pointer by Veney	4:10	108-77	+31
made 3-pointer by Veney	3:21	113-80	+33

20 WINNINGEST PROGRAMS FROM 1990-97

RK.	SCHOOL	W.	L.	PCT.	HEAD COACH(ES)
1.	Kansas	228	46	.832	Roy Williams
2.	Kentucky	218	50	.813	Rick Pitino
3.	Arizona	204	55	.788	Lute Olson
4.	Arkansas	213	63	.772	Nolan Richardson
5.	North Carolina	212	64	.768	Dean Smith
6.	UCLA	194	61	.761	Jim Harrick/Steve Lavin
7.	Massachusetts	202	67	.751	John Calipari/Bruiser Flint
8.	Princeton	161	56	.742	Pete Carril/Bill Carmody
9.	Utah	192	67	.741	Joe Cravens/Rick Majerus
10.	Connecticut	193	68	.739	Jim Calhoun
11.	Duke	202	72	.737	Mike Krzyzewski
12.	Syracuse	195	71	.733	Jim Boeheim
13.	Cincinnati	192	71	.730	Bob Huggins
14.	Indiana	186	71	.724	Bob Knight
15.	Wis.-Green Bay	174	67	.722	Dick Bennett/Mike Heideman
16.	New Mexico State	178	69	.721	Neil McCarthy
17.	Xavier	170	67	.717	Pete Gillen/Skip Prosser
18.	UNLV	175	71	.711	Jerry Tarkanian/Rollie Massimino/Tim Grgurich/Howie Landa/Cleveland Edwards/Bill Bayno
19.	New Mexico	194	80	.708	Dave Bliss
20.	Montana	166	71	.700	Stew Morrill/Blaine Taylor

9/Samaki Walker), Maryland (21-11/Joe Smith), Massachusetts (19-14/Marcus Camby), North Carolina (28-7/Jeff McInnis, Jerry Stackhouse and Rasheed Wallace) might have fared better in the playoffs if standout players had exercised their remaining eligibility instead of defecting to the NBA. . . . Kentucky was also shorthanded because coach Rick Pitino didn't want to jeopardize standout swingman Derek Anderson's NBA prospects after the star swingman underwent major surgery on his right knee and guard Allen Edwards wasn't 100 percent after suffering a hairline fracture in his right ankle. Meanwhile, Cal advanced farther than most observers projected without Ed Gray, the Pac-10 player of the year who broke his right foot. . . . Arkansas (18-13/Darnell Robinson), Connecticut (18-15/Ray Allen) and Memphis (16-15/Loren-

zen Wright) probably would have participated in the NCAA Tournament instead of the NIT if these vital players didn't leave school early for the NBA.

Putting Things in Perspective: UCLA (24-8) defeated Arizona twice by a total of eight points before losing to Minnesota in the Midwest Regional final. . . . Would Arizona have received an at-large invitation if the Wildcats didn't win their first two Pac-10 games by one-point margins?

Scoring Leader: Miles Simon, Arizona (132 points, 22 ppg).

Highest Scoring Average: Austin Croshere, Providence (91 points, 22.8 ppg).

Rebounding Leader: A.J. Bramlett, Arizona (62 rebounds, 10.3 rpg).

Highest Rebounding Average: Tim Duncan, Wake Forest (42 rebounds, 21 rpg).

1997 CHAMPIONSHIP BRACKET

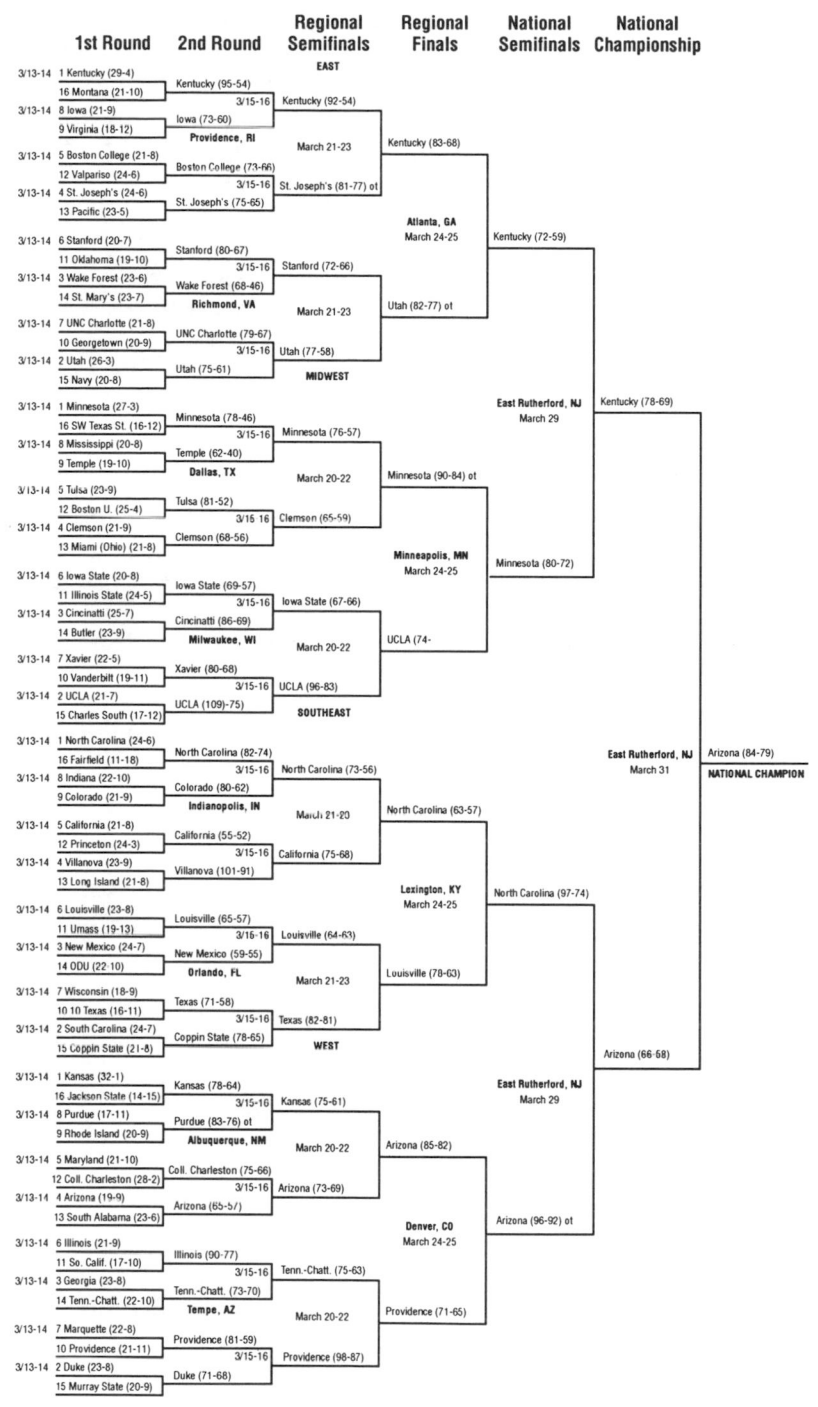

	1st Round	2nd Round	Regional Semifinals	Regional Finals	National Semifinals	National Championship

EAST

- 3/13-14 1 Kentucky (29-4)
- 16 Montana (21-10)
- Kentucky (95-54)
- 3/15-16
- 3/13-14 8 Iowa (21-9)
- 9 Virginia (18-12)
- Iowa (73-60)
- Kentucky (92-54)
- **Providence, RI**
- March 21-23
- Kentucky (83-68)
- 3/13-14 5 Boston College (21-8)
- 12 Valpariso (24-6)
- Boston College (73-66)
- 3/15-16
- 3/13-14 4 St. Joseph's (24-6)
- 13 Pacific (23-5)
- St. Joseph's (75-65)
- St. Joseph's (81-77) ot
- **Atlanta, GA** March 24-25
- Kentucky (72-59)
- 3/13-14 6 Stanford (20-7)
- 11 Oklahoma (19-10)
- Stanford (80-67)
- 3/15-16
- 3/13-14 3 Wake Forest (23-6)
- 14 St. Mary's (23-7)
- Wake Forest (68-46)
- Stanford (72-66)
- **Richmond, VA**
- March 21-23
- Utah (82-77) ot
- 3/13-14 7 UNC Charlotte (21-8)
- 10 Georgetown (20-9)
- UNC Charlotte (79-67)
- 3/15-16
- 3/13-14 2 Utah (26-3)
- 15 Navy (20-8)
- Utah (75-61)
- Utah (77-58)

East Rutherford, NJ March 29

Kentucky (78-69)

MIDWEST

- 3/13-14 1 Minnesota (27-3)
- 16 SW Texas St. (16-12)
- Minnesota (78-46)
- 3/15-16
- 3/13-14 8 Mississippi (20-8)
- 9 Temple (19-10)
- Temple (62-40)
- Minnesota (76-57)
- **Dallas, TX**
- March 20-22
- Minnesota (90-84) ot
- 3/13-14 5 Tulsa (23-9)
- 12 Boston U. (25-4)
- Tulsa (81-52)
- 3/15-16
- 3/13-14 4 Clemson (21-9)
- 13 Miami (Ohio) (21-8)
- Clemson (68-56)
- Clemson (65-59)
- **Minneapolis, MN** March 24-25
- Minnesota (80-72)
- 3/13-14 6 Iowa State (20-8)
- 11 Illinois State (24-5)
- Iowa State (69-57)
- 3/15-16
- 3/13-14 3 Cincinatti (25-7)
- 14 Butler (23-9)
- Cincinatti (86-69)
- Iowa State (67-66)
- **Milwaukee, WI**
- March 20-22
- UCLA (74-
- 3/13-14 7 Xavier (22-5)
- 10 Vanderbilt (19-11)
- Xavier (80-68)
- 3/15-16
- 3/13-14 2 UCLA (21-7)
- 15 Charles South (17-12)
- UCLA (109)-75)
- UCLA (96-83)

SOUTHEAST

- 3/13-14 1 North Carolina (24-6)
- 16 Fairfield (11-18)
- North Carolina (82-74)
- 3/15-16
- 3/13-14 8 Indiana (22-10)
- 9 Colorado (21-9)
- Colorado (80-62)
- North Carolina (73-56)
- **Indianapolis, IN**
- March 21-20
- North Carolina (63-57)
- 3/13-14 5 California (21-8)
- 12 Princeton (24-3)
- California (55-52)
- 3/15-16
- 3/13-14 4 Villanova (23-9)
- 13 Long Island (21-8)
- Villanova (101-91)
- California (75-68)
- **Lexington, KY** March 24-25
- North Carolina (97-74)
- 3/13-14 6 Louisville (23-8)
- 11 Umass (19-13)
- Louisville (65-57)
- 3/15-16
- 3/13-14 3 New Mexico (24-7)
- 14 ODU (22-10)
- New Mexico (59-55)
- Louisville (64-63)
- **Orlando, FL**
- March 21-23
- Louisville (78-63)
- 3/13-14 7 Wisconsin (18-9)
- 10 10 Texas (16-11)
- Texas (71-58)
- 3/15-16
- 3/13-14 2 South Carolina (24-7)
- 15 Coppin State (21-8)
- Coppin State (78-65)
- Texas (82-81)

East Rutherford, NJ March 29

North Carolina (97-74)

Arizona (66-58)

WEST

- 3/13-14 1 Kansas (32-1)
- 16 Jackson State (14-15)
- Kansas (78-64)
- 3/15-16
- 3/13-14 8 Purdue (17-11)
- 9 Rhode Island (20-9)
- Purdue (83-76) ot
- Kansas (75-61)
- **Albuquerque, NM**
- March 20-22
- Arizona (85-82)
- 3/13-14 5 Maryland (21-10)
- 12 Coll. Charleston (28-2)
- Coll. Charleston (75-66)
- 3/15-16
- 3/13-14 4 Arizona (19-9)
- 13 South Alabama (23-6)
- Arizona (65-57)
- Arizona (73-69)
- **Denver, CO** March 24-25
- Arizona (96-92) ot
- 3/13-14 6 Illinois (21-9)
- 11 So. Calif. (17-10)
- Illinois (90-77)
- 3/15-16
- 3/13-14 3 Georgia (23-8)
- 14 Tenn.-Chatt. (22-10)
- Tenn.-Chatt. (73-70)
- Tenn.-Chatt. (75-63)
- **Tempe, AZ**
- March 20-22
- Providence (71-65)
- 3/13-14 7 Marquette (22-8)
- 10 Providence (21-11)
- Providence (81-59)
- 3/15-16
- 3/13-14 2 Duke (23-8)
- 15 Murray State (20-9)
- Duke (71-68)
- Providence (98-87)

East Rutherford, NJ March 31

Arizona (84-79)

NATIONAL CHAMPION

THE SOUTH RISES AGAIN: THE 1990s 413

ALL-DECADE TEAM — 1990 THROUGH 1997

Tim Duncan, C, Wake Forest
Danny Fortson, F, Cincinnati
Grant Hill, F-G, Duke
Jim Jackson, G, Ohio State
Larry Johnson, F, UNLV
Alonzo Mourning, C, Georgetown
Shaquille O'Neal, C, Louisiana State
Glenn Robinson, F, Purdue
Keith Van Horn, F, Utah
Corliss Williamson, F, Arkansas
Co-Coaches: Rick Pitino, Kentucky and Roy Williams, Kansas

Tim Duncan

Wake Forest
6-10 — C
St. Croix, Virgin Islands (Episcopal H.S.)

Named national player of the year by AP and NABC in 1997.... Wooden Award winner in 1997.... NCAA unanimous first-team All-American in 1996 and 1997.... Led the nation in rebounding in 1997 after finishing 5th in 1995 and 4th in 1996.... Ranked among the nation's leaders in blocked shots in 1994 (5th with 3.8 bpg), 1995 (6th with 4.2 bpg), 1996 (8th with 3.8 bpg) and 1997 (9th with 3.3 bpg).... Averaged 17.6 points, 15 rebounds and 4.5 blocked shots in 11 NCAA Tournament games from 1994-97 (7-4 record).

SEASON	G.	FGM-FGA	FG%	FTM-FTA	FT%	REB.	AVG.	PTS.	AVG.
1993-94	33	120-220	.545	82-110	.745	317	9.6	323	9.8
1994-95	32	208-352	.591	118-159	.742	401	12.5	537	16.8
1995-96	32	228-411	.555	149-217	.687	395	12.3	612	19.1
1996-97	31	234-385	.608	171-269	.636	457	14.7	645	20.8
Totals	128	790-1368	.577	520-755	.689	1570	12.3	2117	16.5

Three-point field goals: 1 of 1 (1.000) in 1993-94, 3 of 7 (.429) in 1994-95, 7 of 23 (.304) in 1995-96 and 6 of 22 (.273) in 1996-97. Totals—17 of 53 (.321).

Danny Fortson

Cincinnati
6-7 — F
Pittsburgh, Pa. (Shaler H.S.)

Unanimous NCAA first-team All-American in 1997 and consensus second-team All-American in 1996.... Ranked among the nation's leading scorers in 1996 (49th) and 1997 (19th).... Ranked 7th in the nation in field-goal percentage in 1997.... Averaged 14.9 points and 9.4 rebounds in eight NCAA Tournament games from 1995-97 (5-3 record).

SEASON	G.	FGM-FGA	FG%	FTM-FTA	FT%	REB.	AVG.	PTS.	AVG.
1994-95	34	190-355	.535	134-196	.684	258	7.65	141	5.1
1995-96	33	222-413	.538	220-292	.753	316	9.6	664	20.1
1996-97	33	243-392	.620	217-281	.772	299	9.1	703	21.3
Totals	100	655-1160	.565	571-769	.743	873	8.7	1881	18.8

Three-point field goals: 0 of 1 (.000) in 1994-95, 0 of 1 (.000) in 1995-96 and 0 of 1 in 1996-97. Totals: 0 of 3 (.000).

Grant Hill

Duke
6-8 — G/F
Reston, Va. (South Lakes H.S.)

NCAA unanimous first-team All-American in 1994 and consensus second-team All-American in 1993.... Ranked 17th in the nation in field-goal percentage in 1992.... Fifth-leading scorer and second-leading rebounder for 1991 NCAA championship team (32-7 record), second-leading rebounder and third-leading scorer for 1992 NCAA championship team (34-2), and leading scorer and second-leading rebounder for 1994 NCAA runner-up (28-6).... Named to All-NCAA Tournament team in 1992 and 1994.... Averaged 13.5 points, 6.7 rebounds and 4.3 assists in 20 NCAA Tourna-

ment games from 1991-94 (18-2 record).... Member of 1996 U.S. Olympic team.... Selected by the Detroit Pistons in first round of 1994 NBA draft (3rd pick overall).

SEASON	G.	FGM-FGA	FG%	FTM-FTA	FT%	REB.	AVG.	PTS.	AVG.
1990-91	36	160-310	.516	81-133	.609	183	5.1	402	11.2
1991-92	33	182-298	.611	99-135	.733	187	5.7	463	14.0
1992-93	26	185-320	.578	94-126	.746	166	6.4	468	18.0
1993-94	34	218-472	.462	116-165	.703	233	6.9	591	17.4
Totals	129	745-1400	.532	390-559	.698	769	6.0	1924	14.9

Three-point field goals: 1 of 2 (.500) in 1990-91, 0 of 1 in 1991-92, 4 of 14 (.286) in 1992-93 and 39 of 100 (.390) in 1993-94. Totals—44 of 117 (.376).

Jim Jackson

Ohio State
6-6 — G
Toledo, Ohio (Macomber-Whitney H.S.)

NCAA unanimous first-team All-American in 1992 and consensus first-team All-American in 1991.... Ranked 24th in the nation in scoring in 1992.... Averaged 17.7 points, 6.4 rebounds and 4.4 assists in nine NCAA Tournament games from 1990-92 (6-3 record).... Selected as an undergraduate (after junior season) by the Dallas Mavericks in first round of 1992 NBA draft (4th pick overall).

SEASON	G.	FGM-FGA	FG%	FTM-FTA	FT%	REB.	AVG.	PTS.	AVG.
1989-90	30	194-389	.499	73-93	.785	166	5.5	482	16.1
1990-91	31	228-441	.517	112-149	.752	169	5.5	585	18.9
1991-92	32	264-535	.493	146-180	.811	217	6.8	718	22.4
Totals	93	686-1365	.503	331-422	.784	552	5.9	1785	19.2

Three-point field goals: 21 of 59 (.356) in 1989-90, 17 of 51 (.333) in 1990-91 and 44 of 108 (.407) in 1991-92. Totals—82 of 218 (.376).

Larry Johnson

UNLV
6-7 — F
Dallas, Tex. (Skyline H.S.)

Named national player of the year by NABC and USBWA in 1991.... Naismith Award and Wooden Award winner in 1991.... NCAA unanimous first-team All-American in 1991 and consensus first-team All-American in 1990.... Ranked among the nation's leaders in field-goal percentage in 1990 (11th) and 1991 (8th).... Ranked among the nation's leading scorers in 1990 (61st) and 1991 (34th).... Ranked among the nation's leading rebounders in 1990 (11th) and 1991 (20th).... Leading scorer and rebounder for 1990 NCAA Tournament champion (35-5 record) and 1991 Final Four team (34-1).... Named to 1990 All-NCAA Tournament team.... Averaged 20.2 points and 11.5 rebounds in 11 NCAA Tournament games in 1990 and 1991 (10-1 record).... Averaged 26 points and 11.6 rebounds in two junior college seasons at Odessa (Tex.).... Selected by the Charlotte Hornets in first round of 1991 NBA draft (1st pick overall).

SEASON	G.	FGM-FGA	FG%	FTM-FTA	FT%	REB.	AVG.	PTS.	AVG.
1989-90	40	304-487	.624	201-262	.767	457	11.4	822	20.6
1990-91	35	308-465	.662	162-198	.818	380	10.9	795	22.7
Totals	75	612-952	.643	363-460	.789	837	11.2	1617	21.6

Three-point field goals: 13 of 38 (.342) in 1989-90 and 17 of 48 (.354) in 1990-91. Totals—30 of 86 (.349).

Alonzo Mourning

Georgetown
6-10 — C
Chesapeake, Va. (Indian River H.S.)

NCAA consensus first-team All-American in 1992 and consensus second-team All-American in 1990.... Led the nation in blocked shots (five per game) in 1989 before finishing 26th with 2.2 per game in 1990 and 2nd with five per game in 1992.... Ranked 20th in the nation in rebounding and 37th in scoring in 1992.... Averaged 15.3 points, 8.5 rebounds and 3.7 blocked shots in 10 NCAA Tournament games from 1989-92 (6-4 record).... Selected by the Charlotte Hornets in first round of 1992 NBA draft (2nd pick overall).

SEASON	G.	FGM-FGA	FG%	FTM-FTA	FT%	REB.	AVG.	PTS.	AVG.
1988-89	34	158-262	.603	130-195	.667	248	7.3	447	13.1
1989-90	31	145-276	.525	220-281	.783	265	8.5	510	16.5
1990-91	23	105-201	.522	149-188	.793	176	7.7	363	15.8
1991-92	32	204-343	.595	272-359	.758	343	10.7	681	21.3
Totals	120	612-1082	.566	771-1023	.754	1032	8.6	2001	16.7

Three-point field goals: 1 of 4 (.250) in 1988-89, 0 of 2 in 1989-90, 4 of 13 (.308) in 1990-91 and 6 of 23 (.261) in 1991-92. Totals—11 of 42 (.262).

Shaquille O'Neal

Louisiana State
7-1 — C
San Antonio, Tex. (Cole H.S.)

Named national player of the year by AP and UPI in 1991. . . . NCAA unanimous first-team All-American in 1991 and 1992. . . . Led the nation in rebounding in 1991. Finished 9th in 1990 and 2nd in 1992. . . . Led the nation in blocked shots with 5.2 per game in 1992 after finishing 6th with 3.6 per game in 1990 and 3rd in 1991. . . . Ranked among the nation's leading scorers in 1991 (7th) and 1992 (15th). . . . Ranked among the nation's leaders in field-goal percentage in 1991 (18th) and 1992 (14th). . . . Averaged 24 points, 13.2 rebounds and 5.8 blocked shots in five NCAA Tournament games from 1990-92 (2-3 record). . . . Member of 1996 U.S. Olympic team. . . . Selected as an undergraduate (after junior season) by the Orlando Magic in first round of 1992 NBA draft (1st pick overall).

SEASON	G.	FGM-FGA	FG%	FTM-FTA	FT%	REB.	AVG.	PTS.	AVG.
1989-90	32	180-314	.573	85-153	.556	385	12.0	445	13.9
1990-91	28	312-497	.628	150-235	.638	411	14.7	774	27.6
1991-92	30	294-478	.615	134-254	.528	421	14.0	722	24.1
Totals	90	786-1289	.610	369-642	.575	1217	13.5	1941	21.6

Glenn Robinson

Purdue
6-8 — F
Gary, Ind. (Roosevelt H.S.)

Named national player of the year by AP, UPI, USBWA and NABC in 1994. . . . Wooden Award and Naismith Award winner in 1994. . . . NCAA unanimous first-team All-American in 1994. . . . Led the nation in scoring in 1994 after finishing 9th in 1993. . . . Ranked 27th in the nation in rebounding in 1994. . . . Averaged 31.4 points and 9.8 rebounds in five NCAA Tournament games in 1993 and 1994 (3-2 record). . . . Member of 1996 U.S. Olympic team. . . . Selected by the Milwaukee Bucks in first round of 1994 NBA draft (1st pick overall).

SEASON	G.	FGM-FGA	FG%	FTM-FTA	FT%	REB.	AVG.	PTS.	AVG.
1991-92	Sat out the entire season as a Proposition 48 casualty.								
1992-93	28	246-519	.474	152-205	.741	258	9.2	676	24.1
1993-94	34	368-762	.483	215-270	.796	344	10.1	1030	30.3
Totals	62	614-1281	.479	367-475	.773	602	9.7	1706	27.5

Three-point field goals: 32 of 80 (.400) in 1992-93 and 79 of 208 (.380) in 1993-94. Totals—111 of 288 (.385).

Keith Van Horn

Utah
6-9 — F
Diamond Bar, Calif.

Unanimous NCAA first-team All-American in 1997 and consensus second-team All-American in 1996. . . . Ranked among the nation's leading scorers in 1995 (36th), 1996 (26th) and 1997 (14th). . . . Ranked among the nation's leaders in free-throw percentage in 1995 (20th), 1996 (25th) and 1997 (2nd). . . . Averaged 19.9 points and 7.6 rebounds in eight NCAA Tournament games from 1995-97 (5-3 record; missed 1996 opening-round victory over Canisius because of the flu).

SEASON	G.	FGM-FGA	FG%	FTM-FTA	FT%	REB.	AVG.	PTS.	AVG.
1993-94	25	161-312	.516	100-129	.775	208	8.3	457	18.3
1994-95	33	246-451	.545	143-167	.856	280	8.5	694	21.0
1995-96	32	236-439	.538	160-188	.851	283	8.8	686	21.4
1996-97	32	248-504	.492	151-167	.904	303	9.5	705	22.0

| Totals | 122 | 891-1706 | .522 | 554-651 | .851 | 1074 | 8.8 | 2542 | 20.8 |

Three-point field goals: 35 of 79 (.443) in 1993-94, 59 of 153 (.386) in 1994-95, 54 of 132 (.409) in 1995-96 and 58 of 150 (.387) in 1996-97. Totals—206 of 514 (.401).

Corliss Williamson

Arkansas
6-7 — F
Russellville, Ark.

NCAA consensus second-team All-American in 1994 and 1995. . . . Ranked 7th in the nation in field-goal percentage and 65th in scoring in 1994. Finished 62nd in scoring in 1995. . . . Leading scorer and rebounder for 1994 NCAA Tournament champion (31-3 record) and 1995 NCAA Tournament runner-up (32-7). . . . Final Four Most Outstanding Player in 1994 (52 points, 21 rebounds). . . . Named to All-NCAA Tournament team in 1994 and 1995. . . . Averaged 20.2 points and 7.4 rebounds and shot 59.4 percent from the floor in 15 NCAA Tournament games from 1993-95 (13-2 record). . . . Selected as an undergraduate (after junior season) by the Sacramento Kings in first round of 1995 NBA draft (13th pick overall).

SEASON	G.	FGM-FGA	FG%	FTM-FTA	FT%	REB.	AVG.	PTS.	AVG.
1992-93	18	101-176	.574	61-98	.622	92	5.1	263	14.6
1993-94	34	273-436	.626	149-213	.700	262	7.7	695	20.4
1994-95	39	283-515	.550	203-304	.668	293	7.5	770	19.7
Totals	91	657-1127	.583	413-615	.672	647	7.1	1728	19.0

Three-point field goals: 1 of 6 (.167) in 1994-95.
(Missed several games during freshman season because of a foot injury.)

Rick Pitino

Massachusetts '74
New York, NY

Reached NCAA Final Four on four occasions—once with Providence (1987) and three times with Kentucky (1993, 1996 and 1997). The '96 team won the national title and the '97 squad finished as runner-up. . . . Coach of one North Atlantic Conference Tournament champion (1983) and five SEC Tournament champions (1992 through 1995 and 1997). . . . Compiled a 90-74 regular-season record and 6-7 playoff mark in two seasons as coach of the NBA's New York Knicks (1987-88 and 1988-89). . . . Assistant coach at Hawaii under Bruce O'Neil for two seasons (1974-75 and 1975-76), Syracuse under Jim Boeheim for two seasons (1976-77 and 1977-78) and with the Knicks under Hubie Brown for two seasons (1983-84 and 1984-85).

SEASON	SCHOOL	OVERALL	LEAGUE	FINISH	POSTSEASON
1975-76	Hawaii*	2-4	—	—	DNP
1978-79	Boston Univ.	17-9	—	—	DNP
1979-80	Boston Univ.	21-9	—	—	NIT (0-1)
1980-81	Boston Univ.	13-14	—	—	DNP
1981-82	Boston Univ.	19-9	6-2	4th (N. Atlantic)	DNP
1982-83	Boston Univ.	21-10	8-2	T1st (N. Atlantic)	NCAA (0 1)
1985-86	Providence	17-14	7-9	5th (Big East)	NIT (2-1)
1986-87	Providence	25-9	10-6	T4th (Big East)	NCAA (4-1)
1989-90	Kentucky	14-14	10-8	T4th (SEC)	Probation
1990-91	Kentucky	22-6	14-4	1st (SEC)	Probation
1991-92	Kentucky	29-7	12-4	1st (SEC East)	NCAA (3-1)
1992-93	Kentucky	30-4	13-3	2nd (SEC East)	NCAA (4-1)
1993-94	Kentucky	25-7	12-4	T1st (SEC East)	NCAA (1-1)
1994-95	Kentucky	28-5	14-2	1st (SEC East)	NCAA (3-1)
1995-96	Kentucky	34-2	16-0	1st (SEC East)	NCAA (6-0)
1996-97	Kentucky	34-5	13-3	2nd (SEC East)	NCAA (5-1)

*Pitino was an interim coach when he filled in for Bruce O'Neil with six games remaining.

16-Year College Coaching Record: 351-128 (.733) overall; 2-4 (.333) in a portion of one year at Hawaii; 91-51 (.641) in five years at Boston University; 42-23 (.646) in two years at Providence; 216-50 (.812) in first eight years at Kentucky; 14-4 (.778) in North Atlantic Conference; 17-15 (.531) in Big East Conference; 104-28 (.788) in SEC; 24-6 (.800) in postseason conference tournaments; 26-7 (.788) in NCAA Tournament; 2-2 (.500) in NIT.

Roy Williams

Kansas
(see active coaches' chapter)

FUTURE NCAA DIVISION I TOURNAMENT DATES AND SITES

1998 FIRST AND SECOND ROUNDS

East: Hartford Civic Center, Hartford, CT (March 12 and 14, 1998). USAir Arena, Landover, MD (March 13 and 15, 1998).

Southeast: The Omni, Atlanta (March 12 and 14, 1998). Rupp Arena, Lexington, KY (March 13 and 15, 1998).

Midwest: Myriad Convention Center, Oklahoma City, OK (March 12 and 14, 1998). United Center, Chicago (March 13 and 15, 1998).

West: Arco Arena, Sacramento, CA (March 12 and 14, 1998). Boise State University Pavilion, Boise, ID (March 13 and 15, 1998).

1998 REGIONALS

East: Greensboro Coliseum, Greensboro, NC (March 19 and 21, 1998).

Southeast: ThunderDome, St. Petersburg, FL (March 20 and 22, 1998).

Midwest: Kiel Center, St. Louis (March 20 and 22, 1998).

West: Arrowhead Pond, Anaheim, CA (March 19 and 21, 1998).

1998 FINAL FOUR

Alamodome, San Antonio, TX (March 28 and 30, 1998).

The East Regional winner will oppose the West Regional champion and the Midwest Regional winner will oppose the Southeast Regional champion in the national semifinals.

1999 FIRST AND SECOND ROUNDS

East: FleetCenter, Boston (March 11 and 13, 1999). Charlotte Coliseum, Charlotte, NC (March 12 and 14, 1999).

Southeast: Orlando Arena, Orlando, FL (March 11 and 13, 1999). Louisiana Superdome, New Orleans (March 12 and 14, 1999).

Midwest: Bradley Center, Milwaukee (March 11 and 13, 1999). RCA Dome, Indianapolis (March 12 and 14, 1999).

West: Key Arena, Seattle (March 11 and 13, 1999). McNichols Sports Arena, Denver (March 12 and 14, 1999).

1999 REGIONALS

East: Carrier Dome, Syracuse, NY (March 18 and 20, 1999).

Southeast: Thompson-Boling Arena, Knoxville, TN (March 19 and 21, 1999).

Midwest: Trans World Dome, St. Louis (March 18 and 20, 1999).

West: America West Arena, Phoenix (March 19 and 21, 1999).

1999 FINAL FOUR

ThunderDome, St. Petersburg, FL (March 27 and 29, 1999).

The East Regional winner will oppose the Midwest Regional champion and the West Regional winner will oppose the Southeast Regional champion in the national semifinals.

2000 FIRST AND SECOND ROUNDS

East: Marine Midland Arena, Buffalo (March 17 and 19, 2000). Lawrence Joel Veterans Memorial Coliseum, Winston-Salem, NC (March 17 and 19, 2000).

Southeast: Nashville Arena, Nashville, TN (March 17 and 19, 2000). Birmingham-Jefferson Civic Center, Birmingham, AL (March 17 and 19, 2000).

Midwest: Cleveland State Convocation Center, Cleveland (March 16 and 18, 2000). Hubert H. Humphrey Metrodome, Minneapolis (March 16 and 18, 2000).

West: Jon M. Huntsman Center, Salt Lake City (March 16 and 18, 2000). McKale Center, Tucson, AZ (March 16 and 18, 2000).

2000 REGIONALS

East: Continental Airlines Arena, East Rutherford, NJ (March 24 and 26, 2000).

Southeast: Frank Erwin Center, Austin, TX (March 24 and 26, 2000).

Midwest: The Palace of Auburn Hills, Auburn Hills, MI (March 23 and 25, 2000).

West: University Arena, Albuquerque, NM (March 23 and 25, 2000).

2000 FINAL FOUR

RCA Dome, Indianapolis (April 1 and 3, 2000).

The East Regional winner will oppose the Southeast Regional champion and the West Regional winner will oppose the Midwest Regional champion in the national semifinals.

2001 FIRST AND SECOND ROUNDS

East: Nassau Veterans Memorial Coliseum, Long Island, NY (March 15 and 17, 2001). Greensboro Coliseum, Greensboro, NC (March 15 and 17, 2001).

Southeast: The Pyramid, Memphis, TN (March 16 and 18, 2001). Rupp Arena, Lexington, KY (March 16 and 18, 2001).

Midwest: University of Dayton Arena, Dayton, OH (March 16 and 18, 2001). The Myriad, Oklahoma City, OK (March 16 and 18, 2001).

West: Aztec Bowl Arena, San Diego (March 15 and 17, 2001). Boise State Pavilion, Boise, ID (March 15 and 17, 2001).

2001 REGIONALS

East: CoreStates Center, Philadelphia (March 22 and 24, 2001).

Southeast: Georgia Dome, Atlanta (March 23 and 25, 2001).

Midwest: Alamodome, San Antonio (March 23 and 25, 2001).

West: Arrowhead Pond of Anaheim, Anaheim, CA (March 22 and 24, 2001).

2001 FINAL FOUR

Metrodome, Minneapolis (March 31 and April 2, 2001).

The East Regional winner will oppose the West Regional champion and the Southeast Regional winner will oppose the Midwest Regional champion in the national semifinals.

2002 FINAL FOUR

Georgia Dome, Atlanta (March 30 and April 1, 2002).

The East Regional winner will oppose the Midwest Regional champion and the Southeast Regional winner will oppose the West Regional champion in the national semifinals.

8

THE NATIONAL INVITATION
TOURNAMENT (NIT)

The Final Four hasn't eternally been the final word in national postseason competition, although it appears that's the case. The NCAA playoffs, which previously played second fiddle to the National Invitation Tournament, seems to haughtily look down upon the NIT as little more than an acronymn contest for derisive entries such as National Insignificant Tournament, Not Influential Tournament, Nominally Important Tournament, No Interest Tournament, Nearly Ignominious Tournament, Naturally Impaired Tournament, Never Impressionable Tournament, etc.

But the NIT was once superior to the NCAA during an era when airplanes didn't dominate the transportation industry, television was in its infancy and New York's Madison Square Garden was the place to be if a team wanted extensive national exposure. If ever there was a concept whose time had arrived, it was the NIT in 1938. If ever there was a location to conduct a national tourney at a time when the sports page was the principal place to get sports news, it was in New York because of Gotham's close to 20 daily newspapers.

Too many were saying for too long such provincial comments as the West was best, the

East was least, the North couldn't go forth and the South was all mouth. Finally, basketball could designate a national champion. Originated by the Metropolitan Basketball Writers Association, responsibility for administering the NIT was transferred two years later to local colleges, a group originally known as the Metropolitan Intercollegiate Basketball Committee and in 1948, as the Metropolitan Intercollegiate Basketball Association (MIBA).

And the NIT lived up to billing. In 1939, the NIT final featured two unbeaten teams when Long Island University defeated Loyola of Chicago, 44-32. That game marked the only matchup in major-college history when two undefeated major colleges met in a national postseason tournament (see accompanying box). LIU finished with a 24-0 record and Loyola 21-1.

Long before Michigan's "Fab Five" made headlines as a freshman-dominated team reaching the 1992 NCAA Tournament final, Toledo's similar squad finished runner-up to St. John's in the 1943 NIT. The Rockets were dubbed "Friddle's Freshmen" because first-year coach Berle Friddle had an all-freshman starting lineup.

In the early years, the NIT was an extravaganza so hot the NCAA playoffs were actually scheduled after the NIT to prevent the lukewarm reception given the NCAA from turning completely frigid by going head-to-head against what was clearly basketball's showcase event. Such schedule modifications allowed City College of New York to become the only school to win both titles in the same year (1950) and permitted Utah to win the 1944 NCAA crown after the Utes were eliminated in the opening round of the NIT by eventual third-place finisher Kentucky (46-38). The final year teams participated in both national tournaments was 1952, when Dayton, Duquesne, St. John's and St. Louis doubled up on postseason participation. St. John's was runner-up to Kansas in the NCAA Tournament that year after the Redmen lost their opener in the NIT against La Salle (51-45).

Western Kentucky (28-2, .933), the 1948 NIT third-place finisher, and Seton Hall (31-2, .939), the 1953 NIT champion, led the nation in winning percentage those seasons.

Some observers believe the 1948 NIT, starting the tourney's second decade, was the best from a strength standpoint. If there had been a national poll at the time, it is believed that five of the nation's top seven teams were in the NIT, which was won that year by Ed Macauley-led St. Louis University.

In each of the first two years the Associated Press conducted national rankings (1949 and 1950), five of the top 10 teams participated in the NIT. The four seeded teams in the 1949 NIT all were upset in the quarterfinals after receiving first-round byes—Kentucky, St. Louis, Western Kentucky and Utah. Four of the 12 teams in the 1953 and 1960 NIT fields were schools ranked in the top 10 of the final AP and/or UPI polls. In 1954, the last four NIT survivors (Holy Cross, Duquesne, Niagara and Western Kentucky) combined to win 91 percent of their games entering the semifinals, while their NCAA counterparts (La Salle, Bradley, Penn State and Southern Cal) combined to win barely over 70 percent of their games. Niagara, the third-place finisher in the NIT, defeated 1954

HOW NIT FIELD HAS INCREASED

A committee of New York writers decided that the inaugural NIT would have two local teams, two from elsewhere in the East, and two from the Midwest or Far West. Three years later, the 1941 NIT included three New York area schools in the first eight-team format.

The final year of the 1940s posed a dilemma when local teams failed to compile sterling records, however. Faced with forgoing any local draws, the NIT made a drastic change and expanded the field to 12 teams, adding an opening round to eliminate four entrants. The 1949 opening-round pair of doubleheaders was a dark day and evening for Big Apple hoops as CCNY, Manhattan, NYU, and St. John's dropped their openers by an average of 18.75 points.

Here is how the NIT field has increased over the years:

1938 (6 entrants), 1941 (8), 1949 (12), 1965 (14), 1968 (16), 1979 (24), and 1980 (32).

Note: The NIT went back to a twelve-team field for one year (1976).

TOP 10 BY PERCENTAGE IN NIT

St. John's has compiled more victories in the National Invitation Tournament than any school, but the Red Storm don't rank among the leaders in winning percentage. Here are the top 10 schools by percentage (more than 12 NIT decisions through 1997):

RANK	SCHOOL	APP.	W-L	PCT.
1.	Michigan	5	15-4	.789
2.	Purdue	6	18-5	.783
3.	Virginia Tech	7	17-5	.773
4.	Fresno State	5	11-4	.733
5.	Notre Dame	5	16-6	.727
T6.	Vanderbilt	6	13-5	.722
T6.	Virginia	7	13-5	.722
8.	Xavier	5	10-4	.714
9.	Kentucky	7	11-5	.688
T10.	Minnesota	7	13-6	.684
T10.	Ohio State	6	13-6	.684

NCAA champion La Salle twice during the regular season by a total of 27 points.

The NCAA final was also conducted at Madison Square Garden seven times in eight years from 1943 to 1950. NIT crowds averaged more than 18,000 fans per game from 1945 through 1948. After a point-shaving scandal in 1951 turned New York into a basketball cesspool, however, the Final Four didn't come anywhere close to the Big Apple until the NCAA semifinals and final were held at the Meadowlands in East Rutherford, N.J., in 1996.

NCAA Puts On the Pressure

The NCAA, making it mandatory in the mid-1950s for any team winning its conference to participate in the NCAA playoffs, methodically set in motion the forces pressuring the majority of major schools into selecting its national tournament over the NIT. Xavier, right smack in the middle of a couple of bizarre set of circumstances, is a vivid example of that turbulence. NIT champion-to-be Louisville was ranked 4th in the nation by AP in mid-February when it lost by 40 points at Xavier (99-59). Two years later, Xavier lost 10 of its final 15 regular-season games after a 10-1 start and the NIT asked the Musketeers to give back its NIT bid. But Xavier said "no" and went on to win the 1958 NIT title despite being seeded last under first-year head coach Jim McCafferty.

The issue of "choice" came to a head in 1970 when Marquette, an independent school at the time coached by fiesty Al McGuire, won the NIT after rejecting an NCAA at-large invitation because the Warriors were going to be placed in the NCAA Midwest Regional (Fort Worth, Tex.) instead of closer to home in the Mideast Regional (Dayton, Ohio). McGuire's snub led the NCAA to

RECORD BREAKING

Four NIT games produced the highest-scoring individual outbursts in history for the following schools:

KANSAS STATE—Askia Jones (62 vs. Fresno State in 1994 quarterfinals)
DEPAUL—George Mikan (53 points vs. Rhode Island State in 1945 semifinals)
SIENA—Doremus Bennerman (51 vs. Kansas State in 1994 third-place game)
OREGON—Greg Ballard (43 at Oral Roberts in 1977 first round)

decree any school offered an NCAA bid must accept it or be prohibited from participating in postseason competition.

The NIT, although imperiled by the NCAA's self-serving maneuvers, more than held its own with the NCAA Tournament because of some scintillating storylines. The final NIT at the old Garden in 1967 belonged to a so-called "small" school, Southern Illinois, sparked by a smooth swingman named Walt Frazier. He wasn't Clyde yet, but the future Knick was well on his way.

The competitive NIT, boasting three double overtime games in 1971, was a stark contrast to the "UCLA Invitational." Seemingly invincible UCLA captured seven consecutive NCAA titles from 1967-'73 by winning 28 tournament games by an average of almost 18 points per contest. In 1973, the Bruins' four tournament victories were by an average of 16 points, including a 21-point

POSTSEASON BATTLE OF UNBEATENS On March 22, 1939, the NIT final game, held at New York's Madison Square Garden, featured two unbeaten teams—Loyola of Chicago and Long Island University. That game marked the only time in major-college history that two undefeated major colleges met in a national postseason tournament. LIU defeated Loyola, 44-32. LIU finished with a 24-0 record and Loyola 21-1.

LIU (44)	FG	FT	PTS.
Torgoff	5	2	12
King	0	0	0
Kaplowitz	4	1	9
Schwartz	0	2	2
Scharf	0	0	0
Sewitch	0	1	1
Lobelin	0	0	0
Newman	1	1	3
Shelly	1	0	2
Bromberg	2	1	5
Schechtman	4	1	9
Zeitlin	0	1	1
TOTALS	**17**	**10**	**44**

LOYOLA (32)	FG	FT	PTS.
Hogan	2	0	4
Schell	1	0	2
O'Brien	4	1	9
Graham	1	0	2
Novak	0	1	1
Kautz	3	0	6
Driscoll	0	0	0
Wenskus	4	0	8
TOTALS	**15**	**2**	**32**

St. Louis' Ed Macauley (white uniform, jumping) fights off a defender in a 1949 NIT game.

cipally introduced to hamper the NIT field. The new tourney was called the Collegiate Commissioners Association Tournament in 1974, when Indiana won the title at St. Louis, and then changed to the National Commissioners Invitational Tournament in 1975, when Drake won the title at Louisville (see accompanying box with results of two runner-up tourneys).

The bottom line: Once network television made its move, it left virtually no choice for schools to choose between the national postseason events. The NCAA inflicted another blow to the NIT in 1978 when NCAA Productions started televising all of the NCAA Tournament games. The occasionally acrimonious battle was over as TV made the NCAA playoffs larger, more affluent and more visible than it ever fantasized it could become.

While the NCAA pulled strings like a master puppeteer, the NIT's influence eroded. Prominent active coaches such as Lute Olson and Eddie Sutton have never appeared in the NIT. The last consensus first-team All-America to participate in the NIT was forward Larry Bird of Indiana State, a loser at Rutgers in the 1978 quarterfinals. The last wire-service top 10 team to appear in the NIT was North Carolina, a first-round loser against Purdue in 1974.

triumph over Memphis State in the championship game. Meanwhile, NIT champion Virginia Tech won four exciting postseason games that year by a total of five points, including a game-winning basket at the buzzer in overtime in the final against Notre Dame. The next year, seven of the total of 12 NIT games in the first round and quarterfinals were decided by four points or less.

Exacerbating the tug of war between the two events was a short-lived, eight-team tournament ostensibly to showcase league runners-up but prin-

NIT in Recent Years

The NIT championship games the first half of the 1980s were precursors to bigger things to come. In a five-year span from 1980 through 1984 when the NCAA field ranged from 48 to 52 teams, Virginia (1980 NIT champion), DePaul (1983 run-

Western Kentucky has made 11 NIT appearances, including a second-place finish in 1942. Shown here are members of the 1947–48 team, which took third place in the NIT (from left): Don Ray, John Oldham, Odie Spears, coach E. A. Diddle, Oran McKinney, Dee Gibson, and assistant coach Ted Hornback.

ner-up) and Michigan (1984 champion) became NCAA regional No. 1 seeds the year after reaching an NIT final. Tulsa was a No. 3 seed under coach Nolan Richardson in the 1982 NCAA Tournament after capturing the '81 NIT by winning its last three games by a total of five points.

Nonetheless, when the NCAA bracket was increased to 64 in 1985, the move effectively denied the NIT access to the vast majority of up-and-coming teams. In effect, the NIT champion was reduced to proclaiming "We're No. 65!" although anywhere from 10 to 12 teams out of the NIT draw usually make the NCAA field the following year since the NCAA expanded to 64 entrants.

The NIT has made several strategic alterations over the years, but they've had little impact on how the event is perceived from a national scope. Attendance slipped to an all-time low in 1976 although national power Kentucky won the title. In 1977, former executive director Pete Carlesimo, the father of former Seton Hall coach P.J. Carlesimo, saved the NIT by implementing a plan whereby early-round games were played at campus sites and locations across the country before the four semifinalists advanced to New York.

In 1985, the NIT started a preseason tournament, which evolved into the nation's premier in-season tourney and now probably carries as much

Lenny Wilkens (#14) was a star for the Providence Friars when they were a dominant team in the early 1960s NIT tournaments.

clout, if not more, than the postseason NIT. Coaches are fond of the preseason NIT because those games are exempt from counting against their regular-season limit of contests. For whatever reason, however, none of the first 12 Preseason NIT titlists won the NCAA crown, and the last 10 didn't reach the Final Four. In 1997, Indiana became the first Preseason NIT kingpin to be eliminated in the opening round of the NCAA playoffs. The Hoosiers, however, were the only Preseason NIT champion this decade (1993) to reach a regional final.

The memories and tradition of the NIT are marvelous yet one occasionally wonders how much longer the postseason event can survive when it has become so contrived that second- and third-round matchups aren't announced until after the previous games are played. Although the NIT has tinkered with a rule making certain every semifinalist played at least one road game before getting to New York, it is perceived as a tournament awarding home games on the basis of gate-receipt potential or to favor teams bringing the most fans or publicity or both to Madison Square Garden for the tourney's semifinals and final.

NIT FINAL GAME SUMMARY

YEAR	CHAMPION	RUNNER-UP	MOST VALUABLE PLAYER
1938	Temple	Colorado	Don Shields, Temple
1939	Long Island Univ.	Loyola of Chicago	Bill Lloyd, St. John's
1940	Colorado	Duquesne	Bob Doll, Colorado
1941	Long Island Univ.	Ohio University	Frank Baumholtz, Ohio
1942	West Virginia	Western Kentucky	Rudy Baric, West Virginia
1943	St. John's	Toledo	Harry Boykoff, St. John's
1944	St. John's	DePaul	Bill Kotsores, St. John's
1945	DePaul	Bowling Green St.	George Mikan, DePaul
1946	Kentucky	Rhode Island	Ernie Calverley, Rhode Island
1947	Utah	Kentucky	Vern Gardner, Utah
1948	St. Louis	New York Univ.	Ed Macauley, St. Louis
1949	San Francisco	Loyola of Chicago	Don Lofgan, San Francisco
1950	CCNY	Bradley	Ed Warner, CCNY
1951	Brigham Young	Dayton	Roland Minson, Brigham Young
1952	La Salle	Dayton	Tom Gola and Norm Grekin, La Salle
1953	Seton Hall	St. John's	Walter Dukes, Seton Hall
1954	Holy Cross	Duquesne	Togo Palazzi, Holy Cross
1955	Duquesne	Dayton	Maurice Stokes, St. Francis (Pa.)
1956	Louisville	Dayton	Charlie Tyra, Louisville
1957	Bradley	Memphis St.	Win Wilfong, Memphis St.
1958	Xavier	Dayton	Hank Stein, Xavier
1959	St. John's	Bradley	Tony Jackson, St. John's
1960	Bradley	Providence	Lenny Wilkens, Providence
1961	Providence	St. Louis	Vin Ernst, Providence
1962	Dayton	St. John's	Bill Chmielewski, Dayton
1963	Providence	Canisius	Ray Flynn, Providence
1964	Bradley	New Mexico	Lavern Tart, Bradley
1965	St. John's	Villanova	Ken McIntyre, St. John's
1966	Brigham Young	New York Univ.	Bill Melchionni, Villanova
1967	Southern Illinois	Marquette	Walt Frazier, Southern Illinois
1968	Dayton	Kansas	Don May, Dayton
1969	Temple	Boston College	Terry Driscoll, Boston College
1970	Marquette	St. John's	Dean Meminger, Marquette
1971	North Carolina	Georgia Tech	Bill Chamberlain, N. Carolina
1972	Maryland	Niagara	Tom McMillen, Maryland
1973	Virginia Tech	Notre Dame	John Shumate, Notre Dame
1974	Purdue	Utah	Mike Sojourner, Utah
1975	Princeton	Providence	Ron Lee, Oregon
1976	Kentucky	UNC Charlotte	Cedric Maxwell, UNC Charlotte
1977	St. Bonaventure	Houston	Greg Sanders, St. Bonaventure
1978	Texas	N.C. State	Jim Krivacs and Ron Baxter, Texas
1979	Indiana	Purdue	Butch Carter and Ray Tolbert, Indiana
1980	Virginia	Minnesota	Ralph Sampson, Virginia
1981	Tulsa	Syracuse	Greg Stewart, Tulsa
1982	Bradley	Purdue	Mitchell Anderson, Bradley
1983	Fresno St.	DePaul	Ron Anderson, Fresno St.
1984	Michigan	Notre Dame	Tim McCormick, Michigan
1985	UCLA	Indiana	Reggie Miller, UCLA
1986	Ohio State	Wyoming	Brad Sellers, Ohio State
1987	Southern Miss.	La Salle	Randolph Keys, Southern Miss.
1988	Connecticut	Ohio State	Phil Gamble, Connecticut
1989	St. John's	St. Louis	Jayson Williams, St. John's
1990	Vanderbilt	St. Louis	Scott Draud, Vanderbilt
1991	Stanford	Oklahoma	Adam Keefe, Stanford
1992	Virginia	Notre Dame	Bryant Stith, Virginia
1993	Minnesota	Georgetown	Voshon Lenard, Minnesota
1994	Villanova	Vanderbilt	Doremus Bennerman, Siena
1995	Virginia Teach	Marquette	Shawn Smith, Virgina Tech
1996	Nebraska	St. Joseph's	Erick Strickland, Nebraska
1997	Michigan	Florida State	Robert Traylor, Michigan

MOST NIT APPEARANCES (THROUGH 1997):

St. John's (26), Bradley (18), Dayton (17), Duquesne (16), Fordham (16), Manhattan (16), Saint Louis (16), Providence (14), New Mexico (13), DePaul (12), Louisville (12), Memphis (12), St. Bonaventure (12), St. Peter's (12), Temple (12), Villanova (12), West Virginia (12), Bowling Green State (11), Holy Cross (11), La Salle (11), Marquette (11), Nebraska (11), St. Joseph's (11), Seton Hall (11), Utah (11), Western Kentucky (11).

MOST NIT VICTORIES BY SCHOOL:

St. John's (41), Dayton (29), Providence (28), Bradley (25), Nebraska (19), Villanova (19), Marquette (18), Purdue (18), Saint Louis (18), Duquesne (17), St. Bonaventure (17), Virginia Tech (17).

MOST NIT VICTORIES BY COACH:

Joe Lapchick (21-10), Tom Blackburn (20-10), Bob Knight (15-8), Danny Nee (13-4), Joe Mullaney (13-5), C.M. Newton (12-8), Jim Calhoun (11-3), Dudley Moore (11-8).

ACTIVE COACHES WITH NIT TITLES:

Jim Calhoun (Connecticut '88), Don DeVoe (Virginia Tech '73), Lefty Driesell (Maryland '72), Steve Fisher (Michigan '97), Eddie Fogler (Vanderbilt '90), Bill Frieder (Michigan '84), Clem Haskins (Minnesota '93), Jeff Jones (Virginia '92), Bob Knight (Indiana '79), Steve Lappas (Villanova '94), Eldon Miller (Ohio State '86), Mike Montgomery (Stanford '91), Danny Nee (Nebraska '96), Nolan Richardson (Tulsa '81), Dean Smith (North Carolina '71).

PRESEASON NIT FINALS

1985
Consolation: St. John's 86, Louisville 79
Championship: Duke 92, Kansas 86

1986
Consolation: Temple 67, Memphis State 59
Championship: UNLV 96, Western Kentucky 95 (2ot)

1987
Consolation: Iowa State 107, New Mexico 96
Championship: Florida 70, Seton Hall 68

1988
Consolation: North Carolina 106, Indiana 92
Championship: Syracuse 86, Missouri 84 (ot)

1989
Consolation: UNLV 88, DePaul 53
Championship: Kansas 66, St. John's 57

1990
Consolation: Duke 85, Notre Dame 77
Championship: Arizona 89, Arkansas 77

1991
Consolation: Pittsburgh 91, Texas 87
Championship: Oklahoma State 78, Georgia Tech 71

1992
Consolation: UCLA 86, Florida State 83
Championship: Indiana 78, Seton Hall 74

1993
Consolation: North Carolina 90, Minnesota 76
Championship: Kansas 86, Massachusetts 75

1994
Consolation: Ohio 84, New Mexico State 80 (ot)
Championship: George Washington 69, Memphis 60

1995
Consolation: Georgia Tech 77, Michigan 61
Championship: Arizona 91, Georgetown 81

1996
Consolation: Tulsa 55, Evansville 51
Championship: Indiana 85, Duke 69

Oregon's Ron Lee was Most Valuable Player of the 1975 NIT.

BOMBS AWAY

March 24, 1994
Fresno State at Kansas State

The NCAA postseason record of 14 three-point field goals was set by Kansas State guard Askia Jones in a 115-77 victory over Fresno State in the 1994 NIT quarterfinals. Jones poured in 28 of his Big Eight-record 45 second-half points in the first 7:12 after intermission. His final total of 62 points, spurred by nine consecutive successful three-point shots bridging the first and second halves, was the second-highest scoring output in major-college postseason history. Jones' running point total is in parentheses in the following play-by-play rundown of his three-pointers:

HOME TEAM: KANSAS STATE	TIME	SCORE	MAR
FIRST HALF (3)			
made 3-pointer by Jones (3)	16:25	11-2	+9
made 3-pointer by Jones (8)	10:03	23-14	+9
made 3-pointer by Jones (11)	8:53	28-14	+14
SECOND HALF (11)			
made 3-pointer by Jones (26)	17:21	56-33	+23
made 3-pointer by Jones (29)	15:09	61-37	+24
made 3-pointer by Jones (32)	14:44	64-39	+25
made 3-pointer by Jones (37)	14:22	69-42	+27
made 3-pointer by Jones (40)	13:50	72-45	+27
made 3-pointer by Jones (43)	13:11	75-45	+30
made 3-pointer by Jones (46)	12:38	78-48	+30
made 3-pointer by Jones (51)	7:47	95-56	+39
made 3-pointer by Jones (54)	6:03	98-60	+38
made 3-pointer by Jones (57)	5:35	101-60	+41
made 3-pointer by Jones (60)	2:20	108-72	+36

Texas-El Paso coach Don Haskins was irked in 1993 when the Miners were consigned to Georgetown's on-campus, 2,200-seat McDonough Gym for a second-round game after UTEP had a near-capacity crowd of 11,800 for a first-round contest against Houston. Haskins, according to AP, called the decision political. "They (NIT officials) want to have Georgetown in New York (for the semifinals and final)," he said. "It's all politics." In 1994, Coppin State, undefeated in the Mid-Eastern Athletic Conference for the second consecutive season and 22-8 overall with a difficult non-league schedule, rightfully thought the selection process was unjust when it was left out of the NIT.

The NIT's first nine champions lost a total of 25 games, but its 12 titlists from 1986 through 1997 combined to go 24 games below .500 in conference competition, including a 4-12 league mark compiled by 1988 Big East cellar dweller Connecticut and a 4-10 league record registered by 1996 Big Eight seventh-place team Nebraska. The NIT's "final four" participants combined to average more than 13 defeats per team in the first 13 years after the NCAA field expanded to 64 entrants, including a grim 19-18 mark by 1985 NIT fourth-place finisher Louisville.

It's not beneath the dignity of most high profile schools to appear in the NIT, however. Louisville was the only school to win two NCAA titles from 1977-'86. The 1985 NIT finalists (UCLA and Indiana) have combined for 16 NCAA championships.

"NIT!, NIT!, NIT!" is chanted at some games by unsportsmanlike crowds seeking to ridicule opponents with potential to participate in the NCAA Tournament but on the fence to make it and apparently bound for settling for the NIT. CBS analyst Billy Packer called the NIT "a gerrymandering tournament with no accountability."

Although NIT-picking observers think the postseason NIT should be taken off life support, the mood in New York is to retain a stiff upper lip. "We think the NIT is still a service to college basketball," said Jack Powers, the NIT's Executive Director. "Our early-round games frequently play to packed arenas and we still draw reasonably well in the Garden. Because of parity all across the country, there is a place for the teams in our tournament."

1998 NIT SCHEDULE

First Round (March 11-12-13 on campus sites)
Second Round (March 16-17 on campus sites)
Third Round (March 18-19-20 on campus sites)
Semifinals (March 24 at Madison Square Garden in New York)
Final/Third Place (March 26 at Madison Square Garden in New York)

1938

Quarterfinals
Temple 53, Bradley 40
NYU 39, LIU 37
Semifinals
Temple 56, Oklahoma A&M 44
Colorado 48, NYU 47
Third-Place Game
Oklahoma A&M 37, NYU 24
Championship Game
Temple 60, Colorado 36

1939

Quarterfinals
LIU 52, New Mexico A&M 45
St. John's 71, Roanoke 47
Semifinals
LIU 36, Bradley 32
Loyola (Ill.) 51, St. John's 46
Third-Place Game
Bradley 40, St. John's 35
Championship Game
LIU 44, Loyola (Ill.) 32

1940

Quarterfinals
DePaul 45, LIU 38
Duquesne 38, St. John's 31
Semifinals
Colorado 52, DePaul 37
Duquesne 34, Oklahoma A&M 30
Third-Place Game
Oklahoma A&M 23, DePaul 22
Championship Game
Colorado 51, Duquesne 40

1941

Quarterfinals
CCNY 64, Virginia 35
Ohio U. 55, Duquesne 40
Seton Hall 70, Rhode Island 54
LIU 48, Westminster 36
Semifinals
LIU 49, Seton Hall 26
Ohio U. 45, CCNY 43
Third-Place Game
CCNY 42, Seton Hall 27
Championship Game
LIU 56, Ohio U. 42

1942

Quarterfinals
West Virginia 58, LIU 49
Creighton 59, West Texas State 58
Western Kentucky 49, CCNY 46
Toledo 82, Rhode Island 71
Semifinals
West Virginia 51, Toledo 39
Western Kentucky 49, Creighton 36
Third-Place Game
Creighton 48, Toledo 46
Championship Game
West Virginia 47, Western Kentucky 45

1943

Quarterfinals
St. John's 51, Rice 49
Fordham 60, Western Kentucky 58
Toledo 54, Manhattan 47
Washington & Jefferson 43, Creighton 42
Semifinals
Toledo 46, Washington & Jefferson 39

St. John's 69, Fordham 43
Third-Place Game
Washington & Jefferson 39, Fordham 34
Championship Game
St. John's 48, Toledo 27

1944

Quarterfinals
Oklahoma A&M 43, Canisius 29
Kentucky 46, Utah 38
St. John's 44, Bowling Green 40
DePaul 68, Muhlenberg 45
Semifinals
St. John's 48, Kentucky 45
DePaul 41, Oklahoma A&M 38
Third-Place Game
Kentucky 45, Oklahoma A&M 29
Championship Game
St. John's 47, DePaul 39

1945

Quarterfinals
Rhode Island 51, Tennessee 44
Bowling Green 60, Rensselaer Poly 45
DePaul 76, West Virginia 52
St. John's 34, Muhlenberg 33
Semifinals
DePaul 97, Rhode Island 53
Bowling Green 57, St. John's 44
Third-Place Game
St. John's 64, Rhode Island 57
Championship Game
DePaul 71, Bowling Green 54

1946

Quarterfinals
Rhode Island 82, Bowling Green 79 (ot)
West Virginia 70, St. John's 58
Kentucky 77, Arizona 53
Muhlenberg (Pa.) 47, Syracuse 41
Semifinals
Rhode Island 59, Muhlenberg (Pa.) 49
Kentucky 59, West Virginia 51
Third-Place Game
West Virginia 65, Muhlenberg (Pa.) 40
Championship Game
Kentucky 46, Rhode Island 45

1947

Quarterfinals
Utah 45, Duquesne 44
Kentucky 66, LIU 62
N.C. State 61, St. John's 55
West Virginia 69, Bradley 60
Semifinals
Utah 64, West Virginia 62
Kentucky 60, N.C. State 42
Third-Place Game
N.C. State 64, West Virginia 52
Championship Game
Utah 49, Kentucky 45

1948

Quarterfinals
Western Kentucky 68, La Salle 61
St. Louis 69, Bowling Green 53
NYU 45, Texas 43
De7Paul 75, N.C. State 64
Semifinals
NYU 72, DePaul 59
St. Louis 60, Western Kentucky 53

Third-Place Game
Western Kentucky 61, DePaul 59
Championship Game
St. Louis 65, NYU 52

1949

First Round
Bowling Green 77, St. John's 64
San Francisco 68, Manhattan 43
Bradley 89, NYU 67
Loyola (Ill.) 62, CCNY 47
Quarterfinals
Loyola (Ill.) 61, Kentucky 56
Bradley 95, Western Kentucky 86
San Francisco 64, Utah 63
Bowling Green 80, St. Louis 74
Semifinals
San Francisco 49, Bowling Green 39
Loyola (Ill.) 55, Bradley 50
Third-Place Game
Bowling Green 82, Bradley 77
Championship Game
San Francisco 48, Loyola (Ill.) 47

1950

First Round
Western Kentucky 79, Niagara 72
CCNY 65, San Francisco 46
Syracuse 80, LIU 52
La Salle 72, Arizona 66
Quarterfinals
St. John's 69, Western Kentucky 60
Bradley 78, Syracuse 66
Duquesne 49, La Salle 47
CCNY 89, Kentucky 50
Semifinals
CCNY 62, Duquesne 52
Bradley 83, St. John's 72
Third-Place Game
St. John's 69, Duquesne 67 (ot)
Championship Game
CCNY 69, Bradley 61

1951

First Round
Dayton 77, Lawrence Tech 71
Seton Hall 71, Beloit 57
St. Louis 73, La Salle 61
St. Bonaventure 70, Cincinnati 67 (2ot)
Quarterfinals
Brigham Young 75, St. Louis 58
St. John's 60, St. Bonaventure 58
Dayton 74, Arizona 68
Seton Hall 71, N.C. State 59
Semifinals
Dayton 69, St. John's 62 (ot)
Brigham Young 69, Seton Hall 59
Third-Place Game
St. John's 70, Seton Hall 68 (2ot)
Championship Game
Brigham Young 62, Dayton 43

1952

First Round
Dayton 81, NYU 66
Western Kentucky 62, Louisville 59
La Salle 80, Seton Hall 76
Holy Cross 77, Seattle 72
Quarterfinals
St. Bonaventure 70, Western Kentucky 69
La Salle 51, St. John's 45
Duquesne 78, Holy Cross 68
Dayton 68, St. Louis 58

Semifinals
La Salle 59, Duquesne 46
Dayton 69, St. Bonaventure 62
Third-Place Game
St. Bonaventure 48, Duquesne 34
Championship Game
La Salle 75, Dayton 64

1953

First Round
Duquesne 88, Tulsa 69
Louisville 92, Georgetown 79
St. John's 81, St. Louis 66
Niagara 82, Brigham Young 76 (ot)
Quarterfinals
St. John's 75, La Salle 74
Manhattan 79, Louisville 66
Seton Hall 79, Niagara 74
Duquesne 69, Western Kentucky 61
Semifinals
Seton Hall 74, Manhattan 56
St. John's 64, Duquesne 55
Third-Place Game
Duquesne 81, Manhattan 67
Championship Game
Seton Hall 58, St. John's 46

1954

First Round
St. Francis (N.Y.) 60, Louisville 55
Dayton 90, Manhattan 79
Bowling Green 88, Wichita 84
St. Francis (Pa.) 81, Brigham Young 68
Quarterfinals
Western Kentucky 95, Bowling Green 81
Niagara 77, Dayton 74
Duquesne 69, St. Francis (Pa.) 63
Holy Cross 93, St. Francis (N.Y.) 69
Semifinals
Duquesne 66, Niagara 51
Holy Cross 75, Western Kentucky 59
Third-Place Game
Niagara 71, Western Kentucky 65
Championship Game
Holy Cross 71, Duquesne 62

1955

First Round
Louisville 91, Manhattan 86
Niagara 83, Lafayette 70
St. Francis (Pa.) 89, Seton Hall 78
St. Louis 110, Connecticut 103
Quarterfinals
Duquesne 74, Louisville 66
Cincinnati 85, Niagara 83 (2ot)
St. Francis (Pa.) 68, Holy Cross 64
Dayton 97, St. Louis 81
Semifinals
Dayton 79, St. Francis (Pa.) 73 (ot)
Duquesne 65, Cincinnati 51
Third-Place Game
Cincinnati 96, St. Francis (Pa.) 91 (ot)
Championship Game
Duquesne 70, Dayton 58

1956

First Round
St. Francis (N.Y.) 85, Lafayette 74
Duquesne 69, Oklahoma A&M 61

Seton Hall 96, Marquette 78
Xavier 84, St. Louis 80
Quarterfinals
Louisville 84, Duquesne 72
St. Francis (N.Y.) 74, Niagara 72
St. Joseph's 74, Seton Hall 65
Dayton 72, Xavier 68
Semifinals
Dayton 89, St. Francis (N.Y.) 58
Louisville 89, St. Joseph's 79
Third-Place Game
St. Joseph's 93, St. Francis (N.Y.) 82
Championship Game
Louisville 93, Dayton 80

1957
First Round
Memphis State 77, Utah 75
Xavier 85, Seton Hall 79
Dayton 79, St. Peter's 71
St. Bonaventure 90, Cincinnati 72
Quarterfinals
Memphis State 85, Manhattan 73
St. Bonaventure 85, Seattle 68
Bradley 116, Xavier 81
Temple 77, Dayton 66
Semifinals
Memphis State 80, St. Bonaventure 78
Bradley 94, Temple 66
Third-Place Game
Temple 67, St. Bonaventure 50
Championship Game
Bradley 84, Memphis State 83

1958
First Round
St. John's 76, Butler 69
St. Joseph's 83, St. Peter's 76
Xavier 95, Niagara 86
Fordham 83, St. Francis (Pa.) 59
Quarterfinals
St. John's 71, Utah 70
St. Bonaventure 79, St. Joseph's 75
Xavier 72, Bradley 62
Dayton 74, Fordham 70
Semifinals
Dayton 80, St. John's 56
Xavier 74, St. Bonaventure 53
Third-Place Game
St. Bonaventure 84, St. John's 69
Championship Game
Xavier 78, Dayton 74 (ot)

1959
First Round
Butler 94, Fordham 80
NYU 90, Denver 81
Providence 68, Manhattan 66
St. John's 75, Villanova 67
Quarterfinals
Bradley 83, Butler 77
NYU 63, Oklahoma City 48
Providence 75, St. Louis (2ot)
St. John's 82, St. Bonaventure 74
Semifinals
Bradley 59, NYU 57
St. John's 76, Providence 55
Third-Place Game
NYU 71, Providence 57
Championship Game
St. John's 76, Bradley 71 (ot)

1960
First Round
Villanova 88, Detroit 86
Providence 71, Memphis State 70
St. Bonaventure 94, Holy Cross 81
Dayton 72, Temple 51
Quarterfinals
Utah State 73, Villanova 72 (ot)

Providence 64, St. Louis 53
Bradley 78, Dayton 64
St. Bonaventure 106, St. John's 71
Semifinals
Bradley 82, St. Bonaventure 71
Providence 68, Utah State 62
Third-Place Game
Utah State 99, St. Bonaventure 83
Championship Game
Bradley 88, Providence 72

1961
First Round
St. Louis 58, Miami (Fla.) 56
Holy Cross 86, Detroit 82
Temple 79, Army 66
Providence 73, DePaul 67
Quarterfinals
St. Louis 59, Colorado State 53
Holy Cross 81, Memphis State 69
Dayton 62, Temple 60
Providence 71, Niagara 68
Semifinals
St. Louis 67, Dayton 60
Providence 90, Holy Cross 83 (ot)
Third-Place Game
Holy Cross 85, Dayton 67
Championship Game
Providence 62, St. Louis 59

1962
First Round
Dayton 79, Wichita 71
Temple 80, Providence 78
Holy Cross 72, Colorado State 71
Duquesne 70, Navy 58
Quarterfinals
Dayton 94, Houston 77
Loyola (Ill.) 75, Temple 64
Duquesne 88, Bradley 85
St. John's 80, Holy Cross 74
Semifinals
Dayton 98, Loyola (Ill.) 82
St. John's 75, Duquesne 65
Third-Place Game
Loyola (Ill.) 95, Duquesne 84
Championship Game
Dayton 73, St. John's 67

1963
First Round
Villanova 63, DePaul 51
Memphis State 70, Fordham 49
St. Louis 63, La Salle 61
Miami (Fla.) 71, St. Francis (N.Y.) 70
Quarterfinals
Villanova 54, Wichita 53
Canisius 76, Memphis State 67
Marquette 84, St. Louis 69
Providence 106, Miami (Fla.) 96
Semifinals
Providence 70, Marquette 64
Canisius 61, Villanova 46
Third-Place Game
Marquette 66, Villanova 58
Championship Game
Providence 81, Canisius 66

1964
First Round
St. Joseph's 86, Miami (Fla.) 76
NYU 77, Syracuse 68
Army 64, St. Bonaventure 62
Drake 87, Pittsburgh 82
Quarterfinals
Bradley 83, St. Joseph's 81
NYU 79, DePaul 66
New Mexico 65, Drake 60
Army 67, Duquesne 65 (ot)
Semifinals
New Mexico 72, NYU 65

Bradley 67, Army 52
Third-Place Game
Army 60, NYU 59
Championship Game
Bradley 86, New Mexico 54

1965
First Round
St. John's 114, Boston College 92
Manhattan 71, Texas Western 53
Western Kentucky 57, Fordham 53
Army 70, St. Louis 66
NYU 71, Bradley 70
Detroit 93, La Salle 86
Quarterfinals
St. John's 61, New Mexico 54
Villanova 73, Manhattan 71
NYU 87, Detroit 76
Army 58, Western Kentucky 54
Semifinals
Villanova 91, NYU 69
St. John's 67, Army 60
Third-Place Game
Army 75, NYU 74
Championship Game
St. John's 55, Villanova 51

1966
First Round
Temple 88, Virginia Tech 73
NYU 68, DePaul 65
San Francisco 89, Penn State 77
Villanova 63, St. John's 61
Army 71, Manhattan 66
Boston College 96, Louisville 90 (3ot)
Quarterfinals
Brigham Young 90, Temple 78
NYU 90, Wichita State 84 (ot)
Army 80, San Francisco 63
Villanova 86, Boston College 85
Semifinals
Brigham Young 66, Army 60
NYU 69, Villanova 63
Third-Place Game
Villanova 76, Army 65
Championship Game
Brigham Young 97, NYU 84

1967
First Round
Marshall 70, Villanova 68 (ot)
Southern Illinois 103, St. Peter's 58
Providence 77, Memphis State 68
New Mexico 66, Syracuse 64
Marquette 64, Tulsa 60
Rutgers 78, Utah 76
Quarterfinals
Southern Illinois 72, Duke 63
Marshall 119, Nebraska 88
Rutgers 65, New Mexico 60
Marquette 81, Providence 80 (ot)
Semifinals
Marquette 83, Marshall 78
Southern Illinois 79, Rutgers 70
Third-Place Game
Rutgers 93, Marshall 76
Championship Game
Southern Illinois 71, Marquette 56

1968
First Round
St. Peter's 102, Marshall 93 (2ot)
Duke 97, Oklahoma City 81
Kansas 82, Temple 76
Villanova 77, Wyoming 66
Notre Dame 62, Army 58
LIU 80, Bradley 77
Fordham 69, Duquesne 60
Dayton 87, West Virginia 68

Quarterfinals
Kansas 55, Villanova 49
St. Peter's 100, Duke 71
Dayton 61, Fordham 60
Notre Dame 62, LIU 60
Semifinals
Dayton 76, Notre Dame 74 (ot)
Kansas 58, St. Peter's 46
Third-Place Game
Notre Dame 81, St. Peter's 78
Championship Game
Dayton 61, Kansas 48

1969
First Round
Temple 82, Florida 66
St. Peter's 75, Tulsa 71
Ohio U. 82, West Texas State 80
Tennessee 67, Rutgers 51
Army 51, Wyoming 49
South Carolina 72, Southern Illinois 63
Boston College 78, Kansas 62
Louisville 73, Fordham 70
Quarterfinals
Temple 94, St. Peter's 78
Tennessee 75, Ohio U. 64
Army 59, South Carolina 45
Boston College 88, Louisville 83
Semifinals
Temple 63, Tennessee 58
Boston College 73, Army 61
Third-Place Game
Tennessee 64, Army 52
Championship Game
Temple 89, Boston College 76

1970
First Round
Georgia Tech 78, Duquesne 68
St. John's 70, Miami of Ohio 57
Manhattan 95, North Carolina 90
Army 72, Cincinnati 67
Utah 78, Duke 75
Marquette 62, Massachusetts 55
Louisiana State 83, Georgetown 82
Oklahoma 74, Louisville 73
Quarterfinals
Army 77, Manhattan 72
St. John's 56, Georgia Tech 55
Marquette 83, Utah 63
Louisiana State 97, Oklahoma 94
Semifinals
St. John's 60, Army 59
Marquette 101, Louisiana State 79
Third-Place Game
Army 75, Louisiana State 68
Championship Game
Marquette 65, St. John's 53

1971
First Round
North Carolina 90, Massachusetts 49
Duke 68, Dayton 60
Providence 64, Louisville 58
Tennessee 84, St. John's 83 (2ot)
Georgia Tech 70, La Salle 67
Michigan 86, Syracuse 76
St. Bonaventure 94, Purdue 79
Hawaii 87, Oklahoma 86 (2ot)
Quarterfinals
North Carolina 86, Providence 79
Duke 78, Tennessee 64
Georgia Tech 78, Michigan 70
St. Bonaventure 73, Hawaii 64
Semifinals
North Carolina 73, Duke 69
Georgia Tech 76, St. Bonaventure 71 (2ot)
Third-Place Game
St. Bonaventure 92, Duke 88 (ot)

Championship Game
North Carolina 84, Georgia Tech
66

1972

First Round
Lafayette 72, Virginia 71
Jacksonville 94, Fordham 75
Syracuse 81, Davidson 77
Maryland 67, St. Joseph's 55
Oral Roberts 94, Memphis State
74
St. John's 82, Missouri 81 (ot)
Princeton 68, Indiana 60
Niagara 76, Texas-El Paso 57
Quarterfinals
Jacksonville 87, Lafayette 76
Maryland 71, Syracuse 65
St. John's 94, Oral Roberts 78
Niagara 65, Princeton 60
Semifinals
Maryland 91, Jacksonville 77
Niagara 69, St. John's 67
Third-Place Game
Jacksonville 83, St. John's 80
Championship Game
Maryland 100, Niagara 69

1973

First Round
Notre Dame 69, Southern Cal 65
Louisville 97, American U. 84
North Carolina 82, Oral Roberts
65
Massachusetts 78, Missouri 71
Fairfield 80, Marshall 76
Virginia Tech 65, New Mexico 63
Minnesota 68, Rutgers 59
Alabama 87, Manhattan 86
Quarterfinals
North Carolina 73, Massachu-
setts 63
Notre Dame 79, Louisville 71
Virginia Tech 77, Fairfield 76
Alabama 69, Minnesota 65
Semifinals
Virginia Tech 74, Alabama 73
Notre Dame 78, North Carolina
71
Third-Place Game
North Carolina 88, Alabama 69
Championship Game
Virginia Tech 92, Notre Dame 91
(ot)

1974

First Round
Md.-Eastern Shore 84, Manhat-
tan 81
Jacksonville 73, Massachusetts
69
Hawaii 66, Fairfield 65
Purdue 82, North Carolina 71
Memphis State 73, Seton Hall 72
Utah 102, Rutgers 89
Connecticut 82, St. John's 70
Boston College 63, Cincinnati 62
Quarterfinals
Jacksonville 85, Md.-Eastern
Shore 83
Purdue 85, Hawaii 72
Utah 92, Memphis State 78
Boston College 76, Connecticut
75
Semifinals
Purdue 78, Jacksonville 63
Utah 117, Boston College 93
Third-Place Game
Boston College 87, Jacksonville
77
Championship Game
Purdue 87, Utah 81

1975

First Round
Manhattan 68, Massachusetts 51
Providence 91, Clemson 84
Pittsburgh 70, Southern Illinois 65
St. John's 94, Lafayette 76
South Carolina 71, Connecticut
61
Princeton 84, Holy Cross 63
Oral Roberts 97, Memphis State
95
Oregon 85, St. Peter's 79
Quarterfinals
Providence 101, Pittsburgh 80
St. John's 57, Manhattan 56
Oregon 68, Oral Roberts 59
Princeton 86, South Carolina 67
Semifinals
Providence 85, St. John's 72
Princeton 58, Oregon 57
Third-Place Game
Oregon 80, St. John's 76 (ot)
Championship Game
Princeton 80, Providence 69

1976

First Round
UNC Charlotte 79, San Francisco
74
Holy Cross 84, St. Peter's 78
Kentucky 67, Niagara 61
Providence 84, N.C. A&T 68
Quarterfinals
UNC Charlotte 79, Oregon 72
N.C. State 78, Holy Cross 68
Kentucky 81, Kansas State 78
Providence 73, Louisville 67
Semifinals
UNC Charlotte 80, N.C. State 79
Kentucky 79, Providence 78
Third-Place Game
N.C. State 74, Providence 69
Championship Game
Kentucky 71, UNC Charlotte 67

1977

First Round
*Alabama 86, Memphis State 63
*Virginia Tech 83, Georgetown 79
Illinois State 65, *Creighton 58
*Houston 83, Indiana State 82
Villanova 71, *Old Dominion 68
(ot)
*Massachusetts 86, Seton Hall 85
Oregon 90, *Oral Roberts 89
St. Bonaventure 79, *Rutgers 77
Quarterfinals
Alabama 79, Virginia Tech 72
Houston 91, Illinois State 90
Villanova 81, Massachusetts 71
St. Bonaventure 76, Oregon 73
Semifinals
Houston 82, Alabama 76
St. Bonaventure 86, Villanova 82
Third-Place Game
Villanova 102, Alabama 89
Championship Game
St. Bonaventure 94, Houston 91

1978

First Round
Georgetown 70, *Virginia 68 (ot)
*Nebraska 67, Utah State 66
*Texas 72, Temple 58
*Rutgers 72, Army 70
*Indiana State 73, Illinois State 71
*N.C. State 82, South Carolina 70
*Detroit 94, Virginia Common-
wealth 86
*Dayton 108, Fairfield 93
Quarterfinals
Georgetown 71, *Dayton 62
*Texas 67, Nebraska 48
*Rutgers 57, Indiana State 56

*N.C. State 84, Detroit 77
Semifinals
Texas 96, Rutgers 76
N.C. State 86, Georgetown 85
Third-Place Game
Rutgers 85, Georgetown 72
Championship Game
Texas 101, N.C. State 93
*Home team.

1979

First Round
Clemson 68, *Kentucky 67 (ot)
*Virginia 79, Northeast La. 78
*Old Dominion 83, Wagner 81
*Maryland 67, Rhode Island 65
(3ot)
Nevada-Reno 62, *Oregon State
61
*Ohio State 80, St. Joseph's 66
*Alabama 98, St. Bonaventure 89
Indiana 78, *Texas Tech 59
Texas A&M 79, *New Mexico 68
*Dayton 105, Holy Cross 81
*Purdue 97, Central Michigan 80
Alcorn State 80, *Mississippi
State 78
Second Round
Texas A&M 67, *Nevada-Reno 64
*Purdue 84, Dayton 70
Old Dominion 61, *Clemson 59
Ohio State 79, *Maryland 72
*Alabama 90, Virginia 88
*Indiana 73, Alcorn State 69
Third Round
Indiana and Ohio State drew byes
Alabama 72, *Texas A&M 68 at
Houston
*Purdue 67, Old Dominion 59
Semifinals
Indiana 64, Ohio State 55
Purdue 87, Alabama 68
Third-Place Game
Alabama 96, Ohio State 86
Championship Game
Indiana 53, Purdue 52

1980

First Round
St. Peter's 71, *Connecticut 56
*Illinois State 80, West Texas
State 63
*Texas 70, St. Joseph's 61
*Minnesota 64, Bowling Green 50
Murray State 53, *Jacksonville 49
*Virginia 67, Lafayette 56
*Illinois 105, Loyola (Ill.) 87
*Alabama 53, Penn State 49
*Boston College 95, Boston Uni-
versity 74
Texas-El Paso 58, *Wichita State
56
*Duquesne 65, Pittsburgh 63
*Southwestern La. 74, Ala.-Birm-
ingham 72
*Michigan 76, Nebraska 69
*Mississippi 76, Grambling 74
*UNLV 93, Washington 73
Long Beach State 104, Pepper-
dine 87 at Anaheim
Second Round
St. Peter's 34, *Duquesne 33
*Virginia 57, Boston College 55
Southwestern La. 77, *Texas 76
*Minnesota 58, Mississippi 56
Murray State 70, *Alabama 62
*Illinois 75, Illinois State 65
*Michigan 74, Texas-El Paso 65
*UNLV 90, Long Beach State 81
Quarterfinals
*UNLV 67, St. Peter's 62
*Minnesota 94, Southwestern La.
73
*Illinois 65, Murray State 63
*Virginia 79, Michigan 68

Semifinals
Virginia 90, UNLV 71
Minnesota 65, Illinois 63
Third-Place Game
Illinois 84, UNLV 74
Championship Game
Virginia 58, Minnesota 55

1981

First Round
*Dayton 66, Fordham 65 (2ot)
*Georgia 74, Old Dominion 60
*Texas-El Paso 57, San Jose
State 53
*South Alabama 74, Texas-Arling-
ton 71
*Toledo 91, American U. 83
*Minnesota 90, Drake 77
Connecticut 65, *South Florida 55
*Purdue 84, Rhode Island 58
*Michigan 74, Duquesne 58
*Duke 79, N.C. A&T 69
Temple 58, *Clemson 82
Alabama 73, *St. John's 69 (ot)
Holy Cross 56, *Southern Missis-
sippi 54
*Syracuse 88, Marquette 81
*Tulsa 81, Pan American 71
*West Virginia 67, Pennsylvania
64
Second Round
*Michigan 80, Toledo 68
South Alabama 73, *Georgia 72
*Tulsa 76, Texas-El Paso 72
Minnesota 84, *Connecticut 66
*Duke 75, Alabama 70
*West Virginia 77, Temple 76 (ot)
*Syracuse 77, Holy Cross 57
*Purdue 50, Dayton 46
Quarterfinals
*Syracuse 91, Michigan 76
West Virginia 80, *Minnesota 69
*Tulsa 69, South Alabama 68
*Purdue 81, Duke 69
Semifinals
Tulsa 89, West Virginia 87
Syracuse 70, Purdue 63
Third-Place Game
Purdue 75, West Virginia 72 (ot)
Championship Game
Tulsa 86, Syracuse 84 (ot)

1982

First Round
Oklahoma 81, *Oral Roberts 73
*Purdue 72, Western Kentucky 65
*Illinois 126, LIU 78
Washington 66, *Brigham Young
63
*Texas A&M 60, Lamar 58
*Dayton 76, Connecticut 75 (ot)
*UNLV 87, Murray State 61
*Georgia 73, Temple 60
*Rutgers 55, Iona 51
*Bradley 76, American U. 65
Tulane 83, *Louisiana State 72
UC Irvine 70, *San Diego State 69
*Syracuse 84, St. Peter's 75
*Virginia Tech 69, Fordham 58
Maryland 60, *Richmond 50
Mississippi 53, *Clemson 49
Second Round
Tulane 56, *UNLV 51
*Oklahoma 80, UC Irvine 77
Bradley 95, *Syracuse 81
*Georgia 83, Maryland 69
Dayton 61, *Illinois 58
Texas A&M 69, *Washington 65
Virginia Tech 61, *Mississippi 59
*Purdue 98, Rutgers 65
Quarterfinals
*Oklahoma 91, Dayton 82
*Bradley 77, Tulane 61
*Georgia 90, Virginia Tech 73
*Purdue 86, Texas A&M 68

Semifinals
Bradley 84, Oklahoma 68
Purdue 61, Georgia 60
Championship Game
Bradley 67, Purdue 58

1983

First Round
*Vanderbilt 79, East Tenn. State 74
*South Florida 81, Fordham 69
New Orleans 99, *Louisiana State 94 (ot)
*Oregon State 77, Idaho 59
*DePaul 76, Minnesota 73
*South Carolina 100, Old Dominion 90
Texas Christian 64, *Tulsa 62
*Iona 90, St. Bonaventure 76
*Fresno State 71, Texas-El Paso 64
*Virginia Tech 85, William & Mary 79
*Northwestern 71, Notre Dame 57
Wake Forest 87, *Murray State 80
*Nebraska 72, Tulane 65
*Mississippi 87, Alabama State 75
*Arizona State 87, Cal State Fullerton 83
*Michigan State 72, Bowling Green 71
Second Round
*Nebraska 85, Iona 73
*Mississippi 65, South Florida 57
Fresno State 72, *Michigan State 58
Wake Forest 75, *Vanderbilt 68
*South Carolina 75, Virginia Tech 68
Texas Christian 78, *Arizona State 76
*Oregon State 88, New Orleans 71
*DePaul 65, Northwestern 63
Quarterfinals
*Nebraska 67, Texas Christian 57
*Wake Forest 78, South Carolina 61
Fresno State 76, *Oregon State 67
*DePaul 75, Mississippi 67
Semifinals
Fresno State 86, Wake Forest 62
DePaul 68, Nebraska 58
Championship Game
Fresno State 69, DePaul 60

1984

First Round
*Notre Dame 67, Old Dominion 62
*Tenn.-Chattanooga 74, Georgia 69 (ot)
Lamar 64, *New Mexico 61
Southwestern La. 94, *Utah State 92
*South Alabama 88, Florida 87
*Tennessee 54, St. Peter's 40
Nebraska 56, *Creighton 54
*Xavier 60, Ohio State 57
Florida State 74, *N.C. State 71
Marquette 73, *Iowa State 53
*Virginia Tech 77, Georgia Tech 74
*Michigan 94, Wichita State 70
Santa Clara 66, *Oregon 53
*Weber State 75, Fordham 63
Boston College 76, *St. Joseph's 63
Pittsburgh 95, *La Salle 91
Second Round
Pittsburgh 66, Florida State 63 at Greensboro, NC
Virginia Tech 68, South Alabama 66 at Greensboro, NC

Santa Clara 76, *Lamar 74
*Michigan 83, Marquette 70
*Xavier 58, Nebraska 57
*Tennessee 68, Tenn.-Chattanooga 66
*Southwestern La. 74, Weber State 72 (2ot)
Notre Dame 66, *Boston College 52
Quarterfinals
*Southwestern La. 97, Santa Clara 76
*Michigan 63, Xavier 62
Notre Dame 72, *Pittsburgh 64
*Virginia Tech 72, Tennessee 68
Semifinals
Michigan 78, Virginia Tech 75
Notre Dame 65, Southwestern La. 59
Third-Place Game
Virginia Tech 71, Southwestern La. 70
Championship Game
Michigan 83, Notre Dame 63

1985

First Round
*New Mexico 80, Texas A&M 67
*Nebraska 79, Canisius 68
*Cincinnati 77, Kent State 61
*Louisville 77, Alcorn State 75
Tennessee 65, *Tennessee Tech 62
*Southwestern La. 65, Florida 64
Virginia 56, *West Virginia 55
*Fresno State 79, Santa Clara 76
*South Florida 77, Wake Forest 66
St. Joseph's 68, *Missouri 67
*UCLA 78, Montana 47
*Tenn.-Chattanooga 67, Clemson 65
*Lamar 78, Houston 71
*Indiana 79, Butler 57
*Richmond 59, Fordham 57
Second Round
*UCLA 82, Nebraska 63
Marquette 56, *Cincinnati 54
*Fresno State 66, New Mexico 55
*Virginia 68, St. Joseph's 61
*Indiana 75, Richmond 53
*Louisville 68, South Florida 61
*Tennessee 73, Southwestern La. 72
Tenn.-Chattanooga 85, *Lamar 84 (ot)
Quarterfinals
*Tennessee 61, Virginia 54
*UCLA 53, Fresno State 43
*Indiana 94, Marquette 82 (2ot)
*Louisville 71, Tenn.-Chattanooga 66
Semifinals
UCLA 75, Louisville 66
Indiana 74, Tennessee 67
Third-Place Game
Tennessee 100, Louisville 84
Championship Game
UCLA 65, Indiana 62

1986

First Round
Texas Christian 76, *Montana 69
*McNeese State 86, Dayton 75
*Southwest Mo. State 59, Pittsburgh 52
*Providence 72, Boston University 69
George Mason 65, *Lamar 63
*Wyoming 79, Texas A&M 70
Texas 69, *New Mexico 66
*Florida 81, Southern Mississippi 71
Georgia 95, *Tenn.-Chattanooga 81

Louisiana Tech 67, *Northern Arizona 61
Loyola Marymount 80, *California 75
UC Irvine 80, *UCLA 74
*Brigham Young 67, SMU 63
*Marquette 79, Drake 59
*Clemson 99, Middle Tennessee State 81
Ohio State 65, *Ohio University 62
Second Round
*Florida 77, Texas Christian 75
Clemson 77, *Georgia 65
*Providence 90, George Mason 71
*Southwest Mo. State 83, Marquette 69
*Ohio State 71, Texas 65
*Louisiana Tech 77, McNeese State 61
*Wyoming 99, Loyola Marymount 90
*Brigham Young 93, UC Irvine 80
Quarterfinals
Louisiana Tech 64, *Providence 63
*Florida 54, Southwest Mo. State 53
*Wyoming 62, Clemson 57
*Ohio State 79, Brigham Young 68
Semifinals
Ohio State 79, Louisiana Tech 66
Wyoming 67, Florida 58
Third-Place Game
Louisiana Tech 67, Florida 62
Championship Game
Ohio State 73, Wyoming 63

1987

First Round
*Nebraska 78, Marquette 76
*Boise State 62, Utah 61
Washington 98, *Montana State 90
La Salle 86, *Villanova 84
*Florida State 107, Rhode Island 92
Cleveland State 92, *Tenn.-Chattanooga 73
*Arkansas-Little Rock 42, Baylor 41
*Illinois State 79, Akron 72
*Vanderbilt 74, Jacksonville 72
*Stephen F. Austin 70, James Madison 63
*Niagara 74, Seton Hall 65
*Arkansas 67, Arkansas State 64 (ot)
*St. Louis 76, St. Peter's 60
*Southern Mississippi 93, Mississippi 75
Oregon State 85, *New Mexico 82
*California 72, Cal State Fullerton 68
Second Round
Illinois State 79, *Cleveland State 77
*Arkansas-Little Rock 54, Stephen F. Austin 48
*Vanderbilt 109, Florida State 92
*Washington 73, Boise State 68
La Salle 89, *Niagara 81
*Nebraska 78, Arkansas 71
Southern Mississippi 83, *St. Louis 78
California 65, *Oregon State 62
Quarterfinals
*La Salle 70, Illinois State 50
*Arkansas-Little Rock 80, California 73
Southern Mississippi 95, *Vanderbilt 88

*Nebraska 81, Washington 76
Semifinals
La Salle 92, Arkansas-Little Rock 73
Southern Mississippi 82, Nebraska 75
Third-Place Game
Nebraska 76, Arkansas-Little Rock 67
Championship Game
Southern Mississippi 84, La Salle 80

1988

First Round
*Ohio State 86, Old Dominion 73
*Georgia 53, Georgia Southern 48
Connecticut 62, *West Virginia 57 (ot)
*Evansville 66, Utah 55
Louisiana Tech 66, *Arkansas-Little Rock 56
*Boston College 73, Siena 65
*Houston 69, Fordham 61
*New Mexico 86, Pepperdine 75
*Oregon 81, Santa Clara 65
*Cleveland State 89, Illinois State 83 (ot)
*Middle Tenn. State 85, Tennessee 80
Virginia Commonwealth 81, *Marshall 80
*Arkansas State 70, Northeast Louisiana 54
*Southern Mississippi 74, Clemson 69
*Colorado State 63, New Orleans 54
*Stanford 80, Long Beach State 77
Second Round
*Connecticut 65, Louisiana Tech 59
*Va. Commonwealth 93, Southern Mississippi 89
*Ohio State 86, Cleveland State 80
*Middle Tennessee State 69, Georgia 54
Boston College 86, *Evansville 81
*Colorado State 71, Houston 61
Arkansas State 60, *Stanford 59
*New Mexico 78, Oregon 59
Quarterfinals
*Connecticut 69, Va. Commonwealth 60
Ohio State 68, *New Mexico 65
*Colorado State 69, Arkansas State 49
Boston College 78, *Middle Tenn. State 69
Semifinals
Ohio State 64, Colorado State 62
Connecticut 73, Boston College 67
Third-Place Game
Colorado State 58, Boston College 57
Championship Game
Connecticut 72, Ohio State 67

1989

First Round
*Villanova 76, St. Peter's 56
*Ala.-Birmingham 83, Georgia Southern 74
*Richmond 70, Temple 56
*St. John's 70, Mississippi 67
*Wisconsin 63, New Orleans 61
*Penn State 89, Murray State 73
*Ohio State 81, Akron 70
*St. Louis 87, Southern Illinois 54
*Connecticut 67, UNC Charlotte 62
*California 73, Hawaii 57

*New Mexico 91, Santa Clara 76
*Michigan State 83, Kent State 69 at Detroit
*Wichita State 70, UC Santa Barbara 62
Pepperdine 84, *New Mexico State 69
Nebraska 81, Arkansas State 79
*Oklahoma State 69, Boise State 55

Second Round
St. Louis 73, *Wisconsin 68
*Villanova 76, Penn State 67
*Connecticut 73, California 72
*Ohio State 85, Nebraska 74
Ala.-Birmingham 64, *Richmond 61
*Michigan State 79, Wichita State 67
*St. John's 76, Oklahoma State 64
*New Mexico 86, Pepperdine 69

Quarterfinals
Ala.-Birmingham 85, *Connecticut 79
Michigan State 70, *Villanova 63
St. Louis 66, *New Mexico 65
St. John's 83, *Ohio State 80 (ot)

Semifinals
St. Louis 74, Michigan State 64
St. John's 76, Ala.-Birmingham 65

Third-Place Game
Ala.-Birmingham 78, Michigan State 76 (ot)

Championship Game
St. John's 73, St. Louis 65

1990
First Round
*Penn State 57, Marquette 54
New Orleans 78, *James Madison 74
Tennessee 73, *Memphis State 71
*Fordham 106, Southern (La.) 80
*Maryland 91, Massachusetts 81
*Mississippi State 84, Baylor 75
Wisconsin-Green Bay 73, *Southern Illinois 60
*Vanderbilt 98, Louisiana Tech 90 (ot)
*Oklahoma State 83, Tulsa 74
*Hawaii 69, Stanford 57
*Rutgers 87, Holy Cross 78
*Cincinnati 75, Bowling Green 60
*St. Louis 85, Kent State 74
*DePaul 89, Creighton 72
*New Mexico 89, Oregon 78
Long Beach State 86, *Arizona State 71

Second Round
*Vanderbilt 89, Tennessee 85
*Rutgers 81, Fordham 74
*Penn State 80, Maryland 78
*New Orleans 65, Mississippi State 60
*DePaul 61, Cincinnati 59
*St. Louis 58, Wisconsin-Green Bay 54
*New Mexico 90, Oklahoma State 88
*Hawaii 84, Long Beach State 79

Quarterfinals
Penn State 58, *Rutgers 55
*Vanderbilt 88, New Orleans 65
*St. Louis 54, DePaul 47
*New Mexico 80, Hawaii 58

Semifinals
Vanderbilt 75, Penn State 62
St. Louis 80, New Mexico 73

Third-Place Game
Penn State 83, New Mexico 81 (ot)

Championship Game
Vanderbilt 74, St. Louis 72

1991
First Round
*Providence 98, James Madison 93 (2ot)
*Cincinnati 82, Ball State 55
*Wisconsin 87, Bowling Green 79 (ot)
Southern Illinois 75, *Boise State 74
*Colorado 71, Michigan 64
*Stanford 93, Houston 86
*Siena 90, Fairleigh Dickinson 85
*Memphis State 82, Ala.-Birmingham 76
*Oklahoma 111, Tulsa 86
*Southwest Mo. State 57, Coppin State 47
*Arkansas State 78, Rice 71
Fordham 76, *South Florida 66
*West Virginia 86, Furman 67
*South Carolina 69, George Washington 63
*Massachusetts 93, La Salle 90
*Wyoming 63, Butler 61

Second Round
*Providence 85, West Virginia 79
*Oklahoma 89, Cincinnati 81 (ot)
*Colorado 83, Wyoming 75
Southern Illinois 72, *Southwest Mo. State 69
Arkansas State 58, *Memphis State 57
Stanford 80, *Wisconsin 72
Massachusetts 78, *Fordham 74
*Siena 63, South Carolina 58

Quarterfinals
Oklahoma 83, *Providence 74
Massachusetts 82, *Siena 80 (ot)
*Colorado 81, Arkansas State 75
Stanford 78, *Southern Illinois 68

Semifinals
Stanford 73, Massachusetts 71
Oklahoma 88, Colorado 78

Third-Place Game
Colorado 98, Massachusetts 91

Championship Game
Stanford 78, Oklahoma 72

1992
First Round
*Kansas State 85, Western Kentucky 74
Virginia 83, *Villanova 80
Pittsburgh 67, *Penn State 65
*Washington State 72, Minnesota 70
*Tennessee 71, Ala.-Birmingham 68
*Notre Dame 63, Western Michigan 56
*Manhattan 67, Wisconsin-Green Bay 65
*Purdue 82, Butler 56
*Utah 72, Ball State 57
*New Mexico 90, Louisiana Tech 84
Rhode Island 68, *Vanderbilt 63
Arizona State 71, *UC Santa Barbara 65
*Boston College 78, Southern Illinois 69
*Texas Christian 73, Long Beach State 61
*Florida 66, Richmond 52
*Rutgers 73, James Madison 69

Second Round
*Virginia 77, Tennessee 52
*Notre Dame 64, Kansas State 48
Florida 77, *Pittsburgh 74
*Purdue 67, Texas Christian 51
*New Mexico 79, Washington State 71

Manhattan 62, *Rutgers 61
Rhode Island 81, *Boston College 80 (2ot)
Utah 60, *Arizona State 58

Quarterfinals
*Notre Dame 74, Manhattan 58
Florida 74, *Purdue 67 at Indianapolis
*Virginia 76, New Mexico 71 at Richmond
*Utah 84, Rhode Island 72

Semifinals
Virginia 62, Florida 56
Notre Dame 58, Utah 55

Third-Place Game
Utah 81, Florida 78

Championship Game
Virginia 81, Notre Dame 76

1993
First Round
*Old Dominion 74, Va. Commonwealth 68
Boston College 87, *Niagara 83
*Providence 73, James Madison 61
*Clemson 84, Auburn 72
Ala.-Birmingham 58, *Alabama 56
*Southwest Mo. State 56, St. Joseph's 34
Georgetown 78, *Arizona State 68
*Minnesota 74, Florida 66
*West Virginia 95, Georgia 84
Miami of Ohio 56, *Ohio State 53
*Oklahoma 88, Michigan State 86
Southern Cal 90, *UNLV 74
Jackson State 90, *Connecticut 88 (ot)
*Texas-El Paso 67, Houston 61
Pepperdine 53, *UC Santa Barbara 50

Second Round
*Ala.-Birmingham 65, Clemson 64
*Miami of Ohio 60, Old Dominion 58
*Boston College 101, Rice 68
*Providence 68, West Virginia 67
*Minnesota 86, Oklahoma 72
*Georgetown 71, Texas-El Paso 44
Southwest Mo. State 70, *Jackson State 52
*Southern Cal 71, Pepperdine 59

Quarterfinals
Providence 75, *Boston College 58
*Minnesota 76, Southern Cal 58
*Ala.-Birmingham 61, Southwest Mo. State 52
*Georgetown 66, Miami of Ohio 53

Semifinals
Minnesota 76, Providence 70
Georgetown 45, Ala.-Birmingham 41

Third-Place Game
Ala.-Birmingham 55, Providence 52

Championship Game
Minnesota 62, Georgetown 61

1994
First Round
Tulane 76, *Evansville 63
Vanderbilt 77, *Oklahoma 67
*Fresno State 79, Southern Cal 76
*Bradley 66, Murray State 58
*Northwestern 69, DePaul 68
*Xavier 80, Miami of Ohio 68
*Duquesne 75, UNC Charlotte 73
*Siena 76, Georgia Tech 68
*New Orleans 79, Texas A&M 73 (ot)

*Clemson 96, Southern Mississippi 85
*Old Dominion 76, Manhattan 74
*West Virginia 85, Davidson 69
*Villanova 103, Canisius 79
*Brigham Young 74, Arizona State 67
Gonzaga 80, *Stanford 76
*Kansas State 78, Mississippi State 67

Second Round
Xavier 83, *Northwestern 79
Villanova 82, *Duquesne 66
*Vanderbilt 78, New Orleans 59
Clemson 96, *West Virginia 79
*Kansas State 66, Gonzaga 64
*Fresno State 68, Brigham Young 66
*Bradley 79, Old Dominion 75
*Siena 89, Tulane 79

Quarterfinals
*Vanderbilt 89, Clemson 74
*Villanova 76, Xavier 74
*Siena 75, Bradley 62
*Kansas State 115, Fresno State 77

Semifinals
Vanderbilt 82, Kansas State 76
Villanova 66, Siena 58

Third-Place Game
Siena 92, Kansas State 78

Championship Game
Villanova 80, Vanderbilt 73

1995
First Round
*New Mexico State 97, Colorado 83
*Texas-El Paso 90, Montana 60
*Virginia Tech 62, Clemson 54
*Providence 72, Charleston 67
*Washington State 94, Texas Tech 82
Illinois State 93, *Utah State 87 (2ot)
*Canisius 83, Seton Hall 71
*Bradley 86, Eastern Michigan 85 (2ot)
Coppin State 75, *St. Joseph's 68 (ot)
*South Florida 74, St. John's 67
Marquette 68, *Auburn 61
*St. Bonaventure 75, Southern Miss. 70
*Penn State 62, Miami (Fla.) 56
*Nebraska 69, Georgia 63
*Ohio University 83, George Washington 71
Iowa 96, DePaul 87 at Moline, Ill.

Second Round
New Mexico State 92, *Texas-El Paso 89
Virginia Tech 91, *Providence 78
Washington State 83, *Illinois State 80
Canisius 55, *Bradley 53
*South Florida 75, Coppin State 59
*Marquette 70, St. Bonaventure 61
Penn State 65, *Nebraska 59
*Iowa 66, Ohio University 62

Quarterfinals
*Virginia Tech 64, New Mexico State 61
*Canisius 89, Washington State 80
*Marquette 57, South Florida 50 (ot)
Penn State 67, *Iowa 64

Semifinals
Virginia Tech 71, Canisius 59
Marquette 87, Penn State 79

Third-Place Game
Penn State 66, Canisius 62

Championship Game
Virginia Tech 65, Marquette 64 (ot)

1996

First Round
*Rhode Island 82, Marist 77
College of Charleston 55, *Tennessee 49
*South Carolina 100, Davidson 73
*Michigan State 64, Washington 50
*Minnesota 68, Saint Louis 52
*Missouri 89, Murray State 85
*Wisconsin 55, Manhattan 42
Tulane 87, *Auburn 73 (ot)
*Vanderbilt 86, Arkansas-Little Rock 80
Alabama 72, *Illinois 69
*Illinois State 73, Mount St. Mary's 49
*Fresno State 57, Miami of Ohio 56
St. Joseph's 82, *Iona 78
Nebraska 91, *Colorado State 83

*Washington State 92, Gonzaga 73
Providence 91, Fairfield 79 at New Haven, Conn.

Second Round
*South Carolina 80, Vanderbilt 70
Tulane 84, *Minnesota 65
Illinois State 77, *Wisconsin 62
*Alabama 72, Missouri 49
St. Joseph's 82, *Providence 62
*Nebraska 82, Washington State 73
*Fresno State 80, Michigan State 70
*Rhode Island 62, College of Charleston 58 (ot)

Quarterfinals
Alabama 68, *South Carolina 67
*Tulane 83, Illinois State 72
*St. Joseph's 76, Rhode Island 59
Nebraska 83, *Fresno State 71

Semifinals
Nebraska 90, Tulane 78
St. Joseph's 74, Alabama 69 (ot)

Third-Place Game
Tulane 87, Alabama 76

Championship Game
Nebraska 60, St. Joseph's 56

1997

First Round
*West Virginia 98, Bowling Green 95
*Michigan State 65, George Washington 50
Florida State 82, *Syracuse 67
*Notre Dame 74, Oral Roberts 58
*Pittsburgh 82, New Orleans 63
*Connecticut 71, Iona 66
*Arkansas 101, Northern Arizona 75
*Bradley 66, Drexel 53
*Texas Christian 85, UAB 62
*Nebraska 67, Washington 63
*N.C. State 77, Southwest Missouri State 66
Nevada 97, *Fresno State 86
*UNLV 66, Memphis 62
*Hawaii 71, Oregon 61
*Michigan 76, Miami (Fla.) 63
*Oklahoma State 79, Tulane 72

Second Round
West Virginia 76, *N.C. State 73
*Florida State 68, Michigan State 63
*Arkansas 76, Pittsburgh 71
*UNLV 89, Hawaii 80 (ot)
*Michigan 75, Oklahoma State 65
Nebraska 78, *Nevada 68
*Notre Dame 82, Texas Christian 72
*Connecticut 63, Bradley 47

Quarterfinals
Florida State 76, *West Virginia 71
*Arkansas 86, UNLV 73
Michigan 67, *Notre Dame 66
*Connecticut 76, Nebraska 67

Semifinals
Florida State 71, Connecticut 65 (ot)
Michigan 77, Arkansas 62

Third-Place Game
Connecticut 74, Arkansas 64

Championship Game
Michigan 82, Florida State 73

*Home Team

9

ALL-STARS AND ALL-AMERICANS

1997-98 Preseason All-American Teams

FIRST TEAM

G—Mike Bibby, 6-2, Soph., Arizona
G—Cory Carr, 6-4, Sr., Texas Tech
C—Alexander Koul, 7-1, Sr., George Washington
F—Antawn Jamison, 6-8, Jr., North Carolina
F—Raef LaFrentz, 6-11, Sr., Kansas

SECOND TEAM

G—B.J. McKie, 6-2, Jr., South Carolina
G—Kareem Reid, 5-9, Jr., Arkansas
C—Kenny Thomas, 6-9, Jr., New Mexico
F—Pat Garrity, 6-9, Sr., Notre Dame
F—Paul Pierce, 6-7, Jr., Kansas

THIRD TEAM

G—Ed Cota, 6-1, Soph., North Carolina
G—Richard Hamilton, 6-6, Soph., Connecticut
C—Keon Clark, 6-11, Sr., UNLV
F—Matt Harpring, 6-7, Sr., Georgia Tech
F—Jess Settles, 6-7, Sr., Iowa

FOURTH TEAM

G—Toby Bailey, 6-5, Sr., UCLA
G—Miles Simon, 6-4, Sr., Arizona

C—Robert Traylor, 6-9, Jr., Michigan
F—Corey Benjamin, 6-6, Soph., Oregon State
F—DeMarco Johnson, 6-8, Sr., UNC Charlotte

MOST UNDERRATED TEAM

G—Roderick Blakney, 5-10, Sr., South Carolina State
G—Randy Bolden, 6-2, Sr., Texas Southern
C—Danny Moore, 6-11, Jr., Southwest Missouri State
F—Bonzi Wells, 6-5, Sr., Ball State
F—Raymond Tutt, 6-4, Sr., UC Santa Barbara

HONORABLE MENTION

(Listed Alphabetically by Position)

GUARDS

Earl Boykins, 5-5, Sr., Eastern Michigan
Louis Bullock, 6-2, Jr., Michigan
Donnie Carr, 6-4, Soph., La Salle
Anthony Carter, 6-1, Sr., Hawaii
Mateen Cleaves, 6-2, Soph., Michigan State
Arthur Davis, 6-4, Soph., St. Joseph's
Bryce Drew, 6-3, Sr., Valparaiso
A.J. Guyton, 6-1, Soph., Indiana
Eric Harris, 6-3, Sr., Minnesota

Shaheen Holloway, 5-9, Soph., Seton Hall
Charles Jones, 6-3, Sr., Long Island
Mike Jones, 6-3, Sr., Texas Christian
Trajan Langdon, 6-3, Jr., Duke
Pete Lisicky, 6-4, Sr., Penn State
Felipe Lopez, 6-5, Sr., St. John's
Tyronn Lue, 6-0, Jr., Nebraska
Andre Miller, 6-2, Sr., Utah
Johnny Miller, 6-1, Jr., Clemson
Adrian Pledger, 6-3, Sr., West Virginia
Shawnta Rogers, 5-3, Jr., George Washington
Juan Sanchez, 6-0, Soph., Temple
Curtis Staples, 6-2, Sr., Virginia
Jeremy Veal, 6-3, Sr., Arizona State
LaDrell Whitehead, 5-8, Sr., Wyoming
Steve Wojciechowski, 5-11, Sr., Duke

CENTERS

Jason Collier, 7-0, Soph., Indiana
Mike Doleac, 6-11, Sr., Utah
Evan Eschmeyer, 6-11, Sr., Northwestern
Zendon Hamilton, 6-11, Sr., St. John's
Lari Ketner, 6-10, Jr., Massachusetts
T.J. Lux, 6-9, Jr., Northern Illinois
Todd MacCulloch, 7-0, Jr., Washington
Jelani McCoy, 6-10, Jr., UCLA
Brad Miller, 6-11, Sr., Purdue
Michael Olowokandi, 7-0, Sr., Pacific
Guy Rucker, 6-9, Soph., Iowa
Brian Skinner, 6-10, Sr., Baylor
Tim Young, 7-1, Jr., Stanford

FORWARDS

Rico Alderson, 6-5, Sr., South Alabama
Maceo Baston, 6-9, Sr., Michigan
C.J. Black, 6-8, Soph., Tennessee
Ryan Bowen, 6-7, Sr., Iowa
Torraye Braggs, 6-8, Sr., Xavier
Greg Buckner, 6-4, Sr., Clemson
Joe Bunn, 6-6, Sr., Old Dominion
Brian Cardinal, 6-8, Soph., Purdue
Vince Carter, 6-5, Jr., North Carolina
Kris Clack, 6-5, Jr., Texas
Maurice Curtis, 6-8, Sr., Fordham
Bennett Davison, 6-8, Sr., Arizona
Michael Dickerson, 6-5, Sr., Arizona
Venson Hamilton, 6-9, Jr., Nebraska

James Head, 6-7, Sr., Eastern Michigan
J.R. Henderson, 6-9, Sr., UCLA
Rico Hill, 6-6, Jr., Illinois State
Sam Jacobson, 6-6, Sr., Minnesota
Courtney James, 6-6, Jr., Minnesota
Malcolm Johnson, 6-4, Sr., TCU
Landry Kosmalski, 6-7, Soph., Davidson
Corey Louis, 6-9, Sr., Florida State
Erik Nelson, 6-7, Sr., Vermont
Sam Okey, 6-7, Jr., Wisconsin
Richie Parker, 6-5, Soph., Long Island
Andrae Patterson, 6-8, Sr., Indiana
Reuben Patterson, 6-7, Sr., Cincinnati
James Penny, 6-5, Sr., Texas Christian
Ryan Perryman, 6-7, Sr., Dayton
Reginald Poole, 6-8, Sr., Southwestern La.
James Posey, 6-7, Jr., Xavier
Louis Richardson, 6-8, Sr., New Mexico State
Galen Robinson, 6-8, Sr., Houston
Michael Ruffin, 6-8, Jr., Tulsa
Antonio Smith, 6-8, Jr., Michigan State
Shaun Stonerook, 6-7, Jr., Ohio State
Kelly Thames, 6-8, Sr., Missouri
Winfred Walton, 6-9, Fr., Fresno State

To Earn or To Learn

It's not a surprise that Dale Brown and Larry Finch are no longer coaching LSU and Memphis, respectively, after they each lost numerous vital undergraduates to the pros. Brown saw eight stars depart for the pros from 1985 through 1996 while Finch had five standouts bid adieu to play for pay from 1987 through 1996.

Jeers to those so-called experts for second-guessing the majority of college players with eligibility remaining who declare for the National Basketball Association draft. Far too many observers jump to the conclusion that the time isn't right for most of the undergraduates because they still need to mature.

Do skeptics genuinely believe that these younger athletes need additional seasoning that can be gained only in college? Of course, it's a difficult adjustment from amateur hoops to the pros, but it would be that way even if a player had six or more years of college eligibility.

Before accepting the dogma of administrators that undergraduates are making monumental mistakes, remember that the majority of the premier players in the NBA left college early. More than half of the All-NBA first- and second-team selections since the 1979-80 season departed school with eligibility remaining, including all five first-teamers in 1988-89 (Charles Barkley, Magic Johnson, Michael Jordan, Karl Malone and Hakeem Olajuwon).

Since the NBA began drafting players who left college early in 1971, an average of five undergraduates annually were first- or second-round choices. Naturally, many of the players who migrated early to the pros already had become or were possible All-American candidates.

Six of the defectors went straight to the pros from high school—Kobe Bryant, Darryl Dawkins, Kevin Garnett, Moses Malone, Jermaine O'Neal and Bill Willoughby. Only four NCAA titlists, including just one in the last 14 years, promptly lost undergrads who became NBA first-round draft picks—Michigan State '79 (Johnson), Indiana '81 (Isiah Thomas), North Carolina '82 (James Worthy) and Kentucky '96 (Antoine Walker).

Here are year-by-year alphabetical lists of the undergraduate draftees who were high selections by the NBA or ABA (pick overall is in parentheses following the round selected):

UNDERGRADUATE POS.	COLLEGE	YR.	DRAFTED (ROUND)
1971			
Phil Chenier, G	California	Jr.	Baltimore (1st)
Tom Payne, C	Kentucky	So.	Atlanta (1st)
Nate Williams, F	Utah State	Jr.	Cincinnati (1st)

NOTES: These "hardship cases" were selected in a supplementary draft and the franchises that chose them had to surrender their corresponding pick in the regular draft of college seniors. . . . Mickey Davis, who left Duquesne after his junior season, was selected by Denver in ABA special circumstances draft. His rights were traded to Pittsburgh.

1972			
Bob McAdoo, F-C	North Carolina	Jr.	Buffalo (1st/2)
Brian Taylor, G	Princeton	Jr.	Seattle (2nd/23)

NOTE: Jim Chones departed Marquette late in his junior season and was selected by the New York Nets in the ABA draft.

1973			
Bird Averitt, G	Pepperdine	Jr.	Portland (4th/55)
Dwight Jones, F	Houston	Jr.	Atlanta (1st/9)
Larry Kenon, F	Memphis State	Jr.	Detroit (3rd/50)
Larry McNeill, F	Marquette	Jr.	K.C.-Omaha (2nd/25)
John Williamson, G	New Mexico State	Jr.	Atlanta (6th/96)

NOTES: Mel Davis missed his senior season for St. John's because of a knee injury. He was selected by New York in the first round of the 1973 NBA draft. . . . George Gervin, who left Eastern Michigan after his sopho-

more season (1971-72), played with Pontiac in the CBA in 1972-73 before being selected by the Virginia Squires in the first round of the ABA special circumstances draft. . . . Forward Bruce Seals, who left Xavier (La.) after his sophomore season, was selected by the Utah Stars in the first round of ABA undergraduate draft.

1974			
Gary Brokaw, G	Notre Dame	Jr.	Milwaukee (1st/18)
John Drew, F	Gardner-Webb (N.C.)	Jr.	Atlanta (2nd/25)
Maurice Lucas, F	Marquette	Jr.	Chicago (1st/14)
Eric Money, G	Arizona	Jr.	Detroit (2nd/33)
Coniel Norman, G-F	Arizona	So.	Philadelphia (3rd/37)
Cliff Pondexter, F	Long Beach State	So.	Chicago (1st/16)
Campy Russell, F	Michigan	Jr.	Cleveland (1st/8)
Mike Sojourner, F-C	Utah	So.	Atlanta (1st/10)

NOTES: Forward Gus Gerard, who left Virginia after his junior season, was selected by the Carolina Cougars in the second round of ABA draft. The franchise transferred to St. Louis. . . . Center Moses Malone went straight from Petersburg (Va.) High School to the ABA (third-round pick of the Utah Stars). . . . Center David Vaughn, who left UNLV after his redshirt season (1973-74) following a transfer, signed with the ABA's Virginia Squires in August 1974. He had played for 1971-72 Oral Roberts freshman team and 1972-73 ORU varsity. . . . Henry Williams, who had been selected by New York in the first round of the 1973 ABA undergraduate draft, was signed by the ABA's Utah franchise in November after leaving Jacksonville following his junior season.

1975			
Alvan Adams, F-C	Oklahoma	Jr.	Phoenix (1st/4)
Joe Bryant, F	La Salle	Jr.	Golden State (1st/14)
Luther (Ticky) Burden, G	Utah	Jr.	New York (2nd/26)
Darryl Dawkins, C	Maynard Evans, Fla. HS		Philadelphia (1st/5)
Larry Fogle, F	Canisius	So.	New York (2nd/34)
Lloyd Free, G	Guilford (N.C.)	Jr.	Philadelphia (2nd/23)
Bubbles Hawkins, G	Illinois State	Jr.	Golden State (3rd/51)
Frank Oleynick, G	Seattle	Jr.	Seattle (1st/12)
*Joe Pace, C	Coppin State	Jr.	Phoenix (5th/76)
Eugene Short, F	Jackson State	Jr.	New York (1st/9)
Bill Willoughby, F	Dwight Morrow, N.J. HS		Atlanta (2nd/19)

*Pace transferred to Coppin State from Maryland-Eastern Shore.

NOTE: Pitt's Mel Bennett and Minnesota's Mark Olberding left college after their freshman seasons and were selected in the first round of the ABA draft by the Virginia Squires and San Antonio Spurs, respectively.

1976			
Norm Cook, F	Kansas	Jr.	Boston (1st/16)
Adrian Dantley, F	Notre Dame	Jr.	Buffalo (1st/6)
Jacky Dorsey, F	Georgia	So.	New Orleans (2nd/26)
Lonnie Shelton, F-C	Oregon State	Jr.	New York (2nd/25)
Richard Washington, F	UCLA	Jr.	Kansas City (1st/3)
Larry Wright, G	Grambling	Jr.	Washington (1st/14)

1977			
Kenny Carr, F	North Carolina St.	Jr.	L.A. Lakers (1st/6)
Brad Davis, G	Maryland	Jr.	L.A. Lakers (1st/15)
Ray Epps, G-F	Norfolk State	Jr.	Golden State (5th/104)
Bernard King, F	Tennessee	Jr.	New York Nets (1st/7)

1978			
Winford Boynes, G-F	San Francisco	Jr.	New Jersey (1st/13)
James Hardy, F	San Francisco	Jr.	New Orleans (1st/11)
Frankie Sanders, F	Southern (La.)	Jr.	San Antonio (1st/20)
Reggie Theus, G	UNLV	Jr.	Chicago (1st/9)

1979			
Magic Johnson, G	Michigan State	So.	L.A. Lakers (1st/1)
Cliff Robinson, F	Southern Cal	So.	New Jersey (1st/11)
Sly Williams, F	Rhode Island	Jr.	New York (1st/21)

1980			
Wes Matthews, G	Wisconsin	Jr.	Washington (1st/14)
Jeff Ruland, F-C	Iona	Jr.	Golden State (2nd/25)
DeWayne Scales, F	Louisiana State	Jr.	New York (2nd/36)

1981			
Mark Aguirre, F	DePaul	Jr.	Dallas (1st/1)
Isiah Thomas, G	Indiana	So.	Detroit (1st/2)
Buck Williams, F	Maryland	Jr.	New Jersey (1st/3)

1982

John Bagley, G	Boston College	Jr.	Cleveland (1st/12)
Terry Cummings, F	DePaul	Jr.	San Diego (1st/2)
Quintin Dailey, G	San Francisco	Jr.	Chicago (1st/7)
Clark Kellogg, F	Ohio State	Jr.	Indiana (1st/8)
Cliff Levingston, F	Wichita State	Jr.	Detroit (1st/9)
LaSalle Thompson, C	Texas	Jr.	Kansas City (1st/5)
Dominique Wilkins, F	Georgia	Jr.	Utah (1st/3)
Rob Williams, G	Houston	Jr.	Denver (1st/19)
James Worthy, F	North Carolina	Jr.	L.A. Lakers (1st/1)

1983

Russell Cross, F	Purdue	Jr.	Golden State (1st/6)
Clyde Drexler, G-F	Houston	Jr.	Portland (1st/14)
Derek Harper, G	Illinois	Jr.	Dallas (1st/11)
Glenn (Doc) Rivers, G	Marquette	Jr.	Atlanta (1st/31)
Byron Scott, G	Arizona State	Jr.	San Diego (1st/4)
Ennis Whatley, G	Alabama	So.	Kansas City (1st/13)

1984

Charles Barkley, F	Auburn	Jr.	Philadelphia (1st/5)
Cory Blackwell, F	Wisconsin	Jr.	Seattle (2nd/28)
Stuart Gray, C	UCLA	Jr.	Indiana (2nd/29)
Michael Jordan, G	North Carolina	Jr.	Chicago (1st/3)
Tim McCormick, C-F	Michigan	Jr.	Cleveland (1st/12)
Hakeem Olajuwon, C	Houston	Jr.	Houston (1st/1)

1985

Benoit Benjamin, C	Creighton	Jr.	L.A. Clippers (1st/3)
Manute Bol, C	Bridgeport (Conn.)	Fr.	Washington (2nd/31)
Kenny Green, F	Wake Forest	Jr.	Washington (1st/12)
Karl Malone, F	Louisiana Tech	Jr.	Utah (1st/13)
Jerry Reynolds, G-F	Louisiana State	Jr.	Milwaukee (1st/22)
Wayman Tisdale, F	Oklahoma	Jr.	Indiana (1st/2)

1986

William Bedford, C	Memphis State	Jr.	Phoenix (1st/6)
Walter Berry, F	St. John's	Jr.	Portland (1st/14)
Cedric Henderson, F	Georgia	So.	Atlanta (2nd/32)
Chris Washburn, C	North Carolina St.	So.	Golden State (1st/3)
Pearl Washington, G	Syracuse	So.	New Jersey (1st/13)
John Williams, F	Louisiana State	So.	Washington (1st/12)

1987

Vincent Askew, G-F	Memphis State	Jr.	Philadelphia (2nd/39)
Norris Coleman, F	Kansas State	So.	L.A. Clippers (2nd/38)
Derrick McKey, F	Alabama	Jr.	Seattle (1st/9)
Olden Polynice, C	Virginia	Jr.	Chicago (1st/8)

1988

Rex Chapman, G	Kentucky	So.	Charlotte (1st/8)
Sylvester Gray, F	Memphis State	So.	Miami (2nd/35)
Tito Horford, C	Miami (Fla.)	So.	Milwaukee (2nd/39)
Jerome Lane, F	Pittsburgh	Jr.	Denver (1st/23)
Charles Shackleford, F	N.C. State	Jr.	New Jersey (2nd/32)
Rod Strickland, G	DePaul	Jr.	New York (1st/19)

1989

Nick Anderson, G-F	Illinois	Jr.	Orlando (1st/11)
Jay Edwards, G	Indiana	So.	L.A. Clippers (2nd/33)
*Shawn Kemp, F	Trinity Valley JC	Fr.	Seattle (1st/17)
J.R. Reid, F	North Carolina	Jr.	Charlotte (1st/5)

*Kemp attended Kentucky in the fall of 1988 before dropping out of school because of off-the-court problems. He attended but did not play in junior college.

1990

Carl Herrera, F	Houston	Jr.	Miami (2nd/30)
Sean Higgins, G-F	Michigan	Jr.	San Antonio (2nd/54)
Chris Jackson, G	Louisiana State	So.	Denver (1st/3)
Marcus Liberty, G-F	Illinois	Jr.	Denver (2nd/42)
Jerrod Mustaf, F	Maryland	So.	New York (1st/17)
Dennis Scott, G-F	Georgia Tech	Jr.	Orlando (1st/4)
Kenny Williams, F	Elizabeth City St.	So.	Indiana (2nd/46)

1991

Kenny Anderson, G	Georgia Tech	So.	New Jersey (1st/2)
Terrell Brandon, G	Oregon	Jr.	Cleveland (1st/11)
Donald Hodge, C	Temple	Jr.	Dallas (2nd/33)
Billy Owens, F-G	Syracuse	Jr.	Sacramento (1st/3)
Brian Williams, C-F	Arizona	Jr.	Orlando (1st/10)

1992

Jim Jackson, G	Ohio State	Jr.	Dallas (1st/4)
Harold Miner, G	Southern Cal	Jr.	Miami (1st/12)
Tracy Murray, F	UCLA	Jr.	San Antonio (1st/18)
Shaquille O'Neal, C	Louisiana State	Jr.	Orlando (1st/1)

1993

Shawn Bradley, C	Brigham Young	So.	Philadelphia (1st/2)
Anfernee Hardaway, G	Memphis State	Jr.	Golden State (1st/3)
Jamal Mashburn, F	Kentucky	Jr.	Dallas (1st/4)
James Robinson, G	Alabama	Jr.	Portland (1st/21)
Rodney Rogers, F	Wake Forest	Jr.	Denver (1st/9)
Chris Webber, F	Michigan	So.	Orlando (1st/1)
Luther Wright, C	Seton Hall	Jr.	Utah (1st/18)

1994

Yinka Dare, C	George Washington	So.	New Jersey (1st/14)
Darrin Hancock, G-F	Kansas*	Jr.	Charlotte (2nd/38)
Juwan Howard, F-C	Michigan	Jr.	Washington (1st/5)
Jason Kidd, G	California	So.	Dallas (1st/2)
Donyell Marshall, F	Connecticut	Jr.	Minnesota (1st/4)
Lamond Murray, F	California	Jr.	L.A. Clippers (1st/7)
Glenn Robinson, F	Purdue	Jr.	Milwaukee (1st/1)
Jalen Rose, G	Michigan	Jr.	Denver (1st/13)
Cliff Rozier, F	Louisville	Jr.	Golden State (1st/16)
Dontonio Wingfield, F	Cincinnati	Fr.	Seattle (2nd/37)
Sharone Wright, F	Clemson	Jr.	Philadelphia (1st/6)

*Hancock had transferred to Indiana State but dropped out of school before the season to play professionally in France.

1995

Cory Alexander, G	Virginia	Jr.	San Antonio (1st/29)
Mario Bennett, F	Arizona State	Jr.	Phoenix (1st/27)
Chris Carr, F	Southern Illinois	Jr.	Phoenix (2nd/56)
*Kevin Garnett, F	Farragut, Ill.	HS	Minnesota (1st/5)
Rashard Griffith, C	Wisconsin	So.	Milwaukee (2nd/38)
Antonio McDyess, C-F	Alabama	So.	L.A. Clippers (1st/2)
Joe Smith, F-C	Maryland	So.	Golden State (1st/1)
Jerry Stackhouse, F	North Carolina	So.	Philadelphia (1st/3)
Gary Trent, F	Ohio University	Jr.	Milwaukee (1st/11)
David Vaughn, F	Memphis	Jr.	Orlando (1st/25)
Rasheed Wallace, C-F	North Carolina	So.	Washington (1st/4)
Corliss Williamson, F	Arkansas	Jr.	Sacramento (1st/13)

*Garnett attended high school in South Carolina before moving to Chicago for his senior season.

1996

Shareef Abdur-Rahim, F-C	California	Fr.	Vancouver (1st/3)
Ray Allen, G	Connecticut	Jr.	Minnesota (1st/5)
Kobe Bryant, G	Philadelphia, Pa.	HS	Charlotte (1st/13)
Marcus Camby, C	Massachusetts	Jr.	Toronto (1st/2)
Erick Dampier, C	Mississippi State	Jr.	Indiana (1st/10)
Ronnie Henderson, G	Louisiana State	Jr.	Washington (2nd/55)
Allen Iverson, G	Georgetown	So.	Philadelphia (1st/1)
Dontae' Jones, F	Mississippi State	Jr.	New York (1st/21)
Randy Livingston, G	Louisiana State	So.	Houston (2nd/42)
Stephon Marbury, G	Georgia Tech	Fr.	Milwaukee (1st/4)
Jeff McInnis, G	North Carolina	Jr.	Denver (2nd/37)
Jermaine O'Neal, C	Columbia, S.C.	HS	Portland (1st/17)
Victor Potapenko, C	Wright State	Jr.	Cleveland (1st/12)
Darnell Robinson, C	Arkansas	Jr.	Dallas (2nd/58)
Antoine Walker, F-G	Kentucky	So.	Boston (1st/6)
Samaki Walker, C	Louisville	Jr.	Dallas (1st/9)
Lorenzen Wright, F	Memphis	So.	L.A. Clippers (1st/7)

1997

Tony Battie, C	Texas Tech	Jr.	Denver (1st/5)
Chauncey Billups, G	Colorado	So.	Boston (1st/3)
Mark Blount, C	Pittsburgh	So.	Seattle (2nd/55)
C.J. Bruton, G	Indian Hills CC	Jr.	Vancouver (2nd/53)
James Cotton, G	Long Beach State	Jr.	Denver (2nd/33)
Danny Fortson, F	Cincinnati	Jr.	Milwaukee (1st/10)
Adonal Foyle, C	Colgate	Jr.	Golden State (1st/8)
Marc Jackson, C	Temple	Jr.	Golden State (2nd/38)
Gordon Malone, F	West Virginia	Jr.	Minnesota (2nd/44)
Tracy McGrady, G-F	Mount Zion, N.C.	HS	Toronto (1st/9)
Ron Mercer, G-F	Kentucky	So.	Boston (1st/6)
Paul Rogers, C	Gonzaga	Jr.	L.A. Lakers (2nd/54)
Olivier Saint-Jean, F	San Jose State	Jr.	Sacramento (1st/11)
Mark Sanford, F	Washington	Jr.	Miami (2nd/31)
God Shammgod, G	Providence	So.	Washington (2nd/46)
Maurice Taylor, F	Michigan	Jr.	L.A. Clippers (1st/14)
Tim Thomas, F	Villanova	Fr.	New Jersey (1st/7)

Kings of the Hill

Coastal Carolina forward Tony Dunkin is the only four-time conference player of the year in Division I history. Dunkin achieved the feat in the Big South. Here is a list of individuals who were named league player of the year three consecutive seasons:

CONFERENCE	PLAYER, SCHOOL	MVP YEARS
Atlantic Coast	David Thompson, North Carolina State	1973-74-75
Atlantic Coast	Ralph Sampson, Virginia	1981-82-83
Big East	Chris Mullin, St. John's	1983-84-85
Big Eight	Wayman Tisdale, Oklahoma	1983-84-85
Big Eight	Danny Manning, Kansas	1986-87-88
Big Sky	Larry Krystowiak, Montana	1984-85-86
Big South	Tony Dunkin, Coastal Carolina	1990-91-92-93
Big Ten	Jerry Lucas, Ohio State	1960-61-62
Metro	Clarence Weatherspoon, South. Miss.	1990-91-92
Metro Atlantic	Lionel Simmons, La Salle	1988-89-90
Mid-American	Gary Trent, Ohio University	1993-94-95
Mid-Eastern Athletic	Joe Binion, North Carolina A&T	1982-83-84
Ohio Valley	Clem Haskins, Western Kentucky	1965-66-67
Southeastern	Pete Maravich, Louisiana State	1968-69-70
Southern	Fred Hetzel, Davidson	1963-64-65
Trans America	Willie Jackson, Centenary	1982-83-84
West Coast	Bill Cartwright, San Francisco	1977-78-79

NOTES: Mullin shared Big East player of the year honors with Georgetown's Patrick Ewing in 1984 and 1985. . . . Tisdale left school with one season of eligibility remaining.

Somebody's All-American

School sports information directors have a tendency to water down All-American picks by including every Tom, Dick and Harry ever included from some obscure outlet. Nonetheless, Inside Sports College Basketball has taken on the task of citing the cream of the crop.

Forgoing the sometimes extensive lists of honorable mention selections, following is the key for an ultimate All-American list that focuses on the most prestigious teams.

AP: Associated Press (1948 through 1997—5-man first team, 5-man second team, 5-man third team until 1997; 6-player first team in 1965).

C: Converse (1932 and 1933—5-man first team; 1934 through 1948—5-5-5; 1949 through 1955—5-5-5-5; 1956 through 1979—10-15; 1980—10-13; 1981—10-16; 1982 and 1983—10-15).

NABC: National Association of Basketball Coaches (1947—5-man first team, 5-man second team, 5-man third team; 1948 and 1950 through 1952—5-5; 1949—5; 1954—6-6; 1955—8-8-7; 1956—8-7-7; 1957 through 1970, 1976, 1978 and 1980 through 1997—5-5-5; 1971 through 1973 and 1979—5-5-5-5; 1974 and 1975—5-5-5-5-5; 1977—5-5-5-5-6).

UPI: United Press International* (1949 through 1996—5-man first team, 5-man second team, 5-man third team).

*Known as United Press from 1949 through 1958.

USBWA: United States Basketball Writers Association (1957 through 1983—10-man first team; 1984 through 1997—5-5).

The NCAA has periodically utilized other groups to help determine its consensus All-American teams. Here is a comprehensive checklist of All-American selections with NCAA consensus choices cited if they didn't earn spots on the AP, Converse, NABC, UPI and USBWA teams (years shown denote season ended):

PLAYER, POS., COLLEGE	ALL-AMERICAN RECOGNITION

A

PLAYER, POS., COLLEGE	ALL-AMERICAN RECOGNITION
Shareef Abdur-Rahim, F-C, California	1996 (AP3, NABC3)
Alvan Adams, C, Oklahoma	1974 (NABC4) and 1975 (C2, NABC3)
John Adams, F, Arkansas	1941 (C2)
Mark Aguirre, F, DePaul	1979 (C2), 1980 (AP1, C1, NABC1, UPI1, USBWA1) and 1981 (AP1, C1, NABC1, UPI1, USBWA1)
Danny Ainge, G, Brigham Young	1979 (NABC4), 1980 (NABC3) and 1981 (AP1, C1, NABC1, UPI1, USBWA1)
Mark Alarie, F, Duke	1986 (UPI3)
Lew Alcindor, C, UCLA	1967 (AP1, C1, NABC1, UPI1, USBWA1), 1968 (AP1, C1, NABC1, UPI1, USBWA1) and 1969 (AP1, C1, NABC1, UPI1, USBWA1)
Steve Alford, G, Indiana	1986 (AP1, NABC1, UPI2) and 1987 (AP1, NABC1, UPI1, USBWA1)
Lucius Allen, G, UCLA	1968 (C1, AP2, NABC2, UPI2)
Ray Allen, G-F, Connecticut	1995 (AP3, NABC3, UPI3) and 1996 (AP1, NABC1, UPI1, USBWA1)
Tom Amaker, G, Duke	1987 (NABC3)
Cliff Anderson, C, St. Joseph's	1967 (NABC3)
Harry Anderson, G, Tennessee	1936 (C2)
Kenny Anderson, G, Georgia Tech	1990 (NABC1, AP3) and 1991 (AP1, NABC1, UPI1, USBWA1)
Ernie Andres, G, Indiana	1938 (C2) and 1939 (C2)
Bobby Anet, G, Oregon	1939 (C1)
Paul Arizin, F, Villanova	1950 (AP1, C1, UP1, NABC2)
Jesse Arnelle, C, Penn State	1955 (NABC2)

Jay Arnette, G, Texas	1960 (C1)
Jim Ashmore, G, Mississippi State	1957 (C2, AP3, UP3)
Chester Aubuchon, G, Michigan State	1940 (C3)
Stacey Augmon, F, UNLV	1991 (AP1, NABC2, UPI2, USBWA2)
John Austin, G, Boston College	1965 (USBWA1, C2, AP3, NABC3) and 1966 (C2, NABC2, UPI2)
Dennis Awtrey, C, Santa Clara	1969 (C2) and 1970 (C2)
John Azary, F, Columbia	1951 (NABC2, UP2, AP3, C4)

B

James Babcock, G, Denver	1937 (C1)
Forrest (Whitey) Baccus, ?, SMU	1935 (C3)
John Bagley, G, Boston College	1982 (NABC3)
Damon Bailey, G, Indiana	1994 (NABC2, AP3)
James Bailey, C, Rutgers	1978 (C2, NABC3) and 1979 (C2, UPI3, NABC4)
Greg Ballard, F, Oregon	1977 (USBWA1, C2, NABC3)
Gene Banks, F, Duke	1979 (UPI3) and 1981 (C2, NABC3)
Mike Bantom, F, St. Joseph's	1973 (C2, AP3, NABC4)
Charles Barkley, F, Auburn	1984 (NABC3)
Don Barksdale, C, UCLA	1947 (C3, NABC3)
Jim Barnes, C, Texas Western	1964 (C1, NABC2, AP3, UPI3)
Marvin Barnes, C, Providence	1972 (NABC4), 1973 (C2, UPI3, NABC4) and 1974 (AP1, C1, NABC1, UPI1, USBWA1)
Dick Barnett, G, Tennessee State	1958 (C1) and 1959 (C1)
Leo Barnhorst, C-G, Notre Dame	1949 (C3)
John Barr, ?, Penn State	1941 (C3)
Ernie Barrett, G, Kansas State	1951 (AP2, C2, UP3)
Rick Barry, F, Miami (Fla.)	1964 (C2) and 1965 (AP1, C1, NABC1, UPI1, USBWA1)
Frank Baumholtz, F, Ohio University	1941 (C1)
Elgin Baylor, C, Seattle	1957 (USBWA1, AP2, C2, NABC2, UP2) and 1958 (AP1, C1, NABC1, UPI1, USBWA1)
Alfred (Butch) Beard, G, Louisville	1967 (UPI2, AP3) and 1969 (C2, UPI3)
Ralph Beard, G, Kentucky	1947 (C1, NABC1), 1948 (AP1, C1, NABC1) and 1949 (AP1, NABC1, UP1, C2)
Zelmo Beaty, C, Prairie View (Tex.)	1962 (C1)
Ernie Beck, F, Sr., Pennsylvania	1951 (C4) and 1953 (AP1, C1, NABC1, UP1)
Lew Beck, G, Oregon State	1947 (C2)
William Bedford, C, Memphis State	1986 (AP3)
Ron Behagen, F, Minnesota	1973 (C2, UPI3, NABC4)
Ed Beisser, C, Creighton	1943 (C2)
Walt Bellamy, C, Indiana	1960 (C1, USBWA1, UPI3)
Irv Bemoras, F, Illinois	1953 (C2)
Jules Bender, G, Long Island	1937 (C1)
Benoit Benjamin, C, Creighton	1985 (NABC3)
A.L. Bennett, F, Oklahoma A&M	1948 (AP3)
Kent Benson, C, Indiana	1975 (C2, NABC4), 1976 (AP1, C1, NABC1, UPI1, USBWA1) and 1977 (AP1, C1, NABC1, UPI1)
Louis (Bosey) Berger, F, Maryland	1932 (C1)
Walter Berry, F, St. John's	1986 (AP1, NABC1, UPI1, USBWA1)
Len Bias, F, Maryland	1985 (AP2, USBWA2, NABC3) and 1986 (AP1, NABC1, UPI1, USBWA1)
Henry Bibby, G, UCLA	1972 (C1, NABC1, UPI1, USBWA1, AP2)
Chauncey Billups, G, Colorado	1997 (AP2, NABC2, USBWA2)
Dave Bing, G, Syracuse	1965 (C2, NABC3) and 1966 (AP1, C1, NABC1, UPI1, USBWA1)
Paul Birch, F, Duquesne	1935 (C1)
Larry Bird, F, Indiana State	1977 (NABC3, UPI3), 1978 (AP1, C1, NABC1, UPI1, USBWA1) and 1979 (AP1, C1, NABC1, UPI1, USBWA1)
Otis Birdsong, G, Houston	1977 (C1, NABC1, UPI1, USBWA1, AP2)
Gale Bishop, F, Washington State	1943 (NCAA2)
Ralph Bishop, C, Washington	1936 (C2)
Charles Black, F, Kansas	1943 (C2) and 1946 (C3)
Rolando Blackman, G, Kansas State	1980 (C1, AP3) and 1981 (C1, NABC3)
Nate Blackwell, G, Temple	1987 (UPI3)
Daron (Mookie) Blaylock, G, Oklahoma	1989 (NABC1, AP2, USBWA2, UPI3)
Meyer (Mike) Bloom, C, Temple	1938 (C3)
Ray Blume, G, Oregon State	1980 (AP2) and 1981 (UPI3)
Bruno Boin, C, Washington	1957 (NABC3)
Ron Bonham, F, Cincinnati	1963 (AP1, C1, NABC1, UPI1, USBWA1) and 1964 (AP2, NABC2, UPI2, NABC3)
George BonSalle, C, Illinois	1957 (NABC2)
Melvin Booker, G, Missouri	1994 (AP2, UPI2, USBWA2)
Keith Booth, F, Maryland	1997 (AP3, NABC3)
Bob Boozer, F, Kansas State	1958 (NABC1, USBWA1, AP2, C2, UPI2) and 1959 (AP1, C1, NABC1, UPI1, USBWA1)
Wally Borrevik, C, Oregon	1944 (C3)
Fred (Buzz) Borries, F, Navy	1934 (C2)
Vince Boryla, F, Denver	1949 (AP1, NABC1, UP2, C3)
Roosevelt Bouie, C, Syracuse	1980 (USBWA1, NABC3, UPI3)
Dick Boushka, G-F, St. Louis	1955 (AP3)
Sam Bowie, C, Kentucky	1981 (C1, USBWA1, NABC2, AP3, UPI3) and 1984 (AP2)
Fred Boyd, G, Oregon State	1982 (C2)
Harry Boykoff, C, St. John's	1943 (C1)
Winford Boynes, F, San Francisco	1978 (NABC3)
Gary Bradds, C, Ohio State	1963 (AP1, C1, UPI1, NABC3)
Bill Bradley, F, Princeton	1963 (AP2, C2, UPI2, NABC3), 1964 (AP1, C1, NABC1, UPI1, USBWA1) and 1965 (AP1, C1, NABC1, UPI1, USBWA1)
Charles Bradley, F, Wyoming	1981 (C2)
Clyde Bradshaw, G, DePaul	1980 (C2) and 1981 (UPI3)
Bob Brannum, C, Kentucky	1944 (C2)
Jim Bredar, G, Illinois	1953 (AP3)
Pete Brennan, F, North Carolina	1958 (C1, USBWA1, AP2, NABC3, USBWA3)
Jim Brewer, F, Minnesota	1973 (C1, USBWA1, AP2, NABC2, UPI2)
Ron Brewer, G, Arkansas	1978 (C1, USBWA1, AP2)
Ulysses (Junior) Bridgeman, G-F, Louisville	1975 (C1, USBWA1, UPI3, NABC4)
Bill Bridges, C, Kansas	1961 (C1)

Audley Brindley, C, Dartmouth	1944 (C1)
Gus Broberg, G-F, Dartmouth	1940 (C2) and 1941 (C1)
Tal Brody, G, Illinois	1965 (C2)
Gary Brokaw, G, Notre Dame	1974 (C2, UPI3, NABC5)
Price Brookfield, C, West Texas State	1941 (C3) and 1942 (C1)
Michael Brooks, F, La Salle	1980 (C1, NABC1, UPI1, USBWA1, AP2)
Charley Brown, G, Seattle	1958 (C2) and 1959 (C2, UPI3)
Fred Brown, G, Iowa	1981 (C2, AP3)
Gene Brown, G, San Francisco	1958 (NABC3)
John Brown, F, Missouri	1973 (C2, AP3, NABC3)
Skip Brown, G, Wake Forest	1977 (NABC4)
Omar (Bud) Browning, G, Oklahoma	1935 (C2)
Quinn Buckner, G, Indiana	1974 (NABC4), 1975 (C2, UPI2, NABC3) and 1976 (C2)
Art Bunte, C, Utah	1955 (NABC3) and 1956 (NABC2)
Bill Buntin, C, Michigan	1964 (C2, AP3, NABC3, UPI3) and 1965 (AP2, C2, NABC2, UPI2)
Luther (Ticky) Burden, G, Utah	1975 (AP1, C1, USBWA1, NABC2, UPI2)
Frank Burgess, G, Gonzaga	1961 (AP2, C2, NABC3, UPI3)
Tom Burleson, C, North Carolina State	1973 (USBWA1, C2, NABC3, UPI3) and 1974 (C1, UPI2, AP3, NABC3)
Don Burness, F, Stanford	1942 (NCAA2)
Jim Burns, G, Northwestern	1967 (C2, AP3, NABC3)
Bob Burrow, C, Kentucky	1955 (AP3) and 1956 (C1, NABC1, AP3, UP3)
Lawrence Butler, G, Idaho State	1979 (C2)
Leo Byrd, F, Marshall	1959 (C1, AP2, UPI2)

C

Michael Cage, F-C, San Diego State	1984 (AP2, UPI2)
Carl Cain, F, Iowa	1956 (NABC3)
Joe Caldwell, F, Arizona State	1963 (NABC3)
David (Corky) Calhoun, F, Pennsylvania	1973 (C2)
Bob Calihan, F-C, Detroit	1939 (NCAA2)
Dan Callandrillo, G, Seton Hall	1982 (C2, AP3, NABC3, UPI3)
Ernie Calverley, G, Rhode Island State	1945 (C3) and 1946 (C3)
Marcus Camby, C, Massachusetts	1996 (AP1, NABC1, UPI1, USBWA1)
Larry Cannon, G-F, La Salle	1969 (C2)
Joe Capua, G, Wyoming	1956 (C2)
Howie Carl, G, DePaul	1961 (C2)
Bob Carney, G, Bradley	1954 (C4)
Antoine Carr, F, Wichita State	1983 (AP3)
Austin Carr, G, Notre Dame	1970 (C1, USBWA1, AP2, NABC2, UPI2) and 1971 (AP1, C1, NABC1, UPI1, USBWA1)
Kenny Carr, F, North Carolina State	1976 (C2, AP3, NABC3, UPI3) and 1977 (C2, UPI3, NABC4)
Joe Barry Carroll, C, Purdue	1979 (C2, AP3, NABC3) and 1980 (AP1, C1, NABC1, UPI1, USBWA1)
Howard Carter, F-G, Louisiana State	1982 (C2) and 1983 (C2)
Reggie Carter, G, St. John's	1980 (AP2, UPI2)
Bill Cartwright, C, San Francisco	1977 (AP2, UPI2, NABC3), 1978 (C2) and 1979 (AP1, C1, USBWA1, NABC2, UPI2)
Joseph Cavanaugh, G, Canisius	1937 (C3)
Wilt Chamberlain, C, Kansas	1957 (AP1, C1, NABC1, UPI1, USBWA1) and 1958 (AP1, C1, NABC1, UPI1, USBWA1)
Jerry Chambers, F-C, Utah	1966 (C1)
Rex Chapman, G, Kentucky	1988 (NABC3)
Len Chappell, C, Wake Forest	1961 (C1) and 1962 (AP1, C1, USBWA1, NABC2, UPI2)
Lorenzo Charles, F, N.C. State	1984 (AP3)
Ken Charlton, F, Colorado	1963 (USBWA1)
Calbert Cheaney, F, Indiana	1991 (USBWA2, AP3, NABC3, UPI3), 1992 (AP3, NABC3, UPI3) and 1993 (AP1, NABC1, UPI1, USBWA1)
Derrick Chievous, F, Missouri	1987 (UPI2, AP3)
Randolph Childress, G, Wake Forest	1995 (AP2, NABC2, USBWA2, UPI3)
Tom Chilton, F, East Tennessee State	1961 (C2)
Bill Chmielewski, C, Dayton	1962 (C2)
Jim Chones, C, Marquette	1972 (AP1, C1, UPI1)
Chuck Chuckovits, F, Toledo	1938 (C2)
Tom Churchill, F-C, Oklahoma	1929 (NCAA)
Jim Cleamons, F-G, Ohio State	1971 (C2)
Charles Cleveland, G, Alabama	1975 (NABC5)
Bill Closs, C-F, Rice	1943 (C2)
Vinnie Cohen, C, Syracuse	1957 (C2)
Derrick Coleman, F, Syracuse	1989 (UPI2, NABC3) and 1990 (AP1, NABC1, UPI1, USBWA1)
Marvin Colen, ?, Loyola (III.)	1937 (C2)
Don Collins, F, Washington State	1980 (AP2)
Doug Collins, G, Illinois State	1983 (C1, NABC1, UPI1, USBWA1, AP2)
Jimmy Collins, G, New Mexico State	1970 (USBWA1, C2)
Dallas Comegys, F-C, DePaul	1987 (NABC2, AP3, UPI3)
Ed Conlin, C, Fordham	1954 (C4) and 1955 (NABC2, C3)
Lester Conner, G, Oregon State	1982 (AP2, UPI3)
Bob Cook, F, Wisconsin	1947 (NABC2, C3)
Chuck Cooper, C, Duquesne	1950 (C1, UP3)
Michael Cooper, G, New Mexico	1978 (USBWA1)
Vern Corbin, F, California	1929 (NCAA)
Chris Corchiani, G, North Carolina State	1991 (NABC3)
Dave Corzine, C, DePaul	1978 (C2, NABC2, UPI3)
Kresimir Cosic, C, Brigham Young	1972 (C2, UPI3, NABC4) and 1973 (NABC4)
Norm Cottom, F, Purdue	1934 (C3) and 1935 (C3)
Mel Counts, C, Oregon State	1963 (C2, NABC2) and 1964 (USBWA1, AP2, C2, NABC2, UPI2)
Bob Cousy, G, Holy Cross	1948 (NABC2, AP3), 1949 (AP2, UP2, C4) and 1950 (AP1, NABC1, UP1, C2)
Dave Cowens, C, Florida State	1970 (C2)
Johnny Cox, F, Kentucky	1957 (UP3) and 1959 (AP1, C1, NABC1, UP2)
Wesley Cox, F, Louisville	1977 (C1)
Cliff Crandall, G, Oregon State	1949 (C4)
Claire Cribbs, G-C, Pittsburgh	1934 (C1) and 1935 (C1)

Russ Critchfield, G, California	1967 (C2)
Terry Cummings, F-C, DePaul	1982 (AP1, C1, NABC1, UPI1, USBWA1)
Billy Cunningham, F, North Carolina	1964 (USBWA1, C2) and 1965 (C1, NABC2, UPI2, AP3)
Bill Curley, F, Boston College	1994 (NABC3)
Dell Curry, G, Virginia Tech	1986 (AP2, USBWA2, NABC3, UPI3)

D

Quintin Dailey, G, San Francisco	1982 (AP1, UPI1, USBWA1, NABC2)
Howie Dallmar, G, Pennsylvania	1945 (C2)
Irwin Dambrot, F, CCNY	1950 (C3)
Louie Dampier, G, Kentucky	1966 (AP1, C1, NABC2, UPI2) and 1967 (AP2, C2, NABC3, UPI3)
Mel Daniels, C, New Mexico	1967 (USBWA1, C2, NABC2, UPI2, AP3)
Adrian Dantley, F, Notre Dame	1975 (AP1, C1, NABC1, UPI1, USBWA1) and 1976 (AP1, C1, NABC1, UPI1, USBWA1)
Chuck Darling, C, Iowa	1952 (AP1, NABC1, UPI1, C2)
Jim Darrow, G, Bowling Green	1960 (C1, UPI2, NABC3)
Brad Daugherty, C, North Carolina	1986 (USBWA1, AP2, NABC2, UPI2)
Bob Davies, G, Seton Hall	1941 (C3) and 1942 (C2)
A.W. Davis, F, Tennessee	1965 (USBWA1, C2, AP3, UPI3)
Bill Davis, G, Kentucky	1934 (C3)
Charlie Davis, G, Wake Forest	1971 (C2, NABC4)
Dwight Davis, F, Houston	1972 (AP2, C2)
Mel Davis, F, St. John's	1972 (NABC3)
Ralph Davis, G, Cincinnati	1960 (C2)
Johnny Dawkins, G, Duke	1985 (NABC1, UPI1, AP2) and 1986 (AP1, NABC1, UPI1, USBWA1)
Todd Day, F, Arkansas	1991 (AP2, NABC3) and 1992 (NABC2, AP3, UPI3)
Dave DeBusschere, F, Detroit	1960 (C2, UPI3), 1961 (C2, NABC2, UPI3) and 1962 (C2, AP3, NABC3, UPI3)
Archie Dees, C, Indiana	1957 (C2, AP3, NABC3, UP3) and 1958 (C1, USBWA1, AP2, NABC2, UP2)
Terry Dehere, G, Seton Hall	1993 (AP2, UPI2, NABC3)
Lewis (Pick) Dehner, C, Illinois	1938 (C3) and 1939 (C3)
Tony Delk, G, Kentucky	1996 (UPI1, USBWA1, AP2, NABC2)
Marvin Delph, F, Arkansas	1978 (C2)
Fennis Dembo, F, Wyoming	1988 (AP3)
Walt (Corky) Devlin, F, George Washington	1955 (B3)
John Dick, F, Oregon	1940 (C2)
Dick Dickey, F, North Carolina State	1948 (C2, AP3) and 1950 (AP2, C2, UP3)
Ernie DiGregorio, G, Providence	1972 (NABC4) and 1973 (AP1, C1, USBWA1, NABC2, UPI2)
Bob Dille, F, Valparaiso	1944 (NCAA2)
John (Hook) Dillon, F, North Carolina	1946 (C2) and 1947 (NABC2)
Terry Dischinger, F, Purdue	1960 (C1, USBWA1, AP2, NABC2, UPI1), 1961 (AP1, C1, NABC1, UPI1, USBWA1) and 1962 (AP1, C1, NABC1, UPI1, USBWA1)
Wilfred Doerner, F, Evansville	1942 (C1)
Bob Doll, C, Colorado	1942 (NCAA2)
Bruce Douglas, G, Illinois	1984 (UPI3)
Leon Douglas, C, Alabama	1975 (C1, USBWA1, AP2, NABC2, UPI3) and 1976 (C1, NABC2, AP3, UPI3)
Sherman Douglas, G, Syracuse	1988 (UPI2, AP3) and 1989 (AP1, NABC3)
Lloyd (Sonny) Dove, C, St. John's	1967 (C2, NABC2, UPI2, AP3)
Dave Downey, F, Illinois	1963 (C2)
Steve Downing, C, Indiana	1973 (C2)
Clyde Drexler, F, Houston	1983 (C1, USBWA1, AP2, UPI3)
Terry Driscoll, C, Boston College	1969 (C2, NABC3)
Walter Dukes, C, Seton Hall	1952 (UP3) and 1953 (AP1, C1, NABC1, UP1)
Louis Dunbar, F-G, Houston	1974 (NABC5)
Tim Duncan, C, Wake Forest	1995 (AP3, NABC3), 1996 (AP1, NABC1, UPI1, USBWA1) and 1997 (AP1, NABC1, USBWA1)
T.R. Dunn, G, Alabama	1977 (C2)
Devin Durrant, F, Brigham Young	1984 (AP2, NABC2, USBWA2, UPI3)
Ken Durrett, F-C, La Salle	1981 (C1, USBWA1, NABC2, UPI2)
Dennis DuVal, G, Syracuse	1974 (C2, AP3, NABC5)

E

Bill Ebben, F, Detroit	1957 (C2, AP3)
Paul Ebert, C, Ohio State	1952 (C3), 1953 (AP2, C3, UP3) and 1954 (C3, UP3)
Dwight Eddleman, F, Illinois	1948 (AP2, C3) and 1949 (C1, AP2, UP2)
Keith Edmonson, G, Purdue	1982 (C2)
Jay Edwards, G, Indiana	1989 (UPI1, AP2, NABC2)
LeRoy (Cowboy) Edwards, C, Kentucky	1935 (C2)
Frank Ehmann, F, Northwestern	1955 (C4)
Bob Elliott, F-C, Arizona	1977 (C2, NABC4)
Sean Elliott, F, Arizona	1988 (AP1, NABC1, UPI1, USBWA1) and 1989 (AP1, NABC1, UPI1, USBWA1)
Dale Ellis, F, Tennessee	1982 (C1, USBWA1, AP2, NABC3) and 1983 (AP1, C1, NABC1, USBWA1, UPI2)
Leroy Ellis, C, St. John's	1962 (C2)
Maurice (Bo) Ellis, F, Marquette	1975 (C2, NABC4), 1976 (C2) and 1977 (C2, NABC2, AP3)
Pervis Ellison, C, Louisville	1989 (NABC1, USBWA1, AP2, UPI2)
Len Elmore, C, Maryland	1974 (C1, USBWA1, AP2, NABC2, UPI2)
Howard Engleman, F, Kansas	1941 (NCAA1)
Gene Englund, C, Wisconsin	1941 (C2)
Bill Erickson, G, Illinois	1949 (NABC1, UP3, C4)
Keith Erickson, F, UCLA	1965 (C2, AP3, UPI3)
Vinnie Ernst, G, Providence	1963 (C2)
Julius Erving, F, Massachusetts	1971 (C2, NABC3, UPI3)
Wayne Estes, F, Utah State	1964 (C2, NABC3) and 1965 (AP1, C1, UPI1, USBWA1, NABC2)
Brian Evans, F, Indiana	1996 (AP3, NABC3, UPI3)
Mike Evans, G, Kansas State	1978 (AP3)
Patrick Ewing, C, Georgetown	1982 (C2), 1983 (AP1, C1, NABC1, USBWA1, UPI2), 1984 (AP1, NABC1, UPI1, USBWA1) and 1985 (AP1, NABC1, UPI1, USBWA1)

F

Name	Year(s)
John Fairchild, C, Brigham Young	1965 (NABC3)
Bob Faris, ?, George Washington	1939 (C3)
Mike Farmer, F-C, San Francisco	1958 (USBWA1, C2, NABC2, UP2, AP3)
Robert Faught, C, Notre Dame	1942 (C3)
Ron Feireisel, G, DePaul	1953 (C3, UP3)
Arnie Ferrin, F, Utah	1944 (C1), 1945 (C1), 1947 (C2, NABC3) and 1948 (B1, AP2)
Bob Ferry, C, St. Louis	1959 (USBWA1, C2, AP3, NABC3, UPI3)
Danny Ferry, F-C, Duke	1988 (UPI1, AP2, NABC2, USBWA2) and 1989 (AP1, NABC1, UPI1, USBWA1)
Wes Fesler, G, Ohio State	1931 (NCAA)
Kenny Fields, F, UCLA	1983 (AP3)
Larry Finch, G, Memphis State	1973 (USBWA1, C2)
Henry Finkel, C, Dayton	1966 (C2, AP3, NABC3, UPI3)
Eddie Finnigan, ?, Western Reserve	1933 (C1)
William Fleishman, ?, Western Reserve	1936 (C3)
Vern Fleming, G, Georgia	1984 (NABC3)
Rod Fletcher, G, Illinois	1952 (C1, AP2, NABC2, UP2)
Ken Flower, G, Southern California	1953 (C2)
Darrell Floyd, G-F, Furman	1955 (AP1, NABC2, UP2) and 1956 (AP1, C1, UP1, NABC2)
Eric (Sleepy) Floyd, G, Georgetown	1981 (AP2) and 1982 (AP1, C1, NABC1, UPI1, USBWA1)
Larry Fogle, F, Canisius	1974 (USBWA1, AP2, C2, UPI2, NABC3)
Jack Foley, F, Holy Cross	1962 (USBWA1, C2, NABC2, UPI2, AP3)
Phil Ford, G, North Carolina	1975 (C2), 1976 (C1, NABC1, AP2, UPI2), 1977 (AP1, C1, NABC1, UPI1, USBWA1) and 1978 (AP1, C1, NABC1, UPI1, USBWA1)
Don Forman, G, New York University	1948 (NABC2, AP3)
Chet Forte, G, Columbia	1957 (AP1, C1, UP1, USBWA1, NABC2)
Danny Fortson, F, Cincinnati	1996 (AP2, NABC2, UPI2, USBWA2) and 1997 (AP1, NABC1, USBWA1)
Rod Foster, G, UCLA	1981 (UPI2) and 1983 (C2)
Adonal Foyle, C, Colgate	1997 (USBWA2, AP3)
Clarence (Bevo) Francis, C, Rio Grande (O.)	1953 (UP2, AP3) and 1954 (AP1, NABC2, UP2)
Ricky Frazier, F, Missouri	1982 (C1, AP3, NABC3, UPI3)
Walt Frazier, G-F, Southern Illinois	1967 (C2)
Don Freeman, F, Illinois	1966 (C2)
Robin Freeman, G, Ohio State	1955 (AP1, NABC1, UP2) and 1956 (AP1, C1, NABC1, UP1)
Larry Friend, F, California	1957 (C1, AP3)
Richie Fuqua, G, Oral Roberts	1972 (USBWA1, C2, AP3) and 1973 (C2, AP3)
Terry Furlow, F, Michigan State	1976 (C2, AP3, UPI3)

G

Name	Year(s)
Dave Gambee, F, Oregon State	1958 (C2, UP2)
Vern Gardner, C, Utah	1948 (C3) and 1949 (AP2, NABC2, UP2)
Dick Garmaker, F, Minnesota	1954 (C3) and 1955 (UP1, AP2, NABC2, C3)
Bill Garnett, F, Wyoming	1982 (USBWA1, C2)
Bill Garrett, C, Indiana	1951 (AP2, C2, UP2, C3)
Eric (Hank) Gathers, C, Loyola Marymount	1989 (USBWA2, AP3, UPI3) and 1990 (NABC2, USBWA2, AP3)
Ed Gayda, F, Washington State	1950 (C4)
Harold Gensichen, F, Western Michigan	1943 (C3)
Bob Gerber, C, Toledo	1942 (C2)
John Gianelli, C, Pacific	1972 (NABC4)
Ralph Giannini, G, Santa Clara	1940 (C3)
Joe Gibbon, F, Mississippi	1957 (C2, UP2)
Chet Giermak, C, William & Mary	1950 (NABC2)
Kendall Gill, G, Illinois	1990 (UPI1, AP3, NABC3)
Armon Gilliam, F-C, UNLV	1987 (AP2, NABC2, UPI2, USBWA2)
Artis Gilmore, C, Jacksonville	1970 (C1, AP2, NABC2, UPI2) and 1971 (AP1, C1, UP1, USBWA1)
Jack Givens, F, Kentucky	1977 (NABC4) and 1978 (C1, USBWA1, AP2, NABC2, UPI2)
George Glamack, C, North Carolina	1940 (C2)
Mike Gminski, C, Duke	1978 (C2), 1979 (NABC1, UPI1, USBWA1, AP2, C2) and 1980 (AP2, NABC2, UPI2)
Tom Gola, C-F, La Salle	1952 (C1), 1953 (AP1, C1, NABC1, UP1), 1954 (AP1, C1, NABC1, UP1) and 1955 (AP1, C1, NABC1, UP1)
Moe Goldman, ?, CCNY	1934 (C2)
Don Goldstein, F, Louisville	1959 (C2)
Gail Goodrich, G, UCLA	1964 (C2) and 1965 (AP1, C1, NABC1, UP1, USBWA1)
Hy Gotkin, G, St. John's	1944 (C3)
Mal Graham, G, New York University	1967 (UPI3)
Otto Graham, F, Northwestern	1943 (C3) and 1944 (C2)
Gary Grant, G, Michigan	1987 (USBWA2) and 1988 (AP1, NABC1, UP1, USBWA1)
Harvey Grant, F, Oklahoma	1988 (NABC3, UPI3)
Horace Grant, F, Clemson	1987 (AP2, NABC2, UPI3)
Josh Grant, F, Utah	1993 (UPI3)
Travis Grant, F, Kentucky State	1972 (C1)
Don Grate, F, Ohio State	1944 (C2) and 1945 (C3)
Ed Gray, G, California	1997 (AP3, NABC3)
Gary Gray, G, Oklahoma City	1967 (C2)
Jack Gray, F, Texas	1934 (C2) and 1935 (C1)
Wyndol Gray, F, Bowling Green	1945 (C1)
Jeff Grayer, F, Iowa State	1988 (AP2, UPI3)
A.C. Green, F, Oregon State	1985 (AP3, UPI3)
Al Green, G, Louisiana State	1979 (C2)
Bill Green, F, Colorado State	1963 (NABC1, USBWA1, AP3, UPI3)
Cornell Green, F, Utah State	1962 (NABC3)
John Green, G, UCLA	1962 (C2)
Johnny Green, C, Michigan State	1958 (C2, NABC2, AP3, UP3) and 1959 (C1, USBWA1, AP2, NABC2, UPI2)
Rickey Green, G, Michigan	1976 (C1) and 1977 (AP1, NABC1, UPI1, USBWA1, C2)
Si Green, G, Duquesne	1954 (C4), 1955 (C1, NABC1, UP1, AP2) and 1956 (AP1, NABC1, UP1, C2)
Sidney Green, F-C, UNLV	1983 (USBWA1, C2, NABC3, UPI3)

Steve Green, F, Indiana — 1975 (C2, NABC3, UPI3)
David Greenwood, F, UCLA — 1978 (AP1, C1, NABC1, UP1, USBWA1) and 1979 (AP1, C1, NABC1, UP1)
George Gregory, C, Columbia — 1931 (NCAA)
Kevin Grevey, F, Kentucky — 1974 (NABC5) and 1975 (USBWA1, AP2, C2, NABC2, UPI2)
Rod Griffin, F, Wake Forest — 1977 (USBWA1, AP3, UPI3, NABC5) and 1978 (C1, USBWA1, NABC2, AP3, UPI3)
Darrell Griffith, G, Louisville — 1978 (C2), 1979 (C1, NABC3) and 1980 (AP1, C1, NABC1, UP1, USBWA1)
Dick Groat, G, Duke — 1951 (C1, AP2, NABC2, UP2) and 1952 (AP1, C1, NABC1, UP1)
Frank Groves, C, Kansas State — 1937 (C3)
Alex Groza, C, Kentucky — 1947 (NABC1, C2), 1948 (C1, AP2, NABC2) and 1949 (AP1, C1, UP1)
Ernie Grunfeld, F, Tennessee — 1976 (C2, NABC3, UPI2) and 1977 (USBWA1, AP2, C2, NABC2, UPI2)
Thomas Guerrero, F, UC Santa Barbara — 1941 (C2)
Tom Gugliotta, F, N.C. State — 1992 (NABC3)
Matt Guokas, G, St. Joseph's — 1966 (AP2, C2, NABC2, UPI2)
Lee Guttero, C, Southern California — 1934 (C3) and 1935 (C1)
Tony Guy, G, Kansas — 1982 (C2)

H

Bill Haarlow, F, University of Chicago — 1935 (C2) and 1936 (C2)
Rudy Hackett, F-C, Syracuse — 1975 (AP2, C2)
Cliff Hagan, F, Kentucky — 1952 (AP1, NABC1, UP1, C2) and 1954 (AP1, NABC1, UP1, C2)
Jimmy Hagan, C, Tennessee Tech — 1959 (C2, AP3)
Ron Haigler, F, Pennsylvania — 1975 (NABC5)
Charles Halbert, C, West Texas — 1942 (C3)
Dale Hall, G-F, Army — 1945 (C3)
Forrest Hamilton, F, Southwest Missouri — 1952 (C4)
Ralph Hamilton, F, Indiana — 1947 (C1, NABC3)
Roy Hamilton, G, UCLA — 1979 (AP3)
Tom Hammonds, F, Georgia Tech — 1989 (NABC3)
Bill Hanson, F-C, Washington — 1962 (C2)
Tony Hanson, F-G, Connecticut — 1977 (NABC5)
Vince Hanson, C, Washington State — 1945 (C3)
Bill Hapac, F, Illinois — 1940 (C1)
Anfernee Hardaway, G, Memphis State — 1993 (AP1, NABC1, UPI1, USBWA1)
Charles Hardnett, C, Grambling — 1961 (C2) and 1962 (C1)
John Hargis, F, Texas — 1947 (C3, NABC3)
Jerry Harkness, F, Loyola (Ill.) — 1963 (AP1, C1, NABC1, UP1, USBWA1)
Jules (Skip) Harlicka, G, South Carolina — 1968 (C2)
Derek Harper, G, Illinois — 1983 (AP2, C2)
Jerry Harper, C-F, Alabama — 1956 (C2, NABC3)
Ron Harper, G-F, Miami of Ohio — 1986 (AP2, NABC2, UPI2, USBWA2)
Bob Harris, C, Oklahoma A&M — 1949 (AP2, UP2, C3)
Steve Harris, G, Tulsa — 1985 (UPI2)
Jack Harvey, C-F, Colorado — 1940 (C1)
Clem Haskins, G-F, Western Kentucky — 1966 (C2) and 1967 (AP1, C1, USBWA1, NABC2, UPI2)
Hal Haskins, F, Hamline (Minn.) — 1948 (C1) and 1949 (C3)
Billy Hassett, G, Notre Dame — 1945 (C2)
Joe Hassett, G, Providence — 1977 (NABC3)
Bob Hassmiller, F-G, Fordham — 1939 (NCAA2)
Vern Hatton, G, Kentucky — 1958 (C1)
John Havlicek, F, Ohio State — 1961 (C2, UPI2,AP3) and 1962 (C1, UPI1, USBWA1, AP2, NABC2)
Hersey Hawkins, G, Bradley — 1988 (AP1, NABC1, UPI1, USBWA1)
Tom Hawkins, F, Notre Dame — 1958 (C2, NABC2, UP2, AP3) and 1959 (USBWA1, AP2, C2, NABC2, UPI2)
Elvin Hayes, F-C, Houston — 1966 (C2), 1967 (AP1, C1, NABC1, UP1, USBWA1) and 1968 (AP1, C1, NABC1, UP1, USBWA1)
Spencer Haywood, F-C, Detroit — 1969 (AP1, C1, NABC1, UP1, USBWA1)
Walt Hazzard, G, UCLA — 1963 (USBWA1, AP2, C2, UPI3) and 1964 (AP1, C1, NABC1, UP1, USBWA1)
Tom Heinsohn, F, Holy Cross — 1955 (NABC1, AP3, C3, UP3) and 1956 (AP1, C1, NABC1, UP2)
Ned (Dickie) Hemric, F-C, Wake Forest — 1954 (AP3) and 1955 (NABC1, AP2, UP2, C4)
Alan Henderson, F, Indiana — 1995 (NABC3)
Tom Henderson, G, Hawaii — 1974 (C2, AP3, NABC4)
Larry Hennessy, G, Villanova — 1952 (NABC2, AP3, C4) and 1953 (AP3, UP3, C4)
Don Hennon, G, Pittsburgh — 1958 (AP1, C1, UP1, USBWA1, NABC2) and 1959 (UPI1, C2, NABC2)
Bill Henry, C-F, Rice — 1945 (C2)
Fred Hetzel, F-C, Davidson — 1963 (C2), 1964 (C1, AP2, UPI2, NABC3) and 1965 (AP1, C1, NABC1, UP1, USBWA1)
Art Heyman, F, Duke — 1961 (C2, AP3, UPI3), 1962 (USBWA1, AP2, C2, NABC2, UPI2) and 1963 (AP1, C1, NABC1, UP1, USBWA1)
Wayne Hightower, F, Kansas — 1960 (C2) and 1961 (NABC3)
Bobby Joe Hill, G, Texas Western — 1966 (C1)
Grant Hill, F, Duke — 1992 (UPI2), 1993 (NABC2, UPI2, USBWA2, AP3) and 1994 (AP1, NABC1, UP1, USBWA1)
Simmie Hill, F, West Texas State — 1969 (C2)
Joe Hobbs, G, Florida — 1958 (C1)
Paul Hoffman, F-C, Purdue — 1947 (C3)
Paul Hogue, C, Cincinnati — 1961 (C2) and 1962 (C1, USBWA1, NABC2, AP3, UPI3)
Lionel Hollins, G, Arizona State — 1975 (C1, AP3, NABC3)
Joe Holup, C, George Washington — 1956 (C2, NABC2, AP3)
William (Red) Holzman, G, CCNY — 1942 (C3)
Jerald Honeycutt, F, Tulane — 1997 (NABC3)
Dennis Hopson, G, Ohio State — 1987 (AP2, NABC2, UPI2, USBWA2)
John Horan, F, Dayton — 1955 (C3, NABC3, UP3)
Allan Hornyak, G, Ohio State — 1972 (C2, UPI2, NABC3) and 1973 (C2, NABC3)
Bill Hosket, C, Ohio State — 1968 (C1)
Bob Houbregs, F-C, Washington — 1952 (NABC2, AP3, UP3) and 1953 (AP1, C1, NABC1, UP1)
Allan Houston, G, Tennessee — 1992 (NABC3) and 1993 (AP3, NABC3)
Byron Houston, F, Oklahoma State — 1992 (AP2, NABC2, UPI2, USBWA2)
Kevin Houston, G, Army — 1987 (NABC3)
Frank Howard, C, Ohio State — 1957 (C1, USBWA1, AP2, NABC3, UP3)
Juwan Howard, C, Michigan — 1994 (NABC2, AP3)
Bailey Howell, F, Mississippi State — 1958 (USBWA1, AP2, C2, NABC3, UP3) and 1959 (AP1, C1, NABC1, UP1, USBWA1)

Phil Hubbard, C, Michigan	1977 (USBWA1, C2, NABC2, AP3)
Lou Hudson, F, Minnesota	1965 (C2) and 1966 (C2, NABC3)
Wendell Hudson, F, Alabama	1973 (C2)
Marv Huffman, G, Indiana	1940 (C1)
Vern Huffman, G, Indiana	1936 (C1)
Alfrederick Hughes, F, Loyola (Ill.)	1985 (AP3, UPI3)
Jimmy Hull, F, Ohio State	1939 (C2)
Rod Hundley, G-F, West Virginia	1955 (C4), 1956 (AP2, C2, NABC2, UP2) and 1957 (AP1, C1, NABC1, UP1, USBWA1)
Bobby Hurley, G, Duke	1992 (NABC1, AP3, UPI3) and 1993 (AP1, NABC1, UP1, USBWA1)
Paul Huston, G, Ohio State	1946 (C3)
Mel Hutchins, C, Brigham Young	1951 (C1, AP3, UP3)
Chuck Hyatt, F, Pittsburgh	1929 (NCAA) and 1930 (NCAA)

I

Dan Issel, C, Kentucky	1969 (C1, USBWA1, AP2, NABC2, UPI3) and 1970 (AP1, C1, NABC1, UP1, USBWA1)
Allen Iverson, G, Georgetown	1996 (AP1, NABC1, UP1, USBWA1)
Dick Ives, F, Iowa	1944 (C3) and 1945 (C2)

J

Bobby Jackson, G, Minnesota	1997 (AP2, NABC2, USBWA2)
Chris Jackson, G, Louisiana State	1989 (AP1, UPI1, USBWA1, NABC2) and 1990 (AP1, NABC1, UP1, USBWA1)
Jim Jackson, G-F, Ohio State	1991 (UPI1, USBWA1, AP2, NABC2) and 1992 (AP1, NABC1, UP1, USBWA1)
Mark Jackson, G, St. John's	1987 (AP2, NABC2, UP2, USBWA2)
Mervin Jackson, G, Utah	1968 (USBWA1, C2, NABC3)
Tony Jackson, F, St. John's	1959 (NABC3), 1960 (AP1, C2, NABC2, UPI2) and 1961 (AP2, C2, NABC2, UPI2)
Antawn Jamison, F, North Carolina	1997 (AP2, NABC2)
Thad Jaracz, C, Kentucky	1966 (AP3)
Jim Jarvis, G, Oregon State	1965 (C2)
Chet Jaworski, G, Rhode Island State	1939 (C2)
Keith (Mister) Jennings, G, East Tenn. St.	1991 (NABC2, USBWA2, AP3, UPI3)
Earvin (Magic) Johnson, G, Michigan State	1978 (NABC2, AP3, UPI3) and 1979 (AP1, C1, NABC1, UP1)
Ervin Johnson, C, New Orleans	1993 (UPI3)
Frank Johnson, G, Wake Forest	1981 (C2)
John Johnson, F, Iowa	1970 (C2, AP3, UPI3)
Larry Johnson, F, UNLV	1990 (AP1, UPI1, USBWA1, NABC2) and 1991 (AP1, NABC1, UP1, USBWA1)
Marques Johnson, F, UCLA	1976 (C2, NABC2) and 1977 (AP1, C1, NABC1, UP1, USBWA1)
Ollie Johnson, C, San Francisco	1965 (NABC2, UPI3)
Reggie Johnson, F, Tennessee	1980 (C2)
Ron Johnson, C, Minnesota	1959 (AP3) and 1960 (C2, NABC3)
Steve Johnson, C, Oregon State	1980 (C2) and 1981 (NABC1, USBWA1, AP2, C2)
Vinnie Johnson, G, Baylor	1979 (AP2, C2)
Bobby Jones, F, North Carolina	1974 (C1, USBWA1, AP2, NABC2, UPI2)
Jeff Jones, G, Virginia	1977 (NABC5)
K.C. Jones, G, San Francisco	1956 (C1, NABC1, UP1, AP2)
Wali Jones, G, Villanova	1964 (C2, UPI3)
Wallace (Wah Wah) Jones, F-C, Kentucky	1947 (C2), 1948 (C3) and 1949 (C1, UP2, AP2)
Michael Jordan, G, North Carolina	1983 (AP1, C1, NABC1, UP1, USBWA1) and 1984 (AP1, NABC1, UP1, USBWA1)
Harry Jorgenson, F, Wyoming	1955 (NABC3)
Kevin Joyce, G, South Carolina	1973 (C1, AP2, NABC2, UPI2)
Paul Judson, G, Illinois	1956 (C2, NABC3, UP3)

K

George Kaftan, F-C, Holy Cross	1947 (C1) and 1948 (C1, AP2)
Roger Kaiser, G, Georgia Tech	1960 (C1, USBWA1, AP2, NABC2, UPI2) and 1961 (AP1, UPI1, USBWA1, C2, NABC2)
Bob Kauffman, C, Guilford (N.C.)	1968 (C2)
Wilbert Kautz, G, Loyola (Ill.)	1939 (C2)
Tommy Kearns, G, North Carolina	1957 (C2) and 1958 (AP3)
Adam Keefe, F, Stanford	1992 (AP2, NABC3, UPI3)
Dean Kelley, G, Kansas	1953 (C4)
Rich Kelley, C, Stanford	1975 (UPI3, NABC4)
Clark Kellogg, F, Ohio State	1982 (C1)
Greg Kelser, F, Michigan State	1979 (C1, AP3)
Bill (Pickles) Kennedy, G, Temple	1960 (C2, AP3)
Larry Kenon, F, Memphis State	1973 (C2)
John (Red) Kerr, C, Illinois	1954 (AP3, UP3, C4)
Steve Kerr, G, Arizona	1988 (AP2, NABC3)
Jack Kerris, C, Loyola (Ill.)	1949 (C3)
Alec Kessler, F, Georgia	1990 (UPI2)
Bob Kessler, F, Purdue	1936 (C1)
Earl Keth, F, Central Missouri	1938 (C3)
Jason Kidd, G, California	1994 (AP1, NABC1, UP1, USBWA1)
Greg (Bo) Kimble, G, Loyola Marymount	1990 (AP2, USBWA2, NABC3, UPI3)
Albert King, F, Maryland	1980 (AP1, C2, NABC2, UPI2) and 1981 (UPI2, NABC3)
Bernard King, F, Tennessee	1975 (C2, UPI2, NABC3), 1976 (USBWA1, C2, UPI2, AP3, NABC3) and 1977 (AP1, C1, UPI1, USBWA1, NABC2)
Reggie King, F, Alabama	1978 (AP2, C2) and 1979 (C1, NABC2)
Stacey King, C, Oklahoma	1989 (AP1, NABC1, UPI1, USBWA1)
Bill Kinner, C-F, Utah	1935 (C3)
Bob Kinney, C, Rice	1941 (C1) and 1942 (C1)
H.E. Kirchner, C, Texas Christian	1959 (C2)
Walt Kirk, G, Illinois	1945 (C1)
Ted Kitchel, F, Indiana	1982 (NABC3, UPI3)
Kerry Kittles, G-F, Villanova	1995 (AP2, NABC2, UPI2, USBWA2) and 1996 (AP1, NABC1, UPI2, USBWA2)
Leo Klier, F, Notre Dame	1944 (C1) and 1946 (C1)
Duane Klueh, F, Indiana State	1948 (NCAA2)
Billy Knight, F, Pittsburgh	1974 (USBWA1, AP2, C2, NABC2, UPI3)

Brevin Knight, G, Stanford — 1997 (AP2, NABC2, USBWA2)
Dick Knostman, C, Kansas State — 1952 (AP3) and 1953 (AP2, NABC2, UP2, C4)
Ed Koffenberger, F, Duke — 1946 (C2) and 1947 (C3)
Don Kojis, F, Marquette — 1961 (C1)
George Kok, C, Arkansas — 1948 (AP3)
Milo Komenich, C, Wyoming — 1943 (C3)
Howard Komives, G, Bowling Green — 1964 (C1, AP3, UPI3)
Jon Koncak, C, Southern Methodist — 1985 (AP2, NABC2, UPI2, USBWA2)
Tom Kondla, C, Minnesota — 1967 (C2)
Bud Koper, F, Oklahoma City — 1964 (USBWA1)
William Kotsores, F, St. John's — 1944 (C3)
John Kotz, F, Wisconsin — 1942 (C1) and 1943 (C3)
Barry Kramer, F, NYU — 1963 (AP1, C1, USBWA1, UPI2, NABC3) and 1964 (C2, AP3, NABC3)
Ron Kramer, C, Michigan — 1957 (C2, NABC3)
Ed (Moose) Krause, C, Notre Dame — 1932 (C1), 1933 (C1) and 1934 (C1)
Jim Krebs, C, Southern Methodist — 1957 (C1, NABC1, USBWA1, AP2, UP2)
Jim Krivacs, G, Texas — 1979 (C2)
Mitch Kupchak, F-C, North Carolina — 1975 (C2) and 1976 (USBWA1, AP2, C2, NABC2, UPI2)
Bob Kurland, C, Oklahoma A&M — 1944 (C2), 1945 (C1) and 1946 (C1)

L

George Lacy, G, Richmond — 1935 (C2)
Christian Laettner, C-F, Duke — 1991 (AP2, NABC2, UPI2, USBWA2) and 1992 (AP1, NABC1, UPI1, USBWA1)
Raef LaFrentz, F, Kansas — 1997 (AP1, NABC1, USBWA1)
Tom LaGarde, C, North Carolina — 1977 (C2)
Dwight (Bo) Lamar, G, Southwestern La. — 1972 (AP1, C1, UPI1, NABC2) and 1973 (C1, UPI1, USBWA1, AP2, NABC2)
Jeff Lamp, G, Virginia — 1980 (UPI3) and 1981 (USBWA1,UPI2, AP3, NABC3)
Jerome Lane, F, Pittsburgh — 1987 (AP3, NABC3, UPI3) and 1988 (AP2, USBWA2)
Bob Lanier, C, St. Bonaventure — 1968 (USBWA1, AP2, C2, NABC2, UPI2), 1969 (AP2, C2, NABC2, UPI2) and 1970 (AP1, C1, NABC1, UP1, USBWA1)
York Larese, G, North Carolina — 1959 (AP3), 1960 (C2, NABC3) and 1961 (NABC2, AP3, UPI3)
Barry Larkin, G, Xavier — 1988 (UPI2, AP3)
David Lattin, C, Texas Western — 1967 (C2, AP3, NABC3)
Tony Lavelli, F, Yale — 1946 (C3), 1947 (NABC2), 1948 (NABC1, AP2, C2) and 1949 (AP1, UP1, C2)
Dennis Layton, G, Southern California — 1971 (USBWA1, C2)
Hal Lear, G, Temple — 1956 (C1, NABC2)
Alfred (Butch) Lee, G, Marquette — 1977 (C1, AP2, UPI2, NABC3) and 1978 (AP1, C1, NABC1, UP1, USBWA1)
Clyde Lee, C, Vanderbilt — 1965 (C1, USBWA1, AP2, UPI2) and 1966 (AP1, C1, NABC1, UP1, USBWA1)
Hal Lee, G, Washington — 1934 (C2)
Keith Lee, C, Memphis State — 1982 (C1, AP2), 1983 (C1, UPI1, USBWA2, AP2, NABC2), 1984 (NABC2, UPI2, USBWA2, AP3) and 1985 (AP1, NABC1, UP1, USBWA1)
Ron Lee, G, Oregon — 1974 (C2, NABC4), 1975 (NABC1, C2, UPI2, AP3) and 1976 (AP2, C2, NABC3, UPI3)
Russell Lee, F, Marshall — 1972 (C2)
Bob Leonard, G, Indiana — 1953 (C1, AP3) and 1954 (C1, NABC1, AP2, UP2)
Ronnie Lester, G, Iowa — 1979 (AP2, NABC3, UPI3) and 1980 (C2)
Bob Lewis, F-G, North Carolina — 1966 (AP3, NABC3, UPI3) and 1967 (NABC3)
Mike Lewis, C, Duke — 1968 (C2, AP3, NABC3, UPI3)
Todd Lichti, G, Stanford — 1989 (NABC2, UPI2, USBWA2, AP3)
Paul Lindemann, C, Washington State — 1941 (C1)
Jim Line, F, Kentucky — 1950 (UP3)
Cleo Littleton, F, Wichita — 1955 (NABC3)
Bob Lloyd, G, Rutgers — 1967 (C1, UPI1, USBWA1, AP2, C2)
Lewis Lloyd, F, Drake — 1980 (AP3, UPI3) and 1981 (AP3, UPI3)
Kevin Loder, F, Alabama State — 1981 (C2)
Don Lofgran, F-C, San Francisco — 1949 (C1) and 1950 (AP2, NABC2, UP2)
Bill Logan, C, Iowa — 1956 (C2)
Henry Logan, G, Western Carolina — 1968 (C2)
Elliott Loughlin, G, Navy — 1933 (C1)
Stan Love, C, Oregon — 1971 (C2, NABC4)
Clyde Lovellette, C, Kansas — 1950 (C2, AP3), 1951 (AP1, NABC1, UP1, C2) and 1952 (AP1, C1, NABC1, UP1)
Jerry Lucas, C, Ohio State — 1960 (AP1, C1, NABC1, UP1, USBWA1), 1961 (AP1, C1, NABC1, UP1, USBWA1) and 1962 (AP1, C1, NABC1, UP1, USBWA1)
John Lucas, G, Maryland — 1974 (AP2, C2, NABC3), 1975 (C1, NABC1, UPI1, USBWA1, AP2) and 1976 (AP1, C1, UPI1, USBWA1)
Maurice Lucas, C, Marquette — 1974 (C2, NABC3)
Hank Luisetti, F, Stanford — 1936 (C1), 1937 (C1) and 1938 (C1)

M

Ed Macauley, C-F, St. Louis — 1948 (AP1, NABC1, C2) and 1949 (AP1, C1, NABC1, UP1)
Durand (Rudy) Macklin, F, LSU — 1980 (C1) and 1981 (C1, USBWA1, NABC2, UPI2)
Don MacLean, F, UCLA — 1992 (AP2, NABC2, USBWA2, UPI3)
Mark Macon, G, Temple — 1988 (AP2, NABC2)
Kyle Macy, G, Kentucky — 1978 (UPI3), 1979 (C2, NABC3) and 1980 (AP1, C1, NABC1, UP1, USBWA1)
Kevin Magee, F, UC Irvine — 1981 (AP1, C2) and 1982 (AP1, C1, USBWA1, NABC2, UPI2)
Jeff Malone, G, Mississippi State — 1983 (NABC3)
Karl Malone, F, Louisiana Tech — 1985 (NABC2)
Mike Maloy, C, Davidson — 1968 (C2), 1969 (C1, USBWA1, AP2, UPI2, NABC3) and 1970 (C2, AP3, NABC3, UPI3)
John Mandic, C, Oregon State — 1942 (C1)
Danny Manning, F, Kansas — 1986 (AP2, NABC2, UPI2, USBWA2), 1987 (AP1, NABC1, UP1, USBWA1) and 1988 (AP1, NABC1, UP1, USBWA1)
Pete Maravich, G, Louisiana State — 1968 (AP1, C1, NABC1, UP1, USBWA1), 1969 (AP1, C1, NABC1, UP1, USBWA1) and 1970 (AP1, C1, NABC1, UP1, USBWA1)
Stephon Marbury, G, Georgia Tech — 1996 (AP3, NABC3)
Jack Marin, F, Duke — 1966 (C1, USBWA2, AP2, NABC3, UPI3)
Donyell Marshall, F, Connecticut — 1994 (AP1, NABC1, UP1, USBWA1)
Tom Marshall, F, Western Kentucky — 1954 (AP2, C2, UP2)
Merlin Marty, ?, Loras (Iowa) — 1948 (C2)
Jamal Mashburn, F, Kentucky — 1993 (AP1, NABC1, UP1, USBWA1)

Bobby Joe Mason, G, Bradley	1960 (NABC2)
Bob Mattick, C, Oklahoma A&M	1954 (NABC2, AP3, UP3, C4)
Cedric (Cornbread) Maxwell, F-C, UNCC	1977 (C1, UPI3, NABC5)
Don May, F, Dayton	1967 (C1, USBWA1, UPI3) and 1968 (C1, AP2, NABC2, UPI2)
Scott May, F, Indiana	1975 (AP1, C1, UP1, USBWA1, NABC2) and 1976 (AP1, C1, NABC1, UP1, USBWA1)
Lee Mayberry, G, Arkansas	1992 (AP3, NABC3)
Clyde Mayes, F, Furman	1975 (C2, AP3, NABC4)
Bob McAdoo, C, North Carolina	1972 (C1, USBWA1, AP2, UPI2, NABC3)
Gale McArthur, G, Oklahoma A&M	1951 (AP2, C2, NABC2, UP2)
Billy McCaffrey, G, Vanderbilt	1993 (USBWA2, AP3, NABC3, UPI3)
Willie McCarter, G, Drake	1969 (C2)
John McCarthy, G, Canisius	1956 (C2)
George McCloud, F, Florida State	1989 (AP3, NABC3, UPI3)
Julius McCoy, F, Michigan State	1956 (C2, AP3, NABC3, UP3)
E. (Branch) McCracken, F, Indiana	1930 (NCAA)
Rodney McCray, F-C, Louisville	1983 (C2)
William (Red) McCrocklin, C, Western Ky.	1938 (C3)
Bob McCurdy, F-C, Richmond	1975 (AP3)
Xavier McDaniel, F, Wichita State	1985 (AP1, USBWA1, UPI2, NABC3)
Jim McDaniels, C, Western Kentucky	1970 (C2) and 1971 (AP1, C1, NABC1, USBWA1, UPI2)
Banks McFadden, C, Clemson	1939 (C1)
Mike McGee, F, Michigan	1981 (C2)
Billy McGill, C, Utah	1960 (AP3, NABC3), 1961 (USBWA1, AP2, C2, NABC2, UPI2) and 1962 (AP1, C1, UP1, USBWA1, NABC2)
George McGinnis, F, Indiana	1971 (C2, AP3, NABC3, UPI3)
Dick McGuire, G, St. John's	1947 (NABC2) and 1949 (UP3, C4)
Jim McIntyre, C, Minnesota	1948 (AP1, NABC2) and 1949 (NABC1, AP3)
Derrick McKey, F, Alabama	1987 (UPI2, AP3, NABC3)
Tom McMillen, F, Maryland	1972 (C2, AP3, UPI3), 1973 (C1, NABC2, UPI2, AP3) and 1974 (C1, NABC2, UPI2, AP3)
Jim McMillian, F, Columbia	1968 (UPI3), 1969 (USBWA1, C2, NABC2, UPI3) and 1970 (C2, AP3)
Mark McNamara, C, California	1982 (UPI3)
Jimmy McNatt, F, Oklahoma	1939 (C3) and 1940 (C1)
Carl McNulty, C, Purdue	1952 (C4)
Cliff Meely, C-F, Colorado	1971 (USBWA1, C2, AP3, NABC4)
Don Meineke, C, Dayton	1951 (C4) and 1952 (AP3, C3, UP3)
Bill Melchionni, G, Villanova	1966 (C2)
Gene Melchiorre, G, Bradley	1950 (UP2, C3) and 1951 (AP1, C1, UP1)
Dean Meminger, G, Marquette	1970 (C2) and 1971 (AP1, C1, NABC1, UP1, USBWA1)
Chuck Mencel, G, Minnesota	1953 (UP3, C4) and 1955 (C1, NABC3)
Bill Menke, C, Indiana	1940 (C3)
Ron Mercer, F, Kentucky	1997 (AP1, NABC1, USBWA1)
Joe C. Meriweather, C, Southern Ill.	1975 (NABC5)
Porter Merriweather, G, Tennessee State	1960 (C2)
Tom Meschery, F, St. Mary's (Calif.)	1960 (NABC3) and 1961 (C1, USBWA1)
Dave Meyers, F, UCLA	1975 (AP1, C1, NABC1, UP1, USBWA1)
George Mikan, C, DePaul	1944 (C1), 1945 (C1) and 1946 (C1)
Vern Mikkelsen, C, Hamline (Minn.)	1949 (C2)
Eddie Miles, G, Seattle	1963 (C2, AP3, UPI3)
Larry Miller, F, North Carolina	1967 (C1, USBWA1, AP2, NABC2, UPI3) and 1968 (AP1, C1, NABC1, USBWA1, UPI2)
Reggie Miller, F, UCLA	1986 (UPI3)
Chris Mills, F, Arizona	1993 (AP3, NABC3, UPI3)
Harold Miner, G, Southern California	1992 (AP1, NABC1, UP1, USBWA1)
Ryan Minor, F, Oklahoma	1995 (UPI3) and 1996 (NABC3)
Roland Minson, C, Brigham Young	1951 (C4)
Mike Mitchell, F, Auburn	1978 (C2)
Todd Mitchell, F, Purdue	1988 (NABC3)
Bill Mlkvy, F, Temple	1951 (AP1, C1, NABC1, UP1)
Stan Modzelewski, G, Rhode Island State	1942 (C2)
Doug Moe, F, North Carolina	1961 (USBWA1, AP2, NABC3)
John Moir, F, Notre Dame	1936 (C2), 1937 (C1) and 1938 (C1)
Vic Molodet, G, North Carolina State	1956 (NABC3)
Sidney Moncrief, G-F, Arkansas	1978 (UPI2, AP3, NABC3) and 1979 (AP1, C1, NABC1, USBWA1, UPI2)
Earl Monroe, G, Winston-Salem State	1967 (C1)
Rodney Monroe, G, North Carolina State	1991 (NABC2, UPI2, AP3)
Eric Montross, C, North Carolina	1993 (AP2, NABC2, UPI3) and 1994 (NABC1, AP2)
Bill Morris, G, Washington	1944 (C3)
Max Morris, F-C, Northwestern	1945 (C3) and 1946 (C1)
Bob Morse, C, Pennsylvania	1972 (C2, NABC2)
Lawrence Moten, G-F, Syracuse	1995 (AP3, NABC3)
Rick Mount, G, Purdue	1968 (C1, UPI2, AP3, NABC3), 1969 (AP1, C1, NABC1, UP1, USBWA1) and 1970 (AP1, C1, NABC1, UP1, USBWA1)
Alonzo Mourning, C, Georgetown	1989 (AP3, UPI3), 1990 (NABC1, AP2) 1991 (NABC3) and 1992 (AP1, UPI1, USBWA1, NABC2)
Ed Mullen, G, Marquette	1934 (C1)
Chris Mullin, G-F, St. John's	1983 (C2, UPI3), 1984 (NABC1, UPI1, AP2, USBWA2) and 1985 (AP1, NABC1, UP1, USBWA1)
Jeff Mullins, F, Duke	1963 (C2), 1964 (C1, USBWA1, AP2, NABC2, UPI2)
George Munroe, F, Dartmouth	1942 (C2)
Eric Murdock, G, Providence	1991 (AP2, NABC2, UPI2, USBWA2)
Jack Murdock, G, Wake Forest	1957 (C2)
Allen Murphy, G-F, Louisville	1975 (C2)
Calvin Murphy, G, Niagara	1968 (UPI1, USBWA1, AP2, C2, NABC2), 1969 (AP1, C1, UPI1, USBWA1, NABC2) and 1970 (AP1, C1, UPI1, USBWA1, NABC2)
Charles (Stretch) Murphy, C, Purdue	1929 (NCAA) and 1930 (NCAA)
Lamond Murray, F, California	1994 (USBWA2, AP3, NABC3, UPI3)
Phil (Red) Murrell, F, Drake	1958 (C2)
Willie Murrell, F, Kansas State	1964 (C2)
Dikembe Mutombo, C, Georgetown	1991 (AP3, UPI3)

N

Larry Nance, F, Clemson	1981 (C2)
Charles (Cotton) Nash, F-C, Kentucky	1962 (USBWA1, AP2, C2, UPI2, NABC3), 1963 (USBWA1, AP2, C2, NABC2, UPI2) and 1964 (AP1, C1, NABC1, UP1, USBWA1)
Calvin Natt, F, Northeast Louisiana	1979 (C1, USBWA1, AP2, NABC4)
Willie Naulls, C, UCLA	1956 (C1, NABC2, AP3, UP3)
Don Nelson, F, Iowa	1961 (C2) and 1962 (C2, AP3, NABC3, UPI3)
Dick Nemelka, G, Brigham Young	1966 (C1, USBWA1, NABC3, UPI3)
Jerry Nemer, F, Southern California	1933 (NCAA)
Johnny Neumann, F-G, Mississippi	1971 (C1, USBWA1, AP2, NABC2, UPI2)
Paul Neumann, G, Stanford	1959 (C2)
Ab Nicholas, G, Wisconsin	1952 (C3)
Jack Nichols, C, Washington	1948 (NCAA2)
Gordon Norman, C, Minnesota	1934 (C3)
Ken Norman, F, Illinois	1987 (AP2, USBWA2, NABC3)
Mike Novak, C, Loyola of Chicago	1938 (C2) and 1939 (C2)
Paul Nowak, C, Notre Dame	1936 (C1) and 1937 (C1)

O

Ed O'Bannon, F, UCLA	1994 (NABC3) and 1995 (AP1, NABC1, UP1, USBWA1)
Eddie O'Brien, G, Seattle	1953 (C3, UP3)
Jim O'Brien, G, Boston College	1971 (NABC4)
Johnny O'Brien, G, Seattle	1952 (C2, UP2, AP3) and 1953 (AP1, NABC1, UP1, C3)
Bud Ogden, F, Santa Clara	1969 (USBWA1, C2, UPI2, NABC3)
Don Ohl, G, Illinois	1958 (C2)
Mike O'Koren, F, North Carolina	1978 (C2, NABC3), 1979 (C1, USBWA1, NABC2, UPI2) and 1980 (C1, USBWA1, NABC2, UPI2)
Hakeem Olajuwon, C, Houston	1983 (C2) and 1984 (AP1, NABC1, USBWA1, UPI2)
John Oldham, G, Western Kentucky	1949 (UP3)
Frank Oleynick, G, Seattle	1975 (NABC5)
Mike Olliver, G, Lamar	1981 (C2)
Oscar Olson, F, Carleton (Minn.)	1939 (C3)
Dick O'Neal, C, Texas Christian	1957 (NABC3)
Shaquille O'Neal, C, Louisiana State	1991 (AP1, NABC1, UP1, USBWA1) and 1992 (AP1, NABC1, UP1, USBWA1)
Bernie Opper, G, Kentucky	1939 (C1)
Eddie Oram, G, Southern California	1937 (C2)
Chuck Orebaugh, G, Drake	1937 (C2)
Kevin O'Shea, G, Notre Dame	1947 (NABC3), 1948 (AP1, C1, NABC1), 1949 (AP3) and 1950 (AP1, UP1, C2)
Don Otten, C, Bowling Green	1946 (C2)
Billy Owens, F, Syracuse	1990 (NABC3, UPI3) and 1991 (AP1, NABC1, UP1, USBWA1)
Eddie Owens, F, UNLV	1977 (C2)
Ken Owens, G, Idaho	1982 (C2)

P

Alva (Allie) Paine, G, Oklahoma	1944 (C1)
Togo Palazzi, F, Holy Cross	1953 (C4) and 1954 (C2, NABC2, AP3, UP3)
Wally Palmberg, F, Oregon	1936 (C1)
Robert Parish, C, Centenary	1974 (NABC5), 1975 (NABC5) and 1976 (AP2, C2)
Barry Parkhill, G, Virginia	1972 (C1, USBWA1, AP2, UPI2, NABC3) and 1973 (C2, NABC3)
Jack Parkinson, G, Kentucky	1946 (C1)
Jack Parr, C, Kansas State	1957 (C2) and 1958 (NABC3)
Bob Patterson, F, Tulsa	1955 (C2)
Jim Paxson, G, Dayton	1979 (USBWA1, NABC3)
John Paxson, G, Notre Dame	1982 (C2, UPI2) and 1983 (NABC1, UPI1, C2)
Gary Payton, G, Oregon State	1990 (AP1, NABC1, UP1, USBWA1)
Anthony Peeler, G, Missouri	1990 (UPI3) and 1991 (AP2, NABC2, UP2, USBWA2)
Will Perdue, C, Vanderbilt	1988 (AP3, NABC3)
Sam Perkins, F-C, North Carolina	1982 (USBWA1, C2, NABC2, UPI2), 1983 (C1, UPI1, USBWA1, NABC2, AP3) and 1984 (AP1, UPI1, USBWA1, NABC2)
Ronnie Perry, G, Holy Cross	1977 (C2), 1978 (C2) and 1979 (C2)
Chuck Person, F, Auburn	1986 (NABC3)
Bob Pettit, C, Louisiana State	1952 (AP2, UP2, C4), 1953 (AP2, NABC2, UP2, C3) and 1954 (AP1, C1, NABC1, UP1)
Roger Phegley, G, Bradley	1978 (C2, UPI3)
Milton Phelps, ?, San Diego State	1940 (C3)
Andy Phillip, F, Illinois	1942 (C3), 1943 (C1) and 1947 (NABC1)
Eddie Phillips, F, Alabama	1980 (C2) and 1982 (C2)
Gary Phillips, G, Houston	1961 (C1, USBWA1)
Ricky Pierce, F, Rice	1982 (USBWA1, C2, AP3, NABC3)
John Pilch, G, Wyoming	1950 (NABC2, C3)
John Pinone, C, Villanova	1983 (C2, AP3, UPI3)
H.L. (Ike) Poole, F-C, Arkansas	1936 (C2)
Howard Porter, F, Villanova	1969 (C2, AP3, NABC3, UPI3), 1970 (C2) and 1971 (C1, NABC2, UPI2, AP3)
Rolf Poser, G, Wisconsin	1935 (C3)
Fred Pralle, G, Kansas	1938 (C1)
Mike Pratt, F, Kentucky	1970 (C2)
Paul Pressey, G-F, Tulsa	1982 (USBWA1, NABC2, UPI2, AP3)
Jim Price, G, Louisville	1972 (C1, NABC1, USBWA1, AP2, UPI2)
Mark Price, G, Georgia Tech	1984 (UPI3), 1985 (AP2, NABC2, UPI3) and 1986 (NABC2, AP3, UPI3)
Lou Pucillo, G, North Carolina State	1959 (USBWA1, AP2, C2, NABC3, UPI3)
Bennie Purcell, G, Murray State	1952 (C4)

Q

David Quabius, G, Marquette	1939 (C3)
Art Quimby, C, Connecticut	1955 (NABC2)

R

Ray Ragelis, F, Northwestern	1951 (C2)

Frank Ramsey, F, Kentucky	1951 (AP3, C3, UP3), 1952 (C1, AP2, UP2) and 1953 (C1, AP2, NABC2, UP2)
Terry Rand, C, Marquette	1956 (NABC3)
Mark Randall, F-C, Kansas	1990 (NABC3)
Kelvin Ransey, G, Ohio State	1979 (C2, UPI3) and 1980 (USBWA1, UPI2, NABC3)
Sam Ranzino, F-G, North Carolina State	1950 (C1, AP2) and 1951 (NABC1, UP1, C3)
Bobby Rascoe, G, Western Kentucky	1962 (C1)
Ed Ratleff, F-G, Long Beach State	1972 (AP1, C1, NABC1, UP1, USBWA1) and 1973 (AP1, C1, NABC1, UP1, USBWA1)
James Ray, C, Jacksonville	1980 (C1)
Jimmy Rayl, G, Indiana	1962 (C2, AP3, UPI3) and 1963 (C2, AP3)
Dexter Reed, G, Memphis State	1977 (C2)
Hub Reed, C, Oklahoma City	1958 (C2)
Bryant Reeves, C, Oklahoma State	1994 (UPI2, AP3) and 1995 (UPI2, AP3, NABC3)
Khalid Reeves, G, Arizona	1994 (AP2, UPI2, USBWA2, NABC3)
Don Rehfeldt, C, Wisconsin	1950 (NABC2, UP2, AP3, C4)
J.R. Reid, C, North Carolina	1988 (AP1, NABC1, USBWA1, UPI2) and 1989 (NABC3)
Joe Reiff, F, Northwestern	1931 (NCAA) and 1933 (NCAA)
Jesse (Cab) Renick, G, Oklahoma A&M	1940 (C2)
Bob Rensberger, G, Notre Dame	1943 (C2)
Shawn Respert, G, Michigan State	1994 (UPI3) and 1995 (AP1, NABC1, UP1, USBWA1)
Glen Rice, F, Michigan	1989 (AP2, NABC2, USBWA2, UPI3)
Joe Richey, F, Brigham Young	1953 (NABC2)
Mitch Richmond, F-G, Kansas State	1988 (UPI2, USBWA2)
John Richter, C, North Carolina State	1959 (C1, NABC2)
Dick Ricketts, F-C, Duquesne	1954 (AP2, NABC2, UP2, C3) and 1955 (AP1, NABC1, UP1, C2)
Isaiah (J.R.) Rider, F, UNLV	1993 (AP2, NABC2, UPI2, USBWA2)
Bill Ridley, G, Illinois	1956 (C2, AP3, NABC3, UP3)
Tom Riker, C-F, South Carolina	1972 (AP1, C1, NABC1, USBWA1, UPI2)
Pat Riley, F, Kentucky	1966 (USBWA1, C2, AP3)
Arnie Risen, C, Ohio State	1945 (C2)
Ed Riska, F, Notre Dame	1941 (C3)
David Rivers, G, Notre Dame	1988 (NABC2)
Glenn (Doc) Rivers, G, Marquette	1982 (C2) and 1983 (C2)
Anthony Roberts, F, Oral Roberts	1977 (C1, NABC5)
Alvin Robertson, G, Arkansas	1984 (UPI2, AP3)
Oscar Robertson, F, Cincinnati	1958 (AP1, C1, NABC1, UP1, USBWA1), 1959 (AP1, C1, NABC1, UP1, USBWA1) and 1960 (AP1, C1, NABC1, UP1, USBWA1)
Rick Robey, F-C, Kentucky	1977 (C1, NABC4) and 1978 (C1, NABC1, UPI2, AP3)
David Robinson, C, Navy	1986 (NABC2, USBWA2, AP3, UPI3) and 1987 (AP1, NABC1, UP1, USBWA1)
Flynn Robinson, G, Wyoming	1965 (C2)
Glenn Robinson, F, Purdue	1993 (AP2, NABC2, UPI2, USBWA2) and 1994 (AP1, NABC1, UP1, USBWA1)
Mike Robinson, G, Michigan State	1974 (C2)
Rumeal Robinson, G, Michigan	1990 (AP2, NAC2, UPI2, USBWA2)
Wil Robinson, G, West Virginia	1972 (C2, AP3)
Dave Robisch, C, Kansas	1971 (AP2, C2, NABC3, UPI3)
John Roche, G, South Carolina	1969 (C2), 1970 (C1, USBWA1, AP2, UPI2, NABC3) and 1971 (C1, UPI1, USBWA1, AP2, NABC2)
Gene Rock, F, Southern California	1943 (C2)
Guy Rodgers, G, Temple	1957 (USBWA1, C2, NAC2, AP3, UP3) and 1958 (AP1, C1, NABC1, UP1, USBWA1)
Lou Roe, F, Massachusetts	1994 (NABC3) and 1995 (AP2, NABC2, UPI2, USBWA2)
Carlos Rogers, C, Tennessee State	1994 (UPI2)
Marshall Rogers, G, Pan American	1976 (C2)
Rodney Rogers, F, Wake Forest	1993 (AP2, NABC2, UPI2, USBWA2)
Martin Rolek, G, Minnesota	1937 (C3) and 1938 (C2)
Wayne (Tree) Rollins, C, Clemson	1977 (C2, AP3, NABC5)
Elwood (Woody) Romney, F-C, Brigham Young	1931 (NCAA)
Jalen Rose, G, Michigan	1994 (AP2, NABC2, UPI2, USBWA2)
Malik Rose, C, Drexel	1996 (UPI3)
Lennie Rosenbluth, F, North Carolina	1956 (AP2, C2, NABC2, UP2) and 1957 (AP1, C1, NABC1, UP1, USBWA1)
Dick Rosenthal, C-F, Notre Dame	1954 (C3)
Curtis Rowe, F, UCLA	1970 (C2) and 1971 (C1, AP2, UPI2, NABC3)
Clifford Rozier, C-F, Louisville	1994 (AP1, UPI1, USBWA1, NABC2)
John Rudometkin, C, Southern California	1961 (C2, UPI2, AP3, NABC3) and 1962 (NABC1, AP2, C2, UPI3)
Joe Ruklick, C, Northwestern	1959 (C2, AP3, NABC3)
Jeff Ruland, C, Iona	1980 (NABC3)
Bill Russell, C, San Francisco	1955 (AP1, C1, NABC1, UP1) and 1956 (AP1, C1, NABC1, UP1)
Cazzie Russell, G, Michigan	1964 (C1, USBWA1, AP2, NABC2, UPI2), 1965 (AP1, C1, NABC1, UP1, USBWA1) and 1966 (AP1, C1, NABC1, UP1, USBWA1)
Michael (Campy) Russell, F, Michigan	1974 (C1, USBWA1, NABC2, AP3, UPI3)
Kent Ryan, F, Utah State	1936 (C3)

S

Kenny Sailors, G, Wyoming	1943 (C1) and 1946 (C2)
Forest (Aggie) Sale, F-C, Kentucky	1932 (C1) and 1933 (C1)
John Salley, C-F, Georgia Tech	1986 (NABC3)
Ralph Sampson, C, Virginia	1980 (C2), 1981 (AP1, C1, NABC1, UP1, USBWA1), 1982 (AP1, C1, NABC1, UP1, USBWA1) and 1983 (AP1, C1, NABC1, UP1, USBWA1)
Tom Sanders, C, New York University	1960 (C2, UPI3)
Jason Sasser, F, Texas Tech	1996 (AP3, UPI3)
Joe Schaaf, F, Pennsylvania	1929 (NCAA)
Billy Schaeffer, F, St. John's	1973 (C2, AP3, NABC3, UPI3)
Oscar Schechtman, G, Long Island	1941 (C1)
Steve Scheffler, C, Purdue	1990 (AP3, UPI3)
Dave Schellhase, F, Purdue	1965 (AP2, C2) and 1966 (AP1, C1, NABC1, UP1, USBWA1)
Don Schlundt, C, Indiana	1953 (AP2, C2, NABC2, UP2), 1954 (AP1, NABC1, UP1, C2) and 1955 (NABC1, AP2, UP2, C4)
Harv Schmidt, F, Illinois	1957 (C2)
Dick Schnittker, F, Ohio State	1949 (AP3, UP3) and 1950 (AP1, C1, NABC1, UP1)
Dave Scholz, F, Illinois	1969 (AP3)

Detlef Schrempf, F, Washington	1985 (NABC3)
Danny Schultz, G, Tennessee	1964 (C2)
Charlie Scott, G-F, North Carolina	1968 (C2), 1969 (C1, NABC1, USBWA1, AP2, UPI2) and 1970 (C1, NABC1, USBWA1, AP2, UPI2)
Dennis Scott, G-F, Georgia Tech	1990 (AP2, UPI2, USBWA2, NABC3)
Shea Seals, F, Tulsa	1997 (AP3, NABC3)
Malik Sealy, F, St. John's	1992 (UPI2, USBWA2, AP3)
Ken Sears, F, Santa Clara	1955 (C2, NABC3, UP3)
Alan Seiden, G, St. John's	1959 (USBWA1, C2, NABC2, UPI2)
Rony Seikaly, C, Syracuse	1988 (NABC2, USBWA2, UPI3)
Phil Sellers, F, Rutgers	1975 (AP3) and 1976 (AP1, C1, USBWA1, NABC2, UPI2)
Rollie Seltz, F, Hamline (Minn.)	1946 (C2)
Frank Selvy, F, Furman	1952 (C3) and 1953 (AP2, C2, UP2)
Ben Selzer, G, Iowa	1934 (C2)
George Senesky, F, St. Joseph's	1943 (C1)
Lee Shaffer, F, North Carolina	1959 (NABC3) and 1960 (USBWA1, C2, AP3, UPI3)
Chuck Share, C, Bowling Green	1950 (AP3, C3, UP3)
Bill Sharman, G, Southern California	1950 (NABC1, AP2, C2, UP2)
Lloyd Sharrar, C, West Virginia	1958 (AP2, NABC3, UP3)
Ed Shaver, G-F, Purdue	1935 (C2)
Ronnie Shavlik, C, North Carolina State	1955 (AP2, NABC2, UP2, C3) and 1956 (NABC1, AP2, C2, UP2)
Doron Sheffer, G, Connecticut	1996 (UPI3)
Arnold Short, F, Oklahoma City	1954 (NABC2, AP3, C3, UP3)
Gene Shue, F, Maryland	1953 (C2) and 1954 (C2)
John Shumate, C-F, Notre Dame	1974 (AP1, C1, NABC1, UP1, USBWA1)
Larry Siegfried, G, Ohio State	1960 (C2) and 1961 (C1, USBWA1, AP3, NABC3, UPI3)
Paul Silas, C, Creighton	1962 (C2), 1963 (C2) and 1964 (C2, NABC2, AP3, UPI3)
Mike Silliman, F, Army	1966 (C2)
Gary Simmons, G, Idaho	1958 (C2)
Lionel Simmons, F, La Salle	1988 (UPI3) and 1989 (NABC2, UPI2, USBWA2, AP3)
Ralph Simpson, G, Michigan State	1970 (NABC3)
Emilio Sinicola, G, Niagara	1951 (C4)
Charlie Sitton, F, Oregon State	1983 (C2) and 1984 (NABC3)
Scott Skiles, G, Michigan State	1986 (UPI2, AP2, USBWA2)
Meyer (Whitey) Skoog, G, Minnesota	1949 (AP3), 1950 (AP2) and 1951 (C2, NABC2, AP3, UP3)
Jerry Sloan, F, Evansville	1965 (C1)
Doug Smart, C, Washington	1957 (C2), 1958 (C2) and 1959 (C2)
Jack Smiley, G, Illinois	1943 (C3)
Bobby (Bingo) Smith, F, Tulsa	1969 (C2, AP3)
Charles Smith, G, Georgetown	1989 (AP2, UPI2)
Chris Smith, C, Virginia Tech	1960 (C2)
Don Smith, C, Iowa State	1968 (C2, NABC3)
Don Smith, G-F, Pittsburgh	1933 (C1)
Doug Smith, F, Missouri	1990 (AP2, NABC2, UPI2, USBWA2) and 1991 (UPI2, AP3)
Elmore Smith, C, Kentucky State	1971 (C2)
Glenn Smith, F, Utah	1952 (B1)
Joe Smith, C, Maryland	1994 (UPI3) and 1995 (AP1, NABC1, UP1, USBWA1)
Kenny Smith, G, North Carolina	1987 (AP1, NABC1, UP1, USBWA1)
Michael Smith, C-F, Brigham Young	1988 (UPI2, USBWA2, AP3)
Steve Smith, G, Michigan State	1990 (AP3, UPI3) and 1991 (NABC1, AP2, UPI3)
Willie Smith, G, Missouri	1976 (C1, USBWA1, NABC3)
Dick Snyder, F, Davidson	1966 (C1, USBWA1, AP2)
Ron Sobieszczyk, F, DePaul	1956 (C2)
Mike Sojourner, C, Utah	1974 (C2)
Willie Sojourner, C, Weber State	1971 (C2, NABC4)
Dale Solomon, C, Virginia Tech	1982 (C2)
Willie Somerset, G, Duquesne	1965 (C2)
Edgar Sonderman, ?, Syracuse	1936 (C3)
Dave Sorenson, C, Ohio State	1969 (C2, AP3) and 1970 (C2)
Ken Spain, C, Houston	1968 (C2)
Jim Spanarkel, G, Duke	1978 (C1) and 1979 (UPI1, C2, NABC2)
Wayne Sparks, F, Carleton (Minn.)	1937 (C3)
Odie Spears, F, Western Kentucky	1948 (C2)
Bobby Speight, C, North Carolina State	1953 (NABC2, AP3, C3)
Robert Spessard, C, Washington & Lee	1937 (C2) and 1938 (C2)
Bill Spivey, C, Kentucky	1950 (AP3, UP3) and 1951 (AP1, C1, NABC1, UP1)
Jim Spivey, C, Southeastern Oklahoma	1957 (C2)
Forrest Sprowl, F, Purdue	1942 (C2)
Jerry Stackhouse, F, North Carolina	1995 (AP1, NABC1, UP1, USBWA1)
Kevin Stacom, G, Providence	1974 (C2, NABC3, UPI3)
Dave Stallworth, F, Wichita State	1963 (C1, UPI3), 1964 (AP1, C1, NABC1, UP1, USBWA1) and 1965 (C1, USBWA1, AP2, NABC2, UPI2)
Isaac (Bud) Stallworth, G, Kansas	1972 (C2, AP3)
George Stanich, G, UCLA	1950 (C1)
Terence Stansbury, G, Temple	1984 (NABC3)
Bill Stauffer, G, Missouri	1952 (C2)
Scott Steagall, F, Millikin (Ill.)	1951 (C1)
Hank Stein, G, Xavier	1958 (C2)
Ray Steiner, G, St. Louis	1952 (AP3, C3, UP3)
Jack Stephens, F-G, Notre Dame	1955 (C2, NABC2, UP3)
Steve Stipanovich, C, Missouri	1982 (C2) and 1983 (C1, AP2, NABC2)
Tom Stith, F, St. Bonaventure	1960 (NABC1, UPI1, USBWA1, AP2, C2) and 1961 (AP1, C1, NABC1, UP1, USBWA1)
Maurice Stokes, C, St. Francis (Pa.)	1955 (C2, NABC2, AP3, UP3)
Damon Stoudamire, G, Arizona	1995 (AP1, NABC1, UP1, USBWA1)
Rod Strickland, G, DePaul	1988 (UPI3)
Roger Strickland, F, Jacksonville	1962 (C2) and 1963 (C2)
John Stroud, F, Mississippi	1980 (AP3)
William (Red) Stroud, G, Mississippi St.	1962 (C2) and 1963 (C2)

Don Sunderlage, G, Illinois	1951 (C3, UP3)
Jon Sundvold, G, Missouri	1983 (C2, NABC2, UPI2)
Keith Swagerty, C, Pacific	1967 (C2)
Dan Swartz, C, Morehead State	1956 (C2)
Ben Swain, C, Texas Southern	1958 (C2)

T

Sid Tannenbaum, G, New York University	1946 (C3) and 1947 (NABC1, C2)
Roy Tarpley, C-F, Michigan	1985 (USBWA2, AP3, UPI3) and 1986 (AP3, NABC3)
Earl Tatum, G-F, Marquette	1976 (USBWA1, C2, NABC2, UPI2, AP3)
Brian Taylor, G, Princeton	1972 (C2, NABC2, AP3, UPI3)
Terry Teagle, F, Baylor	1982 (AP2)
Tom Thacker, F-G, Cincinnati	1963 (C1, NABC1, UP1, USBWA1, AP2)
Isiah Thomas, G, Indiana	1981 (AP1, C1, NABC1, UP1, USBWA1)
Kurt Thomas, F-C, Texas Christian	1995 (AP3, NABC3, UPI3)
Chris Thomforde, C, Princeton	1967 (C2)
David Thompson, F, North Carolina State	1973 (AP1, C1, NABC1, UP1, USBWA1), 1974 (AP1, C1, NABC1, UP1, USBWA1) and 1975 (AP1, C1, NABC1, UP1, USBWA1)
Gary Thompson, G, Iowa State	1957 (AP1, C1, USBWA1, NABC2, UP2)
George Thompson, F, Marquette	1969 (C2)
Jim Thompson, F, Duke	1934 (C3)
John (Cat) Thompson, F, Montana State	1929 (NCAA) and 1930 (NCAA)
John Thompson, C, Providence	1964 (C2)
Mychal Thompson, F-C, Minnesota	1977 (USBWA1, AP2, C2, NABC2, UPI2) and 1978 (AP1, C1, UPI1, USBWA1)
Skip Thoren, C, Illinois	1965 (AP2, C2, NABC3, UPI3)
Rod Thorn, G-F, West Virginia	1962 (AP2, C2, UPI2, NABC3) and 1963 (C1, USBWA1, AP2, NABC2, UPI2)
Nate Thurmond, C, Bowling Green	1963 (C2, UPI2)
Jack Tingle, F, Kentucky	1947 (NABC2)
Wayman Tisdale, C-F, Oklahoma	1983 (AP1, C1, USbWA, UPI2, NABC3), 1984 (AP1, NABC1, UP1, USBWA1) and 1985 (AP1, NABC1, UP1, USBWA1)
Ray Tolbert, C, Indiana	1981 (C2)
Rudy Tomjanovich, F-C, Michigan	1969 (C2) and 1970 (C1, AP2, UPI2, NABC3)
Freddie Tompkins, F, South Carolina	1934 (C1)
Andrew Toney, G, Southwestern Louisiana	1980 (C2)
Bernard Toone, F, Marquette	1979 (NABC4)
Irv Torgoff, F, Long Island	1939 (C1)
Gene Tormohlen, C, Tennessee	1959 (C2)
Walt Torrence, G, UCLA	1959 (C1, UPI3)
Monte Towe, G, North Carolina State	1974 (C2)
Carlyle Towery, C, Western Kentucky	1940 (C3) and 1941 (C2)
John Townsend, F, Michigan	1937 (C2) and 1938 (C1)
Victor Townsend, F, Oregon	1941 (C3)
Dick Triptow, G, DePaul	1944 (C2)
Kelly Tripucka, F-G, Notre Dame	1979 (USBWA1, NABC2, UPI2, AP3), 1980 (UPI3) and 1981 (UPI1, NABC2)
Albert Tucker, C, Oklahoma Baptist	1966 (C2) and 1967 (C1)
Gerry Tucker, C, Oklahoma	1943 (C1) and 1947 (C1, NABC1)
Jim Tucker, C, Duquesne	1952 (UP3)
Melvin Turpin, C, Kentucky	1984 (NABC2, USBWA2, AP3, UPI3)
Jack Twyman, F-C, Cincinnati	1955 (C4)
B.J. Tyler, G, Texas	1994 (AP3, UPI3)
Charlie Tyra, C, Louisville	1956 (C1) and 1957 (C1, NABC1, USBWA1, AP2, UPI2)

U

Bill Uhl, C, Dayton	1956 (NABC1, AP2, UP2)
Paul Unruh, F, Bradley	1949 (C4) and 1950 (AP1, NABC1, UP1, C4)
Wes Unseld, C, Louisville	1966 (C2), 1967 (AP1, C1, NABC1, UP1, USBWA1) and 1968 (AP1, C1, NABC1, UP1, USBWA1)

V

Darnell Valentine, G, Kansas	1978 (C2), 1979 (C2), 1980 (C1) and 1981 (C1, AP2)
John Vallely, G, UCLA	1970 (C2, AP3, NABC3, UPI3)
Dick Van Arsdale, F, Indiana	1965 (C2, UPI3)
Tom Van Arsdale, F, Indiana	1965 (C2)
Jan van Breda Kolff, C, Vanderbilt	1974 (C2, NABC4)
Ernie Vandeweghe, F, Colgate	1949 (NABC1, C2, AP3, UP3)
Nick Van Exel, G, Cincinnati	1993 (AP3, NABC3)
Keith Van Horn, F, Utah	1996 (AP2, NABC2, UPI2, USBWA2) and 1997 (AP1, NABC1, USBWA1)
Jacque Vaughn, G, Kansas	1995 (UPI3), 1996 (AP2, NABC2, UPI, USBWA2) and 1997 (AP2, NABC2, USBWA2)
Ralph Vaughn, F, Southern California	1940 (C1)
Bob Verga, G, Duke	1966 (AP2, C2, NABC2, UPI2) and 1967 (NABC1, USBWA1, AP2, C2, UPI2)
Sam Vincent, G, Michigan State	1985 (NABC2, AP3, UPI3)
Danny Vranes, F, Utah	1981 (USBWA1, AP2, C2, NABC2, UPI3)

W

Malcolm (Sparky) Wade, G, Louisiana St.	1935 (C1)
Charles Wagner, F, Washington	1936 (C3)
George Wahlquist, F, Nebraska	1936 (C3)
Mel Waits, ?, Tarkio (Mo.)	1940 (C2)
Neal Walk, C, Florida	1968 (AP2, C2, NABC3, UPI3) and 1969 (C1, AP3, NABC3, UPI3)
Chet Walker, F, Bradley	1960 (AP2, C2, NABC2, UPI2), 1961 (AP1, NABC1, UPI1, USBWA1, C2) and 1962 (AP1, C1, NABC1, UP1, USBWA1)
Darrell Walker, G, Arkansas	1983 (AP2, C2, UPI2)
Horace Walker, F-C, Michigan State	1960 (C2, AP3, UPI3)
Jimmy Walker, G, Providence	1965 (C2, AP3, NABC3), 1966 (UPI1, USBWA1, AP2, C2) and 1967 (AP1, C1, NABC1, UP1, USBWA1)
Kenny Walker, F, Kentucky	1985 (AP2, NABC2, UPI2, USBWA2) and 1986 (AP1, NABC1, UP1, USBWA1)

Wally Walker, F, Virginia	1976 (C2)
Grady Wallace, F, South Carolina	1957 (C1, UP1, AP2)
John Wallace, F, Syracuse	1996 (AP2, NABC2, USBWA2, UPI3)
Rasheed Wallace, C, North Carolina	1995 (AP2, NABC2, UPI2, USBWA2)
Bill Walton, C, UCLA	1972 (AP1, C1, NABC1, UP1, USBWA1), 1973 (AP1, C1, NABC1, UP1, USBWA1) and 1974 (AP1, C1, NABC1, UP1, USBWA1)
Lloyd Walton, G, Marquette	1976 (C2)
Frank Ward, C, Montana State	1930 (NCAA)
Mike Warren, G, UCLA	1967 (C2) and 1968 (C1, USBWA1, AP3, UPI3)
Bryan Warrick, G, St. Joseph's	1981 (C2) and 1982 (C2)
Dwayne (Pearl) Washington, G, Syracuse	1985 (UPI2, USBWA2, AP3, NABC3) and 1986 (UPI2, AP3, NABC3)
Kermit Washington, C-F, American Univ.	1973 (AP1, C2, NABC4)
Richard Washington, C-F, UCLA	1975 (C2) and 1976 (C1, NABC1, UPI1, USBWA1, AP2)
Lou Watson, G, Indiana	1950 (C4)
Clarence Weatherspoon, F, Southern Miss.	1991 (UPI3)
Chris Webber, F, Michigan	1993 (AP1, NABC1, UP1, USBWA1)
Marvin Webster, C, Morgan State	1974 (C2) and 1975 (C2)
Waldo Wegner, F, Iowa State	1935 (C3)
Nick Werkman, F, Seton Hall	1963 (NABC2, AP3, UPI3)
Walt Wesley, C, Kansas	1966 (C1, USBWA1, NABC2, UPI2, AP3)
Jerry West, F-G, West Virginia	1958 (C2, AP3, UP3), 1959 (AP1, C1, NABC1, UP1, USBWA1) and 1960 (AP1, C1, NABC1, UP1, USBWA1)
Mark West, C, Old Dominion	1983 (C2)
Paul Westphal, G, Southern California	1971 (AP2, C2, NABC3, UPI3) and 1972 (C2, NABC2, UPI3)
Ennis Whatley, G, Alabama	1983 (C2, NABC2, AP3, UPI3)
DeJuan Wheat, G, Louisville	1997 (NABC3)
Joseph (Jo Jo) White, G, Kansas	1967 (C2), 1968 (USBWA1, C2, NABC2, AP3, UPI3) and 1969 (C1, AP2, NABC2, UPI2)
Sherman White, C, Long Island	1950 (NABC1, UP2, AP3, C3)
Tony White, G, Tennessee	1987 (AP3, UPI3)
Jerome Whitehead, C, Marquette	1978 (C2, NABC3)
Charles (Hawkeye) Whitney, F, N.C. State	1980 (USBWA1, C2, NABC3)
Sidney Wicks, F, UCLA	1970 (USBWA1, C2, NABC2, AP3, UPI3) and 1971 (AP1, C1, NABC1, UP1, USBWA1)
Ron Widby, F, Tennessee	1967 (AP2, C2, UPI3)
Murray Wier, G, Iowa	1948 (AP1, NABC2, C3)
Bob Wiesenhahn, F, Cincinnati	1961 (C1)
Win Wilfong, F, Memphis State	1957 (C2)
Lenny Wilkens, G, Providence	1960 (C1, USBWA1, AP2)
Keith Wilkes, F, UCLA	1973 (C1, NABC1, USBWA1, AP2, UPI2) and 1974 (AP1, C1, NABC1, UP1, USBWA1)
Dominique Wilkins, F, Georgia	1981 (C2) and 1982 (C1, NABC2, UPI2, AP3)
Herb Wilkinson, G-F, Iowa	1945 (NCAA2)
Richard (Buzz) Wilkinson, G, Virginia	1955 (C1, AP3)
Charles (Buck) Williams, C-F, Maryland	1981 (C2)
Freeman Williams, G, Portland State	1977 (C2, AP3, UPI3) and 1978 (USBWA1, AP2, C2, NABC2, UPI2)
Chuckie Williams, G, Kansas State	1976 (C2)
Gus Williams, G, Southern California	1975 (USBWA1, AP2, C2, USBWA2, UPI3)
Herb Williams, C, Ohio State	1980 (C2, AP3) and 1981 (C1)
James (Fly) Williams, G, Austin Peay St.	1973 (C2, UPI3)
Max Williams, G, Southern Methodist	1960 (AP3)
Reggie Williams, F-G, Georgetown	1987 (AP1, NABC1, UP1, USBWA1)
Ron Williams, G, West Virginia	1968 (C2)
Sam Williams, F, Iowa	1968 (C2, AP3)
Sylvester (Sly) Williams, F, Rhode Island	1978 (C2) and 1979 (USBWA1, C2, AP3, UPI3)
Walt Williams, G-F, Maryland	1992 (AP2, UPI2, USBWA2)
Corliss Williamson, F, Arkansas	1994 (AP2, NABC2, UPI2, USBWA2) and 1995 (AP2, NABC2, UPI2, USBWA2)
Henry Wilmore, F, Michigan	1971 (C2) and 1972 (USBWA1, C2, NABC3, UPI3)
George Wilson, C, Cincinnati	1963 (C2)
Tony Windis, G, Wyoming	1959 (C2)
Urgel (Slim) Wintermute, C, Oregon	1938 (C3) and 1939 (C1)
Les Witte, F, Wyoming	1932 (C1) and 1934 (C1)
Luke Witte, C, Ohio State	1972 (NABC4)
Randy Wittman, G, Indiana	1983 (USBWA1, NABC3)
Andy Wolfe, G, California	1948 (C3)
Al Wood, F, North Carolina	1980 (C2) and 1981 (C1, USBWA1, AP2, NABC2)
Howard Wood, C, Tennessee	1981 (C2)
Leon Wood, G, Cal State Fullerton	1983 (C1) and 1984 (AP2, NABC2, UPI2, USBWA2)
John Wooden, G, Purdue	1932 (C1)
Mike Woodson, F, Indiana	1979 (C2, NABC4) and 1980 (C2, NABC2)
Andre Woolridge, G, Iowa	1997 (AP3)
Mark Workman, C, West Virginia	1951 (AP3) and 1952 (AP1, UP1, NABC2)
Sam Worthen, G, Marquette	1980 (AP3, UPI3)
James Worthy, F, North Carolina	1981 (C2) and 1982 (C1, NABC1, UPI1, USBWA1, AP2)
Lorenzen Wright, C, Memphis	1996 (UPI2, AP3, NABC3)
Dennis Wuycik, F, North Carolina	1972 (C2, NABC2)

Y

George Yardley, F, Stanford	1950 (C4)
Tony Yates, G, Cincinnati	1963 (AP3, NABC3)
Charles Yelverton, G-F, Fordham	1971 (C2, UPI3)
Jewell Young, F, Purdue	1937 (C3) and 1938 (C1)
Michael Young, F, Houston	1984 (AP3, NABC3, UPI3)
Rich Yunkus, C, Georgia Tech	1970 (C2, UPI3) and 1971 (C2, NABC2, AP3)

Z

Bob Zawoluk, C, St. John's	1951 (AP2, UP2, C3) and 1952 (AP2, NABC2, UP2)
Andy Zimmer, C, Indiana	1942 (C3)

NOTE: Converse All-American selections also included small-college players.

Where the Stars Are

College basketball undeniably was recognized as a "city" game in the 1950s and 1960s when New York (Lew Alcindor), Philadelphia (Wilt Chamberlain, Tom Gola and Guy Rodgers), Indianapolis (Oscar Robertson), Oakland (Bill Russell), Washington, D.C. (Elgin Baylor and Dave Bing), Chicago (Cazzie Russell), Detroit (Spencer Haywood) and Boston (Jimmy Walker) accounted for a majority of the biggest names in hoopdom.

But the landscape changed somewhat in the next two decades when towns with populations of fewer than 60,000 supplied a high percentage of the NBA's premier players such as Charles Barkley (from Leeds, Ala.), Larry Bird (French Lick, Ind.), Joe Dumars (Natchitoches, La.), Michael Jordan (Wilmington, N.C.), Karl Malone (Summerfield, La.), Moses Malone (Petersburg, Va.), Kevin McHale (Hibbing, Minn.), Dominique Wilkins (Washington, N.C.) and James Worthy (Gastonia, N.C.).

In the last couple of years, hamlets with little more than a post office and gas station furnished college standouts—Gans, Okla. (Oklahoma State center Bryant Reeves); Hammon, Okla. (Oklahoma forward Ryan Minor), and Pilot Knob, Mo. (Southern Illinois forward Chris Carr).

Whether or not the influence of big cities on big-time hoops might be waning is a subject for debate frequently hinging on provincialism.

"There are still more good players in the big cities," said New Yorker Howard Garfinkel, the creator of the prestigious Five Star Summer Camp. "We used to own the game, but we don't any longer. It's not like it was 40 to 50 years ago. It's no longer just a city game. Now it's national. It's everywhere."

Here is a state-by-state breakdown sizing up the high school hometowns of NCAA consensus first-team All-Americans since the 1928-29 season:

Arizona (1), Arkansas (4), California (23), Colorado (3), Connecticut (4), District of Columbia (6), Florida (3), Georgia (4), Illinois (19), Indiana (27), Iowa (3), Kansas (4), Kentucky (11), Louisiana (4), Maryland (4), Massachusetts (4), Michigan (6), Minnesota (2), Mississippi (1), Missouri (5), Nebraska (2), New Jersey (8), New York (29), North Carolina (11), Ohio (13), Oklahoma (5), Oregon (4), Pennsylvania (26), Rhode Island (2), South Carolina (2), Tennessee (5), Texas (8), Utah (5), Virginia (7), Washington (3), West Virginia (2), Wisconsin (3)

NOTE: Fourteen states never have supplied an NCAA consensus All-American: Alabama, Alaska, Delaware, Hawaii, Idaho, Maine, Montana, Nevada, New Hampshire, New Mexico, North Dakota, South Dakota, Vermont and Wyoming.

*Gilmore (Alabama) and Manning (Kansas) attended high schools in other states their senior seasons.

Off Mainland U.S. (3): Tim Duncan (Virgin Islands), Hakeem Olajuwon (Nigeria), Mychal Thompson (Bahamas).

10

COACH DIRECTORY

Determining the country's best active coaches is an inexact science. Actually, many of the most efficient coaches toil in anonymity at obscure schools with inferior talent. Nonetheless, here is a look at the achievements of major-college coaches who met any of the following criteria:

- At least one NCAA championship team.
- Directed two or more teams to the Final Four.
- Total of 600 victories (minimum of 20 seasons in Division I).
- At least 20 decisions in national postseason tournament competition.

DAVE BLISS

Cornell '65
Binghamton, NY

Coach of fourth-place NIT team in 1990. . . . Coach of four conference tournament champions—1979 (Big Eight), 1988 (SWC), 1993 (WAC) and 1996 (WAC). . . . Assistant coach at Army (1967-68 and 1968-69) and Indiana (1971-72 through 1974-75) under Bob Knight and at Cornell (1969-70 and 1970-71) under Jerry Lace.

Season	School	Overall	League	Finish	Postseason
1975-76	Oklahoma	9-17	6-8	4th (Big Eight)	DNP
1976-77	Oklahoma	18-10	9-5	2nd (Big Eight)	DNP
1977-78	Oklahoma	14-13	7-7	4th (Big Eight)	DNP
1978-79	Oklahoma	21-10	10-4	1st (Big Eight)	NCAA (1-1)
1979-80	Oklahoma	15-12	6-8	6th (Big Eight)	DNP
1980-81	SMU	7-20	3-13	9th (SWC)	DNP
1981-82	SMU	6-21	1-15	9th (SWC)	DNP
1982-83	SMU	19-11	9-7	T4th (SWC)	DNP
1983-84	SMU	25-8	12-4	3rd (SWC)	NCAA (1-1)

1984-85	SMU	23-10	10-6	T2nd (SWC)	NCAA (1-1)
1985-86	SMU	18-11	10-6	4th (SWC)	NIT (0-1)
1986-87	SMU	16-13	7-9	T6th (SWC)	DNP
1987-88	SMU	28-7	12-4	1st (SWC)	NCAA (1-1)
1988-89	New Mex.	22-11	11-5	T2nd (WAC)	NIT (2-1)
1989-90	New Mex.	20-14	9-7	5th (WAC)	NIT (3-2)
1990-91	New Mex.	20-10	10-6	3rd (WAC)	NCAA (0-1)
1991-92	New Mex.	20-13	11-5	3rd (WAC)	NIT (2-1)
1992-93	New Mex.	24-7	13-5	3rd (WAC)	NCAA (0-1)
1993-94	New Mex.	23-8	14-4	1st (WAC)	NCAA (0-1)
1994-95	New Mex.	15-15	9-9	T4th (WAC)	DNP
1995-96	New Mex.	28-5	14-4	2nd (WAC)	NCAA (1-1)
1996-97	New Mex.	25-8	11-5	3rd (WAC/Mountain)	NCAA (1-1)

22-Year Coaching Record: 416-254 (.621) overall; 77-62 (.554) in five years at Oklahoma; 142-101 (.584) in eight years at SMU; 197-91 (.684) in first nine years at New Mexico; 38-32 (.543) in Big Eight Conference; 64-64 (.500) in Southwest Conference; 102-50 (.671) in Western Athletic Conference; 4-3 (.571) in Big Eight Tournament; 6-7 (.462) in SWC Tournament; 12-7 (.632) in WAC Tournament; 6-9 (.400) in NCAA Tournament; 7-5 (.583) in NIT.

JIM BOEHEIM

Syracuse '66
Lyons, NY

Coach of 1987 and 1996 NCAA Tournament runner-up. . . . Coach of 1981 NIT runner-up. . . . Coach of three Big East Tournament champions—1981, 1988 and 1992. . . . Assistant coach at Syracuse under Roy Danforth for seven seasons from 1970-76.

Season	School	Overall	League	Finish	Postseason
1976-77	Syracuse	26-4	—	—	NCAA (1-1)
1977-78	Syracuse	22-6	—	—	NCAA (0-1)
1978-79	Syracuse	26-4	—	—	NCAA (1-1)
1979-80	Syracuse	26-4	5-1	T1st (Big East)	NCAA (1-1)
1980-81	Syracuse	22-12	6-8	6th (Big East)	NIT (4-1)
1981-82	Syracuse	16-13	7-7	T5th (Big East)	NIT (1-1)
1982-83	Syracuse	21-10	9-7	5th (Big East)	NCAA (1-1)
1983-84	Syracuse	23-9	12-4	T2nd (Big East)	NCAA (1-1)
1984-85	Syracuse	22-9	9-7	T3rd (Big East)	NCAA (1-1)
1985-86	Syracuse	26-6	14-2	T1st (Big East)	NCAA (1-1)
1986-87	Syracuse	31-7	12-4	T1st (Big East)	NCAA (5-1)
1987-88	Syracuse	26-9	11-5	2nd (Big East)	NCAA (1-1)
1988-89	Syracuse	30-8	10-6	3rd (Big East)	NCAA (3-1)
1989-90	Syracuse	26-7	12-4	T1st (Big East)	NCAA (2-1)

1990-91	Syracuse	26-6	12-4	1st (Big East)	NCAA (0-1)
1991-92	Syracuse	22-10	10-8	T5th (Big East)	NCAA (1-1)
1992-93	Syracuse	20-9	10-8	3rd (Big East)	Probation
1993-94	Syracuse	23-7	13-5	2nd (Big East)	NCAA (2-1)
1994-95	Syracuse	20-10	12-6	3rd (Big East)	NCAA (1-1)
1995-96	Syracuse	29-9	12-6	2nd (Big East)	NCAA (5-1)
1996-97	Syracuse	19-13	9-9	T4th (Big East 7)	NIT (0-1)

21-Year Coaching Record: 502-172 (.745) at Syracuse; 185-101 (.647) in Big East; 27-15 (.643) in Big East Tournament; 27-17 (.614) in NCAA Tournament; 5-3 (.625) in NIT.

JIM CALHOUN

American International '67
Braintree, MA

Coach of 1988 NIT champion and 1997 third-place team. . . . Coach of five North Atlantic Conference Tournament champions—1981, 1982, 1984, 1985 and 1986. . . . Coach of two Big East Tournament champions—1990 and 1996. . . . Assistant coach at his alma mater for two seasons (1966-67 and 1967-68).

Season	School	Overall	League	Finish	Postseason
1972-73	Northeast.	19-7	—	—	DNP
1973-74	Northeast.	14-11	—	—	DNP
1974-75	Northeast.	12-12	—	—	DNP
1975-76	Northeast.	12-13	—	—	DNP
1976-77	Northeast.	12-14	—	—	DNP
1977-78	Northeast.	14-12	—	—	DNP
1978-79	Northeast.	13-13	—	—	DNP
1979-80	Northeast.	19-8	—	—	DNP
1980-81	Northeast.	24-6	—	—	NCAA (1-1)
1981-82	Northeast.	23-7	8-1	1st (NAC)	NCAA (1-1)
1982-83	Northeast.	13-15	4-6	6th (NAC)	DNP
1983-84	Northeast.	27-5	14-0	1st (NAC)	NCAA (1-1)
1984-85	Northeast.	22-9	13-3	T1st (NAC)	NCAA (0-1)
1985-86	Northeast.	26-5	16-2	1st (NAC)	NCAA (0-1)
1986-87	Conn.	9-19	3-13	T8th (Big East)	DNP
1987-88	Conn.	20-14	4-12	9th (Big East)	NIT (5-0)
1988-89	Conn.	18-13	6-10	T7th (Big East)	NIT (2-1)
1989-90	Conn.	31-6	12-4	T1st (Big East)	NCAA (3-1)
1990-91	Conn.	20-11	9-7	T3rd (Big East)	NCAA (2-1)
1991-92	Conn.	20-10	10-8	T5th (Big East)	NCAA (1-1)
1992-93	Conn.	15-13	9-9	T4th (Big East)	NIT (0-1)
1993-94	Conn.	29-5	16-2	1st (Big East)	NCAA (2-1)
1994-95	Conn.	28-5	16-2	1st (Big East)	NCAA (3-1)
1995-96	Conn.	32-3	17-1	1st (Big East 6)	NCAA (2-1)
1996-97	Conn.	18-15	7-11	6th (Big East 6)	NIT (4-1)

25-Year Coaching Record: 490-251 (.661) overall; 250-137 (.646) in 14 years at Northeastern; 240-114 (.678) in first 11 years at Connecticut; 55-12 (.821) in five years in North Atlantic Conference; 109-79 (.580) in Big East Conference; 13-2 (.867) in NAC Tournament; 10-9 (.526) in Big East Tournament; 16-11 (.593) in NCAA Tournament; 11-3 in NIT (.786).

GALE CATLETT

West Virginia '63
Hedgesville, WV

Winningest coach in West Virginia and Atlantic 10 Conference history. . . . Directed West Virginia to NIT semifinals (4th) in 1981. . . . Coached Cincinnati to two Metro Tournament titles (1976 and 1977). . . . Directed West Virginia to back-to-back Atlantic 10 Tournament championships in 1983 and 1984. . . . Assistant coach under Richmond's Lew Mills, Davidson's Lefty Driesell, Kansas' Ted Owens and Kentucky's Adolph Rupp.

Season	School	Overall	League	Finish	Postseason
1972-73	Cincinnati	17-9	—	—	DNP
1973-74	Cincinnati	19-8	—	—	NIT (0-1)
1974-75	Cincinnati	23-6	—	—	NCAA (2-1)
1975-76	Cincinnati	25-6	2-1	(Metro 6)	NCAA (0-1)
1976-77	Cincinnati	25-5	4-2	2nd (Metro 7)	NCAA (0-1)
1977-78	Cincinnati	17-10	6-6	T4th (Metro 7)	DNP
1978-79	West Va.	16-12	7-3	T2nd (Eastern 8)	DNP
1979-80	West Va.	15-14	4-6	7th (Eastern 8)	DNP
1980-81	West Va.	23-10	9-4	3rd (Eastern 8)	NIT (3-2)
1981-82	West Va.	27-4	13-1	1st (Eastern 8)	NCAA (1-1)
1982-83	West Va.	23-8	10-4	T1st-W (Atl. 10)	NCAA (0-1)
1983-84	West Va.	20-12	9-9	T4th (Atlantic 10)	NCAA (1-1)
1984-85	West Va.	20-9	9-4	1st (Atlantic 10)	NIT (0-1)
1985-86	West Va.	22-11	15-3	T2nd (Atlantic 10)	NCAA (0-1)
1986-87	West Va.	23-8	15-3	2nd (Atlantic 10)	NCAA (0-1)
1987-88	West Va.	18-14	12-6	3rd (Atlantic 10)	NIT (0-1)
1988-89	West Va.	26-5	17-1	1st (Atlantic 10)	NCAA (1-1)
1989-90	West Va.	16-12	11-7	T3rd (Atlantic 10)	DNP
1990-91	West Va.	17-14	10-8	T3rd (Atlantic 10)	NIT (1-1)
1991-92	West Va.	20-12	10-6	3rd (Atlantic 10)	NCAA (0-1)
1992-93	West Va.	17-12	7-7	6th (Atlantic 10)	NIT (1-1)
1993-94	West Va.	17-12	8-8	T3rd (Atlantic 10)	NIT (1-1)
1994-95	West Va.	13-13	7-9	T6th (Atlantic 10)	DNP
1995-96	West Va.	12-15	7-11	4th (Big East 6)	DNP
1996-97	West Va.	21-10	11-7	3rd (Big East 6)	NIT (2-1)

25-Year Coaching Record: 492-251 (.662) overall; 126-44 (.741) in six years at Cincinnati; 345-197 (.637) in first 18 years at West Virginia; 12-9 (.571) in Metro Conference; 180-87 (.674) in Atlantic 10 Conference; 18-18 (.500) in Big East Conference; 5-1 (.833) in Metro Tournament; 21-15 (.583) in Atlantic 10 Tournament; 1-2 (.333) in Big East Tournament; 5-10 (.333) in NCAA Tournament; 8-9 (.471) in NIT.

JOHN CHANEY

Bethune-Cookman '55
Philadelphia, PA

Earned national coach of the year awards from the USBWA in 1987 and from AP, UPI, NABC and USBWA in 1988. . . . Coach of NCAA Division II champion in 1978 and third-place finisher in 1979. . . . Won four Atlantic 10 Conference Tournament titles (1985, 1987, 1988, 1990).

Season	School	Overall	League	Finish	Postseason
1972-73	Cheyney St.	23-5	12-2	1st-E (Pa. Conf.)	NCAA DII (1-1)
1973-74	Cheyney St.	19-7	11-1	T1st-E (Pa. Conf.)	DNP
1974-75	Cheyney St.	16-9	9-5	2nd-E (Pa. Conf.)	DNP
1975-76	Cheyney St.	24-5	11-1	1st-E (Pa. Conf.)	NCAA DII (2-1)
1976-77	Cheyney St.	20-8	10-2	1st-E (Pa. Conf.)	NCAA DII (2-1)
1977-78	Cheyney St.	27-2	12-0	1st-E (Pa. Conf.)	NCAA DII (5-0)
1978-79	Cheyney St.	24-7	10-2	1st-E (Pa. Conf.)	NCAA DII (4-1)
1979-80	Cheyney St.	23-5	12-0	1st-E (Pa. Conf.)	NCAA DII (1-1)
1980-81	Cheyney St.	21-8	9-3	T1st-E (Pa. Conf.)	NCAA DII (1-1)
1981-82	Cheyney St.	28-3	11-1	1st-E (Pa. Conf.)	NCAA DII (2-1)
1982-83	Temple	14-15	5-9	3rd (A10 East)	DNP
1983-84	Temple	26-5	18-0	1st (Atl. 10)	NCAA (1-1)
1984-85	Temple	25-6	15-3	2nd (Atl. 10)	NCAA (1-1)
1985-86	Temple	25-6	15-3	T2nd (Atl. 10)	NCAA (1-1)
1986-87	Temple	32-4	17-1	1st (Atl. 10)	NCAA (1-1)
1987-88	Temple	32-2	18-0	1st (Atl. 10)	NCAA (3-1)
1988-89	Temple	18-12	15-3	2nd (Atl. 10)	NIT (0-1)
1989-90	Temple	20-11	15-3	1st (Atl. 10)	NCAA (0-1)
1990-91	Temple	24-10	15-3	2nd (Atl. 10)	NCAA (3-1)
1991-92	Temple	17-13	11-5	2nd (Atl. 10)	NCAA (1-1)
1992-93	Temple	20-13	8-6	T2nd (Atl. 10)	NCAA (3-1)
1993-94	Temple	23-8	12-4	2nd (Atl. 10)	NCAA (1-1)
1994-95	Temple	19-11	10-6	T2nd (Atl. 10)	NCAA (1-1)
1995-96	Temple	20-13	12-4	2nd (A10 East)	NCAA (1-1)
1996-97	Temple	20-11	10-6	4th (A10 East)	NCAA (1-1)

25-Year Coaching Record: 560-199 (.738) overall; 225-59 (.792) in 10 years at Cheyney State; 315-129 (.709) in first 14 years at Temple; 107-17 (.863) in Pennsylvania Conference; 194-58 (.770) in Atlantic 10 Conference; 29-11 (.725) in Atlantic 10 Tournament; 16-13 (.552) in NCAA Division I Tournament; 0-1 in NIT; 18-7 (.720) in NCAA Division II Tournament.

BOBBY CREMINS

South Carolina '70
Bronx, NY

Led Georgia Tech to Final Four appearance in 1990. . . . Naismith national coach of the year in 1990. . . . His three ACC Tournament championships (1985, 1990 and 1993) are second only to Dean Smith's among active ACC coaches. . . . Led Appalachian State to 1979 Southern Conference Tournament title. . . . Served as an assistant coach at Point Park (Pa.) and under Frank McGuire at South Carolina.

Season	School	Overall	League	Finish	Postseason
1975-76	Appal. St.	13-14	6-6	5th (Southern)	DNP
1976-77	Appal. St.	17-12	8-4	3rd (Southern)	DNP
1977-78	Appal. St.	15-13	9-3	1st (Southern)	DNP
1978-79	Appal. St.	23-6	11-3	1st (Southern)	NCAA (0-1)
1979-80	Appal. St.	12-16	6-10	T6th (Southern)	DNP
1980-81	Appal. St.	20-9	11-5	T1st (Southern)	DNP
1981-82	Ga. Tech	10-16	3-11	8th (ACC)	DNP
1982-83	Ga. Tech	13-15	4-10	6th (ACC)	DNP
1983-84	Ga. Tech	18-11	6-8	T5th (ACC)	NIT (0-1)
1984-85	Ga. Tech	27-8	9-5	T1st (ACC)	NCAA (3-1)

1985-86	Ga. Tech	27-7	11-3	2nd (ACC)	NCAA (2-1)
1986-87	Ga. Tech	16-13	7-7	5th (ACC)	NCAA (0-1)
1987-88	Ga. Tech	22-10	8-6	4th (ACC)	NCAA (1-1)
1988-89	Ga. Tech	20-12	8-6	5th (ACC)	NCAA (0-1)
1989-90	Ga. Tech	28-7	8-6	T3rd (ACC)	NCAA (4-1)
1990-91	Ga. Tech	17-13	6-8	T5th (ACC)	NCAA (1-1)
1991-92	Ga. Tech	23-12	8-8	T4th (ACC)	NCAA (2-1)
1992-93	Ga. Tech	19-11	8-8	6th (ACC)	NCAA (0-1)
1993-94	Ga. Tech	16-13	7-9	6th (ACC)	NIT (0-1)
1994-95	Ga. Tech	18-12	8-8	5th (ACC)	DNP
1995-96	Ga. Tech	24-12	13-3	1st (ACC)	NCAA (2-1)
1996-97	Ga. Tech	9-18	3-13	9th (ACC)	DNP

22-Year Coaching Record: 407-260 (.610) overall; 100-70 (.588) in six years at Appalachian State; 307-190 (.618) in first 16 years at Georgia Tech; 51-31 (.622) in Southern Conference; 117-119 (.496) in Atlantic Coast Conference; 10-5 (.667) in Southern Conference Tournament; 15-13 (.536) in ACC Tournament; 15-11 (.577) in NCAA Tournament; 0-2 (.000) in NIT.

DENNY CRUM

UCLA '58
San Fernando, CA

Reached NCAA Final Four six times—1972 (fourth), 1975 (third), 1980 (champion), 1982 (tied for third), 1983 (tied for third) and 1986 (champion). . . . Coach of 1985 NIT fourth-place team. . . . Coach of 11 Metro Conference Tournament champions—1978, 1980, 1981, 1983, 1986, 1988, 1989, 1990, 1993, 1994 and 1995. . . . Holds an NCAA record by winning at least 20 games each of his first 13 seasons as a head coach. . . . Assistant coach at UCLA for six seasons under John Wooden from 1959-'71 sandwiched around six-year stint at Pierce (Calif.) Community College. . . . Elected to Naismith Memorial Basketball Hall of Fame in 1994.

Season	School	Overall	League	Finish	Postseason
1971-72	Louisville*	26-5	12-2	T1st (MVC)	NCAA (2-2)
1972-73	Louisville	23-7	11-3	2nd (MVC)	NIT (1-1)
1973-74	Louisville	21-7	11-1	1st (MVC)	NCAA (0-2)
1974-75	Louisville	28-3	12-2	1st (MVC)	NCAA (4-1)
1975-76	Louisville	20-8	2-1	... (Metro)	NIT (0-1)
1976-77	Louisville	21-7	6-1	1st (Metro)	NCAA (0-1)
1977-78	Louisville	23-7	9-3	2nd (Metro)	NCAA (1-1)
1978-79	Louisville	24-8	9-1	1st (Metro)	NCAA (1-1)
1979-80	Louisville	33-3	12-0	1st (Metro)	NCAA (5-0)
1980-81	Louisville	21-9	11-1	1st (Metro)	NCAA (0-1)
1981-82	Louisville	23-10	8-4	T2nd (Metro)	NCAA (3-1)
1982-83	Louisville	32-4	12-0	1st (Metro)	NCAA (3-1)
1983-84	Louisville	24-11	11-3	T1st (Metro)	NCAA (2-1)
1984-85	Louisville	19-18	6-8	T4th (Metro)	NIT (3-2)
1985-86	Louisville	32-7	10-2	1st (Metro)	NCAA (6-0)
1986-87	Louisville	18-14	9-3	1st (Metro)	DNP
1987-88	Louisville	24-11	9-3	1st (Metro)	NCAA (2-1)
1988-89	Louisville	24-9	8-4	T2nd (Metro)	NCAA (1-1)
1989-90	Louisville	27-8	12-2	1st (Metro)	NCAA (1-1)
1990-91	Louisville	14-16	4-10	8th (Metro)	DNP
1991-92	Louisville	19-11	7-5	T2nd (Metro)	NCAA (1-1)
1992-93	Louisville	22-9	11-1	1st (Metro)	NCAA (2-1)
1993-94	Louisville	26-6	10-2	1st (Metro)	NCAA (2-1)
1994-95	Louisville	19-14	7-5	T2nd (Metro)	NCAA (0-1)
1995-96	Louisville	22-12	10-4	2nd (C-USA White)	NCAA (2-1)
1996-97	Louisville	26-9	9-5	3rd (C-USA White)	NCAA (3-1)

*Won Missouri Valley Conference playoff game against regular-season co-champion Memphis State (83-72) to earn invitation to NCAA Tournament.

26-Year Coaching Record: 611-233 (.723) at Louisville; 46-8 (.852) in four years in Missouri Valley Conference; 173-59 (.746) in 20 years in Metro Conference; 19-9 (.679) in Conference USA; 33-9 (.786) in Metro Conference Tournament; 2-2 (.500) in C-USA Tournament; 42-21 (.667) in NCAA Tournament; 4-4 (.500) in NIT.

TOM DAVIS

Wisconsin-Platteville '60
Ridgeway, WI

Named AP national coach of the year in 1987. . . . Assistant coach at Maryland under Lefty Driesell and at American University under Tom Young.

Season	School	Overall	League	Finish	Postseason
1971-72	Lafayette	21-6	7-3	T2nd (Mid. Atl./W)	NIT (1-1)
1972-73	Lafayette	16-10	7-3	1st (Mid. Atl./W)	DNP
1973-74	Lafayette	17-9	7-3	T2nd (Mid. Atl./W)	DNP
1974-75	Lafayette	22-6	7-1	1st (ECC/W)	NIT (0-1)
1975-76	Lafayette	19-7	9-1	1st (ECC/W)	DNP
1976-77	Lafayette	21-6	9-1	1st (ECC/W)	DNP
1977-78	Bos. Coll.	15-11	—	—	DNP
1978-79	Bos. Coll.	21-9	—	—	DNP
1979-80	Bos. Coll.	19-10	2-4	5th (Big East)	NIT (0-1)
1980-81	Bos. Coll.	23-7	10-4	1st (Big East)	NCAA (2-1)
1981-82	Bos. Coll.	22-10	8-6	4th (Big East)	NCAA (3-1)
1982-83	Stanford	14-14	6-12	8th (Pac-10)	DNP
1983-84	Stanford	19-12	8-10	T5th (Pac-10)	DNP
1984-85	Stanford	11-17	3-15	10th (Pac-10)	DNP
1985-86	Stanford	14-16	8-10	T5th (Pac-10)	DNP
1986-87	Iowa	30-5	14-4	3rd (Big Ten)	NCAA (3-1)
1987-88	Iowa	24-10	12-6	T3rd (Big Ten)	NCAA (2-1)
1988-89	Iowa	23-10	10-8	4th (Big Ten)	NCAA (1-1)
1989-90	Iowa	12-16	4-14	T8th (Big Ten)	DNP
1990-91	Iowa	21-11	9-9	T5th (Big Ten)	NCAA (1-1)
1991-92	Iowa	19-11	10-8	5th (Big Ten)	NCAA (1-1)
1992-93	Iowa	23-9	11-7	T3rd (Big Ten)	NCAA (1-1)
1993-94	Iowa	11-16	5-13	T10th (Big Ten)	DNP
1994-95	Iowa	21-12	9-9	T7th (Big Ten)	NIT (2-1)
1995-96	Iowa	23-9	11-7	4th (Big Ten)	NCAA (1-1)
1996-97	Iowa	22-10	12-6	T2nd (Big Ten)	NCAA (1-1)

26-Year Coaching Record: 503-269 (.652) overall; 116-44 (.725) in six years at Lafayette; 100-47 (.680) in five years at Boston College; 58-59 (.496) in four years at Stanford; 229-119 (.658) in first 11 years at Iowa; 46-12 (.793) in Middle Atlantic/East Coast Conference; 20-14 (.588) in Big East Conference; 25-47 (.347) in Pacific-10 Conference; 107-91 (.540) in Big Ten Conference; 1-3 (.250) in Big East Conference Tournament; 16-10 (.615) in NCAA Tournament; 3-4 (.429) in NIT.

DON DEVOE

Ohio State '64
Sabina, OH

Directed Virginia Tech to 1973 NIT title and Tennessee to a third-place finish in 1985. . . . Coach of three conference tournament champions—SEC (1979 with Tennessee) and Patriot League (1994 and 1997 with Navy). . . . Served as an assistant coach at Army under Bob Knight and at Ohio State under Fred Taylor.

Season	School	Overall	League	Finish	Postseason
1971-72	Va. Tech	16-10	—	—	DNP
1972-73	Va. Tech	22-5	—	—	NIT (4-0)
1973-74	Va. Tech	13-13	—	—	DNP
1974-75	Va. Tech	16-10	—	—	DNP
1975-76	Va. Tech	21-7	—	—	NCAA (0-1)
1976-77	Wyoming	17-10	8-6	T3rd (WAC)	DNP
1977-78	Wyoming	12-15	3-11	7th (WAC)	DNP
1978-79	Tennessee	21-12	12-6	T2nd (SEC)	NCAA (1-1)
1979-80	Tennessee	18-11	12-6	T3rd (SEC)	NCAA (1-1)
1980-81	Tennessee	21-8	12-6	3rd (SEC)	NCAA (1-1)
1981-82	Tennessee	20-10	13-5	T1st (SEC)	NCAA (1-1)
1982-83	Tennessee	20-12	9-9	T4th (SEC)	NCAA (1-1)
1983-84	Tennessee	21-14	9-9	6th (SEC)	NIT (2-1)
1984-85	Tennessee	22-15	8-10	T7th (SEC)	NIT (4-1)
1985-86	Tennessee	12-16	5-13	8th (SEC)	DNP
1986-87	Tennessee	14-15	7-11	T8th (SEC)	DNP
1987-88	Tennessee	16-13	9-9	6th (SEC)	NIT (0-1)
1988-89	Tennessee	19-11	11-7	T4th (SEC)	NCAA (0-1)
1989-90	Florida*	7-21	3-15	10th (SEC)	DNP
1992-93	Navy	8-19	5-9	5th (Patriot)	DNP
1993-94	Navy	17-13	9-5	T1st (Patriot)	NCAA (0-1)
1994-95	Navy	20-9	10-4	3rd (Patriot)	DNP
1995-96	Navy	15-12	9-3	T1st (Patriot)	DNP
1996-97	Navy	20-9	10-2	1st (Patriot)	NCAA (0-1)

*Served as an interim coach at Florida.

24-Year Coaching Record: 408-290 (.585) overall; 88-45 (.662) in five years at Virginia Tech; 29-25 (.537) in two years at Wyoming; 204-137 (.598)

in 11 years at Tennessee; 7-21 (.250) in one year at Florida; 80-62 (.563) in first five years at Navy; 11-17 (.393) in Western Athletic Conference; 110-106 (.509) in Southeastern Conference; 43-23 (.652) in Patriot League; 9-10 (.474) in SEC Tournament; 7-3 (.700) in Patriot League Tournament; 5-9 (.357) in NCAA Tournament; 10-3 (.769) in NIT.

CHARLES (LEFTY) DRIESELL

Duke '54
Norfolk, VA

Coach of 1972 NIT champion. . . . Coach of five conference tournament champions—three in Southern Conference (1966, 1968 and 1969), one in ACC (1984) and one in Colonial Athletic Association (1994).

Season	School	Overall	League	Finish	Postseason
1960-61	Davidson	9-14	2-10	9th (Southern)	DNP
1961-62	Davidson	14-11	5-6	5th (Southern)	DNP
1962-63	Davidson	20-7	8-3	2nd (Southern)	DNP
1963-64	Davidson	22-4	9-2	1st (Southern)	DNP
1964-65	Davidson	24-2	12-0	1st (Southern)	DNP
1965-66	Davidson	21-7	11-1	1st (Southern)	NCAA (1-2)
1966-67	Davidson	15-12	8-4	2nd (Southern)	DNP
1967-68	Davidson	24-5	9-1	1st (Southern)	NCAA (2-1)
1968-69	Davidson	27-3	9-0	1st (Southern)	NCAA (2-1)
1969-70	Maryland	13-13	5-9	6th (ACC)	DNP
1970-71	Maryland	14-12	5-9	T6th (ACC)	DNP
1971-72	Maryland	27-5	8-4	T2nd (ACC)	NIT (4-0)
1972-73	Maryland	23-7	7-5	3rd (ACC)	NCAA (1-1)
1973-74	Maryland	23-5	9-3	T2nd (ACC)	DNP
1974-75	Maryland	24-5	10-2	1st (ACC)	NCAA (2-1)
1975-76	Maryland	22-6	7-5	T2nd (ACC)	DNP
1976-77	Maryland	19-8	7-5	4th (ACC)	DNP
1977-78	Maryland	15-13	3-9	T6th (ACC)	DNP
1978-79	Maryland	19-11	6-6	4th (ACC)	NIT (1-1)
1979-80	Maryland	24-7	11-3	1st (ACC)	NCAA (1-1)
1980-81	Maryland	21-10	8-6	4th (ACC)	NCAA (1-1)
1981-82	Maryland	16-13	5-9	5th (ACC)	NIT (1-1)
1982-83	Maryland	20-10	8-6	T3rd (ACC)	DNP
1983-84	Maryland	24-8	9-5	2nd (ACC)	NCAA (1-1)
1984-85	Maryland	25-12	8-6	T4th (ACC)	NCAA (2-1)
1985-86	Maryland	19-14	6-8	6th (ACC)	NCAA (1-1)
1988-89	James Mad.	16-14	6-8	T5th (CAA)	DNP
1989-90	James Mad.	20-11	11-3	1st (CAA)	NIT (0-1)
1990-91	James Mad.	19-10	12-2	1st (CAA)	NIT (0-1)
1991-92	James Mad.	21-11	12-2	T1st (CAA)	NIT (0-1)
1992-93	James Mad.	21-9	11-3	T1st (CAA)	NIT (0-1)
1993-94	James Mad.	20-10	10-4	T1st (CAA)	NCAA (0-1)
1994-95	James Mad.	16-13	9-5	3rd (CAA)	DNP
1995-96	James Mad.	10-20	6-10	T6th (CAA)	DNP
1996-97	James Mad.	16-13	8-8	T5th (CAA)	DNP

35-Year Coaching Record: 683-335 (.671) overall; 176-65 (.730) in nine years at Davidson; 348-159 (.686) in 17 years at Maryland; 159-111 (.589) in nine years at James Madison; 73-27 (.730) in Southern Conference; 122-100 (.550) in Atlantic Coast Conference; 85-45 (.654) in Colonial Athletic Association; 15-5 (.750) in Southern Conference Tournament; 17-16 (.515) in ACC Tournament; 13-8 (.619) in CAA Tournament; 15-13 (.536) in NCAA Tournament; 6-6 (.500) in NIT.

HUGH DURHAM

Florida State '59
Louisville, KY

One of only three coaches in NCAA history to win at least 225 games at two Division I schools. . . . His Florida State squad was runner-up to UCLA in the 1972 NCAA Tournament finals and his 1983 Georgia team reached the national semifinals. . . . Guided Georgia to 1982 NIT semifinals (T3rd). . . . Led Georgia to 1983 SEC Tournament title. . . . Assistant coach at his alma mater under Bud Kennedy.

Season	School	Overall	League	Finish	Postseason
1966-67	Florida St.	11-15	—	—	DNP
1967-68	Florida St.	19-8	—	—	NCAA (0-1)
1968-69	Florida St.	18-8	—	—	Probation
1969-70	Florida St.	23-3	—	—	Probation
1970-71	Florida St.	17-9	—	—	Probation
1971-72	Florida St.	27-6	—	—	NCAA (4-1)
1972-73	Florida St.	18-8	—	—	DNP
1973-74	Florida St.	18-8	—	—	DNP
1974-75	Florida St.	18-8	—	—	DNP
1975-76	Florida St.	22-5	—	—	DNP
1976-77	Florida St.	16-11	2-4	5th (Metro)	DNP

Season	School	Overall	League	Finish	Postseason
1977-78	Florida St.	23-6	11-1	1st (Metro)	NCAA (0-1)
1978-79	Georgia	14-14	7-11	7th (SEC)	DNP
1979-80	Georgia	14-13	7-11	T6th (SEC)	DNP
1980-81	Georgia	19-12	9-9	5th (SEC)	NIT (1-1)
1981-82	Georgia	19-12	10-8	6th (SEC)	NIT (3-1)
1982-83	Georgia	24-10	9-9	T4th (SEC)	NCAA (3-1)
1983-84	Georgia	17-13	8-10	T7th (SEC)	NIT (0-1)
1984-85*	Georgia	22-9	12-6	2nd (SEC)	NCAA (1-1)
1985-86	Georgia	17-13	9-9	T5th (SEC)	NIT (1-1)
1986-87	Georgia	18-12	10-8	T3rd (SEC)	NCAA (0-1)
1987-88	Georgia	20-16	8-10	7th (SEC)	NIT (1-1)
1988-89	Georgia	15-16	6-12	9th (SEC)	DNP
1989-90	Georgia	20-9	13-5	1st (SEC)	NCAA (0-1)
1990-91	Georgia	17-13	9-9	5th (SEC)	NCAA (0-1)
1991-92	Georgia	15-14	7-9	4th-E (SEC)	DNP
1992-93	Georgia	15-14	8-8	4th-E (SEC)	NIT (0-1)
1993-94	Georgia	14-16	7-9	4th-E (SEC)	DNP
1994-95	Georgia	18-10	9-7	2nd-E (SEC)	NIT (0-1)

*NCAA Tournament games later vacated by action of the NCAA.

29-Year Coaching Record: 528-311 (.629) overall; 230-95 (.708) in 12 years at Florida State; 298-216 (.580) in 17 years at Georgia; 13-5 (.722) in Metro Conference; 148-150 (.497) in Southeastern Conference; 1-2 (.333) in Metro Tournament; 17-16 (.515) in SEC Tournament; 8-8 (.500) in NCAA Tournament; 6-7 (.462) in NIT.

CLIFF ELLIS

Florida State '68
Chipley, FL

Compiled a 78-12 record (.867) in three junior college seasons for Cumberland (Tenn.) from 1972-73 through 1974-75.

Season	School	Overall	League	Finish	Postseason
1975-76	South Ala.	18-9	—	—	DNP
1976-77	South Ala.	17-10	3-3	3rd (Sun Belt)	DNP
1977-78	South Ala.	18-10	3-7	4th (Sun Belt)	DNP
1978-79	South Ala.	20-7	10-0	1st (Sun Belt)	NCAA (0-1)
1979-80	South Ala.	23-6	12-2	1st (Sun Belt)	NCAA (0-1)
1980-81	South Ala.	25-6	9-3	T1st (Sun Belt)	NIT (2-1)
1981-82	South Ala.	22-6	2-8	6th (Sun Belt)	DNP
1982-83	South Ala.	16-12	6-8	5th (Sun Belt)	DNP
1983-84	South Ala.	22-8	9-5	T2nd (Sun Belt)	NIT (1-1)
1984-85	Clemson	16-13	5-9	T6th (ACC)	NIT (1-1)
1985-86	Clemson	19-15	3-11	7th (ACC)	NIT (2-1)
1986-87	Clemson	25-6	10-4	2nd (ACC)	NCAA (0-1)
1987-88	Clemson	14-15	4-10	7th (ACC)	NIT (0-1)
1988-89	Clemson	19-11	7-7	6th (ACC)	NCAA (1-1)
1989-90	Clemson	26-9	10-4	2nd (ACC)	NCAA (2-1)
1990-91	Clemson	11-17	2-12	7th (ACC)	DNP
1991-92	Clemson	14-14	4-12	9th (ACC)	DNP
1992-93	Clemson	17-13	5-11	7th (ACC)	NIT (1-1)
1993-94	Clemson	18-16	6-10	T7th (ACC)	NIT (2-1)
1994-95	Auburn	16-13	7-9	4th (SEC Western)	NIT (0-1)
1995-96	Auburn	19-13	6-10	T4th (SEC Western)	NIT (0-1)
1996-97	Auburn	16-15	6-10	T3rd (SEC Western)	DNP

22-Year Coaching Record: 401-254 (.612) overall; 171-84 (.671) in nine years at South Alabama; 179-129 (.581) in 10 years at Clemson; 51-41 (.554) in first three years at Auburn; 54-36 (.600) in Sun Belt Conference; 56-90 (.384) in Atlantic Coast Conference; 19-29 (.396) in SEC; 5-8 (.385) in Sun Belt Tournament; 3-10 (.231) in ACC Tournament; 3-3 (.500) in SEC Tournament; 3-5 (.375) in NCAA Tournament; 8-9 (.471) in NIT.

STEVE FISHER

Illinois State '67
Herrin, IL

Reached NCAA Final Four three times—1989 (champion), 1992 (runner-up) and 1993 (runner-up). . . . Coach of 1997 NIT champion. . . . Assistant coach at Western Michigan under Les Wothke for three seasons from 1980-82 and at Michigan under Bill Frieder for seven seasons from 1983-89.

Season	School	Overall	League	Finish	Postseason
1988-89	Michigan	*6-0	—	—	NCAA (6-0)
1989-90	Michigan	23-8	12-6	3rd (Big Ten)	NCAA (1-1)
1990-91	Michigan	14-15	7-11	8th (Big Ten)	NIT (0-1)
1991-92	Michigan	25-9	11-7	3rd (Big Ten)	NCAA (5-1)
1992-93	Michigan	31-5	15-3	2nd (Big Ten)	NCAA (5-1)
1993-94	Michigan	24-8	13-5	2nd (Big Ten)	NCAA (3-1)
1994-95	Michigan	17-14	11-7	3rd (Big Ten)	NCAA (0-1)

| 1995-96 | Michigan | 20-12 | 10-8 | T5th (Big Ten) | NCAA (0-1) |
| 1996-97 | Michigan | 23-11 | 9-9 | T6th (Big Ten) | NIT (5-0) |

*Promoted from assistant to head coach just before the start of the 1989 playoffs after Frieder announced he had accepted the head coaching position at Arizona State.

Nine-Year Coaching Record: 183-82 (.691) at Michigan; 88-56 (.611) in Big Ten Conference; 20-6 (.769) in NCAA Tournament; 5-1 (.833) in NIT.

TIM FLOYD

Louisiana Tech '77
Hattiesburg, MS

Won two conference tournament titles—American South (1990 with New Orleans) and Big Eight (1996 with Iowa State). . . . Student assistant coach at Louisiana Tech in 1976-77 under Emmett Hendricks and assistant coach at Texas-El Paso under Don Haskins.

Season	School	Overall	League	Finish	Postseason
1986-87	Idaho	16-14	5-9	T5th (Big Sky)	DNP
1987-88	Idaho	19-11	11-5	2nd (Big Sky)	DNP
1988-89	New Orl.	19-11	7-3	1st (American S.)	NIT (0-1)
1989-90	New Orl.	21-11	8-2	1st (American S.)	NIT (2-1)
1990-91	New Orl.	23-8	9-3	T1st (American S.)	NCAA (0-1)
1991-92	New Orl.	18-14	9-7	T5th (Sun Belt)	DNP
1992-93	New Orl.	26-4	18-0	1st (Sun Belt)	NCAA (0-1)
1993-94	New Orl.	20-10	12-6	3rd (Sun Belt)	NIT (1-1)
1994-95	Iowa State	23-11	6-8	5th (Big Eight)	NCAA (1-1)
1995-96	Iowa State	24-9	9-5	2nd (Big Eight)	NCAA (1-1)
1996-97	Iowa State	22-9	10-6	3rd (Big 12/N)	NCAA (2-1)

11-Year Coaching Record: 231-112 (.673) overall; 35-25 (.583) in two years at Idaho; 127-58 (.686) in six years at New Orleans; 69-29 (.704) in first three years at Iowa State; 16-14 (.533) in Big Sky Conference; 24-8 (.750) in American South Conference; 39-13 (.750) in Sun Belt Conference; 15-13 (.536) in Big Eight Conference; 10-6 (.625) in Big 12 Conference; 1-2 (.333) in Big Sky Tournament; 4-2 (.667) in American South Tournament; 4-3 (.571) in Sun Belt Tournament; 5-1 (.833) in Big Eight Tournament; 1-1 (.500) in Big 12 Tournament; 4-5 (.444) in NCAA Tournament; 3-3 (.500) in NIT.

BILL FRIEDER

Michigan '64
Saginaw, MI

Coach of 1984 NIT champion. . . . Assistant under Johnny Orr for seven years at Michigan.

Season	School	Overall	League	Finish	Postseason
1980-81	Michigan	19-11	8-10	7th (Big Ten)	NIT (2-1)
1981-82	Michigan	8-19	7-11	T7th (Big Ten)	DNP
1982-83	Michigan	16-12	7-11	9th (Big Ten)	DNP
1983-84	Michigan	24-9	11-7	4th (Big Ten)	NIT (5-0)
1984-85	Michigan	26-4	16-2	1st (Big Ten)	NCAA (1-1)
1985-86	Michigan	28-5	14-4	1st (Big Ten)	NCAA (1-1)
1986-87	Michigan	20-12	10-8	5th (Big Ten)	NCAA (1-1)
1987-88	Michigan	26-8	13-5	2nd (Big Ten)	NCAA (2-1)
1988-89	Michigan	24-7	12-6	3rd (Big Ten)	NCAA*
1989-90	Arizona St.	15-16	6-12	T7th (Pac-10)	NIT (0-1)
1990-91	Arizona St.	20-10	10-8	3rd (Pac-10)	NCAA (1-1)
1991-92	Arizona St.	19-14	9-9	5th (Pac-10)	NIT (1-1)
1992-93	Arizona St.	18-10	11-7	T3rd (Pac-10)	NIT (0-1)
1993-94	Arizona St.	15-13	10-8	T4th (Pac-10)	NIT (0-1)
1994-95	Arizona St.	24-9	12-6	3rd (Pac-10)	NCAA (2-1)
1995-96	Arizona St.	11-16	6-12	8th (Pac-10)	DNP
1996-97	Arizona St.	10-20	2-16	10th (Pac-10)	DNP

*Replaced by Michigan assistant Steve Fisher just before the start of the 1989 playoffs after announcing he had accepted the head coaching position at Arizona State.

17-Year Coaching Record: 323-195 (.624) overall; 191-87 (.687) in nine years at Michigan; 132-108 (.550) in first eight years at Arizona State; 98-64 (.605) in Big Ten Conference; 66-78 (.458) in Pacific-10 Conference; 2-1 (.667) in Pacific-10 Tournament; 8-6 (.571) in NCAA Tournament; 8-5 (.615) in NIT.

PETE GILLEN

Fairfield '68
Brooklyn, NY

Won five Midwestern Collegiate Conference tournament titles (1986, 1987, 1988, 1989 and 1991). . . . Assistant coach at Hawaii under Bruce O'Neil in 1975-76, VMI under Charlie Schmaus in 1976-77 and 1977-78, Villanova under Rollie Massimino in 1978-79 and 1979-80, and Notre Dame under Digger Phelps from 1980-81 through 1984-85.

Season	School	Overall	League	Finish	Postseason
1985-86	Xavier	25-5	10-2	1st (MCC)	NCAA (0-1)
1986-87	Xavier	19-13	7-5	T3rd (MCC)	NCAA (1-1)
1987-88	Xavier	26-4	9-1	1st (MCC)	NCAA (0-1)
1988-89	Xavier	21-12	7-5	3rd (MCC)	NCAA (0-1)
1989-90	Xavier	28-5	12-2	1st (MCC)	NCAA (2-1)
1990-91	Xavier	22-10	11-3	1st (MCC)	NCAA (1-1)
1991-92	Xavier	15-12	7-3	T2nd (MCC)	DNP
1992-93	Xavier	24-6	12-2	T1st (MCC)	NCAA (1-1)
1993-94	Xavier	22-8	8-2	1st (MCC)	NIT (2-1)
1994-95	Providence	17-13	7-11	T6th (Big East)	NIT (1-1)
1995-96	Providence	18-12	9-9	3rd (Big East 7)	NIT (1-1)
1996-97	Providence	24-12	10-8	T2nd (Big East 7)	NCAA (3-1)

12-Year Coaching Record: 261-112 (.700) overall; 202-75 (.729) in nine years at Xavier; 59-37 (.615) in first three years at Providence; 83-25 (.769) in Midwestern Collegiate Conference; 26-28 (.481) in Big East Conference; 17-4 (.810) in Midwestern Collegiate Tournament; 4-3 (.571) in Big East Tournament; 8-8 (.500) in NCAA Tournament; 4-3 (.571) in NIT.

JIM HARRICK

Charleston '60
Charleston, W. Va.

Earned national coach of the year awards from NABC and Naismith in 1995. . . . Coach of UCLA's NCAA Tournament champion in 1995. . . . Assistant under Dutch Belnap for four years from 1973-74 through 1976-77 at Utah State and under Gary Cunningham for two years in 1977-78 and 1978-79 at UCLA.

Season	School	Overall	League	Finish	Postseason
1979-80	Pepperdine	17-11	9-7	T5th (WCAC)	NIT (0-1)
1980-81	Pepperdine	16-12	11-3	T1st (WCAC)	DNP
1981-82	Pepperdine	22-7	14-0	1st (WCAC)	NCAA (1-1)
1982-83	Pepperdine	20-9	10-2	1st (WCAC)	NCAA (0-1)
1983-84	Pepperdine	15-13	8-4	T4th (WCAC)	DNP
1984-85	Pepperdine	23-9	11-1	1st (WCAC)	NCAA (0-1)
1985-86	Pepperdine	25-5	13-1	1st (WCAC)	NCAA (0-1)
1986-87	Pepperdine	12-18	5-9	7th (WCAC)	DNP
1987-88	Pepperdine	17-13	8-6	4th (WCAC)	NIT (0-1)
1988-89	UCLA	21-10	13-5	T3rd (Pac-10)	NCAA (1-1)
1989-90	UCLA	22-11	11-7	4th (Pac-10)	NCAA (2-1)
1990-91	UCLA	23-9	11-7	2nd (Pac-10)	NCAA (0-1)
1991-92	UCLA	28-5	16-2	1st (Pac-10)	NCAA (3-1)
1992-93	UCLA	22-11	11-7	T3rd (Pac-10)	NCAA (0-1)
1993-94	UCLA	21-7	13-5	T2nd (Pac-10)	NCAA (0-1)
1994-95	UCLA	31-2	16 2	1st (Pac-10)	NCAA (6-0)
1995-96	UCLA	23-8	16-2	1st (Pac-10)	NCAA (0-1)

17-Year Coaching Record: 358-160 (.691) overall; 167-97 (.633) in nine years at Pepperdine; 191-63 (.752) in first eight years at UCLA; 87-35 (.713) in West Coast Athletic Conference; 107-37 (.743) in Pacific-10 Conference; 3-2 (.600) in WCAC Tournament; 3-2 (.600) in Pacific-10 Tournament; 14-11 (.560) in NCAA Tournament; 0-2 (.000) in NIT.

CLEM HASKINS

Western Kentucky '67
Campbellsville, KY

Named national coach of the year by all of the major awards in 1997. . . . Guided Minnesota to Final Four in 1997 NCAA Tournament and to 1993 NIT championship. . . . Won Ohio Valley Conference Tournament in 1981. . . . Assistant coach at Western Kentucky under Gene Keady from 1977-78 through 1979-80.

Season	School	Overall	League	Finish	Postseason
1980-81	West. Ky.	21-8	12-2	1st (Ohio Valley)	NCAA (0-1)
1981-82	West. Ky.	19-10	13-3	T1st (Ohio Valley)	NIT (0-1)
1982-83	West. Ky.	12-16	4-10	7th (Sun Belt)	DNP
1983-84	West. Ky.	12-17	5-9	6th (Sun Belt)	DNP
1984-85	West. Ky.	14-14	5-9	7th (Sun Belt)	DNP

1985-86	West. Ky.	23-8	10-4	2nd (Sun Belt)	NCAA (1-1)
1986-87	Minnesota	9-19	2-16	T9th (Big Ten)	DNP
1987-88	Minnesota	10-18	4-14	9th (Big Ten)	DNP
1988-89	Minnesota	19-12	9-9	5th (Big Ten)	NCAA (2-1)
1989-90	Minnesota	23-9	11-7	T4th (Big Ten)	NCAA (3-1)
1990-91	Minnesota	12-16	5-13	9th (Big Ten)	DNP
1991-92	Minnesota	16-16	8-10	T6th (Big Ten)	NIT (0-1)
1992-93	Minnesota	22-10	9-9	T5th (Big Ten)	NIT (5-0)
1993-94	Minnesota	21-12	10-8	T4th (Big Ten)	NCAA (1-1)
1994-95	Minnesota	19-12	10-8	T5th (Big Ten)	NCAA (0-1)
1995-96	Minnesota	19-13	10-8	T5th (Big Ten)	NIT (1-1)
1996-97	Minnesota	31-4	16-2	1st (Big Ten)	NCAA (4-1)

17-Year Coaching Record: 302-214 (.585) overall; 101-73 (.580) in six years at Western Kentucky; 201-141 (.588) in 11 years at Minnesota; 25-5 (.833) in Ohio Valley Conference; 24-32 (.429) in Sun Belt Conference; 94-104 (.475) in Big Ten Conference; 3-1 (.750) in OVC Tournament; 2-4 (.333) in Sun Belt Tournament; 11-7 (.611) in NCAA Tournament; 6-3 (.667) in NIT.

DON HASKINS

Oklahoma State '53
Enid, OK

Coach of 1966 NCAA Tournament champion. . . . Coach of four Western Athletic Conference Tournament champions—1984, 1986, 1989 and 1990. . . . U.S. Olympic team assistant coach in 1972. . . . Elected to Naismith Memorial Basketball Hall of Fame in 1997.

Season	School	Overall	League	Finish	Postseason
1961-62	Tx-El Paso	18-6	5-3	2nd (Border)	DNP
1962-63	Tx-El Paso	19-7	—	—	NCAA (0-1)
1963-64	Tx-El Paso	25-3	—	—	NCAA (2-1)
1964-65	Tx-El Paso	16-9	—	—	NIT (0-1)
1965-66	Tx-El Paso	28-1	—	—	NCAA (5-0)
1966-67	Tx-El Paso	22-6	—	—	NCAA (2-1)
1967-68	Tx-El Paso	14-9	—	—	DNP
1968-69	Tx-El Paso	16-9	—	—	DNP
1969-70	Tx-El Paso	17-8	10-4	1st (WAC)	NCAA (0-1)
1970-71	Tx-El Paso	15-10	9-5	T2nd (WAC)	DNP
1971-72	Tx-El Paso	20-7	9-5	T2nd (WAC)	NIT (0-1)
1972-73	Tx-El Paso	16-10	6-8	5th (WAC)	DNP
1973-74	Tx-El Paso	18-7	8-6	5th (WAC)	DNP
1974-75	Tx-El Paso	20-6	10-4	2nd (WAC)	NCAA (0-1)
1975-76	Tx-El Paso	19-7	9-5	T2nd (WAC)	DNP
1976-77	Tx-El Paso	11-15	3-11	8th (WAC)	DNP
1977-78	Tx-El Paso	10-16	2-12	8th (WAC)	DNP
1978-79	Tx-El Paso	11-15	3-9	T6th (WAC)	DNP
1979-80	Tx-El Paso	20-8	10-4	T2nd (WAC)	NIT (1-1)
1980-81	Tx-El Paso	18-12	9-7	4th (WAC)	NIT (1-1)
1981-82	Tx-El Paso	20-8	11-5	T2nd (WAC)	DNP
1982-83	Tx-El Paso	19-10	11-5	T1st (WAC)	NIT (0-1)
1983-84	Tx-El Paso	27-4	13-3	1st (WAC)	NCAA (0-1)
1984-85	Tx-El Paso	22-10	12-4	1st (WAC)	NCAA (1-1)
1985-86	Tx-El Paso	27-6	12-4	T1st (WAC)	NCAA (0-1)
1986-87	Tx-El Paso	25-7	13-3	1st (WAC)	NCAA (1-1)
1987-88	Tx-El Paso	23-10	10-6	4th (WAC)	NCAA (0-1)
1988-89	Tx-El Paso	26-7	11-5	2nd (WAC)	NCAA (1-1)
1989-90	Tx-El Paso	21-11	10-6	T3rd (WAC)	NCAA (0-1)
1990-91	Tx-El Paso	16-13	7-9	T5th (WAC)	DNP
1991-92	Tx-El Paso	27-7	12-4	T1st (WAC)	NCAA (2-1)
1992-93	Tx-El Paso	21-13	10-8	4th (WAC)	NIT (1-1)
1993-94	Tx-El Paso	18-12	8-10	T5th (WAC)	DNP
1994-95	Tx-El Paso	20-10	13-5	T2nd (WAC)	NIT (1-1)
1995-96	Tx-El Paso	13-16	4-14	9th (WAC)	DNP
1996-97	Tx-El Paso	13-13	6-10	T6th (WAC/Mountain)	DNP

(School's official name was Texas Western until 1967.)

NOTE: UTEP had a 10-3 record in the 1995-96 season when he was sidelined by a heart ailment for the remainder of the year.

36-Year Coaching Record: 691-327 (.679) at Texas-El Paso; 5-3 (.625) in Border Conference; 251-183 (.578) in Western Athletic Conference; 21-8 (.724) in WAC Tournament; 14-13 (.519) in NCAA Tournament; 4-7 (.364) in NIT.

BOB HUGGINS

West Virginia '77
Gnadenhutten, OH

Guided Cincinnati to Final Four in 1992. . . . Captured a total of six conference tournaments—one with Akron (OVC in 1986) and five with Cincinnati (all four Great Midwest from 1992 through 1995 and first of Conference USA in 1996). . . . Served as an assistant coach under Joedy Gardner for one season at West Virginia and under Eldon Miller for two seasons at Ohio State.

Season	School	Overall	League	Finish	Postseason
1980-81	Walsh (O.)	14-16	9-5	T3rd (Mid-Ohio)	DNP
1981-82	Walsh (O.)	23-9	11-3	1st (Mid-Ohio)	DNP
1982-83	Walsh (O.)	34-1	14-0	1st (Mid-Ohio)	NAIA (0-1)
1984-85	Akron	12-14	6-8	6th (OVC)	DNP
1985-86	Akron	22-8	10-4	T1st (OVC)	NCAA (0-1)
1986-87	Akron	21-9	9-5	T2nd (OVC)	NIT (0-1)
1987-88	Akron	21-7	—	—	DNP
1988-89	Akron	21-8	—	—	NIT (0-1)
1989-90	Cincinnati	20-14	9-5	T2nd (Metro)	NIT (1-1)
1990-91	Cincinnati	18-12	8-6	3rd (Metro)	NIT (1-1)
1991-92	Cincinnati	29-5	8-2	T1st (GMC)	NCAA (4-1)
1992-93	Cincinnati	27-5	8-2	1st (GMC)	NCAA (3-1)
1993-94	Cincinnati	22-10	4-5	4th (GMC)	NCAA (0-1)
1994-95	Cincinnati	22-12	7-5	T3rd (GMC)	NCAA (1-0)
1995-96	Cincinnati	28-5	11-3	1st (C-USA Blue)	NCAA (2-1)
1996-97	Cincinnati	26-8	12-2	1st (C-USA Blue)	NCAA (1-1)

16-Year Coaching Record: 360-143 (.716) overall; 71-26 (.732) in three years at Walsh (O.); 97-46 (.693) in five years at Akron; 192-71 (.730) in first eight years at Cincinnati; 34-8 (.810) in Mid-Ohio Conference; 25-17 (.595) in Ohio Valley Conference; 17-11 (.607) in Metro Conference; 30-14 (.682) in Great Midwest Conference; 23-5 (.821) in Conference USA; 3-1 (.750) in Ohio Valley Tournament; 1-2 (.333) in Metro Tournament; 10-0 (1.000) in Great Midwest Tournament; 4-1 (.800) in C-USA Tournament; 12-7 (.632) in NCAA Tournament; 2-4 (.333) in NIT; 0-1 in NAIA Tournament.

GENE KEADY

Kansas State '58
Larned, KS

Named national coach of the year by all of the major awards in 1996, by USBWA in 1984 and co-coach of the year (with Nolan Richardson) by the NABC in 1994. . . . Member of National Junior College Basketball Hall of Fame (as player and coach). Compiled 187-48 record (.796) in eight seasons at Hutchinson (Kan.) Community College. . . . Guided three Purdue teams to NIT semifinal round—1981 (3rd), 1982 (2nd) and 1993 (4th). . . . Assistant coach at Arkansas under Eddie Sutton for four seasons from 1975-78.

Season	School	Overall	League	Finish	Postseason
1978-79	Western Ky.	17-11	7-5	T2nd (OVC)	DNP
1979-80	Western Ky.	21-8	10-2	T1st (OVC)	NCAA (0-1)
1980-81	Purdue	21-11	10-8	4th (Big Ten)	NIT (4-1)
1981-82	Purdue	18-14	11-7	5th (Big Ten)	NIT (4-1)
1982-83	Purdue	21-9	11-7	T2nd (Big Ten)	NCAA (0-1)
1983-84	Purdue	22-7	15-3	T1st (Big Ten)	NCAA (0-1)
1984-85	Purdue	20-9	11-7	T3rd (Big Ten)	NCAA (0-1)
1985-86	Purdue	25-10	11-7	T4th (Big Ten)	NCAA (1-1)
1986-87	Purdue	25-5	15-3	T1st (Big Ten)	NCAA (1-1)
1987-88	Purdue	29-4	16-2	1st (Big Ten)	NCAA (2-1)
1988-89	Purdue	15-16	8-10	T6th (Big Ten)	DNP
1989-90	Purdue	22-8	13-5	2nd (Big Ten)	NCAA (1-1)
1990-91	Purdue	17-12	9-9	T5th (Big Ten)	NCAA (0-1)
1991-92	Purdue	18-15	8-10	T6th (Big Ten)	NIT (2-1)
1992-93	Purdue	18-10	9-9	T5th (Big Ten)	NCAA (0-1)
1993-94	Purdue	29-5	14-4	1st (Big Ten)	NCAA (3-1)
1994-95	Purdue	25-7	15-3	1st (Big Ten)	NCAA (1-1)
1995-96	Purdue	26-6	15-3	1st (Big Ten)	NCAA (1-1)
1996-97	Purdue	18-12	12-6	T2nd (Big Ten)	NCAA (1-1)

19-Year Coaching Record: 404-179 (.692) overall; 38-19 (.667) in two years at Western Kentucky; 366-160 (.696) in first 17 years at Purdue; 17-7 (.708) in Ohio Valley Conference; 203-103 (.663) in Big Ten Conference; 11-14 (.440) in NCAA Tournament; 10-3 (.769) in NIT.

PAT KENNEDY

King's College (Pa.) '76
Keyport, NJ

Coach of Florida State's 1997 NIT runner-up. . . . Won four conference tournament titles—three with Iona (1982, 1984 and 1985) and one with Florida State (1991). . . . Assistant coach at King's College, Lehigh and Iona (under Jim Valvano).

Season	School	Overall	League	Finish	Postseason
1980-81	Iona	15-14	—	—	DNP
1981-82	Iona	24-9	7-3	3rd (MAAC)	NIT (0-1)
1982-83	Iona	22-9	8-2	1st (MAAC)	NIT (1-1)
1983-84	Iona	23-8	11-3	T1st (MAAC)	NCAA (0-1)
1984-85	Iona	26-5	11-3	1st (MAAC)	NCAA (0-1)
1985-86	Iona	14-15	9-5	2nd (MAAC)	DNP
1986-87	Florida St.	19-11	6-6	T3rd (Metro)	NIT (1-1)
1987-88	Florida St.	19-11	7-5	2nd (Metro)	NCAA (0-1)
1988-89	Florida St.	22-8	9-3	1st (Metro)	NCAA (0-1)
1989-90	Florida St.	16-15	6-8	T5th (Metro)	DNP
1990-91	Florida St.	21-11	9-5	2nd (Metro)	NCAA (1-1)
1991-92	Florida St.	22-10	11-5	2nd (ACC)	NCAA (2-1)
1992-93	Florida St.	25-10	12-4	2nd (ACC)	NCAA (3-1)
1993-94	Florida St.	13-14	6-10	T7th (ACC)	DNP
1994-95	Florida St.	12-15	5-11	T6th (ACC)	DNP
1995-96	Florida St.	13-14	5-11	8th (ACC)	DNP
1996-97	Florida St.	20-12	6-10	7th (ACC)	NIT (4-1)

17-Year Coaching Record: 326-191 (.631) overall; 124-60 (.674) in six years at Iona; 202-131 (.607) in first 11 years at Florida State; 46-16 (.742) in Metro Atlantic Athletic Conference; 37-27 (.578) in Metro Conference; 45-51 (.469) in Atlantic Coast Conference; 11-2 (.846) in MAAC Tournament; 5-4 (.556) in Metro Conference Tournament; 1-6 (.143) in ACC Tournament; 6-7 (.462) in NCAA Tournament; 6-4 (.600) in NIT.

BOB KNIGHT

Ohio State '62
Orrville, OH

Named national coach of the year by NABC in 1975; by AP and USBWA in 1975, 1976 and 1989; by UPI in 1976 and 1989, and by Naismith in 1987. . . . Reached NCAA Final Four five times—1973 (third), 1976 (champion), 1981 (champion), 1987 (champion) and 1992 (tied for third). . . . Coach of five NIT semifinalists—1966 (fourth), 1969 (fourth), 1970 (third), 1979 (champion) and 1985 (runner-up). . . . Coach of 1974 Collegiate Commissioners Association Tournament champion. . . . Winningest coach in Big Ten Conference history. . . . U.S. Olympic team coach in 1984. . . . Assistant coach at Army under Tates Locke for two seasons (1963-64 and 1964-65). . . . Elected to Naismith Memorial Basketball Hall of Fame in 1990.

Season	School	Overall	League	Finish	Postseason
1965-66	Army	18-8	—	—	NIT (2-2)
1966-67	Army	13-8	—	—	DNP
1967-68	Army	20-5	—	—	NIT (0-1)
1968-69	Army	18-10	—	—	NIT (2-2)
1969-70	Army	22-6	—	—	NIT (3-1)
1970-71	Army	11-13	—	—	DNP
1971-72	Indiana	17-8	9-5	T3rd (Big Ten)	NIT (0-1)
1972-73	Indiana	22-6	11-3	1st (Big Ten)	NCAA (3-1)
1973-74	Indiana	23-5	12-2	T1st (Big Ten)	CCAT (3-0)
1974-75	Indiana	31-1	18-0	1st (Big Ten)	NCAA (2-1)
1975-76	Indiana	32-0	18-0	1st (Big Ten)	NCAA (5-0)
1976-77	Indiana*	14-13	9-9	5th (Big Ten)	DNP
1977-78	Indiana	21-8	12-6	T2nd (Big Ten)	NCAA (1-1)
1978-79	Indiana	22-12	10-8	5th (Big Ten)	NIT (4-0)
1979-80	Indiana	21-8	13-5	1st (Big Ten)	NCAA (1-1)
1980-81	Indiana	26-9	14-4	1st (Big Ten)	NCAA (5-0)
1981-82	Indiana	19-10	12-6	T2nd (Big Ten)	NCAA (1-1)
1982-83	Indiana	24-6	13-5	1st (Big Ten)	NCAA (1-1)
1983-84	Indiana	22-9	13-5	3rd (Big Ten)	NCAA (2-1)
1984-85	Indiana	19-14	7-11	7th (Big Ten)	NIT (4-1)
1985-86	Indiana	21-8	13-5	2nd (Big Ten)	NCAA (0-1)
1986-87	Indiana	30-4	15-3	T1st (Big Ten)	NCAA (6-0)
1987-88	Indiana	19-10	11-7	5th (Big Ten)	NCAA (0-1)
1988-89	Indiana	27-8	15-3	1st (Big Ten)	NCAA (2-1)
1989-90	Indiana	18-11	8-10	7th (Big Ten)	NCAA (0-1)
1990-91	Indiana	29-5	15-3	T1st (Big Ten)	NCAA (2-1)
1991-92	Indiana	27-7	14-4	2nd (Big Ten)	NCAA (4-1)
1992-93	Indiana	31-4	17-1	1st (Big Ten)	NCAA (3-1)
1993-94	Indiana	21-9	12-6	3rd (Big Ten)	NCAA (2-1)
1994-95	Indiana	19-12	11-7	T3rd (Big Ten)	NCAA (0-1)
1995-96	Indiana	19-12	12-6	T2nd (Big Ten)	NCAA (0-1)
1996-97	Indiana	22-11	9-9	T6th (Big Ten)	NCAA (0-1)

*Overall record is 16-11 and Big Ten mark is 11-7 in fourth place if include two forfeit victories awarded from Minnesota after the season.

32-Year Coaching Record: 698-260 (.729) overall; 102-50 (.671) in six years at Army; 596-210 (.739) in first 26 years at Indiana; 323-133 (.708) in Big Ten Conference; 40-18 (.690) in NCAA Tournament; 15-8 (.652) in NIT; 3-0 in Collegiate Commissioners Association Tournament.

LON KRUGER

Kansas State '75
Silver Lake, KS

Guided Florida to Final Four in 1994 NCAA Tournament. . . . Directed Florida to fourth-place finish in 1992 NIT. . . . Only coach to take three different schools to the Top 20 of a final wire-service poll. . . . Assistant coach at Pittsburg (Kan.) State (1976-77) and Kansas State (1977-78 through 1981-82) under Jack Hartman.

Season	School	Overall	League	Finish	Postseason
1982-83	Pan Am.	7-21	—	—	DNP
1983-84	Pan Am.	13-14	—	—	DNP
1984-85	Pan Am.	12-16	—	—	DNP
1985-86	Pan Am.	20-8	—	—	DNP
1986-87	Kansas St.	20-11	8-6	4th (Big Eight)	NCAA (1-1)
1987-88	Kansas St.	25-11	11-3	2nd (Big Eight)	NCAA (3-1)
1988-89	Kansas St.	19-11	8-6	3rd (Big Eight)	NCAA (0-1)
1989-90	Kansas St.	17-15	7-7	4th (Big Eight)	NCAA (0-1)
1990-91	Florida	11-17	7-11	6th (SEC)	DNP
1991-92	Florida	19-14	9-7	2nd (SEC East)	NIT (3-2)
1992-93	Florida	16-12	9-7	3rd (SEC East)	NIT (0-1)
1993-94	Florida	29-8	12-4	T1st (SEC East)	NCAA (4-1)
1994-95	Florida	17-13	8-8	3rd (SEC East)	NCAA (0-1)
1995-96	Florida	12-16	6-10	T5th (SEC East)	DNP
1996-97	Illinois	22-10	11-7	T4th (Big Ten)	NCAA (1-1)

15-Year Coaching Record: 259-195 (.570) overall; 52-59 (.468) in four years at Pan American; 81-47 (.633) in four years at Kansas State; 104-80 (.565) in six years at Florida; 22-10 (.688) in first year at Illinois; 34-22 (.607) in Big Eight Conference; 51-47 (.520) in Southeastern Conference; 11-7 (.611) in Big Ten Conference; 4-4 (.500) in Big Eight Tournament; 5-6 (.455) in SEC Tournament; 9-7 (.563) in NCAA Tournament; 3-3 (.500) in NIT.

MIKE KRZYZEWSKI

Army '69
Chicago, IL

UPI national coach of the year in 1986. . . . Naismith national coach of the year in 1989 and NABC national coach of the year in 1991. . . . Coach of 1991 and 1992 NCAA champions. . . . Reached NCAA Final Four seven times in nine years from 1986-94. . . . Coach of three ACC Tournament champions—1986, 1988 and 1992. . . . U.S. Olympic team assistant coach in 1992. . . . Assistant coach at Indiana under Bob Knight for one season in 1974-75.

Season	School	Overall	League	Finish	Postseason
1975-76	Army	11-14	—	—	DNP
1976-77	Army	20-8	—	—	DNP
1977-78	Army	19-9	—	—	NIT (0-1)
1978-79	Army	14-11	—	—	DNP
1979-80	Army	9-17	—	—	DNP
1980-81	Duke	17-13	6-8	6th (ACC)	NIT (2-1)
1981-82	Duke	10-17	4-10	T6th (ACC)	DNP
1982-83	Duke	11-17	3-11	7th (ACC)	DNP
1983-84	Duke	24-10	7-7	3rd (ACC)	NCAA (0-1)
1984-85	Duke	23-8	8-6	4th (ACC)	NCAA (1-1)
1985-86	Duke	37-3	12-2	1st (ACC)	NCAA (5-1)
1986-87	Duke	24-9	9-5	3rd (ACC)	NCAA (2-1)
1987-88	Duke	28-7	9-5	4th (ACC)	NCAA (4-1)
1988-89	Duke	28-8	9-5	T2nd (ACC)	NCAA (4-1)
1989-90	Duke	29-9	9-5	2nd (ACC)	NCAA (5-1)
1990-91	Duke	32-7	11-3	1st (ACC)	NCAA (6-0)
1991-92	Duke	34-2	14-2	1st (ACC)	NCAA (6-0)
1992-93	Duke	24-8	10-6	T3rd (ACC)	NCAA (1-1)
1993-94	Duke	28-5	12-4	1st (ACC)	NCAA (5-1)
1994-95	Duke*	9-3	0-1	9th (ACC)	DNP
1995-96	Duke	18-13	8-8	T4th (ACC)	NCAA (0-1)
1996-97	Duke	24-9	12-4	1st (ACC)	NCAA (1-1)

*Missed the last 19 games of 1994-95 season because of a back ailment.

22-Year Coaching Record: 473-207 (.696) overall; 73-59 (.553) in five years at Army; 400-148 (.730) in first 17 years at Duke; 143-92 (.609) in Atlantic Coast Conference; 17-13 (.567) in ACC Tournament; 40-11 (.784) in NCAA Tournament; 2-2 (.500) in NIT.

Season	School	Overall	League	Finish	Postseason
1969-70	Stony Brk.	19-6	9-0	1st (Knicker.)	NCAA DIII (0-1)
1970-71	Stony Brk.	15-10	7-2	T2nd (Knicker.)	DNP
1973-74	Villanova	7-19	—	—	DNP
1974-75	Villanova	9-18	—	—	DNP
1975-76	Villanova	16-11	—	—	DNP
1976-77	Villanova	23-10	6-1	2nd (ECBL East)	NIT (3-1)
1977-78	Villanova	23-9	7-3	T1st (Eastern 8)	NCAA (2-1)
1978-79	Villanova	15-13	9-1	1st (Eastern 8)	DNP
1979-80	Villanova	23-8	7-3	T1st (Eastern 8)	NCAA (1-1)
1980-81	Villanova	20-11	8-6	T3rd (Big East)	NCAA (1-1)
1981-82	Villanova	24-8	11-3	1st (Big East)	NCAA (2-1)
1982-83	Villanova	24-8	12-4	T1st (Big East)	NCAA (2-1)
1983-84	Villanova	19-12	12-4	T2nd (Big East)	NCAA (1-1)
1984-85	Villanova	25-10	9-7	T3rd (Big East)	NCAA (6-0)
1985-86	Villanova	23-14	10-6	4th (Big East)	NCAA (1-1)
1986-87	Villanova	15-16	6-10	6th (Big East)	NIT (0-1)
1987-88	Villanova	24-13	9-7	T3rd (Big East)	NCAA (3-1)
1988-89	Villanova	18-16	7-9	T5th (Big East)	NIT (2-1)
1989-90	Villanova	18-15	8-8	T5th (Big East)	NCAA (0-1)
1990-91	Villanova	17-15	7-9	T7th (Big East)	NCAA (1-1)
1991-92	Villanova	14-15	11-7	4th (Big East)	NIT (0-1)
1992-93	UNLV	21-8	13-5	2nd (Big West)	NIT (0-1)
1993-94	UNLV	15-12	10-8	T5th (Big West)	DNP
1996-97	Clevel. St.	9-19	6-10	T6th (MCC)	DNP

24-Year Coaching Record: 434-295 (.595) overall; 34-16 (.680) in two years at SUNY-Stony Brook; 357-241 (.597) in 19 years at Villanova; 36-20 (.643) in two years at UNLV; 9-19 (.321) in first year at Cleveland State; 16-2 (.889) in Knickerbocker Conference; 29-8 (.784) in Eastern 8 Conference; 110-80 (.579) in Big East Conference; 23-13 (.639) in Big West Conference; 6-10 (.375) in Midwestern Collegiate Conference; 9-2 (.818) in Eastern 8 Tournament; 13-12 (.520) in Big East Tournament; 2-2 (.500) in Big West Tournament; 1-1 (.500) in MCC Tournament; 0-1 in NCAA Division III Tournament; 20-10 (.667) in NCAA Division I Tournament; 5-5 (.500) in NIT.

Future coaching success story: Mike Krzyzewski

RICK MAJERUS

Marquette '70
Sheboygan, WI

Coach of third-place team in 1992 NIT. . . . Won three conference tournament titles—one in Mid-American with Ball State (1989) and two in Western Athletic with Utah (1995 and 1997). . . . Assistant coach at Marquette under Al McGuire and Hank Raymonds from 1971-72 through 1982-83 and with the Milwaukee Bucks under Don Nelson in 1986-87.

Season	School	Overall	League	Finish	Postseason
1983-84	Marquette	17-13	—	—	NIT (1-1)
1984-85	Marquette	20-11	—	—	NIT (2-1)
1985-86	Marquette	19-11	—	—	NIT (1-1)
1987-88	Ball State	14-14	8-8	4th (Mid-American)	DNP
1988-89	Ball State	29-3	14-2	1st (Mid-American)	NCAA (1-1)
1989-90	Utah*	4-2	—	—	DNP
1990-91	Utah	30-4	15-1	1st (WAC)	NCAA (2-1)
1991-92	Utah	24-11	9-7	T4th (WAC)	NIT (4-1)
1992-93	Utah	24-7	15-3	T1st (WAC)	NCAA (1-1)
1993-94	Utah	14-14	8-10	T5th (WAC)	DNP
1994-95	Utah	28-6	15-3	1st (WAC)	NCAA (1-1)
1995-96	Utah	27-7	15-3	1st (WAC)	NCAA (2-1)
1996-97	Utah	29-4	15-1	1st (WAC/Mountain)	NCAA (3-1)

*Missed majority of first season with Utah after undergoing heart surgery.

13-Year Coaching Record: 279-107 (.723) overall; 56-35 (.615) in three years at Marquette; 43-17 (.717) in two years at Ball State; 180-55 (.766) in first eight years at Utah; 22-10 (.688) in Mid-American Conference; 92-28 (.767) in Western Athletic Conference; 3-1 (.750) in Mid-American Tournament; 12-5 (.706) in WAC Tournament; 10-6 (.583) in NCAA Tournament; 8-4 (.667) in NIT.

ROLLIE MASSIMINO

Vermont '56
Hillside, NJ

Coach of NCAA national champion in 1985. . . . Coach of 1977 NIT third-place team. . . . Coach of two Eastern Athletic Association Tournament champions—1978 and 1980. . . . Assistant coach at Penn under Chuck Daly for three seasons from 1972-'74.

NEIL McCARTHY

Sacramento State '65
San Francisco, CA

Coach of four Big Sky Conference Tournament champions—1978, 1979, 1980 and 1983. . . . Coach of two Big West Conference Tournament champions—1992 and 1994. . . . Assistant coach at Weber State under Gene Visscher for four seasons from 1971-72 through 1974-75.

Season	School	Overall	League	Finish	Postseason
1975-76	Weber St.	21-11	9-5	T1st (Big Sky)	DNP
1976-77	Weber St.	20-8	11-3	2nd (Big Sky)	DNP
1977-78	Weber St.	19-10	9-5	3rd (Big Sky)	NCAA (0-1)
1978-79	Weber St.	25-9	10-4	1st (Big Sky)	NCAA (1-1)
1979-80	Weber St.	26-3	13-1	1st (Big Sky)	NCAA (0-1)
1980-81	Weber St.	8-19	5-9	T5th (Big Sky)	DNP
1981-82	Weber St.	15-13	6-8	T4th (Big Sky)	DNP
1982-83	Weber St.	23-8	10-4	T1st (Big Sky)	NCAA (0-1)
1983-84	Weber St.	23-8	12-2	1st (Big Sky)	NIT (1-1)
1984-85	Weber St.	20-9	9-5	3rd (Big Sky)	DNP
1985-86	N. Mex. St.	18-12	10-8	3rd (PCAA)	DNP
1986-87	N. Mex. St.	15-15	9-9	T4th (PCAA)	DNP
1987-88	N. Mex. St.	15-14	8-10	T6th (PCAA)	DNP
1988-89	N. Mex. St.	21-11	12-6	2nd (Big West)	NIT (0-1)
1989-90	N. Mex. St.	26-5	16-2	T1st (Big West)	NCAA (0-1)
1990-91	N. Mex. St.	23-6	15-3	2nd (Big West)	NCAA (0-1)
1991-92	N. Mex. St.	25-8	12-6	3rd (Big West)	NCAA (2-1)
1992-93	N. Mex. St.	26-8	15-3	1st (Big West)	NCAA (1-1)
1993-94	N. Mex. St.	23-8	12-6	1st (Big West)	NCAA (0-1)
1994-95	N. Mex. St.	25-10	13-5	T2nd (Big West)	NIT (2-1)
1995-96	N. Mex. St.	11-15	8-10	T7th (Big West)	DNP
1996-97	N. Mex. St.	19-9	12-4	T1st (Big West/E)	DNP

NOTE: McCarthy was 5-7 during the 1974-75 campaign after taking over for Gene Visscher, but the mark went on Visscher's record because McCarthy was designated as an interim coach and wasn't appointed head coach until the next season.

22-Year Coaching Record: 448-221 (.670) overall; 200-98 (.671) in 10 years at Weber State; 248-123 (.668) in first 12 years at New Mexico State; 94-46 (.671) in Big Sky Conference; 142-72 (.664) in Big West Conference; 11-4 (.733) in Big Sky Tournament; 15-9 (.625) in Big West Tournament; 4-9 (.308) in NCAA Tournament; 3-3 (.500) in NIT.

ELDON MILLER

Wittenberg (Ohio) '61
Gnadenhutten, OH

Coach of 1986 NIT champion and 1979 NIT fourth-place team. . . . Coach of 1990 Mid-Continent Conference Tournament champion. . . . Coach of NCAA Division II Tournament runner-up in 1963. . . . Assistant coach at Wittenberg (Ohio) for one season in 1961-62.

Season	School	Overall	League	Finish	Postseason
1962-63	Wittenberg	26-2	—	—	DII (4-1)
1963-64	Wittenberg	18-5	—	—	DNP
1964-65	Wittenberg	17-5	—	—	DNP
1965-66	Wittenberg	12-11	—	—	DNP
1966-67	Wittenberg	17-7	—	—	DNP
1967-68	Wittenberg	13-13	—	—	DNP
1968-69	Wittenberg	19-6	—	—	DII (0-2)
1969-70	Wittenberg	20-6	—	—	DNP
1970-71	West. Mich.	14-10	5-5	3rd (Mid-American)	DNP
1971-72	West. Mich.	10-14	5-5	4th (Mid-American)	DNP
1972-73	West. Mich.	8-18	2-10	7th (Mid-American)	DNP
1973-74	West. Mich.	13-13	5-7	6th (Mid-American)	DNP
1974-75	West. Mich.	16-10	8-6	5th (Mid-American)	DNP
1975-76	West. Mich.	25-3	15-1	1st (Mid-American)	NCAA (1-1)
1976-77	Ohio State*	9-18	4-14	10th (Big Ten)	DNP
1977-78	Ohio State	16-11	9-9	6th (Big Ten)	DNP
1978-79	Ohio State	19-12	12-6	4th (Big Ten)	NIT (2-2)
1979-80	Ohio State	21-8	12-6	2nd (Big Ten)	NCAA (1-1)
1980-81	Ohio State	14-13	9-9	T5th (Big Ten)	DNP
1981-82	Ohio State	21-10	12-6	T2nd (Big Ten)	NCAA (0-1)
1982-83	Ohio State	20-10	11-7	T2nd (Big Ten)	NCAA (1-1)
1983-84	Ohio State	15-14	8-10	6th (Big Ten)	NIT (0-1)
1984-85	Ohio State	20-10	11-7	T3rd (Big Ten)	NCAA (1-1)
1985-86	Ohio State	19-14	8-10	7th (Big Ten)	NIT (5-0)
1986-87	N. Iowa	13-15	7-7	5th (Mid-Continent)	DNP
1987-88	N. Iowa	10-18	4-10	T6th (Mid-Continent)	DNP
1988-89	N. Iowa	19-9	8-4	2nd (Mid-Continent)	DNP
1989-90	N. Iowa	23-9	6-6	T3rd (Mid-Continent)	NCAA (1-1)
1990-91	N. Iowa	13-19	8-8	T3rd (Mid-Continent)	DNP
1991-92	N. Iowa	10-18	6-12	T7th (Mo. Valley)	DNP
1992-93	N. Iowa	12-15	8-10	6th (Mo. Valley)	DNP
1993-94	N. Iowa	16-13	10-8	5th (Mo. Valley)	DNP
1994-95	N. Iowa	8-20	4-14	T9th (Mo. Valley)	DNP
1995-96	N. Iowa	14-13	8-10	T7th (Mo. Valley)	DNP
1996-97	N. Iowa	16-12	11-7	T4th (Mo. Valley)	DNP

*Record in his first season with Ohio State is 11-16 overall and 6-12 in the Big Ten if include two forfeit victories awarded over Minnesota.

35-Year Coaching Record: 558-402 (.581) overall; 142-55 (.721) in eight years at Wittenberg; 86-68 (.558) in six years at Western Michigan; 176-118 (.607) in 10 years at Ohio State; 154-161 (.489) in first 11 years at Northern Iowa; ??-?? (.???) in Ohio Conference; 40-34 (.541) in Mid-American Conference; 96-84 (.533) in Big Ten Conference; 33-35 (.485) in Mid-Continent Conference; 47-61 (.435) in Missouri Valley Conference; 3-2 (.600) in Mid-Continent Tournament; 3-5 (.375) in MVC Tournament; 4-3 (.571) in NCAA Division II Tournament; 5-6 (.455) in NCAA Division I Tournament; 7-3 (.700) in NIT.

MIKE MONTGOMERY

Long Beach State '68
Long Beach, CA

Coach of 1991 NIT champion. . . . Assistant coach at U.S. Coast Guard Academy, Colorado State, The Citadel, Florida and Boise State.

Season	School	Overall	League	Finish	Postseason
1978-79	Montana	14-13	7-7	T4th (Big Sky)	DNP
1979-80	Montana	17-11	8-6	3rd (Big Sky)	DNP
1980-81	Montana	19-9	11-3	T2nd (Big Sky)	DNP
1981-82	Montana	17-10	10-4	2nd (Big Sky)	DNP
1982-83	Montana	21-8	9-5	T3rd (Big Sky)	DNP
1983-84	Montana	23-7	9-5	2nd (Big Sky)	DNP
1984-85	Montana	22-8	10-4	2nd (Big Sky)	NIT (0-1)
1985-86	Montana	21-11	9-5	T1st (Big Sky)	NIT (0-1)
1986-87	Stanford	15-13	9-9	6th (Pacific-10)	DNP
1987-88	Stanford	21-12	11-7	4th (Pacific-10)	NIT (1-1)
1988-89	Stanford	26-7	15-3	2nd (Pacific-10)	NCAA (0-1)
1989-90	Stanford	18-12	9-9	6th (Pacific-10)	NIT (0-1)
1990-91	Stanford	20-13	8-10	T5th (Pacific-10)	NIT (5-0)
1991-92	Stanford	18-11	10-8	4th (Pacific-10)	NCAA (0-1)
1992-93	Stanford	7-23	2-16	10th (Pacific-10)	DNP
1993-94	Stanford	17-11	10-8	T4th (Pacific-10)	NIT (0-1)
1994-95	Stanford	20-9	10-8	T5th (Pacific-10)	NCAA (1-1)
1995-96	Stanford	20-9	12-6	3rd (Pacific-10)	NCAA (1-1)
1996-97	Stanford	22-8	12-6	T2nd (Pacific-10)	NCAA (2-1)

19-Year Coaching Record: 358-205 (.636) overall; 154-77 (.652) in eight years at Montana; 204-128 (.614) in first 11 years at Stanford; 73-39 (.652) in Big Sky Conference; 108-90 (.545) in Pacific-10 Conference; 6-8 (.429) in Big Sky Tournament; 4-4 (.500) in Pacific-10 Tournament; 4-5 (.444) in NCAA Tournament; 6-5 (.545) in NIT.

DANNY NEE

St. Mary of the Plains (Kan.) '71
Brooklyn, NY

Coach of 1987 NIT runner-up and 1996 NIT champion. . . . Won two Mid-American Conference tournament titles (1983 and 1985). . . . Assistant coach at St. Mary of the Plains (Kan.) and Notre Dame (four years under Digger Phelps).

Season	School	Overall	League	Finish	Postseason
1980-81	Ohio Univ.	7-20	6-10	T7th (Mid-American)	DNP
1981-82	Ohio Univ.	13-14	8-8	4th (Mid-American)	DNP
1982-83	Ohio Univ.	23-9	12-6	2nd (Mid-American)	NCAA (1-1)
1983-84	Ohio Univ.	20-8	14-4	2nd (Mid-American)	DNP
1984-85	Ohio Univ.	22-8	14-4	1st (Mid-American)	NCAA (0-1)
1985-86	Ohio Univ.	22-8	14-4	2nd (Mid-American)	NIT (0-1)
1986-87	Nebraska	21-12	7-7	5th (Big Eight)	NIT (4-1)
1987-88	Nebraska	13-18	4-10	T6th (Big Eight)	DNP
1988-89	Nebraska	17-16	4-10	7th (Big Eight)	NIT (1-1)
1989-90	Nebraska	10-18	3-11	7th (Big Eight)	DNP
1990-91	Nebraska	26-8	9-5	3rd (Big Eight)	NCAA (0-1)
1991-92	Nebraska	19-10	7-7	5th (Big Eight)	NCAA (0-1)
1992-93	Nebraska	20-11	8-6	T2nd (Big Eight)	NCAA (0-1)
1993-94	Nebraska	20-10	7-7	4th (Big Eight)	NCAA (0-1)
1994-95	Nebraska	18-14	4-10	7th (Big Eight)	NIT (1-1)
1995-96	Nebraska	21-14	4-10	7th (Big Eight)	NIT (5-0)
1996-97	Nebraska	19-14	7-9	4th (Big 12/N)	NIT (2-1)

17-Year Coaching Record: 311-212 (.595) overall; 107-67 (.615) in six years at Ohio University; 204-145 (.585) in first 11 years at Nebraska; 68-36 (.654) in Mid-American Conference; 57-83 (.407) in Big Eight Conference; 7-9 (.438) in Big 12 Conference; 6-4 (.600) in Mid-American Tournament; 4-10 (.286) in Big Eight Tournament; 0-1 (.000) in Big 12 Tournament; 1-6 (.143) in NCAA Tournament; 13-4 (.765) in NIT.

ROBERT (LUTE) OLSON

Augsburg, Minn. '57
Mayville, ND

Named national coach of the year by NABC in 1980. . . . Reached NCAA Final Four four times—1980 (fourth with Iowa), 1988 (tied for third with Arizona), 1994 (tied for third with Arizona) and 1997 (first with Arizona). . . . Coach of three Pacific-10 Conference Tournament champions—1988, 1989 and 1990. . . . Coached at Long Beach City College, including the 1971 California community college champion.

Season	School	Overall	League	Finish	Postseason
1973-74	L. Beach St.	24-2	12-0	1st (PCAA)	Probation
1974-75	Iowa	10-16	7-11	7th (Big Ten)	DNP
1975-76	Iowa	19-10	9-9	5th (Big Ten)	DNP
1976-77	Iowa	20-7	12-6	4th (Big Ten)	DNP
1977-78	Iowa	12-15	5-13	8th (Big Ten)	DNP
1978-79	Iowa	20-8	13-5	T1st (Big Ten)	NCAA (0-1)
1979-80	Iowa	23-10	10-8	4th (Big Ten)	NCAA (4-2)
1980-81	Iowa	21-7	13-5	2nd (Big Ten)	NCAA (1-1)
1981-82	Iowa	21-8	12-6	T2nd (Big Ten)	NCAA (1-1)
1982-83	Iowa	21-10	10-8	5th (Big Ten)	NCAA (2-1)
1983-84	Arizona	11-17	8-10	T5th (Pac-10)	DNP
1984-85	Arizona	21-10	12-6	T3rd (Pac-10)	NCAA (0-1)
1985-86	Arizona	23-9	14-4	1st (Pac-10)	NCAA (0-1)
1986-87	Arizona	18-12	13-5	2nd (Pac-10)	NCAA (0-1)
1987-88	Arizona	35-3	17-1	1st (Pac-10)	NCAA (4-1)
1988-89	Arizona	29-4	17-1	1st (Pac-10)	NCAA (2-1)
1989-90	Arizona	25-7	15-3	T1st (Pac-10)	NCAA (1-1)
1990-91	Arizona	28-7	14-4	1st (Pac-10)	NCAA (2-1)
1991-92	Arizona	24-7	13-5	3rd (Pac-10)	NCAA (2-1)
1992-93	Arizona	24-4	17-1	1st (Pac-10)	NCAA (0-1)
1993-94	Arizona	29-6	14-4	1st (Pac-10)	NCAA (4-1)
1994-95	Arizona	23-8	13-5	2nd (Pac-10)	NCAA (0-1)
1995-96	Arizona	26-7	13-5	2nd (Pac-10)	NCAA (2-1)
1996-97	Arizona	24-9	11-7	5th (Pac-10)	NCAA (6-0)

24-Year Coaching Record: 531-203 (.723) overall; 24-2 (.943) in one year at Long Beach State; 167-91 (.647) in nine years at Iowa; 340-110 (.756) in first 14 years at Arizona; 12-0 in Pacific Coast Athletic Association; 91-71 (.562) in Big Ten Conference; 191-59 (.764) in Pacific-10 Conference; 9-1 (.900) in Pacific-10 Tournament; 28-18 (.609) in NCAA Tournament.

TOM PENDERS

Connecticut '67
Stratford, CT

Won three league tournament titles—one in Metro Atlantic Athletic with Fordham (1983) and two in Southwest Conference (1994 and 1995). . . . Never served as an assistant coach.

Season	School	Overall	League	Finish	Postseason
1971-72	Tufts	12-8	—	—	DNP
1972-73	Tufts	22-4	—	—	DNP
1973-74	Tufts	20-6	—	—	DNP
1974-75	Columbia	4-22	2-12	T7th (Ivy League)	DNP
1975-76	Columbia	8-17	6-8	T4th (Ivy League)	DNP
1976-77	Columbia	16-10	8-6	3rd (Ivy League)	DNP
1977-78	Columbia	15-11	11-3	T2nd (Ivy League)	DNP
1978-79	Fordham	7-22	—	—	DNP
1979-80	Fordham	11-17	—	—	DNP
1980-81	Fordham	19-9	—	—	NIT (0-1)
1981-82	Fordham	18-11	8-2	2nd (MAAC)	NIT (0-1)
1982-83	Fordham	19-11	7-3	T2nd (MAAC)	NIT (0-1)
1983-84	Fordham	19-15	7-7	4th (MAAC)	NIT (0-1)
1984-85	Fordham	19-12	9-5	2nd (MAAC)	NIT (0-1)
1985-86	Fordham	13-17	7-7	T4th (MAAC)	DNP
1986-87	Rhode Is.	20-10	12-6	3rd (Atlantic 10)	NIT (0-1)
1987-88	Rhode Is.	28-7	14-4	2nd (Atlantic 10)	NCAA (2-1)
1988-89	Texas	25-9	12-4	2nd (SWC)	NCAA (1-1)
1989-90	Texas	24-9	12-4	3rd (SWC)	NCAA (3-1)
1990-91	Texas	23-9	13-3	2nd (SWC)	NCAA (1-1)
1991-92	Texas	23-12	11-3	T1st (SWC)	NCAA (0-1)
1992-93	Texas	11-17	4-10	7th (SWC)	DNP
1993-94	Texas	26-8	12-2	1st (SWC)	NCAA (1-1)
1994-95	Texas	23-7	11-3	T1st (SWC)	NCAA (1-1)
1995-96	Texas	21-10	10-4	3rd (SWC)	NCAA (1-1)
1996-97	Texas	18-12	10-6	T1st (Big 12/S)	NCAA (2-1)

26-Year Coaching Record: 464-302 (.606) overall; 54-18 (.750) in three years at Tufts; 43-60 (.417) in four years at Columbia; 125-114 (.523) in eight years at Fordham; 48-17 (.738) in two years at Rhode Island; 194-93 (.676) in first nine years at Texas; 27-29 (.482) in Ivy League; 38-24 (.613) in Metro Atlantic Athletic Conference; 26-10 (.722) in Atlantic 10 Conference; 85-33 (.720) in Southwest Conference; 10-6 (.625) in Big 12 Conference; 7-4 (.636) in MAAC Tournament; 3-2 (.600) in Atlantic 10 Tournament; 15-6 (.714) in SWC Tournament; 0-1 (.000) in Big 12 Tournament; 12-9 (.571) in NCAA Tournament; 0-6 (.000) in NIT.

NOLAN RICHARDSON

Texas-El Paso '65
El Paso, TX

Received Naismith Award as national coach of the year and shared similar NABC award in 1994. . . . Coach of three Final Four teams—1990 (tied for third place), 1994 (champion) and 1995 (runner-up). . . . Coach of 1981 NIT champion and 1997 fourth-place team. . . . Coach of five conference tournament champions—Missouri Valley (1982 and 1984) and Southwest Conference (1989, 1990 and 1991). . . . Coach at Western Texas Junior College for three seasons, including the 1980 NJCAA championship team that compiled a 37-0 record.

Season	School	Overall	League	Finish	Postseason
1980-81	Tulsa	26-7	11-5	T2nd (Mo. Valley)	NIT (5-0)
1981-82	Tulsa	24-6	12-4	T2nd (Mo. Valley)	NCAA (0-1)
1982-83	Tulsa	19-12	11-7	T3rd (Mo. Valley)	NIT (0-1)
1983-84	Tulsa	27-4	13-3	T1st (Mo. Valley)	NCAA (0-1)
1984-85	Tulsa	23-8	12-4	1st (Mo. Valley)	NCAA (0-1)
1985-86	Arkansas	12-16	4-12	7th (SWC)	DNP
1986-87	Arkansas	19-14	8-8	5th (SWC)	NIT (1-1)
1987-88	Arkansas	21-9	11-5	T2nd (SWC)	NCAA (0-1)
1988-89	Arkansas	25-7	13-3	1st (SWC)	NCAA (1-1)
1989-90	Arkansas	30-5	14-2	1st (SWC)	NCAA (4-1)
1990-91	Arkansas	34-4	15-1	1st (SWC)	NCAA (3-1)
1991-92	Arkansas	26-8	13-3	1st (SEC West)	NCAA (1-1)
1992-93	Arkansas	22-9	10-6	1st (SEC West)	NCAA (2-1)
1993-94	Arkansas	31-3	14-2	1st (SEC West)	NCAA (6-0)
1994-95	Arkansas	32-7	12-4	T1st (SEC West)	NCAA (5-1)
1995-96	Arkansas	20-13	9-7	T2nd (SEC West)	NCAA (2-1)
1996-97	Arkansas	18-14	8-8	2nd (SEC West)	NIT (3-2)

17-Year Coaching Record: 409-146 (.737) overall; 119-37 (.763) in five years at Tulsa; 290-109 (.727) in first 12 years at Arkansas; 59-23 (.720) in Missouri Valley Conference; 65-31 (.677) in Southwest Conference; 66-30 (.688) in Southeastern Conference; 11-3 (.786) in MVC Tournament; 10-3 (.769) in SWC Tournament; 6-6 (.500) in SEC Tournament; 24-11 (.686) in NCAA Tournament; 9-4 (.692) in NIT.

WINFREY (WIMP) SANDERSON

North Alabama '59
Florence, AL

Only the second coach in SEC history (Kentucky's Adolph Rupp) to win three consecutive SEC Tournament titles (1989-91). Also, led 'Bama to SEC postseason tournament titles in 1982 and 1987 for a total of five. . . . Served as an assistant for 20 years at Alabama under Hayden Riley and C.M. Newton.

Season	School	Overall	League	Finish	Postseason
1980-81	Alabama	18-11	10-8	4th (SEC)	NIT (1-1)
1981-82	Alabama	24-7	12-6	3rd (SEC)	NCAA (1-1)
1982-83	Alabama	20-12	8-10	T8th (SEC)	NCAA (0-1)
1983-84	Alabama	18-12	10-8	5th (SEC)	NCAA (0-1)
1984-85	Alabama	23-10	11-7	T3rd (SEC)	NCAA (2-1)
1985-86	Alabama	24-9	13-5	T2nd (SEC)	NCAA (2-1)
1986-87*	Alabama	28-5	16-2	1st (SEC)	NCAA (2-1)
1987-88	Alabama	14-17	6-12	T8th (SEC)	DNP
1988-89	Alabama	23-8	12-6	T2nd (SEC)	NCAA (0-1)
1989-90	Alabama	26-9	12-6	T2nd (SEC)	NCAA (2-1)
1990-91	Alabama	23-10	12-6	3rd (SEC)	NCAA (2-1)
1991-92	Alabama	26-9	10-6	3rd (SEC)	NCAA (1-1)
1994-95	UALR	17-12	9-9	T5th (Sun Belt)	DNP
1995-96	UALR	23-7	14-4	T1st (Sun Belt)	NIT (0-1)
1996-97	UALR	18-11	11-7	3rd (Sun Belt)	DNP

*NCAA Tournament games later vacated by action of the NCAA.

15-Year Coaching Record: 325-149 (.686) overall; 267-119 (.692) in 12 years at Alabama; 58-30 (.659) in first three years at Arkansas-Little Rock; 17-12 (.586); 132-82 (.617) in Southeastern Conference; 34-20 (.630) in Sun Belt Conference; 25-7 (.781) in SEC Tournament; 5-3 (.625) in Sun Belt Tournament; 12-10 (.545) in NCAA Tournament; 1-2 (.333) in NIT.

DEAN SMITH

Kansas '53
Topeka, KS

NABC national coach of the year in 1977 and USBWA national coach of the year in 1979. . . . All-time winningest coach in NCAA Tournament competition. . . . Reached NCAA Final Four 11 times—1967 (fourth), 1968 (runner-up), 1969 (fourth), 1972 (third), 1977 (runner-up), 1981 (runner-up), 1982 (champion), 1991 (tied for third), 1993 (champion), 1995 (tied for third) and 1997 (tied for third). . . . Coach of 1971 NIT champion and 1973 third-place team. . . . Coach of 13 ACC Tournament champions—1967, 1968, 1969, 1972, 1975, 1977, 1979, 1981, 1982, 1989, 1991, 1994 and 1997. . . . U.S. Olympic team coach in 1976. . . . Assistant coach under Kansas' Dick Harp, Air Force's Bob Spear and North Carolina's Frank McGuire. . . . Elected to Naismith Memorial Basketball Hall of Fame in 1982.

Season	School	Overall	League	Finish	Postseason
1961-62	N.C.	8-9	7-7	T4th (ACC)	DNP
1962-63	N.C.	15-6	10-4	3rd (ACC)	DNP
1963-64	N.C.	12-12	6-8	5th (ACC)	DNP
1964-65	N.C.	15-9	10-4	T2nd (ACC)	DNP
1965-66	N.C.	16-11	8-6	T3rd (ACC)	DNP
1966-67	N.C.	26-6	12-2	1st (ACC)	NCAA (2-2)
1967-68	N.C.	28-4	12-2	1st (ACC)	NCAA (3-1)
1968-69	N.C.	27-5	12-2	1st (ACC)	NCAA (2-2)
1969-70	N.C.	18-9	9-5	T2nd (ACC)	NIT (0-1)
1970-71	N.C.	26-6	11-3	1st (ACC)	NIT (4-0)
1971-72	N.C.	26-5	9-3	1st (ACC)	NCAA (3-1)
1972-73	N.C.	25-8	8-4	2nd (ACC)	NIT (3-1)
1973-74	N.C.	22-6	9-3	T2nd (ACC)	NIT (0-1)
1974-75	N.C.	23-8	8-4	T2nd (ACC)	NCAA (2-1)
1975-76	N.C.	25-4	11-1	1st (ACC)	NCAA (0-1)
1976-77	N.C.	28-5	9-3	1st (ACC)	NCAA (4-1)
1977-78	N.C.	23-8	9-3	1st (ACC)	NCAA (0-1)
1978-79	N.C.	23-6	9-3	T1st (ACC)	NCAA (0-1)
1979-80	N.C.	21-8	9-5	T2nd (ACC)	NCAA (0-1)
1980-81	N.C.	29-8	10-4	2nd (ACC)	NCAA (4-1)
1981-82	N.C.	32-2	12-2	T1st (ACC)	NCAA (5-0)
1982-83	N.C.	28-8	12-2	T1st (ACC)	NCAA (2-1)
1983-84	N.C.	28-3	14-0	1st (ACC)	NCAA (1-1)

DEAN'S ALMOST ATOP LIST

Dean Smith, entering his 36th year as North Carolina's head coach with 851 victories, is on a pace to bypass Kentucky legend Adolph Rupp and become the all-time winningest major-college coach late in the 1996-97 season or early in the 1997-98 campaign. Smith entered this season needing 26 triumphs to move atop the list. The Tar Heels averaged 26 wins annually the previous 30 seasons. Here is a list of the coaches with more than 600 victories through 1995-96:

RANK	COACH	WINS
1.	Adolph Rupp	876
2.	Dean Smith*	851
3.	Henry Iba	767
4.	Ed Diddle	759
5.	Phog Allen	746
6.	Ray Meyer	724
T7.	Don Haskins*	678
T7.	Norm Stewart*	678
9.	Bob Knight*	676
10.	Ralph Miller	674
11.	Lefty Driesell*	667
12.	John Wooden	664
13.	Lou Henson	661
T14.	Marv Harshman	653
T14.	Jerry Tarkanian*	653
16.	Gene Bartow	646
17.	Cam Henderson	630
18.	Norman Sloan	627

*Active coaches.

Notes: Miller was forced to forfeit 17 of his victories with Oregon State. . . . Six NCAA Tournament victories for Tarkanian at Long Beach State were voided by the NCAA. . . . Forfeit victories are not included for Knight (two), Henson (two), Bartow (one) and Harshman (one). . . . Louisville's Denny Crum is expected to crack the 600-win plateau sometime during the 1996-97 season.

1984-85	N.C.	27-9	9-5	T1st (ACC)	NCAA (3-1)
1985-86	N.C.	28-6	10-4	3rd (ACC)	NCAA (2-1)
1986-87	N.C.	32-4	14-0	1st (ACC)	NCAA (3-1)
1987-88	N.C.	27-7	11-3	1st (ACC)	NCAA (3-1)
1988-89	N.C.	29-8	9-5	T2nd (ACC)	NCAA (2-1)
1989-90	N.C.	21-13	8-6	T3rd (ACC)	NCAA (2-1)
1990-91	N.C.	29-6	10-4	2nd (ACC)	NCAA (4-1)
1991-92	N.C.	23-10	9-7	3rd (ACC)	NCAA (2-1)
1992-93	N.C.	34-4	14-2	1st (ACC)	NCAA (6-0)
1993-94	N.C.	28-7	11-5	2nd (ACC)	NCAA (1-1)
1994-95	N.C.	28-6	12-4	T1st (ACC)	NCAA (4-1)
1995-96	N.C.	21-11	10-6	3rd (ACC)	NCAA (1-1)
1996-97	N.C.	28-7	11-5	T2nd (ACC)	NCAA (4-1)

36-Year Coaching Record: 879-254 (.776) at North Carolina; 364-136 (.728) in Atlantic Coast Conference; 58-23 (.716) in ACC Tournament; 65-27 (.699) in NCAA Tournament; 7-3 (.700) in NIT.

ORLANDO (TUBBY) SMITH

High Point, N.C. '73
Scotland, MD

Only coach to take three consecutive teams seeded sixth or worse to the Sweet 16 of the NCAA playoffs (1994 through 1996). . . . Assistant coach for seven seasons from 1979-80 through 1985-86 at Virginia Commonwealth (six under J.D. Barnett and one under Mike Pollio), three seasons from 1986-87 through 1988-89 at South Carolina (under George Felton) and two seasons in 1989-90 and 1990-91 at Kentucky (under Rick Pitino).

Season	School	Overall	League	Finish	Postseason
1991-92	Tulsa	17-13	12-6	T4th (Mo. Valley)	DNP
1992-93	Tulsa	15-14	10-8	4th (Mo. Valley)	DNP
1993-94	Tulsa	23-8	15-3	1st (Mo. Valley)	NCAA (2-1)
1994-95	Tulsa	24-8	15-3	1st (Mo. Valley)	NCAA (2-1)
1995-96	Georgia	21-10	9-7	2nd (SEC/East)	NCAA (2-1)
1996-97	Georgia	23-9	10-6	3rd (SEC/East)	NCAA (0-1)

Six-Year Coaching Record: 123-62 (.665) overall; 79-43 (.648) in four seasons at Tulsa; 44-19 (.698) in two seasons at Georgia; 52-20 (.722) in Missouri Valley Conference; 19-13 (.594) in Southeastern Conference; 5-3 (.625) in MVC Tournament; 4-2 (.667) in SEC Tournament; 6-4 (.600) in NCAA Tournament.

NORM STEWART

Missouri '56
Shelbyville, MO

UPI national coach of the year in 1982 and 1994. Also named by AP in 1994. . . . Coach of six Big Eight Tournament champions—1978, 1982, 1987, 1989, 1991 and 1993. . . . Winningest coach in Big Eight Conference history. . . . Coach of NCAA Division II fourth-place team in 1964. . . . Assistant coach at Missouri under Sparky Stalcup for four seasons from 1958-'61.

Season	School	Overall	League	Finish	Postseason
1961-62	N. Iowa	19-5	8-4	T1st (N. Central)	DNP
1962-63	N. Iowa	15-8	8-4	2nd (N. Central)	DNP
1963-64	N. Iowa	23-4	11-1	1st (N. Central)	NCAA DII (3-2)
1964-65	N. Iowa	16-7	8-4	2nd (N. Central)	DNP
1965-66	N. Iowa	13-7	9-3	2nd (N. Central)	DNP
1966-67	N. Iowa	11-11	6-6	T2nd (N. Central)	DNP
1967-68	Missouri	10-16	5-9	6th (Big Eight)	DNP
1968-69	Missouri	14-11	7-7	5th (Big Eight)	DNP
1969-70	Missouri	15-11	7-7	T3rd (Big Eight)	DNP
1970-71	Missouri	17-9	9-5	T2nd (Big Eight)	DNP
1971-72	Missouri	21-6	10-4	2nd (Big Eight)	NIT (0-1)
1972-73	Missouri	21-6	9-5	T2nd (Big Eight)	NIT (0-1)
1973-74	Missouri	12-14	3-11	T7th (Big Eight)	DNP
1974-75	Missouri	18-9	9-5	3rd (Big Eight)	NCIT (0-1)
1975-76	Missouri	26-5	12-2	1st (Big Eight)	NCAA (0-1)
1976-77	Missouri	21-8	9-5	T2nd (Big Eight)	DNP
1977-78	Missouri	14-16	4-10	T6th (Big Eight)	NCAA (0-1)
1978-79	Missouri	13-15	8-6	T2nd (Big Eight)	DNP
1979-80	Missouri	25-6	11-3	1st (Big Eight)	NCAA (2-1)
1980-81	Missouri	22-10	10-4	1st (Big Eight)	NCAA (0-1)
1981-82	Missouri	27-4	12-2	1st (Big Eight)	NCAA (1-1)
1982-83	Missouri	26-8	12-2	1st (Big Eight)	NCAA (0-1)
1983-84	Missouri	16-14	5-9	6th (Big Eight)	DNP
1984-85	Missouri	18-14	7-7	T3rd (Big Eight)	NIT (0-1)
1985-86	Missouri	21-14	8-6	T3rd (Big Eight)	NCAA (0-1)
1986-87	Missouri	24-10	11-3	1st (Big Eight)	NCAA (0-1)
1987-88	Missouri	19-11	7-7	4th (Big Eight)	NCAA (0-1)
1988-89	Missouri	29-8	10-4	2nd (Big Eight)	NCAA (2-1)
1989-90	Missouri	26-6	12-2	1st (Big Eight)	NCAA (0-1)
1990-91	Missouri	20-10	8-6	4th (Big Eight)	Probation
1991-92	Missouri	21-9	8-6	T2nd (Big Eight)	NCAA (1-1)
1992-93	Missouri	19-14	5-9	7th (Big Eight)	NCAA (0-1)
1993-94	Missouri	28-4	14-0	1st (Big Eight)	NCAA (3-1)
1994-95	Missouri	20-9	8-6	4th (Big Eight)	NCAA (1-1)
1995-96	Missouri	18-15	6-8	6th (Big Eight)	NIT (1-1)
1996-97	Missouri	16-17	5-11	5th (Big 12/N)	DNP

36-Year Coaching Record: 694-351 (.664) overall; 97-42 (.698) in six years at Northern Iowa; 597-309 (.659) in first 30 years at Missouri; 50-22 (.694) in North Central Conference; 246-160 (.606) in Big Eight Conference; 5-11 (.313) in Big 12 Conference; 29-14 (.674) in Big Eight Tournament; 3-1 (.750) in Big 12 Tournament; 12-15 (.444) in NCAA Division I Tournament; 1-4 (.200) in NIT; 0-1 in National Commissioners Invitational Tournament; 3-2 (.600) in NCAA Division II Tournament.

EDDIE SUTTON

Oklahoma State '58
Bucklin, KS

Named national coach of the year by USBWA in 1977, by AP and UPI in 1978, and by AP and NABC in 1986. . . . Coach of two NCAA Tournament Final Four teams—1978 with Arkansas (3rd) and 1995 with Oklahoma State (tied for third). . . . Only coach to guide four different colleges to the NCAA playoffs. . . . Coach of six conference tournament champions—SWC (1977, 1979 and 1982 with Arkansas), SEC (1986 and 1988 with Kentucky) and Big Eight (1995 with Oklahoma State). . . . Assistant coach at Oklahoma State under Henry Iba for one season (1958-59). . . . Coach at Southern Idaho Junior College for three seasons from 1967-'69.

Season	School	Overall	League	Finish	Postseason
1969-70	Creighton	15-10	—	—	DNP
1970-71	Creighton	14-11	—	—	DNP
1971-72	Creighton	15-11	—	—	DNP
1972-73	Creighton	15-12	—	—	DNP
1973-74	Creighton	23-6	—	—	NCAA (2-1)

Season	School	Overall	League	Finish	Postseason
1974-75	Arkansas	17-9	11-3	T2nd (SWC)	DNP
1975-76	Arkansas	19-9	9-7	4th (SWC)	DNP
1976-77	Arkansas	26-2	16-0	1st (SWC)	NCAA (0-1)
1977-78	Arkansas	32-4	14-2	T1st (SWC)	NCAA (4-1)
1978-79	Arkansas	25-5	13-3	T1st (SWC)	NCAA (2-1)
1979-80	Arkansas	21-8	13-3	2nd (SWC)	NCAA (0-1)
1980-81	Arkansas	24-8	13-3	1st (SWC)	NCAA (2-1)
1981-82	Arkansas	23-6	12-4	1st (SWC)	NCAA (0-1)
1982-83	Arkansas	26-4	14-2	2nd (SWC)	NCAA (1-1)
1983-84	Arkansas	25-7	14-2	2nd (SWC)	NCAA (0-1)
1984-85	Arkansas	22-13	10-6	T2nd (SWC)	NCAA (1-1)
1985-86	Kentucky	32-4	17-1	1st (SEC)	NCAA (3-1)
1986-87	Kentucky	18-11	10-8	T3rd (SEC)	NCAA (1-1)
1987-88	Kentucky	27-6	13-5	1st (SEC)	NCAA (2-1)
1988-89	Kentucky	13-19	8-10	T6th (SEC)	DNP
1990-91	Okla. State	24-8	10-4	T1st (Big Eight)	NCAA (2-1)
1991-92	Okla. State	28-8	8-6	T2nd (Big Eight)	NCAA (1-1)
1992-93	Okla. State	20-9	8-6	T2nd (Big Eight)	NCAA (1-1)
1993-94	Okla. State	24-10	10-4	2nd (Big Eight)	NCAA (1-1)
1994-95	Okla. State	27-10	10-4	2nd (Big Eight)	NCAA (4-1)
1995-96	Okla. State	17-10	7-7	T4th (Big Eight)	DNP
1996-97	Okla. State	19-13	7-9	4th (Big 12/S)	NIT (1-1)

27-Year Coaching Record: 591-233 (.717) overall; 82-50 (.621) in five years at Creighton; 260-75 (.776) in 11 years at Arkansas; 90-40 (.692) in four years at Kentucky; 159-68 (.700) in first seven years at Oklahoma State; 139-35 (.799) in Southwest Conference; 48-24 (.667) in Southeastern Conference; 53-31 (.631) in Big Eight Conference; 7-9 (.438) in Big 12 Conference; 13-7 (.650) in SWC Tournament; 6-2 (.750) in SEC Tournament; 8-5 (.615) in Big Eight Tournament; 1-1 (.500) in Big 12 Tournament; 27-18 (.600) in NCAA Tournament; 1-1 (.500) in NIT.

JERRY TARKANIAN

Fresno State '55
Pasadena, CA

UPI national coach of the year in 1983. . . . Coach of 1990 NCAA champion. . . . Reached NCAA Final Four four times in 15 years from 1977-91. . . . Compiled highest career winning percentage in Division I history. . . . Coach of seven Big West Tournament champions—1983, 1985, 1986, 1987, 1989, 1990 and 1991. . . . Compiled a 9-11 record in brief stint with NBA's San Antonio Spurs at the start of 1992-93 season. . . . Compiled a 212-26 (.891) record in seven seasons as coach at two community colleges in California.

Season	School	Overall	League	Finish	Postseason
1968-69	L. Beach St.	23-3	11-1	1st (CCAA)	DNP
1969-70	L. Beach St.	24-5	10-0	1st (PCAA)	NCAA (1-2)
1970-71	L. Beach St.	24-5	10-0	1st (PCAA)	NCAA (2-1)
1971-72	L. Beach St.	25-4	10-2	1st (PCAA)	NCAA (2-1)
1972-73	L. Beach St.	26-3	10-2	1st (PCAA)	NCAA (2-1)
1973-74	UNLV	20-6	10-4	3rd (WCAC)	DNP
1974-75	UNLV	24-5	13-1	1st (WCAC)	NCAA (2-1)
1975-76	UNLV	29-2	—	—	NCAA (1-1)
1976 77	UNLV	29-3	—	—	NCAA (4-1)
1977-78	UNLV	20-8	—	—	Probation
1978-79	UNLV	21-8	—	—	Probation
1979-80	UNLV	23-9	—	—	NIT (3-2)
1980-81	UNLV	16-12	—	—	DNP
1981-82	UNLV	20-10	—	—	NIT (1-1)
1982-83	UNLV	28-3	15-1	1st (PCAA)	NCAA (0-1)
1983-84	UNLV	29-6	16-2	1st (PCAA)	NCAA (2-1)
1984-85	UNLV	28-4	17-1	1st (PCAA)	NCAA (1-1)
1985-86	UNLV	33-5	16-2	1st (PCAA)	NCAA (1-1)
1986-87	UNLV	37-2	18-0	1st (PCAA)	NCAA (4-1)
1987-88	UNLV	28-6	15-3	1st (PCAA)	NCAA (1-1)
1988-89	UNLV	29-8	16-2	1st (Big West)	NCAA (3-1)
1989-90	UNLV	35-5	16-2	T1st (Big West)	NCAA (6-0)
1990-91	UNLV	34-1	18-0	1st (Big West)	NCAA (4-1)
1991-92	UNLV	26-2	18-0	1st (Big West)	Probation
1995-96	Fresno St.	22-11	13-5	3rd (WAC)	NIT (2-1)
1996-97	Fresno St.	20-12	12-4	T1st (WAC/Pacific)	NIT (0-1)

26-Year College Coaching Record: 673-148 (.820) overall; 122-20 (.859) in five years at Long Beach State; 509-105 (.829) in 19 years at UNLV; 42-23 (.646) in first two years at Fresno State; 23-5 (.821) in West Coast Athletic Conference; 205-17 (.923) in Pacific Coast Athletic Association/Big West Conference; 25-9 (.735) in Western Athletic Conference; 24-2 (.923) in Big West Tournament; 1-2 (.333) in WAC Tournament; 37-16 (.698) in NCAA Tournament; 6-5 (.545) in NIT.

TARK ALERT

If Fresno State competes in 30 games in the 1996-97 season, the Bulldogs need to win at least 24 contests to keep Jerry Tarkanian atop the list of winningest coaches by percentage in NCAA history. Here are the coaches with the five highest winning percentages:

COACH,	SCHOOLS	RECORD	PCT.
1. **Jerry Tarkanian,**	Long Beach St./UNLV/Fresno St.	653-136	.828

The only year he failed to win at least 20 games was 1980-81 (16-12 mark).

2. **Clair Bee,**	Rider/Long Island University	412-87	.826

Lost more than five games in a season just once in his first 14 years.

3. **Adolph Rupp,**	Kentucky	876-190	.822

Never compiled a losing won-loss record in his 41 seasons as a head coach.

4. **John Wooden,**	Indiana State/UCLA	664-162	.804

Worst mark was 14-12 in 1959-60 before winning 10 NCAA titles in 12 years.

5. **Dean Smith,**	North Carolina	851-247	.775

Won at least 25 games an amazing 21 seasons with a high of 34 in 1992-93.

JOHN THOMPSON

Providence '64
Washington, D.C.

Named national coach of year by USBWA in 1982, by the NABC in 1985 and by UPI in 1987. . . . Reached NCAA Final Four three times—1982 (runner-up), 1984 (champion) and 1985 (runner-up). . . . Coach of two NIT semifinalists—1978 (fourth) and 1993 (runner-up). . . . Coach of six Big East Conference Tournament champions—1980, 1982, 1984, 1985, 1987 and 1989. . . . U.S. Olympic head coach in 1988 and assistant coach in 1976.

Season	School	Overall	League	Finish	Postseason
1972-73	Georgetwn.	12-15	—	—	DNP
1973-74	Georgetwn.	13-13	—	—	DNP
1974-75	Georgetwn.	18-10	—	—	NCAA (0-1)
1975-76	Georgetwn.	21-7	—	—	NCAA (0-1)
1976-77	Georgetwn.	19-9	—	—	NIT (0-1)
1977-78	Georgetwn.	23-8	—	—	NIT (2-2)
1978-79	Georgetwn.	24-5	—	—	NCAA (0-1)
1979-80	Georgetwn.	26-6	5-1	T1st (Big East)	NCAA (2-1)
1980-81	Georgetwn.	20-12	9-5	2nd (Big East)	NCAA (0-1)
1981-82	Georgetwn.	30-7	10-4	2nd (Big East)	NCAA (4-1)
1982-83	Georgetwn.	22-10	11-5	4th (Big East)	NCAA (1-1)
1983-84	Georgetwn.	34-3	14-2	1st (Big East)	NCAA (5-0)
1984-85	Georgetwn.	35-3	14-2	2nd (Big East)	NCAA (5-1)
1985-86	Georgetwn.	24-8	11-5	3rd (Big East)	NCAA (1-1)
1986-87	Georgetwn.	29-5	12-4	T1st (Big East)	NCAA (3-1)
1987-88	Georgetwn.	20-10	9-7	T3rd (Big East)	NCAA (1-1)
1988-89	Georgetwn.	29-5	13-3	1st (Big East)	NCAA (3-1)
1989-90	Georgetwn.	24-7	11-5	3rd (Big East)	NCAA (1-1)
1990-91	Georgetwn.	19-13	8-8	6th (Big East)	NCAA (1-1)
1991-92	Georgetwn.	22-10	12-6	T1st (Big East)	NCAA (1-1)
1992-93	Georgetwn.	20-13	8-10	8th (Big East)	NIT (4-1)
1993-94	Georgetwn.	19-12	10-8	T4th (Big East)	NCAA (1-1)
1994-95	Georgetwn.	21-10	11-7	4th (Big East)	NCAA (2-1)
1995-96	Georgetwn.	29-8	13-5	1st (Big East 7)	NCAA (3-1)
1996-97	Georgetwn.	20-10	11-7	1st (Big East 7)	NCAA (0-1)

25-Year Coaching Record: 573-218 (.724) at Georgetown; 192-94 (.671) in Big East Conference; 32-12 (.727) in Big East Tournament; 34-19 (.642) in NCAA Tournament; 6-4 (.600) in NIT.

BILLY TUBBS

Lamar '58
Tulsa, OK

Directed Oklahoma to 12 consecutive 20-win seasons (1982-93), a Big Eight best. . . . Took the Sooners to postseason play his last 13 years with them (9 NCAA/4 NIT) before moving to TCU. . . . His '88 OU squad advanced to the national championship game against Kansas. . . . OU teams advanced to NIT semifinals in 1982 (T3rd) and 1991 (2nd). . . . Led Oklahoma to three Big Eight Tournament championships—1985, 1988 and 1990.

Season	School	Overall	League	Finish	Postseason
1971-72	Sthwestn.	12-14	—	—	DNP
1972-73	Sthwestn.	19-8	9-3	2nd (Big State)	DNP
1976-77	Lamar	12-17	6-4	3rd (Southland)	DNP
1977-78	Lamar	18-9	8-2	T1st (Southland)	DNP
1978-79	Lamar	23-9	8-1	1st (Southland)	NCAA (1-1)
1979-80	Lamar	22-11	8-2	1st (Southland)	NCAA (2-1)
1980-81	Oklahoma	9-18	4-10	7th (Big Eight)	DNP
1981-82	Oklahoma	22-11	8-6	3rd (Big Eight)	NIT (3-1)
1982-83	Oklahoma	24-9	10-4	2nd (Big Eight)	NCAA (1-1)
1983-84	Oklahoma	29-5	13-1	1st (Big Eight)	NCAA (3-1)
1984-85	Oklahoma	31-6	13-1	1st (Big Eight)	NCAA (3-1)
1985-86	Oklahoma	26-9	8-6	T3rd (Big Eight)	NCAA (2-1)
1986-87	Oklahoma	24-10	9-5	T2nd (Big Eight)	NCAA (2-1)
1987-88	Oklahoma	35-4	12-2	1st (Big Eight)	NCAA (5-1)
1988-89	Oklahoma	30-6	12-2	1st (Big Eight)	NCAA (2-1)
1989-90	Oklahoma	27-5	11-3	2nd (Big Eight)	NCAA (1-1)
1990-91	Oklahoma	20-15	5-9	T6th (Big Eight)	NIT (4-1)
1991-92	Oklahoma	21-9	8-6	T2nd (Big Eight)	NCAA (0-1)
1992-93	Oklahoma	20-12	7-7	T5th (Big Eight)	NIT (1-1)
1993-94	Oklahoma	15-13	6-8	5th (Big Eight)	NIT (0-1)
1994-95	TCU	16-11	8-6	T3rd (SWC)	DNP
1995-96	TCU	15-15	6-8	4th (SWC)	DNP
1996-97	TCU	22-13	7-9	T4th (WAC/Mtn.)	NIT (1-1)

23-Year Coaching Record: 492-239 (.673) overall; 31-22 (.585) in two years at Southwestern (Tex.); 75-46 (.620) in four years at Lamar; 333-132 (.716) in 14 years at Oklahoma; 53-39 (.576) in first three years at Texas Christian; 30-9 (.769) in Southland Conference; 126-70 (.643) in Big Eight Conference; 14-14 (.500) in Southwest Conference; 7-9 (.438) in Western Athletic Conference; 18-11 (.621) in Big Eight Tournament; 0-2 (.000) in SWC Tournament; 3-1 (.750) in WAC Tournament; 18-11 (.621) in NCAA Tournament; 9-5 (.643) in NIT.

GARY WILLIAMS

Maryland '67
Collingsworth, MD

Coach of 1988 NIT runner-up. . . . Assistant coach at Maryland (freshman team), Lafayette and Boston College under Tom Davis.

Season	School	Overall	League	Finish	Postseason
1978-79	American	14-13	7-4	4th (East Coast)	DNP
1979-80	American	13-14	5-6	5th (East Coast)	DNP
1980-81	American	24-6	11-0	1st (East Coast)	NIT (0-1)
1981-82	American	21-9	8-3	3rd (East Coast)	NIT (0-1)
1982-83	Bos. Coll.	25-7	12-4	T1st (Big East)	NCAA (1-1)
1983-84	Bos. Coll.	18-12	8-8	4th (Big East)	NIT (1-1)
1984-85	Bos. Coll.	20-11	7-9	6th (Big East)	NCAA (2-1)
1985-86	Bos. Coll.	13-15	4-12	7th (Big East)	DNP
1986-87	Ohio State	20-13	9-9	6th (Big Ten)	NCAA (1-1)
1987-88	Ohio State	20-13	9-9	6th (Big Ten)	NIT (4-1)
1988-89	Ohio State	19-15	6-12	8th (Big Ten)	NIT (2-1)
1989-90	Maryland	19-14	6-8	T5th (ACC)	NIT (1-1)
1990-91	Maryland	16-12	5-9	7th (ACC)	DNP
1991-92	Maryland	14-14	5-11	8th (ACC)	DNP
1992-93	Maryland	12-16	2-14	8th (ACC)	DNP
1993-94	Maryland	18-12	8-8	T4th (ACC)	NCAA (2-1)
1994-95	Maryland	26-8	12-4	T1st (ACC)	NCAA (2-1)
1995-96	Maryland	17-13	8-8	T4th (ACC)	NCAA (0-1)
1996-97	Maryland	21-11	9-7	T4th (ACC)	NCAA (2-1)

19-Year Coaching Record: 350-229 (.604) overall; 72-42 (.631) in four years at American; 76-45 (.628) in four years at Boston College; 59-41 (.590) in three years at Ohio State; 143-101 (.586) in first eight years at Maryland; 31-13 (.705) in East Coast Conference; 31-33 (.484) in Big East Conference; 24-30 (.444) in Big Ten Conference; 55-69 (.444) in Atlantic Coast Conference; 4-4 (.500) in ECC Tournament; 2-4 (.333) in Big East Tournament; 5-7 (.417) in ACC Tournament; 8-7 (.533) in NCAA Tournament; 8-6 (.571) in NIT.

ROY WILLIAMS

North Carolina '72
Skyland, NC

USBWA national coach of the year in 1990. . . . Reached NCAA Final Four two times—1991 (runner-up) and 1993 (tied for third). . . . Coach of 1992 Big Eight Tournament champion. . . . Assistant coach at North Carolina under Dean Smith for 10 seasons from 1979-88.

Season	School	Overall	League	Finish	Postseason
1988-89	Kansas	19-12	6-8	6th (Big Eight)	Probation
1989-90	Kansas	30-5	11-3	T2nd (Big Eight)	NCAA (1-1)
1990-91	Kansas	27-8	10-4	T1st (Big Eight)	NCAA (5-1)
1991-92	Kansas	27-5	11-3	1st (Big Eight)	NCAA (1-1)
1992-93	Kansas	29-7	11-3	1st (Big Eight)	NCAA (4-1)
1993-94	Kansas	27-8	9-5	3rd (Big Eight)	NCAA (2-1)
1994-95	Kansas	25-6	11-3	1st (Big Eight)	NCAA (2-1)
1995-96	Kansas	29-5	12-2	1st (Big Eight)	NCAA (3-1)
1996-97	Kansas	34-2	15-1	1st (Big 12/N)	NCAA (2-1)

Nine-Year Coaching Record: 247-58 (.810) at Kansas; 81-31 (.723) in Big Eight Conference; 15-1 (.938) in Big 12 Conference; 10-7 (.588) in Big Eight Tournament; 3-0 (1.000) in Big 12 Tournament; 20-8 (.714) in NCAA Tournament.

STERLING START

Kansas' Roy Williams (213-56, .792) tied former North Carolina State coach Everett Case (1947-54) for most victories in a head coach's first eight seasons. Williams needs to guide the Jayhawks to 28 triumphs in the 1996-97 campaign to keep pace with Case. Here is a list of Case and the three other coaches before Williams to register more than 200 wins through their first nine seasons:

COACH, TEAM	SEASONS	W.	L.	PCT.
Everett Case, N.C. State	1947-55	241	56	.811
Jerry Tarkanian, Long Beach St./UNLV	1969-77	224	36	.862
Denny Crum, Louisville	1972-80	219	55	.799
Jim Boeheim, Syracuse	1977-85	204	71	.742

COACHING RECORDS IN NATIONAL POSTSEASON COMPETITION

(Minimum of 20 tournament games through 1997)

COACH	APP.	NCAA W-L	PCT.	APP.	NIT W-L	PCT.	APP.	OVERALL W-L	PCT.
1. John Wooden	16	47-10	.825	—	—	—	16	47-10	.825
2. Steve Fisher	7	20-6	.769	2	5-1	.833	9	25-7	.781
3. Mike Krzyzewski	13	40-11	.784	2	2-2	.500	15	42-13	.764
4. Larry Brown	7	19-6	.760	—	—	—	7	19-6	.760
5. Rick Pitino	8	26-7	.788	2	2-2	.500	10	28-9	.757
6. Al McGuire	9	20-9	.690	2	7-1	.875	11	27-10	.730
7. Roy Williams	8	20-8	.714	—	—	—	8	20-8	.714
8. Joe B. Hall	10	20-9	.690	2	4-1	.800	12	24-10	.706
9. Dean Smith	27	65-27	.707	4	7-3	.700	31	72-30	.706
10. Bob Knight*	21	40-18	.690	7	15-8	.652	29	58-26	.690
11. Nolan Richardson	12	24-11	.686	4	9-4	.692	16	33-15	.688
12. Lee Rose	2	8-3	.727	5	9-5	.643	7	17-8	.680
13. Jerry Tarkanian	16	37-16	.698	4	6-5	.545	20	43-21	.672
14. Bill E. Foster	3	6-3	.667	4	8-4	.667	7	14-7	.667
15. Jim Calhoun	11	16-11	.593	4	11-3	.786	15	27-14	.659
16. Tom Blackburn	1	1-1	.500	10	20-10	.667	11	21-11	.656
17. Joe Lapchick	1	0-1	.000	12	21-10	.677	13	21-11	.656
18. Joe Mullaney	3	2-3	.400	6	13-5	.722	9	15-8	.652
19. Denny Crum	21	42-21	.667	3	4-4	.500	24	46-25	.648
20. Rick Majerus	6	10-6	.583	4	8-4	.667	10	18-10	.643
21. John Calipari	5	11-5	.688	2	3-3	.500	7	14-8	.636
22. John Thompson	20	34-19	.642	3	6-4	.600	23	40-23	.635
23. Clem Haskins	7	11-7	.611	4	6-3	.667	11	17-10	.630
24. Billy Tubbs	11	18-11	.621	5	9-5	.643	16	27-16	.628
25. Adolph Rupp	20	30-18	.625	5	7-4	.636	25	37-22	.627
26. Rollie Massimino	11	20-10	.667	5	5-5	.500	16	25-15	.625
27. Jim Valvano	9	15-8	.652	1	0-1	.000	10	15-9	.625
28. Terry Holland	10	15-10	.600	5	8-4	.667	15	23-14	.622
29. Forddy Anderson	4	9-5	.643	2	4-3	.571	6	13-8	.619
30. Jim Boeheim	17	27-17	.614	3	5-3	.625	20	32-20	.615
31. Lute Olson	18	28-18	.609	..	.....	....	18	28-18	.609
32. Norman Sloan	6	8-5	.615	5	9-6	.600	11	17-11	.607
33. P.J. Carlesimo	6	12-6	.667	2	0-2	.000	8	12-8	.600
34. Jack Hartman*	7	11-7	.611	3	4-2	.667	10	15-10	.600
35. Hank Iba	8	15-7	.682	4	3-5	.375	12	18-12	.600
36. Eddie Sutton	18	27-18	.600	1	1-1	.500	19	28-19	.596
37. Bill Frieder	6	8-6	.571	6	8-5	.615	12	16-11	.593
38. Frank McGuire	8	14-8	.636	6	6-6	.500	14	20-14	.588
39. Danny Nee	6	1-6	.143	5	13-4	.765	11	14-10	.583
40. Guy Lewis	14	26-18	.591	3	3-3	.500	17	29-21	.580
41. Tom Davis	10	16-10	.615	4	3-4	.429	14	19-14	.576
42. Jud Heathcote	10	15-10	.600	3	4-4	.500	13	19-14	.576
43. Harry Litwack	6	7-6	.538	7	9-6	.600	13	16-12	.571
44. Eldon Miller	6	5-6	.455	3	7-3	.700	9	12-9	.571
45. Dudey Moore	1	1-1	.500	7	11-8	.579	8	12-9	.571
46. Bob Huggins	7	12-7	.632	4	2-4	.333	11	14-11	.560
47. Don DeVoe	9	5-9	.357	4	10-3	.769	13	15-12	.556
48. Don Donoher	8	11-10	.524	7	9-6	.600	15	20-16	.556
49. C.M. Newton	4	3-4	.429	6	12-8	.600	10	15-12	.556
50. Gene Keady	14	11-14	.440	3	10-3	.769	17	21-17	.553

11

FASCINATION
WITH FRESHMEN

Fresh men. As in new. Just like the more than one thousand male teenagers who attempt each season to survive in the dog-eat-dog world of major-college basketball less than one year after being among the top dogs at the high school level. It is, for many of the yearlings, a situation where the "rookies" are thrown in the Division I ocean and asked to sink or swim.

The 1997-98 season marks the 25th anniversary of freshmen playing varsity college basketball although they also were used in wartime years during the 1940s and early '50s because of manpower shortages (see 1951-52 highlights), and at earlier times when eligibility requirements were lax.

Prior to the 1972-73 campaign, colleges fielded freshman teams that required extra scholarships and operating expenses. Consequently, the introduction of freshman eligibility has trimmed costs and, of course, given eager coaches instant access to high school phenoms who are immediately placed under the glare of the spotlight to help keep elite programs on a pedestal or possibly give struggling teams a chance to climb the ladder of success.

Here is a summary of the sudden impact of freshmen:

TOP 10 FRESHMAN SEASONS NATIONALLY

(From 1972-73 through 1996-97)

1. Bernard King, F, Tennessee (1974-75)
2. Wayman Tisdale, C, Oklahoma (1982-83)
3. Robert Parish, C, Centenary (1972-73)
4. Chris Jackson, G, Louisiana State (1988-89)
5. Kenny Anderson, G, Georgia Tech (1989-90)
6. Jeff Ruland, C, Iona (1977-78)
7. Jacky Dorscy, F, Georgia (1974-75)
8. Mark Aguirre, F, DePaul (1978-79)
9. Keith Lee, C, Memphis State (1981-82)
10. Magic Johnson, G, Michigan State (1977-78)

NATIONAL ALL-FRESHMAN TEAMS

(From 1972-73 through 1996-97)

FIRST TEAM

Kenny Anderson, Georgia Tech
1989-90   20.6 ppg   5.5 rpg   8.1 apg
Only freshman ever to score more than 20 points in four straight NCAA playoff games.

Chris Jackson, LSU
1988-89   30.2 ppg   4.1 apg   81.5 FT%

Exploded for 53 points vs. Florida and 55 vs. Ole Miss en route to setting NCAA freshman scoring records with 965 points and 30.2 average. Consensus SEC player of the year was an AP and USBWA first-team All-America.

Bernard King, Tennessee
1974-75   26.4 ppg   12.3 rpg   62.2 FG%
No freshman has matched his overall statistical figures.

Robert Parish, Centenary
1972-73   23 ppg   18.7 rpg   57.9 FG%
Scored school-record 50 points vs. Lamar. Collected 31 points and 33 rebounds vs. Southern Mississippi and 38 points and 29 rebounds vs. Texas-Arlington.

Wayman Tisdale, Oklahoma
1982-83   24.5 ppg   10.3 rpg   58.0 FG%
NCAA consensus first-team All-America. Big Eight Conference player of the year broke Wilt Chamberlain's league scoring record with 810 points, including 46 vs. Iowa State.

SECOND TEAM

Mark Aguirre, DePaul
1978-79   24 ppg   7.6 rpg   52.0 FG%
Top freshman scorer in the nation broke the Blue Demons' scoring record with 767 points. He had a 29-point, eight-rebound performance vs. UCLA in his college debut and finished the season by being named to the All-Final Four team.

Jacky Dorsey, Georgia
1974-75   25.8 ppg   11.8 rpg
His freshman scoring average remains an all-time school single-season record.

Magic Johnson, Michigan State
1977-78   17 ppg   7.9 rpg   7.4 apg
Led the Big Ten Conference in league play in assists (6.8 apg), tied for third in scoring (19.8 ppg) and finished sixth in rebounding (8.2 rpg) to help the Spartans go from 10-17 the previous year to 25-5 and capture the Big Ten title.

Keith Lee, Memphis State
1981-82   18.3 ppg   11 rpg   53.8 FG%

Led the Tigers in scoring, rebounding and blocked shots as they improved their record from 13-14 the previous season to 24-5. Set Metro Conference record with 11.5 rebounds per game in league competition.

Jeff Ruland, Iona
1977-78   22.3 ppg   12.8 rpg   59.4 FG%
Led the nation's freshmen in scoring, rebounding, and field-goal percentage despite being hampered by a sprained ankle suffered in the opening game of the season.

THIRD TEAM

Shareef Abdur-Rahim, Cal
1995-96   21.1 ppg   8.4 rpg   51.8 FG%
The first freshman ever to be named Pacific-10 Conference player of the year led the Bears in steals with 52. His best game overall was a 32-point, 18-rebound performance at Washington State.

Rickey Brown, Mississippi St.
1976-77   19.3 ppg   10.8 rpg   50.8 FG%
Converted a school-record 18 field goals in 22 attempts vs. Auburn en route to a Humphrey Coliseum-record (for an MSU player) 40-point outing.

Adrian Dantley, Notre Dame
1973-74   18.3 ppg   9.7 rpg   55.8 FG%
Led the Irish in free-throw shooting (82.6 percent) and was second on the team in scoring and rebounding. He had a 41-point outing vs. West Virginia. Notre Dame improved its record from 18-12 the previous season to 26-3.

Mark Macon, Temple
1987-88   20.6 ppg   5.6 rpg   2.9 apg
Scored in double figures in 33 of 34 games. Led the 32-2 Owls in scoring and was second in assists.

Mark Price, Georgia Tech
1982-83   20.3 ppg   4.3 apg   87.7 FT%
First freshman ever to lead the vaunted Atlantic Coast Conference in scoring. Also led the ACC in free-throw percentage and three-point field goals.

TOP FRESHMAN SEASONS BY CONFERENCE

AMERICA EAST: Eddie Benton, G, Vermont (1992-93)

ATLANTIC COAST: Kenny Anderson, G, Georgia Tech (1989-90)

ATLANTIC 10: Mark Macon, G, Temple (1987-88)

BIG EAST: Allen Iverson, G, Georgetown (1994-95)

BIG EIGHT: Wayman Tisdale, C, Oklahoma (1982-83)

BIG SKY: Steve Conner, G, Boise State (1974-75)

BIG SOUTH: Tony Dunkin, F, Coastal Carolina (1989-90)

BIG TEN: Magic Johnson, G, Michigan State (1977-78)

BIG 12: Eduardo Najera, F, Oklahoma (1996-97)

BIG WEST: Cliff Pondexter, C, Long Beach State (1973-74)

COLONIAL: Odell Hodge, C, Old Dominion (1992-93)

CONFERENCE USA: Nate Johnson, F, Louisville (1996-97)

EAST COAST: Michael Brooks, F, La Salle (1976-77)

GREAT MIDWEST: Lorenzen Wright, C, Memphis (1994-95)

INDEPENDENTS: Jeff Ruland, C, Iona (1977-78)

IVY LEAGUE: Butch Graves, G, Yale (1980-81)

METRO: Keith Lee, C, Memphis State (1981-82)

METRO ATLANTIC: Lionel Simmons, F, La Salle (1986-87)

MID-AMERICAN: Gary Trent, F, Ohio University (1992-93)

MID-CONTINENT: Tony Bennett, G, Wis.-Green Bay (1988-89)

MID-EASTERN ATHLETIC: Tom Davis, F, Delaware State (1987-88)

MIDWESTERN COLLEGIATE: Kenny Miller, C, Loyola of Chicago (1987-88)

MISSOURI VALLEY: Mitchell Anderson, F, Bradley (1978-79)

NORTHEAST: Chris McGuthrie, G, Mount St. Mary's (1992-93)

OHIO VALLEY: Fly Williams, G, Austin Peay (1972-73)

PACIFIC-10: Shareef Abdur-Rahim, F, California (1995-96)

PATRIOT LEAGUE: Adonal Foyle, C, Colgate (1994-95)

SOUTHEASTERN: Bernard King, F, Tennessee (1974-75)

SOUTHERN: Jonathan Moore, F, Furman (1976-77)

SOUTHLAND: Karl Malone, F, Louisiana Tech (1982-83)

SOUTHWEST: Ira Terrell, C, Southern Methodist (1972-73)

SOUTHWESTERN ATHLETIC: Harry Kelly, F, Texas Southern (1979-80)

SUN BELT: Jarvis Lang, C, UNC Charlotte (1990-91)

TRANS AMERICA ATHLETIC: Willie Jackson, F, Centenary (1980-81)

WEST COAST: Pete Padgett, C, Nevada-Reno (1972-73)

WESTERN ATHLETIC: Coniel Norman, G, Arizona (1972-73)

TOP FRESHMAN SEASONS IN MAJOR CONFERENCES

ACC

Mark Alarie, Duke

1982-83	13 ppg	6.5 rpg	81.3 FT%

Kenny Anderson, Georgia Tech

1989-90	20.6 ppg	5.5 rpg	8.1 apg

Clyde Austin, N.C. State

1976-77	12.2 ppg	5 apg

Gene Banks, Duke

1977-78	17.1 ppg	8.6 rpg	52.8 FG%

Adrian Branch, Maryland

1981-82	15.2 ppg	4.3 rpg

Skip Brown, Wake Forest

1973-74	13.2 ppg	2.7 rpg	3 apg

Junior Burrough, Virginia

1991-92	13.2 ppg	5.8 rpg

Randolph Childress, Wake Forest

1990-91	14 ppg

Bruce Dalrymple, Georgia Tech
1983-84   13.6 ppg   6.9 rpg

Brad Davis, Maryland
1974-75   12.6 ppg   3.3 rpg   4.6 apg   58.0 FG%

Walter Davis, North Carolina
1973-74   14.3 ppg   4.7 rpg

Johnny Dawkins, Duke
1982-83   18.1 ppg   4.1 rpg   4.8 apg

Harold Deane, Virginia
1993-94   12.3 ppg   3.5 rpg

Phil Ford, North Carolina
1974-75   16.4 ppg   5.2 apg   51.6 FG%

James Forrest, Georgia Tech
1991-92   13.3 ppg   6.4 rpg   50.9 FG%

Mike Gminski, Duke
1976-77   15.3 ppg   10.7 rpg   51.5 FG%

Rod Griffin, Wake Forest
1974-75   13.9 ppg   7.6 rpg

Tom Hammonds, Georgia Tech
1985-86   12.2 ppg   6.4 rpg   60.9 FG%

Grant Hill, Duke
1990-91   11.2 ppg   5.1 rpg

Steve Hood, Maryland
1986-87   14.2 ppg   3.9 rpg

Bobby Hurley, Duke
1989-90   8.8 ppg   7.6 apg

Marc Iavaroni, Virginia
1974-75   10.8 ppg   7.9 rpg

Sam Ivy, Wake Forest
1986-87   13.2 ppg   6.1 rpg   56.5 FG%

Albert King, Maryland
1977-78   13.6 ppg   6.7 rpg

Michael Jordan, N. Carolina
1981-82   13.5 ppg   4.4 rpg   53.4 FG%

Chris King, Wake Forest
1988-89   14.4 ppg   6.1 rpg   54.0 FG%

Jeff Lamp, Virginia
1977-78   17.3 ppg   4.4 rpg   84.4 FT%

John Lucas, Maryland
1972-73   14.2 ppg   5.9 apg   53.8 FG%

Greg Manning, Maryland
1977-78   12.1 ppg   57.2 FG%   85.2 FT%

Stephon Marbury, Ga. Tech
1995-96   18.9 ppg   4.5 apg

Jerrod Mustaf, Maryland
1988-89   14.3 ppg   7.8 rpg   52.0 FG%

Mike O'Koren, North Carolina
1976-77   13.9 ppg   6.6 rpg   57.7 FG%

Sam Perkins, North Carolina
1980-81   14.9 ppg   7.8 rpg   62.6 FG%

Mark Price, Georgia Tech
1982-83   20.3 ppg   4.3 apg   87.7 FT%

J.R. Reid, North Carolina
1986-87   14.7 ppg   7.4 rpg   58.4 FG%

Alvis Rogers, Wake Forest
1978-79   13.5 ppg   6.2 rpg

Rodney Rogers, Wake Forest
1990-91   16.3 ppg   7.9 rpg   57.0 FG%

Tree Rollins, Clemson
1973-74   12.4 ppg   12.2 rpg

John Salley, Georgia Tech
1982-83   11.5 ppg   5.7 rpg   50.2 FG%

Ralph Sampson, Virginia
1979-80   14.9 ppg   11.2 rpg   4.6 bpg, 54.7 FG%

Dennis Scott, Georgia Tech
1987-88   15.5 ppg   5 rpg   47.1 3FG%

Joe Smith, Maryland
1993-94   19.4 ppg   10.7 rpg   3.1 bpg

Jerry Stackhouse, N. Carolina
1993-94   12.2 ppg   5 rpg

Bryant Stith, Virginia
1988-89   15.5 ppg   6.5 rpg   54.8 FG%

Bob Sura, Florida State
1991-92   12.3 ppg   3.5 rpg

Wally Walker, Virginia
1972-73   13.7 ppg   6.8 rpg   56.3 FG%

Rasheed Wallace, N. Carolina
1993-94   9.5 ppg   6.6 rpg   1.8 bpg, 60.4 FG%

Hawkeye Whitney, N.C. State
1976-77   14.6 ppg   5.8 rpg   51.4 FG%

Brian Williams, Maryland*
1987-88   12.5 ppg   6 rpg   60.0 FG%

Buck Williams, Maryland
1978-79   10 ppg   10.8 rpg   58.3 FG%

Skip Wise, Clemson
1974-75   18.5 ppg   3.1 rpg

James Worthy, North Carolina
1979-80   12.5 ppg   7.4 rpg   58.7 FG%

Sharone Wright, Clemson
1991-92   12 ppg   8.1 rpg   2.3 bpg
*Brian Williams transferred to Arizona following the season.

ATLANTIC 10

Bruce Atkins, Duquesne
1978-79   13.8 ppg   9.8 rpg

Bernard Blunt, St. Joseph's
1990-91   18.8 ppg

Mike Boyd, West Virginia
1990-91   12.4 ppg   5.8 apg   2.1 spg

Chris Brooks, West Virginia
1987-88   12.6 ppg   5.8 rpg

Mike Brown, George Washington
1981-82   15.6 ppg   8.5 rpg

Marcus Camby, Massachusetts
1993-94   10.2 ppg   6.4 rpg   3.6 bpg

Sam Clancy, Pittsburgh
1977-78   14 ppg   12.1 rpg

Yinka Dare, George Washington
1992-93   12.2 ppg   10.3 rpg

Arthur Davis, St. Joseph's
1996-97   14.7 ppg   4.3 rpg

Edwin Green, Massachusetts
1980-81   14.3 ppg   7.7 rpg

Kenny Green, Rhode Island
1986-87   12.2 ppg   8.3 rpg   2.1 bpg

Alexander Koul, George Wash.
1994-95   12.8 ppg   6.6 rpg   63.2 FG%

Alvin Lott, St. Bonaventure
1983-84   12.7 ppg   4.4 apg   2.6 spg

Mark Macon, Temple
1987-88   20.6 ppg   5.6 rpg   2.9 apg

Jim McCoy, Massachusetts
1988-89   19.8 ppg   3.5 rpg

John Pinone, Villanova
1979-80   14.5 ppg   7.1 rpg   57.3 FG%

Antonio Reynolds-Dean, URI
1995-96   12.1 ppg   8.7 rpg   1.6 bpg

Donald Russell, Massachusetts
1981-82   16.4 ppg

Troy Webster, George Washington
1982-83   16.9 ppg

BIG EAST

Dana Barros, Boston College
1985-86   13.7 ppg   3.5 apg

Derrick Coleman, Syracuse
1986-87   11.9 ppg   8.8 rpg   56.0 FG%

Billy Curley, Boston College
1990-91   12.6 ppg   6.9 rpg   54.2 FG%

Terry Dehere, Seton Hall
1989-90   16.1 ppg   3.4 rpg

Steve Edwards, Miami (Fla.)
1992-93   15.9 ppg

Patrick Ewing, Georgetown
1981-82   12.7 ppg   7.5 rpg   63.1 FG%

Sleepy Floyd, Georgetown
1978-79   16.6 ppg   4.1 rpg   81.3 FT%

Richard Hamilton, Connecticut
1996-97   15.9 ppg

Othella Harrington, Georgetown
1992-93   16.8 ppg   8.8 rpg   57.3 FG%

Nadav Henefeld, Connecticut
1989-90   11.6 ppg   5.6 rpg   3.7 spg

Shaheen Holloway, Seton Hall
1996-97   17.3 ppg

Allen Iverson, Georgetown
1994-95   20.4 ppg   3.3 rpg   4.5 apg

Earl Kelley, Connecticut
1982-83   16.7 ppg

Felipe Lopez, St. John's
1994-95   17.8 ppg

Donyell Marshall, Connecticut
1991-92   11.1 ppg   6.1 rpg

Andre McCloud, Seton Hall
1982-83   16.6 ppg

Lawrence Moten, Syracuse
1991-92   18.2 ppg   6 rpg

Alonzo Mourning, Georgetown
1988-89   13.1 ppg   7.3 rpg   4.9 bpg   60.3 FG%

Chris Mullin, St. John's
1981-82   16.6 ppg   3.2 rpg   53.4 FG%

Eric Murdock, Providence
1987-88   10.7 ppg   3 rpg   3 apg   3.2 spg

Billy Owens, Syracuse
1988-89   13 ppg   6.9 rpg   3.1 apg

Scoonie Penn, Boston College
1995-96   13.2 ppg   3.4 rpg   3.5 apg

Ed Pinckney, Villanova
1981-82   14.2 ppg   7.8 rpg   64.0 FG%

David Russell, St. John's
1979-80   10.8 ppg   5.5 rpg   62.4 FG%

Malik Sealy, St. John's
1988-89   12.9 ppg   6.4 rpg

Charles Smith, Pittsburgh
1984-85   15 ppg   8 rpg   50.2 FG%

Tim Thomas, Villanova
1996-97   16.9 ppg

Pearl Washington, Syracuse
1983-84   14.4 ppg   6.2 apg   2.4 spg

David Wingate, Georgetown
1982-83   12 ppg   3 rpg

BIG EIGHT

Alvan Adams, Oklahoma
1972-73   22.1 ppg   13.2 rpg   54.7 FG%

Chauncey Billups, Colorado
1995-96   17.9 ppg   6.3 rpg   5.5 apg   86.1 FT%

Rolando Blackman, Kansas St.
1977-78   10.9 ppg   6.5 rpg

Kerry Boagni, Kansas*
1982-83   14.1 ppg   4.7 rpg

Donnie Boyce, Colorado
1991-92   14.9 ppg   4.8 rpg   3.1 apg

Matt Bullard, Colorado**
1985-86   12.7 ppg   6.4 rpg   60.4 FG%

Derrick Chievous, Missouri
1984-85   13.1 ppg   5.3 rpg   51.1 FG%

Matt Clark, Oklahoma State
1978-79   13.3 ppg   5.2 rpg

Norris Coleman, Kansas State
1985-86   21.8 ppg   8 rpg   51.8 FG%

Norm Cook, Kansas
1973-74   11.4 ppg   6.5 rpg

Jevon Crudup, Missouri
1990-91   12 ppg   7.1 rpg   52.6 FG%

Richard Dumas, Oklahoma State
1987-88   17.4 ppg   6.4 rpg   54.6 FG%

Mike Evans, Kansas State
1974-75   17 ppg   3.6 rpg   81.5 FT%

Jerry Fort, Nebraska
1972-73   14.5 ppg   4 rpg

Jeff Grayer, Iowa State
1984-85   12.2 ppg   6.5 rpg   52.9 FG%

Ron Harris, Iowa State
1980-81   13.7 ppg   5.9 rpg

Olus Holder, Oklahoma State
1974-75   11.1 ppg   7.2 rpg

Dave Hoppen, Nebraska
1982-83   13.9 ppg   5 rpg   52.4 FG%

Byron Houston, Oklahoma State
1988-89   13 ppg   8.4 rpg   58.3 FG%

Raef LaFrentz, Kansas
1994-95   11.4 ppg   7.5 rpg   53.4 FG%

Emmett Lewis, Colorado
1975-76   15 ppg

Danny Manning, Kansas
1984-85   14.6 ppg   7.6 rpg   56.6 FG%

Curtis Redding, Kansas St.***
1976-77   16.6 ppg   6.8 rpg   83.2 FT%

Doug Smith, Missouri
1987-88   11.3 ppg   6.6 rpg   50.3 FG%

Barry Stevens, Iowa State
1981-82   13 ppg   4.5 rpg

Steve Stipanovich, Missouri
1979-80   14.4 ppg   6.4 rpg   59.8 FG%

Kelly Thames, Missouri
1993-94   12.2 ppg   7.1 rpg   51.4 FG%

Wayman Tisdale, Oklahoma
1982-83   24.5 ppg   10.3 rpg   58.0 FG%

Dean Uthoff, Iowa State
1976-77   11.5 ppg   11.3 rpg

Darnell Valentine, Kansas
1977-78   13.5 ppg   2.8 rpg   4.5 apg

Steve Wallace, Missouri
1978-79   13.4 ppg

Jeff Webster, Oklahoma
1990-91   18.3 ppg   5.5 rpg   56.5 FG%

Corey Williams, Okla. State
1988-89   12.4 ppg   3.5 rpg

*Boagni transferred to Cal State Fullerton.
**Bullard transferred to Iowa.
***Redding transferred to St. John's.

BIG TEN

Steve Alford, Indiana
1983-84   15.5 ppg   91.3 FT%

Eric Anderson, Indiana
1988-89   11.9 ppg   6.1 rpg   54.5 FG%

Cory Blackwell, Wisconsin
1981-82   13.5 ppg   5.1 rpg

Quinn Buckner, Indiana
1972-73   10.8 ppg   4.8 rpg

Calbert Cheaney, Indiana
1989-90   17.1 ppg   4.6 rpg   57.2 FG%

Russell Cross, Purdue
1980-81   16.9 ppg   6.3 rpg   56.6 FG%

Jay Edwards, Indiana
1987-88   15.6 ppg   53.6 3FG%   90.8 FT%

Michael Finley, Wisconsin
1991-92   12.3 ppg   4.9 rpg

Kiwane Garris, Illinois
1993-94   15.9 ppg   3.5 rpg   3.8 apg

Gary Grant, Michigan
1984-85   12.9 ppg   4.7 apg   55.0 FG%

James Gregory, Wisconsin
1976-77   15.9 ppg   10 rpg

Rashard Griffith, Wisconsin
1993-94   13.9 ppg   8.5 rpg   53.8 FG%

Steve Grote, Michigan
1973-74   13 ppg

A.J. Guyton, Indiana
1996-97   13.8 ppg   3.3 rpg   4 apg

Juwan Howard, Michigan
1991-92   11.1 ppg   6.2 rpg

Phil Hubbard, Michigan
1975-76   15.1 ppg   11 rpg   54.6 FG%

Jim Jackson, Ohio State
1989-90   16.1 ppg   5.5 rpg   3.7 apg

Magic Johnson, Michigan State
1977-78   17 ppg   7.9 rpg   7.4 apg

Walter Jordan, Purdue
1974-75   14.1 ppg   7.3 rpg   51.9 FG%

Clark Kellogg, Ohio State
1979-80   11.6 ppg   8 rpg

Greg Kelser, Michigan State
1975-76   11.7 ppg   9.5 rpg   51.7 FG%

Ronnie Lester, Iowa
1976-77   13.4 ppg

Mike McGee, Michigan
1977-78   19.7 ppg   4.9 rpg

Kevin McHale, Minnesota
1976-77   12 ppg   8.1 rpg   55.2 FG%

Billy McKinney, Northwestern
1973-74   15.8 ppg

Cedric Neloms, Northwestern
1991-92   14.4 ppg

Sam Okey, Wisconsin
1995-96   13.2 ppg   6.8 rpg   3.1 apg

Shawn Respert, Michigan State
1991-92   15.8 ppg

Jalen Rose, Michigan
1991-92   17.6 ppg   4.3 rpg   4 apg

Brad Sellers, Wisconsin*
1981-82   14 ppg   9.4 rpg

Jess Settles, Iowa
1993-94   15.3 ppg   7.5 rpg   57.4 FG%

Scott Skiles, Michigan State
1982-83   12.5 ppg   4.9 apg   83.1 FT%

Deon Thomas, Illinois
1990-91   15.1 ppg   6.8 rpg   57.7 FG%

Isiah Thomas, Indiana
1979-80   14.6 ppg   4 rpg   5.5 apg   51.0 FG%

Eric Turner, Michigan
1981-82   14.7 ppg

Sam Vincent, Michigan State
1981-82   11.7 ppg

Chris Webber, Michigan
1991-92   15.5 ppg   10 rpg   55.6 FG%

Herb Williams, Ohio State
1977-78   16.7 ppg   11.4 rpg

Efrem Winters, Illinois
1982-83   12.4 ppg   6.9 rpg

Mike Woodson, Indiana
1976-77   18.5 ppg   52.1 FG%
*Sellers transferred to Ohio State.

COLONIAL

Vernon Butler, Navy
1982-83   11.6 ppg   10.2 rpg

Kent Culuko, James Madison
1991-92   13.6 ppg

William Davis, James Madison
1988-89   15.7 ppg   3.2 rpg

Gus Hill, East Carolina
1987-88   19.3 ppg   5.5 rpg

Odell Hodge, Old Dominion
1992-93   14.7 ppg   9.1 rpg   56.0 FG%

Lester Lyons, East Carolina
1990-91   17.5 ppg   3.3 rpg

Curtis McCants, George Mason
1993-94   14.6 ppg   4.6 apg

Johnny Newman, Richmond
1982-83   12.2 ppg   3.1 rpg   52.8 FG%

Thomas Roberts, William & Mary
1989-90   14 ppg   4.6 rpg

Kenny Sanders, George Mason
1985-86   17.9 ppg   7 rpg   52.2 FG%

Peter Woolfolk, Richmond
1984-85   9.8 ppg   6 rpg

IVY LEAGUE

Jerome Allen, Pennsylvania
1991-92   12.2 ppg   3.6 rpg   3.2 apg

John Bajusz, Cornell
1983-84   10.7 ppg   80.8 FT%

Jim Barton, Dartmouth
1985-86   13.6 ppg   2.8 rpg   94.2 FT%

Joe Carrabino, Harvard
1980-81   14.6 ppg   4.1 rpg

Butch Graves, Yale
1980-81   15.8 ppg

Ralph James, Harvard
1987-88   14.5 ppg   5.7 rpg

Steve Leondis, Yale
1979-80   15.9 ppg   5.5 rpg   3.4 apg   53.6 FG%

Kit Mueller, Princeton
1987-88   12.7 ppg   58.1 FG%

Ed Petersen, Yale
1988-89   16.4 ppg   3.8 apg

Mike Waitkus, Brown
1982-83   14 ppg   5.4 apg   1.8 spg   89.8 FT%

Carlos Williams, Brown
1989-90   11 ppg   8 rpg   57 FG%

METRO

Willie Becton, St. Louis*
1980-81   13.9 ppg   7.3 rpg

Bobby Beecher, Virginia Tech
1982-83   12.7 ppg   6.1 rpg   57 FG%   91.3 FG%

James Bradley, Memphis State
1976-77   15.3 ppg   8.7 rpg

Dell Curry, Virginia Tech
1982-83   14.5 ppg   3 rpg   3.3 apg

Ace Custis, Virginia Tech
1993-94   10.9 ppg   9.1 rpg   52.3 FG%

Andre Davis, UNC Charlotte
1992-93   13.5 ppg

Terry Dozier, South Carolina
1985-86   13.8 ppg   4.9 rpg

Pervis Ellison, Louisville
1985-86   13.1 ppg   8.2 rpg   55.4 FG%

Ricky Frazier, St. Louis**
1977-78   13.7 ppg

Sylvester Gray, Memphis State
1986-87   12.2 ppg   7.6 rpg   53.9 FG%

Darrell Griffith, Louisville
1976-77   12.8 ppg   3.8 rpg   50.2 FG%

Jerald Honeycutt, Tulane
1993-94   15.3 ppg   6.7 rpg

Roger McClendon, Cincinnati
1984-85   12.3 ppg   3.7 rpg   52.3 FG%

Elliot Perry, Memphis State
1987-88   13.1 ppg   3.5 rpg   4.1 apg

Anthony Reed, Tulane
1989-90   18.4 ppg   8.4 rpg   53.3 FG%

Ernest Smith, Memphis State
1988-89   12.9 ppg   4.4 rpg   56.2 FG%

LaBradford Smith, Louisville
1987-88   12.7 ppg   4.5 apg   90.5 FT%

Dale Solomon, Virginia Tech
1978-79   17.8 ppg   7.7 rpg   56.6 FG%

Paul Thompson, Tulane
1979-80   15 ppg   8.2 rpg

Samaki Walker, Louisville
1994-95   13.7 ppg   7.2 rpg   54.6 FG%

Clarence Weatherspoon, USM
1988-89   14.7 ppg   10.7 rpg   54.5 FG%

DeJuan Wheat, Louisville
1993-94   12.6 ppg   3.2 apg

John Williams, Tulane
1981-82   14.8 ppg   7.2 rpg   58.4 FG%

*Becton transferred to Memphis State.
**Frazier transferred to Missouri.

MID-AMERICAN

Jimmal Ball, Akron
1996-97   17.1 ppg

Kenny Battle, Northern Ill.*
1984-85   20.1 ppg   6.2 rpg   52.8 FG%

Dirk Dunbar, Central Mich.
1972-73   18.2 ppg

Ken Epperson, Toledo
1981-82   16.2 ppg   8.5 rpg

Paul Graham, Ohio Univ.
1985-86   15.9 ppg   4.7 rpg

Ron Harper, Miami of Ohio
1982-83   12.9 ppg   7 rpg

Trimill Haywood, Miami of Ohio
1986-87   17.1 ppg

Colin Irish, Bowling Green
1979-80   12.9 ppg   8.2 rpg

Dave Jamerson, Ohio Univ.
1985-86   14 ppg   3 rpg   57.5 FG%

Booker James, Western Michigan
1983-84   14.3 ppg

Tom Kilgore, Central Michigan
1994-95   18.9 ppg

Dan Majerle, Central Michigan
1984-85   18.6 ppg   6.7 rpg   56.8 FG%

Ray McCallum, Ball State
1979-80   16.5 ppg

Craig Michaclis, Miami of Ohio
1989-90   12.8 ppg

Anthony Stacey, Bowling Green
1995-96   16 ppg

Gary Trent, Ohio University
1992-93   19 ppg   9.3 rpg   65.1 FG%

Bonzi Wells, Ball State
1994-95   15.8 ppg   6.1 rpg   2.8 spg
*Battle transferred to Illinois.

MIDWESTERN COLLEGIATE

Jeff Acres, Oral Roberts
1980-81   13.1 ppg   8 rpg

Mark Acres, Oral Roberts
1981-82   14.6 ppg   8.1 rpg   58.6 FG%

Parrish Casebier, Evansville
1990-91   15 ppg

Monroe Douglass, St. Louis
1985-86   14.5 ppg

Brian Grant, Xavier
1990-91   11.6 ppg   8.5 rpg   57.2 FG%

Alfredrick Hughes, Loyola (Ill.)
1981-82   17.3 ppg   6.1 rpg

Byron Larkin, Xavier
1984-85   17 ppg   53.1 FG%

T.J. Lux, Northern Illinois
1995-96   15.2 ppg

Kenny Miller, Loyola (Ill.)
1987-88   14.7 ppg   13.6 rpg   59.5 FG%

Tony Warren, Butler
1979-80   17.6 ppg   60.1 FG%

MISSOURI VALLEY

Mitchell Anderson, Bradley
1978-79   21 ppg

Benoit Benjamin, Creighton
1982-83   14.8 ppg   9.6 rpg   55.5 FG%

Eddie Bird, Indiana State
1987-88   15.3 ppg   4.6 rpg

Rodney Buford, Creighton
1995-96   14.5 ppg   4.2 rpg

Antoine Carr, Wichita State
1979-80   15.2 ppg   5.9 rpg

Wesley Cox, Louisville
1973-74   14.1 ppg

Hersey Hawkins, Bradley
1984-85   14.6 ppg   6.1 rpg   58.1 FG%

Cliff Levingston, Wichita St.
1979-80   15.7 ppg   10.1 rpg   54.6 FG%

Dexter Reed, Memphis State
1973-74   18.4 ppg   4.6 rpg

Shea Seals, Tulsa
1993-94   16.8 ppg   6.5 rpg   3.5 apg

John Williams, Indiana State
1982-83   18.6 ppg

OHIO VALLEY

Frank Allen, Murray State
1989-90   14.6 ppg

Anthony Avery, Tennessee Tech
1985-86   12.3 ppg   3.4 rpg   5.3 apg

Dave Bootcheck, Eastern Kentucky
1976-77   19.7 ppg

Kerry Hammonds, Middle Tenn.
1984-85   13.8 ppg   8 rpg

Chris Harris, Middle Tenn.
1978-79   11.9 ppg   6.5 rpg   54.0 FG%

Geoff Herman, Austin Peay*
1990-91   14.5 ppg

Tim Horton, Tennessee State
1991-92   14.7 ppg

Stephen Kite, Tennessee Tech
1982-83   12.9 ppg   6.6 rpg   59.1 FG%

Antonio Parris, Eastern Ky.
1983-84   18.8 ppg

Herb Stamper, Morehead State
1975-76   18 ppg

Claude Taylor, Middle Tenn.
1974-75   15.8 ppg   7.1 rpg   81.1 FT%

James Williams, Austin Peay
1972-73   29.4 ppg

Monty Wilson, Tennessee State
1992-93   13.4 ppg   5.7 rpg

Earl Wise, Tennessee Tech
1986-87   18.6 ppg   7.6 rpg   51.4 FG%

*Herman transferred to East Tennessee State.

PACIFIC-10

Shareef Abdur-Rahim, Cal
1995-96   21.1 ppg   8.4 rpg   51.8 FG%

Mario Bennett, Arizona State
1991-92   12.5 ppg   6.8 rpg   57.4 FG%

Sean Elliott, Arizona
1985-86   15.6 ppg   5.3 rpg

Jamal Faulkner, Arizona St.*
1990-91   15.4 ppg   6.2 rpg

Rod Foster, UCLA
1979-80   11.5 ppg   54.8 FG%   84.2 FT%

Tremaine Fowlkes, California
1994-95   13.4 ppg   6.7 rpg

Jelani Gardner, California
1994-95   10.7 ppg   6.5 apg

Rickie Hawthorne, California
1972-73   14.2 ppg   5.9 rpg

Mike Hayward, Washington
1987-88   14 ppg   5 rpg   80.7 FT%

Brian Hendrick, California
1989-90   14.9 ppg   7.6 rpg   59.3 FG%

Steve Johnson, Oregon State
1976-77   13.5 ppg   5.6 rpg   59.6 FG%

Jason Kidd, California
1992-93   13 ppg   4.9 rpg   7.7 apg   3.8 spg

Brevin Knight, Stanford
1993-94   11.1 ppg   3.9 rpg   5.4 apg   2.8 spg

Ron Lee, Oregon
1972-73   18.7 ppg   6.6 rpg   4.3 apg

Todd Lichti, Stanford
1985-86   17.2 ppg   4.7 rpg   53.3 FG%

Don MacLean, UCLA
1988-89   18.6 ppg   7.5 rpg   55.5 FG%

Harold Miner, Southern Cal
1989-90   20.6 ppg   3.6 rpg   84.1 FT%

Lamond Murray, California
1991-92   13.8 ppg   6.1 rpg

Tracy Murray, UCLA
1989-90   12.3 ppg   5.5 rpg

Gary Payton, Oregon State
1986-87   12.5 ppg   4 rpg   7.6 apg

Michael Pitts, California
1979-80   13.1 ppg

Steve Puidokas, Washington St.
1973-74   16.8 ppg   8.9 rpg

Gene Ransom, California**
1975-76   13.2 ppg

Pooh Richardson, UCLA
1985-86   10.6 ppg   4.5 rpg   6.2 apg

Cliff Robinson, Southern Cal
1977-78   18.4 ppg   9.6 rpg   52.0 FG%

Byron Scott, Arizona State
1979-80   13.6 ppg   2.7 rpg

Lonnie Shelton, Oregon State
1973-74   12.2 ppg   7.8 rpg   51.8 FG%

Leonard Taylor, California
1984-85   12.4 ppg   6.1 rpg   53.2 FG%

Christian Welp, Washington
1983-84   16.8 ppg   6.2 rpg

*Faulkner transferred to Alabama.
**Ransom transferred to Nevada-Reno.

SEC

Dwight Anderson, Kentucky*
1978-79   13.3 ppg

Charles Barkley, Auburn
1981-82   12.7 ppg   9.8 rpg   59.5 FG%

Ronnie Battle, Auburn
1989-90   17 ppg

Pepto Bolden, Auburn
1973-74   10.5 ppg   11.6 rpg

Sam Bowie, Kentucky
1979-80   12.9 ppg   8.1 rpg

Rickey Brown, Mississippi St.
1976-77   19.3 ppg   10.8 rpg   50.8 FG%

Rex Chapman, Kentucky
1986-87   16 ppg   3.6 apg

Phil Cox, Vanderbilt
1981-82   13.5 ppg   86.9 FT%

Charles Davis, Vanderbilt
1976-77   15.3 ppg   7 rpg

Vernon Delancy, Florida
1980-81   17.8 ppg   5 rpg   54.2 FG%

Jacky Dorsey, Georgia
1974-75   25.8 ppg   11.8 rpg

Litterial Green, Georgia
1988-89   15.5 ppg   4.3 apg

Ernie Grunfeld, Tennessee
1973-74   17.4 ppg   7.2 rpg

Reggie Hannah, Florida
1977-78   13.6 ppg   9.2 rpg   57.7 FG%

Joe Harvell, Mississippi
1989-90   13.2 ppg   5.4 rpg

Cedric Henderson, Georgia
1984-85   15.5 ppg   7.1 rpg

Ronnie Henderson, LSU
1993-94   15.9 ppg

Kenny Higgs, LSU
1974-75   18.1 ppg

Gary Hooker, Mississippi State
1975-76   17.7 ppg

Allan Houston, Tennessee
1989-90   20.3 ppg   2.9 rpg   4.2 apg

Chris Jackson, LSU
1988-89   30.2 ppg   4.1 apg   81.5 FT%

Eddie Johnson, Auburn
1973-74   21.8 ppg

Reggie Johnson, Tennessee
1976-77   11 ppg   8.1 rpg   64.5 FG%

Tim Jumper, Mississippi
1987-88   13.6 ppg

Bernard King, Tennessee
1974-75   26.4 ppg   12.3 ppg   62.2 FG%

Rich Knarr, Mississippi State
1972-73   18 ppg   3.3 rpg   84.3 FT%

Randy Livingston, LSU
1994-95   14 ppg   4 rpg   9.4 apg

Rudy Macklin, LSU
1976-77   14.8 ppg   11.8 rpg   51.9 FG%

Jamal Mashburn, Kentucky
1990-91   12.9 ppg   7 rpg

Vernon Maxwell, Florida
1984-85   13.3 ppg

B.J. McKie, South Carolina
1995-96   15.4 ppg   3.1 rpg   2.8 apg

Chris Mills, Kentucky**
1988-89   14.3 ppg   8.7 rpg

Leonard Mitchell, LSU
1980-81   10.8 ppg   7.2 rpg   51.1 FG%

Mike Mitchell, Auburn
1974-75   18.4 ppg   11.4 rpg

Shaquille O'Neal, LSU
1989-90   13.9 ppg   12 rpg   3.6 bpg   57.3 FG%

Wes Person, Auburn
1990-91   15.4 ppg   5.7 rpg

Eddie Phillips, Alabama
1978-79   14.5 ppg   7.4 rpg

Mike Rhodes, Vanderbilt
1977-78   18.8 ppg   3.7 rpg

Rick Robey, Kentucky
1974-75   10.4 ppg   6.9 rpg   54.4 FG%

James Robinson, Alabama
1989-90   16.8 ppg   3.9 rpg

John Stroud, Mississippi
1976-77   14.5 ppg

Scotty Thurman, Arkansas
1992-93   17.4 ppg   4.4 rpg

Ennis Whatley, Alabama
1981-82   12.1 ppg   5.7 apg

Ray White, Mississippi State
1975-76   18.3 ppg   5.5 rpg   50.6 FG%

Dominique Wilkins, Georgia
1979-80   18.6 ppg   6.5 rpg   52.5 FG%

John Williams, LSU
1984-85   13.4 ppg   6.6 rpg   3 apg   53.4 FG%

Ronnie Williams, Florida
1980-81   19.4 ppg   9 rpg   57.8 FG%

Corliss Williamson, Arkansas
1992-93   14.6 ppg   5.1 rpg   57.4 FG%

*Anderson transferred to Southern Cal.
**Mills transferred to Arizona.

SOUTHERN

Brent Corley, VMI
1995-96   15.8 ppg

Greg Dennis, East Tenn. State
1987-88   16.4 ppg

Chris Dodds, Davidson
1977-78   18.5 ppg

John Gerdy, Davidson
1975-76   17.9 ppg

Skip Henderson, Marshall
1984-85   17.7 ppg

Keith Jennings, E. Tenn. St.
1987-88   12.9 ppg   4.1 rpg   6.3 apg

Troy Lee Mikell, East Tenn. St.
1979-80   16.6 ppg

Jonathan Moore, Furman
1976-77   20 ppg   11.2 rpg   55.4 FG%

Carey Rich, Western Carolina
1990-91   13 ppg

Derek Rucker, Davidson
1984-85   12.8 ppg

George Singleton, Furman
1980-81   16.1 ppg   10.1 rpg   53.5 FG%

George Washington, Marshall
1978-79   16.2 ppg

SOUTHWEST

Billy Allen, SMU*
1978-79   13.4 ppg

Ron Baxter, Texas
1976-77   16.7 ppg

Juan Bragg, TCU
1994-95   15.6 ppg

Darrell Browder, TCU
1980-81   19.4 ppg   4.8 rpg   83.0 FT%

Larry Davis, SMU
1981-82   11.9 ppg   5.7 rpg

Todd Day, Arkansas
1988-89   13.3 ppg   4 rpg

Clyde Drexler, Houston
1980-81   11.9 ppg   10.5 rpg

Carven Holcombe, TCU
1983-84   13.4 ppg

Damon Johnson, Texas A&M
1991-92   15.6 ppg   7.7 rpg   56.4 FG%

Lee Mayberry, Arkansas
1988-89   12.9 ppg

Sidney Moncrief, Arkansas
1975-76   12.6 ppg   7.6 rpg   66.5 FG%

Johnny Moore, Texas
1975-76   13.6 ppg   4.4 apg

Terrence Rencher, Texas
1991-92   19.1 ppg   4.3 rpg   3.6 apg

Brent Scott, Rice
1989-90   15.3 ppg

Vernon Smith, Texas A&M
1977-78   14 ppg   8.4 rpg

Terry Teagle, Baylor
1978-79   14.6 ppg   6.5 rpg   52.9 FG%

Ira Terrell, SMU
1972-73   19.4 ppg   14.1 rpg

LaSalle Thompson, Texas
1979-80   12.8 ppg   9.7 rpg   55.8 FG%

Craig Upchurch, Houston
1987-88   12.1 ppg   5.3 rpg   56.5 FG%

Damion Walker, TCU
1995-96   20.5 ppg   8.8 rpg   50.3 FG%

Micheal Williams, Baylor
1984-85   14.6 ppg

Rob Williams, Houston
1979-80   16.3 ppg

Rudy Woods, Texas A&M
1978-79   13.9 ppg   8.7 rpg   59.8 FG%

Michael Young, Houston
1982-83   17.3 ppg
*Transferred to Nevada-Reno.

SUN BELT

Jorge Azcoitia, South Florida
1978-79   12.9 ppg   5.7 rpg

Anthony Carver, Old Dominion
1986-87   15.5 ppg   7.1 rpg

Radenko Dobras, South Florida
1988-89   16.2 ppg   3.8 rpg   4.5 apg

Chuck Evans, Old Dominion*
1989-90   5.1 ppg   6.9 apg

Clinton Hinton, UNC Charlotte
1984-85   16.8 ppg   7.4 rpg

Jeff Hodge, South Alabama
1985-86   12.2 ppg   2.7 rpg   3.3 apg

Melvin Johnson, UNC Charlotte
1980-81   11.9 ppg   5.4 rpg

Chad Kinch, UNC Charlotte
1976-77   15.4 ppg   3.8 rpg

Jarvis Lang, UNC Charlotte
1990-91   19.6 ppg   10.6 rpg

Ronnie Murphy, Jacksonville
1983-84   17.9 ppg

Otis Smith, Jacksonville
1982-83   14.3 ppg   8.7 rpg

Keith Veney, Lamar**
1992-93   16.6 ppg

Kendrick Warren, Va. Commonwealth
1990-91   15.7 ppg   8.5 rpg   54.1 FG%

Henry Williams, UNC Charlotte
1988-89   17.4 ppg   3.6 rpg
*Transferred to junior college before enrolling at Mississippi State.
**Transferred to Marshall.

WEST COAST

Greg Anthony, Portland*
1986-87   15.3 ppg   4.3 rpg   4 apg

Winford Boynes, San Francisco
1975-76   18.1 ppg   5.3 rpg

Bill Cartwright, San Francisco
1975-76   12.5 ppg   6.9 rpg   53.0 FG%

Darwin Cook, Portland
1976-77   13.2 ppg

Quintin Dailey, San Francisco
1979-80   13.6 ppg   3.7 rpg   52.7 FG%

James Hardy, San Francisco
1975-76   10.7 ppg   9 rpg

Robert Haugen, St. Mary's
1985-86   13.1 ppg   64.5 FG%

Edgar Jones, Nevada-Reno
1975-76   17.6 ppg   10 rpg

Marcos Leite, Pepperdine
1973-74   17.3 ppg   10.4 rpg

Ollie Matson, Pepperdine
1974-75   14.2 ppg   8.3 rpg   52 FG%

Frank Oleynick, Seattle
1972-73   14.5 ppg

Pete Padgett, Nevada-Reno
1972-73   16 ppg   17.8 rpg

Rick Raivio, Portland
1976-77   13 ppg

Kurt Rambis, Santa Clara
1976-77   15 ppg   11.6 rpg   52.7 FG%

Clint Richardson, Seattle
1975-76   18.5 ppg   7.4 rpg

Jose Slaughter, Portland
1978-79   14.7 ppg

David Vann, St. Mary's
1978-79   13 ppg
*Anthony transferred to UNLV.

WAC

Danny Ainge, Brigham Young
1977-78   21.1 ppg   5.8 rpg   86.4 FT%

Shawn Bradley, Brigham Young
1990-91   14.8 ppg   7.7 rpg   5.2 bpg

Gary Brewster, Texas-El Paso
1972-73   11.8 ppg   6.6 rpg   52.4 FG%

Luther (Tickey) Burden, Utah
1972-73   13.8 ppg   3.1 rpg

Michael Cage, San Diego State
1980-81   10.9 ppg   13.1 rpg   55.8 FG%

Fennis Dembo, Wyoming
1984-85   13.5 ppg   7.3 rpg   3 apg

Raymond Dudley, Air Force
1986-87   13.6 ppg   46.2 3FG%

Devin Durrant, Brigham Young
1978-79   13.2 ppg   5.2 rpg   54.0 FG%

Bob Elliott, Arizona
1973-74   16.5 ppg   10.7 rpg

Al Fleming, Arizona
1972-73   12.8 ppg   9.9 rpg   53.7 FG%

Chris Gaines, Hawaii
1986-87   17.1 ppg

Eddie Hughes, Colorado State
1978-79   15.4 ppg

Eric Money, Arizona
1972-73   18.9 ppg

Coniel Norman, Arizona
1972-73   24 ppg

Fred Roberts, Brigham Young
1978-79   14.3 ppg   6.8 rpg   54.3 FG%

Tony Ross, San Diego State
1986-87   16.3 ppg

Mike Sojourner, Utah
1972-73   12.3 rpg

Kenny Thomas, New Mexico
1995-96   14.7 ppg   7.8 rpg   57.8 FG%

Keith Van Horn, Utah
1993-94   18.3 ppg   8.3 rpg

Danny Vranes, Utah
1977-78   12.2 ppg   7.2 rpg

LaDrell Whitehead, Wyoming
1994-95   14.9 ppg   3.5 apg   2 spg

INDEPENDENT SCHOOLS

Mark Aguirre, DePaul
1978-79   24 ppg   7.6 rpg   52.0 FG%

Warren Baker, West Virginia
1973-74   16.6 ppg   11.2 rpg

Otis Birdsong, Houston
1973-74   14.3 ppg   4.2 rpg

Kevin Brooks, Southwestern La.
1987-88   16.8 ppg   6.3 rpg   56.5 FG%

Eric Brown, Miami (Fla.)
1985-86   16.4 ppg

Reggie Carter, Hawaii*
1975-76   16.6 ppg

Dave Corzine, DePaul
1974-75   12.2 ppg   8.6 rpg

Terry Cummings, DePaul
1979-80   14.2 ppg   9.4 rpg

Adrian Dantley, Notre Dame
1973-74   18.3 ppg   9.7 rpg   55.8 FG%

Frank Edwards, Cleveland St.
1977-78   18.7 ppg

Bo Ellis, Marquette
1973-74   12.2 ppg   8.5 rpg   53.5 FG%

LaPhonso Ellis, Notre Dame
1988-89   13.5 ppg   9.4 rpg   56.3 FG%

Alex English, South Carolina
1972-73   14.6 ppg   10.6 rpg

Jimmy Foster, South Carolina
1980-81   14.2 ppg   11 rpg   58.0 FG%

Mike Glenn, Southern Ill.
1973-74   15.3 ppg   53.7 FG%

Jim Graziano, South Carolina
1976-77   13.2 ppg

Sidney Green, UNLV
1979-80   15.6 ppg   11.1 rpg

Tito Horford, Miami (Fla.)
1986-87   14.3 ppg   9.6 rpg

Joe C. Meriweather, SIU
1972-73   17.1 ppg   12.3 rpg   54.2 FG%

David Rivers, Notre Dame
1984-85   15.8 ppg   4.2 apg

Doc Rivers, Marquette
1980-81   14 ppg   3.2 rpg   3.6 apg   55.3 FG%

Phil Sellers, Rutgers
1972-73   19.5 ppg   10.2 rpg

Rod Strickland, DePaul
1985-86   14.1 ppg   5.1 apg

Kelly Tripucka, Notre Dame
1977-78   11.7 ppg   5.2 rpg   57.1 FG%
*Carter transferred to St. John's.

MOST OVERLOOKED

Andy Bolden, George Mason
1980-81   16.9 ppg

Atiim Browne, Lamar
1990-91   15.4 ppg   4.9 apg, 2.2 spg

Steve Burtt, Iona
1980-81   13.6 ppg

Bruce Campbell, Providence
1974-75   11 ppg   6.7 rpg

Jamie Ciampaglio, Wagner
1976-77   19.4 ppg

Bob Cooper, Providence
1973-74   12 ppg   7.2 rpg   3.2 bpg   57.1 FG%

Hollis Copeland, Rutgers
1974-75   13.6 ppg   7 rpg   50.3 FG%

Mike Dabney, Rutgers
1972-73   12.3 ppg   6.1 rpg

Nick Daniels, Xavier
1975-76   15 ppg   7.1 rpg

Tony Dumas, Mo.-Kansas City
1990-91   16.5 ppg   4.8 rpg

Bill Edwards, Wright State
1989-90   15.4 ppg   6.9 rpg

Bruce Elder, Davidson*
1988-89   17.2 ppg

Manny Figueroa, St. Francis (NY)
1975-76   18.6 ppg

Tim Gill, Oral Roberts
1994-95   16.3 ppg

Rick Gilliam, West Chester St.
1979-80   20.3 ppg

Keith Herron, Villanova
1974-75   17.9 ppg   5.1 rpg

Ben Hinson, Baptist
1983-84   15 ppg

Essie Hollis, St. Bonaventure
1973-74   14.7 ppg

George Johnson, St. John's
1974-75   10.1 ppg   9.2 rpg   52.9 FG%

Garry Jordan, Niagara
1977-78   18 ppg

Stan Kimbrough, Central Fla.**
1984-85   18.1 ppg

John Long, Detroit
1974-75   17.1 ppg

Kenneth Lyons, North Texas
1979-80   17.7 ppg   9.5 rpg

Jon Manning, Oklahoma City
1974-75   21.7 ppg

Ronnie McAdoo, Old Dominion
1978-79   15.2 ppg   8.7 rpg

Mike McKay, Connecticut
1978-79   15.9 ppg   5.4 rpg

Dan McLaughlin, Fairleigh Dickinson
1978-79   19.4 ppg

Glenn Mosley, Seton Hall
1973-74   13.8 ppg   14.2 rpg

Calvin Natt, Northeast La.
1975-76   20.6 ppg   11 rpg   55.8 FG%

Tony Parker, Loyola (Ill.)
1973-74   17.1 ppg

Mike Payne, Fairleigh Dickinson
1980-81   16.5 ppg

Mike Perry, Richmond
1977-78   19 ppg

Ronnie Perry, Holy Cross
1976-77   23 ppg   88.1 FT%

Greg Sanders, St. Bonaventure
1974-75   17.5 ppg   6 rpg   51.8 FG%

Ronnie Schmitz, UMKC
1989-90   16.8 ppg

Dale Shackleford, Syracuse
1975-76   11.4 ppg   8.8 rpg

Gary Springer, Iona
1980-81   19.9 ppg   8.5 rpg

Dwight Stewart, Fla. International
1988-89   17.3 ppg

Steve Stielper, James Madison
1976-77   20.9 ppg

Corny Thompson, Connecticut
1978-79   18.6 ppg   10 rpg

Ronnie Valentine, Old Dominion
1976-77   22.4 ppg   9.3 rpg   53.0 FG%

Bob Warner, Maine
1972-73   18.6 ppg

Ken Webb, Fairleigh Dickinson
1976-77   21.8 ppg

Sly Williams, Rhode Island
1976-77   20 ppg   8.1 rpg

Merlin Wilson, Georgetown
1972-73   12.7 ppg   14.1 rpg

Gary Winton, Army
1974-75   19.7 ppg

Carlos Yates, George Mason
1981-82   15.9 ppg

*Elder transferred to Vanderbilt.
**Kimbrough transferred to Xavier following the season.

FRESHMEN OF INFLUENCE

An exclusive list of six freshmen who earned conference player of the year honors.

Freshman, School Conference	Key Statistics	(Season)
Keith Lee, Memphis State Metro	18.3 ppg	11 rpg (1981-82)
Karl Malone, Louisiana Tech Southland	20.9 ppg	10.3 rpg (1982-83)
Wayman Tisdale, Oklahoma Big Eight	24.5 ppg	10.3 rpg (1982-83)
Tony Dunkin, Coastal Carolina Big South	18.1 ppg	6.6 rpg (1989-90)
Gary Trent, Ohio University Mid-American	19.0 ppg	9.3 rpg (1992-93)
Shareef Abdur-Rahim, Cal Pacific-10	21.1 ppg	8.4 rpg (1995-96)

FIRST-YEAR FLASHES

In the first season of freshman eligibility in 1972-73, two yearlings set school single-game scoring records that still exist.

Freshman   Pos.   School
Scoring Record

Fly Williams, G, Austin Peay
51 points vs. Georgia Southern, 51 vs. Tennessee
    Tech
Robert Parish, C, Centenary
    50 at Lamar

Parish joined two other players in the original freshman class to establish school single-game rebounding marks that remain intact.

Freshman, Pos., School

Rebounding Record

Robert Parish, C, Centenary
  33 vs. Southern Mississippi
Pete Padgett, C, Nevada-Reno
  30 at Loyola Marymount
Alvan Adams, C, Oklahoma
  28 vs. Indiana State

RAGS TO RICHES

Here are the players with the greatest increases between their freshman scoring average and senior scoring average since the introduction of freshman eligibility:

Player Fr. Avg.	Final School Sr. Avg.	Increase
Anthony Roberts 5.2	Oral Roberts '77 34.0	28.8 ppg
Zam Fredrick 1.9	South Carolina '81 28.9	27.0 ppg
Mike Ferrara* 2.1	Colgate '81 28.6	26.5 ppg
John Best 3.1	Tennessee Tech '93 28.5	25.4 ppg
Kevin Bradshaw* 12.9	U.S. International '91 37.6	24.7 ppg
Steve Rogers* 3.1	Alabama State '92 27.3	24.2 ppg
Darrin Archbold 0.9	Butler '92 24.8	23.9 ppg
Vin Baker 4.7	Hartford '93 28.3	23.6 ppg
Steve Middleton 1.9	Southern Illinois '88 25.4	23.5 ppg
Bo Kimble* 12.1	Loyola Marymount '90 35.3	23.2 ppg
Scott Haffner* 1.7	Evansville '89 24.5	22.8 ppg
Phil Stinnie 1.1	Va. Commonwealth '88 23.6	22.5 ppg

*Ferrara (Niagara), Bradshaw (Bethune-Cookman), Rogers (Middle Tennessee State), Kimble (Southern Cal) and Haffner (Illinois) played their freshman seasons for other universities.

SLOW STARTERS

NBA regular rotation players Tyrone Bogues (1.2 points per game/Wake Forest), Antonio Davis (1.3/Texas-El Paso), Vinny Del Negro (2.1/North Carolina State), Tom Gugliotta (2.7/North Carolina State), Joe Kleine (2.6/Notre Dame), Andrew Lang (2.6/Arkansas), Will Perdue (2.7/Vanderbilt), Tim Perry (2.3/Temple), Terry Porter (2.0/Wisconsin-Stevens Point) and Brian Shaw (2.9/St. Mary's) averaged fewer than three points per game when they were a college freshman.

HIGHLY-RECRUITED FRESHMEN WHOSE POTENTIAL EXCEEDED COLLEGE ACHIEVEMENTS

1972-73
Mickey Heard, Louisiana State
Danny Moses, Wake Forest
Nino Samuel, Kansas

1973-74
Melvin Baker, Oklahoma
Paul Berwanger, Boston College
Jim Webb, Cincinnati

1974-75
Terry Drake, Iowa
Tim Marshall, Arizona
Mark Wulfemeyer, Southern Cal

1975-76
Irv Chatman, Tennessee
Otis Fulton, Virginia
Alan Hardy, Michigan
Rodney Lee, Memphis State

1976-77
Bill Bryant, Maryland
Alonzo Campbell, Oregon State
Glen Grunwald, Indiana
Tyrone Ladson, Kansas State

1977-78
Tommy Baker, Indiana
Tom Freeman, Kansas State
Craig Harris, Tulane
Bob Lowrie, Tennessee

1978-79
Gordy Bryan, Virginia Tech
Reggie Jackson, Maryland
Leonel Marquetti, Southern Cal
Mike Mitchell, Notre Dame
Chuck Verderber, Kentucky

1979-80
Ron Burns, Oregon
Charles Hurt, Kentucky
Bill Varner, Notre Dame
Ray Whiting, Oregon

1980-81
Bret Bearup, Kentucky
Pete Holbert, Maryland
Mike LaFavre, Indiana
Ricky Norton, Arkansas
Barry Spencer, Notre Dame

1981-82
John Flowers, Indiana
Billy Jordan, Arizona State
Winston Morgan, Indiana
Walter (Dinky) Proctor, N.C. State
Leslie Rockymore, Michigan

1982-83
Pat Ford, Michigan State
Robert Henderson, Michigan
Lloyd Moore, Marquette
Rob Valentine, Louisville

1983-84
John Bowen, Notre Dame
Kenny Hutchinson, Arkansas
Terry Long, Maryland
Carl Pollard, Brigham Young
Barry Sumpter, Louisville

1984-85
Craig Jackson, UCLA
Robert Lock, Kentucky
Richard Madison, Kentucky
Steve Stoyko, Michigan

1985-86
Tyrone Mitchell, Arizona State
Earl Moore, George Mason
Irving Thomas, Kentucky

1986-87
Dwayne Bryant, Georgetown
Quinton Burton, Providence
Ricky Jones, Clemson
James Munlyn, Georgia Tech

1987-88
Lyndon Jones, Indiana
Greg Koubek, Duke
David White, Florida State

1988-89
Milton Bell, Georgetown
Marc Dowdell, Villanova
Cesar Portillo, Florida
Chuck Sproling, St. John's

1989-90
Calvin Byrd, Villanova
Deryl Cunningham, DePaul
Deron Johnson, Arizona
Michael Tait, Georgetown

1990-91
Lee Green, St. John's
Andy Penick, Michigan State
Luther Wright, Seton Hall
Thomas Wyatt, Utah

1991-92
Herb Dove, Purdue
Silas Mills, Utah
Howard Nathan, DePaul
Bubba Wilson, Mississippi State

1992-93
Steve Frazier, Miami (Fla.)
LaMarcus Golden, Tennessee
Chuck Kornegay, N.C. State

1993-94
Chuck Gelatt, Syracuse
Avondre Jones, Southern Cal
Jamal Robinson, Virginia
Michael Stewart, California

1994-95
omm'A Givens, UCLA
Willie Mitchell, Michigan
Lynard Stewart, Temple

Jerod Ward, Michigan
Jahidi White, Georgetown

1995-96
Ryan Blackwell, Illinois
Taymon Domzalski, Duke
Antric Klaber, Connecticut
Melvin Levett, Cincinnati

1996-97
Lucas Barnes, Miami (Fla.)
Mike Chappell, Duke
Willie Dersch, Virginia
Ronnie Fields, DePaul
Ramel Lloyd, Syracuse

CLASSIEST CLASSES IN LAST 25 YEARS

The jury is still out on a couple of Michigan's acclaimed freshman recruiting crops this decade. Duke's class of 2000 is also highly regarded. But will they stand the test of time and earn recognition among the best classes in college basketball history? Here is one view of the top 10 recruiting crops (excluding junior college signees) since the introduction of freshman eligibility in 1972-73:

School/Sr. Class
Recruiting Class Members
College Achievements

1. Indiana '76
Tom Abernethy, Quinn Buckner, Jim Crews, Scott May, Bobby Wilkerson

Last NCAA champion to go undefeated compiled a 63-1 record in last two seasons this class was together, climaxing a run of four Big Ten titles. Reached '73 Final Four with freshmen Buckner and Crews as starting guards under coach Bob Knight (May was ineligible as a freshman for academic reasons).

2. Michigan '96
Juwan Howard, Ray Jackson, Jimmy King, Jalen Rose, Chris Webber

NCAA Tournament runnerup in 1992 and 1993 as freshman and sophomore starters. Howard, Rose and Webber became NBA first-round draft choices as undergraduates. Principal drawback is that none of this group was a member of a Big Ten title team under coach Steve Fisher.

3. Georgetown '85
Ralph Dalton, Pat Ewing, Anthony Jones (transfer/UNLV), Bill Martin

Won NCAA title in 1984, runnerup in '85 and reached Final Four in '82. Went 30-7, 22-10, 34-3, 35-3 under coach John Thompson. Worst Big East record in that span was 11-5 in 1982-83.

4. Notre Dame '81
Tracy Jackson, Kelly Tripucka, Orlando Woolridge

Final Four in 1978 and Midwest Regional runnerup in '79. Irish went 23-8, 24-6, 22-6, 23-6 under coach Digger Phelps. Tripucka and Woolridge had long NBA careers.

5. Michigan State '81
Mike Brkovich, Magic Johnson, Rick Kaye, Jay Vincent

Won 1979 NCAA championship under coach Jud Heathcote. Went 25-5 and 26-6 and captured Big Ten titles in Johnson's two seasons before going 12-15 and 13-14 after he turned pro.

6. Louisville '82
Wiley Brown, Jerry Eaves, Scooter McCray, Derek Smith, Pancho Wright

Won NCAA title in 1980 with Brown, Eaves and Smith starting and McCray sidelined with a knee injury. Reached Final Four in 1982 under coach Denny Crum. Went 24-8, 33-3, 21-9 and 23-10 with Metro Conference crowns the first three years.

7. Kentucky '83
Sam Bowie, Derrick Hord, Charles Hunt, Dirk Minniefield

Oft-injured Bowie played five years, reaching Final Four in 1984. Others had respective records of 29-6, 22-6, 22-8, 23-8, but never advanced beyond second game of NCAA playoffs. Captured three SEC championships in that span under coach Joe B. Hall.

8. UCLA '77
Marques Johnson, Wilbert Olinde, Gavin Smith (transfer/Hawaii), Jim Spillane, Richard Washington

Won John Wooden's final NCAA title in 1975. Washington left for NBA a year early. Bruins went 26-4, 28-3, 28-4 and 25-4 with four Pacific-8 crowns. Reached Final Four in '76 under coach Gene Bartow.

9. North Carolina '77
Bruce Buckley, Walter Davis, John Kuester, Tom LaGarde

Lost 1977 NCAA final (28-5 record) after posting similar marks (composite of 70-18) the previous three years. Captured ACC regular-season championships their last two seasons under coach Dean Smith.

10. North Carolina '94
Eric Montross, Derrick Phelps, Brian Reese, Clifford Rozier (transfer/Louisville), Pat Sullivan

Won NCAA title in 1993 after reaching Final Four in '91 as freshmen. Compiled records of 29-6, 23-10, 34-4 and 28-7 under coach Dean Smith.

Special Mention

Alcorn State '85
Eddie Archer, Aaron Brandon, Tommy Collier, Michael Phelps

Archer, Brandon, Collier and Phelps all finished their careers with more than 1,200 points. The Braves won three SWAC championships in four years from 1982-85 under coach Davey Whitney.

Arizona '76
Al Fleming, John Irving (transfer/Hofstra), Eric Money, Coniel Norman, Jim Rappis

Started off 16-10 before members of the original group went 19-7, 22-7 and 24-9 under coach Fred Snowden. Norman averaged 23.9 ppg and Money averaged 18.5 before they turned pro after two seasons. Irving played one season with the Wildcats before transferring to Hofstra, where he led the nation in rebounding in 1975. Fleming became the school's all-time leading rebounder.

Duke '86
Mark Alarie, Jay Bilas, Johnny Dawkins, David Henderson

Runner-up in 1986 NCAA playoffs with a 37-3 record after going 24-10 and 23-8 the previous two years following 11-17 mark as freshmen under coach Mike Krzyzewski.

East Tenn. State '91
Greg Dennis, Major Geer, Keith Jennings, Alvin West

All four players became 1,000-point scorers in their careers. ETSU coasted to three Southern Conference Tournament titles from 1989-91 under coaches Les Robinson and Alan LeForce.

Maryland '81
Ernest Graham, Albert King, Greg Manning

Graham, King and Manning all finished their careers with more than 1,500 points. The Terrapins went 15-13, 19-11, 24-7 (won 1980 ACC regular-season title) and 21-10 under coach Lefty Driesell.

Pitt '91
Bobby Martin, Jason Matthews, Sean Miller (RS in '89-90), Darelle Porter, Brian Shorter (Prop 48)

All five players became 1,000-point scorers in their careers. The Panthers went 24-7 in 1987-88 when they were freshmen before struggling the next couple of seasons under coach Paul Evans.

Purdue '88
Jeff Arnold, Troy Lewis, Todd Mitchell, Dave Stack, Everette Stephens

"The Three Amigos" (Lewis, Mitchell and Stephens) were instrumental in helping the Boilermakers compile a four-year record of 96-28 (.774), including a glittering 29-4 mark as seniors under coach Gene Keady. Lewis and Mitchell still rank among the school's all-time top 10 scorers.

San Francisco '79
Winford Boynes, Bill Cartwright, Erik Gilberg, Raymond Hamilton (left after two seasons), James Hardy

Went 22-8, 29-2, 22-5 and 22-7 with WCAC championships the last three years. Boynes and

Hardy left school after their junior season when Dan Belluomini succeeded Bob Gaillard as coach.

Southern Cal '89
Jeff Connelly (transfer/Santa Clara), Hank Gathers (transfer/LMU), Bo Kimble (transfer/LMU), Tom Lewis (transfer/Pepperdine)

The nucleus of USC's class, recruited by Stan Morrison, left to become stars in the WCC after a modest freshman season (11-17) when George Raveling arrived as coach.

Southern Mississippi '88
Casey Fisher, Derrick Hamilton, Randolph Keys, John White

Keys, Fisher, Hamilton and White all finished their careers with more than 1,300 points. The Golden Eagles won the 1987 NIT under coach M.K. Turk.

UCLA '83
Darren Daye, Rod Foster, Michael Holton, Cliff Pruitt

NCAA Tournament runnerup in 1980 as freshmen under coach Larry Brown. Won Pacific-10 title in '83 under Brown's successor (Larry Farmer). Compiled records of 22-10, 20-7, 21-6 and 23-6.

Wake Forest '82
Mike Helms, Jim Johnstone, Guy Morgan, Alvis Rogers (RS in '81-82)

All four players finished their careers with more than 1,100 points under coach Carl Tacy. Morgan, Rogers and Johnstone each grabbed more than 550 rebounds. The Demon Deacons posted back-to-back 20-win seasons for the first time in school history (22-7 in 1980-81 and 21-9 in 1981-82).

Wichita State '83
Antoine Carr, James Gibbs, Ozell Jones (transfer/Cal State Fullerton), Cliff Levingston

Posted marks of 17-12, 26-7, 23-6 and 25-3 under coach Gene Smithson. Bogged down by being on NCAA probation in 1982 and 1983. Levingston left after his junior year.

GONE BUT NOT COMPLETELY FORGOTTEN

Excluding Indiana's excellence in the mid-1970s, the premier freshman class in major college history might not have been Michigan's "Fab Five" in the early 1990s but Alabama's portion of the "Rocket 8" in the mid-1950s. The 'Bama group compiled a 68-25 record in four years, including a 14-0 SEC mark and 21-3 overall record as seniors with a 101-77 victory over mighty Kentucky.

Comprising the five-man Crimson Tide class were center Jerry Harper, forwards George Linn and Dennis O'Shea and guards Leon Marlaire and Dick Gunder. Their achievements are often overlooked because they didn't appear in the NCAA Tournament. Harper was the school's leading scorer and rebounder all four years from 1952-53 through 1955-56. The quintet represented Alabama's top five scorers their last two seasons.

Here is a look at their year-by-year won-loss records and cumulative statistics:

Yr.	Overall (SEC)	PPG.	RPG.
Fr.	12-9 (6-7)	30.8	27.8
So.	16-8 (10-4)	50.1	31.0
Jr.	19-5 (11-3)	66.5	42.3
Sr.	21-3 (14-0)	79.0	48.0

STRINGS ATTACHED?

Steve Fisher, upon entering his second full season as Michigan's head coach in 1990-91, began to face a groundswell of criticism that he was inefficient in a coach's most important quality—recruiting. But as the Wolverines muddled through a losing record that year, Fisher was in the process of a major transformation. He was making an about-face from being labeled a poor recruiter to assembling what may be one of the greatest recruiting classes in history.

A key element in Fisher's master plan was adding longtime Detroit high school coach Perry Watson to his staff. Of course, it didn't hurt that Watson's high school star, Jalen Rose, tagged along with him to Michigan. Rose, the leading scorer for the Wolverines' Fab Five Final Four team, went on to the NBA while Watson became coach at the University of Detroit Mercy.

The Watson/Rose connection raised questions regarding the ethics of hiring the coach of a high school phenom. But it has been a relatively common practice.

Michigan was the 10th different school in a 20-year span to reach the Final Four with the help of a "coattail" franchise. There also were 10 first- and second-team consensus All-Americans in that stretch stemming from such associations.

There are unique cases, however. Consensus first-team All-America Danny Manning was recruited by Kansas' Larry Brown, who brought in Manning's father as an assistant although he had been working as a truck driver.

Here is an alphabetical list of NCAA Division I schools that have had star players whose high school coach was reunited with that standout as a college assistant:

ALABAMA-BIRMINGHAM: Joe Evans joined Gene Bartow's staff three years after Eddie Collins enrolled in 1984, which was two years before former high school teammate Larry Rembert arrived on campus. Collins, a two-year starter, was selected to the All-Sun Belt Conference Tournament team in his junior season. Rembert, a three-year starter, led the Blazers in rebounding in his sophomore and senior seasons. . . . Jim Armstrong helped monitor UAB's strength and fitness program for Bartow when Alan Ogg enrolled. Ogg, who set school and Sun Belt single-season and career blocked shot records and led the Blazers in rebounding in 1990, was on the Miami Heat's roster the past two seasons.

BAYLOR: Harry Miller joined Darrel Johnson's staff directly with his son, Roddrick, and teammate Brian Skinner in 1994. Harry Miller became interim head coach shortly before the start of that season and then was given a five-year contract two months later.

BETHUNE-COOKMAN: Owen Harris, Kevin Bradshaw's high school assistant coach, joined Cy McClairen's staff with Bradshaw in

1984. Bradshaw was the Wildcats' second-leading scorer with a 19-point average as a sophomore. He subsequently enrolled at U.S. International after a hitch in the Navy and led the nation in scoring in 1990-91 with 37.6 points per game.

BOSTON COLLEGE: Kevin Mackey joined Tom Davis' staff directly with Joe Beaulieu in 1977, which was one year before former high school teammate Dwan Chandler enrolled. Beaulieu, a transfer from Harvard, led the Eagles in rebounding in 1979 and 1980 and has the third-highest career field-goal percentage (57.1) in school history. Chandler, a two-year starter, was runner-up to John Bagley in assists in 1981 and held the school record for most games played when his eligibility expired.

CAL STATE FULLERTON: Phil Matthews joined George McQuarn's staff directly with Tony Neal in 1981. Neal, the Titans' all-time leader in rebounding and steals, was their No. 3 career scorer in Division I when his eligibility expired. He was a sixth-round draft choice of the Lakers in 1985.

CENTENARY: Ron Kestenbaum joined Riley Wallace's staff directly with Kevin Starke in 1976, which was the same year former high school teammate George Lett transferred from Hawaii. Lett, the Gents' No. 2 all-time leading rebounder (behind Robert Parish) and No. 3 scorer (behind Parish and former NBA player Tom Kerwin) when his eligibility expired, was a fifth-round draft choice of the Warriors in 1979. Starke led the Gents in assists as a freshman before transferring back home to St. Francis (N.Y.).

DAYTON: Larry Miller joined Jim O'Brien's staff one year before Chip Jones and Derrick Dukes enrolled in 1990. Jones, a junior college transfer, was Midwestern Collegiate Conference Newcomer of the Year in 1991 but didn't play as a senior because of academic problems. Dukes led the Flyers in assists for two seasons.

DELAWARE: Larry Davis joined Steve Steinwedel's staff one year before Elsworth Bowers enrolled in 1986. Bowers was the Blue Hens' leading scorer and rebounder in his senior season.

DETROIT: Charlie Coles joined Don Sicko's staff directly with Kevin McAdoo in 1982, which was one year before former high school teammate Brian Humes enrolled. McAdoo is the Titans' all-time assists leader. Humes was the Titans' 11th all-time leading scorer when his eligibility expired in 1987. . . . Jim Boyce joined Dick Vitale's staff with Terry Tyler, who averaged 15 points and 10.5 rebounds per game for the Titans from 1974-75 through 1977-78.

DUKE: Mike Brey, Danny Ferry's high school assistant coach, joined Mike Krzyzewski's staff two years after Ferry enrolled in 1985. Ferry, a first-team consensus All-America in 1989 after being a second-teamer in 1988, is the Blue Devils' No. 4 all-time leading scorer and No. 5 rebounder. Ferry, the second pick overall in the 1989 NBA draft, played the last three seasons with the Cavaliers after spending one year in Italy.

DUQUESNE: Barry Brodzinski joined Mike Satalin's staff one year before Clayton Adams enrolled in 1987, which was one year before former high school teammate Mark Stevenson transferred from Notre Dame. Adams passed Norm Nixon to become the Dukes' all-time assists leader. Stevenson set an Atlantic 10 Conference record for scoring average two years ago. . . . Mike Rice joined John Cinicola's staff directly with Baron (B.B.) Flenory in 1976. Flenory was the Dukes' No. 5 all-time leading scorer and No. 2 in assists when his eligibility expired in 1980.

ILLINOIS STATE: Ron Ferguson joined Will Robinson's staff three years after Mike Bonczyk enrolled in 1972. Bonczyk was the Redbirds' all-time leader in assists when his eligibililty expired in 1976.

INDIANA STATE: James Martin joined Tates Locke's staff directly with Darrin Hancock in 1993 when the forward transferred from Kansas. But Hancock, who played for Martin in Griffin, Ga., before attending junior college, dropped out of school to play professionally in Europe before winding up in the NBA.

IOWA: Rick Moss joined Tom Davis' staff directly with Ray Thompson in 1988. Thompson scored more points than any freshman in Hawkeyes' history except for Roy Marble and was their leading scorer two years ago when he was suspended. Thompson subsequently enrolled at Oral Roberts.

JAMES MADISON: Ernie Nestor joined Lou Campanelli's staff three years after Sherman Dillard enrolled in 1973. Dillard, the Dukes' No. 2 all-time leading scorer, was a sixth-round draft choice of the Pacers in 1978.

KANSAS: Duncan Reid joined Ted Owens' staff directly with Norm Cook in 1973. Cook, who declared early for the NBA draft after leading the Jayhawks in scoring in his junior season, still ranks among the top 10 rebounders in school history. Cook, a first-round draft choice of the Celtics in 1976, also played briefly with the Nuggets. . . . Lafayette Norwood joined Owens' staff directly with Darnell Valentine in 1977. Valentine, the Jayhawks' all-time No. 3 scorer and second-leading assists man, was a first-round draft choice of the Blazers in 1981. He played nine seasons in the NBA with four different teams.

KANSAS STATE: Mark Reiner joined Jack Hartman's staff directly with Curtis Redding and Tyrone Ladson in 1976. Redding was the Wildcats' No. 2 scorer (behind former pro Mike Evans) in 1977 and 1978 before transferring to St. John's. Redding was an eighth-round draft choice of the Nuggets in 1981. Ladson received one letter at Kansas State before transferring to Texas A&M.

KENTUCKY: Bob Chambers joined Joe B. Hall's staff one year after Derrick Hord enrolled in 1979. Hord, the Wildcats' leading scorer as a junior, was a third-round draft choice of the Cavaliers in 1983.

LONG BEACH STATE: Bobby Braswell joined Joe Harrington's staff directly with Lucious Harris in 1989, which was one year after Tyrone Mitchell transferred from Arizona. Harris became the Big West Conference's all-time leading scorer. Mitchell led Long Beach State in assists in 1990 and 1991.

LOUISIANA STATE: Ron Abernathy joined Dale Brown's staff directly with Rudy Macklin in

1976. Macklin, a second-team consensus All-America in 1981, is the Tigers' No. 2 all-time rebounder (behind Shaquille O'Neal) and is second in career scoring (behind Pete Maravich). Macklin, a third-round draft choice of the Hawks in 1981, also played briefly for the Knicks in his three-year NBA career. . . . Rick Huckabay joined Brown's staff directly with Howard Carter in 1979. Carter, the Tigers' No. 4 all-time scorer, was a first-round draft choice of the Nuggets in 1983. He also played briefly with the Mavericks in his two-year NBA career. . . . Gary Duhe joined Brown's staff two years after Derrick Taylor enrolled in 1981. Taylor, who ranks among the Tigers' top 10 in career scoring and assists, was a fourth-round draft choice of the Pacers in 1986. . . . Mike Mallett joined LSU's athletic department as an aide directly with Nikita Wilson in 1983. Wilson, who ranks 10th in career scoring for the Tigers, was a second-round draft choice of the Trail Blazers in 1987. . . . Jim Childers joined Brown's staff directly with Stanley Roberts in 1989. Roberts was the Tigers' No. 2 scorer and rebounder (behind Shaquille O'Neal) in his only season with them before turning pro. Roberts spent one year in Spain before going to the NBA.

LOUISVILLE: Wade Houston joined Denny Crum's staff directly with Darrell Griffith and Bobby Turner in 1976. Griffith, a first-team consensus All-America as a senior, is the Cardinals' all-time leading scorer. Griffith played 10 seasons with the Jazz after being its first-round draft choice in 1980. Turner was a two-year starter before succumbing to scholastic shortcomings. . . . Scott Davenport joined Crum's staff in standout guard DeJuan Wheat's senior season (1996-97).

MASSACHUSETTS: Ray Wilson joined Jack Leaman's staff one year after Julius Erving enrolled in 1968. Erving was the Minutemen's all-time leading scorer when he left college early for the ABA in 1971. He played 11 seasons in the NBA with the 76ers after five years in the ABA.

MICHIGAN: Bill Frieder joined Johnny Orr's staff one year after Wayman Britt enrolled in 1972. Britt, the Wolverines' all-time leader in

assists when his eligibility expired, was the Lakers' fourth-round draft choice in 1976.

MISSOURI: Rich Grawer joined Norm Stewart's staff two years after Mark Dressler enrolled in 1978, which was one year before former high school teammate Steve Stipanovich arrived on campus. Dressler was the "super sub" for three Big Eight Conference championship teams. Stipanovich, a second-team consensus All-America as a senior, ranks No. 2 among the Tigers' all-time leading rebounders and is No. 4 in scoring. Stipanovich, the second pick overall in the 1983 draft, played five seasons with the Pacers before his pro career was curtailed by a knee ailment.

NEW ORLEANS: Joey Stiebing joined Tim Floyd's staff directly with Melvin Simon in 1990, which was one year after high school teammate Darren Laiche enrolled and two years before high school teammates Gerald Williams and Dedric Willoughby arrived on campus. Simon, hailed as the top freshman prospect in the country, didn't attend a school in a high profile conference that year. He was the Privateers' No. 2 rebounder and No. 3 scorer for two seasons. Laiche was a spot starter as a swingman. Williams was a starter after playing for Tyler (Tex.) Junior College. Willoughby became a star at Iowa State after transferring there with Floyd.

NORTH CAROLINA STATE: Mark Phelps joined Herb Sendek's staff directly with Damon Thornton in 1996, which was one year before former high school teammate Kenny Inge arrived on campus.

NORTHEAST LOUISIANA: Mike Vining joined Lenny Fant's staff three years after Calvin Natt and Jamie Mayo enrolled in 1975, which was one year before high school teammates Kenny Natt and Eugene Robinson arrived on campus. Calvin Natt, a second-team consensus All-America as a senior, is the Indians' all-time leading scorer and rebounder. He was a first-round draft choice of the Nets in 1979 and played 10 seasons in the NBA with four different teams. Mayo is one of the school's all-time leaders in assists. Kenny Natt, who led the Indians in scoring in his senior season, was a second-round draft choice of the Pacers in 1980 and played briefly in three seasons with three different NBA teams. Robinson is the school's all-time leader in field-goal percentage and led the Indians in rebounding in his senior season.

NORTH TEXAS: Jimmy Gales joined Bill Blakeley's staff one year after Kenneth Williams enrolled in 1974. Williams, the Eagles' all-time leading rebounder, led the nation in rebounding as a senior.

OKLAHOMA: Mike Mims joined Billy Tubbs' staff one year before Wayman Tisdale enrolled in 1983. Tisdale, a first-team consensus All-America in 1983-84-85, is the Sooners' all-time leader in scoring, rebounding and field-goal shooting despite leaving school a year early. Tisdale, the second pick overall in the 1985 draft, played the last seven seasons in the NBA with the Pacers and Kings.

OKLAHOMA STATE: Steve Henson joined Leonard Hamilton's staff directly with Royce Jeffries in 1986. In his senior season, Jeffries was the Cowboys' No. 2 scorer and rebounder (behind Byron Houston).

PROVIDENCE: Nick Macarchuk joined Dave Gavitt's staff three years after Ernie DiGregorio enrolled in 1969. DiGregorio, a first-team consensus All-America as a senior, is the Friars' all-time assists leader and is fifth in scoring. DiGregorio, the third pick overall in the 1973 draft, played five seasons in the NBA with three different teams. . . . Jimmy Adams joined Gavitt's staff two years after Marvin Barnes enrolled in 1970. Barnes, a first-team consensus All-America as a senior when he led the nation in rebounding, is the Friars' all-time leading rebounder and is second in scoring. Barnes, the second pick overall in the 1974 NBA draft, played four seasons in the NBA with four different teams after spending two years in the ABA with the Spirits of St. Louis.

ROBERT MORRIS: Jim Elias joined Matt Furjanic's staff two years after Chipper Harris enrolled in 1980. Harris is the Colonials' all-time leading scorer and ranks third in career assists.

SAINT LOUIS: Dick Versace joined Bob Polk's staff directly with Leartha Scott in 1973. Scott was the Billikens' No. 2 scorer as a freshman before encountering academic problems and transferring to Wisconsin-Parkside. . . . Mitch Haskins joined Ron Coleman's staff directly with Ricky Frazier in 1977. Frazier, the Billikens' leading scorer as a freshman before transferring to Missouri, was a second-round draft choice of the Bulls in 1982. . . . Larry Hughes, the Bills' top recruit for 1997-98, rejoined Derek Thomas, who had coached him early in his career at a local high school.

SAN FRANCISCO: Don Risley joined Bob Gaillard's staff directly with Bill Cartwright in 1975. Cartwright, a second-team consensus All-America as a sophomore and senior, is the Dons' all-time leading scorer and is third in rebounding. Cartwright, the third overall pick in the 1979 draft, played the last 12 seasons with the Knicks and Bulls.

SOUTHERN CAL: Rudy Washington joined Bob Boyd's staff one year before Leonel Marquetti and Maurice Williams enrolled in 1978. Marquetti, who transferred to Hampton (Va.) Institute after two seasons with the Trojans, was a ninth-round draft choice as an undergraduate by the Spurs in 1981. Williams, whose last-second basket beat UCLA in Pauley Pavilion in 1981, was a two-year All-Pacific-10 first-team forward.

UNLV: George McQuarn joined Jerry Tarkanian's staff three years after Lewis Brown enrolled in 1973. Brown, who ranks second in school history in rebounding (behind Sidney Green), was a fourth-round draft choice of the Bucks in 1977. Brown played briefly with the Bullets in the 1980-81 season.

UTAH STATE: Jim Harrick joined Dutch Belnap's staff one year before Mike Santos and high school teammate Oscar Williams enrolled in 1974. Santos, the Aggies' all-time No. 12 scorer, was a third-round draft choice of the Buffalo Braves in 1978. Williams still holds school assists records for a game, season and career.

VILLANOVA: Jimmy Salmon joined Steve Lappas' staff directly with star forward Tim Thomas, who averaged 16.9 points per game in 1996-97 as a freshman before turning pro early.

VIRGINIA: Richard Schmidt joined Terry Holland's staff directly with Jeff Lamp and Lee Raker in 1977. Lamp, a consensus second-team All-America as a senior, is the Cavaliers' all-time No. 2 scorer (behind Bryant Stith). Lamp, a first-round draft choice of the Trail Blazers in 1981, played six years in the NBA with four different teams. Raker, the seventh-leading scorer in school history when his eligibility expired, was a fourth-round draft pick of San Diego.

VIRGINIA TECH: Bob Schneider joined Charlie Moir's staff directly with his son, Jeff Schneider, in 1978. Jeff was the 11th-leading scorer in the Hokies' history when his eligibility expired.

SUDDEN IMPACT

Here is a year-by-year list of the top 10 freshman scorers from 1972-73 through 1996-97:

1972-73

PLAYER, SCHOOL	G	PTS.	AVG.
James Williams, Austin Peay	29	854	29.4
Coniel Norman, Arizona	24	576	24.0
Robert Parish, Centenary	27	620	23.0
Alvan Adams, Oklahoma	21	464	22.1
Phil Sellers, Rutgers	26	506	19.5
Ira Terrell, SMU	25	484	19.4
Eric Money, Arizona	26	492	18.9
Ron Lee, Oregon	26	486	18.7
Bob Warner, Maine	23	427	18.6
Dirk Dunbar, Central Michigan	26	473	18.2

1973-74

PLAYER, SCHOOL	G	PTS.	AVG.
Eddie Johnson, Auburn	26	567	21.8
Rich Laurel, Hofstra	22	414	18.8
Dexter Reed, Memphis State	30	551	18.4
Adrian Dantley, Notre Dame	28	511	18.3
Ernie Grunfeld, Tennessee	26	453	17.4
Tony Parker, Loyola (Ill.)	26	445	17.1
Steve Puidokas, Washington St.	27	454	16.8

Warren Baker, West Virginia	25	415	16.6
Bob Elliott, Arizona	26	429	16.5
Essie Hollis, St. Bonaventure	30	440	14.7

1974-75

PLAYER, SCHOOL	G	PTS.	AVG.
Bernard King, Tennessee	25	661	26.4
Jacky Dorsey, Georgia	25	646	25.8
Jon Manning, Oklahoma City	26	563	21.7
Gary Winton, Army	24	472	19.7
Skip Wise, Clemson	25	462	18.5
Mike Mitchell, Auburn	25	461	18.4
Kenny Higgs, Louisiana State	26	470	18.1
Keith Herron, Villanova	26	465	17.9
Steve Conner, Boise State	26	459	17.7
Greg Sanders, St. Bonaventure	27	473	17.5

1975-76

PLAYER, SCHOOL	G	PTS.	AVG.
Calvin Natt, NE Louisiana	25	516	20.6
Manny Figueroa, St. Francis (N.Y.)	18	334	18.6
Clint Richardson, Seattle	26	481	18.5
Ray White, Mississippi State	26	475	18.3
Winfred Boynes, San Francisco	30	542	18.1
Herb Stamper, Morehead State	25	450	18.0
John Gerdy, Davidson	26	465	17.9
Gary Hooker, Mississippi State	26	461	17.7
Edgar Jones, Nevada-Reno	26	457	17.6
Norman Black, St. Joseph's	26	440	16.9

1976-77

PLAYER, SCHOOL	G	PTS.	AVG.
Ronne Perry, Holy Cross	25	574	23.0
Ronnie Valentine, Old Dominion	29	650	22.4
Ken Webb, Fairleigh Dickinson	25	546	21.8
Andrew Toney, Southwestern La.	29	608	21.0
Steve Stielper, James Madison	26	543	20.9
Jonathan Moore, Furman	28	561	20.0
Sylvester Williams, Rhode Island	26	520	20.0
Michael Brooks, La Salle	29	579	20.0

PLAYER, SCHOOL	G	PTS.	AVG.
Dave Bootcheck, Eastern Kentucky	24	473	19.7
Jamie Ciampaglio, Wagner	22	427	19.4

1977-78

PLAYER, SCHOOL	G	PTS.	AVG.
Jeff Ruland, Iona	26	580	22.3
Danny Ainge, Brigham Young	30	632	21.1
Mike McGee, Michigan	27	531	19.7
Mike Perry, Richmond	26	494	19.0
Mike Rhodes, Vanderbilt	27	507	18.8
Franklin Edwards, Cleveland State	25	467	18.7
Chris Dodds, Davidson	27	500	18.5
Cliff Robinson, Southern Cal	24	442	18.4
Garry Jordan, Niagara	26	467	18.0
B.B. Davis, Lamar	27	474	17.6

1978-79

PLAYER, SCHOOL	G	PTS.	AVG.
Mark Aguirre, DePaul	32	767	24.0
Mitchell Anderson, Bradley	26	545	21.0
Dan McLaughlin, Fairleigh Dickinson	25	485	19.4
Corny Thompson, Connecticut	29	538	18.6
Dale Solomon, Virginia Tech	30	534	17.8
Sleepy Floyd, Georgetown	29	480	16.6
George Washington, Marshall	27	438	16.2
Mike McKay, Connecticut	28	444	15.9
Steve Barker, Samford	27	422	15.6
Eddie Hughes, Colorado State	27	416	15.4

1979-80

PLAYER, SCHOOL	G	PTS.	AVG.
Harry Kelly, Texas Southern	26	753	29.0
Rick Gilliam, West Chester State	17	345	20.3
Dominique Wilkins, Georgia	16	297	18.6
Kenneth Lyons, North Texas State	27	478	17.7
Tony Warren, Butler	27	476	17.6
David Taylor, Hofstra	28	492	17.6
Troy Lee Mikell, East Tennessee St.	27	447	16.6

PLAYER, SCHOOL	G	PTS.	AVG.
Ray McCallum, Ball State	28	463	16.5
Rob Williams, Houston	28	456	16.3
Cliff Levingston, Wichita State	29	457	15.8

1980-81

PLAYER, SCHOOL	G	PTS.	AVG.
Gary Springer, Iona	29	577	19.9
Ronnie Williams, Florida	28	542	19.4
Al McClain, New Hampshire	26	492	18.9
Vernon Delancey, Florida	28	497	17.8
Willie Jackson, Centenary	28	482	17.2
Andy Bolden, George Mason	26	440	16.9
Russell Cross, Purdue	32	540	16.9
Mike Payne, Fairleigh Dickinson	26	428	16.5
George Singleton, Furman	27	435	16.1
Butch Graves, Yale	26	411	15.8

1981-82

PLAYER, SCHOOL	G	PTS.	AVG.
Steve Black, La Salle	28	561	20.0
Keith Lee, Memphis State	29	532	18.3
Joe Dumars, McNeese State	29	527	18.2
Alfredrick Hughes, Loyola (Ill.)	29	494	17.0
Ray Hall, Canisius	27	454	16.8
Chris Mullin, St. John's	30	498	16.6
Donald Russell, Massachusetts	27	444	16.4
Ken Epperson, Toledo	26	420	16.2
Carlos Yates, George Mason	27	429	15.9
Mike Brown, George Washington	27	421	15.6

1982-83

PLAYER, SCHOOL	G	PTS.	AVG.
Wayman Tisdale, Oklahoma	33	810	24.5
Karl Malone, Louisiana Tech	28	586	20.9
Mark Price, Georgia Tech	28	568	20.3
John Williams, Indiana State	28	520	18.6
Johhny Dawkins, Duke	28	506	18.1
Michael Young, Houston	34	588	17.3
Mike Alexander, Boston Univ.	31	525	16.9
Troy Webster, George Washington	27	457	16.9
Earl Kelley, Connecticut	27	451	16.7
Andre McCloud, Seton Hall	29	481	16.6

1983-84

PLAYER, SCHOOL	G	PTS.	AVG.
Antonio Parris, Eastern Kentucky	26	489	18.8
Ronnie Murphy, Jacksonville	26	465	17.9
Reggie Lewis, Northeastern	32	571	17.8
Tim McAlister, Oklahoma	31	498	16.1
Steve Alford, Indiana	31	479	15.5
Terrance Bailey, Wagner	26	403	15.5
Ben Hinson, Baptist	28	420	15.0
Dwayne Washington, Syracuse	32	460	14.4
Booker James, Western Michigan	26	371	14.3
Bruce Dalrymple, Georgia Tech	29	394	13.6

1984-85

PLAYER, SCHOOL	G	PTS.	AVG.
Kenny Battle, Northern Illinois	27	544	20.1
Dan Majerle, Central Michigan	12	223	18.6
Daren Queenan, Lehigh	30	546	18.2
Stan Kimbrough, Central Florida	28	507	18.1
Skip Henderson, Marshall	33	584	17.7
Byron Larkin, Xavier	29	492	17.0
Clinton Hinton, UNC Charlotte	28	471	16.8
David Rivers, Notre Dame	30	474	15.8
Cedric Henderson, Georgia	28	433	15.5
George Jones, Northwestern State	28	429	15.3

1985-86

PLAYER, SCHOOL	G	PTS.	AVG.
Norris Coleman, Kansas State	28	609	21.8
Charles Price, Grambling	26	469	18.0
Kenny Sanders, George Mason	22	394	17.9
Tom Lewis, Southern Cal	27	475	17.6
Todd Lichti, Stanford	30	516	17.2
Eric Brown, Miami (Fla.)	28	460	16.4
Paul Graham, Ohio U.	29	461	15.9
Sean Elliott, Arizona	32	499	15.6
Otis Ellis, Lafayette	23	358	15.6
John Rankin, Drexel	31	466	15.0

1986-87

PLAYER, SCHOOL	G	PTS.	AVG.
Lionel Simmons, La Salle	33	670	20.3
Earl Wise, Tennessee Tech	27	503	18.6
Chris Gaines, Hawaii	28	480	17.1
Trimill Hayward, Miami (Ohio)	27	462	17.1
Tony Ross, San Diego State	28	455	16.3
Rex Chapman, Kentucky	29	464	16.0
Anthony Carver, Old Dominion	28	433	15.5
Greg Anthony, Portland	28	432	15.4
J.R. Reid, North Carolina	36	528	14.7
Tito Horford, Miami (Fla.)	25	358	14.3

1987-88

PLAYER, SCHOOL	G	PTS.	AVG.
Mark Macon, Temple	34	699	20.6
Gus Hill, East Carolina	26	503	19.3
Paul Newman, Delaware State	26	455	17.5
Richard Dumas, Oklahoma State	30	521	17.4
Kevin Brooks, Southwestern La.	27	453	16.8
Derreck Orr, Coppin State	26	435	16.7
Greg Dennis, East Tennessee State	29	475	16.4
Willie Brand, Texas-Arlington	29	472	16.3
James Scott, Arkansas-Little Rock	31	497	16.0
Jay Edwards, Indiana	23	358	15.6

1988-89

PLAYER, SCHOOL	G	PTS.	AVG.
Chris Jackson, Louisiana State	32	965	30.2
Tony Bennett, Wisconsin-Green Bay	27	516	19.1
Jim McCoy, Massachusetts	28	555	19.8
Dwight Stewart, Fla. International	28	484	17.3
Bruce Elder, Davidson	20	343	17.2

Henry Williams, UNC			
Charlotte	29	505	17.4
Don MacLean, UCLA	31	577	18.6
Lamont Middleton, Hartford	28	460	16.4
Ed Petersen, Yale	28	458	16.4
Radenko Dobras, South Florida	28	453	16.2

1989-90

PLAYER, SCHOOL	G	PTS.	AVG.
Alphonso Ford, Miss. Valley			
State	27	808	29.9
Harold Miner, Southern Cal	28	578	20.6
Kenny Anderson, Georgia Tech	35	721	20.6
Allan Houston, Tennessee	30	609	20.3
Matt O'Brien, Georgia State	28	515	18.4
Anthony Reed, Tulane	28	514	18.4
Tony Dunkin, Coastal Carolina	23	416	18.1
Calbert Cheaney, Indiana	29	495	17.1
Ronnie Battle, Auburn	31	527	17.0
Ronnie Schmitz, Missouri-K.C.	28	471	16.8

1990-91

PLAYER, SCHOOL	G	PTS.	AVG.
Jarvis Lang, UNC Charlotte	28	548	19.6
Jeff Webster, Oklahoma	35	640	18.3
Bernard Blunt, St. Joseph's	30	563	18.8
Lester Lyons, East Carolina	28	494	17.6
James Robinson, Alabama	33	554	16.8
Tony Dumas, Missouri-K.C.	28	462	16.5
Rodney Rogers, Wake Forest	30	489	16.3
Myron Walker, Robert Morris	21	342	16.3
Kendrick Warren, Va.			
Commonwealth	31	488	15.7
Jamal Faulkner, Arizona State	30	462	15.4

1991-92

PLAYER, SCHOOL	G	PTS.	AVG.
Tim Roberts, Southern U.	30	654	21.8
Terrence Rencher, Texas	34	648	19.1
Lawrence Moten, Syracuse	32	583	18.2
Jalen Rose, Michigan	34	597	17.6
Reggie Jackson, Nicholls State	28	460	16.4
Miladin Mutavdzic, Wagner	28	460	16.4
Shawn Respert, Michigan State	30	474	15.8
Damon Johnson, Texas A&M	17	266	15.6

Chris Webber, Michigan	34	528	15.5
Kirby Fortenberry, Alabama			
State	28	425	15.2

1992-93

PLAYER, SCHOOL	G	PTS.	AVG.
Eddie Benton, Vermont	26	619	23.8
Chris McGuthrie, Mount St.			
Mary's	28	553	19.8
Gary Trent, Ohio U.	27	514	19.0
Scotty Thurman, Arkansas	31	540	17.4
Othella Harrington,			
Georgetown	33	554	16.8
Kerry Blackshear, Stetson	27	451	16.7
Keith Veney, Lamar	27	449	16.6
Steve Edwards, Miami (Fla.)	27	430	15.9
Jimmy Lunsford, Alabama St.	22	346	15.7
Odell Hodge, Old Dominion	29	426	14.7

1993-94

PLAYER, SCHOOL	G	PTS.	AVG.
Joe Smith, Maryland	30	582	19.4
Tunji Awojobi, Boston Univ.	27	510	18.9
Keith Van Horn, Utah	25	457	18.3
Charles Smith, Rider	30	507	16.9
Shea Seals, Tulsa	28	470	16.8
Dontonio Wingfield,			
Cincinnati	29	465	16.0
Kiwane Garris, Illinois	28	446	15.9
Ronnie Henderson, Louisiana			
State	27	429	15.9
Jess Settles, Iowa	27	414	15.3
Jerald Honeycutt, Tulane	29	444	15.3

1994-95

PLAYER, SCHOOL	G	PTS.	AVG.
Allen Iverson, Georgetown	30	613	20.4
Ronnell Williams, Southern U.	24	482	20.1
Tom Kilgore, Central			
Michigan	16	303	18.9
Felipe Lopez, St. John's	28	498	17.8
Adonal Foyle, Colgate	30	509	17.0
Tim Gill, Oral Roberts	26	424	16.3
Bonzi Wells, Ball State	30	474	15.8
Juan Bragg, Texas Christian	26	405	15.6

| Danny Fortson, Cincinnati | 34 | 514 | 15.1 |
| Kevin Simmons, UC Irvine | 29 | 433 | 14.9 |

1995-96

PLAYER, SCHOOL	G	PTS.	AVG.
Shareef Abdur-Rahim, California	28	590	21.1
Damion Walker, Texas Christian	30	616	20.5
Stephon Marbury, Georgia Tech	36	679	18.9
Chauncey Billups, Colorado	26	465	17.9
Jabari Outtz, Howard	27	472	17.5
Troy Green, Southeastern La.	27	449	16.6
Anthony Stacey, Bowling Green	27	433	16.0

Brent Corley, VMI	28	441	15.8
B.J. McKie, South Carolina	31	478	15.4
T.J. Lux, Northern Illinois	30	457	15.2

1996-97

PLAYER, SCHOOL	G	PTS.	AVG.
Donnie Carr, La Salle	27	646	23.9
Shaheen Holloway, Seton Hall	28	485	17.3
Jimmal Ball, Akron	26	444	17.1
Tim Thomas, Villanova	32	542	16.9
Ricky Bellinger, St. Peter's	27	440	16.3
Richie Parker, Long Island	29	466	16.1
Richard Hamilton, Connecticut	32	509	15.9
Xavier Singletary, Howard	27	421	15.6
Mike Wozniak, Cal Poly-SLO	30	461	15.4
Craig Claxton, Hofstra	27	406	15.0

12

WOMEN'S HOOPS

As the 1980s drew to a close, an influential sportswriter took a gander at the state of women's athletics and wondered why, with more females than ever taking up sports and fitness activities, there wasn't more interest in women's team sports. Figure skating, gymnastics, tennis, swimming and golf were more identifiable with women participants and spectators, who easily related to the personality factor in individual sports. Where were the matinee idols in women's basketball? After the bodacious Cheryl Miller completed her career at Southern Cal in 1986, the sport lacked a personality to drive it. Before the Magic Johnson-Larry Bird rivalry that emerged in the 1980s, for example, the NBA didn't have any particular sizzle. Women's basketball without Miller continued to grow both on the court and in the stands, but something was missing. The game's biggest supporters and those in the media sensed that it could reach a point of breaking out, of emerging more into the mainstream of sports. But when? And how? And who would do it? The questions got a decisive answer during the 1994-95 season, when a band of unlikely heroines from the University of Connecticut stormed to a perfect 35-0 champi-

onship season, giving women's college basketball a higher profile. As a result, the game has exploded onto the scene with Final Four sellouts, broader corporate sponsorship and professional marketing and generous television that promises to yield more going into the 21st century.

"We've put women's basketball into the minds of a lot of people," said UConn coach Geno Auriemma, a relentless chatterbox and amateur stand-up comic, in the moments after winning the title over favored Tennessee. "We went 35-0 and won the national championship. I can't be eloquent at this time. I'm sure it was a great show today. It was great basketball." Actually, the keys to the Huskies' success, and the reasons why they became a national sports story, are loaded into his comments. For only the third time, a women's team won a national title undefeated, with UConn joining Louisiana Tech in 1981 and the 1986 Texas team. No other team has won as many games en route to a spotless record and an NCAA championship. That in itself gets attention, no matter where you play. That UConn is in the backyard of the New York media market is no coincidence. Once the newspapers began picking up the story as

The 1996 U.S. Women's Olympic Basketball Team.

the season went along, the television stations followed. That bred spoof treatment on "Saturday Night Live," and post-title appearances on David Letterman, Regis & Kathie Lee, and other yak-yak shows. Why such a fuss? Auriemma originally drew the attention of the media several years ago, and still has a difficult time pulling himself away from postgame press conferences. Sarcastic one-liners and articulate, lucid remarks on the game keep scribes happy and writing.

In Connecticut, the state the size of a bread box, UConn basketball is big-time. Fans who couldn't get tickets to men's games ended up selling out Gampel Pavilion for the women. But lots of teams have good players, top-notch coaches

and loyal fans. Why this team? As UConn began drawing national notice, the players became more than athletes. Like Cheryl Miller a decade before, they became personalities, sweethearts to some, who identified with their visible enjoyment of the game on the court and their example away from it. The 1995 national player of the year, Rebecca Lobo, is a classic example. A finesse forward with great outside shooting range and terrific passing ability, Lobo exemplified everything UConn was all about: unselfishness, teamwork, hustle and enthusiasm. Point guard Jennifer Rizzotti and strong forward Jamelle Elliott manifested those qualities in a blue-collar fashion. Kara Wolters, a 6-7 enforcer, is probably the most dominating post player in the game since Anne Donovan played for

Old Dominion in the early 1980s. With the Gotham and New England press chronicling every game and the team having to hide from reporters and fans on occasion to get some privacy, UConn tapped into something few other women's teams ever have done. "I don't think you can top this," Auriemma said. "Thirty-five-and-oh and national champions is about as well as you can do."

The signs of an explosion were apparent in the years leading up to Lobo & Co. In UConn's first Final Four trip in 1991, the exciting, and excitable Virginia guard tandem of Dawn Staley and Tammi Reiss generated vast media attention, although the Cavaliers fell short of getting the brass ring. Upsets were abounding in the NCAA tournament, which for many years was a predictable exercise in which the top women's teams advanced with little suspense. New programs were getting through to the Sweet 16 and making their entries into the national rankings. The supply of gifted athletes with exciting games kept increasing. In the two years before UConn made its historic, dazzling run, the Final Four was loaded with players who helped elevate public perception about women players. Not since Miller has a single player attracted the raves as Sheryl Swoopes did during the two seasons she played for Texas Tech. From 1991 to 1993, the junior college transfer scored 1,645 points, grabbed 597 rebounds and turned heads with her smooth, complete offensive game and full-court talents. The Lady Raiders won the 1993 national championship as she broke Bill Walton's NCAA title game record by scoring 47 points against Ohio State. At halftime of that game, women's media guru Mel Greenberg, who has seen every championship since the early 1970s, made a bold declaration: "This is better than Miller." A year later, an unheralded North Carolina team faced the unenviable task in the title contest of trying to topple Louisiana Tech, which shocked No. 1 Tennessee in the regionals. Charlotte Smith had been enjoying a sterling year after an inauspicious start to her college career, but not even she could have imagined how the basketball gods would annoint her. With less than a second remaining and Tech leading by 57-56 in a rather lackluster contest, Smith set up for a three-point shot, found herself wide open on a fake off the inbounds pass, and nailed the trey at the buzzer. Never had there been such an ending for a women's title game.

Building on the excitement from the close of the 1995-96 season and the best women's TV ratings, as ESPN took over exclusive coverage of the NCAA Tournament, another major development took place. Following the end of an undefeated tour by the U.S. National team against college squads, the National Basketball Association announced that by the summer of 1997, it would launch a summer professional league for women. The announcement came on the heels of the organization of the American Basketball League (ABL) by several Silicon Valley investors, who were tentatively scheduling to begin play in the fall of 1996. The ABL had signed 10 of the national team (later Olympic) players to contracts, promising an average salary of $70,000. But the NBA league, endorsed heartily by Commissioner David Stern, might be the one that sticks. After many failed efforts at a women's pro league in the late 1970s and early 1980s, very little has happened in that direction. The TV sports marketplace has become even more crowded, and comparisons between men's and women's basketball haven't gone away. However, the national team has been able to show how much better women (like men) become as they grow into their late 20s and beyond. To see a beefy Lisa Leslie, an even quicker and more well-rounded Sheryl Swoopes and the 30ish veterans Teresa Edwards and Katrina McClain is to see what a women's pro league would look like. As these players become more well-known to average sports fans, and as they are on television and written about in the papers more frequently, the fan base is expected to grow. The NBA has a built-in system for its league to make it and even make a profit. Starting up, there will be eight teams, all in NBA cities and playing in NBA arenas with the staff of that NBA franchise managing daily operations. Throw in a national TV contract, the league's phenomenal marketing and promotional divisions as well as its licensed merchandise line, and this is perhaps the best, and maybe the best last chance, for a women's league to last in the United States.

The Early Years

To understand how women have gotten to this point in their basketball development, it's necessary to look back at the beginnings. Those origins coincided with the invention of basketball itself, but progress lagged for many decades until the 1970s.

Just months after Dr. James Naismith put up his first peach basket in Springfield, Mass., a physical education teacher at a nearby women's college asked him to explain the new game of "basket ball" in hopes of introducing it to her students. In early 1892, Lithuanian-born Senda Berenson adopted the same general concept of the game as Naismith, but rewrote a substantial portion of his original rule book to suit prevailing Victorian assumptions of femininity and the kind of physical stress that females could endure. Not surprisingly, the first contests that Berenson organized at Smith College limited players to one of three sections of the court and prohibited them from snatching the ball from an opponent.

Other women teachers flocked to write their own rules. Games sprung up at Mount Holyoke College and at Sophie Newcomb College (now part of Tulane University), where women played 11 to a side, and all were restricted to a small portion of the floor. Players could guard opponents only vertically, and the no-snatch rule, which would dominate most women's rules for years, continued to apply. In some places dribbling was not allowed and defenders could not try to steal or bat away an opponent's pass. Bounce passes also were taboo for many years. All these rules were part of an effort to eliminate the roughness that Berenson and her peers found appalling in the basketball games they saw men play.

The controls on women's rules, which fit like the typical corset of the day, began a pattern of events that steered women's basketball for more than 70 years, until women began playing the five-player version that exists today. Women physical educators steadfastly believed that the purpose of basketball and any other sport was for the fitness and well-being of the athlete, and not for competition's sake. Basketball simply was too rough for societal acceptance and their own ideals of physical activity, so future rules revisions that opened up the game came slowly and in some instances, with great reluctance.

As a result, the experience of women in basketball has been drastically different from that of men, although they've been playing just as long. It also explains women's delayed entry into more competitive brands of basketball, and why the women's college game today, despite dramatic progress in the last 20 years, lacks the overt commercialization of men's basketball. The perspective and approach of women leaders, both in the physical education realm through the 1960s and by feminist-minded coaches and athletic administrators since then, in some ways resonate with the values and aspirations of the founders of the women's game.

In addition to the restrictive rules, Berenson and colleagues emphasized the importance of only women teaching and coaching female athletes. This issue has become a highly volatile aspect of the contentious gender equity debate currently roaring through college athletic departments, in which male coaching candidates occasionally are bypassed in favor of women.

One other turn-of-the-century issue still has delicate ramifications and is a hot-button topic that surfaces in larger question of women's rights in sports. Arguments raged for years about whether females would be made more masculine if they undertook athletic pursuits. Then and now, women coaches and teachers pleaded that such activity ideally fosters the well-being, health, vitality, self-image, and confidence of young women. Discussions of women, sports, and sexuality often are laced with connotations of what constitutes feminine nature. Ardent women's sports leaders now contend that health benefits from sports are necessary for all girls and women, and charge their critics routinely engage in homophobic scare tactics to stunt women's advances in athletics.

In April 1896, four years after Berenson published the first Spalding rules for women, the first known women's intercollegiate varsity basketball game was played. Stanford defeated California 2-1 after playing two 20-minute halves, precisely the same time rules that govern the current women's college game. Each team played with nine players and although 700 people cheered with interest, they all were women. At California's request, men were strictly forbidden from watching women compete. Women teachers across the country feared a co-ed audience would prevent them from fulfilling their educational ideals, which did not include spectators who may be interested in something besides their athletic abilities. This philosophy, rooted in the creed of universal participation, rather than elite competition by a talented few, did not pass easily from the scene.

But there was more than a sporadic staging of women's basketball in colleges and high schools between 1900 and 1920. This reflected a new-found sense of independence by some women and a desire by others to strive for more competition than what was offered in intramural programs. While they are the forerunners of the pro-competition feminists in the 1970s and 1980s, and descended from the earliest American women's rights leaders, neither were they terribly interested in upsetting the societal equilibrium of the time. Ironically, as many American women were expressing some limited social freedoms by adopting a Jazz Age flapper lifestyle, women physical education teachers took steps to force female athletic participation into a very narrow domain. They worried that women would not be allowed to take part in sports activities at all if they veered too far away from traditional cultural prescriptions that still dominated educational institutions. Throughout the first half of the 20th century, women's athletic experiences in the educational realm consisted mostly of "play days," large intramural events that emphasized the values their teachers held dear.

Women's collegiate competition whittled away quickly in the 1920s and did not return on a significant national scale until the late 1960s.

High school teams were more commonplace and were most popular in the South and some parts of the Midwest. But the Amateur Athletic Union, which was virtually all male, eyed women's basketball and other women's sports to increase its membership and offerings for athletes. Naturally, the women teachers resisted, and in the early 1920s, tenaciously fought the AAU's efforts. They feared a pro-competition avenue opening for women that they regarded as exploitive and exclusive. Some leaders quickly met to form organizations that worked to oppose women's participation in the Olympic games and denied attempts by the AAU to be affiliated with them.

The AAU fanned the flames by proposing to nationalize women's basketball rules and speed up the game to augment high-level competition. It wasn't until the 1930s that the AAU was allowed membership in women's sports groups. By then, pockets of basketball hotbeds were creating unprecedented opportunities for girls and women. The earliest national-caliber players hailed not from college campuses but from factory and mill towns and thousands of high school communities that placed their female basketball teams on a rare pedestal of respect and admiration.

Women's Basketball Tournaments Increase

That tradition was especially passionate in Iowa, where the famous girls high school basketball tournament got its start in the mid-1920s. The Iowa Girls High School Athletic Union (IGHSAU) was set up expressly to offer interscholastic basketball competition at the same time other states were moving in the opposite direction. Eventually, the girls tournament would come to outdraw the boys and offer a fervent rallying point for fans in Des Moines all the way down to the smallest farming villages. It was as if all the controversies about how females should play basketball missed Iowa completely; the men who set up the IGHSAU firmly believed that girls would benefit from the experience regardless of their life's ambitions. In 1985, however, the six-player tournament got some competition when a five-player option was offered for the first time. By 1993, six-player basketball had been phased out altogether. All across the South, industrial leagues sprang up between the world wars, providing substantial competition for working women and others who wanted to continue playing after high school. Between 1927 and 1932, a Dallas insurance firm, Employers Casualty Company, built a powerful team called the Golden Cyclones that won an AAU national tournament and featured future Olympic champion and golfing legend Babe Didrikson. Two other Dallas teams, the Sunoco Oil Company Oilers and the Schepps Aces, also won national titles, fueling rivalries that were widely reported in the local papers. The Depression forced numerous companies to disband their teams, and the Golden Cyclones were an early victim.

Southern industrial teams continued to dominate the AAUs in the post-war period, producing most of the players on the first American women's national teams. However, a number of college teams cropped up into the fray, signalling the very earliest calls for a pro-varsity existence that was still at least a generation away.

Another Texas school, Wayland Baptist in the Panhandle region, was one of the first institutions to offer basketball scholarships to women. Claude Hutcherson, who sponsored the team, known as the Flying Queens, also arranged for first class travel. They flew to major competition in such places as Mexico and Madison Square Garden in a fleet of Beechcraft Bonanzas he owned. During the 1950s, the Flying Queens locked horns for national supremacy with Nashville Business College (NBC), which boasted Nera White, who later would be inducted into the Naismith Memorial Basketball Hall of Fame. The United States won the first two women's World Championship tournaments in 1953 and 1957, primarily with players from NBC and Hutcherson's Flying Queens.

Away from the playing courts, women's sports leaders actively debated the possibility of strengthening interscholastic competition. Some more traditionally-minded women balked, arguing that women would adopt male patterns of athletic behavior they believed were corrupting and contrary to the best interests of student-athletes. A host of rules changes opened the doors even further. By 1961, the six-player game allowed two players on each side to rove full-court, and an unlimited dribble was permitted five years later. And in 1969, as the first organization devoted to women's varsity collegiate competition was formed, another dramatic new set of rules, ironically introduced on an experimental basis, permanently changed the look of women's basketball. The five-player, full-court game also was played with a 30-second shot clock to speed up the tempo. Not only was this a reward for elite players, but it symbolized the advent of modern college basketball for women.

AIAW and Title IX

As the women's liberation movement gathered steam in the late 1960s, the first major intercollegiate women's basketball tournament set off a wave of activity that permanently changed the game. Although disputes continued for the rest of the decade over how scholarships, recruiting, professional coaches, and competition would be implemented, women had decided firmly that intercollegiate play was a positive and necessary development in increasing women's opportunities in sports.

The National Collegiate Athletic Association had refused repeatedly to sponsor championships for women. In 1966, however, a group of women's sports leaders created the Commission on Intercollegiate Athletics for Women (CIAW) to look into that possibility, piquing the interest of the NCAA. The two groups would clash for 15 years until the NCAA usurped women's separate administration of varsity sports in 1981.

In 1969, a physical education teacher at West Chester (Pa.) State College quietly planted the seeds for championship-oriented competition. Carol Eckman organized the first women's invitational tournament, attracting top college teams from around the nation and showcasing the college game for the first time. Her West Chester team won the title and the event continued for two more years. The CIAW evolved into the Association of Intercollegiate Athletics for Women (AIAW), which first offered a national basketball championship tournament for the 1971—72 season.

But the biggest instrument toward full competition for women came in 1972 when Congress passed a package of laws to order sex equity in education. Title IX of those Education Amendments strictly prohibited federal funds to schools, colleges, and universities that practiced sex discrimination, whether it was in the biology lab or on the basketball court. The most celebrated Title IX cases, however, involved women's athletics, and many of those controversies rage today. It was not until the late 1970s, as the NCAA's interest in sponsoring women's sports soared, that nominal enforcement of Title IX began.

Reflecting the education-oriented philosophies of the AIAW, small colleges coached by prominent women physical education teachers dominated the early years. Immaculata College, a tiny, all-women's institution outside Philadelphia, won the first three titles behind the play of center Theresa Shank; now Theresa Grentz, she is the respected coach at Rutgers and of the 1992 U.S. Olympic team. Two of her teammates also would become leading coaches: Rene Portland of Penn State, and Marianne Stanley, who led Old Dominion to three national titles. Immaculata's coach was Cathy Rush, who like her peers received little or no stipend for coaching. However, after leaving coaching in the late 1970s, she opened up a girls sports camp business and has been a color analyst on women's television games.

Delta State University in Cleveland, Miss., won the next three titles, from 1975 to 1977. Alumna Margaret Wade was brought in to start the program from scratch in 1973, and she relied on a supremely talented local player, 6-3 Lusia Harris, the first true athletic center in the women's college game, to help lead the way. Both are in the Naismith Memorial Basketball Hall of Fame.

The early AIAW years weren't lost on a sports media intrigued by chronicling what was then a novelty. When Queens College played host to the 1973 AIAW national tournament, reporters from all the New York papers, including the *New York Times,* profiled players and coaches and ran box scores. Players congregated in a hospitality room to enjoy juice, cookies, and fellowship after games.

Two years later, New York again was the center of attention as Madison Square Garden officials invited Queens and Immaculata to face off in what became at the time the largest crowd in the United States to watch a women's game. Nearly 12,000 spectators saw Immaculata win in a preliminary to a men's game, a normal practice in women's basketball until the 1980s. Players warmed up to Helen Reddy's popular song that began: "I Am Woman, Hear Me Roar." The Garden was the site for in-season tournaments sponsored by Manufacturers Hanover that featured top college teams throughout the 1970s. The first Kodak All-American team, started by Rush, was unveiled in 1975, and is considered the most prestigious women's All-American honor today.

Although women played with a shot clock to speed up the game, it generally remained mechanical and lacked widespread athleticism for a number of years. The AIAW's first guidelines prohibited females who received athletic scholarships from competing in its sanctioned events. This ban eventually was struck down after a female college tennis player went to court. Scholarships were awarded in limited quantities beginning in 1974, a practice that eventually would benefit large, public universities. The smaller schools, with limited resources, would be pushed out of the national scope by the end of the decade.

Other AIAW policies reflected the leaders' beliefs that the interests of athletes should come first. Student-athletes had to maintain academic averages required of all students at their schools. Women players also could transfer and play immediately at their new college, since other students who transferred could participate in other extracurricular activities once they became academically eligible. No women's basketball team took greater advantage of this rule than Tennessee, which emerged nationally in large part because of transfers. Coach Pat Head persuaded 1976 Olympic teammates Pat Roberts and Cindy Brogdon to transfer to her program. They closed out their careers with the Lady Volunteers and helped Tennessee reach the upper echelon of the AIAW tournament for the first time.

The Olympic team, which won a silver medal, was perhaps the most telling indicator of how women's basketball in the United States had progressed. After being throttled by the Soviets, who boasted a starting lineup with a 7-2 center and a 6-8 forward, American coaches began searching for taller, more athletically-inclined players. They found one in Anne Donovan, a thin 6-8 player from a strong high school program in New Jersey. She joined Old Dominion in time to help win a national championship and later became a national player of the year and a three-time Olympian.

By 1978, big schools were becoming fixtures on the national scene and at the first AIAW Final Four played at UCLA. The home team, led by All-American Ann Meyers, won the title by defeating Maryland in the finals. This ushered in a new period of women's basketball as the recruiting of female players and the professionalization of coaches began in earnest. Many of the women physical education teachers who pioneered the college game were going back to the classroom. Their protégés, in many cases former players barely out of college, filled full-time positions and took the initial steps toward emulating their men's counterparts. They attended camps and tournaments that showcased top high school players, went on publicity tours, and informally organized for their professional common good.

Media attention stepped up that same season, when *Philadelphia Inquirer* reporter Mel Greenberg began the first Associated Press women's basketball poll. Those rankings framed the sport for reporters and gave schools fodder for press releases and brochures. *Parade Magazine* also began choosing girls' high school All-American basketball teams that served as a useful recruiting resource.

UCLA All-American Ann Meyers celebrates her team's 1978 AIAW national championship.

The 1978 Final Four also marked the end of the remarkable career of Carol Blazejowski, who set a women's record by averaging 38.6 points per game that season for Montclair (N.J.) State College. She is widely considered the finest jump shooter ever to play women's basketball and once scored 52 points in a game at Madison Square Garden. As she bowed out, the most decorated women's player ever jumped into prominence. Lynette Woodard of Kansas was the first true all-around athlete to play women's college basketball, starting at all five positions during her career. She scored 3,649 points, only 18 behind Pete Maravich's all-time college mark and became an All-American, Olympian, and the first woman to suit up for the Harlem Globetrotters.

Old Dominion's 1979 and 1980 national title teams exemplified more than basketball supremacy; they were an entertaining band of players who captured the attention of basketball fans in general. Flashy guard Nancy Lieberman was a street-tough New Yorker who learned the game playing against men in the playgrounds of Harlem. Center Inge Nissen, a native of Denmark, was a worldly traveler who occasionally smoked cigarettes and drank coffee during halftime. Their coach, Marianne Stanley, came on the scene after her predecessor, the fiery Pam Parsons, was the subject of complaints from players.

By the time Old Dominion rose to the top, televised women's games were not unprecedented. The first TV game was carried by NBC in 1975 between Immaculata and Maryland. NBC also carried the national title game beginning in 1978 through the early 1980s, although regular season games virtually were non-existent on the tube.

And it was over television that the final rifts between the AIAW and the NCAA erupted, resulting in an ugly, visible dispute marked by the lawsuits, intense rhetoric, and power struggles that highlight recent battles over gender equity. Title IX had forced initial compliance with its provisions in regard to use of facilities, travel and recruiting budgets, and more playing opportunities for athletes, but they hardly amounted to a drop in the basket of what women's sports leaders expected and later would demand.

AIAW leaders were optimistic as the 1970s drew to a close that a lucrative TV contract and other corporate sponsorships could lead to greater self-sufficiency. In 1980, the AIAW signed a four-year contract with NBC that amounted to $200,000 per year in television rights alone and worked other deals to help pay for partial travel expenses for national tournament teams, something it declined to do previously. But the very progress of the AIAW, and of Title IX, led to the ultimate demise of the women-dominated group. Greater demand for scholarship aid, calls from outspoken feminists for equity to match the exact level of support for men's programs, and takeover caveats from the NCAA forced their hand.

The NCAA offered a women's basketball tournament for the 1981—82 season that included promises for more television exposure and program expansion and full reimbursement for travel and expenses to the championships. That last pledge prompted most athletic directors to go with the NCAA, since their costs would be minimized and they were under Title IX threats to broaden women's offerings. Even many women basketball coaches, especially from bigger schools, thought the change would enhance the sport.

The AIAW staged its final basketball tournament the same year, but lost nearly $10,000 in the process. Rutgers defeated Texas in the Palestra in Philadelphia, but only a handful of the nation's top teams remained with the AIAW. Louisiana Tech won the first NCAA women's title on live TV and before a sold-out crowd of more than 10,000 in Norfolk, Va.

Trying to stay alive, the AIAW filed an antitrust lawsuit soon after, but later its members voted to disband. The novel experiment of a student-centered model of college sports was in place for only 11 seasons, but it opened the doors to high-level competition and produced many of the elite coaches who have controlled women's basketball since the 1980s. How they handled their new association with the NCAA proved to be an exciting experience although somewhat contentious.

The NCAA Digs In: Coming of Age in a Time of Transition

With the bitter breakup of the AIAW still fresh in their minds, women's sports leaders looked ahead to a future under the NCAA umbrella with some trepidation. Title IX was nowhere closer to being enforced, and large numbers of women coaches were leaving their positions. Men began filling many of those jobs, especially in basketball, and women feared they were losing their grip on the control of women's athletics.

But on the court, women's basketball experienced a virtual explosion of growth and interest in the 1980s. Players with superb athletic as well as basketball skills were starring in all parts of the country. Many would become Olympic stars later in the decade, as the United States replaced the Soviet Union as the dominant force in international women's basketball.

Just months after Louisiana Tech won the first NCAA title in 1982, elite coaches awaited the recruiting decision of a California teenager who came to personify the sport in an unprecedented fashion. Cheryl Miller finally cast her lot with USC, noting its major media market and academic program in public relations. Not only was Miller one of the most gifted women ever to play basketball, but her personal flair and theatrics attracted national attention and gave the sport an unmistakable identity.

She would become the first four-time Kodak All-American, and in her first two seasons guided USC to national championships. USC fans loved her emotional fury, as she pumped her fists in the air after a spectacular play. Opposing coaches and fans were infuriated when she blew kisses to the crowd or slammed down a ball after a call didn't go her way. However she was perceived by individual supporters or foes, Miller meant one thing to women's basketball. She injected personality, pizazz, and a sense of the dramatic. For once, the game was the viable entertainment option its leaders hoped it would be.

USC reached the title game in Miller's senior season, but lost to Texas in 1986. She was the leading scorer for the 1984 Olympic team that won the gold medal in Los Angeles, and continued a sports career in broadcasting after graduation. In late 1993, she took over the coaching reins at her alma mater.

There was no lack of exciting players and teams to challenge USC. In the Deep South, the Southeastern Conference asserted itself as the best league in the nation. Tennessee had been strong since the 1970s, but with the NCAA era came an increase in funding and commitment at schools like Auburn and

TRACK STAR JOYNER-KERSEE WAS CAGER, TOO

There's an argument in some sexist quarters that women's basketball is inferior because of an absence of female players with all-around athletic skills. It's easy to refute that stance, however, when one recalls Jackie Joyner-Kersee, acknowledged as the greatest female athlete in history.

Joyner, a four-year starter, averaged 9.6 points and 6.2 rebounds per game in her UCLA basketball career from 1980–81 through 1982–83 and 1984–85.

Later, she earned national acclaim with an extraordinary track and field career. Her achievements include:

• Won five medals in Olympic track and field competition, including the gold medal in the heptathlon in 1988 and 1992 and the long jump in 1988.

• Established women's world heptathlon record (7,290 points) and women's American long jump record (24 feet, 5 1/2 inches).

• Earned Sullivan Award as the nation's premier amateur athlete in 1986.

• Named Female Athlete of the Year by the Associated Press in 1987.

Georgia. LSU, Vanderbilt, and Mississippi also were regular contenders for postseason play.

Georgia turned heads by recruiting some of the top high school players in the country. In 1981, Janet Harris, a 6-3 center from Chicago, headed to Georgia to begin a migration that continues today. In the next two years, homegrown talent in guard Teresa Edwards and center Katrina McClain would join forces on one of the most talented teams ever to play. Georgia reached the Final Four in 1983 and in 1985 was favored to win the national title, but was tripped up by Old Dominion in the championship game.

What Georgia and other SEC schools embodied was the full acceptance of recruiting as a tool to advance the game. As gifted athletes who played nearly year-round on national teams and in summer leagues, these players represented the kind of student-athlete that AIAW leaders abhorred. These young women were tied down to their athletic obligations like male athletes had been for years, and there were no signs of turning back. Even more women coaches with physical education backgrounds left the profession, leaving the door open to men and women who fit the new prototype.

A win-at-all-costs recruiting mentality began to materialize at the highest levels of women's basketball, since there aren't nearly the numbers of blue chip players as come out of boys high school ranks. Toward the end of the AIAW era, a scandal rocked women's basketball badly enough to illustrate that women could fall victim to the corrupting influences the game's pioneers dreaded would happen.

When coach Pam Parsons left Old Dominion in 1977 because of protests from her players, she latched on at South Carolina, turning that school into an instant power. She embarked on a national recruiting effort—landing Evelyn Johnson, the talented younger sister of Magic Johnson, among others—to build her program. South Carolina reached the AIAW Final Four in 1980 and was a favorite to get back. But allegations of illegal recruiting, financial and academic activities, and sexual improprieties jolted the school and the sport and led to Parsons' resignation early in the 1980-81 season. A *Sports Illustrated* article detailing the situation included accusations that she was personally involved with one of her players, a charge she vehemently denied. Parsons sued the magazine for libel, but later was convicted of perjury.

The AIAW believed in self-policing of rules violations, but the South Carolina imbroglio clearly demonstrated that approach could not control flagrant abuses. The only major recruiting scandal during the NCAA era was widely reported around the country. Northeast Louisiana made the national rankings in the mid-1980s because of aggressive, nationwide recruiting. When a Mississippi high school star, 6-4 Chana Perry, caught college coaches' attention in 1983, Northeast Louisiana boosters allegedly offered her use of automobiles and other gifts and promised her jobs after graduation. An assistant provided illegal transportation and lodging during a recruiting trip and Perry was given an illegal tryout while still in high school.

Perry signed with Northeast Louisiana and in 1985 helped her team to the Final Four. But soon after, the NCAA placed the school on probation, giving it the maximum penalty for a women's pro-gram: it was not eligible for postseason play. Perry also was not allowed to play there any longer and finished her career at San Diego State.

A host of new schools reached prominent levels during the 1980s, especially from the major conferences. In the Atlantic Coast Conference, Maryland and North Carolina State received a new rival in Virginia, which dominated into the early 1990s behind the guard play of Dawn Staley. The Big Ten featured annual clashes between Ohio State and Iowa, and Purdue entered the fray toward the end of the decade. Colorado and Kansas were the most solid programs in the Big Eight. USC owned the Pacific-10 during the Miller years, but budding programs at Washington and Stanford would shift the balance northward in years to come.

Texas had the Southwest Conference all to itself, winning 188 consecutive league games and leading the nation in attendance for most of the 1980s. In 1986, the Lady Longhorns became the only NCAA champion to go undefeated, posting a 34-0 record and featuring the play of freshman forward Clarissa Davis, who earned Final Four MVP honors. She was one of four players on that team later to become an All-American, and one of three from Texas to make an Olympic team. Injuries cut short Davis' career, but not before she scored 45 points at Tennessee before a world record crowd of nearly 25,000 fans in early 1987.

And Tennessee, after several tries without success, finally won a national title in 1987, the first of three in five seasons for coach Pat Head Summitt, who had learned the recruiting game very well. She developed a pipeline to Michigan to sign the best of that state's deep talent base, and went to Florida to get Bridgette Gordon, a smooth forward who keyed her first title and a repeat performance in 1989. The Lady Volunteers won the crown again in 1991, making Summitt the only women's coach to earn three NCAA championships.

The advent of tougher academic requirements, such as Proposition 48, also changed the national picture. Tara VanDerveer left Ohio State to revive the Stanford program in 1985. She also recruited nationwide for top prep athletes, but many of them were class valedictorians and honor students. Five years later, Stanford won the national title and duplicated the feat in 1992. The 1990 Final Four, played in the spacious 25,000-seat arena on the Tennessee campus, marked another women's watershed. Although Tennessee had been ousted in the regionals, Summitt and other school officials persuaded partisan fans to come. More than 20,000 spectators watched Stanford, led by Knoxville-area native Jennifer Azzi, take the crown.

The Final Four's first advance sellout in 1993 was a fitting finale for Texas Tech senior Sheryl Swoopes, who electrified the crowd of more than 15,000 in Atlanta with a 47-point performance against Ohio State in the title game. That broke Bill Walton's Final Four record of 44 points in 1973 and made her a household name in basketball circles.

Off-the-court issues dominated news stories and NCAA policies in the early 1990s. Women sports activists stepped up efforts to push women coaches for plum jobs, and men coaches complained of reverse discrimination. And the concept of gender equity became a major source of controversy. The NCAA Task Force on Gender Equity mapped out a plan to make athletic programs comply with Title IX toward the end of the decade. But feminist demands for resources proportionate to female student enrollment placed women at severe odds with some athletic directors and football coaches, who saw their revenue-producing programs threatened.

Several basketball programs faced extinction as the 1990s opened. Oklahoma suddenly dropped its women's team during the 1990 Final Four, but threats of a lawsuit forced a change in plans. Similar pressure was put on athletic administrators at William & Mary, which proposed cutting women's basketball for financial reasons. That decision also was reversed after extensive reports appeared in major newspapers and magazines.

In 1984, Title IX was imperiled when the U.S. Supreme Court ruled that the law did not apply if

Southeastern Louisiana's Robin Roberts (right) is now a successful ESPN reporter.

specific departments of an educational institution received no federal funds. The ruling threatened to remove athletics from the realm of Title IX, but Congress overrode the court's action in 1988 by passing the Civil Rights Restoration Act, which mandated universal Title IX compliance.

Women's basketball coaches began to enter the high rent district in terms of salary and benefits in the early 1990s. No less than a half dozen coaches received six-figure contracts following the 1992—93 season, with the equal pay component of gender equity a major factor. Summitt, VanDerveer, Virginia's Debbie Ryan, and several others received the same base pay as the men's coaches at their schools. Others came close to the male standard. After coaching Texas Tech to the 1993 title, Marsha Sharp received a Lexus automobile from the school as a bonus. It was featured on the cover of the school's media guide the next

WOMEN'S CHAMPIONSHIPS, ATTENDANCE, AND TV

With judicious placement of host schools in the bracket, the NCAA women's championship almost doubled in attendance in a 10-year span from 2,455 per session in 1983 to 4,800 in 1992. There has also been an increase in the size of the field. In an era of gender equality, the bracket expanded from 32 to 40 teams in 1988, from 40 to 48 the next year, and from 48 to the same size as the men's tournament (64) in 1994. Another possible change is moving the dates of the women's tourney so it isn't overshadowed as much by the men's event.

Prior to the NCAA's first women's tournament in 1982, several alterations occurred under the auspices of the former governing body, the Association of Intercollegiate Athletics for Women (AIAW). In 1978, the 16-team, one-site event (games were played morning, noon, and night) was transformed into sectional play (four at each regional). A year later, the AIAW field was increased to 24. It decreased to 16 in its 11th and final competition in 1982, when the majority of noteworthy Division I schools chose to compete in the first NCAA championship.

Women's basketball, with few national personalities, is a difficult sell for the television networks. But NCAA executives, terrified of strident cries from Title IX muckrakers, mandated that a women's package be part of CBS' billion dollar deal to carry the men's Final Four. One of the tradeoffs, however, was forcing the women's semifinals and final to be played on back-to-back days. The format is rigorous for any athlete to endure and can be a deterrent to the women putting their best foot forward on national TV in the championship game. The lack of time to physically recuperate didn't stop Texas Tech's Sheryl Swoopes from scoring more points, 47, than any player, male or female, ever managed in an NCAA final in 1993 when she helped the Red Raiders outlast Ohio State (84-82). Swoopes was acknowledged as the best women's player since Southern Cal's Cheryl Miller in the mid-1980s.

The women's championship game has been telecast on CBS since 1987 although it hasn't generated the audience a network needs to keep it going and growing. The ratings for the first six finals were abysmal, starting with a somewhat promising 6.1 (18 share) in 1987 but falling to as low as a 3.7 (11 share) in 1990. But Swoopes' performance in a close game in 1993 helped the women notch a 5.5 rating, a 34 percent increase from the previous year and the highest since 1987. The highest-rated women's basketball game came in 1982, when Louisiana Tech defeated Cheyney on CBS in the NCAA's first female championship game. It drew a 7.3 rating.

In addition to Swoopes' pristine performance, here are other factors demonstrating why women's basketball might be on the horizon of becoming a legitimate form of sports entertainment:

• The four teams at Atlanta in 1993 were Final Four first-timers, showing perhaps the women's game could be on the verge of extensive parity similar to the men.

• In 1993, there was the first advance sellout since the women embraced a Final Four format in 1978.

• The ladies generated enough attention to make the Las Vegas bookmakers' lines.

on the cover of the school's media guide the next season.

But an equal pay dispute at USC erupted into a full-scale controversy in late 1993. Marianne Stanley, who had retooled the program into a winner, demanded the same salary as men's coach George Raveling during contract negotiations. The school offered her slightly less, near the $100,000 mark, a figure she rejected. Her contract expired and Cheryl Miller was hired, but Stanley filed an $8 million sex discrimination lawsuit. She sought reinstatement for the 1993—94 season, but her petition was rejected by the U.S. Supreme Court.

Women's coaches rushed to Stanley's side, publicly blasting USC and suggesting boycotts against the Miller-coached team. But the school contended that since Raveling's team produces revenue and the women lose money, the pressures on them to produce are different and therefore their job descriptions were not the same.

Despite the internal squabbles, women's college basketball continued to attract more fans and media interest. Attendance records have been set every season during the NCAA period, to more than four million for the 1992—93 season. The NCAA tournament was expanded three times and now matches the men's 64-team field. Television exposure also increased, as various schools and conferences signed their own deals and the NCAA

Coach Sylvia Hatchell and her North Carolina team won the 1994 NCAA Championship.

demanded several women's games as part of its men's tournament package awarded to CBS.

Marketing, promotions, and business deals will dictate the viability of women's basketball in the sports marketplace. Coaches sign endorsement contracts, speak before civic and business groups, and are positioning themselves to administer the sport when their coaching days are concluded. Recruiting and evaluation camps and tournaments have helped prepare high school players for the rigors of the college game. Developmental programs have been started by USA Basketball to foster intense competition at a younger age and instill a wider range of basketball skills. International events such as the Olympics and professional leagues for women in Europe have continued the playing careers of elite players, some of whom are competing into their 30s.

The chaste beginnings of women's basketball 100 years ago have given way completely to a modern sport that reflects the emancipation of women in society. For instance, Robin Roberts, who still ranks among the top five scorers and rebounders in Southeastern Louisiana women's history, became one of ESPN's top announcers. In

their struggles to achieve full equality, however, women in basketball still cling to some of the educational precepts that have formed the game's heritage. Finding a balance between those ideals will continue to be their biggest challenge as women's basketball moves into its second century.

Women's Preview for 1997-98

For the last two seasons, the Tennessee Lady Volunteers have had their doubters. After losing a gut-wrenching contest to Connecticut in the 1995 NCAA championship game coach Pat Summitt also said goodbye to a stellar group of seniors who had compiled one of the best four-year records in women's basketball annals. But Summitt has had the last laugh since then, winning back-to-back titles with unlikely and underrated rosters. Now, others once again will be trembling in fear of a Lady Vol machine that's on the verge of being one of the sport's most dominating dynasties. Not only does she have All-American Chamique Holdsclaw, the consensus pre-season player of the year, for two more seasons, but Summitt also assembled perhaps the best women's recruiting class ever to join her this fall.

Tennessee lost just two regulars off a 27-10 team that finished in the middle of the pack in the rugged Southeastern Conference and appeared headed for one of its most disappointing finishes in Summitt's 24 seasons in Knoxville. The Lady Vols fell out of the Top 10 for the first time in 11 years, suffered humilating losses, some by more than 20 points, many of them on national television. But a grueling victory over Old Dominion before a packed Riverfront Coliseum at the end of March capped perhaps Summitt's most improbable of title runs. She now has a women's record of five championships, and trails only John Wooden in NCAA history. A women's team hasn't completed a three-peat since Delta State pulled off the feat from 1975-77, in the AIAW era.

That feat certainly will be threatened with the return of Holdsclaw, a fluid, multi-talented 6-2 forward who is drawing comparisons to Hall of Famer Cheryl Miller. Both players won national championships in their first two collegiate seasons, and Holdsclaw said plainly after her second that she wouldn't mind having four. Add an experienced cast to go with her—point guard Kellie Jolly, center Pashen Thompson, and sophomore utility players Kyra Elzy and Niya Butts, and the Lady Vols have plenty of experience to make another run. In addition there are the freshmen—forward Tamika Catchings and guards Semeka Randall and Kristen Clement, all first-team prep All-Americans—who will step into orange uniforms amid high expectations.

Unlike the last two seasons, however, Tennessee will be the target, and the burden clearly will be on Summitt and her team. They struggled with that role earlier in this decade, when the Nikki McCray-Dana Johnson teams managed just one Final Four trip, that in 1995. And the balance in the sport is more shaky. Louisiana Tech, which beat Tennessee twice last season, has all five starters back and has a physical, athletic lineup that usually gives the Lady Vols fits. North Carolina returns the bulk of its lineup and welcomes a talented recruiting class. And Big Ten co-champion Illinois, the surprise of the Sweet 16 last year, also has most of its key players back and should make a run for higher national acclaim.

Beyond that, many of the usual contenders are in flux. Old Dominion got good news in April when point guard Ticha Penicheiro received another year of eligibility. She has been among the nation's assists leaders the last two seasons and delivered the Lady Monarchs in the NCAA tournament with crafty play. Stanford lost both its guards, including player of the year Kate Starbird, but has enough firepower in the front line to be the Pac 10 favorite once again. Kara Wolters leaves a huge void in the middle for Connecticut, which went into the Midwest Regional finals with a 33-0 record and was trampled by Tennessee, its hopes for another undefeated title season shattered. Nykesha Sales and Shea Ralph will carry the Huskies on to their typical Eastern supremacy.

Tennessee's toughest competition once again could come from within the SEC. Georgia had what some consider the second-best recruiting class, but the Lady Bulldogs have to find five new

starters. Florida reached the Elite 8 for the first time but Kodak All-American center DeLisha Milton has moved on to the pros. Alabama has enough talent to contend but is missing Shalonda Enis and a shocking upset to Notre Dame in the Sweet 16 have strengthened the Tide's occasional reputation for not showing up in big games. Vanderbilt is inconsistent but talented and Arkansas, which beat Tennessee, is unreliable. Auburn, which went from NCAA bubble team to SEC tournament champion after three shocking upsets, has to retool. Coach Joe Ciampi decided to stay after flirting with the available Nebraska job.

Numerous coaching vacancies arose because of the onset of two professional women's leagues. Angela Beck left Nebraska for the San Jose Lasers of the ABL, while Ole Miss veteran coach Van Chancellor departed to lead the WNBA's Houston Comets. Two Big 10 coaches who were fired at the end of the season—Nancy Darsch at Ohio State and Linda McDonald-Hill at Minnesota—latched on with WNBA franchises in New York and Cleveland, respectively. Other high-profile college coaches opted to stay put however. The New York Liberty approached UConn's Geno Auriemma, Jim Foster of Vanderbilt and Joe McKeown of George Washington, but they declined the offers, which were six figures but couldn't match the perks and security of the college level.

The ABL clearly got the better of the college playing talent, largely because of its winter season and average salary of $80,000. Wolters, Starbird, Milton, Enis, Georgia's La'Keshia Frett, Tracy Henderson and Kedra Holland-Corn were among the most coveted seniors who went that route. The WNBA, which played a 10-week summer season with an average salary of around $20,000, attracted Tamecka Dixon of Kansas, but the featured players were Olympic team stars Sheryl Swoopes, Lisa Leslie, Rebecca Lobo and Ruthie Bolton-Holifield and some veteran international players.

The 1998 Women's Final Four will be played in Kansas City's Kemper Arena, and for the first time the NCAA distributed ticket lottery applications to meet the demand for an event that has been a sellout for the past four years.

1997-98 WOMEN'S PRESEASON ALL-AMERICA TEAM

PLAYER	SCHOOL	YR.	POS.	HT.	HOMETOWN
Chamique Holdsclaw	Tennessee	Jr.	F-C	6-2	Astoria, N.Y.
Ticha Penicheiro	Old Dominion	Sr.	G	5-11	Figueira Da Foz, Portugal
Tracy Reid	North Carolina	Sr.	G-F	5-11	Miami, Fla.
Nykesha Sales	Connecticut	Sr.	G-F	6-0	Bloomfield, Conn.
Alisa Burras	Lousiana Tech	Sr.	C	6-3	Chicago, IL

AIAW CHAMPIONS

YEAR	CHAMPION	COACH	RUNNER-UP	SITE
1972	Immaculata	Cathy Rush	West Chester	West Chester, Pa.
1973	Immaculata	Cathy Rush	Queens (N.Y.)	Flushing, N.Y.
1974	Immaculata	Cathy Rush	Miss. College	Manhattan, Kans.
1975	Delta St.	Margaret Wade	Immaculata	Harrisonburg, Va.
1976	Delta St.	Margaret Wade	Immaculata	University Park, Pa.
1977	Delta St.	Margaret Wade	LSU	Minneapolis
1978	UCLA	Billie Moore	Maryland	Los Angeles
1979	Old Dominion	Marianne Stanley	La. Tech	Greensboro, N.C.
1980	Old Dominion	Marianne Stanley	Tenn.	Mt. Pleasant, Mich.
1981	Louisiana Tech	Sonja Hogg	Tenn.	Eugene, Ore.
1982	Rutgers	Theresa Grentz	Texas	Philadelphia

NCAA WOMEN'S CHAMPIONS

YEAR	CHAMPION	COACH	RUNNER-UP	SITE
1982	La. Tech	Sonja Hogg	Cheyney (Pa.)	Norfolk, Va.
1983	Southern Cal	Linda Sharp	La. Tech	Norfolk, Va.
1984	Southern Cal	Linda Sharp	Tennessee	Los Angeles
1985	Old Dominion	Marianne Stanley	Georgia	Austin, Tex.
1986	Texas	Jody Conradt	Southern Cal	Lexington, Ky.
1987	Tennessee	Pat Summitt	La. Tech	Austin, Tex.
1988	La. Tech	Leon Barmore	Auburn	Tacoma, Wash.
1989	Tennessee	Pat Summitt	Auburn	Tacoma, Wash.
1990	Stanford	Tara VanDerveer	Auburn	Knoxville, Tenn.
1991	Tennessee	Pat Summitt	Virginia	New Orleans
1992	Stanford	Tara VanDerveer	W. Kentucky	Los Angeles
1993	Texas Tech	Marsha Sharp	Ohio State	Atlanta
1994	N. Carolina	Sylvia Hatchell	La. Tech	Richmond, Va.
1995	Connecticut	Geno Auriemma	Tennessee	Minneapolis, MN
1996	Tennessee	Pat Summitt	Georgia	Charlotte, NC
1997	Tennessee	Pat Summitt	Old Dominion	Cincinatti, OH

NCAA OUTSTANDING PLAYER AWARD WINNERS

1982—Janice Lawrence, Louisiana Tech
1983—Cheryl Miller, Southern Cal
1984—Cheryl Miller, Southern Cal
1985—Tracy Claxton, Old Dominion
1986—Clarissa Davis, Texas
1987—Tonya Edwards, Tennessee
1988—Erica Westbrooks, Louisiana Tech
1989—Bridgette Gordon, Tennessee
1990—Jennifer Azzi, Stanford
1991—Dawn Staley, Virginia
1992—Molly Goodenbour, Stanford
1993—Sheryl Swoopes, Texas Tech
1994—Charlotte Smith, North Carolina
1995—Rebecca Lobo, Connecticut
1996—Michelle Marciniak, Tennessee
1997—Chamique Holdsclaw, Tennessee

WOMEN'S AWARDS

BRODERICK AWARD

Voted on by a national panel of women's collegiate athletic directors. First presented by the late Thomas Broderick, an athletic outfitter.

1977: Lucy Harris, Delta State
1978: Ann Meyers, UCLA
1979: Nancy Lieberman, Old Dominion
1980: Nancy Lieberman, Old Dominion
1981: Lynette Woodward, Kansas
1982: Pam Kelly, Louisiana Tech
1983: Anne Donovan, Old Dominion
1984: Cheryl Miller, Southern Cal
1985: Cheryl Miller, Southern Cal
1986: Kamie Ethridge, Texas
1987: Katrina McClain, Georgia
1988: Teresa Weatherspoon, La. Tech
1989: Bridgette Gordon, Tennessee
1990: Jennifer Azzi, Stanford
1991: Dawn Staley, Virginia
1992: Dawn Staley, Virginia
1993: Sheryl Swoopes, Texas Tech
1994—Lisa Leslie, Southern Cal
1995—Rebecca Lobo, Connecticut
1996—Jennifer Rizzotti, Connecticut

WADE TROPHY

Voted on by the National Association for Girls and Women in Sports (NAGWS) and awarded for academics and community service as well as player performance. Presented in the name of former Delta State coach Margaret Wade.

1978: Carol Blazejowski, Montclair State
1979: Nancy Lieberman, Old Dominion
1980: Nancy Lieberman, Old Dominion
1981: Lynette Woodward, Kansas
1982: Pam Kelly, Louisiana Tech
1983: LaTaunya Pollard, Long Beach State
1984: Janice Lawrence, Louisiana Tech
1985: Cheryl Miller, Southern Cal
1986: Kamie Ethridge, Texas
1987: Shelly Pennefather, Villanova
1988: Teresa Weatherspoon, Louisiana Tech
1989: Clarissa Davis, Texas
1990: Jennifer Azzi, Stanford
1991: Daedra Charles, Tennessee
1992: Susan Robinson, Penn State
1993: Karen Jennings, Nebraska
1994: Carol Ann Shudlick, Minnesota
1995: Rebecca Lobo, Connecticut
1996—Jennifer Rizzotti, Connecticut
1997—DeLisha Milton, Florida

NAISMITH TROPHY

Voted on by a panel of coaches, sportswriters and broadcasters. Presented by the Atlanta Tip-Off Club in the name of Dr. James Naismith, the inventor of basketball.

1983: Anne Donovan, Old Dominion
1984: Cheryl Miller, Southern Cal
1985: Cheryl Miller, Southern Cal
1986: Cheryl Miller, Southern Cal
1987: Clarissa Davis, Texas
1988: Sue Wicks, Rutgers
1989: Clarissa Davis, Texas
1990: Jennifer Azzi, Stanford
1991: Dawn Staley, Virginia
1992: Dawn Staley, Virginia
1993: Sheryl Swoopes, Texas Tech
1994: Lisa Leslie, Southern Cal
1995: Rebecca Lobo, Connecticut
1996: Saudia Roundtree, Georgia
1997—Kate Starbird, Stanford

WOMEN'S BASKETBALL COACHES ASSOCIATION

Voted on by WBCA members and presented by Rawlings.

1983: Anne Donovan, Old Dominion
1984: Janice Lawrence, Louisiana Tech
1985: Cheryl Miller, Southern Cal
1986: Cheryl Miller, Southern Cal
1987: Katrina McClain, Georgia
1988: Michelle Edwards, Iowa
1989: Clarissa Davis, Texas
1990: Venus Lacey, Louisiana Tech
1991: Dawn Staley, Virginia
1992: Dawn Staley, Virginia
1993: Sheryl Swoopes, Texas Tech
1994: Lisa Leslie, Southern Cal
1995: Rebecca Lobo, Connecticut
1996—Saudia Roundtree, Georgia
1997—Kate Starbird, Stanford

CONVERSE COACH OF THE YEAR

Award voted on by the Women's Basketball Coaches Association and presented by Converse athletic outfitters.

1983: Pat Summitt, Tennessee
1984: Jody Conradt, Texas
1985: Jim Foster, St. Joseph's
1986: Jody Conradt, Texas
1987: Theresa Grentz, Rutgers
1988: Vivian Stringer, Iowa
1989: Tara VanDerveer, Stanford
1990: Kay Yow, North Carolina State
1991: Rene Portland, Penn State
1992: Ferne Labati, Miami (Fla.)
1993: Vivian Stringer, Iowa
1994: Marsha Sharp, Texas Tech
1995: Pat Summitt, Tennessee
1996—Leon Barmore, Louisiana Tech
1997—Geno Auriemma, Connecticut

NAISMITH COACH OF THE YEAR

1987: Pat Summitt, Tennessee
1988: Leon Barmore, Louisiana Tech
1989: Pat Summitt, Tennessee
1990: Tara VanDerveer, Stanford
1991: Debbie Ryan, Virginia
1992: Chris Weller, Maryland
1993: Vivian Stringer, Iowa
1994: Pat Summitt, Tennessee
1995: Geno Auriemma, Connecticut
1996: Andy Landers, Georgia
1997—Geno Auriemma, Connecticut

KODAK ALL-AMERICAN SELECTIONS

Voted on by the Women's Basketball Coaches Association. Selections broken down by major and small schools started in 1983.

1974-75

Carolyn Bush, Wayland Baptist (Tex.); Marianne Crawford, Immaculata (Pa.); Nancy Dunkle, Cal State Fullerton; Lusia Harris, Delta State (Miss.); Jan Irby, William Penn (Iowa); Ann Meyers, UCLA; Brenda Moeller, Wayland Baptist (Tex.); Debbie Oing, Indiana; Sue Rojcewicz, Southern Connecticut State; Susan Yow, Elon (N.C.).

1975-76

Carol Blazejowski, Montclair State (N.J.); Cindy Brogdon, Mercer (Ga.); Nancy Dunkle, Cal State Fullerton; Doris Felderhoff, Stephen F. Austin (Tex.); Lusia Harris, Delta State (Miss.); Susie Kudma, William Penn (Iowa); Ann Meyers, UCLA; Marianne Crawford Stanley, Immaculata (Pa.); Pearl Worrell, Wayland Baptist (Tex.); Susan Yow, North Carolina State.

1976-77

Carol Blazejowski, Montclair State (N.J.); Nancy Dunkle, Cal State Fullerton; Rita Easterling, Mississippi College; Susie Snider Eppers, Baylor; Doris Felderhoff, Stephen F. Austin (Tex.); Lusia Harris, Delta State (Miss.); Charlotte Lewis, Illinois State; Ann Meyers, UCLA; Patricia Roberts, Tennessee; Mary Scharff, Immaculata (Pa.).

1977-78

Genia Beasley, North Carolina State; Carol Blazejowski, Montclair State (N.J.); Debbie Brock, Delta State (Miss.); Cindy Brogdon, Tennessee; Julie Gross, Louisiana State; Althea Gwyn, Queens (N.Y.); Kathy Harston, Wayland Baptist (Tex.); Nancy Lieberman, Old Dominion; Ann Meyers, UCLA; Lynette Woodard, Kansas.

1978-79

Cindy Brogdon, Tennessee; Carol Chason, Valdosta State (Ga.); Pat Colasardo, Montclair State (N.J.); Denise Curry, UCLA; Nancy Lieberman, Old Dominion; Jill Rankin, Wayland Baptist (Tex.); Susan Taylor, Valdosta State (Ga.); Rosie Walker, Stephen F. Austin (Tex.); Franci Washington, Ohio State; Lynette Woodard, Kansas.

1979-80

Denise Curry, UCLA; Tina Gunn, Brigham Young; Pam Kelly, Louisiana Tech; Nancy Lieberman, Old Dominion; Inge Nissen, Old Dominion; Jill Rankin, Wayland Baptist (Tex.); Susan Taylor, Valdosta State (Ga.); Rosie Walker, Stephen F. Austin (Tex.); Holly Warlick, Tennessee; Lynette Woodard, Kansas.

1980-81

Denise Curry, UCLA; Anne Donovan, Old Dominion; Pam Kelly, Louisiana; Kris Kirchner, Rutgers; Carol Menken, Oregon State; Cindy Noble, Tennessee; LaTaunya Pollard, Long Beach State; Bev Smith, Oregon; Valerie Walker, Cheyney (Pa.); Lynette Woodard, Kansas.

1981-82

Jerilynn Harper, Tennessee Tech; Janet Harris, Georgia; Pam Kelly, Louisiana Tech; Barbara Kennedy, Clemson; June Olkowski, Rutgers; Mary Ostrowski, Tennessee; Bev Smith, Oregon; Valerie Still, Kentucky; Angela Turner, Louisiana Tech; Valerie Walker, Cheyney (Pa.).

1982-83

Priscilla Gary, Kansas State; Tanya Haave, Tennessee; Anne Donovan, Old Dominion; Janice Lawrence, Louisiana Tech; Paula McGee, Southern California; Cheryl Miller, Southern California; Jasmina Perazic, Maryland; LaTaunya Pollard, Long Beach State; Valerie Still, Kentucky; Joyce Walker, Louisiana State.

1983-84

Tresa Brown, North Carolina; Janet Harris, Georgia; Becky Jackson, Auburn; Yolanda Laney, Cheyney (Pa.); Janice Lawrence, Louisiana Tech; Pam McGee, Southern California; Cheryl Miller, Southern California; Arnette Smith, Texas; Marilyn Stephens, Temple; Joyce Walker, Louisiana State.

1984-85

Anucha Browne, Northwestern; Sheila Collins, Tennessee; Kirsten Cummings, Long Beach State; Medina Dixon, Old Dominion; Teresa Edwards, Georgia; Kamie Ethridge, Texas; Pam Gant, Louisiana Tech; Janet Harris, Georgia; Eun Jung Lee, Northeast Louisiana; Cheryl Miller, Southern California.

1985-86

Cindy Brown, Long Beach State; Teresa Edwards, Georgia; Kamie Ethridge, Texas; Wanda Ford, Drake; Jennifer Gillom, Mississippi; Pam Leake, North Carolina; Lillie Mason, Western Kentucky; Katrina McClain, Georgia; Cheryl Miller, Southern California; Sue Wicks, Rutgers.

1986-87

Cindy Brown, Long Beach State; Clarissa Davis, Texas; Tracey Hall, Ohio State; Donna Holt, Virginia; Andrea Lloyd, Texas; Katrina McClain, Georgia; Vickie Orr, Auburn; Shelly Pennefather, Villanova; Teresa Weatherspoon, Louisiana Tech; Sue Wicks, Rutgers.

1987-88

Michelle Edwards, Iowa; Bridgette Gordon, Tennessee; Tracey Hall, Ohio State; Donna Holt, Virginia; Suzie McConnell, Penn State; Vickie Orr, Auburn; Penny Toler, Long Beach State; Teresa Weatherspoon, Louisiana Tech; Sue Wicks, Rutgers; Beverly Williams, Texas.

1988-89

Jennifer Azzi, Stanford; Vicky Bullett, Maryland; Clarissa Davis, Texas; Bridgette Gordon, Tennessee; Nora Lewis, Louisiana Tech; Nikita Lowry, Ohio State; Vickie Orr, Auburn; Chana Perry, San Diego State; Deanna Tate, Maryland; Penny Toler, Long Beach State.

1989-90

Jennifer Azzi, Stanford; Daedra Charles, Tennessee; Portia Hill, Stephen F. Austin (Tex.); Dale Hodges, St. Joseph's; Carolyn Jones, Auburn; Venus Lacy, Louisiana Tech; Franthea Price, Iowa; Wendy Scholtens, Vanderbilt; Dawn Staley, Virginia; Andrea Stinson, North Carolina State.

1990-91

Kerry Bascom, Connecticut; Daedra Charles, Tennessee; Dana Chatman, Louisiana State; Delmonica DeHorney, Arkansas; Sonja Henning, Stanford; Joy Holmes, Purdue; Carolyn Jones, Auburn; Genia Miller, Cal State Fullerton; Dawn Staley, Virginia; Andrea Stinson, North Carolina State.

1991-92

Shannon Cate, Montana; Dena Head, Tennessee; MaChelle Joseph, Purdue; Rosemary Kasiorek, West Virginia; Tammi Reiss, Virginia; Susan Robinson, Penn State; Frances Savage, Miami (Fla.); Dawn Staley, Virginia; Sheryl Swoopes, Texas Tech; Val Whiting, Stanford.

1992-93

Andrea Congreaves, Mercer (Ga.); Toni Foster, Iowa; Lauretta Freeman, Auburn; Heidi Gillingham, Vanderbilt; Lisa Harrison, Tennessee; Katie Smith, Ohio State; Karen Jennings, Nebraska; Sheryl Swoopes, Texas Tech; Milica Vukadinovic, California; Val Whiting, Stanford.

1993-94

Jessica Barr, Clemson; Janice Felder, Southern Mississippi; Niesa Johnson, Alabama; Lisa Leslie, Southern California; Rebecca Lobo, Connecticut; Nikki McCray, Tennessee; Andrea Nagy, Florida International; Tonya Sampson, North Carolina; Carol Ann Shudlick, Minnesota; Natalie Williams, UCLA.

1994-95

Angela Aycock, Kansas; Niesa Johnson, Alabama; Vickie Johnson, Louisiana Tech; Rebecca Lobo, Connecticut; Stacey Lovelace, Purdue; Nikki McCray, Tennessee; Wendy Palmer, Virginia; Jennifer Rizzotti, Connecticut; Shelley Sheetz, Colorado; Charlotte Smith, North Carolina.

1995-96

Shalonda Enis, Alabama; Chamique Holdsclaw, Tennessee; Vickie Johnson, Louisiana Tech; Wendy Palmer, Virginia; Jennifer Rizzotti, Connecticut; Saudia Roundtree, Georgia; Sheri Sam, Vanderbilt; Katie Smith, Ohio State; Kate Starbird, Stanford; Debra Williams, Louisiana Tech.

1996-97

Tajama Abraham, George Washington; Tamecka Dixon, Kansas; Chamique Holdsclaw, Tennessee; Clarisse Machanguana, Old Dominion; DeLisha Milton, Florida; Ticha Penicheiro, Old Dominion; Tracy Reid, North Carolina; Nykesha Sales, Connecticut; Kate Starbird, Stanford; Kara Wolters, Connecticut.

INDIVIDUAL RECORDS

MOST POINTS IN A SINGLE GAME

60—Cindy Brown, Long Beach State vs. San Jose State, Feb. 16, 1987 (20 field goals, 20 free throws).

MOST POINTS IN A SINGLE SEASON

974—Cindy Brown, Long Beach State, 1986-87 (362 field goals and 250 free throws in 35 games).

MOST POINTS IN A CAREER

3,122—Patricia Hoskins, Mississippi Valley State, 1985-86 through 1988-89 (1,196 field goals overall, 24 three-point field goals and 706 free throws in 110 games).

HIGHEST SEASON SCORING AVERAGE

33.6—Patricia Hoskins, Mississippi Valley State, 1988-89 (908 points in 27 games).

HIGHEST CAREER SCORING AVERAGE

28.4—Patricia Hoskins, Mississippi Valley State, 1985-86 through 1988-89 (3,122 points in 110 games).

MOST FIELD GOALS IN A SINGLE GAME

27—Lorri Bauman, Drake vs. Southwest Missouri State, Jan. 6, 1984 (33 attempts).

MOST FIELD GOALS IN A SINGLE SEASON

392—Barbara Kennedy, Clemson, 1981-82 (760 attempts).

MOST FIELD GOALS IN A CAREER

1,259—Joyce Walker, Louisiana State, 1980-81 through 1983-84 (2,238 attempts).

CONSECUTIVE SUCCESSFUL FIELD GOALS IN A GAME

17—Dorinda Lindstrom, Santa Clara vs. Fresno State, Nov. 30, 1986.

MOST FIELD GOALS IN A GAME WITHOUT A MISS

16 of 16—Kelly Mago, Southwest Missouri State vs. Bradley, Feb. 18, 1988.

HIGHEST FIELD-GOAL PERCENTAGE IN A SEASON

71.7%—Renay Adams, Tennessee Tech, 1990-91 (185 of 258).

HIGHEST FIELD-GOAL PERCENTAGE IN A CAREER

65.1%—Regina Days, Georgia Southern, 1984-85 through 1987-88 (835 of 1,282).

CONSECUTIVE SUCCESSFUL THREE-POINT FIELD GOALS IN A GAME

9—Susan Smith, Eastern Washington vs. Weber State, Feb. 13, 1988 (made 9 of 10 three-point attempts).

MOST THREE-POINT FIELD GOALS IN A GAME WITHOUT A MISS

8 of 8—Kristi Brown, Middle Tennessee State vs. Tennessee Tech, Feb. 15, 1992.

MOST FREE THROWS IN A GAME

23—Shaunda Greene, Washington vs. Northern Illinois, Nov. 30, 1991 (27 attempts).

MOST FREE THROWS IN A SEASON

275—Lori Bauman, Drake, 1981-82 (325 attempts).

MOST FREE THROWS IN A CAREER

907—Lori Bauman, Drake, 1980-81 through 1983-84 (1,090 attempts).

CONSECUTIVE SUCCESSFUL FREE THROWS IN A SEASON

60—Ginny Doyle, Richmond, 1991-92.

HIGHEST FREE-THROW PERCENTAGE IN A SEASON

95.0%—Ginny Doyle, Richmond, 1991-92 (96 of 101).

HIGHEST FREE-THROW PERCENTAGE IN A CAREER

87.6%—Karen Murray, Washington, 1980-81 through 1983-84 (269 of 307).

MOST REBOUNDS IN A SINGLE GAME

40—Deborah Temple, Delta State vs. UAB, Feb. 14, 1983.

MOST REBOUNDS IN A SINGLE SEASON

534—Wanda Ford, Drake, 1984-85 (30 games).

MOST REBOUNDS IN A CAREER

1,887—Wanda Ford, Drake, 1982-83 through 1985-86 (16.1 average in 117 games).

HIGHEST SEASON REBOUNDING AVERAGE

18.5—Rosina Pearson, Bethune-Cookman, 1984-85 (480 in 26 games).

HIGHEST CAREER REBOUNDING AVERAGE

16.1—Wanda Ford, Drake, 1982-83 through 1985-86 (1,887 in 117 games).

MOST ASSISTS IN A SINGLE GAME

23—Michele Burden, Kent vs. Ball State, Feb. 6, 1991.

HIGHEST SEASON ASSISTS AVERAGE

11.8—Suzie McConnell, Penn State, 1986-87 (355 in 30 games).

HIGHEST CAREER ASSISTS AVERAGE

10.3—Neacole Hall, Alabama State, 1985-86 through 1988-89 (869 in 84 games).

TEAM RECORDS

MOST POINTS BY ONE TEAM IN A SINGLE GAME

149—Long Beach State vs. San Jose State (69), Feb. 16, 1987.

MOST POINTS BY BOTH TEAMS IN A SINGLE GAME

243—Virginia (123) vs. North Carolina State (120), Jan. 12, 1991 (triple overtime).

WIDEST MARGIN OF VICTORY BETWEEN TWO DIVISION I TEAMS

101—Louisiana Tech (126) vs. Texas-Pan American (25), Feb. 18, 1989.

HIGHEST SEASON SCORING AVERAGE

96.7—Providence, 1990-91 (3,095 points in 32 games).

MOST GAMES SCORING 100 POINTS IN A SINGLE SEASON

15—Long Beach State, 1986-87.

MOST CONSECUTIVE GAMES SCORING AT LEAST 100 POINTS

6—Louisiana Tech, 1981-82.

HIGHEST AVERAGE SCORING MARGIN

33.0—Louisiana Tech, 1981-82 (87.3 offense, 54.3 defense).

MOST CONSECUTIVE VICTORIES

54—Louisiana Tech (Dec. 1, 1980 through Jan. 27, 1982; ended Jan. 29, 1982, at Old Dominion, 61-58; last Louisiana Tech defeat before streak came vs. South Carolina, 77-69).

MOST CONSECUTIVE REGULAR-SEASON VICTORIES

52—Vermont (from 1991 to 1993).

MOST CONSECUTIVE HOMECOURT VICTORIES

69—Tennessee.

MOST CONSECUTIVE DEFEATS

58—Brooklyn (Feb. 7, 1987 to Feb. 22, 1989).

All-Time Great Women's Players

JENNIFER AZZI
Stanford
5-8 – G
Oak Ridge, Tenn.

1990 recipient of Wade Trophy and Naismith National Player of the Year Award. . . . Two-time Pacific-10 Player of the Year when she was also a Kodak All-American first team selection (1989 and 1990). . . . Named MVP of the 1990 NCAA Final Four when she led Stanford to a 32-1 record and the NCAA Tournament title. . . . The Cardinal compiled a 101-23 mark during her four seasons.

Year	G	FGM	FGA	FG%	FTM	FTA	FT%	Reb.	Avg.	Pts.	Avg.
86-87	27	91	201	.453	65	95	.684	100	3.7	247	9.2
87-88	32	139	321	.433	57	72	.792	126	3.9	405	12.7
88-89	31	180	331	.544	100	127	.787	129	4.2	513	16.6
89-90	32	159	320	.497	83	104	.798	121	3.8	469	14.7
Totals	122	569	1173	.485	305	398	.766	476	3.9	1634	13.4

Three-point shooting: 70 of 172 (.407) in 1987-88, 53 of 107 (.495) in 1988-89 and 68 of 154 (.442) in 1989-90. Totals: 191 of 433 (.441).

LORRI BAUMAN
Drake
6-3 – C
Des Moines, Iowa

The first woman to score 3,000 points while playing a majority of her games under NCAA auspices. . . . Still holds seven NCAA tournament marks, including 50 points in a game in the 1982 West Regional final in a loss to Maryland. . . . Only one of nine women to score more than 3,000 points and collect more than 1,000 rebounds. . . . Drake qualified for three NCAA Tournament trips during her career. . . . In 120 games, she missed double figures in scoring only four times. . . . Played six-on-six basketball in high school in Iowa, averaging 48 points per game as a senior.

Year	G	FGM	FGA	FG%	FTM	FTA	FT%	Reb.	Avg.	Pts.	Avg.
80-81	28	263	465	.566	212	264	.803	248	8.9	738	26.4
81-82	35	273	513	.532	275	325	.846	372	9.2	821	23.5
82-83	28	264	445	.593	209	251	.833	264	9.4	737	26.3
83-84	29	304	508	.598	211	250	.844	216	7.4	819	28.2
Totals	120	1104	1931	.572	907	1090	.832	1050	8.8	3115	26.0

CAROL BLAZEJOWSKI
Montclair State
5-11 – F
Cranford, N.J.

Still holds women's career scoring average (31.7 points) and season average (38.6) and is third on the all-time women's scoring charts (3,199 points). . . . Was inducted in the Naismith Hall of Fame in 1993. . . . Owns the women's single-season scoring mark with 1,235 points as a senior. . . . A three-time Kodak All-American and the first Wade Trophy winner. . . . Helped Montclair State reach the first AIAW Final Four in 1978. . . . Montclair also played in two other AIAW national tournaments. . . . Continues to play on barnstorming teams in the Northeast. . . . Currently is director of licensing for the National Basketball Association.

Year	G	FGM	FGA	FG%	FTM	FTA	FT%	Reb.	Avg.	Pts.	Avg.
74-75	17	138	320	.430	57	80	.711	171	10.0	333	19.6
75-76	25	298	540	.551	116	150	.773	255	10.2	712	28.5
76-77	27	393	695	.565	133	167	.796	272	10.1	919	34.0
77-78	32	515	905	.569	205	245	.837	317	9.9	1235	38.6
Totals	101	1344	2460	.550	511	642	.795	1015	10.4	3199	31.7

CATHY BOSWELL
Illinois State
5-11 – F
Joliet, Ill.

Illinois State's all-time leading women's scorer (2,005 points) holds six school records and is the only woman athlete at the school to have her number retired. . . . Twice a finalist for the Wade Trophy.

Year	G	FGM	FGA	FG%	FTM	FTA	FT%	Reb.	Avg.	Pts.	Avg.
79-80	33	242	490	.494	51	84	.607	301	9.1	535	16.2
80-81	36	274	537	.510	101	119	.849	343	9.5	649	18.0
81-82	22	165	347	.476	28	44	.636	159	7.2	358	16.3
82-83	30	208	444	.468	47	62	.758	257	8.6	463	15.4
Totals	121	889	1818	.489	227	309	.735	1060	8.8	2005	16.6

DEBBIE BROCK
Delta State
4-11 – G
Forest City, Miss.

The tiny guard played for three AIAW national championship teams from 1975 to 1977. . . . Averaged only 7 points a game during her career, but was known for her excellent passing to future Hall of Fame teammate Lusia Harris. . . . An All-American her final two seasons. . . . Scored 22 points in the 1977 national title game against LSU from what now is the 3-point range.

Year	G	FGM	FGA	FG%	FTM	FTA	FT%	Reb.	Avg.	Pts.	Avg.
74-75	25	63	119	.529	65	77	.844	60	2.4	191	7.6
75-76	34	65	128	.507	62	78	.794	111	3.2	192	5.6
76-77	35	100	221	.452	65	77	.844	78	2.2	95	7.6
77-78	32	85	200	.425	85	103	.825	94	2.9	255	7.9
Totals	126	313	668	.469	277	335	.827	343	2.7	903	7.1

CINDY BROGDON
Mercer/Tennessee
5-10 – F
Buford, Ga.

The second all-time leading women's scorer with 3,240 points. . . . Tennessee made its first trip to the Final Four in her senior year in 1979. . . . Played her first two seasons for Mercer before transferring. . . . Was a two-time Kodak All-American, once at each school.

Year	G	FGM	FGA	FG%	FTM	FTA	FT%	Reb.	Avg.	Pts.	Avg.
75-76	30	348	706	.490	206	247	.830	319	10.6	902	30.1
76-77	28	335	690	.490	174	216	.810	286	10.2	844	30.1
77-78	31	286	593	.482	102	118	.864	238	7.6	674	21.7
78-79	39	344	639	.538	96	118	.813	185	4.7	784	20.1
Totals	128	1313	2628	.500	578	699	.827	1028	8.3	3240	25.0

ANUCHA BROWNE
Northwestern
6-1 – F
Brooklyn, N.Y.

Holds 24 school records and is Northwestern's first Kodak All-American (1985). . . . As a senior, she led the country in scoring with 30.5 points a game. . . . Set an NCAA record by scoring 30 points or more in six consecutive games. . . . The second all-time leading scorer in Big Ten history with 2,307 points, she was a three-time all-league pick and twice was its Player of the Year. . . . A finalist for the Wade Trophy and the Naismith Award.

Year	G	FGM	FGA	FG%	FTM	FTA	FT%	Reb.	Avg.	Pts.	Avg.
81-82	29	136	266	.511	74	116	.638	174	6.0	346	11.9
82-83	27	221	396	.558	110	170	.647	249	9.2	552	20.4
83-84	26	221	481	.459	112	179	.651	271	10.4	554	21.3
84-85	28	341	666	.512	173	254	.681	257	9.2	855	30.5
Totals	110	919	1809	.508	469	719	.652	951	8.6	2307	21.0

VICKY BULLETT
Maryland
6-2 – F/C
Martinsburg, W.V.

A two-time Kodak All-American.... The leading scorer and rebounder in school history.... Leading scorer and rebounder on Maryland's 1989 Final Four team.... Helped team to two Atlantic Coast Conference titles.... A three-time All-ACC pick.

Year	G	FGM	FGA	FG%	FTM	FTA	FT%	Reb.	Avg.	Pts.	Avg.
85–86	21	87	175	.470	44	61	.721	135	6.4	218	10.4
86–87	29	197	357	.552	49	77	.636	243	8.4	443	15.3
87–88	32	243	404	.602	95	134	.709	303	9.6	581	18.2
88–89	32	289	503	.675	108	136	.794	287	9.0	688	21.4
Totals	114	816	1439	.567	296	408	.725	888	7.8	1928	16.9

DENISE CURRY
UCLA
6-1 – F
Davis, Calif.

UCLA's all-time leading scorer (3,198 points) and rebounder (1,310 boards) who played on 1978 AIAW national championship team as a freshman.... Set a collegiate record by scoring in double figures in all 130 games of her career.... A three-time Kodak All-American who helped the Bruins to two West Coast Athletic Association titles and two AIAW national appearances.... Holds 14 UCLA career records.... Currently an assistant coach at the University of California.

Year	G	FGM	FGA	FG%	FTM	FTA	FT%	Reb.	Avg.	Pts.	Avg.
77–78	30	280	451	.621	50	65	.769	273	9.1	610	20.3
78–79	34	355	586	.606	93	115	.809	340	10.0	803	23.6
79–80	30	361	599	.604	133	149	.893	337	11.2	855	28.5
80–81	36	390	647	.603	150	192	.781	360	10.0	930	25.8
Totals	130	1386	2283	.607	426	521	.818	1310	10.1	3198	24.6

CLARISSA DAVIS-WRIGHTSIL
Texas
6-1 – F
San Antonio, Tex.

The all-time Southwest Conference career scoring and third-best scorer in school history despite being cut down by injuries during her career (knee injury as junior).... Was MVP of the 1986 Final Four as a freshman as Texas won the NCAA title.... A two-time Kodak All-American and Wade Trophy winner.... Also named National Player of the Year as a senior by Naismith, Champion Products, and the USBWA/Mercedes.... Scored 45 points in 97-78 Texas win at Tennessee in which a world attendance record (24,563) was set.... Established a Texas record by scoring 843 points during senior year.... Currently playing professional basketball in Turkey, where her husband also is a pro player.

Year	G	FGM	FGA	FG%	FTM	FTA	FT%	Reb.	Avg.	Pts.	Avg.
85–86	34	180	309	.583	99	150	.660	262	7.7	459.	13.5
86–87	26	196	340	.576	91	146	.632	217	8.3	483	18.6
87–88	9	93	145	.641	37	50	.740	87	9.7	223	24.8
88–89	32	324	585	.559	188	262	.718	316	9.9	843	26.3
Totals	101	793	1379	.580	415	608	.680	882	8.7	2008	19.8

ANNE DONOVAN
Old Dominion
6-8 – C
Ridgewood, N.J.

Old Dominion's all-time leading scorer and rebounder played for a national championship squad and two gold medal Olympic squads.... The first exceptionally tall impact player in women's college basketball.... A four-year starter, she was leading scorer and rebounder as a freshman, playing alongside All-Americans Nancy Lieberman and Inge Nissen on national title team.... A three-time Kodak All-American and the 1983 National Player of the Year.

Year	G	FGM	FGA	FG%	FTM	FTA	FT%	Reb.	Avg.	Pts.	Avg.
79–80	38	290	460	.630	68	126	.539	491	12.9	648	17.0
80–81	35	377	591	.638	125	175	.714	569	16.2	879	25.1
81–82	28	240	375	.640	99	142	.697	412	14.7	579	14.7
82–83	35	263	428	.614	87	130	.669	504	14.4	613	17.5
Totals	136	1170	1854	.631	379	573	.661	1976	14.5	2719	19.9

TERESA EDWARDS
Georgia
5-11 – G
Cairo, Ga.

A two-time Kodak All-American and three-time Olympian. . . . Played on Georgia's Final Four teams in 1983 and 1985. . . . Jersey number was the first to be retired for a Georgia basketball player, male or female. . . . Named all-SEC three times. . . . Has played professionally in Italy, Japan, Spain and France. . . . Her international play has spanned from 1981 to the 1996 Olympics and she has participated in 13 major competitions.

Year	G	FGM	FGA	FG%	FTM	FTA	FT%	Reb.	Avg.	Pts.	Avg.
82–83	33	189	412	.459	52	82	.634	73	2.2	430	13.0
83–84	33	207	397	.521	51	65	.785	81	2.5	465	14.1
84–85	30	203	385	.527	58	79	.734	84	2.8	464	15.5
85–86	32	274	491	.558	82	104	.788	146	4.6	630	19.7
Totals	128	873	1685	.518	243	330	.736	384	3.0	1989	15.5

PEGGIE GILLOM
Mississippi
6-0 – F
Abbeville, Miss.

The leading scorer and rebounder in school history.... Led Ole Miss to two AIAW regional tournament trips.... Was a finalist for the Wade Trophy in 1980... Drafted by the Dallas Diamonds of the Women's Professional Basketball League in 1980 and played one season before returning to Ole Miss, where she has been an assistant coach since 1981.... Her younger sister, Jennifer, also scored more than 2,000 points for the Lady Rebels, earned a gold medal with the 1988 U.S. Olympic team, and is the school's only Kodak All-American.

Year	G	FGM	FGA	FG%	FTM	FTA	FT%	Reb.	Avg.	Pts.	Avg.
76–77	28	159	314	.506	41	67	.612	240	8.6	359	12.8
77–78	40	312	583	.535	97	132	.735	329	8.2	721	8.0
78–79	39	288	571	.504	116	152	.763	341	8.7	692	17.7
79–80	37	293	652	.449	128	181	.707	361	9.8	714	19.3
Totals	144	1052	2120	.496	382	532	.718	1271	8.8	2486	17.3

BRIDGETTE GORDON
Tennessee
6-0 – F
DeLand, Fla.

The all-time leading scorer and most decorated player in school history.... Led Tennessee to its first two national championships in 1987 and 1989, and is one of three Lady Volunteers to reach the Final Four in all four of her college seasons. No other women's program holds that distinction.... A two-time Kodak All-American and MVP of the 1989 Final Four.... The all-time leading scorer in NCAA women's tournament history with 388 points and a 21.6 average.... Tennessee was 115-21 during her career, winning two SEC titles, and she was the league's Player of the Year twice.... Led her professional team to the Italian League championship in 1991.

Year	G	FGM	FGA	FG%	FTM	FTA	FT%	Reb.	Avg.	Pts.	Avg.
85–86	34	206	429	.480	69	109	.633	209	6.2	418	14.2
86–87	34	222	459	.484	115	160	.719	232	6.8	559	16.4
87–88	33	286	529	.541	106	151	.702	225	6.8	687	20.8
88–89	36	298	557	.535	131	188	.697	251	7.0	733	20.4
Totals	137	1012	1974	.513	421	608	.692	917	6.1	2460	18.0

JERILYNN HARPER
Tennessee/Tennessee Tech
6-1 – F
Jefferson City, Tenn.

The second all-time career scorer for one of the early powers from the Southeast.... Helped Tech to appearances in the National Women's Invitational Tournament and the first NCAA tournament in 1982.... Owns 10 of the top 11 individual single-game scoring records at Tech.... Scored 40 or more points six different times in her career and in 32 games scored 30 points or more.... Played her freshman year at Tennessee, where she was a reserve on the 1979 Final Four team, before transferring to Tennessee Tech.

Year	G	FGM	FGA	FG%	FTM	FTA	FT%	Reb.	Avg.	Pts.	Avg.
78–79	37	152	271	.561	61	84	.726	170	4.6	365	9.9
79–80	27	159	293	.543	78	100	.780			396	14.7
80–81	34	410	653	.628	191	242	.789			1011	29.7
81–82	31	343	601	.571	191	242	.784			831	26.8
Totals	129	1064	1818	.585	521	668	.780	961	7.4	2603	20.2

JANET HARRIS
Georgia
6-3 – F/C
Chicago, Ill.

Georgia's all-time leading scorer and rebounder, a three-time Kodak All-American, and a member of two U.S. National Sports teams.... Took Georgia to the NCAA Final Four in 1983 and 1985.... Is one of three Georgia women's players to have a jersey number retired.... While at Georgia, the team earned four straight NCAA Tournament trips.... A three-time All-SEC selection, she led Georgia to consecutive league crowns in 1983 and 1984.

Year	G	FGM	FGA	FG%	FTM	FTA	FT%	Reb.	Avg.	Pts.	Avg.
81–82	30	281	517	.533	101	160	.631	371	12.4	663	22.1
82–83	34	299	537	.557	94	155	.606	397	11.7	692	20.4
83–84	33	249	472	.528	88	126	.698	279	8.5	586	17.8
84–85	34	298	503	.592	104	147	.707	351	10.3	700	20.6
Totals	131	1127	2029	.555	387	588	.658	1398	10.7	2641	20.2

LUSIA HARRIS STEWART
Delta State
6-3 – C
Minter City, Miss.

The first female college player to be inducted into the Naismith Basketball Hall of Fame in 1992.... The first prototypical modern center in the women's college game.... Led the Lady Statesmen to three consecutive AIAW national titles from 1975 to 1977. She was MVP of all three national tournaments.... A member of the 1976 silver medal U.S. Olympic team, she scored the first points ever by a female player in the Olympics.... The Olympians' top scorer (15.0) and rebounder (7.0).... A three-time All-American and two-time national Player of the Year.... The nation's top scorer as a junior, averaging 31.2 points.... Delta State's first women's basketball recruit after a 40-year layoff.... Currently a high school teacher and coach in Ruleville, Miss.

Year	G	FGM	FGA	FG%	FTM	FTA	FT%	Reb.	Avg.	Pts.	Avg.
73–74	18	147	226	.650	58	103	.563	252	14.0	352	19.6
74–75	28	300	458	.655	107	145	.738	400	14.3	707	25.3
75–76	34	457	738	.619	146	217	.672	514	15.1	1060	31.2
76–77	35	363	579	.627	136	200	.680	496	14.2	862	24.6
Totals	115	1266	2001	.633	447	665	.672	1662	14.5	2979	25.9

PAM KELLY
Louisiana Tech
6-0 – F
Columbia, La.

Captained Louisiana Tech to national titles in 1981 and 1982 as the Lady Techsters rolled up a dominating record of 69-1 over those seasons, prompting one coach to proclaim they had the two best teams in America.... The school's career leader in points (2,979) and rebounds (1,511) as well as in 19 other categories.... A three-time Kodak All-American and the 1982 Wade Trophy winner.... A member of the Louisiana Tech Hall of Fame and the Louisiana College Athlete of the Year in 1981.... Scored in double figures in 140 of her 153 college games, and notched rebounding double-figure games 80 times.... Had a career-high of 41 points against UCLA as a senior.... The Lady Techsters were 143-10 during her career.

Year	G	FGM	FGA	FG%	FTM	FTA	FT%	Reb.	Avg.	Pts.	Avg.
78–79	38	273	564	.484	62	92	.674	372	9.8	721	19.0
79–80	45	369	710	.520	79	114	.693	491	10.9	932	20.7
80–81	34	204	449	.454	53	70	.757	322	9.5	595	17.5
81–82	36	280	435	.644	171	247	.692	326	9.1	732	20.3
Totals	153	1126	2158	.522	365	531	.687	1511	9.8	2979	19.4

BARBARA KENNEDY
Clemson
6-1 – F/C
Rome, Ga.

A Kodak All-American selection in 1981–82, when she averaged 29 points a game, currently the 10th best seasonal average in NCAA history.... Still holds the Atlantic Coast Conference record for career scoring average and is the league's career rebounding leader... Clemson was 84-42 during her career, qualifying for three AIAW tournaments and the first NCAA women's tournament.... She scored the first points in NCAA women's tournament history against Penn State on March 12, 1982.... A member of the Clemson Athletic Hall of Fame, she also was a Clemson assistant coach and is now an athletic academic counselor at the school.

Year	G	FGM	FGA	FG%	FTM	FTA	FT%	Reb.	Avg.	Pts.	Avg.
78–79	29	227	477	.476	87	130	.669	248	8.6	541	18.7
79–80	36	382	729	.524	89	137	.650	298	8.3	853	23.7
80–81	31	348	722	.482	115	175	.657	306	9.9	811	26.2
81–82	31	392	760	.516	124	172	.721	400	12.9	908	29.3
Totals	127	1349	2688	.502	415	614	.676	1252	9.9	3113	24.5

JANICE LAWRENCE
Louisiana Tech
6-3 – C
Lucedale, Miss.

A three-time Kodak All-American and a national Player of the Year who guided the Lady Techsters to two national titles in 1980–81 and 1981–82. Those title teams were among the most dominating in women's college annals, going a collective 69-1.... The MVP of the first NCAA Women's Final Four in 1982.... The national player of the year in 1984 as well as the Wade Trophy winner.

Year	G	FGM	FGA	FG%	FTM	FTA	FT%	Reb.	Avg.	Pts.	Avg.
80–81	34	192	326	.589	123	189	.651	283	8.3	507	14.9
81–82	36	202	363	.556	124	174	.713	253	7.0	528	14.7
82–83	33	272	455	.598	141	222	.635	301	9.1	685	20.7
83–84	32	268	433	.619	147	207	.710	301	8.1	683	21.3
Totals	135	934	1577	.592	535	792	.676	1097	8.1	2403	17.8

LISA LESLIE
Southern Cal
6-5 – F/C
Inglewood, Calif.

The first four-time All-Pac-10 selection since Cheryl Miller and the 1994 national player of the year. . . . A three-time All-American. . . . Third in USC scoring charts (2,414 points), scoring average (20.1 per game) and fourth in rebounds (1,214). . . . Developed from a thin, gangly high school star into a muscular, strong, dominating post player for the 1996 U.S. Olympic team. . . . Scored 101 points in the first half of a high school game before the opposing team left the court at halftime.

Year	G	FGM	FGA	FG%	FTM	FTA	FT%	Reb.	Avg.	Pts.	Avg.
90-91	30	241	504	.478	98	145	.676	299	10.0	582	19.4
91-92	31	262	476	.550	106	152	.697	261	8.4	632	20.4
92-93	29	211	378	.558	119	162	.735	285	9.8	543	18.7
94-94	30	259	464	.558	138	201	.687	369	12.3	657	21.9
Totals	120	973	1822	.534	461	660	.698	1214	10.1	2414	20.1

NANCY LIEBERMAN CLINE
Old Dominion
5-10 – G
Far Rockaway, N.Y.

One of the first flash-and-dash players of the modern women's era.... She was captain of two national championship teams and a three-time Kodak All-American.... The 1980 national Player of the Year.... Named to the 1976 U.S. Olympic team as an 18-year-old high school graduate.... A first-round draft choice of the Dallas Diamonds in 1980, leading them to a league title.... Was a physical trainer and confidante of tennis champion Martina Navratilova.... Has played in the U.S. Basketball League and currently has several basketball and sports marketing businesses in operation.... Wrote an autobiography entitled *Lady Magic* for the nickname she earned because of her fancy passing abilities.

Year	G	FGM	FGA	FG%	FTM	FTA	FT%	Reb.	Avg.	Pts.	Avg.
76–77	27	240	507	.473	88	117	.709	272	10.1	563	20.9
77–78	34	281	651	.432	119	163	.730	325	9.6	681	20.2
78–79	36	243	500	.478	139	176	.790	276	7.7	625	17.4
79–80	37	203	390	.533	145	186	.779	294	7.9	561	15.2
Totals	134	973	2056	.472	486	642	.757	1167	8.7	2430	18.1

REBECCA LOBO
Connecticut
6-4 – F
Southwick, Mass.

The most-decorated player in Big East history helped Connecticut to a historic 35-0 record and NCAA championship in 1995. . . . A member of the 1996 U.S. Olympic team. . . . Made appearances on David Letterman and other shows and was a magazine cover girl during the Huskies' stretch drive for the title. . . . Was national player of the year as a senior and was an academic Phi Beta Kappa. . . . Has written a book with her mother, whose fight with cancer earned national headlines during Lobo's final two seasons. . . . Big East's career rebounding leader (1,268) and second in UConn scoring (2,133). . . . A two-time All-American and four-time All-Big East pick.

Year	G	FGM	FGA	FG%	FTM	FTA	FT%	Reb.	Avg.	Pts.	Avg.
91-92	29	167	338	.494	82	117	.701	228	7.9	416	14.3
92-93	29	189	421	.449	77	119	.647	326	11.2	484	16.7
93-94	33	243	445	.546	138	187	.738	371	11.2	635	19.2
94-95	35	238	476	.500	104	154	.675	343	9.8	598	17.1
Totals	126	837	1680	.498	401	577	.695	1268	10.1	2133	16.9

Three-point shooting: 0 of 1 in 1991-92, 29 of 85 (.341) in 1992-93, 11 of 34 (.324) in 1993-94 and 18 of 51 (.353) in 1994-95. Totals: 58 of 171 (.339).

KATRINA MCCLAIN
Georgia
6-2 – C
Charleston, S.C.

The 1987 Player of the Year by Champion Products, the Women's Basketball News Service, the American Women's Sports Foundation, and the *Shreveport Journal*.... A two-time All-American and two-time Olympian.... Was named to two All-SEC teams.... Starting center on Georgia team that reached the 1985 national title game.

Year	G	FGM	FGA	FG%	FTM	FTA	FT%	Reb.	Avg.	Pts.	Avg.
83–84	33	137	197	.695	66	95	.695	254	7.7	340	10.3
84–85	29	164	262	.626	70	105	.667	234	8.1	398	13.7
85–86	31	262	396	.662	137	176	.778	314	10.1	661	21.3
86–87	32	310	552	.562	176	240	.733	391	12.2	796	24.9
Totals	125	873	1407	.620	449	616	.729	1193	9.5	2195	17.6

SUZIE MCCONNELL SERIO
Penn State
5-5 – G
Pittsburgh, Pa.

A 1988 Kodak All-American and a two-time Olympian.... The NCAA's all-time women's assists leader, totaling 1,307 for an average of 10.2 a game.... Guided the Nittany Lions to four NCAA Tournament berths.... Named the Frances Pomeroy Naismith winner in 1988 as the top small player in the country .... Had 71 double-figure assist games.... Currently a high school and AAU coach in Pittsburgh.

Year	G	FGM	FGA	FG%	FTM	FTA	FT%	Reb.	Avg.	Pts.	Avg.
84–85	33	157	343	.458	101	136	.743	93	2.8	415	12.6
85–86	32	148	335	.442	86	109	.789	94	2.9	382	11.9
86–87	30	169	337	.502	68	94	.723	141	4.7	418	13.9
87–88	33	255	511	.499	116	143	.811	165	5.0	682	20.6
Totals	128	729	1526	.478	371	482	.770	493	3.9	1897	14.8

NIKKI MCCRAY
Tennessee
5-11 – G/F
Collierville, Tenn.

The leader and defensive ace of a Lady Vol program that during her career had a record of 122-11, the best four-year stretch in school history, and reached the NCAA title game in 1995. . . . A two-time SEC player of the year and All-American. . . . A two-time Naismith player of the year finalist. . . . Ranks among the Top 20 in Tennessee records in steals (second with 292) and points (seventh with 1,572). . . . Tennessee went undefeated in the SEC during her last three seasons, going 33-0 during the regular season and won two SEC tournament titles. . . . Originally signed as a Proposition 48 non-qualifier, but gained an extra season of eligibility following NCAA academic revisions. . . . A member of the 1996 U.S. Olympic team.

Year	G	FGM	FGA	FG%	FTM	FTA	FT%	Reb.	Avg.	Pts.	Avg.
91-92	31	87	174	.500	39	53	.736	114	3.7	215	6.9
92-93	32	133	286	.465	83	115	.722	145	4.5	349	10.9
93-94	33	213	421	.506	111	158	.703	231	7.0	537	16.3
94-95	31	193	392	.492	83	122	.680	182	5.9	471	15.2
Totals	127	626	1273	.492	316	448	.705	672	5.3	1572	12.4

Three-point shooting: 2 of 10 (.200) in 1991-92 and 2 of 15 (.133) in 1994-95.
Totals: 4 of 25 (.160).

PAM MCGEE
Southern Cal
6-3 – F/C
Flint, Mich.

A Kodak All-American in 1984 as a senior.... Member of national title teams in 1983 and 1984.... The identical twin of USC forward Paula McGee.... Was a finalist for the Wade Trophy in 1983 and the Naismith Award in 1984.... USC's all-time leader in career field-goal shooting.

Year	G	FGM	FGA	FG%	FTM	FTA	FT%	Reb.	Avg.	Pts.	Avg.
80–81	34	217	398	.545	75	148	.506	294	8.6	509	14.8
81–82	27	219	381	.575	91	143	.636	312	11.6	529	19.6
82–83	33	249	408	.610	110	174	.632	329	10.0	608	18.4
83–84	33	250	420	.595	68	131	.519	320	8.7	568	17.2
Totals	127	935	1607	.582	365	596	.613	1255	9.9	2214	17.4

PAULA MCGEE
Southern Cal
6-3 – F/C
Flint, Mich.

Was a Kodak All-American in 1981 and 1983.... Helped the Trojans to national titles in 1983 and 1984.... The identical twin of USC forward Pam McGee.... No other USC freshman, including Cheryl Miller, scored as many points (683).

Year	G	FGM	FGA	FG%	FTM	FTA	FT%	Reb.	Avg.	Pts.	Avg.
80–81	34	289	567	.510	105	165	.636	318	9.4	683	20.1
81–82	27	226	461	.490	94	130	.723	278	10.3	546	20.2
82–83	33	282	493	.572	68	91	.747	305	9.2	632	19.2
83–84	33	207	393	.527	71	110	.645	259	7.8	485	14.7
Totals	127	993	1941	.524	338	496	.681	1160	9.1	2346	17.5

CAROL MENKEN SCHAUDT
Oregon State
6-5 – C
Jefferson, Ore.

A 1981 Kodak All-American and 1984 U.S. Olympian.... Owns a majority of Oregon State's individual women's records, despite playing only three seasons for the Beavers after one year of junior college ball.... As a senior, led the nation in field-goal percentage, hitting 75 percent of her shots and helping OSU to a 22-6 record, one of its best ever.... Once scored 51 points in a game.... A three-time all-conference selection of the Northwest College Women's Sports Association.

Year	G	FGM	FGA	FG%	FTM	FTA	FT%	Reb.	Avg.	Pts.	Avg.
78–79	22	239	379	.630	106	173	.612	274	12.5	584	26.5
79–80	31	353	518	.681	125	217	.576	325	10.5	831	26.8
80–81	28	363	484	.750	102	161	.634	302	10.9	828	29.6
Totals	81	955	1381	.692	333	551	.604	901	11.1	2243	27.7

ANN MEYERS
UCLA
5-8 – G
LaHabra, Calif.

Inducted into the Naismith Basketball Hall of Fame in 1993.... With late husband, baseball great Don Drysdale, made history by becoming part of first married couple to both be elected into the halls of fame of their respective sports.... Team captain of 1978 AIAW national championship as a senior.... First woman awarded an athletic scholarship at UCLA.... Older brother Dave Meyers played on national title teams at UCLA in early 1970s.... Drafted by the Indiana Pacers in 1978, the first woman ever selected by an NBA team... Played two seasons for the New Jersey Gems of the Women's Professional Basketball League.

Year	G	FGM	FGA	FG%	FTM	FTA	FT%	Reb.	Avg.	Pts.	Avg.
74–75	23	183	346	.529	56	73	.767	191	8.3	422	18.3
75–76	23	129	303	.426	65	89	.730	189	8.2	323	14.0
76–77	22	160	317	.505	82	99	.828	161	7.3	402	18.3
77–78	29	221	420	.526	96	120	.800	278	9.6	538	18.6
Totals	97	693	1386	.500	299	381	.785	819	8.4	1685	17.4

CHERYL MILLER
Southern Cal
6-3 – F
Riverside, Calif.

A four-time All-American and three-time Naismith Award winner.... Led USC to national titles in 1983 and 1984 and the championship game in 1986.... Named 1980s Player of the Decade by the WBCA and the U.S. Basketball Writers Association.... USC career leader in points, rebounds, field goals, free throws, and steals.... Scored a state-record 105 points in a high school game.... The first four-time *Parade* high school All-American, male or female.... The only USC basketball player, male or female, to have her number retired.... Was a sports commentator for ABC-TV and ESPN before being named USC's head coach in September 1993.... Grew up in an athletic family, with an older brother formerly a major league baseball prospect and younger brother, Reggie, currently starring for the NBA's Indiana Pacers.

Year	G	FGM	FGA	FG%	FTM	FTA	FT%	Reb.	Avg.	Pts.	Avg.
82–83	33	268	486	.551	137	186	.737	320	9.7	673	20.4
83–84	33	281	493	.570	164	218	.752	350	10.6	726	22.0
84–85	30	302	572	.528	201	289	.753	474	15.8	805	26.8
85–86	32	308	506	.609	198	263	.753	390	12.2	814	25.4
Totals	128	1159	2057	.563	702	956	.734	1534	12.0	3018	23.6

KIM MULKEY ROBERTSON
Louisiana Tech
5-4 – G
Hammond, La.

Piloted Lady Techsters to national titles in 1981 and 1982.... A two-time Kodak All-American, she won 1984 Francis Pomeroy Naismith Award as the best women's player under 5-6.... Also selected as an Academic All-American twice.... Currently an assistant coach at Louisiana Tech.

Year	G	FGM	FGA	FG%	FTM	FTA	FT%	Reb.	Avg.	Pts.	Avg.
80–81	34	88	172	.512	76	118	.644	46	1.4	252	7.4
81–82	36	77	158	.487	46	76	.605	56	1.6	200	5.6
82–83	31	78	159	.491	53	85	.624	55	1.8	209	6.7
83–84	32	101	205	.493	81	120	.675	72	2.3	283	8.8
Totals	133	344	694	.496	256	399	.642	229	1.7	944	7.1

INGE NISSEN
Old Dominion
6-5 – C
Randers, Denmark

Member of dominating Old Dominion national title teams in 1979 and 1980.... Second-leading scorer and rebounder in school history.... A two-time Kodak All-American.... Currently an assistant coach at Florida International.... Lady Monarch MVP three times.... Established a school single-game record with 28 rebounds.... One of the first foreign female players to excel in the college game, she recruits many European players as a coach.... Played on professional title teams in Denmark, Norway, and France.... Holds the National Women's Invitational Tournament mark with 20 field goals in a game.... Played briefly in the now-defunct U.S. women's pro leagues.

Year	G	FGM	FGA	FG%	FTM	FTA	FT%	Reb.	Avg.	Pts.	Avg.
76–77	32	255	408	.523	82	152	.539	410	12.8	592	18.5
77–78	32	257	544	.472	148	209	.708	378	11.8	662	20.7
78–79	34	300	576	.521	148	198	.747	339	9.9	749	22.0
79–80	37	252	576	.437	140	199	.703	382	10.3	644	17.4
Totals	135	1064	2184	.487	518	758	.683	1509	11.2	2647	19.6

JUNE OLKOWSKI
Rutgers
6-0 – F
Philadelphia, Pa.

The only Rutgers player to have her jersey number retired.... Was captain and second-leading scorer of 1982 team that won the final AIAW national championship... A two-time Kodak All-American.... Has been an assistant coach at Auburn and Maryland and a head coach at Arizona and Butler, where she has been since the 1993–94 season.

Year	G	FGM	FGA	FG%	FTM	FTA	FT%	Reb.	Avg.	Pts.	Avg.
78–79	32	197	426	.462	102	152	.671	304	9.5	496	15.5
79–80	30	186	379	.491	91	138	.659	225	7.5	463	15.4
80–81	17	101	190	.532	54	78	.692	95	5.6	256	15.1
81–82	24	116	261	.444	53	73	.726	156	6.5	285	11.9
Totals	103	600	1256	.480	300	441	.680	780	7.7	1500	14.8

VICKIE ORR
Auburn
6-3 – C
Decatur, Ala.

A three-time Kodak All-American.... Was a finalist for the Champion/WBCA and Naismith Player of the Year Awards.... Led Auburn to national championship games in 1988 and 1989 ... Was SEC Player of the Year in 1988 ... Was named an assistant coach at Auburn in 1992.

Year	G	FGM	FGA	FG%	FTM	FTA	FT%	Reb.	Avg.	Pts.	Avg.
85–86	30	165	297	.555	65	98	.663	233	7.8	395	13.2
86–87	33	239	396	.604	72	110	.656	252	7.6	550	16.7
87–88	35	248	461	.538	69	90	.767	237	6.8	565	16.1
88–89	33	212	374	.567	101	135	.748	284	8.6	525	15.9
Totals	131	864	1528	.565	307	433	.709	1006	7.7	2035	15.5

SHELLY PENNEFATHER
Villanova
6-1 – F
Utica, N.Y.

The all-time leading career scorer (2,408 points) in school history and for the Philadelphia Big Five .... A two-time All-American and the 1987 Wade Trophy winner.... Named to the All-Big East team three times, and was the league's MVP three times as well.... Is the Big East's women's career scoring and rebounding leader.... Villanova won two Big East regular-season crowns and averaged 23 wins a season during her career.... The first Big East player, male or female, to earn the conference's player of the week award three consecutive times.... Was inducted into the Big Five Hall of Fame in 1993.... She played professionally in Japan for four seasons.... Currently is a member of the Order of St. Claire, a cloistered nunnery in Virginia.

Year	G	FGM	FGA	FG%	FTM	FTA	FT%	Reb.	Avg.	Pts.	Avg.
83–84	29	220	411	.535	64	82	.780	253	9.7	504	19.4
84–85	29	245	459	.534	54	73	.740	317	10.9	544	18.8
85–86	31	302	527	.573	81	99	.818	293	9.5	685	22.1
86–87	31	306	523	.585	68	82	.768	308	9.9	675	21.8
Totals	120	1073	1920	.558	262	336	.779	1171	9.7	2408	20.0

LATAUNYA POLLARD
Long Beach State
5-10 – G/F
East Chicago, Ind.

One of just 13 women players with 3,000 career points or more.... Instrumental in turning Long Beach State into a national power in the early 1980s.... The 1983 Wade Trophy winner and a three-time All-American....

Villanova's Shelly Pennefather maneuvers around the opposition's defense.

Twice named the player of the year by the West Coast Athletic Association.... Holds four major career and three single season school records, including scoring, scoring average, and field goals made.... Guided the 49ers to four postseason bids (three AIAW and one NCAA).... A prototype full-court athlete who helped speed up the transition game in women's basketball.... Was such a popular figure during her college days that she once rode on the City of Long Beach float at the Tournament of Roses parade.

Year	G	FGM	FGA	FG%	FTM	FTA	FT%	Reb.	Avg.	Pts.	Avg.
79–80	34	295	570	.518	70	94	.745	176	5.1	660	19.4
80–81	34	325	602	.540	83	121	.686	193	5.8	733	21.6
81–82	29	292	540	.541	117	154	.760	177	6.1	701	24.2
82–83	31	376	721	.521	155	201	.771	275	8.9	907	29.2
Totals	128	1288	2433	.530	425	570	.745	821	6.4	3001	23.5

JILL RANKIN
Wayland Baptist/Tennessee
6-3 – C
Phillips, Tex.

A Kodak All-American in her only season at Tennessee, which went 35-5 and finished second in the AIAW national tournament.... The last national caliber player at Wayland Baptist, a tiny Texas Panhandle school that was one of the first institutions to give women basketball scholarships as early as the 1950s.... Helped Wayland reach three AIAW national tournaments during its college-era heyday in the late 1970s and was a Kodak choice as a junior.... Scored 81 points in a high school game.

Year	G	FGM	FGA	FG%	FTM	FTA	FT%	Reb.	Avg.	Pts.	Avg.
76–77	36	218	368	.592	91	131	.695	257	7.0	527	14.6
77–78	38	259	426	.607	76	121	.628	262	6.9	594	15.6
78–79	34	410	698	.587	180	234	.769	305	9.0	1000	29.4
79–80	38	296	536	.552	138	172	.802	277	7.3	730	19.2
Totals	146	1183	2028	.583	485	658	.737	1101	7.6	2851	19.2

THERESA SHANK GRENTZ
Immaculata
5-10 – C
Springfield, Pa.

The first dominating center in women's college basketball.... A two-time All-American who paced Immaculata to the first three AIAW national championships from 1972 to 1974.... Bypassed an opportunity to try out for the 1976 Olympic team to get married and begin a family.... One of the first women's coaches to earn a professional salary that did not include teaching duties.... Taught elementary school after graduation before being named head coach at St. Joseph's.... Went to Rutgers in 1977 and coached the last AIAW national championship team in 1982.

Year	G	FGM	FGA	FG%	FTM	FTA	FT%	Reb.	Avg.	Pts.	Avg.
70–71	3	58	101	.574	8	11	.727	44	14.6	66	22.0
71–72	20	188	321	.585	120	170	.705	389	19.4	496	24.8
72–73	16	124	247	.500	59	90	.655	269	16.8	307	19.1
73–74	20	123	257	.478	76	114	.660	263	13.1	322	16.1
Totals	59	493	926	.532	263	385	.683	965	16.3	1191	20.2

BEV SMITH
Oregon
5-11 – F
Salmon Arm, B.C.

The only Oregon player to be named a Kodak All-American (1981 and 1982).... Is the school's career rebounding leader and second leading all-time scorer.... Owns or shares 12 school records.... A four-year starter, she led the Ducks to a 103-20 record, two AIAW national tournament appearances, and one trip to the NCAA tourney.... Was nominated for the Wade Trophy twice.... MVP of the National Women's Invitational Tournament as a freshman.... Played for the 1984 Canadian Olympic team and in the 1979 World Championships.

Year	G	FGM	FGA	FG%	FTM	FTA	FT%	Reb.	Avg.	Pts.	Avg.
78–79	25	166	356	.466	47	86	.547	323	12.9	379	15.2
79–80	27	240	441	.544	99	129	.767	389	13.6	579	21.4
80–81	32	259	485	.534	114	157	.726	376	11.8	632	19.8
81–82	26	192	400	.480	89	119	.748	296	11.4	473	18.2
Totals	110	857	1682	.510	349	491	.711	1362	12.4	2063	18.8

DAWN STALEY
Virginia
5-6 – G
Philadelphia, Pa.

Named national player of the year as a junior and senior by a variety of organizations.... Was a three-time Kodak All-American.... Led Virginia to three Final Four appearances.... Named the 1991 Honda-Broderick Cup Award winner, signifying the top collegiate woman athlete.... Was MVP of the 1991 Final Four, sharing a single-game record of 28 points in a losing effort against Tennessee in the national title game.... The NCAA career steals leader with 454.... The only player in ACC history, male or female, to register at least 2,000 points, 700 rebounds, 700 assists and 400 steals.... The first woman in school history to score 2,000 points.... Led

Virginia to an ACC tournament title and was a two-time league Player of the Year.... Learned the game on the same playgrounds as former Loyola Marymount All-Americans Hank Gathers and Bo Kimble.

Year	G	FGM	FGA	FG%	FTM	FTA	FT%	Reb.	Avg.	Pts.	Avg.
88–89	31	197	431	.457	147	177	.831	158	5.1	574	18.5
89–90	32	203	449	.452	132	169	.781	214	6.7	574	17.9
90–91	34	176	391	.450	108	131	.824	209	6.1	495	14.6
91–92	34	177	366	.484	118	146	.808	191	5.6	492	14.5
Totals	131	753	1637	.460	505	623	.811	772	5.9	2135	16.3

Three-point shooting: 33 of 93 (.355) in 1988-89, 36 of 104 (.346) in 1989-90, 35 of 108 (.324) in 1990-91 and 20 of 66 (.303) in 1991-92. Totals: 124 of 371 (.334).

MARIANNE CRAWFORD STANLEY
Immaculata
5-6 – G
Upper Darby, Pa.

A two-time All-American who played on two AIAW national championship teams.... Considered one of the first guards to speed up the game with a full-court transition game and heady point guard play.... Played on the same Immaculata team with Theresa Grentz, head coach at Rutgers, and Rene Portland of Penn State.... Averaged nearly six assists a game during her career.... Was an assistant coach at Immaculata for one season before beginning her head coaching career at Old Dominion, where she coached three national championship teams.... Moved to USC in 1989 before suing the school on equal pay grounds.

Year	G	FGM	FGA	FG%	FTM	FTA	FT%	Reb.	Avg.	Pts.	Avg.
72–73	16	74	158	.468	56	81	.691	83	5.1	204	12.7
73–74	20	65	168	.386	41	65	.630	62	3.1	171	8.5
74–75	26	86	219	.392	45	70	.642	80	3.0	217	8.3
75–76	27	60	147	.408	34	51	.666	63	2.3	154	5.7
Totals	89	692	285	.418	176	267	.659	288	3.2	746	8.3

VALERIE STILL
Kentucky
6-1 – F/C
Cherry Hill, N.J.

The all-time leading scorer, male or female, in Kentucky basketball history with 2,763 points.... A two-time All-American and finalist for the Wade Trophy.... Led the Lady Kats to their best season ever as a senior, reaching the NCAA Tournament and achieving a No. 4 national ranking.... Guided Kentucky to its only SEC tournament championship in 1982 by averaging 30 points and 11 rebounds in three games and earning MVP honors.... She holds nearly a dozen school career records.... The only woman at Kentucky to have her jersey retired.... Began her playing career in Europe shortly after graduation and is currently playing there, perhaps with the most longevity of any American female.... The younger sister of former Kansas City Chiefs All-Pro lineman Art Still.

Year	G	FGM	FGA	FG%	FTM	FTA	FT%	Reb.	Avg.	Pts.	Avg.
79–80	29	256	463	.553	129	183	.700	403	13.9	641	22.1
80–81	30	260	447	.581	108	154	.701	329	10.9	628	20.9
81–82	32	329	565	.582	136	199	.683	457	14.3	794	24.8
82–83	28	273	456	.599	154	212	.726	336	12.0	700	25.0
Totals	119	1118	1931	.580	527	748	.700	1525	12.8	2763	23.2

SHERYL SWOOPES
Texas Tech
6-0 – F
Brownfield, Tex.

Played just two years of major college basketball, but as a senior guided Texas Tech to the NCAA championship in 1993.... She shattered Bill

Walton's Final Four single-game scoring record of 44 points by tallying 47 against Ohio State in the title contest.... Was a unanimous national Player of the Year and twice earned Kodak All-American honors.... Scored in double figures in all but two of her 66 games at Texas Tech and finished as the school's second all-time scoring leader with 1,645 points.... Was the national Junior College Player of the Year at South Plains Junior College in Texas, where she holds 28 school records.

Year	G	FGM	FGA	FG%	FTM	FTA	FT%	Reb.	Avg.	Pts.	Avg.
91–92	32	275	527	.503	135	167	.808	285	8.9	690	21.6
92–93	34	356	652	.546	211	243	.868	312	9.2	955	28.0
Totals	66	631	1179	.535	346	410	.843	597	9.0	1645	24.9

Three-point shooting: 25 of 61 (.410) in 1991-92 and 32 of 78 (.410) in 1992-93. Totals: 57 of 139 (.410).

JOYCE WALKER
LSU
5-8 – G
Seattle, Wash.

A two-time Kodak All-American and the school's career scoring leader with 2,906 points.... The only player in LSU history to rank in the Top 10 in scoring, rebounding, assists, steals, and blocked shots.... Second-leading SEC career scoring leader at 24.9 points, she also leads the league in career field goals made and attempted.... Helped LSU to an AIAW national tournament appearance as a freshman and to the NCAA regionals in her senior season.

Year	G	FGM	FGA	FG%	FTM	FTA	FT%	Reb.	Avg.	Pts.	Avg.
80–81	30	274	489	.566	67	107	.626	157	5.2	621	20.7
81–82	30	340	500	.576	67	99	.677	136	4.5	747	24.9
82–83	27	312	540	.578	120	161	.745	186	6.9	744	27.6
83–84	30	330	619	.533	134	165	.812	119	4.0	794	26.5
Totals	117	1259	2238	.562	388	532	.729	598	5.1	2906	24.8

ROSIE WALKER
Stephen F. Austin
6-1 – F
Dallas, Tex.

Despite playing only two years, is one of the most decorated players in school history.... A two-time All-American at Stephen F. Austin after being named a junior college All-American.... Holds seven school records in all.... The Ladyjacks recorded a 57-11 during her two seasons and one national AIAW tournament trip.... Scored 30 or more points in 18 different games.

Year	G	FGM	FGA	FG%	FTM	FTA	FT%	Reb.	Avg.	Pts.	Avg.
78–79	35	395	607	.650	122	174	.701	448	12.8	912	26.0
79–80	31	263	390	.674	123	170	.724	354	11.4	649	20.9
Totals	66	658	997	.660	245	344	.712	802	12.2	1561	23.7

TERESA WEATHERSPOON
Louisiana Tech
5-8 – G
Pineland, Tex.

The all-time assists leader in Louisiana Tech history who guided the Lady Techsters to their third national title in 1988.... A two-time Kodak All-

American and the 1988 Wade Trophy Winner.... Also the 1988 recipient of the Honda/Broderick Cup, awarded to the top collegiate female athlete in all sports.... Named to the all-Women's Final Four team twice.... In 1993 became one of the first two Americans to play professional basketball in Russia as a member of the Moscow Red Army team.

Year	G	FGM	FGA	FG%	FTM	FTA	FT%	Reb.	Avg.	Pts.	Avg.
84–85	33	72	140	.514	51	100	.510	127	3.8	195	5.9
85–86	32	110	226	.487	61	112	.545	125	3.9	281	8.7
86–87	33	122	234	.521	67	95	.705	137	4.2	311	9.4
87–88	33	119	249	.478	57	86	.663	144	4.4	300	9.1
Totals	131	423	849	.498	236	393	.601	533	4.1	1087	8.3

LYNETTE WOODARD
Kansas
6-0 – F
Wichita, Kans.

The all-time women's scoring leader, with 3,649 points, only 18 points shy of Pete Maravich's career college record... A four-time All-American and two-time Olympian, captaining the 1984 U.S. gold medal squad.... The 1981 Wade Trophy Winner, awarded to the top female collegian.... Selected the Big Eight's Player of the Decade for the 1980s.... A member of the Kansas and National High School Athletic Halls of Fame.... Paced Kansas to a 108-32 record and three AIAW national tournament appearances.... Holds eight career, eight single-season, and five single-game school records.... Was the first woman to play for the Harlem Globetrotters.... Played professionally in Italy and Japan and briefly was a Kansas assistant coach.... Currently is athletic director for Kansas City public schools.... The first female inducted into the GTE Academic All-American Hall of Fame in 1992.

Year	G	FGM	FGA	FG%	FTM	FTA	FT%	Reb.	Avg.	Pts.	Avg.
77–78	33	366	736	.497	101	152	.664	490	14.8	833	25.2
78–79	38	519	924	.562	139	212	.656	545	14.3	1177	31.0
79–80	37	372	738	.504	137	192	.714	389	10.5	881	23.8
80–81	31	315	594	.533	128	186	.688	310	10.0	758	24.5
Totals	139	1572	2992	.525	505	742	.681	1734	12.4	3649	26.3

All-Time Great Women's Coaches

GENO AURIEMMA
West Chester '80

A two-time national coach of the year who guided Connecticut to a perfect 35-0 national championship season in 1995. . . . The Huskies have won 30 games in a row for the last four seasons, only the second time a college program, men's or women's has done that. The Louisiana Tech women did it in the late 1980s. . . . UConn has won five Big East titles and the last four conference tournament titles. . . . After reaching the Final Four as an upstart in 1991, Auriemma began building a powerhouse with the recruitment of Rebecca Lobo, and followed that with the addition of 6-7 center Kara Wolters in 1993. . . . Glib, personable and media-conscious, Auriemma has been at the center of an East Coast media tidal wave of interest in the Huskies, who sell out most of their home games and have a contract with Connecticut Public TV. . . . Before arriving at UConn, he was a long-time assistant coach at Virginia.

Year	School	Record	Postseason
85-86	Connecticut	12-15	
86-87	Connecticut	14-13	
87-88	Connecticut	17-11	
88-89	Connecticut	24-6	NCAA Tournament
89-90	Connecticut	25-6	NCAA Tournament
90-91	Connecticut	29-5	NCAA Final Four
91-92	Connecticut	23-11	NCAA Tournament
92-93	Connecticut	18-11	NCAA Tournament
93-94	Connecticut	30-3	NCAA Elite 8
94-95	Connecticut	35-0	NCAA Champions
95-96	Connecticut	34-4	NCAA Final Four
96-97	Connecticut	33-1	NCAA Elite 8

12-Year Coaching Record: 294-86 (.773) at Connecticut.

LEON BARMORE
Louisiana Tech '67

The winningest coach by percentage in women's college basketball history.... Served as an assistant and associate head coach and was co-head coach with Sonja Hogg for three seasons before getting the job to himself in 1985.... Tech won two national titles while he was an assistant and again in 1988.... Named co-Coach of the Decade for the 1980s by the U.S. Basketball Writers Association.... Named Naismith National Coach of the Year in 1988.... Until 1990–91, Tech had never finished lower than fifth in the final regular-season AP poll.... Lady Techsters upset No. 1 Tennessee and Southern Cal to reach the 1994 Final Four, losing only on a last-second shot by North Carolina in the finals.

Year	School	Overall	League	Postseason
82–83	La. Tech	26-6		NCAA Runnerup
83–84	La. Tech	30-3		NCAA Final Four
84–85	La. Tech	29-4		NCAA Regional
85–86	La. Tech	27-5		NCAA Regional
86–87	La. Tech	30-3		NCAA Runnerup
87–88	La. Tech	32-2	8-0 (ASC)	NCAA Champion
88–89	La. Tech	32-4	12-0 (ASC)	NCAA Final Four
89–90	La. Tech	32-1	14-0 (ASC)	NCAA Final Four
90–91	La. Tech	18-12	10-4 (ASC)	NCAA 1st Round
91–92	La. Tech	20-10	11-3 (SBC)	NCAA 1st Round
92–93	La. Tech	26-6	13-1 (SBC)	NCAA Regional
93–94	La. Tech	32-3	14-0 (SBC)	NCAA Runnerup
93–94	La. Tech	31-4	14-0 (SBC)	NCAA Runnerup
94–95	La. Tech	28-5	14-0 (SBC)	NCAA Sweet 16
95–96	La. Tech	32-2	14-0 (SBC)	NCAA Elite

14-Year Coaching Record: 398-63 (.863) at Louisiana Tech; 35-13 (.729) in NCAA Tournament.

JOE CIAMPI
Mansfield '68

The 12th winningest active Division I coach who led the Lady Tigers to the NCAA title game in 1988, 1989 and 1990.... National coach of the year in 1987, 1989 and 1993.... He has coached four All-Americans and three Olympians: Vickie Orr in 1988, Carolyn Jones in 1992 and Ruthie Bolton-Holifield in 1996.... Coached Auburn to SEC regular-season titles in 1987, 1988 and 1989 and the SEC Tournment championship in 1981, 1987 and 1990.... The fourth-winningest coach in NCAA tournament history had had 12 teams qualify for the NCAA Tournament.... Coached at Army when Mike Krzyzewski was the men's coach there.... Auburn held an NCAA homecourt winning streak at 68 games from 1986-91 that was broken by Tennessee.

Year	School	Overall	League	Postseason
77-78	Army	19-6		
78-79	Army	20-4		
79-80	Auburn	17-13		
80-81	Auburn	26-7		SEC Tr. Champs
81-82	Auburn	24-5		NCAA Tournament
82-83	Auburn	24-8	6-2 (SEC)	NCAA 2nd Round
83-84	Auburn	19-10	5-3 (SEC)	
84-85	Auburn	25-6	5-3 (SEC)	NCAA 2nd Round
85-86	Auburn	24-6	6-3 (SEC)	NCAA Sweet 16
86-87	Auburn	31-2	8-1 (SEC)	NCAA Elite 8
87-88	Auburn	32-3	9-0 (SEC)	NCAA Runner-up
88-89	Auburn	32-2	9-0 (SEC)	NCAA Runner-up
89-90	Auburn	28-7	7-2 (SEC)	NCAA Runner-up
90-91	Auburn	26-6	7-2 (SEC)	NCAA Elite 8
91-92	Auburn	17-12	4-7 (SEC)	
92-93	Auburn	25-4	9-2 (SEC)	NCAA Sweet 16
93-94	Auburn	20-10	6-5 (SEC)	NCAA 2nd Round
94-95	Auburn	17-10	5-6 (SEC)	
95-96	Auburn	23-9	6-5 (SEC)	NCAA Elite 8

19-Year Coaching Record: 421-72 (.853) overall; 39-10 (.795) in two years at Army; 410-120 (.773) in first 17 years at Auburn; 92-41 (.691) in SEC.

JODY CONRADT
Baylor '63

The all-time winningest coach in women's college basketball history and the only coach with more than 600 career victories.... Her 1986 Texas team went 34-0 and finished as the only undefeated women's NCAA title team

ever.... Earned Southwest Conference Coach of the Year honors four times and was the National Coach of the Year in 1980 and 1986.... Texas won a record 188 consecutive SWC victories until Arkansas snapped the string during the 1989–90 season.... Texas also was the national attendance leader during the 1980s.... Coached the U.S. to a gold medal in the 1987 Pan American Games.... Women's athletic director at Texas since 1992.... A young 1993–94 Lady Longhorn team upset defending NCAA champion Texas Tech with a last-second shot to win the Southwest Conference Tournament.

Year	School	Overall	League	Postseason
69–70	Sam Houston St.	15-4		
70–71	Sam Houston St.	20-6		
71–72	Sam Houston St.	19-6		
72–73	Sam Houston St.	20-7		
73–74	UT-Arlington	9-14		
74–75	UT-Arlington	11-14		
75–76	UT-Arlington	23-11		
76–77	Texas	36-10		AIAW Regional
77–78	Texas	29-10		AIAW Regional
78–79	Texas	37-4		AIAW Regional
79–80	Texas	33-4		5th AIAW
80–81	Texas	28-8		AIAW Nationals
81–82	Texas	35-4		2nd AIAW
82–83	Texas	30-3	8-0 (SWC)	NCAA Regional
83–84	Texas	32-3	16-0 (SWC)	NCAA Regional
84–85	Texas	28-3	16-0 (SWC)	NCAA Regional
85–86	Texas	34-0	16-0 (SWC)	NCAA Champion
86–87	Texas	31-2	16-0 (SWC)	NCAA Final Four
87–88	Texas	32-3	16-0 (SWC)	NCAA Regional
88–89	Texas	27-5	16-0 (SWC)	NCAA Regional
89–90	Texas	27-5	15-1 (SWC)	NCAA Regional
90–91	Texas	21-9	14-2 (SWC)	NCAA 1st Round
91–92	Texas	21-10	13-4 (SWC)	NCAA 2nd Round
92–93	Texas	22-8	13-1 (SWC)	NCAA 2nd Round
93–94	Texas	22-9	10-4 (SWC)	NCAA 2nd Round
94–95	Texas	12-16	7-7 (SWC)	
95–96	Texas	21-9	13-1 (SWC)	NCAA 1st Round

27-Year Coaching Record: 675-187 (.783) overall; 64-23 (.736) in four years at Sam Houston State; 43-39 (.524) in three years at Texas-Arlington; 558-125 (.816) in first 20 years at Texas; 189-19 (.908) in Southwest Conference; 69-25 (.739) in postseason.

SUE GUNTER
Peabody '62

She is the only women's coach with as many as 30 years of heading coaching experience.... Was an All-American AAU player in 1960 for Nashville Business College.... The first women's coach to earn 200 career victories at two different schools.... Coached LSU to the SEC Tournament championship in 1991.... Her LSU team won the National Women's Invitational Tournament in 1985.

Year	School	Overall	League	Postseason
62–63	Middle Tenn. St.	N/A		
63–64	Middle Tenn. St.	N/A		
64–65	Stephen F. Austin	N/A		
65–66	Stephen F. Austin	N/A		
66–67	Stephen F. Austin	N/A		
67–68	Stephen F. Austin	N/A		
69–70	Stephen F. Austin	6-4		
70–71	Stephen F. Austin	12-2		
71–72	Stephen F. Austin	19-9		
72–73	Stephen F. Austin	21-6		
73–74	Stephen F. Austin	27-7		AIAW Tr.
74–75	Stephen F. Austin	32-8		AIAW Tr.
75–76	Stephen F. Austin	30-4		
76–77	Stephen F. Austin	28-6		AIAW Regional
77–78	Stephen F. Austin	25-13		AIAW Tr.
78–79	Stephen F. Austin	30-5		AIAW Regional
79–80	Stephen F. Austin	27-6		AIAW Regional
82–83	LSU	20-7	6-2 (SEC)	
83–84	LSU	23-7	5-3 (SEC)	NCAA Regional
84–85	LSU	20-9	4-4 (SEC)	NWIT Champion
85–86	LSU	27-6	6-3 (SEC)	NCAA Regionals
86–87	LSU	20-8	6-3 (SEC)	NCAA 2nd Round
87–88	LSU	18-11	6-3 (SEC)	NCAA 1st Round
88–89	LSU	19-11	5-4 (SEC)	NCAA Regional
89–90	LSU	21-9	4-5 (SEC)	NCAA 1st Round
90–91	LSU	24-7	5-4 (SEC)	NCAA 2nd Round

91–92	LSU	16-13	4-7 (SEC)
92–93	LSU	9-18	0-11 (SEC)
93–94	LSU	11-16	2-9 (SEC)
94-95	LSU	7-20	1-10 (SEC)
95-96	LSU	21-11	4-7 (SEC)

32-Year Coaching Record: 522-240 (.685) overall; 266-87 (.704) at Stephen F. Austin State; 256-153 (.625) in first 14 years at LSU; 58-75 (.436) in Southeastern Conference; 33-31 (.516) in postseason.

SONJA HOGG
Louisiana Tech '70

Began the famed Louisiana Tech program and coached it to national titles in 1981 and 1982.... Set a women's single-season record of 40 victories in 1979–90.... The 1980–81 team that went 34-0 is only one of two women's teams to go undefeated in a season.... In her later years at Tech, became a marketing and public relations ambassador for the team, leaving Leon Barmore to handle on-court responsibilities.... Left Tech in 1985 and became a high school coach in Texas briefly in the late 1980s.... Was director of marketing for the women's athletic department at Texas and also was the chief fundraiser for a women's basketball hall of fame to be built near Jackson, Tenn.... Named head coach at Baylor in April 1994.

Year	School	Overall	League	Postseason
74–75	La. Tech	13-9		
75–76	La. Tech	19-10		
76–77	La. Tech	22-9		AIAW Regional
77–78	La. Tech	20-8		AIAW Regional
78–79	La. Tech	34-4		AIAW Tr.
79–80	La. Tech	40-5		AIAW Final Four
80–81	La. Tech	34-0		AIAW Champions
81–82	La. Tech	35-1		NCAA Champions
82–83	La. Tech	31-2		NCAA Final Four
83–84	La. Tech	30-3		NCAA Final Four
84–85	La. Tech	29-4		NCAA Regional
94–95	Baylor	13-14	4-10 (SWC)	
95–96	Baylor	11-19	3-11 (SWC)	

13-Year Coaching Record: 331-88 (.689) overall; 307-55 (.848) in 11 years at Louisiana Tech; 24-33 (.421) in first two years at Baylor; 37-11 (.771) in postseason.

LUCILLE KYVALLOS
Springfield College

One of the pioneering college coaches of the early 1970s.... Queens participated in the earliest National Invitation Tournament and later became an AIAW runnerup under her tutelage.... The college coach of former Immaculata mentor Cathy Rush.... Helped organize the first women's college game at Madison Square Garden in 1975 in which her team was defeated by Immaculata before a crowd of more than 12,000 spectators.... Was named the first recipient of the U.S. Basketball Writers Association's Pioneer Award in 1990.... Still a member of the physical education faculty at Queens.

Year	School	Overall	League	Postseason
62–66	W. Chester St.	54-2		
68–69	Queens	N/A		
69–70	Queens	N/A		W. Carolina Inv.
70–71	Queens	N/A		
71–72	Queens	27-2		AIAW Tournament
72–73	Queens	22-5		2nd AIAW Tr.
73–74	Queens	22-4		
74–75	Queens	19-8		
75–76	Queens	20-5		
76–77	Queens	18-13		
77–78	Queens	24-3		
78–79	Queens	N/A		
79–80	Queens	23-6		

Incomplete 16-Year Coaching Record: 229-48 (.826) overall; 54-2 (.964) at West Chester State; 175-46 (.791) at Queens.

ANDY LANDERS
Tennessee Tech '74

Only one of four coaches to take team to Final Four four times. Georgia reached it the last two seasons, but lost to SEC rival Tennessee both times. ... Built Lady Bulldogs from scratch into a contending program largely on recruiting.... One of the first women's coaches to actively recruit from around the country.... Georgia got to NCAA title game in 1985 with future Olympians Teresa Edwards and Teresa McClain.... Seventh among active Division I coaches in winning percentage.... Registered 82 wins at Roane State (Tenn.) Junior College.... Has earned Naismith national coach of the year honors in 1986, 1987 and 1996.... Georgia is seventh in NCAA Tournament wins and 10th in winning percentage in the postseason. . . . SEC coach of the year in 1984 and 1991. . . . The Lady Dogs have gone to 13 NCAA Tournaments and have won five SEC titles under Landers. . . . He has coached eight Kodak All-Americans.

Year	School	Overall	League	Postseason
79-80	Georgia	16-12		
80-81	Georgia	27-10		NWIT Champions
81-82	Georgia	21-9	4-3 (SEC)	NCAA Tournament
82-83	Georgia	27-7	4-5 (SEC)	NCAA Final Four
83-84	Georgia	30-3	8-1 (SEC)	NCAA Sweet 16
84-85	Georgia	29-5	7-1 (SEC)	NCAA Runner-up
85-86	Georgia	30-2	9-0 (SEC)	NCAA Sweet 16
86-87	Georgia	27-5	7-2 (SEC)	NCAA Sweet 16
87-88	Georgia	21-10	5-4 (SEC)	NCAA Sweet 16
88-89	Georgia	23-7	6-3 (SEC)	NCAA Sweet 16
89-90	Georgia	25-5	6-3 (SEC)	NCAA 2nd Round
90-91	Georgia	28-4	9-0 (SEC)	NCAA Elite 8
91-92	Georgia	19-11	6-5 (SEC)	
92-93	Georgia	21-13	5-6 (SEC)	NCAA 2nd Round
93-94	Georgia	17-11	5-6 (SEC)	
94-95	Georgia	28-5	9-2 (SEC)	NCAA Final Four
95-96	Georgia	28-5	10-1 (SEC)	NCAA Runner-up

17-Year Coaching Career: 417-124 (.770) at Georgia; 100-41 (.709) in SEC.

DARLENE MAY
Cal State Fullerton '67

The winningest coach in Division II history, topping the 500-victory mark early in the 1993–94 season and is third among all active women's coaches.... Coached three national championship teams and eight AIAW and NCAA Final Four teams.... Cal Poly-Pomona has never finished below first place in conference play.... Has won the Converse national Division II Coach of the Year award two times.... Also has had a distinguished officiating career, becoming the first woman to referee a women's Olympic contest during the 1984 games in Los Angeles, including the bronze medal game.... Died in 1996 after a battle with cancer that prompted her retirement following the 1993-94 season.

Year	School	Overall	League	Postseason
74–75	Cal Poly-Pomona	16-6		5th AIAW
75–76	Cal Poly-Pomona	20-6		8th AIAW
76–77	Cal Poly-Pomona	28-6	10-0 (SCAA)	5th AIAW
77–78	Cal Poly-Pomona	31-4	10-0 (SCAA)	
78–79	Cal Poly-Pomona	24-7	10-0 (SCAA)	
79–80	Cal Poly-Pomona	27-13	9-1 (SCAA)	6th AIAW
80–81	Cal Poly-Pomona	30-9	12-0 (CCAA)	AIAW Final Four
81–82	Cal Poly-Pomona	29-7	12-0 (CCAA)	NCAA Champion
82–83	Cal Poly-Pomona	29-3	11-0 (CCAA)	NCAA Final Four
83–84	Cal Poly-Pomona	22-7	11-1 (CCAA)	
84–85	Cal Poly-Pomona	26-7	11-1 (CCAA)	NCAA Champion
85–86	Cal Poly-Pomona	30-3	12-0 (CCAA)	NCAA Champion
86–87	Cal Poly-Pomona	29-3	11-1 (CCAA)	NCAA Final Four
87–88	Cal Poly-Pomona	28-4	12-0 (CCAA)	NCAA Regional
88–89	Cal Poly-Pomona	28-6	11-1 (CCAA)	NCAA Final Four
89–90	Cal Poly-Pomona	29-4	12-0 (CCAA)	NCAA Final Four
90–91	Cal Poly-Pomona	22-9	11-1 (CCAA)	NCAA Regional
91–92	Cal Poly-Pomona	23-6	12-0 (CCAA)	
92–93	Cal Poly-Pomona	27-3	11-1 (CCAA)	NCAA Regional
93–94	Cal Poly-Pomona	21-6	9-1 (CCAA)	NCAA 1st Round

19-Year Coaching Record: 519-119 (.813) overall; 195-8 (.961) in the Southern California Athletic Association and California Collegiate Athletic Association.

BILLIE JEAN MOORE
Washburn '66

Coached Cal State Fullerton and UCLA to national championships during a 24-year career that culminated with her retirement in April 1993.... Won the first AIAW Final Four in 1978 in her first year at UCLA.... Her Fullerton team won a national crown in her first year on the job there, predating the official beginning of the AIAW tournament.... Also coached the first U.S. women's Olympic team to a silver medal in 1976.... Teams went to postseason play 16 out of 24 seasons, winning nine conference titles and eight national Top 10 finishes.

Year	School	Overall	League	Postseason
69–70	CS Fullerton	17-1		NIT Champion
70–71	CS Fullerton	20-1		
71–72	CS Fullerton	19-1		3rd AIAW
72–73	CS Fullerton	13-1		
73–74	CS Fullerton	19-2		
74–75	CS Fullerton	19-2		3rd AIAW
75–76	CS Fullerton	14-5		
76–77	CS Fullerton	19-2		
77–78	UCLA	27-3	8-0 (WCAA)	AIAW Champion
78–79	UCLA	24-10	7-1 (WCAA)	4th AIAW
79–80	UCLA	18-12	9-3 (WCAA)	AIAW Regional
80–81	UCLA	29-7	9-3 (WCAA)	5th AIAW
81–82	UCLA	16-14	7-5 (WCAA)	
82–83	UCLA	18-11	9-5 (WCAA)	NCAA Regional
83–84	UCLA	17-12	6-8 (WCAA)	
84–85	UCLA	20-10	10-4 (WCAA)	NCAA Regional
85–86	UCLA	12-16	3-5 (Pac West)	
86–87	UCLA	18-10	11-7 (Pac-10)	
87–88	UCLA	19-11	12-6 (Pac-10)	
88–89	UCLA	12-16	8-10 (Pac-10)	
89–90	UCLA	17-12	12-6 (Pac-10)	NCAA 1st Round
90–91	UCLA	15-13	10-8 (Pac-10)	
91–92	UCLA	21-10	12-6 (Pac-10)	NCAA Regional
92–93	UCLA	13-14	8-10 (Pac-10)	

24-Year Coaching Record: 436-196 (.689) overall; 140-15 (.903) at Cal State Fullerton; 296-181 (.620) at UCLA; 73-35 (.579) in Pacific-10 games; 59-18 (.766) in postseason games.

CATHY RUSH
West Chester State

A women's coaching pioneer who led Immaculata to the first three AIAW national titles... Three of her former players are distinguished college coaches—Theresa Grentz (Rutgers), Rene Portland (Penn State), and Marianne Stanley (formerly of Old Dominion, Pennsylvania, and USC).... Made history in 1975 when Immaculata played Queens in Madison Square Garden, drawing nearly 12,000 spectators.... After retiring in 1977, got into sports camp business for girls, her current occupation.... She runs the camps with her husband, NBA referee Ed Rush.... Is a commentator on women's TV games.... Named the 1994 recipient of the U.S. Basketball Writers Association's Pioneer Award.

Year	School	Overall	League	Postseason
70–71	Immaculata	12-2		
71–72	Immaculata	20-1		AIAW champion
72–73	Immaculata	20-0		AIAW champion
73–74	Immaculata	20-1		AIAW champion
74–75	Immaculata	23-3		AIAW runnerup
75–76	Immaculata	25-3		AIAW nationals
76–77	Immaculata	29-6		AIAW nationals

7-Year Coaching Record: 149-16 (.903) overall.

MARSHA SHARP
Wayland Baptist '75

Bumped Texas out of the top spot in the Southwest Conference for most of the 1990s, culminating with the NCAA championship in 1993. In fact, she used a former Lady Longhorn signee Sheryl Swoopes to guide Tech to the top.... Received a $1 million, five-year contract following the 1995-96 season. . . . Lady Raiders usually outdraw the men's team and filled the Tech football stadium with 40,000 fans for a post-title pep rally. . . . National coach of the year in 1993. . . . Tech has gone to five straight Sweet 16 trips in the NCAA Tournament. . . . SWC coach of the year six times, including

five of the last seven years. . . . Tech has gone to 11 postseason tournaments and has had 11 20-win-plus seasons. . . . Has recruited most of her players from Texas, especially the Panhandle region, but is starting to attract national prep stars. . . . Was a graduate assistant at Wayland for renowned coach Dean Weese. Weese's brother, Linden, has been on Tech's staff for all of her 14 seasons.

Year	School	Overall	League	Postseason
82-83	Texas Tech	22-9	6-2 (SWC)	Women's NIT
83-84	Texas Tech	23-7	13-3 (SWC)	NCAA Tournament
84-85	Texas Tech	24-8	12-4 (SWC)	Women's NIT
85-86	Texas Tech	21-9	13-3 (SWC)	NCAA 2nd Round
86-87	Texas Tech	18-11	10-6 (SWC)	
87-88	Texas Tech	17-13	9-7 (SWC)	
88-89	Texas Tech	17-13	9-7 (SWC)	
89-90	Texas Tech	20-11	11-5 (SWC)	NCAA 2nd Round
90-91	Texas Tech	23-8	12-4 (SWC)	NCAA 2nd Round
91-92	Texas Tech	27-5	13-1 (SWC)	NCAA Sweet 16
92-93	Texas Tech	31-3	13-1 (SWC)	NCAA Champion
93-94	Texas Tech	28-5	12-2 (SWC)	NCAA Sweet 16
94-95	Texas Tech	33-4	13-1 (SWC)	NCAA Sweet 16
95-96	Texas Tech	27-4	13-1 (SWC)	NCAA Sweet 16

14-Year Coaching Record: 331-110 (.751) at Texas Tech; 159-47 (.771) in SWC.

BOB SPENCER
Parsons College '57

Retired following 1992–93 season with 578 wins, the second most of any women's coach ever, trailing only Jody Conradt of Texas.... A native of Iowa, a girls high school hotbed where he coached some of the first women's intercollegiate teams in the mid-1960s.... Started programs at John F. Kennedy College and William Penn College, two of the earliest Midwestern college powers.... William Penn won seven Iowa AIAW titles, six regional crowns, and a national ranking in each of his eight seasons. The 1973 team finished fourth in the AIAW national tournament.

Year	School	Overall	League	Postseason
66–70	JFK	73-42		
71–73	Parsons	67-39		
73–81	William Penn	40-43		
81–82	Fresno St.	8-17		
82–83	Fresno St.	15-12		
83–84	Fresno St.	18-11		
84–85	Fresno St.	20-9		
85–86	Fresno St.	21-9		
86–87	Fresno St.	22-8	12-6	(Big W.)
87–88	Fresno St.	16-12	11-7	(Big W.)
88–89	Fresno St.	18-12	9-9	(Big W.)
89–90	Fresno St.	21-12	11-7	(Big W.)
90–91	Fresno St.	16-13	9-9	(Big W.)
91–92	Fresno St.	13-15	7-11	(Big W.)
92–93	Fresno St.	10-17	4-10	(WAC)

27-Year Coaching Record: 578-274 (.678) overall; 198-137 (.591) at Fresno State.

MARIANNE STANLEY
Immaculata '76

A three-time national championship coach who left USC in an equal pay dispute in September 1993 and sued the institution.... Won two AIAW and one NCAA title at Old Dominion, becoming the only women's coach to win crowns in both associations.... Revived the USC program in her final two seasons, as the Trojans reached the regional finals and regionals.... Two-time national Coach of the Year (1979, 1985).... Old Dominion won titles in 1979 and 1980 and the NCAA crown in 1985.... In her first season of college coaching, Old Dominion won the National Women's Invitational Tournament.... An All-American player at Immaculata (Pa.) College, which won two national titles while she was there.... Hired to market women's basketball at Stanford while her lawsuit was pending.

Year	School	Overall	League	Postseason
77–78	Old Dominion	30-4		NWIT Champion
78–79	Old Dominion	35-1		AIAW Champion
79–80	Old Dominion	37-1		AIAW Champion

UCLA coach Billie Moore hoists the 1978 AIAW trophy, cheered on by her team.

80–81	Old Dominion	28-7		AIAW Final Four
81–82	Old Dominion	22-6		AIAW Regional
82–83	Old Dominion	29-6		NCAA Final Four
83–84	Old Dominion	24-5		NCAA Regional
84–85	Old Dominion	31-3		NCAA Champion
85–86	Old Dominion	15-13		
86–87	Old Dominion	18-13		NCAA Regional
87–88	Pennsylvania	6-20		
88–89	Pennsylvania	5-21		
89–90	USC	8-19	6-12 (Pac-10)	
90–91	USC	18-12	11-7 (Pac-10)	NCAA 2nd Round
91–92	USC	23-8	14-4 (Pac-10)	NCAA Regional
92–93	USC	22-7	14-4 (Pac 10)	NCAA Regional

16-Year Coaching Record: 351-146 (.706) overall; 269-59 (.820) at Old Dominion; 11-41 (.212) at Pennsylvania; 71-46 (.606) at USC; 56-27 (.674) in the Pacific-10 Conference; 17-7 (.708) in the NCAA Tournament. . . Served as interim co-coach at Stanford during 1995-96 season, helping Cardinal to Final Four, then named head coach at California in April 1996.

C. VIVIAN STRINGER
Slippery Rock '70

The 1993 Converse National Coach of the Year after guiding Iowa to its first Final Four appearance and overcoming the death of her husband early in the season.... Coached Cheyney State (Pa.) College to the first women's NCAA title game in 1982.... Also Converse Coach of the Year in 1988.... Iowa has won outright or shared six Big Ten championships since she arrived in 1983.

Year	School	Overall	League	Postseason
71–83	Cheyney St.	251-51		
83–84	Iowa	17-10	11-7 (Big 10)	
84–85	Iowa	20-8	14-4 (Big 10)	
85–86	Iowa	22-7	15-3 (Big 10)	NCAA 2nd Round
86–87	Iowa	26-5	17-1 (Big 10)	NCAA Regional
87–88	Iowa	29-2	17-1 (Big 10)	NCAA Regional
88–89	Iowa	27-5	16-2 (Big 10)	NCAA Regional
89–90	Iowa	23-6	15-3 (Big 10)	NCAA 2nd Round
90–91	Iowa	21-9	13-5 (Big 10)	NCAA 2nd Round
91–92	Iowa	25-4	16-2 (Big 10)	NCAA 2nd Round
92–93	Iowa	27-4	16-2 (Big 10)	NCAA Final Four
93–94	Iowa	21-7	13-5 (Big 10)	NCAA 2nd Round
94–95	Iowa	11-17	6-10 (Big 10)	
95–96	Rutgers	13-15	8-10 (Big East)	

25-Year Coaching Record: 533-150 (.780) overall; 269-84 (.762) in 12 years at Iowa; 13-15 (.464) in first year at Rutgers; 141-45 (.758) in Big Ten; 8-10 (.400) in Big East; 11-9 (.550) in NCAA tournament.

PAT HEAD SUMMITT
Tennessee-Martin '74

Only women's coach to win four national titles (1987, 1989, 1991, 1996)…. Earned her 500th career win in the first game of the 1993–94 season, becoming the second winningest active Division I coach behind Jody Conradt of Texas…. Coached the U.S. women to the 1984 Olympic gold medal, and played on the first Olympic team in 1976 that won a silver medal…. Her teams have qualified for 11 Final Fours and have won 20 or more games 17 consecutive seasons…. The Naismith National Coach of the Year in 1987, 1989, and 1994…. Named co-coach of the decade for the 1980s by the U.S. Basketball Writers Association…. The first woman to receive the John Bunn Award given by the Naismith Basketball Hall of Fame in 1990…. An inductee of the Women's Sports Foundation Hall of Fame in 1990.

Year	School	Overall	League	Postseason
74–75	Tennessee	16-8		
75–76	Tennessee	16-11		
76–77	Tennessee	28-5		3rd AIAW
77–78	Tennessee	27-4		1st AIAW Poll
78–79	Tennessee	30-9		AIAW Final Four
79–80	Tennessee	33-5		2nd AIAW
80–81	Tennessee	25-6		2nd AIAW
81–82	Tennessee	22-10		NCAA Final Four
82–83	Tennessee	25-8	7-1 (SEC)	NCAA Regional
83–84	Tennessee	23-10	7-1 (SEC)	2nd Final Four
84–85	Tennessee	22-10	4-4 (SEC)	NCAA Regional

85–86	Tennessee	24-10	5-4 (SEC)	NCAA Final Four
86–87	Tennessee	28-6	6-3 (SEC)	NCAA Champion
87–88	Tennessee	31-3	8-1 (SEC)	NCAA Final Four
88–89	Tennessee	35-2	8-1 (SEC)	NCAA Champion
89–90	Tennessee	27-6	8-1 (SEC)	NCAA Regional
90–91	Tennessee	30-5	6-3 (SEC)	NCAA Champion
91–92	Tennessee	28-3	10-1 (SEC)	NCAA Regional
92–93	Tennessee	29-3	11-0 (SEC)	NCAA Regional
93–94	Tennessee	31-2	11-0 (SEC)	NCAA Regionals
94–95	Tennessee	31-3	11-0 (SEC)	NCAA Runner-up
95–96	Tennessee	31-4	9-2 (SEC)	NCAA Champion

22-Year Coaching Record: 492-133 (.787) at Tennesseee; 111-22 (.834) in Southeastern Conference; 118-31 (.791) in postseason play; 63-4 (.940) in international play.

TARA VANDERVEER
Indiana '76

The 1996 U.S. Olympic coach who turned Stanford from a downtrodden Pac-10 program to a two-time national champion. . . . Cardinal have reached five Final Fours during her tenure, even in the 1995-96 season, when she was away preparing for the Olympics. Amy Tucker, her long-time assistant, and Marianne Stanley were co-coaches in 1995-96. . . . The national coach of the year in 1990, when Stanford won its first national title, and previously in 1988. . . . Considered one of the best strategists in the women's game, has been talked about as a professional men's coach. . . . Stanford has excelled with top-notch players who also are academic standouts in the classroom. . . . Cardinal have won seven Pac-10 titles and been to the NCAA Sweet 16 or better the last nine seasons. . . . At Ohio State, the Buckeyes won the Big Ten four times. . . . Played for Indiana and watched Bobby Knight's practices intently. . . . During high school, became the team mascot so she could watch the boys' teams and follow its strategy.

Year	School	Overall	League	Postseason
78-79	Idaho	17-8		
79-80	Idaho	25-6		AIAW Tournament
80-81	Ohio State	17-15		
81-82	Ohio State	20-7		
82-83	Ohio State	23-5		
83-84	Ohio State	22-7		NCAA Tournament
84-85	Ohio State	28-3		NCAA Elite 8
85-86	Stanford	13-15	1-7 (Pac-10)	
86-87	Stanford	14-14	8-10 (Pac-10)	
87-88	Stanford	17-5	14-4 (Pac-10)	NCAA Sweet 16
88-89	Stanford	28-3	18-0 (Pac-10)	NCAA Elite 8
89-90	Stanford	32-1	17-1 (Pac-10)	NCAA Champion
90-91	Stanford	26-6	16-2 (Pac-10)	NCAA Final Four
91-92	Stanford	30-3	15-3 (Pac-10)	NCAA Champion
92-93	Stanford	26-6	15-3 (Pac-10)	NCAA Sweet 16
93-94	Stanford	25-6	15-3 (Pac-10)	NCAA Elite 8
94-95	Stanford	30-3	17-1 (Pac-10)	NCAA Final Four

17-Year Coaching Record: 403-113 (.781) overall; 42-14 (.750) in two years at Idaho; 110-37 (.748) in five years at Ohio State; 251-62 (.802) in 10 years at Stanford.

MARGARET WADE
Delta State

Became the first woman college coach inducted into the Naismith Basketball Hall of Fame in 1984…. Coached Delta State to three AIAW national titles from 1975 to 1977, and collected a career record of 157-23 in six seasons…. Revived a dormant Delta State program and retired from coaching in 1979. Her star player, Lusia Harris Stewart, also is a member of the Hall of Fame…. Came to Delta State to teach physical education in 1959 and began a women's varsity program there 14 years later…. Her Delta State team, nicknamed the "Cadillac Kids," once posed for a *Sports Illustrated* photograph along with Wade seated on the hood of a Cadillac…. The Wade Trophy, given to the top woman player each season, is named after her. After a long illness, she died in a Mississippi nursing home in 1996.

Year	School	Overall	League	Postseason
73–74	Delta State	16-2		
74–75	Delta State	28-0		AIAW Champion
75–76	Delta State	33-1		AIAW Champion
76–77	Delta State	32-3		AIAW Champion
77–78	Delta State	27-5		AIAW Tournament
78–79	Delta State	21-12		AIAW Tournament

6-Year Coaching Record: 157-23 (.872) overall.

DEAN WEESE
Wayland Baptist College

Ushered tiny Wayland Baptist College from an AAU powerhouse into a national contender on the women's college scene during the mid-1980s. Wayland won two AAU championships and finished fifth or higher in the AIAW nationals five times in his six seasons.... Wayland was one of the first colleges to offer basketball scholarships to women and his teams were instantly dominant in Texas when the AIAW era began.... Was honored with the 1991 Pioneer Award by the U.S. Basketball Writers Association.... Since leaving Wayland, has been a successful high school coach in west Texas, currently coaching at Levelland High School.

Year	School	Overall	League	Postseason
73–74	Wayland Baptist	37-5		AAU Champion; 5th AIAW
74–75	Wayland Baptist	34-1		AAU Champion; 5th AIAW
75–76	Wayland Baptist	34-5		2nd AAU; 3rd AIAW
76–77	Wayland Baptist	31-5		
77–78	Wayland Baptist	33-5		4th AIAW
78–79	Wayland Baptist	24-10		AIAW Quarterfinals

6-Year College Coaching Record: 193-91 (.862) overall.

CHRIS WELLER
Maryland '66

Has spent most of her adult life at Maryland as a student, coach, and administrator.... The Naismith and U.S. Basketball Writers Association national Coach of the Year in 1992.... A two-time ACC Coach of the Year whose teams have won a record eight ACC titles.... Has missed coaching in a national tournament only twice.... Played basketball and lacrosse and swam during college career.... Coach of the U.S. Jones Cup team in 1992 and the 1994 U.S. Select Team.

Year	School	Overall	League	Postseason
75–76	Maryland	20-4		
76–77	Maryland	17-6		
77–78	Maryland	27-4	5-1 (ACC)	2nd AIAW
78–79	Maryland	22-7	6-1 (ACC)	AIAW Regional
79–80	Maryland	21-9	5-2 (ACC)	AIAW Regional
80–81	Maryland	19-9	5-2 (ACC)	AIAW Regional
81–82	Maryland	25-7	6-1 (ACC)	NCAA Final Four
82–83	Maryland	26-5	10-3 (ACC)	NCAA Regional
83–84	Maryland	19-10	10-4 (ACC)	NCAA Regional
84–85	Maryland	9-18	4-10 (ACC)	
85–86	Maryland	17-13	6-8 (ACC)	NCAA Regional
86–87	Maryland	15-14	6-8 (ACC)	
87–88	Maryland	26-6	12-2 (ACC)	NCAA Regional
88–89	Maryland	29-3	13-1 (ACC)	NCAA Final Four
89–90	Maryland	19-11	7-7 (ACC)	NCAA Regional
90–91	Maryland	17-13	9-5 (ACC)	NCAA Regional
91–92	Maryland	25-6	13-3 (ACC)	NCAA Regional
92–93	Maryland	22-8	11-5 (ACC)	NCAA 2nd Round
93–94	Maryland	15-13	8-8 (ACC)	
94–95	Maryland	11-18	2-14 (ACC)	
95–96	Maryland	13-14	7-9 (ACC)	

21-Year Coaching Record: 414-198 (.676) at Maryland; 145-94 (.606) in Atlantic Coast Conference.

KAY YOW
East Carolina '64

The second-winningest coach in ACC history trails only Maryland's Chris Weller. . . . Coached the 1988 U.S. Olympic team to the gold medal in Seoul. . . . The Wolfpack have won four ACC crowns and have gone to postseason play 17 times. . . . Only five other women's coaches have won 400 games or more at one school. . . . N.C. State has gotten to 11 ACC Tournament title games. . .. Has coached eight All-Americans and 21 All-ACC players. . . . From a coaching family. Her sister, Debbie, coached at Kentucky and Florida and is now the athletic director at Maryland. Another sister, Susan, coached at Drake and Kansas State and played for Kay one season at N.C. State. . . . Had a mastectomy after being diagnosed with breast cancer but then went on to her Olympic duties. . . . Only Jody Conradt, Pat Summitt, Vivian Stringer, and Sue Gunter have won more games in their careers. . . . The WBCA coach of the year in 1990. . . . Pack has gone to Sweet 16 seven times.

Year	School	Overall	League	Postseason
71–72	Elon (N.C.)	5-11		
72–73	Elon (N.C.)	13-3		
73–74	Elon (N.C.)	20-1		
74–75	Elon (N.C.)	19-4		
75–76	N.C. State	19-7		Women's NIT
76–77	N.C. State	21-3		AIAW Tournament
77–78	N.C. State	29-5		AIAW Tournament
78–79	N.C. State	27-7		AIAW Regionals
79–80	N.C. State	28-8		AIAW 2nd Round
80–81	N.C. State	21-10		AIAW Tournament
81–82	N.C. State	24-7		NCAA Sweet 16
82–83	N.C. State	22-8		NCAA 1st Round
83–84	N.C. State	23-9		NCAA Sweet 16
84–85	N.C. State	25-6		NCAA 2nd Round
85–86	N.C. State	18-11		NCAA 1st Round
86–87	N.C. State	24-7		NCAA Sweet 16
87–88	N.C. State	10-17		
88–89	N.C. State	24-7		NCAA Sweet 16
89–90	N.C. State	25-6		NCAA Sweet 16
90–91	N.C. State	27-6		NCAA Sweet 16
91–92	N.C. State	16-12		
92–93	N.C. State	14-13		
93–94	N.C. State	13-14		
94–95	N.C. State	21-10		NCAA Sweet 16
95–96	N.C. State	20-10		NCAA 2nd Round

25-Year Coaching Record: 508-202 (.715) overall; 57-19 (.750) in four years at Elon; 451-183 (.679) in 21 years at N.C. State.

WOMEN'S FINAL NATIONAL RANKINGS

1996-97

AP	USA/CNN	SCHOOL (RECORD)	HEAD COACH
1	4	Connecticut (33-1)	Geno Auriemma
2	2	Old Dominion (34-2)	Wendy Larry
3	3	Stanford (34-2)	Tara VanDerveer
4	9	North Carolina (29-3)	Sylvia Hatchell
5	8	Louisiana Tech (31-4)	Leon Barmore
6	6	Florida (24-9)	Carol Ross
7	7	Georgia (25-6)	Andy Landers
8	11	Alabama (25-7)	Rick Moody
9	16	Kansas (25-6)	Marian Washington
10	12	Louisiana State (25-5)	Sue Gunter
11	1	Tennessee (29-10)	Pat Summitt
12	18	Texas (22-8)	Jody Conradt
13	5	Notre Dame (31-7)	Muffet McGraw
14	14	Virginia (23-8)	Debbie Ryan
15	19	Texas Tech (20-9)	Marsha Sharp
16	13	Illinois (24-8)	Theresa Grentz
17	22	Stephen F. Austin (28-5)	Royce Chadwick
18	10	George Washington (27-6)	Joe McKeown
19	20	Auburn (22-10)	Joe Ciampi
20	17	Vanderbilt (20-11)	Jim Foster
21	25	Clemson (19-11)	Jim Davis
22	—	Western Kentucky (??-?)	Paul Sanderford
23	21	Michigan State (22-8)	Karen Langeland
24	24	Tulane (27-5)	Lisa Stockton
25	—	Duke (??-?)	Gail Goestenkors
—	15	Colorado (23-9)	Ceal Barry
—	23	Purdue (17-11)	Lin Dunn

1995-96

AP	USA/CNN	SCHOOL (RECORD)	HEAD COACH
1	5	Louisiana Tech (31-2)	Leon Barmore
2	3	Connecticut (34-4)	Geno Auriemma
3	4	Stanford (29-3)	Any Tucker/Marianne Stanley
4	1	Tennessee (32-4)	Pat Summitt
5	2	Georgia (28-5)	Andy Landers
6	10	Old Dominion (29-3)	Wendy Larry
7	9	Iowa (27-4)	Angie Lee
8	13	Penn State (27-7)	Rene Portland
9	12	Texas Tech (27-5)	Marsha Sharp
10	11	Alabama (24-8)	Rick Moody
11	6	Virginia (26-7)	Debbie Ryan
12	7	Vanderbilt (23-8)	Jim Foster
13	19	Duke (26-7)	Gail Goestenkors
14	17	Clemson (23-8)	Jim Davis
15	—	Purdue (20-11)	Lin Dunn
16	22	Florida (21-9)	Carol Ross
17	18	Colorado (26-9)	Ceal Barry
18	20	Wisconsin (21-8)	Jane Albright-Dieterle
19	8	Auburn (23-9)	Joe Ciampi
20	—	Kansas (22-10)	Marian Washington
21	—	Oregon State (19-9)	Aki Hill
22	—	Notre Dame (23-8)	Muffet McGraw
23	—	N.C. State (20-10)	Kay Yow
T24	—	Mississippi (18-11)	Van Chancellor
T24	25	Texas (21-9)	Jody Conradt
—	14	Stephen F. Austin (27-4)	Royce Chadwick
—	16	San Francisco (24-8)	Mary Hile and Bill Nepfel
—	23	DePaul (21-10)	Doug Bruno
—	24	Colorado State (26-5)	Greg Williams

1994-95

AP	USA/CNN	SCHOOL (RECORD)	HEAD COACH
1	1	Connecticut (35-0)	Geno Auriemma
2	5	Colorado (30-3)	Ceal Barry
3	2	Tennessee (34-3)	Pat Summitt
4	3	Stanford (30-3)	Tara VanDerveer
5	7	Texas Tech (33-4)	Marsha Sharp
6	8	Vanderbilt (28-7)	Jim Foster
7	16	Penn State (26-5)	Rene Portland
8	10	Louisiana Tech (28-5)	Leon Barmore
9	12	Western Kentucky (28-4)	Paul Sanderford
10	6	Virginia (27-5)	Debbie Ryan
11	11	North Carolina (30-5)	Sylvia Rhyne Hatchell
12	4	Georgia (28-5)	Andy Landers
13	14	Alabama (22-9)	Rick Moody
14	13	Washington (25-9)	Chris Gabrecht
15	20	Arkansas (23-7)	Gary Blair
16	9	Purdue (24-8)	Lin Dunn
17	18	Florida (24-9)	Carol Ross
18	15	George Washington (26-6)	Joe McKeown
19	22	Mississippi (21-8)	Van Chancellor
20	17	Duke (22-9)	Gail Goestenkors
21	21	Oregon State (21-8)	Judy Spoelstra
22	—	San Diego State (24-6)	Beth Burns
23	23	Kansas (20-11)	Marian Washington
24	19	N.C. State (21-10)	Kay Yow
25	—	Old Dominion (27-6)	Wendy Larry
—	24	Drake (25-6)	Lisa Bluder
—	25	Montana (26-7)	Robin Selvig

1993-94

AP	USA/CNN	SCHOOL (RECORD)	HEAD COACH
1	5	Tennessee (31-2)	Pat Summitt
2	6	Penn State (28-3)	Rene Portland
3	7	Connecticut (30-3)	Geno Auriemma
4	1	North Carolina (33-2)	Sylvia Hatchell
5	10	Colorado (27-5)	Ceal Barry
6	2	Louisiana Tech (31-4)	Leon Barmore
7	9	Southern Cal (26-4)	Cheryl Miller
8	3	Purdue (29-5)	Lin Dunn
9	11	Texas Tech (28-5)	Marsha Sharp
10	12	Virginia (27-5)	Debbie Ryan
11	8	Stanford (25-6)	Tara VanDerveer
12	13	Vanderbilt (25-8)	Jim Foster
13	15	Iowa (21-7)	Vivian Stringer
14	14	Seton Hall (27-5)	Phyllis Mangina
15	17	Kansas (22-6)	Marian Washington
16	4	Alabama (26-7)	Rick Moody
17	18	Montana (25-5)	Robin Selvig
18	21	Washington (21-8)	Chris Gabrecht
19	24	Fla. International (25-4)	Cindy Russo
20	25	Florida (22-7)	Carol Ross
21	—	Boise State (23-6)	June Daugherty
22	16	Southern Miss. (26-5)	Kay James
23	20	Mississippi (24-9)	Van Chancellor
24	—	Bowling Green (26-4)	Jaci Clark
25	23	Texas (22-8)	Jody Conradt
—	19	Texas A&M (23-8)	Candi Harvey
—	22	Clemson (20-10)	Jim Davis

1992-93

AP	USA/CNN	SCHOOL (RECORD)	HEAD COACH
1	4	Vanderbilt (30-3)	Jim Foster
2	5	Tennessee (29-3)	Pat Summitt
3	2	Ohio State (28-4)	Nancy Darsch
4	3	Iowa (27-4)	Vivian Stringer
5	1	Texas Tech (31-3)	Marsha Sharp
6	7	Stanford (26-6)	Tara VanDerveer
7	10	Auburn (25-4)	Joe Ciampi
8	13	Penn State (22-6)	Rene Portland
9	6	Virginia (26-6)	Debbie Ryan
10	9	Colorado (27-4)	Ceal Barry
11	18	Maryland (22-8)	Chris Weller
12	11	Stephen F. Austin (28-5)	Gary Blair
13	12	Western Kentucky (24-7)	Paul Sanderford
14	8	Louisiana Tech (26-6)	Leon Barmore
15	14	Southern Cal (22-7)	Marianne Stanley
16	19	Texas (22-8)	Jody Conradt
17	15	North Carolina (23-7)	Sylvia Hatchell
18	23	Vermont (28-1)	Cathy Inglese
19	—	Bowling Green (25-5)	Jaci Clark
20	20	Miami, Fla. (24-7)	Ferne Labati
21	21	Georgia (21-13)	Andy Landers
22	22	Nebraska (23-8)	Angela Beck
23	24	Hawaii (??-?)	Vince Goo
24	—	Kansas (21-9)	Marian Washington
25	—	Northern Illinois (24-6)	Jane Albright-Dieterle
25	—	Oklahoma State (23-9)	Dick Haterman
—	16	Georgetown (23-7)	Patrick Knapp
—	17	SW Missouri State (23-9)	Cheryl Burnett
—	25	Alabama (22-9)	Rick Moody

1991-92

AP	USA/CNN	SCHOOL (RECORD)	HEAD COACH
1	2	Virginia (32-2)	Debbie Ryan
2	5	Tennessee (28-3)	Pat Summitt
3	1	Stanford (30-3)	Tara VanDerveer
4	13	Stephen F. Austin (28-3)	Gary Blair
5	6	Mississippi (29-3)	Van Chancellor
6	9	Miami, Fla. (30-2)	Ferne Labati
7	10	Iowa (25-4)	Vivian Stringer
8	8	Maryland (25-6)	Chris Weller
9	14	Penn State (24-7)	Rene Portland
10	4	SW Missouri State (31-3)	Cheryl Burnett
11	16	Purdue (23-7)	Lin Dunn
12	15	Texas Tech (27-5)	Marsha Sharp
13	7	Vanderbilt (22-9)	Jim Foster
14	11	West Virginia (26-4)	Scott Harrelson
15	3	Western Kentucky (27-8)	Paul Sanderford
16	20	George Washington (25-7)	Joe McKeown
17	25	Kansas (25-6)	Marian Washington
18	17	Alabama (23-7)	Rick Moody
19	23	Texas (21-10)	Jody Conradt
20	19	Clemson (21-10)	Jim Davis
21	24	Creighton (28-4)	Bruce Rasmussen
22	–	Houston (22-8)	Jessie Kenlaw
23	12	Southern Cal (23-8)	Marianne Stanley
24	21	UC Santa Barbara (27-5)	Mark French
25	22	Vermont (29-1)	Cathy Inglese
–	18	UCLA (21-10)	Billie Jean Moore

1990-91

AP	USA/CNN	SCHOOL (RECORD)	HEAD COACH
1	9	Penn State (29-2)	Rene Portland
2	2	Virginia (31-3)	Debbie Ryan
3	6	Georgia (28-4)	Andy Landers
4	1	Tennessee (30-5)	Pat Summitt
5	14	Purdue (26-3)	Lin Dunn
6	5	Auburn (26-6)	Joe Ciampi
7	10	N.C. State (27-6)	Kay Yow
8	18	Louisiana State (24-7)	Sue Gunter
9	12	Arkansas (28-4)	John Sutherland
10	11	Western Kentucky (29-3)	Paul Sanderford
11	3	Stanford (26-6)	Tara VanDerveer
12	13	Washington (24-5)	Chris Gobrecht
13	4	Connecticut (29-5)	Geno Auriemma
14	19	Stephen F. Austin (26-5)	Gary Blair
15	24	Providence (26-6)	Bob Foley
16	25	Texas (21-9)	Jody Conradt
17	22	UNLV (25-7)	Jim Bolla
18	17	Long Beach State (24-8)	Joan Bonvicini
19	–	Mississippi (20-9)	Van Chancellor
20	–	Rutgers (23-7)	Theresa Grentz
21	8	Clemson (22-11)	Jim Davis
22	23	Northwestern (21-9)	Don Perrelli
23	21	Iowa (21-9)	Vivian Stringer
24	7	Lamar (29-4)	Al Barbre
25	16	Oklahoma State (27-6)	Dick Haterman
–	15	James Madison (26-5)	Sheila Moorman
–	20	Vanderbilt (19-12)	Phil Lee

1989-90

AP	USA/CNN	SCHOOL (RECORD)	HEAD COACH
1	4	Louisiana Tech (32-1)	Leon Barmore
2	1	Stanford (32-1)	Tara VanDerveer
3	7	Washington (28-3)	Chris Gobrecht
4	5	Tennessee (27-6)	Pat Summitt
5	15	UNLV (27-3)	Jim Bolla
6	9	Stephen F. Austin (28-3)	Gary Blair
7	13	Georgia (25-5)	Andy Landers
8	6	Texas (27-5)	Jody Conradt
9	2	Auburn (28-7)	Joe Ciampi
10	18	Iowa (23-6)	Vivian Stringer
11	10	N.C. State (25-6)	Kay Yow
12	3	Virginia (29-6)	Debbie Ryan
13	22	Northwestern (24-5)	Don Perrelli
14	20	Long Beach State (25-8)	Joan Bonvicini
15	14	Purdue (23-7)	Lin Dunn
16	24	Hawaii (26-4)	Vince Goo
17	21	Northern Illinois (26-5)	Jane Albright-Dieterle
18	11	Providence (27-5)	Bob Foley
19	16	South Carolina (24-9)	Nancy Wilson
20	23	Southern Miss. (27-5)	Kay James
21	25	Tennessee Tech (26-5)	Bill Worrell
22	8	Arkansas (25-5)	John Sutherland
23	–	Louisiana State (21-9)	Sue Gunter
24	12	Mississippi (22-10)	Van Chancellor
25	–	St. Joseph's (24-7)	Jim Foster
–	17	Vanderbilt (23-11)	Phil Lee
–	19	Clemson (22-10)	Jim Davis

1988-89

AP	USA/CNN	SCHOOL (RECORD)	HEAD COACH
1	1	Tennessee (35-2)	Pat Summitt
2	2	Auburn (32-2)	Joe Ciampi
3	4	Louisiana Tech (32-4)	Leon Barmore
4	5	Stanford (28-3)	Tara VanDerveer
5	3	Maryland (29-3)	Chris Weller
6	6	Texas (27-5)	Jody Conradt
7	7	Long Beach State (30-5)	Joan Bonvicini
8	11	Iowa (27-5)	Vivian Stringer
9	19	Colorado (27-4)	Ceal Barry
10	18	Georgia (23-7)	Andy Landers
11	16	Stephen F. Austin (30-4)	Gary Blair
12	8	Mississippi (23-8)	Van Chancellor
13	10	N.C. State (24-7)	Kay Yow
14	9	Ohio State (24-6)	Nancy Darsch
15	17	Purdue (24-6)	Lin Dunn
16	12	UNLV (27-6)	Jim Bolla
17	22	South Carolina (23-7)	Nancy Wilson
18	–	La Salle (28-3)	John Miller
19	–	Western Kentucky (22-9)	Paul Sanderford
20	21	Old Dominion (23-9)	Wendy Larry
–	13	Clemson (20-11)	Jim Davis
–	14	Louisiana State (19-11)	Sue Gunter
–	15	Virginia (21-10)	Debbie Ryan
–	20	Rutgers (24-7)	Theresa Grentz
–	23	St. Joseph's (23-8)	Jim Foster
–	24	Tennessee Tech (22-8)	Bill Worrell
–	25	James Madison (26-4)	Sheila Moorman

1987-88

AP	USA/CNN	SCHOOL (RECORD)	HEAD COACH
1	3	Tennessee (31-3)	Pat Summitt
2	6	Iowa (29-2)	Vivian Stringer
3	2	Auburn (32-3)	Joe Ciampi
4	5	Texas (32-3)	Jody Conradt
5	1	Louisiana Tech (32-2)	Leon Barmore
6	9	Ohio State (25-5)	Nancy Darsch
7	4	Long Beach State (28-6)	Joan Bonvicini
8	11	Rutgers (27-5)	Theresa Grentz
9	8	Maryland (26-6)	Chris Weller
10	7	Virginia (27-5)	Debbie Ryan
11	16	Washington (25-5)	Chris Gobrecht
12	12	Mississippi (24-7)	Van Chancellor
13	14	Stanford (27-5)	Tara VanDerveer
14	15	James Madison (27-4)	Sheila Moorman
15	13	Southern Cal (22-8)	Linda Sharp
16	17	Montana (28-2)	Robin Selvig
17	10	Georgia (21-10)	Andy Landers
18	23	New Mexico State (26-3)	Joe McKeown
19	18	Stephen F. Austin (29-5)	Gary Blair
20	–	La Salle (25-5)	John Miller
–	19	Western Kentucky (26-8)	Paul Sanderford
–	20	Clemson (21-9)	Jim Davis
–	21	St. Joseph's (24-8)	Jim Foster
–	22	DePaul (27-4)	Doug Bruno
–	24	South Carolina (23-11)	Nancy Wilson
–	25	Houston (22-7)	Greg Williams

1986–87

AP	USA/CNN	SCHOOL (RECORD)	HEAD COACH
1	3	Texas (31-2)	Jody Conradt
2	6	Auburn (31-2)	Joe Ciampi
3	2	Louisiana Tech (30-3)	Leon Barmore
4	4	Long Beach State (33-3)	Joan Bonvicini
5	5	Rutgers (30-3)	Theresa Grentz
6	9	Georgia (27-5)	Andy Landers

7	1	Tennessee (28-6)	Pat Summitt
8	11	Mississippi (25-5)	Van Chancellor
9	7	Iowa (26-5)	Vivian Stringer
10	8	Ohio State (26-5)	Nancy Darsch
11	10	Virginia (26-5)	Debbie Ryan
12	15	James Madison (27-4)	Sheila Moorman
13	12	N.C. State (24-7)	Kay Yow
14	19	Louisiana State (20-8)	Sue Gunter
15	16	Penn State (23-7)	Rene Portland
16	13	Southern Illinois (28-3)	Cindy Scott
17	22	Villanova (27-4)	Harry Perretta
18	21	Vanderbilt (23-10)	Phil Lee
19	14	Southern Cal (22-8)	Linda Sharp
20	18	Washington (23-7)	Chris Gobrecht
–	17	Old Dominion (18-13)	Marianne Stanley
–	20	Oregon (23-7)	Elwin Heiny
–	23	Western Kentucky (24-9)	Paul Sanderford
–	24	St. Joseph's (23-9)	Jim Foster
–	25	Drake	Susan Yow

1985-86

AP	USA/CNN	SCHOOL (RECORD)	HEAD COACH
1	1	Texas (34-0)	Jody Conradt
2	4	Georgia (30-2)	Andy Landers
3	2	Southern Cal (31-5)	Linda Sharp
4	7	Louisiana Tech (27-5)	Leon Barmore
5	3	Western Kentucky (32-4)	Paul Sanderford
6	14	Virginia (26-3)	Debbie Ryan
7	9	Auburn (24-6)	Joe Ciampi
8	12	Long Beach State (29-5)	Joan Bonvicini
9	8	Louisiana State (27-6)	Sue Gunter
10	10	Rutgers (29-4)	Theresa Grentz
11	6	Mississippi (24-8)	Van Chancellor
12	17	Ohio State (23-7)	Nancy Darsch
13	13	Penn State (24-8)	Rene Portland
14	19	Iowa (22-7)	Vivian Stringer
15	5	Tennessee (24-10)	Pat Summitt
16	15	North Carolina (23-9)	Jennifer Alley
17	16	James Madison (28-4)	Sheila Moorman
18	22	Southern Illinois (25-4)	Cindy Scott
19	18	Oklahoma (24-7)	Maura McHugh
20	25	Vanderbilt (22-9)	Phil Lee
–	11	NE Louisiana (26-3)	Linda Harper
–	20	Montana (27-4)	Robin Selvig
–	21	Texas Tech (21-9)	Marsha Sharp
–	23	Drake (22-8)	Carole Baumgarten
–	24	St. Joseph's (22-7)	Jim Foster

1984-85

AP	SCHOOL (RECORD)	HEAD COACH
1	Texas (28-3)	Jody Conradt
2	NE Louisiana (30-2)	Linda Harper
3	Long Beach State (28-3)	Joan Bonvioini
4	Louisiana Tech (29-4)	Leon Barmore
5	Old Dominion (31-3)	Marianne Stanley
6	Mississippi (29-3)	Van Chancellor
7	Ohio State (28-3)	Tara VanDerveer
8	Georgia (29-5)	Andy Landers
9	Penn State (28-5)	Rene Portland
10	Auburn (25-7)	Joe Ciampi
11	Washington (26-2)	Joyce Sake
12	N.C. State (25-6)	Kay Yow
13	Tennessee (22-10)	Pat Summitt
14	Western Kentucky (29-6)	Paul Sanderford
15	Southern Cal (20-9)	Linda Sharp
16	UNLV (25-5)	Jim Bolla
17	St. Joseph's (25-5)	Jim Foster
18	UCLA (20-10)	Billie Jean Moore
19	Texas Tech (24-8)	Marsha Sharp
20	San Diego State (21-9)	Earnest Riggins

1983-84

AP	SCHOOL (RECORD)	HEAD COACH
1	Texas (32-3)	Jody Conradt
2	Louisiana Tech (30-3)	Leon Barmore
3	Georgia (30-3)	Andy Landers
4	Old Dominion (24-5)	Marianne Stanley
5	Southern Cal (29-4)	Linda Sharp
6	Long Beach State (25-6)	Joan Bonvicini
7	Kansas State (25-6)	Lynn Hickey
8	Louisiana State (23-7)	Sue Gunter
9	Cheyney, Pa. (25-5)	Winthrop McGriff
10	Mississippi (24-6)	Van Chancellor
11	Missouri (25-6)	Joann Rutherford
12	Alabama (23-9)	Ken Weeks
13	NE Louisiana (23-4)	Linda Harper
14	North Carolina (24-8)	Jennifer Alley
15	Tennessee (23-10)	Pat Summitt
16	N.C. State (23-9)	Kay Yow
17	Maryland (19-10)	Chris Weller
18	Virginia (22-7)	Debbie Ryan
19	Ohio State (22-7)	Tara VanDerveer
20	UT-Chattanooga (26-5)	Sharon Fanning

1982-83

AP	SCHOOL (RECORD)	HEAD COACH
1	Southern Cal (30-2)	Linda Sharp
2	Louisiana Tech (26-6)	Leon Barmore
3	Texas (30-3)	Jody Conradt
4	Old Dominion (29-6)	Marianne Stanley
5	Cheyney, Pa. (27-3)	Vivian Stringer
6	Long Beach State (24-7)	Joan Bonvicini
7	Maryland (26-5)	Chris Weller
8	Penn State (26-7)	Rene Portland
9	Georgia (27-7)	Andy Landers
10	Tennessee (25-8)	Pat Summitt
11	Arizona State (23-7)	Juliene Simpson
12	Kentucky (23-5)	Terry Hall
13	Mississippi (26-6)	Van Chancellor
14	Auburn (24-8)	Joe Ciampi
15	Missouri (23-6)	Joann Rutherford
16	N.C. State (22-8)	Kay Yow
17	Kansas State (25-6)	Lynn Hickey
18	North Carolina (22-8)	Jennifer Alley
19	Oregon State (24-6)	Aki Hill
20	Louisiana State (20-7)	Sue Gunter

1981-82

AP	SCHOOL (RECORD)	HEAD COACH
1	Louisiana Tech (35-1)	Sonja Hogg
2	Cheyney, Pa. (26-3)	Vivian Stringer
3	Maryland (25-7)	Chris Weller
4	Tennessee (22-10)	Pat Summitt
5	Texas (35-4)	Jody Conradt
6	Southern Cal (22-4)	Linda Sharp
7	Old Dominion (22-6)	Marianne Stanley
8	Rutgers	Theresa Grentz
9	Long Beach State (23-6)	Joan Bonvicini
10	Penn State (24-6)	Rene Portland
11	Villanova	Harry Perretta
12	N.C. State (24-6)	Kay Yow
13	Kentucky (24-8)	Terry Hall
14	Kansas State (26-6)	Lynn Hickey
15	South Carolina (22-8)	Terry Kelly
16	Drake (28-7)	Carole Baumgarten
17	Memphis State (26-5)	Mary Lou Johns
18	Arizona State (24-7)	Juliene Simpson
19	Oregon (20-5)	Elwin Heiny
20	Missouri (24-9)	Joann Rutherford

1980-81

AP	SCHOOL
1	Louisiana Tech
2	Tennessee
3	Old Dominion
4	Southern Cal
5	Cheyney, Pa.
6	Long Beach State
7	UCLA
8	Maryland
9	Rutgers
10	Kansas
11	Kentucky
12	Oregon

AP	SCHOOL
13	N.C. State
14	Stephen F. Austin
15	Illinois State
16	Texas
17	Jackson State
18	Minnesota
19	Oregon
20	Clemson

1979-80

AP	SCHOOL
1	Old Dominion
2	Tennessee
3	Louisiana Tech
4	South Carolina
5	Stephen F. Austin
6	Maryland
7	Texas
8	Rutgers
9	Long Beach State
10	N.C. State
11	Kansas
12	Cheyney, Pa.
13	Kansas State
14	Kentucky
15	Northwestern
16	Mercer
17	Oregon
18	Central Mo. State
19	San Francisco
20	Brigham Young

1978-79

AP	SCHOOL
1	Old Dominion
2	Louisiana Tech
3	Tennessee
4	Texas
5	Stephen F. Austin
6	UCLA
7	Rutgers
8	Maryland
9	Cheyney, Pa.
10	Wayland Baptist
11	N.C. State
12	Valdosta State
13	Penn State
14	Kansas
15	South Carolina
16	Northwestern
17	UNLV
18	Long Beach State
19	Fordham
20	Montclair State

1977-78

AP	SCHOOL
1	Tennessee
2	Wayland Baptist
3	N.C. State
4	Montclair State
5	UCLA
6	Maryland
7	Queens, N.Y.
8	Valdosta State
9	Delta State
10	Louisiana State
11	St. Joseph's
12	Old Dominion
13	Missouri
14	Stephen F. Austin
15	Texas
16	Ohio State
17	Penn State
18	Southern Conn. St.
19	Memphis State
20	Mississippi

1976-77

AP	SCHOOL
1	Delta State
2	Immaculata
3	St. Joseph's
4	Cal St. Fullerton
5	Tennessee
6	Tennessee Tech
7	Wayland Baptist
8	Montclair State
9	Stephen F. Austin
10	N.C. State
11	Louisiana State
12	Baylor
13	UCLA
14	Old Dominion
15	Southeastern La.
16	Maryland
17	Michigan State
18	Miss. College
19	Southern Conn. St.
20	Kansas State

13

SMALL COLLEGES:
J.C., DIVISIONS I & II, AND NAIA

Junior College Action

Junior college players were perceived by many observers for an extended period as the rogues of recruiting. They are now in vogue throughout the vast majority of major four-year universities, however, because of an improved image amid the advent of stiffer academic requirements for Division I freshman eligibility.

Although many tunnel-vision Division I coaches were once standoffish, it seems as if virtually everyone except Ivy League schools are flocking toward J.C. recruits these days, especially after "juco" signees frequented the rosters of recent Final Four teams—Arizona (1997), Arkansas (1990, 1994 and 1995), Cincinnati (1992), Indiana (1987), Kansas (1988, 1991 and 1993), Kentucky (1993), Minnesota (1997), Mississippi State (1996), Oklahoma (1988), Oklahoma State (1995), Syracuse (1996) and UNLV (1987, 1990 and 1991). For instance, five of Cincinnati's nine regulars in 1992 were former junior college players.

It wasn't too long ago when only a splinter group of maverick coaches were bold enough to liberally dot their rosters with J.C. players stereo-

typed as discipline problems, academic risks or simply unsuitable to go directly from high school to major college programs. "Jucoland" was labeled by misguided observers as little more than basketball rehabilitation where free-lance players enjoyed free rein to make Great Plains arenas their own personal H-O-R-S-E stables.

However, major colleges aren't nearly so reluctant any longer to bring "quick fix" junior college players aboard for two or possibly three seasons. It is no longer demeaning to recruit at the juco level because the entire recruiting process is based on the law of supply and demand and harsher academic requirements at the NCAA level increase the amount of talent at the J.C. level.

The talent pool in the NJCAA Tournament might have never been greater than in 1968, when eight of the 10 members of the All-Tournament Team either eventually played or were at least drafted by the NBA and/or ABA, and a ninth All-Tournament Team member played several years with the Harlem Globetrotters.

The misconceptions regarding junior college basketball aren't helped when network TV pulls a snafu such as when it was mistakenly inferred that recent Kentucky guard Dale Brown was the first instance of the Wildcats recruiting a junior college player. Actually, Hall of Fame coach Adolph Rupp, a Kansas native, regularly attended the NJCAA Tournament at Hutchinson, Kan., in the 1950s and recruited four tournament MVPs or leading scorers. Two of the four didn't play much for Kentucky or transferred, but the other two— Bob Burrow (Lon Morris) and Sid Cohen (Kilgore)—proved to be pivotal players for the Wildcats and were selected in the NBA draft. Burrow, an NCAA consensus second-team All-America in 1956, still holds the school record for rebound average in a career (16.1 rpg). Guard Adrian Smith, a key member of Kentucky's 1958 NCAA champion, was also a junior college recruit.

Two decades earlier, Alabama, after finishing 12th in the 13-team SEC in 1937-38 with a 4-12 record, topped the league's regular-season standings the next year with a 13-4 mark. Bama's squad included three junior college graduates, led by center George Prather, who was named to the SEC All-Tournament first five.

The Big Ten Conference has never had an abundance of junior college players, but J.C. transfer Dick Garmaker scored 37 points for Minnesota in his first league game in 1954 before becoming an NCAA consensus All-America the next year.

Success has not been limited to just basketball ability. The most notable student-athlete to come out of junior college might be Nolan Archibald, an Academic All-American selection as a senior and player for Weber State's first NCAA Tournament team in 1968. An All-American selection at Dixie Junior College in his native state of Utah, Archibald graduated cum laude from Weber State before earning an M.S. degree in business administration from the Harvard Business School in 1970. As Black & Decker's chairman of the board, president and chief executive officer since 1986, he heads a $5 billion corporation. Archibald is one of the youngest CEOs of a publicly held Fortune 100 company and has been recognized by Fortune and Business Week as one of the nation's outstanding managers.

Southeastern Oklahoma's Dennis Rodman slams one home, though he went on to become an NBA rebounding machine.

A glance at NBA rosters and the backgrounds of many of the nation's prominent Division I coaches suggests there probably never should have been a stigma attached to the J.C. ranks. One seldom hears NBA commentators credit a J.C. beginning, but approximately 40 NBA players annually played for a two-year school at some point in their college careers, including recent regulars Mookie Blaylock, Anthony Bowie, Sam Cassell, Cedric Ceballos, Blue Edwards, Kevin Edwards, Craig Ehlo, Kevin Gamble, Winston Garland, Armon Gilliam, Harvey Grant, Avery Johnson, Larry Johnson, Dontae' Jones, Nate McMillan, Ken Norman, Robert Pack, Ricky Pierce, Mitch Richmond, J.R. Rider, Alvin Robertson, Dennis Rodman, Latrell Sprewell, John Starks, Nick Van Exel, Spud Webb, Gerald Wilkins, Jerome Williams, Kenny Williams and Kevin Willis. Embellishing junior college credentials even more are all-time pro greats with a J.C. connection such as Tiny Archibald, Ron Boone, Fred Brown, Mack Calvin, Michael Cooper, Mel Daniels, Artis Gilmore, Spencer Haywood, Lionel Hollins, Dennis Johnson, Gus Johnson, Vinnie Johnson, Jim Loscutoff, Bob McAdoo and Paul Pressey.

Former Riverside (Calif.) City and Pasadena (Calif.) City coach Jerry Tarkanian, who wound up at his alma mater (Fresno State) after leaving UNLV, is among about 40 active Division I head coaches who previously served in a similar capacity at a junior college. The list includes the following high profile coaches: Louisville's Denny Crum (Pierce, CA), Purdue's Gene Keady (Hutchinson, KS), Arizona's Lute Olson (Long Beach City, CA), Arkansas' Nolan Richardson (Western Texas), Saint Louis' Charlie Spoonhour (Moberly, MO, and Southeastern, IA), and Oklahoma State's Eddie Sutton (Southern Idaho). Among the former major-college mentors who guided teams to the NCAA Tournament after coaching at the J.C. level are Dick Motta (Weber, UT), Maury John (Moberly, MO) and Jack Hartman (Coffeyville, KS). Hartman took two of his J.C. stars (Paul Henry and Lou Williams) with him to Southern Illinois, where he coached eight years before moving to Kansas State.

Southern Idaho has produced more NCAA Division I head coaches than any other junior college. Joining Sutton at that level were Boyd Grant (Fresno State and Colorado State), Jerry Hale (Oral Roberts) and Fred Trenkle (San Diego State).

Tarkanian, Crum and Olson never coached in the NJCAA Tournament. California community college administrators conduct an in-state tournament because they don't want athletes from their more than 90 men's programs to participate in national competition. The NJCAA Tournament is

NJCAA CHAMPIONS

YEAR	CHAMPION	(RECORD/COACH)
1949	Tyler, TX	(36-1/Floyd Wagstaff)
1950	L.A. City, CA	(24-10/Art Williams)
1951	Tyler, TX	(36-3/Floyd Wagstaff)
1952	Wharton, TX	(34-4/Johnnie Frankie)
1953	El Dorado, KS	(24-7/Dave Weatherby)
1954	Moberly, MO	(22-8/Maury John)
1955	Moberly, MO	(29-4/Maury John)
1956	Kilgore, TX	(27-5/Joe Turner)
1957	San Angelo, TX	(31-2/Phil George)
1958	Kilgore, TX	(27-2/Joe Turner)
1959	Weber, UT	(34-3/Bruce Larson)
1960	Parsons, KS	(25-6/Gene Schickel)
1961	Pueblo, CO	(31-2/Harry Simmons)
1962	Coffeyville, KS	(32-0/Jack Hartman)
1963	Independence, KS	(26-3/Bob Sneller)
1964	Dodge City, KS	(29-2/Chuck Brehm)
1965	Vincennes, IN	(28-6/Allen Bradfield)
1966	Moberly, MO	(29-5/Cotton Fitzsimmons)
1967	Moberly, MO	(31-2/Cotton Fitzsimmons)
1968	San Jacinto, TX	(44-2/Ron Rucker)
1969	Paducah, KY	(23-5/Sonny Haws)
1970	Vincennes, IN	(29-4/Allen Bradfield)
1971	Ellsworth, IA	(26-7/Jim Carey)
1972	Vincennes, IN	(33-0/Allen Bradfield)
1973	Mercer County, NJ	(34-3/Howie Landa)
1974	Mercer County, NJ	(32-2/Howie Landa)
1975	Western Texas	(36-1/Mike Mitchell)
1976	Southern Idaho	(34-1/Boyd Grant)
1977	Independence, KS	(34-2/Dan Wall)
1978	Independence, KS	(28-7/Lynn Cundiff)
1979	Three Rivers, MO	(37-3/Gene Bess)
1980	Western Texas	(37-0/Nolan Richardson)
1981	Westark, AR	(32-5/Gayle Kaundart)
1982	Midland, TX	(34-4/Jerry Stone)
1983	San Jacinto, TX	(35-2/Ronnie Arrow)
1984	San Jacinto, TX	(35-2/Ronnie Arrow)
1985	Dixie, UT	(35-1/Neil Roberts)
1986	San Jacinto, TX	(37-0/Ronnie Arrow)
1987	Southern Idaho	(37-1/Fred Trenkle)
1988	Hutchinson, KS	(36-2/Dave Farrar)
1989	Northeastern Oklahoma A&M	(36-4/Larry Gipson)
1990	Connors State, OK	(35-2/Ed Stepp)
1991	Aquinas, TN	(32-3/Charles Anderson)
1992	Three Rivers, MO	(35-3/Gene Bess)
1993	Pensacola, FL	(31-5/Bob Marlin)
1994	Hutchinson, KS	(35-4/Steve McClain)
1995	Okaloosa-Walton, FL	(31-6/Murray Arnold)
1996	Sullivan, KY	(27-10/Gary Shourds)
1997	Indian Hills, IA	(38-1/Terry Carroll)

Multiple NJCAA titles by school: Moberly (4), San Jacinto (4), Independence (3), Vincennes (3), Hutchinson (2), Kilgore (2), Mercer County (2), Southern Idaho (2), Three Rivers (2), Tyler (2), Western Texas (2).

Most NJCAA titles by state: Texas (13/seven different schools), Kansas (9/six different schools), Missouri (6/two different schools).

a five-day, 16-team, 26-game double-elimination affair that has been played in Hutchinson, Kansas since 1949.

JUNIOR CIRCUIT

Robert Morris (Pa.) is the only school ever to make the move from the junior-college ranks to NCAA Division I in the span of one year. Here is an alphabetical list of current NCAA Division I schools that previously were junior colleges:

Arkansas-Little Rock
Boise State
Campbell (N.C.)
Jacksonville
Lamar
McNeese State
Nicholls State (La.)
UNC Charlotte
UNC Wilmington
Portland State
Robert Morris (Pa.)
San Diego State
Southeastern Louisiana
Southern Utah State
Texas-Arlington
Weber State

JUNIOR COLLEGE JEWELS

Junior college products have made a difference for NCAA Tournament titlists. Keith Erickson (El Camino, CA), Jack Hirsch (Los Angeles Valley, CA), John Vallely (Orange Coast, CA) and Sidney Wicks (Santa Monica, CA) were instrumental in helping UCLA win five of its NCAA championships (1964, 1965, 1969, 1970, 1971) and mighty mite Bobby Joe Hill (Burlington, IA) was the sparkplug for Texas Western when the Miners captured the 1966 title. Wicks is the only individual to become a member of three NCAA champions after playing in junior college.

Here is an alphabetical list of key Final Four team members who previously played for junior colleges:

PLAYER, POS.	FINAL FOUR TEAM(S)	JUNIOR COLLEGE
George Ackles, C	UNLV '91	Garden City (Kan.)
Rex Bailey, G	Western Kentucky '71	Vincennes (Ind.)
Jarvis Basnight, F	UNLV '87	Mount San Antonio (Calif.)
Warren Baxter, G	San Francisco '55 & '56	San Francisco City
Walter Berry, F	St. John's '85	San Jacinto (Tex.)
Mookie Blaylock, G	Oklahoma '88	Midland (Tex.)
Corie Blount, C	Cincinnati '92	Rancho Santiago (Calif.)
Carl Boldt, F	San Francisco '56	Glendale (Calif.)
Kenny Booker, F-G	UCLA '70 and '71	Long Beach (Calif.)
Ron Brewer, G	Arkansas '78	Westark (Ark.)
Karl Brown, G	Georgia Tech '90	Chipola (Fla.)
Terry Brown, G	Kansas '91	Erie (Pa.) & NE Okla. A&M
Pembrook Burrows, F	Jacksonville '70	Brevard (Fla.)
Ron Brewer, G	Arkansas '78	Westark (Ark.)
David Butler, G	UNLV '90	San Jacinto (Tex.)
Chet Carr, F	Southern California '54	Vallejo (Calif.)
Jerry Chambers, F-C	Utah '66	Trinidad (Colo.)
Jason Cipolla, G	Syracuse '96	Tallahassee (Fla.)
Charlie Criss, G	New Mexico State '70	New Mexico J.C.
Howie Dallmar, F	Stanford '42	Menlo (Calif.)
Bennett Davison, F	Arizona '97	West Valley (Calif.)
Art Day, C	San Francisco '57	Hannibal-LaGrange (Mo.)
Alex Dillard, G	Arkansas '94 and '95	Southern Union (Ala.)
Don Draper, G	Drake '69	Coffeyville (Kan.)
Al Dunbar, G	San Francisco '57	Hannibal-LaGrange (Mo.)
Jerry Dunn, F	Western Kentucky '71	Vincennes (Ind.)
Denny Fitzpatrick, G	California '59	Orange Coast (Calif.)
Jerry Frizzell, F	Seattle '58	Grays Harbor (Wash.)
Dean Garrett, C	Indiana '87	City College of San Francisco
Alex Gilbert, F	Indiana State '79	Coffeyville (Kan.)
Armon Gilliam, F-C	UNLV '87	Independence (Kan.)
Artis Gilmore, C	Jacksonville '70	Gardner-Webb (N.C.)
Ricky Grace, G	Oklahoma '88	Midland (Tex.)
Harvey Grant, F	Oklahoma '88	Independence (Kan.)
Evric Gray, F	UNLV '91	Riverside (Calif.)
Rickey Green, G	Michigan '76	Vincennes (Ind.)
Arnette Hallman, F	Purdue '80	Joliet (Ill.)
Dick Hammer, F	Southern California '54	Fullerton (Calif.)
Darrin Hancock, F	Kansas '93	Garden City (Kan.)
Lenzie Howell, F	Arkansas '90	San Jacinto (Tex.)
Roy Irvin, C	Southern California '54	Fullerton (Calif.)
Bobby Jackson, G	Minnesota '97	Western Nebraska
David Johanning, C	Kansas '91	Hutchinson (Kan.)
Larry Johnson, F	UNLV '90 and '91	Odessa (Tex.)
Dontae' Jones, F	Mississippi State '96	Northeast Mississippi
Herb Jones, F	Cincinnati '92	Butler County (Kan.)
John Keller, F-G	Kansas '52	Garden City (Kan.)
Larry Kenon, F	Memphis State '73	Amarillo (Tex.)
Don Kruse, C	Houston '67	Kilgore (Tex.)
Vernon Lewis, G	Houston '67 & '68	Tyler (Tex.)
Archie Marshall, F	Kansas '86	Seminole (Okla.)
Erik Martin, F	Cincinnati '92	Rancho Santiago (Calif.)
Bob McAdoo, C	North Carolina '72	Vincennes (Ind.)
Bill McClintock, F	California '59 and '60	Monterey Peninsula (Calif.)
Johnny McNeil, C	Georgia Tech '90	Chowan (N.C.)
Lincoln Minor, G	Kansas '88	Midland (Tex.)
Larry Moffett, C	UNLV '77	Compton (Calif.)
Rex Morgan, G	Jacksonville '70	Lake Land (Ill.)
Roger Morningstar, F	Kansas '74	Olney (Ill.) Central
Willie Murrell, F	Kansas State '64	Eastern Oklahoma A&M
Swen Nater, C	UCLA '72 and '73	Cypress (Calif.)
Carl Nicks, G	Indiana State '79	Gulf Coast (Fla.)
Jim Nielsen, F	UCLA '67 & '68	Pierce (Calif.)
*Andre Owens, G	Oklahoma State '95	Midland (Tex.)
Gerald Paddio, F	UNLV '87	Seminole (Okla.)
Hal Patterson, F	Kansas '53	Garden City (Kan.)
Morris (Moe) Rivers, G	North Carolina State '74	Gulf Coast (Fla.)
Randy Rutherford, G	Oklahoma State '95	Bacone (Okla.)
Greg Samuel, G	Florida State '72	Broward (Fla.)
Terry Schofield, G	UCLA '69, '70 and '71	Santa Monica (Calif.)
Moses Scurry, F	UNLV '90	San Jacinto (Tex.)
Keith Smart, G	Indiana '87	Garden City (Kan.)
Odie Smith, G	Kentucky '58	Northeast Mississippi
Robert Smith, G	UNLV '77	Arizona Western
Sam Smith, F	UNLV '77	Seminole (Okla.)
Phil Spence, F	North Carolina State '74	Vincennes (Ind.)
Elmore Spencer, C	UNLV '91	Connors (Okla.) State
Leroy Staley, F	Indiana State '79	Florida J.C.
Dwight Stewart, C	Arkansas '94 and '95	South Plains (Tex.)
Rich Tate, G	Utah '66	Trinidad (Colo.)
Ron Thomas, F	Louisville '72	Henderson County (Tex.)
Tom Tolbert, F	Arizona '88	Cerritos (Calif.)
Nick Van Exel, G	Cincinnati '92	Trinity Valley (Tex.)
Mark Wade, G	UNLV '87	El Camino (Calif.)
Russell Walters, F	Mississippi State '96	Jones County (Miss.)
Lloyd Walton, G	Marquette '74	Moberly (Mo.)
Jerome Whitehead, C	Marquette '77	Riverside (Calif.) City
Andre Wiley, F	Oklahoma '88	Compton (Calif.)
David Willard, C	UNLV '87	Laredo (Tex.)
Willie Wise, F	Drake '69	San Francisco City
Gary Zeller, G	Drake '69	Long Beach (Calif.)

*Owens played his first year for Tallahassee Community College.

SIZZLING SCORERS

Last season, California guard Ed Gray became the latest junior college product to set a single-game or single-season scoring record for a Division I school. Here is an alphabetical list of J.C. recruits who set existing Division I school single-game or single-season scoring average standards (type of scoring record in parentheses):

PLAYER, POS.	FOUR-YEAR COLLEGE	JUNIOR COLLEGE
Jim Barnes, F-C	Texas-El Paso (both)	Cameron (Okla.)
Chris Cheeks, G	VCU (DI game)	Lon Morris (Tex.)
Chris Collier, G	Georgia State (game)	North Greenville (S.C.)
Ledell Eackles, G-F	New Orleans (DI game)	San Jacinto (Tex.)
Ed Gray, G	California (game)	Southern Idaho
Spencer Haywood, F	Detroit (season)	Trinidad St. (Colo.)
Willie Humes, F	Idaho (game)	Vincennes (Ind.)
George Jackson, G	UNC Charlotte (game)	Dalton (Ga.)
John Johnson, F	Iowa (game)	Northwest (Wyo.)
Marvin Johnson, F	New Mexico (game)	Howard County (Tex.)
Tommie Johnson, G	Central Michigan (game)	Mott (Mich.)
Vinnie Johnson, G	Baylor (game)	McLennan (Tex.)
Orlando Lightfoot, F	Idaho (game)	Hiwassee (Tenn.)
Lewis Lloyd, F	Drake (season)	New Mexico Military
Kevin Magee, F	UC Irvine (both)	Saddleback (Calif.)
Stan Mayhew, F	Weber State (game)	Trinidad (Colo.)
Von McDade, G	Wis.-Milwaukee (game)	Iowa Lakes
Red Murrell, F	Drake (game)	Moberly (Mo.)
Eugene Oliver, F-G	South Alabama (game)	Brevard (Fla.)
David Peed, F	Eastern Wash. (game)	Skyline (Calif.)
Ricky Pierce, F	Rice (season)	Walla Walla (Wash.)
J.R. Rider, F	UNLV (season)	Allen County (Kan.)
Willie Smith, G	Missouri (season)	Seminole (Okla.)
Martin Terry, G	Arkansas (both)	Hutchinson (Kan.)
Grady Wallace, F	South Carolina (season)	Pikeville (Ky.)

TWO-YEAR SCHOOL START

Last season, Arizona's Lute Olson joined Denny Crum, Jerry Tarkanian and Nolan Richardson in the group of former junior college coaches who guided teams to NCAA Tournament titles. Here is an alphabetical list of prominent active major-college coaches who previously held a similar job in junior college:

DIVISION I COACH, CURRENT SCHOOL	JUNIOR COLLEGE(S)
Ron Abegglen, Weber State	Snow (Utah)
Dana Altman, Creighton	Fairbury (Neb.) and Moberly (Mo.)
Murray Arnold, Stetson	Okaloosa-Walton (Fla.)
*Steve Cleveland, Brigham Young	Fresno (Calif.) City
*Denny Crum, Louisville	Pierce (Calif.)
Mike Deane, Marquette	Delhi A&T (N.Y.)
*Cliff Ellis, Auburn	Cumberland (Tenn.)
*Larry Eustachy, Utah State	Citrus (Calif.)
Dave Farrar, Idaho	Hutchinson (Kan.)
*Gene Keady, Purdue	Hutchinson (Kan.)
Phil Mathews, San Francisco	Ventura (Calif.)
*Fang Mitchell, Coppin State	Gloucester County (N.J.)
Lute Olson, Arizona	Long Beach (Calif.) City
Kevin O'Neill, Northwestern	North County (N.Y.)
Eddie Payne, Oregon State	Truett-McConnell (Ga.)
*Nolan Richardson, Arkansas	Western Texas
*Randy Smithson, Wichita State	Butler County (Kan.)
Charlie Spoonhour, Saint Louis	Moberly (Mo.) and Southeastern (Ia.)
Eddie Sutton, Oklahoma State	Southern Idaho
*Jerry Tarkanian, Fresno State	Riverside City and Pasadena City
Bob Thomason, Pacific	Columbia (Calif.)
Fred Trenkle, San Diego State	Southern Idaho
Riley Wallace, Hawaii	Seminole (Okla.)
Richard Williams, Mississippi St.	Copiah-Lincoln (Miss.)

*Also attended junior college along with other high-profile active head coaches such as Houston's Alvin Brooks, Butler's Barry Collier, SMU's Mike Dement, Mississippi's Rob Evans, Miami's Leonard Hamilton, Alabama's David Hobbs, New Mexico State's Neil McCarthy, Baylor's Harry Miller, Colorado State's Stew Morrill, UC Santa Barbara's Jerry Pimm, Illinois State's Kevin Stallings and TCU's Billy Tubbs.

CALIFORNIA STATE CHAMPIONS

YEAR—CHAMPION	RUNNER-UP	SITE
1952—Ventura	College of Sequoias	Sequoias
1953—College of Sequoias	Fullerton College	Long Beach
1954—Fullerton College	Grant Tech	Sacramento
1955—Fresno City	Mt. San Antonio	Fresno
1956—Los Angeles Harbor	Antelope Valley	Fullerton
1957—Allan Hancock	Vallejo	San Jose
1958—Long Beach City	Oakland	Bakersfield
1959—Long Beach City	Santa Ana	Long Beach
1960—San Jose City	Fullerton	College San Jose
1961—Fullerton College	San Jose College	Allan Hancock
1962—City Coll/ of San Fran.	Citrus College	Orange Coast
1963—Fresno City College	San Diego City	Sacramento
1964—Riverside City College	Allan Hancock	Mt. San Antonio
1965—Riverside City College	Fresno City	San Mateo
1966—Riverside City College	City Col. of San Fran.	Bakersfield
1967—Pasadena City College	Long Beach City	Santa Monica
1968—Cerritos College	Pasadena City College	Cerritos
1969—Pasadena City College	Imperial Valley	Fresno
1970—Compton College	Long Beach City	Long Beach
1971—Long Beach City	Cerritos College	Allan Hancock
1972—Santa Monica College	Laney College	Ventura
1973—Compton College	Long Beach City	Ventura
1974—Allan Hancock	Long Beach City	Fresno
1975—Los Angeles Harbor	Cerritos College	Fresno
1976—Long Beach City	Compton College	Fresno
1977—Cypress College	Santa Barbara City	Fresno
1978—Bakersfield City	City Col. of San Fran.	Long Beach
1979—Orange Coast College	Saddleback College	Fullerton
1980—Cypress College	Chabot College	Pomona
1981—El Camino College	City Col. of San Fran.	Fullerton
1982—Coll. of the Sequoias	Compton College	Santa Clara
1983—Cerritos College	Pasadena City	Santa Clara
1984—San Joaquin Delta	Santa Barbara City	Fresno
1985—El Camino College	San Jose City	Fresno
1986—Sacramento City	City Col. of San Fran.	Cerritos
1987—Ventura College	Saddleback College	Los Angeles
1988—El Camino College	Columbia College	Santa Clara
1989—Cerritos College	Chabot College	Santa Clara
1990—Rancho Santiago Coll.	Chabot College	Irvine
1991—Rancho Santiago Coll.	Long Beach City	Irvine
1992—Cerritos College	West Valley College	San Jose
1993—Columbia College	Ventura College	San Francisco
1994—Long Beach City	Ventura College	Irvine
1995—Ventura College	West Valley	Irvine
1996—Ventura College	West Valley	San Jose

Divisions II and III: Bevo and Friends

The spotlight on Division I leaves the vast majority of Division II and III players toiling in virtual obscurity. That's unless, of course, a school such as Rutgers-Camden considers dropping its program in the midst of establishing an NCAA record for most consecutive defeats with 117 from January 18, 1992 to January 7, 1997, or a player such as sophomore guard Jeff Clement of Grinnell (Iowa) goes 16 for 26 from beyond the three-point arc in just 19 minutes of a 151-112 victory over Monmouth (Ill.) on February 8, 1997, or a player like Paul Cluxton of Northern Kentucky sets an NCAA record last season for consecutive successful free throws.

Still, perhaps the greatest folk hero in college basketball history was a small-college player named Clarence "Bevo" Francis, who set an all-time collegiate scoring record with 113 points for Rio Grande (Ohio) College in a 134-95 victory over Hillsdale on February 2, 1954 (see accompanying box). Francis' revolutionary jump shot helped him average 46.5 points per game that season, when he earned spots on AP, UPI and NABC All-American teams as a small-college player.

Francis proved he could score against major-college opponents by pouring in 39 points vs. Villanova, 41 vs. Providence, 48 vs. Miami (Fla.), 34 vs. North Carolina State, 32 vs. Wake Forest, 48 vs. Butler and 49 and 41 vs. Creighton. Rio Grande won the Providence, Miami, Wake Forest and Butler games and the first Creighton contest.

"I really don't remember much about the 113-point game," said Francis, a factory worker who was selected by the Philadelphia Warriors in the 1956 draft but couldn't reach a contract agreement with them and never played in the NBA. "It was just another time when I was double- and triple-teamed. Their coach told me after the game that if he could have dressed out, he would have guarded me, too."

No stat sheet exists to detail how many shots the 6-9 Francis attempted en route to his 37 field goals against Hillsdale. "Most of them were outside," he said. "With the three-pointer, I know I would have come close to 150 points."

The scoring outburst might not have had much of an impact on him because he scored even more points—116—as a freshman the previous season against Ashland (Ky.) Junior College. Francis averaged 50.1 points that year for a 39-0 team that reportedly generated sufficient gate receipts to save the school from bankruptcy. However, his single-game total against Ashland and his season average were later expunged from the NCAA record book because 27 of the opponents for Rio Grande (pronounced RYE-o Grand) were junior colleges, military teams and vocational schools.

Bevo's nickname stemmed from his father's fondness for Beve Beer, a root beer-type soft drink. Francis rejected offers from larger universities to follow his Wellsville, Ohio, high school coach, Newt Oliver, to a college with an enrollment of 92 full-time students. Francis, who had a wife and an infant when he arrived at Rio Grande, left school after his sophomore season and signed a three-year contract worth $13,000 annually to play on a national barnstorming tour for a team that opposed the Harlem Globetrotters.

Francis' scoring exploits completely overshadowed the rebounding records established by Tom Hart, a 6-4 center for Middlebury. Hart finished his career in 1955-56 with an average of 27.6 rebounds per game, including an average of 29.5 in each of the previous two years. His career average and his season standards are still NCAA marks.

The most recognizable small-college coach in history probably is Clarence "Bighouse" Gaines, who compiled 828 victories in 47 seasons at Winston-Salem State. Gaines' prize pupil was future Hall of Famer Earl "The Pearl" Monroe, a 6-3 guard who averaged 41.5 points per game for the Rams' 1967 College Division titlist. Winston-Salem was the first historically black college to win an NCAA basketball championship. Monroe's presence at Winston-Salem overshadowed one of the most remarkable achievements in hoop history. The next season, 6-6 William English outscored the opposition by himself with 77 points for the Rams in a 146-74 victory over Fayetteville.

Joining Monroe among the most memorable players in the small-college ranks were George Gervin (Eastern Michigan), Walt Frazier (Southern Illinois), Don Buse (Evansville) and Jerry Sloan (Evansville), but many were lost in the shuffle as schools shed small-college status to be classified as major colleges or had a dual affiliation with the NAIA.

Any doubt that some small schools could compete with major universities should be erased when assessing Evansville's undefeated season in 1965. Coach Arad McCutchan's crew opened with a 90-83 victory over eventual Big Ten first-division finisher Iowa and followed that triumph with five consecutive victories over major colleges by an average margin of almost 20 points—North-

---

BEVO BREAKS LOOSE! On February 2, 1954, Hillsdale visited Rio Grande in a game that featured the amazing scoring of Clarence "Bevo" Francis. In an era where there was no three-point zone, Francis wowed the crowd with an all-time scoring total of 113 points (see accompanying text for more details).

HILLSDALE (91)	FG	FT	PTS.	RIO GRANDE (134)	FG	FT	PTS.
Lowry	4	1	9	Wiseman	1	2	4
Helsted	6	7	19	Barr	1	0	2
Kincannon	0	3	3	Ripperger	2	5	9
Wagner	1	0	2	Francis	38	37	113
Davis	7	11	25	McKenzie	0	0	0
Sewell	0	3	3	Vyhnalek	0	0	0
Fake	0	2	2	Moses	1	0	2
Neff	4	4	12	Gossett	0	1	1
Check	1	1	3	Weiher	1	0	2
Allinder	1	2	4	Myers	0	1	1
Thiendeck	1	0	2	**TOTALS**	**44**	**46**	**134**
Vushan	2	0	4				
Tallmen	1	1	3				
TOTALS	**28**	**35**	**91**				

Pan American's Luke Jackson (far right) comes down hard with a rebound, accidentally kicking Rockhurst College's Dick Hennier in an NAIA tournament game in the mid-1960s.

NCAA DIVISION II CHAMPIONS

NOTE: Known as college division from 1957 through 1973.

YEAR CHAMPION	COACH	YEAR CHAMPION	COACH
1957—Wheaton, IL (28-1)	Lee Pfund	1978—Cheyney State, PA (27-2)	John Chaney
1958—South Dakota (22-5)	Duane Clodfelter	1979—North Alabama (22-9)	Bill Jones
1959—Evansville, IN (21-6)	Arad McCutchan	1980—Virginia Union (26-4)	Dave Robbins
1960—Evansville, IN (25-4)	Arad McCutchan	1981—Florida Southern (24-8)	Hal Wissel
1961—Wittenberg, OH (25-4)	Ray Mears	1982—District of Columbia (25-5)	Wil Jones
1962—Mount St. Mary's, MD (24-6)	Jim Phelan	1983—Wright State, OH (28-4)	Ralph Underhill
1963—South Dakota State (22-5)	Jim Iverson	1984—Central Missouri State (29-3)	Lynn Nance
1964—Evansville, IN (26-3)	Arad McCutchan	1985—Jacksonville State, AL (30-1)	Bill Jones
1965—Evansville, IN (29-0)	Arad McCutchan	1986—Sacred Heart, CT (30-4)	Dave Bike
1966—Kentucky Wesleyan (24-6)	Guy Strong	1987—Kentucky Wesleyan (28-5)	Wayne Chapman
1967—Winston-Salem State, NC (30-2)	Clarence Gaines	1988—Lowell, MA (27-7)	Don Doucette
1968—Kentucky Wesleyan (28-3)	Bob Daniels	1989—North Carolina Central (28-4)	Michael Bernard
1969—Kentucky Wesleyan (25-5)	Bob Daniels	1990—Kentucky Wesleyan (31-2)	Wayne Chapman
1970—Philadelphia Textile (29-2)	Herb Magee	1991—North Alabama (29-4)	Gary Elliott
1971—Evansville, IN (22-8)	Arad McCutchan	1992—Virginia Union (30-3)	Dave Robbins
1972—Roanoke, VA (28-4)	Charlie Moir	1993—Cal State-Bakersfield (33-0)	Pat Douglass
1973—Kentucky Wesleyan (24-6)	Bob Jones	1994—Cal State-Bakersfield (27-6)	Pat Douglass
1974—Morgan State, MD (28-5)	Nat Frazier	1995—Southern Indiana (29-4)	Bruce Pearl
1975—Old Dominion, VA (25-6)	Sonny Allen	1996—Fort Hays State, KS (34-0)	Gary Garner
1976—Puget Sound, WA (27-7)	Don Zech	1997—Cal State-Bakersfield (29-4)	Pat Douglass
1977—Tennessee-Chattanooga (27-5)	Ron Shumate		

NOTE: Known as college division from 1957 through 1973.

Most Division II titles by school: Kentucky Wesleyan (6), Evansville (5).

NCAA DIVISION III CHAMPIONS

YEAR CHAMPION	COACH	YEAR CHAMPION	COACH
1975 Lemoyne-Owen, TN (27-5)	Jerry Johnson	1987 North Park, IL (28-3)	Bosko Djurickovic
1976 Scranton, PA (27-5)	Bob Bessoir	1988 Ohio Wesleyan (27-5)	Gene Mehaffey
1977 Wittenberg, OH (23-5)	Larry Hunter	1989 Wisconsin-Whitewater (29-2)	Dave Vander Meulen
1978 North Park, IL (29-2)	Dan McCarrell	1990 Rochester, NY (27-5)	Mike Neer
1979 North Park, IL (26-5)	Dan McCarrell	1991 Wisconsin-Platteville (28-3)	Bo Ryan
1980 North Park, IL (28-3)	Dan McCarrell	1992 Calvin, MI (31-1)	Ed Douma
1981 Potsdam State, NY (30-2)	Jerry Welsh	1993 Ohio Northern (28-2)	Joe Campoli
1982 Wabash, OH (24-4)	Mac Petty	1994 Lebanon Valley, PA (28-4)	Pat Flannery
1983 Scranton, PA (19-7)	Bob Bessoir	1995 Wisconsin-Platteville (31-0)	Bo Ryan
1984 Wisconsin-Whitewater (27-4)	Dave Vander Meulen	1996 Rowan, NJ (28-4)	John Giannini
1985 North Park, IL (26-4)	Bosko Djurickovic	1997 Illinois Wesleyan (29-2)	Dennie Bridges
1986 Potsdam State, NY (32-0)	Jerry Welsh		

Most Division III titles by school: North Park (5), Potsdam State (2), Scranton (2), Wisconsin Platteville (2), Wisconsin-Whitewater (2).

western, Notre Dame, George Washington, LSU and Massachusetts.

After several unsuccessful attempts to restructure its membership in the early 1970s, the NCAA conducted its first ever special convention at Chicago in August, 1973, to realign schools for legislative and competitive purposes. The outcome was to divide the membership by creating Divisions I, II and III. Division III schools were grouped together because they don't award athletic scholarships. Division II has in the neighborhood of 220 members while Division III usually has between 310 and 325.

The 32-team Division II Tournament introduced an "Elite Eight" finals format in 1989, with quarterfinal pairings at one site featuring teams from eight regions (East, Great Lakes, New England, North Central, South, South Atlantic, South Central and West). Springfield, Mass., was the site of the finals for 14 consecutive seasons until the event was moved to Louisville in 1995.

Division III has a 40-team bracket. Wittenberg, the only school to win national titles at both Division II (1961) and Division III (1977), was host of four Division III Tournament semifinals and finals from 1989 through 1992. Buffalo State was designated as host of the event from 1993 through 1995.

Working Their Way Up the Ladder

Cash cow or not, no one should be able to accuse the NCAA's hierarchy of unabashed favoritism for the Division I ranks. After all, a couple of the NCAA's key administrators—Executive Director Cedric Dempsey and Assistant Executive Director for Enforcement and Eligibility Appeals David Berst—have prominent small-college backgrounds.

Dempsey was a former basketball coach at Albion (Mich.), his alma mater. He was named Michigan Intercollegiate Athletic Association Most Valuable Player in basketball in 1953-54. The 6-3 forward finished second in the nation in the 1951-52 NCAA small college rebounding statistics with 21.6 per game. The next season, he finished eighth with 19.5 per game.

Berst was a starting center in basketball and pitcher in baseball for MacMurray (Ill.) from 1965-68. The 6-5 Berst averaged 6.3 points and four rebounds per game in basketball and still holds the school's baseball record for best earned-run average in a career (2.15). He subsequently became a coach in both sports at his alma mater.

NAIA Tournament

Perhaps no postseason competition factors in endurance in such a brief span as much as the National Association of Intercollegiate Athletics Tournament. When 32 of the finest small colleges in the country converge, a champion emerges after winning five games in one week. The NAIA Tournament is also a grueling test for spectators. How fond are you of attending basketball games? You'll discover your absolute limit when you test your royal cushion by sitting through more than 12 hours of basketball each of three consecutive days covering the first two rounds of the 32-team event.

Despite being called for goaltending 12 times in a late 1960s game, Kentucky State's Elmore Smith (right) holds the collegiate record for most rebounds in a season.

There have been numerous NAIA players to warrant such attention, however. Here is an alphabetical list of former NAIA Tournament standouts to go on to play at least three seasons in the NBA and/or ABA: Dick Barnett (Tennessee State), John Barnhill (Tennessee State), Billy Ray Bates (Kentucky State), Zelmo Beaty (Prairie View A&M), M.L. Carr (Guilford), World B. Free (Guilford), Joe Fulks (Murray State), Travis Grant (Kentucky State), Luke Jackson (Pan American), Kevin Loder (Alabama State), Vern Mikkelsen (Hamline), Earl Monroe (Winston-Salem State), Terry Porter (Wisconsin-Stevens Point), Willis Reed (Grambling), Dennis Rodman (Southeastern Oklahoma), Jack Sikma (Illinois Wesleyan), Elmore Smith (Kentucky State), Al Tucker (Oklahoma Baptist) and Foots Walker (West Georgia).

"We're Goin' to Kansas City" served as the theme song for countless small schools across the country for the final time in 1993. After being a fixture for more than 40 years as the Kansas City masterpiece, the week-long marathon shifted along with the NAIA headquarters to Tulsa, beginning in 1994. Attendance had waned in Kansas City for more than a decade, but the principal reason for the move was to escape what had overshadowed the NAIA for years: the nearby headquarters of the NCAA, the Big Eight Conference Tournament, the NFL (Chiefs) and major league baseball (Royals).

The NAIA split into two divisions in 1992. NAIA Division II schools, which conduct a 24-team national tournament, are institutions that distribute no more than five scholarships.

John Barnhill (left) and Dick Barnett—each of whom went on to NBA careers—were members of Tennessee State, the first historically black institution to participate in post-season competition.

NAIA/NAIB CHAMPIONS

YEAR	CHAMPION (RECORD)	COACH
1937	Central Missouri State (17-3)	Tad C. Reid
1938	Central Missouri State (24-3)	Tad C. Reid
1939	Southwestern, KS (21-2)	George Gardner
1940	Tarkio, MO (20-4)	N.P. Kyle
1941	San Diego State (24-7)	Morris Gross
1942	Hamline, MN (20-2)	Joe Hutton
1943	Southeast Missouri State (19-6)	Charles P. Harris
1944	No tournament (WWII)	No tourney
1945	Loyola, LA (19-5)	Jack Orsley
1946	Southern Illinois (20-6)	Abe Martin
1947	Marshall, WV (32-5)	Cam Henderson
1948	Louisville, KY (29-6)	Peck Hickman
1949	Hamline, MN (29-1)	Joe Hutton
1950	Indiana State (27-8)	John Longfellow
1951	Hamline, MN (27-2)	Joe Hutton
1952	Southwest Missouri State (27-5)	Bob Vanatta
1953	Southwest Missouri State (24-4)	Bob Vanatta
1954	St. Benedict's, KS* (24-5)	Ralph Nolan
1955	East Texas State (29-5)	Bob Rogers
1956	McNeese State, LA (33-3)	Ralph Ward
1957	Tennessee State (31-4)	John McLendon
1958	Tennessee State (31-3)	John McLendon
1959	Tennessee State (32-1)	John McLendon
1960	Southwest Texas State (28-3)	Milt Jowers
1961	Grambling, LA (30-4)	Fred Hobdy
1962	Prairie View A&M, TX (27-3)	Leroy Moore
1963	Pan American, TX (26-6)	Sam Williams
1964	Rockhurst, MO (27-6)	Joe (Buddy) Brehmer
1965	Central State, OH (30-0)	William Lucas
1966	Oklahoma Baptist (26-7)	Bob Bass
1967	St. Benedict's, KS* (27-2)	Ralph Nolan
1968	Central State, OH (29-4)	William Lucas
1969	Eastern New Mexico (24-7)	Harry Miller
1970	Kentucky State (29-3)	Lucias Mitchell
1971	Kentucky State (31-2)	Lucias Mitchell
1972	Kentucky State (28-5)	Lucias Mitchell
1973	Guilford, NC (29-5)	Jack Jensen
1974	West Georgia (29-4)	Roger Kaiser
1975	Grand Canyon, AZ (30-3)	Ben Lindsey
1976	Coppin State, MD (39-2)	John Bates
1977	Texas Southern (31-5)	Robert Moreland
1978	Grand Canyon, AZ (30-3)	Ben Lindsey
1979	Drury, MO (33-2)	Jerry Kirksey
1980	Cameron, OK (36-3)	Lonnie Nichols
1981	Bethany Nazarene, OK (36-6)	Loren Gresham
1982	Spartanburg, SC (27-5)	Jerry Waters
1983	Charleston, SC (33-5)	John Kresse
1984	Fort Hays State, KS (35-2)	Bill Morse
1985	Fort Hays State, KS (35-3)	Bill Morse
1986	David Lipscomb, TN (35-4)	Don Meyer
1987	Washburn, KS (35-4)	Bob Chipman
1988	Grand Canyon, AZ (37-6)	Paul Westphal
1989	St. Mary's, TX (28-5)	Buddy Meyer
1990	Birmingham Southern, AL (31-3)	Duane Reboul
1991	Oklahoma City (34-3)	Darrel Johnson
1992	Oklahoma City (38-0)	Darrel Johnson
1993	Hawaii Pacific (30-4)	Tony Sellitto
1994	Oklahoma City (28-7)	Win Case
1995	Birmingham Southern, AL (35-2)	Duane Reboul
1996	Oklahoma City (32-6)	Win Case
1997	Life, GA (34-1)	Roger Kaiser

*St. Benedict's is now known as Benedictine College.

Current Iowa coach Tom Davis graduated from small college Wisconsin-Platteville in 1960.

DIVISION II

YEAR	CHAMPION (RECORD)	COACH
1992	Grace, IN (32-5)	Jim Kessler
1993	Willamette, OR (29-4)	Gordie James
1994	Eureka, IL (27-4)	Dave Darnall
1995	Bethel, IN (38-2)	Mike Lightfoot
1996	Albertson, ID (31-3)	Marty Holly
1997	Bethel, IN (34-5)	Mike Lightfoot

Most NAIA titles by school: Grand Canyon (3), Hamline (3), Kentucky State (3), Oklahoma City (3), Tennessee State (3).

Most NAIA Tournament appearances: Central Washington (24), Wisconsin-Eau Claire (20).

Modest Backgrounds

Small colleges have supplied many of the biggest names in coaching. Recently retired Gene Bartow began his coaching career at Central Missouri State, a Division II power that lists Division I championship coaches Phog Allen of Kansas and Joe B. Hall of Kentucky among its former head coaches. Allen posted an 84-31 record in seven seasons at Central Missouri from 1913-'19, Bartow was 47-21 in three seasons from 1962-'64 and Hall was 19-6 in one season (1964-65).

Central Missouri, winner of the first two NAIA Tournaments in 1937 and 1938, captured the NCAA Division II crown in 1984 under Lynn Nance, the coach at St. Mary's (Calif.) in 1989 when the Gaels made their first NCAA Tournament appearance in 30 years. Another former CMSU coach, Louisiana Tech's Jim Wooldridge, directed Southwest Texas State to its first-ever NCAA playoff appearance in 1994.

The last 12 Final Fours have had at least one coach who graduated from a non-Division I university. Here is an alphabetical list of prominent active major-college coaches who graduated from a small school:

DIVISION I COACH	ALMA MATER
Dana Altman	Eastern New Mexico '80
Rick Barnes	Lenoir-Rhyne (N.C.) '76
J.D. Barnett	Winona (Minn.) State '66
Bill Bayno	Sacred Heart (Conn.) '85
Dick Bennett	Ripon (Wis.) '65
John Brady	Belhaven (Miss.) '76
Jim Calhoun	American International (Mass.) '67
Jeff Capel	Fayetteville (N.C.) State '77
John Chaney	Bethune-Cookman (Fla.) '55
Rob Chavez	Mesa (Colo.) College '80
Perry Clark	Gettysburg (Pa.) '74
Tom Davis	Wisconsin-Platteville '60
Mike Deane	Potsdam (N.Y.) State '74
James Dickey	Central Arkansas '76
Bob Donewald	Hanover (Ind.) '64
Scott Edgar	Pittsburgh-Johnstown '78
Steve Fisher	Illinois State '67
Jerry Green	UNC Asheville '67
Leonard Hamilton	Tennessee-Martin '71
Jim Harrick	Morris Harvey (W. Va.) '60
Rich Herrin	McKendree (Ill.) '56
Bobby Hussey	Appalachian State (N.C.) '62
Pat Kennedy	King's (Pa.) '75
Steve Lappas	City College of New York '77
Steve Lavin	Chapman (Calif.) '88
Nick Macarchuk	Fairfield (Conn.) '63
John MacLeod	Bellarmine (Ky.) '59
Phil Martelli	Widener (Pa.) '76
Neil McCarthy	Sacramento (Calif.) State '65
Eldon Miller	Wittenberg (O.) '61
Harry Miller	Texas Lutheran '74
Jim Molinari	Illinois Wesleyan '77
Bill Musselman	Wittenberg (O.) '62
Danny Nee	St. Mary of the Plains (Kan.) '71
Dave Odom	Guilford (N.C.) '65
Lute Olson	Augsburg (Minn.) '56
Kevin O'Neill	McGill (Montreal, Canada) '79
Ricardo Patton	Belmont (Tenn.) '80
Skip Prosser	Merchant Marine (N.Y.) '72
Oliver Purnell	Old Dominion (Va.) '75
Steve Robinson	Radford (Va.) '81
Kelvin Sampson	Pembroke (N.C.) State '78
Wimp Sanderson	Florence (Ala.) State '59
Herb Sendek	Carnegie-Mellon (Pa.) '85
Sonny Smith	Milligan (Tenn.) '58
Tubby Smith	High Point (N.C.) '73
Charlie Spoonhour	Ozarks (Ark.) '61
Jerry Tarkanian	Fresno (Calif.) State '56
Billy Tubbs	Lamar (Tex.) '58

NOTES: Appalachian State, Bethune-Cookman, Fairfield, Fresno State, Illinois State, Lamar, UNC Asheville, Old Dominion and Radford are now classified as NCAA Division I colleges. . . . Several of these coaches who graduated from small colleges started their careers at major universities before transferring—Barnett (Missouri), Molinari (Kansas State) and Nee (Marquette). . . . Florence State is now the University of North Alabama and Morris Harvey is now the University of Charleston. . . . Lavin attended San Francisco State before transferring to Chapman.

FROM PEON TO PEDESTAL

UC Santa Barbara's Raymond Tutt, the nation's fourth-leading scorer last season in NCAA Division I, is the latest prominent major-college player who started his career and played for a four-year small college before transferring. Consider this alphabetical list:

PLAYER	(SMALL COLLEGE/MAJOR COLLEGE)
Henry Akin	(William Carey, Miss./Morehead State)
Kenny Ammann	(Cal State Bakersfield/Stanford)
Sandy Anderson	(Belmont Abbey/UNC Wilmington)
Scott Barnes	(Eastern Montana/Fresno State)
Elgin Baylor	(College of Idaho/Seattle)
Tyrus Baynham	(District of Columbia/Middle Tenn. St.)
Larry Bergh	(Tuskegee, Ala./Weber State)
Anthony Bethune	(Lock Haven, Pa./Hartford)
Don Boldebuck	(Nebraska Wesleyan/Houston)
Jimmy Bolden	(St. Mary's, Mich./Wichita State)
Mike Born	(Nebraska-Omaha/Iowa State)
Tom Boswell	(South Carolina State/South Carolina)
Jim Boylan	(Assumption, Mass./Marquette)
Dion Brown	(Chaminade/Washington)
Jeff Condill	(SIU-Edwardsville/Gonzaga)
Terry Connolly	(Shepherd, W. Va./Richmond)
Bob Davies	(Franklin & Marshall, Pa./Seton Hall)
Don Delgardo	(Mass.-Boston/Boston University)
Dick Dickey	(DePauw, Ind./North Carolina State)
Khris Fortson	(UC Riverside/UC Santa Barbara)
Chris Gardler	(Widener, Pa./St. Joseph's)
Thomas Garner	(Johnson C. Smith, N.C./N.C. A&T)
Gerald Glass	(Delta State, Miss./Ole Miss)
Chuck Guittar	(New Haven, Conn./Drexel)
David Hallums	(BYU-Hawaii/Hawaii)
Sherman Hamilton	(Florida Tech/Va. Commonwealth)
Mike Hanson	(Tennessee-Martin/Louisiana State)
John Harrell	(North Carolina Central/Duke)
Marcelle Henry	(St. Andrews, N.C./East Carolina)
Rich Henry	(North Dakota State/Maine)
Curtis High	(Tennessee-Martin/Nevada-Reno)
Roy Howard	(Tarleton State, Tex./Texas-El Paso
Avery Johnson	(Cameron, Okla./Southern, La.)
Maynard Johnson	(Macalester, Minn./Minnesota)
Oscar Jones	(Winston-Salem State, N.C./Delaware)
Willie Jones	(Buffalo State/Vanderbilt)
Marcus Kennedy	(Ferris State, Mich./Eastern Michigan)
LeRoy King	(Monmouth, Ill./Northwestern)
Fred Lewis	(Tampa/South Florida)
Tony Massop	(Sacramento State/Kansas State)
Jim McCaffrey	(St. Michael's, Vt./Holy Cross)
Bob McCann	(Upsala, N.J./Morehead State)
Marc Mitchell	(UW-Oshkosh/UW-Milwaukee)
Bret Mundt	(Bethel, Tenn./Memphis State)
Tucker Neale	(Ashland, O./Colgate)
Ime Oduok	(Pacific Christian, Calif./Loyola Marymount)
Donald Petties	(Wayne State, Mich./Western Michigan)
Phenizee Ransom	(Winston-Salem State, N.C./Georgia)
Troy Richardson	(North Dakota/Eastern Illinois)
Arnie Risen	(Eastern Kentucky/Ohio State)
Frank Schade	(Wisconsin-Eau Claire/Texas-El Paso)
Dwayne Scholten	(Seattle Pacific/Washington State)
Willie Scott	(Hillsdale, Mich./Bradley)
Bill Sherwood	(Oglethorpe, Ga./Oregon State)
Bill Simonovich	(Hamline, Minn./Minnesota)
Ron Simpson	(Adelphi, N.Y./Rider)
Anthony Smith*	(Clark, Ga./Western Kentucky)
Scott Snider	(Pacific Lutheran/Gonzaga)
David Stevens	(Voorhees, S.C./The Citadel)
Derek Thompkins	(Davis & Elkins, W. Va./Va. Commonwealth)
Chad Townsend	(St. Edwards, Tex./Murray State)
Joel Tribblehorn	(Fort Lewis, Colo./Colorado State)
Andrew Tunstill	(W. Va. Wesleyan/Middle Tenn. State)
Raymond Tutt	(Azusa Pacific, Calif./UC Santa Barbara)
Brian Vaughns	(Montana Tech/UC Santa Barbara)
Tom Wahl	(Mankato State, Minn./Nebraska)
Tony Walker	(Kean College, N.J./St. Peter's)
Roosevelt Wallace	(Virginia Union/Arkansas)
Kevin Whitted	(Pfeiffer, N.C./Tennessee)
Haywoode Workman	(Winston-Salem State, N.C./Oral Roberts)
Dave Ziegler	(Youngstown State/Kent State)

*Smith served in the U.S. Army and played against WKU while with the Ft. Hood Tankers military team before joining the Hilltoppers.

HUMBLE PIE

Many of the biggest names in coaching have had to rebound from embarrassing defeats that won't be cited on their resumes. Here is an alphabetical list of high-profile active coaches who lost games to non-Division I colleges at some point in their careers.

COACH, SCHOOL	GAMES LOST
Rick Barnes, Clemson	Lost at Chaminade (Hawaii) in 1991-92 while coaching Providence.
Dave Bliss, New Mexico	Lost to Eastern New Mexico in 1991-92.
Jim Calhoun, Connecticut	Lost to American International (Mass.), Bridgeport (Mass.) and Assumption (Mass.) in 1972-73 and Brandeis (Mass.) in 1974-75 while coaching Northeastern.
Bobby Cremins, Georgia Tech	Lost to Lenoir-Rhyne (N.C.) in 1975-76 and 1977-78 while coaching Appalachian State.
Denny Crum, Louisville	Lost at Chaminade (Hawaii) in 1983-84 and 1984-85.
Tom Davis, Iowa	Lost to Chico State in 1982-83 while coaching Stanford and to UC Riverside in 1988-89.
Lefty Driesell, Georgia State	Lost to Catawba (N.C.) twice in 1960-61 and to Carson-Newman (Tenn.) and Erskine (S.C.) in 1961-62 while coaching Davidson.
Bill Frieder, Arizona State	Lost to Alaska-Anchorage on a neutral court in 1988-89 while coaching Michigan.
Leonard Hamilton, Miami (Fla.)	Lost at BYU-Hawaii in 1987-88 while coaching Oklahoma State.
Jim Harrick, Rhode Island	Lost at Abilene (Tex.) Christian in 1984-85 while coaching Pepperdine.
Don Haskins, Texas-El Paso	Lost to Louisiana College in 1977-78.
Mike Krzyzewski, Duke	Lost to SUNY-Buffalo, Scranton (Pa.) and King's College (Pa.) in 1975-76 while coaching Army.
John MacLeod, Notre Dame	Lost to Samford (Ala.) in 1971-72 while coaching Oklahoma.
Jim O'Brien, Ohio State	Lost at Florida Tech in 1988-89 while coaching Boston College.
Dave Odom, Wake Forest	Lost at Alaska-Anchorage in 1993-94.
Rick Pitino, Kentucky	Lost to Adelphi (N.Y.) in 1978-79 while coaching Boston University.
Norm Stewart, Missouri	Lost at Alaska-Anchorage in 1985-86.
John Thompson, Georgetown	Lost to Assumption (Mass.) in 1973-74, Gannon (Pa.) in 1975-76, Randolph-Macon (Va.) in 1974-75, and Roanoke (Va.) in 1972-73.
Billy Tubbs, TCU	Lost to Ohio Northern in 1980-81 while coaching Oklahoma.

Purvis Short was a standout for Jackson State University.

SMALL-SCHOOL STANDOUTS

PLAYER, SCHOOL	LAST YEAR	G.	FG%	FT%	RPG	PPG
Brooms Abramovic, Salem (W. Va.)	1943	97	—	—	—	22.2
Jerry Anderson, Southwest Missouri	1955	106	—	.657	—	9.4
Al Attles, North Carolina A&T	1960	53	.561	.636	—	13.1
Dick Barnett, Tennessee State	1959	136	—	—	—	23.6
John Barnhill, Tennessee State	1959	103	—	—	—	13.8
Billy Ray Bates, Kentucky State	1978	107	.560	.772	7.3	16.1
Zelmo Beaty, Prairie View (Tex.)	1962	108	.655	.775	19.0	24.7
Manute Bol, Bridgeport (Conn.)	1985	31	.611	.595	13.5	22.5
Ron Bontemps, Beloit (Wis.)	1951	83	—	—	—	21.3
Don Buse, Evansville (Ind.)	1972	84	.497	.784	6.3	17.0
M.L. Carr, Guilford (N.C.)	1973	111	.573	.618	11.4	18.0
Fred Carter, Mount St. Mary's	1969	84	.429	.581	10.8	21.9
Barry Clemens, Ohio Wesleyan	1965	94	.466	.719	13.1	20.3
Sweetwater Clifton, Xavier (La.)	1943	18	—	—	—	18.7
E.C. Coleman, Houston Baptist	1973	94	.585	.640	13.6	19.0
Bob Dandridge, Norfolk (Va.) St.	1969	77	.578	.745	13.0	22.6
Mike Davis, Virginia Union	1969	89	—	—	—	31.0
John Drew, Gardner-Webb (N.C.)	1974	51	.518	.692	11.0	25.2
Mario Elie, American International	1985	120	.555	.767	8.3	17.7
Clarence "Bevo" Francis, Rio Grande	1954	66	—	—	—	48.6
Walt Frazier, Southern Illinois	1967	50	.471	.751	10.6	17.7
Lloyd Free, Guilford (N.C.)	1975	85	.485	.731	6.5	23.6
Joe Fulks, Murray (Ky.) State	1943	47	—	.665	—	13.2
Mike Gale, Elizabeth City State	1971	62	.522	.678	15.6	19.6
Harry Gallatin, Northeast Missouri	1948	62	—	—	—	13.2
George Gervin, Eastern Michigan	1972	39	.582	.776	14.4	26.8
Travis Grant, Kentucky State	1972	121	.638	.774	9.4	33.4
Mike Green, Louisiana Tech	1973	102	.580	.723	15.4	22.9
Hal Haskins, Hamline (Minn.)	1950	120	—	—	—	17.1
Cleo Hill, Winston-Salem State	1961	108	.444	.743	6.8	23.2
Wilbur Holland, New Orleans	1975	59	.471	.787	4.6	22.8
Bob Hopkins, Grambling (La.)	1956	126	.423	.738	17.4	29.8
Phil Hutcheson, Lipscomb (Tenn.)	1990	155	—	—	—	26.5
Luke Jackson, Pan American (Tex.)	1964	77	.544	.730	18.5	24.1
Phil Jackson, North Dakota	1967	86	.510	.738	12.9	19.9
Aaron James, Grambling (La.)	1974	106	.581	.697	10.9	22.2
Clemon Johnson, Florida A&M	1978	109	.528	.589	13.7	12.7
George Johnson, Dillard (La.)	1970	90	.472	.590	15.0	12.3
Mickey Johnson, Aurora (Ill.)	1974	94	.561	.660	20.9	26.1
Caldwell Jones, Albany (Ga.) State	1973	109	.506	.674	20.3	20.5
Earl Jones, District of Columbia	1984	109	.541	.776	10.7	23.4
James Jones, Grambling (La.)	1967	104	—	—	—	20.3
Sam Jones, North Carolina Central	1957	100	.463	.697	9.0	17.7
Wilbert Jones, Albany (Ga.) State	1969	117	.481	.687	14.2	17.2
Bob Kauffman, Guilford (N.C.)	1968	113	—	—	15.9	22.8
Jerome Kersey, Longwood (Va.)	1984	103	.507	.607	11.3	17.0
George King, Morris Harvey (W.Va.)	1950	105	—	—	—	24.1
Bob Love, Southern (La.)	1965	104	.561	.749	11.2	23.1
Bob Mabry, Rio Grande (O.)	1970	104	—	—	21.8	22.7
Rick Mahorn, Hampton (Va.) Institute	1980	119	.534	.682	12.3	20.3
Peter Martin, Midamerica Nazarene	1992	56	.696	.756	10.1	34.0
Vern Mikkelsen, Hamline (Minn.)	1949	104	—	—	—	13.6
Earl Monroe, Winston-Salem State	1967	110	—	—	—	26.7
Otto Moore, Pan American (Tex.)	1968	105	.486	.616	16.0	17.9
Jackie Moreland, Louisiana Tech	1960	70	.421	.773	16.5	21.3
Charles Oakley, Virginia Union	1985	117	.609	.627	14.0	20.3
Joe Pace, UMES/Coppin State	1976	116	.545	.657	18.1	18.3
Curtis Perry, Southwest Missouri	1970	105	.460	.623	13.6	17.5
John Pierce, Lipscomb (Tenn.)	1994	148	.658	.771	10.1	28.5
Scottie Pippen, Central Arkansas	1987	93	.563	.695	8.1	17.2
Terry Porter, Wis.-Stevens Point	1985	117	.589	.796	3.8	13.5
Willis Reed, Grambling (La.)	1964	122	.597	.740	15.2	18.7
Len "Truck" Robinson, Tennessee St.	1974	111	.521	.645	13.5	20.3
Dennis Rodman, Southeastern Okla.	1986	96	.637	.625	15.7	25.7
Dan Roundfield, Central Michigan	1975	79	.542	.631	13.1	16.7
Woody Sauldsberry, Texas Southern	1955	29	—	—	—	18.5
Bruce Seals, Xavier (La.)	1973	53	.520	.617	13.0	22.2
Purvis Short, Jackson (Miss.) St.	1978	104	.534	.733	9.3	23.4
Jack Sikma, Illinois Wesleyan	1977	107	.592	.765	13.1	21.2
James Silas, Stephen F. Austin (Tex.)	1972	99	.572	.803	4.7	18.7
Jerry Sloan, Evansville	1965	85	.403	.721	12.4	15.5
Elmore Smith, Kentucky State	1971	85	.584	.566	22.6	21.3
Randy Smith, Buffalo (N.Y.) State	1971	74	.497	.657	13.2	23.1
Scott Steagall, Millikin (Ill.)	1951	98	—	—	—	21.7
Maurice Stokes, St. Francis (Pa.)	1955	102	.448	.655	—	22.4
Sedale Threatt, West Virginia Tech	1983	120	.498	.724	3.7	20.7
Dave Twardzik, Old Dominion (Va.)	1972	82	.506	.799	5.5	20.2
Charles "Chico" Vaughn, Southern Ill.	1962	85	.439	.737	7.8	24.5
Clarence "Foots" Walker, West Ga.	1974	61	.492	.760	7.4	20.9
Ben Warley, Tennessee State	1960	74	.424	.843	10.3	13.8
Don "Slick" Watts, Xavier (La.)	1973	80	.490	.620	4.2	17.6
Marvin Webster, Morgan State (Md.)	1975	114	.524	.658	19.9	17.5
Larry Wright, Grambling (La.)	1976	86	—	.771	—	23.7

NOTES: Statistics for Attles and Gale are available for only their last two of four seasons. . . . The freshman statistics for Barnhill and Sauldsberry are unavailable. . . . L. Jackson (Texas Southern) and E. Smith (Wiley, Tex., College) played for other schools, but those statistics are unavailable. . . . Warley's complete statistics are unavailable and the figures listed are based on available stats. . . . Central Michigan, Coppin State, Eastern Michigan, Evansville, Florida A&M, Grambling, Jackson State, Louisiana Tech, Maryland-Eastern Shore, Morgan State, Mount St. Mary's, Murray State, New Orleans, North Carolina A&T, Old Dominion, Pan American, Prairie View, St. Francis (Pa.), Southern (La.), Southern Illinois, Southwest Missouri State, Stephen F. Austin State, Tennessee State, and Texas Southern subsequently moved up to NCAA Division I status.

SMALL-COLLEGE INDIVIDUAL SCORING RECORD HOLDERS

MOST POINTS IN A SINGLE GAME

NJCAA: 80—Nelson Burrell, Dawson (Mont.) vs. Trinity in 1972-73 season.

NAIA/NCAA DIVISION II: 113—Bevo Francis, Rio Grande (O.) vs. Hillsdale (Mich.), Feb. 2, 1954.

NCAA DIVISION III: 63—Joe DeRoche, Thomas (Me.) vs. St. Joseph's (Me.), Feb. 1, 1988.

MOST POINTS IN A SINGLE SEASON

NJCAA: 1,409—Ollie Taylor, San Jacinto (Tex.), 30.7 average in 46 games in 1967-68.

NAIA: 1,347—Archie Talley, Salem (W.Va.), 40.8 average in 33 games in 1975-76.

NCAA DIVISION II: 1,329—Earl Monroe, Winston-Salem State, 42.9 average in 31 games in 1966-67.

NCAA DIVISION III: 1,044—Greg Grant, Trenton State (N.J.), 32.6 average in 32 games in 1988-89.

MOST POINTS IN A CAREER

NJCAA: 2,456—Ollie Taylor, San Jacinto (Tex.), 26.2 average in 94 games in 1967-68 and 1968-69.

NAIA: 4,230—John Pierce, David Lipscomb (Tenn.), 28.6 average in 148 games from 1990-91 through 1993-94.

NCAA DIVISION II: 4,045—Travis Grant, Kentucky State, 33.4 average in 121 games from 1968-69 through 1971-72.

NCAA DIVISION III: 2,940—Andre Foreman, Salisbury (Md.) State, 27.0 average in 109 games from 1987-88 through 1991-92 (missed 1989-90 season).

HIGHEST SEASON AVERAGE

NJCAA: 47.8—Ron Riordan, Becker (Mass.), 1,387 points in 29 games in 1967-68.

NAIA: 48.3—Bevo Francis, Rio Grande (O.), 580 points in 12 games in 1952-53.

NCAA DIVISION II: 46.5—Bevo Francis, Rio Grande (O.), 1,255 points in 27 games in 1953-54.

NCAA DIVISION III: 36.2—Rickey Sutton, Lyndon State (Vt.), 507 points in 14 games in 1975-76.

HIGHEST CAREER AVERAGE

NJCAA: 34.4—Bobby Gaeta, Bergen (N.J.), 1,752 points in 51 games in 1984-85 and 1986-87.

NAIA: 33.9—Peter Martin, MidAmerica Nazarene (Kan.), 1,906 points in 56 games in 1990-91 and 1991-92 (center from New Zealand originally signed with Hawaii as a freshman in 1986-87 before attending junior college).

NCAA DIVISION II: 33.4—Travis Grant, Kentucky State, 4,045 points in 121 games from 1968-69 through 1971-72.

NCAA DIVISION III: 29.7—Rickey Sutton, Lyndon State (Vt.), 2,379 points in 80 games from 1975-76 through 1978-79.

BRIEF SHINING MOMENT(S)

There's an old adage that everyone gets his 15 minutes of fame. It's more difficult, however, for a small college to get its moment in the sun anymore because many power conferences now have rules disallowing games against non-Division I opponents.

For the following small colleges, victories over major universities since the start of the 1960s were much more than just a line of type in the agate section carried by a wire service:

Small College	Victory Against Major University
Alaska-Anchorage	Defeated Auburn (109-94 in 1989-90), California (88-73 in 1990-91), Dayton (84-70 in 1992-93), Houston (79-78 in 1980-81), Miami, Fla. (78-77 in 1987-88), Michigan (70-66 in 1988-89), Missouri (59-56 in 1985-86), New Mexico (79-72 in 1983-84), Pacific (86-85 in 1979-80), Penn State (79-62 in 1978-79), Santa Clara (72-71 in 1991-92), Tennessee (86-78 in 1990-91), Texas (80-68 in 1986-87), Texas Tech (70-58 in 1990-91), Wake Forest (70-68 in 1993-94) and Washington (77-75 in 1986-87).
Alaska-Fairbanks	Defeated Toledo (66-55 in 1992-93).
Albright (Pa.)	Defeated Rutgers (89-77 in 1964-65) and St. Joseph's (66-56 in 1961-62).
American Int. (Mass.)	Defeated Massachusetts (63-59 in 1961-62, 81-76 in 1966-67, 73-72 in 1969-70 and 70-61 in 1979-80).
Angelo State (Tex.)	Defeated New Mexico State (77-71 in 1971-72).
Aquinas (Mich.)	Defeated Xavier (81-69 in 1970-71).
Ashland (O.)	Defeated Xavier (63-62 in 1976-77).
Assumption (Mass.)	Defeated Georgetown (90-83 in 1971-72 and 72-63 in 1973-74) and Providence (88-80 in 1963-64 and 70-67 in 1984-85).
Bellarmine (Ky.)	Defeated Creighton (81-78 in 1965-66).
Belmont (Tenn.)	Defeated Western Kentucky (52-50 in 1964-65).
Bentley (Mass.)	Defeated Massachusetts (92-72 in 1978-79 and 77-70 in 1979-80).
Biscayne (Fla.)	Defeated Houston (76-74 in 1980-81).
BYU-Hawaii	Defeated Oklahoma State (62-59 in 1987-88).
Cal Poly SLO (Calif.)	Defeated Fresno State (88-81 in 1970-71), Pacific (75-65 in 1974-75), San Francisco (60-51 in 1960-61) and Stanford (79-61 in 1976-77).
UC Riverside	Defeated California (69-63 in 1979-80) and Iowa (110-92 in 1988-89).
UC San Diego	Defeated Utah (60-57 in 1986-87).
Cal State Bakersfield	Defeated Fresno State (92-86 in 1975-76 and 79-70 in 1976-77).
Carnegie Tech (Pa.)	Defeated Duquesne (83-75 in 1959-60) and Penn State (70-57 in 1960-61).
Central State (O.)	Defeated Xavier (76-69 in 1963-64).
Chaminade (Hawaii)	Defeated Louisville (83-72 in 1983-84 and 67-65 in 1984-85), Providence (111-108 in 1991-92), South Carolina (74-66 in 1981-82), SMU (71-70 in 1984-85) and Virginia (77-72 in 1982-83).
Chico (Calif.) State	Defeated Stanford (82-78 in 1982-83).
David Lipscomb (Tenn.)	Defeated Western Kentucky (75-68 in 1962-63).
Defiance (O.)	Defeated Bowling Green (66-64 in 1985-86).
Dillard (La.)	Defeated Tulane (96-85 in 1973-74).
Eastern Montana	Defeated Fresno State (73-71 in 1976-77), Iowa State (66-55 in 1981-82), Texas A&M (39-38 in 1980-81) and Washington State (51-48 in 1981-82).
Eastern New Mexico	Defeated New Mexico (81-76 in 1991-92), New Mexico State (46-43 in 1966-67) and Texas-El Paso (71-67 in 1959-60 and 55-50 in 1960-61).
Fairmont (W.Va.) State	Defeated Southern Mississippi (69-62 in 1984-85).

Florida Southern	Defeated Connecticut (93-85 in 1972-73), Florida (69-58 in 1950-51 and 98-75 in 1979-80), Florida State (78-63 and 73-67 in 1956-57), La Salle (84-73 in 1978-79), South Carolina (70-62 in 1979-80) and Tulane (102-91 in 1966-67).
Florida Tech	Defeated Boston College (77-75 in 1988-89).
Gannon (Pa.)	Defeated Duquesne (79-75 in 1974-75) and Georgetown (57-56 in 1975-76).
Gettysburg (Pa.)	Defeated La Salle (57-44 in 1961-62), Rutgers (83-61 in 1961-62, 72-65 in 1962-63, 60-56 in 1963-64 and 61-60 in 1971-72) and Temple (76-74 in 1959-60).
Hanover (Ind.)	Defeated Xavier (72-71 in 1969-70 and 79-78 in 1977-78).
Hawaii-Hilo	Defeated Creighton (83-76 in 1993-94), Nebraska (71-66 in 1976-77) and New Mexico (81-78 in 1976-77).
Hawaii Pacific	Defeated Fordham (73-59 in 1985-86).
Hayward (Calif.) State	Defeated Pacific (60-57 and 60-53 in 1962-63).
Illinois Wesleyan	Defeated Arizona (67-64 in 1982-83) and Loyola of Chicago (79-74 in 1970-71).
Kentucky Wesleyan	Defeated Arkansas (76-75 in 1969-70), Baylor (98-77 in 1963-64), Mississippi (88-73 in 1969-70), South Carolina (82-74 in 1963-64) and Virginia (62-42 in 1963-64).
King's College (Pa.)	Defeated Seton Hall (76-69 in 1975-76).
LeMoyne (N.Y.)	Defeated Boston College (89-79 in 1976-77).
Louisiana College	Defeated Mississippi State (77-71 in 1969-70), Texas-El Paso (55-54 in 1977-78) and Tulane (85-76 in 1962-63, 86-74 in 1964-65 and 83-76 in 1967-68).
Lowell (Mass.)	Defeated Massachusetts (70-69 in 1989-90).
McKendree (Ill.)	Defeated St. Louis (64-55 in 1980-81).
Metro State (Colo.)	Defeated Mississippi (86-81 in 1989-90).
Midwestern State (Tex.)	Defeated Utah (70-69 in 1979-80).
Mississippi College	Defeated Mississippi State (72-57 in 1964-65).
Missouri-St. Louis	Defeated Arkansas (85-79 in 1971-72), Dayton (66-63 in 1992-93) and St. Louis (89-88 in 1977-78 and 75-70 in 1982-83).
Morris Harvey (W. Va.)	Defeated Pitt (76-72 in 1977-78).
Nebraska-Omaha	Defeated Creighton (56-45 in 1982-83) and Iowa State (84-73 in 1975-76 and 69-68 in 1979-80).
North Dakota	Defeated Creighton (69-64 in 1975-76) and Pacific (72-67 in 1978-79).
Northern Colorado	Defeated Colorado State (58-54 in 1986-87).
Northern Kentucky	Defeated Xavier (63-61 in 1978-79).
North Park (Ill.)	Defeated Jacksonville (78-68 in 1978-79).
Ohio Northern	Defeated Oklahoma (72-69 in 1980-81).
Philadelphia Textile	Defeated St. Joseph's (59-58 in 1977-78), Temple (70-58 in 1975-76) and Villanova (65-59 in 1975-76 and 61-57 in 1976-77).
Puget Sound (Wash.)	Defeated Fresno State (68-53 in 1975-76).
Quincy (Ill.)	Defeated Tulsa (65-59 in 1976-77).
Randolph-Macon (Va.)	Defeated Georgetown (73-72 in 1971-72 and 74-64 in 1974-75).
Rollins (Fla.)	Defeated Georgia (64-60 in 1970-71), Northwestern (66-62 in 1986-87 and 70-68 in 1987-88) and Seton Hall (84-75 in 1973-74).
St. Joseph's (Ind.)	Defeated Tulane (84-77 in 1971-72).
St. Martin's (Wash.)	Defeated Washington State (56-50 in 1980-81).
St. Mary's (Tex.)	Defeated Houston (85-74 in 1974-75) and Tulsa (73-69 in 1975-76 and 62-44 in 1976-77).
St. Norbert (Wis.)	Defeated Loyola of Chicago (80-71 in 1975-76).
San Francisco State	Defeated Arkansas (84-81 in 1971-72) and Pacific (53-47 in 1960-61 and 74-69 in 1961-62).
Santa Fe (N.M.)	Defeated New Mexico State (57-56 in 1962-63) and TCU (71-64 in 1978-79).
Sonoma State (Calif.)	Defeated Fresno State (62-60 in 1989-90).
South Dakota	Defeated Creighton (70-58 in 1959-60), Iowa State (79-75 in 1975-76) and Wyoming (73-72 in 1979-80).
SIU-Edwardsville	Defeated St. Louis (67-64 in 1982-83).
Southern Indiana	Defeated Wisconsin (78-66 in 1990-91).
Springfield (Mass.)	Defeated Massachusetts (63-62 in 1970-71).
Tampa (Fla.)	Defeated Miami, Fla. (113-95 in 1961-62, 78-76 in 1967-68 and 62-61 in 1968-69), N.C. State (67-62 in 1986-87) and South Florida (79-71 in 1987-88).
Texas Lutheran	Defeated TCU (77-76 in 1977-78).
Texas Wesleyan	Defeated SMU (84-83 in 1980-81).
Thomas More (Ky.)	Defeated Xavier (85-64 in 1969-70 and 65-64 in 1972-73).
Union (Tenn.)	Defeated Memphis State (61-53 in 1968-69 and 63-62 in 1969-70).
Upsala (N.J.)	Defeated Rutgers (75-68 in 1959-60).
Wabash (Ind.)	Defeated Creighton (78-77 in 1960-61).
Walsh (O.)	Defeated St. Bonaventure (75-68 in 1992-93).
Washburn (Kan.)	Defeated Arkansas (80-75 in 1970-71).
Wayland Baptist (Tex.)	Defeated TCU (70-68 in 1978-79).
Western New Mexico	Defeated New Mexico State (101-100 in 1965-66 and 69-66 in 1986-87).
West Georgia	Defeated Western Kentucky (89-88 in 1972-73).
Westmont (Calif.)	Defeated TCU (53-52 in 1980-81).
Wheeling (W. Va.)	Defeated Xavier (70-69 in 1978-79).
Whitworth (Wash.)	Defeated New Mexico State (84-78 in 1964-65).
Williams (Mass.)	Defeated Rutgers (75-64 in 1961-62 and 82-70 in 1962-63).
Wilmington (O.)	Defeated Jacksonville (75-73 in 1967-68).
Winona (Minn.) State	Defeated Tulane (83-78 in 1971-72).
Wisconsin-Parkside	Defeated Fresno State (55-46 in 1978-79) and Memphis State (71-69 in 1979-80).
Wisconsin-Stevens Point	Defeated Colorado State (67-56 in 1982-83) and Creighton (57-51 in 1981-82).
Wittenberg (O.)	Defeated Toledo (40-39 in 1959-60).
Xavier (La.)	Defeated Tulane (79-77 in 1972-73).

14

WHAT'S AHEAD
IN 1997-98

efore the 1997-98 season unfolds, it is time to bounce around the country with an insider's guide addressing relevant trends and issues. The following assortment of facts and opinions provides a basket full of pertinent points to ponder from a national perspective.

700 CLUB

In the aftermath of Dean Smith passing Kentucky legend Adolph Rupp to become the all-time winningest major-college coach, the big milestone in the coaching community this season is cracking the 700-win plateau. Five or possibly six mentors will officially join the "700 Club", including Texas' Jody Conradt becoming the first women's coach to reach 700 triumphs.

Here is a list of the men's coaches with more than 600 victories through 1996-97:

RANK	COACH	WINS
1.	Dean Smith*	879
2.	Adolph Rupp	876
3.	Henry Iba	767
4.	Ed Diddle	759
5.	Phog Allen	746
6.	Ray Meyer	724
7.	Bob Knight*	698
8.	Norm Stewart*	694
9.	Lefty Driesell*	693
10.	Don Haskins*	691
11.	Ralph Miller	674
12.	Jerry Tarkanian*	673
13.	John Wooden	664
14.	Lou Henson	661
15.	Marv Harshman	653
16.	Gene Bartow	646
17.	Cam Henderson	630
18.	Norman Sloan	627
19.	Denny Crum	611

*Active coaches.

NOTES: Miller was forced to forfeit 17 of his victories with Oregon State. . . . Six NCAA Tournament victories for Tarkanian at Long Beach State were voided by the NCAA. . . . Forfeit victories are not included for Knight (two), Henson (two), Bartow (one) and Harshman (one). . . . Oklahoma State's Eddie Sutton is expected to become the 20th men's coach to crack the 600-win plateau midway through the 1997-98 season.

TARK ALERT

Jerry Tarkanian's return to his alma mater (Fresno State) likely will prevent him from finishing his career as the all-time winningest coach by percentage in NCAA history. Tarkanian slipped from first place to third after compiling a 20-12 record last season. If the Bulldogs compete in 34 games in the 1997-98 season, they need to win all but one contest to move him back atop the list. Here are the coaches with the five highest winning percentages:

COACH, SCHOOL(S) RECORD	PCT.

COACH, SCHOOL(S)
RECORD   **PCT.**

1. Clair Bee, Rider/Long Island University
       412-87   .826
Lost more than five games in a season just once in his first 14 years.

2. Adolph Rupp, Kentucky
       876-190   .822
Never compiled a losing won-loss record in his 41 seasons as a head coach.

3. Jerry Tarkanian, Long Beach St./UNLV/Fresno St.
       673-148   .820
The only year he failed to win at least 20 games was 1980-81 (16-12 mark).

4. John Wooden, Indiana State/UCLA
       664-162   .804
Worst mark was 14-12 in 1959-60 before winning 10 NCAA titles in 12 years.

5. Dean Smith, North Carolina
       879-254   .776
Won at least 25 games an amazing 22 seasons with a high of 34 in 1992-93.

STERLING START

Roy Williams, entering the 1997-98 season with a 247-58 record (.810) needs to guide Kansas to 19 triumphs this year to remain ahead of former North Carolina State coach Everett Case (1947-55) for most victories in a head coach's first 10 campaigns. Williams' lowest victory total with the Jayhawks was 19 in his first season (1988-89). He averaged 28.5 triumphs annually the previous eight years. Here is a list of Case and the four other coaches before Williams to register more than 225 wins through their first 10 seasons:

COACH	TEAM	SEASONS	W.	L.	PCT.
Everett Case	N.C. State	1947-56	265	60	.815
Jerry Tarkanian	Long Beach St./UNLV	1969-78	244	44	.847
Denny Crum	Louisville	1972-81	240	64	.789
Jim Boeheim	Syracuse	1977-86	230	77	.749
Nolan Richardson	Tulsa/Arkansas	1981-90	226	88	.720

BEST BACKCOURTS IN '97

The following schools possess the most gifted collection of guards:

1. South Carolina
2. Arizona
3. Kentucky
4. Arkansas
5. Duke
6. Connecticut
7. Xavier
8. UCLA
9. North Carolina
10. Virginia.

GREENER PASTURES CAN TURN BROWN

It's doubtful that Cleveland State's Rollie Massimino or Rhode Island's Jim Harrick will break a jinx for NCAA championship coaches. The 1992-93 season with UNLV was a clear indication to Massimino, coach of 1985 NCAA titlist Villanova, that he won't be an exception to a pragmatic rule of thumb. The Rebels' streak of consecutive Big West Conference championships ended at 10 when they compiled a 4-5 league road record, notched a 2-5 mark in games decided by five points or less, endured an academic fiasco involving star player J.R. Rider and lost their NIT opener at home before just 5,000 fans in 19,000-seat Thomas & Mack Center after failing to receive an at-large bid to the NCAA Tournament. And the worst was yet to come for Massimino, who eventually was forced out of Vegas.

It probably didn't enter Massimino's decision-making process while mulling over whether to leave Philadelphia and head West, but NCAA championship coaches who changed jobs and wound up coaching other colleges have never reached the Final Four again.

Perhaps that accounted for some of the gut-level thinking when Don Haskins maneuvered to get out of a deal to coach Detroit after winning the 1966 national title with Texas Western (now Texas-El Paso) and why Bob Knight chose to stay at Indiana rather than accept a lucrative offer from New Mexico. Of the first six coaches to win a Division I title and eventually coach another university, none of them rediscovered what they formerly possessed. Harrick, who guided UCLA to the 1995 NCAA crown, probably will be the seventh.

The experiences of championship coaches who moved to other major schools is chilling. Consider the following track records stacking the odds against Harrick and Massimino compiling a winning tourney mark let alone capturing another title:

COACH, CHAMPIONSHIP TEAM	LAST COLLEGE JOB (NCAA PLAYOFF MARK)
Jim Harrick, UCLA '95	Rhode Island (hired this season)
Howard Hobson, Oregon '39	Yale, 1949-56 (0-2)

Alvin Julian, Holy Cross '47	Dartmouth, 1951-67 (4-3)
Ken Loeffler, La Salle '54	Texas A&M, 1956-57 (did not appear)
Rollie Massimino, Villanova '85	Cleveland State, 1997 (did not appear)
Frank McGuire, North Carolina '57	South Carolina, 1965-1980 (4-5)
*Norman Sloan, N.C. State '74	Florida, 1981-1989 (3-3)

*Sloan also coached Florida from 1961 through 1966.

NOTE: Three individuals to coach a total of five Division I championship teams—Everett Shelton (Wyoming '43), Phil Woolpert (San Francisco '55 and '56) and Ed Jucker (Cincinnati '61 and '62)—ended their college coaching careers at small schools. Shelton, who had just one losing record at Wyoming from 1941 through 1955, incurred five losing marks in nine seasons at Sacramento State although he became the only coach to reach the championship game in both the Division I and Division II Tournaments (Sacramento State was runner-up to Mount St. Mary's in 1962). Woolpert, who didn't sustain more than seven losses with San Francisco in five consecutive years from 1954 through 1958, had at least 10 defeats in all seven of his seasons at San Diego. Jucker, who averaged 22.6 victories annually in his five seasons with Cincinnati, never reached the 20-win plateau in all five of his years at Rollins.

ALL IN THE FAMILY

The Meyer "monarchy" ended at DePaul after Ray and Joey Meyer combined to win 955 games from 1942 through 1997. On the other hand, three other schools this decade hired the son of an individual who previously served as head coach at their institution. Here is a rundown of the father-son coaching combinations at the same school:

MEYERS AT DEPAUL (955-512, .651)

| Ray Meyer | 724-354 (.671) in 42 seasons from 1942-84 |
| Joey Meyer | 231-158 (.594) in 13 seasons from 1985-97 |

BARTOWS AT UAB (383-218, .637)

| Gene Bartow | 365-204 (.641) in 18 seasons from 1979-96 |
| Murry Bartow | 18-14 (.563) in first season last year |

*SMITHSONS AT WICHITA STATE (169-94, .643)

| Gene Smithson | 155-81 (.657) in eight seasons from 1979-86 |
| Randy Smithson | 14-13 (.519) in first season last year |

*SIMONS AT TULANE (120-103, .538)

| Claude Simons Sr. | 101-59 (.631) in nine seasons from 1921-28 & '31 |
| Claude Simons Jr. | 19-44 (.302) in four seasons from 1939-42 |

WELSHS AT IONA (90-79, .533)

| Jerry Welsh | 42-58 (.420) in four seasons from 1992-95 |
| Tim Welsh | 48-21 (.667) in three seasons from 1995-97 |

*There were three coaches between the Smithsons and Simons.

MORE TO THE GAME THAN WINNING

Air Force's Reggie Minton is on the verge of tying Harbin "Red" Lawson for most seasons at a school (14) without posting a winning record. Minton's best mark with the Falcons was 14-14 in 1988-89. Lawson's top record with Georgia while going 112-241 (.317) from 1952-65 was 12-13 in 1959-60.

However, Minton (122-244, .333) is years away from joining the following list of coaches with the longest stints at a school yet finishing with a losing overall record at that institution:

I SHALL RETURN . . . BUT NOT AS SUCCESSFULLY

Kermit Davis and Davey Whitney discovered anew last season at Idaho and Alcorn State, respectively, how difficult it is to resurrect the same level of success they enjoyed in a previous stint at the same school. In the last 50 years, none of the following list of 18 coaches improved their winning percentage after returning to their old major-college stomping grounds (if tenure wasn't interrupted solely because of World War II).

COACH, SCHOOL	1ST STINT	W-L, PCT.	2ND STINT	W-L, PCT.
Lou Carnesecca, St. John's	1966-70	104-35, .748	1974-92	422-165, .719
Kermit Davis, Idaho	1989 & '90	50-12, .806	1997	13-17, .433
Marshall Emery, Delaware State	1977-79	30-50, .375	1986-88	18-66, .214
Dan Fitzgerald, Gonzaga	1979-81	51-29, .638	1986-97	203-140, .592
Lake Kelly, Austin Peay	1972-77	110-52, .679	1986-90	79-70, .530
Joe Lapchick, St. John's	1937-47	181-54, .770	1957-65	154-75, .672
Abe Lemons, Oklahoma City	1956-73	309-181, .631	1984-90	123-84, .594
Dave McDowell, Kent State	1949-51	56-20, .737	1956 & '57	15-29, .341
Joe Mullaney, Providence	1956-69	271-94, .742	1982-85	48-70, .407
Bill Reinhart, George Washington	1936-42	100-38, .725	1950-66	216-201, .518
Jack Rohan, Columbia	1962-74	154-161, .489	1991-95	43-87, .331
Glen Rose, Arkansas	1934-42	154-47, .766	1953-66	171-154, .526
John (Honey) Russell, Seton Hall	1937-43	101-32, .759	1950-60	194-97, .647
Norman Sloan, Florida	1961-66	85-63, .574	1981-89	150-131, .534
Ken Trickey, Oral Roberts	1970-74	118-23 .837	1988-93	96-93, .508
Butch van Breda Kolff, Lafayette	1952-55	68-34, .667	1985-88	64-51, .557
Donald White, Rutgers	1946-56	98-145, .403	1963	7-16, .304
Davey Whitney, Alcorn State	1971-89	395-199, .665	1997	11-17, .393

NOTES: Van Breda Kolff also had two stints at Hofstra, but Hofstra wasn't at the major-college level his first stint there. OCU de-emphasized its program to the NAIA level after Lemons returned. ORU wasn't always at the Division I level for either of Trickey's stints.

COACH, SCHOOL (SEASONS)	TENURE	RECORD	PCT.	BEST SEASON
Harold "Bud" Foster, Wis. (25)	1935-59	265-267	.498	20-3; 1941
John Carpenter, Rider (23)	1967-89	292-328	.471	20-6; 1971
Bill Chandler, Marquette (21)	1931-51	193-198	.494	14-3; 1933
*Lyles Alley, Furman (20)	1946-66	249-257	.492	16-3; 1946
Gerry Friel, New Hampshire (20)	1970-89	200-335	.374	16-9; 1974
Paul Lizzo, Long Island (20)	1976-95	254-308	.451	20-9; 1983
Byron "Buster" Brannon, TCU (19)	1949-67	206-258	.444	24-4; 1952
Joe Vancisin, Yale (19)	1957-75	207-241	.462	18-6; 1962

NOTE: Alley did not coach Furman in the 1949-50 season while completing work to earn his master's degree.

STANDOUT PLAYING AND COACHING

Being a great player has never had anything to do with being a good coach, but occasionally things work out in both endeavors. Although Southwest Missouri State coach Steve Alford, an NCAA first-team All-America in 1986 and 1987, was snubbed by the tournament committee, Southern Cal's Henry Bibby, who excelled as a guard for crosstown rival UCLA, became the 10th individual in history to coach a team to the NCAA Division I Tournament after earning a spot on an NCAA first- or second-team All-America squad. Will Alford or new Morehead State coach Kyle Macy, a first-team All-America in 1980 for Kentucky, be next to join the following alphabetical list of the 10 individuals to achieve the feat?

COACH, SCHOOL (YEARS)	ALMA MATER (ALL-AMERICA YEARS)
Henry Bibby, Southern Cal (1997)	UCLA (1972/1st team selection)
Bob Calihan, Detroit (1962)	Detroit (1939/2nd)
Bob Cousy, Boston College (1967 and 1968)	Holy Cross (1950/1st)
Larry Finch, Memphis (1988-89-92-93-95)	Memphis State (1973/2nd)
Clem Haskins, Western Kentucky (1981 and 1986) and Minnesota (1989-90-94-95-97)	Western Kentucky (1967/1st)
Walt Hazzard, UCLA (1987)	UCLA (1964/1st)
Branch McCracken, Indiana (1940-53-54-58)	Indiana (1930)
Jeff Mullins, UNC Charlotte (1988 and 1992)	Duke (1964/2nd)
John Shumate, SMU (1993)	Notre Dame (1974/1st)
John Wooden, UCLA (1950-52-56-62-63-64-65-67-68-69-70-71-72-73-74-75)	Purdue (1930, 1931 and 1932)

NOTE: The NCAA did not distinguish between first- and second-team All-Americas until 1939.

SELECT CIRCLE

Connecticut coach Jim Calhoun is on his way to becoming the first coach to win 250 games at two different Division I schools. He should reach that plateau with UConn midway through the 1997-98 campaign after earning 250 victories for Northeastern from 1973-86. Here is a look at Calhoun and the five other coaches to win a minimum of 200 games at two different major colleges (victories through 1996-97 in parentheses):

COACH	FIRST SCHOOL	SECOND SCHOOL
Jim Calhoun	Northeastern (250)	Connecticut (240)
Hugh Durham	Florida State (230)	Georgia (298)
Ralph Miller	Wichita State (220)	Oregon State (359)
Johnny Orr	Michigan (209)	Iowa State (218)
Norman Sloan	N.C. State (266)	Florida (235)
Neil McCarthy	Weber State (200)	New Mexico State (248)

SHORT AND SWEET

Xavier's Skip Prosser and Old Dominion's Jeff Capel, ascending stars in the coaching community, are expected to guide their schools to the NCAA Tournament again. In 1993-94, Prosser and Capel took 17-13 Loyola (Md.) and 16-14 North Carolina A&T, respectively, to the NCAA Tournament in their only seasons at those outposts. There have been other coaches, however, who posted even better marks in one-year stints since the generally recognized start of the modern era of college basketball in the early 1950s. Here is a chronological list of 10 coaches who won at least 60 percent of their games in one-year tenures:

COACH, SCHOOL (SEASON)	W-L, PCT.	REASON FOR SHORT STINT
Bob Vanatta, Army (1953-54)	15-7, .682	Became coach at Bradley.
Bill Fitch, Bowling Green (1967-68)	18-7, .720	Became coach at Minnesota.
Jim Harding, La Salle (1967-68)	20-8, .714	Became coach of Minnesota (ABA)
Digger Phelps, Fordham (1970-71)	26-3, .897	Became coach at Notre Dame.
Carl Tacy, Marshall (1971-72)	23-4, .852	Became coach at Wake Forest.
Lute Olson, Long Beach St. (1973-74)	24-2, .923	Became coach at Iowa.
Bill Gibson, South Florida (1974-75)	15-10, .600	Died of a heart attack.
Ron Greene, Miss. State (1977-78)	18-9, .667	Became coach at Murray State.
Rick Barnes, George Mason (1987-88)	20-10, .667	Became coach at Providence.
Art Tolis, New Orleans (1987-88)	21-11, .656	Forced out by administration.

FINEST FRONTCOURTS in '97

The following schools feature collections of the best beasts of the baseline:

1. Kansas
2. UCLA
3. North Carolina
3. Michigan
4. UNLV
5. Florida State
7. Duke
8. Indiana
9. Cincinnati
10. Missouri

TWICE IS NICE

Georgia State's Lefty Driesell (needs 16 triumphs to tie), Auburn's Cliff Ellis (22), Jacksonville's Hugh Durham (27), Fresno State's Jerry Tarkanian (27), Maryland's Gary Williams (27), Rhode Island's Jim Harrick (28) and Illinois' Lon Kruger (31) are in positions where they could become the first active coach to hold three existing school single-season records for most victories.

A coach deserving kudos for standing the test of time is Harold Anderson, who set a pair of records that have remained intact for more than 50 years. Following is a list of coaches who hold current Division I records at two different universities for most victories in a single season:

COACH	FIRST SCHOOL (RECORD/SEASON)	SECOND SCHOOL (RECORD/SEASON)
Harold Anderson	Toledo (24-6/1939-40)	Bowling Green (28-7/1946-47)
Dave Bliss	SMU (28-7/1987-88)	New Mexico (28-5/1995-96)
Jim Calhoun	Northeastern (27-5/1983-84)	Connecticut (32-3/1995-96)
P.J. Carlesimo	Wagner (21-7/1978-79)	Seton Hall (31-7/1988-89)
Bobby Cremins	Appalachian State (23-6/1978-79)	Georgia Tech (28-7/1989-90)
Lefty Driesell	Davidson (27-3/1968-69)	Maryland (27-5/1971-72)
Hugh Durham	Florida State (27-6/1971-72)	Georgia (24-10/1982-83)
Bobby Dye	Cal State Fullerton (23-9/1977-78)	Boise State (24-6/1987-88)
Cliff Ellis	South Alabama (25-6/1980-81)	Clemson (25-6/1986-87)
Paul Evans	Navy (30-5/1985-86)	Pittsburgh* (25-8/1986-87)
Tim Floyd	New Orleans* (26-4/1992-93)	Iowa State (24-9/1995-96)
Smokey Gaines	Detroit* (25-4/1977-78)	San Diego State (23-8/1984-85)
Boyd Grant	Fresno State (27-3/1981-82)	Colorado State (23-10/1988-89)
Jim Harrick	Pepperdine (25-5/1985-86)	UCLA (31-2/1994-95)
Bob Huggins	Akron (22-8/1985-86)	Cincinnati* (29-5/1991-92)
Doggie Julian	Holy Cross (27-3/1946-47)	Dartmouth* (22-5/1957-58)
Jim Killingsworth	Idaho State (25-5/1976-77)	TCU* (24-7/1986-87)
Bob Knight	Army (22-6/1969-70)	Indiana (32-0/1975-76)
Lon Kruger	Kansas State* (25-9/1987-88)	Florida (29-8/1993-94)
Eldon Miller	Western Michigan (25-3/1975-76)	Northern Iowa (23-9/1989-90)
Tom Penders	Rhode Island (28-7/1987-88)	Texas* (26-8/1993-94)
Nolan Richardson	Tulsa (27-4/1983-84)	Arkansas (34-4/1990-91)
Lee Rose	UNC Charlotte (28-5/1976-77)	South Florida (22-10/1982-83)
Jerry Tarkanian	Long Beach State (26-3/1972-73)	UNLV (37-2/1986-87)
Butch van Breda Kolff	Lafayette (23-3/1954-55)	Princeton (25-3/1966-67)
Gary Williams	American (24-6/1980-81)	Boston College (25-7/1982-83)

*Tied school standard.

NEVER NEVER LAND

The list of the nine long-time major colleges to never earn a final AP or UPI top 20 ranking, win an NCAA Tournament or NIT game, or have an NCAA consensus first- or second-team All-America includes Air Force, Brown, Bucknell, The Citadel, Cornell, Harvard, Kent, Lehigh and William & Mary. Air Force, Brown and Harvard have also never had a 20-win season.

TOUGH TO BE A PERFECT EXAMPLE

Here is a breakdown of the conferences that have gone more than 20 years without a member going undefeated in league competition:

LEAGUE (LAST UNBEATEN YEAR)	SCHOOL (CONFERENCE WINS)
Big Sky (1968-69)	Weber State (15)
Big Ten (1975-76)	Indiana (18)
Mid-American (1957-58)	Miami of Ohio (12)
Ohio Valley (1969-70)	Western Kentucky (14)
Western Athletic (never)	First year was 1962-63.

MOVING ON UP

Navy, after improving its Patriot League record each of its first five years under coach Don DeVoe, needs to lose fewer than two conference assignments to keep the string intact. The Midshipmen joined the following three schools in achieving the feat of improving their conference winning percentage five consecutive seasons:

SCHOOL	RECORD	IMPROVING LEAGUE RECORD
Clemson	(2-12 in 1947)	1948 (3-14), 1949 (6-9), 1950 (8-8), 1951 (9-4), 1952 (11-4)
Davidson	(0-10 in 1960)	1961 (2-10), 1962 (5-6), 1963 (8-3), 1964 (9-2), 1965 (12-0)
Georgia Tech	(0-14 in 1981)	1982 (3-11) 1983 (4-10), 1984 (6-8), 1985 (9-5), 1986 (11-3)
Navy	(1-13 in 1992)	1993 (5-9), 1994 (9-5), 1995 (10-4), 1996 (9-3), 1997 (10-2)

SECOND TIME AROUND

Lamar and Northern Illinois became the latest schools to rejoin a conference. Consider:

SCHOOL/CONFERENCE	FIRST STINT	SECOND STINT
Bradley/Missouri Valley	1949-51	Since '56
Creighton/Missouri Valley	1929-48	Since '77
Davidson/Southern	1937-88	Since '93
Drake/Missouri Valley	1908-51	Since '57
Duquesne/Atlantic 10	1977-92	Since '94
Harvard/Ivy League	1902-09	Since '34
Lamar/Southland	1969-87	Since '98
Maryland-Eastern Shore/MEAC	1972-79	Since '83
Morgan State/Mid-Eastern Athletic	1972-80	Since '85
Murray State/Ohio Valley	1949-61	Since '63
New Orleans/Sun Belt	1977-80	Since '92
Northern Illinois/Mid-American	1976-86	Since '98
Oregon/Pacific-10	1916-59	Since '65
Oregon State/Pacific-10	1916-59	Since '65
Penn State/Atlantic 10	1977-79	1983-91
Texas-Arlington/Southland	1969-86	Since '88

MUSICAL CHAIRS

Missouri is the only university to have fewer than five permanent head coaches in the last 70 years—George Edwards (181-172 record in 20 seasons from 1927-46), Wilbur "Sparky" Stalcup (195-179 in 16 seasons from 1947-62), Bob Vanatta (42-80 in five seasons from 1963-67) and Norm Stewart (597-309 in 30 seasons from 1968-97).

Including an interim situation last season, Jacksonville's "revolving door" policy continued when Hugh Durham became the Dolphins' 10th different head coach in the last 25 years.

PICK OF THE LITTER

Fifteen schools have more than 1,500 victories overall, at least 36 NCAA playoff wins or 22 NCAA Tournament appearances, more than 25 NCAA consensus All-America selections or at least 20 final wire-service Top 20 rankings. Only five of the 15 cream-of-the-crop schools have all-time winning records in head-to-head competition in national postseason play, however.

St. John's has compiled more victories in the National Invitation Tournament than any school, but the Red Storm don't rank among the leaders in winning percentage (more than 12 NIT decisions). Michigan's '97 championship enabled the Wolverines to move atop the NIT list (15-4, .789).

North Carolina's NCAA regional final victory over Louisville last season propelled the Tar Heels past Duke on the postseason "pick of the litter" chart. Here is a look at the head-to-head records in national postseason competition through 1997 among the nation's most storied programs:

		NCAA		NIT		OVERALL	
RK.	SCHOOL	W-L	PCT.	W-L	PCT.	W-L	PCT.
1.	UCLA	17-7	.708	2-0	1.000	19-7	.731
2.	North Carolina	19-11	.633	1-1	.500	20-12	.625
3.	Duke	16-9	.640	0-1	.000	16-10	.615
4.	Indiana	13-9	.591	0-1	.000	13-10	.565
5.	Kentucky	15-13	.536	1-1	.500	16-14	.533
6.	Louisville	13-13	.500	1-2	.333	14-15	.483
7.	Arkansas	11-11	.500	0-1	.500	11-12	.478
T8.	Georgetown	5-5	.500	0-1	.000	5-6	.455
T8.	Michigan	6-11	.353	4-1	.800	10-12	.455
10.	St. John's	4-8	.333	3-1	.750	7-9	.438
T11.	Syracuse	5-7	.417	1-1	.500	6-8	.429
T11.	Kansas	8-12	.400	1-0	1.000	9-12	.429
13.	Villanova	7-8	.467	1-3	.250	8-11	.421
14.	Notre Dame	3-11	.214	3-2	.600	6-13	.316
15.	Kansas State	2-9	.182	0-2	.000	2-11	.154

FROM RAGS TO RICHES?

Minnesota, the 1997 Big Ten Conference champion, became the eighth school to make a transformation since the tournament began seeding teams in 1979 from not participating in the NCAA playoffs one year to earning a No. 1 regional seed the next season. Many believe Michigan is capable of duplicating the feat in 1997-98.

One might become convinced the "famine to feast" turnarounds were too unsettling because none of the first eight schools in this category won the national championship. But it should be noted that all of them weren't totally out of the limelight the previous year, as each participated in the NIT.

The only school to be as many as six games below .500 in conference competition one year and earn a No. 1 regional seed the next season was Michigan State. The Spartans, a No. 1 seed in 1990, compiled a 6-12 Big Ten record in 1989. Here is a chronological look at the other about-faces (NCAA playoff record that year is in parentheses):

SCHOOL (REGIONAL)	PREVIOUS YR.	WHAT HAPPENED IN NCAA TOURNAMENT?
Indiana State '79 (Midwest)	23-9	Lost in national final (4-1 mark).
Kentucky '80 (Mideast)	19-12	Lost in regional semifinals (1-1).
Virginia '81 (East)	24-10	Lost in regional semifinals (3-1).
DePaul '84 (Midwest)	21-12	Lost in regional semifinals (1-1).
Michigan '85 (Southeast)	24-9	Lost in second round (1-1).
Connecticut '90 (East)	18-13	Lost in regional final (3-1).
Michigan St. '90 (Southeast)	18-15	Lost in regional semifinals (2-1).
Minnesota (Midwest)	19-13	Lost in national semifinals (4-1).

NOTE: Virginia (1980 champion), DePaul (1983 runner-up), Michigan (1984 champion) and Michigan State (1989 fourth place) reached the NIT "final four" the year before earning a No. 1 seed in the NCAA playoffs.

MISSISSIPPI BURNING

One can prove just about anything with statistics, but it shouldn't be shocking that Mississippi State reached the 1996 Final Four and that Ole Miss made such giant strides last season. The biggest surprise is that it took so long for them to flourish. Mississippi State made only one NCAA Tournament appearance until this decade and Ole Miss participated in the playoffs for just the second time in its history.

It's not a well-known fact, but Mississippi is burning in terms of supplying "premier" players. Mississippi boasts the best ratio population-wise of NCAA consensus first- and second-team All-Americas, Final Four Most Outstanding Players and NBA first-round draft choices from 1988 through 1997 (minimum of two players from these categories).

Yes, the South has risen again. Six of the top 9 states with the best ratios in the previous 10 years come from below the Mason and Dixon line. The following ranking of the top 10 states since 1988 are based on ratios using the 1993 population in thousands (number of NCAA consensus first- and second-team All-Americas, Final Four Most Outstanding Players and NBA first-round draft choices in that span are in parentheses):

RK.	STATE	RATIO
1.	Mississippi (11)	1:240
2.	Michigan (20)	1:474
3.	Maryland/D.C. (11)	1:504
4.	New Jersey (15)	1:525
5.	Georgia (13)	1:532
6.	Tennessee (9)	1:567
7.	Indiana (10)	1:571
8.	Virginia (11)	1:590
9.	Alabama (7)	1:598
10.	Oklahoma (4)	1:808

NOTE: Four of the five states with the highest totals of "premier" players—California (32), New York (16), Pennsylvania (13) and Illinois (14)—didn't have one of the top 10 ratios: Pennsylvania (ranked 16th at 1:927), Illinois (12th at 1:836), California (17th at 1:975), and New York (19th at 1:1,137).

HOW THE MIGHTY HAVE FALLEN

Of the schools to win NCAA Tournament championships since CCNY in 1950, only one of those institutions has not had an NBA first-round draft choice at any point in the last 17 years. The university with that dubious distinction is Marquette, whose only player of note to enter the pros since 1978 is guard Glenn "Doc" Rivers, a second-round draft choice in 1983 as an undergraduate. Marquette, despite two victories in the 1994 NCAA playoffs, has an abysmal 5-9 record in the tourney since capturing the national crown. The Warriors-turned-Golden Eagles went nine consecutive years without appearing in the NCAA playoffs from 1984-92.

DYNAMIC DUOS

Kansas, boasting standouts Raef LaFrentz and Paul Pierce, has a good opportunity to achieve the rare feat of having two NCAA consensus first-team All-Americans in the same season. Here is a chronological list of the first six different sets of teammates named NCAA consensus first-team All-Americans in the same year a total of nine times since the start of the NCAA Tournament in 1939:

SCHOOL	1ST-TEAM ALL-AMERICAN TEAMMATES	YEAR(S)
Kentucky	Ralph Beard and Alex Groza	1947 and 1949
Cincinnati	Ron Bonham and Tom Thacker	1963
UCLA	Henry Bibby and Bill Walton	1972
UCLA	Bill Walton and Keith Wilkes	1973 and 1974
Indiana	Kent Benson and Scott May	1976
North Carolina	Michael Jordan and Sam Perkins	1982 and 1983

TIME WARP

Here is how the 1997-98 preseason All-American team might have shaped up if players hadn't foregone their college eligibility to depart early for the NBA:

FIRST TEAM

G—Allen Iverson
G—Stephon Marbury
C—Shareef Abdur-Rahim
F—Kobe Bryant
F—Kevin Garnett

SECOND TEAM

G—Chauncey Billups
G—Antoine Walker
C—Lorenzen Wright
F—Danny Fortson
F—Ron Mercer

THIRD TEAM

G—Randy Livingston
G—God Shammgod
C—Adonal Foyle

F—Maurice Taylor
F—Tim Thomas

SEE YOU IN SAN ANTONIO

Undergraduate defectors once again played havoc with preseason rankings, but the vast majority of high profile schools will return to the NCAA Tournament. They'll be back among the headliners because whether or not they lost a player early, pinpointing the majority of perennial powers is simply a matter of reshuffling familiar names from the win crowd. After peering into college hoopdom's 1997-98 crystal ball, here is a rundown of the most likely candidates to be battling at the Alamodome in San Antonio by the end of March Madness:

Final Four Bound?

Arizona—Coach Lute Olson has a captivating collection of interchangeable talent at his disposal, especially pristine perimeter players such as Mike Bibby, Michael Dickerson, Miles Simon and Jason Terry. The defending NCAA champion Wildcats, who might possess the most Grade-A talent of any college squad, have stockpiled blue-chippers at every position. The College of Charleston and South Alabama showed in the early rounds of last year's NCAA playoffs that UA isn't invincible, however.

Duke—For all of its weapons, this no-frills brigade faces a difficult time reaching the Final Four if it doesn't receive sufficient output from at least some tough-minded youngsters. Nobody relishes the idea of opposing the Blue Devils, but quality teams can beat them because they are seemingly incapable of asserting the suffocating defensive pressure that previously was their trademark under coach Mike Krzyzewski. Duke will miss Jeff Capel and Greg Newton more than its rabid followers admit.

Kansas—On paper, it appears as if it will be business as usual for the Jayhawks, who have no apparent deficiencies. KU hasn't captured an NCAA title this decade although it is bound for its seventh final Top 10 finish in nine years and boasts the nation's top winning percentage in the

1990s. When Raef LaFrentz plays well, the Jayhawks are virtually unbeatable. Don't be surprised if Paul Pierce unseats LaFrentz as the team's top national player of the year candidate as he continues to hone his game.

North Carolina—Carolina is well-heeled as usual. It will be the end of Western civilization as we know it if UNC doesn't win more than 20 games for the 28th consecutive season or finishes fourth or lower in the mighty ACC for the first time since 1964. The Vince Carter-Ed Cota-Antawn Jamison triumvirate ranks among the top trios in coach Dean Smith's illustrious tenure.

Remainder of Top 10?

Clemson—Tigers loyalists can scarcely restrain themselves because the ingredients for excellence are in place. When you say Greg Buckner, you've said it all. The jack-of-all trades might not be the nation's most valuable player, but he could be the country's MVP of another sort—most versatile player. Observers fond of well-rounded players are enthralled with Buckner's multi-faceted talents. If Iker Iturbe and Terrell McIntyre smooth over some rough edges, Clemson could join Duke and North Carolina and help the ACC duplicate the Big East's 1985 achievement of having three Final Four teams.

Indiana—The Hoosiers have the talent, depth and experience to rebound from the embarrassment of three consecutive first-round losses in the NCAA playoffs and a negative off-season feature about coach Bob Knight's program in Sports Illustrated. It's inexcusable for a team with Jason Collier, A.J. Guyton and Andrae Patterson not to be in the top 20 and contending for a Big Ten title.

Kentucky—The loss of five NBA first-round draft choices the past two years and elegant craftsman Rick Pitino would cripple most programs, but the Wildcats have more than enough reinforcements to compensate this season. Look for redshirt guard Jeff Sheppard to become the Wildcats' big scorer. The problem for new mentor Tubby Smith will be down the road because Pitino had two mediocre recruiting classes in the last three years.

Michigan—The Wolverines have been bewilderingly inconsistent of late, and this year's edition will continue that trend if someone doesn't surface as an adequate playmaker. Off-the-court distractions have taken a toll and might further erode the focus of already inconsistent players such as Robert Traylor and Jerod Ward.

South Carolina—The Gamecocks, showcasing one of the premier backcourts in the country, are poised to set a school single-season record for most victories. Gifted guards B.J. McKie and Melvin Watson are a pleasure to watch.

UCLA—Erratic perimeter shooting is a blemish, but the outlook appears so promising that anything less than dominance will be deemed failure. A squad boasting the likes of Toby Bailey, J.R. Henderson and Jelani McCoy should not have too much difficulty challenging for the Pacific-10 championship despite defending NCAA kingpin Arizona's roster returning unscathed.

Top 25 Candidates

Arkansas—It would border on heresy to ignore this traditional power when assembling a list of top teams. Penetrator deluxe Kareem Reid and long-range marksman Pat Bradley are as potent a backcourt tandem as you can find. The Razorbacks will have trouble in the rugged SEC, however, if they don't develop a better defensive team than they've had the last couple of years.

Florida State—The talented Seminoles suffer from an occasional case of self-absorption, common to a young team unfamiliar with the unselfish teamwork needed to be the cream of the crop. Some of the finer points of the game escape this crew—like converting free throws at key moments, giving a consistent team-oriented effort, and not forcing silly passes and shots. Twin towers Corey Louis and Randell Jackson need to understand that "Me Generation" play is foolhardy.

Fresno State—Devoid of defects after bolstering their bench, the Bulldogs feature more athleticism than probably any roster in the nation. Whether coach Jerry Tarkanian's persistent problems with the NCAA stem from a "Shark Attack"

vendetta or not is questionable. But one thing is not: Tarkanian's renegade reputation will remain intact as long as he embraces a halfway-house mentality. Tarkanian's recruiting of suspect students leaves suspicion lingering that FSU has embraced a win-at-all-costs philosophy comparable to his previous programs at Long Beach State and UNLV.

Georgia—How will the Bulldogs respond after coach Tubby Smith's departure? Their success hinges on how junior college recruits respond to new mentor Ron Jirsa.

Illinois—With Lon Kruger at the helm, it will be a fluke if the resourceful Illini don't prosper. The continued development of Kevin Turner is paramount to helping offset the loss of standout guard Kiwane Garris.

Illinois State—If one accepts the premise that last season's undergraduates should automatically be better with a year of experience, then 25 victories is not out of the question for the Redbirds. Kevin Stallings, knowing he has something special on the horizon, will show outsiders why he rejected coaching jobs at more influential institutions.

Memphis—"Team Transition" has undergone an overhaul under new coach Tic Price, who should keep the Tigers among the nation's elite if a couple of junior college jewels shine.

Minnesota—The Gophers could remain in the driver's seat of the Big Ten if Sam Jacobson continues to hold his own with more heralded players in the league.

Mississippi—No appraisal of elite squads is complete without including the Rebels, despite the fact that they played in just their second NCAA Tournament last year. Ole Miss won't miss the NCAA playoffs this season.

New Mexico—The Lobos' chances of prospering are linked to Kenny Thomas' inside bravado. With a dynamic player such as Thomas on hand, UNM should post another standout season.

Purdue—Purists are infatuated with the Boilermakers, principally because of their unselfishness and willingness to play team defense. Purdue might be bound for its fourth outright Big Ten title in five years.

UNLV—Big things are expected of this squad, and it should challenge for a NCAA berth unless its old playground image during key games resurfaces. Center Keon Clark has pro written all over him.

Vanderbilt—The Commodores boast the firepower to move to the upper level of the SEC. They might have the finest frontcourt in the league.

Wisconsin—The Badgers won't be as one-dimensional as many observers think. Forward Sam Okey is capable of becoming the school's first Big Ten Player of the Year since 1950.

Xavier—Could wind up in the Top 10 if everything falls into place. The Musketeers rule in Cincinnati. They have a dependable backcourt and tough frontcourt.

25 At-Large Invitees?

Cincinnati—Coach Bob Huggins has signed far too many suspect students who can't spell graduation. UC looks more and more like the "UNLV of the Midwest."

Colorado State—If you're fond of darkhorses, take a ride this year with the Rams.

Connecticut—The big question mark for UConn is whether swingman Richard Hamilton becomes the Huskies' player to turn to in the clutch.

George Washington—Returning a strong nucleus, there should be a federal investigation if GWU doesn't emerge as the premier team among universities near the nation's capital. Alexander Koul could become the talk of the nation by the end of the season as the next great foreign center, especially if he earns a spot as the school's first NCAA consensus All-American. Diminutive Shawnta Rogers (5-3) could eventually challenge former Wake Forest sensation Tyrone Bogues (5-3) as the best mighty mite in college history.

Iowa—The Hawkeyes stand on the threshold of their first undisputed Big Ten title in 28 years.

They won't excel, however, unless forward Jess Settles returns in a big way from the injured list and becomes the school's first NCAA consensus first- or second-team All-American since 1952.

Louisville—Traditionally lethal attack could stall if no one steps forward to adequately replace DeJuan Wheat.

Marquette—Under coach Mike Deane's tutelage, the Golden Eagles have initiative and ferocity, two qualities not easily instilled. They'll rely on those characteristics in their quest for the school's first final Top 10 finish since 1979.

Maryland—Will coach Gary Williams ever win a conference tournament?

Michigan State—Keep an eye on guard Mateen Cleaves, a budding All-American.

N.C. State—Was the Wolfpack's sterling ACC Tournament performance last season an illusion?

Oklahoma—Should be one of the nation's most entertaining teams. Coach Kelvin Sampson won't generate the national respect he deserves until he wins at least one NCAA playoff game.

Oklahoma State—Expect another exceptionally strong defensive squad with just enough scoring to contend in the Big 12's South Division.

Rhode Island—Playmaker deluxe Tyson Wheeler can turn any game into his showcase.

St. John's—For all its promising talent, the Red Storm remains a questionable commodity.

St. Joseph's—Rashid Bey is one of the premier backcourters in the guard-dominated Atlantic 10.

Southwest Missouri State—If the Bears can offset the departure of forward Coleco Buie, they could claw their way into the Top 25.

Stanford—In an era practically devoid of intimidating big men, Tim Young will be the difference between a middle-of-the-pack team in a prestigious league and a strong tourney team if he gets any help at all from the perimeter.

Syracuse—For all their assets, the Orangemen won't challenge for a Big East championship unless Todd Burgan plays like he did at the 1996 Final Four.

Temple—Never underestimate the Owls' fighting spirit.

Texas—Coach Tom Penders averaged 22 victories annually in his first nine seasons with the Longhorns and there's no reason to expect things to change.

TCU—The Horned Frogs, perhaps the country's best-kept secret, play with confidence or arrogance, depending on your point of view. When Mike Jones and James Penny are at the top of their games, TCU can compete with anybody.

Utah—All-America Keith Van Horn is gone, but center Michael Doleac and guard Andre Miller comprise one of the best inside-outside combinations in the country.

Virginia—Courtney Alexander and Curtis Staples are capable of becoming All-Americans although there are times they seem to play like All-Underachievers.

Washington—Anyone with an ounce of hoop expertise can tell that this squad will be a national force one day under coach Bob Bender.

West Virginia—Forward Damian Owens could blossom into Big East player of the year.

25 Sleepers

Arizona State—Guard Jeremy Veal is as explosive as any player in the country.

Baylor—Center Brian Skinner and guard Roddrick Miller remain undiscovered treasures, but they could blossom into one of the nation's foremost inside-outside combinations.

Butler—The Bulldogs should successfully defending their Midwestern Collegiate Conference crown unless some seniors turn stale.

Eastern Michigan—Diminutive Earl Boykins brings a unique dimension of creativity to the Eagles.

Hawaii—The Rainbows still need to exhibit an ability to win on the road, which is easier said than done inasmuch as the shortest WAC trip for them is more than 2,000 miles one way.

Long Island—Welcoming back a solid core of experienced players, LIU is even better than advertised.

Miami (Fla.)—It's time for coach Leonard Hamilton to finally deliver the Hurricanes' first NCAA tourney team since 1960.

Missouri—Optimism is high that Mizzou won't be bothered by the absence of an intimidating center.

Montana State—Could help the Big Sky Conference gain an at-large berth in the NCAA Tournament for the first time.

Nebraska—Mexico, Mo., products Tyronn Lue and Cookie Belcher keep the Cornhuskers competitive in the rugged Big 12.

UNC Charlotte—DeMarco Johnson shows signs of becoming Conference USA player of the year.

Northern Arizona—One of the premier outside shooting teams in the country.

Northern Iowa—The Panthers will make a strong showing in the Missouri Valley if they can offset the loss of guard Jason Daisy.

Notre Dame—Irish eyes will be crying if Pat Garrity doesn't lead the glamour boys of the Midwest to the school's first NCAA Tournament triumph this decade.

Ohio State—Jim O'Brien has inherited more talent than most observers know about.

Old Dominion—Despite the departure of standout center Odell Hodge, it's easy to understand why ODU is the prohibitive favorite in the Colonial Athletic Association.

Oral Roberts—High-scoring guard Tim Gill is expected to help the Titans challenge Valparaiso for conference supremacy in their first year in the Mid-Continent.

Oregon State—Don't be surprised if the Beavers perform far beyond expectations.

Pacific—The Tigers are earmarked to dominate again in the West Division of the Big West Conference.

Pepperdine—"Transfer Tech" has the assets to surpass the Waves' total of 10 WCC victories the previous three years.

Princeton—The Tigers have got the Ivy League by the tail and could go undefeated in conference competition for the second straight season.

Tennessee—Kevin O'Neill did not leave the cupboard completely bare for new coach Jerry Green.

Tulsa—Forward Michael Ruffin will challenge for WAC Player of the Year honors if he improves his free-throw shooting.

Utah State—The Aggies should thrive behind the nation's most underrated backcourt (Justin Jones and Duane Rogers).

Valparaiso—Guard Bryce Drew would be bound for All-American honors if he played in a more prestigious league.

REGULAR-SEASON LEAGUE CHAMPION PROJECTIONS

AMERICA EAST—Hartford
ATLANTIC COAST—North Carolina
ATLANTIC 10 (EAST)—Rhode Island
ATLANTIC 10 (WEST)—Xavier
BIG EAST 7—Syracuse
BIG EAST 6—West Virginia
BIG SKY—Northern Arizona

BIG SOUTH—UNC Asheville
BIG TEN—Iowa
BIG 12 (NORTH)—Kansas
BIG 12 (SOUTH)—Oklahoma
BIG WEST (EAST)—New Mexico State
BIG WEST (WEST)—Pacific
COLONIAL—Old Dominion
CONFERENCE USA (AMERICAN)—Marquette
CONFERENCE USA (NATIONAL)—UNC Charlotte
IVY LEAGUE—Princeton
METRO ATLANTIC—Iona
MID-AMERICAN—Bowling Green
MID-CONTINENT—Valparaiso
MID-EASTERN ATHLETIC—Coppin State
MIDWESTERN COLLEGIATE—Butler
MISSOURI VALLEY—Illinois State
NORTHEAST—Long Island
OHIO VALLEY—Austin Peay
PACIFIC-10—Arizona
PATRIOT LEAGUE—Navy
SOUTHEASTERN (EAST)—South Carolina
SOUTHEASTERN (WEST)—Mississippi
SOUTHERN (NORTH)—Davidson
SOUTHERN (SOUTH)—The Citadel
SOUTHLAND—Northeast Louisiana
SOUTHWESTERN ATHLETIC—Alcorn State
SUN BELT—New Orleans
TRANS AMERICA ATHLETIC (EAST)—Fla. International
TRANS AMERICA ATHLETIC (WEST)—Samford

15

CONFERENCE DIRECTORY

The nation's NCAA Division I schools have been in a frenetic restructuring of conferences although the quest for megaleagues might be a delusion because they're vying for television revenue that simply doesn't exist anymore as network sports divisions operate at ample deficits.

Only three Division I conferences remained intact since the late 1980s—the Ivy League, Pacific-10 and West Coast. Although the TV well is dry and no amount of realigning will alter the marketplace, almost one-third of the more than 300 Division I schools changed conferences or shed independent status so far in the 1990s.

A time-honored argument rages each season on the court: Which conference plays the best basketball? The debate attained new heights since the Big East's initial campaign, 1980, the year the NCAA Tournament expanded its field to 48 teams. Naturally, the NCAA playoffs are an accurate barometer to determine the longstanding or recent strength of a league. Consider the following postseason achievements:

• The ACC is the only league to have each of its members play at least 10 games in the NCAA

playoffs. Incredibly, all nine ACC members have winning NCAA Tournament records and advanced to the Sweet 16 since the field expanded to 64 teams. Perhaps the greatest testimony to the ACC's consistent brilliance is the league's average of 11 tournament victories annually from 1983 through 1995.

• The Big East is the only league to have three representatives at a single Final Four—Georgetown, St. John's and Villanova in 1985 after they all defeated ACC members in regional finals. The Big East has had eight different schools win undisputed league titles since its formation in 1980. In 1995-96, the Big East became the only conference ever to have three different members represented on the NCAA consensus first-team All-American squad.

• Entering the 1998 NCAA Tournament, the Big Ten had the most Final Four teams (34) and most different members win the NCAA title (five).

• The Big Eight portion of the fledgling Big 12 sent more teams (six) to the 1992 NCAA Tournament than any league and tied the ACC for the most playoff delegates in 1993 with six. In 1988,

Kansas and Oklahoma enabled the Big Eight to become the only league to have two members meet in the NCAA final from 1986-97.

• The Atlantic 10 and Conference USA were the only leagues to have five 20-win teams in 1995-96. Current A10 members combined to win more NIT titles than any league (11). C-USA is the only league with all of its members having reached the national semifinals of the NCAA Tournament or NIT at some point in their history.

• The Pacific-10, with nine of its 10 schools advancing to the NCAA semifinals at least once, boasts the highest percentage of present league members to reach the Final Four. Pac-10 schools captured two of the last three NCAA crowns.

• In 1994, the SEC compiled the best winning percentage in a single tourney for a league with at least three entrants (12-3 record, .800). The SEC won more NCAA Tournament games than any conference from 1994 through 1996.

1997-98 Preseason League Ratings

1. ATLANTIC COAST—Poised to have five top 20 to 25 teams. At least one of them WILL probably reach the Final Four, where the league has been represented in nine of the previous 10 seasons. The ACC has had more national players of the year than any league since its formation in the mid-1950s. North Carolina's Antawn Jamison might be next in line for such acclaim after Wake Forest center Tim Duncan became the 10th such honoree last year.

2. PACIFIC-10—Could challenge the ACC as the nation's premier league if Arizona State and Oregon State make strong turnarounds as some observers project. With nine of its 10 schools advancing to the NCAA Tournament semifinals at least once, the Pac-10 boasts the highest percentage of present league members to reach the Final Four.

3. SOUTHEASTERN—The SEC, despite a modest 5-5 mark in 1997, compiled more NCAA playoff victories (50) than any league the previous five seasons. Averaged almost nine NBA draft choices annually the past 15 years, including an amazing 13 choices in the two rounds of the 1996 draft. The lack of media centers is the main reason why the league did not have a national coach of the year outside Kentucky until Vanderbilt's Eddie Fogler in 1993 and also why it has captured only two of the principal national player of the year awards since UPI's initial winner in 1955.

4. BIG TEN—Restoring damaged prestige is on the horizon even if no member reaches the Final Four. The Big Ten has had more individuals than any other league earn national coach of the year acclaim. Nonetheless, its reputation has been tarnished this decade despite having four consecutive national players of the year from 1992 through 1995. The league came within eight points of going 0-11 in the NCAA playoffs in 1995 and 1996.

5. BIG 12—Will anyone join Kansas among the nation's top 20 to 25 teams? The Jayhawks could be alone among the elite because Colorado, Iowa State and Texas Tech appear bound for significant nosedives from a year ago.

6. BIG EAST—In 1995-96, the Big East became the only league ever to have three different members represented among the NCAA consensus first-team All-America selections. This year, it might not possess a Top 25 team.

7. ATLANTIC 10—Remains consistently on par, if not superior, to the Big East even after the Big East lured three members away. Don't be surprised if the A10 has three teams rated higher than anyone from the Big East this season.

8. WESTERN ATHLETIC—Rugged road trips test your mettle in this underrated alliance. How potent would the WAC be if perennial powers Brigham Young and Texas-El Paso hadn't fallen on hard times?

9. CONFERENCE USA—If Cincinnati, Louisville and Marquette fall off much, the C-USA might not have a Top 40 club.

10. MISSOURI VALLEY—Potent one-two punch in Illinois State and Southwest Missouri State enables MVC to continue steady but slow ascension up the league ladder. How much longer

will the league be able to retain young turk coaches Kevin Stallings of ISU and Steve Alford of SWMS?

11. MID-AMERICAN—Perennial winner of unofficial award as the biggest overachiever. Who'll be the next up-and-coming coach to depart after Herb Sendek, who left for N.C. State, and Ben Braun, who left for Cal?

12. COLONIAL—Could possess one of the best collection of coaches in the country if overhaul since last season pans out.

13. WEST COAST—It's time for another WCC program to burst upon the national scene like Loyola Marymount did several years ago.

14. SUN BELT—Departure of rising stars in the coaching ranks such as Tim Floyd (from New Orleans to Iowa State), Tic Price (UNO to Memphis) and Ralph Willard (Western Kentucky to Pitt) thwarts league's chances of earning ranking among Top 10.

15. BIG WEST—Defections of Fresno State and UNLV to the WAC plus New Mexico State's off-the-court problems have done immeasurable damage.

16. MIDWESTERN COLLEGIATE—Exits this decade of Dayton, Duquesne, Evansville, La Salle, Marquette, Saint Louis and Xavier to other leagues have been devastating.

17. AMERICA EAST—Drexel coach Bill Herrion is a name to remember.

18. METRO ATLANTIC—Vibrancy stems from more than half of the league's coaches being at their outposts less than four years.

19. IVY LEAGUE—Would consistently be ranked among the top 10 of 12 conferences if another cerebral school or two joined the prosperous programs at Penn and Princeton.

20. MID-CONTINENT—Making giant strides while members, including newcomer, Oral Roberts, try to keep up with Valparaiso's resurgence.

21. SOUTHERN—Tennessee-Chattanooga showed in the 1997 NCAA playoffs that the league deserved an at-large bid.

22. NORTHEAST—Could rank among the top 15 leagues if another school or two can keep pace with lethal LIU.

23. BIG SOUTH—Lack of quality competition reflected by four different schools earning undisputed back-to-back titles in the league's first 12 seasons.

24. BIG SKY—Defections of Boise State and Idaho to the Big West and Weber State's travails have damaged this loop.

25. OHIO VALLEY—Entertaining league proved it's capable of duplicating its feat when it won three consecutive NCAA Tournament first-round games from 1987 through 1989.

26. SOUTHLAND—Return of Lamar could help spur a revival.

27. MID-EASTERN ATHLETIC—No member seems capable of challenging Coppin State, which captured seven of the last eight regular-season titles.

28. PATRIOT LEAGUE—Headlines will be scarce since Adonal Foyle left Colgate early.

29. SOUTHWESTERN ATHLETIC—Return of coach Davey Whitney to Alcorn State isn't enough to rekindle glory years.

30. TRANS AMERICA ATHLETIC—There is little else to brag about other than the College of Charleston.

Putting provincialism aside, here are vital facts on Division I conferences. Each season is denoted by a single year. For example, the ACC's first season in 1953-54 is listed as 1954. The numbers in parentheses after schools with regular-season champions denote undisputed titles first and then ties. Totals for NCAA Tournament records reflect actual conference membership for each season.

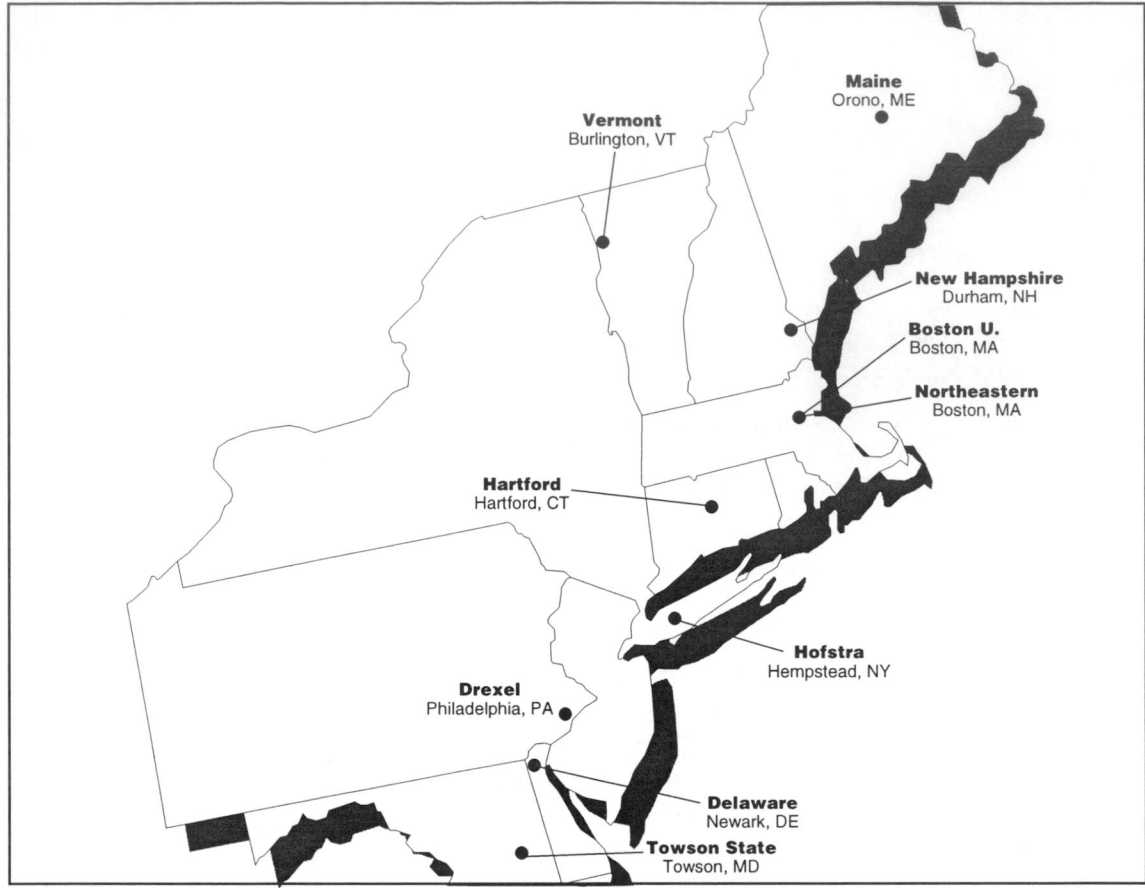

Maine
Orono, ME

Vermont
Burlington, VT

New Hampshire
Durham, NH

Boston U.
Boston, MA

Northeastern
Boston, MA

Hartford
Hartford, CT

Hofstra
Hempstead, NY

Drexel
Philadelphia, PA

Delaware
Newark, DE

Towson State
Towson, MD

AMERICA EAST

ADDRESS: 32 Main Street, P.O. Box 69, Orono, ME 04473 (relocating to Boston area).

PHONE/FAX: (207) 866-2383/7524.

PREVIOUS NAMES: ECAC North (1980-82), ECAC North Atlantic (1983-89), North Atlantic (1990-96).

CURRENT MEMBERS: Boston University (1980-98), Delaware (1992-98), Drexel (1992-98), Hartford (1986-98), Hofstra (1995-98), Maine (1980-98), New Hampshire (1980-98), Northeastern (1980-98), Towson State (1996-98), Vermont (1980-98).

FORMER MEMBERS: Canisius (1980-89), Colgate (1980-90), Holy Cross (1980-83), Niagara (1980-89), Rhode Island (1980), Siena (1985-89).

NCAA TOURNAMENT RECORD: 5-18 (.217).

ALL-TIME SCORING LEADER: Reggie Lewis, Northeastern (2,709 points from 1984-87).

SINGLE-SEASON SCORING LEADERS: Vin Baker, Hartford (792 points in 1992-93) and Mike Ferrara, Colgate (28.6 points per game in 1980-81).

REGULAR-SEASON CHAMPIONS: Boston University (1 outright-2 ties), Canisius (0-1), Delaware (1-0), Drexel (3-1), New Hampshire (0-1), Northeastern (6-4), Siena (2-0).

AEC Tournament Titles: Northeastern (7; 1981-82-84-85-86-87-91), Boston University (4; 1983-88-90-97), Drexel (3; 1994-95-96), Delaware (2; 1992 and 1993), Holy Cross (1; 1980), Siena (1; 1989).

YEAR-BY-YEAR CHAMPIONS (incl. conference records): **1982**—Northeastern (8-1); **1983**—Boston U. (8-2), New Hampshire (8-2); **1984**—Northeastern (14-0); **1985**—Canisius (13-3), Northeastern (13-3); **1986**—Northeastern (16-2); **1987**—Northeastern (17-1); **1988**—Siena (16-2); **1989**—Siena (16-1); **1990**—Boston U. (9-3), Northeastern (9-3); **1991**—Northeastern (8-2); **1992**—Delaware (14-0); **1993**—Drexel (12-2), Northeastern (12-2); **1994**—Drexel (12-2); **1995**—Drexel (12-4); **1996**—Drexel (17-1); **1997**-Boston University (17-1)

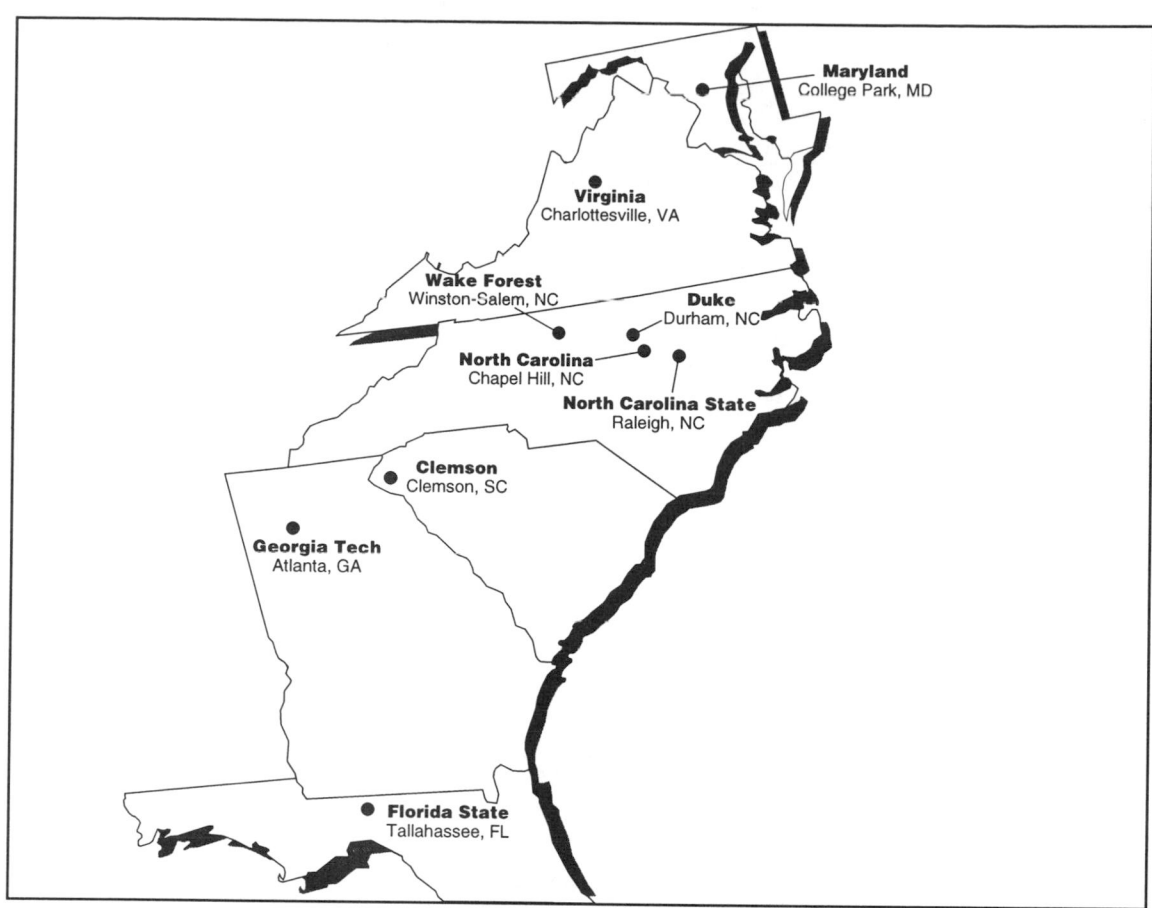

ATLANTIC COAST

ADDRESS: 6011 Landmark Center Boulevard, Post Office Drawer ACC, Greensboro, NC 27419-6999.

PHONE/FAX: (910) 854-8787/8797.

INTERNET ADDRESS: www.acc.com

CURRENT MEMBERS: Clemson (1954-98), Duke (1954-98), Florida State (1992-98), Georgia Tech (1980-98), Maryland (1954-98), North Carolina (1954-98), North Carolina State (1954-98), Virginia (1954-98), Wake Forest (1954-98).

Former Member: South Carolina (1954-71).

NCAA TOURNAMENT RECORD: 237-120 (.664).

NCAA TITLES (7): Duke (1991 and 1992), North Carolina (1957-82-93), North Carolina State (1974 and 1983).

NIT TITLES (4): Maryland (1972), North Carolina (1971), Virginia (1980 and 1992).

ALL-TIME SCORING LEADER: Johnny Dawkins, Duke (2,556 points from 1983-86). Dickie Hemric of Wake Forest (1952-55) scored 2,587 points, but the first two seasons of his career preceded the formation of the ACC.

SINGLE-SEASON SCORING LEADERS: Buzz Wilkinson, Virginia (32.1 points per game in 1954-55) and Dennis Scott, Georgia Tech (960 points in 1989-90).

REGULAR-SEASON CHAMPIONS: Clemson (1 outright-0 ties), Duke (12-0), Georgia Tech (1-1), Maryland (2-1), North Carolina (14-8), North Carolina State (4-3), South Carolina (1-0), Virginia (1-3), Wake Forest (1-2).

ACC TOURNAMENT TITLES: North Carolina (14; 1957-67-68-69-72-75-77-79-81-82-89-91-94-97), N.C. State (10; 1954-55-56-59-65-70-73-74-83-87), Duke (9; 1960-63-64-66-78-80-86-88-92), Wake Forest (4; 1961-62-95-96), Georgia Tech (3; 1985-90-93), Maryland (2; 1958 and 1984), South Carolina (1; 1971), Virginia (1; 1976).

YEAR-BY-YEAR CHAMPIONS (incl. conference records): 1954—Duke (9-1); **1955**—N.C. State (12-2); **1956**—North Carolina (11-3), N.C. State (11-3); **1957**—North Carolina (14-0); **1958**—Duke (11-3); **1959**—North Carolina (12-2), N.C. State (12-2); **1960**—North Carolina (12-2), Wake Forest (12-2); **1961**—North Carolina (12-2); **1962**—Wake Forest (12-2); **1963**—Duke (14-0); **1964**—Duke (13-1); **1965**—Duke (11-3); **1966**—Duke (12-2); **1967**—North Carolina (12-2); **1968**—North Carolina (12-2); **1969**—North Carolina (12-2); **1970**—South Carolina (14-0); **1971**—North Carolina (11-3); **1972**—North Carolina (9-3); **1973**—N.C. State (12-0); **1974**—N.C. State (12-0); **1975**—Maryland (10-2); **1976**—North Carolina (11-1); **1977**—North Carolina (9-3); **1978**—North Carolina (9-3); **1979**—Duke (9-3), North Carolina (9-3); **1980**—Maryland (11-3); **1981**—Virginia (13-1); **1982**—North Carolina (12-2), Virginia (12-2); **1983**—North Carolina (12-2), Virginia (12-2); **1984**—North Carolina (14-0); **1985**—Georgia Tech (9-5), North Carolina (9-5), N.C. State (9-5); **1986**—Duke (12-2); **1987**—North Carolina (14-0); **1988**—North Carolina (11-3); **1989**—N.C. State (10-4); **1990**—Clemson (10-4); **1991**—Duke (11-3); **1992**—Duke (14-2); **1993**—North Carolina (14-2); **1994**—Duke (12-4); **1995**—Maryland (12-4), North Carolina (12-4), Virginia (12-4), Wake Forest (12-4); **1996**—Georgia Tech (13-3); **1997**—Duke (12-4).

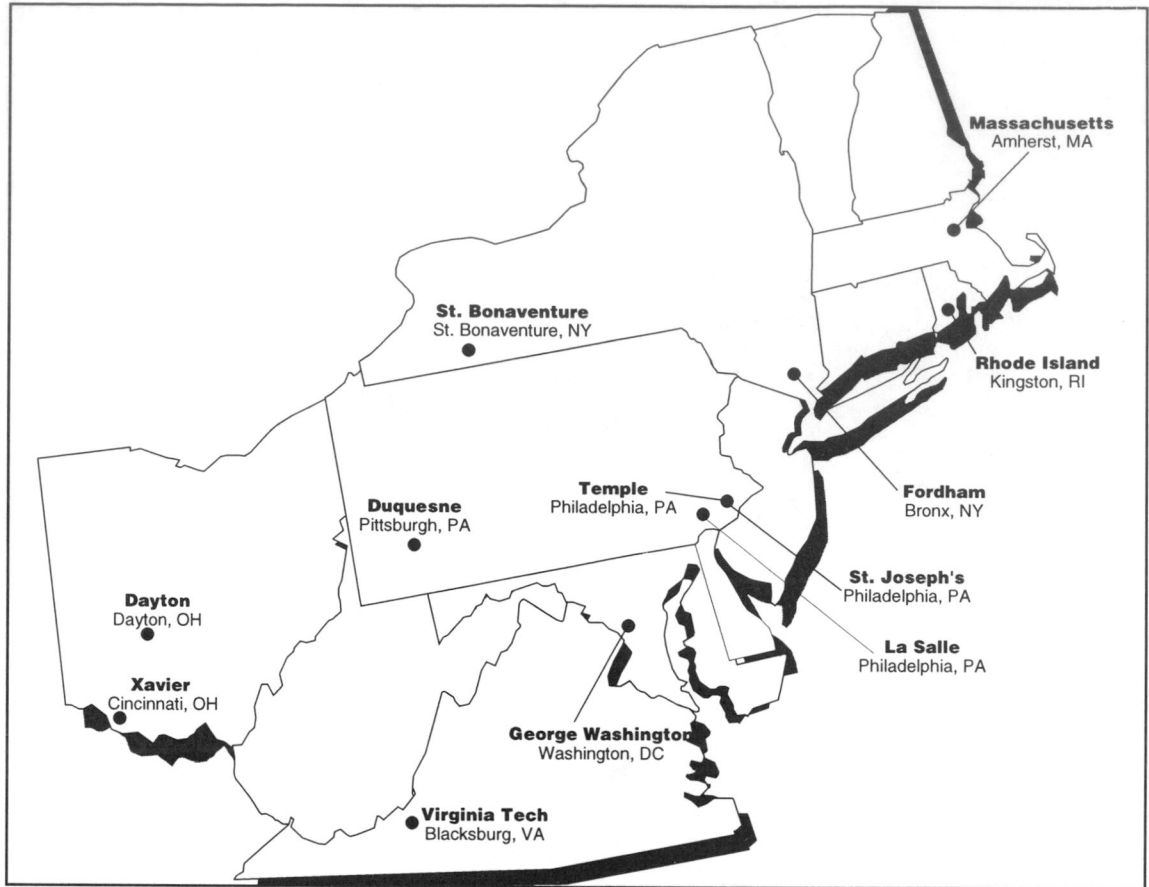

ATLANTIC 10

ADDRESS: 2 Penn Center Plaza, Suite 1410, Philadelphia, PA 19102.

PHONE/FAX: (215) 751-0500/0770.

INTERNET ADDRESS: www.atlantic10.org

PREVIOUS NAMES: Eastern Collegiate Basketball League (1977), Eastern Athletic Association or Eastern 8 (1978 through 1982).

CURRENT MEMBERS: Dayton (1996-98), Duquesne (1977-98 except for 1993), Fordham (1996-98), George Washington (1977-98), La Salle (1996-98), Massachusetts (1977-98), Rhode Island (1981-98), St. Bonaventure (1980-98), St. Joseph's (1983-98), Temple (1983-98), Virginia Tech (1996-98), Xavier (1996-98).

FORMER MEMBERS: Penn State (1977-79 and 1983-91), Pittsburgh (1977-82), Rutgers (1977-95), West Virginia (1977-95), Villanova (1977-80).

NCAA TOURNAMENT RECORD: 48-46 (.511).

NCAA TITLES (1): La Salle (1954) won championship before the conference was formed.

NIT TITLES (11): Dayton (1962 and 1968), Duquesne (1955), La Salle (1952), St. Bonaventure (1977), Temple (1938 and 1969), Virginia Tech (1973 and 1995), West Virginia (1942) and Xavier (1958) won before joining Atlantic 10.

ALL-TIME SCORING LEADER: Mark Macon, Temple (2,609 points from 1988-91).

SINGLE-SEASON SCORING LEADER: Mark Stevenson, Duquesne (788 points and 27.2 ppg in 1989-90).

REGULAR-SEASON CHAMPIONS: Duquesne (0 outright-2 ties), George Washington (0-1), Massachusetts (5-0), Penn State (0-1), Rhode Island (0-1), Rutgers (3-2), St. Bonaventure (0-1), St. Joseph's (2-0), Temple (4-0), Villanova (1-2), Virginia Tech (0-1), West Virginia (3-2), Xavier (1-0).

ATLANTIC 10 TOURNAMENT TITLES: Massachusetts (5; 1992-93-94-95-96), Temple (4; 1985-87-88-90), Pittsburgh (2; 1981 and 1982), Rutgers (2; 1979 and 1989), St. Joseph's (2; 1986 and 1997), Villanova (2; 1978 and 1980), West Virginia (2; 1983 and 1984), Duquesne (1; 1977), Penn State (1; 1991).

YEAR-BY-YEAR CHAMPIONS (incl. conference records): 1977—Rutgers (7-1/E), Penn State (5-5/W), West Virginia (5-5/W); **1978**—Rutgers (7-3), Villanova (7-3); 1979—Villanova (9-1); **1980**—Duquesne (7-3), Rutgers (7-3), Villanova (7-3); **1981**—Duquesne (10-3), Rhode Island (10-3); **1982**—West Virginia (13-1); **1983**—Rutgers (11-3/E), St. Bonaventure (10-4/W), West Virginia (10-4/W); **1984**—Temple (18-0); **1985**—West Virginia (16-2); **1986**—St. Joseph's (16-2); **1987**—Temple (17-1); **1988**—Temple (18-0); **1989**—West Virginia (17-1); **1990**—Temple (15-3); **1991**—Rutgers (14-4); **1992**—Massachusetts (13-3); **1993**—Massachusetts (11-3); **1994**—Massachusetts (14-2); **1995**—Massachusetts (13-3); **1996**—Massachusetts (15-1/E), George Washington (13-3/W), Virginia Tech (13-3/W); **1997**—St. Joseph's (13-3/E); Xavier (13-3/W).

NOTE: The Atlantic 10 had Eastern and Western Divisions for one season in 1982-83. The league resumed divisional play in 1996.

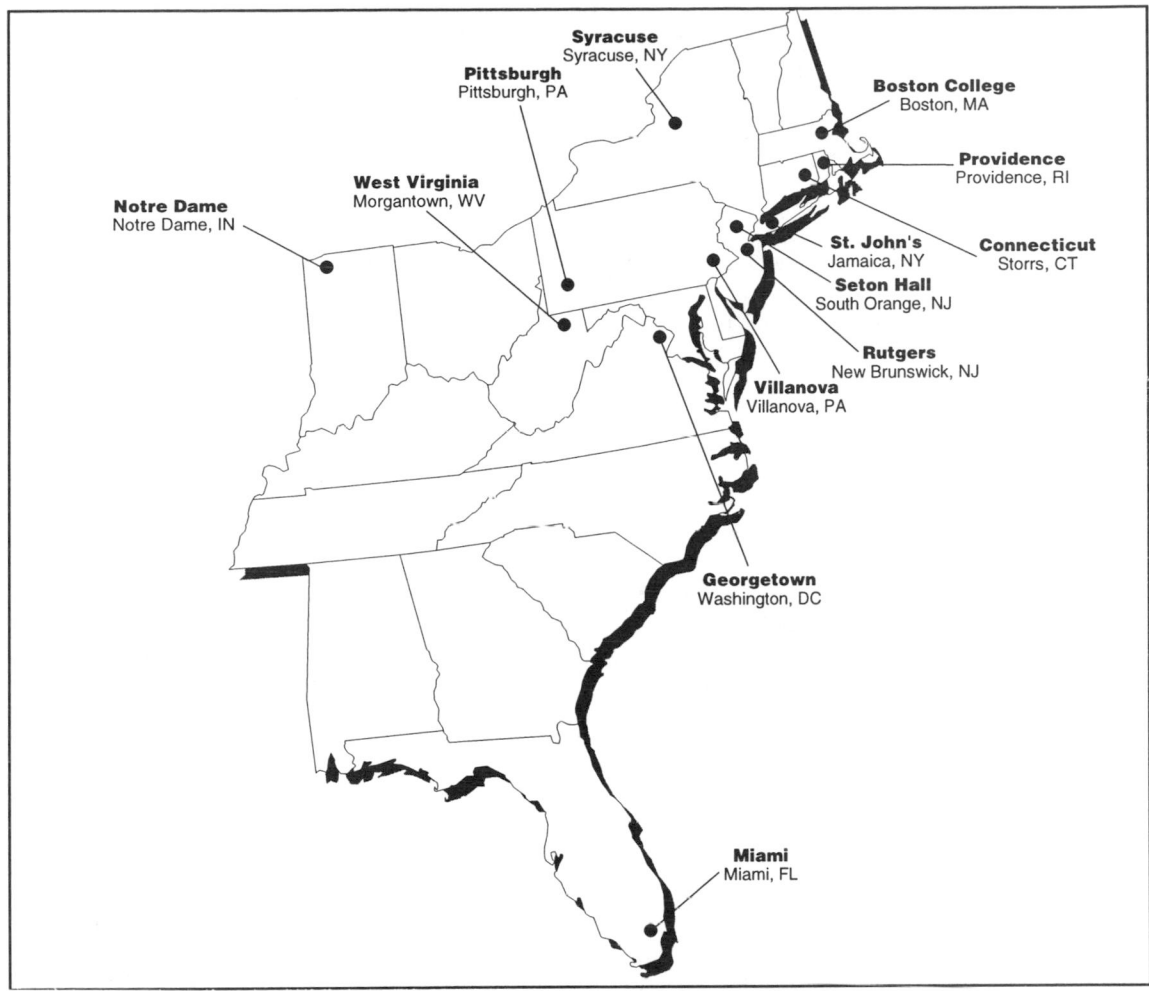

Syracuse
Syracuse, NY

Pittsburgh
Pittsburgh, PA

Boston College
Boston, MA

Providence
Providence, RI

West Virginia
Morgantown, WV

Notre Dame
Notre Dame, IN

St. John's
Jamaica, NY

Connecticut
Storrs, CT

Seton Hall
South Orange, NJ

Rutgers
New Brunswick, NJ

Villanova
Villanova, PA

Georgetown
Washington, DC

Miami
Miami, FL

BIG EAST

ADDRESS: 56 Exchange Terrace, Providence, RI 02903.

PHONE/FAX: (401) 453-0660, 272-9108/751-8540.

INTERNET ADDRESS: To be determined .

CURRENT MEMBERS: Boston College (1980-98), Connecticut (1980-98), Georgetown (1980-98), Miami, Fla. (1992-98), Notre Dame (1996-98), Pittsburgh (1983-98), Providence (1980-98), Rutgers (1996-98), St. John's (1980-98), Seton Hall (1980-98), Syracuse (1980-98), Villanova (1981-98), West Virginia (1996-98).

NCAA TOURNAMENT RECORD: 139-83 (.626).

NCAA TITLES (2): Georgetown (1984) and Villanova (1985).

NIT TITLES (10): Connecticut (1988), Providence (1961 and 1963), St. John's (1943-44-59-65-89), Seton Hall (1953), Villanova (1994). Three of the titles were earned since the formation of the league.

ALL-TIME SCORING LEADER: Terry Dehere, Seton Hall (2,494 points from 1990-93).

REGULAR-SEASON CHAMPIONS: Boston College (1 outright-2 ties), Connecticut (3-1), Georgetown (4-3), Pittsburgh (1-1), St. John's (1-4), Seton Hall (1-1), Syracuse (1-4), Villanova (1-2).

BIG EAST TOURNAMENT TITLES: Georgetown (6; 1980-82-84-85-87-89), Syracuse (3; 1981-88-92), Connecticut (2; 1990 and 1996), St. John's (2; 1983 and 1986), Seton Hall (2; 1991 and 1993), Boston College (1; 1997), Providence (1; 1994), Villanova (1; 1995).

YEAR-BY-YEAR CHAMPIONS (incl. conference records): 1980—Georgetown (5-1), St. John's (5-1), Syracuse (5-1); **1981**—Boston College (10-4); **1982**—Villanova (11-3); **1983**—Boston College (12-4), St. John's (12-4), Villanova (12-4); **1984**—Georgetown (14-2); **1985**—St. John's (15-1); **1986**—St. John's (14-2), Syracuse (14-2); **1987**—Georgetown (12-4), Pittsburgh (12- 4), Syracuse (12-4); **1988**—Pittsburgh (12-4); **1989**—Georgetown (13-3); **1990**—Connecticut (12-4), Syracuse (12-4); **1991**—Syracuse (12-4); **1992**—Georgetown (12-6), St. John's (12-6), Seton Hall (12-6); **1993**—Seton Hall (14-4); **1994**—Connecticut (16-2); **1995**—Connecticut (16-2); **1996**—Connecticut (17-1/BE 6), Georgetown (13-5/BE 7); **1997**—Boston College (12-6/BE 6), Villanova (12-6/BE 6); Georgetown (11-7/BE 7).

NOTE: League split into two divisions in 1996—Big East 7 (Georgetown, Miami, Pittsburgh, Providence, Rutgers, Seton Hall and Syracuse) and Big East 6 (Boston College, Connecticut, Notre Dame, St. John's, Villanova and West Virginia).

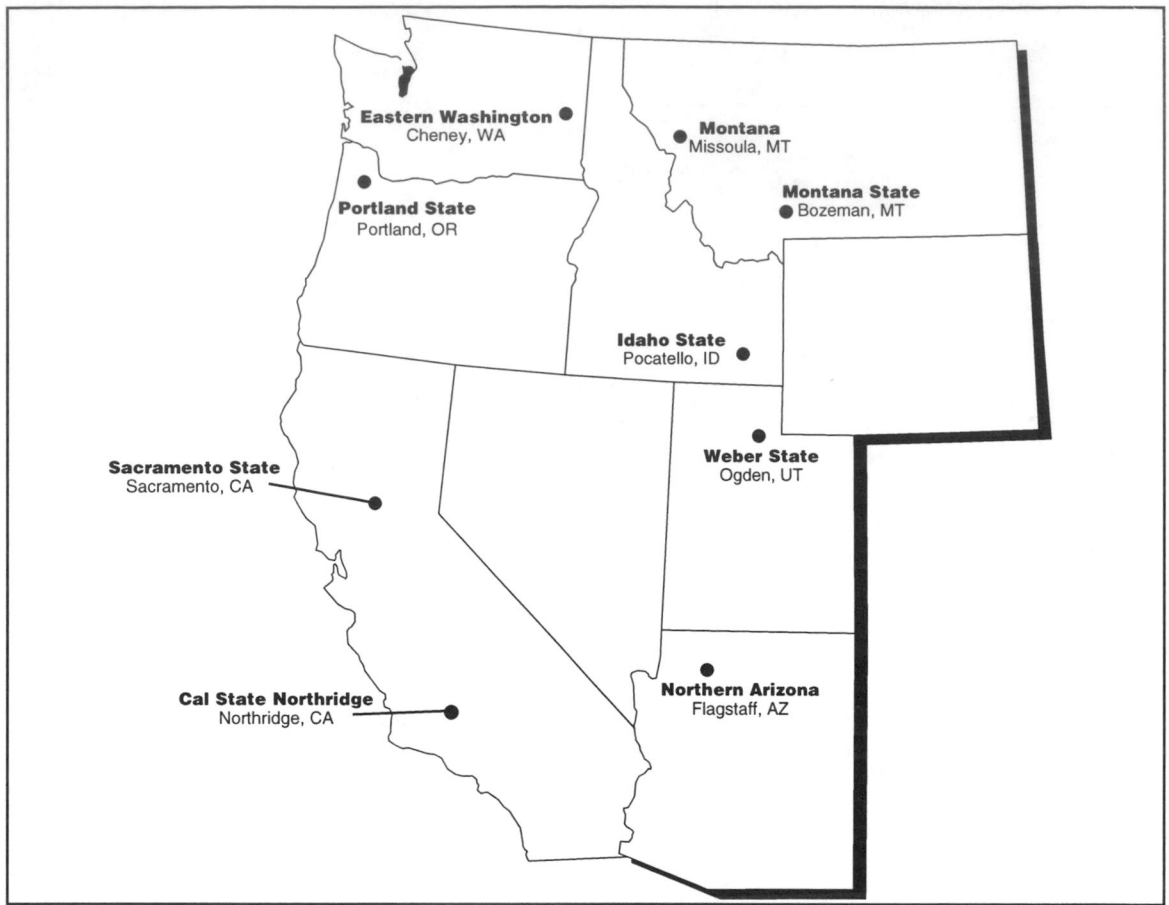

BIG SKY

ADDRESS: Post Office Box 1459, Ogden, UT 84402.

PHONE/FAX: (801) 392-1978/5568.

INTERNET ADDRESS: www.bigskyconf.com

CURRENT MEMBERS: Cal State Northridge (1997 and 1998), Eastern Washington (1988-98), Idaho State (1964-98), Montana (1964-98), Montana State (1964-98), Northern Arizona (1971-98), Portland State (1997 and 1998), Sacramento State (1997 and 1998), Weber State (1964-98).

FORMER MEMBERS: Boise State (1971-96), Gonzaga (1964-79), Idaho (1964-96), Nevada-Reno (1980-92).

NCAA TOURNAMENT RECORD: 9-32 (.220).

ALL-TIME SCORING LEADER: Orlando Lightfoot, Idaho (2,102 points from 1992-94).

SINGLE-SEASON SCORING LEADER: Dave Wagnon, Idaho State (32.5 points per game in 1965-66).

REGULAR-SEASON CHAMPIONS: Boise State (1 outright-2 ties), Gonzaga (0-2), Idaho (4-1), Idaho State (1-3), Montana (4-3), Montana State (3-1), Nevada-Reno (1-1), Northern Arizona (1-1), Weber State (10-5).

BIG SKY TOURNAMENT TITLES: Boise State (4; 1976-88-93-94), Idaho (4; 1981-82-89-90), Weber State (5; 1978-79-80-83-95), Montana (3; 1991-92-97), Idaho State (2; 1977 and 1987), Montana State (2; 1986 and 1996), Nevada (2; 1984 and 1985).

YEAR-BY-YEAR CHAMPIONS (incl. conference records): 1964—Montana State (8-2); **1965**—Weber State (8-2); **1966**—Gonzaga (8-2), Weber State (8-2); **1967**—Gonzaga (7-3), Montana State (7-3); **1968**—Weber State (12-3); **1969**—Weber State (12-3); **1970**—Weber State (12-3); **1971**—Weber State (12-2); **1972**—Weber State (10-4); **1973**—Weber State (13-1); **1974**—Idaho State (11-3)*, Montana (11-3); **1975**—Montana (13-1); **1976**—Boise State (9-5), Idaho State (9-5), Weber State (9-5); **1977**—Idaho State (13-1); **1978**—Montana (12-2); **1979**—Weber State (10-4); **1980**—Weber State (13-1); **1981**—Idaho (12-2); **1982**—Idaho (13-1); **1983**—Nevada (10-4), Weber State (10-4); **1984**—Weber State (12-2); **1985**—Nevada (11-3); **1986**—Montana (9-5), Northern Arizona (9-5); **1987**—Montana State (12-2); **1988**—Boise State (13-3); **1989**—Boise State (13-3), Idaho (13-3); **1990**—Idaho (13-3); **1991**—Montana (13-3); **1992**—Montana (14-2); **1993**—Idaho (11-3); **1994**—Idaho State (10-4), Weber State (10-4); **1995**—Montana (11-3), Weber State (11-3); **1996**—Montana State (11-3); **1997**—Northern Arizona (14-2).

*Won playoff.

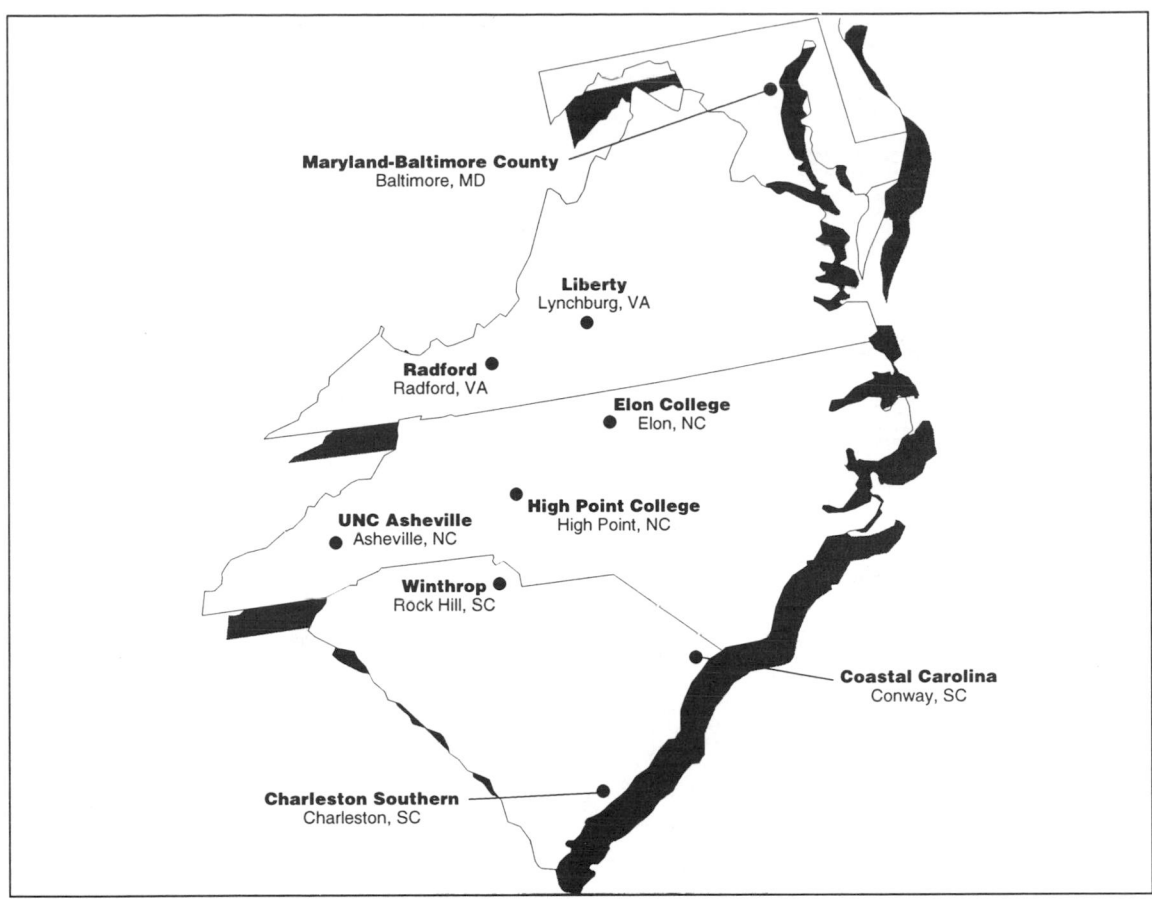

Maryland-Baltimore County
Baltimore, MD

Liberty
Lynchburg, VA

Radford
Radford, VA

Elon College
Elon, NC

UNC Asheville
Asheville, NC

High Point College
High Point, NC

Winthrop
Rock Hill, SC

Coastal Carolina
Conway, SC

Charleston Southern
Charleston, SC

BIG SOUTH

TEMPORARY ADDRESS: c/o Winthrop University, Winthrop Coliseum, Rock Hill, SC 29733 (relocating to Charlotte area).

TEMPORARY PHONE/FAX: (803) 817-6340/817-6578.

CURRENT MEMBERS: Charleston Southern (1986-98), Coastal Carolina (1986-98), Elon (since 1998), High Point College (since 1998), Liberty (1992-98), Maryland-Baltimore County (1993-98; slated to join the Northeast Conference in 1999), UNC Asheville (1986-98), Radford (1986-98), Winthrop (1986-98). High Point is slated to join the Big South in 2000.

FORMER MEMBERS: Armstrong State (1986 and 1987), Augusta (1986-91), Campbell (1986-94), Davidson (1991 and 1992), North Carolina-Greensboro (1993-97), Towson State (1993-95).

NCAA TOURNAMENT RECORD: 0-6 (.000).

ALL-TIME SCORING LEADER: Tony Dunkin, Coastal Carolina (2,151 points from 1990-93).

REGULAR-SEASON CHAMPIONS: Charleston Southern (2 outright-0 ties), Coastal Carolina (4-0), Liberty (0-1), UNC Asheville (0-1), UNC Greensboro (2-0), Radford (1-0), Towson State (2-0).

BIG SOUTH TOURNAMENT TITLES: Charleston Southern (4; 1986-87-95-97), Coastal Carolina (3; 1990-91-93), Liberty (1; 1994), Campbell (1; 1992), UNC Asheville (1; 1989), UNC Greensboro (1; 1996), Winthrop (1; 1988).

YEAR-BY-YEAR CHAMPIONS (incl. conference records): 1986—Charleston Southern (5-1); **1987—**Charleston Southern (12-2); **1988—**Coastal Carolina (9-3); **1989—**Coastal Carolina (9-3); **1990—**Coastal Carolina (11-1); **1991—**Coastal Carolina (13-1); **1992—**Radford (12-2); **1993—**Towson State (14-2); **1994—**Towson State (16-2); **1995—**UNC Greensboro (14-2); **1996—**UNC Greensboro (11-3); **1997—**Liberty (11-3), UNC Asheville (11-3).

BIG TEN

ADDRESS: 1500 West Higgins Road, Park Ridge, IL 60068-6300.

PHONE/FAX: (847) 696-1010/1110.

INTERNET ADDRESS: www.bigten.org

PREVIOUS NAMES: Intercollegiate Conference of Faculty Representatives or Western Conference, Big Nine (1947 and 1948).

CURRENT MEMBERS: Illinois (1896-1998), Indiana (1899-1998), Iowa (1899-1998), Michigan (1896-1998), Michigan State (1949-98), Minnesota (1896-1998), Northwestern (1896-1998), Ohio State (1912-98), Penn State (1993-98), Purdue (1896-1998), Wisconsin (1896-1998).

FORMER MEMBER: University of Chicago (1906-46).

NCAA TOURNAMENT RECORD: 220-133 (.623).

NCAA TITLES (9): Indiana (1940-53-76-81-87), Michigan (1989), Michigan State (1979), Ohio State (1960), Wisconsin (1941).

NIT TITLES (6): Indiana (1979), Michigan (1984 and 1997), Minnesota (1993), Ohio State (1986), Purdue (1974).

ALL-TIME SCORING LEADER: Calbert Cheaney, Indiana (2,613 points from 1990-93).

SINGLE-SEASON SCORING LEADER: Rick Mount, Purdue (35.4 points per game in 1969-70).

REGULAR-SEASON CHAMPIONS: Chicago (3 outright-3 ties), Illinois (6-6), Indiana (11-8), Iowa (4-4), Michigan (7-5), Michigan State (3-3), Minnesota (5-4), Northwestern (1-1), Ohio State (10-5), Purdue (12-9), Wisconsin (7-7).

YEAR-BY-YEAR CHAMPIONS (incl. conference records): 1923—Iowa (11-1), Wisconsin (11-1); **1924**—Chicago (8-4), Illinois (8-4), Wisconsin (8-4); **1925**—Ohio State (11-1); **1926**—Indiana (8-4), Iowa (8-4), Michigan (8-4), Purdue (8-4); **1927**—Michigan (10-2); **1928**—Indiana (10-2), Purdue (10-2); **1929**—Michigan (10-2), Wisconsin (10-2); **1930**—Purdue (10-0); **1931**—Northwestern (11-1); **1932**—Purdue (11-1); **1933**—Northwestern (10-2), Ohio State (10-2); **1934**—Purdue (10-2); **1935**—Illinois (9-3), Purdue (9-3), Wisconsin (9-3); **1936**—Indiana (11-1), Purdue (11-1); **1937**—Illinois (10-2), Minnesota (10-2); **1938**—Purdue (10-2); **1939**—Ohio State (10-2); **1940**—Purdue (10-2); **1941**—Wisconsin (11-1); **1942**—Illinois (13-2); **1943**—Illinois (12-0); **1944**—Ohio State (10-2); **1945**—Iowa (11-1); **1946**—Ohio State (10-2); **1947**—Wisconsin (9-3); **1948**—Michigan (10-2); **1949**—Illinois (10-2); **1950**—Ohio State (11-1); **1951**—Illinois (13-1); **1952**—Illinois (12-2); **1953**—Indiana (17-1); **1954**—Indiana (12-2); **1955**—Iowa (11-3); **1956**—Iowa (13-1); **1957**—Indiana (10-4), Michigan State (10-4); **1958**—Indiana (10-4); **1959**—Michigan State (12-2); **1960**—Ohio State (13-1); **1961**—Ohio State (14-0); **1962**—Ohio State (13-1); **1963**—Illinois (11-3), Ohio State (11-3); **1964**—Michigan (11-3), Ohio State (11-3); **1965**—Michigan (13-1); **1966**—Michigan (11-3); **1967**—Indiana (10-4), Michigan State (10-4); **1968**—Iowa (10-4), Ohio State (10-4); **1969**—Purdue (13-1); **1970**—Iowa (14-0); **1971**—Ohio State (13-1); **1972**—Minnesota (11-3); **1973**—Indiana (11-3); **1974**—Indiana (12-2), Michigan (12-2); **1975**—Indiana (18-0); **1976**—Indiana (18-0); **1977**—Michigan (16-2); **1978**—Michigan State (15-3); **1979**—Iowa (13-5), Michigan State (13-5), Purdue (13-5); **1980**—Indiana (13-5); **1981**—Indiana (14-4); **1982**—Minnesota (14-4); **1983**—Indiana (13-5); **1984**—Illinois (15-3), Purdue (15-3); **1985**—Michigan (16-2); **1986**—Michigan (14-4); **1987**—Indiana (15-3), Purdue (15-3); **1988**—Purdue (16-2); **1989**—Indiana (15-3); **1990**—Michigan State (15-3); **1991**—Indiana (15-3), Ohio State (15-3); **1992**—Ohio State (15-3); **1993**—Indiana (17-1); **1994**—Purdue (14-4); **1995**—Purdue (15-3); **1996**—Purdue (15-3); **1997**—Minnesota (16-2).

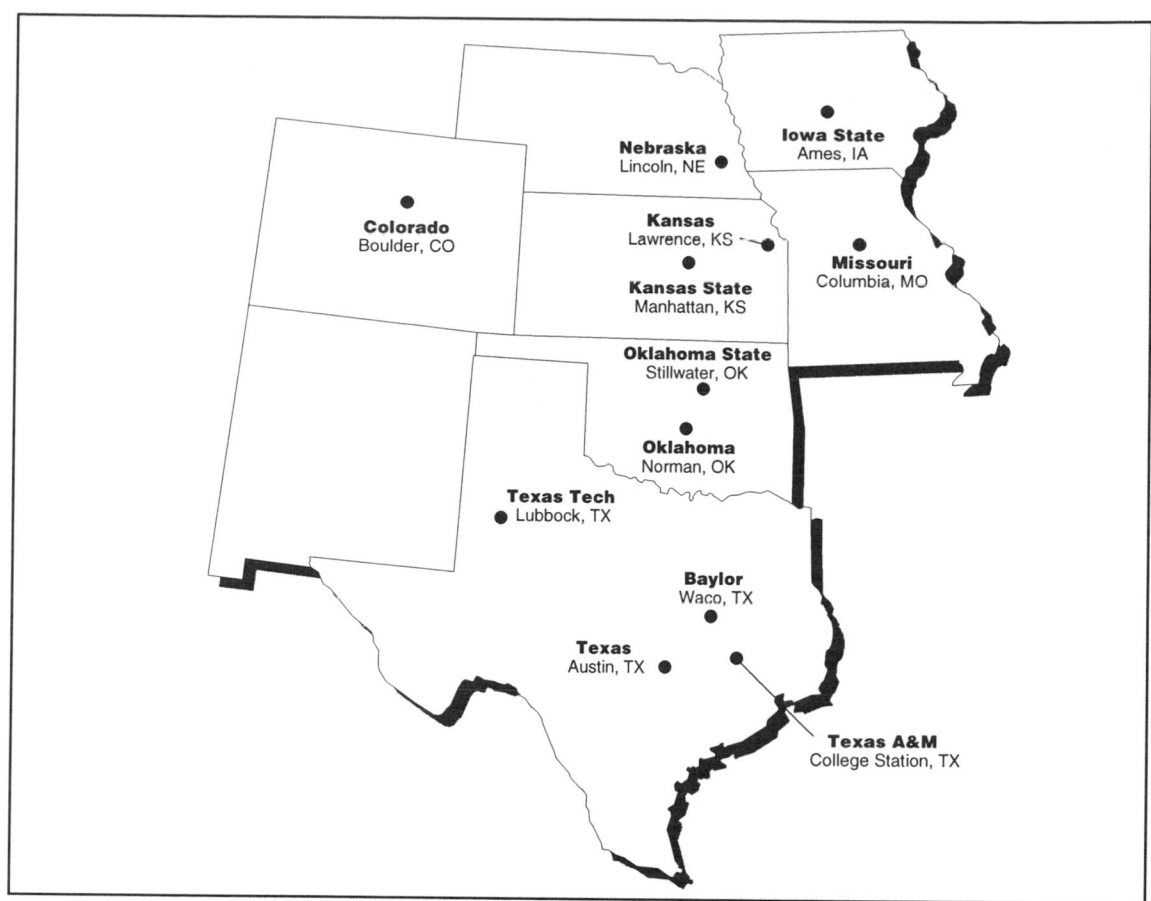

BIG TWELVE

TEMPORARY ADDRESS: 2201 Stemmons Freeway, 28th Floor, Dallas, TX 75207.

PHONE/FAX: (214) 742-1212/2046.

INTERNET ADDRESS: www.big12conf.com

CURRENT MEMBERS: Baylor (1997 and 1998), Colorado (1997 and 1998), Iowa State (1997 and 1998), Kansas (1997 and 1998), Kansas State (1997 and 1998), Missouri (1997 and 1998), Nebraska (1997 and 1998), Oklahoma (1997 and 1998), Oklahoma State (1997 and 1998), Texas (1997 and 1998), Texas A&M (1997 and 1998), Texas Tech (1997 and 1998).

NCAA TOURNAMENT RECORD: 7-5 (.583).

NCAA TITLES (2): Kansas (1952 and 1988) won championships as a member of the Big Eight before the Big 12 was formed.

NIT TITLES (2): Texas (1978) and Nebraska (1996) won championships while members of the SWC and Big Eight, respectively, before the Big 12 was formed.

REGULAR-SEASON CHAMPIONS: Kansas (1 outright-0 ties), Texas (0 1), Texas Tech (0-1).

BIG 12 TOURNAMENT TITLES: Kansas (1; 1997).

YEAR-BY-YEAR CHAMPIONS: 1997—Kansas (15-1/N); Texas and Texas Tech (10-6/S).

NOTE: The Big 12 introduced divisional play from its inception (North and South).

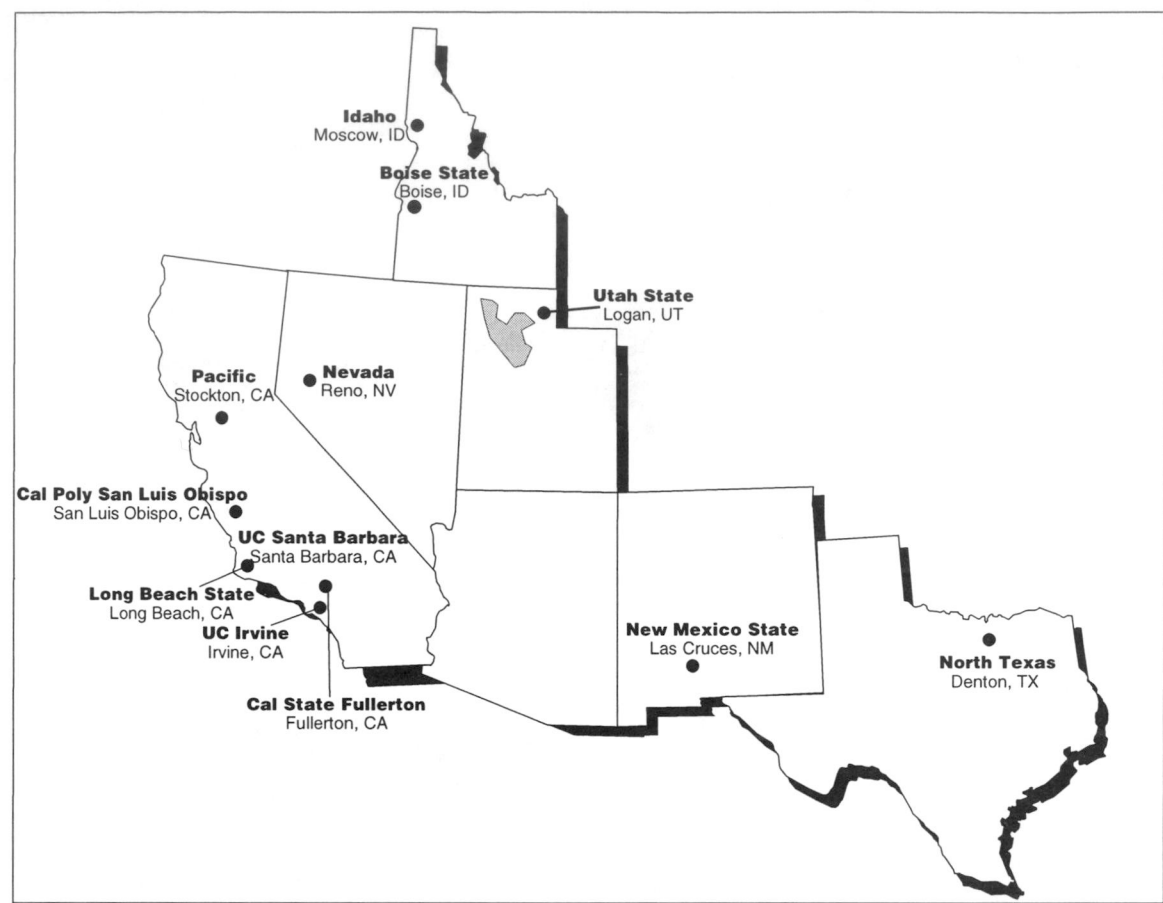

BIG WEST

ADDRESS: 2 Corporate Park, Suite 206, Irvine, CA 92714.

PHONE/FAX: (714) 261-2525/2528.

INTERNET ADDRESS: www.igeneration.com/bigwest

PREVIOUS NAME: Pacific Coast Athletic Association (1970-88).

CURRENT MEMBERS: Boise State (1997 and 1998), UC Irvine (1978-98), Cal Poly San Luis Obispo (1997 and 1998), UC Santa Barbara (1970-74 and 1977-98), Cal State Fullerton (1975-98), Idaho (1997 and 1998), Long Beach State (1970-98), Nevada (1993-98), New Mexico State (1984-98), North Texas (1997 and 1998), Pacific (1972-98), Utah State (1979-98).

FORMER MEMBERS: Cal State Los Angeles (1970-74), Fresno State (1970-92), San Diego State (1970-78), San Jose State (1970-96), UNLV (1983-96).

NCAA TOURNAMENT RECORD: 37-38 (.493).

NCAA TITLES: (1): UNLV (1990).

ALL-TIME SCORING LEADER: Lucious Harris, Long Beach State (2,312 points from 1990-93).

SINGLE-SEASON SCORING LEADERS: Armon Gilliam, UNLV (903 points in 1986-87) and Raymond Lewis, Cal State Los Angeles (32.9 points per game in 1972-73).

REGULAR-SEASON CHAMPIONS: Cal State Fullerton (0 outright-1 tie), Fresno State (2-1), Long Beach State (7-2), Nevada (0-1), New Mexico State (2-2), Pacific (2-0), San Diego State (0-2), UNLV (9-1), Utah State (2-1).

BIG WEST TOURNAMENT TITLES: UNLV (7; 1983-85-86-87-89-90-91), Fresno State (3; 1981-82-84), Long Beach State (3; 1977, 1993 and 1995), New Mexico State (2; 1992 and 1994), Pacific (2; 1979 and 1997), San Jose State (2; 1980 and 1996), Cal State Fullerton (1; 1978), San Diego State (1; 1976), Utah State (1; 1988).

YEAR-BY-YEAR CHAMPIONS (incl. conference records): 1970—Long Beach State (10-0); **1971**—Long Beach State (10-0); **1972**—Long Beach State (10-2); **1973**—Long Beach State (10-2); **1974**—Long Beach State (12-0); **1975**—Long Beach State (8-2); **1976**—Cal State Fullerton (6-4), Long Beach State (6-4); **1977**—Long Beach State (9-3), San Jose State (9-3); **1978**—Fresno State (11-3), San Diego State (11-3); **1979**—Pacific (11-3); **1980**—Utah State (11-2); **1981**—Fresno State (12-2); **1982**—Fresno State (13-1); **1983**—UNLV (15-1); **1984**—UNLV (16-2); **1985**—UNLV (17-1); **1986**—UNLV (16-2); **1987**—UNLV (18-0); **1988**—UNLV (15-3); **1989**—UNLV (16-2); **1990**—New Mexico State (16-2), UNLV (16-2); **1991**—UNLV (18-0); **1992**—UNLV (18-0); **1993**—New Mexico State (15-3); **1994**—New Mexico State (12-6); **1995**—Utah State (14-4); **1996**—Long Beach State (12-6); **1997**—Nevada (12-4/E), New Mexico State (12-4/E), Utah State (12-4/E); Pacific (12-4/W).

NOTE: League split into two divisions (Eastern and Western) for the 1996-97 season.

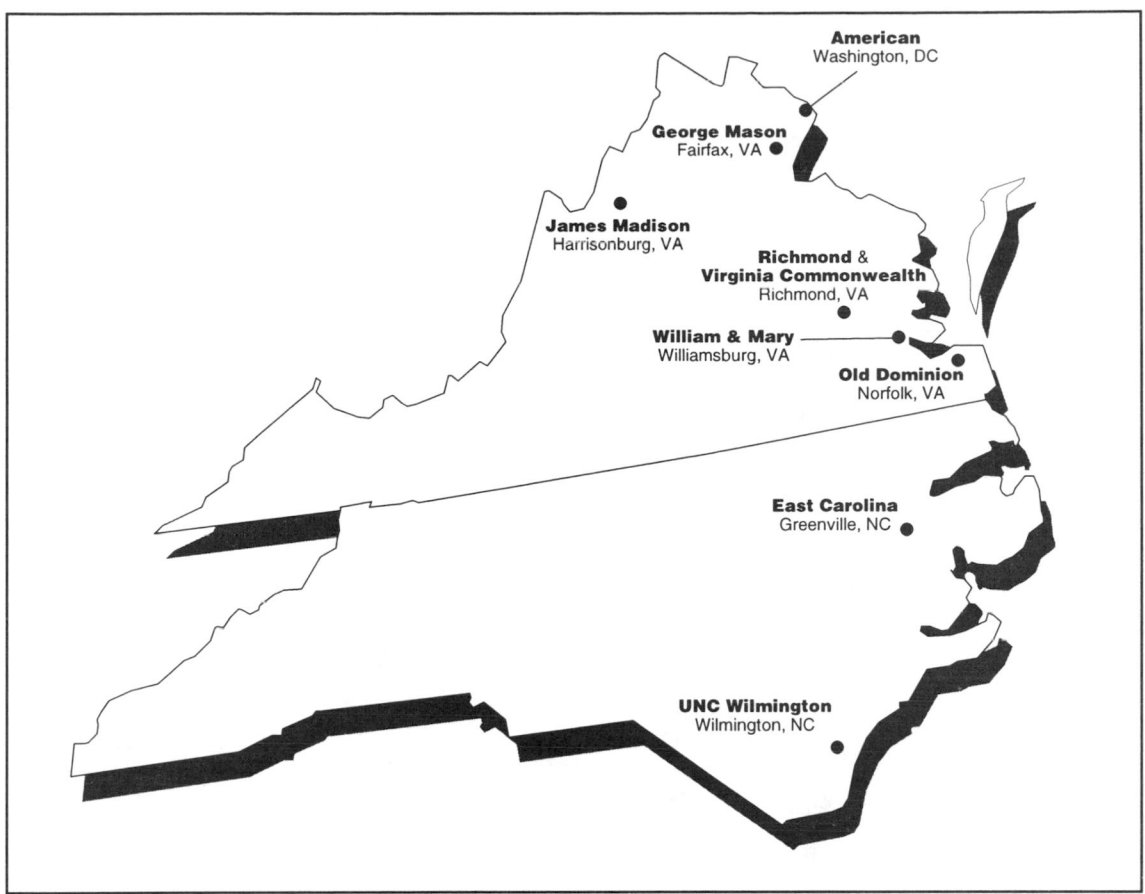

COLONIAL ATHLETIC ASSOCIATION

ADDRESS: 8625 Patterson Avenue, Richmond, VA 23229-6349.

PHONE/FAX: (804) 754-1616/1830.

INTERNET ADDRESS: www.urich.edu/~caa/

PREVIOUS NAME: ECAC South (1983-86).

CURRENT MEMBERS: American (1985-98), East Carolina (1983-98), George Mason (1983-98), James Madison (1983-98), UNC Wilmington (1985-98), Old Dominion (1992-98), Richmond (1983-98), Virginia Commonwealth (1996-98), William & Mary (1983-98).

FORMER MEMBER: Navy (1983-91).

NCAA TOURNAMENT RECORD: 11-16 (.407).

ALL-TIME SCORING LEADER: David Robinson, Navy (2,669 points from 1984-87).

REGULAR-SEASON CHAMPIONS: James Madison (2 outright-3 ties), Navy (2-1), UNC Wilmington (0-1), Old Dominion (1-3), Richmond (3-2), Virginia Commonwealth (1-0), William & Mary (1-0).

CAA TOURNAMENT TITLES: Richmond (4; 1984-88-90-91), Navy (3; 1985-86-87), Old Dominion (3; 1992-95-97), James Madison (2; 1983 and 1994), East Carolina (1; 1993), George Mason (1; 1989), Virginia Commonwealth (1; 1996).

YEAR-BY-YEAR CHAMPIONS (incl. conference records): 1983—William & Mary (9-0); **1984**—Richmond (7-3); **1985**—Navy (11-3), Richmond (11-3); **1986**—Navy (13-1); **1987**—Navy (13-1); **1988**—Richmond (11-3); **1989**—Richmond (13-1); **1990**—James Madison (11-3); **1991**—James Madison (12-2); **1992**—James Madison (12-2), Richmond (12-2); **1993**—James Madison (11-3), Old Dominion (11-3); **1994**—James Madison (10-4), Old Dominion (10-4); **1995**—Old Dominion (12-2); **1996**—Virginia Commonwealth (14-2); **1997**—UNC Wilmington (10-6), Old Dominion (10-6).

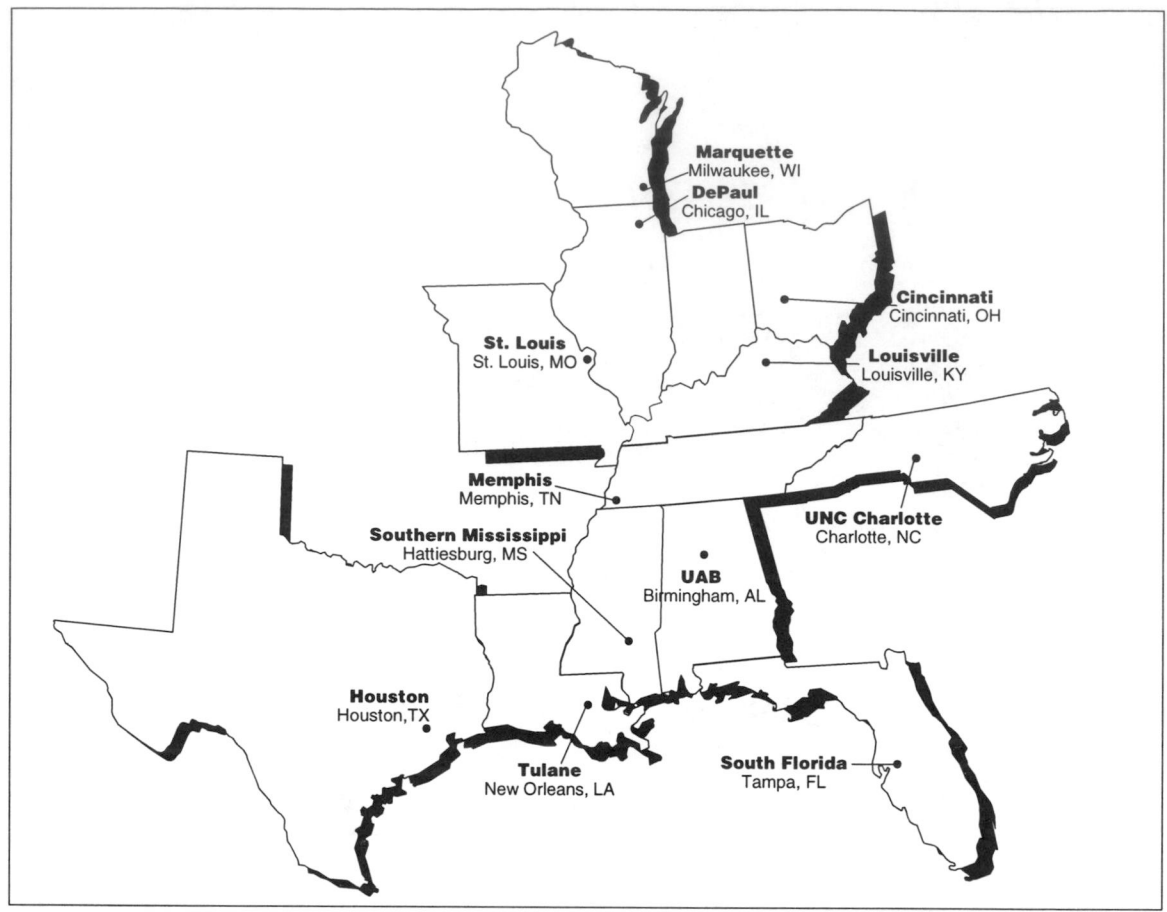

CONFERENCE USA

ADDRESS: 35 East Wacker Drive, Suite 650, Chicago, IL 60601.

PHONE/FAX: (312) 553-0483/0495, 0496.

INTERNET ADDRESS: www.c-usa.org

CURRENT MEMBERS: UAB (1996-98), Cincinnati (1996-98), DePaul (1996-98), Houston (1997 and 1998), Louisville (1996-98), Marquette (1996-98), Memphis (1996-98), UNC Charlotte (1996-98), Saint Louis (1996-98), South Florida (1996-98), Southern Mississippi (1996-98), Tulane (1996-98).

NCAA TOURNAMENT RECORD: 11-8 (.579).

NCAA TITLES (5): Cincinnati (1961 and 1962), Louisville (1980 and 1986) and Marquette (1977) won championships before the C-USA was formed.

NIT TITLES (5): DePaul (1945), Louisville (1956), Marquette (1970), Saint Louis (1948) and Southern Mississippi (1987) won championships before the C-USA was formed.

REGULAR-SEASON CHAMPIONS: Cincinnati (1 outright-1 tie), Memphis (0-1).

C-USA TOURNAMENT TITLES: Cincinnati (1; 1996), Marquette (1; 1997).

YEAR-BY-YEAR CHAMPIONS (incl. conference records): 1996—Cincinnati (11-3/Blue), Memphis (11-3/White); **1997**—Cincinnati (12-2/Blue).

NOTE: Conference started with three divisions—Red, White and Blue. Team with the best overall league record was considered its regular-season champion in 1996 and 1997 before the conference went to two divisions (American and National).

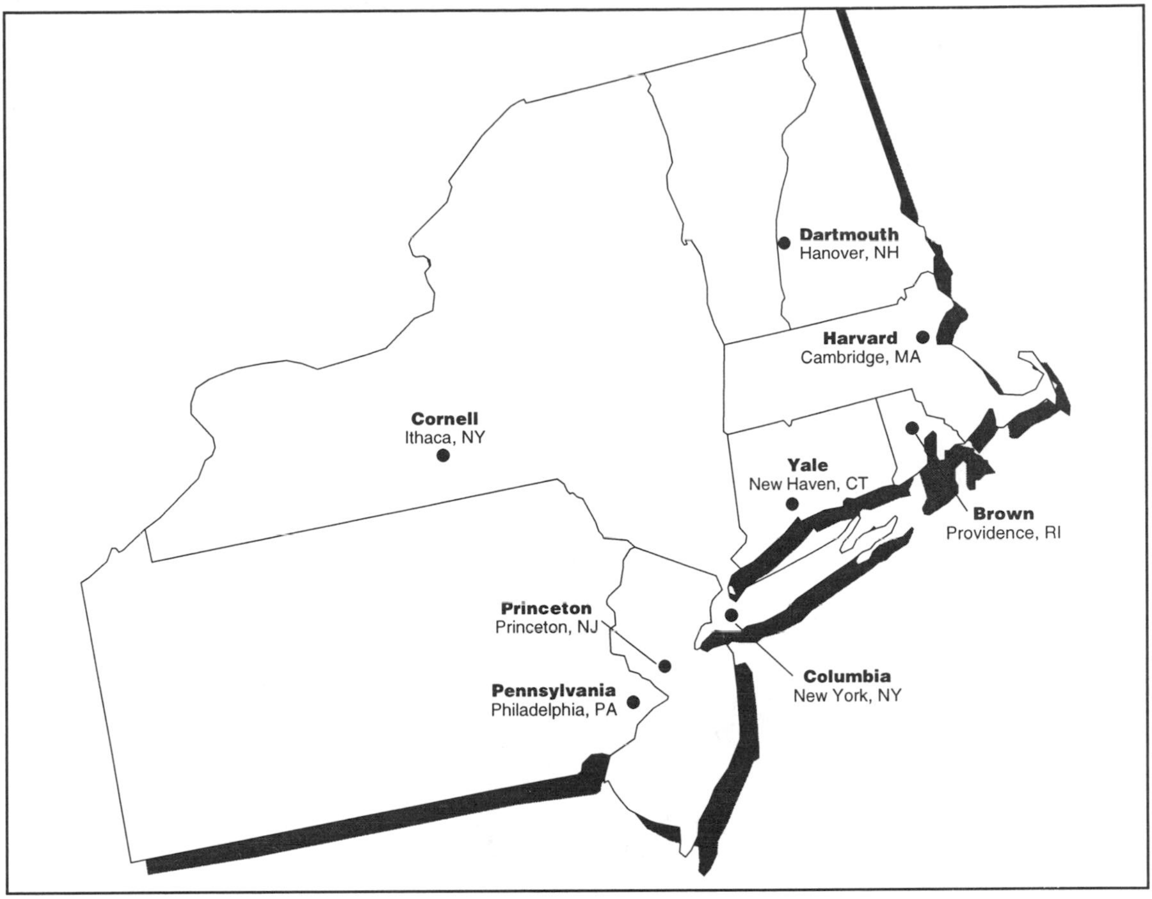

Map showing Ivy League member locations: Dartmouth (Hanover, NH), Harvard (Cambridge, MA), Cornell (Ithaca, NY), Yale (New Haven, CT), Brown (Providence, RI), Princeton (Princeton, NJ), Columbia (New York, NY), Pennsylvania (Philadelphia, PA).

IVY LEAGUE

ADDRESS: 120 Alexander Street, Princeton, NJ 08544.

PHONE/FAX: (609) 258-6426/1690.

INTERNET ADDRESS: www.ivyleague.princeton.edu/

PREVIOUS NAME: Eastern Intercollegiate Basketball League (1902-54).

CURRENT MEMBERS: Brown (1954-98), Columbia (1902-98), Cornell (1902-98), Dartmouth (1912-98), Harvard (1902-09 and 1934-98), Pennsylvania (1904-98), Princeton (1902-98), Yale (1902-98).

NCAA TOURNAMENT RECORD: 37-61 (.378).

NIT TITLES (1): Princeton (1975).

ALL-TIME SCORING LEADER: Bill Bradley, Princeton (2,503 points from 1963-65).

SINGLE-SEASON SCORING LEADER: Bill Bradley, Princeton (32.3 points per game in 1963-64).

REGULAR-SEASON CHAMPIONS: Brown (1 outright-0 ties), Columbia (12-5), Cornell (3-2), Dartmouth (9-3), Penn (25-7), Princeton (19-13), Yale (9-1).

YEAR-BY-YEAR CHAMPIONS (incl. conference records): 1902—Yale (6-2); **1903**—Yale (7-1); **1904**—Columbia (10-0); **1905**—Columbia (8-0); **1906**—Pennsylvania (9-1); **1907**—Yale (9-1); **1908**—Pennsylvania (8-0); **1909**—Columbia (7-1)*; **1910**—Columbia (6-0)*; **1911**—Columbia (7-1); **1912**—Columbia (8-2); **1913**—Cornell (7-1); **1914**—Columbia (8-2), Cornell (8-2); **1915**—Yale (8-2); **1916**—Pennsylvania (8-2), Princeton (8-2); **1917**—Yale (9-1); **1918**—Pennsylvania (9-1); **1919**—Pennsylvania (7-1); **1920**—Pennsylvania (10-0); **1921**—Pennsylvania (9-1); **1922**—Princeton (9-2); **1923**—Yale (7-3); **1924**—Cornell (8-2); **1925**—Princeton (9-1); **1926**—Columbia (9-1); **1927**—Dartmouth (7-3), Princeton (7-3); **1928**—Pennsylvania (7-3), Princeton (7-3); **1929**—Pennsylvania (8-2); **1930**—Columbia (9-1); **1931**—Columbia (10-0); **1932**—Columbia (8-2), Princeton (8-2); **1933**—Yale (8-2); **1934**—Pennsylvania (10-2); **1935**—Columbia (10-2), Pennsylvania (10-2); **1936**—Columbia (12-0); **1937**—Pennsylvania (12-0); **1938**—Dartmouth (8-4); **1939**—Dartmouth (10-2); **1940**—Dartmouth (11-1); **1941**—Dartmouth (10-2); **1942**—Dartmouth (10-2), Princeton (10-2); **1943**—Dartmouth (11-1); **1944**—Dartmouth (8-0); **1945**—Pennsylvania (5-1); **1946**—Dartmouth (7-1); **1947**—Columbia (11-1); **1948**—Columbia (11-1); **1949**—Yale (9-3); **1950**—Princeton (11-1); **1951**—Columbia (12-0); **1952**—Princeton (10-2); **1953**—Pennsylvania (10-2); **1954**—Cornell (12-3); **1955**—Princeton (11-4); **1956**—Dartmouth (10-4); **1957**—Yale (12-2); **1958**—Dartmouth (11-3); **1959**—Dartmouth (14-1); **1960**—Princeton (11-3); **1961**—Princeton (11-3); **1962**—Yale (13-1); **1963**—Princeton (12-3); **1964**—Princeton (12-2); **1965**—Princeton (13-1); **1966**—Pennsylvania (12-2); **1967**—Princeton (13-1); **1968**—Columbia (13-2); **1969**—Princeton (14-0); **1970**—Pennsylvania (14-0); **1971**—Pennsylvania (14-0); **1972**—Pennsylvania (13-1); **1973**—Pennsylvania (12-2); **1974**—Pennsylvania (13-1); **1975**—Pennsylvania (13-1); **1976**—Princeton (14-0); **1977**—Princeton (13-1); **1978**—Pennsylvania (12-2); **1979**—Pennsylvania (13-1); **1980**—Pennsylvania (11-3), Princeton (11-3); **1981**—Pennsylvania (13-1), Princeton (13-1); **1982**—Pennsylvania (12-2); **1983**—Princeton (12-2); **1984**—Princeton (10-4); **1985**—Pennsylvania (10-4); **1986**—Brown (10-4); **1987**—Pennsylvania (10-4); **1988**—Cornell (11-3); **1989**—Princeton (11-3); **1990**—Princeton (11-3); **1991**—Princeton (14-0); **1992**—Princeton (12-2); **1993**—Pennsylvania (14-0); **1994**—Pennsylvania (14-0); **1995**—Pennsylvania (14-0); **1996**—Pennsylvania (12-2), Princeton* (12-2); **1997**—Princeton (14-0)

*Won playoff.

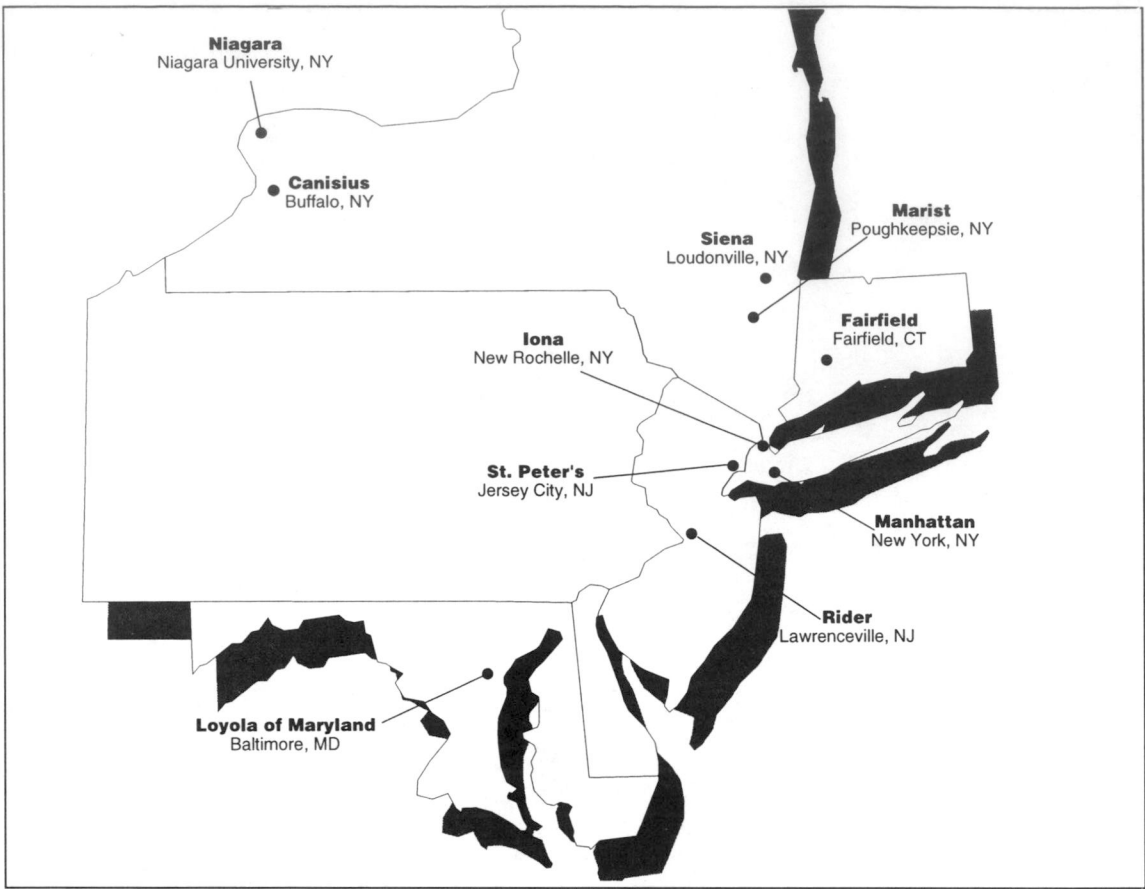

Map showing locations:

Niagara — Niagara University, NY

Canisius — Buffalo, NY

Marist — Poughkeepsie, NY

Siena — Loudonville, NY

Fairfield — Fairfield, CT

Iona — New Rochelle, NY

St. Peter's — Jersey City, NJ

Manhattan — New York, NY

Rider — Lawrenceville, NJ

Loyola of Maryland — Baltimore, MD

METRO ATLANTIC ATHLETIC

ADDRESS: 1090 Amboy Avenue, Edison, NJ 08837-2847.

PHONE/FAX: (908) 225-0202/5440.

CURRENT MEMBERS: Canisius (1990-98), Fairfield (1982-98), Iona (1982-98), Loyola, Md. (1990-98), Manhattan (1982-98), Marist (since 1998), Niagara (1990-98), Rider (since 1998), St. Peter's (1982-98), Siena (1990-98).

FORMER MEMBERS: Army (1982-90), Fordham (1982-90), Holy Cross (1984-90), La Salle (1984-92).

NCAA TOURNAMENT RECORD: 2-15 (.118).

ALL-TIME SCORING LEADER: Lionel Simmons, La Salle (3,217 points from 1987-90).

REGULAR-SEASON CHAMPIONS: Canisius (1 outright-0 ties), Fairfield (1-1), Holy Cross (1-0), Iona (3-2), La Salle (3-1), Manhattan (3-0), St. Peter's (2-1), Siena (1-0).

MAAC TOURNAMENT TITLES: La Salle (4; 1988-89-90-92), Fairfield (3; 1986-87-97), Iona (3; 1982-84-85), St. Peter's (2; 1991 and 1995), Canisius (1; 1996), Fordham (1; 1983), Loyola, Md. (1; 1994), Manhattan (1; 1993).

YEAR-BY-YEAR CHAMPIONS (incl. conference records): 1982—St. Peter's (9-1); **1983**—Iona (8-2); **1984**—Iona (11-3), La Salle (11-3), St. Peter's (11-3); **1985**—Iona (11-3); **1986**—Fairfield (13-1); **1987**—St. Peter's (11-3); **1988**—La Salle (14-0); **1989**—La Salle (13-1); **1990**—Holy Cross (14-2/N), La Salle (16-0/S); **1991**—Siena (12-4); **1992**—Manhattan (13-3); **1993**—Manhattan (12-2); **1994**—Canisius (12-2); **1995**—Manhattan (12-2); **1996**—Fairfield (10-4), Iona (10-4); **1997**—Iona (11-3)

NOTE: The MAAC had North and South Divisions for one season in 1989-90.

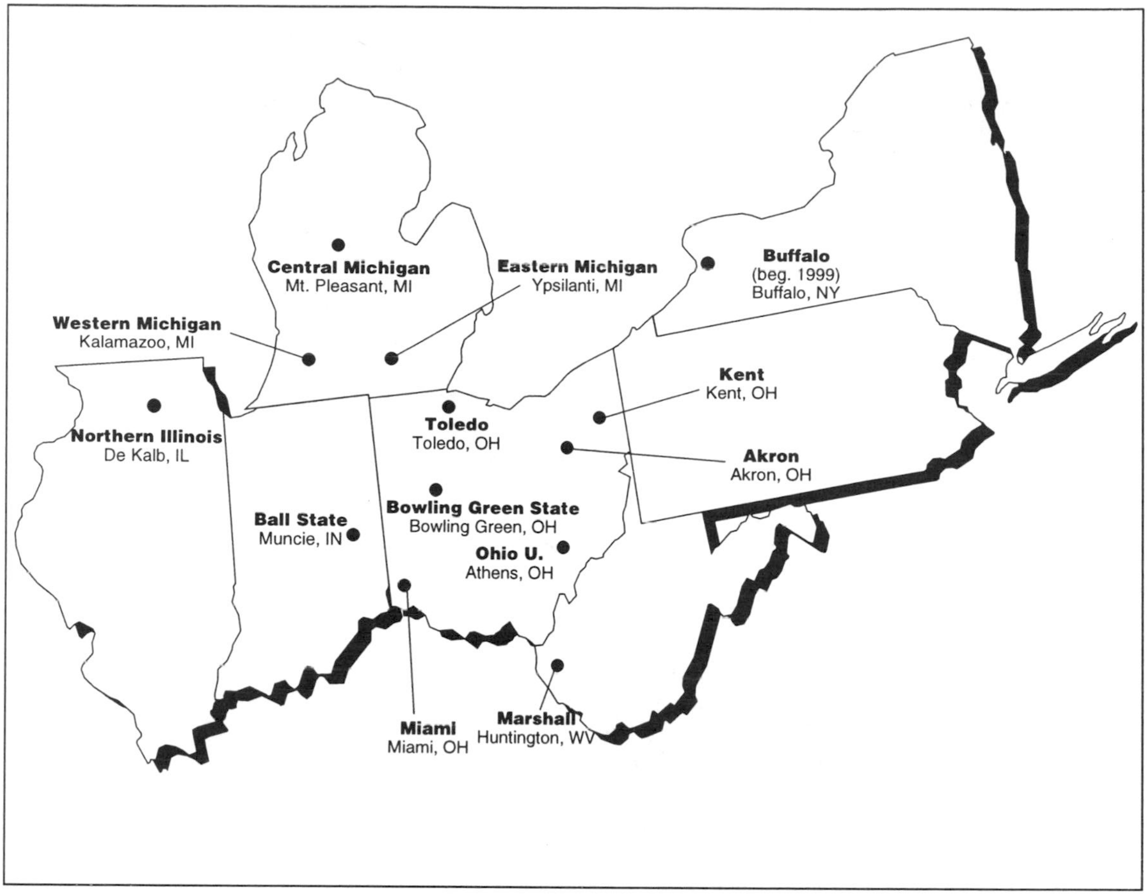

MID-AMERICAN

ADDRESS: Four SeaGate, Suite 102, Toledo, OH 43604.

PHONE/FAX: (419) 249-7177/7199.

INTERNET ADDRESS: To be determined

CURRENT MEMBERS: Akron (1993-98), Ball State (1976-98), Bowling Green State (1954-98), Central Michigan (1973-98), Eastern Michigan (1975-98), Kent (1952-98), Marshall (1954-69 and since 1998), Miami of Ohio (1948-98), Northern Illinois (1976-86 and since 1998), Ohio (1947-98), Toledo (1952-98), Western Michigan (1948-98). Buffalo is slated to join the league in 1999.

FORMER MEMBERS: Butler (1947-50), Cincinnati (1947-53), Wayne State (1947), Western Reserve (1947-55).

NCAA TOURNAMENT RECORD: 19-52 (.268).

ALL-TIME SCORING LEADER: Ron Harper, Miami of Ohio (2,377 points from 1983-86).

SINGLE-SEASON SCORING LEADERS: Dave Jamerson, Ohio (874 points in 1989-90) and Howard Komives, Bowling Green State (36.7 points per game in 1963-64).

REGULAR-SEASON CHAMPIONS: Ball State (3 outright-2 ties), Bowling Green State (4-3), Butler (0-1), Central Michigan (2-2), Cincinnati (4-1), Eastern Michigan (3-0), Marshall (1-0), Miami of Ohio (13-6), Northern Illinois (0-1), Ohio (7-2), Toledo (3-0), Western Michigan (1-2).

MAC TOURNAMENT TITLES: Ball State (6; 1981-86-89-90-93-95), Eastern Michigan (3; 1988-91-96), Miami of Ohio (3; 1984-92-97), Ohio (3; 1983-85-94), Central Michigan (1; 1987), Northern Illinois (1; 1982), Toledo (1; 1980).

YEAR-BY-YEAR CHAMPIONS (incl. conference records): **1947**—Butler (6-2), Cincinnati (6-2); **1948**—Cincinnati (7-2); **1949**—Cincinnati (9-1); **1950**—Cincinnati (10-0); **1951**—Cincinnati (7-1); **1952**—Miami of Ohio (9-3), Western Michigan (9-3); **1953**—Miami of Ohio (10-2); **1954**—Toledo (10-2); **1955**—Miami of Ohio (11-3); **1956**—Marshall (10-2); **1957**—Miami of Ohio (11-1); **1958**—Miami of Ohio (12-0); **1959**—Bowling Green (9-3), Miami of Ohio (9-3); **1960**—Ohio U. (10-2); **1961**—Ohio U. (10-2); **1962**—Bowling Green (11-1); **1963**—Bowling Green (9-3); **1964**—Ohio U. (10-2); **1965**—Miami of Ohio (11-1), Ohio U. (11-1); **1966**—Miami of Ohio (11-1); **1967**—Toledo (11-1); **1968**—Bowling Green (10-2); **1969**—Miami of Ohio (10-2); **1970**—Ohio U. (9-1); **1971**—Miami of Ohio (9-1); **1972**—Ohio U. (7-3), Toledo (7-3); **1973**—Miami of Ohio (9-2); **1974**—Ohio U. (9-3); **1975**—Central Michigan (10-4); **1976**—Western Michigan (15-1); **1977**—Central Michigan (13-3), Miami of Ohio (13-3); **1978**—Miami of Ohio (12-4); **1979**—Central Michigan (13-3), Toledo (13-3)*; **1980**—Toledo (14-2); **1981**—Ball State (10-6), Bowling Green (10-6), Northern Illinois (10-6), Toledo (10-6), Western Michigan (10-6); **1982**—Ball State (12-4); **1983**—Bowling Green (15-3); **1984**—Miami of Ohio (16-2); **1985**—Ohio U. (14-4); **1986**—Miami of Ohio (16-2); **1987**—Central Michigan (14-2); **1988**—Eastern Michigan (14-2); **1989**—Ball State (14-2); **1990**—Ball State (13-3); **1991**—Eastern Michigan (13-3); **1992**—Miami of Ohio (13-3); **1993**—Ball State (14-4), Miami of Ohio (14-4); **1994**—Ohio U. (14-4); **1995**—Miami of Ohio (16-2); **1996**—Eastern Michigan (14-4); **1997**—Bowling Green (13-5), Miami of Ohio (13-5).

*Won playoff.

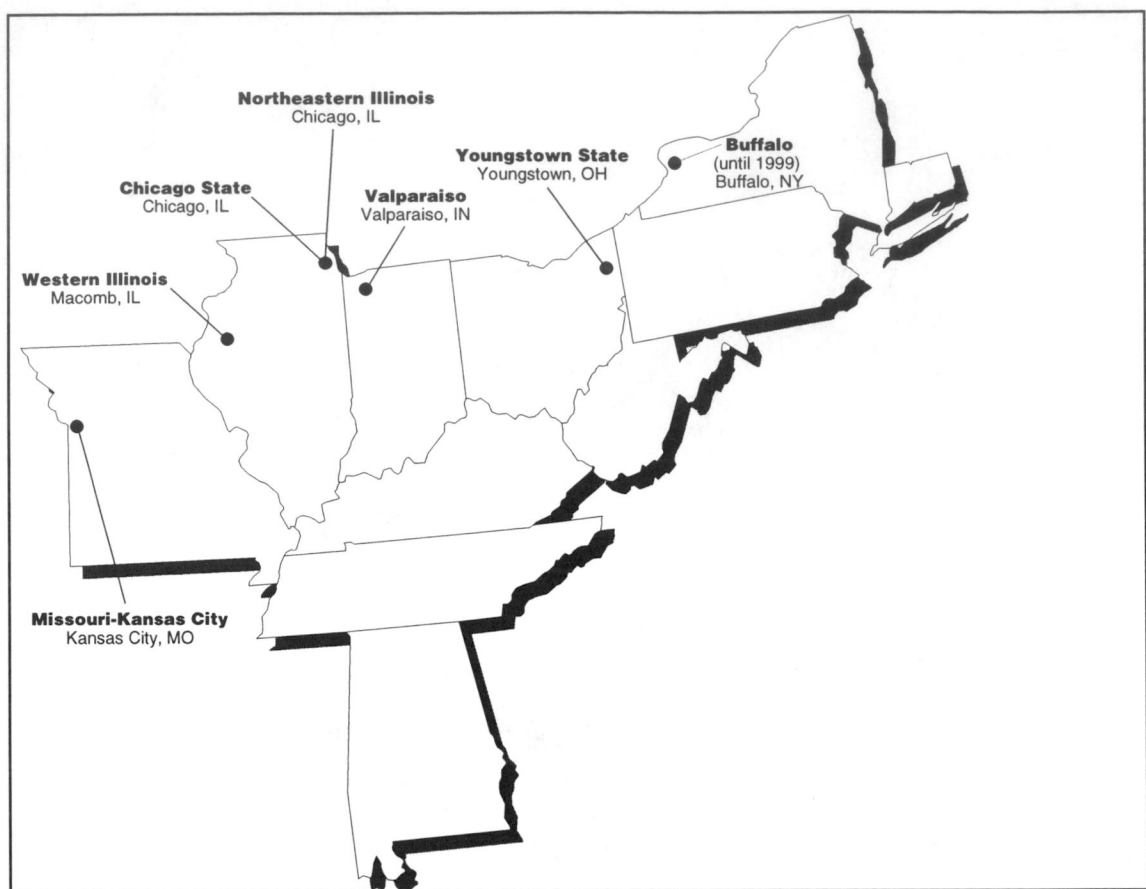

Northeastern Illinois
Chicago, IL

Chicago State
Chicago, IL

Valparaiso
Valparaiso, IN

Youngstown State
Youngstown, OH

Buffalo
(until 1999)
Buffalo, NY

Western Illinois
Macomb, IL

Missouri-Kansas City
Kansas City, MO

MID-CONTINENT

ADDRESS: 40 Shuman Boulevard, Suite 118, Naperville, IL 60563.

PHONE/FAX: (630) 416-7560/7564.

INTERNET ADDRESS: www.mid-con.com

PREVIOUS NAME: Association of Mid-Continent Universities (1983-89).

CURRENT MEMBERS: Buffalo (1995-98; plans to join Mid-American in 1999), Chicago State (1995-98), Missouri-Kansas City (1995-98), Northeastern Illinois (1995-98), Oral Roberts (since 1998), Southern Utah State (since 1998), Valparaiso (1983-98), Western Illinois (1983-98), Youngstown State (1992-98). Oakland University (Mich.)is slated to join in 1999.

FORMER MEMBERS: Akron (1991 and 1992), Central Connecticut State (1995-97), Cleveland State (1983-94), Eastern Illinois (1983-96), Illinois-Chicago (1983-94), Northern Illinois (1991-94), Northern Iowa (1983-91), Southwest Missouri State (1983-90), Troy State (1995-97), Wisconsin-Green Bay (1983-94), Wisconsin-Milwaukee (1993 and 1994), Wright State (1992-94).

NCAA TOURNAMENT RECORD: 5-13 (.278).

ALL-TIME SCORING LEADER: Tony Bennett, Wisconsin-Green Bay (2,285 points from 1989-92).

REGULAR-SEASON CHAMPIONS: Cleveland State (3 outright 0 ties), Illinois-Chicago (1-0), Northern Illinois (1-0), Southwest Missouri State (4-0), Valparaiso (3-0), Western Illinois (1-0), Wisconsin-Green Bay (2-0).

MID-CONTINENT TOURNAMENT TITLES: Valparaiso (3; 1995-96-97), Eastern Illinois (2; 1985 and 1992), Southwest Missouri State (2; 1987 and 1991), Wisconsin-Green Bay (2; 1990 and 1994), Cleveland State (1; 1986), Northern Iowa (1; 1989), Western Illinois (1; 1984), Wright State (1; 1993).

YEAR-BY-YEAR CHAMPIONS (incl. conference records): 1983—Western Illinois (9-3); 1984—Illinois-Chicago (12-2); 1985—Cleveland State (11-3); 1986—Cleveland State (13-1); 1987—Southwest Missouri State (13-1); 1988—Southwest Missouri State (12-2); 1989—Southwest Missouri State (10-2); 1990—Southwest Missouri State (11-1); 1991—Northern Illinois (14-2); 1992—Wisconsin-Green Bay (14-2); 1993—Cleveland State (15-1); 1994—Wisconsin-Green Bay (15-3); 1995—Valparaiso (14-4); 1996—Valparaiso (13-5); 1997—Valparaiso (13-3).

NOTE: Cleveland State would have won 1989 regular-season championship instead of Southwest Missouri State if the Vikings' league games had counted. But Cleveland State was on NCAA probation and declared ineligible by the league so the Mid-Continent wouldn't risk losing its automatic bid to the NCAA Tournament.

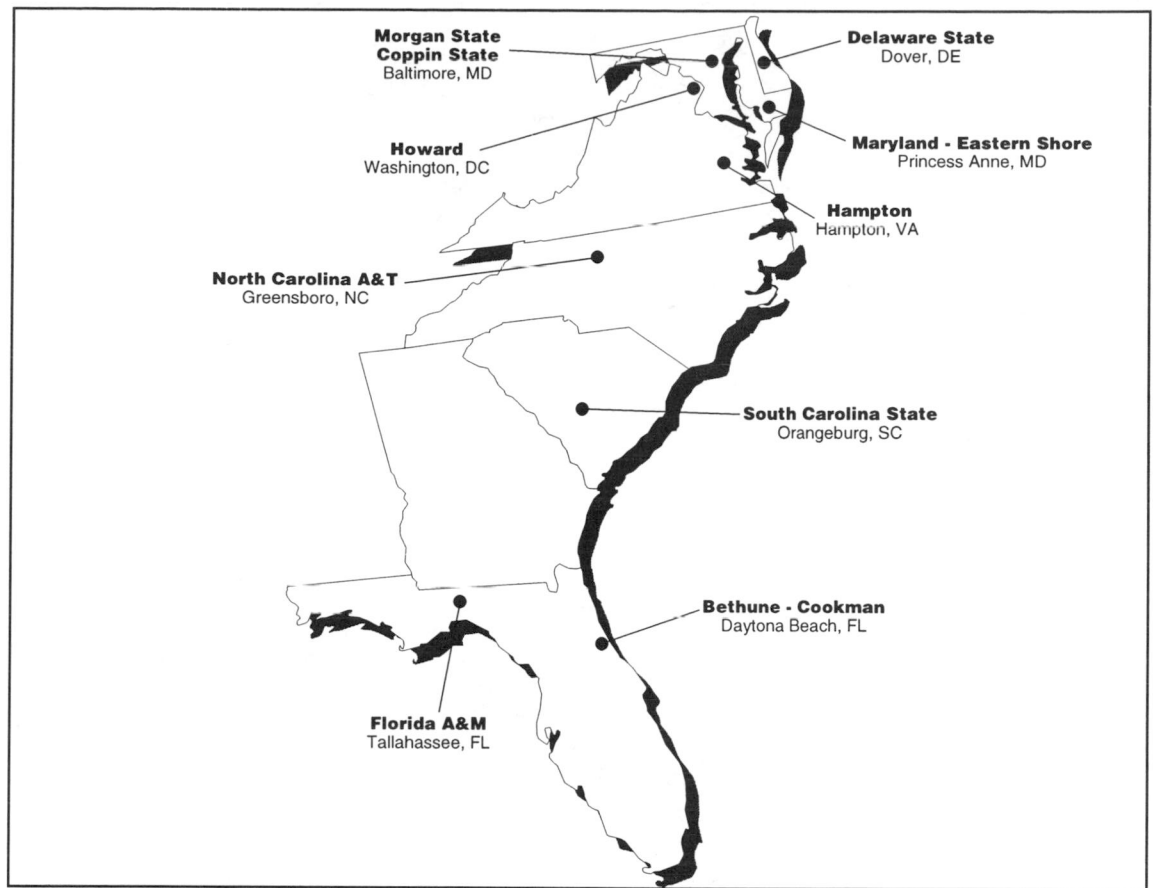

Morgan State
Coppin State
Baltimore, MD

Delaware State
Dover, DE

Howard
Washington, DC

Maryland - Eastern Shore
Princess Anne, MD

Hampton
Hampton, VA

North Carolina A&T
Greensboro, NC

South Carolina State
Orangeburg, SC

Bethune - Cookman
Daytona Beach, FL

Florida A&M
Tallahassee, FL

MID-EASTERN ATHLETIC

ADDRESS: 102 North Elm Street, Suite 401, P.O. Box 21205, Greensboro, NC 27401.

PHONE/FAX: (910) 275-9961/9964.

CURRENT MEMBERS: Bethune-Cookman (1981-98), Coppin State (1986-98), Delaware State (1972-98), Florida A&M (1980-98), Hampton (1996-98), Howard (1972-98), Maryland-Eastern Shore (1972-79 and 1983-98), Morgan State (1972-80 and 1985-98), North Carolina A&T (1972-98), South Carolina State (1972-98).

FORMER MEMBER: North Carolina Central (1972-80).

NCAA TOURNAMENT RECORD: 1-16 (.059).

ALL-TIME SCORING LEADER: Tom Davis, Delaware State (2,274 points from 1988-91).

DIVISION I REGULAR-SEASON CHAMPIONS (since 1972): Coppin State (7 outright-0 ties), Howard (3-1), Maryland-Eastern Shore (1-1), Morgan State (0-2), North Carolina A&T (10-2), South Carolina State (2-0).

MEAC TOURNAMENT TITLES: (since 1981): North Carolina A&T (9; 1982-83-84-85-86-87-88-94-95), Coppin State (3; 1990-93-97), Howard (2; 1981 and 1992), South Carolina State (2; 1989 and 1996), Florida A&M (1; 1991).

YEAR-BY-YEAR CHAMPIONS (incl. conference records): 1972—North Carolina A&T (9-3); **1973**—Maryland-Eastern Shore (10-2); **1974**—Maryland-Eastern Shore (11-1), Morgan State (11-1); **1975**—North Carolina A&T (10-2); **1976**—Morgan State (11-1), North Carolina A&T (11-1); **1977**—South Carolina State (10-2); **1978**—North Carolina A&T (11-1); **1979**—North Carolina A&T (11-1); **1980**—No standings; **1981**—North Carolina A&T (7-3); **1982**—North Carolina A&T (10-2); **1983**—Howard (11-1); **1984**—North Carolina A&T (9-1); **1985**—North Carolina A&T (10-2); **1986**—North Carolina A&T (12-2); **1987**—Howard (13-1); **1988**—North Carolina A&T (16-0); **1989**—South Carolina State (14-2); **1990**—Coppin State (15-1); **1991**—Coppin State (14-2); **1992**—Howard (12-4), North Carolina A&T (12-4); **1993**—Coppin State (16-0); **1994**—Coppin State (16-0); **1995**—Coppin State (15-1); **1996**—Coppin State (14-2); **1997**—Coppin State (15-3).

NOTE: The MEAC moved up to Division I status in 1981.

MIDWESTERN COLLEGIATE

ADDRESS: Pan American Plaza, 201 South Capitol Avenue, Suite 500, Indianapolis, IN 46225.

PHONE/FAX: (317) 237-5622/5620.

INTERNET ADDRESS: www.mccnet.org

PREVIOUS NAME: Midwestern City (1980-85).

CURRENT MEMBERS: Butler (1980-98), Cleveland State (1995-98), Detroit (1981-98), Illinois-Chicago (1995-98), Loyola of Chicago (1980-98), Wisconsin-Green Bay (1995-98), Wisconsin-Milwaukee (1995-98), Wright State (1995-98).

FORMER MEMBERS: Dayton (1989-93), Duquesne (1993), Evansville (1980-94), La Salle (1993-95), Marquette (1990 and 1991), Northern Illinois (1995-97), Oklahoma City (1980-85), Oral Roberts (1980-87), St. Louis (1983-91), Xavier (1980-95).

NCAA TOURNAMENT RECORD: 9-20 (.310).

NCAA TITLES (1): Loyola of Chicago (1963) won its NCAA title before the conference was formed.

ALL-TIME SCORING LEADER: Alfredrick Hughes, Loyola of Chicago (2,906 points from 1982-85).

SINGLE-SEASON SCORING LEADER: Alfredrick Hughes, Loyola of Chicago (868 points in 1984-85 and 27.6 points per game in 1983-84).

REGULAR-SEASON CHAMPIONS: Butler (1 outright-0 ties), Evansville (3-2), Loyola of Chicago (3-1), Oral Roberts (1-0), Wisconsin-Green Bay (1-0), Xavier (7-1).

MCC TOURNAMENT TITLES: Xavier (6; 1983-86-87-88-89-91), Evansville (3; 1982-92-93), Oral Roberts (2; 1980 and 1984), Butler (1; 1997), Dayton (1; 1990), Detroit Mercy (1; 1994), Loyola of Chicago (1; 1985), Northern Illinois (1; 1996), Oklahoma City (1; 1981), Wisconsin-Green Bay (1; 1995).

YEAR-BY-YEAR CHAMPIONS (incl. conference records): 1980—Loyola of Chicago (5-0); **1981**—Xavier (8-3); **1982**—Evansville (10-2); **1983**—Loyola of Chicago (12-2); **1984**—Oral Roberts (11-3); **1985**—Loyola of Chicago (13-1); **1986**—Xavier (10-2); **1987**—Evansville (8-4), Loyola of Chicago (8-4); **1988**—Xavier (9-1); **1989**—Evansville (10-2); **1990**—Xavier (12-2); **1991**—Xavier (11-3); **1992**—Evansville (8-2); **1993**—Evansville (12-2), Xavier (12-2); **1994**—Xavier (8-2); **1995**—Xavier (14-0); **1996**—Wisconsin-Green Bay (16-0).Marco, (add to year-by-year champions) — 1997-Butler (12-4)

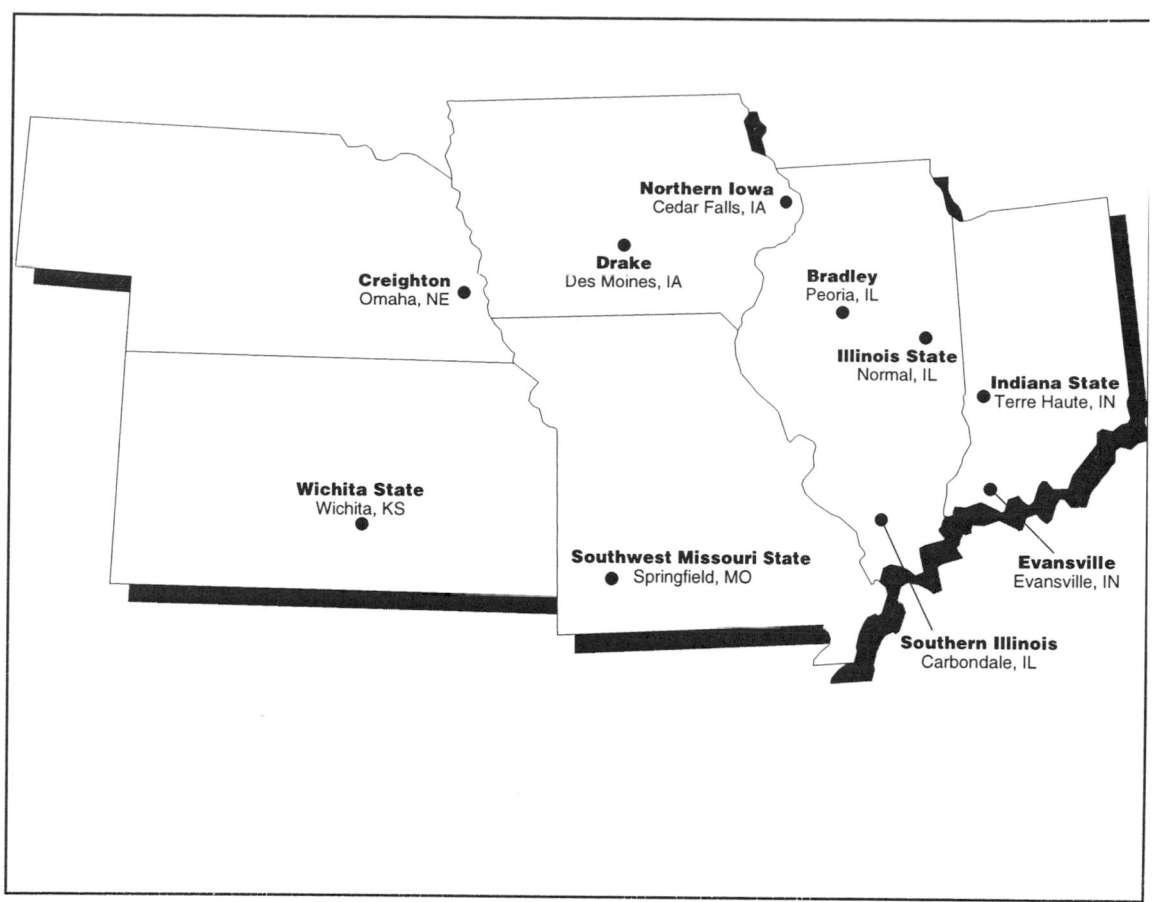

MISSOURI VALLEY

ADDRESS: 1000 St. Louis Union Station, Suite 333, St. Louis, MO 63103.

PHONE/FAX: (314) 421-0339/3505.

INTERNET ADDRESS: www.mvc.org

PREVIOUS NAME: Missouri Valley Intercollegiate Athletic Association.

CURRENT MEMBERS: Bradley (1949-51 and 1956-98), Creighton (1929-48 and 1977-98), Drake (1908-51 and 1957-98), Evansville (1995-98), Illinois State (1981-98), Indiana State (1977-98), Northern Iowa (1992-98), Southern Illinois (1975-98), Southwest Missouri State (1991-98), Wichita State (1946-98).

FORMER MEMBERS: Butler (1933 and 1934), Cincinnati (1958-70), Detroit (1950-57), Grinnell, Ia. (1919-39), Houston (1951-60), Iowa State (1908-28), Kansas (1908-28), Kansas State (1914-28), Louisville (1965-75), Memphis State (1968-73), Missouri (1908-28), Nebraska (1908-28), New Mexico State (1971-83), North Texas State (1958-75), Oklahoma (1920-28), Oklahoma A&M (1926-57), St. Louis (1938-74), Tulsa (1935-96), Washburn, Kan. (1935-41), Washington, Mo. (1908-47), West Texas State (1971-86).

NCAA TOURNAMENT RECORD: 69-68 (.504).

NIT TITLES (5): Bradley (1957-60-64-82), Southern Illinois (1967).

ALL-TIME SCORING LEADER: Hersey Hawkins, Bradley (3,008 points from 1985-88).

SINGLE-SEASON SCORING LEADER: Hersey Hawkins, Bradley (36.3 points per game in 1987-88).

REGULAR-SEASON CHAMPIONS (since 1929): Bradley (6 outright-1 tie), Butler (2-0), Cincinnati (6-1), Creighton (6-5), Drake (1-6), Houston (1-0), Illinois State (2-2), Indiana State (1-0), Louisville (4-3), Memphis State (1-1), New Mexico State (0-1), Oklahoma A&M (9-4), St. Louis (3-2), Southern Illinois (1-2), Tulsa (4-2), Washington, Mo. (1-2), Wichita State (4-1).

MVC TOURNAMENT TITLES: Creighton (4; 1978-81-89-91), Southern Illinois (4; 1977-93-94-95), Tulsa (4; 1982-84-86-96), Illinois State (3; 1983-90-97), Bradley (2; 1980 and 1988), Wichita State (2; 1985 and 1987), Indiana State (1; 1979), Southwest Missouri State (1; 1992).

YEAR-BY-YEAR CHAMPIONS (incl. conference records): 1962—Bradley (10-2), Cincinnati (10-2)*; **1963**—Cincinnati (11-1); **1964**—Drake (10-2), Wichita St. (10-2)*; **1965**—Wichita St. (11-3); **1966**—Cincinnati (10-4); **1967**—Louisville (12-2); **1968**—Louisville (14-2); **1969**—Drake (13-3), Louisville (13-3)*; **1970**—Drake (14-2); **1971**—Drake (9-5)*, Louisville (9-5), St. Louis (9-5); **1972**—Louisville (12-2)*, Memphis (12-2); **1973**—Memphis (12-2); **1974**—Louisville (11-1); **1975**—Louisville (12-2); **1976**—Wichita St. (10-2); **1977**—NM. St. (8-4), SIU (8-4); **1978**—Creighton (12-4); **1979**—Ind. St. (16-0); **1980**—Bradley (13-3); **1981**—Wichita St. (12-4); **1982**—Bradley (13-3); **1983**—Wichita St. (17-1); **1984**—Ill. St. (13-3), Tulsa (13-3); **1985**—Tulsa (12-4); **1986**—Bradley (16-0); **1987**—Tulsa (11-3); **1988**—Bradley (12-2); **1989**—Creighton (11-3); **1990**—SIU (10-4); **1991**—Creighton (12-4); **1992**—Ill. St. (14-4), SIU (14-4); **1993**—Ill. St. (13-5); **1994**—Tulsa (15-3); **1995**—Tulsa (15-3); **1996**—Bradley (15-3); **1997**—Illinois State (14-4).

*Won playoff.

NOTE: The MVIAA had North and South Divisions from 1908-10 and 1912-14. There was no conference competition in 1944 and 1945 because of World War II. The nucleus of what is now the Big Eight Conference split from the other MVIAA's members prior to the start of the 1928-29 season.

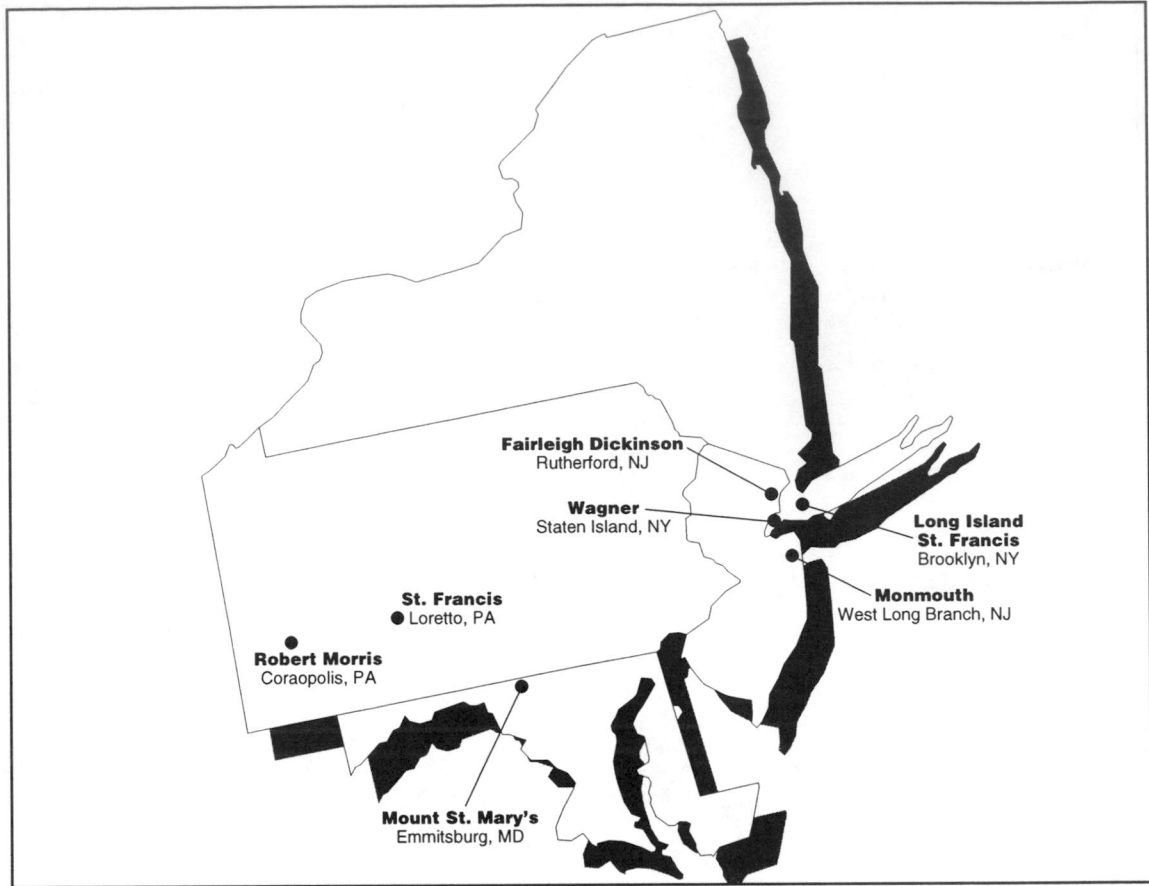

Fairleigh Dickinson
Rutherford, NJ

Wagner
Staten Island, NY

Long Island
St. Francis
Brooklyn, NY

St. Francis
Loretto, PA

Monmouth
West Long Branch, NJ

Robert Morris
Coraopolis, PA

Mount St. Mary's
Emmitsburg, MD

NORTHEAST

ADDRESS: 220 Old New Brunswick Road, Piscataway, NJ 08854.

PHONE/FAX: (908) 562-0877/8838.

PREVIOUS NAME: ECAC Metro (1982-88).

CURRENT MEMBERS: Central Connecticut State (since 1998), Fairleigh Dickinson (1982-98), Long Island (1982-98), Monmouth (1986-98), Mount St. Mary's (1990-98), Robert Morris (1982-98), St. Francis, N.Y. (1982-98), St. Francis, Pa. (1982-98), Wagner (1982-98). Maryland-Baltimore County is slated to join the NEC in 1999, and Quinnipiac (Conn.) and Sacred Heart (Conn.) are slated to join by 2000.

FORMER MEMBERS: Baltimore (1982 and 1983), Loyola, Md. (1982-89), Marist (1982-97), Rider (1993-97), Siena (1982-84), Towson State (1982).

NCAA TOURNAMENT RECORD: 1-16 (.059).

NIT TITLES (2): Long Island (1939 and 1941). Both titles occurred before the league was formed.

ALL-TIME SCORING LEADER: Terrance Bailey, Wagner (2,591 points from 1984-87).

SINGLE-SEASON SCORING LEADER: Charles Jones, LIU (30.1 points per game in 1996-97).

REGULAR-SEASON CHAMPIONS: Fairleigh Dickinson (2 outright-2 ties), Long Island (2-1), Marist (2-1), Mount St. Mary's (1-0), Rider (3-0), Robert Morris (5-1), St. Francis, Pa. (0-1).

NORTHEAST TOURNAMENT TITLES: Robert Morris (5; 1982-83-89-90-92), Fairleigh Dickinson (2; 1985 and 1988), Long Island (2; 1984 and 1997), Marist (2; 1986 and 1987), Rider (2; 1993 and 1994), Mount St. Mary's (1; 1995), Monmouth (1; 1996), St. Francis, Pa. (1; 1991).

YEAR-BY-YEAR CHAMPIONS (incl. conference records): 1982—Fairleigh Dickinson (12-3/North), Robert Morris (9-5/South); **1983**—Long Island (11-3/N), Robert Morris (12-2/S); **1984**—Long Island (11-5), Robert Morris (11-5); **1985**—Marist (11-3); **1986**—Fairleigh Dickinson (13-3); **1987**—Marist (15-1); **1988**—Fairleigh Dickinson (13-3), Marist (13-3); **1989**—Robert Morris (12-4); **1990**—Robert Morris (12-4); **1991**—Fairleigh Dickinson (13-3), St. Francis, Pa. (13-3); **1992**—Robert Morris (12-4); **1993**—Rider (14-4); **1994**—Rider (14-4); **1995**—Rider (13-5); **1996**—Mount St. Mary's (16-2); **1997**—Long Island (15-3).

NOTE: The NEC had North and South Divisions in its first two seasons in 1982 and 1983.

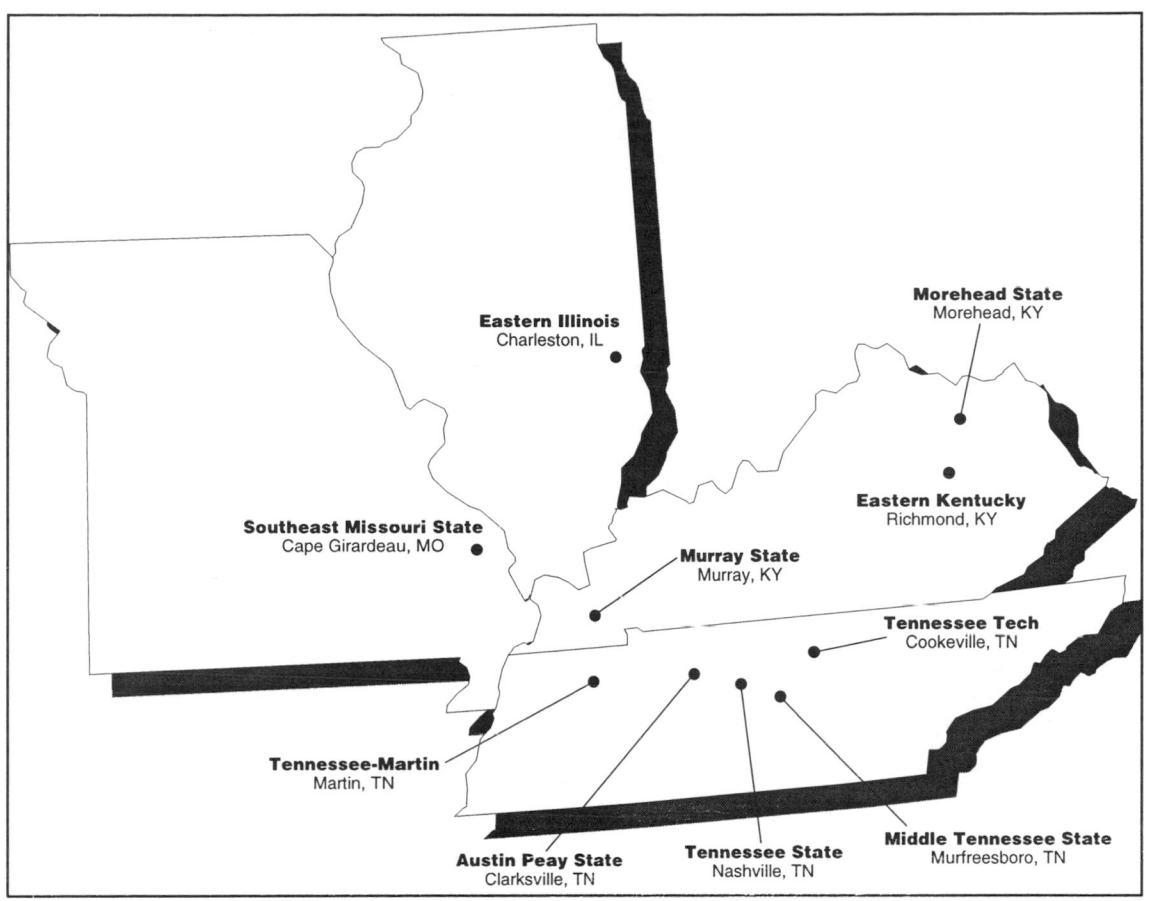

Morehead State Morehead, KY

Eastern Illinois Charleston, IL

Eastern Kentucky Richmond, KY

Southeast Missouri State Cape Girardeau, MO

Murray State Murray, KY

Tennessee Tech Cookeville, TN

Tennessee-Martin Martin, TN

Austin Peay State Clarksville, TN

Tennessee State Nashville, TN

Middle Tennessee State Murfreesboro, TN

OHIO VALLEY

ADDRESS: 278 Franklin Road, Suite 103, Brentwood, TN 37027.

PHONE/FAX: (615) 371-1698/1788.

CURRENT MEMBERS: Austin Peay State (1964-98), Eastern Illinois (1997 and 1998), Eastern Kentucky (1949-98), Middle Tennessee State (1953-98), Morehead State (1949-98), Murray State (1949-61 and 1963-98), Southeast Missouri State (1992-98), Tennessee-Martin (1993-98), Tennessee State (1988-98), Tennessee Tech (1949-98).

FORMER MEMBERS: Akron (1981-87), East Tennessee State (1959-78), Evansville (1949-52), Marshall (1949-52), Western Kentucky (1949-82), Youngstown State (1982-88).

NCAA TOURNAMENT RECORD: 20-48 (.294).

ALL-TIME SCORING LEADER: Joe Jakubick, Akron (2,583 points from 1981-84).

SINGLE-SEASON SCORING LEADERS: Jim McDaniels, Western Kentucky (878 points in 1970-71) and Tom Chilton, east Tennessee State (32.1 points per game in 1960-61).

REGULAR-SEASON CHAMPIONS: Akron (0 outright-1 tie), Austin Peay State (2-2), Eastern Kentucky (4-2), East Tennessee State (0-2), Middle Tennessee State (2-3), Morehead State (1-7), Murray State (9-7), Tennessee State (1-1), Tennessee Tech (2-2), Western Kentucky (13-6).

OVC TOURNAMENT TITLES: Western Kentucky (10; 1949-52-53-54-65-66-76-78-80-81), Murray State (8; 1951-64-88-90-91-92-95-97), Middle Tennessee State (5; 1975-77-82-85-89), Eastern Kentucky (3; 1950-55-79), Austin Peay (2; 1987 and 1996), Morehead State (2; 1983

and 1984), Tennessee State (2; 1993 and 1994), Akron (1; 1986), Tennessee Tech (1; 1967).

YEAR-BY-YEAR CHAMPIONS (incl. conference records): 1949—Western Kentucky (8-2); **1950**—Western Kentucky (8-0); **1951**—Murray State (9-3); **1952**—Western Kentucky (9-1); **1953**—Eastern Kentucky (9-1); **1954**—Western Kentucky (9-1); **1955**—Western Kentucky (8-2); **1956**—Morehead State (7-3), Tennessee Tech (7-3), Western Kentucky (7-3); **1957**—Morehead State (9-1), Western Kentucky (9-1); **1958**—Tennessee Tech (8-2); **1959**—Eastern Kentucky (10-2); **1960**—Western Kentucky (10-2); **1961**—Eastern Kentucky (9-3), Morehead State (9-3), Western Kentucky (9-3); **1962**—Western Kentucky (11-1); **1963**—Morehead State (8-4), Tennessee Tech (8-4); **1964**—Murray State (11-3); **1965**—Eastern Kentucky (13-1); **1966**—Western Kentucky (14-0); **1967**—Western Kentucky (13-1); **1968**—East Tennessee State (10-4), Murray State (10-4); **1969**—Morehead State (11-3), Murray State (11-3); **1970**—Western Kentucky (14-0); **1971**—Western Kentucky (12-2); **1972**—Eastern Kentucky (9-5), Morehead State (9-5), —Western Kentucky (9-5); **1973**—Austin Peay (11-3); **1974**—Austin Peay (10-4), Morehead State (10-4); **1975**—Middle Tennessee State (12-2); **1976**—Western Kentucky (11-3); **1977**—Austin Peay (13-1); **1978**—East Tennessee State (10-4), Middle Tennessee State (10-4); **1979**—Eastern Kentucky (9-3); **1980**—Murray State (10-2), Western Kentucky (10-2); **1981**—Western Kentucky (12-2); **1982**—Murray State (13-3), Western Kentucky (13-3); **1983**—Murray State (11-3); **1984**—Morehead State (12-2); **1985**—Tennessee Tech (11-3); **1986**—Akron (10-4), Middle Tennessee State (10-4); **1987**—Middle Tennessee State (11-3); **1988**—Murray State (13-1); **1989**—Middle Tennessee State (10-2), Murray State (10-2); **1990**—Murray State (10-2); **1991**—Murray State (10-2); **1992**—Murray State (11-3); **1993**—Tennessee State (13-3); **1994**—Murray State (15-1); **1995**—Murray State (11-5), Tennessee State (11-5); **1996**—Murray State (12-4).Marco, (add to year-by-year champions) — 1997-Austin Peay (12-6), Murray State (12-6)

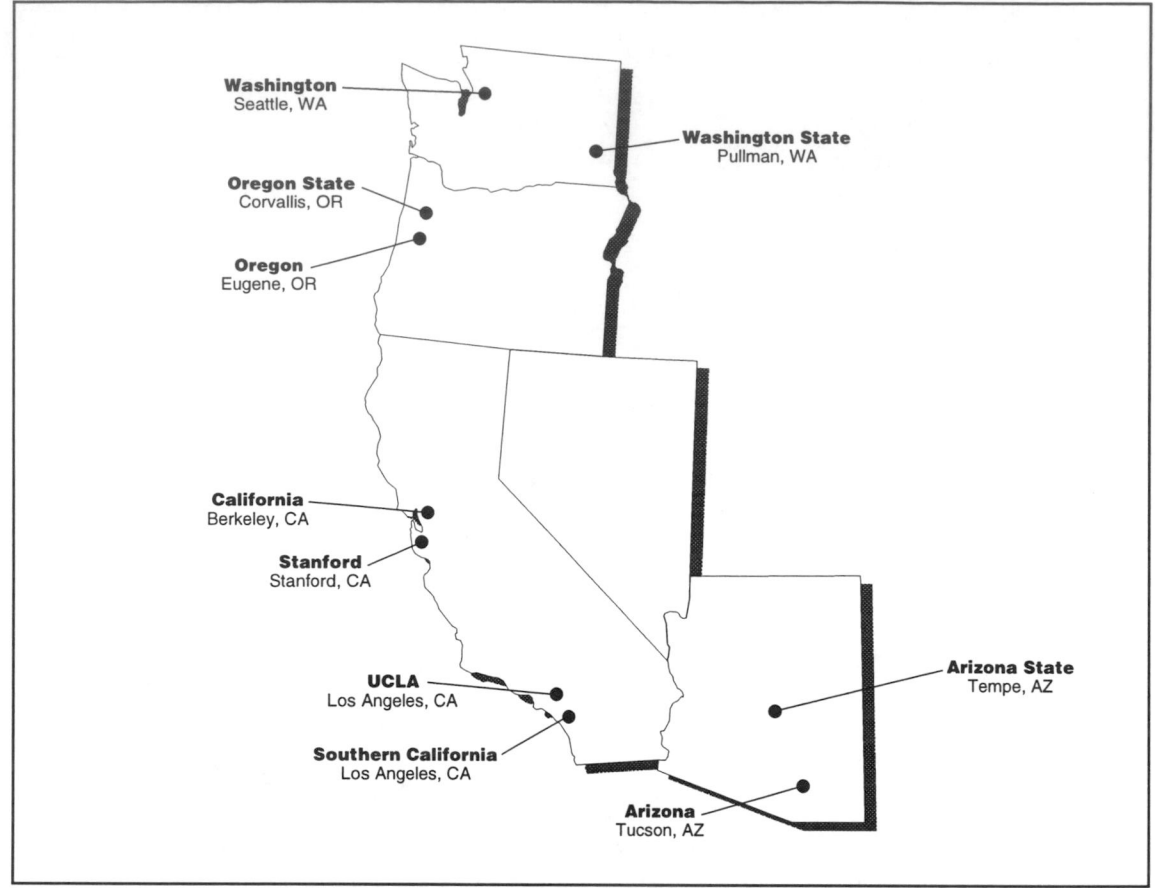

PACIFIC-10

ADDRESS: 800 South Broadway, Suite 400, Walnut Creek, CA 94596.

PHONE/FAX: (510) 932-4411/4601.

INTERNET ADDRESS: www.pac-10.org

PREVIOUS NAMES: Pacific Coast Conference (1916-59), Athletic Association of Western Universities (1960-68), Pacific-8 (1969-78).

CURRENT MEMBERS: Arizona (1979-98), Arizona State (1979-98), California (1916-98), Oregon (1916-59 and 1965-98), Oregon State (1916-59 and 1965-98), Southern California (1922-98), Stanford (1917-98), UCLA (1928-98), Washington (1916-98), Washington State (1917-59 and 1964-98).

FORMER MEMBERS: Idaho (1922-59), Montana (1924-29).

NCAA TOURNAMENT RECORD: 153-99 (.607).

NCAA TITLES (15): Arizona (1997), California (1959), Oregon (1939), UCLA (1964-65-67-68-69-70-71-72-73-75-95), Stanford (1942).

NIT TITLES (2): Stanford (1991), UCLA (1985).

ALL-TIME SCORING LEADER: Don MacLean, UCLA (2,608 points from 1989-92).

SINGLE-SEASON SCORING LEADER: Lew Alcindor, UCLA (29 points per game in 1966-67).

REGULAR-SEASON CHAMPIONS (since 1916): Arizona (6 outright-1 tie), California (10-4), Idaho (2-0), Oregon (2-1), Oregon State (8-4), Southern California (6-1), Stanford (5-2), UCLA (25-2), Washington (6-3), Washington State (2-0).

PACIFIC-10 TOURNAMENT TITLES: Arizona (3; 1988-89-90), UCLA (1; 1987).

YEAR-BY-YEAR CHAMPIONS (incl. conference records): 1933—Oregon St. (12-4/N)*; **1934**—Washington (14-2/N)*; **1935**—Southern Cal (11-1/S)*; **1936**—Stanford (8-4/S)*; **1937**—Stanford (10-2/S)*; **1938**—Stanford (10-2/S)*; **1939**—Oregon (14-2/N)*; **1940**—Southern Cal (10-2/S)*; **1941**—Washington St. (13-3/N)*; **1942**—Stanford (11-1/S)*; **1943**—Washington (12-4/N)*; **1944**—Washington (15-1/N), California (4-0/S); **1945**—Oregon (11-5/N), UCLA (3-1/S); **1946**—California (11-1/S)*; **1947**—Oregon St. (13-3/N)*; **1948**—Washington (10-6/N)*; **1949**—Oregon St. (12-4/N)*; **1950**—UCLA (10-2/S)*; **1951**—Washington (11-5/N)*; **1952**—UCLA (8-4/S)*; **1953**—Washington (15-1/N)*; **1954**—Southern Cal (8-4/S)*; **1955**—Oregon St. (15-1/N)*; **1956**—UCLA (16-0); **1957**—California (14-2); **1958**—California (12-4), Oregon St. (12-4); **1959**—California (14-2); **1960**—California (11-1); **1961**—Southern Cal (9-3); **1962**—UCLA (10-2); **1963**—Stanford (7-5), UCLA (7-5); **1964**—UCLA (15-0); **1965**—UCLA (14-0); **1966**—Oregon St. (12-2); **1967**—UCLA (14-0); **1968**—UCLA (14-0); **1969**—UCLA (13-1); **1970**—UCLA (12-2); **1971**—UCLA (14-0); **1972**—UCLA (14-0); **1973**—UCLA (14-0); **1974**—UCLA (12-2); **1975**—UCLA (12-2); **1976**—UCLA (12-2); **1977**—UCLA (11-3); **1978**—UCLA (14-0); **1979**—UCLA (15-3); **1980**—Oregon St. (16-2); **1981**—Oregon St. (17-1); **1982**—Oregon St. (16-2); **1983**—UCLA (15-3); **1984**—Oregon St. (15-3), Washington (15-3); **1985**—Southern Cal (13-5), Washington (13-5); **1986**—Arizona (14-4); **1987**—UCLA (14-4); **1988**—Arizona (17-1); **1989**—Arizona (17-1); **1990**—Arizona (15-3), Oregon St. (15-3); **1991**—Arizona (14-4); **1992**—UCLA (16-2); **1993**—Arizona (17-1); **1994**—Arizona (14-4); **1995**—UCLA (16-2); **1996**—UCLA (16-2); **1997**—UCLA (15-3).

*Won divisional playoff.

NOTE: The PCC had North and South Divisions from 1923-55. No official league competition in 1917-18.

PATRIOT LEAGUE

ADDRESS: 3897 Adler Place, Building C, Suite 310, Bethlehem, PA 18017.

PHONE/FAX: (610) 691-2414/8414.

CURRENT MEMBERS: Army (1991-98), Bucknell (1991-98), Colgate (1991-98), Holy Cross (1991-98), Lafayette (1991-98), Lehigh (1991-98), Navy (1992-98).

FORMER MEMBER: Fordham (1991-95).

NCAA TOURNAMENT RECORD: 0-6 (.000).

REGULAR-SEASON CHAMPIONS: Bucknell (1 outright-2 ties), Colgate (0-3), Fordham (1-2), Holy Cross (0-1), Navy (1-2).

PATRIOT TOURNAMENT TITLES: Colgate (2; 1995 and 1996), Fordham (2; 1991 and 1992), Navy (2; 1994 and 1997), Holy Cross (1; 1993).

YEAR-BY-YEAR CHAMPIONS (incl. conference records): 1991—Fordham (11-1); **1992**—Bucknell (11-3), Fordham (11-3); **1993**—Bucknell (13-1); **1994**—Colgate (9-5), Fordham (9-5), Holy Cross (9-5), Navy (9-5); **1995**—(11-3); **1996**—Colgate (9-3), Navy (9-3); **1997**—Navy (10-2).

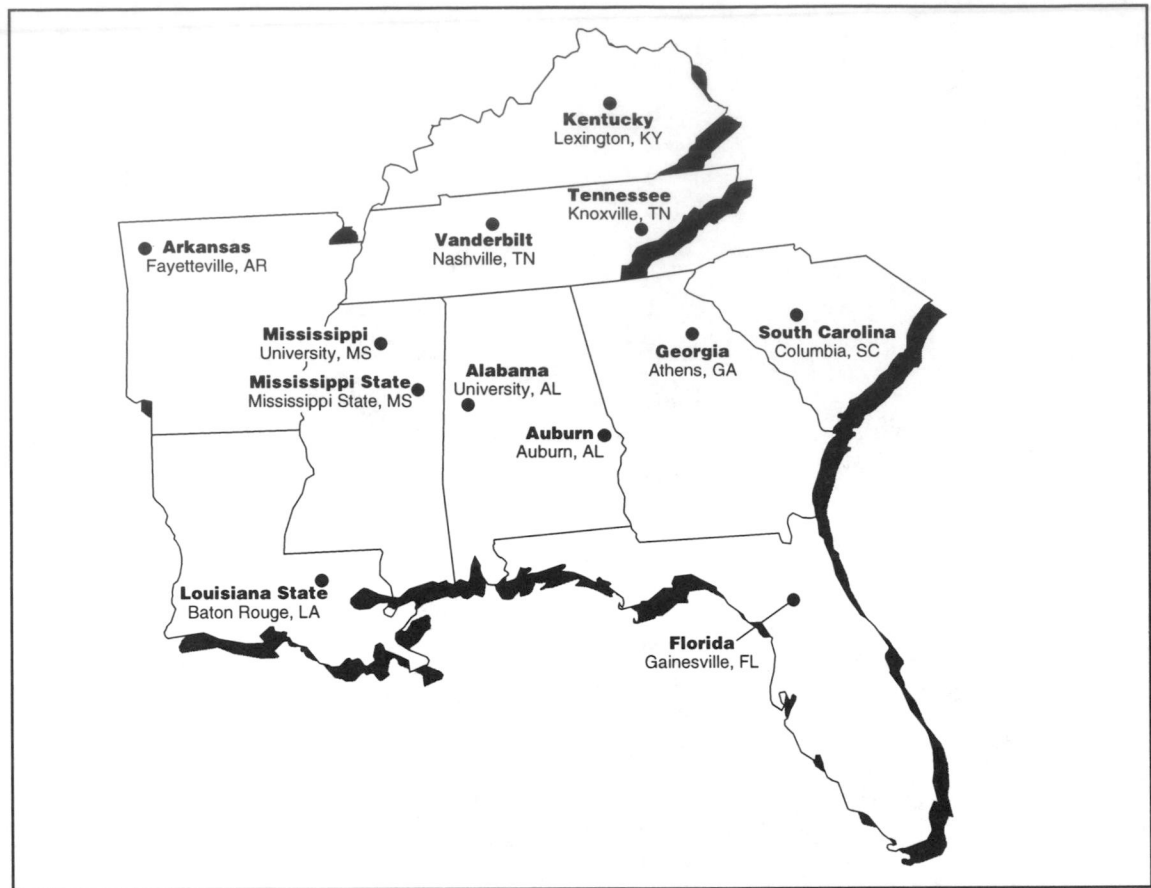

SOUTHEASTERN

ADDRESS: 2201 Civic Center Boulevard, Birmingham, AL 35203-1103.

PHONE/FAX: (205) 458-3010/3031.

INTERNET ADDRESS: www.secsports.com

CURRENT MEMBERS: Alabama (1933-98), Arkansas (1992-98), Auburn (1933-98), Florida (1933-98), Georgia (1933-98), Kentucky (1933-98), Louisiana State (1933-98), Mississippi (1933-98), Mississippi State (1933-98), South Carolina (1992-98), Tennessee (1933-98), Vanderbilt (1933-98).

FORMER MEMBERS: Georgia Tech (1933-64), Sewanee (1933-40), Tulane (1933-66).

NCAA TOURNAMENT RECORD: 163-114 (.588).

NCAA TITLES (7): Arkansas (1994), Kentucky (1948-49-51-58-78-96).

NIT TITLES (3): Kentucky (1946 and 1976), Vanderbilt (1990).

ALL-TIME SCORING LEADER: Pete Maravich, LSU (3,667 points from 1968-70).

SINGLE-SEASON SCORING LEADER: Pete Maravich, LSU (44.5 points per game in 1969-70).

REGULAR-SEASON CHAMPIONS: Alabama (5 outright-2 ties), Arkansas (3-1), Auburn (1-0), Florida (1-1), Georgia (1-0), Georgia Tech (1-0), Kentucky (31-10), Louisiana State (4-4), Mississippi (1-0), Mississippi State (4-3), South Carolina (1-0), Tennessee (2-4), Tulane (1-0), Vanderbilt (2-1).

SEC TOURNAMENT TITLES: Kentucky (21; 1933-37-39-40-42-44-45-46-47-48-49-50-52-84-86-88-92-93-94-95-97), Alabama (6; 1934-1982-87-89-90-91), Tennessee (4; 1936-41-43-79), Auburn (1; 1985), Georgia (1; 1983), Georgia Tech (1; 1938), Louisiana State (1; 1980), Mississippi (1; 1981), Mississippi State (1; 1996), Vanderbilt (1; 1951).

YEAR-BY-YEAR CHAMPIONS (incl. conference records): 1948—Kentucky (9-0); **1949**—Kentucky (13-0); **1950**—Kentucky (11-2); **1951**—Kentucky (14-0); **1952**—Kentucky (14-0); **1953**—Louisiana State (13-0); **1954**—Kentucky (14-0), Louisiana State (14-0); **1955**—Kentucky (12-2); **1956**—Alabama (14-0); **1957**—Kentucky (12-2); **1958**—Kentucky (12-2); **1959**—Mississippi State (13-1); **1960**—Auburn (12-2); **1961**—Mississippi State (11-3); **1962**—Kentucky (13-1), Mississippi State (13-1); **1963**—Mississippi State (12-2); **1964**—Kentucky (11-3); **1965**—Vanderbilt (15-1); **1966**—Kentucky (15-1); **1967**—Tennessee (15-3); **1968**—Kentucky (15-3); **1969**—Kentucky (16-2); **1970**—Kentucky (17-1); **1971**—Kentucky (16-2); **1972**—Kentucky (14-4), Tennessee (14-4); **1973**—Kentucky (14-4); **1974**—Alabama (15-3), Vanderbilt (15-3); **1975**—Alabama (15-3), Kentucky (15-3); **1976**—Alabama (15-3); **1977**—Kentucky (16-2), Tennessee (16-2); **1978**—Kentucky (16-2); **1979**—Louisiana State (14-4); **1980**—Kentucky (15-3); **1981**—Louisiana State (17-1); **1982**—Kentucky (13-5), Tennessee (13-5); **1983**—Kentucky (13-5); **1984**—Kentucky (14-4); **1985**—Louisiana State (13-5); **1986**—Kentucky (17-1); **1987**—Alabama (16-2); **1988**—Kentucky (13-5); **1989**—Florida (13-5); **1990**—Georgia (13-5); **1991**—Louisiana State (13-5), Mississippi State (13-5); **1992**—Kentucky (12-4/E), Arkansas (13-3/W); **1993**—Vanderbilt (14-2/E), Arkansas (10-6/W); **1994**—Florida (12-4/E), Kentucky (12-4/E), Arkansas (14-2/W); **1995**—Kentucky (14-2/E), Arkansas (12-4/W), Mississippi State (12-4/W); **1996**—Kentucky (16-0/E), Mississippi State (10-6/W); **1997**—South Carolina (15-1/E); Mississippi (11-5/W); **1997**—South Carolina (15-1/E); Mississippi (11-5/W)

NOTE: The SEC introduced Eastern and Western Divisions for the first time in the 1991-92 season.

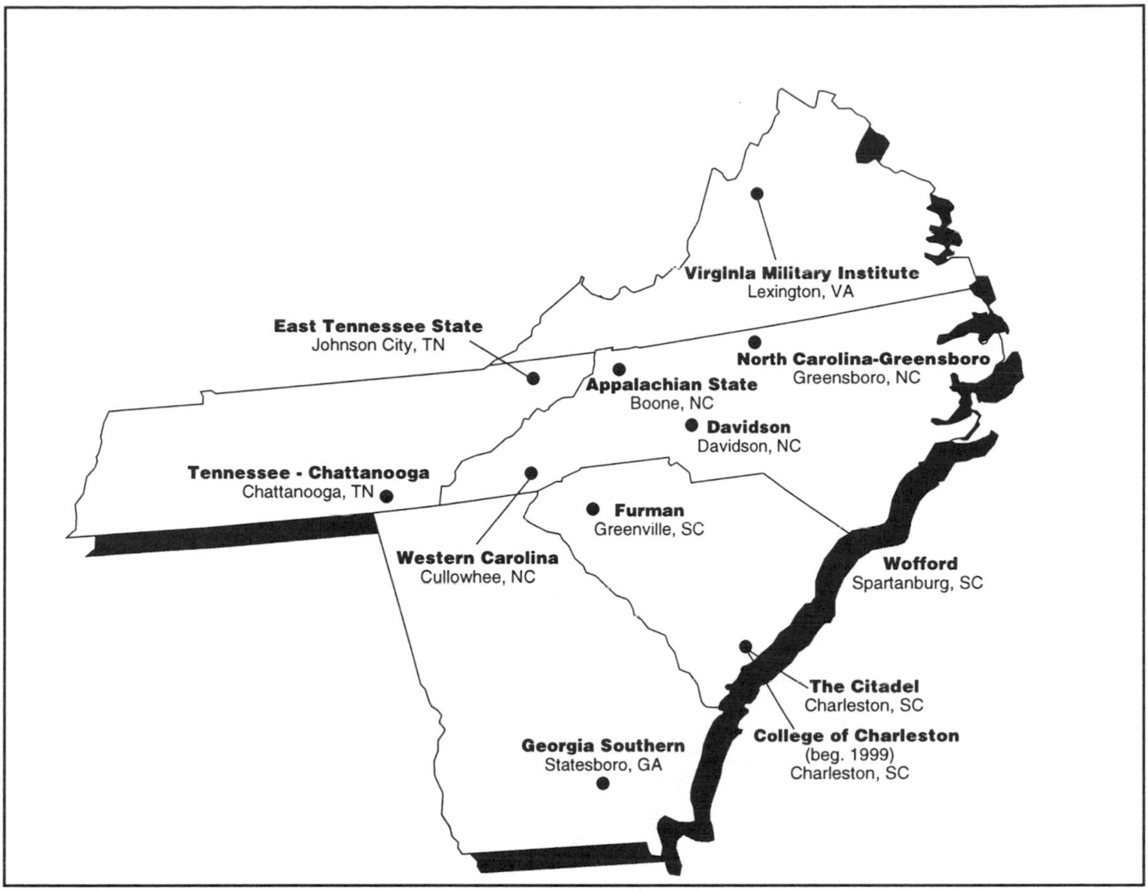

SOUTHERN

ADDRESS: One West Pack Square, Suite 1508, Asheville, NC 28801.

PHONE/FAX: (704) 255-7872/251-5006.

INTERNET ADDRESS: www.socon.org

PREVIOUS NAME: Southern Intercollegiate Athletic.

CURRENT MEMBERS: Appalachian State (1973-98), The Citadel (1937-98), Davidson (1937-88 and 1993-98), East Tennessee State (1980-98), Furman (1937-98), Georgia Southern (1993-98), North Carolina-Greensboro (since 1998), Tennessee-Chattanooga (1978-98), Virginia Military (1926-98), Western Carolina (1978-98), Wofford (since 1998). The College of Charleston is slated to join the league in 1999.

FORMER MEMBERS: Alabama (1922-32), Auburn (1922-32), Clemson (1922-53), Duke (1929-53), East Carolina (1966-77), George Washington (1942 and 1943 and 1946-70), Georgia (1922-32), Georgia Tech (1922-32), Kentucky (1922-32), Louisiana State (1923-32), Marshall (1978-97), Maryland (1924-53), Mississippi (1923-32), Mississippi State (1922-32), North Carolina (1922-53), North Carolina State (1922-53), Richmond (1937-76), University of the South (1924-32), South Carolina (1923-53), Tennessee (1922-32), Tulane (1923-32), Vanderbilt (1923-32), Virginia (1922-37), Virginia Tech (1922-65), Wake Forest (1937-53), Washington & Lee (1922-58), West Virginia (1951-68), William & Mary (1937-77).

NCAA TOURNAMENT RECORD: 28-55 (.337).

ALL-TIME SCORING LEADER: Skip Henderson, Marshall (2,574 points from 1985-88).

SINGLE-SEASON SCORING LEADER: Frank Selvy, Furman (41.7 points per game in 1953-54).

REGULAR-SEASON CHAMPIONS: Alabama (1 outright-0 ties), Appalachian State (2-1), Auburn (1-0), Davidson (10-2), East Tennessee State (1-2), Furman (3-2), George Washington (1-1), Georgia (1-0), Marshall (4-1), Maryland (0-1), North Carolina (7-0), North Carolina State (6-0), South Carolina (4-0), Tennessee-Chattanooga (9-3), Tulane (1-0), Virginia (1-0), Virginia Military (1-1), Virginia Tech (1-0), Wake Forest (1-0), Washington & Lee (3-0), Western Carolina (1-0), West Virginia (9-1).

SC TOURNAMENT TITLES: West Virginia (10; 1955-56-57-58-59-60-62-63-65-67), North Carolina (8; 1922-24-25-26-35-36-40-45), UT-Chattanooga (8; 1981-82-83-88-93-94-95-97), North Carolina State (7; 1929-47-48-49-50-51-52), Furman (6; 1971-73-74-75-78-80), Davidson (5; 1966-68-69-70-86), Duke (5; 1938-41-42-44-46), East Tennessee State (4; 1989-90-91-92), George Washington (3; 1943-54-61), Marshall (3; 1984-85-87), VMI (3; 1964-76-77), Washington & Lee (2; 1934 and 1937), Alabama (1; 1930), Appalachian State (1; 1979), Clemson (1; 1939), East Carolina (1; 1972), Georgia (1; 1932), Maryland (1; 1931), Mississippi (1; 1928), Mississippi State (1; 1923), South Carolina (1; 1933), Vanderbilt (1; 1927), Wake Forest (1; 1953), Western Carolina (1; 1996).

YEAR-BY-YEAR CHAMPIONS (incl. conference records): 1980—Furman (14-1); **1981**—Appalachian St. (11-5), Davidson (11-5), Tenn.-Chat. (11-5); **1982**—Tenn.-Chat. (15-1); **1983**—Tenn.-Chat. (15-1); **1984**—Marshall (13-3); **1985**—Tenn.-Chat. (14-2); **1986**—Tenn.-Chat. (12-4); **1987**—Marshall (15-1); **1988**—Marshall (14-2); **1989**—Tenn.-Chat. (10-4); **1990**—E. Tenn. St. (12-2); **1991**—E. Tenn. St. (11-3), Furman (11-3), Tenn.-Chat. (11-3); **1992**—E. Tenn. St. (12-2), Tenn.-Chat. (12-2); **1993**—Tenn.-Chat. (16-2); **1994**—Tenn.-Chat. (14-4); **1995**—Marshall (10-4/N), UTC (11-3/S), **1996**—Davidson (14-0/N), W. Caro. (10-4/S).Marco, (add to year-by-year champions) — 1997-Davidson (10-4/N), Marshall (10-4/N); UTC (11-3/S)

NOTE: League split into two divisions in 1995—Northern and Southern.

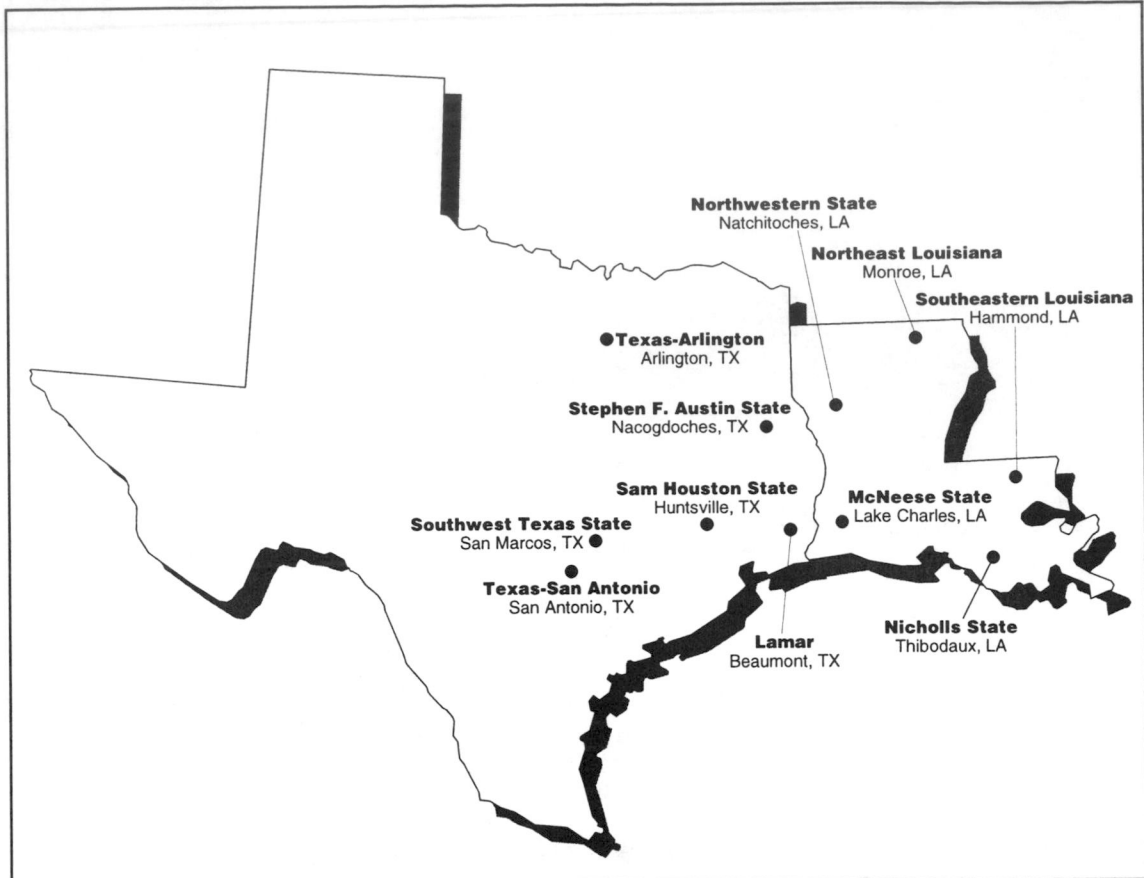

SOUTHLAND

ADDRESS: 8150 North Central Expressway, Suite 930, Dallas, TX 75206.

PHONE/FAX: (214) 750-7522/8077.

CURRENT MEMBERS: Lamar (1969-87 and since 1998), McNeese State (1973-98), Nicholls State (1992-98), Northeast Louisiana (1983-98), Northwestern State, La. (1988-98), Sam Houston State (1988-98), Southeastern Louisiana (since 1998), Southwest Texas State (1988-98), Stephen F. Austin State (1988-98), Texas-Arlington (1969-86 and 1988-98), Texas-San Antonio (1992-98).

FORMER MEMBERS: Abilene Christian (1969-73), Arkansas State (1969-87), Louisiana Tech (1972-87), North Texas (1983-96), Southwestern Louisiana (1972-82), Trinity, Tex. (1969-72).

NCAA TOURNAMENT RECORD: 11-23 (.324).

ALL-TIME SCORING LEADER: Dwight "Bo" Lamar, Southwestern Louisiana (3,493 points from 1970-73).

SINGLE-SEASON SCORING LEADER: Dwight "Bo" Lamar, Southwestern Louisiana (36.3 points per game in 1971-72).

Regular-Season Champions (since 1964): Abilene Christian (2 outright-1 tie), Arkansas State (3-1), Lamar (7-1), Louisiana Tech (5-0), McNeese State (1-2), Nicholls State (1-0), Northeast Louisiana (6-1), North Texas (2-0), Southwest Texas State (0-1), Southwestern Louisiana (2-0), Texas-San Antonio (1-0), Trinity (1-0).

SLC TOURNAMENT TITLES: Northeast Louisiana (6; 1986-90-91-92-93-96), Louisiana Tech (3; 1984-85-87), Lamar (2; 1981 and 1983), Southwest Texas State (2; 1994 and 1997), McNeese State (1; 1989), Nicholls State (1; 1995), North Texas (1; 1988), Southwestern Louisiana (1; 1982).

YEAR-BY-YEAR CHAMPIONS (incl. conference records): 1964—Lamar (7-1); **1965**—Abilene Christian (6-2), Arkansas State (6-2); **1966**—Abilene Christian (8-0); **1967**—Arkansas State (8-0); **1968**—Abilene Christian (6-2); **1969**—Trinity, Tex. (7-1); **1970**—Lamar (7-1); **1971**—Arkansas State (6-2); **1972**—Southwestern Louisiana (8-0); **1973**—Southwestern Louisiana (12-0); **1974**—Arkansas State (4-0); **1975**—McNeese State (6-2); **1976**—Louisiana Tech (9-1); **1977**—Southwestern Louisiana (8-2); **1978**—Lamar (8-2), McNeese State (8-2); **1979**—Lamar (9-1); **1980**—Lamar (8-2); **1981**—Lamar (8-2); **1982**—Southwestern Louisiana (8-2); **1983**—Lamar (9-3); **1984**—Lamar (11-1); **1985**—Louisiana Tech (11-1); **1986**—Northeast Louisiana (9-3); **1987**—Louisiana Tech (9-1); **1988**—North Texas (12-2); **1989**—North Texas (10-4); **1990**—Northeast Louisiana (13-1); **1991**—Northeast Louisiana (13-1); **1992**—Texas-San Antonio (15-3); **1993**—Northeast Louisiana (17-1); **1994**—Northeast Louisiana (15-3); **1995**—Nicholls State (17-1); **1996**—Northeast Louisiana (13-5); **1997**—McNeese State (10-6), Northeast Louisiana (10-6), Southwest Texas State (10-6).

NOTE: The SLC moved up to Division I status in 1976.

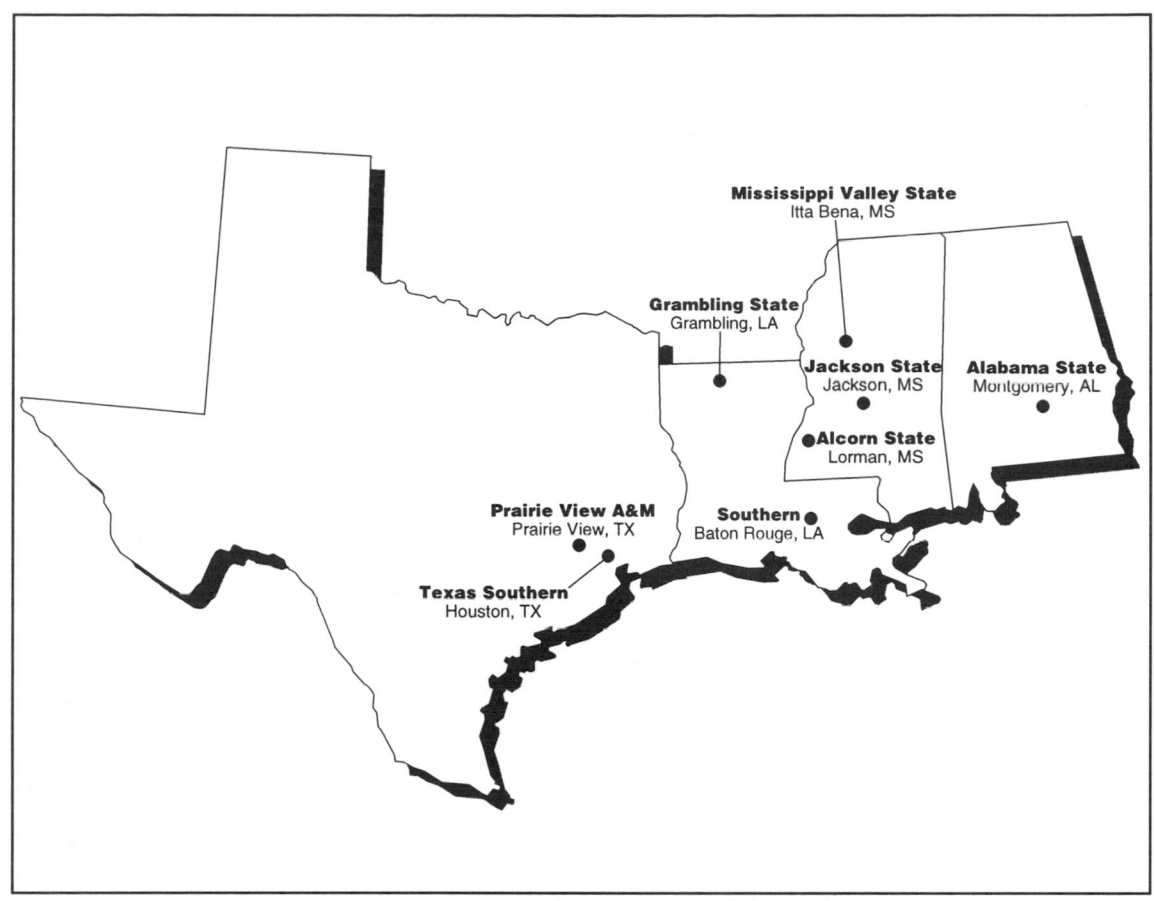

Mississippi Valley State
Itta Bena, MS

Grambling State
Grambling, LA

Jackson State
Jackson, MS

Alabama State
Montgomery, AL

Alcorn State
Lorman, MS

Prairie View A&M
Prairie View, TX

Southern
Baton Rouge, LA

Texas Southern
Houston, TX

SOUTHWESTERN ATHLETIC

ADDRESS: 1500 Sugar Bowl Drive, Louisiana Superdome, New Orleans, LA 70112.

PHONE/FAX: (504) 523-7573/7513.

CURRENT MEMBERS: Alabama State (1983-98), Alcorn State (1963-98), Grambling State (1959-98), Jackson State (1959-98), Mississippi Valley State (1969-98), Prairie View A&M (1921-98 except for 1990-91), Southern (1935-98), Texas Southern (1955-98).

FORMER MEMBERS: Arkansas AM&N (1937-70), Bishop (1921-56), Langston (1932-57), Paul Quinn (1921-29), Sam Houston (1921-59), Texas College (1921-61), Wiley (1921-68).

NCAA TOURNAMENT RECORD: 4-17 (.190).

ALL-TIME SCORING LEADER: Harry Kelly, Texas Southern (3,066 points from 1980-83).

REGULAR-SEASON CHAMPIONS (since joining NCAA in 1957): Alcorn State (7 outright-5 ties), Arkansas AM&N (0-1), Grambling (6-3), Jackson State (5-5), Mississippi Valley State (1-2), Prairie View (2-0), Southern (3-4), Texas Southern (6-2).

SWAC TOURNAMENT TITLES: (since 1980): Southern (6; 1981-85-87-88-89-93), Alcorn State (4; 1980-82-83-84), Mississippi Valley State (3; 1986-92-96), Texas Southern (3; 1990-94-95), Jackson State (1; 1997).

YEAR-BY-YEAR CHAMPIONS: 1957—Texas Southern; **1958**—Texas Southern; **1959**—Grambling; **1960**—Grambling; **1961**—Prairie View; **1962**—Prairie View; **1963**—Grambling; **1964**—Grambling, Jackson State; **1965**—Southern; **1966**—Alcorn State, Grambling; **1967**—Alcorn State, Arkansas AM&N, Grambling; **1968**—Alcorn State, Jackson State; **1969**—Alcorn State; **1970**—Jackson State; **1971**—Grambling; **1972**—Grambling; **1973**—Alcorn State; **1974**—Jackson State; **1975**—Jackson State; **1976**—Alcorn State; **1977**—Texas Southern; **1978**—Jackson State, Southern; **1979**—Alcorn State; **1980**—Alcorn State; **1981**—Alcorn State, Southern; **1982**—Alcorn State, Jackson State; **1983**—Texas Southern; **1984**—Alcorn State; **1985**—Alcorn State; **1986**—Alcorn State, Southern; **1987**—Grambling; **1988**—Southern; **1989**—Grambling, Southern, Texas Southern; **1990**—Southern; **1991**—Jackson State; **1992**—Mississippi Valley State, Texas Southern; **1993**—Jackson State; **1994**—Texas Southern; **1995**—Texas Southern; **1996**—Jackson State, Mississippi Valley State.

NOTE: The SWAC, which started in 1921, moved up to Division I status in 1980.

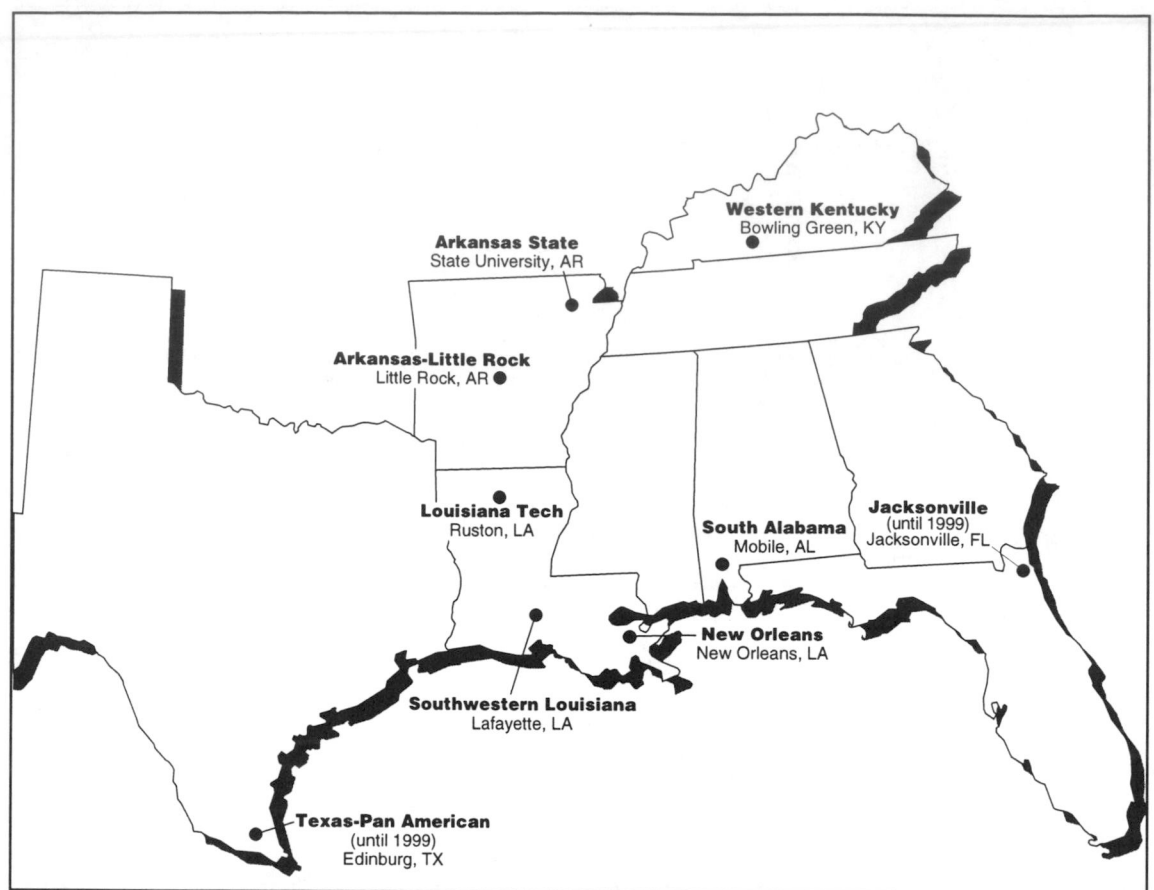

Map labels:

- **Arkansas State** — State University, AR
- **Western Kentucky** — Bowling Green, KY
- **Arkansas-Little Rock** — Little Rock, AR ●
- **Louisiana Tech** — Ruston, LA
- **South Alabama** — Mobile, AL
- **Jacksonville** (until 1999) — Jacksonville, FL
- **New Orleans** — New Orleans, LA
- **Southwestern Louisiana** — Lafayette, LA
- **Texas-Pan American** (until 1999) — Edinburg, TX

SUN BELT

ADDRESS: One Galleria Boulevard, Suite 2115, Metairie, LA 70001.

PHONE/FAX: (504) 834-6600/6806.

INTERNET ADDRESS: www.sports-u.com/sunbelt/

CURRENT MEMBERS: Arkansas-Little Rock (1992-98), Arkansas State (1992-98), Jacksonville (1977-98; plans to join the Trans America in 1999), Louisiana Tech (1992-98), New Orleans (1977-80 and 1992-98), South Alabama (1977-98), Southwestern Louisiana (1992-98), Texas-Pan American (1992-98; plans to drop out of the Sun Belt after this season), Western Kentucky (1983-98).

FORMER MEMBERS: Central Florida (1992), Georgia State (1977-81), Lamar (1992-97), UNC Charlotte (1977-91), Old Dominion (1983-91), South Florida (1977-91), UAB (1980-91), Virginia Commonwealth (1980-91).

NCAA TOURNAMENT RECORD: 21-35 (.375).

ALL-TIME WINNINGEST COACH: Gene Bartow, UAB (111 conference victories from 1980-91).

ALL-TIME SCORING LEADER: Charlie Bradley, South Florida (2,273 points from 1982-85).

SINGLE-SEASON SCORING LEADERS: Charlie Bradley, South Florida (901 points in 1982-83) and Greg Guy, Texas-Pan American (29.3 points per game in 1992-93).

REGULAR-SEASON CHAMPIONS: Arkansas-Little Rock (0 outright-1 tie), Louisiana Tech (0-1), New Orleans (1-2), UNC Charlotte (3-0), Old Dominion (1-1), South Alabama (4-2), Southwestern Louisiana (0-1), UAB (2-1), Virginia Commonwealth (2-2), Western Kentucky (3-0).

SUN BELT TOURNAMENT TITLES: UAB (4; 1982-83-84-87), South Alabama (3; 1989-91-97), Virginia Commonwealth (3; 1980-81-85), Jacksonville (2; 1979 and 1986), New Orleans (2; 1978 and 1996), UNC Charlotte (2; 1977 and 1988), Southwestern Louisiana (2; 1992 and 1994), Western Kentucky (2; 1993 and 1995), South Florida (1; 1990).

YEAR-BY-YEAR CHAMPIONS (incl. conference records): 1977—UNC Charlotte (5-1); **1978**—UNC Charlotte (9-1); **1979**—South Alabama (10-0); **1980**—South Alabama (12-2); **1981**—Alabama-Birmingham (9-3), South Alabama (9-3), Virginia Commonwealth (9-3); **1982**—Alabama-Birmingham (9-1); **1983**—Old Dominion (12-2), Virginia Commonwealth (12-2); **1984**—Virginia Commonwealth (11-3); **1985**—Virginia Commonwealth (12-2); **1986**—Old Dominion (11-3); **1987**—Western Kentucky (12-2); **1988**—UNC Charlotte (11-3); **1989**—South Alabama (11-3); **1990**—Alabama-Birmingham (12-2); **1991**—South Alabama (11-3); **1992**—Louisiana Tech (13-3); **1993**—New Orleans (18-0); **1994**—Western Kentucky (14-4); **1995**—Western Kentucky (17-1); **1996**—Arkansas-Little Rock (14-4), New Orleans (14-4).Marco, (add to year-by-year champions) — 1997-New Orleans (14-4), South Alabama (14-4)

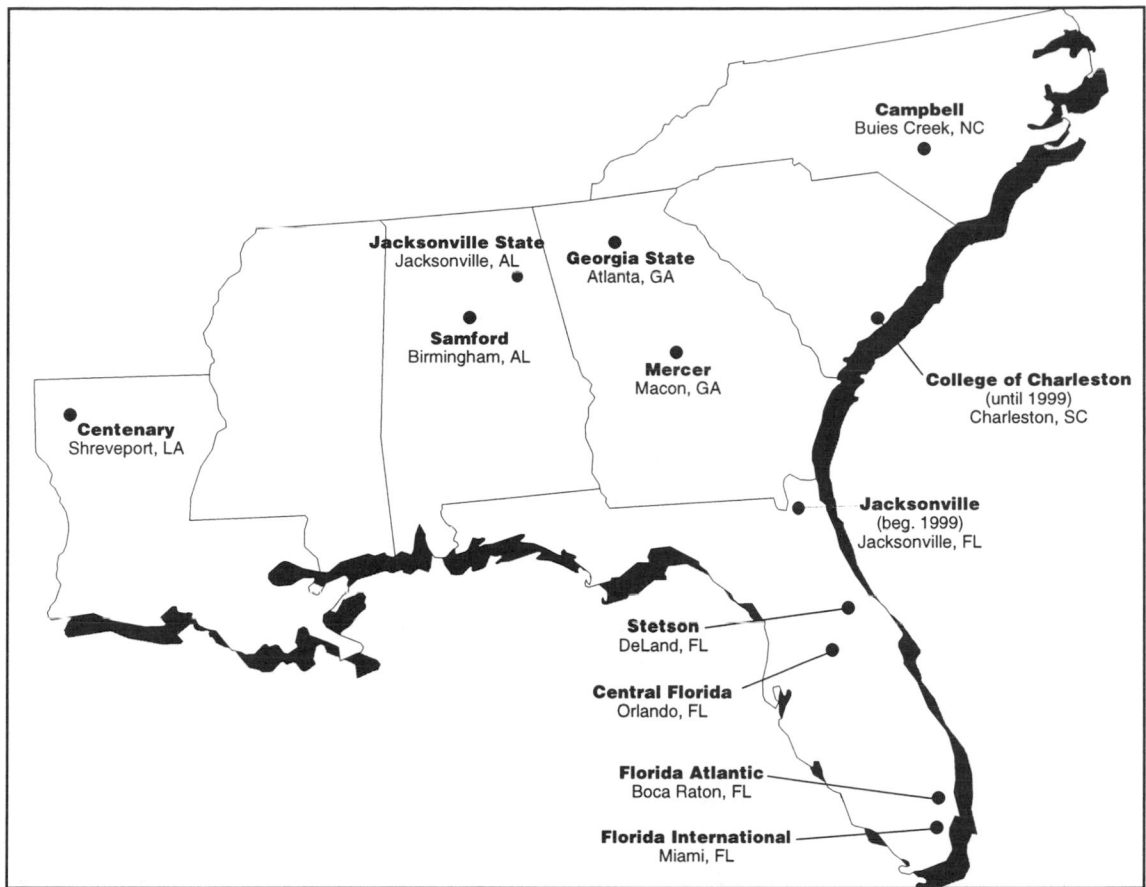

Map labels:

- **Campbell** — Buies Creek, NC
- **Jacksonville State** — Jacksonville, AL
- **Georgia State** — Atlanta, GA
- **Samford** — Birmingham, AL
- **Mercer** — Macon, GA
- **College of Charleston** — (until 1999) Charleston, SC
- **Centenary** — Shreveport, LA
- **Jacksonville** — (beg. 1999) Jacksonville, FL
- **Stetson** — DeLand, FL
- **Central Florida** — Orlando, FL
- **Florida Atlantic** — Boca Raton, FL
- **Florida International** — Miami, FL

TRANS AMERICA ATHLETIC

ADDRESS: The Commons, Suite 108-B, 3370 Vineville Avenue, Macon, GA 31204.

PHONE/FAX: (912) 474-3394/4272.

CURRENT MEMBERS: Campbell (1995-98), Centenary (1980-98), Central Florida (1994-98), College of Charleston, S.C. (1994-98; slated to join the Southern Conference in 1999), Florida Atlantic (1996-98), Florida International (1992-98), Georgia State (1985-98), Jacksonville, Ala., State (1996-98), Mercer (1980-98), Samford (1980-98), Stetson (1987-98), Troy State (since 1998). Jacksonville (Fla.) is slated to join the TAAC in 1999.

FORMER MEMBERS: Arkansas-Little Rock (1981-91), Georgia Southern (1981-92), Hardin-Simmons (1980-90), Houston Baptist (1980-89), Northeast Louisiana (1980-82), Northwestern State, La. (1981-84), Southeastern Louisiana (1992-97), Texas-Pan American (1980), Texas-San Antonio (1987-91).

NCAA TOURNAMENT RECORD: 2-17 (.105).

ALL-TIME SCORING LEADER: Willie Jackson, Centenary (2,535 points from 1981-84).

SINGLE-SEASON SCORING LEADERS: Sam Mitchell, Mercer (774 points in 1984-85) and Ernie Hill, Oklahoma City (26.6 points per game in 1978-79).

REGULAR-SEASON CHAMPIONS: Arkansas-Little Rock (4 outright-1 tie), Centenary (1-0), College of Charleston (4-0), Florida International (1-0), Georgia Southern (3-1), Houston Baptist (2-0), Northeast Louisiana (2-0), Samford (1-0), Texas-San Antonio (1-0).

TAAC TOURNAMENT TITLES: Arkansas-Little Rock (3; 1986-89-90), Georgia Southern (3; 1983-87-92), Central Florida (2; 1994 and 1996), Mercer (2; 1981 and 1985), Northeast Louisiana (2; 1979 and 1982), Centenary (1; 1980), College of Charleston (1; 1997), Florida International (1; 1995), Georgia State (1; 1991), Houston Baptist (1; 1984), Texas-San Antonio (1; 1988).

YEAR-BY-YEAR CHAMPIONS (incl. conference records): 1980—Northeast Louisiana (6-0); **1981**—Houston Baptist (9-3); **1982**—Arkansas-Little Rock (12-4); **1983**—Arkansas-Little Rock (12-2); **1984**—Houston Baptist (11-3); **1985**—Georgia Southern (11-3); **1986**—Arkansas-Little Rock (12-2); **1987**—Arkansas-Little Rock (16-2); **1988**—Arkansas-Little Rock (15-3), Georgia Southern (15-3); **1989**—Georgia Southern (16-2); **1990**—Centenary (14-2); **1991**—Texas-San Antonio (12-2); **1992**—Georgia Southern (13-1); **1993**—Florida International (9-3); **1994**—College of Charleston (14-2); **1995**—College of Charleston (15-1); **1996**—College of Charleston (15-1). Marco, (add to year-by-year champions) — 1997-College of Charleston (16-0/E); Samford (11-5/W)

NOTE: League split into two divisions in 1997—East and West.

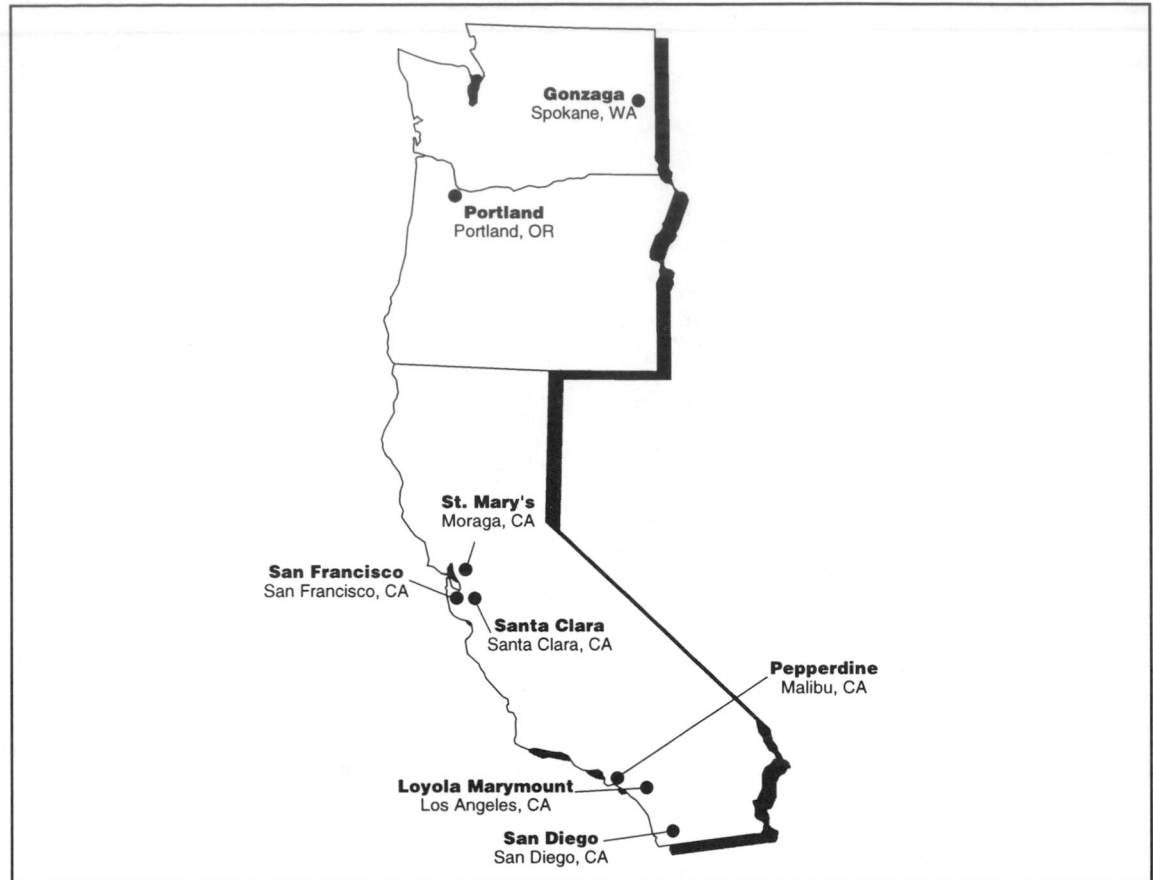

WEST COAST

ADDRESS: 400 Oyster Point Boulevard, Suite 221, South San Francisco, CA 94080.

PHONE/FAX: (415) 873-8622/7846.

INTERNET ADDRESS: www.westcoast.org

PREVIOUS NAMES: California Basketball Association (1953-55) and West Coast Athletic (1956-88).

CURRENT MEMBERS: Gonzaga (1980-98), Loyola Marymount (1956-98), Pepperdine (1956-98), Portland (1977-98), St. Mary's (1953-98), San Diego (1980-98), San Francisco (1953-98), Santa Clara (1953-98).

FORMER MEMBERS: UC Santa Barbara (1965-69), Fresno State (1956 and 1957), Nevada-Reno (1970-79), Pacific (1953-71), San Jose State (1953-69), Seattle (1972-80), UNLV (1970-75).

NCAA TOURNAMENT RECORD: 44-51 (.463).

NCAA TITLES (2): San Francisco (1955 and 1956).

ALL-TIME SCORING LEADER: Eric "Hank" Gathers, Loyola Marymount (2,490 points from 1988-90).

SINGLE-SEASON SCORING LEADERS: Greg "Bo" Kimble, Loyola Marymount (1,131 points in 1989-90) and William "Bird" Averitt, Pepperdine (33.9 points per game in 1972-73).

REGULAR-SEASON CHAMPIONS: Gonzaga (1 outright-1 tie), Loyola Marymount (3-0), Pacific (3-0), Pepperdine (9-1), St. Mary's (2-2), San Diego (2-0), San Francisco (13-2), Santa Clara (7-2), UNLV (1-0).

WCC TOURNAMENT TITLES: Pepperdine (3; 1991-92-94), Loyola Marymount (2; 1988 and 1989), Santa Clara (2; 1987 and 1993), Gonzaga (1; 1995), Portland (1; 1996), St. Mary's (1; 1997).

YEAR-BY-YEAR CHAMPIONS (incl. conference records): 1953—San Francisco (6-2), Santa Clara (6-2)*; **1954**—Santa Clara (9-3); **1955**—San Francisco (12-0); **1956**—San Francisco (14-0); **1957**—San Francisco (12-2); **1958**—San Francisco (12-0); **1959**—St. Mary's (11-1); **1960**—Loyola Marymount (9-3), Santa Clara (9-3)*; **1961**—Loyola Marymount (10-2); **1962**—Pepperdine (11-1); **1963**—San Francisco (10-2); **1964**—San Francisco (12-0); **1965**—San Francisco (13-1); **1966**—Pacific (13-1); **1967**—Pacific (14-0); **1968**—Santa Clara (13-1); **1969**—Santa Clara (13-1); **1970**—Pacific (11-3), Santa Clara (11-3)*; **1971**—Pacific (12-2); **1972**—San Francisco (13-1); **1973**—San Francisco (12-2); **1974**—San Francisco (12-2); **1975**—UNLV (13-1); **1976**—Pepperdine (10-2); **1977**—San Francisco (14-0); **1978**—San Francisco (12-2); **1979**—San Francisco (12-2); **1980**—San Francisco (11-5), St. Mary's (11-5); **1981**—Pepperdine (11-3), San Francisco (11-3); **1982**—Pepperdine (14-0); **1983**—Pepperdine (10-2); **1984**—San Diego (9-3); **1985**—Pepperdine (11-1); **1986**—Pepperdine (13-1); **1987**—San Diego (13-1); **1988**—Loyola Marymount (14-0); **1989**—St. Mary's (12-2); **1990**—Loyola Marymount (13-1); **1991**—Pepperdine (13-1); **1992**—Pepperdine (14-0); **1993**—Pepperdine (11-3); **1994**—Gonzaga (12-2); **1995**—Santa Clara (12-2); **1996**—Gonzaga (10-4), Santa Clara (10-4); **1997**—St. Mary's (10-4), Santa Clara (10-4).

*Won playoff.

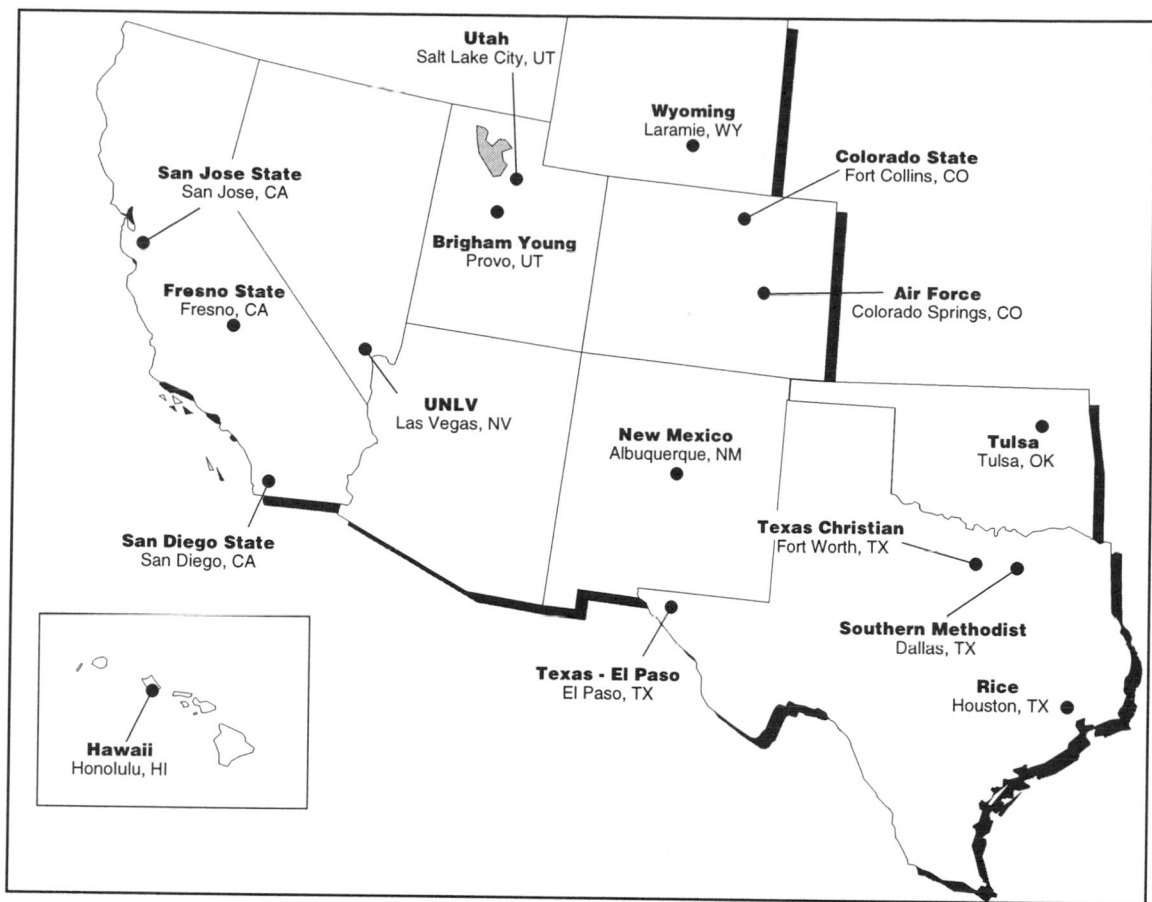

WESTERN ATHLETIC

ADDRESS: 9250 East Costilla Avenue, Suite 300, Englewood, CO 80112-3643.

PHONE/FAX: (303) 799-9221/3888.

INTERNET ADDRESS: www.wac.org

CURRENT MEMBERS: Air Force (1981-98), Brigham Young (1963-98), Colorado State (1970-98), Fresno State (1993-98), Hawaii (1980-98), New Mexico (1963-98), Rice (1997 and 1998), San Diego State (1979-98), San Jose State (1997 and 1998), Southern Methodist (1997 and 1998), Texas Christian (1997 and 1998), Texas-El Paso (1970-98), Tulsa (1997 and 1998), UNLV (1996-98), Utah (1963-98), Wyoming (1963-98).

FORMER MEMBERS: Arizona (1963-78), Arizona State (1963-78).

NCAA TOURNAMENT RECORD: 46-67 (.407).

NCAA TITLES (3): Wyoming (1943), Utah (1944), Texas-El Paso (1966). UTEP, Utah and Wyoming won the championships before joining the WAC.

NIT TITLES (5): Brigham Young (1951 and 1966), Fresno State (1983), Tulsa (1981), Utah (1947). The only one of the four won as a member of the WAC was BYU in 1966.

ALL-TIME SCORING LEADER: Keith Van Horn, Utah (2,542 points from 1994-97).

SINGLE-SEASON SCORING LEADER: Jerry Chambers, Utah (28.8 points per game in 1965-66).

REGULAR-SEASON CHAMPIONS: Arizona (1 outright-0 ties), Arizona State (3-1), Brigham Young (6-6), Colorado State (1-1), Fresno State (0-1), Hawaii (0-1), New Mexico (4-1), Texas-El Paso (4-3), Utah (6-4), Wyoming (1-4).

WAC TOURNAMENT TITLES: Texas-El Paso (4; 1984-86-89-90), Brigham Young (2; 1991 and 1992), New Mexico (2; 1993 and 1996), Utah (2; 1995 and 1997), Wyoming (2; 1987 and 1988), Hawaii (1; 1994), San Diego State (1; 1985).

YEAR-BY-YEAR CHAMPIONS (incl. conference records): **1963**—Arizona State (9-1); **1964**—Arizona State (7-3), New Mexico (7-3); **1965**—Brigham Young (8-2); **1966**—Utah (7-3); **1967**—Brigham Young (8-2); **1968**—New Mexico (8-2); **1969**—Brigham Young (6-4), Wyoming (6-4); **1970**—Texas-El Paso (10-4); **1971**—Brigham Young (10-4); **1972**—Brigham Young (12-2); **1973**—Arizona State (10-4); **1974**—New Mexico (10-4); **1975**—Arizona State (12-2); **1976**—Arizona (11-3); **1977**—Utah (11-3); **1978**—New Mexico (13-1); **1979**—Brigham Young (10-2); **1980**—Brigham Young (13-1); **1981**—Utah (13-3), Wyoming (13-3); **1982**—Wyoming (14-2); **1983**—Brigham Young (11-5), Texas-El Paso (11-5), Utah (11-5); **1984**—Texas-El Paso (13-3); **1985**—Texas-El Paso (12-4); **1986**—Texas-El Paso (12-4), Utah (12-4), Wyoming (12-4); **1987**—Texas-El Paso (13-3); **1988**—Brigham Young (13-3); **1989**—Colorado State (12-4); **1990**—Brigham Young (11-5), Colorado State (11-5); **1991**—Utah (15-1); **1992**—Brigham Young (12-4), Texas-El Paso (12-4); **1993**—Brigham Young (15-3), Utah (15-3); **1994**—New Mexico (14-4); **1995**—Utah (15-3); **1996**—Utah (15-3); **1997**—Utah (15-1/M); Fresno State (12-4/P), Hawaii (12-4/P).

NOTE: League split into two divisions in 1997—Mountain and Pacific.

FORMER MAJOR COLLEGE CONFERENCES

AMERICAN WEST (1995 AND 1996):

Cal Poly joined the Big West and Cal State Northridge and Sacramento State joined Big Sky.

MEMBERS: Cal Poly San Luis Obispo, Cal State Northridge, Sacramento State and Southern Utah.

REGULAR-SEASON CHAMPIONS: Cal Poly SLO (1 outright-0 ties), Southern Utah (1-0).

AWC TOURNAMENT TITLES: Southern Utah (2; 1995 and 1996).

YEAR-BY-YEAR CHAMPIONS (incl. conference records): 1995—Southern Utah (6-0); **1996**—Cal Poly SLO (5-1).

AMERICAN SOUTH (1988-91)

Merged with the Sun Belt.

MEMBERS: Arkansas State (1988-91), Lamar (1988-91), Louisiana Tech (1988-91), New Orleans (1988-91), Southwestern Louisiana (1988-91), Texas-Pan American (1988-91).

NCAA TOURNAMENT RECORD: 1-3 (.250).

REGULAR-SEASON CHAMPIONS: Arkansas State (0 outright-1 tie), Louisiana Tech (0-2), New Orleans (1-3).

AMERICAN SOUTH TOURNAMENT TITLES: Louisiana Tech (3; 1988-89-91), New Orleans (1; 1990).

YEAR-BY-YEAR CHAMPIONS (incl. conference records): 1988—Louisiana Tech (7-3), New Orleans (7-3); **1989**—New Orleans (7-3); **1990**—Louisiana Tech (8-2), New Orleans (8-2); **1991**—Arkansas State (9-3), New Orleans (9-3).

BIG EIGHT (1919-96):

Combined with half of Southwest Conference to form Big 12.

PREVIOUS NAMES: Big Six (1929 through 1947), Big Seven (1948 through 1958).

MEMBERS: Colorado (1948-96), Iowa State (1929-96), Kansas (1929-96), Kansas State (1929-96), Missouri (1929-96), Nebraska (1929-96), Oklahoma (1929-96), Oklahoma State (1959-96).

NCAA TOURNAMENT RECORD: 137-109 (.557).

NCAA TITLES (2) : Kansas (1952 and 1988).

NIT TITLES (1) : Nebraska (1996).

ALL-TIME SCORING LEADER: Danny Manning, Kansas (2,951 points from 1985-88).

SINGLE-SEASON SCORING LEADERS: Danny Manning, Kansas (942 points in 1987-88) and Wilt Chamberlain, Kansas (30.1 points per game in 1957-58).

REGULAR-SEASON CHAMPIONS: Colorado (3 outright-2 ties), Iowa State (2-2), Kansas (22-8), Kansas State (12-3), Missouri (9-2), Nebraska (0-3), Oklahoma (7-5), Oklahoma State (1-1).

BIG EIGHT TOURNAMENT TITLES: Missouri (6; 1978-82-87-89-91-93), Kansas (4; 1981-84-86-92), Oklahoma (4; 1979-85-88-90), Kansas State (2; 1977 and 1980), Iowa State (1; 1996), Nebraska (1; 1994), Oklahoma State (2; 1983 and 1995).

YEAR-BY-YEAR CHAMPIONS (incl. conference records): 1929—Oklahoma (10-0); **1930**—Missouri (8-2); **1931**—Kansas (7-3); **1932**—Kansas (7-3); **1933**—Kansas (8-2); **1934**—Kansas (9-1); **1935**—Iowa State (8-2); **1936**—Kansas (10-0); **1937**—Kansas (8-2), Nebraska (8-2); **1938**—Kansas (9-1); **1939**—Missouri (7-3), Oklahoma (7-3); **1940**—Kansas (8-2)*, Missouri (8-2), Oklahoma (8-2); **1941**—Iowa State (7-3), Kansas (7-3); **1942**—Kansas (8-2), Oklahoma (8-2); **1943**—Kansas (10-0); **1944**—Iowa State (9-1), Oklahoma (9-1); **1945**—Iowa State (8-2); **1946**—Kansas (10-0); **1947**—Oklahoma (8-2); **1948**—Kansas State (9-3); **1949**—Nebraska (9-3), Oklahoma (9-3); **1950**—Kansas (8-4), Kansas State (8-4), Nebraska (8-4); **1951**—Kansas State (11-1); **1952**—Kansas (11-1); **1953**—Kansas (10-2); **1954**—Colorado (10-2), Kansas (10-2); **1955**—Colorado (11-1); **1956**—Kansas State (10-2); **1957**—Kansas (11-1); **1958**—Kansas State (10-2); **1959**—Kansas State (14-0); **1960**—Kansas (10-4)*, Kansas State (10-4); **1961**—Kansas State (13-1); **1962**—Colorado (13-1); **1963**—Colorado (11-3), Kansas State (11-3); **1964**—Kansas State (12-2); **1965**—Oklahoma State (12-

2); **1966**—Kansas (13-1); **1967**—Kansas (13-1); **1968**—Kansas State (11-3); **1969**—Colorado (10-4); **1970**—Kansas State (10-4); **1971**—Kansas (14-0); **1972**—Kansas State (12-2); **1973**—Kansas State (12-2); **1974**—Kansas (13-1); **1975**—Kansas (11-3); **1976**—Missouri (12-2); **1977**—Kansas State (11-3); **1978**—Kansas (13-1); **1979**—Oklahoma (10-4); **1980**—Missouri (11-3); **1981**—Missouri (10-4); **1982**—Missouri (12-2); **1983**—Missouri (12-2); **1984**—Oklahoma (13-1); **1985**—Oklahoma (13-1); **1986**—Kansas (13-1); **1987**—Missouri (11-3); **1988**—Oklahoma (12-2); **1989**—Oklahoma (12-2); **1990**—Missouri (12-2); **1991**—Kansas (10-4), Oklahoma State (10-4); **1992**—Kansas (11-3); **1993**—Kansas (11-3); **1994**—Missouri (14-0); **1995**—Kansas (11-3); **1996**—Kansas (12-2).

*Won playoff.

Note: Kansas won 13 of the 21 Missouri Valley Intercollegiate Athletic Association titles from 1908-28.

BORDER (1932-62):

Disbanded when the WAC was formed.

MEMBERS: Arizona (1932-61), Arizona State (1932-62), Hardin-Simmons (1942-62), New Mexico (1932-42 and 1945-51), New Mexico State (1932-62), Northern Arizona (1932-53), Texas-El Paso (1936-62), Texas Tech (1933-56), West Texas State (1942-62).

NCAA TOURNAMENT RECORD: 2-13 (.133).

REGULAR-SEASON CHAMPIONS: Arizona (7 outright-2 ties), Arizona State (2-2), Hardin-Simmons (0-1), New Mexico (1-0), New Mexico State (4-4), Texas Tech (5-1), Texas Western (2-1), West Texas A&M (2-2).

YEAR-BY-YEAR CHAMPIONS (incl. conference records): 1933—Texas Tech; **1934**—Texas Tech; **1935**—Texas Tech; **1936**—Arizona; **1937**—New Mexico State; **1938**—New Mexico State; **1939**—New Mexico State; **1940**—New Mexico State; **1941**—DNP; **1942**—West Texas A&M; **1943**—West Texas A&M; **1944**—Northern Arizona; **1945**—New Mexico; **1946**—Arizona*; **1947**—Arizona; **1948**—Arizona; **1949**—Arizona; **1950**—Arizona; **1951**—Arizona; **1952**—New Mexico State, West Texas A&M; **1953**—Arizona, Hardin-Simmons; **1954**—Texas Tech; **1955**—Texas Tech, West Texas A&M; **1956**—Texas Tech; **1957**—Texas Western; **1958**—Arizona State; **1959**—Arizona State, New Mexico State, Texas Western; **1960**—New Mexico State; **1961**—Arizona State, New Mexico State; **1962**—Arizona State.

*Won tournament for official title.

EASTERN INTERCOLLEGIATE (1933-39)

REGULAR-SEASON CHAMPIONS: Carnegie Tech (0 outright-2 ties), Georgetown (0-1), Pittsburgh (2-3), Temple (1-1), West Virginia (0-1).

YEAR-BY-YEAR CHAMPIONS (incl. conference records): 1933—Pittsburgh (7-1); **1934**Pittsburgh (8-0); **1935**—Pittsburgh (6-2)*, West Virginia (6-2); **1936**—Carnegie Tech (7-3)*, Pittsburgh (7-3); **1937**—Pittsburgh (7-3)*, Temple (7-3); **1938**—Temple (9-1); **1939**—Carnegie Tech (6-4), Georgetown (6-4).

*Won playoff game.

GREAT MIDWEST (1992-95):

Most of league merged with Metro to form Conference USA.

MEMBERS: Cincinnati (1992-95), Dayton (1994 and 1995), DePaul (1992-95), Marquette (1992-95), Memphis (1992-95), Saint Louis (1992-95), UAB (1992-95).

NCAA TOURNAMENT RECORD: 16-13 (.552).

REGULAR-SEASON CHAMPIONS: Cincinnati (1 outright-1 tie), DePaul (0-1), Marquette (1-0), Memphis (1-0).

GMC TOURNAMENT TITLES: Cincinnati (all 4).

YEAR-BY-YEAR CHAMPIONS (incl. conference records): 1992—Cincinnati (8-2), DePaul (8-2); **1993** —Cincinnati (8-2); **1994**—Marquette (10-2); **1995**—Memphis (9-3).

GULF STAR (1985-87):

Members joined Southland or became independents before joining Trans America Athletic.

MEMBERS: Nicholls State (1985-87), Northwestern State (1985-87), Sam Houston State (1985-87), Southeastern Louisiana (1985-87), Southwest Texas State (1985-87), Stephen F. Austin State (1985-87).

REGULAR-SEASON CHAMPIONS: Sam Houston State (1986), Southeastern Louisiana (1985), Stephen F. Austin State (1987).

YEAR-BY-YEAR CHAMPIONS (incl. conference records): 1985—Southeastern Louisiana (9-1); **1986**—Sam Houston State (9-1); **1987**—Stephen F. Austin (10-0).

METRO (1976-95):

Much of league merged with Great Midwest to form Conference USA.

MEMBERS: Cincinnati (1976-91), Florida State (1977-91), Georgia Tech (1976-78), Louisville (1976-95), Memphis State (1976-91), UNC Charlotte (1992-95), St. Louis (1976-82), South Carolina (1984-91), Southern Mississippi (1983-95), South Florida (1992-95), Tulane (1976-85 and 1990-95), Virginia Commonwealth (1992-95), Virginia Tech (1979-95).

NCAA TITLES (2) : Louisville (1980 and 1986).

NIT TITLES (1) : Southern Mississippi (1987).

ALL-TIME SCORING LEADER: Bimbo Coles, Virginia Tech (2,484 points from 1987-90).

NCAA TOURNAMENT RECORD: 48-42 (.533).

REGULAR-SEASON CHAMPIONS: Florida State (2 outright-0 ties), Louisville (11-1), Memphis State (2-1), UNC Charlotte (1-0), Southern Mississippi (1-0), Tulane (1-0).

METRO TOURNAMENT TITLES: Louisville (11; 1978-80-81-83-86-88-89-90-93-94-95), Memphis State (4; 1982-84-85-87), Cincinnati (2; 1976 and 1977), Florida State (1; 1991), UNC Charlotte (1; 1992), Virginia Tech (1; 1979).

YEAR-BY-YEAR CHAMPIONS (incl. conference records): 1976—Tulane (1-0); **1977**—Louisville (6-1); **1978**—Florida State (11-1); **1979**—Louisville (9-1); **1980**—Louisville (12-0); **1981**—Louisville (11-1); **1982**—Memphis (10-2); **1983**—Louisville (12-0); **1984**—Louisville (11-3), Memphis (11-3); **1985**—Memphis (13-1); **1986**—Louisville (10-2); **1987**—Louisville (9-3); **1988**—Louisville (9-3); **1989**—Florida State (9-3); **1990**—Louisville (12-2); **1991**—Southern Miss. (10-4); **1992**—Tulane (8-4); **1993**—Louisville (11-1); **1994**—Louisville (10-2); **1994**—Louisville (10-2); **1995**—UNC Charlotte (8-4)

Note: Tulane's 1976 "title" is not recognized because the most league games any member played in that inaugural season was three.

METROPOLITAN COLLEGIATE (1966-69):

Disbanded with eight members, including Fairleigh Dickinson, Hofstra, Iona, Long Island, Manhattan, St. Peter's, Seton Hall and Wagner.

MEMBERS: Fairleigh Dickinson (1966-69), Hofstra (1966-69), Iona (1966-69), Long Island (1966-69), Manhattan (1966-69), New York University (1966 and 1967), St. Peter's (1966-69), St. Francis, N.Y. (1966-68), Seton Hall (1966-69), Wagner (1966-69).

REGULAR-SEASON CHAMPIONS: Manhattan (1 outright-2 ties), St. Francis, N.Y. (0-1), St. Peter's (1-2).

YEAR-BY-YEAR CHAMPIONS (incl. conference records): 1966—Manhattan (8-1); **1967**—Manhattan (7-2), St. Francis, N.Y. (7-2), St. Peter's (7-2); **1968**—St. Peter's (8-0); **1969**—Manhattan (7-1), St. Peter's (7-1).

MIDDLE ATLANTIC/EAST COAST (1959-94):

Middle Atlantic (1959-74) split into Eastern and Western sections the last five years of its existence before the majority of members wound up forming the ECC (1975-92 and '94). The ECC, which featured a divisional format its first nine years, merged with the Mid-Continent prior to start of 1994-95 season.

MEMBERS: American (1967-84), Brooklyn (1992), Bucknell (1959-90), Buffalo (1992 and 1994), Central Connecticut State (1991-94), Chicago State (1994), Delaware (1959-91), Drexel (1959-91), Gettysburg (1959-74), Hofstra (1966-94), Lafayette (1959-90), La Salle (1959-90), Lehigh (1959-90), Maryland-Baltimore County (1991 and 1992), Muhlenberg (1959-64), Northeastern Illinois (1994), Rider (1967-92), Rutgers (1959-62), St. Joseph's (1959-82), Temple (1959-82), Towson State (1983-92), Troy State (1994), West Chester State (1966-74).

NCAA TOURNAMENT RECORD: 12-37 (.245).

ECC REGULAR-SEASON CHAMPIONS: American (1 outright-2 ties), Bucknell (5-1), Drexel (1-0), Hofstra (1-3), Lafayette (5-2), La Salle (1-2), Rider (1-1), St. Joseph's (2-0), Temple (2-1), Towson State (1-1), West Chester State (1-0).

ECC TOURNAMENT TITLES: La Salle (4; 1975-78-80-83), Hofstra (3; 1976-77-94), Towson State (3; 1990-91-92), Bucknell (2; 1987 and 1989), Lehigh (2; 1985 and 1988), St. Joseph's (2; 1981 and 1982), Drexel (1; 1986), Rider (1; 1984), Temple (1; 1979).

YEAR-BY-YEAR CHAMPIONS (incl. conference records): 1959—St. Joseph's (7-0); **1960**—St. Joseph's (7-1); **1961**—St. Joseph's (8-0); **1962**—St. Joseph's (9-1); **1963**—St. Joseph's (8-0); **1964**—Temple (6-1); **1965**—St. Joseph's*; **1966**—St. Joseph's*; **1967**—Temple*; **1968**—La Salle*; **1969**—Temple*, St. Joseph's**; **1970**—St. Joseph's (5-0/E), Temple** (E), Lafayette (7-3/W), Lehigh (7-3/W), Rider (7-3/W); **1971**—St. Joseph's** (6-0/E), Lafayette (9-1/W); **972**—Temple** (6-0/E), Rider (8-2/W); **1973**—St. Joseph's** (6-0/E), Lafayette (7-3/W); **1974**—La Salle (5-1/E), St. Joseph's** (5-1/E), Rider (8-2/W); **1975**—American (5-1/E), La Salle (5-1/E), Lafayette (7-1/W); **1976**—St. Joseph's (4-1/E), Lafayette (9-1/W); **1977**—Temple (4-1/E), Hofstra (4-1/E), Lafayette (9-1/W); **1978**—La Salle (5-0/E), Lafayette (10-0/W); **1979**—Temple (10-0/E), Bucknell (11-5/W); **1980**—St. Joseph's (10-1/E), Bucknell (13-3/W), Lafayette (13-3/W); **1981**—American (11-0/E), Lafayette (8-8/W), Rider (8-8/W); **1982**—Temple (11-0/E), West Chester State (8-8/W); **1983**—American (7-2/E), La Salle (7-2/E), Hofstra (7-2/E), Rider (10-3/W); **1984**—Bucknell (14-2); **1985**—Bucknell (10-4); **1986**—Drexel (11-3); **1987**—Bucknell (11-3); **1988**—Lafayette (11-3); **1989**—Bucknell (11-3); **1990**—Towson State (8-6); Hofstra (8-6), Lehigh (8-6), **1991**—Towson State (10-2); **1992**—Hofstra (10-2).

*No formal conference competition. Champion based on best regular-season record.

**Won playoff.

Note: ECC had a four-team playoff from 1970-74 with openers matching No. 1 in East vs. No. 2 in West and No. 1 in West vs. No. 2 in East.

MOUNTAIN STATES (1938-62 EXCEPT FOR 1944 AND 1945):

Seven members dropped out of the Rocky Mountain and formed the Mountain States Intercollegiate Athletic Conference after the 1936-37 season. The Mountain States was also informally known as the Big Seven before being dubbed the Skyline Six and then Eight (after Montana and New Mexico joined in 1952. Four teams from the Skyline and two from the Border Conference formed the Western Athletic Conference in 1962.

MEMBERS: Brigham Young (1938-62), Colorado State (1938-47), Colorado A&M/State (1938-62), Montana (1952-62), Montana State (1952-62), New Mexico (1952-62), Utah (1938-62), Utah State (1938-62), Wyoming (1938-62).

NCAA TOURNAMENT RECORD: 20-34 (.370).

REGULAR-SEASON CHAMPIONS: Brigham Young (4 outright-1 tie), Colorado (3-1), Colorado State (1-1), Utah (6-2), Wyoming (7-1).

YEAR-BY-YEAR CHAMPIONS: 1938—Colorado (10-2); Utah (10-2); **1939**—Colorado (10-2); **1940**—Colorado (11-1); **1941**—Wyoming (10-2); **1942**—Colorado 911-1); **1943**—Wyoming (4-0/E), Brigham Young (7-1/W); **1944**—No conference competition; **1945**—Utah (8-0); **1946**—Wyoming (10-2); **1947**—Wyoming (11-1); **1948**—Brigham Young (8-2); **1949**—Wyoming (15-5); **1950**—Brigham Young (14 6); **1951**—Brigham Young (15-5); **1952**—Wyoming (13-1); **1953**—Wyoming (12-2); **1954**—Colorado A&M (12-2); **1955**—Utah (13-1); **1956**—Utah (12-2); **1957**—Brigham Young (11-3); **1958**—Wyoming (10-4); **1959**—Utah (13-1); **1960**—Utah (13-1); **1961**—Colorado State (12-2), Utah (12-2)* ; **1962**—Utah (13-1).

*Won playoff.

NEW ENGLAND/YANKEE (1937-75):

Rhode Island won first eight championships, Connecticut won 17 titles in 20 years from 1948-67 and Massachusetts won outright or shared seven of last eight titles.

MEMBERS: Boston University (1973-76), Connecticut (1938-43 and 1946-76), Maine (1938-43 and 1946-76), Massachusetts (1947-76), New Hampshire (1938-43 and 1946-76), Northeastern (1938-43 and 1946), Rhode Island (1938-43 and 1946-76), Vermont (1947-76).

NCAA TOURNAMENT RECORD: 3-15 for Yankee (.167).

REGULAR-SEASON CHAMPIONS: Connecticut (15 outright-4 ties), Massachusetts (6-2), Rhode Island (10-4).

YEAR-BY-YEAR CHAMPIONS (incl. conference records): 1937—Rhode Island (8-0); **1938**—Rhode Island (8-0); **1939**—Rhode Island (7-1); **1940**—Rhode Island (8-0); **1941**—Connecticut (7-1), Rhode Island (7-1); **1942**—Rhode Island (8-0); **1943**—Rhode Island (7-1); **1944**—DNP; **1945**—DNP; **1946**—Rhode Island (4-0); **1947**—Vermont (1-0)*; **1948**—

Connecticut (6-1); **1949**—Connecticut (7-1); **1950**—Rhode Island (6-1); **1951**—Connecticut (6-1); **1952**—Connecticut (6-1); **1953**—Connecticut (5-1); **1954**—Connecticut; **1955**—Connecticut; **1956**—Connecticut (6-1); **1957**—Connecticut (8-0); **1958**—Connecticut (10-0); **1959**—Connecticut (8-2); **1960**—Connecticut (8-2); **1961**—Rhode Island (9-1); **1962**—Massachusetts (8-2); **1963**—Connecticut (9-1); **1964**—Connecticut (8-2), Rhode Island (8-2); **1965**—Connecticut (10-0); **1966**—Connecticut (9-1), Rhode Island (9-1); **1967**—Connecticut (9-1); **1968**—Massachusetts (8-2), Rhode Island (8-2); **1969**—Massachusetts (9-1); **1970**—Connecticut (8-2), Massachusetts (8-2); **1971**—Massachusetts (10-0); **1972**—Rhode Island (8-2); **1973**—Massachusetts (10-2); **1974**—Massachusetts (11-1); **1975**—Massachusetts (10-2).

*Connecticut had the most league victories in the 1946-47 campaign with a 6-1 mark when the conference changed its name to Yankee.

ROCKY MOUNTAIN (1922-60):

Divisional format from 1925-37.

MEMBERS: Adams State (1958-63), Brigham Young (1925-37), Colorado (1923-37), Colorado A&M/State (1924-37), Colorado College (1923-63), Colorado School of Mines (1923-63), Colorado Teachers (1925-34) Denver (1923-37), Greeley State/Colorado State College/Northern Colorado (1935-63), Idaho State (1950-60), Montana State (1925-57 except for 1948), Utah (1925-37), Utah Agricultural/State (1925-37), Western State/Colorado Western (1925-63), Wyoming (1923-37).

REGULAR-SEASON CHAMPIONS: Brigham Young (2 outright-2 ties), Colorado (2-1), Colorado College (7-0), Colorado State (5-2), Denver (0-1), Idaho State (8-0), Montana State (8-3), Northern Colorado (5-0), Utah (2-3), Utah State (2-1), Wyoming (5-1).

YEAR-BY-YEAR CHAMPIONS: 1922—Colorado Col.; **1923**—Colorado Col. (7-1); **1924**—Colorado Col. (9-1); **1925**—Colorado Col. (10-3/E), Brigham Young (5-3/W); **1926**—Colorado State Col.(13-1/E), Utah (8-4/W); **1927**—Colorado Col. (12-2/E), Montana State (10-2/W); **1928**—Wyoming (9-3/E), Montana State (11-1/W); **1929**—Colorado (10-2/E), Montana State (11-1); **1930**—Colorado (11-3/E) Montana State (7-5/W), Utah State (7-5/W); **1931**—Wyoming (11-1/E), Utah (8-4/W); **1932**—Wyoming (12-0/E), Brigham Young (8-4/W), Utah (8-4/W); **1933**—Wyoming (12-2/E), Colorado State (12-2/E), Brigham Young (9-3/W), Utah (9-3/W); **1934**—Wyoming (14-0/E), Brigham Young (9-3/W); **1935**—Northern Colorado (9-3/E), Utah State (9-3/W); **1936**—Wyoming (11-3/E), Utah (9-3/W); **1937**—Denver (10-2/E), Colorado (10-2/E), Montana State (7-5/W), Utah (7-5/W); **1938**—Montana State (10-0); **1939**—Northern Colorado (7-3); **1940**—Northern Colorado (3-1); **1941**—Northern Colorado (9-5); **1942**—Northern Colorado (6-2); **1943**—Northern Colorado (5-3); **1944**—Colorado College (6-0); **1945**—Colorado College (2-0); **1946**—Colorado State (7-1); **1947**—Montana State (7-1); **1948**—Colorado State (5-1); **1949**—Colorado State (7-1); **1950**—Montana State (9-1); **1951**—Montana State (9-1); **1952**—Colorado State (8-2), Montana State (8-2); **1953**—Idaho State (10-0); **1954**—Idaho State (9-1); **1955**—Idaho State (9-1); **1956**—Idaho State (9-1); **1957**—Idaho State (12-0); **1958**—Idaho State (10-0); **1959**—Idaho State (9-1); **1960**—Idaho State (8-0).

SOUTHWEST (1915-96):

League disbanded with schools joining three different conferences (Big 12, Conference USA and WAC).

MEMBERS: Arkansas (1924-91), Baylor (1915-96), Houston (1976-96), Oklahoma A&M (1918 and 1922-25), Phillips, Okla. (1920), Rice (1915-96), Southern Methodist (1919-96), Southwestern, Tex. (1915 and 1916), Texas (1915-96), Texas A&M (1915-96), Texas Christian (1924-96), Texas Tech (1958-96).

NCAA TOURNAMENT RECORD: 75-89 (.457).

NIT TITLES (1) : Texas (1978).

ALL-TIME SCORING LEADER: Terrence Rencher, Texas (2,306 points from 1992-95).

SINGLE-SEASON SCORING LEADER: Otis Birdsong, Houston (30.3 points per game in 1976-77).

REGULAR-SEASON CHAMPIONS: Arkansas (14 outright-8 ties), Baylor (3-2), Houston (2-1), Oklahoma A&M (1-0), Rice (4-6), Southern Methodist (8-5), Texas (12-10), Texas A&M (9-2), Texas Christian (8-2), Texas Tech (4-2).

SWC TOURNAMENT TITLES: Arkansas (6; 1977-79-82-89-90-91), Houston (5; 1978-81-83-84-92), Texas Tech (5; 1976-85-86-93-96), Texas (2; 1994 and 1995), Texas A&M (2; 1980 and 1987), SMU (1; 1988).

YEAR-BY-YEAR CHAMPIONS (incl. conference records): 1915—Texas (5-0); **1916**—Texas (6-0); **1917**—Texas (7-1); **1918**—Rice (7-3); **1919**—Texas (11-2); **1920**—Texas A&M (16-0); **1921**—Texas A&M (10-2); **1922**—Texas A&M (13-3); **1923**—Texas A&M (15-3); **1924**—Texas (20-0); **1925**—Oklahoma A&M (12-2); **1926**—Arkansas (11-1); **1927**—Arkansas (8-2); **1928**—Arkansas (12-0); **1929**—Arkansas (11-1); **1930**—Arkansas (10-2); **1931**—Texas Christian (9-3); **1932**—Baylor (10-2); **1933**—Texas (11-1); **1934**—Texas Christian (10-2); **1935**—Arkansas (9-3), Rice (9-3), Southern Methodist (9-3); **1936**—Arkansas (11-1); **1937**—Southern Methodist (10-2); **1938**—Arkansas (11-1); **1939**—Texas (10-2); **1940**—Rice (10-2); **1941**—Arkansas (12-0); **1942**—Arkansas (10-2), Rice (10-2); **1943**—Rice (9-3), Texas (9-3); **1944**—Arkansas (11-1), Rice (11-1); **1945**—Rice (12-0); **1946**—Baylor (11-1); **1947**—Texas (12-0); **1948**—Baylor (11-1); **1949**—Arkansas (9-3)*, Baylor (9-3); Rice (9-3), Southern Methodist (9-3); **1950**—Arkansas (8-4), Baylor (8-4); **1951**—Texas (8-4), Texas A&M (8-4), Texas Christian (8-4); **1952**—Texas Christian (11-1); **1953**—Texas Christian (9-3); **1954**—Rice (9-3)*, Texas (9-3); **1955**—Southern Methodist (9-3); **1956**—Southern Methodist (12-0); **1957**—Southern Methodist (11-1); **1958**—Arkansas (9-5)*, Southern Methodist (9-5); **1959**—Texas Christian (9-3); **1960**—Texas (11-3); **1961**—Texas Tech (11-3); **1962**—Southern Methodist (11-3), Texas Tech (11-3)*; **1963**—Texas (13-1); **1964**—Texas A&M (13-1); **1965**—Southern Methodist (10-4)*, Texas (10-4); **1966**—Southern Methodist (11-3); **1967**—Southern Methodist (12-2); **1968**—Texas Christian (9-5); **1969**—Texas A&M (12-2); **1970**—Rice (10-4); **1971**—Texas Christian (11-3); **1972**—Southern Methodist (10-4), Texas (10-4)*; **1973**—Texas Tech (12-2); **1974**—Texas (11-3); **1975**—Texas A&M (12-2); **1976**—Texas A&M (14-2); **1977**—Arkansas (16-0); **1978**—Arkansas (14-2), Texas (14-2); **1979**—Arkansas (13-3), Texas (13-3); **1980**—Texas A&M (14-2); **1981**—Arkansas (13-3); **1982**—Arkansas (12-4); **1983**—Houston (16-0); **1984**—Houston (15-1); **1985**—Texas Tech (12-4); **1986**—Texas (12-4), Texas A&M (12-4), Texas Christian (12-4); **1987**—Texas Christian (14-2); **1988**—Southern Methodist (12-4); **1989**—Arkansas (13-3); **1990**—Arkansas (15-1); **1991**—Arkansas (15-1); **1992**—Houston (11-3), Texas (11-3); **1993**—Southern Methodist (12-2); **1994**—Texas (12-2); **1995**—Texas (11-3), Texas Tech (11-3); **1996**—Texas Tech (14-0).

*Won playoff.

BASKETBALL ORGANIZATIONS

National Collegiate Athletic Association (NCAA)
6201 College Boulevard
Overland Park, KS 66211-2422
Phone/Fax: (913) 339-1906/1950

National Association of Intercollegiate Athletics (NAIA)
6120 South Yale Avenue, Suite 1450
Tulsa, OK 74136-4223
Phone/Fax: (918) 494-8828/8841

National Junior College Athletic Association (NJCAA)
Post Office Box 7305
Colorado Springs, CO 80933-7305
Phone/Fax: (719) 590-9788/7324

Community College League of California
2017 "O" Street
Sacramento, CA 95814
Phone/Fax: (916) 444-8641/2954

Naismith Memorial Hall of Fame
1150 West Columbus Avenue
Springfield, MA 01101-0179
Phone/Fax: (413) 781-6500/1939

National Invitation Tournament (NIT)
Downtown Athletic Club
19 West Street, Suite 2010
New York, NY 10004
Phone/Fax: (212) 425-6510/785-0594

USA Basketball
5465 Mark Dabling Boulevard
Colorado Springs, CO 80918-3842
Phone/Fax: (719) 590-4800/4811

National Association of Basketball Coaches (NABC)
9300 West 110th Street, Suite 640
Overland Park, KS 66210-1486
Phone/Fax: (913) 469-1001/1390

Black Coaches Association (BCA)
Rudy Washington, Executive Director
1900 13th Street, Suite 200
Boulder, CO 80302
Phone/Fax: (515) 327-1248/(303) 449-3813

Women's Basketball Coaches Association (WBCA)
4646 B Lawrenceville Highway
Lilburn, GA 30247-3620
Phone/Fax: (770) 279-8027/8473

United States Basketball Writers Association (USBWA)
c/o Joe Mitch, Executive Director
1000 St. Louis Union Station, Suite 333
St. Louis, MO 63103
Phone/Fax: (314) 421-0339/3505

College Sports Information Directors of America
c/o Fred Nuesch
Texas A&M-Kingsville
Campus Box 114A
Kingsville, TX 78363
Phone/Fax: (512) 595-3908/0389

Amateur Athletic Union (AAU)
6571 Forum Drive
Suite 200
Orlando, FL 32821
Phone/Fax: (407) 363-6170/6171

International Basketball Federation (FIBA)
Post Office Box 700607
D-81306 Munchen
Germany
Phone/Fax: 011 4989 7481 580/5888

QUALITY ONLINE SERVICES

scbs.sportsline.com
espnet.sportzone.com
foxsports.com
info.totalsports.net
nando.net/sportserver
naia.org
ncaa.org
njcaa.org
sfan.com
sportingnews.com
sportsillustrated.com
usatoday.com/sports

16

SCHOOL DIRECTORY

In 1950, 145 schools were classified as major colleges. Forty years later, the number of NCAA Division I institutions had more than doubled to in excess of 300. Here are vital facts for those schools that meet any of the following criteria:

- Classified as major colleges for more than 40 years.

- At least one player become an NCAA consensus first- or second-team All-American.

- Won at least one NCAA Tournament game.

- Reached the NIT semifinals.

- Member of a conference that supplied an NCAA champion.

- Won a minimum of one NIT game after winning at least one contest in the NCAA Division II Tournament or NAIA Tournament.

- Participated in one of the two national runner-up tournaments in 1974 or 1975.

- Appeared in the NCAA Division I Tournament after reaching the national semifinals in the NCAA Division II Tournament or NAIA Tournament.

- Participated in a total of at least 10 games in the NCAA Tournament and NIT.

AIR FORCE

OFFICIAL NAME: United States Air Force Academy.
NICKNAME: Falcons.
ADDRESS: Building 2169, Room 1050, Colorado Springs, CO 80840-5461.
PHONE/FAX: (719) 333-4263/3798.
ENROLLMENT: 4,400.
ARENA: Clune Arena (Capacity-6,007; Year Opened-1968).
SCHOOL COLORS: Blue and Silver.
CONFERENCE: Western Athletic.
NCAA TOURNAMENT APPEARANCES (2): 1960 and 1962; 0-2 record.
NIT APPEARANCES: None.
6ALL-TIME WINNINGEST COACH: Bob Spear (15 years from 1957-71, 176-176 record, .500).
ALL-TIME SCORING LEADER: Raymond Dudley (2,178 points from 1987-90).
ALL-TIME REBOUNDING LEADER: Reggie Jones (776 from 1978-81).

ALABAMA

OFFICIAL NAME: University of Alabama.
NICKNAME: Crimson Tide.
ADDRESS: Post Office Box 870391, Tuscaloosa, AL 35487-0391.
PHONE/FAX: (205) 348-6084/8841.
ENROLLMENT: 20,000.
ARENA: Coleman Coliseum (Capacity-15,043; Year Opened-1968).
SCHOOL COLORS: Crimson and White.
CONFERENCE: Southeastern.
FINAL AP TOP 10 RANKINGS (4): 1956-75-76-87.
NCAA TOURNAMENT APPEARANCES (14): 1975-76-82-83-84-85-86-87-89-90-91-92-94-95; 15-14 record (.517); never reached regional final.

NIT APPEARANCES (7): 1973-77-79-80-81-93-96; 13-10 record (.565); finished 4th in 1973, 4th in 1977, 3rd in 1979 and 4th in 1996.

ALL-TIME WINNINGEST COACH: Winfrey "Wimp" Sanderson (12 years from 1981-92, 267-119 record, .692).

ALL-TIME SCORING LEADER: Reggie King (2,168 points from 1976-79).

ALL-TIME REBOUNDING LEADER: Jerry Harper (1,688 from 1953-56).

NCAA CONSENSUS SECOND-TEAM ALL-AMERICANS (1): Leon Douglas (1975).

ALCORN STATE

OFFICIAL NAME: Alcorn State University.

NICKNAME: Braves.

ADDRESS: 1000 ASU Drive, Post Office Box 510, Lorman, MS 39096.

PHONE/FAX: (601) 877-6466/3821.

ENROLLMENT: 2,975.

ARENA: Davey L. Whitney Complex (Capacity-7,000; Year Opened-1974).

SCHOOL COLORS: Purple and Old Gold.

CONFERENCE: Southwestern Athletic.

NCAA DIVISION I TOURNAMENT APPEARANCES (4): 1980-82-83-84; 3-4 record (.429).

NCAA DIVISION II TOURNAMENT APPEARANCES (1): 1969; 1-1 record (.500).

NAIA TOURNAMENT APPEARANCES (7): 1967-68-73-74-75-76-77; 11-7 record (.611); finished 2nd in 1974 and 3rd in 1975.

NIT APPEARANCES (2): 1979 and 1985; 1-2 record (.333).

ALL-TIME WINNINGEST COACH: Davey Whitney (20 years from 1971-89 and 1997, 406-216 record, .653).

ALL-TIME SCORING LEADER: Richard Smith (2,527 points from 1953-56 when school was classified at the NAIA level).

ALL-TIME REBOUNDING LEADER: Alfred Milton (1,432 from 1972-75 when school was classified as a small college).

AMERICAN

OFFICIAL NAME: American University.

NICKNAME: Eagles.

ADDRESS: 224 Bender Arena, 4400 Massachusetts Avenue, NW, Washington, DC 20016-8005.

PHONE/FAX: (202) 885-3032/3033.

ENROLLMENT: 11,500.

ARENA: Bender Arena (Capacity-5,000; Year Opened-1988).

SCHOOL COLORS: Red, White and Blue.

CONFERENCE: Colonial Athletic Association.

NCAA DIVISION I TOURNAMENT APPEARANCES: None.

NCAA DIVISION II TOURNAMENT APPEARANCES (3): 1958-59-60; 6-3 record (.667).

NAIA TOURNAMENT APPEARANCES (2): 1950 and 1951; 0-2 record.

NIT APPEARANCES (3): 1973-81-82; 0-3 record.

ALL-TIME WINNINGEST COACH: Ed Tapscott (eight years from 1983-90, 109-117 record, .482).

ALL-TIME SCORING LEADER: Russell "Boo" Bowers (2,065 points from 1978-81).

ALL-TIME REBOUNDING LEADER: Kermit Washington (1,478 from 1971-73).

NCAA CONSENSUS SECOND-TEAM ALL-AMERICANS (1): Kermit Washington (1973).

ARIZONA

OFFICIAL NAME: University of Arizona.

NICKNAME: Wildcats.

ADDRESS: McKale Center, Tucson, AZ 85721.

PHONE/FAX: (602) 621-4163/2681.

ENROLLMENT: 35,305.

ARENA: McKale Center (Capacity-14,257; Year Opened-1973).

SCHOOL COLORS: Cardinal and Navy.

CONFERENCE: Pacific-10.

FINAL AP TOP 10 RANKINGS (6): 1988-89-91-92-93-94.

NCAA TOURNAMENT APPEARANCES (16): 1951-76-77-85-86-87-88-89-90-91-92-93-94-95-96-97; 23-15 record (.605); reached Final Four in 1988 (T3rd), 1994 (T3rd) and 1997 (1st).

NIT APPEARANCES (3): 1946-50-51; 0-3 record.

NCIT Record: 2-1 to finish 2nd in 1975.

ALL-TIME WINNINGEST COACH: Fred Enke (36 years from 1926-61, 511-318 record, .616).

ALL-TIME SCORING LEADER: Sean Elliott (2,535 points from 1986-89).

ALL-TIME REBOUNDING LEADER: Al Fleming (1,190 from 1973-76).

NCAA CONSENSUS FIRST-TEAM ALL-AMERICANS (3): Sean Elliott (1988 and 1989), Damon Stoudamire (1995).

NCAA CONSENSUS SECOND-TEAM ALL-AMERICANS (1): Khalid Reeves (1994)

ARIZONA STATE

OFFICIAL NAME: Arizona State University.

NICKNAME: Sun Devils.

ADDRESS: IAC Building, Room 105, Tempe, AZ 85287-2505.

PHONE/FAX: (602) 965-6592/5408.

ENROLLMENT: 42,625.

ARENA: University Activity Center (Capacity-14,198; Year Opened-1974).

SCHOOL COLORS: Maroon and Gold.

CONFERENCE: Pacific-10.

FINAL AP TOP 10 RANKINGS (3): 1963-75-81.

NCAA TOURNAMENT APPEARANCES (11): 1958-61-62-63-64-73-75-80-81-91-95; 11-12 record (.478); regional runner-up in 1961, 1963 and 1975.

NAIA TOURNAMENT APPEARANCES (2): 1948 and 1953; 2-2 record (.500).

NIT APPEARANCES (5): 1983-90-92-93-94; 2-5 record (.286).

CCAT Record: 0-1 in 1974.

ALL-TIME WINNINGEST COACH: Ned Wulk (25 years from 1958-82, 406-272 record, .599).

ALL-TIME SCORING LEADER: Ron Riley (1,834 points from 1993-96).

ALL-TIME REBOUNDING LEADER: Tony Cerkvenik (1,022 from 1960-63).

ARKANSAS

OFFICIAL NAME: University of Arkansas.

NICKNAME: Razorbacks.

ADDRESS: Post Office Box 7777, Fayetteville, AR 72702.

PHONE/FAX: (501) 575-2751/7481.

ENROLLMENT: 14,600.

ARENA: Bud Walton Arena (Capacity-19,200; Year Opened-1993).

SCHOOL COLORS: Cardinal and White.

CONFERENCE: Southeastern.

FINAL AP TOP 10 RANKINGS (9): 1978-79-83-84-90-91-92-94-95.

NCAA TOURNAMENT APPEARANCES (22): 1941-45-49-58-77-78-79-80-81-82-83-84-85-88-89-90-91-92-93-94-95-96; 37-22 record (.627); reached Final Four in 1941 (T3rd), 1945 (T3rd), 1978 (3rd), 1990 (T3rd), 1994 (1st) and 1995 (2nd).

NIT APPEARANCES (2): 1987 and 1997; 4-3 record (.571); finished 4th in 1997.

ALL-TIME WINNINGEST COACH: Glen Rose (23 years from 1934-42 and 1953-66, 325-201 record, .618).

ALL-TIME SCORING LEADER: Todd Day (2,395 points from 1989-92).

ALL-TIME REBOUNDING LEADER: Sidney Moncrief (1,015 from 1976-79).

NCAA CONSENSUS FIRST-TEAM ALL-AMERICANS (3): Ike Poole (1936), John Adams (1941), Sidney Moncrief (1979).

NCAA CONSENSUS SECOND-TEAM ALL-AMERICANS (4): Ron Brewer (1978), Darrell Walker (1983), Corliss Williamson (1994 and 1995).

ARKANSAS-LITTLE ROCK

OFFICIAL NAME: University of Arkansas at Little Rock (UALR).

NICKNAME: Trojans.

ADDRESS: 2801 South University Avenue, Little Rock, AR 72204.

PHONE/FAX: (501) 569-3449/3030.

ENROLLMENT: 12,420.

ARENA: Barton Coliseum (Capacity-8,303; Year Opened-1952).

SCHOOL COLORS: Maroon and Gold.

CONFERENCE: Sun Belt.

NCAA TOURNAMENT APPEARANCES (3): 1986-89-90; 1-3 record (.250).

NIT APPEARANCES (3): 1987-88-96; 3-4 record (.429); finished 4th in 1987.

ALL-TIME WINNINGEST COACH: Mike Newell (six years from 1985-90, 133-60 record, .689).

ALL-TIME SCORING LEADER: James Scott (1,731 points from 1988-91).

ALL-TIME REBOUNDING LEADER: Larry Johnson (1,315 from 1975-78 when school was classified as a small college).

ARKANSAS STATE

OFFICIAL NAME: Arkansas State University.

NICKNAME: Indians.

ADDRESS: Post Office Box 1000, State University, AR 72467.

PHONE/FAX: (870) 972-2541/3367.

ENROLLMENT: 9,820.

ARENA: Convocation Center (Capacity-10,563; Year Opened-1987).

SCHOOL COLORS: Scarlet and Black.

CONFERENCE: Sun Belt.

NCAA DIVISION I TOURNAMENT APPEARANCES: None.

NCAA DIVISION II TOURNAMENT APPEARANCES (6): 1958-60-62-63-66-67; 5-7 record (.417).

NIT APPEARANCES (4): 1987-88-89-91; 4-4 record (.500).

NAIA TOURNAMENT APPEARANCES (2): 1947 and 1949; 0-2 record.

ALL-TIME WINNINGEST COACH: John Rauth (14 years from 1950-63 when school was classified as a small college, 191-150 record, .560).

ALL-TIME SCORING LEADER: Jerry Rook (2,153 points from 1962-65 when school was classified as a small college).

ALL-TIME REBOUNDING LEADER: John Belcher (1,166 from 1969-72; school was classified as a small college his first two years).

ARMY

OFFICIAL NAME: United States Military Academy.

Nicknames: Black Knights, Cadets.

ADDRESS: 639 Howard Road, West Point, NY 10996-9906.

PHONE/FAX: (914) 938-3512/446-2556.

ENROLLMENT: 4,200.

ARENA: Christl Arena (Capacity-5,043; Year Opened-1985).

SCHOOL COLORS: Black, Gold and Gray.

CONFERENCE: Patriot League.

NCAA TOURNAMENT APPEARANCES: None.

NIT APPEARANCES (8): 1961-64-65-66-68-69-70-78; 13-10 record (.565); finished 3rd in 1964, 3rd in 1965, 4th in 1966, 4th in 1969 and 3rd in 1970.

ALL-TIME WINNINGEST COACH: Leo Novak (13 years from 1927-39, 126-61 record, .674).

ALL-TIME SCORING LEADER: Kevin Houston (2,325 points from 1984-87).

ALL-TIME REBOUNDING LEADER: Gary Winton (1,168 from 1975-78).

NCAA CONSENSUS SECOND-TEAM ALL-AMERICANS (2): Dale Hall (1944 and 1945).

AUBURN

OFFICIAL NAME: Auburn University.

NICKNAME: Tigers.

ADDRESS: Post Office Box 351, Auburn, AL 36831-0351.

PHONE/FAX: (334) 844-9701/9708.

ENROLLMENT: 22,120.

ARENA: Beard-Eaves Memorial Coliseum (Capacity-10,108; Year Opened-1969).

SCHOOL COLORS: Burnt Orange and Navy Blue.

CONFERENCE: Southeastern.

FINAL AP TOP 10 RANKINGS (1): 1959.

NCAA TOURNAMENT APPEARANCES (5): 1984-85-86-87-88; 7-5 record (.583); regional runner-up in 1986.

NIT APPEARANCES (3): 1993-95-96; 0-3 record.

ALL-TIME WINNINGEST COACH: Joel Eaves (14 years from 1950-63, 213-100 record, .681).

ALL-TIME SCORING LEADER: Chuck Person (2,311 points from 1983-86).

ALL-TIME REBOUNDING LEADER: Mike Mitchell (996 from 1975-78).

AUSTIN PEAY STATE

OFFICIAL NAME: Austin Peay State University.

NICKNAME: Governors.

ADDRESS: Box 4515, Clarksville, TN 37044.

PHONE/FAX: (615) 648-7561/7562.

ENROLLMENT: 8,200.

ARENA: Dunn Center (Capacity-9,092; Year Opened-1975).

SCHOOL COLORS: Red and White.

CONFERENCE: Ohio Valley.

NCAA DIVISION I TOURNAMENT APPEARANCES (4): 1973-74-87-96; 2-5 record (.286).

NCAA DIVISION II TOURNAMENT APPEARANCES (4): 1958-60-61-63; 3-6 record (.333).

NAIA TOURNAMENT APPEARANCES (1): 1957; 0-1 record.

NIT APPEARANCES: None.

ALL-TIME WINNINGEST COACH: David B. Aaron (16 years from 1947-62 when school was classified as a small college, 258-174 record, .597).

ALL-TIME SCORING LEADER: Tom Morgan (1,850 points in 1953 and from 1956-58 when school was classified as a small college; Bubba Wells is expected to bypass Morgan during the 1996-97 season).

ALL-TIME REBOUNDING LEADER: Tom Morgan (1,431 in 1953 and from 1956-58 when school was classified as a small college).

BALL STATE

OFFICIAL NAME: Ball State University.
NICKNAME: Cardinals.
ADDRESS: HP 120, Muncie, IN 47306-0929.
PHONE/FAX: (317) 285-8242/8929.
ENROLLMENT: 20,515.

ARENA: University Arena (Capacity-11,500; Year Opened-1992).
SCHOOL COLORS: Cardinal and White.
CONFERENCE: Mid-American.
NCAA DIVISION I TOURNAMENT APPEARANCES (6): 1981-86-89-90-93-95; 3-6 record (.333).
NCAA DIVISION II TOURNAMENT APPEARANCES (1): 1964; 0-2 record.
NAIA TOURNAMENT APPEARANCES (1): 1957; 1-1 record (.500).
NIT APPEARANCES (2): 1991 and 1992; 0-2 record.
ALL-TIME WINNINGEST COACH: Jim Hinga (14 years from 1955-68 when school was classified as a small college, 154-169 record, .477).
ALL-TIME SCORING LEADER: Ray McCallum (2,109 points from 1980-83).
ALL-TIME REBOUNDING LEADER: Ed Butler (1,231 from 1962-64 when school was classified as a small college).

BAYLOR

OFFICIAL NAME: Baylor University.
NICKNAME: Bears.
ADDRESS: 3031 Dutton, Waco, TX 76711.
PHONE/FAX: (817) 755-3066/1369.
ENROLLMENT: 12,500.

ARENA: Ferrell Center (Capacity-10,084; Year Opened-1988).
SCHOOL COLORS: Green and Gold.
CONFERENCE: Big 12.
NCAA TOURNAMENT APPEARANCES (4): 1946-48-50-88; 3-6 record (.333); reached Final Four in 1948 (2nd) and 1950 (4th).
NIT APPEARANCES (2): 1987 and 1990; 0-2 record.
ALL-TIME WINNINGEST COACH: Bill Henderson (18 years from 1942-61, 201-233 record, .463).
ALL-TIME SCORING LEADER: Terry Teagle (2,189 points from 1979-82).
ALL-TIME REBOUNDING LEADER: Jerry Mallett (877 from 1955-57).

BOISE STATE

OFFICIAL NAME: Boise State University.
NICKNAME: Broncos.
ADDRESS: 1910 University Drive, Boise, ID 83725.
PHONE/FAX: (208) 385-3868/3361.
ENROLLMENT: 15,060.
ARENA: BSU Pavilion (Capacity-12,380; Year Opened-1982).
SCHOOL COLORS: Blue and Orange.
CONFERENCE: Big West.
NCAA DIVISION I TOURNAMENT APPEARANCES (4): 1976-88-93-94; 0-4 record.
NCAA DIVISION II TOURNAMENT APPEARANCES (1): 1970; 1-1 record (.500).
NIT APPEARANCES (3): 1987-89-91; 1-3 record (.250).
ALL-TIME WINNINGEST COACH: Bobby Dye (12 years from 1984-95, 213-133 record, .616).
ALL-TIME SCORING LEADER: Tanoka Beard (1,944 points from 1990-93).
ALL-TIME REBOUNDING LEADER: Bill Otey (805 from 1969 and 1970 when school was classified as a small college).

BOSTON COLLEGE

NICKNAME: Eagles.
ADDRESS: Conte Forum 321, Chestnut Hill, MA 02167.
PHONE/FAX: (617) 552-3004/4903.
ENROLLMENT: 9,165.
ARENA: Silvio O. Conte Forum (Capacity-8,606; Year Opened-1988).

SCHOOL COLORS: Maroon and Gold.
CONFERENCE: Big East.
FINAL AP TOP 10 RANKINGS (1): 1967.
NCAA TOURNAMENT APPEARANCES (10): 1958-67-68-75-81-82-83-85-94-96; 16-12 record (.571); regional runner-up in 1967, 1982 and 1994.
NIT APPEARANCES (10): 1965-66-69-74-80-84-88-92-93-97; 15-10 record (.600); finished 2nd in 1969, 3rd in 1974 and 4th in 1988.
ALL-TIME WINNINGEST COACH: Jim O'Brien (11 years from 1987-97, 168-166 record, .503).
ALL-TIME SCORING LEADER: Dana Barros (2,342 points from 1986-89).
ALL-TIME REBOUNDING LEADER: Terry Driscoll (1,071 from 1967-69).

BOSTON UNIVERSITY

NICKNAME: Terriers.
ADDRESS: 285 Babcock Street, Boston, MA 02215.
PHONE/FAX: (617) 353-2872/4286.
ENROLLMENT: 13,665.
ARENA: Case Gym (Capacity-2,500; Year Opened-1971).
SCHOOL COLORS: Scarlet and White.
CONFERENCE: America East.
NCAA TOURNAMENT APPEARANCES (5): 1959-83-88-90-97; 2-5 record (.286); regional runner-up in 1959.
NIT APPEARANCES (2): 1980 and 1986; 0-2 record.
ALL-TIME WINNINGEST COACH: Mike Jarvis (five years from 1986-90, 101-51 record, .664).
ALL-TIME SCORING LEADER: Drederick Irving (1,931 points from 1985-88).
ALL-TIME REBOUNDING LEADER: James Garvin (935 from 1971-73).

BOWLING GREEN STATE

OFFICIAL NAME: Bowling Green State University.
NICKNAME: Falcons.
ADDRESS: BGSU Athletic Department, Bowling Green, OH 43403-0030.
PHONE/FAX: (419) 372-7076/6015.

ENROLLMENT: 17,000.
ARENA: Anderson Arena (Capacity-5,000; Year Opened-1960).
SCHOOL COLORS: Brown and Orange.
CONFERENCE: Mid-American.
FINAL AP TOP 10 RANKINGS (2): 1949 and 1962.
NCAA TOURNAMENT APPEARANCES (4): 1959-62-63-68; 1-5 record (.167).
NIT APPEARANCES (11): 1944-45-46-48-49-54-80-83-90-91-97; 6-11 record (.353); finished 2nd in 1945 and 3rd in 1949.
NCIT Record: 1-1 in 1975.
ALL-TIME WINNINGEST COACH: Harold Anderson (21 years from 1943-63, 367-193 record, .655).
ALL-TIME SCORING LEADER: Howard Komives (1,834 points from 1962-64).
ALL-TIME REBOUNDING LEADER: Nate Thurmond (1,295 from 1961-63).
NCAA CONSENSUS FIRST-TEAM ALL-AMERICANS (1): Wyndol Gray (1945 before playing for Harvard the next season).

NCAA CONSENSUS SECOND-TEAM ALL-AMERICANS (1): Nate Thurmond (1963).

BRADLEY

OFFICIAL NAME: Bradley University.

NICKNAME: Braves.

ADDRESS: 1501 West Bradley Avenue, Peoria, IL 61625.

PHONE/FAX: (309) 677-2624/2626.

ENROLLMENT: 6,000.

ARENA: Carver Arena (Capacity-10,825; Year Opened-1982).

SCHOOL COLORS: Red and White.

CONFERENCE: Missouri Valley.

FINAL AP TOP 10 RANKINGS (8): 1949-50-51-54-59-60-61-62.

NCAA TOURNAMENT APPEARANCES (7): 1950-54-55-80-86-88-96; 9-7 record (.563); reached Final Four in 1950 (2nd) and 1954 (2nd).

NIT APPEARANCES (18): 1938-39-47-49-50-57-58-59-60-62-64-65-68-82-85-94-95-97; 25-15 record (.625); finished 3rd in 1939, 4th in 1949, 2nd in 1950, 1st in 1957, 2nd in 1959, 1st in 1960, 1st in 1964 and 1st in 1982.

CCAT Record: 1-1 in 1974.

ALL-TIME WINNINGEST COACH: A.J. Robertson (26 years from 1921-48, 312-186 record, .627).

ALL-TIME SCORING LEADER: Hersey Hawkins (3,008 points from 1985-88).

ALL-TIME REBOUNDING LEADER: Dick Estergard (1,414 from 1952-54).

NCAA CONSENSUS FIRST-TEAM ALL-AMERICANS (5): Paul Unruh (1950), Gene Melchiorre (1951), Chet Walker (1961 and 1962), Hersey Hawkins (1988).

BRIGHAM YOUNG

OFFICIAL NAME: Brigham Young University.

NICKNAME: Cougars.

ADDRESS: 30 Smith Fieldhouse, Provo, UT 84602.

PHONE/FAX: (801) 378-4911/3520.

ENROLLMENT: 27,000.

ARENA: Marriott Center (Capacity-22,700; Year Opened-1971).

SCHOOL COLORS: Royal Blue and White.

CONFERENCE: Western Athletic.

FINAL AP TOP 10 RANKINGS (2): 1965 and 1972.

NCAA TOURNAMENT APPEARANCES (18): 1950-51-57-65-69-71-72-79-80-81-84-87-88-90-91-92-93-95; 11-21 record (.344); regional runner-up in 1950, 1951 and 1981.

NAIA TOURNAMENT APPEARANCES (2): 1948 and 1949; 2-2 record (.500).

NIT APPEARANCES (7): 1951-53-54-66-82-86-94; 9-5 record (.643); finished 1st in 1951 and 1966.

ALL-TIME WINNINGEST COACH: Stan Watts (23 years from 1950-72, 372-254 record, .594).

ALL-TIME SCORING LEADER: Danny Ainge (2,467 points from 1978-81).

ALL-TIME REBOUNDING LEADER: Michael Smith (922 from 1984-89; missed 1984-85 and 1985-86 seasons while on a LDS mission).

NCAA CONSENSUS FIRST-TEAM ALL-AMERICANS (2): Elwood Romney (1931), Danny Ainge (1981).

NCAA CONSENSUS SECOND-TEAM ALL-AMERICANS (4): Mel Hutchins (1951), Joe Richey (1953), Devin Durrant (1984), Michael Smith (1988).

BROWN

OFFICIAL NAME: Brown University.

NICKNAME: Bears.

ADDRESS: Box 1932, Providence, RI 02912.

PHONE/FAX: (401) 863-2219, 2259/1436.

ENROLLMENT: 5,500.

ARENA: Pizzitola Sports Center (Capacity-2,800; Year Opened-1989).

SCHOOL COLORS: Seal Brown, Cardinal Red and White.

CONFERENCE: Ivy League.

NCAA TOURNAMENT APPEARANCES (2): 1939 and 1986; 0-2 record.

NIT APPEARANCES: None.

ALL-TIME WINNINGEST COACH: Stanley Ward (15 years from 1955-69, 133-261 record, .338).

ALL-TIME SCORING LEADER: Arnie Berman (1,668 points from 1970-72).

ALL-TIME REBOUNDING LEADER: Phil Brown (931 from 1973-75).

BUCKNELL

OFFICIAL NAME: Bucknell University.

NICKNAME: Bison.

ADDRESS: Lewisburg, PA 17837-2005.

PHONE/FAX: (717) 524-1227/1660.

ENROLLMENT: 3,400.

ARENA: Davis Gymnasium (Capacity-2,300; Year Opened-1938).

SCHOOL COLORS: Orange and Blue.

CONFERENCE: Patriot League.

NCAA TOURNAMENT APPEARANCES (2): 1987 and 1989; 0-2 record.

NIT APPEARANCES: None.

ALL-TIME WINNINGEST COACH: Charlie Woollum (19 years from 1976-94, 318-221 record, .590).

ALL-TIME SCORING LEADER: Al Leslie (1,973 points from 1978-81).

ALL-TIME REBOUNDING LEADER: Hal Danzig (1,134 from 1957-59).

BUTLER

OFFICIAL NAME: Butler University.

NICKNAME: Bulldogs.

ADDRESS: 4600 Sunset Avenue, Indianapolis, IN 46208.

PHONE/FAX: (317) 283-9375/9808.

ENROLLMENT: 4,200.

ARENA: Hinkle Fieldhouse (11,043).

SCHOOL COLORS: Blue and White.

CONFERENCE: Midwestern Collegiate.

NCAA TOURNAMENT APPEARANCES (2): 1962 and 1997; 2-2 record (.500).

NIT APPEARANCES (5): 1958-59-85-91-92; 1-5 record (.167).

ALL-TIME WINNINGEST COACH: Tony Hinkle (41 years from 1927-70, 560-392 record, .588).

ALL-TIME SCORING LEADER: Chad Tucker (2,321 points from 1984-88; sat out most of 1986-87 season because of shoulder injury).

ALL-TIME REBOUNDING LEADER: Daryl Mason (961 from 1972-74).

CALIFORNIA

OFFICIAL NAME: University of California (At Berkeley).

NICKNAME: Golden Bears.

ADDRESS: Memorial Stadium, Berkeley, CA 94720.

PHONE/FAX: (510) 642-5363/643-7778.

ENROLLMENT: 31,000.

ARENAS: Harmon Arena (Capacity-6,578 to be upgraded to 12,500 upon refurbishing; Year Opened-1933) and Oakland/Alameda County Coliseum (Capacity-15,025; Year Opened-1966).

SCHOOL COLORS: Blue and Gold.

CONFERENCE: Pacific-10.

FINAL AP TOP 10 RANKINGS (1): 1960.

NCAA TOURNAMENT APPEARANCES (10): 1946-57-58-59-60-90-93-94-96-97; 16-10 record (.615); reached Final Four in 1946 (4th), 1959 (1st) and 1960 (2nd).

NIT APPEARANCES (3): 1986-87-89; 3-3 record (.500).

ALL-TIME WINNINGEST COACH: Clarence "Nibs" Price (30 years from 1925-54, 449-294 record, .604).

ALL-TIME SCORING LEADER: Lamond Murray (1,688 points from 1992-94).

ALL-TIME REBOUNDING LEADER: Bob McKeen (1,019 from 1952-55).

NCAA CONSENSUS FIRST-TEAM ALL-AMERICANS (3): Vern Corbin (1929), Darrall Imhoff (1960), Jason Kidd (1994).

NCAA CONSENSUS SECOND-TEAM ALL-AMERICANS (2): Andy Wolfe (1948), Lamond Murray (1994).

UC IRVINE

OFFICIAL NAME: University of California (At Irvine).

NICKNAME: Anteaters.

ADDRESS: Campus and University Drive, Irvine, CA 92717.

PHONE/FAX: (714) 856-5814/5260.

ENROLLMENT: 16,700.

ARENA: Bren Events Center (Capacity-5,000; Year Opened-1987).

SCHOOL COLORS: Blue and Gold.

CONFERENCE: Big West.

NCAA DIVISION I TOURNAMENT APPEARANCES: None.

NCAA DIVISION II TOURNAMENT APPEARANCES (4): 1968-69-72-75; 2-6 record (.250).

NIT APPEARANCES (2): 1982 and 1986; 2-2 record (.500).

ALL-TIME WINNINGEST COACH: Bill Mulligan (11 years from 1981-91, 163-156 record, .511).

ALL-TIME SCORING LEADER: Tod Murphy (1,778 points from 1983-86).

ALL-TIME REBOUNDING LEADER: Dave Baker (926 from 1972-75 when school was classified as a small college).

NCAA CONSENSUS SECOND-TEAM ALL-AMERICANS (1): Kevin Magee (1982).

UC SANTA BARBARA

OFFICIAL NAME: University of California (At Santa Barbara).

NICKNAME: Gauchos.

ADDRESS: Ward Memorial Freeway, Santa Barbara, CA 93106.

PHONE/FAX: (805) 893-3428/4537.

ENROLLMENT: 18,200.

ARENA: The Thunderdome (Capacity-6,000; Year Opened-1979).

SCHOOL COLORS: Blue and Gold.

CONFERENCE: Big West.

NCAA DIVISION I TOURNAMENT APPEARANCES (2): 1988 and 1990; 1-2 record (.333).

NCAA DIVISION II TOURNAMENT APPEARANCES (2): 1961 and 1963; 3-2 record (.600).

NAIA TOURNAMENT APPEARANCES (1): 1941; finished 4th with 3-2 record (.600).

NIT APPEARANCES (3): 1989-92-93; 0-3 record.

ALL-TIME WINNINGEST COACH: Jerry Pimm (14 years from 1984-97, 215-183 record, .540).

ALL-TIME SCORING LEADER: Carrick DeHart (1,687 points from 1987-90).

ALL-TIME REBOUNDING LEADER: Eric McArthur (904 from 1987-90).

CAL STATE FULLERTON

OFFICIAL NAME: California State University (At Fullerton).

NICKNAME: Titans.

ADDRESS: 800 North State College Boulevard, Fullerton, CA 92634-9480.

PHONE/FAX: (714) 773-3970/3141.

ENROLLMENT: 22,000.

ARENA: Titan Gym (Capacity-4,000; Year Opened-1964).

SCHOOL COLORS: Navy, Orange and White.

CONFERENCE: Big West.

NCAA TOURNAMENT APPEARANCES (1): 1978; reached regional final with a 2-1 record.

NIT APPEARANCES (2): 1983 and 1987; 0-2 record.

NAIA TOURNAMENT APPEARANCES (1): 1962; 2-1 record (.667).

ALL-TIME WINNINGEST COACH: Alex Omalev (12 years from 1961-72 when school was classified as a small college, 138-177 record, .438).

ALL-TIME SCORING LEADER: Leon Wood (1,876 points from 1982-84 after transferring from Arizona).

ALL-TIME REBOUNDING LEADER: Tony Neal (1,115 from 1982-85).

NCAA CONSENSUS SECOND-TEAM ALL-AMERICANS (1): Leon Wood (1984).

CANISIUS

OFFICIAL NAME: Canisius College.

NICKNAME: Golden Griffins.

ADDRESS: 2001 Main Street, Buffalo, NY 14208.

PHONE/FAX: (716) 888-2970/2980.

ENROLLMENT: 4,865.

ARENAS: Koessler Athletic Center (Capacity-1,800; Year Opened-1968) and Marine Midland Arena (Capacity-20,000; Year Opened-1996).

SCHOOL COLORS: Blue and Gold.

CONFERENCE: Metro Atlantic Athletic.

NCAA TOURNAMENT APPEARANCES (4): 1955-56-57-96; 6-4 record (.600); regional runner-up in 1955 and 1956.

NIT APPEARANCES (5): 1944-63-85-94-95; 5-5 record (.500); finished 2nd in 1963 and 4th in 1995.

ALL-TIME WINNINGEST COACH: Nick Macarchuk (10 years from 1978-87, 149-128 record, .538).

ALL-TIME SCORING LEADER: Ray Hall (2,226 points from 1982-85).

ALL-TIME REBOUNDING LEADER: Henry Nowak (880 from 1955-57).

NCAA CONSENSUS SECOND-TEAM ALL-AMERICANS (1): Larry Fogle (1974).

CENTRAL MICHIGAN

OFFICIAL NAME: Central Michigan University.

NICKNAME: Chippewas.

ADDRESS: 100 Rose Arena, Mount Pleasant, MI 48859.

PHONE/FAX: (517) 774-3277/7324.

ENROLLMENT: 16,450.

ARENA: Dan Rose Arena (Capacity-5,200; Year Opened-1973).

SCHOOL COLORS: Maroon and Gold.

CONFERENCE: Mid-American.

NCAA DIVISION I TOURNAMENT APPEARANCES (3): 1975-77-87; 2-3 record (.400).

NCAA DIVISION II TOURNAMENT APPEARANCES (3): 1965-70-71; 3-3 record (.500).

NAIA TOURNAMENT APPEARANCES (2): 1966 and 1967; 2-2 record (.500).

NIT APPEARANCES (1): 1979; 0-1 record.

ALL-TIME WINNINGEST COACH: Ted Kjolhede (15 years from 1957-71 when school was classified as a small college, 215-157 record, .578).

ALL-TIME SCORING LEADER: Melvin McLaughlin (2,071 points from 1980-83).

ALL-TIME REBOUNDING LEADER: Dan Roundfield (1,031 from 1973-75).

CHARLESTON

OFFICIAL NAME: College of Charleston.

NICKNAME: Cougars.

ADDRESS: 26 George Street, Charleston, SC 29424.

PHONE/FAX: (803) 953-5465/6534.

ENROLLMENT: 10,200.

ARENA: F. Mitchell Johnson Center (Capacity-3,052; Year Opened-1983).

SCHOOL COLORS: Maroon and White.

CONFERENCE: Trans America Athletic.

NCAA DIVISION I TOURNAMENT APPEARANCES (2): 1994 and 1997; 1-2 record (.333).

NIT APPEARANCES (2): 1995 and 1996; 1-2 record (.333).

NAIA TOURNAMENT APPEARANCES (6): 1983-85-86-87-88-89; 15-5 record (.750); finished 3rd once and 1st in 1983.

ALL-TIME WINNINGEST COACH: John Kresse (19 years from 1979-97, 441-112 record, .797).

CINCINNATI

OFFICIAL NAME: University of Cincinnati.

NICKNAME: Bearcats.

ADDRESS: 340 Shoemaker Center, Cincinnati, OH 45221-0021.

PHONE/FAX: (513) 556-5191/0619.

ENROLLMENT: 36,000.

ARENA: Myrl Shoemaker Center (Capacity-13,176; Year Opened-1989).

SCHOOL COLORS: Red and Black.

CONFERENCE: Conference USA.

FINAL AP TOP 10 RANKINGS (10): 1958-59-60-61-62-63-66-93-96-97.

NCAA TOURNAMENT APPEARANCES (16): 1958-59-60-61-62-63-66-75-76-77-92-93-94-95-96-97; 32-15 record (.681); reached Final Four in 1959 (3rd), 1960 (3rd), 1961 (1st), 1962 (1st), 1963 (2nd) and 1992 (3rd).

NIT APPEARANCES (8): 1951-55-57-70-74-85-90-91; 5-8 record (.385); finished 3rd in 1955.

ALL-TIME WINNINGEST COACH: Bob Huggins (eight years from 1990-97, 192-71 record, .730).

ALL-TIME SCORING LEADER: Oscar Robertson (2,973 points from 1958-60).

ALL-TIME REBOUNDING LEADER: Oscar Robertson (1,338 from 1958-60).

NCAA CONSENSUS FIRST-TEAM ALL-AMERICANS (6): Oscar Robertson (1958, 1959 and 1960), Ron Bonham (1963), Tom Thacker (1963), Danny Fortson (1997).

NCAA CONSENSUS SECOND-TEAM ALL-AMERICANS (2): Ron Bonham (1964), Danny Fortson (1996).

THE CITADEL

NICKNAME: Bulldogs.

ADDRESS: 171 Moultrie Street, Charleston, SC 29409.

PHONE/FAX: (803) 953-5120/4058.

ENROLLMENT: 2,000.

ARENA: McAlister Field House (Capacity-6,200; Year Opened-1939).

SCHOOL COLORS: Citadel Blue and White.

CONFERENCE: Southern.

NCAA TOURNAMENT APPEARANCES: None.

NIT APPEARANCES: None.

ALL-TIME WINNINGEST COACH: Les Robinson (11 years from 1975-85, 132-162 record, .449).

ALL-TIME SCORING LEADER: Regan Truesdale (1,661 points from 1982-85).

ALL-TIME REBOUNDING LEADER: Ray Graves (924 from 1958-60).

CLEMSON

OFFICIAL NAME: Clemson University.

NICKNAME: Tigers.

ADDRESS: 100 Perimeter Road, Post Office Box 31, Clemson, SC 29633.

PHONE/FAX: (864) 365-2114/656-0299.

ENROLLMENT: 17,665.

ARENA: Littlejohn Coliseum (Capacity-11,020; Year Opened-1968).

SCHOOL COLORS: Purple and Orange.

CONFERENCE: Atlantic Coast.

NCAA TOURNAMENT APPEARANCES (6): 1980-87-89-90-96-97; 8-6 record (.571); regional runner-up in 1980.

NIT APPEARANCES (10): 1975-79-81-82-85-86-88-93-94-95; 6-10 record (.375).

ALL-TIME WINNINGEST COACH: Cliff Ellis (10 years from 1985-94, 177-128 record, .580).

ALL-TIME SCORING LEADER: Elden Campbell (1,880 points from 1987-90).

ALL-TIME REBOUNDING LEADER: Tree Rollins (1,311 from 1974-77).

NCAA CONSENSUS SECOND-TEAM ALL-AMERICANS (1): Horace Grant (1987).

CLEVELAND STATE

OFFICIAL NAME: Cleveland State University.

NICKNAME: Vikings.

ADDRESS: Convocation Center, 2000 Prospect Avenue, Cleveland, OH 44115.

PHONE/FAX: (216) 687-4818/523-7257.

ENROLLMENT: 17,135.

ARENA: Henry J. Goodman Arena (Capacity-13,610; Year Opened-1991).

SCHOOL COLORS: Forest Green and White.

CONFERENCE: Midwestern Collegiate.

NCAA TOURNAMENT APPEARANCES (1): 1986; 2-1 record (.667).

NIT APPEARANCES (2): 1987 and 1988; 2-2 record (.500).

ALL-TIME WINNINGEST COACH: Ray Dieringer (14 years from 1970-83, 151-209 record, .419).

ALL-TIME SCORING LEADER: Ken "Mouse" McFadden (2,256 points from 1986-89).

ALL-TIME REBOUNDING LEADER: Weldon Kytle (1,241 from 1962-65 when school was classified as a small college).

COLGATE

OFFICIAL NAME: Colgate University.

NICKNAME: Red Raiders.

ADDRESS: 13 Oak Drive, Hamilton, NY 13346-1398.

PHONE/FAX: (315) 824-7602/7977.

ENROLLMENT: 2,700.

ARENA: Cotterell Court (Capacity-3,091; Year Opened-1966).

SCHOOL COLORS: Maroon, Gray and White.

CONFERENCE: Patriot League.

NCAA TOURNAMENT APPEARANCES (2): 1995 and 1996; 0-2 record.

NIT APPEARANCES: None.

ALL-TIME WINNINGEST COACH: Howard Hartman (13 years from 1950-62, 137-146 record, .484).

ALL-TIME SCORING LEADER: Tucker Neale (2,075 points from 1993-95; played freshman season for Ashland University, a Division II school in Ohio, before sitting out one year as a medical redshirt).

ALL-TIME REBOUNDING LEADER: Jack Nichols (1,082 from 1955-57).

NCAA CONSENSUS SECOND-TEAM ALL-AMERICANS (1): Ernie Vandeweghe (1949).

COLORADO

OFFICIAL NAME: University of Colorado.

NICKNAME: Buffaloes.

ADDRESS: CU Fieldhouse Annex, Box 357, Boulder, CO 80309.

PHONE/FAX: (303) 492-5626/3811.

ENROLLMENT: 25,090.

ARENA: Coors Events/Conference Center (Capacity-11,198; Year Opened-1979).

SCHOOL COLORS: Silver, Gold and Black.

CONFERENCE: Big 12.

FINAL AP TOP 10 RANKINGS (2): 1962 and 1963.

NCAA TOURNAMENT APPEARANCES (9): 1940-42-46-54-55-62-63-69-97; 9-11 record (.450); reached Final Four in 1942 (T3rd) and 1955 (3rd).

NIT APPEARANCES (4): 1938-40-91-95; 7-3 record (.700); finished 2nd in 1938, 1st in 1940 and 3rd in 1991.

ALL-TIME WINNINGEST COACH: Russell "Sox" Walseth (20 years from 1957-76 record, 261-245 record, .516).

ALL-TIME SCORING LEADER: Donnie Boyce (1,995 points from 1992-95).

ALL-TIME REBOUNDING LEADER: Cliff Meely (971 from 1969-71).

NCAA CONSENSUS SECOND-TEAM ALL-AMERICANS (3): Jack Harvey (1940), Bob Doll (1942), Chauncey Billups (1997).

COLORADO STATE

OFFICIAL NAME: Colorado State University.

NICKNAME: Rams.

ADDRESS: 202 B Moby Arena, Fort Collins, CO 80523.

PHONE/FAX: (970) 491-5067/1348.

ENROLLMENT: 20,600.

ARENA: Moby Arena (Capacity-10,000; Year Opened-1966).

SCHOOL COLORS: Green and Gold.

CONFERENCE: Western Athletic.

NCAA TOURNAMENT APPEARANCES (7): 1954-63-65-66-69-89-90; 3-8 record (.273); regional runner-up in 1969.

NIT APPEARANCES (4): 1961-62-88-96; 4-4 record (.500); finished 3rd in 1988.

ALL-TIME WINNINGEST COACH: Jim Williams (26 years from 1955-80, 352-283 record, .556).

ALL-TIME SCORING LEADER: Pat Durham (1,980 points from 1986-89).

ALL-TIME REBOUNDING LEADER: Pat Durham (851 from 1986-89).

NCAA CONSENSUS SECOND-TEAM ALL-AMERICANS (1): Bill Green (1963).

COLUMBIA

OFFICIAL NAME: Columbia University.

NICKNAME: Lions.

ADDRESS: 406 Dodge Physical Fitness Center, New York, NY 10027.

PHONE/FAX: (212) 854-2534/8168.

ENROLLMENT: 4,000.

ARENA: Levien Gymnasium (Capacity-3,408; Year Opened-1974).

SCHOOL COLORS: Columbia Blue and White.

CONFERENCE: Ivy League.

FINAL AP TOP 10 RANKINGS (2): 1951 and 1968.

NCAA TOURNAMENT APPEARANCES (3): 1948-51-68; 2-4 record (.333).

NIT APPEARANCES: None.

ALL-TIME WINNINGEST COACH: Jack Rohan (18 years from 1962-74 and 1991-95, 197-248 record, .443).

ALL-TIME SCORING LEADER: Leonard "Buck" Jenkins (1,766 points from 1990-93).

ALL-TIME REBOUNDING LEADER: Frank Thomas (1,022 from 1954-56).

NCAA CONSENSUS FIRST-TEAM ALL-AMERICANS (2): George Gregory (1931), Chet Forte (1957).

CONNECTICUT

OFFICIAL NAME: University of Connecticut.

NICKNAMES: Huskies, UConn.

ADDRESS: 2095 Hillside Road, U-78, Storrs, CT 06269-3078.

PHONE/FAX: (860) 486-3531/5085.

ENROLLMENT: 25,885.

ARENAS: Harry A. Gampel Pavilion (Capacity-8,241; Year Opened-1990) and Hartford Civic Center (Capacity-16,294; Year Opened-1981).

SCHOOL COLORS: National Flag Blue and White.

CONFERENCE: Big East.

FINAL AP TOP 10 RANKINGS (4): 1990-94-95-96.

NCAA TOURNAMENT APPEARANCES (19): 1951-54-56-57-58-59-60-63-64-65-67-76-79-90-91-92-94-95-96; 17-20 record (.459); regional runner-up in 1964, 1990 and 1995.

NIT APPEARANCES (10): 1955-74-75-80-81-82-88-89-93-97; 13-9 record (.591); finished 1st in 1988 and 3rd in 1997.

ALL-TIME WINNINGEST COACH: Hugh Greer (17 years from 1947-63, 286-112 record, .718).

ALL-TIME SCORING LEADER: Chris Smith (2,145 points from 1989-92).

ALL-TIME REBOUNDING LEADER: Art Quimby (1,716 from 1952-55).

NCAA CONSENSUS FIRST-TEAM ALL-AMERICANS (2): Donyell Marshall (1994), Ray Allen (1996).

COPPIN STATE

OFFICIAL NAME: Coppin State College.

NICKNAME: Eagles.

ADDRESS: 2500 West North Avenue, Baltimore, MD 21216.

PHONE/FAX: (410) 383-5688/669-6154.

ENROLLMENT: 3,650.

ARENA: Coppin Center-Pullen Gym (Capacity-3,000; Year Opened-1987).

SCHOOL COLORS: Royal Blue and Gold.

CONFERENCE: Mid-Eastern Athletic.

NCAA DIVISION I TOURNAMENT APPEARANCES (3): 1990-93-97; 1-3 record (.250).

NIT APPEARANCES (2): 1991 and 1995; 1-2 record (.333).

NAIA TOURNAMENT APPEARANCES (1): 1976; 5-0 record; finished 1st.

CORNELL

OFFICIAL NAME: Cornell University.

NICKNAME: Big Red.

ADDRESS: Teagle Hall, Ithaca, NY 14853-6501.

PHONE/FAX: (607) 255-3752/9791.

ENROLLMENT: 12,900.

ARENA: Newman Arena (Capacity-4,750; Year Opened-1989).

SCHOOL COLORS: Carnellian Red and White.

CONFERENCE: Ivy League.

NCAA TOURNAMENT APPEARANCES (2): 1954 and 1988; 0-3 record.

NIT APPEARANCES: None.

ALL-TIME WINNINGEST COACH: Royner Greene (13 years from 1947-59, 168-145 record, .537).

ALL-TIME SCORING LEADER: John Bajusz (1,663 points from 1984-87).

ALL-TIME REBOUNDING LEADER: George Farley (1,089 from 1958-60).

CREIGHTON

OFFICIAL NAME: Creighton University.

NICKNAME: Bluejays.

ADDRESS: Vinardi Athletic Center, 2500 California Plaza, Omaha, NE 68178-0810.

PHONE/FAX: (402) 280-2720/5596.

ENROLLMENT: 6,240.

ARENA: Omaha Civic Auditorium (Capacity-9,481; Year Opened-1954).

SCHOOL COLORS: Blue and White.

CONFERENCE: Missouri Valley.

NCAA TOURNAMENT APPEARANCES (9): 1941-62-64-74-75-78-81-89-91; 7-10 record (.412); regional runner-up in 1941.

NIT APPEARANCES (5): 1942-43-77-84-90; 2-5 record (.286); finished 3rd in 1942.

ALL-TIME WINNINGEST COACH: Arthur Schabinger (13 years from 1923-35, 163-66 record, .712).

ALL-TIME SCORING LEADER: Bob Harstad (2,110 points from 1988-91).

ALL-TIME REBOUNDING LEADER: Paul Silas (1,751 from 1962-64).

NCAA CONSENSUS FIRST-TEAM ALL-AMERICANS (1): Ed Beisser (1943).

DARTMOUTH

OFFICIAL NAME: Dartmouth College.

NICKNAME: Big Green.

ADDRESS: 6083 Alumni Gym, Hanover, NH 03755-3512.

PHONE/FAX: (603) 646-2468/1286.

ENROLLMENT: 4,200.

ARENA: Leede Arena (Capacity-2,100; Year Opened-1986).

SCHOOL COLORS: Dartmouth Green and White.

CONFERENCE: Ivy League.

NCAA TOURNAMENT APPEARANCES (7): 1941-42-43-44-56-58-59; 10-7 record (.588); reached Final Four in 1942 (2nd) and 1944 (2nd).

NIT APPEARANCES: None.

ALL-TIME WINNINGEST COACH: Alvin "Doggie" Julian (17 years from 1951-67, 183-236 record, .437).

ALL-TIME SCORING LEADER: Jim Barton (2,158 points from 1986-89).

ALL-TIME REBOUNDING LEADER: Rudy LaRusso (1,239 from 1957-59).

NCAA CONSENSUS FIRST-TEAM ALL-AMERICANS (3): Gus Broberg (1940 and 1941), Audley Brindley (1944).

NCAA CONSENSUS SECOND-TEAM ALL-AMERICANS (1): George Munroe (1942).

DAVIDSON

OFFICIAL NAME: Davidson College.

NICKNAME: Wildcats.

ADDRESS: Post Office Box 1750, Davidson, NC 28036.

PHONE/FAX: (704) 892-2374/2636.

ENROLLMENT: 1,550.

ARENA: John M. Belk Arena (Capacity-5,700; Year Opened-1989).

SCHOOL COLORS: Red and Black.

CONFERENCE: Southern.

FINAL AP TOP 10 RANKINGS (4): 1964-65-68-69.

NCAA TOURNAMENT APPEARANCES (5): 1966-68-69-70-86; 5-6 record (.455); regional runner-up in 1968 and 1969.

NIT APPEARANCES (3): 1972-94-96; 0-3 record.

ALL-TIME WINNINGEST COACH: Charles "Lefty" Driesell (nine years from 1961-69, 176-65 record, .730).

ALL-TIME SCORING LEADER: John Gerdy (2,487 points from 1976-79).

ALL-TIME REBOUNDING LEADER: Mike Maloy (1,111 from 1968-70).

NCAA CONSENSUS FIRST-TEAM ALL-AMERICANS (1): Fred Hetzel (1965).

NCAA CONSENSUS SECOND-TEAM ALL-AMERICANS (3): Fred Hetzel (1964), Dick Snyder (1966), Mike Maloy (1969).

DAYTON

OFFICIAL NAME: University of Dayton.

NICKNAME: Flyers.

ADDRESS: 300 College Park, Dayton, OH 45469-1238.

PHONE/FAX: (513) 229-4460/4461.

ENROLLMENT: 6,300.

ARENA: University of Dayton Arena (Capacity-13,455; Year Opened-1969).

SCHOOL COLORS: Red and Blue.

CONFERENCE: Atlantic 10.

FINAL AP TOP 10 RANKINGS (2): 1955 and 1956.

NCAA TOURNAMENT APPEARANCES (10): 1952-65-66-67-69-70-74-84-85-90; 13-12 record (.520); reached Final Four in 1967 (2nd).

NIT APPEARANCES (17): 1951-52-54-55-56-57-58-60-61-62-68-71-78-79-81-82-86; 29-16 record (.644); finished 2nd in 1951, 2nd in 1952, 2nd in 1955, 2nd in 1956, 2nd in 1958, 4th in 1961, 1st in 1962 and 1st in 1968.

ALL-TIME WINNINGEST COACH: Don Donoher (26 years from 1964-89, 437-275 record, .614).

ALL-TIME SCORING LEADER: Roosevelt Chapman (2,233 points from 1981-84).

ALL-TIME REBOUNDING LEADER: John Horan (1,341 from 1952-55).

NCAA CONSENSUS SECOND-TEAM ALL-AMERICANS (5): Don Meineke (1952), Bill Uhl (1956), Don May (1967 and 1968), Jim Paxson (1979).

DEPAUL

OFFICIAL NAME: DePaul University.

NICKNAME: Blue Demons.

ADDRESS: 1011 West Belden Avenue, Chicago, IL 60614.

PHONE/FAX: (773) 325-7525/7531.

ENROLLMENT: 16,745.

ARENA: Rosemont Horizon (Capacity-17,500; Year Opened-1980).

SCHOOL COLORS: Royal Blue and Scarlet.

CONFERENCE: Conference USA.

FINAL AP TOP 10 RANKINGS (8): 1964-78-79-80-81-82-84-87.

NCAA TOURNAMENT APPEARANCES (20): 1943-53-56-59-60-65-76-78-79-80-81-82-84-85-86-87-88-89-91-92; 20-23 record (.465); reached Final Four in 1943 (T3rd) and 1979 (3rd).

NIT APPEARANCES (12): 1940-44-45-48-61-63-64-66-83-90-94-95; 13-13 record (.500); finished 4th in 1940, 2nd in 1944, 1st in 1945, 4th in 1948 and 2nd in 1983.

ALL-TIME WINNINGEST COACH: Ray Meyer (42 years from 1943-84, 724-354 record, .671).

ALL-TIME SCORING LEADER: Mark Aguirre (2,182 points from 1979-81).

ALL-TIME REBOUNDING LEADER: Dave Corzine (1,151 from 1975-78).

NCAA CONSENSUS FIRST-TEAM ALL-AMERICANS (6): George Mikan (1944, 1945 and 1946), Mark Aguirre (1980 and 1981), Terry Cummings (1982).

NCAA CONSENSUS SECOND-TEAM ALL-AMERICANS (1): Dick Triptow (1944).

DETROIT

OFFICIAL NAME: University of Detroit.

NICKNAME: Titans.

ADDRESS: 4001 West McNichols Road, Post Office Box 19900, Detroit, MI 48219-0900.

PHONE/FAX: (313) 993-1745/1765.

ENROLLMENT: 7,800.

ARENAS: Calihan Hall (Capacity-8,837; Year Opened-1952) and Cobo Arena (Capacity-11,143; Year Opened-1960).

SCHOOL COLORS: Red, White and Blue.

CONFERENCE: Midwestern Collegiate.

NCAA TOURNAMENT APPEARANCES (3): 1962-77-79; 1-3 record (.250).

NIT APPEARANCES (4): 1960-61-65-78; 2-4 record (.333).

ALL-TIME WINNINGEST COACH: Bob Calihan (21 years from 1949-69, 306-237 record, .564).

ALL-TIME SCORING LEADER: John Long (2,167 points from 1975-78).

ALL-TIME REBOUNDING LEADER: Dave DeBusschere (1,552 from 1960-62).

NCAA CONSENSUS FIRST-TEAM ALL-AMERICANS (1): Spencer Haywood (1969).

NCAA CONSENSUS SECOND-TEAM ALL-AMERICANS (1): Bob Calihan (1939).

DRAKE

OFFICIAL NAME: Drake University.

NICKNAME: Bulldogs.

ADDRESS: Drake Fieldhouse, Des Moines, IA 50311.

PHONE/FAX: (515) 271-3012/3015.

ENROLLMENT: 4,000.

ARENA: Knapp Center (Capacity-7,002; Year Opened-1992).

SCHOOL COLORS: Blue and White.

NCAA TOURNAMENT APPEARANCES (3): 1969-70-71; 5-3 record (.625); reached Final Four in 1969 (3rd).

NAIA TOURNAMENT APPEARANCES (1): 1938; 0-1 record.

NIT APPEARANCES (3): 1964-81-86; 1-3 record (.250).

NCIT RECORD: 3-0 to finish 1st in 1975.

ALL-TIME WINNINGEST COACH: Maury John (13 years from 1959-71, 211-131 record, .617).

ALL-TIME SCORING LEADER: Phillip "Red" Murrell (1,657 points from 1956-58).

ALL-TIME REBOUNDING LEADER: Melvin Mathis (854 from 1983-86).

DREXEL

OFFICIAL NAME: Drexel University.

NICKNAME: Dragons.

ADDRESS: 32nd and Chestnut Streets, Philadelphia, PA 19104.

PHONE/FAX: (215) 590-8945/8668.

ENROLLMENT: 4,703.

ARENA: Physical Education Athletic Center (Capacity-2,300; Year Opened-1975).

SCHOOL COLORS: Navy Blue and Gold.

CONFERENCE: America East.

NCAA DIVISION I TOURNAMENT APPEARANCES (4): 1986-94-95-96; 1-4 record (.200).

NCAA DIVISION II TOURNAMENT APPEARANCES (4): 1957-60-66-67; 0-7 record.

NIT APPEARANCES (1): 1997; 0-1 record.

ALL-TIME WINNINGEST COACH: Sam Cozen (16 years from 1953-68 when school was classified as a small college, 213-94 record, .694).

ALL-TIME SCORING LEADER: Michael Anderson (2,208 points from 1985-88).

ALL-TIME REBOUNDING LEADER: Malik Rose (1,514 from 1993-96).

DUKE

OFFICIAL NAME: Duke University.

NICKNAME: Blue Devils.

ADDRESS: Post Office Box 90555, 118 Cameron Indoor Stadium, Durham, NC 27708-0555.

PHONE/FAX: (919) 684-2633/2489.

ENROLLMENT: 6,130.

ARENA: Cameron Indoor (Capacity-9,314; Year Opened-1939).

SCHOOL COLORS: Royal Blue and White.

CONFERENCE: Atlantic Coast.

FINAL AP TOP 10 RANKINGS (18): 1958-61-62-63-64-65-66-68-78-85-86-88-89-91-92-93-94-97.

NCAA TOURNAMENT APPEARANCES (21): 1955-60-63-64-66-78-79-80-84-85-86-87-88-89-90-91-92-93-94-96-97; 57-19 record (.750); reached Final Four in 1963 (3rd), 1964 (2nd), 1966 (2nd), 1978 (2nd), 1986 (2nd), 1988 (T3rd), 1989 (T3rd), 1990 (2nd), 1991 (1st), 1992 (1st) and 1994 (2nd).

NIT APPEARANCES (5): 1967-68-70-71-81; 5-6 record (.455); finished 4th in 1971.

ALL-TIME WINNINGEST COACH: Mike Krzyzewski (17 years from 1981-97, 400-148 record, .730).

ALL-TIME SCORING LEADER: Johnny Dawkins (2,556 points from 1983-86).

ALL-TIME REBOUNDING LEADER: Mike Gminski (1,242 from 1977-80).

NCAA CONSENSUS FIRST-TEAM ALL-AMERICANS (10): Dick Groat (1952), Art Heyman (1963), Bob Verga (1967), Mike Gminski (1979), Johnny Dawkins (1985 and 1986), Danny Ferry (1989), Christian Laettner (1992), Bobby Hurley (1993), Grant Hill (1994).

NCAA CONSENSUS SECOND-TEAM ALL-AMERICANS (11): Ed Koffenberger (1947), Dick Groat (1951), Art Heyman (1962), Jeff Mullins (1964), Jack Marin (1966), Bob Verga (1966), Jim Spanarkel (1979), Mike Gminski (1980), Danny Ferry (1988), Christian Laettner (1991), Grant Hill (1993).

DUQUESNE

OFFICIAL NAME: Duquesne University.

NICKNAME: Dukes.

ADDRESS: A.J. Palumbo Center, 600 Forbes Avenue, Pittsburgh, PA 15282.

PHONE/FAX: (412) 396-6560/6210.

ENROLLMENT: 8,600.

ARENA: A.J. Palumbo Center (Capacity-6,200; Year Opened-1988).

SCHOOL COLORS: Red and Blue.

CONFERENCE: Atlantic 10.

FINAL AP TOP 10 RANKINGS (6): 1950-52-53-54-55-69.

NCAA TOURNAMENT APPEARANCES (5): 1940-52-69-71-77; 4-5 record (.444); reached Final Four in 1940 (T3rd).

NIT APPEARANCES (16): 1940-41-47-50-52-53-54-55-56-62-64-68-70-80-81-94; 17-18 record (.486); finished 2nd in 1940, 4th in 1950, 4th in 1952, 3rd in 1953, 2nd in 1954, 1st in 1955 and 4th in 1962.

ALL-TIME WINNINGEST COACH: Charles "Chick" Davies (21 years from 1925-48, 314-106 record, .748).

ALL-TIME SCORING LEADER: Dick Ricketts (1,963 points from 1952-55).

ALL-TIME REBOUNDING LEADER: Dick Ricketts (1,496 from 1952-55).

NCAA CONSENSUS FIRST-TEAM ALL-AMERICANS (3): Dick Ricketts (1955), Si Green (1955 and 1956).

NCAA CONSENSUS SECOND-TEAM ALL-AMERICANS (2): Chuck Cooper (1950), Dick Ricketts (1954).

EAST CAROLINA

OFFICIAL NAME: East Carolina University.

NICKNAME: Pirates.

ADDRESS: Ward Sports Medicine Building, Greenville, NC 27858-4353.

PHONE/FAX: (919) 328-4522/4528.

ENROLLMENT: 17,570.

ARENA: Williams Arena at Minges Coliseum (Capacity-7,500; Year Opened-1995).

SCHOOL COLORS: Purple and Gold.

CONFERENCE: Colonial Athletic Association.

NCAA TOURNAMENT APPEARANCES (2): 1972 and 1993; 0-2 record.

NAIA TOURNAMENT APPEARANCES (2): 1953 and 1954; 0-2 record.

NIT APPEARANCES: None.

NCIT RECORD: 0-1 in 1975.

ALL-TIME WINNINGEST COACH: Howard Porter (12 years from 1948-59 when school was classified as a small college, 182-102 record, .641).

ALL-TIME SCORING LEADER: Bobby Hodges (2,018 points from 1951-54 when school was classified as a small college).

ALL-TIME REBOUNDING LEADER: Bill Otte (969 from 1961-64 when school was classified as a small college).

EAST TENNESSEE STATE

OFFICIAL NAME: East Tennessee State University.

NICKNAME: Buccaneers.

ADDRESS: Post Office Box 70707, University Drive & State of Franklin Road, Johnson City, TN 37614.

PHONE/FAX: (423).439-4220/6138.

ENROLLMENT: 12,105.

ARENA: Memorial Center (Capacity-12,000; Year Opened-1977).

SCHOOL COLORS: Blue and Gold.

CONFERENCE: Southern.

NCAA DIVISION I TOURNAMENT APPEARANCES (5): 1968-89-90-91-92; 2-6 record (.250).

NCAA DIVISION II TOURNAMENT APPEARANCES (1): 1957; 1-1 record (.500).

NAIA TOURNAMENT APPEARANCES (3): 1953-54-56; 0-3 record.

NIT APPEARANCES (1): 1983; 0-1 record.

ALL-TIME WINNINGEST COACH: Madison Brooks (25 years from 1949-73, 370-263 record, .585).

ALL-TIME SCORING LEADER: Greg Dennis (2,204 points from 1989-92).

NCAA CONSENSUS SECOND-TEAM ALL-AMERICANS (1): Keith "Mister" Jennings (1991).

EASTERN KENTUCKY

OFFICIAL NAME: Eastern Kentucky University.

NICKNAMES: Colonels, Maroons.

ADDRESS: 205 Begley Building, Richmond, KY 40475-3105.

PHONE/FAX: (606) 622-1253/1230.

ENROLLMENT: 15,725.

ARENA: McBrayer Arena (Capacity-6,500; Year Opened-1962).

SCHOOL COLORS: Maroon and White.

CONFERENCE: Ohio Valley.

NCAA TOURNAMENT APPEARANCES (5): 1953-59-65-72-79; 0-5 record.

NAIA TOURNAMENT APPEARANCES (2): 1945 and 1946; 3-2 record (.600); finished 3rd in 1945.

NIT APPEARANCES: None.

ALL-TIME WINNINGEST COACH: Paul McBrayer (16 years from 1947-62, 219-144 record, .603).

ALL-TIME SCORING LEADER: Antonio Parris (1,723 points from 1984-87).

ALL-TIME REBOUNDING LEADER: Mike Smith (977 from 1989-92).

EASTERN MICHIGAN

OFFICIAL NAME: Eastern Michigan University.

NICKNAME: Eagles.

ADDRESS: 200 Bowen Field House, Ypsilanti, MI 48197.

PHONE/FAX: (313) 487-0317/485-3840.

ENROLLMENT: 25,835.

ARENA: Bowen Field House (Capacity-5,600; Year Opened-1955).

SCHOOL COLORS: Dark Green and White.

CONFERENCE: Mid-American.

NCAA DIVISION I TOURNAMENT APPEARANCES (3): 1988-91-96; 3-3 record (.500).

NCAA DIVISION II TOURNAMENT APPEARANCES (1): 1972; 3-2 record (.600); finished 4th in 1972.

NAIA TOURNAMENT APPEARANCES (4): 1968-69-70-71; 8-4 record (.667); finished 2nd in 1971.

NIT APPEARANCES (1): 1995; 0-1 record.

ALL-TIME WINNINGEST COACH: Ben Braun (11 years from 1986-96, 185-132 record, .584).

ALL-TIME SCORING LEADER: Kennedy McIntosh (2,219 points from 1968-71 when school was classified Division II).

ALL-TIME REBOUNDING LEADER: Kennedy McIntosh (1,426 from 1968-71 when school was classified Division II).

EVANSVILLE

OFFICIAL NAME: University of Evansville.

NICKNAME: Aces.

ADDRESS: 1800 Lincoln Avenue, Evansville, IN 47722.

PHONE/FAX: (812) 479-2350/2199.

ENROLLMENT: 2,600.

ARENA: Roberts Stadium (Capacity-12,300; Year Opened-1956).

SCHOOL COLORS: Purple and White.

CONFERENCE: Missouri Valley.

NCAA DIVISION I TOURNAMENT APPEARANCES (4): 1982-89-92-93; 1-4 record (.200).

NCAA DIVISION II TOURNAMENT APPEARANCES (15): 1957-58-59-60-61-62-63-64-65-66-68-71-72-74-76; 40-10 record (.800); finished first five times (1959-60-64-65-71) and third once (1958).

NAIA TOURNAMENT APPEARANCES (4): 1941-42-51-55; 3-4 record (.429).

NIT APPEARANCES (2): 1988 and 1994; 1-2 record (.333).

ALL-TIME WINNINGEST COACH: Arad McCutchan (31 years from 1947-77 when school was classified as a small college, 514-314 record, .622).

ALL-TIME SCORING LEADER: Larry Humes (2,236 points from 1964-66 when school was classified as a small college).

ALL-TIME REBOUNDING LEADER: Dale Wise (1,197 from 1959-61 when school was classified as a small college).

NCAA CONSENSUS SECOND-TEAM ALL-AMERICANS (1): Wilfred Doerner (1942).

FAIRFIELD

OFFICIAL NAME: Fairfield University.

NICKNAME: Stags.

ADDRESS: Fairfield, CT 06430-7524.

PHONE/FAX: (203) 254-4000/4117.

ENROLLMENT: 2,900.

ARENA: Alumni Hall (Capacity-2,479; Year Opened-1959).

SCHOOL COLOR: Cardinal Red.

CONFERENCE: Metro Atlantic Athletic.

NCAA DIVISION I TOURNAMENT APPEARANCES (3): 1986-87-97; 0-3 record.

NCAA DIVISION II TOURNAMENT APPEARANCES (3): 1960-61-62; 2-4 record (.333).

NIT APPEARANCES (4): 1973-74-78-96; 1-4 record (.200).

ALL-TIME WINNINGEST COACH: Fred Barakat (11 years from 1971-81, 160-128 record, .556).

ALL-TIME SCORING LEADER: Tony George (2,006 points from 1983-86).

ALL-TIME REBOUNDING LEADER: Drew Henderson (1,080 from 1990-93).

FLORIDA

OFFICIAL NAME: University of Florida.

NICKNAME: Gators.

ADDRESS: Post Office Box 14485, Gainesville, FL 32604.

PHONE/FAX: (352) 375-4683/4809.

ENROLLMENT: 40,000.

ARENA: Stephen C. O'Connell Center (Capacity-12,000; Year Opened-1980).

SCHOOL COLORS: Orange and Blue.

CONFERENCE: Southeastern.

NCAA TOURNAMENT APPEARANCES (5): 1987-88-89-94-95; 7-5 record (.583); reached Final Four in 1994 (T3rd).

NIT APPEARANCES (6): 1969-84-85-86-92-93; 6-8 record (.429); finished 4th in 1986 and 1992.

ALL-TIME WINNINGEST COACH: Norman Sloan (15 years from 1961-66 and 1981-89, 235-194 record, .548).

ALL-TIME SCORING LEADER: Ronnie Williams (2,090 points from 1981-84).

ALL-TIME REBOUNDING LEADER: Neal Walk (1,181 from 1967-69).

FLORIDA STATE

OFFICIAL NAME: Florida State University.

NICKNAME: Seminoles.

ADDRESS: Moore Athletic Center, Post Office Drawer 2195, Tallahassee, FL 32316, or West Pensacola & Stadium Drive, 32306-4043.

PHONE/FAX: (904) 644-1403/3820.

ENROLLMENT: 29,000.

ARENA: Tallahassee-Leon County Civic Center (Capacity-12,500; Year Opened-1981).

SCHOOL COLORS: Garnet and Gold.

CONFERENCE: Atlantic Coast.

FINAL AP TOP 10 RANKINGS (1): 1972.

NCAA TOURNAMENT APPEARANCES (9): 1968-72-78-80-88-89-91-92-93; 11-9 record (.550); reached Final Four in 1972 (2nd).

NAIA TOURNAMENT APPEARANCES (2): 1951 and 1955; 3-2 record (.600).

NIT APPEARANCES (3): 1984-87-97; 6-3 record (.667); finished 2nd in 1997.

ALL-TIME WINNINGEST COACH: J.K. "Bud" Kennedy (18 years from 1949-66, 237-208 record, .532).

ALL-TIME SCORING LEADER: Bob Sura (2,130 points from 1992-95).

ALL-TIME REBOUNDING LEADER: Dave Cowens (1,340 from 1968-70).

FORDHAM

OFFICIAL NAME: Fordham University.

NICKNAME: Rams.

ADDRESS: Rose Hill Gym, Bronx, NY 10458-9993.

PHONE/FAX: (718) 817-4240/4244.

ENROLLMENT: 14,500.

ARENA: Rose Hill Gym (Capacity-3,470; Year Opened-1926).

SCHOOL COLORS: Maroon and White.

CONFERENCE: Atlantic 10.

FINAL AP TOP 10 RANKINGS (1): 1971.

NCAA TOURNAMENT APPEARANCES (4): 1953-54-71-92; 2-4 record (.333).

NIT APPEARANCES (16): 1943-58-59-63-65-68-69-72-81-82-83-84-85-88-90-91; 5-17 record (.227); finished 4th in 1943.

ALL-TIME WINNINGEST COACH: John Bach (18 years from 1951-68, 263-193 record, .576).

ALL-TIME SCORING LEADER: Ed Conlin (1,886 points from 1952-55).

ALL-TIME REBOUNDING LEADER: Ed Conlin (1,930 from 1952-55).

NCAA CONSENSUS SECOND-TEAM ALL-AMERICANS (1): Bob Hass-miller (1939).

FRESNO STATE

OFFICIAL NAME: Fresno State University.

NICKNAME: Bulldogs.

ADDRESS: 5305 North Campus Drive, Fresno, CA 93740-0027.

PHONE/FAX: (209) 278-2509/4689.

ENROLLMENT: 19,600.

ARENA: Selland Arena (Capacity-10,159; Year Opened-1966).

SCHOOL COLORS: Cardinal and Blue.

CONFERENCE: Western Athletic.

NCAA DIVISION I TOURNAMENT APPEARANCES (3): 1981-82-84; 1-3 record (.250).

NCAA DIVISION II TOURNAMENT APPEARANCES (7): 1958-60-62-63-64-65-66; 8-8 record (.500).

NIT APPEARANCES (5): 1983-85-94-96-97; 11-4 record (.733); finished 1st in 1983.

ALL-TIME WINNINGEST COACH: Boyd Grant (nine years from 1978-86, 194-74 record, .724).

ALL-TIME SCORING LEADER: Wil Hooker (1,739 points from 1989-92).

ALL-TIME REBOUNDING LEADER: Gary Alcorn (1,080 from 1957-59).

FURMAN

OFFICIAL NAME: Furman University.

NICKNAME: Paladins.

ADDRESS: 3300 Poinsett Highway, Greenville, SC 29613.

PHONE/FAX: (864) 294-2061/3061.

ENROLLMENT: 2,500.

ARENA: Greenville Memorial Auditorium (Capacity-5,344; Year Opened-1958).

SCHOOL COLORS: Purple and White.

CONFERENCE: Southern.

NCAA TOURNAMENT APPEARANCES (6): 1971-73-74-75-78-80; 1-7 record (.125).

NIT APPEARANCES (1): 1991; 0-1 record.

ALL-TIME WINNINGEST COACH: Lyles Alley (20 years from 1946-49 and 1951-66, 249-257 record, .492).

ALL-TIME SCORING LEADER: Frank Selvy (2,538 points from 1952-54).

ALL-TIME REBOUNDING LEADER: Jonathan Moore (1,242 from 1977-80).

NCAA CONSENSUS FIRST-TEAM ALL-AMERICANS (1): Frank Selvy (1954).

NCAA CONSENSUS SECOND-TEAM ALL-AMERICANS (3): Frank Selvy (1953), Darrell Floyd (1955 and 1956).

GEORGE WASHINGTON

OFFICIAL NAME: George Washington University.

NICKNAME: Colonials.

ADDRESS: Smith Center, Room 107, 600 22nd Street NW, Washington, DC 20052.

PHONE/FAX: (202) 994-8604/2713.

ENROLLMENT: 17,000.

ARENA: Charles E. Smith Center (Capacity-5,000; Year Opened-1975).

SCHOOL COLORS: Buff and Blue.

CONFERENCE: Atlantic 10.

NCAA TOURNAMENT APPEARANCES (5): 1954-61-93-94-96; 3-5 record (.375).

NIT APPEARANCES (3): 1991-95-97; 0-3 record.

ALL-TIME WINNINGEST COACH: Bill Reinhart (24 years from 1936-42 and 1950-66, 316-239 record, .569).

ALL-TIME SCORING LEADER: Joe Holup (2,226 points from 1953-56).

ALL-TIME REBOUNDING LEADER: Joe Holup (2,030 from 1953-56).

GEORGETOWN

OFFICIAL NAME: Georgetown University.

NICKNAME: Hoyas.

ADDRESS: McDonough Arena, Box 571124, Washington, DC 20057-1124.

PHONE/FAX: (202) 687-2492/2491.

ENROLLMENT: 6,180.

ARENA: USAir Arena (Capacity-19,500; Year Opened-1973).

SCHOOL COLORS: Blue and Gray.

CONFERENCE: Big East.

FINAL AP TOP 10 RANKINGS (7): 1982-84-85-87-89-90-96.

NCAA TOURNAMENT APPEARANCES (21): 1943-75-76-79-80-81-82-83-84-85-86-87-88-89-90-91-92-94-95-96-97; 36-20 record (.643); reached Final Four in 1943 (2nd), 1982 (2nd), 1984 (1st) and 1985 (2nd).

NIT APPEARANCES (5): 1953-70-77-78-93; 6-6 record (.500); finished 4th in 1978 and 2nd in 1993.

ALL-TIME WINNINGEST COACH: John Thompson (25 years from 1973-97, 573-218 record, .724).

ALL-TIME SCORING LEADER: Eric Floyd (2,304 points from 1979-82).

ALL-TIME REBOUNDING LEADER: Patrick Ewing (1,316 from 1982-85).

NCAA CONSENSUS FIRST-TEAM ALL-AMERICANS (7): Sleepy Floyd (1982), Patrick Ewing (1983, 1984 and 1985), Reggie Williams (1987), Alonzo Mourning (1992), Allen Iverson (1996).

NCAA CONSENSUS SECOND-TEAM ALL-AMERICANS (1): Alonzo Mourning (1990).

GEORGIA

OFFICIAL NAME: University of Georgia.

NICKNAME: Bulldogs.

ADDRESS: Post Office Box 1472, Athens, GA 30613.

PHONE/FAX: (706) 542-1621/1140.

ENROLLMENT: 28,690.

ARENA: Georgia Coliseum (Capacity-10,512; Year Opened-1963).

SCHOOL COLORS: Red and Black.

CONFERENCE: Southeastern.

NCAA TOURNAMENT APPEARANCES (7): 1983-85-87-90-91-96-97; 6-7 record (.462); reached Final Four in 1983 (T3rd).

NIT APPEARANCES (7): 1981-82-84-86-88-93-95; 6-7 record (.462); reached semifinals in 1982.

ALL-TIME WINNINGEST COACH: Hugh Durham (17 years from 1979-95, 298-216 record, .580).

ALL-TIME SCORING LEADER: Litterial Green (2,111 points from 1989-92).

ALL-TIME REBOUNDING LEADER: Bob Lienhard (1,116 from 1968-70).

GEORGIA TECH

OFFICIAL NAME: Georgia Institute of Technology.

NICKNAMES: Yellow Jackets, Rambling Wreck.

ADDRESS: 150 Bobby Dodd Way, N.W., Atlanta, GA 30332-0455.

PHONE/FAX: (404) 894-5445/853-2674.

ENROLLMENT: 13,000.

ARENA: Alexander Memorial Coliseum (Capacity-10,026; Year Opened-1957).

SCHOOL COLORS: Old Gold and White.

CONFERENCE: Atlantic Coast.

FINAL AP TOP 10 RANKINGS (3): 1985-86-90.

NCAA TOURNAMENT APPEARANCES (11): 1960-85-86-87-88-89-90-91-92-93-96; 16-11 record (.593); reached Final Four in 1990 (T3rd).

NIT APPEARANCES (4): 1970-71-84-94; 4-4 record (.500); finished 2nd in 1971.

ALL-TIME WINNINGEST COACH: Bobby Cremins (16 years from 1982-97, 307-190 record, .618).

ALL-TIME SCORING LEADER: Rich Yunkus (2,232 points from 1969-71).

ALL-TIME REBOUNDING LEADER: Malcolm Mackey (1,205 from 1990-93).

NCAA CONSENSUS FIRST-TEAM ALL-AMERICANS (2): Roger Kaiser (1961), Kenny Anderson (1991).

NCAA CONSENSUS SECOND-TEAM ALL-AMERICANS (3): Roger Kaiser (1960), Mark Price (1985), Dennis Scott (1990).

GONZAGA

OFFICIAL NAME: Gonzaga University.

NICKNAME: Zags.

ADDRESS: East 502 Boone Avenue, Spokane, WA 99258.

PHONE/FAX: (509) 328-4220/484-2830.

ENROLLMENT: 5,000.

ARENA: Charlotte Y. Martin Centre (Capacity-4,000; Year Opened-1965).

SCHOOL COLORS: Blue, Red and White.

CONFERENCE: West Coast.

NCAA TOURNAMENT APPEARANCES (1): 1995; 0-1 record.

NAIA TOURNAMENT APPEARANCES (2): 1948 and 1953; 1-2 record (.333).

NIT APPEARANCES (2): 1994 and 1996; 1-2 record (.333).

ALL-TIME WINNINGEST COACH: Hank Anderson (21 years from 1952-72, 290-272 record, .516).

ALL-TIME SCORING LEADER: Frank Burgess (2,196 points from 1959-61).

ALL-TIME REBOUNDING LEADER: Jerry Vermillion (1,670 from 1952-55).

NCAA CONSENSUS SECOND-TEAM ALL-AMERICANS (1): Frank Burgess (1961).

HARVARD

OFFICIAL NAME: Harvard University.

NICKNAME: Crimson.

ADDRESS: 60 John F. Kennedy Street, Cambridge, MA 02138.

PHONE/FAX: (617) 495-2206/2130.

ENROLLMENT: 6,675.

ARENA: Lavicks Pavilion at the Briggs Athletic Center (Capacity-2,083; Year Opened-1995).

SCHOOL COLORS: Crimson, Black and White.

CONFERENCE: Ivy League.

NCAA TOURNAMENT APPEARANCES (1): 1946; 0-2 record.

NIT APPEARANCES: None.

ALL-TIME WINNINGEST COACH: Floyd Wilson (14 years from 1955-68, 144-181 record, .443).

ALL-TIME SCORING LEADER: Joe Carrabino (1,880 points from 1982-85).

ALL-TIME REBOUNDING LEADER: Ron Mitchell (803 from 1989-92).

HAWAII

OFFICIAL NAME: University of Hawaii.

NICKNAME: Rainbows.

ADDRESS: 1337 Lower Campus Road, Honolulu, HI 96822.

PHONE/FAX: (808) 956-7523/4470.

ENROLLMENT: 19,810.

ARENA: Special Events Arena (Capacity-10,225; Year Opened-1994).

SCHOOL COLORS: Green and White.

CONFERENCE: Western Athletic.

NCAA TOURNAMENT APPEARANCES (2): 1972 and 1994; 0-2 record.

NAIA TOURNAMENT APPEARANCES (1): 1949; 0-1 record.

NIT APPEARANCES (5): 1971-74-89-90-97; 5-5 record (.500).

ALL-TIME WINNINGEST COACH: Riley Wallace (10 years from 1988-97, 156-142 record, .523).

ALL-TIME SCORING LEADER: Chris Gaines (1,734 points from 1987-90).

ALL-TIME REBOUNDING LEADER: Melton Werts (1,098 from 1973-76).

HOLY CROSS

OFFICIAL NAME: Holy Cross College.

NICKNAME: Crusaders.

ADDRESS: 1 College Street, Worcester, MA 01610-2395.

PHONE/FAX: (508) 793-2583/2309.

ENROLLMENT: 2,600.

ARENA: Hart Recreation Center (Capacity-3,600; Year Opened-1975).

SCHOOL COLORS: Royal Purple and White.

CONFERENCE: Patriot League.

FINAL AP TOP 10 RANKINGS (2): 1950 and 1954.

NCAA TOURNAMENT APPEARANCES (8): 1947-48-50-53-56-77-80-93; 7-8 record (.467); reached Final Four in 1947 (1st) and 1948 (3rd).

NIT APPEARANCES (11): 1952-54-55-60-61-62-75-76-79-81-90; 10-10 record (.500); finished 1st in 1954 and 3rd in 1961.

ALL-TIME WINNINGEST COACH: George Blaney (22 years from 1973-94, 357-276 record, .564).

ALL-TIME SCORING LEADER: Ronnie Perry (2,524 points from 1977-80).

ALL-TIME REBOUNDING LEADER: Tom Heinsohn (1,254 from 1954-56).

NCAA CONSENSUS FIRST-TEAM ALL-AMERICANS (2): Bob Cousy (1950), Tom Heinsohn (1956).

NCAA CONSENSUS SECOND-TEAM ALL-AMERICANS (3): George Kaftan (1947 and 1948), Jack Foley (1962).

HOUSTON

OFFICIAL NAME: University of Houston.

NICKNAME: Cougars.

ADDRESS: Department of Athletics, Houston, TX 77204-6742.

PHONE/FAX: (713) 743-9404/9411.

ENROLLMENT: 30,755.

ARENA: Hofheinz Pavilion (Capacity-10,132; Year Opened-1969).

SCHOOL COLORS: Scarlet and White.

CONFERENCE: Conference USA.

FINAL AP TOP 10 RANKINGS (4): 1967-68-83-84.

NCAA TOURNAMENT APPEARANCES (18): 1956-61-65-66-67-68-70-71-72-73-78-81-82-83-84-87-90-92; 26-23 record (.531); reached Final Four in 1967 (3rd), 1968 (4th), 1982 (T3rd), 1983 (2nd) and 1984 (2nd).

NAIA TOURNAMENT APPEARANCES (2): 1946 and 1947; 2-2 record (.500).

NIT APPEARANCES (6): 1962-77-85-88-91-93; 4-6 record (.400); finished 2nd in 1977.

ALL-TIME WINNINGEST COACH: Guy Lewis (30 years from 1957-86, 592-279 record, .680).

ALL-TIME SCORING LEADER: Elvin Hayes (2,884 points from 1966-68).

ALL-TIME REBOUNDING LEADER: Elvin Hayes (1,602 from 1966-68).

NCAA CONSENSUS FIRST-TEAM ALL-AMERICANS (4): Elvin Hayes (1967 and 1968), Otis Birdsong (1977), Hakeem Olajuwon (1984).

NCAA CONSENSUS SECOND-TEAM ALL-AMERICANS (1): Clyde Drexler (1983).

IDAHO

OFFICIAL NAME: University of Idaho.

NICKNAME: Vandals.

ADDRESS: East End Kibbie Dome, Moscow, ID 83843.

PHONE/FAX: (208) 885-0211/0255.

ENROLLMENT: 14,395.

ARENA: Kibbie ASUI Dome (Capacity-10,000; Year Opened-1975).

SCHOOL COLORS: Silver and Gold.

CONFERENCE: Big West.

FINAL AP TOP 10 RANKINGS (1): 1982.

NCAA TOURNAMENT APPEARANCES (4): 1981-82-89-90; 1-4 record (.200).

NIT APPEARANCES (1): 1983; 0-1 record.

ALL-TIME WINNINGEST COACH: Charles Finley (seven years from 1948-54, 113-94 record, .546).

ALL-TIME SCORING LEADER: Orlando Lightfoot (2,102 points from 1992-94).

ALL-TIME REBOUNDING LEADER: Deon Watson (877 from 1991-94).

IDAHO STATE

OFFICIAL NAME: Idaho State University.

NICKNAME: Bengals.

ADDRESS: Post Office Box 8124, Pocatello, ID 83209.

PHONE/FAX: (208) 236-3651/3659.

ENROLLMENT: 12,450.

ARENA: Holt Arena (Capacity-8,721; Year Opened-1970).

SCHOOL COLORS: Orange and Black.

CONFERENCE: Big Sky.

NCAA TOURNAMENT APPEARANCES (11): 1953-54-55-56-57-58-59-60-74-77-87; 8-13 record (.381); regional runner-up in 1977.

NAIA TOURNAMENT APPEARANCES (1): 1938; 1-1 record (.500).

NIT APPEARANCES: None.

ALL-TIME WINNINGEST COACH: Guy Wicks (10 years from 1932-41 when school was classified as a small college, 168-71 record, .703).

ALL-TIME SCORING LEADER: Les Roh (1,964 points from 1953-56 when school was classified as a small college).

ALL-TIME REBOUNDING LEADER: Steve Hayes (1,147 from 1974-77).

ILLINOIS

OFFICIAL NAME: University of Illinois.

NICKNAME: Fighting Illini.

ADDRESS: Bielfeldt Athletic Administration Building, 1700 South Fourth Street, Champaign, IL 61820.

PHONE/FAX: (217) 333-1390/5540.

ENROLLMENT: 35,000.

ARENA: Assembly Hall (Capacity-16,450; Year Opened-1963).

SCHOOL COLORS: Orange and Blue.

CONFERENCE: Big Ten.

FINAL AP TOP 10 RANKINGS (7): 1949-51-52-56-63-84-89.

NCAA TOURNAMENT APPEARANCES (18): 1942-49-51-52-63-81-83-84-85-86-87-88-89-90-93-94-95-97; 22-19 record (.537); reached Final Four in 1949 (3rd), 1951 (3rd), 1952 (3rd) and 1989 (T3rd).

NIT APPEARANCES (3): 1980-82-96; 5-3 record (.625); finished 3rd in 1980.

ALL-TIME WINNINGEST COACH: Lou Henson (21 years from 1976-96, 421-226 record, .651).

ALL-TIME SCORING LEADER: Deon Thomas (2,129 points from 1991-94).

ALL-TIME REBOUNDING LEADER: Efrem Winters (853 from 1983-86).

NCAA CONSENSUS FIRST-TEAM ALL-AMERICANS (5): Bill Hapac (1940), Andy Phillip (1942 and 1943), Walt Kirk (1945), Rod Fletcher (1952).

NCAA CONSENSUS SECOND-TEAM ALL-AMERICANS (4): Andy Phillip (1947), Bill Erickson (1949), Ken Norman (1987), Kendall Gill (1990).

ILLINOIS STATE

OFFICIAL NAME: Illinois State University.

NICKNAME: Redbirds.

ADDRESS: Horton Field House 133, College at Delaine, Normal, IL 61790-7130.

PHONE/FAX: (309) 438-3825/5634.

ENROLLMENT: 21,000.

ARENA: Redbird Arena (Capacity-10,600; Year Opened-1989).

SCHOOL COLORS: Red and White.

CONFERENCE: Missouri Valley.

NCAA DIVISION I TOURNAMENT APPEARANCES (5): 1983-84-85-90-97; 2-5 record (.286).

NCAA DIVISION II TOURNAMENT APPEARANCES (5): 1957-62-67-68-69; 6-7 record (.462); finished 4th in 1967.

NAIA TOURNAMENT APPEARANCES (1): 1959; 2-1 record (.667).

NIT APPEARANCES (7): 1977-78-80-87-88-95-96; 7-7 record (.500).

ALL-TIME WINNINGEST COACH: Joseph Cogdal (22 years from 1928-49 when school was classified as a small college, 280-177 record, .613).

ALL-TIME SCORING LEADER: Doug Collins (2,240 points from 1971-73).

ALL-TIME REBOUNDING LEADER: Ron deVries (1,033 from 1972-74).

NCAA CONSENSUS FIRST-TEAM ALL-AMERICANS (1): Doug Collins (1973).

INDIANA

OFFICIAL NAME: Indiana University.

NICKNAME: Hoosiers.

ADDRESS: Assembly Hall, Bloomington, IN 47405.

PHONE/FAX: (812) 855-2421/9401.

ENROLLMENT: 35,000.

ARENA: Assembly Hall (Capacity-17,357; Year Opened-1971).

SCHOOL COLORS: Cream and Crimson.

CONFERENCE: Big Ten.

FINAL AP TOP 10 RANKINGS (16): 1951-53-54-60-73-74-75-76-80-81-83-87-89-91-92-93.

NCAA TOURNAMENT APPEARANCES (26): 1940-53-54-58-67-73-75-76-78-80-81-82-83-84-86-87-88-89-90-91-92-93-94-95-96-97; 50-21 record (.704); reached Final Four in 1940 (1st), 1953 (1st), 1973 (3rd), 1976 (1st), 1981 (1st), 1987 (1st) and 1992 (T3rd).

NIT APPEARANCES (3): 1972-79-85; 8-2 record (.800); finished 1st in 1979 and 2nd in 1985.

CCAT RECORD: 3-0 to finish 1st in 1974.

ALL-TIME WINNINGEST COACH: Bob Knight (26 years from 1972-97, 598-208 record, .742).

ALL-TIME SCORING LEADER: Calbert Cheaney (2,613 points from 1990-93).

ALL-TIME REBOUNDING LEADER: Alan Henderson (1,091 from 1992-95).

NCAA CONSENSUS FIRST-TEAM ALL-AMERICANS (13): Branch McCracken (1930), Vern Huffman (1936), Ernie Andres (1939), Ralph Hamilton (1947), Don Schlundt (1954), Scott May (1975 and 1976), Kent Benson (1976 and 1977), Isiah Thomas (1981), Steve Alford (1986 and 1987), Calbert Cheaney (1993).

NCAA CONSENSUS SECOND-TEAM ALL-AMERICANS (9): Marv Huffman (1940), Bill Garrett (1951), Don Schlundt (1953 and 1955), Bob Leonard (1954), Archie Dees (1958), Walt Bellamy (1961), Randy Wittman (1983), Jay Edwards (1989).

INDIANA STATE

OFFICIAL NAME: Indiana State University.

NICKNAME: Sycamores.

ADDRESS: ISU Arena, 4th & Chestnut, Terre Haute, IN 47809.

PHONE/FAX: (812) 237-4160/4157.

ENROLLMENT: 11,570.

ARENA: Hulman Center (Capacity-10,200; Year Opened-1972).

SCHOOL COLORS: Blue and White.

CONFERENCE: Missouri Valley.

FINAL AP TOP 10 RANKINGS (1): 1979.

NCAA DIVISION I TOURNAMENT APPEARANCES (1): 1979; finished 2nd with a 4-1 record.

NCAA DIVISION II TOURNAMENT APPEARANCES (3): 1966-67-68; 5-4 record (.556); finished 2nd in 1968.

NAIA TOURNAMENT APPEARANCES (12): 1942-43-46-48-49-50-52-53-54-59-62-63; 25-12 record (.676); finished 1st in 1950, 2nd in 1946 and 1948, 3rd in 1953, and 4th in 1949.

NIT APPEARANCES (2): 1977 and 1978; 1-2 record (.333).

ALL-TIME WINNINGEST COACH: Duane Klueh (12 years from 1956-67 when school was classified as a small college, 182-121 record, .602).

ALL-TIME SCORING LEADER: Larry Bird (2,850 points from 1977-79).

ALL-TIME REBOUNDING LEADER: Larry Bird (1,247 from 1977-79).

NCAA CONSENSUS FIRST-TEAM ALL-AMERICANS (2): Larry Bird (1978 and 1979).

NCAA CONSENSUS SECOND-TEAM ALL-AMERICANS (2): Duane Klueh (1948).

IONA

OFFICIAL NAME: Iona College.

NICKNAME: Gaels.

ADDRESS: 715 North Avenue, New Rochelle, NY 10801-1890.

PHONE/FAX: (914) 633-2334/2072.

ENROLLMENT: 7,500.

ARENA: Mulcahy Center (Capacity-3,200; Year Opened-1975).

SCHOOL COLORS: Maroon and Gold.

CONFERENCE: Metro Atlantic Athletic.

NCAA TOURNAMENT APPEARANCES (4): 1979-80-84-85; 1-4 record (.200).

NIT APPEARANCES (4): 1982-83-96-97; 1-4 record (.200).

ALL-TIME WINNINGEST COACH: Jim McDermott (26 years from 1948-73, 319-253 record, .558).

ALL-TIME SCORING LEADER: Steve Burtt (2,534 points from 1981-84).

ALL-TIME REBOUNDING LEADER: Warren Isaac (1,124 from 1963-65).

IOWA

OFFICIAL NAME: University of Iowa.

NICKNAME: Hawkeyes.

ADDRESS: 205 Carver-Hawkeye Arena, Iowa City, IA 52242.

PHONE/FAX: (319) 335-9411/9417.

ENROLLMENT: 28,000.

ARENA: Carver-Hawkeye Arena (Capacity-15,500; Year Opened-1983).

SCHOOL COLORS: Old Gold and Black.

CONFERENCE: Big Ten.

FINAL AP TOP 10 RANKINGS (6): 1952-55-56-61-70-87.

NCAA TOURNAMENT APPEARANCES (18): 1955-56-70-79-80-81-82-83-85-86-87-88-89-91-92-93-96-97; 24-20 record (.545); reached Final Four in 1955 (4th), 1956 (2nd) and 1980 (4th).

NIT APPEARANCES (1): 1995; 2-1 record (.667).

ALL-TIME WINNINGEST COACH: Tom Davis (11 years from 1987-97, 229-119 record, .658).

ALL-TIME SCORING LEADER: Roy Marble (2,116 points from 1986-89).

ALL-TIME REBOUNDING LEADER: Kevin Kunnert (914 from 1971-73).

NCAA CONSENSUS FIRST-TEAM ALL-AMERICANS (2): Murray Wier (1948), Chuck Darling (1952).

NCAA CONSENSUS SECOND-TEAM ALL-AMERICANS (2): Richard Ives (1945), Herb Wilkinson (1945).

IOWA STATE

OFFICIAL NAME: Iowa State University.

NICKNAME: Cyclones.

ADDRESS: Olsen Building Annex, Ames, IA 50011.

PHONE/FAX: (515) 294-3372/0558.

ENROLLMENT: 22,755.

ARENA: James H. Hilton Coliseum (Capacity-14,020; Year Opened-1971).

SCHOOL COLORS: Cardinal and Gold.

CONFERENCE: Big 12.

NCAA TOURNAMENT APPEARANCES (10): 1944-85-86-88-89-92-93-95-96-97; 8-10 record (.444); reached Final Four in 1944 (T3rd).

NIT APPEARANCES (1): 1984; 0-1 record.

ALL-TIME WINNINGEST COACH: Johnny Orr (14 years from 1981-94, 218-200 record, .522).

ALL-TIME SCORING LEADER: Jeff Grayer (2,502 points from 1985-88).

ALL-TIME REBOUNDING LEADER: Dean Uthoff (1,233 from 1977-80).

NCAA CONSENSUS SECOND-TEAM ALL-AMERICANS (1): Gary Thompson (1957).

JACKSONVILLE

OFFICIAL NAME: Jacksonville University.

NICKNAME: Dolphins.

ADDRESS: 2800 University Boulevard North, Jacksonville, FL 32211.

PHONE/FAX: (904) 744-7402/743-0067.

ENROLLMENT: 2,400.

ARENA: Jacksonville Coliseum (Capacity-9,150; Year Opened-1960).

SCHOOL COLORS: Green and White.

CONFERENCE: Sun Belt.

FINAL AP TOP 10 RANKINGS (1): 1970.

NCAA TOURNAMENT APPEARANCES (5): 1970-71-73-79-86; 4-5 record (.444); reached Final Four in 1970 (2nd).

NAIA TOURNAMENT APPEARANCES (1): 1965; 0-1 record.

NIT APPEARANCES (4): 1972-74-80-87; 5-5 record (.500); finished 3rd in 1972 and 4th in 1974.

ALL-TIME WINNINGEST COACH (Division I level): Joe Williams (six years from 1965-70, 92-61 record, .601).

ALL-TIME SCORING LEADER: Ralph Tiner (2,184 points from 1962-65 when school was classified as a small college).

ALL-TIME REBOUNDING LEADER: Artis Gilmore (1,224 in 1970 and 1971).

NCAA CONSENSUS FIRST-TEAM ALL-AMERICANS (1): Artis Gilmore (1971).

JAMES MADISON

OFFICIAL NAME: James Madison University.

NICKNAME: Dukes.

ADDRESS: Harrisonburg, VA 22807.

PHONE/FAX: (703) 568-6154/3703.

ENROLLMENT: 11,500.

ARENA: JMU Convocation Center (Capacity-7,612; Year Opened-1982).

SCHOOL COLORS: Purple and Gold.

CONFERENCE: Colonial Athletic Association.

NCAA DIVISION I TOURNAMENT APPEARANCES (4): 1981-82-83-94; 3-4 record (.429).

NCAA DIVISION II TOURNAMENT APPEARANCES (2): 1974 and 1976; 0-3 record.

NIT APPEARANCES (5): 1987-90-91-92-93; 0-5 record.

ALL-TIME WINNINGEST COACH: Lou Campanelli (13 years from 1973-85, 238-118 record, .669).

ALL-TIME SCORING LEADER: Steve Stiepler (2,126 points from 1977-80).

ALL-TIME REBOUNDING LEADER: Steve Stiepler (917 from 1977-80).

KANSAS

OFFICIAL NAME: University of Kansas.

NICKNAME: Jayhawks.

ADDRESS: 104 Allen Fieldhouse, Lawrence, KS 66045.

PHONE/FAX: (913) 864-3417/7944.

ENROLLMENT: 25,240.

ARENA: Allen Fieldhouse (Capacity-16,300; Year Opened-1955).

SCHOOL COLORS: Crimson and Blue.

CONFERENCE: Big 12.

FINAL AP TOP 10 RANKINGS (16): 1952-53-57-58-66-67-71-74-78-86-90-92-93-95-96-97.

NCAA TOURNAMENT APPEARANCES (26): 1940-42-52-53-57-60-66-67-71-74-75-78-81-84-85-86-87-88-90-91-92-93-94-95-96-97; 56-26 record (.683); reached Final Four in 1940 (2nd), 1952 (1st), 1953 (2nd), 1957 (2nd), 1971 (4th), 1974 (4th), 1986 (T3rd), 1988 (1st), 1991 (2nd) and 1993 (T3rd).

NIT APPEARANCES (2): 1968 and 1969; 3-2 record (.600); finished 2nd in 1968.

ALL-TIME WINNINGEST COACH: Dr. Forrest C. (Phog) Allen (39 years—1908, 1909 and 1920-56; 590-219 record, .729).

ALL-TIME SCORING LEADER: Danny Manning (2,951 points from 1985-88).

ALL-TIME REBOUNDING LEADER: Danny Manning (1,187 from 1985-88).

NCAA CONSENSUS FIRST-TEAM ALL-AMERICANS (10): Fred Pralle (1938), Howard Engleman (1941), Charles Black (1943), Clyde Lovellette (1951 and 1952), Wilt Chamberlain (1957 and 1958), Danny Manning (1987 and 1988), Raef LaFrentz (1997).

NCAA CONSENSUS SECOND-TEAM ALL-AMERICANS (8): Charles Black (1946), Walt Wesley (1966), Joseph "Jo Jo" White (1968 and 1969), Isaac "Bud" Stallworth (1972), Danny Manning (1986), Jacque Vaughn (1996 and 1997).

KANSAS STATE

OFFICIAL NAME: Kansas State University.

NICKNAME: Wildcats.

ADDRESS: 144 Bramlage Coliseum, 1800 College Avenue, Manhattan, KS 66502.

PHONE/FAX: (913) 532-6735/6093.

ENROLLMENT: 20,775.

ARENA: Fred Bramlage Coliseum (Capacity-13,500; Year Opened-1988).

SCHOOL COLORS: Purple and White.

CONFERENCE: Big 12.

FINAL AP TOP 10 RANKINGS (7): 1951-52-58-59-61-62-73.

NCAA TOURNAMENT APPEARANCES (22): 1948-51-56-58-59-61-64-68-70-72-73-75-77-80-81-82-87-88-89-90-93-96; 27-26 record (.509); reached Final Four in 1948 (4th), 1951 (2nd), 1958 (4th) and 1964 (4th).

NIT APPEARANCES (3): 1976-92-94; 4-4 record (.500); finished 4th in 1994.

CCAT RECORD: 0-1 in 1974.

ALL-TIME WINNINGEST COACH: Jack Hartman (16 years from 1971-86, 295-169 record, .643).

ALL-TIME SCORING LEADER: Mike Evans (2,115 points from 1975-78).

ALL-TIME REBOUNDING LEADER: Ed Nealy (1,071 from 1979-82).

NCAA CONSENSUS FIRST-TEAM ALL-AMERICANS (2): Bob Boozer (1958 and 1959).

NCAA CONSENSUS SECOND-TEAM ALL-AMERICANS (3): Ernie Barrett (1951), Dick Knostman (1953), Mitch Richmond (1988).

KENT

OFFICIAL NAME: Kent University.

NICKNAME: Golden Flashes.

ADDRESS: MAC Center, Kent, OH 44242-0001.

PHONE/FAX: (216) 672-2110/2112.

ENROLLMENT: 29,785.

ARENA: Memorial Athletic and Convocation Center (Capacity-6,327; Year Opened-1950).

SCHOOL COLORS: Blue and Gold.

CONFERENCE: Mid-American.

NCAA TOURNAMENT APPEARANCES: None.

NIT APPEARANCES (3): 1985-89-90; 0-3 record.

ALL-TIME WINNINGEST COACH: Jim McDonald (10 years from 1983-92, 148-138 record, .517).

ALL-TIME SCORING LEADER: Burrell McGhee (1,710 points from 1977-79).

ALL-TIME REBOUNDING LEADER: Trent Grooms (1,012 from 1977-80).

KENTUCKY

OFFICIAL NAME: University of Kentucky.

NICKNAME: Wildcats.

ADDRESS: Memorial Coliseum, Avenue of Champions, Lexington, KY 40506-0019.

PHONE/FAX: (606) 257-8000/323-4310.

ENROLLMENT: 24,000.

ARENA: Rupp Arena (Capacity-23,000; Year Opened-1976).

SCHOOL COLORS: Blue and White.

CONFERENCE: Southeastern.

FINAL AP TOP 10 RANKINGS (32): 1949-50-51-52-54-55-56-57-58-59-62-64-66-68-69-70-71-75-77-78-80-81-84-86-88-91-92-93-94-95-96-97.

NCAA TOURNAMENT APPEARANCES (39): 1942-45-48-49-51-52-55-56-57-58-59-61-62-64-66-68-69-70-71-72-73-75-77-78-80-81-82-83-84-85-86-87-88-92-93-94-95-96-97; 77-35 record (.688); reached Final Four in 1942 (T3rd), 1948 (1st), 1949 (1st), 1951 (1st), 1958 (1st), 1966 (2nd), 1975 (2nd), 1978 (1st), 1984 (T3rd), 1993 (T3rd), 1996 (1st) and 1997 (2nd).

NIT APPEARANCES (7): 1944-46-47-49-50-76-79; 11-5 record (.688); finished 3rd in 1944, 1st in 1946, 2nd in 1947 and 1st in 1976.

ALL-TIME WINNINGEST COACH: Adolph Rupp (42 years from 1931-72, 875-190 record, .822).

ALL-TIME SCORING LEADER: Dan Issel (2,138 points from 1968-70).

ALL-TIME REBOUNDING LEADER: Dan Issel (1,078 from 1968-70).

NCAA CONSENSUS FIRST-TEAM ALL-AMERICANS (20): Forest Sale (1932 and 1933), LeRoy Edwards (1935), Bob Brannum (1944), Ralph Beard (1947, 1948 and 1949), Alex Groza (1947 and 1949), Bill Spivey (1951), Cliff Hagan (1952 and 1954), Johnny Cox (1959), Charles "Cotton" Nash (1964), Dan Issel (1970), Kyle Macy (1980), Kenny Walker (1986), Jamal Mashburn (1993), Tony Delk (1996), Ron Mercer (1997).

NCAA CONSENSUS SECOND-TEAM ALL-AMERICANS (17): Bernie Opper (1939), Jack Parkinson (1946), Alex Groza (1948), Wallace Jones (1949), Frank Ramsey (1954), Bob Burrow (1956), Charles "Cotton" Nash (1962 and 1963), Louie Dampier (1966 and 1967), Dan Issel (1969), Kevin Grevey (1975), Jack Givens (1978), Rick Robey (1978), Sam Bowie (1981), Mel Turpin (1984), Kenny Walker (1985).

LAFAYETTE

OFFICIAL NAME: Lafayette College.

NICKNAME: Leopards.

ADDRESS: Easton, PA 18042-1768.

PHONE/FAX: (610) 250-5122/5519.

ENROLLMENT: 2,000.

ARENA: Allan P. Kirby Field House (Capacity-3,500; Year Opened-1973).

SCHOOL COLORS: Maroon and White.

CONFERENCE: Patriot League.

NCAA TOURNAMENT APPEARANCES (1): 1957; 0-2 record.

NIT APPEARANCES (5): 1955-56-72-75-80; 1-5 record (.167).

ALL-TIME WINNINGEST COACH: George Davidson (12 years from 1956-67, 170-116 record, .594).

ALL-TIME SCORING LEADER: Tracy Tripucka (1,973 points from 1970-72).

ALL-TIME REBOUNDING LEADER: Jim Radcliff (1,148 from 1955-57).

LAMAR

OFFICIAL NAME: Lamar University.

NICKNAME: Cardinals.

ADDRESS: Post Office Box 10066, Beaumont, TX 77710.

PHONE/FAX: (409) 880-2323/2338.

ENROLLMENT: 9,110.

ARENA: Montagne Center (Capacity-10,080; Year Opened-1984).

SCHOOL COLORS: Red and White.

CONFERENCE: Southland.

NCAA DIVISION I TOURNAMENT APPEARANCES (4): 1979-80-81-83; 5-4 record (.556).

NCAA DIVISION II TOURNAMENT APPEARANCES (5): 1960-62-63-64-66; 5-5 record (.500).

NIT APPEARANCES (4): 1982-84-85-86; 2-4 record (.333).

ALL-TIME WINNINGEST COACH: Jack Martin (25 years from 1952-76, 334-283 record, .541).

ALL-TIME SCORING LEADER: Mike Olliver (2,518 points from 1978-81).

ALL-TIME REBOUNDING LEADER: Clarence Kea (1,143 from 1977-80).

LA SALLE

OFFICIAL NAME: La Salle University.

NICKNAME: Explorers.

ADDRESS: 1900 West Olney Avenue, Box 805, Philadelphia, PA 19141-1199.

PHONE/FAX: (215) 951-1513/1694.

ENROLLMENT: 5,800.

ARENA: CoreStates Spectrum (Capacity-8,952; Year Opened-1967).

SCHOOL COLORS: Blue and Gold.

CONFERENCE: Atlantic 10.

FINAL AP TOP 10 RANKINGS (5): 1950-53-54-55-69.

NCAA TOURNAMENT APPEARANCES (11): 1954-55-68-75-78-80-83-88-89-90-92; 11-10 record (.524); reached Final Four in 1954 (1st) and 1955 (2nd).

NIT APPEARANCES (11): 1948-50-51-52-53-63-65-71-84-87-91; 9-10 record (.474); finished 1st in 1952 and 2nd in 1987.

ALL-TIME WINNINGEST COACH: Bill "Speedy" Morris (11 years from 1987-97, 193-136 record, .587).

ALL-TIME SCORING LEADER: Lionel Simmons (3,217 points from 1987-90).

ALL-TIME REBOUNDING LEADER: Tom Gola (2,201 from 1952-55).

NCAA CONSENSUS FIRST-TEAM ALL-AMERICANS (5): Tom Gola (1953, 1954 and 1955), Michael Brooks (1980), Lionel Simmons (1990).

NCAA CONSENSUS SECOND-TEAM ALL-AMERICANS (2): Ken Durrett (1971), Lionel Simmons (1989).

LEHIGH

OFFICIAL NAME: Lehigh University.

NICKNAMES: Engineers, Mountain Hawks.

ADDRESS: 641 Taylor Street, Bethlehem, PA 18015-3187.

PHONE/FAX: (610) 758-3174/4407.

ENROLLMENT: 4,400.

ARENA: Stabler Arena (Capacity-5,600; Year Opened-1979).

SCHOOL COLORS: Brown and White.

CONFERENCE: Patriot League.

NCAA TOURNAMENT APPEARANCES (2): 1985 and 1988; 0-2 record.

NIT APPEARANCES: None.

ALL-TIME WINNINGEST COACH: Tony Packer (16 years from 1951-66, 112-213 record, .345).

ALL-TIME SCORING LEADER: Daren Queenan (2,703 points from 1985-88).

ALL-TIME REBOUNDING LEADER: Daren Queenan (1,013 from 1985-88).

LONG BEACH STATE

OFFICIAL NAME: California State University (At Long Beach).

NICKNAME: 49ers.

ADDRESS: 1250 Bellflower Boulevard, Long Beach, CA 90840.

PHONE/FAX: (310) 985-7978/8197.

ENROLLMENT: 27,445.

ARENA: The Pyramid (Capacity-5,000; Year Opened-1994).

SCHOOL COLORS: Black and Gold.

CONFERENCE: Big West.

FINAL AP TOP 10 RANKINGS (3): 1972-73-74.

NCAA DIVISION I TOURNAMENT APPEARANCES (7): 1970-71-72-1973-77-93-95; 7-8 record (.467); regional runner-up in 1971 and 1972.

NCAA DIVISION II TOURNAMENT APPEARANCES (1): 1961; 1-1 record (.500).

NIT APPEARANCES (3): 1980-88-90; 2-3 record (.400).

ALL-TIME WINNINGEST COACH: Jerry Tarkanian (five years from 1969-73, 121-20 record, .858).

ALL-TIME SCORING LEADER: Lucious Harris (2,312 points from 1990-93).

ALL-TIME REBOUNDING LEADER: Francois Wise (896 from 1977-80).

NCAA CONSENSUS FIRST-TEAM ALL-AMERICANS (2): Ed Ratleff (1972 and 1973).

LONG ISLAND

OFFICIAL NAME: Long Island University.

NICKNAME: Blackbirds.

ADDRESS: University Plaza, Brooklyn, NY 11201.

PHONE/FAX: (718) 488-1420/780-4046.

ENROLLMENT: 9,500.

ARENA: Schwartz Athletic Center (Capacity-1,700; Year Opened-1963).

SCHOOL COLORS: Blue and White.

CONFERENCE: Northeast.

NCAA DIVISION I TOURNAMENT APPEARANCES (3): 1981-84-97; 0-3 record.

NCAA DIVISION II TOURNAMENT APPEARANCES (3): 1965-66-67; 6-3 record (.667).

NIT APPEARANCES (9): 1938-39-40-41-42-47-50-68-82; 7-7 record (.500); finished 1st in 1939 and 1941.

ALL-TIME WINNINGEST COACH: Clair Bee (18 years from 1932-43 and 1946-51, 359-80 record, .818).

ALL-TIME SCORING LEADER: Joe Griffin (1,830 points from 1992-95).

ALL-TIME REBOUNDING LEADER: Carey Scurry (1,013 from 1983-85; played freshman season in junior college).

NCAA CONSENSUS FIRST-TEAM ALL-AMERICANS (2): Jules Bender (1937), Irving Torgoff (1939).

NCAA CONSENSUS SECOND-TEAM ALL-AMERICANS (2): Oscar Schechtman (1941), Sherman White (1950).

LOUISIANA STATE

OFFICIAL NAME: Louisiana State University.

NICKNAME: Tigers.

ADDRESS: Post Office Box 25095, Baton Rouge, LA 70894-5095.

PHONE/FAX: (504) 388-8226/1861.

ENROLLMENT: 24,750.

ARENA: Pete Maravich Assembly Center (Capacity-14,164; Year Opened-1972).

SCHOOL COLORS: Purple and Gold.

CONFERENCE: Southeastern.

FINAL AP TOP 10 RANKINGS (4): 1953-79-80-81.

NCAA TOURNAMENT APPEARANCES (15): 1953-54-79-80-81-84-85-86-87-88-89-90-91-92-93; 17-18 record (.486); reached Final Four in 1953 (4th), 1981 (4th) and 1986 (T3rd).

NIT APPEARANCES (3): 1970-82-83; 2-4 record (.333); finished 4th in 1970.

ALL-TIME WINNINGEST COACH: Dale Brown (25 years from 1973-97, 448-301 record, .598).

ALL-TIME SCORING LEADER: Pete Maravich (3,667 points from 1968-70).

ALL-TIME REBOUNDING LEADER: Durand "Rudy" Macklin (1,276 from 1977-81; missed 1978-79 season because of a broken leg).

NCAA CONSENSUS FIRST-TEAM ALL-AMERICANS (8): Bob Pettit (1954), Pete Maravich (1968, 1969 and 1970), Chris Jackson (1989 and 1990), Shaquille O'Neal (1991 and 1992).

NCAA CONSENSUS SECOND-TEAM ALL-AMERICANS (2): Bob Pettit (1953), Durand "Rudy" Macklin (1981).

LOUISIANA TECH

OFFICIAL NAME: Louisiana Tech University.

NICKNAME: Bulldogs.

ADDRESS: Post Office Box 3166TS, Ruston, LA 71272.

PHONE/FAX: (318) 257-3144/3757.

ENROLLMENT: 10,380.

ARENA: Thomas Assembly Center (Capacity-8,000; Year Opened-1982).

SCHOOL COLORS: Columbia Blue and Red.

CONFERENCE: Sun Belt.

FINAL AP TOP 10 RANKINGS (1): 1985.

NCAA DIVISION I TOURNAMENT APPEARANCES (5): 1984-85-87-89-91; 4-5 record (.444).

NCAA DIVISION II TOURNAMENT APPEARANCES (2): 1967 and 1971; 2-2 record (.500).

NAIA TOURNAMENT APPEARANCES (4): 1942-46-53-55; 1-4 record (.200).

NIT APPEARANCES (4): 1986-88-90-92; 5-4 record (.556); finished 3rd in 1986.

ALL-TIME WINNINGEST COACH: Cecil C. Crowley (21 years in 1941, 1942 and from 1946-64 when school was classified as a small college, 269-221 record, .549).

ALL-TIME SCORING LEADER: Mike Green (2,340 points from 1970-73 when school was classified as a small college).

ALL-TIME REBOUNDING LEADER: Mike Green (1,575 from 1970-73 when school was classified as a small college).

LOUISVILLE

OFFICIAL NAME: University of Louisville.

NICKNAME: Cardinals.

ADDRESS: Belknap Campus, Louisville, KY 40292.

PHONE/FAX: (502) 852-6581/7401.

ENROLLMENT: 23,000.

ARENA: Freedom Hall (Capacity-18,865; Year Opened-1956).

SCHOOL COLORS: Red, Black and White.

CONFERENCE: Conference USA.

FINAL AP TOP 10 RANKINGS (11): 1956-57-67-68-72-75-78-80-83-86-94.

NCAA TOURNAMENT APPEARANCES (27): 1951-59-61-64-67-68-72-74-75-77-78-79-80-81-82-83-84-86-88-89-90-92-93-94-95-96-97; 48-29 record (.623); reached Final Four in 1959 (4th), 1972 (4th), 1975 (3rd), 1980 (1st), 1982 (T3rd), 1983 (T3rd) and 1986 (1st).

NAIA TOURNAMENT APPEARANCES (1): 1948; won title with a 5-0 record.

NIT APPEARANCES (12): 1952-53-54-55-56-66-69-70-71-73-76-85; 10-12 record (.455); finished 1st in 1956 and 4th in 1985.

ALL-TIME WINNINGEST COACH: Denny Crum (26 years from 1972-97, 613-233 record, .725).

ALL-TIME SCORING LEADER: Darrell Griffith (2,333 points from 1977-80).

ALL-TIME REBOUNDING LEADER: Charlie Tyra (1,617 from 1954-57).

NCAA CONSENSUS FIRST-TEAM ALL-AMERICANS (6): Charlie Tyra (1957), Wes Unseld (1967 and 1968), Darrell Griffith (1980), Pervis Ellison (1989), Clifford Rozier (1994).

NCAA CONSENSUS SECOND-TEAM ALL-AMERICANS (1): Jim Price (1972).

LOYOLA (ILL.)

OFFICIAL NAME: Loyola University.

NICKNAME: Ramblers.

ADDRESS: 6525 North Sheridan Road, Chicago, IL 60626.

PHONE/FAX: (773) 508-2575/3884.

ENROLLMENT: 15,885.

ARENAS: Alumni Gym (Capacity-2,975; Year Opened-1926) and Rosemont Horizon (Capacity-17,500; Year Opened-1980).

SCHOOL COLORS: Maroon and Gold.

CONFERENCE: Midwestern Collegiate.

FINAL AP TOP 10 RANKINGS (3): 1963-64-66.

NCAA TOURNAMENT APPEARANCES (5): 1963-64-66-68-85; 9-4 record (.692); reached Final Four in 1963 (1st).

NAIA TOURNAMENT APPEARANCES (1): 1943; 0-1 record.

NIT APPEARANCES (4): 1939-49-62-80; 6-4 record (.600); finished 2nd in 1939, 2nd in 1949 and 3rd in 1962.

ALL-TIME WINNINGEST COACH: George Ireland (24 years from 1952-75, 321-255 record, .557).

ALL-TIME SCORING LEADER: Alfredrick Hughes (2,914 points from 1982-85).

ALL-TIME REBOUNDING LEADER: LaRue Martin (1,062 from 1970-72).

NCAA CONSENSUS FIRST-TEAM ALL-AMERICANS (1): Jerry Harkness (1963).

NCAA CONSENSUS SECOND-TEAM ALL-AMERICANS (1): Michael Novak (1939).

LOYOLA MARYMOUNT

OFFICIAL NAME: Loyola Marymount University.

NICKNAME: Lions.

ADDRESS: 7900 Loyola Boulevard, Los Angeles, CA 90045-2699.

PHONE/FAX: (310) 338-7643/2703.

ENROLLMENT: 3,900.

ARENA: Albert Gersten Pavilion (Capacity-4,156; Year Opened-1982).

SCHOOL COLORS: Crimson and Blue.

CONFERENCE: West Coast.

NCAA TOURNAMENT APPEARANCES (5): 1961-80-88-89-90; 5-5 record (.500); regional runner-up in 1990.

NAIA TOURNAMENT APPEARANCES (1): 1955; 0-1 record.

NIT APPEARANCES (1): 1986; 1-1 record (.500).

ALL-TIME WINNINGEST COACH: William Donovan (eight years from 1954-61, 107-101 record, .514).

ALL-TIME SCORING LEADER: Eric "Hank" Gathers (2,490 points from 1988-90; played his freshman season at Southern Cal in 1985-86).

ALL-TIME REBOUNDING LEADER: Jim Haderlein (1,161 from 1969-71).

NCAA CONSENSUS SECOND-TEAM ALL-AMERICANS (2): Eric "Hank" Gathers (1990), Greg "Bo" Kimble (1990).

MANHATTAN

OFFICIAL NAME: Manhattan College.

NICKNAME: Jaspers.

ADDRESS: Manhattan College Parkway, Riverdale, NY 10471-4098.

PHONE/FAX: (718) 920-0228/543-8802.

ENROLLMENT: 3,400.

ARENA: Draddy Gymnasium (Capacity-3,000; Year Opened-1979).

SCHOOL COLORS: Kelly Green and White.

CONFERENCE: Metro Atlantic Athletic.

NCAA TOURNAMENT APPEARANCES (4): 1956-58-93-95; 2-5 record (.286).

NAIA TOURNAMENT APPEARANCES (1): 1948; 2-1 record (.667).

NIT APPEARANCES (16): 1943-49-53-54-55-57-59-65-66-70-73-74-75-92-94-96; 6-17 record (.261); finished 4th in 1953.

ALL-TIME WINNINGEST COACH: Kenneth Norton (22 years from 1947-68, 310-205 record, .602).

ALL-TIME SCORING LEADER: Keith Bullock (1,992 points from 1990-93).

ALL-TIME REBOUNDING LEADER: Bill Campion (1,070 from 1973-75).

MARQUETTE

OFFICIAL NAME: Marquette University.

NICKNAME: Golden Eagles.

ADDRESS: 1212 West Wisconsin Avenue, Milwaukee, WI 53233.

PHONE/FAX: (414) 288-7447/6519.

ENROLLMENT: 10,750.

ARENA: Bradley Center (Capacity-18,592; Year Opened-1988).

SCHOOL COLORS: Blue and Gold.

CONFERENCE: Conference USA.

FINAL AP TOP 10 RANKINGS (10): 1955-70-71-72-73-74-76-77-78-79.

NCAA TOURNAMENT APPEARANCES (21): 1955-59-61-68-69-71-72-73-74-75-76-77-78-79-80-82-83-93-94-96-97; 28-22 record (.560); reached Final Four in 1974 (2nd) and 1977 (1st).

NIT APPEARANCES (11): 1956-63-67-70-81-84-85-86-87-90-95; 18-9 record (.667); finished 3rd in 1963, 2nd in 1967 and 1995, and 1st in 1970.

ALL-TIME WINNINGEST COACH: Al McGuire (13 years from 1965-77, 295-80 record, .787).

ALL-TIME SCORING LEADER: George Thompson (1,773 points from 1967-69).

ALL-TIME REBOUNDING LEADER: Don Kojis (1,222 from 1959-61).

NCAA CONSENSUS FIRST-TEAM ALL-AMERICANS (3): Dean Meminger (1971), Jim Chones (1972), Alfred "Butch" Lee (1978).

NCAA CONSENSUS SECOND-TEAM ALL-AMERICANS (3): Earl Tatum (1976), Alfred "Butch" Lee (1977), Sam Worthen (1980).

MARSHALL

OFFICIAL NAME: Marshall University.

NICKNAME: Thundering Herd.

ADDRESS: Post Office Box 1360, 400 Hal Greer Boulevard, Huntington, WV 25715-1360.

PHONE/FAX: (304) 696-5275/2325.

ENROLLMENT: 12,530.

ARENA: Henderson Center (Capacity-10,250; Year Opened-1981).

SCHOOL COLORS: Green and White.

CONFERENCE: Mid-American.

NCAA TOURNAMENT APPEARANCES (5): 1956-72-84-85-87; 0-5 record.

NAIA TOURNAMENT APPEARANCES (3): 1938-47-48; 7-2 record (.778); finished 1st in 1947.

NIT APPEARANCES (4): 1967-68-73-88; 2-5 record (.286); finished 4th in 1967.

ALL-TIME WINNINGEST COACH: Cam Henderson (20 years from 1936-55, 361-160 record, .693).

ALL-TIME SCORING LEADER: Skip Henderson (2,574 points from 1985-88).

ALL-TIME REBOUNDING LEADER: Charlie Slack (1,916 from 1953-56).

NCAA CONSENSUS SECOND-TEAM ALL-AMERICANS (1): Leo Byrd (1959).

MARYLAND

OFFICIAL NAME: University of Maryland.

Nicknames: Terrapins, Terps.

ADDRESS: Post Office Box 295, College Park, MD 20741-0295, or 1102 Cole Field House, Campus Drive, 20742.

PHONE/FAX: (301) 314-7064/9094.

ENROLLMENT: 30,370.

ARENA: Cole Field House (Capacity-14,500; Year Opened-1955).

SCHOOL COLORS: Red, White, Black and Gold.

CONFERENCE: Atlantic Coast.

FINAL AP TOP 10 RANKINGS (6): 1958-73-74-75-80-95.

NCAA TOURNAMENT APPEARANCES (14): 1958-73-75-80-81-83-84-85-86-88-94-95-96-97; 17-14 record (.548); regional runner-up in 1973 and 1975.

NIT APPEARANCES (4): 1972-79-82-90; 7-3 record (.700); finished 1st in 1972.

ALL-TIME WINNINGEST COACH: Charles "Lefty" Driesell (17 years from 1970-86, 348-159 record, .686).

ALL-TIME SCORING LEADER: Len Bias (2,149 points from 1983-86).

ALL-TIME REBOUNDING LEADER: Len Elmore (1,053 from 1972-74).

NCAA CONSENSUS FIRST-TEAM ALL-AMERICANS (5): Louis Berger (1932), John Lucas (1975 and 1976), Len Bias (1986), Joe Smith (1995).

NCAA CONSENSUS SECOND-TEAM ALL-AMERICANS (5): Tom McMillen (1973), Len Elmore (1974), Albert King (1980), Len Bias (1985), Walt Williams (1992).

MASSACHUSETTS

OFFICIAL NAME: University of Massachusetts-Amherst.

Nicknames: Minutemen, UMass.

ADDRESS: Boyden Building, Mullins Center, Amherst, MA 01003.

PHONE/FAX: (413) 545-2439/1556.

ENROLLMENT: 16,825.

ARENA: William D. Mullins Memorial Center (Capacity-9,493; Year Opened-1992).

SCHOOL COLORS: Maroon and White.

CONFERENCE: Atlantic 10.

FINAL AP TOP 10 RANKINGS (3): 1994-95-96.

NCAA TOURNAMENT APPEARANCES (7): 1962-92-93-94-95-96-97; 11-7 record (.611); reached Final Four in 1996 (T3rd).

NIT APPEARANCES (8): 1970-71-73-74-75-77-90-91; 5-9 record (.357); finished 4th in 1991.

ALL-TIME WINNINGEST COACH: Jack Leaman (13 years from 1967-79, 217-126 record, .632).

ALL-TIME SCORING LEADER: Jim McCoy (2,374 points from 1989-92).

ALL-TIME REBOUNDING LEADER: Lou Roe (1,070 from 1992-95).

NCAA CONSENSUS FIRST-TEAM ALL-AMERICANS (1): Marcus Camby (1996).

NCAA CONSENSUS SECOND-TEAM ALL-AMERICANS (1): Lou Roe (1995).

MEMPHIS

OFFICIAL NAME: University of Memphis.

NICKNAME: Tigers.

ADDRESS: Athletic Office Building, Memphis, TN 38152.

PHONE/FAX: (901) 678-2337/4134.

ENROLLMENT: 21,500.

ARENA: The Pyramid (Capacity-20,142; Year Opened-1991).

SCHOOL COLORS: Blue and Gray.

CONFERENCE: Conference USA.

FINAL AP TOP 10 RANKINGS (2): 1982 and 1985.

NCAA TOURNAMENT APPEARANCES (16): 1955-56-62-73-76-82-83-84-85-86-88-89-92-93-95-96; 18-16 record (.529); reached Final Four in 1973 (2nd) and 1985 (T3rd).

NAIA TOURNAMENT APPEARANCES (2): 1951 and 1952; 3-2 record (.600).

NIT APPEARANCES (12): 1957-60-61-63-67-72-74-75-77-90-91-97; 6-12 record (.333); finished 2nd in 1957.

ALL-TIME WINNINGEST COACH: Larry Finch (11 years from 1987-97, 220-130 record, .629).

ALL-TIME SCORING LEADER: Keith Lee (2,408 points from 1982-85).

ALL-TIME REBOUNDING LEADER: Keith Lee (1,336 from 1982-85).

NCAA CONSENSUS FIRST-TEAM ALL-AMERICANS (3): Keith Lee (1983 and 1985), Anfernee Hardaway (1993).

NCAA CONSENSUS SECOND-TEAM ALL-AMERICANS (3): Larry Finch (1973), Keith Lee (1984), Lorenzen Wright (1996).

MIAMI (FLA.)

OFFICIAL NAME: University of Miami.

NICKNAME: Hurricanes.

ADDRESS: Post Office Box 248167, Coral Gables, FL 33124-0814.

PHONE/FAX: (305) 284-3244/2807.

ENROLLMENT: 13,155.

ARENA: Miami Arena (Capacity-15,388; Year Opened-1988).

SCHOOL COLORS: Orange, Green and White.

CONFERENCE: Big East.

FINAL AP TOP 10 RANKINGS (1): 1960.

NCAA TOURNAMENT APPEARANCES (1): 1960; 0-1 record.

NAIA TOURNAMENT APPEARANCES (1): 1949; 0-1 record.

NIT APPEARANCES (5): 1961-63-64-95-97; 1-5 record (.167).

ALL-TIME WINNINGEST COACH: Bruce Hale (13 years from 1955-67, 220-112 record, .663).

ALL-TIME SCORING LEADER: Rick Barry (2,298 points from 1963-65).

ALL-TIME REBOUNDING LEADER: Rick Barry (1,274 from 1963-65).

NCAA CONSENSUS FIRST-TEAM ALL-AMERICANS (1): Rick Barry (1965).

MIAMI (OHIO)

OFFICIAL NAME: Miami University.

NICKNAME: Red Hawks.

ADDRESS: 230 Millett Hall, Oxford, OH 45056.

PHONE/FAX: (513) 529-4327/6729.

ENROLLMENT: 16,000.

ARENA: Millett Hall (Capacity-9,200; Year Opened-1968).

SCHOOL COLORS: Red and White.

CONFERENCE: Mid-American.

NCAA TOURNAMENT APPEARANCES (15): 1953-55-57-58-66-69-71-73-78-84-85-86-92-95-97; 4-17 record (.190).

NIT APPEARANCES (4): 1970-93-94-96; 2-4 record (.333).

ALL-TIME WINNINGEST COACH: Darrell Hedric (14 years from 1971-84, 216-157 record, .579).

ALL-TIME SCORING LEADER: Ron Harper (2,377 points from 1983-86).

ALL-TIME REBOUNDING LEADER: Ron Harper (1,119 from 1983-86).

NCAA CONSENSUS SECOND-TEAM ALL-AMERICANS (1): Ron Harper (1986).

MICHIGAN

OFFICIAL NAME: University of Michigan.

NICKNAME: Wolverines.

ADDRESS: 1000 South State Street, Ann Arbor, MI 48109-2201.

PHONE/FAX: (313) 763-1381/747-1188.

ENROLLMENT: 36,845.

ARENA: Crisler Arena (Capacity-13,562; Year Opened-1967).

SCHOOL COLORS: Maize and Blue.

CONFERENCE: Big Ten.

FINAL AP TOP 10 RANKINGS (11): 1964-65-66-74-76-77-85-86-88-89-93.

NCAA TOURNAMENT APPEARANCES (19): 1948-64-65-66-74-75-76-77-85-86-87-88-89-90-92-93-94-95-96; 40-18 record (.690); reached Final Four in 1964 (3rd), 1965 (2nd), 1976 (2nd), 1989 (1st), 1992 (2nd) and 1993 (2nd).

NIT APPEARANCES (6): 1971-80-81-84-91-97; 15-4 record (.789); finished 1st in 1984 and 1997.

ALL-TIME WINNINGEST COACH: Johnny Orr (12 years from 1969-80, 209-113 record, .649).

ALL-TIME SCORING LEADER: Glen Rice (2,442 points from 1986-89).

ALL-TIME REBOUNDING LEADER: Rudy Tomjanovich (1,039 from 1968-70).

NCAA CONSENSUS FIRST-TEAM ALL-AMERICANS (5): Cazzie Russell (1965 and 1966), Rickey Green (1977), Gary Grant (1988), Chris Webber (1993).

NCAA CONSENSUS SECOND-TEAM ALL-AMERICANS (8): Cazzie Russell (1964), Bill Buntin (1965), Henry Wilmore (1972), Michael "Campy" Russell (1974), Phil Hubbard (1977), Glen Rice (1989), Rumeal Robinson (1990), Jalen Rose (1994).

MICHIGAN STATE

OFFICIAL NAME: Michigan State University.

NICKNAME: Spartans.

ADDRESS: Fourth Floor, Olds Hall, East Lansing, MI 48824-1044.

PHONE/FAX: (517) 355-2271/353-9636.

ENROLLMENT: 40,645.

ARENA: Jack Breslin Student Events Center (Capacity-15,138; Year Opened-1989).

SCHOOL COLORS: Green and White.

CONFERENCE: Big Ten.

FINAL AP TOP 10 RANKINGS (4): 1959-78-79-90.

NCAA TOURNAMENT APPEARANCES (11): 1957-59-78-79-85-86-90-91-92-94-95; 17-11 record (.607); reached Final Four in 1957 (4th) and 1979 (1st).

NIT APPEARANCES (5): 1983-89-93-96-97; 6-6 record (.500); finished 4th in 1989.

ALL-TIME WINNINGEST COACH: George "Jud" Heathcote (19 years from 1977-95, 340-220 record, .607).

ALL-TIME SCORING LEADER: Shawn Respert (2,531 points from 1991-95; missed majority of 1990-91 season recovering from knee injury sustained in high school playoffs).

ALL-TIME REBOUNDING LEADER: Greg Kelser (1,092 from 1976-79).

NCAA CONSENSUS FIRST-TEAM ALL-AMERICANS (2): Earvin "Magic" Johnson (1979), Shawn Respert (1995).

NCAA CONSENSUS SECOND-TEAM ALL-AMERICANS (3): Johnny Green (1959), Scott Skiles (1986), Steve Smith (1991).

MIDDLE TENNESSEE STATE

OFFICIAL NAME: Middle Tennessee State University.

NICKNAME: Blue Raiders.

ADDRESS: Box 20, Murfreesboro, TN 37132.

PHONE/FAX: (615) 898-2450/5626.

ENROLLMENT: 17,385.

ARENA: Hale Arena (Capacity-11,520; Year Opened-1972).

SCHOOL COLORS: Navy Blue and White.

CONFERENCE: Ohio Valley.

NCAA TOURNAMENT APPEARANCES (6): 1975-77-82-85-87-89; 2-6 record (.250).

NAIA TOURNAMENT APPEARANCES (1): 1955; 0-1 record.

NIT APPEARANCES (2): 1986 and 1988; 2-2 record (.500).

ALL-TIME WINNINGEST COACH: Jimmy Earle (10 years from 1970-79, 165-101 record, .620).

ALL-TIME SCORING LEADER: Robert Taylor (1,622 points from 1990-93).

ALL-TIME REBOUNDING LEADER: Warren Kidd (1,048 from 1990-93).

MINNESOTA

OFFICIAL NAME: University of Minnesota.

NICKNAME: Golden Gophers.

ADDRESS: 208 Bierman Athletic Building, 516 15th Avenue SE, Minneapolis, MN 55455-0101.

PHONE/FAX: (612) 625-4090/0359.

ENROLLMENT: 39,000.

ARENA: Williams Arena (Capacity-14,300; Year Opened-1928).

SCHOOL COLORS: Maroon and Gold.

CONFERENCE: Big Ten.

FINAL AP TOP 10 RANKINGS (5): 1949-65-73-82-97.

NCAA TOURNAMENT APPEARANCES (7): 1972-82-89-90-94-95-97; 12-7 record (.632); reached Final Four in 1997 (T3rd).

NIT APPEARANCES (7): 1973-80-81-83-92-93-96; 13-6 record (.684); finished 2nd in 1980 and 1st in 1993.

ALL-TIME WINNINGEST COACH: Louis J. Cooke (27 years from 1898-1924, 245-135-2 record, .644).

ALL-TIME SCORING LEADER: Voshon Lenard (2,103 points from 1992-95).

ALL-TIME REBOUNDING LEADER: Mychal Thompson (956 from 1975-78).

NCAA CONSENSUS FIRST-TEAM ALL-AMERICANS (3): Jim McIntyre (1948), Dick Garmaker (1955), Mychal Thompson (1978).

NCAA CONSENSUS SECOND-TEAM ALL-AMERICANS (4): Jim McIntyre (1949), Jim Brewer (1973), Mychal Thompson (1977), Bobby Jackson (1997).

MISSISSIPPI

OFFICIAL NAME: University of Mississippi.

NICKNAME: Rebels.

ADDRESS: Fraternity Row, Post Office Box 217, University, MS 38677.

PHONE/FAX: (601) 232-7522/7006.

ENROLLMENT: 12,540.

ARENA: C.M. "Tad" Smith Coliseum (Capacity-8,135; Year Opened-1966).

SCHOOL COLORS: Cardinal Red and Navy Blue.

CONFERENCE: Southeastern.

NCAA TOURNAMENT APPEARANCES (2): 1981 and 1997; 0-2 record.

NIT APPEARANCES (5): 1980-82-83-87-89; 4-5 record (.444).

ALL-TIME WINNINGEST COACH: Bonnie Graham (13 years from 1950-62, 144-168 record, .462).

ALL-TIME SCORING LEADER: John Stroud (2,328 points from 1977-80).

ALL-TIME REBOUNDING LEADER: Walter Actwood (945 from 1974-77).

NCAA CONSENSUS SECOND-TEAM ALL-AMERICANS (1): Johnny Neumann (1971).

MISSISSIPPI STATE

OFFICIAL NAME: Mississippi State University.

NICKNAME: Bulldogs.

ADDRESS: Post Office Drawer 5308, Mississippi State, MS 39762.

PHONE/FAX: (601) 325-2703/2563.

ENROLLMENT: 13,575.

ARENA: Humphrey Coliseum (Capacity-9,419; Year Opened-1975).

SCHOOL COLORS: Maroon and White.

CONFERENCE: Southeastern.

FINAL AP TOP 10 RANKINGS (3): 1959-62-63.

NCAA TOURNAMENT APPEARANCES (4): 1963-91-95-96; 7-4 record (.636); reached Final Four in 1996 (T3rd).

NIT APPEARANCES (3): 1979-90-94; 1-3 record (.250).

ALL-TIME WINNINGEST COACH: Richard Williams (11 years from 1987-97, 176-148 record, .543).

ALL-TIME SCORING LEADER: Jeff Malone (2,142 points from 1980-83).

ALL-TIME REBOUNDING LEADER: Bailey Howell (1,277 from 1957-59).

NCAA CONSENSUS FIRST-TEAM ALL-AMERICANS (1): Bailey Howell (1959).

NCAA CONSENSUS SECOND-TEAM ALL-AMERICANS (1): Bailey Howell (1958).

MISSOURI

OFFICIAL NAME: University of Missouri.

NICKNAMES: Tigers, Mizzou.

ADDRESS: Box 677, Hearnes Center, Columbia, MO 65205.

PHONE/FAX: (573) 882-3241/4720.

ENROLLMENT: 23,440.

ARENA: Hearnes Center (Capacity-13,349; Year Opened-1972); new 16,500- to 17,000-seat arena is slated to open in 2000.

SCHOOL COLORS: Old Gold and Black.

CONFERENCE: Big 12.

FINAL AP TOP 10 RANKINGS (4): 1982-83-89-94.

NCAA TOURNAMENT APPEARANCES (16): 1944-76-78-80-81-82-83-86-87-88-89-90-92-93-94-95; 13-16 record (.448); regional runner-up in 1944, 1976 and 1994.

NIT APPEARANCES (4): 1972-73-85-96; 1-4 record (.200).

NCIT RECORD: 0-1 in 1975.

ALL-TIME WINNINGEST COACH: Norm Stewart (30 years from 1968-97, 597-309 record, .659).

ALL-TIME SCORING LEADER: Derrick Chievous (2,580 points from 1985-88).

ALL-TIME REBOUNDING LEADER: Doug Smith (1,053 from 1988-91).

NCAA CONSENSUS SECOND-TEAM ALL-AMERICANS (5): Steve Stipanovich (1983), Jon Sundvold (1983), Doug Smith (1990), Anthony Peeler (1992), Melvin Booker (1994).

MONTANA

OFFICIAL NAME: University of Montana.

NICKNAME: Grizzlies.

ADDRESS: Adams Fieldhouse, Missoula, MT 59812.

PHONE/FAX: (406) 243-6899/6859.

ENROLLMENT: 11,755.

ARENA: Dahlberg Arena (Capacity-8,950; Year Opened-1953).

SCHOOL COLORS: Copper, Silver and Gold.

CONFERENCE: Big Sky.

NCAA TOURNAMENT APPEARANCES (4): 1975-91-92-97; 1-5 record (.167).

NAIA TOURNAMENT APPEARANCES (2): 1948 and 1950; 0-2 record.

NIT APPEARANCES (3): 1985-86-95; 0-3 record.

ALL-TIME WINNINGEST COACH: George "Jiggs" Dahlberg (16 years from 1938-42 and 1945-55 when school was classified as a small college most of that span, 222-224 record, .498).

ALL-TIME SCORING LEADER: Larry Krystkowiak (2,017 points from 1983-86).

ALL-TIME REBOUNDING LEADER: Larry Krystkowiak (1,105 from 1983-86).

MONTANA STATE

OFFICIAL NAME: Montana State University.

NICKNAME: Bobcats.

ADDRESS: 426 Culbertson Hall, Bozeman, MT 59717.

PHONE/FAX: (406) 994-5133/4102.

ENROLLMENT: 10,400.

ARENA: Worthington Arena (Capacity-7,828; Year Opened-1956).

SCHOOL COLORS: Blue and Gold.

CONFERENCE: Big Sky.

NCAA TOURNAMENT APPEARANCES (3): 1951-86-96; 0-3 record.

NAIA TOURNAMENT APPEARANCES (6): 1946-47-52-54-55-56; 1-6 record (.143).

NIT APPEARANCES (1): 1987; 0-1 record.

ALL-TIME WINNINGEST COACH: John "Brick" Breeden (17 years from 1936-47 and 1949-54 when school was classified as a small college most of that span, 283-198 record, .588).

ALL-TIME SCORING LEADER: Larry Chanay (2,034 points from 1957-60).

ALL-TIME REBOUNDING LEADER: Jack Gillespie (1,011 from 1967-69).

NCAA CONSENSUS FIRST-TEAM ALL-AMERICANS (3): John Thompson (1929 and 1930), Frank Ward (1930).

MOREHEAD STATE

OFFICIAL NAME: Morehead State University.

NICKNAME: Eagles.

ADDRESS: Morehead, KY 40351.

PHONE/FAX: (606) 783-2500/2550.

ENROLLMENT: 8,340.

ARENA: Ellis T. Johnson Arena (Capacity-6,500; Year Opened-1981).

SCHOOL COLORS: Blue and Gold.

CONFERENCE: Ohio Valley.

NCAA TOURNAMENT APPEARANCES (5): 1956-57-61-83-84; 4-6 record (.400).

NAIA TOURNAMENT APPEARANCES (2): 1942 and 1951; 0-2 record.

NIT APPEARANCES: None.

ALL-TIME WINNINGEST COACH: Ellis T. Johnson (15 years from 1937-43 and 1946-53 when school was classified as a small college, 196-158 record, .554).

ALL-TIME SCORING LEADER: Herbie Stamper (2,072 points from 1976-79).

ALL-TIME REBOUNDING LEADER: Steve Hamilton (1,675 from 1955-58).

MURRAY STATE

OFFICIAL NAME: Murray State University.

NICKNAME: Racers.

ADDRESS: Stewart Stadium, Murray, KY 42071.

PHONE/FAX: (502) 762-4270/6814.

ENROLLMENT: 8,190.

ARENA: Cutchin Fieldhouse/Racer Arena (Capacity-5,550; Year Opened-1954); construction is underway for a new MSU Regional Special Events Center slated to be ready midway through the 1997-98 season.

SCHOOL COLORS: Blue and Gold.

CONFERENCE: Ohio Valley.

NCAA TOURNAMENT APPEARANCES (8): 1964-69-88-90-91-92-95-97; 1-8 record (.111).

NAIA TOURNAMENT APPEARANCES (7): 1938-39-41-42-43-50-52; 16-8 record (.667); finished 2nd in 1941 and 1952, 3rd in 1938 and 4th in 1943.

NIT APPEARANCES (6): 1980-82-83-89-94-96; 2-6 record (.250).

ALL-TIME WINNINGEST COACH: Carlisle Cutchin (17 years from 1925-41 when school was classified as a small college, 267-101 record, .726).

ALL-TIME SCORING LEADER: Jeff Martin (2,484 points from 1986-89).

ALL-TIME REBOUNDING LEADER: Ronald "Popeye" Jones (1,374 from 1989-92).

NAVY

OFFICIAL NAME: United States Naval Academy.

NICKNAME: Midshipmen.

ADDRESS: 566 Brownson Road, Ricketts Hall, Annapolis, MD 21402-5000.

PHONE/FAX: (410) 268-6226/269-6779.

ENROLLMENT: 4,200.

ARENA: Alumni Hall (Capacity-5,710; Year Opened-1991).

SCHOOL COLORS: Navy Blue and Gold.

CONFERENCE: Patriot League.

NCAA TOURNAMENT APPEARANCES (10): 1947-53-54-59-60-85-86-87-94-97; 8-11 record (.421); regional runner-up in 1947, 1954 and 1986.

NIT APPEARANCES (1): 1962; 0-1 record.

ALL-TIME WINNINGEST COACH: Ben Carnevale (20 years from 1947-66, 257-160 record, .616).

ALL-TIME SCORING LEADER: David Robinson (2,669 points from 1984-87).

ALL-TIME REBOUNDING LEADER: David Robinson (1,314 from 1984-87).

NCAA CONSENSUS FIRST-TEAM ALL-AMERICANS (2): Elliott Loughlin (1933), David Robinson (1987).

NCAA CONSENSUS SECOND-TEAM ALL-AMERICANS (1): David Robinson (1986).

NEBRASKA

OFFICIAL NAME: University of Nebraska.

NICKNAMES: Cornhuskers, Huskers.

ADDRESS: 116 South Stadium, Post Office Box 880123, Lincoln, NE 68588-0123.

PHONE/FAX: (402) 472-2263/2005.

ENROLLMENT: 25,000.

ARENA: Devaney Sports Center (Capacity-14,200; Year Opened-1976).

SCHOOL COLORS: Scarlet and Cream.

CONFERENCE: Big 12.

NCAA TOURNAMENT APPEARANCES (5): 1986-91-92-93-94; 0-5 record.

NIT APPEARANCES (11): 1967-78-80-83-84-85-87-89-95-96-97; 19-10 record (.655); finished tied for 3rd in 1983, 3rd in 1987 and 1st in 1996.

ALL-TIME WINNINGEST COACH: Joe Cipriano (17 years from 1964-80, 253-197 record, .562).

ALL-TIME SCORING LEADER: Dave Hoppen (2,167 points from 1983-86).

ALL-TIME REBOUNDING LEADER: Leroy Chalk (782 from 1969-71).

NEVADA

OFFICIAL NAME: University of Nevada.

NICKNAME: Wolf Pack.

ADDRESS: 1664 North Virginia Street, Lawlor Annex/232, Reno, NV 89557-0041.

PHONE: (702) 784-4600.

ENROLLMENT: 12,500.

ARENA: Lawlor Events Center (Capacity-11,200; Year Opened-1983).

SCHOOL COLORS: Silver and Blue.

CONFERENCE: Big West.

NCAA DIVISION I TOURNAMENT APPEARANCES (2): 1984 and 1985; 0-2 record.

NCAA DIVISION II TOURNAMENT APPEARANCES (4): 1957-61-64-66; 1-6 record (.143).

NIT APPEARANCES (2): 1979 and 1997; 2-2 record (.500).

NAIA TOURNAMENT APPEARANCES (1): 1946; 2-1 record (.667).

ALL-TIME WINNINGEST COACH: Glenn "Jake" Lawlor (15 years in 1943 and from 1946-59 when school was classified as a small college, 201-168 record, .545).

ALL-TIME SCORING LEADER: Edgar Jones (1,877 points from 1976-79).

ALL-TIME REBOUNDING LEADER: Pete Padgett (1,464 from 1973-76).

NEW MEXICO

OFFICIAL NAME: University of New Mexico.

NICKNAME: Lobos.

ADDRESS: South Campus, Albuquerque, NM 87131.

PHONE/FAX: (505) 277-2026/0142.

ENROLLMENT: 23,755.

ARENA: University Arena/The Pit (Capacity-18,018; Year Opened-1966).

SCHOOL COLORS: Cherry and Silver.

CONFERENCE: Western Athletic.

FINAL AP TOP 10 RANKINGS (1): 1968.

NCAA TOURNAMENT APPEARANCES (8): 1968-74-78-91-93-94-96-97; 4-9 record (.308).

NAIA TOURNAMENT APPEARANCES (1): 1947; 0-1 record.

NIT APPEARANCES (13): 1964-65-67-73-79-84-85-86-87-88-89-90-92; 13-14 record (.481); finished 2nd in 1964 and 4th in 1990.

ALL-TIME WINNINGEST COACH: Dave Bliss (nine years from 1989-97, 197-91 record, .686).

ALL-TIME SCORING LEADER: Charles Smith (1,800-plus points from 1994-97).

ALL-TIME REBOUNDING LEADER: Luc Longley (922 from 1988-91).

NCAA CONSENSUS SECOND-TEAM ALL-AMERICANS (1): Mel Daniels (1967).

NEW MEXICO STATE

OFFICIAL NAME: New Mexico State University.

NICKNAME: Aggies.

ADDRESS: Box 30001, Department 3145, Las Cruces, NM 88003-8001.

PHONE/FAX: (505) 646-3929/2425.

ENROLLMENT: 15,165.

ARENA: Pan American Center (Capacity-13,071; Year Opened-1968).

SCHOOL COLORS: Crimson and White.

CONFERENCE: Big West.

FINAL AP TOP 10 RANKINGS (1): 1970.

NCAA TOURNAMENT APPEARANCES (15): 1952-59-60-67-68-69-70-71-75-79-90-91-92-93-94; 10-17 record (.370); reached Final Four in 1970 (3rd).

NAIA TOURNAMENT APPEARANCES (4): 1938-50-51-52; 5-4 record (.556).

NIT APPEARANCES (3): 1939-89-95; 3-3 record (.500).

ALL-TIME WINNINGEST COACH: Neil McCarthy (12 years from 1986-97, 248-123 record, .668).

ALL-TIME SCORING LEADER: Albert "Slab" Jones (1,758 points from 1977-80).

ALL-TIME REBOUNDING LEADER: Sam Lacey (1,265 from 1968-70).

NCAA CONSENSUS SECOND-TEAM ALL-AMERICANS (1): Jimmy Collins (1970).

NEW ORLEANS

OFFICIAL NAME: University of New Orleans.

NICKNAME: Privateers.

ADDRESS: Lakefront Arena, New Orleans, LA 70148.

PHONE/FAX: (504) 280-6284, 7027/7240.

ENROLLMENT: 15,570.

ARENA: Kiefer UNO Lakefront Arena (Capacity-10,000; Year Opened-1983).

SCHOOL COLORS: Royal Blue and Silver.

CONFERENCE: Sun Belt.

NCAA DIVISION I TOURNAMENT APPEARANCES (4): 1987-91-93-96; 1-4 record (.200).

NCAA DIVISION II TOURNAMENT APPEARANCES (4): 1971-72-74-75; 9-6 record (.600); finished 2nd in 1975 and 4th in 1974.

NIT APPEARANCES (6): 1983-88-89-90-94-97; 4-6 record (.400).

ALL-TIME WINNINGEST COACH: Ron Greene (eight years from 1970-77 when school was classified as a small college most of that span, 146-65 record, .692).

ALL-TIME SCORING LEADER: Mel Henderson (1,854 points from 1970-73 when school was classified as a small college).

ALL-TIME REBOUNDING LEADER: Ervin Johnson (1,287 from 1990-93).

NIAGARA

OFFICIAL NAME: Niagara University.

NICKNAME: Purple Eagles.

ADDRESS: LL O'Shea Hall, Niagara University, NY 14109-2009.

PHONE/FAX: (716) 286-8588/8581.

ENROLLMENT: 3,000.

ARENAS: Marine Midland Arena (Capacity-21,000; Year Opened-1996); Niagara Falls Convention Center (Capacity-6,000; Year Opened-1974) and Gallagher Center (Capacity-3,200; Year Opened-1949).

SCHOOL COLORS: Purple, White and Gold.

CONFERENCE: Metro Atlantic Athletic.

NCAA TOURNAMENT APPEARANCES (1): 1970; 1-2 record (.333).

NIT APPEARANCES (11): 1950-53-54-55-56-58-61-72-76-87-93; 8-11 record (.421); finished 3rd in 1954 and 2nd in 1972.

ALL-TIME WINNINGEST COACH: John J. "Taps" Gallagher (31 years from 1932-43 and 1947-65, 465-261 record, .640).

ALL-TIME SCORING LEADER: Calvin Murphy (2,548 points from 1968-70).

ALL-TIME REBOUNDING LEADER: Alex Ellis (1,533 from 1956-58).

NCAA CONSENSUS FIRST-TEAM ALL-AMERICANS (2): Calvin Murphy (1969 and 1970).

NCAA CONSENSUS SECOND-TEAM ALL-AMERICANS (1): Calvin Murphy (1968).

NORTH CAROLINA

OFFICIAL NAME: University of North Carolina (At Chapel Hill).

NICKNAME: Tar Heels.

ADDRESS: Post Office Box 2126, Chapel Hill, NC 27515-2126, or Smith Center, Skipper Bowles Drive, 27514.

PHONE/FAX: (919) 962-2123/0612.

ENROLLMENT: 24,063.

ARENA: Smith Center (Capacity-21,572; Year Opened-1986).

SCHOOL COLORS: Carolina Blue and White.

CONFERENCE: Atlantic Coast.

FINAL AP TOP 10 RANKINGS (25): 1957-59-61-67-68-69-72-75-76-77-79-81-82-83-84-85-86-87-88-89-91-93-94-95-97.

NCAA TOURNAMENT APPEARANCES (31): 1941-46-57-59-67-68-69-72-75-76-77-78-79-80-81-82-83-84-85-86-87-88-89-90-91-92-93-94-95-96-97; 72-31 record (.699); reached Final Four in 1946 (2nd), 1957 (1st), 1967 (4th), 1968 (2nd), 1969 (4th), 1972 (3rd), 1977 (2nd), 1981 (2nd), 1982 (1st), 1991 (T3rd), 1993 (1st), 1995 (T3rd) and 1997 (T3rd).

NIT APPEARANCES (4): 1970-71-73-74; 7-3 record (.700); finished 1st in 1971 and 3rd in 1973.

ALL-TIME WINNINGEST COACH: Dean Smith (36 years from 1962-97, 879-254 record, .776).

ALL-TIME SCORING LEADER: Phil Ford (2,290 points from 1975-78).

ALL-TIME REBOUNDING LEADER: Sam Perkins (1,167 from 1981-84).

NCAA CONSENSUS FIRST-TEAM ALL-AMERICANS (15): George Glamack (1940 and 1941), Lennie Rosenbluth (1957), Larry Miller (1968), Bob McAdoo (1972), Phil Ford (1977 and 1978), James Worthy (1982), Michael Jordan (1983 and 1984), Sam Perkins (1983 and 1984), Kenny Smith (1987), J.R. Reid (1988), Jerry Stackhouse (1995).

NCAA CONSENSUS SECOND-TEAM ALL-AMERICANS (18): John Dillon (1946), Pete Brennan (1958), Lee Shaffer (1960), Larry Miller (1967), Charlie Scott (1969 and 1970), Bobby Jones (1974), Phil Ford (1976), Mitch Kupchak (1976), Mike O'Koren (1979 and 1980), Al Wood (1981), Sam Perkins (1982), Brad Daugherty (1986), Eric Montross (1993 and 1994), Rasheed Wallace (1995), Antawn Jamison (1997).

NC CHARLOTTE

NICKNAME: 49ers.

ADDRESS: 9201 University City Boulevard, Charlotte, NC 28223-0001.

PHONE/FAX: (704) 547-4937/4918.

ENROLLMENT: 15,650.

ARENA: Dale F. Halton Arena (Capacity-9,600; Year Opened-1996).

SCHOOL COLORS: Green and White.

CONFERENCE: Conference USA.

NCAA TOURNAMENT APPEARANCES (5): 1977-88-92-95-97; 4-6 record (.400); reached Final Four in 1977 (4th).

NIT APPEARANCES (3): 1976-89-94; 3-3 record (.500); finished 2nd in 1976.

ALL-TIME WINNINGEST COACH: Jeff Mullins (11 years from 1986-96, 182-142 record, .562).

ALL-TIME SCORING LEADER: Henry Williams (2,383 points from 1989-92).

ALL-TIME REBOUNDING LEADER: Cedric "Cornbread" Maxwell (1,117 from 1974-77).

NORTH CAROLINA STATE

OFFICIAL NAME: North Carolina State University.

NICKNAME: Wolfpack.

ADDRESS: Post Office Box 8501, Case Athletic Center, Cates Avenue, Raleigh, NC 27695-8501.

PHONE/FAX: (919) 515-2102/2898.

ENROLLMENT: 26,685.

ARENA: Entertainment and Sports Arena (Capacity-21,660; Year Opened-1998).

SCHOOL COLORS: Red and White.

CONFERENCE: Atlantic Coast.

FINAL AP TOP 10 RANKINGS (9): 1950-51-55-56-59-70-73-74-75.

NCAA TOURNAMENT APPEARANCES (17): 1950-51-52-54-56-65-70-74-80-82-83-85-86-87-88-89-91; 27-16 record (.628); reached Final Four in 1950 (3rd), 1974 (1st) and 1983 (1st).

NIT APPEARANCES (7): 1947-48-51-76-78-84-97; 8-7 record (.533); finished 3rd in 1947, 3rd in 1976 and 2nd in 1978.

ALL-TIME WINNINGEST COACH: Everett Case (19 years from 1947-65, 377-134 record, .738).

ALL-TIME SCORING LEADER: Rodney Monroe (2,551 points from 1988-91).

ALL-TIME REBOUNDING LEADER: Ronnie Shavlik (1,598 from 1954-56).

NCAA CONSENSUS FIRST-TEAM ALL-AMERICANS (5): Sam Ranzino (1951), Ronnie Shavlik (1956), David Thompson (1973, 1974 and 1975).

NCAA CONSENSUS SECOND-TEAM ALL-AMERICANS (3): Dick Dickey (1948), Ronnie Shavlik (1955), Tom Burleson (1973).

NORTHEASTERN

OFFICIAL NAME: Northeastern University.

NICKNAME: Huskies.

ADDRESS: 360 Huntington Avenue, Boston, MA 02115.

PHONE/FAX: (617) 373-2691/3152.

ENROLLMENT: 11,500.

ARENA: Matthews Arena (Capacity-6,000; Year Opened-1910).

SCHOOL COLORS: Red and Black.

CONFERENCE: America East.

NCAA DIVISION I TOURNAMENT APPEARANCES (7): 1981-82-84-85-86-87-91; 3-7 record (.300).

NCAA DIVISION II TOURNAMENT APPEARANCES (6): 1962-63-64-66-67-68; 8-6 record (.571).

NIT APPEARANCES: None.

ALL-TIME WINNINGEST COACH: Jim Calhoun (14 years from 1973-86, 250-137 record, .646).

ALL-TIME SCORING LEADER: Reggie Lewis (2,709 points from 1984-87).

ALL-TIME REBOUNDING LEADER: Mark Halsel (1,115 from 1981-84).

NORTHEAST LOUISIANA

OFFICIAL NAME: Northeast Louisiana University.

NICKNAME: Indians.

ADDRESS: Malone Stadium, Monroe, LA 71209-2500.

PHONE/FAX: (318) 342-5460/5464.

ENROLLMENT: 11,555.

ARENA: Ewing Coliseum (Capacity-8,000; Year Opened-1971).

SCHOOL COLORS: Maroon and Gold.

CONFERENCE: Southland.

NCAA DIVISION I TOURNAMENT APPEARANCES (7): 1982-86-90-91-92-93-96; 0-7 record.

NAIA TOURNAMENT APPEARANCES (1): 1970; 1-1 record (.500).

NIT APPEARANCES (2): 1979 and 1988; 0-2 record.

ALL-TIME WINNINGEST COACH: Lenny Fant (22 years from 1958-79 when school was classified as a small college most of that span, 326-221 record, .596).

ALL-TIME SCORING LEADER: Calvin Natt (2,581 points from 1976-79).

ALL-TIME REBOUNDING LEADER: Calvin Natt (1,285 from 1976-79).

NCAA CONSENSUS SECOND-TEAM ALL-AMERICANS (1): Calvin Natt (1979).

NORTHERN IOWA

OFFICIAL NAME: University of Northern Iowa.

NICKNAME: Panthers.

ADDRESS: UNI-Dome, Cedar Falls, IA 50614.

PHONE/FAX: (319) 273-6354/3602.

ENROLLMENT: 12,800.

ARENA: UNI-Dome (Capacity-10,000; Year Opened-1976).

SCHOOL COLORS: Purple and Old Gold.

CONFERENCE: Missouri Valley.

NCAA DIVISION I TOURNAMENT APPEARANCES (1): 1990; 1-1 record (.500).

NCAA DIVISION II TOURNAMENT APPEARANCES (3): 1962-64-79; 5-4 record (.556); finished 4th in 1964.

NAIA TOURNAMENT APPEARANCES (4): 1946-48-49-53; 2-4 record (.333).

NIT APPEARANCES: None.

ALL-TIME WINNINGEST COACH: Eldon Miller (11 years from 1987-97, 154-161 record, .489).

ALL-TIME SCORING LEADER: Jason Reese (2,033 points from 1987-90).

ALL-TIME REBOUNDING LEADER: Pete Spoden (1,104 from 1961-64 when school was classified as a small college).

NORTHWESTERN

OFFICIAL NAME: Northwestern University.

NICKNAME: Wildcats.

ADDRESS: 1501 Central Street, Evanston, IL 60201-1699.

PHONE/FAX: (847) 491-7503/8818.

ENROLLMENT: 7,400.

ARENA: Welsh-Ryan Arena (Capacity-8,117; Year Opened-1952).

SCHOOL COLORS: Purple and White.

CONFERENCE: Big Ten.

NCAA TOURNAMENT APPEARANCES: None.

NIT APPEARANCES (2): 1983 and 1994; 2-2 record (.500).

ALL-TIME WINNINGEST COACH: Arthur "Dutch" Lonborg (23 years from 1928-50, 236-203-1 record, .538).

ALL-TIME SCORING LEADER: Billy McKinney (1,900 points from 1974-77).

ALL-TIME REBOUNDING LEADER: Joe Ruklick (868 from 1957-59).

NCAA CONSENSUS FIRST-TEAM ALL-AMERICANS (4): Joe Reiff (1931 and 1933), Otto Graham (1944/also played with Colgate), Max Morris (1946).

NCAA CONSENSUS SECOND-TEAM ALL-AMERICANS (2): Otto Graham (1943), Max Morris (1945).

NOTRE DAME

OFFICIAL NAME: University of Notre Dame.

NICKNAME: Fighting Irish.

ADDRESS: Joyce Athletic and Convocation Center, Notre Dame, IN 46556.

PHONE/FAX: (219) 631-7516/7941.

ENROLLMENT: 9,850.

ARENA: Joyce Athletic and Convocation Center (Capacity-11,418; Year Opened-1968).

SCHOOL COLORS: Gold and Blue.

CONFERENCE: Big East.

FINAL AP TOP 10 RANKINGS (12): 1953-54-58-70-74-76-77-78-79-80-81-86.

NCAA TOURNAMENT APPEARANCES (24): 1953-54-57-58-60-63-65-69-70-71-74-75-76-77-78-79-80-81-85-86-87-88-89-90; 25-28 record (.472); reached Final Four in 1978 (4th).

NIT APPEARANCES (6): 1968-73-83-84-92-97; 16-6 record (.727); finished 3rd in 1968, 2nd in 1973, 2nd in 1984 and 2nd in 1992.

ALL-TIME WINNINGEST COACH: Richard "Digger" Phelps (20 years from 1972-91, 393-197 record, .666).

ALL-TIME SCORING LEADER: Austin Carr (2,560 points from 1969-71).

ALL-TIME REBOUNDING LEADER: Tom Hawkins (1,318 from 1957-59).

NCAA CONSENSUS FIRST-TEAM ALL-AMERICANS (17): Ed "Moose" Krause (1932, 1933 and 1934), John Moir (1936, 1937 and 1938), Paul Nowak (1936, 1937 and 1938), Leo Klier (1944 and 1946), Billy Hassett (1945), Kevin O'Shea (1948), Austin Carr (1971), John Shumate (1974), Adrian Dantley (1975 and 1976).

NCAA CONSENSUS SECOND-TEAM ALL-AMERICANS (9): Bob Rensberger (1943), Billy Hassett (1946), Kevin O'Shea (1950), Tom Hawkins (1959), Austin Carr (1970), Kelly Tripucka (1979 and 1981), John Paxson (1982 and 1983).

OHIO UNIVERSITY

NICKNAME: Bobcats.

ADDRESS: Convocation Center, Athens, OH 45701-2979.

PHONE/FAX: (614) 593-1298/2420.

ENROLLMENT: 18,500.

ARENA: Convocation Center (Capacity-13,000; Year Opened-1968).

SCHOOL COLORS: Hunter Green and White.

CONFERENCE: Mid-American.

NCAA TOURNAMENT APPEARANCES (10): 1960-61-64-65-70-72-74-83-85-94; 4-11 record (.267); regional runner-up in 1964.

NIT APPEARANCES (3): 1941-69-95; 4-3 record (.571); finished 2nd in 1941.

ALL-TIME WINNINGEST COACH: Jim Snyder (25 years from 1950-74, 355-245 record, .592).

ALL-TIME SCORING LEADER: Dave Jamerson (2,336 points from 1986-90; missed 1986-87 season because of a knee injury).

ALL-TIME REBOUNDING LEADER: John Deveraux (957 from 1981-84).

NCAA CONSENSUS SECOND-TEAM ALL-AMERICANS (1): Frank Baumholtz (1941).

OHIO STATE

OFFICIAL NAME: Ohio State University.

NICKNAME: Buckeyes.

ADDRESS: 410 Woody Hayes Drive, 124 St. John Arena, Columbus, OH 43210-1166.

PHONE/FAX: (614) 292-6861/8547.

ENROLLMENT: 52,180.

ARENA: St. John Arena (Capacity-13,276; Year Opened-1956); new 19,560-seat facility is scheduled to open in 1998-99.

SCHOOL COLORS: Scarlet and Gray.

CONFERENCE: Big Ten.

FINAL AP TOP 10 RANKINGS (9): 1950-60-61-62-63-71-80-91-92.

NCAA TOURNAMENT APPEARANCES (18): 1939-44-45-46-50-60-61-62-68-71-80-82-83-85-87-90-91-92; 31-17 record (.646); reached Final Four in 1939 (2nd), 1944 (T3rd), 1945 (T3rd), 1946 (3rd), 1960 (1st), 1961 (2nd), 1962 (2nd) and 1968 (3rd).

NIT APPEARANCES (6): 1979-84-86-88-89-93; 13-6 record (.684); finished 4th in 1979, 1st in 1986 and 2nd in 1988.

ALL-TIME WINNINGEST COACH: Fred Taylor (18 years from 1959-76, 297-158 record, .653).

ALL-TIME SCORING LEADER: Dennis Hopson (2,096 points from 1984-87).

ALL-TIME REBOUNDING LEADER: Jerry Lucas (1,411 from 1960-62).

NCAA CONSENSUS FIRST-TEAM ALL-AMERICANS (10): Wes Fesler (1931), Jimmy Hull (1939), Dick Schnittker (1950), Robin Freeman (1956), Jerry Lucas (1960, 1961 and 1962), Gary Bradds (1964), Jim Jackson (1991 and 1992).

NCAA CONSENSUS SECOND-TEAM ALL-AMERICANS (9): Don Grate (1944 and 1945), Robin Freeman (1955), Frank Howard (1957), Larry Siegfried (1961), John Havlicek (1962), Gary Bradds (1963), Kelvin Ransey (1980), Dennis Hopson (1987).

OKLAHOMA

OFFICIAL NAME: University of Oklahoma.

NICKNAME: Sooners.

ADDRESS: 180 West Brooks, Room 235, Norman, OK 73019.

PHONE/FAX: (405) 325-8231/7623.

ENROLLMENT: 24,500.

ARENA: Lloyd Noble Center (Capacity-11,100; Year Opened-1975).

SCHOOL COLORS: Crimson and Cream.

CONFERENCE: Big 12.

FINAL AP TOP 10 RANKINGS (5): 1984-85-88-89-90.

NCAA TOURNAMENT APPEARANCES (16): 1939-43-47-79-83-84-85-86-87-88-89-90-92-95-96-97; 20-16 record (.556); reached Final Four in 1939 (3rd), 1947 (2nd) and 1988 (2nd).

NIT APPEARANCES (6): 1970-71-82-91-93-94; 9-6 record (.600); finished in tie for 3rd in 1982 and 2nd in 1991.

ALL-TIME WINNINGEST COACH: Billy Tubbs (14 years from 1981-94, 333-132 record, .716).

ALL-TIME SCORING LEADER: Wayman Tisdale (2,661 points from 1983-85).

ALL-TIME REBOUNDING LEADER: Wayman Tisdale (1,048 from 1983-85).

NCAA CONSENSUS FIRST-TEAM ALL-AMERICANS (8): Thomas Churchill (1929), Omar "Bud" Browning (1935), Allie Paine (1944), Gerry Tucker (1947), Wayman Tisdale (1983, 1984 and 1985), Stacey King (1989).

NCAA CONSENSUS SECOND-TEAM ALL-AMERICANS (3): James McNatt (1940), Gerry Tucker (1943), Daron "Mookie" Blaylock (1989).

OKLAHOMA STATE

OFFICIAL NAME: Oklahoma State University.

NICKNAME: Cowboys.

ADDRESS: Gallagher-Iba Arena, Stillwater, OK 74078.

PHONE/FAX: (405) 744-5749/7754.

ENROLLMENT: 18,500.

ARENA: Gallagher-Iba Arena (Capacity-6,381; Year Opened-1938).

SCHOOL COLORS: Orange and Black.

CONFERENCE: Big 12.

FINAL AP TOP 10 RANKINGS (4): 1949-51-53-54.

NCAA TOURNAMENT APPEARANCES (14): 1945-46-49-51-53-54-58-65-83-91-92-93-94-95; 25-13 record (.658); reached Final Four in 1945 (1st), 1946 (1st), 1949 (2nd), 1951 (4th) and 1995 (T3rd).

NIT APPEARANCES (7): 1938-40-44-56-89-90-97; 6-8 record (.429); finished 3rd in 1938, 3rd in 1940 and 4th in 1944.

ALL-TIME WINNINGEST COACH: Hank Iba (36 years from 1935-70, 655-316 record, .675).

ALL-TIME SCORING LEADER: Byron Houston (2,374 points from 1989-92).

ALL-TIME REBOUNDING LEADER: Byron Houston (1,190 from 1989-92).

NCAA CONSENSUS FIRST-TEAM ALL-AMERICANS (3): Bob Kurland (1944, 1945 and 1946).

NCAA CONSENSUS SECOND-TEAM ALL-AMERICANS (4): Jesse "Cab" Renick (1940), Gale McArthur (1951), Bob Mattick (1954), Byron Houston (1992).

OLD DOMINION UNIVERSITY

OLD DOMINION

OFFICIAL NAME: Old Dominion University.

NICKNAME: Monarchs.

ADDRESS: Athletic Administration Building, Norfolk, VA 23529-0201.

PHONE/FAX: (757) 683-3372/3119.

ENROLLMENT: 17,000.

ARENA: Norfolk Scope (Capacity-10,253; Year Opened-1971).

SCHOOL COLORS: Slate Blue and Silver.

CONFERENCE: Colonial Athletic Association.

NCAA DIVISION I TOURNAMENT APPEARANCES (7): 1980-82-85-86-92-95-97; 2-7 record (.222).

NCAA DIVISION II TOURNAMENT APPEARANCES (7): 1969-70-71-73-74-75-76; 15-8 record (.652); finished 1st in 1975, 2nd in 1971 and 4th in 1976.

NIT APPEARANCES (8): 1977-79-81-83-84-88-93-94; 4-8 record (.333).

ALL-TIME WINNINGEST COACH: Bud Metheny (17 years from 1949-65 when school was classified as a small college, 198-163 record, .548).

ALL-TIME SCORING LEADER: Ronnie Valentine (2,204 points from 1977-80).

ALL-TIME REBOUNDING LEADER: Randy Leddy (1,153 from 1963-66 when school was classified as a small college).

ORAL ROBERTS

OFFICIAL NAME: Oral Roberts University.

NICKNAME: Golden Eagles.

ADDRESS: 7777 South Lewis Avenue, Tulsa, OK 74171.

PHONE/FAX: (918) 495-7102/7123.

ENROLLMENT: 4,515.

ARENA: Mabee Center (Capacity-10,575; Year Opened-1972).

SCHOOL COLORS: Navy Blue, Vegas Gold and White.

CONFERENCE: Mid-Continent.

NCAA TOURNAMENT APPEARANCES (2): 1974 and 1984; 2-2 record (.500); regional runner-up in 1974.

NAIA TOURNAMENT APPEARANCES (1): 1990; 2-1 record (.667).

NIT APPEARANCES (6): 1972-73-75-77-82-97; 2-6 record (.250).

ALL-TIME WINNINGEST COACH: Ken Trickey (11 years from 1970-74 and 1988-93, 214-116 record, .648).

ALL-TIME SCORING LEADER: Greg Sutton (3,070 points from 1989-91 when school spent his last two seasons at the NAIA level; played freshman season for Langston in 1986-87).

ALL-TIME REBOUNDING LEADER: Eddie Woods (1,365 from 1971-74).

NCAA CONSENSUS SECOND-TEAM ALL-AMERICANS (1): Richie Fuqua (1972).

OREGON

OFFICIAL NAME: University of Oregon.

NICKNAME: Ducks.

ADDRESS: Len Casanova Athletic Center, 2727 Leo Harris Parkway, Eugene, OR 97401-8835.

PHONE/FAX: (541) 346-5488/5449.

ENROLLMENT: 17,100.

ARENA: McArthur Court (Capacity-9,738; Year Opened-1927).

SCHOOL COLORS: Emerald Green and Lemon Yellow.

CONFERENCE: Pacific-10.

NCAA TOURNAMENT APPEARANCES (5): 1939-45-60-61-95; 6-4 record (.600); reached Final Four in 1939 (1st).

NIT APPEARANCES (7): 1975-76-77-84-88-90-97; 5-7 record (.417); finished 3rd in 1975.

ALL-TIME WINNINGEST COACH: Howard Hobson (11 years from 1936-44, 1946 and 1947; 212-124 record, .631).

ALL-TIME SCORING LEADER: Ron Lee (2,085 points from 1973-76).

ALL-TIME REBOUNDING LEADER: Greg Ballard (1,114 from 1974-77).

NCAA CONSENSUS FIRST-TEAM ALL-AMERICANS (2): Urgel "Slim" Wintermute (1939), John Dick (1940).

NCAA CONSENSUS SECOND-TEAM ALL-AMERICANS (3): Bob Anet (1939), Ron Lee (1975), Greg Ballard (1977).

OREGON STATE

OFFICIAL NAME: Oregon State University.

NICKNAME: Beavers.

ADDRESS: 209 Gill Coliseum, Corvallis, OR 97331.

PHONE/FAX: (503) 737-3720/3072.

ENROLLMENT: 15,550.

ARENA: Gill Coliseum (Capacity-10,400; Year Opened-1949).

SCHOOL COLORS: Orange and Black.

CONFERENCE: Pacific-10.

FINAL AP TOP 10 RANKINGS (5): 1955-64-80-81-82.

NCAA TOURNAMENT APPEARANCES (16): 1947-49-55-62-63-64-66-75-80-81-82-84-85-88-89-90; 12-19 record (.387); reached Final Four in 1949 (4th) and 1963 (4th).

NIT APPEARANCES (3): 1979-83-87; 3-3 record (.500).

ALL-TIME WINNINGEST COACH: Amory "Slats" Gill (36 years from 1929-64, 599-392 record, .604).

ALL-TIME SCORING LEADER: Gary Payton (2,172 points from 1987-90).

ALL-TIME REBOUNDING LEADER: Mel Counts (1,375 from 1962-64).

NCAA CONSENSUS FIRST-TEAM ALL-AMERICANS (2): Steve Johnson (1981), Gary Payton (1990).

NCAA CONSENSUS SECOND-TEAM ALL-AMERICANS (3): John Mandic (1942), Dave Gambee (1958), Mel Counts (1964).

PACIFIC

OFFICIAL NAME: University of the Pacific.

NICKNAME: Tigers.

ADDRESS: 3601 Pacific Avenue, Stockton, CA 95211.

PHONE/FAX: (209) 946-2479/2757.

ENROLLMENT: 4,000.

ARENA: Alex G. Spanos Center (Capacity-6,150; Year Opened-1981).

SCHOOL COLORS: Orange and Black.

CONFERENCE: Big West.

NCAA TOURNAMENT APPEARANCES (5): 1966-67-71-79-97; 2-6 record (.250); regional runner-up in 1967.

NAIA TOURNAMENT APPEARANCES (1): 1951; 0-1 record.

NIT APPEARANCES: None.

ALL-TIME WINNINGEST COACH: Dick Edwards (nine years from 1964-72, 169-72 record, .701).

ALL-TIME SCORING LEADER: Ron Cornelius (2,065 points from 1978-81).

ALL-TIME REBOUNDING LEADER: Keith Swagerty (1,505 from 1965-67).

PENN

OFFICIAL NAME: University of Pennsylvania.

NICKNAME: Quakers.

ADDRESS: 235 South 33rd Street, Weightman Hall South, Philadelphia, PA 19104-6322.

PHONE/FAX: (215) 898-6128/1747.

ENROLLMENT: 9,300.

ARENA: Palestra (Capacity-8,700; Year Opened-1927).

SCHOOL COLORS: Red and Blue.

CONFERENCE: Ivy League.

FINAL AP TOP 10 RANKINGS (2): 1971 and 1972.

NCAA TOURNAMENT APPEARANCES (16): 1953-70-71-72-73-74-75-78-79-80-82-85-87-93-94-95; 13-18 record (.419); reached Final Four in 1979 (4th).

NIT APPEARANCES (1): 1981; 0-1 record.

ALL-TIME WINNINGEST COACH: Lon Jourdet (19 years from 1915-20 and 1931-43, 227-143 record, .614).

ALL-TIME SCORING LEADER: Ernie Beck (1,827 points from 1951-53).

ALL-TIME REBOUNDING LEADER: Ernie Beck (1,557 from 1951-53).

NCAA CONSENSUS FIRST-TEAM ALL-AMERICANS (3): Joe Schaaf (1929), Howie Dallmar (1945), Ernie Beck (1953).

PENN STATE

OFFICIAL NAME: Penn State University.

NICKNAME: Nittany Lions.

ADDRESS: 101D Bryce Jordan Center, University Park, PA 16802-7101.

PHONE/FAX: (814) 865-1757/863-3165.

ENROLLMENT: 31,400.

ARENA: Bryce Jordan Center (Capacity-15,300; Year Opened-1996).

SCHOOL COLORS: Blue and White.

CONFERENCE: Big Ten.

FINAL AP TOP 10 RANKINGS (1): 1954.

NCAA TOURNAMENT APPEARANCES (7): 1942-52-54-55-65-91-96; 7-9 record (.438); reached Final Four in 1954 (3rd).

NIT APPEARANCES (6): 1966-80-89-90-92-95; 9-6 record (.600); finished 3rd in 1990 and 1995.

ALL-TIME WINNINGEST COACH: John Egli (14 years from 1955-68, 187-135 record, .581).

ALL-TIME SCORING LEADER: Jesse Arnelle (2,138 points from 1952-55).

ALL-TIME REBOUNDING LEADER: Jesse Arnelle (1,238 from 1952-55).

PEPPERDINE

OFFICIAL NAME: Pepperdine University.

NICKNAME: Waves.

ADDRESS: 24255 Pacific Coast Highway, Malibu, CA 90263.

PHONE/FAX: (310) 456-4333/4322.

ENROLLMENT: 7,450.

ARENA: Firestone Fieldhouse (Capacity-3,104; Year Opened-1973).

SCHOOL COLORS: Blue, Orange and White.

CONFERENCE: West Coast.

NCAA TOURNAMENT APPEARANCES (11): 1944-62-76-79-82-83-85-86-91-92-94; 4-12 record (.250).

NAIA TOURNAMENT APPEARANCES (7): 1942-43-45-46-50-51-52; 11-7 record (.611); finished 2nd in 1945 and 3rd in 1946.

NIT APPEARANCES (4): 1980-88-89-93; 2-4 record (.333).

ALL-TIME WINNINGEST COACH: Robert Dowell (20 years from 1949-68, 263-263 record, .500).

ALL-TIME SCORING LEADER: Dane Suttle (1,702 points from 1980-83).

ALL-TIME REBOUNDING LEADER: Dana Jones (1,031 from 1991-94).

PITTSBURGH

OFFICIAL NAME: University of Pittsburgh.

NICKNAME: Panthers.

ADDRESS: Post Office Box 7436, Pittsburgh, PA 15213.

PHONE/FAX: (412) 648-8240/8248.

ENROLLMENT: 13,500.

ARENAS: Fitzgerald Field House (Capacity-6,798; Year Opened-1951) and Civic Arena (Capacity-17,500; Year Opened-1961).

SCHOOL COLORS: Blue and Gold.

CONFERENCE: Big East.

FINAL AP TOP 10 RANKINGS (1): 1988.

NCAA TOURNAMENT APPEARANCES (13): 1941-57-58-63-74-81-82-85-87-88-89-91-93; 8-14 record (.364); reached Final Four in 1941 (T3rd).

NIT APPEARANCES (7): 1964-75-80-84-86-92-97; 5-7 record (.417).

ALL-TIME WINNINGEST COACH: Dr. H.C. "Doc" Carlson (31 years from 1923-53, 366-248 record, .596).

ALL-TIME SCORING LEADER: Charles Smith (2,045 points from 1985-88).

ALL-TIME REBOUNDING LEADER: Sam Clancy (1,342 from 1978-81).

NCAA CONSENSUS FIRST-TEAM ALL-AMERICANS (6): Chuck Hyatt (1929 and 1930), Don Smith (1933), Claire Cribbs (1934 and 1935), Don Hennon (1958).

NCAA CONSENSUS SECOND-TEAM ALL-AMERICANS (3): Don Hennon (1959), Billy Knight (1974), Jerome Lane (1988).

PORTLAND

OFFICIAL NAME: University of Portland.

NICKNAME: Pilots.

ADDRESS: 5000 North Willamette Boulevard, Portland, OR 97203-5798.

PHONE/FAX: (503) 283-7117/7242.

ENROLLMENT: 2,700.

ARENA: Earle A. Chiles Center (Capacity-5,000; Year Opened-1984).

SCHOOL COLORS: Purple and White.

CONFERENCE: West Coast.

NCAA TOURNAMENT APPEARANCES (2): 1959 and 1996; 0-2 record.

NAIA TOURNAMENT APPEARANCES (9): 1942-49-50-51-52-53-54-57-58; 5-10 record (.333); finished 4th in 1952.

NIT APPEARANCES: None.

ALL-TIME WINNINGEST COACH: Jack Avina (17 years from 1971-87, 222-243 record, .477).

ALL-TIME SCORING LEADER: Jose Slaughter (1,940 points, 1979-82).

ALL-TIME REBOUNDING LEADER: Rick Raivio (910, 1977-80).

PRINCETON

OFFICIAL NAME: Princeton University.

NICKNAME: Tigers.

ADDRESS: Post Office Box 71, Jadwin Gymnasium, Princeton, NJ 08544.

PHONE/FAX: (609) 258-3568/4477.

ENROLLMENT: 4,500.

ARENA: Jadwin Gymnasium (Capacity-7,500; Year Opened-1969).

SCHOOL COLORS: Orange and Black.

CONFERENCE: Ivy League.

FINAL AP TOP 10 RANKINGS (1): 1967.

NCAA TOURNAMENT APPEARANCES (20): 1952-55-60-61-63-64-65-67-69-76-77-81-83-84-89-90-91-92-96-97; 12-24 record (.333); reached Final Four in 1965 (3rd).

NIT APPEARANCES (2): 1972 and 1975; 5-1 record (.833); finished 1st in 1975.

ALL-TIME WINNINGEST COACH: Pete Carril (29 years from 1968-96, 514-261 record, .663).

ALL-TIME SCORING LEADER: Bill Bradley (2,503 points from 1963-65).

ALL-TIME REBOUNDING LEADER: Bill Bradley (1,008 from 1963-65).

NCAA CONSENSUS FIRST-TEAM ALL-AMERICANS (2): Bill Bradley (1964 and 1965).

PROVIDENCE

OFFICIAL NAME: Providence College.

NICKNAME: Friars.

ADDRESS: River Avenue & Eaton Street, Providence, RI 02918.

PHONE/FAX: (401) 865-2272/2583.

ENROLLMENT: 3,545.

ARENA: Civic Center (Capacity-13,106; Year Opened-1972).

SCHOOL COLORS: Black and White.

CONFERENCE: Big East.

FINAL AP TOP 10 RANKINGS (3): 1965-73-74.

NCAA TOURNAMENT APPEARANCES (13): 1964-65-66-72-73-74-77-78-87-89-90-94-97; 14-14 record (.500); reached Final Four in 1973 (4th) and 1987 (T3rd).

NAIA TOURNAMENT APPEARANCES (1): 1951; 0-1 record.

NIT APPEARANCES (14): 1959-60-61-62-63-67-71-75-76-86-91-93-95-96; 28-15 record (.651); finished 4th in 1959, 2nd in 1960, 1st in 1961, 1st in 1963, 4th in 1976 and 4th in 1993.

ALL-TIME WINNINGEST COACH: Joe Mullaney (18 years from 1956-69 and 1982-85, 319-164 record, .660).

ALL-TIME SCORING LEADER: Jimmy Walker (2,045 points from 1964-67).

ALL-TIME REBOUNDING LEADER: Marvin Barnes (1,592 from 1971-74).

NCAA CONSENSUS FIRST-TEAM ALL-AMERICANS (4): Jimmy Walker (1966 and 1967), Ernie DiGregorio (1973), Marvin Barnes (1974).

NCAA CONSENSUS SECOND-TEAM ALL-AMERICANS (2): Lenny Wilkens (1960), Eric Murdock (1991).

PURDUE

OFFICIAL NAME: Purdue University.

NICKNAME: Boilermakers.

ADDRESS: Room 15 - Mackey Arena, West Lafayette, IN 47907-1790.

PHONE/FAX: (317) 494-3200/5447.

ENROLLMENT: 34,685.

ARENA: Mackey Arena (Capacity-14,123; Year Opened-1967).

SCHOOL COLORS: Old Gold and Black.

CONFERENCE: Big Ten.

FINAL AP TOP 10 RANKINGS (7): 1969-84-87-88-90-94-96.

NCAA TOURNAMENT APPEARANCES (16): 1969-77-80-83-84-85-86-87-88-90-91-93-94-95-96-97; 19-16 record (.543); reached Final Four in 1969 (2nd) and 1980 (3rd).

NIT APPEARANCES (6): 1971-74-79-81-82-92; 18-5 record (.783); finished 1st in 1974, 2nd in 1979, 3rd in 1981 and 2nd in 1982.

NCIT RECORD: 1-1 in 1975.

ALL-TIME WINNINGEST COACH: Ward "Piggy" Lambert (29 years from 1917-46, 371-152 record, .709). Gene Keady is expected to break Lambert's mark in 1997-98.

ALL-TIME SCORING LEADER: Rick Mount (2,323 points from 1968-70).

ALL-TIME REBOUNDING LEADER: Joe Barry Carroll (1,148 from 1977-80).

NCAA CONSENSUS FIRST-TEAM ALL-AMERICANS (16): Charles "Stretch" Murphy (1929 and 1930), John Wooden (1930, 1931 and 1932), Norman Cottom (1934), Bob Kessler (1936), Jewell Young (1937 and 1938), Terry Dischinger (1961 and 1962), Dave Schellhase (1966), Rick Mount (1969 and 1970), Joe Barry Carroll (1980), Glenn Robinson (1994).

NCAA CONSENSUS SECOND-TEAM ALL-AMERICANS (3): Terry Dischinger (1960), Dave Schellhase (1965), Glenn Robinson (1993).

RHODE ISLAND

OFFICIAL NAME: University of Rhode Island.

NICKNAME: Rams.

ADDRESS: Mackal Fieldhouse, Kingston, RI 02881.

PHONE/FAX: (401) 874-2409/5354.

ENROLLMENT: 11,500.

ARENAS: Keaney Gymnasium (Capacity-4,000; Year Opened-1953) and Providence Civic Center (Capacity-13,106; Year Opened-1972).

SCHOOL COLORS: Light Blue, Dark Blue and White.

CONFERENCE: Atlantic 10.

NCAA TOURNAMENT APPEARANCES (6): 1961-66-78-88-93-97; 3-6 record (.333).

NIT APPEARANCES (9): 1941-42-45-46-79-81-87-92-96; 7-10 record (.412); finished 4th in 1945 and 2nd in 1946.

ALL-TIME WINNINGEST COACH: Frank Keaney (27 years from 1922-48, 403-124 record, .765).

ALL-TIME SCORING LEADER: Steve Chubin (2,154 points from 1963-66; missed 1964-65 season because he was academically ineligible).

ALL-TIME REBOUNDING LEADER: Art Stephenson (1,048 from 1966-68).

NCAA CONSENSUS FIRST-TEAM ALL-AMERICANS (1): Chet Jaworski (1939).

NCAA CONSENSUS SECOND-TEAM ALL-AMERICANS (2): Stan Modzelewski (1941 and 1942).

RICE

OFFICIAL NAME: Rice University.

NICKNAME: Owls.

ADDRESS: Post Office Box 1892, 6100 South Main, Houston, TX 77251-1892.

PHONE/FAX: (713) 527-4034/6019.

ENROLLMENT: 2,600.

ARENA: Autry Court (Capacity-5,000; Year Opened-1950).

SCHOOL COLORS: Blue and Gray.

CONFERENCE: Western Athletic.

NCAA TOURNAMENT APPEARANCES (4): 1940-42-54-70; 2-5 record (.286); regional runner-up in 1940 and 1942.

NIT APPEARANCES (3): 1943-91-93; 1-3 record (.250).

ALL-TIME WINNINGEST COACH: Don Suman (10 years from 1950-59, 132-106 record, .555).

ALL-TIME SCORING LEADER: Brent Scott (1,906 points from 1990-93).

ALL-TIME REBOUNDING LEADER: Brent Scott (1,049 from 1990-93).

NCAA CONSENSUS FIRST-TEAM ALL-AMERICANS (3): Bob Kinney (1942), Bill Closs (1943), Bill Henry (1945).

NCAA CONSENSUS SECOND-TEAM ALL-AMERICANS (2): Bob Kinney (1941), Bill Henry (1944).

RICHMOND

OFFICIAL NAME: University of Richmond.

NICKNAME: Spiders.

ADDRESS: Robins Center, Richmond, VA 23173.

PHONE/FAX: (804) 289-8365/8820.

ENROLLMENT: 2,800.

ARENA: Robins Center (Capacity-9,171; Year Opened-1972).

SCHOOL COLORS: Blue and Red.

CONFERENCE: Colonial Athletic Association.

NCAA TOURNAMENT APPEARANCES (5): 1984-86-88-90-91; 5-5 record (.500).

NIT APPEARANCES (4): 1982-85-89-92; 2-4 record (.333).

ALL-TIME WINNINGEST COACH: Dick Tarrant (12 years from 1982-93, 239-126 record, .655).

ALL-TIME SCORING LEADER: John Newman (2,383 points from 1983-86).

ALL-TIME REBOUNDING LEADER: Ken Daniel (1,255 from 1953-56).

ROBERT MORRIS

OFFICIAL NAME: Robert Morris College.

NICKNAME: Colonials.

ADDRESS: Narrows Run Road, Coraopolis, PA 15108-1189.

PHONE/FAX: (412) 262-8314/8557.

ENROLLMENT: 5,300.

ARENA: Charles L. Sewall Center (Capacity-3,056; Year Opened-1985).

SCHOOL COLORS: Blue and White.

CONFERENCE: Northeast.

NCAA TOURNAMENT APPEARANCES (5): 1982-83-89-90-92; 1-5 record (.167).

NIT APPEARANCES: None.

ALL-TIME WINNINGEST COACH: Jarrett Durham (12 years from 1985-96, 157-183 record, .462).

ALL-TIME SCORING LEADER: Myron Walker (1,965 points from 1991-94).

ALL-TIME REBOUNDING LEADER: Anthony Dickens (751 from 1986-90; missed 1986-87 season because of a hip injury).

RUTGERS

OFFICIAL NAME: Rutgers, The State University of New Jersey.

NICKNAME: Scarlet Knights.

ADDRESS: Post Office Box 1149, Piscataway, NJ 08855-1149.

PHONE/FAX: (908) 445-4200/3063.

ENROLLMENT: 33,585.

ARENA: Louis Brown Athletic Center (Capacity-9,000; Year Opened-1978).

SCHOOL COLORS: Scarlet and White.

CONFERENCE: Big East.

FINAL AP TOP 10 RANKINGS (1): 1976.

NCAA TOURNAMENT APPEARANCES (6): 1975-76-79-83-89-91; 5-7 record (.417); reached Final Four in 1976 (4th).

NIT APPEARANCES (9): 1967-69-73-74-77-78-82-90-92; 10-9 record (.526); finished 3rd in 1967 and 1978.

ALL-TIME WINNINGEST COACH: Tom Young (12 years from 1974-85, 239-117 record, .671).

ALL-TIME SCORING LEADER: Phil Sellers (2,399 points from 1973-76).

ALL-TIME REBOUNDING LEADER: Phil Sellers (1,115 from 1973-76).

NCAA CONSENSUS FIRST-TEAM ALL-AMERICANS (1): Bob Lloyd (1967).

NCAA CONSENSUS SECOND-TEAM ALL-AMERICANS (1): Phil Sellers (1976).

ST. BONAVENTURE

OFFICIAL NAME: St. Bonaventure University.

NICKNAME: Bonnies.

ADDRESS: Reilly Center, St. Bonaventure, NY 14778.

PHONE/FAX: (716) 375-2319/2383.

ENROLLMENT: 2,700.

ARENA: Reilly Center (Capacity-6,000; Year Opened-1966).

SCHOOL COLORS: Brown and White.

CONFERENCE: Atlantic 10.

FINAL AP TOP 10 RANKINGS (4): 1960-61-68-70.

NCAA TOURNAMENT APPEARANCES (4): 1961-68-70-78; 6-6 record (.500); reached Final Four in 1970 (4th).

NIT APPEARANCES (12): 1951-52-57-58-59-60-64-71-77-79-83-95; 17-13 record (.567); finished 3rd in 1952, 4th in 1957, 3rd in 1958, 4th in 1960, 3rd in 1971 and 1st in 1977.

ALL-TIME WINNINGEST COACH: Larry Weise (12 years from 1962-73, 202-90 record, .692).

ALL-TIME SCORING LEADER: Greg Sanders (2,238 points from 1975-78).

ALL-TIME REBOUNDING LEADER: Bob Lanier (1,180 from 1968-70).

NCAA CONSENSUS FIRST-TEAM ALL-AMERICANS (3): Tom Stith (1960 and 1961), Bob Lanier (1970).

NCAA CONSENSUS SECOND-TEAM ALL-AMERICANS (1): Bob Lanier (1968).

ST. FRANCIS (N.Y.)

OFFICIAL NAME: St. Francis College.

NICKNAME: Terriers.

ADDRESS: 180 Remsen Street, Brooklyn Heights, NY 11201.

PHONE/FAX: (718) 522-2300/1274.

ENROLLMENT: 1,910.

ARENA: Physical Education Center (Capacity-1,400; Year Opened-1971).

SCHOOL COLORS: Royal Blue, Red and White.

CONFERENCE: Northeast.

NCAA TOURNAMENT APPEARANCES: None.

NAIA TOURNAMENT APPEARANCES (1): 1955; 0-1 record.

NIT APPEARANCES (3): 1954-56-63; 3-4 record (.429); finished 4th in 1956.

ALL-TIME WINNINGEST COACH: Daniel Lynch (21 years from 1949-69, 282-237 record, .543).

ALL-TIME SCORING LEADER: Darwin Purdie (1,613 points from 1986-89).

ALL-TIME REBOUNDING LEADER: Jerome Williams (1,018 from 1972-74).

ST. FRANCIS (PA.)

OFFICIAL NAME: St. Francis College of Pennsylvania.

NICKNAME: Red Flash.

ADDRESS: Maurice Stokes Athletics Center, Loretto, PA 15940.

PHONE/FAX: (814) 472-3128/3044.

ENROLLMENT: 1,200.

ARENA: DeGol Arena, Stokes Center (Capacity-3,500; Year Opened-1972).

SCHOOL COLORS: Red and White.

CONFERENCE: Northeast.

NCAA TOURNAMENT APPEARANCES (1): 1991; 0-1 record.

NAIA TOURNAMENT APPEARANCES (1): 1948; 0-1 record.

NIT APPEARANCES (3): 1954-55-58; 3-4 record (.429); finished 4th in 1955.

ALL-TIME WINNINGEST COACH: Dr. William Hughes (21 years from 1946-66, 293-206-1 record, .587).

ALL-TIME SCORING LEADER: Joe Anderson (2,301 points from 1988-91).

ALL-TIME REBOUNDING LEADER: Maurice Stokes (1,819 from 1953-55 when school was classified as a small college; rebounding statistics weren't kept in 1951-52).

ST. JOHN'S

OFFICIAL NAME: St. John's University.

NICKNAME: Red Storm.

ADDRESS: 8000 Utopia Parkway, Jamaica, NY 11439.

PHONE/FAX: (718) 990-6367/969-8468.

ENROLLMENT: 19,500.

ARENAS: Alumni Hall (Capacity-6,008; Year Opened-1961) and Madison Square Garden (Capacity-19,876).

SCHOOL COLORS: Red and White.

CONFERENCE: Big East.

FINAL AP TOP 10 RANKINGS (8): 1950-51-52-53-69-83-85-86.

NCAA TOURNAMENT APPEARANCES (23): 1951-52-61-67-68-69-73-76-77-78-79-80-82-83-84-85-86-87-88-90-91-92-93; 23-25 record (.479); reached Final Four in 1952 (2nd) and 1985 (T3rd).

NIT APPEARANCES (26): 1939-40-43-44-45-46-47-49-50-51-52-53-58-59-60-62-65-66-70-71-72-74-75-81-89-95; 41-29 record (.586); finished 4th in 1939, 1st in 1943, 1st in 1944, 3rd in 1945, 3rd in 1950, 3rd in 1951, 2nd in 1953, 4th in 1958, 1st in 1959, 2nd in 1962, 1st in 1965, 2nd in 1970, 4th in 1972, 4th in 1975 and 1st in 1989.

ALL-TIME WINNINGEST COACH: Lou Carnesecca (24 years from 1966-70 and 1974-92, 526-200 record, .725).

ALL-TIME SCORING LEADER: Chris Mullin (2,440 points from 1982-85).

ALL-TIME REBOUNDING LEADER: George Johnson (1,240 from 1975-78).

NCAA CONSENSUS FIRST-TEAM ALL-AMERICANS (3): Harry Boykoff (1943), Chris Mullin (1985), Walter Berry (1986).

NCAA CONSENSUS SECOND-TEAM ALL-AMERICANS (8): Bob Zawoluk (1952), Alan Seiden (1959), Tony Jackson (1960 and 1961), Lloyd "Sonny" Dove (1967), Chris Mullin (1984), Mark Jackson (1987), Malik Sealy (1992).

ST. JOSEPH'S

OFFICIAL NAME: St. Joseph's University.

NICKNAME: Hawks.

ADDRESS: 5600 City Avenue, Philadelphia, PA 19131.

PHONE/FAX: (610) 660-1707/1727.

ENROLLMENT: 2,700.

ARENA: Alumni Memorial Fieldhouse (Capacity-3,200; Year Opened-1949).

SCHOOL COLORS: Crimson and Gray.

CONFERENCE: Atlantic 10.

FINAL AP TOP 10 RANKINGS (2): 1965 and 1966.

NCAA TOURNAMENT APPEARANCES (15): 1959-60-61-62-63-65-66-69-71-73-74-81-82-86-97; 14-19 record (.424); reached Final Four in 1961 (3rd).

NIT APPEARANCES (11): 1956-58-64-72-79-80-84-85-93-95-96; 9-11 record (.450); finished 3rd in 1956 and 2nd in 1996.

ALL-TIME WINNINGEST COACH: Bill Ferguson (25 years from 1929-53, 309-208 record, .598).

ALL-TIME SCORING LEADER: Bernard Blunt (1,985 points from 1991-95; missed majority of 1993-94 season because of kneecap injury).

ALL-TIME REBOUNDING LEADER: Cliff Anderson (1,288 from 1965-67).

NCAA CONSENSUS FIRST-TEAM ALL-AMERICANS (1): George Senesky (1943).

NCAA CONSENSUS SECOND-TEAM ALL-AMERICANS (1): Matt Guokas (1966).

SAINT LOUIS

OFFICIAL NAME: Saint Louis University.

NICKNAME: Billikens.

ADDRESS: 3672 West Pine Boulevard, St. Louis, MO 63108.

PHONE/FAX: (314) 977-2524/7193.

ENROLLMENT: 11,300.

ARENA: Kiel Center (Capacity-20,000; Year Opened-1994).

SCHOOL COLORS: Blue and White.

CONFERENCE: Conference USA.

FINAL AP TOP 10 RANKINGS (4): 1949-51-52-57.

NCAA TOURNAMENT APPEARANCES (4): 1952-57-94-95; 2-5 record (.286); regional runner-up in 1952.

NIT APPEARANCES (16): 1948-49-51-52-53-55-56-59-60-61-63-65-87-89-90-96; 18-15 record (.545); finished 1st in 1948, 2nd in 1961, 2nd in 1989 and 2nd in 1990.

ALL-TIME WINNINGEST COACH: Eddie Hickey (11 years from 1948-58, 211-89 record, .703).

ALL-TIME SCORING LEADER: Anthony Bonner (1,972 points from 1987-90).

ALL-TIME REBOUNDING LEADER: Anthony Bonner (1,424 from 1987-90).

NCAA CONSENSUS FIRST-TEAM ALL-AMERICANS (2): Ed Macauley (1948 and 1949).

ST. MARY'S

OFFICIAL NAME: St. Mary's College.

NICKNAME: Gaels.

ADDRESS: Post Office Box 5100, Moraga, CA 94575.

PHONE/FAX: (510) 631-4402/4405.

ENROLLMENT: 4,000.

ARENA: McKeon Pavilion (Capacity-3,500; Year Opened-1978).

SCHOOL COLORS: Blue and Red.

CONFERENCE: West Coast.

NCAA TOURNAMENT APPEARANCES (3): 1959-89-97; 1-3 record (.250); regional runner-up in 1959.

NIT APPEARANCES: None.

ALL-TIME WINNINGEST COACH: James Weaver (seven years from 1956-62, 110-67 record, .621).

ALL-TIME SCORING LEADER: David Vann (1,738 points from 1979-82).

ALL-TIME REBOUNDING LEADER: Tom Meschery (916 from 1959-61).

ST. PETER'S

OFFICIAL NAME: St. Peter's College.

NICKNAME: Peacocks.

ADDRESS: 2641 Kennedy Boulevard, Jersey City, NJ 07306-5997.

PHONE/FAX: (201) 915-9101/9102.

ENROLLMENT: 3,355.

ARENA: Yanitelli Center (Capacity-3,200; Year Opened-1975).

SCHOOL COLORS: Blue and White.

CONFERENCE: Metro Atlantic Athletic.

NCAA TOURNAMENT APPEARANCES (2): 1991 and 1995; 0-2 record.

NAIA TOURNAMENT APPEARANCES (2): 1953 and 1954; 3-2 record (.600).

NIT APPEARANCES (12): 1957-58-67-68-69-75-76-80-82-84-87-89; 5-13 record (.278); finished 4th in 1968.

ALL-TIME WINNINGEST COACH: Don Kennedy (22 years from 1951-72 when school was classified as a small college most of that span, 323-195 record, .624).

ALL-TIME SCORING LEADER: Willie Haynes (1,730 points from 1986-89).

ALL-TIME REBOUNDING LEADER: Pete O'Dea (1,033 from 1966-68).

SAN DIEGO

OFFICIAL NAME: University of San Diego.

NICKNAME: Toreros.

ADDRESS: 5998 Alcala Park, San Diego, CA 92110-2492.

PHONE/FAX: (619) 260-4745/292-0388.

ENROLLMENT: 6,200.

ARENA: USD Sports Center (Capacity-2,500; Year Opened-1963).

SCHOOL COLORS: Columbia Blue, Navy and White.

CONFERENCE: West Coast.

NCAA DIVISION I TOURNAMENT APPEARANCES (2): 1984 and 1987; 0-2 record.

NCAA DIVISION II TOURNAMENT APPEARANCES (5): 1966-73-74-78-79; 4-6 record (.400).

NIT APPEARANCES: None.

ALL-TIME WINNINGEST COACH: Jim Brovelli (11 years from 1974-84, 160-131 record, .550).

ALL-TIME SCORING LEADER: Stan Washington (1,472 points from 1972-74 when school was classified as a small college).

ALL-TIME REBOUNDING LEADER: Gus Magee (948 from 1967-70 when school was classified as a small college).

SAN DIEGO STATE

OFFICIAL NAME: San Diego State University.

NICKNAME: Aztecs.

ADDRESS: Athletics Building, Room 109, San Diego, CA 92182.

PHONE/FAX: (619) 594-5547/6541.

ENROLLMENT: 27,000.

ARENA: San Diego Sports Arena (Capacity-13,741); a new 12,000-seat on-campus facility called the Student Activities Center is slated to open in 1997.

SCHOOL COLORS: Scarlet and Black.

CONFERENCE: Western Athletic.

NCAA DIVISION I TOURNAMENT APPEARANCES (3): 1975-76-85; 0-3 record.

NCAA DIVISION II TOURNAMENT APPEARANCES (3): 1957-67-68; 5-3 record (.625).

NAIA TOURNAMENT APPEARANCES (5): 1939-40-41-42-56; 15-4 record (.789); finished 1st in 1941 and 2nd in 1939 and 1940.

NIT APPEARANCES (1): 1982; 0-1 record.

ALL-TIME WINNINGEST COACH: George Ziegenfuss (21 years from 1949-69 when school was classified as a small college, 316-229 record, .580).

ALL-TIME SCORING LEADER: Michael Cage (1,846 points from 1981-84).

ALL-TIME REBOUNDING LEADER: Michael Cage (1,317 from 1981-84).

NCAA CONSENSUS SECOND-TEAM ALL-AMERICANS (1): Michael Cage (1984).

SAN FRANCISCO

OFFICIAL NAME: University of San Francisco.
NICKNAME: Dons.
ADDRESS: 2130 Fulton, San Francisco, CA 94117-1080.
PHONE/FAX: (415) 422-6161/2929.
ENROLLMENT: 7,000.

ARENA: Memorial Gymnasium (Capacity-5,300; Year Opened-1958).
SCHOOL COLORS: Green and Gold.
CONFERENCE: West Coast.
FINAL AP TOP 10 RANKINGS (5): 1949-55-56-58-77.
NCAA TOURNAMENT APPEARANCES (15): 1955-56-57-58-63-64-65-72-73-74-77-78-79-81-82; 21-13 record (.618); reached Final Four in 1955 (1st), 1956 (1st) and 1957 (3rd).
NIT APPEARANCES (4): 1949-50-66-76; 5-3 record (.625); finished 1st in 1949.
ALL-TIME WINNINGEST COACH: Bob Gaillard (eight years from 1971-78, 165-57 record, .743).
ALL-TIME SCORING LEADER: Bill Cartwright (2,116 points from 1976-79).
ALL-TIME REBOUNDING LEADER: Bill Russell (1,606 from 1954-56).
NCAA CONSENSUS FIRST-TEAM ALL-AMERICANS (3): Bill Russell (1955 and 1956), Quintin Dailey (1982).
NCAA CONSENSUS SECOND-TEAM ALL-AMERICANS (5): Don Lofgran (1950), K.C. Jones (1956), Mike Farmer (1958), Bill Cartwright (1977 and 1979).

SAN JOSE STATE

OFFICIAL NAME: San Jose State University.
NICKNAME: Spartans.
ADDRESS: 1 Washington Square, San Jose, CA 95192.
PHONE/FAX: (408) 924-1217/1291.
ENROLLMENT: 30,000.

ARENA: The Event Center (Capacity-5,000; Year Opened-1989).
SCHOOL COLORS: Gold, White and Blue.
CONFERENCE: Western Athletic.
NCAA TOURNAMENT APPEARANCES (3): 1951-80-96; 0-3 record.
NAIA TOURNAMENT APPEARANCES (2): 1948 and 1949; 3-2 record (.600).
NIT APPEARANCES (1): 1981; 0-1 record.
ALL-TIME WINNINGEST COACH: Walt McPherson (17 years in 1941, 1942 and from 1946-60, 251-197 record, .560).
ALL-TIME SCORING LEADER: Ricky Berry (1,767 points from 1986-88 after transferring from Oregon State).
ALL-TIME REBOUNDING LEADER: Marv Branstrom (864 from 1956-58).

SANTA CLARA

OFFICIAL NAME: Santa Clara University.
NICKNAME: Broncos.
ADDRESS: Toso Pavilion, Santa Clara, CA 95053.
PHONE/FAX: (408) 554-4661/6942.

ENROLLMENT: 7,800.
ARENA: Toso Pavilion (Capacity-5,000; Year Opened-1975).
SCHOOL COLORS: Bronco Red and White.
CONFERENCE: West Coast.
FINAL AP TOP 10 RANKINGS (1): 1969.
NCAA TOURNAMENT APPEARANCES (10): 1952-53-54-60-68-69-70-87-95-96; 10-12 record (.455); reached Final Four in 1952 (4th).
NIT APPEARANCES (4): 1984-85-88-89; 2-4 record (.333).
ALL-TIME WINNINGEST COACH: Carroll Williams (22 years from 1971-92, 344-274 record, .557).
ALL-TIME SCORING LEADER: Kurt Rambis (1,735 points from 1977-80).
ALL-TIME REBOUNDING LEADER: Dennis Awtrey (1,135 from 1968-70).
NCAA CONSENSUS SECOND-TEAM ALL-AMERICANS (1): Bud Ogden (1969).

SETON HALL

OFFICIAL NAME: Seton Hall University.
NICKNAME: Pirates.
ADDRESS: 400 South Orange Avenue, South Orange, NJ 07079.
PHONE/FAX: (201) 761-9497/9493.

ENROLLMENT: 10,540.
ARENAS: Continental Airlines Arena (Capacity-20,029; Year Opened-1981) and Walsh Gym (Capacity-3,200; Year Opened-1940).
SCHOOL COLORS: Blue and White.
CONFERENCE: Big East.
FINAL AP TOP 10 RANKINGS (2): 1953 and 1993.
NCAA TOURNAMENT APPEARANCES (6): 1988-89-91-92-93-94; 12-6 record (.667); reached Final Four in 1989 (2nd).
NIT APPEARANCES (11): 1941-51-52-53-55-56-57-74-77-87-95; 7-12 record (.316); finished 4th in 1941, 4th in 1951 and 1st in 1953.
ALL-TIME WINNINGEST COACH: John "Honey" Russell (18 years from 1937-43 and 1950-60, 295-129 record, .696).
ALL-TIME SCORING LEADER: Terry Dehere (2,494 points from 1990-93).
ALL-TIME REBOUNDING LEADER: Walter Dukes (1,697 from 1951-53).
NCAA CONSENSUS FIRST-TEAM ALL-AMERICANS (2): Bob Davies (1942), Walter Dukes (1953).
NCAA CONSENSUS SECOND-TEAM ALL-AMERICANS (1): Terry Dehere (1993).

SIENA

OFFICIAL NAME: Siena College.
NICKNAME: Saints.
ADDRESS: 515 Loudon Road, Loudonville, NY 12211-1462.
PHONE/FAX: (518) 783-2411/2992.
ENROLLMENT: 2,700.
ARENAS: Alumni Recreation Center (Capacity-4,000; Year Opened-1974) and Knickerbocker Arena (Capacity-15,500).
SCHOOL COLORS: Green and Gold.
CONFERENCE: Metro Atlantic Athletic.
NCAA DIVISION I TOURNAMENT APPEARANCES (1): 1989; 1-1 record (.500).
NCAA DIVISION II TOURNAMENT APPEARANCES (1): 1974; 2-1 record (.667).
NIT APPEARANCES (3): 1988-91-94; 6-3 record (.667); finished 3rd in 1994.
ALL-TIME WINNINGEST COACH: Dan Cunha (21 years from 1942-65, 246-225 record, .522).
ALL-TIME SCORING LEADER: Marc Brown (2,284 points from 1988-91).
ALL-TIME REBOUNDING LEADER: Lee Matthews (1,037 from 1990-93).

SOUTH ALABAMA

OFFICIAL NAME: University of South Alabama.
NICKNAME: Jaguars.
ADDRESS: 1107 HPELS Building, Mobile, AL 36688-0002.
PHONE/FAX: (334) 460-7121/7297.
ENROLLMENT: 12,465.
ARENA: Mobile Civic Center (Capacity-10,000; Year Opened-1964).
SCHOOL COLORS: Red, Blue and White.
CONFERENCE: Sun Belt.
NCAA TOURNAMENT APPEARANCES (5): 1979-80-89-91-97; 1-5 record (.167).
NIT APPEARANCES (2): 1981 and 1984; 3-2 record (.600).
ALL-TIME WINNINGEST COACH: Cliff Ellis (nine years from 1976-84, 171-84 record, .671).
ALL-TIME SCORING LEADER: Jeff Hodge (2,221 points from 1986-89).
ALL-TIME REBOUNDING LEADER: Terry Catledge (932 from 1983-85).

SOUTH CAROLINA

OFFICIAL NAME: University of South Carolina.
NICKNAME: Gamecocks.
ADDRESS: Rex Enright Athletic Center, 1300 Rosewood Drive, Columbia, SC 29208.
PHONE/FAX: (803) 777-5204/2967.
ENROLLMENT: 26,130.
ARENA: Carolina Coliseum/Frank McGuire Arena (Capacity-12,401; Year Opened-1968).
SCHOOL COLORS: Garnet and Black.
CONFERENCE: Southeastern.
FINAL AP TOP 10 RANKINGS (4): 1970-71-72-97.
NCAA TOURNAMENT APPEARANCES (6): 1971-72-73-74-89-97; 4-7 record (.364); never reached regional final.
NIT APPEARANCES (6): 1969-75-78-83-91-96; 7-6 record (.538).
ALL-TIME WINNINGEST COACH: Frank McGuire (16 years from 1965-80, 283-142 record, .666).
ALL-TIME SCORING LEADER: Alex English (1,972 points from 1973-76).
ALL-TIME REBOUNDING LEADER: Lee Collins (1,159 from 1953-56).
NCAA CONSENSUS FIRST-TEAM ALL-AMERICANS (1): Tom Riker (1972).
NCAA CONSENSUS SECOND-TEAM ALL-AMERICANS (4): Grady Wallace (1957), John Roche (1970 and 1971), Kevin Joyce (1973).

SOUTH FLORIDA

OFFICIAL NAME: University of South Florida.
NICKNAME: Bulls.
ADDRESS: 4202 East Fowler Avenue, PED 214, Tampa, FL 33620.
PHONE/FAX: (813) 974-4086/5328.
ENROLLMENT: 37,000.
ARENA: Sun Dome (Capacity-10,411; Year Opened-1980).
SCHOOL COLORS: Green and Gold.
CONFERENCE: Conference USA.
NCAA TOURNAMENT APPEARANCES (2): 1990 and 1992; 0-2 record.
NIT APPEARANCES (5): 1981-83-85-91-95; 4-5 record (.444).
ALL-TIME WINNINGEST COACH: Bobby Paschal (10 years from 1987-96, 127-159 record, .443).
ALL-TIME SCORING LEADER: Charlie Bradley (2,319 points from 1982-85).
ALL-TIME REBOUNDING LEADER: Hakim Shahid (893 from 1987-90).

SOUTHERN

OFFICIAL NAME: Southern University & A&M.
NICKNAME: Jaguars.
ADDRESS: Post Office Box 9942, Baton Rouge, LA 70813.
PHONE/FAX: (504) 771-2601/4400.
ENROLLMENT: 9,500.
ARENA: F.G. Clark Activity Center (Capacity-7,500; Year Opened-1976).
SCHOOL COLORS: Columbia Blue and Gold.
CONFERENCE: Southwestern Athletic.
NCAA DIVISION I TOURNAMENT APPEARANCES (6): 1981-85-87-88-89-93; 1-6 record (.143).
NCAA DIVISION II TOURNAMENT APPEARANCES (3): 1974-75-77; 1-5 record (.167).
NAIA TOURNAMENT APPEARANCES (1): 1965; 2-1 record (.667).
NIT APPEARANCES (1): 1990; 0-1 record.
ALL-TIME WINNINGEST COACH:
ALL-TIME SCORING LEADER: Frankie Sanders (2,141 points from 1976-78).
ALL-TIME REBOUNDING LEADER: Jervaughn Scales (1,099 from 1992-94).

SOUTHERN CALIFORNIA

OFFICIAL NAME: University of Southern California.
NICKNAME: Trojans.
ADDRESS: Heritage Hall, Los Angeles, CA 90089-0602.
PHONE/FAX: (213) 740-8480/7584.
ENROLLMENT: 28,375.
ARENA: Los Angeles Sports Arena (Capacity-15,509; Year Opened-1959).
SCHOOL COLORS: Cardinal and Gold.
CONFERENCE: Pacific-10.
FINAL AP TOP 10 RANKINGS (3): 1961-71-92.
NCAA TOURNAMENT APPEARANCES (10): 1940-54-60-61-79-82-85-91-92-97; 6-12 record (.333); reached Final Four in 1940 (T3rd) and 1954 (4th).
NIT APPEARANCES (3): 1973-93-94; 2-3 record (.400).
CCAT/NCIT RECORD: 2-2 in 1974 (runner-up) and 1975 (eliminated in first round).
ALL-TIME WINNINGEST COACH: Justin "Sam" Barry (17 years from 1930-41 and 1946-50, 260-138 record, .653).
ALL-TIME SCORING LEADER: Harold Miner (2,048 points from 1990-92).
ALL-TIME REBOUNDING LEADER: Ron Riley (1,067 from 1970-72).
NCAA CONSENSUS FIRST-TEAM ALL-AMERICANS (5): Jerry Nemer (1933), Lee Guttero (1935), Ralph Vaughn (1940), Bill Sharman (1950), Harold Miner (1992).
NCAA CONSENSUS SECOND-TEAM ALL-AMERICANS (3): Gene Rock (1943), John Rudometkin (1962), Gus Williams (1975).

SOUTHERN ILLINOIS

OFFICIAL NAME: Southern Illinois University (At Carbondale).
NICKNAME: Salukis.
ADDRESS: SIU Arena, Carbondale, IL 62901.
PHONE/FAX: (618) 453-7235/2648.
ENROLLMENT: 24,870.
ARENA: SIU Arena (Capacity-10,014; Year Opened-1964).
SCHOOL COLORS: Maroon and White.
CONFERENCE: Missouri Valley.

NCAA DIVISION I TOURNAMENT APPEARANCES (4): 1977-93-94-95; 1-4 record (.200).

NCAA DIVISION II TOURNAMENT APPEARANCES (7): 1959-61-62-63-64-65-66; 17-9 record (.654); finished 2nd in 1965 and 1966, 3rd in 1962 and 4th in 1963.

NAIA TOURNAMENT APPEARANCES (5): 1945-46-47-48-60; 8-5 record (.615); finished 1st in 1946 and 4th in 1945.

NIT APPEARANCES (7): 1967-69-75-89-90-91-92; 6-6 record (.500); finished 1st in 1967.

ALL-TIME WINNINGEST COACH: William McAndrew (28 years from 1914-18 and 1921-43 when school was classified as a small college, 303-210 record, .591).

ALL-TIME SCORING LEADER: Charlie Vaughn (2,088 points from 1959-62 when school was classified as a small college).

ALL-TIME REBOUNDING LEADER: Seymour Bryson (1,244 from 1956-59 when school was classified as a small college).

SOUTHERN METHODIST

OFFICIAL NAME: Southern Methodist University.

NICKNAME: Mustangs.

ADDRESS: SMU Box 216, 6024 Airline, Dallas, TX 75275-0216.

PHONE/FAX: (214) 768-2883/2044.

ENROLLMENT: 5,435.

ARENA: Moody Coliseum (Capacity-8,998; Year Opened-1956).

SCHOOL COLORS: Red and Blue.

CONFERENCE: Western Athletic.

FINAL AP TOP 10 RANKINGS (2): 1956 and 1957.

NCAA TOURNAMENT APPEARANCES (10): 1955-56-57-65-66-67-84-85-88-93; 10-12 record (.455); reached Final Four in 1956 (4th).

NIT APPEARANCES (1): 1986; 0-1 record.

CCAT RECORD: 0-1 in 1974.

ALL-TIME WINNINGEST COACH: E.O. "Doc" Hayes (20 years from 1948-67, 299-191 record, .610).

ALL-TIME SCORING LEADER: Gene Phillips (1,931 points from 1969-71).

ALL-TIME REBOUNDING LEADER: Jon Koncak (1,169 from 1982-85).

NCAA CONSENSUS FIRST-TEAM ALL-AMERICANS (1): Jim Krebs (1957).

NCAA CONSENSUS SECOND-TEAM ALL-AMERICANS (1): Jon Koncak (1985).

SOUTHERN MISSISSIPPI

OFFICIAL NAME: University of Southern Missis-sippi.

NICKNAME: Golden Eagles.

ADDRESS: Southern Station, Box 5161, Hattiesburg, MS 39406-5161.

PHONE/FAX: (601) 266-4503/4507.

ENROLLMENT: 13,000.

ARENA: Reed Green Coliseum (Capacity-8,095; Year Opened-1965).

SCHOOL COLORS: Black and Gold.

CONFERENCE: Conference USA.

NCAA TOURNAMENT APPEARANCES (2): 1990 and 1991; 0-2 record.

NAIA TOURNAMENT APPEARANCES (4): 1952-53-54-55; 2-4 record (.333).

NIT APPEARANCES (6): 1981-86-87-88-94-95; 6-5 record (.545); finished 1st in 1987.

ALL-TIME WINNINGEST COACH: M.K. Turk (20 years from 1977-96, 300-267 record, .529).

ALL-TIME SCORING LEADER: Nick Revon (2,135 points from 1951-54 when school was classified as a small college).

ALL-TIME REBOUNDING LEADER: Clarence Weatherspoon (1,320 from 1989-92).

SOUTHWEST MISSOURI STATE

OFFICIAL NAME: Southwest Missouri State University.

NICKNAME: Bears.

ADDRESS: 901 South National, Springfield, MO 65804.

PHONE/FAX: (417) 836-5402/4868.

ENROLLMENT: 17,440.

ARENA: Hammons Student Center (Capacity-8,858; Year Opened-1976).

SCHOOL COLORS: Maroon and White.

CONFERENCE: Missouri Valley.

NCAA DIVISION I TOURNAMENT APPEARANCES (5): 1987-88-89-90-92; 1-5 record (.167).

NCAA DIVISION II TOURNAMENT APPEARANCES (10): 1958-59-66-67-68-69-70-73-74-78; 23-10 record (.697); finished 2nd in 1959, 1967, 1969 and 1974.

NAIA TOURNAMENT APPEARANCES (6): 1939-43-49-52-53-54; 15-4 record (.789); finished 1st in 1952 and 1953, and 3rd in 1954.

NIT APPEARANCES (4): 1986-91-93-97; 5-4 record (.556).

ALL-TIME WINNINGEST COACH: Andrew McDonald (23 years from 1926-43 and 1946-50 when school was classified as a small college, 301-166 record, .644).

ALL-TIME SCORING LEADER: Daryel Garrison (1,975 points from 1972-75 when school was classified as a small college).

ALL-TIME REBOUNDING LEADER: Curtis Perry (1,424 from 1967-70 when school was classified as a small college).

SOUTHWESTERN LOUISIANA

OFFICIAL NAME: University of Southwestern Louisiana.

NICKNAME: Ragin' Cajuns.

ADDRESS: 201 Reinhardt Drive, Lafayette, LA 70506-4297.

PHONE/FAX: (318) 482-6331/6649.

ENROLLMENT: 16,500.

ARENA: Cajundome (Capacity-12,000; Year Opened-1985).

SCHOOL COLORS: Vermilion and White.

CONFERENCE: Sun Belt.

FINAL AP TOP 10 RANKINGS (2): 1972 and 1973.

NCAA TOURNAMENT APPEARANCES (6): 1972-73-82-83-92-94; 4-7 record (.364).

NIT APPEARANCES (3): 1980-84-85; 6-4 record (.600); finished 4th in 1984.

ALL-TIME WINNINGEST COACH: Beryl Shipley (16 years from 1958-73 when school was classified as a small college most of that span, 296-129 record, .696).

ALL-TIME SCORING LEADER: Dwight "Bo" Lamar (3,493 points from 1970-73).

ALL-TIME REBOUNDING LEADER: Roy Ebron (1,064 from 1971-73).

NCAA CONSENSUS FIRST-TEAM ALL-AMERICANS (2): Dwight "Bo" Lamar (1972 and 1973).

STANFORD

OFFICIAL NAME: Stanford University.

NICKNAME: Cardinal.

ADDRESS: Encina Gym, Stanford, CA 94305.

PHONE/FAX: (415) 723-4418/725-2957.

ENROLLMENT: 13,075.

ARENA: Maples Pavilion (Capacity-7,391; Year Opened-1968).

SCHOOL COLORS: Cardinal and White.

CONFERENCE: Pacific-10.

NCAA TOURNAMENT APPEARANCES (6): 1942-89-92-95-96-97; 7-5 record (.583); reached Final Four in 1942 (1st).

NIT APPEARANCES (4): 1988-90-91-94; 6-3 record (.667); finished 1st in 1991.

ALL-TIME WINNINGEST COACH: Howie Dallmar (21 years from 1955-75, 264-264 record, .500).

ALL-TIME SCORING LEADER: Todd Lichti (2,336 points from 1986-89).

ALL-TIME REBOUNDING LEADER: Adam Keefe (1,119 from 1989-92).

NCAA CONSENSUS FIRST-TEAM ALL-AMERICANS (3): Hank Luisetti (1936, 1937 and 1938).

NCAA CONSENSUS SECOND-TEAM ALL-AMERICANS (3): Don Burness (1942), Todd Lichti (1989), Brevin Knight (1997).

SYRACUSE

OFFICIAL NAME: Syracuse University.

NICKNAME: Orangemen.

ADDRESS: Manley Field House, Syracuse, NY 13244-5020.

PHONE/FAX: (315) 443-2608/2076.

ENROLLMENT: 10,200.

ARENA: Carrier Dome (Capacity-33,000; Year Opened-1980).

SCHOOL COLOR: Orange.

CONFERENCE: Big East.

FINAL AP TOP 10 RANKINGS (10): 1975-77-79-80-86-87-88-89-90-91.

NCAA TOURNAMENT APPEARANCES (23): 1957-66-73-74-75-76-77-78-79-80-83-84-85-86-87-88-89-90-91-92-94-95-96; 35-24 record (.593); reached Final Four in 1975 (4th), 1987 (2nd) and 1996 (2nd).

NIT APPEARANCES (9): 1946-50-64-67-71-72-81-82-97; 7-9 record (.438); finished 2nd in 1981.

ALL-TIME WINNINGEST COACH: Jim Boeheim (21 years from 1977-97, 502-172 record, .745).

ALL-TIME SCORING LEADER: Lawrence Moten (2,334 points from 1992-95).

ALL-TIME REBOUNDING LEADER: Derrick Coleman (1,537 from 1987-90).

NCAA CONSENSUS FIRST-TEAM ALL-AMERICANS (3): Dave Bing (1966), Derrick Coleman (1990), Billy Owens (1991).

NCAA CONSENSUS SECOND-TEAM ALL-AMERICANS (4): Dwayne "Pearl" Washington (1985), Rony Seikaly (1988), Sherman Douglas (1989), John Wallace (1996).

TEMPLE

OFFICIAL NAME: Temple University.

NICKNAME: Owls.

ADDRESS: 1900 North Broad Street-109-00, McGonigle Hall-047-00, Philadelphia, PA 19122.

PHONE/FAX: (215) 204-7445/7499.

ENROLLMENT: 33,000.

ARENA: McGonigle Hall (Capacity-3,900; Year Opened-1969).

SCHOOL COLORS: Cherry and White.

CONFERENCE: Atlantic 10.

FINAL AP TOP 10 RANKINGS (3): 1958-87-88.

NCAA TOURNAMENT APPEARANCES (21): 1944-56-58-64-67-70-72-79-84-85-86-87-88-90-91-92-93-94-95-96-97; 24-21 record (.533); reached Final Four in 1956 (3rd) and 1958 (3rd).

NIT APPEARANCES (12): 1938-57-60-61-62-66-68-69-78-81-82-89; 13-10 record (.565); finished 1st in 1938, 3rd in 1957 and 1st in 1969.

ALL-TIME WINNINGEST COACH: Harry Litwack (21 years from 1953-73, 373-193 record, .659).

ALL-TIME SCORING LEADER: Mark Macon (2,609 points from 1988-91).

ALL-TIME REBOUNDING LEADER: John Baum (1,042 from 1967-69).

NCAA CONSENSUS FIRST-TEAM ALL-AMERICANS (3): Meyer "Mike" Bloom (1938), Bill Mlkvy (1951), Guy Rodgers (1958).

NCAA CONSENSUS SECOND-TEAM ALL-AMERICANS (2): Guy Rodgers (1957), Mark Macon (1988).

TENNESSEE

OFFICIAL NAME: University of Tennessee.

NICKNAME: Volunteers.

ADDRESS: Post Office Box 15016, 1720 Volunteer Boulevard, Knoxville, TN 37901.

PHONE/FAX: (423) 974-1212/1269.

ENROLLMENT: 26,580.

ARENA: Thompson-Boling Arena (Capacity-24,535; Year Opened-1987).

SCHOOL COLORS: Orange and White.

CONFERENCE: Southeastern.

FINAL AP TOP 10 RANKINGS (1): 1967.

NCAA TOURNAMENT APPEARANCES (9): 1967-76-77-79-80-81-82-83-89; 5-10 record (.333); never reached regional final.

NIT APPEARANCES (9): 1945-69-71-84-85-88-90-92-96; 12-9 record (.571); finished 3rd in 1969 and 1985.

CCAT/NCIT RECORD: 0-2 in 1974 and 1975.

ALL-TIME WINNINGEST COACH: Ray Mears (15 years from 1963-77, 278-112 record, .713).

ALL-TIME SCORING LEADER: Allan Houston (2,801 points from 1990-93).

ALL-TIME REBOUNDING LEADER: Gene Tormohlen (1,113 from 1957-59).

NCAA CONSENSUS FIRST-TEAM ALL-AMERICANS (2): Bernard King (1977), Dale Ellis (1983).

NCAA CONSENSUS SECOND-TEAM ALL-AMERICANS (3): Bernard King (1976), Ernie Grunfeld (1977), Dale Ellis (1982).

TENNESSEE-CHATTANOOGA

OFFICIAL NAME: University of Tennessee-Chattanooga.

NICKNAME: Moccasins.

ADDRESS: 615 McCallie Avenue, Chattanooga, TN 37403.

PHONE/FAX: (615) 755-4618/4610.

ENROLLMENT: 8,325.

ARENA: UTC Arena (Capacity-11,218; Year Opened-1982).

SCHOOL COLORS: Navy Blue and Old Gold.

CONFERENCE: Southern.

NCAA DIVISION I TOURNAMENT APPEARANCES (8): 1981-82-83-88-93-94-95-97; 3-8 record (.273).

NCAA DIVISION II TOURNAMENT APPEARANCES (5): 1961-73-75-76-77; 11-5 record (.688); finished 1st in 1977 and 2nd in 1976.

NIT APPEARANCES (4): 1984-85-86-87; 3-4 record (.429).

ALL-TIME WINNINGEST COACH: Mack McCarthy (12 years from 1986-97, 243-122 record, .666).

ALL-TIME SCORING LEADER: Wayne Goldon (2,384 points from 1974-77 when school was classified as a small college).

ALL-TIME REBOUNDING LEADER: David Bryan (1,059 from 1966-69 when school was classified as a small college).

TENNESSEE STATE

OFFICIAL NAME: Tennessee State University.

NICKNAME: Tigers.

ADDRESS: P.O. Box 343, 3500 John A. Merritt Boulevard, Nashville, TN 37209-1561.

PHONE/FAX: (615) 963-5851/5895.

ENROLLMENT: 8,450.

ARENA: Howard Gentry Complex (Capacity-10,150; Year Opened-1977).

SCHOOL COLORS: Blue and White.

CONFERENCE: Ohio Valley.

NCAA DIVISION I TOURNAMENT APPEARANCES (2): 1993 and 1994; 0-2 record.

NCAA DIVISION II TOURNAMENT APPEARANCES (8): 1963-67-70-71-72-73-74-75; 19-9 record (.679); reached national semifinals in 1970 (2nd), 1972 (3rd), 1973 (2nd) and 1975 (4th).

NAIA TOURNAMENT APPEARANCES (7): 1953-54-56-57-58-59-60; 23-4 record (.852); finished 1st three times (1957, 1958 and 1959) and 3rd in 1960.

ALL-TIME WINNINGEST COACH: Ed Martin (17 years from 1969-85, 284-154 record, .648).

ALL-TIME SCORING LEADER: Dick Barnett (3,209 points from 1956-59 when school was classified as a small college).

ALL-TIME REBOUNDING LEADER: Lloyd Neal (1,667 from 1969-71 when school was classified as a small college).

TENNESSEE TECH

OFFICIAL NAME: Tennessee Tech University.

NICKNAME: Golden Eagles.

ADDRESS: Box 5057, Cookeville, TN 38505.

PHONE/FAX: (615) 372-3088/6139.

ENROLLMENT: 8,240.

ARENA: Eblen Center (Capacity-10,152; Year Opened-1977).

SCHOOL COLORS: Purple and Gold.

CONFERENCE: Ohio Valley.

NCAA TOURNAMENT APPEARANCES (2): 1958 and 1963; 0-2 record.

NIT APPEARANCES (1): 1985; 0-1 record.

ALL-TIME WINNINGEST COACH: Putty Overall (22 seasons in 1925 and from 1927-47 when school was classified as a small college, 164-134 record, .550).

ALL-TIME SCORING LEADER: Earl Wise (2,196 points from 1987-90).

ALL-TIME REBOUNDING LEADER: Jimmy Hagan (1,108 from 1958-60).

TEXAS

OFFICIAL NAME: University of Texas-Austin.

NICKNAME: Longhorns.

ADDRESS: Post Office Box 7399, Austin, TX 78713.

PHONE/FAX: (512) 471-7437/6040.

ENROLLMENT: 47,905.

ARENA: Frank Erwin Center (Capacity-16,042; Year Opened-1977).

SCHOOL COLORS: Burnt Orange and White.

CONFERENCE: Big 12.

NCAA TOURNAMENT APPEARANCES (16): 1939-43-47-60-63-72-74-79-89-90-91-92-94-95-96-97; 16-19 record (.457); reached Final Four in 1943 (3rd) and 1947 (3rd).

NIT APPEARANCES (4): 1948-78-80-86; 6-3 record (.667); finished 1st in 1978.

ALL-TIME WINNINGEST COACH: Tom Penders (nine years from 1989-97, 194-93 record, .676).

ALL-TIME SCORING LEADER: Terrence Rencher (2,306 points from 1992-95).

ALL-TIME REBOUNDING LEADER: LaSalle Thompson (1,027 from 1980-82).

NCAA CONSENSUS FIRST-TEAM ALL-AMERICANS (1): Jack Gray (1935).

NCAA CONSENSUS SECOND-TEAM ALL-AMERICANS (1): John Hargis (1947).

TEXAS A&M

OFFICIAL NAME: Texas A&M University.

NICKNAME: Aggies.

ADDRESS: Koldus Building, Room 222, College Station, TX 77843-1228.

PHONE/FAX: (409) 845-5725/0564.

ENROLLMENT: 43,255.

ARENA: G. Rollie White Coliseum (Capacity-7,500; Year Opened-1954); Reed Arena is slated to open in the 1997-98 season (12,500).

SCHOOL COLORS: Maroon and White.

CONFERENCE: Big 12.

NCAA TOURNAMENT APPEARANCES (6): 1951-64-69-75-80-87; 3-7 record (.300); never reached regional final.

NIT APPEARANCES (5): 1979-82-85-86-94; 4-5 record (.444).

ALL-TIME WINNINGEST COACH: Shelby Metcalf (27 years from 1964-90, 438-306 record, .589).

ALL-TIME SCORING LEADER: Vernon Smith (1,778 points from 1978-81).

ALL-TIME REBOUNDING LEADER: Vernon Smith (978 from 1978-81).

TEXAS CHRISTIAN

OFFICIAL NAME: Texas Christian University.

NICKNAME: Horned Frogs.

ADDRESS: TCU Box 32924, Ft. Worth, TX 76129.

PHONE/FAX: (817) 921-7969/7964.

ENROLLMENT: 6,990.

ARENA: Daniel-Meyer Coliseum (Capacity-7,166; Year Opened-1961).

SCHOOL COLORS: Purple and White.

CONFERENCE: Western Athletic.

NCAA TOURNAMENT APPEARANCES (6): 1952-53-59-68-71-87; 5-6 record (.455); regional runner-up in 1968.

NIT APPEARANCES (4): 1983-86-92-97; 5-4 record (.556).

ALL-TIME WINNINGEST COACH: Byron "Buster" Brannon (19 years from 1949-67, 206-258 record, .444).

ALL-TIME SCORING LEADER: Darrell Browder (1,886 points from 1980-83).

ALL-TIME REBOUNDING LEADER: Reggie Smith (966 from 1989-92).

TEXAS-EL PASO

OFFICIAL NAME: University of Texas-El Paso.

NICKNAME: Miners.

ADDRESS: 201 Baltimore, El Paso, TX 79968.

PHONE/FAX: (915) 747-5330/5444.

ENROLLMENT: 17,500.

ARENA: Special Events Center (Capacity-12,222; Year Opened-1977).

SCHOOL COLORS: Orange, Blue and White.

CONFERENCE: Western Athletic.

FINAL AP TOP 10 RANKINGS (3): 1966-67-84.

NCAA TOURNAMENT APPEARANCES (14): 1963-64-66-67-70-75-84-85-86-87-88-89-90-92; 14-13 record (.519); reached Final Four in 1966 (1st).

NAIA TOURNAMENT APPEARANCES (1): 1941; 0-1 record.

NIT APPEARANCES (7): 1965-72-80-81-83-93-95; 4-7 record (.364).

ALL-TIME WINNINGEST COACH: Don Haskins (36 years from 1962-97, 691-326 record, .679).

ALL-TIME SCORING LEADER: Antoine Gillespie (1,706 points from 1993-95; missed 1991-92 season after failing to meet the academic requirements of Proposition 48).

ALL-TIME REBOUNDING LEADER: Jim Barnes (965 in 1963 and 1964).

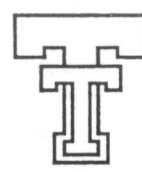

TEXAS TECH

OFFICIAL NAME: Texas Tech University.

NICKNAME: Red Raiders.

ADDRESS: Post Office Box 43021, Lubbock, TX 79409-3021.

PHONE/FAX: (806) 742-2770/1970.

ENROLLMENT: 25,000.

ARENA: United Spirit Arena (Capacity-12,600; Year Opened-1998).

SCHOOL COLORS: Red and Black.

CONFERENCE: Big 12.

FINAL AP TOP 10 RANKINGS (1): 1996.

NCAA TOURNAMENT APPEARANCES (9): 1954-56-61-62-73-76-85-86-96; 5-10 record (.333); never reached regional final.

NAIA TOURNAMENT APPEARANCES (2): 1942 and 1949; 3-2 record (.600).

NIT APPEARANCES (2): 1979 and 1995; 0-2 record.

ALL-TIME WINNINGEST COACH: Gerald Myers (21 years from 1971-91, 326-261 record, .555).

ALL-TIME SCORING LEADER: Rick Bullock (2,118 points from 1973-76).

ALL-TIME REBOUNDING LEADER: Jim Reed (1,330 from 1954-56).

TOLEDO

OFFICIAL NAME: University of Toledo.

NICKNAME: Rockets.

ADDRESS: Glass Bowl Stadium, Toledo, OH 43606.

PHONE/FAX: (419) 530-3790/3795.

ENROLLMENT: 24,540.

ARENA: John F. Savage Hall (Capacity-9,000; Year Opened-1976).

SCHOOL COLORS: Midnight Blue and Gold.

CONFERENCE: Mid-American.

NCAA TOURNAMENT APPEARANCES (4): 1954-67-79-80; 1-4 record (.200).

NIT APPEARANCES (3): 1942-43-81; 4-4 record (.500); finished 4th in 1942 and 2nd in 1943.

CCAT RECORD: 1-1 in 1974.

ALL-TIME WINNINGEST COACH: Bob Nichols (22 years from 1966-87, 375-213 record, .638).

ALL-TIME SCORING LEADER: Ken Epperson (2,016 points from 1982-85).

ALL-TIME REBOUNDING LEADER: Ken Epperson (960 from 1982-85).

TULANE

OFFICIAL NAME: Tulane University.

NICKNAME: Green Wave.

ADDRESS: James W. Wilson Jr. Center for Athletics, New Orleans, LA 70118.

PHONE/FAX: (504) 865-5506/5512.

ENROLLMENT: 11,485.

ARENA: Avron B. Fogelman Arena (Capacity-3,600; Year Opened-1933).

SCHOOL COLORS: Olive Green and Sky Blue.

CONFERENCE: Conference USA.

FINAL AP TOP 10 RANKINGS (1): 1949.

NCAA TOURNAMENT APPEARANCES (3): 1992-93-95; 3-3 record (.500).

NIT APPEARANCES (5): 1982-83-94-96-97; 7-5 record (.583); finished 3rd in 1996.

ALL-TIME WINNINGEST COACH: Clifford Wells (18 years from 1946-63, 259-169 record, .605).

ALL-TIME SCORING LEADER: Jerald Honeycutt (2,209 points from 1994-97).

ALL-TIME REBOUNDING LEADER: Jack Ardon (1,062 from 1960-62).

TULSA

OFFICIAL NAME: The University of Tulsa.

NICKNAME: Golden Hurricane.

ADDRESS: 600 South College, Tulsa, OK 74104-3189.

PHONE/FAX: (918) 631-2395/3913.

ENROLLMENT: 4,600.

ARENA: Maxwell Convention Center (Capacity-8,659; Year Opened-1964); a $28 million on-campus Student Life and Convocation Complex is expected to be completed by fall 1998.

SCHOOL COLORS: Old Gold, Royal Blue and Crimson.

CONFERENCE: Western Athletic.

FINAL AP TOP 10 RANKINGS (1): 1982.

NCAA TOURNAMENT APPEARANCES (10): 1955-82-84-85-86-87-94-95-96-97; 6-10 record (.375).

NIT APPEARANCES (7): 1953-67-69-81-83-90-91; 5-6 record (.455); finished 1st in 1981.

ALL-TIME WINNINGEST COACH: Clarence Iba (11 years from 1950-60, 137-147 record, .482).

ALL-TIME SCORING LEADER: Shea Seals (2,288 points from 1994-97).

ALL-TIME REBOUNDING LEADER: Bob Goodall (776 from 1958-60).

NCAA CONSENSUS SECOND-TEAM ALL-AMERICANS (1): Paul Pressey (1982).

UAB

OFFICIAL NAME: University of Alabama at Birmingham.

NICKNAME: Blazers.

ADDRESS: 115 UAB Arena, Birmingham, AL 35294-1160.

PHONE/FAX: (205) 934-0722/7505.

ENROLLMENT: 16,660.

ARENA: UAB Arena (Capacity-8,500; Year Opened-1988).

SCHOOL COLORS: Green, Gold and White.

CONFERENCE: Conference USA.

NCAA TOURNAMENT APPEARANCES (9): 1981-82-83-84-85-86-87-90-94; 6-9 record (.400); reached regional final in 1982.

NIT APPEARANCES (6): 1980-89-91-92-93-97; 8-6 record (.571); finished 3rd in 1989 and 1993.

ALL-TIME WINNINGEST COACH: Gene Bartow (18 years from 1979-96, 365-204 record, .641).

ALL-TIME SCORING LEADER: Steve Mitchell (1,867 points from 1983-86).

ALL-TIME REBOUNDING LEADER: Jerome Mincy (933 from 1983-86).

UCLA

NICKNAME: Bruins.

ADDRESS: J.D. Morgan Center, 405 Hilgard Avenue, Los Angeles, CA 90024.

PHONE/FAX: (310) 206-6831/825-8664.

ENROLLMENT: 35,500.

ARENA: Pauley Pavilion (Capacity-12,819; Year Opened-1965).

SCHOOL COLORS: Navy Blue and Gold.

CONFERENCE: Pacific-10.

FINAL AP TOP 10 RANKINGS (22): 1950-56-64-65-67-68-69-70-71-72-73-74-75-76-77-78-79-81-83-92-95-97.

NCAA TOURNAMENT APPEARANCES (33): 1950-52-56-62-63-64-65-67-68-69-70-71-72-73-74-75-76-77-78-79-80-81-83-87-89-90-91-92-93-94-95-96-97; 77-26 record (.748); reached Final Four in 1962 (4th), 1964 (1st), 1965 (1st), 1967 (1st), 1968 (1st), 1969 (1st), 1970 (1st), 1971 (1st), 1972 (1st), 1973 (1st), 1974 (3rd), 1975 (1st), 1976 (3rd), 1980 (2nd) and 1995 (1st).

NIT APPEARANCES (2): 1985 and 1986; 5-1 record (.833); finished 1st in 1985.

ALL-TIME WINNINGEST COACH: John Wooden (27 years from 1949-75, 620-147 record, .808).

ALL-TIME SCORING LEADER: Don MacLean (2,608 points from 1989-92).

ALL-TIME REBOUNDING LEADER: Bill Walton (1,370 from 1972-74).

NCAA CONSENSUS FIRST-TEAM ALL-AMERICANS (18): Walt Hazzard (1964), Gail Goodrich (1965), Lew Alcindor (1967, 1968 and 1969), Sidney Wicks (1971), Henry Bibby (1972), Bill Walton (1972, 1973 and 1974), Keith Wilkes (1973 and 1974), Dave Meyers (1975), Richard Washington (1976), Marques Johnson (1977), David Greenwood (1978 and 1979), Ed O'Bannon (1995).

NCAA CONSENSUS SECOND-TEAM ALL-AMERICANS (4): Don Barksdale (1947), Lucius Allen (1968), Sidney Wicks (1970), Don MacLean (1992).

UNLV

NICKNAME: Runnin' Rebels.

ADDRESS: 4505 Maryland Parkway, Las Vegas, NV 89154.

PHONE/FAX: (702) 895-3207/0989.

ENROLLMENT: 20,240.

ARENA: Thomas & Mack Center (Capacity-18,500; Year Opened-1983).

SCHOOL COLORS: Scarlet and Gray.

CONFERENCE: Western Athletic.

FINAL AP TOP 10 RANKINGS (8): 1976-77-83-85-87-90-91-92.

NCAA DIVISION I TOURNAMENT APPEARANCES (12): 1975-76-77-83-84-85-86-87-88-89-90-91; 30-11 record (.732); reached Final Four in 1977 (3rd), 1987 (T3rd), 1990 (1st) and 1991 (T3rd).

NCAA DIVISION II TOURNAMENT APPEARANCES (4): 1965-67-68-69; 4-5 record (.444).

NIT APPEARANCES (4): 1980-82-93-97; 6-5 record (.545); finished 4th in 1980.

ALL-TIME WINNINGEST COACH: Jerry Tarkanian (19 years from 1974-92, 509-105 record, .829).

ALL-TIME SCORING LEADER: Eddie Owens (2,221 points from 1974-77).

ALL-TIME REBOUNDING LEADER: Sidney Green (1,276 from 1980-83).

NCAA CONSENSUS FIRST-TEAM ALL-AMERICANS (2): Larry Johnson (1990 and 1991).

NCAA CONSENSUS SECOND-TEAM ALL-AMERICANS (4): Sidney Green (1983), Armon Gilliam (1987), Stacey Augmon (1991), Isaiah "J.R." Rider (1993).

RUNNIN' UTES

UTAH

OFFICIAL NAME: University of Utah.

NICKNAME: Utes.

ADDRESS: Jon Huntsman Center, Salt Lake City, UT 84112.

PHONE/FAX: (801) 581-3510/4358.

ENROLLMENT: 26,600.

ARENA: Jon Huntsman Center (Capacity-15,000; Year Opened-1969).

SCHOOL COLORS: Crimson and White.

CONFERENCE: Western Athletic.

FINAL AP TOP 10 RANKINGS (5): 1955-60-62-91-97.

NCAA TOURNAMENT APPEARANCES (19): 1944-45-55-56-59-60-61-66-77-78-79-81-83-86-91-93-95-96-97; 25-22 record (.532); reached Final Four in 1944 (1st), 1961 (4th) and 1966 (4th).

NIT APPEARANCES (10): 1944-47-49-57-58-70-74-87-88-92; 11-9 record (.550); finished 1st in 1947, 2nd in 1974 and 3rd in 1992.

ALL-TIME WINNINGEST COACH: Vadal Peterson (26 years from 1928-53, 384-224 record, .631).

ALL-TIME SCORING LEADER: Keith Van Horn (2,542 points from 1994-97).

ALL-TIME REBOUNDING LEADER: Billy McGill (1,106 from 1960-62).

NCAA CONSENSUS FIRST-TEAM ALL-AMERICANS (4): Bill Kinner (1936), Arnie Ferrin (1945), Billy McGill (1962), Keith Van Horn (1997).

NCAA CONSENSUS SECOND-TEAM ALL-AMERICANS (9): Arnie Ferrin (1944, 1947 and 1948), Vern Gardner (1947 and 1949), Billy McGill (1961), Luther "Ticky" Burden (1975), Danny Vranes (1981), Keith Van Horn (1996).

AGGIES

UTAH STATE

OFFICIAL NAME: Utah State University.

NICKNAME: Aggies.

ADDRESS: 700 North & 800 East, Logan, UT 84322.

PHONE/FAX: (801) 797-1361/2615.

ENROLLMENT: 17,435.

ARENA: Smith Spectrum (Capacity-10,270; Year Opened-1970).

SCHOOL COLORS: Navy Blue and White.

CONFERENCE: Big West.

FINAL AP TOP 10 RANKINGS (1): 1960.

NCAA TOURNAMENT APPEARANCES (11): 1939-62-63-64-70-71-75-79-80-83-88; 5-13 record (.278); regional runner-up in 1939 and 1970.

NAIA TOURNAMENT APPEARANCES (1): 1952; 1-1 record (.500).

NIT APPEARANCES (5): 1960-67-78-84-95; 2-5 record (.286); finished 3rd in 1960.

ALL-TIME WINNINGEST COACH: E. Lowell "Dick" Romney (22 years from 1920-41, 225-157 record, .589).

ALL-TIME SCORING LEADER: Greg Grant (2,127 points from 1983-86).

ALL-TIME REBOUNDING LEADER: Cornell Green (1,067 from 1960-62).

NCAA CONSENSUS SECOND-TEAM ALL-AMERICANS (1): Wayne Estes (1965).

VALPARAISO

OFFICIAL NAME: Valparaiso University.

NICKNAME: Crusaders.

ADDRESS: Athletics-Recreation Center (ARC), Valparaiso, IN 46383.

PHONE/FAX: (219) 464-5232/5762.

ENROLLMENT: 3,760.

ARENA: Athletics-Recreation Center (Capacity-4,500; Year Opened-1984).

SCHOOL COLORS: Brown and Gold.

CONFERENCE: Mid-Continent.

NCAA DIVISION I TOURNAMENT APPEARANCES (2): 1996 and 1997; 0-2 record.

NCAA DIVISION II TOURNAMENT APPEARANCES (5): 1962-66-67-69-73; 7-5 record (.583).

NAIA TOURNAMENT APPEARANCES (2): 1938 and 1943; 1-2 record (.333).

ALL-TIME WINNINGEST COACH: Homer Drew (nine years from 1989-97, 121-137 record, .469).

ALL-TIME SCORING LEADER: Tracy Gipson (1,785 points from 1990-93).

ALL-TIME REBOUNDING LEADER: Chris Ensminger (910 from 1993-96).

NCAA CONSENSUS SECOND-TEAM ALL-AMERICANS (1): Bob Dille (1944).

VANDERBILT

OFFICIAL NAME: Vanderbilt University.

NICKNAME: Commodores.

ADDRESS: Post Office Box 120158, Nashville, TN 37212.

PHONE/FAX: (615) 322-4121/343-7064.

ENROLLMENT: 9,300.

ARENA: Memorial Gymnasium (Capacity-15,311; Year Opened-1952).

SCHOOL COLORS: Black and Gold.

CONFERENCE: Southeastern.

FINAL AP TOP 10 RANKINGS (4): 1957-65-66-93.

NCAA TOURNAMENT APPEARANCES (7): 1965-74-88-89-91-93-97; 5-8 record (.385); regional runner-up in 1965.

NIT APPEARANCES (6): 1983-87-90-92-94-96; 13-5 record (.722); finished 1st in 1990 and 2nd in 1994.

ALL-TIME WINNINGEST COACH: Roy Skinner (16 years from 1959 and 1962-76, 278-135 record, .673).

ALL-TIME SCORING LEADER: Phil Cox (1,725 points from 1982-85).

ALL-TIME REBOUNDING LEADER: Clyde Lee (1,223 from 1964-66).

NCAA CONSENSUS FIRST-TEAM ALL-AMERICANS (1): Clyde Lee (1966).

NCAA CONSENSUS SECOND-TEAM ALL-AMERICANS (2): Clyde Lee (1965), Billy McCaffrey (1993).

VILLANOVA

OFFICIAL NAME: Villanova University.

NICKNAME: Wildcats.

ADDRESS: Jake Nevin Field House, 800 Lancaster Avenue, Villanova, PA 19085-1674.

PHONE/FAX: (610) 519-4120/7323.

ENROLLMENT: 5,995.

ARENAS: The Pavilion (Capacity-6,500; Year Opened-1986) and CoreStates Spectrum (Capacity-18,060).

SCHOOL COLORS: Blue and White.

CONFERENCE: Big East.

FINAL AP TOP 10 RANKINGS (5): 1964-65-69-95-96.

NCAA TOURNAMENT APPEARANCES (24): 1939-49-51-55-62-64-69-70-71-72-78-80-81-82-83-84-85-86-88-90-91-95-96-97; 37-24 record (.607); reached Final Four in 1939 (T3rd), 1971 (2nd) and 1985 (1st).

NIT APPEARANCES (12): 1959-60-63-65-66-67-68-77-87-89-92-94; 19-12 record (.613); finished 4th in 1963, 2nd in 1965, 3rd in 1966, 3rd in 1977 and 1st in 1994.

ALL-TIME WINNINGEST COACH: Alexander G. Severance (25 years from 1937-61, 413-201 record, .673).

ALL-TIME SCORING LEADER: Kerry Kittles (2,243 points from 1993-96).

ALL-TIME REBOUNDING LEADER: Howard Porter (1,317 from 1969-71).

NCAA CONSENSUS FIRST-TEAM ALL-AMERICANS (2): Paul Arizin (1950), Kerry Kittles (1996).

NCAA CONSENSUS SECOND-TEAM ALL-AMERICANS (2): Howard Porter (1971), Kerry Kittles (1995).

VIRGINIA

OFFICIAL NAME: University of Virginia.

NICKNAME: Cavaliers.

ADDRESS: Post Office Box 3785, University Hall, Alderman & Massie Roads, Charlottesville, VA 22903.

PHONE/FAX: (804) 982-5500/5525.

ENROLLMENT: 18,010.

ARENA: University Hall (Capacity-8,457; Year Opened-1965).

SCHOOL COLORS: Orange and Blue.

CONFERENCE: Atlantic Coast.

FINAL AP TOP 10 RANKINGS (3): 1981-82-83.

NCAA TOURNAMENT APPEARANCES (14): 1976-81-82-83-84-86-87-89-90-91-93-94-95-97; 21-14 record (.600); reached Final Four in 1981 (3rd) and 1984 (T3rd).

NIT APPEARANCES (7): 1941-72-78-79-80-85-92; 13-5 record (.722); finished 1st in 1980 and 1992.

ALL-TIME WINNINGEST COACH: Terry Holland (16 years from 1975-90, 326-173 record, .653).

ALL-TIME SCORING LEADER: Bryant Stith (2,516 points from 1989-92).

ALL-TIME REBOUNDING LEADER: Ralph Sampson (1,511 from 1980-83).

NCAA CONSENSUS FIRST-TEAM ALL-AMERICANS (3): Ralph Sampson (1981, 1982 and 1983).

NCAA CONSENSUS SECOND-TEAM ALL-AMERICANS (2): Barry Parkhill (1972), Jeff Lamp (1981).

VIRGINIA COMMONWEALTH

OFFICIAL NAME: Virginia Commonwealth University.

NICKNAME: Rams.

ADDRESS: VCU Box 2003, Richmond, VA 23284-2003.

PHONE/FAX: (804) 828-7000/9723.

ENROLLMENT: 22,000.

ARENA: Richmond Coliseum (Capacity-12,500; Year Opened-1971); Stuart C. Sigel Convocation and Recreation Center is slated to open in the 1998-99 season (Capacity-7,500).

SCHOOL COLORS: Black and Gold.

CONFERENCE: Colonial Athletic Association.

NCAA TOURNAMENT APPEARANCES (6): 1980-81-83-84-85-96; 4-6 record (.400).

NIT APPEARANCES (3): 1978-88-93; 2-3 record (.400).

ALL-TIME WINNINGEST COACH: J.D. Barnett (six years from 1980-85, 132-48 record, .733). Sonny Smith is expected to break Barnett's mark in 1997-98.

ALL-TIME SCORING LEADER: Len Creech (2,019 points from 1965-69 when school was classified as a small college; missed 1967-68 season).

ALL-TIME REBOUNDING LEADER: Lorenza Watson (1,143 from 1976-79).

VIRGINIA MILITARY

OFFICIAL NAME: Virginia Military Institute.

NICKNAME: Keydets.

ADDRESS: Lexington, VA 24450.

PHONE/FAX: (540) 464-7253/7583.

ENROLLMENT: 1,300.

ARENA: Cameron Hall (Capacity-5,800; Year Opened-1981).

SCHOOL COLORS: Red, White and Yellow.

CONFERENCE: Southern.

NCAA TOURNAMENT APPEARANCES (3): 1964-76-77; 3-3 record (.500); regional runner-up in 1976.

NIT APPEARANCES: None.

ALL-TIME WINNINGEST COACH: Joe Cantafio (eight years from 1987-94, 79-147 record, .350).

ALL-TIME SCORING LEADER: Gay Elmore (2,423 points from 1983-87; missed majority of 1982-83 season because of leg and wrist injuries).

ALL-TIME REBOUNDING LEADER: Dave Montgomery (1,068 from 1975-78).

VIRGINIA TECH

OFFICIAL NAME: Virginia Polytechnic Institute & State University.

NICKNAME: Hokies.

ADDRESS: Jamerson Athletic Center, Blacksburg, VA 24061-0502.

PHONE/FAX: (703) 231-6725/6984.

ENROLLMENT: 22,235.

ARENA: Cassell Coliseum (Capacity-9,971; Year Opened-1962).

SCHOOL COLORS: Chicago Maroon and Burnt Orange.

CONFERENCE: Atlantic 10.

NCAA TOURNAMENT APPEARANCES (7): 1967-76-79-80-85-86-96; 5-7 record (.417); regional runner-up in 1967.

NIT APPEARANCES (7): 1966-73-77-82-83-84-95; 17-5 record (.773); finished 1st in 1973 and 1995, and 3rd in 1984.

ALL-TIME WINNINGEST COACH: Charles Moir (11 years from 1977-87, 213-119 record, .642).

ALL-TIME SCORING LEADER: Vernell "Bimbo" Coles (2,484 points from 1987-90).

ALL-TIME REBOUNDING LEADER: Chris Smith (1,508 from 1958-61).

NCAA CONSENSUS SECOND-TEAM ALL-AMERICANS (1): Dell Curry (1986).

WAKE FOREST

OFFICIAL NAME: Wake Forest University.

NICKNAME: Demon Deacons.

ADDRESS: Post Office Box 7265, Athletic Center, Wingate Drive, Winston-Salem, NC 27109.

PHONE/FAX: (910) 759-5640/5140.

ENROLLMENT: 3,600.

ARENA: Lawrence Joel Memorial Coliseum (Capacity-14,407; Year Opened-1989).

SCHOOL COLORS: Old Gold and Black.

CONFERENCE: Atlantic Coast.

FINAL AP TOP 10 RANKINGS (4): 1977-95-96-97.

NCAA TOURNAMENT APPEARANCES (15): 1939-53-61-62-77-81-82-84-91-92-93-94-95-96-97; 22-15 record (.595); reached Final Four in 1962 (3rd).

NIT APPEARANCES (2): 1983 and 1985; 3-2 record (.600); finished in tie for 3rd in 1983.

ALL-TIME WINNINGEST COACH: Murray Greason (23 years from 1934-43 and 1945-57, 288-243 record, .542).

ALL-TIME SCORING LEADER: Dickie Hemric (2,587 points from 1952-55).

ALL-TIME REBOUNDING LEADER: Dickie Hemric (1,802 from 1952-55).

NCAA CONSENSUS FIRST-TEAM ALL-AMERICANS (3): Len Chappell (1962), Tim Duncan (1996 and 1997).

NCAA CONSENSUS SECOND-TEAM ALL-AMERICANS (5): Dickie Hemric (1955), Rod Griffin (1977 and 1978), Rodney Rogers (1993), Randolph Childress (1995).

WASHINGTON

OFFICIAL NAME: University of Washington.

NICKNAME: Huskies.

ADDRESS: Graves Building, Seattle, WA 98195.

PHONE/FAX: (206) 543-2230/5000.

ENROLLMENT: 34,000.

ARENA: Hec Edmundson Pavilion (Capacity-7,900; Year Opened-1927).

SCHOOL COLORS: Purple and Gold.

CONFERENCE: Pacific-10.

FINAL AP TOP 10 RANKINGS (2): 1952 and 1953.

NCAA TOURNAMENT APPEARANCES (8): 1943-48-51-53-76-84-85-86; 8-9 record (.471); reached Final Four in 1953 (3rd).

NIT APPEARANCES (5): 1980-82-87-96-97; 3-5 record (.375).

ALL-TIME WINNINGEST COACH: Clarence "Hec" Edmundson (27 years from 1921-47, 488-195 record, .714).

ALL-TIME SCORING LEADER: Christian Welp (2,073 points from 1984-87).

ALL-TIME REBOUNDING LEADER: Doug Smart (1,051 from 1957-59).

NCAA CONSENSUS FIRST-TEAM ALL-AMERICANS (2): Hal Lee (1934), Bob Houbregs (1953).

NCAA CONSENSUS SECOND-TEAM ALL-AMERICANS (2): Jack Nichols (1948), Bob Houbregs (1952).

WASHINGTON STATE

OFFICIAL NAME: Washington State University.

NICKNAME: Cougars.

ADDRESS: Bohler Gym, Room M-8, Pullman, WA 99164-1602.

PHONE/FAX: (509) 335-2684/0267.

ENROLLMENT: 17,500.

ARENA: Friel Court (Capacity-12,058; Year Opened-1973).

SCHOOL COLORS: Crimson and Gray.

CONFERENCE: Pacific-10.

NCAA TOURNAMENT APPEARANCES (4): 1941-80-83-94; 3-4 record (.429); reached Final Four in 1941 (2nd).

NIT APPEARANCES (3): 1992-95-96; 4-3 record (.571).

ALL-TIME WINNINGEST COACH: Jack Friel (30 years from 1929-58, 495-377 record, .568).

ALL-TIME SCORING LEADER: Steve Puidokas (1,894 points from 1974-77).

ALL-TIME REBOUNDING LEADER: Steve Puidokas (992 from 1974-77).

NCAA CONSENSUS SECOND-TEAM ALL-AMERICANS (3): Paul Lindemann (1941), Gale Bishop (1943), Vince Hanson (1945).

WEBER STATE

OFFICIAL NAME: Weber State University.

NICKNAME: Wildcats.

ADDRESS: Wildcat Stadium, Ogden, UT 84408-2702.

PHONE/FAX: (801) 626-6010/6490.

ENROLLMENT: 14,500.

ARENA: Dee Events Center (Capacity-12,000; Year Opened-1977).

SCHOOL COLORS: Royal Purple and White.

CONFERENCE: Big Sky.

NCAA TOURNAMENT APPEARANCES (11): 1968-69-70-71-72-73-78-79-80-83-95; 5-12 record (.294).

NIT APPEARANCES (1): 1984; 1-1 record (.500).

ALL-TIME WINNINGEST COACH: Neil McCarthy (11 years from 1975-85, 200-98 record, .671).

ALL-TIME SCORING LEADER: Bruce Collins (2,019 points from 1977-80).

ALL-TIME REBOUNDING LEADER: Willie Sojourner (1,143 from 1969-71).

WEST VIRGINIA

OFFICIAL NAME: West Virginia University.

NICKNAME: Mountaineers.

ADDRESS: Post Office Box 0877, Morgantown, WV 26507-0877.

PHONE/FAX: (304) 293-2821/4105.

ENROLLMENT: 22,710.

ARENA: WVU Coliseum (Capacity-14,000; Year Opened-1970).

SCHOOL COLORS: Old Gold and Blue.

CONFERENCE: Big East.

FINAL AP TOP 10 RANKINGS (6): 1952-57-58-59-60-61.

NCAA TOURNAMENT APPEARANCES (17): 1955-56-57-58-59-60-62-63-65-67-82-83-84-86-87-89-92; 11-17 record (.393); reached Final Four in 1959 (2nd).

NIT APPEARANCES (12): 1942-45-46-47-68-81-85-88-91-93-94-97; 14-13 record (.519); finished 1st in 1942, 3rd in 1946, 4th in 1947 and 4th in 1981.

ALL-TIME WINNINGEST COACH: Gale Catlett (19 years from 1979-97, 366-207 record, .639).

ALL-TIME SCORING LEADER: Jerry West (2,309 points from 1958-60).

ALL-TIME REBOUNDING LEADER: Jerry West (1,240 from 1958-60).

NCAA CONSENSUS FIRST-TEAM ALL-AMERICANS (3): Rod Hundley (1957), Jerry West (1959 and 1960).

NCAA CONSENSUS SECOND-TEAM ALL-AMERICANS (4): Mark Workman (1952), Rod Hundley (1956), Rod Thorn (1962 and 1963).

WESTERN CAROLINA

OFFICIAL NAME: Western Carolina University.

NICKNAME: Catamounts.

ADDRESS: Ramsey Center, Cullowhee, NC 28723.

PHONE/FAX: (704) 227-7171/7688.

ENROLLMENT: 6,500.

ARENA: Ramsey Center (Capacity-7,826; Year Opened-1987).

SCHOOL COLORS: Purple and Gold.

CONFERENCE: Southern.

NCAA TOURNAMENT APPEARANCES (1): 1996; 0-1 record.

NAIA TOURNAMENT APPEARANCES (3): 1947-63-72; 4-3 record (.571); finished runner-up in 1963.

ALL-TIME WINNINGEST COACH: Jim Gudger (19 years from 1951-69 when the school was classified as a small college, 311-222 record, .583).

ALL-TIME SCORING LEADER: Henry Logan (3,290 points from 1965-68 when school was classified as a small college).

ALL-TIME REBOUNDING LEADER: Greg Wittman (1,354 from 1966-69 when school was classified as a small college).

WESTERN KENTUCKY

OFFICIAL NAME: Western Kentucky University.

NICKNAME: Hilltoppers.

ADDRESS: College Heights, Bowling Green, KY 42101.

PHONE/FAX: (502) 745-4298/3444.

ENROLLMENT: 15,400.

ARENA: E.A. Diddle Arena (Capacity-11,300; Year Opened-1963).

SCHOOL COLORS: Red and White.

CONFERENCE: Sun Belt.

FINAL AP TOP 10 RANKINGS (6): 1949-50-54-66-67-71.

NCAA TOURNAMENT APPEARANCES (16): 1940-60-62-66-67-70-71-76-78-80-81-86-87-93-94-95; 15-17 record (.469); reached Final Four in 1971 (3rd).

NAIA TOURNAMENT APPEARANCES (1): 1938; 0-1 record.

NIT APPEARANCES (11): 1942-43-48-49-50-52-53-54-65-82-92; 8-12 record (.400); finished 2nd in 1942, 3rd in 1948 and 4th in 1954.

ALL-TIME WINNINGEST COACH: Ed Diddle (42 years from 1923-64, 759-302 record, .715).

ALL-TIME SCORING LEADER: Jim McDaniels (2,238 points from 1969-71).

ALL-TIME REBOUNDING LEADER: Ralph Crosthwaite (1,309 from 1955-59; missed 1955-56 season for disciplinary reasons).

NCAA CONSENSUS FIRST-TEAM ALL-AMERICANS (2): Clem Haskins (1967), Jim McDaniels (1971).

NCAA CONSENSUS SECOND-TEAM ALL-AMERICANS (1): Tom Marshall (1954).

WESTERN MICHIGAN

OFFICIAL NAME: Western Michigan University.

NICKNAME: Broncos.

ADDRESS: University Arena, Kalamazoo, MI 49008-5166.

PHONE/FAX: (616) 387-4138/4139.

ENROLLMENT: 26,675.

ARENA: University Arena (Capacity-5,800; Year Opened-1957 as Read Fieldhouse; renovated as University Arena for 1995).

SCHOOL COLORS: Brown and Gold.

CONFERENCE: Mid-American.

FINAL AP TOP 10 RANKINGS (1): 1976.

NCAA TOURNAMENT APPEARANCES (1): 1976; 1-1 record (.500).

NIT APPEARANCES (1): 1992; 0-1 record.

ALL-TIME WINNINGEST COACH: Herbert "Buck" Read (27 years from 1923-49, 351-171 record, .672).

ALL-TIME SCORING LEADER: Manny Newsome (1,786 points from 1962-64).

ALL-TIME REBOUNDING LEADER: Paul Griffin (1,008 from 1973-76).

WICHITA STATE

OFFICIAL NAME: Wichita State University.

NICKNAME: Shockers.

ADDRESS: Campus Box 18, Wichita, KS 67260-0018.

PHONE/FAX: (316) 689-3265/3336.

ENROLLMENT: 15,000.

ARENA: Levitt Arena (Capacity-10,656; Year Opened-1955).

SCHOOL COLORS: Yellow and Black.

CONFERENCE: Missouri Valley.

FINAL AP TOP 10 RANKINGS (2): 1963 and 1964.

NCAA TOURNAMENT APPEARANCES (7): 1964-65-76-81-85-87-88; 6-8 record (.429); reached Final Four in 1965 (4th).

NAIA TOURNAMENT APPEARANCES (2): 1945 and 1946; 0-2 record.

NIT APPEARANCES (7): 1954-62-63-66-80-84-89; 1-7 record (.125).

ALL-TIME WINNINGEST COACH: Ralph Miller (13 years from 1952-64, 220-133 record, .623).

ALL-TIME SCORING LEADER: Cleo Littleton (2,164 points from 1952-55).

ALL-TIME REBOUNDING LEADER: Xavier McDaniel (1,359 from 1982-85).

NCAA CONSENSUS FIRST-TEAM ALL-AMERICANS (2): Dave Stallworth (1964), Xavier McDaniel (1985).

NCAA CONSENSUS SECOND-TEAM ALL-AMERICANS (1): Dave Stallworth (1965).

WILLIAM & MARY

OFFICIAL NAME: College of William & Mary.

NICKNAME: Tribe.

ADDRESS: Post Office Box 399, Williamsburg, VA 23187.

PHONE/FAX: (757) 221-3344/3412.

ENROLLMENT: 5,300.

ARENA: William & Mary Hall (Capacity-10,000; Year Opened-1969).

SCHOOL COLORS: Green, Gold and Silver.

CONFERENCE: Colonial Athletic Association.

NCAA TOURNAMENT APPEARANCES: None.

NIT APPEARANCES (1): 1983; 0-1 record.

ALL-TIME WINNINGEST COACH: William B. Chambers (nine years from 1958-66, 113-110 record, .507).

ALL-TIME SCORING LEADER: Chet Giermak (2,052 points from 1947-50).

ALL-TIME REBOUNDING LEADER: Jeff Cohen (1,679 from 1958-61).

WISCONSIN

OFFICIAL NAME: University of Wisconsin (At Madison).

NICKNAME: Badgers.

ADDRESS: 1440 Monroe Street, Madison, WI 53711.

PHONE/FAX: (608) 262-1811/8184.

ENROLLMENT: 40,305.

ARENA: Kohl Center (Capacity-16,500; Year Opened-1998).

SCHOOL COLORS: Cardinal and White.

CONFERENCE: Big Ten.

NCAA TOURNAMENT APPEARANCES (4): 1941-47-94-97; 5-3 record (.625); reached Final Four in 1941 (1st).

NIT APPEARANCES (4): 1989-91-93-96; 3-4 record (.429).

ALL-TIME WINNINGEST COACH: Harold "Bud" Foster (25 years from 1935-59, 265-267 record, .498).

ALL-TIME SCORING LEADER: Michael Finley (2,147 points from 1992-95).

ALL-TIME REBOUNDING LEADER: Claude Gregory (904 from 1978-81).

NCAA CONSENSUS FIRST-TEAM ALL-AMERICANS (2): Gene Englund (1941), John Kotz (1942).

NCAA CONSENSUS SECOND-TEAM ALL-AMERICANS (2): John Kotz (1943), Don Rehfeldt (1950).

WISCONSIN-GREEN BAY

OFFICIAL NAME: University of Wisconsin (At Green Bay).

NICKNAME: Phoenix.

ADDRESS: Phoenix Sports Center, 2420 Nicolet Drive, Green Bay, WI 54311-7001.

PHONE/FAX: (414) 465-2145/2357.

ENROLLMENT: 5,000.

ARENA: Brown County Veterans Memorial Arena (Capacity-5,600; Year Opened-1958).

SCHOOL COLORS: Red, Green and White.

CONFERENCE: Midwestern Collegiate.

NCAA DIVISION I TOURNAMENT APPEARANCES (4): 1991-94-95-96; 1-4 record (.200).

NCAA DIVISION II TOURNAMENT APPEARANCES (6): 1974-76-77-78-79-81; 13-8 record (.619); finished 2nd in 1978 and 1979, and 4th in 1981.

NAIA TOURNAMENT APPEARANCES (1): 1973; 2-1 record (.667).

NIT APPEARANCES (2): 1990 and 1992; 1-2 record (.333).

ALL-TIME WINNINGEST COACH: Dave Buss (13 years from 1970-82 when school was classified as a small college most of that span, 271-94 record, .742).

ALL-TIME SCORING LEADER: Tony Bennett (2,285 points from 1989-92).

ALL-TIME REBOUNDING LEADER: Dennis Woelffer (947 from 1970-73 when school was classified as a small college).

WRIGHT STATE

OFFICIAL NAME: Wright State University.

NICKNAME: Raiders.

ADDRESS: 3640 Col. Glenn Highway, Dayton, OH 45435.

PHONE/FAX: (937) 775-2816/2368.

ENROLLMENT: 16,490.

ARENA: Ervin J. Nutter Center (Capacity-10,632; Year Opened-1990).

SCHOOL COLORS: Green and Gold.

CONFERENCE: Midwestern Collegiate.

NCAA DIVISION I TOURNAMENT APPEARANCES (1): 1993; 0-1 record.

NCAA DIVISION II TOURNAMENT APPEARANCES (8): 1976-79-80-81-82-83-85-86; 12-7 record (.632); finished 1st in 1983.

ALL-TIME WINNINGEST COACH: Ralph Underhill (18 years from 1979-96, 356-162 record, .687).

ALL-TIME SCORING LEADER: Bill Edwards (2,303 points from 1990-93).

ALL-TIME REBOUNDING LEADER: Bill Edwards (907 from 1990-93).

WYOMING

OFFICIAL NAME: University of Wyoming.

NICKNAME: Cowboys.

ADDRESS: Post Office Box 3414, Fieldhouse-North Addition, Laramie, WY 82071-3414.

PHONE/FAX: (307) 766-2256/2346.

ENROLLMENT: 11,000.

ARENA: Arena-Auditorium (Capacity-15,028; Year Opened-1982).

SCHOOL COLORS: Brown and Yellow.

CONFERENCE: Western Athletic.

NCAA TOURNAMENT APPEARANCES (13): 1941-43-47-48-49-52-53-58-67-81-82-87-88; 8-18 record (.308); reached Final Four in 1943 (1st).

NIT APPEARANCES (4): 1968-69-86-91; 5-4 record (.556); finished 2nd in 1986.

ALL-TIME WINNINGEST COACH: Everett Shelton (19 years from 1940-43 and 1945-59, 328-201 record, .620).

ALL-TIME SCORING LEADER: Fennis Dembo (2,311 points from 1985-88).

ALL-TIME REBOUNDING LEADER: Reginald Slater (1,197 from 1989-92).

NCAA CONSENSUS FIRST-TEAM ALL-AMERICANS (3): Les Witte (1932 and 1934), Ken Sailors (1943).

NCAA CONSENSUS SECOND-TEAM ALL-AMERICANS (1): Ken Sailors (1946).

XAVIER

OFFICIAL NAME: Xavier University.

NICKNAME: Musketeers.

ADDRESS: 3800 Victory Parkway, Cincinnati, OH 45207-6114.

PHONE/FAX: (513) 745-3416/2825.

ENROLLMENT: 6,125.

ARENA: Cincinnati Gardens (Capacity-10,400; Year Opened-1949); school trustees approved construction of a $39 million, 10,700-seat on-campus arena to be ready for the 1999-2000 season.

SCHOOL COLORS: Blue and White.

CONFERENCE: Atlantic 10.

NCAA TOURNAMENT APPEARANCES (11): 1961-83-86-87-88-89-90-91-93-95-97; 6-11 record (.353).

NAIA TOURNAMENT APPEARANCES (1): 1948; finished 4th with 3-2 record (.600).

NIT APPEARANCES (5): 1956-57-58-84-94; 10-4 record (.714); finished 1st in 1958.

ALL-TIME WINNINGEST COACH: Pete Gillen (nine years from 1986-94, 202-75 record, .729).

ALL-TIME SCORING LEADER: Byron Larkin (2,696 points from 1985-88).

ALL-TIME REBOUNDING LEADER: Tyrone Hill (1,380 from 1987-90).

YALE

OFFICIAL NAME: Yale University.
NICKNAMES: Elis, Bulldogs.
ADDRESS: Box 208216, New Haven, CT 06520-8216.
PHONE/FAX: (203) 432-1455/1454.
ENROLLMENT: 5,200.
ARENA: John J. Lee Amphitheater (Capacity-3,100; Year Opened-1932).
SCHOOL COLORS: Yale Blue and White.
CONFERENCE: Ivy League.
NCAA TOURNAMENT APPEARANCES (3): 1949-57-62; 0-4 record.
NIT APPEARANCES: None.
ALL-TIME WINNINGEST COACH: Joe Vancisin (19 years from 1957-75, 207-241 record, .462).
ALL-TIME SCORING LEADER: Butch Graves (2,090 points from 1981-84).
ALL-TIME REBOUNDING LEADER: Ed Robinson (1,182 from 1955-57).
NCAA CONSENSUS FIRST-TEAM ALL-AMERICANS (1): Tony Lavelli (1949).
NCAA CONSENSUS SECOND-TEAM ALL-AMERICANS (2): Tony Lavelli (1946 and 1948).

FORMER MAJOR COLLEGES WITH AN NCAA CONSENSUS FIRST TEAM ALL-AMERICAN

Denver: Vince Boryla (1949 after playing two previous seasons for Notre Dame)
New York University: Sid Tannenbaum (1946 and 1947), Barry Kramer (1963)
Seattle: Johnny O'Brien (1953), Elgin Baylor (1957)
West Texas State: Price Brookfield (1942)
Note: Denver, which de-emphasized its program in 1980, is slated to ready to NCAA Division I status in the 1998-1999 season.

FORMER MAJOR COLLEGES WITH AT LEAST ONE NATIONAL POSTSEASON VICTORY

SCHOOL/LAST YEAR IN DIVISION I NCAA	NIT	CURRENT STATUS
City College of New York/1953 4-2	6-3	Division III
Muhlenberg (Pa.)/1963 0-0	1-4	Division III
New York University/1971 9-9	13-10	Division III
Oklahoma City/1985 8-13	0-2	NAIA
Seattle/1980 10-13	0-2	NAIA
Washington and Jefferson (Pa.) 0-0	2-1	Division III
Wayne State (Mich.)/1950 1-2	0-0	Division II

Note: Three of these schools finished at least two seasons ranked among the Top 20 in a final AP or UPI poll—NYU (1960 and 1963), Oklahoma City (1953-57-59) and Seattle (1952-53-54-56-57-58-59-63).

THE NAME GAME

Here is a look at some of the name changes since 1930 of current Division I schools:

- Alcorn State (formerly Alcorn A&M)
- Arizona State (Tempe Normal until 1925 and Tempe Teachers until 1945)
- Arkansas-Little Rock (formerly Little Rock University)
- Auburn (formerly Alabama Poly)
- Boise State (Boise College until 1974)
- Bradley (formerly Bradley Tech)
- UC Santa Barbara (formerly Santa Barbara State College)
- Cal State Fullerton (formerly Orange County State College, Orange State College and California State College at Fullerton)
- Cal State Northridge (San Fernando Valley State from 1958 to 1972)
- Central Florida (Florida Tech until 1978)
- Central Michigan (formerly Central Michigan Normal and Business Institute)
- Charleston Southern (formerly Baptist College)
- Cleveland State (Fenn College until 1965)
- Colorado State (Colorado Agriculture until 1935, Colorado State College until 1941, and Colorado A&M until 1957)
- Detroit Mercy (University of Detroit and Mercy College of Detroit merged in 1990)
- Duke (Trinity until 1925)
- Georgia Southern (formerly Georgia Teachers College)
- Grambling State (formerly Grambling College)
- Idaho State (Idaho-Southern Branch until 1946 and Idaho State College until 1963)
- Iowa State (formerly Iowa Agricultural College)
- James Madison (Madison College from 1938 until 1977)
- Kent (formerly Kent State)
- Liberty (formerly Lynchburg Baptist College and Liberty Baptist College)
- Loyola Marymount (Loyola University until 1930, merged with Marymount College in 1968, and name changed in 1973)
- Massachusetts (Massachusetts Agricultural College until 1931 and Massachusetts State College until 1947)
- Memphis (West Tennessee State Normal School until 1925, West Tennessee State Teachers College until 1941, Memphis State College until 1957 and Memphis State University until 1994)
- Missouri-Kansas City (formerly University of Kansas City)
- Montana (formerly Montana State College)
- Nevada (formerly Nevada-Reno)
- New Mexico State (New Mexico Agriculture until 1933, New Mexico State College until 1942, and New Mexico A&M until 1960)
- New Orleans (LSU in New Orleans—LSUNO—until 1974)
- North Carolina State (formerly North Carolina College of Agriculture and Mechanic Arts)
- Northern Arizona (Northern Arizona State Teachers College until 1945 and Arizona State College at Flagstaff until 1966)
- Northern Colorado (formerly Colorado State College)
- Northern Iowa (Iowa State Teachers College from 1909 to 1961 and State College of Iowa until 1967)
- North Texas (formerly North Texas State)
- Northwestern State (Louisiana State Normal College until mid-1940s)
- Oklahoma State (Oklahoma A&M until 1957)
- Oregon State (Oregon Agriculture until 1927)
- Portland (Columbia University until 1935)
- Rhode Island (formerly Rhode Island State College)
- Sam Houston State (formerly Sam Houston Normal Institute and Sam Houston State Teachers College)
- San Francisco (St. Ignatius until 1930)
- Southeastern Louisiana University (Southeastern Louisiana College from 1928 to 1970)
- Southern Mississippi (Hattiesburg Teachers until 1940 and Mississippi Southern until 1962)
- Southern Utah State (formerly Branch Agricultural College)
- Southwest Missouri State (formerly Southwest Missouri State Teachers College and Southwest Missouri State College until 1972)

- Tennessee State (Tennessee A&I until merger with University of Tennessee at Nashville in 1979)
- Tennessee Tech (Tennessee Polytechnic Institute until 196?)
- Texas-El Paso (Texas Mines until 1949 and Texas Western College until 1967; tried to implement acronymn UTEP, but it wasn't accepted)
- Texas-Pan American (formerly Pan American)
- Tulsa (Henry Kendall College until 1921)
- UAB (formerly Alabama-Birmingham)
- UCLA (Los Angeles Normal until 1919 and UC Southern Branch until 1930)
- UNLV (Nevada Southern until 1969)
- Utah State (Utah Agricultural College until 1932)
- Virginia Commonwealth (Richmond Professional Institute until 1968)
- Wichita State (Fairmount until 1927 and Wichita until 1964)
- Wisconsin-Milwaukee (Wisconsin State Normal School until 1927, Milwaukee State Teachers College until 1951 and Wisconsin State College-Milwaukee until 1956)

RECORDS IN NATIONAL POSTSEASON COMPETITION
(Minimum of 25 tournament games through 1997)

SCHOOL	NCAA APP.	NCAA W-L	NCAA PCT.	NIT APP.	NIT W-L	NIT PCT.	OVERALL APP.	OVERALL W-L	OVERALL PCT.
UCLA	33	77-26	.748	2	5-1	.833	35	82-27	.752
Indiana*	26	50-21	.704	3	8-2	.800	30	61-23	.726
Michigan	19	40-18	.690	6	15-4	.789	25	55-22	.714
Duke	21	57-19	.750	5	5-6	.455	26	62-25	.713
North Carolina	31	72-31	.699	4	7-3	.700	35	79-34	.699
UNLV	12	30-11	.732	4	6-5	.545	16	36-16	.692
Kentucky	39	77-35	.688	7	11-5	.688	46	88-40	.688
Kansas	26	56-26	.683	2	3-2	.600	28	59-28	.678
Minnesota	7	12-7	.632	7	13-6	.684	14	25-13	.658
Ohio State	18	31-17	.646	6	13-6	.684	24	44-23	.657
Virginia Tech	7	5-7	.417	7	17-5	.773	14	22-12	.647
Virginia	14	21-14	.600	7	13-5	.722	21	34-19	.642
Purdue*	16	19-16	.543	6	18-5	.783	23	38-22	.633
Arkansas	22	37-22	.627	2	4-3	.571	24	41-25	.621
San Francisco	15	21-13	.618	4	5-3	.625	19	26-16	.619
Georgetown	21	36-20	.643	5	6-6	.500	26	42-26	.618
Cincinnati	16	32-15	.681	8	5-8	.385	24	37-23	.617
Villanova	24	37-24	.607	12	19-12	.613	36	56-36	.609
Bradley*	7	9-7	.563	18	25-15	.625	26	35-23	.603
N.C. State	17	27-16	.628	7	8-7	.533	24	35-23	.603
Dayton	10	13-12	.520	17	29-16	.644	27	42-28	.600
Marquette	21	28-22	.560	11	18-9	.667	32	46-31	.597
Oklahoma State	14	25-13	.658	7	6-8	.429	21	31-21	.596
Wake Forest	15	22-15	.595	2	3-2	.600	17	25-17	.595
California	10	16-10	.615	3	3-3	.500	13	19-13	.594
Providence	13	14-14	.500	14	28-15	.651	27	42-29	.592
Florida State	9	11-9	.550	3	6-3	.667	12	17-12	.586
Louisville	27	48-29	.623	12	10-12	.455	39	58-41	.586
Maryland	14	17-14	.548	7	7-3	.700	21	24-17	.585
Boston College	11	16-12	.571	9	15-10	.600	20	31-22	.585
Vanderbilt	7	5-8	.385	6	13-5	.722	13	18-13	.581
Michigan State	11	17-11	.607	5	6-6	.500	16	23-17	.575
Georgia Tech	11	16-11	.593	4	4-4	.500	15	20-15	.571
Oklahoma	16	20-16	.556	6	9-6	.600	22	29-22	.569
Arizona*	16	23-15	.605	3	0-3	.000	20	25-19	.568
Syracuse	23	35-24	.593	9	7-9	.438	32	42-33	.560
Nebraska	5	0-5	.000	11	19-10	.655	16	19-15	.559
Iowa	18	24-20	.545	1	2-1	.667	19	26-21	.553
Illinois	18	22-19	.537	3	5-3	.625	21	27-22	.551
St. Bonaventure	4	6-6	.500	12	17-13	.567	16	23-19	.548
Notre Dame	24	25-28	.472	6	16-6	.727	30	41-34	.547
Temple	21	24-21	.533	12	13-10	.565	33	37-31	.544
St. John's	23	23-25	.479	26	41-29	.586	49	64-54	.542
Alabama	14	15-14	.517	7	13-10	.565	21	28-24	.538
Utah	19	25-22	.532	11	11-9	.550	30	36-31	.537
Colorado	9	9-11	.450	4	7-3	.700	13	16-14	.533
Penn State	7	7-9	.438	6	9-6	.600	13	16-15	.516
Xavier	11	6-11	.353	5	10-4	.714	16	16-15	.516
Connecticut	19	17-20	.459	10	13-9	.591	29	30-29	.508
Houston	18	26-23	.531	6	4-6	.400	24	30-29	.508
Florida	5	7-5	.583	6	6-8	.429	11	13-13	.500
Kansas State*	22	27-26	.509	3	4-4	.500	26	31-31	.500
La Salle	11	11-10	.524	11	9-10	.474	22	20-20	.500
Massachusetts	7	11-7	.611	8	5-9	.357	15	16-16	.500
Saint Louis	4	2-5	.286	16	18-15	.545	20	20-20	.500
Texas	16	16-19	.457	4	6-3	.667	20	22-22	.500
Seton Hall	6	12-6	.667	11	6-13	.316	17	18-19	.486
Holy Cross	8	7-8	.467	11	10-10	.500	19	17-18	.486
Rutgers	6	5-7	.417	9	10-9	.526	15	15-16	.484
UAB	9	6-9	.400	6	8-6	.571	15	14-15	.483
DePaul	20	20-23	.465	12	13-13	.500	32	33-36	.478
Duquesne	5	4-5	.444	16	17-18	.486	21	21-23	.477

Team										
Texas-El Paso	14	14-13	.519	7	4-7	.364	21	18-20	.474
Clemson	6	8-6	.571	10	6-10	.375	16	14-16	.467
Louisiana State	15	17-18	.486	3	2-4	.333	18	19-22	.463
Georgia	7	6-7	.462	7	6-7	.462	14	12-14	.462
Memphis	16	18-16	.529	12	6-12	.333	28	24-28	.462
West Virginia	17	11-17	.393	12	14-13	.519	29	25-30	.455
Tennessee*	9	5-10	.333	9	12-9	.571	20	17-21	.447
Western Kentucky	16	15-17	.469	11	8-12	.400	27	23-29	.442
Washington	8	8-9	.471	5	3-5	.375	13	11-14	.440
Brigham Young	18	11-21	.344	7	9-5	.643	25	20-26	.435
St. Joseph's	15	14-19	.424	11	9-11	.450	26	23-30	.434
Santa Clara	10	10-12	.455	4	2-4	.333	14	12-16	.429
New Mexico	8	4-9	.308	13	13-14	.481	21	17-23	.425
Arizona State*	11	11-12	.478	5	2-5	.286	17	13-18	.419
Tulsa	10	6-10	.375	7	5-6	.455	17	11-16	.407
Penn	16	13-18	.419	1	0-1	.000	17	13-19	.406
Oregon State	16	12-19	.387	3	3-3	.500	19	15-22	.405
Princeton	20	12-24	.333	2	5-1	.833	22	17-25	.405
Missouri*	16	13-16	.448	4	1-4	.200	21	14-21	.400
New Mexico State	15	10-17	.370	3	3-3	.500	18	13-20	.394
Rhode Island	6	3-6	.333	9	7-10	.412	15	10-16	.385
Pitt	13	8-14	.364	7	5-7	.417	20	13-21	.382
Wyoming	13	8-18	.308	4	5-4	.556	17	13-22	.371
Southern Cal*	10	6-12	.333	3	2-3	.400	15	10-17	.370
Bowling Green*	4	1-5	.167	11	6-11	.353	16	8-17	.320
Utah State	11	5-13	.278	5	2-5	.286	16	7-18	.280
Manhattan	4	2-5	.286	16	6-17	.261	20	8-22	.267
Fordham	4	2-4	.333	16	5-17	.227	20	7-21	.250
Miami of Ohio	15	4-17	.190	4	2-4	.333	19	6-21	.222

*In the mid-1970s, the NCAA introduced a short-lived, eight-team tournament ostensibly to showcase league runners-up but principally to erode the NIT's influence. The tourney was called the Collegiate Commissioners Association Tournament in 1974, when Indiana won the title at St. Louis, and then changed to the National Commissioners Invitational Tournament in 1975, when Drake won the title at Louisville. High-profile school records in the event included: Arizona (2-1), Arizona State (0-1), Bowling Green (1-1), Bradley (1-1), Drake (3-0), Indiana (3-0), Kansas State (0-1), Missouri (0-1), Purdue (1-1), Southern Cal (2-2), SMU (0-1), Tennessee (0-2) and Toledo (1-1).

17

PIONEERS OF THE GAME

I n the aftermath of the 50th anniversary celebration of Jackie Robinson beginning his major league baseball career, it is easy to forget there was a time when the now 75 percent African American National Basketball Association was 100 percent white. It's also easy to forget that Robinson was instrumental in college basketball's "civil rights" movement.

In 1930-31, Columbia's George Gregory became the first African American to gain college All-America honors. The first black to appear in the NBA, however, didn't occur until 20 years later.

UCLA's Don Barksdale, one of the first seven African Americans to play in the NBA, was the first black U.S. Olympic basketball player (1948) as well as the first black to play in an NBA All-Star Game (1952). UCLA's initial all-conference basketball player in the 1940s had been the multi-talented Robinson, a forward who compiled the highest scoring average in the Pacific Coast Conference both of his seasons with the Bruins (12.3 points per league game in 1939-40 and 11.1 in 1940-41) after transferring from Pasadena (Calif.) City College.

There are ramifications when assessing the issue of race and it would be nice if we were all color blind. Nonetheless, it's impossible to properly evaluate the history of college basketball without adressing the sensitive topic.

The integration of college basketball, waiting primarily on the South to emerge from the "Jim Crow" dark ages, wasn't complete until the mid-1970s. Although overt racism probably wasn't quite as pervasive as in professional sports, many of the African American players who broke the color barriers at colleges during the post-World War II era faced more than their share of hardships and hostility.

"They (opposing fans) were all just rabid," recalls Perry Wallace, Vanderbilt's standout forward who became the first black varsity player in the all-white Southeastern Conference in 1967-68. "I'm talking racial stuff, people threatening your life ... calling you 'nigger,' 'coon,' 'shoe polish.' The first time I played Ole Miss I got spat on at halftime by four generations of one family."

Wallace, a local product of Nashville who went on to become a tenured law professor at the University of Baltimore, encountered raucous road trips through the Deep South, where belligerent spectators drenched him with their drinks and cheerleaders led the crowd in racist chants. In Mississippi, he was punched in the eye by an opposing player whom he knew he couldn't fight back.

Wallace told the Nashville Business & Lifestyles that "I'm not one of these historical revisionists who tries to claim he was all-smart and all-seeing back in those days. Everybody knew that what was happening was important. You've got to understand that this was post-legal segregation, but it was de facto segregation."

In an interview with The Tennessean, Wallace spoke of also feeling alienated from classmates at Vandy, of being informed by members of the campus church that elders there would withhold contributions if he attended.

"I can't say it any other way," Wallace confided. "I have been there by myself. It's been a very lonesome thing. People knew my name but weren't interested in knowing me. They respected my basketball ability but still considered me as a person who sweeps floors."

Henry Harris, the first black athlete at Auburn and, for a while, the only black Wallace played against in the SEC, took his own life by jumping off a building in New York soon after he left college. And Tom Payne, who broke the color barrier at Kentucky a year after Wallace graduated, has been in prison for an extended period. "Tom Payne had a tragic life and it wasn't all owing to playing in the SEC, but that didn't help," Wallace asserts. "You have to take the time that it requires to recover from an experience like that. You have to heal right. And fortunately, I think I have. I'm not destroyed. I've wrestled with the emotional effect that experience has had on my life. That was a process that was not easy those first few years, but I did it."

To be sure, things have changed drastically in society for minority groups. Robinson and Wallace could only do so much. The following list of individuals who broke the color barrier at schools since the start of the 1950s, the generally accepted introduction of the modern era of college basketball, deserve special mention for paving the path for thousands of black athletes by taking giant steps toward bridging the racial chasm:

SCHOOL	FIRST AFRICAN AMERICAN PLAYER (FIRST VARSITY SEASON)
Air Force	Jimmy Love (1960-61)
	Statistics are unavailable.
Alabama	Wendell Hudson (1970-71)
	Averaged 19.2 ppg and 12 rpg in his career, finishing as Bama's fourth-leading scorer and second-leading rebounder. The two-time first-team All-SEC selection was a Helms All-America choice as a senior in 1972-73.
Arizona	Hadie Redd (1953-54)
	Led the Wildcats in scoring (13.2 ppg and 13.6) and rebounding (7 rpg and 9.4) in both of his varsity seasons.
Arizona State	John Burton/Carl Miller (1953-54)
	Burton averaged 7.1ppg in three seasons. Miller averaged 4.4 ppg in his lone season while playing on the varsity as a freshman.
Arkansas	Thomas Johnson (1968-69)
	Averaged 15.5 ppg for 1967-68 freshman squad.
Arkansas State	Milton Sullivan (1966-67 when school was a small college)
Auburn	Henry Harris (1969-70)
	Averaged 11.8 ppg, 6.7 rpg and 2.5 apg in three-year varsity career. Standout defensive player was captain of Auburn's team as a senior.
Austin Peay St.	L.M. Ellis (1963-64)
Ball State	Stan Davis (1951-52 when school was a small college)
	All-Indiana Collegiate Conference choice as a senior when he averaged a team-high 18.5 ppg.
Baylor	Tommy Bowman (1967-68)
	Led the Bears in scoring (13.5 ppg) and rebounding (9.4 rpg) in his first varsity season. All-Southwest Conference choice in '67-68 and '68-69.
Bowling Green	Chrystal "Boo" Ellis (1951-52)
	Averaged 7.3 ppg in two varsity seasons.
Bradley	Curly Johnson/Shellie McMillon (1955-56)
	Members of 1957 NIT champion. Johnson averaged 4.8 ppg in three varsity seasons. McMillon averaged 14.1 ppg and 9.3 rpg in three varsity seasons, including a team-high 16.4 ppg in 1956-57. McMillon, who scored 42 points vs. Detroit, was an All-Missouri Valley Conference choice as a senior.
Brigham Young	*Gary Batiste (1974-75)
	Statistics are unavailable.
Butler	Henry Foster (1954-55)
	Scored 316 points in three seasons despite not having played basketball in high school. Led the Bulldogs in rebounding in 1955-56.
Centenary	*Jesse Marshall (1968-69)
	Led the Gents in scoring (16 ppg) and rebounding (9.6 rpg) as a senior after being their second-leading scorer (15.9 ppg) and leading rebounder (10.2 rpg) as a junior.
Central Michigan	Charles Pruitt (1952-53 when school was a small college)
	Averaged 6.3 ppg in two seasons.
The Citadel	*Oscar Scott (1971-72)
	Three-year service veteran averaged 11.8 ppg and 7 rpg in two seasons. He led the Bulldogs in rebounding as a senior.
Clemson	Craig Mobley (1970-71)
	Played sparingly in his only season.
Colorado	Billy Lewis (1957-58)
	Averaged 3.6 ppg and 2.9 rpg in three seasons.
Colorado State	Waymon Anderson (1955-56)
	Forward-center played sparingly in his two varsity seasons.

Cornell   Henry Buncom (1952-53)

Scored 209 points in three seasons. He was the team's second-leading rebounder as a sophomore.

Creighton   Bob Gibson (1954-55)

Future Baseball Hall of Famer was the school's first player to average at least 20 points per game in his career (20.2).

Dartmouth   Dick Fairley (1952-53)

Averaged 5.7 ppg in three seasons. Led the team in rebounding as a junior (8.7 ppg).

Davidson   Mike Maloy (1967-68)

Three-time All-America averaged 19.3 ppg and 12.4 rpg in his career. Southern Conference Player of the Year as a junior and senior. He was the leading scorer (24.6 ppg) and rebounder (14.3 rpg) on the winningest team in school history (27-3 in 1968-69).

Delaware   Charley Parnell (1966-67)

First-team All-East Coast Conference choice led the Blue Hens in scoring with 18.5 ppg.

Drake   Johnny Bright (1949-50)

All-America football halfback and future member of the Canadian Football Hall of Fame scored 35 points in 17 games for the Bulldogs' basketball team.

Duke   C.B. Claiborne (1966-67)

Averaged 4.1 ppg in three seasons.

East Carolina   *Vince Colbert (1966-67)

Averaged 14.3 ppg and 7.3 rpg in two seasons. He led the team in rebounding as a junior (7.1 rpg).

Eastern Kentucky   Garfield Smith (1965-66)

Averaged 14.5 ppg and 13.2 rpg in three seasons. He was an All-Ohio Valley Conference choice as a senior when he finished second in the nation in rebounding (19.7 rpg).

East Tenn. State   Tommy Woods (1964-65)

Two-time All-Ohio Valley Conference choice averaged 15.3 ppg and 16.2 rpg in three seasons. He grabbed 38 rebounds in a game vs. Middle Tennessee en route to finishing third in the nation in rebounding as a sophomore (19.6 rpg).

Evansville   Jim Smallins (1954-55 when school was a small college)

Averaged 10.3 ppg in three varsity seasons. Smallins had a school-record 31 rebounds in a game vs. Kentucky Wesleyan as a senior, when he averaged 16.3 ppg.

Florida   Malcolm Meeks/Steve Williams (1971-72)

Meeks played sparingly in two seasons. Williams, who averaged 8 ppg and 5.2 rpg in three varsity seasons, was the Gators' second-leading scorer as a sophomore (12.8 ppg).

Florida State   John Burt/*Willie Williams/Skip Young (1968-69)

Burt averaged 3.6 ppg and 2.4 rpg in three seasons. Williams averaged 12.5 ppg and 10.3 rpg in two seasons and led the nation in field-goal shooting as a senior (63.6%). Young averaged 11.7 ppg in three seasons, including 15 ppg as a sophomore.

Furman   *Liscio Thomas (1969-70)

Averaged 17 ppg and 9.9 rpg in two seasons. He led the Paladins in scoring as a junior (17.7 ppg) and was the second-leading scorer and rebounder for the 1971 Southern Conference champion.

George Washington   Garland Pinkston (1967-68)

Second-leading scorer (12.5 ppg) and rebounder (7.3 rpg) in his only varsity season for GWU.

Georgia   Ronnie Hogue (1970-71)

Finished three-year varsity career as the second-leading scorer in school history (17.8 ppg). He was an All-SEC choice with 20.5 ppg as a junior, when he set the school single-game scoring record with 46 points vs. LSU.

Georgia Tech   *Karl Binns (1971-72)

He was the leading rebounder (6.5 rpg) and fourth-leading scorer (8.8 ppg) in his only season with the Yellow Jackets.

Gonzaga   Blake Elliott (1956-57)

Air Force veteran averaged 6 ppg and 5.7 rpg in four seasons. He was the school's third-leading scorer as a senior in 1959-60 with 8.5 ppg.

Houston   Don Chaney/Elvin Hayes (1965-66)

Chaney, an All-America as a senior, averaged 12.6 ppg in three seasons and was a member of Final Four teams in 1967 and 1968. Hayes, a three-time All-America, averaged 31 ppg and 17.2 rpg in three seasons. The Hall of Famer led the Cougars in scoring and rebounding all three years.

Idaho   *John Sullivan (1954-55)

Saw limited action in two seasons after joining team following football season. His free throw with seven seconds remaining gave the Vandals an 80-79 victory over Washington in 1954-55.

Illinois   Walt Moore (1951-52)

Scored five points while playing in only four games.

Iowa State   John Crawford (1955-56)

Averaged 13.4 ppg and 9.7 rpg in three seasons. He led the Cyclones in rebounding all three years and paced them in scoring as a senior (14.1 ppg).

Jacksonville   Chip Dublin (1967-68)

Averaged 7.1 ppg in three seasons, including an 8.3 mark for the Dolphins' team that reached the 1970 Final Four. He scored 19 points in a 106-100 victory over top-ranked Kentucky in the 1970 NCAA Tournament.

Kansas   LaVannes Squires (1951-52)

Totaled 32 points and 17 rebounds in 33 games in three seasons. Member of Final Four teams with the Jayhawks in 1952 and 1953.

Kansas State   Gene Wilson (1951-52)

Averaged 5 ppg in three seasons of a career interrupted by military service (missed 1952-53 and 1953-54).

Kentucky   Tom Payne (1970-71)

Led the Wildcats in rebounding (10.1 rpg) and was their second-leading scorer (16.9 ppg) in his only varsity season before turning pro. He had a 39-point, 19-rebound performance vs. LSU.

Lafayette   Earl Brown (1966-67)

La Salle   Jackie Moore (1951-52)

Averaged 10.3 ppg and 12.1 rpg in two seasons. Second-leading rebounder both years for the Explorers behind All-America Tom Gola.

Lehigh   Gene Brown/Harold Lambert (1972-73)

Brown average4d 2.5ppg in two varsity seasons. Lambert averaged 4.6 ppg and 5.1 rpg in two varsity seasons and was captain of the team in 1973-74.

Louisiana State   Collis Temple (1971-72)

Averaged 10.1 ppg and 8.1 rpg in three seasons. Ranked second in the SEC in rebounding (11.1 rpg) and seventh in field-goal shooting (54.9%) as a senior.

Louisville   Wade Houston/Sam Smith/Eddie Whitehead (1963-64)

Houston averaged 6.1 ppg and 3.5 rpg in three seasons. Smith averaged 9.2 ppg and team-high 11 rpg in his only varsity season with the Cardinals before transferring to Kentucky Wesleyan. Whitehead, Louisville's second-leading rebounder as a senior (7.6 rpg), averaged 5.8 ppg and 5.2 rpg in three seasons.

Loyola Marymount   Robert Cox (1953-54)

Averaged 16.9 ppg and 11.1 rpg in two seasons while leading the Lions in both categories each year.

Marquette   Ralph Wilson (1951-52)

Averaged 5.7 ppg in three seasons.

Marshall   Hal Greer (1955-56)

Averaged 19.4 ppg in three sesons. Hall of Famer led the Thundering Herd in rebounding as a junior (13.8 rpg) and senior (11.7 rpg).

Maryland   Billy Jones (1965-66)

Averaged 8.9 ppg and 4.5 rpg in three seasons. He was the Terrapins' third-leading scorer and rebounder as both a junior and senior.

Memphis   Herb Hilliard (1966-67)

Averaged 2.5 ppg and 3.7 rpg in three seasons. He was the Tigers' second-leading rebounder as a junior (5.2 rpg).

Miami (Fla.)   Willie Allen (1968-69)

Averaged 17.2 ppg and 12.2 rpg in three seasons. Led the Hurricanes in scoring (19.9 ppg) and rebounding (17.2 rpg) as a senior.

Michigan   John Codwell/Don Eaddy (1951-52)

Codwell, the Wolverines' second-leading scorer as a junior (10.5 ppg), averaged 6.4 ppg in three seasons. Eaddy, Michigan's top scorer in Big Ten competition as a sophomore (13.8 ppg), averaged 11.4 ppg in four seasons.

Michigan State   Rickey Ayala (1951-52)

One of the smallest players in college history (5-5) averaged 4 ppg in 1951-52 and 5 ppg in 1952-53.

Middle Tenn. State   Willie Brown/Art Polk (1966-67)

Brown, an All-Ohio Valley Conference choice as junior and senior, averaged 20.3 ppg and 7.4 rpg in three seasons en route to finishing his career as the school's all-time scoring leader (1,524 points). Polk, MTSU's second-leading rebounder as a junior and senior, averaged 12.3 ppg and 9.2 rpg in three seasons.

Minnesota   Bobby Bell (1960-61)

Future All-America football tackle and Pro Football Hall of Famer collected four points and four rebounds in three games.

Mississippi   Coolidge Ball (1971-72)

Two-time All-SEC selection (sophomore and junior years) averaged 14.1 ppg and 9.9 rpg in three seasons. He led the Rebels in scoring (16.8 ppg) and was second in rebounding (10.3 rpg) as a sophomore.

Mississippi State   Larry Fry/Jerry Jenkins (1972-73)

Fry averaged 13.8 ppg and 8.1 rpg in three seasons. Jenkins, an All-SEC selection as a junior and senior when he was the Bulldogs' leading scorer each year, averaged 19.3 ppg and 7 rpg in three seasons.

Missouri   Al Abram (1956-57)

Averaged 11 ppg over four seasons. He led the Tigers in scoring (16.1 ppg), rebounding (8.9 rpg) and field-goal shooting (45%) in 1958-59.

Montana State   Larry Chanay (1956-57)

Four-year Air Force veteran finished his four-year college career as the school's all-time leading scorer (2,034 points). He led the Bobcats in scoring all four seasons.

Murray State   Stew Johnson (1963-64)

Averaged 16.8 ppg and 12.9 rpg in three seasons on his way to finishing his career as the school's all-time fourth-leading scorer (1,275 points) and second-leading rebounder (981).

New Mexico   Dean Dorsey/*Fred Sims (1958-59)

Dorsey was the Lobos' second-leading scorer (9.6 ppg) in his only season. Sims was UNM's top rebounder (9.5 rpg) and third-leading scorer (8.3 ppg) in his only season.

New Mexico State   Joe Kelly (1956-57)

Averaged 7 ppg in three seasons, including 9.2 as a senior in 1958-59.

Niagara   Ed Fleming/Charlie Hoxie (1951-52)

Fleming averaged 15 ppg and 8.7 rpg in four seasons to finish No. 1 on the school's all-time scoring (1,682) and rebounding (975) lists. Hoxie averaged 11.7 ppg and 8.4 rpg in four seasons to finish his career as the school's third-leading scorer (1,274) and second-leading rebounder (916).

North Carolina   Charlie Scott (1967-68)

Averaged 22.1 ppg and 7.1 rpg in three seasons. He was a consensus second-team All-America choice in his last two years.

N.C. State   Al Heartley (1968-69)

Averaged 4.8 ppg in three seasons.

Northwestern   Fred DuHart (1954-55)

Averaged 2.4 ppg in three seasons.

Notre Dame   Joe Bertrand/Entee Shine (1951-52)

Bertrand averaged 14.6 ppg in three seasons, including 16.5 as a senior when the Irish finished the year ranked sixth in the final AP poll. Shine averaged 6.3 ppg in 13 games in his only season.

Ohio University   Bunk Adams (1958-59)

Averaged 16.4 ppg and 11.8 rpg in three seasons, including a team-high 12.8 rpg as a senior. He led the team in scoring as a sophomore (14.4 ppg) and junior (16.4) and was second as a senior (18.2) en route to finishing as OU's career leader in points (1,196). All-MAC first team as a junior and senior after earning second-team status as a sophomore.

Ohio State   Cleo Vaughn (1953-54)

Averaged 3.6 ppg in his only varsity season with the Buckeyes.

Oklahoma   Buddy Hudson/Joe Lee Thompson (1958-59)

Hudson, a transfer from Oklahoma Baptist, averaged 5.1 ppg and 3 rpg in two seasons. Thompson averaged 2.5 ppg in three seasons.

Oklahoma State   L.C. Gordon (1958-59)

Averaged 2.4 ppg and 2.3 rpg in three seasons.

Oregon State   *Charlie White (1964-65)

Led the Beavers in rebounding (7 rpg) and was their second-leading scorer (9.6 ppg) as a junior. The next year as first five pick on the All-Pac-8 team, he was OSU's second-leading scorer (11.7 ppg) and rebounder (6.6 rpg) and led the team in field-goal shooting (49.4%) and free-throw shooting (81.4%).

Pacific   John Thomas (1954-55)

Averaged 15.1 ppg and 11.3 rpg in three seasons while leading the team in scoring and rebounding all three years. Finished career as the school's all-time scoring leader (1,178 points). He set Pacific single-season records for points (480) and rebounds (326) in 1955-56.

Pepperdine   Larry Dugan (1952-53)

Averaged 13.5 ppg in three seasons, leading the team in scoring as both a junior (15.4 ppg) and senior (17.4 ppg). He was a third-team NAIA All-America choice in 1954-55.

Pittsburgh   Julius Pegues (1955-56)

Averaged 13.6 ppg in three seasons, finishing as the school's second-leading scorer (17.6 ppg) as a senior behind All-America Don Hennon. Pegues scored a game-high 31 points in an 82-77 loss to Miami of Ohio in the 1958 NCAA Tournament.

Providence   Lionel Jenkins (1955-56)

Averaged 4.8 ppg in three seasons. His best year was as a sophomore when he averaged 7.8 ppg.

Purdue   *Ernie Hall (1951-52)

Averaged 12.4 ppg in nine games before being dropped from the team.

Rhode Island   Bernard "Slick" Pina (1953-54)

Averaged 9 ppg in his only varsity season.

Rice   Leroy Marion (1969-70)

Averaged 5.6 ppg and 3.3 rpg in a three-year varsity career marred by a knee injury.

Richmond   Carlton Mack (1971-72)

Averaged 4.4 ppg in three varsity seasons.

St. John's   Solly Walker (1951-52)

Averaged 7.8 ppg and 6.8 rpg in three seasons. Member of 1952 NCAA runnerup and 1953 NIT runnerup. Led the team in scoring (14 ppg) and rebounding (12.2 rpg) as a senior.

St. Joseph's   John Tiller (1961-62)

Averaged 2.6 ppg and 3.3 rpg in three seasons.

St. Louis   Larry Sykes (1952-53)

Transfer who previously attended Morgan State and LIU collected 14 points and four rebounds in 12 games in his only season.

St. Mary's   LaRoy Doss (1956-57)

Averaged 14.8 ppg and 9.2 rpg in three seasons, leading the squad in rebounding as a sophomore and in scoring as a junior and senior. Second-team All-WCAC as a sophomore and junior and first five pick as a senior. Finished third on the school's career scoring list with 1,139 points.

San Francisco   K.C. Jones/Carl Lawson (1951-52)

Jones, a member of the 1955 NCAA champion and 1956 Olympic champion, averaged 8.8 ppg in five seasons (played only one game in 1953-54 before undergoing an appendectomy). Lawson averaged 2.4 ppg in three seasons.

Santa Clara   Leroy Jackson (1960-61)

Averaged 10.1 ppg and 8.3 rpg in three seasons, leading the team in rebounding all three years. Named to second five on All-WCAC team as a senior when he averaged 11.9 ppg and 10.9 rpg.

Seton Hall   Walter Dukes (1950-51)

Averaged 19.9 ppg and 18.9 rpg in three seasons. Consensus first-team All-America as a senior when he averaged 26.1 ppg and 22.2 rpg to lead the Dukes to a 31-2 record and NIT title.

South Alabama   *Cliff McKay/*Eugene Oliver/*Darius Segure/*Leon Williams (1972-73)

Oliver averaged 17.9 ppg and 5.1 rpg in two seasons, leading the team in scoring both years and setting a school single-game record with 46 points vs. Southern Mississippi. McKay, Segure and Williams were also J.C. recruits.

South Carolina   Casey Manning (1970-71)

Averaged 2.6 ppg and 1.8 rpg in three seasons.

Southern Illinois   Harvey Welch (1951-52)

Averaged 11 ppg and 6.5 rpg in three seasons, including a team-high 12.3 ppg as a senior.

Southern Methodist   *Ruben Triplett (1971-72)

Averaged 14.9 ppg and 9 rpg in two seasons. Named All-SWC as a junior when he led the Mustangs in scoring (18.2 ppg) and rebounding (10.8 rpg).

Southern Miss.   Wilbert Jordan (1969-70)

Averaged 4 ppg and 2.8 rpg in three varsity seasons.

Southwestern La.   Leslie Scott (1966-67)

Averaged 6.1 ppg in his only varsity season.

Stanford   *Ed Tucker (1951-52)

Averaged 15.8 ppg in two seasons, leading the team in scoring both years. Led the PCC Southern Division in scoring in 1951-52 when he was an all-league pick.

Tennessee   *Larry Robinson (1971-72)

Averaged 10.9 ppg and 8.8 rpg in two seasons. Led the Volunteers in rebounding and field-goal shooting both years.

Tennessee Tech   Marv Beidleman/Joe Hilson/Henry Jordan (1965-66)

Beidleman scored 27 points in 12 games in his only varsity season. Hilson, the team's second-leading scorer in 1966-67 (17 ppg), averaged 13.9 ppg and 3.7 rpg in two seasons. Jordan, an All-OVC selection, averaged 16.1 ppg and 13.1 rpg (ranking 25th in the nation) in his only varsity season.

Texas   Sam Bradley (1968-69)

Averaged 6.5 ppg in his only varsity season.

Texas A&M   *Mario Brown (1971-72)

Averaged 13 ppg and 4.3 apg in two seasons, leading the team in assists both years.

Texas Christian   James Cash (1966-67)

Averaged 13.9 ppg and 11.6 rpg in three seasons. All-SWC selection as a senior when the led the Horned Frogs in scoring (16.3 ppg) and rebounding (11.6 rpg). He had six games with at least 20 rebounds.

Texas-El Paso   Charlie Brown (1956-57)

Three-time All-Border Conference choice led the league in scoring as a sophomore (23.4 ppg). He averaged 17.5 ppg in three varsity seasons, leading the Miners in scoring each year.

Texas Tech   *Gene Knolle/*Greg Lowery (1969-70)

Knolle, a two-time All-SWC selection, averaged 21.5 ppg and 8.4 rpg in two seasons. Lowery, who averaged 19.7 ppg in his three-year

career, was first-team All-SWC as a sophomore and senior and a second-team choice as a junior en route to finishing as the school's career scoring leader (1,476 points).

Tulane   Harold Sylvester (1968-69)

Averaged 12.5 ppg and 9.1 rpg in three varsity seasons. He led the Green Wave in rebounding as a sophomore and was its second-leading rebounder and scorer as a junior and senior.

Tulsa   *Herman Callands/*Sherman Dillard/*Julian Hammond (1964-65)

Callands, Tulsa's leading rebounder as a junior (11.2 rpg), averaged 7.9 ppg and 8.8 rpg in two seasons. Dillard, the team's second-leading scorer as a senior (15.4), averaged 10.6 ppg and 5.1 rpg in two years. Hammond, who averaged 12.2 ppg and 7.6 rpg in two seasons, led Tulsa in scoring (16.4 ppg) and rebounding (7.6 rpg) as a senior when he was an All-MVC choice and paced the nation in field-goal shooting (65.9%).

UNLV   Silas Stepp (1962-63)

Averaged 18.3 ppg and 10.8 rpg in four seasons. He led the team in scoring all four years and was its top rebounder his last three seasons.

Utah   *Jim Thomas (1957-58)

Averaged 2.7 ppg and 2.7 rpg in three seasons.

Utah State   Sam Haggerty/Hal Theus (1956-57)

Haggerty averaged 3.6 ppg in two seasons. Theus, the team's leading rebounder as a junior, averaged 14.4 ppg and 10.7 rpg in three seasons.

Vanderbilt   Perry Wallace (1967-68)

Averaged 12.9 ppg and 11.5 rpg in three varsity seasons. He was the Commodores' leading rebounder as a junior (10.2 rpg) and leading scorer as a senior (13.4 ppg).

Villanova   Kenneth Harrison (1956-57)

Averaged 6.2 ppg and 4.4 rpg in three varsity seasons. His best season was as a sophomore when he averaged 8 ppg and 5.8 rpg.

Virginia   Al Drummond (1971-72)

Averaged 5.2 ppg in three varsity seasons.

Virginia Military   Charlie Tyler (1971-72)

Averaged 9 ppg and 6.8 rpg in three varsity seasons. He led VMI in scoring as a sophomore (12.6 ppg) and in rebounding as a junior (6.8 rpg) and senior (6.6 rpg).

Virginia Tech   Charlie Lipscomb (1969-70)

Averaged 11.4 ppg and 9.4 rpg in three varsity seasons. He led the team in rebounding (10.4 rpg) and was its second-leading scorer (12.1 ppg) as a sophomore.

Wake Forest   Norwood Todmann (1967-68)

Averaged 10.5 ppg and 4.1 rpg in three seasons, including 13.3 ppg as a sophomore.

Washington State   Howard Allen McCants (1952-53)

The 6-8, 235-pound multi-sport athlete averaged 3.9 ppg and 6.1 rpg in two seasons. He was the PCC high jump outdoor champion in 1953.

Western Kentucky   Clem Haskins/Dwight Smith (1964-65)

Haskins, a three-time OVC Player of the Year who was a consensus first-team All-America as a senior, averaged 22.1 ppg and 10.6 rpg in three varsity seasons. Smith, a three-time all-conference choice who averaged 14.6 ppg and 10.9 rpg in his college career, led the Hilltoppers in rebounding as a sophomore (11.3 rpg) and as a senior (11.9 rpg).

West Virginia   Ed Harvard/*Carl Head/Norman Holmes/Ron "Fritz" Williams (1965-66)

Harvard (1.3 ppg) and Holmes (2.7 ppg) played sparingly while Head averaged 13.9 ppg in 1965-66. Head, who averaged 17.1 ppg and 7.9 rpg in two seasons, paced the team in field-goal shooting as a junior (53.5%) and in scoring as a senior (20.5 ppg). Williams, the Southern Conference's player of the year as a senior, led the Mountaineers in scoring and assists all three varsity seasons on his way to finishing with averages of 20.1 ppg and 6 apg.

Wichita State   Cleo Littleton (1951-52)

Averaged 19 ppg and 7.7 rpg in four seasons, leading the Shockers in scoring each year. Wichita State's career scoring leader (2,164 points) is the only player to be a four-time first-team All-Missouri Valley Conference choice.

William & Mary   Ron Satterthwaite (1973-74)

Averaged 13.2 ppg in four seasons. He led the Tribe in scoring as a sophomore and junior, averaging 16.9 ppg each year. Named to All-Southern Conference team as a sophomore.

Wisconsin   Ivan Jefferson (1958-59)

Averaged 6.3 ppg and 3.6 rpg in his only varsity season with the Badgers before transferring to Southern Illinois.

Wyoming   *Curt Jimerson (1960-61)

Averaged 14.6 ppg in two seasons, including a team-high 17.5 ppg as a senior.

Xavier   Ray Tomlin (1954-55)

Scored 66 points in 41 varsity games in three seasons.

*Junior college recruit.

NOTES: Transfer Andre Polly practiced with the William & Mary varsity in 1971-72, but the accomplished musician transferred again to a better music school. . . . USL's Leslie Scott sat out one season after transferring from Loyola of Chicago. . . . Stephen Pitters was a member of Centenary's freshman squad in 1967-68, but wasn't on the varsity team the next season.

18

THE QUESTIONS & ANSWERS
OF 1997-98

Instead of subjecting yourself to about 4,000 college basketball games involving more than 300 NCAA Division I schools before receiving the answers, there's got to be a better way to gain a handle on the state of the game. Well, you can get a sharper perspective of what's ahead in the 1997-98 campaign by just bouncing around the country answering the following germane queries concerning conferences, teams, coaches, players and issues.

Division I men's teams know they have 35 seconds in each possession to befuddle their opponents with creative defenses and offenses. As the clock ticks down off the court before the start of the season, any college fan who reads the following 35 thought-provoking questions and answers can become a self-proclaimed expert and befuddle friends with his or her knowledge.

35. Which conference will be the best in the nation this year?

The ACC's second-division teams aren't as potent as they are normally, but the league gains a slight nod over the Big Ten, Big 12, Pacific-10 and SEC because of three members are capable of finishing among the country's top five squads—Clemson, Duke, North Carolina.

The Big Ten is on the verge of recapturing much of its lost prestige. The league that will be surprisingly strong is the Missouri Valley, where Illinois State and Southwest Missouri State could end up in the Top 25.

34. Which conference isn't living up to billing?

Conference USA still has some rebuilding to do unless several junior college recruits blossom in a hurry.

33. Which teams are poised to make the biggest turnarounds from last year?

Seven teams capable of going from losing records last season to 20 victories this year include Arizona State (10-20 mark last year), Mississippi State (12-18), Missouri (16-17), Ohio State (10-17), Oregon State (7-20), Penn State (10-17) and St. John's (13-14).

Conversely, seven teams that are good bets to regress from a minimum of 22 victories, including at least one NCAA Tournament triumph, to possibly a losing record this season are Boston College (22-9 mark last year), California (23-9), Colorado (22-10), Iowa State (22-9), Tennessee-Chattanooga (24-12), Villanova (24-10) and Wake Forest (24-7).

32. Which schools are on the verge of cracking a final Top 10 poll for the first time?

A surprising number of longtime mediocre programs are in the process of joining the elite. Good bets to soon discard their traditional nondescript status are Fresno State, George Washington, Iowa State, Mississippi, Oregon and Texas. Whether it's this season or the not-too-distant future, it appears as though at least a couple of these six schools will finish in the Top 10.

31. Which tournament-tested school won't appear in the 1998 NCAA playoffs instead of challenging for the title?

The University of California Golden Bears could have been contenders for the national championship if they had not suffered major personnel losses. Instead, UC wound up on probation because of irregularities under former coach Todd Bozeman. If Shareef Abdur-Rahim had stuck around for more than just one season before leaping to the NBA, Cal would definitely be a contender. Tony Gonzalez was lost to the NFL where he will play tight end; up-and-comer Tremaine Fowlkes transferred to Fresno St. and Jelani Gardner chose to be the big fish in the little pond of Pepperdine. With these four standouts, Cal might have been facing Kansas for the national title this coming March.

30. Which schools are poised to shed their March Sadness and return to the NCAA Tournament after prolonged absences?

Three universities with good reasons to be optimistic that they can end their NCAA playoff dry spells this season or in the near future are Bowling Green (last NCAA Tournament appearance was in 1968), Miami, Fla. (1960) and Rice (1970).

29. How many schools should consider dropping out of Division I and entering the small-college ranks?

Elon (N.C.) is moving up this year and schools such as Albany (N.Y.), Quinnipiac (Conn.) and Sacred Heart (Conn.) are upgrading their programs by the end of the century. Frankly, about 80 or so of the more than 300 Division I institutions have little or no business at this level year in and year out. Many of them would be better off by performing in Division II or the NAIA, where they would be powers. The majority of independent schools aren't as proficient as Northwestern, which has finished in the Big Ten Conference basement 12 of the last 13 seasons. The following eight conferences are behind the eight ball because they just don't measure up to most Division I athletic standards: America East, Big South, Mid-Continent, Mid-Eastern Athletic, Northeast, Southland, Southwestern Athletic and Trans America Athletic.

28. Which coaches deserve more national publicity?

There are coaches who have made cameo appearances in the spotlight, but should become fixtures on the national landscape if they continue to prosper. Five "coming attractions" who've never reached the Final Four yet appear capable of succeeding luminaries Denny Crum, Bob Knight, Dean Smith and Jerry Tarkanian by the turn of the century among the cream of the crop in the coaching profession include:

• Jim Calhoun, Connecticut—Averaged almost 30 victories for three seasons from 1993-94 through 1995-96 before last year's mediocre campaign.

• Tim Floyd, Iowa State—He has been at least eight games above .500 nine of the previous 10 seasons.

• Pete Gillen, Providence—Notre Dame would still be a perennial NCAA Tournament team if the Irish had made more of an effort to hire him as Digger Phelps' successor.

• Mike Jarvis, George Washington—Entering his 13th major-college season, he shows signs of being the type of coach who'll never have a losing record.

• Rick Majerus, Utah—Won at least 24 games seven of his last eight full seasons.

27. Which coaches are in jeopardy of losing their jobs?

At least 33 Division I schools incurred a head coaching change in 24 of the last 25 years. Pat Kennedy saw the handwriting on the wall and took off for DePaul. It took a good deal of gall for him to demand a contract extension after Florida State's four consecutive second-division finishes in the ACC.

Here are possible scenarios whereby the following seven high profile coaches on hot seats in major conferences could be endangered species unless their teams make dramatic about-faces:

Tony Barone—On shaky ground if he loses at least 16 games for the sixth time in seven seasons with Texas A&M.

Alvin Brooks—In trouble if Houston loses as many as 16 games for the fourth time in five seasons.

Bill Frieder—In hot water if Arizona State finishes eighth or lower in the Pacific-10 for the third straight season.

Jeff Jones—Big trouble looms if Virginia posts its sixth non-winning ACC record in his eight years at the Cavaliers' helm.

Eldon Miller—Can't afford to come close to his average of 16 defeats annually over the previous seven seasons with Northern Iowa.

Danny Nee—In trouble if Nebraska compiles its fourth consecutive losing league record. His 4-11 conference tournament record and 0-4 mark in the NCAA playoffs with the Huskers don't help him any.

Ralph Willard—In trouble if Pitt loses as many as 15 games for the fourth time in as many seasons since he assumed control of the program.

26. What is the most impressive achievement by an active coach few people know about?

It is believed that new Richmond coach John Beilein is the only active mentor in the country to register 20-win seasons at the junior college, NAIA, NCAA Division II and NCAA Division I levels. A 22-7 record in 1993-94 in his second year at the major-college level with Canisius was

the winningest in school history and came just two seasons after the Golden Griffins suffered an all-time high in losses (8-22 mark in 1991-92).

25. Who is the top candidate for national player of the year?

The field in the race for national player of the year was reduced considerably after a bevy of brilliant undergraduates left college early for the NBA. Naturally, team success often determines individual honors. Only four national players of the year from schools in a conference didn't play on squads that finished in first or second place in their league—Chet Forte (Columbia tied for third in the Ivy League in 1957), Michael Brooks (La Salle was third in the ECC in 1980), Danny Ainge (Brigham Young was third in the WAC in 1981) and Danny Manning (Kansas was third in the Big Eight in 1988).

Raef LaFrentz will be the odds-on favorite in 1997-98 if Kansas wins at least 29 games for the third consecutive season and the Iowa native builds upon last year when he became the first player in Roy Williams' nine seasons as KU coach to top 20 points in eight straight games.

24. What are the nation's best-kept secrets?

Drexel's Bill Herrion is the latest coaching phenom out of the America East Conference, which previously was known as the North Atlantic. Luminaries Jim Calhoun and Rick Pitino preceded Herrion in the NAC.

Darkhorses among the nation's teams might be Colorado State and George Washington, which could be bound for their first final Top 20 appearance since 1969 and 1955, respectively.

The nation's all-underrated team might be comprised of the following players:

G—Roderick Blakney, 5-10, Sr., South Carolina State

G—Randy Bolden, 6-2, Sr., Texas Southern

C—Danny Moore, 6-11, Jr., Southwest Missouri State

F—Bonzi Wells, 6-5, Sr., Ball State

F—Raymond Tutt, 6-4, Sr., UC Santa Barbara

23. Who are the most influential new recruits?

Duke is acknowledged as having one of the top freshman recruiting classes of all time. UNLV's Lamar Odom should excel as a yearling, while the most versatile new kid on the block who will immediately be the top player on his team is 6-5 guard Larry Hughes of Saint Louis.

Elsewhere, junior college jewels are expected to make a major impact at Memphis and UNC Charlotte.

22. Are coaches too concerned with issues instead of taking care of business?

Coaches should quit crying about having to trim their overkill staff, bemoaning stiffer scholastic standards for recruits and portraying NCAA poohbahs as uncaring louts because players aren't permitted air fare to fly home for the holidays and some parents can't afford to fly in to watch their sons play. Why don't the coaches quit recruiting poor kids from hundreds, if not thousands, of miles away and just concentrate a little harder on prospects within a radius a wee bit closer to home?

21. Has the game passed them by?

Is there a changing of the guard among much of the nation's coaching elite? Respected coaches with fading stars include:

Gale Catlett—He is two games below .500 in conference competition the five previous seasons and compiled just one NCAA Tournament victory with West Virginia since the field expanded to 64 in 1985.

Bobby Cremins—Just one winning record in ACC competition the previous seven seasons with Georgia Tech and only two victories in national postseason play the last five years.

Lefty Driesell—Winless in national postseason competition in his nine seasons with James Madison before departing for Georgia State.

Hugh Durham—Devoid of official NCAA Tournament victories since 1983, his predicament isn't likely to change in the immediate future after surfacing at Jacksonville.

Steve Fisher—No Big Ten Conference championships in his first eight full seasons with Michigan and recently had his program immersed in suspect off-the-court activities.

Bill Frieder—A total of only four national postseason tournament victories this decade with Arizona State.

Don Haskins—Sporting a 14-13 tourney mark with Texas-El Paso, he is in danger of becoming the only NCAA championship team coach other than Wyoming's Everett Shelton to finish his career with a non-winning Division I playoff record.

Bob Knight—Six NCAA playoff first-round defeats with Indiana since 1986, including each of the last three years.

Rollie Massimino—Blemish of only one victory in national postseason competition this decade probably won't change with Cleveland State.

Norm Stewart—Missouri mentor ranks dead last among the more than 40 active coaches with at least 20 decisions in national postseason competition (13-20).

Billy Tubbs—Winless in the NCAA Tournament in the previous seven years with Oklahoma and TCU.

20. Whose hiring by a prominent school brought to mind what could become one of the biggest blunders this century?

Virginia Commonwealth's program might have been anything but common if the Rams had promoted Tubby Smith to head coach after he served six seasons as an assistant there under J.D. Barnett from 1979-80 through 1984-85. Smith, immersed in the pressure cooker at Kentucky as Rick Pitino's successor, was an assistant to Mike Pollio at VCU in 1985-86 before serving three seasons from 1986-87 through 1988-89 at South Carolina under George Felton and two campaigns in 1989-90 and 1990-91 at UK under Pitino.

VCU, after getting off to a rousing start with a 71.6 winning percentage in its first 12 seasons at the Division I level under coaches Chuck Noe,

Dana Kirk and Barnett, has won a modest 53.8 percent of its games the last 12 years under Pollio (1986-89) and Sonny Smith (1990-97).

19. Shouldn't schools give transfers more of a break?

Administrators should stop pulling strings with kids' lives when they seek to transfer and automatically give a player a release whatever the circumstances of his departure so the athlete can immediately receive an athletic scholarship at another school. After all, it shouldn't be a one-way street and numerous coaches had contractual obligations to schools when they left for greener pastures. Furthermore, a player who leaves under suspicious circumstances isn't worth the time and trouble of keeping around anyway.

Incidentally, the most influential transfer, if he's eligible, this season probably will be Lester Earl, who is attending Kansas after departing LSU.

18. Which high profile coaches still have something to prove?

Glaring holes remain in the resumes of New Mexico's Dave Bliss, Iowa State's Tim Floyd, South Carolina's Eddie Fogler, Villanova's Steve Lappas, Stanford's Mike Montgomery, Oklahoma's Kelvin Sampson and Maryland's Gary Williams because they've never guided a team to an NCAA regional final. Williams has also never won a conference tournament.

17. Which name schools have been absent from the national rankings lately.

Around 80 different schools have finished the last 12 seasons or so in a final AP or UPI Top 20 poll, but five prominent schools that haven't been on that long list are UAB (out since 1982), Auburn (1984), Fresno State (1982), Houston (1984) and Providence (1977).

16. Who is the most recognized coach to never receive one of the major national coach of the year awards?

It doesn't seem possible, but Louisville's Denny Crum has been shut out of the national coaching awards.

15. Why is it so difficult to compare teams from different eras?

Seven of the last 10 NCAA champions—Kansas '88, Michigan '89, Duke '91, North Carolina '93, Arkansas '94, Kentucky '96 and Arizona '97—wouldn't have been invited to participate in the playoffs prior to 1975. The NCAA Tournament bracket never included more than 25 entrants until it expanded to 32 teams in 1975 when schools other than the conference champion could be chosen on an at-large basis from the same league for the first time.

14. What is the most outrageous prediction that still makes good sense?

Of the more than 30 schools with at least five final AP Top 10 rankings, the only one to never reach the Final Four is Maryland. Don't be surprised if the Terrapins, Clemson, Connecticut, South Carolina or Xavier arrives at the Final Four in a great long-shot bet as the national semifinals has a newcomer for the third consecutive season.

13. Why hasn't the principal state university in a hoop hotbed such as Illinois ever had a team reach the championship game of the NCAA Tournament?

Illinois hasn't supplied an NCAA consensus first-team All-America since Rod Fletcher in 1952. The Fighting Illini had just two NCAA consensus second-team All-Americas in that span—forward Ken Norman (1987) and guard Kendall Gill (1990). This year isn't expected to be any different.

Illinois, Princeton, Temple and Texas are four of the 10 snakebitten schools among the 25 winningest institutions in major-college history to never reach the title game of an NCAA Tournament, let alone win an NCAA crown.

12. Which schools should be ashamed of themselves for ducking nearby quality opponents?

It defies logic as to why the following schools forsake entertaining games with natural rivals while scheduling several meaningless "rout-a-matics" at home:

• Alabama (shuns UAB and South Alabama).

• Arkansas (shuns Arkansas-Little Rock and Arkansas State).

• Illinois (shuns Bradley, DePaul, Illinois State and Southern Illinois).

• LSU (shuns Louisiana Tech, New Orleans, Southwestern Louisiana and Tulane).

• Missouri (shuns St. Louis and Southwest Missouri State).

• Notre Dame (shuns Purdue).

• Ohio State (shuns Cincinnati and competent Mid-American Conference members).

11. Which former coach continues to have the most impact?

No, it isn't one-of-a-kind John Wooden. Last year's NCAA Tournament was yet another testimony to the influence of the late Henry (Hank) Iba, who coached 36 seasons at Oklahoma State from 1935-'70 and passed away last year. Arkansas coach Nolan Richardson played at UTEP under Don Haskins, a former player under Iba. Florida's Kruger played at Kansas State under Jack Hartman, who is one of seven former Oklahoma State players to eventually coach teams into the NCAA playoffs.

All four head coaches at the 1994 Final Four would have been Iba descendants if Missouri (coached by Norm Stewart) had defeated Arizona in the West Regional final and if Purdue (Gene Keady) had defeated Duke in the Southeast Regional final.

10. What does the Big Ten need to do to recapture some of its prestige?

Introducing the money-making gimmick otherwise known as a postseason tournament isn't the remedy to get the Big Ten "tourney tough" again. A mixture of several or all of the items on the following checklist must unfold for the Big Ten in order for the conference to regain its luster and rank among the nation's elite leagues:

• Continued influx of influential "fortysomething" coaches to alleviate aging coaching community.

• Recruit more efficiently outside the Midwest, especially overseas and in the junior college ranks.

• Lure a school from the Big Twelve or Conference USA and go to divisional play.

9. Was Dean Smith's achievement of passing Kentucky legend Adolph Rupp as the all-time winningest major-college coach blown out of proportion?

Of course it wasn't just another day at the beach, but what was all the fuss about? Smith himself doesn't believe his greatest achievement is the NCAA career victory total, 23 consecutive playoff appearances or record 13 consecutive trips to the regional semifinals from 1981-93. "I'm most proud of reaching the Final Four four times in six years from 1967-72," Smith says. "Back in the old days (before 1975), we had to win the ACC Tournament just to go to the (NCAA) playoffs. That's real pressure!"

The opinion from this corner concurs with the modest Smith that he has attained several greater milestones. Here is one observer's view of the 10 more significant achievements in major-college basketball coaching history:

1. John Wooden: UCLA had only two winning records in the 18 years prior to his arrival. The Bruins never had a losing mark in his 27 seasons at their helm, including an unprecedented 10 NCAA titles in a 12-year span (seven in a row from 1967-73).

2. John Wooden: NCAA-record 88-game winning streak from Jan. 30, 1971 through Jan. 17, 1974.

3. Adolph Rupp: Never compiled a losing won-loss record in 41 seasons, including an average annual mark of 27-3 in a 15-year span from 1944-59 with seven straight SEC Tournament titles (1944-50). He garnered an incredible 27 SEC regular-season championships.

4. Dean Smith: Twenty-three consecutive NCAA Tournament appearances, including 13 straight years of directing Carolina to regional semifinals from 1981-93.

5. Dean Smith: Thirty-three consecutive years finishing among the top three in the regular-season standings of the prestigious ACC, including 19 straight seasons finishing first or second from 1967 through 1985.

6. Bob Knight: Directed the last undefeated Division I team (1975-76) en route to a 57-game regular-season winning streak, including a league-record 37-game winning string in regular-season Big Ten competition.

7. Jerry Tarkanian: Ten straight 25-win seasons and conference championships with UNLV from 1982-83 through 1991-92. The only year he failed to win at least 20 games was 1980-81 (16-12 mark).

8. Hank Iba: Only coach with six or more NCAA playoff appearances to reach the regional finals every time. Oklahoma A&M became the only school to reach the NCAA championship game in its first three playoff appearances, winning national titles in 1945 and 1946. The Aggies won the national team defense crown 15 times in a 20-year stretch.

9. Dean Smith: Three consecutive Final Four appearances from 1967-69 when North Carolina had to win the pressure-packed ACC Tournament in order to participate in the NCAA playoffs when the field consisted of 23 to 25 teams.

10. Clair Bee: Lost fewer than four games seven times in nine campaigns from 1934-42, including two undefeated seasons in a four-year span with LIU.

8. Which school could have been defending its NCAA championship this season if everything had fallen into place?

South Carolina, not Kansas, would have been the nation's No. 1 team entering last year's NCAA Tournament if Ray Allen, Kevin Garnett and Jermaine O'Neal had remained in their home state and exercised all of their college eligibility with the Gamecocks. They might have become the first undefeated team since Indiana '76 instead of tarnishing an excellent regular-season performance

by suffering an embarassing first-round loss to Coppin State in the NCAA Tournament.

7. How much credence should observers put in first-rate coaches with dime-store playoff results?

High-profile coaches such as New Mexico State's Neil McCarthy (4-9), West Virginia's Gale Catlett (5-10), New Mexico's Dave Bliss (6-9 mark), Purdue's Gene Keady (11-14) and Missouri's Norm Stewart (12-15) occasionally have to cover their assets amid grilling because of their dismal NCAA Tournament resumes. They're due, however, to eventually turn things around and shouldn't be written off altogether. Remember: Legendary John Wooden lost his first five playoff games as coach at UCLA by an average of more than 11 points and compiled an anemic 3-9 record from 1950 through 1963 before the Bruins won an unprecedented 10 national titles in 12 years from 1964 through 1975.

6. Which coach is under the biggest microscope?

Kansas coach Roy Williams appears to be enduring the same "Great Expectations" syndrome that hovered around Dean Smith, Williams' mentor at North Carolina. Smith, of course, was roundly criticized in some misguided quarters while compiling a 16-12 NCAA playoff record through his first 10 appearances until capturing his initial NCAA Tournament title in 1982. It's of little solace to Williams, but he has a significantly better tournament record than Smith at the same juncture (20-8).

5. What is the most intriguing family connection affecting college hoops this season?

Arizona benefits from having a link to perhaps two of the 10 or so best father-son combinations in college basketball history. You've been living in a closet if you haven't heard about Wildcat standout Mike Bibby and the estranged relationship he has with Southern Cal coach Henry Bibby, a first-team All-America for UCLA in 1972.

Lost in the shuffle, however, is Wildcats backcourtmate Miles Simon, the 1997 Final Four

Most Outstanding Player. His father, Walt Simon, averaged 12.4 ppg for Utah in 1966-67 and 1967-68 after averaging 27.5 ppg for Fullerton Junior College. Walt outscored Lew Alcindor, 31-26, in a 102-74 victory for the acclaimed undefeated baby Bruins in 1965-66.

4. Should defending champion Arizona be held in such high esteem?

Senior-less Arizona's work-in-progress improvement last season exceeded expectations although many observers felt the Wildcats should have finished higher than fifth place in the Pacific-10 Conference standings. Their youthful innocence will be a distant memory this year, however.

The pressure on them to excel in postseason competition will be as intense as it was for Michigan's prodigies in 1993 after the Wolverines, showcasing the Fab Five freshmen, reached the NCAA Tournament championship game the previous year before bowing to Duke.

If Michigan's quintet with panache had regressed and become the Fraud Five by losing its opening playoff game in 1993 instead of reaching the national final again, the Wolverines would have been the biggest bust for a team to return a Final Four squad intact since Duke lost its East Regional opener against St. John's (80-78) as a No. 2 seed in 1979.

Three players who finished their Blue Devil careers with more than 2,000 points (Gene Banks, Mike Gminski and Jim Spanarkel) each compiled lower scoring averages in 1979 than they manufactured the previous year, when Duke was national runner-up. In 1978, Banks, Gminski and Spanarkel became the only trio to each score at least 20 points in both Final Four games (total of 71 points in 90-86 victory over Notre Dame in the semifinals and 63 in 94-88 setback against Kentucky in the championship game). Duke is the only national runner-up to score more than 85 points in an NCAA final. Banks, Gminski and Spanarkel all scored at least 16 points when they combined to shoot 53.5 percent from the floor against St. John's in 1979, but none of their team-mates managed more than seven points as the Blue Devils blew a five-point halftime lead.

There have been other overtly disappointing playoff teams although they returned the nucleus of a Final Four squad. Arizona doesn't want to join the following list of three teams since the tournament field went permanently to at least 25 entrants in 1969 to reach the national final one year and not win a playoff game the next season despite losing no more than one starter who wasn't the leading scorer for the Final Four squad:

TEAM (RECORD)	NEXT YEAR	KEY PLAYER LOSS
Jacksonville '70 (27-2)	22-4	Rex Morgan

1971 NCAA Performance: The Dolphins blew a 14-point halftime cushion and lost in the first round of the Mideast Regional against eventual Final Four team Western Kentucky (74-72). Western Kentucky's Jim McDaniels outscored Jacksonville's Artis Gilmore, 23-12, in a battle of seven-foot first-team All-Americas. A "hidden man/shoelace" trick by WKU's Clarence Glover set up the winning basket in the final seconds.

North Carolina State '74 (30-1)	22-6	Tom Burleson

1975 NCAA Performance: Despite the presence of national player of the year David Thompson, the ACC Tournament runner-up Wolfpack did not compete in the NCAA playoffs after losing twice against regular-season champion Maryland in league play.

Marquette '77 (25-7)	24-4	Bo Ellis

1978 NCAA Performance: The Warriors, making their eighth of 10 consecutive tournament appearances, wasted a five-point, halftime lead and lost in the first round of the Mideast Regional against Miami of Ohio (84-81 in overtime). Current Ohio State coach Randy Ayers collected 20 points and 10 rebounds for the Redskins to help offset national player of the year Butch Lee's 27 points for Marquette.

NOTES: Jacksonville '71 (Tom Wasdin succeeded Joe Williams) and Marquette '78 (Hank Raymonds succeeded Al McGuire) had new coaches. North Carolina State's coach both seasons was Norman Sloan . . . The six schools other than Marquette to participate in the NCAA play-offs as defending champions but lose their opening-round game were UCLA '95 (defeated by Princeton in Southeast Regional the next year), Indiana '87 (Richmond in East Regional), Louisville '80 (Arkansas in Midwest Regional), Kentucky '58 (Louisville in Mideast Regional), Indiana '53 (Notre Dame in East Regional) and Utah '44 (Oklahoma State in Western Regional).

3. What's the biggest trend among coaches?

Across America, there are low and mid-level Division I programs that have lured high profile coaches to their universities—Fresno State's Jerry Tarkanian, Arkansas-Little Rock's Wimp Sanderson, Navy's Don DeVoe, San Jose State's Stan Morrison, Georgia State's Lefty Driesell, Jacksonville's Hugh Durham, South Alabama's Bill Musselman and Northwestern (La.) State's J.D. Barnett. Each has his own ambitions now. Some want to find their way back into major college basketball, and some, such as Driesell and Tarkanian, simply want to turn a loser into a winner, and redeem themselves before retirement.

2. What is the most unusual coaching arrangement?

Southwest Missouri State coach Steve Alford didn't arrive in Springfield, Mo., to try to outdo his father, Sam, a legendary coach at Chrysler High in New Castle, Ind. In an unusual twist, the father's footsteps are right there on the sideline as the son's top assistant.

1. Who are the nation's premier players from foreign countries?

Gone is unanimous player of the year Tim Duncan, a product of the Virgin Islands, a territory of the United States. There are still numerous impact players from off the mainland U.S. Here is a ranking of the nation's top 10 international players at U.S. universities:

RANK PLAYER	POS.	COLLEGE NATIVE	COUNTRY
1. Alexander Koul,	C	George Washington	Soviet Republics
2. *Ademola Okulaja	F	North Carolina	Germany
3. Juan "Pepe" Sanchez	G	Temple	Argentina
4. Sarunas Jasikevicius	G	Maryland	Lithuania
5. Rodrigo de la Fuente	G	Washington State	Spain
6. Obinna Ekezie	C	Maryland	Nigeria
7. Kirill Misyuchenko	C	The Citadel	Russia
8. Elvir Ovcina	F-C	Syracuse	Bosnia
9. Jacky Kaba	C	Seton Hall	Liberia
10. Marius Janulis	G	Syracuse	Lithuania

*Born in Nigeria.

19

NCAA HONORS

Excluding specialty publications, there are six nationally-recognized Player of the Year awards. None of them, however, comes anywhere close to being the equivalent to college football's undisputed most prestigious honor, the Heisman Trophy. The basketball stalemate stems from essentially the same people voting on the major awards (writers or coaches or a combination) and the announcements coming one after another right around the Final Four when the games dominate the sports page.

United Press International, on the verge of extinction in recent years, got all of this started back in 1955. Four years later, the United States Basketball Writers Association, having chosen All-American teams in each of the two previous seasons, added a Player of the Year award to its postseason honors. In recent years, the USBWA award was sponsored by Mercedes and then RCA.

The third oldest of the awards comes from the most dominant wire service, the Associated Press. Perhaps because of its vast network of media outlets, the AP award gets more print and broadcast attention than the other honors. The AP award started in 1961 before affiliating in 1972 with the

Commonwealth Athletic Club of Lexington, Ky., which was looking for a way to honor Hall of Fame coach Adolph Rupp. The result of their merger is the Rupp Trophy.

The Atlanta Tipoff Club initially was associated with UPI before starting its own Naismith Award in 1969. Six years later, the National Association of Basketball Coaches initiated its award, which was sponsored from the outset by the Eastman Kodak Company. In 1977, the Los Angeles Athletic Club began honoring Hall of Fame UCLA coach John Wooden with the Wooden Award.

POWER CONFERENCES

UCLA has had six different individuals earn national player of the year acclaim. Incredibly, perennial power Kentucky has never had a player win one of the six principal national player of the year awards. Here is a look at the six conferences with at least two different individuals capturing one of the six principal national player of the year awards since UPI's initial winner in 1955:

ACC (10)—Johnny Dawkins (Duke), Tim Duncan (Wake Forest), Danny Ferry (Duke), Phil Ford (North Carolina), Art Heyman (Duke), Michael Jordan (North Carolina), Christian Laettner (Duke), Ralph Sampson (Virginia), Joe Smith (Maryland), David Thompson (North Carolina State).

Big Ten (8)—Gary Bradds (Ohio State), Calbert Cheaney (Indiana), Jim Jackson (Ohio State), Jerry Lucas (Ohio State), Scott May (Indiana), Shawn Respert (Michigan State), Glenn Robinson (Purdue), Cazzie Russell (Michigan).

Pacific-10 (7)—Lew Alcindor (UCLA), Sean Elliott (Arizona), Walt Hazzard (UCLA), Marques Johnson (UCLA), Ed O'Bannon (UCLA), Bill Walton (UCLA), Sidney Wicks (UCLA).

Big East (4)—Ray Allen (Connecticut), Walter Berry (St. John's), Patrick Ewing (Georgetown), Chris Mullin (St. John's).

Missouri Valley (3)—Larry Bird (Indiana State), Hersey Hawkins (Bradley), Oscar Robertson (Cincinnati).

SEC (2)—Pete Maravich (Louisiana State), Shaquille O'Neal (Louisiana State).

NATIONAL PLAYER OF THE YEAR AWARDS

1955: Tom Gola, La Salle, 6-6, Sr. (24.2 ppg, 19.9 rpg/UPI)
The Explorers (26-5) were runner-ups in the NCAA Tournament.

1956: Bill Russell, San Francisco, 6-9, Sr. (20.6 ppg, 21 rpg, 51.3 FG%/UPI)
The Dons (29-0) captured the NCAA championship after winning all 14 of their conference games by more than 10 points.

1957: Chet Forte, Columbia, 5-9, Sr. (28.9 ppg, 4.5 rpg, 85.2 FT%/UPI)
The Lions (18-6) did not appear in postseason competition after finishing in a tie for third place in the Ivy League.

1958: Oscar Robertson, Cincinnati, 6-5, Soph. (35.1 ppg, 15.2 rpg, 57.1 FG%/UPI)
The Bearcats (25-3) lost their NCAA Tournament opener after winning the Missouri Valley title (13-1 mark) in their first year in the conference.

1959: Oscar Robertson, Cincinnati, 6-5, Jr. (32.6 ppg, 16.3 rpg, 50.9 FG%/UPI, USBWA)
The Bearcats (26-4) finished in third place in the NCAA Tournament after compiling a 13-1 Missouri Valley record to win the league title.

1960: Oscar Robertson, Cincinnati, 6-5, Sr. (33.7 ppg, 14.1 rpg, 52.6 FG%/UPI, USBWA)
The Bearcats (28-2), third-place finisher in the NCAA Tournament, captured their third consecutive Missouri Valley title with a 13-1 record.

1961: Jerry Lucas, Ohio State, 6-8, Jr. (24.9 ppg, 17.4 rpg, 62.3 FG%/AP, UPI, USBWA)
The Buckeyes (27-1) became the first team in 18 years to go undefeated in Big Ten competition (14-0) before finishing runner-up in the NCAA Tournament.

1962: Jerry Lucas, Ohio State, 6-8, Sr. (21.8 ppg, 17.8 rpg, 61.1 FG%/AP, UPI, USBWA)
The Buckeyes (26-2) lost in the NCAA Championship Game after becoming the first Big Ten school to win three consecutive undisputed league titles since Wisconsin from 1912 to 1914.

1963: Art Heyman, Duke, 6-5, Sr. (24.9 ppg, 10.8 rpg/AP, UPI, USBWA)
The Blue Devils (27-3), third-place finisher in the NCAA Tournament, went undefeated (14-0) in ACC competition.

1964: Gary Bradds, Ohio State, 6-8, Sr. (30.6 ppg, 13.4 rpg, 52.4 FG%/AP, UPI)
The Buckeyes (16-8) did not participate in postseason competition after compiling an 11-3 Big Ten record to finish in a tie for first place with Michigan.

Walt Hazzard, UCLA, 6-2, Sr. (18.6 ppg, 4.7 rpg/USBWA)
The NCAA champion Bruins (30-0) compiled a 15-0 record in the Athletic Association of Western Universities.

1965: Bill Bradley, Princeton, 6-5, Sr. (30.5 ppg, 11.8 rpg, 53.3 FG%, 88.6 FT%/AP, UPI, USBWA)
The Tigers (23-6) finished in third place in the NCAA Tournament after winning the Ivy League title with a 13-1 mark.

1966: Cazzie Russell, Michigan, 6-5, Sr. (30.8 ppg, 8.4 rpg, 51.8 FG%, 82.5 FT%/AP, UPI, USBWA)
The Wolverines (18-8) lost the NCAA Tournament Mideast

Regional final after winning the Big Ten title with an 11-3 record.

1967: Lew Alcindor, UCLA, 7-2, Soph. (29 ppg, 15.5 rpg, 66.7 FG%/AP, UPI, USBWA)
The NCAA champion Bruins (30-0) compiled a 14-0 record in the Pacific-8 Conference.

1968: Elvin Hayes, Houston, 6-8, Sr. (36.8 ppg, 18.9, 54.9 FG%/AP, UPI, USBWA)
The independent Cougars (31-2) finished in fourth place in the NCAA Tournament.

1969: Lew Alcindor, UCLA, 7-2, Sr. (24 ppg, 14.7 rpg, 63.5 FG%/AP, UPI, USBWA, Naismith)
The NCAA champion Bruins (29-1) compiled a 13-1 Pacific-8 record.

1970: Pete Maravich, Louisiana State, 6-5, Sr. (44.5 ppg, 5.3 rpg/AP, UPI, USBWA, Naismith)
The Tigers (22-10), fourth-place finisher in the NIT, posted their highest SEC finish (runner-up with a 13-5 record) since going undefeated in league play in 1954.

1971: Austin Carr, Notre Dame, 6-3, Sr. (38 ppg, 7.4 rpg, 51.7 FG%, 81.1 FT%/AP, UPI, Naismith)
The independent Irish (20-9) lost in the NCAA Tournament Midwest Regional semifinals.

Sidney Wicks, UCLA, 6-8, Sr. (21.3 ppg, 12.8 rpg, 52.4 FG%/USBWA)
The NCAA champion Bruins (29-1) went undefeated (14-0) in Pacific-8 competition.

1972: Bill Walton, UCLA, 6-11, Soph. (21.1 ppg, 15.5 rpg, 64.0 FG%/AP, UPI, USBWA, Naismith)
The NCAA champion Bruins (30-0) compiled an unbeaten record (14-0) in Pacific-8 play.

1973: Bill Walton, UCLA, 6-11, Jr. (20.4 ppg, 16.9 rpg, 65.0 FG%/AP, UPI, USBWA, Naismith)
The NCAA champion Bruins (30-0) went undefeated (14-0) in Pacific-8 competition for the seventh time in 10 years.

1974: Bill Walton, UCLA, 6-11, Sr. (19.3 ppg, 14.7 rpg, 66.5 FG%/UPI, USBWA, Naismith)
The Bruins (26-4) finished in third place in the NCAA Tournament after winning the Pacific-8 title with a 12-2 record.

David Thompson, North Carolina State, 6-4, Jr. (26 ppg, 7.9 rpg, 54.7 FG%/AP)
The Wolfpack (30-1) won the NCAA Tournament after becoming the only school to have back-to-back undefeated records in ACC competition.

1975: David Thompson, North Carolina State, 6-4, Sr. (29.9 ppg, 8.2 rpg, 54.6 FG%/AP, UPI, NABC, USBWA, Naismith)
The Wolfpack (22-6) did not participate in national postseason play after finishing in a three-way tie for second place in the ACC and losing in the ACC Tournament final.

1976: Scott May, Indiana, 6-7, Sr. (23.5 ppg, 7.7 rpg, 52.7 FG%/AP, UPI, NABC, Naismith)
The NCAA champion Hoosiers (32-0) captured their fourth consecutive Big Ten title.

Adrian Dantley, Notre Dame, 6-5, Jr. (28.6 ppg, 10.1 rpg, 58.8 FG%/USBWA)
The independent Irish (23-6) lost in the NCAA Tournament Midwest Regional semifinals.

1977: Marques Johnson, UCLA, 6-7, Sr. (21.4 ppg, 11.1 rpg, 59.1 FG%/AP, UPI, NABC, USBWA, Naismith, Wooden)
The Bruins (24-5) lost in the NCAA Tournament West Regional semifinals after winning the Pacific-8 title with an 11-3 record.

1978: Phil Ford, North Carolina, 6-2, Sr. (20.8 ppg, 52.7 FG%, 81.0 FT%/NABC, USBWA, Wooden)
The Tar Heels (23-8) lost their NCAA Tournament West Regional opener after finishing atop the ACC standings with a 9-3 league record.

Butch Lee, Marquette, 6-2, Sr. (17.7 ppg, 3.1 rpg, 50.6 FG%, 87.9

FT%/AP, UPI, Naismith)

The independent Warriors (24-4) lost their NCAA Tournament Mideast Regional opener.

1979: Larry Bird, Indiana State, 6-9, Sr. (28.6 ppg, 14.9 rpg, 53.2 FG%, 83.1 FT%/AP, UPI, NABC, USBWA, Naismith, Wooden)

The Sycamores (33-1), NCAA Tournament runner-up, became the first Missouri Valley school to go undefeated in league competition (16-0) since Oklahoma A&M went 10-0 in 1948.

1980: Mark Aguirre, DePaul, 6-7, Soph. (26.8 ppg, 7.6 rpg, 54.0 FG%/AP, UPI, USBWA, Naismith)

The independent Blue Demons (26-2) lost their NCAA Tournament opener in the West Regional.

Michael Brooks, La Salle, 6-7, Sr. (24.1 ppg, 11.5 rpg, 52.4 FG%/NABC)

The Explorers (22-9) lost in the first round of the NCAA Tournament Mideast Regional after winning the East Coast Conference Tournament following a third-place finish in the ECC's Eastern Section.

Darrell Griffith, Louisville, 6-4, Sr. (22.9 ppg, 4.8 rpg, 55.3 FG%/Wooden).

The NCAA champion Cardinals (33-3) were undefeated in Metro Conference competition (12-0).

1981: Ralph Sampson, Virginia, 7-4, Soph. (17.7 ppg, 11.5 rpg, 55.7 FG%/AP, UPI, USBWA, Naismith)

The Cavaliers (29-4) lost in the NCAA Tournament national semifinals after winning their first ACC regular-season title with a 13-1 league record.

Danny Ainge, Brigham Young, 6-5, Sr. (24.4 ppg, 4.8 rpg, 51.8 FG%, 82.4 FT%/NABC, Wooden)

The Cougars (25-7) lost the NCAA Tournament East Regional final after finishing in third place in the WAC with a 12-4 league record.

1982: Ralph Sampson, Virginia, 7-4, Jr. (15.8 ppg, 11.4 rpg, 56.1 FG%/AP, UPI, NABC, USBWA, Naismith, Wooden)

The Cavaliers (30-4) lost in the NCAA Tournament Mideast Regional semifinals after tying North Carolina for first place in the ACC with a 12-2 record.

1983: Ralph Sampson, Virginia, 7-4, Sr. (19 ppg, 11.7 rpg, 60.4 FG%/AP, UPI, NABC, USBWA, Naismith, Wooden)

The Cavaliers (29-5) lost the NCAA Tournament West Regional final after tying North Carolina for first place in the ACC with a 12-2 record.

1984: Michael Jordan, North Carolina, 6-6, Jr. (19.6 ppg, 5.3 rpg, 55.1 FG%/AP, UPI, NABC, USBWA, Naismith, Wooden)

The Tar Heels (28-3) lost in the NCAA Tournament East Regional semifinals after becoming the first ACC team to go undefeated in league play (14-0) since North Carolina State in 1974.

1985: Chris Mullin, St. John's, 6-6, Sr. (19.8 ppg, 4.8 rpg, 52.1 FG%, 82.4 FT%/UPI, USBWA, Wooden)

The Redmen (31-4) lost in the NCAA Tournament national semifinals after winning the Big East title with a 15-1 mark.

Patrick Ewing, Georgetown, 7-0, Sr. (14.6 ppg, 9.2 rpg, 62.5 FG%/AP, NABC, Naismith)

The Hoyas (35-3) lost the NCAA Tournament final after finishing runner-up in the Big East standings with a 14-2 record.

1986: Walter Berry, St. John's, 6-8, Jr. (23 ppg, 11.1 rpg, 59.8 FG%/AP, UPI, NABC, USBWA, Wooden)

The Redmen (31-5) lost in the second round of the NCAA Tournament West Regional after tying for first place in the Big East with a 14-2 record.

Johnny Dawkins, Duke, 6-2, Sr. (20.2 ppg, 3.6 rpg, 54.9 FG%, 81.2 FT%/Naismith)

The Blue Devils (37-3) lost in the NCAA Tournament final after compiling a 12-2 ACC record to win their second regular-season league title in 20 years.

1987: David Robinson, Navy, 6-11, Sr. (28.2 ppg, 11.8 rpg, 59.1 FG%/AP,

UCLA's Walt Hazzard (left) handles the ball against Duke.

UPI, NABC, USBWA, Naismith, Wooden)

The Midshipmen (26-6) lost in the first round of the NCAA Tournament East Regional after winning the Colonial Athletic Association with a 13-1 mark.

1988: Hersey Hawkins, Bradley, 6-3, Sr. (36.3 ppg, 7.8 rpg, 52.4 FG%, 84.8 FT%/AP, UPI, USBWA)

The Braves (26-5) lost in the first round of the NCAA Tournament Southeast Regional after winning the Missouri Valley title with a 12-2 league record.

Danny Manning, Kansas, 6-10, Sr. (24.8 ppg, 9 rpg, 58.3 FG%/NABC, Naismith, Wooden)

The Jayhawks (27-11) won the NCAA Tournament after finishing in third place in the Big Eight with a 9-5 league record.

1989: Danny Ferry, Duke, 6-10, Sr. (22.6 ppg, 7.4 rpg, 52.2 FG%/UPI, USBWA, Naismith)

The Blue Devils (28-8) lost in the NCAA Tournament national semifinals after finishing in a three-way tie for first in the ACC standings with a 9-5 league record.

Sean Elliott, Arizona, 6-8, Sr. (22.3 ppg, 7.2 rpg, 84.1 FT%/AP, NABC, Wooden)

The Wildcats (29-4) lost in the NCAA Tournament West Regional semifinals after winning the Pacific-10 title with a 17-1 league record.

1990: Lionel Simmons, La Salle, 6-7, Sr. (26.5 ppg, 11.1 rpg, 51.3 FG%/AP, UPI, NABC, USBWA, Naismith, Wooden)

The Explorers (30-2) lost in the second round of the NCAA Tournament East Regional after compiling the best record in the Metro Atlantic Athletic Conference (16-0 in South Division).

1991: Larry Johnson, UNLV, 6-7, Sr. (22.7 ppg, 10.9 rpg, 66.2 FG%, 81.8 FT%/NABC, USBWA, Naismith, Wooden)

The Rebels (34-1) lost in the NCAA Tournament national semifinals after going undefeated (18-0) in the Big West Conference.

Shaquille O'Neal, Louisiana State, 7-1, Soph. (27.6 ppg, 14.7 rpg, 62.8 FG%/AP, UPI)

The Tigers (20-10) lost in the first round of the NCAA Tournament Midwest Regional after tying for first place in the SEC standings with a 13-5 league mark.

1992: Christian Laettner, Duke, 6-11, Sr. (21.5 ppg, 7.9 rpg, 57.5 FG%, 81.5 FT%/AP, NABC, USBWA, Naismith, Wooden)

The Blue Devils (35-2) won the NCAA Tournament after winning the ACC regular-season title with a 14-2 league record.

Jim Jackson, Ohio State, 6-6, Jr. (22.4 ppg, 6.8 rpg, 81.1 FT%/UPI)

The Buckeyes (26-6) lost the NCAA Tournament Southeast Regional final after compiling a 15-3 Big Ten record to win their first undisputed league title since 1971.

1993: Calbert Cheaney, Indiana, 6-7, Sr. (22.4 ppg, 6.4 rpg, 54.9 FG%/AP, UPI, NABC, USBWA, Naismith, Wooden)

The Hoosiers (31-4) lost the NCAA Tournament Midwest Regional final after compiling the best record in Big Ten competition (17-1) since they went undefeated in 1976.

1994: Glenn Robinson, Purdue, 6-8, Jr. (30.3 ppg, 10.1 rpg/AP, UPI, NABC, USBWA, Naismith, Wooden)

The Boilermakers (29-5) lost the NCAA Tournament Southeast Regional final after winning the Big Ten championship with their first winning league record in four years (14-4).

1995: Ed O'Bannon, UCLA, 6-8, Sr. (20.4 ppg, 8.3 rpg, 1.9 spg, 53.3 FG%/USBWA, Wooden)

The Bruins (31-2) reached the Final Four for the first time since 1980 and captured the national title for the first time since 1975.

Shawn Respert, Michigan State, 6-3, Sr. (25.6 ppg, 4 rpg, 86.9 FT%, 47.4 3FG%/NABC)

The Spartans (22-6) finished at least eight games above .500 in Big Ten competition (14-4) for the first time since winning the NCAA championship with Magic Johnson in 1979.

Joe Smith, Maryland, 6-10, Soph. (20.8 ppg, 10.6 rpg, 2.9 bpg, 57.8 FG%/AP, UPI, Naismith)

The Terrapins (26-8) compiled a winning record in ACC competition (12-4) for the first time since 1985 en route to their first regular-season crown since 1980.

1996: Marcus Camby, Massachusetts, 6-11, Jr. (20.5 ppg, 8.1 rpg, 3.9 bpg/AP, NABC, USBWA, Naismith, Wooden)

The Minutemen (35-2) won 26 consecutive games in one stretch before reaching the Final Four for the first time in school history. Camby copped the honor despite missing four games after mysteriously collapsing before a contest in mid-January.

Ray Allen, Connecticut, 6-5, Jr. (23.4 ppg, 6.5 rpg/UPI)

The Huskies (32-3) became the first Big East team to post the league's undisputed best record in back-to-back seasons.

1997: Tim Duncan, Wake Forest, 6-10, Sr. (20.8 ppg, 14.7 rpg, 3.2 apg, 3.3 bpg, 60.8 FG%/AP, NABC, Naismith, USBWA, Wooden)

The Demon Deacons (24-7) post a school-record fifth consecutive 20-win season by improving their mark to 42-14 in their last 56 contests against ACC competition. Duncan, the nation's leading career rebounder in the previous 24 years, had the unusual statistic for a center of not only leading his team in blocked shots but also assists.

NATIONAL COACH OF THE YEAR AWARDS

1955: Phil Woolpert, San Francisco (28-1 overall record; 12-0 in California Basketball Association/UPI)

The Dons ascended to an NCAA title after absorbing three consecutive losing seasons from 1951 to 1953.

1956: Phil Woolpert, San Francisco (29-0; 14-0 in West Coast Athletic/UPI)

The Dons extended their winning streak to 55 consecutive games en route to another NCAA championship.

1957: Frank McGuire, North Carolina (27-0; 14-0 in ACC/UPI)

The Tar Heels captured their first ACC regular-season championship. They won 22 games by at least nine points.

1958: Tex Winter, Kansas State (22-5; 10-2 in Big Seven/UPI)

The Wildcats won the Big Seven championship one year before entering the NCAA Tournament ranked No. 1 in the country.

1959: Eddie Hickey, Marquette (23-6/USBWA)

The Warriors, after losing more than 10 games in 11 of their 12 previous seasons, had a 22-3 record in Hickey's first year at their helm until dropping three of their last four outings.

Adolph Rupp, Kentucky (24-3; 12-2 in SEC/UPI)

The Wildcats extended their streak of 20-win seasons to 14.

1960: Pete Newell, California (28-2; 11-1 in AAWU/UPI, USBWA)

The Bears' bid to win back-to-back NCAA championships was thwarted by Ohio State in the tourney final.

1961: Fred Taylor, Ohio State (27-1; 14-0 in Big Ten/UPI, USBWA)

The Buckeyes became the first team to go undefeated in Big Ten competition since Illinois in 1943.

1962: Fred Taylor, Ohio State (26-2; 13-1 in Big Ten/UPI, USBWA)

The Buckeyes captured their third of five consecutive Big Ten championships.

1963: Ed Jucker, Cincinnati (26-2; 11-1 in Missouri Valley/UPI, USBWA)

The Bearcats captured their sixth MVC championship in as many seasons as a member of the league.

1964: John Wooden, UCLA (30-0; 15-0 in AAWU/UPI, USBWA)

The Bruins went undefeated to capture their first of 10 NCAA championships.

1965: Dave Strack, Michigan (24-4; 13-1 in Big Ten/UPI)

The Wolverines won their first undisputed Big Ten title since 1948.

Butch van Breda Kolff, Princeton (23-6; 13-1 in Ivy League/USBWA)

The Tigers won their third consecutive conference title before reaching the Final Four.

1966: Adolph Rupp, Kentucky (27-2; 15-1 in SEC/UPI, USBWA)

The Wildcats' only regular-season defeat was at Tennessee before bowing to Texas Western in the NCAA Tournament final.

1967: John Wooden, UCLA (30-0; 14-0 in AAWU/AP, UPI, USBWA)

Only one of the Bruins' last 14 opponents scored more than 16 points.

1968: Guy Lewis, Houston (31-2/AP, UPI, NABC, USBWA)

The Cougars were ranked No. 1 in the country entering the NCAA Tournament.

1969: John Wooden, UCLA (29-1; 13-1 in Pacific-8/AP, UPI, NABC)

The Bruins' lone setback was to Southern Cal, 46-44.

Maury John, Drake (26-5; 13-3 in Missouri Valley/USBWA)

The Bulldogs set a school record for victories just two years after compiling an unsightly 9-16 mark.

1970: John Wooden, UCLA (28-2; 12-2 in Pacific-8/AP, UPI, NABC, USBWA)

The Bruins yielded 87.5 points per game while absorbing both of their losses in a late four-game stretch in league play before recovering.

1971: Al McGuire, Marquette (28-1/AP, UPI, USBWA)

The Warriors entered the NCAA Tournament undefeated before losing by one point to Ohio State.

Jack Kraft, Villanova (23-6/NABC)

The Wildcats reached the Final Four for the first time since 1939.

1972: John Wooden, UCLA (30-0; 14-0 in Pacific-8/AP, UPI, NABC, USBWA)

The Bruins scored at least 105 points in their first seven outings and never look back.

1973: John Wooden, UCLA (30-0; 14-0 in Pacific-8/AP, UPI, USBWA)

The Bruins, going undefeated for the fourth time in 10 years, captured their seventh consecutive NCAA championship.

Gene Bartow, Memphis State (24-6; 12-2 in Missouri Valley/NABC)

The Tigers reached the Final Four for the first time just three years after going 6-20.

1974: Al McGuire, Marquette (26-5/NABC)

The Warriors, with only one senior starter, ranked among the top five in both wire-service polls before finishing runner-up in the NCAA Tournament.

Digger Phelps, Notre Dame (26-3/UPI)

The Fighting Irish, two years after compiling a 6-20 record, won more than 25 games for one of only two times in school history.

Norman Sloan, North Carolina State (30-1; 12-0 in ACC/AP, USBWA)

The Wolfpack won the NCAA Tournament after going undefeated in ACC competition for the second consecutive season.

1975: Bob Knight, Indiana (31-1; 18-0 in Big Ten/AP, UPI, NABC, USBWA)

The Hoosiers were unbeaten until they were eliminated in the NCAA Tournament by Kentucky (92-90).

1976: Bob Knight, Indiana (32-0; 18-0 in Big Ten/AP, USBWA)

The Hoosiers became the last undefeated Division I team.

Johnny Orr, Michigan (25-7; 14-4 in Big Ten/NABC)

The Wolverines reached the NCAA Tournament championship game just three years after compiling a 6-8 league record.

Tom Young, Rutgers (31-2/UPI)

The Scarlet Knights arrived at the Final Four with an undefeated record.

1977: Bob Gaillard, San Francisco (29-2; 14-0 in WCAC/AP, UPI)

The Dons won their first 29 games before bowing to Notre Dame in their regular-season finale and UNLV in the opening round of the playoffs.

Dean Smith, North Carolina (28-5; 9-3 in ACC/NABC)

The Tar Heels reached the Final Four for the fifth time in 11 seasons.

Eddie Sutton, Arkansas (26-2; 16-0 in SWC/USBWA)

The Razorbacks became the first team to go undefeated in SWC competition since SMU in 1956.

1978: Eddie Sutton, Arkansas (32-4; 14-2 in SWC/AP, UPI)

The Razorbacks became the first SWC in 22 years to reach the Final Four.

Ray Meyer, DePaul (27-3/USBWA)

The Blue Demons won more than one NCAA Tournament game for the first time since 1960.

Bill Foster, Duke (27-7; 8-4 in ACC/shared NABC)

The Blue Devils compiled their first winning record in ACC competition since 1971 before making their first NCAA Tournament appearance since 1966.

Abe Lemons, Texas (26-5; 14-2 in SWC/shared NABC)

The NIT champion Longhorns won more than 25 games for the first time in school history.

1979: Bill Hodges, Indiana State (33-1; 16-0 in Missouri Valley/AP, UPI)

The Sycamores reached the championship game in its first NCAA Tournament appearance.

Ray Meyer, DePaul (26-6/NABC)

The Blue Demons reached the Final Four for the first time since 1943.

Dean Smith, North Carolina (23-6; 9-3 in ACC/USBWA)

The Tar Heels won their fourth consecutive ACC regular-season championship.

1980: Ray Meyer, DePaul (26-2/AP, UPI, USBWA)

The Blue Demons' only regular-season defeat was in double overtime at Notre Dame.

Lute Olson, Iowa (23-10; 10-8 in Big Ten/NABC)

The Hawkeyes reached the Final Four for the first time since 1956.

1981: Ralph Miller, Oregon State (26-2; 17-1 in Pacific-10/AP, UPI, shared NABC, USBWA)

The Beavers were undefeated until their regular-season finale.

Jack Hartman, Kansas State (24-9; 9-5 in Big Eight/shared NABC)

The Wildcats won their most games in a season since 1959.

1982: Ralph Miller, Oregon State (25-5; 16-2 in Pacific-10/AP)

The Beavers captured their third consecutive conference crown.

Don Monson, Idaho (27-3; 13-1 in Big Sky/NABC)

The Vandals' victories included decisions by at least 19 points away from home against Washington, Washington State, Iowa State, Oregon State, and Oregon.

Norm Stewart, Missouri (27-4; 12-2 in Big Eight/UPI)

The Tigers captured their third of four consecutive outright Big Eight Conference regular-season championships.

John Thompson, Georgetown (30-7; 10-4 in Big East/USBWA)

The Hoyas reached the Final Four for the first time since 1943.

1983: Lou Carnesecca, St. John's (28-5; 12-4 in Big East/NABC, USBWA)

The Redmen won at least 28 games for the first of three times in four seasons.

Guy Lewis, Houston (31-3; 16-0 in SWC/AP)

The Cougars won 26 consecutive games until they were upset in the NCAA Tournament final.

Jerry Tarkanian, UNLV (28-3; 15-1 in PCAA/UPI)

The Rebels won their first of 10 regular-season conference titles in as many years.

1984: Ray Meyer, DePaul (27-3/AP, UPI)

The Blue Demons, in Meyer's swan song, registered their seventh consecutive season with more than 20 victories.

Marv Harshman, Washington (24-7; 15-3 in Pacific-10/NABC)

The Huskies won their first conference crown since 1953.

Gene Keady, Purdue (22-7; 15-3 in Big Ten/USBWA)

The Boilermakers compiled their 12th consecutive winning league record.

1985: Lou Carnesecca, St. John's (31-4; 15-1 in Big East/UPI, USBWA)

The Redmen captured their lone undisputed conference championship.

Bill Frieder, Michigan (26-4; 16-2 in Big Ten/AP)

The Wolverines won the Big Ten title just two years after compiling a 7-11 league record.

John Thompson, Georgetown (35-3; 14-2 in Big East/NABC)

The Hoyas won at least 30 games for the third time in four seasons.

1986: Eddie Sutton, Kentucky (32-4; 17-1 in SEC/AP, NABC)

Three of the Wildcats' four defeats were by a total of just nine points.

Mike Krzyzewski, Duke (37-3; 12-2 in ACC/UPI)

The Blue Devils established an ACC record for most victories in a single season.

Dick Versace, Bradley (32-3; 16-0 in Missouri Valley/USBWA)

The Braves won their first NCAA Tournament game in more than 30 years.

1987: John Chaney, Temple (32-4; 17-1 in Atlantic 10/USBWA)

The Owls became the first Atlantic 10 team to win more than 30 games in a single season.

Tom Davis, Iowa (30-5; 14-4 in Big Ten/AP)

The Hawkeyes set a school standard for victories just three years after compiling a losing record.

Bob Knight, Indiana (30-4; 15-3 in Big Ten/Naismith)

The Hoosiers finished among the top three in league standings for the seventh time in eight seasons.

Rick Pitino, Providence (25-9; 10-6 in Big East/NABC)

The Friars reached the Final Four two years after posting an 11-20 record.

John Thompson, Georgetown (29-5; 12-4 in Big East/UPI)

The Hoyas ranked among the top 10 in the final AP poll for one of six times in a nine-year span.

1988: John Chaney, Temple (32-2; 18-0 in Atlantic 10/AP, UPI, NABC, USBWA)

The Owls, leading the nation in field-goal percentage defense, won 32 games for the second consecutive campaign.

Larry Brown, Kansas (27-11; 9-5 in Big Eight/Naismith)

The Jayhawks finished at least four games above .500 in Big Eight play for the fifth time in as many seasons under Brown before becoming the first Big Eight team to win a Final Four game in more than 30 years.

1989: Bob Knight, Indiana (27-8; 15-3 in Big Ten/AP, UPI, USBWA)

The Hoosiers won 21 of 22 games in one stretch.

P. J. Carlesimo, Seton Hall (31-7; 11-5 in Big East/NABC)

The Pirates posted their first winning record in conference competition en route to reaching the NCAA Tournament championship game.

Mike Krzyzewski, Duke (28-8; 9-5 in ACC/Naismith)

The Blue Devils won at least 28 games for the second time in five consecutive seasons.

1990: Jim Calhoun, Connecticut (31-6; 12-4 in Big East/AP, UPI)

The Huskies, after finishing at least four games below .500 in league play the previous seven seasons, tied Syracuse for first place.

Bobby Cremins, Georgia Tech (28-7; 8-6 in ACC/Naismith)

The Yellow Jackets reached the Final Four for the only time in school history.

Jud Heathcote, Michigan State (28-6; 15-3 in Big Ten/NABC)

The Spartans won the Big Ten title just one year after finishing next to last place.

Roy Williams, Kansas (30-5; 11-3 in Big Eight/USBWA)

The Jayhawks reached the Final Four just one year after posting a losing record in league play.

1991: Randy Ayers, Ohio State (27-4; 15-3 in Big Ten/AP, Naismith, USBWA)

The Buckeyes captured their first league title since 1971.

Mike Krzyzewski, Duke (32-7; 11-3 in ACC/NABC)

The Blue Devils ended their streak of eight trips to the Final Four without a national championship.

Rick Majerus, Utah (30-4; 15-1 in WAC/UPI)

The Utes, 32-31 over the previous two years, became the only WAC team ever to win 30 games in a single season.

1992: Perry Clark, Tulane (21-8; 8-4 in Metro/UPI, USBWA)

The Green Wave won a conference title two years after compiling a 4-24 record.

Mike Krzyzewski, Duke (34-2; 14-2 in ACC/Naismith)

The Blue Devils reached the Final Four for the fifth consecutive season.

George Raveling, Southern Cal (24-6; 15-3 in Pacific-10/NABC)

The Trojans won more than 20 games for the first time since 1974.

Roy Williams, Kansas (27-5; 11-3 in Big Eight/AP)

Kansas State coach Jack Hartman.

The Jayhawks captured their first outright Big Eight crown since 1986.

1993: Eddie Fogler, Vanderbilt (28-6; 14-2 in SEC/AP, UPI, NABC, USBWA)

The Commodores shattered their school record for most victories in a single season.

Dean Smith, North Carolina (34-4; 14-2 in ACC/Naismith)

The Tar Heels won the NCAA title after reaching the Sweet 16 of the NCAA Tournament for the 13th consecutive season.

1994: Norm Stewart, Missouri (28-4; 14-0 in Big Eight/AP, UPI)

The Tigers became the first undefeated team in Big Eight competition since Kansas in 1971.

Nolan Richardson, Arkansas (31-3; 14-2 in SEC/Naismith, shared NABC)

The NCAA champion Razorbacks reached the 30-win plateau for the third time in five seasons.

Charlie Spoonhour, St. Louis (23-6; 8-4 in Great Midwest/USBWA)

The Billikens participated in the NCAA Tournament for the first time since 1957.

Gene Keady, Purdue (29-5; 14-4 in Big Ten/shared NABC)

The Boilermakers won the Big Ten title after three consecutive non-winning records in conference competition.

1995: Jim Harrick, UCLA (31-2; 16-2 in Pacific-10/NABC, Naismith)

The Bruins set a school record for most victories in a season en route to their first Final Four appearance since 1980.

Kelvin Sampson, Oklahoma (23-9; 9-5 in Big Eight/AP, USBWA)

The Sooners post their best league record (9-5) and overall mark since 1990.

Leonard Hamilton, Miami, Fla. (15-13; 9-9 in Big East/UPI)

The Hurricanes, winless in conference play the previous year, snap a 29-game league losing streak on the road en route to finishing with the greatest one-season turnaround in Big East history. Hamilton is the first coach of the year not to crack the 20-win plateau.

1996: Gene Keady, Purdue (26-6; 15-3 in Big Ten/AP, UPI, USBWA)

The Boilermakers become the first school since Ohio State in the early 1960s to win three consecutive Big Ten titles.

John Calipari, Massachusetts (35-2, 15-1 in Eastern Division of Atlantic 10/NABC, Naismith)

The Minutemen captured their fifth consecutive Atlantic regular-season and conference tournament championship before reaching the Final Four for the first time in school history. It was light years removed from Calipari's first season as a head coach in 1988-89 when UMass registered its 11th consecutive losing record. He went to the pros after the '96 Final Four.

1997: Clem Haskins, Minnesota (31-4; 16-2 in Big Ten to finish first/AP, NABC, Naismith, USBWA)

The Gophers' first league title in 15 years enables Clem The Gem to become the only former NCAA consensus first-team All-American other than legendary John Wooden to later be named national coach of the year.

NCAA CONSENSUS ALL-AMERICANS SINCE 1928-29

1928-29: Tom Churchill, F-C, Jr., Oklahoma; Vern Corbin, F, Sr., California; Chuck Hyatt, F, Jr., Pittsburgh; Charles (Stretch) Murphy, C, Jr., Purdue; Joe Schaaf, F, Sr., Pennsylvania; John (Cat) Thompson, F, Jr., Montana State.

1929-30: Chuck Hyatt, F, Sr., Pittsburgh; Charles (Stretch) Murphy, C, Sr., Purdue; E. (Branch) McCracken, F, Sr., Indiana; John (Cat) Thompson, F, Sr., Montana State; Frank Ward, C, Sr., Montana State; John Wooden, G, Soph., Purdue.

1930-31: Wes Fesler, G, Sr., Ohio State; George Gregory, C, Sr., Columbia; Joe Reiff, F, Soph., Northwestern; Elwood (Woody) Romney, F-C, Jr., Brigham Young; John Wooden, G, Jr., Purdue.

1931-32: Louis (Bosey) Berger, F, Sr., Maryland; Ed (Moose) Krause, C, Soph., Notre Dame; Forest (Aggie) Sale, F-C, Jr., Kentucky; Les Witte, F, Soph., Wyoming; John Wooden, G, Sr., Purdue.

1932-33: Ed (Moose) Krause, C, Jr., Notre Dame; Elliott Loughlin, G, Sr., Navy; Jerry Nemer, F, Sr., Southern California; Joe Reiff, F, Sr., Northwestern; Forest (Aggie) Sale, F-C, Sr., Kentucky; Don Smith, G-F, Soph., Pittsburgh.

1933-34: Norm Cottom, F, Jr., Purdue; Claire Cribbs, G-C, Jr., Pittsburgh; Ed (Moose) Krause, C, Sr., Notre Dame; Hal Lee, G, Sr., Washington; Les Witte, F, Sr., Wyoming.

1934-35: Omar (Bud) Browning, G, Sr., Oklahoma; Claire Cribbs, G-C, Sr., Pittsburgh; LeRoy (Cowboy) Edwards, C, Soph., Kentucky; Jack Gray, F, Sr., Texas; Lee Guttero, C, Sr., Southern California.

1935-36: Vern Huffman, G, Jr., Indiana; Bob Kessler, F, Sr., Purdue; Bill Kinner, C-F, Sr., Utah; Hank Luisetti, F, Soph., Stanford; John Moir, F, Soph., Notre Dame; Paul Nowak, C, Soph., Notre Dame; H.L. (Ike) Poole, F-C, Sr., Arkansas.

1936-37: Jules Bender, G, Sr., Long Island; Hank Luisetti, F, Jr., Stanford; John Moir, F, Jr., Notre Dame; Paul Nowak, C, Jr., Notre Dame; Jewell Young, F, Jr., Purdue.

1937-38: Meyer (Mike) Bloom, C, Sr., Temple; Hank Luisetti, F, Sr., Stanford; John Moir, F, Sr., Notre Dame; Paul Nowak, C, Sr., Notre Dame; Fred Pralle, G, Sr., Kansas; Jewell Young, F, Sr., Purdue.

1938-39: First Team: Ernie Andres, G, Sr., Indiana; Jimmy Hull, F, Sr., Ohio State; Chet Jaworski, G, Sr., Rhode Island; Irv Torgoff, F, Sr., Long Island; Urgel (Slim) Wintermute, C, Sr., Oregon.

Second Team: Bobby Anet, G, Sr., Oregon; Bob Calihan, F-C, Jr., Detroit; Bob Hassmiller, F-G, Sr., Fordham; Mike Novak, C, Sr., Loyola of Chicago; Bernie Opper, G, Sr., Kentucky.

1939-40: First Team: Gus Broberg, G-F, Jr., Dartmouth; John Dick, F, Sr., Oregon; George Glamack, C, Jr., North Carolina; Bill Hapac, F, Sr., Illinois; Ralph Vaughn, F, Sr., Southern California.

Second Team: Jack Harvey, C, Sr., Colorado; Marv Huffman, G, Sr., Indiana; Jimmy McNatt, F, Sr., Oklahoma; Jesse (Cab) Renick, G, Sr., Oklahoma A&M.

1940-41: First Team: John Adams, F, Sr., Arkansas; Gus Broberg, G-F, Jr., Dartmouth; Howard Engleman, F, Sr., Kansas; Gene Englund, C, Sr., Wisconsin; George Glamack, C, Sr., North Carolina.

Second Team: Frankie Baumholtz, F, Sr., Ohio University; Bob Kinney, C, Jr., Rice; Paul Lindemann, C, Sr., Washington State; Stan Modzelewski, G, Jr., Rhode Island State; Oscar Schechtman, G, Sr., Long Island.

1941-42: First Team: Price Brookfield, C, Sr., West Texas State; Bob Davies, G, Sr., Seton Hall; Bob Kinney, C, Sr., Rice; John Kotz, F, Jr., Wisconsin; Andy Phillip, F, Soph., Illinois.

Second Team: Don Burness, F, Sr., Stanford; Wilfred Doerner, F, Jr., Evansville; Bob Doll, C, Sr., Colorado; John Mandic, C, Sr., Oregon State; Stan Modzelewski, G, Sr., Rhode Island State; George Munroe, F, Jr., Dartmouth.

1942-43: First Team: Ed Beisser, C, Sr., Creighton; Charles Black, F, Soph., Kansas; Harry Boykoff, C, Soph., St. John's; Bill Closs, C-F, Sr., Rice; Andy Phillip, F, Jr., Illinois; George Senesky, F, Sr., St. Joseph's.

Second Team: Gale Bishop, F, Jr., Washington State; Otto Graham, F, Jr., Northwestern; John Kotz, F, Sr., Wisconsin; Bob Rensberger, G, Sr., Notre Dame; Gene Rock, F, Jr., Southern California; Gerry Tucker, C, Jr., Oklahoma.

1943-44: First Team: Bob Brannum, C, Fr., Kentucky; Audley Brindley, C, Jr., Dartmouth; Otto Graham, F, Sr., Northwestern*; Leo Klier, F, Jr., Notre Dame; Bob Kurland, C, Soph., Oklahoma A&M; George Mikan, C, Soph., DePaul; Alva (Allie) Paine, G, Jr., Oklahoma.

Second Team: Bob Dille, F, Jr., Valparaiso; Arnie Ferrin, F, Fr., Utah; Don Grate, F, Soph., Ohio State; Dale Hall, G-F, Jr., Army; Bill Henry, C-F, Jr., Rice; Dick Triptow, G, Sr., DePaul.

*Graham also played four games for Colgate.

1944-45: First Team: Howie Dallmar, G, Sr., Pennsylvania; Arnie Ferrin, F, Soph., Utah; Wyndol Gray, F, Soph., Bowling Green; Billy Hassett, G, Jr., Notre Dame; Bill Henry, C-F, Sr., Rice; Walt Kirk, G, Jr., Illinois; Bob Kurland, C, Jr., Oklahoma A&M; George Mikan, C, Jr., DePaul.

Second Team: Don Grate, F, Jr., Ohio State; Dale Hall, G-F, Jr., Army; Vince Hanson, C, Soph., Washington State; Dick Ives, F, Soph., Iowa; Max Morris, F-C, Jr., Northwestern; Herb Wilkinson, G-F, Soph., Iowa.

1945-46: First Team: Leo Klier, F, Sr., Notre Dame; Bob Kurland, C, Sr., Oklahoma A&M; George Mikan, C, Sr., DePaul; Max Morris, F-C, Sr., Northwestern; Sid Tannenbaum, G, Jr., NYU.

Second Team: Charles Black, F, Jr., Kansas; John Dillon, F, Soph., North Carolina; Billy Hassett, G, Sr., Notre Dame; Tony Lavelli, F, Fr., Yale; Jack Parkinson, G, Jr., Kentucky; Kenny Sailors, G, Sr., Wyoming.

1946-47: First Team: Ralph Beard, G, Soph., Kentucky; Alex Groza, C, Soph., Kentucky; Ralph Hamilton, F, Sr., Indiana; Sid Tannenbaum, G, Sr., NYU; Gerry Tucker, C, Sr., Oklahoma.

Second Team: Don Barksdale, C, Sr., UCLA; Arnie Ferrin, F, Jr., Utah; Vern Gardner, C, Soph., Utah; John Hargis, F, Sr., Texas; George Kaftan, F-C, Soph., Holy Cross; Ed Koffenberger, F, Sr., Duke; Andy Phillip, F, Sr., Illinois.

1947-48: First Team: Ralph Beard, G, Jr., Kentucky; Ed Macauley, C-F, Jr., St. Louis; Jim McIntyre, C, Jr., Minnesota; Kevin O'Shea, G, Soph., Notre Dame; Murray Wier, G, Sr., Iowa.

Second Team: Dick Dickey, F, Soph., North Carolina State; Arnie Ferrin, F, Sr., Utah; Alex Groza, C, Jr., Kentucky; Hal Haskins, F, Soph., Hamline (Minn.); George Kaftan, F-C, Jr., Holy Cross; Duane Klueh, F, Jr., Indiana State; Tony Lavelli, F, Jr., Yale; Jack Nichols, C, Sr., Washington; Andy Wolfe, G, Sr., California.

1948-49: First Team: Ralph Beard, G, Sr., Kentucky; Vince Boryla, F, Sr., Denver; Alex Groza, C, Sr., Kentucky; Tony Lavelli, F, Sr., Yale; Ed Macauley, C-F, Sr., St. Louis.

Second Team: Bill Erickson, G, Jr., Illinois; Vern Gardner, C, Sr., Utah; Wallace Jones, F-C, Sr., Kentucky; Jim McIntyre, C, Sr., Minnesota; Ernie Vandeweghe, F, Sr., Colgate.

1949-50: First Team: Paul Arizin, F, Sr., Villanova; Bob Cousy, G, Sr., Holy Cross; Dick Schnittker, F, Sr., Ohio State; Bill Sharman, G, Sr., Southern California; Paul Unruh, F, Sr., Bradley.

Second Team: Chuck Cooper, C, Sr., Duquesne; Don Lofgran, F-C, Sr., San Francisco; Kevin O'Shea, G, Sr., Notre Dame; Don Rehfeldt, C, Sr., Wisconsin; Sherman White, C, Jr., Long Island.

1950-51: First Team: Clyde Lovellette, C, Jr., Kansas; Gene Melchiorre, G, Sr., Bradley; Bill Mlkvy, F, Jr., Temple; Sam Ranzino, F, Sr., North Carolina State; Bill Spivey, C, Jr., Kentucky.

Second Team: Ernie Barrett, G, Sr., Kansas State; Bill Garrett, C, Sr., Indiana; Dick Groat, G, Jr., Duke; Mel Hutchins, C, Sr., Brigham Young; Gale McArthur, G, Sr., Oklahoma A&M.

1951-52: First Team: Chuck Darling, C, Sr., Iowa; Rod Fletcher, G, Sr., Illinois; Dick Groat, G, Sr., Duke; Cliff Hagan, F, Jr., Kentucky; Clyde Lovellette, C, Sr., Kansas.

Second Team: Bob Houbregs, F-C, Jr., Washington; Don Meineke, C, Sr., Dayton; Johnny O'Brien, G, Jr., Seattle; Mark Workman, C, Sr., West Virginia; Bob Zawoluk, C, Sr., St. John's.

1952-53: First Team: Ernie Beck, F, Sr., Pennsylvania; Walter Dukes, C, Jr., Seton Hall; Tom Gola, C-F, Soph., La Salle; Bob Houbregs, C, Sr., Washington; Johnny O'Brien, G, Sr., Seattle.

Second Team: Dick Knostman, C, Sr., Kansas State; Bob Pettit, C, Jr., Louisiana State; Joe Richey, F, Sr., Brigham Young; Don Schlundt, C, Soph., Indiana; Frank Selvy, F, Jr., Furman.

1953-54: First Team: Tom Gola, C-F, Jr., La Salle; Cliff Hagan, F, Sr., Kentucky; Bob Pettit, C, Sr., Louisiana State; Don Schlundt, C, Jr., Indiana; Frank Selvy, F, Sr., Furman.

Second Team: Bob Leonard, G, Sr., Indiana; Tom Marshall, F, Sr., Western Kentucky; Bob Mattick, C, Sr., Oklahoma A&M; Frank Ramsey, F, Sr., Kentucky; Dick Ricketts, F-C, Jr., Duquesne.

1954-55: First Team: Dick Garmaker, F, Sr., Minnesota; Tom Gola, C-F, Sr., La Salle; Si Green, G, Jr., Duquesne; Dick Ricketts, F-C, Sr., Duquesne; Bill Russell, C, Jr., San Francisco.

Second Team: Darrell Floyd, G-F, Jr., Furman; Robin Freeman, G, Jr., Ohio State; Ned (Dickie) Hemric, F-C, Sr., Wake Forest; Don Schlundt, C, Sr., Indiana; Ron Shavlik, C, Jr., North Carolina State.

1955-56: First Team: Robin Freeman, G, Sr., Ohio State; Si Green, G, Sr., Duquesne; Tom Heinsohn, F, Sr., Holy Cross; Bill Russell, C, Sr., San Francisco; Ron Shavlik, C, Sr., North Carolina State.

Second Team: Bob Burrow, C, Sr., Kentucky; Darrell Floyd, G-F, Sr., Furman; Rod Hundley, G-F, Jr., West Virginia; K.C. Jones, G, Sr., San Francisco; Willie Naulls, C, Sr., UCLA; Bill Uhl, C, Sr., Dayton.

1956-57: First Team: Wilt Chamberlain, C, Soph., Kansas; Chet Forte, G, Sr., Columbia; Rod Hundley, G-F, Sr., West Virginia; Jim Krebs, C, Sr., Southern Methodist; Lennie Rosenbluth, F, Sr., North Carolina; Charlie Tyra, C, Sr., Louisville.

Second Team: Elgin Baylor, C, Soph., Seattle; Frank Howard, C, Jr., Ohio State; Guy Rodgers, G, Jr., Temple; Gary Thompson, G, Sr., Iowa State; Grady Wallace, F, Sr., South Carolina.

1957-58: First Team: Elgin Baylor, F-C, Jr., Seattle; Bob Boozer, F, Jr., Kansas State; Wilt Chamberlain, C, Jr., Kansas; Don Hennon, G, Jr., Pittsburgh; Oscar Robertson, F, Soph., Cincinnati; Guy Rodgers, G, Sr., Temple.

Second Team: Pete Brennan, F, Sr., North Carolina; Archie Dees, C, Sr., Indiana; Mike Farmer, F-C, Sr., San Francisco; Dave Gambee, F, Sr., Oregon State; Bailey Howell, F, Jr., Mississippi State.

1958-59: First Team: Bob Boozer, F, Sr., Kansas State; Johnny Cox, F, Sr., Kentucky; Bailey Howell, F, Sr., Mississippi State; Oscar Robertson, F, Jr., Cincinnati; Jerry West, F, Jr., West Virginia.

Second Team: Leo Byrd, F, Sr., Marshall; Johnny Green, C, Sr., Michigan State; Tom Hawkins, F, Sr., Notre Dame; Don Hennon, G, Sr., Pittsburgh; Alan Seiden, G, Sr., St. John's.

1959-60: First Team: Darrall Imhoff, C, Sr., California; Jerry Lucas, C, Soph., Ohio State; Oscar Robertson, F, Sr., Cincinnati; Tom Stith, F, Jr., St. Bonaventure; Jerry West, F, Sr., West Virginia.

Second Team: Terry Dischinger, F, Soph., Purdue; Tony Jackson, F, Jr., St. John's; Roger Kaiser, G, Jr., Georgia Tech; Lee Shaffer, F, Sr., North Carolina; Lenny Wilkens, G, Sr., Providence.

1960-61: First Team: Terry Dischinger, F, Jr., Purdue; Roger Kaiser, G, Sr., Georgia Tech; Jerry Lucas, C, Jr., Ohio State; Tom Stith, F, Sr., St. Bonaventure; Chet Walker, F, Jr., Bradley.

Second Team: Walt Bellamy, C, Sr., Indiana; Frank Burgess, G, Sr., Gonzaga; Tony Jackson, F, Sr., St. John's; Billy McGill, C, Jr., Utah; Larry Siegfried, G, Sr., Ohio State.

1961-62: First Team: Len Chappell, C, Sr., Wake Forest; Terry Dischinger, F, Sr., Purdue; Jerry Lucas, C, Sr., Ohio State; Billy McGill, C, Sr., Utah; Chet Walker, F, Sr., Bradley.

Second Team: Jack Foley, F, Sr., Holy Cross; John Havlicek, F, Sr., Ohio State; Art Heyman, F, Jr., Duke; Charles (Cotton) Nash, F-C, Soph., Kentucky; John Rudometkin, C, Sr., Southern California; Rod Thorn, G-F, Jr., West Virginia.

1989–90 All-American Syracuse forward Derrick Coleman brings down a rebound.

1962-63: First Team: Ron Bonham, F, Jr., Cincinnati; Jerry Harkness, F, Sr., Loyola (Ill.); Art Heyman, F, Sr., Duke; Barry Kramer, F, Jr., NYU; Tom Thacker, F-G, Sr., Cincinnati.

Second Team: Gary Bradds, C, Jr., Ohio State; Bill Green, F, Sr., Colorado State; Charles (Cotton) Nash, F-C, Jr., Kentucky; Rod Thorn, G-F, Sr., West Virginia; Nate Thurmond, C, Sr., Bowling Green.

1963-64: First Team: Gary Bradds, C, Sr., Ohio State; Bill Bradley, F, Jr., Princeton; Walt Hazzard, G, Sr., UCLA; Charles (Cotton) Nash, F, Sr., Kentucky; Dave Stallworth, F, Jr., Wichita State.

Second Team: Ron Bonham, F, Sr., Cincinnati; Mel Counts, C, Sr., Oregon State; Fred Hetzel, F-C, Jr., Davidson; Jeff Mullins, F, Sr., Duke; Cazzie Russell, G, Soph., Michigan.

1964-65: First Team: Rick Barry, F, Sr., Miami (Fla.); Bill Bradley, F, Sr., Princeton; Gail Goodrich, G, Sr., UCLA; Fred Hetzel, F-C, Sr., Davidson; Cazzie Russell, G, Jr., Michigan.

Second Team: Bill Buntin, C, Sr., Michigan; Wayne Estes, F, Sr., Utah State; Clyde Lee, C, Jr., Vanderbilt; Dave Schellhase, F, Jr., Purdue; Dave Stallworth, F, Sr., Wichita State.

1965-66: First Team: Dave Bing, G, Sr., Syracuse; Clyde Lee, C, Sr., Vanderbilt; Cazzie Russell, G, Sr., Michigan; Dave Schellhase, F, Sr., Purdue; Jimmy Walker, G, Jr., Providence.

Second Team: Louie Dampier, G, Jr., Kentucky; Matt Guokas, G, Sr., St. Joseph's; Jack Marin, F, Sr., Duke; Dick Snyder, F, Sr., Davidson; Bob Verga, G, Jr., Duke; Walt Wesley, C, Sr., Kansas.

1966-67: First Team: Lew Alcindor, C, Soph., UCLA; Clem Haskins, G-F, Sr., Western Kentucky; Elvin Hayes, F-C, Jr., Houston; Bob Lloyd, G, Sr., Rutgers; Wes Unseld, C, Jr., Louisville; Bob Verga, G, Sr., Duke; Jimmy Walker, G, Sr., Providence.

Second Team: Louie Dampier, G, Sr., Kentucky; Mel Daniels, C, Sr., New Mexico; Lloyd (Sonny) Dove, C, Sr., St. John's; Don May, F, Jr., Dayton; Larry Miller, F, Jr., North Carolina.

1967-68: First Team: Lew Alcindor, C, Jr., UCLA; Elvin Hayes, F-C, Sr., Houston; Pete Maravich, G, Soph., Louisiana State; Larry Miller, F, Sr., North Carolina; Wes Unseld, C, Sr., Louisville.

Second Team: Lucius Allen, G, Jr., UCLA; Bob Lanier, C, Soph., St. Bonaventure; Don May, F, Sr., Dayton; Calvin Murphy, G, Soph., Niagara; Joseph (Jo Jo) White, G, Jr., Kansas.

1968-69: First Team: Lew Alcindor, C, Sr., UCLA; Spencer Haywood, F-C, Jr., Detroit; Pete Maravich, G, Jr., Louisiana State; Rick Mount, G, Jr., Purdue; Calvin Murphy, G, Jr., Niagara.

Second Team: Dan Issel, C, Jr., Kentucky; Mike Maloy, C, Jr., Davidson; Bud Ogden, F, Sr., Santa Clara; Charlie Scott, G-F, Jr., North Carolina; Joseph (Jo Jo) White, G, Sr., Kansas.

1969-70: First Team: Dan Issel, F-C, Sr., Kentucky; Bob Lanier, C, Sr., St. Bonaventure; Pete Maravich, G, Sr., Louisiana State; Rick Mount, G, Sr., Purdue; Calvin Murphy, G, Sr., Niagara.

Second Team: Austin Carr, G, Jr., Notre Dame; Jimmy Collins, G, Sr., New Mexico State; John Roche, G, Jr., South Carolina; Charlie Scott, G-F, Sr., North Carolina; Sidney Wicks, F, Jr., UCLA.

1970-71: First Team: Austin Carr, G, Sr., Notre Dame; Artis Gilmore, C, Sr., Jacksonville; Jim McDaniels, C, Sr., Western Kentucky; Dean Meminger, G, Sr., Marquette; Sidney Wicks, F, Sr., UCLA.

Second Team: Ken Durrett, F-C, Sr., La Salle; Johnny Neumann, F-G, Soph., Mississippi; Howard Porter, F, Sr., Villanova; John Roche, G, Jr., South Carolina; Curtis Rowe, F, Sr., UCLA.

1971-72: First Team: Henry Bibby, G, Sr., UCLA; Jim Chones, C, Jr., Marquette; Dwight (Bo) Lamar, G, Jr., Southwestern Louisiana; Bob McAdoo, C, Jr., North Carolina; Ed Ratleff, F-G, Jr., Long Beach State; Tom Riker, C, Sr., South Carolina; Bill Walton, C, Soph., UCLA.

Second Team: Richie Fuqua, G, Jr., Oral Roberts; Barry Parkhill, G, Jr., Virginia; Jim Price, G, Sr., Louisville; Bud Stallworth, G, Sr., Kansas; Henry Wilmore, F, Jr., Michigan.

1972-73: First Team: Doug Collins, G, Sr., Illinois State; Ernie DiGregorio, G, Sr., Providence; Dwight (Bo) Lamar, G, Sr., Southwestern Louisiana; Ed Ratleff, F-G, Sr., Long Beach State; David Thompson, F, Soph., North Carolina State; Bill Walton, C, Jr., UCLA; Keith Wilkes, F, Jr., UCLA.

Second Team: Jim Brewer, F, Sr., Minnesota; Tom Burleson, C, Jr., North Carolina State; Larry Finch, G, Sr., Memphis State; Kevin Joyce, G, Sr., South Carolina; Tom McMillen, F, Jr., Maryland; Kermit Washington, C-F, Sr., American University.

1973-74: First Team: Marvin Barnes, C, Sr., Providence; John Shumate, C-F, Soph., Notre Dame; David Thompson, F, Jr., North Carolina State; Bill Walton, C, Sr., UCLA; Keith Wilkes, F, Sr., UCLA.

Second Team: Len Elmore, C, Sr., Maryland; Larry Fogle, F, Soph., Canisius; Bobby Jones, F, Sr., North Carolina; Billy Knight, F, Sr., Pittsburgh; Michael (Campy) Russell, F, Jr., Michigan.

1974-75: First Team: Adrian Dantley, F, Soph., Notre Dame; John Lucas, G, Jr., Maryland; Scott May, F, Jr., Indiana; Dave Meyers, F, Sr., UCLA; David Thompson, F, Sr., North Carolina State.

Second Team: Luther (Ticky) Burden, G, Jr., Utah; Leon Douglas, C, Jr., Alabama; Kevin Grevey, F, Sr., Kentucky; Ron Lee, G, Jr., Oregon; Gus Williams, G, Sr., Southern California.

1975-76: First Team: Kent Benson, C, Jr., Indiana; Adrian Dantley, F, Jr., Notre Dame; John Lucas, G, Sr., Maryland; Scott May, F, Sr., Indiana; Richard Washington, C-F, Jr., UCLA.

Second Team: Phil Ford, G, Soph., North Carolina; Bernard King, F, Soph., Tennessee; Mitch Kupchak, F-C, Sr., North Carolina; Phil Sellers, F, Sr., Rutgers; Earl Tatum, G-F, Sr., Marquette.

1976-77: First Team: Kent Benson, C, Sr., Indiana; Otis Birdsong, G, Sr., Houston; Phil Ford, G, Jr., North Carolina; Rickey Green, G, Sr., Michigan; Marques Johnson, F, Sr., UCLA; Bernard King, F, Jr., Tennessee.

Second Team: Greg Ballard, F, Sr., Oregon; Bill Cartwright, C, Soph., San Francisco; Rod Griffin, F, Jr., Wake Forest; Ernie Grunfeld, F, Sr., Tennessee; Phil Hubbard, C, Soph., Michigan; Alfred (Butch) Lee, G, Jr., Marquette; Mychal Thompson, F-C, Jr., Minnesota.

1977-78: First Team: Larry Bird, F, Jr., Indiana State; Phil Ford, G, Sr., North Carolina; David Greenwood, F, Jr., UCLA; Alfred (Butch) Lee, G, Sr., Marquette; Mychal Thompson, C, Sr., Minnesota.

1995-96 All-American UMass center Marcus Camby.

Second Team: Ron Brewer, G, Sr., Arkansas; Jack Givens, F, Sr., Kentucky; Rod Griffin, F, Sr., Wake Forest; Rick Robey, F-C, Sr., Kentucky; Freeman Williams, G, Sr., Portland State.

1978-79: First Team: Larry Bird, F-C, Sr., Indiana State; Mike Gminski, C, Jr., Duke; David Greenwood, F, Sr., UCLA; Earvin (Magic) Johnson, G, Soph., Michigan State; Sidney Moncrief, G-F, Sr., Arkansas.

Second Team: Bill Cartwright, C, Sr., San Francisco; Calvin Natt, F, Sr., Northeast Louisiana; Mike O'Koren, F, Jr., North Carolina; Jim Paxson, G, Sr., Dayton; Jim Spanarkel, G, Sr., Duke; Kelly Tripucka, F-G, Soph., Notre Dame; Sylvester (Sly) Williams, F, Jr., Rhode Island.

1979-80: First Team: Mark Aguirre, F, Soph., DePaul; Michael Brooks, F, Sr., La Salle; Joe Barry Carroll, C, Sr., Purdue; Darrell Griffith, G, Sr., Louisville; Kyle Macy, G, Sr., Kentucky.

Second Team: Mike Gminski, C, Sr., Duke; Albert King, F, Jr., Maryland; Mike O'Koren, F, Sr., North Carolina; Kelvin Ransey, G, Sr., Ohio State; Sam Worthen, G, Sr., Marquette.

1980-81: First Team: Mark Aguirre, F, Jr., DePaul; Danny Ainge, G, Sr., Brigham Young; Steve Johnson, C, Sr., Oregon State; Ralph Sampson, C, Soph., Virginia; Isiah Thomas, G, Soph., Indiana.

Second Team: Sam Bowie, C, Soph., Kentucky; Jeff Lamp, G, Sr., Virginia; Durand (Rudy) Macklin, F, Sr., Louisiana State; Kelly Tripucka, F-G, Sr., Notre Dame; Danny Vranes, F, Sr., Utah; Al Wood, F, Sr., North Carolina.

1981-82: First Team: Terry Cummings, F-C, Jr., DePaul; Quintin Dailey, G, Jr., San Francisco; Eric (Sleepy) Floyd, G, Sr., Georgetown; Ralph Sampson, C, Jr., Virginia; James Worthy, F, Jr., North Carolina.

Second Team: Dale Ellis, F, Jr., Tennessee; Kevin Magee, F, Sr., UC Irvine; John Paxson, G, Jr., Notre Dame; Sam Perkins, F-C, Soph., North Carolina; Paul Pressey, G-F, Sr., Tulsa.

1982-83: First Team: Dale Ellis, F, Sr., Tennessee; Patrick Ewing, C, Soph., Georgetown; Michael Jordan, G, Soph., North Carolina; Keith Lee, C,

Soph., Memphis State; Sam Perkins, C, Jr., North Carolina; Ralph Sampson, C, Sr., Virginia; Wayman Tisdale, C-F, Fr., Oklahoma.

Second Team: Clyde Drexler, F, Jr., Houston; Sidney Green, F-C, Sr., UNLV; John Paxson, G, Sr., Notre Dame; Steve Stipanovich, C, Sr., Missouri; Jon Sundvold, G, Sr., Missouri; Darrell Walker, G, Sr., Arkansas; Randy Wittman, G, Sr., Indiana.

1983-84: First Team: Patrick Ewing, C, Jr., Georgetown; Michael Jordan, G, Jr., North Carolina; Hakeem Olajuwon, C, Jr., Houston; Sam Perkins, C, Sr., North Carolina; Wayman Tisdale, C-F, Soph., Oklahoma.

Second Team: Michael Cage, F-C, Sr., San Diego State; Devin Durrant, F, Sr., Brigham Young; Keith Lee, C-F, Jr., Memphis State; Chris Mullin, G-F, Jr., St. John's; Melvin Turpin, C, Sr., Kentucky; Leon Wood, G, Sr., Cal State Fullerton.

1984-85: First Team: Johnny Dawkins, G, Jr., Duke; Patrick Ewing, C, Sr., Georgetown; Keith Lee, C, Sr., Memphis State; Xavier McDaniel, F, Sr., Wichita State; Chris Mullin, G-F, Sr., St. John's; Wayman Tisdale, C-F, Jr., Oklahoma.

Second Team: Len Bias, F, Jr., Maryland; Jon Koncak, C, Sr., Southern Methodist; Mark Price, G, Jr., Georgia Tech; Kenny Walker, F, Jr., Kentucky; Dwayne (Pearl) Washington, G, Soph., Syracuse.

1985-86: First Team: Steve Alford, G, Jr., Indiana; Walter Berry, F, Jr., St. John's; Len Bias, F, Sr., Maryland; Johnny Dawkins, G, Sr., Duke; Kenny Walker, F, Sr., Kentucky.

Second Team: Dell Curry, G, Sr., Virginia Tech; Brad Daugherty, C, Sr., North Carolina; Ron Harper, G-F, Sr., Miami of Ohio; Danny Manning, F, Soph., Kansas; David Robinson, C, Jr., Navy; Scott Skiles, G, Sr., Michigan State.

1986-87: First Team: Steve Alford, G, Sr., Indiana; Danny Manning, F-C, Jr., Kansas; David Robinson, C, Sr., Navy; Kenny Smith, G, Sr., North Carolina; Reggie Williams, F-G, Sr., Georgetown.

Second Team: Armon Gilliam, F-C, Sr., UNLV; Horace Grant, F, Sr., Clemson; Dennis Hopson, G, Sr., Ohio State; Mark Jackson, G, Sr., St. John's; Ken Norman, F, Sr., Illinois.

1987-88: First Team: Sean Elliott, F, Jr., Arizona; Gary Grant, G, Sr., Michigan; Hersey Hawkins, G, Sr., Bradley; Danny Manning, F-C, Sr., Kansas; J.R. Reid, C, Soph., North Carolina.

Second Team: Danny Ferry, F-C, Jr., Duke; Jerome Lane, F, Jr., Pittsburgh; Mark Macon, G, Fr., Temple; Mitch Richmond, F-G, Sr., Kansas State; Rony Seikaly, C, Sr., Syracuse; Michael Smith, C-F, Jr., Brigham Young.

1988-89: First Team: Sean Elliott, F, Sr., Arizona; Pervis Ellison, C, Sr., Louisville; Danny Ferry, F-C, Sr., Duke; Chris Jackson, G, Fr., Louisiana State; Stacey King, C, Sr., Oklahoma.

Second Team: Daron (Mookie) Blaylock, G, Sr., Oklahoma; Sherman Douglas, G, Sr., Syracuse; Jay Edwards, G, Soph., Indiana; Todd Lichti, G, Sr., Stanford; Glen Rice, F, Sr., Michigan; Lionel Simmons, F, Jr., La Salle.

1989-90: First Team: Derrick Coleman, F, Sr., Syracuse; Chris Jackson, G, Soph., Louisiana State; Larry Johnson, F, Jr., UNLV; Gary Payton, G, Sr., Oregon State; Lionel Simmons, F, Sr., La Salle.

Second Team: Eric (Hank) Gathers, C, Sr., Loyola Marymount; Kendall Gill, G, Sr., Illinois; Greg (Bo) Kimble, G, Sr., Loyola Marymount; Alonzo Mourning, C, Soph., Georgetown; Rumeal Robinson, G, Sr., Michigan; Dennis Scott, G-F, Jr., Georgia Tech; Doug Smith, F, Jr., Missouri.

1990-91: First Team: Kenny Anderson, G, Soph., Georgia Tech; Jim Jackson, G-F, Soph., Ohio State; Larry Johnson, F, Sr., UNLV; Shaquille O'Neal, C, Soph., Louisiana State; Billy Owens, F, Jr., Syracuse.

Second Team: Stacey Augmon, F, Sr., UNLV; Keith (Mister) Jennings, G, Sr., East Tennessee State; Christian Laettner, C-F, Jr., Duke; Eric Murdock, G, Sr., Providence; Steve Smith, G, Sr., Michigan State.

1991-92: First Team: Jim Jackson, G-F, Jr., Ohio State; Christian Laettner, F-C, Sr., Duke; Harold Miner, G, Jr., Southern California; Alonzo Mourning, C, Sr., Georgetown; Shaquille O'Neal, C, Jr., Louisiana State.

Second Team: Byron Houston, F, Sr., Oklahoma State; Don MacLean, F, Sr., UCLA; Anthony Peeler, G, Sr., Missouri; Malik Sealy, F, Sr., St. John's; Walt Williams, G-F, Sr., Maryland.

1992-93: First Team: Calbert Cheaney, F, Sr., Indiana; Anfernee Hardaway, G, Jr., Memphis State; Bobby Hurley, G, Sr., Duke; Jamal Mashburn, F, Jr., Kentucky; Chris Webber, F, Soph., Michigan.

Second Team: Terry Dehere, G, Sr., Seton Hall; Grant Hill, F, Jr., Duke; Billy McCaffrey, G, Jr., Vanderbilt; Eric Montross, C, Jr., North Carolina; Isaiah

(J.R.) Rider, F, Sr., UNLV; Glenn Robinson, F, Soph., Purdue; Rodney Rogers, F, Jr., Wake Forest.

1993-94: First Team: Grant Hill, F-G, Sr., Duke; Jason Kidd, G, Soph., California; Donyell Marshall, F, Jr., Connecticut; Glenn Robinson, F, Jr., Purdue; Clifford Rozier, C-F, Jr., Louisville.

Second Team: Melvin Booker, G, Sr., Missouri; Eric Montross, C, Sr., North Carolina; Lamond Murray, F, Jr., California; Khalid Reeves, G, Sr., Arizona; Jalen Rose, G, Jr., Michigan; Corliss Williamson, F, Soph., Arkansas.

1994-95: First Team: Ed O'Bannon, F, Sr., UCLA; Shawn Respert, G, Sr., Michigan State; Joe Smith, C, Soph., Maryland; Jerry Stackhouse, F, Soph., North Carolina; Damon Stoudamire, G, Sr., Arizona.

Second Team: Randolph Childress, G, Sr., Wake Forest; Kerry Kittles, G-F, Jr., Villanova; Lou Roe, F, Sr., Massachusetts; Rasheed Wallace, C, Soph., North Carolina; Corliss Williamson, F, Jr., Arkansas.

1995-96: First Team: Ray Allen, G-F, Jr., Connecticut; Marcus Camby, C, Jr., Massachusetts; Tony Delk, G, Sr., Kentucky; Tim Duncan, C, Jr., Wake Forest; Allen Iverson, G, Soph., Georgetown; Kerry Kittles, G-F, Sr., Villanova.

Second Team: Danny Fortson, F, Soph., Cincinnati; Keith Van Horn, F, Jr., Utah; Jacque Vaughn, G, Jr., Kansas; John Wallace, F, Sr., Syracuse; Lorenzen Wright, C, Soph., Memphis.

1996-97: First Team: Tim Duncan, C, Sr., Wake Forest; Danny Fortson, F, Jr., Cincinnati; Raef LaFrentz, F, Jr., Kansas; Ron Mercer, F, Soph., Kentucky; Keith Van Horn, F, Sr., Utah.

Second Team: Chauncey Billups, G, Soph., Colorado; Bobby Jackson, G, Sr., Minnesota; Antawn Jamison, F, Soph., North Carolina; Brevin Knight, G, Sr., Stanford; Jacque Vaughn, G, Sr., Kansas.

SELECTIONS CITED FOR NCAA CONSENSUS ALL-AMERICAN TEAMS

Christy Walsh Syndicate: 1929 and 1930
College Humor Magazine: 1929–33, 1936
Helms Foundation: 1929–48
Converse Yearbook: 1932–48
Literary Digest Magazine: 1934
Omaha World Newspaper: 1937
Madison Square Garden: 1937–42
Newspaper Enterprises Association: 1938, 1953–63
Colliers (Basketball Coaches): 1939, 1949–56
Pic Magazine: 1942–44
The Sporting News: 1943–46
Argosy Magazine: 1945
True Magazine: 1946 and 1947
Associated Press: 1948–
Look Magazine: 1949–63
United Press International: 1949–
International News Service: 1950–58
National Association of Basketball Coaches: 1957–
United States Basketball Writers Association: 1960–

INDEX

This index includes all persons, associations, leagues, and teams appearing in all sections of the *Inside Sports College Basketball*, except for box scores, individual and team statistics boxes, long lists of names, and material of general statistical nature.

A

AAU *see* Amateur Athletic Union
ABA 233, 439
Abdul Jabbar, Kareem *see* Alcindor, Lew
Abdur-Rahim, Shareef 350, 411, 470, 484, 656
Aberdeen, Stu 264
Abernathy, Ron 491
Abernethy, Tom 236, 487
Abilene Christian 221
ABL *see* American Basketball League
ACC *see* Atlantic Coast Conference
Aces *see* Evansville
Acres, Dick 299
Acres, Mark 299, 306
Adams, Alvan 221, 485
Adams, Clayton 491
Adams, Frank 70
Adams, Jack 102
Adams, Jimmy 493
Adams, John 40
Adams, Luke 204
Adebayo, Sunday 399
Adrion, Charlie 181
Aggies *see* New Mexico State, Texas A&M, Utah State
Aguirre, Mark 265, 275, 276, 285, 292, 346, 469, 470

AIAW *see* Association of Intercollegiate Athletics for Women
Ainge, Danny 281, 657
Air Force Falcons 102, 114, 243, 258, 369, 555, 603
Akron Zips 318
Alabama-Birmingham Blazers 290, 291, 292, 320, 325, 342, 490, 640, 659
Alabama Crimson Tide 29, 31, 72, 95-6, 101, 102, 198, 206, 228, 235, 235, 237, 244, 244, 308, 315, 325, 334, 344, 369, 390, 396, 403, 538, 603-4, 659
Alabama Crimson Tide (women's team) 513
Alabama State 297, 303
Alaimo, Gerald 228
Alarie, Mark 320, 488
Albany (NY) 656
Albion (MI) 545
Alcindor, Lew 129, 168, 171, 173-4, 177, 179, 183, 186, 189, 190, 191, 192, 204, 218, 395, 453, 662
Alcorn State Braves 264, 277, 306, 488, 567, 604
Alexander, Cory 390, 396, 405
Alexander, Courtney 563
Alexander, Cy 342
Alexander, Gary 356, 358
Alford, Sam 400, 663
Alford, Steve 322, 326, 329, 346, 400, 556, 567, 663
All-Border Conference 28
Allen, Bob 37
Allen, Forrest "Phog" 10, 11, 28, 34, 37, 58, 61, 80, 104, 124, 547
Allen, Frankie 376
Allen, George 30
Allen, Lucius 168, 183

Allen, Ray 412, 660
Allen, Sonny 310
Alley, Lyles 72, 83
Allums, Darrell 279
Alosa, Matt 398
Alston, Bailey 351
Amaker, Tommy 322
Amateur Athletic Union (AAU) 6, 9, 17, 503, 601
America East Conference 567, 568, 656
America West Conference 598
American Basketball Association *see* ABA
American Basketball League (ABL) 501, 513
American Conference 121
American Eagles 221, 262, 284, 604
American South Conference 598
Ames *see* Iowa State
Amherst 7
Anderson, Bill 63
Anderson, Cliff 174
Anderson, Derek 394, 412
Anderson, Eric 373
Anderson, Forddy 70, 76
Anderson, Glen 132
Anderson, Harold 36, 57, 63
Anderson, John 7
Anderson, Kenny 234, 351, 355, 356, 360, 373, 380, 469
Anderson, Michael 332
Anderson, Nick 323, 344, 356
Anderson, W. H. 4
Andreas, Lew 13, 45
Anet, Bobby 32
Angell, Emmett 7
Anteaters *see* California-Irvine
Anthony, Greg 358
Antigua, Orlando 394
Antinelli, Al 79
Appalachian State 262
Archbold, Darrin 366, 485
Archer, Eddie 488
Archibald, Nolan 538
Arizin, Paul 63, 66, 69, 70, 399
Arizona State Sun Devils 84, 104, 121, 142, 149, 165, 198,
     206, 238, 249, 255, 281, 285, 287, 380, 400, 563, 566,
     604, 655, 657, 658
Arizona Wildcats 41, 63, 77, 79, 104, 121, 156, 165, 220, 221,
     235, 238, 242, 244, 245, 255, 263-4, 329, 330, 332, 341,
     367, 371, 373, 378, 399, 406, 410, 411, 412, 488, 537,
     560, 604, 659, 660, 662
Arkansas-Little Rock Trojans 304, 319, 325, 605
Arkansas Razorbacks 40, 46, 47, 51, 61, 79, 116, 206, 227,
     250, 256, 261, 276, 284, 302, 326, 344, 361, 376, 386,
     390, 392, 395, 399, 403, 412, 537, 561, 604-5, 659, 660
Arkansas Razorbacks (women's team) 513
Arkansas State Indians 234, 361, 605

Armstrong, Jack 274
Armstrong, Jim 490
Army Cadets 11, 38, 48, 169, 182, 199, 206, 243, 311, 605
Arnelle, Jesse 78, 92, 96, 97
Arnold, Frank 264
Arnold, Jeff 488
Arnold, Jerome 262
Arnold, Murray 290, 297
Arrow, Ronnie 362
Arthurs, Johnny 188
Artman, Bob 26
Ashmore, Jim 108
Askew, Vincent 334
Associated Press 663
Association of Intercollegiate Athletics for Women (AIAW)
     505, 507, 509
Atkinson, Joe 300
Atlanta Tipoff Club 663
Atlantic Athletic Conference 310
Atlantic Coast Conference (ACC) 70, 85, 88, 90, 102, 114,
     129, 142, 149, 156, 180, 197, 206, 212, 214, 223, 227,
     228, 233, 234, 235, 236, 242, 259, 263, 273, 274, 281,
     288, 302, 308, 318, 323, 325, 349, 380, 392, 399, 408,
     471-3, 509, 565, 566, 569, 655
Atlantic Ten Conference 303, 325, 349, 363, 473, 566, 570
Aubrey, Sam 55
Auburn Tigers 8, 116, 118, 119, 120, 131, 138, 198, 204, 235,
     264, 273, 304, 306, 310, 315, 318, 391, 605, 650, 659
Auburn Tigers (women's team) 508, 513
Auerbach, Arnold "Red" 35, 71
Augmon, Stacey 358, 360, 363
Auriemma, Geno 499, 500, 501, 513, 525
Austin, John 155, 156
Austin Peay State Governors 218, 249, 327, 605
Austin, Ron 204
Avina, Jack 258
Awtrey, Dennis 191
Ayers, Randy 259, 361, 362, 662
Azary, John 77
Aztecs *see* San Diego State
Azzi, Jennifer 510, 518

B

Badgers *see* Wisconsin
Bagley, John 300, 490
Bailey, Bobby 88
Bailey, Charles 227
Bailey, Terrance 318
Bailey, Toby 395, 561
Baker, Cecil 132
Baker, Jimmie 221
Baker, Lamar 298
Baker, Tay 169
Baker, Terry 152

Baker University 10
Baker, Vin 366, 376, 485
Balanis, George 250
Baldwin, Oscar "Red" 27
Baldwin-Wallace (OH) 85
Balentine, Charles 302
Ball State Cardinals 342, 606
Ballard, Greg 249
Baltimore 299
Banks, Freddie 329
Banks, Gene 267, 662
Bannon, Kevin 384
Baptiste, Cyril 196
Barber, John 82
Barker, Bud 27
Barker, Cliff 62, 65
Barkley, Charles 315, 437, 453
Barksdale, Don 45, 57, 649
Barmore, Leon 526
Barnes, Jim "Bad News" 155, 156, 160
Barnes, Ken 163
Barnes, Marvin 214, 223, 226, 231, 493
Barnett, Dick 546
Barnett, J. D. 310, 658, 659, 663
Barnhill, John 546
Barnstable, Dale 62, 65, 66
Baron, Jim 361, 363
Barone, Tony 288, 361, 657
Barrett, Ernie 77
Barry, Jim 163
Barry, Rick 162, 163, 166
Barton, Jim 325, 332
Bartow, Gene 195, 206, 234, 251, 290-1, 400, 490, 547
Basile, Danny 383
Bauman, Lorri 518
Bavetta, Dick 121
Baxter, Lionel 48
Baylor Bears 31, 51, 54, 71, 73, 120, 391, 490, 563, 606
Baylor, Elgin 69, 109, 113, 115, 118, 126, 370, 453
Bearcats see Cincinnati
Beard, Butch 179
Beard, Frank 74
Beard, Ralph 50, 57, 62, 66, 67
Bears see Baylor, Brown, Southwest Missouri State
Beasley, Charles 179
Beasley, John 168
Beaulieu, Joe 490
Beavers see Oregon State
Beck, Angela 513
Beck, Corey 392
Beck, Ernie 69, 84
Beckel, Bob 102, 118
Becton, Benny 150

Bee, Clair 14, 15, 16, 34, 35, 41, 72, 74, 75, 660
Begovich, Matty 14
Behagen, Ron 214
Beilein, John 384, 657
Beisser, Ed 45
Belcher, Cookie 563
Belko, Steve 80
Bell, Melvin 186
Bellamy, Walt 136
Belluomini, Dan 489
Belnap, Dutch 493
Belz, Carl 118
Bemus, Charles 4
Bender, Bob 261, 563
Bender, Jules 15
Bengals see Idaho State
Benington, John 119
Bennerman, Doremus 383
Bennett, Dick 384
Bennett, Mario 380
Benson, Kent 236, 244
Benton, Eddie 383, 393, 399
Benton, Terry 206
Berenson, Senda 502, 503
Berman, Arnie 211
Berry, Bill 279, 284
Berry, Curtis 279
Berry, Ricky 332
Berry, Walter 329
Berst, David 545
Best, John 376, 485
Bethune-Cookman Wildcats 490
Bevely, Tilman 318
Bey, Rashid 562
Bialosuknia, Wes 174
Bias, Len 316, 322
Bibb, Bill 310
Bibby, Henry 201, 556, 660
Bibby, Mike 410, 560, 660
Big East Conference 263, 274, 288, 315, 316, 327, 332, 342, 374, 379, 398, 408, 473-4, 565, 566, 571
Big Eight Conference 107, 113, 148, 150, 156, 164, 190, 211, 242, 263, 274, 276, 325, 330, 333, 349, 380, 474-5, 509, 565-6, 598
Big Green see Dartmouth
Big Red see Cornell
Big Seven Conference 61, 71, 82
Big Six Conference 38
Big Sky Conference 189, 204, 221, 235, 242, 567, 572
Big South Conference 376, 439, 567, 573, 656
Big Ten Conference 28, 40, 43, 48, 53, 54, 56, 57, 79, 85, 108, 129, 150, 156, 177, 183, 188-9, 196, 198, 199, 205, 212, 214, 235, 240, 244, 249, 251, 256, 258, 264, 265, 264,

274, 275, 282, 287, 304, 306, 310, 344, 346, 349, 362, 363, 396, 400, 402, 475-6, 509, 565, 566, 574, 655, 660

Big Twelve Conference 349, 566, 575, 655

Big West Conference 214, 218, 365, 491, 554, 567, 576

Bilas, Jay 488

Biles, Willie 218, 219, 226

Billikens see St. Louis

Billups, Chauncey 410

Bing, Dave 168, 453

Binion, Joe 291

Bird, Larry 248, 249, 258, 261, 262, 264, 265, 269, 422, 453, 499

Birdsong, Otis 249, 380

Bison see Bucknell

Black, Charles 26

Black Coaches Association (BCA) 350, 601

Black, Leon 230

Black, Steve 300

Black, W. O. 4

Blackbirds see Long Island

Blackburn, Tom 79, 145, 157

Blair, Bill 243, 264

Blakeley, Bill 240, 258, 493

Blakney, Roderick 410, 657

Blaney, George 214, 235

Blanton, Ricky 337

Blaylock, Mookie 330, 333

Blazejowski, Carol 506, 518

Blazers see Alabama-Birmingham

Bliss, Dave 235, 266, 332, 333, 398, 455, 659, 660

Block, John 168

Blocker, Randy 383

Blue Demons see DePaul

Blue Devils see Duke

Blue Raiders see Middle Tennessee State

Bluejays see Creighton

Blye, Sylvester 137

Bobcats see Montana State, Ohio

Boeheim, Jim 195, 276, 325, 401, 455-6

Bogues, Tyrone "Mugsy" 274, 485, 562

Bohler, George 29

Boilermakers see Purdue

Boise State Broncos 204, 332, 567, 606

Bol, Manute 363

Bolden, Randy 657

Bolton-Holifield, Ruthie 513

Bonczyk, Mike 491

Bond, Phillip 236

Bonner, Anthony 351

Bonnies see St. Bonaventure

Booker, Hassan 409

Boozer, Bob 118

Border Conference 77, 146, 598

Born, Bertram "B.H." 85, 86

Boryla, Vince 26

Bossert, Gary 323

Boston Celtics 305

Boston College Eagles 54, 103, 219, 262, 291, 297, 300, 332, 408, 490, 606, 655

Boston University Terriers 121, 198, 215, 409, 606

Boswell, Cathy 518

Boudreau, Lou 28

Bouldin, Carl 140

Bowers, Elsworth 490

Bowers, Russell 276

Bowie, Sam 294, 300, 306, 308, 398, 487

Bowling Green Falcons 27, 41, 57, 65, 97, 154, 606-7, 656

Bowman, Nate 166

Boyce, Donnie 383, 392

Boyce, Jim 491

Boyd, Bob 206, 228, 266, 493

Boyd, Devin 376

Boyd, Mike 362

Boyer, Tommy 142, 149

Boykins, Earl 563

Boykoff, Harry 52, 57

Boyle, Jim 318

Boynes, Winford 267, 488

Bozeman, Todd 377

Bradds, Gary 149, 155

Bradford, Troy 325

Bradley, Bill 155, 163-4, 166, 168, 192

Bradley Braves 70, 74, 76, 77, 92, 100, 109, 129, 138, 149, 150, 247-8, 277, 288, 317, 318, 333, 420, 607

Bradley, Charlie 297

Bradley, Dudley 263

Bradley, Harold 75, 132, 149

Bradley, Jim 215

Bradley, Joe 55

Bradley, Pat 561

Bradley, Ron 367

Bradley, Shawn 362, 390, 396

Bradshaw, Kevin 358, 360, 485, 490

Bramlett, A. J. 411, 412

Brandeis 103

Brandenburg, Jim 299, 318

Brandon, Aaron 488

Brandon, Terrell 360

Branham, Melvin 383

Brannon, Buster 36, 79

Branstrom, Marv 108

Braswell, Bobby 491

Braun, Ben 361, 567

Braves see Alcorn State, Bradley

Brennan, Pete 109, 110

Brennan, Tom 362

Brent, David 196, 205

Brewer, Jim 212, 216

Brewer, Ron 250, 256, 261

Brey, Mike 491

Brickey, Robert 334

Bridgeman, Junior 236, 237

Bridges, Warren 281

Brigham Young Cougars 41, 76, 146, 151, 200, 207, 210, 211, 215, 264, 281, 284, 308, 390, 396, 406, 566, 607

Brindley, Aud 50

Brisker, John 179

Bristow, Allan 218

Britt, Wayman 492

Brittman, Darron 316

Brkovich, Mike 487

Broadnax, Horace 312

Broberg, Gus 26, 38, 67

Brock, Debbie 518

Broderick Award 514

Brodzinski, Barry 491

Brogdon, Cindy 506, 518

Brokaw, Gary 238

Broncos see Boise State, Santa Clara, Western Michigan

Brookin, Rod 332

Brooklyn 52

Brooklyn College of Pharmacy 12

Brooklyn YMCA 2

Brooks, Alvin 657

Brooks, Chris 323

Brooks, Michael 275, 376, 657

Broussard, Rickey 393

Browder, Darrell 281

Brown Bears 30, 190, 219, 228, 263, 316, 388, 390, 607

Brown, Carl 342

Brown, Craig 360

Brown, Dale 195, 284, 311, 406, 436, 491, 492, 538

Brown, Earl 48

Brown, Fred 197, 291

Brown, Larry 70, 318, 333, 489, 490, 253, 493,

Brown, Lou 70

Brown, Marc 344

Brown, Marcus 398, 399

Brown, Owen 228

Brown, Rickey 470

Brown, Roger 136

Brown, Russell 263

Brown, Skip 233

Brown, Wiley 278, 487

Brown, Willie 188

Browne, Anucha 518

Bruen, Jack 376

Bruins see UCLA

Brundy, Stanley 346

Bryant, Ernie 86

Bryant, Kobe 350, 437

Bubas, Vic 77, 156, 190

Buccaneers see East Tennessee State

Buchanan, Izett 383

Buck, Mike 344

Buckeyes see Ohio State

Buckley, Bruce 488

Bucknell Bison 108, 303, 607

Buckner, Greg 560

Buckner, Quinn 236, 243, 244, 487

Budd, Dave 130

Buffalo 250

Buffaloes see Colorado

Buie, Coleco 562

Bullard, Gerald 100

Bulldogs see Butler, Citadel, Drake, Fresno State, Georgia, Louisiana Tech, Mississippi State, Yale

Bullett, Vicky 519

Bullington, Larry 227

Bulls see South Florida

Bunte, Art 78

Buntin, Bill 160, 164

Buonaguro, Mitch 318

Burden, Luther "Ticky" 221, 245

Burdette, Floyd 72

Burgan, Todd 405, 562

Burgess, Frank 136

Burleson, Tom 227, 230, 231, 355

Burness, Don 42

Burrell, Nelson 550

Burrell, Scott 374

Burrow, Bob 103, 105, 538

Burwell, Clyde 228

Buse, Don 542

Bush, Jerry 114

Butler Bulldogs 145, 198, 201, 410, 411, 563, 607

Butler, Lawrence 262

Butts, Niya 513

Buzolich, Nick 50

Byhre, Ed 262

Byrd, Leo 118

Byrdsong, Ricky 385

C

Cable, Barney 103

Cadets see Army

Cage, Michael 302

Cain, Bill 201

Cain, Carl 105

Cal Poly-San Luis Obispo 399

Cal State-Fullerton Titans 243, 258, 259, 261, 290, 299, 342, 490, 608

Caldwell, Joe 156

Calhoun, Corkie 208

Calhoun, Jim 303, 393, 398, 456, 556, 656, 657

California Basketball Association 95, 98

California Golden Bears 9, 11, 53, 54, 121, 133, 135, 136, 289, 316, 379-80, 383, 393, 396, 411, 412, 607-8, 655, 656

California Golden Bears (women's team) 503

California-Irvine Anteaters 281, 288, 290, 354, 608

California-Santa Barbara Gauchos 332, 333, 608

Caligaris, Dave 258

Calihan, Bob 156

Calipari, John 354, 367, 370, 398, 399, 405

Calkins, Bob "Ace" 29

Callandrillo, Dan 288

Calloway, Ricky 326

Calverley, Ernie 48, 140

Calvert, Paul 30

Camby, Marcus 398, 400, 412, 671

Cameron, Eddie 35

Campanelli, Lou 290, 377, 491

Campbell, Marc 298

Campion, Bill 221

Canisius Golden Griffins 108, 114, 226, 384, 393, 402, 408, 608, 657

Cann, Howard 11, 13, 115

Canty, Bob 96

Capel, Jeff 556, 560

Capua, Joe 102

Cardinals see Ball State, Lamar, Louisville, Stanford

Carey, Jim 250, 262

Carlesimo, P. J. 262, 334, 342, 423

Carlesimo, Pete 423

Carlson, Doc 11

Carlson, H. C. 85-6

Carlton, Jerry 142

Carlton, Rahsaan 405

Carnegie Tech 28, 29

Carnesecca, Lou 170, 310, 318, 332, 369

Carnevale, Ben 75, 157

Carney, Bob 95

Carney, Steve 332

Carpenter, Kareem 394

Carr, Antoine 296, 489

Carr, Austin 189, 197, 198, 201, 203, 204, 210, 269

Carr, Chris 453

Carr, Cory 410

Carr, Ronnie 284, 298

Carril, Pete 360, 377, 400, 401

Carroll, Joe Barry 279

Carter, Howard 492

Carter, Perry 365

Carter, Ron 258

Carter, Vince 560

Cartwright, Bill 269, 488, 493

Case, Everett 58, 75, 80, 90, 102, 119, 120, 128, 164, 554

Case Western Reserve 98

Casey, Don 263

Casey, Dwane 341

Casey, Mike 201

Cash, James 176

Cassell, Sam 374, 380

Castellani, John 109

Catalina, Nelson 361

Catamounts see Western Carolina

Catchings, Tamika 513

Catholic 284

Catledge, Terry 310

Catlett, Gale 290, 456, 658, 660

Cavaliers see Virginia

CCNY see City College of New York

Centenary 235, 242, 243, 490

Central Florida 384, 402

Central Michigan Chippewas 235, 325, 608-9

Central Missouri State 547

Chamberlain, Wilt 69, 104, 107, 109, 111, 113, 114, 118, 124, 126, 376, 453

Chambers, Bill 83

Chambers, Bob 491

Chambers, Jerry 168, 171, 173

Chaminade 294

Chanay, Larry 130

Chancellor, Van 513

Chandler, Dwan 490

Chandler, Happy 28

Chaney, John 303, 325, 332, 380, 456

Chapman, Gib 393

Chapman, Roosevelt 305, 308

Chappell, Len 142, 148

Charles, Ken 219

Charles, Lorenzo 299

Charleston Cougars 609

Charleston Southern 325

Chavez, Rob 377, 393, 403

Cheaney, Calbert 370, 373, 380

Cheeks, Chris 338

Chelette, Newton 310

Chicago 4, 8, 48, 54, 83, 362

Chiesa, Gordon 299

Childers, Jim 492

Childress, Mike 206

Childress, Randolph 373, 374, 392

Chilton, Tom 136

Chipman, Roy 258

Chippewas see Central Michigan

Chones, Jim 195, 216

Christl, Edward C. 48

Ciampi, Joe 513, 526

Cincinnati Bearcats 57, 70, 75, 76, 83, 116, 135, 139, 140, 142, 146, 148, 149, 152, 155, 169, 196, 200, 238, 250, 288, 311, 367, 396, 406-7, 411, 537, 562, 566, 609

Cinicola, John 491
Cipriano, Joe 169, 281
Cirino, Brad 398
Citadel Bulldogs 102, 243, 262, 342, 609
City College of New York (CCNY) 7, 11, 13, 16, 72-3, 74, 77, 85, 132, 420, 559
Clark, Arlen 118
Clark, Keon 562
Clark, Perry 367, 373
Clark, Rusty 181
CLAW see Commission on Intercollegiate Athletics for Women
Clay, Dwight 218, 225
Cleamons, Jim 199
Cleaves, Mateen 562
Clement, Jeff 541
Clement, Kristen 513
Clemson Tigers 29, 40, 55, 75, 80, 102, 108, 156, 165, 180, 234, 235, 265, 273, 277, 298, 323, 325, 327, 349, 385, 396, 405, 560, 609, 655, 659
Cleveland State Vikings 310, 318, 320, 362, 383, 554, 609, 658
Clifton, Jeff 383
Cline, Nancy Lieberman see Lieberman-Cline, Nancy
Closs, Keith 393, 400
Clune, Jack 95
Cluxton, Paul 541
Coast Guard 54
Coastal Carolina 439
Cobb, Ernie 262
Cofield, Bill 249
Cohen, Fred 104
Cohen, Jeff 136
Cohen, Sid 538
Coker, Lee 27
Colangelo, Jerry 138
Coleman, Derrick 323, 329, 670
Coleman, Mike 234
Coleman, Norris 334, 344
Coleman, Ron 493
Coles, Bimbo 332, 338
Coles, Charles 325
Coles, Charlie 491
Colgate Red Raiders 281, 282, 325, 376, 567, 609-10
College of Charleston 409, 411, 560, 567
College Sports Information Directors of America 601
Collegiate Commissioners Association Tournament 422
Collier, Barry 410
Collier, Chris 360
Collier, Gary 390
Collier, Jason 560
Collier, Tommy 488
Collins, Chris 387
Collins, Craig 310
Collins, Don 276

Collins, Doug 211, 218, 387
Collins, Eddie 490
Colonels see Eastern Kentucky
Colonial Athletic Association 325, 380, 476, 567, 577
Colonials see George Washington, Robert Morris
Colorado Buffaloes 38, 42, 100, 148, 190, 204, 264, 299, 325, 366, 410, 566, 610, 655
Colorado Buffaloes (women's team) 509
Colorado State Rams 91, 139, 206, 255, 342, 562, 610, 657
Colson, Gary 243
Columbia College of Pharmacy 12
Columbia Lions 7, 12, 13, 62, 75, 77, 181, 377, 610, 649
Combes, Harry 79, 108, 138
Commission on Intercollegiate Athletics for Women (CLAW) 504
Commodores see Vanderbilt
Community College League of California 601
Condie, Lyman 50
Conference USA 349, 566, 578, 655
Conforti, John 188, 198
Conley, Gene 70-1
Conley, Larry 171
Conlin, Ed 84
Connecticut Huskies 30, 54, 98, 132, 137, 152, 214, 247, 332, 342, 360, 393, 396, 398, 405, 407, 412, 427, 556, 562, 610, 659
Connecticut Huskies (women's team) 499, 500, 501, 512, 513
Connelly, Jeff 489
Conner, Jimmy Dan 236, 237
Conner, Nick 211
Conradt, Jody 526, 553
Cook, Norm 253, 491
Cooper, Michael 261
Cope, Bob 62
Coppin State Eagles 411, 427, 567, 610-11
Corbett, Don 332
Corbin, Max 30
Corell, Ed 145
Corley, Bill 76, 180
Cornell Big Red 4, 76, 176, 304, 334, 611
Cornhuskers see Nebraska
Corpus Christi 221
Corzine, Dave 259, 261
Cosic, Kresimir 210, 211
Costello, Larry 83
Costner, Tony 302
Cota, Ed 560
Cotton, James 410
Cottrell, Steve 290
Cougars see Brigham Young, Charleston, Houston, Washington State
Counts, Mel 148, 154, 156
Cousy, Bob 62, 73
Cowboys see Oklahoma State, Wyoming

Cowden, Bill 42
Cowens, Dave 203
Cowles, Ozzie 41, 54, 60, 62
Cox, Frosty 38
Cox, Johnny 115, 116
Crake, Eric 84
Cratsley, Melvin 28
Creighton Bluejays 9, 11, 39, 45, 57, 72, 81, 109, 220, 361, 611
Cremins, Bobby 197, 262, 318, 378, 456-7, 658
Crews, Jim 342, 487
Crimson see Harvard
Crimson Tide see Alabama
Crisp, Hank 31
Croshere, Austin 408, 411, 412
Cross, Russell 308
Crum, Denny 195, 215, 233, 276, 311, 457, 487, 492, 539, 656, 659
Crusaders see Holy Cross, Valparaiso
Culton, Albert 284
Cummings, Terry 300
Cunningham, Billy 156, 258
Cunningham, Dick 176
Cunningham, Gary 132, 195, 263
Cunningham, Jim 114
Curran, Joseph 108
Curry, Denise 519
Cutright, Michael 338
Cyclones see Iowa State

D

Dabney, Mike 244
Dailey, Quintin 289-90
Daisy, Jason 563
Dallmar, Howie 42-3, 51, 235
Dalton, Ralph 487
Daly, Chuck 235, 258, 263
Dambrot, Irwin 73
Daniels, Antonio 399
Daniels, Chris 399
Daniels, Gary 144
Daniels, Mel 249
Dantley, Adrian 238, 253, 269, 470
Dare, Yinka 211, 396
Darling, Charles 79
Darrow, James 131
Darsch, Nancy 513
Dartmouth Big Green 35, 41, 47, 48, 49, 50, 52, 54, 62, 63, 114, 119, 190, 214, 383, 611
Davenport, Scott 492
Davidson, George 111
Davidson Wildcats 45, 52, 129, 142, 165, 177, 180, 189, 200, 220, 243, 385, 398, 611
Davies, Bob 56
Davies, Chick 61

Davis & Elkins 10
Davis, Antonio 485
Davis, Charlie 188
Davis, Clarissa 509
Davis, Joe 51
Davis, Kerry 243
Davis, Lardie 41
Davis, Larry 41, 490
Davis, Lucius, Sr. 369
Davis, Lucius. Jr. 369
Davis, Mark 315
Davis, Mel 225
Davis, Mickey 216
Davis, Stan 226
Davis, Tom 325, 338, 457, 490, 491, 547
Davis, Walter 488
Davis-Wrightsil, Clarissa 519
Dawkins, Darryl 437
Dawkins, Johnny 319, 322, 346-7, 488
Dawkins, Paul 262
Day, Doug 360
Daye, Darren 279, 489
Dayton Flyers 9, 36, 78, 79, 82, 85, 114, 145, 157, 179, 229, 285, 305, 385, 420, 490, 567, 611
Dean, Everett 30, 41, 42, 43
Deane, Mike 342, 361, 384, 562
Deaton, Tom 310
DeBernardi, Forrest S. 12
DeBerry, Tom 235
DeBusschere, Dave 132, 146
Dee, Johnny 96, 102
Dees, Benny 325
Deford, Frank 171
Dehere, Terry 365, 374
Del Negro, Vinny 485
Delaware 144, 332, 366, 490
Delaware State 361
Delk, Tony 401
Delph, Marvin 261
Delta State (women's team) 505, 512
Dembo, Fennis 329
Dememt, Mike 334
Dement, Mike 393
Demon Deacons see Wake Forest
Dempsey, Cedric 545
Dennard, Kenny 263
Dennis, Greg 488
Denver 262, 277
DePaul Blue Demons 28, 29, 46, 48, 51, 54, 56, 102, 157, 183, 200, 247, 259, 261, 262, 265, 276, 279, 284, 285, 287, 291, 292, 300, 304, 325, 344, 406, 422, 555, 611-2, 657
DePauw (IN) 52
DeRoche, Joe 550
Detroit Pistons 216

Detroit Titans 102, 108, 156, 212, 249, 258, 490, 491, 612

DeVoe, Don 310, 457-8, 557, 663

Dick, John 32

Dickerson, Michael 410, 560

Dickey, Dick 60

Dickey, James 398

Diddle, E. A. 423

Diddle, Ed 29, 45, 83, 89, 157

Didrikson, Babe 504

Dierking, Connie 108

DiGregorio, Ernie 222, 223, 225, 493

Dillard, Sherman 491

Dillard, Skip 285

Dischinger, Terry 136, 142, 143

Dixon, Malik 410

Dixon, Tamecka 513

Dobard, Rodney 374

Dobbs, Wayne 190

Doleach, Michael 563

Dollar, Cameron 394

Dolphins see Jacksonville

Donches, Steve 168

Donewald, Bob 235, 297, 342, 367

Donnelly, Terry 266

Donoher, Don 157

Donohue, Jack 171

Donovan, Anne 500, 506, 519

Dons see San Francisco

Doogan, John 84

Dorsey, Jacky 234, 469, 470

Douglas, Leon 235, 244

Douglas, Sherman 341

Dowell, Duck 145

Downey, Dave 150

Downing, Steve 221, 225

Downs, Raymond 97, 102, 103

Dragons see Drexel

Drake Bulldogs 8, 59, 137, 156, 189, 191, 200, 210, 362, 422, 612

Dressler, Mark 279, 492

Drew, Bryce 410, 411, 564

Drew, Homer 410

Drexel Dragons 398, 401, 567, 612

Drexler, Clyde 292, 294, 296, 300, 308

Driesell, Charles "Lefty" 142, 165, 189, 200, 215, 233, 302, 316, 349, 392, 398, 458, 488, 658, 663

Driscoll, Terry 190

Dromo, John 215

Drum, Lex 279

Drummond, Troy 391

Ducks see Oregon

Dudley, Demetrius 376

Dudley, Raymond 338

Duff, Mike 255

Duhe, Gary 492

Duhon, Glenn 318

Duke Blue Devils 29, 35, 39, 40, 60, 71, 75, 156, 165, 170, 176, 180, 190, 221, 226, 234, 255, 258, 259, 261, 263, 267, 302, 318, 319, 322, 332, 333, 334, 337, 349, 354-5, 358, 363, 369, 370, 371, 373, 374, 378, 391, 392, 399, 408, 487, 488, 491, 558, 560, 612, 655, 658, 659, 662

Duke, Wayne 310

Dukes, Derrick 490

Dukes see Duquesne, James Madison

Dukes, Walter 83, 84

Dukiet, Bob 276

Dumars, Joe 453

Dumas, Tony 383

Duncan, Tim 211, 396, 399, 405, 411, 412, 414, 454, 566, 663

Dunkin, Tony 376, 439, 484

Dunn, Jerry 400

Duquesne Dukes 27-8, 61, 90, 114, 186-7, 276, 420, 491, 567, 612-3

Durham, Hugh 215, 297, 458, 658, 663

Durrant, Devin 302

Durrenberger, Joe 96

Dutcher, Jim 316

Dwyer, Cliff 70

Dye, Bobby 258, 332

Dye, Tippy 77

Dykstra, Joe 288

E

Eackles, Ledell 330

Eads, Clyde 311

Eagles see American, Boston College, Coppin State, Eastern Michigan, Morehead State

Eagles, Tommy Joe 391

Eaker, Gerald 394

Earl, Lester 659

Earle, Jimmy 235

East Carolina Pirates 235, 380, 613

East Coast Conference 291

East Tennessee State Buccaneers 264, 311, 361, 371, 488, 613

Eastern Intercollegiate Conference 28, 29

Eastern Intercollegiate League 75

Eastern Kentucky Colonels 26, 27, 57, 89, 121, 262, 323, 613

Eastern League 8, 9

Eastern Michigan Eagles 361, 563, 613

Eaves, Jerry 487

Eaves, Joel 119, 131

Ebron, Roy 214, 216

Eckman, Carol 504

Eddleman, Dike 60

Edmundson, Hec 36, 58

Edney, Tyus 394

Edwards, Allen 412

Edwards, Bill 376

Edwards, Cleveland 391

Edwards, Dick 157, 177
Edwards, Doug 373, 374
Edwards, Frank 276, 284
Edwards, George 49, 558
Edwards, Jay 356, 363
Edwards, Ken 235
Edwards, Ozie 218
Edwards, Teresa 501, 508, 519
Egan, Hank 243, 258, 325
Egan, Jack 135, 159
Egan, Johnny 120
Elias, Jim 493
Eliot, Charles 6
Elliott, Jamelle 500
Elliott, Pete 62
Elliott, Sax 82
Elliott, Sean 330, 344
Ellis, Alex 108
Ellis, Bo 249
Ellis, Cliff 263, 284, 325, 458
Ellis, Dale 295
Ellis, LaPhonso 344
Ellis, Leron 341
Ellis, LeRoy 145
Ellison, Pervis 318, 319, 322
Elmore, Len 227, 228, 233
Elon (NC) 656
Elzy, Kyra 513
Embry, Wayne 108
Endacott, Paul 11
Engineers see Lehigh
Engleman, Howard 37, 38, 58
English, William 542
Enis, Shalonda 513
Enke, Fred 41, 77, 121
Erickson, Keith 159
Erving, Julius 149, 199, 204, 206, 208, 492
Estergard, Dick 90
Estes, Butch 362
Estes, Wayne 150, 162, 163
Evans, Joe 490
Evans, John 132
Evans, Mike 237
Evans, Paul 318, 488
Evansville Aces 255, 325, 342, 542, 567, 613-4
Ewing, Patrick 211, 273, 291, 302, 305, 308, 315, 347, 487
Explorers see La Salle

F

Fairfield Stags 318, 408, 411, 614
Fairleigh Dickinson 206, 332, 334
Falcons see Air Force, Bowling Green
Falk, Rich 155, 297

Fant, Lenny 492
Farley, George 131-2
Fater, Joe 48
Faught, Bob 41
Faust, Duane 325
Feaster, Rob 382
Feinstein, John 274
Feldhaus, Allen 131
Feldman, Jon 138
Felton, George 658
Ferguson, Ron 491
Ferrara, Mike 281, 282, 485
Ferrin, Arnie 26, 47, 49, 67
Ferry, Danny 334, 338, 491
Fibbe, Jimmy 131
Fields, Denny 258
Fighting Illini see Illinois
Fighting Irish see Notre Dame
Filipek, Ron 168
Finch, Larry 219, 225, 325, 436
Finkel, Henry 163
Finley, Michael 374, 392
Finney, Jody 199
Fiore, Ted 361
Fish, Matt 367
Fisher, Casey 489
Fisher, George 173
Fisher, Harry 7-8
Fisher, Scott 318
Fisher, Steve 343, 376, 379, 396, 458-9, 487, 489, 658
Fitzgerald, Dan 384, 396
Fitzgerald, Darrin 323, 325
Fitzsimmons, Jim 211
Fleming, Al 488
Fleming, Ed 78, 83
Fleming, Ernie 211
Flenory, Baron "B.B." 491
Fletcher, Rod 659
Florida Gators 40, 165, 189, 198, 273, 329, 334, 337, 342, 344, 384, 614
Florida Gators (women's team) 513
Florida International 396
Florida State Seminoles 203, 204, 215, 216, 225, 339, 343, 344, 374, 561, 614, 657
Floyd, Darrell 88, 97, 102, 107
Floyd, John 201
Floyd, Sleepy 288
Floyd, Tim 376, 385, 398, 459, 492, 567, 656, 659
Flyers see Dayton
Flynn, Mike 236
Flynt, "Parson" Bill 47
Fogel, Karl 325
Fogle, Larry 226
Fogler, Eddie 333, 376, 399, 566, 659

Foley, Jack 144
Ford, Alphonso 374
Ford, Chris 203
Ford, Gene 188
Ford, Phil 245, 253, 270
Ford, Sherell 392
Ford, Sherrell 394
Fordham Rams 13, 70, 204, 206, 210, 310, 377, 614
Foreman, Andre 551
Fortc, Chet 108, 657
Fortenberry, Ken 297
Fortson, Danny 406, 414
Foster, Bill 393, 406
Foster, Fred 181
Foster, Harold "Bud" 12, 25, 40, 57, 72, 121
Foster, Jim 513
Foster, Pat 303
Foster, Rod 279, 489
49ers see Long Beach State, UNC-Charlotte
Fowlkes, Tremaine 656
Foyle, Adonal 408, 567
Francis, Clarence "Bevo" 82, 541-2, 550, 551
Franklin, Joe 183
Franklin, Kenderick 410
Franklin, Kevin 351
Franklin, Mike 238
Fraschilla, Fran 380, 393
Frazier, Nat 342
Frazier, Ricky 493
Frazier, Walt 421, 542
Frederick, Rex 114
Fredrick, Zam 282, 485
Freeman, Buck 13
Freeman, Don 168
Freeman, Robin 102, 103
Fresno State Bulldogs 256, 290, 553, 561, 567, 614-5, 656, 659
Frett, La'Keshia 513
Friars see Providence
Friddle, Berle 419
Frieder, Bill 459, 492, 657, 658
Friel, Gerry 199, 343
Friel, Jack 39, 49, 72
Fryer, Jeff 351, 355
Fuqua, Richie 211
Furjanic, Matt 297, 493
Furlow, Terry 241
Furman Paladins 72, 83, 206, 228, 250, 255, 276, 362, 615

G

Gaeckler, Roger 249
Gaels see Iona, St. Mary's
Gaeta, Bobby 551
Gaillard, Bob 145, 489, 493

Gaines, Clarence "Bighouse" 542
Gaines, Corey 330
Gaines, David 258
Gaines, Smokey 310
Gaither, Tommy 318, 325
Gale, Bob 47
Gales, Jimmy 493
Galiber, Joe 73
Gallagher, Don 136
Gallon, Ricky 236
Gamecocks see South Carolina
Garden City (KS) Community College 326
Gardner, Jack 58, 61, 76, 165, 171, 173, 207
Gardner, Jelani 656
Garfinkel, Howard 453
Garibaldi, Dick 189
Garmaker, Dick 538
Garnett, Kevin 350, 437, 660
Garrett, Dean 326
Garrett, Dick 180
Garrick, Tom 330
Garris, Kiwane 561
Garrity, Pat 563
Gathers, Hank 316, 330, 339, 350-1, 489
Gators see Florida
Gauchos see California-Santa Barbara
Gaudet, Pete 391
Gavitt, Dave 190, 228, 263, 493
Gaze, Andrew 344
Geer, Major 488
Geneva College 4
George Mason 303
George Washington Colonials 35, 54, 55, 75, 89, 98, 103, 138, 190, 250, 376, 380, 396, 399, 562, 615, 656, 657
George Washington Colonials (women's team) 513
Georgetown Hoyas 28, 29, 46, 62, 90, 121, 132, 144, 195, 221, 242, 244, 256, 273, 288, 291, 302, 305, 306, 310, 311, 312, 313, 315, 327, 332, 362, 374, 379, 411, 427, 487, 565, 615
Georgia Bulldogs 8, 72, 131, 176, 180, 242, 273, 273, 297, 300, 329, 334, 337, 561, 615
Georgia Bulldogs (women's team) 508, 513
Georgia Southern 366
Georgia State 227, 360, 658
Georgia Tech Yellow Jackets 8, 95, 108, 135, 154, 198, 204, 206, 298, 302, 308, 315, 318, 349, 351, 355, 356, 363, 373, 374, 378, 380, 399, 615, 658
Gerard, Gerry 71, 75
Gerson, Rip 14
Gervasoni, Mike 394
Gervin, Derrick 310
Gervin, George 310, 542
Gettysburg 221
Gianelli, John 214

Gibbon, Joe 107
Gibbs, James 489
Gibson, Bill 206, 235
Gibson, Dee 423
Giermak, Chet 70
Gilberg, Erik 488
Gill, Kendall 659
Gill, Slats 157
Gill, Tim 563
Gillen, Pete 344, 459, 656
Gillom, Peggie 519
Gilmore, Artis 201, 203, 204, 205, 208, 270, 662
Givens, Jack 237, 258
Glamack, George 26, 35, 40, 67
Glass, Gerald 337
Glenn, Mike 253
Glover, Clarence 210, 662
Gminski, Mike 255, 261, 267, 662
Godfrey, Ron 206
Goheen, Barry 338
Gola, Tom 69, 78, 89, 91-2, 95, 96, 98, 126, 190, 453
Golden Bears *see* California
Golden Eagles *see* Oral Roberts, Southern Mississippi, Tennessee Tech
Golden Flashes *see* Kent
Golden Gophers *see* Minnesota
Golden Griffins *see* Canisius
Golden Hurricane *see* Tulsa
Gondrezick, Glen 253
Gonzaga Zags 221, 284, 384, 396, 616
Gonzalez, Rob 299
Gonzalez, Tony 656
Goodrich, Gail, Jr. 28, 159, 160, 166, 378
Goodrich, Gail, Sr. 28
Gordon, Bridgette 509, 519-20
Gore, Demetreus 332
Governors *see* Austin Peay State
Graham, Chuck 374
Graham, Ernest 262, 488
Graham, Michael 305, 315
Graham, Otto 48
Grambling 276
Granger, Kevin 399
Grant, Boyd 256, 290, 342, 539
Grant, Greg 550
Grant, Horace 323
Grant, Josh 373
Grant, Travis 551
Grate, Don 56
Grawemeyer, Phil 100
Grawer, Rich 317, 342, 492
Gray, Ed 410, 412
Gray, Jack 57

Gray, Kevin 391
Gray, Steve 150
Gray, Stuart 315
Gray, Sylvester 344, 356
Gray, Wyndol 51
Grayson, Doug 174
Great Alaska Shootout 264
Great Midwest Conference 349, 367, 598
Green, Bill 150
Green, Cornell 146
Green, Fred 58
Green, Jerry 396, 564
Green, Johnny 110, 111, 124
Green, Kevin 360
Green, Lionel 269
Green, Rickey 253
Green, Tom 332
Green Wave *see* Tulane
Greenberg, Mel 501, 506
Greene, Ron 276
Greene, Roy 76
Greenwood, Craig 181
Greenwood, David 195, 266
Greer, Hugh 132, 152
Gregor, Gary 176
Gregory, George 12, 649
Grekin, Norm 92
Grentz, Theresa Shank 505, 524
Grevey, Kevin 236, 237
Grgurich, Tim 390
Griffin, Joe 394
Griffin, John 274
Griffin, Rod 250
Griffith, Darrell "Dr. Dunkenstein" 275, 277, 278-9, 492
Grinnell (IA) 31
Grizzlies *see* Montana
Groat, Dick 69, 71, 79
Groom, George 211
Gross, Elmer 82
Groza, Alex 26, 51, 53, 56, 62, 66, 67, 74
Grubar, Dick 191
Grunfeld, Ernie 240, 242
Gugliotta, Tom 485
Guley, Marc 111
Gulf Star Conference 598-9
Gulf States Conference 129
Gulick, Luther 6
Gunder, Dick 489
Gunter, Sue 526-7
Gurein, Richie 89
Guy, Greg 376, 384
Guyton, A. J. 560
Guziak, Ron 180

H

Hackett, Rudy 236-7
Haffner, Scott 342, 485
Hagan, Cliff 79, 89, 91, 126
Hagan, Jimmy 118, 130
Hagan, Joe 28
Hagan, Tom 188
Halbrook, Wade "Swede" 90, 96
Haldorson, Burdette 84
Hale, Bruce 132, 135, 149
Hale, Edwin 51
Hale, Jerry 539
Hall, Dale 48, 79
Hall, David 203, 206
Hall, Joe B. 66, 220, 311, 487, 491, 547
Hamilton, Derrick 489
Hamilton, Leonard 325, 493, 563
Hamilton, Lowell 344
Hamilton, Raymond 488
Hamilton, Richard 562
Hamilton, Roy 251
Hamilton, Steve 107
Hamline (MN) 5, 62
Hampton Institute 12
Hancock, Darrin 491
Handlan, Jay 75
Hankins, Cecil 51
Hankins, Norm 61
Hankinson, Phil 208
Hannon, Bill 79
Hansen, Bob 278
Hansen, Paul 281
Hanson, Victor A. 11
Hardin-Simmons (TX) 354
Hardy, James 267, 488
Hargis, John 46
Harkness, Jerry 152
Harlem Globetrotters 79, 118, 138
Harmon, Jerome 344
Harp, Dick 110, 124
Harper, Derek 308
Harper, Jerilynn 520
Harper, Jerry 102, 103, 489
Harper, Ron 310
Harrick, Jim 318, 393, 406, 459, 493, 554
Harrington, Joe 303, 333, 491
Harrington, Tom 118
Harris, Chipper 493
Harris, Eric 411
Harris, Gene 144
Harris, Henry 650
Harris, Janet 508, 520
Harris, Ken 249

Harris, Kenny 374
Harris, Lucious 491
Harris, Lusia 505, 520
Harris, Owen 490
Harris, Rufus 276
Harrison, Pops 51
Harrison, Robert 206
Harshman, Marv 170, 243, 264, 311
Hart, Henry 118
Hart, Tom 542
Harter, Dick 206, 208, 263
Hartford YMCA 3
Hartman, Jack 201, 237, 287, 491, 539, 660, 668
Hartmann, Dick 139
Harvard Crimson 5, 6, 7, 54, 56, 108, 155, 206, 302, 408, 616
Harvey, Boo 344
Hashley, Doug 290
Haskell Institute 10
Haskins, Clem 163, 179, 284, 409, 411, 459-60
Haskins, Don 171, 201, 235, 349, 354, 427, 460, 658, 660
Haskins, Mitch 493
Hassett, Billy 51
Hatchell, Sylvia 512
Hatfield, Jim 250
Haverford College 4, 5
Havlicek, John 133, 139, 146
Hawaii Rainbows 171, 216, 563, 616
Hawkeyes see Iowa
Hawkins, Connie 136
Hawkins, Darrell 380
Hawkins, Earl 342
Hawkins, Hersey 330, 332, 333
Hawkins, Robert "Bubbles" 226, 245
Hawkins, Tom 119
Hawks see St. Joseph's
Hayes, E. C. "Doc" 177
Hayes, Elvin 173, 174, 179, 180, 181, 183, 184, 186, 192
Hayes, Jim 188, 198
Hayes, Ken 247-8, 299
Hayes, Steve 253
Haynes, Marques 79
Haywood, Spencer 188, 195, 453
Hazzard, Walt 157, 159, 160, 311, 327, 665
Head, Pat see Summitt, Pat Head
Heathcote, Jud 258, 392, 487
Heaton, Bob 265
Heckman, Roy 182
Hedric, Darrell 258, 303
Heinsohn, Tom 96
Heitz, Ken 168, 190
Helmlinger, John 131
Helms, Joe 95
Helms, Mike 489

Hemric, Dick 78, 96
Henderson, Alan 380
Henderson, Bill 54, 71
Henderson, Cam 10-11
Henderson, Cedric 329, 337
Henderson, David 320, 488
Henderson, J. R. 561
Henderson, Phil 334, 355
Henderson, Skip 330, 332
Henderson, Tracy 513
Hennessey, John 48
Hennessy, Larry 84
Hennon, Don 69, 108, 114
Henry, Paul 539
Henson, David 258
Henson, Les 276
Henson, Lou 199, 287, 304, 342, 400
Henson, Steve 493
Herndon, Mack 148
Herndon, William 366
Herrera, Carl 363
Herrin, Rich 211
Herrion, Bill 398, 567, 657
Hess, Doug 206
Hetzel, Fred 156, 163
Heyman, Art 149
Hickey, Eddie 57, 62, 81, 119, 157
Hickey, Howard "Red" 40
Hickman, Jeff 210
Hickman, Peck 177
Higgins, Sean 343, 363
Higgs, Kenny 250
Hightower, Wayne 146
Hildebrand, Matt 383
Hill, Bobby Joe 171, 173, 179
Hill, Ernie 264
Hill, Grant 369-70, 373, 378, 414
Hill, Henry 262
Hill, Seabern 198
Hillhouse, Art 15, 16
Hilltoppers *see* Western Kentucky
Hilton, Chip 15
Hinkle, Tony 201
Hiram College 5
Hobdy, Fred 276
Hobson, Howard 32, 104
Hodge, Donald 373
Hodge, Odell 563
Hodges, Bill 262, 265
Hodges, Harlan 121
Hofstra 132, 249, 385
Hogg, Sonja 527
Hogue, Paul 130, 139, 146

Hogue, Ronnie 211
Hokies *see* Virginia Tech
Holbrook, Eddie 276
Holcomb, Derek 264
Holdsclaw, Chamique 512
Holland, Brad 251
Holland, Joe 57
Holland, Terry 156, 200, 220, 290, 494
Holland-Corn, Kedra 513
Holman, Denny 179
Holman, Nat 13, 16, 73, 132, 223
Holmes, Allen 140
Holton, Michael 279, 489
Holup, Joe 89, 102
Holy Cross Crusaders 7, 27, 57, 59, 62, 63, 70, 73, 91, 121, 171, 215, 235, 253, 420, 616
Holzman, Red 73
Hoosiers *see* Indiana
Hopkins, Phil 400
Hoppen, Dave 310
Hopson, Andy 221
Horan, John 78
Hord, Derrick 487, 491
Horford, Tito 344
Hornback, Ted 423
Horned Frogs *see* Texas Christian
Hornyak, Allan 208
Horvath, Paul 77
Hoskins, Don 554
Houbregs, Bob 84, 88
Houle, Matt 376
Houston, Allan 376, 380
Houston Baptist 342
Houston, Byron 365, 366
Houston Cougars 132, 179, 184, 186, 210, 220, 249, 264, 273, 292, 299, 300, 303, 305, 308, 363, 382, 616, 657, 659
Houston, Kevin 325
Houston, Wade 354, 492
Howard College 8
Howard, Frank 107
Howard, Juwan 373, 387, 396, 487
Howard, Mo 228
Howard, Terry 236
Howard University 12
Howder, Lynn 206
Howell, Bailey 108, 118
Howland, Ben 410
Hoyas see Georgetown
Hubbard, Phil 247, 251, 253, 261,
Huckabay, Rick 303, 325, 492
Huery, Ron 344
Huffman, Marv 37
Huffman, Vern 37
Huggins, Bob 250, 318, 366, 367, 460, 562

Hughes, Alfredrick 302, 310
Hughes, Larry 493, 658
Hull, Bill 146
Hull, Jimmy 32
Humes, Brian 491
Humes, Willie 204
Hundley, Hot Rod 107, 108
Hunt, Anderson 354, 355, 358
Hunt, Charles 487
Hunt, Lee 367
Hunter, Larry 384
Hunter, Les 152, 159
Hunter, Lindsey 376
Hurley, Bobby 355, 369, 370, 371, 374, 378
Hurley, Danny 390
Hurricanes *see* Miami (FL)
Huskies *see* Connecticut, Northeastern, Washington
Hutcherson, Claude 504
Hyatt, Chuck 11, 33
Hyatt, W. C. 7
Hyder, Whack 95, 108, 135, 154

I

Iba, Clarence 72
Iba, Hank 54, 66, 68, 72, 84, 98, 157, 195, 201, 235, 660, 660
Iba, Moe 201, 320
Idaho State Bengals 31, 80, 109, 132, 135, 201, 204, 249, 251, 262, 617
Idaho Vandals 8, 28, 121, 277, 287, 290, 567, 616-7
Illinois-Chicago 303
Illinois Fighting Illini 8, 9, 28, 43, 57, 60, 79, 102, 108, 138, 150, 189, 196, 211, 228, 240, 264, 287, 304, 308, 325, 327, 337, 342, 343, 344, 356, 399, 561, 617, 659, 660
Illinois Fighting Illini (women's team) 513
Illinois State Redbirds 211, 218, 245, 297, 342, 410, 491, 561, 566-7, 617, 655
Imhoff, Darrall 121
Immaculata College 505, 507
Indiana Hoosiers 8, 12, 28, 36, 38, 40, 52, 58, 65, 85, 86, 88, 91, 97, 108, 114, 177, 183, 195, 199, 205, 215, 216, 219, 225, 235, 236, 238, 240, 244, 245, 247, 248, 249, 251, 261, 274, 279, 282, 284, 287, 291, 300, 310, 323, 326, 329, 333, 342, 344, 356, 363, 380, 392, 402, 408, 411, 422, 424, 427, 437, 487, 489, 537, 560, 617, 663
Indiana State Sycamores 196, 248, 258, 261, 262, 264, 265, 266, 278, 279, 342, 360, 422, 491, 617-8
Indians *see* Arkansas State, Northeast Louisiana
Inge, Kenny 492
Inniss, Al 103
Intercollegiate Athletic Association 6
International Basketball Federation (FIBA) 601
Iona Gaels 266, 276, 618
Iowa Girls High School Athetic Union (IGHSAU) 503
Iowa Hawkeyes 5, 8, 41, 50, 51, 54, 104, 105, 121, 198, 205, 228, 275, 278, 279, 287, 310, 325,

327, 344, 374, 392, 491, 562, 618
Iowa Hawkeyes (women's team) 509
Iowa State Cyclones 8, 38, 50, 107, 132, 201, 274, 373, 385, 398, 400, 492, 566,618, 655, 656
Ireland, George 149, 235
Irish, Ned 14
Irving, John 488
Isaac, Warren 163
Isner, Mack 79
Issel, Dan 192-3, 198, 203, 215
Iturbe, Iker 405, 560
Iverson, Allen 398, 405, 411
Ivory, Elvin 439
Ivy, Hercle 234
Ivy League 48, 54, 108, 206, 225, 235, 263, 276, 291, 316, 400, 476, 565, 567, 579

J

Jackson, Chris 337, 363, 373, 469-70
Jackson, Eddie 160
Jackson, Jim 380, 414
Jackson, Keith 330
Jackson, Larry 233
Jackson, Luke 543
Jackson, Mannie 138
Jackson, Mark 316
Jackson, Michael 305
Jackson, Randell 561
Jackson, Ray 487
Jackson, Reggie 394
Jackson, Tracy 279, 487
Jacksonville Dolphins 169, 199, 201, 203, 205, 206, 208, 320, 376, 618, 662
Jacobsen, Adam 409
Jacobson, Sam 561
Jaguars *see* South Alabama, Southern
Jakubick, Joe 296, 302
Jamerson, Dave 339, 351
James Madison Dukes 290, 291, 325, 398, 491, 618-9, 658
James, Ralph 351
Jamison, Antawn 560, 566
Janicki, Bernie 79
Jarvis, Mike 376, 380, 399, 656
Jaspers *see* Manhattan
Jayhawks *see* Kansas
Jeffries, Royce 493
Jenkins, Buck 360
Jennings, Keith 360, 488
Jerome, John 351
Jiminez, Juan 200
Jobe, Ben 383
Johansen, Wally 32
John Carroll 98
John, Maury 156, 189, 210, 539

Johns, Wilbur 65

Johnson, Avery 330

Johnson, Bill 90

Johnson, Dana 513

Johnson, Darrel 391, 490

Johnson, Deckery 281

Johnson, DeMarco 563

Johnson, Earvin "Magic" 196, 261-2, 264, 265, 262, 270, 437, 469, 470, 487, 499, 509

Johnson, Eddie 264

Johnson, Ellis 77

Johnson, Ervin 377

Johnson, Evelyn 509

Johnson, George 261

Johnson, Gus 149, 152

Johnson, John 197, 198

Johnson, Jon 311

Johnson, Larry 355, 358, 363, 365, 414

Johnson, Marques 195, 250, 488

Johnson, Marvin 255

Johnson, Ollie 168

Johnson, Phil 189, 190

Johnson, Roddrick 490

Johnson, Steve 281

Johnson, Tommy 330

Johnson, Vinnie 262

Johnstone, Jim 489

Jolly, Kellie 513

Jones, Anthony 487

Jones, Askia 383

Jones, Ben 46-7

Jones, Billy 170

Jones, Bob 365

Jones, Charles 410

Jones, Chip 490

Jones, Dontae 399

Jones, Dwight 250

Jones, Edgar 249

Jones, Jackie 363, 365

Jones, Jeff 361, 365, 657

Jones, Justin 564

Jones, K. C. 95, 98, 104

Jones, Mike 287, 409, 563

Jones, Ozell 287, 489

Jones, Wallace "Wah Wah" 57, 62

Jordan, Eddie 244

Jordan, John 116

Jordan, Michael 288, 291, 294, 299, 305, 315, 347, 437, 453

Joseph, Cedric 221

Jourdet, Lou 41

Jucker, Ed 139, 146, 154

Julian, Alvin "Doggie" 27, 57, 59, 114, 119

K

Kaftan, George 59

Kaiser, Roger 136

Kajikawa, Bill 84

Kaminsky, Rick 156

Kansas Jayhawks 8, 11, 28, 36, 38, 42, 58, 61, 71-2, 82, 86, 88, 98, 104, 107, 109-10, 111, 118, 150, 173, 210, 211, 219, 227, 237, 253, 261, 263, 276, 285, 287, 304, 316, 318, 319, 322, 327, 332, 333, 334, 337, 343, 407, 410, 411, 420, 491, 537, 554, 559, 560, 566, 619, 659, 660

Kansas Jayhawks (women's team) 506, 509

Kansas State Wildcats 9, 38, 54, 58, 61, 76, 77, 82, 103, 114, 119, 122, 146, 148, 150, 156, 164, 173 203, 206, 207, 219, 237, 253, 258, 276, 285, 287, 332, 334, 337, 344, 491, 619

Karstens, Bob 394

Karver, Elliott 89

Kaye, Rick 487

Kea, Clarence 266

Keady, Gene 284, 332, 384, 460, 488, 539, 660, 660

Keaney, Frank 30

Kearns, Tommy 70, 109

Keefe, Adam 366

Keeling, Rudy 384

Keinath, Charles 8

Kelleher, Ed 13, 48

Keller, Billy 191

Kelley, Allen 88

Kelley, Dale 198

Kelley, Dean 88

Kelley, Rich 228

Kellogg, Clark 300

Kellogg, Junius 69

Kelly, Eamon 311

Kelly, Harry 291, 296, 380

Kelly, Lake 249

Kelly, Pam 520

Kelser, Greg 261, 265, 263

Kelso, Ben 211

Kemp, Shawn 341

Kenna, Doug 48

Kennedy, Andy 360

Kennedy, Barbara 520

Kennedy, Don 181

Kennedy, Eugene "Goo" 206

Kennedy, Pat 461, 657

Kenon, Larry 223, 231

Kent Golden Flashes 383, 619

Kent State 189, 215

Kentucky Wesleyan 365

Kentucky Wildcats 26, 28, 36, 42, 43, 45, 48, 51, 53, 54, 56, 62, 63, 65, 66, 69, 72, 73-5, 77, 81, 88, 89, 91, 95-6, 98, 100, 101, 102, 108, 109, 110, 115, 116, 118, 121-2, 131, 138, 149, 151, 154, 160, 165, 171, 176, 189, 196, 198, 201, 203, 204, 210, 212, 216, 220, 225, 227, 236, 237, 238,

242, 245, 256, 258, 261, 265, 273, 291, 292, 300, 302, 305, 306, 310, 311, 334, 341, 342, 373, 382, 390, 392, 393, 396, 399, 400-1, 402, 403, 406, 410, 411, 412, 420, 423, 437, 487, 491, 537, 538, 560, 619, 650, 659, 663

Kerns, Frank 367

Kerr, Steve 329, 330

Kerwin, Jim 393

Kerwin, Tom 168

Kessinger, Don 154

Kestenbaum, Ron 490

Keydets *see* Virginia Military

Keys, Randolph 489

Kidd, Jason 377, 379-80, 383, 396

Kilcullen, Matt 393

Killick, Tom 48

Killingsworth, Jim 249, 289, 325, 329

Kimball, Tony 166

Kimble, Bo 316, 330, 351, 355, 358, 485, 489

Kimbro, Tony 337

Kinch, Chad 251

King, Albert 488

King, Bernard 234, 242, 247, 469, 470

King, Bob 151, 265

King, Bruce "Sky" 226

King, Dolly 12, 35

King, Frankie 383

King, George 151, 188

King, Jimmy 373, 377, 487

King, Kirk 407

King, Reggie 244, 258

King, Ron 204, 225

King, Stacey 322

King, Tom 132

Kinsbrunner, Mac 14

Kirchner, H. E. 124, 126

Kirk, Dana 310, 325, 659

Kitchel, Ted 282

Kittles, Kerry 393

Kleine, Joe 485

Klenck, Bob 45

Klier, Leo 26

Knight, Bob 74, 169, 182, 195, 196, 199, 206, 215, 219, 225, 235, 236, 240, 244, 274, 310, 326, 349, 374, 402, 461, 462, 487, 554, 560, 656, 658, 660

Knight, Pat 374

Koch, Jerry 90

Komenich, M ilo 46

Komives, Howard 149, 154, 155, 156

Kotz, John 40

Koul, Alexander 562

Kraft, Jack 208, 219

Kramer, Barry 150, 154

Krause, Moose 61

Kresse, John 409

Kribbs, Benton 108

Kruger, Lon 332, 384, 461, 561, 660

Krzyzewski, Mike 235, 243, 302, 318, 363, 369, 388, 391, 399, 461, 462, 488, 491, 560

Kubacki, Jim 113

Kuester, John 253, 488

Kuhn, Rick 262

Kukoy, Bill 77

Kundla, John 28, 157

Kupchak, Mitch 237

Kupec, C. J. 236

Kurland, Bob 26, 51, 52, 53, 54, 55, 56, 67

Kyvallos, Lucille 527

L

La Salle Explorers 54, 78, 91, 92, 95, 96, 98, 100, 103, 191, 275, 300, 351, 385, 420, 567, 620

Lacefield, Reggie 181

Lacey, Edgar 184

Lacey, Sam 200, 203

Lacy, Jim 61, 63

Ladner, Wendell 200

Ladson, Tyrone 491

Laettner, Christian 363, 365, 369, 370, 373

Lafayette Leopards 63, 98, 111, 132, 138 206, 258, 311, 619-20

LaFleur, Andre 323

LaFrentz, Raef 559, 560, 657

LaGarde, Tom 253, 488

Laiche, Darren 492

Laimbeer, Bill 265

Lamar, Bo 211, 216

Lamar Cardinals 204, 264, 266, 279, 302, 303, 376, 558, 567, 620

Lamb, Rolando 315

Lambert, Gene 61

Lambert, Paul 264

Lambert, Ward "Piggy" 38, 53

Lamp, Jeff 494

Landa, Howie 88, 391

Landers, Andy 527

Landsberger, Mark 249

Lane, Jerome 332, 333, 337, 344

Lang, Andrew 485

Lang, Antonio 387

Lange, Bill 48

Langer, Ralph 45

Langley, Nate 409

Lanier, Bob 181, 183, 184, 188, 203

Lapchick, Joe 52, 140, 165

LaPorte, Frank 228

Lappas, Steve 398, 494, 659

Larese, York 70

LaRusso, Rudy 114

Laskowski, John 236
Laurel, Rich 249, 253
Laurie, Barry 279
Lavelli, Tony 63
Lavin, Steve 406
Lawrence, Janice 520
Lawrence Tech (MN) 62
Lawson, Don 176
Lawson, Harbin "Red" 131, 555
Layne, Floyd 73
Leach, Barton 96
Leaman, Jack 492
Lear, Hal 104, 105, 371
Lebanon Valley (PA) 86, 88
Lee, Butch 237, 245, 259, 257
Lee, Clyde 169
Lee, Greg 221
Lee, Jim 238
Lee, Keith 308, 310, 469, 470, 484
Lee, Kurk 351
Lee, Ron 235, 241, 426
LeForce, Alan 361, 488
Leggat, Harry 47
LeGrand, Bob 284
Lehigh Engineers 30, 85, 138, 182 274, 315, 332, 620
Leinhard, Bob 190
Lembo, Larry 156
Lemons, Abe 183, 258, 289
LeMoyne 103
Lenox, Bennie 156
Leonard, Bob 86
Leonard, Fessor 228
Leopards see Lafayette
Leslie, Lisa 501, 513, 521
Leslie, Todd 351
Lester, Ronnie 279
Lett, George 490
Lever, Fat 287
Levingston, Cliff 287, 489
Lewis, Bob 50, 168
Lewis, Dana 201
Lewis, Guy 54, 174, 186, 299, 303, 316, 319
Lewis, Kim 380
Lewis, Larry 188
Lewis, Raymond 196, 218
Lewis, Reggie 306, 318, 320
Lewis, Tom 316, 489
Lewis, Troy 488
Liberty 367, 410
Lichti, Todd 342
Lieberman-Cline, Nancy 507, 521
Lifson, Al 78
Lightfoot, Orlando 383

Lincoln University 12
Lindeman, Paul 40
Line, Jim 62
Linn, George 95, 489
Lions see Columbia, Loyola Marymount
Lister, Alton 287
Litchfield, Terry 136
Little, Larry 235, 243
Little, Willie 303
Littleton, Cleo 78, 98
Litwack, Harry 221
Livingston, Randy 393
Livingston, Ron 91
Lloyd, Bob 168, 174, 187
Lloyd, Lewis "Magic" 276
LoBalbo, Al 206
Lobo, Rebecca 500, 513, 521
Locke, Tates 491
Loeffler, Ken 96
Logan, Bill 105
Lollis, Quadre 403
Lonborg, Dutch 31
Long Beach State 49ers 190, 204, 210, 211, 221, 226, 228, 235, 250, 333, 491, 620
Long, Grant 332
Long Island Blackbirds 15, 16, 28, 29, 30, 35, 41, 48, 72, 74, 75, 182, 406, 419, 563, 567, 620
Longhorns see Texas
Longley, Luc 211
Los Angeles Athletic Club 663
Los Angeles Lakers 265
Los Angeles State 82, 235
Loscutoff, Jim 96
Louis, Corey 561
Louisiana State Tigers 84, 86, 89, 138, 144, 180, 186-7, 195, 198, 201, 250, 256, 263, 264, 267, 279, 284, 287, 298, 310, 313, 319, 320, 322, 329, 334, 337, 363, 373, 380, 382, 390, 406, 436, 491, 621, 660
Louisiana State Tigers (women's team) 508
Louisiana Tech Bulldogs 196, 302, 310, 322, 377, 621
Louisiana Tech Bulldogs (women's team) 499, 507, 508, 513
Louisville Cardinals 126, 177, 179, 195, 196, 215, 216, 236, 237, 253, 276, 278, 279, 284, 300, 302, 311, 315, 319, 320, 322, 326, 337, 339, 344, 362, 376, 392, 396, 411, 421, 427, 487, 492, 562, 566, 621, 663
Lovellette, Clyde 78, 80-1, 86, 127, 395
Lowery, Greg 211
Loyola (MD) 63, 387-8, 556
Loyola Marymount Lions 317, 329, 330, 332, 339, 350-1, 355, 360, 567 621-2
Loyola of Chicago Ramblers 29, 63, 142, 148-9, 152, 154, 159 206, 235, 310, 419, 621
Loyola of Louisiana 215
LSU Tigers see Louisiana State Tigers
Lucas, Jerry 130, 133, 139, 142, 146, 149, 193

Lucas, John 227, 228, 242, 270
Lucas, Maurice 195, 238
Luckett, Walter 196
Luckydo, Phillip 366
Lue, Tyronn 563
Luisetti, Angelo "Hank" 15, 16, 27, 33
Lynch, Daniel 90
Lynch, George 374, 377-8
Lynn, Mike 183
Lyons, Delano 162
Lyons, Kenneth 296
Lysaght, Walt 84

M

MAC *see* Mid-American Conference
Macarchuk, Nick 493
Macauley, Ed 26, 65, 68, 420, 422
Mack, Oliver 258
Mack, Rodney 332
Mackey, Kevin 310, 318, 362, 490
Macklin, Rudy 249, 267, 279, 287, 491
MacLeod, John 201
MacMurray (IL) 545
Macon, Charles 394
Macon, Mark 332, 342, 470
Macy, Kyle 196, 556
Magarity, Dave 398
Magdanz, Eric 144
Magee, Kevin 281, 288
Mahon, Frank 2
Mahoney, Johnny 97
Maine 132, 384, 408
Majerle, Dan 332
Majerus, Rick 342, 361, 462, 656
Malaise, Dub 168
Mallett, Mike 492
Malone, Karl 296, 315, 322, 437, 453, 484
Malone, Moses 233, 437, 453
Maloy, Mike 191
Manhattan Jaspers 29, 45, 54, 69, 98, 115, 116, 137, 299, 380, 393, 622
Mann, Cyrus 196
Mann, Marcus 399
Manning, Danny 316, 327, 333, 335, 337, 347, 490, 657
Manning, Greg 276, 488
Manning, Jon 262-3
Manning, Red 216
Mantz, Bobby 114
Manuel, Eric 341
Maravich, Pete 37, 129, 144, 164, 180, 186-7, 189, 193, 197-8, 201, 380
Maravich, Press 37, 164, 180
Marbury, Don 318
Marbury, Stephon 318, 350, 399

Margenthaler, Jack 297
Marist 398
Marlaire, Leon 489
Marquette, George "Rinso" 86
Marquette Warriors 39, 98, 104, 119, 157, 183, 195, 196, 206, 208, 212, 216, 218, 228, 230, 237, 238, 244, 245, 247, 250, 251, 253, 259, 262, 308, 332, 385, 408, 411, 421, 559, 562, 566, 567, 622, 662
Marquetti, Leonel 493
Marshall, Donyell 382, 383, 396
Marshall, Jack 72
Marshall Thundering Herd 10, 215, 264, 303, 325, 622
Marshall, Tom 90
Martelli, Phil 399, 410
Martin, Bill 487
Martin, Bobby 332, 488
Martin, James 491
Martin, LaRue 206
Martin, Peter 551
Martin, Phil 92
Martin, Slater 65
Martin, Wayne 303
Martinez, Francisco "Kiko" 31
Maryland-Baltimore County 325, 342
Maryland-Eastern Shore 227
Maryland Terrapins 28, 40, 52, 58, 75, 85, 90, 114, 116, 132, 165, 206, 214, 215, 226, 227-8, 233, 236, 242, 250, 263, 292, 300, 302, 316, 320, 323, 332, 354, 388, 392, 403, 408, 412, 562, 622, 659
Maryland Terrapins (women's team) 506, 507, 509
Mashburn, Jamal 373, 390
Mason, Anthony 332
Massachusetts Minutemen 148, 199, 204, 206, 208, 255, 263, 276-7, 302, 304, 354, 367, 370, 393, 396, 398, 399, 400, 412, 492, 622-3
Massimino, R. C. 313
Massimino, Rollie 312, 313, 390, 462, 554, 658
Mathisen, Art 43
Matson, Ollie 235
Matthews, Jason 332, 488
Matthews, Phil 490
Maxwell, Cedric "Cornbread" 249, 253
May, Darlene 527
May, Don 174, 179
May, Scott 238, 243, 244, 247, 487
Mayhew, Stan 249
Mayo, Jamie 492
McAdoo, Bob 223, 491
McArthur, Eric 354
McBrayer, Paul 57, 89, 121
McCafferty, Jim 421
McCaffery, Fran 274, 332
McCaffrey, Billy 376
McCaffrey, Jim 310
McCarthy, Babe 118, 148

McCarthy, John 116
McCarthy, Neil 242, 277, 462, 660
McClain, Katrina 501, 508, 521
McClairen, Cy 490
McConathy, Mike 241, 249
McConnell Serio, Suzie 521
McCormick, Tim 315
McCovey, Smokey 365
McCoy, Jelani 411, 561
McCracken, Branch 12, 36, 58, 85, 88, 114, 165
McCray, Ernie 132
McCray, Nikki 513, 521
McCray, Rodney 278
McCray, Scooter 278, 487
McCreary, Jay 37, 144
McCurdy, Bob 233, 234
McCutchan, Arad 542
McDade, Von 360
McDaniel, Xavier 310
McDaniels, Jim 204, 208, 210, 662
McDonald-Hill, Linda 513
McDyess, Antonio 396, 405
McFadden, Banks 75, 80
McGee, Mike 282
McGee, Pam 522
McGee, Paula 522
McGill, Billy 140, 142, 144, 145
McGinnis, George 216, 225
McGrady, Tracy 350
McGuire, Al 195, 206, 228, 247, 250-1, 252, 271, 421, 662
McGuire, Allie 208
McGuire, Dick 47, 52
McGuire, Frank 70, 79, 84, 110, 174, 199, 210, 277
McHale, Kevin 249, 453
McIlvaine, Jim 376
McInnis, Jeff 412
McIntyre, Terrell 560
McKean, Jim 176
McKeen, Bob 78
McKendrick, Doug 168
McKeown, Joe 513
McKie, B. J. 561
McKinney, Bones 55-6, 140, 142
McKinney, Oran 423
McLain, Gary 312
McLaughlin, Frank 302
McMillan, Tom 227-8, 233
McNeese State 318
McNeill, Larry 195, 230-1
McNulty, Carl 76
McPherson, Herb 168
McPherson, Walt 72
McQuarn, George 290, 490, 493

Mealy, Bob 131
Meanwell, Doc 10, 12-13
Mears, Ray 151, 176, 179, 187, 249, 258
Meely, Cliff 204
Mehen, Bernie 36
Melchiorre, Gene 74
Mele, Sam 46
Melvin, Eddie 132
Meminger, Dean "The Dream" 206, 208
Memphis State 109, 196, 200, 206, 215, 221, 223, 225, 231, 264, 284, 298, 310, 323, 325, 334, 339, 344, 356, 380
Memphis Tigers 401, 403, 412, 436, 561, 623, 658
Mencel, Chuck 78
Mendenhall, Mike 118
Mengelt, John 198, 204
Menke, Ken 43, 58
Menken Schaudt, Carol 522
Menze, Louis 38, 50
Mercer 310
Mercer County (NJ) Community College 88
Mercer, Ron 400, 411
Mercer, Walter 47
Meriweather, Joe C. 228
Merson, Leo 15
Meschery, Tom 137
Metcalf, Shelby 156, 157, 276, 343
Metro Atlantic Athletic Conference 318, 384, 567, 580
Metro Conference 284, 326, 332, 339, 349, 393, 476-7, 599
Metropolitan Basketball Writers Association 17, 419
Metropolitan Collegiate Conference 599
Metropolitan Intercollegiate Basketball Association (MIBA) 419
Metropolitan Intercollegiate Basketball Committee see Metropolitan Intercollegiate
Basketball Association
Meyer, Jeff 410
Meyer, Joey 304, 325, 406, 555
Meyer, Ray 28, 46, 157, 285, 304, 406, 555
Meyers, Ann 506, 522
Meyers, Dave 195
Miami (FL) Hurricanes 58, 132, 135, 149, 166, 169, 206, 317, 333, 344, 367, 393, 563, 623, 656
Miami (OH) Red Hawks 58, 64-5, 183, 259, 258, 303, 623, 662
Micheaux, Larry 300
Michigan State Spartans 9, 70, 110, 196, 205, 214, 219, 258, 261, 264, 264-5, 266, 267, 278, 299, 310, 316, 342, 363, 437, 439, 487, 558, 562, 623-4
Michigan Wolverines 60, 62, 70, 108, 160, 163, 164, 165, 188, 236, 238, 242, 244, 247, 251, 253, 261, 282, 310, 315, 337, 342, 343, 344, 346,355, 362, 363, 369, 373, 376, 378, 390, 396, 402, 411, 423, 487, 489-90, 492, 558, 560, 623, 658, 659, 662
Mid-American Conference 75, 215, 284, 325, 332, 477, 567, 581
Mid-Continent Conference 310, 567, 582, 656
Mid-Eastern Athletic Conference 427, 567, 583, 656
Middle Atlantic Conference 86, 599

Middle Tennessee State Blue Raiders 235, 291, 318, 332, 342, 343-4, 624

Middle West Conference 9

Middleton, Steve 332, 485

Midshipmen *see* Navy

Midwestern City Conference 310

Midwestern Collegiate Conference 325, 400, 477, 567, 584

Mikan, George 7, 26, 50, 51, 56, 68, 188

Mikan, Larry 188, 200

Miklovic, Ned 114

Milholland, Mike 163

Miller, Andre 563

Miller, Cheryl 499, 500, 501, 508, 511, 512, 522

Miller, Dan 201

Miller, Eldon 205, 240, 243, 277, 463, 657

Miller, Floyd 41

Miller, Harry 490

Miller, Kenny 332

Miller, Larry 187, 490

Miller, Ralph 41-2, 78, 90, 149, 198, 342

Miller, Reggie 329

Miller, Roddrick 563

Miller, Ron 159

Miller, Sean 332, 488

Miller, Tom 304

Miller, Tony 211, 394

Millikan, Bud 114, 116, 201

Mills, Chris 341

Mills, Doug 44

Mills, Johnny 211, 219

Mills, Lewis 228

Mills, Nate 256

Mills, Terry 323, 343

Milton, DeLisha 513

Mims, Mike 493

Miner, Harold 366, 380

Miners *see* Texas-El Paso

Minnesota Golden Gophers 7, 8, 9, 28, 97, 157, 200, 204, 212, 214, 216, 241, 249, 251, 253, 256, 277, 316, 400, 409, 411, 537, 558, 561, 624

Minnesota Golden Gophers (women's team) 513

Minnesota School of Agriculture and Mining 5

Minniefield, Dirk 487

Minor, Ryan 453

Minton, Reggie 555

Minutemen *see* Massachusetts

Mississippi Rebels 29, 51, 72, 148, 204, 220, 227, 264, 287, 291, 337, 396, 406, 559, 561, 624, 656

Mississippi Rebels (women's team) 508, 513

Mississippi State Bulldogs 31, 108, 109, 118, 119, 138, 144, 148, 264, 361, 393, 398, 399, 400, 537, 559, 624, 655

Missouri-Kansas City 367

Missouri Tigers 8, 10, 103, 164, 211, 244, 247, 263, 276, 279, 289, 298, 327, 342, 355, 383, 396, 410, 492, 558, 563, 624-5, 655, 658, 660

Missouri Valley Conference (MVC) 8, 10, 11, 28, 31, 38, 45, 63, 109, 129, 132, 148, 149, 156, 169, 196, 200, 262, 277, 299, 477-8, 566-7, 585, 655

Mitchell, Todd 488

Mitchell, Tyrone 491

Mitts, Billy 148

Mix, Steve 179

Mlkvy, Bill 69, 75, 78, 384

Mobley, Cuttino 405

Moccasins *see* Tennessee-Chattanooga

Moe, Doug 70

Moffett, Larry 253

Moir, Charlie 494

Moir, John 28, 33

Molinari, Jim 361

Molinas, Jack 75, 84, 136

Monarchs *see* Old Dominion

Moncrief, Sidney 250, 261

Money, Eric 221, 238, 488

Monroe, Earl 542, 550

Monroe, Rodney 344

Monson, Don 277, 287, 290

Montana Grizzlies 9, 171, 236, 366, 625

Montana State Bobcats 11, 12, 290, 563, 625

Montclair (NJ) State College 506

Montgomery, Mike 463, 659

Montross, Eric 28, 377, 378, 488

Moore, Billie Jean 528, 529

Moore, Danny 657

Moore, Dudey 90

Moore, Ernie 160

Moore, Jim 163

Moore, Lennell 326

Moore, Ricky 405, 407

Moran, Mike 114

Morcau, Daryl 298

Morehead State Eagles 77, 303, 556, 625

Moreland, Tom 157

Morgan, Guy 489

Morgan, Ralph 5,6, 12, 14

Morgan State 342

Morgenthaler, Elmore 54

Morris, Bruce 311

Morrison, Stan 311, 489, 663

Morrow, Paul 84

Mortell, Bob 132

Morton, John 343

Morton, Mike 276

Moss, Perry 291, 294

Moss, Rick 491

Motta, Dick 539

Mount Holyoke 502

Mount, Rick 129, 186, 187, 190, 191, 192, 193, 197, 198, 378

Mount St. Mary's 398

Mount Union (OH) 38

Mountain States Conference 599

Mountaineers *see* West Virginia

Mourning, Alonzo 273, 365, 415

Moyer, Ron 206

Muehlbauer, Anton 136

Muhlenberg (PA) 62, 64, 152

Mulkey Robertson, Kim 522

Mullaney, Joe 182

Mulligan, Bill 290

Mullin, Chris 312, 315

Mullin, Kevin 308

Mullins, Jeff 160

Mullins, Pete 85

Murdock, Eric 360

Murdock, Jackie 108

Murphy, Calvin 129, 181, 187, 198, 203, 399

Murphy, Charles 12

Murray, Lamond 396

Murray State Racers 76, 276, 284, 333, 361, 625

Murray, Tracy 380, 383

Murrell, Red 114

Murtaugh Savages 31

Musketeers *see* Xavier

Musselman, Bill 663

Mustangs *see* Southern Methodist

Mutombo, Dikembe 211, 342

MVC *see* Missouri Valley Conference

N

NABC *see* National Association of Basketball Coaches

NAIA *see* National Association of Intercollegiate Athletics

Naismith, James 1-2, 4, 9, 10, 17, 35, 502

Naismith, Maude 17

Naismith Memorial Hall of Fame 601

Naismith Trophy 514

Nance, Lynn 342, 547

Nash, Bob 214

Nash, Steve 394

Nashville Business College 504

National Association of Basketball Coaches (NABC) 25, 49, 377, 601, 665

National Association of Intercollegiate Athletics (NAIA) 17, 545-6, 601

National Basketball Association *see* NBA

National Collegiate Athletic Association (NCAA) 9, 554, 601

National Commissioners Invitational Tournament 422

National Invitation Tournament *see* NIT

National Junior College Athletic Association (NJCAA) 601

Natt, Calvin 249, 492

Natt, Kenny 492

Naulls, Willie 104

Navy Midshipmen 9, 11, 35, 75, 144, 150, 157, 273, 313, 318, 329, 409, 557,625-6

NBA 195-6, 436, 437, 501

NCAA *see* National Collegiate Athletic Association

Neal, Craig 315

Neal, Tony 490

Neale, Tucker 382

Nebraska Cornhuskers 5, 8, 38, 48, 51, 72, 113, 114, 164, 168, 171, 273, 281, 289, 319, 320, 337, 361, 427, 563, 626, 657

Nebraska Cornhuskers (women's team) 513

Nee, Danny 361, 463, 657

Need, Ricky 385

Neely, Jess 29

Neff, Herb 79

Nelson, Don 142

Nestor, Ernie 491

Nevada-Reno 243, 250, 262, 310

Nevada Wolf Pack 626

New England Conference 48

New England Intercollegiate Basketball League 7

New England League 8, 9, 599

New Hampshire 79, 137, 199, 343, 360, 377, 393

New Mexico A&M *see* New Mexico State

New Mexico Lobos 39, 98, 104, 146, 151-2, 164, 165, 186, 255, 277, 308, 316, 342, 398, 561, 626

New Mexico School of Mines 54

New Mexico State Aggies 28, 31, 36, 39, 81, 186, 199, 200, 203, 247-8, 299, 354, 373, 377, 399, 567, 626

New Orleans Privateers 256, 298, 325, 376, 380, 385, 391, 492, 626

New Orleans State 249

New York Knicks 251, 315

New York University 11, 13, 35, 53, 132, 174, 198, 206

Newell, Mike 325

Newell, Pete 122, 124, 132-3

Newman, Donald 304

Newmann, Johnny 204

Newsome, Manny 155

Newton, C. M. 228, 237, 342

Newton, Greg 560

Newton, Steve 361

Niagara Purple Eagles 83, 95, 198, 274, 282, 420, 627

Nicholls State 393

Nichols, Bob 266-7

Nichols, Deno 46-7

Nichols, Jack 61, 62

Niewierowski, Stan 136

Nike 313

Nissen, Inge 507, 522

NIT 3, 17, 25, 27, 109, 114, 140, 316, 419-33, 558, 601

Nittany Lions *see* Penn State

Nix, Dyron 376

Nixon, Mark 361

NJCAA *see* National Junior College Athletic Association

Noe, Chuck 658

Nolan, Dick 45

Nolan, Jim 54

Nord, Ron 171

Nordholz, Mike 174

Nordmann, Bob "Bevo" 140

Norman, Coniel 221, 238, 245, 488

Norman, Ken 325, 659

Norris, Eugene 46

Norris, Max 51

North Atlantic Conference 303

North Carolina A&T 255, 291, 332, 556

North Carolina-Charlotte 49ers 234, 249, 251, 253, 325, 367, 563, 627, 658

North Carolina-Greensboro 393

North Carolina State Wolfpack 40, 58, 60, 70, 73, 75, 77, 80, 84, 90, 100, 102, 104, 108, 119, 124, 131, 164, 180, 197, 214, 223, 227, 228, 229, 230, 231, 233, 236, 255, 261, 263, 264, 299, 300, 305, 310, 329, 333, 334, 344, 354, 385, 408, 492, 554, 562, 627, 662

North Carolina State Wolfpack (women's team) 509

North Carolina Tar Heels 11, 29, 31, 39, 40, 45, 48, 52, 70, 75, 79, 84, 90, 102, 109-10, 111, 114, 115, 118, 124, 129, 131, 140, 146, 149, 170, 177, 180, 186, 191, 196, 198-9, 206, 208, 211, 214, 220, 223, 226, 228, 233, 234-5, 236, 240, 242, 245, 247, 253, 255, 259, 263, 265, 273, 275, 277, 279, 284, 287, 291, 292, 294, 298, 300, 302, 305, 308, 310, 315, 323, 334, 344, 349, 354, 356, 367, 374, 376, 377-8, 380, 387, 396, 399, 403, 408, 410, 411, 412, 422, 437, 488, 558, 560, 627, 655, 659

North Carolina Tar Heels (women's team) 501, 513

North Texas 258, 493

North Texas State 190, 240

Northeast Conference 406, 567, 586, 656

Northeast Louisiana Indians 325, 376, 492, 628

Northeast Louisiana Indians (women's team) 509

Northeastern Huskies 291, 303, 306, 325, 556, 627

Northeastern Illinois 409

Northern Arizona 84, 235, 410, 563

Northern Colorado 258

Northern Illinois 215, 361, 558

Northern Iowa Panthers 355, 563, 628, 657

Northwest College Conference 8, 9

Northwestern (LA) State 290, 341

Northwestern Wildcats 8, 31, 48, 51, 54, 70, 102, 121, 205, 265, 297, 310, 362, 374, 385, 409, 628, 656

Norton, Ken 137

Norwood, Lafayette 491

Notre Dame Fighting Irish 27, 28, 41, 45, 54, 61, 70, 76, 91, 92, 116, 119, 189, 197, 198, 201, 203, 204, 210, 214, 215, 218, 225, 228, 231, 238, 244, 250, 253, 264, 265, 276, 281, 291, 319-20, 342, 344, 373, 393, 487, 563, 628, 660

Notre Dame Fighting Irish (women's team) 513

Nowak, Paul 28

Nowell, Mel 133

O

Odom, Dave 393, 398

Odom, Ed 276

Odom, Garry 191

Odom, Lamar 658

Oftring, Frank 73

Ogden, Bud 174, 191

Ogden, Ralph 191

Ogg, Alan 490

Ohio State Buckeyes 4, 25, 32, 54, 56, 61, 70, 77, 102, 133, 135, 138, 139, 146, 150, 156, 199, 205, 208, 214, 216, 219, 243, 244, 277, 300, 342, 361, 362, 380, 394, 563, 629, 655, 660

Ohio State Buckeyes (women's team) 509, 510, 513

Ohio University Bobcats 64, 339, 384, 628

Ohio Valley Conference 89, 103, 114, 121, 200, 210, 218, 284, 291, 318, 376, 478, 567, 587

Ohio Wesleyan 36

Okey, Sam 562

Oklahoma A&M 28, 31, 38, 51, 53, 54, 59, 63, 66, 77, 79, 84, 98, 103

Oklahoma City 110, 218, 263, 311

Oklahoma Sooners 11, 32, 38, 59, 103, 114, 177, 201, 263, 266, 274, 296, 319, 322, 330, 332, 333, 337, 356, 363, 366, 371, 493, 537, 562, 629

Oklahoma Sooners (women's team) 510

Oklahoma State Cowboys 108, 136, 146, 157, 164, 258, 281, 297, 300, 304, 363, 493, 537, 562, 629

Olajuwon, Hakeem 211, 273, 292, 298, 300, 302, 305, 308, 437, 454

Olberding, Mark 253

Old Dominion Monarchs 249, 276, 320, 362, 396, 556, 563, 629

Old Dominion Monarchs (women's team) 505, 506, 507, 508, 509, 512, 513

Oldham, John 103, 114, 200, 210, 423

Oleynick, Frank 235

Olinde, Wilbert 488

Oliver, Brian 351, 354, 355

Oliver, Eugene 227

Oliver, James 297

Oliver, John 393

Oliver, Newt 542

Olkowski, June 523

Olliver, Mike 276, 279, 287

Olsen, Harold 25

Olson, Lute 228, 283, 332, 378, 410, 422, 463-4, 539, 560

Oral Roberts Golden Eagles 211, 215, 218, 221, 248, 281, 299, 629-30

Orangemen *see* Syracuse

Oregon Agricultural *see* Oregon State

Oregon Ducks 8, 30, 32, 37, 52, 126, 135, 165, 170-1, 225, 235, 241-2, 244, 247, 318, 354, 393, 396, 563, 567, 630, 656

Oregon State Beavers 9, 32, 36, 100, 152, 157, 197, 198, 216, 225, 275, 281, 284-5, 287, 289, 318, 342, 393, 563, 566, 630, 655

Orr, Johnny 274, 385, 492
Orr, Louis 279
Orr, Vickie 523
Orsborn, Chuck 149
Outlaw, James 227
Overton, Doug 360
Owens, Andy 198
Owens, Billy 373
Owens, Damian 563
Owens, Eddie 253
Owens, Ted 227, 491
Owls *see* Rice, Temple
O'Bannon, Ed 363, 395, 396
O'Brien, Jim 388, 490, 563
O'Brien, Johnny 79, 83, 88
O'Brien, Ralph "Buckshot" 70
O'Connor, Ed 98
O'Koren, Mike 253
O'Neal, Dick 97
O'Neal, Jermaine 350, 437, 660
O'Neal, Shaquille 273, 360, 365, 380, 415
O'Neill, E. P. 7
O'Neill, Kevin 385, 564
O'Shea, Dennis 489

P

Pac-10 Conference 263, 275, 281, 311, 316, 349, 393, 478-9,
    509, 565, 566, 588, 655
Pacific Coast Athletic Association 235, 250, 256
Pacific Coast Athletic Association *see* Big West Conference
Pacific Coast Conference 16, 41, 121
Pacific Eight Conference 210, 225, 244, 263
Pacific Lutheran 311
Pacific Tigers 65, 157, 177, 214, 235, 354, 377, 409, 563, 630
Packer, Billy 85, 130, 132, 427
Packer, Tony 85
Padgett, Pete 221, 243, 485
Page, H. O. "Pat" 8
Page, Kenny 276
Paladins *see* Furman
Palmer, Chet 43
Palombizio, Dan 310
Pan-American 249
Panthers *see* Northern Iowa, Pitt
Panzer College 29
Parfitt, Dick 235
Parish, Robert 219, 221, 242, 469, 470, 484, 485
Parker, Richie 406
Parkhill, Barry 211, 212
Parkinson, Bruce 235
Parks, Cherokee 387, 390
Parrack, Doyle 114, 201
Parsons, Pam 507, 509

Pate, Jesse 399
Patriot League 382, 557, 567, 589
Patterson, Andrae 560
Patterson, Bob 100
Patterson, Steve 204, 208
Patton, Dave 235
Patton, Lee 72
Patton, Ricardo 410
Pauly, Steve 152
Payne, Michael 105
Payne, Tom 104-5, 216, 225, 650
Payton, Gary 351, 354
Payton, Mel 76
Peacocks *see* St. Peter's
Peed, David 338
Pelkington, Bob 157
Pelleta, Pete 152
Pendelton, Anthony 323
Penders, Tom 310, 332, 334, 344, 384, 464, 563
Penicheiro, Ticha 513
Penn Quakers 5, 6, 14, 41, 43, 76, 85, 103, 132, 196, 206, 208,
    212, 225, 235, 258, 263, 264, 265, 276, 291, 316, 396,
    400, 567, 630
Penn State Nittany Lions 11, 29, 30, 82, 92, 349, 363, 400,
    405, 420, 630-1, 655
Penn State Nittany Lions (women's team) 505
Pennefather, Shelly 523
Penny, James 563
Pepperdine Waves 145, 218, 235, 243, 299, 318, 385, 564, 631
Perdue, Will 485
Perigo, Bill 108
Perkins, Sam 288, 347
Perry, Chana 509
Perry, Richard "The Fixer" 262
Perry, Ronnie 253
Perry, Tim 320, 322, 329, 485
Person, Chuck 383
Person, Wesley 383
Peterson, Vadal 50, 85
Pettit, Bob 79, 86, 95, 127
Pflugner, Mike 399
Phelan, Jim 398, 400
Phelps, Derrick 377-8, 488
Phelps, Digger 156, 206, 215, 487,
Phelps, Mark 492
Phelps, Michael 488
Philadelphia 76ers 258
Philadelphia Textile 250
Phillip, Andy 26, 43, 58, 68
Phillips, Gene 198, 204
Phillips, Mike 238
Phoenix *see* Wisconsin-Green Bay
Piatkowski, Eric 383
Pierce, John 550

Pierce, Paul 559, 560

Pierce, Ricky 290

Pilch, John 62

Pilots *see* Portland

Pimm, Jerry 332

Pinckney, Ed 315

Pirates *see* East Carolina, Seton Hall

Pitino, Rick 373, 379, 401, 406, 412, 415-6, 560, 657

Pitt Panthers 11, 26, 29, 40, 85-6, 200, 228, 255, 325, 332, 333, 344, 488, 631, 657

Platt, Harry 27

Polaha, Mike 325

Polite, Michael 344

Polk, Bob 493

Pollard, Jim 16, 42, 43

Pollard, Lataunya 523

Pollard, Scot 407

Pollio, Mike 658, 659

Pondexter, Roscoe 196

Poole, Stacey 344

Porter, Darelle 332, 488

Porter, Howard 206, 207-8

Porter, Terry 485

Portland Pilots 258, 281, 393, 403, 631

Portland, Rene 505

Portland State 235, 249, 255

Portman, Bob 180, 181

Posnack, Mack 14

Potopsky, Dan 97

Power Memorial Academy 171

Powers, Jack 115, 427

Prairie View 367

Pralle, Ferdinand "Fred" 33

Prather, George 538

Presley, Bob 181

Price, Cebe 103

Price, Clarence "Nibs" 53, 54

Price, Jim 216

Price, Mark 308, 470

Price, Tic 561, 567

Price, Tony 265, 269

Princeton Tigers 5, 9, 14, 164, 169, 177, 219, 225, 276, 306, 311, 316, 360, 377, 401, 564, 567, 631, 659

Privateers *see* New Orleans

Proposition 48 323, 509

Prosser, Skip 387-8, 556

Providence Friars 120, 138, 182, 214, 223, 225, 228, 231, 263, 289, 327, 410, 411, 493, 631, 659

Pruitt, Cliff 489

Pryor, Ken 59

Purdue Boilermakers 8, 12, 28, 38, 45, 53, 57, 61, 91, 97, 168, 188, 196, 198, 235, 240, 251, 258, 275, 308, 332, 362, 374, 382, 396, 488, 561, 632, 660

Purdue Boilermakers (women's team) 509

Purnell, Oliver 361, 362

Purple Eagles *see* Niagara

Q

Quakers *see* Pennsylvania

Queenan, Daren 325, 332

Queens College (women's team) 505

Quigg, Joe 110, 115

Quiggle, Jack 110

Quimby, Art 96

Quinnett, Brian 325

Quinnipiac (CT) 656

R

Racers *see* Murray State

Radford 361, 362, 367

Raftery, Bill 228

Ragelis, Ray 76

Raiders *see* Wright State

Rainbows *see* Hawaii

Rajin' Cajuns *see* Southwestern Louisiana

Raker, Lee 494

Ralph, Bill 90

Ralph, Shea 513

Ramblers *see* Loyola of Chicago

Rams *see* Colorado State, Fordham, Rhode Island, Virginia Commonwealth

Ramsay, Jack 108, 140, 165

Ramsey, Cal 108

Ramsey, Frank 89, 91

Rand, Terry 100

Randall, Semeka 513

Rank, Wally 276

Rankin, Jill 523-4

Rankin, John 332

Ransey, Kelvin 279

Ranzino, Sam 73, 77

Rappis, Jim 488

Ratleff, Ed 204, 211, 221

Ratliff, Theo 394

Ratterman, George 54

Raveling, George 120, 279, 367, 390, 489, 511

Ray, Don 423

Ray, Henry 228

Ray, James 276

Ray, Jim 103

Raycroft, Joseph 4, 8, 9

Rayl, Jimmy 142, 144, 150

Raymonds, Hank 250, 662

Razorbacks *see* Arkansas

Rebels *see* Mississippi

Red Flash *see* St. Francis (PA)

Red Hawks *see* Miami (OH)

Red Raiders *see* Colgate, Texas Tech
Red Storm *see* St. John's
Redbirds *see* Illinois State
Redding, Curtis 491
Reed, Jim 103
Reed, Sykes 11
Reese, Brian 488
Reeves, Bryant 374, 393, 453
Reeves, Khalid 383, 388, 390
Regis (CO) 139
Reid, Anthony 338
Reid, Duncan 491
Reid, J. R. 356, 365
Reid, Kareem 561
Reid, Roger 406
Reiff, Joe 33
Reimers, Gary 114
Reiner, Mark 491
Reinhart, Bill 98, 103
Reiss, Tammy 501
Reiter, Bob 96
Rembert, Larry 490
Renick, Jesse "Cab" 31
Rensselaer Polytechnic Institute 52
Respert, Shawn 363
Reveno, Eric 337
Reynolds, Billy 249
Reynolds, Jerry 313, 322
Rhode Island Rams 27, 30, 38, 41, 76, 263, 332, 334, 405,
    554, 562, 632
Rhode Island State 48, 60, 70
Rhodes, Lafester 330
Rice, Glen 343, 346
Rice, Mike 276, 310, 491
Rice Owls 36, 47, 51, 90, 170, 282, 362, 632, 656
Rich, Marvin 218
Richards, Jim 284
Richardson, Michael Ray 236, 241, 258
Richardson, Nolan 281, 292, 303, 319, 361, 386-7, 423, 464,
    539, 660
Richmann, Ivan 114
Richmond, Mitch 332, 337
Richmond Spiders 55, 165, 169, 228, 233, 304, 306, 332, 332,
    363, 632
Richter, John 70
Ricketts, Dick 69, 78, 96
Rider 14, 15, 48, 384
Rider, J. R. 376, 554
Ridings, Gordon 75
Ridl, Buzz 200, 228
Riggins, Eric 325
Riker, Tom 216
Rinaldi, Rich 204
Rio Grande (OH) College 82, 541

Riordan, Ron 551
Risen, Arnie 56
Risley, Don 493
Ritter, John 225
Rivers, Glenn "Doc" 308, 559
Rizzotti, Jennifer 500
Robbins, Rob 354
Roberson, Kevin 365
Robert Morris Colonials 297, 408, 493, 632
Roberts, Anthony 248, 485
Roberts, Bobby 156
Roberts, Brett 366
Roberts, Joe 133
Roberts, Pat 506
Roberts, Robin 510, 512
Roberts, Stanley 492
Roberts, Tim 393
Robertson, Alvin 306
Robertson, Kim Mulkey *see* Mulkey Robertson, Kim
Robertson, Oscar 69, 86, 113, 114, 116, 118, 119, 124, 127,
    130, 135, 210, 453
Robeson, Paul 12
Robey, Rick 238, 245
Robinson, Cliff 258
Robinson, Darnell 412
Robinson, David 273, 310, 313, 316, 320, 325, 329, 347-8, 365
Robinson, Ed 103
Robinson, Eugene 492, 493
Robinson, Flynn 163
Robinson, Glenn 379, 382, 396, 415
Robinson, Jackie 649
Robinson, James 390
Robinson, John 244
Robinson, Keith 323
Robinson, Les 262, 488
Robinson, Mike 214
Robinson, Ronnie 206
Robinson, Rumeal 323, 343
Robinson, Wil 211
Robinson, Will 211, 218, 491
Rocha, Red 216
Roche, John 190, 197, 204
Rockets *see* Toledo
Rocky Mountain Conference 80, 132, 600
Rodgers, Guy 69, 104, 113, 453
Rodman, Dennis 538
Rogers, Alvis 489
Rogers, Bob 118
Rogers, Duane 564
Rogers, George 282
Rogers, Harry 219
Rogers, Marshall 241
Rogers, Rodney 390

Rogers, Roy 399
Rogers, Shawnta 562
Rogers, Steve 366, 485
Roggenburk, Garry 132
Rohan, Jack 181, 377
Rohr, William 121
Rolfe, Red 54
Rolles, Chuck 103
Rollins, Ken 57, 62
Roman, Ed 74
Roosma, John 12
Rose, Jalen 371, 373, 396, 487, 489-90
Rose, Lee 249, 253, 297
Rose, Stan 376
Rosemond, Ken 180
Rosenbluth, Lennie 70, 108, 109, 110, 111
Rosenthal, Dick 91
Ross, Billy 376
Ross, Steve 114
Rossini, Lou 75
Rouse, Vic 152, 154, 159
Rowe, Curtis 201, 204
Rowsom, Brian 325
Rozier, Clifford 382, 396, 488
Ruffin, Michael 564
Ruffner, Bryon 406
Ruklick, Joe 107, 114
Ruland, Jeff 276, 469, 470
Runnin' Rebels see UNLV
Rupp, Adolph 28, 36, 62, 63, 65, 69, 81, 89, 95, 128, 149, 171,
    195, 204, 210, 216 349, 538, 553, 660
Rush, Cathy 505, 528
Russell, Bill 69, 89, 96, 98, 100, 104, 127, 453
Russell, Campy 238
Russell, Cazzie 160, 163, 164, 166, 168, 188, 193, 453
Russell, Honey 35, 38
Russo, Andy 310
Russo, Marius 15
Rutgers-Camden 541
Rutgers Scarlet Knights 132, 137, 169, 174, 228, 237, 240,
    244, 255, 342, 393, 632-3
Rutgers Scarlet Knights (women's team) 505, 507
Rutherford, Randy 393
Rutland, Tony 405
Ryan, Debbie 510

S

Saarelainen, Timo 308
Sacramento State 46, 394
Sacred Heart (CT) 656
Sahm, Walt 165
Sailors, Kenny 45, 46, 371
Saints see Siena
Sale, Forest "Aggie" 33

Sales, Nykesha 513
Salmon, Jimmy 494
Salukis see Southern Illinois
Samford 234
Sampson, Kelvin 562, 659
Sampson, Ralph 273, 281, 288, 292, 294, 302, 348, 365
San Diego State Aztecs 310, 362, 634-5
San Diego Toreros 325, 634
San Francisco Dons 69, 95, 98 100, 104, 110, 136, 152, 159
    221, 235, 250, 261, 267, 289, 317, 488, 493, 635
San Jose State Spartans 72, 77, 136, 279, 325, 385, 635
Sanders, Mike 279
Sanderson, Winfrey "Wimp" 325, 369, 464, 663
Santa Clara Broncos 65, 95, 98, 136, 145, 189, 191, 378,
    394, 635
Santos, Mike 493
Sappleton, Wayne 284
Satalin, Mike 491
Scaife, Don 234
Scales, DeWayne 267, 287
Scarlet Knights see Rutgers
Schaeffer, Billy 219
Schaudt, Carol Menken see Menken Schaudt, Carol
Schaus, Fred 119, 258
Schayes, Dolph 53
Schellhase, Dave 168, 382
Scheuerman, Sharm 105
Schintzius, Dwayne 338
Schlundt, Don 78, 86, 91, 127
Schmaus, Charlie 249
Schmidt, Harv 189, 228
Schmidt, Richard 494
Schmitz, Ronnie 360
Schneider, Bob 494
Schneider, Jeff 494
Schneider, Tom 315
Schnittker, Dick 70
Schommer, John 8
School, Bill 105
Schuckman, Allie 14
Schultz, Dick 228
Schwartz, Willie 15
Scott, Byron 281, 287
Scott, Charlie 190, 191
Scott, Dave 118
Scott, Dennis 351, 355, 358, 363
Scott, George 308
Scott, Joe 136
Scott, Leartha 493
Scott, William 334
Scranton (PA) 62
Scurry, Carey 299
Seaberg, Bill 105
Seals, Shea 411

Searcy, Tony 258
Sears, Ken 78, 96
Seattle 98, 109, 115, 235, 277
SEC *see* Southeastern Conference
Sedran, Barney 7
Seikaly, Rony 329
Seitz, Bob 70
Sellers, Phil 243, 244
Selvy, Frank 83, 88, 89, 91, 107
Seminoles see Florida State
Sendek, Herb 492, 567
Senesky, George 45
Senser, Joe 255-6
Serio, Suzie McConnell *see* McConnell Serio, Suzie
Seton Hall Pirates 27, 35, 38, 56, 91, 113, 114, 228, 258, 273, 288, 334, 337, 342, 343, 344, 367, 390, 420, 635
Settles, Jess 562
Sewanee (TN) 36
Shackelford, Lynn 168, 183, 184
Shackleford, Charles 344
Shank, Theresa *see* Grentz, Theresa Shank
Shannon, Howie 200
Shannon, Ollie 204
Sharman, Bill 71
Sharp, Marsha 510, 528
Shavlik, Ronnie 70, 96, 102
Shaw, Brian 485
Shawver, Kirk 279
Sheary, Buster 70
Shed, Nevil 171
Sheffield, Fred 50
Shelton, Everett 44, 45, 46, 66, 658
Shepherd, Billy 198
Sheppard, Jeff 560
Sheriff, Russ 114
Sherrod, Clarence 204
Shillington, John 5
Shipley, Beryl 215
Shockers *see* Wichita State
Short, Purvis 549
Shorter, Brian 488
Shumate, John 225, 231, 377
Siegfried, Larry 133
Siena Saints 83, 274, 342, 343, 344, 361, 384, 635
Signorile, James 198
Siko, Don 491
Silas, Paul 145, 156, 160, 162
Simmons, Larry 325, 351
Simmons, Lionel 338, 351
Simmons, Marty 332
Simon, Melvin 492
Simon, Miles 410, 412, 560, 660-1
Simon, Walt 662

Simpson, Greg 394
Simpson, Ralph 439
Singh, Sadat 12
Sisler, Dave 81
Skinner, Brian 490, 563
Skinner, Roy 120, 166, 180, 198
Skousen, Bob 144
Skyline Conference 146
Slack, Charlie 90, 96, 103
Slater, Reginald 367
Slaughter, Jose 281
Sloan, Jerry 255, 542
Sloan, Norman 229, 329, 342, 662
Smart, Keith 326, 327
Smiley, Jack 43, 58
Smith, Adrian 538
Smith, Bev 524
Smith, Bill 204
Smith, Charles 332
Smith, Charlotte 501
Smith, Chris 118
Smith College 502
Smith, Curt 376
Smith, Dean 129, 146, 149, 177, 186, 198, 349, 362, 363, 374, 376, 378, 379, 464-5, 488, 553, 560, 656, 660, 660
Smith, Derek 487
Smith, Donald 218
Smith, Elmore 545
Smith, Frank 332
Smith, Garfield 181
Smith, Gavin 249, 488
Smith, Joe 403, 412
Smith, John 285
Smith, LaBradford 355
Smith, Michael 383
Smith, Orlando "Tubby" 465
Smith, Pat 176
Smith, Robert 253
Smith, Sam 253
Smith, Sonny 264, 306, 310, 318, 659
Smith, Tommy 96
Smith, Tony 253, 351
Smith, Tubby 390, 402, 560, 561, 658
Smith, Vernon 276
Smith, Willie 241, 244, 247
Smithson, Gene 489
Smits, Rik 211
SMU Mustangs *see* Southern Methodist Mustangs
Smuin, Dick 50
Sneed, Darnell 376
Snowden, Fred 220, 235, 242, 244
Snowden, Jim 488
Snyder, Brad 394

Sojourner, Mike 221, 245

Sojourner, Willie 201

Somerset, Willie 150

Sooners *see* Oklahoma

Sophie Newcomb College *see* Tulane University

Sorenson, Dave 199

South Alabama Jaguars 256, 263, 284, 344, 362, 560, 636

South Carolina Gamecocks 26, 29, 52, 55, 131, 174, 197, 199, 204, 206, 210, 216, 225, 228, 277, 282, 342, 344, 406, 411, 561, 636, 659, 660

South Carolina Gamecocks (women's team) 509

South Carolina State 342

South Florida Bulls 235, 297, 356, 636

Southeastern Conference (SEC) 36, 38, 63, 89, 118, 129, 148, 154, 169, 196, 227, 250, 265, 266, 267, 311, 334, 344, 349, 354, 386, 399, 402, 406, 479-80, 508, 512, 513, 566, 590, 655

Southeastern Louisiana 297, 310

Southeastern Louisiana (women's team) 512

Southern (LA) 383, 378, 567, 591

Southern Cal Trojans *see* USC Trojans

Southern Conference 9, 35, 49, 58, 75, 80, 85, 88, 103, 119, 138, 151, 165, 177, 180, 200, 228, 243, 250, 284, 325, 362, 398, 480

Southern Idaho 539

Southern Illinois Salukis 211, 212, 264, 421, 636-7

Southern Intercollegiate Athletic Association 8

Southern Jaguars 636

Southern Methodist Mustangs 177, 198, 243, 276, 304, 322, 332, 333, 377, 637

Southern Mississippi Golden Eagles 200, 258, 325, 332, 362, 489, 637

Southern Oregon 249

Southland Conference 338, 567, 592, 656

Southwest Conference 71, 77, 129, 132, 156, 176, 177, 204, 206, 249, 250, 264, 318, 319, 333, 343, 349, 361, 377, 384, 398, 480-1, 509, 600

Southwest Missouri State Bears 325, 327, 400, 556, 562, 566-7, 637, 655

Southwest Texas State 384, 547

Southwestern Athletic Conference 567, 593, 656

Southwestern Louisiana Ragin' Cajuns 129, 211, 215, 216, 218, 226, 249-50, 371, 439, 637

Spanarkcl, Jim 267, 662

Spartans *see* Michigan State, San Jose State

Spear, Bob 114

Spears, Odie 423

Spencer, Bob 528

Spencer, Gamel 325

Speraw, Kirk 384

Spiders *see* Richmond

Spika, Dan 190

Spillane, Jim 488

Spivey, Bill 74, 77

Spoelstra, Art 83

Spoonhour, Charlie 325, 384, 390, 539

Springfield 38

St. Bonaventure Bonnies 76, 103, 137, 139, 184, 199, 203, 299, 311, 393, 633

St. Francis (NY) Terriers 70, 90, 121, 136, 198, 633

St. Francis (PA) Red Flash 86, 361, 363, 633

St. John's Red Storm 13, 27, 35, 48-9, 52, 140, 150, 165, 170, 191, 225, 261, 266, 277, 312, 313, 315, 318, 329, 332, 342, 344, 363, 369, 377, 398, 407, 419, 420, 558, 562, 565, 633, 655

St. Joseph's Hawks 130, 132, 165, 168, 235, 241, 285, 318, 399, 406, 410, 562, 633-4

St. Louis Billikens 38, 45, 61, 63, 90, 119, 138, 140, 165, 196, 317, 342, 384, 390, 420, 493, 634

St. Mary's (CA) Gaels 121, 124, 228, 333, 342, 410, 547, 634

St. Peter's Peacocks 181, 200, 204, 276, 361, 634

Stack, Dave 488

Stackhouse, Jerry 403, 412

Stacom, Kevin 223

Stagg, Amos Alonzo 2, 4

Stags *see* Fairfield

Stahl, Floyd 54, 56

Stalcup, Wilbur "Sparky" 558

Staley, Dawn 501, 509, 524

Stallings, Kevin 410, 561, 567

Stallworth, Bud 211

Stallworth, Dave "The Rave" 149, 162, 163, 166

Stanford Cardinals 4, 16, 27, 30, 39, 42, 43, 45, 50, 171, 235, 337, 342, 343, 344, 405, 562, 637-8

Stanford Cardinals (women's team) 503, 509, 510, 513

Stanley, Ken 136

Stanley, Marianne Crawford 505, 507, 511, 524 528

Staples, Curtis 563

Starbird, Kate 513

Starke, Kevin 490

Starnes, Bob 150

Starrick, Greg 212

Stebbins, Pops 1

Steiner, Joe 136

Steinmetz, Christian 7, 8

Steinwedel, Steve 332, 366, 490

Sten, Greg 221

Stephens, Everette 488

Stephenson, Art 181

Stephenson, Jim 188

Stern, David 501

Stetson 235

Stevenson, Mark 351, 491

Stewart, Bruce 318, 332, 342

Stewart, Lusia Harris *see* Harris, Lusia

Stewart, Norm 103, 241, 289, 298, 342, 349, 383, 465, 492, 558, 658, 660, 660

Stiebing, Joey 492

Stiepler, Steve 262

Still, Valerie 524

Stinnie, Phil 485

Stipanovich, Steve 298, 492
Stith, Sam 130
Stith, Tom 130, 139
Stockton, John 284
Stoddard, Tim 229-30
Stokes, Maurice 86
Stone, Jonathan 366
Storm, Tom 174
Stowell, Joe 248
Stowers, Keith 138
Strannigan, Bill 91, 190
Street, Chris 374
Stricker, Bill 188
Strickland, Rod 344
Stringer, C. Vivian 530
Sullivan, Pat 488
Suman, Don 90
Summitt, Pat Head 506, 509, 510, 512, 513, 530
Sun Belt Conference 190, 256, 263, 276, 320, 332, 362, 367, 393, 481, 567, 594
Sun Devils *see* Arizona State
Sunderlage, Don 77
Sundstrom, Swede 84
Sundvold, Jon 298
Sura, Bob 374
Sutton, Eddie 176, 201, 220, 250, 341, 363, 422, 465-6, 539
Sutton, Rickey 551
Swagerty, Keith 165, 173
Swaim, Johnny 183
Swank, Joe 177
Swanson, Dennis 138
Swartz, Dan 103
SWC *see* Southwest Conference
Sweeney, Jim 262
Swoopes, Sheryl 501, 510, 513, 524-5
Sycamores *see* Indiana State
Syracuse Nationals 216
Syracuse Orangemen 9, 13, 45, 111, 144, 150, 168, 195, 204, 228, 236, 238, 276, 310, 325, 326, 327, 329, 341,363, 367, 367, 373, 379, 400, 401, 402, 405, 537, 562, 638
Sysko, Dave 156

T

Tabbachi, Max 83
Tacy, Carl 215, 489
Tallent, Bob 188
Talley, Archie 550
Tanenbaum, Sid 26, 68
Tar Heels *see* North Carolina
Tarkanian, Jerry 190, 221, 226, 255, 325, 349, 365, 466, 493, 539, 553, 561, 656, 660, 663
Tarrant, Dick 304, 306, 332
Tatum, Goose 79
Taylor, Blaine 366

Taylor, Brian 225
Taylor, Corky 214
Taylor, Derrick 492
Taylor, Fred 135, 138, 156, 199, 243
Taylor, Jay 338
Taylor, Kent 168
Taylor, Maurice 561
Taylor, Ollie 550
TCU *see* Texas Christian Horned Frogs
Teahan, Matt 262
Tebell, Gus 27
Temple Owls 4, 5, 29, 30, 52, 75, 103, 104, 115, 121, 212, 221, 226, 235, 263, 291, 303, 323, 325, 332, 333, 342, 367, 373, 376, 380, 393, 399, 563, 638, 659
Tennessee-Chattanooga Moccasins 290, 297, 411, 567, 638, 655
Tennessee State Tigers 376, 638-9
Tennessee Tech Golden Eagles 103, 114, 121, 310, 639
Tennessee Volunteers 27, 31, 41, 72, 151, 164, 169, 176, 179, 180, 197, 226, 242, 249, 258, 265, 266, 310, 376, 564, 638
Tennessee Volunteers (women's team) 499, 501, 506, 508, 509, 510, 512, 513
Terrapins *see* Maryland
Terrell, Ira 243
Terriers *see* Boston, St. Francis (NY)
Terry, Jason 560
Terry, Martin 219
Texas A&M Aggies 9, 54, 77, 96, 118, 156, 157, 191, 276, 279, 343, 639, 657
Texas-Arlington 284, 361
Texas Christian Horned Frogs 41, 71, 79, 183, 206, 281, 289, 325, 329, 563, 639
Texas-El Paso Miners 36, 63, 171, 173, 235, 238, 249, 277, 289, 315, 354, 362, 369, 427, 566, 568, 639-40
Texas Longhorns (women's team) 499, 507, 508, 509, 509
Texas Longhorns 9, 29, 57, 77, 98, 103, 132, 149, 206, 228, 230, 258, 289, 319, 344, 384, 563, 639, 656, 659
Texas-San Antonio 310
Texas Southern 291
Texas Tech Red Raiders 190, 228, 299, 398, 403, 410, 411, 566, 640
Texas Tech Red Raiders (women's team) 501, 510
Texas Wesleyan 62, 160, 165, 179
Thacker, Tom 146, 154
Thames, Kelly 396
Theus, Reggie 253
Thomas, Daryl 326
Thomas, Derek 493
Thomas, Gary 391
Thomas, Isiah 284, 291, 300, 437
Thomas, Jim 284
Thomas, John 247
Thomas, Kenny 561
Thomas, Kurt 394
Thomas, Steve 155, 156

Thomas, Tim 350, 407, 494

Thompson, Billy 319

Thompson, David 227, 229, 230, 231, 233, 234, 236, 270, 343, 662

Thompson, Gary 166

Thompson, John 156, 195, 221, 244, 256, 288, 305, 310, 362, 374, 466, 487

Thompson, John A. "Cat" 12

Thompson, Mychal 241, 249, 256, 454

Thompson, Pashen 513

Thompson, Paul 298

Thompson, Ray 491

Thompson, Scott 362

Thompson, Stephen 329

Thompson, Tomas 365

Thoren, Skip 154, 165

Thorn, Rod 154

Thornton, Damon 492

Thundering Herd see Marshall

Thurman, Scotty 387, 390, 403

Thurmond, Nate 136, 149, 154

Thurston, John 325

Tigers see Auburn, Clemson, Louisiana State, Memphis, Missouri, Pacific, Princeton, Tennessee State

Tillman, James 276

Timmons, Bob 86

Tindall, Billy 180

Tingle, Jack 57

Tisdale, Wayman 296, 302, 309, 310, 313, 322, 348, 469, 470, 484, 493

Titans see Cal State-Fullerton, Detroit

Title IX 505, 507, 510

Tolbert, Brian 403

Tolbert, Ray 287

Toledo Rockets 27, 36, 45, 48, 132, 177, 179 06, 249, 266, 317, 419, 640

Tomjanovich, Rudy 181, 188

Tooley, Ed 96

Toreros see San Diego

Toronto 4

Towe, Monty 227

Tower, Oswald 9

Townes, Kareem 394

Towson State 384

Trans America Athletic Conference 264, 304 402, 567, 595, 656

Traylor, Robert 561

Trenkle, Fred 539

Trent, Gary 484

Tribe see William and Mary

Triche, Howard 329

Trickey, Ken 215, 218

Trinity 7, 221

Tripucka, Kelly 265, 276, 487

Tripucka, Todd 241

Trojans see Arkansas-Little Rock, USC

Tropf, Glenn 330

Truax, Terry 384

Truitt, Frank 189, 215

Tsioropoulos, Lou 91

Tubbs, Billy 274, 332, 467, 493, 658

Tucker, Gerry 26, 57

Tueller, Rod 299

Tulane Green Wave 8, 40, 64, 71, 114, 156, 169, 242, 298, 311, 367, 373, 380, 640

Tulane Green Wave (women's team) 502

Tullos, Archie 330

Tulsa Golden Hurricane 72, 79, 150, 177, 201, 215, 281, 292, 303, 390, 411, 423, 564, 640

Turk, M. K. 258, 325, 489

Turner, Bobby 492

Turner, Eric 315

Turner, Kevin 561

Turpin, Melvin 302, 306, 308

Tutt, Raymond 410, 657

Twogood, Forrest 28

Tyler, Terry 491

Tyra, Charlie 103

Tyson, Gary 227

U

U.S. International University 316, 339, 360, 490

U.S. Merchant Marines Academy (Kings Point) 54

U.S. Military Academy 12

UCLA Bruins 29, 39, 41, 43, 45, 65, 73, 103, 129, 146, 154, 157, 159, 160, 165, 168, 171, 177, 179, 183-4, 186, 189, 195, 196, 197, 201, 203, 204, 207, 208, 210-1, 216, 218, 221, 225, 226, 229, 230, 233, 235, 236, 238, 244, 245, 250, 251, 253, 261, 263, 266, 273, 275, 277, 278, 279, 281, 284, 311, 315, 316, 327, 354, 363, 380, 393, 394-5, 401, 406, 412, 421, 427, 488, 489, 529, 561, 640-41, 649, 663

UCLA Bruins (women's team) 506

Underhill, Ralph 406

Underwood, Paul 103

Union University 12

United Press International 665

United States Basketball Writers Association (USBWA) 601, 665

University of California-Los Angeles Bruins see UCLA Bruins

University of Havana 48

University of Mexico City 31

University of Nevada-Las Vegas Runnin' Rebels see UNLV Runnin' Rebels

University of Southern California Trojans see USC Trojans

UNLV Runnin' Rebels 88, 226, 235, 242, 244, 253, 255, 263, 299, 325, 327, 328, 333, 342, 354-5, 358, 365, 373, 377, 385, 390, 391, 493, 537, 554, 562, 567, 641

Unseld, Wes 169, 179, 180, 186, 193

Urzetta, Sam 61, 70

USA Basketball 601
USC Trojans 12, 37, 39, 41, 45, 49, 92, 165, 189, 206, 210, 228, 266, 311, 316, 367, 380, 390, 420, 489, 493, 556, 636
USC Trojans (women's team) 508, 509, 511
Usher, Van 367
Usilton, James 30
Utah Jazz 255
Utah State Aggies 132, 146, 299, 385, 493, 564, 641
Utah Utes 46, 47, 48, 49, 53, 85, 100, 104, 135, 140, 148, 152, 165, 171, 173, 207, 221, 245, 289, 361, 373, 420, 563, 641, 663
Utes *see* Utah
Uthoff, Dean 277
Utica 326

V

Vacendak, Steve 170
Valentine, Darnell 491
Valentine, Ronnie 258
Vallely, John 190, 201
Valparaiso Crusaders 45, 342, 385, 409, 564, 567, 641
Valvano, Jim 174, 266, 276, 310, 354
van Breda Kolff, Butch 98, 132, 166, 177, 311, 385
Van Eman, Lanny 146
Van Horn, Keith 406, 415, 563
Vanatta, Bob 558
Vance, Gene 43, 58
Vandals see Idaho
Vanderbilt Commodores 4, 8, 120, 166, 180, 196, 198, 338, 344, 376, 562, 566, 642, 649, 650
Vanderbilt Commodores (women's team) 508, 513
VanDerveer, Tara 509, 510, 530
Vandeweghe, Ernie 64
Vandeweghe, Kiki 64, 279
Varn, Jerry 84
Vaughn, David 221, 380, 403
Vaughn, Jacque 407
Vaught, Loy 343, 355, 358
Veal, Jeremy 563
Veney, Keith 376, 409
Verga, Bob 174
Vermont 362
Versace, Dick 277, 288, 317, 318, 493
Vikings *see* Cleveland State
Villanova Wildcats 48, 54, 62, 63, 64, 70, 103, 114, 120, 203, 206, 207, 208, 210, 219, 235, 250, 298, 299, 311, 312, 313, 315, 319, 342, 396, 398, 494, 565, 642, 656
Vincent, Don 116
Vincent, Jay 310, 487
Vincent, Sam 310, 315
Vining, Mike 376, 492
Virginia Cavaliers 9, 60, 96, 118, 131, 138, 150, 165, 169, 190, 206, 212, 233, 244, 273, 281, 290, 292, 299, 300, 302, 305, 365, 390, 396, 405, 422, 494, 563, 642, 657

Virginia Cavaliers (women's team) 501, 509
Virginia Commonwealth Rams 310, 374, 642, 658-9
Virginia Military Institute Keydets 138, 242, 243, 249, 325, 642
Virginia Polytechnic 9
Virginia Tech Hokies 31, 146, 151, 165, 169, 200, 276, 279, 323, 332, 393, 406, 422, 494, 643
Virostek, Don 84
Visscher, Gene 220
Vitale, Dick 171, 174, 249, 491
VMI *see* Virginia Military Institute Keydets
Voelkel, Ray 262
Volunteers *see* Tennessee
Vrankavich, Russ 156

W

WAC *see* Western Athletic Conference
Wacker, Mike 289
Wade, Bob 325
Wade, Margaret 505, 530-1
Wade, Mark 323, 329
Wade Trophy 514
Wadsworth, Mike 90
Wagner 262
Wagner, Milt 315
Wagnon, Dave 168
Wake Forest Demon Deacons 56, 96, 139, 140, 142, 146, 165, 180, 220, 233, 234, 250, 373, 374, 390, 392, 393, 398, 405, 408, 489, 643, 656
Walk, Neal 180
Walker, Antoine 411, 437
Walker, Chet 193-4
Walker, Damion 563
Walker, Daryll 346
Walker, Horace 132
Walker, Jimmy 14, 173, 174, 453
Walker, Joyce 525
Walker, Kenny 306, 308, 320
Walker, Myron 383
Walker, Rosie 525
Walker, Samaki 392, 412
Walker, Solly 81
Wallace, Grady 107, 108
Wallace, John 398, 405
Wallace, Perry 180, 649-9
Wallace, Rasheed 396, 403, 412
Wallace, Riley 490
Wallace, Steve 279
Walters, Dick 255
Walton, Bill 195, 204, 210, 213, 216, 218, 221, 223, 225, 226, 229, 270, 501, 510
Walton, Lloyd 245
Ward, Jerod 561
Ward, Stanley 190
Ware, Tracey 373

Warner, Bob 228

Warner, Ed 73, 74

Warner, Scott 200

Warren, Jeff 366

Warren, John 52

Warren, Mike 183

Warrensburg see Central Missouri

Warrensburg Teachers College 10

Warriors see Marquette

Warzynski, Ken 200

Wasdin, Tom 662

Washburn (KS) 38

Washburn, Chris 329, 337

Washington (MO) 132

Washington & Lee 28, 121

Washington Huskies 8, 36, 58, 61, 77, 90-1, 121, 233, 244, 264, 311, 399-400, 563, 643

Washington Huskies (women's team) 509

Washington, Kenny 157, 159, 160

Washington, Kermit 221

Washington, Pearl 329

Washington, Richard 195, 236, 238, 244, 253, 488

Washington, Rudy 362, 493

Washington State Cougars 8, 36, 39, 40, 49, 72, 85, 170 277, 279, 297, 311, 643

Waters, Bucky 221

Watson, Anthony 318

Watson, Bobby 255

Watson, Lou 177, 225

Watson, Melvin 561

Watson, Perry 489, 490

Watts, Stan 76, 207, 215

Waves see Pepperdine

Wayland Baptist 504

Wayne State (MI) 72

WCAC see West Coast Athletic Conference

WCC see West Coast Conference

Weatherspoon, Teresa 525

Weaver, James 124

Webb, Paul 249, 276

Webb, Spud 274

Webber, Chris 371, 373, 378-9, 380, 390, 396, 402, 487

Webber, Mayce 378

Weber State Wildcats 189, 201, 220, 242, 277, 567, 643

Webster, Jeff 356

Weese, Dean 531

Weinhauer, Bob 258, 263, 291

Weir, Murray 61

Weise, Larry 199

Welch, Poo 210

Weller, Chris 531

Wells, Bonzi 657

Wells, Bubba 409

Wells, Clifford 64, 71, 114

Weltlich, Bob 235, 287, 319, 396

Werkman, Nick 149, 155

West, Alvin 488

West Chester State 255, 291

West Chester State (women's team) 504

West Coast Athletic Conference 152, 235, 243, 284

West Coast Conference 98, 218, 219, 329, 330, 481-2, 565, 567, 596

West, Jerry 116, 121, 122, 123, 126, 127-8, 130, 135

West, Mark 298

West Texas State 319

West Virginia Mountaineers 29, 41, 64, 72, 115, 116, 119, 121, 130, 138, 146, 151, 165, 180, 250, 258, 284, 290, 299, 302, 398, 563, 643-4, 658

Western Athletic Conference 146, 171, 206, 207, 220-1, 238, 242, 255, 318, 325, 361, 482, 566, 597

Western Carolina Catamounts 284, 290, 400, 401-2, 644

Western Conference 8

Western Illinois 288, 297, 393

Western Illinois State Teacher's College 12

Western Kentucky Hilltoppers 26, 28-9, 41, 45, 58, 63, 83, 89, 98, 157, 179, 200, 204, 206, 208, 210, 279, 284, 291, 320, 376, 393, 420, 423, 644, 662

Western Michigan Broncos 28, 48, 205, 240, 243, 244, 367, 644

Western Texas 281

Westhead, Paul 318, 332, 351

Westminster College 12

Whatley, Ennis 308, 315

Wheat, DeJuan 411, 492, 562

Wheeler, Tyson 562

White, Jo Jo 173

White, John 332, 489

White, Nera 504

White, Sherman 74

White, Tony 325, 376

Whitehead, Jerome 245

Whitehead, LaDrell 410

Whitman College 8

Whitmore, Bob 181

Whitney, Davey 277, 488, 567

Whittaker, Frank 48

Whittenburg, Dereck 299, 300

Wichita 72, 78, 90, 160

Wichita State Shockers 146, 149, 163, 166, 200, 206, 287, 297, 333, 489, 644

Wicks, Sidney 201, 204, 207, 208, 210

Widby, Ron 169

Wiethe, John 57, 70, 75

Wiggins, Ernie 108

Wilbourne, Nate 394

Wildcats see Arizona, Davidson, Kansas State, Kentucky, Northwestern, Villanova, Weber State

Wiley, Gene 138

Wilkens, Lenny 424

Wilkerson, Bobby 236, 244, 487
Wilkes, Glenn 235
Wilkes, James 279
Wilkes, Keith 195, 230, 271
Wilkins, Dick 53
Wilkins, Dominique 300, 453
Wilkins, Gerald 310
Wilkinson, Buzz 90, 97
Wilkinson, Herb 49
Willard, Ralph 376, 567, 657
William and Mary Tribe 64, 70, 83, 130, 200, 250, 644-5
William and Mary Tribe (women's team) 510
Williams 7
Williams, Brian 373
Williams, Buck 279, 292
Williams, Carroll 98
Williams, Donald 378, 380
Williams, Freeman 249, 255, 380
Williams, Gary 284, 297, 388, 467, 562, 659
Williams, Gerald 492
Williams, James "Fly" 218, 219, 226, 484
Williams, Joe 199, 206, 250, 662
Williams, John "Hot Rod" 311, 313, 329, 334
Williams, Kenneth 493
Williams, Larry 253
Williams, Lou 539
Williams, Maurice 493
Williams, Michael 396
Williams, Monty 373
Williams, Oscar 493
Williams, Paul 296
Williams, Ray 249
Williams, Reggie 305
Williams, Richard 398
Williams, Rob 292, 294, 300
Williams, Rollie 41
Williams, Roy 379, 416, 467, 554, 661
Williams, Sam 287
Williams, Sandy 156
Williams, Shammond 411
Williams, Walt 366
Williamson, Corliss 387, 396, 403, 415
Williamson, John 211, 234
Willoughby, Bill 437
Willoughby, Dedric 380, 492
Wilson, Ben 308
Wilson, Bernard 64
Wilson, Darryl 396
Wilson, Desi 360
Wilson, Ed 181
Wilson, Floyd 108
Wilson, Merlin 242
Wilson, Nikita 492

Wilson, Ray 492
Wingfield, Dontonio 350, 396, 411
Winston-Salem State 542
Winter, Tex 119
Winthrop 408
Wirtz, Lenny 370
Wisconsin Badgers 7, 8, 9, 10, 12, 25, 40, 42, 57, 59, 65, 72, 121, 183, 204, 240-1, 249, 262, 277, 342, 362, 388, 390, 408, 562, 645
Wisconsin-Green Bay Phoenix 384, 400, 408, 645
Wise, Skip 234
Wisniewski, Irvin 144
Witte, Les 33
Witte, Luke 214
Wittenberg (OH) 38, 41, 258, 544
Wittman, Randy 279
WNBA 501, 513
Wohl, Dave 208
Wolff, Dennis 409
Wolfpack see Nevada, North Carolina State
Wolters, Kara 500, 513
Wolverines see Michigan
Women's Basketball Coaches Association (WBCA) 601
Women's National Basketball Association see WNBA
Wood, Al 263, 287
Wood, Leon 299, 302
Woodard, Lynette 506, 525
Wooden, John 13, 33, 43, 65, 73, 103, 146, 154, 157, 159, 182, 183, 194, 195, 218, 225, 233, 236, 251, 279, 311, 369, 488, 512, 660, 661, 665
Woods, Randy 360
Woods, Rudy 276
Woods, Tommy 165
Woods, Wilbur 12
Wooldridge, Jim 384, 547
Woollum, Charlie 303
Woolpert, Phil 104, 190
Woolridge, Orlando 265, 281, 487
Word, Jason 383
Worsley, Larry 164
Worthy, James 275, 288, 291, 300, 437, 453
Wothke, Les 311
Wright, Carl 322
Wright, Leroy 121
Wright, Lorenzen 412
Wright, Luther 390
Wright, Pancho 487
Wright, Rynn 276
Wright, Sharone 396
Wright State Raiders 406, 645
Wulk, Ned 121, 149, 206
Wuycik, Dennis 206
Wyoming Cowboys 45, 46, 50, 66, 104, 114, 190, 299, 318, 645, 658

X

Xavier Musketeers 109, 114, 241, 284, 327, 332, 344, 363, 400, 407, 421, 556, 562, 567, 645, 659

Y

Yale Bulldogs 4, 5, 6, 7, 8, 54, 276, 645
Yankee Conference 132
Yankee League 599
Yarborough, Bill 97
Yates, Carlos 297, 310
Yates, Doug 120
Yates, Tony 311
Yates, Wayne 290
Yellow Jackets *see* Georgia Tech
Yelverton, Charlie 204
YMCA 6, 9
YMCA School for Christian Workers 1

Yoest, Mike 330
Young, Jewell 33
Young, Michael 292, 300
Young, Tim 405, 562
Young, Tom 228, 240, 362
Youngblood, Jim 176
Youngstown State 310
Yow, Kay 531
Yunkus, Rich 198, 204

Z

Zags *see* Gonzaga
Zaslofsky, Max 52
Zawoluk, Bob 70, 81
Zunic, Matt 148
Zuppke, Bob 7
Zvosec, Rich 362

PHOTO CREDITS

Photographs appearing in *Inside Sports College Basketball* were received from the following sources:

Bradley University, 330; Dartmouth College, 57; DePaul University, 50, 304; Duke University, 369, 462; Furman University, 91; Georgia Institute of Technology, 136, 351, 354 (right); Indiana University, 243 (left), 322, 371; Jacksonville University, 204; Kansas State University, 670; La Salle University, 89; Louisiana State University, photo by John Titchen, Star Bulletin Photo, 189; Louisiana Tech University, 520; Loyola Marymount University, 350; Marquette University, 249, 252, 257; Michigan State University, 262, 263; National Association of Basketball Coaches, 405; National Association of Intercollegiate Athletics, 537, 543, 545, 546, 547, 549; Niagara University, 203; North Atlantic Conference, 339; North Carolina State University, 229 (left), 352; North Carolina State University, photo copyright Burnie Batchelor Studio, Inc., 120; Oral Roberts University, 211; Pennsylvania State University, 92; Providence College, 173; Providence College, photos by Thomas Maguire, Jr. 222, 226; Purdue University, 13, 143, 197, 382; Rutgers, The State University of New Jersey, photo by Dean Nathans/*Scarlet Letter,* 243 (right); St. Bonaventure University, 183 (right); St. Joseph's University, 140; St. Louis University, 422; Southeastern Louisiana University, 510; Stanford University, 15, 41; Syracuse University 672; Syracuse University, photo by Stephen Parker 323; University of Arizona, 283; University of California, 377; University of California, Los Angeles (UCLA), 157, 160, 171, 177, 182, 208, 213, 229 (right), 234, 506, 529, 667; University of Cincinnati, 86, 119, 366; University of Connecticut, 383; University of Dayton, photo by Ed Morris Photography, 174 (left); University of Houston, 174 (right), 183 (right), 294, 298, 316; University of Idaho, 152; University of Iowa, 547; University of Kansas, 2, 124 (right), 124 (left), 335; University of Louisville, 180, 277, 318; University of Miami, 162; University of Nevada, Las Vegas, 354 (left), 358, 360; University of North Carolina, 512; University of Oklahoma, 309; University of Oregon, 30, 426; University of Tennessee, 240, 247, 295; University of Texas at El Paso, 460; University of Utah, 47; University of Wyoming, 44; USA Basketball, 500, 518, 519, 521, 524, 525, 530; Vanderbilt University, 338; Villanova University, 523; Wake Forest University, 88, 118, 393 (top); West Virginia University, 98, 114; Western Kentucky University, 423; Wichita State University, 149.

School logos appear courtesy of the individual school or conference.